2024/25

THE DIRECTORY OF
GRANT MAKING TRUSTS

28th edition

Jessica Threlfall, Muna Farah, Ross Hardy, Kalli Jayasuriya and Ian Pembridge

Additional research by Rhiannon Doherty, Ellen Johnson, Lucy Martin, Hannah Sundell and Judith Turner

dsc
directory of social change

Published by the Directory of Social Change (Registered Charity no. 800517 in England and Wales)
Registered address: Directory of Social Change, First Floor, 10 Queen Street Place, London EC4R 1BE
Tel: 020 4526 5995

Visit www.dsc.org.uk to find out more about our books, subscription funding website and training events. You can also sign up for e-newsletters so that you're always the first to hear about what's new.

The publisher welcomes suggestions and comments that will help to inform and improve future versions of this and all of our titles. Please give us your feedback by emailing publications@dsc.org.uk.

It should be understood that this publication is intended for guidance only and is not a substitute for professional or legal advice. No responsibility for loss occasioned as a result of any person acting or refraining from acting can be accepted by the authors or publisher.

First published by Charities Aid Foundation 1968
Second edition 1971
Third edition 1974
Fourth edition 1975
Fifth edition 1977
Sixth edition 1978
Seventh edition 1981
Eighth edition 1983
Ninth edition 1985
Tenth edition 1987
Eleventh edition 1989
Twelfth edition 1991
Thirteenth edition 1993
Fourteenth edition 1995
Fifteenth edition 1997
Sixteenth edition 1999
Seventeenth edition published by Directory of Social Change 2001
Eighteenth edition 2003
Nineteenth edition 2005
Twentieth edition 2007
Twenty-first edition 2010
Twenty-second edition 2012
Twenty-third edition 2014
Twenty-fourth edition 2015
Twenty-fifth edition 2017
Twenty-sixth edition 2019
Twenty-seventh edition 2021
Twenty-eighth edition 2023

ISBN 978 1 78482 107 4

British Library Cataloguing in Publication Data
A catalogue record for this book is available from the British Library

Cover design by Kate Griffith
Text designed by Eugenie Dodd Typographics, London
Typeset by Marlinzo Services, Frome
Printed and bound by CPI Group (UK) Ltd, Croydon, CRO4YY

FSC
www.fsc.org
MIX
Paper | Supporting
responsible forestry
FSC® C013604

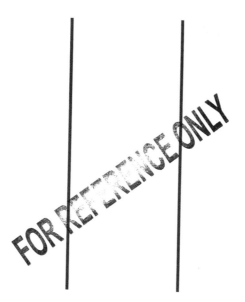

Contents

Foreword

Fundraising is a personal and deeply human endeavour. It is about building relationships, telling powerful stories and creating connections that inspire generosity, care and commitment. Right now, the cost-of-living crisis is affecting individuals, families and communities from all walks of life, and as fundraisers we are challenged to bridge the gaps and enable the charities we love and work for to offer essential support.

In the face of crisis – the impact of the COVID-19 pandemic and now even greater financial pressures – charities have continued with remarkable resilience, adapting programmes and services to meet the evolving needs of their beneficiaries. Yet the strain on resources is real, and many of us are grappling with budget cuts, reduced donations and a challenge of doing more with less.

Since 2020, the giving environment has fundamentally changed. Mass participation events have seen hugely reduced numbers, hybrid working has impacted how we deliver Charity of the Year partnerships and people have become far more discerning in their giving, often reducing the number of charities they support. Competition is real, and as more charities bring new fundraising products to market, the rising costs of buying media space, printing and postage has made it all so much harder for many charities to get a share of voice.

Amidst all these shifts, grant-making charities have remained a reliable constant, with over 2,000 funders listed in *The Directory of Grant Making Trusts*, giving a cumulative £6.9 billion to good causes in the UK annually. While some grant-makers have doubtless faced their own financial constraints, many have continued to stand firm in their dedication to make a difference. With their long-term outlook and strategic approach, grant-making charities continue to enable stability and provide essential funding for both established programmes and innovative projects.

In over 20 years in our wonderful sector, something I consistently hear is that donors want charities to collaborate and reduce duplication. With this in mind, *The Directory of Grant Making Trusts* is a brilliant one-stop-shop for charities and grants fundraisers. There is no need to replicate the research and insight, as here it is – all prepared so you can dive in whenever you need.

Good luck combining your boundless passion with this excellent resource!

Laurie Boult
Executive Fundraising and Engagement
Director, Age UK

About the Directory of Social Change

At the Directory of Social Change (DSC), we believe that the world is made better by people coming together to serve their communities and each other. For us, an independent voluntary sector is at the heart of that social change and we exist to support charities, voluntary organisations and community groups in the work they do. Our role is to:

- **Provide practical information** on a range of topics from fundraising to project management in both our printed publications and our e-books

- **Offer training** through public courses, events and in-house services

- **Research funders** and maintain a subscription database, *Funds Online*, with details on funding from grant-making charities, companies and government sources

- **Offer bespoke research** to voluntary sector organisations in order to evaluate projects, identify new opportunities and help make sense of existing data

- **Stimulate debate and campaign** on key issues that affect the voluntary sector, particularly to champion the concerns of smaller charities

We are a registered charity ourselves but we self-fund most of our work. We charge for services, but cross-subsidise those which charities particularly need and cannot easily afford.

Visit our website **www.dsc.org.uk** to see how we can help you to help others and have a look at **www.fundsonline.org.uk** to see how DSC could improve your fundraising. Alternatively, call our friendly team at **020 4526 5995** to chat about your needs or drop us a line at **cs@dsc.org.uk**.

Introduction

Welcome to the 28th edition of *The Directory of Grant Making Trusts* (DGMT). This book covers over 2,000 of the largest grant-making charities that award grants to UK organisations. Since the previous edition of this guide, the voluntary sector has transitioned from adapting to the challenges presented by the COVID-19 pandemic to navigating the pressures caused by the cost-of-living crisis. Rising everyday costs, increasing demand for services and financial pressure on donors all present difficulties for charities striving to serve their beneficiaries. We hope the meticulously researched information in this directory will help your organisation find the necessary funding to achieve your aims in these difficult times.

The Charities Aid Foundation published the first edition of DGMT in 1968 and the guide has been researched and published by DSC since 2001. Over this time, the title has gained a notable reputation as a comprehensive guide to UK grant-makers and their funding policies. DSC's other guides include independent, sometimes critical, comments on and analysis of funders' activities. DGMT does not. Rather, it is a concise and to-the-point guide to UK grant-makers. It is designed to provide a bridge between the grant-making and fundraising communities in the UK. Today, it is hard to imagine the difficulties which must have been encountered and the amount of time spent trying to obtain funds from these organisations before DGMT brought together so many of them in one place.

This edition welcomes over 120 grant-makers that are completely new to DGMT. Each individual funder listed in this guide has the capacity to give over £50,000 annually, with some funders giving significantly more, up to a staggering £906.6 million awarded by Arts Council England. Together, the grant-makers in this guide awarded around £6.9 billion to organisations. This figure marks a considerable increase of around £1.3 billion from the previous edition.

Although the vast majority of funders in this guide are registered grant-making charities, there are a number which are not. For example, some of the largest funders, such as the four UK arts councils, are non-departmental public bodies. Excluding the funding awarded by such bodies, the total awarded by grant-making charities in this guide amounted to almost £5 billion.

In the course of our research, we scrutinised each grant-maker's annual reports and accounts, mainly for the 2021 and 2021/22 financial years. We also examined the content of other resources, such as funders' websites, social media accounts and application guidelines, in order to provide the most relevant information for our readers. In some cases we also made direct contact with the funders themselves.

Each record in this guide includes a figure for the total grants awarded by the funder to organisations. The record may also include a figure for grants awarded to individuals, where this information was available. In a small number of cases, we were unable to determine the breakdown of grants awarded to organisations and to individuals. In these cases, this is noted in the record.

Some charities had not filed their 2021 or 2021/22 accounts by the time our research concluded. For these records, we used the latest available accounts and have noted this in the narrative.

We value the opinions of our readers on all aspects of our work, including this directory. We are always looking to improve our guides and welcome any feedback – positive or negative – which could be useful for future editions. Please email any comments you would like to make to research@dsc.org.uk.

All in the Research Team at DSC wish you the very best of luck with your fundraising!

The grant-makers we have listed

This directory aims to include the majority of UK-based grant-makers that are capable of giving at least around £50,000 a year to organisations. Many of their trustees and/or staff are extremely helpful, and we have been able to access comprehensive information on current policies via their websites, published material or direct communication. However, not all grant-makers are so open. Where we have found this to be the case and information is not readily available, the funder's details have been updated, where possible, using the information on the appropriate regulator's website. Grant-makers have been included in the indexes under the appropriate headings according to their own published guidelines, grant-making practices and/or annual reports. We have placed those for which we do not have such information under what we believe to be the most suitable categories based on the information available.

In general we have included:

- funders with a grant-making capacity of at least around £50,000 per year which make grants to charities and voluntary organisations in the UK. Please note that while the grant totals of some of the funders listed here could be below £50,000 in the given year, their grant-making activities either have the potential to exceed this amount or vary significantly each year.

We have excluded:

- grant-makers which fund individuals only;

- grant-makers which fund one organisation exclusively;

- grant-makers which generally have a grant-making capacity of less than £50,000 (smaller grant-making charities are included on our funding website fundsonline.org.uk);

- grant-makers which only fund work overseas;

- grant-makers which have ceased to exist or are being wound up with any remaining funds fully committed.

We continue to include grant-making charities which state that they do not respond to unsolicited applications. We believe that their inclusion benefits fundraisers by giving a broader overview of the grant-making community, and that the information could be important in building relationships with funders. We feel it benefits grant-makers in helping them to communicate that they do not wish to receive applications, which fundraisers might not know if they identified that particular grant-maker through another avenue. Where possible, we include the reasons why the grant-maker is not awarding grants, cannot accept applications or is not seeking unsolicited requests. We believe this is more helpful than letting the funder remain an obscure name in the sea of funders. Perhaps most importantly, making this information available to fundraisers helps to reduce the number of ineligible applications that are submitted to very busy and often over-stretched grant-makers. As outlined in DSC's Responsible Giving policy principle, clear and accessible information is essential for both funders and applicants and ensures effective use of time and charitable resources (please visit www.dsc.org.uk/our-policy-principles for more information).

Acknowledgements

We would like to thank Laurie Boult, Director of Fundraising and Engagement at Age UK, for contributing the foreword to this edition.

We would also like to thank all those trustees and staff of grant-making organisations who strive to make their information openly available, and all those who have helped our research by responding to our communications and providing helpful comments.

How to use DGMT

The directory starts with four indexes:

- grant-makers by geographical area;
- grant-makers by field of interest and type of beneficiary;
- grant-makers by type of organisation;
- grant-makers by type of grant.

There is also an alphabetical listing of the top 150 grant-makers by grant total on page xix.

Using these indexes, readers should be able to make a shortlist of grant-makers whose funding policies match their needs.

Grant-makers by geographical area

This index enables you to see which grant-makers will consider applications from a charity or project in a particular geographical area. It contains the following:

LIST OF GEOGRAPHICAL AREA HEADINGS

This lists the geographical area headings used in DGMT.

LIST OF GRANT-MAKERS BY GEOGRAPHICAL AREA

Funders are listed under the geographical areas where they will consider funding.

Grant-makers by field of interest and type of beneficiary

This index enables you to see which grant-makers are likely to fund a particular type of work to benefit a particular type of person. It lists grant-makers according to:

- the type of activity or work they are willing to fund – their fields of interest;
- who they want to benefit – their preferred beneficiaries.

These pages contain the following:

LIST OF FIELDS OF INTEREST AND TYPES OF BENEFICIARY

This lists the headings used in DGMT to categorise fields of interest and types of beneficiary.

LIST OF GRANT-MAKERS BY FIELD OF INTEREST AND TYPE OF BENEFICIARY

Funders are listed under their fields of interest and types of beneficiary where there is a stated preference, or where our research suggests the grant-maker may have a preference.

The index is structured hierarchically. This means that the general heading comes first, followed by more specific subject areas. For example, under 'Beneficial groups' you can find the 'Social and economic circumstances' category which is then split into further sub-headings, including 'People who are homeless/at risk of homelessness', 'Carers' and 'Victims of disasters and famine'.

So, if your project falls under a specific heading such as 'Victims of disasters and famine', it is also worth looking at the grant-makers which have expressed a general interest in funding 'Social and economic circumstances'. Grant-makers might be interested in funding your project even if they have not specifically expressed a preference for a particular field as long as it falls within the broad area they are supporting.

Grant-makers by type of organisation

This index enables you to see which grant-makers will consider funding a particular type of organisation. As all the grant-makers in this guide will fund registered, excepted or exempt charities, we have not included specific listings for these types of organisation. The index contains the following:

LIST OF TYPES OF ORGANISATION

This lists the headings used in DGMT to categorise types of organisation.

LIST OF GRANT-MAKERS BY TYPE OF ORGANISATION

Funders are listed under the types of organisation for which they have expressed a funding preference.

Grant-makers by type of grant

This index enables you to see which grant-makers can consider making the types of grant you are looking for. Grant-makers are listed under the type of grant that our research suggests they are willing or likely to make. These pages contain the following:

LIST OF TYPES OF GRANT

This lists the headings used in DGMT to categorise types of grant.

LIST OF GRANT-MAKERS BY TYPE OF GRANT

Funders are listed under the types of grant that they are willing or likely to make.

The largest grant-makers

On page xix we have listed the largest 150 grant-makers by the total of grants awarded to organisations in alphabetical order. Between them they account for around £5.6 billion, or about 82% of the funds available in the book. Please *do not* use this simply as a mailing list: these grant-makers cover a wide range of specialist interests and many of them will not fund your work.

We strongly recommend that you read each record carefully and compile your own list of those major grant-makers relevant to you. You can then set this list alongside the other lists generated from the other indexes in the directory. We believe this list should only be used as an effective way of ensuring that you do not omit any major grant-makers.

How to use DGMT
Key steps

STEP 1

Define the project, programme or work for which you are seeking funding.

STEP 2

Geographical area: find the area most local to your requirements (the geographical location of the people who will benefit from any funding received). Identify the relevant section of the index.

STEP 3

Field of interest and type of beneficiary: identify the categories that match your project. What charitable activities, facilities or services will the funding provide? What are the characteristics which best describe the people who will benefit from any funding received? Find the relevant sections of the index and funders listed there.

▼

STEP 4

Type of organisation: identify the type of your organisation (or, if you are searching for funding on behalf of someone else, the type of organisation which would be receiving the funds). Find the relevant section of the index.

▼

STEP 5

Type of grant: identify the type of grant you are looking for. Find the relevant section of the index and grant-makers listed there.

▼

STEP 6

Compare the relevant sections of grant-makers identified through all of the indexes to find the funders which appear in more than one section. This way, you will produce a list of those whose funding policies most closely match the characteristics of the project for which you are seeking funding.

To expand your list of potential funders, you could include grant-makers that have a general interest in funding your area of work – while these may not define a specific field as a priority or preference, they will consider applications as long as they fall within the broad category.

▼

STEP 7

Look up the records for the grant-makers identified, study their details carefully and pay close attention to 'What is funded', 'What is not funded' and the preferred method of communication or where further details may be found.

▼

Look at the list of the top 150 grant-makers to make sure you do not miss any major funders. Look up the records for the grant-makers identified, study their details carefully and, again, pay particularly close attention to 'What is funded' and 'What is not funded'. Remember that these funders are likely to be more well-known and, consequently, the application process may be more competitive.

▼

EXAMPLE

Funding is being sought to purchase equipment for a children's hospice in North Wales.

■ The geographical location is: United Kingdom → Wales → North Wales. You may want to look at the grant-makers listed under the broader region (Wales) as well, and it is also worth looking at grant-makers listed under United Kingdom. A grant-maker listed under a more general heading may be just as willing to fund activity in a specific region as another which states that it has a specific interest in that area.

■ The service to be provided is: health. If you were looking for funding for a children's hospice, you would probably first look under 'Community health services' which can be found under 'Health'; however, grant-makers listed under the broader area of interest (health) are also worth looking at.

■ The key characteristic of the people to benefit is that they are: children. If you look under 'Beneficial groups', you will find 'Children and young people', which is under 'Age'.

■ The type of organisation is: hospice.

■ The type of grant being sought is: capital costs.

The list you produce by following these steps will contain the grant-makers that match your project criteria most accurately; however, it is also worth considering funders that give for general charitable purposes, especially if they give in your local area.

A typical DGMT record

The example below shows the information that typically appears in a DGMT record. An explanation of the information in each field is given alongside.

CC NO
Charity registration number

WHERE FUNDING CAN BE GIVEN
The village, town, borough, parish or other geographical area in which the grant-maker is prepared to fund

WHAT IS FUNDED
Details of the types of project or activity the grant-maker plans to fund and the groups it intends to ultimately benefit

WHAT IS NOT FUNDED
The types of project or causes the grant-maker does not fund, e.g. expeditions, scholarships

SAMPLE GRANTS
Examples of grants previously awarded by the grant-maker

TRUSTEES
Names of the trustees

CONTACT DETAILS
Information on whom to contact for further details or, if applicable, where applications should be sent

ESTABLISHED
The year the grant-maker was established

WHO CAN BENEFIT
The types of organisation that can be supported

TYPE OF GRANT
The types of grant or loan the grant-maker is prepared to give, e.g. one-off grants, core costs, project costs

RANGE OF GRANTS
The typical size of grants awarded

FINANCES
The most recent financial information available, including the total amount given in grants during the year

OTHER INFORMATION
Any other information which might be useful to grant-seekers

HOW TO APPLY
Useful information to those preparing their grant application

■ The Fictitious Trust

CC NO 123456   **ESTABLISHED** 1993
WHERE FUNDING CAN BE GIVEN UK.
WHO CAN BENEFIT Charitable organisations; individuals.
WHAT IS FUNDED Education and training.
WHAT IS NOT FUNDED Gap year activities.
TYPE OF GRANT One-off grants; capital costs; running costs.
RANGE OF GRANTS £250 to £5,000.
SAMPLE GRANTS A registered charity (£5,000); a CIC (£1,000); a museum (£800); a gallery and a university (£500 each); an exempt charity (£400); an excepted charity (£250).
FINANCES *Financial year end 31/03/2022*
Income £55,000
Grants to organisations £50,000
Grants to individuals £10,000
Assets £800,000
TRUSTEES Ernestine Papadopoulos; Samuel Akintola; Grace O'Malley; Alistair Johnson; Dr Angelique Kidjo; Prof. Miriam Masekela.
OTHER INFORMATION Grants were awarded to 46 organisations during the year.
HOW TO APPLY Apply in writing to the address below. An sae should be enclosed if an acknowledgement is required.
CONTACT DETAILS The Trust Secretary, The Old Barn, Main Street, New Town ZC48 2QQ *Tel.* 020 7123 4567 *Email* grantsteam@fictitioustrust.co.uk *Website* www.fictitioustrust.co.uk

The top 150 grant-makers by grant total

This is a list of the largest 150 grant-makers by the total of grants awarded to organisations in alphabetical order. Between them they account for around £5.6 billion, or about 82% of the funds available in the book. *Please do not use this simply as a mailing list: these grant-makers cover a wide range of specialist interests and many of them will not fund your work.*

We recommend that you read each record carefully and compile your own list of major grant-makers relevant to you. You can use this list alongside the other lists generated from the indexes in the directory. We believe this is the most effective way of ensuring that you do not omit any major grant-makers.

The 29th May 1961 Charitable Trust

The A. B. Charitable Trust

A. W. Charitable Trust

The Access to Justice Foundation

Achisomoch Aid Company Ltd

AKO Foundation

Alzheimer's Research UK

Alzheimer's Society

Arcadia Fund

The Architectural Heritage Fund

Armed Forces Covenant Fund Trust

The John Armitage Charitable Trust

Arts Council England

Arts Council of Northern Ireland

Arts Council of Wales (also known as Cyngor Celfyddydau Cymru)

Bank of Scotland Foundation

BBC Children in Need

Becht Foundation

Benefact Trust Ltd

Benesco Charity Ltd

Bloodwise

The Liz and Terry Bramall Foundation

Breast Cancer Now

The British Academy

British Heart Foundation

The Barrow Cadbury Trust

The Calleva Foundation

Cancer Research UK

The City Bridge Trust (Bridge House Estates)

The Clothworkers' Foundation

Denise Coates Foundation

Comic Relief

Corra Foundation

Creative Scotland

The Roger De Haan Charitable Trust

Diabetes UK

Dunard Fund

John Ellerman Foundation

England and Wales Cricket Trust

The Exilarch's Foundation

Esmée Fairbairn Foundation

The February Foundation

The Fidelity UK Foundation

The Football Foundation

The Foyle Foundation

The Gannochy Trust

The Gatsby Charitable Foundation

Goldman Sachs Gives (UK)

The Mike Gooley Trailfinders Charity

The Edward Gostling Foundation

The Grace Trust

Groundwork UK

Paul Hamlyn Foundation

The Helen Hamlyn Trust

The Health Foundation

The Helping Foundation

Heritage Lottery Fund

Historic Environment Scotland

Hospice UK

The Albert Hunt Trust

The Hunter Foundation

The Jabbs Foundation

The Jagclif Charitable Trust

The Elton John AIDS Foundation

The Jordan Charitable Foundation

The Kavli Trust

The Kennedy Trust for Rheumatology Research

The Kentown Wizard Foundation

Keren Association Ltd

Kidney Research UK

The LankellyChase Foundation

The Law Family Charitable Foundation

The Legal Education Foundation

Lempriere Pringle 2015

The Leverhulme Trust

The Linbury Trust

Lloyds Bank Foundation for England and Wales

Lloyd's Register Foundation

The London Community Foundation (LCF)

John Lyon's Charity

Masonic Charitable Foundation

The Master Charitable Trust

Maudsley Charity

Medical Research Foundation

The Mohn Westlake Foundation

Moondance Foundation

The Steve Morgan Foundation

The Alexander Mosley Charitable Trust

Motor Neurone Disease Association

The National Churches Trust

The National Lottery Community Fund

Nesta

NNS Foundation

North London Charities Ltd

Community Foundation for Northern Ireland

The Nuffield Foundation

The Hamish Ogston Foundation

The Pears Family Charitable Foundation

The Jack Petchey Foundation

The Players Foundation

The Portal Trust

The Racing Foundation

The Rank Foundation Ltd

The Julia and Hans Rausing Trust

The Sigrid Rausing Trust

Reuben Foundation

The Robertson Trust

The Gerald and Gail Ronson Family Foundation

The Rothschild Foundation

Rothschild Foundation (Hanadiv) Europe

The Joseph Rowntree Charitable Trust

The Royal British Legion

The Royal Foundation of The Prince and Princess of Wales

The Royal Navy and Royal Marines Charity

The Samworth Foundation

Foundation Scotland

Shetland Charitable Trust

The Henry Smith Charity

Social Investment Business Foundation

Souter Charitable Trust

St James's Place Charitable Foundation

Stewards Company Ltd

The Stoller Charitable Trust

The Stone Family Foundation

Stephen Taylor Foundation

The Thompson Family Charitable Trust

Sir Jules Thorn Charitable Trust

The Tolkien Trust

Trust for London

The Tudor Trust

Community Foundation serving Tyne and Wear and Northumberland

UBS Optimus Foundation UK

UJIA (United Jewish Israel Appeal)

The UK Youth Fund: Thriving Minds

The Michael Uren Foundation

The Veolia Environmental Trust

Versus Arthritis

The Virgin Foundation (Virgin Unite)

The Vodafone Foundation

Volant Charitable Trust

The Waterloo Foundation

The Wellcome Trust

Westminster Foundation

The Garfield Weston Foundation

The Charles Wolfson Charitable Trust

The Wolfson Foundation

The Worwin UK Foundation

Yorkshire Cancer Research

Youth Endowment Fund (YEF)

Youth Music

Other publications and resources

The following publications and resources may also be of interest to readers of DGMT. They are all available directly from DSC by ringing 020 4526 5995 or visiting our website at www.dsc.org.uk.

Publications

The Guide to Grants for Individuals in Need

This best-selling funding guide gives details of a wide range of funds and other support available for the relief of individual poverty and hardship. It remains a key reference book for social workers, as well as the individuals themselves and those concerned with their welfare. It contains:

- Details on national and local charitable grant-makers which collectively give over £373 million a year towards the relief of individual poverty and hardship.

- Essential advice on applications for each source: eligibility; types of grant given; annual grant total; contact details.

- An example of how to make an effective application, and advice on finding the right sources to apply to.

The Guide to UK Company Giving

This invaluable guide offers insight into more than 400 companies in the UK that give a combined total of around £415 million in community contributions to voluntary and community organisations. It contains:

- Essential information on whom to contact within each company.

- Detailed information on cash and in-kind donations, employee-led support, sponsorship and details of CSR programmes.

- A section containing essential details on around 160 corporate charities.

The Guide to the Major Trusts

The in-depth research and independent comment that this flagship title offers has made it an essential reference guide for all fundraisers. This guide is the only source of independent critical analysis of grant-makers in practice. It includes:

- Essential information on the 1,000 largest grant makers which together give a total of over £7.33 billion.

- Clear descriptions of charities' policies and practices, as well as details of grant programmes, contact details, eligibility criteria and information on how to apply.

The Guide to New Trusts This popular guide offers essential details on newly established funders. It is a vital resource for anyone looking for fresh potential sources of funding for their organisation. The guide includes:

■ Research on around 100 newly registered grant-making charities.

■ Key funding guidelines, including grant-makers' aims and objectives, and stated policies.

■ Contact details and any available information that could help tailor your appeal.

Funds Online

DSC's funding website, Funds Online (www.fundsonline.org.uk) contains information on over 8,000 funders which make grants to organisations and individuals.

Some of the great features include:

■ Fast, intelligent and intuitive search function – locate the right funder for you within a few clicks.

■ User dashboard – track funding you have applied for, see new funding opportunities, and save searches and funders with ease.

■ Email alerts to let you know when funders you are interested in have been updated.

■ Great data and insight for multi-user account administrators – see how your subscription is being used to inform your decision-making.

There are four subscription options:

Grant-making charities funding organisations – information on over 4,500 grant-making charities giving a combined total of over £5.8 billion to organisations.

Grant-making charities funding individuals – details on around 3,400 charities that give to individuals for educational and welfare purposes. Collectively they give over £350 million each year.

Company giving for organisations – information on over 460 companies giving over £400 million per year in UK cash donations and in-kind support.

Government and statutory support for organisations – funding from local, regional and central government, and European sources.

Grant-makers by geographical area

This index contains the following:

List of geographical areas: This lists the geographical area headings used in DGMT.

Grant-makers by geographical area: Funders listed under the geographical areas for which they have expressed a funding preference. Asterisks mark funders which have not featured in DGMT before.

Grant-makers by geographical area

Worldwide

The 3Ts Charitable Trust
The A. S. Charitable Trust
ABF The Soldiers' Charity
abrdn Charitable Foundation
Achisomoch Aid Company Ltd
The Bryan Adams Foundation
Adenfirst Ltd
The Adlard Family Charitable
　Foundation
The Aimwell Charitable Trust
AKO Foundation
The Alborada Trust
The Alchemy Foundation
The Aldama Foundation
Al-Fayed Charitable Foundation
The Derrill Allatt Foundation
The Allen & Overy Foundation
The Allen Trust
The Almond Trust
Amabrill Ltd
Amant Foundation
The Anchor Foundation
Andrew Anderson Trust
Andor Charitable Trust
The Apax Foundation
Arcadia Fund
Ardbarron Trust Ltd
The Artemis Charitable
　Foundation
The Ove Arup Foundation
Ove Arup Partnership
　Charitable Trust
Ashburnham Thanksgiving
　Trust
The Ashworth Charitable Trust
The Associated Board of the
　Royal Schools of Music
　(ABRSM)
Atlas Memorial Ltd
The Aurora Trust (formerly The
　Ashden Trust)
The Aziz Foundation
The Austin Bailey Foundation
The Bamford Charitable
　Foundation
Veronica and Lars Bane
　Foundation
Robert Barr's Charitable Trust
The Batchworth Trust
Bay Charitable Trust
BC Partners Foundation
Beauland Ltd
Becht Foundation
Bedfordshire Charitable Trust
　Ltd
The Benham Charitable
　Settlement
The Bestway Foundation
The Michael Bishop
　Foundation
Lady Blakenham's Charity
　Trust
The Blandford Lake Trust
The Sir Victor Blank Charitable
　Settlement

The Blyth Charitable Trust
The Boltini Trust
The Boodle and Dunthorne
　Charitable Trust
The Salo Bordon Charitable
　Trust
The P. G. and N. J. Boulton
　Trust
The Britford Bridge Trust
The British Academy
The British and Foreign Bible
　Society
The British and Foreign School
　Society (BFSS)
The Rory and Elizabeth Brooks
　Foundation
The Brothers Trust
The Mary Brown Memorial
　Trust
The Brown Source Trust
R. S. Brownless Charitable
　Trust
Brushmill Ltd
The Buffini Chao Foundation
Bulb Foundation
The Burberry Foundation
Clara E. Burgess Charity
Burnie's Foundation
The Arnold Burton 1998
　Charitable Trust
The G. W. Cadbury Charitable
　Trust
The Barrow Cadbury Trust
The Candy Foundation
Cannon Charitable Trust
David William Traill Cargill
　Fund
Carlee Ltd
The Antonio Carluccio
　Foundation
The Casey Trust
Catholic Charitable Trust
The Thomas Sivewright Catto
　Charitable Settlement
The Charities Advisory Trust
Charitworth Ltd
The Cheruby Trust
Childs Charitable Trust
Christadelphian Samaritan
　Fund
The André Christian Trust
Chrysalis Trust
The Clarkson Foundation
The Clothworkers' Foundation
The Clover Trust
Clydpride Ltd
Denise Coates Foundation
The Cobalt Trust
The Vivienne and Samuel
　Cohen Charitable Trust
The R. and S. Cohen
　Foundation
The Coles-Medlock Foundation
The Coltstaple Trust
Comic Relief

The Alice Ellen Cooper-Dean
　Charitable Foundation
Marjorie Coote Animal Charity
　Trust
The Gershon Coren Charitable
　Foundation
Michael Cornish Charitable
　Trust
The Evan Cornish Foundation
The CPF Trust
The Cross Trust
Oizer Dalim Trust
The Danson Foundation*
The Davidson Family
　Charitable Trust
The Crispin Davis Family Trust
The Davis Foundation
Dawat-E-Hadiyah Trust (United
　Kingdom)
The Dawe Charitable Trust
The Roger De Haan Charitable
　Trust
The De Laszlo Foundation
The Miriam Dean Refugee
　Trust Fund
The Delves Charitable Trust
The Desmond Foundation
The Laduma Dhamecha
　Charitable Trust
The Dischma Charitable Trust
Donibristle Trust
The Dorfman Foundation
Dr. Martens Foundation
Dromintee Trust
The Mildred Duveen Charitable
　Trust
The James Dyson Foundation
EA Foundation*
Ebenezer Trust
The Ecology Trust
The Gilbert and Eileen Edgar
　Foundation
Edinburgh Trust No2 Account
Edupoor Ltd
The George Elias Charitable
　Trust
The Elie Trust
John Ellerman Foundation
Ellinson Foundation Ltd
The EQ Foundation
The Esfandi Charitable
　Foundation
Joseph Ettedgui Charitable
　Foundation
Euro Quality Foundation
The Beryl Evetts and Robert
　Luff Animal Welfare Trust
　Ltd
The Exilarch's Foundation
The Farthing Trust
Allan and Nesta Ferguson
　Charitable Settlement
Fine & Country Foundation
The Follett Trust
Fonthill Foundation
Forest Hill Charitable Trust

The Forrester Family Trust
The Anna Rosa Forster
 Charitable Trust
The Lord Forte Foundation
The Foster Wood Foundation
Four Acre Trust
Foux Foundation
The Foxglove Trust
The Freshfield Foundation
Friends of Boyan Trust
The Fulmer Charitable Trust
The Funding Network
The Gatsby Charitable
 Foundation
The Generations Foundation
The Gertner Charitable Trust
The Tara Getty Foundation
The Gibbs Charitable Trusts
The G. C. Gibson Charitable
 Trust
The B. and P. Glasser
 Charitable Trust
The Glass-House Trust
The Gloag Foundation
Sydney and Phyllis Goldberg
 Memorial Charitable Trust
The Golden Bottle Trust
The Goldman Sachs Charitable
 Gift Fund (UK)
Goldman Sachs Gives (UK)
The Jane Goodman Charitable
 Trust*
The Goodman Foundation
The Hemraj Goyal Foundation
Grace Charitable Trust
The Grace Trust
The Gisela Graham Foundation
Grahame Charitable
 Foundation Ltd
The Green Hall Foundation
The Green Room Charitable
 Trust
Philip and Judith Green Trust
The Grimmitt Trust
M. and R. Gross Charities Ltd
The Guy Foundation
H. and T. Clients Charitable
 Trust
H. P. Charitable Trust
The Hadley Trust
The Helen Hamlyn Trust
The Kathleen Hannay
 Memorial Charity
The Happold Foundation
The Haramead Trust
Harbinson Charitable Trust
The Harbour Foundation
The Peter and Teresa Harris
 Charitable Trust
The Hasluck Charitable Trust
The Maurice Hatter Foundation
The Dorothy Hay-Bolton
 Charitable Trust
The Heathside Charitable Trust
The Charlotte Heber-Percy
 Charitable Trust

The Michael Heller Charitable
 Foundation
The Simon Heller Charitable
 Settlement
The Highcroft Charitable Trust
Highway One Trust
The Hillier Trust
R. G. Hills Charitable Trust
Hinchley Charitable Trust
The Stuart Hine Trust CIO
The Hintze Family Charity
 Foundation
The Hiscox Foundation
Hockerill Educational
 Foundation
The Jane Hodge Foundation
The Holliday Foundation
Hollyhock Charitable
 Foundation
Sir Harold Hood's Charitable
 Trust
Hope Trust
The Thomas J. Horne
 Memorial Trust
The Sir Joseph Hotung
 Charitable Settlement
Michael and Shirley Hunt
 Charitable Trust
The Hunter Foundation
The Hunting Horn General
 Charitable Trust
The Hutton Foundation
The Harold Hyam Wingate
 Foundation
Ibrahim Foundation Ltd
IGO Foundation Ltd
The Ingram Trust
The Innocent Foundation
The Investindustrial
 Foundation
Investream Charitable Trust
The Invigorate Charitable Trust
The ITF Seafarers Trust
The J. A. R. Charitable Trust
The J. J. Charitable Trust
JAC Trust*
The Jagclif Charitable Trust
The Jephcott Charitable Trust
The Jerusalem Trust
Jewish Child's Day
Joffe Charitable Trust CIO
The Elton John AIDS
 Foundation
John Lewis and Partners
 Foundation
The Christopher and Kirsty
 Johnston Charitable Trust
The Muriel Jones Foundation
The Cyril and Eve Jumbo
 Charitable Trust
The Jusaca Charitable Trust
Kahal Chassidim Bobov
The Kasner Charitable Trust
The Michael and Ilse Katz
 Foundation

The Kennedy Trust for
 Rheumatology Research
The Kentown Wizard
 Foundation
The Nancy Kenyon Charitable
 Trust
Keren Association Ltd
E. and E. Kernkraut Charities
 Ltd
Fraser Kilpatrick Charitable
 Trust
The Kilroot Foundation
King/Cullimore Charitable
 Trust
Laura Kinsella Foundation
The Ernest Kleinwort
 Charitable Trust
Kollel and Co. Ltd
Kolyom Trust Ltd
The K. P. Ladd Charitable
 Trust
Maurice and Hilda Laing
 Charitable Trust
The David Laing Foundation
The Kirby Laing Foundation
The Lancashire Foundation
The Lauffer Family Charitable
 Foundation
Mrs F. B. Laurence Charitable
 Trust
The Law Society Charity
Ana Leaf Foundation*
The William Leech Charity
The Leigh Trust
The Mark Leonard Trust
The Ralph Levy Charitable
 Company Ltd
Cecil and Hilda Lewis
 Charitable Trust
David and Ruth Lewis Family
 Charitable Trust
The Sir Edward Lewis
 Foundation
The Limbourne Trust
The Linbury Trust
The Lister Charitable Trust
The Michael and Betty Little
 Trust*
The Second Joseph Aaron
 Littman Foundation
Jack Livingstone Charitable
 Trust
Lloyd's of London Foundation
Lloyd's Register Foundation
The Lyndal Tree Foundation
The Lyons Trust*
The Macdonald-Buchanan
 Charitable Trust
The Mackintosh Foundation
The John MacLeod Charitable
 Trust
The Mactaggart Third Fund
The Ian Mactaggart Trust
The Mageni Trust
The Mallinckrodt Foundation

The Manoukian Charitable
   Foundation
Marbeh Torah Trust
The Marchig Animal Welfare
   Trust
The Michael Marks Charitable
   Trust
Marmot Charitable Trust
The Martin Charitable Trust
The Master Charitable Trust
Material World Foundation
Mayfair Charities Ltd
Gemma and Chris McGough
   Charitable Foundation CIO
Melodor Ltd
The Melow Charitable Trust
Mercaz Torah Vechesed Ltd
The Brian Mercer Charitable
   Trust
Merchant Navy Welfare Board
Merriman Charitable
   Foundation*
T. and J. Meyer Family
   Foundation Ltd
The Mickel Fund
The Mila Charitable
   Organisation
The Millennium Oak Trust
The Millfield Trust
The Millichope Foundation
The Millward Charitable Trust
The Milne Family Foundation
The MK Charitable Trust
The Henry Moore Foundation
The Morel Charitable Trust
The Morris Charitable Trust
The Mosawi Foundation
Vyoel Moshe Charitable Trust
The Alexander Mosley
   Charitable Trust
Motor Neurone Disease
   Association
The Edwina Mountbatten and
   Leonora Children's
   Foundation
The Frederick Mulder
   Foundation
Brian Murtagh Charitable Trust
The Mutley Foundation
MW (CL) Foundation
MW (GK) Foundation
MW (HO) Foundation
MW (RH) Foundation
The NDL Foundation
Nemoral Ltd
Network for Social Change
   Charitable Trust
NNS Foundation
The Nomura Charitable Trust
The Northwick Trust
The Norton Rose Fulbright
   Charitable Foundation
The Oakdale Trust
Ocean Family Foundation
The Ofenheim Charitable Trust
The Ogle Christian Trust

The Hamish Ogston
   Foundation
The Olwyn Foundation
Open House Trust Ltd
Orange Tree Trust
The Orrin Charitable Trust
Ostro Fayre Share Foundation
Otsar Trust
The Ovo Charitable Foundation
The P27 Trust
The Paget Charitable Trust
The Paphitis Charitable Trust
The Paragon Trust
Susanna Peake Charitable
   Trust
The Pears Family Charitable
   Foundation
Dina Perelman Trust Ltd
Personal Assurance Charitable
   Trust
Petplan Charitable Trust
The Pharsalia Charitable Trust
The Pickwell Foundation
PIMCO Foundation Europe
The Pinchbeck Charitable Trust
Pink Ribbon Foundation
Polden-Puckham Charitable
   Foundation
The Portrack Charitable Trust
The Priory Foundation
The Privy Purse Charitable
   Trust
The Puebla Charitable Trust
Rachel Charitable Trust
The Bishop Radford Trust
The Rainford Trust
The Randal Charitable
   Foundation
The Sigrid Rausing Trust
Reuben Foundation
Rhodi Charitable Trust
The Rhododendron Trust
Riada Trust
Ridgesave Ltd
The River Farm Foundation
Rivers Foundation
The Roan Charitable Trust
The Rock Foundation
The Roddick Foundation
Mrs L. D. Rope's Third
   Charitable Settlement
The Eranda Rothschild
   Foundation
The Roughley Charitable Trust
Rowanville Ltd
The Joseph Rowntree
   Charitable Trust
The Royal Foundation of The
   Prince and Princess of
   Wales
RSM UK Foundation
The RWS Foundation
The S. M. B. Trust
The Dr Mortimer and Theresa
   Sackler Foundation

Erach and Roshan Sadri
   Foundation
The Jean Sainsbury Animal
   Welfare Trust
Saint Sarkis Charity Trust
The M. J. Samuel Charitable
   Trust
The Samworth Foundation
The Sandhu Charitable
   Foundation
The Sands Family Trust
The Sasha Foundation*
The Schmidt-Bodner Charitable
   Trust
The Anthony Scholefield
   Foundation
O. and G. Schreiber Charitable
   Trust
Schroder Charity Trust
The Schroder Foundation
The Scotshill Trust
Scouloudi Foundation
Seedfield Trust
The Segelman Trust
The Seven Fifty Trust
SF Foundation
The Shanley Charitable Trust
The Shears Foundation
The Archie Sherman Charitable
   Trust
Shlomo Memorial Fund Ltd
Shulem B. Association Ltd
The Simmons & Simmons
   Charitable Foundation
The Slaughter and May
   Charitable Trust
Kathleen Beryl Sleigh
   Charitable Trust
Rita and David Slowe
   Charitable Trust
Ruth Smart Foundation
Stanley Smith UK Horticultural
   Trust
Societe Generale UK
   Foundation
Songdale Ltd
The E. C. Sosnow Charitable
   Trust
Souter Charitable Trust
W. F. Southall Trust
Sparquote Ltd
Spears-Stutz Charitable Trust
Michael and Sarah Spencer
   Foundation
The Squires Foundation
St James's Place Charitable
   Foundation
Staples Trust
Starlow Charities Ltd
C. E. K. Stern Charitable Trust
The Sir Sigmund Sternberg
   Charitable Foundation
Stewards Company Ltd
Sir Halley Stewart Trust
The Stobart Newlands
   Charitable Trust

The Stone Family Foundation
Peter Stormonth Darling
    Charitable Trust
The Street Foundation
Sabina Sutherland Charitable
    Trust
Swarovski Foundation
The Hugh Symons Charitable
    Trust
Tabeel Trust
Talteg Ltd
The Tanlaw Foundation
Tanner Trust
C. B. and H. H. T. Taylor 1984
    Trust
Stephen Taylor Foundation
The Tedworth Charitable Trust
Scott Thomson Charitable
    Trust
The Thornton Trust
The Three Oaks Trust
The Thriplow Charitable Trust
Mrs R. P. Tindall's Charitable
    Trust
The Tomoro Foundation
The Tory Family Foundation
The Toy Trust
The Constance Travis
    Charitable Trust
The Trelix Charitable Trust*
Truedene Co. Ltd
The Trysil Charitable Trust
The James Tudor Foundation
Tzedakah
UBS Optimus Foundation UK
The Udlington Trust
Ulting Overseas Trust
The Ulverscroft Foundation
The Michael Uren Foundation
The Utley Foundation
The Valentine Charitable Trust
The Albert Van Den Bergh
    Charitable Trust
The Van Mesdag Fund
The Van Neste Foundation
The Vardy Foundation
Veg Trust Ltd (incorporating
    the Matthew Eyton Animal
    Welfare Trust)
Virgin Atlantic Foundation
The Vodafone Foundation
The Georg and Emily von Opel
    Foundation
The Barbara Ward Children's
    Foundation
The Waterloo Foundation
G. R. Waters Charitable Trust
    2000
The Wellcome Trust
Westhill Endowment
The Norman Whiteley Trust
Whitley Animal Protection Trust
Wickens Family Foundation
The H. D. H. Wills 1965
    Charitable Trust
The Wimbledon Foundation

The Charles Wolfson
    Charitable Trust
Woodlands Green Ltd
WWDP (World Day of Prayer
    National Committee for
    England, Wales and
    Northern Ireland)
Wychville Ltd
The Wyndham Charitable Trust
Yankov Charitable Trust
Zephyr Charitable Trust
The Zochonis Charitable Trust
Zurich Community Trust (UK)
    Ltd

Africa

AKO Foundation
Al Madad Foundation*
Anglo American Foundation
Veronica and Lars Bane
    Foundation
The Baring Foundation
The Boltini Trust
BOOST Charitable Trust
The Brenley Trust
The Noel Buxton Trust
William A. Cadbury Charitable
    Trust
The Childwick Trust
Corra Foundation
Credit Suisse EMEA
    Foundation
The Dashlight Foundation
The Miriam Dean Refugee
    Trust Fund
Didymus
Donibristle Trust
The Ecology Trust
The Gilbert and Eileen Edgar
    Foundation
The Eighty Eight Foundation
The Gatsby Charitable
    Foundation
The James Grace Trust
The Charles Hayward
    Foundation
The Headley Trust
Heb Ffin (Without Frontier)
The Hilden Charitable Fund
The Hunting Horn General
    Charitable Trust
The Indigo Trust
The J. J. Charitable Trust
The Frank Jackson Foundation
The Jerusalem Trust
The Kavli Trust
Maurice and Hilda Laing
    Charitable Trust
The Kirby Laing Foundation
The Beatrice Laing Trust
Lancaster Foundation
The Leeward Trust
Lord and Lady Lurgan Trust
Medical Research Foundation
The Morel Charitable Trust

Morgan Stanley International
    Foundation
NNS Foundation
Parabola Foundation
David and Elaine Potter
    Foundation
The Raindance Charitable
    Trust
The Rambourg Foundation
The Eleanor Rathbone
    Charitable Trust
The Clive Richards Foundation
The Alan and Babette
    Sainsbury Charitable Fund
The Scott Bader
    Commonwealth Ltd
Rita and David Slowe
    Charitable Trust
The Peter Stebbings Memorial
    Charity
The Sterry Family Foundation
Stolkin Foundation
The Stone Family Foundation
The Gay and Keith Talbot Trust
Mrs R. P. Tindall's Charitable
    Trust
The Tolkien Trust
The True Colours Trust
The Tudor Trust
The Union of the Sisters of
    Mercy of Great Britain
The Virgin Foundation (Virgin
    Unite)
The Scurrah Wainwright Charity
The Windfall Foundation
The Wood Foundation
The Edward and Catherine
    Wray Charitable Trust
The Wyfold Charitable Trust
The Zochonis Charitable Trust

Asia (excluding Israel)

AKO Foundation
Al Madad Foundation*
Alliance Family Foundation Ltd
The Arah Foundation
The Asfari Foundation
Bagri Foundation
Bairdwatson Charitable Trust
Bally's Foundation
Veronica and Lars Bane
    Foundation
The Bestway Foundation
The Boltini Trust
Byrne Family Foundation
William A. Cadbury Charitable
    Trust
CareTech Charitable
    Foundation
Credit Suisse EMEA
    Foundation
The Daiwa Anglo-Japanese
    Foundation

The Miriam Dean Refugee
  Trust Fund
Donibristle Trust
The DWF Charitable
  Foundation
The Ecology Trust
Eight Strands Foundation
The Hemraj Goyal Foundation
The James Grace Trust
The Great Britain Sasakawa
  Foundation
The Walter Guinness
  Charitable Trust
Paul Hamlyn Foundation
The Helen Hamlyn Trust
HFC Help for Children UK Ltd
The Hinduja Foundation
The Jerusalem Trust
J. E. Joseph Charitable Fund
The Kavli Trust
The Kiawah Charitable Trust
Kusuma Trust UK
The Kirby Laing Foundation
The Beatrice Laing Trust
The Leeward Trust
The Matliwala Family
  Charitable Trust
The Mittal Foundation
Morgan Stanley International
  Foundation
Open House Trust Ltd
Ostro Fayre Share Foundation
The Parivar Trust
John Pearce Foundation
The Queen Anne's Gate
  Foundation
The Eleanor Rathbone
  Charitable Trust
Rhodi Charitable Trust
The Clive Richards Foundation
Erach and Roshan Sadri
  Foundation
The Scott Bader
  Commonwealth Ltd
The Serco Foundation
The Shoe Zone Trust
The Sino-British Fellowship
  Trust
The Stone Family Foundation
The Gay and Keith Talbot Trust
Mrs R. P. Tindall's Charitable
  Trust
The Union of the Sisters of
  Mercy of Great Britain

Central and South America

Anglo American Foundation
William A. Cadbury Charitable
  Trust
Didymus
The Karlsson Játiva Charitable
  Foundation
The Leeward Trust

The Scott Bader
  Commonwealth Ltd
The Sunrise Foundation CIO
The Virgin Foundation (Virgin
  Unite)

Europe

Al Madad Foundation*
Alliance Family Foundation Ltd
ArtSocial Foundation
Bally's Foundation
Veronica and Lars Bane
  Foundation
William A. Cadbury Charitable
  Trust
The CIBC World Markets
  Children's Foundation
Credit Suisse EMEA
  Foundation
Donibristle Trust
The DWF Charitable
  Foundation
The Ecology Trust
The Peter and Teresa Harris
  Charitable Trust
The Headley Trust
The Investindustrial
  Foundation
The Karlsson Játiva Charitable
  Foundation
Keren Association Ltd
Kusuma Trust UK
The Martin Laing Foundation
The Lyndal Tree Foundation
Merchant Navy Welfare Board
Morgan Stanley International
  Foundation
The Polonsky Foundation
QBE European Operations
  Foundation
The Rambourg Foundation
The Joseph and Lena Randall
  Charitable Trust
Rothschild Foundation
  (Hanadiv) Europe
The Scott Bader
  Commonwealth Ltd
The Serco Foundation
Sofronie Foundation
The T.K. Maxx and
  Homesense Foundation
The Tolkien Trust
The Union of the Sisters of
  Mercy of Great Britain
The Georg and Emily von Opel
  Foundation
The Galen and Hilary Weston
  Foundation
The Maurice Wohl Charitable
  Foundation

Israel

4 Charity Foundation
A. W. Charitable Trust
Alliance Family Foundation Ltd
Atkin Charitable Foundation
Atlas Memorial Ltd
The Max Barney Foundation
The Beaverbrooks Charitable
  Trust
Benesco Charity Ltd
Ruth Berkowitz Charitable
  Trust
The John Black Charitable
  Foundation
The Bertie Black Foundation
Abraham Algy Bloom
  Foundation
The Bluston Charitable
  Settlement
The Salo Bordon Charitable
  Trust
The CH (1980) Charitable
  Trust
Charitworth Ltd
CMZ Ltd
The Vivienne and Samuel
  Cohen Charitable Trust
The R. and S. Cohen
  Foundation
Col-Reno Ltd
The Gershon Coren Charitable
  Foundation
Itzchok Meyer Cymerman Trust
  Ltd
The D. M. Charitable Trust
The Manny and Brigitta
  Davidson Charitable
  Foundation
The Davis Foundation
The Henry and Suzanne Davis
  Foundation
Debmar Benevolent Trust Ltd
The Djanogly Foundation
Dollond Charitable Trust
The Doughty Charity Trust
Dushinsky Trust Ltd
Entindale Ltd
The Esfandi Charitable
  Foundation
The Exilarch's Foundation
Extonglen Ltd
Famos Foundation Trust
The Isaac and Freda Frankel
  Memorial Charitable Trust
Friends of Wiznitz Ltd
The Gatsby Charitable
  Foundation
The Gertner Charitable Trust
M. and R. Gross Charities Ltd
The Harbour Foundation
The Maurice Hatter Foundation
The Humanitarian Trust
The Huntingdon Foundation
  Ltd
Investream Charitable Trust
Jewish Child's Day

J. E. Joseph Charitable Fund
The Jusaca Charitable Trust
The Ian Karten Charitable
    Trust
The Kasner Charitable Trust
The Kennedy Leigh Charitable
    Trust
Keren Association Ltd
Kupath Gemach Chaim
    Bechesed Viznitz Trust
The Lauffer Family Charitable
    Foundation
Joseph Levy Foundation
Cecil and Hilda Lewis
    Charitable Trust
Jack Livingstone Charitable
    Trust
The Locker Foundation
Sir Jack Lyons Charitable Trust
The M. Y. A. Charitable Trust
The Manackerman Charitable
    Trust
The Manson Family Charitable
    Trust
Marbeh Torah Trust
The Stella and Alexander
    Margulies Charitable Trust
Mayfair Charities Ltd
Mayheights Ltd
Melodor Ltd
The Melow Charitable Trust
Mercaz Torah Vechesed Ltd
Vyoel Moshe Charitable Trust
The Mutley Foundation
The Mutual Trust Group
Ner Foundation
Newpier Charity Ltd
The Polonsky Foundation
Porter Foundation
R. S. Charitable Trust
Reuben Foundation
The Rofeh Trust
The Gerald and Gail Ronson
    Family Foundation
The Cecil Rosen Foundation
Rothschild Foundation
    (Hanadiv) Europe
Rowanville Ltd
The Jeremy and John Sacher
    Charitable Trust
The Sam and Bella Sebba
    Charitable Foundation
Sellata Ltd
SF Foundation
Shlomo Memorial Fund Ltd
Songdale Ltd
The E. C. Sosnow Charitable
    Trust
The Steinberg Family
    Charitable Trust
C. E. K. Stern Charitable Trust
The Sir Sigmund Sternberg
    Charitable Foundation
Stervon Ltd
The David Tannen Charitable
    Trust

Mrs R. P. Tindall's Charitable
    Trust
Trumros Ltd
Tzedakah
UJIA (United Jewish Israel
    Appeal)
The Velvet Foundation
VHLT Ltd
The Linda and Michael
    Weinstein Charitable Trust
The Maurice Wohl Charitable
    Foundation
The Charles Wolfson
    Charitable Trust
The Wolfson Family Charitable
    Trust

North America

AKO Foundation
Alliance Family Foundation Ltd
Bally's Foundation
Becht Foundation
Bennett Lowell Ltd
The Brothers Trust
The G. W. Cadbury Charitable
    Trust
CMZ Ltd
The DWF Charitable
    Foundation
The Exilarch's Foundation
Family Philanthropy Ltd
Friends of Wiznitz Ltd
The Investindustrial
    Foundation
The Lauffer Family Charitable
    Foundation
Melodor Ltd
The Mittal Foundation
The Mutual Trust Group
NNS Foundation
The Polonsky Foundation
The Rambourg Foundation
The Gerald and Gail Ronson
    Family Foundation
The Dr Mortimer and Theresa
    Sackler Foundation
The Scott Bader
    Commonwealth Ltd
The Sam and Bella Sebba
    Charitable Foundation
SF Foundation
Shlomo Memorial Fund Ltd
Surgo Foundation UK Ltd

Oceania

Anglo American Foundation
The DWF Charitable
    Foundation
The Girdlers' Company
    Charitable Trust
The Scott Bader
    Commonwealth Ltd

The Virgin Foundation (Virgin
    Unite)

United Kingdom

The 29th May 1961 Charitable Trust
The 3Ts Charitable Trust
4 Charity Foundation
The 4814 Trust
The 64 Trust*
The A Team Foundation Ltd
The A. and J. Charitable Trust
The A. B. Charitable Trust
The A. S. Charitable Trust
The Abbeyfield Research Foundation
ABF The Soldiers' Charity
abrdn Charitable Foundation
abrdn Financial Fairness Trust
The Access to Justice Foundation
Achisomoch Aid Company Ltd
Action Medical Research
The Bryan Adams Foundation
The Adint Charitable Trust
The AIM Foundation
The Aimwell Charitable Trust
Sylvia Aitken's Charitable Trust
AJ Bell Trust
Al Madad Foundation*
The Alborada Trust
The Alchemy Foundation
The Aldama Foundation
Al-Fayed Charitable Foundation
AlixPartners (UK) Charitable Foundation
The Derrill Allatt Foundation
D. C. R. Allen Charitable Trust
Alliance Family Foundation Ltd
The Almond Trust
Alpkit Foundation
Alzheimer's Research UK
Alzheimer's Society
Amabrill Ltd
Amant Foundation
Ambergate Charitable Trust
The Ampersand Foundation
The AMW Charitable Trust
The Anchor Foundation
Andrew Anderson Trust
Andor Charitable Trust
Anglo American Foundation
The Anson Charitable Trust
AO Smile Foundation
The Apax Foundation
The Annabel Arbib Foundation
The Archer Trust
The Architectural Heritage Fund
Ardbarron Trust Ltd
The Ardeola Charitable Trust
Armed Forces Covenant Fund Trust
Armed Forces Education Trust
The Armourers and Brasiers Gauntlet Trust
The Art Fund
The Artemis Charitable Foundation

Douglas Arter Foundation
ArtSocial Foundation
The Ove Arup Foundation
Ove Arup Partnership Charitable Trust
The Asfari Foundation
Ashburnham Thanksgiving Trust
The Ashworth Charitable Trust
The Ian Askew Charitable Trust
The Associated Board of the Royal Schools of Music (ABRSM)
Asthma and Lung UK
The Astor Foundation
Atkin Charitable Foundation
The Atlas Fund
Atlas Memorial Ltd
The Aurelius Charitable Trust
The Aurora Trust (formerly The Ashden Trust)
The Aziz Foundation
B&Q Foundation
Backstage Trust
Bagri Foundation
The Baily Thomas Charitable Fund
Bally's Foundation
The Bamford Charitable Foundation
The Band Trust
Veronica and Lars Bane Foundation
The Banister Charitable Trust
The Barbers' Company General Charities
The Barbour Foundation
Barcapel Foundation Ltd
The Baring Foundation
The Michael Barnard Charitable Trust
Lord Barnby's Foundation
Barnsbury Charitable Trust
Misses Barrie Charitable Trust
Robert Barr's Charitable Trust
Bay Charitable Trust
The Bay Tree Charitable Trust
BBC Children in Need
BC Partners Foundation
Bear Mordechai Ltd
The Beaverbrooks Charitable Trust
Becht Foundation
The David and Ruth Behrend Fund
Benefact Trust Ltd
Benesco Charity Ltd
The Benham Charitable Settlement
Bennett Lowell Ltd
Ruth Berkowitz Charitable Trust
The Bestway Foundation
The Billmeir Charitable Trust
The Percy Bilton Charity
Binks Trust

Birkdale Trust for Hearing Impaired Ltd*
The Michael Bishop Foundation
Maria Bjornson Memorial Fund
The John Black Charitable Foundation
The Sydney Black Charitable Trust
The Bertie Black Foundation
Lady Blakenham's Charity Trust
The Sir Victor Blank Charitable Settlement
Bloodwise
Abraham Algy Bloom Foundation
The Bloomfield Charitable Trust
Bluespark Foundation
The Bluston Charitable Settlement
Blyth Watson Charitable Trust
BNA Charitable Incorporated Organisation
The Boltini Trust
The Bonamy Charitable Trust
The Charlotte Bonham-Carter Charitable Trust
BOOST Charitable Trust
The Salo Bordon Charitable Trust
The Bosson Family Charitable Trust
The Bothwell Charitable Trust
The P. G. and N. J. Boulton Trust
Sir Clive Bourne Family Trust
Bourneheights Ltd
G. and K. Boyes Charitable Trust
The William Brake Charitable Trust
The Liz and Terry Bramall Foundation
Breast Cancer Now
The Brenley Trust
Bristol Charities
The BRIT Trust
The Britford Bridge Trust
The British Academy
The British and Foreign School Society (BFSS)
British Eye Research Foundation (Fight for Sight)
British Heart Foundation (BHF)
British Humane Association
British Motor Sports Training Trust
The Bromley Trust
The Brook Trust
The Rory and Elizabeth Brooks Foundation
The Brothers Trust
The Mary Brown Memorial Trust

The Brown Source Trust
R. S. Brownless Charitable
    Trust
T. B. H. Brunner's Charitable
    Settlement
Brushmill Ltd
Buckingham Trust
The Buffini Chao Foundation
Building and Civil Engineering
    Charitable Trust
Bulb Foundation
The Bulldog Trust Ltd
Bupa Foundation
The Burberry Foundation
The Burden Trust
The Burdett Trust for Nursing
Clara E. Burgess Charity
Burnie's Foundation
The Arnold Burton 1998
    Charitable Trust
C. and F. Charitable Trust
The G. W. Cadbury Charitable
    Trust
William A. Cadbury Charitable
    Trust
The Cadbury Foundation
The Barrow Cadbury Trust
The Cadogan Charity
M. J. Camp Charitable
    Foundation
Cancer Research UK
The Frederick and Phyllis Cann
    Trust
Cannon Charitable Trust
Card Factory Foundation
CareTech Charitable
    Foundation
Carew Pole Charitable Trust
David William Traill Cargill
    Fund
The Antonio Carluccio
    Foundation
The Carpenters Company
    Charitable Trust
The Carrington Charitable
    Trust
The Leslie Mary Carter
    Charitable Trust
The Casey Trust
The Castanea Trust
Catholic Charitable Trust
Catkin Pussywillow Charitable
    Trust
The Thomas Sivewright Catto
    Charitable Settlement
The Cayo Foundation
The B. G. S. Cayzer Charitable
    Trust
Elizabeth Cayzer Charitable
    Trust
The Cazenove Charitable Trust
CEO Sleepout
The CH (1980) Charitable
    Trust
The Amelia Chadwick Trust
Chapman Charitable Trust

The Charities Advisory Trust
Charitworth Ltd
Chartered Accountants' Livery
    Charity (CALC)
The Lorna and Yuti
    Chernajovsky Biomedical
    Research Foundation
The Cheruby Trust
The Chetwode Foundation
Children with Cancer UK
Childs Charitable Trust
CHK Foundation
Christadelphian Samaritan
    Fund
The André Christian Trust
Chrysalis Trust
The Churchill Foundation
The CIBC World Markets
    Children's Foundation
The Roger and Sarah Bancroft
    Clark Charitable Trust
Clinks*
The Clore Duffield Foundation
The Clothworkers' Foundation
The Clover Trust
The Robert Clutterbuck
    Charitable Trust
CMZ Ltd
The Francis Coales Charitable
    Foundation
Denise Coates Foundation
The Cobalt Trust
The Vivienne and Samuel
    Cohen Charitable Trust
The John S. Cohen Foundation
The R. and S. Cohen
    Foundation
The Coles-Medlock Foundation
Sir Jeremiah Colman Gift Trust
Col-Reno Ltd
The Colt Foundation
Colwinston Charitable Trust
Comic Relief
The Comino Foundation
The Company of Actuaries
    Charitable Trust Fund
Congregational and General
    Charitable Trust
The Ernest Cook Trust
The Cooks Charity
The Catherine Cookson
    Charitable Trust
The Keith Coombs Trust
Co-op Foundation
Mabel Cooper Charity
The Alice Ellen Cooper-Dean
    Charitable Foundation
Marjorie Coote Animal Charity
    Trust
The Gershon Coren Charitable
    Foundation
Michael Cornish Charitable
    Trust
The Corporation of Trinity
    House of Deptford Strond

The Costa Family Charitable
    Trust
The Cotton Industry War
    Memorial Trust
The Coulthurst Trust
Countypier Ltd
Coutts Charitable Foundation
The Noel Coward Foundation
Dudley and Geoffrey Cox
    Charitable Trust
The Lord Cozens-Hardy Trust
The CPF Trust
Craignish Trust
CRASH
The Elizabeth Creak Charitable
    Trust
Credit Suisse EMEA
    Foundation
The Cross Trust
CSIS Charity Fund
Cullum Family Trust
Itzchok Meyer Cymerman Trust
    Ltd
The D. G. Charitable
    Settlement
The D. M. Charitable Trust
The Daiwa Anglo-Japanese
    Foundation
Oizer Dalim Trust
The Danson Foundation*
The Dashlight Foundation
The David Family Foundation*
The Manny and Brigitta
    Davidson Charitable
    Foundation
The Davidson Family
    Charitable Trust
Michael Davies Charitable
    Settlement
The Davis Foundation
Dawat-E-Hadiyah Trust (United
    Kingdom)
The Dawe Charitable Trust
The De Laszlo Foundation
William Dean Countryside and
    Educational Trust
Debmar Benevolent Trust Ltd
The Delius Trust
The Delves Charitable Trust
Dentons UK and Middle East
    LLP Charitable Trust
The J. N. Derbyshire Trust
The Desmond Foundation
The Laduma Dhamecha
    Charitable Trust
Diabetes UK
The Alan and Sheila Diamond
    Charitable Trust
Dinwoodie Charitable Company
The Djanogly Foundation
The DLM Charitable Trust
The Ken Dodd Charitable
    Foundation
Dollond Charitable Trust
Donibristle Trust
The Dorcas Trust

The Dorfman Foundation
The Dorus Trust
The Double 'O' Charity Ltd
The D'Oyly Carte Charitable Trust
Dromintee Trust
Dunard Fund
The Dunhill Medical Trust
The Dunn Family Charitable Trust
The Charles Dunstone Charitable Trust
Dushinsky Trust Ltd
The Mildred Duveen Charitable Trust
The DWF Charitable Foundation
The Dyers' Company Charitable Trust
The James Dyson Foundation
E. B. M. Charitable Trust
Audrey Earle Charitable Trust
Sir John Eastwood Foundation
Ebenezer Trust
The Ecology Trust
The Economist Charitable Trust
The Gilbert and Eileen Edgar Foundation
Edinburgh Trust No2 Account
Edupoor Ltd
W. G. Edwards Charitable Foundation
Eight Strands Foundation
The Eighty Eight Foundation
The George Elias Charitable Trust
The Elie Trust
The Ellerdale Trust
John Ellerman Foundation
Emerton-Christie Charity
EMI Music Sound Foundation
Entindale Ltd
Epilepsy Research UK
The EQ Foundation
The Esfandi Charitable Foundation
The Essex Youth Trust
The Ethos Foundation
Joseph Ettedgui Charitable Foundation
Euro Quality Foundation
The Eventhall Family Charitable Trust
The Everard Foundation
Eversheds Sutherland (International) Charitable Trust
The Beryl Evetts and Robert Luff Animal Welfare Trust Ltd
The Exilarch's Foundation
The ExPat Foundation
Extonglen Ltd
G. F. Eyre Charitable Trust
Esmée Fairbairn Foundation

The Fairness Foundation
The Fairstead Trust
Family Philanthropy Ltd
Famos Foundation Trust
The Lord Faringdon Charitable Trust
Samuel William Farmer Trust
Fat Face Foundation*
The February Foundation
The A. M. Fenton Trust
Allan and Nesta Ferguson Charitable Settlement
The Fidelio Charitable Trust
The Fidelity UK Foundation
Doris Field Charitable Trust
The Finborough Foundation
Dixie Rose Findlay Charitable Trust
Fine & Country Foundation
The Finnis Scott Foundation
Sir John Fisher Foundation
Marc Fitch Fund
The Earl Fitzwilliam Charitable Trust
The Joyce Fletcher Charitable Trust
The Mrs Yvonne Flux Charitable Trust
The Follett Trust
The Forbes Charitable Foundation
Oliver Ford Foundation
Fordeve Ltd
Forest Hill Charitable Trust
The Forman Hardy Charitable Trust
The Forrester Family Trust
The Anna Rosa Forster Charitable Trust
The Lord Forte Foundation
The Foster Wood Foundation
Four Acre Trust
The Foyle Foundation
Mrs D. M. France-Hayhurst Foundation
The Isaac and Freda Frankel Memorial Charitable Trust
The Elizabeth Frankland Moore and Star Foundation
The Gordon Fraser Charitable Trust
The Louis and Valerie Freedman Charitable Settlement
The Freelands Foundation Ltd
The Freshfield Foundation
Friarsgate Trust
Friends of Boyan Trust
Friends of the National Libraries
Friends Provident Charitable Foundation
Frognal Trust
The Patrick and Helena Frost Foundation
The Fulmer Charitable Trust

The Funding Network
G. M. C. Trust
The Gale Family Charity Trust
The Garrick Charitable Trust
The Gatsby Charitable Foundation
The Robert Gavron Charitable Trust
Sir Robert Geffery's Almshouse Trust
The Generational Foundation*
The Generations Foundation
The Gertner Charitable Trust
The Tara Getty Foundation
J. Paul Getty Jr General Charitable Trust*
The Gibbs Charitable Trusts
The G. C. Gibson Charitable Trust
The B. and P. Glasser Charitable Trust
The Glass-House Trust
The Gloag Foundation
Global Charities
Sydney and Phyllis Goldberg Memorial Charitable Trust
The Goldcrest Charitable Trust
The Golden Bottle Trust
The Goldman Sachs Charitable Gift Fund (UK)
The Goldsmiths' Company Charity
The Golf Foundation
The Golsoncott Foundation
Matthew Good Foundation*
Nicholas and Judith Goodison's Charitable Settlement
The Goodman Foundation
The Mike Gooley Trailfinders Charity
The Gosling Foundation Ltd
The Edward Gostling Foundation
Gowling WLG (UK) Charitable Trust
The Hemraj Goyal Foundation
Grace Baptist Trust Corporation*
Grace Charitable Trust
The Grace Trust
The James Grace Trust
Graff Foundation
The Gisela Graham Foundation
The Graham Trust
Grahame Charitable Foundation Ltd
GrantScape
The Great Britain Sasakawa Foundation
The Freddie Green and Family Charitable Foundation*
The Kenneth and Susan Green Charitable Foundation
The Green Hall Foundation

The Green Room Charitable
Trust
Philip and Judith Green Trust
The Greenslade Family
Foundation
The Gretna Charitable Trust
The Grocers' Charity
Groundwork UK
The Walter Guinness
Charitable Trust
Calouste Gulbenkian
Foundation – UK Branch
H. and T. Clients Charitable
Trust
H. P. Charitable Trust
The Hadley Trust
Hamamelis Trust
Paul Hamlyn Foundation
The Helen Hamlyn Trust
The Kathleen Hannay
Memorial Charity
The Haramead Trust
Harbinson Charitable Trust
The Harbour Foundation
The Harding Trust
The Harebell Centenary Fund
The Hargreaves Foundation
The Harris Family Charitable
Trust
The Peter Harrison Foundation
The Harrison-Frank Family
Foundation (UK) Ltd
The Hasluck Charitable Trust
The Maurice Hatter Foundation
The Hawthorne Charitable
Trust
The Charles Hayward
Foundation
The Headley Trust
The Health Foundation
Heart Research UK
The Heathside Charitable Trust
The Charlotte Heber-Percy
Charitable Trust
Ernest Hecht Charitable
Foundation
The Percy Hedley 1990
Charitable Trust
The Hedley Foundation
The Michael Heller Charitable
Foundation
The Simon Heller Charitable
Settlement
The Helping Foundation
The Trevor Hemmings
Foundation
Henley Royal Regatta
Charitable Trust
The G. D. Herbert Charitable
Trust
Heritage Lottery Fund
The Highcroft Charitable Trust
Highway One Trust
The Hilden Charitable Fund
The Derek Hill Foundation

The Alison Hillman Charitable
Trust*
R. G. Hills Charitable Trust
Hinchley Charitable Trust
The Hinduja Foundation
The Stuart Hine Trust CIO
The Hinrichsen Foundation
The Hintze Family Charity
Foundation
The Hiscox Foundation
The Henry C. Hoare Charitable
Trust
The Hobson Charity Ltd
Hockerill Educational
Foundation
The Jane Hodge Foundation
The Holbeck Charitable Trust
The Holden Charitable Trust
Hollick Family Foundation
The Holliday Foundation
Hollyhock Charitable
Foundation
Homelands Charitable Trust
Sir Harold Hood's Charitable
Trust
The Thomas J. Horne
Memorial Trust
The Horse Trust
Horwich Shotter Charitable
Trust
The Hosking Charitable Trust*
Hospice UK
The Hospital Saturday Fund
The Sir Joseph Hotung
Charitable Settlement
The Reta Lila Howard
Foundation
James T. Howat Charitable
Trust
The Huggard Charitable Trust
The Humanitarian Trust
Michael and Shirley Hunt
Charitable Trust
The Albert Hunt Trust
The Hunter Foundation
The Hunting Horn General
Charitable Trust
The Huntingdon Foundation
Ltd
The Hutchinson Charitable
Trust
The Hutton Foundation
The Nani Huyu Charitable Trust
The Harold Hyam Wingate
Foundation
Ibrahim Foundation Ltd
The Iceland Foods Charitable
Foundation
The Idlewild Trust
The Iliffe Family Charitable
Trust
Imagine Foundation
Impetus
The Indigo Trust
The Ingram Trust
The Inlight Trust

The Inman Charity
The Institute for Policy
Research
The International Bankers
Charitable Trust
The Inverforth Charitable Trust
Investream Charitable Trust
The Invigorate Charitable Trust
The Ireland Fund of Great
Britain
Irish Youth Foundation (UK)
Ltd (incorporating The
Lawlor Foundation)
The Irving Memorial Trust
The Isla Foundation
The ITF Seafarers Trust
The J. J. Charitable Trust
The Jabbs Foundation
JAC Trust*
The Frank Jackson Foundation
The Jagclif Charitable Trust
The Susan and Stephen
James Charitable
Settlement
Jay Education Trust
JD Foundation
The Jenour Foundation
The Jephcott Charitable Trust
The Jerusalem Trust
Jewish Child's Day
The Jewish Youth Fund
The Elton John AIDS
Foundation
John Lewis and Partners
Foundation
Lillie Johnson Charitable Trust
Johnnie Johnson Trust
The Christopher and Kirsty
Johnston Charitable Trust
The Muriel Jones Foundation
The Joron Charitable Trust
The Cyril and Eve Jumbo
Charitable Trust
Anton Jurgens Charitable Trust
The Jusaca Charitable Trust
The Boris Karloff Charitable
Foundation
The Karlsson Játiva Charitable
Foundation
The Ian Karten Charitable
Trust
The Kasner Charitable Trust
The Michael and Ilse Katz
Foundation
C. S. Kaufman Charitable
Trust
The Kavli Trust
The Emmanuel Kaye
Foundation
The Kelly Family Charitable
Trust
The Kennedy Leigh Charitable
Trust
The Kennel Club Charitable
Trust

The Kentown Wizard Foundation

The Nancy Kenyon Charitable Trust

Keren Association Ltd

E. and E. Kernkraut Charities Ltd

KFC Foundation

The Kiawah Charitable Trust

Kidney Research UK

Fraser Kilpatrick Charitable Trust

The Kilroot Foundation

The Mary Kinross Charitable Trust

Laura Kinsella Foundation

The Graham Kirkham Foundation

The Ernest Kleinwort Charitable Trust

The Kobler Trust

The KPMG Foundation

Kreditor Charitable Trust

The Kreitman Foundation

Kupath Gemach Chaim Bechesed Viznitz Trust

Kusuma Trust UK

The Kyte Charitable Trust

Ladbrokes Coral Trust

The K. P. Ladd Charitable Trust

John Laing Charitable Trust

Maurice and Hilda Laing Charitable Trust

Christopher Laing Foundation

The David Laing Foundation

The Kirby Laing Foundation

The Martin Laing Foundation

The Beatrice Laing Trust

The Lancashire Foundation

Lancaster Foundation

LandAid Charitable Trust Ltd (LandAid)

The Allen Lane Foundation

Langdale Trust

The LankellyChase Foundation

Mrs M. A. Lascelles Charitable Trust

The Lauffer Family Charitable Foundation

Mrs F. B. Laurence Charitable Trust

The Law Family Charitable Foundation

The Law Society Charity

The Richard Lawes Foundation

The Edgar E. Lawley Foundation

Lawson Beckman Charitable Trust

The Leach Fourteenth Trust

Ana Leaf Foundation*

The Leathersellers' Foundation

The Leche Trust

The Arnold Lee Charitable Trust

Leeds Building Society Foundation

The Leeward Trust

The Legal Education Foundation

Sarah Jane Leigh Charitable Trust*

The Leigh Trust

The Mark Leonard Trust

The Leri Charitable Trust

The Leverhulme Trust

Lord Leverhulme's Charitable Trust

The Ralph Levy Charitable Company Ltd

Joseph Levy Foundation

Cecil and Hilda Lewis Charitable Trust

Bernard Lewis Family Charitable Trust

David and Ruth Lewis Family Charitable Trust

The Charles Lewis Foundation

The Sir Edward Lewis Foundation

Liberum Foundation

The Lightbulb Trust*

The Limbourne Trust

Limoges Charitable Trust

The Linbury Trust

The Linder Foundation

The Lister Charitable Trust

The Frank Litchfield Charitable Trust

The Charles Littlewood Hill Trust

The Second Joseph Aaron Littman Foundation

The George John and Sheilah Livanos Charitable Trust

The Livingbridge Foundation*

The Ian and Natalie Livingstone Charitable Trust

Jack Livingstone Charitable Trust

The Elaine and Angus Lloyd Charitable Trust

The Andrew Lloyd Webber Foundation

Localtrent Ltd

The Locker Foundation

The London Marathon Charitable Trust Ltd

Lords Group Foundation*

The Lord's Taverners

The Lower Green Foundation

The C. L. Loyd Charitable Trust

LPW Ltd

Robert Luff Foundation Ltd

Lord and Lady Lurgan Trust

The Lyndal Tree Foundation

Sir Jack Lyons Charitable Trust

The Lyons Trust*

M. and C. Trust

M. B. Foundation

The M. Y. A. Charitable Trust

The Macdonald-Buchanan Charitable Trust

Mace Foundation

The Mackintosh Foundation

The John MacLeod Charitable Trust

The MacRobert Trust 2019

The Mactaggart Third Fund

The Ian Mactaggart Trust

The Magen Charitable Trust

The Mageni Trust

Magnify Foundation*

The Mahoro Charitable Trust

Making a Difference Locally Ltd

The Mallinckrodt Foundation

Man Group plc Charitable Trust

The Manackerman Charitable Trust

The W. M. Mann Foundation

The Manoukian Charitable Foundation

The Manson Family Charitable Trust

The Marandi Foundation

Marbeh Torah Trust

The Marchig Animal Welfare Trust

The Stella and Alexander Margulies Charitable Trust

The Michael Marks Charitable Trust

The Marks Family Charitable Trust

Marmot Charitable Trust

The Marque Foundation

The Marsh Christian Trust

Charlotte Marshall Charitable Trust

The Martin Charitable Trust

The Kristina Martin Charitable Trust

The Dan Maskell Tennis Trust

The Master Charitable Trust

Matchroom Sport Charitable Foundation

Material World Foundation

The Mather Family Charitable Trust

The Matliwala Family Charitable Trust

The Violet Mauray Charitable Trust

Mayfair Charities Ltd

The Mayfield Valley Arts Trust

Mazars Charitable Trust

The Robert McAlpine Foundation

The McCarthy Stone Foundation

D. D. McPhail Charitable Settlement

Medical Research Foundation

The Medlock Charitable Trust

The Melow Charitable Trust

Menuchar Ltd

The Brian Mercer Charitable Trust

Merchant Navy Welfare Board

The Merchant Taylors' Foundation*

T. and J. Meyer Family Foundation Ltd

The Mickleham Trust

The Mila Charitable Organisation

The Millennium Oak Trust

The Ronald Miller Foundation

The Millfield Trust

The Millichope Foundation

Mills and Reeve Charitable Trust

The Millward Charitable Trust

The Milne Family Foundation

The James Milner Foundation

Minton Charitable Trust

The Laurence Misener Charitable Trust

The Mishcon Family Charitable Trust

The Brian Mitchell Charitable Settlement

The MITIE Foundation

The Mittal Foundation

The MK Charitable Trust

Mole Charitable Trust

The Monday Charitable Trust

The Henry Moore Foundation

The Morel Charitable Trust

The Morgan Charitable Foundation

The Morris Charitable Trust

G. M. Morrison Charitable Trust

The Ken and Edna Morrison Charitable Trust

The Mosawi Foundation

The Moshal Charitable Trust

Vyoel Moshe Charitable Trust

The Alexander Mosley Charitable Trust

The Mosselson Charitable Trust

Motability

Moto Foundation

Motor Neurone Disease Association

J. P. Moulton Charitable Foundation

The Edwina Mountbatten and Leonora Children's Foundation

The Mowgli Trust

The MSE Charity

The Mulberry Trust

The Frederick Mulder Foundation

Multiple Sclerosis Society

Edith Murphy Foundation

Murphy-Neumann Charity Company Ltd

The John R. Murray Charitable Trust

Brian Murtagh Charitable Trust

Music Sales Charitable Trust

The Mutley Foundation

The Mutual Trust Group

MW (CL) Foundation

MW (GK) Foundation

MW (RH) Foundation

The National Churches Trust

The National Express Foundation

The National Lottery Community Fund

The National Manuscripts Conservation Trust

The Nationwide Foundation

The NDL Foundation

Near Neighbours

Nemoral Ltd

Ner Foundation

Nesta

Network for Social Change Charitable Trust

Newby Trust Ltd

The Frances and Augustus Newman Foundation

Newpier Charity Ltd

The NFU Mutual Charitable Trust

The Nineveh Charitable Trust

NNS Foundation

The Nomura Charitable Trust

Normanby Charitable Trust

Northcott Trust

Northern Consortium*

The Northwick Trust

The Norton Rose Fulbright Charitable Foundation

The Nuffield Foundation

The Oakdale Trust

The Oakley Charitable Trust

Odin Charitable Trust

The Ofenheim Charitable Trust

The Ogle Christian Trust

The Hamish Ogston Foundation

Oizer Charitable Trust

Old Possum's Practical Trust

The Olwyn Foundation

Open House Trust Ltd

Orange Tree Trust

The Orrin Charitable Trust

Orthopaedic Research UK

Ostro Fayre Share Foundation

The Sir Peter O'Sullevan Charitable Trust

The O'Sullivan Family Charitable Trust

Otsar Trust

The Ovo Charitable Foundation

The Owen Family Trust

The Doris Pacey Charitable Foundation

The Paget Charitable Trust

The Paphitis Charitable Trust

The Paragon Trust

The Parivar Trust

The Samuel and Freda Parkinson Charitable Trust

Parkinson's UK

Peacock Charitable Trust

John Pearce Foundation

David Pearlman Charitable Foundation

The Pears Family Charitable Foundation

The Pell Charitable Trust

The Penchant Foundation

The Pennycress Trust

Dina Perelman Trust Ltd

The Performing Right Society Foundation

Petplan Charitable Trust

The Pets at Home Foundation

The Pharsalia Charitable Trust

The Phillips and Rubens Charitable Trust

Betty Phillips Charitable Trust

The Phillips Family Charitable Trust

The Pickwell Foundation

The Pilgrim Trust

Cecil Pilkington Charitable Trust

Elise Pilkington Charitable Trust

The Austin and Hope Pilkington Trust

Miss A. M. Pilkington's Charitable Trust

The Pinchbeck Charitable Trust

Pink Ribbon Foundation

The Pixel Fund

Charles Plater Trust*

The Players Foundation

Thomas Pocklington Trust

Polden-Puckham Charitable Foundation

The George and Esme Pollitzer Charitable Settlement

The Polonsky Foundation

The Porta Pia 2012 Foundation

Porter Foundation

The Portrack Charitable Trust

David and Elaine Potter Foundation

Poundland Foundation

Premierquote Ltd

The Pret Foundation

The Primrose Trust

The Prince of Wales's Charitable Foundation

The Prince's Countryside Fund

The Princess Anne's Charities

The Priory Foundation

Prison Service Charity Fund

The Privy Purse Charitable Trust

The Progress Foundation

Prostate Cancer UK

The Prudence Trust
The Puebla Charitable Trust
The PwC Foundation
QBE European Operations
  Foundation
The Queen Anne's Gate
  Foundation
Queen Mary's Roehampton
  Trust
The Quilter Foundation
Quintessentially Foundation
R. S. Charitable Trust
The Racing Foundation
The Radcliffe Trust
Richard Radcliffe Trust
The Bishop Radford Trust
The Rainford Trust
The Rambourg Foundation
The Randal Charitable
  Foundation
The Joseph and Lena Randall
  Charitable Trust
Randeree Charitable Trust
The Rank Foundation Ltd
The Joseph Rank Trust
The Ranworth Trust
The Ratcliff Foundation
The Rathbones Group
  Foundation
The Julia and Hans Rausing
  Trust*
The Sigrid Rausing Trust
The Roger Raymond Charitable
  Trust
The Rayne Foundation
The Sir James Reckitt Charity
The Reece Foundation
Rees Jeffreys Road Fund
The Max Reinhardt Charitable
  Trust
The Resolution Trust
Reuben Foundation
Rhodi Charitable Trust
The Rhododendron Trust
Riada Trust
The Sir Cliff Richard Charitable
  Trust
Ridgesave Ltd
Rigby Foundation
The Sir John Ritblat Family
  Foundation
The River Farm Foundation
The River Trust
RNID (The Royal National
  Institute for Deaf People)
The Roan Charitable Trust
The Dezna Robins Jones
  Charitable Foundation
The Rock Foundation
Rockcliffe Charitable Trust
The Roddick Foundation
The Rofeh Trust
The Sir James Roll Charitable
  Trust
The Helen Roll Charity

The Gerald and Gail Ronson
  Family Foundation
Mrs L. D. Rope's Third
  Charitable Settlement
Rosa Fund
The Rose Animal Welfare Trust
  CIO
The Cecil Rosen Foundation
Rosetrees
The Ross Foundation
The Rothermere Foundation
Rothesay Foundation*
The Rothschild Foundation
The Eranda Rothschild
  Foundation
Rothschild Foundation
  (Hanadiv) Europe
Rowanville Ltd
The Rowlands Trust
The Joseph Rowntree
  Charitable Trust
The Joseph Rowntree
  Foundation
Royal Artillery Charitable Fund
The Royal British Legion
The Royal Foundation of The
  Prince and Princess of
  Wales
The Royal Navy and Royal
  Marines Charity
RSM UK Foundation
The Rubin Foundation
  Charitable Trust
The Ruddock Foundation for
  the Arts
Russell Trust
The RWS Foundation
The S. M. B. Trust
The Jeremy and John Sacher
  Charitable Trust
The Michael and Nicola Sacher
  Charitable Trust
The Sackler Trust
The Saddlers' Company
  Charitable Fund
Erach and Roshan Sadri
  Foundation
The Jean Sainsbury Animal
  Welfare Trust
The Alan and Babette
  Sainsbury Charitable Fund
Saint Sarkis Charity Trust
The Saintbury Trust
The Salamander Charitable
  Trust
Salisbury Pool Charity
Salters' Charitable Foundation
The Basil Samuel Charitable
  Trust
The M. J. Samuel Charitable
  Trust
The Peter Samuel Charitable
  Trust
The Samworth Foundation
The Sandhu Charitable
  Foundation

Sandra Charitable Trust
The Sands Family Trust
Santander UK Foundation Ltd
The Sasha Foundation*
The Savoy Educational Trust
The Schmidt-Bodner Charitable
  Trust
The Anthony Scholefield
  Foundation
The Schreib Trust
Schreiber Charitable Trust
O. and G. Schreiber Charitable
  Trust
The Schreier Foundation*
Schroder Charity Trust
The Schroder Foundation
The Scotshill Trust
The Scott Bader
  Commonwealth Ltd
Sir Samuel Scott of Yews
  Trust
The John Scott Trust Fund
ScottishPower Foundation
Scouloudi Foundation
The Screwfix Foundation
Seafarers UK (King George's
  Fund for Sailors)
The Searchlight Electric
  Charitable Trust
The Sam and Bella Sebba
  Charitable Foundation
Seedfield Trust
The Segelman Trust
Leslie Sell Charitable Trust
Sellata Ltd
The Serco Foundation
The Seven Fifty Trust
SF Foundation
The Cyril Shack Trust
The Jean Shanks Foundation
The Shanley Charitable Trust
ShareGift (The Orr Mackintosh
  Foundation)
The Sharp Foundation
The Shears Foundation
The Sheepdrove Trust
The Sheldon Trust
The Sherling Charitable Trust
The Archie Sherman Charitable
  Trust
The Bassil Shippam and
  Alsford Trust
The Shipwrights Charitable
  Fund
Shlomo Memorial Fund Ltd
The Shoe Zone Trust
Shulem B. Association Ltd
The Florence Shute Millennium
  Trust
The Simmons & Simmons
  Charitable Foundation
Singer Foundation
The Sino-British Fellowship
  Trust
The Charles Skey Charitable
  Trust

Skipton Building Society Charitable Foundation
The John Slater Foundation
The Slaughter and May Charitable Trust
Kathleen Beryl Sleigh Charitable Trust
Rita and David Slowe Charitable Trust
Smallwood Trust
Ruth Smart Foundation
The N. Smith Charitable Settlement
The Peter Smith Charitable Trust for Nature
The Henry Smith Charity
The Leslie Smith Foundation
The Martin Smith Foundation
Stanley Smith UK Horticultural Trust
Philip Smith's Charitable Trust
Social Investment Business Foundation
Societe Generale UK Foundation
Sodexo Stop Hunger Foundation
Sofronie Foundation
David Solomons Charitable Trust
The E. C. Sosnow Charitable Trust
Souter Charitable Trust
The Stephen R. and Philippa H. Southall Charitable Trust
W. F. Southall Trust
Peter Sowerby Foundation
SPAR Charitable Fund
The Spear Charitable Trust
The SpeedoMick Foundation
Michael and Sarah Spencer Foundation
The Jessie Spencer Trust
Spurrell Charitable Trust
The Geoff and Fiona Squire Foundation
St James's Place Charitable Foundation
Stadium Charitable Trust
The Stafford Trust
Stanley Foundation Ltd
Staples Trust
Starlow Charities Ltd
The Peter Stebbings Memorial Charity
The Steel Charitable Trust
The Steinberg Family Charitable Trust
C. E. K. Stern Charitable Trust
The Sir Sigmund Sternberg Charitable Foundation
The Sterry Family Foundation
Stervon Ltd
The Stevenson Family's Charitable Trust
Sir Halley Stewart Trust

The Stewarts Law Foundation
The Stobart Newlands Charitable Trust
The Stone Family Foundation
The Stoneygate Trust
The Samuel Storey Family Charitable Trust
Peter Stormonth Darling Charitable Trust
Peter Storrs Trust
The W. O. Street Charitable Foundation
The Street Foundation
Streetsmart – Action for the Homeless
The Sunrise Foundation CIO
Surgo Foundation UK Ltd
Sabina Sutherland Charitable Trust
The Swann-Morton Foundation
Swarovski Foundation
The John Swire (1989) Charitable Trust
The Swire Charitable Trust
The Charles and Elsie Sykes Trust
The Hugh Symons Charitable Trust
The Syncona Foundation
The William Syson Foundation
T. and S. Trust Fund
The T.K. Maxx and Homesense Foundation
The Tabhair Charitable Trust
The Tajtelbaum Charitable Trust
The Gay and Keith Talbot Trust
Talteg Ltd
The Tanlaw Foundation
The David Tannen Charitable Trust
Tanner Trust
The Taurus Foundation
Tay Charitable Trust
C. B. and H. H. T. Taylor 1984 Trust
The Taylor Family Foundation
The Tedworth Charitable Trust
Tegham Ltd
The Tennis Foundation
The Thales Charitable Trust
the7stars Foundation
The Theatres Trust Charitable Fund
The Thompson Family Charitable Trust
Scott Thomson Charitable Trust
The Sue Thomson Foundation
Sir Jules Thorn Charitable Trust
The Thornton Trust
The Three Guineas Trust
The Thriplow Charitable Trust
Mrs R. P. Tindall's Charitable Trust

The Tolkien Trust
The Tomoro Foundation
The Tompkins Foundation
The Toy Trust
Annie Tranmer Charitable Trust
The Constance Travis Charitable Trust
The Triangle Trust (1949) Fund
The True Colours Trust
Truedene Co. Ltd
The Truemark Trust
Truemart Ltd
Trumros Ltd
The Trusthouse Charitable Foundation
The Trysil Charitable Trust
The James Tudor Foundation
The Tudor Trust
The Tufton Charitable Trust
The Tuixen Foundation
The Florence Turner Trust
Tzedakah
UBS Optimus Foundation UK
The Udlington Trust
Ufi VocTech Trust
UJIA (United Jewish Israel Appeal)
The UK Youth Fund: Thriving Minds*
Ulting Overseas Trust
The Ulverscroft Foundation
The Underwood Trust
The Union of Orthodox Hebrew Congregations
The United Reformed Church (Wessex) Trust Ltd
UnLtd (Foundation for Social Entrepreneurs)
UPP Foundation
The Michael Uren Foundation
The Utley Foundation
The Valentine Charitable Trust
The Albert Van Den Bergh Charitable Trust
The Van Mesdag Fund
The Van Neste Foundation
The Vandervell Foundation
The Vardy Foundation
Variety, the Children's Charity
The William and Patricia Venton Charitable Trust
The Veolia Environmental Trust
Versus Arthritis
The Veterans' Foundation
VINCI UK Foundation
Nigel Vinson Charitable Trust
Virgin Atlantic Foundation
The Virgin Money Foundation
Vivdale Ltd
The Vodafone Foundation
The Georg and Emily von Opel Foundation
The VTCT Foundation
Sylvia Waddilove Foundation UK
The Scurrah Wainwright Charity

The Bruce Wake Charity
Wallace and Gromit's
Children's Foundation
War Memorials Trust
The Barbara Ward Children's
Foundation
The Watches of Switzerland
Group Foundation
Mrs Waterhouse Charitable
Trust
The Waterloo Foundation
G. R. Waters Charitable Trust
2000
Wates Family Enterprise Trust
The William Wates Memorial
Trust
The Weavers' Company
Benevolent Fund
The David Webster Charitable
Trust
The Linda and Michael
Weinstein Charitable Trust
The Weinstock Fund
The James Weir Foundation
Wellbeing of Women
The Wellcome Trust
Wellington Management UK
Foundation
The Westfield Health
Charitable Trust
Westhill Endowment
The Galen and Hilary Weston
Foundation
The Garfield Weston
Foundation
The Barbara Whatmore
Charitable Trust
The Which? Fund
The Whinfell Charitable Fund
The Whitaker Charitable Trust
Colonel W. H. Whitbread
Charitable Trust
The Melanie White Foundation
Ltd
Whitley Animal Protection Trust
WHSmith Trust
Wickens Family Foundation
The Felicity Wilde Charitable
Trust
The Will Charitable Trust
The H. D. H. Wills 1965
Charitable Trust
Sumner Wilson Charitable
Trust
The Wimbledon Foundation
The Windfall Foundation
The Benjamin Winegarten
Charitable Trust
W. Wing Yip and Brothers
Foundation
The Michael and Anna Wix
Charitable Trust
The Maurice Wohl Charitable
Foundation
The Charles Wolfson
Charitable Trust

The Wolfson Family Charitable
Trust
The Wolfson Foundation
The Lord Leonard and Lady
Estelle Wolfson Foundation
The Victoria Wood Foundation
Wooden Spoon Society
Woodroffe Benton Foundation
The Woodward Charitable
Trust
The Woosnam Foundation
The Worshipful Company of
Glovers of London
Charitable Trust
The Worshipful Company of
Information Technologists
The Worwin UK Foundation
The Edward and Catherine
Wray Charitable Trust
The Eric Wright Charitable
Trust
Wychville Ltd
The Wyndham Charitable Trust
The Wyseliot Rose Charitable
Trust
Yorkshire Building Society
Charitable Foundation
The Elizabeth and Prince
Zaiger Trust
The Marjorie and Arnold Ziff
Charitable Foundation
The Zochonis Charitable Trust
Zurich Community Trust (UK)
Ltd

England

The A. H. Trust
The Adlard Family Charitable
Foundation
The Aitken Family Charitable
Trust
AKO Foundation
Beryl Alexander Charity
The Arah Foundation
The Ardwick Trust
The John Armitage Charitable
Trust
Arts Council England
The Asda Foundation
The Ashley Family Foundation
The Rachel Baker Memorial
Charity
The Kamini and Vindi Banga
Family Trust
Barchester Healthcare
Foundation
The Max Barney Foundation
The Barratt Developments plc
Charitable Foundation
Bauer Radio's Cash for Kids
Charities
The Beaverbrook Foundation
Belljoe Tzedoko Ltd
Biffa Award
The Bill Family Charitable Trust
The Blakebank Trust
Blakemore Foundation
The Boodle and Dunthorne
Charitable Trust
The Borrows Charitable Trust
The Boshier-Hinton Foundation
British Gas Energy Trust
Bill Brown 1989 Charitable
Trust
Building and Civil Engineering
Charitable Trust
The Noel Buxton Trust
The George Cadbury Trust
The Wilfrid and Constance
Cave Foundation
Chalfords Ltd
The Charman Family Charitable
Trust
Chartered Accountants' Livery
Charity (CALC)
CLA Charitable Trust
F. B. Coales No. 4 (Family)
Trust
The Sir William Coxen Trust
Fund
Michael Crawford Children's
Charity
Crisis UK
The Crucible Foundation
The Peter Cruddas Foundation
The Daniell Trust
The Henry and Suzanne Davis
Foundation
The De Brye Charitable Trust
Didymus

William and Frances Dobie
  Charitable Foundation
The Doughty Charity Trust
Drapers Charitable Fund
The DS Smith Charitable
  Foundation
The Dulverton Trust
The James and Deirdre Dyson
  Trust
John Ellerman Foundation
England and Wales Cricket
  Trust
Esher House Charitable Trust
The Fidelis Foundation*
The Fieldrose Charitable Trust
The Football Association
  National Sports Centre
The Football Foundation
The Fort Foundation
Ian M. Foulerton Charitable
  Trust
The Fraxinus Charitable Trust
The Joseph Strong Frazer Trust
The Patrick and Helena Frost
  Foundation
The G. R. P. Charitable Trust
GambleAware
The Gaudio Family Foundation
  (UK) Ltd
Martin Geddes Charitable
  Trust
The General Nursing Council
  for England and Wales
  Trust
The George Family Foundation
The Girdlers' Company
  Charitable Trust
The Goshen Trust
Grand Charitable Trust of the
  Order of Women
  Freemasons
The Grand Trust CIO
Gordon Gray Trust
The Albert Gubay Charitable
  Foundation
The Lennox Hannay Charitable
  Trust
The Peter and Teresa Harris
  Charitable Trust
The Hearth Foundation
The Trevor Hemmings
  Foundation
Tim Henman Foundation
The Bernhard Heuberger
  Charitable Trust*
Historic Houses Foundation
The Iris Rose Holley Charitable
  Trust
Hurdale Charity Ltd
The Inflexion Foundation
The Investindustrial
  Foundation
The J. Isaacs Charitable Trust
The J. and J. Benevolent
  Foundation

The Kennedy Trust for
  Rheumatology Research
The Lake House Charitable
  Foundation
The Herd Lawson and Muriel
  Lawson Charitable Trust
Little Lives UK*
Lloyds Bank Foundation for
  England and Wales
Lloyd's Patriotic Fund
The Lockwood Charitable
  Foundation
Longleigh Foundation
Lord and Lady Lurgan Trust
The Robin MacLeod Charitable
  Trust
Charity of John Marshall
Masonic Charitable Foundation
The Theodore Maxxy
  Charitable Trust
The Mikheev Charitable Trust
Millie's Watch
The Modiano Charitable Trust
The Mohn Westlake
  Foundation
The Morrisons Foundation
The Mulchand Foundation
The National Garden Scheme
The National Hockey
  Foundation
The Gareth Neame Foundation
The Norwood and Newton
  Settlement
The Ouseley Church Music
  Trust
Ovingdean Hall Foundation
P. F. Charitable Trust
The Pantheon Charitable Trust
Parabola Foundation
The Pargiter Trust
People's Health Trust
The Persimmon Charitable
  Foundation
Q Charitable Trust
The Raindance Charitable
  Trust
C. A. Redfern Charitable
  Foundation
Rentrust Foundation Ltd
The Revere Charitable Trust
Riverside Charitable Trust Ltd
The Rix-Thompson-Rothenberg
  Foundation
RJM Charity Trust
The Rockspring Charitable
  Trust
Royal Masonic Trust for Girls
  and Boys
S. and R. Charitable Trust
The Dr Mortimer and Theresa
  Sackler Foundation
The Sanderson Foundation
The Scorpion Charitable Trust*
Scott (Eredine) Charitable
  Trust

SHINE (Support and Help in
  Education)
Sloane Robinson Foundation
Arabella and Julian Smith
  Family Trust
Songdale Ltd
The Squire Patton Boggs
  Charitable Trust
The St Lazarus Charitable
  Trust*
Stolkin Foundation
The Bernard Sunley
  Foundation
The Syder Foundation
The Ashley Tabor-King
  Foundation
Stephen Taylor Foundation
The Thirty Percy Foundation
The Troutsdale Charitable
  Trust
The Tweed Family Charitable
  Foundation
The Union of the Sisters of
  Mercy of Great Britain
Valencia Communities Fund
The Velvet Foundation
The Virgin Foundation (Virgin
  Unite)
The Welland Trust
Wembley National Stadium
  Trust
The Melanie White Foundation
  Ltd
The Wigoder Family Foundation
The Francis Winham
  Foundation
The Woodstock Family
  Charitable Foundation
The Wyfold Charitable Trust
The Yapp Charitable Trust
Youth Endowment Fund (YEF)*
Youth Music

East Midlands

Axis Foundation
The Edward Cadbury
  Charitable Trust
Church Urban Fund
The Coalfields Regeneration
  Trust
The Helen Jean Cope Charity
The Haramead Trust
The Hearth Foundation
Johnnie Johnson Trust
Edith Murphy Foundation
The Ratcliff Foundation
The Jessie Spencer Trust
The Whitaker Charitable Trust
The Wilmcote Charitrust

....

■ Derbyshire

The Bamford Charitable
  Foundation

The Bingham Trust
The Harry Bottom Charitable
Trust
The Evan Cornish Foundation
William Dean Countryside and
Educational Trust
Foundation Derbyshire
Duke of Devonshire's
Charitable Trust
Gay and Peter Hartley's
Hillards Charitable Trust
The Medicash Foundation
Provincial Grand Charity of the
Province of Derbyshire
Toyota Manufacturing UK
Charitable Trust
Woodroffe Benton Foundation

■ Leicestershire

The Carlton Hayes Mental
Health Charity
The Helen Jean Cope Charity
The J. Reginald Corah
Foundation Fund
Dromintee Trust
The Maud Elkington Charitable
Trust
The Everard Foundation
Gay and Peter Hartley's
Hillards Charitable Trust
P. and C. Hickinbotham
Charitable Trust
The David Laing Foundation
Leicestershire and Rutland
Masonic Charity
Association
Leicestershire, Leicester and
Rutland Community
Foundation
Edith Murphy Foundation
Alderman Newton's
Educational Foundation
The Jack Patston Charitable
Trust
The Shoe Zone Trust
The Vichai Srivaddhanaprabha
Foundation
The Florence Turner Trust

■ Lincolnshire

Alan Boswell Group Charitable
Trust
BNA Charitable Incorporated
Organisation
Michael Cornish Charitable
Trust
The Evan Cornish Foundation
Gay and Peter Hartley's
Hillards Charitable Trust
Help for Health
Lincolnshire Community
Foundation
Charity of John Marshall

The Medlock Charitable Trust
The Mercers Charitable
Foundation
The Rugby Group Benevolent
Fund Ltd
Worth Waynflete Foundation

■ Northamptonshire

The Benham Charitable
Settlement
The Frederick and Phyllis Cann
Trust
The Childwick Trust
The Francis Coales Charitable
Foundation
Douglas Compton James
Charitable Trust
The Maud Elkington Charitable
Trust
Ford Britain Trust
Gay and Peter Hartley's
Hillards Charitable Trust
The David Laing Foundation
The Macdonald-Buchanan
Charitable Trust
The Janet and Brian Moore
Charitable Trust*
Northamptonshire Community
Foundation
The Clive Richards Foundation
The Strangward Trust
The Constance Travis
Charitable Trust

■ Nottinghamshire

BNA Charitable Incorporated
Organisation
Boots Charitable Trust
The Chetwode Foundation
The Evan Cornish Foundation
The J. N. Derbyshire Trust
The Dunn Family Charitable
Trust
Sir John Eastwood Foundation
The Thomas Farr Charity
The Fifty Fund
The Forman Hardy Charitable
Trust
Gay and Peter Hartley's
Hillards Charitable Trust
The Lady Hind Trust
The Jones 1986 Charitable
Trust
The Charles Littlewood Hill
Trust
Nottinghamshire Community
Foundation
The Mary Potter Convent
Hospital Trust
The Clive Richards Foundation
The Skerritt Trust
The Whitaker Charitable Trust

■ Rutland

The Carlton Hayes Mental
Health Charity
The J. Reginald Corah
Foundation Fund
The Maud Elkington Charitable
Trust
P. and C. Hickinbotham
Charitable Trust
Leicestershire and Rutland
Masonic Charity
Association
Leicestershire, Leicester and
Rutland Community
Foundation
The Shoe Zone Trust
The Vichai Srivaddhanaprabha
Foundation

East of England

Cadent Foundation
The Penchant Foundation
Red Hill Charitable Trust
The Strangward Trust

■ Bedfordshire

The John Apthorp Charity
The Bedfordshire and
Hertfordshire Historic
Churches Trust
Bedfordshire and Luton
Community Foundation
Bedfordshire Charitable Trust
Ltd
The Childwick Trust
Church Urban Fund
The Francis Coales Charitable
Foundation
The Connolly Foundation (UK)
Ltd
William Delafield Charitable
Trust
The Gale Family Charity Trust
The Harpur Trust
House of Industry Estate
Near Neighbours
The Panacea Charitable Trust
The Potton Consolidated
Charity
The Eranda Rothschild
Foundation
The Rugby Group Benevolent
Fund Ltd
The Steel Charitable Trust
The Strangward Trust
The Wixamtree Trust

■ Cambridgeshire

Alan Boswell Group Charitable
Trust
The John Apthorp Charity

The Broomton Foundation
Cambridgeshire Community
  Foundation
The Childwick Trust
Church Urban Fund
The John Coates Charitable
  Trust
The Cole Charitable Trust
Douglas Compton James
  Charitable Trust
The Dawe Charitable Trust
Eastern Counties Educational
  Trust Ltd
The Evelyn Trust
The Earl Fitzwilliam Charitable
  Trust
The Simon Gibson Charitable
  Trust
Gay and Peter Hartley's
  Hillards Charitable Trust
The Hudson Foundation
Huntingdon Freemen's Trust
The Hutchinson Charitable
  Trust
The Frank Litchfield Charitable
  Trust
Mills and Reeve Charitable
  Trust
The Jack Patston Charitable
  Trust
The Pye Foundation
The Rugby Group Benevolent
  Fund Ltd
The Mrs Smith and Mount
  Trust
The Strangward Trust
Annie Tranmer Charitable Trust

....

■ Essex

Andrews Charitable Trust
The Boltini Trust
The Broomton Foundation
The Leslie Mary Carter
  Charitable Trust
The Childwick Trust
The Christabella Charitable
  Trust
Colchester Catalyst Charity
Eastern Counties Educational
  Trust Ltd
The Essex and Southend
  Sports Trust
Essex Community Foundation
Ford Britain Trust
Fowler Smith and Jones Trust
Charles S. French Charitable
  Trust
Friends of Essex Churches
  Trust
The Grange Farm Centre Trust
Hockerill Educational
  Foundation
The Martin Laing Foundation
The Frank Litchfield Charitable
  Trust

London Legal Support Trust
  (LLST)
Makers of Playing Cards
  Charity
The Mulberry Trust
The Jack Petchey Foundation
The Priory Foundation
Rosca Trust
The Rugby Group Benevolent
  Fund Ltd
The Mrs Smith and Mount
  Trust
Tabeel Trust
Annie Tranmer Charitable Trust
The Tudwick Foundation

....

■ Hertfordshire

Andrews Charitable Trust
The John Apthorp Charity
The Arsenal Foundation
The Bedfordshire and
  Hertfordshire Historic
  Churches Trust
The Boltini Trust
The Childwick Trust
The Robert Clutterbuck
  Charitable Trust
The Francis Coales Charitable
  Foundation
Eastern Counties Educational
  Trust Ltd
The Follett Trust
The Simon Gibson Charitable
  Trust
The Gretna Charitable Trust
Hertfordshire Community
  Foundation
Hockerill Educational
  Foundation
Christopher Laing Foundation
The Martin Laing Foundation
The Frank Litchfield Charitable
  Trust
London Legal Support Trust
  (LLST)
Makers of Playing Cards
  Charity
The Priory Foundation
Salisbury Pool Charity
The Shanly Foundation
The Mrs Smith and Mount
  Trust
The Stevenage Community
  Trust
The Valiant Charitable Trust
West Herts Charity Trust Ltd

....

■ Norfolk

Alan Boswell Group Charitable
  Trust
Anguish's Educational
  Foundation

The Paul Bassham Charitable
  Trust
The Lord Belstead Charitable
  Settlement*
The Broomton Foundation
The Leslie Mary Carter
  Charitable Trust
The Childwick Trust
The John Coates Charitable
  Trust
The Lord Cozens-Hardy Trust
Eastern Counties Educational
  Trust Ltd
The Ellerdale Trust
Anne French Memorial Trust
The Simon Gibson Charitable
  Trust
The Lady Hind Trust
The Martin Laing Foundation
The Charles Littlewood Hill
  Trust
The Mercers Charitable
  Foundation
The Mickleham Trust
Mills and Reeve Charitable
  Trust
The Norfolk Churches Trust Ltd
Norfolk Community Foundation
Educational Foundation of
  Alderman John Norman
Norwich Consolidated
  Charities
Norwich Town Close Estate
  Charity
The Pennycress Trust
The Ranworth Trust
The Mrs Smith and Mount
  Trust
The R. C. Snelling Charitable
  Trust
Spurrell Charitable Trust
Annie Tranmer Charitable Trust
The Virgin Money Foundation
The Geoffrey Watling Charity

....

■ Suffolk

Alan Boswell Group Charitable
  Trust
Beccles Townlands Charity
The Lord Belstead Charitable
  Settlement*
The Broomton Foundation
The Leslie Mary Carter
  Charitable Trust
The Childwick Trust
Eastern Counties Educational
  Trust Ltd
Ganzoni Charitable Trust
The Simon Gibson Charitable
  Trust
The Frank Jackson Foundation
Music Sales Charitable Trust
The Pargiter Trust
Mrs L. D. Rope's Third
  Charitable Settlement

The Mrs Smith and Mount
Trust
Suffolk Community Foundation
The Suffolk Historic Churches
Trust
Annie Tranmer Charitable Trust
The Tudwick Foundation
The Geoffrey Watling Charity
Alfred Williams Charitable
Trust

Greater London

A. W. Charitable Trust
The Addleshaw Goddard
Charitable Trust
The Allen & Overy Foundation
Andrews Charitable Trust
Anpride Ltd
The Arah Foundation
The Armourers and Brasiers
Gauntlet Trust
The Ashendene Trust
The Astor Foundation
Lawrence Atwell's Charity
(Skinners' Company)
Axis Foundation
The Berkeley Foundation
The Cadogan Charity
The Calleva Foundation
The Carpenters Company
Charitable Trust
The Carr-Gregory Trust
Chapman Charitable Trust
The Charterhouse Charitable
Trust
The Childhood Trust
The Childwick Trust
The Christabella Charitable
Trust
Church Urban Fund
The City Bridge Trust (Bridge
House Estates)
The John Coates Charitable
Trust
The Vivienne and Samuel
Cohen Charitable Trust
The Cooks Charity
Dudley and Geoffrey Cox
Charitable Trust
Drapers Charitable Fund
Ellinson Foundation Ltd
Field Family Charitable Trust
The Goldsmiths' Company
Charity
The Grange Farm Centre Trust
The Greenslade Family
Foundation
The Gretna Charitable Trust
The Heritage of London Trust
Ltd
The Holbeck Charitable Trust
The Horners Charity Fund
Inner London Magistrates
Court Poor Box and Feeder
Charity

The International Bankers
Charitable Trust
The Ithaca Trust
J. E. Joseph Charitable Fund
The Kasner Charitable Trust
William Kendall's Charity (Wax
Chandlers Company)
Robert Kitchin (Saddlers' Co.)
Kusuma Trust UK
The Leathersellers' Foundation
Liberum Foundation
Lloyd's of London Foundation
London Catalyst
The London Community
Foundation (LCF)
London Freemasons Charity
London Housing Foundation
Ltd (LHF)
London Legal Support Trust
(LLST)
The London Marathon
Charitable Trust Ltd
Lord and Lady Lurgan Trust
Makers of Playing Cards
Charity
The Mercers Charitable
Foundation
Mills and Reeve Charitable
Trust
The Morel Charitable Trust
Music Sales Charitable Trust
Near Neighbours
The Nomura Charitable Trust
The Jack Petchey Foundation
PIMCO Foundation Europe
The Progress Foundation
Red Hill Charitable Trust
The Rose Foundation
Salters' Charitable Foundation
The Sheldon Trust
The Mrs Smith and Mount
Trust
The Squire Patton Boggs
Charitable Trust
The Peter Stebbings Memorial
Charity
T. and S. Trust Fund
Tallow Chandlers Benevolent
Fund No 2
Trust for London
VHLT Ltd
The Vintners' Foundation
The Virgin Money Foundation
Vision Foundation
The William Wates Memorial
Trust
Wellington Management UK
Foundation
W. Wing Yip and Brothers
Foundation
The Victoria Wood Foundation
Worshipful Company of Gold
and Silver Wyre Drawers
Second Charitable Trust
Fund

■ Barking and Dagenham

The Essex and Southend
Sports Trust
Ford Britain Trust
Charles S. French Charitable
Trust
Friends of Essex Churches
Trust

■ Barnet

The Arsenal Foundation
The Consuelo and Anthony
Brooke Charitable Trust
Cadent Foundation
The Eighteen Fund
Edward Harvist Trust (The
Harvist Estate)
John Lyon's Charity
Mayheights Ltd
Mercaz Torah Vechesed Ltd
The Mutley Foundation
North London Charities Ltd
The David Tannen Charitable
Trust
Tegham Ltd

■ Bexley

William Kendall's Charity (Wax
Chandlers Company)
Maudsley Charity

■ Brent

Edward Harvist Trust (The
Harvist Estate)
The Huntingdon Foundation
Ltd
Hyde Charitable Trust
The Kingsbury Charity
The Leri Charitable Trust
John Lyon's Charity
The Manackerman Charitable
Trust
Melodor Ltd
Sellata Ltd
Wembley National Stadium
Trust

■ Camden

The Arsenal Foundation
The Consuelo and Anthony
Brooke Charitable Trust
Camden Giving
The Charterhouse Charitable
Trust
Fishmongers' Company's
Charitable Trust
The Hampstead Wells and
Campden Trust

Edward Harvist Trust (The
    Harvist Estate)
Hollick Family Foundation
The Huntingdon Foundation
    Ltd
John Lyon's Charity
North London Charities Ltd
The Portal Trust
Richard Reeve's Foundation
Two Magpies Fund

■ City of London

The Barbers' Company General
    Charities
Cadent Foundation
The Charterhouse Charitable
    Trust
The Childwick Trust
The Company of Actuaries
    Charitable Trust Fund
Cripplegate Foundation
The Dischma Charitable Trust
East End Community
    Foundation
Fishmongers' Company's
    Charitable Trust
Charles S. French Charitable
    Trust
Gowling WLG (UK) Charitable
    Trust
The Greenslade Family
    Foundation
HFC Help for Children UK Ltd
The Sir Joseph Hotung
    Charitable Settlement
The International Bankers
    Charitable Trust
Robert Kitchin (Saddlers' Co.)
John Lyon's Charity
The Portal Trust
Richard Reeve's Foundation
The Saddlers' Company
    Charitable Fund
The Mrs Smith and Mount
    Trust
Tallow Chandlers Benevolent
    Fund No 2
Wakefield and Tetley Trust
The Worshipful Company of
    Glovers of London
    Charitable Trust
Worshipful Company of
    Needlemakers Charitable
    Fund

■ City of Westminster

The Consuelo and Anthony
    Brooke Charitable Trust
The Charterhouse Charitable
    Trust
Fishmongers' Company's
    Charitable Trust
M. and R. Gross Charities Ltd

Edward Harvist Trust (The
    Harvist Estate)
Hyde Park Place Estate Charity
John Lyon's Charity
The Portal Trust
Strand Parishes Trust
Two Magpies Fund
Westminster Almshouses
    Foundation
Westminster Foundation

■ Croydon

The Croydon Relief-in-Need
    Charity
Hyde Charitable Trust
Maudsley Charity
W. Wing Yip and Brothers
    Foundation

■ Ealing

Heathrow Community Trust
Housing Pathways Trust
John Lyon's Charity

■ Greenwich

Sir William Boreman's
    Foundation
Hyde Charitable Trust
Maudsley Charity
The Portal Trust

■ Hackney

The Arsenal Foundation
The Charterhouse Charitable
    Trust
East End Community
    Foundation
The Englefield Charitable Trust
Fishmongers' Company's
    Charitable Trust
Ford Britain Trust
Charles S. French Charitable
    Trust
Friends of Wiznitz Ltd
Hackney Parochial Charities
Jay Education Trust
The Manackerman Charitable
    Trust
Mayheights Ltd
Melodor Ltd
Mercaz Torah Vechesed Ltd
The Merchant Taylors'
    Foundation*
The Portal Trust
Sellata Ltd
The Talmud Torah Machzikei
    Hadass Trust
The David Tannen Charitable
    Trust

■ Hammersmith and Fulham

Dr Edwards and Bishop King's
    Fulham Charity
The Girdlers' Company
    Charitable Trust
Hammersmith United Charities
John Lyon's Charity
The Portal Trust

■ Haringey

Cadent Foundation
Charles S. French Charitable
    Trust
Friends of Wiznitz Ltd
North London Charities Ltd
Sellata Ltd
The David Tannen Charitable
    Trust
The Tottenham Grammar
    School Foundation
Two Magpies Fund

■ Harrow

Edward Harvist Trust (The
    Harvist Estate)
John Lyon's Charity

■ Havering

The Essex and Southend
    Sports Trust
Ford Britain Trust
Charles S. French Charitable
    Trust
Friends of Essex Churches
    Trust
The Norwood and Newton
    Settlement

■ Hillingdon

Heathrow Community Trust

■ Hounslow

Heathrow Community Trust
Housing Pathways Trust

■ Islington

The Arsenal Foundation
The Charterhouse Charitable
    Trust
Cloudesley
Cripplegate Foundation
Fishmongers' Company's
    Charitable Trust
Charles S. French Charitable
    Trust

The Girdlers' Company
  Charitable Trust
Hyde Charitable Trust
The Morris Charitable Trust
North London Charities Ltd
The Portal Trust
Richard Reeve's Foundation
Two Magpies Fund

■ Kensington and Chelsea

The Consuelo and Anthony
  Brooke Charitable Trust
The John Coates Charitable
  Trust
Hollick Family Foundation
The Kensington and Chelsea
  Foundation
John Lyon's Charity
The Portal Trust
Westway Trust

■ Lambeth

The Battersea Power Station
  Foundation
The Charterhouse Charitable
  Trust
The John Coates Charitable
  Trust
Fishmongers' Company's
  Charitable Trust
Hyde Charitable Trust
Maudsley Charity
The Peter Minet Trust
The Portal Trust
Sir Walter St John's
  Educational Charity
The Walcot Foundation

■ Lewisham

Sir William Boreman's
  Foundation
Hyde Charitable Trust
Maudsley Charity
The Merchant Taylors'
  Foundation*
The Portal Trust

■ Merton

The John Coates Charitable
  Trust
The Vernon N. Ely Charitable
  Trust
The Generations Foundation
Maudsley Charity
The Taylor Family Foundation
The Wimbledon Foundation

■ Newham

East End Community
  Foundation
The Essex and Southend
  Sports Trust
Fishmongers' Company's
  Charitable Trust
Ford Britain Trust
Charles S. French Charitable
  Trust
Friends of Essex Churches
  Trust
The Portal Trust
Royal Docks Trust (London)

■ Redbridge

The Essex and Southend
  Sports Trust
Ford Britain Trust
Charles S. French Charitable
  Trust
Friends of Essex Churches
  Trust

■ Richmond

The Barnes Fund
Hampton Fund
Heathrow Community Trust
Maudsley Charity
Richmond Parish Lands Charity
Two Ridings Community
  Foundation

■ Southwark

The Charterhouse Charitable
  Trust
Fishmongers' Company's
  Charitable Trust
The Girdlers' Company
  Charitable Trust
Hyde Charitable Trust
Charity of John Marshall
Maudsley Charity
The Merchant Taylors'
  Foundation*
The Peter Minet Trust
Newcomen Collett Foundation
The Portal Trust
The Alan and Babette
  Sainsbury Charitable Fund
St Olave's and St Saviour's
  Schools Foundation CIO*
United St Saviour's Charity
Wakefield and Tetley Trust

■ Tower Hamlets

The Charterhouse Charitable
  Trust
East End Community
  Foundation

Fishmongers' Company's
  Charitable Trust
Ford Britain Trust
Charles S. French Charitable
  Trust
The Merchant Taylors'
  Foundation*
Morgan Stanley International
  Foundation
The Portal Trust
Tower Hill Trust
Wakefield and Tetley Trust

■ Waltham Forest

The Arsenal Foundation
The Essex and Southend
  Sports Trust
Ford Britain Trust
Charles S. French Charitable
  Trust
Friends of Essex Churches
  Trust

■ Wandsworth

The Battersea Power Station
  Foundation
The John Coates Charitable
  Trust
Maudsley Charity
The Portal Trust
Sir Walter St John's
  Educational Charity
The Wimbledon Foundation

North East England

The Roy and Pixie Baker
  Charitable Trust
The Ballinger Charitable Trust
The Barbour Foundation
The Bernicia Foundation
The Tony Bramall Charitable
  Trust
Bright Red Charity
Chrysalis Trust
The Coalfields Regeneration
  Trust
The Catherine Cookson
  Charitable Trust
The Evan Cornish Foundation
Ellinson Foundation Ltd
The Goshen Trust
The Greggs Foundation
The Hearth Foundation
The Hospital of God at
  Greatham
The William Leech Charity
The Millfield House Foundation
  (1)
The Moulding Foundation
Normanby Charitable Trust
The Reece Foundation
The Roseline Foundation*

The Shears Foundation
SHINE (Support and Help in
Education)
The Squires Foundation
The Vardy Foundation
The Virgin Money Foundation
The William Webster
Charitable Trust
The Victoria Wood Foundation
Sir Graham Wylie Foundation

■ County Durham

The Evan Cornish Foundation
The Coulthurst Trust
County Durham Community
Foundation
The Sir Tom Cowie Charitable
Trust
The Gillian Dickinson Trust
Jill Franklin Trust
The Hadrian Trust
The W. A. Handley Charity
Trust
The Hospital of God at
Greatham
Sir James Knott Trust
Lempriere Pringle 2015
The Mercers Charitable
Foundation
The Millfield House Foundation
(1)
The Northumbria Historic
Churches Trust
The J. G. W. Patterson
Foundation
Sir John Priestman Charity
Trust
The Reece Foundation
The Rothley Trust

■ North Yorkshire (formerly Cleveland)

The Tony Bramall Charitable
Trust
The Brelms Trust CIO
The Jack Brunton Charitable
Trust
The Evan Cornish Foundation
The Coulthurst Trust
The Dashlight Foundation
Duke of Devonshire's
Charitable Trust
The A. M. Fenton Trust
Jill Franklin Trust
Gay and Peter Hartley's
Hillards Charitable Trust
The Holbeck Charitable Trust
The Hospital of God at
Greatham
The Mercers Charitable
Foundation

The George A. Moore
Foundation
The Ken and Edna Morrison
Charitable Trust
The Ken and Lynne Morrison
Charitable Trust
Normanby Charitable Trust
The Rothley Trust
The Shears Foundation
The Sylvia and Colin Shepherd
Charitable Trust
Peter Sowerby Foundation
Tees Valley Community
Foundation
Two Ridings Community
Foundation
The Scurrah Wainwright Charity
Woodsmith Foundation Ltd
Yorkshire Cancer Research
The Yorkshire Historic
Churches Trust

■ Northumberland

The Evan Cornish Foundation
The Gillian Dickinson Trust
Jill Franklin Trust
E. C. Graham Belford
Charitable Settlement
The Hadrian Trust
The W. A. Handley Charity
Trust
The Percy Hedley 1990
Charitable Trust
The Hospital of God at
Greatham
The Joicey Trust
Sir James Knott Trust
R. W. Mann Trust
The Mercers Charitable
Foundation
The Millfield House Foundation
(1)
The Northumbria Historic
Churches Trust
The J. G. W. Patterson
Foundation
The Reece Foundation
The Rothley Trust
Shaftoe Educational
Foundation
The Shears Foundation
The St Hilda's Trust
Community Foundation serving
Tyne and Wear and
Northumberland
Wellbank Foundation*

■ Tyne and Wear

The Evan Cornish Foundation
The Sir Tom Cowie Charitable
Trust
The Gillian Dickinson Trust
Jill Franklin Trust

The Hadrian Trust
The W. A. Handley Charity
Trust
The Hospital of God at
Greatham
The Joicey Trust
Sir James Knott Trust
R. W. Mann Trust
The Mercers Charitable
Foundation
The Millfield House Foundation
(1)
The Pargiter Trust
The J. G. W. Patterson
Foundation
Sir John Priestman Charity
Trust
The Reece Foundation
The Roseline Foundation*
The Rothley Trust
The Shears Foundation
The St Hilda's Trust
T. and S. Trust Fund
Community Foundation serving
Tyne and Wear and
Northumberland
Wellbank Foundation*

North West England

The Tim Bacon Foundation
Philip Barker Charity
The Bonamy Charitable Trust
The Bowland Charitable Trust
The Tony Bramall Charitable
Trust
Bright Red Charity
Cadent Foundation
The Coalfields Regeneration
Trust
The Evan Cornish Foundation
The Eventhall Family
Charitable Trust
The Granada Foundation
The Grand Trust CIO
The Hearth Foundation
The Trevor Hemmings
Foundation
The Medicash Foundation
The Brian Mercer Charitable
Trust
The Moulding Foundation
North West Cancer Research
SHINE (Support and Help in
Education)
The John Slater Foundation
The Steinberg Family
Charitable Trust
The Stoller Charitable Trust
UKH Foundation
United Utilities Trust Fund
The Victoria Wood Foundation
The Eric Wright Charitable
Trust

■ Cheshire

A. W. Charitable Trust
The Addleshaw Goddard
  Charitable Trust
The John Apthorp Charity
Philip Barker Charity
Beauland Ltd
The Marjory Boddy Charitable
  Trust
Barbara and Derek Calrow
  Charitable Foundation
Cheshire Community
  Foundation Ltd
Cheshire Freemasons' Charity
Church Urban Fund
The Robert Clutterbuck
  Charitable Trust
Congleton Inclosure Trust
The Evan Cornish Foundation
CRH Charitable Trust
William Dean Countryside and
  Educational Trust
Duchy of Lancaster Benevolent
  Fund
Ford Britain Trust
Forever Manchester
The Greater Manchester High
  Sheriff's Police Trust
The Hamilton Davies Trust
Horwich Shotter Charitable
  Trust
J. E. Joseph Charitable Fund
The Kasner Charitable Trust
The Peter Kershaw Trust
The Ursula Keyes Trust
The Leri Charitable Trust
Lord Leverhulme's Charitable
  Trust
Jack Livingstone Charitable
  Trust
Localtrent Ltd
The Lyons Trust*
M. B. Foundation
Manchester Airport Community
  Trust Fund
The Manchester Guardian
  Society Charitable Trust
The Mather Family Charitable
  Trust
MBNA General Foundation
Mills and Reeve Charitable
  Trust
Mole Charitable Trust
John Moores Foundation
The Steve Morgan Foundation
The Mutley Foundation
MW (HO) Foundation
Oizer Charitable Trust
The Dowager Countess
  Eleanor Peel Trust
The Pennycress Trust
Samjo Ltd
The Searchlight Electric
  Charitable Trust
The Shears Foundation
The Skelton Bounty

The Squire Patton Boggs
  Charitable Trust
The Stoller Charitable Trust
T. and S. Trust Fund
Toyota Manufacturing UK
  Charitable Trust
The Virgin Money Foundation
We Love MCR Charity
Westminster Foundation
The Whinfell Charitable Fund
The Williams Family
  Foundation
Brian Wilson Charitable Trust
W. Wing Yip and Brothers
  Foundation
The Zochonis Charitable Trust

■ Cumbria

The Harold and Alice Bridges
  Charity
The Evan Cornish Foundation
CRH Charitable Trust
Cumbria Community
  Foundation
Sir John Fisher Foundation
The Hadfield Charitable Trust
The W. A. Handley Charity
  Trust
Kelsick's Educational
  Foundation
The Herd Lawson and Muriel
  Lawson Charitable Trust
The Samuel and Freda
  Parkinson Charitable Trust
The J. G. W. Patterson
  Foundation
The Dowager Countess
  Eleanor Peel Trust
Francis C. Scott Charitable
  Trust
The Frieda Scott Charitable
  Trust
The Squires Foundation
The Norman Whiteley Trust
The Yorkshire Dales
  Millennium Trust

■ Greater Manchester

A. W. Charitable Trust
The Addleshaw Goddard
  Charitable Trust
The John Apthorp Charity
Beauland Ltd
The Booth Charities
Barbara and Derek Calrow
  Charitable Foundation
The Chadwick Educational
  Foundation
Cheshire Freemasons' Charity
Church Urban Fund
The Evan Cornish Foundation
CRH Charitable Trust

Duchy of Lancaster Benevolent
  Fund
Ford Britain Trust
Forever Manchester
The Greater Manchester High
  Sheriff's Police Trust
The Hamilton Davies Trust
Horwich Shotter Charitable
  Trust
J. E. Joseph Charitable Fund
The Kasner Charitable Trust
The Peter Kershaw Trust
The Leri Charitable Trust
Lord Leverhulme's Charitable
  Trust
Jack Livingstone Charitable
  Trust
Localtrent Ltd
The Lyons Trust*
M. B. Foundation
The Manackerman Charitable
  Trust
Manchester Airport Community
  Trust Fund
The Manchester Guardian
  Society Charitable Trust
The Mather Family Charitable
  Trust
Melodor Ltd
Mills and Reeve Charitable
  Trust
Mole Charitable Trust
The Mutley Foundation
MW (HO) Foundation
Oizer Charitable Trust
The Dowager Countess
  Eleanor Peel Trust
Samjo Ltd
The Searchlight Electric
  Charitable Trust
The Shears Foundation
The Skelton Bounty
The Squire Patton Boggs
  Charitable Trust
The Stoller Charitable Trust
T. and S. Trust Fund
The Virgin Money Foundation
We Love MCR Charity
The Whinfell Charitable Fund
W. Wing Yip and Brothers
  Foundation
The Zochonis Charitable Trust

■ Lancashire

The Harold and Alice Bridges
  Charity
The Chadwick Educational
  Foundation
Church Urban Fund
The Evan Cornish Foundation
CRH Charitable Trust
William Dean Countryside and
  Educational Trust
Duchy of Lancaster Benevolent
  Fund

The Fort Foundation
Community Foundations for
Lancashire and Merseyside
Lancashire Environmental
Fund Ltd
Lord Leverhulme's Charitable
Trust
The W. M. and B. W. Lloyd
Trust
The Brian Mercer Charitable
Trust
John Moores Foundation
Near Neighbours
The Samuel and Freda
Parkinson Charitable Trust
The Dowager Countess
Eleanor Peel Trust
Rhodi Charitable Trust
Riverside Charitable Trust Ltd
Francis C. Scott Charitable
Trust
The Skelton Bounty
The W. O. Street Charitable
Foundation
Mrs Waterhouse Charitable
Trust
Westminster Foundation
The Yorkshire Dales
Millennium Trust

....

■ Merseyside

The 64 Trust*
The David and Ruth Behrend
Fund
The Charles Brotherton Trust
The Amelia Chadwick Trust
Cheshire Freemasons' Charity
The Evan Cornish Foundation
William Dean Countryside and
Educational Trust
The Ken Dodd Charitable
Foundation
Duchy of Lancaster Benevolent
Fund
Ford Britain Trust
The Hemby Charitable Trust
P. H. Holt Foundation
Community Foundations for
Lancashire and Merseyside
Lord Leverhulme's Charitable
Trust
Liverpool Charity and Voluntary
Services (LCVS)
MBNA General Foundation
John Moores Foundation
The Steve Morgan Foundation
The Dowager Countess
Eleanor Peel Trust
Pilkington Charities Fund
The Sir Harry Pilkington Fund
The Rainford Trust
The Eleanor Rathbone
Charitable Trust
Elizabeth Rathbone Charity
The Ravensdale Trust

The Clive Richards Foundation
The Skelton Bounty
West Derby Waste Lands
Charity

South East England

The Ammco Trust
Axis Foundation
The Rowan Bentall Charitable
Trust
The Berkeley Foundation
Bill Brown 1989 Charitable
Trust
Chapman Charitable Trust
The Childwick Trust
Dudley and Geoffrey Cox
Charitable Trust
Fonthill Foundation
The Dorothy Hay-Bolton
Charitable Trust
HFC Help for Children UK Ltd
The Roger and Jean Jefcoate
Trust
The Leach Fourteenth Trust
The Pell Charitable Trust
Postcode Society Trust
Red Hill Charitable Trust
Mrs L. D. Rope's Third
Charitable Settlement
Sandra Charitable Trust
The Syder Foundation
The Sue Thomson Foundation
The Wates Foundation
The William Wates Memorial
Trust

....

■ Berkshire

The Ashendene Trust
The Louis Baylis (Maidenhead
Advertiser) Charitable Trust
Berkshire Community
Foundation
The Blagrave Trust
The Boltini Trust
The Wilfrid and Constance
Cave Foundation
The Childwick Trust
Colefax Charitable Trust
The Earley Charity
The Eight Foundation
The Englefield Charitable Trust
Greenham Trust Ltd
The Peter Harrison Foundation
Heathrow Community Trust
Henley Educational Trust
Makers of Playing Cards
Charity
Mobbs Memorial Trust Ltd
The Gerald Palmer Eling Trust
Company
The Pargiter Trust

Payne-Gallwey 1989 Charitable
Trust
The Clive Richards Foundation
The Peter Samuel Charitable
Trust
The Shanly Foundation
Singer Foundation
The Spoore, Merry and Rixman
Foundation
The Syder Foundation
The Tompkins Foundation

....

■ Buckinghamshire

Andrews Charitable Trust
The Anson Charitable Trust
The Louis Baylis (Maidenhead
Advertiser) Charitable Trust
The Boltini Trust
Buckinghamshire Community
Foundation
The Carrington Charitable
Trust
The Childwick Trust
The Francis Coales Charitable
Foundation
William Delafield Charitable
Trust
The Louis and Valerie
Freedman Charitable
Settlement
William Harding's Charity
The Peter Harrison Foundation
Heathrow Community Trust
The Roger and Jean Jefcoate
Trust
London Legal Support Trust
(LLST)
Makers of Playing Cards
Charity
Milton Keynes Community
Foundation Ltd
Mobbs Memorial Trust Ltd
The National Hockey
Foundation
The Pharsalia Charitable Trust
The Rothschild Foundation
The Eranda Rothschild
Foundation
The Shanly Foundation
The Sherling Charitable Trust
The Syder Foundation

....

■ East Sussex

Andrews Charitable Trust
The Ian Askew Charitable Trust
The Isabel Blackman
Foundation
The Blagrave Trust
The Consuelo and Anthony
Brooke Charitable Trust
The Chalk Cliff Trust
The Childwick Trust
Cullum Family Trust

Gatwick Airport Community
Trust
The Peter Harrison Foundation
Hollick Family Foundation
Hyde Charitable Trust
The Ernest Kleinwort
Charitable Trust
The Lawson Trust CIO
London Legal Support Trust
(LLST)
The Magdalen and Lasher
Charity (General Fund)
The Ofenheim Charitable Trust
The Pebbles Trust
The River Trust
The Romney Marsh Historic
Churches Trust
The Rugby Group Benevolent
Fund Ltd
Southover Manor General
Education Trust Ltd
The Sussex Community
Foundation

■ Hampshire

The Blagrave Trust
The Charlotte Bonham-Carter
Charitable Trust
The Calleva Foundation
M. J. Camp Charitable
Foundation
The Childwick Trust
Colefax Charitable Trust
John and Freda Coleman
Charitable Trust
Sir Jeremiah Colman Gift Trust
The Alice Ellen Cooper-Dean
Charitable Foundation
The Dibden Allotments Fund
The Dischma Charitable Trust
The Eight Foundation
Ford Britain Trust
Greenham Trust Ltd
Hampshire and Isle of Wight
Community Foundation
The Peter Harrison Foundation
The Emmanuel Kaye
Foundation
The Michael and Betty Little
Trust*
The Gerald Micklem Charitable
Trust
Northcott Trust
The Gerald Palmer Eling Trust
Company
The William Price Charitable
Trust
Sarum St Michael Educational
Charity
The Selwood Charitable Trust
The Shanly Foundation
The Syder Foundation
Zurich Community Trust (UK)
Ltd

■ Isle of Wight

The Blagrave Trust
Hampshire and Isle of Wight
Community Foundation
The Peter Harrison Foundation
Isle of Wight Foundation
Daisie Rich Trust

■ Kent

The Astor Foundation
Lawrence Atwell's Charity
(Skinners' Company)
The Boltini Trust
The Frank Brake Charitable
Trust
The William Brake Charitable
Trust
The Childwick Trust
The Coalfields Regeneration
Trust
The Cobtree Charity Trust Ltd
The Cole Charitable Trust
Colyer-Fergusson Charitable
Trust
The Roger De Haan Charitable
Trust
The Friends of Kent Churches
Gatwick Airport Community
Trust
The Gibbons Family Trust
The Godinton Charitable Trust
The Great Stone Bridge Trust
of Edenbridge
The Peter Harrison Foundation
R. G. Hills Charitable Trust
The Hollands-Warren Fund
Hollick Family Foundation
Hyde Charitable Trust
Kent Community Foundation
The Lawson Trust CIO
The Elaine and Angus Lloyd
Charitable Trust
London Legal Support Trust
(LLST)
Makers of Playing Cards
Charity
Charity of John Marshall
Henry Oldfield Trust
The Pargiter Trust
The Philip and Connie Phillips
Foundation*
The Romney Marsh Historic
Churches Trust
The Rugby Group Benevolent
Fund Ltd
The Mrs Smith and Mount
Trust
The Tory Family Foundation

■ Oxfordshire

The Ammco Trust
Andrews Charitable Trust
Banbury Charities

Barnsbury Charitable Trust
T. B. H. Brunner's Charitable
Settlement
The Wilfrid and Constance
Cave Foundation
The Childwick Trust
William Delafield Charitable
Trust
The DLM Charitable Trust
The Lord Faringdon Charitable
Trust
Doris Field Charitable Trust
The Peter Harrison Foundation
Henley Educational Trust
Christopher Laing Foundation
The David Laing Foundation
The C. L. Loyd Charitable Trust
The Millfield Trust
The Janet and Brian Moore
Charitable Trust*
The Mosawi Foundation
Oxfordshire Community
Foundation
Oxfordshire Historic Churches
Trust (2016)
The Gerald Palmer Eling Trust
Company
The Pharsalia Charitable Trust
Mr and Mrs J. A. Pye's
Charitable Settlement
The Clive Richards Foundation
The Rugby Group Benevolent
Fund Ltd
Sarum St Michael Educational
Charity
The Shanly Foundation
Singer Foundation
Staples Trust
The Adrian Swire Charitable
Trust
The Syder Foundation
Tanner Trust

■ Surrey

Andrews Charitable Trust
Misses Barrie Charitable Trust
The Billmeir Charitable Trust
The Boltini Trust
The Childwick Trust
The John Coates Charitable
Trust
John and Freda Coleman
Charitable Trust
Cullum Family Trust
The Eight Foundation
Gatwick Airport Community
Trust
Hamamelis Trust
The Peter Harrison Foundation
Heathrow Community Trust
The Ingram Trust
The Sir Edward Lewis
Foundation
The Michael and Betty Little
Trust*

The Elaine and Angus Lloyd
    Charitable Trust
London Legal Support Trust
    (LLST)
Makers of Playing Cards
    Charity
Charity of John Marshall
The Pargiter Trust
The Shanly Foundation
The R. C. Sherriff Rosebriars
    Trust
The Mrs Smith and Mount
    Trust
Community Foundation for
    Surrey
The Syder Foundation
Humphrey Richardson Taylor
    Charitable Trust
Walton-on-Thames Charity

■ West Sussex

Andrews Charitable Trust
The Ian Askew Charitable Trust
The Blagrave Trust
The Boltini Trust
The Consuelo and Anthony
    Brooke Charitable Trust
Byrne Family Foundation
The Childwick Trust
The John Coates Charitable
    Trust
Cullum Family Trust
The Eight Foundation
Friarsgate Trust
Gatwick Airport Community
    Trust
The F. Glenister Woodger Trust
    CIO
The Peter Harrison Foundation
Heathrow Community Trust
Hyde Charitable Trust
The Ernest Kleinwort
    Charitable Trust
The Lawson Trust CIO
The Michael and Betty Little
    Trust*
London Legal Support Trust
    (LLST)
The Gerald Micklem Charitable
    Trust
The River Trust
The Shanly Foundation
The Bassil Shippam and
    Alsford Trust
Southover Manor General
    Education Trust Ltd
The Sussex Community
    Foundation
The Three Oaks Trust
The Tompkins Foundation

South West England

Axis Foundation
The Rowan Bentall Charitable
    Trust
The Berkeley Foundation
Bill Brown 1989 Charitable
    Trust
G. F. Eyre Charitable Trust
The Joyce Fletcher Charitable
    Trust
The Leach Fourteenth Trust
The Clare Milne Trust
The Norman Family Charitable
    Trust
The Pargiter Trust
Susanna Peake Charitable
    Trust
The Pell Charitable Trust
The Pickwell Foundation
The Portishead Nautical Trust
Postcode Local Trust
Postcode Society Trust
The Clive Richards Foundation
Spielman Charitable Trust
St Monica Trust
The Wates Foundation
The Elizabeth and Prince
    Zaiger Trust

■ Bristol

Andrews Charitable Trust
Douglas Arter Foundation
The Avon and Somerset Police
    Community Trust
Bristol Charities
J. and M. Britton Charitable
    Trust
The Burges Salmon Charitable
    Trust
The Carr-Gregory Trust
Denman Charitable Trust
The Gloucestershire Historic
    Churches Trust
The Nani Huyu Charitable Trust
John James Bristol Foundation
The Leonard Laity Stoate
    Charitable Trust
The Merchant Venturers
    Charity
The Morel Charitable Trust
The Nisbet Trust
The Parivar Trust
The Portishead Nautical Trust
Quartet Community Foundation
Singer Foundation
Spielman Charitable Trust
St Monica Trust
The Sunrise Foundation CIO
Dame Violet Wills Will Trust

■ Cornwall and the Scilly Isles

Carew Pole Charitable Trust
The Wilfrid and Constance
    Cave Foundation
Cornwall Community
    Foundation
Duchy Health Charity Ltd
The Duke of Cornwall's
    Benevolent Fund
The Heathcoat Trust
The Leonard Laity Stoate
    Charitable Trust
The Clare Milne Trust
The Norman Family Charitable
    Trust
The Charles Skey Charitable
    Trust
Tanner Trust

■ Devon

Viscount Amory's Charitable
    Trust
The Ashworth Charitable Trust
Bideford Bridge Trust
The Wilfrid and Constance
    Cave Foundation
The John Coates Charitable
    Trust
Mabel Cooper Charity
The Corton Hill Trust
Devon Community Foundation
The Gibbons Family Trust
The David Gibbons Foundation
The Heathcoat Trust
The Leonard Laity Stoate
    Charitable Trust
The Clare Milne Trust
The Norman Family Charitable
    Trust
Sarum St Michael Educational
    Charity
The Charles Skey Charitable
    Trust

■ Dorset

The Burry Charitable Trust
The Wilfrid and Constance
    Cave Foundation
The Clover Trust
The Alice Ellen Cooper-Dean
    Charitable Foundation
The Corton Hill Trust
Dorset Community Foundation
The Dorset Historic Churches
    Trust
The Eight Foundation
The Leonard Laity Stoate
    Charitable Trust
Salisbury Pool Charity
Sarum St Michael Educational
    Charity
The Sherling Charitable Trust

The Adrian Swire Charitable
Trust
The Talbot Village Trust
Mrs R. P. Tindall's Charitable
Trust
The Valentine Charitable Trust
The Elizabeth and Prince
Zaiger Trust

■ Gloucestershire

Andrews Charitable Trust
Douglas Arter Foundation
The Ashendene Trust
The Avon and Somerset Police
Community Trust
Barnwood Trust
Bristol Archdeaconry Charity
The George Cadbury Trust
The Wilfrid and Constance
Cave Foundation
Denman Charitable Trust
Gloucestershire Community
Foundation
The Gloucestershire Historic
Churches Trust
The Nani Huyu Charitable Trust
Sylvanus Lysons Charity
The Nisbet Trust
The Notgrove Trust
The Parivar Trust
Susanna Peake Charitable
Trust
The Portishead Nautical Trust
Quartet Community Foundation
The Rowlands Trust
The Saintbury Trust
The Florence Shute Millennium
Trust
Singer Foundation
Philip Smith's Charitable Trust
St Monica Trust
The Summerfield Charitable
Trust
Dame Violet Wills Will Trust
Zurich Community Trust (UK)
Ltd

■ Somerset

Andrews Charitable Trust
Douglas Arter Foundation
The Avon and Somerset Police
Community Trust
The Brownsword Charitable
Foundation
The Wilfrid and Constance
Cave Foundation
The Roger and Sarah Bancroft
Clark Charitable Trust
The Corton Hill Trust
Denman Charitable Trust
The Dorothy Whitney Elmhirst
Trust
The Foxglove Trust

The Nani Huyu Charitable Trust
The Leonard Laity Stoate
Charitable Trust
The Medlock Charitable Trust
The Nisbet Trust
The Norman Family Charitable
Trust
The Portishead Nautical Trust
Quartet Community Foundation
The Peter Samuel Charitable
Trust
Sarum St Michael Educational
Charity
The Charles Skey Charitable
Trust
Somerset Community
Foundation
The Sperring Charity
St John's Foundation Est.
1174
St Monica Trust
The Adrian Swire Charitable
Trust
Dame Violet Wills Will Trust
The Elizabeth and Prince
Zaiger Trust

■ Wiltshire

The Ashendene Trust
The Blagrave Trust
The Wilfrid and Constance
Cave Foundation
Chippenham Borough Lands
Charity
Community First
The James Dyson Foundation
The Eight Foundation
Samuel William Farmer Trust
The Fulmer Charitable Trust
The Walter Guinness
Charitable Trust
The Gerald Palmer Eling Trust
Company
The Pharsalia Charitable Trust
Sarum St Michael Educational
Charity
Singer Foundation
The Adrian Swire Charitable
Trust
The Syder Foundation
Mrs R. P. Tindall's Charitable
Trust
Wiltshire Community
Foundation
Zurich Community Trust (UK)
Ltd

West Midlands Region

Axis Foundation
The Rachel Baker Memorial
Charity
The Berkeley Foundation

The Edward Cadbury
Charitable Trust
William A. Cadbury Charitable
Trust
The Edward and Dorothy
Cadbury Trust
The George Cadbury Trust
Cadent Foundation
The Coalfields Regeneration
Trust
The Keith Coombs Trust
Baron Davenport's Charity
Dumbreck Charity
The Eveson Charitable Trust
Field Family Charitable Trust
G. M. C. Trust
The Grantham Yorke Trust
Gay and Peter Hartley's
Hillards Charitable Trust
Heart of England Community
Foundation
The Hearth Foundation
The Alan Edward Higgs Charity
The Jabbs Foundation
The Sir Barry Jackson County
Fund
Lillie Johnson Charitable Trust
Johnnie Johnson Trust
The Edgar E. Lawley
Foundation
The Michael Marsh Charitable
Trust
Millie's Watch
The National Express
Foundation
The Oakley Charitable Trust
The Owen Family Trust
The Patrick Trust
Quothquan Trust
The Ratcliff Foundation
The Clive Richards Foundation
The Rowlands Trust
The Saintbury Trust
The Sheldon Trust
C. B. and H. H. T. Taylor 1984
Trust
The Wilmcote Charitrust

■ Herefordshire

E. F. Bulmer Trust
The Edward Cadbury
Charitable Trust
The Elmley Foundation
The Eveson Charitable Trust
The Hawthorne Charitable
Trust
Herefordshire Community
Foundation
The Herefordshire Historic
Churches Trust
The Huntingdon Foundation
Ltd
The Jordan Charitable
Foundation
The Mumford Memorial Trust*

The Parivar Trust
The Rowlands Trust
The Stephen R. and Philippa
   H. Southall Charitable Trust
St Peter's Saltley Trust
The Roger and Douglas Turner
   Charitable Trust

■ Shropshire

The Edward Cadbury
   Charitable Trust
The Daniell Trust
Euro Quality Foundation
The Lady Forester Trust
MBNA General Foundation
The Millichope Foundation
The Rowlands Trust
The Walker Trust

■ Staffordshire

The Bamford Charitable
   Foundation
Consolidated Charity of Burton
   upon Trent
The Edward Cadbury
   Charitable Trust
The Chartley Foundation
William Dean Countryside and
   Educational Trust
The Wilfred and Elsie Elkes
   Charity Fund
The Harding Trust
The Michael Marsh Charitable
   Trust
The Community Foundation for
   Staffordshire
St Peter's Saltley Trust

■ Warwickshire

The 29th May 1961 Charitable
   Trust
Misses Barrie Charitable Trust
The Edward Cadbury
   Charitable Trust
Coventry Building Society
   Charitable Foundation
The Elizabeth Creak Charitable
   Trust
Dumbreck Charity
Heart of England Community
   Foundation
The Alan Edward Higgs Charity
The King Henry VIII Endowed
   Trust – Warwick
The Michael Marsh Charitable
   Trust
The Janet and Brian Moore
   Charitable Trust*
The Norton Foundation
The Rowlands Trust
The Rugby Group Benevolent
   Fund Ltd

The Saintbury Trust
Singer Foundation
Stratford-upon-Avon Town Trust
Warwick Relief-in-Need Charity
The Warwickshire Masonic
   Charitable Association Ltd

■ West Midlands Metropolitan Area

The Lord Austin Trust
The Birmingham Diocesan
   Board of Finance
The Charles Brotherton Trust
The Edward Cadbury
   Charitable Trust
The George Cadbury Trust
The Barrow Cadbury Trust
Church Urban Fund
The Cole Charitable Trust
The George Henry Collins
   Charity
Dumbreck Charity
The Eveson Charitable Trust
George Fentham Birmingham
   Charity
Field Family Charitable Trust
General Charity (Coventry)
Gowling WLG (UK) Charitable
   Trust
The Grimmitt Trust
Harborne Parish Lands Charity
The Alan Edward Higgs Charity
The Sir Barry Jackson County
   Fund
Lillie Johnson Charitable Trust
The Michael Marsh Charitable
   Trust
The Bernard Piggott Charitable
   Trust
Quothquan Trust
The Roughley Charitable Trust
The Rowlands Trust
The Saintbury Trust
The Sheldon Trust
The Squire Patton Boggs
   Charitable Trust
St Peter's Saltley Trust
Sutton Coldfield Charitable
   Trust
The Roger and Douglas Turner
   Charitable Trust
G. J. W. Turner Trust

■ Worcestershire

Misses Barrie Charitable Trust
The Edward Cadbury
   Charitable Trust
The Wilfrid and Constance
   Cave Foundation
Dumbreck Charity
The Elmley Foundation
The Eveson Charitable Trust
Gordon Gray Trust

The Hawthorne Charitable
   Trust
The Kildare Trust
Laslett's (Hinton) Charity
The Michael Marsh Charitable
   Trust
John Martin's Charity
The Rowlands Trust
The Saintbury Trust
Singer Foundation
The Roger and Douglas Turner
   Charitable Trust
Worcestershire Community
   Foundation

Yorkshire and the Humber

The Liz and Terry Bramall
   Foundation
The Arnold Burton 1998
   Charitable Trust
The Keith Howard Foundation
The Lyndal Tree Foundation
The Mayfield Valley Arts Trust
The Ken and Lynne Morrison
   Charitable Trust
The Rose Animal Welfare Trust
   CIO
The Rothley Trust
SHINE (Support and Help in
   Education)
Stadium Charitable Trust
The Charles and Elsie Sykes
   Trust
Tees Valley Community
   Foundation

■ East Riding of Yorkshire

The Tony Bramall Charitable
   Trust
The Brelms Trust CIO
The Joseph and Annie Cattle
   Trust
The Evan Cornish Foundation
The Dashlight Foundation
Help for Health
The Holbeck Charitable Trust
The Hull and East Riding
   Charitable Trust
The Ken and Edna Morrison
   Charitable Trust
The Ken and Lynne Morrison
   Charitable Trust
The Sir James Reckitt Charity
Stadium Charitable Trust
Two Ridings Community
   Foundation
The Scurrah Wainwright Charity
Yorkshire Cancer Research
The Yorkshire Historic
   Churches Trust

■ North Yorkshire

The Tony Bramall Charitable Trust
The Brelms Trust CIO
The Charles Brotherton Trust
The Jack Brunton Charitable Trust
The Evan Cornish Foundation
The Coulthurst Trust
The Dashlight Foundation
Duke of Devonshire's Charitable Trust
The A. M. Fenton Trust
The Feoffees of St Michael's Spurriergate York
Gay and Peter Hartley's Hillards Charitable Trust
The Holbeck Charitable Trust
The Mercers Charitable Foundation
The George A. Moore Foundation
The Ken and Edna Morrison Charitable Trust
The Ken and Lynne Morrison Charitable Trust
Normanby Charitable Trust
Sir John Priestman Charity Trust
The Purey Cust Trust CIO
The Rothley Trust
The Shears Foundation
The Patricia and Donald Shepherd Charitable Trust
The Sylvia and Colin Shepherd Charitable Trust
Peter Sowerby Foundation
Tees Valley Community Foundation
Two Ridings Community Foundation
The Scurrah Wainwright Charity
Woodsmith Foundation Ltd
Yorkshire Cancer Research
The Yorkshire Dales Millennium Trust
The Yorkshire Historic Churches Trust

■ South Yorkshire

The Harry Bottom Charitable Trust
The Tony Bramall Charitable Trust
The Brelms Trust CIO
Church Burgesses Educational Foundation
Church Burgesses Trust
The Evan Cornish Foundation
The Dashlight Foundation
The Earl Fitzwilliam Charitable Trust
The Freshgate Trust Foundation

The J. G. Graves Charitable Trust
Gay and Peter Hartley's Hillards Charitable Trust
The Holbeck Charitable Trust
The Ken and Edna Morrison Charitable Trust
The Ken and Lynne Morrison Charitable Trust
The Sheffield Town Trust
South Yorkshire Community Foundation
The Swann-Morton Foundation
The Talbot Trusts
The Virgin Money Foundation
The Scurrah Wainwright Charity
Yorkshire Cancer Research
The Yorkshire Historic Churches Trust

■ West Yorkshire

The Addleshaw Goddard Charitable Trust
The Tony Bramall Charitable Trust
The Brelms Trust CIO
The Charles Brotherton Trust
Community Foundation for Calderdale
Church Urban Fund
The Evan Cornish Foundation
The Coulthurst Trust
The Dashlight Foundation
The Harry and Mary Foundation
Gay and Peter Hartley's Hillards Charitable Trust
The Holbeck Charitable Trust
Leeds Community Foundation
Sir George Martin Trust
Mills and Reeve Charitable Trust
The George A. Moore Foundation
The Morel Charitable Trust
The Ken and Edna Morrison Charitable Trust
The Ken and Lynne Morrison Charitable Trust
Near Neighbours
One Community Foundation Ltd
The Shears Foundation
The Squire Patton Boggs Charitable Trust
The Squires Foundation
The Virgin Money Foundation
Wade's Charity
The Scurrah Wainwright Charity
Yorkshire Cancer Research
The Yorkshire Historic Churches Trust
The Marjorie and Arnold Ziff Charitable Foundation

Zurich Community Trust (UK) Ltd

Channel Islands

The A. S. Charitable Trust
Michael Cornish Charitable
    Trust
Ana Leaf Foundation*
Lloyds Bank Foundation for the
    Channel Islands
The National Garden Scheme
The Pargiter Trust
The Joseph Rank Trust
Santander UK Foundation Ltd
The W. O. Street Charitable
    Foundation
War Memorials Trust

Isle of Man

The A. S. Charitable Trust
The Albert Gubay Charitable
    Foundation
The Quilter Foundation
Santander UK Foundation Ltd
War Memorials Trust

Scotland

The Aberbrothock Skea Trust
abrdn Financial Fairness Trust
Adam Family Foundation
The AEB Charitable Trust
Age Scotland
Sylvia Aitken's Charitable Trust
The AMW Charitable Trust
The Baird Trust
Bairdwatson Charitable Trust
Bank of Scotland Foundation
Barcapel Foundation Ltd
Barchester Healthcare
    Foundation
The Michael Barnard
    Charitable Trust
The Barratt Developments plc
    Charitable Foundation
Misses Barrie Charitable Trust
Robert Barr's Charitable Trust
Bauer Radio's Cash for Kids
    Charities
Binks Trust
British Gas Energy Trust
Building and Civil Engineering
    Charitable Trust
Miss Margaret Butters Reekie
    Charitable Trust
The Noel Buxton Trust
The Cadogan Charity
William A. Cargill Charitable
    Trust
David William Traill Cargill
    Fund
The Carnegie Trust for the
    Universities of Scotland
Cattanach
The Coalfields Regeneration
    Trust
Corra Foundation
Craignish Trust
Creative Scotland
The Crerar Trust
Crisis UK
Cruden Foundation Ltd
The Cunningham Trust
The Daniell Trust
Digital Extra Fund
The Dulverton Trust
Dunard Fund
Dunlossit and Islay Community
    Trust
The Robert Fleming Hannay
    Memorial Charity
The Gordon Fraser Charitable
    Trust
The Hugh Fraser Foundation
GambleAware
The Gannochy Trust
The Graham Trust
William Grant Foundation*
Dr Guthrie's Association
The Lennox Hannay Charitable
    Trust
Christina Mary Hendrie Trust
Historic Environment Scotland

Hope Trust
Miss Agnes H. Hunter's Trust
Impact Funding Partners Ltd
Lady Eda Jardine Charitable
   Trust
Fraser Kilpatrick Charitable
   Trust
The R. J. Larg Family Trust
Mrs M. A. Lascelles Charitable
   Trust
The Lyndal Tree Foundation
The R. S. Macdonald
   Charitable Trust
The MacRobert Trust 2019
The Manackerman Charitable
   Trust
The W. M. Mann Foundation
The Martin Charitable Trust
Nancie Massey Charitable
   Trust
Medical Research Scotland
The Meikle Foundation
Merchants House of Glasgow
The Mickel Fund
Hugh and Mary Miller Bequest
   Trust
The Ronald Miller Foundation
The Milne Family Foundation
The Morrisons Foundation
P. F. Charitable Trust
Miss M. E. S. Paterson's
   Charitable Trust
People's Health Trust
People's Postcode Trust
The Persimmon Charitable
   Foundation
Miss A. M. Pilkington's
   Charitable Trust
Queen Mary's Roehampton
   Trust
Rentrust Foundation Ltd
The Robertson Trust
The Ryvoan Trust*
Foundation Scotland
Scotland's Garden Scheme*
The Ina Scott Sutherland
   Charitable Foundation
The John Scott Trust Fund
Scottish Coal Industry Special
   Welfare Fund
Scottish Property Industry
   Festival of Christmas
   (SPIFOX)
Souter Charitable Trust
The Stafford Trust
The Hugh Stenhouse
   Foundation
The William Syson Foundation
Tay Charitable Trust
Tenovus Scotland
The Trades House of Glasgow
The Triangle Trust (1949) Fund
The Turtleton Charitable Trust
The Union of the Sisters of
   Mercy of Great Britain
Valencia Communities Fund

Volant Charitable Trust
John Watson's Trust*
The Colin Weir Charitable
   Foundation
The Weir Charitable Trust
The Whitaker Charitable Trust
J. and J. R. Wilson Trust
Women's Fund for Scotland
The James Wood Bequest
   Fund
The Wood Foundation
WPG Charitable Trust*
Youth Music

Ayrshire and Arran

Bairdwatson Charitable Trust
The John Scott Trust Fund
Walton Foundation
The James Weir Foundation

Dumfries and Galloway

Dumfriesshire East Community
   Benefit Group SCIO
The Holywood Trust

Dunbartonshire and Argyll and Bute

Dunlossit and Islay Community
   Trust
Walton Foundation

Fife

The Carnegie Dunfermline
   Trust
The R. J. Larg Family Trust
Mathew Trust
The Meikle Foundation
The Alexander Moncur Trust
Russell Trust

Glasgow

The Addleshaw Goddard
   Charitable Trust
Robert Barr's Charitable Trust
The Bellahouston Bequest
   Fund
W. A. Cargill Fund
The Endrick Trust
James T. Howat Charitable
   Trust
The Martin Charitable Trust
Merchants House of Glasgow
Morgan Stanley International
   Foundation

The Templeton Goodwill Trust
The Trades House of Glasgow
The Virgin Money Foundation
Walton Foundation
The James Weir Foundation
Zurich Community Trust (UK)
   Ltd

Highlands and Western Isles

The Gordon and Ena Baxter
   Foundation*
The Daniell Trust
The Englefield Charitable Trust
The Peter Samuel Charitable
   Trust
Westminster Foundation

Lanarkshire

Bairdwatson Charitable Trust
Walton Foundation

Lothian

The Addleshaw Goddard
   Charitable Trust
The AEB Charitable Trust
Binks Trust
The Castansa Trust
Dunard Fund
Edinburgh Children's Holiday
   Fund
Dr Guthrie's Association
KPE4 Charitable Trust
Nancie Massey Charitable
   Trust
North Berwick Trust
The Row Fogo Charitable Trust
The Virgin Money Foundation
John Watson's Trust*

Orkney and Shetland

Shetland Charitable Trust

Renfrewshire

Walton Foundation

Scottish Borders

The AEB Charitable Trust
The Joicey Trust

Tayside

The Gordon and Ena Baxter
Foundation*
The Gannochy Trust
The R. J. Larg Family Trust
Leng Charitable Trust
Mathew Trust
The Alexander Moncur Trust
The Nine Incorporated Trades
of Dundee General Fund
Charity
Northwood Charitable Trust
The Hugh Stenhouse
Foundation
Tay Charitable Trust

Wales

The A. H. Trust
The Adlard Family Charitable
Foundation
The Aitken Family Charitable
Trust
The Arah Foundation
The Ardwick Trust
The John Armitage Charitable
Trust
Arts Council of Wales (also
known as Cyngor
Celfyddydau Cymru)
The Asda Foundation
The Ashley Family Foundation
Axis Foundation
The Rachel Baker Memorial
Charity
The Kamini and Vindi Banga
Family Trust
Barchester Healthcare
Foundation
Lord Barnby's Foundation
The Max Barney Foundation
The Barratt Developments plc
Charitable Foundation
Bauer Radio's Cash for Kids
Charities
Belljoe Tzedoko Ltd
The Bill Family Charitable Trust
The Blakebank Trust
Blakemore Foundation
The Boodle and Dunthorne
Charitable Trust
The Borrows Charitable Trust
The Boshier-Hinton Foundation
British Gas Energy Trust
Building and Civil Engineering
Charitable Trust
The Noel Buxton Trust
The Wilfrid and Constance
Cave Foundation
Chalfords Ltd
The Charman Family Charitable
Trust
Chartered Accountants' Livery
Charity (CALC)
CLA Charitable Trust
F. B. Coales No. 4 (Family)
Trust
The Coalfields Regeneration
Trust
The John S. Cohen Foundation
Colwinston Charitable Trust
Michael Crawford Children's
Charity
Crisis UK
The Crucible Foundation
The Peter Cruddas Foundation
The Daniell Trust
Margaret Davies Charity
The Henry and Suzanne Davis
Foundation
The De Brye Charitable Trust
Didymus

William and Frances Dobie
Charitable Foundation
The Ken Dodd Charitable
Foundation
Drapers Charitable Fund
The DS Smith Charitable
Foundation
The Dulverton Trust
The James and Deirdre Dyson
Trust
England and Wales Cricket
Trust
Esher House Charitable Trust
The Fieldrose Charitable Trust
The Fort Foundation
Ian M. Foulerton Charitable
Trust
The Fraxinus Charitable Trust
The Joseph Strong Frazer Trust
The Patrick and Helena Frost
Foundation
The G. R. P. Charitable Trust
GambleAware
The Gaudio Family Foundation
(UK) Ltd
Martin Geddes Charitable
Trust
The General Nursing Council
for England and Wales
Trust
The George Family Foundation
The Gibbs Charitable Trusts
The Goshen Trust
Grand Charitable Trust of the
Order of Women
Freemasons
The Grand Trust CIO
The Albert Gubay Charitable
Foundation
The Lennox Hannay Charitable
Trust
The Peter and Teresa Harris
Charitable Trust
The Hearth Foundation
The Trevor Hemmings
Foundation
Tim Henman Foundation
The Bernhard Heuberger
Charitable Trust*
Historic Houses Foundation
The Iris Rose Holley Charitable
Trust
Hurdale Charity Ltd
The Inflexion Foundation
The Investindustrial
Foundation
The J. Isaacs Charitable Trust
The Jenour Foundation
The Herd Lawson and Muriel
Lawson Charitable Trust
The Ian and Natalie
Livingstone Charitable Trust
Lloyds Bank Foundation for
England and Wales
Lloyd's Patriotic Fund

The Lockwood Charitable
    Foundation
The Robin MacLeod Charitable
    Trust
Charity of John Marshall
Masonic Charitable Foundation
The Theodore Maxxy
    Charitable Trust
The Mikheev Charitable Trust
Millennium Stadium Charitable
    Trust (Ymddiriedolaeth
    Elusennol Stadiwm y
    Mileniwm)
Millie's Watch
The Modiano Charitable Trust
The Mohn Westlake
    Foundation
Moondance Foundation
The Morrisons Foundation
The Mulchand Foundation
The National Garden Scheme
The Gareth Neame Foundation
The Norwood and Newton
    Settlement
The Oakdale Trust
The Ofenheim Charitable Trust
The Ouseley Church Music
    Trust
P. F. Charitable Trust
The Pantheon Charitable Trust
The James Pantyfedwen
    Foundation
    (Ymddiriedolaeth James
    Pantyfedwen)
People's Health Trust
The Persimmon Charitable
    Foundation
Postcode Community Trust
Q Charitable Trust
Queen Mary's Roehampton
    Trust
The Raindance Charitable
    Trust
The Ratcliff Foundation
C. A. Redfern Charitable
    Foundation
Rentrust Foundation Ltd
The Revere Charitable Trust
The Clive Richards Foundation
Riverside Charitable Trust Ltd
The Rix-Thompson-Rothenberg
    Foundation
RJM Charity Trust
The Rockspring Charitable
    Trust
Royal Masonic Trust for Girls
    and Boys
The Dr Mortimer and Theresa
    Sackler Foundation
The Sanderson Foundation
The Scorpion Charitable Trust*
Scott (Eredine) Charitable
    Trust
Sloane Robinson Foundation
Arabella and Julian Smith
    Family Trust

The Squire Patton Boggs
    Charitable Trust
The St Lazarus Charitable
    Trust*
Stolkin Foundation
The Bernard Sunley
    Foundation
The Ashley Tabor-King
    Foundation
Stephen Taylor Foundation
The Thirty Percy Foundation
The Triangle Trust (1949) Fund
The Tweed Family Charitable
    Foundation
The Union of the Sisters of
    Mercy of Great Britain
The Velvet Foundation
The Community Foundation in
    Wales
The Waterloo Foundation
The Welland Trust
The Wigoder Family Foundation
The Woodstock Family
    Charitable Foundation
The Wyfold Charitable Trust
The Yapp Charitable Trust
Youth Endowment Fund (YEF)*
Youth Music

Mid and West Wales

The County Council of Dyfed
    Welsh Church Fund
The Daniell Trust
Garthgwynion Charities
The Simon Gibson Charitable
    Trust
The Morel Charitable Trust
Swansea and Brecon Diocesan
    Board of Finance Ltd

North Wales

The Blandford Lake Trust
Chapman Charitable Trust
The Daniell Trust
The Earl Fitzwilliam Charitable
    Trust
P. and C. Hickinbotham
    Charitable Trust
The Isle of Anglesey Charitable
    Association (Cymdeithas
    Elusennol Ynys Môn)
MBNA General Foundation
The Medicash Foundation
The Steve Morgan Foundation
North West Cancer Research
The Bernard Piggott Charitable
    Trust
Toyota Manufacturing UK
    Charitable Trust
The Williams Family
    Foundation

South Wales

The Austin Bailey Foundation
Ford Britain Trust
The Simon Gibson Charitable
    Trust
Heb Ffin (Without Frontier)
The Huggard Charitable Trust
The Monmouthshire County
    Council Welsh Church Act
    Fund
The Dezna Robins Jones
    Charitable Foundation
The Florence Shute Millennium
    Trust
Swansea and Brecon Diocesan
    Board of Finance Ltd
The Virgin Money Foundation
The Welsh Church Act Fund

Northern Ireland	Republic of Ireland
Arts Council of Northern Ireland	B&Q Foundation
The Michael Barnard Charitable Trust	Benefact Trust Ltd
Bauer Radio's Cash for Kids Charities	Breast Cancer Now
Biffa Award	William A. Cadbury Charitable Trust
Maureen Boal Charitable Trust	The Cadbury Foundation
Building and Civil Engineering Charitable Trust	Elizabeth Cayzer Charitable Trust
Church of Ireland Priorities Fund	Church of Ireland Priorities Fund
Donibristle Trust	Dentons UK and Middle East LLP Charitable Trust
Drapers Charitable Fund	Duke of Devonshire's Charitable Trust
The Enkalon Foundation	The DWF Charitable Foundation
The Fermanagh Trust	EMI Music Sound Foundation
Halifax Foundation for Northern Ireland	The Fidelis Foundation*
P. and C. Hickinbotham Charitable Trust	The Finnis Scott Foundation
The Reta Lila Howard Foundation	Marc Fitch Fund
Integrated Education Fund	The Albert Gubay Charitable Foundation
The Ireland Fund of Great Britain	Calouste Gulbenkian Foundation – UK Branch
Lord and Lady Lurgan Trust	The Charles Hayward Foundation
The Esmé Mitchell Trust	Hinchley Charitable Trust
John Moores Foundation	The Hospital Saturday Fund
The National Garden Scheme	The Ireland Fund of Great Britain
Community Foundation for Northern Ireland	The Ian Karten Charitable Trust
Northern Pharmacies Ltd Trust Fund	Ladbrokes Coral Trust
Open House Trust Ltd	The O'Sullivan Family Charitable Trust
The O'Sullivan Family Charitable Trust	The Ouseley Church Music Trust
The Rix-Thompson-Rothenberg Foundation	The Joseph Rank Trust
The T.K. Maxx and Homesense Foundation	The Scott Bader Commonwealth Ltd
The Triangle Trust (1949) Fund	ShareGift (The Orr Mackintosh Foundation)
Ulster Garden Villages Ltd	Sodexo Stop Hunger Foundation
	The T.K. Maxx and Homesense Foundation
	The Tabhair Charitable Trust
	C. B. and H. H. T. Taylor 1984 Trust
	Mrs R. P. Tindall's Charitable Trust
	The Toy Trust
	VINCI UK Foundation
	Wellbeing of Women
	The Galen and Hilary Weston Foundation
	Wooden Spoon Society

Grant-makers by field of interest and type of beneficiary

This index contains the following:

List of fields of interest and types of beneficiary: This lists the headings used in DGMT to categorise fields of interest and types of beneficiary.

Grant-makers by field of interest and type of beneficiary: Funders listed under the fields of interest and types of beneficiary for which they have expressed a funding preference. Asterisks mark funders which have not featured in DGMT before.

Grant-makers by field of interest and type of beneficiary

Animals 44
Animal conservation 44

Animal health care/veterinary practice 45

Animal welfare 45

Arts, culture and heritage 46
Access to the arts 49

Architecture and design 50

Arts and cultures of specific communities 50

Crafts 50

Heritage 50

Literature 51

Media (including TV, film, publishing and radio) 52

Performing arts 52

Visual arts 53

Community services and development 53
Advice and counselling services 56

Citizenship 57

Community enterprise and social entrepreneurship 57

Community transport 58

Rural communities 58

Support services 58

Urban communities 58

Education and training 59
Alternative education 65

Extracurricular activities 65

Higher education 65

Integrated education 66

Preschool education 66

Primary education 66

Secondary education 66

Special educational needs 66

Vocational training and apprenticeships 66

Arts, humanities and social sciences 67

Literacy 67

Sciences (formal) 67

Sciences (natural) 67

Sciences (professional and applied) 67

Skilled crafts 67

Emergency response/relief 68
Air ambulance 68

Emergency relief 68

Lifeboats 68

Mountain rescue 68

Environment 69
Agriculture and farming 71

Biodiversity 71

Climate change 72

Coastal/marine 72

Energy 72

Forestry 72

Fresh water (e.g. streams, rivers and lakes) 72

Waste management and recycling 72

General charitable purposes 73

Health 79
Clinical treatment/care 85

Community health services 87

Complementary and alternative therapies 88

Health advice and support 88

Health awareness/ promotion 89

Mental health and well-being 90

Respite breaks/ convalescence 91

Housing and homelessness 91
Almshouses 92

Homelessness outreach 92

Hostels/shelters 92

Housing advice 92

Social housing 93

Supported accommodation 93

Religion 93
Christianity 94

Interfaith activities/ understanding 95

Islam 96

Judaism 96

Research 98
Environmental research 98

Humanities and social sciences 99

Medical research 99

Social justice 101
Conflict resolution 101

Human rights 102

Social welfare 103

Sports and recreation 110
Recreational activities and clubs 112

Sports 112

Specific sports 112

Work outside the UK 113
Conflict resolution, peace-building and disarmament 114

Education 114

Emergency appeals/aid 114

Humanitarian aid 114

Water, sanitation and hygiene (WASH) 115

Age 115
Children and young people 115

Older people 121

Beneficial groups 125
Disability 125

- People with a cognitive or learning disability 129

- People with a physical disability 129

Gender and sexuality 130

- LGBTQ+ 130

- Women and girls 131

Health 131

- Mental health 135

- People with specific conditions 136

- Substance misuse/abuse 137

Occupation and membership groups 138

- Armed forces 138

- Arts and heritage 138

- Environment, agriculture and animals 139

- Freemasons 139

- Manufacturing 139

- Medicine and health 139

- Seafarers and ex-seafarers 139

- Science, technology and engineering 140

- Service industry 140

- Social or sporting clubs 140

People of a particular heritage/ethnic origin 140

- Gypsy, Roma and Traveller 140

Relationships 140

- Bereavement 141

- Families 141

Animals

The Bryan Adams Foundation
The Adlard Family Charitable
  Foundation
Sylvia Aitken's Charitable Trust
The Alborada Trust
Al-Fayed Charitable Foundation
The Astor Foundation
The Banister Charitable Trust
Lord Barnby's Foundation
Biffa Award
Burnie's Foundation
The Edward and Dorothy
  Cadbury Trust
The Frederick and Phyllis Cann
  Trust
The Leslie Mary Carter
  Charitable Trust
Marjorie Coote Animal Charity
  Trust
The Dorus Trust
Audrey Earle Charitable Trust
The Lord Faringdon Charitable
  Trust
The Gordon Fraser Charitable
  Trust
The Joseph Strong Frazer Trust
The B. and P. Glasser
  Charitable Trust
The Graham Trust
Hamamelis Trust
The Lennox Hannay Charitable
  Trust
The Hawthorne Charitable
  Trust
The Charlotte Heber-Percy
  Charitable Trust
The Henry C. Hoare Charitable
  Trust
The Hobson Charity Ltd
The Keith Howard Foundation
The Muriel Jones Foundation
The Kennel Club Charitable
  Trust
The Graham Kirkham
  Foundation
The Ernest Kleinwort
  Charitable Trust
Langdale Trust
Mrs F. B. Laurence Charitable
  Trust
The Herd Lawson and Muriel
  Lawson Charitable Trust
Limoges Charitable Trust
The Macdonald-Buchanan
  Charitable Trust
The Robin MacLeod Charitable
  Trust
The Marsh Christian Trust
The Martin Charitable Trust
The Master Charitable Trust
The Millennium Oak Trust
The Ronald Miller Foundation
The Millichope Foundation
The Norman Family Charitable
  Trust

The Oakdale Trust
The Paget Charitable Trust
The Jack Patston Charitable
  Trust
Susanna Peake Charitable
  Trust
Petplan Charitable Trust
The Bernard Piggott Charitable
  Trust
The Prince of Wales's
  Charitable Foundation
The Princess Anne's Charities
The Racing Foundation
The Ratcliff Foundation
The Royal Foundation of The
  Prince and Princess of
  Wales
The S. M. B. Trust
The Saddlers' Company
  Charitable Fund
Salisbury Pool Charity
The M. J. Samuel Charitable
  Trust
Sandra Charitable Trust
ShareGift (The Orr Mackintosh
  Foundation)
The Sheepdrove Trust
The John Slater Foundation
Ruth Smart Foundation
The N. Smith Charitable
  Settlement
The Spear Charitable Trust
Sabina Sutherland Charitable
  Trust
The Taurus Foundation
Tay Charitable Trust
The Constance Travis
  Charitable Trust
The Underwood Trust
The Michael Uren Foundation
The Van Mesdag Fund
Veg Trust Ltd (incorporating
  the Matthew Eyton Animal
  Welfare Trust)
Nigel Vinson Charitable Trust
The Virgin Foundation (Virgin
  Unite)
The H. D. H. Wills 1965
  Charitable Trust

Animal conservation

The AEB Charitable Trust
The Derrill Allatt Foundation
The Ian Askew Charitable Trust
The Banister Charitable Trust
Biffa Award
Burnie's Foundation
M. J. Camp Charitable
  Foundation
The Wilfrid and Constance
  Cave Foundation
CLA Charitable Trust

Marjorie Coote Animal Charity
  Trust
Craignish Trust
The Daniell Trust
The Dashlight Foundation
William Dean Countryside and
  Educational Trust
The Earl Fitzwilliam Charitable
  Trust
The B. and P. Glasser
  Charitable Trust
Michael and Shirley Hunt
  Charitable Trust
The Iliffe Family Charitable
  Trust
Langdale Trust
Mrs F. B. Laurence Charitable
  Trust
The R. S. Macdonald
  Charitable Trust
The Marchig Animal Welfare
  Trust
The Michael Marks Charitable
  Trust
The Millennium Oak Trust
The Millichope Foundation
The Esmé Mitchell Trust
The Norman Family Charitable
  Trust
The Oakdale Trust
The Ofenheim Charitable Trust
The Owen Family Trust
The Samuel and Freda
  Parkinson Charitable Trust
The Jack Patston Charitable
  Trust
Cecil Pilkington Charitable
  Trust
The Primrose Trust
The Prince of Wales's
  Charitable Foundation
The Ratcliff Foundation
The Royal Foundation of The
  Prince and Princess of
  Wales
The Michael and Nicola Sacher
  Charitable Trust
The Jean Sainsbury Animal
  Welfare Trust
Ruth Smart Foundation
Tay Charitable Trust
Veg Trust Ltd (incorporating
  the Matthew Eyton Animal
  Welfare Trust)
The David Webster Charitable
  Trust
Whitley Animal Protection Trust
The H. D. H. Wills 1965
  Charitable Trust
J. and J. R. Wilson Trust
The Worwin UK Foundation

Animal health care/veterinary practice

The Alborada Trust
Burnie's Foundation
The Beryl Evetts and Robert Luff Animal Welfare Trust Ltd
Michael and Shirley Hunt Charitable Trust
The Kennel Club Charitable Trust
Petplan Charitable Trust
The Pets at Home Foundation
Betty Phillips Charitable Trust
The Racing Foundation
The Jean Sainsbury Animal Welfare Trust
Veg Trust Ltd (incorporating the Matthew Eyton Animal Welfare Trust)
Sylvia Waddilove Foundation UK

Animal welfare

The Aberbrothock Skea Trust
abrdn Charitable Foundation
The AEB Charitable Trust
Sylvia Aitken's Charitable Trust
Alan Boswell Group Charitable Trust
The Alborada Trust
Al-Fayed Charitable Foundation
The Derrill Allatt Foundation
The Astor Foundation
The Benham Charitable Settlement
The Rowan Bentall Charitable Trust
The Isabel Blackman Foundation
Maureen Boal Charitable Trust
Burnie's Foundation
The Cadogan Charity
The Calleva Foundation
M. J. Camp Charitable Foundation
The Castanea Trust
The Chartley Foundation
The Childwick Trust
The Robert Clutterbuck Charitable Trust
The Catherine Cookson Charitable Trust
Marjorie Coote Animal Charity Trust
The David Family Foundation*
The De Brye Charitable Trust
The Dischma Charitable Trust
Dumbreck Charity
E. B. M. Charitable Trust
The Enkalon Foundation

The Beryl Evetts and Robert Luff Animal Welfare Trust Ltd
The Fairness Foundation
The Anna Rosa Forster Charitable Trust
Mrs D. M. France-Hayhurst Foundation
The Joseph Strong Frazer Trust
The Tara Getty Foundation
The Golden Bottle Trust
The Graham Trust
The Lennox Hannay Charitable Trust
The Harebell Centenary Fund
The Hawthorne Charitable Trust
The Charlotte Heber-Percy Charitable Trust
The Henry C. Hoare Charitable Trust
The Horse Trust
Michael and Shirley Hunt Charitable Trust
The Ithaca Trust
The Jenour Foundation
The Kennel Club Charitable Trust
The Graham Kirkham Foundation
Ladbrokes Coral Trust
Langdale Trust
Mrs F. B. Laurence Charitable Trust
The Herd Lawson and Muriel Lawson Charitable Trust
The Leeward Trust
Lord Leverhulme's Charitable Trust
The Michael and Betty Little Trust*
The R. S. Macdonald Charitable Trust
The Robin MacLeod Charitable Trust
The Marchig Animal Welfare Trust
The Martin Charitable Trust
Matchroom Sport Charitable Foundation
The Gerald Micklem Charitable Trust
The Millward Charitable Trust
The Mumford Memorial Trust*
Edith Murphy Foundation
The Nineveh Charitable Trust
The Oakdale Trust
The Sir Peter O'Sullevan Charitable Trust
P. F. Charitable Trust
The Samuel and Freda Parkinson Charitable Trust
The Jack Patston Charitable Trust
Payne-Gallwey 1989 Charitable Trust

John Pearce Foundation
Petplan Charitable Trust
The Pets at Home Foundation
Betty Phillips Charitable Trust
Elise Pilkington Charitable Trust
The Primrose Trust
The Prince of Wales's Charitable Foundation
The Princess Anne's Charities
The Racing Foundation
The Rhododendron Trust
The Roan Charitable Trust
The Rose Animal Welfare Trust CIO
The Saddlers' Company Charitable Fund
The Jean Sainsbury Animal Welfare Trust
The Scotshill Trust
Ruth Smart Foundation
The Peter Smith Charitable Trust for Nature
Arabella and Julian Smith Family Trust
The Stafford Trust
The Samuel Storey Family Charitable Trust
The Tanlaw Foundation
The Taurus Foundation
Tay Charitable Trust
The Troutsdale Charitable Trust
The Underwood Trust
The Valentine Charitable Trust
The Van Mesdag Fund
Veg Trust Ltd (incorporating the Matthew Eyton Animal Welfare Trust)
The William and Patricia Venton Charitable Trust
Nigel Vinson Charitable Trust
Sylvia Waddilove Foundation UK
Mrs Waterhouse Charitable Trust
The Weir Charitable Trust
Whitley Animal Protection Trust
The H. D. H. Wills 1965 Charitable Trust
J. and J. R. Wilson Trust
The Woosnam Foundation
The Elizabeth and Prince Zaiger Trust

Arts, culture and heritage

The 29th May 1961 Charitable
Trust
The A. and J. Charitable Trust
The Aberdeen Endowments
Trust
Adam Family Foundation
The Adlard Family Charitable
Foundation
The AEB Charitable Trust
Sylvia Aitken's Charitable Trust
AKO Foundation
The Aldama Foundation
The Derrill Allatt Foundation
D. C. R. Allen Charitable Trust
Amant Foundation
The Ammco Trust
The Anchor Foundation
Andor Charitable Trust
The Anson Charitable Trust
The Arah Foundation
The Architectural Heritage
Fund
The Ardeola Charitable Trust
The John Armitage Charitable
Trust
The Armourers and Brasiers
Gauntlet Trust
The Art Fund
Arts Council England
Arts Council of Northern
Ireland
Arts Council of Wales (also
known as Cyngor
Celfyddydau Cymru)
ArtSocial Foundation
The Ashendene Trust
The Ashley Family Foundation
The Associated Board of the
Royal Schools of Music
(ABRSM)
The Astor Foundation
Atkin Charitable Foundation
The Aurelius Charitable Trust
Backstage Trust
Bagri Foundation
The Baird Trust
The Band Trust
Veronica and Lars Bane
Foundation
The Kamini and Vindi Banga
Family Trust
Barchester Healthcare
Foundation
The Baring Foundation
Misses Barrie Charitable Trust
Robert Barr's Charitable Trust
The Gordon and Ena Baxter
Foundation*
BC Partners Foundation
The Beaverbrook Foundation
The Benham Charitable
Settlement
Bennett Lowell Ltd

Biffa Award
The Billmeir Charitable Trust
The Bingham Trust
The Michael Bishop
Foundation
Maria Bjornson Memorial Fund
The Bertie Black Foundation
The Sir Victor Blank Charitable
Settlement
Blyth Watson Charitable Trust
The Boltini Trust
The Charlotte Bonham-Carter
Charitable Trust
The Bowland Charitable Trust
The Liz and Terry Bramall
Foundation
The Brelms Trust CIO
The Britford Bridge Trust
J. and M. Britton Charitable
Trust
The Consuelo and Anthony
Brooke Charitable Trust
The Charles Brotherton Trust
The Brownsword Charitable
Foundation
T. B. H. Brunner's Charitable
Settlement
The Jack Brunton Charitable
Trust
The Bulldog Trust Ltd
The Arnold Burton 1998
Charitable Trust
The Edward Cadbury
Charitable Trust
William A. Cadbury Charitable
Trust
The Edward and Dorothy
Cadbury Trust
The George Cadbury Trust
The Calleva Foundation
Camden Giving
Carew Pole Charitable Trust
William A. Cargill Charitable
Trust
The Carnegie Dunfermline
Trust
The Castansa Trust
The Thomas Sivewright Catto
Charitable Settlement
The Wilfrid and Constance
Cave Foundation
The Cayo Foundation
The B. G. S. Cayzer Charitable
Trust
Elizabeth Cayzer Charitable
Trust
The Amelia Chadwick Trust
The Chalk Cliff Trust
Chapman Charitable Trust
The Charities Advisory Trust
The Chartley Foundation
The Childhood Trust
Chippenham Borough Lands
Charity
Church Burgesses Educational
Foundation

The Roger and Sarah Bancroft
Clark Charitable Trust
The Clore Duffield Foundation
The John Coates Charitable
Trust
The Vivienne and Samuel
Cohen Charitable Trust
The John S. Cohen Foundation
The R. and S. Cohen
Foundation
The Cole Charitable Trust
Sir Jeremiah Colman Gift Trust
Colwinston Charitable Trust
Douglas Compton James
Charitable Trust
The Catherine Cookson
Charitable Trust
The Keith Coombs Trust
The County Council of Dyfed
Welsh Church Fund
County Durham Community
Foundation
Coutts Charitable Foundation
Creative Scotland
Cruden Foundation Ltd
Cumbria Community
Foundation
The Daiwa Anglo-Japanese
Foundation
The David Family Foundation*
The Manny and Brigitta
Davidson Charitable
Foundation
Michael Davies Charitable
Settlement
Margaret Davies Charity
The Roger De Haan Charitable
Trust
The De Laszlo Foundation
Foundation Derbyshire
Devon Community Foundation
The Alan and Sheila Diamond
Charitable Trust
The Gillian Dickinson Trust
Didymus
The Dischma Charitable Trust
The Djanogly Foundation
William and Frances Dobie
Charitable Foundation
The Dorfman Foundation
The Dorus Trust
The D'Oyly Carte Charitable
Trust
Drapers Charitable Fund
The Duke of Cornwall's
Benevolent Fund
The Dulverton Trust
Dumbreck Charity
Dumfriesshire East Community
Benefit Group SCIO
Dunard Fund
Dunlossit and Islay Community
Trust
The Charles Dunstone
Charitable Trust

The Dyers' Company
Charitable Trust
The James and Deirdre Dyson
Trust
The Earley Charity
The Gilbert and Eileen Edgar
Foundation
The Eighty Eight Foundation
John Ellerman Foundation
The Elmley Foundation
Emerton-Christie Charity
The Englefield Charitable Trust
The Enkalon Foundation
Esmée Fairbairn Foundation
The Lord Faringdon Charitable
Trust
The Fidelity UK Foundation
The Finnis Scott Foundation
Sir John Fisher Foundation
The Earl Fitzwilliam Charitable
Trust
The Robert Fleming Hannay
Memorial Charity
The Joyce Fletcher Charitable
Trust
The Follett Trust
Ford Britain Trust
Oliver Ford Foundation
The Fort Foundation
Fowler Smith and Jones Trust
The Foxglove Trust
The Foyle Foundation
The Elizabeth Frankland Moore
and Star Foundation
The Gordon Fraser Charitable
Trust
The Hugh Fraser Foundation
The Joseph Strong Frazer Trust
Charles S. French Charitable
Trust
The Freshgate Trust
Foundation
Friends of the National
Libraries
The Gannochy Trust
Gatwick Airport Community
Trust
The Gibbs Charitable Trusts
The G. C. Gibson Charitable
Trust
The Simon Gibson Charitable
Trust
The Glass-House Trust
The Gloucestershire Historic
Churches Trust
The Golden Bottle Trust
The Goldman Sachs Charitable
Gift Fund (UK)
Goldman Sachs Gives (UK)
The Goldsmiths' Company
Charity
The Golsoncott Foundation
Nicholas and Judith
Goodison's Charitable
Settlement
The Graham Trust

The Granada Foundation
The J. G. Graves Charitable
Trust
The Great Britain Sasakawa
Foundation
The Kenneth and Susan Green
Charitable Foundation
Greenham Trust Ltd
The Grimmitt Trust
The Grocers' Charity
Calouste Gulbenkian
Foundation – UK Branch
The Hadfield Charitable Trust
The Hadrian Trust
Paul Hamlyn Foundation
The Helen Hamlyn Trust
Hampton Fund
The W. A. Handley Charity
Trust
The Lennox Hannay Charitable
Trust
The Kathleen Hannay
Memorial Charity
The Harbour Foundation
William Harding's Charity
The Peter and Teresa Harris
Charitable Trust
The Harrison-Frank Family
Foundation (UK) Ltd
The Hawthorne Charitable
Trust
The Headley Trust
The Heathside Charitable Trust
The Charlotte Heber-Percy
Charitable Trust
Ernest Hecht Charitable
Foundation
The Hedley Foundation
The Hemby Charitable Trust
Herefordshire Community
Foundation
Heritage Lottery Fund
P. and C. Hickinbotham
Charitable Trust
The Derek Hill Foundation
The Hillier Trust
The Lady Hind Trust
The Hinduja Foundation
The Hinrichsen Foundation
The Hintze Family Charity
Foundation
The Hiscox Foundation
The Hobson Charity Ltd
The Holbeck Charitable Trust
Hollick Family Foundation
The Holliday Foundation
P. H. Holt Foundation
The Holywood Trust
The Harold Hyam Wingate
Foundation
The Idlewild Trust
The Inverforth Charitable Trust
The Investindustrial
Foundation
The Invigorate Charitable Trust

The Ireland Fund of Great
Britain
Irish Youth Foundation (UK)
Ltd (incorporating The
Lawlor Foundation)
The Ithaca Trust
Lady Eda Jardine Charitable
Trust
The Jenour Foundation
The Jewish Youth Fund
The Jusaca Charitable Trust
The Kennedy Leigh Charitable
Trust
The Kensington and Chelsea
Foundation
Fraser Kilpatrick Charitable
Trust
Laura Kinsella Foundation
The Graham Kirkham
Foundation
Sir James Knott Trust
The Kobler Trust
Kusuma Trust UK
The Kyte Charitable Trust
The David Laing Foundation
The Kirby Laing Foundation
The Martin Laing Foundation
Langdale Trust
The Lauffer Family Charitable
Foundation
The Law Family Charitable
Foundation
The Edgar E. Lawley
Foundation
The Lawson Trust CIO
The Leach Fourteenth Trust
The Leathersellers' Foundation
The Leeward Trust
The Leri Charitable Trust
The Leverhulme Trust
Lord Leverhulme's Charitable
Trust
The Ralph Levy Charitable
Company Ltd
Cecil and Hilda Lewis
Charitable Trust
Liberum Foundation
The Limbourne Trust
Limoges Charitable Trust
The Linbury Trust
The Linder Foundation
The Lister Charitable Trust
The Michael and Betty Little
Trust*
The Charles Littlewood Hill
Trust
The George John and Sheilah
Livanos Charitable Trust
Liverpool Charity and Voluntary
Services (LCVS)
Jack Livingstone Charitable
Trust
The Elaine and Angus Lloyd
Charitable Trust
The Andrew Lloyd Webber
Foundation

The Lockwood Charitable
Foundation
The London Community
Foundation (LCF)
The C. L. Loyd Charitable Trust
Lord and Lady Lurgan Trust
Sir Jack Lyons Charitable Trust
The Mackintosh Foundation
The Mageni Trust
The Manchester Guardian
Society Charitable Trust
The W. M. Mann Foundation
The Manoukian Charitable
Foundation
The Marandi Foundation
The Stella and Alexander
Margulies Charitable Trust
The Michael Marks Charitable
Trust
The Marks Family Charitable
Trust
The Marsh Christian Trust
Charity of John Marshall
The Martin Charitable Trust
Sir George Martin Trust
Nancie Massey Charitable
Trust
The Master Charitable Trust
Material World Foundation
Mazars Charitable Trust
The Medlock Charitable Trust
The Meikle Foundation
The Merchant Venturers
Charity
Merchants House of Glasgow
The Mickel Fund
The Mikheev Charitable Trust
The Mila Charitable
Organisation
Millennium Stadium Charitable
Trust (Ymddiriedolaeth
Elusennol Stadiwm y
Mileniwm)
The Ronald Miller Foundation
The Millichope Foundation
Milton Keynes Community
Foundation Ltd
The Laurence Misener
Charitable Trust
The Brian Mitchell Charitable
Settlement
The Esmé Mitchell Trust
The Mittal Foundation
The Modiano Charitable Trust
The Mohn Westlake
Foundation
The Alexander Moncur Trust
The Monmouthshire County
Council Welsh Church Act
Fund
The Henry Moore Foundation
The Morel Charitable Trust
The Morris Charitable Trust
G. M. Morrison Charitable
Trust
The Morrisons Foundation

The Mulberry Trust
The John R. Murray Charitable
Trust
Music Sales Charitable Trust
The NDL Foundation
Network for Social Change
Charitable Trust
The Nine Incorporated Trades
of Dundee General Fund
Charity
The Nisbet Trust
Normanby Charitable Trust
Northwood Charitable Trust
The Norton Foundation
Norwich Town Close Estate
Charity
The Norwood and Newton
Settlement
The Notgrove Trust
The Oakdale Trust
The Oakley Charitable Trust
Odin Charitable Trust
The Ofenheim Charitable Trust
The Hamish Ogston
Foundation
Old Possum's Practical Trust
Henry Oldfield Trust
The Owen Family Trust
Oxfordshire Community
Foundation
P. F. Charitable Trust
Parabola Foundation
The Patrick Trust
David Pearlman Charitable
Foundation
People's Postcode Trust
The Performing Right Society
Foundation
The Persimmon Charitable
Foundation
The Phillips and Rubens
Charitable Trust
The Phillips Family Charitable
Trust
The Bernard Piggott Charitable
Trust
The Pilgrim Trust
Cecil Pilkington Charitable
Trust
The Sir Harry Pilkington Fund
The Austin and Hope
Pilkington Trust
The Polonsky Foundation
Porter Foundation
The Portrack Charitable Trust
Postcode Community Trust
Postcode Local Trust
Postcode Society Trust
David and Elaine Potter
Foundation
Quartet Community Foundation
The Radcliffe Trust
Richard Radcliffe Trust
The Rainford Trust
The Rambourg Foundation

The Joseph and Lena Randall
Charitable Trust
The Ranworth Trust
Elizabeth Rathbone Charity
The Julia and Hans Rausing
Trust*
The Ravensdale Trust
The Rayne Foundation
The Max Reinhardt Charitable
Trust
Reuben Foundation
The Revere Charitable Trust
The Rhododendron Trust
Daisie Rich Trust
The Clive Richards Foundation
Rigby Foundation
The Sir John Ritblat Family
Foundation
Rockcliffe Charitable Trust
The Rockspring Charitable
Trust
The Roddick Foundation
The Gerald and Gail Ronson
Family Foundation
The Roseline Foundation*
The Ross Foundation
The Rothermere Foundation
The Rothschild Foundation
The Eranda Rothschild
Foundation
Rothschild Foundation
(Hanadiv) Europe
The Roughley Charitable Trust
The Rowlands Trust
Royal Docks Trust (London)
The Rubin Foundation
Charitable Trust
The Ruddock Foundation for
the Arts
Russell Trust
The Jeremy and John Sacher
Charitable Trust
The Michael and Nicola Sacher
Charitable Trust
The Dr Mortimer and Theresa
Sackler Foundation
The Sackler Trust
The Saddlers' Company
Charitable Fund
The Saintbury Trust
The Salamander Charitable
Trust
The Basil Samuel Charitable
Trust
The M. J. Samuel Charitable
Trust
Schroder Charity Trust
The Schroder Foundation
Foundation Scotland
Scotland's Garden Scheme*
The Scotshill Trust
The Frieda Scott Charitable
Trust
The John Scott Trust Fund
Scottish Coal Industry Special
Welfare Fund

ScottishPower Foundation

Scouloudi Foundation

ShareGift (The Orr Mackintosh Foundation)

The Sharp Foundation

The Shears Foundation

The Sheepdrove Trust

The Sheffield Town Trust

The Sylvia and Colin Shepherd Charitable Trust

The Archie Sherman Charitable Trust

The R. C. Sherriff Rosebriars Trust

Shetland Charitable Trust

The Bassil Shippam and Alsford Trust

The Charles Skey Charitable Trust

Kathleen Beryl Sleigh Charitable Trust

The N. Smith Charitable Settlement

The E. C. Sosnow Charitable Trust

The Stephen R. and Philippa H. Southall Charitable Trust

Peter Sowerby Foundation

Spielman Charitable Trust

The Squire Patton Boggs Charitable Trust

Stanley Foundation Ltd

The Steel Charitable Trust

The Sterry Family Foundation

The Stevenson Family's Charitable Trust

The Samuel Storey Family Charitable Trust

The Summerfield Charitable Trust

Sabina Sutherland Charitable Trust

Sutton Coldfield Charitable Trust

Swarovski Foundation

The John Swire (1989) Charitable Trust

The Swire Charitable Trust

The Charles and Elsie Sykes Trust

The William Syson Foundation

The Taurus Foundation

Tay Charitable Trust

C. B. and H. H. T. Taylor 1984 Trust

Humphrey Richardson Taylor Charitable Trust

The Taylor Family Foundation

The Tedworth Charitable Trust

The Theatres Trust Charitable Fund

The Tolkien Trust

The Tompkins Foundation

The Constance Travis Charitable Trust

The Troutsdale Charitable Trust

The Roger and Douglas Turner Charitable Trust

The Turtleton Charitable Trust

Ulster Garden Villages Ltd

The Underwood Trust

The Valentine Charitable Trust

The Albert Van Den Bergh Charitable Trust

The Vandervell Foundation

The Vardy Foundation

Nigel Vinson Charitable Trust

Sylvia Waddilove Foundation UK

Mrs Waterhouse Charitable Trust

G. R. Waters Charitable Trust 2000

The William Wates Memorial Trust

The Geoffrey Watling Charity

The Weinstock Fund

The Weir Charitable Trust

The Welsh Church Act Fund

Westhill Endowment

The Garfield Weston Foundation

Westway Trust

The Barbara Whatmore Charitable Trust

The Williams Family Foundation

Sumner Wilson Charitable Trust

Wiltshire Community Foundation

The Wixamtree Trust

The Maurice Wohl Charitable Foundation

The Wolfson Family Charitable Trust

The Wolfson Foundation

The Lord Leonard and Lady Estelle Wolfson Foundation

The Victoria Wood Foundation

The Woodward Charitable Trust

Worshipful Company of Gold and Silver Wyre Drawers Second Charitable Trust Fund

The Worwin UK Foundation

WPG Charitable Trust*

The Wyfold Charitable Trust

The Wyseliot Rose Charitable Trust

Youth Music

Access to the arts

The Art Fund

Arts Council of Northern Ireland

Bagri Foundation

Binks Trust

Maria Bjornson Memorial Fund

Elizabeth Cayzer Charitable Trust

Chapman Charitable Trust

The Charities Advisory Trust

The Chetwode Foundation

The Childhood Trust

The Clore Duffield Foundation

The Noel Coward Foundation

Creative Scotland

The Elmley Foundation

Esmée Fairbairn Foundation

The Finnis Scott Foundation

The Joyce Fletcher Charitable Trust

Fowler Smith and Jones Trust

The Foyle Foundation

The Freelands Foundation Ltd

Charles S. French Charitable Trust

The Garrick Charitable Trust

The Gatsby Charitable Foundation

The Robert Gavron Charitable Trust

The Golsoncott Foundation

Halifax Foundation for Northern Ireland

Paul Hamlyn Foundation

The Helen Hamlyn Trust

The Harbour Foundation

The Headley Trust

Ernest Hecht Charitable Foundation

The Heritage of London Trust Ltd

The Derek Hill Foundation

P. H. Holt Foundation

The Idlewild Trust

The Ireland Fund of Great Britain

The Sir Barry Jackson County Fund

The London Community Foundation

John Lyon's Charity

The Mackintosh Foundation

Material World Foundation

The Mayfield Valley Arts Trust

The Brian Mercer Charitable Trust

Millennium Stadium Charitable Trust (Ymddiriedolaeth Elusennol Stadiwm y Mileniwm)

The Mohn Westlake Foundation

The Henry Moore Foundation

The Morel Charitable Trust

Nottinghamshire Community Foundation

Porter Foundation

The Rix-Thompson-Rothenberg Foundation

The Ruddock Foundation for the Arts

The Alan and Babette
    Sainsbury Charitable Fund
Humphrey Richardson Taylor
    Charitable Trust
The Taylor Family Foundation
The Theatres Trust Charitable
    Fund
The Lord Leonard and Lady
    Estelle Wolfson Foundation
The Victoria Wood Foundation
The Woodward Charitable
    Trust
Youth Music

Architecture and design

The Ove Arup Foundation
Dunard Fund
The Granada Foundation
The Lord Leonard and Lady
    Estelle Wolfson Foundation

Arts and cultures of specific communities

Arcadia Fund
The Art Fund
The Ashley Family Foundation
Bagri Foundation
Binks Trust
The Noel Coward Foundation
The Daiwa Anglo-Japanese
    Foundation
William Grant Foundation*
The Great Britain Sasakawa
    Foundation
The Helen Hamlyn Trust
The Ireland Fund of Great
    Britain
The London Community
    Foundation
Material World Foundation
The James Pantyfedwen
    Foundation
    (Ymddiriedolaeth James
    Pantyfedwen)
Rothschild Foundation
    (Hanadiv) Europe
The Ruddock Foundation for
    the Arts
The Sino-British Fellowship
    Trust
The Weir Charitable Trust
W. Wing Yip and Brothers
    Foundation
Youth Music

Crafts

The Armourers and Brasiers
    Gauntlet Trust

The Carpenters Company
    Charitable Trust
The Cotton Industry War
    Memorial Trust
Creative Scotland
The Dyers' Company
    Charitable Trust
The Elmley Foundation
The Headley Trust
The Idlewild Trust
The Kirby Laing Foundation
The Leathersellers' Foundation
The Leche Trust
Lloyd's Register Foundation
The Nine Incorporated Trades
    of Dundee General Fund
    Charity
The Radcliffe Trust
The Saddlers' Company
    Charitable Fund
The Weavers' Company
    Benevolent Fund
The Worshipful Company of
    Glovers of London
    Charitable Trust
Worshipful Company of Gold
    and Silver Wyre Drawers
    Second Charitable Trust
    Fund
Worshipful Company of
    Needlemakers Charitable
    Fund

Heritage

The Adlard Family Charitable
    Foundation
The Aldama Foundation
The Architectural Heritage
    Fund
The Art Fund
The Ian Askew Charitable Trust
The Astor Foundation
Atlas Memorial Ltd
The Baird Trust
The Roy and Pixie Baker
    Charitable Trust
The Barbour Foundation
Barcapel Foundation Ltd
The Beaverbrook Foundation
The Bedfordshire and
    Hertfordshire Historic
    Churches Trust
The Bellahouston Bequest
    Fund
Benefact Trust Ltd
The Benham Charitable
    Settlement
Bennett Lowell Ltd
The Rowan Bentall Charitable
    Trust
The Birmingham Diocesan
    Board of Finance
The Michael Bishop
    Foundation

The Bosson Family Charitable
    Trust
G. and K. Boyes Charitable
    Trust
T. B. H. Brunner's Charitable
    Settlement
Buckingham Trust
The Arnold Burton 1998
    Charitable Trust
Consolidated Charity of Burton
    upon Trent
M. J. Camp Charitable
    Foundation
Carew Pole Charitable Trust
The Leslie Mary Carter
    Charitable Trust
Elizabeth Cayzer Charitable
    Trust
The Charities Advisory Trust
The Francis Coales Charitable
    Foundation
The John Coates Charitable
    Trust
Sir Jeremiah Colman Gift Trust
Colwinston Charitable Trust
Community First
Congregational and General
    Charitable Trust
The County Council of Dyfed
    Welsh Church Fund
Creative Scotland
Cruden Foundation Ltd
The Roger De Haan Charitable
    Trust
William Delafield Charitable
    Trust
The Dischma Charitable Trust
The Dorset Historic Churches
    Trust
The D'Oyly Carte Charitable
    Trust
Drapers Charitable Fund
The Duke of Cornwall's
    Benevolent Fund
The Dulverton Trust
The Charles Dunstone
    Charitable Trust
The Englefield Charitable Trust
The Lord Faringdon Charitable
    Trust
The February Foundation
The Feoffees of St Michael's
    Spurriergate York
Marc Fitch Fund
The Earl Fitzwilliam Charitable
    Trust
Ian M. Foulerton Charitable
    Trust
Fowler Smith and Jones Trust
The Foyle Foundation
Jill Franklin Trust
The Gordon Fraser Charitable
    Trust
The Freshgate Trust
    Foundation

Friends of Essex Churches
Trust
The Friends of Kent Churches
Friends of the National
Libraries
Frognal Trust
J. Paul Getty Jr General
Charitable Trust*
The Simon Gibson Charitable
Trust
The Gloucestershire Historic
Churches Trust
The Goldsmiths' Company
Charity
The Graham Trust
William Grant Foundation*
The J. G. Graves Charitable
Trust
The Helen Hamlyn Trust
The W. A. Handley Charity
Trust
The Charles Hayward
Foundation
The Headley Trust
The Herefordshire Historic
Churches Trust
Heritage Lottery Fund
The Heritage of London Trust
Ltd
The Hintze Family Charity
Foundation
Historic Environment Scotland
Historic Houses Foundation
The Holbeck Charitable Trust
The Hosking Charitable Trust*
The Idlewild Trust
The Investindustrial
Foundation
The Kilroot Foundation
Laura Kinsella Foundation
The Graham Kirkham
Foundation
Sir James Knott Trust
Laslett's (Hinton) Charity
Mrs F. B. Laurence Charitable
Trust
The Lawson Trust CIO
The Leach Fourteenth Trust
The Leche Trust
Limoges Charitable Trust
The Linbury Trust
The Charles Littlewood Hill
Trust
The Andrew Lloyd Webber
Foundation
Lloyd's Register Foundation
The Lockwood Charitable
Foundation
Manchester Airport Community
Trust Fund
The Michael Marks Charitable
Trust
The Marsh Christian Trust
Charity of John Marshall
The Master Charitable Trust

Matchroom Sport Charitable
Foundation
The Millichope Foundation
The Esmé Mitchell Trust
The Monmouthshire County
Council Welsh Church Act
Fund
The Henry Moore Foundation
G. M. Morrison Charitable
Trust
The Alexander Mosley
Charitable Trust
The National Churches Trust
The National Manuscripts
Conservation Trust
The Norfolk Churches Trust Ltd
Normanby Charitable Trust
The Northumbria Historic
Churches Trust
The Norwood and Newton
Settlement
The Hamish Ogston
Foundation
Henry Oldfield Trust
The Owen Family Trust
Oxfordshire Historic Churches
Trust (2016)
The James Pantyfedwen
Foundation
(Ymddiriedolaeth James
Pantyfedwen)
The Jack Patston Charitable
Trust
David Pearlman Charitable
Foundation
The Bernard Piggott Charitable
Trust
The Pilgrim Trust
The Players Foundation
Sir John Priestman Charity
Trust
The Prince of Wales's
Charitable Foundation
The Joseph and Lena Randall
Charitable Trust
The Joseph Rank Trust
Rees Jeffreys Road Fund
The Clive Richards Foundation
Rigby Foundation
The Sir John Ritblat Family
Foundation
The Romney Marsh Historic
Churches Trust
The Ross Foundation
The Rothermere Foundation
Rothschild Foundation
(Hanadiv) Europe
The Roughley Charitable Trust
The Rowlands Trust
Royal Docks Trust (London)
The Royal Navy and Royal
Marines Charity
The Ruddock Foundation for
the Arts
Salisbury Pool Charity
Schroder Charity Trust

The Scorpion Charitable Trust*
ShareGift (The Orr Mackintosh
Foundation)
The Sheffield Town Trust
The Sylvia and Colin Shepherd
Charitable Trust
The Shipwrights Charitable
Fund
The Stephen R. and Philippa
H. Southall Charitable Trust
Stanley Foundation Ltd
Stolkin Foundation
Peter Stormonth Darling
Charitable Trust
The Suffolk Historic Churches
Trust
The Summerfield Charitable
Trust
Sabina Sutherland Charitable
Trust
The Swire Charitable Trust
The Adrian Swire Charitable
Trust
The Charles and Elsie Sykes
Trust
The William Syson Foundation
Tanner Trust
The Theatres Trust Charitable
Fund
The Roger and Douglas Turner
Charitable Trust
The Michael Uren Foundation
Valencia Communities Fund
War Memorials Trust
Mrs Waterhouse Charitable
Trust
The Geoffrey Watling Charity
The David Webster Charitable
Trust
The Welsh Church Act Fund
The Barbara Whatmore
Charitable Trust
Colonel W. H. Whitbread
Charitable Trust
Alfred Williams Charitable
Trust
Wiltshire Community
Foundation
The Wolfson Foundation
Worth Waynflete Foundation
The Yorkshire Dales
Millennium Trust
The Yorkshire Historic
Churches Trust

Literature

Creative Scotland
The Elmley Foundation
Friends of the National
Libraries
The Garrick Charitable Trust
The Granada Foundation
Ernest Hecht Charitable
Foundation
The Derek Hill Foundation

The Harold Hyam Wingate
   Foundation
The Graham Kirkham
   Foundation
The Limbourne Trust
The Marsh Christian Trust
The William Syson Foundation

Media (including TV, film, publishing and radio)

The Bertie Black Foundation
Creative Scotland
The Daiwa Anglo-Japanese
   Foundation
The Elmley Foundation
The J. J. Charitable Trust
The Jerusalem Trust
The Roddick Foundation
G. R. Waters Charitable Trust
   2000

Performing arts

The Aberdeenshire Educational
   Trust Scheme
The Associated Board of the
   Royal Schools of Music
   (ABRSM)
Backstage Trust
Bagri Foundation
The Rachel Baker Memorial
   Charity
The Kamini and Vindi Banga
   Family Trust
Bennett Lowell Ltd
Binks Trust
Maria Bjornson Memorial Fund
Bluespark Foundation
The Marjory Boddy Charitable
   Trust
The Boltini Trust
The BRIT Trust
T. B. H. Brunner's Charitable
   Settlement
The Jack Brunton Charitable
   Trust
Carew Pole Charitable Trust
The Carr-Gregory Trust
The Childhood Trust
Church Burgesses Educational
   Foundation
The Clore Duffield Foundation
The Vivienne and Samuel
   Cohen Charitable Trust
Colwinston Charitable Trust
Douglas Compton James
   Charitable Trust
Coutts Charitable Foundation
The Noel Coward Foundation
Creative Scotland
Margaret Davies Charity
The De Laszlo Foundation

The Delius Trust
The D'Oyly Carte Charitable
   Trust
Dunard Fund
The Gilbert and Eileen Edgar
   Foundation
John Ellerman Foundation
The Elmley Foundation
EMI Music Sound Foundation
The Lord Faringdon Charitable
   Trust
The Fidelio Charitable Trust
The Joyce Fletcher Charitable
   Trust
The Foyle Foundation
The Gordon Fraser Charitable
   Trust
The Freshgate Trust
   Foundation
The Garrick Charitable Trust
The Gatsby Charitable
   Foundation
The G. C. Gibson Charitable
   Trust
The Golsoncott Foundation
The Gisela Graham Foundation
The Granada Foundation
Dr Guthrie's Association
The Helen Hamlyn Trust
The W. A. Handley Charity
   Trust
The Harbour Foundation
The Harding Trust
The Peter and Teresa Harris
   Charitable Trust
Ernest Hecht Charitable
   Foundation
Henley Educational Trust
Tim Henman Foundation
The Derek Hill Foundation
The Hinrichsen Foundation
The Hobson Charity Ltd
The Keith Howard Foundation
The Harold Hyam Wingate
   Foundation
The Idlewild Trust
The Inverforth Charitable Trust
The Sir Barry Jackson County
   Fund
The Boris Karloff Charitable
   Foundation
The Karlsson Játiva Charitable
   Foundation
The Michael and Ilse Katz
   Foundation
The Emmanuel Kaye
   Foundation
The Graham Kirkham
   Foundation
The Kirby Laing Foundation
The Leche Trust
The Mark Leonard Trust
The Limbourne Trust
The Linbury Trust
The Linder Foundation

The Andrew Lloyd Webber
   Foundation
John Lyon's Charity
The Mackintosh Foundation
Material World Foundation
The Mayfield Valley Arts Trust
The Brian Mercer Charitable
   Trust
Merchants House of Glasgow
Millennium Stadium Charitable
   Trust (Ymddiriedolaeth
   Elusennol Stadiwm y
   Mileniwm)
The Millward Charitable Trust
The Esmé Mitchell Trust
The Henry Moore Foundation
The Morel Charitable Trust
G. M. Morrison Charitable
   Trust
The Nisbet Trust
Nottinghamshire Community
   Foundation
The Ofenheim Charitable Trust
The Hamish Ogston
   Foundation
The Ouseley Church Music
   Trust
Parabola Foundation
David Pearlman Charitable
   Foundation
The Pell Charitable Trust
The Performing Right Society
   Foundation
The Bernard Piggott Charitable
   Trust
The Polonsky Foundation
The Portrack Charitable Trust
The Radcliffe Trust
The Rainford Trust
The Max Reinhardt Charitable
   Trust
The Rix-Thompson-Rothenberg
   Foundation
The Ross Foundation
The Rothermere Foundation
The Rowlands Trust
The Ruddock Foundation for
   the Arts
The Saddlers' Company
   Charitable Fund
The Alan and Babette
   Sainsbury Charitable Fund
The Sands Family Trust
The Bassil Shippam and
   Alsford Trust
Kathleen Beryl Sleigh
   Charitable Trust
The Martin Smith Foundation
Stolkin Foundation
The Adrian Swire Charitable
   Trust
The William Syson Foundation
Humphrey Richardson Taylor
   Charitable Trust
The Taylor Family Foundation

The Theatres Trust Charitable Fund

Mrs R. P. Tindall's Charitable Trust

The Utley Foundation

The Vandervell Foundation

Sylvia Waddilove Foundation UK

The Weinstock Fund

Westhill Endowment

The Whitaker Charitable Trust

Alfred Williams Charitable Trust

The Wolfson Foundation

The Lord Leonard and Lady Estelle Wolfson Foundation

The Victoria Wood Foundation

Worshipful Company of Gold and Silver Wyre Drawers Second Charitable Trust Fund

Youth Music

Visual arts

The Ampersand Foundation

The Art Fund

Binks Trust

Maria Bjornson Memorial Fund

The Rory and Elizabeth Brooks Foundation

Carew Pole Charitable Trust

Colwinston Charitable Trust

Douglas Compton James Charitable Trust

The Noel Coward Foundation

Creative Scotland

Margaret Davies Charity

The De Laszlo Foundation

Dunard Fund

The Elmley Foundation

The Finnis Scott Foundation

The Foyle Foundation

The Gordon Fraser Charitable Trust

The Freelands Foundation Ltd

The Gatsby Charitable Foundation

The Golsoncott Foundation

The Granada Foundation

Dr Guthrie's Association

The Idlewild Trust

The Linbury Trust

The Linder Foundation

John Lyon's Charity

Material World Foundation

The Brian Mercer Charitable Trust

Millennium Stadium Charitable Trust (Ymddiriedolaeth Elusennol Stadiwm y Mileniwm)

The Henry Moore Foundation

Nottinghamshire Community Foundation

The Max Reinhardt Charitable Trust

The Ruddock Foundation for the Arts

The Alan and Babette Sainsbury Charitable Fund

Stolkin Foundation

The William Syson Foundation

Sylvia Waddilove Foundation UK

The Lord Leonard and Lady Estelle Wolfson Foundation

The Victoria Wood Foundation

Community services and development

The 4814 Trust

The A. and J. Charitable Trust

abrdn Charitable Foundation

Adam Family Foundation

The Aimwell Charitable Trust

Alan Boswell Group Charitable Trust

The Alchemy Foundation

The Aldama Foundation

Amant Foundation

The Architectural Heritage Fund

The Armourers and Brasiers Gauntlet Trust

Ove Arup Partnership Charitable Trust

The Asda Foundation

The Asfari Foundation

The Ashley Family Foundation

The Astor Foundation

The Avon and Somerset Police Community Trust

The Ballinger Charitable Trust

Bank of Scotland Foundation

Barchester Healthcare Foundation

Philip Barker Charity

The Barnes Fund

Barnwood Trust

The Battersea Power Station Foundation

BBC Children in Need

BC Partners Foundation

The James Beattie Charitable Trust

Bedfordshire and Luton Community Foundation

Benefact Trust Ltd

The Berkeley Foundation

The Bernicia Foundation

Biffa Award

The Birmingham Diocesan Board of Finance

The Bertie Black Foundation

The Blagrave Trust

The Boltini Trust

Boots Charitable Trust

The Liz and Terry Bramall Foundation

The Brelms Trust CIO

The Harold and Alice Bridges Charity

Bristol Archdeaconry Charity

British Gas Energy Trust

British Humane Association

The Consuelo and Anthony Brooke Charitable Trust

The Mary Brown Memorial Trust

R. S. Brownless Charitable Trust

The Brownsword Charitable
  Foundation
The Jack Brunton Charitable
  Trust
Buckinghamshire Community
  Foundation
The Burges Salmon Charitable
  Trust
Consolidated Charity of Burton
  upon Trent
The Edward Cadbury
  Charitable Trust
William A. Cadbury Charitable
  Trust
The Edward and Dorothy
  Cadbury Trust
Cadent Foundation
Community Foundation for
  Calderdale
The Calleva Foundation
Cambridgeshire Community
  Foundation
Camden Giving
Card Factory Foundation
CareTech Charitable
  Foundation
Carew Pole Charitable Trust
W. A. Cargill Fund
The Antonio Carluccio
  Foundation
The Carnegie Dunfermline
  Trust
The Castansa Trust
The Wilfrid and Constance
  Cave Foundation
Cheshire Community
  Foundation Ltd
The Childhood Trust
Chippenham Borough Lands
  Charity
Church Urban Fund
The Churchill Foundation
The Clarkson Foundation
The Clothworkers' Foundation
The John Coates Charitable
  Trust
Denise Coates Foundation
The Cole Charitable Trust
Colyer-Fergusson Charitable
  Trust
Comic Relief
Community First
Congleton Inclosure Trust
Co-op Foundation
The J. Reginald Corah
  Foundation Fund
Michael Cornish Charitable
  Trust
Cornwall Community
  Foundation
Corra Foundation
County Durham Community
  Foundation
Coventry Building Society
  Charitable Foundation
Cripplegate Foundation

The Peter Cruddas Foundation
Cruden Foundation Ltd
Cumbria Community
  Foundation
The Roger De Haan Charitable
  Trust
The Delves Charitable Trust
Foundation Derbyshire
The J. N. Derbyshire Trust
Devon Community Foundation
The Dibden Allotments Fund
Donibristle Trust
Dorset Community Foundation
The Dorus Trust
Duchy of Lancaster Benevolent
  Fund
The Dulverton Trust
Dumfriesshire East Community
  Benefit Group SCIO
Dunlossit and Islay Community
  Trust
The James Dyson Foundation
Dr Edwards and Bishop King's
  Fulham Charity
The Endrick Trust
The Englefield Charitable Trust
The Enkalon Foundation
Esher House Charitable Trust
Essex Community Foundation
Euro Quality Foundation
The Everard Foundation
Esmée Fairbairn Foundation
The Thomas Farr Charity
Fat Face Foundation*
The Fermanagh Trust
Sir John Fisher Foundation
The Follett Trust
The Football Association
  National Sports Centre
Ford Britain Trust
Forever Manchester
Fowler Smith and Jones Trust
The Foyle Foundation
Charles S. French Charitable
  Trust
Friarsgate Trust
Friends Provident Charitable
  Foundation
The Funding Network
The Gannochy Trust
Gatwick Airport Community
  Trust
The Gaudio Family Foundation
  (UK) Ltd
The Tara Getty Foundation
J. Paul Getty Jr General
  Charitable Trust*
The G. C. Gibson Charitable
  Trust
Global Charities
Gloucestershire Community
  Foundation
The Golden Bottle Trust
Goldman Sachs Gives (UK)
The Goldsmiths' Company
  Charity

Matthew Good Foundation*
The Mike Gooley Trailfinders
  Charity
The Gosling Foundation Ltd
The Grace Trust
William Grant Foundation*
The Grantham Yorke Trust
The J. G. Graves Charitable
  Trust
The Great Stone Bridge Trust
  of Edenbridge
The Greater Manchester High
  Sheriff's Police Trust
Greenham Trust Ltd
The Grimmitt Trust
The Grocers' Charity
Groundwork UK
The Hadfield Charitable Trust
Halifax Foundation for
  Northern Ireland
The Hamilton Davies Trust
Hammersmith United Charities
Hampshire and Isle of Wight
  Community Foundation
Hampton Fund
The W. A. Handley Charity
  Trust
The Lennox Hannay Charitable
  Trust
Harborne Parish Lands Charity
William Harding's Charity
Gay and Peter Hartley's
  Hillards Charitable Trust
The Hasluck Charitable Trust
The Hawthorne Charitable
  Trust
The Charles Hayward
  Foundation
Heart of England Community
  Foundation
The Heathcoat Trust
Heathrow Community Trust
The Hemby Charitable Trust
Herefordshire Community
  Foundation
Hertfordshire Community
  Foundation
P. and C. Hickinbotham
  Charitable Trust
The Lady Hind Trust
The Henry C. Hoare Charitable
  Trust
The Hobson Charity Ltd
The Holbeck Charitable Trust
Hollick Family Foundation
P. H. Holt Foundation
The Holywood Trust
Sir Harold Hood's Charitable
  Trust
The Hospital of God at
  Greatham
The Keith Howard Foundation
Hyde Charitable Trust
Hyde Park Place Estate Charity
Ibrahim Foundation Ltd
Imagine Foundation

Impact Funding Partners Ltd
Impetus
The International Bankers
  Charitable Trust
The Inverforth Charitable Trust
Investream Charitable Trust
The Invigorate Charitable Trust
The Ireland Fund of Great
  Britain
Irish Youth Foundation (UK)
  Ltd (incorporating The
  Lawlor Foundation)
The J. Isaacs Charitable Trust
The Isle of Anglesey Charitable
  Association (Cymdeithas
  Elusennol Ynys Môn)
Isle of Wight Foundation
John Lewis and Partners
  Foundation
The Jones 1986 Charitable
  Trust
The Cyril and Eve Jumbo
  Charitable Trust
Kent Community Foundation
The Ursula Keyes Trust
KFC Foundation
Fraser Kilpatrick Charitable
  Trust
The Mary Kinross Charitable
  Trust
Sir James Knott Trust
The KPMG Foundation
Kusuma Trust UK
Ladbrokes Coral Trust
John Laing Charitable Trust
The Martin Laing Foundation
The Leonard Laity Stoate
  Charitable Trust
Community Foundations for
  Lancashire and Merseyside
Lancashire Environmental
  Fund Ltd
The Allen Lane Foundation
Mrs F. B. Laurence Charitable
  Trust
The Edgar E. Lawley
  Foundation
The Lawson Trust CIO
The Leathersellers' Foundation
Leeds Building Society
  Foundation
The Leeward Trust
Lempriere Pringle 2015
The Leri Charitable Trust
Lord Leverhulme's Charitable
  Trust
The Charles Lewis Foundation
The Lightbulb Trust*
The Limbourne Trust
Lincolnshire Community
  Foundation
The Michael and Betty Little
  Trust*
The Charles Littlewood Hill
  Trust

Liverpool Charity and Voluntary
  Services (LCVS)
Jack Livingstone Charitable
  Trust
Lloyds Bank Foundation for the
  Channel Islands
London Catalyst
The London Community
  Foundation (LCF)
The London Marathon
  Charitable Trust Ltd
Longleigh Foundation
Sylvanus Lysons Charity
Mace Foundation
The Mackintosh Foundation
The MacRobert Trust 2019
Making a Difference Locally
  Ltd
Manchester Airport Community
  Trust Fund
The Manchester Guardian
  Society Charitable Trust
R. W. Mann Trust
The Martin Charitable Trust
Sir George Martin Trust
John Martin's Charity
Nancie Massey Charitable
  Trust
The Master Charitable Trust
Matchroom Sport Charitable
  Foundation
Mathew Trust
The McCarthy Stone
  Foundation
The Medlock Charitable Trust
The Mercers Charitable
  Foundation
The Merchant Venturers
  Charity
Merchants House of Glasgow
Millennium Stadium Charitable
  Trust (Ymddiriedolaeth
  Elusennol Stadiwm y
  Mileniwm)
The Milne Family Foundation
Milton Keynes Community
  Foundation Ltd
The Peter Minet Trust
Mobbs Memorial Trust Ltd
The Monmouthshire County
  Council Welsh Church Act
  Fund
The Janet and Brian Moore
  Charitable Trust*
The Steve Morgan Foundation
The Morris Charitable Trust
The Morrisons Foundation
The Mosawi Foundation
The Alexander Mosley
  Charitable Trust
Moto Foundation
The Mulberry Trust
The Mumford Memorial Trust*
The John R. Murray Charitable
  Trust
MW (RH) Foundation

The National Express
  Foundation
The National Garden Scheme
The National Lottery
  Community Fund
The Nationwide Foundation
Near Neighbours
The NFU Mutual Charitable
  Trust
The Nine Incorporated Trades
  of Dundee General Fund
  Charity
The Nisbet Trust
The Nomura Charitable Trust
Norfolk Community Foundation
The Norman Family Charitable
  Trust
North Berwick Trust
Community Foundation for
  Northern Ireland
The Northwick Trust
Northwood Charitable Trust
Norwich Consolidated
  Charities
The Notgrove Trust
Nottinghamshire Community
  Foundation
The Oakdale Trust
One Community Foundation
  Ltd
Open House Trust Ltd
Orange Tree Trust
Ostro Fayre Share Foundation
The Owen Family Trust
The Gerald Palmer Eling Trust
  Company
The Paragon Trust
Susanna Peake Charitable
  Trust
David Pearlman Charitable
  Foundation
The Pears Family Charitable
  Foundation
The Pebbles Trust
The Penchant Foundation
People's Health Trust
The Persimmon Charitable
  Foundation
The Pharsalia Charitable Trust
The Philip and Connie Phillips
  Foundation*
The Bernard Piggott Charitable
  Trust
The Pilgrim Trust
The George and Esme Pollitzer
  Charitable Settlement
The Porta Pia 2012
  Foundation
Postcode Community Trust
Postcode Local Trust
Poundland Foundation
The Prince's Countryside Fund
The Progress Foundation
Provincial Grand Charity of the
  Province of Derbyshire
The Puebla Charitable Trust

QBE European Operations
    Foundation
Queen Mary's Roehampton
    Trust
Richard Radcliffe Trust
The Rainford Trust
The Rambourg Foundation
Randeree Charitable Trust
The Eleanor Rathbone
    Charitable Trust
Elizabeth Rathbone Charity
The Sir James Reckitt Charity
Reuben Foundation
Daisie Rich Trust
The Clive Richards Foundation
Richmond Parish Lands Charity
The River Farm Foundation
The Sir James Roll Charitable
    Trust
The Gerald and Gail Ronson
    Family Foundation
Rosca Trust
The Roseline Foundation*
The Rothley Trust
Rothschild Foundation
    (Hanadiv) Europe
The Roughley Charitable Trust
The Row Fogo Charitable Trust
The Rugby Group Benevolent
    Fund Ltd
Russell Trust
The RWS Foundation
The Sackler Trust
The Saintbury Trust
Salisbury Pool Charity
Salters' Charitable Foundation
Schroder Charity Trust
The Schroder Foundation
Foundation Scotland
Scotland's Garden Scheme*
The Frieda Scott Charitable
    Trust
The Screwfix Foundation
Leslie Sell Charitable Trust
The Shanly Foundation
ShareGift (The Orr Mackintosh
    Foundation)
The Shears Foundation
The Sheffield Town Trust
The Sheldon Trust
Shetland Charitable Trust
The Skelton Bounty
The Charles Skey Charitable
    Trust
Skipton Building Society
    Charitable Foundation
The Mrs Smith and Mount
    Trust
The Henry Smith Charity
South Yorkshire Community
    Foundation
The Stephen R. and Philippa
    H. Southall Charitable Trust
W. F. Southall Trust
Peter Sowerby Foundation
Spurrell Charitable Trust

The Squires Foundation
The Stafford Trust
The Community Foundation for
    Staffordshire
The Peter Stebbings Memorial
    Charity
Stratford-upon-Avon Town Trust
The Street Foundation
Suffolk Community Foundation
The Summerfield Charitable
    Trust
Community Foundation for
    Surrey
Sutton Coldfield Charitable
    Trust
The Talbot Village Trust
Tanner Trust
Tay Charitable Trust
Stephen Taylor Foundation
The Thirty Percy Foundation
Tower Hill Trust
Toyota Manufacturing UK
    Charitable Trust
The Constance Travis
    Charitable Trust
The Truemark Trust
Trust for London
The Trusthouse Charitable
    Foundation
The Tudor Trust
The Roger and Douglas Turner
    Charitable Trust
United St Saviour's Charity
Valencia Communities Fund
The Van Neste Foundation
The Vardy Foundation
Variety, the Children's Charity
The Veolia Environmental Trust
VINCI UK Foundation
Nigel Vinson Charitable Trust
The Virgin Money Foundation
Wade's Charity
Wakefield and Tetley Trust
The Community Foundation in
    Wales
Walton Foundation
Walton-on-Thames Charity
G. R. Waters Charitable Trust
    2000
The Wates Foundation
We Love MCR Charity
The Weavers' Company
    Benevolent Fund
The Weinstock Fund
West Derby Waste Lands
    Charity
Westhill Endowment
Westminster Foundation
The Garfield Weston
    Foundation
Westway Trust
WHSmith Trust
Alfred Williams Charitable
    Trust
Wiltshire Community
    Foundation

The Wimbledon Foundation
W. Wing Yip and Brothers
    Foundation
The Wolfson Family Charitable
    Trust
The James Wood Bequest
    Fund
Wooden Spoon Society
Woodsmith Foundation Ltd
The Woodstock Family
    Charitable Foundation
The Woodward Charitable
    Trust
Worth Waynflete Foundation
The Worwin UK Foundation
The Yorkshire Dales
    Millennium Trust
Youth Endowment Fund (YEF)*
The Zochonis Charitable Trust
Zurich Community Trust (UK)
    Ltd

Advice and counselling services

ABF The Soldiers' Charity
The Access to Justice
    Foundation
The Astor Foundation
Bairdwatson Charitable Trust
Bank of Scotland Foundation
The James Beattie Charitable
    Trust
The Bernicia Foundation
The Liz and Terry Bramall
    Foundation
British Gas Energy Trust
William A. Cadbury Charitable
    Trust
Camden Giving
The Childhood Trust
The Clothworkers' Foundation
Colyer-Fergusson Charitable
    Trust
Cripplegate Foundation
Devon Community Foundation
Dixie Rose Findlay Charitable
    Trust
Jill Franklin Trust
Friends Provident Charitable
    Foundation
The Gannochy Trust
Global Charities
The Goldsmiths' Company
    Charity
The Grantham Yorke Trust
Dr Guthrie's Association
The Hadfield Charitable Trust
The Hadrian Trust
Hammersmith United Charities
Hampshire and Isle of Wight
    Community Foundation
Hampton Fund

The Charles Hayward
Foundation
The Hemby Charitable Trust
The Hobson Charity Ltd
Miss Agnes H. Hunter's Trust
Isle of Wight Foundation
KFC Foundation
Fraser Kilpatrick Charitable
Trust
The Allen Lane Foundation
The Law Society Charity
The Leathersellers' Foundation
The Leigh Trust
The London Community
Foundation (LCF)
London Legal Support Trust
(LLST)
The Mickleham Trust
G. M. Morrison Charitable
Trust
The Alexander Mosley
Charitable Trust
The MSE Charity
The Mulberry Trust
The Norman Family Charitable
Trust
Norwich Consolidated
Charities
The Pixel Fund
The Portishead Nautical Trust
The Progress Foundation
The PwC Foundation
The Queen Anne's Gate
Foundation
The Quilter Foundation
The Rainford Trust
The Sigrid Rausing Trust
The Robertson Trust
The Roughley Charitable Trust
The Royal British Legion
RSM UK Foundation
Santander UK Foundation Ltd
The Simmons & Simmons
Charitable Foundation
Singer Foundation
The Mrs Smith and Mount
Trust
The Henry Smith Charity
The Stewarts Law Foundation
C. B. and H. H. T. Taylor 1984
Trust
Trust for London
The Trusthouse Charitable
Foundation
United Utilities Trust Fund
The Vardy Foundation
The Veterans' Foundation
VINCI UK Foundation
Warwick Relief-in-Need Charity
The Waterloo Foundation
The Wates Foundation
The Which? Fund
The Maurice Wohl Charitable
Foundation
Woodsmith Foundation Ltd

The Woodward Charitable
Trust

Citizenship

The A. B. Charitable Trust
The Aldama Foundation
The Asda Foundation
The Asfari Foundation
The Bernicia Foundation
The Blagrave Trust
The Britford Bridge Trust
The Mary Brown Memorial
Trust
The John Coates Charitable
Trust
Cripplegate Foundation
The Davis Foundation
The Delves Charitable Trust
Dumfriesshire East Community
Benefit Group SCIO
Dunlossit and Islay Community
Trust
The Endrick Trust
The Enkalon Foundation
The Fairness Foundation
The Fort Foundation
The Gannochy Trust
The Golden Bottle Trust
The Lennox Hannay Charitable
Trust
The Hedley Foundation
The Henry C. Hoare Charitable
Trust
The Hunter Foundation
The Invigorate Charitable Trust
Isle of Wight Foundation
Fraser Kilpatrick Charitable
Trust
The KPMG Foundation
The Leeward Trust
The Legal Education
Foundation
The Leigh Trust
The MacRobert Trust 2019
The Martin Charitable Trust
The Master Charitable Trust
The Milne Family Foundation
Near Neighbours
The Nine Incorporated Trades
of Dundee General Fund
Charity
The Northwick Trust
Open House Trust Ltd
Polden-Puckham Charitable
Foundation
Richard Radcliffe Trust
The Sigrid Rausing Trust
The Joseph Rowntree
Charitable Trust
Salters' Charitable Foundation
ScottishPower Foundation
The Simmons & Simmons
Charitable Foundation
The Charles Skey Charitable
Trust

South Yorkshire Community
Foundation
W. F. Southall Trust
Stratford-upon-Avon Town Trust
Sutton Coldfield Charitable
Trust
The Triangle Trust (1949) Fund
Trust for London
Nigel Vinson Charitable Trust

Community enterprise and social entrepreneurship

The Alchemy Foundation
D. C. R. Allen Charitable Trust
Anglo American Foundation
The Apax Foundation
The Asda Foundation
BC Partners Foundation
The James Beattie Charitable
Trust
Ruth Berkowitz Charitable
Trust
The Bingham Trust
The Harold and Alice Bridges
Charity
The Britford Bridge Trust
The Consuelo and Anthony
Brooke Charitable Trust
The Noel Buxton Trust
Camden Giving
The Chalk Cliff Trust
The Cole Charitable Trust
Co-op Foundation
Cripplegate Foundation
The Delves Charitable Trust
East End Community
Foundation
The Ecology Trust
The Englefield Charitable Trust
Esmée Fairbairn Foundation
The Fort Foundation
Friends Provident Charitable
Foundation
The Funding Network
The Goldman Sachs Charitable
Gift Fund (UK)
GrantScape
The Green Room Charitable
Trust
The Grimmitt Trust
The Hadrian Trust
Hammersmith United Charities
Heb Ffin (Without Frontier)
The Alan Edward Higgs Charity
Housing Pathways Trust
The Hunter Foundation
Hyde Charitable Trust
The J. J. Charitable Trust
The Kensington and Chelsea
Foundation
Fraser Kilpatrick Charitable
Trust

Liberum Foundation
The Livingbridge Foundation*
The W. M. and B. W. Lloyd
    Trust
The London Community
    Foundation (LCF)
Making a Difference Locally
    Ltd
The Master Charitable Trust
The Merchant Venturers
    Charity
The MITIE Foundation
The Monmouthshire County
    Council Welsh Church Act
    Fund
Vyoel Moshe Charitable Trust
The MSE Charity
The Nomura Charitable Trust
Norwich Consolidated
    Charities
Henry Oldfield Trust
Oxfordshire Community
    Foundation
The Jack Petchey Foundation
Richmond Parish Lands Charity
The Rothley Trust
Royal Docks Trust (London)
The Rugby Group Benevolent
    Fund Ltd
ScottishPower Foundation
The Shears Foundation
Singer Foundation
Somerset Community
    Foundation
South Yorkshire Community
    Foundation
Stanley Foundation Ltd
Sir Halley Stewart Trust
The Bernard Sunley
    Foundation
The Thirty Percy Foundation
Trust for London
The Trusthouse Charitable
    Foundation
The Tudor Trust
UnLtd (Foundation for Social
    Entrepreneurs)
The Veolia Environmental Trust
VINCI UK Foundation
The Virgin Foundation (Virgin
    Unite)
The Virgin Money Foundation
Wates Family Enterprise Trust
Westway Trust
The Wood Foundation
The Yorkshire Dales
    Millennium Trust
Zephyr Charitable Trust

Community transport

The Liz and Terry Bramall
    Foundation

The Jack Brunton Charitable
    Trust
M. J. Camp Charitable
    Foundation
Community First
Hertfordshire Community
    Foundation
The Lord's Taverners
The Morrisons Foundation
Rees Jeffreys Road Fund
Foundation Scotland
The Serco Foundation
Shetland Charitable Trust
Variety, the Children's Charity
West Herts Charity Trust Ltd

Rural communities

The Aberbrothock Skea Trust
The Ashley Family Foundation
The Astor Foundation
The Ballinger Charitable Trust
The Liz and Terry Bramall
    Foundation
The Noel Buxton Trust
M. J. Camp Charitable
    Foundation
Carew Pole Charitable Trust
Cheshire Community
    Foundation Ltd
Community First
The Dulverton Trust
The Ecology Trust
The Earl Fitzwilliam Charitable
    Trust
The Tara Getty Foundation
J. Paul Getty Jr General
    Charitable Trust*
The Hamilton Davies Trust
The Hawthorne Charitable
    Trust
The Hilden Charitable Fund
Isle of Wight Foundation
The Limbourne Trust
The Janet and Brian Moore
    Charitable Trust*
The NFU Mutual Charitable
    Trust
The Jack Patston Charitable
    Trust
Payne-Gallwey 1989 Charitable
    Trust
The Prince of Wales's
    Charitable Foundation
The Prince's Countryside Fund
The Robertson Trust
The Frieda Scott Charitable
    Trust
The Shears Foundation
The Sheffield Town Trust
Shetland Charitable Trust
The Stephen R. and Philippa
    H. Southall Charitable Trust
Tanner Trust
The Tedworth Charitable Trust

The Trusthouse Charitable
    Foundation
The David Webster Charitable
    Trust
Worth Waynflete Foundation
Zephyr Charitable Trust

Support services

The A. B. Charitable Trust
Barnwood Trust
The Liz and Terry Bramall
    Foundation
The Noel Buxton Trust
The John Coates Charitable
    Trust
Cripplegate Foundation
The Fairness Foundation
The Charles Hayward
    Foundation
Michael and Shirley Hunt
    Charitable Trust
The Allen Lane Foundation
The Leathersellers' Foundation
The London Community
    Foundation (LCF)
The Merchant Venturers
    Charity
The Mickleham Trust
Norwich Consolidated
    Charities
The Rix-Thompson-Rothenberg
    Foundation
The Sheldon Trust
The Skelton Bounty
South Yorkshire Community
    Foundation
The Vardy Foundation
Woodsmith Foundation Ltd
The Woodward Charitable
    Trust

Urban communities

The Alchemy Foundation
The Battersea Power Station
    Foundation
The Liz and Terry Bramall
    Foundation
The Noel Buxton Trust
Community First
Cripplegate Foundation
The Gaudio Family Foundation
    (UK) Ltd
The Hamilton Davies Trust
The Morel Charitable Trust
The Morris Charitable Trust
The Persimmon Charitable
    Foundation
Stephen Taylor Foundation
The Trusthouse Charitable
    Foundation

Education and training

The 29th May 1961 Charitable Trust

4 Charity Foundation

The A. and J. Charitable Trust

The Aberdeen Endowments Trust

The Aberdeenshire Educational Trust Scheme

ABF The Soldiers' Charity

abrdn Charitable Foundation

abrdn Financial Fairness Trust

Adam Family Foundation

The Bryan Adams Foundation

The Addleshaw Goddard Charitable Trust

Adenfirst Ltd

The Aimwell Charitable Trust

The Aitken Family Charitable Trust

Sylvia Aitken's Charitable Trust

AKO Foundation

Al Madad Foundation*

The Alborada Trust

The Aldama Foundation

Al-Fayed Charitable Foundation

The Derrill Allatt Foundation

The Allen & Overy Foundation

D. C. R. Allen Charitable Trust

Alliance Family Foundation Ltd

Alzheimer's Society

Amabrill Ltd

Amant Foundation

Viscount Amory's Charitable Trust

Andrew Anderson Trust

Andor Charitable Trust

Anglo American Foundation

Anguish's Educational Foundation

The Apax Foundation

The John Apthorp Charity

The Arah Foundation

The Annabel Arbib Foundation

Ardbarron Trust Ltd

The Ardwick Trust

Armed Forces Covenant Fund Trust

Armed Forces Education Trust

The John Armitage Charitable Trust

The Armourers and Brasiers Gauntlet Trust

The Arsenal Foundation

The Ove Arup Foundation

Ove Arup Partnership Charitable Trust

The Asda Foundation

The Asfari Foundation

The Ashendene Trust

The Ashley Family Foundation

The Ian Askew Charitable Trust

The Associated Board of the Royal Schools of Music (ABRSM)

The Astor Foundation

Atkin Charitable Foundation

Atlas Memorial Ltd

Lawrence Atwell's Charity (Skinners' Company)

The Lord Austin Trust

The Aziz Foundation

Bagri Foundation

Bairdwatson Charitable Trust

The Roy and Pixie Baker Charitable Trust

The Band Trust

Veronica and Lars Bane Foundation

The Kamini and Vindi Banga Family Trust

The Barbers' Company General Charities

The Barbour Foundation

Philip Barker Charity

The Barnes Fund

Robert Barr's Charitable Trust

Bauer Radio's Cash for Kids Charities

The Gordon and Ena Baxter Foundation*

BC Partners Foundation

The James Beattie Charitable Trust

The Beaverbrooks Charitable Trust

Beccles Townlands Charity

The Bellahouston Bequest Fund

Benesco Charity Ltd

The Benham Charitable Settlement

The Rowan Bentall Charitable Trust

The Berkeley Foundation

Ruth Berkowitz Charitable Trust

The Bestway Foundation

Bideford Bridge Trust

The Billmeir Charitable Trust

The Bingham Trust

Binks Trust

Birkdale Trust for Hearing Impaired Ltd*

The Birmingham Diocesan Board of Finance

The Michael Bishop Foundation

The Sydney Black Charitable Trust

The Bertie Black Foundation

The Isabel Blackman Foundation

The Blagrave Trust

The Sir Victor Blank Charitable Settlement

Abraham Algy Bloom Foundation

Bluespark Foundation

The Bluston Charitable Settlement

The Boltini Trust

The Bonamy Charitable Trust

The Booth Charities

The Salo Bordon Charitable Trust

Sir William Boreman's Foundation

The Boshier-Hinton Foundation

The Bosson Family Charitable Trust

The Harry Bottom Charitable Trust

The Bowland Charitable Trust

G. and K. Boyes Charitable Trust

The Liz and Terry Bramall Foundation

Breast Cancer Now

The Brelms Trust CIO

The Brenley Trust

The Britford Bridge Trust

The British Academy

The British and Foreign School Society (BFSS)

British Heart Foundation (BHF)

British Motor Sports Training Trust

J. and M. Britton Charitable Trust

The Consuelo and Anthony Brooke Charitable Trust

The Charles Brotherton Trust

The Mary Brown Memorial Trust

The Brownsword Charitable Foundation

Brushmill Ltd

Buckingham Trust

The Buffini Chao Foundation

Building and Civil Engineering Charitable Trust

The Bulldog Trust Ltd

The Burberry Foundation

The Burden Trust

The Burdett Trust for Nursing

Clara E. Burgess Charity

The Arnold Burton 1998 Charitable Trust

Consolidated Charity of Burton upon Trent

C. and F. Charitable Trust

The Edward Cadbury Charitable Trust

The G. W. Cadbury Charitable Trust

William A. Cadbury Charitable Trust

The Cadbury Foundation

The Edward and Dorothy Cadbury Trust

The Cadogan Charity

The Calleva Foundation

Camden Giving

The Frederick and Phyllis Cann
Trust
CareTech Charitable
Foundation
William A. Cargill Charitable
Trust
W. A. Cargill Fund
The Antonio Carluccio
Foundation
The Carnegie Dunfermline
Trust
The Carnegie Trust for the
Universities of Scotland
The Carpenters Company
Charitable Trust
The Carr-Gregory Trust
The Castansa Trust
Catkin Pussywillow Charitable
Trust
The Wilfrid and Constance
Cave Foundation
The Cayo Foundation
The B. G. S. Cayzer Charitable
Trust
The Chadwick Educational
Foundation
The Amelia Chadwick Trust
Chalfords Ltd
Charitworth Ltd
Chartered Accountants' Livery
Charity (CALC)
The Charterhouse Charitable
Trust
The Cheruby Trust
Cheshire Community
Foundation Ltd
The Chetwode Foundation
The Childhood Trust
The Childwick Trust
Chippenham Borough Lands
Charity
The André Christian Trust
Church Burgesses Educational
Foundation
Church Burgesses Trust
Church of Ireland Priorities
Fund
The Roger and Sarah Bancroft
Clark Charitable Trust
The Clothworkers' Foundation
The Robert Clutterbuck
Charitable Trust
Clydpride Ltd
The Coalfields Regeneration
Trust
The John Coates Charitable
Trust
Denise Coates Foundation
The Vivienne and Samuel
Cohen Charitable Trust
The John S. Cohen Foundation
The R. and S. Cohen
Foundation
The Cole Charitable Trust
John and Freda Coleman
Charitable Trust

The Coles-Medlock Foundation
Sir Jeremiah Colman Gift Trust
The Comino Foundation
The Company of Actuaries
Charitable Trust Fund
Douglas Compton James
Charitable Trust
The Connolly Foundation (UK)
Ltd
The Ernest Cook Trust
The Cooks Charity
The Catherine Cookson
Charitable Trust
The Keith Coombs Trust
The Alice Ellen Cooper-Dean
Charitable Foundation
The J. Reginald Corah
Foundation Fund
The Evan Cornish Foundation
The Corporation of Trinity
House of Deptford Strond
The County Council of Dyfed
Welsh Church Fund
County Durham Community
Foundation
Dudley and Geoffrey Cox
Charitable Trust
The Lord Cozens-Hardy Trust
The Elizabeth Creak Charitable
Trust
Credit Suisse EMEA
Foundation
Cripplegate Foundation
The Peter Cruddas Foundation
Cruden Foundation Ltd
Cullum Family Trust
Cumbria Community
Foundation
Itzchok Meyer Cymerman Trust
Ltd
The D. M. Charitable Trust
Oizer Dalim Trust
The Daniell Trust
The Danson Foundation*
The Dashlight Foundation
The David Family Foundation*
Michael Davies Charitable
Settlement
Margaret Davies Charity
The Crispin Davis Family Trust
Dawat-E-Hadiyah Trust (United
Kingdom)
The Roger De Haan Charitable
Trust
William Dean Countryside and
Educational Trust
The J. N. Derbyshire Trust
Devon Community Foundation
The Laduma Dhamecha
Charitable Trust
The Alan and Sheila Diamond
Charitable Trust
The Dibden Allotments Fund
Didymus
The Dischma Charitable Trust
The Djanogly Foundation

William and Frances Dobie
Charitable Foundation
Donibristle Trust
The Dorcas Trust
The Dorfman Foundation
The Dorus Trust
The Double 'O' Charity Ltd
Drapers Charitable Fund
The DS Smith Charitable
Foundation
Duchy of Lancaster Benevolent
Fund
The Duke of Cornwall's
Benevolent Fund
Dumfriesshire East Community
Benefit Group SCIO
The DWF Charitable
Foundation
The Dyers' Company
Charitable Trust
The James and Deirdre Dyson
Trust
EA Foundation*
The Earley Charity
East End Community
Foundation
The Economist Charitable
Trust
The Gilbert and Eileen Edgar
Foundation
Edinburgh Trust No2 Account
Edupoor Ltd
The Eight Foundation
Eight Strands Foundation
The Eighteen Fund
The Eighty Eight Foundation
The George Elias Charitable
Trust
The Elie Trust
The Maud Elkington Charitable
Trust
The Dorothy Whitney Elmhirst
Trust
The Elmley Foundation
Emerton-Christie Charity
EMI Music Sound Foundation
England and Wales Cricket
Trust
The Englefield Charitable Trust
The Enkalon Foundation
Entindale Ltd
The EQ Foundation
Esher House Charitable Trust
The Essex Youth Trust
Euro Quality Foundation
The Everard Foundation
The Exilarch's Foundation
Extonglen Ltd
Family Philanthropy Ltd
The Lord Faringdon Charitable
Trust
Samuel William Farmer Trust
The Thomas Farr Charity
The Farthing Trust
George Fentham Birmingham
Charity

The Feoffees of St Michael's
Spurriergate York
Allan and Nesta Ferguson
Charitable Settlement
The Fidelity UK Foundation
The Finborough Foundation
The Finnis Scott Foundation
Sir John Fisher Foundation
Fishmongers' Company's
Charitable Trust
The Follett Trust
Fonthill Foundation
Ford Britain Trust
Oliver Ford Foundation
Forest Hill Charitable Trust
The Forrester Family Trust
The Fort Foundation
The Foster Wood Foundation
Four Acre Trust
Foux Foundation
The Foyle Foundation
The Elizabeth Frankland Moore
and Star Foundation
The Gordon Fraser Charitable
Trust
The Hugh Fraser Foundation
The Joseph Strong Frazer Trust
The Freelands Foundation Ltd
Charles S. French Charitable
Trust
The Freshfield Foundation
The Freshgate Trust
Foundation
Friarsgate Trust
The Fulmer Charitable Trust
The Funding Network
The Gannochy Trust
The Gatsby Charitable
Foundation
The Gaudio Family Foundation
(UK) Ltd
The Robert Gavron Charitable
Trust
Sir Robert Geffery's
Almshouse Trust
General Charity (Coventry)
The Generational Foundation*
The Tara Getty Foundation
The Gibbons Family Trust
The Gibbs Charitable Trusts
The G. C. Gibson Charitable
Trust
The Girdlers' Company
Charitable Trust
The Glass-House Trust
The Gloag Foundation
The Golden Bottle Trust
The Goldman Sachs Charitable
Gift Fund (UK)
Goldman Sachs Gives (UK)
The Goldsmiths' Company
Charity
The Jane Goodman Charitable
Trust*
The Mike Gooley Trailfinders
Charity

The Gosling Foundation Ltd
The Hemraj Goyal Foundation
Grace Charitable Trust
The Grace Trust
The James Grace Trust
The Granada Foundation
The Grantham Yorke Trust
The J. G. Graves Charitable
Trust
The Great Britain Sasakawa
Foundation
The Great Stone Bridge Trust
of Edenbridge
The Greater Manchester High
Sheriff's Police Trust
The Kenneth and Susan Green
Charitable Foundation
Philip and Judith Green Trust
Greenham Trust Ltd
The Greenslade Family
Foundation
The Grimmitt Trust
The Grocers' Charity
M. and R. Gross Charities Ltd
Groundwork UK
The Walter Guinness
Charitable Trust
Dr Guthrie's Association
The Hadrian Trust
Halifax Foundation for
Northern Ireland
The Hamilton Davies Trust
Paul Hamlyn Foundation
The Helen Hamlyn Trust
Hampshire and Isle of Wight
Community Foundation
Hampton Fund
The W. A. Handley Charity
Trust
The Lennox Hannay Charitable
Trust
The Happold Foundation
The Haramead Trust
Harbinson Charitable Trust
Harborne Parish Lands Charity
The Harbour Foundation
William Harding's Charity
The Harebell Centenary Fund
The Hargreaves Foundation
The Harpur Trust
The Peter Harrison Foundation
The Harrison-Frank Family
Foundation (UK) Ltd
The Harry and Mary
Foundation
Gay and Peter Hartley's
Hillards Charitable Trust
Edward Harvist Trust (The
Harvist Estate)
The Maurice Hatter Foundation
The Headley Trust
The Health Foundation
Heart of England Community
Foundation
Heart Research UK
The Heathcoat Trust

Heathrow Community Trust
The Heathside Charitable Trust
Heb Ffin (Without Frontier)
The Charlotte Heber-Percy
Charitable Trust
Ernest Hecht Charitable
Foundation
The Hedley Foundation
The Michael Heller Charitable
Foundation
The Simon Heller Charitable
Settlement
The Hemby Charitable Trust
Henley Educational Trust
Henley Royal Regatta
Charitable Trust
Tim Henman Foundation
Herefordshire Community
Foundation
Hertfordshire Community
Foundation
The Bernhard Heuberger
Charitable Trust*
The Alan Edward Higgs Charity
The Highcroft Charitable Trust
The Hilden Charitable Fund
The Derek Hill Foundation
The Hillier Trust
R. G. Hills Charitable Trust
The Lady Hind Trust
The Hinduja Foundation
The Hintze Family Charity
Foundation
The Hiscox Foundation
The Henry C. Hoare Charitable
Trust
The Hobson Charity Ltd
Hockerill Educational
Foundation
The Jane Hodge Foundation
The Holbeck Charitable Trust
The Holden Charitable Trust
Hollick Family Foundation
The Holliday Foundation
Hollyhock Charitable
Foundation
P. H. Holt Foundation
Sir Harold Hood's Charitable
Trust
Hope Trust
The Horners Charity Fund
The Horse Trust
The Hosking Charitable Trust*
Hospice UK
The Sir Joseph Hotung
Charitable Settlement
House of Industry Estate
Housing Pathways Trust
The Reta Lila Howard
Foundation
The Humanitarian Trust
The Hunter Foundation
Miss Agnes H. Hunter's Trust
The Huntingdon Foundation
Ltd
Huntingdon Freemen's Trust

The Hutchinson Charitable
    Trust
The Nani Huyu Charitable Trust
Hyde Park Place Estate Charity
IGO Foundation Ltd
The Iliffe Family Charitable
    Trust
Impetus
The Institute for Policy
    Research
Integrated Education Fund
The International Bankers
    Charitable Trust
The Inverforth Charitable Trust
The Investindustrial
    Foundation
Investream Charitable Trust
The Invigorate Charitable Trust
The Ireland Fund of Great
    Britain
Irish Youth Foundation (UK)
    Ltd (incorporating The
    Lawlor Foundation)
The J. Isaacs Charitable Trust
Isle of Wight Foundation
The J. A. R. Charitable Trust
The J. and J. Benevolent
    Foundation
The Jabbs Foundation
The Frank Jackson Foundation
John James Bristol Foundation
The Jephcott Charitable Trust
The Jewish Youth Fund
John Lewis and Partners
    Foundation
The Jordan Charitable
    Foundation
The Joron Charitable Trust
J. E. Joseph Charitable Fund
The Jusaca Charitable Trust
The Karlsson Játiva Charitable
    Foundation
The Ian Karten Charitable
    Trust
The Kasner Charitable Trust
C. S. Kaufman Charitable
    Trust
The Emmanuel Kaye
    Foundation
Kelsick's Educational
    Foundation
The Kennedy Leigh Charitable
    Trust
The Kensington and Chelsea
    Foundation
Kent Community Foundation
Keren Association Ltd
E. and E. Kernkraut Charities
    Ltd
The Peter Kershaw Trust
The Kiawah Charitable Trust
The Graham Kirkham
    Foundation
Robert Kitchin (Saddlers' Co.)
Sir James Knott Trust
Kolyom Trust Ltd

KPE4 Charitable Trust
The KPMG Foundation
The Kreitman Foundation
Kusuma Trust UK
The Kyte Charitable Trust
Ladbrokes Coral Trust
John Laing Charitable Trust
The Kirby Laing Foundation
The Beatrice Laing Trust
Community Foundations for
    Lancashire and Merseyside
The Lancashire Foundation
Mrs F. B. Laurence Charitable
    Trust
The Law Family Charitable
    Foundation
The Edgar E. Lawley
    Foundation
Lawson Beckman Charitable
    Trust
The Lawson Trust CIO
Ana Leaf Foundation*
The Leathersellers' Foundation
The Leeward Trust
The Legal Education
    Foundation
The Leigh Trust
The Leri Charitable Trust
The Leverhulme Trust
Lord Leverhulme's Charitable
    Trust
Cecil and Hilda Lewis
    Charitable Trust
Bernard Lewis Family
    Charitable Trust
David and Ruth Lewis Family
    Charitable Trust
Liberum Foundation
The Lightbulb Trust*
The Limbourne Trust
Limoges Charitable Trust
The Linbury Trust
The Linder Foundation
The Lister Charitable Trust
The Michael and Betty Little
    Trust*
The Charles Littlewood Hill
    Trust
The Second Joseph Aaron
    Littman Foundation
Liverpool Charity and Voluntary
    Services (LCVS)
The Livingbridge Foundation*
The Elaine and Angus Lloyd
    Charitable Trust
The W. M. and B. W. Lloyd
    Trust
Lloyd's of London Foundation
Lloyd's Register Foundation
Localtrent Ltd
The Locker Foundation
The Lockwood Charitable
    Foundation
The London Community
    Foundation (LCF)
London Freemasons Charity

Longleigh Foundation
LPW Ltd
Lord and Lady Lurgan Trust
John Lyon's Charity
The Lyons Trust*
The M. Y. A. Charitable Trust
The Macdonald-Buchanan
    Charitable Trust
Mace Foundation
The Mackintosh Foundation
The MacRobert Trust 2019
The Magen Charitable Trust
Makers of Playing Cards
    Charity
Making a Difference Locally
    Ltd
Man Group plc Charitable
    Trust
The Manackerman Charitable
    Trust
The Manchester Guardian
    Society Charitable Trust
The W. M. Mann Foundation
R. W. Mann Trust
The Manoukian Charitable
    Foundation
The Manson Family Charitable
    Trust
The Marandi Foundation
The Stella and Alexander
    Margulies Charitable Trust
The Marks Family Charitable
    Trust
The Marque Foundation
The Michael Marsh Charitable
    Trust
The Marsh Christian Trust
Charity of John Marshall
Charlotte Marshall Charitable
    Trust
The Martin Charitable Trust
John Martin's Charity
Nancie Massey Charitable
    Trust
The Master Charitable Trust
The Matliwala Family
    Charitable Trust
The Robert McAlpine
    Foundation
Gemma and Chris McGough
    Charitable Foundation CIO
The Medlock Charitable Trust
Melodor Ltd
The Mercers Charitable
    Foundation
The Merchant Taylors'
    Foundation*
The Merchant Venturers
    Charity
Merchants House of Glasgow
T. and J. Meyer Family
    Foundation Ltd
The Mickel Fund
The Mikheev Charitable Trust
The Millennium Oak Trust

Hugh and Mary Miller Bequest Trust
The Ronald Miller Foundation
The Millfield Trust
The Millichope Foundation
The Millward Charitable Trust
The Milne Family Foundation
The James Milner Foundation
Milton Keynes Community Foundation Ltd
Minton Charitable Trust
The Brian Mitchell Charitable Settlement
The MITIE Foundation
The Mittal Foundation
The MK Charitable Trust
The Modiano Charitable Trust
The Mohn Westlake Foundation
Mole Charitable Trust
The Alexander Moncur Trust
The Monday Charitable Trust
The Monmouthshire County Council Welsh Church Act Fund
Moondance Foundation
The Henry Moore Foundation
The Steve Morgan Foundation
Morgan Stanley International Foundation
The Morris Charitable Trust
G. M. Morrison Charitable Trust
The Ken and Edna Morrison Charitable Trust
The Ken and Lynne Morrison Charitable Trust
The Morrisons Foundation
The Mosawi Foundation
The Moshal Charitable Trust
Vyoel Moshe Charitable Trust
The Mosselson Charitable Trust
Moto Foundation
Motor Neurone Disease Association
The Moulding Foundation
The Mulberry Trust
The John R. Murray Charitable Trust
Brian Murtagh Charitable Trust
Music Sales Charitable Trust
The Mutley Foundation
The Mutual Trust Group
MW (CL) Foundation
MW (GK) Foundation
MW (HO) Foundation
MW (RH) Foundation
The National Express Foundation
The National Garden Scheme
The NDL Foundation
Ner Foundation
Nesta
Network for Social Change Charitable Trust

Newby Trust Ltd
Newpier Charity Ltd
Alderman Newton's Educational Foundation
The NFU Mutual Charitable Trust
The Nineveh Charitable Trust
The Nisbet Trust
NNS Foundation
The Nomura Charitable Trust
Norfolk Community Foundation
Educational Foundation of Alderman John Norman
The Norman Family Charitable Trust
Normanby Charitable Trust
North Berwick Trust
North West Cancer Research
Northamptonshire Community Foundation
Northcott Trust
Northern Consortium*
Community Foundation for Northern Ireland
Northwood Charitable Trust
The Norton Foundation
The Norton Rose Fulbright Charitable Foundation
Norwich Town Close Estate Charity
The Nuffield Foundation
The Oakley Charitable Trust
The Hamish Ogston Foundation
Oizer Charitable Trust
The Olwyn Foundation
Open House Trust Ltd
Orthopaedic Research UK
The O'Sullivan Family Charitable Trust
Ovingdean Hall Foundation
The Ovo Charitable Foundation
The Owen Family Trust
The Paget Charitable Trust
The Gerald Palmer Eling Trust Company
The Panacea Charitable Trust
The Paragon Trust
The Parivar Trust
Peacock Charitable Trust
Susanna Peake Charitable Trust
David Pearlman Charitable Foundation
The Pears Family Charitable Foundation
Dina Perelman Trust Ltd
The Persimmon Charitable Foundation
Personal Assurance Charitable Trust
The Jack Petchey Foundation
Petplan Charitable Trust
The Phillips and Rubens Charitable Trust

The Phillips Family Charitable Trust
The Bernard Piggott Charitable Trust
The Pilgrim Trust
Cecil Pilkington Charitable Trust
The Sir Harry Pilkington Fund
The Players Foundation
The George and Esme Pollitzer Charitable Settlement
The Polonsky Foundation
The Portal Trust
Porter Foundation
The Portishead Nautical Trust
The Portrack Charitable Trust
Postcode Society Trust
David and Elaine Potter Foundation
The Potton Consolidated Charity
The Pret Foundation
The William Price Charitable Trust
The Prince of Wales's Charitable Foundation
The Priory Foundation
The Progress Foundation
The PwC Foundation
Mr and Mrs J. A. Pye's Charitable Settlement
QBE European Operations Foundation
Quartet Community Foundation
The Queen Anne's Gate Foundation
The Quilter Foundation
Quintessentially Foundation
R. S. Charitable Trust
Rachel Charitable Trust
The Racing Foundation
The Radcliffe Trust
Richard Radcliffe Trust
The Rainford Trust
The Rambourg Foundation
The Randal Charitable Foundation
The Joseph and Lena Randall Charitable Trust
Randeree Charitable Trust
The Ranworth Trust
The Eleanor Rathbone Charitable Trust
Elizabeth Rathbone Charity
The Julia and Hans Rausing Trust*
The Ravensdale Trust
The Roger Raymond Charitable Trust
The Sir James Reckitt Charity
Red Hill Charitable Trust
The Reece Foundation
Rees Jeffreys Road Fund
Richard Reeve's Foundation
The Max Reinhardt Charitable Trust

Rentrust Foundation Ltd
Reuben Foundation
The Clive Richards Foundation
Richmond Parish Lands Charity
Ridgesave Ltd
Rigby Foundation
The River Farm Foundation
Rivers Foundation
Riverside Charitable Trust Ltd
The Rix-Thompson-Rothenberg
    Foundation
The Roan Charitable Trust
The Robertson Trust
The Dezna Robins Jones
    Charitable Foundation
Rockcliffe Charitable Trust
The Rockspring Charitable
    Trust
The Roddick Foundation
The Gerald and Gail Ronson
    Family Foundation
Mrs L. D. Rope's Third
    Charitable Settlement
The Roseline Foundation*
The Cecil Rosen Foundation
The Ross Foundation
The Rothermere Foundation
The Rothley Trust
The Rothschild Foundation
The Eranda Rothschild
    Foundation
Rothschild Foundation
    (Hanadiv) Europe
The Roughley Charitable Trust
Rowanville Ltd
The Rowlands Trust
The Royal British Legion
Royal Docks Trust (London)
Royal Masonic Trust for Girls
    and Boys
RSM UK Foundation
Russell Trust
The RWS Foundation
The S. M. B. Trust
The Sackler Trust
The Saddlers' Company
    Charitable Fund
Erach and Roshan Sadri
    Foundation
The Alan and Babette
    Sainsbury Charitable Fund
The Saintbury Trust
The Salamander Charitable
    Trust
Salters' Charitable Foundation
Samjo Ltd
The Basil Samuel Charitable
    Trust
The M. J. Samuel Charitable
    Trust
The Sanderson Foundation
The Sandhu Charitable
    Foundation
The Sands Family Trust
The Schreib Trust
Schreiber Charitable Trust

O. and G. Schreiber Charitable
    Trust
Schroder Charity Trust
The Schroder Foundation
Foundation Scotland
Scotland's Garden Scheme*
The Scotshill Trust
The Scott Bader
    Commonwealth Ltd
Francis C. Scott Charitable
    Trust
The Ina Scott Sutherland
    Charitable Foundation
Scottish Coal Industry Special
    Welfare Fund
Scottish Property Industry
    Festival of Christmas
    (SPIFOX)
ScottishPower Foundation
Scouloudi Foundation
The Sam and Bella Sebba
    Charitable Foundation
SF Foundation
Shaftoe Educational
    Foundation
The Shanly Foundation
ShareGift (The Orr Mackintosh
    Foundation)
The Shears Foundation
The Sheepdrove Trust
The Sheldon Trust
The Sherling Charitable Trust
The Archie Sherman Charitable
    Trust
SHINE (Support and Help in
    Education)
The Bassil Shippam and
    Alsford Trust
The Shipwrights Charitable
    Fund
Shlomo Memorial Fund Ltd
The Shoe Zone Trust
Shulem B. Association Ltd
Singer Foundation
The Skelton Bounty
The Charles Skey Charitable
    Trust
Skipton Building Society
    Charitable Foundation
Sloane Robinson Foundation
The Mrs Smith and Mount
    Trust
The N. Smith Charitable
    Settlement
Arabella and Julian Smith
    Family Trust
The Leslie Smith Foundation
The Martin Smith Foundation
Philip Smith's Charitable Trust
The R. C. Snelling Charitable
    Trust
Societe Generale UK
    Foundation
Sodexo Stop Hunger
    Foundation
Sofronie Foundation

Somerset Community
    Foundation
Songdale Ltd
The E. C. Sosnow Charitable
    Trust
South Yorkshire Community
    Foundation
The Stephen R. and Philippa
    H. Southall Charitable Trust
Southover Manor General
    Education Trust Ltd
Peter Sowerby Foundation
Sparquote Ltd
The SpeedoMick Foundation
Michael and Sarah Spencer
    Foundation
Spielman Charitable Trust
The Spoore, Merry and Rixman
    Foundation
The Geoff and Fiona Squire
    Foundation
The Squire Patton Boggs
    Charitable Trust
Sir Walter St John's
    Educational Charity
St John's Foundation Est.
    1174
St Olave's and St Saviour's
    Schools Foundation CIO*
Stanley Foundation Ltd
Starlow Charities Ltd
The Peter Stebbings Memorial
    Charity
The Steel Charitable Trust
The Steinberg Family
    Charitable Trust
C. E. K. Stern Charitable Trust
The Sterry Family Foundation
The Stevenson Family's
    Charitable Trust
Sir Halley Stewart Trust
The Stewarts Law Foundation
Stolkin Foundation
The Stoneygate Trust
The Samuel Storey Family
    Charitable Trust
Peter Stormonth Darling
    Charitable Trust
Peter Storrs Trust
Strand Parishes Trust
Stratford-upon-Avon Town Trust
The W. O. Street Charitable
    Foundation
The Street Foundation
Suffolk Community Foundation
The Summerfield Charitable
    Trust
The Bernard Sunley
    Foundation
Surgo Foundation UK Ltd
Sutton Coldfield Charitable
    Trust
The Swann-Morton Foundation
Swarovski Foundation
The John Swire (1989)
    Charitable Trust

The Swire Charitable Trust
The Charles and Elsie Sykes
    Trust
The Tabhair Charitable Trust
The Ashley Tabor-King
    Foundation
The Talbot Village Trust
Tallow Chandlers Benevolent
    Fund No 2
Talteg Ltd
The Tanlaw Foundation
The David Tannen Charitable
    Trust
Tay Charitable Trust
C. B. and H. H. T. Taylor 1984
    Trust
Humphrey Richardson Taylor
    Charitable Trust
The Taylor Family Foundation
Stephen Taylor Foundation
The Thales Charitable Trust
Scott Thomson Charitable
    Trust
The Sue Thomson Foundation
The Thornton Trust
The Thriplow Charitable Trust
Mrs R. P. Tindall's Charitable
    Trust
The Tolkien Trust
The Tomoro Foundation
The Tompkins Foundation
The Tory Family Foundation
The Tottenham Grammar
    School Foundation
Tower Hill Trust
Toyota Manufacturing UK
    Charitable Trust
The Trades House of Glasgow
The Constance Travis
    Charitable Trust
The Troutsdale Charitable
    Trust
Truedene Co. Ltd
Trumros Ltd
The James Tudor Foundation
The Tudwick Foundation
The Tuixen Foundation
The Turtleton Charitable Trust
The Tweed Family Charitable
    Foundation
UBS Optimus Foundation UK
Ufi VocTech Trust
UJIA (United Jewish Israel
    Appeal)
The Underwood Trust
The Union of the Sisters of
    Mercy of Great Britain
UPP Foundation
The Michael Uren Foundation
The Van Mesdag Fund
The Vandervell Foundation
The Vardy Foundation
The Velvet Foundation
The Veterans' Foundation
Nigel Vinson Charitable Trust
The Vintners' Foundation

Virgin Atlantic Foundation
The Vodafone Foundation
The Georg and Emily von Opel
    Foundation
The Walcot Foundation
The Walker Trust
Walton Foundation
The Barbara Ward Children's
    Foundation
The Waterloo Foundation
G. R. Waters Charitable Trust
    2000
Wates Family Enterprise Trust
The Wates Foundation
The William Wates Memorial
    Trust
The Geoffrey Watling Charity
John Watson's Trust*
The Weavers' Company
    Benevolent Fund
The Weinstock Fund
The James Weir Foundation
Wellbank Foundation*
Wellington Management UK
    Foundation
The Welsh Church Act Fund
Westminster Almshouses
    Foundation
The Garfield Weston
    Foundation
Westway Trust
The Barbara Whatmore
    Charitable Trust
The Whinfell Charitable Fund
The Wimbledon Foundation
The Windfall Foundation
The Benjamin Winegarten
    Charitable Trust
W. Wing Yip and Brothers
    Foundation
The Michael and Anna Wix
    Charitable Trust
The Wixamtree Trust
The Maurice Wohl Charitable
    Foundation
The Charles Wolfson
    Charitable Trust
The Wolfson Family Charitable
    Trust
The Wolfson Foundation
The Wood Foundation
Woodroffe Benton Foundation
Woodsmith Foundation Ltd
The Woodward Charitable
    Trust
The Woosnam Foundation
The Worshipful Company of
    Glovers of London
    Charitable Trust
Worshipful Company of Gold
    and Silver Wyre Drawers
    Second Charitable Trust
    Fund
The Worshipful Company of
    Information Technologists

Worshipful Company of
    Needlemakers Charitable
    Fund
The Worwin UK Foundation
WPG Charitable Trust*
The Eric Wright Charitable
    Trust
Wychville Ltd
The Wyfold Charitable Trust
Sir Graham Wylie Foundation
Yankov Charitable Trust
The Yapp Charitable Trust
Youth Endowment Fund (YEF)*
The Elizabeth and Prince
    Zaiger Trust
The Zochonis Charitable Trust

Alternative education

The Cooks Charity
The Pret Foundation
The Shipwrights Charitable
    Fund

Extracurricular activities

The Aberdeenshire Educational
    Trust Scheme
The Childhood Trust
The Ernest Cook Trust
Matchroom Sport Charitable
    Foundation
Newcomen Collett Foundation
The William Price Charitable
    Trust
Red Hill Charitable Trust
St John's Foundation Est.
    1174
The Tottenham Grammar
    School Foundation
John Watson's Trust*
The Woodward Charitable
    Trust

Higher education

The Aberdeenshire Educational
    Trust Scheme
Alzheimer's Society
Binks Trust
Bloodwise
The Harry Bottom Charitable
    Trust
The Rory and Elizabeth Brooks
    Foundation
The G. W. Cadbury Charitable
    Trust
The Carnegie Trust for the
    Universities of Scotland
The Elizabeth Creak Charitable
    Trust

The Foyle Foundation
The Simon Heller Charitable
  Settlement
Henley Educational Trust
The International Bankers
  Charitable Trust
The Ireland Fund of Great
  Britain
The Ian Karten Charitable
  Trust
The Graham Kirkham
  Foundation
Vyoel Moshe Charitable Trust
The National Express
  Foundation
Northcott Trust
The Nuffield Foundation
The James Pantyfedwen
  Foundation
  (Ymddiriedolaeth James
  Pantyfedwen)
David Pearlman Charitable
  Foundation
The Pharsalia Charitable Trust
The Bernard Piggott Charitable
  Trust
The Polonsky Foundation
The William Price Charitable
  Trust
Randeree Charitable Trust
Rees Jeffreys Road Fund
The Ina Scott Sutherland
  Charitable Foundation
The Swann-Morton Foundation
Tay Charitable Trust
Humphrey Richardson Taylor
  Charitable Trust
The Thriplow Charitable Trust
UPP Foundation

Integrated education

Integrated Education Fund

Preschool education

Henley Educational Trust
Northcott Trust
SHINE (Support and Help in
  Education)

Primary education

The G. W. Cadbury Charitable
  Trust
The Chadwick Educational
  Foundation
The Vivienne and Samuel
  Cohen Charitable Trust
The Foyle Foundation
Henley Educational Trust

The J. J. Charitable Trust
Nesta
Newcomen Collett Foundation
Northcott Trust
The Bernard Piggott Charitable
  Trust
The William Price Charitable
  Trust
The Ina Scott Sutherland
  Charitable Foundation
SHINE (Support and Help in
  Education)
Tay Charitable Trust
The Tottenham Grammar
  School Foundation
John Watson's Trust*

Secondary education

The Ina Scott Sutherland
  Charitable Foundation
SHINE (Support and Help in
  Education)
The Swann-Morton Foundation
Tay Charitable Trust
The Tottenham Grammar
  School Foundation
John Watson's Trust*
Colonel W. H. Whitbread
  Charitable Trust

Special educational needs

ArtSocial Foundation
The Boshier-Hinton Foundation
The J. Reginald Corah
  Foundation Fund
Eastern Counties Educational
  Trust Ltd
The Joyce Fletcher Charitable
  Trust
The Forbes Charitable
  Foundation
The Foyle Foundation
The J. G. Graves Charitable
  Trust
The J. J. Charitable Trust
The Ian Karten Charitable
  Trust
The Kasner Charitable Trust
The Lord's Taverners
Hugh and Mary Miller Bequest
  Trust
The Ken and Lynne Morrison
  Charitable Trust
The Morrisons Foundation
Red Hill Charitable Trust
The Rix-Thompson-Rothenberg
  Foundation
The Sheldon Trust
The Leslie Smith Foundation
The Street Foundation

The Tottenham Grammar
  School Foundation
The Barbara Ward Children's
  Foundation
John Watson's Trust*
Westminster Almshouses
  Foundation
The Woodward Charitable
  Trust

Vocational training and apprenticeships

Bairdwatson Charitable Trust
The Max Barney Foundation
Building and Civil Engineering
  Charitable Trust
CareTech Charitable
  Foundation
The Coalfields Regeneration
  Trust
John and Freda Coleman
  Charitable Trust
The Cooks Charity
Cumbria Community
  Foundation
The Finnis Scott Foundation
The Girdlers' Company
  Charitable Trust
Isle of Wight Foundation
John Lewis and Partners
  Foundation
The Ian Karten Charitable
  Trust
The Kirby Laing Foundation
Mathew Trust
The National Garden Scheme
Northern Pharmacies Ltd Trust
  Fund
The Players Foundation
The William Price Charitable
  Trust
The Reece Foundation
Scotland's Garden Scheme*
Seafarers UK (King George's
  Fund for Sailors)
The Shipwrights Charitable
  Fund
Ufi VocTech Trust
Bairdwatson Charitable Trust
The Blagrave Trust
Boots Charitable Trust
Building and Civil Engineering
  Charitable Trust
CareTech Charitable
  Foundation
The Coalfields Regeneration
  Trust
The Cooks Charity
GambleAware
The Lady Hind Trust
Isle of Wight Foundation
The Jerusalem Trust

John Lewis and Partners
Foundation
The London Community
Foundation (LCF)
Mathew Trust
Hugh and Mary Miller Bequest
Trust
John Moores Foundation
The Players Foundation
The Pret Foundation
The Royal British Legion
The Royal Foundation of The
Prince and Princess of
Wales
The Shears Foundation
C. B. and H. H. T. Taylor 1984
Trust
Trust for London
Ufi VocTech Trust

Arts, humanities and social sciences

The Aldama Foundation
The Ove Arup Foundation
The Ashley Family Foundation
The Aurelius Charitable Trust
The Burberry Foundation
The Daiwa Anglo-Japanese
Foundation
The De Laszlo Foundation
The Elmley Foundation
The Finborough Foundation
The Freelands Foundation Ltd
The Great Britain Sasakawa
Foundation
Paul Hamlyn Foundation
The Harbour Foundation
The Institute for Policy
Research
The Leche Trust
The Legal Education
Foundation
The Leverhulme Trust
The Linder Foundation
The MacRobert Trust 2019
The Mayfield Valley Arts Trust
The Mikheev Charitable Trust
The Nuffield Foundation
Orange Tree Trust
The Polonsky Foundation
The Rainford Trust
The Resolution Trust
Rothschild Foundation
(Hanadiv) Europe

Literacy

Ardbarron Trust Ltd
The Elmley Foundation
The Foyle Foundation
The Girdlers' Company
Charitable Trust

The J. J. Charitable Trust
The Cyril and Eve Jumbo
Charitable Trust
The KPMG Foundation
The Lightbulb Trust*
Lloyds Bank Foundation for the
Channel Islands
Man Group plc Charitable
Trust
The Marsh Christian Trust
The Mercers Charitable
Foundation
The Morrisons Foundation
Old Possum's Practical Trust
St John's Foundation Est.
1174
The Adrian Swire Charitable
Trust
WHSmith Trust

Sciences (formal)

The Burberry Foundation
The Finborough Foundation
The Gatsby Charitable
Foundation
The Golden Bottle Trust
The Graham Trust
The Invigorate Charitable Trust
The Graham Kirkham
Foundation
The Kirby Laing Foundation
The Leri Charitable Trust
The Mikheev Charitable Trust
The Mila Charitable
Organisation
The Reece Foundation
The Eranda Rothschild
Foundation
The Rowlands Trust
The Charles Skey Charitable
Trust

Sciences (natural)

The Armourers and Brasiers
Gauntlet Trust
The Burberry Foundation
The Elizabeth Creak Charitable
Trust
The Finborough Foundation
The Gatsby Charitable
Foundation
The Granada Foundation
The Great Britain Sasakawa
Foundation
The Harbour Foundation
The Invigorate Charitable Trust
The Frank Jackson Foundation
The Eranda Rothschild
Foundation
The Rowlands Trust
Salters' Charitable Foundation
The Sylvia and Colin Shepherd
Charitable Trust

Sylvia Waddilove Foundation
UK

Sciences (professional and applied)

The British Academy
British Heart Foundation (BHF)
The Burdett Trust for Nursing
The Antonio Carluccio
Foundation
The Corporation of Trinity
House of Deptford Strond
The Elizabeth Creak Charitable
Trust
The Institute for Policy
Research
The Linder Foundation
Lloyd's Register Foundation
The National Garden Scheme
The Nuffield Foundation
The Racing Foundation
Scotland's Garden Scheme*
Sofronie Foundation

Skilled crafts

The Armourers and Brasiers
Gauntlet Trust
The Cotton Industry War
Memorial Trust
The Dyers' Company
Charitable Trust
The Idlewild Trust
The Kirby Laing Foundation
The Leathersellers' Foundation
The Leche Trust
Lloyd's Register Foundation
The Nine Incorporated Trades
of Dundee General Fund
Charity
The Radcliffe Trust
The Saddlers' Company
Charitable Fund
The Worshipful Company of
Glovers of London
Charitable Trust
Worshipful Company of
Needlemakers Charitable
Fund

Emergency response/relief

The Adlard Family Charitable Foundation
Alan Boswell Group Charitable Trust
Ardbarron Trust Ltd
The Artemis Charitable Foundation
The Astor Foundation
The Barbour Foundation
Blakemore Foundation
The Boltini Trust
Miss Margaret Butters Reekie Charitable Trust
The Clothworkers' Foundation
Devon Community Foundation
The Alan and Sheila Diamond Charitable Trust
Euro Quality Foundation
Dixie Rose Findlay Charitable Trust
Forest Hill Charitable Trust
The Joseph Strong Frazer Trust
The Tara Getty Foundation
The Golden Bottle Trust
The Grace Trust
The Kenneth and Susan Green Charitable Foundation
Greenham Trust Ltd
The Lennox Hannay Charitable Trust
The Hawthorne Charitable Trust
The Hobson Charity Ltd
The Holbeck Charitable Trust
The Innocent Foundation
JD Foundation
The Leeward Trust
Limoges Charitable Trust
The Linbury Trust
The Michael and Betty Little Trust*
London Freemasons Charity
The MacRobert Trust 2019
The Master Charitable Trust
Milton Keynes Community Foundation Ltd
The Monmouthshire County Council Welsh Church Act Fund
The Steve Morgan Foundation
The Morrisons Foundation
The Norman Family Charitable Trust
Oxfordshire Community Foundation
The Parivar Trust
The Samuel and Freda Parkinson Charitable Trust
The Puebla Charitable Trust
Rhodi Charitable Trust
Richmond Parish Lands Charity
The Sir James Roll Charitable Trust

The Royal Foundation of The Prince and Princess of Wales
The S. M. B. Trust
Salters' Charitable Foundation
Scott (Eredine) Charitable Trust
The Ina Scott Sutherland Charitable Foundation
Seafarers UK (King George's Fund for Sailors)
Somerset Community Foundation
South Yorkshire Community Foundation
SPAR Charitable Fund
The Ashley Tabor-King Foundation
Tay Charitable Trust
Community Foundation serving Tyne and Wear and Northumberland
The Welsh Church Act Fund
The Will Charitable Trust
The James Wood Bequest Fund
The Worshipful Company of Glovers of London Charitable Trust
The Zochonis Charitable Trust

Air ambulance

The Liz and Terry Bramall Foundation
Miss Margaret Butters Reekie Charitable Trust
Dixie Rose Findlay Charitable Trust
The Grace Trust
Hampshire and Isle of Wight Community Foundation
The Hawthorne Charitable Trust
The Hospital Saturday Fund
The Notgrove Trust
Spurrell Charitable Trust
The Ashley Tabor-King Foundation
Tay Charitable Trust
The James Wood Bequest Fund

Emergency relief

The Artemis Charitable Foundation
The P. G. and N. J. Boulton Trust
The Clothworkers' Foundation
Denise Coates Foundation
Forest Hill Charitable Trust
House of Industry Estate
The Innocent Foundation
The Leeward Trust

Cecil and Hilda Lewis Charitable Trust
The Ogle Christian Trust
The S. M. B. Trust
South Yorkshire Community Foundation
The Ashley Tabor-King Foundation
The Gay and Keith Talbot Trust
Tay Charitable Trust
Community Foundation serving Tyne and Wear and Northumberland
The Will Charitable Trust
The Worshipful Company of Glovers of London Charitable Trust

Lifeboats

Mrs F. B. Laurence Charitable Trust
The R. S. Macdonald Charitable Trust
The Laurence Misener Charitable Trust
Seafarers UK (King George's Fund for Sailors)
Spurrell Charitable Trust
The Stafford Trust
The Ashley Tabor-King Foundation

Mountain rescue

JD Foundation
The Ashley Tabor-King Foundation

Environment

The 29th May 1961 Charitable Trust
The A Team Foundation Ltd
The A. and J. Charitable Trust
abrdn Charitable Foundation
The Bryan Adams Foundation
The Adlard Family Charitable Foundation
The AEB Charitable Trust
The AIM Foundation
Sylvia Aitken's Charitable Trust
AKO Foundation
Alpkit Foundation
Anglo American Foundation
The Anson Charitable Trust
Arcadia Fund
The Artemis Charitable Foundation
The Ove Arup Foundation
Ove Arup Partnership Charitable Trust
The Ashendene Trust
The Ian Askew Charitable Trust
The Astor Foundation
The Aurora Trust (formerly The Ashden Trust)
The Banister Charitable Trust
The Barbour Foundation
Lord Barnby's Foundation
The Barratt Developments plc Charitable Foundation
The Gordon and Ena Baxter Foundation*
BC Partners Foundation
Becht Foundation
Benefact Trust Ltd
The Benham Charitable Settlement
The Rowan Bentall Charitable Trust
Biffa Award
The Isabel Blackman Foundation
Blakemore Foundation
The Boltini Trust
The Charlotte Bonham-Carter Charitable Trust
The Bowland Charitable Trust
G. and K. Boyes Charitable Trust
The Liz and Terry Bramall Foundation
The Britford Bridge Trust
The Brown Source Trust
Buckinghamshire Community Foundation
The Bulldog Trust Ltd
Consolidated Charity of Burton upon Trent
The Edward Cadbury Charitable Trust
The Edward and Dorothy Cadbury Trust
Cadent Foundation
The Cadogan Charity

The Calleva Foundation
Cambridgeshire Community Foundation
Camden Giving
M. J. Camp Charitable Foundation
Carew Pole Charitable Trust
The Leslie Mary Carter Charitable Trust
The Castansa Trust
The B. G. S. Cayzer Charitable Trust
The Amelia Chadwick Trust
The Chalk Cliff Trust
Chapman Charitable Trust
The Charities Advisory Trust
The Chartley Foundation
CHK Foundation
The City Bridge Trust (Bridge House Estates)
CLA Charitable Trust
The John Coates Charitable Trust
The John S. Cohen Foundation
The Cole Charitable Trust
Community First
County Durham Community Foundation
The Sir Tom Cowie Charitable Trust
Craignish Trust
The Elizabeth Creak Charitable Trust
The D. G. Charitable Settlement
The Daniell Trust
The David Family Foundation*
The Davis Foundation
The Roger De Haan Charitable Trust
William Dean Countryside and Educational Trust
The Delves Charitable Trust
Foundation Derbyshire
The Dischma Charitable Trust
Dorset Community Foundation
The Dorus Trust
The D'Oyly Carte Charitable Trust
Dr. Martens Foundation
The DS Smith Charitable Foundation
The Dulverton Trust
Dumfriesshire East Community Benefit Group SCIO
Dunard Fund
Dunlossit and Islay Community Trust
The DWF Charitable Foundation
EA Foundation*
Audrey Earle Charitable Trust
The Ecology Trust
John Ellerman Foundation
Emerton-Christie Charity
The Everard Foundation

Esmée Fairbairn Foundation
The Fairness Foundation
Family Philanthropy Ltd
The Lord Faringdon Charitable Trust
Samuel William Farmer Trust
Fat Face Foundation*
The February Foundation
The A. M. Fenton Trust
The Fieldrose Charitable Trust
The Finborough Foundation
The Finnis Scott Foundation
The Earl Fitzwilliam Charitable Trust
Ford Britain Trust
Forever Manchester
The Fort Foundation
The Gordon Fraser Charitable Trust
The Hugh Fraser Foundation
The Joseph Strong Frazer Trust
The Freshfield Foundation
The Freshgate Trust Foundation
Frognal Trust
The Funding Network
The Gannochy Trust
The Gatsby Charitable Foundation
Gatwick Airport Community Trust
The Generations Foundation
The Tara Getty Foundation
J. Paul Getty Jr General Charitable Trust*
The G. C. Gibson Charitable Trust
The Simon Gibson Charitable Trust
The B. and P. Glasser Charitable Trust
The Golden Bottle Trust
Matthew Good Foundation*
William Grant Foundation*
GrantScape
Gordon Gray Trust
The Great Britain Sasakawa Foundation
Greenham Trust Ltd
The Grocers' Charity
Groundwork UK
Calouste Gulbenkian Foundation – UK Branch
The Hadfield Charitable Trust
The Hadrian Trust
Hamamelis Trust
The W. A. Handley Charity Trust
The Lennox Hannay Charitable Trust
Harbinson Charitable Trust
The Harrison-Frank Family Foundation (UK) Ltd
The Hawthorne Charitable Trust
Heathrow Community Trust

The Charlotte Heber-Percy
   Charitable Trust
The Hemby Charitable Trust
The G. D. Herbert Charitable
   Trust
Herefordshire Community
   Foundation
P. and C. Hickinbotham
   Charitable Trust
The Lady Hind Trust
The Hinduja Foundation
The Henry C. Hoare Charitable
   Trust
The Hobson Charity Ltd
P. H. Holt Foundation
The Sir Joseph Hotung
   Charitable Settlement
Ibrahim Foundation Ltd
The Iceland Foods Charitable
   Foundation
The Iliffe Family Charitable
   Trust
The Inflexion Foundation
The Investindustrial
   Foundation
The Ireland Fund of Great
   Britain
The Ithaca Trust
The J. J. Charitable Trust
The Jabbs Foundation
JAC Trust*
The Frank Jackson Foundation
Lady Eda Jardine Charitable
   Trust
The Jephcott Charitable Trust
John Lewis and Partners
   Foundation
The Muriel Jones Foundation
Kent Community Foundation
The Kilroot Foundation
The Ernest Kleinwort
   Charitable Trust
Sir James Knott Trust
Kusuma Trust UK
Ladbrokes Coral Trust
Christopher Laing Foundation
The Kirby Laing Foundation
The Martin Laing Foundation
The Leonard Laity Stoate
   Charitable Trust
Community Foundations for
   Lancashire and Merseyside
Lancashire Environmental
   Fund Ltd
Langdale Trust
Mrs F. B. Laurence Charitable
   Trust
The Law Family Charitable
   Foundation
The Lawson Trust CIO
The Leach Fourteenth Trust
The Leeward Trust
The Mark Leonard Trust
The Leri Charitable Trust
Lord Leverhulme's Charitable
   Trust

The Limbourne Trust
Limoges Charitable Trust
The Linbury Trust
Lincolnshire Community
   Foundation
The Linder Foundation
The Lister Charitable Trust
The Michael and Betty Little
   Trust*
The Charles Littlewood Hill
   Trust
Lloyd's Register Foundation
The London Community
   Foundation (LCF)
The Lyndal Tree Foundation
The Mackintosh Foundation
The MacRobert Trust 2019
Manchester Airport Community
   Trust Fund
The Michael Marks Charitable
   Trust
Marmot Charitable Trust
The Marsh Christian Trust
Sir George Martin Trust
The Master Charitable Trust
MBNA General Foundation
Gemma and Chris McGough
   Charitable Foundation CIO
The Medlock Charitable Trust
The Merchant Venturers
   Charity
Merriman Charitable
   Foundation*
T. and J. Meyer Family
   Foundation Ltd
The Gerald Micklem Charitable
   Trust
The Mila Charitable
   Organisation
The Millennium Oak Trust
Millennium Stadium Charitable
   Trust (Ymddiriedolaeth
   Elusennol Stadiwm y
   Mileniwm)
The Millichope Foundation
Moondance Foundation
The Morrisons Foundation
Moto Foundation
The Mulberry Trust
The National Garden Scheme
Nesta
Network for Social Change
   Charitable Trust
The NFU Mutual Charitable
   Trust
The Nineveh Charitable Trust
The Norman Family Charitable
   Trust
The Northwick Trust
The Oakdale Trust
The Ofenheim Charitable Trust
One Community Foundation
   Ltd
The Ovo Charitable Foundation
The Owen Family Trust

Oxfordshire Community
   Foundation
P. F. Charitable Trust
The Paget Charitable Trust
The Paragon Trust
Miss M. E. S. Paterson's
   Charitable Trust
The Jack Patston Charitable
   Trust
Peacock Charitable Trust
Susanna Peake Charitable
   Trust
The Persimmon Charitable
   Foundation
The Bernard Piggott Charitable
   Trust
Cecil Pilkington Charitable
   Trust
PIMCO Foundation Europe
Charles Plater Trust*
Polden-Puckham Charitable
   Foundation
The George and Esme Pollitzer
   Charitable Settlement
Porter Foundation
The Portrack Charitable Trust
Postcode Community Trust
Postcode Local Trust
Postcode Society Trust
The Prince of Wales's
   Charitable Foundation
The Prince's Countryside Fund
The Princess Anne's Charities
Mr and Mrs J. A. Pye's
   Charitable Settlement
Quartet Community Foundation
Richard Radcliffe Trust
The Rainford Trust
The Ranworth Trust
The Ratcliff Foundation
The Sigrid Rausing Trust
The Sir James Reckitt Charity
The Reece Foundation
The Revere Charitable Trust
The Rhododendron Trust
Daisie Rich Trust
The Roddick Foundation
The Roseline Foundation*
The Rothschild Foundation
The Roughley Charitable Trust
The Rowlands Trust
Royal Docks Trust (London)
The Royal Foundation of The
   Prince and Princess of
   Wales
RSM UK Foundation
Russell Trust
The S. M. B. Trust
The Sackler Trust
The Saintbury Trust
Salisbury Pool Charity
The M. J. Samuel Charitable
   Trust
The Samworth Foundation
Sandra Charitable Trust
Schroder Charity Trust

The Schroder Foundation
Foundation Scotland
Scotland's Garden Scheme*
The Scott Bader
   Commonwealth Ltd
ScottishPower Foundation
Scouloudi Foundation
The Sam and Bella Sebba
   Charitable Foundation
ShareGift (The Orr Mackintosh
   Foundation)
The Shears Foundation
The Sheepdrove Trust
The Sheffield Town Trust
The Sylvia and Colin Shepherd
   Charitable Trust
Ruth Smart Foundation
The N. Smith Charitable
   Settlement
The Leslie Smith Foundation
The Martin Smith Foundation
Stanley Smith UK Horticultural
   Trust
Philip Smith's Charitable Trust
South Yorkshire Community
   Foundation
The Stephen R. and Philippa
   H. Southall Charitable Trust
W. F. Southall Trust
Peter Sowerby Foundation
The Spear Charitable Trust
Michael and Sarah Spencer
   Foundation
Staples Trust
The Steel Charitable Trust
The Stevenson Family's
   Charitable Trust
The Samuel Storey Family
   Charitable Trust
The Summerfield Charitable
   Trust
Community Foundation for
   Surrey
Sabina Sutherland Charitable
   Trust
Sutton Coldfield Charitable
   Trust
Swarovski Foundation
The John Swire (1989)
   Charitable Trust
The Swire Charitable Trust
The Hugh Symons Charitable
   Trust
The Talbot Village Trust
The Tanlaw Foundation
The Taurus Foundation
Tay Charitable Trust
C. B. and H. H. T. Taylor 1984
   Trust
Stephen Taylor Foundation
The Tedworth Charitable Trust
The Thirty Percy Foundation
The Tolkien Trust
The Tomoro Foundation
Tower Hill Trust

Toyota Manufacturing UK
   Charitable Trust
The Constance Travis
   Charitable Trust
The Roger and Douglas Turner
   Charitable Trust
UBS Optimus Foundation UK
Ulster Garden Villages Ltd
The Underwood Trust
The Michael Uren Foundation
Valencia Communities Fund
The Valentine Charitable Trust
The Albert Van Den Bergh
   Charitable Trust
The Van Neste Foundation
The Vandervell Foundation
The Veolia Environmental Trust
Nigel Vinson Charitable Trust
The Virgin Foundation (Virgin
   Unite)
The Georg and Emily von Opel
   Foundation
Mrs Waterhouse Charitable
   Trust
The Waterloo Foundation
Wates Family Enterprise Trust
The Wates Foundation
The Geoffrey Watling Charity
The David Webster Charitable
   Trust
The Weinstock Fund
Wellbank Foundation*
The Garfield Weston
   Foundation
Westway Trust
The Barbara Whatmore
   Charitable Trust
The Whitaker Charitable Trust
Colonel W. H. Whitbread
   Charitable Trust
Whitley Animal Protection Trust
Alfred Williams Charitable
   Trust
The H. D. H. Wills 1965
   Charitable Trust
Sumner Wilson Charitable
   Trust
Wiltshire Community
   Foundation
The Windfall Foundation
The Wixamtree Trust
Woodroffe Benton Foundation
Woodsmith Foundation Ltd
Worth Waynflete Foundation
The Yorkshire Dales
   Millennium Trust
Zephyr Charitable Trust

Agriculture and farming

The A Team Foundation Ltd
The Ian Askew Charitable Trust
The Aurora Trust (formerly The
   Ashden Trust)

The Castansa Trust
The Chalk Cliff Trust
CLA Charitable Trust
Community First
Craignish Trust
The Elizabeth Creak Charitable
   Trust
The Ecology Trust
The Englefield Charitable Trust
The Finnis Scott Foundation
The Great Britain Sasakawa
   Foundation
The Hutchinson Charitable
   Trust
The J. J. Charitable Trust
The Mark Leonard Trust
The Limbourne Trust
The MacRobert Trust 2019
The National Garden Scheme
The NFU Mutual Charitable
   Trust
The Nineveh Charitable Trust
Oxfordshire Community
   Foundation
The Prince of Wales's
   Charitable Foundation
Salisbury Pool Charity
Scotland's Garden Scheme*
The Shears Foundation
The Sheepdrove Trust
Tanner Trust
The Thirty Percy Foundation
Sylvia Waddilove Foundation
   UK
The David Webster Charitable
   Trust
The Whitaker Charitable Trust
The H. D. H. Wills 1965
   Charitable Trust

Biodiversity

abrdn Charitable Foundation
Anglo American Foundation
Arcadia Fund
Becht Foundation
Biffa Award
M. J. Camp Charitable
   Foundation
The Delves Charitable Trust
The Ecology Trust
Family Philanthropy Ltd
Fat Face Foundation*
The Finnis Scott Foundation
Hamamelis Trust
John Lewis and Partners
   Foundation
Lancashire Environmental
   Fund Ltd
The Linder Foundation
People's Postcode Trust
Postcode Community Trust
Postcode Local Trust
Postcode Society Trust
The Peter Samuel Charitable
   Trust

Ruth Smart Foundation
The Swire Charitable Trust
The Taurus Foundation
Tower Hill Trust
Valencia Communities Fund
Worth Waynflete Foundation

Ocean Family Foundation
The Shipwrights Charitable
    Fund
The Tomoro Foundation
UBS Optimus Foundation UK
The Waterloo Foundation

The Grocers' Charity
The Kavli Trust

Climate change

AKO Foundation
The Aurora Trust (formerly The
    Ashden Trust)
Becht Foundation
Benefact Trust Ltd
Bulb Foundation
Comic Relief
The Ecology Trust
The Freshfield Foundation
The Funding Network
The Tara Getty Foundation
Calouste Gulbenkian
    Foundation – UK Branch
The Sir Joseph Hotung
    Charitable Settlement
The J. J. Charitable Trust
The Kavli Trust
The Kreitman Foundation
The Mark Leonard Trust
The Limbourne Trust
The Linbury Trust
The Brian Mercer Charitable
    Trust
The Millennium Oak Trust
The Frederick Mulder
    Foundation
The Nineveh Charitable Trust
The Ovo Charitable Foundation
People's Postcode Trust
The Pickwell Foundation
Postcode Community Trust
Postcode Local Trust
Postcode Society Trust
The Samworth Foundation
The Leslie Smith Foundation
The Summerfield Charitable
    Trust
The Talbot Village Trust
The Thirty Percy Foundation
Wates Family Enterprise Trust
The Yorkshire Dales
    Millennium Trust

Coastal/marine

Becht Foundation
M. J. Camp Charitable
    Foundation
Craignish Trust
The Dashlight Foundation
John Ellerman Foundation
Fat Face Foundation*
The Tara Getty Foundation
Calouste Gulbenkian
    Foundation – UK Branch
The Lyndal Tree Foundation

Energy

The Aurora Trust (formerly The
    Ashden Trust)
Cadent Foundation
Co-op Foundation
The David Family Foundation*
The Grocers' Charity
The J. J. Charitable Trust
The Mark Leonard Trust
The Limbourne Trust
Lloyd's Register Foundation
Marmot Charitable Trust
Nesta
The Rothley Trust
South Yorkshire Community
    Foundation
The Thirty Percy Foundation

Forestry

The Aurora Trust (formerly The
    Ashden Trust)
Carew Pole Charitable Trust
Fat Face Foundation*
Hamamelis Trust
The J. J. Charitable Trust
The Jabbs Foundation
The Nineveh Charitable Trust
The Peter Samuel Charitable
    Trust
The Waterloo Foundation
The Whitaker Charitable Trust

Fresh water (e.g. streams, rivers and lakes)

M. J. Camp Charitable
    Foundation
Carew Pole Charitable Trust
Craignish Trust
John Ellerman Foundation
Esmée Fairbairn Foundation
Fat Face Foundation*
The Lyndal Tree Foundation
The Nineveh Charitable Trust
Tay Charitable Trust

Waste management and recycling

The Burberry Foundation
Carew Pole Charitable Trust

General charitable purposes

The 3Ts Charitable Trust
4 Charity Foundation
The 4814 Trust
The 64 Trust*
The A. and J. Charitable Trust
ABF The Soldiers' Charity
abrdn Charitable Foundation
The Addleshaw Goddard Charitable Trust
The Adlard Family Charitable Foundation
The Aitken Family Charitable Trust
Sylvia Aitken's Charitable Trust
The Aldama Foundation
AlixPartners (UK) Charitable Foundation
D. C. R. Allen Charitable Trust
Amant Foundation
The Ammco Trust
Viscount Amory's Charitable Trust
The AMW Charitable Trust
The Anson Charitable Trust
The Arah Foundation
The Annabel Arbib Foundation
The Archer Trust
The Ardeola Charitable Trust
The Ardwick Trust
The John Armitage Charitable Trust
The Arsenal Foundation
Ove Arup Partnership Charitable Trust
The Asda Foundation
Ashburnham Thanksgiving Trust
The Ashendene Trust
The Ian Askew Charitable Trust
Atkin Charitable Foundation
The Atlas Fund
The Lord Austin Trust
Axis Foundation
Bagri Foundation
The Bamford Charitable Foundation
Banbury Charities
The Band Trust
The Barbers' Company General Charities
The Barbour Foundation
Lord Barnby's Foundation
The Barnes Fund
The Max Barney Foundation
Barnsbury Charitable Trust
The Barratt Developments plc Charitable Foundation
Misses Barrie Charitable Trust
Robert Barr's Charitable Trust
The Paul Bassham Charitable Trust
The Battersea Power Station Foundation

The Bay Tree Charitable Trust
The Louis Baylis (Maidenhead Advertiser) Charitable Trust
The James Beattie Charitable Trust
The Beaverbrook Foundation
The Beaverbrooks Charitable Trust
Beccles Townlands Charity
Bedfordshire and Luton Community Foundation
Bedfordshire Charitable Trust Ltd
The David and Ruth Behrend Fund
The Lord Belstead Charitable Settlement*
The Benham Charitable Settlement
Bennett Lowell Ltd
The Rowan Bentall Charitable Trust
Berkshire Community Foundation
Bideford Bridge Trust
The Bill Family Charitable Trust
The Billmeir Charitable Trust
The Bingham Trust
Binks Trust
The Michael Bishop Foundation
The Bertie Black Foundation
The Blakebank Trust
Blakemore Foundation
Lady Blakenham's Charity Trust
The Sir Victor Blank Charitable Settlement
Abraham Algy Bloom Foundation
The Bloomfield Charitable Trust
The Bluston Charitable Settlement
The Blyth Charitable Trust
Blyth Watson Charitable Trust
BNA Charitable Incorporated Organisation
The Charlotte Bonham-Carter Charitable Trust
The Boodle and Dunthorne Charitable Trust
The Borrows Charitable Trust
The Bothwell Charitable Trust
The Bowland Charitable Trust
The Frank Brake Charitable Trust
The William Brake Charitable Trust
The Liz and Terry Bramall Foundation
The Harold and Alice Bridges Charity
Bristol Charities
British Humane Association

J. and M. Britton Charitable Trust
The Broomton Foundation
The Brothers Trust
The Brown Source Trust
R. S. Brownless Charitable Trust
T. B. H. Brunner's Charitable Settlement
The Jack Brunton Charitable Trust
Buckinghamshire Community Foundation
The Bulldog Trust Ltd
The Burges Salmon Charitable Trust
The Burry Charitable Trust
Byrne Family Foundation
The G. W. Cadbury Charitable Trust
The Edward and Dorothy Cadbury Trust
The George Cadbury Trust
Community Foundation for Calderdale
Barbara and Derek Calrow Charitable Foundation
Cambridgeshire Community Foundation
Camden Giving
M. J. Camp Charitable Foundation
The Candy Foundation
The Frederick and Phyllis Cann Trust
Card Factory Foundation
David William Traill Cargill Fund
W. A. Cargill Fund
The Carrington Charitable Trust
The Casey Trust
The Castanea Trust
Catkin Pussywillow Charitable Trust
The Joseph and Annie Cattle Trust
The Thomas Sivewright Catto Charitable Settlement
The Wilfrid and Constance Cave Foundation
The B. G. S. Cayzer Charitable Trust
The Cazenove Charitable Trust
The Amelia Chadwick Trust
The Charities Advisory Trust
The Charman Family Charitable Trust
Chartered Accountants' Livery Charity (CALC)
The Charterhouse Charitable Trust
The Cheruby Trust
Cheshire Community Foundation Ltd
Cheshire Freemasons' Charity

The Chetwode Foundation
Chippenham Borough Lands
  Charity
The Christabella Charitable
  Trust
Church Burgesses Trust
The Roger and Sarah Bancroft
  Clark Charitable Trust
The Clarkson Foundation
The Clover Trust
Clydpride Ltd
The John Coates Charitable
  Trust
The Cobalt Trust
The Cobtree Charity Trust Ltd
The Vivienne and Samuel
  Cohen Charitable Trust
Colefax Charitable Trust
The George Henry Collins
  Charity
Sir Jeremiah Colman Gift Trust
The Company of Actuaries
  Charitable Trust Fund
Douglas Compton James
  Charitable Trust
Congleton Inclosure Trust
The Catherine Cookson
  Charitable Trust
The Keith Coombs Trust
Mabel Cooper Charity
The Alice Ellen Cooper-Dean
  Charitable Foundation
The Helen Jean Cope Charity
The Gershon Coren Charitable
  Foundation
Michael Cornish Charitable
  Trust
Cornwall Community
  Foundation
The Corton Hill Trust
The Costa Family Charitable
  Trust
The Cotton Industry War
  Memorial Trust
The Coulthurst Trust
The County Council of Dyfed
  Welsh Church Fund
County Durham Community
  Foundation
The Sir Tom Cowie Charitable
  Trust
The Lord Cozens-Hardy Trust
The CPF Trust
Craignish Trust
Cripplegate Foundation
The Crucible Foundation
Cullum Family Trust
Cumbria Community
  Foundation
Itzchok Meyer Cymerman Trust
  Ltd
The D. G. Charitable
  Settlement
The Davidson Family
  Charitable Trust

Michael Davies Charitable
  Settlement
Margaret Davies Charity
The Crispin Davis Family Trust
The Henry and Suzanne Davis
  Foundation
The De Brye Charitable Trust
Debmar Benevolent Trust Ltd
Denman Charitable Trust
Dentons UK and Middle East
  LLP Charitable Trust
Foundation Derbyshire
The J. N. Derbyshire Trust
Devon Community Foundation
The Laduma Dhamecha
  Charitable Trust
The Alan and Sheila Diamond
  Charitable Trust
The Dibden Allotments Fund
The Dischma Charitable Trust
The DLM Charitable Trust
William and Frances Dobie
  Charitable Foundation
The Dorfman Foundation
Dorset Community Foundation
The Dorus Trust
The Double 'O' Charity Ltd
Dromintee Trust
Duke of Devonshire's
  Charitable Trust
The Dulverton Trust
Dumbreck Charity
The Dunn Family Charitable
  Trust
The Charles Dunstone
  Charitable Trust
The Mildred Duveen Charitable
  Trust
Audrey Earle Charitable Trust
The Earley Charity
Sir John Eastwood Foundation
Edinburgh Trust No2 Account
Edupoor Ltd
The Eighteen Fund
The Eighty Eight Foundation
The Wilfred and Elsie Elkes
  Charity Fund
The Maud Elkington Charitable
  Trust
The Ellerdale Trust
The Vernon N. Ely Charitable
  Trust
The Englefield Charitable Trust
The EQ Foundation
The Esfandi Charitable
  Foundation
Essex Community Foundation
Joseph Ettedgui Charitable
  Foundation
The Eventhall Family
  Charitable Trust
The Everard Foundation
Eversheds Sutherland
  (International) Charitable
  Trust
G. F. Eyre Charitable Trust

The Fairness Foundation
The Fairstead Trust
The Lord Faringdon Charitable
  Trust
The Farthing Trust
The February Foundation
The A. M. Fenton Trust
The Feoffees of St Michael's
  Spurriergate York
The Fermanagh Trust
The Fidelis Foundation*
Doris Field Charitable Trust
The Fieldrose Charitable Trust
Dixie Rose Findlay Charitable
  Trust
Sir John Fisher Foundation
The Earl Fitzwilliam Charitable
  Trust
The Robert Fleming Hannay
  Memorial Charity
The Mrs Yvonne Flux
  Charitable Trust
The Follett Trust
Fordeve Ltd
Forest Hill Charitable Trust
Forever Manchester
The Forman Hardy Charitable
  Trust
The Forrester Family Trust
The Fort Foundation
Foux Foundation
Fowler Smith and Jones Trust
The Foxglove Trust
The Foyle Foundation
The Elizabeth Frankland Moore
  and Star Foundation
The Gordon Fraser Charitable
  Trust
The Hugh Fraser Foundation
The Fraxinus Charitable Trust
The Joseph Strong Frazer Trust
Anne French Memorial Trust
Frognal Trust
The Patrick and Helena Frost
  Foundation
The Fulmer Charitable Trust
The Funding Network
G. M. C. Trust
The G. R. P. Charitable Trust
The Gale Family Charity Trust
GambleAware
Ganzoni Charitable Trust
Garthgwynion Charities
Gatwick Airport Community
  Trust
The Gaudio Family Foundation
  (UK) Ltd
The Robert Gavron Charitable
  Trust
The Generational Foundation*
The George Family Foundation
The Gertner Charitable Trust
The Tara Getty Foundation
The G. C. Gibson Charitable
  Trust

The Simon Gibson Charitable Trust

The B. and P. Glasser Charitable Trust

The F. Glenister Woodger Trust CIO

Gloucestershire Community Foundation

The Godinton Charitable Trust

The Goldcrest Charitable Trust

The Golden Bottle Trust

The Goldman Sachs Charitable Gift Fund (UK)

Goldman Sachs Gives (UK)

The Goldsmiths' Company Charity

Matthew Good Foundation*

The Jane Goodman Charitable Trust*

The Goodman Foundation

The Gosling Foundation Ltd

Gowling WLG (UK) Charitable Trust

Grace Charitable Trust

The Grace Trust

Graff Foundation

E. C. Graham Belford Charitable Settlement

The Grand Trust CIO

GrantScape

The J. G. Graves Charitable Trust

The Great Stone Bridge Trust of Edenbridge

The Freddie Green and Family Charitable Foundation*

The Green Hall Foundation

The Green Room Charitable Trust

The Gretna Charitable Trust

The Grimmitt Trust

The Grocers' Charity

Groundwork UK

The Walter Guinness Charitable Trust

H. and T. Clients Charitable Trust

Hampshire and Isle of Wight Community Foundation

The W. A. Handley Charity Trust

The Lennox Hannay Charitable Trust

The Kathleen Hannay Memorial Charity

The Haramead Trust

Harbinson Charitable Trust

Harborne Parish Lands Charity

The Harbour Foundation

William Harding's Charity

The Harebell Centenary Fund

The Peter and Teresa Harris Charitable Trust

The Harris Family Charitable Trust

The Harrison-Frank Family Foundation (UK) Ltd

Gay and Peter Hartley's Hillards Charitable Trust

Edward Harvist Trust (The Harvist Estate)

The Hasluck Charitable Trust

The Maurice Hatter Foundation

The Hawthorne Charitable Trust

Heart of England Community Foundation

The Hearth Foundation

The Heathcoat Trust

The Heathside Charitable Trust

The Charlotte Heber-Percy Charitable Trust

The Percy Hedley 1990 Charitable Trust

The Michael Heller Charitable Foundation

The Hemby Charitable Trust

The Trevor Hemmings Foundation

Tim Henman Foundation

The G. D. Herbert Charitable Trust

Herefordshire Community Foundation

Hertfordshire Community Foundation

The Bernhard Heuberger Charitable Trust*

P. and C. Hickinbotham Charitable Trust

The Alan Edward Higgs Charity

R. G. Hills Charitable Trust

The Hiscox Foundation

The Henry C. Hoare Charitable Trust

The Hobson Charity Ltd

The Iris Rose Holley Charitable Trust

Hollick Family Foundation

The Holliday Foundation

P. H. Holt Foundation

Sir Harold Hood's Charitable Trust

The Horners Charity Fund

The Hospital of God at Greatham

The Sir Joseph Hotung Charitable Settlement

House of Industry Estate

The Reta Lila Howard Foundation

James T. Howat Charitable Trust

The Hudson Foundation

The Huggard Charitable Trust

The Hull and East Riding Charitable Trust

Michael and Shirley Hunt Charitable Trust

The Hunting Horn General Charitable Trust

Huntingdon Freemen's Trust

The Hutchinson Charitable Trust

The Hutton Foundation

The Nani Huyu Charitable Trust

The Harold Hyam Wingate Foundation

Ibrahim Foundation Ltd

The Iceland Foods Charitable Foundation

The Iliffe Family Charitable Trust

Impact Funding Partners Ltd

The Inflexion Foundation

The Ingram Trust

The Inman Charity

The Inverforth Charitable Trust

The Investindustrial Foundation

Investream Charitable Trust

The Irving Memorial Trust

The J. Isaacs Charitable Trust

The Isle of Anglesey Charitable Association (Cymdeithas Elusennol Ynys Môn)

The J. and J. Benevolent Foundation

The J. J. Charitable Trust

The Jagclif Charitable Trust

John James Bristol Foundation

The Susan and Stephen James Charitable Settlement

Lady Eda Jardine Charitable Trust

Jay Education Trust

JD Foundation

The Jenour Foundation

The Jephcott Charitable Trust

Lillie Johnson Charitable Trust

The Christopher and Kirsty Johnston Charitable Trust

The Joicey Trust

The Muriel Jones Foundation

The Joron Charitable Trust

J. E. Joseph Charitable Fund

Kahal Chassidim Bobov

The Kasner Charitable Trust

The Michael and Ilse Katz Foundation

The Emmanuel Kaye Foundation

William Kendall's Charity (Wax Chandlers Company)

The Kennedy Leigh Charitable Trust

Kent Community Foundation

The Nancy Kenyon Charitable Trust

Keren Association Ltd

E. and E. Kernkraut Charities Ltd

The Ursula Keyes Trust

The Kildare Trust

Fraser Kilpatrick Charitable Trust

The King Henry VIII Endowed
Trust – Warwick
King/Cullimore Charitable
Trust
The Mary Kinross Charitable
Trust
Laura Kinsella Foundation
The Graham Kirkham
Foundation
Robert Kitchin (Saddlers' Co.)
The Ernest Kleinwort
Charitable Trust
Sir James Knott Trust
The Kobler Trust
Kollel and Co. Ltd
Kreditor Charitable Trust
Kusuma Trust UK
The Kyte Charitable Trust
The David Laing Foundation
The Kirby Laing Foundation
The Martin Laing Foundation
The Leonard Laity Stoate
Charitable Trust
Community Foundations for
Lancashire and Merseyside
Langdale Trust
The R. J. Larg Family Trust
Mrs M. A. Lascelles Charitable
Trust
The Lauffer Family Charitable
Foundation
Mrs F. B. Laurence Charitable
Trust
The Richard Lawes Foundation
The Edgar E. Lawley
Foundation
The Herd Lawson and Muriel
Lawson Charitable Trust
Lawson Beckman Charitable
Trust
The Leach Fourteenth Trust
The Leathersellers' Foundation
The Arnold Lee Charitable
Trust
The William Leech Charity
Leeds Community Foundation
Leicestershire and Rutland
Masonic Charity
Association
Leicestershire, Leicester and
Rutland Community
Foundation
Leng Charitable Trust
The Leri Charitable Trust
The Ralph Levy Charitable
Company Ltd
Cecil and Hilda Lewis
Charitable Trust
Bernard Lewis Family
Charitable Trust
David and Ruth Lewis Family
Charitable Trust
The Charles Lewis Foundation
The Sir Edward Lewis
Foundation
The Limbourne Trust

Limoges Charitable Trust
Lincolnshire Community
Foundation
The Lister Charitable Trust
The Frank Litchfield Charitable
Trust
Little Lives UK*
The Charles Littlewood Hill
Trust
The George John and Sheilah
Livanos Charitable Trust
Liverpool Charity and Voluntary
Services (LCVS)
Jack Livingstone Charitable
Trust
The Elaine and Angus Lloyd
Charitable Trust
The W. M. and B. W. Lloyd
Trust
Lloyd's of London Foundation
Localtrent Ltd
The Lockwood Charitable
Foundation
The London Community
Foundation (LCF)
London Freemasons Charity
The Lower Green Foundation
The C. L. Loyd Charitable Trust
LPW Ltd
Lord and Lady Lurgan Trust
The Lyndal Tree Foundation
The Mackintosh Foundation
The John MacLeod Charitable
Trust
The Mactaggart Third Fund
The Ian Mactaggart Trust
The Magen Charitable Trust
The Mageni Trust
The Mahoro Charitable Trust
Making a Difference Locally
Ltd
The Mallinckrodt Foundation
The Manackerman Charitable
Trust
Manchester Airport Community
Trust Fund
The Manchester Guardian
Society Charitable Trust
The W. M. Mann Foundation
R. W. Mann Trust
The Manson Family Charitable
Trust
The Marque Foundation
The Michael Marsh Charitable
Trust
The Marsh Christian Trust
Charlotte Marshall Charitable
Trust
The Martin Charitable Trust
The Kristina Martin Charitable
Trust
Matchroom Sport Charitable
Foundation
The Mather Family Charitable
Trust

The Violet Mauray Charitable
Trust
The Theodore Maxxy
Charitable Trust
Mayheights Ltd
Mazars Charitable Trust
MBNA General Foundation
The Robert McAlpine
Foundation
The Meikle Foundation
The Merchant Venturers
Charity
Merchants House of Glasgow
The Mikheev Charitable Trust
The Mila Charitable
Organisation
The Millennium Oak Trust
Hugh and Mary Miller Bequest
Trust
The Ronald Miller Foundation
The Millichope Foundation
Millie's Watch
Mills and Reeve Charitable
Trust
The Millward Charitable Trust
The Clare Milne Trust
Milton Keynes Community
Foundation Ltd
The Laurence Misener
Charitable Trust
The Mishcon Family Charitable
Trust
The Esmé Mitchell Trust
The MITIE Foundation
The Mittal Foundation
Mobbs Memorial Trust Ltd
The Modiano Charitable Trust
The Mohn Westlake
Foundation
Mole Charitable Trust
The Alexander Moncur Trust
The Monmouthshire County
Council Welsh Church Act
Fund
The George A. Moore
Foundation
The Morgan Charitable
Foundation
The Steve Morgan Foundation
The Morris Charitable Trust
G. M. Morrison Charitable
Trust
The Ken and Edna Morrison
Charitable Trust
The Ken and Lynne Morrison
Charitable Trust
The Morrisons Foundation
The Moshal Charitable Trust
Vyoel Moshe Charitable Trust
The Alexander Mosley
Charitable Trust
Moto Foundation
The Mowgli Trust
The Mulberry Trust
The Mulchand Foundation
The Mumford Memorial Trust*

Music Sales Charitable Trust
The Mutley Foundation
The National Express
Foundation
The National Lottery
Community Fund
The Gareth Neame Foundation
Norfolk Community Foundation
The Norman Family Charitable
Trust
Normanby Charitable Trust
North London Charities Ltd
Northamptonshire Community
Foundation
Northcott Trust
Community Foundation for
Northern Ireland
The Northwick Trust
The Notgrove Trust
Nottinghamshire Community
Foundation
Odin Charitable Trust
The Ofenheim Charitable Trust
Oizer Charitable Trust
One Community Foundation
Ltd
The Orrin Charitable Trust
Ostro Fayre Share Foundation
The Owen Family Trust
Oxfordshire Community
Foundation
P. F. Charitable Trust
The Paget Charitable Trust
The Pantheon Charitable Trust
The James Pantyfedwen
Foundation
(Ymddiriedolaeth James
Pantyfedwen)
Parabola Foundation
The Paragon Trust
The Samuel and Freda
Parkinson Charitable Trust
Miss M. E. S. Paterson's
Charitable Trust
The Patrick Trust
Peacock Charitable Trust
Susanna Peake Charitable
Trust
David Pearlman Charitable
Foundation
The Penchant Foundation
The Pennycress Trust
People's Health Trust
Dina Perelman Trust Ltd
The Persimmon Charitable
Foundation
Personal Assurance Charitable
Trust
The Pharsalia Charitable Trust
The Phillips Family Charitable
Trust
The Bernard Piggott Charitable
Trust
The Sir Harry Pilkington Fund
Miss A. M. Pilkington's
Charitable Trust

The Pinchbeck Charitable Trust
The Porta Pia 2012
Foundation
Porter Foundation
Postcode Society Trust
Sir John Priestman Charity
Trust
The Primrose Trust
The Princess Anne's Charities
The Priory Foundation
The Privy Purse Charitable
Trust
Provincial Grand Charity of the
Province of Derbyshire
The Puebla Charitable Trust
The PwC Foundation
Mr and Mrs J. A. Pye's
Charitable Settlement
Q Charitable Trust
Quartet Community Foundation
The Queen Anne's Gate
Foundation
Quintessentially Foundation
R. S. Charitable Trust
Rachel Charitable Trust
The Raindance Charitable
Trust
The Rainford Trust
The Joseph and Lena Randall
Charitable Trust
The Ratcliff Foundation
The Rathbones Group
Foundation
The Ravensdale Trust
The Roger Raymond Charitable
Trust
C. A. Redfern Charitable
Foundation
Rentrust Foundation Ltd
The Rhododendron Trust
Riada Trust
Daisie Rich Trust
The Clive Richards Foundation
Richmond Parish Lands Charity
Rigby Foundation
The Sir John Ritblat Family
Foundation
The River Farm Foundation
Riverside Charitable Trust Ltd
RJM Charity Trust
The Roan Charitable Trust
The Dezna Robins Jones
Charitable Foundation
Rockcliffe Charitable Trust
The Rockspring Charitable
Trust
The Rofeh Trust
The Sir James Roll Charitable
Trust
The Helen Roll Charity
The Gerald and Gail Ronson
Family Foundation
Mrs L. D. Rope's Third
Charitable Settlement
Rosca Trust
The Rose Foundation

The Rothermere Foundation
The Rothley Trust
The Rowlands Trust
Royal Artillery Charitable Fund
Royal Docks Trust (London)
The Rubin Foundation
Charitable Trust
The Rugby Group Benevolent
Fund Ltd
Russell Trust
The RWS Foundation
S. and R. Charitable Trust
The S. M. B. Trust
The Jeremy and John Sacher
Charitable Trust
The Saddlers' Company
Charitable Fund
The Salamander Charitable
Trust
Salisbury Pool Charity
The Basil Samuel Charitable
Trust
The M. J. Samuel Charitable
Trust
The Peter Samuel Charitable
Trust
The Sanderson Foundation
The Sandhu Charitable
Foundation
Sandra Charitable Trust
The Sands Family Trust
The Schmidt-Bodner Charitable
Trust
The Anthony Scholefield
Foundation
The Schreib Trust
O. and G. Schreiber Charitable
Trust
Foundation Scotland
Scotland's Garden Scheme*
The Scotshill Trust
Scott (Eredine) Charitable
Trust
The Ina Scott Sutherland
Charitable Foundation
The John Scott Trust Fund
Scottish Property Industry
Festival of Christmas
(SPIFOX)
ScottishPower Foundation
Scouloudi Foundation
The Searchlight Electric
Charitable Trust
The Sam and Bella Sebba
Charitable Foundation
The Selwood Charitable Trust
The Cyril Shack Trust
ShareGift (The Orr Mackintosh
Foundation)
The Sharp Foundation
The Sheepdrove Trust
The Sheffield Town Trust
The Sheldon Trust
The Patricia and Donald
Shepherd Charitable Trust

The Sylvia and Colin Shepherd
   Charitable Trust
The Sherling Charitable Trust
The Archie Sherman Charitable
   Trust
Shlomo Memorial Fund Ltd
Shulem B. Association Ltd
The Florence Shute Millennium
   Trust
The Charles Skey Charitable
   Trust
The John Slater Foundation
The Slaughter and May
   Charitable Trust
Rita and David Slowe
   Charitable Trust
The N. Smith Charitable
   Settlement
Arabella and Julian Smith
   Family Trust
The R. C. Snelling Charitable
   Trust
Social Investment Business
   Foundation
Sodexo Stop Hunger
   Foundation
Somerset Community
   Foundation
South Yorkshire Community
   Foundation
The Stephen R. and Philippa
   H. Southall Charitable Trust
W. F. Southall Trust
SPAR Charitable Fund
Sparquote Ltd
The Spear Charitable Trust
Spears-Stutz Charitable Trust
The Jessie Spencer Trust
The Sperring Charity
Spielman Charitable Trust
Spurrell Charitable Trust
The Geoff and Fiona Squire
   Foundation
The Squire Patton Boggs
   Charitable Trust
The Squires Foundation
The Vichai Srivaddhanaprabha
   Foundation
Stadium Charitable Trust
The Stafford Trust
Starlow Charities Ltd
The Peter Stebbings Memorial
   Charity
The Hugh Stenhouse
   Foundation
The Stevenage Community
   Trust
The Stevenson Family's
   Charitable Trust
The Stoller Charitable Trust
The Stoneygate Trust
The Samuel Storey Family
   Charitable Trust
Peter Stormonth Darling
   Charitable Trust
Peter Storrs Trust

Stratford-upon-Avon Town Trust
Suffolk Community Foundation
Community Foundation for
   Surrey
The Sussex Community
   Foundation
Sabina Sutherland Charitable
   Trust
Sutton Coldfield Charitable
   Trust
The Swann-Morton Foundation
Swarovski Foundation
The John Swire (1989)
   Charitable Trust
The Adrian Swire Charitable
   Trust
The Syder Foundation
The Charles and Elsie Sykes
   Trust
The T.K. Maxx and
   Homesense Foundation
The Talbot Village Trust
Tallow Chandlers Benevolent
   Fund No 2
The Taurus Foundation
Tay Charitable Trust
Stephen Taylor Foundation
The Tedworth Charitable Trust
Tees Valley Community
   Foundation
The Templeton Goodwill Trust
The Thales Charitable Trust
The Thompson Family
   Charitable Trust
Mrs R. P. Tindall's Charitable
   Trust
The Tompkins Foundation
Toyota Manufacturing UK
   Charitable Trust
The Trades House of Glasgow
The Trelix Charitable Trust*
The Troutsdale Charitable
   Trust
The Truemark Trust
Truemart Ltd
The Trysil Charitable Trust
The Tudor Trust
The Tuixen Foundation
G. J. W. Turner Trust
The Florence Turner Trust
Two Ridings Community
   Foundation
Community Foundation serving
   Tyne and Wear and
   Northumberland
Tzedakah
The Udlington Trust
The Utley Foundation
The Valentine Charitable Trust
The Valiant Charitable Trust
The Albert Van Den Bergh
   Charitable Trust
The Van Mesdag Fund
The Vandervell Foundation
The Vardy Foundation
The Velvet Foundation

VHLT Ltd
Virgin Atlantic Foundation
The Virgin Foundation (Virgin
   Unite)
The Community Foundation in
   Wales
The Barbara Ward Children's
   Foundation
The Warwickshire Masonic
   Charitable Association Ltd
G. R. Waters Charitable Trust
   2000
The Geoffrey Watling Charity
We Love MCR Charity
The David Webster Charitable
   Trust
The William Webster
   Charitable Trust
The Linda and Michael
   Weinstein Charitable Trust
The Colin Weir Charitable
   Foundation
The James Weir Foundation
The Welsh Church Act Fund
West Derby Waste Lands
   Charity
Westminster Foundation
The Whinfell Charitable Fund
The Whitaker Charitable Trust
The Melanie White Foundation
   Ltd
WHSmith Trust
The Wigoder Family Foundation
The H. D. H. Wills 1965
   Charitable Trust
Dame Violet Wills Will Trust
The Wilmcote Charitrust
Brian Wilson Charitable Trust
Wiltshire Community
   Foundation
The Benjamin Winegarten
   Charitable Trust
W. Wing Yip and Brothers
   Foundation
The Michael and Anna Wix
   Charitable Trust
The James Wood Bequest
   Fund
The Woodstock Family
   Charitable Foundation
Worcestershire Community
   Foundation
The Worshipful Company of
   Glovers of London
   Charitable Trust
Worshipful Company of Gold
   and Silver Wyre Drawers
   Second Charitable Trust
   Fund
Worshipful Company of
   Needlemakers Charitable
   Fund
Worth Waynflete Foundation
The Worwin UK Foundation
The Edward and Catherine
   Wray Charitable Trust

Wychville Ltd
The Wyfold Charitable Trust
The Wyndham Charitable Trust
Yorkshire Building Society
  Charitable Foundation
Youth Endowment Fund (YEF)*
The Elizabeth and Prince
  Zaiger Trust
The Marjorie and Arnold Ziff
  Charitable Foundation
The Zochonis Charitable Trust
Zurich Community Trust (UK)
  Ltd

Health

The 29th May 1961 Charitable
  Trust
4 Charity Foundation
The 4814 Trust
The A. and J. Charitable Trust
The Aberbrothock Skea Trust
ABF The Soldiers' Charity
The Addleshaw Goddard
  Charitable Trust
Adenfirst Ltd
The Adint Charitable Trust
The AEB Charitable Trust
The AIM Foundation
The Aimwell Charitable Trust
Alan Boswell Group Charitable
  Trust
The Alborada Trust
The Alchemy Foundation
The Aldama Foundation
Al-Fayed Charitable Foundation
The Derrill Allatt Foundation
Alliance Family Foundation Ltd
Alzheimer's Society
Amant Foundation
Ambergate Charitable Trust
The Ammco Trust
The AMW Charitable Trust
The Anchor Foundation
Andrew Anderson Trust
Andor Charitable Trust
Anglo American Foundation
The John Apthorp Charity
Ardbarron Trust Ltd
The Ardeola Charitable Trust
The Ardwick Trust
Armed Forces Covenant Fund
  Trust
The Artemis Charitable
  Foundation
Douglas Arter Foundation
ArtSocial Foundation
Ove Arup Partnership
  Charitable Trust
The Asda Foundation
Asthma and Lung UK
The Astor Foundation
Atkin Charitable Foundation
Atlas Memorial Ltd
The Lord Austin Trust
Bagri Foundation
The Baily Thomas Charitable
  Fund
The Roy and Pixie Baker
  Charitable Trust
The Ballinger Charitable Trust
Veronica and Lars Bane
  Foundation
The Kamini and Vindi Banga
  Family Trust
The Barbour Foundation
Barcapel Foundation Ltd
Barchester Healthcare
  Foundation
The Baring Foundation
The Barnes Fund

Barnwood Trust
Misses Barrie Charitable Trust
Robert Barr's Charitable Trust
The Batchworth Trust
Bauer Radio's Cash for Kids
  Charities
The Gordon and Ena Baxter
  Foundation*
The Bay Tree Charitable Trust
BBC Children in Need
The James Beattie Charitable
  Trust
The Beaverbrook Foundation
The Beaverbrooks Charitable
  Trust
Bedfordshire Charitable Trust
  Ltd
The Bellahouston Bequest
  Fund
Benesco Charity Ltd
The Benham Charitable
  Settlement
The Rowan Bentall Charitable
  Trust
The Bestway Foundation
Bideford Bridge Trust
The Billmeir Charitable Trust
Birkdale Trust for Hearing
  Impaired Ltd*
The Michael Bishop
  Foundation
Maria Bjornson Memorial Fund
The John Black Charitable
  Foundation
The Bertie Black Foundation
The Isabel Blackman
  Foundation
Blakemore Foundation
Lady Blakenham's Charity
  Trust
The Sir Victor Blank Charitable
  Settlement
The Bluston Charitable
  Settlement
Blyth Watson Charitable Trust
Maureen Boal Charitable Trust
The Marjory Boddy Charitable
  Trust
The Boltini Trust
The Booth Charities
Boots Charitable Trust
The Boshier-Hinton Foundation
The Bothwell Charitable Trust
The Harry Bottom Charitable
  Trust
Sir Clive Bourne Family Trust
The Frank Brake Charitable
  Trust
The Tony Bramall Charitable
  Trust
The Liz and Terry Bramall
  Foundation
The Brelms Trust CIO
Bright Red Charity
The Britford Bridge Trust

British Eye Research
   Foundation (Fight for Sight)
British Humane Association
J. and M. Britton Charitable
   Trust
The Consuelo and Anthony
   Brooke Charitable Trust
The Brothers Trust
Bill Brown 1989 Charitable
   Trust
The Mary Brown Memorial
   Trust
R. S. Brownless Charitable
   Trust
T. B. H. Brunner's Charitable
   Settlement
The Jack Brunton Charitable
   Trust
Buckingham Trust
Buckinghamshire Community
   Foundation
The Bulldog Trust Ltd
E. F. Bulmer Trust
The Burden Trust
The Burdett Trust for Nursing
Clara E. Burgess Charity
Consolidated Charity of Burton
   upon Trent
Miss Margaret Butters Reekie
   Charitable Trust
William A. Cadbury Charitable
   Trust
The Cadbury Foundation
The Edward and Dorothy
   Cadbury Trust
The George Cadbury Trust
Camden Giving
Cancer Research UK
CareTech Charitable
   Foundation
Carew Pole Charitable Trust
William A. Cargill Charitable
   Trust
W. A. Cargill Fund
The Antonio Carluccio
   Foundation
The Carr-Gregory Trust
The Leslie Mary Carter
   Charitable Trust
The Castanea Trust
Catkin Pussywillow Charitable
   Trust
The Joseph and Annie Cattle
   Trust
The Thomas Sivewright Catto
   Charitable Settlement
The Wilfrid and Constance
   Cave Foundation
The Charterhouse Charitable
   Trust
Cheshire Community
   Foundation Ltd
The Childhood Trust
Children with Cancer UK
The Childwick Trust
The André Christian Trust

Chrysalis Trust
Church Burgesses Trust
The Churchill Foundation
The Clarkson Foundation
The Clore Duffield Foundation
The Clothworkers' Foundation
Cloudesley
The Clover Trust
F. B. Coales No. 4 (Family)
   Trust
The Coalfields Regeneration
   Trust
The John Coates Charitable
   Trust
Denise Coates Foundation
The Vivienne and Samuel
   Cohen Charitable Trust
The John S. Cohen Foundation
Colchester Catalyst Charity
Sir Jeremiah Colman Gift Trust
The Colt Foundation
Colyer-Fergusson Charitable
   Trust
The Connolly Foundation (UK)
   Ltd
The Catherine Cookson
   Charitable Trust
The Keith Coombs Trust
Co-op Foundation
The Alice Ellen Cooper-Dean
   Charitable Foundation
The J. Reginald Corah
   Foundation Fund
The Gershon Coren Charitable
   Foundation
Michael Cornish Charitable
   Trust
The Evan Cornish Foundation
Corra Foundation
County Durham Community
   Foundation
The Lord Cozens-Hardy Trust
Michael Crawford Children's
   Charity
CRH Charitable Trust
Cripplegate Foundation
The Croydon Relief-in-Need
   Charity
CSIS Charity Fund
Itzchok Meyer Cymerman Trust
   Ltd
The D. G. Charitable
   Settlement
The D. M. Charitable Trust
Baron Davenport's Charity
Margaret Davies Charity
The Crispin Davis Family Trust
Dawat-E-Hadiyah Trust (United
   Kingdom)
The De Brye Charitable Trust
The Roger De Haan Charitable
   Trust
The Delves Charitable Trust
Foundation Derbyshire
The J. N. Derbyshire Trust
Devon Community Foundation

The Laduma Dhamecha
   Charitable Trust
The Alan and Sheila Diamond
   Charitable Trust
The Dibden Allotments Fund
The Dischma Charitable Trust
The Djanogly Foundation
William and Frances Dobie
   Charitable Foundation
Donibristle Trust
The Dorus Trust
The Double 'O' Charity Ltd
The D'Oyly Carte Charitable
   Trust
Dromintee Trust
Duchy Health Charity Ltd
Duchy of Lancaster Benevolent
   Fund
Dumbreck Charity
Dunlossit and Islay Community
   Trust
The Dunn Family Charitable
   Trust
The DWF Charitable
   Foundation
The Dyers' Company
   Charitable Trust
The James and Deirdre Dyson
   Trust
EA Foundation*
Sir John Eastwood Foundation
The Gilbert and Eileen Edgar
   Foundation
Edupoor Ltd
The Eight Foundation
Eight Strands Foundation
The Eighteen Fund
The Eighty Eight Foundation
The Elie Trust
The Wilfred and Elsie Elkes
   Charity Fund
The Ellerdale Trust
Emerton-Christie Charity
The Englefield Charitable Trust
The Enkalon Foundation
The EQ Foundation
Esher House Charitable Trust
Euro Quality Foundation
The Evelyn Trust
The Eventhall Family
   Charitable Trust
The Everard Foundation
The Eveson Charitable Trust
The Exilarch's Foundation
The Fairstead Trust
Family Philanthropy Ltd
The Lord Faringdon Charitable
   Trust
Samuel William Farmer Trust
The Thomas Farr Charity
The Farthing Trust
The February Foundation
George Fentham Birmingham
   Charity
The A. M. Fenton Trust
The Fidelity UK Foundation

The Fieldrose Charitable Trust
Dixie Rose Findlay Charitable
 Trust
Sir John Fisher Foundation
The Earl Fitzwilliam Charitable
 Trust
The Robert Fleming Hannay
 Memorial Charity
The Follett Trust
Forest Hill Charitable Trust
The Lady Forester Trust
Forever Manchester
The Forman Hardy Charitable
 Trust
The Forrester Family Trust
The Fort Foundation
The Foster Wood Foundation
Foux Foundation
Fowler Smith and Jones Trust
The Gordon Fraser Charitable
 Trust
The Joseph Strong Frazer Trust
Charles S. French Charitable
 Trust
The Freshfield Foundation
The Freshgate Trust
 Foundation
Friarsgate Trust
Friends of Wiznitz Ltd
Frognal Trust
The Funding Network
Ganzoni Charitable Trust
The Robert Gavron Charitable
 Trust
Martin Geddes Charitable
 Trust
General Charity (Coventry)
The General Nursing Council
 for England and Wales
 Trust
The Tara Getty Foundation
The David Gibbons Foundation
The Gibbs Charitable Trusts
The G. C. Gibson Charitable
 Trust
The Simon Gibson Charitable
 Trust
The Girdlers' Company
 Charitable Trust
The B. and P. Glasser
 Charitable Trust
The Gloag Foundation
Global Charities
Sydney and Phyllis Goldberg
 Memorial Charitable Trust
The Goldcrest Charitable Trust
The Golden Bottle Trust
The Goldman Sachs Charitable
 Gift Fund (UK)
Goldman Sachs Gives (UK)
The Goldsmiths' Company
 Charity
The Jane Goodman Charitable
 Trust*
The Goodman Foundation

The Edward Gostling
 Foundation
Gowling WLG (UK) Charitable
 Trust
Grace Charitable Trust
The Grace Trust
The Gisela Graham Foundation
The Graham Trust
Grand Charitable Trust of the
 Order of Women
 Freemasons
The J. G. Graves Charitable
 Trust
Gordon Gray Trust
The Great Britain Sasakawa
 Foundation
The Great Stone Bridge Trust
 of Edenbridge
The Kenneth and Susan Green
 Charitable Foundation
The Green Hall Foundation
Philip and Judith Green Trust
Greenham Trust Ltd
The Greenslade Family
 Foundation
The Grimmitt Trust
The Grocers' Charity
The Albert Gubay Charitable
 Foundation
The Hadley Trust
Halifax Foundation for
 Northern Ireland
The Helen Hamlyn Trust
The Hampstead Wells and
 Campden Trust
Hampton Fund
The W. A. Handley Charity
 Trust
The Lennox Hannay Charitable
 Trust
The Kathleen Hannay
 Memorial Charity
The Haramead Trust
Harborne Parish Lands Charity
The Harbour Foundation
The Harding Trust
The Hargreaves Foundation
The Harpur Trust
The Peter and Teresa Harris
 Charitable Trust
The Harris Family Charitable
 Trust
The Harrison-Frank Family
 Foundation (UK) Ltd
The Harry and Mary
 Foundation
Gay and Peter Hartley's
 Hillards Charitable Trust
Edward Harvist Trust (The
 Harvist Estate)
The Hasluck Charitable Trust
The Hawthorne Charitable
 Trust
The Dorothy Hay-Bolton
 Charitable Trust
The Headley Trust

The Health Foundation
Heart of England Community
 Foundation
The Heathcoat Trust
The Heathside Charitable Trust
Heb Ffin (Without Frontier)
The Charlotte Heber-Percy
 Charitable Trust
Ernest Hecht Charitable
 Foundation
The Hedley Foundation
Help for Health
The Trevor Hemmings
 Foundation
Christina Mary Hendrie Trust
Tim Henman Foundation
The G. D. Herbert Charitable
 Trust
Herefordshire Community
 Foundation
The Bernhard Heuberger
 Charitable Trust*
HFC Help for Children UK Ltd
The Alan Edward Higgs Charity
R. G. Hills Charitable Trust
The Lady Hind Trust
The Hinduja Foundation
The Hintze Family Charity
 Foundation
The Henry C. Hoare Charitable
 Trust
The Hobson Charity Ltd
The Jane Hodge Foundation
The Holbeck Charitable Trust
Hollick Family Foundation
Hollyhock Charitable
 Foundation
P. H. Holt Foundation
Sir Harold Hood's Charitable
 Trust
The Thomas J. Horne
 Memorial Trust
The Horners Charity Fund
Hospice UK
The Hospital of God at
 Greatham
The Hospital Saturday Fund
The Sir Joseph Hotung
 Charitable Settlement
The Hudson Foundation
The Huggard Charitable Trust
The Humanitarian Trust
The Albert Hunt Trust
Miss Agnes H. Hunter's Trust
Hurdale Charity Ltd
The Nani Huyu Charitable Trust
Hyde Charitable Trust
Hyde Park Place Estate Charity
The Iceland Foods Charitable
 Foundation
The Iliffe Family Charitable
 Trust
The Indigo Trust
The Inflexion Foundation
The Inman Charity
The Inverforth Charitable Trust

The Ireland Fund of Great
    Britain
John James Bristol Foundation
The Susan and Stephen
    James Charitable
    Settlement
Lady Eda Jardine Charitable
    Trust
The Roger and Jean Jefcoate
    Trust
The Jenour Foundation
The Jephcott Charitable Trust
The Elton John AIDS
    Foundation
John Lewis and Partners
    Foundation
Lillie Johnson Charitable Trust
The Jones 1986 Charitable
    Trust
The Muriel Jones Foundation
J. E. Joseph Charitable Fund
The Jusaca Charitable Trust
The Karlsson Játiva Charitable
    Foundation
The Ian Karten Charitable
    Trust
The Kasner Charitable Trust
The Michael and Ilse Katz
    Foundation
The Emmanuel Kaye
    Foundation
The Kennedy Leigh Charitable
    Trust
The Kennedy Trust for
    Rheumatology Research
Kent Community Foundation
The Kentown Wizard
    Foundation
The Peter Kershaw Trust
The Ursula Keyes Trust
Fraser Kilpatrick Charitable
    Trust
The Kingsbury Charity
The Mary Kinross Charitable
    Trust
The Graham Kirkham
    Foundation
Sir James Knott Trust
The Kobler Trust
The Kreitman Foundation
Kupath Gemach Chaim
    Bechesed Viznitz Trust
Kusuma Trust UK
The Kyte Charitable Trust
Ladbrokes Coral Trust
Christopher Laing Foundation
The David Laing Foundation
The Kirby Laing Foundation
The Martin Laing Foundation
The Leonard Laity Stoate
    Charitable Trust
The Lake House Charitable
    Foundation
Community Foundations for
    Lancashire and Merseyside
The Lancashire Foundation

Lancaster Foundation
The Allen Lane Foundation
Langdale Trust
The R. J. Larg Family Trust
Laslett's (Hinton) Charity
Mrs F. B. Laurence Charitable
    Trust
The Law Family Charitable
    Foundation
The Richard Lawes Foundation
The Edgar E. Lawley
    Foundation
Lawson Beckman Charitable
    Trust
The Lawson Trust CIO
The Leach Fourteenth Trust
Ana Leaf Foundation*
The Leathersellers' Foundation
Leeds Building Society
    Foundation
The Leeward Trust
The Leri Charitable Trust
Lord Leverhulme's Charitable
    Trust
The Ralph Levy Charitable
    Company Ltd
Joseph Levy Foundation
Cecil and Hilda Lewis
    Charitable Trust
Bernard Lewis Family
    Charitable Trust
The Lightbulb Trust*
The Limbourne Trust
Limoges Charitable Trust
The Linbury Trust
The Linder Foundation
The Lister Charitable Trust
The Frank Litchfield Charitable
    Trust
The Michael and Betty Little
    Trust*
The Charles Littlewood Hill
    Trust
The George John and Sheilah
    Livanos Charitable Trust
Liverpool Charity and Voluntary
    Services (LCVS)
The Ian and Natalie
    Livingstone Charitable Trust
Jack Livingstone Charitable
    Trust
The Elaine and Angus Lloyd
    Charitable Trust
The W. M. and B. W. Lloyd
    Trust
Lloyds Bank Foundation for
    England and Wales
Lloyds Bank Foundation for the
    Channel Islands
The Locker Foundation
The Lockwood Charitable
    Foundation
London Catalyst
The London Community
    Foundation (LCF)
London Freemasons Charity

The C. L. Loyd Charitable Trust
Robert Luff Foundation Ltd
The Lyndal Tree Foundation
The Macdonald-Buchanan
    Charitable Trust
Mace Foundation
The Mackintosh Foundation
The John MacLeod Charitable
    Trust
The Robin MacLeod Charitable
    Trust
The Mahoro Charitable Trust
Making a Difference Locally
    Ltd
The Manackerman Charitable
    Trust
The Manchester Guardian
    Society Charitable Trust
R. W. Mann Trust
The Manoukian Charitable
    Foundation
The Manson Family Charitable
    Trust
The Marks Family Charitable
    Trust
The Marque Foundation
The Michael Marsh Charitable
    Trust
The Marsh Christian Trust
Charlotte Marshall Charitable
    Trust
The Martin Charitable Trust
The Kristina Martin Charitable
    Trust
John Martin's Charity
Masonic Charitable Foundation
Nancie Massey Charitable
    Trust
The Master Charitable Trust
Matchroom Sport Charitable
    Foundation
The Matliwala Family
    Charitable Trust
The Violet Mauray Charitable
    Trust
Mayheights Ltd
Mazars Charitable Trust
MBNA General Foundation
The McCarthy Stone
    Foundation
The Medicash Foundation
The Medlock Charitable Trust
The Meikle Foundation
The Brian Mercer Charitable
    Trust
The Merchant Taylors'
    Foundation*
The Merchant Venturers
    Charity
Merchants House of Glasgow
Merriman Charitable
    Foundation*
T. and J. Meyer Family
    Foundation Ltd
The Mickel Fund
The Mickleham Trust

The Gerald Micklem Charitable Trust

The Millennium Oak Trust

Hugh and Mary Miller Bequest Trust

The Ronald Miller Foundation

The Millichope Foundation

The Milne Family Foundation

The Clare Milne Trust

The James Milner Foundation

The Laurence Misener Charitable Trust

The Mishcon Family Charitable Trust

The Brian Mitchell Charitable Settlement

The Esmé Mitchell Trust

The MK Charitable Trust

The Mohn Westlake Foundation

The Alexander Moncur Trust

The Monmouthshire County Council Welsh Church Act Fund

Moondance Foundation

John Moores Foundation

The Morgan Charitable Foundation

The Steve Morgan Foundation

Morgan Stanley International Foundation

The Morris Charitable Trust

G. M. Morrison Charitable Trust

The Ken and Edna Morrison Charitable Trust

The Ken and Lynne Morrison Charitable Trust

The Morrisons Foundation

The Mosawi Foundation

Vyoel Moshe Charitable Trust

Motor Neurone Disease Association

The Moulding Foundation

J. P. Moulton Charitable Foundation

The Edwina Mountbatten and Leonora Children's Foundation

The Mulberry Trust

Edith Murphy Foundation

Murphy-Neumann Charity Company Ltd

The John R. Murray Charitable Trust

Brian Murtagh Charitable Trust

Music Sales Charitable Trust

The Mutley Foundation

The National Garden Scheme

The NDL Foundation

Ner Foundation

Nesta

Network for Social Change Charitable Trust

Newby Trust Ltd

The Nine Incorporated Trades of Dundee General Fund Charity

The Nineveh Charitable Trust

NNS Foundation

Norfolk Community Foundation

The Norman Family Charitable Trust

Normanby Charitable Trust

North Berwick Trust

Northamptonshire Community Foundation

Community Foundation for Northern Ireland

Northern Pharmacies Ltd Trust Fund

The Northwick Trust

Northwood Charitable Trust

The Norton Foundation

The Norton Rose Fulbright Charitable Foundation

Norwich Consolidated Charities

The Notgrove Trust

Nottinghamshire Community Foundation

The Ofenheim Charitable Trust

The Hamish Ogston Foundation

Oizer Charitable Trust

Open House Trust Ltd

The Sir Peter O'Sullevan Charitable Trust

The O'Sullivan Family Charitable Trust

The Ovo Charitable Foundation

The Owen Family Trust

The Paget Charitable Trust

The Panacea Charitable Trust

The Paragon Trust

The Parivar Trust

Miss M. E. S. Paterson's Charitable Trust

Peacock Charitable Trust

Susanna Peake Charitable Trust

David Pearlman Charitable Foundation

The Pears Family Charitable Foundation

The Penchant Foundation

The Persimmon Charitable Foundation

Personal Assurance Charitable Trust

The Pharsalia Charitable Trust

The Phillips and Rubens Charitable Trust

The Philip and Connie Phillips Foundation*

The Bernard Piggott Charitable Trust

The Pilgrim Trust

Cecil Pilkington Charitable Trust

Pilkington Charities Fund

The Sir Harry Pilkington Fund

PIMCO Foundation Europe

Pink Ribbon Foundation

The Pixel Fund

The Players Foundation

Thomas Pocklington Trust

The George and Esme Pollitzer Charitable Settlement

Porter Foundation

The Portrack Charitable Trust

Postcode Community Trust

Postcode Local Trust

Postcode Society Trust

The Mary Potter Convent Hospital Trust

The Prince of Wales's Charitable Foundation

The Princess Anne's Charities

The Priory Foundation

Prison Service Charity Fund

Provincial Grand Charity of the Province of Derbyshire

The Purey Cust Trust CIO

The PwC Foundation

Mr and Mrs J. A. Pye's Charitable Settlement

QBE European Operations Foundation

Quartet Community Foundation

The Queen Anne's Gate Foundation

Queen Mary's Roehampton Trust

The Quilter Foundation

Quintessentially Foundation

Richard Radcliffe Trust

The Rainford Trust

The Rambourg Foundation

The Randal Charitable Foundation

The Joseph and Lena Randall Charitable Trust

The Ranworth Trust

The Ratcliff Foundation

The Eleanor Rathbone Charitable Trust

Elizabeth Rathbone Charity

The Julia and Hans Rausing Trust*

The Ravensdale Trust

The Rayne Foundation

The Sir James Reckitt Charity

C. A. Redfern Charitable Foundation

The Max Reinhardt Charitable Trust

Rentrust Foundation Ltd

Reuben Foundation

The Rhododendron Trust

Riada Trust

Daisie Rich Trust

The Clive Richards Foundation

Richmond Parish Lands Charity

Rigby Foundation

The River Farm Foundation

RNID (The Royal National Institute for Deaf People)

The Roan Charitable Trust

The Dezna Robins Jones Charitable Foundation

Rockcliffe Charitable Trust

The Rockspring Charitable Trust

The Roddick Foundation

The Gerald and Gail Ronson Family Foundation

The Roseline Foundation*

The Cecil Rosen Foundation

Rothesay Foundation*

The Rothley Trust

Rothschild Foundation (Hanadiv) Europe

The Roughley Charitable Trust

The Rowlands Trust

The Royal Foundation of The Prince and Princess of Wales

The Rubin Foundation Charitable Trust

Russell Trust

The Ryvoan Trust*

S. and R. Charitable Trust

The Jeremy and John Sacher Charitable Trust

The Michael and Nicola Sacher Charitable Trust

The Saintbury Trust

The Salamander Charitable Trust

Samjo Ltd

The Basil Samuel Charitable Trust

The M. J. Samuel Charitable Trust

The Sandhu Charitable Foundation

Sandra Charitable Trust

The Sands Family Trust

The Sasha Foundation*

Schroder Charity Trust

The Schroder Foundation

The Scorpion Charitable Trust*

Scotland's Garden Scheme*

The Scotshill Trust

Scott (Eredine) Charitable Trust

The Frieda Scott Charitable Trust

Sir Samuel Scott of Yews Trust

The Ina Scott Sutherland Charitable Foundation

The John Scott Trust Fund

Scouloudi Foundation

Seafarers UK (King George's Fund for Sailors)

The Sam and Bella Sebba Charitable Foundation

The Serco Foundation

The Shanly Foundation

ShareGift (The Orr Mackintosh Foundation)

The Shears Foundation

The Sylvia and Colin Shepherd Charitable Trust

The Sherling Charitable Trust

The Archie Sherman Charitable Trust

Shetland Charitable Trust

The Bassil Shippam and Alsford Trust

The Florence Shute Millennium Trust

The Charles Skey Charitable Trust

Kathleen Beryl Sleigh Charitable Trust

The Mrs Smith and Mount Trust

Arabella and Julian Smith Family Trust

The Leslie Smith Foundation

The R. C. Snelling Charitable Trust

Sodexo Stop Hunger Foundation

Somerset Community Foundation

Songdale Ltd

The E. C. Sosnow Charitable Trust

Souter Charitable Trust

South Yorkshire Community Foundation

The Stephen R. and Philippa H. Southall Charitable Trust

Peter Sowerby Foundation

Sparquote Ltd

The Spear Charitable Trust

Michael and Sarah Spencer Foundation

Spurrell Charitable Trust

The Geoff and Fiona Squire Foundation

The Squire Patton Boggs Charitable Trust

The Squires Foundation

The Vichai Srivaddhanaprabha Foundation

St James's Place Charitable Foundation

St John's Foundation Est. 1174

The St Lazarus Charitable Trust*

St Monica Trust

Stadium Charitable Trust

The Community Foundation for Staffordshire

Stanley Foundation Ltd

The Peter Stebbings Memorial Charity

The Steel Charitable Trust

The Hugh Stenhouse Foundation

The Sterry Family Foundation

The Stevenson Family's Charitable Trust

Sir Halley Stewart Trust

The Stewarts Law Foundation

Stolkin Foundation

The Samuel Storey Family Charitable Trust

Peter Stormonth Darling Charitable Trust

The Strangward Trust

Stratford-upon-Avon Town Trust

The W. O. Street Charitable Foundation

Suffolk Community Foundation

The Bernard Sunley Foundation

The Sunrise Foundation CIO

Surgo Foundation UK Ltd

Community Foundation for Surrey

Sutton Coldfield Charitable Trust

The Swann-Morton Foundation

The John Swire (1989) Charitable Trust

The Swire Charitable Trust

The Charles and Elsie Sykes Trust

The Hugh Symons Charitable Trust

The Syncona Foundation

The T.K. Maxx and Homesense Foundation

The Talbot Trusts

Talteg Ltd

The Tanlaw Foundation

Tanner Trust

The Taurus Foundation

Tay Charitable Trust

C. B. and H. H. T. Taylor 1984 Trust

The Thales Charitable Trust

The Thompson Family Charitable Trust

Sir Jules Thorn Charitable Trust

The Thornton Trust

Mrs R. P. Tindall's Charitable Trust

The Tolkien Trust

The Tomoro Foundation

The Tompkins Foundation

The Tory Family Foundation

The Toy Trust

Toyota Manufacturing UK Charitable Trust

Annie Tranmer Charitable Trust

The Constance Travis Charitable Trust

The Trelix Charitable Trust*

The True Colours Trust

Trumros Ltd

The Trysil Charitable Trust

The James Tudor Foundation

The Tudwick Foundation

The Tufton Charitable Trust

The Tuixen Foundation
The Roger and Douglas Turner Charitable Trust
UBS Optimus Foundation UK
UKH Foundation
Ulster Garden Villages Ltd
The Underwood Trust
The Valentine Charitable Trust
The Albert Van Den Bergh Charitable Trust
The Van Mesdag Fund
The Vardy Foundation
Variety, the Children's Charity
The Velvet Foundation
Versus Arthritis
The Veterans' Foundation
Virgin Atlantic Foundation
Vision Foundation
The Vodafone Foundation
Volant Charitable Trust
The Georg and Emily von Opel Foundation
Sylvia Waddilove Foundation UK
Wakefield and Tetley Trust
The Walker Trust
Walton Foundation
The Barbara Ward Children's Foundation
The Warwickshire Masonic Charitable Association Ltd
Mrs Waterhouse Charitable Trust
The Waterloo Foundation
The Wates Foundation
The Geoffrey Watling Charity
The Weinstock Fund
The Weir Charitable Trust
The James Weir Foundation
Wellbank Foundation*
The Welsh Church Act Fund
The Westfield Health Charitable Trust
The Galen and Hilary Weston Foundation
The Garfield Weston Foundation
The Whinfell Charitable Fund
The Melanie White Foundation Ltd
The Williams Family Foundation
Dame Violet Wills Will Trust
The Wilmcote Charitrust
Sumner Wilson Charitable Trust
Wiltshire Community Foundation
The Wimbledon Foundation
The Windfall Foundation
The Francis Winham Foundation
The Michael and Anna Wix Charitable Trust
The Wixamtree Trust

The Maurice Wohl Charitable Foundation
The Charles Wolfson Charitable Trust
The Wolfson Family Charitable Trust
The Lord Leonard and Lady Estelle Wolfson Foundation
The James Wood Bequest Fund
Wooden Spoon Society
Woodroffe Benton Foundation
Woodsmith Foundation Ltd
The Worshipful Company of Glovers of London Charitable Trust
Worshipful Company of Gold and Silver Wyre Drawers Second Charitable Trust Fund
The Worwin UK Foundation
The Eric Wright Charitable Trust
The Wyfold Charitable Trust
Sir Graham Wylie Foundation
The Wyseliot Rose Charitable Trust
The Yapp Charitable Trust
Yorkshire Building Society Charitable Foundation
Yorkshire Cancer Research
The Elizabeth and Prince Zaiger Trust
Zephyr Charitable Trust
The Marjorie and Arnold Ziff Charitable Foundation
The Zochonis Charitable Trust
Zurich Community Trust (UK) Ltd

Clinical treatment/care

The Abbeyfield Research Foundation
The Aberbrothock Skea Trust
ABF The Soldiers' Charity
Action Medical Research
The Bryan Adams Foundation
The Aimwell Charitable Trust
The Alchemy Foundation
Beryl Alexander Charity
D. C. R. Allen Charitable Trust
Alliance Family Foundation Ltd
Alzheimer's Research UK
Alzheimer's Society
The Annabel Arbib Foundation
The John Armitage Charitable Trust
ArtSocial Foundation
Asthma and Lung UK
The Astor Foundation
The Tim Bacon Foundation
The Baily Thomas Charitable Fund

Bally's Foundation
The Kamini and Vindi Banga Family Trust
The Barbers' Company General Charities
The Baring Foundation
The Barnes Fund
Barnwood Trust
The Barratt Developments plc Charitable Foundation
Maria Bjornson Memorial Fund
The John Black Charitable Foundation
Bloodwise
The Marjory Boddy Charitable Trust
The Boltini Trust
The Boshier-Hinton Foundation
The Harry Bottom Charitable Trust
The P. G. and N. J. Boulton Trust
G. and K. Boyes Charitable Trust
The Tony Bramall Charitable Trust
Breast Cancer Now
Bright Red Charity
British Eye Research Foundation (Fight for Sight)
British Heart Foundation (BHF)
Bill Brown 1989 Charitable Trust
The Brownsword Charitable Foundation
T. B. H. Brunner's Charitable Settlement
The Bulldog Trust Ltd
The Burden Trust
The Burdett Trust for Nursing
Miss Margaret Butters Reekie Charitable Trust
Cancer Research UK
Carew Pole Charitable Trust
The Carlton Hayes Mental Health Charity
The B. G. S. Cayzer Charitable Trust
Chapman Charitable Trust
The Childhood Trust
Children with Cancer UK
The City Bridge Trust (Bridge House Estates)
The Vivienne and Samuel Cohen Charitable Trust
The Colt Foundation
The Connolly Foundation (UK) Ltd
The Keith Coombs Trust
The Sir William Coxen Trust Fund
Cruden Foundation Ltd
The Danson Foundation*
The Dashlight Foundation
Michael Davies Charitable Settlement

The De Laszlo Foundation
The Delves Charitable Trust
Foundation Derbyshire
The J. N. Derbyshire Trust
Dinwoodie Charitable Company
Dr. Martens Foundation
The Dunhill Medical Trust
The Charles Dunstone
   Charitable Trust
The Gilbert and Eileen Edgar
   Foundation
W. G. Edwards Charitable
   Foundation
The Eighty Eight Foundation
The Ellerdale Trust
The Englefield Charitable Trust
Epilepsy Research UK
The Evelyn Trust
The Everard Foundation
The Eveson Charitable Trust
The Fairness Foundation
The Fairstead Trust
Family Philanthropy Ltd
The Lord Faringdon Charitable
   Trust
The February Foundation
The Fieldrose Charitable Trust
Sir John Fisher Foundation
Fishmongers' Company's
   Charitable Trust
The Forbes Charitable
   Foundation
Forest Hill Charitable Trust
The Anna Rosa Forster
   Charitable Trust
Four Acre Trust
Jill Franklin Trust
The Hugh Fraser Foundation
The Joseph Strong Frazer Trust
The Louis and Valerie
   Freedman Charitable
   Settlement
The Freshgate Trust
   Foundation
Frognal Trust
The General Nursing Council
   for England and Wales
   Trust
The David Gibbons Foundation
The Girdlers' Company
   Charitable Trust
Global Charities
Sydney and Phyllis Goldberg
   Memorial Charitable Trust
The Goldsmiths' Company
   Charity
The Grace Trust
The J. G. Graves Charitable
   Trust
The Great Britain Sasakawa
   Foundation
The Walter Guinness
   Charitable Trust
Halifax Foundation for
   Northern Ireland
The Harebell Centenary Fund

The Hargreaves Foundation
The Peter and Teresa Harris
   Charitable Trust
The Harris Family Charitable
   Trust
The Hawthorne Charitable
   Trust
The Health Foundation
Heart Research UK
The Hedley Foundation
The Simon Heller Charitable
   Settlement
Help for Health
The Hemby Charitable Trust
HFC Help for Children UK Ltd
Highway One Trust
The Alison Hillman Charitable
   Trust*
The Hintze Family Charity
   Foundation
The Hobson Charity Ltd
The Holbeck Charitable Trust
The Hollands-Warren Fund
Hollick Family Foundation
Homelands Charitable Trust
Sir Harold Hood's Charitable
   Trust
The Thomas J. Horne
   Memorial Trust
Hospice UK
The Hospital of God at
   Greatham
The Sir Joseph Hotung
   Charitable Settlement
The Albert Hunt Trust
Miss Agnes H. Hunter's Trust
The Nani Huyu Charitable Trust
The Inverforth Charitable Trust
The J. Isaacs Charitable Trust
JD Foundation
The Elton John AIDS
   Foundation
The Ian Karten Charitable
   Trust
The Kavli Trust
The Kennedy Trust for
   Rheumatology Research
Kent Community Foundation
The Peter Kershaw Trust
The Graham Kirkham
   Foundation
The Ernest Kleinwort
   Charitable Trust
Kollel and Co. Ltd
Kupath Gemach Chaim
   Bechesed Viznitz Trust
The Lake House Charitable
   Foundation
Lancaster Foundation
The Allen Lane Foundation
Langdale Trust
The Richard Lawes Foundation
The Leeward Trust
Sarah Jane Leigh Charitable
   Trust*
The Lightbulb Trust*

The Linder Foundation
The Charles Littlewood Hill
   Trust
The Lockwood Charitable
   Foundation
The London Community
   Foundation (LCF)
Robert Luff Foundation Ltd
Lord and Lady Lurgan Trust
The R. S. Macdonald
   Charitable Trust
The W. M. Mann Foundation
The Manoukian Charitable
   Foundation
The Marque Foundation
The Kristina Martin Charitable
   Trust
Sir George Martin Trust
Nancie Massey Charitable
   Trust
Maudsley Charity
MBNA General Foundation
The Robert McAlpine
   Foundation
D. D. McPhail Charitable
   Settlement
The Merchant Taylors'
   Foundation*
The Mickleham Trust
John Moores Foundation
The Ken and Lynne Morrison
   Charitable Trust
The Alexander Mosley
   Charitable Trust
The Mosselson Charitable
   Trust
Motor Neurone Disease
   Association
J. P. Moulton Charitable
   Foundation
The Edwina Mountbatten and
   Leonora Children's
   Foundation
The Mulberry Trust
The National Garden Scheme
Newby Trust Ltd
The Frances and Augustus
   Newman Foundation
North West Cancer Research
Odin Charitable Trust
The Hamish Ogston
   Foundation
Orange Tree Trust
Orthopaedic Research UK
The Panacea Charitable Trust
The Samuel and Freda
   Parkinson Charitable Trust
The J. G. W. Patterson
   Foundation
Payne-Gallwey 1989 Charitable
   Trust
John Pearce Foundation
People's Postcode Trust
The Pharsalia Charitable Trust
The Philip and Connie Phillips
   Foundation*

....

The Pilgrim Trust
The Sir Harry Pilkington Fund
Pink Ribbon Foundation
The Pixel Fund
Thomas Pocklington Trust
The Portrack Charitable Trust
Postcode Local Trust
The Prince of Wales's
　Charitable Foundation
The Priory Foundation
The Prudence Trust
The Purey Cust Trust CIO
Queen Mary's Roehampton
　Trust
The Randal Charitable
　Foundation
The Joseph and Lena Randall
　Charitable Trust
The Ratcliff Foundation
The Rayne Foundation
The Rhododendron Trust
Riverside Charitable Trust Ltd
The Robertson Trust
Rosetrees
The Roughley Charitable Trust
The S. M. B. Trust
The Alan and Babette
　Sainsbury Charitable Fund
The Saintbury Trust
The Peter Samuel Charitable
　Trust
The Sasha Foundation*
The Schreier Foundation*
The Schroder Foundation
Francis C. Scott Charitable
　Trust
The Frieda Scott Charitable
　Trust
Sir Samuel Scott of Yews
　Trust
The Jean Shanks Foundation
The Shanly Foundation
The Sheepdrove Trust
The N. Smith Charitable
　Settlement
The Leslie Smith Foundation
David Solomons Charitable
　Trust
South Yorkshire Community
　Foundation
Peter Sowerby Foundation
The Spear Charitable Trust
Spielman Charitable Trust
St James's Place Charitable
　Foundation
The Community Foundation for
　Staffordshire
The Steinberg Family
　Charitable Trust
The Hugh Stenhouse
　Foundation
Sir Halley Stewart Trust
The Stoller Charitable Trust
The Stone Family Foundation
The Charles and Elsie Sykes
　Trust

The Syncona Foundation
The T.K. Maxx and
　Homesense Foundation
The Gay and Keith Talbot Trust
The Talbot Village Trust
Tallow Chandlers Benevolent
　Fund No 2
Tanner Trust
The Taurus Foundation
Tay Charitable Trust
C. B. and H. H. T. Taylor 1984
　Trust
Sir Jules Thorn Charitable
　Trust
The Three Guineas Trust
The True Colours Trust
The James Tudor Foundation
The Tuixen Foundation
The Roger and Douglas Turner
　Charitable Trust
The UK Youth Fund: Thriving
　Minds*
UKH Foundation
The Ulverscroft Foundation
The Michael Uren Foundation
The Utley Foundation
The Valentine Charitable Trust
The Albert Van Den Bergh
　Charitable Trust
The Vandervell Foundation
The Velvet Foundation
Versus Arthritis
The Veterans' Foundation
VINCI UK Foundation
Vision Foundation
Volant Charitable Trust
Wallace and Gromit's
　Children's Foundation
The Weinstock Fund
Wellbeing of Women
The Wellcome Trust
The Welsh Church Act Fund
The Galen and Hilary Weston
　Foundation
The Felicity Wilde Charitable
　Trust
The Will Charitable Trust
W. Wing Yip and Brothers
　Foundation
The Francis Winham
　Foundation
The Wolfson Foundation
The Lord Leonard and Lady
　Estelle Wolfson Foundation
The James Wood Bequest
　Fund
The Worshipful Company of
　Glovers of London
　Charitable Trust
The Eric Wright Charitable
　Trust
The Yapp Charitable Trust
Yorkshire Cancer Research

Community health services

The Archer Trust
Barchester Healthcare
　Foundation
Barnwood Trust
The Burdett Trust for Nursing
The Coalfields Regeneration
　Trust
The Vivienne and Samuel
　Cohen Charitable Trust
Co-op Foundation
CRASH
The Evelyn Trust
Sir John Fisher Foundation
The Forbes Charitable
　Foundation
Jill Franklin Trust
The Hugh Fraser Foundation
The Louis and Valerie
　Freedman Charitable
　Settlement
Charles S. French Charitable
　Trust
The General Nursing Council
　for England and Wales
　Trust
The Girdlers' Company
　Charitable Trust
Sydney and Phyllis Goldberg
　Memorial Charitable Trust
The Grimmitt Trust
The Hamilton Davies Trust
Gay and Peter Hartley's
　Hillards Charitable Trust
The Hawthorne Charitable
　Trust
The Lady Hind Trust
P. H. Holt Foundation
The Hudson Foundation
Michael and Shirley Hunt
　Charitable Trust
The Albert Hunt Trust
Irish Youth Foundation (UK)
　Ltd (incorporating The
　Lawlor Foundation)
The Kentown Wizard
　Foundation
The Allen Lane Foundation
London Catalyst
The London Community
　Foundation (LCF)
The Mackintosh Foundation
The Merchant Taylors'
　Foundation*
The Gerald Micklem Charitable
　Trust
J. P. Moulton Charitable
　Foundation
The Norman Family Charitable
　Trust
Odin Charitable Trust
People's Health Trust
The Philip and Connie Phillips
　Foundation*

The Pilgrim Trust
The George and Esme Pollitzer
  Charitable Settlement
Postcode Community Trust
The Mary Potter Convent
  Hospital Trust
Richard Radcliffe Trust
Elizabeth Rathbone Charity
Richmond Parish Lands Charity
The Sir James Roll Charitable
  Trust
Salisbury Pool Charity
The Sheldon Trust
The Talbot Trusts
The Three Guineas Trust
The James Tudor Foundation
The Utley Foundation
Valencia Communities Fund
The Vardy Foundation
Variety, the Children's Charity
VINCI UK Foundation
Vision Foundation
The Bruce Wake Charity
The Will Charitable Trust
Yorkshire Cancer Research

Complementary and alternative therapies

J. Paul Getty Jr General
  Charitable Trust*

Health advice and support

ABF The Soldiers' Charity
The AIM Foundation
ArtSocial Foundation
The Asda Foundation
Asthma and Lung UK
The Avon and Somerset Police
  Community Trust
The Baily Thomas Charitable
  Fund
The Ballinger Charitable Trust
The Barbour Foundation
The Barnes Fund
Barnwood Trust
Bill Brown 1989 Charitable
  Trust
Building and Civil Engineering
  Charitable Trust
Bupa Foundation
The Burdett Trust for Nursing
Miss Margaret Butters Reekie
  Charitable Trust
The Noel Buxton Trust
Camden Giving
CareTech Charitable
  Foundation
Carew Pole Charitable Trust
The Carlton Hayes Mental
  Health Charity

The Antonio Carluccio
  Foundation
Chapman Charitable Trust
The Childhood Trust
Children with Cancer UK
The Childwick Trust
The Churchill Foundation
The City Bridge Trust (Bridge
  House Estates)
The Colt Foundation
Colyer-Fergusson Charitable
  Trust
The Connolly Foundation (UK)
  Ltd
Corra Foundation
CRH Charitable Trust
Cripplegate Foundation
The Danson Foundation*
The Delves Charitable Trust
Foundation Derbyshire
The J. N. Derbyshire Trust
The D'Oyly Carte Charitable
  Trust
Dr. Martens Foundation
The Charles Dunstone
  Charitable Trust
Edupoor Ltd
The Evelyn Trust
The Everard Foundation
The Eveson Charitable Trust
Esmée Fairbairn Foundation
The Fairstead Trust
The February Foundation
Fishmongers' Company's
  Charitable Trust
The Joseph Strong Frazer Trust
The Louis and Valerie
  Freedman Charitable
  Settlement
Charles S. French Charitable
  Trust
GambleAware
The Tara Getty Foundation
The Girdlers' Company
  Charitable Trust
The B. and P. Glasser
  Charitable Trust
Global Charities
The Grantham Yorke Trust
The Green Hall Foundation
Philip and Judith Green Trust
Halifax Foundation for
  Northern Ireland
Hammersmith United Charities
The Dorothy Hay-Bolton
  Charitable Trust
HFC Help for Children UK Ltd
The Hobson Charity Ltd
The Jane Hodge Foundation
Hollick Family Foundation
Hope Trust
The Hospital of God at
  Greatham
The Hospital Saturday Fund
Housing Pathways Trust
The Huggard Charitable Trust

The Albert Hunt Trust
Miss Agnes H. Hunter's Trust
Hyde Charitable Trust
The Iceland Foods Charitable
  Foundation
The Inman Charity
The J. Isaacs Charitable Trust
The Roger and Jean Jefcoate
  Trust
The Ian Karten Charitable
  Trust
The Kavli Trust
The Kelly Family Charitable
  Trust
The Kennedy Trust for
  Rheumatology Research
Kent Community Foundation
The Graham Kirkham
  Foundation
The Kirby Laing Foundation
The Allen Lane Foundation
The Leeward Trust
Sarah Jane Leigh Charitable
  Trust*
The Leigh Trust
The Lightbulb Trust*
The Linbury Trust
London Catalyst
The London Community
  Foundation (LCF)
Longleigh Foundation
John Lyon's Charity
The Mackintosh Foundation
Making a Difference Locally
  Ltd
The Kristina Martin Charitable
  Trust
Sir George Martin Trust
Matchroom Sport Charitable
  Foundation
Maudsley Charity
MBNA General Foundation
The Medicash Foundation
The Merchant Taylors'
  Foundation*
The Mickleham Trust
The Millennium Oak Trust
The Monmouthshire County
  Council Welsh Church Act
  Fund
G. M. Morrison Charitable
  Trust
The Morrisons Foundation
Motor Neurone Disease
  Association
J. P. Moulton Charitable
  Foundation
Newby Trust Ltd
The Norman Family Charitable
  Trust
The Northwick Trust
Henry Oldfield Trust
One Community Foundation
  Ltd
The Panacea Charitable Trust
People's Health Trust

People's Postcode Trust
The Bernard Piggott Charitable
    Trust
The Pilgrim Trust
Cecil Pilkington Charitable
    Trust
The Sir Harry Pilkington Fund
The Pixel Fund
The Portishead Nautical Trust
The Portrack Charitable Trust
Postcode Community Trust
Postcode Society Trust
The Prudence Trust
Queen Mary's Roehampton
    Trust
The Randal Charitable
    Foundation
The Joseph and Lena Randall
    Charitable Trust
The Ratcliff Foundation
The Rayne Foundation
RNID (The Royal National
    Institute for Deaf People)
The Robertson Trust
The Dezna Robins Jones
    Charitable Foundation
The Rothley Trust
The Royal British Legion
The Royal Foundation of The
    Prince and Princess of
    Wales
The Michael and Nicola Sacher
    Charitable Trust
Salisbury Pool Charity
The Sasha Foundation*
The Schreier Foundation*
Francis C. Scott Charitable
    Trust
The Frieda Scott Charitable
    Trust
The John Scott Trust Fund
The Sam and Bella Sebba
    Charitable Foundation
The Shanly Foundation
The Sheldon Trust
The Mrs Smith and Mount
    Trust
Sodexo Stop Hunger
    Foundation
David Solomons Charitable
    Trust
St James's Place Charitable
    Foundation
St John's Foundation Est.
    1174
St Monica Trust
The Community Foundation for
    Staffordshire
The Peter Stebbings Memorial
    Charity
The Hugh Stenhouse
    Foundation
The W. O. Street Charitable
    Foundation
The Charles and Elsie Sykes
    Trust

The Talbot Trusts
The Tedworth Charitable Trust
Sir Jules Thorn Charitable
    Trust
The Three Guineas Trust
The True Colours Trust
Trust for London
The Tuixen Foundation
The UK Youth Fund: Thriving
    Minds*
UKH Foundation
The Valentine Charitable Trust
The Velvet Foundation
The Veterans' Foundation
The Vintners' Foundation
Vision Foundation
Volant Charitable Trust
The VTCT Foundation
The Waterloo Foundation
The Wellcome Trust
The Welsh Church Act Fund
The Wolfson Foundation
The James Wood Bequest
    Fund
The Woodward Charitable
    Trust
The Eric Wright Charitable
    Trust
The Yapp Charitable Trust
The Zochonis Charitable Trust

Health awareness/ promotion

ABF The Soldiers' Charity
The AIM Foundation
The Alchemy Foundation
ArtSocial Foundation
The Baily Thomas Charitable
    Fund
The Baring Foundation
The Barnes Fund
British Eye Research
    Foundation (Fight for Sight)
Building and Civil Engineering
    Charitable Trust
The Burdett Trust for Nursing
Miss Margaret Butters Reekie
    Charitable Trust
The Noel Buxton Trust
Camden Giving
Carew Pole Charitable Trust
The Carlton Hayes Mental
    Health Charity
The Antonio Carluccio
    Foundation
Chapman Charitable Trust
The City Bridge Trust (Bridge
    House Estates)
The Vivienne and Samuel
    Cohen Charitable Trust
Colyer-Fergusson Charitable
    Trust
The Connolly Foundation (UK)
    Ltd

CRH Charitable Trust
The Danson Foundation*
The J. N. Derbyshire Trust
Dr. Martens Foundation
The Evelyn Trust
The Eveson Charitable Trust
Jill Franklin Trust
The Joseph Strong Frazer Trust
The Louis and Valerie
    Freedman Charitable
    Settlement
GambleAware
The Girdlers' Company
    Charitable Trust
The B. and P. Glasser
    Charitable Trust
Global Charities
Halifax Foundation for
    Northern Ireland
The Haramead Trust
The Health Foundation
Heart Research UK
HFC Help for Children UK Ltd
The Lady Hind Trust
The Hobson Charity Ltd
Hollick Family Foundation
Sir Harold Hood's Charitable
    Trust
Hope Trust
The Hospital of God at
    Greatham
The Hospital Saturday Fund
Housing Pathways Trust
The Albert Hunt Trust
Impact Funding Partners Ltd
The Inman Charity
The Innocent Foundation
The Roger and Jean Jefcoate
    Trust
The Ian Karten Charitable
    Trust
The Kavli Trust
The Kelly Family Charitable
    Trust
Kent Community Foundation
The Graham Kirkham
    Foundation
The Leeward Trust
Sarah Jane Leigh Charitable
    Trust*
The Leigh Trust
The Lightbulb Trust*
The Linder Foundation
The London Community
    Foundation (LCF)
Making a Difference Locally
    Ltd
The Kristina Martin Charitable
    Trust
Sir George Martin Trust
Maudsley Charity
MBNA General Foundation
The Mickleham Trust
Motor Neurone Disease
    Association

J. P. Moulton Charitable
Foundation
Newby Trust Ltd
Northern Pharmacies Ltd Trust
Fund
Northwood Charitable Trust
Henry Oldfield Trust
The Panacea Charitable Trust
Peacock Charitable Trust
The Pears Family Charitable
Foundation
People's Health Trust
People's Postcode Trust
The Pilgrim Trust
The Sir Harry Pilkington Fund
The Pixel Fund
The Prudence Trust
The Purey Cust Trust CIO
The Rayne Foundation
The Robertson Trust
The Roughley Charitable Trust
The Royal British Legion
The Sasha Foundation*
The Schreier Foundation*
The Frieda Scott Charitable
Trust
The Segelman Trust
The Shanly Foundation
The Shears Foundation
Sodexo Stop Hunger
Foundation
St James's Place Charitable
Foundation
St John's Foundation Est.
1174
The Community Foundation for
Staffordshire
The W. O. Street Charitable
Foundation
The Charles and Elsie Sykes
Trust
The Tedworth Charitable Trust
Sir Jules Thorn Charitable
Trust
The Three Guineas Trust
The James Tudor Foundation
The Tuixen Foundation
The UK Youth Fund: Thriving
Minds*
UKH Foundation
The Ulverscroft Foundation
The Vintners' Foundation
Vision Foundation
Volant Charitable Trust
The VTCT Foundation
The Waterloo Foundation
The Wellcome Trust
The Galen and Hilary Weston
Foundation
Westway Trust
The Wimbledon Foundation
The Wolfson Foundation
The Lord Leonard and Lady
Estelle Wolfson Foundation
The James Wood Bequest
Fund

The Eric Wright Charitable
Trust
The Wyseliot Rose Charitable
Trust
The Yapp Charitable Trust
Yorkshire Cancer Research

Mental health and well-being

ABF The Soldiers' Charity
Alan Boswell Group Charitable
Trust
Beryl Alexander Charity
ArtSocial Foundation
The Asda Foundation
The Baily Thomas Charitable
Fund
Bally's Foundation
The Baring Foundation
The Barnes Fund
Barnwood Trust
The Barratt Developments plc
Charitable Foundation
The Bulldog Trust Ltd
Bupa Foundation
Camden Giving
CareTech Charitable
Foundation
The Carlton Hayes Mental
Health Charity
Chapman Charitable Trust
The Childhood Trust
The Childwick Trust
The Churchill Foundation
The City Bridge Trust (Bridge
House Estates)
The Connolly Foundation (UK)
Ltd
CRH Charitable Trust
Cripplegate Foundation
The Danson Foundation*
The Dashlight Foundation
Foundation Derbyshire
The J. N. Derbyshire Trust
Dr. Martens Foundation
Edupoor Ltd
The Ellerdale Trust
The Evelyn Trust
The Eveson Charitable Trust
The Fairness Foundation
The Fairstead Trust
Fishmongers' Company's
Charitable Trust
Jill Franklin Trust
GambleAware
The Tara Getty Foundation
The Girdlers' Company
Charitable Trust
Global Charities
The J. G. Graves Charitable
Trust
Halifax Foundation for
Northern Ireland
The Hargreaves Foundation

Herefordshire Community
Foundation
Highway One Trust
The Hobson Charity Ltd
The Jane Hodge Foundation
Hollick Family Foundation
The Hospital of God at
Greatham
The Albert Hunt Trust
Hyde Charitable Trust
The Inverforth Charitable Trust
JD Foundation
The Roger and Jean Jefcoate
Trust
The Ian Karten Charitable
Trust
The Kavli Trust
Kent Community Foundation
The Graham Kirkham
Foundation
The Allen Lane Foundation
The Richard Lawes Foundation
Sarah Jane Leigh Charitable
Trust*
The Lightbulb Trust*
The Linbury Trust
The London Community
Foundation (LCF)
Longleigh Foundation
John Lyon's Charity
The Kristina Martin Charitable
Trust
Sir George Martin Trust
Maudsley Charity
MBNA General Foundation
The Medicash Foundation
The Merchant Taylors'
Foundation*
The Millennium Oak Trust
John Moores Foundation
G. M. Morrison Charitable
Trust
The Mulberry Trust
Newby Trust Ltd
Northwood Charitable Trust
One Community Foundation
Ltd
Orange Tree Trust
The Panacea Charitable Trust
Peacock Charitable Trust
The Pears Family Charitable
Foundation
People's Postcode Trust
The Pilgrim Trust
Cecil Pilkington Charitable
Trust
The Sir Harry Pilkington Fund
The Pixel Fund
Postcode Community Trust
Postcode Local Trust
Postcode Society Trust
The Prince of Wales's
Charitable Foundation
The Priory Foundation
The Prudence Trust
The Purey Cust Trust CIO

The Randal Charitable
Foundation
The Rayne Foundation
The Rhododendron Trust
The Robertson Trust
The Roughley Charitable Trust
The Royal Foundation of The
Prince and Princess of
Wales
The Sasha Foundation*
The Schreier Foundation*
Francis C. Scott Charitable
Trust
The Frieda Scott Charitable
Trust
The Sam and Bella Sebba
Charitable Foundation
The Shanly Foundation
The Mrs Smith and Mount
Trust
South Yorkshire Community
Foundation
St James's Place Charitable
Foundation
The Community Foundation for
Staffordshire
The Peter Stebbings Memorial
Charity
The Stone Family Foundation
The T.K. Maxx and
Homesense Foundation
The Talbot Trusts
The Talbot Village Trust
The Taurus Foundation
C. B. and H. H. T. Taylor 1984
Trust
Sir Jules Thorn Charitable
Trust
The Tuixen Foundation
The UK Youth Fund: Thriving
Minds*
UKH Foundation
The Veterans' Foundation
Volant Charitable Trust
The Wellcome Trust
The Wimbledon Foundation
The Wolfson Foundation
The Lord Leonard and Lady
Estelle Wolfson Foundation
The James Wood Bequest
Fund
The Eric Wright Charitable
Trust
The Wyseliot Rose Charitable
Trust
The Yapp Charitable Trust

Respite breaks/
convalescence

The Alchemy Foundation
The Childwick Trust
Edinburgh Children's Holiday
Fund
The Ellerdale Trust

Charles S. French Charitable
Trust
The Girdlers' Company
Charitable Trust
The Edward Gostling
Foundation
The Hampstead Wells and
Campden Trust
The Hedley Foundation
The Linder Foundation
The Gerald Micklem Charitable
Trust
The Millennium Oak Trust
The Eleanor Rathbone
Charitable Trust
The Sheldon Trust
The Will Charitable Trust
The Eric Wright Charitable
Trust

Housing and
homelessness

The 29th May 1961 Charitable
Trust
ABF The Soldiers' Charity
Adam Family Foundation
The Adint Charitable Trust
The Alchemy Foundation
Andrews Charitable Trust
B&Q Foundation
The Barbour Foundation
The Barratt Developments plc
Charitable Foundation
Benefact Trust Ltd
The Berkeley Foundation
Blakemore Foundation
The Brelms Trust CIO
R. S. Brownless Charitable
Trust
Community Foundation for
Calderdale
CEO Sleepout
The Clarkson Foundation
The Clothworkers' Foundation
The Cole Charitable Trust
The Coltstaple Trust
Corra Foundation
CRASH
Michael Crawford Children's
Charity
Crisis UK
The D. G. Charitable
Settlement
Baron Davenport's Charity
The Dawe Charitable Trust
The Dorus Trust
Dr. Martens Foundation
Drapers Charitable Fund
The DWF Charitable
Foundation
The Eveson Charitable Trust
The Thomas Farr Charity
The Feoffees of St Michael's
Spurriergate York
Fine & Country Foundation
Ford Britain Trust
The Forrester Family Trust
The Elizabeth Frankland Moore
and Star Foundation
Global Charities
The Goldsmiths' Company
Charity
The Green Hall Foundation
The Greggs Foundation
The Albert Gubay Charitable
Foundation
The Hadrian Trust
Hammersmith United Charities
Hampshire and Isle of Wight
Community Foundation
Hampton Fund
The Haramead Trust
Harborne Parish Lands Charity
The Harbour Foundation
William Harding's Charity

The Harrison-Frank Family
  Foundation (UK) Ltd
The Hasluck Charitable Trust
The Hemby Charitable Trust
P. and C. Hickinbotham
  Charitable Trust
Highway One Trust
The Lady Hind Trust
The Hobson Charity Ltd
The Jane Hodge Foundation
Hollick Family Foundation
Sir Harold Hood's Charitable
  Trust
The Hospital of God at
  Greatham
The Huggard Charitable Trust
The Albert Hunt Trust
The Nani Huyu Charitable Trust
Irish Youth Foundation (UK)
  Ltd (incorporating The
  Lawlor Foundation)
JD Foundation
The Cyril and Eve Jumbo
  Charitable Trust
The Jusaca Charitable Trust
Kent Community Foundation
The Kingsbury Charity
The Graham Kirkham
  Foundation
Sir James Knott Trust
Ladbrokes Coral Trust
John Laing Charitable Trust
The Beatrice Laing Trust
LandAid Charitable Trust Ltd
  (LandAid)
The LankellyChase Foundation
Laslett's (Hinton) Charity
Mrs F. B. Laurence Charitable
  Trust
The Leathersellers' Foundation
Leeds Building Society
  Foundation
The Linbury Trust
The Michael and Betty Little
  Trust*
The Charles Littlewood Hill
  Trust
Lloyds Bank Foundation for the
  Channel Islands
London Housing Foundation
  Ltd (LHF)
Longleigh Foundation
The Lyons Trust*
Mace Foundation
The Mackintosh Foundation
The Robin MacLeod Charitable
  Trust
Making a Difference Locally
  Ltd
The Medlock Charitable Trust
The Mercers Charitable
  Foundation
The Merchant Taylors'
  Foundation*
Merriman Charitable
  Foundation*

The Monday Charitable Trust
John Moores Foundation
The Morgan Charitable
  Foundation
The Steve Morgan Foundation
G. M. Morrison Charitable
  Trust
The Nationwide Foundation
The Nisbet Trust
The Norman Family Charitable
  Trust
The Norton Foundation
Norwich Consolidated
  Charities
Nottinghamshire Community
  Foundation
Odin Charitable Trust
Henry Oldfield Trust
Orange Tree Trust
The Persimmon Charitable
  Foundation
The Phillips and Rubens
  Charitable Trust
The Philip and Connie Phillips
  Foundation*
The Austin and Hope
  Pilkington Trust
PIMCO Foundation Europe
The George and Esme Pollitzer
  Charitable Settlement
The Pret Foundation
Queen Mary's Roehampton
  Trust
The Raindance Charitable
  Trust
The Eleanor Rathbone
  Charitable Trust
The Rhododendron Trust
Richmond Parish Lands Charity
The River Farm Foundation
The Robertson Trust
Mrs L. D. Rope's Third
  Charitable Settlement
The Royal British Legion
The Sackler Trust
Erach and Roshan Sadri
  Foundation
The Saintbury Trust
The Sam and Bella Sebba
  Charitable Foundation
The Shanly Foundation
Rita and David Slowe
  Charitable Trust
The Mrs Smith and Mount
  Trust
The Henry Smith Charity
The SpeedoMick Foundation
St John's Foundation Est.
  1174
The Peter Stebbings Memorial
  Charity
Streetsmart – Action for the
  Homeless
The Talbot Trusts
C. B. and H. H. T. Taylor 1984
  Trust

The Tolkien Trust
The Tomoro Foundation
The Constance Travis
  Charitable Trust
Trust for London
The Tudor Trust
The Tuixen Foundation
The Albert Van Den Bergh
  Charitable Trust
The Veterans' Foundation
VINCI UK Foundation
The Vintners' Foundation
The Virgin Money Foundation
Sylvia Waddilove Foundation
  UK
Walton-on-Thames Charity
Wates Family Enterprise Trust
Sir Graham Wylie Foundation
Yorkshire Building Society
  Charitable Foundation
The Zochonis Charitable Trust

Almshouses

Baron Davenport's Charity
Hammersmith United Charities
The Hospital of God at
  Greatham
Laslett's (Hinton) Charity
Norwich Consolidated
  Charities

Homelessness outreach

ABF The Soldiers' Charity
The London Community
  Foundation (LCF)
Rita and David Slowe
  Charitable Trust
The Peter Stebbings Memorial
  Charity
Streetsmart – Action for the
  Homeless
The Virgin Money Foundation

Hostels/shelters

CRASH
The Nisbet Trust
Norwich Consolidated
  Charities
Rita and David Slowe
  Charitable Trust
The Mrs Smith and Mount
  Trust
Streetsmart – Action for the
  Homeless

Housing advice

The Charles Littlewood Hill
  Trust

The Nationwide Foundation
The Nisbet Trust
Streetsmart – Action for the
  Homeless
Trust for London

Social housing

Longleigh Foundation
The Nationwide Foundation
Norwich Consolidated
  Charities

Supported accommodation

Baron Davenport's Charity
Harborne Parish Lands Charity
The Hospital of God at
  Greatham
The Allen Lane Foundation
The Charles Littlewood Hill
  Trust
Norwich Consolidated
  Charities
The Skerritt Trust
St Monica Trust

Religion

The A. S. Charitable Trust
Adenfirst Ltd
Sylvia Aitken's Charitable Trust
Alliance Family Foundation Ltd
Amabrill Ltd
Viscount Amory's Charitable
  Trust
Ardbarron Trust Ltd
The John Armitage Charitable
  Trust
The Asda Foundation
The Ashendene Trust
The Astor Foundation
Atkin Charitable Foundation
Atlas Memorial Ltd
The Austin Bailey Foundation
Philip Barker Charity
Bay Charitable Trust
Bear Mordechai Ltd
Beauland Ltd
The Bellahouston Bequest
  Fund
Benesco Charity Ltd
The Billmeir Charitable Trust
The Bingham Trust
Abraham Algy Bloom
  Foundation
The Harry Bottom Charitable
  Trust
Bourneheights Ltd
The Mary Brown Memorial
  Trust
Buckingham Trust
Consolidated Charity of Burton
  upon Trent
C. and F. Charitable Trust
Cannon Charitable Trust
Carew Pole Charitable Trust
W. A. Cargill Fund
The B. G. S. Cayzer Charitable
  Trust
Chalfords Ltd
Charitworth Ltd
Chartered Accountants' Livery
  Charity (CALC)
Church Burgesses Trust
Church of Ireland Priorities
  Fund
The Roger and Sarah Bancroft
  Clark Charitable Trust
The Clore Duffield Foundation
Clydpride Ltd
CMZ Ltd
The Vivienne and Samuel
  Cohen Charitable Trust
The Catherine Cookson
  Charitable Trust
The Alice Ellen Cooper-Dean
  Charitable Foundation
The Costa Family Charitable
  Trust
The Cross Trust
Itzchok Meyer Cymerman Trust
  Ltd
Didymus

The Djanogly Foundation
Duchy of Lancaster Benevolent
  Fund
The Duke of Cornwall's
  Benevolent Fund
The Gilbert and Eileen Edgar
  Foundation
The Eighteen Fund
The Englefield Charitable Trust
The Everard Foundation
The Farthing Trust
The Robert Fleming Hannay
  Memorial Charity
The Fort Foundation
The Gordon Fraser Charitable
  Trust
The Joseph Strong Frazer Trust
Friends of Boyan Trust
Friends of Wiznitz Ltd
The G. C. Gibson Charitable
  Trust
The Simon Gibson Charitable
  Trust
The Gloag Foundation
The Golden Bottle Trust
The Gosling Foundation Ltd
The Hemraj Goyal Foundation
The James Grace Trust
The Great Stone Bridge Trust
  of Edenbridge
The Grimmitt Trust
The Albert Gubay Charitable
  Foundation
Hampshire and Isle of Wight
  Community Foundation
The Lennox Hannay Charitable
  Trust
Harbinson Charitable Trust
The Harbour Foundation
The Peter and Teresa Harris
  Charitable Trust
The Herefordshire Historic
  Churches Trust
The Lady Hind Trust
The Hinduja Foundation
The Henry C. Hoare Charitable
  Trust
The Hobson Charity Ltd
The Jane Hodge Foundation
The Holbeck Charitable Trust
The Holden Charitable Trust
Sir Harold Hood's Charitable
  Trust
The Reta Lila Howard
  Foundation
The Huggard Charitable Trust
The Harold Hyam Wingate
  Foundation
Hyde Park Place Estate Charity
The Inlight Trust
The Invigorate Charitable Trust
Kreditor Charitable Trust
The David Laing Foundation
The Kirby Laing Foundation
Lancaster Foundation

The Lauffer Family Charitable
  Foundation
Mrs F. B. Laurence Charitable
  Trust
Lempriere Pringle 2015
Lord Leverhulme's Charitable
  Trust
Bernard Lewis Family
  Charitable Trust
The Michael and Betty Little
  Trust*
The Locker Foundation
Magnify Foundation*
The Marque Foundation
Charity of John Marshall
The Master Charitable Trust
Mayheights Ltd
Menuchar Ltd
Mercaz Torah Vechesed Ltd
The Mikheev Charitable Trust
The Millward Charitable Trust
The MK Charitable Trust
The Monmouthshire County
  Council Welsh Church Act
  Fund
G. M. Morrison Charitable
  Trust
The Mulberry Trust
Music Sales Charitable Trust
Ner Foundation
Newpier Charity Ltd
The Nine Incorporated Trades
  of Dundee General Fund
  Charity
The Norwood and Newton
  Settlement
P. F. Charitable Trust
The Paragon Trust
The Bernard Piggott Charitable
  Trust
The Potton Consolidated
  Charity
The Privy Purse Charitable
  Trust
R. S. Charitable Trust
The Bishop Radford Trust
The Joseph and Lena Randall
  Charitable Trust
The Joseph Rank Trust
Rentrust Foundation Ltd
The Clive Richards Foundation
The Gerald and Gail Ronson
  Family Foundation
The Roseline Foundation*
The Rothermere Foundation
Rothschild Foundation
  (Hanadiv) Europe
S. and R. Charitable Trust
The S. M. B. Trust
Erach and Roshan Sadri
  Foundation
Samjo Ltd
The Schreib Trust
O. and G. Schreiber Charitable
  Trust
SF Foundation

ShareGift (The Orr Mackintosh
  Foundation)
The Archie Sherman Charitable
  Trust
Shulem B. Association Ltd
The Charles Skey Charitable
  Trust
The Henry Smith Charity
The Martin Smith Foundation
Starlow Charities Ltd
The Hugh Stenhouse
  Foundation
Stewards Company Ltd
Sir Halley Stewart Trust
Sabina Sutherland Charitable
  Trust
Sutton Coldfield Charitable
  Trust
The Tanlaw Foundation
The Taurus Foundation
Tay Charitable Trust
C. B. and H. H. T. Taylor 1984
  Trust
Mrs R. P. Tindall's Charitable
  Trust
The Tompkins Foundation
The Constance Travis
  Charitable Trust
Truedene Co. Ltd
UJIA (United Jewish Israel
  Appeal)
The United Reformed Church
  (Wessex) Trust Ltd
The Velvet Foundation
Nigel Vinson Charitable Trust
The Georg and Emily von Opel
  Foundation
Westhill Endowment
The Garfield Weston
  Foundation
The Wigoder Family Foundation
Sumner Wilson Charitable
  Trust
Worshipful Company of
  Needlemakers Charitable
  Fund

Christianity

The A. S. Charitable Trust
The Almond Trust
Viscount Amory's Charitable
  Trust
The Anchor Foundation
Andrew Anderson Trust
Andrews Charitable Trust
The Archer Trust
Ardbarron Trust Ltd
Ashburnham Thanksgiving
  Trust
The Astor Foundation
The Baird Trust
Philip Barker Charity
Benefact Trust Ltd
The Benham Charitable
  Settlement

The Birmingham Diocesan
  Board of Finance
The Sydney Black Charitable
  Trust
The Isabel Blackman
  Foundation
The Blandford Lake Trust
The Bosson Family Charitable
  Trust
The Harry Bottom Charitable
  Trust
The P. G. and N. J. Boulton
  Trust
The Bowland Charitable Trust
The Liz and Terry Bramall
  Foundation
Bristol Archdeaconry Charity
The British and Foreign Bible
  Society
The Mary Brown Memorial
  Trust
T. B. H. Brunner's Charitable
  Settlement
Buckingham Trust
Carew Pole Charitable Trust
Catholic Charitable Trust
Childs Charitable Trust
The Christabella Charitable
  Trust
The André Christian Trust
Church Burgesses Educational
  Foundation
Church Burgesses Trust
Church of Ireland Priorities
  Fund
Church Urban Fund
The Roger and Sarah Bancroft
  Clark Charitable Trust
Cloudesley
The Clover Trust
Sir Jeremiah Colman Gift Trust
Congregational and General
  Charitable Trust
The Costa Family Charitable
  Trust
The County Council of Dyfed
  Welsh Church Fund
Donibristle Trust
The Dorcas Trust
The Dyers' Company
  Charitable Trust
Ebenezer Trust
The Elie Trust
The Farthing Trust
The Earl Fitzwilliam Charitable
  Trust
Forest Hill Charitable Trust
The Foster Wood Foundation
Anne French Memorial Trust
The Friends of Kent Churches
The Fulmer Charitable Trust
Ganzoni Charitable Trust
The Gibbs Charitable Trusts
The Gloag Foundation
The Goshen Trust

Grace Baptist Trust
Corporation*
Grace Charitable Trust
The Grace Trust
The James Grace Trust
Philip and Judith Green Trust
The Grimmitt Trust
Gay and Peter Hartley's
Hillards Charitable Trust
Heb Ffin (Without Frontier)
Highway One Trust
The Hillier Trust
Hinchley Charitable Trust
The Stuart Hine Trust CIO
The Hintze Family Charity
Foundation
Hockerill Educational
Foundation
The Holbeck Charitable Trust
Hollyhock Charitable
Foundation
Homelands Charitable Trust
Sir Harold Hood's Charitable
Trust
Hope Trust
The Reta Lila Howard
Foundation
The Hunting Horn General
Charitable Trust
Hyde Park Place Estate Charity
The Iliffe Family Charitable
Trust
The Invigorate Charitable Trust
The J. A. R. Charitable Trust
The Jenour Foundation
The Nancy Kenyon Charitable
Trust
The K. P. Ladd Charitable
Trust
Maurice and Hilda Laing
Charitable Trust
The Kirby Laing Foundation
The Martin Laing Foundation
The Leonard Laity Stoate
Charitable Trust
Lancaster Foundation
Langdale Trust
Laslett's (Hinton) Charity
The Herd Lawson and Muriel
Lawson Charitable Trust
Lempriere Pringle 2015
The Charles Littlewood Hill
Trust
The Elaine and Angus Lloyd
Charitable Trust
The Lockwood Charitable
Foundation
Sylvanus Lysons Charity
Magnify Foundation*
The Mallinckrodt Foundation
The Manoukian Charitable
Foundation
Charity of John Marshall
Charlotte Marshall Charitable
Trust
John Martin's Charity

The Millfield Trust
The Milne Family Foundation
The Monmouthshire County
Council Welsh Church Act
Fund
The Mulberry Trust
The National Churches Trust
The Northumbria Historic
Churches Trust
The Norwood and Newton
Settlement
The Ogle Christian Trust
Open House Trust Ltd
Otsar Trust
The Ouseley Church Music
Trust
The Owen Family Trust
Oxfordshire Historic Churches
Trust (2016)
The P27 Trust
The Gerald Palmer Eling Trust
Company
The James Pantyfedwen
Foundation
(Ymddiriedolaeth James
Pantyfedwen)
Miss M. E. S. Paterson's
Charitable Trust
The Jack Patston Charitable
Trust
Payne-Gallwey 1989 Charitable
Trust
The Bernard Piggott Charitable
Trust
Charles Plater Trust*
Sir John Priestman Charity
Trust
Quothquan Trust
The Bishop Radford Trust
The Rank Foundation Ltd
The Joseph Rank Trust
The Sir James Reckitt Charity
Riada Trust
The Sir Cliff Richard Charitable
Trust
The River Trust
The Rock Foundation
Mrs L. D. Rope's Third
Charitable Settlement
The S. M. B. Trust
The Saddlers' Company
Charitable Fund
Saint Sarkis Charity Trust
The Salamander Charitable
Trust
Sarum St Michael Educational
Charity
Seedfield Trust
The Seven Fifty Trust
The Bassil Shippam and
Alsford Trust
The Henry Smith Charity
The R. C. Snelling Charitable
Trust
Souter Charitable Trust
W. F. Southall Trust

The Squires Foundation
St Peter's Saltley Trust
The Hugh Stenhouse
Foundation
Stewards Company Ltd
Sir Halley Stewart Trust
The Stobart Newlands
Charitable Trust
Stolkin Foundation
Stratford-upon-Avon Town Trust
Sabina Sutherland Charitable
Trust
Swansea and Brecon Diocesan
Board of Finance Ltd
Tabeel Trust
Tay Charitable Trust
Scott Thomson Charitable
Trust
The Thornton Trust
Mrs R. P. Tindall's Charitable
Trust
The Tory Family Foundation
The Tufton Charitable Trust
Ulting Overseas Trust
The Union of the Sisters of
Mercy of Great Britain
The Vardy Foundation
Nigel Vinson Charitable Trust
The Georg and Emily von Opel
Foundation
Mrs Waterhouse Charitable
Trust
The Welsh Church Act Fund
The Whinfell Charitable Fund
The Norman Whiteley Trust
The Wilmcote Charitrust
The James Wood Bequest
Fund
WWDP (World Day of Prayer
National Committee for
England, Wales and
Northern Ireland)
The Yorkshire Historic
Churches Trust

Interfaith activities/ understanding

The Arah Foundation
The Edward Cadbury
Charitable Trust
The Davis Foundation
Didymus
The Doughty Charity Trust
Anne French Memorial Trust
The Hemraj Goyal Foundation
The Hinduja Foundation
The Humanitarian Trust
The Harold Hyam Wingate
Foundation
The Inlight Trust
The Kennedy Leigh Charitable
Trust
The Leeward Trust

The Mulberry Trust
Near Neighbours
Ostro Fayre Share Foundation
Randeree Charitable Trust
The Sir James Roll Charitable
  Trust
The Jeremy and John Sacher
  Charitable Trust
The Alan and Babette
  Sainsbury Charitable Fund
The Sir Sigmund Sternberg
  Charitable Foundation

Islam

Dawat-E-Hadiyah Trust (United
  Kingdom)
The Matliwala Family
  Charitable Trust
Randeree Charitable Trust

Judaism

4 Charity Foundation
The A. H. Trust
A. W. Charitable Trust
Achisomoch Aid Company Ltd
Adenfirst Ltd
The Aimwell Charitable Trust
Alliance Family Foundation Ltd
Amabrill Ltd
Anpride Ltd
The Ardwick Trust
Atlas Memorial Ltd
Bay Charitable Trust
Bear Mordechai Ltd
Beauland Ltd
Belljoe Tzedoko Ltd
Benesco Charity Ltd
Ruth Berkowitz Charitable
  Trust
The Bertie Black Foundation
The Sir Victor Blank Charitable
  Settlement
Abraham Algy Bloom
  Foundation
The Bluston Charitable
  Settlement
The Bonamy Charitable Trust
The Salo Bordon Charitable
  Trust
Sir Clive Bourne Family Trust
Bourneheights Ltd
Brushmill Ltd
C. and F. Charitable Trust
Cannon Charitable Trust
Carlee Ltd
The CH (1980) Charitable
  Trust
Chalfords Ltd
Charitworth Ltd
The Childwick Trust
The Clore Duffield Foundation
Clydpride Ltd
CMZ Ltd

The Vivienne and Samuel
  Cohen Charitable Trust
The R. and S. Cohen
  Foundation
Col-Reno Ltd
The Gershon Coren Charitable
  Foundation
Countypier Ltd
Itzchok Meyer Cymerman Trust
  Ltd
The D. M. Charitable Trust
Oizer Dalim Trust
The Davidson Family
  Charitable Trust
The Davis Foundation
Debmar Benevolent Trust Ltd
The Desmond Foundation
The Alan and Sheila Diamond
  Charitable Trust
The Djanogly Foundation
Dollond Charitable Trust
The Dorfman Foundation
The Doughty Charity Trust
Dushinsky Trust Ltd
The George Elias Charitable
  Trust
Ellinson Foundation Ltd
Entindale Ltd
The Esfandi Charitable
  Foundation
Esher House Charitable Trust
The Eventhall Family
  Charitable Trust
The Exilarch's Foundation
Extonglen Ltd
Famos Foundation Trust
Fordeve Ltd
The Isaac and Freda Frankel
  Memorial Charitable Trust
Friends of Boyan Trust
Friends of Wiznitz Ltd
The G. R. P. Charitable Trust
The Gertner Charitable Trust
The Jane Goodman Charitable
  Trust*
Grahame Charitable
  Foundation Ltd
M. and R. Gross Charities Ltd
H. P. Charitable Trust
The Harbour Foundation
The Maurice Hatter Foundation
The Heathside Charitable Trust
The Simon Heller Charitable
  Settlement
The Helping Foundation
The Bernhard Heuberger
  Charitable Trust*
The Highcroft Charitable Trust
The Holden Charitable Trust
Horwich Shotter Charitable
  Trust
The Humanitarian Trust
The Huntingdon Foundation
  Ltd
Hurdale Charity Ltd

The Harold Hyam Wingate
  Foundation
IGO Foundation Ltd
Investream Charitable Trust
The J. and J. Benevolent
  Foundation
The Susan and Stephen
  James Charitable
  Settlement
Jay Education Trust
Jewish Child's Day
The Jewish Youth Fund
J. E. Joseph Charitable Fund
The Jusaca Charitable Trust
Kahal Chassidim Bobov
The Kasner Charitable Trust
The Michael and Ilse Katz
  Foundation
C. S. Kaufman Charitable
  Trust
The Kennedy Leigh Charitable
  Trust
Keren Association Ltd
E. and E. Kernkraut Charities
  Ltd
The Kobler Trust
Kollel and Co. Ltd
Kolyom Trust Ltd
Kreditor Charitable Trust
Kupath Gemach Chaim
  Bechesed Viznitz Trust
The Kyte Charitable Trust
The Lauffer Family Charitable
  Foundation
Lawson Beckman Charitable
  Trust
The Arnold Lee Charitable
  Trust
Bernard Lewis Family
  Charitable Trust
David and Ruth Lewis Family
  Charitable Trust
The Second Joseph Aaron
  Littman Foundation
Jack Livingstone Charitable
  Trust
Localtrent Ltd
The Locker Foundation
LPW Ltd
Sir Jack Lyons Charitable Trust
M. and C. Trust
M. B. Foundation
The M. Y. A. Charitable Trust
The Magen Charitable Trust
The Manackerman Charitable
  Trust
The Manson Family Charitable
  Trust
Marbeh Torah Trust
The Stella and Alexander
  Margulies Charitable Trust
The Marks Family Charitable
  Trust
The Marque Foundation
The Violet Mauray Charitable
  Trust

Mayfair Charities Ltd
Mayheights Ltd
Melodor Ltd
The Melow Charitable Trust
Menuchar Ltd
Mercaz Torah Vechesed Ltd
The Mishcon Family Charitable
Trust
The MK Charitable Trust
The Modiano Charitable Trust
Mole Charitable Trust
The Morgan Charitable
Foundation
The Moshal Charitable Trust
Vyoel Moshe Charitable Trust
The Mosselson Charitable
Trust
The Mutley Foundation
The Mutual Trust Group
MW (CL) Foundation
MW (GK) Foundation
MW (HO) Foundation
MW (RH) Foundation
Nemoral Ltd
Ner Foundation
Newpier Charity Ltd
North London Charities Ltd
Oizer Charitable Trust
The Doris Pacey Charitable
Foundation
David Pearlman Charitable
Foundation
The Pears Family Charitable
Foundation
Dina Perelman Trust Ltd
The Phillips and Rubens
Charitable Trust
The Phillips Family Charitable
Trust
The Polonsky Foundation
Porter Foundation
Premierquote Ltd
R. S. Charitable Trust
Rachel Charitable Trust
The Joseph and Lena Randall
Charitable Trust
Rentrust Foundation Ltd
Ridgesave Ltd
The Sir John Ritblat Family
Foundation
The Roan Charitable Trust
The Rofeh Trust
The Gerald and Gail Ronson
Family Foundation
The Cecil Rosen Foundation
Rothschild Foundation
(Hanadiv) Europe
Rowanville Ltd
The Rubin Foundation
Charitable Trust
S. and R. Charitable Trust
The Jeremy and John Sacher
Charitable Trust
The Michael and Nicola Sacher
Charitable Trust
Samjo Ltd

The Peter Samuel Charitable
Trust
The Schmidt-Bodner Charitable
Trust
The Schreib Trust
Schreiber Charitable Trust
O. and G. Schreiber Charitable
Trust
The Searchlight Electric
Charitable Trust
The Sam and Bella Sebba
Charitable Foundation
Sellata Ltd
SF Foundation
The Archie Sherman Charitable
Trust
Shlomo Memorial Fund Ltd
Shulem B. Association Ltd
Songdale Ltd
The E. C. Sosnow Charitable
Trust
Sparquote Ltd
Starlow Charities Ltd
The Steinberg Family
Charitable Trust
C. E. K. Stern Charitable Trust
The Sir Sigmund Sternberg
Charitable Foundation
Stervon Ltd
T. and S. Trust Fund
The Tajtelbaum Charitable
Trust
The Talmud Torah Machzikei
Hadass Trust
Talteg Ltd
The David Tannen Charitable
Trust
The Taurus Foundation
Tegham Ltd
Truedene Co. Ltd
Truemart Ltd
Trumros Ltd
Tzedakah
UJIA (United Jewish Israel
Appeal)
The Union of Orthodox Hebrew
Congregations
The Velvet Foundation
VHLT Ltd
Vivdale Ltd
Walton Foundation
The Linda and Michael
Weinstein Charitable Trust
The Wigoder Family Foundation
The Benjamin Winegarten
Charitable Trust
The Michael and Anna Wix
Charitable Trust
The Maurice Wohl Charitable
Foundation
The Charles Wolfson
Charitable Trust
The Wolfson Family Charitable
Trust
Woodlands Green Ltd
Wychville Ltd

Yankov Charitable Trust
The Marjorie and Arnold Ziff
Charitable Foundation

Research

The Abbeyfield Research Foundation
abrdn Financial Fairness Trust
The AIM Foundation
The Anson Charitable Trust
Arcadia Fund
The Armourers and Brasiers Gauntlet Trust
ArtSocial Foundation
The Ove Arup Foundation
The Asfari Foundation
Asthma and Lung UK
The Baily Thomas Charitable Fund
Maria Bjornson Memorial Fund
The John Black Charitable Foundation
Bloodwise
The Bluston Charitable Settlement
The Harry Bottom Charitable Trust
Breast Cancer Now
Bright Red Charity
The British Academy
British Heart Foundation (BHF)
The Rory and Elizabeth Brooks Foundation
Buckingham Trust
Building and Civil Engineering Charitable Trust
Miss Margaret Butters Reekie Charitable Trust
The Edward Cadbury Charitable Trust
Cancer Research UK
The Childwick Trust
Christadelphian Samaritan Fund
The Elizabeth Creak Charitable Trust
Cripplegate Foundation
The Delves Charitable Trust
The Eighty Eight Foundation
The Evelyn Trust
The Eveson Charitable Trust
Marc Fitch Fund
The Joseph Strong Frazer Trust
The Freelands Foundation Ltd
Friends of Wiznitz Ltd
Friends Provident Charitable Foundation
The Gatsby Charitable Foundation
The Tara Getty Foundation
The Grace Trust
The Hawthorne Charitable Trust
The Health Foundation
The Michael Heller Charitable Foundation
The Simon Heller Charitable Settlement
HFC Help for Children UK Ltd
The Holbeck Charitable Trust

The Humanitarian Trust
The Institute for Policy Research
The ITF Seafarers Trust
The Frank Jackson Foundation
The Jusaca Charitable Trust
The Kennedy Trust for Rheumatology Research
The Mary Kinross Charitable Trust
The Graham Kirkham Foundation
The Legal Education Foundation
The Leverhulme Trust
Cecil and Hilda Lewis Charitable Trust
The Frank Litchfield Charitable Trust
Lloyd's Register Foundation
Longleigh Foundation
The Mackintosh Foundation
The Robert McAlpine Foundation
The Millennium Oak Trust
The Mohn Westlake Foundation
Edith Murphy Foundation
The Nineveh Charitable Trust
North West Cancer Research
The Nuffield Foundation
Orange Tree Trust
P. F. Charitable Trust
Parkinson's UK
The J. G. W. Patterson Foundation
Peacock Charitable Trust
David Pearlman Charitable Foundation
The Pears Family Charitable Foundation
The Pilgrim Trust
David and Elaine Potter Foundation
Queen Mary's Roehampton Trust
The Racing Foundation
The Rainford Trust
Randeree Charitable Trust
The Ratcliff Foundation
The Resolution Trust
Rothschild Foundation (Hanadiv) Europe
The Rowlands Trust
The Joseph Rowntree Foundation
The Dr Mortimer and Theresa Sackler Foundation
The Schroder Foundation
The Scorpion Charitable Trust*
The Shears Foundation
Smallwood Trust
Stanley Smith UK Horticultural Trust
Peter Sowerby Foundation

The Peter Stebbings Memorial Charity
The Charles and Elsie Sykes Trust
The Syncona Foundation
Tay Charitable Trust
Sir Jules Thorn Charitable Trust
The Thriplow Charitable Trust
Trust for London
The Ulverscroft Foundation
The Underwood Trust
The Albert Van Den Bergh Charitable Trust
Nigel Vinson Charitable Trust
Vision Foundation
The Waterloo Foundation
The Wellcome Trust
The Galen and Hilary Weston Foundation
The Which? Fund
The Wolfson Family Charitable Trust
Yorkshire Cancer Research
Youth Endowment Fund (YEF)*

Environmental research

The A Team Foundation Ltd
The Ove Arup Foundation
The Ian Askew Charitable Trust
The Aurora Trust (formerly The Ashden Trust)
Cadent Foundation
The Castansa Trust
The Chalk Cliff Trust
CLA Charitable Trust
Community First
The Elizabeth Creak Charitable Trust
The Ecology Trust
The Gatsby Charitable Foundation
The Tara Getty Foundation
The Great Britain Sasakawa Foundation
Hamamelis Trust
The Jabbs Foundation
The Frank Jackson Foundation
Lloyd's Register Foundation
Marmot Charitable Trust
The NFU Mutual Charitable Trust
The Nineveh Charitable Trust
Oxfordshire Community Foundation
Porter Foundation
The Scott Bader Commonwealth Ltd
The Shears Foundation
The Sheepdrove Trust
The Martin Smith Foundation
The Thirty Percy Foundation

The David Webster Charitable Trust

Humanities and social sciences

The Aldama Foundation
The Ove Arup Foundation
The Ashley Family Foundation
The Aurelius Charitable Trust
The Burberry Foundation
The Daiwa Anglo-Japanese Foundation
The De Laszlo Foundation
The Elmley Foundation
The Finborough Foundation
The Freelands Foundation Ltd
The Great Britain Sasakawa Foundation
Paul Hamlyn Foundation
The Harbour Foundation
The Institute for Policy Research
The Leche Trust
The Legal Education Foundation
The Leverhulme Trust
The Linder Foundation
The MacRobert Trust 2019
The Mayfield Valley Arts Trust
The Mikheev Charitable Trust
The Nuffield Foundation
Orange Tree Trust
The Polonsky Foundation
The Rainford Trust
The Resolution Trust
Rothschild Foundation (Hanadiv) Europe

Medical research

The Abbeyfield Research Foundation
The Aberbrothock Skea Trust
Action Medical Research
The Bryan Adams Foundation
Sylvia Aitken's Charitable Trust
The Alborada Trust
The Alchemy Foundation
The Aldama Foundation
D. C. R. Allen Charitable Trust
Alzheimer's Research UK
Alzheimer's Society
Andor Charitable Trust
The Anson Charitable Trust
The Annabel Arbib Foundation
The John Armitage Charitable Trust
The Armourers and Brasiers Gauntlet Trust
Asthma and Lung UK
The Astor Foundation
The Tim Bacon Foundation
The Baily Thomas Charitable Fund

The Roy and Pixie Baker Charitable Trust
The Kamini and Vindi Banga Family Trust
The Barbour Foundation
Robert Barr's Charitable Trust
The Batchworth Trust
Ruth Berkowitz Charitable Trust
The Bestway Foundation
The Bingham Trust
Maria Bjornson Memorial Fund
The John Black Charitable Foundation
Blakemore Foundation
Lady Blakenham's Charity Trust
Bloodwise
The Bluston Charitable Settlement
Maureen Boal Charitable Trust
The Boltini Trust
The Bothwell Charitable Trust
The Harry Bottom Charitable Trust
The P. G. and N. J. Boulton Trust
G. and K. Boyes Charitable Trust
The Tony Bramall Charitable Trust
Breast Cancer Now
Bright Red Charity
British Eye Research Foundation (Fight for Sight)
British Heart Foundation (BHF)
Bill Brown 1989 Charitable Trust
The Brownsword Charitable Foundation
Buckingham Trust
The Burden Trust
Miss Margaret Butters Reekie Charitable Trust
William A. Cadbury Charitable Trust
The Cadogan Charity
The Calleva Foundation
Cancer Research UK
The Cayo Foundation
The B. G. S. Cayzer Charitable Trust
The Charities Advisory Trust
The Lorna and Yuti Chernajovsky Biomedical Research Foundation
Children with Cancer UK
The Childwick Trust
Christadelphian Samaritan Fund
Denise Coates Foundation
The Vivienne and Samuel Cohen Charitable Trust
The Colt Foundation
The Connolly Foundation (UK) Ltd

Dudley and Geoffrey Cox Charitable Trust
CRH Charitable Trust
Cruden Foundation Ltd
The Cunningham Trust
Michael Davies Charitable Settlement
The De Laszlo Foundation
The Delves Charitable Trust
Diabetes UK
The Alan and Sheila Diamond Charitable Trust
Dinwoodie Charitable Company
Dromintee Trust
The Dunhill Medical Trust
The James Dyson Foundation
The Gilbert and Eileen Edgar Foundation
The Eighty Eight Foundation
The Englefield Charitable Trust
Epilepsy Research UK
The Evelyn Trust
The Eveson Charitable Trust
The Exilarch's Foundation
The Fairness Foundation
The Fieldrose Charitable Trust
Sir John Fisher Foundation
The Follett Trust
The Anna Rosa Forster Charitable Trust
The Elizabeth Frankland Moore and Star Foundation
The Joseph Strong Frazer Trust
The Louis and Valerie Freedman Charitable Settlement
The Freshfield Foundation
Friends of Wiznitz Ltd
Frognal Trust
The Gatsby Charitable Foundation
General Charity (Coventry)
The Generational Foundation*
The Tara Getty Foundation
The G. C. Gibson Charitable Trust
The B. and P. Glasser Charitable Trust
Sydney and Phyllis Goldberg Memorial Charitable Trust
The Mike Gooley Trailfinders Charity
The Grace Trust
The Gisela Graham Foundation
The Great Britain Sasakawa Foundation
The Albert Gubay Charitable Foundation
The Walter Guinness Charitable Trust
The Guy Foundation
H. and T. Clients Charitable Trust
Hamamelis Trust
The Harbour Foundation

The Peter and Teresa Harris Charitable Trust

The Maurice Hatter Foundation

The Hawthorne Charitable Trust

The Health Foundation

The Michael Heller Charitable Foundation

The Simon Heller Charitable Settlement

Help for Health

The Alison Hillman Charitable Trust*

The Hinduja Foundation

The Henry C. Hoare Charitable Trust

The Hobson Charity Ltd

The Jane Hodge Foundation

The Holbeck Charitable Trust

Homelands Charitable Trust

The Hospital Saturday Fund

The Sir Joseph Hotung Charitable Settlement

The Harold Hyam Wingate Foundation

The Iceland Foods Charitable Foundation

The Inman Charity

The Jabbs Foundation

The Elton John AIDS Foundation

The Joron Charitable Trust

The Cyril and Eve Jumbo Charitable Trust

The Emmanuel Kaye Foundation

The Kennedy Trust for Rheumatology Research

Kidney Research UK

Fraser Kilpatrick Charitable Trust

The Mary Kinross Charitable Trust

The Graham Kirkham Foundation

The Ernest Kleinwort Charitable Trust

Kollel and Co. Ltd

The Kirby Laing Foundation

The Richard Lawes Foundation

The Leach Fourteenth Trust

Ana Leaf Foundation*

The William Leech Charity

Cecil and Hilda Lewis Charitable Trust

David and Ruth Lewis Family Charitable Trust

The Linbury Trust

The Linder Foundation

The Frank Litchfield Charitable Trust

The Michael and Betty Little Trust*

The Charles Littlewood Hill Trust

The Second Joseph Aaron Littman Foundation

Robert Luff Foundation Ltd

Lord and Lady Lurgan Trust

The Lyndal Tree Foundation

The Mackintosh Foundation

The W. M. Mann Foundation

The Manoukian Charitable Foundation

The Stella and Alexander Margulies Charitable Trust

Masonic Charitable Foundation

Nancie Massey Charitable Trust

Mazars Charitable Trust

The Robert McAlpine Foundation

D. D. McPhail Charitable Settlement

Medical Research Foundation

Medical Research Scotland

The Mikheev Charitable Trust

The Millennium Oak Trust

Hugh and Mary Miller Bequest Trust

Mills and Reeve Charitable Trust

G. M. Morrison Charitable Trust

The Mosselson Charitable Trust

Motor Neurone Disease Association

J. P. Moulton Charitable Foundation

Multiple Sclerosis Society

Edith Murphy Foundation

Newby Trust Ltd

The Frances and Augustus Newman Foundation

The Norman Family Charitable Trust

North West Cancer Research

Northern Pharmacies Ltd Trust Fund

The Norton Rose Fulbright Charitable Foundation

The Nuffield Foundation

The Ofenheim Charitable Trust

Open House Trust Ltd

Orange Tree Trust

The O'Sullivan Family Charitable Trust

P. F. Charitable Trust

The Paragon Trust

Parkinson's UK

The J. G. W. Patterson Foundation

Payne-Gallwey 1989 Charitable Trust

Peacock Charitable Trust

David Pearlman Charitable Foundation

The Dowager Countess Eleanor Peel Trust

The Pharsalia Charitable Trust

The Phillips and Rubens Charitable Trust

The Bernard Piggott Charitable Trust

Cecil Pilkington Charitable Trust

The George and Esme Pollitzer Charitable Settlement

Prostate Cancer UK

The Prudence Trust

Queen Mary's Roehampton Trust

The Rainford Trust

The Joseph and Lena Randall Charitable Trust

The Ranworth Trust

The Ratcliff Foundation

The Revere Charitable Trust

RNID (The Royal National Institute for Deaf People)

The Roan Charitable Trust

The Cecil Rosen Foundation

Rosetrees

The Rothermere Foundation

The Rothley Trust

The Eranda Rothschild Foundation

The Row Fogo Charitable Trust

The Rowlands Trust

The S. M. B. Trust

The Dr Mortimer and Theresa Sackler Foundation

The Sackler Trust

The Alan and Babette Sainsbury Charitable Fund

The Salamander Charitable Trust

The Peter Samuel Charitable Trust

The Schroder Foundation

Sir Samuel Scott of Yews Trust

The John Scott Trust Fund

The Jean Shanks Foundation

The Shears Foundation

The Sheepdrove Trust

The Bassil Shippam and Alsford Trust

The Florence Shute Millennium Trust

The Charles Skey Charitable Trust

The N. Smith Charitable Settlement

The Leslie Smith Foundation

Peter Sowerby Foundation

The Stafford Trust

The Peter Stebbings Memorial Charity

The Hugh Stenhouse Foundation

Sir Halley Stewart Trust

The Stoller Charitable Trust

The Stoneygate Trust

Peter Stormonth Darling Charitable Trust

The Swann-Morton Foundation
The Charles and Elsie Sykes
    Trust
The Syncona Foundation
The Gay and Keith Talbot Trust
Tallow Chandlers Benevolent
    Fund No 2
The Tanlaw Foundation
Tay Charitable Trust
The Taylor Family Foundation
Tenovus Scotland
Sir Jules Thorn Charitable
    Trust
The Tolkien Trust
Toyota Manufacturing UK
    Charitable Trust
The Troutsdale Charitable
    Trust
The James Tudor Foundation
The Roger and Douglas Turner
    Charitable Trust
The Ulverscroft Foundation
The Underwood Trust
The Michael Uren Foundation
The Albert Van Den Bergh
    Charitable Trust
The Vandervell Foundation
The Velvet Foundation
Versus Arthritis
Vision Foundation
The VTCT Foundation
Sylvia Waddilove Foundation
    UK
Wellbeing of Women
The Wellcome Trust
The Welsh Church Act Fund
The Galen and Hilary Weston
    Foundation
The Felicity Wilde Charitable
    Trust
W. Wing Yip and Brothers
    Foundation
The Maurice Wohl Charitable
    Foundation
The Charles Wolfson
    Charitable Trust
The Wolfson Family Charitable
    Trust
The Lord Leonard and Lady
    Estelle Wolfson Foundation
The Woosnam Foundation
Yorkshire Cancer Research

Social justice

The A. B. Charitable Trust
The A. S. Charitable Trust
The Alchemy Foundation
The Allen & Overy Foundation
The John Armitage Charitable
    Trust
The Asfari Foundation
The Aziz Foundation
The Baring Foundation
Benefact Trust Ltd
The Michael Bishop
    Foundation
The Blagrave Trust
Blyth Watson Charitable Trust
The Rory and Elizabeth Brooks
    Foundation
The Bulldog Trust Ltd
The Barrow Cadbury Trust
Camden Giving
W. A. Cargill Fund
The Cayo Foundation
Clinks*
Comic Relief
The Evan Cornish Foundation
Craignish Trust
Cripplegate Foundation
Didymus
Dr. Martens Foundation
John Ellerman Foundation
Emerton-Christie Charity
Esmée Fairbairn Foundation
The Fairness Foundation
The Robert Fleming Hannay
    Memorial Charity
The Forrester Family Trust
The Funding Network
The Golden Bottle Trust
The Goldsmiths' Company
    Charity
The Hadley Trust
Paul Hamlyn Foundation
The Lennox Hannay Charitable
    Trust
The Charles Hayward
    Foundation
Highway One Trust
Michael and Shirley Hunt
    Charitable Trust
Impact Funding Partners Ltd
The Indigo Trust
The Invigorate Charitable Trust
The Ireland Fund of Great
    Britain
Joffe Charitable Trust CIO
The Muriel Jones Foundation
The Emmanuel Kaye
    Foundation
The Kiawah Charitable Trust
The Mary Kinross Charitable
    Trust
The Kreitman Foundation
The Allen Lane Foundation
The LankellyChase Foundation
The Law Society Charity
The Leathersellers' Foundation

The Leeward Trust
The Legal Education
    Foundation
The Leigh Trust
The Leri Charitable Trust
The Livingbridge Foundation*
The Millennium Oak Trust
John Moores Foundation
The Frederick Mulder
    Foundation
Network for Social Change
    Charitable Trust
The Nuffield Foundation
The Oakdale Trust
The Olwyn Foundation
Polden-Puckham Charitable
    Foundation
The Portrack Charitable Trust
David and Elaine Potter
    Foundation
The Eleanor Rathbone
    Charitable Trust
The Sigrid Rausing Trust
The Roddick Foundation
Rosa Fund
The Joseph Rowntree
    Charitable Trust
The Joseph Rowntree
    Foundation
The Samworth Foundation
The Sam and Bella Sebba
    Charitable Foundation
The Serco Foundation
The Simmons & Simmons
    Charitable Foundation
The Stewarts Law Foundation
C. B. and H. H. T. Taylor 1984
    Trust
Stephen Taylor Foundation
The Three Guineas Trust
Trust for London
The Tudor Trust
United St Saviour's Charity
The Van Neste Foundation
Nigel Vinson Charitable Trust
The Scurrah Wainwright Charity
G. R. Waters Charitable Trust
    2000
Sumner Wilson Charitable
    Trust
Youth Endowment Fund (YEF)*
Zephyr Charitable Trust

Conflict resolution

The A. S. Charitable Trust
William A. Cadbury Charitable
    Trust
The Barrow Cadbury Trust
The Charities Advisory Trust
Craignish Trust
The Daiwa Anglo-Japanese
    Foundation
The Dulverton Trust
Allan and Nesta Ferguson
    Charitable Settlement

The Follett Trust
J. Paul Getty Jr General
    Charitable Trust*
The Golden Bottle Trust
The Great Britain Sasakawa
    Foundation
The Hadrian Trust
The Ireland Fund of Great
    Britain
Irish Youth Foundation (UK)
    Ltd (incorporating The
    Lawlor Foundation)
The J. Isaacs Charitable Trust
The Kennedy Leigh Charitable
    Trust
The Leeward Trust
The Leri Charitable Trust
Marmot Charitable Trust
The Morel Charitable Trust
Near Neighbours
Network for Social Change
    Charitable Trust
The Northwick Trust
Ostro Fayre Share Foundation
Polden-Puckham Charitable
    Foundation
Randeree Charitable Trust
The Sigrid Rausing Trust
The Rayne Foundation
The Joseph Rowntree
    Charitable Trust
The Sino-British Fellowship
    Trust
W. F. Southall Trust
The Tolkien Trust
The Worwin UK Foundation
Youth Endowment Fund (YEF)*

Human rights

The A. B. Charitable Trust
The Arah Foundation
The Asfari Foundation
The Aziz Foundation
Veronica and Lars Bane
    Foundation
The Baring Foundation
The Michael Bishop
    Foundation
The Sydney Black Charitable
    Trust
The Blagrave Trust
Blyth Watson Charitable Trust
The Bromley Trust
The Brook Trust
The Bulldog Trust Ltd
The Noel Buxton Trust
The Barrow Cadbury Trust
Clinks*
The Evan Cornish Foundation
Coutts Charitable Foundation
Craignish Trust
The Peter Cruddas Foundation
The D. G. Charitable
    Settlement
The Davis Foundation

Didymus
Dr. Martens Foundation
John Ellerman Foundation
Emerton-Christie Charity
Esmée Fairbairn Foundation
The Fairness Foundation
The Farthing Trust
The Robert Fleming Hannay
    Memorial Charity
The Elizabeth Frankland Moore
    and Star Foundation
Jill Franklin Trust
The Funding Network
The Robert Gavron Charitable
    Trust
The Golden Bottle Trust
The Goldsmiths' Company
    Charity
The Hemraj Goyal Foundation
The Green Room Charitable
    Trust
Greenham Trust Ltd
The Hadrian Trust
The Helen Hamlyn Trust
The Lennox Hannay Charitable
    Trust
The Harrison-Frank Family
    Foundation (UK) Ltd
The Charles Hayward
    Foundation
Highway One Trust
The Hilden Charitable Fund
The Hiscox Foundation
The Sir Joseph Hotung
    Charitable Settlement
Michael and Shirley Hunt
    Charitable Trust
The Invigorate Charitable Trust
The ITF Seafarers Trust
Joffe Charitable Trust CIO
The Muriel Jones Foundation
The Emmanuel Kaye
    Foundation
The Kennedy Leigh Charitable
    Trust
The Kiawah Charitable Trust
The Mary Kinross Charitable
    Trust
Laura Kinsella Foundation
The Kreitman Foundation
The Allen Lane Foundation
The LankellyChase Foundation
The Leathersellers' Foundation
The Leeward Trust
The Legal Education
    Foundation
The Leigh Trust
The Leri Charitable Trust
The Michael and Betty Little
    Trust*
Lloyds Bank Foundation for
    England and Wales
The Master Charitable Trust
Gemma and Chris McGough
    Charitable Foundation CIO
The Millennium Oak Trust

John Moores Foundation
The Morel Charitable Trust
G. M. Morrison Charitable
    Trust
Network for Social Change
    Charitable Trust
Odin Charitable Trust
The Olwyn Foundation
P. F. Charitable Trust
The Pargiter Trust
PIMCO Foundation Europe
Polden-Puckham Charitable
    Foundation
The Portrack Charitable Trust
David and Elaine Potter
    Foundation
The Rambourg Foundation
Randeree Charitable Trust
The Eleanor Rathbone
    Charitable Trust
The Sigrid Rausing Trust
The Roddick Foundation
Rosa Fund
The Joseph Rowntree
    Charitable Trust
The Alan and Babette
    Sainsbury Charitable Fund
Saint Sarkis Charity Trust
The Samworth Foundation
Francis C. Scott Charitable
    Trust
The Sam and Bella Sebba
    Charitable Foundation
The Simmons & Simmons
    Charitable Foundation
Smallwood Trust
Staples Trust
The Peter Stebbings Memorial
    Charity
The Street Foundation
Swarovski Foundation
The T.K. Maxx and
    Homesense Foundation
The Three Guineas Trust
The Tolkien Trust
The Triangle Trust (1949) Fund
Trust for London
Nigel Vinson Charitable Trust
Volant Charitable Trust
G. R. Waters Charitable Trust
    2000
Women's Fund for Scotland
The Worwin UK Foundation
The Wyndham Charitable Trust
Zephyr Charitable Trust

Social welfare

The 29th May 1961 Charitable
Trust
4 Charity Foundation
The 4814 Trust
The A. and J. Charitable Trust
The A. H. Trust
A. W. Charitable Trust
ABF The Soldiers' Charity
abrdn Financial Fairness Trust
Adam Family Foundation
The Bryan Adams Foundation
The Addleshaw Goddard
Charitable Trust
Adenfirst Ltd
The Adint Charitable Trust
The AEB Charitable Trust
Age Scotland
Sylvia Aitken's Charitable Trust
AJ Bell Trust
Alan Boswell Group Charitable
Trust
The Alchemy Foundation
The Aldama Foundation
Al-Fayed Charitable Foundation
The Derrill Allatt Foundation
D. C. R. Allen Charitable Trust
The Allen Trust
Alliance Family Foundation Ltd
Amabrill Ltd
Ambergate Charitable Trust
The Ammco Trust
Viscount Amory's Charitable
Trust
The AMW Charitable Trust
Andrew Anderson Trust
Andrews Charitable Trust
Anpride Ltd
The Apax Foundation
The John Apthorp Charity
The Annabel Arbib Foundation
The Archer Trust
Ardbarron Trust Ltd
The Ardwick Trust
Armed Forces Covenant Fund
Trust
The John Armitage Charitable
Trust
The Armourers and Brasiers
Gauntlet Trust
The Arsenal Foundation
The Artemis Charitable
Foundation
ArtSocial Foundation
Ove Arup Partnership
Charitable Trust
The Asda Foundation
The Asfari Foundation
Ashburnham Thanksgiving
Trust
The Ashendene Trust
The Ashworth Charitable Trust
Atkin Charitable Foundation
Atlas Memorial Ltd
The Lord Austin Trust
Axis Foundation

B&Q Foundation
The Austin Bailey Foundation
The Roy and Pixie Baker
Charitable Trust
The Ballinger Charitable Trust
Bank of Scotland Foundation
The Barbour Foundation
Barcapel Foundation Ltd
Barchester Healthcare
Foundation
Philip Barker Charity
The Michael Barnard
Charitable Trust
Lord Barnby's Foundation
The Barnes Fund
Barnwood Trust
Robert Barr's Charitable Trust
The Batchworth Trust
Bauer Radio's Cash for Kids
Charities
The Gordon and Ena Baxter
Foundation*
Bay Charitable Trust
The Bay Tree Charitable Trust
BBC Children in Need
Beauland Ltd
The Beaverbrook Foundation
The Beaverbrooks Charitable
Trust
Beccles Townlands Charity
Bedfordshire and Luton
Community Foundation
Bedfordshire Charitable Trust
Ltd
The Bellahouston Bequest
Fund
Belljoe Tzedoko Ltd
Benefact Trust Ltd
Benesco Charity Ltd
The Benham Charitable
Settlement
The Rowan Bentall Charitable
Trust
The Berkeley Foundation
The Bernicia Foundation
The Bestway Foundation
Bideford Bridge Trust
The Billmeir Charitable Trust
The Percy Bilton Charity
The Bingham Trust
Binks Trust
Birkdale Trust for Hearing
Impaired Ltd*
The Birmingham Diocesan
Board of Finance
Maria Bjornson Memorial Fund
The Sydney Black Charitable
Trust
The Bertie Black Foundation
The Isabel Blackman
Foundation
Lady Blakenham's Charity
Trust
The Sir Victor Blank Charitable
Settlement

The Bluston Charitable
Settlement
Blyth Watson Charitable Trust
Maureen Boal Charitable Trust
The Marjory Boddy Charitable
Trust
The Bonamy Charitable Trust
The Booth Charities
Boots Charitable Trust
The Salo Bordon Charitable
Trust
The Bothwell Charitable Trust
The Harry Bottom Charitable
Trust
Bourneheights Ltd
The Tony Bramall Charitable
Trust
The Liz and Terry Bramall
Foundation
The Brelms Trust CIO
The Brenley Trust
Bristol Charities
The Britford Bridge Trust
British Gas Energy Trust
British Humane Association
J. and M. Britton Charitable
Trust
The Brook Trust
The Brothers Trust
The Charles Brotherton Trust
Bill Brown 1989 Charitable
Trust
The Mary Brown Memorial
Trust
R. S. Brownless Charitable
Trust
Brushmill Ltd
Buckingham Trust
Buckinghamshire Community
Foundation
Building and Civil Engineering
Charitable Trust
The Bulldog Trust Ltd
E. F. Bulmer Trust
The Burberry Foundation
The Burden Trust
Clara E. Burgess Charity
The Arnold Burton 1998
Charitable Trust
Consolidated Charity of Burton
upon Trent
Byrne Family Foundation
The Edward Cadbury
Charitable Trust
The Barrow Cadbury Trust
The Edward and Dorothy
Cadbury Trust
Cadent Foundation
The Cadogan Charity
Community Foundation for
Calderdale
The Calleva Foundation
Cambridgeshire Community
Foundation
Cannon Charitable Trust
Carew Pole Charitable Trust

William A. Cargill Charitable
Trust
W. A. Cargill Fund
The Carpenters Company
Charitable Trust
The Carr-Gregory Trust
The Leslie Mary Carter
Charitable Trust
The Casey Trust
The Castanea Trust
Catkin Pussywillow Charitable
Trust
Cattanach
The Joseph and Annie Cattle
Trust
The Cayo Foundation
The B. G. S. Cayzer Charitable
Trust
The Amelia Chadwick Trust
Chalfords Ltd
The Chalk Cliff Trust
The Charities Advisory Trust
Charitworth Ltd
Chartered Accountants' Livery
Charity (CALC)
The Charterhouse Charitable
Trust
The Cheruby Trust
Cheshire Community
Foundation Ltd
The Childhood Trust
Children with Cancer UK
The Childwick Trust
Chippenham Borough Lands
Charity
CHK Foundation
The André Christian Trust
Chrysalis Trust
Church Burgesses Trust
Church Urban Fund
The Churchill Foundation
The City Bridge Trust (Bridge
House Estates)
The Clarkson Foundation
Clinks*
The Clore Duffield Foundation
The Clothworkers' Foundation
Cloudesley
The Clover Trust
Clydpride Ltd
CMZ Ltd
Denise Coates Foundation
The Vivienne and Samuel
Cohen Charitable Trust
The John S. Cohen Foundation
The R. and S. Cohen
Foundation
The Cole Charitable Trust
The Coles-Medlock Foundation
The Coltstaple Trust
Colyer-Fergusson Charitable
Trust
Comic Relief
Douglas Compton James
Charitable Trust

The Connolly Foundation (UK)
Ltd
The Cooks Charity
The Alice Ellen Cooper-Dean
Charitable Foundation
The J. Reginald Corah
Foundation Fund
The Evan Cornish Foundation
Cornwall Community
Foundation
The Corporation of Trinity
House of Deptford Strond
Corra Foundation
The County Council of Dyfed
Welsh Church Fund
County Durham Community
Foundation
Countypier Ltd
Coutts Charitable Foundation
Coventry Building Society
Charitable Foundation
The Sir Tom Cowie Charitable
Trust
Dudley and Geoffrey Cox
Charitable Trust
The Lord Cozens-Hardy Trust
CRASH
Michael Crawford Children's
Charity
The Crerar Trust
CRH Charitable Trust
Cripplegate Foundation
Crisis UK
The Cross Trust
The Croydon Relief-in-Need
Charity
The Peter Cruddas Foundation
Cruden Foundation Ltd
CSIS Charity Fund
Cumbria Community
Foundation
Itzchok Meyer Cymerman Trust
Ltd
The D. M. Charitable Trust
Oizer Dalim Trust
The Dashlight Foundation
Baron Davenport's Charity
The Manny and Brigitta
Davidson Charitable
Foundation
Margaret Davies Charity
The Crispin Davis Family Trust
The Davis Foundation
Dawat-E-Hadiyah Trust (United
Kingdom)
The Dawe Charitable Trust
The De Brye Charitable Trust
The Roger De Haan Charitable
Trust
The Delves Charitable Trust
Foundation Derbyshire
The J. N. Derbyshire Trust
The Desmond Foundation
Devon Community Foundation
The Dibden Allotments Fund
The Dischma Charitable Trust

The Djanogly Foundation
The Ken Dodd Charitable
Foundation
Donibristle Trust
The Dorcas Trust
Dorset Community Foundation
The Dorus Trust
The Double 'O' Charity Ltd
Dr. Martens Foundation
Drapers Charitable Fund
Dromintee Trust
Duchy of Lancaster Benevolent
Fund
The Duke of Cornwall's
Benevolent Fund
The Dulverton Trust
Dumbreck Charity
Dunlossit and Islay Community
Trust
The Dunn Family Charitable
Trust
Dushinsky Trust Ltd
The Dyers' Company
Charitable Trust
The James Dyson Foundation
E. B. M. Charitable Trust
EA Foundation*
The Earley Charity
East End Community
Foundation
Ebenezer Trust
The Ecology Trust
The Gilbert and Eileen Edgar
Foundation
Edupoor Ltd
Dr Edwards and Bishop King's
Fulham Charity
W. G. Edwards Charitable
Foundation
The Eight Foundation
Eight Strands Foundation
The Eighteen Fund
The Eighty Eight Foundation
The George Elias Charitable
Trust
The Elie Trust
The Maud Elkington Charitable
Trust
The Ellerdale Trust
The Endrick Trust
The Englefield Charitable Trust
The Enkalon Foundation
Entindale Ltd
The EQ Foundation
Esher House Charitable Trust
Essex Community Foundation
The Essex Youth Trust
The Ethos Foundation
Euro Quality Foundation
The Everard Foundation
The Exilarch's Foundation
The ExPat Foundation
Esmée Fairbairn Foundation
The Fairstead Trust
Family Philanthropy Ltd

The Lord Faringdon Charitable
  Trust
Samuel William Farmer Trust
The Thomas Farr Charity
The Farthing Trust
Fat Face Foundation*
George Fentham Birmingham
  Charity
The A. M. Fenton Trust
The Feoffees of St Michael's
  Spurriergate York
The Fermanagh Trust
The Fidelity UK Foundation
Field Family Charitable Trust
The Fifty Fund
Dixie Rose Findlay Charitable
  Trust
Sir John Fisher Foundation
The Earl Fitzwilliam Charitable
  Trust
The Robert Fleming Hannay
  Memorial Charity
Ford Britain Trust
Forest Hill Charitable Trust
Forever Manchester
The Forman Hardy Charitable
  Trust
The Forrester Family Trust
The Fort Foundation
The Foster Wood Foundation
Four Acre Trust
Foux Foundation
The Isaac and Freda Frankel
  Memorial Charitable Trust
The Elizabeth Frankland Moore
  and Star Foundation
The Hugh Fraser Foundation
The Joseph Strong Frazer Trust
The Louis and Valerie
  Freedman Charitable
  Settlement
Charles S. French Charitable
  Trust
The Freshfield Foundation
The Freshgate Trust
  Foundation
Friarsgate Trust
Friends of Wiznitz Ltd
Frognal Trust
The Fulmer Charitable Trust
The Gannochy Trust
Ganzoni Charitable Trust
The Gaudio Family Foundation
  (UK) Ltd
Martin Geddes Charitable
  Trust
General Charity (Coventry)
The Generations Foundation
The Tara Getty Foundation
J. Paul Getty Jr General
  Charitable Trust*
The Gibbons Family Trust
The David Gibbons Foundation
The Gibbs Charitable Trusts
The Simon Gibson Charitable
  Trust

The Girdlers' Company
  Charitable Trust
The B. and P. Glasser
  Charitable Trust
The Gloag Foundation
Global Charities
Gloucestershire Community
  Foundation
Sydney and Phyllis Goldberg
  Memorial Charitable Trust
The Golden Bottle Trust
The Goldman Sachs Charitable
  Gift Fund (UK)
Goldman Sachs Gives (UK)
The Goldsmiths' Company
  Charity
The Goodman Foundation
The Gosling Foundation Ltd
The Edward Gostling
  Foundation
Gowling WLG (UK) Charitable
  Trust
The Hemraj Goyal Foundation
Grace Charitable Trust
The Grace Trust
The James Grace Trust
The Graham Trust
Grand Charitable Trust of the
  Order of Women
  Freemasons
The Grand Trust CIO
William Grant Foundation*
The Grantham Yorke Trust
GrantScape
Gordon Gray Trust
The Greater Manchester High
  Sheriff's Police Trust
The Kenneth and Susan Green
  Charitable Foundation
The Green Hall Foundation
The Green Room Charitable
  Trust
Greenham Trust Ltd
The Greenslade Family
  Foundation
The Greggs Foundation
The Grocers' Charity
M. and R. Gross Charities Ltd
The Albert Gubay Charitable
  Foundation
The Walter Guinness
  Charitable Trust
Dr Guthrie's Association
Hackney Parochial Charities
The Hadfield Charitable Trust
The Hadley Trust
The Hadrian Trust
Halifax Foundation for
  Northern Ireland
Paul Hamlyn Foundation
The Helen Hamlyn Trust
Hammersmith United Charities
Hampshire and Isle of Wight
  Community Foundation
The Hampstead Wells and
  Campden Trust

Hampton Fund
The W. A. Handley Charity
  Trust
The Haramead Trust
Harbinson Charitable Trust
Harborne Parish Lands Charity
The Harbour Foundation
William Harding's Charity
The Harpur Trust
The Peter Harrison Foundation
The Harrison-Frank Family
  Foundation (UK) Ltd
The Harry and Mary
  Foundation
Gay and Peter Hartley's
  Hillards Charitable Trust
Edward Harvist Trust (The
  Harvist Estate)
The Hasluck Charitable Trust
The Maurice Hatter Foundation
The Hawthorne Charitable
  Trust
The Charles Hayward
  Foundation
The Headley Trust
Heart of England Community
  Foundation
The Heathcoat Trust
The Heathside Charitable Trust
Heb Ffin (Without Frontier)
The Charlotte Heber-Percy
  Charitable Trust
Ernest Hecht Charitable
  Foundation
The Hedley Foundation
The Hemby Charitable Trust
The Trevor Hemmings
  Foundation
Christina Mary Hendrie Trust
Tim Henman Foundation
The G. D. Herbert Charitable
  Trust
Herefordshire Community
  Foundation
Hertfordshire Community
  Foundation
HFC Help for Children UK Ltd
The Alan Edward Higgs Charity
The Highcroft Charitable Trust
Highway One Trust
The Hilden Charitable Fund
The Hillier Trust
R. G. Hills Charitable Trust
The Lady Hind Trust
The Hinduja Foundation
The Hiscox Foundation
The Henry C. Hoare Charitable
  Trust
The Hobson Charity Ltd
The Jane Hodge Foundation
The Holbeck Charitable Trust
Hollyhock Charitable
  Foundation
The Holywood Trust
Homelands Charitable Trust

Sir Harold Hood's Charitable
Trust
The Hosking Charitable Trust*
The Hospital of God at
Greatham
House of Industry Estate
Housing Pathways Trust
The Reta Lila Howard
Foundation
The Hudson Foundation
The Humanitarian Trust
The Hunter Foundation
Huntingdon Freemen's Trust
Hurdale Charity Ltd
The Hutchinson Charitable
Trust
The Nani Huyu Charitable Trust
Hyde Charitable Trust
Hyde Park Place Estate Charity
IGO Foundation Ltd
The Iliffe Family Charitable
Trust
Imagine Foundation
Impact Funding Partners Ltd
The Inman Charity
Inner London Magistrates
Court Poor Box and Feeder
Charity
Investream Charitable Trust
The Invigorate Charitable Trust
The Ireland Fund of Great
Britain
Irish Youth Foundation (UK)
Ltd (incorporating The
Lawlor Foundation)
The Isla Foundation
The Isle of Anglesey Charitable
Association (Cymdeithas
Elusennol Ynys Môn)
The ITF Seafarers Trust
The J. A. R. Charitable Trust
The J. and J. Benevolent
Foundation
The Jabbs Foundation
John James Bristol Foundation
The Jenour Foundation
Jewish Child's Day
John Lewis and Partners
Foundation
Johnnie Johnson Trust
The Jones 1986 Charitable
Trust
The Muriel Jones Foundation
The Cyril and Eve Jumbo
Charitable Trust
Anton Jurgens Charitable Trust
The Jusaca Charitable Trust
The Karlsson Játiva Charitable
Foundation
The Ian Karten Charitable
Trust
The Kasner Charitable Trust
The Michael and Ilse Katz
Foundation
The Emmanuel Kaye
Foundation

The Kelly Family Charitable
Trust
William Kendall's Charity (Wax
Chandlers Company)
The Kennedy Leigh Charitable
Trust
The Kensington and Chelsea
Foundation
Kent Community Foundation
The Kentown Wizard
Foundation
The Nancy Kenyon Charitable
Trust
The Peter Kershaw Trust
The Ursula Keyes Trust
KFC Foundation
The Kiawah Charitable Trust
The Kingsbury Charity
The Mary Kinross Charitable
Trust
Laura Kinsella Foundation
The Graham Kirkham
Foundation
The Ernest Kleinwort
Charitable Trust
Kollel and Co. Ltd
Kolyom Trust Ltd
KPE4 Charitable Trust
The KPMG Foundation
Kupath Gemach Chaim
Bechesed Viznitz Trust
Ladbrokes Coral Trust
John Laing Charitable Trust
Maurice and Hilda Laing
Charitable Trust
Christopher Laing Foundation
The David Laing Foundation
The Martin Laing Foundation
The Beatrice Laing Trust
The Leonard Laity Stoate
Charitable Trust
The Lake House Charitable
Foundation
Community Foundations for
Lancashire and Merseyside
The Lancashire Foundation
Lancaster Foundation
The Allen Lane Foundation
Langdale Trust
The LankellyChase Foundation
The R. J. Larg Family Trust
Laslett's (Hinton) Charity
Mrs F. B. Laurence Charitable
Trust
The Herd Lawson and Muriel
Lawson Charitable Trust
Lawson Beckman Charitable
Trust
The Lawson Trust CIO
The Leathersellers' Foundation
The William Leech Charity
Leeds Building Society
Foundation
The Leeward Trust
The Leri Charitable Trust

The Ralph Levy Charitable
Company Ltd
Joseph Levy Foundation
Cecil and Hilda Lewis
Charitable Trust
Bernard Lewis Family
Charitable Trust
David and Ruth Lewis Family
Charitable Trust
Liberum Foundation
The Limbourne Trust
The Linbury Trust
Lincolnshire Community
Foundation
The Linder Foundation
The Lister Charitable Trust
The Michael and Betty Little
Trust*
The Charles Littlewood Hill
Trust
The Second Joseph Aaron
Littman Foundation
The George John and Sheilah
Livanos Charitable Trust
Liverpool Charity and Voluntary
Services (LCVS)
The Livingbridge Foundation*
The Ian and Natalie
Livingstone Charitable Trust
The Elaine and Angus Lloyd
Charitable Trust
The W. M. and B. W. Lloyd
Trust
Lloyds Bank Foundation for
England and Wales
Lloyds Bank Foundation for the
Channel Islands
Lloyd's of London Foundation
Lloyd's Patriotic Fund
Localtrent Ltd
The Locker Foundation
London Catalyst
The London Community
Foundation (LCF)
London Freemasons Charity
Lords Group Foundation*
The C. L. Loyd Charitable Trust
LPW Ltd
The Lyndal Tree Foundation
John Lyon's Charity
The Lyons Trust*
Sylvanus Lysons Charity
M. and C. Trust
M. B. Foundation
The M. Y. A. Charitable Trust
The R. S. Macdonald
Charitable Trust
The Mackintosh Foundation
The John MacLeod Charitable
Trust
The Robin MacLeod Charitable
Trust
The MacRobert Trust 2019
The Magdalen and Lasher
Charity (General Fund)
The Magen Charitable Trust

Magnify Foundation*
The Mahoro Charitable Trust
Makers of Playing Cards
   Charity
The Manackerman Charitable
   Trust
Manchester Airport Community
   Trust Fund
The Manchester Guardian
   Society Charitable Trust
The W. M. Mann Foundation
R. W. Mann Trust
The Manoukian Charitable
   Foundation
Marbeh Torah Trust
The Marque Foundation
The Michael Marsh Charitable
   Trust
The Marsh Christian Trust
Charlotte Marshall Charitable
   Trust
The Martin Charitable Trust
Sir George Martin Trust
John Martin's Charity
Masonic Charitable Foundation
Nancie Massey Charitable
   Trust
The Master Charitable Trust
Material World Foundation
Mathew Trust
The Matliwala Family
   Charitable Trust
Mayfair Charities Ltd
Mayheights Ltd
Mazars Charitable Trust
MBNA General Foundation
The Robert McAlpine
   Foundation
The McCarthy Stone
   Foundation
The Medlock Charitable Trust
Melodor Ltd
The Melow Charitable Trust
Mercaz Torah Vechesed Ltd
The Brian Mercer Charitable
   Trust
The Mercers Charitable
   Foundation
Merchant Navy Welfare Board
The Merchant Taylors'
   Foundation*
The Merchant Venturers
   Charity
Merchants House of Glasgow
Merriman Charitable
   Foundation*
The Mickel Fund
The Mickleham Trust
The Gerald Micklem Charitable
   Trust
The Millennium Oak Trust
The Ronald Miller Foundation
The Millfield House Foundation
   (1)
Mills and Reeve Charitable
   Trust

The Millward Charitable Trust
The Milne Family Foundation
Milton Keynes Community
   Foundation Ltd
The Peter Minet Trust
Minton Charitable Trust
The Mishcon Family Charitable
   Trust
The Brian Mitchell Charitable
   Settlement
The Esmé Mitchell Trust
The Mittal Foundation
The Mohn Westlake
   Foundation
The Alexander Moncur Trust
The Monday Charitable Trust
The Monmouthshire County
   Council Welsh Church Act
   Fund
Moondance Foundation
John Moores Foundation
The Morel Charitable Trust
The Morgan Charitable
   Foundation
The Steve Morgan Foundation
The Morris Charitable Trust
G. M. Morrison Charitable
   Trust
The Morrisons Foundation
The Mosawi Foundation
Vyoel Moshe Charitable Trust
The Mosselson Charitable
   Trust
Motability
The Moulding Foundation
The Mulberry Trust
The Frederick Mulder
   Foundation
Edith Murphy Foundation
Murphy-Neumann Charity
   Company Ltd
The John R. Murray Charitable
   Trust
Brian Murtagh Charitable Trust
Music Sales Charitable Trust
The Mutley Foundation
The Mutual Trust Group
MW (CL) Foundation
MW (GK) Foundation
MW (HO) Foundation
MW (RH) Foundation
The National Express
   Foundation
The National Lottery
   Community Fund
The Nationwide Foundation
Nemoral Ltd
Ner Foundation
Nesta
Network for Social Change
   Charitable Trust
Newby Trust Ltd
The Frances and Augustus
   Newman Foundation
Newpier Charity Ltd

The NFU Mutual Charitable
   Trust
The Nine Incorporated Trades
   of Dundee General Fund
   Charity
The Nineveh Charitable Trust
Norfolk Community Foundation
The Norman Family Charitable
   Trust
Normanby Charitable Trust
North Berwick Trust
Northamptonshire Community
   Foundation
Community Foundation for
   Northern Ireland
The Northwick Trust
Northwood Charitable Trust
The Norton Foundation
The Norton Rose Fulbright
   Charitable Foundation
Norwich Consolidated
   Charities
Nottinghamshire Community
   Foundation
The Nuffield Foundation
The Oakdale Trust
The Oakley Charitable Trust
Odin Charitable Trust
The Ofenheim Charitable Trust
Henry Oldfield Trust
One Community Foundation
   Ltd
Open House Trust Ltd
The Sir Peter O'Sullevan
   Charitable Trust
The O'Sullivan Family
   Charitable Trust
Otsar Trust
The Owen Family Trust
Oxfordshire Community
   Foundation
The Paget Charitable Trust
The Gerald Palmer Eling Trust
   Company
The Panacea Charitable Trust
The Paragon Trust
The Pargiter Trust
The Parivar Trust
Miss M. E. S. Paterson's
   Charitable Trust
The Patrick Trust
Payne-Gallwey 1989 Charitable
   Trust
Peacock Charitable Trust
David Pearlman Charitable
   Foundation
The Pears Family Charitable
   Foundation
The Pebbles Trust
The Dowager Countess
   Eleanor Peel Trust
The Penchant Foundation
People's Health Trust
People's Postcode Trust
The Persimmon Charitable
   Foundation

Personal Assurance Charitable
    Trust
The Pharsalia Charitable Trust
The Phillips and Rubens
    Charitable Trust
The Phillips Family Charitable
    Trust
The Philip and Connie Phillips
    Foundation*
The Pickwell Foundation
The Bernard Piggott Charitable
    Trust
The Pilgrim Trust
Cecil Pilkington Charitable
    Trust
Elise Pilkington Charitable
    Trust
Pilkington Charities Fund
The Sir Harry Pilkington Fund
PIMCO Foundation Europe
Charles Plater Trust*
The Players Foundation
The George and Esme Pollitzer
    Charitable Settlement
The Porta Pia 2012
    Foundation
Porter Foundation
The Portishead Nautical Trust
The Portrack Charitable Trust
Postcode Community Trust
Postcode Local Trust
Postcode Society Trust
The Potton Consolidated
    Charity
Premierquote Ltd
The Pret Foundation
Sir John Priestman Charity
    Trust
The Prince of Wales's
    Charitable Foundation
The Princess Anne's Charities
Provincial Grand Charity of the
    Province of Derbyshire
The Puebla Charitable Trust
The Purey Cust Trust CIO
The Pye Foundation
Mr and Mrs J. A. Pye's
    Charitable Settlement
QBE European Operations
    Foundation
Quartet Community Foundation
The Queen Anne's Gate
    Foundation
Quintessentially Foundation
Quothquan Trust
R. S. Charitable Trust
Rachel Charitable Trust
The Racing Foundation
The Raindance Charitable
    Trust
The Rainford Trust
The Randal Charitable
    Foundation
The Joseph and Lena Randall
    Charitable Trust
The Rank Foundation Ltd

The Ranworth Trust
The Eleanor Rathbone
    Charitable Trust
Elizabeth Rathbone Charity
The Julia and Hans Rausing
    Trust*
The Ravensdale Trust
The Sir James Reckitt Charity
C. A. Redfern Charitable
    Foundation
The Max Reinhardt Charitable
    Trust
Rentrust Foundation Ltd
The Revere Charitable Trust
The Rhododendron Trust
Daisie Rich Trust
The Sir Cliff Richard Charitable
    Trust
Richmond Parish Lands Charity
Ridgesave Ltd
Rigby Foundation
The River Farm Foundation
The River Trust
Rivers Foundation
Riverside Charitable Trust Ltd
The Roan Charitable Trust
The Robertson Trust
Rockcliffe Charitable Trust
The Roddick Foundation
The Gerald and Gail Ronson
    Family Foundation
Mrs L. D. Rope's Third
    Charitable Settlement
Rosca Trust
The Roseline Foundation*
The Cecil Rosen Foundation
Rothesay Foundation*
The Rothschild Foundation
The Eranda Rothschild
    Foundation
The Roughley Charitable Trust
The Row Fogo Charitable Trust
The Rowlands Trust
The Joseph Rowntree
    Foundation
Royal Artillery Charitable Fund
Royal Docks Trust (London)
The Royal Foundation of The
    Prince and Princess of
    Wales
Royal Masonic Trust for Girls
    and Boys
The Royal Navy and Royal
    Marines Charity
RSM UK Foundation
The Rugby Group Benevolent
    Fund Ltd
Russell Trust
The RWS Foundation
The Ryvoan Trust*
S. and R. Charitable Trust
The S. M. B. Trust
The Michael and Nicola Sacher
    Charitable Trust
The Sackler Trust

The Saddlers' Company
    Charitable Fund
Erach and Roshan Sadri
    Foundation
The Saintbury Trust
The Salamander Charitable
    Trust
Samjo Ltd
The Basil Samuel Charitable
    Trust
The M. J. Samuel Charitable
    Trust
The Peter Samuel Charitable
    Trust
Sandra Charitable Trust
The Schreib Trust
Schreiber Charitable Trust
O. and G. Schreiber Charitable
    Trust
Schroder Charity Trust
The Schroder Foundation
The Scorpion Charitable Trust*
Foundation Scotland
The Scotshill Trust
The Scott Bader
    Commonwealth Ltd
Francis C. Scott Charitable
    Trust
The Frieda Scott Charitable
    Trust
The Ina Scott Sutherland
    Charitable Foundation
The John Scott Trust Fund
Scottish Coal Industry Special
    Welfare Fund
Scottish Property Industry
    Festival of Christmas
    (SPIFOX)
ScottishPower Foundation
Scouloudi Foundation
Seafarers UK (King George's
    Fund for Sailors)
The Searchlight Electric
    Charitable Trust
The Sam and Bella Sebba
    Charitable Foundation
Seedfield Trust
The Segelman Trust
Sellata Ltd
The Serco Foundation
SF Foundation
The Shanley Charitable Trust
The Shanly Foundation
The Shears Foundation
The Sheldon Trust
The Sylvia and Colin Shepherd
    Charitable Trust
The Archie Sherman Charitable
    Trust
The Bassil Shippam and
    Alsford Trust
Shlomo Memorial Fund Ltd
The Shoe Zone Trust
The Simmons & Simmons
    Charitable Foundation
The Skelton Bounty

The Charles Skey Charitable
Trust
Skipton Building Society
Charitable Foundation
The John Slater Foundation
Kathleen Beryl Sleigh
Charitable Trust
Rita and David Slowe
Charitable Trust
Smallwood Trust
The Mrs Smith and Mount
Trust
The N. Smith Charitable
Settlement
The Henry Smith Charity
Arabella and Julian Smith
Family Trust
The Leslie Smith Foundation
The Martin Smith Foundation
Philip Smith's Charitable Trust
The R. C. Snelling Charitable
Trust
Sodexo Stop Hunger
Foundation
Somerset Community
Foundation
Songdale Ltd
The E. C. Sosnow Charitable
Trust
Souter Charitable Trust
South Yorkshire Community
Foundation
W. F. Southall Trust
Sparquote Ltd
The SpeedoMick Foundation
Michael and Sarah Spencer
Foundation
Spielman Charitable Trust
Spurrell Charitable Trust
The Geoff and Fiona Squire
Foundation
The Squire Patton Boggs
Charitable Trust
The Squires Foundation
The St Hilda's Trust
St James's Place Charitable
Foundation
St John's Foundation Est.
1174
The St Lazarus Charitable
Trust*
St Monica Trust
The Stafford Trust
The Community Foundation for
Staffordshire
Stanley Foundation Ltd
Starlow Charities Ltd
The Peter Stebbings Memorial
Charity
The Steel Charitable Trust
The Steinberg Family
Charitable Trust
The Hugh Stenhouse
Foundation
Stervon Ltd
Sir Halley Stewart Trust

The Stewarts Law Foundation
Stolkin Foundation
The Stone Family Foundation
Strand Parishes Trust
Stratford-upon-Avon Town Trust
The W. O. Street Charitable
Foundation
The Street Foundation
Streetsmart – Action for the
Homeless
Suffolk Community Foundation
The Summerfield Charitable
Trust
The Bernard Sunley
Foundation
The Sunrise Foundation CIO
Community Foundation for
Surrey
Sabina Sutherland Charitable
Trust
Sutton Coldfield Charitable
Trust
The Swann-Morton Foundation
The John Swire (1989)
Charitable Trust
The Swire Charitable Trust
The Charles and Elsie Sykes
Trust
The Hugh Symons Charitable
Trust
The T.K. Maxx and
Homesense Foundation
The Tabhair Charitable Trust
The Tajtelbaum Charitable
Trust
The Talbot Trusts
The Talbot Village Trust
Tallow Chandlers Benevolent
Fund No 2
Talteg Ltd
The Tanlaw Foundation
The David Tannen Charitable
Trust
Tanner Trust
The Taurus Foundation
Tay Charitable Trust
C. B. and H. H. T. Taylor 1984
Trust
The Taylor Family Foundation
Tegham Ltd
the7stars Foundation
Scott Thomson Charitable
Trust
The Sue Thomson Foundation
Sir Jules Thorn Charitable
Trust
The Three Oaks Trust
Mrs R. P. Tindall's Charitable
Trust
The Tomoro Foundation
The Tompkins Foundation
The Tory Family Foundation
Tower Hill Trust
The Toy Trust
Toyota Manufacturing UK
Charitable Trust

The Trades House of Glasgow
Annie Tranmer Charitable Trust
The Constance Travis
Charitable Trust
The Trelix Charitable Trust*
The Troutsdale Charitable
Trust
Truedene Co. Ltd
The Truemark Trust
Trumros Ltd
Trust for London
The Trusthouse Charitable
Foundation
The Trysil Charitable Trust
The Tudor Trust
The Tudwick Foundation
The Tuixen Foundation
The Roger and Douglas Turner
Charitable Trust
The Turtleton Charitable Trust
The Tweed Family Charitable
Foundation
Two Magpies Fund
Tzedakah
UBS Optimus Foundation UK
UJIA (United Jewish Israel
Appeal)
Ulster Garden Villages Ltd
The Underwood Trust
The Union of the Sisters of
Mercy of Great Britain
United St Saviour's Charity
United Utilities Trust Fund
The Valentine Charitable Trust
The Albert Van Den Bergh
Charitable Trust
The Van Mesdag Fund
The Van Neste Foundation
The Vandervell Foundation
The Vardy Foundation
The Velvet Foundation
The William and Patricia
Venton Charitable Trust
The Veterans' Foundation
VHLT Ltd
VINCI UK Foundation
The Vintners' Foundation
Virgin Atlantic Foundation
The Virgin Foundation (Virgin
Unite)
The Virgin Money Foundation
The Vodafone Foundation
Volant Charitable Trust
The Georg and Emily von Opel
Foundation
The Scurrah Wainwright Charity
Wakefield and Tetley Trust
The Walcot Foundation
The Walker Trust
Walton-on-Thames Charity
The Barbara Ward Children's
Foundation
Warwick Relief-in-Need Charity
The Warwickshire Masonic
Charitable Association Ltd

The Watches of Switzerland
Group Foundation
Mrs Waterhouse Charitable
Trust
The Waterloo Foundation
Wates Family Enterprise Trust
The Wates Foundation
The William Wates Memorial
Trust
The Geoffrey Watling Charity
We Love MCR Charity
The Weinstock Fund
The Welland Trust
Wellbank Foundation*
The Welsh Church Act Fund
West Derby Waste Lands
Charity
Westhill Endowment
Westminster Almshouses
Foundation
Westminster Foundation
The Garfield Weston
Foundation
Westway Trust
The Melanie White Foundation
Ltd
The Norman Whiteley Trust
Wickens Family Foundation
The Felicity Wilde Charitable
Trust
The Williams Family
Foundation
The Wilmcote Charitrust
J. and J. R. Wilson Trust
Wiltshire Community
Foundation
The Wimbledon Foundation
The Windfall Foundation
The Benjamin Winegarten
Charitable Trust
W. Wing Yip and Brothers
Foundation
The Francis Winham
Foundation
The Michael and Anna Wix
Charitable Trust
The Wixamtree Trust
The Maurice Wohl Charitable
Foundation
The Charles Wolfson
Charitable Trust
Women's Fund for Scotland
The James Wood Bequest
Fund
The Wood Foundation
Wooden Spoon Society
Woodlands Green Ltd
Woodroffe Benton Foundation
Woodsmith Foundation Ltd
The Woodstock Family
Charitable Foundation
The Woodward Charitable
Trust
The Worshipful Company of
Glovers of London
Charitable Trust

Worshipful Company of Gold
and Silver Wyre Drawers
Second Charitable Trust
Fund
Worshipful Company of
Needlemakers Charitable
Fund
The Eric Wright Charitable
Trust
Wychville Ltd
The Wyfold Charitable Trust
Sir Graham Wylie Foundation
The Wyseliot Rose Charitable
Trust
The Yapp Charitable Trust
Yorkshire Building Society
Charitable Foundation
The Elizabeth and Prince
Zaiger Trust
Zephyr Charitable Trust
The Marjorie and Arnold Ziff
Charitable Foundation
The Zochonis Charitable Trust
Zurich Community Trust (UK)
Ltd

Sports and recreation

The 29th May 1961 Charitable
Trust
The Aberdeenshire Educational
Trust Scheme
Adam Family Foundation
The Bryan Adams Foundation
Alan Boswell Group Charitable
Trust
Alpkit Foundation
The Ammco Trust
Armed Forces Covenant Fund
Trust
The Arsenal Foundation
The Astor Foundation
The Barnes Fund
Robert Barr's Charitable Trust
Bauer Radio's Cash for Kids
Charities
The James Beattie Charitable
Trust
Beccles Townlands Charity
Bideford Bridge Trust
Biffa Award
The Isabel Blackman
Foundation
Blakemore Foundation
Bluespark Foundation
BOOST Charitable Trust
The Booth Charities
The Bowland Charitable Trust
The Brelms Trust CIO
British Motor Sports Training
Trust
The Jack Brunton Charitable
Trust
Consolidated Charity of Burton
upon Trent
Camden Giving
The Carnegie Dunfermline
Trust
The Chartley Foundation
The Childhood Trust
Chippenham Borough Lands
Charity
Church Burgesses Trust
The Robert Clutterbuck
Charitable Trust
The Vivienne and Samuel
Cohen Charitable Trust
Community First
Michael Cornish Charitable
Trust
County Durham Community
Foundation
Cruden Foundation Ltd
Cumbria Community
Foundation
The Roger De Haan Charitable
Trust
Foundation Derbyshire
The James and Deirdre Dyson
Trust
The Earley Charity

Edinburgh Children's Holiday Fund

The Vernon N. Ely Charitable Trust

England and Wales Cricket Trust

The Englefield Charitable Trust

The Enkalon Foundation

The Essex and Southend Sports Trust

The Essex Youth Trust

The Lord Faringdon Charitable Trust

Dixie Rose Findlay Charitable Trust

The Football Association National Sports Centre

The Football Foundation

The Foxglove Trust

The Joseph Strong Frazer Trust

Charles S. French Charitable Trust

The Freshgate Trust Foundation

Gatwick Airport Community Trust

The Granada Foundation

The Grange Farm Centre Trust

The Grantham Yorke Trust

GrantScape

The J. G. Graves Charitable Trust

Greenham Trust Ltd

The Greenslade Family Foundation

The Albert Gubay Charitable Foundation

Dr Guthrie's Association

The Hadrian Trust

The Hamilton Davies Trust

Hampshire and Isle of Wight Community Foundation

The Lennox Hannay Charitable Trust

The Hargreaves Foundation

The Harpur Trust

The Peter Harrison Foundation

Edward Harvist Trust (The Harvist Estate)

The Dorothy Hay-Bolton Charitable Trust

The Hedley Foundation

Henley Educational Trust

Henley Royal Regatta Charitable Trust

Tim Henman Foundation

The Holbeck Charitable Trust

The Holywood Trust

Huntingdon Freemen's Trust

The Isle of Anglesey Charitable Association (Cymdeithas Elusennol Ynys Môn)

John Lewis and Partners Foundation

Johnnie Johnson Trust

The Ursula Keyes Trust

Fraser Kilpatrick Charitable Trust

Sir James Knott Trust

The Kyte Charitable Trust

The Leathersellers' Foundation

The Leeward Trust

The Michael and Betty Little Trust*

The Charles Littlewood Hill Trust

The George John and Sheilah Livanos Charitable Trust

The London Marathon Charitable Trust Ltd

The Lord's Taverners

Making a Difference Locally Ltd

The Martin Charitable Trust

Sir George Martin Trust

The Dan Maskell Tennis Trust

The Master Charitable Trust

Matchroom Sport Charitable Foundation

MBNA General Foundation

The Mickel Fund

Millennium Stadium Charitable Trust (Ymddiriedolaeth Elusennol Stadiwm y Mileniwm)

The James Milner Foundation

Minton Charitable Trust

The Mohn Westlake Foundation

The John R. Murray Charitable Trust

The National Express Foundation

The Norman Family Charitable Trust

North Berwick Trust

Northamptonshire Community Foundation

Norwich Town Close Estate Charity

One Community Foundation Ltd

Oxfordshire Community Foundation

Miss M. E. S. Paterson's Charitable Trust

Payne-Gallwey 1989 Charitable Trust

People's Postcode Trust

The Persimmon Charitable Foundation

The Players Foundation

The Porta Pia 2012 Foundation

Postcode Community Trust

Postcode Local Trust

Postcode Society Trust

Poundland Foundation

The Priory Foundation

The Racing Foundation

Randeree Charitable Trust

The Ratcliff Foundation

Riada Trust

Richmond Parish Lands Charity

The Ross Foundation

The Rothermere Foundation

Royal Docks Trust (London)

The Rugby Group Benevolent Fund Ltd

Russell Trust

The Saddlers' Company Charitable Fund

The Saintbury Trust

The Frieda Scott Charitable Trust

Scottish Coal Industry Special Welfare Fund

The Sheffield Town Trust

The Sherling Charitable Trust

The Shipwrights Charitable Fund

The Charles Skey Charitable Trust

The Martin Smith Foundation

The Squire Patton Boggs Charitable Trust

St Olave's and St Saviour's Schools Foundation CIO*

Stadium Charitable Trust

The Community Foundation for Staffordshire

The Sterry Family Foundation

Peter Stormonth Darling Charitable Trust

Stratford-upon-Avon Town Trust

The Summerfield Charitable Trust

Sutton Coldfield Charitable Trust

Tay Charitable Trust

The Tompkins Foundation

The Tottenham Grammar School Foundation

Tower Hill Trust

The Toy Trust

The Constance Travis Charitable Trust

The Troutsdale Charitable Trust

The Trusthouse Charitable Foundation

The Albert Van Den Bergh Charitable Trust

The Georg and Emily von Opel Foundation

Wade's Charity

The Bruce Wake Charity

The Barbara Ward Children's Foundation

The William Wates Memorial Trust

The Geoffrey Watling Charity

The Weir Charitable Trust

Wellbank Foundation*

The Welsh Church Act Fund

Wembley National Stadium Trust

Westway Trust

The Wimbledon Foundation
The Wixamtree Trust
Wooden Spoon Society
Woodsmith Foundation Ltd
WPG Charitable Trust*
Sir Graham Wylie Foundation

Recreational activities and clubs

The 29th May 1961 Charitable
   Trust
The Aberdeenshire Educational
   Trust Scheme
The Ammco Trust
The Astor Foundation
Barnwood Trust
Robert Barr's Charitable Trust
The James Beattie Charitable
   Trust
Bideford Bridge Trust
The Jack Brunton Charitable
   Trust
Carew Pole Charitable Trust
The Childhood Trust
The Peter Cruddas Foundation
The J. N. Derbyshire Trust
Edinburgh Children's Holiday
   Fund
The Essex Youth Trust
The Thomas Farr Charity
Dixie Rose Findlay Charitable
   Trust
The Freshgate Trust
   Foundation
The Grange Farm Centre Trust
The Grantham Yorke Trust
The Peter Harrison Foundation
The Holbeck Charitable Trust
The Holywood Trust
Sir Harold Hood's Charitable
   Trust
The Jewish Youth Fund
Kelsick's Educational
   Foundation
KFC Foundation
The Leeward Trust
The Charles Littlewood Hill
   Trust
The Lord's Taverners
R. W. Mann Trust
Matchroom Sport Charitable
   Foundation
The Millennium Oak Trust
The Monmouthshire County
   Council Welsh Church Act
   Fund
One Community Foundation
   Ltd
The Jack Petchey Foundation
Postcode Community Trust
Postcode Local Trust
Postcode Society Trust
The Ratcliff Foundation

Daisie Rich Trust
The Roughley Charitable Trust
The Rugby Group Benevolent
   Fund Ltd
Scottish Coal Industry Special
   Welfare Fund
The Shanly Foundation
The Sheldon Trust
The Shipwrights Charitable
   Fund
The Skelton Bounty
The R. C. Snelling Charitable
   Trust
St Olave's and St Saviour's
   Schools Foundation CIO*
Humphrey Richardson Taylor
   Charitable Trust
Stephen Taylor Foundation
The UK Youth Fund: Thriving
   Minds*
Variety, the Children's Charity
The Barbara Ward Children's
   Foundation
The Weir Charitable Trust
The Welsh Church Act Fund
The Wimbledon Foundation
Wooden Spoon Society
The Woodward Charitable
   Trust

Sports

The Gordon and Ena Baxter
   Foundation*
The Benham Charitable
   Settlement
The Britford Bridge Trust
British Motor Sports Training
   Trust
The Chetwode Foundation
The Childhood Trust
The Clover Trust
The Vernon N. Ely Charitable
   Trust
England and Wales Cricket
   Trust
The Essex Youth Trust
The Thomas Farr Charity
The Football Association
   National Sports Centre
The Football Foundation
The Fort Foundation
The Freshgate Trust
   Foundation
The Great Britain Sasakawa
   Foundation
Henley Educational Trust
Henley Royal Regatta
   Charitable Trust
The Keith Howard Foundation
The Kyte Charitable Trust
The London Marathon
   Charitable Trust Ltd
The Lord's Taverners
Matchroom Sport Charitable
   Foundation

Mazars Charitable Trust
Minton Charitable Trust
The National Hockey
   Foundation
One Community Foundation
   Ltd
P. F. Charitable Trust
The Players Foundation
The Racing Foundation
Randeree Charitable Trust
The Ratcliff Foundation
The Sheffield Town Trust
Peter Stormonth Darling
   Charitable Trust
The Constance Travis
   Charitable Trust
The Welsh Church Act Fund
Colonel W. H. Whitbread
   Charitable Trust
Wooden Spoon Society

Specific sports

British Motor Sports Training
   Trust
The Childwick Trust
The Vernon N. Ely Charitable
   Trust
England and Wales Cricket
   Trust
The Football Association
   National Sports Centre
The Football Foundation
The Golf Foundation
Henley Royal Regatta
   Charitable Trust
The Keith Howard Foundation
Johnnie Johnson Trust
The Boris Karloff Charitable
   Foundation
The Lord's Taverners
The Dan Maskell Tennis Trust
The Sir Peter O'Sullevan
   Charitable Trust
Payne-Gallwey 1989 Charitable
   Trust
The Players Foundation
The Racing Foundation
Riada Trust
The Saddlers' Company
   Charitable Fund
The Shipwrights Charitable
   Fund
The Tennis Foundation
The Wimbledon Foundation
Wooden Spoon Society

Work outside the UK

The A. S. Charitable Trust
The Bryan Adams Foundation
Al Madad Foundation*
The Alborada Trust
The Allen & Overy Foundation
Andrew Anderson Trust
Arcadia Fund
The Archer Trust
Armed Forces Covenant Fund Trust
The Artemis Charitable Foundation
The Asfari Foundation
The Ashworth Charitable Trust
The Austin Bailey Foundation
The Baring Foundation
The Bestway Foundation
Lady Blakenham's Charity Trust
The Boltini Trust
The Rory and Elizabeth Brooks Foundation
The Brown Source Trust
Buckingham Trust
The Noel Buxton Trust
The G. W. Cadbury Charitable Trust
William A. Cadbury Charitable Trust
The Calleva Foundation
The Thomas Sivewright Catto Charitable Settlement
The André Christian Trust
The Clothworkers' Foundation
The R. and S. Cohen Foundation
The Coles-Medlock Foundation
Comic Relief
The Alice Ellen Cooper-Dean Charitable Foundation
Corra Foundation
Credit Suisse EMEA Foundation
The D. G. Charitable Settlement
The Dashlight Foundation
The Miriam Dean Refugee Trust Fund
The Delves Charitable Trust
Donibristle Trust
Dromintee Trust
The Dulverton Trust
EA Foundation*
The Englefield Charitable Trust
Euro Quality Foundation
Allan and Nesta Ferguson Charitable Settlement
The Fieldrose Charitable Trust
The Follett Trust
Forest Hill Charitable Trust
The Foxglove Trust
The Freshfield Foundation
The Fulmer Charitable Trust

The Gatsby Charitable Foundation
The Generations Foundation
The Gibbs Charitable Trusts
The Gloag Foundation
Sydney and Phyllis Goldberg Memorial Charitable Trust
The Golden Bottle Trust
The Goldman Sachs Charitable Gift Fund (UK)
The Goodman Foundation
The Hemraj Goyal Foundation
The Grace Trust
The Great Britain Sasakawa Foundation
The Green Hall Foundation
The Green Room Charitable Trust
The Grimmitt Trust
The Hadley Trust
The Helen Hamlyn Trust
Harbinson Charitable Trust
The Peter and Teresa Harris Charitable Trust
The Hasluck Charitable Trust
The Charles Hayward Foundation
The Headley Trust
The Charlotte Heber-Percy Charitable Trust
The Jane Hodge Foundation
Sir Harold Hood's Charitable Trust
The Hunting Horn General Charitable Trust
The Innocent Foundation
The Inverforth Charitable Trust
The Invigorate Charitable Trust
The J. J. Charitable Trust
The Frank Jackson Foundation
The Jephcott Charitable Trust
The Jerusalem Trust
The Elton John AIDS Foundation
John Lewis and Partners Foundation
The Cyril and Eve Jumbo Charitable Trust
The Nancy Kenyon Charitable Trust
The Kiawah Charitable Trust
The Kyte Charitable Trust
Maurice and Hilda Laing Charitable Trust
The Kirby Laing Foundation
The Martin Laing Foundation
The Beatrice Laing Trust
The Lancashire Foundation
Langdale Trust
The Leach Fourteenth Trust
The William Leech Charity
The Linbury Trust
The Michael and Betty Little Trust*
Lloyd's of London Foundation
The Mageni Trust

The Manson Family Charitable Trust
Marmot Charitable Trust
Gemma and Chris McGough Charitable Foundation CIO
The Brian Mercer Charitable Trust
Merriman Charitable Foundation*
T. and J. Meyer Family Foundation Ltd
The Mikheev Charitable Trust
The Millennium Oak Trust
The Millichope Foundation
The Morel Charitable Trust
The Morgan Charitable Foundation
The Alexander Mosley Charitable Trust
The Edwina Mountbatten and Leonora Children's Foundation
Music Sales Charitable Trust
The NDL Foundation
Network for Social Change Charitable Trust
The Northwick Trust
The Norton Rose Fulbright Charitable Foundation
The Olwyn Foundation
Open House Trust Ltd
Susanna Peake Charitable Trust
The Pears Family Charitable Foundation
The Pharsalia Charitable Trust
The Portrack Charitable Trust
David and Elaine Potter Foundation
The Priory Foundation
The Puebla Charitable Trust
The Quilter Foundation
The Raindance Charitable Trust
The Rainford Trust
The Rambourg Foundation
The Randal Charitable Foundation
The Joseph and Lena Randall Charitable Trust
Randeree Charitable Trust
The Ranworth Trust
The Eleanor Rathbone Charitable Trust
The Rhododendron Trust
Riada Trust
The Roddick Foundation
Mrs L. D. Rope's Third Charitable Settlement
The RWS Foundation
The S. M. B. Trust
The M. J. Samuel Charitable Trust
The Sandhu Charitable Foundation
The Schroder Foundation

Seedfield Trust
The Archie Sherman Charitable
   Trust
Rita and David Slowe
   Charitable Trust
The N. Smith Charitable
   Settlement
Souter Charitable Trust
W. F. Southall Trust
Spears-Stutz Charitable Trust
The Squire Patton Boggs
   Charitable Trust
The Stafford Trust
Stewards Company Ltd
The Stone Family Foundation
The Sunrise Foundation CIO
Sabina Sutherland Charitable
   Trust
The Hugh Symons Charitable
   Trust
The Tanlaw Foundation
Tanner Trust
C. B. and H. H. T. Taylor 1984
   Trust
The Tolkien Trust
The Toy Trust
The James Tudor Foundation
The Ulverscroft Foundation
The Albert Van Den Bergh
   Charitable Trust
The Van Neste Foundation
The Vodafone Foundation
The Waterloo Foundation
G. R. Waters Charitable Trust
   2000
The Norman Whiteley Trust
The Wimbledon Foundation
The Windfall Foundation
The Wood Foundation
The Zochonis Charitable Trust
Zurich Community Trust (UK)
   Ltd

Conflict resolution, peace-building and disarmament

The A. S. Charitable Trust
William A. Cadbury Charitable
   Trust
The Dulverton Trust
Allan and Nesta Ferguson
   Charitable Settlement
The Follett Trust
The Golden Bottle Trust
Marmot Charitable Trust
Network for Social Change
   Charitable Trust
The Northwick Trust
Randeree Charitable Trust
W. F. Southall Trust
The Tolkien Trust

Education

The Bestway Foundation
The Coles-Medlock Foundation
The Dashlight Foundation
EA Foundation*
Allan and Nesta Ferguson
   Charitable Settlement
The Follett Trust
The Gloag Foundation
The Grace Trust
The Green Room Charitable
   Trust
The Headley Trust
Sir Harold Hood's Charitable
   Trust
The Frank Jackson Foundation
The Jephcott Charitable Trust
John Lewis and Partners
   Foundation
The Kiawah Charitable Trust
Merriman Charitable
   Foundation*
The Northwick Trust
David and Elaine Potter
   Foundation
The Rainford Trust
Riada Trust
C. B. and H. H. T. Taylor 1984
   Trust
The Vodafone Foundation

Emergency appeals/aid

The Alborada Trust
The Allen & Overy Foundation
The Bestway Foundation
The Boltini Trust
CHK Foundation
Christadelphian Samaritan
   Fund
The Clarkson Foundation
Denise Coates Foundation
The Alan and Sheila Diamond
   Charitable Trust
Forest Hill Charitable Trust
The Forrester Family Trust
The Anna Rosa Forster
   Charitable Trust
The B. and P. Glasser
   Charitable Trust
Sydney and Phyllis Goldberg
   Memorial Charitable Trust
The Grace Trust
Harbinson Charitable Trust
The Hasluck Charitable Trust
The Leeward Trust
The Linbury Trust
Lloyd's of London Foundation
Masonic Charitable Foundation
The Millichope Foundation
G. M. Morrison Charitable
   Trust
The Northwick Trust

The Norton Rose Fulbright
   Charitable Foundation
The Privy Purse Charitable
   Trust
The Quilter Foundation
Randeree Charitable Trust
Seedfield Trust
The Tanlaw Foundation
The Toy Trust
The Utley Foundation

Humanitarian aid

The A. and J. Charitable Trust
The Alborada Trust
Andrew Anderson Trust
Ove Arup Partnership
   Charitable Trust
The Asfari Foundation
The Ashworth Charitable Trust
The Bestway Foundation
The Brown Source Trust
CHK Foundation
Christadelphian Samaritan
   Fund
The Coles-Medlock Foundation
The Alan and Sheila Diamond
   Charitable Trust
Donibristle Trust
The Dulverton Trust
EA Foundation*
The Fieldrose Charitable Trust
The Forrester Family Trust
The Anna Rosa Forster
   Charitable Trust
Four Acre Trust
The Foxglove Trust
The Fulmer Charitable Trust
The B. and P. Glasser
   Charitable Trust
The Goldman Sachs Charitable
   Gift Fund (UK)
The Goodman Foundation
The Grace Trust
The Green Room Charitable
   Trust
The Helen Hamlyn Trust
Harbinson Charitable Trust
The Peter and Teresa Harris
   Charitable Trust
The Michael Heller Charitable
   Foundation
Sir Harold Hood's Charitable
   Trust
The Hunting Horn General
   Charitable Trust
The Innocent Foundation
The Ithaca Trust
The Kyte Charitable Trust
The Linbury Trust
The Michael and Betty Little
   Trust*
Lloyd's of London Foundation
The Lyndal Tree Foundation
Sir Jack Lyons Charitable Trust
The Mageni Trust

Masonic Charitable Foundation
Gemma and Chris McGough
  Charitable Foundation CIO
Merriman Charitable
  Foundation*
The Mikheev Charitable Trust
The Millichope Foundation
The Morel Charitable Trust
G. M. Morrison Charitable
  Trust
Music Sales Charitable Trust
The Northwick Trust
The Norton Rose Fulbright
  Charitable Foundation
Open House Trust Ltd
The Paragon Trust
The Pharsalia Charitable Trust
PIMCO Foundation Europe
The Portrack Charitable Trust
The Privy Purse Charitable
  Trust
Randeree Charitable Trust
The Eleanor Rathbone
  Charitable Trust
The Rhododendron Trust
The Roddick Foundation
Mrs L. D. Rope's Third
  Charitable Settlement
The Rothley Trust
The S. M. B. Trust
The Salamander Charitable
  Trust
The John Scott Trust Fund
Seedfield Trust
The Archie Sherman Charitable
  Trust
The N. Smith Charitable
  Settlement
The Stevenson Family's
  Charitable Trust
The Tanlaw Foundation
Tanner Trust
The Tolkien Trust
The Utley Foundation
The Norman Whiteley Trust

Water, sanitation and hygiene (WASH)

EA Foundation*
The Charles Hayward
  Foundation
The Headley Trust
The Jephcott Charitable Trust
Open House Trust Ltd
The Eleanor Rathbone
  Charitable Trust
Seedfield Trust
The Stone Family Foundation
The Waterloo Foundation

Age

Children and young people

The 4814 Trust
The A. and J. Charitable Trust
The Aberbrothock Skea Trust
The Aberdeenshire Educational
  Trust Scheme
abrdn Charitable Foundation
Action Medical Research
Adam Family Foundation
The Bryan Adams Foundation
The Adint Charitable Trust
The AIM Foundation
The Aimwell Charitable Trust
Sylvia Aitken's Charitable Trust
AJ Bell Trust
Al Madad Foundation*
Alan Boswell Group Charitable
  Trust
The Alchemy Foundation
Al-Fayed Charitable Foundation
The Derrill Allatt Foundation
D. C. R. Allen Charitable Trust
Ambergate Charitable Trust
Viscount Amory's Charitable
  Trust
Anguish's Educational
  Foundation
AO Smile Foundation
The John Apthorp Charity
The Archer Trust
The Ardwick Trust
Armed Forces Covenant Fund
  Trust
Armed Forces Education Trust
The John Armitage Charitable
  Trust
The Armourers and Brasiers
  Gauntlet Trust
Arts Council of Wales (also
  known as Cyngor
  Celfyddydau Cymru)
ArtSocial Foundation
Ove Arup Partnership
  Charitable Trust
The Asda Foundation
The Asfari Foundation
The Ashendene Trust
The Astor Foundation
Lawrence Atwell's Charity
  (Skinners' Company)
The Lord Austin Trust
The Aziz Foundation
Backstage Trust
The Austin Bailey Foundation
Bairdwatson Charitable Trust
The Roy and Pixie Baker
  Charitable Trust
The Ballinger Charitable Trust
The Band Trust
Veronica and Lars Bane
  Foundation
Bank of Scotland Foundation

The Barbour Foundation
Barcapel Foundation Ltd
Philip Barker Charity
Lord Barnby's Foundation
The Barnes Fund
Barnsbury Charitable Trust
Barnwood Trust
Misses Barrie Charitable Trust
The Batchworth Trust
Bauer Radio's Cash for Kids
  Charities
The Gordon and Ena Baxter
  Foundation*
Bay Charitable Trust
BBC Children in Need
The James Beattie Charitable
  Trust
The Beaverbrooks Charitable
  Trust
Bedfordshire Charitable Trust
  Ltd
The Benham Charitable
  Settlement
The Rowan Bentall Charitable
  Trust
The Berkeley Foundation
Ruth Berkowitz Charitable
  Trust
Berkshire Community
  Foundation
The Bernicia Foundation
Bideford Bridge Trust
The Percy Bilton Charity
Binks Trust
Birkdale Trust for Hearing
  Impaired Ltd*
The Birmingham Diocesan
  Board of Finance
The Sydney Black Charitable
  Trust
The Isabel Blackman
  Foundation
The Blagrave Trust
Lady Blakenham's Charity
  Trust
The Blandford Lake Trust
Bluespark Foundation
The Bluston Charitable
  Settlement
The Boltini Trust
The Bonamy Charitable Trust
The Charlotte Bonham-Carter
  Charitable Trust
The Boodle and Dunthorne
  Charitable Trust
The Salo Bordon Charitable
  Trust
Sir William Boreman's
  Foundation
The Borrows Charitable Trust
The Boshier-Hinton Foundation
The Bothwell Charitable Trust
The Bowland Charitable Trust
The Brelms Trust CIO
The Brenley Trust
Bristol Charities

The BRIT Trust
The British and Foreign School
 Society (BFSS)
The Brook Trust
The Brothers Trust
The Charles Brotherton Trust
The Brownsword Charitable
 Foundation
The Jack Brunton Charitable
 Trust
Buckingham Trust
Buckinghamshire Community
 Foundation
The Buffini Chao Foundation
Bupa Foundation
Clara E. Burgess Charity
The Burry Charitable Trust
Consolidated Charity of Burton
 upon Trent
Miss Margaret Butters Reekie
 Charitable Trust
Byrne Family Foundation
The G. W. Cadbury Charitable
 Trust
William A. Cadbury Charitable
 Trust
The Cadogan Charity
The Calleva Foundation
Cambridgeshire Community
 Foundation
The Frederick and Phyllis Cann
 Trust
Carew Pole Charitable Trust
William A. Cargill Charitable
 Trust
W. A. Cargill Fund
The Carnegie Dunfermline
 Trust
The Carpenters Company
 Charitable Trust
The Casey Trust
The Castanea Trust
The Castansa Trust
Cattanach
The Joseph and Annie Cattle
 Trust
The Cayo Foundation
The Chadwick Educational
 Foundation
The Chalk Cliff Trust
Chapman Charitable Trust
Chartered Accountants' Livery
 Charity (CALC)
Cheshire Community
 Foundation Ltd
The Chetwode Foundation
The Childhood Trust
Children with Cancer UK
The Childwick Trust
Chippenham Borough Lands
 Charity
CHK Foundation
Church Burgesses Educational
 Foundation
Church Burgesses Trust
The Churchill Foundation

The CIBC World Markets
 Children's Foundation
The City Bridge Trust (Bridge
 House Estates)
CLA Charitable Trust
The Roger and Sarah Bancroft
 Clark Charitable Trust
The Clore Duffield Foundation
The Clothworkers' Foundation
The Robert Clutterbuck
 Charitable Trust
F. B. Coales No. 4 (Family)
 Trust
The Vivienne and Samuel
 Cohen Charitable Trust
Colchester Catalyst Charity
The Cole Charitable Trust
John and Freda Coleman
 Charitable Trust
The Coles-Medlock Foundation
Colyer-Fergusson Charitable
 Trust
Community First
Douglas Compton James
 Charitable Trust
The Connolly Foundation (UK)
 Ltd
The Ernest Cook Trust
The Catherine Cookson
 Charitable Trust
The Keith Coombs Trust
Co-op Foundation
The J. Reginald Corah
 Foundation Fund
Michael Cornish Charitable
 Trust
The Evan Cornish Foundation
The Corporation of Trinity
 House of Deptford Strond
Corra Foundation
Coutts Charitable Foundation
The Sir Tom Cowie Charitable
 Trust
Dudley and Geoffrey Cox
 Charitable Trust
Michael Crawford Children's
 Charity
Creative Scotland
Credit Suisse EMEA
 Foundation
CRH Charitable Trust
Cripplegate Foundation
The Peter Cruddas Foundation
Cullum Family Trust
Cumbria Community
 Foundation
Itzchok Meyer Cymerman Trust
 Ltd
Oizer Dalim Trust
The Daniell Trust
Baron Davenport's Charity
Margaret Davies Charity
The Crispin Davis Family Trust
The Davis Foundation
The De Brye Charitable Trust

The Roger De Haan Charitable
 Trust
Dentons UK and Middle East
 LLP Charitable Trust
Foundation Derbyshire
The J. N. Derbyshire Trust
The Desmond Foundation
The Alan and Sheila Diamond
 Charitable Trust
The Dibden Allotments Fund
The Gillian Dickinson Trust
Digital Extra Fund
Donibristle Trust
The Dorfman Foundation
Dorset Community Foundation
The Double 'O' Charity Ltd
The D'Oyly Carte Charitable
 Trust
Drapers Charitable Fund
Dromintee Trust
The DS Smith Charitable
 Foundation
Duchy of Lancaster Benevolent
 Fund
The Dulverton Trust
Dumbreck Charity
Dunlossit and Islay Community
 Trust
The Charles Dunstone
 Charitable Trust
The Dyers' Company
 Charitable Trust
E. B. M. Charitable Trust
East End Community
 Foundation
Eastern Counties Educational
 Trust Ltd
Sir John Eastwood Foundation
The Gilbert and Eileen Edgar
 Foundation
Edinburgh Children's Holiday
 Fund
Dr Edwards and Bishop King's
 Fulham Charity
The Eight Foundation
The Eighteen Fund
The Elie Trust
The Wilfred and Elsie Elkes
 Charity Fund
The Maud Elkington Charitable
 Trust
The Ellerdale Trust
EMI Music Sound Foundation
England and Wales Cricket
 Trust
The Englefield Charitable Trust
The EQ Foundation
Esher House Charitable Trust
The Essex and Southend
 Sports Trust
The Essex Youth Trust
The Evelyn Trust
The Everard Foundation
The Eveson Charitable Trust
The ExPat Foundation
Extonglen Ltd

Esmée Fairbairn Foundation
The Fairness Foundation
The Fairstead Trust
The Thomas Farr Charity
George Fentham Birmingham
Charity
The Fidelity UK Foundation
Field Family Charitable Trust
The Finborough Foundation
Dixie Rose Findlay Charitable
Trust
The Robert Fleming Hannay
Memorial Charity
The Joyce Fletcher Charitable
Trust
The Follett Trust
Fonthill Foundation
Ford Britain Trust
Forest Hill Charitable Trust
Forever Manchester
The Forrester Family Trust
Four Acre Trust
Foux Foundation
Fowler Smith and Jones Trust
The Isaac and Freda Frankel
Memorial Charitable Trust
The Elizabeth Frankland Moore
and Star Foundation
Jill Franklin Trust
The Gordon Fraser Charitable
Trust
The Hugh Fraser Foundation
The Joseph Strong Frazer Trust
The Louis and Valerie
Freedman Charitable
Settlement
Charles S. French Charitable
Trust
Friarsgate Trust
Frognal Trust
The Patrick and Helena Frost
Foundation
The Fulmer Charitable Trust
The Gale Family Charity Trust
The Gannochy Trust
Gatwick Airport Community
Trust
The Gaudio Family Foundation
(UK) Ltd
Martin Geddes Charitable
Trust
Sir Robert Geffery's
Almshouse Trust
General Charity (Coventry)
The Generational Foundation*
The Generations Foundation
The Tara Getty Foundation
The Gibbons Family Trust
The Simon Gibson Charitable
Trust
The B. and P. Glasser
Charitable Trust
The Glass-House Trust
Gloucestershire Community
Foundation
The Golden Bottle Trust

The Goldsmiths' Company
Charity
The Golf Foundation
The Golsoncott Foundation
The Goodman Foundation
The Mike Gooley Trailfinders
Charity
Gowling WLG (UK) Charitable
Trust
The Hemraj Goyal Foundation
The Grace Trust
The Gisela Graham Foundation
Grand Charitable Trust of the
Order of Women
Freemasons
The Grantham Yorke Trust
Gordon Gray Trust
The Great Britain Sasakawa
Foundation
The Great Stone Bridge Trust
of Edenbridge
The Green Hall Foundation
The Green Room Charitable
Trust
Philip and Judith Green Trust
Greenham Trust Ltd
The Greenslade Family
Foundation
The Greggs Foundation
The Grimmitt Trust
The Grocers' Charity
The Walter Guinness
Charitable Trust
Dr Guthrie's Association
Hackney Parochial Charities
The Hadfield Charitable Trust
The Hadley Trust
The Hadrian Trust
Halifax Foundation for
Northern Ireland
The Hamilton Davies Trust
Paul Hamlyn Foundation
The Helen Hamlyn Trust
Hammersmith United Charities
Hampton Fund
The W. A. Handley Charity
Trust
The Lennox Hannay Charitable
Trust
The Kathleen Hannay
Memorial Charity
The Happold Foundation
The Haramead Trust
Harborne Parish Lands Charity
William Harding's Charity
The Harebell Centenary Fund
The Hargreaves Foundation
The Harpur Trust
The Peter Harrison Foundation
The Harry and Mary
Foundation
Gay and Peter Hartley's
Hillards Charitable Trust
The Hasluck Charitable Trust
The Hawthorne Charitable
Trust

The Dorothy Hay-Bolton
Charitable Trust
The Charles Hayward
Foundation
The Headley Trust
Heart of England Community
Foundation
The Hearth Foundation
Heathrow Community Trust
The Charlotte Heber-Percy
Charitable Trust
Ernest Hecht Charitable
Foundation
The Percy Hedley 1990
Charitable Trust
The Hedley Foundation
The Hemby Charitable Trust
Christina Mary Hendrie Trust
Henley Educational Trust
Henley Royal Regatta
Charitable Trust
Tim Henman Foundation
The G. D. Herbert Charitable
Trust
Herefordshire Community
Foundation
Hertfordshire Community
Foundation
HFC Help for Children UK Ltd
P. and C. Hickinbotham
Charitable Trust
The Alan Edward Higgs Charity
R. G. Hills Charitable Trust
The Lady Hind Trust
The Hiscox Foundation
The Henry C. Hoare Charitable
Trust
The Hobson Charity Ltd
The Holbeck Charitable Trust
Hollick Family Foundation
The Holliday Foundation
The Holywood Trust
Homelands Charitable Trust
Sir Harold Hood's Charitable
Trust
The Horners Charity Fund
The Hosking Charitable Trust*
The Hospital of God at
Greatham
Housing Pathways Trust
The Reta Lila Howard
Foundation
James T. Howat Charitable
Trust
The Hull and East Riding
Charitable Trust
The Humanitarian Trust
The Albert Hunt Trust
The Hunter Foundation
Miss Agnes H. Hunter's Trust
The Huntingdon Foundation
Ltd
Huntingdon Freemen's Trust
The Nani Huyu Charitable Trust
Hyde Charitable Trust

The Iceland Foods Charitable
Foundation
The Iliffe Family Charitable
Trust
Impetus
The Inlight Trust
The Innocent Foundation
Integrated Education Fund
The International Bankers
Charitable Trust
The Inverforth Charitable Trust
Investream Charitable Trust
The Invigorate Charitable Trust
The Ireland Fund of Great
Britain
Irish Youth Foundation (UK)
Ltd (incorporating The
Lawlor Foundation)
The Isle of Anglesey Charitable
Association (Cymdeithas
Elusennol Ynys Môn)
The J. A. R. Charitable Trust
The J. J. Charitable Trust
The Sir Barry Jackson County
Fund
The Frank Jackson Foundation
Lady Eda Jardine Charitable
Trust
The JD Foundation
The Jerusalem Trust
Jewish Child's Day
The Jewish Youth Fund
John Lewis and Partners
Foundation
Lillie Johnson Charitable Trust
Johnnie Johnson Trust
The Jones 1986 Charitable
Trust
The Jordan Charitable
Foundation
The Joron Charitable Trust
J. E. Joseph Charitable Fund
The Cyril and Eve Jumbo
Charitable Trust
The Boris Karloff Charitable
Foundation
The Karlsson Játiva Charitable
Foundation
The Ian Karten Charitable
Trust
The Kasner Charitable Trust
The Kavli Trust
The Emmanuel Kaye
Foundation
Kelsick's Educational
Foundation
The Kensington and Chelsea
Foundation
Kent Community Foundation
The Kentown Wizard
Foundation
Keren Association Ltd
The Peter Kershaw Trust
KFC Foundation
The Kiawah Charitable Trust

Fraser Kilpatrick Charitable
Trust
The Kilroot Foundation
The Mary Kinross Charitable
Trust
Robert Kitchin (Saddlers' Co.)
The Ernest Kleinwort
Charitable Trust
The Kobler Trust
Kolyom Trust Ltd
KPE4 Charitable Trust
The KPMG Foundation
The Kreitman Foundation
Kupath Gemach Chaim
Bechesed Viznitz Trust
Kusuma Trust UK
The Kyte Charitable Trust
Ladbrokes Coral Trust
John Laing Charitable Trust
Maurice and Hilda Laing
Charitable Trust
Christopher Laing Foundation
The David Laing Foundation
The Kirby Laing Foundation
The Martin Laing Foundation
The Leonard Laity Stoate
Charitable Trust
The Lake House Charitable
Foundation
Community Foundations for
Lancashire and Merseyside
The Lancashire Foundation
Lancaster Foundation
LandAid Charitable Trust Ltd
(LandAid)
The Allen Lane Foundation
Langdale Trust
Laslett's (Hinton) Charity
Mrs F. B. Laurence Charitable
Trust
The Law Family Charitable
Foundation
The Edgar E. Lawley
Foundation
Lawson Beckman Charitable
Trust
The Lawson Trust CIO
The Leathersellers' Foundation
The William Leech Charity
Leeds Community Foundation
Leicestershire and Rutland
Masonic Charity
Association
The Leigh Trust
Lempriere Pringle 2015
The Mark Leonard Trust
The Leri Charitable Trust
Joseph Levy Foundation
Cecil and Hilda Lewis
Charitable Trust
Bernard Lewis Family
Charitable Trust
David and Ruth Lewis Family
Charitable Trust
The Charles Lewis Foundation
Liberum Foundation

Limoges Charitable Trust
The Linbury Trust
The Linder Foundation
The Lister Charitable Trust
The Frank Litchfield Charitable
Trust
Little Lives UK*
The Michael and Betty Little
Trust*
Liverpool Charity and Voluntary
Services (LCVS)
The Ian and Natalie
Livingstone Charitable Trust
Jack Livingstone Charitable
Trust
The Elaine and Angus Lloyd
Charitable Trust
The Andrew Lloyd Webber
Foundation
Lloyds Bank Foundation for
England and Wales
Lloyds Bank Foundation for the
Channel Islands
Lloyd's of London Foundation
Localtrent Ltd
The Locker Foundation
London Freemasons Charity
The London Marathon
Charitable Trust Ltd
The Lord's Taverners
LPW Ltd
Lord and Lady Lurgan Trust
The Lyndal Tree Foundation
John Lyon's Charity
Sylvanus Lysons Charity
M. and C. Trust
M. B. Foundation
The R. S. Macdonald
Charitable Trust
The Macdonald-Buchanan
Charitable Trust
Mace Foundation
The MacRobert Trust 2019
Makers of Playing Cards
Charity
Man Group plc Charitable
Trust
The Manackerman Charitable
Trust
The Manchester Guardian
Society Charitable Trust
R. W. Mann Trust
The Manson Family Charitable
Trust
The Marandi Foundation
Marbeh Torah Trust
The Marks Family Charitable
Trust
Marmot Charitable Trust
The Michael Marsh Charitable
Trust
The Martin Charitable Trust
Sir George Martin Trust
The Dan Maskell Tennis Trust
Masonic Charitable Foundation
The Master Charitable Trust

Matchroom Sport Charitable
Foundation
The Matliwala Family
Charitable Trust
Mayfair Charities Ltd
Mayheights Ltd
MBNA General Foundation
The Robert McAlpine
Foundation
Gemma and Chris McGough
Charitable Foundation CIO
D. D. McPhail Charitable
Settlement
The Medlock Charitable Trust
The Meikle Foundation
Melodor Ltd
Menuchar Ltd
The Mercers Charitable
Foundation
The Merchant Venturers
Charity
Merchants House of Glasgow
Merriman Charitable
Foundation*
T. and J. Meyer Family
Foundation Ltd
The Mickleham Trust
The Gerald Micklem Charitable
Trust
The Millennium Oak Trust
Hugh and Mary Miller Bequest
Trust
The Ronald Miller Foundation
The James Milner Foundation
Milton Keynes Community
Foundation Ltd
The Peter Minet Trust
Minton Charitable Trust
The Mishcon Family Charitable
Trust
The Esmé Mitchell Trust
The Mittal Foundation
The Mohn Westlake
Foundation
Mole Charitable Trust
The Monday Charitable Trust
The Monmouthshire County
Council Welsh Church Act
Fund
Moondance Foundation
John Moores Foundation
The Steve Morgan Foundation
Morgan Stanley International
Foundation
The Morris Charitable Trust
G. M. Morrison Charitable
Trust
The Mosawi Foundation
Vyoel Moshe Charitable Trust
The Mosselson Charitable
Trust
The Moulding Foundation
The Edwina Mountbatten and
Leonora Children's
Foundation
The Mowgli Trust

The MSE Charity
The Mulberry Trust
The Mulchand Foundation
Edith Murphy Foundation
Murphy-Neumann Charity
Company Ltd
Brian Murtagh Charitable Trust
Music Sales Charitable Trust
The Mutley Foundation
The National Express
Foundation
The NDL Foundation
Nemoral Ltd
Ner Foundation
Nesta
Newby Trust Ltd
Newcomen Collett Foundation
Newpier Charity Ltd
Alderman Newton's
Educational Foundation
The NFU Mutual Charitable
Trust
The Nisbet Trust
The Nomura Charitable Trust
Norfolk Community Foundation
Educational Foundation of
Alderman John Norman
The Norman Family Charitable
Trust
Normanby Charitable Trust
Northamptonshire Community
Foundation
Northcott Trust
The Norton Foundation
Nottinghamshire Community
Foundation
Odin Charitable Trust
The Ofenheim Charitable Trust
Oizer Charitable Trust
Old Possum's Practical Trust
Henry Oldfield Trust
The Olwyn Foundation
Open House Trust Ltd
Ostro Fayre Share Foundation
The Sir Peter O'Sullevan
Charitable Trust
The O'Sullivan Family
Charitable Trust
Ovingdean Hall Foundation
The Ovo Charitable Foundation
The Doris Pacey Charitable
Foundation
The Paget Charitable Trust
The James Pantyfedwen
Foundation
(Ymddiriedolaeth James
Pantyfedwen)
The Paphitis Charitable Trust
The Paragon Trust
The Parivar Trust
Miss M. E. S. Paterson's
Charitable Trust
The Patrick Trust
Payne-Gallwey 1989 Charitable
Trust
Peacock Charitable Trust

Susanna Peake Charitable
Trust
The Pears Family Charitable
Foundation
The Pebbles Trust
People's Postcode Trust
The Persimmon Charitable
Foundation
The Jack Petchey Foundation
The Phillips and Rubens
Charitable Trust
The Bernard Piggott Charitable
Trust
The Pilgrim Trust
The Sir Harry Pilkington Fund
The Austin and Hope
Pilkington Trust
Miss A. M. Pilkington's
Charitable Trust
PIMCO Foundation Europe
The Pixel Fund
The Players Foundation
Thomas Pocklington Trust
The George and Esme Pollitzer
Charitable Settlement
The Porta Pia 2012
Foundation
The Portal Trust
The Portishead Nautical Trust
The Portrack Charitable Trust
Postcode Community Trust
Postcode Local Trust
Postcode Society Trust
The Potton Consolidated
Charity
Poundland Foundation
Premierquote Ltd
Sir John Priestman Charity
Trust
The Princess Anne's Charities
The Priory Foundation
Prison Service Charity Fund
The Privy Purse Charitable
Trust
The Progress Foundation
Provincial Grand Charity of the
Province of Derbyshire
The Prudence Trust
QBE European Operations
Foundation
The Queen Anne's Gate
Foundation
The Quilter Foundation
Quintessentially Foundation
The Radcliffe Trust
Richard Radcliffe Trust
The Raindance Charitable
Trust
The Rainford Trust
The Rambourg Foundation
The Joseph and Lena Randall
Charitable Trust
Randeree Charitable Trust
The Ratcliff Foundation
The Eleanor Rathbone
Charitable Trust

Elizabeth Rathbone Charity

The Rathbones Group Foundation

The Ravensdale Trust

The Roger Raymond Charitable Trust

The Rayne Foundation

The Sir James Reckitt Charity

Red Hill Charitable Trust

The Reece Foundation

Richard Reeve's Foundation

The Revere Charitable Trust

The Rhododendron Trust

Riada Trust

Richmond Parish Lands Charity

The River Farm Foundation

Rivers Foundation

The Rix-Thompson-Rothenberg Foundation

The Robertson Trust

Rockcliffe Charitable Trust

The Sir James Roll Charitable Trust

Rosa Fund

Rosca Trust

The Roseline Foundation*

The Ross Foundation

The Rothermere Foundation

The Rothley Trust

The Eranda Rothschild Foundation

The Roughley Charitable Trust

Royal Docks Trust (London)

The Royal Foundation of The Prince and Princess of Wales

Royal Masonic Trust for Girls and Boys

The Royal Navy and Royal Marines Charity

The Ryvoan Trust*

The Jeremy and John Sacher Charitable Trust

The Saddlers' Company Charitable Fund

The Alan and Babette Sainsbury Charitable Fund

The Saintbury Trust

The Salamander Charitable Trust

Samjo Ltd

The Sandhu Charitable Foundation

Sandra Charitable Trust

Sarum St Michael Educational Charity

The Sasha Foundation*

The Savoy Educational Trust

The Schreier Foundation*

Schroder Charity Trust

Foundation Scotland

The Scott Bader Commonwealth Ltd

Francis C. Scott Charitable Trust

The Frieda Scott Charitable Trust

The Ina Scott Sutherland Charitable Foundation

The John Scott Trust Fund

Scottish Property Industry Festival of Christmas (SPIFOX)

Scouloudi Foundation

Seedfield Trust

The Segelman Trust

Leslie Sell Charitable Trust

Shaftoe Educational Foundation

The Shanly Foundation

ShareGift (The Orr Mackintosh Foundation)

The Sheffield Town Trust

The Sheldon Trust

The Patricia and Donald Shepherd Charitable Trust

The Sylvia and Colin Shepherd Charitable Trust

The R. C. Sherriff Rosebriars Trust

Shetland Charitable Trust

SHINE (Support and Help in Education)

The Bassil Shippam and Alsford Trust

The Shipwrights Charitable Fund

The Shoe Zone Trust

The Skelton Bounty

The Charles Skey Charitable Trust

Skipton Building Society Charitable Foundation

The Slaughter and May Charitable Trust

Kathleen Beryl Sleigh Charitable Trust

Sloane Robinson Foundation

The Mrs Smith and Mount Trust

The N. Smith Charitable Settlement

The Henry Smith Charity

Arabella and Julian Smith Family Trust

The Leslie Smith Foundation

Sofronie Foundation

Somerset Community Foundation

South Yorkshire Community Foundation

Southover Manor General Education Trust Ltd

Spielman Charitable Trust

The Spoore, Merry and Rixman Foundation

Spurrell Charitable Trust

The Geoff and Fiona Squire Foundation

The Squire Patton Boggs Charitable Trust

The Squires Foundation

The St Hilda's Trust

St James's Place Charitable Foundation

Sir Walter St John's Educational Charity

St John's Foundation Est. 1174

St Olave's and St Saviour's Schools Foundation CIO*

Stadium Charitable Trust

The Stafford Trust

The Community Foundation for Staffordshire

The Steinberg Family Charitable Trust

The Hugh Stenhouse Foundation

The Stevenson Family's Charitable Trust

Stolkin Foundation

The Stoller Charitable Trust

The Stone Family Foundation

The Stoneygate Trust

The Samuel Storey Family Charitable Trust

Peter Storrs Trust

Strand Parishes Trust

Stratford-upon-Avon Town Trust

The W. O. Street Charitable Foundation

The Street Foundation

Suffolk Community Foundation

The Bernard Sunley Foundation

The Sussex Community Foundation

Sabina Sutherland Charitable Trust

Sutton Coldfield Charitable Trust

The Swann-Morton Foundation

The Swire Charitable Trust

The Adrian Swire Charitable Trust

The Charles and Elsie Sykes Trust

The T.K. Maxx and Homesense Foundation

The Ashley Tabor-King Foundation

The Talbot Trusts

The Talbot Village Trust

Tallow Chandlers Benevolent Fund No 2

Tanner Trust

Tay Charitable Trust

C. B. and H. H. T. Taylor 1984 Trust

Humphrey Richardson Taylor Charitable Trust

The Taylor Family Foundation

Stephen Taylor Foundation

The Tedworth Charitable Trust

The Thales Charitable Trust

the7stars Foundation

The Thornton Trust
The Three Guineas Trust
Mrs R. P. Tindall's Charitable
  Trust
The Tolkien Trust
The Tomoro Foundation
The Tompkins Foundation
The Tottenham Grammar
  School Foundation
Tower Hill Trust
The Toy Trust
The Trades House of Glasgow
Annie Tranmer Charitable Trust
The Triangle Trust (1949) Fund
The Troutsdale Charitable
  Trust
The True Colours Trust
Truedene Co. Ltd
Truemart Ltd
Trumros Ltd
The Trusthouse Charitable
  Foundation
The Trysil Charitable Trust
The Tudor Trust
The Tuixen Foundation
The Roger and Douglas Turner
  Charitable Trust
The Tweed Family Charitable
  Foundation
Two Magpies Fund
Two Ridings Community
  Foundation
Community Foundation serving
  Tyne and Wear and
  Northumberland
Tzedakah
UBS Optimus Foundation UK
UJIA (United Jewish Israel
  Appeal)
The UK Youth Fund: Thriving
  Minds*
Ulster Garden Villages Ltd
The Ulverscroft Foundation
The Union of the Sisters of
  Mercy of Great Britain
The Utley Foundation
The Valentine Charitable Trust
The Albert Van Den Bergh
  Charitable Trust
The Van Mesdag Fund
The Van Neste Foundation
The Vardy Foundation
Variety, the Children's Charity
VHLT Ltd
The Vintners' Foundation
The Virgin Money Foundation
Vivdale Ltd
Volant Charitable Trust
Wade's Charity
Wallace and Gromit's
  Children's Foundation
The Barbara Ward Children's
  Foundation
Warwick Relief-in-Need Charity
The Waterloo Foundation
Wates Family Enterprise Trust

The William Wates Memorial
  Trust
John Watson's Trust*
We Love MCR Charity
The Weavers' Company
  Benevolent Fund
The Weinstock Fund
Wellington Management UK
  Foundation
Wembley National Stadium
  Trust
West Derby Waste Lands
  Charity
Westhill Endowment
Westminster Almshouses
  Foundation
Westminster Foundation
The Garfield Weston
  Foundation
Westway Trust
The Barbara Whatmore
  Charitable Trust
Colonel W. H. Whitbread
  Charitable Trust
WHSmith Trust
Wickens Family Foundation
The Felicity Wilde Charitable
  Trust
Alfred Williams Charitable
  Trust
The Williams Family
  Foundation
Dame Violet Wills Will Trust
The Wilmcote Charitrust
The Wimbledon Foundation
The Michael and Anna Wix
  Charitable Trust
The Wolfson Foundation
The Lord Leonard and Lady
  Estelle Wolfson Foundation
The Wood Foundation
Wooden Spoon Society
Woodlands Green Ltd
Woodroffe Benton Foundation
Woodsmith Foundation Ltd
The Woodward Charitable
  Trust
Worshipful Company of
  Glovers of London
  Charitable Trust
Worshipful Company of Gold
  and Silver Wyre Drawers
  Second Charitable Trust
  Fund
Worth Waynflete Foundation
The Worwin UK Foundation
The Eric Wright Charitable
  Trust
The Wyfold Charitable Trust
Sir Graham Wylie Foundation
The Wyndham Charitable Trust
The Wyseliot Rose Charitable
  Trust
The Yapp Charitable Trust
Yorkshire Building Society
  Charitable Foundation

Youth Endowment Fund (YEF)*
Youth Music
The Elizabeth and Prince
  Zaiger Trust
The Zochonis Charitable Trust
Zurich Community Trust (UK)
  Ltd

Older people

The 29th May 1961 Charitable
  Trust
The 4814 Trust
The Abbeyfield Research
  Foundation
Adam Family Foundation
The Bryan Adams Foundation
The Adint Charitable Trust
The AEB Charitable Trust
Age Scotland
The Aimwell Charitable Trust
Sylvia Aitken's Charitable Trust
Alan Boswell Group Charitable
  Trust
Andor Charitable Trust
The John Apthorp Charity
The Archer Trust
Armed Forces Covenant Fund
  Trust
The John Armitage Charitable
  Trust
The Asda Foundation
The Ashendene Trust
The Astor Foundation
The Lord Austin Trust
The Avon and Somerset Police
  Community Trust
The Austin Bailey Foundation
The Ballinger Charitable Trust
The Band Trust
Bank of Scotland Foundation
The Barbour Foundation
Barchester Healthcare
  Foundation
Lord Barnby's Foundation
The Barnes Fund
Misses Barrie Charitable Trust
The Batchworth Trust
The Gordon and Ena Baxter
  Foundation*
Bay Charitable Trust
The Beaverbrook Foundation
The Beaverbrooks Charitable
  Trust
Bedfordshire Charitable Trust
  Ltd
The Benham Charitable
  Settlement
The Rowan Bentall Charitable
  Trust
Berkshire Community
  Foundation
Bideford Bridge Trust
The Percy Bilton Charity
The Sydney Black Charitable
  Trust

The Bertie Black Foundation
The Isabel Blackman
   Foundation
Lady Blakenham's Charity
   Trust
The Boltini Trust
The Charlotte Bonham-Carter
   Charitable Trust
The Booth Charities
The Borrows Charitable Trust
The Boshier-Hinton Foundation
The Bosson Family Charitable
   Trust
The Bothwell Charitable Trust
The Harry Bottom Charitable
   Trust
The Brelms Trust CIO
Bristol Charities
The Charles Brotherton Trust
Bill Brown 1989 Charitable
   Trust
R. S. Brownless Charitable
   Trust
The Brownsword Charitable
   Foundation
The Jack Brunton Charitable
   Trust
Buckingham Trust
The Burden Trust
The Burry Charitable Trust
Consolidated Charity of Burton
   upon Trent
Miss Margaret Butters Reekie
   Charitable Trust
William A. Cadbury Charitable
   Trust
Carew Pole Charitable Trust
William A. Cargill Charitable
   Trust
W. A. Cargill Fund
The Carpenters Company
   Charitable Trust
The Castanea Trust
The Castansa Trust
The Joseph and Annie Cattle
   Trust
The Chalk Cliff Trust
Chartered Accountants' Livery
   Charity (CALC)
Cheshire Community
   Foundation Ltd
The Childwick Trust
Chippenham Borough Lands
   Charity
Church Burgesses Trust
The Churchill Foundation
The City Bridge Trust (Bridge
   House Estates)
The Roger and Sarah Bancroft
   Clark Charitable Trust
The Clothworkers' Foundation
The Clover Trust
The Robert Clutterbuck
   Charitable Trust
The Vivienne and Samuel
   Cohen Charitable Trust

Colchester Catalyst Charity
The Cole Charitable Trust
Douglas Compton James
   Charitable Trust
The Connolly Foundation (UK)
   Ltd
The J. Reginald Corah
   Foundation Fund
The Evan Cornish Foundation
Cripplegate Foundation
The Cross Trust
Cullum Family Trust
Cumbria Community
   Foundation
Itzchok Meyer Cymerman Trust
   Ltd
The D. G. Charitable
   Settlement
Oizer Dalim Trust
Baron Davenport's Charity
The Davis Foundation
The De Brye Charitable Trust
The Roger De Haan Charitable
   Trust
Dentons UK and Middle East
   LLP Charitable Trust
The J. N. Derbyshire Trust
The Alan and Sheila Diamond
   Charitable Trust
Dorset Community Foundation
Drapers Charitable Fund
Dromintee Trust
Duchy Health Charity Ltd
Duchy of Lancaster Benevolent
   Fund
The Dulverton Trust
Dumbreck Charity
The Dunhill Medical Trust
Dunlossit and Islay Community
   Trust
The Earley Charity
Sir John Eastwood Foundation
The Gilbert and Eileen Edgar
   Foundation
Edupoor Ltd
W. G. Edwards Charitable
   Foundation
The Eight Foundation
The Eighteen Fund
The Eighty Eight Foundation
The Elie Trust
The Wilfred and Elsie Elkes
   Charity Fund
The Maud Elkington Charitable
   Trust
The Englefield Charitable Trust
The EQ Foundation
The Evelyn Trust
The Everard Foundation
The Eveson Charitable Trust
The ExPat Foundation
Extonglen Ltd
The Fairness Foundation
The Lord Faringdon Charitable
   Trust
The Thomas Farr Charity

George Fentham Birmingham
   Charity
Field Family Charitable Trust
The Robert Fleming Hannay
   Memorial Charity
The Follett Trust
Forever Manchester
The Forrester Family Trust
The Isaac and Freda Frankel
   Memorial Charitable Trust
The Elizabeth Frankland Moore
   and Star Foundation
Jill Franklin Trust
The Hugh Fraser Foundation
The Joseph Strong Frazer Trust
Charles S. French Charitable
   Trust
Friarsgate Trust
Frognal Trust
The Fulmer Charitable Trust
The Gale Family Charity Trust
Gatwick Airport Community
   Trust
Martin Geddes Charitable
   Trust
General Charity (Coventry)
The David Gibbons Foundation
The Simon Gibson Charitable
   Trust
The B. and P. Glasser
   Charitable Trust
Gloucestershire Community
   Foundation
The Golden Bottle Trust
The Goldsmiths' Company
   Charity
The Goodman Foundation
Gowling WLG (UK) Charitable
   Trust
The Graham Trust
Grand Charitable Trust of the
   Order of Women
   Freemasons
Gordon Gray Trust
The Green Hall Foundation
Greenham Trust Ltd
The Greggs Foundation
The Grimmitt Trust
The Grocers' Charity
The Albert Gubay Charitable
   Foundation
The Walter Guinness
   Charitable Trust
Hackney Parochial Charities
The Hadfield Charitable Trust
The Hadrian Trust
Halifax Foundation for
   Northern Ireland
The Helen Hamlyn Trust
The Hampstead Wells and
   Campden Trust
Hampton Fund
The W. A. Handley Charity
   Trust
The Lennox Hannay Charitable
   Trust

Harborne Parish Lands Charity

William Harding's Charity

Gay and Peter Hartley's Hillards Charitable Trust

Edward Harvist Trust (The Harvist Estate)

The Hasluck Charitable Trust

The Hawthorne Charitable Trust

The Dorothy Hay-Bolton Charitable Trust

The Charles Hayward Foundation

The Headley Trust

Heart of England Community Foundation

Ernest Hecht Charitable Foundation

The Percy Hedley 1990 Charitable Trust

The Hedley Foundation

The Helping Foundation

The Hemby Charitable Trust

Christina Mary Hendrie Trust

The G. D. Herbert Charitable Trust

Herefordshire Community Foundation

R. G. Hills Charitable Trust

The Lady Hind Trust

The Hiscox Foundation

The Henry C. Hoare Charitable Trust

The Hobson Charity Ltd

The Jane Hodge Foundation

The Hollands-Warren Fund

Sir Harold Hood's Charitable Trust

The Hospital of God at Greatham

Housing Pathways Trust

James T. Howat Charitable Trust

The Hudson Foundation

The Huggard Charitable Trust

The Huntingdon Foundation Ltd

Huntingdon Freemen's Trust

The Nani Huyu Charitable Trust

The Iliffe Family Charitable Trust

The Inlight Trust

The Inman Charity

Investream Charitable Trust

The Invigorate Charitable Trust

The Ireland Fund of Great Britain

The J. Isaacs Charitable Trust

The Isle of Anglesey Charitable Association (Cymdeithas Elusennol Ynys Môn)

The J. A. R. Charitable Trust

John James Bristol Foundation

The Roger and Jean Jefcoate Trust

Lillie Johnson Charitable Trust

The Jones 1986 Charitable Trust

The Joron Charitable Trust

J. E. Joseph Charitable Fund

The Michael and Ilse Katz Foundation

The Kensington and Chelsea Foundation

Kent Community Foundation

Keren Association Ltd

The Peter Kershaw Trust

Fraser Kilpatrick Charitable Trust

The Kingsbury Charity

The Ernest Kleinwort Charitable Trust

Kolyom Trust Ltd

Kupath Gemach Chaim Bechesed Viznitz Trust

Ladbrokes Coral Trust

The Kirby Laing Foundation

The Martin Laing Foundation

The Beatrice Laing Trust

The Lake House Charitable Foundation

Community Foundations for Lancashire and Merseyside

Lancaster Foundation

The Allen Lane Foundation

Langdale Trust

Laslett's (Hinton) Charity

Mrs F. B. Laurence Charitable Trust

The Edgar E. Lawley Foundation

The Herd Lawson and Muriel Lawson Charitable Trust

Lawson Beckman Charitable Trust

The Lawson Trust CIO

Leeds Community Foundation

The Leeward Trust

Leicestershire and Rutland Masonic Charity Association

Lempriere Pringle 2015

The Leri Charitable Trust

Cecil and Hilda Lewis Charitable Trust

Bernard Lewis Family Charitable Trust

David and Ruth Lewis Family Charitable Trust

The Linbury Trust

The Frank Litchfield Charitable Trust

The Michael and Betty Little Trust*

Jack Livingstone Charitable Trust

Lloyds Bank Foundation for England and Wales

Lloyds Bank Foundation for the Channel Islands

Lloyd's of London Foundation

Localtrent Ltd

The Locker Foundation

London Freemasons Charity

The London Marathon Charitable Trust Ltd

The C. L. Loyd Charitable Trust

LPW Ltd

Lord and Lady Lurgan Trust

M. and C. Trust

M. B. Foundation

The Macdonald-Buchanan Charitable Trust

The Magdalen and Lasher Charity (General Fund)

The Manchester Guardian Society Charitable Trust

R. W. Mann Trust

Marbeh Torah Trust

Marmot Charitable Trust

The Michael Marsh Charitable Trust

The Martin Charitable Trust

Sir George Martin Trust

The Dan Maskell Tennis Trust

Masonic Charitable Foundation

The Master Charitable Trust

Matchroom Sport Charitable Foundation

The Matliwala Family Charitable Trust

Mayfair Charities Ltd

Mayheights Ltd

MBNA General Foundation

The Robert McAlpine Foundation

The McCarthy Stone Foundation

D. D. McPhail Charitable Settlement

The Medlock Charitable Trust

The Meikle Foundation

Melodor Ltd

Menuchar Ltd

The Mercers Charitable Foundation

The Merchant Venturers Charity

Merchants House of Glasgow

T. and J. Meyer Family Foundation Ltd

The Mickleham Trust

The Gerald Micklem Charitable Trust

The Millennium Oak Trust

Milton Keynes Community Foundation Ltd

The Peter Minet Trust

Mole Charitable Trust

The Monday Charitable Trust

The Monmouthshire County Council Welsh Church Act Fund

Moondance Foundation

John Moores Foundation

The Steve Morgan Foundation

The Morris Charitable Trust

G. M. Morrison Charitable Trust

The Ken and Lynne Morrison Charitable Trust

Vyoel Moshe Charitable Trust

The Mulberry Trust

Edith Murphy Foundation

Murphy-Neumann Charity Company Ltd

The Mutley Foundation

Nemoral Ltd

Ner Foundation

Newby Trust Ltd

Newpier Charity Ltd

Norfolk Community Foundation

The Norman Family Charitable Trust

Normanby Charitable Trust

Northamptonshire Community Foundation

Nottinghamshire Community Foundation

Odin Charitable Trust

The Ofenheim Charitable Trust

Oizer Charitable Trust

Old Possum's Practical Trust

Otsar Trust

The Paget Charitable Trust

The Paragon Trust

The Pargiter Trust

Miss M. E. S. Paterson's Charitable Trust

The Patrick Trust

Susanna Peake Charitable Trust

The Dowager Countess Eleanor Peel Trust

The Persimmon Charitable Foundation

The Phillips and Rubens Charitable Trust

The Phillips Family Charitable Trust

The Philip and Connie Phillips Foundation*

The Bernard Piggott Charitable Trust

Elise Pilkington Charitable Trust

Pilkington Charities Fund

The Sir Harry Pilkington Fund

Miss A. M. Pilkington's Charitable Trust

The George and Esme Pollitzer Charitable Settlement

The Porta Pia 2012 Foundation

The Portrack Charitable Trust

Postcode Community Trust

Postcode Local Trust

Postcode Society Trust

The Potton Consolidated Charity

Premierquote Ltd

Sir John Priestman Charity Trust

Quothquan Trust

The Rainford Trust

The Joseph and Lena Randall Charitable Trust

The Rank Foundation Ltd

The Ratcliff Foundation

The Ravensdale Trust

The Rayne Foundation

The Sir James Reckitt Charity

The Rhododendron Trust

Richmond Parish Lands Charity

Riverside Charitable Trust Ltd

Rockcliffe Charitable Trust

Rosca Trust

Rothesay Foundation*

The Rothley Trust

The Eranda Rothschild Foundation

The Roughley Charitable Trust

The Row Fogo Charitable Trust

The Rowlands Trust

Royal Masonic Trust for Girls and Boys

The Royal Navy and Royal Marines Charity

The Saddlers' Company Charitable Fund

The Saintbury Trust

The Salamander Charitable Trust

Samjo Ltd

The Scott Bader Commonwealth Ltd

The Frieda Scott Charitable Trust

The Searchlight Electric Charitable Trust

The Shanly Foundation

The Sheffield Town Trust

The Sheldon Trust

The Sylvia and Colin Shepherd Charitable Trust

The R. C. Sherriff Rosebriars Trust

Shetland Charitable Trust

The Bassil Shippam and Alsford Trust

The Skelton Bounty

The Skerritt Trust

The Charles Skey Charitable Trust

Skipton Building Society Charitable Foundation

Kathleen Beryl Sleigh Charitable Trust

The Mrs Smith and Mount Trust

Philip Smith's Charitable Trust

Somerset Community Foundation

South Yorkshire Community Foundation

Spielman Charitable Trust

The Squire Patton Boggs Charitable Trust

The Squires Foundation

St John's Foundation Est. 1174

St Monica Trust

Stadium Charitable Trust

The Community Foundation for Staffordshire

The Steinberg Family Charitable Trust

Stratford-upon-Avon Town Trust

The W. O. Street Charitable Foundation

Suffolk Community Foundation

The Bernard Sunley Foundation

The Sussex Community Foundation

Sutton Coldfield Charitable Trust

The John Swire (1989) Charitable Trust

The Charles and Elsie Sykes Trust

T. and S. Trust Fund

The Talbot Trusts

Tanner Trust

Tay Charitable Trust

C. B. and H. H. T. Taylor 1984 Trust

The Tennis Foundation

Tenovus Scotland

Sir Jules Thorn Charitable Trust

The Thornton Trust

The Tolkien Trust

The Tomoro Foundation

Tower Hill Trust

Truedene Co. Ltd

Truemart Ltd

Trumros Ltd

The Trusthouse Charitable Foundation

The Tudor Trust

The Roger and Douglas Turner Charitable Trust

Two Ridings Community Foundation

Community Foundation serving Tyne and Wear and Northumberland

Tzedakah

The Union of the Sisters of Mercy of Great Britain

United St Saviour's Charity

UnLtd (Foundation for Social Entrepreneurs)

The Albert Van Den Bergh Charitable Trust

The William and Patricia Venton Charitable Trust

VHLT Ltd

Vivdale Ltd

Wade's Charity

Walton-on-Thames Charity

Warwick Relief-in-Need Charity

The Weinstock Fund

Wellbank Foundation*

The Welsh Church Act Fund
West Derby Waste Lands
Charity
Westminster Almshouses
Foundation
The Galen and Hilary Weston
Foundation
The Williams Family
Foundation
The Wilmcote Charitrust
J. and J. R. Wilson Trust
The Francis Winham
Foundation
The Michael and Anna Wix
Charitable Trust
The Wolfson Family Charitable
Trust
The Wolfson Foundation
The Lord Leonard and Lady
Estelle Wolfson Foundation
Woodlands Green Ltd
Woodroffe Benton Foundation
Woodsmith Foundation Ltd
Worth Waynflete Foundation
The Eric Wright Charitable
Trust
The Wyfold Charitable Trust
The Wyseliot Rose Charitable
Trust
The Yapp Charitable Trust
Yorkshire Building Society
Charitable Foundation
The Elizabeth and Prince
Zaiger Trust
The Zochonis Charitable Trust
Zurich Community Trust (UK)
Ltd

Beneficial groups

Disability

The 29th May 1961 Charitable
Trust
The 4814 Trust
The Aberbrothock Skea Trust
The Adint Charitable Trust
The Aimwell Charitable Trust
Sylvia Aitken's Charitable Trust
The Alchemy Foundation
The Aldama Foundation
D. C. R. Allen Charitable Trust
Alzheimer's Society
Ambergate Charitable Trust
The Ammco Trust
Andor Charitable Trust
The Anson Charitable Trust
The John Apthorp Charity
The Archer Trust
The Ardwick Trust
The Arsenal Foundation
Douglas Arter Foundation
ArtSocial Foundation
The Astor Foundation
Axis Foundation
B&Q Foundation
The Baily Thomas Charitable
Fund
The Band Trust
Bank of Scotland Foundation
Barchester Healthcare
Foundation
The Barnes Fund
Barnsbury Charitable Trust
Barnwood Trust
Misses Barrie Charitable Trust
The Batchworth Trust
Bauer Radio's Cash for Kids
Charities
The Gordon and Ena Baxter
Foundation*
The James Beattie Charitable
Trust
The Benham Charitable
Settlement
The Rowan Bentall Charitable
Trust
The Berkeley Foundation
Bideford Bridge Trust
The Percy Bilton Charity
Birkdale Trust for Hearing
Impaired Ltd*
The Michael Bishop
Foundation
The Bertie Black Foundation
Lady Blakenham's Charity
Trust
The Marjory Boddy Charitable
Trust
BOOST Charitable Trust
The Boshier-Hinton Foundation
The Bothwell Charitable Trust
The Harry Bottom Charitable
Trust

The P. G. and N. J. Boulton
Trust
The Liz and Terry Bramall
Foundation
The Brelms Trust CIO
Bristol Charities
The Britford Bridge Trust
British Eye Research
Foundation (Fight for Sight)
Bill Brown 1989 Charitable
Trust
R. S. Brownless Charitable
Trust
The Brownsword Charitable
Foundation
The Jack Brunton Charitable
Trust
The Bulldog Trust Ltd
Miss Margaret Butters Reekie
Charitable Trust
William A. Cadbury Charitable
Trust
CareTech Charitable
Foundation
Carew Pole Charitable Trust
The Leslie Mary Carter
Charitable Trust
The Casey Trust
The Joseph and Annie Cattle
Trust
The Thomas Sivewright Catto
Charitable Settlement
The Amelia Chadwick Trust
Cheshire Community
Foundation Ltd
The Childhood Trust
The Childwick Trust
Chippenham Borough Lands
Charity
Chrysalis Trust
The Churchill Foundation
The City Bridge Trust (Bridge
House Estates)
CLA Charitable Trust
The Clothworkers' Foundation
Cloudesley
The Clover Trust
The Vivienne and Samuel
Cohen Charitable Trust
Colchester Catalyst Charity
The Catherine Cookson
Charitable Trust
The J. Reginald Corah
Foundation Fund
Michael Cornish Charitable
Trust
Cornwall Community
Foundation
Corra Foundation
The Cotton Industry War
Memorial Trust
The Sir William Coxen Trust
Fund
The Lord Cozens-Hardy Trust
Michael Crawford Children's
Charity

CRH Charitable Trust
Cruden Foundation Ltd
Cullum Family Trust
The Daniell Trust
The David Family Foundation*
The De Brye Charitable Trust
The Roger De Haan Charitable
  Trust
The Delves Charitable Trust
Foundation Derbyshire
The J. N. Derbyshire Trust
Devon Community Foundation
The Alan and Sheila Diamond
  Charitable Trust
The Dibden Allotments Fund
The Gillian Dickinson Trust
The Dischma Charitable Trust
William and Frances Dobie
  Charitable Foundation
Dorset Community Foundation
The Dorus Trust
The D'Oyly Carte Charitable
  Trust
Drapers Charitable Fund
Duchy of Lancaster Benevolent
  Fund
Dumbreck Charity
Dunlossit and Islay Community
  Trust
The Charles Dunstone
  Charitable Trust
Eastern Counties Educational
  Trust Ltd
Sir John Eastwood Foundation
Edupoor Ltd
The Eight Foundation
The Eighteen Fund
The Elie Trust
The Wilfred and Elsie Elkes
  Charity Fund
The Ellerdale Trust
Emerton-Christie Charity
The EQ Foundation
The Everard Foundation
The Eveson Charitable Trust
The Fairness Foundation
The Fairstead Trust
The Lord Faringdon Charitable
  Trust
Samuel William Farmer Trust
The Thomas Farr Charity
The February Foundation
George Fentham Birmingham
  Charity
The A. M. Fenton Trust
The Fieldrose Charitable Trust
Dixie Rose Findlay Charitable
  Trust
Sir John Fisher Foundation
The Earl Fitzwilliam Charitable
  Trust
The Robert Fleming Hannay
  Memorial Charity
The Joyce Fletcher Charitable
  Trust
The Follett Trust

The Forbes Charitable
  Foundation
Ford Britain Trust
Forest Hill Charitable Trust
The Lady Forester Trust
The Forman Hardy Charitable
  Trust
Foux Foundation
Fowler Smith and Jones Trust
The Gordon Fraser Charitable
  Trust
The Hugh Fraser Foundation
The Joseph Strong Frazer Trust
The Louis and Valerie
  Freedman Charitable
  Settlement
Charles S. French Charitable
  Trust
Friarsgate Trust
Frognal Trust
The Patrick and Helena Frost
  Foundation
The Fulmer Charitable Trust
Gatwick Airport Community
  Trust
The Robert Gavron Charitable
  Trust
General Charity (Coventry)
The Generations Foundation
The Tara Getty Foundation
J. Paul Getty Jr General
  Charitable Trust*
The David Gibbons Foundation
The B. and P. Glasser
  Charitable Trust
Global Charities
Gloucestershire Community
  Foundation
Sydney and Phyllis Goldberg
  Memorial Charitable Trust
The Goldcrest Charitable Trust
The Golden Bottle Trust
The Goldsmiths' Company
  Charity
The Goodman Foundation
The Gosling Foundation Ltd
The Edward Gostling
  Foundation
Gowling WLG (UK) Charitable
  Trust
The Hemraj Goyal Foundation
The Grace Trust
The Graham Trust
Grand Charitable Trust of the
  Order of Women
  Freemasons
The Green Hall Foundation
Greenham Trust Ltd
The Greggs Foundation
The Grocers' Charity
The Walter Guinness
  Charitable Trust
The Hadley Trust
The Hadrian Trust
Halifax Foundation for
  Northern Ireland

Hampshire and Isle of Wight
  Community Foundation
The Hampstead Wells and
  Campden Trust
Hampton Fund
The W. A. Handley Charity
  Trust
The Lennox Hannay Charitable
  Trust
The Haramead Trust
Harborne Parish Lands Charity
William Harding's Charity
The Harebell Centenary Fund
The Hargreaves Foundation
The Harris Family Charitable
  Trust
The Peter Harrison Foundation
The Harrison-Frank Family
  Foundation (UK) Ltd
Gay and Peter Hartley's
  Hillards Charitable Trust
The Hasluck Charitable Trust
The Maurice Hatter Foundation
The Hawthorne Charitable
  Trust
The Dorothy Hay-Bolton
  Charitable Trust
The Headley Trust
Heart of England Community
  Foundation
The Hedley Foundation
Help for Health
The Hemby Charitable Trust
Tim Henman Foundation
The G. D. Herbert Charitable
  Trust
Herefordshire Community
  Foundation
P. and C. Hickinbotham
  Charitable Trust
The Hillier Trust
R. G. Hills Charitable Trust
The Lady Hind Trust
The Henry C. Hoare Charitable
  Trust
The Hobson Charity Ltd
The Jane Hodge Foundation
Hollick Family Foundation
The Holywood Trust
Sir Harold Hood's Charitable
  Trust
The Thomas J. Horne
  Memorial Trust
The Horners Charity Fund
The Hospital of God at
  Greatham
The Hospital Saturday Fund
Housing Pathways Trust
The Hudson Foundation
The Huggard Charitable Trust
The Humanitarian Trust
Miss Agnes H. Hunter's Trust
The Iliffe Family Charitable
  Trust
The Indigo Trust
The Inflexion Foundation

The Inman Charity
The Invigorate Charitable Trust
Irish Youth Foundation (UK)
    Ltd (incorporating The
    Lawlor Foundation)
The J. and J. Benevolent
    Foundation
Lady Eda Jardine Charitable
    Trust
The Roger and Jean Jefcoate
    Trust
Lillie Johnson Charitable Trust
Johnnie Johnson Trust
The Jones 1986 Charitable
    Trust
The Muriel Jones Foundation
J. E. Joseph Charitable Fund
The Cyril and Eve Jumbo
    Charitable Trust
Anton Jurgens Charitable Trust
The Ian Karten Charitable
    Trust
The Michael and Ilse Katz
    Foundation
The Kennedy Leigh Charitable
    Trust
The Kennedy Trust for
    Rheumatology Research
The Kensington and Chelsea
    Foundation
Kent Community Foundation
The Kentown Wizard
    Foundation
The Peter Kershaw Trust
The Ursula Keyes Trust
Fraser Kilpatrick Charitable
    Trust
The Graham Kirkham
    Foundation
The Ernest Kleinwort
    Charitable Trust
The Kobler Trust
Ladbrokes Coral Trust
Maurice and Hilda Laing
    Charitable Trust
Christopher Laing Foundation
The David Laing Foundation
The Beatrice Laing Trust
The Leonard Laity Stoate
    Charitable Trust
The Lake House Charitable
    Foundation
Community Foundations for
    Lancashire and Merseyside
The LankellyChase Foundation
Mrs F. B. Laurence Charitable
    Trust
The Edgar E. Lawley
    Foundation
The Lawson Trust CIO
The Leach Fourteenth Trust
The Leathersellers' Foundation
Leeds Building Society
    Foundation
The Leeward Trust

Leicestershire and Rutland
    Masonic Charity
    Association
The Mark Leonard Trust
The Leri Charitable Trust
Cecil and Hilda Lewis
    Charitable Trust
David and Ruth Lewis Family
    Charitable Trust
The Linbury Trust
The Linder Foundation
The Frank Litchfield Charitable
    Trust
Little Lives UK*
The Michael and Betty Little
    Trust*
The Charles Littlewood Hill
    Trust
The George John and Sheilah
    Livanos Charitable Trust
Jack Livingstone Charitable
    Trust
The Elaine and Angus Lloyd
    Charitable Trust
The W. M. and B. W. Lloyd
    Trust
Lloyds Bank Foundation for
    England and Wales
Lloyds Bank Foundation for the
    Channel Islands
The Locker Foundation
London Catalyst
The London Community
    Foundation (LCF)
London Freemasons Charity
The Lord's Taverners
Lord and Lady Lurgan Trust
The Lyndal Tree Foundation
John Lyon's Charity
The R. S. Macdonald
    Charitable Trust
The Macdonald-Buchanan
    Charitable Trust
The Manackerman Charitable
    Trust
The Manchester Guardian
    Society Charitable Trust
R. W. Mann Trust
The Manson Family Charitable
    Trust
The Michael Marsh Charitable
    Trust
The Marsh Christian Trust
Charlotte Marshall Charitable
    Trust
The Martin Charitable Trust
Sir George Martin Trust
John Martin's Charity
The Dan Maskell Tennis Trust
The Master Charitable Trust
Matchroom Sport Charitable
    Foundation
Material World Foundation
MBNA General Foundation
The Robert McAlpine
    Foundation

D. D. McPhail Charitable
    Settlement
The Medicash Foundation
The Medlock Charitable Trust
Merchants House of Glasgow
The Mickleham Trust
The Gerald Micklem Charitable
    Trust
The Millennium Oak Trust
Hugh and Mary Miller Bequest
    Trust
The Ronald Miller Foundation
The Clare Milne Trust
Milton Keynes Community
    Foundation Ltd
The Laurence Misener
    Charitable Trust
The Mishcon Family Charitable
    Trust
The Brian Mitchell Charitable
    Settlement
The Esmé Mitchell Trust
The MITIE Foundation
The MK Charitable Trust
Mobbs Memorial Trust Ltd
The Modiano Charitable Trust
Mole Charitable Trust
The Monmouthshire County
    Council Welsh Church Act
    Fund
The Morgan Charitable
    Foundation
The Steve Morgan Foundation
The Morris Charitable Trust
G. M. Morrison Charitable
    Trust
The Ken and Edna Morrison
    Charitable Trust
The Ken and Lynne Morrison
    Charitable Trust
The Morrisons Foundation
The Mosselson Charitable
    Trust
Motability
Moto Foundation
The Moulding Foundation
The MSE Charity
The Mulberry Trust
Edith Murphy Foundation
Murphy-Neumann Charity
    Company Ltd
Brian Murtagh Charitable Trust
Music Sales Charitable Trust
The Mutley Foundation
Newby Trust Ltd
Norfolk Community Foundation
The Norman Family Charitable
    Trust
Northamptonshire Community
    Foundation
The Northwick Trust
The Norton Foundation
Norwich Consolidated
    Charities
The Oakdale Trust
Odin Charitable Trust

Oizer Charitable Trust
Old Possum's Practical Trust
One Community Foundation
    Ltd
The Sir Peter O'Sullevan
    Charitable Trust
The O'Sullivan Family
    Charitable Trust
Otsar Trust
Ovingdean Hall Foundation
The Owen Family Trust
Oxfordshire Community
    Foundation
The Paragon Trust
Miss M. E. S. Paterson's
    Charitable Trust
Payne-Gallwey 1989 Charitable
    Trust
Peacock Charitable Trust
Susanna Peake Charitable
    Trust
The Pears Family Charitable
    Foundation
The Pharsalia Charitable Trust
The Phillips and Rubens
    Charitable Trust
The Phillips Family Charitable
    Trust
The Philip and Connie Phillips
    Foundation*
The Bernard Piggott Charitable
    Trust
The Austin and Hope
    Pilkington Trust
The Players Foundation
The George and Esme Pollitzer
    Charitable Settlement
The Portishead Nautical Trust
The Portrack Charitable Trust
Prison Service Charity Fund
Provincial Grand Charity of the
    Province of Derbyshire
The Purey Cust Trust CIO
QBE European Operations
    Foundation
Queen Mary's Roehampton
    Trust
The Radcliffe Trust
Richard Radcliffe Trust
The Rainford Trust
The Joseph and Lena Randall
    Charitable Trust
Elizabeth Rathbone Charity
Red Hill Charitable Trust
C. A. Redfern Charitable
    Foundation
The Revere Charitable Trust
The Rhododendron Trust
Riada Trust
Richmond Parish Lands Charity
Rigby Foundation
RNID (The Royal National
    Institute for Deaf People)
The Roan Charitable Trust
The Robertson Trust

The Dezna Robins Jones
    Charitable Foundation
The Sir James Roll Charitable
    Trust
The Gerald and Gail Ronson
    Family Foundation
Mrs L. D. Rope's Third
    Charitable Settlement
Rosca Trust
The Rothley Trust
The Roughley Charitable Trust
The Rowlands Trust
Royal Docks Trust (London)
The Ryvoan Trust*
S. and R. Charitable Trust
The Jeremy and John Sacher
    Charitable Trust
The Saddlers' Company
    Charitable Fund
The Saintbury Trust
The Salamander Charitable
    Trust
Samjo Ltd
The Basil Samuel Charitable
    Trust
Scott (Eredine) Charitable
    Trust
The John Scott Trust Fund
Scottish Property Industry
    Festival of Christmas
    (SPIFOX)
Scouloudi Foundation
The Sam and Bella Sebba
    Charitable Foundation
The Shanly Foundation
The Shears Foundation
The Sheffield Town Trust
The Sheldon Trust
The R. C. Sherriff Rosebriars
    Trust
The Shipwrights Charitable
    Fund
The Skelton Bounty
The Charles Skey Charitable
    Trust
Kathleen Beryl Sleigh
    Charitable Trust
The Mrs Smith and Mount
    Trust
The N. Smith Charitable
    Settlement
The Leslie Smith Foundation
David Solomons Charitable
    Trust
Songdale Ltd
Spielman Charitable Trust
Spurrell Charitable Trust
The Geoff and Fiona Squire
    Foundation
The Squire Patton Boggs
    Charitable Trust
St James's Place Charitable
    Foundation
St Monica Trust
Stadium Charitable Trust

The Peter Stebbings Memorial
    Charity
The Steinberg Family
    Charitable Trust
The Sir Sigmund Sternberg
    Charitable Foundation
Sir Halley Stewart Trust
The Stewarts Law Foundation
Strand Parishes Trust
The Strangward Trust
Stratford-upon-Avon Town Trust
The W. O. Street Charitable
    Foundation
The Street Foundation
The Bernard Sunley
    Foundation
The Sunrise Foundation CIO
Sutton Coldfield Charitable
    Trust
The Swann-Morton Foundation
The Swire Charitable Trust
The Charles and Elsie Sykes
    Trust
The T.K. Maxx and
    Homesense Foundation
The Talbot Trusts
Tallow Chandlers Benevolent
    Fund No 2
The Tanlaw Foundation
Tanner Trust
Tay Charitable Trust
C. B. and H. H. T. Taylor 1984
    Trust
The Tennis Foundation
The Thales Charitable Trust
Sir Jules Thorn Charitable
    Trust
The Three Guineas Trust
The Three Oaks Trust
The Tory Family Foundation
Tower Hill Trust
The Toy Trust
Annie Tranmer Charitable Trust
The Constance Travis
    Charitable Trust
The True Colours Trust
The James Tudor Foundation
The Tudor Trust
The Tuixen Foundation
The Roger and Douglas Turner
    Charitable Trust
UKH Foundation
The Ulverscroft Foundation
The Albert Van Den Bergh
    Charitable Trust
The Van Mesdag Fund
Variety, the Children's Charity
VINCI UK Foundation
Vision Foundation
The Vodafone Foundation
Sylvia Waddilove Foundation
    UK
The Bruce Wake Charity
The Walker Trust
The Barbara Ward Children's
    Foundation

The Warwickshire Masonic
  Charitable Association Ltd
Mrs Waterhouse Charitable
  Trust
G. R. Waters Charitable Trust
  2000
The Wates Foundation
John Watson's Trust*
The William Webster
  Charitable Trust
The Weinstock Fund
The James Weir Foundation
The Welsh Church Act Fund
Wembley National Stadium
  Trust
The Westfield Health
  Charitable Trust
The Whinfell Charitable Fund
The Will Charitable Trust
The Williams Family
  Foundation
The Francis Winham
  Foundation
The Michael and Anna Wix
  Charitable Trust
The Wolfson Family Charitable
  Trust
The Wolfson Foundation
The Lord Leonard and Lady
  Estelle Wolfson Foundation
Wooden Spoon Society
The Woodward Charitable
  Trust
The Worshipful Company of
  Glovers of London
  Charitable Trust
Worth Waynflete Foundation
The Worwin UK Foundation
The Wyseliot Rose Charitable
  Trust
The Yapp Charitable Trust
Yorkshire Building Society
  Charitable Foundation
The Elizabeth and Prince
  Zaiger Trust
Zurich Community Trust (UK)
  Ltd

....

■ **People with a
  cognitive or
  learning disability**

The Aldama Foundation
Douglas Arter Foundation
The Baily Thomas Charitable
  Fund
Bank of Scotland Foundation
The Percy Bilton Charity
The Boshier-Hinton Foundation
CareTech Charitable
  Foundation
Carew Pole Charitable Trust
The Childwick Trust
The City Bridge Trust (Bridge
  House Estates)
The Clothworkers' Foundation

The Vivienne and Samuel
  Cohen Charitable Trust
The J. Reginald Corah
  Foundation Fund
Cornwall Community
  Foundation
CRH Charitable Trust
Cullum Family Trust
The Daniell Trust
The David Family Foundation*
The Delves Charitable Trust
Eastern Counties Educational
  Trust Ltd
The Ellerdale Trust
The Eveson Charitable Trust
The Fieldrose Charitable Trust
Dixie Rose Findlay Charitable
  Trust
The Forbes Charitable
  Foundation
The Joseph Strong Frazer Trust
J. Paul Getty Jr General
  Charitable Trust*
The Gisela Graham Foundation
The Albert Gubay Charitable
  Foundation
Halifax Foundation for
  Northern Ireland
Hampton Fund
The Peter Harrison Foundation
The Hawthorne Charitable
  Trust
The Hedley Foundation
Help for Health
Miss Agnes H. Hunter's Trust
The Inman Charity
The J. J. Charitable Trust
The Ian Karten Charitable
  Trust
Fraser Kilpatrick Charitable
  Trust
The Mark Leonard Trust
Lloyds Bank Foundation for
  England and Wales
London Freemasons Charity
The Lord's Taverners
John Lyon's Charity
Sir George Martin Trust
The Dan Maskell Tennis Trust
Matchroom Sport Charitable
  Foundation
Material World Foundation
The Gerald Micklem Charitable
  Trust
The Millennium Oak Trust
Hugh and Mary Miller Bequest
  Trust
The MSE Charity
Norfolk Community Foundation
The Norman Family Charitable
  Trust
Odin Charitable Trust
Old Possum's Practical Trust
Payne-Gallwey 1989 Charitable
  Trust

The Philip and Connie Phillips
  Foundation*
The Bernard Piggott Charitable
  Trust
The Portishead Nautical Trust
The Purey Cust Trust CIO
QBE European Operations
  Foundation
Queen Mary's Roehampton
  Trust
The Rainford Trust
Red Hill Charitable Trust
The Rix-Thompson-Rothenberg
  Foundation
The Robertson Trust
The Sir James Roll Charitable
  Trust
The Roughley Charitable Trust
The Ryvoan Trust*
The Saddlers' Company
  Charitable Fund
The Saintbury Trust
Scottish Property Industry
  Festival of Christmas
  (SPIFOX)
The Sheldon Trust
The Mrs Smith and Mount
  Trust
The Leslie Smith Foundation
David Solomons Charitable
  Trust
The Strangward Trust
The Swann-Morton Foundation
The Charles and Elsie Sykes
  Trust
The Tanlaw Foundation
The Three Guineas Trust
The True Colours Trust
The Tuixen Foundation
Variety, the Children's Charity
The Barbara Ward Children's
  Foundation
John Watson's Trust*
The Weinstock Fund
Wickens Family Foundation
The Will Charitable Trust
The Lord Leonard and Lady
  Estelle Wolfson Foundation

....

■ **People with a
  physical disability**

The 29th May 1961 Charitable
  Trust
The Aldama Foundation
Douglas Arter Foundation
ArtSocial Foundation
Bank of Scotland Foundation
Barnsbury Charitable Trust
The Benham Charitable
  Settlement
The Percy Bilton Charity
Birkdale Trust for Hearing
  Impaired Ltd*
Lady Blakenham's Charity
  Trust

The Boshier-Hinton Foundation
British Eye Research
 Foundation (Fight for Sight)
Miss Margaret Butters Reekie
 Charitable Trust
CareTech Charitable
 Foundation
Carew Pole Charitable Trust
The Childwick Trust
The City Bridge Trust (Bridge
 House Estates)
The Clothworkers' Foundation
The J. Reginald Corah
 Foundation Fund
Cornwall Community
 Foundation
CRH Charitable Trust
The De Brye Charitable Trust
The Delves Charitable Trust
The Dibden Allotments Fund
The Wilfred and Elsie Elkes
 Charity Fund
The Ellerdale Trust
The Eveson Charitable Trust
The Fieldrose Charitable Trust
Dixie Rose Findlay Charitable
 Trust
The Joseph Strong Frazer Trust
Frognal Trust
J. Paul Getty Jr General
 Charitable Trust*
The B. and P. Glasser
 Charitable Trust
The Greggs Foundation
Hampton Fund
The Peter Harrison Foundation
The Hawthorne Charitable
 Trust
The Dorothy Hay-Bolton
 Charitable Trust
The Hedley Foundation
Help for Health
Highway One Trust
Miss Agnes H. Hunter's Trust
The Indigo Trust
The Inman Charity
The Roger and Jean Jefcoate
 Trust
The Ian Karten Charitable
 Trust
The Beatrice Laing Trust
Cecil and Hilda Lewis
 Charitable Trust
The Frank Litchfield Charitable
 Trust
The Michael and Betty Little
 Trust*
Lloyds Bank Foundation for
 England and Wales
London Freemasons Charity
The Lord's Taverners
John Lyon's Charity
The R. S. Macdonald
 Charitable Trust
Sir George Martin Trust
The Dan Maskell Tennis Trust

Matchroom Sport Charitable
 Foundation
Material World Foundation
The Gerald Micklem Charitable
 Trust
The Millennium Oak Trust
Hugh and Mary Miller Bequest
 Trust
Brian Murtagh Charitable Trust
Newby Trust Ltd
Norfolk Community Foundation
The Norman Family Charitable
 Trust
Old Possum's Practical Trust
Payne-Gallwey 1989 Charitable
 Trust
The Philip and Connie Phillips
 Foundation*
The Bernard Piggott Charitable
 Trust
The Purey Cust Trust CIO
Queen Mary's Roehampton
 Trust
Richard Radcliffe Trust
The Rainford Trust
The Joseph and Lena Randall
 Charitable Trust
Riada Trust
The Robertson Trust
Rosca Trust
The Ryvoan Trust*
The Saddlers' Company
 Charitable Fund
The Saintbury Trust
Scottish Property Industry
 Festival of Christmas
 (SPIFOX)
Kathleen Beryl Sleigh
 Charitable Trust
The Leslie Smith Foundation
The Strangward Trust
The Swann-Morton Foundation
The Charles and Elsie Sykes
 Trust
The Talbot Trusts
The Tanlaw Foundation
The True Colours Trust
The Tuixen Foundation
The Ulverscroft Foundation
Variety, the Children's Charity
Vision Foundation
The Bruce Wake Charity
The Barbara Ward Children's
 Foundation
The Weinstock Fund
The Welsh Church Act Fund
The Will Charitable Trust
The Worshipful Company of
 Glovers of London
 Charitable Trust
The Elizabeth and Prince
 Zaiger Trust

Gender and sexuality

Bank of Scotland Foundation
The Baring Foundation
The Barrow Cadbury Trust
The Coles-Medlock Foundation
Cornwall Community
 Foundation
Coutts Charitable Foundation
Cripplegate Foundation
The J. N. Derbyshire Trust
The Dischma Charitable Trust
Dr. Martens Foundation
The Fairness Foundation
J. Paul Getty Jr General
 Charitable Trust*
The Hemraj Goyal Foundation
The Hadrian Trust
The Charles Hayward
 Foundation
Hollick Family Foundation
Impact Funding Partners Ltd
The Kasner Charitable Trust
The Kiawah Charitable Trust
The Kreitman Foundation
The Mishcon Family Charitable
 Trust
Moondance Foundation
John Moores Foundation
The Mosselson Charitable
 Trust
Norfolk Community Foundation
The Parivar Trust
The Pilgrim Trust
PIMCO Foundation Europe
The Players Foundation
The Joseph and Lena Randall
 Charitable Trust
The Eleanor Rathbone
 Charitable Trust
Elizabeth Rathbone Charity
Rosa Fund
The Alan and Babette
 Sainsbury Charitable Fund
The Scott Bader
 Commonwealth Ltd
Smallwood Trust
Staples Trust
The Peter Stebbings Memorial
 Charity
The T.K. Maxx and
 Homesense Foundation
Two Magpies Fund
Volant Charitable Trust
Wembley National Stadium
 Trust
The Woodward Charitable
 Trust

....

■ LGBTQ+

Bank of Scotland Foundation
The Baring Foundation
Dr. Martens Foundation
The Fairness Foundation

The Kreitman Foundation
The London Community
Foundation (LCF)
Sir George Martin Trust
The Mishcon Family Charitable
Trust
Norfolk Community Foundation
The Sigrid Rausing Trust
The T.K. Maxx and
Homesense Foundation

....

■ Women and girls

The Barrow Cadbury Trust
The Coles-Medlock Foundation
Cornwall Community
Foundation
Coutts Charitable Foundation
Cripplegate Foundation
Dentons UK and Middle East
LLP Charitable Trust
The J. N. Derbyshire Trust
The Dischma Charitable Trust
The Fairness Foundation
J. Paul Getty Jr General
Charitable Trust*
The Hemraj Goyal Foundation
The Hadrian Trust
The Charles Hayward
Foundation
The Hilden Charitable Fund
Hollick Family Foundation
P. H. Holt Foundation
Impact Funding Partners Ltd
The Kasner Charitable Trust
The Kiawah Charitable Trust
The LankellyChase Foundation
The Leathersellers' Foundation
The London Community
Foundation (LCF)
The Marsh Christian Trust
Moondance Foundation
John Moores Foundation
The Mosselson Charitable
Trust
Norfolk Community Foundation
The Olwyn Foundation
The Parivar Trust
The Pilgrim Trust
PIMCO Foundation Europe
The Joseph and Lena Randall
Charitable Trust
The Eleanor Rathbone
Charitable Trust
Elizabeth Rathbone Charity
The Sigrid Rausing Trust
The Robertson Trust
Rosa Fund
The Alan and Babette
Sainsbury Charitable Fund
The Sasha Foundation*
The Scott Bader
Commonwealth Ltd
Smallwood Trust
Staples Trust

The Peter Stebbings Memorial
Charity
Tay Charitable Trust
Two Magpies Fund
Volant Charitable Trust
Wembley National Stadium
Trust
Women's Fund for Scotland
The Woodward Charitable
Trust
Zephyr Charitable Trust

Health

The 29th May 1961 Charitable
Trust
4 Charity Foundation
The 4814 Trust
The Aberbrothock Skea Trust
Achisomoch Aid Company Ltd
The Adint Charitable Trust
The AEB Charitable Trust
The Aimwell Charitable Trust
The Alchemy Foundation
The Aldama Foundation
Al-Fayed Charitable Foundation
The Derrill Allatt Foundation
D. C. R. Allen Charitable Trust
Alliance Family Foundation Ltd
Alzheimer's Society
Amant Foundation
Ambergate Charitable Trust
The AMW Charitable Trust
Andor Charitable Trust
The Anson Charitable Trust
The Annabel Arbib Foundation
The Ardeola Charitable Trust
The Ardwick Trust
The Arsenal Foundation
The Artemis Charitable
Foundation
ArtSocial Foundation
Ove Arup Partnership
Charitable Trust
Asthma and Lung UK
The Lord Austin Trust
B&Q Foundation
The Ballinger Charitable Trust
The Band Trust
Bank of Scotland Foundation
The Barbers' Company General
Charities
The Barbour Foundation
Barcapel Foundation Ltd
The Baring Foundation
The Barnes Fund
Barnsbury Charitable Trust
Barnwood Trust
Misses Barrie Charitable Trust
The Batchworth Trust
Bauer Radio's Cash for Kids
Charities
The Gordon and Ena Baxter
Foundation*
The Bay Tree Charitable Trust
The Beaverbrook Foundation

The Beaverbrooks Charitable
Trust
The Bellahouston Bequest
Fund
Benesco Charity Ltd
The Benham Charitable
Settlement
Ruth Berkowitz Charitable
Trust
The Bestway Foundation
Bideford Bridge Trust
The Percy Bilton Charity
The Bingham Trust
The John Black Charitable
Foundation
The Bertie Black Foundation
The Isabel Blackman
Foundation
Lady Blakenham's Charity
Trust
Bloodwise
The Bluston Charitable
Settlement
Blyth Watson Charitable Trust
Maureen Boal Charitable Trust
The Marjory Boddy Charitable
Trust
The Boltini Trust
The Booth Charities
The Harry Bottom Charitable
Trust
Sir Clive Bourne Family Trust
The Tony Bramall Charitable
Trust
The Liz and Terry Bramall
Foundation
Breast Cancer Now
The Brelms Trust CIO
Bristol Charities
The Britford Bridge Trust
British Heart Foundation (BHF)
Bill Brown 1989 Charitable
Trust
R. S. Brownless Charitable
Trust
T. B. H. Brunner's Charitable
Settlement
Buckingham Trust
E. F. Bulmer Trust
Bupa Foundation
The Burden Trust
Consolidated Charity of Burton
upon Trent
Miss Margaret Butters Reekie
Charitable Trust
The Edward and Dorothy
Cadbury Trust
Cancer Research UK
Carew Pole Charitable Trust
William A. Cargill Charitable
Trust
The Carr-Gregory Trust
The Leslie Mary Carter
Charitable Trust
The Castanea Trust
The Castansa Trust

The Joseph and Annie Cattle
   Trust
The Thomas Sivewright Catto
   Charitable Settlement
The Wilfrid and Constance
   Cave Foundation
The B. G. S. Cayzer Charitable
   Trust
The Amelia Chadwick Trust
The Chalk Cliff Trust
The Chetwode Foundation
The Childhood Trust
Children with Cancer UK
The Childwick Trust
Chippenham Borough Lands
   Charity
CHK Foundation
The Churchill Foundation
The Clarkson Foundation
The Clothworkers' Foundation
The Clover Trust
F. B. Coales No. 4 (Family)
   Trust
The John Coates Charitable
   Trust
The Cobtree Charity Trust Ltd
The Vivienne and Samuel
   Cohen Charitable Trust
Colchester Catalyst Charity
Colyer-Fergusson Charitable
   Trust
Douglas Compton James
   Charitable Trust
The J. Reginald Corah
   Foundation Fund
The Gershon Coren Charitable
   Foundation
Cornwall Community
   Foundation
Corra Foundation
Dudley and Geoffrey Cox
   Charitable Trust
The Sir William Coxen Trust
   Fund
The Lord Cozens-Hardy Trust
CRASH
Michael Crawford Children's
   Charity
CRH Charitable Trust
Cripplegate Foundation
The Cross Trust
The Croydon Relief-in-Need
   Charity
Cruden Foundation Ltd
The Cunningham Trust
The D. G. Charitable
   Settlement
The D. M. Charitable Trust
The Roger De Haan Charitable
   Trust
The Delves Charitable Trust
Dentons UK and Middle East
   LLP Charitable Trust
The J. N. Derbyshire Trust
The Laduma Dhamecha
   Charitable Trust

The Alan and Sheila Diamond
   Charitable Trust
The Dischma Charitable Trust
Donibristle Trust
The Dorcas Trust
The Dorus Trust
The D'Oyly Carte Charitable
   Trust
Dromintee Trust
Duchy Health Charity Ltd
Duchy of Lancaster Benevolent
   Fund
Dunlossit and Islay Community
   Trust
The Earley Charity
Eastern Counties Educational
   Trust Ltd
Edupoor Ltd
The Eight Foundation
The Eighteen Fund
The Elie Trust
The Wilfred and Elsie Elkes
   Charity Fund
The Ellerdale Trust
The Englefield Charitable Trust
The Enkalon Foundation
The Evelyn Trust
The Everard Foundation
The Eveson Charitable Trust
The Exilarch's Foundation
G. F. Eyre Charitable Trust
The Fairness Foundation
The Fairstead Trust
The Lord Faringdon Charitable
   Trust
Samuel William Farmer Trust
The Thomas Farr Charity
The February Foundation
George Fentham Birmingham
   Charity
The A. M. Fenton Trust
Dixie Rose Findlay Charitable
   Trust
Sir John Fisher Foundation
Fishmongers' Company's
   Charitable Trust
The Earl Fitzwilliam Charitable
   Trust
The Follett Trust
Forest Hill Charitable Trust
The Lady Forester Trust
The Forman Hardy Charitable
   Trust
The Forrester Family Trust
The Fort Foundation
Foux Foundation
Fowler Smith and Jones Trust
The Elizabeth Frankland Moore
   and Star Foundation
The Gordon Fraser Charitable
   Trust
The Hugh Fraser Foundation
The Joseph Strong Frazer Trust
The Louis and Valerie
   Freedman Charitable
   Settlement

Charles S. French Charitable
   Trust
The Freshgate Trust
   Foundation
Friarsgate Trust
The Patrick and Helena Frost
   Foundation
The Fulmer Charitable Trust
G. M. C. Trust
Ganzoni Charitable Trust
Martin Geddes Charitable
   Trust
General Charity (Coventry)
The Generations Foundation
The Tara Getty Foundation
J. Paul Getty Jr General
   Charitable Trust*
The David Gibbons Foundation
The Girdlers' Company
   Charitable Trust
The B. and P. Glasser
   Charitable Trust
The Gloag Foundation
Global Charities
Sydney and Phyllis Goldberg
   Memorial Charitable Trust
The Goldsmiths' Company
   Charity
The Goodman Foundation
The Gosling Foundation Ltd
The Edward Gostling
   Foundation
Gowling WLG (UK) Charitable
   Trust
Grace Charitable Trust
The Grace Trust
The Graham Trust
Grand Charitable Trust of the
   Order of Women
   Freemasons
The Green Hall Foundation
Philip and Judith Green Trust
Greenham Trust Ltd
The Grimmitt Trust
The Albert Gubay Charitable
   Foundation
H. and T. Clients Charitable
   Trust
The Hadley Trust
The Hadrian Trust
Halifax Foundation for
   Northern Ireland
Hamamelis Trust
The Helen Hamlyn Trust
Hampshire and Isle of Wight
   Community Foundation
The Hampstead Wells and
   Campden Trust
Hampton Fund
The W. A. Handley Charity
   Trust
The Lennox Hannay Charitable
   Trust
The Kathleen Hannay
   Memorial Charity
The Haramead Trust

The Harding Trust
The Harebell Centenary Fund
The Hargreaves Foundation
The Harris Family Charitable
 Trust
The Harrison-Frank Family
 Foundation (UK) Ltd
Gay and Peter Hartley's
 Hillards Charitable Trust
Edward Harvist Trust (The
 Harvist Estate)
The Hasluck Charitable Trust
The Hawthorne Charitable
 Trust
The Charles Hayward
 Foundation
The Headley Trust
The Health Foundation
Heart of England Community
 Foundation
Heart Research UK
The Heathcoat Trust
Heb Ffin (Without Frontier)
The Hedley Foundation
Help for Health
The Hemby Charitable Trust
Tim Henman Foundation
The G. D. Herbert Charitable
 Trust
Herefordshire Community
 Foundation
The Alison Hillman Charitable
 Trust*
R. G. Hills Charitable Trust
The Hintze Family Charity
 Foundation
The Henry C. Hoare Charitable
 Trust
The Hobson Charity Ltd
The Jane Hodge Foundation
The Holbeck Charitable Trust
The Hollands-Warren Fund
Hollick Family Foundation
P. H. Holt Foundation
Sir Harold Hood's Charitable
 Trust
Hope Trust
The Thomas J. Horne
 Memorial Trust
Hospice UK
The Hospital of God at
 Greatham
The Hospital Saturday Fund
The Hudson Foundation
The Hull and East Riding
 Charitable Trust
The Humanitarian Trust
Huntingdon Freemen's Trust
The Nani Huyu Charitable Trust
Hyde Park Place Estate Charity
The Iliffe Family Charitable
 Trust
The Inflexion Foundation
The Inman Charity
The Inverforth Charitable Trust

The Ireland Fund of Great
 Britain
The J. Isaacs Charitable Trust
The J. and J. Benevolent
 Foundation
The Susan and Stephen
 James Charitable
 Settlement
The JD Foundation
The Roger and Jean Jefcoate
 Trust
The Jenour Foundation
The Elton John AIDS
 Foundation
Lillie Johnson Charitable Trust
The Jones 1986 Charitable
 Trust
Anton Jurgens Charitable Trust
The Jusaca Charitable Trust
The Ian Karten Charitable
 Trust
The Michael and Ilse Katz
 Foundation
The Kennedy Leigh Charitable
 Trust
The Kennedy Trust for
 Rheumatology Research
The Kensington and Chelsea
 Foundation
Kent Community Foundation
The Kentown Wizard
 Foundation
The Peter Kershaw Trust
The Ursula Keyes Trust
Fraser Kilpatrick Charitable
 Trust
The Mary Kinross Charitable
 Trust
The Graham Kirkham
 Foundation
The Ernest Kleinwort
 Charitable Trust
The Kobler Trust
Kollel and Co. Ltd
Kupath Gemach Chaim
 Bechesed Viznitz Trust
Kusuma Trust UK
Ladbrokes Coral Trust
Christopher Laing Foundation
The Kirby Laing Foundation
The Martin Laing Foundation
The Leonard Laity Stoate
 Charitable Trust
The Lake House Charitable
 Foundation
Community Foundations for
 Lancashire and Merseyside
Lancaster Foundation
The Allen Lane Foundation
Laslett's (Hinton) Charity
Mrs F. B. Laurence Charitable
 Trust
The Richard Lawes Foundation
The Edgar E. Lawley
 Foundation
The Leach Fourteenth Trust

The Leathersellers' Foundation
Leeds Building Society
 Foundation
The Leeward Trust
Leicestershire and Rutland
 Masonic Charity
 Association
The Leigh Trust
Lord Leverhulme's Charitable
 Trust
Limoges Charitable Trust
The Linder Foundation
The Lister Charitable Trust
The Frank Litchfield Charitable
 Trust
The Charles Littlewood Hill
 Trust
Liverpool Charity and Voluntary
 Services (LCVS)
The Ian and Natalie
 Livingstone Charitable Trust
Jack Livingstone Charitable
 Trust
The Elaine and Angus Lloyd
 Charitable Trust
Lloyds Bank Foundation for
 England and Wales
Lloyds Bank Foundation for the
 Channel Islands
The Locker Foundation
London Catalyst
London Freemasons Charity
Longleigh Foundation
The Lord's Taverners
The C. L. Loyd Charitable Trust
Lord and Lady Lurgan Trust
The Lyndal Tree Foundation
John Lyon's Charity
The R. S. Macdonald
 Charitable Trust
Mace Foundation
The Manackerman Charitable
 Trust
The Manchester Guardian
 Society Charitable Trust
R. W. Mann Trust
The Manoukian Charitable
 Foundation
The Manson Family Charitable
 Trust
The Marsh Christian Trust
Charlotte Marshall Charitable
 Trust
The Martin Charitable Trust
Sir George Martin Trust
John Martin's Charity
Masonic Charitable Foundation
The Master Charitable Trust
Matchroom Sport Charitable
 Foundation
The Matliwala Family
 Charitable Trust
Maudsley Charity
The Violet Mauray Charitable
 Trust
MBNA General Foundation

The Robert McAlpine
  Foundation
D. D. McPhail Charitable
  Settlement
The Medicash Foundation
The Merchant Taylors'
  Foundation*
The Merchant Venturers
  Charity
Merchants House of Glasgow
The Mickleham Trust
The Gerald Micklem Charitable
  Trust
The Millennium Oak Trust
Hugh and Mary Miller Bequest
  Trust
The Ronald Miller Foundation
The James Milner Foundation
Milton Keynes Community
  Foundation Ltd
The Laurence Misener
  Charitable Trust
The Mishcon Family Charitable
  Trust
The Brian Mitchell Charitable
  Settlement
The Esmé Mitchell Trust
The MK Charitable Trust
The Monmouthshire County
  Council Welsh Church Act
  Fund
Moondance Foundation
John Moores Foundation
The Morris Charitable Trust
G. M. Morrison Charitable
  Trust
The Ken and Lynne Morrison
  Charitable Trust
The Morrisons Foundation
Motor Neurone Disease
  Association
The Moulding Foundation
The Edwina Mountbatten and
  Leonora Children's
  Foundation
The MSE Charity
The Mulberry Trust
Multiple Sclerosis Society
Edith Murphy Foundation
Murphy-Neumann Charity
  Company Ltd
Brian Murtagh Charitable Trust
Music Sales Charitable Trust
The National Garden Scheme
Ner Foundation
Newby Trust Ltd
The Frances and Augustus
  Newman Foundation
Norfolk Community Foundation
The Norman Family Charitable
  Trust
Normanby Charitable Trust
North West Cancer Research
Northern Pharmacies Ltd Trust
  Fund

The Norton Rose Fulbright
  Charitable Foundation
Norwich Consolidated
  Charities
Nottinghamshire Community
  Foundation
The Nuffield Foundation
The Oakdale Trust
Henry Oldfield Trust
One Community Foundation
  Ltd
Open House Trust Ltd
Orthopaedic Research UK
The O'Sullivan Family
  Charitable Trust
Otsar Trust
Ovingdean Hall Foundation
P. F. Charitable Trust
The Paget Charitable Trust
The Panacea Charitable Trust
The Paragon Trust
The Parivar Trust
Parkinson's UK
Miss M. E. S. Paterson's
  Charitable Trust
The J. G. W. Patterson
  Foundation
Peacock Charitable Trust
Susanna Peake Charitable
  Trust
David Pearlman Charitable
  Foundation
The Pears Family Charitable
  Foundation
The Dowager Countess
  Eleanor Peel Trust
Personal Assurance Charitable
  Trust
The Pharsalia Charitable Trust
The Philip and Connie Phillips
  Foundation*
The Bernard Piggott Charitable
  Trust
Cecil Pilkington Charitable
  Trust
Pilkington Charities Fund
The Sir Harry Pilkington Fund
Pink Ribbon Foundation
The Pixel Fund
The Players Foundation
Thomas Pocklington Trust
Porter Foundation
The Portrack Charitable Trust
The Mary Potter Convent
  Hospital Trust
The Priory Foundation
Prison Service Charity Fund
Prostate Cancer UK
Provincial Grand Charity of the
  Province of Derbyshire
Mr and Mrs J. A. Pye's
  Charitable Settlement
QBE European Operations
  Foundation
Quartet Community Foundation
Quothquan Trust

Richard Radcliffe Trust
The Rainford Trust
The Randal Charitable
  Foundation
The Joseph and Lena Randall
  Charitable Trust
The Ratcliff Foundation
Elizabeth Rathbone Charity
The Ravensdale Trust
The Rayne Foundation
Red Hill Charitable Trust
C. A. Redfern Charitable
  Foundation
The Rhododendron Trust
Riada Trust
Daisie Rich Trust
Richmond Parish Lands Charity
Rigby Foundation
Riverside Charitable Trust Ltd
RNID (The Royal National
  Institute for Deaf People)
The Dezna Robins Jones
  Charitable Foundation
Rockcliffe Charitable Trust
The Gerald and Gail Ronson
  Family Foundation
The Cecil Rosen Foundation
The Rothermere Foundation
The Roughley Charitable Trust
The Rowlands Trust
The Royal Foundation of The
  Prince and Princess of
  Wales
The Jeremy and John Sacher
  Charitable Trust
The Michael and Nicola Sacher
  Charitable Trust
The Alan and Babette
  Sainsbury Charitable Fund
The Salamander Charitable
  Trust
Samjo Ltd
The Basil Samuel Charitable
  Trust
The Sands Family Trust
The Sasha Foundation*
Schroder Charity Trust
The Scotshill Trust
The Scott Bader
  Commonwealth Ltd
Sir Samuel Scott of Yews
  Trust
The Ina Scott Sutherland
  Charitable Foundation
The John Scott Trust Fund
Scouloudi Foundation
The Searchlight Electric
  Charitable Trust
The Sam and Bella Sebba
  Charitable Foundation
The Jean Shanks Foundation
The Shanly Foundation
The Shears Foundation
The Bassil Shippam and
  Alsford Trust

The Florence Shute Millennium
   Trust
Skipton Building Society
   Charitable Foundation
The Mrs Smith and Mount
   Trust
The N. Smith Charitable
   Settlement
The Henry Smith Charity
Arabella and Julian Smith
   Family Trust
The Leslie Smith Foundation
Philip Smith's Charitable Trust
Somerset Community
   Foundation
Songdale Ltd
The E. C. Sosnow Charitable
   Trust
South Yorkshire Community
   Foundation
The Stephen R. and Philippa
   H. Southall Charitable Trust
Sparquote Ltd
Spielman Charitable Trust
The Squire Patton Boggs
   Charitable Trust
The Squires Foundation
St James's Place Charitable
   Foundation
The Peter Stebbings Memorial
   Charity
The Hugh Stenhouse
   Foundation
The Sir Sigmund Sternberg
   Charitable Foundation
The Sterry Family Foundation
Sir Halley Stewart Trust
The Stoller Charitable Trust
The Stone Family Foundation
Stratford-upon-Avon Town Trust
The W. O. Street Charitable
   Foundation
The Sunrise Foundation CIO
Community Foundation for
   Surrey
Sutton Coldfield Charitable
   Trust
The Swann-Morton Foundation
The Charles and Elsie Sykes
   Trust
The Tajtelbaum Charitable
   Trust
The Gay and Keith Talbot Trust
The Talbot Trusts
Tallow Chandlers Benevolent
   Fund No 2
Tanner Trust
The Taurus Foundation
Tay Charitable Trust
C. B. and H. H. T. Taylor 1984
   Trust
The Thales Charitable Trust
Sir Jules Thorn Charitable
   Trust
The Thornton Trust
The Three Guineas Trust

The Tolkien Trust
The Tompkins Foundation
The Tory Family Foundation
The Toy Trust
Toyota Manufacturing UK
   Charitable Trust
The Constance Travis
   Charitable Trust
The True Colours Trust
The Trusthouse Charitable
   Foundation
The James Tudor Foundation
The Tudor Trust
The Tuixen Foundation
UKH Foundation
Ulster Garden Villages Ltd
The Ulverscroft Foundation
The Union of the Sisters of
   Mercy of Great Britain
The Utley Foundation
The Valentine Charitable Trust
The Albert Van Den Bergh
   Charitable Trust
The Van Mesdag Fund
The Vandervell Foundation
Variety, the Children's Charity
The Velvet Foundation
The Vintners' Foundation
Virgin Atlantic Foundation
The Vodafone Foundation
The Georg and Emily von Opel
   Foundation
The VTCT Foundation
Wallace and Gromit's
   Children's Foundation
The Warwickshire Masonic
   Charitable Association Ltd
Mrs Waterhouse Charitable
   Trust
The Geoffrey Watling Charity
Wellbank Foundation*
The Welsh Church Act Fund
The Westfield Health
   Charitable Trust
The Galen and Hilary Weston
   Foundation
The Garfield Weston
   Foundation
The Whinfell Charitable Fund
The Melanie White Foundation
   Ltd
The Felicity Wilde Charitable
   Trust
The Will Charitable Trust
The Wilmcote Charitrust
Sumner Wilson Charitable
   Trust
The Michael and Anna Wix
   Charitable Trust
The Wolfson Family Charitable
   Trust
The Wolfson Foundation
The Lord Leonard and Lady
   Estelle Wolfson Foundation
The James Wood Bequest
   Fund

The Woodward Charitable
   Trust
Worshipful Company of Gold
   and Silver Wyre Drawers
   Second Charitable Trust
   Fund
The Eric Wright Charitable
   Trust
Sir Graham Wylie Foundation
The Wyseliot Rose Charitable
   Trust
The Yapp Charitable Trust
Yorkshire Building Society
   Charitable Foundation
Yorkshire Cancer Research
The Elizabeth and Prince
   Zaiger Trust
Zephyr Charitable Trust
The Zochonis Charitable Trust
Zurich Community Trust (UK)
   Ltd

....

■ Mental health

The Aldama Foundation
Beryl Alexander Charity
ArtSocial Foundation
Bally's Foundation
Bank of Scotland Foundation
The Baring Foundation
Barnwood Trust
The Benham Charitable
   Settlement
The Percy Bilton Charity
Bupa Foundation
The Carlton Hayes Mental
   Health Charity
The Childhood Trust
CHK Foundation
The City Bridge Trust (Bridge
   House Estates)
F. B. Coales No. 4 (Family)
   Trust
Douglas Compton James
   Charitable Trust
Cornwall Community
   Foundation
CRH Charitable Trust
Cripplegate Foundation
The Danson Foundation*
The Dashlight Foundation
The J. N. Derbyshire Trust
The Dischma Charitable Trust
Dr. Martens Foundation
Eastern Counties Educational
   Trust Ltd
Edupoor Ltd
The Ellerdale Trust
The Evelyn Trust
The Eveson Charitable Trust
The Fairness Foundation
Fishmongers' Company's
   Charitable Trust
The Joseph Strong Frazer Trust
G. M. C. Trust

J. Paul Getty Jr General
    Charitable Trust*
The Girdlers' Company
    Charitable Trust
Global Charities
Hampshire and Isle of Wight
    Community Foundation
The Hargreaves Foundation
The Charles Hayward
    Foundation
Highway One Trust
The Hospital of God at
    Greatham
The Albert Hunt Trust
The Ireland Fund of Great
    Britain
The JD Foundation
The Roger and Jean Jefcoate
    Trust
The Ian Karten Charitable
    Trust
The Kavli Trust
The Kensington and Chelsea
    Foundation
The Mary Kinross Charitable
    Trust
The Graham Kirkham
    Foundation
The Allen Lane Foundation
The LankellyChase Foundation
The Richard Lawes Foundation
Sarah Jane Leigh Charitable
    Trust*
The Michael and Betty Little
    Trust*
Lloyds Bank Foundation for
    England and Wales
The London Community
    Foundation (LCF)
Longleigh Foundation
John Lyon's Charity
Mace Foundation
The Kristina Martin Charitable
    Trust
Sir George Martin Trust
Maudsley Charity
MBNA General Foundation
The Millennium Oak Trust
John Moores Foundation
G. M. Morrison Charitable
    Trust
The MSE Charity
Newby Trust Ltd
Norfolk Community Foundation
The Norman Family Charitable
    Trust
The Northwick Trust
Norwich Consolidated
    Charities
Nottinghamshire Community
    Foundation
One Community Foundation
    Ltd
The Paragon Trust
Peacock Charitable Trust
People's Postcode Trust

The Philip and Connie Phillips
    Foundation*
Cecil Pilkington Charitable
    Trust
The Sir Harry Pilkington Fund
The Pixel Fund
The Priory Foundation
The Prudence Trust
The Purey Cust Trust CIO
The PwC Foundation
QBE European Operations
    Foundation
The Randal Charitable
    Foundation
The Rayne Foundation
Red Hill Charitable Trust
The Rhododendron Trust
The Royal Foundation of The
    Prince and Princess of
    Wales
The Ryvoan Trust*
The Schreier Foundation*
Francis C. Scott Charitable
    Trust
The Sam and Bella Sebba
    Charitable Foundation
The Mrs Smith and Mount
    Trust
Arabella and Julian Smith
    Family Trust
South Yorkshire Community
    Foundation
The Peter Stebbings Memorial
    Charity
The Stone Family Foundation
Community Foundation for
    Surrey
The Charles and Elsie Sykes
    Trust
The Talbot Trusts
The Taurus Foundation
The Tudor Trust
The Tuixen Foundation
The UK Youth Fund: Thriving
    Minds*
UKH Foundation
The Valentine Charitable Trust
Volant Charitable Trust
Wakefield and Tetley Trust
The Lord Leonard and Lady
    Estelle Wolfson Foundation
The James Wood Bequest
    Fund
The Eric Wright Charitable
    Trust
The Wyseliot Rose Charitable
    Trust
The Yapp Charitable Trust

....

■ People with specific conditions

The 4814 Trust
Achisomoch Aid Company Ltd
The AEB Charitable Trust
The Aldama Foundation

Al-Fayed Charitable Foundation
The Anson Charitable Trust
The Ardeola Charitable Trust
ArtSocial Foundation
Asthma and Lung UK
The Bellahouston Bequest
    Fund
The Benham Charitable
    Settlement
The Bingham Trust
Binks Trust
Birkdale Trust for Hearing
    Impaired Ltd*
Bloodwise
Maureen Boal Charitable Trust
The Marjory Boddy Charitable
    Trust
The Harry Bottom Charitable
    Trust
Sir Clive Bourne Family Trust
Bright Red Charity
British Eye Research
    Foundation (Fight for Sight)
British Heart Foundation (BHF)
Buckingham Trust
Miss Margaret Butters Reekie
    Charitable Trust
Cancer Research UK
The Castansa Trust
The Childhood Trust
Children with Cancer UK
F. B. Coales No. 4 (Family)
    Trust
The Cobtree Charity Trust Ltd
The Vivienne and Samuel
    Cohen Charitable Trust
Douglas Compton James
    Charitable Trust
The Keith Coombs Trust
Cornwall Community
    Foundation
The Cross Trust
The D. G. Charitable
    Settlement
The Delves Charitable Trust
The Elie Trust
The Wilfred and Elsie Elkes
    Charity Fund
The Evelyn Trust
Dixie Rose Findlay Charitable
    Trust
The Joseph Strong Frazer Trust
The B. and P. Glasser
    Charitable Trust
Sydney and Phyllis Goldberg
    Memorial Charitable Trust
Philip and Judith Green Trust
The Albert Gubay Charitable
    Foundation
H. and T. Clients Charitable
    Trust
The Hawthorne Charitable
    Trust
The Headley Trust
Heart Research UK
Highway One Trust

The Alison Hillman Charitable
Trust*
Sir Harold Hood's Charitable
Trust
The Albert Hunt Trust
The Inman Charity
The Roger and Jean Jefcoate
Trust
The Elton John AIDS
Foundation
The Ian Karten Charitable
Trust
The Kennedy Trust for
Rheumatology Research
The Kentown Wizard
Foundation
Fraser Kilpatrick Charitable
Trust
The Kirby Laing Foundation
The Leeward Trust
Joseph Levy Foundation
The Frank Litchfield Charitable
Trust
London Freemasons Charity
The R. S. Macdonald
Charitable Trust
The Martin Charitable Trust
Matchroom Sport Charitable
Foundation
Merchants House of Glasgow
The Mickleham Trust
The Gerald Micklem Charitable
Trust
The Millennium Oak Trust
Hugh and Mary Miller Bequest
Trust
The Ken and Edna Morrison
Charitable Trust
The Ken and Lynne Morrison
Charitable Trust
Motor Neurone Disease
Association
The MSE Charity
Multiple Sclerosis Society
Murphy-Neumann Charity
Company Ltd
North West Cancer Research
Norwich Consolidated
Charities
The Nuffield Foundation
The O'Sullivan Family
Charitable Trust
Otsar Trust
Ovingdean Hall Foundation
The Paragon Trust
Parkinson's UK
The J. G. W. Patterson
Foundation
Peacock Charitable Trust
The Dowager Countess
Eleanor Peel Trust
The Philip and Connie Phillips
Foundation*
The Bernard Piggott Charitable
Trust

Cecil Pilkington Charitable
Trust
The Sir Harry Pilkington Fund
Pink Ribbon Foundation
Thomas Pocklington Trust
The Portrack Charitable Trust
Prison Service Charity Fund
Prostate Cancer UK
The Purey Cust Trust CIO
Richard Radcliffe Trust
The Rainford Trust
The Joseph and Lena Randall
Charitable Trust
Red Hill Charitable Trust
Riada Trust
The Dezna Robins Jones
Charitable Foundation
The Alan and Babette
Sainsbury Charitable Fund
Sir Samuel Scott of Yews
Trust
The Ina Scott Sutherland
Charitable Foundation
The Bassil Shippam and
Alsford Trust
Skipton Building Society
Charitable Foundation
The Leslie Smith Foundation
South Yorkshire Community
Foundation
St James's Place Charitable
Foundation
The W. O. Street Charitable
Foundation
The Swann-Morton Foundation
The Charles and Elsie Sykes
Trust
The Syncona Foundation
The Talbot Trusts
Tanner Trust
Tay Charitable Trust
The Three Guineas Trust
The True Colours Trust
The James Tudor Foundation
The Ulverscroft Foundation
The Utley Foundation
The Valentine Charitable Trust
The VTCT Foundation
The Galen and Hilary Weston
Foundation
The Will Charitable Trust
The Lord Leonard and Lady
Estelle Wolfson Foundation
The James Wood Bequest
Fund
The Wyseliot Rose Charitable
Trust
Yorkshire Cancer Research
Zephyr Charitable Trust

....

■ Substance misuse/abuse

Bank of Scotland Foundation
The Brelms Trust CIO
The Chetwode Foundation

The Clothworkers' Foundation
Colyer-Fergusson Charitable
Trust
Corra Foundation
Dixie Rose Findlay Charitable
Trust
Forest Hill Charitable Trust
Martin Geddes Charitable
Trust
J. Paul Getty Jr General
Charitable Trust*
The Greater Manchester High
Sheriff's Police Trust
Halifax Foundation for
Northern Ireland
P. and C. Hickinbotham
Charitable Trust
Hope Trust
The Hospital of God at
Greatham
Inner London Magistrates
Court Poor Box and Feeder
Charity
The Kelly Family Charitable
Trust
The Graham Kirkham
Foundation
The LankellyChase Foundation
Laslett's (Hinton) Charity
The Leigh Trust
Lloyds Bank Foundation for
England and Wales
Lloyds Bank Foundation for the
Channel Islands
Longleigh Foundation
Merchants House of Glasgow
The Mickleham Trust
Norfolk Community Foundation
The Norman Family Charitable
Trust
Norwich Consolidated
Charities
Henry Oldfield Trust
Open House Trust Ltd
The Players Foundation
The Randal Charitable
Foundation
The Rhododendron Trust
The Roughley Charitable Trust
The Sasha Foundation*
The Frieda Scott Charitable
Trust
The Henry Smith Charity
The Peter Stebbings Memorial
Charity
the7stars Foundation
The Trusthouse Charitable
Foundation
The Vintners' Foundation
Volant Charitable Trust
The Woodward Charitable
Trust

Occupation and membership groups

■ Armed forces

The Aberbrothock Skea Trust
ABF The Soldiers' Charity
The AEB Charitable Trust
Alan Boswell Group Charitable Trust
Armed Forces Covenant Fund Trust
Armed Forces Education Trust
The Armourers and Brasiers Gauntlet Trust
The Astor Foundation
The Band Trust
The Barratt Developments plc Charitable Foundation
The Benham Charitable Settlement
The Michael Bishop Foundation
Blakemore Foundation
T. B. H. Brunner's Charitable Settlement
The Cadogan Charity
Carew Pole Charitable Trust
The Castanea Trust
The Cayo Foundation
Chartered Accountants' Livery Charity (CALC)
The Childwick Trust
The Robert Clutterbuck Charitable Trust
Drapers Charitable Fund
The Dyers' Company Charitable Trust
Edinburgh Trust No2 Account
The Englefield Charitable Trust
The Everard Foundation
The Forrester Family Trust
The Elizabeth Frankland Moore and Star Foundation
The Joseph Strong Frazer Trust
The Golden Bottle Trust
The Mike Gooley Trailfinders Charity
The Gosling Foundation Ltd
Greenham Trust Ltd
The Grocers' Charity
The Walter Guinness Charitable Trust
The W. A. Handley Charity Trust
The Lennox Hannay Charitable Trust
Christina Mary Hendrie Trust
The Hintze Family Charity Foundation
The Hobson Charity Ltd
The Inman Charity
The Inverforth Charitable Trust
The Michael and Ilse Katz Foundation

The Graham Kirkham Foundation
Sir James Knott Trust
The Beatrice Laing Trust
Mrs F. B. Laurence Charitable Trust
The Lawson Trust CIO
The Michael and Betty Little Trust*
The Charles Littlewood Hill Trust
Lloyd's Patriotic Fund
The MacRobert Trust 2019
The Master Charitable Trust
The Laurence Misener Charitable Trust
The Alexander Mosley Charitable Trust
The Norman Family Charitable Trust
P. F. Charitable Trust
The Paragon Trust
Payne-Gallwey 1989 Charitable Trust
Susanna Peake Charitable Trust
The Bernard Piggott Charitable Trust
The George and Esme Pollitzer Charitable Settlement
The Princess Anne's Charities
Queen Mary's Roehampton Trust
The Joseph and Lena Randall Charitable Trust
Riada Trust
Rigby Foundation
The Rothermere Foundation
The Rothley Trust
The Rowlands Trust
Royal Artillery Charitable Fund
The Royal British Legion
The Royal Navy and Royal Marines Charity
The Saddlers' Company Charitable Fund
Salters' Charitable Foundation
Schroder Charity Trust
Scott (Eredine) Charitable Trust
Scouloudi Foundation
The Serco Foundation
The Charles Skey Charitable Trust
Philip Smith's Charitable Trust
The Stafford Trust
The Swire Charitable Trust
The Michael Uren Foundation
The Utley Foundation
The Albert Van Den Bergh Charitable Trust
The Veterans' Foundation
G. R. Waters Charitable Trust 2000
Colonel W. H. Whitbread Charitable Trust

The Wilmcote Charitrust
The Worshipful Company of Glovers of London Charitable Trust
Worshipful Company of Gold and Silver Wyre Drawers Second Charitable Trust Fund
The Zochonis Charitable Trust

■ Arts and heritage

The Aldama Foundation
The Architectural Heritage Fund
The John Armitage Charitable Trust
The Art Fund
Arts Council England
Arts Council of Northern Ireland
Bagri Foundation
The Band Trust
Maria Bjornson Memorial Fund
The British Academy
The Rory and Elizabeth Brooks Foundation
William A. Cargill Charitable Trust
Colwinston Charitable Trust
Creative Scotland
The Daiwa Anglo-Japanese Foundation
The Delius Trust
The D'Oyly Carte Charitable Trust
The Gilbert and Eileen Edgar Foundation
The Eighty Eight Foundation
The Elmley Foundation
EMI Music Sound Foundation
The Fidelio Charitable Trust
Sir John Fisher Foundation
Oliver Ford Foundation
The Golsoncott Foundation
The Helen Hamlyn Trust
The Hinrichsen Foundation
Historic Houses Foundation
The Hobson Charity Ltd
P. H. Holt Foundation
The Hull and East Riding Charitable Trust
The Idlewild Trust
The Inverforth Charitable Trust
The Sir Barry Jackson County Fund
The Boris Karloff Charitable Foundation
The David Laing Foundation
The Leche Trust
Limoges Charitable Trust
Lord and Lady Lurgan Trust
The Mackintosh Foundation
The Henry Moore Foundation
G. M. Morrison Charitable Trust

The Bernard Piggott Charitable
Trust
The Pilgrim Trust
The Polonsky Foundation
The Radcliffe Trust
The Max Reinhardt Charitable
Trust
The William Syson Foundation
Humphrey Richardson Taylor
Charitable Trust
The Theatres Trust Charitable
Fund
The Michael Uren Foundation
Sumner Wilson Charitable
Trust
The Lord Leonard and Lady
Estelle Wolfson Foundation

■ Environment, agriculture and animals

The A Team Foundation Ltd
Ove Arup Partnership
Charitable Trust
Burnie's Foundation
The Frederick and Phyllis Cann
Trust
The Wilfrid and Constance
Cave Foundation
The Elizabeth Creak Charitable
Trust
The Ecology Trust
Groundwork UK
Harbinson Charitable Trust
The Hobson Charity Ltd
P. H. Holt Foundation
The Hutchinson Charitable
Trust
The Graham Kirkham
Foundation
The MacRobert Trust 2019
The Martin Charitable Trust
The Master Charitable Trust
The National Garden Scheme
The NFU Mutual Charitable
Trust
The Nineveh Charitable Trust
One Community Foundation
Ltd
The Paragon Trust
The Pets at Home Foundation
Betty Phillips Charitable Trust
Elise Pilkington Charitable
Trust
The Primrose Trust
The Prince's Countryside Fund
The Princess Anne's Charities
The Racing Foundation
Scotland's Garden Scheme*
The Underwood Trust
The Michael Uren Foundation
Sumner Wilson Charitable
Trust

■ Freemasons

Douglas Compton James
Charitable Trust
Leicestershire and Rutland
Masonic Charity
Association
London Freemasons Charity
Provincial Grand Charity of the
Province of Derbyshire

■ Manufacturing

The Cotton Industry War
Memorial Trust
The Horners Charity Fund
Makers of Playing Cards
Charity
Daisie Rich Trust
Riverside Charitable Trust Ltd
The Rugby Group Benevolent
Fund Ltd
The Savoy Educational Trust
South Yorkshire Community
Foundation
The Worshipful Company of
Glovers of London
Charitable Trust
Worshipful Company of
Needlemakers Charitable
Fund

■ Medicine and health

Action Medical Research
The Aldama Foundation
Asthma and Lung UK
The Barbers' Company General
Charities
The Michael Bishop
Foundation
The John Black Charitable
Foundation
Bloodwise
The Boltini Trust
Breast Cancer Now
British Heart Foundation (BHF)
The Burdett Trust for Nursing
Cancer Research UK
CareTech Charitable
Foundation
The Cunningham Trust
Dinwoodie Charitable Company
The James Dyson Foundation
The Gilbert and Eileen Edgar
Foundation
The General Nursing Council
for England and Wales
Trust
Harbinson Charitable Trust
The Health Foundation
The Jane Hodge Foundation
Sir Harold Hood's Charitable
Trust
Hospice UK

The Inman Charity
The Linder Foundation
G. M. Morrison Charitable
Trust
Motor Neurone Disease
Association
The Edwina Mountbatten and
Leonora Children's
Foundation
The National Garden Scheme
Northern Pharmacies Ltd Trust
Fund
Orthopaedic Research UK
The Paragon Trust
Susanna Peake Charitable
Trust
The Pharsalia Charitable Trust
The Purey Cust Trust CIO
The Royal Foundation of The
Prince and Princess of
Wales
Sandra Charitable Trust
Sir Samuel Scott of Yews
Trust
The Jean Shanks Foundation
The Swann-Morton Foundation
The James Tudor Foundation
The Underwood Trust
The Michael Uren Foundation
The Velvet Foundation
The Melanie White Foundation
Ltd
The Lord Leonard and Lady
Estelle Wolfson Foundation
The Worshipful Company of
Glovers of London
Charitable Trust

■ Seafarers and ex-seafarers

The Astor Foundation
The Frederick and Phyllis Cann
Trust
Carew Pole Charitable Trust
The Clarkson Foundation
The Corporation of Trinity
House of Deptford Strond
Sir John Fisher Foundation
The Joseph Strong Frazer Trust
The Gosling Foundation Ltd
The W. A. Handley Charity
Trust
The ITF Seafarers Trust
Sir James Knott Trust
Mrs F. B. Laurence Charitable
Trust
Lloyd's Register Foundation
The MacRobert Trust 2019
Merchant Navy Welfare Board
The Laurence Misener
Charitable Trust
The Royal Navy and Royal
Marines Charity
Scouloudi Foundation

Seafarers UK (King George's
Fund for Sailors)
The Shipwrights Charitable
Fund

■ Science, technology and engineering

Building and Civil Engineering
Charitable Trust
The James Dyson Foundation
Lloyd's Register Foundation

■ Service industry

The Cooks Charity
The Lord Forte Foundation
Daisie Rich Trust
Riverside Charitable Trust Ltd
The Savoy Educational Trust
Worshipful Company of
Needlemakers Charitable
Fund

■ Social or sporting clubs

The James Beattie Charitable
Trust
British Motor Sports Training
Trust
The Jack Brunton Charitable
Trust
The Chartley Foundation
Cheshire Freemasons' Charity
The Childhood Trust
The Football Association
National Sports Centre
The Fort Foundation
The Grange Farm Centre Trust
The Grantham Yorke Trust
Henley Educational Trust
Henley Royal Regatta
Charitable Trust
The Lady Hind Trust
Leicestershire and Rutland
Masonic Charity
Association
The Charles Littlewood Hill
Trust
Making a Difference Locally
Ltd
Matchroom Sport Charitable
Foundation
Oxfordshire Community
Foundation
The Jack Petchey Foundation
The Racing Foundation
Daisie Rich Trust
Toyota Manufacturing UK
Charitable Trust
The Georg and Emily von Opel
Foundation

People of a particular heritage/ethnic origin

abrdn Charitable Foundation
Bagri Foundation
The Barrow Cadbury Trust
The Clothworkers' Foundation
The Daiwa Anglo-Japanese
Foundation
The Eighty Eight Foundation
The Grace Trust
The Great Britain Sasakawa
Foundation
The Hadrian Trust
The Hinduja Foundation
The Ireland Fund of Great
Britain
Irish Youth Foundation (UK)
Ltd (incorporating The
Lawlor Foundation)
The Kiawah Charitable Trust
The LankellyChase Foundation
Lloyds Bank Foundation for
England and Wales
The Manoukian Charitable
Foundation
John Moores Foundation
The Mutley Foundation
Near Neighbours
Network for Social Change
Charitable Trust
Norfolk Community Foundation
Odin Charitable Trust
The Austin and Hope
Pilkington Trust
The Eleanor Rathbone
Charitable Trust
The Sigrid Rausing Trust
Rentrust Foundation Ltd
The Robertson Trust
Rosca Trust
The Joseph Rowntree
Charitable Trust
Saint Sarkis Charity Trust
The Scott Bader
Commonwealth Ltd
The Sino-British Fellowship
Trust
Staples Trust
The Talbot Trusts
Tees Valley Community
Foundation
Volant Charitable Trust
Wakefield and Tetley Trust
The Wates Foundation
W. Wing Yip and Brothers
Foundation
Youth Endowment Fund (YEF)*

■ Gypsy, Roma and Traveller

The Allen Lane Foundation
Near Neighbours
Odin Charitable Trust
The Sigrid Rausing Trust
The Woodward Charitable
Trust

Relationships

Al-Fayed Charitable Foundation
The Barnes Fund
The Brook Trust
Clara E. Burgess Charity
The Noel Buxton Trust
Cambridgeshire Community
Foundation
Cattanach
Colyer-Fergusson Charitable
Trust
Corra Foundation
Cripplegate Foundation
The De Brye Charitable Trust
The Ellerdale Trust
Esmée Fairbairn Foundation
Global Charities
Gloucestershire Community
Foundation
The Grantham Yorke Trust
The Walter Guinness
Charitable Trust
The Hadley Trust
Halifax Foundation for
Northern Ireland
Hammersmith United Charities
Hampshire and Isle of Wight
Community Foundation
The Headley Trust
The Alan Edward Higgs Charity
The Hobson Charity Ltd
Inner London Magistrates
Court Poor Box and Feeder
Charity
The Jabbs Foundation
The Kelly Family Charitable
Trust
The Kensington and Chelsea
Foundation
The Graham Kirkham
Foundation
Kollel and Co. Ltd
The KPMG Foundation
Laslett's (Hinton) Charity
The Richard Lawes Foundation
Lloyds Bank Foundation for
England and Wales
John Lyon's Charity
The Marsh Christian Trust
Charlotte Marshall Charitable
Trust
Masonic Charitable Foundation
John Moores Foundation
The Steve Morgan Foundation

G. M. Morrison Charitable
Trust
The MSE Charity
The Mulberry Trust
The George and Esme Pollitzer
Charitable Settlement
The Rainford Trust
The Eleanor Rathbone
Charitable Trust
The Roughley Charitable Trust
The Segelman Trust
The Henry Smith Charity
The Leslie Smith Foundation
Somerset Community
Foundation
South Yorkshire Community
Foundation
St John's Foundation Est.
1174
The Peter Stebbings Memorial
Charity
Sir Halley Stewart Trust
The W. O. Street Charitable
Foundation
The Tedworth Charitable Trust
The Trusthouse Charitable
Foundation
The Walker Trust
The Woodward Charitable
Trust
The Worshipful Company of
Glovers of London
Charitable Trust
The Eric Wright Charitable
Trust
The Zochonis Charitable Trust

....

■ **Bereavement**

The Ellerdale Trust
Global Charities
Halifax Foundation for
Northern Ireland
The Hobson Charity Ltd
The Richard Lawes Foundation
The Kristina Martin Charitable
Trust
The MSE Charity
The Roughley Charitable Trust
The Leslie Smith Foundation
The Worshipful Company of
Glovers of London
Charitable Trust

....

■ **Families**

The Aberdeenshire Educational
Trust Scheme
Adam Family Foundation
Atlas Memorial Ltd
The Barnes Fund
The Brook Trust
The Noel Buxton Trust
Cambridgeshire Community
Foundation

Carew Pole Charitable Trust
Cattanach
The Childhood Trust
The Vivienne and Samuel
Cohen Charitable Trust
Colyer-Fergusson Charitable
Trust
Corra Foundation
Cripplegate Foundation
Cumbria Community
Foundation
Foundation Derbyshire
Devon Community Foundation
The Ellerdale Trust
Esmée Fairbairn Foundation
The Fifty Fund
Gloucestershire Community
Foundation
The Grantham Yorke Trust
The Walter Guinness
Charitable Trust
Hackney Parochial Charities
The Hadley Trust
Halifax Foundation for
Northern Ireland
Hammersmith United Charities
Hampshire and Isle of Wight
Community Foundation
The Headley Trust
The Alan Edward Higgs Charity
Highway One Trust
Ibrahim Foundation Ltd
Imagine Foundation
Inner London Magistrates
Court Poor Box and Feeder
Charity
The Jabbs Foundation
The Kelly Family Charitable
Trust
The Kensington and Chelsea
Foundation
The Graham Kirkham
Foundation
The KPMG Foundation
Maurice and Hilda Laing
Charitable Trust
Laslett's (Hinton) Charity
The Michael and Betty Little
Trust*
Lloyds Bank Foundation for
England and Wales
The London Community
Foundation (LCF)
John Lyon's Charity
Charlotte Marshall Charitable
Trust
Masonic Charitable Foundation
The Mercers Charitable
Foundation
John Moores Foundation
The Steve Morgan Foundation
G. M. Morrison Charitable
Trust
The MSE Charity
The Mulberry Trust

Norwich Consolidated
Charities
The George and Esme Pollitzer
Charitable Settlement
The Rainford Trust
The Robertson Trust
The Royal British Legion
The Frieda Scott Charitable
Trust
Scottish Coal Industry Special
Welfare Fund
The Segelman Trust
The Henry Smith Charity
Somerset Community
Foundation
South Yorkshire Community
Foundation
St John's Foundation Est.
1174
The Peter Stebbings Memorial
Charity
Sir Halley Stewart Trust
The W. O. Street Charitable
Foundation
Suffolk Community Foundation
The Tedworth Charitable Trust
The Trusthouse Charitable
Foundation
The Walker Trust
The Wates Foundation
The Woodward Charitable
Trust
The Worshipful Company of
Glovers of London
Charitable Trust
The Eric Wright Charitable
Trust

....

■ **Orphans**

Al-Fayed Charitable Foundation
Clara E. Burgess Charity
The De Brye Charitable Trust
Kollel and Co. Ltd
The Eleanor Rathbone
Charitable Trust
The Leslie Smith Foundation
The Walker Trust
The Worshipful Company of
Glovers of London
Charitable Trust

Religion

4 Charity Foundation
The A. H. Trust
A. W. Charitable Trust
Achisomoch Aid Company Ltd
Adenfirst Ltd
The Aimwell Charitable Trust
Alliance Family Foundation Ltd
The Almond Trust
Amabrill Ltd
Viscount Amory's Charitable
Trust

The Anchor Foundation
Andrews Charitable Trust
Anpride Ltd
The Ardwick Trust
The John Armitage Charitable
    Trust
Ashburnham Thanksgiving
    Trust
Atlas Memorial Ltd
The Aziz Foundation
The Baird Trust
Bay Charitable Trust
Bear Mordechai Ltd
Beauland Ltd
The Beaverbrooks Charitable
    Trust
The Bellahouston Bequest
    Fund
Belljoe Tzedoko Ltd
Benefact Trust Ltd
Benesco Charity Ltd
The Benham Charitable
    Settlement
Ruth Berkowitz Charitable
    Trust
The Sydney Black Charitable
    Trust
The Bertie Black Foundation
The Blandford Lake Trust
Abraham Algy Bloom
    Foundation
The Bluston Charitable
    Settlement
The Bonamy Charitable Trust
The Harry Bottom Charitable
    Trust
The P. G. and N. J. Boulton
    Trust
Sir Clive Bourne Family Trust
Bourneheights Ltd
Bristol Archdeaconry Charity
The British and Foreign Bible
    Society
The Mary Brown Memorial
    Trust
T. B. H. Brunner's Charitable
    Settlement
Brushmill Ltd
Buckingham Trust
The Arnold Burton 1998
    Charitable Trust
Consolidated Charity of Burton
    upon Trent
C. and F. Charitable Trust
Carew Pole Charitable Trust
Carlee Ltd
Catholic Charitable Trust
The CH (1980) Charitable
    Trust
Chalfords Ltd
Chartered Accountants' Livery
    Charity (CALC)
The Childwick Trust
Church Burgesses Trust
Church of Ireland Priorities
    Fund

The Roger and Sarah Bancroft
    Clark Charitable Trust
The Clore Duffield Foundation
Cloudesley
The Clover Trust
Clydpride Ltd
CMZ Ltd
The Vivienne and Samuel
    Cohen Charitable Trust
Col-Reno Ltd
Congregational and General
    Charitable Trust
The Gershon Coren Charitable
    Foundation
The Costa Family Charitable
    Trust
The County Council of Dyfed
    Welsh Church Fund
The Cross Trust
Itzchok Meyer Cymerman Trust
    Ltd
The D. M. Charitable Trust
Oizer Dalim Trust
The Manny and Brigitta
    Davidson Charitable
    Foundation
The Davidson Family
    Charitable Trust
The Davis Foundation
Dawat-E-Hadiyah Trust (United
    Kingdom)
Debmar Benevolent Trust Ltd
The Desmond Foundation
The Alan and Sheila Diamond
    Charitable Trust
The Djanogly Foundation
Donibristle Trust
The Dorcas Trust
The Dorfman Foundation
The Dorset Historic Churches
    Trust
The Doughty Charity Trust
The Gilbert and Eileen Edgar
    Foundation
The George Elias Charitable
    Trust
The Elie Trust
Ellinson Foundation Ltd
The Esfandi Charitable
    Foundation
The Eventhall Family
    Charitable Trust
The Exilarch's Foundation
Famos Foundation Trust
The Fieldrose Charitable Trust
The Robert Fleming Hannay
    Memorial Charity
Fordeve Ltd
Forest Hill Charitable Trust
The Foster Wood Foundation
The Isaac and Freda Frankel
    Memorial Charitable Trust
Anne French Memorial Trust
Friends of Boyan Trust
The Friends of Kent Churches
The G. R. P. Charitable Trust

Ganzoni Charitable Trust
The Gertner Charitable Trust
The Gibbs Charitable Trusts
The B. and P. Glasser
    Charitable Trust
The Gloag Foundation
The Goshen Trust
Grace Baptist Trust
    Corporation*
Grace Charitable Trust
The Grace Trust
Philip and Judith Green Trust
M. and R. Gross Charities Ltd
Heb Ffin (Without Frontier)
The Helping Foundation
The Herefordshire Historic
    Churches Trust
The Bernhard Heuberger
    Charitable Trust*
The Highcroft Charitable Trust
The Hinduja Foundation
The Hintze Family Charity
    Foundation
Hockerill Educational
    Foundation
The Holbeck Charitable Trust
The Holden Charitable Trust
Homelands Charitable Trust
Sir Harold Hood's Charitable
    Trust
Hope Trust
Horwich Shotter Charitable
    Trust
The Humanitarian Trust
The Huntingdon Foundation
    Ltd
The Harold Hyam Wingate
    Foundation
The Inlight Trust
Investream Charitable Trust
The J. Isaacs Charitable Trust
The J. A. R. Charitable Trust
The J. and J. Benevolent
    Foundation
Jay Education Trust
The Jerusalem Trust
Jewish Child's Day
The Jewish Youth Fund
J. E. Joseph Charitable Fund
The Jusaca Charitable Trust
Kahal Chassidim Bobov
The Kasner Charitable Trust
The Michael and Ilse Katz
    Foundation
C. S. Kaufman Charitable
    Trust
Keren Association Ltd
E. and E. Kernkraut Charities
    Ltd
The Kobler Trust
Kollel and Co. Ltd
Kolyom Trust Ltd
Kupath Gemach Chaim
    Bechesed Viznitz Trust
The Kirby Laing Foundation

The Leonard Laity Stoate
Charitable Trust
Lancaster Foundation
The Lauffer Family Charitable
Foundation
The Herd Lawson and Muriel
Lawson Charitable Trust
Lawson Beckman Charitable
Trust
The Arnold Lee Charitable
Trust
The Leeward Trust
Leicestershire and Rutland
Masonic Charity
Association
Cecil and Hilda Lewis
Charitable Trust
Bernard Lewis Family
Charitable Trust
David and Ruth Lewis Family
Charitable Trust
The Charles Littlewood Hill
Trust
The Second Joseph Aaron
Littman Foundation
Jack Livingstone Charitable
Trust
Localtrent Ltd
The Locker Foundation
LPW Ltd
M. and C. Trust
M. B. Foundation
The Magen Charitable Trust
The Mallinckrodt Foundation
The Manackerman Charitable
Trust
The Manson Family Charitable
Trust
Marbeh Torah Trust
The Marks Family Charitable
Trust
Charity of John Marshall
Charlotte Marshall Charitable
Trust
John Martin's Charity
The Matliwala Family
Charitable Trust
The Violet Mauray Charitable
Trust
Mayfair Charities Ltd
Mayheights Ltd
Melodor Ltd
The Melow Charitable Trust
Menuchar Ltd
Mercaz Torah Vechesed Ltd
The Millfield Trust
The Milne Family Foundation
The Mishcon Family Charitable
Trust
The MK Charitable Trust
The Modiano Charitable Trust
Mole Charitable Trust
Vyoel Moshe Charitable Trust
The Mosselson Charitable
Trust
The Mulberry Trust

The Mutley Foundation
The Mutual Trust Group
MW (CL) Foundation
MW (GK) Foundation
MW (HO) Foundation
MW (RH) Foundation
Near Neighbours
Nemoral Ltd
Ner Foundation
Newpier Charity Ltd
North London Charities Ltd
The Northumbria Historic
Churches Trust
The Norwood and Newton
Settlement
Oizer Charitable Trust
Open House Trust Ltd
The Ouseley Church Music
Trust
Oxfordshire Historic Churches
Trust (2016)
The Doris Pacey Charitable
Foundation
The Gerald Palmer Eling Trust
Company
Miss M. E. S. Paterson's
Charitable Trust
David Pearlman Charitable
Foundation
The Pears Family Charitable
Foundation
The Phillips and Rubens
Charitable Trust
The Phillips Family Charitable
Trust
The Bernard Piggott Charitable
Trust
The George and Esme Pollitzer
Charitable Settlement
The Potton Consolidated
Charity
Premierquote Ltd
Sir John Priestman Charity
Trust
The Privy Purse Charitable
Trust
Quothquan Trust
R. S. Charitable Trust
Rachel Charitable Trust
The Bishop Radford Trust
The Joseph and Lena Randall
Charitable Trust
Randeree Charitable Trust
The Joseph Rank Trust
The Rayne Foundation
The Sir James Reckitt Charity
Rentrust Foundation Ltd
Riada Trust
Richmond Parish Lands Charity
Ridgesave Ltd
RJM Charity Trust
The Gerald and Gail Ronson
Family Foundation
Mrs L. D. Rope's Third
Charitable Settlement
The Rothermere Foundation

Rothschild Foundation
(Hanadiv) Europe
Rowanville Ltd
S. and R. Charitable Trust
The S. M. B. Trust
The Jeremy and John Sacher
Charitable Trust
The Saddlers' Company
Charitable Fund
Erach and Roshan Sadri
Foundation
Samjo Ltd
Sarum St Michael Educational
Charity
The Schmidt-Bodner Charitable
Trust
The Schreib Trust
Schreiber Charitable Trust
O. and G. Schreiber Charitable
Trust
The Searchlight Electric
Charitable Trust
The Sam and Bella Sebba
Charitable Foundation
Seedfield Trust
Sellata Ltd
The Seven Fifty Trust
SF Foundation
The Cyril Shack Trust
The Archie Sherman Charitable
Trust
The Bassil Shippam and
Alsford Trust
Shlomo Memorial Fund Ltd
Shulem B. Association Ltd
The Henry Smith Charity
Songdale Ltd
The E. C. Sosnow Charitable
Trust
Souter Charitable Trust
The Stephen R. and Philippa
H. Southall Charitable Trust
W. F. Southall Trust
Sparquote Ltd
The Squires Foundation
St Peter's Saltley Trust
Starlow Charities Ltd
The Steinberg Family
Charitable Trust
C. E. K. Stern Charitable Trust
Stervon Ltd
Stewards Company Ltd
Sir Halley Stewart Trust
Sabina Sutherland Charitable
Trust
Swansea and Brecon Diocesan
Board of Finance Ltd
T. and S. Trust Fund
The Tajtelbaum Charitable
Trust
The Talmud Torah Machzikei
Hadass Trust
Talteg Ltd
The David Tannen Charitable
Trust
Tay Charitable Trust

C. B. and H. H. T. Taylor 1984 Trust

The Thornton Trust

Mrs R. P. Tindall's Charitable Trust

The Tory Family Foundation

Truedene Co. Ltd

Truemart Ltd

Trumros Ltd

The Tufton Charitable Trust

Tzedakah

UJIA (United Jewish Israel Appeal)

Ulting Overseas Trust

The Union of Orthodox Hebrew Congregations

The Union of the Sisters of Mercy of Great Britain

The United Reformed Church (Wessex) Trust Ltd

VHLT Ltd

Nigel Vinson Charitable Trust

Vivdale Ltd

The Georg and Emily von Opel Foundation

The Welsh Church Act Fund

Westhill Endowment

The Wigoder Family Foundation

Sumner Wilson Charitable Trust

The Benjamin Winegarten Charitable Trust

The Maurice Wohl Charitable Foundation

The Charles Wolfson Charitable Trust

The Wolfson Family Charitable Trust

The James Wood Bequest Fund

Woodlands Green Ltd

WWDP (World Day of Prayer National Committee for England, Wales and Northern Ireland)

Wychville Ltd

Yankov Charitable Trust

The Yorkshire Historic Churches Trust

The Marjorie and Arnold Ziff Charitable Foundation

■ **People of the Christian faith**

The Almond Trust

The Anchor Foundation

Andrews Charitable Trust

Ardbarron Trust Ltd

Ashburnham Thanksgiving Trust

The Baird Trust

The Bellahouston Bequest Fund

Benefact Trust Ltd

The Benham Charitable Settlement

Binks Trust

The Sydney Black Charitable Trust

The Harry Bottom Charitable Trust

The P. G. and N. J. Boulton Trust

The Liz and Terry Bramall Foundation

Bristol Archdeaconry Charity

The Mary Brown Memorial Trust

T. B. H. Brunner's Charitable Settlement

Buckingham Trust

Carew Pole Charitable Trust

Catholic Charitable Trust

Childs Charitable Trust

The Christabella Charitable Trust

Church of Ireland Priorities Fund

The Roger and Sarah Bancroft Clark Charitable Trust

Cloudesley

The Clover Trust

Congregational and General Charitable Trust

The Costa Family Charitable Trust

The County Council of Dyfed Welsh Church Fund

The Cross Trust

Donibristle Trust

The Dorset Historic Churches Trust

Ebenezer Trust

The Elie Trust

Forest Hill Charitable Trust

The Foster Wood Foundation

The Joseph Strong Frazer Trust

The Friends of Kent Churches

Ganzoni Charitable Trust

The Gibbs Charitable Trusts

The Gloag Foundation

The Goshen Trust

Grace Baptist Trust Corporation*

Grace Charitable Trust

The Grace Trust

Philip and Judith Green Trust

The Herefordshire Historic Churches Trust

Hinchley Charitable Trust

The Stuart Hine Trust CIO

The Hintze Family Charity Foundation

Hockerill Educational Foundation

The Holbeck Charitable Trust

Sir Harold Hood's Charitable Trust

Hope Trust

The Hunting Horn General Charitable Trust

The J. A. R. Charitable Trust

The Jerusalem Trust

The K. P. Ladd Charitable Trust

The Kirby Laing Foundation

The Leonard Laity Stoate Charitable Trust

Lancaster Foundation

The Herd Lawson and Muriel Lawson Charitable Trust

The Charles Littlewood Hill Trust

Magnify Foundation*

The Mallinckrodt Foundation

Charity of John Marshall

Charlotte Marshall Charitable Trust

John Martin's Charity

The Millfield Trust

The Milne Family Foundation

The Mulberry Trust

The Norfolk Churches Trust Ltd

The Northumbria Historic Churches Trust

The Norwood and Newton Settlement

The Ogle Christian Trust

Open House Trust Ltd

Otsar Trust

The Ouseley Church Music Trust

Oxfordshire Historic Churches Trust (2016)

The P27 Trust

The Gerald Palmer Eling Trust Company

Miss M. E. S. Paterson's Charitable Trust

The Bernard Piggott Charitable Trust

Charles Plater Trust*

The Potton Consolidated Charity

Sir John Priestman Charity Trust

The Privy Purse Charitable Trust

Quothquan Trust

The Bishop Radford Trust

The Joseph Rank Trust

The Sir James Reckitt Charity

Riada Trust

The River Trust

The Rock Foundation

Mrs L. D. Rope's Third Charitable Settlement

The Rothermere Foundation

The S. M. B. Trust

The Saddlers' Company Charitable Fund

Sarum St Michael Educational Charity

Seedfield Trust

The Seven Fifty Trust

The Bassil Shippam and
Alsford Trust
Souter Charitable Trust
The Stephen R. and Philippa
H. Southall Charitable Trust
W. F. Southall Trust
The Squires Foundation
St Peter's Saltley Trust
The Hugh Stenhouse
Foundation
Stewards Company Ltd
Sir Halley Stewart Trust
The Stobart Newlands
Charitable Trust
Sabina Sutherland Charitable
Trust
Swansea and Brecon Diocesan
Board of Finance Ltd
Tay Charitable Trust
C. B. and H. H. T. Taylor 1984
Trust
The Thornton Trust
The Tory Family Foundation
The Tufton Charitable Trust
The Union of the Sisters of
Mercy of Great Britain
Nigel Vinson Charitable Trust
The Georg and Emily von Opel
Foundation
The Welsh Church Act Fund
Westhill Endowment
The Norman Whiteley Trust
The James Wood Bequest
Fund
WWDP (World Day of Prayer
National Committee for
England, Wales and
Northern Ireland)
The Yorkshire Historic
Churches Trust

■ People of the Jewish faith

4 Charity Foundation
The A. H. Trust
A. W. Charitable Trust
Achisomoch Aid Company Ltd
Adenfirst Ltd
The Aimwell Charitable Trust
Alliance Family Foundation Ltd
Amabrill Ltd
Andrew Anderson Trust
Anpride Ltd
The Ardwick Trust
Atkin Charitable Foundation
Atlas Memorial Ltd
Bay Charitable Trust
Bear Mordechai Ltd
Beauland Ltd
The Beaverbrooks Charitable
Trust
Belljoe Tzedoko Ltd
Benesco Charity Ltd
Ruth Berkowitz Charitable
Trust

The Bertie Black Foundation
Abraham Algy Bloom
Foundation
The Bluston Charitable
Settlement
The Bonamy Charitable Trust
The Salo Bordon Charitable
Trust
Sir Clive Bourne Family Trust
Bourneheights Ltd
Brushmill Ltd
The Arnold Burton 1998
Charitable Trust
C. and F. Charitable Trust
Carlee Ltd
The CH (1980) Charitable
Trust
Chalfords Ltd
Charitworth Ltd
The Childwick Trust
The Clore Duffield Foundation
Clydpride Ltd
CMZ Ltd
The Vivienne and Samuel
Cohen Charitable Trust
Col-Reno Ltd
The Gershon Coren Charitable
Foundation
Countypier Ltd
Itzchok Meyer Cymerman Trust
Ltd
The D. M. Charitable Trust
Oizer Dalim Trust
The Manny and Brigitta
Davidson Charitable
Foundation
The Davidson Family
Charitable Trust
The Davis Foundation
Debmar Benevolent Trust Ltd
The Desmond Foundation
The Alan and Sheila Diamond
Charitable Trust
The Djanogly Foundation
Dollond Charitable Trust
The Dorfman Foundation
The Doughty Charity Trust
Dushinsky Trust Ltd
The George Elias Charitable
Trust
Ellinson Foundation Ltd
Entindale Ltd
The Esfandi Charitable
Foundation
Esher House Charitable Trust
The Eventhall Family
Charitable Trust
The Exilarch's Foundation
Extonglen Ltd
Famos Foundation Trust
Fordeve Ltd
The Isaac and Freda Frankel
Memorial Charitable Trust
Friends of Boyan Trust
Friends of Wiznitz Ltd
The G. R. P. Charitable Trust

The Gertner Charitable Trust
The B. and P. Glasser
Charitable Trust
The Jane Goodman Charitable
Trust*
Grahame Charitable
Foundation Ltd
M. and R. Gross Charities Ltd
H. P. Charitable Trust
The Maurice Hatter Foundation
The Simon Heller Charitable
Settlement
The Helping Foundation
The Bernhard Heuberger
Charitable Trust*
The Highcroft Charitable Trust
The Holden Charitable Trust
Homelands Charitable Trust
Horwich Shotter Charitable
Trust
The Humanitarian Trust
The Huntingdon Foundation
Ltd
Hurdale Charity Ltd
The Harold Hyam Wingate
Foundation
IGO Foundation Ltd
Investream Charitable Trust
The J. Isaacs Charitable Trust
The J. and J. Benevolent
Foundation
The Susan and Stephen
James Charitable
Settlement
Jay Education Trust
Jewish Child's Day
The Jewish Youth Fund
J. E. Joseph Charitable Fund
The Jusaca Charitable Trust
Kahal Chassidim Bobov
The Kasner Charitable Trust
The Michael and Ilse Katz
Foundation
C. S. Kaufman Charitable
Trust
The Kennedy Leigh Charitable
Trust
Keren Association Ltd
E. and E. Kernkraut Charities
Ltd
The Kobler Trust
Kollel and Co. Ltd
Kolyom Trust Ltd
Kreditor Charitable Trust
Kupath Gemach Chaim
Bechesed Viznitz Trust
The Kyte Charitable Trust
The Lauffer Family Charitable
Foundation
Lawson Beckman Charitable
Trust
The Arnold Lee Charitable
Trust
Cecil and Hilda Lewis
Charitable Trust

Bernard Lewis Family
   Charitable Trust
David and Ruth Lewis Family
   Charitable Trust
The Second Joseph Aaron
   Littman Foundation
Jack Livingstone Charitable
   Trust
Localtrent Ltd
The Locker Foundation
LPW Ltd
Sir Jack Lyons Charitable Trust
M. and C. Trust
M. B. Foundation
The M. Y. A. Charitable Trust
The Magen Charitable Trust
The Manackerman Charitable
   Trust
The Manson Family Charitable
   Trust
Marbeh Torah Trust
The Stella and Alexander
   Margulies Charitable Trust
The Marks Family Charitable
   Trust
The Violet Mauray Charitable
   Trust
Mayfair Charities Ltd
Mayheights Ltd
Melodor Ltd
The Melow Charitable Trust
Menuchar Ltd
Mercaz Torah Vechesed Ltd
The Mishcon Family Charitable
   Trust
The MK Charitable Trust
The Modiano Charitable Trust
Mole Charitable Trust
The Morgan Charitable
   Foundation
The Moshal Charitable Trust
Vyoel Moshe Charitable Trust
The Mosselson Charitable
   Trust
The Mutley Foundation
The Mutual Trust Group
MW (CL) Foundation
MW (GK) Foundation
MW (HO) Foundation
MW (RH) Foundation
Nemoral Ltd
Ner Foundation
Newpier Charity Ltd
North London Charities Ltd
Oizer Charitable Trust
The Doris Pacey Charitable
   Foundation
David Pearlman Charitable
   Foundation
The Pears Family Charitable
   Foundation
Dina Perelman Trust Ltd
The Phillips and Rubens
   Charitable Trust
The Phillips Family Charitable
   Trust

The George and Esme Pollitzer
   Charitable Settlement
Porter Foundation
Premierquote Ltd
R. S. Charitable Trust
Rachel Charitable Trust
The Joseph and Lena Randall
   Charitable Trust
The Rayne Foundation
Rentrust Foundation Ltd
Richmond Parish Lands Charity
Ridgesave Ltd
The Rofeh Trust
The Gerald and Gail Ronson
   Family Foundation
Rothschild Foundation
   (Hanadiv) Europe
Rowanville Ltd
The Rubin Foundation
   Charitable Trust
S. and R. Charitable Trust
The Jeremy and John Sacher
   Charitable Trust
The Michael and Nicola Sacher
   Charitable Trust
Samjo Ltd
The Peter Samuel Charitable
   Trust
The Schmidt-Bodner Charitable
   Trust
The Schreib Trust
Schreiber Charitable Trust
O. and G. Schreiber Charitable
   Trust
The Searchlight Electric
   Charitable Trust
The Sam and Bella Sebba
   Charitable Foundation
Sellata Ltd
SF Foundation
The Cyril Shack Trust
The Archie Sherman Charitable
   Trust
Shlomo Memorial Fund Ltd
Shulem B. Association Ltd
Songdale Ltd
The E. C. Sosnow Charitable
   Trust
Sparquote Ltd
Starlow Charities Ltd
The Steinberg Family
   Charitable Trust
C. E. K. Stern Charitable Trust
Stervon Ltd
T. and S. Trust Fund
The Tajtelbaum Charitable
   Trust
The Talmud Torah Machzikei
   Hadass Trust
Talteg Ltd
The David Tannen Charitable
   Trust
The Taurus Foundation
Tegham Ltd
Truedene Co. Ltd
Truemart Ltd

Trumros Ltd
Tzedakah
UJIA (United Jewish Israel
   Appeal)
The Union of Orthodox Hebrew
   Congregations
The Velvet Foundation
VHLT Ltd
Vivdale Ltd
Walton Foundation
The Linda and Michael
   Weinstein Charitable Trust
The Wigoder Family Foundation
The Benjamin Winegarten
   Charitable Trust
The Maurice Wohl Charitable
   Foundation
The Charles Wolfson
   Charitable Trust
The Wolfson Family Charitable
   Trust
Woodlands Green Ltd
Wychville Ltd
Yankov Charitable Trust
The Marjorie and Arnold Ziff
   Charitable Foundation

....

■ People of the Muslim faith

The Aziz Foundation
Dawat-E-Hadiyah Trust (United
   Kingdom)
The Matliwala Family
   Charitable Trust
Randeree Charitable Trust

....

■ People of other faiths

Erach and Roshan Sadri
   Foundation

Social and economic circumstances

The 29th May 1961 Charitable
   Trust
The 4814 Trust
The A. B. Charitable Trust
The A. S. Charitable Trust
The Aberdeenshire Educational
   Trust Scheme
abrdn Charitable Foundation
abrdn Financial Fairness Trust
The Access to Justice
   Foundation
Achisomoch Aid Company Ltd
Adam Family Foundation
The Addleshaw Goddard
   Charitable Trust
The Adint Charitable Trust
Sylvia Aitken's Charitable Trust

The Alchemy Foundation
The Aldama Foundation
The Derrill Allatt Foundation
The Allen & Overy Foundation
D. C. R. Allen Charitable Trust
The Allen Trust
Alliance Family Foundation Ltd
Alpkit Foundation
Amant Foundation
Ambergate Charitable Trust
The AMW Charitable Trust
Andrews Charitable Trust
Anguish's Educational
   Foundation
The Apax Foundation
The John Apthorp Charity
The Annabel Arbib Foundation
The Archer Trust
Ardbarron Trust Ltd
The Ardwick Trust
The John Armitage Charitable
   Trust
The Arsenal Foundation
The Artemis Charitable
   Foundation
Ove Arup Partnership
   Charitable Trust
The Asda Foundation
Ashburnham Thanksgiving
   Trust
The Ashworth Charitable Trust
The Astor Foundation
The Lord Austin Trust
Axis Foundation
The Aziz Foundation
The Austin Bailey Foundation
Bairdwatson Charitable Trust
The Roy and Pixie Baker
   Charitable Trust
The Ballinger Charitable Trust
B&Q Foundation
Bank of Scotland Foundation
The Barbers' Company General
   Charities
The Barbour Foundation
The Michael Barnard
   Charitable Trust
The Barnes Fund
Barnsbury Charitable Trust
Barnwood Trust
Misses Barrie Charitable Trust
The Batchworth Trust
Bauer Radio's Cash for Kids
   Charities
The Gordon and Ena Baxter
   Foundation*
Bay Charitable Trust
The Bay Tree Charitable Trust
BBC Children in Need
The James Beattie Charitable
   Trust
Beauland Ltd
The Beaverbrooks Charitable
   Trust
Beccles Townlands Charity

Bedfordshire and Luton
   Community Foundation
Bedfordshire Charitable Trust
   Ltd
The Bellahouston Bequest
   Fund
Benefact Trust Ltd
Benesco Charity Ltd
The Benham Charitable
   Settlement
The Rowan Bentall Charitable
   Trust
The Berkeley Foundation
The Bernicia Foundation
The Bestway Foundation
Bideford Bridge Trust
The Percy Bilton Charity
The Bingham Trust
The Sydney Black Charitable
   Trust
The Bertie Black Foundation
The Isabel Blackman
   Foundation
The Blagrave Trust
Lady Blakenham's Charity
   Trust
The Blandford Lake Trust
Blyth Watson Charitable Trust
Maureen Boal Charitable Trust
The Marjory Boddy Charitable
   Trust
The Boltini Trust
BOOST Charitable Trust
The Booth Charities
Boots Charitable Trust
The Salo Bordon Charitable
   Trust
The Boshier-Hinton Foundation
The Harry Bottom Charitable
   Trust
The P. G. and N. J. Boulton
   Trust
The Liz and Terry Bramall
   Foundation
The Brelms Trust CIO
The Brenley Trust
Bristol Charities
The Britford Bridge Trust
The British and Foreign School
   Society (BFSS)
British Gas Energy Trust
British Humane Association
J. and M. Britton Charitable
   Trust
The Brook Trust
Bill Brown 1989 Charitable
   Trust
R. S. Brownless Charitable
   Trust
Brushmill Ltd
Buckingham Trust
Buckinghamshire Community
   Foundation
Building and Civil Engineering
   Charitable Trust
E. F. Bulmer Trust

The Arnold Burton 1998
   Charitable Trust
Consolidated Charity of Burton
   upon Trent
Miss Margaret Butters Reekie
   Charitable Trust
The Noel Buxton Trust
Byrne Family Foundation
William A. Cadbury Charitable
   Trust
The Barrow Cadbury Trust
The Edward and Dorothy
   Cadbury Trust
Cadent Foundation
Community Foundation for
   Calderdale
Cambridgeshire Community
   Foundation
Camden Giving
CareTech Charitable
   Foundation
Carew Pole Charitable Trust
The Antonio Carluccio
   Foundation
The Carr-Gregory Trust
The Joseph and Annie Cattle
   Trust
The Thomas Sivewright Catto
   Charitable Settlement
The Wilfrid and Constance
   Cave Foundation
The Cayo Foundation
The B. G. S. Cayzer Charitable
   Trust
The Amelia Chadwick Trust
The Chalk Cliff Trust
The Charterhouse Charitable
   Trust
Cheshire Community
   Foundation Ltd
The Chetwode Foundation
The Childhood Trust
Chippenham Borough Lands
   Charity
CHK Foundation
Christadelphian Samaritan
   Fund
The André Christian Trust
Chrysalis Trust
The City Bridge Trust (Bridge
   House Estates)
CLA Charitable Trust
The Roger and Sarah Bancroft
   Clark Charitable Trust
The Clarkson Foundation
The Clore Duffield Foundation
The Clothworkers' Foundation
Cloudesley
The Clover Trust
The John Coates Charitable
   Trust
The Vivienne and Samuel
   Cohen Charitable Trust
The John S. Cohen Foundation
The R. and S. Cohen
   Foundation

The Cole Charitable Trust
The Coltstaple Trust
Colyer-Fergusson Charitable
    Trust
Comic Relief
Community First
Douglas Compton James
    Charitable Trust
The Cooks Charity
Co-op Foundation
The Alice Ellen Cooper-Dean
    Charitable Foundation
The Gershon Coren Charitable
    Foundation
The Evan Cornish Foundation
Cornwall Community
    Foundation
Corra Foundation
County Durham Community
    Foundation
Coventry Building Society
    Charitable Foundation
The Lord Cozens-Hardy Trust
Craignish Trust
Michael Crawford Children's
    Charity
The Crerar Trust
CRH Charitable Trust
Cripplegate Foundation
Crisis UK
The Cross Trust
The Croydon Relief-in-Need
    Charity
Cruden Foundation Ltd
Cumbria Community
    Foundation
The D. G. Charitable
    Settlement
The D. M. Charitable Trust
Dawat-E-Hadiyah Trust (United
    Kingdom)
The Dawe Charitable Trust
The Roger De Haan Charitable
    Trust
The Delves Charitable Trust
Foundation Derbyshire
The J. N. Derbyshire Trust
The Gillian Dickinson Trust
Didymus
The Ken Dodd Charitable
    Foundation
Donibristle Trust
The Dorcas Trust
Dorset Community Foundation
The Dorus Trust
The Double 'O' Charity Ltd
The Doughty Charity Trust
The D'Oyly Carte Charitable
    Trust
Dr. Martens Foundation
Drapers Charitable Fund
Dromintee Trust
Duchy of Lancaster Benevolent
    Fund
The Dulverton Trust

The Charles Dunstone
    Charitable Trust
The Dyers' Company
    Charitable Trust
EA Foundation*
The Earley Charity
Ebenezer Trust
Edinburgh Children's Holiday
    Fund
Edupoor Ltd
Dr Edwards and Bishop King's
    Fulham Charity
The Eight Foundation
The George Elias Charitable
    Trust
The Elie Trust
The Wilfred and Elsie Elkes
    Charity Fund
The Ellerdale Trust
The Endrick Trust
The Englefield Charitable Trust
The Enkalon Foundation
Entindale Ltd
The EQ Foundation
The Eventhall Family
    Charitable Trust
The Everard Foundation
The Eveson Charitable Trust
The Exilarch's Foundation
The ExPat Foundation
G. F. Eyre Charitable Trust
The Fairness Foundation
The Lord Faringdon Charitable
    Trust
Samuel William Farmer Trust
The Farthing Trust
The February Foundation
George Fentham Birmingham
    Charity
The Fifty Fund
The Finborough Foundation
Dixie Rose Findlay Charitable
    Trust
Fine & Country Foundation
Fishmongers' Company's
    Charitable Trust
The Earl Fitzwilliam Charitable
    Trust
The Robert Fleming Hannay
    Memorial Charity
The Follett Trust
Forest Hill Charitable Trust
Forever Manchester
The Forman Hardy Charitable
    Trust
The Forrester Family Trust
The Anna Rosa Forster
    Charitable Trust
Foux Foundation
The Elizabeth Frankland Moore
    and Star Foundation
Jill Franklin Trust
The Gordon Fraser Charitable
    Trust
The Hugh Fraser Foundation

The Louis and Valerie
    Freedman Charitable
    Settlement
Charles S. French Charitable
    Trust
Friends of Wiznitz Ltd
The Patrick and Helena Frost
    Foundation
The Fulmer Charitable Trust
The Gannochy Trust
General Charity (Coventry)
The Generations Foundation
The Tara Getty Foundation
J. Paul Getty Jr General
    Charitable Trust*
The David Gibbons Foundation
The Gibbs Charitable Trusts
The Girdlers' Company
    Charitable Trust
The B. and P. Glasser
    Charitable Trust
The Gloag Foundation
Global Charities
Gloucestershire Community
    Foundation
Sydney and Phyllis Goldberg
    Memorial Charitable Trust
The Golden Bottle Trust
The Goldsmiths' Company
    Charity
The Goodman Foundation
The Gosling Foundation Ltd
The Edward Gostling
    Foundation
Gowling WLG (UK) Charitable
    Trust
The Hemraj Goyal Foundation
Grace Charitable Trust
The Grace Trust
The Graham Trust
The Grand Trust CIO
William Grant Foundation*
The Grantham Yorke Trust
The J. G. Graves Charitable
    Trust
The Green Hall Foundation
The Green Room Charitable
    Trust
Philip and Judith Green Trust
Greenham Trust Ltd
The Greggs Foundation
The Grocers' Charity
The Walter Guinness
    Charitable Trust
Hackney Parochial Charities
The Hadfield Charitable Trust
The Hadley Trust
The Hadrian Trust
Halifax Foundation for
    Northern Ireland
Paul Hamlyn Foundation
The Helen Hamlyn Trust
Hammersmith United Charities
Hampshire and Isle of Wight
    Community Foundation

The Hampstead Wells and
Campden Trust
Hampton Fund
The W. A. Handley Charity
Trust
The Lennox Hannay Charitable
Trust
The Haramead Trust
Harbinson Charitable Trust
Harborne Parish Lands Charity
The Harbour Foundation
William Harding's Charity
The Hargreaves Foundation
The Harpur Trust
The Peter Harrison Foundation
The Harrison-Frank Family
Foundation (UK) Ltd
The Harry and Mary
Foundation
Edward Harvist Trust (The
Harvist Estate)
The Hasluck Charitable Trust
The Hawthorne Charitable
Trust
The Charles Hayward
Foundation
The Headley Trust
Heart of England Community
Foundation
Heb Ffin (Without Frontier)
Ernest Hecht Charitable
Foundation
The Hedley Foundation
The Hemby Charitable Trust
Henley Educational Trust
Tim Henman Foundation
Herefordshire Community
Foundation
Hertfordshire Community
Foundation
P. and C. Hickinbotham
Charitable Trust
The Alan Edward Higgs Charity
The Highcroft Charitable Trust
Highway One Trust
The Hillier Trust
R. G. Hills Charitable Trust
The Lady Hind Trust
The Hinduja Foundation
The Hiscox Foundation
The Henry C. Hoare Charitable
Trust
The Hobson Charity Ltd
The Holbeck Charitable Trust
Hollick Family Foundation
P. H. Holt Foundation
The Holywood Trust
Sir Harold Hood's Charitable
Trust
The Hosking Charitable Trust*
The Hospital of God at
Greatham
House of Industry Estate
Housing Pathways Trust
The Huggard Charitable Trust

The Hull and East Riding
Charitable Trust
The Humanitarian Trust
The Albert Hunt Trust
The Hunter Foundation
Miss Agnes H. Hunter's Trust
Huntingdon Freemen's Trust
The Nani Huyu Charitable Trust
Hyde Charitable Trust
Hyde Park Place Estate Charity
IGO Foundation Ltd
Imagine Foundation
Impact Funding Partners Ltd
Impetus
The Inflexion Foundation
Inner London Magistrates
Court Poor Box and Feeder
Charity
The Innocent Foundation
The International Bankers
Charitable Trust
The Invigorate Charitable Trust
The Ireland Fund of Great
Britain
Irish Youth Foundation (UK)
Ltd (incorporating The
Lawlor Foundation)
The Isla Foundation
Isle of Wight Foundation
The J. A. R. Charitable Trust
The J. and J. Benevolent
Foundation
The Jabbs Foundation
The Frank Jackson Foundation
Jay Education Trust
The JD Foundation
The Roger and Jean Jefcoate
Trust
The Jenour Foundation
The Jerusalem Trust
John Lewis and Partners
Foundation
Johnnie Johnson Trust
The Jones 1986 Charitable
Trust
J. E. Joseph Charitable Fund
Anton Jurgens Charitable Trust
The Jusaca Charitable Trust
The Ian Karten Charitable
Trust
The Michael and Ilse Katz
Foundation
The Emmanuel Kaye
Foundation
The Kelly Family Charitable
Trust
William Kendall's Charity (Wax
Chandlers Company)
The Kennedy Leigh Charitable
Trust
The Kensington and Chelsea
Foundation
Kent Community Foundation
The Nancy Kenyon Charitable
Trust
The Peter Kershaw Trust

KFC Foundation
Fraser Kilpatrick Charitable
Trust
The Mary Kinross Charitable
Trust
The Graham Kirkham
Foundation
Sir James Knott Trust
Kollel and Co. Ltd
Kolyom Trust Ltd
KPE4 Charitable Trust
The KPMG Foundation
Kupath Gemach Chaim
Bechesed Viznitz Trust
Kusuma Trust UK
Ladbrokes Coral Trust
Maurice and Hilda Laing
Charitable Trust
The Martin Laing Foundation
The Leonard Laity Stoate
Charitable Trust
The Lake House Charitable
Foundation
Community Foundations for
Lancashire and Merseyside
The Lancashire Foundation
Lancaster Foundation
LandAid Charitable Trust Ltd
(LandAid)
The Allen Lane Foundation
The LankellyChase Foundation
The R. J. Larg Family Trust
Laslett's (Hinton) Charity
Mrs F. B. Laurence Charitable
Trust
The Edgar E. Lawley
Foundation
The Herd Lawson and Muriel
Lawson Charitable Trust
Lawson Beckman Charitable
Trust
The Lawson Trust CIO
The Leach Fourteenth Trust
The Leathersellers' Foundation
Leeds Building Society
Foundation
Leeds Community Foundation
The Leeward Trust
The Legal Education
Foundation
Leicestershire and Rutland
Masonic Charity
Association
The Leigh Trust
The Mark Leonard Trust
The Leri Charitable Trust
Cecil and Hilda Lewis
Charitable Trust
Bernard Lewis Family
Charitable Trust
David and Ruth Lewis Family
Charitable Trust
Liberum Foundation
The Lightbulb Trust*
The Limbourne Trust
The Linbury Trust

The Linder Foundation
The Lister Charitable Trust
The Frank Litchfield Charitable
Trust
The Charles Littlewood Hill
Trust
The Second Joseph Aaron
Littman Foundation
The Ian and Natalie
Livingstone Charitable Trust
The Elaine and Angus Lloyd
Charitable Trust
The W. M. and B. W. Lloyd
Trust
Lloyds Bank Foundation for
England and Wales
Lloyds Bank Foundation for the
Channel Islands
Lloyd's of London Foundation
Lloyd's Patriotic Fund
Localtrent Ltd
London Catalyst
London Freemasons Charity
London Legal Support Trust
(LLST)
Longleigh Foundation
The Lord's Taverners
The C. L. Loyd Charitable Trust
The Lyndal Tree Foundation
John Lyon's Charity
The Lyons Trust*
Sylvanus Lysons Charity
M. and C. Trust
The R. S. Macdonald
Charitable Trust
Mace Foundation
The Mackintosh Foundation
The Magdalen and Lasher
Charity (General Fund)
The Magen Charitable Trust
The Manchester Guardian
Society Charitable Trust
R. W. Mann Trust
The Manoukian Charitable
Foundation
Marbeh Torah Trust
Marmot Charitable Trust
The Michael Marsh Charitable
Trust
The Marsh Christian Trust
Charlotte Marshall Charitable
Trust
The Martin Charitable Trust
Sir George Martin Trust
John Martin's Charity
Nancie Massey Charitable
Trust
The Master Charitable Trust
Mathew Trust
The Matliwala Family
Charitable Trust
Mayfair Charities Ltd
MBNA General Foundation
The Medlock Charitable Trust
Melodor Ltd
The Melow Charitable Trust

Mercaz Torah Vechesed Ltd
The Brian Mercer Charitable
Trust
The Mercers Charitable
Foundation
The Merchant Taylors'
Foundation*
The Merchant Venturers
Charity
Merchants House of Glasgow
Merriman Charitable
Foundation*
The Mickel Fund
The Mickleham Trust
The Gerald Micklem Charitable
Trust
The Millennium Oak Trust
The Millfield House Foundation
(1)
Mills and Reeve Charitable
Trust
The James Milner Foundation
Milton Keynes Community
Foundation Ltd
The Peter Minet Trust
Minton Charitable Trust
The Mishcon Family Charitable
Trust
The Brian Mitchell Charitable
Settlement
The MK Charitable Trust
The Modiano Charitable Trust
The Monday Charitable Trust
The Monmouthshire County
Council Welsh Church Act
Fund
Moondance Foundation
John Moores Foundation
The Morgan Charitable
Foundation
The Steve Morgan Foundation
The Morris Charitable Trust
G. M. Morrison Charitable
Trust
The Morrisons Foundation
Moto Foundation
The Moulding Foundation
The MSE Charity
The Mulberry Trust
Edith Murphy Foundation
Murphy-Neumann Charity
Company Ltd
Brian Murtagh Charitable Trust
The National Express
Foundation
The Nationwide Foundation
The NDL Foundation
Near Neighbours
Nemoral Ltd
Ner Foundation
Network for Social Change
Charitable Trust
Newby Trust Ltd
Newpier Charity Ltd
The NFU Mutual Charitable
Trust

The Nisbet Trust
The Nomura Charitable Trust
Norfolk Community Foundation
The Norman Family Charitable
Trust
Normanby Charitable Trust
Northamptonshire Community
Foundation
Northern Consortium*
Community Foundation for
Northern Ireland
The Northwick Trust
The Norton Foundation
The Norton Rose Fulbright
Charitable Foundation
Norwich Consolidated
Charities
Nottinghamshire Community
Foundation
The Nuffield Foundation
Odin Charitable Trust
Old Possum's Practical Trust
Henry Oldfield Trust
One Community Foundation
Ltd
Otsar Trust
Oxfordshire Community
Foundation
P. F. Charitable Trust
The Paget Charitable Trust
The Gerald Palmer Eling Trust
Company
The Panacea Charitable Trust
The Paragon Trust
The Pargiter Trust
The Parivar Trust
Peacock Charitable Trust
David Pearlman Charitable
Foundation
The Pebbles Trust
The Dowager Countess
Eleanor Peel Trust
People's Health Trust
People's Postcode Trust
Personal Assurance Charitable
Trust
The Pharsalia Charitable Trust
The Bernard Piggott Charitable
Trust
The Pilgrim Trust
Cecil Pilkington Charitable
Trust
Pilkington Charities Fund
The Sir Harry Pilkington Fund
PIMCO Foundation Europe
The Players Foundation
Polden-Puckham Charitable
Foundation
The George and Esme Pollitzer
Charitable Settlement
The Porta Pia 2012
Foundation
Porter Foundation
The Portishead Nautical Trust
The Portrack Charitable Trust
Postcode Community Trust

Postcode Local Trust
Postcode Society Trust
The Potton Consolidated
    Charity
Premierquote Ltd
The Pret Foundation
Sir John Priestman Charity
    Trust
The Princess Anne's Charities
The Privy Purse Charitable
    Trust
The Progress Foundation
The PwC Foundation
The Pye Foundation
Mr and Mrs J. A. Pye's
    Charitable Settlement
QBE European Operations
    Foundation
Quartet Community Foundation
The Queen Anne's Gate
    Foundation
The Quilter Foundation
Quothquan Trust
R. S. Charitable Trust
Rachel Charitable Trust
Richard Radcliffe Trust
The Rainford Trust
The Joseph and Lena Randall
    Charitable Trust
The Eleanor Rathbone
    Charitable Trust
Elizabeth Rathbone Charity
The Ravensdale Trust
The Rayne Foundation
C. A. Redfern Charitable
    Foundation
The Resolution Trust
Rhodi Charitable Trust
The Rhododendron Trust
Riada Trust
Daisie Rich Trust
Richmond Parish Lands Charity
Rigby Foundation
The River Farm Foundation
Riverside Charitable Trust Ltd
The Rix-Thompson-Rothenberg
    Foundation
The Robertson Trust
The Sir James Roll Charitable
    Trust
The Gerald and Gail Ronson
    Family Foundation
Mrs L. D. Rope's Third
    Charitable Settlement
Rosca Trust
The Eranda Rothschild
    Foundation
The Roughley Charitable Trust
The Rowlands Trust
The Joseph Rowntree
    Charitable Trust
The Royal British Legion
Royal Docks Trust (London)
The Rugby Group Benevolent
    Fund Ltd
The RWS Foundation

S. and R. Charitable Trust
The S. M. B. Trust
The Jeremy and John Sacher
    Charitable Trust
The Michael and Nicola Sacher
    Charitable Trust
The Saddlers' Company
    Charitable Fund
Erach and Roshan Sadri
    Foundation
The Alan and Babette
    Sainsbury Charitable Fund
The Salamander Charitable
    Trust
Samjo Ltd
The Basil Samuel Charitable
    Trust
The Samworth Foundation
The Savoy Educational Trust
The Schreib Trust
O. and G. Schreiber Charitable
    Trust
Schroder Charity Trust
Foundation Scotland
The Scott Bader
    Commonwealth Ltd
The Frieda Scott Charitable
    Trust
The Ina Scott Sutherland
    Charitable Foundation
The John Scott Trust Fund
Scottish Coal Industry Special
    Welfare Fund
ScottishPower Foundation
Scouloudi Foundation
The Sam and Bella Sebba
    Charitable Foundation
Seedfield Trust
The Segelman Trust
The Serco Foundation
SF Foundation
The Shanley Charitable Trust
The Shanly Foundation
The Shears Foundation
The Sheldon Trust
Shetland Charitable Trust
SHINE (Support and Help in
    Education)
The Bassil Shippam and
    Alsford Trust
The Shipwrights Charitable
    Fund
Shlomo Memorial Fund Ltd
The Shoe Zone Trust
The Simmons & Simmons
    Charitable Foundation
The Skelton Bounty
The Charles Skey Charitable
    Trust
Rita and David Slowe
    Charitable Trust
The Mrs Smith and Mount
    Trust
The Henry Smith Charity
Arabella and Julian Smith
    Family Trust

The Leslie Smith Foundation
Philip Smith's Charitable Trust
Sodexo Stop Hunger
    Foundation
Sofronie Foundation
Somerset Community
    Foundation
Songdale Ltd
The E. C. Sosnow Charitable
    Trust
Souter Charitable Trust
South Yorkshire Community
    Foundation
W. F. Southall Trust
Sparquote Ltd
The SpeedoMick Foundation
Spielman Charitable Trust
The Squires Foundation
The St Hilda's Trust
Sir Walter St John's
    Educational Charity
St John's Foundation Est.
    1174
The Community Foundation for
    Staffordshire
The Peter Stebbings Memorial
    Charity
The Hugh Stenhouse
    Foundation
Stervon Ltd
Sir Halley Stewart Trust
The Stone Family Foundation
Strand Parishes Trust
Stratford-upon-Avon Town Trust
The W. O. Street Charitable
    Foundation
The Street Foundation
Streetsmart – Action for the
    Homeless
Suffolk Community Foundation
The Bernard Sunley
    Foundation
The Sunrise Foundation CIO
Community Foundation for
    Surrey
Sabina Sutherland Charitable
    Trust
Sutton Coldfield Charitable
    Trust
The Swann-Morton Foundation
The Swire Charitable Trust
The Charles and Elsie Sykes
    Trust
The Tabhair Charitable Trust
The Talbot Trusts
The Talbot Village Trust
Tallow Chandlers Benevolent
    Fund No 2
The Taurus Foundation
Tay Charitable Trust
C. B. and H. H. T. Taylor 1984
    Trust
The Tedworth Charitable Trust
Tegham Ltd
the7stars Foundation

Scott Thomson Charitable
Trust
Sir Jules Thorn Charitable
Trust
The Thornton Trust
The Three Guineas Trust
The Three Oaks Trust
The Tolkien Trust
Tower Hill Trust
The Toy Trust
Toyota Manufacturing UK
Charitable Trust
The Trades House of Glasgow
Annie Tranmer Charitable Trust
The Constance Travis
Charitable Trust
The Triangle Trust (1949) Fund
The Truemark Trust
Trust for London
The Trusthouse Charitable
Foundation
The Tudor Trust
The Tuixen Foundation
The Turtleton Charitable Trust
Two Magpies Fund
Two Ridings Community
Foundation
Tzedakah
Ufi VocTech Trust
Ulster Garden Villages Ltd
The Underwood Trust
The Union of the Sisters of
Mercy of Great Britain
United St Saviour's Charity
United Utilities Trust Fund
The Valentine Charitable Trust
The Albert Van Den Bergh
Charitable Trust
The Van Mesdag Fund
The Van Neste Foundation
The Vandervell Foundation
The Vardy Foundation
The Velvet Foundation
The Vintners' Foundation
Virgin Atlantic Foundation
The Virgin Money Foundation
The Vodafone Foundation
Volant Charitable Trust
The Georg and Emily von Opel
Foundation
Sylvia Waddilove Foundation
UK
The Scurrah Wainwright Charity
Wakefield and Tetley Trust
The Walcot Foundation
The Walker Trust
Walton-on-Thames Charity
Warwick Relief-in-Need Charity
The Warwickshire Masonic
Charitable Association Ltd
The Watches of Switzerland
Group Foundation
Mrs Waterhouse Charitable
Trust
The Waterloo Foundation
The Wates Foundation

The William Wates Memorial
Trust
The Geoffrey Watling Charity
We Love MCR Charity
The Weavers' Company
Benevolent Fund
The William Webster
Charitable Trust
Wellbank Foundation*
Wellington Management UK
Foundation
The Welsh Church Act Fund
West Derby Waste Lands
Charity
Westminster Almshouses
Foundation
Westminster Foundation
The Garfield Weston
Foundation
Westway Trust
The Melanie White Foundation
Ltd
Wickens Family Foundation
The Wimbledon Foundation
The Benjamin Winegarten
Charitable Trust
The Michael and Anna Wix
Charitable Trust
The Wixamtree Trust
The James Wood Bequest
Fund
The Wood Foundation
Wooden Spoon Society
Woodlands Green Ltd
The Woodward Charitable
Trust
The Worshipful Company of
Glovers of London
Charitable Trust
The Worshipful Company of
Information Technologists
The Worwin UK Foundation
The Eric Wright Charitable
Trust
Sir Graham Wylie Foundation
The Wyseliot Rose Charitable
Trust
The Yapp Charitable Trust
Yorkshire Building Society
Charitable Foundation
The Elizabeth and Prince
Zaiger Trust
Zephyr Charitable Trust
The Zochonis Charitable Trust
Zurich Community Trust (UK)
Ltd

....

■ Asylum seekers/ internally displaced peoples/refugees

The A. B. Charitable Trust
Al Madad Foundation*
The Alborada Trust
The Apax Foundation
The Noel Buxton Trust

William A. Cadbury Charitable
Trust
The City Bridge Trust (Bridge
House Estates)
The Roger and Sarah Bancroft
Clark Charitable Trust
The Evan Cornish Foundation
Craignish Trust
The Dashlight Foundation
Dentons UK and Middle East
LLP Charitable Trust
The J. N. Derbyshire Trust
Dr. Martens Foundation
EA Foundation*
Emerton-Christie Charity
The Fairness Foundation
The Forrester Family Trust
Jill Franklin Trust
The Fulmer Charitable Trust
The Gloag Foundation
The Golden Bottle Trust
Paul Hamlyn Foundation
Harbinson Charitable Trust
The Harbour Foundation
P. and C. Hickinbotham
Charitable Trust
The Hilden Charitable Fund
P. H. Holt Foundation
The Hospital of God at
Greatham
Imagine Foundation
Inner London Magistrates
Court Poor Box and Feeder
Charity
JAC Trust*
KFC Foundation
Maurice and Hilda Laing
Charitable Trust
The Allen Lane Foundation
The Leigh Trust
The Mark Leonard Trust
The Leri Charitable Trust
The Limbourne Trust
The Linbury Trust
Lloyds Bank Foundation for
England and Wales
London Catalyst
The London Community
Foundation (LCF)
The Lyndal Tree Foundation
The Robin MacLeod Charitable
Trust
The Marks Family Charitable
Trust
The Marsh Christian Trust
The Mercers Charitable
Foundation
The Mickleham Trust
Near Neighbours
Network for Social Change
Charitable Trust
The Northwick Trust
Norwich Consolidated
Charities
Odin Charitable Trust
Orange Tree Trust

The Pickwell Foundation
The Eleanor Rathbone
    Charitable Trust
The Sigrid Rausing Trust
The Rayne Foundation
The Robertson Trust
Rosca Trust
The Roughley Charitable Trust
The Joseph Rowntree
    Charitable Trust
The Alan and Babette
    Sainsbury Charitable Fund
The Sam and Bella Sebba
    Charitable Foundation
The Gay and Keith Talbot Trust
The Talbot Trusts
The Tolkien Trust
The Union of the Sisters of
    Mercy of Great Britain
The Vodafone Foundation
Volant Charitable Trust
Wakefield and Tetley Trust
Wickens Family Foundation
The Woodward Charitable
    Trust

....

■ Carers

The Alchemy Foundation
The Astor Foundation
The Ballinger Charitable Trust
The Barnes Fund
The Charlotte Bonham-Carter
    Charitable Trust
The Brelms Trust CIO
The British and Foreign School
    Society (BFSS)
Miss Margaret Butters Reekie
    Charitable Trust
Carew Pole Charitable Trust
The Clothworkers' Foundation
The D'Oyly Carte Charitable
    Trust
The Ellerdale Trust
The Forbes Charitable
    Foundation
Jill Franklin Trust
The Girdlers' Company
    Charitable Trust
Global Charities
The Goldsmiths' Company
    Charity
The Greggs Foundation
The Albert Gubay Charitable
    Foundation
The Hadrian Trust
Hampshire and Isle of Wight
    Community Foundation
Hampton Fund
The Hawthorne Charitable
    Trust
The Hedley Foundation
The Alan Edward Higgs Charity
The Hobson Charity Ltd
Hospice UK
The Albert Hunt Trust

The Roger and Jean Jefcoate
    Trust
KFC Foundation
The Leach Fourteenth Trust
The Linder Foundation
Lloyds Bank Foundation for the
    Channel Islands
The Lord's Taverners
The Lyndal Tree Foundation
The Mercers Charitable
    Foundation
The Mickleham Trust
John Moores Foundation
The Morrisons Foundation
The MSE Charity
Norfolk Community Foundation
Norwich Consolidated
    Charities
The Austin and Hope
    Pilkington Trust
The Portrack Charitable Trust
The Quilter Foundation
The Rayne Foundation
The Rhododendron Trust
The Rix-Thompson-Rothenberg
    Foundation
The Roughley Charitable Trust
The Frieda Scott Charitable
    Trust
The Tedworth Charitable Trust
the7stars Foundation
The Triangle Trust (1949) Fund
Wakefield and Tetley Trust
Walton-on-Thames Charity
The Waterloo Foundation
The Will Charitable Trust
The Eric Wright Charitable
    Trust

....

■ Disadvantaged and socially excluded people

The 29th May 1961 Charitable
    Trust
The 4814 Trust
The Aberdeenshire Educational
    Trust Scheme
abrdn Charitable Foundation
abrdn Financial Fairness Trust
Adam Family Foundation
AJ Bell Trust
The Derrill Allatt Foundation
D. C. R. Allen Charitable Trust
The AMW Charitable Trust
The Anchor Foundation
Anpride Ltd
The John Apthorp Charity
The Annabel Arbib Foundation
The Ardwick Trust
The John Armitage Charitable
    Trust
The Arsenal Foundation
The Ashworth Charitable Trust
The Astor Foundation
Axis Foundation

The Aziz Foundation
Backstage Trust
The Austin Bailey Foundation
The Ballinger Charitable Trust
Bank of Scotland Foundation
The Baring Foundation
Barnwood Trust
Bauer Radio's Cash for Kids
    Charities
The Gordon and Ena Baxter
    Foundation*
Bay Charitable Trust
The Bay Tree Charitable Trust
BBC Children in Need
The James Beattie Charitable
    Trust
Beauland Ltd
Bedfordshire and Luton
    Community Foundation
Bedfordshire Charitable Trust
    Ltd
The Benham Charitable
    Settlement
The Berkeley Foundation
The Bernicia Foundation
Bideford Bridge Trust
The Percy Bilton Charity
The Bingham Trust
The Blagrave Trust
Blyth Watson Charitable Trust
Maureen Boal Charitable Trust
Boots Charitable Trust
The Salo Bordon Charitable
    Trust
The Liz and Terry Bramall
    Foundation
The Brelms Trust CIO
The Brenley Trust
Bristol Charities
British Gas Energy Trust
British Humane Association
Bill Brown 1989 Charitable
    Trust
R. S. Brownless Charitable
    Trust
Buckingham Trust
Buckinghamshire Community
    Foundation
The Bulldog Trust Ltd
Consolidated Charity of Burton
    upon Trent
Byrne Family Foundation
C. and F. Charitable Trust
William A. Cadbury Charitable
    Trust
The Edward and Dorothy
    Cadbury Trust
Community Foundation for
    Calderdale
CareTech Charitable
    Foundation
Carew Pole Charitable Trust
The Antonio Carluccio
    Foundation
The Carr-Gregory Trust
The Amelia Chadwick Trust

The Charterhouse Charitable
 Trust
The Chetwode Foundation
The Childhood Trust
Chippenham Borough Lands
 Charity
The Roger and Sarah Bancroft
 Clark Charitable Trust
The Clore Duffield Foundation
The Clothworkers' Foundation
Cloudesley
The John Coates Charitable
 Trust
The Vivienne and Samuel
 Cohen Charitable Trust
Comic Relief
The Cooks Charity
Co-op Foundation
Cornwall Community
 Foundation
Corra Foundation
County Durham Community
 Foundation
The Lord Cozens-Hardy Trust
Craignish Trust
The Crerar Trust
CRH Charitable Trust
The Cross Trust
The Croydon Relief-in-Need
 Charity
Cumbria Community
 Foundation
Dentons UK and Middle East
 LLP Charitable Trust
Foundation Derbyshire
The J. N. Derbyshire Trust
The Gillian Dickinson Trust
Didymus
Donibristle Trust
The Dorcas Trust
The Double 'O' Charity Ltd
Dr. Martens Foundation
Drapers Charitable Fund
The Dulverton Trust
The Charles Dunstone
 Charitable Trust
The Dyers' Company
 Charitable Trust
EA Foundation*
The Earley Charity
Edinburgh Children's Holiday
 Fund
Edupoor Ltd
The Eight Foundation
The Elie Trust
The EQ Foundation
The Eventhall Family
 Charitable Trust
The Everard Foundation
Dixie Rose Findlay Charitable
 Trust
The Robert Fleming Hannay
 Memorial Charity
The Follett Trust
Foux Foundation

The Elizabeth Frankland Moore
 and Star Foundation
Charles S. French Charitable
 Trust
Friends of Wiznitz Ltd
The Gannochy Trust
General Charity (Coventry)
The Tara Getty Foundation
J. Paul Getty Jr General
 Charitable Trust*
The Gibbs Charitable Trusts
The Girdlers' Company
 Charitable Trust
The B. and P. Glasser
 Charitable Trust
Global Charities
Gloucestershire Community
 Foundation
The Hemraj Goyal Foundation
Grace Charitable Trust
The Grace Trust
The Graham Trust
The Grand Trust CIO
William Grant Foundation*
The Grantham Yorke Trust
The J. G. Graves Charitable
 Trust
The Green Hall Foundation
The Green Room Charitable
 Trust
Greenham Trust Ltd
The Greggs Foundation
Hackney Parochial Charities
Halifax Foundation for
 Northern Ireland
Hammersmith United Charities
Hampshire and Isle of Wight
 Community Foundation
Hampton Fund
Harbinson Charitable Trust
Harborne Parish Lands Charity
William Harding's Charity
The Hargreaves Foundation
The Peter Harrison Foundation
The Harrison-Frank Family
 Foundation (UK) Ltd
Ernest Hecht Charitable
 Foundation
The Hedley Foundation
Hertfordshire Community
 Foundation
P. and C. Hickinbotham
 Charitable Trust
The Alan Edward Higgs Charity
The Highcroft Charitable Trust
The Hillier Trust
The Lady Hind Trust
The Hiscox Foundation
P. H. Holt Foundation
The Holywood Trust
Sir Harold Hood's Charitable
 Trust
The Hosking Charitable Trust*
House of Industry Estate
The Huggard Charitable Trust
The Albert Hunt Trust

The Hunter Foundation
Miss Agnes H. Hunter's Trust
The Harold Hyam Wingate
 Foundation
Hyde Charitable Trust
Hyde Park Place Estate Charity
IGO Foundation Ltd
Imagine Foundation
Impact Funding Partners Ltd
Impetus
The Inflexion Foundation
Inner London Magistrates
 Court Poor Box and Feeder
 Charity
The Invigorate Charitable Trust
The Ireland Fund of Great
 Britain
Irish Youth Foundation (UK)
 Ltd (incorporating The
 Lawlor Foundation)
The Isla Foundation
Isle of Wight Foundation
The Frank Jackson Foundation
Johnnie Johnson Trust
The Jones 1986 Charitable
 Trust
Anton Jurgens Charitable Trust
The Kelly Family Charitable
 Trust
The Kensington and Chelsea
 Foundation
The Graham Kirkham
 Foundation
Sir James Knott Trust
Kolyom Trust Ltd
KPE4 Charitable Trust
Ladbrokes Coral Trust
The Martin Laing Foundation
The Leonard Laity Stoate
 Charitable Trust
The Lancashire Foundation
LandAid Charitable Trust Ltd
 (LandAid)
The Allen Lane Foundation
Laslett's (Hinton) Charity
Mrs F. B. Laurence Charitable
 Trust
The Lawson Trust CIO
The Leathersellers' Foundation
Leeds Building Society
 Foundation
Leeds Community Foundation
The Leeward Trust
The Mark Leonard Trust
Bernard Lewis Family
 Charitable Trust
Liberum Foundation
The Lightbulb Trust*
The Charles Littlewood Hill
 Trust
The Ian and Natalie
 Livingstone Charitable Trust
The Elaine and Angus Lloyd
 Charitable Trust
The W. M. and B. W. Lloyd
 Trust

Lloyds Bank Foundation for
England and Wales
London Catalyst
The London Community
Foundation (LCF)
London Freemasons Charity
London Legal Support Trust
(LLST)
The Lord's Taverners
The Lyons Trust*
Sylvanus Lysons Charity
The R. S. Macdonald
Charitable Trust
Mace Foundation
R. W. Mann Trust
The Martin Charitable Trust
Sir George Martin Trust
The Master Charitable Trust
The Brian Mercer Charitable
Trust
The Mercers Charitable
Foundation
The Merchant Taylors'
Foundation*
The Mickleham Trust
The Millennium Oak Trust
The Millfield House Foundation
(1)
Mills and Reeve Charitable
Trust
Milton Keynes Community
Foundation Ltd
The Peter Minet Trust
The Esmé Mitchell Trust
The Modiano Charitable Trust
John Moores Foundation
The Morgan Charitable
Foundation
The Steve Morgan Foundation
The Moulding Foundation
The Mulberry Trust
Murphy-Neumann Charity
Company Ltd
Near Neighbours
Ner Foundation
Newby Trust Ltd
Northern Consortium*
Community Foundation for
Northern Ireland
The Norton Foundation
The Norton Rose Fulbright
Charitable Foundation
Norwich Consolidated
Charities
The Nuffield Foundation
Old Possum's Practical Trust
Henry Oldfield Trust
Open House Trust Ltd
Otsar Trust
Oxfordshire Community
Foundation
The Gerald Palmer Eling Trust
Company
The Panacea Charitable Trust
The Pargiter Trust
Peacock Charitable Trust

David Pearlman Charitable
Foundation
The Pebbles Trust
People's Health Trust
People's Postcode Trust
Personal Assurance Charitable
Trust
The Pharsalia Charitable Trust
The Bernard Piggott Charitable
Trust
The Pilgrim Trust
Cecil Pilkington Charitable
Trust
The Players Foundation
The George and Esme Pollitzer
Charitable Settlement
The Portrack Charitable Trust
Postcode Community Trust
Postcode Local Trust
Postcode Society Trust
The Potton Consolidated
Charity
The Progress Foundation
The PwC Foundation
The Pye Foundation
The Rainford Trust
The Randal Charitable
Foundation
The Joseph and Lena Randall
Charitable Trust
Randeree Charitable Trust
The Eleanor Rathbone
Charitable Trust
Elizabeth Rathbone Charity
The Rayne Foundation
Rhodi Charitable Trust
The Rhododendron Trust
Daisie Rich Trust
Rigby Foundation
The River Farm Foundation
The Robertson Trust
The Sir James Roll Charitable
Trust
Rosca Trust
The Roughley Charitable Trust
The Joseph Rowntree
Charitable Trust
The RWS Foundation
S. and R. Charitable Trust
The Jeremy and John Sacher
Charitable Trust
The Michael and Nicola Sacher
Charitable Trust
Samjo Ltd
Santander UK Foundation Ltd
The Schreib Trust
Foundation Scotland
The Frieda Scott Charitable
Trust
The Ina Scott Sutherland
Charitable Foundation
The John Scott Trust Fund
Scottish Coal Industry Special
Welfare Fund
The Segelman Trust
The Serco Foundation

The Shanly Foundation
The Shears Foundation
The Sheldon Trust
SHINE (Support and Help in
Education)
The Bassil Shippam and
Alsford Trust
The Shipwrights Charitable
Fund
Shlomo Memorial Fund Ltd
The Simmons & Simmons
Charitable Foundation
The Skelton Bounty
The Charles Skey Charitable
Trust
The Henry Smith Charity
The Leslie Smith Foundation
Sofronie Foundation
Somerset Community
Foundation
Souter Charitable Trust
W. F. Southall Trust
The SpeedoMick Foundation
The St Hilda's Trust
Sir Walter St John's
Educational Charity
The Community Foundation for
Staffordshire
The Hugh Stenhouse
Foundation
Strand Parishes Trust
The Bernard Sunley
Foundation
The Sunrise Foundation CIO
Sabina Sutherland Charitable
Trust
The Swire Charitable Trust
The Adrian Swire Charitable
Trust
The Charles and Elsie Sykes
Trust
The Tabhair Charitable Trust
The Talbot Village Trust
Tallow Chandlers Benevolent
Fund No 2
The Taurus Foundation
Tay Charitable Trust
C. B. and H. H. T. Taylor 1984
Trust
The Taylor Family Foundation
the7stars Foundation
Sir Jules Thorn Charitable
Trust
The Three Oaks Trust
The Tomoro Foundation
Tower Hill Trust
The Constance Travis
Charitable Trust
The Trusthouse Charitable
Foundation
The Turtleton Charitable Trust
The Tweed Family Charitable
Foundation
Ulster Garden Villages Ltd
The Valentine Charitable Trust
The Van Mesdag Fund

The Vandervell Foundation
The Velvet Foundation
VINCI UK Foundation
The Vintners' Foundation
The Virgin Money Foundation
The Vodafone Foundation
Volant Charitable Trust
Sylvia Waddilove Foundation
   UK
The Scurrah Wainwright Charity
Wakefield and Tetley Trust
Walton-on-Thames Charity
The Watches of Switzerland
   Group Foundation
Mrs Waterhouse Charitable
   Trust
The Wates Foundation
The William Wates Memorial
   Trust
The Geoffrey Watling Charity
We Love MCR Charity
The Weavers' Company
   Benevolent Fund
The William Webster
   Charitable Trust
Wellbank Foundation*
Wellington Management UK
   Foundation
Westway Trust
The Which? Fund
Wickens Family Foundation
The Benjamin Winegarten
   Charitable Trust
The Wixamtree Trust
The James Wood Bequest
   Fund
Wooden Spoon Society
The Woodward Charitable
   Trust
The Worshipful Company of
   Glovers of London
   Charitable Trust
The Worshipful Company of
   Information Technologists
The Wyseliot Rose Charitable
   Trust
The Yapp Charitable Trust
Youth Endowment Fund (YEF)*
Zephyr Charitable Trust
The Zochonis Charitable Trust
Zurich Community Trust (UK)
   Ltd

....

■ Ex-offenders/ offenders/people at risk of offending

The 29th May 1961 Charitable
   Trust
The A. B. Charitable Trust
The Alchemy Foundation
The John Armitage Charitable
   Trust
The Sydney Black Charitable
   Trust
The Bowland Charitable Trust

The Bromley Trust
The Noel Buxton Trust
William A. Cadbury Charitable
   Trust
The Barrow Cadbury Trust
The Cayo Foundation
The Chetwode Foundation
CHK Foundation
The City Bridge Trust (Bridge
   House Estates)
The Roger and Sarah Bancroft
   Clark Charitable Trust
Clinks*
The Clothworkers' Foundation
Colyer-Fergusson Charitable
   Trust
The Evan Cornish Foundation
Dentons UK and Middle East
   LLP Charitable Trust
Dr. Martens Foundation
Drapers Charitable Fund
Emerton-Christie Charity
The Fairness Foundation
Fishmongers' Company's
   Charitable Trust
The Forrester Family Trust
Jill Franklin Trust
The Robert Gavron Charitable
   Trust
The Girdlers' Company
   Charitable Trust
The Golden Bottle Trust
The Goldsmiths' Company
   Charity
The Greater Manchester High
   Sheriff's Police Trust
The Grocers' Charity
The Albert Gubay Charitable
   Foundation
The Walter Guinness
   Charitable Trust
The Hadley Trust
The Hadrian Trust
Halifax Foundation for
   Northern Ireland
The Helen Hamlyn Trust
The Charles Hayward
   Foundation
Heb Ffin (Without Frontier)
The Hedley Foundation
P. and C. Hickinbotham
   Charitable Trust
The Hilden Charitable Fund
The Lady Hind Trust
P. H. Holt Foundation
Sir Harold Hood's Charitable
   Trust
The Hospital of God at
   Greatham
Michael and Shirley Hunt
   Charitable Trust
The Albert Hunt Trust
Imagine Foundation
Impetus

Inner London Magistrates
   Court Poor Box and Feeder
   Charity
The Jabbs Foundation
The Jerusalem Trust
The Emmanuel Kaye
   Foundation
The Kelly Family Charitable
   Trust
The Kensington and Chelsea
   Foundation
KFC Foundation
The Mary Kinross Charitable
   Trust
Maurice and Hilda Laing
   Charitable Trust
The Beatrice Laing Trust
The Allen Lane Foundation
The LankellyChase Foundation
The Leathersellers' Foundation
The Leigh Trust
The Mark Leonard Trust
The Linder Foundation
Lloyds Bank Foundation for
   England and Wales
Lloyds Bank Foundation for the
   Channel Islands
The Merchant Taylors'
   Foundation*
The Merchant Venturers
   Charity
G. M. Morrison Charitable
   Trust
The MSE Charity
The Norman Family Charitable
   Trust
The Northwick Trust
The Oakdale Trust
Odin Charitable Trust
Henry Oldfield Trust
The Austin and Hope
   Pilkington Trust
The Players Foundation
The Portishead Nautical Trust
The Sigrid Rausing Trust
The Rayne Foundation
The Rhododendron Trust
The Sir James Roll Charitable
   Trust
The Roughley Charitable Trust
Saint Sarkis Charity Trust
The Frieda Scott Charitable
   Trust
The SpeedoMick Foundation
The Peter Stebbings Memorial
   Charity
The Swire Charitable Trust
C. B. and H. H. T. Taylor 1984
   Trust
The Tolkien Trust
The Triangle Trust (1949) Fund
Volant Charitable Trust
The Weavers' Company
   Benevolent Fund
The Welsh Church Act Fund

The Woodward Charitable
Trust
Youth Endowment Fund (YEF)*

....

■ Migrants

The Barrow Cadbury Trust
The City Bridge Trust (Bridge
House Estates)
The Roger and Sarah Bancroft
Clark Charitable Trust
The Evan Cornish Foundation
EA Foundation*
The Fairness Foundation
Paul Hamlyn Foundation
The Allen Lane Foundation
The Linbury Trust
The London Community
Foundation (LCF)
G. M. Morrison Charitable
Trust
The MSE Charity
Near Neighbours
The Sigrid Rausing Trust
The Roughley Charitable Trust
The Tolkien Trust
The Union of the Sisters of
Mercy of Great Britain
Wakefield and Tetley Trust

....

■ People who are educationally disadvantaged

The 29th May 1961 Charitable
Trust
The 4814 Trust
abrdn Charitable Foundation
The Addleshaw Goddard
Charitable Trust
AJ Bell Trust
The Allen & Overy Foundation
Anguish's Educational
Foundation
The John Armitage Charitable
Trust
Lawrence Atwell's Charity
(Skinners' Company)
Bank of Scotland Foundation
The Max Barney Foundation
The Berkeley Foundation
The Bernicia Foundation
The Bestway Foundation
The Boshier-Hinton Foundation
The Chetwode Foundation
Church Burgesses Educational
Foundation
The Roger and Sarah Bancroft
Clark Charitable Trust
The Clothworkers' Foundation
The John Coates Charitable
Trust
Colyer-Fergusson Charitable
Trust

Cornwall Community
Foundation
The Danson Foundation*
The David Family Foundation*
EA Foundation*
The Eight Foundation
The Elie Trust
Allan and Nesta Ferguson
Charitable Settlement
The Hugh Fraser Foundation
The Girdlers' Company
Charitable Trust
The Gloag Foundation
The Grace Trust
The Grantham Yorke Trust
The Green Room Charitable
Trust
The Hadfield Charitable Trust
Paul Hamlyn Foundation
Harbinson Charitable Trust
Harborne Parish Lands Charity
The Peter Harrison Foundation
The Hemby Charitable Trust
Henley Educational Trust
The Alan Edward Higgs Charity
The Holbeck Charitable Trust
The Hosking Charitable Trust*
Housing Pathways Trust
The Hunter Foundation
Miss Agnes H. Hunter's Trust
Hyde Park Place Estate Charity
Impetus
The International Bankers
Charitable Trust
The Ireland Fund of Great
Britain
Isle of Wight Foundation
John Lewis and Partners
Foundation
The Ian Karten Charitable
Trust
Kelsick's Educational
Foundation
The Kensington and Chelsea
Foundation
Fraser Kilpatrick Charitable
Trust
Robert Kitchin (Saddlers' Co.)
KPE4 Charitable Trust
The KPMG Foundation
Community Foundations for
Lancashire and Merseyside
Cecil and Hilda Lewis
Charitable Trust
Lloyds Bank Foundation for the
Channel Islands
The London Community
Foundation (LCF)
London Freemasons Charity
The Lyons Trust*
Man Group plc Charitable
Trust
The Mercers Charitable
Foundation
The Merchant Taylors'
Foundation*

The Merchant Venturers
Charity
Merriman Charitable
Foundation*
The James Milner Foundation
John Moores Foundation
The Ken and Edna Morrison
Charitable Trust
The Ken and Lynne Morrison
Charitable Trust
The Morrisons Foundation
The Moulding Foundation
Newby Trust Ltd
Norfolk Community Foundation
Northern Consortium*
The Nuffield Foundation
Open House Trust Ltd
Peacock Charitable Trust
The Players Foundation
The Progress Foundation
The PwC Foundation
Richard Radcliffe Trust
Elizabeth Rathbone Charity
Richmond Parish Lands Charity
The Robertson Trust
The Alan and Babette
Sainsbury Charitable Fund
Foundation Scotland
The Sheldon Trust
SHINE (Support and Help in
Education)
Arabella and Julian Smith
Family Trust
Sofronie Foundation
St John's Foundation Est.
1174
The Stewarts Law Foundation
The Swire Charitable Trust
The Trusthouse Charitable
Foundation
Ufi VocTech Trust
The Velvet Foundation
The Vintners' Foundation
The Virgin Money Foundation
The Vodafone Foundation
The Waterloo Foundation
Wellington Management UK
Foundation
Westminster Almshouses
Foundation
The Wolfson Foundation
Zephyr Charitable Trust

....

■ People who are homeless/at risk of homelessness

The 29th May 1961 Charitable
Trust
The 4814 Trust
Adam Family Foundation
The Addleshaw Goddard
Charitable Trust
The Alchemy Foundation
Andrews Charitable Trust
Bank of Scotland Foundation

The Barbour Foundation
Barnsbury Charitable Trust
The Berkeley Foundation
The Brelms Trust CIO
Community Foundation for
    Calderdale
CEO Sleepout
The Clothworkers' Foundation
The Cole Charitable Trust
The Coltstaple Trust
The Evan Cornish Foundation
Corra Foundation
CRASH
Crisis UK
The D. G. Charitable
    Settlement
The Dawe Charitable Trust
Dentons UK and Middle East
    LLP Charitable Trust
Foundation Derbyshire
Dorset Community Foundation
Dr. Martens Foundation
Drapers Charitable Fund
The Eveson Charitable Trust
The Finborough Foundation
Dixie Rose Findlay Charitable
    Trust
Fine & Country Foundation
The Follett Trust
The Elizabeth Frankland Moore
    and Star Foundation
The Goldsmiths' Company
    Charity
The Greggs Foundation
The Albert Gubay Charitable
    Foundation
The Hadrian Trust
Halifax Foundation for
    Northern Ireland
Hammersmith United Charities
Hampshire and Isle of Wight
    Community Foundation
The Haramead Trust
The Harbour Foundation
Heb Ffin (Without Frontier)
The Hedley Foundation
P. and C. Hickinbotham
    Charitable Trust
Highway One Trust
The Hilden Charitable Fund
The Hobson Charity Ltd
Hollick Family Foundation
Sir Harold Hood's Charitable
    Trust
Housing Pathways Trust
The Huggard Charitable Trust
Inner London Magistrates
    Court Poor Box and Feeder
    Charity
Irish Youth Foundation (UK)
    Ltd (incorporating The
    Lawlor Foundation)
The JD Foundation
The Cyril and Eve Jumbo
    Charitable Trust
The Jusaca Charitable Trust

The Kensington and Chelsea
    Foundation
Kent Community Foundation
KFC Foundation
The Graham Kirkham
    Foundation
Sir James Knott Trust
Ladbrokes Coral Trust
John Laing Charitable Trust
Maurice and Hilda Laing
    Charitable Trust
The Beatrice Laing Trust
LandAid Charitable Trust Ltd
    (LandAid)
The LankellyChase Foundation
Laslett's (Hinton) Charity
Mrs F. B. Laurence Charitable
    Trust
The Leathersellers' Foundation
Leeds Building Society
    Foundation
The Linbury Trust
Lloyds Bank Foundation for
    England and Wales
Lloyds Bank Foundation for the
    Channel Islands
The London Community
    Foundation (LCF)
London Housing Foundation
    Ltd (LHF)
The Mackintosh Foundation
The Mercers Charitable
    Foundation
The Merchant Venturers
    Charity
Merriman Charitable
    Foundation*
The Mickleham Trust
The Monday Charitable Trust
John Moores Foundation
G. M. Morrison Charitable
    Trust
The MSE Charity
The Nationwide Foundation
The Nisbet Trust
Norfolk Community Foundation
The Norman Family Charitable
    Trust
Norwich Consolidated
    Charities
Nottinghamshire Community
    Foundation
Odin Charitable Trust
Henry Oldfield Trust
Orange Tree Trust
The Philip and Connie Phillips
    Foundation*
PIMCO Foundation Europe
The Portishead Nautical Trust
The Portrack Charitable Trust
The Pret Foundation
Quartet Community Foundation
Richard Radcliffe Trust
The Rhododendron Trust
Richmond Parish Lands Charity
The River Farm Foundation

The Robertson Trust
Mrs L. D. Rope's Third
    Charitable Settlement
The Roughley Charitable Trust
The Royal British Legion
Royal Docks Trust (London)
Erach and Roshan Sadri
    Foundation
The Salamander Charitable
    Trust
The Shanly Foundation
Rita and David Slowe
    Charitable Trust
The Mrs Smith and Mount
    Trust
The Henry Smith Charity
The SpeedoMick Foundation
The Peter Stebbings Memorial
    Charity
Sir Halley Stewart Trust
Streetsmart – Action for the
    Homeless
The Swire Charitable Trust
The Talbot Trusts
Tay Charitable Trust
C. B. and H. H. T. Taylor 1984
    Trust
the7stars Foundation
Sir Jules Thorn Charitable
    Trust
The Tolkien Trust
The Tuixen Foundation
The Albert Van Den Bergh
    Charitable Trust
VINCI UK Foundation
The Virgin Money Foundation
Walton-on-Thames Charity
Wickens Family Foundation
The Worshipful Company of
    Glovers of London
    Charitable Trust
Yorkshire Building Society
    Charitable Foundation

....

■ People who are isolated

abrdn Charitable Foundation
Camden Giving
The Goldsmiths' Company
    Charity
The Greggs Foundation
Hammersmith United Charities
The Harpur Trust
Inner London Magistrates
    Court Poor Box and Feeder
    Charity
The Ireland Fund of Great
    Britain
The Kensington and Chelsea
    Foundation
Community Foundations for
    Lancashire and Merseyside
The Lancashire Foundation
The Linbury Trust

The London Community
Foundation (LCF)
The Mercers Charitable
Foundation
The Janet and Brian Moore
Charitable Trust*
Nesta
Norfolk Community Foundation
The Philip and Connie Phillips
Foundation*
The Prince of Wales's
Charitable Foundation
Foundation Scotland
SHINE (Support and Help in
Education)
South Yorkshire Community
Foundation
Community Foundation for
Surrey
The Trusthouse Charitable
Foundation
Wakefield and Tetley Trust
Walton-on-Thames Charity
The Woodward Charitable
Trust

■ People who are on low incomes and/or benefits

The 29th May 1961 Charitable
Trust
The Aberdeenshire Educational
Trust Scheme
abrdn Charitable Foundation
abrdn Financial Fairness Trust
Achisomoch Aid Company Ltd
Adam Family Foundation
AJ Bell Trust
The Aldama Foundation
Ambergate Charitable Trust
The Archer Trust
The Artemis Charitable
Foundation
Atlas Memorial Ltd
B&Q Foundation
The Barnes Fund
The Bellahouston Bequest
Fund
The Berkeley Foundation
The Sydney Black Charitable
Trust
The Bertie Black Foundation
The Salo Bordon Charitable
Trust
The Harry Bottom Charitable
Trust
The P. G. and N. J. Boulton
Trust
British Gas Energy Trust
J. and M. Britton Charitable
Trust
Brushmill Ltd
Buckingham Trust
The Barrow Cadbury Trust
Carew Pole Charitable Trust

The Chetwode Foundation
The Childhood Trust
Chippenham Borough Lands
Charity
CLA Charitable Trust
The Roger and Sarah Bancroft
Clark Charitable Trust
Cloudesley
The R. and S. Cohen
Foundation
The Cole Charitable Trust
Colyer-Fergusson Charitable
Trust
Community First
Douglas Compton James
Charitable Trust
Michael Crawford Children's
Charity
Cripplegate Foundation
The J. N. Derbyshire Trust
Donibristle
The Double 'O' Charity Ltd
The Doughty Charity Trust
EA Foundation*
Dr Edwards and Bishop King's
Fulham Charity
The George Elias Charitable
Trust
The Elie Trust
The Ellerdale Trust
The Enkalon Foundation
The Fifty Fund
The Robert Fleming Hannay
Memorial Charity
The Follett Trust
The Hugh Fraser Foundation
The Tara Getty Foundation
The B. and P. Glasser
Charitable Trust
The Gloag Foundation
Gloucestershire Community
Foundation
The Goodman Foundation
The Gosling Foundation Ltd
The Graham Trust
The Green Room Charitable
Trust
Hackney Parochial Charities
The Hadley Trust
The Hadrian Trust
Harbinson Charitable Trust
Harborne Parish Lands Charity
The Harpur Trust
Edward Harvist Trust (The
Harvist Estate)
The Hawthorne Charitable
Trust
The Heathcoat Trust
Henley Educational Trust
Tim Henman Foundation
Herefordshire Community
Foundation
The Highcroft Charitable Trust
Highway One Trust
The Hinduja Foundation

The Henry C. Hoare Charitable
Trust
The Hobson Charity Ltd
The Holbeck Charitable Trust
The Hospital of God at
Greatham
Housing Pathways Trust
The Hunter Foundation
Huntingdon Freemen's Trust
IGO Foundation Ltd
Impetus
Inner London Magistrates
Court Poor Box and Feeder
Charity
The Innocent Foundation
The Ireland Fund of Great
Britain
The J. A. R. Charitable Trust
The J. and J. Benevolent
Foundation
Jay Education Trust
J. E. Joseph Charitable Fund
The Jusaca Charitable Trust
William Kendall's Charity (Wax
Chandlers Company)
The Peter Kershaw Trust
Fraser Kilpatrick Charitable
Trust
The Graham Kirkham
Foundation
Kolyom Trust Ltd
KPE4 Charitable Trust
Kupath Gemach Chaim
Bechesed Viznitz Trust
Community Foundations for
Lancashire and Merseyside
The Allen Lane Foundation
The LankellyChase Foundation
Lawson Beckman Charitable
Trust
The Lawson Trust CIO
The Leeward Trust
The Leri Charitable Trust
Cecil and Hilda Lewis
Charitable Trust
The Linder Foundation
The Frank Litchfield Charitable
Trust
Localtrent Ltd
London Catalyst
London Freemasons Charity
The Magdalen and Lasher
Charity (General Fund)
The Magen Charitable Trust
Marbeh Torah Trust
The Martin Charitable Trust
Mayfair Charities Ltd
Melodor Ltd
The Melow Charitable Trust
Mercaz Torah Vechesed Ltd
The Merchant Venturers
Charity
Merchants House of Glasgow
The Esmé Mitchell Trust
The MK Charitable Trust

The Monmouthshire County
Council Welsh Church Act
Fund
The Morris Charitable Trust
The MSE Charity
Edith Murphy Foundation
Ner Foundation
Newpier Charity Ltd
Norfolk Community Foundation
Norwich Consolidated
Charities
The Nuffield Foundation
Open House Trust Ltd
Otsar Trust
Peacock Charitable Trust
David Pearlman Charitable
Foundation
The Bernard Piggott Charitable
Trust
Pilkington Charities Fund
The Players Foundation
The Portishead Nautical Trust
The Portrack Charitable Trust
Premierquote Ltd
The Pret Foundation
Quartet Community Foundation
Rachel Charitable Trust
Richard Radcliffe Trust
The Eleanor Rathbone
Charitable Trust
Richmond Parish Lands Charity
Riverside Charitable Trust Ltd
Mrs L. D. Rope's Third
Charitable Settlement
The RWS Foundation
Samjo Ltd
The Schreib Trust
The Ina Scott Sutherland
Charitable Foundation
The Sam and Bella Sebba
Charitable Foundation
SF Foundation
SHINE (Support and Help in
Education)
The Bassil Shippam and
Alsford Trust
Shlomo Memorial Fund Ltd
The Leslie Smith Foundation
Songdale Ltd
Sparquote Ltd
The Squires Foundation
The Peter Stebbings Memorial
Charity
Stervon Ltd
The W. O. Street Charitable
Foundation
Sabina Sutherland Charitable
Trust
Sutton Coldfield Charitable
Trust
The Swire Charitable Trust
Tay Charitable Trust
Tegham Ltd
Scott Thomson Charitable
Trust
The Thornton Trust

The Tomoro Foundation
The Trusthouse Charitable
Foundation
The Tuixen Foundation
Tzedakah
The Union of the Sisters of
Mercy of Great Britain
United Utilities Trust Fund
The Valentine Charitable Trust
The Van Mesdag Fund
The Velvet Foundation
Wakefield and Tetley Trust
The Walcot Foundation
The Walker Trust
The Welsh Church Act Fund
West Derby Waste Lands
Charity
Westminster Almshouses
Foundation
The Benjamin Winegarten
Charitable Trust
The James Wood Bequest
Fund
Woodlands Green Ltd
The Worwin UK Foundation
Zephyr Charitable Trust

....

■ **People who are
unemployed**

abrdn Charitable Foundation
abrdn Financial Fairness Trust
Bairdwatson Charitable Trust
The Max Barney Foundation
The James Beattie Charitable
Trust
The Berkeley Foundation
Building and Civil Engineering
Charitable Trust
Colyer-Fergusson Charitable
Trust
Cornwall Community
Foundation
The Enkalon Foundation
Dr Guthrie's Association
The Hadfield Charitable Trust
Housing Pathways Trust
Inner London Magistrates
Court Poor Box and Feeder
Charity
Isle of Wight Foundation
The Kensington and Chelsea
Foundation
Fraser Kilpatrick Charitable
Trust
The KPMG Foundation
The Leathersellers' Foundation
The London Community
Foundation (LCF)
Mathew Trust
The MSE Charity
The Players Foundation
The Progress Foundation
The Henry Smith Charity
Arabella and Julian Smith
Family Trust

The Trusthouse Charitable
Foundation
Ufi VocTech Trust
VINCI UK Foundation

....

■ **People who have
been affected by
crime**

The Avon and Somerset Police
Community Trust
The Michael Barnard
Charitable Trust
The Cayo Foundation
The Greater Manchester High
Sheriff's Police Trust
The Hadley Trust
The Charles Hayward
Foundation
Inner London Magistrates
Court Poor Box and Feeder
Charity
The Kensington and Chelsea
Foundation
The LankellyChase Foundation
The Leathersellers' Foundation
The London Community
Foundation (LCF)
The Players Foundation
The Trusthouse Charitable
Foundation

....

■ **People who have
been affected by
violence, abuse or
neglect**

The Michael Barnard
Charitable Trust
The Brelms Trust CIO
The Bromley Trust
The Brook Trust
The Noel Buxton Trust
The Chetwode Foundation
The City Bridge Trust (Bridge
House Estates)
The Roger and Sarah Bancroft
Clark Charitable Trust
The Clothworkers' Foundation
Cripplegate Foundation
The Ellerdale Trust
The Fairness Foundation
The Finborough Foundation
Forest Hill Charitable Trust
The Forrester Family Trust
The Tara Getty Foundation
J. Paul Getty Jr General
Charitable Trust*
The Gloag Foundation
Global Charities
Sydney and Phyllis Goldberg
Memorial Charitable Trust
The Albert Gubay Charitable
Foundation
The Hadrian Trust

Halifax Foundation for
Northern Ireland
Hampshire and Isle of Wight
Community Foundation
The Charles Hayward
Foundation
Heb Ffin (Without Frontier)
HFC Help for Children UK Ltd
The Hospital of God at
Greatham
Housing Pathways Trust
Inner London Magistrates
Court Poor Box and Feeder
Charity
The Jabbs Foundation
The Emmanuel Kaye
Foundation
The Kelly Family Charitable
Trust
The Lake House Charitable
Foundation
The Allen Lane Foundation
The LankellyChase Foundation
The Leathersellers' Foundation
Lloyds Bank Foundation for
England and Wales
Lloyds Bank Foundation for the
Channel Islands
The London Community
Foundation (LCF)
London Freemasons Charity
Longleigh Foundation
The R. S. Macdonald
Charitable Trust
The Merchant Taylors'
Foundation*
The Mickleham Trust
The MSE Charity
The Norton Foundation
The Pilgrim Trust
The Portishead Nautical Trust
The Portrack Charitable Trust
The Sigrid Rausing Trust
The Robertson Trust
The Roughley Charitable Trust
The Samworth Foundation
The Frieda Scott Charitable
Trust
The Mrs Smith and Mount
Trust
The Henry Smith Charity
South Yorkshire Community
Foundation
The Peter Stebbings Memorial
Charity
The Swire Charitable Trust
The Talbot Trusts
Tay Charitable Trust
the7stars Foundation
The Three Guineas Trust
The Trusthouse Charitable
Foundation
Two Magpies Fund
The Vodafone Foundation
Volant Charitable Trust
Wakefield and Tetley Trust

Wickens Family Foundation
The Woodward Charitable
Trust
The Yapp Charitable Trust

....

■ Sex workers

P. and C. Hickinbotham
Charitable Trust
The Emmanuel Kaye
Foundation
The London Community
Foundation (LCF)
The Samworth Foundation
The Swire Charitable Trust
Volant Charitable Trust

....

■ Victims of disasters and famine

The A. S. Charitable Trust
The Alchemy Foundation
The Allen & Overy Foundation
Ove Arup Partnership
Charitable Trust
The Ashworth Charitable Trust
The Austin Bailey Foundation
The Roy and Pixie Baker
Charitable Trust
The Michael Barnard
Charitable Trust
The Rowan Bentall Charitable
Trust
The Bestway Foundation
Lady Blakenham's Charity
Trust
The Blandford Lake Trust
Christadelphian Samaritan
Fund
The R. and S. Cohen
Foundation
The Coltstaple Trust
The Dulverton Trust
EA Foundation*
The Anna Rosa Forster
Charitable Trust
The Tara Getty Foundation
The Goodman Foundation
The Grace Trust
The Harbour Foundation
The Holbeck Charitable Trust
Lloyd's of London Foundation
Gemma and Chris McGough
Charitable Foundation CIO
The Millichope Foundation
The Monmouthshire County
Council Welsh Church Act
Fund
The Parivar Trust
The Pharsalia Charitable Trust
The Privy Purse Charitable
Trust
Rhodi Charitable Trust
The S. M. B. Trust
Seedfield Trust

The Constance Travis
Charitable Trust
Sumner Wilson Charitable
Trust

Grant-makers by type of organisation

This index contains the following:

List of types of organisation: This lists the headings used in DGMT to categorise types of organisation.

Grant-makers by type of organisation: Funders listed under the types of organisation for which they have expressed a funding preference. Asterisks mark funders which have not featured in DGMT before.

Grant-makers by type of organisation

Community interest companies (CICs) 165

Hospices 167

Hospitals 171

Museums, libraries and galleries 174

Non-registered charities/ voluntary groups 175

Places of worship 179

Schools and colleges 183

Social enterprises 187

Statutory authorities 190

Uniformed groups 190

Universities 191

Community interest companies (CICs)

The 4814 Trust
The A. and J. Charitable Trust
ABF The Soldiers' Charity
abrdn Financial Fairness Trust
Age Scotland
The Allen & Overy Foundation
Anguish's Educational Foundation
The Architectural Heritage Fund
The Art Fund
Arts Council England
Arts Council of Wales (also known as Cyngor Celfyddydau Cymru)
The Ove Arup Foundation
Ove Arup Partnership Charitable Trust
The Ashley Family Foundation
The Tim Bacon Foundation
The Baily Thomas Charitable Fund
The Roy and Pixie Baker Charitable Trust
Bally's Foundation
The Bamford Charitable Foundation
The Barbour Foundation
Barchester Healthcare Foundation
The Baring Foundation
The Barnes Fund
Barnwood Trust
Robert Barr's Charitable Trust
BBC Children in Need
Bedfordshire and Luton Community Foundation
The Rowan Bentall Charitable Trust
The Berkeley Foundation
Berkshire Community Foundation
The Bernicia Foundation
Bideford Bridge Trust
Biffa Award
The Percy Bilton Charity
The Bingham Trust
The Birmingham Diocesan Board of Finance
The Blagrave Trust
Bluespark Foundation
The Boshier-Hinton Foundation
The Harold and Alice Bridges Charity
Buckinghamshire Community Foundation
The Bulldog Trust Ltd
E. F. Bulmer Trust
Bupa Foundation
Cadent Foundation
Community Foundation for Calderdale

Cambridgeshire Community Foundation
Camden Giving
The Frederick and Phyllis Cann Trust
Card Factory Foundation
Carew Pole Charitable Trust
Cheshire Community Foundation Ltd
Church Urban Fund
The City Bridge Trust (Bridge House Estates)
CLA Charitable Trust
The Clothworkers' Foundation
The Coalfields Regeneration Trust
The Cobalt Trust
Colchester Catalyst Charity
John and Freda Coleman Charitable Trust
Sir Jeremiah Colman Gift Trust
Colyer-Fergusson Charitable Trust
Community First
The Catherine Cookson Charitable Trust
Co-op Foundation
The Evan Cornish Foundation
Cornwall Community Foundation
The Corporation of Trinity House of Deptford Strond
Corra Foundation
County Durham Community Foundation
Cripplegate Foundation
Cumbria Community Foundation
Baron Davenport's Charity
The Roger De Haan Charitable Trust
The Delves Charitable Trust
Foundation Derbyshire
Devon Community Foundation
The Gillian Dickinson Trust
Digital Extra Fund
Dorset Community Foundation
Duchy of Lancaster Benevolent Fund
The Duke of Cornwall's Benevolent Fund
Duke of Devonshire's Charitable Trust
The Dulverton Trust
Dumfriesshire East Community Benefit Group SCIO
The Dunhill Medical Trust
Dunlossit and Islay Community Trust
East End Community Foundation
The Ellerdale Trust
The EQ Foundation
The Essex and Southend Sports Trust
Essex Community Foundation

The Evelyn Trust
Esmée Fairbairn Foundation
The Thomas Farr Charity
The Fermanagh Trust
Doris Field Charitable Trust
The Finnis Scott Foundation
Sir John Fisher Foundation
Fishmongers' Company's Charitable Trust
The Earl Fitzwilliam Charitable Trust
The Football Foundation
Forever Manchester
The Freelands Foundation Ltd
The Freshgate Trust Foundation
Friends Provident Charitable Foundation
The Funding Network
The Gibbs Charitable Trusts
The Simon Gibson Charitable Trust
Gloucestershire Community Foundation
The Golden Bottle Trust
Goldman Sachs Gives (UK)
The Golsoncott Foundation
Matthew Good Foundation*
The Grace Trust
The Grand Trust CIO
The Grantham Yorke Trust
GrantScape
The J. G. Graves Charitable Trust
The Greggs Foundation
Groundwork UK
Calouste Gulbenkian Foundation – UK Branch
Dr Guthrie's Association
Hackney Parochial Charities
The Hadfield Charitable Trust
The Hadrian Trust
The Hamilton Davies Trust
Paul Hamlyn Foundation
Hammersmith United Charities
Hampshire and Isle of Wight Community Foundation
Hampton Fund
The Happold Foundation
Harborne Parish Lands Charity
William Harding's Charity
The Harpur Trust
Edward Harvist Trust (The Harvist Estate)
Heart of England Community Foundation
Heart Research UK
The Hearth Foundation
Heathrow Community Trust
Herefordshire Community Foundation
Hertfordshire Community Foundation
The Hilden Charitable Fund
The Lady Hind Trust
The Holywood Trust

The Hosking Charitable Trust*
The Hospital of God at
    Greatham
Housing Pathways Trust
Hyde Charitable Trust
Impact Funding Partners Ltd
The Isla Foundation
The Isle of Anglesey Charitable
    Association (Cymdeithas
    Elusennol Ynys Môn)
Isle of Wight Foundation
JAC Trust*
The Sir Barry Jackson County
    Fund
John James Bristol Foundation
John Lewis and Partners
    Foundation
The Joicey Trust
The Jones 1986 Charitable
    Trust
The Kelly Family Charitable
    Trust
The Kensington and Chelsea
    Foundation
KFC Foundation
The Mary Kinross Charitable
    Trust
Sir James Knott Trust
John Laing Charitable Trust
Community Foundations for
    Lancashire and Merseyside
Lancashire Environmental
    Fund Ltd
The Allen Lane Foundation
The LankellyChase Foundation
The Law Family Charitable
    Foundation
The Law Society Charity
The Legal Education
    Foundation
Leicestershire, Leicester and
    Rutland Community
    Foundation
Lincolnshire Community
    Foundation
The W. M. and B. W. Lloyd
    Trust
The Andrew Lloyd Webber
    Foundation
Lloyds Bank Foundation for the
    Channel Islands
Lloyd's of London Foundation
London Catalyst
The London Community
    Foundation (LCF)
The London Marathon
    Charitable Trust Ltd
The R. S. Macdonald
    Charitable Trust
Making a Difference Locally
    Ltd
Manchester Airport Community
    Trust Fund
R. W. Mann Trust
The Michael Marsh Charitable
    Trust

Mathew Trust
Maudsley Charity
The Merchant Taylors'
    Foundation*
The Merchant Venturers
    Charity
Millennium Stadium Charitable
    Trust (Ymddiriedolaeth
    Elusennol Stadiwm y
    Mileniwm)
The Clare Milne Trust
Milton Keynes Community
    Foundation Ltd
Moondance Foundation
John Moores Foundation
The Steve Morgan Foundation
Moto Foundation
The MSE Charity
The National Express
    Foundation
The National Garden Scheme
The National Hockey
    Foundation
The National Lottery
    Community Fund
Near Neighbours
Nesta
Network for Social Change
    Charitable Trust
Newcomen Collett Foundation
The NFU Mutual Charitable
    Trust
The Nine Incorporated Trades
    of Dundee General Fund
    Charity
The Nineveh Charitable Trust
The Nisbet Trust
Norfolk Community Foundation
The Norman Family Charitable
    Trust
North Berwick Trust
Northamptonshire Community
    Foundation
Community Foundation for
    Northern Ireland
Northwood Charitable Trust
Norwich Consolidated
    Charities
Norwich Town Close Estate
    Charity
Nottinghamshire Community
    Foundation
The Oakdale Trust
One Community Foundation
    Ltd
Oxfordshire Community
    Foundation
The Parivar Trust
The Pears Family Charitable
    Foundation
The Pebbles Trust
People's Health Trust
People's Postcode Trust
The Persimmon Charitable
    Foundation

Personal Assurance Charitable
    Trust
The Pets at Home Foundation
The Pickwell Foundation
Pilkington Charities Fund
The Sir Harry Pilkington Fund
Pink Ribbon Foundation
Polden-Puckham Charitable
    Foundation
Postcode Community Trust
Postcode Local Trust
Postcode Society Trust
The Mary Potter Convent
    Hospital Trust
Poundland Foundation
The Prince's Countryside Fund
The Prudence Trust
The Purey Cust Trust CIO
The PwC Foundation
Quartet Community Foundation
The Radcliffe Trust
The Eleanor Rathbone
    Charitable Trust
The Sir James Reckitt Charity
Rees Jeffreys Road Fund
Richard Reeve's Foundation
Rhodi Charitable Trust
Richmond Parish Lands Charity
Rigby Foundation
The Rix-Thompson-Rothenberg
    Foundation
The Robertson Trust
Rosa Fund
Rosca Trust
Rothesay Foundation*
The Rothley Trust
The Rothschild Foundation
The Rowlands Trust
The Joseph Rowntree
    Charitable Trust
The Joseph Rowntree
    Foundation
The Royal Navy and Royal
    Marines Charity
Russell Trust
Santander UK Foundation Ltd
Foundation Scotland
Francis C. Scott Charitable
    Trust
Seafarers UK (King George's
    Fund for Sailors)
The Sheffield Town Trust
The Sheldon Trust
The R. C. Sherriff Rosebriars
    Trust
SHINE (Support and Help in
    Education)
The Shipwrights Charitable
    Fund
Smallwood Trust
The Henry Smith Charity
Social Investment Business
    Foundation
Somerset Community
    Foundation

South Yorkshire Community Foundation
Peter Sowerby Foundation
The Jessie Spencer Trust
The St Hilda's Trust
Sir Walter St John's Educational Charity
St John's Foundation Est. 1174
The Community Foundation for Staffordshire
Staples Trust
Stratford-upon-Avon Town Trust
The W. O. Street Charitable Foundation
Streetsmart – Action for the Homeless
Suffolk Community Foundation
The Summerfield Charitable Trust
Community Foundation for Surrey
The Sussex Community Foundation
Sutton Coldfield Charitable Trust
The William Syson Foundation
The Talbot Trusts
Tanner Trust
The Tedworth Charitable Trust
Tees Valley Community Foundation
The Theatres Trust Charitable Fund
The Thirty Percy Foundation
The Triangle Trust (1949) Fund
The True Colours Trust
Trust for London
The Trusthouse Charitable Foundation
The Tudor Trust
Two Magpies Fund
Two Ridings Community Foundation
Community Foundation serving Tyne and Wear and Northumberland
Ufi VocTech Trust
The UK Youth Fund: Thriving Minds*
The Ulverscroft Foundation
United St Saviour's Charity
UPP Foundation
The Valentine Charitable Trust
The Vardy Foundation
Variety, the Children's Charity
The Veolia Environmental Trust
The Veterans' Foundation
VINCI UK Foundation
The Virgin Money Foundation
Vision Foundation
Volant Charitable Trust
Sylvia Waddilove Foundation UK
The Scurrah Wainwright Charity
The Bruce Wake Charity

Wakefield and Tetley Trust
The Community Foundation in Wales
Walton-on-Thames Charity
The Waterloo Foundation
Wates Family Enterprise Trust
The Wates Foundation
The Weavers' Company Benevolent Fund
The Welsh Church Act Fund
Wembley National Stadium Trust
Westminster Foundation
The Garfield Weston Foundation
Westway Trust
Alfred Williams Charitable Trust
Wiltshire Community Foundation
Woodsmith Foundation Ltd
The Woodward Charitable Trust
Worcestershire Community Foundation
The Worshipful Company of Information Technologists
Worshipful Company of Needlemakers Charitable Fund
Youth Endowment Fund (YEF)*
Youth Music
Zurich Community Trust (UK) Ltd

Hospices

The 3Ts Charitable Trust
The 64 Trust*
The A. and J. Charitable Trust
ABF The Soldiers' Charity
Age Scotland
Al-Fayed Charitable Foundation
The Almond Trust
Andor Charitable Trust
The Annabel Arbib Foundation
The Ardwick Trust
The Armourers and Brasiers Gauntlet Trust
The Arsenal Foundation
Ove Arup Partnership Charitable Trust
The Asda Foundation
The Ian Askew Charitable Trust
The Astor Foundation
Atkin Charitable Foundation
The Lord Austin Trust
The Baily Thomas Charitable Fund
The Band Trust
Bank of Scotland Foundation
The Barbers' Company General Charities
The Barbour Foundation
Misses Barrie Charitable Trust
Robert Barr's Charitable Trust
The Paul Bassham Charitable Trust
The Batchworth Trust
Bauer Radio's Cash for Kids Charities
The Louis Baylis (Maidenhead Advertiser) Charitable Trust
The Beaverbrook Foundation
The Beaverbrooks Charitable Trust
Bedfordshire Charitable Trust Ltd
The Bellahouston Bequest Fund
The Lord Belstead Charitable Settlement*
Benesco Charity Ltd
The Rowan Bentall Charitable Trust
The Bestway Foundation
Bideford Bridge Trust
The Percy Bilton Charity
Binks Trust
The Birmingham Diocesan Board of Finance
The Sydney Black Charitable Trust
The Isabel Blackman Foundation
Blakemore Foundation
The Sir Victor Blank Charitable Settlement
Blyth Watson Charitable Trust
The Marjory Boddy Charitable Trust
The Boltini Trust

The Booth Charities
Boots Charitable Trust
The Borrows Charitable Trust
The Boshier-Hinton Foundation
The Bothwell Charitable Trust
The Frank Brake Charitable
Trust
The Tony Bramall Charitable
Trust
The Liz and Terry Bramall
Foundation
The Brenley Trust
The Harold and Alice Bridges
Charity
Bright Red Charity
J. and M. Britton Charitable
Trust
Bill Brown 1989 Charitable
Trust
R. S. Brownless Charitable
Trust
The Jack Brunton Charitable
Trust
Buckingham Trust
Buckinghamshire Community
Foundation
E. F. Bulmer Trust
The Burdett Trust for Nursing
Clara E. Burgess Charity
The Burry Charitable Trust
Miss Margaret Butters Reekie
Charitable Trust
Byrne Family Foundation
William A. Cadbury Charitable
Trust
The Cadbury Foundation
The Edward and Dorothy
Cadbury Trust
The George Cadbury Trust
Community Foundation for
Calderdale
Cambridgeshire Community
Foundation
The Frederick and Phyllis Cann
Trust
Carew Pole Charitable Trust
William A. Cargill Charitable
Trust
David William Traill Cargill
Fund
W. A. Cargill Fund
The Carlton Hayes Mental
Health Charity
The Carrington Charitable
Trust
The Leslie Mary Carter
Charitable Trust
The Castanea Trust
The Wilfrid and Constance
Cave Foundation
The Amelia Chadwick Trust
Cheshire Freemasons' Charity
The Childhood Trust
Children with Cancer UK
The Childwick Trust

Chippenham Borough Lands
Charity
The Churchill Foundation
The Roger and Sarah Bancroft
Clark Charitable Trust
Denise Coates Foundation
The Cobtree Charity Trust Ltd
The Vivienne and Samuel
Cohen Charitable Trust
Colchester Catalyst Charity
Sir Jeremiah Colman Gift Trust
Colyer-Fergusson Charitable
Trust
The Company of Actuaries
Charitable Trust Fund
Douglas Compton James
Charitable Trust
The Connolly Foundation (UK)
Ltd
The Catherine Cookson
Charitable Trust
The Helen Jean Cope Charity
The Gershon Coren Charitable
Foundation
Michael Cornish Charitable
Trust
The Sir Tom Cowie Charitable
Trust
The Sir William Coxen Trust
Fund
CRASH
The Crerar Trust
The Croydon Relief-in-Need
Charity
Cullum Family Trust
Cumbria Community
Foundation
Baron Davenport's Charity
The David Family Foundation*
Michael Davies Charitable
Settlement
Margaret Davies Charity
The Roger De Haan Charitable
Trust
The De Laszlo Foundation
Dentons UK and Middle East
LLP Charitable Trust
Foundation Derbyshire
Devon Community Foundation
The Laduma Dhamecha
Charitable Trust
The Dibden Allotments Fund
The Ken Dodd Charitable
Foundation
The D'Oyly Carte Charitable
Trust
Duchy Health Charity Ltd
Duchy of Lancaster Benevolent
Fund
The Duke of Cornwall's
Benevolent Fund
The Mildred Duveen Charitable
Trust
Sir John Eastwood Foundation
Ebenezer Trust

The Gilbert and Eileen Edgar
Foundation
W. G. Edwards Charitable
Foundation
The Wilfred and Elsie Elkes
Charity Fund
Esher House Charitable Trust
Essex Community Foundation
The Evelyn Trust
The Eveson Charitable Trust
The Exilarch's Foundation
G. F. Eyre Charitable Trust
The Fairstead Trust
The Lord Faringdon Charitable
Trust
Samuel William Farmer Trust
The February Foundation
George Fentham Birmingham
Charity
The A. M. Fenton Trust
Doris Field Charitable Trust
The Fifty Fund
Dixie Rose Findlay Charitable
Trust
The Finnis Scott Foundation
Sir John Fisher Foundation
The Earl Fitzwilliam Charitable
Trust
Ford Britain Trust
The Lady Forester Trust
The Foster Wood Foundation
Fowler Smith and Jones Trust
The Elizabeth Frankland Moore
and Star Foundation
Jill Franklin Trust
The Hugh Fraser Foundation
The Joseph Strong Frazer Trust
Charles S. French Charitable
Trust
The Freshgate Trust
Foundation
Friarsgate Trust
The Patrick and Helena Frost
Foundation
The Funding Network
Ganzoni Charitable Trust
Gatwick Airport Community
Trust
General Charity (Coventry)
The Generations Foundation
The Gibbons Family Trust
The Simon Gibson Charitable
Trust
The B. and P. Glasser
Charitable Trust
The F. Glenister Woodger Trust
CIO
The Godinton Charitable Trust
The Golden Bottle Trust
Goldman Sachs Gives (UK)
The Goshen Trust
Gowling WLG (UK) Charitable
Trust
The Grace Trust

Grand Charitable Trust of the Order of Women Freemasons

The Grantham Yorke Trust

The J. G. Graves Charitable Trust

Gordon Gray Trust

The Green Hall Foundation

Greenham Trust Ltd

The Greggs Foundation

The Grimmitt Trust

The Walter Guinness Charitable Trust

Hackney Parochial Charities

The Hadfield Charitable Trust

The Hadley Trust

The Hadrian Trust

Hampshire and Isle of Wight Community Foundation

Hampton Fund

The W. A. Handley Charity Trust

The Lennox Hannay Charitable Trust

The Kathleen Hannay Memorial Charity

The Harding Trust

The Harebell Centenary Fund

The Peter and Teresa Harris Charitable Trust

The Harris Family Charitable Trust

Edward Harvist Trust (The Harvist Estate)

The Hasluck Charitable Trust

The Hawthorne Charitable Trust

The Health Foundation

Heathrow Community Trust

The Charlotte Heber-Percy Charitable Trust

Ernest Hecht Charitable Foundation

Help for Health

Christina Mary Hendrie Trust

Tim Henman Foundation

The G. D. Herbert Charitable Trust

Herefordshire Community Foundation

The Heritage of London Trust Ltd

The Lady Hind Trust

The Hiscox Foundation

The Hobson Charity Ltd

The Jane Hodge Foundation

The Hollands-Warren Fund

Hollyhock Charitable Foundation

The Holywood Trust

Homelands Charitable Trust

Sir Harold Hood's Charitable Trust

The Thomas J. Horne Memorial Trust

Horwich Shotter Charitable Trust

Hospice UK

The Hospital of God at Greatham

The Hospital Saturday Fund

The Albert Hunt Trust

Hyde Park Place Estate Charity

The Iceland Foods Charitable Foundation

The Iliffe Family Charitable Trust

The Inman Charity

The Inverforth Charitable Trust

John James Bristol Foundation

The Susan and Stephen James Charitable Settlement

Lady Eda Jardine Charitable Trust

The Roger and Jean Jefcoate Trust

The Jenour Foundation

John Lewis and Partners Foundation

Lillie Johnson Charitable Trust

The Christopher and Kirsty Johnston Charitable Trust

The Jones 1986 Charitable Trust

Anton Jurgens Charitable Trust

The Jusaca Charitable Trust

Kahal Chassidim Bobov

The Michael and Ilse Katz Foundation

The Kensington and Chelsea Foundation

The Kentown Wizard Foundation

The Ursula Keyes Trust

The Kildare Trust

Fraser Kilpatrick Charitable Trust

The King Henry VIII Endowed Trust – Warwick

The Kingsbury Charity

The Graham Kirkham Foundation

The Ernest Kleinwort Charitable Trust

Sir James Knott Trust

The Kobler Trust

Kusuma Trust UK

Ladbrokes Coral Trust

Christopher Laing Foundation

The Beatrice Laing Trust

Langdale Trust

The R. J. Larg Family Trust

Laslett's (Hinton) Charity

Mrs F. B. Laurence Charitable Trust

The Edgar E. Lawley Foundation

The Herd Lawson and Muriel Lawson Charitable Trust

The Lawson Trust CIO

Leicestershire and Rutland Masonic Charity Association

Leicestershire, Leicester and Rutland Community Foundation

Leng Charitable Trust

The Ralph Levy Charitable Company Ltd

Limoges Charitable Trust

Lincolnshire Community Foundation

The Linder Foundation

The Frank Litchfield Charitable Trust

The Michael and Betty Little Trust*

The Charles Littlewood Hill Trust

The Second Joseph Aaron Littman Foundation

The Elaine and Angus Lloyd Charitable Trust

The W. M. and B. W. Lloyd Trust

The Locker Foundation

The Lockwood Charitable Foundation

London Catalyst

The C. L. Loyd Charitable Trust

Robert Luff Foundation Ltd

Lord and Lady Lurgan Trust

The Lyndal Tree Foundation

M. and C. Trust

Making a Difference Locally Ltd

The Manchester Guardian Society Charitable Trust

The W. M. Mann Foundation

R. W. Mann Trust

The Michael Marsh Charitable Trust

Charlotte Marshall Charitable Trust

The Martin Charitable Trust

Sir George Martin Trust

Masonic Charitable Foundation

Nancie Massey Charitable Trust

The Master Charitable Trust

Matchroom Sport Charitable Foundation

The Mather Family Charitable Trust

Maudsley Charity

The Violet Mauray Charitable Trust

Mazars Charitable Trust

MBNA General Foundation

The Robert McAlpine Foundation

D. D. McPhail Charitable Settlement

The Medicash Foundation

The Medlock Charitable Trust

Merriman Charitable
   Foundation*
The Gerald Micklem Charitable
   Trust
The Millennium Oak Trust
The Millichope Foundation
The Millward Charitable Trust
The Clare Milne Trust
Milton Keynes Community
   Foundation Ltd
The Laurence Misener
   Charitable Trust
The Brian Mitchell Charitable
   Settlement
Mobbs Memorial Trust Ltd
Moondance Foundation
The George A. Moore
   Foundation
G. M. Morrison Charitable
   Trust
The Ken and Lynne Morrison
   Charitable Trust
The Alexander Mosley
   Charitable Trust
Moto Foundation
The Edwina Mountbatten and
   Leonora Children's
   Foundation
The Mulberry Trust
The National Garden Scheme
The National Hockey
   Foundation
The National Lottery
   Community Fund
The NFU Mutual Charitable
   Trust
Norfolk Community Foundation
Educational Foundation of
   Alderman John Norman
The Norman Family Charitable
   Trust
Normanby Charitable Trust
North Berwick Trust
Northern Pharmacies Ltd Trust
   Fund
Norwich Consolidated
   Charities
Norwich Town Close Estate
   Charity
The Notgrove Trust
Nottinghamshire Community
   Foundation
Odin Charitable Trust
The Ofenheim Charitable Trust
Henry Oldfield Trust
The Orrin Charitable Trust
The Sir Peter O'Sullevan
   Charitable Trust
The Paget Charitable Trust
The Paphitis Charitable Trust
The Paragon Trust
Miss M. E. S. Paterson's
   Charitable Trust
The Patrick Trust
The Jack Patston Charitable
   Trust

The J. G. W. Patterson
   Foundation
Payne-Gallwey 1989 Charitable
   Trust
Peacock Charitable Trust
Susanna Peake Charitable
   Trust
John Pearce Foundation
The Pears Family Charitable
   Foundation
The Pebbles Trust
The Dowager Countess
   Eleanor Peel Trust
The Persimmon Charitable
   Foundation
Personal Assurance Charitable
   Trust
Elise Pilkington Charitable
   Trust
The Sir Harry Pilkington Fund
Miss A. M. Pilkington's
   Charitable Trust
Pink Ribbon Foundation
The George and Esme Pollitzer
   Charitable Settlement
The Mary Potter Convent
   Hospital Trust
Sir John Priestman Charity
   Trust
The Prince of Wales's
   Charitable Foundation
Prison Service Charity Fund
Provincial Grand Charity of the
   Province of Derbyshire
The Purey Cust Trust CIO
Mr and Mrs J. A. Pye's
   Charitable Settlement
Quartet Community Foundation
Richard Radcliffe Trust
The Rainford Trust
The Rambourg Foundation
The Joseph and Lena Randall
   Charitable Trust
The Ratcliff Foundation
The Rathbones Group
   Foundation
The Ravensdale Trust
The Sir James Reckitt Charity
C. A. Redfern Charitable
   Foundation
The Revere Charitable Trust
Riada Trust
The Clive Richards Foundation
Richmond Parish Lands Charity
Rigby Foundation
The Roan Charitable Trust
Rockcliffe Charitable Trust
The Gerald and Gail Ronson
   Family Foundation
Rosca Trust
The Rose Foundation
The Ross Foundation
The Rothermere Foundation
The Row Fogo Charitable Trust
The Rowlands Trust

The Rugby Group Benevolent
   Fund Ltd
S. and R. Charitable Trust
The Saintbury Trust
Salisbury Pool Charity
Samjo Ltd
The Basil Samuel Charitable
   Trust
Sandra Charitable Trust
Schroder Charity Trust
Foundation Scotland
The John Scott Trust Fund
Scouloudi Foundation
The Sam and Bella Sebba
   Charitable Foundation
The Sheffield Town Trust
The Sylvia and Colin Shepherd
   Charitable Trust
The Sherling Charitable Trust
The Bassil Shippam and
   Alsford Trust
The Shoe Zone Trust
The Charles Skey Charitable
   Trust
Skipton Building Society
   Charitable Foundation
The John Slater Foundation
The Leslie Smith Foundation
Philip Smith's Charitable Trust
The R. C. Snelling Charitable
   Trust
Societe Generale UK
   Foundation
Somerset Community
   Foundation
The Stephen R. and Philippa
   H. Southall Charitable Trust
Peter Sowerby Foundation
The Spear Charitable Trust
The Jessie Spencer Trust
Spielman Charitable Trust
Spurrell Charitable Trust
The Geoff and Fiona Squire
   Foundation
The Squires Foundation
The Vichai Srivaddhanaprabha
   Foundation
St James's Place Charitable
   Foundation
St John's Foundation Est.
   1174
St Monica Trust
The Community Foundation for
   Staffordshire
The Peter Stebbings Memorial
   Charity
The Steel Charitable Trust
The Hugh Stenhouse
   Foundation
The Stevenage Community
   Trust
The Stevenson Family's
   Charitable Trust
The Stoneygate Trust
The Samuel Storey Family
   Charitable Trust

Peter Stormonth Darling
Charitable Trust
Strand Parishes Trust
Stratford-upon-Avon Town Trust
The Summerfield Charitable
Trust
The Bernard Sunley
Foundation
Community Foundation for
Surrey
The Sussex Community
Foundation
The Swann-Morton Foundation
The John Swire (1989)
Charitable Trust
The Adrian Swire Charitable
Trust
The Charles and Elsie Sykes
Trust
The Hugh Symons Charitable
Trust
The Talbot Village Trust
Tanner Trust
C. B. and H. H. T. Taylor 1984
Trust
The Thompson Family
Charitable Trust
Sir Jules Thorn Charitable Trust
The Tompkins Foundation
The Toy Trust
Toyota Manufacturing UK
Charitable Trust
The Trades House of Glasgow
Annie Tranmer Charitable Trust
The True Colours Trust
The Truemark Trust
The James Tudor Foundation
The Tudwick Foundation
The Tufton Charitable Trust
The Tuixen Foundation
The Roger and Douglas Turner
Charitable Trust
Two Ridings Community
Foundation
Ulster Garden Villages Ltd
The Ulverscroft Foundation
The Underwood Trust
The Union of the Sisters of
Mercy of Great Britain
The Valentine Charitable Trust
The Valiant Charitable Trust
The Albert Van Den Bergh
Charitable Trust
Variety, the Children's Charity
Sylvia Waddilove Foundation
UK
The Bruce Wake Charity
The Walker Trust
Wallace and Gromit's
Children's Foundation
The Warwickshire Masonic
Charitable Association Ltd
The Watches of Switzerland
Group Foundation
Mrs Waterhouse Charitable
Trust

Wates Family Enterprise Trust
The Geoffrey Watling Charity
The Wellcome Trust
West Herts Charity Trust Ltd
The Westfield Health
Charitable Trust
The Garfield Weston
Foundation
Westway Trust
The Whinfell Charitable Fund
WHSmith Trust
The Felicity Wilde Charitable
Trust
The Will Charitable Trust
The Williams Family
Foundation
Dame Violet Wills Will Trust
Brian Wilson Charitable Trust
Sumner Wilson Charitable
Trust
J. and J. R. Wilson Trust
Wiltshire Community
Foundation
The Francis Winham
Foundation
The Charles Wolfson
Charitable Trust
The Wolfson Family Charitable
Trust
The Wolfson Foundation
The Woodstock Family
Charitable Foundation
Worcestershire Community
Foundation
Worshipful Company of Gold
and Silver Wyre Drawers
Second Charitable Trust
Fund
Worshipful Company of
Needlemakers Charitable
Fund
Worth Waynflete Foundation
The Wyseliot Rose Charitable
Trust
Yorkshire Building Society
Charitable Foundation
Yorkshire Cancer Research
The Elizabeth and Prince
Zaiger Trust
Zurich Community Trust (UK)
Ltd

Hospitals

The 29th May 1961 Charitable
Trust
The A. and J. Charitable Trust
The Abbeyfield Research
Foundation
ABF The Soldiers' Charity
Action Medical Research
Al-Fayed Charitable Foundation
Alzheimer's Research UK
Alzheimer's Society
The Annabel Arbib Foundation
The Ardwick Trust
The John Armitage Charitable
Trust
The Armourers and Brasiers
Gauntlet Trust
Ove Arup Partnership
Charitable Trust
Asthma and Lung UK
The Astor Foundation
Atkin Charitable Foundation
The Lord Austin Trust
B&Q Foundation
Banbury Charities
The Barbers' Company General
Charities
Lord Barnby's Foundation
Robert Barr's Charitable Trust
The Batchworth Trust
Bauer Radio's Cash for Kids
Charities
The James Beattie Charitable
Trust
The Beaverbrook Foundation
The Beaverbrooks Charitable
Trust
Benesco Charity Ltd
The Rowan Bentall Charitable
Trust
The Bestway Foundation
The Percy Bilton Charity
The Bingham Trust
Binks Trust
The Birmingham Diocesan
Board of Finance
The Sydney Black Charitable
Trust
The Isabel Blackman
Foundation
Bloodwise
The Bluston Charitable
Settlement
The Marjory Boddy Charitable
Trust
The Boltini Trust
The Boshier-Hinton Foundation
The Harry Bottom Charitable
Trust
The Tony Bramall Charitable
Trust
Breast Cancer Now
Bright Red Charity
British Eye Research
Foundation (Fight for Sight)
British Heart Foundation (BHF)

T. B. H. Brunner's Charitable
Settlement
The Jack Brunton Charitable
Trust
The Burden Trust
The Burry Charitable Trust
Miss Margaret Butters Reekie
Charitable Trust
Cambridgeshire Community
Foundation
The Frederick and Phyllis Cann
Trust
Carew Pole Charitable Trust
David William Traill Cargill
Fund
W. A. Cargill Fund
The Carlton Hayes Mental
Health Charity
The Carrington Charitable
Trust
The Wilfrid and Constance
Cave Foundation
Cheshire Freemasons' Charity
Children with Cancer UK
The Clore Duffield Foundation
The Vivienne and Samuel
Cohen Charitable Trust
Colchester Catalyst Charity
Colefax Charitable Trust
Sir Jeremiah Colman Gift Trust
The Costa Family Charitable
Trust
Dudley and Geoffrey Cox
Charitable Trust
The Sir William Coxen Trust
Fund
The Croydon Relief-in-Need
Charity
The Cunningham Trust
The Roger De Haan Charitable
Trust
The Laduma Dhamecha
Charitable Trust
The Alan and Sheila Diamond
Charitable Trust
The Dibden Allotments Fund
Dinwoodie Charitable Company
The Ken Dodd Charitable
Foundation
The Dorfman Foundation
Duchy Health Charity Ltd
Dumbreck Charity
The Dunhill Medical Trust
The Charles Dunstone
Charitable Trust
The Mildred Duveen Charitable
Trust
Sir John Eastwood Foundation
Ebenezer Trust
The Gilbert and Eileen Edgar
Foundation
The Maud Elkington Charitable
Trust
The Ellerdale Trust
Epilepsy Research UK
Esher House Charitable Trust

Joseph Ettedgui Charitable
Foundation
The Evelyn Trust
The Eventhall Family
Charitable Trust
The Everard Foundation
The Eveson Charitable Trust
The Exilarch's Foundation
The Fairstead Trust
The Lord Faringdon Charitable
Trust
Samuel William Farmer Trust
The Thomas Farr Charity
George Fentham Birmingham
Charity
The Fifty Fund
The Follett Trust
The Lady Forester Trust
The Fort Foundation
The Foster Wood Foundation
Fowler Smith and Jones Trust
The Elizabeth Frankland Moore
and Star Foundation
Jill Franklin Trust
The Hugh Fraser Foundation
The Joseph Strong Frazer Trust
The Freshgate Trust
Foundation
The Patrick and Helena Frost
Foundation
The Funding Network
The Gale Family Charity Trust
GambleAware
The Robert Gavron Charitable
Trust
General Charity (Coventry)
The Generations Foundation
The Gibbs Charitable Trusts
The Simon Gibson Charitable
Trust
The B. and P. Glasser
Charitable Trust
The F. Glenister Woodger Trust
CIO
Sydney and Phyllis Goldberg
Memorial Charitable Trust
Goldman Sachs Gives (UK)
Grace Charitable Trust
The Grace Trust
Grand Charitable Trust of the
Order of Women
Freemasons
The Green Hall Foundation
The Greggs Foundation
The Grimmitt Trust
The Walter Guinness
Charitable Trust
Hackney Parochial Charities
The Hadfield Charitable Trust
Hampton Fund
The Peter and Teresa Harris
Charitable Trust
The Harris Family Charitable
Trust
The Harry and Mary
Foundation

The Dorothy Hay-Bolton
Charitable Trust
The Health Foundation
Heart Research UK
Help for Health
The Heritage of London Trust
Ltd
The Hintze Family Charity
Foundation
The Hiscox Foundation
The Hobson Charity Ltd
Homelands Charitable Trust
Sir Harold Hood's Charitable
Trust
The Hospital Saturday Fund
The Sir Joseph Hotung
Charitable Settlement
The Albert Hunt Trust
The Iliffe Family Charitable
Trust
The Inverforth Charitable Trust
The Susan and Stephen
James Charitable
Settlement
Lillie Johnson Charitable Trust
The Joron Charitable Trust
Kahal Chassidim Bobov
The Kennedy Trust for
Rheumatology Research
The Kensington and Chelsea
Foundation
The Kentown Wizard
Foundation
The Ursula Keyes Trust
Kidney Research UK
Fraser Kilpatrick Charitable
Trust
The King Henry VIII Endowed
Trust – Warwick
Kusuma Trust UK
Ladbrokes Coral Trust
The William Leech Charity
The Leverhulme Trust
Lord Leverhulme's Charitable
Trust
David and Ruth Lewis Family
Charitable Trust
The Linder Foundation
The Michael and Betty Little
Trust*
The Second Joseph Aaron
Littman Charitable Trust
The Elaine and Angus Lloyd
Charitable Trust
The W. M. and B. W. Lloyd
Trust
London Catalyst
Robert Luff Foundation Ltd
Lord and Lady Lurgan Trust
M. and C. Trust
The Manackerman Charitable
Trust
The W. M. Mann Foundation
R. W. Mann Trust
The Michael Marsh Charitable
Trust

Matchroom Sport Charitable Foundation

Maudsley Charity

The Robert McAlpine Foundation

T. and J. Meyer Family Foundation Ltd

The Laurence Misener Charitable Trust

The Modiano Charitable Trust

Moondance Foundation

The George A. Moore Foundation

G. M. Morrison Charitable Trust

Motor Neurone Disease Association

J. P. Moulton Charitable Foundation

The Edwina Mountbatten and Leonora Children's Foundation

The National Garden Scheme

The National Hockey Foundation

The Frances and Augustus Newman Foundation

The Norman Family Charitable Trust

Normanby Charitable Trust

The Orrin Charitable Trust

Orthopaedic Research UK

The Paragon Trust

Parkinson's UK

The J. G. W. Patterson Foundation

Payne-Gallwey 1989 Charitable Trust

The Pears Family Charitable Foundation

Miss A. M. Pilkington's Charitable Trust

Pink Ribbon Foundation

Thomas Pocklington Trust

The George and Esme Pollitzer Charitable Settlement

The Mary Potter Convent Hospital Trust

Sir John Priestman Charity Trust

Prison Service Charity Fund

Prostate Cancer UK

Mr and Mrs J. A. Pye's Charitable Settlement

Queen Mary's Roehampton Trust

The Joseph and Lena Randall Charitable Trust

The Ratcliff Foundation

The Julia and Hans Rausing Trust*

The Sir James Reckitt Charity

Riada Trust

The Clive Richards Foundation

Rigby Foundation

RNID (The Royal National Institute for Deaf People)

The Dezna Robins Jones Charitable Foundation

Rockcliffe Charitable Trust

The Gerald and Gail Ronson Family Foundation

Rosca Trust

The Cecil Rosen Foundation

Rosetrees

The Rothermere Foundation

The Row Fogo Charitable Trust

Samjo Ltd

The Basil Samuel Charitable Trust

Sandra Charitable Trust

Sir Samuel Scott of Yews Trust

The Jean Shanks Foundation

The Charles Skey Charitable Trust

Somerset Community Foundation

Peter Sowerby Foundation

The Jessie Spencer Trust

The Sperring Charity

The Geoff and Fiona Squire Foundation

The Squires Foundation

The Vichai Srivaddhanaprabha Foundation

St Monica Trust

The Peter Stebbings Memorial Charity

The Steel Charitable Trust

The Stoller Charitable Trust

The Stoneygate Trust

Peter Stormonth Darling Charitable Trust

Stratford-upon-Avon Town Trust

Sutton Coldfield Charitable Trust

The Swann-Morton Foundation

The Adrian Swire Charitable Trust

The Charles and Elsie Sykes Trust

The Talbot Trusts

Tenovus Scotland

The Thompson Family Charitable Trust

The Sue Thomson Foundation

Sir Jules Thorn Charitable Trust

The Tompkins Foundation

Annie Tranmer Charitable Trust

The Tuixen Foundation

Ulster Garden Villages Ltd

The Ulverscroft Foundation

The Underwood Trust

The Valentine Charitable Trust

The Valiant Charitable Trust

Variety, the Children's Charity

The Veterans' Foundation

Sylvia Waddilove Foundation UK

Wallace and Gromit's Children's Foundation

The Warwickshire Masonic Charitable Association Ltd

Mrs Waterhouse Charitable Trust

The Wellcome Trust

The Westfield Health Charitable Trust

The Galen and Hilary Weston Foundation

The Garfield Weston Foundation

WHSmith Trust

Dame Violet Wills Will Trust

The Francis Winham Foundation

The Charles Wolfson Charitable Trust

The Wolfson Family Charitable Trust

The Lord Leonard and Lady Estelle Wolfson Foundation

The Worshipful Company of Glovers of London Charitable Trust

Worshipful Company of Needlemakers Charitable Fund

The Wyndham Charitable Trust

The Wyseliot Rose Charitable Trust

Yorkshire Cancer Research

The Elizabeth and Prince Zaiger Trust

Zurich Community Trust (UK) Ltd

Museums, libraries and galleries

The 29th May 1961 Charitable Trust
The 4814 Trust
The Bryan Adams Foundation
The Alborada Trust
The Aldama Foundation
Viscount Amory's Charitable Trust
The Ampersand Foundation
The John Armitage Charitable Trust
The Art Fund
Arts Council of Wales (also known as Cyngor Celfyddydau Cymru)
ArtSocial Foundation
The Ashley Family Foundation
Atkin Charitable Foundation
The Austin Bailey Foundation
The Kamini and Vindi Banga Family Trust
The Baring Foundation
Barnsbury Charitable Trust
Robert Barr's Charitable Trust
The Louis Baylis (Maidenhead Advertiser) Charitable Trust
The Beaverbrook Foundation
The Beaverbrooks Charitable Trust
Bennett Lowell Ltd
Bideford Bridge Trust
The Michael Bishop Foundation
The Sir Victor Blank Charitable Settlement
The Boltini Trust
The William Brake Charitable Trust
The Liz and Terry Bramall Foundation
J. and M. Britton Charitable Trust
T. B. H. Brunner's Charitable Settlement
The Arnold Burton 1998 Charitable Trust
The G. W. Cadbury Charitable Trust
Community Foundation for Calderdale
Catkin Pussywillow Charitable Trust
The Wilfrid and Constance Cave Foundation
Elizabeth Cayzer Charitable Trust
Chapman Charitable Trust
The Clore Duffield Foundation
Denise Coates Foundation
The John S. Cohen Foundation
Colwinston Charitable Trust
The Helen Jean Cope Charity

The County Council of Dyfed Welsh Church Fund
The Sir Tom Cowie Charitable Trust
The Daiwa Anglo-Japanese Foundation
Margaret Davies Charity
The Roger De Haan Charitable Trust
The Delius Trust
The Alan and Sheila Diamond Charitable Trust
The Gillian Dickinson Trust
The Dorfman Foundation
The D'Oyly Carte Charitable Trust
Duchy of Lancaster Benevolent Fund
John Ellerman Foundation
The Elmley Foundation
Esmée Fairbairn Foundation
Family Philanthropy Ltd
The Lord Faringdon Charitable Trust
The Thomas Farr Charity
The Finnis Scott Foundation
Sir John Fisher Foundation
Fishmongers' Company's Charitable Trust
Marc Fitch Fund
Oliver Ford Foundation
Ian M. Foulerton Charitable Trust
Fowler Smith and Jones Trust
The Foyle Foundation
The Freelands Foundation Ltd
Friends of the National Libraries
J. Paul Getty Jr General Charitable Trust*
Nicholas and Judith Goodison's Charitable Settlement
The Grantham Yorke Trust
The J. G. Graves Charitable Trust
The Helen Hamlyn Trust
Hampshire and Isle of Wight Community Foundation
The Lennox Hannay Charitable Trust
The Charles Hayward Foundation
The Headley Trust
The Heathcoat Trust
The Charlotte Heber-Percy Charitable Trust
Heritage Lottery Fund
The Heritage of London Trust Ltd
The Derek Hill Foundation
The Lady Hind Trust
The Hinduja Foundation
The Hintze Family Charity Foundation
Historic Environment Scotland

The Hobson Charity Ltd
The Harold Hyam Wingate Foundation
The Idlewild Trust
The Ireland Fund of Great Britain
Sir James Knott Trust
Kusuma Trust UK
The Kirby Laing Foundation
Langdale Trust
Mrs M. A. Lascelles Charitable Trust
Lord Leverhulme's Charitable Trust
Cecil and Hilda Lewis Charitable Trust
The Linbury Trust
The Linder Foundation
Jack Livingstone Charitable Trust
The W. M. and B. W. Lloyd Trust
The Andrew Lloyd Webber Foundation
The Lockwood Charitable Foundation
The Ian Mactaggart Trust
The W. M. Mann Foundation
The Michael Marks Charitable Trust
The Marks Family Charitable Trust
Sir George Martin Trust
Nancie Massey Charitable Trust
Mathew Trust
The Mickel Fund
The Mikheev Charitable Trust
The Laurence Misener Charitable Trust
The Esmé Mitchell Trust
The Monmouthshire County Council Welsh Church Act Fund
The Henry Moore Foundation
G. M. Morrison Charitable Trust
The Alexander Mosley Charitable Trust
The John R. Murray Charitable Trust
The National Manuscripts Conservation Trust
Near Neighbours
Normanby Charitable Trust
Norwich Town Close Estate Charity
The Ofenheim Charitable Trust
Old Possum's Practical Trust
Henry Oldfield Trust
The Orrin Charitable Trust
The Owen Family Trust
Oxfordshire Community Foundation
Parabola Foundation
The Patrick Trust

David Pearlman Charitable
 Foundation
The Pears Family Charitable
 Foundation
The Phillips and Rubens
 Charitable Trust
The Pilgrim Trust
Miss A. M. Pilkington's
 Charitable Trust
The Polonsky Foundation
The Julia and Hans Rausing
 Trust*
Richmond Parish Lands Charity
The River Farm Foundation
The Rix-Thompson-Rothenberg
 Foundation
Rockcliffe Charitable Trust
The Gerald and Gail Ronson
 Family Foundation
The Rose Foundation
The Roseline Foundation*
The Rothschild Foundation
Rothschild Foundation
 (Hanadiv) Europe
The Rowlands Trust
Royal Artillery Charitable Fund
The Ruddock Foundation for
 the Arts
The Jeremy and John Sacher
 Charitable Trust
The Michael and Nicola Sacher
 Charitable Trust
The Sackler Trust
The Alan and Babette
 Sainsbury Charitable Fund
Saint Sarkis Charity Trust
Salisbury Pool Charity
Schroder Charity Trust
The Sharp Foundation
The Sheffield Town Trust
The Charles Skey Charitable
 Trust
Kathleen Beryl Sleigh
 Charitable Trust
Stanley Smith UK Horticultural
 Trust
Philip Smith's Charitable Trust
The Stephen R. and Philippa
 H. Southall Charitable Trust
Stanley Foundation Ltd
Staples Trust
The Steel Charitable Trust
The Stevenson Family's
 Charitable Trust
The Samuel Storey Family
 Charitable Trust
Peter Stormonth Darling
 Charitable Trust
Suffolk Community Foundation
The Bernard Sunley
 Foundation
Tay Charitable Trust
C. B. and H. H. T. Taylor 1984
 Trust
The Roger and Douglas Turner
 Charitable Trust

Two Ridings Community
 Foundation
The Ulverscroft Foundation
The Valentine Charitable Trust
The Welsh Church Act Fund
The Garfield Weston
 Foundation
The Wolfson Family Charitable
 Trust
The Wolfson Foundation
The Lord Leonard and Lady
 Estelle Wolfson Foundation
Worcestershire Community
 Foundation

Non-registered charities/ voluntary groups

The 64 Trust*
The A. and J. Charitable Trust
ABF The Soldiers' Charity
Adam Family Foundation
The Aimwell Charitable Trust
Sylvia Aitken's Charitable Trust
AJ Bell Trust
Al Madad Foundation*
Alan Boswell Group Charitable
 Trust
Alpkit Foundation
The Ampersand Foundation
The Arsenal Foundation
Arts Council England
Ove Arup Partnership
 Charitable Trust
The Asda Foundation
The Asfari Foundation
The Ashendene Trust
The Ashley Family Foundation
The Associated Board of the
 Royal Schools of Music
 (ABRSM)
The Aurelius Charitable Trust
The Avon and Somerset Police
 Community Trust
The Austin Bailey Foundation
The Roy and Pixie Baker
 Charitable Trust
The Ballinger Charitable Trust
Bally's Foundation
The Bamford Charitable
 Foundation
Barcapel Foundation Ltd
Barchester Healthcare
 Foundation
Philip Barker Charity
The Barnes Fund
The Max Barney Foundation
Barnwood Trust
Misses Barrie Charitable Trust
Robert Barr's Charitable Trust
The Battersea Power Station
 Foundation
Bauer Radio's Cash for Kids
 Charities
The Gordon and Ena Baxter
 Foundation*
BBC Children in Need
The James Beattie Charitable
 Trust
Beccles Townlands Charity
Bedfordshire and Luton
 Community Foundation
The Rowan Bentall Charitable
 Trust
Berkshire Community
 Foundation
The Bernicia Foundation
The Bestway Foundation
Bideford Bridge Trust
Biffa Award

The Percy Bilton Charity
Binks Trust
Birkdale Trust for Hearing Impaired Ltd*
The Birmingham Diocesan Board of Finance
The Blakebank Trust
Blakemore Foundation
Bluespark Foundation
BOOST Charitable Trust
Boots Charitable Trust
The Harold and Alice Bridges Charity
British Gas Energy Trust
British Motor Sports Training Trust
The Mary Brown Memorial Trust
The Jack Brunton Charitable Trust
Buckingham Trust
Buckinghamshire Community Foundation
Building and Civil Engineering Charitable Trust
The Bulldog Trust Ltd
E. F. Bulmer Trust
Burnie's Foundation
Consolidated Charity of Burton upon Trent
Byrne Family Foundation
The Cadbury Foundation
Cadent Foundation
Community Foundation for Calderdale
Cambridgeshire Community Foundation
Camden Giving
The Frederick and Phyllis Cann Trust
Card Factory Foundation
William A. Cargill Charitable Trust
The Carnegie Dunfermline Trust
The Carpenters Company Charitable Trust
Chalfords Ltd
The Chartley Foundation
Cheshire Community Foundation Ltd
The Childhood Trust
Chippenham Borough Lands Charity
CHK Foundation
Cloudesley
The Coalfields Regeneration Trust
John and Freda Coleman Charitable Trust
Comic Relief
The Comino Foundation
Community First
The Ernest Cook Trust
The Catherine Cookson Charitable Trust

Mabel Cooper Charity
Michael Cornish Charitable Trust
The Evan Cornish Foundation
Cornwall Community Foundation
County Durham Community Foundation
Coventry Building Society Charitable Foundation
Creative Scotland
Cripplegate Foundation
Crisis UK
The Cross Trust
CSIS Charity Fund
Cullum Family Trust
Cumbria Community Foundation
The D. G. Charitable Settlement
Baron Davenport's Charity
The Roger De Haan Charitable Trust
William Delafield Charitable Trust
The Delius Trust
Foundation Derbyshire
The J. N. Derbyshire Trust
Devon Community Foundation
The Dibden Allotments Fund
Digital Extra Fund
Dorset Community Foundation
Duchy of Lancaster Benevolent Fund
The Duke of Cornwall's Benevolent Fund
Dumfriesshire East Community Benefit Group SCIO
Dunlossit and Islay Community Trust
The Earley Charity
East End Community Foundation
Eastern Counties Educational Trust Ltd
Dr Edwards and Bishop King's Fulham Charity
The Eighty Eight Foundation
The Elmley Foundation
The Vernon N. Ely Charitable Trust
England and Wales Cricket Trust
The Enkalon Foundation
Essex Community Foundation
The Essex Youth Trust
Euro Quality Foundation
The Evelyn Trust
The Everard Foundation
Esmée Fairbairn Foundation
George Fentham Birmingham Charity
Doris Field Charitable Trust
The Finnis Scott Foundation
The Football Association National Sports Centre

The Football Foundation
Ford Britain Trust
Forever Manchester
The Forman Hardy Charitable Trust
The Fort Foundation
Fowler Smith and Jones Trust
Jill Franklin Trust
The Joseph Strong Frazer Trust
The Freshgate Trust Foundation
Friends Provident Charitable Foundation
The Funding Network
GambleAware
Gatwick Airport Community Trust
The Generations Foundation
The B. and P. Glasser Charitable Trust
The F. Glenister Woodger Trust CIO
Gloucestershire Community Foundation
The Grace Trust
Graff Foundation
The Granada Foundation
The Grange Farm Centre Trust
William Grant Foundation*
Greenham Trust Ltd
The Greggs Foundation
The Grimmitt Trust
Groundwork UK
Calouste Gulbenkian Foundation – UK Branch
The Hamilton Davies Trust
Hammersmith United Charities
Hampshire and Isle of Wight Community Foundation
The Hampstead Wells and Campden Trust
The Happold Foundation
The Harding Trust
William Harding's Charity
The Harpur Trust
Gay and Peter Hartley's Hillards Charitable Trust
Edward Harvist Trust (The Harvist Estate)
The Health Foundation
Heart of England Community Foundation
Heart Research UK
The Hearth Foundation
The Heathcoat Trust
Heathrow Community Trust
The Hemby Charitable Trust
Henley Educational Trust
Henley Royal Regatta Charitable Trust
Herefordshire Community Foundation
The Heritage of London Trust Ltd
Hertfordshire Community Foundation

The Hilden Charitable Fund
The Lady Hind Trust
The Hiscox Foundation
Historic Environment Scotland
Hockerill Educational
Foundation
Hollyhock Charitable
Foundation
The Holywood Trust
The Hospital of God at
Greatham
The Sir Joseph Hotung
Charitable Settlement
House of Industry Estate
Housing Pathways Trust
The Hull and East Riding
Charitable Trust
Huntingdon Freemen's Trust
Hyde Charitable Trust
Ibrahim Foundation Ltd
Imagine Foundation
Impact Funding Partners Ltd
The Institute for Policy
Research
Integrated Education Fund
The Ireland Fund of Great
Britain
The Isla Foundation
The Isle of Anglesey Charitable
Association (Cymdeithas
Elusennol Ynys Môn)
Isle of Wight Foundation
JAC Trust*
The Sir Barry Jackson County
Fund
John James Bristol Foundation
Lady Eda Jardine Charitable
Trust
The Elton John AIDS
Foundation
John Lewis and Partners
Foundation
The Christopher and Kirsty
Johnston Charitable Trust
The Joicey Trust
Kahal Chassidim Bobov
The Karlsson Játiva Charitable
Foundation
The Kavli Trust
The Kensington and Chelsea
Foundation
Kent Community Foundation
KFC Foundation
Kidney Research UK
Fraser Kilpatrick Charitable
Trust
The King Henry VIII Endowed
Trust – Warwick
The Graham Kirkham
Foundation
Robert Kitchin (Saddlers' Co.)
Sir James Knott Trust
The Kreitman Foundation
John Laing Charitable Trust
The Martin Laing Foundation

Community Foundations for
Lancashire and Merseyside
Lancashire Environmental
Fund Ltd
The Allen Lane Foundation
The LankellyChase Foundation
Mrs M. A. Lascelles Charitable
Trust
The Lauffer Family Charitable
Foundation
The Richard Lawes Foundation
The Edgar E. Lawley
Foundation
Ana Leaf Foundation*
The William Leech Charity
Leeds Community Foundation
Leicestershire and Rutland
Masonic Charity
Association
Leicestershire, Leicester and
Rutland Community
Foundation
Leng Charitable Trust
David and Ruth Lewis Family
Charitable Trust
Lincolnshire Community
Foundation
The Frank Litchfield Charitable
Trust
The Michael and Betty Little
Trust*
The Second Joseph Aaron
Littman Foundation
The W. M. and B. W. Lloyd
Trust
London Catalyst
The London Community
Foundation (LCF)
London Housing Foundation
Ltd (LHF)
London Legal Support Trust
(LLST)
The London Marathon
Charitable Trust Ltd
Lords Group Foundation*
The Lord's Taverners
The Ian Mactaggart Trust
The Magen Charitable Trust
Magnify Foundation*
Making a Difference Locally
Ltd
Manchester Airport Community
Trust Fund
The Manchester Guardian
Society Charitable Trust
R. W. Mann Trust
The Dan Maskell Tennis Trust
The Master Charitable Trust
Maudsley Charity
MBNA General Foundation
The McCarthy Stone
Foundation
The Mercers Charitable
Foundation
The Merchant Taylors'
Foundation*

The Millennium Oak Trust
Millennium Stadium Charitable
Trust (Ymddiriedolaeth
Elusennol Stadiwm y
Mileniwm)
The Millichope Foundation
Milton Keynes Community
Foundation Ltd
Mobbs Memorial Trust Ltd
The Monmouthshire County
Council Welsh Church Act
Fund
The Janet and Brian Moore
Charitable Trust*
The Henry Moore Foundation
John Moores Foundation
The Alexander Mosley
Charitable Trust
Moto Foundation
The Frederick Mulder
Foundation
The National Express
Foundation
The National Garden Scheme
The National Hockey
Foundation
The Nationwide Foundation
Near Neighbours
Ner Foundation
Nesta
Newcomen Collett Foundation
The NFU Mutual Charitable
Trust
The Nine Incorporated Trades
of Dundee General Fund
Charity
The Nomura Charitable Trust
Norfolk Community Foundation
Educational Foundation of
Alderman John Norman
The Norman Family Charitable
Trust
North Berwick Trust
Northamptonshire Community
Foundation
Community Foundation for
Northern Ireland
Northern Pharmacies Ltd Trust
Fund
The Norton Foundation
Norwich Town Close Estate
Charity
The Notgrove Trust
Nottinghamshire Community
Foundation
The Nuffield Foundation
The Oakdale Trust
Ocean Family Foundation
Henry Oldfield Trust
One Community Foundation
Ltd
Orthopaedic Research UK
The Sir Peter O'Sullevan
Charitable Trust
Otsar Trust

The Ouseley Church Music
    Trust
Ovingdean Hall Foundation
The James Pantyfedwen
    Foundation
    (Ymddiriedolaeth James
    Pantyfedwen)
The Parivar Trust
The Jack Patston Charitable
    Trust
John Pearce Foundation
The Pears Family Charitable
    Foundation
The Pell Charitable Trust
People's Health Trust
People's Postcode Trust
The Performing Right Society
    Foundation
The Persimmon Charitable
    Foundation
The Jack Petchey Foundation
The Pets at Home Foundation
The Pharsalia Charitable Trust
Miss A. M. Pilkington's
    Charitable Trust
The Portal Trust
Postcode Community Trust
Postcode Local Trust
Postcode Society Trust
The Mary Potter Convent
    Hospital Trust
The Potton Consolidated
    Charity
Poundland Foundation
Quartet Community Foundation
The Racing Foundation
The Rainford Trust
The Rambourg Foundation
The Eleanor Rathbone
    Charitable Trust
The Sigrid Rausing Trust
The Sir James Reckitt Charity
The Reece Foundation
Rees Jeffreys Road Fund
Richard Reeve's Foundation
The Revere Charitable Trust
Rhodi Charitable Trust
Riada Trust
Daisie Rich Trust
Richmond Parish Lands Charity
Rigby Foundation
The Sir John Ritblat Family
    Foundation
Riverside Charitable Trust Ltd
The Rix-Thompson-Rothenberg
    Foundation
The Rock Foundation
The Sir James Roll Charitable
    Trust
Mrs L. D. Rope's Third
    Charitable Settlement
Rosca Trust
The Ross Foundation
The Rothley Trust
The Rowlands Trust

The Joseph Rowntree
    Charitable Trust
Royal Docks Trust (London)
The Rugby Group Benevolent
    Fund Ltd
Russell Trust
Santander UK Foundation Ltd
The Schreier Foundation*
Foundation Scotland
Francis C. Scott Charitable
    Trust
The Frieda Scott Charitable
    Trust
The John Scott Trust Fund
The Screwfix Foundation
Seafarers UK (King George's
    Fund for Sailors)
The Sam and Bella Sebba
    Charitable Foundation
Leslie Sell Charitable Trust
The Serco Foundation
The Seven Fifty Trust
Shaftoe Educational
    Foundation
The Shanly Foundation
The Sheffield Town Trust
The Bassil Shippam and
    Alsford Trust
The Shipwrights Charitable
    Fund
The Skelton Bounty
Skipton Building Society
    Charitable Foundation
The Slaughter and May
    Charitable Trust
Kathleen Beryl Sleigh
    Charitable Trust
Smallwood Trust
The Henry Smith Charity
The R. C. Snelling Charitable
    Trust
Sofronie Foundation
Somerset Community
    Foundation
South Yorkshire Community
    Foundation
Southover Manor General
    Education Trust Ltd
The SpeedoMick Foundation
The Sperring Charity
The Spoore, Merry and Rixman
    Foundation
The St Hilda's Trust
St John's Foundation Est.
    1174
St Olave's and St Saviour's
    Schools Foundation CIO*
St Peter's Saltley Trust
The Community Foundation for
    Staffordshire
The Stevenage Community
    Trust
Stewards Company Ltd
Stratford-upon-Avon Town Trust
The W. O. Street Charitable
    Foundation

Suffolk Community Foundation
The Summerfield Charitable
    Trust
The Sunrise Foundation CIO
Community Foundation for
    Surrey
The Sussex Community
    Foundation
Sutton Coldfield Charitable
    Trust
Swarovski Foundation
The William Syson Foundation
The Talbot Trusts
Humphrey Richardson Taylor
    Charitable Trust
Tees Valley Community
    Foundation
Tenovus Scotland
The Theatres Trust Charitable
    Fund
The Tottenham Grammar
    School Foundation
Tower Hill Trust
The Toy Trust
Toyota Manufacturing UK
    Charitable Trust
The Troutsdale Charitable
    Trust
Trust for London
The Trusthouse Charitable
    Foundation
The Tudor Trust
The Tudwick Foundation
The Tuixen Foundation
Two Magpies Fund
Two Ridings Community
    Foundation
Community Foundation serving
    Tyne and Wear and
    Northumberland
Ufi VocTech Trust
UJIA (United Jewish Israel
    Appeal)
The UK Youth Fund: Thriving
    Minds*
Ulster Garden Villages Ltd
The Ulverscroft Foundation
United St Saviour's Charity
UPP Foundation
Valencia Communities Fund
Variety, the Children's Charity
The Veolia Environmental Trust
The Veterans' Foundation
The Virgin Foundation (Virgin
    Unite)
The Virgin Money Foundation
Vision Foundation
The Vodafone Foundation
Sylvia Waddilove Foundation
    UK
Wade's Charity
The Scurrah Wainwright Charity
Wakefield and Tetley Trust
The Walcot Foundation
The Walker Trust
War Memorials Trust

The Waterloo Foundation
Wates Family Enterprise Trust
The Wates Foundation
The William Wates Memorial Trust
The Geoffrey Watling Charity
We Love MCR Charity
The William Webster Charitable Trust
The Linda and Michael Weinstein Charitable Trust
The Weir Charitable Trust
The Welsh Church Act Fund
Wembley National Stadium Trust
The Westfield Health Charitable Trust
The Garfield Weston Foundation
Westway Trust
The Whitaker Charitable Trust
The Wigoder Family Foundation
Wiltshire Community Foundation
The Wimbledon Foundation
The Wolfson Family Charitable Trust
The Wolfson Foundation
Women's Fund for Scotland
The Victoria Wood Foundation
Woodroffe Benton Foundation
Woodsmith Foundation Ltd
The Woodward Charitable Trust
Worcestershire Community Foundation
Worshipful Company of Needlemakers Charitable Fund
Worth Waynflete Foundation
Sir Graham Wylie Foundation
The Yorkshire Dales Millennium Trust
Youth Music
Zurich Community Trust (UK) Ltd

Places of worship

The A. and J. Charitable Trust
The A. H. Trust
The A. S. Charitable Trust
Age Scotland
The Almond Trust
Viscount Amory's Charitable Trust
The AMW Charitable Trust
The Anchor Foundation
Andrew Anderson Trust
Andrews Charitable Trust
The John Armitage Charitable Trust
The Armourers and Brasiers Gauntlet Trust
Ashburnham Thanksgiving Trust
The Ashendene Trust
The Astor Foundation
The Atlas Fund
Atlas Memorial Ltd
The Aurelius Charitable Trust
The Baily Thomas Charitable Fund
Bairdwatson Charitable Trust
The Band Trust
Lord Barnby's Foundation
The Barnes Fund
Barnsbury Charitable Trust
The Paul Bassham Charitable Trust
The Louis Baylis (Maidenhead Advertiser) Charitable Trust
BBC Children in Need
The James Beattie Charitable Trust
The Bedfordshire and Hertfordshire Historic Churches Trust
The Bellahouston Bequest Fund
Benefact Trust Ltd
The Benham Charitable Settlement
The Rowan Bentall Charitable Trust
Bideford Bridge Trust
Biffa Award
The Bingham Trust
Binks Trust
The Birmingham Diocesan Board of Finance
The Isabel Blackman Foundation
The Blakebank Trust
Abraham Algy Bloom Foundation
The Bluston Charitable Settlement
The Boltini Trust
The Bonamy Charitable Trust
The Booth Charities
The Salo Bordon Charitable Trust

The Bosson Family Charitable Trust
The Harry Bottom Charitable Trust
The P. G. and N. J. Boulton Trust
The Bowland Charitable Trust
The Liz and Terry Bramall Foundation
The Harold and Alice Bridges Charity
Bristol Archdeaconry Charity
The British and Foreign Bible Society
T. B. H. Brunner's Charitable Settlement
The Jack Brunton Charitable Trust
Buckingham Trust
Consolidated Charity of Burton upon Trent
William A. Cadbury Charitable Trust
The Edward and Dorothy Cadbury Trust
Community Foundation for Calderdale
Cambridgeshire Community Foundation
The Frederick and Phyllis Cann Trust
Cannon Charitable Trust
Carew Pole Charitable Trust
The Carrington Charitable Trust
The Leslie Mary Carter Charitable Trust
Catholic Charitable Trust
CEO Sleepout
The Chadwick Educational Foundation
Chippenham Borough Lands Charity
The André Christian Trust
Church Burgesses Educational Foundation
Church Burgesses Trust
Church of Ireland Priorities Fund
Church Urban Fund
The Roger and Sarah Bancroft Clark Charitable Trust
The Clore Duffield Foundation
Cloudesley
The Robert Clutterbuck Charitable Trust
CMZ Ltd
The Francis Coales Charitable Foundation
The Coalfields Regeneration Trust
The Cobtree Charity Trust Ltd
The Vivienne and Samuel Cohen Charitable Trust
Sir Jeremiah Colman Gift Trust

Colyer-Fergusson Charitable
  Trust
Community First
Congleton Inclosure Trust
Congregational and General
  Charitable Trust
The Catherine Cookson
  Charitable Trust
The Helen Jean Cope Charity
The Costa Family Charitable
  Trust
The County Council of Dyfed
  Welsh Church Fund
The Sir Tom Cowie Charitable
  Trust
The Cross Trust
The Croydon Relief-in-Need
  Charity
Baron Davenport's Charity
Margaret Davies Charity
The Davis Foundation
The De Brye Charitable Trust
The Roger De Haan Charitable
  Trust
William Delafield Charitable
  Trust
The Alan and Sheila Diamond
  Charitable Trust
Donibristle Trust
Dorset Community Foundation
The Dorset Historic Churches
  Trust
Dromintee Trust
Duchy of Lancaster Benevolent
  Fund
The Duke of Cornwall's
  Benevolent Fund
Duke of Devonshire's
  Charitable Trust
The Dulverton Trust
Dumbreck Charity
Dumfriesshire East Community
  Benefit Group SCIO
The Dyers' Company
  Charitable Trust
Ebenezer Trust
The Gilbert and Eileen Edgar
  Foundation
Edinburgh Trust No2 Account
The Eighteen Fund
The Elie Trust
The Maud Elkington Charitable
  Trust
The Englefield Charitable Trust
The Enkalon Foundation
Entindale Ltd
Esher House Charitable Trust
The Everard Foundation
The Eveson Charitable Trust
G. F. Eyre Charitable Trust
Famos Foundation Trust
The Thomas Farr Charity
The Farthing Trust
The A. M. Fenton Trust
The Feoffees of St Michael's
  Spurriergate York

Allan and Nesta Ferguson
  Charitable Settlement
Doris Field Charitable Trust
The Fifty Fund
The Foster Wood Foundation
Ian M. Foulerton Charitable
  Trust
Fowler Smith and Jones Trust
Jill Franklin Trust
The Joseph Strong Frazer Trust
Friends of Essex Churches
  Trust
The Friends of Kent Churches
Friends of Wiznitz Ltd
The Gale Family Charity Trust
Ganzoni Charitable Trust
Gatwick Airport Community
  Trust
General Charity (Coventry)
The Gibbs Charitable Trusts
The Simon Gibson Charitable
  Trust
The Gloucestershire Historic
  Churches Trust
The Godinton Charitable Trust
The Golsoncott Foundation
The Jane Goodman Charitable
  Trust*
The Goshen Trust
Grace Baptist Trust
  Corporation*
Grace Charitable Trust
The Grace Trust
The Grantham Yorke Trust
The J. G. Graves Charitable
  Trust
The Green Hall Foundation
Philip and Judith Green Trust
The Grimmitt Trust
The Grocers' Charity
Hackney Parochial Charities
The Hamilton Davies Trust
Hampshire and Isle of Wight
  Community Foundation
Hampton Fund
The W. A. Handley Charity
  Trust
The Lennox Hannay Charitable
  Trust
Harborne Parish Lands Charity
The Peter and Teresa Harris
  Charitable Trust
Gay and Peter Hartley's
  Hillards Charitable Trust
The Hawthorne Charitable
  Trust
The Headley Trust
The Heathcoat Trust
The Charlotte Heber-Percy
  Charitable Trust
The Helping Foundation
The Herefordshire Historic
  Churches Trust
Heritage Lottery Fund
The Heritage of London Trust
  Ltd

The Hillier Trust
The Lady Hind Trust
The Stuart Hine Trust CIO
The Hintze Family Charity
  Foundation
Historic Environment Scotland
Hockerill Educational
  Foundation
The Jane Hodge Foundation
The Holbeck Charitable Trust
The Holden Charitable Trust
Hollyhock Charitable
  Foundation
Homelands Charitable Trust
Sir Harold Hood's Charitable
  Trust
Hope Trust
The Hospital of God at
  Greatham
Housing Pathways Trust
The Hudson Foundation
The Humanitarian Trust
The Hunting Horn General
  Charitable Trust
Hyde Park Place Estate Charity
The Idlewild Trust
IGO Foundation Ltd
The Iliffe Family Charitable
  Trust
The Isla Foundation
The J. and J. Benevolent
  Foundation
John James Bristol Foundation
Lady Eda Jardine Charitable
  Trust
The Jenour Foundation
The Jerusalem Trust
The Joicey Trust
The Jusaca Charitable Trust
The Kasner Charitable Trust
The Nancy Kenyon Charitable
  Trust
The Kildare Trust
The King Henry VIII Endowed
  Trust – Warwick
Sir James Knott Trust
Kollel and Co. Ltd
Kolyom Trust Ltd
Kupath Gemach Chaim
  Bechesed Viznitz Trust
The K. P. Ladd Charitable
  Trust
Maurice and Hilda Laing
  Charitable Trust
The Kirby Laing Foundation
The Martin Laing Foundation
The Beatrice Laing Trust
The Leonard Laity Stoate
  Charitable Trust
Lancashire Environmental
  Fund Ltd
Lancaster Foundation
The R. J. Larg Family Trust
Laslett's (Hinton) Charity
Mrs F. B. Laurence Charitable
  Trust

The Herd Lawson and Muriel Lawson Charitable Trust

The Leche Trust

The William Leech Charity

Leicestershire and Rutland Masonic Charity Association

Leicestershire, Leicester and Rutland Community Foundation

Lempriere Pringle 2015

Leng Charitable Trust

Lord Leverhulme's Charitable Trust

Limoges Charitable Trust

The Linbury Trust

Lincolnshire Community Foundation

The Michael and Betty Little Trust*

The Charles Littlewood Hill Trust

The Second Joseph Aaron Littman Foundation

Jack Livingstone Charitable Trust

The Elaine and Angus Lloyd Charitable Trust

The W. M. and B. W. Lloyd Trust

The Locker Foundation

The Lockwood Charitable Foundation

London Catalyst

The C. L. Loyd Charitable Trust

Sylvanus Lysons Charity

The Mactaggart Third Fund

The Magdalen and Lasher Charity (General Fund)

Magnify Foundation*

Making a Difference Locally Ltd

R. W. Mann Trust

The Manoukian Charitable Foundation

The Michael Marsh Charitable Trust

Charity of John Marshall

Charlotte Marshall Charitable Trust

The Martin Charitable Trust

The Kristina Martin Charitable Trust

Sir George Martin Trust

John Martin's Charity

Nancie Massey Charitable Trust

Maudsley Charity

Mayheights Ltd

The Medlock Charitable Trust

Menuchar Ltd

The Mercers Charitable Foundation

The Merchant Venturers Charity

The Mikheev Charitable Trust

The Millfield Trust

The Millichope Foundation

The Millward Charitable Trust

The Milne Family Foundation

Milton Keynes Community Foundation Ltd

The Esmé Mitchell Trust

The MK Charitable Trust

Mobbs Memorial Trust Ltd

The Modiano Charitable Trust

Mole Charitable Trust

The Monmouthshire County Council Welsh Church Act Fund

The Morel Charitable Trust

G. M. Morrison Charitable Trust

Vyoel Moshe Charitable Trust

The Alexander Mosley Charitable Trust

The Mumford Memorial Trust*

Music Sales Charitable Trust

The National Churches Trust

The National Express Foundation

The National Hockey Foundation

The National Lottery Community Fund

Near Neighbours

Ner Foundation

The Nine Incorporated Trades of Dundee General Fund Charity

The Norfolk Churches Trust Ltd

Norfolk Community Foundation

Normanby Charitable Trust

Northamptonshire Community Foundation

The Northumbria Historic Churches Trust

Northwood Charitable Trust

Norwich Town Close Estate Charity

The Norwood and Newton Settlement

The Notgrove Trust

The Ofenheim Charitable Trust

The Ogle Christian Trust

Old Possum's Practical Trust

Henry Oldfield Trust

Open House Trust Ltd

The Orrin Charitable Trust

Otsar Trust

The Ouseley Church Music Trust

The Owen Family Trust

Oxfordshire Historic Churches Trust (2016)

The P27 Trust

The Gerald Palmer Eling Trust Company

The James Pantyfedwen Foundation (Ymddiriedolaeth James Pantyfedwen)

The Paragon Trust

Miss M. E. S. Paterson's Charitable Trust

The Jack Patston Charitable Trust

Payne-Gallwey 1989 Charitable Trust

Susanna Peake Charitable Trust

David Pearlman Charitable Foundation

The Pears Family Charitable Foundation

Dina Perelman Trust Ltd

The Persimmon Charitable Foundation

The Phillips and Rubens Charitable Trust

The Pilgrim Trust

The Sir Harry Pilkington Fund

Miss A. M. Pilkington's Charitable Trust

Charles Plater Trust*

The Mary Potter Convent Hospital Trust

The Potton Consolidated Charity

Sir John Priestman Charity Trust

The Privy Purse Charitable Trust

Quothquan Trust

R. S. Charitable Trust

The Bishop Radford Trust

The Rank Foundation Ltd

The Joseph Rank Trust

The Ratcliff Foundation

The Rathbones Group Foundation

The Julia and Hans Rausing Trust*

The Sir James Reckitt Charity

Daisie Rich Trust

The Clive Richards Foundation

Richmond Parish Lands Charity

Rigby Foundation

The River Trust

The Rock Foundation

The Romney Marsh Historic Churches Trust

Mrs L. D. Rope's Third Charitable Settlement

Rosca Trust

The Rose Foundation

The Roseline Foundation*

The Cecil Rosen Foundation

The Rothermere Foundation

The Rowlands Trust

The Joseph Rowntree Charitable Trust

The Rugby Group Benevolent Fund Ltd

S. and R. Charitable Trust

The Saddlers' Company Charitable Fund

Saint Sarkis Charity Trust

The Salamander Charitable Trust
Salisbury Pool Charity
The Basil Samuel Charitable Trust
The Peter Samuel Charitable Trust
The Sanderson Foundation
Sandra Charitable Trust
Sarum St Michael Educational Charity
Schroder Charity Trust
Foundation Scotland
Seedfield Trust
The Seven Fifty Trust
The Shanly Foundation
The Sheffield Town Trust
The Sylvia and Colin Shepherd Charitable Trust
The Bassil Shippam and Alsford Trust
The Skelton Bounty
The Charles Skey Charitable Trust
The Henry Smith Charity
The R. C. Snelling Charitable Trust
The Stephen R. and Philippa H. Southall Charitable Trust
The Jessie Spencer Trust
The Sperring Charity
Spurrell Charitable Trust
The St Hilda's Trust
St Peter's Saltley Trust
Starlow Charities Ltd
The Hugh Stenhouse Foundation
Stewards Company Ltd
The Stobart Newlands Charitable Trust
Stolkin Foundation
The Samuel Storey Family Charitable Trust
Stratford-upon-Avon Town Trust
The Suffolk Historic Churches Trust
The Summerfield Charitable Trust
The Bernard Sunley Foundation
Sabina Sutherland Charitable Trust
Sutton Coldfield Charitable Trust
Swansea and Brecon Diocesan Board of Finance Ltd
The John Swire (1989) Charitable Trust
The Adrian Swire Charitable Trust
Tabeel Trust
The Tajtelbaum Charitable Trust
The Talbot Village Trust
Tallow Chandlers Benevolent Fund No 2

Tanner Trust
C. B. and H. H. T. Taylor 1984 Trust
Scott Thomson Charitable Trust
Mrs R. P. Tindall's Charitable Trust
The Tompkins Foundation
The Constance Travis Charitable Trust
The Troutsdale Charitable Trust
The Truemark Trust
Trust for London
The Tudor Trust
The Tufton Charitable Trust
Community Foundation serving Tyne and Wear and Northumberland
UJIA (United Jewish Israel Appeal)
Ulting Overseas Trust
The Union of the Sisters of Mercy of Great Britain
The United Reformed Church (Wessex) Trust Ltd
United St Saviour's Charity
Valencia Communities Fund
The Albert Van Den Bergh Charitable Trust
The Vardy Foundation
Nigel Vinson Charitable Trust
Warwick Relief-in-Need Charity
Wates Family Enterprise Trust
The Wates Foundation
The Geoffrey Watling Charity
The William Webster Charitable Trust
The Linda and Michael Weinstein Charitable Trust
The Welsh Church Act Fund
West Derby Waste Lands Charity
Westhill Endowment
Westminster Foundation
The Garfield Weston Foundation
The Whinfell Charitable Fund
The Whitaker Charitable Trust
The Norman Whiteley Trust
The Wilmcote Charitrust
The Benjamin Winegarten Charitable Trust
The Wixamtree Trust
The Wolfson Family Charitable Trust
The Wolfson Foundation
The James Wood Bequest Fund
The Worshipful Company of Glovers of London Charitable Trust
Worshipful Company of Needlemakers Charitable Fund
Worth Waynflete Foundation

WWDP (World Day of Prayer National Committee for England, Wales and Northern Ireland)
The Yorkshire Historic Churches Trust
The Marjorie and Arnold Ziff Charitable Foundation
Zurich Community Trust (UK) Ltd

Schools and colleges

The 29th May 1961 Charitable Trust
The A. and J. Charitable Trust
The A. H. Trust
The Aberdeenshire Educational Trust Scheme
The Bryan Adams Foundation
The Adlard Family Charitable Foundation
Age Scotland
The Alborada Trust
Al-Fayed Charitable Foundation
Alpkit Foundation
Viscount Amory's Charitable Trust
Andrews Charitable Trust
Anguish's Educational Foundation
The Annabel Arbib Foundation
The Ardwick Trust
Armed Forces Education Trust
The John Armitage Charitable Trust
The Armourers and Brasiers Gauntlet Trust
Arts Council of Wales (also known as Cyngor Celfyddydau Cymru)
The Ove Arup Foundation
The Asda Foundation
The Asfari Foundation
The Ian Askew Charitable Trust
The Associated Board of the Royal Schools of Music (ABRSM)
The Atlas Fund
Lawrence Atwell's Charity (Skinners' Company)
The Avon and Somerset Police Community Trust
The Tim Bacon Foundation
The Baird Trust
The Band Trust
The Baring Foundation
Lord Barnby's Foundation
The Barnes Fund
Barnsbury Charitable Trust
Barnwood Trust
Bauer Radio's Cash for Kids Charities
Bay Charitable Trust
The Louis Baylis (Maidenhead Advertiser) Charitable Trust
BC Partners Foundation
Bear Mordechai Ltd
The James Beattie Charitable Trust
Beauland Ltd
The Beaverbrooks Charitable Trust
Beccles Townlands Charity
The Lord Belstead Charitable Settlement*

Benefact Trust Ltd
Benesco Charity Ltd
The Rowan Bentall Charitable Trust
Berkshire Community Foundation
The Bestway Foundation
Bideford Bridge Trust
Biffa Award
The Percy Bilton Charity
The Bingham Trust
Binks Trust
Birkdale Trust for Hearing Impaired Ltd*
The Birmingham Diocesan Board of Finance
The Michael Bishop Foundation
The Sydney Black Charitable Trust
The Isabel Blackman Foundation
Blakemore Foundation
Abraham Algy Bloom Foundation
Bluespark Foundation
The Bluston Charitable Settlement
The Boltini Trust
The Bonamy Charitable Trust
The Booth Charities
The Salo Bordon Charitable Trust
Sir William Boreman's Foundation
The Boshier-Hinton Foundation
The P. G. and N. J. Boulton Trust
Bourneheights Ltd
The Bowland Charitable Trust
The Liz and Terry Bramall Foundation
The Brenley Trust
The Harold and Alice Bridges Charity
Bristol Charities
The BRIT Trust
The British and Foreign Bible Society
The British and Foreign School Society (BFSS)
J. and M. Britton Charitable Trust
R. S. Brownless Charitable Trust
The Jack Brunton Charitable Trust
Buckingham Trust
The Buffini Chao Foundation
E. F. Bulmer Trust
The Burden Trust
Clara E. Burgess Charity
The Burry Charitable Trust
Consolidated Charity of Burton upon Trent
Byrne Family Foundation

The G. W. Cadbury Charitable Trust
The Edward and Dorothy Cadbury Trust
The George Cadbury Trust
Community Foundation for Calderdale
Cambridgeshire Community Foundation
Camden Giving
Cannon Charitable Trust
CareTech Charitable Foundation
W. A. Cargill Fund
The Carnegie Dunfermline Trust
The Carpenters Company Charitable Trust
The Carrington Charitable Trust
The Wilfrid and Constance Cave Foundation
The Chadwick Educational Foundation
Chalfords Ltd
Chapman Charitable Trust
Charitworth Ltd
Chartered Accountants' Livery Charity (CALC)
Cheshire Freemasons' Charity
The Childhood Trust
Chippenham Borough Lands Charity
Church Burgesses Educational Foundation
The Clore Duffield Foundation
The Clothworkers' Foundation
The Robert Clutterbuck Charitable Trust
Clydpride Ltd
CMZ Ltd
The Coalfields Regeneration Trust
Denise Coates Foundation
The Cobtree Charity Trust Ltd
The Vivienne and Samuel Cohen Charitable Trust
The John S. Cohen Foundation
Colefax Charitable Trust
John and Freda Coleman Charitable Trust
Sir Jeremiah Colman Gift Trust
Col-Reno Ltd
Colyer-Fergusson Charitable Trust
Douglas Compton James Charitable Trust
Congleton Inclosure Trust
The Connolly Foundation (UK) Ltd
The Ernest Cook Trust
The Cooks Charity
The Catherine Cookson Charitable Trust
The Helen Jean Cope Charity

The J. Reginald Corah
Foundation Fund
The Corporation of Trinity
House of Deptford Strond
The Costa Family Charitable
Trust
County Durham Community
Foundation
The Sir Tom Cowie Charitable
Trust
The Cross Trust
Cullum Family Trust
Cumbria Community
Foundation
The D. M. Charitable Trust
The Daiwa Anglo-Japanese
Foundation
The Daniell Trust
Margaret Davies Charity
The Crispin Davis Family Trust
The Davis Foundation
The Roger De Haan Charitable
Trust
William Delafield Charitable
Trust
The Alan and Sheila Diamond
Charitable Trust
The Dibden Allotments Fund
Digital Extra Fund
The Dischma Charitable Trust
Dorset Community Foundation
The Double 'O' Charity Ltd
Drapers Charitable Fund
Duchy of Lancaster Benevolent
Fund
The Duke of Cornwall's
Benevolent Fund
Duke of Devonshire's
Charitable Trust
Dumbreck Charity
Dumfriesshire East Community
Benefit Group SCIO
The Dyers' Company
Charitable Trust
The James Dyson Foundation
East End Community
Foundation
Eastern Counties Educational
Trust Ltd
Sir John Eastwood Foundation
The Gilbert and Eileen Edgar
Foundation
Edinburgh Children's Holiday
Fund
Dr Edwards and Bishop King's
Fulham Charity
The Maud Elkington Charitable
Trust
The Ellerdale Trust
The Elmley Foundation
EMI Music Sound Foundation
The Englefield Charitable Trust
The Enkalon Foundation
Entindale Ltd
The Essex and Southend
Sports Trust

The Essex Youth Trust
The Eveson Charitable Trust
The Exilarch's Foundation
Family Philanthropy Ltd
Famos Foundation Trust
Samuel William Farmer Trust
George Fentham Birmingham
Charity
The Fidelio Charitable Trust
Doris Field Charitable Trust
The Fifty Fund
The Finnis Scott Foundation
Sir John Fisher Foundation
Fishmongers' Company's
Charitable Trust
The Earl Fitzwilliam Charitable
Trust
The Mrs Yvonne Flux
Charitable Trust
The Football Foundation
Ford Britain Trust
Forever Manchester
The Forman Hardy Charitable
Trust
The Lord Forte Foundation
Four Acre Trust
The Foyle Foundation
The Hugh Fraser Foundation
The Joseph Strong Frazer Trust
The Freshgate Trust
Foundation
Friends of Wiznitz Ltd
The Funding Network
The Gale Family Charity Trust
Ganzoni Charitable Trust
Gatwick Airport Community
Trust
The Robert Gavron Charitable
Trust
Sir Robert Geffery's
Almshouse Trust
The Generations Foundation
The Gibbons Family Trust
The Gibbs Charitable Trusts
The Simon Gibson Charitable
Trust
The F. Glenister Woodger Trust
CIO
Gloucestershire Community
Foundation
The Goldman Sachs Charitable
Gift Fund (UK)
Goldman Sachs Gives (UK)
The Goldsmiths' Company
Charity
The Golf Foundation
Grace Charitable Trust
The Grace Trust
Grahame Charitable
Foundation Ltd
The Grange Farm Centre Trust
William Grant Foundation*
The Grantham Yorke Trust
GrantScape
The J. G. Graves Charitable
Trust

The Great Britain Sasakawa
Foundation
The Great Stone Bridge Trust
of Edenbridge
Greenham Trust Ltd
The Greenslade Family
Foundation
The Greggs Foundation
The Grimmitt Trust
The Grocers' Charity
Groundwork UK
Dr Guthrie's Association
Hackney Parochial Charities
The Hadrian Trust
The Hamilton Davies Trust
Paul Hamlyn Foundation
The Helen Hamlyn Trust
Hammersmith United Charities
Hampshire and Isle of Wight
Community Foundation
The W. A. Handley Charity
Trust
The Happold Foundation
Harbinson Charitable Trust
Harborne Parish Lands Charity
William Harding's Charity
The Harebell Centenary Fund
The Harpur Trust
The Peter Harrison Foundation
Edward Harvist Trust (The
Harvist Estate)
The Hawthorne Charitable
Trust
The Heathcoat Trust
Heathrow Community Trust
The Charlotte Heber-Percy
Charitable Trust
Ernest Hecht Charitable
Foundation
The Helping Foundation
Henley Educational Trust
Tim Henman Foundation
Herefordshire Community
Foundation
The Heritage of London Trust
Ltd
The Highcroft Charitable Trust
The Hilden Charitable Fund
The Lady Hind Trust
The Hinduja Foundation
The Hintze Family Charity
Foundation
The Hobson Charity Ltd
The Jane Hodge Foundation
The Holbeck Charitable Trust
The Holden Charitable Trust
The Holywood Trust
Sir Harold Hood's Charitable
Trust
The Horners Charity Fund
Horwich Shotter Charitable
Trust
Housing Pathways Trust
The Keith Howard Foundation
The Hudson Foundation

The Hull and East Riding
Charitable Trust
The Hunter Foundation
The Huntingdon Foundation
Ltd
Huntingdon Freemen's Trust
Hurdale Charity Ltd
Hyde Charitable Trust
Hyde Park Place Estate Charity
IGO Foundation Ltd
Imagine Foundation
Integrated Education Fund
The International Bankers
Charitable Trust
The Ireland Fund of Great
Britain
Irish Youth Foundation (UK)
Ltd (incorporating The
Lawlor Foundation)
The ITF Seafarers Trust
The Frank Jackson Foundation
John James Bristol Foundation
The Jenour Foundation
The Jerusalem Trust
Johnnie Johnson Trust
The Jones 1986 Charitable
Trust
The Muriel Jones Foundation
The Jusaca Charitable Trust
Kahal Chassidim Bobov
The Karlsson Játiva Charitable
Foundation
The Ian Karten Charitable
Trust
The Kasner Charitable Trust
C. S. Kaufman Charitable
Trust
Kelsick's Educational
Foundation
William Kendall's Charity (Wax
Chandlers Company)
The Kensington and Chelsea
Foundation
The Nancy Kenyon Charitable
Trust
The Ursula Keyes Trust
The Kilroot Foundation
The King Henry VIII Endowed
Trust – Warwick
Robert Kitchin (Saddlers' Co.)
Sir James Knott Trust
Kollel and Co. Ltd
KPE4 Charitable Trust
The KPMG Foundation
Kusuma Trust UK
The Kyte Charitable Trust
The Kirby Laing Foundation
The Beatrice Laing Trust
Community Foundations for
Lancashire and Merseyside
The Lancashire Foundation
Lancaster Foundation
The R. J. Larg Family Trust
The Lauffer Family Charitable
Foundation

Mrs F. B. Laurence Charitable
Trust
The Law Society Charity
The Edgar E. Lawley
Foundation
Lawson Beckman Charitable
Trust
The Lawson Trust CIO
The Leathersellers' Foundation
The Legal Education
Foundation
Leicestershire, Leicester and
Rutland Community
Foundation
The Leverhulme Trust
Lord Leverhulme's Charitable
Trust
Cecil and Hilda Lewis
Charitable Trust
The Linbury Trust
Lincolnshire Community
Foundation
The Michael and Betty Little
Trust*
The Charles Littlewood Hill
Trust
The Second Joseph Aaron
Littman Foundation
Jack Livingstone Charitable
Trust
The Elaine and Angus Lloyd
Charitable Trust
The W. M. and B. W. Lloyd
Trust
Localtrent Ltd
The Locker Foundation
The London Marathon
Charitable Trust Ltd
The Lord's Taverners
Lord and Lady Lurgan Trust
Sir Jack Lyons Charitable Trust
John Lyon's Charity
M. and C. Trust
M. B. Foundation
The Mackintosh Foundation
The MacRobert Trust 2019
The Mactaggart Third Fund
The Magdalen and Lasher
Charity (General Fund)
The Magen Charitable Trust
Making a Difference Locally
Ltd
Man Group plc Charitable
Trust
The Manackerman Charitable
Trust
Manchester Airport Community
Trust Fund
The Manchester Guardian
Society Charitable Trust
R. W. Mann Trust
The Manson Family Charitable
Trust
Marbeh Torah Trust
The Michael Marsh Charitable
Trust

Charlotte Marshall Charitable
Trust
The Kristina Martin Charitable
Trust
Sir George Martin Trust
John Martin's Charity
The Dan Maskell Tennis Trust
Nancie Massey Charitable
Trust
The Master Charitable Trust
Mathew Trust
Maudsley Charity
Mayfair Charities Ltd
The Mayfield Valley Arts Trust
Mayheights Ltd
Mazars Charitable Trust
MBNA General Foundation
The McCarthy Stone
Foundation
The Medlock Charitable Trust
Melodor Ltd
The Melow Charitable Trust
The Brian Mercer Charitable
Trust
The Mercers Charitable
Foundation
The Merchant Venturers
Charity
Merchants House of Glasgow
The Mickel Fund
The Mikheev Charitable Trust
The Millennium Oak Trust
Millennium Stadium Charitable
Trust (Ymddiriedolaeth
Elusennol Stadiwm y
Mileniwm)
The Millichope Foundation
The Clare Milne Trust
The Esmé Mitchell Trust
Mobbs Memorial Trust Ltd
Mole Charitable Trust
The Monmouthshire County
Council Welsh Church Act
Fund
Moondance Foundation
The George A. Moore
Foundation
The Morel Charitable Trust
Morgan Stanley International
Foundation
The Morris Charitable Trust
The Moshal Charitable Trust
Vyoel Moshe Charitable Trust
The Alexander Mosley
Charitable Trust
Moto Foundation
The John R. Murray Charitable
Trust
MW (CL) Foundation
MW (GK) Foundation
MW (HO) Foundation
MW (RH) Foundation
The National Express
Foundation
The National Hockey
Foundation

The National Lottery
   Community Fund
Near Neighbours
Ner Foundation
Nesta
Newcomen Collett Foundation
Alderman Newton's
   Educational Foundation
The Nine Incorporated Trades
   of Dundee General Fund
   Charity
The Nineveh Charitable Trust
Norfolk Community Foundation
Educational Foundation of
   Alderman John Norman
The Norman Family Charitable
   Trust
Normanby Charitable Trust
North Berwick Trust
Northcott Trust
Community Foundation for
   Northern Ireland
The Norton Foundation
Norwich Town Close Estate
   Charity
The Notgrove Trust
Nottinghamshire Community
   Foundation
The Ogle Christian Trust
Oizer Charitable Trust
Old Possum's Practical Trust
One Community Foundation
   Ltd
Open House Trust Ltd
The O'Sullivan Family
   Charitable Trust
The Ouseley Church Music
   Trust
The Ovo Charitable Foundation
The Owen Family Trust
Susanna Peake Charitable
   Trust
David Pearlman Charitable
   Foundation
The Pears Family Charitable
   Foundation
The Pebbles Trust
People's Postcode Trust
Dina Perelman Trust Ltd
The Persimmon Charitable
   Foundation
The Jack Petchey Foundation
The Phillips and Rubens
   Charitable Trust
Miss A. M. Pilkington's
   Charitable Trust
The Portal Trust
The Portrack Charitable Trust
Postcode Community Trust
Postcode Local Trust
Postcode Society Trust
The Mary Potter Convent
   Hospital Trust
The Potton Consolidated
   Charity
Premierquote Ltd

The Prince's Countryside Fund
The Priory Foundation
The Privy Purse Charitable
   Trust
The Purey Cust Trust CIO
Mr and Mrs J. A. Pye's
   Charitable Settlement
Quartet Community Foundation
R. S. Charitable Trust
The Radcliffe Trust
The Joseph and Lena Randall
   Charitable Trust
Randeree Charitable Trust
The Rathbones Group
   Foundation
The Ravensdale Trust
The Sir James Reckitt Charity
Red Hill Charitable Trust
The Reece Foundation
Richard Reeve's Foundation
Reuben Foundation
Rhodi Charitable Trust
Daisie Rich Trust
The Clive Richards Foundation
Richmond Parish Lands Charity
The Dezna Robins Jones
   Charitable Foundation
The Gerald and Gail Ronson
   Family Foundation
Rosca Trust
The Rose Foundation
The Cecil Rosen Foundation
The Ross Foundation
The Rothermere Foundation
Rowanville Ltd
The Rowlands Trust
The Rugby Group Benevolent
   Fund Ltd
Russell Trust
S. and R. Charitable Trust
Salisbury Pool Charity
The Basil Samuel Charitable
   Trust
The Sands Family Trust
Sarum St Michael Educational
   Charity
The Savoy Educational Trust
Schreiber Charitable Trust
Foundation Scotland
Scottish Property Industry
   Festival of Christmas
   (SPIFOX)
Shaftoe Educational
   Foundation
The Shanly Foundation
The Shears Foundation
The Sheepdrove Trust
The Sheffield Town Trust
The Sheldon Trust
The Sylvia and Colin Shepherd
   Charitable Trust
The R. C. Sherriff Rosebriars
   Trust
SHINE (Support and Help in
   Education)

The Bassil Shippam and
   Alsford Trust
The Shipwrights Charitable
   Fund
Shulem B. Association Ltd
The Sino-British Fellowship
   Trust
The Charles Skey Charitable
   Trust
The John Slater Foundation
The Slaughter and May
   Charitable Trust
Sloane Robinson Foundation
The Henry Smith Charity
The Leslie Smith Foundation
Stanley Smith UK Horticultural
   Trust
The R. C. Snelling Charitable
   Trust
Societe Generale UK
   Foundation
David Solomons Charitable
   Trust
Somerset Community
   Foundation
South Yorkshire Community
   Foundation
Southover Manor General
   Education Trust Ltd
The Spear Charitable Trust
The Sperring Charity
Spielman Charitable Trust
The Spoore, Merry and Rixman
   Foundation
St James's Place Charitable
   Foundation
Sir Walter St John's
   Educational Charity
St John's Foundation Est.
   1174
St Olave's and St Saviour's
   Schools Foundation CIO*
St Peter's Saltley Trust
The Community Foundation for
   Staffordshire
Starlow Charities Ltd
The Steel Charitable Trust
The Stevenage Community
   Trust
Stolkin Foundation
The Samuel Storey Family
   Charitable Trust
Peter Stormonth Darling
   Charitable Trust
Strand Parishes Trust
Stratford-upon-Avon Town Trust
Suffolk Community Foundation
The Summerfield Charitable
   Trust
The Bernard Sunley
   Foundation
The Sunrise Foundation CIO
Community Foundation for
   Surrey
The Sussex Community
   Foundation

Sutton Coldfield Charitable Trust
The Swann-Morton Foundation
The John Swire (1989) Charitable Trust
The Adrian Swire Charitable Trust
The Charles and Elsie Sykes Trust
The Tajtelbaum Charitable Trust
The Talbot Village Trust
Tallow Chandlers Benevolent Fund No 2
The David Tannen Charitable Trust
Tanner Trust
Tay Charitable Trust
C. B. and H. H. T. Taylor 1984 Trust
Humphrey Richardson Taylor Charitable Trust
Stephen Taylor Foundation
The Tedworth Charitable Trust
Tees Valley Community Foundation
The Tennis Foundation
The Thompson Family Charitable Trust
The Sue Thomson Foundation
Mrs R. P. Tindall's Charitable Trust
The Tompkins Foundation
The Tottenham Grammar School Foundation
Tower Hill Trust
The Toy Trust
Toyota Manufacturing UK Charitable Trust
Trumros Ltd
The Tufton Charitable Trust
The Tuixen Foundation
Ufi VocTech Trust
UJIA (United Jewish Israel Appeal)
Ulster Garden Villages Ltd
Ulting Overseas Trust
The Ulverscroft Foundation
The Valentine Charitable Trust
The Vandervell Foundation
Variety, the Children's Charity
The Vintners' Foundation
Vivdale Ltd
The Walcot Foundation
The Waterloo Foundation
G. R. Waters Charitable Trust 2000
Wates Family Enterprise Trust
John Watson's Trust*
The Linda and Michael Weinstein Charitable Trust
Wembley National Stadium Trust
West Derby Waste Lands Charity
West Herts Charity Trust Ltd

Westhill Endowment
Westminster Foundation
The Garfield Weston Foundation
Westway Trust
WHSmith Trust
Brian Wilson Charitable Trust
W. Wing Yip and Brothers Foundation
The Maurice Wohl Charitable Foundation
The Charles Wolfson Charitable Trust
The Wolfson Family Charitable Trust
The Wolfson Foundation
The Wood Foundation
Wooden Spoon Society
Woodroffe Benton Foundation
Woodsmith Foundation Ltd
The Worshipful Company of Glovers of London Charitable Trust
Worshipful Company of Gold and Silver Wyre Drawers Second Charitable Trust Fund
The Worshipful Company of Information Technologists
Worshipful Company of Needlemakers Charitable Fund
Worth Waynflete Foundation
Youth Endowment Fund (YEF)*
Youth Music
Zurich Community Trust (UK) Ltd

Social enterprises

The 29th May 1961 Charitable Trust
The A. and J. Charitable Trust
The Aberdeen Endowments Trust
ABF The Soldiers' Charity
abrdn Financial Fairness Trust
Age Scotland
AKO Foundation
Al Madad Foundation*
Anguish's Educational Foundation
The Apax Foundation
The Armourers and Brasiers Gauntlet Trust
The Art Fund
Arts Council England
Arts Council of Wales (also known as Cyngor Celfyddydau Cymru)
The Asfari Foundation
The Roy and Pixie Baker Charitable Trust
Bally's Foundation
The Bamford Charitable Foundation
The Barbour Foundation
Lord Barnby's Foundation
The Barnes Fund
The Max Barney Foundation
Barnwood Trust
Misses Barrie Charitable Trust
Robert Barr's Charitable Trust
The Gordon and Ena Baxter Foundation*
BBC Children in Need
Bedfordshire and Luton Community Foundation
Benesco Charity Ltd
Berkshire Community Foundation
The Bernicia Foundation
Biffa Award
The Percy Bilton Charity
The Bingham Trust
The Birmingham Diocesan Board of Finance
The Blagrave Trust
Bluespark Foundation
BOOST Charitable Trust
Boots Charitable Trust
The Harold and Alice Bridges Charity
The Jack Brunton Charitable Trust
Buckinghamshire Community Foundation
The Bulldog Trust Ltd
E. F. Bulmer Trust
Bupa Foundation
Consolidated Charity of Burton upon Trent
Community Foundation for Calderdale

Cambridgeshire Community
Foundation
Camden Giving
Card Factory Foundation
CareTech Charitable
Foundation
Cheshire Community
Foundation Ltd
Church Urban Fund
The City Bridge Trust (Bridge
House Estates)
CLA Charitable Trust
The Clothworkers' Foundation
The Coalfields Regeneration
Trust
The Cobalt Trust
The Cobtree Charity Trust Ltd
Colchester Catalyst Charity
John and Freda Coleman
Charitable Trust
Comic Relief
The Comino Foundation
Community First
The Catherine Cookson
Charitable Trust
Co-op Foundation
The Evan Cornish Foundation
Cornwall Community
Foundation
Corra Foundation
County Durham Community
Foundation
Cripplegate Foundation
Crisis UK
Cumbria Community
Foundation
Baron Davenport's Charity
Foundation Derbyshire
Devon Community Foundation
Digital Extra Fund
Dorset Community Foundation
The Duke of Cornwall's
Benevolent Fund
The Dunhill Medical Trust
Dunlossit and Islay Community
Trust
East End Community
Foundation
Eastern Counties Educational
Trust Ltd
The Elmley Foundation
The Enkalon Foundation
Essex Community Foundation
The Evelyn Trust
Esmée Fairbairn Foundation
The Finnis Scott Foundation
Fishmongers' Company's
Charitable Trust
The Follett Trust
The Football Foundation
The Forbes Charitable
Foundation
Forever Manchester
The Forman Hardy Charitable
Trust

The Freshgate Trust
Foundation
Friends Provident Charitable
Foundation
The Funding Network
Gatwick Airport Community
Trust
The F. Glenister Woodger Trust
CIO
Gloucestershire Community
Foundation
Sydney and Phyllis Goldberg
Memorial Charitable Trust
Matthew Good Foundation*
The Grace Trust
The Granada Foundation
The Green Room Charitable
Trust
The Greggs Foundation
Groundwork UK
Calouste Gulbenkian
Foundation – UK Branch
The Hadfield Charitable Trust
The Hadrian Trust
Halifax Foundation for
Northern Ireland
The Hamilton Davies Trust
Hampshire and Isle of Wight
Community Foundation
Hampton Fund
The Happold Foundation
Harbinson Charitable Trust
Harborne Parish Lands Charity
William Harding's Charity
The Harpur Trust
Edward Harvist Trust (The
Harvist Estate)
Heart of England Community
Foundation
Heart Research UK
Heathrow Community Trust
Herefordshire Community
Foundation
Heritage Lottery Fund
The Heritage of London Trust
Ltd
Hertfordshire Community
Foundation
Highway One Trust
The Hilden Charitable Fund
Historic Environment Scotland
The Holywood Trust
The Hospital of God at
Greatham
Housing Pathways Trust
The Hunter Foundation
Hyde Charitable Trust
Ibrahim Foundation Ltd
Imagine Foundation
Impact Funding Partners Ltd
Impetus
The Innocent Foundation
The Isla Foundation
Isle of Wight Foundation
John James Bristol Foundation

The Kensington and Chelsea
Foundation
Kent Community Foundation
King/Cullimore Charitable
Trust
The Mary Kinross Charitable
Trust
Sir James Knott Trust
Kusuma Trust UK
Community Foundations for
Lancashire and Merseyside
Lancashire Environmental
Fund Ltd
Lancaster Foundation
The Allen Lane Foundation
The LankellyChase Foundation
Leeds Community Foundation
The Legal Education
Foundation
Lincolnshire Community
Foundation
The Frank Litchfield Charitable
Trust
The W. M. and B. W. Lloyd
Trust
Lloyd's of London Foundation
The London Community
Foundation (LCF)
The London Marathon
Charitable Trust Ltd
Making a Difference Locally
Ltd
R. W. Mann Trust
Mathew Trust
Maudsley Charity
MBNA General Foundation
The Mercers Charitable
Foundation
The Millennium Oak Trust
Millennium Stadium Charitable
Trust (Ymddiriedolaeth
Elusennol Stadiwm y
Mileniwm)
The Monmouthshire County
Council Welsh Church Act
Fund
Moondance Foundation
John Moores Foundation
The Steve Morgan Foundation
The MSE Charity
The Frederick Mulder
Foundation
The John R. Murray Charitable
Trust
The National Express
Foundation
The National Hockey
Foundation
The National Lottery
Community Fund
The Nationwide Foundation
Near Neighbours
Nesta
Network for Social Change
Charitable Trust
Newcomen Collett Foundation

The NFU Mutual Charitable
  Trust
The Nineveh Charitable Trust
The Nisbet Trust
Norfolk Community Foundation
The Norman Family Charitable
  Trust
Northamptonshire Community
  Foundation
Norwich Town Close Estate
  Charity
Nottinghamshire Community
  Foundation
Orthopaedic Research UK
Ovingdean Hall Foundation
Oxfordshire Community
  Foundation
The Pears Family Charitable
  Foundation
People's Health Trust
People's Postcode Trust
Pilkington Charities Fund
Pink Ribbon Foundation
Polden-Puckham Charitable
  Foundation
Postcode Community Trust
Postcode Local Trust
Postcode Society Trust
The Mary Potter Convent
  Hospital Trust
The Prince's Countryside Fund
The PwC Foundation
Quartet Community Foundation
The Eleanor Rathbone
  Charitable Trust
The Sigrid Rausing Trust
The Reece Foundation
Richard Reeve's Foundation
Richmond Parish Lands Charity
The Roddick Foundation
Rosca Trust
The Joseph Rowntree
  Charitable Trust
The Joseph Rowntree
  Foundation
Royal Docks Trust (London)
Russell Trust
The RWS Foundation
Santander UK Foundation Ltd
The Savoy Educational Trust
Foundation Scotland
Francis C. Scott Charitable
  Trust
The Cyril Shack Trust
The Sheffield Town Trust
The John Slater Foundation
Smallwood Trust
The Henry Smith Charity
Social Investment Business
  Foundation
Societe Generale UK
  Foundation
Sodexo Stop Hunger
  Foundation
Somerset Community
  Foundation

South Yorkshire Community
  Foundation
Spurrell Charitable Trust
The St Hilda's Trust
Sir Walter St John's
  Educational Charity
The Community Foundation for
  Staffordshire
The Stone Family Foundation
Stratford-upon-Avon Town Trust
The W. O. Street Charitable
  Foundation
Streetsmart – Action for the
  Homeless
Suffolk Community Foundation
The Summerfield Charitable
  Trust
Surgo Foundation UK Ltd
Community Foundation for
  Surrey
The Sussex Community
  Foundation
The William Syson Foundation
Tallow Chandlers Benevolent
  Fund No 2
Tees Valley Community
  Foundation
The Theatres Trust Charitable
  Fund
The Thirty Percy Foundation
Tower Hill Trust
The Triangle Trust (1949) Fund
Trust for London
The Trusthouse Charitable
  Foundation
The Tudor Trust
The Tuixen Foundation
Two Ridings Community
  Foundation
Community Foundation serving
  Tyne and Wear and
  Northumberland
Ufi VocTech Trust
The UK Youth Fund: Thriving
  Minds*
The Ulverscroft Foundation
United St Saviour's Charity
UnLtd (Foundation for Social
  Entrepreneurs)
UPP Foundation
The Vardy Foundation
The Veolia Environmental Trust
VINCI UK Foundation
The Virgin Foundation (Virgin
  Unite)
The Virgin Money Foundation
Vision Foundation
The Vodafone Foundation
The Scurrah Wainwright Charity
The Bruce Wake Charity
The Walcot Foundation
The Community Foundation in
  Wales
Walton-on-Thames Charity
The Warwickshire Masonic
  Charitable Association Ltd

The Waterloo Foundation
Wates Family Enterprise Trust
The Wates Foundation
The William Wates Memorial
  Trust
The Geoffrey Watling Charity
Wembley National Stadium
  Trust
The Garfield Weston
  Foundation
Westway Trust
The Wilmcote Charitrust
The Wood Foundation
Wooden Spoon Society
Woodsmith Foundation Ltd
The Woodward Charitable
  Trust
Worshipful Company of Gold
  and Silver Wyre Drawers
  Second Charitable Trust
  Fund
Worshipful Company of
  Needlemakers Charitable
  Fund
Youth Music
Zurich Community Trust (UK)
  Ltd

Statutory authorities

The A. and J. Charitable Trust
Age Scotland
The Almond Trust
The Architectural Heritage
  Fund
The Birmingham Diocesan
  Board of Finance
The Booth Charities
T. B. H. Brunner's Charitable
  Settlement
Buckingham Trust
Buckinghamshire Community
  Foundation
Cambridgeshire Community
  Foundation
William A. Cargill Charitable
  Trust
The Catherine Cookson
  Charitable Trust
Crisis UK
The Davis Foundation
Dumfriesshire East Community
  Benefit Group SCIO
Edinburgh Children's Holiday
  Fund
The Enkalon Foundation
The Eveson Charitable Trust
The Follett Trust
The Football Foundation
The Forman Hardy Charitable
  Trust
The Joseph Strong Frazer Trust
Friends Provident Charitable
  Foundation
The F. Glenister Woodger Trust
  CIO
GrantScape
The Hamilton Davies Trust
Heritage Lottery Fund
The Heritage of London Trust
  Ltd
Historic Environment Scotland
Historic Houses Foundation
The Henry C. Hoare Charitable
  Trust
The Hunter Foundation
The Iliffe Family Charitable
  Trust
Inner London Magistrates
  Court Poor Box and Feeder
  Charity
The Isle of Anglesey Charitable
  Association (Cymdeithas
  Elusennol Ynys Môn)
The King Henry VIII Endowed
  Trust – Warwick
The Law Society Charity
Limoges Charitable Trust
The London Marathon
  Charitable Trust Ltd
The C. L. Loyd Charitable Trust
John Lyon's Charity
The Dan Maskell Tennis Trust

Mathew Trust
Maudsley Charity
The Medlock Charitable Trust
The National Hockey
  Foundation
The National Lottery
  Community Fund
The National Manuscripts
  Conservation Trust
Norfolk Community Foundation
Normanby Charitable Trust
Northamptonshire Community
  Foundation
Norwich Town Close Estate
  Charity
Orthopaedic Research UK
The Mary Potter Convent
  Hospital Trust
Richard Reeve's Foundation
Foundation Scotland
The Bassil Shippam and
  Alsford Trust
Swarovski Foundation
The Talbot Trusts
Tanner Trust
Nigel Vinson Charitable Trust
War Memorials Trust
Wembley National Stadium
  Trust
Worshipful Company of
  Needlemakers Charitable
  Fund
Yorkshire Cancer Research
Youth Endowment Fund (YEF)*

Uniformed groups

The Band Trust
Misses Barrie Charitable Trust
The Louis Baylis (Maidenhead
  Advertiser) Charitable Trust
Bideford Bridge Trust
The Marjory Boddy Charitable
  Trust
The Harold and Alice Bridges
  Charity
T. B. H. Brunner's Charitable
  Settlement
The Jack Brunton Charitable
  Trust
Carew Pole Charitable Trust
The Leslie Mary Carter
  Charitable Trust
Church Burgesses Trust
The Catherine Cookson
  Charitable Trust
Cornwall Community
  Foundation
The Corporation of Trinity
  House of Deptford Strond
The Roger De Haan Charitable
  Trust
The Dibden Allotments Fund
Duchy of Lancaster Benevolent
  Fund
Dumfriesshire East Community
  Benefit Group SCIO
Essex Community Foundation
Sir John Fisher Foundation
The Gibbons Family Trust
The Gosling Foundation Ltd
Dr Guthrie's Association
Hampshire and Isle of Wight
  Community Foundation
Edward Harvist Trust (The
  Harvist Estate)
Heathrow Community Trust
The Lady Hind Trust
The Hudson Foundation
Sir James Knott Trust
Lancashire Environmental
  Fund Ltd
The R. J. Larg Family Trust
Mrs F. B. Laurence Charitable
  Trust
Limoges Charitable Trust
Lincolnshire Community
  Foundation
The London Marathon
  Charitable Trust Ltd
The MacRobert Trust 2019
The Magdalen and Lasher
  Charity (General Fund)
Manchester Airport Community
  Trust Fund
The Manchester Guardian
  Society Charitable Trust
The W. M. Mann Foundation
R. W. Mann Trust
MBNA General Foundation
Milton Keynes Community
  Foundation Ltd

Mobbs Memorial Trust Ltd
Moondance Foundation
Moto Foundation
The Nine Incorporated Trades
of Dundee General Fund
Charity
Norfolk Community Foundation
Normanby Charitable Trust
The Notgrove Trust
The Patrick Trust
Susanna Peake Charitable
Trust
The Persimmon Charitable
Foundation
Miss A. M. Pilkington's
Charitable Trust
The Sir James Reckitt Charity
Rigby Foundation
The Rowlands Trust
The Royal Foundation of The
Prince and Princess of
Wales
The Rugby Group Benevolent
Fund Ltd
Foundation Scotland
The Frieda Scott Charitable
Trust
Leslie Sell Charitable Trust
Shaftoe Educational
Foundation
The Shanly Foundation
The Sheffield Town Trust
The Sheldon Trust
The Patricia and Donald
Shepherd Charitable Trust
The Skelton Bounty
The Henry Smith Charity
The R. C. Snelling Charitable
Trust
South Yorkshire Community
Foundation
Spielman Charitable Trust
St Olave's and St Saviour's
Schools Foundation CIO*
Community Foundation for
Surrey
The Charles and Elsie Sykes
Trust
The Talbot Village Trust
The Tudwick Foundation
Two Ridings Community
Foundation
Variety, the Children's Charity
The Veolia Environmental Trust
Wembley National Stadium
Trust
West Derby Waste Lands
Charity
West Herts Charity Trust Ltd
WHSmith Trust
Wiltshire Community
Foundation
Woodsmith Foundation Ltd

Worshipful Company of Gold
and Silver Wyre Drawers
Second Charitable Trust
Fund
The Yapp Charitable Trust

Universities

The 29th May 1961 Charitable
Trust
The 3Ts Charitable Trust
The A. and J. Charitable Trust
The Abbeyfield Research
Foundation
The Aberdeenshire Educational
Trust Scheme
abrdn Financial Fairness Trust
Action Medical Research
The AIM Foundation
The Alborada Trust
Alliance Family Foundation Ltd
Alzheimer's Research UK
Alzheimer's Society
The AMW Charitable Trust
Anglo American Foundation
The Annabel Arbib Foundation
Arcadia Fund
The Ardeola Charitable Trust
The Ardwick Trust
The John Armitage Charitable
Trust
The Armourers and Brasiers
Gauntlet Trust
The Art Fund
The Ove Arup Foundation
The Asfari Foundation
The Associated Board of the
Royal Schools of Music
(ABRSM)
Asthma and Lung UK
The Astor Foundation
Atkin Charitable Foundation
The Atlas Fund
The Aurelius Charitable Trust
The Aziz Foundation
The Baird Trust
The Kamini and Vindi Banga
Family Trust
The Barbers' Company General
Charities
The Baring Foundation
Philip Barker Charity
Misses Barrie Charitable Trust
Robert Barr's Charitable Trust
BC Partners Foundation
The Bellahouston Bequest
Fund
The Lord Belstead Charitable
Settlement*
Benefact Trust Ltd
Benesco Charity Ltd
The Bestway Foundation
Binks Trust
The Birmingham Diocesan
Board of Finance
The John Black Charitable
Foundation
Blakemore Foundation
The Sir Victor Blank Charitable
Settlement
Bloodwise
Abraham Algy Bloom
Foundation

The Bluston Charitable
Settlement
The Boltini Trust
The Salo Bordon Charitable
Trust
Sir William Boreman's
Foundation
The Borrows Charitable Trust
The Boshier-Hinton Foundation
The Harry Bottom Charitable
Trust
The P. G. and N. J. Boulton
Trust
The Tony Bramall Charitable
Trust
The Liz and Terry Bramall
Foundation
Breast Cancer Now
The Harold and Alice Bridges
Charity
Bright Red Charity
The British Academy
The British and Foreign Bible
Society
British Eye Research
Foundation (Fight for Sight)
British Heart Foundation (BHF)
The Rory and Elizabeth Brooks
Foundation
Building and Civil Engineering
Charitable Trust
E. F. Bulmer Trust
The Burdett Trust for Nursing
The G. W. Cadbury Charitable
Trust
The Barrow Cadbury Trust
The Calleva Foundation
Cancer Research UK
Cannon Charitable Trust
CareTech Charitable
Foundation
William A. Cargill Charitable
Trust
W. A. Cargill Fund
The Carnegie Trust for the
Universities of Scotland
The Carpenters Company
Charitable Trust
Chapman Charitable Trust
Chartered Accountants' Livery
Charity (CALC)
The Lorna and Yuti
Chernajovsky Biomedical
Research Foundation
Children with Cancer UK
The Roger and Sarah Bancroft
Clark Charitable Trust
The Clore Duffield Foundation
Denise Coates Foundation
The Vivienne and Samuel
Cohen Charitable Trust
The John S. Cohen Foundation
Colchester Catalyst Charity
The Colt Foundation
The Comino Foundation

Marjorie Coote Animal Charity
Trust
The Costa Family Charitable
Trust
Dudley and Geoffrey Cox
Charitable Trust
The Elizabeth Creak Charitable
Trust
CRH Charitable Trust
Cullum Family Trust
The Cunningham Trust
The D. M. Charitable Trust
The Daiwa Anglo-Japanese
Foundation
Michael Davies Charitable
Settlement
Margaret Davies Charity
The Davis Foundation
The De Laszlo Foundation
William Delafield Charitable
Trust
Diabetes UK
The Alan and Sheila Diamond
Charitable Trust
Digital Extra Fund
Dinwoodie Charitable Company
The Dischma Charitable Trust
The Djanogly Foundation
The Dorfman Foundation
The Double 'O' Charity Ltd
Drapers Charitable Fund
Duchy of Lancaster Benevolent
Fund
The Dunhill Medical Trust
The Mildred Duveen Charitable
Trust
The Dyers' Company
Charitable Trust
The James Dyson Foundation
Eastern Counties Educational
Trust Ltd
The Gilbert and Eileen Edgar
Foundation
The Elmley Foundation
Entindale Ltd
Epilepsy Research UK
The Evelyn Trust
The Eveson Charitable Trust
The Exilarch's Foundation
The Lord Faringdon Charitable
Trust
The Thomas Farr Charity
Allan and Nesta Ferguson
Charitable Settlement
The Fidelio Charitable Trust
Doris Field Charitable Trust
The Finnis Scott Foundation
Sir John Fisher Foundation
Marc Fitch Fund
The Mrs Yvonne Flux
Charitable Trust
The Football Foundation
The Forman Hardy Charitable
Trust
The Fort Foundation
The Lord Forte Foundation

The Foyle Foundation
The Hugh Fraser Foundation
The Joseph Strong Frazer Trust
The Freelands Foundation Ltd
The Freshgate Trust
Foundation
Friends of the National
Libraries
Friends Provident Charitable
Foundation
The Funding Network
GambleAware
The Gatsby Charitable
Foundation
The Robert Gavron Charitable
Trust
The General Nursing Council
for England and Wales
Trust
J. Paul Getty Jr General
Charitable Trust*
The F. Glenister Woodger Trust
CIO
The Golden Bottle Trust
The Goldman Sachs Charitable
Gift Fund (UK)
Goldman Sachs Gives (UK)
The Goldsmiths' Company
Charity
The Golsoncott Foundation
Nicholas and Judith
Goodison's Charitable
Settlement
The Mike Gooley Trailfinders
Charity
Gowling WLG (UK) Charitable
Trust
The Grace Trust
The Great Britain Sasakawa
Foundation
Philip and Judith Green Trust
The Grimmitt Trust
The Grocers' Charity
Calouste Gulbenkian
Foundation – UK Branch
The Guy Foundation
The Hadfield Charitable Trust
Hamamelis Trust
The Hamilton Davies Trust
The Helen Hamlyn Trust
The Lennox Hannay Charitable
Trust
The Happold Foundation
The Harbour Foundation
The Harpur Trust
The Peter Harrison Foundation
The Maurice Hatter Foundation
The Health Foundation
Heart Research UK
The Michael Heller Charitable
Foundation
Help for Health
The Helping Foundation
Heritage Lottery Fund
The Heritage of London Trust
Ltd

The Lady Hind Trust
The Hinduja Foundation
The Hintze Family Charity
 Foundation
Historic Houses Foundation
The Hobson Charity Ltd
The Jane Hodge Foundation
The Holbeck Charitable Trust
P. H. Holt Foundation
Sir Harold Hood's Charitable
 Trust
Hope Trust
The Horse Trust
The Sir Joseph Hotung
 Charitable Settlement
Housing Pathways Trust
The Keith Howard Foundation
The Humanitarian Trust
The Hunter Foundation
The Huntingdon Foundation
 Ltd
The Harold Hyam Wingate
 Foundation
Hyde Park Place Estate Charity
Ibrahim Foundation Ltd
The Inman Charity
The Innocent Foundation
The Institute for Policy
 Research
The International Bankers
 Charitable Trust
The Ireland Fund of Great
 Britain
Irish Youth Foundation (UK)
 Ltd (incorporating The
 Lawlor Foundation)
The ITF Seafarers Trust
The Jabbs Foundation
The Frank Jackson Foundation
John James Bristol Foundation
The Susan and Stephen
 James Charitable
 Settlement
Lady Eda Jardine Charitable
 Trust
The Jerusalem Trust
The Elton John AIDS
 Foundation
The Jusaca Charitable Trust
The Ian Karten Charitable
 Trust
C. S. Kaufman Charitable
 Trust
The Kennedy Trust for
 Rheumatology Research
The Kennel Club Charitable
 Trust
Kidney Research UK
The Kilroot Foundation
The Mary Kinross Charitable
 Trust
Robert Kitchin (Saddlers' Co.)
Sir James Knott Trust
Kollel and Co. Ltd
The KPMG Foundation
Kusuma Trust UK

The Kirby Laing Foundation
The Martin Laing Foundation
The R. J. Larg Family Trust
The Lauffer Family Charitable
 Foundation
The Law Family Charitable
 Foundation
The Law Society Charity
The Edgar E. Lawley
 Foundation
The Lawson Trust CIO
The Leathersellers' Foundation
The Leche Trust
The William Leech Charity
The Legal Education
 Foundation
Leicestershire and Rutland
 Masonic Charity
 Association
Leng Charitable Trust
The Leverhulme Trust
Cecil and Hilda Lewis
 Charitable Trust
David and Ruth Lewis Family
 Charitable Trust
Limoges Charitable Trust
The Linbury Trust
The Linder Foundation
The Charles Littlewood Hill
 Trust
The Second Joseph Aaron
 Littman Foundation
The W. M. and B. W. Lloyd
 Trust
Lloyd's Register Foundation
Lord and Lady Lurgan Trust
Sir Jack Lyons Charitable Trust
The R. S. Macdonald
 Charitable Trust
The MacRobert Trust 2019
The Mactaggart Third Fund
The Ian Mactaggart Trust
The Magen Charitable Trust
The Mallinckrodt Foundation
The W. M. Mann Foundation
R. W. Mann Trust
Marbeh Torah Trust
The Marchig Animal Welfare
 Trust
The Michael Marks Charitable
 Trust
The Michael Marsh Charitable
 Trust
Sir George Martin Trust
Masonic Charitable Foundation
Nancie Massey Charitable
 Trust
The Master Charitable Trust
Mathew Trust
Maudsley Charity
Mayfair Charities Ltd
D. D. McPhail Charitable
 Settlement
Medical Research Foundation
Medical Research Scotland
The Medlock Charitable Trust

Melodor Ltd
The Mercers Charitable
 Foundation
The Merchant Venturers
 Charity
Merchants House of Glasgow
The Mickel Fund
The Mikheev Charitable Trust
The Millfield House Foundation
 (1)
The Millichope Foundation
Mills and Reeve Charitable
 Trust
The Millward Charitable Trust
The Esmé Mitchell Trust
The Mittal Foundation
Mole Charitable Trust
The Henry Moore Foundation
G. M. Morrison Charitable
 Trust
The Moshal Charitable Trust
The Alexander Mosley
 Charitable Trust
Motor Neurone Disease
 Association
J. P. Moulton Charitable
 Foundation
Multiple Sclerosis Society
Edith Murphy Foundation
The John R. Murray Charitable
 Trust
The National Express
 Foundation
The National Hockey
 Foundation
The National Manuscripts
 Conservation Trust
The Nationwide Foundation
Near Neighbours
Ner Foundation
Nesta
The Frances and Augustus
 Newman Foundation
The NFU Mutual Charitable
 Trust
The Nine Incorporated Trades
 of Dundee General Fund
 Charity
The Nineveh Charitable Trust
The Norman Family Charitable
 Trust
Normanby Charitable Trust
North West Cancer Research
Northern Pharmacies Ltd Trust
 Fund
Northwood Charitable Trust
The Nuffield Foundation
Orange Tree Trust
Orthopaedic Research UK
The O'Sullivan Family
 Charitable Trust
The Panacea Charitable Trust
Parabola Foundation
Parkinson's UK
The J. G. W. Patterson
 Foundation

David Pearlman Charitable Foundation

The Pears Family Charitable Foundation

The Dowager Countess Eleanor Peel Trust

Petplan Charitable Trust

The Pharsalia Charitable Trust

The Pilgrim Trust

Thomas Pocklington Trust

The Polonsky Foundation

The Portal Trust

The Mary Potter Convent Hospital Trust

David and Elaine Potter Foundation

Prostate Cancer UK

Mr and Mrs J. A. Pye's Charitable Settlement

Queen Mary's Roehampton Trust

The Racing Foundation

Randeree Charitable Trust

The Sir James Reckitt Charity

The Reece Foundation

Rees Jeffreys Road Fund

The Resolution Trust

Reuben Foundation

The Rix-Thompson-Rothenberg Foundation

RNID (The Royal National Institute for Deaf People)

The Roan Charitable Trust

The Dezna Robins Jones Charitable Foundation

Rockcliffe Charitable Trust

The Gerald and Gail Ronson Family Foundation

The Rose Foundation

The Cecil Rosen Foundation

Rosetrees

The Rothermere Foundation

The Rothschild Foundation

The Eranda Rothschild Foundation

Rothschild Foundation (Hanadiv) Europe

The Row Fogo Charitable Trust

The Rowlands Trust

The Joseph Rowntree Charitable Trust

The Joseph Rowntree Foundation

The Royal Foundation of The Prince and Princess of Wales

The Rubin Foundation Charitable Trust

The Ruddock Foundation for the Arts

Russell Trust

The Dr Mortimer and Theresa Sackler Foundation

The Sackler Trust

The Saintbury Trust

The Basil Samuel Charitable Trust

Sarum St Michael Educational Charity

The Savoy Educational Trust

Sir Samuel Scott of Yews Trust

ScottishPower Foundation

The Sam and Bella Sebba Charitable Foundation

The Jean Shanks Foundation

The Sheepdrove Trust

The Sheffield Town Trust

The Sylvia and Colin Shepherd Charitable Trust

SHINE (Support and Help in Education)

The Shipwrights Charitable Fund

The Sino-British Fellowship Trust

The Charles Skey Charitable Trust

The John Slater Foundation

Sloane Robinson Foundation

Stanley Smith UK Horticultural Trust

Peter Sowerby Foundation

The Spear Charitable Trust

Michael and Sarah Spencer Foundation

St Peter's Saltley Trust

Stanley Foundation Ltd

Staples Trust

The Steel Charitable Trust

The Sir Sigmund Sternberg Charitable Foundation

The Stevenson Family's Charitable Trust

Sir Halley Stewart Trust

Stolkin Foundation

The Stoneygate Trust

The Samuel Storey Family Charitable Trust

Peter Stormonth Darling Charitable Trust

The Summerfield Charitable Trust

Surgo Foundation UK Ltd

The Swann-Morton Foundation

The John Swire (1989) Charitable Trust

The Adrian Swire Charitable Trust

The Charles and Elsie Sykes Trust

The Talbot Village Trust

Tallow Chandlers Benevolent Fund No 2

Tay Charitable Trust

C. B. and H. H. T. Taylor 1984 Trust

Humphrey Richardson Taylor Charitable Trust

Stephen Taylor Foundation

The Tedworth Charitable Trust

Tenovus Scotland

The Thirty Percy Foundation

The Thompson Family Charitable Trust

Sir Jules Thorn Charitable Trust

The Thriplow Charitable Trust

The Tolkien Trust

The James Tudor Foundation

The Tuixen Foundation

Ufi VocTech Trust

UJIA (United Jewish Israel Appeal)

Ulster Garden Villages Ltd

Ulting Overseas Trust

The Ulverscroft Foundation

UPP Foundation

The Valentine Charitable Trust

The Vandervell Foundation

Versus Arthritis

Nigel Vinson Charitable Trust

The VTCT Foundation

Walton Foundation

The Waterloo Foundation

Wates Family Enterprise Trust

The Linda and Michael Weinstein Charitable Trust

Wellbeing of Women

The Wellcome Trust

The Galen and Hilary Weston Foundation

The Garfield Weston Foundation

The Which? Fund

WHSmith Trust

W. Wing Yip and Brothers Foundation

The Maurice Wohl Charitable Foundation

The Charles Wolfson Charitable Trust

The Wolfson Family Charitable Trust

The Wolfson Foundation

The Lord Leonard and Lady Estelle Wolfson Foundation

The Wood Foundation

Woodroffe Benton Foundation

The Worshipful Company of Glovers of London Charitable Trust

Worshipful Company of Gold and Silver Wyre Drawers Second Charitable Trust Fund

The Worshipful Company of Information Technologists

Worshipful Company of Needlemakers Charitable Fund

Yorkshire Cancer Research

Youth Endowment Fund (YEF)*

The Marjorie and Arnold Ziff Charitable Foundation

Zurich Community Trust (UK) Ltd

Grant-makers by type of grant

This index contains the following:

List of types of grant: This lists the headings used in DGMT to categorise types of grant.

Grant-makers by type of grant: Funders listed under the types of grant for which they have expressed a funding preference. Asterisks mark funders which have not featured in DGMT before.

Grant-makers by type of grant

Campaigning

abrdn Financial Fairness Trust
Achisomoch Aid Company Ltd
The AIM Foundation
Friends Provident Charitable
    Foundation
The Olwyn Foundation
The Seven Fifty Trust
Trust for London

Capacity-building

ArtSocial Foundation
The Berkeley Foundation
The Childhood Trust
Children with Cancer UK
The Dunhill Medical Trust
Friends Provident Charitable
    Foundation
The Jerusalem Trust
The Kiawah Charitable Trust
The Graham Kirkham
    Foundation
The Kirby Laing Foundation
John Lyon's Charity
John Moores Foundation
Norwich Town Close Estate
    Charity
The Robertson Trust
The Royal British Legion
The Sam and Bella Sebba
    Charitable Foundation
The Theatres Trust Charitable
    Fund
The VTCT Foundation
Walton-on-Thames Charity
Westhill Endowment
The Eric Wright Charitable
    Trust

Capital costs

The 29th May 1961 Charitable
    Trust
The Aberdeenshire Educational
    Trust Scheme
Achisomoch Aid Company Ltd
The Bryan Adams Foundation
The Adint Charitable Trust
Age Scotland
Alan Boswell Group Charitable
    Trust
Al-Fayed Charitable Foundation
D. C. R. Allen Charitable Trust
Alpkit Foundation
Amabrill Ltd
The Ammco Trust
The Anchor Foundation
Anguish's Educational
    Foundation
The Anson Charitable Trust
The John Apthorp Charity
Arts Council of Wales (also
    known as Cyngor
    Celfyddydau Cymru)
The Ashley Family Foundation
Atlas Memorial Ltd
Backstage Trust
The Baily Thomas Charitable
    Fund
The Baird Trust
Bairdwatson Charitable Trust
The Rachel Baker Memorial
    Charity
The Ballinger Charitable Trust
Banbury Charities
The Banister Charitable Trust
Bank of Scotland Foundation
The Barbers' Company General
    Charities
Barchester Healthcare
    Foundation
The Barnes Fund
Barnwood Trust
Robert Barr's Charitable Trust
The Paul Bassham Charitable
    Trust
Bauer Radio's Cash for Kids
    Charities
The Gordon and Ena Baxter
    Foundation*
BBC Children in Need
BC Partners Foundation
The James Beattie Charitable
    Trust
The Beaverbrook Foundation
Beccles Townlands Charity
The Bedfordshire and
    Hertfordshire Historic
    Churches Trust
The Bellahouston Bequest
    Fund
The Lord Belstead Charitable
    Settlement*
Benefact Trust Ltd
Benesco Charity Ltd

Berkshire Community Foundation

Biffa Award

The Percy Bilton Charity

The Bingham Trust

Birkdale Trust for Hearing Impaired Ltd*

The Michael Bishop Foundation

The John Black Charitable Foundation

Blakemore Foundation

Bloodwise

Bluespark Foundation

The Bluston Charitable Settlement

BNA Charitable Incorporated Organisation

The Marjory Boddy Charitable Trust

BOOST Charitable Trust

The Booth Charities

Boots Charitable Trust

The Boshier-Hinton Foundation

The Bosson Family Charitable Trust

The Harry Bottom Charitable Trust

The Harold and Alice Bridges Charity

Bristol Charities

The British and Foreign Bible Society

The British and Foreign School Society (BFSS)

British Eye Research Foundation (Fight for Sight)

British Gas Energy Trust

British Heart Foundation (BHF)

British Motor Sports Training Trust

The Broomton Foundation

The Mary Brown Memorial Trust

The Jack Brunton Charitable Trust

Buckinghamshire Community Foundation

The Buffini Chao Foundation

E. F. Bulmer Trust

Consolidated Charity of Burton upon Trent

Community Foundation for Calderdale

Cambridgeshire Community Foundation

The Frederick and Phyllis Cann Trust

Card Factory Foundation

The Leslie Mary Carter Charitable Trust

The Joseph and Annie Cattle Trust

The Wilfrid and Constance Cave Foundation

Elizabeth Cayzer Charitable Trust

CEO Sleepout

The Chadwick Educational Foundation

Chalfords Ltd

The Chalk Cliff Trust

The Chetwode Foundation

The Childwick Trust

Chippenham Borough Lands Charity

Chrysalis Trust

Church Burgesses Educational Foundation

Church Burgesses Trust

Church of Ireland Priorities Fund

The City Bridge Trust (Bridge House Estates)

CLA Charitable Trust

The Clothworkers' Foundation

Cloudesley

The Robert Clutterbuck Charitable Trust

The Francis Coales Charitable Foundation

The John Coates Charitable Trust

Denise Coates Foundation

Colchester Catalyst Charity

The Cole Charitable Trust

Community First

Congregational and General Charitable Trust

The Cooks Charity

The Catherine Cookson Charitable Trust

The Helen Jean Cope Charity

The Corporation of Trinity House of Deptford Strond

The County Council of Dyfed Welsh Church Fund

County Durham Community Foundation

The Sir Tom Cowie Charitable Trust

The Lord Cozens-Hardy Trust

CRASH

The Crerar Trust

Cruden Foundation Ltd

Cullum Family Trust

Cumbria Community Foundation

The Daniell Trust

Baron Davenport's Charity

The Manny and Brigitta Davidson Charitable Foundation

The Davidson Family Charitable Trust

Margaret Davies Charity

The Roger De Haan Charitable Trust

The De Laszlo Foundation

The Miriam Dean Refugee Trust Fund

Foundation Derbyshire

Diabetes UK

The Gillian Dickinson Trust

Dorset Community Foundation

Duchy Health Charity Ltd

The Dulverton Trust

Dunard Fund

The Dunhill Medical Trust

The Earley Charity

Dr Edwards and Bishop King's Fulham Charity

W. G. Edwards Charitable Foundation

The Elmley Foundation

EMI Music Sound Foundation

England and Wales Cricket Trust

The Englefield Charitable Trust

The Enkalon Foundation

The Essex and Southend Sports Trust

Essex Community Foundation

The Essex Youth Trust

The Evelyn Trust

The Eventhall Family Charitable Trust

The Eveson Charitable Trust

Samuel William Farmer Trust

The February Foundation

The Feoffees of St Michael's Spurriergate York

The Fidelity UK Foundation

Field Family Charitable Trust

Fine & Country Foundation

The Finnis Scott Foundation

Sir John Fisher Foundation

The Joyce Fletcher Charitable Trust

The Football Association National Sports Centre

The Football Foundation

The Forbes Charitable Foundation

Ford Britain Trust

Oliver Ford Foundation

The Forrester Family Trust

Ian M. Foulerton Charitable Trust

Fowler Smith and Jones Trust

The Foyle Foundation

Mrs D. M. France-Hayhurst Foundation

The Gordon Fraser Charitable Trust

The Hugh Fraser Foundation

Anne French Memorial Trust

The Freshgate Trust Foundation

Friarsgate Trust

The Friends of Kent Churches

G. M. C. Trust

The Gannochy Trust

Ganzoni Charitable Trust

Gatwick Airport Community Trust

General Charity (Coventry)

The Generations Foundation

J. Paul Getty Jr General Charitable Trust*

The Gibbons Family Trust

The Gibbs Charitable Trusts

The G. C. Gibson Charitable Trust

The F. Glenister Woodger Trust CIO

Global Charities

The Gloucestershire Historic Churches Trust

The Godinton Charitable Trust

Nicholas and Judith Goodison's Charitable Settlement

The Gosling Foundation Ltd

Grace Baptist Trust Corporation*

Grace Charitable Trust

The Granada Foundation

The Grantham Yorke Trust

GrantScape

The J. G. Graves Charitable Trust

The Great Stone Bridge Trust of Edenbridge

The Green Hall Foundation

Groundwork UK

The Hadfield Charitable Trust

The Hadley Trust

The Hadrian Trust

Halifax Foundation for Northern Ireland

The Hamilton Davies Trust

The Hampstead Wells and Campden Trust

Harborne Parish Lands Charity

The Harebell Centenary Fund

The Hargreaves Foundation

The Harpur Trust

The Peter Harrison Foundation

Edward Harvist Trust (The Harvist Estate)

The Charles Hayward Foundation

The Headley Trust

Heart of England Community Foundation

Heart Research UK

Heathrow Community Trust

Ernest Hecht Charitable Foundation

The Percy Hedley 1990 Charitable Trust

Help for Health

The Hemby Charitable Trust

Henley Educational Trust

Tim Henman Foundation

Herefordshire Community Foundation

The Herefordshire Historic Churches Trust

Heritage Lottery Fund

Hertfordshire Community Foundation

P. and C. Hickinbotham Charitable Trust

The Alan Edward Higgs Charity

Highway One Trust

The Hinduja Foundation

The Hintze Family Charity Foundation

Historic Environment Scotland

Historic Houses Foundation

P. H. Holt Foundation

The Holywood Trust

Hospice UK

The Hospital Saturday Fund

House of Industry Estate

The Hudson Foundation

The Hull and East Riding Charitable Trust

The Albert Hunt Trust

Huntingdon Freemen's Trust

Hyde Park Place Estate Charity

Ibrahim Foundation Ltd

The Iceland Foods Charitable Foundation

The Ingram Trust

Integrated Education Fund

Irish Youth Foundation (UK) Ltd (incorporating The Lawlor Foundation)

The Isla Foundation

The Isle of Anglesey Charitable Association (Cymdeithas Elusennol Ynys Môn)

Isle of Wight Foundation

The ITF Seafarers Trust

The Jabbs Foundation

The Sir Barry Jackson County Fund

John James Bristol Foundation

The Roger and Jean Jefcoate Trust

The Jenour Foundation

The Jephcott Charitable Trust

Jewish Child's Day

The Jewish Youth Fund

Johnnie Johnson Trust

The Joicey Trust

The Jones 1986 Charitable Trust

The Jordan Charitable Foundation

The Joron Charitable Trust

The Cyril and Eve Jumbo Charitable Trust

The Jusaca Charitable Trust

The Ian Karten Charitable Trust

The Kelly Family Charitable Trust

The Kennedy Leigh Charitable Trust

The Kennel Club Charitable Trust

Kent Community Foundation

Keren Association Ltd

The Ursula Keyes Trust

KFC Foundation

Fraser Kilpatrick Charitable Trust

The King Henry VIII Endowed Trust – Warwick

King/Cullimore Charitable Trust

The Mary Kinross Charitable Trust

The Ernest Kleinwort Charitable Trust

Sir James Knott Trust

Kollel and Co. Ltd

The K. P. Ladd Charitable Trust

John Laing Charitable Trust

Maurice and Hilda Laing Charitable Trust

Christopher Laing Foundation

The David Laing Foundation

The Kirby Laing Foundation

The Martin Laing Foundation

The Beatrice Laing Trust

The Leonard Laity Stoate Charitable Trust

Lancashire Environmental Fund Ltd

LandAid Charitable Trust Ltd (LandAid)

The LankellyChase Foundation

The Richard Lawes Foundation

The Leathersellers' Foundation

Leeds Building Society Foundation

Leeds Community Foundation

The Legal Education Foundation

The Mark Leonard Trust

Joseph Levy Foundation

The Sir Edward Lewis Foundation

The Limbourne Trust

The Linbury Trust

Lincolnshire Community Foundation

The Charles Littlewood Hill Trust

Liverpool Charity and Voluntary Services (LCVS)

The Ian and Natalie Livingstone Charitable Trust

The W. M. and B. W. Lloyd Trust

Lloyds Bank Foundation for the Channel Islands

London Catalyst

The London Community Foundation (LCF)

London Legal Support Trust (LLST)

The London Marathon Charitable Trust Ltd

Longleigh Foundation

The Lord's Taverners

John Lyon's Charity

The R. S. Macdonald Charitable Trust

The Mackintosh Foundation
The MacRobert Trust 2019
Manchester Airport Community Trust Fund
R. W. Mann Trust
The Marchig Animal Welfare Trust
The Michael Marsh Charitable Trust
Charity of John Marshall
Sir George Martin Trust
John Martin's Charity
The Dan Maskell Tennis Trust
Mayfair Charities Ltd
The Robert McAlpine Foundation
Medical Research Foundation
Merchant Navy Welfare Board
The Merchant Venturers Charity
Merchants House of Glasgow
The Mickel Fund
The Gerald Micklem Charitable Trust
Millennium Stadium Charitable Trust (Ymddiriedolaeth Elusennol Stadiwm y Mileniwm)
Milton Keynes Community Foundation Ltd
Minton Charitable Trust
Mobbs Memorial Trust Ltd
The Monmouthshire County Council Welsh Church Act Fund
The Janet and Brian Moore Charitable Trust*
John Moores Foundation
The Steve Morgan Foundation
Morgan Stanley International Foundation
The Morris Charitable Trust
The Morrisons Foundation
Motability
Motor Neurone Disease Association
J. P. Moulton Charitable Foundation
Murphy-Neumann Charity Company Ltd
The National Churches Trust
The National Hockey Foundation
The National Lottery Community Fund
The Nationwide Foundation
Network for Social Change Charitable Trust
Newby Trust Ltd
Newcomen Collett Foundation
The Frances and Augustus Newman Foundation
Alderman Newton's Educational Foundation
The Nineveh Charitable Trust
The Nisbet Trust

The Norfolk Churches Trust Ltd
The Norman Family Charitable Trust
North West Cancer Research
Northamptonshire Community Foundation
The Northumbria Historic Churches Trust
The Norton Foundation
Norwich Town Close Estate Charity
The Norwood and Newton Settlement
The Oakdale Trust
The Oakley Charitable Trust
One Community Foundation Ltd
Orange Tree Trust
The Sir Peter O'Sullevan Charitable Trust
The Ouseley Church Music Trust
Ovingdean Hall Foundation
Oxfordshire Historic Churches Trust (2016)
P. F. Charitable Trust
The Paget Charitable Trust
The Panacea Charitable Trust
Miss M. E. S. Paterson's Charitable Trust
The Jack Patston Charitable Trust
John Pearce Foundation
The Pears Family Charitable Foundation
The Pebbles Trust
The Dowager Countess Eleanor Peel Trust
People's Health Trust
The Persimmon Charitable Foundation
Petplan Charitable Trust
The Pets at Home Foundation
The Pilgrim Trust
Elise Pilkington Charitable Trust
Pilkington Charities Fund
Pink Ribbon Foundation
The Players Foundation
The Portal Trust
Porter Foundation
Postcode Community Trust
Postcode Local Trust
The Mary Potter Convent Hospital Trust
The Potton Consolidated Charity
Sir John Priestman Charity Trust
The Primrose Trust
The Prince's Countryside Fund
The Prudence Trust
The Purey Cust Trust CIO
Quartet Community Foundation
Queen Mary's Roehampton Trust

The Racing Foundation
The Rainford Trust
The Joseph Rank Trust
The Rathbones Group Foundation
The Rayne Foundation
The Sir James Reckitt Charity
Red Hill Charitable Trust
Rees Jeffreys Road Fund
Riada Trust
The Clive Richards Foundation
Richmond Parish Lands Charity
Rivers Foundation
The Robertson Trust
The Roddick Foundation
The Gerald and Gail Ronson Family Foundation
Rosca Trust
The Rose Foundation
The Cecil Rosen Foundation
The Rothley Trust
The Rowlands Trust
Royal Artillery Charitable Fund
The Royal British Legion
Royal Docks Trust (London)
The Royal Foundation of The Prince and Princess of Wales
The Royal Navy and Royal Marines Charity
The Rugby Group Benevolent Fund Ltd
The Ryvoan Trust*
The Saddlers' Company Charitable Fund
The Jean Sainsbury Animal Welfare Trust
The Alan and Babette Sainsbury Charitable Fund
The Savoy Educational Trust
Foundation Scotland
Scott (Eredine) Charitable Trust
The Scott Bader Commonwealth Ltd
Francis C. Scott Charitable Trust
The Frieda Scott Charitable Trust
Scottish Property Industry Festival of Christmas (SPIFOX)
ScottishPower Foundation
The Screwfix Foundation
Seafarers UK (King George's Fund for Sailors)
The Sam and Bella Sebba Charitable Foundation
Leslie Sell Charitable Trust
Shaftoe Educational Foundation
The Shanly Foundation
The Sheldon Trust
The Archie Sherman Charitable Trust

The R. C. Sherriff Rosebriars Trust

Shetland Charitable Trust

The Shipwrights Charitable Fund

Shulem B. Association Ltd

The Skelton Bounty

The Skerritt Trust

The Charles Skey Charitable Trust

The Mrs Smith and Mount Trust

The R. C. Snelling Charitable Trust

Somerset Community Foundation

South Yorkshire Community Foundation

W. F. Southall Trust

Southover Manor General Education Trust Ltd

Peter Sowerby Foundation

The Jessie Spencer Trust

The Sperring Charity

The Spoore, Merry and Rixman Foundation

St James's Place Charitable Foundation

Sir Walter St John's Educational Charity

St Monica Trust

The Stafford Trust

Staples Trust

The Steel Charitable Trust

The Stevenage Community Trust

Stolkin Foundation

Strand Parishes Trust

Stratford-upon-Avon Town Trust

Streetsmart – Action for the Homeless

Suffolk Community Foundation

The Suffolk Historic Churches Trust

The Summerfield Charitable Trust

The Bernard Sunley Foundation

Community Foundation for Surrey

The Sussex Community Foundation

Swansea and Brecon Diocesan Board of Finance Ltd

The Swire Charitable Trust

The Adrian Swire Charitable Trust

The Syder Foundation

Tabeel Trust

The Gay and Keith Talbot Trust

The Talbot Trusts

The Talbot Village Trust

Tanner Trust

Humphrey Richardson Taylor Charitable Trust

Stephen Taylor Foundation

The Tennis Foundation

Tenovus Scotland

The Theatres Trust Charitable Fund

Sir Jules Thorn Charitable Trust

Mrs R. P. Tindall's Charitable Trust

The Tory Family Foundation

The Tottenham Grammar School Foundation

Tower Hill Trust

The Toy Trust

The Trades House of Glasgow

The Constance Travis Charitable Trust

The True Colours Trust

Truemart Ltd

Trumros Ltd

Trust for London

The Tudor Trust

The Roger and Douglas Turner Charitable Trust

Two Magpies Fund

Community Foundation serving Tyne and Wear and Northumberland

Ulster Garden Villages Ltd

The Ulverscroft Foundation

The Underwood Trust

The United Reformed Church (Wessex) Trust Ltd

United St Saviour's Charity

Valencia Communities Fund

The Valiant Charitable Trust

Variety, the Children's Charity

The Velvet Foundation

The Veolia Environmental Trust

Versus Arthritis

The Veterans' Foundation

VINCI UK Foundation

Virgin Atlantic Foundation

Sylvia Waddilove Foundation UK

Wade's Charity

The Scurrah Wainwright Charity

The Walker Trust

G. R. Waters Charitable Trust 2000

John Watson's Trust*

The Weavers' Company Benevolent Fund

The William Webster Charitable Trust

The Weinstock Fund

The Weir Charitable Trust

The James Weir Foundation

The Wellcome Trust

The Welsh Church Act Fund

Wembley National Stadium Trust

The Westfield Health Charitable Trust

Westminster Almshouses Foundation

The Garfield Weston Foundation

Westway Trust

The Will Charitable Trust

Alfred Williams Charitable Trust

The Williams Family Foundation

The H. D. H. Wills 1965 Charitable Trust

Sumner Wilson Charitable Trust

J. and J. R. Wilson Trust

Wiltshire Community Foundation

The Charles Wolfson Charitable Trust

The Wolfson Family Charitable Trust

The Wolfson Foundation

Wooden Spoon Society

The Eric Wright Charitable Trust

The Wyndham Charitable Trust

Yorkshire Building Society Charitable Foundation

The Yorkshire Dales Millennium Trust

The Yorkshire Historic Churches Trust

Youth Music

Zephyr Charitable Trust

The Marjorie and Arnold Ziff Charitable Foundation

Zurich Community Trust (UK) Ltd

Collection and acquisition

The Art Fund
The Beaverbrook Foundation
Denise Coates Foundation
The Manny and Brigitta
    Davidson Charitable
    Foundation
The De Laszlo Foundation
The Lord Faringdon Charitable
    Trust
The Linbury Trust
The Henry Moore Foundation
The Ruddock Foundation for
    the Arts

Core/revenue costs

The 29th May 1961 Charitable
    Trust
The A. B. Charitable Trust
ABF The Soldiers' Charity
abrdn Financial Fairness Trust
The Access to Justice
    Foundation
The Adint Charitable Trust
The AEB Charitable Trust
The AIM Foundation
AKO Foundation
Alan Boswell Group Charitable
    Trust
The Alborada Trust
Al-Fayed Charitable Foundation
The Allen & Overy Foundation
Amabrill Ltd
The Ammco Trust
The Anchor Foundation
Anguish's Educational
    Foundation
The Anson Charitable Trust
Armed Forces Covenant Fund
    Trust
The Armourers and Brasiers
    Gauntlet Trust
The Asfari Foundation
The Ashley Family Foundation
The Aurora Trust (formerly The
    Ashden Trust)
The Avon and Somerset Police
    Community Trust
Backstage Trust
The Baily Thomas Charitable
    Fund
Bairdwatson Charitable Trust
The Ballinger Charitable Trust
The Banister Charitable Trust
Bank of Scotland Foundation
The Barbour Foundation
Barcapel Foundation Ltd
The Baring Foundation
Philip Barker Charity
The Barnes Fund
The Battersea Power Station
    Foundation
BBC Children in Need
BC Partners Foundation
The James Beattie Charitable
    Trust
The Beaverbrook Foundation
The Berkeley Foundation
The Bernicia Foundation
Bideford Bridge Trust
The Bingham Trust
The Michael Bishop
    Foundation
Maria Bjornson Memorial Fund
The Blagrave Trust
Blakemore Foundation
The Blandford Lake Trust
Bloodwise

The Marjory Boddy Charitable
    Trust
BOOST Charitable Trust
Boots Charitable Trust
Sir William Boreman's
    Foundation
The Harry Bottom Charitable
    Trust
The Brelms Trust CIO
The British and Foreign Bible
    Society
British Eye Research
    Foundation (Fight for Sight)
British Gas Energy Trust
British Heart Foundation (BHF)
The Brook Trust
The Mary Brown Memorial
    Trust
Buckinghamshire Community
    Foundation
E. F. Bulmer Trust
Consolidated Charity of Burton
    upon Trent
The Noel Buxton Trust
William A. Cadbury Charitable
    Trust
Community Foundation for
    Calderdale
Cambridgeshire Community
    Foundation
Camden Giving
The Carnegie Trust for the
    Universities of Scotland
Cattanach
The Wilfrid and Constance
    Cave Foundation
The B. G. S. Cayzer Charitable
    Trust
Elizabeth Cayzer Charitable
    Trust
Chalfords Ltd
The Chalk Cliff Trust
Chartered Accountants' Livery
    Charity (CALC)
The Chetwode Foundation
Chippenham Borough Lands
    Charity
CHK Foundation
Chrysalis Trust
Church Burgesses Educational
    Foundation
The City Bridge Trust (Bridge
    House Estates)
Cloudesley
The Robert Clutterbuck
    Charitable Trust
The John Coates Charitable
    Trust
Denise Coates Foundation
The Cole Charitable Trust
The Colt Foundation
Community First
Corra Foundation
The County Council of Dyfed
    Welsh Church Fund

County Durham Community
Foundation
The Lord Cozens-Hardy Trust
Creative Scotland
Credit Suisse EMEA
Foundation
Cripplegate Foundation
The Croydon Relief-in-Need
Charity
Cruden Foundation Ltd
CSIS Charity Fund
Cumbria Community
Foundation
The Daniell Trust
The Danson Foundation*
Baron Davenport's Charity
The Miriam Dean Refugee
Trust Fund
Foundation Derbyshire
Devon Community Foundation
The Gillian Dickinson Trust
Dorset Community Foundation
The D'Oyly Carte Charitable
Trust
Drapers Charitable Fund
The Dulverton Trust
East End Community
Foundation
The Ecology Trust
Dr Edwards and Bishop King's
Fulham Charity
The George Elias Charitable
Trust
John Ellerman Foundation
The Elmley Foundation
The Endrick Trust
England and Wales Cricket
Trust
The Englefield Charitable Trust
The Enkalon Foundation
Essex Community Foundation
The Essex Youth Trust
The Eveson Charitable Trust
The ExPat Foundation
Esmée Fairbairn Foundation
The February Foundation
The Feoffees of St Michael's
Spurriergate York
The Fidelity UK Foundation
Field Family Charitable Trust
Fine & Country Foundation
The Finnis Scott Foundation
Sir John Fisher Foundation
The Joyce Fletcher Charitable
Trust
The Forbes Charitable
Foundation
Forest Hill Charitable Trust
Forever Manchester
The Forrester Family Trust
Four Acre Trust
Fowler Smith and Jones Trust
The Foyle Foundation
The Gordon Fraser Charitable
Trust
The Hugh Fraser Foundation

The Freshgate Trust
Foundation
Friarsgate Trust
Friends Provident Charitable
Foundation
G. M. C. Trust
The Gannochy Trust
The Gatsby Charitable
Foundation
General Charity (Coventry)
J. Paul Getty Jr General
Charitable Trust*
The G. C. Gibson Charitable
Trust
The Simon Gibson Charitable
Trust
The Glass-House Trust
Global Charities
Gloucestershire Community
Foundation
Grace Charitable Trust
The Great Stone Bridge Trust
of Edenbridge
The Greggs Foundation
The Grimmitt Trust
The Grocers' Charity
Groundwork UK
Calouste Gulbenkian
Foundation – UK Branch
Hackney Parochial Charities
The Hadfield Charitable Trust
The Hadley Trust
The Hadrian Trust
Halifax Foundation for
Northern Ireland
The Hamilton Davies Trust
The Helen Hamlyn Trust
Hammersmith United Charities
The Hampstead Wells and
Campden Trust
Harborne Parish Lands Charity
William Harding's Charity
The Harebell Centenary Fund
The Peter Harrison Foundation
The Headley Trust
Heathrow Community Trust
Ernest Hecht Charitable
Foundation
The Percy Hedley 1990
Charitable Trust
The Hemby Charitable Trust
Herefordshire Community
Foundation
The Herefordshire Historic
Churches Trust
The Alan Edward Higgs Charity
Highway One Trust
The Hilden Charitable Fund
Hinchley Charitable Trust
The Hintze Family Charity
Foundation
The Holbeck Charitable Trust
The Holywood Trust
Hospice UK
House of Industry Estate
Housing Pathways Trust

James T. Howat Charitable
Trust
The Hudson Foundation
The Hull and East Riding
Charitable Trust
The Albert Hunt Trust
Miss Agnes H. Hunter's Trust
Ibrahim Foundation Ltd
Impetus
The Indigo Trust
The Inlight Trust
Irish Youth Foundation (UK)
Ltd (incorporating The
Lawlor Foundation)
The Isla Foundation
The Isle of Anglesey Charitable
Association (Cymdeithas
Elusennol Ynys Môn)
The ITF Seafarers Trust
The J. J. Charitable Trust
The Jabbs Foundation
The Jerusalem Trust
Joffe Charitable Trust CIO
The Joicey Trust
The Jones 1986 Charitable
Trust
The Jordan Charitable
Foundation
The Joron Charitable Trust
The Jusaca Charitable Trust
The Kelly Family Charitable
Trust
The Kennedy Leigh Charitable
Trust
The Kennel Club Charitable
Trust
Kent Community Foundation
The Kentown Wizard
Foundation
The King Henry VIII Endowed
Trust – Warwick
King/Cullimore Charitable
Trust
The Mary Kinross Charitable
Trust
The Graham Kirkham
Foundation
The Ernest Kleinwort
Charitable Trust
Sir James Knott Trust
The K. P. Ladd Charitable
Trust
John Laing Charitable Trust
Christopher Laing Foundation
The Leonard Laity Stoate
Charitable Trust
The Lake House Charitable
Foundation
Community Foundations for
Lancashire and Merseyside
The Allen Lane Foundation
The LankellyChase Foundation
The Law Society Charity
The Herd Lawson and Muriel
Lawson Charitable Trust
The Leathersellers' Foundation

Leeds Community Foundation
The Legal Education
Foundation
The Mark Leonard Trust
Joseph Levy Foundation
The Charles Lewis Foundation
The Sir Edward Lewis
Foundation
The Linbury Trust
Lincolnshire Community
Foundation
The Michael and Betty Little
Trust*
The Charles Littlewood Hill
Trust
Liverpool Charity and Voluntary
Services (LCVS)
The Ian and Natalie
Livingstone Charitable Trust
Lloyds Bank Foundation for the
Channel Islands
London Catalyst
The London Community
Foundation (LCF)
London Freemasons Charity
London Legal Support Trust
(LLST)
The London Marathon
Charitable Trust Ltd
John Lyon's Charity
The R. S. Macdonald
Charitable Trust
The Mackintosh Foundation
The MacRobert Trust 2019
Man Group plc Charitable
Trust
Marmot Charitable Trust
The Marsh Christian Trust
Sir George Martin Trust
Masonic Charitable Foundation
The McCarthy Stone
Foundation
The Mercers Charitable
Foundation
The Merchant Venturers
Charity
Merchants House of Glasgow
T. and J. Meyer Family
Foundation Ltd
The Mickel Fund
The Gerald Micklem Charitable
Trust
The Millfield House Foundation
(1)
Milton Keynes Community
Foundation Ltd
The Alexander Moncur Trust
The Monmouthshire County
Council Welsh Church Act
Fund
The Steve Morgan Foundation
G. M. Morrison Charitable
Trust
Motor Neurone Disease
Association

The Frederick Mulder
Foundation
The National Lottery
Community Fund
The Nationwide Foundation
Network for Social Change
Charitable Trust
Newby Trust Ltd
Newcomen Collett Foundation
The Frances and Augustus
Newman Foundation
The Nisbet Trust
The Norman Family Charitable
Trust
The Oakdale Trust
The Oakley Charitable Trust
The Olwyn Foundation
One Community Foundation
Ltd
Orange Tree Trust
P. F. Charitable Trust
The Paget Charitable Trust
The Panacea Charitable Trust
The Pears Family Charitable
Foundation
The Pets at Home Foundation
The Pickwell Foundation
The Pilgrim Trust
Pilkington Charities Fund
Pink Ribbon Foundation
Polden-Puckham Charitable
Foundation
The Portal Trust
Postcode Society Trust
The Mary Potter Convent
Hospital Trust
David and Elaine Potter
Foundation
The Primrose Trust
The Prince of Wales's
Charitable Foundation
The Prince's Countryside Fund
The Privy Purse Charitable
Trust
The Progress Foundation
The Prudence Trust
Quartet Community Foundation
Queen Mary's Roehampton
Trust
The Racing Foundation
The Rainford Trust
The Joseph Rank Trust
The Eleanor Rathbone
Charitable Trust
The Sigrid Rausing Trust
The Ravensdale Trust
The Rayne Foundation
The Sir James Reckitt Charity
Richmond Parish Lands Charity
The Robertson Trust
The Roddick Foundation
Rosa Fund
The Rothschild Foundation
Rothschild Foundation
(Hanadiv) Europe
The Roughley Charitable Trust

The Joseph Rowntree
Charitable Trust
The Royal British Legion
Royal Masonic Trust for Girls
and Boys
The Royal Navy and Royal
Marines Charity
The Ryvoan Trust*
The Jean Sainsbury Animal
Welfare Trust
The Alan and Babette
Sainsbury Charitable Fund
Salters' Charitable Foundation
The Samworth Foundation
Schroder Charity Trust
Foundation Scotland
The Scott Bader
Commonwealth Ltd
Francis C. Scott Charitable
Trust
The Frieda Scott Charitable
Trust
Seafarers UK (King George's
Fund for Sailors)
The Sam and Bella Sebba
Charitable Foundation
The Segelman Trust
Shaftoe Educational
Foundation
ShareGift (The Orr Mackintosh
Foundation)
The Shears Foundation
SHINE (Support and Help in
Education)
The Shipwrights Charitable
Fund
Shulem B. Association Ltd
The Charles Skey Charitable
Trust
The Mrs Smith and Mount
Trust
Sofronie Foundation
Somerset Community
Foundation
Souter Charitable Trust
South Yorkshire Community
Foundation
W. F. Southall Trust
The Jessie Spencer Trust
St James's Place Charitable
Foundation
The Stafford Trust
The Community Foundation for
Staffordshire
Staples Trust
The Peter Stebbings Memorial
Charity
The Steel Charitable Trust
The Hugh Stenhouse
Foundation
The Stone Family Foundation
Strand Parishes Trust
Stratford-upon-Avon Town Trust
Suffolk Community Foundation
The Bernard Sunley
Foundation

The Sunrise Foundation CIO
Community Foundation for
Surrey
The Sussex Community
Foundation
The Swire Charitable Trust
The Adrian Swire Charitable
Trust
The Tabhair Charitable Trust
The Talbot Village Trust
The Tedworth Charitable Trust
The Tennis Foundation
The Thirty Percy Foundation
Sir Jules Thorn Charitable
Trust
The Three Guineas Trust
The Three Oaks Trust
The Thriplow Charitable Trust
Mrs R. P. Tindall's Charitable
Trust
The Constance Travis
Charitable Trust
The Triangle Trust (1949) Fund
The True Colours Trust
Trust for London
The Trusthouse Charitable
Foundation
The James Tudor Foundation
The Tudor Trust
The Tudwick Foundation
The Tuixen Foundation
The Roger and Douglas Turner
Charitable Trust
Two Magpies Fund
The Underwood Trust
The United Reformed Church
(Wessex) Trust Ltd
United St Saviour's Charity
The Valentine Charitable Trust
The Virgin Money Foundation
Vision Foundation
Volant Charitable Trust
The Scurrah Wainwright Charity
Wakefield and Tetley Trust
The Walcot Foundation
Walton-on-Thames Charity
G. R. Waters Charitable Trust
2000
Wates Family Enterprise Trust
The Wates Foundation
The Weavers' Company
Benevolent Fund
The Weinstock Fund
The Weir Charitable Trust
The James Weir Foundation
Wembley National Stadium
Trust
Westminster Foundation
The Garfield Weston
Foundation
Westway Trust
Whitley Animal Protection Trust
The H. D. H. Wills 1965
Charitable Trust
J. and J. R. Wilson Trust

Wiltshire Community
Foundation
Wooden Spoon Society
Woodroffe Benton Foundation
The Woodward Charitable
Trust
Worth Waynflete Foundation
The Eric Wright Charitable
Trust
WWDP (World Day of Prayer
National Committee for
England, Wales and
Northern Ireland)
The Wyndham Charitable Trust
The Yapp Charitable Trust
The Yorkshire Dales
Millennium Trust
Youth Music
Zurich Community Trust (UK)
Ltd

Development funding

Achisomoch Aid Company Ltd
The Architectural Heritage
Fund
The Art Fund
ArtSocial Foundation
Backstage Trust
Philip Barker Charity
The Paul Bassham Charitable
Trust
Benesco Charity Ltd
The Berkeley Foundation
The Buffini Chao Foundation
William A. Cadbury Charitable
Trust
CEO Sleepout
The Corporation of Trinity
House of Deptford Strond
Credit Suisse EMEA
Foundation
CSIS Charity Fund
The Roger De Haan Charitable
Trust
The Dunhill Medical Trust
The Elie Trust
The Elmley Foundation
England and Wales Cricket
Trust
The Fidelity UK Foundation
The Forbes Charitable
Foundation
Friends Provident Charitable
Foundation
The Generations Foundation
The Glass-House Trust
The Hadley Trust
The Helen Hamlyn Trust
Harborne Parish Lands Charity
Tim Henman Foundation
Hinchley Charitable Trust
Hospice UK
The Hunter Foundation
The Harold Hyam Wingate
Foundation
The Iceland Foods Charitable
Foundation
The Innocent Foundation
Integrated Education Fund
Irish Youth Foundation (UK)
Ltd (incorporating The
Lawlor Foundation)
The J. J. Charitable Trust
Joffe Charitable Trust CIO
Keren Association Ltd
The Kiawah Charitable Trust
The Kirby Laing Foundation
The Mark Leonard Trust
The Linbury Trust
London Legal Support Trust
(LLST)
The James Milner Foundation
Milton Keynes Community
Foundation Ltd
The Henry Moore Foundation

The Mutual Trust Group
The National Garden Scheme
Nesta
The Nineveh Charitable Trust
The Pilgrim Trust
The Players Foundation
Thomas Pocklington Trust
The Portal Trust
Porter Foundation
The Progress Foundation
The Rathbones Group
　Foundation
The Rothley Trust
The Sam and Bella Sebba
　Charitable Foundation
The Segelman Trust
Shaftoe Educational
　Foundation
The Mrs Smith and Mount
　Trust
Peter Sowerby Foundation
St Peter's Saltley Trust
The Stone Family Foundation
The W. O. Street Charitable
　Foundation
Swansea and Brecon Diocesan
　Board of Finance Ltd
The Gay and Keith Talbot Trust
Tanner Trust
C. B. and H. H. T. Taylor 1984
　Trust
Stephen Taylor Foundation
The Tedworth Charitable Trust
The Thirty Percy Foundation
The Triangle Trust (1949) Fund
The True Colours Trust
Truemart Ltd
Trumros Ltd
The Tudor Trust
Community Foundation serving
　Tyne and Wear and
　Northumberland
Ufi VocTech Trust
The Valentine Charitable Trust
Virgin Atlantic Foundation
Walton-on-Thames Charity
WWDP (World Day of Prayer
　National Committee for
　England, Wales and
　Northern Ireland)
Yorkshire Cancer Research
Youth Music
Zephyr Charitable Trust

Loan finance/ social investment

Esmée Fairbairn Foundation
The Maurice Hatter Foundation
The Herefordshire Historic
　Churches Trust
The Jewish Youth Fund
Kupath Gemach Chaim
　Bechesed Viznitz Trust
The William Leech Charity
The Lightbulb Trust*
Nesta
The Rayne Foundation
The Romney Marsh Historic
　Churches Trust
Social Investment Business
　Foundation
Ulster Garden Villages Ltd
UnLtd (Foundation for Social
　Entrepreneurs)
The Virgin Foundation (Virgin
　Unite)
The Charles Wolfson
　Charitable Trust

Project funding

The A. B. Charitable Trust
The Abbeyfield Research
　Foundation
The Aberdeenshire Educational
　Trust Scheme
abrdn Charitable Foundation
abrdn Financial Fairness Trust
Achisomoch Aid Company Ltd
Action Medical Research
The Bryan Adams Foundation
The Adint Charitable Trust
The AEB Charitable Trust
AKO Foundation
Al Madad Foundation*
Alan Boswell Group Charitable
　Trust
The Alchemy Foundation
Al-Fayed Charitable Foundation
The Allen & Overy Foundation
D. C. R. Allen Charitable Trust
Alpkit Foundation
The Ampersand Foundation
The Anchor Foundation
Andrews Charitable Trust
Anguish's Educational
　Foundation
The Anson Charitable Trust
The John Apthorp Charity
The Archer Trust
The Architectural Heritage
　Fund
Armed Forces Covenant Fund
　Trust
Armed Forces Education Trust
The John Armitage Charitable
　Trust
The Armourers and Brasiers
　Gauntlet Trust
Douglas Arter Foundation
Arts Council England
Arts Council of Wales (also
　known as Cyngor
　Celfyddydau Cymru)
ArtSocial Foundation
The Ove Arup Foundation
The Asfari Foundation
The Ashley Family Foundation
The Ashworth Charitable Trust
The Associated Board of the
　Royal Schools of Music
　(ABRSM)
The Astor Foundation
Lawrence Atwell's Charity
　(Skinners' Company)
The Aurelius Charitable Trust
The Aurora Trust (formerly The
　Ashden Trust)
The Avon and Somerset Police
　Community Trust
Backstage Trust
The Austin Bailey Foundation
The Baily Thomas Charitable
　Fund
Bairdwatson Charitable Trust

The Rachel Baker Memorial Charity

The Ballinger Charitable Trust

Banbury Charities

Veronica and Lars Bane Foundation

The Banister Charitable Trust

Bank of Scotland Foundation

The Barbers' Company General Charities

Barchester Healthcare Foundation

Philip Barker Charity

The Barnes Fund

Barnwood Trust

Robert Barr's Charitable Trust

The Paul Bassham Charitable Trust

The Battersea Power Station Foundation

Bauer Radio's Cash for Kids Charities

The Gordon and Ena Baxter Foundation*

BBC Children in Need

BC Partners Foundation

The James Beattie Charitable Trust

The Beaverbrook Foundation

Beccles Townlands Charity

Becht Foundation

The Lord Belstead Charitable Settlement*

Benefact Trust Ltd

Benesco Charity Ltd

The Berkeley Foundation

Berkshire Community Foundation

Biffa Award

The Bingham Trust

Birkdale Trust for Hearing Impaired Ltd*

The Michael Bishop Foundation

Maria Bjornson Memorial Fund

The John Black Charitable Foundation

The Blagrave Trust

The Blandford Lake Trust

Bloodwise

The Bloomfield Charitable Trust

Bluespark Foundation

The Bluston Charitable Settlement

BNA Charitable Incorporated Organisation

The Charlotte Bonham-Carter Charitable Trust

BOOST Charitable Trust

The Booth Charities

Boots Charitable Trust

Sir William Boreman's Foundation

The Brelms Trust CIO

The Harold and Alice Bridges Charity

Bristol Archdeaconry Charity

Bristol Charities

The BRIT Trust

The British and Foreign Bible Society

The British and Foreign School Society (BFSS)

British Eye Research Foundation (Fight for Sight)

British Gas Energy Trust

British Heart Foundation (BHF)

British Motor Sports Training Trust

The Brook Trust

The Broomton Foundation

Bill Brown 1989 Charitable Trust

The Mary Brown Memorial Trust

The Brown Source Trust

R. S. Brownless Charitable Trust

The Jack Brunton Charitable Trust

Buckinghamshire Community Foundation

The Buffini Chao Foundation

Building and Civil Engineering Charitable Trust

Bulb Foundation

Bupa Foundation

The Burden Trust

The Burdett Trust for Nursing

The Burges Salmon Charitable Trust

Burnie's Foundation

Consolidated Charity of Burton upon Trent

The Noel Buxton Trust

The Edward Cadbury Charitable Trust

William A. Cadbury Charitable Trust

The Barrow Cadbury Trust

The Edward and Dorothy Cadbury Trust

Community Foundation for Calderdale

The Calleva Foundation

Cambridgeshire Community Foundation

Camden Giving

Cancer Research UK

Card Factory Foundation

The Carlton Hayes Mental Health Charity

The Antonio Carluccio Foundation

The Leslie Mary Carter Charitable Trust

The Casey Trust

Cattanach

The Joseph and Annie Cattle Trust

The Wilfrid and Constance Cave Foundation

The B. G. S. Cayzer Charitable Trust

Elizabeth Cayzer Charitable Trust

CEO Sleepout

Chalfords Ltd

The Chalk Cliff Trust

Chartered Accountants' Livery Charity (CALC)

The Charterhouse Charitable Trust

The Chetwode Foundation

The Childhood Trust

Children with Cancer UK

Childs Charitable Trust

The Childwick Trust

Chippenham Borough Lands Charity

The Christabella Charitable Trust

Church Burgesses Educational Foundation

Church of Ireland Priorities Fund

Church Urban Fund

CLA Charitable Trust

Cloudesley

The John Coates Charitable Trust

Denise Coates Foundation

Colchester Catalyst Charity

The Cole Charitable Trust

John and Freda Coleman Charitable Trust

The George Henry Collins Charity

The Colt Foundation

Colwinston Charitable Trust

Colyer-Fergusson Charitable Trust

The Comino Foundation

Community First

Douglas Compton James Charitable Trust

Congregational and General Charitable Trust

The Cooks Charity

The Catherine Cookson Charitable Trust

The Alice Ellen Cooper-Dean Charitable Foundation

Marjorie Coote Animal Charity Trust

Michael Cornish Charitable Trust

The Evan Cornish Foundation

The Corporation of Trinity House of Deptford Strond

Corra Foundation

The County Council of Dyfed Welsh Church Fund

County Durham Community Foundation

The Noel Coward Foundation

The Sir Tom Cowie Charitable
    Trust
Creative Scotland
Credit Suisse EMEA
    Foundation
The Crerar Trust
Cripplegate Foundation
The Croydon Relief-in-Need
    Charity
Cruden Foundation Ltd
Cullum Family Trust
Cumbria Community
    Foundation
The Cunningham Trust
The Daiwa Anglo-Japanese
    Foundation
The Danson Foundation*
Baron Davenport's Charity
The Davidson Family
    Charitable Trust
The Roger De Haan Charitable
    Trust
The De Laszlo Foundation
The Miriam Dean Refugee
    Trust Fund
The Delius Trust
The Delves Charitable Trust
Denman Charitable Trust
Devon Community Foundation
Digital Extra Fund
Dinwoodie Charitable Company
The Djanogly Foundation
Dorset Community Foundation
The Dorus Trust
The D'Oyly Carte Charitable
    Trust
Drapers Charitable Fund
Duchy Health Charity Ltd
The Dulverton Trust
Dumfriesshire East Community
    Benefit Group SCIO
Dunard Fund
The Dunhill Medical Trust
The DWF Charitable
    Foundation
The Dyers' Company
    Charitable Trust
The James Dyson Foundation
E. B. M. Charitable Trust
The Earley Charity
East End Community
    Foundation
The Ecology Trust
The Economist Charitable
    Trust
The Gilbert and Eileen Edgar
    Foundation
Dr Edwards and Bishop King's
    Fulham Charity
W. G. Edwards Charitable
    Foundation
The George Elias Charitable
    Trust
The Elie Trust
The Maud Elkington Charitable
    Trust

John Ellerman Foundation
The Elmley Foundation
Emerton-Christie Charity
The Endrick Trust
England and Wales Cricket
    Trust
The Enkalon Foundation
Epilepsy Research UK
The EQ Foundation
Essex Community Foundation
The Essex Youth Trust
Euro Quality Foundation
The Evelyn Trust
The Eventhall Family
    Charitable Trust
The Eveson Charitable Trust
The ExPat Foundation
Esmée Fairbairn Foundation
The Lord Faringdon Charitable
    Trust
The Thomas Farr Charity
The February Foundation
George Fentham Birmingham
    Charity
The Feoffees of St Michael's
    Spurriergate York
Allan and Nesta Ferguson
    Charitable Settlement
The Fidelio Charitable Trust
The Fidelity UK Foundation
Field Family Charitable Trust
Fine & Country Foundation
Sir John Fisher Foundation
Fishmongers' Company's
    Charitable Trust
Marc Fitch Fund
Ford Britain Trust
Oliver Ford Foundation
Forever Manchester
The Forrester Family Trust
The Lord Forte Foundation
Fowler Smith and Jones Trust
The Foyle Foundation
Mrs D. M. France-Hayhurst
    Foundation
The Gordon Fraser Charitable
    Trust
The Hugh Fraser Foundation
The Louis and Valerie
    Freedman Charitable
    Settlement
The Freelands Foundation Ltd
Friarsgate Trust
Friends Provident Charitable
    Foundation
The Fulmer Charitable Trust
The Funding Network
The Gale Family Charity Trust
The Gannochy Trust
Ganzoni Charitable Trust
The Garrick Charitable Trust
The Gatsby Charitable
    Foundation
Gatwick Airport Community
    Trust

Martin Geddes Charitable
    Trust
Sir Robert Geffery's
    Almshouse Trust
General Charity (Coventry)
The Generations Foundation
The Gibbons Family Trust
The Gibbs Charitable Trusts
The G. C. Gibson Charitable
    Trust
The Simon Gibson Charitable
    Trust
The Glass-House Trust
Global Charities
Gloucestershire Community
    Foundation
Sydney and Phyllis Goldberg
    Memorial Charitable Trust
Goldman Sachs Gives (UK)
The Golsoncott Foundation
Nicholas and Judith
    Goodison's Charitable
    Settlement
The Goshen Trust
The Gosling Foundation Ltd
The Edward Gostling
    Foundation
The Granada Foundation
The Grand Trust CIO
GrantScape
The Great Stone Bridge Trust
    of Edenbridge
The Greater Manchester High
    Sheriff's Police Trust
The Green Hall Foundation
Greenham Trust Ltd
The Greenslade Family
    Foundation
The Greggs Foundation
The Grimmitt Trust
The Grocers' Charity
Groundwork UK
Calouste Gulbenkian
    Foundation – UK Branch
The Guy Foundation
Hackney Parochial Charities
The Hadfield Charitable Trust
The Hadley Trust
The Hadrian Trust
Halifax Foundation for
    Northern Ireland
The Helen Hamlyn Trust
Hammersmith United Charities
The Hampstead Wells and
    Campden Trust
The Happold Foundation
Harborne Parish Lands Charity
The Harding Trust
The Hargreaves Foundation
The Harpur Trust
The Peter Harrison Foundation
Edward Harvist Trust (The
    Harvist Estate)
The Charles Hayward
    Foundation
The Headley Trust

The Health Foundation
Heart of England Community
Foundation
Heart Research UK
Heathrow Community Trust
Heb Ffin (Without Frontier)
Ernest Hecht Charitable
Foundation
The Hedley Foundation
The Michael Heller Charitable
Foundation
The Simon Heller Charitable
Settlement
Help for Health
The Helping Foundation
Henley Educational Trust
Henley Royal Regatta
Charitable Trust
Tim Henman Foundation
Herefordshire Community
Foundation
The Herefordshire Historic
Churches Trust
Heritage Lottery Fund
Hertfordshire Community
Foundation
HFC Help for Children UK Ltd
Highway One Trust
The Hilden Charitable Fund
Hinchley Charitable Trust
The Hinduja Foundation
The Hinrichsen Foundation
Historic Environment Scotland
Historic Houses Foundation
The Hobson Charity Ltd
Hockerill Educational
Foundation
The Jane Hodge Foundation
The Holbeck Charitable Trust
Hollick Family Foundation
P. H. Holt Foundation
The Holywood Trust
The Horse Trust
Hospice UK
The Hospital of God at
Greatham
The Hospital Saturday Fund
House of Industry Estate
Housing Pathways Trust
The Reta Lila Howard
Foundation
James T. Howat Charitable
Trust
The Hudson Foundation
The Huggard Charitable Trust
The Hull and East Riding
Charitable Trust
The Humanitarian Trust
The Albert Hunt Trust
The Hunter Foundation
Miss Agnes H. Hunter's Trust
Huntingdon Freemen's Trust
The Harold Hyam Wingate
Foundation
Hyde Charitable Trust
Ibrahim Foundation Ltd

The Idlewild Trust
Imagine Foundation
The Indigo Trust
The Ingram Trust
The Inlight Trust
The Innocent Foundation
The Institute for Policy
Research
Integrated Education Fund
The International Bankers
Charitable Trust
The Investindustrial
Foundation
The Ireland Fund of Great
Britain
The Isla Foundation
Isle of Wight Foundation
The ITF Seafarers Trust
The J. J. Charitable Trust
The Sir Barry Jackson County
Fund
The Roger and Jean Jefcoate
Trust
The Jenour Foundation
The Jephcott Charitable Trust
The Jerusalem Trust
Jewish Child's Day
The Jewish Youth Fund
Joffe Charitable Trust CIO
The Joron Charitable Trust
The Cyril and Eve Jumbo
Charitable Trust
Anton Jurgens Charitable Trust
The Ian Karten Charitable
Trust
The Kennel Club Charitable
Trust
The Kensington and Chelsea
Foundation
Kent Community Foundation
The Kentown Wizard
Foundation
Keren Association Ltd
The Peter Kershaw Trust
KFC Foundation
The Kiawah Charitable Trust
Fraser Kilpatrick Charitable
Trust
The King Henry VIII Endowed
Trust – Warwick
The Mary Kinross Charitable
Trust
Robert Kitchin (Saddlers' Co.)
The Ernest Kleinwort
Charitable Trust
Kollel and Co. Ltd
The KPMG Foundation
The Kreitman Foundation
Kusuma Trust UK
The K. P. Ladd Charitable
Trust
John Laing Charitable Trust
Maurice and Hilda Laing
Charitable Trust
Christopher Laing Foundation
The Kirby Laing Foundation

The Martin Laing Foundation
The Beatrice Laing Trust
The Lake House Charitable
Foundation
Community Foundations for
Lancashire and Merseyside
Lancashire Environmental
Fund Ltd
LandAid Charitable Trust Ltd
(LandAid)
The LankellyChase Foundation
The Law Society Charity
The Richard Lawes Foundation
The Herd Lawson and Muriel
Lawson Charitable Trust
The Lawson Trust CIO
The Leach Fourteenth Trust
The Leathersellers' Foundation
The Leche Trust
The William Leech Charity
Leeds Community Foundation
The Legal Education
Foundation
Leicestershire, Leicester and
Rutland Community
Foundation
The Leverhulme Trust
Joseph Levy Foundation
The Charles Lewis Foundation
The Limbourne Trust
The Linbury Trust
Lincolnshire Community
Foundation
The Linder Foundation
The Lister Charitable Trust
The Frank Litchfield Charitable
Trust
The Michael and Betty Little
Trust*
Liverpool Charity and Voluntary
Services (LCVS)
The Ian and Natalie
Livingstone Charitable Trust
The Andrew Lloyd Webber
Foundation
Lloyds Bank Foundation for the
Channel Islands
Lloyd's of London Foundation
Lloyd's Patriotic Fund
Lloyd's Register Foundation
The Locker Foundation
London Catalyst
The London Community
Foundation (LCF)
London Housing Foundation
Ltd (LHF)
The London Marathon
Charitable Trust Ltd
Longleigh Foundation
Lords Group Foundation*
The Lord's Taverners
John Lyon's Charity
The R. S. Macdonald
Charitable Trust
Mace Foundation
The Mackintosh Foundation

The MacRobert Trust 2019
The Magdalen and Lasher
  Charity (General Fund)
Man Group plc Charitable
  Trust
R. W. Mann Trust
The Marandi Foundation
The Marchig Animal Welfare
  Trust
Marmot Charitable Trust
The Michael Marsh Charitable
  Trust
Sir George Martin Trust
John Martin's Charity
Masonic Charitable Foundation
Mathew Trust
Maudsley Charity
The Robert McAlpine
  Foundation
D. D. McPhail Charitable
  Settlement
The Medlock Charitable Trust
The Brian Mercer Charitable
  Trust
The Mercers Charitable
  Foundation
Merchants House of Glasgow
The Mickel Fund
The Gerald Micklem Charitable
  Trust
Millennium Stadium Charitable
  Trust (Ymddiriedolaeth
  Elusennol Stadiwm y
  Mileniwm)
The Millfield House Foundation
  (1)
The Millfield Trust
Mills and Reeve Charitable
  Trust
The Clare Milne Trust
The James Milner Foundation
Milton Keynes Community
  Foundation Ltd
Minton Charitable Trust
Mobbs Memorial Trust Ltd
The Mohn Westlake
  Foundation
Moondance Foundation
The George A. Moore
  Foundation
John Moores Foundation
The Morel Charitable Trust
Morgan Stanley International
  Foundation
The Morris Charitable Trust
The Morrisons Foundation
Motor Neurone Disease
  Association
J. P. Moulton Charitable
  Foundation
The Edwina Mountbatten and
  Leonora Children's
  Foundation
The MSE Charity
The Frederick Mulder
  Foundation

Multiple Sclerosis Society
Edith Murphy Foundation
The Mutley Foundation
The National Express
  Foundation
The National Garden Scheme
The National Hockey
  Foundation
The National Lottery
  Community Fund
The Nationwide Foundation
Near Neighbours
Nesta
Network for Social Change
  Charitable Trust
Newby Trust Ltd
Alderman Newton's
  Educational Foundation
The NFU Mutual Charitable
  Trust
The Nineveh Charitable Trust
The Nisbet Trust
The Nomura Charitable Trust
North Berwick Trust
North West Cancer Research
Northamptonshire Community
  Foundation
Northern Consortium*
Northern Pharmacies Ltd Trust
  Fund
The Norton Foundation
Norwich Consolidated
  Charities
Norwich Town Close Estate
  Charity
The Norwood and Newton
  Settlement
The Nuffield Foundation
The Oakdale Trust
The Oakley Charitable Trust
Ocean Family Foundation
The Hamish Ogston
  Foundation
Old Possum's Practical Trust
The Olwyn Foundation
One Community Foundation
  Ltd
Orange Tree Trust
Orthopaedic Research UK
The Sir Peter O'Sullevan
  Charitable Trust
The O'Sullivan Family
  Charitable Trust
Ovingdean Hall Foundation
The Ovo Charitable Foundation
P. F. Charitable Trust
The Gerald Palmer Eling Trust
  Company
Parabola Foundation
Miss M. E. S. Paterson's
  Charitable Trust
The J. G. W. Patterson
  Foundation
John Pearce Foundation
The Pebbles Trust

The Dowager Countess
  Eleanor Peel Trust
People's Health Trust
People's Postcode Trust
The Performing Right Society
  Foundation
The Persimmon Charitable
  Foundation
The Jack Petchey Foundation
Petplan Charitable Trust
The Pets at Home Foundation
The Philip and Connie Phillips
  Foundation*
The Pickwell Foundation
The Pilgrim Trust
Elise Pilkington Charitable
  Trust
Pilkington Charities Fund
The Austin and Hope
  Pilkington Trust
Pink Ribbon Foundation
The Pixel Fund
The Players Foundation
Thomas Pocklington Trust
Polden-Puckham Charitable
  Foundation
The Portal Trust
Porter Foundation
Postcode Community Trust
Postcode Local Trust
Postcode Society Trust
The Mary Potter Convent
  Hospital Trust
David and Elaine Potter
  Foundation
The Potton Consolidated
  Charity
The Pret Foundation
Sir John Priestman Charity
  Trust
The Primrose Trust
The Prince of Wales's
  Charitable Foundation
The Prince's Countryside Fund
The Progress Foundation
Prostate Cancer UK
QBE European Operations
  Foundation
Quartet Community Foundation
The Queen Anne's Gate
  Foundation
Queen Mary's Roehampton
  Trust
Quintessentially Foundation
Quothquan Trust
The Racing Foundation
The Radcliffe Trust
The Bishop Radford Trust
The Rainford Trust
The Rambourg Foundation
The Joseph Rank Trust
The Eleanor Rathbone
  Charitable Trust
The Rathbones Group
  Foundation
The Sigrid Rausing Trust

The Ravensdale Trust
The Rayne Foundation
The Sir James Reckitt Charity
Red Hill Charitable Trust
Rees Jeffreys Road Fund
Richard Reeve's Foundation
The Resolution Trust
The Rhododendron Trust
Daisie Rich Trust
Richmond Parish Lands Charity
Rivers Foundation
The Robertson Trust
The Roddick Foundation
The Helen Roll Charity
The Gerald and Gail Ronson
  Family Foundation
Rosa Fund
Rosca Trust
The Rose Foundation
Rosetrees
The Rothley Trust
The Rothschild Foundation
Rothschild Foundation
  (Hanadiv) Europe
The Rowlands Trust
The Joseph Rowntree
  Charitable Trust
The Joseph Rowntree
  Foundation
The Royal British Legion
Royal Docks Trust (London)
The Royal Foundation of The
  Prince and Princess of
  Wales
Royal Masonic Trust for Girls
  and Boys
The Royal Navy and Royal
  Marines Charity
The Ruddock Foundation for
  the Arts
The Rugby Group Benevolent
  Fund Ltd
Russell Trust
The Ryvoan Trust*
The Saddlers' Company
  Charitable Fund
Erach and Roshan Sadri
  Foundation
The Jean Sainsbury Animal
  Welfare Trust
The Alan and Babette
  Sainsbury Charitable Fund
Salters' Charitable Foundation
The Samworth Foundation
Santander UK Foundation Ltd
Sarum St Michael Educational
  Charity
The Sasha Foundation*
The Savoy Educational Trust
Schroder Charity Trust
Foundation Scotland
The Scotshill Trust
Scott (Eredine) Charitable
  Trust
Francis C. Scott Charitable
  Trust

The Frieda Scott Charitable
  Trust
Scottish Property Industry
  Festival of Christmas
  (SPIFOX)
ScottishPower Foundation
Seafarers UK (King George's
  Fund for Sailors)
The Sam and Bella Sebba
  Charitable Foundation
Seedfield Trust
The Segelman Trust
The Seven Fifty Trust
The Shanly Foundation
The Shears Foundation
The Sheffield Town Trust
The Sheldon Trust
The Sylvia and Colin Shepherd
  Charitable Trust
The Archie Sherman Charitable
  Trust
The R. C. Sherriff Rosebriars
  Trust
Shetland Charitable Trust
SHINE (Support and Help in
  Education)
The Shipwrights Charitable
  Fund
The Skelton Bounty
Smallwood Trust
The Mrs Smith and Mount
  Trust
The Henry Smith Charity
Arabella and Julian Smith
  Family Trust
Stanley Smith UK Horticultural
  Trust
The R. C. Snelling Charitable
  Trust
Societe Generale UK
  Foundation
Sofronie Foundation
Somerset Community
  Foundation
The E. C. Sosnow Charitable
  Trust
Souter Charitable Trust
South Yorkshire Community
  Foundation
Southover Manor General
  Education Trust Ltd
Peter Sowerby Foundation
The Sperring Charity
The Spoore, Merry and Rixman
  Foundation
The St Hilda's Trust
St James's Place Charitable
  Foundation
Sir Walter St John's
  Educational Charity
St Peter's Saltley Trust
The Stafford Trust
The Community Foundation for
  Staffordshire
Staples Trust

The Peter Stebbings Memorial
  Charity
The Steel Charitable Trust
The Hugh Stenhouse
  Foundation
The Stevenage Community
  Trust
Sir Halley Stewart Trust
Stolkin Foundation
The Stone Family Foundation
The Stoneygate Trust
Strand Parishes Trust
Stratford-upon-Avon Town Trust
The W. O. Street Charitable
  Foundation
Streetsmart – Action for the
  Homeless
Suffolk Community Foundation
The Suffolk Historic Churches
  Trust
The Sunrise Foundation CIO
Surgo Foundation UK Ltd
Community Foundation for
  Surrey
The Sussex Community
  Foundation
Sabina Sutherland Charitable
  Trust
Sutton Coldfield Charitable
  Trust
The Swann-Morton Foundation
Swansea and Brecon Diocesan
  Board of Finance Ltd
Swarovski Foundation
The Swire Charitable Trust
The T.K. Maxx and
  Homesense Foundation
The Tabhair Charitable Trust
The Gay and Keith Talbot Trust
The Talbot Trusts
Tanner Trust
C. B. and H. H. T. Taylor 1984
  Trust
Humphrey Richardson Taylor
  Charitable Trust
The Taylor Family Foundation
Stephen Taylor Foundation
The Tedworth Charitable Trust
The Tennis Foundation
Tenovus Scotland
the7stars Foundation
The Thirty Percy Foundation
Sir Jules Thorn Charitable
  Trust
The Three Guineas Trust
The Three Oaks Trust
The Thriplow Charitable Trust
Mrs R. P. Tindall's Charitable
  Trust
The Tottenham Grammar
  School Foundation
Tower Hill Trust
The Toy Trust
The Trades House of Glasgow
The Constance Travis
  Charitable Trust

The True Colours Trust
Truemart Ltd
Trumros Ltd
Trust for London
The Trusthouse Charitable
Foundation
The James Tudor Foundation
The Tudor Trust
The Tudwick Foundation
The Tuixen Foundation
Two Magpies Fund
Community Foundation serving
Tyne and Wear and
Northumberland
Ufi VocTech Trust
Ulster Garden Villages Ltd
The Ulverscroft Foundation
The Underwood Trust
The United Reformed Church
(Wessex) Trust Ltd
United St Saviour's Charity
UnLtd (Foundation for Social
Entrepreneurs)
UPP Foundation
The Michael Uren Foundation
Valencia Communities Fund
The Valentine Charitable Trust
The Valiant Charitable Trust
The Veolia Environmental Trust
Versus Arthritis
The Veterans' Foundation
The Vintners' Foundation
Virgin Atlantic Foundation
The Virgin Money Foundation
Vision Foundation
The Vodafone Foundation
Volant Charitable Trust
The VTCT Foundation
Wade's Charity
Wakefield and Tetley Trust
The Walcot Foundation
Walton-on-Thames Charity
The Barbara Ward Children's
Foundation
Warwick Relief-in-Need Charity
The Waterloo Foundation
G. R. Waters Charitable Trust
2000
Wates Family Enterprise Trust
The Wates Foundation
The William Wates Memorial
Trust
The Geoffrey Watling Charity
We Love MCR Charity
The Weavers' Company
Benevolent Fund
The William Webster
Charitable Trust
The Weir Charitable Trust
The Welland Trust
Wellbank Foundation*
Wellbeing of Women
The Welsh Church Act Fund
Wembley National Stadium
Trust

The Westfield Health
Charitable Trust
Westhill Endowment
Westminster Almshouses
Foundation
Westminster Foundation
The Garfield Weston
Foundation
Westway Trust
The Barbara Whatmore
Charitable Trust
The Which? Fund
Whitley Animal Protection Trust
WHSmith Trust
The Will Charitable Trust
The Williams Family
Foundation
The H. D. H. Wills 1965
Charitable Trust
J. and J. R. Wilson Trust
Wiltshire Community
Foundation
The Charles Wolfson
Charitable Trust
The Wolfson Family Charitable
Trust
The Lord Leonard and Lady
Estelle Wolfson Foundation
Women's Fund for Scotland
The Wood Foundation
Wooden Spoon Society
Woodroffe Benton Foundation
The Worshipful Company of
Glovers of London
Charitable Trust
The Worshipful Company of
Information Technologists
The Eric Wright Charitable
Trust
WWDP (World Day of Prayer
National Committee for
England, Wales and
Northern Ireland)
Yorkshire Building Society
Charitable Foundation
Yorkshire Cancer Research
The Yorkshire Dales
Millennium Trust
Youth Endowment Fund (YEF)*
Youth Music
Zephyr Charitable Trust
Zurich Community Trust (UK)
Ltd

Research funding

The Aberdeenshire Educational
Trust Scheme
abrdn Financial Fairness Trust
Action Medical Research
The Bryan Adams Foundation
The AEB Charitable Trust
The AIM Foundation
The Aimwell Charitable Trust
The Alborada Trust
The Alchemy Foundation
Alzheimer's Society
The Ove Arup Foundation
Asthma and Lung UK
The Astor Foundation
The Aurora Trust (formerly The
Ashden Trust)
The Tim Bacon Foundation
The Baily Thomas Charitable
Fund
Robert Barr's Charitable Trust
The Paul Bassham Charitable
Trust
Bloodwise
The Bluston Charitable
Settlement
Breast Cancer Now
Bright Red Charity
Bill Brown 1989 Charitable
Trust
Building and Civil Engineering
Charitable Trust
The Edward Cadbury
Charitable Trust
The Barrow Cadbury Trust
Cancer Research UK
The Lorna and Yuti
Chernajovsky Biomedical
Research Foundation
Children with Cancer UK
Childs Charitable Trust
The Childwick Trust
Denise Coates Foundation
Marjorie Coote Animal Charity
Trust
The Cunningham Trust
Margaret Davies Charity
The De Laszlo Foundation
Diabetes UK
Dinwoodie Charitable Company
The Dunhill Medical Trust
The James Dyson Foundation
E. B. M. Charitable Trust
The EQ Foundation
The Evelyn Trust
The Lord Faringdon Charitable
Trust
Sir John Fisher Foundation
Marc Fitch Fund
The Louis and Valerie
Freedman Charitable
Settlement
The Freelands Foundation Ltd
Friends Provident Charitable
Foundation
GambleAware

The Gatsby Charitable
Foundation
The General Nursing Council
for England and Wales
Trust
The Glass-House Trust
The Great Britain Sasakawa
Foundation
The Guy Foundation
The Helen Hamlyn Trust
The Happold Foundation
The Health Foundation
Heart Research UK
The Michael Heller Charitable
Foundation
Help for Health
HFC Help for Children UK Ltd
The Hinduja Foundation
The Hinrichsen Foundation
Hockerill Educational
Foundation
The Jane Hodge Foundation
The Horse Trust
The Hospital Saturday Fund
James T. Howat Charitable
Trust
The Iceland Foods Charitable
Foundation
The Innocent Foundation
The Institute for Policy
Research
Integrated Education Fund
The ITF Seafarers Trust
The Jabbs Foundation
The Frank Jackson Foundation
The Kennedy Trust for
Rheumatology Research
The Kennel Club Charitable
Trust
The Graham Kirkham
Foundation
Kusuma Trust UK
The Kirby Laing Foundation
The William Leech Charity
The Leverhulme Trust
Joseph Levy Foundation
David and Ruth Lewis Family
Charitable Trust
The Linder Foundation
The Frank Litchfield Charitable
Trust
The Second Joseph Aaron
Littman Foundation
Lloyd's Register Foundation
London Housing Foundation
Ltd (LHF)
Longleigh Foundation
Robert Luff Foundation Ltd
The Mackintosh Foundation
The MacRobert Trust 2019
The Robert McAlpine
Foundation
D. D. McPhail Charitable
Settlement
Medical Research Foundation

The Millfield House Foundation
(1)
Mills and Reeve Charitable
Trust
The Henry Moore Foundation
Motor Neurone Disease
Association
J. P. Moulton Charitable
Foundation
Multiple Sclerosis Society
Edith Murphy Foundation
Murphy-Neumann Charity
Company Ltd
The Nationwide Foundation
Nesta
The Frances and Augustus
Newman Foundation
The Nineveh Charitable Trust
North West Cancer Research
Northern Consortium*
Northern Pharmacies Ltd Trust
Fund
The Nuffield Foundation
The Oakley Charitable Trust
Orthopaedic Research UK
The O'Sullivan Family
Charitable Trust
Ovingdean Hall Foundation
P. F. Charitable Trust
Parkinson's UK
The J. G. W. Patterson
Foundation
John Pearce Foundation
The Dowager Countess
Eleanor Peel Trust
Petplan Charitable Trust
The Bernard Piggott Charitable
Trust
The Pilgrim Trust
Pink Ribbon Foundation
Thomas Pocklington Trust
Prostate Cancer UK
The Racing Foundation
The Resolution Trust
RNID (The Royal National
Institute for Deaf People)
The Gerald and Gail Ronson
Family Foundation
Rosetrees
Rothschild Foundation
(Hanadiv) Europe
The Rowlands Trust
The Joseph Rowntree
Foundation
The Ruddock Foundation for
the Arts
The Alan and Babette
Sainsbury Charitable Fund
Sir Samuel Scott of Yews
Trust
Scouloudi Foundation
The Sam and Bella Sebba
Charitable Foundation
The Jean Shanks Foundation
The Sino-British Fellowship
Trust

Arabella and Julian Smith
Family Trust
Stanley Smith UK Horticultural
Trust
Peter Sowerby Foundation
The Steel Charitable Trust
Sir Halley Stewart Trust
The Stoneygate Trust
The Swann-Morton Foundation
The Gay and Keith Talbot Trust
Tenovus Scotland
Sir Jules Thorn Charitable
Trust
The Three Guineas Trust
The Tory Family Foundation
Trust for London
The Michael Uren Foundation
The Valentine Charitable Trust
Versus Arthritis
The VTCT Foundation
The Waterloo Foundation
Wellbeing of Women
The Wellcome Trust
The Galen and Hilary Weston
Foundation
The Which? Fund
The Lord Leonard and Lady
Estelle Wolfson Foundation
The Woosnam Foundation
Yorkshire Cancer Research
Youth Endowment Fund (YEF)*

Salaries

The AIM Foundation
AKO Foundation
The Alchemy Foundation
The Aurora Trust (formerly The Ashden Trust)
The Baily Thomas Charitable Fund
Philip Barker Charity
The Blandford Lake Trust
The Booth Charities
CEO Sleepout
Corra Foundation
Credit Suisse EMEA Foundation
Drapers Charitable Fund
The Ecology Trust
The Essex Youth Trust
Oliver Ford Foundation
Four Acre Trust
The Gatsby Charitable Foundation
J. Paul Getty Jr General Charitable Trust*
The Glass-House Trust
Gloucestershire Community Foundation
The Hadrian Trust
Harborne Parish Lands Charity
The Charles Hayward Foundation
The Headley Trust
Heart of England Community Foundation
Heritage Lottery Fund
P. and C. Hickinbotham Charitable Trust
Hinchley Charitable Trust
The Hintze Family Charity Foundation
The Holbeck Charitable Trust
The Holywood Trust
The Inlight Trust
Integrated Education Fund
Irish Youth Foundation (UK) Ltd (incorporating The Lawlor Foundation)
Isle of Wight Foundation
The Jabbs Foundation
The Jerusalem Trust
The Peter Kershaw Trust
Sir James Knott Trust
The LankellyChase Foundation
The Legal Education Foundation
The Leverhulme Trust
Joseph Levy Foundation
Liverpool Charity and Voluntary Services (LCVS)
Lloyds Bank Foundation for the Channel Islands
The London Community Foundation (LCF)
Man Group plc Charitable Trust

The Mercers Charitable Foundation
The Janet and Brian Moore Charitable Trust*
The National Manuscripts Conservation Trust
The Frances and Augustus Newman Foundation
The Nineveh Charitable Trust
Northern Pharmacies Ltd Trust Fund
The Olwyn Foundation
Ovingdean Hall Foundation
The Philip and Connie Phillips Foundation*
The Pilgrim Trust
Elise Pilkington Charitable Trust
The Prudence Trust
The Rayne Foundation
Richmond Parish Lands Charity
The Robertson Trust
Rosetrees
Royal Masonic Trust for Girls and Boys
The Shears Foundation
The Sheldon Trust
The Henry Smith Charity
South Yorkshire Community Foundation
St James's Place Charitable Foundation
The Stafford Trust
Sir Halley Stewart Trust
The Sunrise Foundation CIO
The Swire Charitable Trust
The Adrian Swire Charitable Trust
The Tedworth Charitable Trust
Tenovus Scotland
Trust for London
The Trusthouse Charitable Foundation
Community Foundation serving Tyne and Wear and Northumberland
Versus Arthritis
The Wates Foundation
The Weir Charitable Trust
Wooden Spoon Society
Youth Music
Zurich Community Trust (UK) Ltd

Seed funding/ start-up funding

ABF The Soldiers' Charity
Achisomoch Aid Company Ltd
Age Scotland
AKO Foundation
The Ove Arup Foundation
The Astor Foundation
The Austin Bailey Foundation
The Barbour Foundation
Barcapel Foundation Ltd
Barnwood Trust
The Michael Bishop Foundation
The Boshier-Hinton Foundation
The Harry Bottom Charitable Trust
Bristol Archdeaconry Charity
Bristol Charities
Buckinghamshire Community Foundation
Bulb Foundation
E. F. Bulmer Trust
Community Foundation for Calderdale
The Casey Trust
The Wilfrid and Constance Cave Foundation
The Christabella Charitable Trust
The André Christian Trust
Church Burgesses Trust
Church of Ireland Priorities Fund
Church Urban Fund
County Durham Community Foundation
Cumbria Community Foundation
The Dulverton Trust
The Elmley Foundation
The Essex and Southend Sports Trust
Samuel William Farmer Trust
The Gordon Fraser Charitable Trust
The Hugh Fraser Foundation
The Freshgate Trust Foundation
The Funding Network
G. M. C. Trust
Gatwick Airport Community Trust
The F. Glenister Woodger Trust CIO
Grace Charitable Trust
The J. G. Graves Charitable Trust
The Great Stone Bridge Trust of Edenbridge
The Hadrian Trust
William Harding's Charity
Heart of England Community Foundation

Herefordshire Community
  Foundation
P. and C. Hickinbotham
  Charitable Trust
The Alan Edward Higgs Charity
Hockerill Educational
  Foundation
Hollick Family Foundation
P. H. Holt Foundation
Housing Pathways Trust
James T. Howat Charitable
  Trust
The Hunter Foundation
The Indigo Trust
Integrated Education Fund
Irish Youth Foundation (UK)
  Ltd (incorporating The
  Lawlor Foundation)
The J. J. Charitable Trust
John James Bristol Foundation
The Jewish Youth Fund
Joffe Charitable Trust CIO
The Jusaca Charitable Trust
The Kennedy Leigh Charitable
  Trust
The Peter Kershaw Trust
The King Henry VIII Endowed
  Trust – Warwick
King/Cullimore Charitable
  Trust
The Mary Kinross Charitable
  Trust
The Ernest Kleinwort
  Charitable Trust
Sir James Knott Trust
The K. P. Ladd Charitable
  Trust
The Leonard Laity Stoate
  Charitable Trust
Community Foundations for
  Lancashire and Merseyside
The Allen Lane Foundation
The Mark Leonard Trust
Joseph Levy Foundation
Lincolnshire Community
  Foundation
The Linder Foundation
The Charles Littlewood Hill
  Trust
Lloyds Bank Foundation for the
  Channel Islands
London Catalyst
The London Community
  Foundation (LCF)
London Legal Support Trust
  (LLST)
The R. S. Macdonald
  Charitable Trust
The Michael Marsh Charitable
  Trust
Merchant Navy Welfare Board
Milton Keynes Community
  Foundation Ltd
The Frederick Mulder
  Foundation

The National Lottery
  Community Fund
Network for Social Change
  Charitable Trust
Newcomen Collett Foundation
The Nuffield Foundation
The Oakdale Trust
Orthopaedic Research UK
The Ouseley Church Music
  Trust
Pink Ribbon Foundation
Polden-Puckham Charitable
  Foundation
The Mary Potter Convent
  Hospital Trust
Quartet Community Foundation
The Eleanor Rathbone
  Charitable Trust
The Rayne Foundation
The Sir James Reckitt Charity
The Clive Richards Foundation
Richmond Parish Lands Charity
The Helen Roll Charity
Rosetrees
The Rothley Trust
The Roughley Charitable Trust
The Joseph Rowntree
  Charitable Trust
Royal Docks Trust (London)
The Royal Foundation of The
  Prince and Princess of
  Wales
The Royal Navy and Royal
  Marines Charity
Sarum St Michael Educational
  Charity
Francis C. Scott Charitable
  Trust
Seafarers UK (King George's
  Fund for Sailors)
The Segelman Trust
SHINE (Support and Help in
  Education)
The Shipwrights Charitable
  Fund
The Charles Skey Charitable
  Trust
The R. C. Snelling Charitable
  Trust
Somerset Community
  Foundation
W. F. Southall Trust
Sir Walter St John's
  Educational Charity
Sir Halley Stewart Trust
Strand Parishes Trust
The Summerfield Charitable
  Trust
The Sunrise Foundation CIO
Community Foundation for
  Surrey
The Sussex Community
  Foundation
Swansea and Brecon Diocesan
  Board of Finance Ltd
Tabeel Trust

Tenovus Scotland
The Thriplow Charitable Trust
The Triangle Trust (1949) Fund
Ufi VocTech Trust
The VTCT Foundation
Wade's Charity
The Scurrah Wainwright Charity
Wakefield and Tetley Trust
Walton-on-Thames Charity
The Wellcome Trust
Alfred Williams Charitable
  Trust
J. and J. R. Wilson Trust
Zurich Community Trust (UK)
  Ltd

Strategic funding

Achisomoch Aid Company Ltd
Backstage Trust
The Michael Bishop
Foundation
Bloodwise
British Motor Sports Training
Trust
The Buffini Chao Foundation
Cloudesley
Colwinston Charitable Trust
Douglas Compton James
Charitable Trust
The Corporation of Trinity
House of Deptford Strond
Dorset Community Foundation
The Evelyn Trust
The Funding Network
The Grand Trust CIO
The Harding Trust
Hinchley Charitable Trust
The Hunter Foundation
The International Bankers
Charitable Trust
The Kiawah Charitable Trust
Mace Foundation
Nesta
The Nuffield Foundation
People's Health Trust
The Players Foundation
The Potton Consolidated
Charity
The Prince of Wales's
Charitable Foundation
The Sam and Bella Sebba
Charitable Foundation
The Seven Fifty Trust
Social Investment Business
Foundation
The Tedworth Charitable Trust
The Thirty Percy Foundation
Truemart Ltd
Trumros Ltd
The United Reformed Church
(Wessex) Trust Ltd
United St Saviour's Charity
The Valentine Charitable Trust
Wembley National Stadium
Trust
Yorkshire Cancer Research
Zephyr Charitable Trust

Unrestricted funding

The 29th May 1961 Charitable
Trust
ABF The Soldiers' Charity
The Adint Charitable Trust
D. C. R. Allen Charitable Trust
The Anson Charitable Trust
The Artemis Charitable
Foundation
The Asfari Foundation
The Ballinger Charitable Trust
The Band Trust
The Barbour Foundation
Berkshire Community
Foundation
Bideford Bridge Trust
The Sydney Black Charitable
Trust
The Blagrave Trust
The British and Foreign School
Society (BFSS)
The Bromley Trust
The Brown Source Trust
The Bulldog Trust Ltd
E. F. Bulmer Trust
The Thomas Sivewright Catto
Charitable Settlement
The Wilfrid and Constance
Cave Foundation
The Chartley Foundation
CHK Foundation
The CIBC World Markets
Children's Foundation
Co-op Foundation
Countypier Ltd
CSIS Charity Fund
The Dulverton Trust
Esmée Fairbairn Foundation
The Fidelis Foundation*
The Forrester Family Trust
Friends Provident Charitable
Foundation
G. M. C. Trust
The Gale Family Charity Trust
The Goldman Sachs Charitable
Gift Fund (UK)
The Edward Gostling
Foundation
The Grimmitt Trust
Calouste Gulbenkian
Foundation – UK Branch
William Harding's Charity
The Harebell Centenary Fund
The Hilden Charitable Fund
The Hiscox Foundation
Ibrahim Foundation Ltd
Impetus
The Indigo Trust
The Frank Jackson Foundation
John James Bristol Foundation
Joffe Charitable Trust CIO
The King Henry VIII Endowed
Trust – Warwick

King/Cullimore Charitable
Trust
The Mary Kinross Charitable
Trust
The K. P. Ladd Charitable
Trust
The Allen Lane Foundation
The Edgar E. Lawley
Foundation
The Leathersellers' Foundation
Lincolnshire Community
Foundation
The Charles Littlewood Hill
Trust
Lloyds Bank Foundation for
England and Wales
John Lyon's Charity
The R. S. Macdonald
Charitable Trust
The Marsh Christian Trust
The Millfield Trust
The Peter Minet Trust
The National Lottery
Community Fund
Network for Social Change
Charitable Trust
Newby Trust Ltd
The Oakdale Trust
One Community Foundation
Ltd
The Paget Charitable Trust
The James Pantyfedwen
Foundation
(Ymddiriedolaeth James
Pantyfedwen)
The Pears Family Charitable
Foundation
People's Postcode Trust
The Pickwell Foundation
Pink Ribbon Foundation
Polden-Puckham Charitable
Foundation
David and Elaine Potter
Foundation
The Eleanor Rathbone
Charitable Trust
The Sir James Reckitt Charity
Richard Reeve's Foundation
The Robertson Trust
Rosa Fund
The Roseline Foundation*
Rothschild Foundation
(Hanadiv) Europe
The Joseph Rowntree
Charitable Trust
Royal Masonic Trust for Girls
and Boys
The Samworth Foundation
The Sandhu Charitable
Foundation
Scotland's Garden Scheme*
Seafarers UK (King George's
Fund for Sailors)
ShareGift (The Orr Mackintosh
Foundation)

Somerset Community
  Foundation
The Summerfield Charitable
  Trust
The Sunrise Foundation CIO
The Sussex Community
  Foundation
The Swire Charitable Trust
The Adrian Swire Charitable
  Trust
The Taurus Foundation
The Tuixen Foundation
The Roger and Douglas Turner
  Charitable Trust
Wade's Charity
The Scurrah Wainwright Charity
Wakefield and Tetley Trust
Wates Family Enterprise Trust
The Weinstock Fund
Wellington Management UK
  Foundation
J. and J. R. Wilson Trust
Wiltshire Community
  Foundation
The Michael and Anna Wix
  Charitable Trust
The Wyndham Charitable Trust

The alphabetical register of grant-makers

This section lists the individual records for the grant-makers.

■ The 29th May 1961 Charitable Trust

CC NO 200198　　　　**ESTABLISHED** 1961
WHERE FUNDING CAN BE GIVEN UK, with a preference for the Warwickshire and Coventry areas.
WHO CAN BENEFIT Registered charities; social enterprises; universities.
WHAT IS FUNDED The arts; museums; conservation; employment, education and training; homelessness and housing; leisure and recreation; young people; health; offenders; social welfare.
WHAT IS NOT FUNDED Individuals; unregistered charities.
TYPE OF GRANT Capital costs; core/revenue costs; unrestricted funding.
RANGE OF GRANTS Up to £270,000 but typically £6,000 to £40,000.
SAMPLE GRANTS University of Warwick (£271,000); Shelter (£75,000); Resurgo (£15,000); Birmingham Repertory Theatre, Oxford Philharmonic Orchestra and Northern Ballet (£5,000 each).
FINANCES *Financial year end 05/04/2022*
Income £6,150,000
Grants to organisations £5,070,000
Assets £131,030,000
TRUSTEES Paul Varney; Andrew Jones; Elizabeth Rantzen; Geoffrey Cox; Charles Martin.
OTHER INFORMATION Grants were awarded to 397 organisations during the year. Grants were distributed as follows: social welfare (£1.52 million); art and museums (£889,500); leisure, recreation and youth (£739,000); homelessness and housing (£577,500); employment, education and training (£519,000); medical causes (£314,000); conservation and protection (£157,000). Beneficiaries that received under £5,000 were not listed in the 2021/22 accounts.
HOW TO APPLY Apply in writing to the correspondent, enclosing your organisation's most recent annual report and accounts. Follow-up visits to charities may be requested to better understand applicants' requirements. The trustees typically meet in February, May, August and November. Due to the large number of applications received, applications are not acknowledged and unsuccessful applicants are not notified.
CONTACT DETAILS The Trustees, One Eastwood, Binley Business Park, Coventry CV3 2UB *Tel.* 020 7024 9034 *Email* enquiries@29may1961charity.org.uk

■ The 3Ts Charitable Trust

CC NO 1109733　　　　**ESTABLISHED** 2005
WHERE FUNDING CAN BE GIVEN UK and overseas.
WHO CAN BENEFIT Registered charities.
WHAT IS FUNDED General charitable purposes.
RANGE OF GRANTS Between £500 and £190,000.
SAMPLE GRANTS Médecins Sans Frontières (£190,000); Marie Curie Cancer Care (£130,000); St Giles Trust (£85,000); Supporting Dalit Children (£50,000); Envision (£1,000); Cerebral Palsy Alliance Research (£510).
FINANCES *Financial year end 31/03/2022*
Income £3,290,000
Grants to organisations £1,640,000
Assets £13,650,000
TRUSTEES William Medlicott; Charles Sherwood; Tim Sherwood; Tabitha Sherwood; Tatiana Sherwood; Rosemary Sherwood.
OTHER INFORMATION In 2021/22 the trust made grants to 27 organisations.

HOW TO APPLY The trustees adopt a proactive approach in seeking worthy causes requiring support.
CONTACT DETAILS The Trustees, PO Box 68, Knebworth, Hertfordshire SG3 6UZ *Tel.* 01892 701743 *Email* info@3tscharitabletrust.com

■ 4 Charity Foundation

CC NO 1077143　　　　**ESTABLISHED** 1999
WHERE FUNDING CAN BE GIVEN UK and Israel.
WHO CAN BENEFIT Mainly Jewish charities and causes.
WHAT IS FUNDED General charitable purposes; social welfare; education; health; Jewish causes.
RANGE OF GRANTS Up to £200,000.
SAMPLE GRANTS The Marque Foundation (£200,000); Ahavat Yisrael UK (£145,600); KKL Charity Accounts (£142,000); British Friends of Yeshivat Har Etzion (£108,000); JNF Charitable Trust (£42,800); Conference of European Rabbis (£36,100); American Jewish Joint Distribution Committee UK Trust (£33,100).
FINANCES *Financial year end 31/03/2022*
Income £167,800
Grants to organisations £715,500
Assets £3,680,000
TRUSTEES Jacob Schimmel; Verette Schimmel; Johnathan Schimmel.
OTHER INFORMATION Grants for 2021/22 were broken down as follows: advancement of education (£459,500); advancement of health or saving lives (£12,000); prevention or relief of poverty (£44,900); other (£200,000). Only grants of £10,000 or more were listed in the beneficiaries, with grants of under £10,000 totalling £7,900.
HOW TO APPLY Apply in writing to the correspondent.
CONTACT DETAILS Jacob Schimmel, Trustee, 121 Princes Park Avenue, London NW11 0JS *Tel.* 020 8455 0100 *Email* four4charities@gmail.com

■ The 4814 Trust

CC NO 1162714
WHERE FUNDING CAN BE GIVEN UK.
WHO CAN BENEFIT Small UK charities.
WHAT IS FUNDED Social welfare; health; children and young people; general charitable purposes.
RANGE OF GRANTS Typically up to £10,000.
SAMPLE GRANTS St Giles Trust (£45,000); The Trussell Trust (£40,000); Climbing Out (£15,000); The Amber Foundation (£12,000).
FINANCES *Financial year end 31/12/2021*
Income £2,960,000
Grants to organisations £112,000
Grants to individuals £3,600
Assets £7,450,000
TRUSTEES Chris Bedwell; Carole Bedwell; Chris Gardner; Francis Bedwell.
OTHER INFORMATION The trust's income for 2021 was increased from its typical level by capital (valued at £2.87 million) donated by the Bestobell-Meggitt Welfare Trust (Charity Commission no. 284376) with which The 4814 Trust shares trustees and on whose behalf awards grants. Typically The 4814 Trust has a much lower annual income of around £200,000. Grants were awarded to four organisations during the year. An additional £3,600 was awarded to individuals.
HOW TO APPLY Applications should be made in writing and sent via email or post to the correspondent. The trustees ask that you include a copy of your latest accounts, any

supporting literature and an overview of your plans for the next 12 months. The trustees will contact successful applicants or applicants from whom more information is required.

CONTACT DETAILS Chris Bedwell, Chair of Trustees, PO Box 96, Somerton TA11 9BS *Email* grants@the4814trust.org *Website* www.the4814trust.com

....

■ The 64 Trust

CC NO 1190683

WHERE FUNDING CAN BE GIVEN UK, with a preference for Merseyside.

WHO CAN BENEFIT Charitable organisations.

WHAT IS FUNDED General charitable purposes.

SAMPLE GRANTS A list of beneficiaries was not included in the annual report and accounts.

FINANCES *Financial year end* 31/12/2021
Income £503,000
Grants to organisations £461,000
Assets £17,500

TRUSTEES John Nelson; Anne Lundon; Ramesh Kumar Jagota; Pauline Connolly.

HOW TO APPLY Apply in writing to the correspondent.

CONTACT DETAILS The Trustees, 64 Mount Pleasant, Liverpool L3 5SD *Tel.* 0151 318 9931 *Email* the64trust@outlook.com

■ The A Team Foundation Ltd

CC NO 1077094   **ESTABLISHED** 1999
WHERE FUNDING CAN BE GIVEN UK.
WHO CAN BENEFIT Charitable organisations.
WHAT IS FUNDED Food and land projects that are ecologically, economically and socially conscious.
RANGE OF GRANTS Typically £1,000 to £50,000.
SAMPLE GRANTS Prism the Gift Fund (£179,200); The Gaia Foundation (£50,000); Sustainable Food Trust (£20,000); Fairwild Foundation (£5,000).
FINANCES *Financial year end 05/04/2022*
Income £420,200
Grants to organisations £785,500
Assets £17,740,000
TRUSTEES Benjamin Arbib; Paul Reynolds; Marina Arbib.
OTHER INFORMATION In 2021/22, the foundation awarded grants to 21 organisations.
HOW TO APPLY Unsolicited applications are not accepted.
CONTACT DETAILS The Trustees, 61 Grosvenor Street, London W1K 3JE *Tel.* 020 3011 1100 *Email* info@ateamfoundation.org *Website* www. ateamfoundation.org

■ The A. and J. Charitable Trust

CC NO 1058058   **ESTABLISHED** 1996
WHERE FUNDING CAN BE GIVEN UK.
WHO CAN BENEFIT Medical organisations.
WHAT IS FUNDED Medical research.
SAMPLE GRANTS Game and Wildlife Conservation Trust (£50,000); Turquoise Mountain Trust (£50,000); Somerville College (£25,000); Dragon School Trust (£10,000); Royal Marsden Cancer (£5,000); Atlantic Salmon Trust (£5,000); St Peter's PCC (£1,500).
FINANCES *Financial year end 05/04/2022*
Income £256,300
Grants to organisations £384,500
Assets £216,000
TRUSTEES Lady Jane Parker; Sir Alan Parker; Graham Chambers.
HOW TO APPLY Apply in writing to the correspondent.
CONTACT DETAILS Suzanne Rose, c/o Dixon Wilson, 22 Chancery Lane, London WC2A 1LS *Tel.* 020 7680 8100 *Email* suzannerose@dixonwilson.co. uk

■ The A. B. Charitable Trust

CC NO 1000147   **ESTABLISHED** 1990
WHERE FUNDING CAN BE GIVEN UK.
WHO CAN BENEFIT Registered charities. The trustees favour charities that have an annual income of between £150,000 and £1.5 million and do not have substantial free reserves.
WHAT IS FUNDED Migrants and refugees; criminal justice and penal reform; human rights, particularly access to justice.
WHAT IS NOT FUNDED Individuals; organisations that are not registered charities.
TYPE OF GRANT Project funding; core costs.
RANGE OF GRANTS Typically £10,000 to £50,000.

SAMPLE GRANTS Refugee Action (£200,000); Legal Education Foundation (£125,000); Action for Race Equality (£100,000); Refugees at Home (£50,000); Central England Law Centre and Doctors of the World (£30,000 each); Safe Passage International (£20,000); Transform Justice (£20,000); Public Law Project (£3,750); Centre for Knowledge Equity (£500).
FINANCES *Financial year end 30/04/2022*
Income £4,740,000
Grants to organisations £5,030,000
Assets £1,390,000
TRUSTEE ABCT Trustee Ltd.
OTHER INFORMATION In 2021/22, the trust ran three programmes: the Open Programme (£2.53 million); the Special Initiatives Programme (invitation only; £1.48 million); and the Anchor Programme (invitation only; £500,000). Grants were distributed by cause as follows: human rights (£1.4 million), migrants and refugees (£2.26 million) and the justice system (£1.08 million).
HOW TO APPLY Applications can be completed online via the trust's website. Application deadlines are typically in January, April, July and October. Full guidelines and answers to FAQs are available on the trust's website.
CONTACT DETAILS Havva Hassan, Grants Administrator, c/o Woodsford, 3rd Floor, 8 Bloomsbury Street, London WC1B 3SR *Tel.* 020 7313 8070 *Email* mail@ abcharitabletrust.org.uk *Website* www. abcharitabletrust.org.uk

■ The A. H. Trust

CC NO 1101843   **ESTABLISHED** 2003
WHERE FUNDING CAN BE GIVEN England and Wales.
WHO CAN BENEFIT Jewish charitable organisations and members of the Jewish community who are in need.
WHAT IS FUNDED Advancement of the Jewish religion; social welfare; education.
SAMPLE GRANTS Kollel Beis Aharon (£35,000).
FINANCES *Financial year end 31/03/2022*
Income £199,400
Grants to organisations £143,300
Assets £1,240,000
TRUSTEES Elisabeth Smith; Arye Grossnass; Sarah Smith.
OTHER INFORMATION The grant total includes grants awarded to organisations and individuals; a breakdown was not available. Only grants of £25,000 and above were listed in the annual report and accounts. Grants of below £25,000 totalled £108,300.
HOW TO APPLY Apply in writing to the correspondent.
CONTACT DETAILS Ivor Smith, Trustee, New Burlington House, 1075 Finchley Road, London NW11 0PU *Tel.* 020 8203 9991 *Email* mail@ cohenarnold.com

■ The A. S. Charitable Trust

CC NO 242190   **ESTABLISHED** 1965
WHERE FUNDING CAN BE GIVEN UK and overseas.
WHO CAN BENEFIT Christian causes; places of worship; charitable organisations.
WHAT IS FUNDED Christian causes; Christianity; overseas aid; overseas development; peace and reconciliation; social justice.
WHAT IS NOT FUNDED Individuals.
RANGE OF GRANTS Typically £5,000 to £50,000.
SAMPLE GRANTS Friends of Bix Church (£50,000); St Martin's House Project (£40,000); GRACE Organisation (£29,800); Langley House Trust

(£15,000); Lambeth Trust (£10,000); Bibles for Children and Cross Rhythms (£5,000 each); Hope Coventry (£2,500).

FINANCES *Financial year end 05/04/2021*
Income £410,300
Grants to organisations £216,600
Assets £19,610,000

TRUSTEES Caroline Eady; George Calvocoressi; Simon Sampson.

OTHER INFORMATION The 2020/21 accounts were the latest available at the time of writing (May 2023). During the year, grants were given to over 11 organisations totalling £216,600. Only grants of over £1,000 were listed in the beneficiaries, with grants of less than £1,000 totalling £400.

HOW TO APPLY Apply in writing to the correspondent.

CONTACT DETAILS The Trustees, Bix Bottom Farm, Henley-on-Thames, Oxfordshire RG9 6BH

■ A. W. Charitable Trust

CC NO 283322 **ESTABLISHED** 1961
WHERE FUNDING CAN BE GIVEN London; Gateshead; Manchester; Salford; Israel.
WHO CAN BENEFIT Registered charities.
WHAT IS FUNDED Orthodox Jewish causes; social welfare.
SAMPLE GRANTS A list of beneficiaries was not included in the annual report and accounts.
FINANCES *Financial year end 30/06/2022*
Income £16,010,000
Grants to organisations £5,220,000
Assets £288,010,000
TRUSTEES Rabbi Aubrey Weis; Rachel Weis; Sir Weis.
HOW TO APPLY Apply in writing to the correspondent.
CONTACT DETAILS The Trustees, 66 Waterpark Road, Manchester M7 4JL *Tel.* 0161 740 0116

■ The Abbeyfield Research Foundation

CC NO 1167685 **ESTABLISHED** 2016
WHERE FUNDING CAN BE GIVEN UK.
WHO CAN BENEFIT Organisations, mainly universities.
WHAT IS FUNDED Research relating to the quality of life and provision of care for older people.
WHAT IS NOT FUNDED Research using animals.
TYPE OF GRANT PhD studentships; project costs.
RANGE OF GRANTS PhD studentships of up to £30,000 per year; small project grants of up to £50,000 per year; pump-priming grants of up to £20,000 for one year.
SAMPLE GRANTS Nottinghamshire NHS Trust (£46,000); Leeds University (£37,600); University of York (£21,600); Sheffield Hospitals NHS Trust (£17,400); University of Sheffield (£8,000); King's College (£1,600); University of Edinburgh (£344); University of the West of Scotland (£234).
FINANCES *Financial year end 31/03/2022*
Income £100,000
Grants to organisations £144,000
Assets £49,300
TRUSTEES Prof. Brian Williams; Robin Means; Kenneth Staveley.
OTHER INFORMATION During 2021/22, the foundation awarded one new grant of £114,000 to the University of Worcester, as well as making payments for grants awarded in previous years.
HOW TO APPLY The foundation invites applications annually, typically in October. Application forms can be downloaded from the foundation's website and returned via email. Successful applicants at stage one are invited to complete a second-stage application.
CONTACT DETAILS The Trustees, St Peter's House, 2 Bricket Road, St Albans, Hertfordshire AL1 3JW *Tel.* 01727 734067 *Email* research@ abbeyfield.com *Website* www. abbeyfieldresearchfoundation.org

■ The Aberbrothock Skea Trust

OSCR NO SC039202 **ESTABLISHED** 2007
WHERE FUNDING CAN BE GIVEN The east of Scotland, north of the Firth of Tay.
WHO CAN BENEFIT Charitable organisations.
WHAT IS FUNDED General charitable purposes, including: health; children and young people; wildlife; the armed forces.
RANGE OF GRANTS Usually up to £2,500.
SAMPLE GRANTS A list of beneficiaries was not included in the annual report and accounts.
FINANCES *Financial year end 31/01/2022*
Income £208,500
Grants to organisations £93,500
Assets £5,150,000
OTHER INFORMATION Forty-four organisations were supported during the year, all of which received a grant of under £5,000. The 2021/22 accounts state that the trust normally limits grants paid to a charitable organisation in any calendar year to a maximum of £2,500.
HOW TO APPLY Apply in writing to the correspondent.
CONTACT DETAILS The Trustees, c/o Thorntons Law LLP, Brothockbank House, Arbroath, Angus DD11 1NE

■ The Aberdeen Endowments Trust

OSCR NO SC010507 **ESTABLISHED** 1909
WHERE FUNDING CAN BE GIVEN The former City and Royal Burgh of Aberdeen (i.e. pre-1975).
WHO CAN BENEFIT Organisations and individuals.
WHAT IS FUNDED Education and the arts. The main purpose of the trust is to give financial assistance to individuals for educational purposes.
WHAT IS NOT FUNDED People or organisations from outside the former City and Royal Burgh of Aberdeen.
TYPE OF GRANT One-off grants; bursaries.
RANGE OF GRANTS Typically £1,000.
SAMPLE GRANTS A list of beneficiaries was not included in the annual report and accounts.
FINANCES *Financial year end 31/12/2021*
Income £1,220,000
Grants to organisations £843,000
Assets £43,270,000
TRUSTEES Three people elected by Aberdeen City Council; one by the Senatus Academicus of the University of Aberdeen; two by the governors of Robert Gordon's College, Aberdeen; two by the Church of Scotland Presbytery of Aberdeen; one by the churches of Aberdeen other than the Church of Scotland; one by the Society of Advocates in Aberdeen; one by the Convener Court of the Seven Incorporated Trades of Aberdeen; one by the trade unions with branches in Aberdeen; one by the Aberdeen Local Association of the Educational Institute of Scotland; and between two and four co-optees.
OTHER INFORMATION The grant total includes amounts awarded to individuals and organisations.
HOW TO APPLY Application forms are available from the correspondent. The trust's Benefactions Committee, which makes financial awards, normally meets nine or ten times a year.

CONTACT DETAILS The Trustees, 19 Albert Street, Aberdeen, Aberdeenshire AB25 1QF *Tel.* 01224 640194 *Email* aet1909@btopenworld.com *Website* www.aberdeenendowmentstrust.co.uk

---

■ The Aberdeenshire Educational Trust Scheme

OSCR NO SC028382   **ESTABLISHED** 1999
WHERE FUNDING CAN BE GIVEN Aberdeenshire.
WHO CAN BENEFIT Individuals; schools and colleges; universities; charitable organisations.
WHAT IS FUNDED Further education, including bursaries or grants, fees and equipment or books; school trips; sports clubs and facilities; the promotion of education in art, music or drama.
TYPE OF GRANT Capital costs; research funding; project funding; bursaries.
RANGE OF GRANTS Small grants of £200 to £540.
SAMPLE GRANTS A list of beneficiaries was not included in the annual report and accounts.
FINANCES *Financial year end 31/03/2022*
Income £152,000
Grants to organisations £116,000
Grants to individuals £73,000
Assets £4,450,000
TRUSTEES Isobel Davidson; Judy Whyte; Susan Padfield.
OTHER INFORMATION The 2021/22 annual report states that the maximum grant for individuals for school trips or further education has been increased to £540. Grants were broken down as follows: special equipment £90,000; further education (£52,000); sports facilities (£26,000); travel (£16,000); preference grants – schools (£4,000); prizes (£1,000).
HOW TO APPLY Apply via the application form on the trust's website.
CONTACT DETAILS The Administrator, Aberdeenshire Council, Woodhill House, Westburn Road, Aberdeen, Aberdeenshire AB16 5GB *Email* asataet@aberdeenshire.gov.uk *Website* www.aberdeenshire.gov.uk/benefits-and-grants/educational-grants

---

■ ABF The Soldiers' Charity

CC NO 1146420   **ESTABLISHED** 1944
WHERE FUNDING CAN BE GIVEN UK and overseas.
WHO CAN BENEFIT Charitable organisations with a preference for members of COBSEO/Veterans Scotland; other not-for-profit organisations; community projects; housing associations.
WHAT IS FUNDED Support for British Army soldiers, veterans and their immediate families, including in the following areas: welfare; employment; education and training; care of older people; housing; disability; and well-being.
WHAT IS NOT FUNDED Organisations that do not support serving soldiers, veterans and their immediate families, and/or the wider Army community; funding requests made within 12 months of the outcome of a previous application; gap years, study trips, fundraising expeditions or sponsorship; specific posts and salaries (however, the trustees will consider contributing to an organisation's core operating costs); full cost recovery; multi-year grants; umbrella organisations.
TYPE OF GRANT Core/revenue costs; seed funding/start-up funding; unrestricted funding.
RANGE OF GRANTS Up to £150,000.
SAMPLE GRANTS Defence Medical Welfare Service (£150,000); Regular Forces Employment

Association (RFEA) (£100,000); The Not Forgotten Association (£35,000); The Warrior Programme (£20,000); Mission Motorsport (£7,000).
FINANCES *Financial year end 31/03/2022*
Income £11,160,000
Grants to organisations £3,430,000
Assets £100,110,000
TRUSTEES Simon Hale; Christopher Hughes; Paul Carney; Maj. General Paul Griffiths; Rowena Fell; Rachel Booth; David London; Anthony Scott; Amanda Metcalfe; James Rous; Mary Fagan.
OTHER INFORMATION Grants were made under the following headings: employment, education and training; family; housing; older people; well-being.
HOW TO APPLY Apply via the application form on the charity's website.
CONTACT DETAILS The Trustees, Mountbarrow House, 12 Elizabeth Street, London SW1W 9RB *Tel.* 020 7901 8900 *Email* externalgrants@soldierscharity.org *Website* https://soldierscharity.org/need-our-help/charity-grants

---

■ abrdn Charitable Foundation

OSCR NO SC042597   **ESTABLISHED** 2011
WHERE FUNDING CAN BE GIVEN UK and overseas where the company has a presence.
WHO CAN BENEFIT Registered charities.
WHAT IS FUNDED There are two categories: People and Planet. The People category focuses on enabling education, employment and financial wellness. The Planet category focuses on protecting nature and addressing climate change.
WHAT IS NOT FUNDED Projects or organisations that promote religious or political views, or discriminate against protected characteristics such as sexual orientation or gender; applications from crowdfunding initiatives or individuals; projects with capital build costs.
TYPE OF GRANT Project costs.
RANGE OF GRANTS Between £5,000 and £25,000.
SAMPLE GRANTS A list of beneficiaries was not included in the annual report and accounts.
FINANCES *Financial year end 31/12/2021*
Income £2,220,000
Grants to organisations £1,280,000
Assets £1,310,000
TRUSTEES Stephanie Bruce; Stephen Whitehead; René Buehlmann; Paul Aggett; David Gorman.
OTHER INFORMATION The foundation also develops partnerships with charities tackling the educational needs of disadvantaged young people in emerging market countries. Grants were distributed as follows: local community support (£1.05 million) and emerging markets projects (£238,800).
HOW TO APPLY Complete an expression of interest form on the foundation's website. The board of directors meets and reviews funding requests on a quarterly basis.
CONTACT DETAILS The Trustees, 10 Queen's Terrace, Aberdeen AB10 1XL *Email* charitablefoundation@abrdn.com *Website* www.abrdn.com/corporate/corporate-sustainability/abrdn-charitable-foundation

■ abrdn Financial Fairness Trust

OSCR NO SC040877 **ESTABLISHED** 2009

WHERE FUNDING CAN BE GIVEN UK, with a preference for Scotland.

WHO CAN BENEFIT Registered charities; voluntary organisations; think tanks; campaigning groups; research bodies; universities.

WHAT IS FUNDED Research, policy and campaigning on structural and individual issues relating to financial well-being.

WHAT IS NOT FUNDED See the online funding guide for a comprehensive list of exclusions, which includes individuals.

TYPE OF GRANT Project funding; core costs; research; campaigning.

RANGE OF GRANTS Mostly between £50,000 and £120,000.

SAMPLE GRANTS University of York (£147,200 in two grants); University of Oxford (£123,000); University of Southampton (£90,800); Parenting NI (£77,000); Gingerbread (£74,800); Centrepoint (£60,100); Coventry University (£59,800); Resolution Foundation (£12,000).

FINANCES *Financial year end 31/12/2021*
Income £2,590,000
Grants to organisations £754,300
Assets £103,510,000

TRUSTEES Alistair Darling; James Daunt; Naomi Eisenstadt; Prof. David Hall; Prof. Wendy Loretto; Graeme McEwan; Keith Skeoch; Euan Stirling; Lucy Heller; Ella Hugh. Matthew Upton; Kate Bell; Jenny Marra.

OTHER INFORMATION During 2021, grants were awarded via the trust's three programmes as follows: Income (£405,900); Assets (£198,000); Spending (£135,000). A further £15,500 was awarded through a category titled 'Cross cutting'.

HOW TO APPLY Application forms and guidelines can be downloaded from the trust's website. When completed, applications should be sent to applications@financialfairness.org.uk. The trust has two annual deadlines, in February and June. See the website for details of upcoming deadlines.

CONTACT DETAILS The Trustees, 1 George Street, Edinburgh EH2 2LL *Tel.* 0131 528 4243 *Email* enquiries@financialfairness.org.uk *Website* www.financialfairness.org.uk/en

■ The Access to Justice Foundation

CC NO 1126147 **ESTABLISHED** 2008

WHERE FUNDING CAN BE GIVEN UK.

WHO CAN BENEFIT Legal advice charities.

WHAT IS FUNDED The provision of legal assistance to people in need.

TYPE OF GRANT Core costs.

RANGE OF GRANTS Typically up to £60,000.

SAMPLE GRANTS Support Through Court (£684,100); Central England Law Centre (£168,600); Friends, Families and Travellers (£60,000); Dostiyo Asian Women and Girls Organisation (£60,000); Disability North (£42,300); Special Educational Needs Advice Centre (£25,500); Wanstead and Woodford Migrant Support (£10,000); Citizens Advice Cornwall (£2,900); Barrow Cadbury Trust (£500).

FINANCES *Financial year end 31/12/2021*
Income £7,700,000
Grants to organisations £6,450,000
Assets £1,360,000

TRUSTEES Laurence Harris; Nicola Sawford; Joe Snape; Andrew Seager; Sarah Stephens; Audrey Haaxman; Maura McGowan; Gavin Mansfield; Simon Davis; Maxcine Akinsowon; Carol Storer; Sacha Rose.

OTHER INFORMATION Grants were awarded to 94 organisations in 2021.

HOW TO APPLY Visit the foundation's website for the latest information on funding opportunities.

CONTACT DETAILS Grants Team, PO Box 64162, London WC2A 9AN *Tel.* 020 7092 3973 *Email* enquiries@atjf.org.uk *Website* https://atjf.org.uk

■ Achisomoch Aid Company Ltd

CC NO 278387 **ESTABLISHED** 1979

WHERE FUNDING CAN BE GIVEN UK and overseas.

WHO CAN BENEFIT Jewish schools and charities.

WHAT IS FUNDED The advancement of religion in accordance with the Jewish faith.

TYPE OF GRANT Project funding; strategic funding; capital costs; development funding; campaigning; seed funding.

RANGE OF GRANTS Up to £1.28 million.

SAMPLE GRANTS Yeshivas Beis Hillel (£2 million); Hasmonean High School Charitable Trust (£1.28 million); Michtav Oz (£740,000); North London Welfare and Educational Foundation (£530,400); Mercaz Hatorah Netzach Yisroel (£377,900); Noa Girls (£201,200); Vishnitz Girls School Ltd (£100,000).

FINANCES *Financial year end 31/03/2022*
Income £50,450,000
Grants to organisations £46,060,000
Assets £15,770,000

TRUSTEES Jack Emanuel; Michael Hackenbroch; Richard Denton; Anthony Katz.

OTHER INFORMATION The following information about how the charity operates is given on the its website: 'Achisomoch is a charity voucher agency – it is like a bank. You open an account with us and then pay money into the account. You are given a cheque (voucher) book and can then make (charitable) payments by using these vouchers. As a charity in its own right, we can reclaim the tax rebate under Gift Aid to increase the money in your account and available for distribution to charities. Donations, via vouchers can be made only to registered charities. You get regular statements and can arrange to speak to client services for any help or special instructions.'.

HOW TO APPLY Charity applications and guidelines are available on the charity's website.

CONTACT DETAILS The Trustees, Enterprise House, 2 The Crest, London NW4 2HN *Tel.* 020 8731 8988 *Email* admin@achisomoch.org *Website* www.achisomoch.org

■ Action Medical Research

CC NO 208701 **ESTABLISHED** 1952

WHERE FUNDING CAN BE GIVEN UK.

WHO CAN BENEFIT University departments; hospitals; research institutions.

WHAT IS FUNDED Medical research focusing on children's health including research into premature birth, cerebral palsy, childhood infections, juvenile arthritis, leukaemia and other rare conditions. Research into medical engineering is also supported.

WHAT IS NOT FUNDED A full list of exclusions can be found on the charity's website.

TYPE OF GRANT Project funding; research training fellowships.

RANGE OF GRANTS Up to £250,000.

SAMPLE GRANTS A list of research projects funded by the charity can be found on it's website.

Think carefully about every application. Is it justified?

225

FINANCES *Financial year end* 31/12/2022
Income £6,110,000
Grants to organisations £2,550,000
Assets £6,540,000

TRUSTEES Luke Bordewich; Prof. David Edwards; Richard Wild; Kathy Harvey; Prof. David Rowitch; Richard Stoneham-Buck; Karen Last; Prof. Stephanie Schorge; Rajat Sharma.

HOW TO APPLY Full details of applying for both project and research grants are given on the charity's website along with current closing dates.

CONTACT DETAILS The Trustees, 5th Floor, 167–169 Great Portland Street, London W1W 5PF *Tel.* 01403 210406 *Email* info@action.org.uk *Website* www.action.org.uk

....

■ Adam Family Foundation

OSCR NO SC046468　　**ESTABLISHED** 2016
WHERE FUNDING CAN BE GIVEN Scotland, mainly Moray.
WHO CAN BENEFIT Charitable organisations; individuals.
WHAT IS FUNDED Community facilities; community development; social welfare; homelessness and housing; education; sport; the arts; older people; children and young people.
SAMPLE GRANTS A list of beneficiaries was not included in the annual report and accounts.
FINANCES *Financial year end* 30/04/2022
Income £140,000
Grants to organisations £171,400
Assets £115,300
OTHER INFORMATION The grant total includes amounts awarded to 23 organisations and 4 individuals during the year. We were unable to determine a breakdown.
HOW TO APPLY Apply in writing to the correspondent.
CONTACT DETAILS The Trustees, Alexander Fleming House, 8 Southfield Drive, Elgin, Morayshire IV30 6GR

....

■ The Bryan Adams Foundation

CC NO 1117863
WHERE FUNDING CAN BE GIVEN UK and overseas.
WHO CAN BENEFIT Registered charities.
WHAT IS FUNDED Education of children and young people; older people; animal welfare; conservation; disaster relief; museums and galleries; recreational facilities; health; medical research.
TYPE OF GRANT Capital costs; project funding; research.
RANGE OF GRANTS Mostly £1,000 to £5,000.
SAMPLE GRANTS Hoping Foundation (£25,000); Thomas's Foundation (£20,500); Place2Be (£15,000); Big Issue Foundation and Help Musicians UK (£10,000 each); Dusty Yak Foundation (£5,000); St Benedict Day Nursery (£3,000); MEI Schools Canada (£580).
FINANCES *Financial year end* 31/03/2022
Income £144,100
Grants to organisations £109,100
Assets £461,700
TRUSTEES Bryan Adams; Alicia Grimaldi; Rafi Manoukian; Andrew Trotter.
OTHER INFORMATION Grants were made to 12 organisations during the year.
HOW TO APPLY At the time of writing (February 2022) the foundation was closed for applications. Check the foundation's website for the latest information.

CONTACT DETAILS The Trustees, 8 Apollo Place, London SW10 0ET *Tel.* 020 7376 3819 *Email* foundation@bryanadams.com *Website* www.thebryanadamsfoundation.com

....

■ The Addleshaw Goddard Charitable Trust

CC NO 286887　　**ESTABLISHED** 1983
WHERE FUNDING CAN BE GIVEN Aberdeen; Edinburgh; Glasgow; Greater London; Leeds; Manchester; Doha, Dubai; Hamburg; Hong Kong; Muscat; Paris; Singapore; Tokyo.
WHO CAN BENEFIT Local, national and international charities.
WHAT IS FUNDED General charitable purposes; education; health; legal education and the legal profession; social welfare.
SAMPLE GRANTS A list of beneficiaries was not included in the annual report and accounts. Previous beneficiaries have included: Centrepoint; Changing Faces; NSPCC; Street League.
FINANCES *Financial year end* 05/04/2022
Income £82,800
Grants to organisations £175,600
Assets £230,200
TRUSTEES Bruce Lightbody; Louise Cliffe; Jonathan Cheney; Lisa Rodgers; Pervinder Kaur.
OTHER INFORMATION The following breakdown of grants awarded was provided: national and other donations (£100,000); speculative applications (£50,000); COVID-19 response (£17,000); matching staff fundraising (£8,600).
HOW TO APPLY Apply in writing to the correspondent.
CONTACT DETAILS Jonathan Cheney, Trustee, Addleshaw Goddard LLP, 3 Sovereign Square, Sovereign Street, Leeds LS1 4ER *Tel.* 0113 209 2578 *Email* jonathan.cheney@addleshawgoddard.com

....

■ Adenfirst Ltd

CC NO 291647　　**ESTABLISHED** 1984
WHERE FUNDING CAN BE GIVEN Worldwide.
WHO CAN BENEFIT Mainly Jewish organisations.
WHAT IS FUNDED Education; health; the relief of poverty; the advancement of religion.
RANGE OF GRANTS £1,000 to £24,000.
SAMPLE GRANTS Russian Immigrant Aid Fund Ltd (£24,000); Colel Kupath Ramban Ltd (£20,500); Rosecare Foundation (£11,600); Kol Yom Trust (£10,000); North London Welfare and Educational Foundation (£9,000); Tchabe Kollel Ltd (£8,000).
FINANCES *Financial year end* 31/12/2021
Income £289,700
Grants to organisations £163,700
Assets £5,510,000
TRUSTEES Mrs H. F. Bondi; Leonard Bondi; Ian Heitner; Sarah Heitner; Sylvia Cymerman; Michael Cymerman; Chaim Friedmann.
HOW TO APPLY Apply in writing to the correspondent.
CONTACT DETAILS Mrs H. F. Bondi, Company Secretary, c/o 479 Holloway Road, London N7 6LE *Tel.* 020 7272 2255 *Email* mail@cohenarnold.com

■ The Adint Charitable Trust

CC NO 265290   **ESTABLISHED** 1973
WHERE FUNDING CAN BE GIVEN UK.
WHO CAN BENEFIT Registered charities.
WHAT IS FUNDED General charitable purposes, with a preference for health and medical research, social welfare, disability, and housing and homelessness.
WHAT IS NOT FUNDED Individuals; non-registered charities.
TYPE OF GRANT Capital costs; core/revenue costs; project funding; unrestricted funding.
RANGE OF GRANTS Typically £5,000 to £10,000.
SAMPLE GRANTS ABF The Soldiers' Charity and British Red Cross (£20,000 each); Alzheimer's Society, Canine Partners, Hospice UK, Listening Books, Meningitis Now and Support Through Court (£10,000 each); Clowns in the Sky, Dystonia Society and Prostate Cancer UK (£5,000 each).
FINANCES *Financial year end* 05/04/2022
Income £189,900
Grants to organisations £490,000
Assets £9,880,000
TRUSTEES Anthony Edwards; Douglas Oram; Brian Pate; Claire Edwards.
OTHER INFORMATION According to the 2021/22 annual report, during the year the trust made additional awards 'well above the run rate of recent years' to help smaller charities negatively affected by the economic climate. The trustees anticipated to continue this higher rate of grants in 2022/23. The trust made grants to 53 organisations in 2021/22.
HOW TO APPLY Apply in writing to the correspondent, including full details of the charity for which the funding is requested. Unsuccessful applicants will not be notified.
CONTACT DETAILS The Trustees, c/o Hazlewoods, Windsor House, Bayshill Road, Cheltenham, Gloucestershire GL50 3AT *Email* adintct@ btinternet.com

■ The Adlard Family Charitable Foundation

CC NO 1164276   **ESTABLISHED** 2015
WHERE FUNDING CAN BE GIVEN Worldwide, predominantly England and Wales.
WHO CAN BENEFIT Charitable organisations.
WHAT IS FUNDED General charitable purposes; the environment, conservation and heritage.
RANGE OF GRANTS £1,000 to £30,000.
SAMPLE GRANTS Greenpeace Environmental Trust (£20,000); Ellesmere College (£10,000); Hmm Arts Ltd, The Hive and Lakes International Comic Art Festivals Ltd (£5,000 each); RNLI (£2,000); Disability Arts in Shropshire, Monduli Green and Pentabus Arts Ltd (£1,000 each).
FINANCES *Financial year end* 09/09/2021
Income £41,900
Grants to organisations £61,000
Assets £157,700
TRUSTEES Elsa Adlard; Charles Adlard; Ludlow Trust Company Ltd.
OTHER INFORMATION The 2020/21 accounts were the latest available at the time of writing (June 2023). During the year, the foundation awarded 11 grants to charitable organisations.
HOW TO APPLY Apply in writing to the correspondent. The trustees meet regularly to consider grants.
CONTACT DETAILS The Trustees, 1st Floor, Tower Wharf, Cheese Lane, Bristol BS2 0JJ *Tel.* 0117 313 8200 *Email* charitabletrusts@ludlowtrust.com

■ The AEB Charitable Trust

OSCR NO SC028858   **ESTABLISHED** 1998
WHERE FUNDING CAN BE GIVEN Scotland, with a preference for the Lothian and Borders regions.
WHO CAN BENEFIT Registered charities; galleries; museums; hospitals; universities.
WHAT IS FUNDED Wildlife, ecology and nature; health, particularly research into and the treatment of Alzheimer's and the care of older people; museums and galleries; music and the arts; emergency services and the armed forces.
WHAT IS NOT FUNDED Individuals.
TYPE OF GRANT Research costs; project funding; core/revenue costs. One-off and multi-year grants.
RANGE OF GRANTS Mostly £1,000 to £10,000. Larger grants are awarded occasionally, at the trustees' discretion.
SAMPLE GRANTS Horatio's Garden – Scotland (£20,000); University of Aberdeen Development Trust (£15,000); The Royal School of Veterinary Studies (£10,000); Sepsis Research and Haddington Garden Trust (£5,000); Butterfly Conservation Trust (£3,000); Royal Society for the Protection of Birds (£1,300).
FINANCES *Financial year end* 31/03/2022
Income £118,200
Grants to organisations £111,300
Assets £3,140,000
OTHER INFORMATION In 2021/22, grants were distributed as follows: health (£46,000); wildlife and nature (£37,300); older and retired people (£15,000); arts, museums and historic sites (£13,000).
HOW TO APPLY Apply in writing or via email to the correspondent by the deadline stated on the trust's website (typically in November). The trustees meet once a year in spring and normally pay grants prior to 31 March.
CONTACT DETAILS The Trustees, c/o Turcan Connell, Princes Exchange, 1 Earl Grey Street, Edinburgh EH3 9EE *Tel.* 0131 228 8111 *Email* enquiries@turcanconnell.com *Website* www.turcanconnell.com/the-aeb-charitable-trust

■ Age Scotland

OSCR NO SC010100   **ESTABLISHED** 2009
WHERE FUNDING CAN BE GIVEN Scotland.
WHO CAN BENEFIT Registered charities and community groups.
WHAT IS FUNDED Projects benefitting older people.
WHAT IS NOT FUNDED Statutory authorities; commercial organisations; individuals.
TYPE OF GRANT Capital costs; one-off grants; seed funding/start-up costs.
RANGE OF GRANTS Typically up to £2,500.
SAMPLE GRANTS Kirrie Connections (£100,000); The Royal British Legion Scotland (£64,600); FARES4FREE (£41,500); St John Red Cross Defence Medical Welfare (£50,400); Luminate (£5,500); West Granton Community (£2,500); Tarbert Soup Group (£2,000); Elder Voice (£1,000).
FINANCES *Financial year end* 31/03/2022
Income £6,710,000
Grants to organisations £370,800
Assets £8,170,000
TRUSTEES Stuart Purdy; Prof. Marion McMurdo; Robert Hare; Pennie Taylor; Prof. Brendan McCormack; Kenneth Nicholson; Alison Harrington; Graham Reece; Faith Jayne; Kate Smith.
OTHER INFORMATION During 2021/22, £24,200 was awarded in grants of less than £1,000, the

recipients of which were not listed in the charity's annual report and accounts.

HOW TO APPLY Details of current grant programmes and how to apply can be found on the charity's website.

CONTACT DETAILS The Trustees, Causewayside House, 160 Causewayside, Edinburgh EH9 1PR *Tel.* 0333 323 2400 *Email* members@ agescotland.org.uk *Website* www.ageuk.org.uk/ scotland

■ The AIM Foundation

CC NO 263294   **ESTABLISHED** 1971
WHERE FUNDING CAN BE GIVEN UK.
WHO CAN BENEFIT Charitable organisations.
WHAT IS FUNDED Nutrition for health and well-being; children and young people; the environment.
TYPE OF GRANT Revenue grants: core costs and salaries; campaigning and research.
RANGE OF GRANTS Mostly up to £30,000.
SAMPLE GRANTS Esmée Fairbairn Foundation (£100,000); Impetus – The Private Equity Foundation (£55,000); Culinary Medicine (£41,000); The Food Foundation (£25,000); International Rescue Committee (£5,000); The Outward Bound Trust (£3,000); The Christie Charitable Fund (£1,500); Charlie Waller Trust (£1,000).
FINANCES *Financial year end* 31/08/2022
Income £9,840,000
Grants to organisations £986,500
Assets £11,900,000
TRUSTEES Philippa Bailey; Caroline Marks; Joanna Barrett; Sophie Jones; Alison Prout.
OTHER INFORMATION Grants awarded to organisations were broken down in the foundation's annual report and accounts as follows: nutrition and well-being (£287,200); young people (£252,700); the environment (£252,100); early years (£181,000); other (£13,500).
HOW TO APPLY The foundation does not accept unsolicited applications.
CONTACT DETAILS The Trustees, c/o Albert Goodman LLP, Goodwood House, Blackbrook Park Avenue, Taunton, Somerset TA1 2PX *Tel.* 01823 286096 *Email* collaborate@theaimfoundation. org.uk *Website* https://theaimfoundation.org.uk

■ The Aimwell Charitable Trust

CC NO 1039415   **ESTABLISHED** 1994
WHERE FUNDING CAN BE GIVEN UK and overseas.
WHO CAN BENEFIT Charitable organisations; educational organisations.
WHAT IS FUNDED Education; social welfare; health; community development and services; Jewish causes.
TYPE OF GRANT Research funding.
RANGE OF GRANTS Mostly up to £50,000.
SAMPLE GRANTS British Friends of the Hebrew University (£223,100); Portland Trust (£144,900); UJIA (£127,900) Jewish Care (£50,000).
FINANCES *Financial year end* 31/03/2022
Income £133,200
Grants to organisations £1,110,000
Assets £14,500,000
TRUSTEES Isaac Kaye; Steven Kaye; Geoffrey Jayson; Warren Roiter; Craig Cowan.
OTHER INFORMATION Grants were awarded to 46 organisations in 2021/22. Only the five beneficiaries that received a grant of more than £50,000 were listed in the annual report.
HOW TO APPLY Apply in writing to the correspondent.

CONTACT DETAILS Geoffrey Jayson, Trustee, c/o Baystone Associates, 3rd Floor, 52 Conduit Street, London W1S 2YX *Tel.* 020 7317 8980 *Email* geoffrey@jaysonconsulting.co.uk

■ The Aitken Family Charitable Trust

CC NO 1168153   **ESTABLISHED** 2016
WHERE FUNDING CAN BE GIVEN England and Wales.
WHO CAN BENEFIT Charities; educational organisations; hospitals.
WHAT IS FUNDED General charitable purposes; education.
RANGE OF GRANTS Up to £100,000.
SAMPLE GRANTS Chelsea and Westminster Hospital (£100,000); St Paul's Girls' School Bursary Fund (£50,000); First Story (£15,000); The Black Curriculum (£5,000).
FINANCES *Financial year end* 16/02/2022
Income £238,300
Grants to organisations £170,000
TRUSTEES Peter Aitken; Jane Aitken; Katharine Aitken; Anna Aitken; Lucy Aitken; Alexandra Aitken; Ludlow Trust Company Ltd.
OTHER INFORMATION During 2021/22, grants were made to four organisations.
HOW TO APPLY The trust does not accept unsolicited applications.
CONTACT DETAILS The Trustees, Ludlow Trust Co. Ltd, Tower Wharf, Cheese Lane, Bristol BS2 0JJ *Tel.* 0117 313 8200 *Email* charitabletrusts@ ludlowtrust.com

■ Sylvia Aitken's Charitable Trust

OSCR NO SC010556   **ESTABLISHED** 1985
WHERE FUNDING CAN BE GIVEN UK, with a preference for Scotland.
WHO CAN BENEFIT Charitable organisations.
WHAT IS FUNDED Medical research; children and young people; older people; the environment; wildlife and animals; education; culture; religion; disability; social welfare.
SAMPLE GRANTS A list of beneficiaries was not included in the annual report and accounts. Previous beneficiaries have included: Association for International Cancer Research; Barn Owl Trust; British Lung Foundation; British Stammering Association; Disabled Living Foundation; Epilepsy Research Trust; Friends of the Lake District; Motor Neurone Disease Association; Network for Surviving Stalking; Roy Castle Lung Cancer Foundation; Royal Scots Dragoon Guards Museum Trust; Scottish Child Psychotherapy Trust; Sense Scotland; Tall Ships Youth Trust; Tenovus Scotland; Wood Green Animal Shelters; YoungMinds.
FINANCES *Financial year end* 05/04/2022
Income £758,100
Grants to organisations £371,000
Assets £4,420,000
OTHER INFORMATION Grants payable during 2021/22 were categorised as follows: medical causes (£127,500); children and young people (£87,500); people who are older, who have disabilities or who are facing disadvantage (£75,500); the countryside, wildlife and animals (£71,000); educational, cultural and religious causes (£9,500). In addition, the annual report and accounts note that £30,000 was expended on 'general grant activities'.
HOW TO APPLY Apply in writing to the correspondent.

CONTACT DETAILS The Trustees, c/o Fergusons Chartered Accountants, 24 Woodside, Houston, Renfrewshire PA6 7DD

■ AJ Bell Trust

CC NO 1141269   **ESTABLISHED** 2011
WHERE FUNDING CAN BE GIVEN UK.
WHO CAN BENEFIT Individuals and organisations that promote social welfare, skills development, education, and training.
WHAT IS FUNDED Social welfare with a focus on children and young adults under 25 years of age.
SAMPLE GRANTS A list of beneficiaries was not included in the annual report and accounts.
FINANCES *Financial year end* 30/09/2021
Income £292,900
Grants to organisations £191,200
Assets £2,330,000
TRUSTEES Tracey Bell; Andrew Bell; Paul Clements; Paul Barrow.
OTHER INFORMATION The 2020/21 annual accounts were the latest available at the time of writing (June 2023).
HOW TO APPLY Apply in writing to the correspondent.
CONTACT DETAILS Esther Speksnijder, Secretary, Blythe Hall, Blythe Lane, Lathom, Ormskirk, Lancashire L40 5TY *Email* moorhall@outlook.com *Website* www.ajbell.co.uk/group/about-us/corporate-social-responsibility

■ AKO Foundation

CC NO 1151815   **ESTABLISHED** 2013
WHERE FUNDING CAN BE GIVEN UK, particularly North London; Norway; Germany; Denmark; Sri Lanka; USA; Africa.
WHO CAN BENEFIT Registered charities.
WHAT IS FUNDED Education; the arts; the environment.
TYPE OF GRANT Project funding, including salaries and core costs; seed funding.
SAMPLE GRANTS AKO Kunststiftelse (£15.9 million); European Climate Foundation (£3.84 million); Foundation for International Law for the Environment (£1.07 million); OnSide Youth Zones (£400,000); The Courtauld Institute (£255,000); Feeding Britain (£116,000); Doorstep Homeless Families Project (£85,000); Literacy Pirates (£75,000); United Borders (£54,000); Julie's Bicycle (£5,000).
FINANCES *Financial year end* 31/12/2021
Income £268,500,000
Grants to organisations £40,890,000
Assets £1,071,000,000
TRUSTEES Henrik Syse; David Woodburn; Sally Procopis.
OTHER INFORMATION Grants were distributed as follows: art (£18 million); climate change (£11.48 million); education (£9.6 million); AKO Give Back Initiative (£897,000); local projects (£881,000).
HOW TO APPLY Unsolicited applications are not accepted.
CONTACT DETAILS The Trustees, One Newman Street, London W1T 1PB *Tel.* 020 7070 2400 *Email* enquiries@akofoundation.org *Website* www.akofoundation.org

■ Al Madad Foundation

CC NO 1101574   **ESTABLISHED** 2004
WHERE FUNDING CAN BE GIVEN UK, the Middle East and Europe. See the foundation's website for a full list of eligible countries.
WHO CAN BENEFIT Registered charities; social enterprises; CIOs; companies limited by guarantee which have charitable purposes.
WHAT IS FUNDED The education of refugee children.
WHAT IS NOT FUNDED Individuals.
TYPE OF GRANT Project costs, including indirect associated costs, e.g. general overhead and administration expenses.
RANGE OF GRANTS Up to £100,000.
SAMPLE GRANTS A list of beneficiaries was not included in the annual report and accounts.
FINANCES *Financial year end* 31/12/2022
Income £328,200
Grants to organisations £325,400
Assets £346,400
TRUSTEES Faiza Meyassar; Basma Alireza; Yasmin Alireza.
OTHER INFORMATION We were unable to determine the amount awarded to organisations in the UK.
HOW TO APPLY Calls for proposals are advertised on the foundation's website and on social media. Guidance on how to write a concept note and eligibility criteria are published in the 'Grant Seeker FAQs' section of the website.
CONTACT DETAILS The Trustees, 52 Mount Street, London W1K 2SF *Tel.* 020 7408 7896 *Email* contact@almadadfoundation.org *Website* www.almadadfoundation.org

■ Alan Boswell Group Charitable Trust

CC NO 1183272   **ESTABLISHED** 2019
WHERE FUNDING CAN BE GIVEN Primarily areas where Alan Boswell Group operates (Norfolk, Suffolk, Cambridgeshire and Lincolnshire).
WHO CAN BENEFIT Charitable organisations.
WHAT IS FUNDED Causes that benefit the wider public and communities in the beneficial area, with a focus on the following areas: community resources; health care and mental health; sports teams and foundations; older people; veterans; vulnerable communities; animal welfare; disaster recovery.
TYPE OF GRANT Capital costs; project funding; core costs.
SAMPLE GRANTS A list of beneficiaries was not included in the annual report and accounts.
FINANCES *Financial year end* 31/03/2022
Income £522,600
Grants to organisations £520,200
Assets £34,400
TRUSTEES Christopher Gibbs; Alexandra Bartram; Alan Boswell; Sarah Lusher; Alastair Drew; Lisa Adams.
OTHER INFORMATION Grants were broken down as follows: social and welfare (£207,800); health and medical causes (£173,400); youth and education (£85,000); heritage (£30,000); community sport and leisure (£24,000).
HOW TO APPLY An application form, together with eligibility criteria and guidance, can be found on the Alan Boswell Group website.
CONTACT DETAILS The Trustees, Prospect House, Rouen Road, Norwich NR1 1RE *Tel.* 01603 218000 *Email* contact@alanboswelltrust.com *Website* www.alanboswell.com/about/environmental-social-governance/the-alan-boswell-group-charitable-trust-abgct

Think carefully about every application. Is it justified?

229

■ The Alborada Trust

CC NO 1091660   **ESTABLISHED** 2001
WHERE FUNDING CAN BE GIVEN UK and overseas.
WHO CAN BENEFIT Charitable organisations; universities; colleges.
WHAT IS FUNDED Medical and veterinary research and education; animal welfare; disaster relief; refugees; conservation and wildlife.
WHAT IS NOT FUNDED Charities that receive substantial government aid; charities involved in pet welfare; the arts and culture; marriage guidance; children's welfare charities (in the UK); zoos; charities involved in political or media lobbying.
TYPE OF GRANT Research funding; general funding; revenue costs.
RANGE OF GRANTS Typically £25,000 to £500,000.
SAMPLE GRANTS Alzheimer's Research UK (£1 million); Médecins Sans Frontières (£657,600 in seven grants); David Shepherd Wildlife Foundation (£232,500); Priscilla Bacon Hospice and University of Cambridge (£100,000 each); Mercy Ships UK (£35,000); Horatio's Garden (£25,000); Medical Detection Dogs and The British Racing School (£10,000 each).
FINANCES *Financial year end* 31/12/2021
Income £25,080,000
Grants to organisations £4,900,000
Assets £19,760,000
TRUSTEES Roland Lerner; Capt. James Nicholson; Eva Rausing; Alison Traub; Robert Goff; Larry Pillard.
HOW TO APPLY Details of how to apply can be found on the trust's website.
CONTACT DETAILS Grant Harris, Director, Lanwades Stud, Moulton Road, Kennett, Newmarket, Suffolk CB8 8QS *Email* director@alboradatrust.com *Website* www.alboradatrust.com

■ The Alchemy Foundation

CC NO 292500   **ESTABLISHED** 1985
WHERE FUNDING CAN BE GIVEN UK and overseas.
WHO CAN BENEFIT Community projects; voluntary organisations; registered charities.
WHAT IS FUNDED Disability (particularly mobility, access, helplines and communications); social welfare (inner-city community projects, disaffected young people, family mediation, homelessness); penal reform (work with prisoners, especially young prisoners and their families); medical research and aid (especially in areas of 'blindness and disfigurement'); individual enterprise (by helping Raleigh International and similar organisations to give opportunities to young people according to need); respite for carers; water projects in the financially developing world. The foundation also delivers the Alchemist Scheme, which funds the costs of fundraisers assigned to other charities to assist with their fundraising efforts.
TYPE OF GRANT Salaries; project funding; medical research.
SAMPLE GRANTS A list of beneficiaries was not included in the annual report and accounts.
FINANCES *Financial year end* 05/04/2022
Income £50,600
Grants to organisations £268,600
Assets £995,500
TRUSTEES Alexander Armitage; Antoun Elias; Andrew Murison; Sir Richard Stilgoe; Dr Jemima Stilgoe; Lady Annabel Stilgoe; Prof. Dr Jack Stilgoe; Holly Stilgoe; Joseph Stilgoe; Rufus Stilgoe; Caroline Pedley.
OTHER INFORMATION In 2021/22, grants were distributed as follows: disability (£76,800); the Alchemist Scheme (£76,500); social welfare (£51,300); penal reform and work with prisoners and their families (£31,000); other (£27,000); individuals (£3,900); respite for carers (£2,300).
HOW TO APPLY Apply in writing to the correspondent.
CONTACT DETAILS The Trustees, Trevereux Manor, Trevereux Hill, Limpsfield Chart, Oxted, Surrey RH8 0TL

■ The Aldama Foundation

CC NO 1126791   **ESTABLISHED** 2008
WHERE FUNDING CAN BE GIVEN UK and overseas.
WHO CAN BENEFIT Charitable organisations; registered, excepted or exempt charities; museums, libraries and galleries.
WHAT IS FUNDED Social welfare; education; medical research/medical care; citizenship and community development; arts, culture, heritage or science.
TYPE OF GRANT One-off and recurrent.
RANGE OF GRANTS Mostly up to £20,000, with the occasional larger grant.
SAMPLE GRANTS The listed beneficiaries include: National Gallery (£1.3 million); Science Museum (£500,000); The Francis Crick Institute and The Institute of Cancer Research (£240,000 each); FareShare and The Trussell Trust (£120,000 each); Save Britain's Heritage (£25,000).
FINANCES *Financial year end* 05/04/2022
Income £797,000
Grants to organisations £3,260,000
Assets £3,320,000
TRUSTEE The Dickinson Trust Ltd.
OTHER INFORMATION Only organisations that received grants of over £20,000 were listed as beneficiaries in the foundation's 2021/22 accounts. Grants of under £20,000 totalled £191,300. Grants were broken down as follows: advancement of the arts, culture, heritage or science (£2.42 million); medical research/medical care (£485,300); social welfare (£334,800); advancement of citizenship or community development (£11,000); education (£10,000). In previous years, the foundation has also awarded grants for amateur sport and the environment. No grants were awarded to individuals during the year. According to its 2021/22 annual report and accounts, the foundation awards grants 'both on a one-off and recurring basis'.
HOW TO APPLY Apply in writing to the correspondent.
CONTACT DETAILS The Trustees, 4th Floor, 7 Swallow Street, London W1B 4DE *Tel.* 020 7907 2100 *Email* charity@mfs.co.uk

■ Beryl Alexander Charity

CC NO 1179895
WHERE FUNDING CAN BE GIVEN England.
WHO CAN BENEFIT Registered charities.
WHAT IS FUNDED Mental health.
SAMPLE GRANTS University College London: Mental Health of Children and Young People with Long COVID (£110,100).
FINANCES *Financial year end* 31/12/2021
Income £25,600
Grants to organisations £110,100
Assets £2,330,000
TRUSTEES Joshua Alton; Jeremy Alton; Ruby Alton; Dr Laurence Lions.
HOW TO APPLY Apply in writing to the correspondent.
CONTACT DETAILS The Trustees, 4 London Road, Stanmore, HA7 4NZ *Tel.* 020 8958 8970

■ Al-Fayed Charitable Foundation

CC NO 297114   **ESTABLISHED** 1987
WHERE FUNDING CAN BE GIVEN Mainly the UK, but also worldwide.
WHO CAN BENEFIT Registered charities; schools; hospices; hospitals; medical centres; individuals.
WHAT IS FUNDED The health, well-being and education of disadvantaged children and young people; animal welfare.
TYPE OF GRANT Project funding; capital costs; core costs.
RANGE OF GRANTS Typically £500 to £10,000.
SAMPLE GRANTS Zoë's Place (£82,500); Face for Children in Need (£55,000); West Heath 2000 Ltd (£28,000); World Animal Protection (£10,000); Harrods Ltd (£2,400); Heart Cells Foundation (£500).
FINANCES *Financial year end* 31/12/2021
Income £174,800
Grants to organisations £188,400
Assets £18,700
TRUSTEES Mohamed Fayed; Camilla Fayed; Heini Fayed; Omar Fayed.
OTHER INFORMATION During 2021, the foundation awarded seven grants.
HOW TO APPLY Apply in writing to the correspondent via email or post. Include an sae if applying by post.
CONTACT DETAILS The Trustees, 55 Park Lane, London W1K 1NA *Tel.* 020 7409 9350 *Email* acf@alfayed.com *Website* www.the-acf.com

■ AlixPartners (UK) Charitable Foundation

CC NO 1134913   **ESTABLISHED** 2010
WHERE FUNDING CAN BE GIVEN UK.
WHO CAN BENEFIT Registered charities.
WHAT IS FUNDED General charitable purposes.
RANGE OF GRANTS £1,000 to £10,000.
SAMPLE GRANTS Garwood and Open Palm (£10,000 each); Magic Breakfast (£7,300); RESTART (£6,200); Healthcare Workers' Foundation (£5,000); Institute of Cancer Research (£4,000); Great Ormond Street Hospital Children's Charity (£2,200); Combat Stress (£1,400); Art and Soul (£1,000).
FINANCES *Financial year end* 31/03/2022
Income £76,200
Grants to organisations £68,700
Assets £103,000
TRUSTEES Alastair Beveridge; Ruth Nutman; Timothy Roberts; John Bruce; Derek Holt; Stylianos Fragkos; Timothy Gray.
OTHER INFORMATION Grants totalling £68,700 were made to 14 organisations during 2021/22.
HOW TO APPLY Apply in writing to the correspondent.
CONTACT DETAILS The Trustees, AlixPartners, 6 New Street Square, London EC4A 3BF *Tel.* 020 7098 7400 *Email* fviti@alixpartners.com *Website* www.alixpartners.com/about-alixpartners

■ The Derrill Allatt Foundation

CC NO 1148440   **ESTABLISHED** 2012
WHERE FUNDING CAN BE GIVEN Worldwide.
WHO CAN BENEFIT Registered charities.
WHAT IS FUNDED Social welfare; social inclusion; health; training; the arts; animals.
RANGE OF GRANTS £490 to £23,500.
SAMPLE GRANTS Previous beneficiaries have included: The Calvert Trust (£23,500); Central

School of Ballet Charitable Trust (£18,000); Normandy Community Therapy Garden (£12,000); Enham Appeals and Global Giving for Marefat School (£1,000 each); The Berkeley Ensemble (£490).
FINANCES *Financial year end* 05/04/2022
Income £10,800
Grants to organisations £172,000
TRUSTEES Diana Hargreaves; Clare Matthews; Payne Hicks Beach Trust Corporation Ltd.
OTHER INFORMATION Full accounts were not available to view on the Charity Commission's website due to the foundation's low income. We have therefore estimated the foundation's grant total based on its total expenditure.
HOW TO APPLY Unsolicited applications are not accepted.
CONTACT DETAILS The Trustees, Payne Hicks Beach, 10 New Square, Lincoln's Inn, London WC2A 3QG *Tel.* 020 7465 4300

■ The Allen & Overy Foundation

CC NO 1153738   **ESTABLISHED** 2013
WHERE FUNDING CAN BE GIVEN London; UK; worldwide.
WHO CAN BENEFIT Registered charities.
WHAT IS FUNDED Disaster relief; access to justice; access to education, employment and training.
TYPE OF GRANT Project and core costs.
RANGE OF GRANTS Local Grants Programme: typically between £5,000 and £10,000. Global Grants Programme: typically £50,000.
SAMPLE GRANTS Hope and Homes for Children (£430,400); Ceasefire Centre (£50,000); Action Tutoring (£25,000); Transport for All (£5,000).
FINANCES *Financial year end* 30/04/2022
Income £1,530,000
Grants to organisations £1,770,000
Assets £566,100
TRUSTEES Philip Mansfield; Andrew Wedderburn-Day; Mark Mansell; Brendan Hannigan; Angela Clist; Joanna Page; Mary Johnston; Hilde Baan; Franz Ranero.
OTHER INFORMATION The foundation has two grant programmes: The Global Grants Programme, which supports three or four charities each year under core themes; and Local Charitable Giving (London) programme, which awards average grants of £5,000 to £10,000 that may be given for projects or core costs. The foundation also makes a large annual donation to its global charity partner. For further information on each grants programme see the foundation's helpful website.
HOW TO APPLY Application guidelines and up-to-date information on application submission dates for each grants programme are available on the foundation's website.
CONTACT DETAILS The Trustees, One Bishops Square, London E1 6AD *Tel.* 020 3088 0000 *Email* allenoveryfoundation@allenovery.com *Website* www.allenovery.com/en-gb/global/about_us/responsible_business/our_pro_bono_and_community_work/who_we_support

■ D. C. R. Allen Charitable Trust

CC NO 277293   **ESTABLISHED** 1979
WHERE FUNDING CAN BE GIVEN UK.
WHO CAN BENEFIT Registered charities.
WHAT IS FUNDED General charitable purposes, especially disadvantaged young people. There is a preference for small to medium-sized charities.
WHAT IS NOT FUNDED Individuals; services usually provided by statutory sources; causes outside

the UK; evangelical or worship-related activities; animal welfare; medical research; heritage conservation/preservation; arts or collections; performing arts.

TYPE OF GRANT Capital costs; project funding; unrestricted funding.

RANGE OF GRANTS From £1,000 to £20,000. Larger amounts may be considered, especially for innovative or capital projects.

SAMPLE GRANTS A list of beneficiaries was not included in the annual report and accounts. Previous beneficiaries have included: Centrepoint and Northamptonshire Parent Infant Partnership (£25,000 each); Designability (£20,000); Greenham Community Trust and Operation New World (£10,000 each); Bright Ideas Trust (£5,000); Young Asian Voices (£2,000); Great Ormond Street Hospital Children's Charity (£1,000); St Leonard's Church – Aston-le-Walls (£500).

FINANCES *Financial year end 05/04/2022*
Income £176,800
Grants to organisations £131,700
Assets £323,100

TRUSTEES Julie Frusher; Tristram Allen; Colin Allen.

OTHER INFORMATION In 2021/22, grants were broken down as follows: youth projects (£63,000); education (£33,000); disability (£9,000); medical causes (£7,600).

HOW TO APPLY Applications should be made by email to the correspondent and should include a copy of your latest accounts and your official charity number. The trustees normally meet monthly, so decisions can be made promptly. It is not possible for the trustees to respond to unsuccessful applicants, so if no positive response has been received within eight weeks of the application date, then applicants may assume that they have not been successful.

CONTACT DETAILS Julie Frusher, Trustee, Edgcote House, Edgcote, Banbury, Oxfordshire OX17 1AG *Tel.* 01295 660077 *Email* julie.frusher@edgecote.com

■ The Allen Trust

CC NO 1146388   **ESTABLISHED** 2012

WHERE FUNDING CAN BE GIVEN Worldwide.

WHO CAN BENEFIT Registered charities.

WHAT IS FUNDED Social welfare.

RANGE OF GRANTS Up to £62,000 but mostly £500 to £8,000.

SAMPLE GRANTS African Revival (£61,800); Cinnamon Network (£7,500); Mission Aviation (£5,000); Hospices of Hope (£3,000); George Twist and New Bridge Foundation (£1,000 each).

FINANCES *Financial year end 31/03/2022*
Income £29,300
Grants to organisations £96,800
Assets £2,170,000

TRUSTEES Tony Allen; Melanie Pollitt.

OTHER INFORMATION Grants were awarded to ten organisations during the year.

HOW TO APPLY Apply in writing to the correspondent.

CONTACT DETAILS The Trustees, Oakmead Farm, Ockham Lane, Cobham, Surrey KTLL 1LY *Tel.* 07764 475257

■ Alliance Family Foundation Ltd

CC NO 258721   **ESTABLISHED** 1968

WHERE FUNDING CAN BE GIVEN UK; Israel; Iran; Serbia; USA.

WHO CAN BENEFIT Charitable organisations, particularly Jewish organisations benefitting

young people and people disadvantaged by poverty; individuals.

WHAT IS FUNDED Jewish causes; the relief of poverty; the advancement of religion; education.

RANGE OF GRANTS Up to £50,000.

SAMPLE GRANTS Weizmann Institute (£50,000); Jewish Care (£12,500).

FINANCES *Financial year end 31/03/2022*
Income £1,810,000
Grants to organisations £84,300
Grants to individuals £28,400
Assets £2,350,000

TRUSTEES The Hon. Sara Esterkin; The Hon. Joshua Alliance; Lord David Alliance.

OTHER INFORMATION There were 29 grants made to organisations and individuals during the year. Grants to individuals were awarded for educational and medical/care costs.

HOW TO APPLY Apply in writing to the correspondent.

CONTACT DETAILS The Trustees, Spencer House, 27 St James's Place, London SW1A 1NR *Tel.* 020 7493 7735 *Email* aff@alliance.me

■ The Almond Trust

CC NO 328583   **ESTABLISHED** 1990

WHERE FUNDING CAN BE GIVEN UK and overseas.

WHO CAN BENEFIT Mostly organisations of which the trustees have personal knowledge, particularly those benefitting Christians and evangelists.

WHAT IS FUNDED Christian evangelism; the advancement of the translation, reading, study and teaching of the Bible.

RANGE OF GRANTS Typically £5,000 to £15,000.

SAMPLE GRANTS Warbleton PCC (£15,000); BMS World Mission, Christian Solidarity Worldwide and Tearfund (£10,000 each); Arab Vision and The Bible Network (£5,000 each); Oxford Inter-Collegiate Christian Union (£4,000).

FINANCES *Financial year end 31/03/2022*
Income £656,500
Grants to organisations £300,000
Assets £960,500

TRUSTEES Lady Cooke; Sir Jeremy Cooke; Samuel Cooke.

OTHER INFORMATION Grants were awarded to 27 organisations during the year.

HOW TO APPLY The trust's accounts state that it rarely responds to uninvited applications.

CONTACT DETAILS Jeremy Cooke, Trustee, White Birch Farm, White Birch Lane, Warbleton, East Sussex, TN21 9BE *Tel.* 01435 830883

■ Alpkit Foundation

CC NO 1162585   **ESTABLISHED** 2015

WHERE FUNDING CAN BE GIVEN UK.

WHO CAN BENEFIT Individuals; groups; schools; organisations.

WHAT IS FUNDED Outdoor experiences; outdoor educational programs and training (i.e. first aid or mountain leader training); the environment and conservation.

WHAT IS NOT FUNDED Charity challenges; commercially led travel expeditions that are not focused on the great outdoors (e.g. rebuilding schools, overseas medicine); scout jamborees; holidays; retrospective applications.

TYPE OF GRANT Transport costs; capital costs (equipment); project costs.

SAMPLE GRANTS A list of beneficiaries was not included in the annual report and accounts.

FINANCES *Financial year end 31/10/2021*
Income £167,300
Grants to organisations £140,000
Assets £40,900

TRUSTEES David Hanney; Kenneth Stocker; Colin Stocker; Nicholas Smith; Adge Last; Eloise Cundill; Rehna Yaseen; Pete Whittaker; Yazan Abbas; Joshua Manley.

OTHER INFORMATION This is the charitable foundation of Alpkit, an outdoor clothing and equipment company. The website provides examples of activities likely to be supported. The 2020/21 annual report and accounts were the latest available at the time of writing (June 2023). Note that the grant total may include amounts awarded to individuals.

HOW TO APPLY Apply via the application form on the website.

CONTACT DETAILS The Trustees, Alpkit Ltd, Unit 12–14 Oak House, Moorgreen Industrial Park, Engine Lane, Newthorpe, Nottinghamshire NG16 3QU *Email* akf@alpkit.com *Website* www.alpkit.com/foundation

■ Alzheimer's Research UK

CC NO 1077089   **ESTABLISHED** 1998

WHERE FUNDING CAN BE GIVEN UK.

WHO CAN BENEFIT Universities; charities; hospitals; research institutions.

WHAT IS FUNDED Research into the cause, diagnosis/detection of, prevention and treatment of Alzheimer's disease and other forms of dementia.

SAMPLE GRANTS University College London (£4.36 million); University of Oxford (£2.88 million); The University of Manchester (£107,000); Crawford Works (£15,000).

FINANCES *Financial year end 31/03/2022*
Income £42,190,000
Grants to organisations £20,880,000
Assets £15,820,000

TRUSTEES David Mayhew; Rupert Evenett; Michael Cooper; Nicholas Antill; Christopher Carter; Caroline Brul; Giles Dennison; Prof. Rob Howard; Dr Ruth McKernan; Divya Manek; Amanda Farnsworth; Kathryn Swann; Shirley Cramer.

HOW TO APPLY Full details of all available grant schemes including deadlines, eligibility criteria and application procedures are available on the charity's website.

CONTACT DETAILS The Trustees, 3 Riverside, Granta Park, Cambridge CB21 6AD *Tel.* 0300 111 5333 *Email* enquiries@alzheimersresearchuk.org *Website* www.alzheimersresearchuk.org

■ Alzheimer's Society

CC NO 296645   **ESTABLISHED** 1987

WHERE FUNDING CAN BE GIVEN UK.

WHO CAN BENEFIT Universities; hospitals; research institutions.

WHAT IS FUNDED Research into dementia.

WHAT IS NOT FUNDED Refer to the website for exclusions for individual funding schemes.

TYPE OF GRANT Research funding; fellowships, studentships, bursaries.

SAMPLE GRANTS University of Southampton (£273,000); University of Oxford (£256,000); University of Strathclyde (£190,000); Sheffield Institute for Neuroscience (£14,000); University of Sussex (£10,000); University of Salford (£9,000); University of Stirling (£8,000); University of St Andrews (£6,000).

FINANCES *Financial year end 31/03/2022*
Income £116,540,000
Grants to organisations £7,060,000
Assets £93,400,000

TRUSTEES Manish Shah; Stephen Hill; Caroline Fawcett; Andrew Lynch; Prof. Hugh McKenna; Prof. Subrata Banerjee; Susan Allen; Andrew Cornwall; Patrick Figgis; Christine Maddocks.

HOW TO APPLY For information on how to apply to one of Alzheimer's Society's current grant schemes, refer to the website. Funding calls are advertised on the website and applications should be submitted online.

CONTACT DETAILS Research Team, 43–44 Crutched Friars, London EC3N 2AE *Tel.* 020 7423 5136 *Email* grantenquiries@alzheimer's.org.uk *Website* www.alzheimer's.org.uk

■ Amabrill Ltd

CC NO 1078968   **ESTABLISHED** 2000

WHERE FUNDING CAN BE GIVEN UK and overseas.

WHO CAN BENEFIT Jewish charities.

WHAT IS FUNDED The advancement of education and religious practice in accordance with the teachings of the Orthodox Jewish faith; social welfare.

TYPE OF GRANT Capital costs; core costs.

RANGE OF GRANTS Generally around £50,000, with some larger grants.

SAMPLE GRANTS Amud Hatzdokoh Trust (£383,900); Achisomoch Aid Company Ltd (£239,100); Kahal Chasidim Bobov (£188,400); Beis Hillel Trust (£81,000); Moreshet Hatorah (£56,000); The M. Y. A. Charitable Trust and Yesamach Levav (£50,000 each).

FINANCES *Financial year end 28/02/2022*
Income £3,200,000
Grants to organisations £3,290,000
Assets £26,200,000

TRUSTEES Israel Grossnass; Frances Lerner; Mr C. Lerner; Irving Lerner.

OTHER INFORMATION Grants were distributed as follows: educational grants (£1.27 million); relief of poverty (£1.13 million); advancement of the Jewish faith (£892,400). Grants of under £50,000 totalled £1.9 million.

HOW TO APPLY Apply in writing to the correspondent. The 2021/22 annual report explains: 'Appeal letters are received from, and personal visits made by representatives of Jewish charitable, religious and educational institutions. These requests are then considered by the trustees and grants are made in accordance with the trustees' decisions.'

CONTACT DETAILS The Trustees, 1 Golders Manor Drive, London NW11 9HU *Tel.* 020 8455 6785 *Email* mail@venittandgreaves.com

■ Amant Foundation

CC NO 1177721   **ESTABLISHED** 2018

WHERE FUNDING CAN BE GIVEN UK and overseas.

WHO CAN BENEFIT Registered charities.

WHAT IS FUNDED General charitable purposes; arts, culture, heritage and science.

RANGE OF GRANTS Mostly under £100,000.

SAMPLE GRANTS Museum of Modern Art — New York (£4.19 million); Memorial-Sloan Kettering Cancer Centre – New York (£123,000); Tate Modern Art Gallery – London (£50,000); HRH Prince Charles Royal Drawing School – London (£15,000); Delfina Foundation for Art – London (£9,000); Artists Space – New York (£3,500).

FINANCES *Financial year end 31/12/2021*
Income £2,850,000
Grants to organisations £4,410,000
Assets £3,440,000

TRUSTEES Lonti Ebers; James Flatt; Ian Flatt.

Think carefully about every application. Is it justified?

233

OTHER INFORMATION The foundation recently changed its name from Partners Global Foundation to Amant Foundation. In 2021, nine grants were awarded to organisations.

HOW TO APPLY Apply in writing to the correspondent.

CONTACT DETAILS The Trustees, Apartment 5406, 1 Park Drive, London E14 9LX *Tel.* 07850 088910

■ Ambergate Charitable Trust

CC NO 1187659   **ESTABLISHED** 2020

WHERE FUNDING CAN BE GIVEN UK.

WHO CAN BENEFIT Registered charities.

WHAT IS FUNDED Social welfare; health; children and young people; disability.

RANGE OF GRANTS Up to £50,000, but mostly £500 to £5,000.

SAMPLE GRANTS Rise UK (£50,000); Centrepoint and The Trussell Trust (£5,000 each); Multiple Sclerosis Trust (£2,500); The Dash Charity (£1,000); Hot Line Meal Service (£500).

FINANCES *Financial year end 31/12/2021*
Income £530,000
Grants to organisations £151,000
Assets £1,300,000

TRUSTEES Catherine Cullen; Daniella Cullen; Francesca Cullen; John Cullen; Luke Cullen.

HOW TO APPLY Apply in writing to the correspondent.

CONTACT DETAILS Darran Fawcett, c/o Irwin Mitchell LLP, Thomas Eggar House, Friary Lane, Chichester PO19 1UF *Tel.* 01243 813208 *Email* darran.fawcett@irwinmitchell.com

■ The Ammco Trust

CC NO 327962   **ESTABLISHED** 1988

WHERE FUNDING CAN BE GIVEN Oxfordshire and its adjoining counties.

WHO CAN BENEFIT Registered charities.

WHAT IS FUNDED General charitable purposes, with a preference for disability-related causes.

WHAT IS NOT FUNDED Individuals; students; research.

TYPE OF GRANT Capital costs; core/revenue costs.

RANGE OF GRANTS Between £500 and £2,000.

SAMPLE GRANTS The 3H Foundation; Carers UK; Happy Days; Horatio's Garden; James Hopkins Trust; Maggies; MERU; Parasol Project; Parkinson's UK; Support Dogs; RAW; Thrive; Thumbs Up.

FINANCES *Financial year end 05/04/2022*
Income £58,200
Grants to organisations £72,100
Assets £2,590,000

TRUSTEES Nicholas Cobbold; Esther Lewis; Rowena Vickers; Clare Luck.

OTHER INFORMATION The trust's annual report and accounts provide the following breakdown of grants awarded: disability (£42,500); welfare (£27,500); other (£2,100). A list of beneficiaries was available in the accounts but grant totals were not included.

HOW TO APPLY Apply in writing to the correspondent. Applications are reviewed quarterly.

CONTACT DETAILS The Trustees, Wallon, Drewsteignton, Exeter, Devon EX6 6PZ *Tel.* 01647 272847

■ Viscount Amory's Charitable Trust

CC NO 204958   **ESTABLISHED** 1962

WHERE FUNDING CAN BE GIVEN Devon.

WHO CAN BENEFIT Registered charities; churches; schools.

WHAT IS FUNDED General charitable purposes, with a preference for education and religion.

WHAT IS NOT FUNDED Applications from individuals for poverty relief; applications for grants or short-term loans for individuals.

RANGE OF GRANTS Mainly under £30,000.

SAMPLE GRANTS Rona Sailing Project (£96,500); Blundell's School (£40,200); Exeter Cathedral School (£39,800); Westcountry Rivers Trust (£15,000); Exeter Paediatric Integrated Care Solutions (£9,000); Exeter School and Royal Ballet School (£6,000 each).

FINANCES *Financial year end 05/04/2022*
Income £405,300
Grants to organisations £406,500
Grants to individuals £19,100
Assets £14,140,000

TRUSTEES Mrs C. E. Cavender; Sir Ian Amory.

OTHER INFORMATION Grants are awarded to individuals for education and health-related needs. Grants totalling £19,100 were made to 22 individuals during 2021/22. Only organisations that received grants of over £5,000 were listed as beneficiaries in the trust's accounts.

HOW TO APPLY Apply in writing to the correspondent – applications should not be sent by email. Applications should include: the applicant organisation's address and email, general background information of the appeal, the nature of the sponsoring or associated organisation, the total amount to be raised, how much has been raised, a proposal for any shortfall and any other relevant information.

CONTACT DETAILS S. Curtis, The Island, Lowman Green, Tiverton, Devon EX16 4LA *Tel.* 01884 242200 *Email* office@vact.org.uk *Website* www.vact.org.uk

■ The Ampersand Foundation

CC NO 1167018   **ESTABLISHED** 2011

WHERE FUNDING CAN BE GIVEN UK.

WHO CAN BENEFIT Arts organisations; museums and galleries.

WHAT IS FUNDED Visual arts projects including exhibitions, acquisitions and commissions.

TYPE OF GRANT Project funding; exhibitions; acquisitions.

RANGE OF GRANTS £5,000 to £50,000.

SAMPLE GRANTS DASH (£150,000); Graves Gallery (£89,000); Art UK (£50,000); Roche Court Educational Trust (£25,000); The Common Guild (£15,000); National Museums of Wales (£10,000); Focal Point Gallery (£5,000).

FINANCES *Financial year end 31/03/2022*
Income £599,000
Grants to organisations £462,500
Grants to individuals £15,000
Assets £4,940,000

TRUSTEES John Kirkland; Simon Conway; Thiago Carvalho; Alastair Sooke; Victoria Siddall.

HOW TO APPLY Apply in writing to the correspondent. Full details of the application process including deadlines can be found on the foundation's website.

CONTACT DETAILS The Trustees, Waltons Clark Whitehill, Maritime House, Harbour Walk, Hartlepool TS24 0UX *Tel.* 01429 234414 *Email* info@theampersandfoundation.com *Website* www.theampersandfoundation.com

■ The AMW Charitable Trust

OSCR NO SC006959   ESTABLISHED 1974
WHERE FUNDING CAN BE GIVEN UK, with a preference for the west of Scotland.
WHO CAN BENEFIT Charitable organisations; universities.
WHAT IS FUNDED General charitable purposes, with a focus on health and social welfare.
RANGE OF GRANTS Mostly grants of £10,000.
SAMPLE GRANTS Age Concern, Bowel Cancer UK, Highland Hospice, Sepsis Research, Strathclyde University and Stroke Association (£10,000 each).
FINANCES *Financial year end* 05/04/2022 *Income* £173,600 *Grants to organisations* £140,000 *Assets* £5,360,000
OTHER INFORMATION The trust awarded 14 grants during the year.
HOW TO APPLY Apply in writing to the correspondent. The trustees normally meet twice a year to consider applications.
CONTACT DETAILS The Trustees, c/o KPMG LLP, 319 St Vincent Street, Glasgow G2 5AS

■ The Anchor Foundation

CC NO 1082485   ESTABLISHED 2000
WHERE FUNDING CAN BE GIVEN UK and overseas.
WHO CAN BENEFIT Christian charities.
WHAT IS FUNDED Christian charities addressing social inclusion, particularly though healing and the arts.
WHAT IS NOT FUNDED No grants are awarded to individuals. It is not the normal practice of the charity to support the same project for more than three years (projects which have had three years of funding may apply again two years after the payment of the last grant).
TYPE OF GRANT Applications for capital and revenue funding are considered; however, only in very exceptional circumstances will grants be given for building work.
RANGE OF GRANTS £500 to £20,000.
SAMPLE GRANTS Riding Lights Theatre Company (£9,200); Castlemilk Parish Church (£7,500); Christian Solidarity Worldwide, Embracing Age and The Toybox Charity (£5,000 each); Hope Into Action (£3,000); Art Action UK (£2,000); Church Pastoral Aid Society (£1,000).
FINANCES *Financial year end* 31/03/2022 *Income* £205,300 *Grants to organisations* £239,700 *Assets* £9,080,000
TRUSTEES The Revd Robin Anker-Petersen; Nina Stewart; The Revd Canon Michael Mitton; Sue Mayfield.
OTHER INFORMATION The trustees look favourably on organisations whose boards demonstrate equal opportunities.
HOW TO APPLY An initial application form can be completed on the foundation's website, where full guidelines for applicants are also available.
CONTACT DETAILS The Secretary, PO Box 7689, Perth, Perthshire PH2 1JX *Email* secretary@ theanchorfoundation.org.uk *Website* www. theanchorfoundation.org.uk

■ Andrew Anderson Trust

CC NO 212170   ESTABLISHED 1954
WHERE FUNDING CAN BE GIVEN UK and overseas.
WHO CAN BENEFIT Charitable organisations.
WHAT IS FUNDED General charitable purposes, with a focus on religious activities, education and training, health and overseas aid.
SAMPLE GRANTS A list of beneficiaries was not included in the annual report and accounts.
FINANCES *Financial year end* 05/04/2022 *Income* £418,100 *Grants to organisations* £379,300 *Grants to individuals* £81,000 *Assets* £14,050,000
TRUSTEES Andrew Anderson; Margaret Anderson; Fiona West; Colleen Rosser.
HOW TO APPLY The charity is fully committed and does not accept unsolicited applications.
CONTACT DETAILS The Trustees, 1 Cote House Lane, Bristol BS9 3UW *Email* andrew_r_anderson@ yahoo.co.uk

■ Andor Charitable Trust

CC NO 1083572   ESTABLISHED 1996
WHERE FUNDING CAN BE GIVEN UK and overseas.
WHO CAN BENEFIT Charitable organisations.
WHAT IS FUNDED Health; medical research; the arts; social welfare; education; older people; people with disabilities.
RANGE OF GRANTS Up to £5,000 but mostly £1,000 to £3,000.
SAMPLE GRANTS The Chickenshed Theatre Trust (£5,000); Carers UK (£4,000); City of Birmingham Symphony Orchestra (£3,000), The Virtual Doctors (£2,000); Brain Research Trust and The Epilepsy Society (£1,000 each).
FINANCES *Financial year end* 05/04/2022 *Income* £88,000 *Grants to organisations* £160,500 *Assets* £3,470,000
TRUSTEES Nicholas Lederer; David Rothenberg; Dr Claire Walford; Karen Andor.
OTHER INFORMATION There were 78 grants made during the year.
HOW TO APPLY Contact the correspondent for further information.
CONTACT DETAILS The Trustees, c/o Blick Rothenberg Chartered Accountants, 16 Great Queen Street, Covent Garden, London WC2B 5AH *Tel.* 020 7544 8865 *Email* robin@ blickrothenberg.com

■ Andrews Charitable Trust

CC NO 1174706   ESTABLISHED 1965
WHERE FUNDING CAN BE GIVEN Bath and North East Somerset; Bristol; Buckinghamshire; East Sussex; Essex; Gloucestershire; Hertfordshire; London; Oxfordshire; South Gloucester; Surrey; West Sussex.
WHO CAN BENEFIT Christian organisations; churches.
WHAT IS FUNDED Housing; social welfare; Christian community projects supporting disadvantaged or marginalised people.
TYPE OF GRANT Project funding.
SAMPLE GRANTS A list of beneficiaries was not included in the annual report and accounts. Previous beneficiaries have included: Lighthouse (£92,000); The Cinnamon Network (£70,000); Carers Worldwide (£45,300); The Archbishop of Canterbury's Council (£20,500); 1625 Independent People (£17,000); Christian Funders Forum (£2,000).

FINANCES *Financial year end* 31/12/2021
Income £24,440,000
Grants to organisations £350,200
Assets £15,460,000
TRUSTEES Alison Kelly; Ami Davis; Elizabeth Hughes; Nicholas Wright; Paul Heal; Ruth Knagg; Helen Battrick; Alexandra McDonald; Carl Tomlin; Nathan Moore.
OTHER INFORMATION During the year, the trust awarded 172 grants to organisations. Grants were broken down as follows: relief of poverty (£177,700); Christian projects (£72,000); carers (£45,000); youth (£36,700); speaking volumes (£18,900).
HOW TO APPLY The trust only accepts applications for its Christian Innovation Grants programme, which provides small grants to Christian organisations that promote the Christian faith and provide practical help for disadvantaged and marginalised people within communities. Applications to this programme can be made online via The Cinnamon Network's website (https://cinnamonnetwork.co.uk/).
CONTACT DETAILS The Trustees, The Clockhouse, Bath Hill, Keynsham, Bristol BS31 1HL *Tel.* 0117 946 1834 *Email* info@andrewscharitabletrust.org.uk *Website* www.andrewscharitabletrust.org.uk

■ Anglo American Foundation

CC NO 1111719   ESTABLISHED 2005
WHERE FUNDING CAN BE GIVEN UK; Australia; Botswana; Brazil; Canada; Chile; Colombia; Ecuador; Ireland; Namibia; Peru; Sierra Leone; Singapore; South Africa; Zimbabwe.
WHO CAN BENEFIT Registered charities.
WHAT IS FUNDED Community development; education and training; the environment; health (particularly HIV/AIDS); social welfare.
RANGE OF GRANTS £1,000 to £1 million.
SAMPLE GRANTS Pyxera Global (£1.02 million); Anglo American Foundation (£953,700); Transparency International Australia (£611,300); Early Childcare Education Learning Centre Canada (£211,200); Gems and Jewellery Export Promotion Council (£97,100).
FINANCES *Financial year end* 31/12/2021
Income £80,300,000
Grants to organisations £3,410,000
Assets £77,330,000
TRUSTEES Jonathan Samuel; Anik Michaud-Ahmed; Norman Mbazima; Yvonne Mfolo.
OTHER INFORMATION The foundation was established in 2005 by Anglo American plc, a large multinational mining company. The foundation has six funding programmes. In 2021, grants were broken down as follows: community development (£2.05 million); capacity development (£611,300); education and training (£569,200); health and welfare (£151,500); employee matched funding (£22,300); other social investment (£2,500).
HOW TO APPLY The foundation does not accept unsolicited applications. Contact the correspondent for more information.
CONTACT DETAILS The Trustees, 17 Charterhouse Street, London EC1N 6RA *Tel.* 020 7968 8888 *Email* aagf@angloamerican.com *Website* www.angloamericangroupfoundation.org

■ Anguish's Educational Foundation

CC NO 311288   ESTABLISHED 1605
WHERE FUNDING CAN BE GIVEN Norwich and the parishes of Costessey, Hellesdon, Catton, Sprowston, Thorpe-next-Norwich and Corpusty.
WHO CAN BENEFIT Registered charities; schools; individuals.
WHAT IS FUNDED The education of children and young people (under 25 years old).
TYPE OF GRANT Core costs; capital costs; project funding.
SAMPLE GRANTS St Edmunds Society (£67,600); Mile Cross Primary School (£44,500); The SAW Trust (£22,100); Mancroft Advice Project (£21,000); BREAK (£15,000); Corpusty Primary School (£14,600); Norwich International Youth Project (£12,500); Reflex Theatre (£2,300).
FINANCES *Financial year end* 31/03/2022
Income £1,000,000
Grants to organisations £260,500
Grants to individuals £388,100
Assets £27,340,000
TRUSTEES David Fullman; Jeanne Southgate; Michael Flynn; Cllr Karen Davis; Boyd Taylor; Philip Davies; John Garside; Prof. Eneida Mioshi; Jacqueline Hanlon; Laura McCartney-Gray; Cllr Adam Giles; Sally Button; Vivien Thomas; Ashley Ford-McAllister.
HOW TO APPLY The foundation shares its administration with the Norwich Consolidated Charites and Norwich Freemen's Charity (also known as the Norwich Town Close Estate Charity). Applicants must first read the information on the Norwich Charitable Trusts website (www.norwichcharitabletrusts.org.uk/) and then contact the correspondent. If successful, applicants will be invited to make an application via the 'Flexigrant' application portal.
CONTACT DETAILS David Hynes, CEO of Norwich Charitable Trusts, c/o Norwich Charitable Trusts, 1 Woolgate Court, St Benedicts Street, Norwich, Norfolk NR2 4AP *Tel.* 01603 621023 *Email* david.hynes@norwichcharitabletrusts.org.uk *Website* www.anguishseducationalfoundation.org.uk

■ Anpride Ltd

CC NO 288978   ESTABLISHED 1984
WHERE FUNDING CAN BE GIVEN London.
WHO CAN BENEFIT Registered charities.
WHAT IS FUNDED Advancement of the Jewish faith; social welfare.
RANGE OF GRANTS Mostly up to £5,000.
SAMPLE GRANTS A list of beneficiaries was not included in the annual report and accounts.
FINANCES *Financial year end* 30/09/2021
Income £194,500
Grants to organisations £97,900
Assets £1,600,000
TRUSTEES Golda Benedikt; Chaim Benedikt; Aron Geldzahler.
OTHER INFORMATION Only grants of £5,000 and over were listed in the charity's annual report and accounts. Unlisted grants of less than £5,000 totalled £48,800. The 2020/21 accounts were the latest available at the time of writing (May 2023).
HOW TO APPLY Apply in writing to the correspondent.
CONTACT DETAILS The Trustees, 99 Geldeston Road, London E5 8RS *Tel.* 020 8806 1011

■ The Anson Charitable Trust

CC NO 1111010   **ESTABLISHED** 2005
WHERE FUNDING CAN BE GIVEN UK, with a preference for Buckinghamshire.
WHO CAN BENEFIT Registered charities; social enterprises; hospices.
WHAT IS FUNDED Arts and culture; medical research and the sciences; community development; the environment and ecology.
WHAT IS NOT FUNDED Individuals.
TYPE OF GRANT Capital costs; core/revenue costs; project funding; unrestricted funding.
SAMPLE GRANTS Garsington Opera (£21,800); Changing Faces (£6,000); BucksVision (£3,000); Blesma (£1,000); The National Trust (£120).
FINANCES *Financial year end 05/04/2022*
Income £250,000
Grants to organisations £365,900
Assets £51,500
TRUSTEES Kirsty Anson; George Anson.
HOW TO APPLY Application forms can be downloaded from the charity's website.
CONTACT DETAILS The Trustees, The Lilies, High Street, Weedon, Aylesbury, Buckinghamshire HP22 4NS *Tel.* 01296 640331 *Email* mail@ansoncharitabletrust.org.uk *Website* www.ansoncharitabletrust.org.uk

■ AO Smile Foundation

CC NO 1157111   **ESTABLISHED** 2014
WHERE FUNDING CAN BE GIVEN UK, in areas local to the company's offices.
WHO CAN BENEFIT Charitable organisations.
WHAT IS FUNDED Children and young people.
SAMPLE GRANTS A list of beneficiaries was not included in the annual report and accounts. Previous beneficiaries have included: Onside Youth Zones (£139,200); Derian House (£56,000); Duke of Edinburgh Award Scheme (£50,000).
FINANCES *Financial year end 31/03/2022*
Income £37,400
Grants to organisations £102,200
Assets £227,000
TRUSTEES John Roberts; David Wilkinson; Julie Finnemore.
OTHER INFORMATION The foundation is the corporate charity of AO World plc, an online retailer specialising in household appliances.
HOW TO APPLY Contact the correspondent or your nearest AO site for further information.
CONTACT DETAILS Justin Packman, Foundation and Partnerships Manager, AO Smile Foundation, 5A The Parklands, Lostock, Bolton BL6 4SD *Email* justin.packman@ao.com *Website* www.ao-world.com/responsibility/ao-smile-foundation

■ The Apax Foundation

CC NO 1112845   **ESTABLISHED** 2006
WHERE FUNDING CAN BE GIVEN UK and overseas, with a focus on disadvantaged communities.
WHO CAN BENEFIT Registered charities and community groups.
WHAT IS FUNDED Social entrepreneurship; social mobility; welfare; education; support for refugees.
TYPE OF GRANT One-off and multi-year grants.
RANGE OF GRANTS Mostly under £10,000, but larger grants of £10,000 to £100,000 are also awarded.
SAMPLE GRANTS Breaking Barriers; Opportunity Network; Sponsors for Educational Opportunity.

FINANCES *Financial year end 31/12/2021*
Income £1,930,000
Grants to organisations £2,090,000
Assets £78,760,000
TRUSTEES Sir Ronald Cohen; Dr Peter Englander; David Marks; Simon Cresswell; Mitch Truwit; Shashank Singh; Rohan Haldea; Jason Wright; Roxana-Viorica Mirica.
OTHER INFORMATION The foundation is the corporate charity of Apax Partners LLP, a private equity firm, and receives a share of its profits.
HOW TO APPLY Apply in writing to the correspondent.
CONTACT DETAILS Kate Albert, Foundation Manager, 33 Jermyn Street, London SW1Y 6DN *Tel.* 020 7872 6300 *Email* foundation@apax.com *Website* www.apax.com/responsibility/apax-foundation

■ The John Apthorp Charity

CC NO 1102472   **ESTABLISHED** 2003
WHERE FUNDING CAN BE GIVEN Bedfordshire; Cambridgeshire; Greater Manchester; Hertfordshire.
WHO CAN BENEFIT Registered charities.
WHAT IS FUNDED Children and young people; older people; people with disabilities; social welfare.
WHAT IS NOT FUNDED Charities outside the geographic catchment area; charities that have large unrestricted reserves (in excess of 25%, or three months of annual spending); core funding; retrospective expenditure; any organisation which is not a registered charity; statutory organisations; individuals; any organisation which has recently received funding from the charity.
TYPE OF GRANT Capital costs; project funding.
RANGE OF GRANTS Grants range from £500 to £100,000.
SAMPLE GRANTS Ride High (£30,500); Viva Arts and Community (£20,000); Wheathampstead United Church (£17,000); Kids in Action (£15,000); Potton Hall for All (£10,000); Ross Park Scout Group (£4,400); Hatfield House Chamber Music Festival (£2,000); Bucks Search and Rescue (£1,700); Macintyre Care (£750).
FINANCES *Financial year end 31/12/2021*
Income £381,300
Grants to organisations £252,700
Assets £12,970,000
TRUSTEES Duncan Apthorp; John Apthorp; Kate Arnold; Dr Christina Apthorp.
OTHER INFORMATION In total, 26 organisations were awarded grants during the year.
HOW TO APPLY Applicants are asked to read the eligibility criteria on the charity's website before applying. The charity recommends that applications are sent via email. Upcoming deadlines are published on the website.
CONTACT DETAILS The Trustees, 29 Newlands Avenue, Radlett, Hertfordshire WD7 8 EJ *Email* johnapthorpcharity@hotmail.com *Website* www.johnapthorpcharity.org

■ The Arah Foundation

CC NO 1154244   **ESTABLISHED** 2013
WHERE FUNDING CAN BE GIVEN England and Wales; St Vincent and the Grenadines; Turkey.
WHO CAN BENEFIT Registered charities.
WHAT IS FUNDED General charitable purposes; education and training; arts and culture; human rights; religious and racial harmony.
SAMPLE GRANTS A list of beneficiaries was not available.

FINANCES *Financial year end* 31/03/2022
Income £810
Grants to organisations £236,100
TRUSTEES William Arah; Asli Arah.
OTHER INFORMATION Full accounts were not available to view on the Charity Commission's website due to the foundation's low income. We have therefore estimated the grant total based on the foundation's total expenditure.
HOW TO APPLY Applications can be made in writing to the correspondent.
CONTACT DETAILS The Trustees, c/o MacFarlanes LLP, 10 Norwich Street, London EC4A 1BD *Tel.* 07435 883224 *Email* info@arahfoundation.org

■ The Annabel Arbib Foundation

CC NO 296358   **ESTABLISHED** 1987
WHERE FUNDING CAN BE GIVEN UK.
WHO CAN BENEFIT Registered charities and local organisations with charitable purposes.
WHAT IS FUNDED Social welfare; children's welfare; medical causes; education.
WHAT IS NOT FUNDED Individuals.
TYPE OF GRANT Recurrent and one-off grants.
RANGE OF GRANTS From £250 to £348,800.
SAMPLE GRANTS Arbib Educational Trust (£348,800); University of Bristol – Lyons (£4,500); A Better America Foundation (£3,800); Lady Garden Foundation (£2,000); Ace Africa (£500); Rotary Club of Henley (£250).
FINANCES *Financial year end* 05/04/2022
Income £380,800
Grants to organisations £422,400
Assets £15,760,000
TRUSTEES Annabel Nicoll; Paddy Nicoll; Rory Nicoll; Phoebe Nicoll; Sam Nicoll.
OTHER INFORMATION Grants were distributed as follows: medical causes (£2,000), education (£353,300); other (£6,100).
HOW TO APPLY Apply in writing to the correspondent. However, note that the trustees have stressed that grants are largely made to organisations with which they have a connection; therefore, unsolicited applications are unlikely to be successful.
CONTACT DETAILS Paula Doraisamy, 61 Grosvenor Street, London W1K 3JE *Tel.* 020 3011 1100 *Email* admin@61grosvenorstreet.com

■ Arcadia Fund

                    ESTABLISHED 2001
WHERE FUNDING CAN BE GIVEN Worldwide.
WHO CAN BENEFIT Registered charities; educational organisations.
WHAT IS FUNDED Preserving endangered culture; protecting endangered nature; promoting open access to information.
WHAT IS NOT FUNDED Individuals.
SAMPLE GRANTS Re:wild (£4.8 million); Creative Commons (£3.2 million); University of Cambridge (£2.4 million); Bournemouth University (£69,600).
FINANCES *Financial year end* 31/12/2022
Grants to organisations £67,770,000
TRUSTEE Talvik Trust Services AG.
OTHER INFORMATION Arcadia Fund is not registered with the Charity Commission. The grant total was taken from the grant-maker's Grant Directory page on its website and converted to GBP using the exchange rate at the time of writing (May 2023).
HOW TO APPLY Unsolicited applications are not accepted.

CONTACT DETAILS Grants Team, 6th Floor, 40 Villiers Street, London WC2N 6NJ *Email* info@arcadiafund.org.uk *Website* www.arcadiafund.org.uk

■ The Archer Trust

CC NO 1033534   **ESTABLISHED** 1994
WHERE FUNDING CAN BE GIVEN UK. Overseas projects can be supported but only via a UK charity.
WHO CAN BENEFIT Small UK-registered charities. According to the trust's website, preference is given to organisations working in areas with high unemployment and deprivation in the UK, and organisations that make 'good use' of volunteers.
WHAT IS FUNDED Provision of aid or support to defined groups of people who are disadvantaged or marginalised.
WHAT IS NOT FUNDED Individuals; conservation, heritage and environmental projects; conversions for disabled access; charities supporting animals; research; evangelism; umbrella charities; hospices; charities whose cash balance exceeds nine months' expenditure.
TYPE OF GRANT Project funding.
RANGE OF GRANTS £500 to £5,000.
SAMPLE GRANTS Mission Without Borders (£5,000); St Paul's Hostel (£4,000); Autism UK (£3,000); Independent Provider of Special Education Advice and Prison Fellowship (£2,500 each); Joy Foundation (£1,500); Christ Church Lancaster (£1,000); Sefton Support Group (£500).
FINANCES *Financial year end* 05/04/2022
Income £1,330,000
Grants to organisations £263,500
Assets £3,400,000
TRUSTEES James Archer; Michael Baker; Robert Mellors; Helen Green; Clare Atkins.
HOW TO APPLY Apply in writing to the correspondent. Unsuccessful applicants will not receive a response, even if an sae is enclosed.
CONTACT DETAILS The Secretary, Oakford, Stortford, Standon, Ware, Hertfordshire SG11 1LT *Tel.* 01920 462312 *Website* www.archertrust.org.uk

■ The Architectural Heritage Fund

CC NO 266780   **ESTABLISHED** 1976
WHERE FUNDING CAN BE GIVEN UK.
WHO CAN BENEFIT Registered charities; not-for-profit organisations; CICs; benefit societies; parish and town councils; community councils (in Scotland and Wales).
WHAT IS FUNDED Historic buildings; conservation; encouraging the use of historic buildings for public benefit.
WHAT IS NOT FUNDED Individuals; unincorporated trusts or associations; local authorities and other public sector bodies; for-profit companies unless in a partnership led by incorporated charity community business or social enterprise; churches or other places of worship where the building will remain in use primarily as a place of religious worship.
TYPE OF GRANT Project funding; development funding.
RANGE OF GRANTS Grants range from £2,000 to £350,000.
SAMPLE GRANTS Heritage Lincolnshire (£350,000); Creative Land Trust (£100,000); Heritage Lab CIC (£15,000); Newhampton Arts Centre (£8,300); Banana Enterprise Network (£2,100).

FINANCES *Financial year end 31/03/2022*
Income £7,090,000
Grants to organisations £5,080,000
Assets £17,620,000
TRUSTEES Myra Barnes; David Hunter; Suzanne
Snowden; Adebayo Alao; Karen Latimer; Roy
Hodson; Graham Fisher; James Bowdidge;
Gregory Pickup; Dr Neal Sashore; Esther Wild;
Audrey Carlin; Rosaleen Kerslake.
HOW TO APPLY Expression of interest forms and
further guidance can be found on the fund's
website.
CONTACT DETAILS The Trustees, 3 Spital Yard,
Spitalfields, London E1 6AQ *Tel.* 020 7925
0199 *Email* ahf@ahfund.org.uk *Website* www.
ahfund.org.uk

■ Ardbarron Trust Ltd

CCNI NO NIC101111
WHERE FUNDING CAN BE GIVEN UK and financially
developing countries.
WHO CAN BENEFIT Registered charities.
WHAT IS FUNDED Awareness and understanding of
the Christian gospel; social welfare; health care;
literacy.
SAMPLE GRANTS A list of beneficiaries was not
available in the charity's annual report and
accounts. Previous beneficiaries have included:
Christian Missions Charitable Trust; Echoes of
Service; Operation Mobilisation; Strategic
Resource Group; Tearfund; Youth for Christ.
FINANCES *Financial year end 31/12/2021*
Income £5,360,000
Grants to organisations £4,890,000
Grants to individuals £92,100
Assets £219,110,000
TRUSTEES Martin Agnew; Geoffrey Agnew; John
Agnew; Malcolm Johnston.
OTHER INFORMATION Grants were made to 319
organisations during the year.
HOW TO APPLY Apply in writing to the correspondent.
CONTACT DETAILS The Trustees, 9 Hightown Avenue,
Newtownabbey, Co Antrim BT36 4RT *Tel.* 028
9034 2733

■ The Ardeola Charitable Trust

CC NO 1124380   ESTABLISHED 2008
WHERE FUNDING CAN BE GIVEN UK.
WHO CAN BENEFIT Registered charities.
WHAT IS FUNDED General charitable purposes,
including education, the arts and health.
RANGE OF GRANTS £5,000 to £60,000.
SAMPLE GRANTS Garsington Opera (£200,000);
Royal National Theatre (£161,000); Target
Ovarian Cancer (£100,000); University of
Southampton (£64,000); British Museum
(£40,000); Durham Cathedral (£35,000);
Ashmolean Museum (£30,000); Thames
Hospice (£25,000); Windsor Festival Society
and Macmillan Cancer Support (£10,000 each);
The Art Fund (£2,000).
FINANCES *Financial year end 31/05/2022*
Income £1,340,000
Grants to organisations £1,170,000
Assets £6,150,000
TRUSTEES Graham Barker; Joanna Barker; William
Hiscocks; Prof. John Cornwall; Zedra Trust
Company (UK) Ltd.
OTHER INFORMATION Typically, but not always, the
same organisations are supported each year.
HOW TO APPLY Unsolicited applications are not
accepted.
CONTACT DETAILS The Trustees, Zedra UK Trusts,
Booths Hall, Booths Park, Chelford Road,

Knutsford, Cheshire WA16 8GS *Tel.* 01565
748829

■ The Ardwick Trust

CC NO 266981   ESTABLISHED 1975
WHERE FUNDING CAN BE GIVEN England and Wales.
WHO CAN BENEFIT Charitable organisations.
WHAT IS FUNDED General charitable purposes with a
focus on: Jewish causes; social welfare; health;
disability; older people; children and young
people.
RANGE OF GRANTS Up to £1,000, but mostly £100 to
£500.
SAMPLE GRANTS Nightingale Hammerson and
Technion UK (£1,000 each); Magen David Adorn
UK (£700); Bowel Research UK and Headway
North London (£500 each); Afghanistan and
Central Asian Association and Asthma UK (£200
each); Computer Aid International (£100).
FINANCES *Financial year end 05/04/2022*
Income £91,100
Grants to organisations £62,000
Assets £1,370,000
TRUSTEES Janet Bloch; Dominic Flynn; Judith
Portrait.
OTHER INFORMATION In 2021/22, the trust awarded
326 grants to projects in England and Wales.
HOW TO APPLY Apply in writing to the correspondent.
CONTACT DETAILS The Trustees, Office Suite 1,
Haslemere House, Lower Street, Haslemere,
Surrey GU27 2PE *Tel.* 01428 652788
Email haslemere@knoxcropper.com

■ Armed Forces Covenant Fund Trust

CC NO 1177627   ESTABLISHED 2018
WHERE FUNDING CAN BE GIVEN UK.
WHO CAN BENEFIT Organisations that support the
armed forces community.
WHAT IS FUNDED Support for the armed forces
community, including: social welfare; mental and
physical health; education; employment;
criminal justice.
WHAT IS NOT FUNDED Individuals.
TYPE OF GRANT Typically core and project costs.
RANGE OF GRANTS Programme dependent.
SAMPLE GRANTS A full list of beneficiaries can be
found on the website.
FINANCES *Financial year end 31/03/2022*
Income £28,150,000
Grants to organisations £25,960,000
Assets £1,910,000
TRUSTEE The Armed Forces Covenant Fund Trustee.
OTHER INFORMATION Open funding programmes are
advertised on the charity's website.
HOW TO APPLY Check the charity's website for
current programmes and to apply.
CONTACT DETAILS Grants Team, 95 Horseferry Road,
London SW1P 2DX *Tel.* 020 7154 1725
Email info@covenantfund.org.uk *Website* www.
covenantfund.org.uk

■ Armed Forces Education Trust

CC NO 1167682   ESTABLISHED 2016
WHERE FUNDING CAN BE GIVEN UK.
WHO CAN BENEFIT Schools/education providers
(must be a registered charity or not-for-profit
organisation); individuals.
WHAT IS FUNDED The education of people under 25
who are or were dependants of serving or
former members of the armed forces.

WHAT IS NOT FUNDED Capital projects; activities that should be funded by the Service Pupil Premium (in England); activities that the state has a legal obligation to provide.

TYPE OF GRANT Project funding.

RANGE OF GRANTS Up to £48,000.

SAMPLE GRANTS Service Children's Progression Alliance (£48,000); Supporting Service Children in Education Cymru (£34,200); Forres (£29,000); Firhill (£20,000); Oxfordshire County Council (£13,200); Credenhill Primary School (£7,500); Peel Primary (£4,000); Gateway School (£1,500).

FINANCES *Financial year end 31/08/2022*
Income £425,500
Grants to organisations £186,900
Grants to individuals £256,600
Assets £13,980,000

TRUSTEES Merrick Willis; Alan Behagg; Jenny Lycett; Maria Clohessy; Tim Flesher; Iain Buckle; Dominic Toriati; Lucy Robinson.

OTHER INFORMATION Grants were paid to 12 organisations during the year.

HOW TO APPLY Eligible organisations can submit applications via the trust's website.

CONTACT DETAILS The Trustees, PO Box 684, Farnham, Surrey GU9 1LP *Tel.* 07464 732000 *Email* admin@armedforceseducation.org *Website* www.armedforceseducation.org

■ The John Armitage Charitable Trust

CC NO 1079688   **ESTABLISHED** 2000

WHERE FUNDING CAN BE GIVEN England and Wales.

WHO CAN BENEFIT Registered charitable organisations.

WHAT IS FUNDED Support for disadvantaged children and young people; education; medical care; research; arts and culture, prisoners and young offenders; religion.

TYPE OF GRANT Project funding.

RANGE OF GRANTS Up to £300,000.

SAMPLE GRANTS The five largest grants were: Pembroke College Cambridge (£2.5 million); Harris Foundation (£330,000); Fight for Peace (£150,000); The Forward Trust (£120,000); Home-Start Westminster (£105,000).

FINANCES *Financial year end 05/04/2022*
Income £16,290,000
Grants to organisations £7,240,000
Assets £170,650,000

TRUSTEES John Armitage; Catherine Armitage; William Francklin; Celina Francklin; Robert MacInnes.

OTHER INFORMATION Only the beneficiaries of the five largest grants were listed in the accounts. In total, 104 organisations were awarded grants. Grants were broken down as follows: education (£3,470,000); youth support (£983,500); general charitable purposes (£830,000); parenting support (£657,000); support for former offenders (£466,000); museum and arts (£354,500); medical research and care (£321,000); religion (£154,000).

HOW TO APPLY Unsolicited applications are not accepted.

CONTACT DETAILS The Trustees, c/o Sampson West, Forum House, 1st Floor, 15–18 Lime Street, London EC3M 7AN *Tel.* 020 7404 5040

■ The Armourers and Brasiers Gauntlet Trust

CC NO 279204   **ESTABLISHED** 1979

WHERE FUNDING CAN BE GIVEN UK, with some preference for London.

WHO CAN BENEFIT Registered charities; small charities; schools; colleges; universities.

WHAT IS FUNDED Materials science; community projects; the armed forces; children and young people; education; health and medical research; the arts; arms or armour.

WHAT IS NOT FUNDED The maintenance, repair or restoration of buildings; individuals; projects outside the UK.

TYPE OF GRANT Core costs; project funding.

RANGE OF GRANTS Typically up to £4,000.

SAMPLE GRANTS Industrial Experience Awards – University of Swansea (£19,000); Secondary Schools Science Programme (£12,000); The Mason Fund Summer Placements (£10,000); The Rodolfus Foundation (£9,000); Salter's Festivals of Chemistry (£4,200); The Ulysses Trust (£2,000); St Margaret Lothbury (£1,000); University of Nottingham (£250).

FINANCES *Financial year end 31/03/2022*
Income £361,600
Grants to organisations £262,000
Grants to individuals £35,300
Assets £9,850,000

TRUSTEES Prof. William Bonfield; Nicola Davies; Edward Pitt; Jonathan Hale; Prof. Emma Ream; Dr Roger Bowdler.

OTHER INFORMATION In 2021/22 grants were awarded to 71 organisations, totalling £262,000, and a further 74 grants totalling £35,300 were awarded to individuals.

HOW TO APPLY The trust's three grant programmes have separate application processes. Online application forms are available on the website, alongside guidelines and deadlines. Applicants who are shortlisted for the Small Charities Programme will be interviewed, and the trust may request to visit your charity before the interview.

CONTACT DETAILS The Trustees, Armourers' Hall, 81 Coleman Street, London EC2R 5BJ *Tel.* 020 7374 4000 *Email* charities@armourershall.co.uk *Website* www.armourershall.co.uk/funding-grants

■ The Arsenal Foundation

CC NO 1145668   **ESTABLISHED** 2012

WHERE FUNDING CAN BE GIVEN Barnet; Camden; Hackney; Hertsmere; Islington; Walthamstow.

WHO CAN BENEFIT Organisations and individuals.

WHAT IS FUNDED Education; sport; health; medical; disability; social welfare; children and young people.

SAMPLE GRANTS Save the Children (£340,400); Islington Giving (£50,000); Willow (£43,100).

FINANCES *Financial year end 31/05/2022*
Income £153,200
Grants to organisations £694,700
Grants to individuals £2,000
Assets £1,350,000

TRUSTEES Svenja Geissmar; Alan Sefton; Andrew Jolly; Vinaichandra Venkatesham; Frederick Hudson.

OTHER INFORMATION The Gunners Fund supports local projects and good causes in the boroughs of Islington, Camden and Hackney by offering small grants of up to £2,500.

HOW TO APPLY Application forms are available to download from the foundation's website, along with grant-making guidelines. The foundation states that it is unable to respond to all of the applications it receives, due to the high volume, so if you do not receive a response within one month, you should assume that you have been unsuccessful. Gunners Fund application guidelines are available online at: www.arsenal.com/arsenalfoundation/local-giving/gunners-fund.

CONTACT DETAILS Samir Singh, Highbury House, 75 Drayton Park, London N5 1BU *Tel.* 020 7704 4406 *Email* ssingh@arsenal.co.uk *Website* www.arsenal.com/thearsenalfoundation

....

■ The Art Fund

CC NO 209174   **ESTABLISHED** 1903
WHERE FUNDING CAN BE GIVEN UK.
WHO CAN BENEFIT Public museums, galleries, historic houses, libraries and archives that are: open for at least half the week for at least six months a year; are fully or provisionally accredited under the Arts Council Scheme; charities; CIOs; CICs; charitable community benefit societies.
WHAT IS FUNDED Museums and galleries, including the acquisition of works of art; supporting professional development; connecting more people with art.
WHAT IS NOT FUNDED A list of exclusions can be found on the charity's website.
TYPE OF GRANT Collections and acquisitions; training and development; display of art through tours and exhibitions.
RANGE OF GRANTS Programme dependent.
SAMPLE GRANTS Hepworth Wakefield (£500,000); National Gallery – London (£300,000); Stained Glass Museum – East Anglia (£106,500); Imperial War Museum – London (£85,000); British Museum – London (£45,000); Nottingham Castle (£11,200); Leicester Museum and Art Gallery (£2,700); The Seaside Museum – Herne Bay (£620).
FINANCES *Financial year end* 31/12/2021
Income £17,590,000
Grants to organisations £3,000,000
Assets £62,000,000
TRUSTEES Jeremy Palmer; Axel Ruger; Prof. Marcia Pointon; Richard Deacon; Monisha Shah; Tessa Jackson; Katrina Brown; Anupam Ganguli; Susan Rees; Satish Padiyar; Madeleine Kennedy; Stella Osunsade; Clare Gough; Desmond Shawe-Taylor; Dr David Dibosa; Chris Smith.
OTHER INFORMATION The charity has a number of grant programmes, information of which can be found on its website.
HOW TO APPLY Applications can be made via the charity's online portal.
CONTACT DETAILS Museum Services, 2 Granary Square, King's Cross, London N1C 4BH *Tel.* 020 7225 4800 *Email* museums@artfund.org *Website* www.artfund.org

....

■ The Artemis Charitable Foundation

OSCR NO SC037857   **ESTABLISHED** 2007
WHERE FUNDING CAN BE GIVEN UK and overseas.
WHO CAN BENEFIT UK-registered charities.
WHAT IS FUNDED Health; social welfare; education and training; the environment; global disasters and emergency appeals.
TYPE OF GRANT Typically one-off grants, but multi-year grants may be given if a partnership develops into a multi-year relationship. The foundation will consider unrestricted funding.
RANGE OF GRANTS Up to £60,000.

SAMPLE GRANTS Shivia Microfinance (£60,000); Client Earth (£57,500); City Harvest (£50,500); Reach Academy (£50,000); Mary's Meals (£21,200); Beaver Trust (£2,500); The Trussell Trust (£250).
FINANCES *Financial year end* 31/12/2021
Income £1,020,000
Grants to organisations £924,800
Assets £659,400
OTHER INFORMATION According to its 2021 accounts, 'the foundation aims to have a primary core charity in each category and a junior core charity receiving less funding, with the option more that this level of funding may be split over more than one junior charity in that activity.' The foundation is the charitable arm of Artemis Investment Management LLP.
HOW TO APPLY Apply in writing via email. Full details of what should be included in an application can be found on the foundation's website.
CONTACT DETAILS Marisa Charosky, Foundation Coordinator, 6th Floor, Exchange Plaza, 50 Lothian Road, Edinburgh EH3 9BY *Email* charitablefoundation@artemisfunds.com *Website* www.artemisfunds.com/en/about-artemis/artemis-charitable-foundation

....

■ Douglas Arter Foundation

CC NO 201794   **ESTABLISHED** 1960
WHERE FUNDING CAN BE GIVEN UK, with a preference for Bristol, Somerset and Gloucestershire.
WHO CAN BENEFIT Registered charities only.
WHAT IS FUNDED Projects supporting people with disabilities.
WHAT IS NOT FUNDED Research; core costs; major funding appeals.
TYPE OF GRANT Project funding.
RANGE OF GRANTS £250 to £2,500.
SAMPLE GRANTS A list of beneficiaries was not included in the annual report and accounts. Previous beneficiaries have included: Assist Trust; Build Charity; Challenge; Climbing Out; Deafway; Hamlet; Listening Books; React (Rapid Effective Assistance for Children with potentially Terminal illness); Wheely Boat; Willow Foundation.
FINANCES *Financial year end* 31/12/2021
Income £105,500
Grants to organisations £64,000
Assets £3,940,000
TRUSTEES John Gurney; John Hudd; Geoffrey Arter; Peter Yardley; Belinda Arter.
OTHER INFORMATION In 2021 the foundation received 377 appeals, 118 of which were successful.
HOW TO APPLY Apply in writing by post to the correspondent. Applications must include: the objectives of the appeal; funding already available; details of self-help; a timetable for the project; and a copy of your organisation's latest audited accounts. Appeals should be for specific projects. Only successful applicants will be acknowledged. The trustees meet four times a year, in the first week of March, June, September and December, and cheques for grants will be sent by the second week of those months.
CONTACT DETAILS Belinda Arter, The Secretary, Fern Villa, Melksham Road, Patterdown, Chippenham, Wiltshire SN15 2NR *Tel.* 01249 448252 *Email* dafbristol@aol.com

■ Arts Council England

cc no 1036733   established 1994
where funding can be given England.
who can benefit Arts organisations; galleries; museums; libraries; artists and creative professionals.
what is funded Developing, sustaining and promoting the arts.
what is not funded Exclusions may vary depending upon the specific grants programme.
type of grant Mostly project funding.
range of grants £1,000 to £100,000.
sample grants A list of beneficiaries was not included in the annual report and accounts.
finances *Financial year end 31/03/2022*
Income £941,850,000
Grants to organisations £906,640,000
trustees Sir Nicholas Serota; Sukhbinder Johal; Elizabeth Murdoch; Andrew Miller; David Roberts; Kathryn Willard; Dr Veronica Brown; Ruth Mackenzie; Michael Eakin; Ciara Eastell; Catherine Mallyon; Helen Birchenough.
how to apply There is a helpful funding finder facility on the Arts Council's website which allows users to browse its funding programmes. Applications can made via the Grantium grants portal.
contact details Customer Services, Bloomsbury Street, Bloomsbury, London WC1B 3HF *Tel.* 0161 934 4317 *Email* use the contact form on the website *Website* www.artscouncil.org.uk

■ Arts Council of Northern Ireland

established 1995
where funding can be given Northern Ireland.
who can benefit Artists; arts organisations.
what is funded The Arts Council of Northern Ireland (ACNI) is the development and funding agency for the Arts in Northern Ireland. It distributes public money and National Lottery funds to develop and deliver a wide variety of arts projects, events and initiatives across Northern Ireland.
sample grants Examples of projects supported by the council can be found on its website.
finances *Financial year end 31/03/2021*
Income £1,710,000
Grants to organisations £35,720,000
Assets (£3,260,000)
trustees Liam Hannaway; William Leatham; Julie Andrews; Lynne Best; Paul Boyle; Paul Brolly; Joe Dougan; Sean Kelly; Laura McCorry; Ray Hall; Dr Gearoid Trimble.
other information The 2020/21 accounts were the latest available at the time of writing (May 2023). We have taken the figure for 'expenditure on arts' as the grant total. Note that this figure may include grants to individuals.
how to apply Information on what funding is currently available, guidelines and full details of how to apply can be found on the Arts Council of Northern Ireland's website.
contact details The Arts Development Department, Linen Hill House, 23 Linenhall Street, Lisburn, County Antrim BT28 1FJ *Tel.* 028 9262 3555 *Email* info@artscouncil-ni.org *Website* www.artscouncil-ni.org

■ Arts Council of Wales (Cyngor Celfyddydau Cymru)

cc no 1034245   established 1994
where funding can be given Wales.
who can benefit Arts organisations; schools; individuals.
what is funded Arts activities and projects including: theatre; arts centres; opera; visual arts; dance; music; arts and young people; community arts; literature; circuses and carnivals; disability arts.
type of grant Project funding; capital costs; training costs.
sample grants Welsh National Opera (£4.58 million); Theatr Clwyd (£1.82 million); National Theatre Wales (£1.62 million); Pontardawe Arts Centre (£63,900); Blackwood Miners' Institute (£20,000); The River Centre (£1,000).
finances *Financial year end 31/03/2022*
Income £66,240,000
Grants to organisations £42,430,000
Grants to individuals £238,000
Assets £2,420,000
trustees Margaret-Anne Russell; Elen Robert; Ruth Fabby; Tafsila Khan; Ceri Davies; Prudence Thimbleby; Keith Murrell; Lhosa Daly; Dr Sarah Younan; Gwennan Jones; Yr Athro Tudur Hallam; Victoria Provis; Alison Mears; Devinda de Silva; Kate Eden.
how to apply Details of the application process and application deadlines for each programme can be found on the council's website.
contact details Grants Team, Bute Place, Cardiff CF10 5AL *Tel.* 0330 124 2733 *Email* use the contact form on the website *Website* www.arts.wales

■ ArtSocial Foundation

cc no 1163100   established 2015
where funding can be given UK and Russia.
who can benefit Non-profit organisations.
what is funded The use of arts and art therapy to improve the lives of vulnerable children and young people with special educational needs and disabilities, life-limiting and chronic medical conditions, and mental health conditions and trauma (including those who are refugees, asylum seekers or displaced).
what is not funded Individuals; building funds; bursaries or scholarships; capital campaigns; deficit financing; emergency funding; endowments; festivals or events; film projects; land acquisition, match funding; seed funding; sponsorships.
type of grant Service/programme delivery; capacity-building.
range of grants £900 to £22,000.
sample grants ANPO 'Centre of Psychology and Art Therapy' Studio SAMO (£22,800); Otakar Kraus Music Trust (£22,400); ANPO 'Diaconal Centre' Prikosnovenie ('Touch') (£7,100); APNO Koleso Obozrenia (£4,300); Charity Fund Here and Now ('Zdes' i Seychas') (£1,000).
finances *Financial year end 31/08/2021*
Income £68,100
Grants to organisations £57,800
Assets £107,200
trustees Alina Davey; Anna Siakotos; Alina Uspenskaya; Lali Margania; Areta Hryschuk; Jacqueline Hall.
other information Five organisations were awarded grants during the year. The 2020/21 accounts were the latest available at the time of writing (May 2023).

HOW TO APPLY An application form, together with full guidelines and FAQs, is available on the website.

CONTACT DETAILS Liza Oliver, Charity Programmes Advisor, LCLB Suite 1756, Ground Floor, 95 Mortimer Street, London W1W 7GB *Tel.* 07599 714773 *Email* info@ArtSocial.uk or Liza@ArtSocial.uk *Website* http://artsocial.uk

■ The Ove Arup Foundation

CC NO 328138　　　　**ESTABLISHED** 1989
WHERE FUNDING CAN BE GIVEN UK and overseas.
WHO CAN BENEFIT Charitable organisations; universities; research organisations; CICs.
WHAT IS FUNDED The built environment; engineering; architecture; education.
WHAT IS NOT FUNDED Individuals for private study.
TYPE OF GRANT Research and project grants, including start-up and feasibility costs.
RANGE OF GRANTS Up to £55,000.
SAMPLE GRANTS Sydney Opera House (£161,800); City Space Architecture (£70,000); The Glass House (£60,000); Arts Depot (£5,000); The Anglo Danish Society (£2,500).
FINANCES *Financial year end 31/03/2022*
Income £479,500
Grants to organisations £403,200
Assets £6,130,000
TRUSTEES Caroline Cole; Terry Hill; Gregory Hodkinson; Tim Chapman; Faith Wainwright; Alan Belfield; Kate West; Ricky Tsui.
HOW TO APPLY Application forms are available to download from the website. The trustees' meetings are held quarterly,in early December, March, June and September. The trustees will consider applications received by the Secretary by the middle of the preceding month.
CONTACT DETAILS John Ward, Secretary, Ove Arup Foundation, 8 Fitzroy Street, London W1T 4BJ *Tel.* 020 7636 1531 *Email* foundation@ ovearupfoundation.org *Website* www. ovearupfoundation.org

■ Ove Arup Partnership Charitable Trust

CC NO 1038737　　　　**ESTABLISHED** 1978
WHERE FUNDING CAN BE GIVEN UK and overseas.
WHO CAN BENEFIT Registered charities; non-profit organisations in the UK and overseas; hospices; hospitals.
WHAT IS FUNDED Education; social care; health and welfare; disaster relief and poverty alleviation; local community development; sustainability; the environment and technology.
WHAT IS NOT FUNDED Individuals.
RANGE OF GRANTS Typically £500 to £60,000.
SAMPLE GRANTS The Ove Arup Foundation (£400,000); Unicef (£98,000); World Vision (£34,000); The Line (£5,000); The Myton Hospices (£500).
FINANCES *Financial year end 31/03/2022*
Income £1,320,000
Grants to organisations £1,330,000
Assets £28,400
TRUSTEE Ove Arup Partnership Trust Corporation Ltd.
OTHER INFORMATION Only organisations that received grants of over £500 were listed as beneficiaries in the charity's accounts. Grants of under £500 totalled £2,700.
HOW TO APPLY Apply in writing to the correspondent. Grants are reviewed at least once per annum

and funding may be committed for multiple (typically three) years.
CONTACT DETAILS Stephanie Wilde, Ove Arup and Partners Ltd, 8 Fitzroy Street, London W1T 4BJ *Tel.* 020 7636 1531 *Email* stephanie.wilde@ arup.com

■ The Asda Foundation

CC NO 1124268　　　　**ESTABLISHED** 2008
WHERE FUNDING CAN BE GIVEN England and Wales.
WHO CAN BENEFIT Registered charities and voluntary sector organisations.
WHAT IS FUNDED Community development.
WHAT IS NOT FUNDED Each programme has specific exclusions – see the relevant guidance on the foundation's website.
RANGE OF GRANTS Up to £250,000.
SAMPLE GRANTS University of Leeds (£180,000); Jane Tomlinson's Run for All (£139,000); Duke of Edinburgh Award Charter (£127,500); Breast Cancer Now (£17,500); Moordown Community Association (£15,000).
FINANCES *Financial year end 31/12/2021*
Income £3,750,000
Grants to organisations £3,960,000
Grants to individuals £45,000
Assets £4,470,000
TRUSTEES John Cookman; Jane Earnshaw; Jason Martin; Jodie Tate; Simon Lewis; Patricia Mitchell; Susan Hennessey; Helen Selby.
OTHER INFORMATION The Asda Foundation is Asda's charitable trust. It supplements the good causes that Asda employees support locally, as well as a number of bigger ad hoc projects in local communities.
HOW TO APPLY Further information on how to apply for grants can be found on the foundation's website.
CONTACT DETAILS Grants Team, Asda House, Great Wilson Street, Leeds, West Yorkshire LS11 5AD *Email* asdafoundation@asda.co.uk *Website* www.asdafoundation.org

■ The Asfari Foundation

CC NO 1116751　　　　**ESTABLISHED** 2006
WHERE FUNDING CAN BE GIVEN UK; Jordan; Lebanon; Palestine; Syria.
WHO CAN BENEFIT Registered charities; universities.
WHAT IS FUNDED Youth enterprise; civil society capacity development; policy research into social and economic change in the Levant region; humanitarian aid and disaster relief.
TYPE OF GRANT Core (or operational) costs; innovation and project testing costs; existing project costs. Funding is flexible but not unrestricted.
RANGE OF GRANTS £50,000 to £100,000 per partner per year for three years.
SAMPLE GRANTS Grants made in the UK included: International Rescue Committee (£672,800); Galilee Foundation and Year Here (£75,000 each); Good Chance Theatre and The Voices Project (£10,000 each); Centre for Lebanese Studies (£5,000).
FINANCES *Financial year end 31/12/2021*
Income £3,030,000
Grants to organisations £2,600,000
Assets £16,290,000
TRUSTEES Adeeb Asfari; Ayman Asfari; Sawsan Asfari; John Ferguson; Dr Marwan Muasher; Rasha Elmasry; Kareem Asfari; Saba Almubaslat.
OTHER INFORMATION Grants made in the UK totalled approximately £895,100.

HOW TO APPLY The foundation invites applications for funding once a year through an open call, usually in January. Eligibility and application criteria vary from year to year – check the foundation's website for up-to-date information.

CONTACT DETAILS Programmes Team, Unit A, 1–3 Canfield Place, London NW6 3BT *Tel.* 020 7372 3889 *Email* admin@asfarifoundation.org.uk or programmes@asfarifoundation.org.uk *Website* www.asfarifoundation.org.uk

■ Ashburnham Thanksgiving Trust

CC NO 249109   **ESTABLISHED** 1965

WHERE FUNDING CAN BE GIVEN UK and worldwide.

WHO CAN BENEFIT Individuals and Christian missions.

WHAT IS FUNDED Only Christian work already known to the trustees, particularly evangelical overseas missionary work.

WHAT IS NOT FUNDED Building costs.

RANGE OF GRANTS Typically under £1,000.

SAMPLE GRANTS St Stephen's Society (£4,600); Links International (£3,000); Micah Trust (£2,300); Open Doors (£1,500); Ashburnham Chapel (£1,000); Disasters Emergency Committee – Ukraine Humanitarian Appeal (£10).

FINANCES *Financial year end 05/04/2022* *Income* £270,300 *Grants to organisations* £71,000 *Grants to individuals* £14,800 *Assets* £9,070,000

TRUSTEES Robert Bickersteth; Edward Bickersteth; Dr Charles Warren.

OTHER INFORMATION In 2021/22, grants were awarded to 66 organisations and 14 individuals.

HOW TO APPLY Unsolicited applications are not accepted.

CONTACT DETAILS The Trustees, Agmerhurst House, Kitchenham Road, Ashburnham, Battle, East Sussex TN33 9NB *Tel.* 01424 892253 *Email* att@lookingforward.biz

■ The Ashendene Trust

CC NO 270749   **ESTABLISHED** 1975

WHERE FUNDING CAN BE GIVEN Gloucestershire; London; West Berkshire; Wiltshire.

WHO CAN BENEFIT Registered charities.

WHAT IS FUNDED General charitable purposes; arts, culture, heritage and science; the environment and conservation; education and training; social welfare; religious activities; children and young people; older people.

WHAT IS NOT FUNDED Buildings; individuals.

RANGE OF GRANTS Generally up to £7,000.

SAMPLE GRANTS Alzheimer's Society (£6,000); Tetbury Music Festival (£5,000); Bath Festival Orchestra (£3,000).

FINANCES *Financial year end 05/04/2022* *Income* £38,400 *Grants to organisations* £68,900 *Assets* £1,170,000

TRUSTEES Nicholas Hornby; Camilla Pugh; James Spence.

OTHER INFORMATION Only organisations that received grants of over £2,000 were listed as beneficiaries in the charity's accounts. Grants of under £2,000 totalled £3,400 and grants of over £2,000 totalled £65,500.

HOW TO APPLY Apply in writing to the correspondent.

CONTACT DETAILS The Trustees, 34 Sackville Street, London W1S 3ED *Tel.* 020 7036 4110

■ The Ashley Family Foundation

CC NO 288099   **ESTABLISHED** 1985

WHERE FUNDING CAN BE GIVEN England and Wales, with a preference for Wales.

WHO CAN BENEFIT Registered charities; unregistered charities supported by a registered charity.

WHAT IS FUNDED Development of rural communities; participation in the arts; community projects.

WHAT IS NOT FUNDED Individuals; business ventures; overseas projects; religious projects; direct funding for schools; retrospective expenditure. The foundation is also unlikely to fund sports-focused projects and well-supported causes (such as cancer and animal welfare).

TYPE OF GRANT Revenue proposals are favoured over capital requests. Funding is generally awarded to one-off projects but the trustees will consider funding a project over a number of years (up to three).

RANGE OF GRANTS Mostly under £10,000.

SAMPLE GRANTS British Red Cross (£100,000); Awel Aman Tawe Cyf (£25,000); Abram Wilson Foundation for Creative Arts (£10,000); Bristol Music Trust (£8,000); Shakespeare Link (£5,700); Down Syndrome Cheshire (£3,300); Women's Centre Sutton (£1,900); Newton-le-Willows Community Library (£500).

FINANCES *Financial year end 30/09/2022* *Income* £357,300 *Grants to organisations* £615,100 *Assets* £13,000,000

TRUSTEES Emma Shuckburgh; Jeremy McIlroy; Alexis Korner; Julian Ashley; Anita George; Meirion Rees; Mandy Davies.

HOW TO APPLY Applications can be made online through the foundation's website when funding rounds are open. Details of upcoming funding rounds can be found on the website. Applicants are encouraged to read the grant criteria on the website and speak to the foundation before applying. To discuss an application in Welsh, contact Ffion Roberts at the Community Foundation in Wales, on 029 2037 9580.

CONTACT DETAILS The Administrator, 6 Trull Farm Buildings, Trull, Tetbury, Gloucestershire GL8 8SQ *Tel.* 0303 040 1005 *Email* info@ashleyfamilyfoundation.org.uk *Website* www.ashleyfamilyfoundation.org.uk

■ The Ashworth Charitable Trust

CC NO 1045492   **ESTABLISHED** 1995

WHERE FUNDING CAN BE GIVEN UK; Devon; overseas.

WHO CAN BENEFIT Registered charities.

WHAT IS FUNDED Humanitarian causes; social welfare.

WHAT IS NOT FUNDED Charities which are not UK-registered; individuals; charities with a turnover of over £1 million; charities with disproportionately large reserves, unless there is an exceptional reason; animal welfare; projects promoting religion or party political activities; charities mainly involved in research; heritage; museums; UK hospices.

TYPE OF GRANT Project funding.

RANGE OF GRANTS Mainly between £2,500 and £5,000.

SAMPLE GRANTS BASED UK (£6,000); Impact Trust (£5,700); MYTIME Young Carers and Transitions UK (£5,000 each); Skiggle (£4,000); Bikes for Refugees, Stop Abuse for Everyone – SAFE and The Virtual Doctors (£3,000 each).

FINANCES *Financial year end 05/04/2022* *Income* £179,700 *Grants to organisations* £167,300 *Assets* £6,250,000

TRUSTEES Katherine Gray; Sharareh Rouhipour; Kian Golestani; Dr Wendi Momen; Ian Miles.

OTHER INFORMATION Grants were awarded to 49 organisations.

HOW TO APPLY Apply online via the trust's website. The trustees hold biannual meetings, usually in May and November. Successful applicants will be informed within six weeks of the relevant meeting. Note the following statement from the trust's website: 'our solicitors should only be contacted as a last resort in the event of a genuine complication or crisis, as they are not in a position to comment on the progress of an application or the decision of the trustees.'

CONTACT DETAILS Sarah Higgins, Veale Wasbrough Vizards LLP, PO Box 3501, Bristol BS2 2FL *Email* admin@ashworthtrust.org *Website* www.ashworthtrust.org

....

■ The Ian Askew Charitable Trust

CC NO 264515 **ESTABLISHED** 1972

WHERE FUNDING CAN BE GIVEN UK, with a preference for Sussex.

WHO CAN BENEFIT Charitable organisations; schools; churches, chapels and other historically significant buildings.

WHAT IS FUNDED General charitable purposes; education; the conservation and restoration of historic buildings; agriculture, horticulture and arboriculture.

RANGE OF GRANTS Generally up to £2,000.

SAMPLE GRANTS Sussex Community Foundation (£15,000); ABF The Soldiers' Charity (£2,000); Asthma UK and British Lung Foundation Partnership, Deafblind UK, Care for Veterans and St George's Church – West Grinstead (£1,000 each); The Frozen Ark Project (£500); The Sussex Historic Churches Trust (£100).

FINANCES *Financial year end* 05/04/2022
Income £607,400
Grants to organisations £210,500
Assets £25,170,000

TRUSTEES Rory Askew; James Rank; Henrietta Marshall; Venetia Harrison; Keith Buckland.

OTHER INFORMATION In 2021/22, the trust made grants to 172 organisations. Grants were awarded from the Estate Fund (£190,400) and the Conservation Fund (£20,100). The trust made a larger grant of £15,000 to Sussex Community Foundation which was then distributed to several beneficiaries.

HOW TO APPLY Apply in writing to the correspondent. Applications are reviewed by the trustees every third month.

CONTACT DETAILS The Trustees, Coney Hall, Sharpsbridge Lane, Newick, East Sussex BN8 4SA *Tel.* 01825 723302 *Email* carruthers@mistral.co.uk

....

■ The Associated Board of the Royal Schools of Music (ABRSM)

CC NO 292182 **ESTABLISHED** 1985

WHERE FUNDING CAN BE GIVEN UK and overseas.

WHO CAN BENEFIT Registered charities.

WHAT IS FUNDED Music education.

TYPE OF GRANT Project funding.

RANGE OF GRANTS £5,000 to £25,000.

SAMPLE GRANTS The UK Association for Music Education (£34,000); National Youth Jazz Orchestra (£30,000); National Youth Orchestra (£26,000); London Music Fund (£20,000);

National Children's Orchestra (£18,000); Royal Philharmonic Society (£11,000).

FINANCES *Financial year end* 31/01/2022
Income £42,500,000
Grants to organisations £2,000,000
Assets £19,070,000

TRUSTEES Prof. Jonathan Freeman-Attwood; Prof. Colin Lawson; Kevin Porter; Prof. Linda Merrick; Prof. Jeffrey Sharkey; Damian Wisniewski; Antony Hales; Frances Anderson; Bronwyn Syiek; Veronica Wadley; Leslie Kwan; Abdul Bhanji; Karen Lorenzo; Nicola Irvine.

OTHER INFORMATION Grants were broken down as follows: support for the four Royal Schools of Music (£5.6 million); scholarships (£1.05 million); music education (£382,000).

HOW TO APPLY Contact the correspondent for more information.

CONTACT DETAILS The Trustees, Associated Board of the Royal Schools of Music, 4 London Wall Place, London EC2Y 5AU *Tel.* 020 7467 8223 *Email* abrsm@abrsm.ac.uk *Website* www.abrsm.org

....

■ Asthma and Lung UK

CC NO 326730 **ESTABLISHED** 1984

WHERE FUNDING CAN BE GIVEN UK.

WHO CAN BENEFIT Hospitals; universities; other research institutions; charitable organisations involved with lung disease/respiratory diseases.

WHAT IS FUNDED Research into lung disease, including its causes, cure, improved treatment, diagnostics and care.

WHAT IS NOT FUNDED Exclusion criteria may vary according to the programme being applied to. See the charity's website for further information.

TYPE OF GRANT Research funding.

RANGE OF GRANTS Programme dependent.

SAMPLE GRANTS A list of beneficiaries was not included in the annual report and accounts.

FINANCES *Financial year end* 30/06/2022
Income £13,900,000
Grants to organisations £3,800,000
Assets £13,160,000

TRUSTEES John Graham; Emily Bushby; Prof. Edwin Chilvers; James Bowes; Prof. Ian Hall; Prof. Ian Sabroe; Katherine Morgan; Niren Patel; Michael O'Connor; Caroline Karlsen; Tamara Ingram.

HOW TO APPLY Details of the application process can be found on the charity's website. All applications must be completed through the Flexi-Grant portal.

CONTACT DETAILS Research Team, 18 Mansell Street, London E1 8AA *Tel.* 0300 222 5800 *Email* info@asthmaandlung.org.uk *Website* www.asthmaandlung.org.uk

....

■ The Astor Foundation

CC NO 225708 **ESTABLISHED** 1962

WHERE FUNDING CAN BE GIVEN UK.

WHO CAN BENEFIT Medical research organisations; registered charities; hospices; hospitals.

WHAT IS FUNDED Medical research; children and young people; people with disabilities; rural communities; culture and art; sports and recreation; carers; education; advice and counselling; animal welfare; the armed forces; heritage; older people; emergency response/relief; the environment; maritime causes; religion.

WHAT IS NOT FUNDED Core costs; direct costs; international charities; non-registered UK charities.

TYPE OF GRANT Research; start-up funding; project funding; in-kind support.

RANGE OF GRANTS Mostly between £1,000 and £1,500, with the occasional smaller or larger grant.

SAMPLE GRANTS League of Friends – University College London Hospitals (£5,000); Hospice UK (£4,000); Alzheimer's Society, London's Air Ambulance and Samaritans (£3,000 each); Eton College and RNLI (£2,500 each); Cancer Support Wiltshire, Daisies Kids Club and Go Beyond (£1,500 each); Animal Free Research, MahaDevi Yoga Centre and Phoebe (£1,000 each); The Jean Freedman Music Foundation and Silver Links (£500 each).

FINANCES *Financial year end 05/04/2022 Income* £119,900 *Grants to organisations* £113,500 *Assets* £4,730,000

TRUSTEES Charles Astor; Thomas Catchpole; Dr Matthew Gibbins; Hon. Tania Astor; Prof. Sir John Cunningham; Robert Astor.

OTHER INFORMATION Grants were broken down as follows: medical causes (£36,000 to 15 organisations); regular and rolling grants (£32,500 to 10 organisations); people with disabilities (£10,000 to 9 organisations); children and youth (£6,500 to 6 organisations); carers (£4,500 to 4 organisations); social welfare for disadvantaged people (£4,500 to 4 organisations); education (£2,500 to 2 organisations); advice and counselling (£2,000 to 2 organisations); animal welfare (£2,000 to 2 organisations); the armed forces (£2,000 to 2 organisations); community (£2,000 to 2 organisations); maritime causes (£2,000 to 2 organisations); sports and recreation (£2,000 to 2 organisations); arts and heritage (£1,500 to 2 organisations); older people (£1,500 to 2 organisations); emergency response/relief (£1,000 to 1 organisation); VIP (£1,000 to 1 organisation).

HOW TO APPLY Apply via the application form on the foundation's website.

CONTACT DETAILS B. Doyle, Secretary, 9 Hamilton Mews, London SW18 5AY *Tel.* 07957 954507 *Email* astor.foundation@gmail.com *Website* www.astorfoundation.co.uk

■ Atkin Charitable Foundation

CC NO 1112925   **ESTABLISHED** 2006
WHERE FUNDING CAN BE GIVEN UK and Israel.
WHO CAN BENEFIT Registered charities; hospices; hospitals; museums and galleries; universities.
WHAT IS FUNDED General charitable purposes; Jewish causes.
RANGE OF GRANTS Mostly up to £10,000, with some larger grants.
SAMPLE GRANTS Previous beneficiaries have included: Roundhouse Trust (£85,000); Jami (£50,000); Jewish Care (£35,000); Great Ormond Street Hospital Children's Charity (£20,000); Design Museum and National Holocaust Centre and Museum (£10,000 each); Royal Academy of Art (£8,400).
FINANCES *Financial year end 05/04/2022 Income* £290 *Grants to organisations* £851,900
TRUSTEES Edward Atkin; Lara Atkin; Celia Atkin; Ross Atkin; Barry Gold.
OTHER INFORMATION Full accounts from 2021/22 were not available to view on the Charity Commission's website due to the foundation's low income. We have therefore estimated the foundation's grant total based on its total

expenditure. Barry Gold is also a trustee for the Catkin Pussywillow Charitable Trust.
HOW TO APPLY Apply in writing to the correspondent via email.
CONTACT DETAILS The Trustees, 16 Rosemont Road, London NW3 6NE *Tel.* 07932 279494 *Email* info@atkinfoundation.org

■ The Atlas Fund

CC NO 278030   **ESTABLISHED** 1979
WHERE FUNDING CAN BE GIVEN UK.
WHO CAN BENEFIT Registered charities; churches; schools.
WHAT IS FUNDED General charitable purposes.
RANGE OF GRANTS Generally £1,000 to £5,000.
SAMPLE GRANTS Samaritans (£6,000); The Salvation Army (£5,000); Bridewell Organic Gardens (£3,500); Baby Lifeline and NSPCC (£2,000 each); Age UK, Ashmolean Museum and Marie Curie (£1,000 each).
FINANCES *Financial year end 31/03/2022 Income* £88,800 *Grants to organisations* £82,000 *Assets* £3,270,000
TRUSTEES Sir William Touche; Lady Hester Touche; Helen Hofmann; Peter Touche.
OTHER INFORMATION Grants were awarded to 38 organisations during the year.
HOW TO APPLY Contact the correspondent for further information.
CONTACT DETAILS The Trustees, Stane House, Stane Street, Ockley, Dorking, Surrey RH5 5TQ *Tel.* 01306 627397 *Email* toucheockley@btinternet.com

■ Atlas Memorial Ltd

CCNI NO NIC101043   **ESTABLISHED** 2015
WHERE FUNDING CAN BE GIVEN Worldwide, with a preference for Israel and the UK.
WHO CAN BENEFIT Jewish organisations; places of worship.
WHAT IS FUNDED The Jewish religion and religious education; relief of poverty for Jewish communities; maintenance of buildings used for religious practice; the advancement of health; the advancement of education.
TYPE OF GRANT General funding; capital costs (including maintenance).
RANGE OF GRANTS Mostly up to £20,000 with the occasional larger grant.
SAMPLE GRANTS Asser Bishvil Foundation (£294,000) and Notzar Chesed (£242,000).
FINANCES *Financial year end 31/01/2022 Income* £115,700 *Grants to organisations* £590,500 *Assets* £3,360,000
TRUSTEES Joel Gross; Abraham Gross; Israel Gross; Berish Gross.
OTHER INFORMATION Only beneficiaries of grants of over £20,000 were listed in the annual report and accounts. Grants of under £20,000 totalled £54,500.
HOW TO APPLY Apply in writing to the correspondent.
CONTACT DETAILS Michael Salomon, Correspondent, 86 Filey Avenue, London N16 6JJ *Tel.* 020 8806 0088

■ Lawrence Atwell's Charity (Skinners' Company)

CC NO 210773   **ESTABLISHED** 1988
WHERE FUNDING CAN BE GIVEN London and Kent.
WHO CAN BENEFIT Charitable organisations; individuals.
WHAT IS FUNDED Projects that support young people not in education, employment or training to move into employment.
WHAT IS NOT FUNDED See the grant-maker's website for a full list of exclusions.
TYPE OF GRANT Project funding, for up to three years.
RANGE OF GRANTS Up to £10,000.
SAMPLE GRANTS Circle Community (£10,000); Young Lives Foundation (£9,900); The Gifted Organisation Ltd (£9,300); Pathways for All People (£6,000).
FINANCES *Financial year end* 30/06/2022
Income £431,900
Grants to organisations £211,400
Grants to individuals £221,000
Assets £18,390,000
TRUSTEE The Worshipful Company of Skinners.
HOW TO APPLY Applicants should first contact the charity by email with a short outline of the project. If you are eligible, the charity will be in touch with full details of how to apply. Further information including application deadlines can be found on the charity's website.
CONTACT DETAILS Grants Officer, Skinners' Hall, 8 Dowgate Hill, London EC4R 2SP *Tel.* 020 7213 0561 *Email* charities@skinners.org.uk *Website* www.skinners.org.uk/grants-and-trusts/atwell

■ The Aurelius Charitable Trust

CC NO 271333   **ESTABLISHED** 1975
WHERE FUNDING CAN BE GIVEN UK.
WHO CAN BENEFIT Registered charities; non-registered charities; universities; religious bodies/institutions.
WHAT IS FUNDED The conservation and preservation of culture inherited from the past; the dissemination of knowledge, particularly in the humanities field; research or publications.
WHAT IS NOT FUNDED Individuals.
TYPE OF GRANT Project costs.
RANGE OF GRANTS Mostly £2,000 to £5,000.
SAMPLE GRANTS Royal Museums Greenwich (£5,000); Manchester Museum (£4,000); Durham School (£2,700); Hampshire Cultural Trust (£2,000); The British Academy (£1,000).
FINANCES *Financial year end* 05/04/2022
Income £66,500
Grants to organisations £77,200
Assets £2,540,000
TRUSTEES Philip Haynes; William Wallis.
OTHER INFORMATION In 2021/22, grants were awarded to 27 organisations to fund specific projects.
HOW TO APPLY Apply in writing to the correspondent. Grants are generally made on the recommendation of the trust's board of advisors. Unsolicited applications will only be responded to if an sae is included. The trustees meet twice a year.
CONTACT DETAILS The Trustees, Briarsmead, Old Road, Buckland, Betchworth, Surrey RH3 7DU *Tel.* 01737 842186 *Email* philip.haynes@tiscali.co.uk

■ The Aurora Trust (formerly The Ashden Trust)

CC NO 802623   **ESTABLISHED** 1989
WHERE FUNDING CAN BE GIVEN UK and overseas.
WHO CAN BENEFIT Registered charities.
WHAT IS FUNDED Tackling climate change. The trust has four programme areas: connecting people with nature; sustainable farming; stopping deforestation; aligning financial markets with the Paris Agreement.
WHAT IS NOT FUNDED Individuals.
TYPE OF GRANT Project funding; core costs, including salaries; research.
RANGE OF GRANTS Typically £1,000 to £60,000.
SAMPLE GRANTS Green Finance Institute (£80,000); Peers for the Planet (£60,000); Platform (£52,000); Linking Environment and Farming – LEAF (£40,000); People and Planet (£30,000); Stop Ecocide Foundation (£15,250); The Social Change Nest (£10,000); Harmony Project (£4,000); Inspiring Minds (£500).
FINANCES *Financial year end* 05/04/2022
Income £1,800,000
Grants to organisations £1,260,000
Assets £45,690,000
TRUSTEES Sarah Butler-Sloss; Claire Birch; Grace Yu.
OTHER INFORMATION The trust is one of the Sainsbury Family Charitable Trusts, which share a common administration – see www.sftc.org.uk for more information.
HOW TO APPLY The trust does not generally accept unsolicited applications. However, the trust's website states: 'We may put out a 'Call for Proposals' to expand one of our programme areas – this will set out what activities and type and size of organisation we are looking to fund.' Guidelines for proposals can be found on the trust's website.
CONTACT DETAILS The Trustees, The Peak, 5 Wilton Road, London SW1V 1AP *Tel.* 020 7410 0330 *Email* info@sfct.org.uk or aurora@sfct.org.uk *Website* https://auroratrust.org.uk/

■ The Lord Austin Trust

CC NO 208394   **ESTABLISHED** 1937
WHERE FUNDING CAN BE GIVEN Birmingham City; Dudley; Sandwell; Solihull; Walsall.
WHO CAN BENEFIT Hospitals, medical organisations and charities in Birmingham and West Midlands; national organisations (but not their provincial branches).
WHAT IS FUNDED General charitable purposes; health; medical research; the welfare and education of disadvantaged children; older people; community projects.
WHAT IS NOT FUNDED Individuals.
RANGE OF GRANTS Mostly around £6,000.
SAMPLE GRANTS City of Birmingham Symphony Orchestra (£6,500); Acorns Children's Hospice and St Mary's Hospice (£6,000 each).
FINANCES *Financial year end* 31/03/2022
Income £115,100
Grants to organisations £93,500
Assets £4,380,000
TRUSTEES Neil Andrews; Rodney Kettel; Keith Dudley; Robert Hunt; Sarah Wood.
OTHER INFORMATION Only grants of over £5,000 were listed as beneficiaries. Grants of under £5,000 totalled £75,000 in 2022.
HOW TO APPLY Apply in writing to the correspondent, including a set of recent accounts. The trustees meet twice a year to consider grants.
CONTACT DETAILS Chrissy Norgrove, Administrator, The Estate Office, Wharf Cottage, Broombank,

Tenbury Wells, Worcestershire WR15 8NY
Tel. 07940 160844 *Email* chrissy@
lordaustintrust.org.uk

....

■ The Avon and Somerset Police Community Trust

CC NO 1076770   **ESTABLISHED** 1999
WHERE FUNDING CAN BE GIVEN The Avon and
Somerset Constabulary area.
WHO CAN BENEFIT Charitable organisations;
community and voluntary organisations.
WHAT IS FUNDED Crime reduction and public safety;
road safety.
TYPE OF GRANT Project funding; core/revenue costs.
RANGE OF GRANTS Usually up to £50,000.
SAMPLE GRANTS Lifeskills and The Wheels Project
(£30,000 each); Be Home Safe Scheme; Life
Education Centre Bristol and Wessex.
FINANCES *Financial year end* 31/03/2021
Income £329,800
Grants to organisations £414,600
TRUSTEES Paul Hooper; Sue Mountstevens; Andy
Marsh; James Makepeace; David Wood; Roger
Opie; Robert Bernays.
OTHER INFORMATION The 2020/21 accounts were
the latest available at the time of writing (May
2023). Grants of £5,000 or less totalled
£330,500, and grants of over £5,000 totalled
£84,200. A full list of beneficiaries was not
included in the trust's 2020/21 accounts. The
trust's net assets for the year were illegible in
the accounts.
HOW TO APPLY Applications are made through the
funder's website. See each fund's page for
criteria, guidance and deadlines.
CONTACT DETAILS Rachael Callow, Trust Officer, PO
Box 37, Valley Road, Portishead, Bristol
BS20 8QJ *Tel.* 01278 646650
Email policecommunitytrust@avonandsomerset.
police.uk *Website* www.avonandsomerset.
police.uk/apply/police-community-trust

....

■ Axis Foundation

CC NO 1126117   **ESTABLISHED** 2009
WHERE FUNDING CAN BE GIVEN The Midlands; London;
the south of England; Wales.
WHO CAN BENEFIT Registered charities; community
organisations; schools; individuals.
WHAT IS FUNDED General charitable purposes; small/
local projects or causes.
WHAT IS NOT FUNDED National appeals; projects that
are non-inclusive and are not open to all
individuals and communities irrespective of
gender, race or faith; the advancement of
religion or religious groups unless they offer a
non-religious service to the local community;
work outside the UK; replacement of statutory
funding; projects of a political nature; animal
welfare.
RANGE OF GRANTS Generally to £10,000.
SAMPLE GRANTS Demelza House (£35,000);
Disabled Sailors Association (£10,000); Swale
Gloves (£6,000); Dads Lane Community
Association (£5,000).
FINANCES *Financial year end* 31/03/2022
Income £375,100
Grants to organisations £180,600
Assets £313,300
TRUSTEES Maurice Gertski; John Hayes; Timothy
Hayes; Michael Hayes; Yusuf Ibrahim; Peter
Varney; Sandra Ryan.
HOW TO APPLY Applications can be made via the
foundation's website.

CONTACT DETAILS The Trustees, Tramway House,
3 Tramway Avenue, Stratford E15 4PN
Tel. 0330 045 0030 *Email* info@
axisfoundation.com *Website* www.
axisfoundation.org

....

■ The Aziz Foundation

CC NO 1169558   **ESTABLISHED** 2016
WHERE FUNDING CAN BE GIVEN UK and overseas.
WHO CAN BENEFIT Universities; registered charities.
WHAT IS FUNDED Disadvantaged communities, with a
current focus on educational support for British
Muslims (master's scholarships and bursaries);
general charitable purposes.
TYPE OF GRANT Scholarships (tuition fees);
bursaries; general funding.
SAMPLE GRANTS A list of beneficiaries was not
included in the annual report and accounts.
FINANCES *Financial year end* 31/03/2022
Income £1,480,000
Grants to organisations £1,300,000
TRUSTEES Hussein Aziz; Talat Malik; Asif Aziz;
Rahima Aziz.
OTHER INFORMATION During 2021/22, 50
scholarships and bursaries were awarded to
students starting postgraduate courses at over
20 different UK universities. In addition, 32
grants were awarded to other organisations. The
foundation's 2021/22 annual reported stated:
'In the financial year the Foundation awarded 32
grants, which were used to support work in its
priority areas including media, creative content
and law.'
HOW TO APPLY Contact the foundation for further
information. For universities wishing to join the
foundation's Preferred Partner scheme, contact
the correspondent. The following statement was
taken from the foundation's Institutional
Partnerships Brochure, which is available on its
website: 'We are looking to partner with forward
looking, inclusive institutions that take the
principle of widening participation seriously and
are taking the necessary steps to diversify their
student cohorts at the postgraduate level.'
CONTACT DETAILS The Trustees, 16 Babmaes Street,
London SW1Y 6HD *Tel.* 020 7432 2444
Email enquiries@azizfoundation.org.uk
Website http://azizfoundation.org.uk

■ B&Q Foundation

CC NO 1183275/OSCR no. SC051154
WHERE FUNDING CAN BE GIVEN UK and the Republic of Ireland.
WHO CAN BENEFIT Registered charities.
WHAT IS FUNDED Projects that improve housing and community spaces and help people who are experiencing poor-quality housing or homelessness.
WHAT IS NOT FUNDED Individuals.
TYPE OF GRANT One-off.
SAMPLE GRANTS A list of beneficiaries was not included in the annual report and accounts.
FINANCES *Financial year end* 31/01/2022
Income £1,720,000
Grants to organisations £1,070,000
Assets £73,800
TRUSTEES Paul Crisp; Andrew Moat; Catherine Burge; Antony Purnell; Anna Peters; Vicki Carroll; Aleah Truscott; Simon Hewett-Avison.
HOW TO APPLY Register your interest by filling out the form linked on the website.
CONTACT DETAILS The Trustees, B&Q. House, Chestnut Avenue, Chandler's Ford, Eastleigh SO53 3LE *Tel.* 023 8069 0000 *Email* BandQFoundation@b-and-q.co.uk *Website* www.diy.com/corporate/bandq-foundation

■ Backstage Trust

CC NO 1145887 **ESTABLISHED** 2012
WHERE FUNDING CAN BE GIVEN UK.
WHO CAN BENEFIT Registered charities; theatres.
WHAT IS FUNDED Theatre, music and the performing arts for disadvantaged and young people.
WHAT IS NOT FUNDED Non-registered charities; individuals.
TYPE OF GRANT Core costs; pro bono support; capital costs; project funding; strategic funding; development funding.
RANGE OF GRANTS Mostly up to £50,000, with the occasional larger grant.
SAMPLE GRANTS The Old Vic (£300,000); Leeds Playhouse and Theatre Development Trust (£250,000); Hall for Cornwall (£150,000); Belarus Free Theatre and Reading Rep Theatre (£100,000 each); Royal Academy of Music and Watershed (£75,000 each); National Theatre (£50,500).
FINANCES *Financial year end* 05/04/2022
Income £3,130,000
Grants to organisations £4,510,000
Assets £1,150,000
TRUSTEES Lady Susie Sainsbury; David Wood; Dominic Flynn.
OTHER INFORMATION Only organisations that received grants of over £50,000 were listed as beneficiaries in the trust's accounts. Grants of under £50,000 totalled £1.54 million and were given to 63 organisations. The trust's 2021/22 annual report states that: '3 grants totalling £375,000 were awarded for Covid-19 emergency support with a further 85 grants totalling £4,140,000 awarded for core and project support and for capital programmes'.
HOW TO APPLY Apply in writing to the correspondent.

CONTACT DETAILS The Trustees, North House, 27 Great Peter Street, London SW1P 3LN *Tel.* 020 7072 4498 *Email* info@ backstagetrust.org.uk

■ The Tim Bacon Foundation

CC NO 1173108 **ESTABLISHED** 2017
WHERE FUNDING CAN BE GIVEN The North West.
WHO CAN BENEFIT Registered charities.
WHAT IS FUNDED Cancer research.
TYPE OF GRANT Research grants.
SAMPLE GRANTS Blood Cancer UK (£17,500) and Maggie's (£1,400).
FINANCES *Financial year end* 31/03/2022
Income £81,600
Grants to organisations £18,900
Assets £159,000
TRUSTEES Jeremy Roberts; David Mansbridge; Alec Gutherie; Michelle Gandy; Chris Hill; Peter Martin; Lucy Blake; Thom Hetherington.
OTHER INFORMATION In 2021/22 the foundation's grant total was £18,900; however, in previous years, it has been much higher, so we believe it has the capacity to give more.
HOW TO APPLY Applications can be made via the foundation's website at any time. Applications are reviewed annually. The deadline for receipt of applications is 31 December.
CONTACT DETAILS The Trustees, 98 King Street, Knutsford, Cheshire WA16 6HQ *Tel.* 01565 631234 *Email* info@timbaconfoundation.co.uk *Website* www.timbaconfoundation.co.uk

■ Bagri Foundation

CC NO 1000219 **ESTABLISHED** 1990
WHERE FUNDING CAN BE GIVEN Mainly the UK and India.
WHO CAN BENEFIT Charitable organisations; individuals.
WHAT IS FUNDED Artistic, cultural, research and digital projects that celebrate and promote Asian culture; innovative cross-disciplinary projects that examine traditional and contemporary Asian culture; support for emerging artists from Asia; education; health.
RANGE OF GRANTS £5,000 to £150,000.
SAMPLE GRANTS Details of previous beneficiaries and current projects can be found on the website.
FINANCES *Financial year end* 31/08/2022
Income £2,470,000
Grants to organisations £910,200
Grants to individuals £5,400
Assets £13,210,000
TRUSTEES Lady Bagri; The Hon. Apurv Bagri; The Hon. Alka Bagri; Amisha Bagri; Aditi Malhotra.
OTHER INFORMATION In 2021/22, grants were distributed in the following categories: education (£547,000); culture (£360,400); health (£2,800).
HOW TO APPLY Application forms can be downloaded from the foundation's website and should be submitted by email. The trustees meet twice a year to consider applications. Details of funding rounds can be found on the foundation's website but typically run from 1 December to 31 May (round one) and 1 June to 15 November (round two).
CONTACT DETAILS The Trustees, 25–27 Lorne Close, London NW8 7JJ *Tel.* 020 7280 0000 *Email* enquiries@bagrifoundation.org *Website* http://bagrifoundation.org

■ The Austin Bailey Foundation

CC NO 514912   **ESTABLISHED** 1984

WHERE FUNDING CAN BE GIVEN Swansea and overseas.

WHO CAN BENEFIT Registered charities; CICs; hospices; churches.

WHAT IS FUNDED Social welfare and Christian churches in Swansea; overseas aid and relief.

WHAT IS NOT FUNDED Medical research, apart from in exceptional circumstances; individuals; organisations which are not registered charities or churches; building or refurbishment projects.

TYPE OF GRANT Project funding; seed funding/start-up funding.

RANGE OF GRANTS £500 to £2,000.

SAMPLE GRANTS Send a Cow (£4,000); Parklands Church – Swansea (£2,500); Swansea Mind (£2,000); Matthew's House (£1,2000); Neath Port Talbot Stroke Group (£1,000); Faith in Families – Bonymaen (£600); HangOut (£500); Swansea Music Art Digital (£400).

FINANCES *Financial year end* 05/04/2022
Income £505,900
Grants to organisations £142,100
Assets £2,010,000

TRUSTEES Clive Bailey; Sandra Morton; Sian Popper; James Leach; Eleanor Norton; Dr Ashraf Mikhail; Sally Goldstone; The Revd Steven Buting.

HOW TO APPLY Application forms are available to download from the foundation's website and should be submitted by email. The trustees usually meet in April, September and December. The deadline for applications is one month before the meeting or two months before for work overseas. The dates of upcoming meetings can be found on the foundation's website.

CONTACT DETAILS Sandra Morton, Trustee, St Thomas Church, Lewis Street, St Thomas, Swansea SA1 8BP *Tel.* 01792 473569 *Email* localcharities@austinbaileyfoundation.org *Website* www.austinbaileyfoundation.org

■ The Baily Thomas Charitable Fund

CC NO 262334   **ESTABLISHED** 1971

WHERE FUNDING CAN BE GIVEN UK.

WHO CAN BENEFIT Registered and exempt charities; schools and parent–teacher associations. Applications for research grants will only be considered from university departments.

WHAT IS FUNDED Research into learning disabilities (mainly the development of initial-stage research projects); the care and relief of people affected by learning disabilities.

WHAT IS NOT FUNDED Individuals; CICs; statutory funding. A full list of exclusions is available on the fund's helpful website.

TYPE OF GRANT Capital and revenue costs for both specific projects and for general running/core costs; research costs, including salaries; fellowships.

RANGE OF GRANTS Small grants: £250 to £10,000; general grants: £10,000 to £100,000.

SAMPLE GRANTS University of Glasgow (£197,800); Aston University (£91,700); University College London (£88,200); University of Surrey (£70,300); University of Sheffield (£59,900); Jolly Josh (£28,000); Down's Syndrome Scotland (£25,000); The Hextol Foundation (£20,000).

FINANCES *Financial year end* 30/09/2022
Income £1,790,000
Grants to organisations £2,470,000
Assets £82,820,000

TRUSTEES Prof. Anne Farmer; Suzanne Marriott; Kenneth Young; Prof. Sally-Ann Cooper; Jonathan Snow.

OTHER INFORMATION Only beneficiaries of grants of £20,000 and above were listed in the accounts. Grants of under £20,000 totalled £1.23 million. See the fund's website for up-to-date details of its funding programmes.

HOW TO APPLY Applications should be made using the fund's online application form. There are no submission deadlines for applicants seeking funding of up to £10,000. Grants of under £5,000 are considered solely by the Chair. Grants of above £10,000 are considered at Main Grant Board meetings, details of which can be found on the website along with comprehensive guidelines for each grant scheme.

CONTACT DETAILS Ann Cooper, Secretary to the Trustees, c/o TMF Global Services (UK) Ltd, 960 Capability Green, Luton, Bedfordshire LU1 3PE *Tel.* 01582 439225 *Email* info@bailythomas.org.uk *Website* www.bailythomas.org.uk

■ The Baird Trust

OSCR NO SC016549   **ESTABLISHED** 1873

WHERE FUNDING CAN BE GIVEN Scotland.

WHO CAN BENEFIT Churches.

WHAT IS FUNDED Maintenance and repair of churches; educational activities of churches.

WHAT IS NOT FUNDED Churches with adequate unrestricted and/or designated funds that could cover the costs; work that is already underway or has already taken place; applications without some contribution from the congregation.

TYPE OF GRANT Capital costs; general funding.

RANGE OF GRANTS Up to £10,000.

SAMPLE GRANTS 3D Drumchapel (£10,000); Street Connect (£8,000); St Columbkille's Roman Catholic Church (£7,000); Carloway Free Church and Creich Parish Church (£5,000 each); Newburgh United Reformed Church (£3,000); St Anne's Episcopal Church (£2,000).

FINANCES *Financial year end* 31/12/2022
Income £470,400
Grants to organisations £169,300
Grants to individuals £87,100
Assets £12,500,000

TRUSTEES Cmdr Charles Ball; The Hon. Mary Coltman; Col. J. M. K. Erskine; Dr Alison Elliot; Luke Borwick; Walter Barbour; Lt. Col. Richard Callander; Ms M. E. Davis.

HOW TO APPLY Application forms can be downloaded from the website and must be accompanied by your organisation's most recent annual accounts. At the time of writing (May 2023), the trust's website stated that postal applications were not being received due to the closure of its office in response to the COVID-19 pandemic. Please check the trust's website for the most up-to-date information.

CONTACT DETAILS The Trustees, 182 Bath Street, Glasgow G2 4HG *Tel.* 0141 332 0476 *Email* info@bairdtrust.org.uk *Website* www.bairdtrust.org.uk

■ Bairdwatson Charitable Trust

OSCR NO SC038468   **ESTABLISHED** 2007

WHERE FUNDING CAN BE GIVEN Scotland, with a strong preference for Ayr and Airdrie; West Bengal.

WHO CAN BENEFIT Registered charities; social enterprises; charitable organisations; individuals.

WHAT IS FUNDED Education or training for employment; re-training; supporting people into work; vocational training, especially for young people.

WHAT IS NOT FUNDED Hospices and palliative care; appliances for illness or disability; organisations concerned with specific diseases; medical research; animal charities; projects in England, Wales or Northern Ireland, large projects where the trust's contribution would not make a material difference.

TYPE OF GRANT Revenue/core costs; capital funding, project funding.

RANGE OF GRANTS Generally up to £20,000.

SAMPLE GRANTS Citizens Advice Motherwell and Wishaw (£19,300); South Asia Voluntary Enterprise (£10,600); Action for Children (£10,000); Bazooka Arts (£9,900).

FINANCES *Financial year end* 31/03/2022
Income £75,700
Grants to organisations £70,800
Assets £2,620,000

TRUSTEES Robert Kerr; Jane Wylie-Roberts; Jacqueline Leslie.

HOW TO APPLY Applications can be made via the trust's website. Application forms are also available from the trust's website and can be returned by email.

CONTACT DETAILS Linda Anderson, Grant Assessor, 27 Balfour Terrace, Murray, East Kilbride, Lanarkshire G75 0JQ *Tel.* 07982 915666 *Email* linda@bairdwatson.org.uk *Website* www.bairdwatson.org.uk

---

■ The Roy and Pixie Baker Charitable Trust

CC NO 1101988   **ESTABLISHED** 1995

WHERE FUNDING CAN BE GIVEN The North East.

WHO CAN BENEFIT Registered charities.

WHAT IS FUNDED Health and medical research; education of young people; heritage; social welfare; disaster relief.

WHAT IS NOT FUNDED According to our previous research, grants are not given to individuals.

RANGE OF GRANTS Up to £5,000.

SAMPLE GRANTS A list of beneficiaries was not included in the annual report and accounts. Previous beneficiaries have included: Daft as a Brush (£10,000); NE Youth (£5,000); Washington Riding Centre for the Disabled (£4,000); Durham Association of Boys and Girls Clubs (£2,500); Northumberland Rugby Union (£1,500); Be Inspired To (£1,000); Northumbria Deaf Mission (£500); SAFE (£200).

FINANCES *Financial year end* 05/04/2022
Income £54,100
Grants to organisations £40,500
Assets £3,520,000

TRUSTEES Leslie Caisley; Tony Glenton; George Straker; Bill Dryden.

OTHER INFORMATION In 2021/22, grants were awarded in the following categories: health and medicine (£17,000); education (£13,500); architectural preservation (£6,000) people in need (£4,000). In previous years, the grant total has exceeded £50,000; therefore, we believe it has the capacity to give more.

HOW TO APPLY Apply in writing to the correspondent, providing full back-up information. The trustees meet twice a year.

CONTACT DETAILS The Trustees, c/o Ryecroft Glenton, 32 Portland Terrace, Newcastle upon Tyne, Tyne and Wear NE2 1QP *Tel.* 0191 281 1292 *Email* bakercharitabletrust@ryecroftglenton.com

---

■ The Rachel Baker Memorial Charity

CC NO 1162913   **ESTABLISHED** 2009

WHERE FUNDING CAN BE GIVEN England and Wales.

WHO CAN BENEFIT Charitable organisations; individuals.

WHAT IS FUNDED Classical music.

WHAT IS NOT FUNDED Retrospective funds.

TYPE OF GRANT Long-term capital projects.

SAMPLE GRANTS A list of beneficiaries was not available.

FINANCES *Financial year end* 05/04/2022
Income £0
Grants to organisations £250,000

TRUSTEES Robin Daniels; Nicholas Moxon; Kirsten McEwen.

OTHER INFORMATION Full accounts were not available to view on the Charity Commission's website due to the charity's low income. We have therefore estimated the grant total based on the charity's total expenditure.

HOW TO APPLY Apply in writing to the correspondent.

CONTACT DETAILS The Trustees, c/o Higgs LLP, Unit 3, Waterfront Business Park, Dudley Road, Brierley Hill, West Midlands DY5 1LX *Tel.* 01384 327322 *Email* charity.administration@higgsllp.co.uk

---

■ The Ballinger Charitable Trust

CC NO 1121739   **ESTABLISHED** 2007

WHERE FUNDING CAN BE GIVEN The North East.

WHO CAN BENEFIT Registered charities; social enterprises; CICs; voluntary groups.

WHAT IS FUNDED The health, development and well-being of children and young people; older people; rural or coastal isolation; dementia; carers.

WHAT IS NOT FUNDED Individuals.

TYPE OF GRANT Core/revenue costs; capital costs; project funding; unrestricted funding. Typically awarded for up to three years.

RANGE OF GRANTS Typically less than £20,000.

SAMPLE GRANTS Neighbourhood Youth Projects (£166,300); Sunderland All Together Consortium (£80,000); Kinship (£20,000); Dry Water Arts CIC, North East Young Dads and Lads Project and Young Women's Outreach Project (£15,000 each); Young Asian Voices (£11,900); Community Counselling Co-operative (£7,200); Friends of Fawdon Community Library (£5,000); Hope Church East Cleveland (£750).

FINANCES *Financial year end* 31/12/2021
Income £1,200,000
Grants to organisations £1,580,000
Assets £28,300,000

TRUSTEES Andrew Ballinger; Diana Ballinger; Nicola Crowther; John Flynn.

OTHER INFORMATION Grants of less than £20,000 totalled £1.13 million.

HOW TO APPLY Applications can be made through the trust's website.

CONTACT DETAILS Joanne Thomas, Co-ordinator, PO Box 166, Ponteland, Newcastle upon Tyne, Tyne and Wear NE20 2BL *Tel.* 07578 197886 *Email* info@ballingercharitabletrust.org.uk *Website* www.ballingercharitabletrust.org.uk

---

■ Bally's Foundation

CC NO 1188099

WHERE FUNDING CAN BE GIVEN UK; Canada; Hong Kong; Gibraltar; Malta; Manilla; Sweden; Ukraine; USA.

WHO CAN BENEFIT The foundation gives grants to charitable organisations that protect the well-being of individuals suffering from mental health issues.

WHAT IS FUNDED Mental health.

WHAT IS NOT FUNDED According to the foundation website, grants are not awarded to/for the following: organisations that deal with physical health care, treatment and rehabilitation, or research; applications relating to sports; religious or political organisations; one-off conferences and workshops; organisations or applications focused solely or primarily on raising public awareness of mental health issues via marketing campaigns.

RANGE OF GRANTS £5,000 to £600,000.

SAMPLE GRANTS Mental Health Innovations (£600,000); Ambitious about Autism (£200,000); Women's Aid (£150,000); Kinetic Foundation – Smiles Campaign (£89,100); Orchard OCD (£40,000); Body and Soul (£10,000); Child Bereavement (£5,000).

FINANCES *Financial year end 31/12/2021*
Income £1,820,000
Grants to organisations £2,100,000
Assets £525,100

TRUSTEES Neil Goulden; Kevin Hopgood; Holly Spiers; Christina Southall; Anita Iwugo.

OTHER INFORMATION The Bally's Foundation was established in February 2020 by Gamesys Group, which is now owned by Bally's Corporation.

HOW TO APPLY At the time of writing (July 2023) the foundation was not accepting applications. Its website stated: 'From 2024, the Bally's Foundation will reflect the wider scope of the Bally's Group, consequently the Foundation is focusing on initiatives within North America. In support of this increased remit, we are currently not processing new funding applications.'

CONTACT DETAILS The Trustees, 10 Piccadilly, London WJ10 0DD *Email* info@gamesysfoundation.org *Website* www.ballysfoundation.org

■ The Bamford Charitable Foundation

CC NO 279848   **ESTABLISHED** 1979

WHERE FUNDING CAN BE GIVEN UK and overseas, but mainly within a 40-mile radius of Rocester.

WHO CAN BENEFIT Charitable organisations.

WHAT IS FUNDED General charitable purposes.

RANGE OF GRANTS Up to £100,000.

SAMPLE GRANTS A list of beneficiaries was not included in the annual report and accounts. Previous beneficiaries have included: Medical Detection Dogs (£100,000); Child Bereavement UK (£50,000); Lakeland Autistic Charity (£20,000); Help for Heroes (£10,000); Alabare Christian Care Centres (£5,000); Morton in Marsh Croquet Club (£1,000); YoungMinds (£500).

FINANCES *Financial year end 31/03/2022*
Income £17,400
Grants to organisations £1,330,000

TRUSTEES Lord Bamford; Lady Bamford.

OTHER INFORMATION Full accounts were not available to view on the Charity Commission's website due to the foundation's low income. We have therefore estimated the grant total based on the foundation's total expenditure.

HOW TO APPLY Apply in writing to the correspondent.

CONTACT DETAILS The Trustees, J. C. Bamford Excavators Ltd, Lakeside Works, Denstone Road, Rocester, Uttoxeter, Staffordshire ST14 5JP *Tel.* 01889 593140

■ Banbury Charities

CC NO 201418   **ESTABLISHED** 1961

WHERE FUNDING CAN BE GIVEN Within either a five or ten-mile radius of Banbury.

WHO CAN BENEFIT Charitable organisations; schools; churches; uniformed groups; individuals.

WHAT IS FUNDED General charitable purposes.

TYPE OF GRANT Project funding; capital costs.

RANGE OF GRANTS Generally up to £26,000.

SAMPLE GRANTS Banbury Welfare Trust (£26,000); Katharine House Hospice (£20,000); Banbury and District Canoe Club (£9,000); Oxford Hospitals Charity – Injury Minimisation Programme for Schools (£8,300); Style Acre Banbury and Tooley's Boatyard Trust (£5,000 each); Julie Bruce Dance Academy (£1,000).

FINANCES *Financial year end 31/12/2021*
Income £504,100
Grants to organisations £133,800
Grants to individuals £47,500
Assets £9,140,000

TRUSTEES Judy May; Julia Colegrave; Angela Heritage; Colin Clarke; Martin Humphris; Valerie Fisher; Jamie Briggs; Tom Blinkhorn; John Donaldson; Sandra Williams; Phillip Chapman; Ian Harwood.

OTHER INFORMATION Grants were awarded to 23 organisations. Only organisations that received grants of over £1,000 were listed as beneficiaries in the charity's accounts. No grants of less than £1,000 were made.

HOW TO APPLY Apply in writing to the correspondent.

CONTACT DETAILS Mrs M. Tarrant, Clerk to the Trustees, 36 West Bar, Banbury, Oxfordshire OX16 9RU *Tel.* 01295 251234

■ The Band Trust

CC NO 279802   **ESTABLISHED** 1976

WHERE FUNDING CAN BE GIVEN UK.

WHO CAN BENEFIT UK-registered charities; individuals.

WHAT IS FUNDED General charitable purposes including: the armed forces; children and young people; disability; education; the arts; older people; nursing care.

WHAT IS NOT FUNDED Political activities; commercial ventures or publications; retrospective grants or loans; direct replacement of statutory funding or activities that are primarily the responsibility of central or local government.

TYPE OF GRANT Unrestricted funding.

RANGE OF GRANTS Typically under £150,000.

SAMPLE GRANTS Seashell Trust (£500,000); The British Exploring Society (£150,000); The PACE Centre Ltd (£120,000); The Royal Academy of Culinary Arts' Adopt a School Trust (£30,000); The Sick Children's Trust (£25,000); The Bolingbroke Trust (£10,000); Friends of the Courtauld Institute (£1,100).

FINANCES *Financial year end 31/03/2022*
Income £719,000
Grants to organisations £3,560,000
Grants to individuals £17,600
Assets £23,090,000

TRUSTEES Richard Mason; The Hon. Nicholas Wallop; The Hon. Nicholas Wallop; Victoria Wallop; Bartholomew Peerless; Henry Wallop.

OTHER INFORMATION In 2021/22, grants were awarded to 38 organisations and 1 individual. Grants to organisations were broken down as follows: education (£775,000); disadvantaged

(£720,000); children and young people (£655,000); hospice and hospital (£600,000); disability (£465,000); older people (£287,000); miscellaneous (£20,000); miscellaneous up to £2,000 (£18,600).

HOW TO APPLY Unsolicited applications are not accepted – only make an application if you have been invited to do so.

CONTACT DETAILS Richard Mason, Trustee, BM Box 2144, London WC1N 3XX *Tel.* 020 7702 4243 *Email* rjsmason32@gmail.com *Website* www.bandtrust.co.uk

■ Veronica and Lars Bane Foundation

CC NO 1183391 **ESTABLISHED** 2019

WHERE FUNDING CAN BE GIVEN UK; overseas including Europe, Kenya, Nepal and South Africa.

WHO CAN BENEFIT Registered charities.

WHAT IS FUNDED Young people and education; livelihoods and human rights; health and well-being; arts and culture.

TYPE OF GRANT Project funding.

SAMPLE GRANTS Biteback2030; EMpower; Fistula Foundation; Hand-in-Hand; London Academy of Excellence; Roundhouse.

FINANCES *Financial year end 31/12/2021* *Income* £0 *Grants to organisations* £145,000 *Assets* £4,060,000

TRUSTEES Lars Bane; Veronica Bane; Georg Kjallgren; Martin Wiwen-Nilsson.

HOW TO APPLY Unsolicited applications are not accepted.

CONTACT DETAILS The Trustees, 98 Frognal, London NW3 6XB *Tel.* 07921 894842 *Email* grants@banefoundation.org *Website* https://banefoundation.org

■ The Kamini and Vindi Banga Family Trust

CC NO 1171409 **ESTABLISHED** 2017

WHERE FUNDING CAN BE GIVEN England and Wales.

WHO CAN BENEFIT Charitable organisations; universities.

WHAT IS FUNDED General charitable purposes; cancer research; education through the performing arts.

RANGE OF GRANTS £500 to £50,000.

SAMPLE GRANTS Teamwork Fine Arts Society (£28,000); The Poetry School (£10,000); Royal National Theatre (£1,500); Bharatiya Vidya Bhavan London (£3,000); Alzheimer's Research UK (£250).

FINANCES *Financial year end 05/04/2021* *Income* £980,200 *Grants to organisations* £161,000 *Assets* £5,400,000

TRUSTEES Kamini Banga; Manvinder Banga; Baroness Patience Wheatcroft; Prof. Roy Anderson.

OTHER INFORMATION Ten beneficiaries of grants were listed in the annual report and accounts (£111,000). In addition, grants under 'major giving and appeals' totalled £50,000. The 2020/21 accounts were the latest available at the time of writing (June 2023).

HOW TO APPLY Apply in writing to the correspondent. The trustees hold at least two meetings each year.

CONTACT DETAILS The Trustees, c/o Handelsbanken Wealth Management, 77 Mount Ephraim, Tunbridge Wells, Kent TN4 8BS *Tel.* 01892 701801

■ The Banister Charitable Trust

CC NO 1102320 **ESTABLISHED** 2004

WHERE FUNDING CAN BE GIVEN UK.

WHO CAN BENEFIT Charitable organisations.

WHAT IS FUNDED Conservation, protection and improvement of the physical and natural environment.

TYPE OF GRANT Core costs; project costs; capital costs.

RANGE OF GRANTS From £500 to £200,000.

SAMPLE GRANTS Woodland Trust – Pepper Wood (£200,000); Amphibian and Reptile Conservation Trust (£50,000); West Cumbria Rivers Trust (£10,000); The Moorland Mousie Trust (£5,000); APE Project (£500).

FINANCES *Financial year end 31/12/2021* *Income* £907,500 *Grants to organisations* £623,600 *Assets* £11,140,000

TRUSTEES Huw Banister; Christopher Banister; Ludlow Trust Company Ltd.

HOW TO APPLY Apply in writing to the correspondent.

CONTACT DETAILS The Trustees, Ludlow Trust Co. Ltd, Tower Wharf, Cheese Lane, Bristol BS2 0JJ *Tel.* 0117 313 8200 *Email* charitabletrusts@ludlowtrust.com

■ Bank of Scotland Foundation

OSCR NO SC032942 **ESTABLISHED** 2002

WHERE FUNDING CAN BE GIVEN Scotland.

WHO CAN BENEFIT OSCR-registered charities.

WHAT IS FUNDED Social disadvantage or exclusion; developing and improving local communities; financial literacy and financial inclusion.

WHAT IS NOT FUNDED Political organisations; animal welfare; the promotion of religion; medical research; organisations that redistribute funding for subsequent grant-making to other organisations and/or individuals; individuals; advertising; sponsorship; foreign travel; overseas projects; newly registered charities that have been operating for less than one year.

TYPE OF GRANT Core costs; capital costs; project funding; one-off and multi-year.

RANGE OF GRANTS Programme dependent.

SAMPLE GRANTS LGBT Youth Scotland (£172,500); St Andrews Environmental Network (£134,600); Healthy 'n' Happy Community Development Trust (£107,600); Families Like Us (£70,500); Home-Start Lorn (£25,000); Street Soccer Scotland (£24,500); Cruse Bereavement Care Scotland (£23,200); Epilepsy Connections (£20,000).

FINANCES *Financial year end 31/12/2021* *Income* £5,310,000 *Grants to organisations* £5,020,000 *Assets* £2,270,000

TRUSTEES Graham Blair; Alison Macdonald; Graeme Thompson; Karen Watt; Donald MacKechnie; Julianne Reddin; Jackie Leiper; Ken MacIntosh; Laura Armstrong; Jon Alexander.

OTHER INFORMATION The foundation also operates a matched giving programme whereby Lloyds Banking Group colleagues can receive matched funding for their fundraising activities. In 2021, the foundation made 168 grants totalling £4.75 million under the theme of social exclusion and disadvantage. These grants ranged from £1,300 to £176,200. In addition, it awarded matched funding totalling £270,400. Only organisations that received grants of over £20,000 were listed as beneficiaries in the foundation's accounts. A full list of beneficiaries can be found on the foundation's website.

Think carefully about every application. Is it justified?

253

HOW TO APPLY Check the foundation's website for current deadlines and fund opening dates. Further information on each grants programme is available on the website.

CONTACT DETAILS The Trustees, The Mound, Edinburgh EH1 1YZ *Tel.* 07385 024428 *Email* enquiries@bankofscotlandfoundation.co.uk *Website* www.bankofscotlandfoundation.org

---

■ The Barbers' Company General Charities

CC NO 265579   **ESTABLISHED** 1973
WHERE FUNDING CAN BE GIVEN UK, with a preference for the City of London.
WHO CAN BENEFIT Hospitals; hospices; educational organisations; charitable organisations; individuals.
WHAT IS FUNDED Education, particularly medical education; social welfare.
WHAT IS NOT FUNDED Medical research; large, well-endowed charities; large projects.
TYPE OF GRANT Project costs; capital costs.
RANGE OF GRANTS Typically less than £25,000.
SAMPLE GRANTS King's College London (£88,800); Royal College of Surgeons (£50,000); Phyllis Tuckwell Hospice (£30,000); ABF The Soldiers' Charity (£6,500); London Symphony Orchestra (£4,000); British Society of Gastroenterology (£3,000); Calibre Audio (£2,000); Medical Artists' Association, St Giles Cripplegate and Tooting and Balham Sea Cadets (£1,000 each).
FINANCES *Financial year end* 31/08/2022
Income £259,100
Grants to organisations £271,700
Grants to individuals £5,700
Assets £1,900,000
TRUSTEE Worshipful Company of Barbers.
HOW TO APPLY Apply in writing, directly to the Worshipful Company of Barbers. Guidelines are provided on the website.
CONTACT DETAILS Malachy Doran, Clerk, The Worshipful Company of Barbers, Barber-Surgeons' Hall, 1A Monkwell Square, London EC2Y 5BL *Tel.* 020 7606 0741 *Email* clerk@barberscompany.org *Website* http://barberscompany.org.uk

---

■ The Barbour Foundation

CC NO 328081   **ESTABLISHED** 1988
WHERE FUNDING CAN BE GIVEN UK, but primarily the North East (Tyne and Wear, Northumberland, Durham and South Tyneside).
WHO CAN BENEFIT Registered charities; CICs; social enterprises; sports clubs; hospices.
WHAT IS FUNDED Relief in need due to social circumstances, financial hardship or distress; education and employability; homelessness; research into the cause and treatment of chronic illness or disease and the provision of medical equipment; protection and preservation of buildings and countryside of environmental, historical or architectural interest; national and international disaster relief.
WHAT IS NOT FUNDED Applications from outside the geographical area of benefit; applications from educational organisations; capital grants for building projects; applications from individuals.
TYPE OF GRANT Core/revenue costs; seed funding/start-up funding; unrestricted funding.
RANGE OF GRANTS Up to £150,000 but mainly between £1,000 to £5,000.
SAMPLE GRANTS International Centre for Life (£100,000); British Red Cross – Ukraine Crisis Appeal (£50,000); Action for Children (£20,000); Action for Medical Research (£10,000); Go Kids Go (£1,000).
FINANCES *Financial year end* 05/04/2022
Income £1,020,000
Grants to organisations £1,060,000
Assets £13,320,000
TRUSTEES Dame Margaret Barbour; Helen Barbour; Nichola Bellaby.
OTHER INFORMATION According to the foundation's annual accounts, 362 grants were awarded during the year.
HOW TO APPLY Apply in writing to the correspondent. Full details of what should be included in an application can be found on the foundation's website. Applications for Main Grants are considered at quarterly meetings and applications for Small Grants are considered at meetings every six weeks.
CONTACT DETAILS Edith Howse, Executive Secretary, Simonside, South Shields, Tyne and Wear NE34 9PD *Tel.* 0191 427 4217 *Email* barbour.foundation@barbour.com *Website* www.barbour.com/uk/the-barbour-foundation

---

■ Barcapel Foundation Ltd

OSCR NO SC009211   **ESTABLISHED** 1964
WHERE FUNDING CAN BE GIVEN UK, mainly Scotland.
WHO CAN BENEFIT Registered charities.
WHAT IS FUNDED Health, particularly complementary and alternative therapies; arts, culture and heritage, particularly the built environment; young people from socially disadvantaged backgrounds.
WHAT IS NOT FUNDED Individual applications for travel or similar; organisations or individuals engaged in promoting religious or political beliefs; applications for funding costs for feasibility studies or similar; charities whose work is delivered outside the British Isles.
TYPE OF GRANT Core/revenue costs; seed funding/start-up funding.
RANGE OF GRANTS Up to £100,000.
SAMPLE GRANTS National Galleries of Scotland and Young Enterprise Scotland (£25,000 each); Guts UK Charity (£20,000); Royal Conservatoire of Scotland (£15,000); Compass Community Board (£11,500); Hearts and Minds (£7,500); Eighteen and Under (£5,000); KIND Scotland (£2,000).
FINANCES *Financial year end* 31/12/2021
Income £52,800
Grants to organisations £235,100
Assets £3,220,000
TRUSTEES Robert Wilson; Amanda Richards; Jed Wilson; Clement Wilson; Hermione Wilson.
OTHER INFORMATION The foundation awarded grants to 46 organisations during the year. Grants to unlisted organisations totalled £10,000.
HOW TO APPLY Application forms are available from the foundation's website. They should be returned by post with a covering letter and a copy of your annual accounts, but note that the trustees ask that you do not send any additional information at this stage. If you have any additional documents or information you feel is particularly important, refer to them in the covering letter so the trustees can request them if required. The foundation does not accept applications by email. Application deadlines are posted on the foundation's website.
CONTACT DETAILS The Trustees, 3rd Floor, 3 Hill Street, New Town, Edinburgh EH2 3JP *Tel.* 0131 381 8111 *Email* admin@barcapelfoundation.org *Website* www.barcapelfoundation.org

■ Barchester Healthcare Foundation

CC NO 1083272   **ESTABLISHED** 2000

WHERE FUNDING CAN BE GIVEN England; Scotland; Wales.

WHO CAN BENEFIT Charitable organisations; CICs; individuals.

WHAT IS FUNDED Health; social welfare; recreation and community services; older people; people with disabilities.

WHAT IS NOT FUNDED Core/running costs; salaries; indirect services such as helplines, newsletters, leaflets or research; major building projects or large capital projects; minibuses; training of staff and volunteers; food/food bank provision (unless part of an activity or project); activities for residents in a care home operated by Barchester Healthcare or any other care home company.

TYPE OF GRANT One-off; capital costs; project funding.

RANGE OF GRANTS Typically £100 to £2,000.

SAMPLE GRANTS Wenlo Riding for the Disabled (£2,500); People and Gardens CIC (£2,000); Shopmobility Paisley and District (£1,500); Normandy Community Therapy Garden and Plymouth Wheelchair Basketball (£1,300 each); Bootle Tool Shed (£1,200); Face Front Inclusive Theatre, Salford Refugee Link and The Widows Empowerment Trust (£1,000 each).

FINANCES *Financial year end 31/12/2021*
Income £235,000
Grants to organisations £82,000
Grants to individuals £65,000
Assets £108,000

TRUSTEES Ann Mackay; Dr Pete Calveley; Fiona McGill; Jamie Hodgson; Andy Tilden; Julia Scott; Shannon Cullen.

OTHER INFORMATION In 2021, 88 grants were awarded to organisations and a further 110 grants were awarded to individuals.

HOW TO APPLY Applications can be made via the foundation's website.

CONTACT DETAILS Grants Management Team, 3rd Floor, The Aspect, 12 Finsbury Square, London EC2A 1AS *Tel.* 0800 328 3328 *Email* info@bhcfoundation.org.uk *Website* www.bhcfoundation.org.uk

■ The Baring Foundation

CC NO 258583   **ESTABLISHED** 1969

WHERE FUNDING CAN BE GIVEN UK and Africa.

WHO CAN BENEFIT Charitable organisations; UK charities working with NGO partners in financially developing countries.

WHAT IS FUNDED The foundation has three grant programmes: Arts – promoting the role of creativity in the lives of people with mental health problems; International Development – empowering LGBTQ+ communities in sub-Saharan Africa; Strengthening the Voluntary Sector – supporting human rights and legal initiatives.

TYPE OF GRANT Core costs.

RANGE OF GRANTS Grants range from £500 to £300,000.

SAMPLE GRANTS The Other Foundation (£175,000); The Civil Liberties Trust and SOS Special Educational Needs (£150,000 each); Environmental Rights Centre for Scotland (£65,400); Racial Justice Network (£50,000) ; APPEAL (£14,600); Sheila McKechnie Foundation (£10,000); Latin American Women's Rights Service (£5,000).

FINANCES *Financial year end 31/12/2021*
Income £2,280,000
Grants to organisations £3,960,000
Assets £124,780,000

TRUSTEES David Elliott; Dr Robert Berkeley; Shauneen Lambe; Lucy Groot; Victoria Amedume; James Jenkins; Samuel Thorne; Rhys Pullen; Emebet Wuhib-Mutungi; Jillian Popkins; Asif Afridi; Ashley Coombes; Dipuo Magwaza; Judith Robertson; Pontso Mafethe.

HOW TO APPLY Check the foundation's website for the latest information on open programmes. Applicants may wish to sign up to the foundation's e-newsletter, to be notified when funding rounds open.

CONTACT DETAILS The Trustees, 8–10 Moorgate, London EC2R 6DA *Tel.* 020 7767 1348 *Email* baring.foundation@ing.com *Website* https://baringfoundation.org.uk

■ Philip Barker Charity

CC NO 1000227   **ESTABLISHED** 1990

WHERE FUNDING CAN BE GIVEN Cheshire.

WHO CAN BENEFIT Registered charities; community organisations; universities.

WHAT IS FUNDED General charitable purposes; young people and youth activities; community development; social welfare; education and employment; Christianity.

TYPE OF GRANT Core costs; salaries; project funding; development funding.

SAMPLE GRANTS University of Chester (£100,000); The Youth Federation (£40,000 in two grants).

FINANCES *Financial year end 31/10/2021*
Income £41,800
Grants to organisations £140,000
Assets £1,970,000

TRUSTEES Sir Edmund Burton; Janet Groves; Terry Groves.

OTHER INFORMATION The 2020/21 annual report and accounts were the latest available to view at the time of writing (June 2023). A small number of grants are made each year.

HOW TO APPLY Apply in writing to the correspondent.

CONTACT DETAILS The Trustees, Bay Tree Cottage, Barbary Close, South Cheriton, Templecombe, Somerset BA8 0BG *Tel.* 07967 204685

■ The Michael Barnard Charitable Trust

CC NO 1157878   **ESTABLISHED** 2014

WHERE FUNDING CAN BE GIVEN UK, with a preference for Northern Ireland and Scotland.

WHO CAN BENEFIT Charitable organisations; individuals.

WHAT IS FUNDED Social welfare.

SAMPLE GRANTS A list of beneficiaries was not included in the annual report and accounts. Previous beneficiaries have included: The Alex Lewis Trust; Homeless Help – Basildon; Mustard Tree – Greater Manchester; One Love Soup Kitchen – Southend.

FINANCES *Financial year end 31/03/2022*
Income £21,500
Grants to organisations £66,800
Grants to individuals £14,000
Assets £1,100,000

TRUSTEES John Summerton; Michael Barnard; John Caulcutt.

HOW TO APPLY Apply in writing to the correspondent.

CONTACT DETAILS The Trustees, Brown Heath Park, Gregory Lane, Durley, Southampton SO32 2BS *Tel.* 07977 403704

■ Lord Barnby's Foundation

CC NO 251016   **ESTABLISHED** 1966

WHERE FUNDING CAN BE GIVEN UK and Wales.

WHO CAN BENEFIT Registered charities.

WHAT IS FUNDED General charitable purposes.

WHAT IS NOT FUNDED Individuals.

TYPE OF GRANT One-off and recurrent.

RANGE OF GRANTS £500 to £10,000.

SAMPLE GRANTS Polish Knights of Malta (£50,000); Countryside Learning, Turquoise Mountain and Young Lives vs Cancer (£10,000 each); Horsley Riding for the Disabled (£5,000); Outward Bound Trust (£4,000); Jumbulance (£3,000); Bradford South Scouts (£2,500); Ring and Ride (£2,000); Oxfordshire Youth (£1,750); Halo Trust, Only A Payment Away and Your Emotional Support Services [YESS] (£1,000 each); Cavell Nurses (£500).

FINANCES *Financial year end 31/03/2022*
Income £264,700
Grants to organisations £260,500
Assets £5,700,000

TRUSTEES Laura Greenall; The Hon. George Lopes; The Countess Peel; Mr E. J. Smith-Maxwell; David Cecil.

HOW TO APPLY Applications will only be considered if received in writing accompanied by a set of your latest accounts.

CONTACT DETAILS The Trustees, PO Box 442, Market Drayton, Shropshire TF9 9EQ *Tel.* 07835 441168 *Email* lordbarnbyfoundation@gmail.com

■ The Barnes Fund

CC NO 200103   **ESTABLISHED** 1970

WHERE FUNDING CAN BE GIVEN The ancient parish of Barnes only (broadly the SW13 postal district).

WHO CAN BENEFIT Charitable organisations.

WHAT IS FUNDED Social welfare; older people and their carers; disability; physical and mental health; carers; recreational facilities; educational facilities and opportunities. Grants are also made to individuals through referral agencies for educational purposes and for the relief of hardship.

WHAT IS NOT FUNDED National organisations.

TYPE OF GRANT Capital revenue grants; core funding; grants for specific one-off projects, schemes or equipment.

RANGE OF GRANTS Organisational grants: up to £40,000, but mostly below £10,000. Welfare grants for individuals: generally up to £500 per year for up to three years.

SAMPLE GRANTS Castelnau Centre Project (£45,200); Richmond Citizens Advice (£38,600); Crossroads Care (£20,200); FiSH Neighbourhood Care (£14,500); Richmond Mind (£8,500); Richmond Mencap (£5,000); MID Mediation and Counselling (£3,000); Barnes Music Society (£2,000); Crossway Pregnancy Crisis Centre (£1,500); Barnes Music Festival (£750).

FINANCES *Financial year end 31/12/2021*
Income £721,500
Grants to organisations £245,500
Grants to individuals £28,400
Assets £13,510,000

TRUSTEE The Barnes Fund Trustee Ltd.

OTHER INFORMATION Grants were awarded to 37 organisations and 113 individuals during the year. Grants were broken down as follows: relief of sickness and distress (£97,400); education (£76,800); relief of poverty (£62,900); relief of older people (£22,200); capital projects (£7,800); leisure facilities (£3,800).

HOW TO APPLY Organisations can apply using an online form on the fund's website and are advised to first read the eligibility guidelines. There are separate application forms for core funding and project funding. Applications from organisations are considered at trustees' meetings in February, May, July, and October each year. Applications must be received by the 6th of the month preceding a meeting to be considered.

CONTACT DETAILS Katy Makepeace-Gray, Executive Director, PO Box 347, Hampton TW12 9ED *Tel.* 07484 146 802 (Monday to Thursday) *Email* executivedirector@thebarnesfund.org.uk *Website* https://thebarnesfund.org.uk

■ The Max Barney Foundation

CC NO 1164583   **ESTABLISHED** 2014

WHERE FUNDING CAN BE GIVEN England and Wales; Israel.

WHO CAN BENEFIT Registered charities; social enterprises; Jewish organisations.

WHAT IS FUNDED General charitable purposes; relief of unemployment through vocational training and job creation, particularly within the Jewish community.

RANGE OF GRANTS Typically between £60,000 and £100,000.

SAMPLE GRANTS Laniado Hospital (£172,000); Central British Fund for World Jewish Relief (£100,000); The Kemach Foundation and Tikva UK (£80,000 each); American Jewish Joint Distribution Committee (UK) Trust and Gvahim NGO (£75,000 each); The Work Avenue Foundation (£70,000); The Prince's Trust (£65,000).

FINANCES *Financial year end 31/05/2022*
Income £2,550,000
Grants to organisations £1,340,000
Assets £1,860,000

TRUSTEES Alexander Bard; Michael Goldstein; Gary Phillips.

HOW TO APPLY Contact the correspondent for further information.

CONTACT DETAILS The Trustees, 4th Floor, 168 Shoreditch High Street, London E1 6HU *Tel.* 020 7583 5555 *Email* shraga@maxbarney.com

■ Barnsbury Charitable Trust

CC NO 241383   **ESTABLISHED** 1964

WHERE FUNDING CAN BE GIVEN UK, but no local charities outside Oxfordshire.

WHO CAN BENEFIT Charitable organisations.

WHAT IS FUNDED General charitable purposes.

WHAT IS NOT FUNDED Individuals.

RANGE OF GRANTS Typically less than £11,000.

SAMPLE GRANTS Oxfordshire VCH Trust (£10,000); Landmark Trust (£6,500); St Luke's Hospital – Oxford (£5,000); Dorchester Festival (£3,000); Oxfordshire Youth (£2,500); London Library (£1,000); Growing Well (£500); Oxford Oratory Trust (£100).

FINANCES *Financial year end 05/04/2022*
Income £174,500
Grants to organisations £170,400
Assets £8,220,000

TRUSTEES Mary Brunner; Isabel Sharp; Sir Hugo Brunner.

OTHER INFORMATION The trust awarded grants to 47 organisations.

HOW TO APPLY Apply in writing to the correspondent.

CONTACT DETAILS The Trustees, 26 Norham Road, Oxford, Oxfordshire OX2 6SF *Tel.* 01865 554821 *Email* hmrbrunner@gmail.com

■ Barnwood Trust

CC NO 1162855   **ESTABLISHED** 1792
WHERE FUNDING CAN BE GIVEN Gloucestershire.
WHO CAN BENEFIT Registered charities; CICs; social enterprises; schools and colleges; unconstituted voluntary groups; individuals.
WHAT IS FUNDED People with disabilities; people experiencing mental health problems; community services and spaces; holiday and play schemes.
TYPE OF GRANT Project costs; start-up costs; equipment costs; capital costs.
RANGE OF GRANTS Up to £50,000.
SAMPLE GRANTS GL11 Community Hub (£50,000); Gloucestershire VCS Alliance (£40,000); Gloucestershire Counselling Services (£20,000); Cotswolds Boatmobility (£18,000); Longhope Recreation Ground (£14,000); Greenwood's Therapeutic Horticulture CIC (£14,500); Forest Furniture Bank (£10,000).
FINANCES *Financial year end* 31/12/2021
Income £2,780,000
Grants to organisations £997,000
Grants to individuals £1,220,000
Assets £105,850,000
TRUSTEES Dr Jean Waters; Suzanne Beech; Shaun Parsons; Benjamin Preece-Smith; Ann Santry; Patricia Jay; Philippa Jones; Colin Smith.
OTHER INFORMATION Only beneficiaries of organisational grants of over £10,000 were listed in the accounts. Grants of under £10,000 totalled £367,800.
HOW TO APPLY Applicants must first contact their local Strategic Development Manager (listed on the trust's website) to discuss their ideas. Applications can then be made via an online portal on the trust's website. Be aware that applications are considered first by Gloucestershire Funders, a partnership of funding organisations that works together to support local initiatives in Gloucestershire's communities. Further information on the trust's funding policies can be found on its website.
CONTACT DETAILS Funding Team, Overton House, Overton Road, Cheltenham GL50 3BN *Tel.* 01242 539935 *Email* grants@barnwoodtrust.org *Website* www.barnwoodtrust.org

■ The Barratt Developments plc Charitable Foundation

CC NO 1188447   **ESTABLISHED** 2020
WHERE FUNDING CAN BE GIVEN England; Scotland; Wales.
WHO CAN BENEFIT Charitable organisations.
WHAT IS FUNDED General charitable purposes including: diversity and inclusion; the environment; mental health and well-being; homelessness; veterans.
SAMPLE GRANTS Outward Bound Trust (£1 million); Whizz-Kidz (£631,000); Magic Breakfast (£100,000); The Prince's Trust (£68,200); Action for Kids Charitable Trust (£60,000).
FINANCES *Financial year end* 30/06/2022
Income £4,540,000
Grants to organisations £3,830,000
Assets £1,300,000

TRUSTEES David Thomas; Jeremy Hipkiss; Kamalprit Bains; Tim Collins; Mark Rolfe; Lord Gavin Barwell; Ugochukwu Ikokwu; Philippa Charles.
OTHER INFORMATION Only beneficiaries of grants of over £50,000 were included in the annual report and accounts. Grants of under £50,000 totalled (£1.97 million).
HOW TO APPLY At the time of writing (August 2023) the foundation's website stated that it was 'revamping' its grants programme; charities were being invited to submit an online Expression of Interest form. Visit the website for updates.
CONTACT DETAILS The Trustees, Barratt House, Cartwright Way, Forest Business Park, Bardon Hill LE67 1UF *Tel.* 01530 278278 *Email* cf@barrattplc.co.uk *Website* https://barrattfoundation.org.uk

■ Misses Barrie Charitable Trust

CC NO 279459   **ESTABLISHED** 1979
WHERE FUNDING CAN BE GIVEN UK, with a particular interest in Scotland, Surrey, Warwickshire and Worcestershire.
WHO CAN BENEFIT Registered charities.
WHAT IS FUNDED General charitable purposes.
WHAT IS NOT FUNDED Individuals.
RANGE OF GRANTS Usually £1,000 to £10,000.
SAMPLE GRANTS National Youth Orchestra of Great Britain (£10,000); University of Oxford (£7,500); Broadway Youth Club (£4,000); National Youth Choirs of Great Britain (£3,500); Bowel Cancer UK (£3,000); Warwickshire Social Inclusion Partnership (£2,000); Tunnell Trust (£1,000).
FINANCES *Financial year end* 05/04/2022
Income £214,900
Grants to organisations £194,900
Assets £7,810,000
TRUSTEES John Carter; Rachel Fraser; Sally Abell; Charlotte Carter; Suzanne Fraser.
OTHER INFORMATION The trustees prefer to support small to medium-sized charities.
HOW TO APPLY Apply in writing to the correspondent accompanied by up-to-date accounts or financial information. The trustees are unable to notify unsuccessful applicants.
CONTACT DETAILS The Trustees, 34 Victoria Road, Dartmouth, Devon TQ6 9SA *Tel.* 01737 248065 *Email* charlotte@raymondcarter.co.uk

■ Robert Barr's Charitable Trust

OSCR NO SC007613   **ESTABLISHED** 1970
WHERE FUNDING CAN BE GIVEN UK and overseas.
WHO CAN BENEFIT Charitable organisations; hospitals; schools; universities; CICs.
WHAT IS FUNDED General charitable purposes; social welfare; health; education; the arts, culture and heritage; recreation; medical research.
TYPE OF GRANT Capital costs; project funding; research grants.
RANGE OF GRANTS £5,000 to £50,000, with the occasional larger grant.
SAMPLE GRANTS RNLI (£250,000); Abernethy Trust (£50,000); George Watson's Family Foundation and Venture Trust (£5,000 each).
FINANCES *Financial year end* 05/04/2022
Income £648,000
Grants to organisations £310,000
Assets £30,000,000
OTHER INFORMATION Grants were broken down as follows: social welfare (£305,000) and conservation (£5,000). Four organisations were awarded grants.
HOW TO APPLY Apply in writing to the correspondent.

CONTACT DETAILS The Trustees, c/o Shepherd and Wedderburn LLP, 1 West Regent Street, Glasgow G2 1RW

■ The Paul Bassham Charitable Trust

CC NO 266842   **ESTABLISHED** 1973
WHERE FUNDING CAN BE GIVEN Norfolk.
WHO CAN BENEFIT UK-registered charities; charitable bodies that are exempt from registration.
WHAT IS FUNDED General charitable purposes.
WHAT IS NOT FUNDED Individuals.
TYPE OF GRANT Capital costs; development funding; project costs; research grants.
RANGE OF GRANTS Up to £50,000.
SAMPLE GRANTS Norfolk Wildlife Trust (£20,000); Norwich Preservation Trust (£12,000); Norfolk and Norwich Festival (£10,000); Norfolk Heart Trust – Norfolk Community Foundation (£5,000); Save our Spaniels (£5,000); The Woodland Trust (£5,000).
FINANCES *Financial year end* 05/04/2022
  Income £396,600
  Grants to organisations £355,200
  Assets £15,470,000
TRUSTEES Alexander Munro; Graham Tuttle; Patrick Harris; Morris Peacock.
OTHER INFORMATION Only organisations that received grants of over £5,000 were listed as beneficiaries in the trust's accounts. Grants of under £5,000 totalled £163,300.
HOW TO APPLY Apply in writing to the correspondent. The trustees will only consider written applications and do so on a quarterly basis.
CONTACT DETAILS The Trustees, c/o Howes Percival LLP, Flint Buildings, 1 Bedding Lane, Norwich, Norfolk NR3 1RG *Tel.* 01603 762103

■ The Batchworth Trust

CC NO 245061   **ESTABLISHED** 1965
WHERE FUNDING CAN BE GIVEN Worldwide.
WHO CAN BENEFIT Major UK and international charities.
WHAT IS FUNDED General charitable purposes, with a preference for health and social welfare.
RANGE OF GRANTS Up to £100,000 but generally £2,000 to £25,000.
SAMPLE GRANTS Disasters Emergency Committee (£100,000); Educate for Africa (£60,000); Crisis UK (£25,000), The Trussell Trust (£20,000); Age Scotland and Literacy Pirates (£10,000 each); WaterAid (£5,000), Diabetes UK (£2,000).
FINANCES *Financial year end* 05/04/2022
  Income £587,600
  Grants to organisations £1,360,000
  Assets £2,500,000
TRUSTEE Lockwell Trustees Ltd.
OTHER INFORMATION Grants were made to 101 charities during the year.
HOW TO APPLY Contact the correspondent for further information.
CONTACT DETAILS James Peach, c/o Kreston Reeves LLP, Springfield House, Springfield Road, Horsham, West Sussex RH12 2RG *Tel.* 01293 776152 *Email* james.peach@krestonreeves.com

■ The Battersea Power Station Foundation

CC NO 1161232   **ESTABLISHED** 2014
WHERE FUNDING CAN BE GIVEN Lambeth and Wandsworth.
WHO CAN BENEFIT Charitable organisations.
WHAT IS FUNDED General charitable purposes; community services and development.
TYPE OF GRANT Core/revenue costs; project funding.
SAMPLE GRANTS A list of beneficiaries was not included in the annual report and accounts. Previous beneficiaries have included: Walcot Foundation (£25,000); Hestia (£9,600); Caius House and Junction Community Trust (£5,000 each); Providence House (£2,000); NSPCC (£1,000).
FINANCES *Financial year end* 31/12/2021
  Income £546,700
  Grants to organisations £71,400
  Assets £537,400
TRUSTEES The Rt Hon. Lord Strathclyde; Dato' Jaganath Derek Steven Sabapathy; Madonna Kinsey.
HOW TO APPLY The foundation is no longer accepting applications for new grants.
CONTACT DETAILS Barbra Mazur, Foundation Secretary, 1 Village Courtyard, Circus West Village, Battersea Power Station, London SW11 8AH *Tel.* 020 7501 0713 *Email* CommunitiesTeam@bpsdc.co.uk *Website* http://bpsfoundation.org.uk

■ Bauer Radio's Cash for Kids Charities

CC NO 1122062   **ESTABLISHED** 2007
WHERE FUNDING CAN BE GIVEN UK.
WHO CAN BENEFIT Registered charities; schools; community groups; health organisations; individuals.
WHAT IS FUNDED Disadvantaged children and young people up to the age of 18.
WHAT IS NOT FUNDED A list of exclusions is available in the Eligibility Criteria document, accessible via the website.
TYPE OF GRANT Capital costs; project costs.
RANGE OF GRANTS Typically from £1,000 to £3,000.
SAMPLE GRANTS A list of beneficiaries was not included in the annual report and accounts.
FINANCES *Financial year end* 31/12/2021
  Income £13,500,000
  Grants to organisations £1,920,000
  Assets £3,650,000
TRUSTEES Sally Aitchison; Martin Ball; Sean Marley; Danny Simpson; Susan Voss; Gary Stein; David Tighe.
OTHER INFORMATION This is the umbrella charity for Bauer Radio, which owns radio stations in 23 areas of the UK. Each station has its own charity and operates a grant-making strategy to benefit children in the local area. The grant total includes grants made to individuals and organisations, but we were unable to determine the exact amount awarded to individuals. The charity gave a further £8.82 million in gifts in kind through its Mission Christmas appeal.
HOW TO APPLY To apply for a grant, first visit the locations page of the charity's website to find your local radio station and grants team. Application forms, eligibility criteria and deadlines are available on the local websites.
CONTACT DETAILS The Trustees, Hampdon House, Unit 3 Falcon Court, Preston Farm, Stockton-on-Tees, County Durham TS18 3TS *Email* info@

cashforkids.uk.com *Website* https://cashforkids.org.uk

■ The Gordon and Ena Baxter Foundation

OSCR NO SC003211
WHERE FUNDING CAN BE GIVEN North-east Scotland; the Highlands and Islands of Scotland.
WHO CAN BENEFIT Registered charities; constituted community or sporting groups.
WHAT IS FUNDED Education and training; health; social welfare; sport; arts and heritage; conservation and the environment.
WHAT IS NOT FUNDED Running costs or salary/wages overheads; training costs, including volunteer training; individual sponsorship agreements; retrospective expenditure; routine repairs and maintenance; the promotion of religious or political beliefs; general circulars; research; animal welfare; start-up costs; grant-making charities; projects generally understood to be the responsibility of a statutory authority.
TYPE OF GRANT Capital projects; capital costs.
RANGE OF GRANTS £100 to £25,000.
SAMPLE GRANTS Huntly Development Trust (£25,000); Cromdale Village Hall (£5,000); Outfit Moray (£3,000); Sue Ryder – Dee View Court (£2,800); 1st Mosstodloch Scout Group (£2,100).
FINANCES *Financial year end 31/03/2022*
Income £110,700
Grants to organisations £179,200
Assets £107,100
HOW TO APPLY Applications can be made via the foundation's website.
CONTACT DETAILS The Trustees, c/o Baxters Food Group, Fochabers, Moray IV32 7LD *Email* sarah@gebfoundation.com *Website* www.gebfoundation.com

■ Bay Charitable Trust

CC NO 1060537 **ESTABLISHED** 1997
WHERE FUNDING CAN BE GIVEN UK and overseas.
WHO CAN BENEFIT Registered charities; Orthodox Jewish organisations.
WHAT IS FUNDED Social welfare; the advancement of traditions of the Orthodox Jewish religion and the study of Torah.
SAMPLE GRANTS A list of beneficiaries was not included in the annual report and accounts.
FINANCES *Financial year end 31/12/2021*
Income £421,000
Grants to organisations £411,900
Assets £53,800
TRUSTEES Ian Kreditor; Michael Lisser.
OTHER INFORMATION The grant total includes awards made to individuals.
HOW TO APPLY Apply in writing to the correspondent.
CONTACT DETAILS Ian Kreditor, Trustee, 21 Woodlands Close, London NW11 9QR *Tel.* 020 8810 4321

■ The Bay Tree Charitable Trust

CC NO 1044091 **ESTABLISHED** 1994
WHERE FUNDING CAN BE GIVEN UK.
WHO CAN BENEFIT Charitable organisations.
WHAT IS FUNDED General charitable purposes including: development work; health; social welfare.
WHAT IS NOT FUNDED Grants are not made to individuals.

RANGE OF GRANTS Grants range from £5,000 to £20,000.
SAMPLE GRANTS Shelter (£50,000); Disasters Emergency Committee Afghanistan Crisis Appeal and Unicef UK (£25,000 each); Disasters Emergency Committee – Coronavirus Appeal (£10,000).
FINANCES *Financial year end 31/12/2021*
Income £104,600
Grants to organisations £110,000
Assets £7,690,000
TRUSTEES Paul Benton; Emma Benton; Ian Benton.
OTHER INFORMATION Grants were made to four organisations during the year.
HOW TO APPLY Apply in writing to the correspondent. All appeals should contain the following: your charity's aims and objectives; your charity's registration number; the nature of your appeal; if for a specific project, your total target and any contributions received against that target; and any other relevant factors. Applications should include a copy of your latest accounts.
CONTACT DETAILS The Trustees, PO Box 53983, London SW15 1VT *Tel.* 020 7465 4300

■ The Louis Baylis (Maidenhead Advertiser) Charitable Trust

CC NO 210533 **ESTABLISHED** 1962
WHERE FUNDING CAN BE GIVEN Berkshire and South Buckinghamshire (the areas served by the publications of Baylis Media Ltd).
WHO CAN BENEFIT Registered charities.
WHAT IS FUNDED General charitable purposes.
RANGE OF GRANTS Grants are typically of less than £3,000.
SAMPLE GRANTS Re:Charge R and R (£6,000); Great Ormond Street Hospital Children's Charity (£2,000); Berkshire Care Trust (£1,500); Home Park Lawn Tennis Club (£1,000); Leisure Focus Trust (£600).
FINANCES *Financial year end 30/06/2022*
Income £1,650,000
Grants to organisations £192,800
Assets £14,120,000
TRUSTEES Patricia Lattimer; Peter Murcott; John Robertson; Peter Sands.
OTHER INFORMATION The grants were broken down as follows: local charities and organisations (£159,900 in 81 grants); regional charities and organisations (£21,400 in 11 grants); national charities (£11,500 in 9 grants).
HOW TO APPLY Application forms are available to download on the website and should be returned to the trust by email or post.
CONTACT DETAILS The Administrator, PO Box 4832, Maidenhead, Berkshire SL60 1JQ *Email* info@louisbaylistrust.org.uk *Website* www.louisbaylistrust.org.uk

■ BBC Children in Need

CC NO 802052 **ESTABLISHED** 1989
WHERE FUNDING CAN BE GIVEN UK, including the Channel Islands and the Isle of Man.
WHO CAN BENEFIT Voluntary projects; community groups; registered charities; not-for-profit organisations; churches; schools.
WHAT IS FUNDED Children and young people under the age of 18 experiencing disadvantage through illness, distress, abuse or neglect, any kind of disability, behavioural or psychological difficulties, or who are living in poverty and/or experiencing deprivation.

TYPE OF GRANT Capital costs; project funding; core/revenue funding.

RANGE OF GRANTS Generally up to £15,000.

SAMPLE GRANTS A list of beneficiaries was not included in the annual report and accounts.

FINANCES *Financial year end* 30/06/2022
Income £69,420,000
Grants to organisations £65,730,000
Assets £37,460,000

TRUSTEES Rosemary Millard; James Fairclough; Sandeep Bhamra; Randel Bryan; Cherrie Bija; Leigh Tavaziva; Kenny Imafidon; Trevor Bradley; Kieran Clifton; Rhona Burns; Jonathan Munro; Suzy Lamb; Matthew Baker.

HOW TO APPLY Applications can be made via the charity's website, which also has information on eligibility criteria, application deadlines and exclusions. If you have a general enquiry, are unsure about anything you have read or are looking for support regarding your application, contact the charity via phone or email. You can also contact your local, regional or national office.

CONTACT DETAILS Grants Team, Grants, PO Box 649, Salford M5 0LD *Tel.* 0345 609 0015 (select option 2) *Email* pudseygrants@bbc.co.uk *Website* www.bbcchildreninneed.co.uk

■ BC Partners Foundation

CC NO 1136956   **ESTABLISHED** 2010

WHERE FUNDING CAN BE GIVEN UK and overseas.

WHO CAN BENEFIT Registered charities; schools; universities; hospitals; local authorities.

WHAT IS FUNDED Community development; conservation of the environment; arts; education.

TYPE OF GRANT Capital costs; project funding; core/revenue costs.

RANGE OF GRANTS Mostly up to £100,000.

SAMPLE GRANTS Private Equity Foundation (£119,500); Right to Play (£12,000); Fine Cell Work (£10,000); The Haemophilia Society (£100).

FINANCES *Financial year end* 31/12/2021
Income £44,200
Grants to organisations £368,300
Assets £585,300

TRUSTEES Nikos Stathopoulos; Cedric Dubourdieu; Francesco Loredan; Laurian Douin; Matthew Evans.

OTHER INFORMATION This is the foundation of the private equity firm BC Partners.

HOW TO APPLY The foundation does not accept unsolicited applications. Charities are nominated by BC Partners employees or trustees of the foundation.

CONTACT DETAILS The Trustees, BC Partners LLP, 40 Portman Square, London W1H 6DA *Tel.* 020 7009 4800 *Website* www.bcpartners.com/about/foundation

■ Bear Mordechai Ltd

CC NO 286806   **ESTABLISHED** 1982

WHERE FUNDING CAN BE GIVEN UK.

WHO CAN BENEFIT Registered charities.

WHAT IS FUNDED Projects and organisations benefitting Jewish people.

RANGE OF GRANTS Up to £50,000.

SAMPLE GRANTS Yad Yemin (£32,800); Tzedaka Bchol Eis (£13,800); Almat Ltd (£6,500); Forty Ltd (£1,000); Amud Hatzdokoh Trust (£360).

FINANCES *Financial year end* 31/03/2022
Income £201,900
Grants to organisations £100,100
Assets £396,100

TRUSTEES Eliezer Benedikt; Yechiel Benedikt; Chaim Benedikt.

OTHER INFORMATION Only beneficiaries of grants of £1,000 and over were listed in the 2019/20 accounts (13 organisations). Small grants of less than £1,000 totalled £1,100.

HOW TO APPLY Apply in writing to the correspondent.

CONTACT DETAILS The Trustees, 29 Fountayne Road, London N16 7EA *Tel.* 0161 792 9461 *Email* dp.whiteside@gmail.com

■ The James Beattie Charitable Trust

CC NO 265654   **ESTABLISHED** 1972

WHERE FUNDING CAN BE GIVEN Wolverhampton.

WHO CAN BENEFIT Local projects and organisations, hospitals, churches, schools, clubs (including Scout and Guide groups) and support services benefitting the people of Wolverhampton.

WHAT IS FUNDED General charitable purposes, particularly children and young people and community benefit.

WHAT IS NOT FUNDED Individuals. The trust is unlikely to donate to national charities, even those that offer ringfencing for Wolverhampton.

TYPE OF GRANT Capital costs; project funding; revenue costs; one-off or recurring grants.

RANGE OF GRANTS £100 to £25,000.

SAMPLE GRANTS A list of beneficiaries was not included in the annual report and accounts. Previous beneficiaries have included: Bilbrook Initiatives Hub; Canal and River Trust; Edward's Trust; Hands On Wednesfield; Listening Books; Oasis Soup Kitchen; The Haven Wolverhampton; Theodora Children's Charity; West Midlands CARE Team; Wolverhampton Mencap.

FINANCES *Financial year end* 05/04/2022
Income £86,700
Grants to organisations £132,400
Assets £4,530,000

TRUSTEES Kenneth Dolman; Susannah Norbury; Jane Redshaw; Michael Redshaw; Michael Boyce.

OTHER INFORMATION In total, 54 grants were awarded in 2021/22.

HOW TO APPLY Apply in writing to the correspondent, including a recent set of accounts, contact details, the grant size required and information about what the funding will be used for. Eligible applications are considered by the trustees once per month.

CONTACT DETAILS The Trustees, PO Box 12, Bridgnorth, Shropshire WV15 5LQ *Tel.* 0121 551 6021 *Website* https://jamesbeattietrust.org.uk

■ Beauland Ltd

CC NO 511374   **ESTABLISHED** 1981

WHERE FUNDING CAN BE GIVEN Worldwide, with some preference for the Manchester area.

WHO CAN BENEFIT Registered charities; Jewish educational and religious institutions.

WHAT IS FUNDED Advancement of the Orthodox Jewish faith and Jewish religious education; social welfare.

RANGE OF GRANTS Up to £95,000.

SAMPLE GRANTS Pesach Project (£95,000); Kehal Charedim Trust (£90,000); CMZ (£85,000); Ner

Foundation (£31,000); Beis Aharon Trust (£10,000); Keren Charity (£2,000).
FINANCES *Financial year end* 05/04/2022
Income £1,090,000
Grants to organisations £714,600
Assets £15,020,000
TRUSTEES Henry Neumann; Pinchas Neumann; Maurice Neumann; Mr Neumann; Esther Henry; Janet Bleier; Miriam Friedlander; Rebecca Delange; Hannah Roseman.
HOW TO APPLY Contact the correspondent for further information.
CONTACT DETAILS Maurice Neumann, Trustee, 32 Stanley Road, Salford M7 4ES *Tel.* 0161 720 6188

■ The Beaverbrook Foundation

CC NO 1153470   **ESTABLISHED** 1954
WHERE FUNDING CAN BE GIVEN England.
WHO CAN BENEFIT Registered charities.
WHAT IS FUNDED General charitable purposes with a focus on: the improvement of church buildings; the purchase of books, papers, manuscripts or works of art; care of older people and people with illnesses; arts, culture and heritage.
WHAT IS NOT FUNDED Retrospective costs.
TYPE OF GRANT Capital costs; revenue and running costs; project funding; collections and acquisitions.
RANGE OF GRANTS Up to £40,000.
SAMPLE GRANTS London Screen Academy (£40,000); Place2Be (£25,000); English National Ballet (£20,000); Bristol Music Trust (£16,000); T21 (£12,000); Cardinal Hume Centre (£10,000); World Horse Welfare (£5,000); BASMOM (£500).
FINANCES *Financial year end* 30/09/2021
Income £76,200
Grants to organisations £291,900
Assets £15,190,000
TRUSTEES Lord Beaverbrook; Lady Beaverbrook; John Kidd; Max Aitken; The Hon. Laura Levi; Rory Aitken; The Hon. Charlotte Aitken.
OTHER INFORMATION Grants of less than £5,000 totalled £104,200 and were not listed in the foundation's accounts. The 2020/21 accounts were the latest available at the time of writing (June 2023).
HOW TO APPLY Applications can be made via the foundation's website.
CONTACT DETAILS Jane Ford, Secretary, 19 Crown Passage, London SW1Y 6PP *Tel.* 020 3325 3987 *Email* jane@beaverbrookfoundation.org *Website* www.beaverbrookfoundation.org

■ The Beaverbrooks Charitable Trust

CC NO 1142857   **ESTABLISHED** 2011
WHERE FUNDING CAN BE GIVEN UK and Israel.
WHO CAN BENEFIT Charitable organisations.
WHAT IS FUNDED General charitable purposes including: education, welfare, health, mentoring and self-development.
RANGE OF GRANTS Typically up to £50,000.
SAMPLE GRANTS The Fed (£300,000); Prevent Breast Cancer (£50,000); North West Air Ambulance Charity (£36,000); Jewish Leadership Council (£30,000); Jewish Futures Trust (£20,000); Jewish Learning Exchange (£15,000); King David Schools (£10,000); Langdon (£5,000).

FINANCES *Financial year end* 30/04/2022
Income £443,500
Grants to organisations £1,480,000
Assets £6,300,000
TRUSTEES Mark Adlestone; Anna Blackburn; Susie Nicholas; Paul Holly.
OTHER INFORMATION Only grants of £5,000 or more were listed in the trust's annual report and accounts. Unlisted grants of less than £5,000 totalled £252,300.
HOW TO APPLY Apply in writing to the correspondent.
CONTACT DETAILS The Trustees, Adele House, Park Road, St Annes-on-Sea, Lancashire FY8 1RE *Tel.* 01253 721262 *Email* Charitable.Trust@ beaverbrooks.co.uk *Website* www.beaverbrooks. co.uk/100/enriching-lives

■ Beccles Townlands Charity

CC NO 210714   **ESTABLISHED** 1544
WHERE FUNDING CAN BE GIVEN Beccles.
WHO CAN BENEFIT Organisations and individuals.
WHAT IS FUNDED General charitable purposes, including social welfare, sport and education.
WHAT IS NOT FUNDED Applications that do not benefit Beccles and its inhabitants. Requests from national/regional organisations will only be considered if the sum requested will be used for the benefit of Beccles residents.
TYPE OF GRANT Project and capital costs.
SAMPLE GRANTS Bungay Area Community Transport (£30,000); St Luke's Church (£12,000); Beccles Royales Gymnastics Club (£10,000); Beccles Volunteer Centre (£3,000).
FINANCES *Financial year end* 31/10/2021
Income £153,000
Grants to organisations £79,200
Assets £6,890,000
TRUSTEES Gillian Campbell; Keith Gregory; James Hartley; Kenneth Leggett; Jennifer Langeskov; Robert Seppings; Fay Baldry; Mark Jermey; Dr Timothy Morton; James Cook; Neil Hickman.
OTHER INFORMATION The 2020/21 accounts were the latest available at the time of writing (June 2023). No grants were made to individuals during the year.
HOW TO APPLY Applications can be made via the charity's website.
CONTACT DETAILS The Secretary, Leman House, Ballygate, Beccles, Suffolk NR34 9ND *Tel.* 07584 322845 *Website* http:// becclestownlandscharity.org.uk

■ Becht Foundation

CC NO 1116657   **ESTABLISHED** 2006
WHERE FUNDING CAN BE GIVEN Worldwide.
WHO CAN BENEFIT Charitable organisations.
WHAT IS FUNDED Biodiversity and the environment, with a focus on marine conservation.
WHAT IS NOT FUNDED Individuals; scholarships or tuition assistance for undergraduate or postgraduate students.
TYPE OF GRANT Project funding.
SAMPLE GRANTS Save the Children (£1.66 million); Blue Ventures Conservation (£809,700); Client Earth (£450,200); Elemental Water Foundation (£254,600); Oceans North Conservation (£202,400); Irish Environmental Network and Mangrove Action Project (£81,000 each); High Seas Alliance (£40,500); Oxford Hospitals (£5,700); Tiny Lives (£2,700).
FINANCES *Financial year end* 31/12/2021
Income £3,150,000
Grants to organisations £7,140,000
Assets £434,200,000

TRUSTEES Lambertus Becht; Ann Becht; David Poulter; R&H Trust Co. (UK) Ltd.

OTHER INFORMATION The financial figures were converted from USD to pounds using the exchange rate at the time of writing (May 2023). During the year, grants were awarded to 28 organisations.

HOW TO APPLY An online application form is available on the foundation's website. The trustees only reply to successful applicants.

CONTACT DETAILS The Trustees, c/o Rawlinson and Hunter, 6 New Street Square, London EC4A 3AQ *Tel.* 020 7842 2000 *Email* thebfct@rawlinson-hunter.com *Website* https://bfct.org

....

■ The Bedfordshire and Hertfordshire Historic Churches Trust

CC NO 1005697   ESTABLISHED 1991

WHERE FUNDING CAN BE GIVEN Bedfordshire, Hertfordshire and the part of Barnet which falls within the Diocese of St Albans.

WHO CAN BENEFIT Places of active Christian worship.

WHAT IS FUNDED The restoration, maintenance, preservation, repair and reconstruction of churches and chapels.

WHAT IS NOT FUNDED Individuals.

TYPE OF GRANT Capital costs.

RANGE OF GRANTS Typically £1,000 to £5,000.

SAMPLE GRANTS St Mary the Virgin – Clophill (£13,000); All Saints – Houghton Conquest (£10,000); All Saints – Bedford (£8,000); St Peter – Harrold (£1,500).

FINANCES *Financial year end 31/03/2022*
Income £247,500
Grants to organisations £155,500
Assets £469,000

TRUSTEES Richard Genochio; Dr Christopher Green; William Marsterson; Stuart Russell; Jim May; Madeline Russell; Judith Howard; The Revd Malcolm Grant; The Revd Thomas Sander; Theresa Britt; The Revd Paul Hughes; Sir Timothy Clifford; Trevor Groom.

OTHER INFORMATION The trust also acts as a distributive agent for church grants made by the Wixamtree Trust, Bedfordshire.

HOW TO APPLY Initial enquiries should be made to the Grants Secretary.

CONTACT DETAILS Archie Russell, Grants Secretary, Wychbrook, 31 Ivel Gardens, Biggleswade, Bedfordshire SG18 0AN *Tel.* 01767 312966 *Email* grants@bedshertshct.org.uk *Website* www.bedshertshct.org.uk

....

■ Bedfordshire and Luton Community Foundation

CC NO 1086516   ESTABLISHED 2001

WHERE FUNDING CAN BE GIVEN The county of Bedfordshire and the borough of Luton.

WHO CAN BENEFIT Registered charities or other not-for-profit organisations (community groups/PTAs/sports groups, etc.). CICs and social enterprises should contact the foundation or review the specific guidance document on the community foundation's website.

WHAT IS FUNDED General charitable purposes; community welfare.

WHAT IS NOT FUNDED Criteria for each of the foundation's grant programmes are available on the website, as well as a list of general exclusions.

TYPE OF GRANT Programme dependent.

RANGE OF GRANTS Mostly under £10,000, with the average grant being £5,000.

SAMPLE GRANTS Luton Access (£475,800); Autism Bedfordshire (£281,100); Keech Hospice Care (£30,000); Signposts (£3,500); Cruse Bereavement Care (£950).

FINANCES *Financial year end 31/03/2022*
Income £5,870,000
Grants to organisations £2,930,000
Assets £3,870,000

TRUSTEES Vivianne Vayssieres; Dr Joan Bailey; Grafton Barbour; Rory Herbert; Bina Briggs; Judith Barker; Attiq Malik; Thanbirul Haque; Susan Hughes.

OTHER INFORMATION This is one of the 47 UK community foundations, which distribute funding for a wide range of purposes. As with all community foundations, there are a number of donor-advised funds managed on behalf of individuals, families and charitable trusts. Grant schemes tend to change frequently – consult the foundation's website for details of current programmes and up-to-date deadlines.

HOW TO APPLY Application forms for the various funds are available on the foundation's website. If you wish to apply for more than one fund at the same time, you should first contact the foundation. The panel meets around five times a year.

CONTACT DETAILS Grants Administrator, Room 130, Enterprise House, Wrest Park, Silsoe, Bedfordshire MK45 4HS *Tel.* 01525 306690 *Email* administrator@blcf.org.uk *Website* www.blcf.org.uk

....

■ Bedfordshire Charitable Trust Ltd

CC NO 234329   ESTABLISHED 1964

WHERE FUNDING CAN BE GIVEN Mainly local charities in Bedford and overseas.

WHO CAN BENEFIT Charitable organisations.

WHAT IS FUNDED General charitable purposes, especially health and social welfare for older people and children.

RANGE OF GRANTS Up to £50,000.

SAMPLE GRANTS Chellington Centre (£50,000); Bedford Daycare Hospice (£43,300); School Readers (£33,000); Impakt Housing and Support (£10,000); BRASS (£5,000); Goldington Green Academy (£3,200); New Life, Keech Hospice and Transitions UK (£2,500 each).

FINANCES *Financial year end 31/03/2022*
Income £283,900
Grants to organisations £202,000
Assets £16,230,000

TRUSTEES Christopher Kilroy; Christina Beddoes; Margaret Ibbett; Mark Thompson; Peter Ibbett; Dr Vicki Ibbett.

OTHER INFORMATION Grants of less than £2,000 totalled £21,500 in 2021/22.

HOW TO APPLY Apply in writing to the correspondent.

CONTACT DETAILS Christina Beddoes, Trustee and Secretary, Ladyslaude Court, Bramley Way, Bedford MK41 7FX *Tel.* 01234 352840 *Email* secretary@bedsct.co.uk

....

■ The David and Ruth Behrend Fund

CC NO 261567   ESTABLISHED 1969

WHERE FUNDING CAN BE GIVEN UK, with a preference for Merseyside.

WHO CAN BENEFIT Registered charities.

WHAT IS FUNDED General charitable purposes. The charity only gives funding to charities known to the settlors.

RANGE OF GRANTS Up to £40,000 but mostly under £10,000.

SAMPLE GRANTS St Elizabeth's PCC (£40,000); LCVS Everyday Changes Fund (£7,200); Big Help Project, Porchfield Community Association and Women's Health Info and Support (£2,000 each); National Youth Advocacy Service, St Andrew's Community Network and West Everton Community Council (£1,000 each).

FINANCES *Financial year end* 31/03/2022
Income £112,400
Grants to organisations £101,900
Assets £1,870,000

TRUSTEES Michael Behrend; Andrew Behrend; Liverpool Charity and Voluntary Services.

HOW TO APPLY The charity's 2021/22 annual report and accounts state: 'Grants are only made to charities known to the settlor and unsolicited applications are therefore not considered.'

CONTACT DETAILS The Trustees, 151 Dale Street, Liverpool L2 2AH *Tel.* 0151 227 5177

■ The Bellahouston Bequest Fund

OSCR NO SC011781 **ESTABLISHED** 1888

WHERE FUNDING CAN BE GIVEN Glasgow and district, but not more than five miles beyond the Glasgow city boundary.

WHO CAN BENEFIT Churches; registered charities; universities and educational institutions; hospices.

WHAT IS FUNDED Education; Protestant evangelical churches and associated schools, halls and clergy; social welfare; health.

WHAT IS NOT FUNDED Organisations or churches which do not fall within the geographical remit of the fund.

TYPE OF GRANT Capital costs.

RANGE OF GRANTS Usually between £2,000 and £5,000.

SAMPLE GRANTS University of Glasgow (£6,000); Positive Action in Housing Ltd. (£5,000); Carnwadric Project (£4,000); Glasgow Street Pastors (£3,000); Maryhill Parish Church and Flourish House (£2,000 each).

FINANCES *Financial year end* 30/06/2022
Income £158,100
Grants to organisations £164,700
Assets £5,480,000

OTHER INFORMATION The fund awarded 38 grants to organisations during the year.

HOW TO APPLY Apply in writing to the correspondent. The trustees meet on a regular basis.

CONTACT DETAILS The Trustees, c/o Mitchells Roberton Solicitors, George House, 36 North Hanover Street, Glasgow G1 2AD *Tel.* 0141 552 3422 *Email* emb@mitchells-roberton.co.uk

---

■ Belljoe Tzedoko Ltd

CC NO 282726 **ESTABLISHED** 1981

WHERE FUNDING CAN BE GIVEN England and Wales.

WHO CAN BENEFIT Registered charities.

WHAT IS FUNDED Advancement of the Orthodox Jewish faith; relief of poverty.

RANGE OF GRANTS Up to £30,000.

SAMPLE GRANTS Viznitz Ltd (£36,000); Hatzola (£30,000); Jewish Learning Exchange (£20,000); Ohr Someach (£15,000); Steps Ahead (£12,000); Teshuvoh Tefilloh Tzedokoh (£10,000).

FINANCES *Financial year end* 31/12/2021
Income £662,400
Grants to organisations £519,900
Assets £8,820,000

TRUSTEES Karen Lobenstein; Morris Lobenstein; Benjamin Lobenstein.

OTHER INFORMATION During the year, grants of less than £10,000 totalled £307,900.

HOW TO APPLY Contact the correspondent for further information.

CONTACT DETAILS The Trustees, 92 Fairholt Road, London N16 5NH *Tel.* 020 8455 6789

■ The Lord Belstead Charitable Settlement

CC NO 1053321 **ESTABLISHED** 1996

WHERE FUNDING CAN BE GIVEN Norfolk and Suffolk.

WHO CAN BENEFIT Registered charities.

WHAT IS FUNDED General charitable purposes.

TYPE OF GRANT Mostly capital projects.

RANGE OF GRANTS Up to £250,000 but mostly £1,000 to £5,000.

SAMPLE GRANTS East Anglia's Children's Hospices (£250,000); Ipswich School (£50,000); University of Suffolk (£5,000); Hadleigh Foodbank (£2,000); Suffolk Owl Sanctuary (£500).

FINANCES *Financial year end* 05/04/2022
Income £327,500
Grants to organisations £839,000
Assets £13,290,000

TRUSTEES Louise Long; John Pickering; Hon. Charles Boscawen.

OTHER INFORMATION Grants were made to 115 organisations during the year.

HOW TO APPLY Apply in writing to the correspondent.

CONTACT DETAILS Bill White, c/o Birketts LLP, Providence House, 141–145 Princes Street, Ipswich IP1 1QJ *Email* bill-white@birketts.co.uk

---

■ Benefact Trust Ltd

CC NO 263960 **ESTABLISHED** 1972

WHERE FUNDING CAN BE GIVEN UK and Ireland.

WHO CAN BENEFIT Registered charities; schools; hospitals; hospices; religious bodies/organisations.

WHAT IS FUNDED The repair, restoration and protection of Churches and Christian places of worship; social issues such as homelessness, poverty, climate change and cultural cohesion; promoting the Christian faith.

WHAT IS NOT FUNDED Overseas projects or charities; running costs (i.e. salaries and overheads), except when assisting the launch of new or transformative projects; charities with a political association; individuals or causes that will benefit only one person (e.g. student grants and scholarships); healthcare projects, although hospices can apply for funding towards the provision of chapel and chaplaincy space; animal welfare or rescue; work that is primarily the responsibility of statutory authorities including residential, respite, day care and housing provision; retrospective grants, although the trust may consider applications for work already done which was urgent (e.g. essential emergency roof repairs) or for major capital projects (where work has started before all funding has been raised); more than one application from the same organisation within a 24-month period; one-off events that benefit only a few people.

TYPE OF GRANT Capital costs; project funding.

RANGE OF GRANTS Mostly £1,000 to £15,000 but larger grants are considered.

SAMPLE GRANTS Methodist Connexion (£1.4 million); The Diocese of London (£385,000); The Diocese of Leeds (£285,000); The Cinnamon Network (£201,000); Betel UK – Birmingham (£120,000); Just Finance Foundation and The Keswick Convention Trust (£100,000 each).

FINANCES *Financial year end 31/12/2021*
Income £28,660,000
Grants to organisations £19,330,000
Assets £542,440,000

TRUSTEES Timothy Carroll; Stephen Hudson; Caroline Banszky; The Ven. Karen Lund; The Very Revd Jane Hedges; Chris Moulder; The Revd Paul Davis; Sir Stephen Lamport; David Smart; David Paterson.

OTHER INFORMATION The trust's income is derived from its wholly owned subsidiary company Ecclesiastical Insurance Office plc.

HOW TO APPLY Applications should be submitted online via the trust's website. Applications can be submitted at any time.

CONTACT DETAILS Iain Hearn, Correspondent, Benefact House, 2000 Pioneer Avenue, Gloucester Business Park, Brockworth, Gloucestershire GL3 4AW *Tel.* 01452 873189 *Email* info@benefacttrust.co.uk *Website* https://benefacttrust.co.uk

■ Benesco Charity Ltd

CC NO 269181   **ESTABLISHED** 1970
WHERE FUNDING CAN BE GIVEN UK and Israel.
WHO CAN BENEFIT Registered charities; hospitals; schools.
WHAT IS FUNDED Medical causes; education; welfare; causes benefitting the Jewish community.
WHAT IS NOT FUNDED Individuals.
TYPE OF GRANT General funding; development funding; capital costs; project funding.
RANGE OF GRANTS Mostly up to £50,000, with the occasional larger grant.
SAMPLE GRANTS The Charles Wolfson Charitable Trust (£23.4 million) and Broughton Jewish Opportunity Fund (£90,000).
FINANCES *Financial year end 05/04/2022*
Income £8,000,000
Grants to organisations £23,600,000
Assets £187,680,000
TRUSTEES Jonathan Ragol-Levy; Hon. Andrew Wolfson; David Wolfson; Mikael Breuer-Weil.
OTHER INFORMATION Each year, the charity makes a significant donation to The Charles Wolfson Charitable Trust. In 2021/22, the grant to The Charles Wolfson Charitable Trust represented 99% of the charity's grant total. A further £197,000 was distributed to other organisations, as follows: social welfare (£191,900); medicine (£5,000). No grants were awarded towards education during this period.
HOW TO APPLY Apply in writing to the correspondent.
CONTACT DETAILS The Trustees, c/o Benesco Charity Ltd, 8–10 Hallam Street, London W1W 6NS *Tel.* 020 7079 2506

■ The Benham Charitable Settlement

CC NO 239371   **ESTABLISHED** 1965
WHERE FUNDING CAN BE GIVEN UK, with a special emphasis on Northamptonshire, and overseas.
WHO CAN BENEFIT Registered charities; churches; schools.

WHAT IS FUNDED General charitable purposes; medical charities; Christian mission; disability; overseas aid; older people; children, schools and young people; conservation; art and sport; animal welfare.

WHAT IS NOT FUNDED Individuals.

RANGE OF GRANTS Typically £1,000 to £2,000.

SAMPLE GRANTS Northampton Association of Youth Clubs (£45,000); The Filling Station Trust (£10,000); Sunningdale Hope Trust (£3,000); Katharine House Hospice, SportsAble and Voluntary Impact Northamptonshire (£2,000 each); Action on Poverty, Church Homeless Trust, Huntington's Disease Association and Samaritans (£1,000 each).

FINANCES *Financial year end 05/04/2022*
Income £304,900
Grants to organisations £204,500
Assets £9,600,000

TRUSTEES Lady Rosalind Hutton; The Revd J. A. Nickols; Mrs M. M. Tittle; Sarah Elsom.

OTHER INFORMATION In 2021/22, the charity made 70 grants to organisations. Grants were broken down as follows: medical charities (£36,000); disability (£26,000); good causes (general) (£24,500); young people (£19,000); vulnerable older people (£18,000); overseas aid (£15,000); churches (£2,000); wildlife/conservation (£2,000); arts and sports (£1,000).

HOW TO APPLY Apply in writing to the correspondent.

CONTACT DETAILS The Trustees, Norfolk Cottage, 1 Virginia Drive, Virginia Water, Surrey GU25 4RX *Tel.* 020 7631 4754

■ Bennett Lowell Ltd

CC NO 1149726   **ESTABLISHED** 2012
WHERE FUNDING CAN BE GIVEN UK and USA.
WHO CAN BENEFIT Registered charities; museums, theatres and arts organisations; US tax-exempt organisations working in the UK.
WHAT IS FUNDED General charitable purposes, with a particular focus on arts institutions.
WHAT IS NOT FUNDED Individuals.
RANGE OF GRANTS Mostly up to £35,000, with some larger grants.
SAMPLE GRANTS Previous beneficiaries have included: Ark Franklin Primary School; The British Museum; The Brunel Museum; The Israel Philharmonic Orchestra; London Library; The Old Royal Naval College; The Royal Horticultural Society; Selwyn College; The Swan Sanctuary; Yorkshire Ballet Summer School.
FINANCES *Financial year end 31/12/2021*
Income £310
Grants to organisations £65,000
TRUSTEES John Attree; David Borthwick; William Borthwick; Molly Borthwick.
OTHER INFORMATION The charity's annual report and accounts were not available to view on the Charity Commission's website due to its low income. We have therefore estimated the grant total based on the charity's total expenditure.
HOW TO APPLY Apply in writing to the correspondent.
CONTACT DETAILS The Trustees, c/o Charles Russell Speechlys LLP, 5 Fleet Place, London EC4M 7RD *Tel.* 020 7203 5000 *Email* information@crsblaw.com

The Rowan Bentall Charitable Trust

cc no 273818   **established** 1972
where funding can be given Southern England.
who can benefit Registered charities; churches; CICs.
what is funded Health and well-being; churches (repair, maintenance and improvement); children and young people; older people; people with disabilities; education; the environment; animal welfare; relief for natural disasters.
range of grants Mostly £250 to £1,000.
sample grants Kingston and District Sea Cadet Corps (£3,000); Rotary Club of Kingston upon Thames (£1,000); Greyhound Trust (£500); Chobham Cricket Club (£190).
finances *Financial year end* 05/04/2022
Income £58,100
Grants to organisations £56,700
Assets £3,220,000
trustees L. Edward Bentall; Kate Bentall; Alastair Bentall; Sarah Thompson; Sarah Haines; Holly Hunter; Abigail Shaw.
other information The trust also supports any former Bentall's employee (including employees of any subsidiary or associated company) and their widows, widowers, children and dependents. Grants were awarded to 121 charitable organisations during the year. They were broken down as follows: the relief of people in need (£21,900); the advancement of education (£15,200); the advancement of health or saving of lives (£12,300); other purposes (£2,300); the advancement of animal welfare (£2,100); the advancement of the environment (£1,800); local churches (£1,300).
how to apply Contact the correspondent for further information.
contact details The Trustees, PO Box 109, Haslemere, Surrey GU27 9GW *Tel.* 01223 259043 *Email* rowanbentallcharitabletrust@hotmail.co.uk

The Berkeley Foundation

cc no 1152596   **established** 2013
where funding can be given Berkshire; Birmingham; Buckinghamshire; Greater London; Hampshire; Hertfordshire; Kent; Oxfordshire; Surrey; Warwickshire; West Sussex.
who can benefit Registered charities; CICs.
what is funded Supporting young people and their communities in the following areas: housing and homelessness; education, training and employment; health and well-being.
what is not funded Individuals.
type of grant Project funding; core/revenue costs; development funding; capacity building.
sample grants The Lord's Taverners (£1.04 million); Association of British Neurologists (£210,000); The Change Foundation (£135,100).
finances *Financial year end* 30/04/2022
Income £2,630,000
Grants to organisations £2,160,000
Assets £1,850,000
trustees Robert Perrins; Wendy Pritchard; Alison Dowsett.
other information The fund makes grants to its strategic partners and designated charities. It also invites applications to its Community Investment Fund, which makes smaller grants to innovative programmes in line with its key areas: housing, education, employment, health and well-being. Only beneficiaries of grants of over £50,000 were included in the accounts.

how to apply Applications are typically made online through the foundation's website. The foundation welcomes Expressions of Interest at any time during the year.
contact details The Trustees, Berkeley House, 19 Portsmouth Road, Cobham, Surrey KT11 1JG *Tel.* 01932 584551 *Email* info@berkeleyfoundation.org.uk *Website* www.berkeleyfoundation.org.uk

Ruth Berkowitz Charitable Trust

cc no 1111673   **established** 2005
where funding can be given UK and Israel.
who can benefit Mainly Jewish charitable organisations.
what is funded General charitable purposes; welfare, education and security needs in the Jewish community; research by major UK cancer charities. Grants are usually distributed between the following categories: medical causes; children, young people and education; community.
range of grants £5,000 to £50,000.
sample grants Previous beneficiaries have included: University Jewish Chaplaincy (£50,000); World Jewish Relief (£45,000); Community Security Trust (£40,000); London School of Jewish Studies (£30,000); Marie Curie Cancer Care (£15,000); Aleh Charitable Foundation and Camp Simcha (£10,000 each); British Friends of United Hatzalah Israel and The Z.S.V. Trust (£7,500); Jewish Deaf Association and Rimon Jewish Primary School (£5,000 each).
finances *Financial year end* 05/04/2022
Income £5,700
Grants to organisations £418,300
trustees Brian Beckman; Philip Goodman.
other information Full accounts were not available to view on the Charity Commission's website due to the trust's low income. We have therefore estimated the grant total based on the trust's total expenditure.
how to apply Our previous research suggests that the trustees generally only support charities known to them and do not usually respond to unsolicited applications.
contact details The Trustees, PO Box 864, Gillingham ME8 1FE *Tel.* 020 7408 8888 *Email* admin@ruthberkowitztrust.org

Berkshire Community Foundation

cc no 1155173   **established** 1985
where funding can be given Berkshire (the unitary authorities of Bracknell, Reading, Slough, Windsor and Maidenhead, West Berkshire and Wokingham).
who can benefit Registered charities; unregistered charities; CICs; social enterprises; schools; PTAs; amateur sports clubs; individuals.
what is funded General charitable purposes.
what is not funded Refer to the website for specific exclusions under each grants programme.
type of grant Capital costs; project funding; unrestricted funding.
sample grants A list of beneficiaries was not included in the annual report and accounts. Previous beneficiaries have included: Creativity in Sport; Destiny Support CIC; Home-Start Reading; Living Paintings Trust; Recovering in Mind; Slough Refugee Support.

FINANCES *Financial year end* 31/03/2022
Income £1,840,000
Grants to organisations £1,210,000
Assets £13,730,000

TRUSTEES Sean Taylor; Alexander Barfield; Debra Allcock Tyler; Stephen Howard; Margaret Haines; Susan Roberts; Darren Browne; Camilla Horwood; Jane Potter; Julie Elliott; Nicholas Burrows.

OTHER INFORMATION This is one of the 47 UK community foundations, which distribute funding for a wide range of purposes. As with all community foundations, there are a number of donor-advised funds managed on behalf of individuals, families and charitable trusts. Grant schemes tend to change frequently – consult the foundation's website for details of current programmes and up-to-date deadlines.

HOW TO APPLY Potential applicants are advised to visit the community foundation's website or contact its grants team to find the most suitable funding stream.

CONTACT DETAILS Grants Team, 100 Longwater Avenue, Green Park, Reading, Berkshire RG2 6GP *Tel.* 0118 930 3021 *Email* info@berkshirecf.org *Website* www.berkshirecf.org

■ The Bernicia Foundation

CC NO 1190094
WHERE FUNDING CAN BE GIVEN The North East.
WHO CAN BENEFIT Registered charities; constituted voluntary or community organisations; individuals.
WHAT IS FUNDED Initiatives that aim to increase social or economic inclusion; charitable causes including poverty, young people and social welfare.
WHAT IS NOT FUNDED Organisations with an annual income of over £750,000; organisations with unrestricted reserves that exceed six months' running costs; contributions to general appeals or circulars; religious/political activity, which is not for the wider public benefit; routine building or equipment repairs and maintenance; activities that have already taken place/retrospective funding; grant-making by other organisations/third-party funding; privately owned and profit-distributing companies or limited partnerships; projects and initiatives operating outside the North East; CICs and other non-charitable social enterprises, except in very specific circumstances (see the website for details).
TYPE OF GRANT Core costs; one-off grants.
RANGE OF GRANTS Grants for individuals: up to £1,000; grants for organisations: up to £10,000.
SAMPLE GRANTS Clean Slate Solutions and The Recruitment Junction (£10,000 each); Hextol Foundation (£5,000); Northumberland Badminton Association and Renaissance Arts (£1,000 each); Hartlepool Gymnastics Club (£660); Real Lives Real Choices (£600).
FINANCES *Financial year end* 31/03/2022
Income £300,000
Grants to organisations £190,900
Grants to individuals £1,600
Assets £73,000
TRUSTEES Avril Gibson; Carol Meredith; Beth Hazon; Claire-Jane Rewcastle.
OTHER INFORMATION Twenty-eight grants were awarded to organisations and three grants were awarded to individuals.
HOW TO APPLY Applications can be made via the foundation's website.

CONTACT DETAILS The Trustees, Oakwood Way, Ashwood Business Park, Ashington NE63 0XF *Tel.* 0344 800 3800 *Email* foundation@berniciafoundation.com *Website* https://berniciafoundation.com

■ The Bestway Foundation

CC NO 297178 **ESTABLISHED** 1987
WHERE FUNDING CAN BE GIVEN UK and overseas, particularly India, Pakistan, Bangladesh and Sri Lanka.
WHO CAN BENEFIT Registered charities; unregistered organisations; overseas charitable bodies; individuals; educational establishments.
WHAT IS FUNDED Education and training; social welfare; health; emergency relief.
TYPE OF GRANT The majority of grants are made on an annual basis.
RANGE OF GRANTS £500 to £100,000.
SAMPLE GRANTS Previous beneficiaries have included: Crimestoppers (£40,000); Queen Elizabeth's Foundation for Disabled People (£20,000); The Duke of Edinburgh's Award (£15,000); The Drink Trust (£1,000).
FINANCES *Financial year end* 30/06/2022
Income £21,800
Grants to organisations £290,000
TRUSTEES Lord Zameer Choudrey; Sir Anwar Pervez; Mohammed Younus Sheikh; Dawood Pervez; Rizwan Pervez; The Hon. Haider Choudrey.
OTHER INFORMATION Full accounts were not available to view on the Charity Commission's website due to the foundation's low income. We have therefore estimated the grant total based on the foundation's total expenditure.
HOW TO APPLY Apply in writing to the correspondent. The foundation has previously noted that telephone calls are not invited.
CONTACT DETAILS Mohammed Younus Sheikh, Secretary and Trustee, Bestway Foundation, 2 Abbey Road, London NW10 7BW *Tel.* 020 8453 1234 *Email* zulfikaur.wajid-hasan@bestway.co.uk *Website* www.bestwaygroup.co.uk/responsibility/bestway-foundation

■ Bideford Bridge Trust

CC NO 204536 **ESTABLISHED** 1973
WHERE FUNDING CAN BE GIVEN The parish of Bideford, Devon and the immediate neighbourhood.
WHO CAN BENEFIT Charitable organisations; individuals.
WHAT IS FUNDED General charitable purposes including: education; social welfare; health; amateur sports; business start-up schemes.
TYPE OF GRANT Core costs; running costs; unrestricted funding.
RANGE OF GRANTS £1,500 to £25,000.
SAMPLE GRANTS North Devon Hospice (£16,000); Appledore Maritime Heritage Trust (£12,500); Bideford Methodist Church (£10,000); Appledore Book Festival and Bideford Baptist Church (£5,000 each); Appledore Football Club (£3,000); 1st Woolsery Scouts (£2,700); Bideford and District Sea Cadets (£2,000); Buckland Brewer Methodist Church (£1,000).
FINANCES *Financial year end* 31/12/2021
Income £865,800
Grants to organisations £529,900
Grants to individuals £25,600
Assets £20,730,000
TRUSTEES Oliver Chope; Peter Christie; Eric Hubber; William Isaac; Elizabeth Junkison; Sally Ellis; Jamie McKenzie; Jude Gubb; Peter Sims; Sadie Green; Shirley Langford.

OTHER INFORMATION The 2021 accounts were the latest available to view at the time of writing (June 2023).

HOW TO APPLY Application forms for each grants programme are available to download on the funder's website. Completed forms should be returned by post.

CONTACT DETAILS The Steward, 23A The Quay, Bideford, Devon EX39 2EZ *Tel.* 01237 473184 *Email* info@bidefordbridgetrust.org.uk *Website* www.bidefordbridgetrust.org.uk

---

■ Biffa Award

ESTABLISHED 1997
WHERE FUNDING CAN BE GIVEN England and Northern Ireland. Projects should be located near a Biffa operation and any licensed landfill site; there is a postcode checker on the website.
WHO CAN BENEFIT Charitable organisations.
WHAT IS FUNDED Biodiversity; community buildings; recreation; cultural facilities.
WHAT IS NOT FUNDED Each theme has specific exclusions. Check the website for details.
TYPE OF GRANT Capital costs; project funding.
RANGE OF GRANTS Grants range from £10,000 to £75,000.
SAMPLE GRANTS Lincolnshire Wildlife Trust and The Woodland Trust (£750,000 each); Froglife Trust (£51,300); 306th Manchester Scouts (£39,900); Grant Dalby Playground Project (£24,700).
FINANCES *Financial year end* 31/03/2022 *Grants to organisations* £3,610,000
TRUSTEES Andrew Moffat; Patience Thody; Simon Rutledge; Jackie Doone; Mick Davis; Debbie Tann.
OTHER INFORMATION Full financial information was not available as the Biffa Award is not a registered charity. The grant total has been taken from the Biffa Award's Annual Review 2021–2022. Partnership grants were broken down as follows: natural environment (£1.5 million in two grants); built environment (£771,300 in two grants). Main grants were distributed as follows: community buildings (£699,500 in 21 grants); recreation (£509,900 in 12 grants); rebuilding biodiversity (£127,800 in four grants).
HOW TO APPLY Applications can be made through the Biffa Award website. Check the website for application deadlines.
CONTACT DETAILS The Grants Team, The Wildlife Trusts, The Kiln, Mather Road, Newark, Nottinghamshire NG24 1WT *Tel.* 01636 670000 *Email* biffa-award@wildlifetrusts.org *Website* www.biffa-award.org

---

■ The Bill Family Charitable Trust

CC NO 1187639   **ESTABLISHED** 2020
WHERE FUNDING CAN BE GIVEN England and Wales.
WHO CAN BENEFIT Registered.
WHAT IS FUNDED General charitable purposes.
TYPE OF GRANT Mostly one-off; occasionally, three-year grants are considered.
SAMPLE GRANTS A list of beneficiaries was not available.
FINANCES *Financial year end* 31/10/2022 *Income* £17,200 *Grants to organisations* £75,600
TRUSTEES Christine Brown; Berenice Morris.
OTHER INFORMATION Full accounts were not available to view on the Charity Commission's website due to the trust's low income. We have

therefore estimated the trust's grant total based on its total expenditure.
HOW TO APPLY Apply in writing to the correspondent.
CONTACT DETAILS The Trustees, Browns Solicitors, 51 Tweedy Road, Bromley, BR1 3NH *Tel.* 020 8464 7432 *Email* info@brownsols.co.uk

---

■ The Billmeir Charitable Trust

CC NO 208561   **ESTABLISHED** 1956
WHERE FUNDING CAN BE GIVEN UK, with a preference for the Surrey area.
WHO CAN BENEFIT Charitable organisations.
WHAT IS FUNDED General charitable purposes; arts and culture; education; medical research and aid; religious activities; social welfare.
RANGE OF GRANTS Typically between £1,000 and £10,000.
SAMPLE GRANTS Marlborough College (£20,000); Reed's School, Cobham (£15,000); ABF The Soldiers' Charity (£10,000); Surrey Community Foundation (£5,000); Crohn's and Colitis UK (£2,000); Three Pillars Project (£1,000).
FINANCES *Financial year end* 05/04/2022 *Income* £208,300 *Grants to organisations* £187,700 *Assets* £7,730,000
TRUSTEES Suzanne Marriott; Jason Whitaker; Max Whitaker.
OTHER INFORMATION In 2020/21, the trust made grants to around 40 organisations. They were distributed as follows: education (£66,100); medical research/aid (£47,000); relief of people in need (£28,600); arts and culture (£24,800); other (£13,500); religious activities (£7,600).
HOW TO APPLY Unsolicited applications are not invited and are rarely successful. Many of the trust's grants are to organisations that it supports on a regular basis.
CONTACT DETAILS Martin Fernandopulle, BDO LLP, 55 Baker Street, London W1U 7EU *Tel.* 020 7486 5888 *Email* charity.correspondence@bdo.co.uk

---

■ The Percy Bilton Charity

CC NO 1094720   **ESTABLISHED** 1962
WHERE FUNDING CAN BE GIVEN UK.
WHO CAN BENEFIT Registered charities; unregistered charities; social enterprises; CICs; PTAs; hospitals; hospices; individuals.
WHAT IS FUNDED Disadvantaged/underprivileged young people (under 25 years of age); people with disabilities (physical or learning disabilities) or mental health problems; older people (aged over 60).
WHAT IS NOT FUNDED A full list of exclusions can be found on the charity's website.
TYPE OF GRANT Capital costs.
RANGE OF GRANTS Large grants: £2,000 to £5,000; small grants: up to £750.
SAMPLE GRANTS A list of beneficiaries was not included in the annual report and accounts.
FINANCES *Financial year end* 31/03/2022 *Income* £829,100 *Grants to organisations* £382,800 *Grants to individuals* £390,000 *Assets* £32,820,000
TRUSTEES Hayley Bilton; Kim Lansdown; James Lee; Charles Sosna; Benjamin Chance.
OTHER INFORMATION Grants are also made to individuals who have a physical or learning disability, enduring mental health problem or who are over 65 and are in financial hardship.

HOW TO APPLY Applications can be made online on the website and supporting documentation should be emailed or sent by post. Applicants should consult the charity's website for detailed guidance on how to make an application for each of the grant schemes.

CONTACT DETAILS The Trustees, Bilton House, 7 Culmington Road, Ealing, London W13 9NB *Tel.* 020 8579 2829 *Email* information@ percybiltoncharity.org *Website* www.percy-bilton-charity.org

■ The Bingham Trust

CC NO 287636   **ESTABLISHED** 1977

WHERE FUNDING CAN BE GIVEN Buxton and the surrounding SK17 postcode area.

WHO CAN BENEFIT Charitable organisations; individuals.

WHAT IS FUNDED General charitable purposes; social welfare; education; religious activity; community development.

WHAT IS NOT FUNDED Repayment of existing debts; businesses or profit-making organisations; higher education (university and college level); retrospective expenditure; revenue costs; organisations that have previously applied within the last 12 months; salaries; fitted carpets (only carpet squares).

TYPE OF GRANT One-off grants. The trustees prefer to fund capital projects rather than revenue expenses.

RANGE OF GRANTS The standard grant size is £1,000.

SAMPLE GRANTS A list of beneficiaries was not included in the annual report and accounts. Previous beneficiaries have included: Good News Family Care (£37,500); Warslow Village Hall (£5,000); High Peak Foodbank (£4,900); Step By Step (£4,000); Buxton Community School and High Peak CVS (£3,100 each); Samaritans and Volunteer Centre Buxton (£2,000 each); Buxton Well Dressing and Churches Together (£1,000 each); PDSA (£50).

FINANCES *Financial year end* 05/04/2022
Income £126,000
Grants to organisations £85,300
Assets £5,280,000

TRUSTEES Roger Horne; Alexandra Hurst; Helen Mirtle; Christine McMullen; Eric Butterley.

OTHER INFORMATION The grant total also includes the amount awarded in grants to individuals; a breakdown was not included in the annual report and accounts.

HOW TO APPLY Application forms can be downloaded from the trust's website and returned via email or post. All applications are acknowledged and are typically reviewed in January, April, July and October – closing dates for the next funding round can be found on the trust's website. Refer to the trust's guidelines and FAQs before applying.

CONTACT DETAILS The Trustees, Unit 1, Tongue Lane Industrial Estate, Dew Pond Lane, Buxton SK17 7LN *Tel.* 07966 738546 *Email* binghamtrust@aol.com *Website* www.binghamtrust.org.uk

■ Binks Trust

OSCR NO SC008849   **ESTABLISHED** 1973

WHERE FUNDING CAN BE GIVEN UK.

WHO CAN BENEFIT Registered, excepted or exempt charities; non-registered charities/voluntary groups; hospitals; hospices; universities; schools and colleges; places of worship.

WHAT IS FUNDED General charitable purposes with a preference for the arts, music, social welfare and education.

RANGE OF GRANTS Mostly up to £10,000, with the occasional larger grant.

SAMPLE GRANTS University of Oxford Development Trust (£1.01 million); Greyfriars Kirk Charteris (£865,000); EMMS International and New College – Oxford (£100,000 each); Edinburgh International Festival (£60,000); Cross Reach (£30,000); Centre for Young Musicians, The Book Whisperers and L'Arche (£10,000 each).

FINANCES *Financial year end* 05/04/2022
Income £5,940,000
Grants to organisations £2,630,000
Assets £14,560,000

OTHER INFORMATION Only organisations that received grants of over £8,000 were listed as beneficiaries in the trust's accounts. Grants of under £8,000 totalled £117,000.

HOW TO APPLY Apply in writing to the correspondent.

CONTACT DETAILS The Trustees, 61 Dublin Street, Edinburgh EH3 6NL

■ Birkdale Trust for Hearing Impaired Ltd

CC NO 1103074

WHERE FUNDING CAN BE GIVEN UK.

WHO CAN BENEFIT Charities; individuals.

WHAT IS FUNDED Children and young people (under the age of 25) with hearing impairments.

WHAT IS NOT FUNDED Retrospective expenditure.

TYPE OF GRANT Project costs; specialist equipment.

RANGE OF GRANTS Mostly under £10,000.

SAMPLE GRANTS Down Syndrome Training and Support Service (£10,800); Audenshaw Primary School (£5,000); Deaf Active (£4,000); The Galaxy Trust (£3,000); Toy Like Me (£2,000); Walthew House (£1,500); Swain House – Deaf Children's Fund (£750); St Cecilia's (£540).

FINANCES *Financial year end* 05/04/2022
Income £760,400
Grants to organisations £85,400
Grants to individuals £125,800
Assets £7,020,000

TRUSTEES Colin Pennington; Dr Imran Mulla; Christopher Bevan; Lucy Riding; Mrs H. Sills; Mrs S. Turner; Sandra Unsworth; Christine Watkinson; Barbara Pattison; Pauline Coventry; Mr D. Albert.

HOW TO APPLY Application forms are available to download from the charity's website. Completed application forms should be returned by post enclosing an sae for the trust's reply. The trustees meet six times per year to consider applications.

CONTACT DETAILS Karen Fleetwood, Administrator, 21 Gleneagles Drive, Ainsdale, Southport PR8 3PP *Tel.* 07736 539111 *Email* karen_ fleetwood@hotmail.com *Website* www.grantsforthedeaf.co.uk

■ The Birmingham Diocesan Board of Finance

CC NO 249403

WHERE FUNDING CAN BE GIVEN The Diocese of Birmingham.

WHO CAN BENEFIT National church organisations; church schools; individuals.

WHAT IS FUNDED Christianity; mission activities; church maintenance; community regeneration; education.

SAMPLE GRANTS A list of beneficiaries was not included in the annual report and accounts.

FINANCES *Financial year end* 31/12/2021
Income £11,690,000
Grants to organisations £683,000
Grants to individuals £360,000
Assets £47,740,000

TRUSTEES Julian Phillips; Deirdre Moll; Steven Skakel; The Revd Anne Hollinghurst; Trevor Lewis; The Revd Catherine Grylls; Matt Thompson; The Revd Rebecca Stephens; The Revd Bamidele Sotonwa; Jennifer Clark; Jonathan Goll; The Revd Jeremy Allcock; Guy Hordern; The Revd Geoffrey Lanham; Anesu Mayambi; Christine Price; The Revd Louise Shaw; Patricia Williams; The Revd Toby Crowe; The Revd Sarah Hayes; The Ven. Jennifer Tomlinson.

OTHER INFORMATION A total of 178 grants were made to organisations and individuals during the year.

HOW TO APPLY Apply in writing to the correspondent. The trustees meet regularly throughout the year.

CONTACT DETAILS Jan Smart, Diocesan Secretary, Citadel, 190 Corporation Street, Birmingham, West Midlands B4 6QD *Tel.* 0121 426 4000 *Email* diocesansecretary@cofebirmingham.com *Website* www.cofebirmingham.com

---

■ The Michael Bishop Foundation

CC NO 297627   **ESTABLISHED** 1987

WHERE FUNDING CAN BE GIVEN Worldwide.

WHO CAN BENEFIT Registered charities.

WHAT IS FUNDED General charitable purposes; arts, culture and heritage; human rights, social justice and equality; the advancement of health and medicine; education and training.

TYPE OF GRANT Project funding; capital costs; core/revenue costs; seed funding/start-up funding; strategic funding.

RANGE OF GRANTS Mostly up to £150,000, with the occasional larger grant.

SAMPLE GRANTS The English Heritage Trust (£1 million); International Bomber Command Centre and NSPCC (£250,000 each); ABF The Soldiers' Charity and Mill Hill (£50,000 each); Lord Lyon Society (£25,000); RNLI Brighton (£5,000); Royal Flying Doctor Service of Australia Friends in the UK (£150).

FINANCES *Financial year end* 05/04/2022
Income £2,130,000
Grants to organisations £3,010,000
Assets £45,400,000

TRUSTEES Grahame Elliott; Baron Glendonbrook of Bowdon; Timothy Bye; Martin Ritchie.

OTHER INFORMATION During the year, the foundation awarded grants to 26 organisations. Grants were broken down as follows: heritage (£1 million); education and training (£778,400); arts and culture (£645,000); human rights and social justice (£250,000); general charitable purposes (£232,500); the advancement of health and medicine (£100,500). Other focus areas may be considered from time to time. The foundation gives a grant to The Glendonbrook Foundation every year.

HOW TO APPLY Unsolicited applications are not accepted.

CONTACT DETAILS The Trustees, Staunton House, Staunton Harold, Ashby-de-la-Zouch, Leicestershire LE65 1RW *Tel.* 01530 564388 *Email* jo.furlong@btconnect.com

---

■ Maria Bjornson Memorial Fund

CC NO 1126096   **ESTABLISHED** 2008

WHERE FUNDING CAN BE GIVEN UK.

WHO CAN BENEFIT Registered charities; individuals.

WHAT IS FUNDED Medical and scientific research; the performing, visual and creative arts; social welfare for artists and people in the creative industries.

TYPE OF GRANT Project funding; core costs.

RANGE OF GRANTS Typically less than £20,000.

SAMPLE GRANTS Continuo Foundation (£150,000); Freelancers Make Theatre Work (£60,000); Concerts in the West (£45,000); Academy of Ancient Music (£18,000); Two Moors Festival (£10,000); Fertile Ground Dance Company (£8,000); Autism Bedfordshire (£5,000); Garage Art Group (£1,000).

FINANCES *Financial year end* 31/12/2021
Income £320,800
Grants to organisations £907,000
Grants to individuals £28,500
Assets £14,600,000

TRUSTEES Simon Weil; Sir Richard Eyre; Robert Crowley; Ida Levine.

OTHER INFORMATION Grants were made to 48 organisations and six individuals.

HOW TO APPLY Apply in writing to the correspondent.

CONTACT DETAILS The Trustees, c/o Charles Russell Speechlys LLP, 5 Fleet Place, London EC4M 7RD *Tel.* 020 7438 2101 *Website* www.mbmf.org.uk

---

■ The John Black Charitable Foundation

CC NO 1143431   **ESTABLISHED** 2011

WHERE FUNDING CAN BE GIVEN UK and Israel.

WHO CAN BENEFIT Universities; charitable organisations.

WHAT IS FUNDED Medical research (particularly Parkinson's disease and prostate cancer); general charitable purposes.

TYPE OF GRANT Capital costs; project funding.

RANGE OF GRANTS Up to £1.62 million.

SAMPLE GRANTS A list of beneficiaries was not included in the annual report and accounts.

FINANCES *Financial year end* 31/03/2022
Income £4,890,000
Grants to organisations £3,620,000
Assets £83,550,000

TRUSTEES Stephen Conway; David Taglight.

OTHER INFORMATION During the year, long-term grants were awarded to Oxford University and University College London for specific research into Parkinson's disease and prostate cancer. Grants were awarded for the following purposes: prostate cancer (£1.62 million); Parkinson's disease (£1.25 million); other charitable purposes (£744,600).

HOW TO APPLY Apply in writing to the correspondent.

CONTACT DETAILS The Trustees, 24 Old Burlington Street, London W1S 3AW *Tel.* 020 7734 0424

■ The Sydney Black Charitable Trust

CC NO 219855   **ESTABLISHED** 1949

WHERE FUNDING CAN BE GIVEN UK.

WHO CAN BENEFIT Registered charities; schools; amateur sports clubs; hospitals; hospices.

WHAT IS FUNDED Christianity; social welfare; older people; young people; education; prisoners' rights.

TYPE OF GRANT Unrestricted funding.

Think carefully about every application. Is it justified?

269

RANGE OF GRANTS £300 to £10,000.

SAMPLE GRANTS A list of beneficiaries was not included in the annual report and accounts.

FINANCES *Financial year end 05/04/2022*
Income £62,100
Grants to organisations £69,300
Assets £4,330,000

TRUSTEES Philip Crabtree; Stephen Crabtree; Hilary Dickenson.

OTHER INFORMATION Grants were made to 147 organisations in the following categories: education and children (£36,000); people who are older or in financial need (£13,800); prisoners (£10,000); religion (£9,500).

HOW TO APPLY Applications should be made in writing to the correspondent.

CONTACT DETAILS The Trustees, PO Box 1251, St Albans, Hertfordshire AL1 9JU *Tel.* 07814 009039

....

■ The Bertie Black Foundation

CC NO 245207   ESTABLISHED 1965
WHERE FUNDING CAN BE GIVEN UK and Israel.
WHO CAN BENEFIT Registered charities.
WHAT IS FUNDED General charitable purposes; social welfare; education; medical assistance; community; focus on Jewish causes and culture.
RANGE OF GRANTS Up to £15,000.
SAMPLE GRANTS Jewish Care (£15,000); JW3 Development (£10,000); Chai Cancer Care and UK Jewish Film (£7,500 each); GIFT and World Jewish Relief (£5,000 each).
FINANCES *Financial year end 05/04/2022*
Income £111,700
Grants to organisations £75,700
Assets £5,010,000
TRUSTEES Doris Black; Harry Black; Carolyn Black; Isabelle Seddon; Ivor Seddon.
OTHER INFORMATION Grants were broken down as follows: community (£37,700); health (£24,800); culture (£13,200). Only organisations that received grants of over £5,000 were listed as beneficiaries in the 2021/22 accounts. Grants of under £5,000 totalled £25,700.
HOW TO APPLY Unsolicited applications are not accepted.
CONTACT DETAILS The Trustees, Ground Floor, 4 Portsdown Mews, London NW11 7HD *Tel.* 020 3848 1360 *Email* harry@ yelvertonproperties.co.uk

....

■ The Isabel Blackman Foundation

CC NO 313577   ESTABLISHED 1966
WHERE FUNDING CAN BE GIVEN Hastings and St Leonards-on-Sea.
WHO CAN BENEFIT Charitable organisations; hospices; churches; schools; individuals.
WHAT IS FUNDED General charitable purposes including: health; social services; education; culture and recreation; youth clubs and organisations; religion; the environment.
WHAT IS NOT FUNDED Applications will only be considered from organisations based in Hastings and St Leonards district unless the applicant is able to satisfy the trustees that there is a direct or genuine connection with the people of Hastings and St Leonards-on-Sea.
RANGE OF GRANTS Up to £60,000 but generally from £500 to £5,000.
SAMPLE GRANTS Isabel Blackman Centre (£75,000); Hastings Area Community Trust (£15,000); Little Gate Farm (£5,000); Archive Resource Centre and Starlight Children's Foundation

(£2,000 each); Hearing Dogs for Deaf People (£1,500); Barbarians Swimmers, Dame Vera Lynn Children's Charity and FareShare Sussex (£1,000).

FINANCES *Financial year end 05/04/2022*
Income £297,700
Grants to organisations £219,800
Grants to individuals £14,300
Assets £9,640,000

TRUSTEES Patricia Connolly; Christine Deacon; Martin Holgate; David Harding; Michael Cornes.

OTHER INFORMATION Grants to organisations and individuals were broken down as follows: social services (£140,800); health (£55,800); education (£20,000); culture and recreation (£11,500); youth clubs (£3,000); the environment (£2,000); religion (£1,000).

HOW TO APPLY Apply in writing to the correspondent.

CONTACT DETAILS The Trustees, Stonehenge, 13 Laton Road, Hastings, East Sussex TN34 2ES *Tel.* 01424 431756 *Email* ibfoundation@uwclub.net

....

■ The Blagrave Trust

CC NO 1164021   ESTABLISHED 2015
WHERE FUNDING CAN BE GIVEN Berkshire; Hampshire; Isle of Wight; Sussex; Wiltshire.
WHO CAN BENEFIT Registered charities; social enterprises; voluntary groups; CICs; individuals.
WHAT IS FUNDED Disadvantaged young people (aged 12–25); young people's social change efforts; social justice.
WHAT IS NOT FUNDED Each funding programme has its own exclusion criteria – see the trust's website for more information.
TYPE OF GRANT Core/revenue costs; project funding; unrestricted funding.
RANGE OF GRANTS Typically under £30,000.
SAMPLE GRANTS No Limits (£117,300); Peace First (£40,000); Friends, Families and Travellers (£33,400 in two grants); Young Women's Trust (£30,400); Prison Reform Trust (£30,000); Gendered Intelligence (£23,000); ASD Family Support (£10,400); Homeless Link, Mandala Theatre Company and Our Streets Now (£400 each).
FINANCES *Financial year end 31/12/2021*
Income £2,870,000
Grants to organisations £2,300,000
Grants to individuals £52,000
Assets £44,560,000
TRUSTEES Clare Cannock; Segun Olowookere; Adaeze Aghaji; Boudicca Pepper; Victor Azubuike; Naomi Ambrose; Barbara Agwaziam; Edward Jacobs.
OTHER INFORMATION In 2021 the trust made grants totalling £2.3 million to 108 organisations.
HOW TO APPLY Applicants should complete the brief outline proposal form on the trust's website. Within a month, successful applicants will be invited to complete the next steps, including attending a (virtual) meeting and sharing business, planning and financial documentation. Applications for amounts over £20,000 are reviewed by trustees in January, April, June, September and November; applications for amounts under £2,000 are reviewed monthly.
CONTACT DETAILS Emine Arabaci, Team and Grants Assistant, c/o Cripplegate Foundation, 13 Elliott's Place, London N1 8HX *Email* grants@blagravetrust.org *Website* www. blagravetrust.org

■ The Blakebank Trust

CC NO 1189954 **ESTABLISHED** 2020

WHERE FUNDING CAN BE GIVEN England and Wales.

WHO CAN BENEFIT Registered charities; universities; church councils.

WHAT IS FUNDED General charitable purposes, with a focus on Christian causes and the relief of poverty.

SAMPLE GRANTS All Saints Church PCC Underbarrow with Helsington (£15,000); Safe Families and Hospice of St Mary Ulverston (£10,000 each); Southampton City Mission (£5,000).

FINANCES *Financial year end* 19/05/2022
Income £619,700
Grants to organisations £100,000
Assets £1,280,000

TRUSTEES Dr Hilary Crowe; Sarah de Mars; Elizabeth Kirsch; Dr Daniel Butler.

HOW TO APPLY Apply in writing to the correspondent. The trust's Charity Commission record states that it is open to applications.

CONTACT DETAILS The Trustees, Middle Blakebank, Underbarrow, Kendal, Cumbria LA8 8HP *Tel.* 07713 608963

■ Blakemore Foundation

CC NO 1015938 **ESTABLISHED** 1992

WHERE FUNDING CAN BE GIVEN England and Wales, excluding parts of the South West and northern England. There is a map on the foundation's website.

WHO CAN BENEFIT Local and national charitable organisations; community groups; sports clubs; schools; hospices and hospitals.

WHAT IS FUNDED General charitable purposes, including: sport and recreation; health; medical research; housing and homelessness; emergency services and the armed forces; the environment.

WHAT IS NOT FUNDED Salaries; national charities (unless directly linked to an A.F. Blakemore employee or local branch); grants for an individual; good causes that fall outside A.F. Blakemore's trading area; overseas appeals; expeditions or overseas travel; sponsorship and marketing promotions; endowment and hardship funds; political causes.

TYPE OF GRANT Capital costs; core costs.

RANGE OF GRANTS Up to £200.

SAMPLE GRANTS A list of beneficiaries was not included in the annual report and accounts.

FINANCES *Financial year end* 30/04/2022
Income £401,800
Grants to organisations £101,600
Assets £191,200

TRUSTEES Peter Blakemore; Ita McAuley.

OTHER INFORMATION Charities can also apply for in-kind support in the form of goods for local charity and community events.

HOW TO APPLY Applications can be made through the foundation's website.

CONTACT DETAILS Kate Senter, Community Affairs Officer, A. F. Blakemore and Son Ltd, Longacre, Willenhall, West Midlands WV13 2JP *Tel.* 0121 568 2910 *Email* Blakemore.Foundation@ afblakemore.co.uk *Website* www.afblakemore. com/blakemore-foundation/blakemore-foundation

■ Lady Blakenham's Charity Trust

CC NO 266198 **ESTABLISHED** 1973

WHERE FUNDING CAN BE GIVEN Worldwide.

WHO CAN BENEFIT Charitable organisations.

WHAT IS FUNDED General charitable purposes; disability; medical welfare and research; overseas.

RANGE OF GRANTS Mostly £3,000 each.

SAMPLE GRANTS Previous beneficiaries have included: 3H Fund; 4Sight Vision Support; Blind Veterans UK; Dodford Children's Holiday Farm; Maggie's Cancer Caring Centre; Marie Curie Cancer Care; The National Brain Appeal; Zane – Zimbabwe a National Emergency.

FINANCES *Financial year end* 05/04/2022
Income £12,800
Grants to organisations £56,000

TRUSTEES Hon. Mary-Anne Sergison-Brooke; Simon Cowell; Nicholas Brooke.

OTHER INFORMATION Full accounts were not available to view on the Charity Commission's website due to the charity's low income. The grant total has been estimated based on the charity's total expenditure.

HOW TO APPLY Apply in writing to the correspondent.

CONTACT DETAILS The Trustees, Chipping Warden Manor, Banbury, Oxfordshire OX17 1LB *Tel.* 01295 660227 *Email* Blakenham_Charity@ tmf-group.com

■ The Blandford Lake Trust

CC NO 1069630 **ESTABLISHED** 1998

WHERE FUNDING CAN BE GIVEN North Wales and overseas.

WHO CAN BENEFIT Registered charities.

WHAT IS FUNDED Overseas aid and development; Christian outreach work in North Wales.

TYPE OF GRANT Project funding; core/revenue costs; salaries.

RANGE OF GRANTS Typically £1,000 to £10,000.

SAMPLE GRANTS Christian Aid (£30,000); Peace Direct, Ripple Effect and VIVA (£10,000 each); Urban Saints (£2,000).

FINANCES *Financial year end* 31/12/2022
Income £70,000
Grants to organisations £83,000
Assets £1,200

TRUSTEES Mr J. R. Lake; Mrs L. E. Lake; Mr M. C. Lake; Mr R. M. Lake.

HOW TO APPLY Apply in writing to the correspondent.

CONTACT DETAILS The Trustees, The Courts, Park Street, Denbigh, Denbighshire LL16 3DE *Tel.* 01745 813174

■ The Sir Victor Blank Charitable Settlement

CC NO 1084187 **ESTABLISHED** 1979

WHERE FUNDING CAN BE GIVEN UK and overseas.

WHO CAN BENEFIT Jewish organisations; registered charities.

WHAT IS FUNDED Jewish causes; general charitable purposes.

RANGE OF GRANTS Up to £266,700.

SAMPLE GRANTS University of Oxford (£266,700); UJIA (£25,000); Wellbeing of Women (£13,000); Royal Papworth Hospital Charity (£11,600); Proms at St Jude's (£6,000); Noah's Ark Children's Hospice (£1,000).

FINANCES *Financial year end* 05/04/2022
Income £200,600
Grants to organisations £930,200
Assets £2,090,000

TRUSTEES Lady Sylvia Blank; Simon Blank; Sir Maurice Blank.

OTHER INFORMATION Grants of less than £1,000 totalled £2,500.

HOW TO APPLY Contact the correspondent for further information.

CONTACT DETAILS The Trustees, 2nd Floor, Regis House, 45 King William Street, London EC4R 9AN *Tel.* 020 7403 1877 *Email* enquiries@ sirvictorblankcharitablesettlement.com

■ Bloodwise

CC NO 216032/SC037529 **ESTABLISHED** 1960

WHERE FUNDING CAN BE GIVEN UK.

WHO CAN BENEFIT Universities; hospitals; research institutions.

WHAT IS FUNDED Research into blood cancers, including: laboratory-based research projects; training; career development awards; clinical trials.

TYPE OF GRANT Capital costs; core costs; project funding; strategic funding; research.

RANGE OF GRANTS Project grants of up to £280,000 are awarded, for up to three years for clearly defined research projects.

SAMPLE GRANTS The University of Cambridge (£749,000); Medical Research Council (£499,000) University of Southampton (£456,000); Francis Crick Institute (£379,000); Cardiff University (£203,000); Newcastle University (£159,000); Imperial College Healthcare NHS Trust (£75,000); King's College London (£66,000).

FINANCES *Financial year end* 31/03/2022 *Income* £13,270,000 *Grants to organisations* £5,090,000 *Assets* £12,980,000

TRUSTEES Steven Prescott-Jones; Julia Whittaker; Prof. Frances Balkwill; John Ormerod; Tim Gillbanks; Simon Guild; Gemma Peters; Amir Sethu; Jasmine Handford; Louise Lai; Prof. Christine Harrison; Juliet Hillier; Claude Littner; Alastair Boyle.

HOW TO APPLY Applications must be submitted via Grant Tracker. Further information on how to apply can be found on the charity's website.

CONTACT DETAILS Research Team, Blood Cancer UK, Suite 31 Bonnington Bond, 2 Anderson Place, Edinburgh EH6 5NP *Tel.* 020 7269 9018 *Email* research@bloodwise.org.uk *Website* https://bloodcancer.org.uk/research/funding/apply

■ Abraham Algy Bloom Foundation

CC NO 207071 **ESTABLISHED** 1958

WHERE FUNDING CAN BE GIVEN UK and Israel.

WHO CAN BENEFIT Charitable organisations; Jewish educational institutions; places of worship.

WHAT IS FUNDED Jewish causes including: religion; education; general charitable purposes.

WHAT IS NOT FUNDED Individuals.

SAMPLE GRANTS Previous beneficiaries have included: Manchester Talmudical College and Yeshivah Shaarei Torah.

FINANCES *Financial year end* 05/04/2022 *Income* £3,200 *Grants to organisations* £248,500

TRUSTEES Barrie Bloom; Joshua Bloom.

OTHER INFORMATION Full accounts were not available to view on the Charity Commission's website due to the charity's low income. We have therefore estimated the charity's grant total based on its total expenditure.

HOW TO APPLY Apply in writing to the correspondent.

CONTACT DETAILS The Trustees, Onward Buildings, 207 Deansgate, Manchester, M3 3NW *Tel.* 0161 834 0026

■ The Bloomfield Charitable Trust

CC NO 1145866 **ESTABLISHED** 2012

WHERE FUNDING CAN BE GIVEN UK.

WHO CAN BENEFIT Registered charities.

WHAT IS FUNDED General charitable purposes.

TYPE OF GRANT Project funding.

SAMPLE GRANTS The Raspberry Pi Foundation (£166,900 in two grants); The National Autistic Society (£166,800 in five grants); Action for Kids Charitable Trust (£87,500 in seven grants); School-Home Support (£86,100 in five grants); The Markfield Project (£15,500); Lancaster University (£1,200).

FINANCES *Financial year end* 06/02/2022 *Income* £581,800 *Grants to organisations* £556,000 *Assets* £6,050,000

TRUSTEES Martin Hellawell; Mandy Hellawell; Ludlow Trust Company Ltd.

OTHER INFORMATION The trust made grants to nine organisations.

HOW TO APPLY Apply in writing to the correspondent.

CONTACT DETAILS The Trustees, Ludlow Trust Company Ltd, Tower Wharf, Cheese Lane, Bristol BS2 0JJ *Tel.* 0117 313 8200 *Email* charitabletrusts@ludlowtrust.com

■ Bluespark Foundation

CC NO 1167172 **ESTABLISHED** 2016

WHERE FUNDING CAN BE GIVEN UK.

WHO CAN BENEFIT Charitable organisations; schools and education institutions; drama and music organisations; amateur sports clubs; youth organisations; individuals.

WHAT IS FUNDED Projects that support the education and development of children and young people. In previous years the following types of project have been supported: academic activities; drama; sport; outdoor activities; music, dance and singing; leadership and team building; educational excursions.

WHAT IS NOT FUNDED Projects for children or young people under the age of 5 or over the age of 22; life-skill mentoring services; counselling services; holiday clubs or playgroups; construction, maintenance or repair of buildings; training adults who work with children or young people; student fees or maintenance.

TYPE OF GRANT Project funding; capital costs.

RANGE OF GRANTS Up to £5,000 but typically under £2,000.

SAMPLE GRANTS The Centre School; Colchester Sea Cadet Corps; Court Moor School; Dorset Children's Foundation; Drama Express; Gosforth Amateur Dramatic Society; Rosedale Primary School; Space Science Engineering Foundation.

FINANCES *Financial year end* 31/03/2022 *Income* £104,100 *Grants to organisations* £100,200 *Assets* £601,000

TRUSTEES Robert Bartlett; Sarah Budnik; Tim Davies.

OTHER INFORMATION During 2021/22, the foundation awarded 71 grants to organisations and 3 grants to individuals. A financial breakdown of these grants was not available.

HOW TO APPLY Applications can be made through the foundation's website.

CONTACT DETAILS The Trustees, 84A Upland Road, Sutton, Surrey SM2 5JB *Tel.* 020 8661 9997 *Email* contact@bluesparkfoundation.org.uk *Website* http://bluesparkfoundation.org.uk

■ The Bluston Charitable Settlement

CC NO 256691   **ESTABLISHED** 1968
WHERE FUNDING CAN BE GIVEN Mostly UK.
WHO CAN BENEFIT Registered charities; places of worship; educational establishments; medical institutions.
WHAT IS FUNDED General charitable purposes; education of children; social welfare; health; research; Jewish causes.
TYPE OF GRANT General funding; capital project costs; research funding.
RANGE OF GRANTS Typically £10,000 to £50,000.
SAMPLE GRANTS British Institute of International and Comparative Law and Chief Rabbinate Trust (£50,000 each); Ohel Torah Beth David (£30,000); Marie Curie and Prisoners Abroad (£25,000 each); Beit Halochem UK (£18,000); British Library, Camden Psychotherapy Unit, Childhood Trust and Jewish Council for Racial Equality (£10,000 each); Maccabi GB (£5,000).
FINANCES *Financial year end* 05/04/2022
Income £528,900
Grants to organisations £393,000
Assets £26,275,000
TRUSTEES Anna Jose; Daniel Dover; Martin Paisner.
OTHER INFORMATION In 2021/22 the charity made grants to 18 organisations.
HOW TO APPLY Apply in writing to the correspondent. The trustees meet twice a year to consider applications.
CONTACT DETAILS The Trustees, 20 Gloucester Place, London W1U 8HA *Tel.* 020 7486 7760

■ The Blyth Charitable Trust

CC NO 1176537   **ESTABLISHED** 2018
WHERE FUNDING CAN BE GIVEN Worldwide.
WHO CAN BENEFIT Charitable organisations.
WHAT IS FUNDED General charitable purposes.
RANGE OF GRANTS Generally £1,000 to £25,000.
SAMPLE GRANTS Blesma (£68,000); Injured Jockey's Fund (£50,000); World Horse Welfare (£25,000); Maggie's Centre (£10,000); Habitat for Humanity (£7,500); The Countryside Alliance Foundation (£5,000); Todenham Church – Gloucestershire (£1,000).
FINANCES *Financial year end* 18/12/2021
Income £178,800
Grants to organisations £291,500
Assets £10,820,000
TRUSTEES Lord James Blyth; The Hon. Abigail Beng; Lady Pamela Blyth; Ludlow Trust Company Ltd.
OTHER INFORMATION The 2020/21 accounts were the latest available at the time of writing (June 2023). During the year, grants were awarded to 14 organisations.
HOW TO APPLY Apply in writing to the correspondent.
CONTACT DETAILS The Trustees, 1st Floor, Tower Wharf, Cheese Lane, Bristol BS2 0JJ *Tel.* 0117 313 8200 *Email* charitabletrusts@ludlowtrust.com

■ Blyth Watson Charitable Trust

CC NO 1071390   **ESTABLISHED** 1996
WHERE FUNDING CAN BE GIVEN UK.
WHO CAN BENEFIT Registered charities.
WHAT IS FUNDED Humanitarian causes based in the UK and other general charitable purposes.
TYPE OF GRANT One-off and recurrent.
RANGE OF GRANTS Up to £7,000.
SAMPLE GRANTS St John's Hospice (£10,000); South West London Law Centre (£6,000); Streets of London (£5,000); Merton Music Foundation (£4,000); YoungMinds (£3,000); The Old Vic and The Stroke Association (£2,000 each); Chronic Disease (£1,000).
FINANCES *Financial year end* 30/06/2022
Income £159,700
Grants to organisations £104,000
Assets £5,220,000
TRUSTEES Alastair Collett; Elizabeth Neale.
OTHER INFORMATION Grants were made to 36 organisations during 2021/22.
HOW TO APPLY Apply in writing to the correspondent. The trustees meet twice a year, usually in June and December, to consider applications.
CONTACT DETAILS The Trustees, c/o BDB Pitmans, One Bartholomew Close, London EC1A 7BL *Tel.* 020 7227 7000

■ BNA Charitable Incorporated Organisation

CC NO 1182500   **ESTABLISHED** 2019
WHERE FUNDING CAN BE GIVEN UK, with a strong preference for Newark and Nottinghamshire, Lincoln and Lincolnshire, and the surrounding area.
WHO CAN BENEFIT Registered charities.
WHAT IS FUNDED General charitable purposes.
WHAT IS NOT FUNDED Projects outside the UK; statutory authorities; projects which are primarily intended to promote political or religious beliefs; general appeals or circulars, including contributions to endowment funds.
TYPE OF GRANT Project funding; capital costs.
RANGE OF GRANTS Typically less than £10,000.
SAMPLE GRANTS Macmillan Cancer Support (£100,000); Well Homeless Support (£54,000); Beanblock (£29,500); Children's Bereavement Centre (£26,200); Newark Women's Aid (£7,900); Barnby Road Academy (£2,000); Newark Dementia (£1,000); Abbey Access Training (£800).
FINANCES *Financial year end* 30/06/2022
Income £283,000
Grants to organisations £887,200
Grants to individuals £7,500
Assets £19,330,000
TRUSTEES Richard Vigar; Herman Kok; Susan Fisher; Keith Girling; Paul Simpson.
HOW TO APPLY Applications can be made via the charity's website.
CONTACT DETAILS The Trustees, c/o Wright Vicar Ltd, 15 Newland, Lincoln LN1 1XG *Tel.* 01522 531341 *Email* phillipa.cridland@wrightvigar.co.uk *Website* www.bnacharity.com

■ Maureen Boal Charitable Trust

CCNI NO NIC105862   **ESTABLISHED** 1997
WHERE FUNDING CAN BE GIVEN Northern Ireland.
WHO CAN BENEFIT Charitable organisations.
WHAT IS FUNDED Health and saving lives; social welfare; animal welfare.
SAMPLE GRANTS Guide Dogs NI; Independence at Home; Prostate Cancer UK.

Think carefully about every application. Is it justified?

273

FINANCES *Financial year end* 05/04/2022
Income £127,700
Grants to organisations £123,300
Assets £2,880,000

TRUSTEE Northern Bank Executor and Trustee Company Ltd.

HOW TO APPLY Apply in writing to the correspondent.

CONTACT DETAILS The Trustees, c/o Northern Bank Executor and Trustee Company Ltd, PO Box 183, Donegall Square West, Belfast BT1 6JS *Tel.* 028 9004 8125 *Email* philip.donnan@danskebank.co.uk

■ The Marjory Boddy Charitable Trust

CC NO 1091356 **ESTABLISHED** 2002

WHERE FUNDING CAN BE GIVEN Chester, West Cheshire and the surrounding areas.

WHO CAN BENEFIT Registered charities; uniformed groups; hospices; hospitals.

WHAT IS FUNDED Health; education; social welfare; the arts.

TYPE OF GRANT Capital costs; core/revenue costs.

SAMPLE GRANTS A list of beneficiaries was not included in the annual report and accounts.

FINANCES *Financial year end* 05/04/2022
Income £1,920,000
Grants to organisations £228,700
Assets £5,770,000

TRUSTEES Edward Walton; Elizabeth Roberts; William Benoy; Clare Harrison; Michael Mills; Peter Catherall.

OTHER INFORMATION Grants were distributed as follows: support groups (£119,300); hospices and hospitals (£68,000); theatre groups (£17,500); youth clubs (£15,100); disability charities (£8,800).

HOW TO APPLY Applications can be submitted via the form on the trust's website, by post or email. Full details of what should be included in an application can be found on the trust's website. The trustees meet three times a year, in February, June and October. Successful applicants will be notified within 28 days of the meetings.

CONTACT DETAILS The Trustees, c/o Morris and Co., Chester House, Lloyd Drive, Ellesmere Port, Cheshire CH65 9HQ *Tel.* 0151 348 8400 *Email* marjoryboddytrust@moco.co.uk *Website* https://marjoryboddy.co.uk

■ The Boltini Trust

CC NO 1123129 **ESTABLISHED** 2008

WHERE FUNDING CAN BE GIVEN UK, particularly Surrey and West Sussex but also other home counties; overseas, including Africa, Asia and the West Indies.

WHO CAN BENEFIT Charitable organisations; hospitals; hospices; schools and colleges; universities; museums; churches.

WHAT IS FUNDED General charitable purposes; overseas causes; disadvantaged people; people with disabilities; community development; education; medical research and institutions; disaster relief; environmental causes.

WHAT IS NOT FUNDED Individuals.

RANGE OF GRANTS Typically £2,000 to £100,000.

SAMPLE GRANTS Sound and Music (£100,000); Unicef (£30,000); Alike (£20,000); Rother Valley Together (£15,000); Hope for Tomorrow (£10,000); Midhurst Green and RNIB (£2,000 each).

FINANCES *Financial year end* 31/03/2022
Income £587,200
Grants to organisations £570,100
Assets £14,810,000

TRUSTEES Sarah Bolton; Benjamin Bolton; Oliver Bolton; Anthony Bolton; James Nelson; Emma Nelson; Fiona Bolton; Phoebe Bolton.

OTHER INFORMATION A total of 53 grants were made in 2021/22.

HOW TO APPLY Apply in writing to the correspondent.

CONTACT DETAILS The Trustees, Woolbeding Glebe, Woolbeding, Midhurst, West Sussex GU29 9RR *Tel.* 01730 817324 *Email* boltinitrust@gmail.com

■ The Bonamy Charitable Trust

CC NO 326424 **ESTABLISHED** 1983

WHERE FUNDING CAN BE GIVEN UK, with a preference for the North West.

WHO CAN BENEFIT Charitable organisations.

WHAT IS FUNDED Advancement of the Jewish faith; Jewish education; social welfare.

RANGE OF GRANTS Generally £6,000 to £12,000.

SAMPLE GRANTS Federation of Jewish Community (£12,500); Community Security Trust (£12,000); UJIA (£10,000); SMS Foundation (£10,000); Aish UK (£6,000).

FINANCES *Financial year end* 31/12/2021
Income £164,800
Grants to organisations £107,200
Assets £613,300

TRUSTEES James Moryoussef; Robert Moryoussef; Max Moryoussef.

OTHER INFORMATION Grants to organisations were broken down as follows: Jewish outreach and continuity (£32,600); general poverty and welfare (£26,900); Jewish education (£24,700); Jewish welfare (£15,300); synagogues (£7,800).

HOW TO APPLY Contact the correspondent for further information.

CONTACT DETAILS The Trustees, Flat 2, Forrest Hills, South Downs Road, Altrincham, Cheshire WA14 3HD *Tel.* 01706 345868

■ The Charlotte Bonham-Carter Charitable Trust

CC NO 292839 **ESTABLISHED** 1985

WHERE FUNDING CAN BE GIVEN UK, with some preference for Hampshire.

WHO CAN BENEFIT Registered charities.

WHAT IS FUNDED General charitable purposes which were of particular concern to Lady Charlotte Bonham-Carter during her lifetime including: arts and culture; countryside preservation; young carers; older people; early intervention for children and young people.

WHAT IS NOT FUNDED Charities with religious or political objectives; uniformed groups; animal charities; large medical research charities; applications by/for the benefit of individuals, or sponsorship for individuals fundraising for charities; projects outside the UK.

TYPE OF GRANT Project funding.

RANGE OF GRANTS Mostly under £5,000.

SAMPLE GRANTS The British Museum (£6,000); Ashmolean Museum (£4,500); Clifton College (£3,000); City and Guilds of London Art School (£2,000); Birmingham Royal Ballet (£1,000).

FINANCES *Financial year end* 05/04/2022
Income £164,400
Grants to organisations £125,800
Assets £6,570,000

TRUSTEES David Bonham-Carter; Eliza Bonham-Carter; Sir Matthew Farrer; Georgina Nayler; Mary Grimond.

OTHER INFORMATION Grants were awarded to 44 charities during the year. The trust supports a number of charities on a regular basis, as well in response to applications.

HOW TO APPLY According to the website, applications must be made by letter accompanied by a completed Application Covering Sheet (available to download from the website) and should explain what your charity does, the purpose of the application, funds raised so far and the timescale involved. The application should include a copy of your latest accounts. Applications should be sent by post, with supporting documents printed single sided (with the exception of accounts, for which this may not be possible) and should be submitted by 1 January or 1 September, for meetings in March and October, respectively. Applications are not acknowledged on receipt and successful applicants will be notified by the end of March or October.

CONTACT DETAILS Jenny Cannon, Charity Administrator, Chelwood, Rectory Road, East Carleton, Norwich, Norfolk NR14 8HT *Tel.* 01508 571230 *Email* admin@charlottebonhamcartercharitabletrust.org.uk *Website* https://charlottebonhamcartercharitabletrust.org.uk

■ The Boodle and Dunthorne Charitable Trust

CC NO 1077748   **ESTABLISHED** 1999
WHERE FUNDING CAN BE GIVEN UK and overseas.
WHO CAN BENEFIT Registered charities.
WHAT IS FUNDED General charitable purposes.
WHAT IS NOT FUNDED Individuals.
TYPE OF GRANT One-off and recurrent.
RANGE OF GRANTS Typically around £5,000 to £20,000.
SAMPLE GRANTS Street Child (£110,000); I Can and I Am (£70,000); Rainbow Trust (£25,800); Alder Hey Children's Hospital (£15,000); Seashell Trust (£10,000).
FINANCES *Financial year end* 05/04/2022
Income £1,520,000
Grants to organisations £385,700
Assets £2,340,000
TRUSTEES Nicholas Wainwright; Michael Wainwright.
OTHER INFORMATION Established in 1999, this is the charitable trust of Boodles, a family jewellers based in the North West.
HOW TO APPLY Contact the correspondent for further information. The 2021/22 annual report states: 'The Trustees have discretion over where and when grants [are] made. Grants will be made by the Trustees as and when they identify a suitable and deserving cause.'
CONTACT DETAILS The Trustees, Boodles House, 35 Lord Street, Liverpool, Merseyside L2 9SQ *Tel.* 0151 224 0580

■ BOOST Charitable Trust

CC NO 1111961   **ESTABLISHED** 2005
WHERE FUNDING CAN BE GIVEN England; Wales; Eswatini.
WHO CAN BENEFIT Registered charities; not-for-profit organisations involved in sports.
WHAT IS FUNDED Access to sport for disadvantaged individuals and people with disabilities.

TYPE OF GRANT Project funding; core costs; capital costs.
RANGE OF GRANTS Mostly up to £10,000.
SAMPLE GRANTS Running Charity (£12,000); Goalball (£10,000); Sport in Mind (£7,500); Raider Braves (£6,600); Level Water (£5,000); Better Things (£3,000); RISE (£2,000); Whitstable Lawn Tennis Club (£1,200).
FINANCES *Financial year end* 30/09/2022
Income £186,100
Grants to organisations £186,100
Assets £1,350,000
TRUSTEES Oliver Bartrum; Alurie Dutton; Robert Houston; Philippa Fine.
OTHER INFORMATION In 2021/22, grants of over £1,000 were awarded to 26 organisations. Twenty-six small awards of £750 or less were also awarded, totalling £16,600.
HOW TO APPLY Contact the correspondent via email or letter. Information on what to include can be found on the trust's website.
CONTACT DETAILS Sarah Johnson, Trust Manager, 5 St Bride Street, London EC4A 4AS *Tel.* 020 7078 1966 *Email* sarah.johnson@boostct.org *Website* www.boostct.org

■ The Booth Charities

CC NO 221800   **ESTABLISHED** 1963
WHERE FUNDING CAN BE GIVEN Salford.
WHO CAN BENEFIT Organisations supporting the inhabitants of the City of Salford, especially older people; individuals.
WHAT IS FUNDED General charitable purposes; social welfare; recreation and leisure; education.
TYPE OF GRANT Capital costs; project funding; salaries; one-off grants. Funding is awarded for up to three years.
RANGE OF GRANTS £100 to £60,000.
SAMPLE GRANTS Salford Citizens Advice (£45,000); Broughton House Veteran Care Village (£20,000); Special Spirits (£16,100); Henshaw's Society for Blind People (£10,800); YMCA Manchester (£9,900); Beech Court Tenant and Residents Association (£1,400); The Salvation Army – Swinton (£900); Healthy Hearts Exercise Group (£500).
FINANCES *Financial year end* 31/03/2022
Income £1,630,000
Grants to organisations £452,600
Grants to individuals £1,200
Assets £50,400
TRUSTEES Alan Dewhurst; Richard Kershaw; Roger Weston; William Whittle; John Willis; Richard Fildes; Philip Okell; Barbara Griffin; James Tully; Patrick Loftus; Stephen Cheshire.
OTHER INFORMATION Grants were awarded to 63 organisations during 2021/22 in the following categories: relief of distress and sickness (£219,000); educational facilities (£109,100); recreation/leisure facilities (£72,000); relief of older people or those experiencing financial hardship (£24,000); other (£7,500). A further £21,000 was awarded to Sacred Trinity Church. In addition, grants totalling £1,200 were made to 22 individuals.
HOW TO APPLY Apply in writing to the correspondent.
CONTACT DETAILS The Trustees, c/o Butcher and Barlow LLP, 3 Royal Mews, Gadbrook Road, Northwich, Cheshire CW9 7UD *Tel.* 01606 334309 *Email* jaldersley@butcher-barlow.co.uk

■ Boots Charitable Trust

CC NO 1045927   **ESTABLISHED** 1971
WHERE FUNDING CAN BE GIVEN Nottinghamshire.
WHO CAN BENEFIT Registered charities; voluntary organisations that are too small to qualify for charitable status.
WHAT IS FUNDED Health; lifelong learning; community development; social care.
WHAT IS NOT FUNDED Projects benefitting people outside Nottinghamshire; individuals; organisations which are not registered charities and which have an income or expenditure of more than £5,000 per year; charities seeking funds to redistribute to other charities; projects for which there is a legal statutory obligation or which replace statutory funding.
TYPE OF GRANT Project funding; capital costs; core costs.
RANGE OF GRANTS £100 to £10,000.
SAMPLE GRANTS Dance4, Nidas and Refugee Roots (£10,000 each); Framework (£8,800); Home-Start Nottingham (£7,000); Good Vibrations (£6,200); Good Companions (£4,400); Read Easy Nottingham (£2,000).
FINANCES *Financial year end 31/08/2021*
Income £266,800
Grants to organisations £250,000
Assets £0
TRUSTEES Lavinia Moxley; Felicity Walton-Bateson; Stuart Buchanan; Lucy Reynolds; Beneeta Shah.
OTHER INFORMATION In 2020/21 the trust made a total of 31 grants which were broken down as follows: social care (£117,600); health (£61,200); lifelong learning (£39,600); community development (£31,600). The 2020/21 accounts were the latest available at the time of writing (June 2023).
HOW TO APPLY There is an online application form on the website alongside guidance on eligibility. Paper application forms can also be requested from the correspondent.
CONTACT DETAILS The Trustees, Boots UK Ltd, D90E S09, 1 Thane Road West, Nottingham, Nottinghamshire NG90 1BS
Email feelgoodworks@boots.co.uk
Website www.boots-uk.com/corporate_social_responsibility/boots-charitable-trust.aspx

■ The Salo Bordon Charitable Trust

CC NO 266439   **ESTABLISHED** 1973
WHERE FUNDING CAN BE GIVEN UK and overseas.
WHO CAN BENEFIT Charitable organisations, primarily Jewish organisations; Jewish educational institutions; places of worship.
WHAT IS FUNDED Jewish causes; religious education; social welfare.
RANGE OF GRANTS Mostly up to around £5,000, with the occasional larger grant.
SAMPLE GRANTS Achisomoch Aid Company (£31,000); North London Welfare and Educational Foundation (£11,000); Project SEED Ltd (£7,500); Golders Green Beth Hamedrash Congregation and Menorah Grammar School Charitable Trust (£5,000 each); Beis Soroh Schnierer School (£2,500).
FINANCES *Financial year end 05/04/2022*
Income £110,900
Grants to organisations £108,900
Assets £7,300,000
TRUSTEES Marcel Bordon; Lilly Bordon.
OTHER INFORMATION Only organisations that received grants of over £2,000 were listed as beneficiaries in the trust's 2021/22 accounts. Grants of under £2,000 totalled £5,800.

HOW TO APPLY Apply in writing to the correspondent.
CONTACT DETAILS The Trustees, 39 Gresham Gardens, London NW11 8PA *Tel.* 020 8458 6622

■ Sir William Boreman's Foundation

CC NO 312796   **ESTABLISHED** 1962
WHERE FUNDING CAN BE GIVEN Greenwich and Lewisham.
WHO CAN BENEFIT Registered charities; individuals; educational establishments.
WHAT IS FUNDED Educational projects for young people under the age of 25.
TYPE OF GRANT Project funding; bursaries; core costs.
RANGE OF GRANTS Up to £5,000.
SAMPLE GRANTS Young Lewisham Project (£10,000); New Woodlands School (£6,000); National Youth Jazz Orchestra (£5,000); Thomas Tallis School (£900).
FINANCES *Financial year end 31/07/2022*
Income £148,100
Grants to organisations £90,100
Grants to individuals £36,700
Assets £4,820,000
TRUSTEE The Drapers' Company.
HOW TO APPLY Application forms can be downloaded from The Drapers' Company website.
CONTACT DETAILS The Trustees, The Drapers Company, Drapers' Hall, Throgmorton Avenue, London EC2N 2DQ *Tel.* 020 7588 5001
Email mail@thedrapers.co.uk *Website* https://thedrapers.co.uk/sir-william-boremans-foundation

■ The Borrows Charitable Trust

CC NO 1140591   **ESTABLISHED** 2011
WHERE FUNDING CAN BE GIVEN England and Wales.
WHO CAN BENEFIT Registered charities.
WHAT IS FUNDED General charitable purposes.
RANGE OF GRANTS Between £5,000 and £16,000, with some larger grants.
SAMPLE GRANTS Community Foundation for Surrey (£60,300); Footsteps International (£32,700); Royal Opera House (£27,500); Rossall Foundation (£24,000); Collaborative Schools Network (£16,600); The Elkon Charity (£16,000); Carers UK, Mind and Orpheus (£5,000 each).
FINANCES *Financial year end 31/03/2022*
Income £295,100
Grants to organisations £422,100
Assets £7,970,000
TRUSTEES Sally Borrows; Simon Borrows.
OTHER INFORMATION Grants were made to 29 organisations throughout the year, with only grants of over £5,000 being listed in the accounts. Grants of less than £5,000 totalled £89,000.
HOW TO APPLY Apply in writing to the correspondent.
CONTACT DETAILS The Trustees, c/o Kingston Smith and Partners LLP, Devonshire House, 60 Goswell Road, London EC1M 7AD *Tel.* 020 7566 4000

■ The Boshier-Hinton Foundation

CC NO 1108886   **ESTABLISHED** 2005
WHERE FUNDING CAN BE GIVEN England and Wales.
WHO CAN BENEFIT Registered charities; CICs; schools; universities; PTAs; hospitals; hospices.

WHAT IS FUNDED Work with children and adults with special educational needs.

WHAT IS NOT FUNDED Repeat grants within two years; retrospective expenditure; salaries; capital projects.

TYPE OF GRANT Capital costs; seed funding/start-up funding.

RANGE OF GRANTS Generally between £1,000 and £2,000.

SAMPLE GRANTS Deaf Academy (£10,000); Snowdon Trust (£5,000); Young Enterprise (£2,500); Mobility Trust (£2,000); Calvert Trust Exmoor (£1,500); Get Set 4 Tennis CIC (£1,300); Brighton and Hove Speak Out (£800); Autism Early Support Trust (£300).

FINANCES *Financial year end 31/03/2022*
Income £76,600
Grants to organisations £196,700
Assets £1,030,000

TRUSTEES Dr Peter Boshier; Thea Boshier; Colin Flint; Susanne McEwen.

OTHER INFORMATION The foundation awarded 123 grants during 2021/22.

HOW TO APPLY Application forms can be downloaded from the foundation's website and should be returned by post. Guidance can be found on the application form. The correspondent can also be contacted via telephone or email for further information. There are no deadlines.

CONTACT DETAILS The Trustees, Whitegates, 32 Lower Street, Horning, Norfolk NR12 8AA *Tel.* 01692 630695 *Email* boshierhinton@yahoo.co.uk *Website* www.boshierhintonfoundation.org.uk

■ The Bosson Family Charitable Trust

CC NO 1146096   **ESTABLISHED** 2012
WHERE FUNDING CAN BE GIVEN UK.

WHO CAN BENEFIT Registered charities and churches.

WHAT IS FUNDED Education and training and religious activities.

TYPE OF GRANT Capital costs.

SAMPLE GRANTS A list of beneficiaries was not available.

FINANCES *Financial year end 31/03/2022*
Income £22,900
Grants to organisations £92,900

TRUSTEES Dr Alison Bosson; Paul Bosson; George Bosson.

OTHER INFORMATION Registered in February 2012, the trust's objects are education, training and religious activities, with capital grants being given to registered charities and churches. The settlors of the trust are Paul Bosson, chief financial officer at Sophis, and his wife. Full accounts for 2021/22 were not available to view on the Charity Commission's website due to the trust's low income. We have therefore estimated the grant total based on the trust's total expenditure.

HOW TO APPLY Unsolicited applications are not considered.

CONTACT DETAILS Paul Bosson, Trustee, 7 Seer Mead, Seer Green, Beaconsfield, Buckinghamshire HP9 2QL *Tel.* 01494 680148 *Email* paulbosson@aol.com

■ The Bothwell Charitable Trust

CC NO 299056   **ESTABLISHED** 1987
WHERE FUNDING CAN BE GIVEN UK.

WHO CAN BENEFIT Registered charities; hospices.

WHAT IS FUNDED General charitable purposes including: children's causes; hospices; medical research; disability and social welfare.

WHAT IS NOT FUNDED Individuals.

SAMPLE GRANTS A list of beneficiaries was not included in the annual report and accounts.

FINANCES *Financial year end 05/04/2022*
Income £126,100
Grants to organisations £359,000
Assets £3,800,000

TRUSTEES Crispian Howard; Paul James; Theresa McGregor.

OTHER INFORMATION During the year, grants were distributed as follows: medical research (£127,000); disability/social work (£106,000); children's causes (£47,000); other causes (£45,000); hospices (£34,000).

HOW TO APPLY Apply in writing to the correspondent.

CONTACT DETAILS The Trustees, 69 Burrell Road, Compton, Newbury, Berkshire RG20 6QX *Tel.* 01925 757702 *Email* bct1987aa@gmail.com

■ The Harry Bottom Charitable Trust

CC NO 204675   **ESTABLISHED** 1960
WHERE FUNDING CAN BE GIVEN Barnsley; North East Derbyshire; Rotherham; Sheffield.

WHO CAN BENEFIT Registered charities; hospitals; universities; places of worship.

WHAT IS FUNDED Religion; social welfare; medical causes and health; education; general charitable purposes.

WHAT IS NOT FUNDED Structural works; salaries; organisations with large cash reserves; national organisations; individuals.

TYPE OF GRANT Capital costs; core/revenue costs; seed funding/start-up funding; bursaries.

RANGE OF GRANTS Typically between £2,000 and £10,000.

SAMPLE GRANTS A list of beneficiaries was not included in the annual report and accounts. Previous beneficiaries have included: Ashgate Hospice (£12,000); The Cavendish Hip Foundation (£10,000); University of Sheffield (£9,000); Snowdrop Project (£6,500); Homeless at Christmas (£3,000); Sheffield Methodist Church (£2,500); Stocksbridge Dementia (£2,000).

FINANCES *Financial year end 30/06/2022*
Income £249,300
Grants to organisations £125,400
Assets £7,040,000

TRUSTEES Prof. Andrew Rawlinson; Helen Woolley; Derek Handforth; Revd William Shaw; Jonathan Hattersley.

OTHER INFORMATION Grants were broken down as follows: education and general charitable purposes (£76,700); religion (£33,500); medical causes (£15,200).

HOW TO APPLY Apply in writing to the correspondent by email or post. See the website for full guidance, including a list of details that applications must include.

CONTACT DETAILS The Trustees, c/o Lishmans LLP, 16–18 Station Road, Chapeltown, Sheffield, South Yorkshire S35 2XH *Tel.* 0114 246 5348 *Email* harrybottomtrust@lishmansllp.com *Website* www.theharrybottomtrust.co.uk

■ The P. G. and N. J. Boulton Trust

CC NO 1158431   ESTABLISHED 1976

WHERE FUNDING CAN BE GIVEN Worldwide.

WHO CAN BENEFIT Registered charities, particularly smaller charities.

WHAT IS FUNDED Christian missionary work; social welfare and disaster relief; medical research and health care.

WHAT IS NOT FUNDED Individuals; the environment and conservation; culture and heritage; sports and leisure; animal welfare; church building repairs.

RANGE OF GRANTS £500 to £20,000.

SAMPLE GRANTS Longcroft Church (£23,000); Vision for China (£22,000); Wycliffe UK (£6,000); Christian Institute and Slavic Gospel Association (£3,000 each); Anglo-Peruvian Child Care Mission and New Tribes Mission (£1,000 each); Asia Link (£500).

FINANCES *Financial year end 31/03/2022*
Income £1,050,000
Grants to organisations £68,500
Assets £5,850,000

TRUSTEES Mr Perry; Mrs Perry; Miss Jardine-Smith; Mr Stafford.

OTHER INFORMATION Grants were awarded to 16 organisations during the year.

HOW TO APPLY Note the following statement from the trust's website: 'Due to ongoing changes in policy...we are now largely unable to honour unsolicited requests for grants. If you would however like to share something of your work with us, then we are happy for you to do so but would be grateful if you would do so by conventional post, rather than by email. We are unable to respond to all correspondence, but as a general guideline, the trustees meet every three months and if you do not receive any response within that timeframe, then you may reasonably assume that we are unable to provide any help at the present time'.

CONTACT DETAILS The Trustees, P. G. and N. J. Boulton Trust, PO Box 72, Wirral, Merseyside CH28 9AE *Tel.* 0151 677 7729 *Website* www.boultontrust.org.uk

■ Sir Clive Bourne Family Trust

CC NO 290620   ESTABLISHED 1984

WHERE FUNDING CAN BE GIVEN UK.

WHO CAN BENEFIT Charities and voluntary bodies.

WHAT IS FUNDED The trustees favour Orthodox Jewish causes. A number of health and medical charities, particularly relating to cancer, have also benefitted.

SAMPLE GRANTS A list of beneficiaries was not included in the annual report and accounts. Previous beneficiaries have included: Prostate Cancer (£16,700); Jewish Care (£15,500); MDA UK (£10,000); Norwood (£9,300); Chai Community Care (£5,000); Chana (£1,800); Viscardi Center (£1,000); WIZO UK (£900); Simon Marks Primary School (£500).

FINANCES *Financial year end 05/04/2022*
Income £70,900
Grants to organisations £80,100
Assets £5,410,000

TRUSTEES Lady Joy Bourne; Katie Cohen; Lucy Furman; Merryl Flitterman; Claire Lefton.

OTHER INFORMATION The trust supports Jewish charitable causes.

HOW TO APPLY Apply in writing to the correspondent.

CONTACT DETAILS J. Bater, Correspondent, Gardiner House, 6B Hemnall Street, Epping, Essex CM16 4LW *Tel.* 01992 560500 *Email* jbater@seabourne-group.com

■ Bourneheights Ltd

CC NO 298359   ESTABLISHED 1984

WHERE FUNDING CAN BE GIVEN UK.

WHO CAN BENEFIT Orthodox Jewish organisations and registered charities.

WHAT IS FUNDED Orthodox Jewish causes including education, welfare and advancement of the Orthodox Jewish faith.

RANGE OF GRANTS From £10,000 to £147,000.

SAMPLE GRANTS Mosdos Chernobil (£146,600); Chasdei Aharon Ltd (£130,700); Tchabe Kollel Ltd (£80,000); The Gevurath Ari Torah Academy Trust (£45,000); College for Higher Rabbinical Studies (£30,000); The Happy and Healthy Trust (£10,000).

FINANCES *Financial year end 30/11/2021*
Income £2,490,000
Grants to organisations £1,330,000
Assets £10,180,000

TRUSTEES Chaskel Rand; Erno Berger; Yechiel Chersky; Schloime Rand.

OTHER INFORMATION The 2020/21 accounts were the latest available at the time of writing (June 2023). Organisations that received grants of less than £10,000 were not identified in the accounts. In 2020/21, grants of under £10,000 amounted to £145,000.

HOW TO APPLY Contact the correspondent for further information.

CONTACT DETAILS Schloime Rand, Trustee and Secretary, Flat 10, Palm Court, Queen Elizabeth's Walk, London N16 5XA *Tel.* 020 8800 1572

■ The Bowland Charitable Trust

CC NO 292027   ESTABLISHED 1985

WHERE FUNDING CAN BE GIVEN The North West.

WHO CAN BENEFIT Registered charities; charitable organisations.

WHAT IS FUNDED Religion; education; culture; rehabilitation of offenders; recreation; the environment; young people.

RANGE OF GRANTS Up to £100,000.

SAMPLE GRANTS A list of beneficiaries was not included in the annual report and accounts. Previous beneficiaries have included: Blackburn Cathedral Trust; Bowland High School; The Brantwood Trust; LEB Partnership; The Lowry Centre Trust; Nazareth Unitarian Chapel; North Music Trust; Ribble FM; Ron Clark Academy; The Rosemere Cancer Foundation.

FINANCES *Financial year end 31/12/2021*
Income £2,310,000
Grants to organisations £175,600
Grants to individuals £5,400
Assets £3,840,000

TRUSTEES Tony Cann; Carole Fahy; Hugh Turner.

OTHER INFORMATION The 2020/21 accounts were the latest available at the time of writing (May 2023). Grants were broken down as follows: religious activities (£100,800); educational activities (£45,000); support for activities of young people (£25,000); donations to other charities (£10,200).

HOW TO APPLY The charity invites applications for the funding of projects from individuals, institutions and charitable organisations. Applications should be made directly to the trustees, who meet regularly to assess them.

CONTACT DETAILS Carole Fahy, Bowland House, Philips Road, Blackburn, Lancashire BB1 5NA *Tel.* 01254 688051 *Email* carole.fahy@cannco.co.uk

■ G. and K. Boyes Charitable Trust

CC NO 1166015
WHERE FUNDING CAN BE GIVEN UK.
WHO CAN BENEFIT Charitable organisations.
WHAT IS FUNDED The environment; education; medical research, in particular dementia and brain tumours; health; heritage.
RANGE OF GRANTS Up to £260,000.
SAMPLE GRANTS Previous beneficiaries have included: Cherubim; David Shepherd Wildlife Trust; English National Ballet; Holland Park Opera; London Zoological Society; Royal Marsden Cancer Charity; Susan's Farm.
FINANCES *Financial year end 05/04/2022*
Income £2,500
Grants to organisations £165,000
TRUSTEES Mark Cannon-Brookes; Mrs A. Dalmahoy; Mr R. A. Henderson; Cripps Trust Corporation Ltd.
OTHER INFORMATION The 2021/22 annual report and accounts were not available to view on the Charity Commission's website due to the charity's low income. We have therefore estimated the charity's grant total.
HOW TO APPLY Apply in writing to the correspondent.
CONTACT DETAILS Joanne Lee, c/o Cripps Harries Hall LLP, 22 Mount Ephraim, Tunbridge Wells, Kent TN4 8AS *Tel.* 01892 765431 *Email* joanne.lee@cripps.co.uk

■ The Frank Brake Charitable Trust

CC NO 1023245   **ESTABLISHED** 1993
WHERE FUNDING CAN BE GIVEN Kent.
WHO CAN BENEFIT Registered charities.
WHAT IS FUNDED General charitable purposes.
RANGE OF GRANTS £4,000 to £400,000.
SAMPLE GRANTS Parkinson's UK (£400,000); Kent Community Foundation (£130,000); Kent Multiple Sclerosis Society Therapy Centre (£60,000); Alexander Devine Children's Hospice (£7,500) The Kent Foundation (£4,100).
FINANCES *Financial year end 31/03/2022*
Income £2,430,000
Grants to organisations £898,100
Assets £33,260,000
TRUSTEES Richard Brake; Michelle Leveridge; Michael Trigg; Philip Wilson; Stephanie Senior.
OTHER INFORMATION Grants were awarded to 20 organisations during the year.
HOW TO APPLY The 2021/22 accounts state that 'unsolicited direct applications to the Trust are not encouraged.'
CONTACT DETAILS Michael Trigg, Trustee, c/o Gill Turner Tucker, 2 Country Gate, Staceys Street, Maidstone, Kent ME14 1ST *Tel.* 01622 759051 *Email* michael.trigg@gillturnertucker.com

■ The William Brake Charitable Trust

CC NO 1023244   **ESTABLISHED** 1993
WHERE FUNDING CAN BE GIVEN UK, with a preference for Kent.
WHO CAN BENEFIT Registered charities; universities; hospices.
WHAT IS FUNDED General charitable purposes.
RANGE OF GRANTS Mostly £1,000 to £25,000, with some larger grants of up to £60,000.
SAMPLE GRANTS The Whitley Fund for Nature (£60,000); The Natural History Museum (£50,000); The National Portrait Gallery (£39,000); Child Bereavement UK (£35,000); Scotch College Adelaide (£32,800); The Duke of Edinburgh's Award (£30,000); Motor Neurone Disease Association (£25,000); The Kent MS Therapy Unit (£16,000); Barnardo's (£15,000); CWPLUS (£10,000); Parkinson's UK (£9,500); The Rosemary Foundation (£8,000); The Mike Collingwood Memorial Fund (£5,000); Petersfield Youth Theatre (£1,000).
FINANCES *Financial year end 31/03/2022*
Income £208,100
Grants to organisations £727,500
Assets £13,830,000
TRUSTEES Philip Wilson; Deborah Isaac; Penelope Lang; Michael Trigg.
OTHER INFORMATION Grants were awarded to 114 organisations during the year totalling £727,500.
HOW TO APPLY Apply in writing to the correspondent. The 2021/22 accounts note: 'The charity invites applications from the William Brake family for funding of worthy registered charities each year, with a particular emphasis on local charities where the family know the charity's representative.' The trustees hold two formal meetings each year to consider grants.
CONTACT DETAILS Michael Trigg, Chair and Trustee, c/o Gill Turner Tucker Solicitors, Colman House, King Street, Maidstone, Kent ME14 1JE *Tel.* 01622 759051 *Email* michael.trigg@gillturnertucker.com

■ The Tony Bramall Charitable Trust

CC NO 1001522   **ESTABLISHED** 1988
WHERE FUNDING CAN BE GIVEN Northern England, with some preference for Yorkshire.
WHO CAN BENEFIT Charities; medical organisations; hospices; individuals.
WHAT IS FUNDED Medical research; ill health; social welfare.
RANGE OF GRANTS Up to £200,000 but mostly under £5,000.
SAMPLE GRANTS University of Leeds (£207,000); North Yorkshire Hospice Care (£5,000); Hope for Tomorrow (£3,000); Spinal Research (£1,000); Connect Yorkshire (£100).
FINANCES *Financial year end 05/04/2022*
Income £75,000
Grants to organisations £231,700
Assets £4,930,000
TRUSTEES Karen Ogden; Tony Bramall; Anna Bramall; Geoffrey Tate.
OTHER INFORMATION Grants were made to 16 organisations during the year.
HOW TO APPLY Apply in writing to the correspondent. The trustees review all applications. According to the 2021/22 annual report, 'certain fund requests are assessed by personal visits and discussions with the applicants.'
CONTACT DETAILS Alison Lockwood, 12 Cardale Court, Cardale Park, Beckwith Head Road, Harrogate, North Yorkshire HG3 1RY *Tel.* 01423 535300 *Email* alison.lockwood@bramallproperties.co.uk

■ The Liz and Terry Bramall Foundation

CC NO 1121670   **ESTABLISHED** 2007
WHERE FUNDING CAN BE GIVEN UK, with a strong preference for Yorkshire.
WHO CAN BENEFIT Charitable organisations; churches; hospices; schools; universities; cultural organisations.

WHAT IS FUNDED Christian causes; the promotion of urban or rural regeneration in areas of social and economic deprivation; the environment; social welfare; health; education and training; arts and culture; preservation of historic buildings; prevention of crime. A detailed list of supported areas can be found on the foundation's website.

SAMPLE GRANTS Leeds University (£398,800); The National Railway Museum (£250,000); St Michael's Hospice (£100,000); Leeds Lieder Festival (£45,000); One In A Million – Bradford (£20,000); Walking With The Wounded (£10,000); Sprotbrough Community Christmas Lights (£2,000); RAF Benevolent Fund (£1,000).

FINANCES *Financial year end 05/04/2022*
Income £2,160,000
Grants to organisations £5,470,000
Assets £114,820,000

TRUSTEES Dr Terence Bramall; Elizabeth Bramall; Suzannah Allard; Rebecca Bletcher; Rachel Tunnicliffe; Anthony Sharp.

OTHER INFORMATION During 2021/22 the foundation awarded 184 grants. Some organisations received more than one grant.

HOW TO APPLY Applications should be made in writing to the correspondent and should be no more than 120 words. Details of what to include can be found on the website. Applications should be sent via post or email and they will be acknowledged within ten working days. The trustees meet four times a year, usually in January, April, August and November. The foundation's 2021/22 annual report states: 'Unsolicited requests from national charities will generally only be considered if there is some public benefit to the Yorkshire region.'

CONTACT DETAILS The Trustees, c/o Raworths LLP, Eton House, 89 Station Parade, Harrogate, North Yorkshire HG1 1HF *Tel.* 01423 566666 *Email* bramallfoundation@raworths.co.uk *Website* www.bramallfoundation.org

■ Breast Cancer Now

CC NO 1160558   **ESTABLISHED** 2014
WHERE FUNDING CAN BE GIVEN UK; Republic of Ireland; USA.
WHO CAN BENEFIT Research institutions.
WHAT IS FUNDED Breast cancer research.
TYPE OF GRANT Research grants; PhD studentships; fellowships.
RANGE OF GRANTS Project grants: up to £250,000; catalyst grants: up to £400,000.
SAMPLE GRANTS Institute of Cancer Research (£8.86 million); King's College London (£694,000); Bart's Health NHS Trust (£514,000); University of Cambridge (£415,000); University of Edinburgh (£302,000); University of Leeds (£215,000).
FINANCES *Financial year end 31/07/2022*
Income £66,880,000
Grants to organisations £12,200,000
Assets £49,190,000
TRUSTEES Pascale Alvanitakis-Guely; Ann Pickering; Christopher Copeland; Andrew Moore; Mark Astaire; Sonia Gayle; Barbara Brown; Jill Thompson; Dr Nisha Sharma; Prof. Mitch Dowsett; Prof. Ingunn Holen; Dr Andreas Makris; Georgette Oni; Claire Ryan.
OTHER INFORMATION Ten beneficiaries that received over £200,000 were listed in the charity's accounts. Grants awarded to unlisted beneficiaries totalled £123,000.
HOW TO APPLY Applications can be made through the charity's website. Refer to the website for application deadlines and guidelines.

CONTACT DETAILS The Trustees, 5th Floor, Ibex House, 42–47 Minories, London EC3N 1DY *Tel.* 0333 207 0300 *Email* grants_admin@breastcancernow.org *Website* www.breastcancernow.org

■ The Brelms Trust CIO

CC NO 1153372   **ESTABLISHED** 2013
WHERE FUNDING CAN BE GIVEN Yorkshire.
WHO CAN BENEFIT Registered charities. Mainly small to medium-sized charities with an income of less than £500,000 and usually with unrestricted reserves of six months or less.
WHAT IS FUNDED Arts, education and sport; carers; conservation; debt and benefits advice; people affected by domestic abuse and sexual violence; excluded young people; homelessness; older people facing isolation; people with physical or learning disabilities; prevention of re-offending; refugees, asylum seekers and ethnic minorities; rural isolation; people affected by substance misuse; support in bereavement; support for disadvantaged communities.
WHAT IS NOT FUNDED Organisations without charitable status; organisations not registered at the Charity Commission; large charitable organisations with an annual income of more than £500,000; national charities, unless the project is based in Yorkshire and for the specific benefit of the Yorkshire community, with clear evidence of embedded local management and financial control of budgetary spending and grant funding, usually evidenced by a set of accounts; applications from individuals or for student gap-year costs; charities which send out general appeal letters for donations; organisations which advance religion or promote faith-based activities; party-political organisations; animal welfare; medical research; retrospective expenditure.
TYPE OF GRANT Core costs and projects funding.
RANGE OF GRANTS Up to £15,000.
SAMPLE GRANTS Together We Grow (£18,000); Streetbikes (£15,000); Irise International (£12,000); Active Independence (£8,900); Artistic Attic Trust (£6,000); Happy Tears Foundation (£5,000); Bridlington Pride (£4,100); Gwennie's Getaways (£3,000).
FINANCES *Financial year end 30/11/2022*
Income £440,700
Grants to organisations £494,100
Assets £2,190,000
TRUSTEES Mary Cornish; Stephen Stroud; Lesley Faithful; Juliet Kemp; Alan Wallace; Susan Brown; Jillian Malcomson.
OTHER INFORMATION Grants were made to 42 organisations during the year and were broken down into 20 grants in West Yorkshire, 15 in South Yorkshire, 4 in East Yorkshire and 3 in North Yorkshire.
HOW TO APPLY Applications can be made via the trust's website.
CONTACT DETAILS The Trustees, Stringer House, 34 Lupton Street, Leeds, West Yorkshire LS10 2RU *Email* admin@brelmstrust.org.uk *Website* www.brelmstrust.org.uk

■ The Brenley Trust

CC NO 1151128   **ESTABLISHED** 2013
WHERE FUNDING CAN BE GIVEN UK and southern Africa.
WHO CAN BENEFIT Charitable organisations.
WHAT IS FUNDED Social welfare; education.

RANGE OF GRANTS Between £1,000 and £250,000.
SAMPLE GRANTS Church of the Holy Spirit (SA) (£250,000); Tayntons (£101,100); Bruton School (£15,000); Lourdes Pilgrimage (£5,000) Churches in Wynchcombe (£1,000).
FINANCES *Financial year end 31/01/2022*
Income £76,400
Grants to organisations £750,000
Grants to individuals £131,900
Assets £12,250,000
TRUSTEES Patrick Riley; Mary-Louise Brennickmeyer; Robbert Zoet.
HOW TO APPLY Apply in writing to the correspondent.
CONTACT DETAILS The Trustees, 17 Princes Drive, Oxshott, Leatherhead, Surrey KT22 0UL *Tel.* 01372 841801 *Email* patrick.riley@ btinternet.com

■ The Harold and Alice Bridges Charity

CC NO 236654   **ESTABLISHED** 1963
WHERE FUNDING CAN BE GIVEN Lancashire and south Cumbria (particularly the River Ribble area and northwards, the Blackburn area and the South Lakes).
WHO CAN BENEFIT Registered charities; village halls; churches; voluntary/local organisations; CICs; hospices; scout groups. Charitable status is preferred.
WHAT IS FUNDED General charitable purposes, with a preference for projects supporting rural and village life.
WHAT IS NOT FUNDED Grants are not normally awarded for running expenses.
TYPE OF GRANT Capital projects.
RANGE OF GRANTS Mostly up to £5,000.
SAMPLE GRANTS Aighton, Bailey and Chaigley Village Hall (£5,000); Longton Victory Memorial Sports and Social (£3,500); Ingleton Allotment Association (£3,000); Penwortham Cricket Club and Rosemere Cancer Foundation (£2,000 each); Lytham Cricket Club (£1,000); Ireby with Leck Parish Council (£500).
FINANCES *Financial year end 05/04/2022*
Income £132,300
Grants to organisations £110,400
Assets £4,300,000
TRUSTEES John Hinchliffe; Christopher Calvert.
OTHER INFORMATION During the year, grants were made to 70 organisations.
HOW TO APPLY Refer to the charity's website for full details, including a downloadable application form. Completed forms should be sent to the correspondent by post. The charity's website states: 'The application form has been designed to be straightforward to complete and it would be appreciated if the application could be confined to the application form itself and not include any attachments.' The application deadlines are 15 January, 15 May and 15 September each year.
CONTACT DETAILS The Trustees, c/o Linder Myers Solicitors, 21–23 Park Street, Lytham, Lancashire FY8 5LU *Tel.* 0844 984 6001 *Email* david.hinchliffe@lindermyers.co.uk *Website* www.haroldandalicebridgescharity.co.uk

■ Bright Red Charity

CC NO 1178566   **ESTABLISHED** 1988
WHERE FUNDING CAN BE GIVEN The north of England.
WHO CAN BENEFIT Charitable organisations; universities; research organisations; hospitals.

WHAT IS FUNDED Blood cancer research; the care of patients with blood cancer; education and training of healthcare professionals caring for patients with blood cancers.
TYPE OF GRANT Research; fellowships; studentships.
SAMPLE GRANTS A list of beneficiaries was not included in the annual report and accounts.
FINANCES *Financial year end 31/12/2021*
Income £128,400
Grants to organisations £89,400
Assets £345,100
TRUSTEES David Tompkins; Gail Jones; Matthew Collin; Mark Thompson; Victoria Hervey; Charlotte Dickinson; Kathryn McRae.
OTHER INFORMATION Grants were broken down as follows: research (£89,400); education (£50).
HOW TO APPLY Application forms for research grants can be downloaded from the charity's website. Contact the correspondent for any other funding enquiries.
CONTACT DETAILS The Trustees, Ward 33, Northern Centre for Cancer Care, Freeman Hospital, Newcastle upon Tyne NE7 7DN *Email* info@ brightred.org.uk *Website* https://brightred.org. uk

■ Bristol Archdeaconry Charity

CC NO 1058853   **ESTABLISHED** 1996
WHERE FUNDING CAN BE GIVEN The Archdeaconry of Bristol and the surrounding area (including the Deanery of Kingswood in South Gloucestershire, and the Benefice of Marshfield with Cold Ashton and Tormarton with West Littleton).
WHO CAN BENEFIT Churches and religious bodies.
WHAT IS FUNDED Church of England ministry and community projects.
TYPE OF GRANT Project funding; start-up funding.
RANGE OF GRANTS £1,000 to £100,000.
SAMPLE GRANTS Diocese of Bristol (£60,000); St Martin's – Knowle (£5,600); All Saints – Fishponds (£5,000); Encounter Christianity (£2,500); St Helen's – Alveston (£1,000).
FINANCES *Financial year end 31/12/2021*
Income £137,100
Grants to organisations £148,000
Assets £4,240,000
TRUSTEES Roger Metcalfe; Peter Woolf; David Worthington; Stephen Gisby; The Revd Richard Croft; Nicholas Bacon; The Ven. Neil Warwick; Adrian Howkins; Ben Silvey; Gene Joyner; Caroline Jowett-Ive; Caroline Duckworth.
HOW TO APPLY Apply in writing to the correspondent. The trustees meet twice during the year.
CONTACT DETAILS A. Maddox, Clerk to the Trustees, All Saints Centre, 1 All Saints Court, Bristol BS1 1JN *Tel.* 0117 929 2709 *Email* ascl. charity@btconnect.com

■ Bristol Charities

CC NO 1109141   **ESTABLISHED** 1960
WHERE FUNDING CAN BE GIVEN In practice, the City of Bristol, North Somerset and South Gloucestershire, mainly within a ten-mile radius of Bristol city centre.
WHO CAN BENEFIT Registered charities; schools; individuals; carers.
WHAT IS FUNDED Social welfare; disability; health; relief of carers; education.
TYPE OF GRANT Capital costs; project funding; start-up funding.
RANGE OF GRANTS Up to £75,000, but mainly under £15,000.
SAMPLE GRANTS Bristol Grammar School (£62,300 in two grants); Carers Support Centre (£9,900);

Queen Elizabeth's Hospital School (£7,800); Khaas (£4,600); Cabot Learning Federation (£2,700).

FINANCES *Financial year end* 31/03/2022
Income £2,100,000
Grants to organisations £90,400
Grants to individuals £211,500
Assets £40,510,000

TRUSTEES Richard Gore; Michelle Meredith; Nolan Webber; Rachel Howell; Andrew Mennell; Olivia Spencer; Keith Low; Ian Dunn; Elizabeth Carrington-Porter; Keith Hicks.

OTHER INFORMATION In total, seven grants were awarded to organisations during 2021/22. The charity also provides almshouse accommodation for older people.

HOW TO APPLY Application forms for each grants programme are available to download from the charity's website, together with full criteria and guidelines.

CONTACT DETAILS The Trustees, 17 St Augustine's Parade, Bristol BS1 4UL *Tel.* 0117 930 0301 *Email* info@bristolcharities.org.uk *Website* www.bristolcharities.org.uk

■ The BRIT Trust

CC NO 1000413   **ESTABLISHED** 1989
WHERE FUNDING CAN BE GIVEN UK.
WHO CAN BENEFIT Charitable organisations.
WHAT IS FUNDED The BRIT Trust considers all applications which meet the criteria within its mission statement: 'improving lives through the power of music and the creative arts.'
TYPE OF GRANT Project funding.
RANGE OF GRANTS Mostly £5,000 to £60,000.
SAMPLE GRANTS The BRIT School (£452,000); Nordoff Robbins Music Therapy (£400,000); BPI BRITs Apprentice Scheme (£194,300).
FINANCES *Financial year end* 31/12/2021
Income £1,690,000
Grants to organisations £1,070,000
Assets £12,620,000
TRUSTEES Geoff Taylor; Tony Wadsworth; David Sharpe; William Rowe; David Munns; Angela Watts; Gerald Doherty; Rita Broe; Henry Semmence; Paul Burger; Caroline Dollimore; Mulika Sannie; Kwame Kwaten.
OTHER INFORMATION The trust mainly supports The Brit School and Nordoff Robbins. However, when possible, the trustees make smaller donations to support additional charitable organisations and activities. These applications are considered at their meeting in November. Only organisations that received grants of over £10,000 were listed as beneficiaries in the trust's accounts. Grants of under £10,000 totalled £25,000.
HOW TO APPLY See the trust's website for the latest information on applications.
CONTACT DETAILS The Trustees, Level 21, 40 Bank Street, Canary Wharf, London E14 5DS *Email* brittrust@bpi.co.uk *Website* www.brittrust.co.uk

■ The Britford Bridge Trust

CC NO 1160012   **ESTABLISHED** 2014
WHERE FUNDING CAN BE GIVEN UK and overseas.
WHO CAN BENEFIT Registered charities.
WHAT IS FUNDED Social welfare; education; health; arts, science, culture and heritage; community development; sport; the environment.
RANGE OF GRANTS Up to £150,000, but mostly from £5,000 to £20,000.

SAMPLE GRANTS Museum of London (£150,000); Addenbrooke's Charitable Trust (£75,000); London Handel Society (£50,000); Tom's Trust (£30,000); RNLI and Seashell Trust (£20,000 each); Friends of the Elderly (£10,000); British Epilepsy Association (£5,000); Derbyshire Wildlife Trust (£3,000).
FINANCES *Financial year end* 05/04/2022
Income £584,100
Grants to organisations £943,500
Assets £30,330,000
TRUSTEES Dr Margaret MacDougall; Adrian Frost; Brodies and Co. (Trustees) Ltd.
OTHER INFORMATION Grants were awarded to 78 organisations during the year.
HOW TO APPLY Contact the correspondent to request an application form. The trustees meet to review applications every three months.
CONTACT DETAILS The Trustees, c/o Brodies LLP, Brodies House, 14–17 Atholl Crescent, Edinburgh EH3 8HA *Tel.* 01224 392264 *Email* thebritfordbridgetrust@brodies.com *Website* https://thebritfordbridgetrust.org

■ The British Academy

CC NO 233176   **ESTABLISHED** 1902
WHERE FUNDING CAN BE GIVEN UK and overseas.
WHO CAN BENEFIT Postdoctoral scholars in the humanities and social sciences, ordinarily resident in the UK.
WHAT IS FUNDED Research grants, international joint activities, appointments, research projects and conferences.
WHAT IS NOT FUNDED Loans for graduate studies.
TYPE OF GRANT All awards are at postdoctoral level only.
RANGE OF GRANTS Up to £5.1 million.
SAMPLE GRANTS University of Oxford (£5.08 million); University of Cambridge (£2.15 million); University of Bristol (£1.2 million); Newcastle University (£1.05 million); University of Nottingham (£816,500); University of Northumbria (£528,700); University of Cardiff (£302,800); University of the West of England (£209,100).
FINANCES *Financial year end* 31/03/2022
Income £54,990,000
Grants to organisations £42,320,000
Grants to individuals £218,300
Assets £39,990,000
TRUSTEES Prof. Aditi Lahiri; Prof. Hamish Scott; Prof. Charles Tripp; Prof. Simon Goldhill; Prof. Simon Swain; Prof. Sarah Birch; Prof. Tony Manstead; Prof. Jane Millar; Prof. Chakravarthi Ram-Prasad; Prof. Annett Volfing; Prof. Sally Shuttleworth; Prof. Conor Gearty; Prof. Isobel Armstrong; Prof. Andrew Hurrell; Prof. Bencie Woll; Prof. Dauvit Bron; Prof. Felix Driver; Prof. Ian Christie; Prof. Angela McRobbie; Prof. Julia Black; Prof. Graeme Barker; Prof. Rana Mitter; Prof. Marianne Elliott; Prof. Christina Boswell.
OTHER INFORMATION Only the 50 largest total payments to single institutions were available to view.
HOW TO APPLY Comprehensive details of grants and awards are available from the academy's website.
CONTACT DETAILS Grants Team, 10 Carlton House Terrace, London SW1Y 5AH *Tel.* 020 7969 5200 *Email* finance@thebritishacademy.ac.uk *Website* www.britac.ac.uk

■ The British and Foreign Bible Society

CC NO 232759   **ESTABLISHED** 1804
WHERE FUNDING CAN BE GIVEN Worldwide.
WHO CAN BENEFIT Registered charities; prisons; immigration centres; schools; universities; places of worship.
WHAT IS FUNDED Projects that make the Bible available and accessible to people around the world.
TYPE OF GRANT Capital costs; project funding; core/revenue costs.
SAMPLE GRANTS A list of beneficiaries was not included in the annual report and accounts.
FINANCES *Financial year end 31/03/2022*
    Income £23,040,000
    Grants to organisations £4,080,000
    Assets £34,590,000
TRUSTEES Catherine Pepinster; Paul Chandler; Ian Dighe; Paul Williams; Keith Starling; Leanne Long; Ramez Atallah; Brenden Thompson; Rosemary Williams; Rochelle Bond; Alan Eccles; Dr Olubunmi Olayisade; Fidelis Omozuapo; Chittoor George.
OTHER INFORMATION A total of 229 grants were made during the year, distributed as follows: engagement and advocacy grants (£1.68 million); capacity-building grants (£1.23 million); production and distribution grants (£553,000); translation grants (£344,000); national grants (£140,000); literacy grants (£104,000).
HOW TO APPLY For international grants: contact the correspondent for further information. For academic grants: application forms can be found at the charity's website. Completed forms should be returned to the Grants Team via email at elaine.young@biblesociety.org.uk, or returned to the correspondent by post.
CONTACT DETAILS Grants Team, Stonehill Green, Westlea, Swindon, Wiltshire SN5 7DG *Tel.* 01793 418100 *Email* info@biblesociety.org.uk *Website* www.biblesociety.org.uk

■ The British and Foreign School Society (BFSS)

CC NO 314286   **ESTABLISHED** 1964
WHERE FUNDING CAN BE GIVEN UK and overseas.
WHO CAN BENEFIT UK-registered charities; educational institutions.
WHAT IS FUNDED Access to education or the quality of education for vulnerable or deprived children and young people under the age of 25. In the UK the BFSS will support access to education or the quality of education for vulnerable or deprived children and young people under the age of 25. Internationally the BFSS supports projects to improve the quality, sustainability, and access to education for young people within international marginalised and deprived communities.
TYPE OF GRANT Capital costs; project funding; unrestricted funding.
RANGE OF GRANTS £5,000 to £30,000.
SAMPLE GRANTS Carefree Fostering Ind (£30,600); YMCA Sutton Coldfield (£29,900); Sheffield Young Carers (£28,300); Royal Caledonian Education Trust (£15,000); Parents and Children Together (£11,200); Northants Music and Performing Arts Trust (£6,000); Kinship Care NI (£5,700).

FINANCES *Financial year end 31/12/2021*
    Income £649,700
    Grants to organisations £876,200
    Grants to individuals £884,300
    Assets £29,570,000
TRUSTEES Peter Miller; Prof. Joy Cooper; Vic Craggs; Jane Creasy; David Baron; Charlotte Cashman; Janice Miller; Anood Al-Samerai; Amy Barnecutt; Dr John Kanyaru.
OTHER INFORMATION The charity awarded grants totalling £1.76 million during the year. Grants to UK projects amounted to £212,600.
HOW TO APPLY Apply via the BFSS website.
CONTACT DETAILS The Trustees, 7–14 Great Dover Street, London SE1 4YR *Email* grants@bfss.org.uk *Website* www.bfss.org.uk

■ British Eye Research Foundation (Fight for Sight)

CC NO 1111438   **ESTABLISHED** 2005
WHERE FUNDING CAN BE GIVEN UK.
WHO CAN BENEFIT Universities; hospitals; other academic or medical organisations.
WHAT IS FUNDED Ophthalmology and research that addresses sight loss across all eye diseases and conditions.
WHAT IS NOT FUNDED Each individual scheme has its own exclusion criteria. See the charity's website for further information.
TYPE OF GRANT Project funding; core costs; capital costs; studentships.
RANGE OF GRANTS Programme dependent.
SAMPLE GRANTS University of Liverpool (£600,000); University College London Institute of Ophthalmology (£465,000); Birmingham Children's Hospital (£245,000); University College London (£99,000); University of Manchester (£52,000); University of Birmingham (£22,000); University of Nottingham (£10,000); Anglia Ruskin University (£10,000).
FINANCES *Financial year end 31/03/2022*
    Income £3,510,000
    Grants to organisations £2,260,000
    Assets £8,010,000
TRUSTEES Dr Amit Patel; Victoria Currey; Darren Barker; Elizabeth Honer; Ly Lam; Heather Goodhew; Roy Quinlan; Louisa Vincent; Prof. Maria Cordeiro; Alina Kessel; Sylvester Oppong; Keith Felton.
OTHER INFORMATION Several grant programmes are offered by the grant-maker each year for research teams who are attached to recognised UK academic or medical institutions. According to its website these include: Small Grants (up to £15,000); Small Grant Awards (delivered in collaboration with other research partners); PhD Studentships (up to £100,000). See the grant-maker's website for further information on current grant programmes. Grants were awarded to 23 organisations during the year.
HOW TO APPLY Information on how to apply can be found on the grant-maker's website.
CONTACT DETAILS Andy Cottell, Director of Finance and Operations, 18 Mansell Street, London E1 8AA *Tel.* 020 7264 3900 *Email* grants@fightforsight.org.uk *Website* www.fightforsight.org.uk

■ British Gas Energy Trust

cc no 1179578   **ESTABLISHED** 2004
WHERE FUNDING CAN BE GIVEN England; Wales; Scotland.
WHO CAN BENEFIT Charitable organisations offering financial/debt advice; individuals.
WHAT IS FUNDED Emergency hardship relief for individuals in the form of clearing gas and electricity debts; financial and debt advice; support for individuals experiencing financial difficulty in addition to health concerns; grants to organisations that provide fuel debt advice services.
WHAT IS NOT FUNDED The following individuals will not be supported: those living outside England, Scotland or Wales; those without electric and/or gas debt; those with savings above £5,000; those who have not received help from a money advice agency; those who have received a grant from the trust within the last two years; those who do not have a current energy account in their name or who are not a member of the household.
TYPE OF GRANT Project funding; capital costs; core costs.
SAMPLE GRANTS A list of beneficiaries was not included in the annual report and accounts.
FINANCES *Financial year end 31/03/2022*
Income £8,300,000
Grants to organisations £3,790,000
Grants to individuals £1,860,000
Assets £2,620,000
TRUSTEES Helen Charlton; Albert Chong; Laurie Lee; Sheila Wheeler; William Gillis; Mark McGillicuddy; Hardial Bhogal; Susan Deacon; Christina Thwaite.
OTHER INFORMATION The trust supports individuals through a hardship fund. Both British Gas customers and non-customers can apply for grants to clear domestic gas and electricity debts owed to British Gas or other suppliers. The trust also funds advice organisations across England, Wales and Scotland.
HOW TO APPLY Applications can be made online via the trust's website.
CONTACT DETAILS The Trustees, Farrer and Co., 65–66 Lincoln's Inn Fields, London WC2A 3LH *Tel.* 020 3375 7496 *Email* contact@ britishgasenergytrust.org.uk *Website* www. britishgasenergytrust.org.uk

■ British Heart Foundation (BHF)

cc no 225971   **ESTABLISHED** 1961
WHERE FUNDING CAN BE GIVEN UK.
WHO CAN BENEFIT Universities; hospitals; charitable organisations related to cardiovascular research.
WHAT IS FUNDED Support for clinical and non-clinical cardiovascular researchers at all stages of their career.
TYPE OF GRANT Capital costs; core costs; project funding; fellowships; partnership funding.
RANGE OF GRANTS Programme dependent.
SAMPLE GRANTS University of Oxford (£9.8 million in ten grants); Imperial College London (£5.8 million in six grants); University of Edinburgh (£3.5 million in five grants); Cambridge University (£2.7 million in three grants); University of Bristol (£1.4 million in two grants); University of Strathclyde (£700,000); University of Glasgow and University of Leicester (£400,000 each).

FINANCES *Financial year end 31/03/2022*
Income £150,000,000
Grants to organisations £72,300,000
Assets £117,000,000
TRUSTEES Prof. David Lomas; Peter Phippen; Daryl Fielding; Dr Sarah Clarke; Timothy Howe; Karen Frank; Prof. Jill Pell; Mark Fitzpatrick; Prof. Sir Munir Pirmohamed; Sir John Hood; Dr Annalisa Jenkins; Wendy Becker; Prof. Brian Walker; Prof. Ismaa Farooqi.
OTHER INFORMATION The foundation has several grant programmes with different levels of funding available. Further details can be found on the foundation's website. In 2021/22, the foundation awarded new research grants worth £72.3 million, including supplements made to new and existing grants. Only the top 50 grants to organisations were listed in the foundation's accounts. Other grants not listed in the accounts can be found in the grants report available on the foundation's website. Grants not listed in the accounts totalled £31.5 million.
HOW TO APPLY Details on how to apply can be found on the foundation's website, along with guidelines and other useful information on the application process.
CONTACT DETAILS Research Funds Department, Greater London House (4th Floor), 180 Hampstead Road, London NW1 7AW *Tel.* 020 7554 0434 *Email* research@bhf.org.uk *Website* www.bhf.org.uk

■ British Humane Association

cc no 207120   **ESTABLISHED** 1922
WHERE FUNDING CAN BE GIVEN UK.
WHO CAN BENEFIT Charitable organisations.
WHAT IS FUNDED General charitable purposes, with a preference for social welfare and human rights.
RANGE OF GRANTS £1,500 to £10,000.
SAMPLE GRANTS Karibuni Trust and Order of St John – St John of Jerusalem Eye Hospital (£10,000 each); InterAct Stroke Support and Sebastian Action Trust (£6,000 each); BlindAid and Child Autism UK (£5,000 each); React (Rapid Effective Assistance for Children with potentially Terminal illness) and Teen Action (£4,000 each); Carousel (£1,600).
FINANCES *Financial year end 31/12/2021*
Income £141,300
Grants to organisations £160,000
Assets £6,010,000
TRUSTEES Anthony Chignell; Philip Gee; Michael Nemko; Rachel Campbell-Johnston; Edward Campbell-Johnston; Dr John Smail; Anna Campbell-Johnston; Anne Holden; Duncan Cantlay.
OTHER INFORMATION Grants totalling £160,000 were awarded to 34 organisations in 2021.
HOW TO APPLY Applications made directly to the grant-maker are not considered. The 2021 annual report states: 'The directors of the Association have decided, that in order to increase the amount available for grant distribution to beneficiaries, they will transfer funds to other charitable organisations, which have in place systems for identifying and assisting deserving cases in need.'
CONTACT DETAILS Sarah Fox, Company Secretary, Suite One, 4 Bessemer Road, Cardiff CF11 8BA *Tel.* 029 2002 2143 *Email* secretary@ britishhumaneassociation.co.uk

■ British Motor Sports Training Trust

CC NO 273828   **ESTABLISHED** 1977
WHERE FUNDING CAN BE GIVEN UK.
WHO CAN BENEFIT Organisations involved with four-wheeled motor sports.
WHAT IS FUNDED Education and training, mainly for volunteer marshals and officials; grants for additional or enhanced safety improvements which comply with Motorsport UK requirements of regulations.
TYPE OF GRANT Capital costs; project funding; strategic funding.
SAMPLE GRANTS Motorsport UK Association Ltd (£117,000); CAM Rescue (£4,000); Association of Motorsport Recovery Operators (£3,600); Ballynahinch and District Motor Club (£2,600); Trent Valley Kart Club (£2,500); Calder Rescue (£1,500); Scottish Association of Motor Sports Clubs (£1,100).
FINANCES *Financial year end* 31/12/2021
Income £129,700
Grants to organisations £140,500
Assets £3,880,000
TRUSTEES Nicky Moffitt; Jim Morris; Dominic Ostrowski; Hugh Chambers; Katherine Traxton; Roderick Parkin; Dr Benjamin Shippey; Philip Foster.
OTHER INFORMATION The trust has two main grant programmes: the Safety Development Fund, which awards grants for safety at closed road and rally events, and the Volunteer and Marshals Training Day Programme, which funds safety training projects. Further information on each programme can be found on the trust's website. Only organisations that received grants of over £1,000 were listed as beneficiaries in the trust's accounts. Grants of under £1,000 totalled £240.
HOW TO APPLY Application forms and further information on the application process can be found on the trust's website. Application forms can either be downloaded and sent to the correspondent or be filled out online.
CONTACT DETAILS Allan Dean-Lewis, Secretary, Birds Nest, 28 Tan y Bryn Road, Llandudno LL30 1UU *Tel.* 07801 591332 *Email* gensec@bmstt.org *Website* www.bmstt.org

■ J. and M. Britton Charitable Trust

CC NO 1081979   **ESTABLISHED** 1996
WHERE FUNDING CAN BE GIVEN Bristol.
WHO CAN BENEFIT Local charitable organisations; individuals; hospices; educational organisations.
WHAT IS FUNDED General charitable purposes; education; relief of poverty.
RANGE OF GRANTS Typically up to £20,000 but mostly under £5,000.
SAMPLE GRANTS A list of beneficiaries was not included in the annual report and accounts. Previous beneficiaries have included: Bristol Music Trust (£20,000); Jessie May (£10,000); Access Sport (£5,000); Gympanzees (£5,000); SENSE (£3,000) Royal Forestry Society (£1,000); Disabled Travel Service (£1,000); Badminton School (£1,000).
FINANCES *Financial year end* 05/04/2022
Income £82,400
Grants to organisations £162,800
Assets £3,690,000
TRUSTEES Robert Bernays; Annie Bernays; Richard Bernays; Caroline Duckworth; Alison Bernays; Lady Merrison.

OTHER INFORMATION During the year, grants of over £1,000 were awarded to 54 organisations. Grants of less than £1,000 totalled £28,800. No grants were awarded to individuals during the year.
HOW TO APPLY Apply in writing to the correspondent. The trustees meet regularly to consider applications.
CONTACT DETAILS The Trustees, 3A Merlin Haven, Wotton-under-Edge, Gloucestershire GL12 7BA *Tel.* 01453 498044

■ The Bromley Trust

CC NO 801875   **ESTABLISHED** 1989
WHERE FUNDING CAN BE GIVEN UK.
WHO CAN BENEFIT UK-registered charities with an annual turnover of between £100,000 and £5 million.
WHAT IS FUNDED Human rights; prison reform.
WHAT IS NOT FUNDED See the trust's website for a full list of exclusions.
TYPE OF GRANT Unrestricted.
RANGE OF GRANTS Mostly £5,000 to £20,000.
SAMPLE GRANTS Prison Reform Trust (£40,000); Detention Action (£20,000); Article 39 (£15,000); Hear Me Out and Women In Prison (£10,000 each); Koestler Trust (£9,000).
FINANCES *Financial year end* 31/03/2022
Income £251,100
Grants to organisations £774,500
Assets £17,430,000
TRUSTEES Fiona Cramb; Adam McCormack; Helen Curtis; Rod Clark; Phillip Everett; Dr Jamie Bennett; Dr Eleanor Brown; Alison McGinley.
OTHER INFORMATION Grants were broken down as follows: human rights (£395,000); prison reform (£349,500).
HOW TO APPLY Application forms and guidelines are available from the trust's helpful website.
CONTACT DETAILS The Trustees, Studio 5, Unit G03, The Leather Market, 11/13 Weston Street, London SE1 3ER *Email* enquiries@thebromleytrust.org.uk. *Website* www.thebromleytrust.org.uk

■ The Brook Trust

CC NO 1123562   **ESTABLISHED** 2008
WHERE FUNDING CAN BE GIVEN UK.
WHO CAN BENEFIT Registered charities.
WHAT IS FUNDED Support for people affected by domestic and sexual abuse; early intervention programmes with children and families aiming to break cycles of social and economic deprivation and dysfunction.
TYPE OF GRANT Core costs; front-line projects. Often multi-year grants.
SAMPLE GRANTS Refuge (£125,000); Disasters Emergency Committee (£70,000); Twins Trust (£26,000); Northamptonshire Rape Crisis (£10,000); Child Autism UK (£5,000).
FINANCES *Financial year end* 05/04/2022
Income £588,400
Grants to organisations £1,280,000
Assets £4,670,000
TRUSTEES Tim Bull; Rosalind Riley; Dr Elinor Cleghorn.
OTHER INFORMATION Grants are also made via The Brook Trust Fund for Kent, which is administered by Kent Community Foundation. The trust's website states: 'The Brook Trust Fund for Kent will make grants to organisations and individuals working to achieve positive social outcomes, using early intervention where possible, tackling disadvantage, deprivation and

social exclusion, particularly in areas such as the elderly, offenders, women's groups, parenting support for vulnerable families. Grants range from £500 to £5,000.'

HOW TO APPLY The Brook Trust will not consider unsolicited funding applications. See the Kent Community Foundation website for further information on The Brook Trust Fund for Kent.

CONTACT DETAILS The Trustees, PO Box 161, Cranbrook, Kent TN17 9BL *Email* info@brooktrust.org *Website* www.brooktrust.org

■ The Consuelo and Anthony Brooke Charitable Trust

CC NO 1150569   **ESTABLISHED** 2013

WHERE FUNDING CAN BE GIVEN Barnet; Camden; City of Westminster; East Sussex; Kensington and Chelsea; West Sussex.

WHO CAN BENEFIT Charitable organisations.

WHAT IS FUNDED Education; the arts; community development; health.

SAMPLE GRANTS A list of beneficiaries was not included in the annual report and accounts.

FINANCES *Financial year end* 05/04/2022
Income £94,600
Grants to organisations £115,500
Assets £3,800

TRUSTEES Anthony Brooke; Carol Brooke; Charlotte Eade; Alexander Brooke.

HOW TO APPLY Apply in writing to the correspondent.

CONTACT DETAILS The Trustees, 20 Caroline Place, London W2 4AN *Tel.* 07802 796416 *Email* anthonylbrooke@btinternet.com

■ The Rory and Elizabeth Brooks Foundation

CC NO 1111587   **ESTABLISHED** 2005

WHERE FUNDING CAN BE GIVEN UK and overseas.

WHO CAN BENEFIT Charitable organisations.

WHAT IS FUNDED International development; poverty research; higher education; social justice; visual arts.

RANGE OF GRANTS £20,000 to £100,000.

SAMPLE GRANTS Platinum Jubilee (£100,000); Justice and Care (£35,000); Tate Foundation (£27,200).

FINANCES *Financial year end* 31/01/2022
Income £820,100
Grants to organisations £199,300
Assets £862,900

TRUSTEES Elizabeth Brooks; Roderick Brooks; Bridget Fury.

OTHER INFORMATION During the year, grants were awarded to 12 organisations. Only three beneficiaries were listed in the annual report.

HOW TO APPLY Apply in writing to the correspondent.

CONTACT DETAILS Robyn Bryson, Correspondent, Orion House, 5 Upper St Martin's Lane, London WC2H 9EA *Tel.* 020 7024 2217 *Email* RBryson@mmlcapital.com

■ The Broomton Foundation

CC NO 1125386   **ESTABLISHED** 2008

WHERE FUNDING CAN BE GIVEN East Anglia.

WHO CAN BENEFIT Charitable organisations.

WHAT IS FUNDED General charitable purposes.

TYPE OF GRANT Capital and project costs.

RANGE OF GRANTS From £210 to £500,000.

SAMPLE GRANTS University of Pennsylvania (USA) Foundation Ltd (£50,000): Riding for the Disabled Foundation (£80,000); Feeding Britain,

Maggie's Centre (£50,000 each); Pancreatic Cancer UK (£10,000); Service Dogs UK (£210).

FINANCES *Financial year end* 05/04/2022
Income £3,560,000
Grants to organisations £834,800
Assets £19,140,000

TRUSTEES Benedicta Chamberlain; Julius Chamberlain; Robert Chamberlain; Kate Lewis.

HOW TO APPLY Contact the correspondent for further information.

CONTACT DETAILS The Trustees, Providence House, 141–145 Princes Street, Ipswich, Suffolk IP1 1QJ *Tel.* 01473 232300 *Email* admin@broomton.org

■ The Brothers Trust

CC NO 1172675   **ESTABLISHED** 2017

WHERE FUNDING CAN BE GIVEN UK and overseas, including the USA.

WHO CAN BENEFIT Registered charities.

WHAT IS FUNDED General charitable purposes; social welfare; health.

SAMPLE GRANTS Momentum (£110,300); DEBRA (£75,000); John Foundation (£46,900); Stem 4 (£27,500); Storybook Dads (£13,000); Warm Heart (£7,600); Mind Step Foundation (£3,800); Spark School Book Grant (£1,500).

FINANCES *Financial year end* 31/03/2022
Income £732,300
Grants to organisations £612,900
Assets £172,800

TRUSTEES Dominic Holland; Thomas Holland; Nicola Holland; Gregory Cook; Janine Cook; Andrea Coates; Lena Hoon Koay.

HOW TO APPLY Apply in writing to the correspondent. The trust's Charity Commission record states that it 'identifies needs itself and considers unsolicited applications for funds.'

CONTACT DETAILS The Trustees, c/o SA Ledgers Ltd, 57 Canbury Park Road, Kingston upon Thames, Surrey KT2 6LQ *Tel.* 020 3649 1665 *Website* www.thebrotherstrust.org

■ The Charles Brotherton Trust

CC NO 227067   **ESTABLISHED** 1940

WHERE FUNDING CAN BE GIVEN The cities of Birmingham, Leeds, Liverpool, Wakefield and York, and Bebington in Wirral.

WHO CAN BENEFIT Charitable organisations.

WHAT IS FUNDED Education; organised recreational activities; older people; social welfare; children and young people.

WHAT IS NOT FUNDED Individuals.

RANGE OF GRANTS Generally up to £500.

SAMPLE GRANTS University of Leeds – Brotherton Library (£6,000); Brotherton Charity Trust (£1,300); PDSA Student Training Scheme (£350); Meanwood Valley Urban Farm (£300); Conservation Volunteers (£275); Shaftesbury Youth Club (£250); Support Dogs (£230); Helplink Community Support (£180); Northfield ECO Centre (£150).

FINANCES *Financial year end* 31/03/2022
Income £66,600
Grants to organisations £70,000
Assets £2,240,000

TRUSTEES Christopher Brotherton-Ratcliffe; David Brotherton; Helen Brotherton-Lloyd; Dominic Jones.

OTHER INFORMATION During 2021/22, the trust awarded grants to 276 beneficiaries. The grants were distributed as follows: Leeds (£26,000); Birmingham (£13,000); Bebington and Wirral

(£6,500); Liverpool (£6,500); Wakefield (£6,500); York (£6,500).

HOW TO APPLY Apply in writing to the correspondent. The application should clearly show your organisation's activities, geographical area of operations and for what the funds are required. Applications should be accompanied by your organisation's most recent set of accounts. There is no formal application form and applications are not acknowledged. Grants are considered by the trustees at the start of the trust's accounting year in April and a single payment is made to successful applicants in October.

CONTACT DETAILS The Secretary, PO Box 374, Harrogate, North Yorkshire HG1 4YW *Email* admin@charlesbrothertontrust.com *Website* www.charlesbrothertontrust.com

■ Bill Brown 1989 Charitable Trust

CC NO 801756   **ESTABLISHED** 1989

WHERE FUNDING CAN BE GIVEN England, with a strong preference for the south of England.

WHO CAN BENEFIT UK-registered charities; hospices.

WHAT IS FUNDED Research into blindness; medical research; deaf and blind people; older people; people with disabilities; social welfare.

WHAT IS NOT FUNDED Individuals; animal welfare; small (local) charitable causes; appeals from regional branches of national charitable organisations; wildlife and environmental conservation; maintenance of buildings; religious charities.

TYPE OF GRANT Research funding; project funding.

RANGE OF GRANTS Typically less than £15,000.

SAMPLE GRANTS Charities Aid Foundation (£75,000); University of Bristol (£30,000); Macmillan Cancer Support (£15,000); BRACE (£10,000); Marie Curie Cancer Care (£7,500); Fight Against Blindness (£5,000); Richmond Borough Mind (£3,800).

FINANCES *Financial year end* 30/06/2021
Income £495,400
Grants to organisations £974,100
Assets £13,580,000

TRUSTEE Bill Brown Charity Trustees.

OTHER INFORMATION In 2020/21 the charity awarded £750,000 in eight payments to Churchill College, Cambridge, which funds the interdisciplinary Bill Brown Creative Workshop programme. The 2020/21 accounts were the latest available at the time of writing (June 2023).

HOW TO APPLY Applications should be sent in writing via email to the correspondent with a copy of your organisation's latest annual report and accounts. Applications must be received by the end of April or the end of September to be sure of consideration at the summer or winter trustees' meeting. Information on what to include in the application can be found on the charity's website.

CONTACT DETAILS The Trustees, 10 New Square, Lincolns Inn, London WC2A 3QG *Tel.* 020 7465 4300 *Email* appeals@billbrowncharity.org *Website* www.billbrowncharity.org

■ The Mary Brown Memorial Trust

OSCR NO SC048591

WHERE FUNDING CAN BE GIVEN UK and overseas.

WHO CAN BENEFIT Charitable organisations.

WHAT IS FUNDED Advancement of the Christian faith; education; social welfare; health; citizenship

and community development; religious and racial harmony; equality and diversity.

WHAT IS NOT FUNDED Non-charitable organisations; charities whose main aim is influencing policy or lobbying; general running costs of a project; political parties.

TYPE OF GRANT Project funding; capital costs; core costs.

RANGE OF GRANTS Small grants of up to £5,000; large grants of up to £50,000.

SAMPLE GRANTS Glasgow City Mission (£15,000); Auldhouse Community Church (£10,000); Cathcart Youth Ministry Partnership (£6,000); Disasters Emergency Committee – Afghanistan Crisis Appeal, Exodus Trust and Prison Fellowship England (£5,000 each); Hearts and Minds (£4,700); Mosaic Middle East (£4,400).

FINANCES *Financial year end* 31/12/2021
Income £5,600
Grants to organisations £109,800
Assets £656,600

OTHER INFORMATION Fifteen grants were awarded to organisations during the year.

HOW TO APPLY Apply via the trust's website. The trustees meet three times per year.

CONTACT DETAILS The Trustees, 51 Netherauldhouse Road, Glasgow G43 2XG *Email* use the contact form on the website *Website* http://marybrowntrust.com

■ The Brown Source Trust

CC NO 1165158   **ESTABLISHED** 2016

WHERE FUNDING CAN BE GIVEN UK and overseas.

WHO CAN BENEFIT Charitable organisations.

WHAT IS FUNDED General charitable purposes, including social welfare, humanitarian aid and environmental needs.

TYPE OF GRANT Project funding; multi-year grants; unrestricted funding.

RANGE OF GRANTS Typically up to £15,000.

SAMPLE GRANTS Ebony Horse Club and Snowdrop Project (£15,000 each); The Charitable Trust for the Tongabezi Trust School (£11,800); RSPB (£10,000); The British Asian Trust, Catch 22 Charity Ltd and Kindred Studios CIC (£5,000 each); Christ's College Cambridge (£1,400).

FINANCES *Financial year end* 21/11/2021
Income £16,700
Grants to organisations £68,200
Assets £204,200

TRUSTEES Nicola Brown; Alan Brown; Hannah Brown; Harry Brown; Chloe Noble; Jack Brown; Ludlow Trust Company Ltd.

OTHER INFORMATION The 2020/21 accounts were the latest available at the time of writing (June 2023). The trust awarded grants to eight organisations during the period.

HOW TO APPLY The trust's website states the following: 'In general, we source most of the organisations we provide grants to from our own research. However, if you email harry@brown-source.com with some basic information about yourself then we will do our best to get back to you soon.'

CONTACT DETAILS The Trustees, Ludlow Trust Co. Ltd, Tower Wharf, Cheese Lane, Bristol BS2 0JJ *Tel.* 0117 313 8200 *Email* harry@brown-source.com *Website* http://brownsourcetrust.org.uk

■ R. S. Brownless Charitable Trust

CC NO 1000320 **ESTABLISHED** 1990

WHERE FUNDING CAN BE GIVEN Mainly UK, but occasionally overseas.

WHO CAN BENEFIT Registered charities; schools; amateur sports clubs; hospices.

WHAT IS FUNDED General charitable purposes including: disability, illness, social welfare; older people.

TYPE OF GRANT Project funding.

RANGE OF GRANTS Normally under £1,000.

SAMPLE GRANTS A list of beneficiaries was not included in the annual report and accounts.

FINANCES *Financial year end 09/07/2022*
Income £37,600
Grants to organisations £52,700
Assets £1,380,000

TRUSTEES Philippa Nicolai; Frances Plummer.

HOW TO APPLY Apply in writing to the correspondent.

CONTACT DETAILS The Trustees, Hennerton Holt, Hennerton, Wargrave, Reading, Berkshire RG10 8PD *Tel.* 0118 940 4029

■ The Brownsword Charitable Foundation

CC NO 1012615 **ESTABLISHED** 1992

WHERE FUNDING CAN BE GIVEN Bath and the surrounding areas.

WHO CAN BENEFIT Charitable organisations.

WHAT IS FUNDED Children and young people; the arts; older people; community work; people with learning difficulties; education; medical research.

RANGE OF GRANTS Between £1,000 and £200,000.

SAMPLE GRANTS Forever Friends Appeal – Royal United Hospital (£200,000); Arts Taunton (£45,000); Bath Abbey (£25,000); Bath Festivals Ltd and Royal Horticultural Society (£5,000 each); Merchant Venturers (£2,000).

FINANCES *Financial year end 31/12/2021*
Income £234,800
Grants to organisations £283,000
Assets £11,270,000

TRUSTEES Andrew Brownsword; Robert Calleja; Peter Matthews; Allesandra Brownsword-Matthews.

OTHER INFORMATION Grants were made to seven organisations.

HOW TO APPLY Apply in writing to the correspondent.

CONTACT DETAILS The Trustees, 4 Queen Square, Bath, Somerset BA1 2HA *Tel.* 01225 339661

■ T. B. H. Brunner's Charitable Settlement

CC NO 260604 **ESTABLISHED** 1969

WHERE FUNDING CAN BE GIVEN UK, with some preference for Oxfordshire.

WHO CAN BENEFIT Registered charities; individuals; places of worship; statutory authorities; uniformed groups; hospitals; museums, galleries and libraries.

WHAT IS FUNDED Church of England preservation projects; historical preservation; arts and culture, including music; the armed forces; health; general charitable purposes.

RANGE OF GRANTS Between £100 and £7,200.

SAMPLE GRANTS Rotherfield Greys PCC (£20,000 in six grants); The National Trust (£14,400 in two grants); Institute of Economic Affairs (£5,000); Oxford Historic Churches Trust (£4,000); Dorchester Festival (£3,000); British Red Cross and The London Library (£1,000 each); Royal British Legion and The Listening Library (£500

each); Moorfield Eye Hospital, St Paul's Cathedral and Venice Peril Fund (£100 each).

FINANCES *Financial year end 05/04/2022*
Income £80,600
Grants to organisations £72,400
Assets £4,200,000

TRUSTEES Helen Brunner; Dr Imogen Brunner; Timothy Brunner.

HOW TO APPLY Apply in writing to the correspondent.

CONTACT DETAILS The Trustees, 2 Inverness Gardens, London W8 4RN *Tel.* 020 7727 6277 *Email* p.roberts@robco.uk.com

■ The Jack Brunton Charitable Trust

CC NO 518407 **ESTABLISHED** 1986

WHERE FUNDING CAN BE GIVEN The North Riding area of Yorkshire (prior to the boundary changes in 1974).

WHO CAN BENEFIT Charities and community organisations, including: churches; Scouts and Girl Guide groups; village halls; amateur sports clubs; social enterprises; hospital departments; drama, theatre and music groups; mountain rescue teams; schools; accessible transport services.

WHAT IS FUNDED General charitable purposes.

TYPE OF GRANT Capital costs, including medical, sports and leisure equipment; refurbishment and building costs for churches; project funding.

RANGE OF GRANTS Up to £10,000.

SAMPLE GRANTS Disasters Emergency Committee – Ukraine Humanitarian Appeal (£100,000); Great North Air Ambulance and Yorkshire Air Ambulance (£75,000 each); Leeds Hospital Charity (£10,000); House of Mercy – Middlesbrough (£7,000); St Catherine's Hospice – Scarborough (£5,000); Teenage Cancer Trust (£4,000); Open Country – York (£3,000); Great Ayton Dramatic Society (£2,250).

FINANCES *Financial year end 05/04/2022*
Income £340,700
Grants to organisations £453,900
Assets £12,070,000

TRUSTEES James Lumb; Derek Noble; David Swallow; Caroline Dickinson; Andrew Dickins.

OTHER INFORMATION Grants were awarded to 77 organisations during the year. This includes 41 grants of £2,000 or less. Only the beneficiaries of grants of above £2,000 were listed in the accounts.

HOW TO APPLY Application forms can be downloaded from the trust's website and should be signed before returning to the correspondent. The trustees meet on a quarterly basis to consider applications.

CONTACT DETAILS David Swallow, Administrator and Trustee, Commercial House, 10 Bridge Road, Stokesley, North Yorkshire TS9 5AA *Tel.* 01642 711407 *Email* margaretc@swallco.co.uk *Website* www.jackbruntontrust.co.uk

■ Brushmill Ltd

CC NO 285420 **ESTABLISHED** 1982

WHERE FUNDING CAN BE GIVEN UK and overseas.

WHO CAN BENEFIT Organisations benefitting Jewish people.

WHAT IS FUNDED Jewish education and places of worship for the Jewish community; social welfare; education.

RANGE OF GRANTS Up to £178,500.

SAMPLE GRANTS Friends of Boyan Trust (£178,400); Chasdei Aharon Ltd (£46,800); Zoreya Tzedokos

(£17,100); Yad Shlomo Trust (£11,800); Bais Rizhin Trust (£8,600); YTV London (£4,500); Friends of Zichron Dovid (£3,300); Amud Hatzdokoh Trust (£3,000).

FINANCES *Financial year end 31/03/2022*
Income £314,900
Grants to organisations £296,200
Assets £18,800

TRUSTEES Mr C. Getter; Mrs E. Weinberger; Mr J. Weinberger.

OTHER INFORMATION Only beneficiaries that received grants of over £3,000 were listed in the accounts. Grants of less than £3,000 totalled £22,700, Grants of over £3,000 were awarded to eight organisations and totalled £273,500.

HOW TO APPLY Apply in writing to the correspondent. The charity's 2021/22 accounts state: 'The Trustees consider all requests which they receive and make donations based on the level of funds available.'

CONTACT DETAILS M. Getter, Secretary, 76 Fairholt Road, London N16 5HN *Tel.* 020 8731 0777 *Email* mail@cohenarnold.com

---

■ Buckingham Trust

CC NO 237350 **ESTABLISHED** 1962
WHERE FUNDING CAN BE GIVEN UK.
WHO CAN BENEFIT Charitable organisations; schools and colleges; places of worship; statutory authorities; hospices; individuals.
WHAT IS FUNDED Christianity, including missionary activities; secular and religious education; social welfare; health and medical; work outside the UK.
RANGE OF GRANTS Mostly up to around £10,000, with the occasional larger grant.
SAMPLE GRANTS Langham Partnership (£61,100); St Andrew's PCC (£25,500); Global Clubfoot International (£13,200); European Christian Mission (£9,000); Liverpool One (£5,900); Care for the Family (£2,500).
FINANCES *Financial year end 05/04/2022*
Income £319,800
Grants to organisations £457,200
Grants to individuals £2,200
Assets £636,400
TRUSTEES Richard Foot; Christina Clay.
OTHER INFORMATION Only organisations that received grants of over £2,500 were listed as beneficiaries. Grants of under £2,500 totalled £81,400. The 2021/22 accounts state that the trust was "working towards closing" and consequently, the trustees had begun "disposing of investments, and giving the funds to other charities."
HOW TO APPLY Apply in writing to the correspondent.
CONTACT DETAILS Christina Clay, Trustee, c/o Foot Davson Ltd, 17 Church Road, Tunbridge Wells, Kent TN1 1LG *Tel.* 01892 774774

■ Buckinghamshire Community Foundation

CC NO 1073861 **ESTABLISHED** 1998
WHERE FUNDING CAN BE GIVEN The administrative county of Buckinghamshire, excluding Milton Keynes.
WHO CAN BENEFIT Registered charities; unregistered charities; CICs limited by guarantee; social enterprises; clubs and societies; associations; amateur sports clubs; hospices; individuals; local authorities.
WHAT IS FUNDED General charitable purposes; community development; social welfare; the environment; health; children and young people; community safety.
TYPE OF GRANT Capital costs; core/revenue costs; seed funding/start-up funding; project funding. Different types of grants are available through the funding programmes.
RANGE OF GRANTS Up to £20,000, but mostly between £1,000 and £5,000.
SAMPLE GRANTS Youth Concern (£46,500); Wycombe Women's Aid (£24,500); Children in Care (£12,000); NEST – Aylesbury Vale (£10,000).
FINANCES *Financial year end 31/03/2022*
Income £2,520,000
Grants to organisations £981,300
Grants to individuals £351,600
Assets £10,570,000
TRUSTEES Lynda Marston-Weston; Philip Manktelow; Robert Taylor; Annalise Smith; Lucy Wood; Moir Stewart; Richard Collins; Mark Bradbury; Philippa Kirkbride; George Anson; Annie Beadle.
OTHER INFORMATION This is one of the 47 UK community foundations, which distribute funding for a wide range of purposes. As with all community foundations, there are a number of donor-advised funds managed on behalf of individuals, families and charitable trusts. Grant schemes tend to change frequently – consult the foundation's website for details of current programmes and up-to-date deadlines.
HOW TO APPLY Potential applicants are advised to visit the community foundation's website or contact its grants team to find the most suitable funding stream.
CONTACT DETAILS The Trustees, New Road, Weston Turville, Aylesbury, Buckinghamshire HP22 5QT *Tel.* 01296 330134 *Email* info@buckscf.org *Website* http://heartofbucks.org

---

■ The Buffini Chao Foundation

CC NO 1111022 **ESTABLISHED** 2005
WHERE FUNDING CAN BE GIVEN UK and overseas.
WHO CAN BENEFIT Charitable organisations.
WHAT IS FUNDED Enhancing education and opportunity for children and young people.
TYPE OF GRANT Capital costs; project funding; development funding; strategic funding.
RANGE OF GRANTS Up to £100,000.
SAMPLE GRANTS Royal National Theatre (£250,000); Victoria and Albert Museum (£125,000); Seaview (£40,000); Sporting Way (£4,100).
FINANCES *Financial year end 05/04/2022*
Income £2,710,000
Grants to organisations £683,300
Assets £13,060,000
TRUSTEES Lady Buffini; Sir Damon Buffini; Maria Hindmarsh; Sue Gutierrez.
HOW TO APPLY The foundation's support is primarily determined through the trustees' experience, personal networks and research. Charities that meet the foundation's core objectives can get in touch with the correspondent.
CONTACT DETAILS Alison Taylor, Foundation Secretary, PO Box 1427, Northampton, Northamptonshire NN1 9FP *Email* trustees@ buffinichao.com *Website* www.buffinichao.com

■ Building and Civil Engineering Charitable Trust

CC NO 1004732 **ESTABLISHED** 1991
WHERE FUNDING CAN BE GIVEN UK.
WHO CAN BENEFIT Charitable organisations; not-for-profit organisations; research organisations; individuals.
WHAT IS FUNDED Education, training and retraining for operatives, past operatives and young people who want to start working in the construction industry; education, training and research for occupational health and safety initiatives in the construction industry; hardship grants for individuals who work, or have worked, in the construction industry.
WHAT IS NOT FUNDED Public sector bodies; overheads; project management fees; non-UK based organisations.
TYPE OF GRANT Project funding; annual awards; research; pro bono support for individuals.
RANGE OF GRANTS Up to £25,000.
SAMPLE GRANTS Mates in Mind and Institute for Employment Studies (£25,000 for a joint research project); Construction Youth Trust (£20,000 from the Mowlem Award); Crawley Open House and Smart Business Assistance (£5,000 each).
FINANCES *Financial year end 30/09/2021*
Income £363,900
Grants to organisations £122,200
Grants to individuals £74,300
Assets £72,900
TRUSTEES Jeremy Swain; Vaughan Hart; Stephen Terrell; Patrick Heath-Lay; Robert Miosh.
OTHER INFORMATION Grants were broken down as follows: education and retraining – organisations (£97,200) and individuals (£3,400); social welfare – individuals (£57,000) and organisations (£0); research and training for occupational safety – organisations (£25,000) and individuals (£13,900). The 2020/21 accounts were the latest available at the time of writing (May 2023).
HOW TO APPLY Contact the correspondent for further information and an application form.
CONTACT DETAILS Alena Aliokhna, Secretary, Manor Royal, Crawley, West Sussex RH10 9QP *Tel.* 0300 200 0600 *Email* charitabletrust@bandce.co.uk *Website* https://bandce.co.uk/corporate-responsibility/the-charitable-trust

■ Bulb Foundation

CC NO 1183235
WHERE FUNDING CAN BE GIVEN UK and overseas.
WHO CAN BENEFIT Charitable organisations.
WHAT IS FUNDED Climate change.
TYPE OF GRANT Project funding; seed funding.
SAMPLE GRANTS Carbon Tracker Initiative and Third Generation Environmentalism (£100,000 each); Anthropocene Fixed Income Institute, Boston University Global Development Policy Center, Energy Unlocked and Climate Foundation (£75,000 each); Overseas Development Institute (£15,000).
FINANCES *Financial year end 31/03/2022*
Income £636,800
Grants to organisations £940,000
Assets £397,600
TRUSTEES Hayden Wood; Amit Gudka; Dr Alexander Edwards; Sophie Pullan; Dr Amal-Lee Amin.
OTHER INFORMATION The foundation is associated with green energy supplier Bulb Energy Ltd.
HOW TO APPLY The foundation seeks out organisations it wishes to fund.
CONTACT DETAILS The Trustees, 155 Bishopsgate, London EC2M 3TQ *Tel.* 020 7256 5992 *Email* allisonrobertshaw@bulbfoundation.org *Website* https://bulb.co.uk/foundation

■ The Bulldog Trust Ltd

CC NO 1123081 **ESTABLISHED** 2008
WHERE FUNDING CAN BE GIVEN UK.
WHO CAN BENEFIT Registered charities; CICs; community benefit societies.
WHAT IS FUNDED General charitable purposes. Grants are given in the following categories: youth and education; arts and culture; health and well-being; human rights, law and justice; the environment; poverty and disadvantage; disability.
TYPE OF GRANT Unrestricted.
RANGE OF GRANTS Up to £30,000.
SAMPLE GRANTS Escape2Make and Tempus Novo (£30,000 each); Powerhouse Creative CIC (£29,400); Red Hen Project and WAM Youth (£15,000 each); Safe Soulmates (£14,500); Cambridge Community Arts (£12,800); Agnes Smith Advice Centre (£10,000).
FINANCES *Financial year end 30/06/2022*
Income £2,060,000
Grants to organisations £941,400
Assets £9,140,000
TRUSTEES Charles Hoare; Hamish McPherson; Stephen Sacks.
OTHER INFORMATION The Fore is a grant-making initiative of The Bulldog Trust. The trust's 2021/22 annual report notes that The Fore is in the process of becoming independent from the trust; however, the organisations will remain closely linked. Grants awarded in 2021/22 in conjunction with The Fore totalled £893,600. Grants awarded by The Bulldog Trust totalled £47,800.
HOW TO APPLY Contact the trust for more information. Applications for The Fore can be made via its website at www.thefore.org.
CONTACT DETAILS The Trustees, 2 Temple Place, London WC2R 3BD *Tel.* 020 7240 6044 *Email* info@bulldogtrust.org *Website* https://twotempleplace.org/about-us/the-bulldog-trust

■ E. F. Bulmer Trust

CC NO 1188978 **ESTABLISHED** 1938
WHERE FUNDING CAN BE GIVEN Herefordshire.
WHO CAN BENEFIT Registered charities; unregistered charities; social enterprises; CICs; schools; universities; hospices; individuals.
WHAT IS FUNDED Social welfare; health. Former employees of H. P. Bulmer Holdings plc and individuals who are in need.
WHAT IS NOT FUNDED A list of exclusions can be found on the trust's website.
TYPE OF GRANT Capital costs; core and revenue costs; seed funding and start-up funding; unrestricted funding.
RANGE OF GRANTS Mostly under £5,000.
SAMPLE GRANTS The Cartshed (£7,000); Livability (£5,000); Growing Point (£6,000); Midlands Air Ambulance (£5,000); Royal National College (£4,000); Hereford Yoga (£3,500); Herefordshire Riding for the Disabled and Marches Counselling Service (£3,000 each).
FINANCES *Financial year end 31/03/2022*
Income £396,400
Grants to organisations £91,700
Grants to individuals £38,700
Assets £17,880,000

TRUSTEES Andrew Murray; Gillian Bulmer; Andrew Patten; Penelope Murray.

OTHER INFORMATION A total of 27 organisations were supported during 2021/22.

HOW TO APPLY Application forms are available to download from the trust's website. Once completed, they should be returned by email. The trustees meet four times a year to consider grant applications. Check the website for application deadlines.

CONTACT DETAILS Paddy Nugent, Chief Operating Officer, Fred Bulmer Centre, Wall Street, Hereford, Herefordshire HR4 9HP *Tel.* 01432 271293 *Email* efbulmer@gmail.com *Website* www.efbulmer.co.uk

■ Bupa Foundation

CC NO 1162759   **ESTABLISHED** 2015

WHERE FUNDING CAN BE GIVEN UK.

WHO CAN BENEFIT Registered charities; social enterprises; CICs; for-profit organisations.

WHAT IS FUNDED Children and young people's mental health.

TYPE OF GRANT Project funding.

SAMPLE GRANTS A list of beneficiaries was not included in the annual report and accounts. Previous beneficiaries have included: Asthma UK (£115,000); Muscular Dystrophy UK (£45,300); Single Homeless Project (£23,000); Cruse Bereavement Care (£22,800); Salford Foundation (£22,300); Bike for Good and Cardiff Community Trust (£1,000 each).

FINANCES *Financial year end 31/12/2021*
Income £1,190,000
Grants to organisations £984,400
Assets £138,800

TRUSTEES Dr Paula Franklin; Andrea Spyropoulos; Dr Helen Cliffe; Sally Pain; Thomas Hoosen-Webber; Mark Callister-Davies; Alexandra Cole; Robert Edmundson; Siobhan Moynihan.

OTHER INFORMATION Grants were made to 82 organisations during the year.

HOW TO APPLY Contact the correspondent or your local Community Committee for further information.

CONTACT DETAILS The Trustees, Battle Bridge House, 300–306 Gray's Inn Road, London WC1X 8DU *Email* bupafoundation@bupa.com *Website* www.bupaukfoundation.org

■ The Burberry Foundation

CC NO 1154468   **ESTABLISHED** 2013

WHERE FUNDING CAN BE GIVEN Worldwide, with a strong preference for communities where Burberry employees live and work.

WHO CAN BENEFIT Registered charities.

WHAT IS FUNDED STEAM education; educational equality; waste reduction; social and economic development.

SAMPLE GRANTS Teach First (£485,300); Ideas (£400,000); Unicef (£320,000); MyKindaCrowd (£132,100); King's College London (£50,600).

FINANCES *Financial year end 31/03/2022*
Income £1,800,000
Grants to organisations £2,700,000
Assets £2,350,000

TRUSTEES Christopher Holmes; Edward Rash; Dr Gerard Murphy.

OTHER INFORMATION Grants to UK organisations totalled £2.1 million.

HOW TO APPLY Apply in writing to the correspondent.

CONTACT DETAILS Pamela Batty, Secretary, Burberry Ltd, Horseferry House, Horseferry Road, London SW1P 2AW *Tel.* 020 7806 1328

Email enquiries@burberryfoundation.com
Website www.burberryplc.com/en/responsibility/policies/communities/the-burberry-foundation.html

■ The Burden Trust

CC NO 235859   **ESTABLISHED** 1913

WHERE FUNDING CAN BE GIVEN UK, mainly Bristol.

WHO CAN BENEFIT Charitable organisations; hospitals; retirement homes; schools and training institutions.

WHAT IS FUNDED Medical research; social welfare.

TYPE OF GRANT Project funding.

RANGE OF GRANTS Up to £15,000.

SAMPLE GRANTS Bristol Hospitality Network (£15,000); Changing Tunes and Feelgood Community (£10,000 each); Bristol Schools Connection, Encounter Christianity and Trauma Breakthrough (£5,000 each); Bristol After Stroke (£4,300); CHAS (£2,500).

FINANCES *Financial year end 31/03/2022*
Income £175,500
Grants to organisations £143,100
Assets £5,420,000

TRUSTEES Prof. Andrew Halestrap; Anthony Miles; Colin Havill; Annie Crawley; Dr Sheena Tranter.

OTHER INFORMATION In 2021/22, grants were distributed as follows: supporting marginalised people (£76,800); schools and training institutions (£50,000); organisations for the care and training of young people (£15,000); research (£1,300).

HOW TO APPLY Applications can be made using the online form available on the trust's website and should be submitted, usually, by 31 March each year in preparation for the trustees' meeting in June.

CONTACT DETAILS The Trustees, 51 Downs Park West, Westbury Park, Bristol BS6 7QL *Tel.* 0117 962 8611 *Email* use the contact form on the website. *Website* www.burdentrustbristol.co.uk

■ The Burdett Trust for Nursing

CC NO 1089849   **ESTABLISHED** 2001

WHERE FUNDING CAN BE GIVEN UK.

WHO CAN BENEFIT Registered charities; universities.

WHAT IS FUNDED Nursing and health care.

TYPE OF GRANT Project funding.

RANGE OF GRANTS Programme dependent.

SAMPLE GRANTS Wellbeing of Women (£218,300); Council of Deans of Health (£90,000); East London NHS Foundation Trust (£25,000); Abigail's Footsteps, Jaya Mental Health and Richard's House Children's Hospice (£10,000 each); Caring for Carers (£8,000); Zimbabwe Life Project (£7,200); University of the Highlands and Islands (£4,700); Midwife-led Community Transformation (£1,200).

FINANCES *Financial year end 31/12/2021*
Income £950,100
Grants to organisations £3,400,000
Grants to individuals £206,900
Assets £89,330,000

TRUSTEES Dame Christine Beasley; Alan Gibbs; Andrew Smith; Evy Hambro; Prof. David Sines; Andrew Gibbs; Audrey Ardern-Jones; Dame Donna Kinnair; Rachael Corser; Janice Stevens.

OTHER INFORMATION In 2021 the trust awarded grants to 65 organisations and 259 individuals.

HOW TO APPLY See the trust's website for information on the current grant programmes and details on how to apply.

CONTACT DETAILS Lauren George, Charity Administrator, c/o Rathbone Trust Company Ltd, 8 Finsbury Circus, London EC2M 7AZ *Tel.* 020 7399 0102 *Email* Lauren.George@rathbones. com *Website* www.btfn.org.uk

■ The Burges Salmon Charitable Trust

CC NO 272522   ESTABLISHED 1976
WHERE FUNDING CAN BE GIVEN Priority is given to Bristol and the surrounding area.
WHO CAN BENEFIT Registered charities. The trustees will generally support small to medium-sized charities rather than large national charities.
WHAT IS FUNDED Community projects.
TYPE OF GRANT Project funding.
RANGE OF GRANTS Mostly up to £3,000.
SAMPLE GRANTS Quartet Community Foundation (£36,000); Gympanzees (£3,400); One25 and The Yard (£3,000 each); Anchor Society and Grateful Society (£1,000); North Bristol Advice Centre (£700); Bristol Children's Help Society (£600).
FINANCES *Financial year end 31/10/2021*
Income £79,000
Grants to organisations £79,300
Assets £39,000
TRUSTEES John Houlden; Mark Shepherd; Thomas Hewitt; Camilla Usher-Clark; Alice Honeywill; Catherine Maid; Robert Forman.
OTHER INFORMATION Grants were awarded to 84 organisations. The trust's accounts named 14 beneficiaries, which received £60,700 in total. The remaining £18,600 was awarded to unnamed beneficiaries in grants of less than £500 each. The 2020/21 accounts were the latest available at the time of writing (May 2023).
HOW TO APPLY Apply in writing to the correspondent.
CONTACT DETAILS Alison Preece, Trust Secretary, Burges Salmon LLP, 1 Glass Wharf, Bristol BS2 0ZX *Tel.* 0117 902 2731 *Email* alison. preece@burges-salmon.com

■ Clara E. Burgess Charity

CC NO 1072546   ESTABLISHED 1998
WHERE FUNDING CAN BE GIVEN UK and overseas.
WHO CAN BENEFIT Registered charities; schools; hospices.
WHAT IS FUNDED Children and young people, particularly facilities and assistance for their education, health and physical well-being. Preference may be given to younger children under the age of ten and children who have lost one or both parents.
RANGE OF GRANTS Mostly £1,000 to £5,000.
SAMPLE GRANTS Children's Heart Surgery Fund (£9,000); Alderley Edge School, Bolton Lads and Girls Club, Playskill, Railway Children and Sunrise Partnership (£4,500 each); Duchy Preschool (£2,000).
FINANCES *Financial year end 20/10/2021*
Income £237,200
Grants to organisations £56,000
Assets £12,240,000
TRUSTEE Ludlow Trust Company Ltd.
OTHER INFORMATION Grants were awarded to 12 organisations, representing a substantial reduction on the previous year in both number and the total grant expenditure. The 2020/21 accounts were the latest available at the time of writing (June 2023).

HOW TO APPLY Applications can be made in writing to the correspondent and are considered in January, April, July and October.
CONTACT DETAILS The Trustees, c/o Ludlow Trust Company Ltd, 1st Floor, Tower Wharf, Cheese Lane, Bristol BS2 0JJ *Tel.* 0117 313 8200 *Email* charitabletrusts@ludlowtrust.com

■ Burnie's Foundation

CC NO 1167997   ESTABLISHED 2016
WHERE FUNDING CAN BE GIVEN UK and overseas.
WHO CAN BENEFIT Charitable organisations.
WHAT IS FUNDED Animal welfare.
TYPE OF GRANT Project funding.
RANGE OF GRANTS £3,000 to £145,000.
SAMPLE GRANTS Sa Cleda Farm – Spain (£69,200); SOS Dogs – Netherlands (£28,500); Cat Protection Pollensa – Spain (£8,300).
FINANCES *Financial year end 31/05/2022*
Income £87,700
Grants to organisations £118,100
Assets £910,000
TRUSTEES Kenneth Tonkin; Bethann Sells; Richard Thoburn.
OTHER INFORMATION Grants were made to 31 organisations.
HOW TO APPLY Unsolicited applications are not accepted.
CONTACT DETAILS The Trustees, 45 Britton Street, London EC1M 5NA *Tel.* 020 7250 7000 *Email* burnie@burniesfoundation.com *Website* www.burniesfoundation.com

■ The Burry Charitable Trust

CC NO 281045   ESTABLISHED 1961
WHERE FUNDING CAN BE GIVEN Mainly Highcliffe in Dorset and the surrounding areas.
WHO CAN BENEFIT Charities, voluntary groups and other not-for-profit organisations.
WHAT IS FUNDED General charitable purposes.
RANGE OF GRANTS Up to £36,000 but mostly £1,000 to £5,000.
SAMPLE GRANTS New Forest Basics Bank (£36,300); Diverse Abilities Plus (£25,400); Oakhaven Hospital Trust (£24,900); The Salvation Army (£5,000); New Forest Mencap (£2,000); Myeloma UK (£1,500).
FINANCES *Financial year end 05/04/2022*
Income £84,300
Grants to organisations £129,700
Assets £2,980,000
TRUSTEES Adrian Osman; Sarah Teague; John Butters; Timothy Knight.
OTHER INFORMATION In 2021/22, grants were awarded to 13 local charitable organisations.
HOW TO APPLY Contact the correspondent for further information.
CONTACT DETAILS Sarah Teague, Trustee, 10 Hoburne Lane, Highcliffe, Christchurch, Dorset BH23 4HP *Tel.* 01425 277661 *Email* sarah.teague@hoburne.com

■ The Arnold Burton 1998 Charitable Trust

CC NO 1074633   ESTABLISHED 1998
WHERE FUNDING CAN BE GIVEN UK, with a strong preference for Yorkshire, and overseas.
WHO CAN BENEFIT Registered charities.
WHAT IS FUNDED Arts and amenities; education; health; heritage; social welfare; work overseas; Jewish causes.

RANGE OF GRANTS Up to £35,000 but mostly under £20,000.

SAMPLE GRANTS Leeds Community Foundation (£35,000); Disasters Emergency Committee – Ukraine Humanitarian Appeal (£20,000); Garsington Opera (£15,000); Opera North (£10,000); Laser Trust Fund Moghissi, Love Leeds Parks and Yorkshire Air Museum (£5,000 each); Merchant Taylors' (£150).

FINANCES *Financial year end* 05/04/2022
Income £163,700
Grants to organisations £163,500
Assets £5,850,000

TRUSTEES Jeremy Burton; Mark Burton; Nicholas Burton.

OTHER INFORMATION There were 17 grants made during 2021/22. Grants were broken down as follows: social and welfare (£68,500); arts and amenities (£50,000); international causes (£30,000); health (£10,000); heritage (£5,000).

HOW TO APPLY Apply in writing to the correspondent.

CONTACT DETAILS The Trustees, Castlegarth, Scott Lane, Wetherby LS22 6LH *Tel.* 01937 585558

■ Consolidated Charity of Burton upon Trent

CC NO 239072   **ESTABLISHED** 2001

WHERE FUNDING CAN BE GIVEN Burton upon Trent and the parishes of Branston, Stretton and Outwoods.

WHO CAN BENEFIT Registered charities; voluntary groups; churches; individuals.

WHAT IS FUNDED General charitable purposes including: health; social welfare; recreation and leisure; education and youth development; faith; the environment; heritage; community development.

TYPE OF GRANT Capital costs; core/revenue costs; project funding.

SAMPLE GRANTS A list of beneficiaries was not included in the annual report and accounts. Previous beneficiaries have included: SARAC (£18,000); 16th Burton Scout Group (£6,600); St Mary's Church (£5,000); St Giles Hospice (£4,500); Fishing in Safe Hands, Little Theatre Company and Tutbury Pre-School (£2,000 each); Asthma Relief (£1,900).

FINANCES *Financial year end* 31/12/2021
Income £628,800
Grants to organisations £87,300
Grants to individuals £125,700
Assets £16,930,000

TRUSTEES Patricia Ackroyd; Dennis Fletcher; Margaret Heather; The Revd Robert Styles; David Leese; Cllr Beryl Toon; Ben Robinson; Geoffrey Brown; George Fargher; Sandra Phillips; Ronald Clarke; Simon Gaskin; Keith Williamson; Cecilia Mahon; Danielle Upton.

HOW TO APPLY Applications can be made through the charity's website.

CONTACT DETAILS Clerk of Trustees, 1st Floor, Gibraltar House, Crown Square, First Avenue, First Avenue, Burton-on-Trent DE14 2WE *Tel.* 01283 527067 *Email* use the contact form on the website *Website* www.consolidatedcharityburton.org.uk

■ Miss Margaret Butters Reekie Charitable Trust

OSCR NO SC024696   **ESTABLISHED** 1996

WHERE FUNDING CAN BE GIVEN Scotland.

WHO CAN BENEFIT Registered charities; hospices.

WHAT IS FUNDED Health and medical research; people with disabilities; older people; air ambulance services; carers.

RANGE OF GRANTS Mostly £5,000, with the occasional larger or smaller grant.

SAMPLE GRANTS Ayrshire Hospice and Bone Cancer Research Trust (£10,000 each); Alzheimer's Research UK, Care for Carers and Scotland's Charity Air Ambulance (£5,000 each); Highland Hospice and St Vincent's Hospice (£2,500 each).

FINANCES *Financial year end* 08/04/2022
Income £158,000
Grants to organisations £113,000
Assets £4,840,000

HOW TO APPLY Apply in writing to the correspondent.

CONTACT DETAILS The Trustees, c/o Lindsays, Caledonian Exchange, 19A Canning Street, Edinburgh EH3 8HE *Tel.* 0131 229 1212

■ The Noel Buxton Trust

CC NO 220881   **ESTABLISHED** 1919

WHERE FUNDING CAN BE GIVEN UK, eastern and southern Africa.

WHO CAN BENEFIT Registered charities.

WHAT IS FUNDED Families affected by domestic violence; offenders and ex-offenders; sustainable and regenerative projects in Africa.

TYPE OF GRANT Project funding; core/revenue costs.

RANGE OF GRANTS Grants range from £1,000 to £11,000.

SAMPLE GRANTS Garden of Hope (£5,000); New Leaf Support (£4,000); New Bridge Foundation and The Dash Charity (£3,000 each); Staying Put (£2,000); LifeCycle UK (£1,500).

FINANCES *Financial year end* 31/12/2021
Income £112,500
Grants to organisations £110,100
Assets £2,790,000

TRUSTEES Katie Aston; Simon Buxton; Brendan Gormley; Emma Compton-Burnett; Jo Tunnard; Katie Buxton; Tahera Aanchawan; James Buckley.

OTHER INFORMATION Grants were made to 32 organisations during the year under the following themes: African communities (£40,100); prisoners (£38,000); families affected by domestic abuse (£32,000).

HOW TO APPLY Visit the trust's website for guidance on how to apply to each programme.

CONTACT DETAILS The Administrator, PO Box 520, Fleet, Hampshire GU51 9GX *Email* admin@noelbuxtontrust.org.uk *Website* www.noelbuxtontrust.org.uk

■ Byrne Family Foundation

CC NO 1137878   **ESTABLISHED** 2010

WHERE FUNDING CAN BE GIVEN West Sussex and Bangladesh.

WHO CAN BENEFIT Charitable organisations. The charity has previously supported local hospices (St Wilfred and Chestnut Tree House), Christmas hamper appeals, self-defence classes for local Selsey residents, and a charity fun run. The trustees continue to split their donations between local causes and the Hope House project for children in Bangladesh.

Think carefully about every application. Is it justified?

293

WHAT IS FUNDED General charitable purposes, including disadvantaged children and young people and Christian causes.

RANGE OF GRANTS Mostly £1,000 to £20,000.

SAMPLE GRANTS Hope House – Bangladesh (£159,600); Global Compassion (£15,300); Wholesome Warehouse (£7,100); St Barnabas Hospice (£3,800); Chestnut Tree House (£2,000).

FINANCES *Financial year end 31/05/2022*
Income £171,000
Grants to organisations £194,900
Assets £5,124,000

TRUSTEES Kevin Byrne; Ruth Byrne; Lisa Byrne; David Harland; Emily Styles; Rachel Byrne.

OTHER INFORMATION The foundation was formerly know as the Checkatrade Foundation. Grants of less than £1,000 each totalled £1,800 during the year.

HOW TO APPLY Contact the correspondent for further information.

CONTACT DETAILS Kevin Byrne, Trustee, Richmond House, The Apple Building, Ellis Square, Selsey, West Sussex PO20 0AF *Tel.* 07967 350212 *Email* kevin@byrneproperty.co.uk

294

Does the funder you have chosen match your needs? Haphazard applications waste postage and time

■ C. and F. Charitable Trust

cc no 274529 **ESTABLISHED** 1977
WHERE FUNDING CAN BE GIVEN UK.
WHO CAN BENEFIT Orthodox Jewish charities.
WHAT IS FUNDED Relief of poverty within the Jewish community; Orthodox Jewish causes.
RANGE OF GRANTS £10,000 to £30,000.
SAMPLE GRANTS Friends of Beis Soroh Schneier and Friends of Merkaz Torah Belz Machnovka (£30,000 each); Mifal Hachesed Vehatzedokoh (£25,000); Friends of Beis Chinuch Lebonos Ltd (£20,000); One Heart – Lev Echod (£10,000).
FINANCES *Financial year end 22/04/2022*
Income £125,000
Grants to organisations £115,000
Assets £1,430,000
TRUSTEES Fradel Kaufman; Simon Kaufman.
OTHER INFORMATION The trust awarded five grants to organisations.
HOW TO APPLY Apply in writing to the correspondent.
CONTACT DETAILS Simon Kaufman, Trustee, 50 Keswick Street, Gateshead, Tyne and Wear NE8 1TQ *Tel.* 0191 490 0138

■ The Edward Cadbury Charitable Trust

cc no 1160334 **ESTABLISHED** 2015
WHERE FUNDING CAN BE GIVEN The Midlands region, including Herefordshire, Shropshire, Staffordshire Warwickshire and Worcestershire.
WHO CAN BENEFIT Registered charities.
WHAT IS FUNDED Arts and culture; community projects and integration; compassionate support; conservation and the environment; interfaith and multifaith relations; education and training; research.
TYPE OF GRANT Project costs and research.
RANGE OF GRANTS Up to £100,000 but mainly between £500 and £10,000.
SAMPLE GRANTS Father Hudson's Society (£50,000); Coventry City of Culture Trust (£25,000); British Heart Foundation (£10,000); Clean Rivers Trust (£5,000); West Mercia Women's Aid (£3,000).
FINANCES *Financial year end 05/04/2022*
Income £1,240,000
Grants to organisations £926,000
Assets £55,200,000
TRUSTEES Nigel Cadbury; Dr William Southall; Charles Gillett; Andrew Littleboy; Robert Marriott.
HOW TO APPLY Applications can be made by writing to the correspondent by post or email. Alternatively, applications can be made online through the trust's website. Applications are accepted all year round and are normally considered within a three-month timescale. Letters of application should provide a clear and concise description of the project requiring funding as well as the outcomes and benefits that are likely to be achieved. The trustees also require an outline budget and explanation of how the project is to be funded initially and in the future together with the latest annual report and accounts for the charity.
CONTACT DETAILS Susan Anderson, Trust Manager, Rokesley, University of Birmingham – Selly Oak, Bristol Road, Selly Oak, Birmingham, West Midlands B29 6QF *Tel.* 0121 472 1838
Email ecadburytrust@btconnect.com
Website www.edwardcadburytrust.org.uk

■ The G. W. Cadbury Charitable Trust

cc no 231861 **ESTABLISHED** 1922
WHERE FUNDING CAN BE GIVEN Worldwide, with a preference for the UK and the USA.
WHO CAN BENEFIT Registered charities; schools and colleges; universities; museums and libraries.
WHAT IS FUNDED General charitable purposes; work outside the UK.
RANGE OF GRANTS Mostly between £1,000 and £5,000, with the occasional smaller or larger grant.
SAMPLE GRANTS Gender and Development Network (£40,000); Retina UK (£27,500); Pacific Northwest Ballet (£21,000); Babbasa (£10,000); Haverford College and Sixty One (£5,000 each); Cornell University, Highgate International Chamber Music Festival and Sex Education Forum (£2,000 each); In These Times, Massachusetts Bar Foundation and Plymouth Housing Group (£1,000 each).
FINANCES *Financial year end 05/04/2022*
Income £243,500
Grants to organisations £135,800
Assets £8,690,000
TRUSTEES Nick Woodroffe; Lyndall Boal; Jessica Woodroffe; Caroline Woodroffe; Jennifer Boal; Peter Boal.
OTHER INFORMATION Grants were broken down as follows by location: UK (£92,800); USA (£43,000). Of the grant total, 88% was composed of grants of £5,000 or more, and 12% was composed of grants of £1,000 to £5,000. During this period, no grants were made that were under £1,000.
HOW TO APPLY Apply in writing to the correspondent.
CONTACT DETAILS The Trustees, c/o Saffery Champness, St Catherines Court, Berkeley Place, Bristol, Somerset BS8 1BQ *Tel.* 0117 915 1617

■ William A. Cadbury Charitable Trust

cc no 213629 **ESTABLISHED** 1923
WHERE FUNDING CAN BE GIVEN Birmingham and the West Midlands; the UK; Ireland; financially developing countries in Africa, Asia, Eastern Europe and South America, with a particular focus on West Africa.
WHO CAN BENEFIT Registered charities; CICs.
WHAT IS FUNDED Birmingham and the West Midlands: community action; vulnerable groups; advice, mediation and counselling; education and training; the environment and conservation; medical research and health care; the arts; people affected by the criminal justice system. UK: projects clearly linked to the Quaker movement that support the work of the Religious Society of Friends. Ireland: peace and reconciliation. International development (mainly focused on West Africa).
WHAT IS NOT FUNDED Individuals (whether for research, expeditions, educational purposes or medical treatment); projects concerned with travel, adventure, sports or recreation; organisations which are based outside the UK.
TYPE OF GRANT Core costs; development funding; project funding. Grants are normally one-off.

RANGE OF GRANTS Small grants: up to £2,000; large grants: usually from £10,000 to £20,000.

SAMPLE GRANTS Extern NI (£30,000); Nishkam Civic Association (£25,000); The Jericho Foundation (£20,000); Paper Boat (£15,000).

FINANCES *Financial year end 31/03/2022*
Income £1,240,000
Grants to organisations £949,800
Assets £58,850,000

TRUSTEES Sophy Blandy; Rupert Cadbury; Janine Cobain; John Penny; Margaret Salmon; Sarah Stafford; Adrian Thomas; Katherine Cadbury; Victoria Mohan.

HOW TO APPLY Grant applications can be submitted online (preferred) or by post. Applications should include the following information: the charity's registration number; a description of the charity's aims and achievements; an outline and budget for the project; the grants programme to which the charity is applying; details of projects previously funded by the trust (if applicable); and details of funds raised to date and the current shortfall.

CONTACT DETAILS The Trustees, Rokesley, University of Birmingham, Bristol Road, Selly Oak, Birmingham, West Midlands B29 6QF *Tel.* 0121 472 1464 *Email* info@wa-cadbury.org.uk *Website* www.wa-cadbury.org.uk

··

■ The Cadbury Foundation

CC NO 1050482   **ESTABLISHED** 1935

WHERE FUNDING CAN BE GIVEN Charities close to Cadbury sites in the UK and Ireland.

WHO CAN BENEFIT Registered charities and voluntary organisations.

WHAT IS FUNDED Skills development; sustainability; disability sport.

SAMPLE GRANTS Health for Life in Primary Schools (£100,000); Grocery Aid (£50,000); St Francis Hospice (£43,700); Age Action, Cardiac Risk in the Young, Mountain Rescue, Sense and The Turning Tides Project (£5,000 each).

FINANCES *Financial year end 31/12/2021*
Income £649,400
Grants to organisations £484,700
Assets £380,700

TRUSTEES Eoin Kellett; Lisa Crane; Louise Stigant; Clive Jones; Joshua Townson; Denise Chester.

OTHER INFORMATION The Cadbury Foundation was set up in 1935 in recognition of the company's founders, George and Richard Cadbury, and their investment in the welfare of their employees and wider communities. In 2010 Kraft Foods Inc. gained control of Cadbury plc. In 2012 Kraft Foods Inc. was split into Kraft Food Group plc and Mondelēz, which now funds The Cadbury Foundation.

HOW TO APPLY The trustees actively seek out projects to support and therefore cannot accept any unsolicited requests for funding.

CONTACT DETAILS The Trustees, PO Box 12, Bourneville, Birmingham, West Midlands B30 2LU *Tel.* 0121 787 2421 *Email* kelly.farrell@mdlz.com *Website* www.cadbury.co.uk/cadbury-foundation

··

■ The Barrow Cadbury Trust

CC NO 1115476   **ESTABLISHED** 1920

WHERE FUNDING CAN BE GIVEN UK and overseas, with a preference for Birmingham and the Black Country (Dudley, Sandwell, Smethwick, West Bromwich and Wolverhampton).

WHO CAN BENEFIT Charities and voluntary organisations, preferably grassroots community groups and user-led projects.

WHAT IS FUNDED Criminal justice; migration; social and economic justice.

TYPE OF GRANT Projects; recurring costs; running expenditure; research.

SAMPLE GRANTS A list of the trust's funded projects is provided on its website.

FINANCES *Financial year end 31/03/2022*
Income £3,190,000
Grants to organisations £5,060,000
Assets £85,430,000

TRUSTEES Nicola Cadbury; Erica Cadbury; Tamsin Rupprecheter; Henry Serle; Anna Southall; John Serle; Steven Skakel; Catherina Pharoah; Esther McConnell; Omar Khan; Alice Hickinbotham.

OTHER INFORMATION Grants were awarded to 74 organisations in 2021/22. Additionally, the trust provided use of premises to the voluntary sector to the value of £68,000; however, this has not been included in the grant total. The trust also provides social investment. It will consider investments which further its aim to promote social justice.

HOW TO APPLY Applicants should initially complete an enquiry form, which is available on the trust's website. Applicants can complete the application form once they have discussed the project with the trust and have been asked to make an application. Applications can be made at any time.

CONTACT DETAILS The Trustees, The Foundry, 17 Oval Way, London SE11 5RR *Tel.* 020 7632 9060 *Email* general@barrowcadbury.org.uk *Website* www.barrowcadbury.org.uk

··

■ The Edward and Dorothy Cadbury Trust

CC NO 1107327   **ESTABLISHED** 1928

WHERE FUNDING CAN BE GIVEN There is a particular focus on the West Midlands and Worcestershire.

WHO CAN BENEFIT Registered charities.

WHAT IS FUNDED The trust continues to support, where appropriate, the interests of the founders and the particular charitable interests of the trustees. Grants are made under five main headings: arts and culture; community projects and integration; compassionate support; education and training; and conservation and the environment.

TYPE OF GRANT Grants are usually made on a one-off basis for a specific purpose or part of a project.

RANGE OF GRANTS From £500 to £5,000. Significant projects or capital appeals may occasionally receive grants of up to £20,000.

SAMPLE GRANTS Birmingham Hippodrome and Douglas Macmillan Hospice – Stoke (£5,000 each); Living Paintings Trust (£2,500); Birmingham Centre for Arts Therapies (£3,000); Young People First (£2,000); Kidney Care (£1,400); Albany Theatre Trust and All Saints Youth Project (£1,000 each).

FINANCES *Financial year end 05/04/2022*
Income £213,600
Grants to organisations £209,800
Assets £9,970,000

TRUSTEES Susan Anfilogoff; Julie Cadbury; Julia Gillett; Philippa Ward; Dr Johanna Russell; Jayne Higgins.

OTHER INFORMATION Grants were awarded to 123 organisations during 2021/22 from a total of 180 grant applications.

HOW TO APPLY Application forms can be downloaded from the trust's website and may be submitted at any time either online, by post or by email. The website states that application forms must be supported with the following: a letter detailing the funding required, the outcomes and benefits the project is intended to achieve, a project budget and a copy of the latest annual report and accounts (if these are not available on the Charity Commission's website). Applications are usually considered within three months. Applications that fall outside the trust's areas of interest may not be considered or acknowledged.

CONTACT DETAILS Susan Anderson, Trust Manager, Rokesley, University of Birmingham – Selly Oak, Bristol Road, Selly Oak, Birmingham, West Midlands B29 6QF *Tel.* 0121 472 1838 *Email* e-dcadburytrust@btconnect.com *Website* www.e-dcadburytrust.org.uk

■ The George Cadbury Trust

CC NO 1040999   **ESTABLISHED** 1924

WHERE FUNDING CAN BE GIVEN England, with a preference for the West Midlands and Gloucestershire.

WHO CAN BENEFIT Registered charities.

WHAT IS FUNDED General charitable purposes.

RANGE OF GRANTS Up to £12,500.

SAMPLE GRANTS Macmillan Cancer Support (£12,500); English Schools Orchestra and Red Cross Northampton (£10,000 each); Roald Dahl's Marvellous Children's Charity and Shelter (£5,000 each); Alcohol Change UK and Canine Partners (£1,000 each).

FINANCES *Financial year end* 05/04/2022 *Income* £422,500 *Grants to organisations* £367,900 *Assets* £19,350,000

TRUSTEES Angela Cadbury; Mark Cadbury; Roger Cadbury; Benedict Cadbury; Timothy Cadbury.

OTHER INFORMATION Grants were made to 89 organisations during the year. Beneficiaries of grants of under £999 were not recorded in the charity's accounts and totalled £2,900.

HOW TO APPLY Contact the correspondent for further information.

CONTACT DETAILS The Trustees, c/o BDO LLP, 2 Snow Hill, Birmingham B4 6GA *Tel.* 0121 265 7288

■ Cadent Foundation

ESTABLISHED 2019

WHO CAN BENEFIT Charitable organisations.

WHAT IS FUNDED Projects which address the root causes and impacts of fuel poverty. Projects should have at least one of the following outputs: practical energy efficiency solutions; energy efficiency information; income maximisation information; education and training.

WHAT IS NOT FUNDED Animal groups; individuals; loan repayment; sponsorship of events or activities; religious or faith groups; overseas travel or groups; political or lobbying groups; sports groups; natural disaster relief; heritage and historic buildings; projects that are not sustainable; building refurbishment (although support for community spaces may be considered); schools; medical projects located outside Cadent's region.

SAMPLE GRANTS A list of beneficiaries was not available.

FINANCES *Financial year end* 31/12/2022 *Grants to organisations* £2,940,000

OTHER INFORMATION Full financial information was not available as the foundation is administered by the Charities Trust (Charity Commission no. 327489) and is not a registered charity. The foundation's grant total has been taken from its 2022 Impact Report.

HOW TO APPLY The foundation's website states: 'Grant applications are by invitation only. If you have a project you think we might be able to support, we'd like to hear from you. Please email a project outline to: enquiries@cadentfoundation.com.'

CONTACT DETAILS Julia Dwyer, Cadent Foundation Director, Pilot Way, Ansty Park, Coventry CV7 9JU *Email* enquiries@cadentfoundation.com *Website* https://cadentgas.com/cadent-foundation

■ The Cadogan Charity

CC NO 247773   **ESTABLISHED** 1966

WHERE FUNDING CAN BE GIVEN UK, with a preference for London and Scotland.

WHO CAN BENEFIT Registered charities.

WHAT IS FUNDED Social welfare; medical research; military charities; conservation and the environment; education; animal welfare.

TYPE OF GRANT Support is usually given over one to two years, although some one-off grants may be made.

RANGE OF GRANTS Up to £250,000.

SAMPLE GRANTS Game and Wildlife Trust (£175,000); Heathfield School (£100,000); Missing Salmon Alliance (£50,000); British Heart Foundation (£10,000); Gurkha Welfare Trust (£5,000).

FINANCES *Financial year end* 05/04/2022 *Income* £2,090,000 *Grants to organisations* £2,740,000 *Assets* £52,350,000

TRUSTEES The Rt Hon. Earl Cadogan; Viscount Chelsea; William Cadogan; Countess Cadogan; Lady Anna-Karina Thomson.

OTHER INFORMATION Grants were broken down as follows: social welfare (£1.36 million); animal welfare (£366,000); education (£344,000); medical research (£292,000); military charities (£291,000); the environment (£90,000).

HOW TO APPLY The charity's 2021/22 annual report states: 'Although the trustees make some grants with no formal applications, they normally require organisations to submit a request saying how the funds could be used, what would be achieved, and how this would add to public benefit.'

CONTACT DETAILS Paul Loutit, Secretary to Trustees, 10 Duke of York Square, London SW3 4LY *Tel.* 020 7730 4567 *Email* paul.loutit@cadogan.co.uk

■ Community Foundation for Calderdale

CC NO 1002722   **ESTABLISHED** 1991

WHERE FUNDING CAN BE GIVEN Calderdale.

WHO CAN BENEFIT Registered charities; unregistered charities; CICs; social enterprises; hospices; places of worship; schools; individuals; PTAs.

WHAT IS FUNDED General charitable purposes including: homelessness and housing; poverty and disadvantage; community cohesion.

WHAT IS NOT FUNDED A list of exclusions can be found on the foundation's website.

TYPE OF GRANT Capital costs; project funding; seed funding/start-up funding; core/revenue costs.

SAMPLE GRANTS Royd Regeneration (£35,000); St Augustine's Centre (£15,800); Calderdale College (£10,100); WomenCentre Ltd (£8,000); Tuesday 2 O'clock Club (£300).

FINANCES *Financial year end* 30/06/2022
Income £3,060,000
Grants to organisations £2,270,000
Grants to individuals £14,100
Assets £14,070,000

TRUSTEES Christopher Harris; Brenda Hodgson; Alison Haskins; Heidi Bingham; Dr Roger Moore; Richard Blackburn; Zohrah Zancudi; Neil Wright; Nigel Cliffe; Preet Sandhu.

OTHER INFORMATION This is one of the 47 UK community foundations, which distribute funding for a wide range of purposes. As with all community foundations, there are a number of donor-advised funds managed on behalf of individuals, families and charitable trusts. Grant schemes tend to change frequently – consult the foundation's website for details of current programmes and up-to-date deadlines.

HOW TO APPLY Potential applicants are advised to visit the community foundation's website or contact its grants team to find the most suitable funding stream.

CONTACT DETAILS The Trustees, The 1855 Building (First Floor), Discovery Road, Halifax, West Yorkshire HX1 2NG *Tel.* 01422 439700 *Email* grants@cffc.co.uk *Website* www.cffc.co.uk

■ The Calleva Foundation

CC NO 1078808   **ESTABLISHED** 1999

WHERE FUNDING CAN BE GIVEN London and Hampshire.

WHO CAN BENEFIT Charitable organisations.

WHAT IS FUNDED Education and academic research; children's holidays; social services; medical research; international relief; the environment; animal welfare.

TYPE OF GRANT Project funding.

RANGE OF GRANTS From £51,000 to £6.67 million.

SAMPLE GRANTS Jenner Institute (£6.67 million); Kew Gardens – Plant and Fungal Trees of Life Project (£400,000); Portsmouth Grammar School Bursaries (£160,000); West London Zone Literacy Catch Up (£75,000); Royal Academy of Music Bursary – Calleva Foundation Scholars (£51,000).

FINANCES *Financial year end* 31/12/2021
Income £3,750,000
Grants to organisations £8,570,000
Assets (£990,000)

TRUSTEES Caroline Butt; Stephen Butt.

OTHER INFORMATION Grants payable during the year were distributed as follows: medical research (£6.68 million); education (£507,600); academic research (£425,000); social services (£404,500); overseas/international relief (£288,100); education – international (£198,400); children's holidays (£55,000); the environment (£11,600); animal welfare/other (£1,000).

HOW TO APPLY The foundation does not accept unsolicited applications.

CONTACT DETAILS The Trustees, The Calleva Foundation, PO Box 22554, London W8 5GN *Tel.* 020 8638 8653 *Email* contactcalleva@btopenworld.com

■ Barbara and Derek Calrow Charitable Foundation

CC NO 1178695

WHERE FUNDING CAN BE GIVEN Manchester and Bolton.

WHO CAN BENEFIT Charitable organisations.

WHAT IS FUNDED General charitable purposes.

SAMPLE GRANTS A list of beneficiaries was not included in the annual report and accounts.

FINANCES *Financial year end* 31/03/2022
Income £177,300
Grants to organisations £206,900
Assets £6,100

TRUSTEES Robert Calrow; Barbara Calrow; Robert Campbell; Julie Jones.

HOW TO APPLY Apply in writing to the correspondent.

CONTACT DETAILS The Trustees, 2 Stonehouse, Chapeltown Road, Bromley Cross, Bolton BL7 9NB *Tel.* 01204 309523 *Email* derekcalrow@me.com

■ Cambridgeshire Community Foundation

CC NO 1103314   **ESTABLISHED** 2003

WHERE FUNDING CAN BE GIVEN Cambridgeshire.

WHO CAN BENEFIT Registered charities; CICs; social enterprises; schools; PTAs; hospitals; hospices; religious bodies/institutions; local authorities; individuals.

WHAT IS FUNDED General charitable purposes including: social welfare; community development; health; children and young people; families; the environment.

WHAT IS NOT FUNDED See the foundation's website for a full list of exclusions.

TYPE OF GRANT Capital costs; core/revenue costs; project funding.

RANGE OF GRANTS Mostly up to £10,000.

SAMPLE GRANTS A list of beneficiaries was not included in the annual report and accounts.

FINANCES *Financial year end* 31/03/2022
Income £7,650,000
Grants to organisations £2,630,000
Grants to individuals £146,200
Assets £15,160,000

TRUSTEES Simon Humphrey; Alison Griffiths; Linda Sinclair; Caroline Stenner; Stuart Thompson; Dr Joanna Slota-Newson; Claire Davis; Elizabeth Damazer; Dr Gareth Thomas; Christopher Parkhouse; Stephen Catling; Jonathan Jelley; Alric Blake; Jennifer Millard; Paul Lewis.

OTHER INFORMATION This is one of the 47 UK community foundations, which distribute funding for a wide range of purposes. As with all community foundations, there are a number of donor-advised funds managed on behalf of individuals, families and charitable trusts. Grant schemes tend to change frequently – consult the foundation's website for details of current programmes and up-to-date deadlines.

HOW TO APPLY Potential applicants are advised to visit the community foundation's website or contact its grants team to find the most suitable funding stream.

CONTACT DETAILS The Grants Team, Hangar One, The Airport, Newmarket Road, Cambridge CB5 8TG *Tel.* 01223 410535 *Email* info@cambscf.org.uk *Website* www.cambscf.org.uk

■ Camden Giving

CC NO 1174463   **ESTABLISHED** 2017
WHERE FUNDING CAN BE GIVEN Camden.
WHO CAN BENEFIT Registered charities; not-for-profit organisations; CICs; CIOs; schools; social enterprises.
WHAT IS FUNDED Activities that benefit the people who live and work in Camden including those that address: poverty and inequality; social isolation; employment; improving mental and physical health.
WHAT IS NOT FUNDED A full list of exclusions for each grants programme can be found on the website.
TYPE OF GRANT Project funding; core costs.
RANGE OF GRANTS Up to £100,000.
SAMPLE GRANTS Newham Refugee Consortium (£30,000); Somers Town Community Association (£29,800); Doorstep Homeless Project (£7,500); Swiss Church (£4,000); The Screen Film Community (£3,000): Platform Cricket (£1,500); The Wellness Action Alliance (£100); Performing Productions (£70).
FINANCES *Financial year end* 31/03/2022
Income £1,010,000
Grants to organisations £817,400
Grants to individuals £63,400
Assets £856,500
TRUSTEES Simon Pitkeathley; Sue Wilby; Allan Sutherland; Dominic Pinkney; Tom Holliss; Graham Dyer; Nathan Dyke; Rose Alexander; Hafsa Mohammed; Vanessa Browne.
OTHER INFORMATION During 2021/22, 151 grants were awarded, with the majority of funding going to social cohesion projects. The charity acts as a hyperlocal community foundation for Camden, providing additional in-kind support for charities in the area.
HOW TO APPLY Information on eligibility and opening dates for funding rounds can be found on the website. The charity strongly advises that prospective applicants get in touch before making an application, to talk through the criteria for funding. This can be done by attending one of the charity's events, booking an appointment or by emailing admin@camdengiving.org.uk.
CONTACT DETAILS The Grants Team, 5–7 Buck Street, Camden Town, London NW1 8NJ *Tel.* 07979 996462 *Email* admin@camdengiving.org.uk *Website* www.camdengiving.org.uk

■ M. J. Camp Charitable Foundation

CC NO 1085654   **ESTABLISHED** 2000
WHERE FUNDING CAN BE GIVEN UK, with a preference for Hayling Island.
WHO CAN BENEFIT Charitable organisations; registered UK charities.
WHAT IS FUNDED Conservation of the UK's natural, historical, archaeological and scientific heritage; canals and inland waterways; the welfare of horses, ponies and donkeys; the preservation of historical vehicles, particularly steam trains; community transport; general charitable purposes.
RANGE OF GRANTS Mostly between £1,000 and £2,000, with the occasional larger grant.
SAMPLE GRANTS Hampshire and Isle of Wight Air Ambulance (£180,000); The Wey and Arun Canal Trust (£120,000); RNLI (£30,000); Rowans Hospice (£20,000); Forest of Avon Trust, People4ponies and Surfers Against Sewage (£2,000 each); Clean Up UK, Friends of the Cromford Canal and WWF-UK (£1,000 each).

FINANCES *Financial year end* 30/09/2022
Income £1,740,000
Grants to organisations £398,000
Assets £16,860,000
TRUSTEES Ann Rogers; Christopher Driscoll; Richard Weekes.
HOW TO APPLY Apply in writing to the correspondent.
CONTACT DETAILS The Trustees, Lower Tye Farm, Copse Lane, Hayling Island, Hampshire PO11 0RQ *Tel.* 023 9246 4276 *Email* richard@sthermans.co.uk

■ Cancer Research UK

CC NO 1089464
WHERE FUNDING CAN BE GIVEN UK.
WHO CAN BENEFIT Research institutions; universities; hospitals.
WHAT IS FUNDED Research focused on understanding cancer; therapeutic innovation; public health and behavioural research.
WHAT IS NOT FUNDED See the charity's website for details of exclusions under each specific funding scheme.
TYPE OF GRANT Research funding; project costs.
SAMPLE GRANTS Francis Crick Institute (£60.4 million); University of Cambridge (£54.82 million); University of Manchester (£36.14 million); Imperial College London (£11.24 million); Newcastle University (£4.37 million); King's College London (£3.17 million); Dana Farber Cancer Institute (£1.66 million); University of Strathclyde (£831,000).
FINANCES *Financial year end* 31/03/2022
Income £668,500,000
Grants to organisations £310,300,000
Assets £378,000,000
TRUSTEES Catherine Brown; Prof. Sir Leszek Borysiewicz; Peter Chambre; Prof. Sir Michael Richards; Tracy Groose; Prof. Nicholas Jones; Prof. Moira Whyte; Joanne Shaw; Dr Robert Easton; Prof. Pamela Kearns; Bomonlu Adelaja; Prof. Doreen Cantrell; Prof. Gerard Evan; Hitesh Thakrar; Rakshit Kapoor.
HOW TO APPLY Applications can be made on the charity's online grants management system. Each funding scheme has its own application guidelines and deadlines, which are detailed on the charity's website.
CONTACT DETAILS The Trustees, 2 Redman Place, London E20 1JQ *Tel.* 020 7242 0200 *Email* grants.helpline@cancer.org.uk *Website* www.cancerresearchuk.org

■ The Candy Foundation

CC NO 1176337   **ESTABLISHED** 2017
WHERE FUNDING CAN BE GIVEN Worldwide.
WHO CAN BENEFIT Registered charities.
WHAT IS FUNDED General charitable purposes.
WHAT IS NOT FUNDED Individuals.
SAMPLE GRANTS Supporting Wounded Veterans (£150,000); UBS Optimus Foundation (for Disability Rights International) (£100,000); Northern Counties School and Woman's Trust (£10,000 each).
FINANCES *Financial year end* 31/12/2021
Income £281,700
Grants to organisations £280,000
Assets £30
TRUSTEES Nicholas Candy; Holly Vukadinovic; Christopher Sullivan; Kevin Cahill; David Williams.
HOW TO APPLY Unsolicited applications are not accepted.

CONTACT DETAILS The Trustees, 49 Upper Brook Street, London W1K 2BR *Tel.* 020 3841 9608

....

■ The Frederick and Phyllis Cann Trust

CC NO 1087863   **ESTABLISHED** 1998
WHERE FUNDING CAN BE GIVEN UK, with a preference for Northamptonshire.
WHO CAN BENEFIT Registered charities; CICs; hospices; hospitals.
WHAT IS FUNDED Animal welfare; children's welfare; safety at sea.
TYPE OF GRANT Capital costs.
RANGE OF GRANTS £500 to £7,000.
SAMPLE GRANTS Northampton Saints Foundation (£7,000); RNLI (£5,000); Battersea Dogs and Cats Home and Lakeland Day Care Hospice (£2,000 each); British Stammering Association (£1,000); Emmanuel Group of Churches (£500).
FINANCES *Financial year end* 05/04/2022
Income £55,400
Grants to organisations £61,000
Assets £2,870,000
TRUSTEES Keith Panter; Michael Percival; Philip Saunderson; David Sharp; Ian James; Gillian Evans.
HOW TO APPLY Contact the correspondent for further information.
CONTACT DETAILS Angela Moon, Correspondent, c/o Hewitsons, Elgin House, Billing Road, Northampton, Northamptonshire NN1 5AU *Tel.* 01604 233233 *Email* angelamoon@ hewitsons.com

....

■ Cannon Charitable Trust

CC NO 1080818   **ESTABLISHED** 2000
WHERE FUNDING CAN BE GIVEN UK and overseas.
WHO CAN BENEFIT Charitable organisations; individuals.
WHAT IS FUNDED Religious education; social welfare.
RANGE OF GRANTS Up to £120,000.
SAMPLE GRANTS One Heart – Lev Echod (£120,000); Friends of Mercaz Hatorah Belz Macnivka (£90,000); Tchabe Kollel (£65,000); United Talmudical Association (£28,500); Hatzola Trust Ltd (£25,000).
FINANCES *Financial year end* 31/01/2022
Income £581,800
Grants to organisations £1,230,000
Assets £64,100
TRUSTEES Robert Tauber; Juliana Tauber.
HOW TO APPLY Contact the correspondent for further information.
CONTACT DETAILS The Trustees, Unit 2A Berol House, 25 Ashley Road, Tottenham Hale, London N17 9LJ *Tel.* 020 8885 9430

....

■ Card Factory Foundation

CC NO 1180081   **ESTABLISHED** 2018
WHERE FUNDING CAN BE GIVEN UK.
WHO CAN BENEFIT Not-for-profit organisations; community groups; individuals.
WHAT IS FUNDED General charitable purposes.
TYPE OF GRANT Project funding; capital costs.
RANGE OF GRANTS Up to £2,500.
SAMPLE GRANTS A list of beneficiaries was not included in the annual report and accounts. Previous beneficiaries have included: Alzheimer's Society; British Heart Foundation; Macmillan Cancer Support; NSPCC.

FINANCES *Financial year end* 31/01/2022
Income £1,000,000
Grants to organisations £281,600
Assets £2,350,000
TRUSTEES Julie Hardy; Jane Rowney; Susan Glass; Nicola Rogerson; Stephen Gleadall; Brian Waring.
OTHER INFORMATION The foundation's Community Grant Fund supports charitable causes that benefit the communities of the company's employees and stores.
HOW TO APPLY Applications can be made via the foundation's website.
CONTACT DETAILS The Trustees, Century House, Brunel Road, Wakefield 41 Industrial Estate, Wakefield, West Yorkshire WF2 0XG *Tel.* 07933 399645 *Email* trustees@cardfactoryfoundation. org *Website* www.cardfactoryinvestors.com/ foundation

....

■ CareTech Charitable Foundation

CC NO 1182567   **ESTABLISHED** 2017
WHERE FUNDING CAN BE GIVEN UK and Pakistan.
WHO CAN BENEFIT Registered charities; social enterprises; current and former employees of CareTech Holdings plc.
WHAT IS FUNDED Disability; skills development; local community poverty relief projects.
SAMPLE GRANTS Alzheimer's Society (£125,000); British Asian Trust (£100,000); Whizz-Kidz (£49,300); Social Care Leaders Scheme (£15,000).
FINANCES *Financial year end* 30/09/2022
Income £2,380,000
Grants to organisations £1,940,000
Assets £8,080,000
TRUSTEES Charles Cheffings; Sheikh Farouq Rashid; Sheikh Haroon Rashid; Navshir Jaffer; Jessica Taplin; Christopher Dickinson; Farzana Ali; Sheikh Hamza Rashid; Dr Moira Livingston; Claire Marshall; Lisa Stafford.
HOW TO APPLY Each grants programme has an eligibility test, which should be completed by prospective applicants before making an application. For organisations deemed eligible, applications can be made online. Paper or digital/Word copies of the application form can be requested by email.
CONTACT DETAILS The Trustees, Metropolitan House, 3 Darkes Lane, Potters Bar, Hertfordshire EN6 1AG *Tel.* 01707 601800 *Email* info@ caretechfoundation.org.uk *Website* www. caretechfoundation.org.uk

....

■ Carew Pole Charitable Trust

CC NO 255375   **ESTABLISHED** 1968
WHERE FUNDING CAN BE GIVEN UK, with a preference for Cornwall.
WHO CAN BENEFIT Registered charities; CICs; hospices; hospitals; places of worship; uniformed groups.
WHAT IS FUNDED Social welfare; heritage; the environment; horticulture; the armed services; the arts; Christianity; rural community.
WHAT IS NOT FUNDED Individuals for full-time education; churches and village halls not local to Antony House and Torpoint, or without a connection with Carew Pole Baronetcy.
RANGE OF GRANTS £250 to £5,000.
SAMPLE GRANTS The Fishmongers' Company and Wild Young Parents Project (£5,000 each); Battling On, CLEAR and Holy Trinity Parish Church (£2,000 each); Liskerrett Centre (£1,500); Deviock Activities Group, Linking

Environment and Farming and Royal Cornwall Hospital (£1,000 each); Falmouth Food Co-op, Forest Pathways and Kreslu (£750 each); 2nd Bude and Jacobstow Scout Group, Millbrook Skatepark Project and Royal West of England Academy (£500 each); Crafts Council, Fishermen's Mission and RNLI (£250 each).

FINANCES *Financial year end 05/04/2022*
Income £85,000
Grants to organisations £63,200
Assets £2,360,000

TRUSTEES Tremayne Pole; James Williams; Clare Coode.

HOW TO APPLY Apply in writing to the correspondent.

CONTACT DETAILS The Trustees, The Antony Estate Office, Antony, Torpoint, Cornwall PL11 3AB *Tel.* 01752 815303 *Email* william@antonyestate.com

■ William A. Cargill Charitable Trust

OSCR NO SC012076　　**ESTABLISHED** 1992
WHERE FUNDING CAN BE GIVEN Scotland.
WHO CAN BENEFIT Registered charities.
WHAT IS FUNDED Care of older people; care and support of children; medical research; education; arts, culture and heritage; science.
SAMPLE GRANTS A list of beneficiaries was not included in the annual report and accounts.
FINANCES *Financial year end 30/11/2021*
Income £157,800
Grants to organisations £124,500
Assets £6,520,000
OTHER INFORMATION The 2020/21 accounts were the latest available at the time of writing (May 2023).
HOW TO APPLY Contact the correspondent for further information.
CONTACT DETAILS The Trustees, c/o Miller Beckett and Jackson Solicitors, 190 St Vincent Street, Glasgow G2 5SP

■ David William Traill Cargill Fund

OSCR NO SC012703　　**ESTABLISHED** 1939
WHERE FUNDING CAN BE GIVEN UK and overseas.
WHO CAN BENEFIT Registered charities; universities; hospices.
WHAT IS FUNDED General charitable purposes.
WHAT IS NOT FUNDED Individuals.
SAMPLE GRANTS A list of beneficiaries was not included in the annual report and accounts. Previous beneficiaries have included: City of Glasgow Society of Social Service; Colquhoun Bequest Fund for Incurables; Crathie Opportunity Holidays; Glasgow and West of Scotland Society for the Blind; Glasgow City Mission; Greenock Medical Aid Society; Lead Scotland; North Glasgow Community Forum; Scottish Maritime Museum – Irvine; Scottish Episcopal Church; Scottish Motor Neurone Disease Association; Three Towns Blind Bowling/Social Club.
FINANCES *Financial year end 30/11/2021*
Income £381,100
Grants to organisations £311,800
Assets £11,930,000
OTHER INFORMATION The 2020/21 accounts were the latest available at the time of writing (May 2023).
HOW TO APPLY Apply in writing to the correspondent.
CONTACT DETAILS The Trustees, c/o Miller Beckett and Jackson Ltd, 190 St Vincent Street, Glasgow G2 5SP

■ W. A. Cargill Fund

OSCR NO SC008456　　**ESTABLISHED** 1962
WHERE FUNDING CAN BE GIVEN Glasgow and the west of Scotland.
WHO CAN BENEFIT Registered charities; charitable organisations; hospices; hospitals; schools.
WHAT IS FUNDED The prevention or relief of poverty; education; religion; the advancement of health; citizenship or community development; arts/culture/heritage; science; relief of older people; ill health; disability; social and economic disadvantage.
WHAT IS NOT FUNDED Individuals.
RANGE OF GRANTS Up to £50,000 but generally from £500 to £5,000.
SAMPLE GRANTS A list of beneficiaries was not included in the annual report and accounts.
FINANCES *Financial year end 30/11/2021*
Income £516,000
Grants to organisations £538,300
Assets £23,370,000
OTHER INFORMATION The 2021 accounts were the latest available at the time of writing (May 2023). The range is an estimation based on previous accounts. The most recent accounts (2021) do not give a full breakdown of grants made to organisations.
HOW TO APPLY Apply in writing to the correspondent.
CONTACT DETAILS The Trustees, c/o Miller Beckett and Jackson Ltd, 190 St Vincent Street, Glasgow G2 5SP

■ Carlee Ltd

CC NO 282873　　**ESTABLISHED** 1981
WHERE FUNDING CAN BE GIVEN Worldwide.
WHO CAN BENEFIT Jewish organisations.
WHAT IS FUNDED The advancement of religion in accordance with the Orthodox Jewish faith; the relief of poverty; general charitable purposes.
RANGE OF GRANTS £12,000 to £50,000.
SAMPLE GRANTS Achisomoch Aid Company (£40,900); A T.I.M.E. Ltd and Amud Hatzdokoh Trust (£20,000); Bayis Lepleitos (£18,000); Beis Aharon TT Activity Centre and Friends of Beis Chinuch Lebonos Trust (£12,000).
FINANCES *Financial year end 31/03/2022*
Income £505,900
Grants to organisations £465,600
Assets £1,520,000
TRUSTEES Bernard Stroh; Alexander Singer; Ephraim Bleier; Esther Kahn.
OTHER INFORMATION Grants were awarded to more than 20 organisations during the year.
HOW TO APPLY Apply in writing to the correspondent.
CONTACT DETAILS The Trustees, 32 Paget Road, London N16 5NQ *Tel.* 020 8802 4782 *Email* admin@carleeltd.org

■ The Carlton Hayes Mental Health Charity

CC NO 219783　　**ESTABLISHED** 1834
WHERE FUNDING CAN BE GIVEN Leicester City; Leicestershire; Rutland.
WHO CAN BENEFIT Charitable organisations.
WHAT IS FUNDED Mental health.
TYPE OF GRANT Project funding.
RANGE OF GRANTS Small grants: up to £5,000; large grants: over £5,000.
SAMPLE GRANTS Raising Health (£55,000); Leicester Charity Link (£30,000); Active Wesley Hall (£16,000); Schizophrenia Support Group (£2,000); Mosaic (£1,500).

FINANCES *Financial year end 31/03/2022*
Income £196,800
Grants to organisations £198,800
Assets £6,530,000
TRUSTEES Mark Newcombe; Rachael Stembridge; Richard Foster; Neil Bannister; Gale Waller; Rashmikant Joshi; Dr Susan Smith; Carole Eastwood; Mark Dunkley.
OTHER INFORMATION Grants were awarded to 14 organisations during the year.
HOW TO APPLY Application forms are available to download from the charity's website.
CONTACT DETAILS Helen Pole, Assistant to the Clerk, Shakespeare Martineau, Two Colton Square, Leicester LE1 1QH *Tel.* 0116 254 5454 ext. 6235 *Email* use the contact form on the website *Website* www.carltonhayes.co.uk

....

■ The Antonio Carluccio Foundation

CC NO 1167646
WHERE FUNDING CAN BE GIVEN UK and overseas.
WHO CAN BENEFIT Charities; individuals.
WHAT IS FUNDED Prevention and relief of poverty and hunger; the training of chefs and cooks.
TYPE OF GRANT Project funding.
RANGE OF GRANTS Typically £5,000 to £10,000, with some larger grants.
SAMPLE GRANTS St Petrock's (£35,500); Action Through Enterprise (£17,600); Hospitality Action and Ulster University (£10,000 each); The Good Kitchen Mussomelli (£6,000). FoodBlessed (£5,000).
FINANCES *Financial year end 30/06/2022*
Income £430,400
Grants to organisations £98,900
Assets £568,800
TRUSTEES Andrea Stevenson; Steven Berry; Simon Kossoff.
OTHER INFORMATION During 2021/22 grants were awarded to eight organisations during the year. The grants were broken down into the following categories: education/nutrition (51%) and feeding (49%).
HOW TO APPLY Apply in writing to the correspondent.
CONTACT DETAILS The Trustees, Chamberlain Berry, 27–28 New Road, Chippenham SN15 1HS *Tel.* 01249 461999 *Email* trustees@theantoniocarlucciofoundation.org

....

■ The Carnegie Dunfermline Trust

OSCR NO SC015710   ESTABLISHED 1903
WHERE FUNDING CAN BE GIVEN Dunfermline and the surrounding areas.
WHO CAN BENEFIT Registered charities; voluntary sector organisations; schools; amateur sports clubs; societies.
WHAT IS FUNDED Projects, activities and schemes with social, community, educational, cultural, sport and recreational purposes.
WHAT IS NOT FUNDED Individuals; closed groups (with the exception of those catering for specialist needs); political, military or sectarian bodies; activities outside the geographic scope of the trust; medical organisations; routine running or salary costs; costs which are the responsibility of a government body.
RANGE OF GRANTS Between £300 and £10,000.
SAMPLE GRANTS Duloch Primary School (£10,000); Archaeology Scotland (£7,000); Dunfermline Bowling Club (£5,000); Dunfermline Water Polo Club (£4,000); Fife Festival of Music (£1,500); Real Life Options (£1,000); TURN Project (£850); Plastic-Free Dunfermline (£250).
FINANCES *Financial year end 31/12/2021*
Income £480,400
Grants to organisations £110,000
Assets £17,820,000
TRUSTEES Andrew Croxford; Dr Colin Firth; Danny McArthur; Janet McCauslin; Gillian Mann; George Murray; The Revd MaryAnn Rennie; Mike Reid; Fiona Robertson; J. Douglas Scott; David Walker; Ian Wilson; Thomas Docherty; Rachel Doyle; Victoria Simpson; Dr Ruth Strain.
OTHER INFORMATION The trust awarded 52 grants for the causes of: schools (£45,500); community and general grants (£33,100); sport (£21,200); emergency grants (£6,800); creative arts (£3,200).
HOW TO APPLY Application forms are available to download from the trust's website.
CONTACT DETAILS The Trustees, Andrew Carnegie House, Pittencrieff Street, Dunfermline, Fife KY12 8AW *Tel.* 01383 749789 *Email* grants@carnegietrust.com *Website* www.andrewcarnegie.co.uk

....

■ The Carnegie Trust for the Universities of Scotland

OSCR NO SC015600   ESTABLISHED 1901
WHERE FUNDING CAN BE GIVEN Scotland.
WHO CAN BENEFIT Universities.
WHAT IS FUNDED Enrichment of the scholarly capability of Scotland's Universities and assistance for people of limited means to benefit from higher education. The trust operates a number of funding streams to achieve this, which are: fee support for Scottish students unable to fund their course at a Scottish university; Vacation Scholarships for undergraduates who have a talent and an interest for research; bursaries to cover the cost of tuition fees of one year of postgraduate study at a Scottish university; scholarships for PhD study; Research Incentive Grants to fund high-quality research in any academic field; Collaborative Research Grants to encourage academic researchers to initiate joint research projects to the benefit of Scottish universities as a whole; the Centenary Professorship scheme to support visits to Scotland from leading international researchers.
WHAT IS NOT FUNDED See the website for exclusions of individual schemes.
TYPE OF GRANT Core/revenue costs.
SAMPLE GRANTS University of Aberdeen; University of Dundee; University of Edinburgh; University of the Highlands and Islands; University of Stirling.
FINANCES *Financial year end 30/09/2022*
Income £2,890,000
Grants to organisations £1,770,000
Assets £71,850,000
TRUSTEES Dr Alison Fieldin; The Rt Hon. Lord Eassie; Dr Alison Fielding; Prof. Andrea Nolan; Prof. Sally Mapstone; Prof. George Boyne; Ray Perman; Dr Bridget McConnell; Sara Parkin; Dr Mary Duffy; Ronnie Bowie; Prof. Richard Williams; Prof. Sir Gerry McCormac; Graeme Johnston.
OTHER INFORMATION The grant total includes funding awarded to universities and individuals.
HOW TO APPLY Details of the various schemes operated by the trust are available from its website.

CONTACT DETAILS The Trustees, Andrew Carnegie House, Pittencrieff Street, Dunfermline, Fife KY12 8AW *Tel.* 01383 724990 *Email* use the contact form on the website. *Website* www. carnegie-trust.org

■ The Carpenters Company Charitable Trust

CC NO 276996 **ESTABLISHED** 1978
WHERE FUNDING CAN BE GIVEN UK, with a preference for Greater London.
WHO CAN BENEFIT Individuals and schools, colleges, universities and other charitable organisations promoting the craft of carpentry.
WHAT IS FUNDED Education; crafts; children and young people; older people; homelessness.
WHAT IS NOT FUNDED Grants are not normally made to individual churches or cathedrals, or to educational establishments with no association to the Carpenters' Company. Funds are usually only available to charities registered with the Charity Commission or exempt from registration.
SAMPLE GRANTS Building Crafts College (£1.27 million); Norton Folgate Trust (£48,600); Creative Dimension (£15,000); No Going Back (£10,000).
FINANCES *Financial year end* 30/06/2022
Income £1,430,000
Grants to organisations £1,410,000
Assets £34,720,000
TRUSTEES Michael Mathews; Martin Samuel; Alistair Gregory-Smith; Rachel Bower.
OTHER INFORMATION The majority of the trust's income each year goes to the Building Crafts College, but the trust also maintains long-standing commitments to numerous other organisations, mainly in the Greater London area.
HOW TO APPLY At the time of writing (May 2023) the trust's website stated: 'All funds are currently committed and we are not considering any applications. The website will be updated should this position change.'
CONTACT DETAILS Brig. T. J. Gregson, Clerk to the Carpenters Company, Carpenters' Hall, 1 Throgmorton Avenue, London EC2N 2JJ *Tel.* 020 7588 7001 *Email* info@carpentersco. com *Website* www.carpentersco.com/charities/carpenters-company-charitable-trust

■ The Carr-Gregory Trust

CC NO 1085580 **ESTABLISHED** 2001
WHERE FUNDING CAN BE GIVEN London and Bristol.
WHO CAN BENEFIT Charitable organisations.
WHAT IS FUNDED Performing arts; health; social welfare; education.
WHAT IS NOT FUNDED Individuals.
RANGE OF GRANTS £1,000 to £22,500.
SAMPLE GRANTS A list of beneficiaries was not included in the annual report and accounts. Previous beneficiaries have included: Royal Academy of Music (£22,500); Alzheimer's Research UK (£10,000); Prisoners' Education Trust (£7,500); National Opera Studio (£5,000); Barbican Centre Trust (£3,000); Great Western Air Ambulance (£2,500); Sound World (£1,000).
FINANCES *Financial year end* 31/12/2022
Income £191,100
Grants to organisations £620,400
Assets £596,000
TRUSTEES Linda Carr; Russ Carr; Heather Wheelhouse.

OTHER INFORMATION Grants of over £1,000 were made to 32 organisations during the year. Grants were broken down as follows: education (£539,600); social needs (£35,000); health (£27,000); arts/culture (£18,700).
HOW TO APPLY Apply in writing to the correspondent.
CONTACT DETAILS The Trustees, 56 Pembroke Road, Clifton, Bristol BS8 3DT *Tel.* 0117 973 7605

■ The Carrington Charitable Trust

CC NO 265824 **ESTABLISHED** 1973
WHERE FUNDING CAN BE GIVEN UK, with a preference for Buckinghamshire.
WHO CAN BENEFIT Registered charities.
WHAT IS FUNDED General charitable purposes.
RANGE OF GRANTS Mostly up to £1,000.
SAMPLE GRANTS Bledlow Village Hall Appeal (£10,000); Priscilla Bacon Centre for Palliative Care (£5,000); Bledlow PCC (£1,300); Autism Early Support Trust (£1,000); Alexander Devine Children's Hospice (£500); Buckinghamshire Garden Trust (£150).
FINANCES *Financial year end* 05/04/2022
Income £95,600
Grants to organisations £66,300
Assets £7,620,000
TRUSTEES The Hon. Virginia Carrington; Jeffrey Cloke; Lord Carrington.
OTHER INFORMATION In 2021/22, grants were awarded to 57 organisations across the UK, with the majority operating in Buckinghamshire.
HOW TO APPLY Apply in writing to the correspondent.
CONTACT DETAILS Jeffrey Cloke, The Courtyard, Manor House Estate Office, Perry Lane, Bledlow, Buckinghamshire HP27 9PA *Tel.* 01844 273508 *Email* angienuttall@carington.co.uk

■ The Leslie Mary Carter Charitable Trust

CC NO 284782 **ESTABLISHED** 1982
WHERE FUNDING CAN BE GIVEN UK, with a strong preference for Norfolk, north Essex and Suffolk.
WHO CAN BENEFIT Registered charities; hospices; churches; uniformed groups.
WHAT IS FUNDED Conservation and restoration; the environment; social welfare; health.
WHAT IS NOT FUNDED Individuals.
TYPE OF GRANT Capital and project costs.
RANGE OF GRANTS Typically £1,000 to £5,000.
SAMPLE GRANTS Suffolk Wildlife Trust (£7,500); Action Medical Research, British Heart Foundation and Samaritans (£5,000 each); Age UK, Bone Cancer Research and Parkinson's UK (£3,000 each); National Maritime Museum (£2,000); Our Special Friends (£1,000).
FINANCES *Financial year end* 31/12/2021
Income £1,120,000
Grants to organisations £147,000
Assets £6,050,000
TRUSTEES Martyn Carr; Sam Wilson; Marycita Wilson; Sara Carr.
OTHER INFORMATION During 2021 the trust awarded grants to 47 organisations.
HOW TO APPLY Apply in writing to the correspondent. The trustees meet every six months to consider applications.
CONTACT DETAILS The Trustees, c/o Birketts LLP, Providence House, 141–145 Princes Street, Ipswich, Suffolk IP1 1QJ *Tel.* 01473 232300

■ The Casey Trust

CC NO 1055726   **ESTABLISHED** 1996
WHERE FUNDING CAN BE GIVEN UK and financially developing countries.
WHO CAN BENEFIT UK-registered charities.
WHAT IS FUNDED Children (up to the age of 18).
WHAT IS NOT FUNDED Individuals; unregistered organisations; projects that are not exclusively for children.
TYPE OF GRANT Project funding; seed funding/start-up funding. The trustees look to support start-up projects or identifiable new initiatives within existing projects rather than recurring events or continuing events.
SAMPLE GRANTS A list of beneficiaries was not included in the annual report and accounts. Previous beneficiaries have included: Raw Material (£12,500); World Monuments Fund (£11,000); Buttle UK (£2,500); Acorns (£2,400); The Children's Adventure Farm Trust (£2,300); Lifelites (£2,100); Malaika Kids UK, Motability and Sightsavers (£2,000 each); Street Child – Liberia (£1,800); Perthes Association (£1,600); Sunny Days Children's Fund (£1,500); Edinburgh Young Carers Project and St Luke's Cares (£1,000 each).
FINANCES *Financial year end 30/06/2022*
Income £106,400
Grants to organisations £90,000
Assets £4,020,000
TRUSTEES Kenneth Howard; Benjamin Shorten; Sam Howard; Alex Krikler.
OTHER INFORMATION Grants were awarded to 57 organisations during 2021/22.
HOW TO APPLY Appeals may be made in writing to the correspondent, providing a brief outline of the work and project for which the money is required as well as a clear budget and a recent set of accounts, if possible. An sae should be enclosed if a response is required.
CONTACT DETAILS The Trustees, 27 Arkwright Road, London NW3 6BJ *Tel.* 020 7794 2523 *Email* caseytrust@icloud.com *Website* www.caseytrust.org

■ The Castanea Trust

CC NO 1136180   **ESTABLISHED** 2010
WHERE FUNDING CAN BE GIVEN UK.
WHO CAN BENEFIT Registered charities.
WHAT IS FUNDED Ex-Service personnel and their families; children who are sick; animal welfare; older people.
RANGE OF GRANTS Up to £18,000.
SAMPLE GRANTS Combat Stress (£18,000); SSAFA, the Armed Forces charity (£12,000); National Museums Liverpool and St Luke's Cheshire Hospice (£6,000 each); The Woodland Trust (£3,000); Outward Bound (£1,000); Abbeyfield (£750).
FINANCES *Financial year end 05/04/2022*
Income £217,200
Grants to organisations £224,000
Assets £12,160,000
TRUSTEES Ian Duncan; Mark Feeny; Geoffrey Wall.
OTHER INFORMATION Grants were made to 36 organisations during 2021/22.
HOW TO APPLY Contact the correspondent for further information.
CONTACT DETAILS Mark Feeny, Trustee, c/o Brabners LLP, Horton House, Exchange Flags, Liverpool L2 3YL *Email* mark.feeny@brabners.com

■ The Castansa Trust

OSCR NO SC037414   **ESTABLISHED** 2008
WHERE FUNDING CAN BE GIVEN The Lothians, Glasgow and Dumfries and Galloway.
WHO CAN BENEFIT Registered charities.
WHAT IS FUNDED Education; children and young people; people with dementia or cancer; social inclusion; arts and culture; health; the environment.
WHAT IS NOT FUNDED Individuals.
RANGE OF GRANTS Typically £5,000 to £15,000, but some larger grants may be available.
SAMPLE GRANTS The Big Green Give (£52,500); Reform Scotland (£40,000); Dogs Trust (£10,000); John Muir Trust (£5,000); The Orchard Project (£1,000).
FINANCES *Financial year end 25/07/2022*
Income £36,300
Grants to organisations £362,000
Assets £1,440,000
HOW TO APPLY According to its webpage, the trust no longer accepts unsolicited applications 'due to [having] a significant number of existing commitments'.
CONTACT DETAILS The Trustees, c/o Turcan Connell, Princes Exchange, 1 Earl Grey Street, Edinburgh EH3 9EE *Website* www.turcanconnell.com/the-castansa-trust

■ Catholic Charitable Trust

CC NO 215553   **ESTABLISHED** 1935
WHERE FUNDING CAN BE GIVEN UK and overseas.
WHO CAN BENEFIT Catholic organisations.
WHAT IS FUNDED The traditional teachings of the Roman Catholic faith.
RANGE OF GRANTS Up to £20,000.
SAMPLE GRANTS Academy of Sacred Music and Society of Saint Pius X – England (£20,000 each); Little Sisters of the Poor (£8,000); Catholic Trust for England and Wales and Chavagnes International College (£5,000 each); St Francis Leprosy Guild and St James Church Spanish Place (£3,000 each); Latin Mass Society (£2,000).
FINANCES *Financial year end 31/12/2021*
Income £94,700
Grants to organisations £109,900
Assets £3,560,000
TRUSTEES John Vernor-Miles; Wilfrid Vernor-Miles; David Orr; Jennifer Vernor-Miles.
OTHER INFORMATION During 2021 the trust made grants to 19 charities.
HOW TO APPLY Apply in writing to the correspondent. The trust's 2021 annual report and accounts state: 'The charity does not invite applications for grants but does consider unsolicited appeals.'
CONTACT DETAILS Wilfrid Vernor-Miles, Trustee, c/o Hunters Solicitors, 9 New Square, London WC2A 3QN *Tel.* 020 7412 0050 *Email* wilfrid.vernor-miles@hunterslaw.com

■ Catkin Pussywillow Charitable Trust

CC NO 1100036   **ESTABLISHED** 2003
WHERE FUNDING CAN BE GIVEN UK.
WHO CAN BENEFIT Charitable organisations.
WHAT IS FUNDED Health; social welfare; education; general charitable purposes.
RANGE OF GRANTS From £3,750 to £100,000.
SAMPLE GRANTS Hampstead Theatre (£100,000); Caring Matters Now (£25,000); St Ann's College (£10,000); Guildhall School Trust and HVP UK

(£5,000 each); Sir John Soames Museum (£3,750).

FINANCES *Financial year end* 05/04/2022
Income £150,000
Grants to organisations £148,800
Assets £29,900

TRUSTEES Celia Atkin; Barry Gold; Raymond Harris.

OTHER INFORMATION Grants were awarded to six organisations during 2021/22.

HOW TO APPLY Contact the correspondent for further information.

CONTACT DETAILS The Trustees, c/o Adler Shine LLP, Aston House, Cornwall Avenue, Church End, London N3 1LF *Tel.* 020 8371 3000

■ Cattanach

OSCR NO SC049833　　　**ESTABLISHED** 1992

WHERE FUNDING CAN BE GIVEN Scotland.

WHO CAN BENEFIT Registered charities.

WHAT IS FUNDED Prenatal care; projects for children under the age of three; social welfare.

WHAT IS NOT FUNDED Individuals; personal study or travel; hospices or palliative care; animal charities; appliances for illness or disability; organisations concerned with specific diseases; large capital projects (more than £100,000); projects costing less than £3,000; crèches where parents are not involved; organisations or activities where religious content is compulsory for users; general appeals.

TYPE OF GRANT Project funding; core/revenue costs. Grants are often multi-year.

RANGE OF GRANTS From £3,000 to £25,000 with most grants being around £10,000.

SAMPLE GRANTS Rock Community Church (£74,100); Queen's Nursing Institute (£40,000); Family Journeys (£38,800); Govan HELP (£30,000); Isle of Jura Development Trust (£2,800).

FINANCES *Financial year end* 31/12/2021
Income £303,100
Grants to organisations £1,360,000
Assets £24,880,000

TRUSTEES Andrew Millington; Mafe Marwick; Steven Murray; Rory Marsh; Heather Coady; Jennifer Corrigan; Patricia Jackson; Caroline Murray; Trisha Hall; Rachel Mathers.

HOW TO APPLY Details of how to apply can be found on the charity's website. The charity recommends that potential applicants make an informal enquiry to check the suitability of their project before starting the application process.

CONTACT DETAILS Jemma Slater, Grants and Relationships Officer, Mansfield Traquair Centre, 15 Mansfield Place, 502 Gorgie Road, Edinburgh EH3 6BB *Tel.* 0131 474 6155 *Email* info@cattanach.org.uk *Website* www.cattanach.org.uk

■ The Joseph and Annie Cattle Trust

CC NO 262011　　　**ESTABLISHED** 1970

WHERE FUNDING CAN BE GIVEN Hull and East Yorkshire.

WHO CAN BENEFIT Charitable organisations.

WHAT IS FUNDED General charitable purposes including: older people; people with disabilities; health; social welfare; children with dyslexia.

TYPE OF GRANT Capital costs; project funding; one-off and recurring grants.

RANGE OF GRANTS Up to £1,000.

SAMPLE GRANTS A list of beneficiaries was not included in the annual report and accounts.

FINANCES *Financial year end* 30/06/2022
Income £354,300
Grants to organisations £351,500
Assets £12,260,000

TRUSTEES Mr S. C. Jowers; Paul Edwards; Christopher Munday; Ann Hughes.

HOW TO APPLY Application forms are available from the trust's website. Application forms should be printed, completed in handwriting and submitted to the trust by post or fax.

CONTACT DETAILS The Administrator, PO Box 23, Patrington, Hull, East Yorkshire HU12 0WF *Tel.* 01964 671742 *Email* rogercattletrust@protonmail.com *Website* www.jacattletrust.co.uk

■ The Thomas Sivewright Catto Charitable Settlement

CC NO 279549　　　**ESTABLISHED** 1979

WHERE FUNDING CAN BE GIVEN UK and overseas.

WHO CAN BENEFIT Registered charities.

WHAT IS FUNDED General charitable purposes.

TYPE OF GRANT Unrestricted funding.

RANGE OF GRANTS Typically between £500 and £1,000. Occasionally, larger grants are awarded.

SAMPLE GRANTS Unicef COVAX Appeal (£50,000); Royal College of Music – SGC Scholarship (£15,500); Royal Conservatoire of Scotland (£12,000); British Liver Trust (£3,000); Cure Parkinson's Trust (£2,000); Cystic Fibrosis Trust (£750); British Eye Research Foundation (£500).

FINANCES *Financial year end* 05/04/2022
Income £547,000
Grants to organisations £363,900
Assets £10,740,000

TRUSTEES Lord Catto; Olivia Marchant; Zoe Richmond-Watson.

HOW TO APPLY Apply in writing to the correspondent. The trustees meet quarterly to consider applications and distribute funding.

CONTACT DETAILS The Trustees, PO Box 47408, London N21 1YW *Tel.* 07836 247913 *Email* office@tscatto.org.uk

■ The Wilfrid and Constance Cave Foundation

CC NO 241900　　　**ESTABLISHED** 1965

WHERE FUNDING CAN BE GIVEN England and Wales, with a preference for Berkshire, Cornwall, Devon, Dorset, Gloucestershire, Oxfordshire, Somerset, Wiltshire and Worcestershire.

WHO CAN BENEFIT Charitable organisations; registered charities; hospices; hospitals; schools and colleges; museums.

WHAT IS FUNDED General charitable purposes; education; the arts; culture; science; health; community development; animal conservation.

TYPE OF GRANT Capital costs; core/revenue costs; seed funding/start-up funding; project funding; unrestricted funding.

RANGE OF GRANTS Up to £20,000 but typically between £1,000 and £10,000.

SAMPLE GRANTS Exmoor Young Voices (£20,000); The Farmer's Club Pinnacle Award (£14,000); Disasters Emergency Committee – Ukraine Appeal (£10,000); The Story Museum (£5,000); Two Moors Festival (£3,000); Westcountry Rivers Trust (£2,000); Swan Support (£1,000).

FINANCES *Financial year end* 05/04/2022
Income £133,500
Grants to organisations £162,000
Assets £5,020,000

TRUSTEES Mark Pickin; Emily Pickin; Melanie Howells; Joshua Thorne.

OTHER INFORMATION According to the foundation's 2021/22 annual report, it awarded 40 grants to organisations during the year.

HOW TO APPLY The foundation does not accept or respond to unsolicited applications.

CONTACT DETAILS Michelle Allen, Secretary, Clewer Boatyard Ltd, Clewer Court Road, Winkfield, Windsor, Berkshire SL4 5JD *Tel.* 01753 859274 *Email* secretary@cavefoundation.org.uk *Website* www.cavefoundation.org.uk

······································

■ The Cayo Foundation

CC NO 1080607   **ESTABLISHED** 1999
WHERE FUNDING CAN BE GIVEN UK.
WHO CAN BENEFIT Registered charities.
WHAT IS FUNDED General charitable purposes; medical research; crime prevention; children and young people; performing arts.
RANGE OF GRANTS £1,000 to £125,000.
SAMPLE GRANTS Crimestoppers Trust (£148,200). A full list of beneficiaries is not available.
FINANCES *Financial year end* 30/09/2021
Income £59,900
Grants to organisations £365,700
Assets £3,740,000
TRUSTEES Angela McCarville; Stewart Harris.
OTHER INFORMATION The foundation awarded one grant totalling £148,200 to Crimestoppers Trust and seven other grants to charities that were not listed in the foundation's annual report and accounts. The 2020/21 accounts were the latest available at the time of writing (March 2023).
HOW TO APPLY Apply in writing to the correspondent.
CONTACT DETAILS The Trustees, 59 Loampit Vale, London SE13 7FR *Tel.* 020 7248 6700 *Website* http://cayofoundation.org.uk

······································

■ The B. G. S. Cayzer Charitable Trust

CC NO 286063   **ESTABLISHED** 1982
WHERE FUNDING CAN BE GIVEN UK.
WHO CAN BENEFIT Registered charities.
WHAT IS FUNDED General charitable purposes; heritage, conservation and the environment; arts and culture; medical research, treatment and care; education and training; social welfare.
TYPE OF GRANT Project funding; core/revenue costs. One-off and multi-year grants.
RANGE OF GRANTS Up to £90,000.
SAMPLE GRANTS Independence from Drugs and Alcohol Scotland – River Garden (£80,000); Fourth Feathers Youth and Community Centre (£28,500); Royal Horticultural Society Rosemoor – Peter Buckley Learning Centre (£17,500); Charlie Waller Memorial Trust, Mission to Seafarers and MND Scotland (£5,000 each); Centre Stage Community Theatre (£3,000); Teapot Trust (£2,000).
FINANCES *Financial year end* 05/04/2022
Income £185,700
Grants to organisations £167,500
Assets £6,000,000
TRUSTEES Mary Buckley; Arabella Hunter; Roseanna Leslie; Sonia Barry.
OTHER INFORMATION In 2021/22 the trust made grants to 20 organisations, distributed across the following areas: medical research, treatment and care (£95,000); arts and culture (£32,500); heritage, conservation and the environment (£17,500); education and training (£13,500);

general charitable purposes (£8,000); relief of poverty (£1,000). Only organisations that received grants of over £2,000 were listed as beneficiaries in the trust's accounts.

HOW TO APPLY Unsolicited applications are not accepted and will not be responded to; the trustees identify the projects and organisations they wish to support.

CONTACT DETAILS The Trustees, The Cayzer Trust Company Ltd, 30 Buckingham Gate, London SW1E 6NN *Tel.* 020 7802 8439 *Email* admin@ cayzertrust.com

······································

■ Elizabeth Cayzer Charitable Trust

CC NO 1059265   **ESTABLISHED** 1996
WHERE FUNDING CAN BE GIVEN The British Isles.
WHO CAN BENEFIT Museums, galleries and other arts organisations and projects.
WHAT IS FUNDED Support to and promotion of the work of museums, galleries and the architectural heritage of the British Isles. This includes academic research and art history publications.
TYPE OF GRANT Project funding; capital costs; core costs.
RANGE OF GRANTS Up to £65,000.
SAMPLE GRANTS Wentworth Woodhouse Preservation Trust (£65,000); The National Gallery – One Gallery Accommodation Hub (£50,000); The Wallace Collection (£46,500); Sir John Soane's Museum (£20,000); The British Institute of Florence (£1,000).
FINANCES *Financial year end* 31/03/2022
Income £163,400
Grants to organisations £236,000
Assets £8,630,000
TRUSTEES Dominic Gibbs; The Hon. Elizabeth Gilmour; Sonia Barry; George Ponsonby.
OTHER INFORMATION In 2021/22 the trust made grants to eight organisations.
HOW TO APPLY Unsolicited applications are not accepted.
CONTACT DETAILS Elizabeth Gilmour, Trustee, The Cayzer Trust Company Ltd, Cayzer House, 30 Buckingham Gate, London SW1E 6NN *Tel.* 020 7802 8080 *Email* admin@cayzertrust. com

······································

■ The Cazenove Charitable Trust

CC NO 1086899   **ESTABLISHED** 1969
WHERE FUNDING CAN BE GIVEN UK.
WHO CAN BENEFIT Charitable organisations.
WHAT IS FUNDED General charitable purposes.
RANGE OF GRANTS £1,000 to £7,500.
SAMPLE GRANTS Cancer Research UK (£7,600); Duchenne and St Mary's Parents Association (£3,000 each); Walking With The Wounded (£2,000); Myeloma UK, PMGY Foundation and St Nicholas Church of England School PTA (£1,500 each); REACH, St Margaret's Lothbury and The Willow Foundation (£1,000 each).
FINANCES *Financial year end* 31/12/2021
Income £56,900
Grants to organisations £60,400
Assets £3,490,000
TRUSTEES Michael Power; Michael Wentworth-Stanley; David Mayhew; Lucinda Napier; James Barker; John Mayne; Nicholas Hall; Damian Robinson.
OTHER INFORMATION Only organisations that received grants of over £1,000 were listed as beneficiaries in the charity's accounts. Grants of

under £1,000 totalled £26,400. The trust primarily supports fundraising activities by employees and ex-employees of JPMorgan Cazenove and Cazenove Capital Management via a matched giving scheme.

HOW TO APPLY Apply in writing to the correspondent.

CONTACT DETAILS The Trustees, Cazenove Capital Management Ltd, 12 Moorgate, London EC2R 6DA *Tel.* 020 7658 1178

■ CEO Sleepout

CC NO 1154963   **ESTABLISHED** 2013

WHERE FUNDING CAN BE GIVEN UK.

WHO CAN BENEFIT Charitable organisations; CICs; registered charities.

WHAT IS FUNDED Homelessness.

TYPE OF GRANT Running costs (including salaries); project funding; equipment; capital developments.

RANGE OF GRANTS Mostly up to £5,000.

SAMPLE GRANTS Walking With The Wounded (£30,500); MCC Foundation (£19,600); Charity Begins at Home (£13,000); The Hope Foundation (£1,500); Greater Change (£500).

FINANCES *Financial year end 31/03/2022*
Income £440,300
Grants to organisations £255,300
Assets £148,800

TRUSTEES Andy Preston; Niklas Tunley; Abu Ali.

OTHER INFORMATION Grants are available for activities in areas where a CEO Sleepout event has been held.

HOW TO APPLY Applications can be made via the charity's website.

CONTACT DETAILS The Trustees, Boho Number One, Bridge Street West, Middlesbrough, North Yorkshire TS2 1AE *Tel.* 07922 478994 *Email* info@ceosleepoutuk.com *Website* www.ceosleepoutuk.com

■ The CH (1980) Charitable Trust

CC NO 279481   **ESTABLISHED** 1980

WHERE FUNDING CAN BE GIVEN UK and Israel.

WHO CAN BENEFIT Jewish organisations.

WHAT IS FUNDED Jewish causes.

WHAT IS NOT FUNDED Individuals.

RANGE OF GRANTS £500 to £37,000.

SAMPLE GRANTS Previous beneficiaries have included: Jerusalem Foundation (£38,000); Oxford Centre for Hebrew and Jewish Studies (£37,000); Jewish Care (£20,000); Anglo-Israel Association (£16,600); UJIA (£10,000); Israel Diaspora Trust and West London Synagogue Charitable Fund (£3,000 each); Anne Frank Trust and Israel Guide Dogs for the Blind (£500 each); Friends of the Hebrew University (£200).

FINANCES *Financial year end 05/10/2021*
Income £1,700
Grants to organisations £326,200

TRUSTEE SG Kleinwort Hambros Trust Company (UK) Ltd.

OTHER INFORMATION Full accounts were not available to view on the Charity Commission's website. We have therefore estimated the trust's grant total based on its total expenditure. The trust's 2021 annual report and accounts were the latest available information at the time of writing (May 2023).

HOW TO APPLY Unsolicited applications are not considered.

CONTACT DETAILS The Trustees, SG Kleinwort Hambros Trust Company (UK) Ltd, 1 Bank Street, London E14 4SG *Tel.* 020 3207 7232

■ The Chadwick Educational Foundation

CC NO 526373   **ESTABLISHED** 1963

WHERE FUNDING CAN BE GIVEN The borough of Bolton and former urban district of Turton.

WHO CAN BENEFIT Schools; individuals.

WHAT IS FUNDED Education.

TYPE OF GRANT Mainly capital grants.

SAMPLE GRANTS Egerton Primary School (£36,000); Sharples Primary School (£31,000); St Paul's Church of England Primary School (£8,000); Lever Edge Primary School (£5,000); Bolton Parish Church (£160).

FINANCES *Financial year end 31/12/2021*
Income £207,100
Grants to organisations £459,200
Assets £95,000

TRUSTEES Peter Liptrott; Esther Gelling; Ian Tomkin; The Revd Canon Dr Chris Bracegirdle; Diane Abbott; Kathryn Hodgkiss.

OTHER INFORMATION Grants were awarded to 33 organisations during the year.

HOW TO APPLY The 2021 annual report and accounts state: 'The Charity invites applications for grants through headteachers at Bolton schools and with the co-operation of Bolton's Local Education Authority. Preference is given to the underprivileged.'

CONTACT DETAILS The Trustees, c/o R. P. Smith and Co. Ltd, Hamill House, 112–116 Chorley New Road, Bolton BL1 4DH *Tel.* 01204 534421

■ The Amelia Chadwick Trust

CC NO 213795   **ESTABLISHED** 1960

WHERE FUNDING CAN BE GIVEN UK, with a preference for Merseyside.

WHO CAN BENEFIT Registered charities; hospices.

WHAT IS FUNDED General charitable purposes; education; health; the arts; social welfare; the environment.

WHAT IS NOT FUNDED Individuals.

RANGE OF GRANTS Mostly below £3,000.

SAMPLE GRANTS Unicef (£10,000); Alzheimer's Research UK (£4,000); Alzheimer's Society (£3,000); Fortune Centre and Young Persons Advisory Service (£1,000 each).

FINANCES *Financial year end 05/04/2022*
Income £175,600
Grants to organisations £149,300
Assets £5,370,000

TRUSTEES Matthew Dawson; Andrew Behrend; Alice Turner; Liverpool Charity and Voluntary Services.

OTHER INFORMATION Only beneficiaries of grants of £1,000 and above were listed in the accounts.

HOW TO APPLY Grants are only made to charities known to the trustees and unsolicited applications are not considered.

CONTACT DETAILS The Trustees, c/o Liverpool Charity and Voluntary Services, 151 Dale Street, Liverpool L2 2AH *Tel.* 0151 227 5177 *Email* info@lcvs.org.uk

■ Chalfords Ltd

CC NO 287322   **ESTABLISHED** 1983

WHERE FUNDING CAN BE GIVEN England and Wales.

WHO CAN BENEFIT Jewish Orthodox institutions.

WHAT IS FUNDED Advancement of the Orthodox Jewish religion; advancement of Jewish religious education; social welfare.

TYPE OF GRANT Capital projects; revenue funding.

RANGE OF GRANTS Up to £464,900 but mostly £86,000 or less.

SAMPLE GRANTS LPW Ltd (£464,900); Rise and Shine Ltd (£80,000); Care All Ltd (£58,000); Edupoor Ltd and Support The Charity Worker (£30,000 each); Community Concern London (£33,200).

FINANCES *Financial year end 31/12/2021*
Income £3,090,000
Grants to organisations £1,370,000
Assets £64,370,000

TRUSTEES Irwin Weiler; Riki Weiler; Mr A. Weiler; Mr M. Weiler.

OTHER INFORMATION Grants were distributed as follows: advancement of education (£1.41 million); advancement of the Jewish religion (£731,800); relief of poverty (£113,800); other general purposes (£62,900); grants to other grant-making charities (£40,200). Only organisations that received grants of over £20,000 were listed as beneficiaries in the charity's accounts. Grants of £20,000 or less totalled £187,100.

HOW TO APPLY Apply in writing to the correspondent. The trustees consider all requests which they receive and make donations based on the level of funds available.

CONTACT DETAILS The Trustees, New Burlington House, 1075 Finchley Road, London NW11 0PU *Tel.* 020 8455 6075

■ The Chalk Cliff Trust

CC NO 1139102   **ESTABLISHED** 2010
WHERE FUNDING CAN BE GIVEN East Sussex.
WHO CAN BENEFIT Registered charities. Organisations pending registration and pressure groups will also be considered.
WHAT IS FUNDED Youth schemes and activities; social welfare; older people; people with learning difficulties or disabilities; overseas aid, particularly projects concerned with education, malnutrition or health; the environment; arts and culture.
TYPE OF GRANT Project funding; capital grants; core administration costs.
RANGE OF GRANTS £3,000 to £5,000.
SAMPLE GRANTS De La Warr Pavilion Charitable Trust (£25,000); East Sussex (£12,000); Rwanda Aid (£10,000); Wonder Foundation (£9,500); Christ Church and St Peter and St James Hospice (£5,000 each).
FINANCES *Financial year end 31/03/2022*
Income £8,000,000
Grants to organisations £980,700
Assets £19,590,000
TRUSTEES Sarah Hunter; Robert Senior; Justine Senior; Rachel Senior; Hannah Senior.
OTHER INFORMATION In 2021/22, only organisations that received grants of £5,000 or over were listed as beneficiaries in the trust's accounts. Grants of under £5,000 totalled £879,300.
HOW TO APPLY Application forms can be downloaded from the trust's website and should be sent with supporting documents by email.
CONTACT DETAILS The Trustees, 18 Keere Street, Lewes, East Sussex BN7 1TY *Tel.* 01273 525354 *Email* apply@chalkclifftrust.org *Website* www.chalkclifftrust.org

---

■ Chapman Charitable Trust

CC NO 232791   **ESTABLISHED** 1963
WHERE FUNDING CAN BE GIVEN National charities operating across the UK; local charities operating in North Wales or the South East.
WHO CAN BENEFIT Registered charities; educational or research establishments with charitable

status. The trust prefers to support charities which address the root causes of problems and it welcomes applications for research projects.
WHAT IS FUNDED Physical and mental well-being; conservation of the natural environment; sustainability; improving access to the arts, especially for young people.
WHAT IS NOT FUNDED Non-UK-registered charities; individuals, including for sponsorship or education, research or travel; CICs; community amateur sports clubs; co-operative societies and not-for-profit organisations.
RANGE OF GRANTS Mostly £1,000 to £2,000.
SAMPLE GRANTS PAN UK (£10,000); Methodist Homes (£6,000); The Woodland Trust (£2,000); We Are GROW (£1,000).
FINANCES *Financial year end 05/04/2022*
Income £2,180,000
Grants to organisations £300,000
Assets £8,190,000
TRUSTEES Guy Chapman; Richard Chapman; Bryony Chapman; Thomas Williams; Gregory Chapman.
OTHER INFORMATION According to the trust's annual report and accounts, it awarded £300,000 in grants to charities. Grants are broken down as follows: well-being (£162,500); nature conservation (£72,000); arts (£65,500).
HOW TO APPLY Apply online via the trust's website. The trustees meet twice a year, in March and September.
CONTACT DETAILS Richard Chapman, Trustee, c/o RPG Crouch Chapman LLP, 5th Floor 14–16 Dowgate Hill, London EC4R 2SU *Tel.* 020 3697 7147 *Email* cct@ chapmancharitabletrust.org.uk *Website* www. chapmancharitabletrust.org.uk

---

■ The Charities Advisory Trust

CC NO 1040487   **ESTABLISHED** 1994
WHERE FUNDING CAN BE GIVEN UK and overseas.
WHO CAN BENEFIT Charitable organisations.
WHAT IS FUNDED General charitable purposes.
WHAT IS NOT FUNDED Individuals; large fundraising charities.
SAMPLE GRANTS A list of beneficiaries was not included in the annual report and accounts.
FINANCES *Financial year end 30/06/2022*
Income £714,500
Grants to organisations £355,000
Assets £2,800,000
TRUSTEES Leila Mohamed; David Russell; Rowena Dunn.
OTHER INFORMATION Grants were broken down as follows in 2021/22: Good Gifts Catalogue (£339,500); Direct Awards Programme (£15,500).
HOW TO APPLY Apply in writing to the correspondent.
CONTACT DETAILS The Trustees, Radius Works, Back Lane, Hampstead, London NW3 1HL *Tel.* 020 7794 9835 *Email* people@ charitiesadvisorytrust.org.uk *Website* www. charitiesadvisorytrust.org.uk

---

■ Charitworth Ltd

CC NO 286908   **ESTABLISHED** 1983
WHERE FUNDING CAN BE GIVEN Worldwide, mainly the UK and Israel.
WHO CAN BENEFIT Charitable organisations; educational institutions.
WHAT IS FUNDED The advancement of the Orthodox Jewish faith and education; the relief of poverty.
RANGE OF GRANTS Up to £190,000.
SAMPLE GRANTS Moreshet Hatorah Ltd and The ABC Trust (£190,000 each); Zichron Nachum

(Europe) Trust (£120,000); Vishnitz Girls School Ltd (£75,000); Rise and Shine (£50,000); Comet Charities Ltd (£27,000); Sassov Beis Hamedrash (£25,000); Amud Hatzdokoh Trust (£21,000); Kef Kids (£20,000).

FINANCES *Financial year end 31/03/2022*
Income £2,220,000
Grants to organisations £868,000
Assets £41,390,000

TRUSTEES Samuel Halpern; Sidney Halpern; David Halpern; Relly Halpern.

OTHER INFORMATION During the year, grants were awarded to 12 organisations totalling £868,000. Sundry donations totalled £176,200.

HOW TO APPLY Apply in writing to the correspondent.

CONTACT DETAILS The Trustees, New Burlington House, 1075 Finchley Road, London NW11 0PU *Tel.* 020 8731 0777

■ The Charman Family Charitable Trust

CC NO 1179004　　　**ESTABLISHED** 2018
WHERE FUNDING CAN BE GIVEN England and Wales.
WHO CAN BENEFIT Charitable organisations.
WHAT IS FUNDED General charitable purposes.
SAMPLE GRANTS A list of beneficiaries was not available.

FINANCES *Financial year end 27/04/2022*
Income £7,400
Grants to organisations £80,000

TRUSTEES Christine Brown; Berenice Morris.

OTHER INFORMATION The annual report and accounts for 2021/22 were not available to view on the Charity Commission's website due to the charity's low income. We have therefore estimated the grant total based on the charity's total expenditure.

HOW TO APPLY Apply in writing to the correspondent.

CONTACT DETAILS The Trustees, Browns Solicitors, 51 Tweedy Road, Bromley, BR1 3NH *Tel.* 020 8464 7432

■ Chartered Accountants' Livery Charity (CALC)

CC NO 327681　　　**ESTABLISHED** 1988
WHERE FUNDING CAN BE GIVEN Unrestricted but primarily within England and Wales.
WHO CAN BENEFIT Registered charities; schools; universities.
WHAT IS FUNDED General charitable purposes including social welfare and education.
WHAT IS NOT FUNDED Causes that promote a single religion; political causes; animal welfare; medical research. The charity is unlikely to support individuals, sports events or projects where the grant will not make a significant difference to the cause supported.
TYPE OF GRANT Core/revenue costs; project funding.
RANGE OF GRANTS Generally, £250 to £3,000, but up to £250,000 for Major Project Awards.
SAMPLE GRANTS Change Matters (£75,000); Life Cycle UK (£5,000); The Access Project (£3,000); Treloar Trust (£2,000); Make Them Smile (£1,600); Jubilee Sailing Trust (£1,000); ICAEW (£300); Christie Charity (£100).

FINANCES *Financial year end 30/09/2022*
Income £235,900
Grants to organisations £185,700
Assets £2,120,000

TRUSTEES William Robinson; Sally-Ann Orton; Neeraj Kapur; Stephen Maslin; Dr Hilary Lindsay; Richard Green; Susan Field; David Watson.

OTHER INFORMATION In total, 46 grants were awarded to organisations during the year.

HOW TO APPLY Completed forms (available on the website) and accompanying applications may be sent by email to the Clerk to the Trustees, Claire Ferrar, at charity@accountantslivery.org, or by post. The trustees meet quarterly, generally at the end of March, June, September and December, to consider applications.

CONTACT DETAILS Claire Ferrar, Clerk to the Trustees, 35 Ascot Way, Bicester, Oxfordshire OX26 1AG *Tel.* 01865 582350 *Email* charity@accountantslivery.org *Website* www.accountantslivery.org

---

■ The Charterhouse Charitable Trust

CC NO 210894　　　**ESTABLISHED** 1962
WHERE FUNDING CAN BE GIVEN London boroughs on the City of London perimeter.
WHO CAN BENEFIT Registered charities.
WHAT IS FUNDED Social welfare; health and well-being; education; general charitable purposes.
TYPE OF GRANT Mainly project funding or where it is thought a donation would make a difference.
RANGE OF GRANTS Up to £10,000.
SAMPLE GRANTS Disasters Emergency Committee – Ukraine Humanitarian Appeal (£35,000); Right to Play and Street Doctors (£10,000 each); Live Unlimited and The Trussell Trust (£5,000 each).

FINANCES *Financial year end 30/06/2022*
Income £51,500
Grants to organisations £95,000
Assets £2,100,000

TRUSTEES Thomas Patrick; Willem Toit; Mirja Weidner; Laalithya Vadlamani.

OTHER INFORMATION This trust is managed by people nominated by Charterhouse Development Capital Ltd.

HOW TO APPLY Apply in writing to the correspondent.

CONTACT DETAILS Irina Watson, Secretary, 6th Floor, Belgrave House, 76 Buckingham Palace Road, London SW1W 9TQ *Tel.* 020 7334 5322 *Email* irina.watson@charterhouse.co.uk *Website* www.charterhouse.co.uk

---

■ The Chartley Foundation

CC NO 1154637　　　**ESTABLISHED** 2013
WHERE FUNDING CAN BE GIVEN Staffordshire.
WHO CAN BENEFIT Charitable organisations; sports teams.
WHAT IS FUNDED General charitable purposes; the arts; amateur sport; the environment.
TYPE OF GRANT Unrestricted funding.
RANGE OF GRANTS Up to £230,000.
SAMPLE GRANTS Stone Hockey Club (£222,300); The Outward Bound Trust (£215,900); The Duke of Edinburgh's Award (£100,000); Game and Wildlife Conservation Trust (£30,000); Staffordshire Wildlife Trust (£10,000); Staffordshire Clubs for Young People (£5,000).

FINANCES *Financial year end 31/12/2021*
Income £155,900
Grants to organisations £242,800
Assets £11,450,000

TRUSTEES David Johnson; Lord Stafford; Richard Poole.

OTHER INFORMATION Grants were awarded to ten organisations during the year.

HOW TO APPLY Apply in writing to the correspondent.

CONTACT DETAILS David Johnson, Trustee, The Bradshaws, Codsall, Wolverhampton, Staffordshire WV8 2HU *Tel.* 01902 754855 *Email* tcf@sorbus.com

■ The Lorna and Yuti Chernajovsky Biomedical Research Foundation

CC NO 1184405 **ESTABLISHED** 2019
WHERE FUNDING CAN BE GIVEN UK.
WHO CAN BENEFIT Research institutions; universities.
WHAT IS FUNDED Biomedical research into autoimmunity, inflammation, infectious diseases and ageing.
TYPE OF GRANT Research grants.
RANGE OF GRANTS Up to £150,000.
SAMPLE GRANTS University of Glasgow (£106,700); Sheffield University (£98,100); Surrey University (£83,500).
FINANCES *Financial year end* 05/04/2022
Income £545,300
Grants to organisations £725,600
Assets £1,940,000
TRUSTEES Dr Lorna Chernajovsky; Prof. Paul-Peter Tak; Prof. Yuti Chernajovsky.
HOW TO APPLY See the foundation's website for information on its latest grant calls.
CONTACT DETAILS The Trustees, PO Box 1198, Whitstable, Kent, CT5 9DW *Email* use the contact form on the website *Website* www.chernajovskyfoundation.org.uk

■ The Cheruby Trust

CC NO 327069 **ESTABLISHED** 1986
WHERE FUNDING CAN BE GIVEN UK and overseas.
WHO CAN BENEFIT Registered charities.
WHAT IS FUNDED General charitable purposes, including social welfare and education.
RANGE OF GRANTS Mostly under £5,000.
SAMPLE GRANTS Street Child (£7,000); Concern Worldwide (£5,000); Mobile Education Partnerships (£4,000); Arts 4 Dementia (£3,800); FareShare (£3,000); National Autistic Society (£2,000); The Stuart Low Trust (£1,000); Rainforest Concern (£500).
FINANCES *Financial year end* 05/04/2022
Income £75,000
Grants to organisations £79,800
Assets £1,700
TRUSTEES Christopher Cook; Alison Corob; Tricia Corob; Laura Corob; Sheila Wechsler.
OTHER INFORMATION Grants were awarded to 40 organisations during the year.
HOW TO APPLY Apply in writing to the correspondent.
CONTACT DETAILS The Trustees, 62 Grosvenor Street, London W1K 3JF *Tel.* 020 7499 4301

■ Cheshire Community Foundation Ltd

CC NO 1143711 **ESTABLISHED** 2011
WHERE FUNDING CAN BE GIVEN Cheshire.
WHO CAN BENEFIT Registered charities; community and voluntary organisations; CICs; social enterprises.
WHAT IS FUNDED General charitable purposes including: mental health and well-being; poverty and disadvantage; education, skills and employment; stronger communities.
WHAT IS NOT FUNDED Check the foundation's website for programme-specific exclusions.
TYPE OF GRANT Programme dependent.
RANGE OF GRANTS Programme dependent.
SAMPLE GRANTS Warrington Youth Club Ltd (£37,600); Dementia UK (£30,000); Cheshire East Citizens Advice (£19,700); Family Ties CIC (£15,000); Community Recycle Cycles CIC (£13,000); St Wilfrid's Church – Grappenhall (£10,000); Sandwell Homeless and Resettlement Project, St Oswald's Hospice and Survive (£5,000 each); Cheshire Young Carers (£2,500); Bridge Wellness Gardens (£1,000); The Boaty Theatre Company (£760).
FINANCES *Financial year end* 31/12/2021
Income £1,990,000
Grants to organisations £1,850,000
Assets £10,070,000
TRUSTEES Howard Platt; David Wootton; Nicola Owen; Jake Ankers; Sean Humphreys; Andrew Butters; Terry Inns; Diane Brown; Sarah Callander-Beckett; Jeannie France-Hayhurst.
OTHER INFORMATION This is one of the 47 UK community foundations, which distribute funding for a wide range of purposes. As with all community foundations, there are a number of donor-advised funds managed on behalf of individuals, families and charitable trusts. Grant schemes tend to change frequently – consult the foundation's website for details of current programmes and up-to-date deadlines. The foundation processed 561 applications in 2021 and awarded 338 grants.
HOW TO APPLY Potential applicants are advised to visit the community foundation's website or contact its grants team to find the most suitable funding stream.
CONTACT DETAILS Angela Richardson, Grants Director, c/o The Challenge Academy Trust, Bridgewater High School, Broomfields Road, Warrington, Cheshire WA4 3AE *Tel.* 01606 330607 *Email* grants@cheshirecommunityfoundation.org.uk *Website* www.cheshirecommunityfoundation.org.uk

■ Cheshire Freemasons' Charity

CC NO 219177 **ESTABLISHED** 1963
WHERE FUNDING CAN BE GIVEN Cheshire; Stockport; Tameside; Trafford; Wirral.
WHO CAN BENEFIT Individuals; organisations benefitting Masons and their families; registered charities.
WHAT IS FUNDED General charitable purposes; social welfare; children and young people.
SAMPLE GRANTS A list of beneficiaries was not included in the annual report and accounts.
FINANCES *Financial year end* 30/04/2022
Income £469,200
Grants to organisations £571,600
Assets £5,240,000
TRUSTEES Michael Ireland; Dennis Talbot; Jonathan Shasha; Paul Crudge; Michael Leese.
OTHER INFORMATION The charity's 2021/22 annual report and accounts state that grants totalling £571,600 were made to 'individuals, organisations and other charities'; however, a breakdown was not available.
HOW TO APPLY Contact the correspondent for further information.
CONTACT DETAILS The Trustees, Ashcroft House, 36 Clay Lane, Timperley, Altrincham, Cheshire WA15 7AB *Tel.* 0161 980 6090 *Email* enquiries@cheshiremasons.co.uk *Website* www.cheshiremasons.co.uk

■ The Chetwode Foundation

cc no 265950   **established** 1973
where funding can be given UK, with a preference for Nottinghamshire.
who can benefit Registered charities.
what is funded General charitable purposes; disadvantaged children and young people (including education, employability, sport and art); training for youth workers; prisoners and ex-offenders.
what is not funded Individuals; national charities without a local focus; organisations outside the UK.
type of grant Project funding; capital costs; core costs; recurrent grants may be considered.
range of grants Up to £10,000 but mostly under £5,000.
sample grants Framework (£10,000); Reach Learning (£8,000); Kidscape (£6,900); The Access Project (£5,000); Pintsize Theatre Company (£3,900); Lifespring Church – Warsop (£3,500); St Ann's Allotments (£1,700); Tall Ships Youth Trust (£1,500).
finances *Financial year end 05/04/2022*
Income £81,200
Grants to organisations £70,800
Assets £3,120,000
trustees Russell Price; Lesley Samworth; Fiona Johnson.
other information Grants were awarded to 16 organisations during 2021/22.
how to apply An application form is available to download from the website or by contacting the trustees via email or post. Applications can be submitted at any time by email or post. The trustees aim to acknowledge all relevant applications within four weeks.
contact details Administrator, Farm Office, Stragglethorpe Grainstore, Nottingham Road, Cropwell Bishop, Nottingham NG12 2JU *Tel.* 0115 989 3722 *Email* info@thechetwodefoundation.co.uk *Website* www.thechetwodefoundation.co.uk

■ The Childhood Trust

cc no 1154032   **established** 2013
where funding can be given Greater London.
who can benefit Registered charities; hospices; educational institutions; community groups.
what is funded Children and young people causes, including: social welfare; well-being and health; raising awareness about poverty; education; arts and culture; sports and recreation.
what is not funded Statutory funding; capital costs; religious groups; accommodation for homeless children or families; trips abroad; repayment of loans or payment of debts; retrospective expenditure; payment for areas that are the responsibility of statutory authorities; awareness raising work, such as research projects; individuals, including hardship grants and educational bursaries. Full exclusions are available in the trust's grant-making policy, which is available to download from the website.
type of grant Project funding; matched funding; pro bono work; capacity building.
range of grants Up to £50,000 but mostly under £20,000.
sample grants Bookmark Reading Charity, Jamie's Farm and Step by Step London (£50,000 each); Power2 (£30,000); Alexandra Rose Charity, Greenhouse Sports Ltd and UK Music Masters Ltd (£25,000 each); Restore the Music UK, West London Action for Children and West London Zone (£15,000 each); Place2Be, Spark Inside and ThinkForward – UK (£12,500 each); Children Ahead Ltd, Lyric Hammersmith and Up 'n Away (£10,000 each); Abram Wilson Foundation for Creative Arts, Solace Women's Aid and Unicorn Theatre (£5,000 each); Embrace Child Victims of Crime (£3,000); Home-Start Wandsworth, St Vincent's Family Project and Strength and Learning Through Horses (£1,000 each); City Gateway (£90).
finances *Financial year end 30/06/2022*
Income £3,100,000
Grants to organisations £1,520,000
Assets £1,390,000
trustees Grant Gordon; Neha Mahendru; Jonathon Kelly; Andrei Popescu; David Rhodes; Nicola Horlick; Rebecca Jacques; Lesley O'Mara; Galiema Cloete; Dr Mathias Hink.
other information During this period, the trust's volunteering and pro bono services totalled £292,300 in value. The trust also raised £6.83 million through its campaigns, the Christmas Challenge and Champions for Children.
how to apply Visit the trust's website to apply.
contact details Laurence Guinness, Chief Executive and Secretary, 18 Buckingham Palace Road, London SW1W 0QP *Tel.* 07507 880109 *Email* info@childhoodtrust.org *Website* www.childhoodtrust.org.uk

■ Children with Cancer UK

cc no 298405   **established** 2003
where funding can be given UK.
who can benefit UK-based medical and scientific research centres; universities; hospitals; charities.
what is funded Research into childhood cancer; welfare projects for young cancer patients and their families.
type of grant Research; project costs; capacity building; studentships.
range of grants Up to £350,000.
sample grants Birmingham Women's and Children's Hospital Charity (£1.07 million); Newcastle University – INSTINCT-MB (£712,000); Beads of Courage – 2021 (£225,000); British Neuro-Oncology Society Annual Meeting 2021 (£1,200); International Family Nursing Association Meeting 2021 (£180).
finances *Financial year end 31/12/2021*
Income £14,840,000
Grants to organisations £2,240,000
Assets £14,460,000
trustees Caroline Randerson; David Gibbs; Alex Leitch; Phil Hall; Dr Bruce Morland; Georgie Wolfinden.
other information During 2021, grants were broken down as follows: welfare (£1.42 million); research into treatment (£813,300); raising awareness (£11,900).
how to apply For information on current research funding opportunities and how to apply, refer to the charity's website. There is no open application process for welfare grants – the trustees determine which organisations are to be supported. Check the charity's website for the latest information.
contact details The Trustees, 21–27 Lamb's Conduit Street, London WC1N 3NL *Tel.* 020 7404 0808 *Email* research@childrenwithcancer.org.uk; info@childrenwithcancer.org.uk *Website* www.childrenwithcancer.org.uk

■ Childs Charitable Trust

CC NO 1153327   **ESTABLISHED** 1962

WHERE FUNDING CAN BE GIVEN UK and overseas.

WHO CAN BENEFIT Christian UK-registered charities.

WHAT IS FUNDED Evangelical work; humanitarian projects; Christian gospel projects.

WHAT IS NOT FUNDED Building works; repairs; refurbishment or renovation projects; fixtures and fittings; food banks; street pastors/wardens; gap year projects; churches; uniformed youth organisations; new organisations with a turnover of less than £100,000.

TYPE OF GRANT Project funding; research.

SAMPLE GRANTS Off the Fence (£165,000); Bible Reading Fellowship (£45,000); Emmanuel Press (£35,000); Mission Aviation Fellowship (MAF) UK (£20,000); International Needs, Lifeworks and Wycliffe Bible Translators (£15,000 each); The Soldiers' and Airmen's Scripture Readers Association (£10,000).

FINANCES *Financial year end 31/12/2021*
Income £378,900
Grants to organisations £652,500
Assets £10,470,000

TRUSTEES Christopher Large; Steve Puttock; Melanie Churchyard; Robert Peake; Janice Kalyan.

OTHER INFORMATION Only beneficiaries of grants of over £10,000 were listed in the accounts. We were unable to determine the exact amount for grants awarded in the UK. During the year, the trust received 287 applications and made grants to 63 organisations.

HOW TO APPLY If you have been funded by the trust in the past five years, contact the correspondent to request an application form. If you meet the qualifying criteria but have not been awarded a grant from the trust in the last five years, complete the online enquiry form or call to discuss your eligibility. You will be sent an application form if you are successful. Application deadlines can be found on the trust's website.

CONTACT DETAILS Melanie Churchyard, Chief Executive Officer, 40 Chapel Road, Pawlett, Bridgwater, Somerset TA6 4SH *Tel.* 01323 417944 *Email* info@childstrust.org *Website* http://childscharitabletrust.org

■ The Childwick Trust

CC NO 1150413   **ESTABLISHED** 1985

WHERE FUNDING CAN BE GIVEN Southern and south-eastern UK. A full list of the counties supported can be found on the trust's website. The trust also operates in South Africa.

WHO CAN BENEFIT Registered charities.

WHAT IS FUNDED In the UK: health, people with disabilities and older people; welfare in connection with the (horse) bloodstock industry; Jewish causes. In South Africa: education; childhood development.

WHAT IS NOT FUNDED A full list of exclusions can be found on the trust's helpful website.

TYPE OF GRANT Mainly one-off, project and capital funding for research and medical equipment.

RANGE OF GRANTS Typically £5,000 to £20,000.

SAMPLE GRANTS Racing Welfare (£150,000); National Horseracing Museum (£90,000); British Racing School (£75,000); Hospice of St Francis (£30,000); Langdon Foundation (£25,000); Keech Hospice Care (£20,000); Child Bereavement UK (£15,000).

FINANCES *Financial year end 31/03/2022*
Income £1,900,000
Grants to organisations £2,880,000
Assets £88,340,000

TRUSTEES Peter Anwyl-Harris; John Wood; Dr Alan Stranders; Clare Maurice; Mark Farmar; Michael Fiddes.

OTHER INFORMATION In 2021/22, grants totalling £3.27 million were awarded to charities in the UK and South Africa. Grants were broken down as follows: health – UK (£2.12 million); education – South Africa (£804,700); racing – UK (£325,000); Jewish charities (£308,100); pensioners welfare (£34,400). A full list of beneficiaries of grants of above £15,000 is available on the website.

HOW TO APPLY Applications can be made through the trust's website. Applications windows are normally open in October and April each year and close at midnight on the 31st of the month.

CONTACT DETAILS Kirsty Jones, Trust Administrator, 9 Childwick Green, Childwicksbury, St Albans, Hertfordshire AL3 6JJ *Tel.* 01727 844666 *Email* kirsty@childwicktrust.org *Website* www.childwicktrust.org

■ Chippenham Borough Lands Charity

CC NO 270062   **ESTABLISHED** 1990

WHERE FUNDING CAN BE GIVEN Chippenham parish.

WHO CAN BENEFIT Individuals; community/charitable organisations.

WHAT IS FUNDED General charitable purposes; community projects, including arts projects; social welfare; education and training; work with young people.

WHAT IS NOT FUNDED Individual sportspeople; local authorities; retrospective applications; first degrees; the advancement of religion; animal welfare; political activities; salaries (except the proportion related to the delivery of a project); anything that can be obtained from statutory sources.

TYPE OF GRANT Project funding; capital costs; core costs.

RANGE OF GRANTS Typically under £10,000.

SAMPLE GRANTS Doorway Wiltshire (£15,000); Refashion My Town (£14,400); Fringe February (£13,900); Children's Hospice South West (£10,000); Wiltshire College Chippenham (£6,000); Wilts and Berks Canal Trust (£4,800); Chippenham Town Council (£3,000); Wiltshire Outdoor Learning Team (£1,000).

FINANCES *Financial year end 31/03/2022*
Income £504,800
Grants to organisations £115,800
Grants to individuals £43,300
Assets £17,320,000

TRUSTEES David Sandberg; Donald Steele; Jim Cook; Philip Wren; Susan Lenihan; Geraldine McKibbin; Richard Squires; Annette Foster; Linda Candy; Fiona Young; Sue Linacre; Jenny Budgell.

OTHER INFORMATION Grants to organisations were broken down as follows: education and work with young people (£58,200); social welfare (£39,600); other charitable purposes (£61,200). The charity also rents out two community centres in the centre of Chippenham.

HOW TO APPLY Apply via a form available from the correspondent. Visit the charity's website for further guidelines. The trustees meet monthly.

CONTACT DETAILS The Trustees, Jubilee Building, Bank House, Bath Road, Chippenham, Wiltshire SN15 2SA *Tel.* 01249 658180 *Email* admin@cblc.org.uk *Website* www.cblc.org.uk

■ CHK Foundation

CC NO 1050900   **ESTABLISHED** 1995
WHERE FUNDING CAN BE GIVEN UK.
WHO CAN BENEFIT Registered charities.
WHAT IS FUNDED At risk young people aged 11 to 24. Priority is given to organisations supporting young people affected by addiction, the criminal justice system or the care system.
TYPE OF GRANT Core costs; unrestricted funding.
RANGE OF GRANTS Up to £250,000.
SAMPLE GRANTS The Door (£247,400); The Avenues Youth Project (£200,000); The Baca Charity (£154,000); Esmée Fairbairn Foundation (£100,000); World Land Trust (£75,000); Into University (£50,000); The Friendship Café (£10,000); Choose Love (£5,000).
FINANCES *Financial year end 31/01/2022*
Income £3,130,000
Grants to organisations £3,720,000
Assets £150,840,000
TRUSTEES Joanna Prest; Katharine Loyd; Lucy Morris; Rupert Prest; Dr Edward Peake; Diana Acland; Pandora Morris; Charles Kirwan-Taylor; Camilla Peake; Elisalex Jewell.
OTHER INFORMATION CHK Foundation was formerly CHK Charities Ltd.
HOW TO APPLY The foundation's website states the following: 'Applications for funding are not invited. CHK Foundation undertakes its own research to identify the charities it wishes to support.'
CONTACT DETAILS The Trustees, PO Box 277, Royston, 8 St James's Square, London SG8 1EX *Tel.* 07592 806521 *Email* admin@chkcharities.co.uk *Website* www.chkcharities.co.uk

■ The Christabella Charitable Trust

CC NO 800610   **ESTABLISHED** 1988
WHERE FUNDING CAN BE GIVEN Essex and East London.
WHO CAN BENEFIT Registered charities; local organisations; individuals.
WHAT IS FUNDED General charitable purposes; Christian causes.
WHAT IS NOT FUNDED General running costs or building refurbishment; UK-wide or international charities.
TYPE OF GRANT Seedcorn funding of projects involving volunteers.
RANGE OF GRANTS Up to £10,000.
SAMPLE GRANTS LDF Charitable Trust (£10,000); The Children's Society (£9,200); The Basildon Community Resource Centre (£5,500); Sightsavers (£1,000).
FINANCES *Financial year end 31/12/2021*
Income £244,000
Grants to organisations £51,500
Grants to individuals £27,600
Assets £7,910,000
TRUSTEES Robert Folwell; Richard Hilburn; Ian Elliott; Christine Turner; Mark Wentworth; Marc Humphreys.
OTHER INFORMATION This trust's primary objective is to maintain the charity's property at Barnards Farm in West Horndon as the house of the National Malus Collection. Only beneficiaries that received grants of over £1,000 were listed in the accounts.
HOW TO APPLY A limited number of grants are awarded each year. Contact the correspondent by post if you believe your project would be of relevance or interest to the trust.
CONTACT DETAILS Robert Folwell, Trustee and Trust Administrator, Warth Business Centre, Warth Road, Bury BL9 9TB *Email* bobfolwell@hotmail.com *Website* https://barnardsfarm.eu/christabella-charitable-trust

■ Christadelphian Samaritan Fund

CC NO 1004457   **ESTABLISHED** 1991
WHERE FUNDING CAN BE GIVEN UK and overseas.
WHO CAN BENEFIT Registered charities, with preference given to small charities.
WHAT IS FUNDED Social welfare; humanitarian aid/emergency relief; medical research.
RANGE OF GRANTS Mostly up to £400.
SAMPLE GRANTS Save the Children (£17,000); Oxfam (£5,000); ShelterBox Trust and The Trussell Trust (£3,000 each); ActionAid (£2,000); Yemen Crisis Appeal (£1,300); WaterAid (£200).
FINANCES *Financial year end 31/12/2021*
Income £120,700
Grants to organisations £96,000
Assets £121,700
TRUSTEES John Buckler; David Ensell; Roger Miles; Pauline Bromage; Elisabeth Briley; Ruth Deedman; Mark Halstead; Mark Leinster.
HOW TO APPLY Apply in writing by post and include details of what the charity does and what the appeal is for. The trustees meet quarterly. The charity is unable to respond to all requests.
CONTACT DETAILS Mark Halstead, Secretary, Westhaven House, Arleston Way, Shirley, Solihull, West Midlands B90 4LH *Tel.* 0121 713 7100 *Email* use the contact form on the website. *Website* https://christadelphiansf.com

■ The André Christian Trust

CC NO 248466   **ESTABLISHED** 1950
WHERE FUNDING CAN BE GIVEN UK and overseas.
WHO CAN BENEFIT Registered charities; religious bodies/institutions.
WHAT IS FUNDED Christian missionary work; promotion of Christianity; the relief of sickness and poverty; the advancement of education.
TYPE OF GRANT Seed funding/start-up funding.
RANGE OF GRANTS £1,000 to £11,000.
SAMPLE GRANTS Tiverton Vineyard Church (£11,500); Choices Pregnancy Centre (£11,200); Care for the Family (£9,000); Palm Tree Associates (£7,000); Life Words (£4,000).
FINANCES *Financial year end 31/12/2021*
Income £60,500
Grants to organisations £86,800
Assets £2,270,000
TRUSTEES Stephen Daykin; Andrew Mowll; Peter Appleby.
OTHER INFORMATION Grants were awarded to 15 organisations during the year.
HOW TO APPLY Apply in writing to the correspondent.
CONTACT DETAILS Andrew Mowll, Trustee, 24 Hellings Gardens, Broadclyst, Exeter, Devon EX5 3DX *Tel.* 01392 759836

■ Chrysalis Trust

CC NO 1133525   **ESTABLISHED** 2010
WHERE FUNDING CAN BE GIVEN Local projects in the North East; national organisations providing benefit across the UK; overseas.
WHO CAN BENEFIT Registered charities.
WHAT IS FUNDED The trust's current priorities are: the relief of poverty and disability; provision of access to shelter, education, health care and water.
WHAT IS NOT FUNDED Research – academic or medical; holidays or outings; arts or

entertainment activities; animal welfare; local appeals outside the North East; general appeals.

TYPE OF GRANT Capital costs; core/revenue costs.

RANGE OF GRANTS £1,000 to £10,000.

SAMPLE GRANTS A list of beneficiaries was not included in the annual report and accounts. Previous beneficiaries have included: 700 Club and Walkabout Foundation (£10,000 each); Re-Cycle (£8,300); Huntington's Disease Association (£6,500); Children and Families Across Borders, Gregg's Foundation, Impact, Wamba Community Trust and YMCA North Tyneside (£5,000 each); Freedom from Torture (£4,000).

FINANCES *Financial year end 31/03/2022*
Income £45,700
Grants to organisations £55,500
Assets £2,150,000

TRUSTEES Mark Evans; Sarah Evans; Andrew Playle; Thomas Evans; Hannah Evans.

HOW TO APPLY Application forms are can be downloaded from the trust's website. Applications are considered twice a year, usually in June and January. The deadline for submissions are 15 May and 15 December, respectively.

CONTACT DETAILS Sarah Evans, Trustee, Piper Close House, Aydon Road, Corbridge, Northumberland NE45 5PW *Email* info@chrysalis-trust.co.uk *Website* www.chrysalis-trust.co.uk

■ Church Burgesses Educational Foundation

CC NO 529357   **ESTABLISHED** 1963

WHERE FUNDING CAN BE GIVEN Sheffield.

WHO CAN BENEFIT Charitable organisations; churches; individuals.

WHAT IS FUNDED Education for young people under the age of 25.

WHAT IS NOT FUNDED Higher education courses.

TYPE OF GRANT Project funding; core costs; capital costs.

SAMPLE GRANTS A list of beneficiaries was not included in the annual report and accounts.

FINANCES *Financial year end 31/12/2021*
Income £223,500
Grants to organisations £68,600
Grants to individuals £25,800
Assets £445,400

TRUSTEES The Revd Stephen Hunter; Mr D. Stanley; The Revd W. H. Thomas; David Booker; David Quinney; Dr Linda Kirk; Stephen Eccleston.

OTHER INFORMATION Grants were broken down as follows: church school grants (£36,000); families, young people and children (£19,000); special individual grants (£18,700); special organisational one-off grants (£7,600); music in the city (£6,000).

HOW TO APPLY Application forms are available to download, together with criteria and guidelines, from the foundation's website. Forms should be returned to the correspondent by post.

CONTACT DETAILS Ian Potter, The Law Clerk, Derwent House, 150 Arundel Gate, Sheffield S1 2FN *Tel.* 0114 267 5588 *Email* ian.potter@wrigleys. co.uk *Website* www.sheffieldchurchburgesses. org.uk/educational.htm

■ Church Burgesses Trust

CC NO 221284   **ESTABLISHED** 1554

WHERE FUNDING CAN BE GIVEN Sheffield.

WHO CAN BENEFIT Registered charities; religious bodies/institutions.

WHAT IS FUNDED Social welfare; health; recreational facilities; Anglican churches.

TYPE OF GRANT Capital costs; seed funding/start-up funding.

RANGE OF GRANTS £500 to £10,000.

SAMPLE GRANTS Paces High Green (£5,000); Age UK – Sheffield and The Sick Children's Trust (£3,000 each); Crystal Peaks Church (£1,000); The Salvation Army (£400).

FINANCES *Financial year end 31/12/2021*
Income £1,970,000
Grants to organisations £306,800
Assets £42,330,000

TRUSTEES Dr Julie Banham; Mr D. F. Booker; The Revd S. A. P. Hunter; Nicholas Hutton; Mr D. Stanley; Ian Walker; David Quinney; Stephen Eccleston; Elizabeth Brownhill; Dr Susan Gentle.

OTHER INFORMATION The trust is connected to the Church Burgesses Educational Foundation.

HOW TO APPLY Application forms can be downloaded from the relevant page on the trust's website.

CONTACT DETAILS Ian Potter, The Law Clerk, c/o Wrigleys Solicitors LLP, Derwent House, 150 Arundel Gate, Sheffield S1 2FN *Tel.* 0114 267 5588 *Email* ian.potter@wrigleys.co.uk *Website* www.sheffieldchurchburgesses.org.uk

■ Church of Ireland Priorities Fund

ESTABLISHED 1980

WHERE FUNDING CAN BE GIVEN The island of Ireland.

WHO CAN BENEFIT Church of Ireland churches.

WHAT IS FUNDED Training (lay and ordained); Christian education; outreach initiatives; innovative ministry projects in rural areas.

WHAT IS NOT FUNDED Projects which are still at the planning stage; recurrent grant aid; funding for salaries; financing debts; funding for cathedrals and churches; routine renovations and repairs.

TYPE OF GRANT Project funding; capital costs. Applications for seed funding are encouraged.

RANGE OF GRANTS Up to £40,000.

SAMPLE GRANTS House of Bishops (£34,700); St Saviour's Parish Church – Craigavon (£14,500); Lisburn Cathedral (£11,600); Mother's Union (£7,100); Solas Project (£6,900); Crosslink (£1,400); Church of Ireland Clergy Pensions Fund (£390).

FINANCES
Grants to organisations £395,600

TRUSTEES The committee members are: Roy Totten; Joan Bruton; Hazel Corrigan; Bishop George Davison; The Revd Peter Ferguson; Glenn Moore; The Revd Lynda Peilow.

OTHER INFORMATION All financial information was converted from EUR using the exchange rate at the time of writing (May 2023). Financial information was not available as the charity is based in the Republic of Ireland. The grant total has been taken from the 2023 Allocations document, located on the grant-maker's website.

HOW TO APPLY Application forms are available from the grant-maker's website along with criteria and guidelines. Applications must be made by 31 October each year.

CONTACT DETAILS The Administrator, Church of Ireland House, Church Avenue, Rathmines,

Dublin DO6 CF67 *Tel.* +353 (0)1 4125607 *Email* priorities@ireland.anglican.org or use the contact form on the website *Website* www. priorities.ireland.anglican.org

■ Church Urban Fund

cc no 297483   **established** 1988
where funding can be given Birmingham; The Black Country; East London; East Midlands; Greater Manchester; Lancashire; Luton; Peterborough; West London; West Yorkshire.
who can benefit Local faith-based organisations; voluntary groups; charities.
what is funded Community cohesion and development; social welfare.
what is not funded See the website for specific exclusions.
type of grant Seed funding; project funding.
range of grants Typically £250 to £5,000.
sample grants A list of beneficiaries was not included in the annual report and accounts. Previous beneficiaries have included: Centre for Theology and Community – London (£128,000); King's Centre – West London (£98,000); Faithful Neighbours – Bradford (£76,000); Transforming Communities Together – Black Country (£58,000); St Philip's Centre – Leicester (£55,000); Thrive Together Birmingham (£21,000).
finances *Financial year end 31/12/2021*
Income £5,130,000
Grants to organisations £841,000
Assets £2,030,000
trustees Alison Grieve; Andrew Barnett; Alec Spencer; The Revd Canon Dr Anderson Jeremiah; Robert Hallam; Christina Rees; Susan Chalkley.
other information The charity's Near Neighbours grants programme funds local groups which are working to bring together neighbours to develop relationships and to improve their communities. Grants were broken down as follows: community (£500,000) and homelessness/housing (£23,000).
how to apply Details of the application procedure for each programme can be found on the charity's website. Contact details of local Near Neighbours co-ordinators can be found on the Near Neighbours website.
contact details The Near Neighbours Team, The Foundry, 17 Oval Way, London SE11 5RR *Tel.* 020 3752 5655 *Email* hello@cuf.org.uk *Website* www.cuf.org.uk

■ The Churchill Foundation

cc no 1164320   **established** 2015
where funding can be given UK.
who can benefit Local charities; community groups; national charities.
what is funded Social welfare; health; older people; children and young people.
range of grants Typically less than £2,000.
sample grants Macmillan Cancer Support (£54,600); Muscular Dystrophy (£5,100); Brain Tumour Research (£2,000); Alzheimer's Society, The Brain Charity and Keech Hospice Care (£1,000 each).
finances *Financial year end 31/12/2021*
Income £120,000
Grants to organisations £80,400
Grants to individuals £2,400
Assets £212,700
trustees Suzanne Revell; Clinton McCarthy; John Hatchard; Spencer McCarthy; Lindsay Matthews.

other information The foundation has two programmes: the Annual Partnership Programme, which supports organisations chosen by the trustees, and the Small Grants programme, which makes grants of between £50 and £2,000 for applicants referred by Churchill Retirement colleagues, owners or business partners. Grants were awarded to 46 organisations during the year.
how to apply Applications should be made in writing and be returned by email. The Annual Partnership Programme is usually open for applications between August and September, with applicants being informed if they have been shortlisted by 1 November. The Small Grants application process is open all year round but applicants must be referred by Churchill Retirement colleagues, owners or business partners.
contact details Nicola Wallace-Walton, Foundation Manager, Churchill Retirement Living Ltd, Churchill House, Parkside, Ringwood, Hampshire BH24 3SG *Tel.* 01425 462100 *Email* enquiries@churchillfoundation.co.uk *Website* www.churchillfoundation.co.uk

■ The CIBC World Markets Children's Foundation

cc no 1105094   **established** 2004
where funding can be given UK and Europe.
who can benefit UK or European-registered charities.
what is funded Children and young people.
type of grant Two-year partnerships; unrestricted funding.
range of grants Up to £52,000.
sample grants XLP and STEM4 (£52,000 each); Go Beyond and Honeypot (£26,000 each).
finances *Financial year end 31/03/2022*
Income £202,700
Grants to organisations £161,000
Assets £35,600
trustees Andrew Ryde; Samantha Orozco; Sarah Heavey; Sonia Beardsmore; Thomas Broad.
other information This is the UK corporate charity of the Canadian Imperial Bank of Commerce (CIBC). During the year, grants were awarded to four UK-registered 'Charities of the Year'.
how to apply Apply in writing to the correspondent. The foundation's website states: 'In Europe, the Miracle Day Campaign begins early in the year when we start accepting requests from charities wishing to be considered for donations from the upcoming year's fundraising efforts.'
contact details Andrew Ryde, Chairperson, c/o Canadian Imperial Bank of Commerce, 150 Cheapside, London EC2V 6ET *Email* ukchildrensmiracle@cibc.co.uk *Website* www.cibc.com/ca/miracleday/ international/childrens-foundation.html

■ The City Bridge Trust (Bridge House Estates)

cc no 1035628   **established** 1995
where funding can be given Greater London.
who can benefit Registered charities; CICs; CIOs; charitable companies; exempt or excepted charities; registered industrial and provident societies or co-operatives.
what is funded Children and young people; criminal justice; people with disabilities; the environment; mental health; older people; social welfare and food poverty; migrants, refugees

and people seeking asylum; tackling abuse, exploitation and hatred.

TYPE OF GRANT Capital and core/revenue costs. Revenue grants can be for up to five years.

SAMPLE GRANTS A list of beneficiaries was not included in the annual report and accounts. Previous beneficiaries have included: Federation of London Youth Clubs (£390,000 over three years); Kingston Voluntary Action (£303,600 over two years); British Refugee Council (£220,800 over three years); Afghanistan and Central Asian Association (£121,000 over three years); Magpie Dance (£100,000 over three years); Fulham Good Neighbour Service (£28,200); Cripplegate Foundation (£25,000); The Spitz Charitable Trust (£9,400); Migrants Rights Network (£5,050); St Barnabas PCC (£980).

FINANCES *Financial year end 31/03/2022*
Income £34,100,000
Grants to organisations £33,300,000
Assets £1,720,000,000

TRUSTEE The Mayor and Commonalty and Citizens of the City of London.

OTHER INFORMATION The City Bridge Trust is the grant-making arm of the Bridge House Estates charity.

HOW TO APPLY Applications have to be made through the online portal on the trust's website. To access the online form, you must first complete the eligibility quiz.

CONTACT DETAILS The Grants Team, City of London Corporation, PO Box 270, Guildhall, London EC2P 2EJ *Tel.* 020 7332 3710
Email citybridgetrust@cityoflondon.gov.uk
Website www.citybridgetrust.org.uk

■ CLA Charitable Trust

CC NO 280264   **ESTABLISHED** 1980
WHERE FUNDING CAN BE GIVEN England and Wales.
WHO CAN BENEFIT Registered charities; CICs.
WHAT IS FUNDED The advancement of physical and mental health (particularly of disadvantaged young people) by providing recreational/educational opportunities in the countryside.
WHAT IS NOT FUNDED Individuals; retrospective costs; non-educational holidays.
TYPE OF GRANT One-off grants; project costs; running costs; capital costs.
RANGE OF GRANTS Mostly under £5,000.
SAMPLE GRANTS The Country Trust (£6,000); We are Grow (£5,000); Wild Things Ecological Education Collective (£4,300); Bryntail Cottage and Youth on the Move (£3,000 each); Stonebridge City Farm (£2,500); Chaos Group Cornwall (£2,200); The Holly Lodge Centre (£2,000).
FINANCES *Financial year end 30/11/2021*
Income £225,600
Grants to organisations £144,500
Assets £484,300
TRUSTEES Bridget Biddell; Andrew Grant; Robin Clarke; Jane Lane; Giles Bowring; Roger Douglas; Caroline Wilson.
OTHER INFORMATION The 2020/21 accounts were the latest available to view at the time of writing (June 2023). Only organisations that received grants of over £2,000 were listed as beneficiaries in the trust's accounts.
HOW TO APPLY Application forms can be downloaded from the trust's website. The trustees meet three times a year to consider applications.
CONTACT DETAILS The Trustees, 16 Belgrave Square, London SW1X 8PQ *Tel.* 020 7235 0511 *Email* charitabletrust@cla.org.uk *Website* www.cla.org.uk

■ The Roger and Sarah Bancroft Clark Charitable Trust

CC NO 211513   **ESTABLISHED** 1960
WHERE FUNDING CAN BE GIVEN UK, with a preference for Somerset.
WHO CAN BENEFIT Charitable organisations; universities.
WHAT IS FUNDED General charitable purposes with a preference for Quaker causes, heritage; education.
WHAT IS NOT FUNDED Individuals.
RANGE OF GRANTS Mostly under £10,000.
SAMPLE GRANTS The Alfred Gillett Trust (£4.25 million); Quaker Peace and Social Witness (£4,500); Architectural Heritage Society of Scotland (£4,000); Quaker Service (£3,000); The Society for the Protection of Ancient Buildings and Quaker Council for European Affairs (£2,000 each); Medical Aid for Palestinians (£1,000).
FINANCES *Financial year end 31/12/2021*
Income £80,100
Grants to organisations £4,290,000
Assets £2,770,000
TRUSTEES Alice Clark; Caroline Gould; Martin Lovell; Robert Robertson; Priscilla Goldby.
OTHER INFORMATION Grants were made to 25 organisations during 2021. Grants were distributed within the following categories: restricted grants (£4.25 million to one organisation); other grants (£13,000); religion (£12,000); education (£6,000); Somerset (£2,000).
HOW TO APPLY Apply in writing to the correspondent. The trustees meet regularly to consider applications.
CONTACT DETAILS The Trustees, c/o C. and J. Clark Ltd, Box 1, 40 High Street, Street, Somerset BA16 0EQ *Tel.* 01458 842121 *Email* mel.park@clarks.com

■ The Clarkson Foundation

CC NO 1191357   **ESTABLISHED** 2020
WHERE FUNDING CAN BE GIVEN Worldwide.
WHO CAN BENEFIT Registered charities.
WHAT IS FUNDED General charitable purposes including: people affected by COVID-19; social welfare; health; homelessness; community development; maritime charities; disaster relief.
SAMPLE GRANTS Samaritans; Street Child; The Valley Hospital Charity; The Wave Project; The Whitechapel Mission; Willow Foundation.
FINANCES *Financial year end 31/12/2021*
Income £381,800
Grants to organisations £86,500
Assets £294,600
TRUSTEES Jeffrey Woyda; Richard Haines; Dharani Sridharan; Alexander Gray; Lily-Rose Bagshaw; Robert Knight; Katharine Thompson.
OTHER INFORMATION The foundation is the corporate charity of Clarkson plc, a provider of shipping services headquartered in London. Grants were made to 16 organisations during the year.
HOW TO APPLY The foundation's website states: 'If you think the foundation can help with charitable causes you are involved with, or you have an idea of ways the foundation can help – get in touch.'
CONTACT DETAILS The Trustees, Commodity Quay, St Katharine Docks, London E1W 1BF *Email* foundation@clarksons.com *Website* www.theclarksonfoundation.com

■ Clinks

CC NO 1074546   **ESTABLISHED** 1998
WHERE FUNDING CAN BE GIVEN UK.
WHO CAN BENEFIT Voluntary sector organisations.
WHAT IS FUNDED Criminal justice, including work with individuals in the criminal justice system and their families, discrimination and equality.
SAMPLE GRANTS Paul Hamlyn Foundation Inspiring Futures (£89,600); Criminal Justice Board for Wales (£50,400); Department for Health and Social Care – Voluntary, Community and Social Enterprise Health and Wellbeing Alliance (£33,800).
FINANCES *Financial year end 31/03/2022*
Income £1,630,000
Grants to organisations £173,800
Assets £462,000
TRUSTEES Jessica Southgate; Roma Hooper; Simon Alsop; Simon Ruding; Richard Booty; Amina Ditta; Donna Everett; Maisie Hulbert; Salim Baba; Kelly Loftus.
OTHER INFORMATION During 2021/22, grants were awarded to three organisations.
HOW TO APPLY At the time of writing (April 2023), the charity's website stated the following: 'The funding portal is no longer a service provided to Clinks members. Clinks is reviewing what we hear from voluntary organisations via our sector support survey and will look to provide member-specific routes to funding opportunities in the future. If you have any concerns or queries contact membership@clinks.org'.
CONTACT DETAILS The Trustees, 82A James Carter Road, Mildenhall, Suffolk IP28 7DE *Tel.* 020 4502 6774 *Email* info@clinks.org *Website* www.clinks.org

■ The Clore Duffield Foundation

CC NO 1084412   **ESTABLISHED** 1964
WHERE FUNDING CAN BE GIVEN UK.
WHO CAN BENEFIT Registered charities.
WHAT IS FUNDED The cultural sector, in particular museums, galleries, and performing arts spaces. Support is also given to the Jewish community and to health organisations.
WHAT IS NOT FUNDED Projects outside the UK; individuals; general appeals or circulars.
TYPE OF GRANT Programme dependent.
RANGE OF GRANTS Programme dependent.
SAMPLE GRANTS Royal Opera House Covent Garden Foundation (£1.5 million); The Old Vic and Nightingale Hammerson (£100,000 each); Oxford Institute for Population Ageing (£93,400); Community Security Trust (£60,000); Anna Freud Centre for Children and Families (£25,000); Young Musicians Symphony Orchestra (£10,000); Elias Ashmole Trust (£2,000); Blue Marine Foundation (£500).
FINANCES *Financial year end 31/12/2021*
Income £27,800
Grants to organisations £3,020,000
Assets £47,930,000
TRUSTEES Dame Vivien Duffield; David Harrel; James Harding; Richard Oldfield; Jeremy Sandelson; Melanie Clore.
OTHER INFORMATION Grants were awarded to 32 organisations in 2021. The Clore Leadership Programme received £330,000 from the foundation.
HOW TO APPLY Unsolicited applications are not accepted unless the foundation advertises a specific call for funding.

CONTACT DETAILS The Trustees, Studio 3, Chelsea Manor Studios, Flood Street, London SW3 5SR *Tel.* 020 7351 6061 *Email* info@cloreduffield. org.uk *Website* www.cloreduffield.org.uk

■ The Clothworkers' Foundation

CC NO 274100   **ESTABLISHED** 1977
WHERE FUNDING CAN BE GIVEN UK and financially developing countries.
WHO CAN BENEFIT Registered charities; social enterprises; CICs; special schools.
WHAT IS FUNDED People with disabilities; disadvantaged young people and minority communities; older people; domestic and sexual violence; homelessness; visual impairment; alcohol and substance misuse; prisoners and ex-offenders.
WHAT IS NOT FUNDED Refer to the foundation's website for a full list exclusions.
TYPE OF GRANT Capital costs.
RANGE OF GRANTS The grant size depends on a number of factors, including the project size. See the foundation's website for further information.
SAMPLE GRANTS All details of the foundation's past grantees can be found on its website.
FINANCES *Financial year end 31/12/2021*
Income £11,640,000
Grants to organisations £6,990,000
Assets £265,290,000
TRUSTEES Michael Jarvis; Dr Lucy Rawson; Andrew Blessley; Hanif Virji; Susanna O'Leary; Philip Portal; Denis Clough; Thomas Stoddart-Scott; Charles Hutchins; Neel Patani; Emma Clark; Chloe Holness; Ola Opoosun; Dhruv Patel.
HOW TO APPLY Applications can be made through the foundation's website, where guidelines and an eligibility quiz can also be found.
CONTACT DETAILS The Trustees, Clothworkers' Hall, Dunster Court, Mincing Lane, London EC3R 7AH *Tel.* 020 7623 7041 *Email* foundation@ clothworkers.co.uk *Website* www. clothworkersfoundation.org.uk

■ Cloudesley

CC NO 205959   **ESTABLISHED** 1517
WHERE FUNDING CAN BE GIVEN Islington.
WHO CAN BENEFIT Voluntary and charitable organisations; individuals; churches.
WHAT IS FUNDED Health; social welfare; people with disabilities; Church of England churches in the Islington Deanery.
TYPE OF GRANT Projects costs; strategic; small one-off grants; large multi-year grants; core funding; capital costs.
RANGE OF GRANTS Programme dependent.
SAMPLE GRANTS Disability Action in Islington (£90,000); Healthwatch Islington (£50,000); Islington People's Rights (£30,000); Centre 404 (£12,000); One True Voice (£2,000).
FINANCES *Financial year end 30/06/2022*
Income £1,620,000
Grants to organisations £1,350,000
Grants to individuals £191,000
Assets £57,050,000
TRUSTEE Richard Cloudesley Trustee Ltd.
OTHER INFORMATION Grants to churches totalled £777,000 and health and welfare grants to organisations totalled £572,000. Health and welfare grants to individuals totalled £191,000.
HOW TO APPLY Applications can be completed online during open funding periods.
CONTACT DETAILS Grants Committee, Office 1.1, Resource for London, 356 Holloway Road,

London, N7 6PA *Tel.* 020 7697 4094
Email info@cloudesley.org.uk *Website* www.
cloudesley.org.uk

■ The Clover Trust

CC NO 213578   **ESTABLISHED** 1961
WHERE FUNDING CAN BE GIVEN UK, with a slight
preference for West Dorset, and occasionally
overseas.
WHO CAN BENEFIT Registered charities.
WHAT IS FUNDED Older people; young people;
Catholicism; health; people with disabilities.
TYPE OF GRANT Up to three years.
RANGE OF GRANTS £1,500 to £40,000.
SAMPLE GRANTS Friends of Children in Romania
(£40,000); Farms of City Children (£16,000);
999 Club (£8,000); Kate's Nursing Home
(£7,000); The JOLT Trust (£5,000); Brainwave
(£3,000); The MPS Society (£1,500).
FINANCES *Financial year end* 31/12/2021
Income £196,400
Grants to organisations £190,000
Assets £6,120,000
TRUSTEES Sara Woodhouse; Charlotte Morrison;
Ben Woodhouse.
OTHER INFORMATION Grants were awarded to 34
organisations during the year.
HOW TO APPLY The trust's Charity Commission
record states: 'The Trustees prefer to make
regular donations to a designated selection of
recipients and intend to continue with this policy
for the foreseeable future. The trustees are
currently not accepting any further applications
for grant funding from other individuals or
organisations.'
CONTACT DETAILS The Trustees, Box Tree House,
22 Martingale Road, Burbage, Marlborough,
Wiltshire SN8 3TY

■ The Robert Clutterbuck Charitable Trust

CC NO 1010559   **ESTABLISHED** 1992
WHERE FUNDING CAN BE GIVEN UK, with a preference
for Cheshire and Hertfordshire.
WHO CAN BENEFIT Registered charities; schools;
places of worship.
WHAT IS FUNDED Current and former Service
personnel; sport and recreational facilities for
young people in Cheshire and Hertfordshire; the
welfare, protection and preservation of domestic
animal life in Cheshire and Hertfordshire;
natural history and wildlife.
WHAT IS NOT FUNDED Individuals; charities with an
annual turnover exceeding £1 million (unless
they are primarily concerned with the welfare of
ex-Service personnel or have previously received
a grant from the trust).
TYPE OF GRANT Capital costs; core and revenue
costs.
RANGE OF GRANTS £1,000 to £3,000.
SAMPLE GRANTS East Cheshire Hospice and
Northchurch Sports Association (£3,000 each);
Clean Rivers Trust and Hounds for Heroes
(£2,000 each); Autism Inclusive and Botanical
Society of Great Britain and Ireland (£1,000
each).
FINANCES *Financial year end* 05/04/2022
Income £48,200
Grants to organisations £63,500
Assets £2,460,000
TRUSTEES Ian Pearson; Lucy Pitman; Tessa
Lydekker.

OTHER INFORMATION Grants were made to 43
organisations during 2021/22.
HOW TO APPLY The trust's website states: 'There are
no application forms and charities wishing to
apply should write to the Secretary giving details
of what they propose to do with any grant made
and of their current financial position.' The
trustees usually meet twice a year in March and
September to consider grants. The deadlines for
the application rounds are 30 June and
31 December each year.
CONTACT DETAILS George Wolfe, Secretary,
28 Brookfields, Calver, Hope Valley, Derbyshire
S32 3XB *Tel.* 01433 631308 *Email* secretary@
clutterbucktrust.org.uk *Website* www.
clutterbucktrust.org.uk

■ Clydpride Ltd

CC NO 295393   **ESTABLISHED** 1982
WHERE FUNDING CAN BE GIVEN Worldwide.
WHO CAN BENEFIT Individuals and institutions
benefitting Jewish people and people
disadvantaged by poverty.
WHAT IS FUNDED Advancement of the Orthodox
Jewish faith; relief of poverty; general charitable
purposes.
RANGE OF GRANTS Generally up to £35,000.
SAMPLE GRANTS North London Welfare and
Educational Foundation (£35,000); Friends of
Mir and Gateshead Talmudical College
(£25,000 each); Beis Soroh Schneirer of
Golders Green Ltd (£15,000); Torah Vodaas Ltd
(£10,000); Side by Side (Children) Ltd (£7,500).
FINANCES *Financial year end* 24/12/2021
Income £2,970,000
Grants to organisations £549,800
Grants to individuals £330
Assets £46,030,000
TRUSTEES Mr A. Faust; Jonathan Weinstein; Jacob
Halpern; Leon Faust.
OTHER INFORMATION The 2020/21 accounts were
the latest available at the time of writing (June
2023). Grants were broken down as follows: the
advancement of religion through education
(£342,800); relief of poverty (£152,300);
benefit of the Jewish community (£55,100).
Only organisations that received grants of over
£25,000 were listed as beneficiaries in the
charity's accounts. Grants of under £25,000
totalled £337,600.
HOW TO APPLY Apply in writing to the correspondent.
The charity considers all grant requests from
organisations that fall within the criteria of the
charity's objects.
CONTACT DETAILS T. Faust, Secretary, c/o Rayner
Essex LLP, Entrance D, Tavistock House South,
Tavistock Square, London WC1H 9LG *Tel.* 020
8731 7744

■ CMZ Ltd

CC NO 1087870   **ESTABLISHED** 2001
WHERE FUNDING CAN BE GIVEN London; Israel; USA.
WHO CAN BENEFIT Charitable organisations.
WHAT IS FUNDED Orthodox Jewish education and
social welfare.
RANGE OF GRANTS Generally from £70,000 to
£191,500.
SAMPLE GRANTS One Heart Lev Echod (£191,500);
Lehachzikom (£134,000); Edupoor Ltd
(£117,300); Friends of Beis Chinuch Lebonos
Trust (£107,500); Tchabe Kollel Ltd
(£105,900); Chasdei Sholom (£85,000); Amud
Hatzdokoh Trust (£78,500); Care All Ltd
(£74,700).

FINANCES *Financial year end* 31/03/2022
Income £3,840,000
Grants to organisations £3,660,000
Grants to individuals £147,400
Assets £333,700

TRUSTEES Mr P. Schneebalg; Samuel Steinmetz; Chaim Gottesfeld.

OTHER INFORMATION The charity offered 15 grants to organisations during the year.

HOW TO APPLY The charity awards grants and donations to registered charitable organisations and individuals, provided that a letter of approbation from a qualified Rabbi or Vaad Hatzdokoh is produced.

CONTACT DETAILS B. Goldberg, Secretary, 206 High Road, London N15 4NP *Tel.* 020 8801 6038

....

■ The Francis Coales Charitable Foundation

CC NO 270718   **ESTABLISHED** 1975

WHERE FUNDING CAN BE GIVEN UK, with a preference for Bedfordshire, Buckinghamshire, Hertfordshire and Northamptonshire (including the Diocese of Peterborough).

WHO CAN BENEFIT Old buildings open to the public, usually churches, monuments and monumental brasses.

WHAT IS FUNDED The structural repair of ecclesiastical buildings (built before 1875) which are open to the public (preference is given to churches in the counties of Buckinghamshire, Bedfordshire, Hertfordshire and Northamptonshire); the conservation of monuments and monumental brasses (no geographical restriction); the publication of architectural and architectural books and papers; the purchase of documents and items for record offices and museums; archaeological research and related causes.

WHAT IS NOT FUNDED Domestic items such as heating, lighting, wiring, installation of facilities, etc.

TYPE OF GRANT Largely one-off; capital costs (fabric repairs only).

RANGE OF GRANTS Mostly £500 to £5,000.

SAMPLE GRANTS A list of beneficiaries was not included in the annual report and accounts. Previous beneficiaries have included: Northamptonshire Victoria County History (£6,000); Smisby Derbyshire (£4,500); Hertfordshire Building Trust (£3,000); Chiltern Open Air Museum – Buckinghamshire (£1,000); London Record Society (£750); Monumental Brass Society (£500).

FINANCES *Financial year end* 31/12/2021
Income £134,400
Grants to organisations £99,700
Assets £5,590,000

TRUSTEES Matthew Saunders; Martin Stuchfield; Pamela Ward; The Revd Brian Wilcox; John Barker.

OTHER INFORMATION In 2021, a total of 26 applications were considered and 24 received support.

HOW TO APPLY Application forms can be downloaded from the foundation's website. Once completed, these should be submitted to the foundation by post. The trustees normally meet three times a year to consider grants. The foundation's website offers the following guidance: 'In respect of a building or contents, include a copy of the relevant portion only of the architect's (or conservator's) specification showing the actual work proposed. Photographs illustrating this are a necessity, and only in exceptional circumstances will an application be considered without supporting photographs here. It is of help if six copies of any supporting documentation are submitted in order that each trustee may have a copy in advance of the meeting.'

CONTACT DETAILS David Edworthy, Administrator, The Old Rectory, Rectory Way, Lympsham, Weston-super-Mare, Somerset BS24 0EW *Tel.* 01934 750817 *Email* administrator@franciscoales.uk *Website* http://franciscoales.co.uk

....

■ F. B. Coales No. 4 (Family) Trust

CC NO 1179856   **ESTABLISHED** 1964

WHERE FUNDING CAN BE GIVEN England and Wales.

WHO CAN BENEFIT Charitable organisations.

WHAT IS FUNDED Physical and mental health; children and young people.

SAMPLE GRANTS A list of beneficiaries was not included in the annual report and accounts.

FINANCES *Financial year end* 05/04/2022
Income £350,000
Grants to organisations £149,900
Assets £1,000,000

TRUSTEES John Burton; Christopher Winn; Sarah Hashmi.

HOW TO APPLY Apply in writing to the correspondent.

CONTACT DETAILS The Trustees, c/o Winn and Coales (Denso) Ltd, Denso House, 33–35 Chapel Road, London SE27 0TR

....

■ The Coalfields Regeneration Trust

CC NO 1074930   **ESTABLISHED** 1999

WHERE FUNDING CAN BE GIVEN Coalfield and former coalfield communities in England, Scotland and Wales.

WHO CAN BENEFIT Most voluntary and community organisations and groups working to regenerate coalfield communities are eligible to apply for funding as long as they are not for personal profit. These include registered charities, companies limited by guarantee, community benefit societies, CICs, CIOs and community amateur sports clubs.

WHAT IS FUNDED Health and well-being; skills; employment.

WHAT IS NOT FUNDED Check the trust's website for programme-specific exclusions.

RANGE OF GRANTS Up to £200,000.

SAMPLE GRANTS A list of beneficiaries was not included in the annual report and accounts. Previous beneficiaries have included: Aylesham Neighbourhood Project (£210,000); Haswell and District Mencap Society (£98,000); Derbyside Rural Community Council – Wheels to Work (£89,000); The Cornforth Partnership (£75,000); Nottinghamshire Independent Domestic Abuse Link Workers (£66,000); Stoke-on-Trent and District Gingerbread Centre Ltd (£37,000); St John's Church (£10,000); Mansfield and Dukeries Irish Association (£5,000); City of Durham Air Cadets (£3,800); Thornycroft Art Club (£520).

FINANCES *Financial year end* 31/03/2022
Income £2,180,000
Grants to organisations £1,440,000
Assets £41,260,000

TRUSTEES Dawn Davies; Peter McNestry; Wayne Thomas; Nicolas Wilson; Michael Clapham; Robert Young; Nicky Stubbs; Trudie McGuinness; Linda Rutter; Judith Kirton-Darling; Keith Cunliffe.

OTHER INFORMATION The trust provides advice, support and financial assistance to community and voluntary organisations which are working to tackle problems at a grassroots level within coalfield communities. Grants were made to 392 organisations during the year.

HOW TO APPLY Details on how to make an application to each programme can be found on the trust's website, where guidance notes are also available. Applicants can contact their regional teams to find out more information or to discuss an application.

CONTACT DETAILS The Trustees, 1 Waterside Park, Valley Way, Wombwell, Barnsley, South Yorkshire S73 0BB *Tel.* 01226 270800 *Email* info@coalfields-regen.org.uk *Website* www.coalfields-regen.org.uk

■ The John Coates Charitable Trust

CC NO 262057   ESTABLISHED 1969
WHERE FUNDING CAN BE GIVEN Cambridge, Devon, London, Norfolk, Surrey and West Sussex.
WHO CAN BENEFIT Registered charities.
WHAT IS FUNDED Education for people with disabilities; outdoors education; prisoners' well-being; the arts; medicine/health care, including supporting service-users and funding research; heritage, conservation and the environment; societal and community cohesion.
WHAT IS NOT FUNDED Individuals; regional offices of national organisations; projects delivered overseas.
TYPE OF GRANT Capital costs; core/revenue costs; project funding.
RANGE OF GRANTS Typically between £5,000 and £10,000.
SAMPLE GRANTS Disasters Emergency Committee – Afghanistan Crisis Appeal (£15,000); Magic Breakfast (£10,000); Katherine Low Settlement Ltd (£5,000); Kangaroos Mid Sussex (£3,000); Lighthouse Relief (£2,500); Golden Oldies (£2,000).
FINANCES *Financial year end* 05/04/2022 *Income* £367,600 *Grants to organisations* £485,000 *Assets* £16,290,000
TRUSTEES Claire Cartledge; Catharine Kesley; Rebecca Lawes; Susan Down; Antonia Youngman; Elspeth McGregor.
OTHER INFORMATION In 2021/22, grants were awarded to 90 organisations.
HOW TO APPLY Applications can be made through the trust's website. The trustees meet twice a year usually in January and July to consider applications. See the website for application deadlines.
CONTACT DETAILS The Trustees, c/o The Trust Partnership Ltd, 6 Trull Farm Buildings, Trull, Tetbury, Gloucestershire GL8 8SQ *Tel.* 01285 719595 *Email* johncoates@thetrustpartnership.com *Website* https://johncoatescharitabletrust.org.uk

■ Denise Coates Foundation

CC NO 1149110   ESTABLISHED 2012
WHERE FUNDING CAN BE GIVEN UK and overseas.
WHO CAN BENEFIT Charities and community groups.
WHAT IS FUNDED Education and training; health and welfare; arts and culture; medical research and development; community development; disaster recovery.

TYPE OF GRANT Project funding; core costs; capital costs; research; collections and acquisitions.
SAMPLE GRANTS University Hospitals of North Midlands Charity (£8.36 million); Douglas Macmillan Hospice (£2.19 million); The Stonyhurst Foundation (£1.6 million); The Royal Marsden Cancer Charity (£1.35 million); New Vic Theatre (£1.11 million); Midlands Air Ambulance Charity (£1.09 million); Thrive at Five (£1 million).
FINANCES *Financial year end* 27/03/2022 *Income* £105,120,000 *Grants to organisations* £17,650,000 *Assets* £667,960,000
TRUSTEES John Coates; Peter Coates; Denise Coates; James White; Simon Galletley; Oliver Adams.
OTHER INFORMATION In 2021/22, grants were distributed as follows: medical research and development (£10 million); health and welfare (£3.19 million); education and training (£2.01 million); community development (£1.45 million); arts and culture (£993,000).
HOW TO APPLY Apply in writing to the correspondent.
CONTACT DETAILS The Trustees, bet365 House, Media Way, Stoke-on-Trent, Staffordshire ST1 5SZ *Tel.* 0845 600 0365

■ The Cobalt Trust

CC NO 1096342   ESTABLISHED 2002
WHERE FUNDING CAN BE GIVEN UK and overseas.
WHO CAN BENEFIT Registered charities known to the trustees.
WHAT IS FUNDED General charitable purposes.
SAMPLE GRANTS A list of beneficiaries was not included in the annual report and accounts.
FINANCES *Financial year end* 31/03/2022 *Income* £332,600 *Grants to individuals* £442,000 *Assets* £415,200
TRUSTEES Stephen Dawson; Brigitte Dawson.
OTHER INFORMATION In 2021/22 only grants to individuals were recorded in the accounts.
HOW TO APPLY The trustees do not respond to unsolicited applications.
CONTACT DETAILS Stephen Dawson, Trustee, Hillside Farm, Church Lane, Freshford, Bath BA2 7WD *Tel.* 07720 345880

■ The Cobtree Charity Trust Ltd

CC NO 208455   ESTABLISHED 1951
WHERE FUNDING CAN BE GIVEN Maidstone and district.
WHO CAN BENEFIT Registered charities; churches; hospices.
WHAT IS FUNDED General charitable purposes by other charities in the Maidstone and district area.
RANGE OF GRANTS Typically between £1,000 and £5,000.
SAMPLE GRANTS A list of beneficiaries was not included in the annual report and accounts. Previous beneficiaries have included: Young Farmers (£15,900); Young Lives (£12,000); Teenage Cancer Trust (£6,000); Heart of Kent Hospice and Maidstone Winter Shelter (£5,000 each); Rainbow Trust Children's Charity (£2,000). Connect Church Maidstone (£800).
FINANCES *Financial year end* 05/04/2022 *Income* £201,800 *Grants to organisations* £176,300 *Assets* £8,630,000
TRUSTEES John Fletcher; Lawrence Martin; David Wigg; Stephen Beck; Stefan Jordan; Mike Sharp; Michael Startup; Sandra Knatchbull.

HOW TO APPLY An application form is available to download from the charity's website. The website states that 'trustees hold quarterly meetings in January, April, July, and October, and review applications at each meeting. Applications should reach the Secretary to the Trustees by the first of the month prior to the next quarterly meeting.'

CONTACT DETAILS The Trustees, 3 Thurnham Oast, Aldington Lane, Thurnham, Maidstone, Kent ME14 3LL *Tel.* 01622 736865
Email cobtreecharitytrust@outlook.com
Website www.cobtreecharitytrust.org

■ The Vivienne and Samuel Cohen Charitable Trust

CC NO 255496   **ESTABLISHED** 1965
WHERE FUNDING CAN BE GIVEN UK; overseas, with a focus on Israel.
WHO CAN BENEFIT Charitable organisations; hospices; hospitals; places of worship; educational institutions.
WHAT IS FUNDED Jewish causes; health; education; religion; social welfare; culture and recreation; general charitable purposes.
WHAT IS NOT FUNDED Individuals.
RANGE OF GRANTS Mostly between £1,000 and £3,000, with the occasional larger grant.
SAMPLE GRANTS Yeshaya Adler Memorial Fund (£16,500); Yeshivat Ohr Torah Stone (£10,000); Israel Free Loan Association, Mesila UK (£5,000 each); Mosaica Center for Conflict Resolution, Shaare Zadek UK and University College London – Development Office (£2,000 each); Disabled Living Foundation, Simon Marks Jewish Primary School and UK Toremet (£1,000 each).
FINANCES *Financial year end* 05/04/2022
Income £156,300
Grants to organisations £191,100
Assets £4,630,000
TRUSTEES Michael Ben-Gershon; Gershon Cohen; Gideon Lauffer; Jonathan Lauffer; Elizabeth Hacohen.
OTHER INFORMATION Grants were broken down as follows: education (£59,800 to 20 organisations); care and welfare (£54,400 to 34 organisations); religion (£40,000 to 10 organisations); medical and health (£26,000 to 22 organisations); culture and recreation (£10,900 to 9 organisations). Only organisations that received grants of over £1,000 were listed as beneficiaries in the trust's 2021/22. Grants of under £1,000 totalled £9,000 and were awarded to 29 organisations.
HOW TO APPLY Apply in writing to the correspondent.
CONTACT DETAILS The Trustees, c/o Hentons (London) Ltd, Ground Floor, 31 Kentish Town Road, London NW1 8NL *Tel.* 020 7637 3210
Email csco@hentons.com

■ The John S. Cohen Foundation

CC NO 241598   **ESTABLISHED** 1965
WHERE FUNDING CAN BE GIVEN UK and Wales.
WHO CAN BENEFIT Registered charities; colleges and universities; museums.
WHAT IS FUNDED Arts; conservation and the environment; education and academia; social welfare and medical research.
RANGE OF GRANTS Mostly £1,000 to £15,000, with one larger payment of £65,000.

SAMPLE GRANTS New Writing North (£65,000); Birmingham Repertory Theatre and Royal National Theatre (£15,000 each); Ragged School Museum and Royal Academy of Arts (£10,000 each); Academy of Ancient Music (£9,000); Welsh National Opera (£8,000); Royal Albert Hall (£7,500); Royal Academy of Dramatic Art (RADA) and Royal Academy of Music (£5,000); Camden Art Centre (£3,000); Dartington Hall Trust (£2,000); Orion Orchestra (£1,500).
FINANCES *Financial year end* 31/03/2022
Income £641,600
Grants to organisations £565,000
Assets £11,610,000
TRUSTEES Olivia Qizilbash; Dr Imogen Cohen; Jillian Barker.
OTHER INFORMATION Grants were broken down as follows: conservation and the environment (£349,000); the arts (£212,000); education and academia (£35,000).
HOW TO APPLY Apply in writing to the correspondent.
CONTACT DETAILS Diana Helme, Administrator, PO Box 21277, London W9 2YH *Tel.* 020 7286 6921

■ The R. and S. Cohen Foundation

CC NO 1078225   **ESTABLISHED** 1999
WHERE FUNDING CAN BE GIVEN Worldwide, particularly the UK and Israel.
WHO CAN BENEFIT Jewish charitable organisations; registered charities.
WHAT IS FUNDED Education; social welfare; the arts, particularly the performing arts.
WHAT IS NOT FUNDED Individuals.
RANGE OF GRANTS £1,000 to £495,800.
SAMPLE GRANTS The Portland Trust (£495,800); Ben Gurion University Foundation (£45,400); Community Security Trust (£20,000); Southbank Centre (£1,000).
FINANCES *Financial year end* 31/12/2021
Income £36,800
Grants to organisations £644,900
Assets £1,220,000
TRUSTEES Lady Sharon Harel-Cohen; Sir Ronald Cohen; Tamara Harel-Cohen; Jonathan Harel-Cohen; David Marks.
HOW TO APPLY Unsolicited applications are not accepted.
CONTACT DETAILS The Trustees, 3–4 Stanley Crescent, London, W11 2NB *Tel.* 020 7182 7800

■ Colchester Catalyst Charity

CC NO 228352   **ESTABLISHED** 1963
WHERE FUNDING CAN BE GIVEN Colchester (the CO postcode).
WHO CAN BENEFIT Registered charities; CICs; social enterprises; universities; hospitals; hospices; individuals.
WHAT IS FUNDED Health care; respite breaks for carers.
WHAT IS NOT FUNDED Retrospective expenditure.
TYPE OF GRANT Project funding; capital costs.
SAMPLE GRANTS HIVE (£30,000); Mind (£25,000); Open Road (£10,000); Sailship (£9,000); Bright Lives (£3,500); Edensor (£2,600).
FINANCES *Financial year end* 31/12/2021
Income £360,800
Grants to organisations £225,500
Grants to individuals £209,100
Assets £12,940,000
TRUSTEES Peter Fitt; Christine Hayward; Dr Max Hickman; Mark Pertwee; Dr Naomi Busfield;

Think carefully about every application. Is it justified?

321

Elizabeth Thrower; Keith Songhurst; Iain Turner; Dr Sean MacDonnell.

OTHER INFORMATION Grants were broken down as follows: charities (£225,500); special individual needs (£85,300); respite care (£123,800).

HOW TO APPLY Apply online via the charity's website. Application forms can also be sent out by post on request. Application deadlines can be found on the charity's website.

CONTACT DETAILS The Trustees, 14 Dedham Vale Business Centre, Manningtree Road, Dedham, Colchester, Essex CO7 6BL *Tel.* 01206 323420 *Email* info@colchestercatalyst.co.uk *Website* www.colchestercatalyst.co.uk

■ The Cole Charitable Trust

CC NO 264033   **ESTABLISHED** 1972

WHERE FUNDING CAN BE GIVEN Cambridge; Greater Birmingham; Kent.

WHO CAN BENEFIT Registered charities.

WHAT IS FUNDED Social welfare; community development; environmental development; young people; community development.

WHAT IS NOT FUNDED National or regional organisations; non-registered charities; large building appeals; animal charities; research or further education; individuals.

TYPE OF GRANT Small capital or project grants; normally one-off; core costs.

RANGE OF GRANTS Typically between £500 and £1,200.

SAMPLE GRANTS Hope Projects West Midlands Ltd (£53,100); Entraide Mutual Aid (£3,000); Birmingham Centre for Arts Therapies (£2,000); Afghanistan and Central Asian Association (£1,500); Hands of Hope and Street Teams (£1,000 each); Life and Soul Youth Work (£750); Churches Together in Earlsdon and Chapelfields (£500).

FINANCES *Financial year end* 05/04/2022 *Income* £150,000 *Grants to organisations* £172,400 *Assets* £5,420,000

TRUSTEES Dr James Cole; George Cole; Tom Cole; Tim Cole; Jont Cole; Ranjit Sondhi; Katie Cole; Jacqui Francis; Angie Cole.

OTHER INFORMATION In 2021/22, grants were distributed as follows: trustee requests/special interest (£62,200): care and social welfare (£55,800); children and young people (£21,900); arts and culture (£13,000); personal and community empowerment (£10,500); disability (£5,600); education and training (£3,500).

HOW TO APPLY Application forms are available to download from the trust's website. Completed forms should be returned by email (preferred) or post along with a one-page letter and a copy of your latest accounts if they are not available to view on the Charity Commission's website. The trustees meet to consider applications twice a year, usually in April/May and October/November. Applications should be received six weeks before the relevant meeting and precise deadlines are available on the website. Applicants will be notified of the outcome in writing within six weeks of the meeting.

CONTACT DETAILS Lise Jackson, Administrator, PO Box 955, Haslingfield, Cambridge CB23 1WX *Tel.* 01223 871676 *Email* thecoletrust@gmail.com *Website* www.colecharitabletrust.org.uk

■ Colefax Charitable Trust

CC NO 1017285   **ESTABLISHED** 1993

WHERE FUNDING CAN BE GIVEN Berkshire and Hampshire.

WHO CAN BENEFIT Registered charities; hospitals; schools; charitable organisations.

WHAT IS FUNDED General charitable purposes.

WHAT IS NOT FUNDED Individuals.

RANGE OF GRANTS Mostly between £500 and £30,000.

SAMPLE GRANTS The Harbour Project (£30,000), Full Fact (£25,000); Newbury Spring Festival (£20,100); West Berkshire Mencap (£6,100); Wiltshire Air Ambulance (£5,000); The Salvation Army (£2,000); Wessex Heritage Trust (£1,000); Crohn's and Colitis (£500).

FINANCES *Financial year end* 05/04/2022 *Income* £355,700 *Grants to organisations* £139,000 *Assets* £20,200,000

TRUSTEES John Heath; Hans Krohn; Daniela Fiennes-Cox.

HOW TO APPLY The annual report for 2021/22 states: 'The trustees decide jointly which charitable institutions are to receive donations from the Trust. No invitations are sought from eligible institutions.'

CONTACT DETAILS Hans Krohn, Trustee, Westbrook House, St Helens Gardens, The Pitchens, Wroughton, Swindon, Wiltshire SN4 0RD *Tel.* 01635 200415 *Email* colefaxtrust@outlook.com

■ John and Freda Coleman Charitable Trust

CC NO 278223   **ESTABLISHED** 1979

WHERE FUNDING CAN BE GIVEN Hampshire and Surrey.

WHO CAN BENEFIT Registered charities; unregistered charities; CICs; social enterprises; schools.

WHAT IS FUNDED Education and training for young people.

TYPE OF GRANT Project funding.

RANGE OF GRANTS Up to £25,000.

SAMPLE GRANTS Previous beneficiaries have included: Surrey SATRO (£25,000); Surrey Care Trust (£10,000); Therapy Garden – Green School (£6,000); Surrey Silkway (£4,000); Linkable (£3,000); Second Chance and Surrey Youth Focus (£2,500 each); Alton College STEM Outreach (£1,500); Ro-Ro Sailing(£1,000).

FINANCES *Financial year end* 05/04/2022 *Income* £13,000 *Grants to organisations* £87,100

TRUSTEES Jeanette Bird; Paul Coleman; Brian Coleman; Nicole Coleman.

OTHER INFORMATION Full accounts were not available to view on the Charity Commission's website due to the trust's low income. We have therefore estimated the grant total based on the trust's total expenditure.

HOW TO APPLY The trust's website states: 'If you would like to make an application for a grant either call us on 01428 681333 or email jeanette@thecolemantrust.co.uk.'

CONTACT DETAILS Jeanette Bird, Trustee, The Nest, 3 Gasden Drive, Witley, Godalming, Surrey GU8 5QQ *Tel.* 01428 681333 *Email* jeanette@thecolemantrust.co.uk *Website* https://thecolemantrust.co.uk

■ The Coles-Medlock Foundation

CC NO 1132780   **ESTABLISHED** 2009
WHERE FUNDING CAN BE GIVEN Projects must be in financially developing countries.
WHO CAN BENEFIT UK-registered charities.
WHAT IS FUNDED Projects that alleviate hardship or poverty in financially developing countries. See the website for the foundation's current focus area within this theme.
WHAT IS NOT FUNDED Individuals; organisations not registered in the UK.
RANGE OF GRANTS Mostly up to £25,000.
SAMPLE GRANTS Salford University (£150,000); UBS (£50,000); Pipal Tree (£25,000); CHASE Africa (£15,000); Hope for Justice and Pratham UK (£10,000 each); Children on the Edge (£9,000).
FINANCES *Financial year end 31/07/2022*
Income £294,000
Grants to organisations £669,900
Assets £15,920,000
TRUSTEES Mark Goodman; David Medlock; Jacqueline Medlock; Peter Medlock.
OTHER INFORMATION Only grants of £10,000 and over were listed in the foundation's annual report and accounts. Unlisted grants of less than £10,000 totalled £123,000.
HOW TO APPLY Applications can be made using an online form on the foundation's website. The trustees meet quarterly.
CONTACT DETAILS The Trustees, St George's Lodge, 33 Oldfield Road, Bath, Somerset BA2 3ND *Tel.* 01225 946226 *Email* office@coles-medlock.org *Website* www.coles-medlock.org

■ The George Henry Collins Charity

CC NO 212268   **ESTABLISHED** 1959
WHERE FUNDING CAN BE GIVEN Within a 25-mile radius of Birmingham.
WHO CAN BENEFIT Local charitable organisations and local branches of registered national charities in Birmingham.
WHAT IS FUNDED General charitable purposes, with a preference for health, older people and projects tackling loneliness.
TYPE OF GRANT One-off project funding.
RANGE OF GRANTS £250 to £1,000.
SAMPLE GRANTS A list of beneficiaries was not included in the annual report and accounts. Previous beneficiaries have included: Edward's Trust, Restore and Sutton Coldfield YMCA (£1,000 each); Acorns Children's Hospice, Bentley Beginnings, Birmingham Asian Resources Centre, Birmingham Royal Ballet, Coventry Resource Centre for the Blind, Martineau Gardens and Whole Person Health Trust (£500 each); Birmingham Repertory Theatre and Warwickshire Social Inclusion Partnership (£250 each).
FINANCES *Financial year end 05/04/2022*
Income £72,700
Grants to organisations £95,500
Assets £2,360,000
TRUSTEES Peter Coggan; Anthony Collins; Roger Otto; Sally Botteley; Simon Field.
HOW TO APPLY Apply in writing to the correspondent. The trustees usually meet in March, July and November.
CONTACT DETAILS Chrissy Norgrove, Clerk to the Trustees, c/o Shakespeare Martineau, 1 Colmore Square, Birmingham B4 6AA *Tel.* 07940 160844 *Email* chrissy@ georgehenrycollinscharity.org.uk

■ Sir Jeremiah Colman Gift Trust

CC NO 229553   **ESTABLISHED** 1920
WHERE FUNDING CAN BE GIVEN UK, with a preference for Hampshire, especially Basingstoke.
WHO CAN BENEFIT Registered charities; churches.
WHAT IS FUNDED General charitable purposes, with a preference for health, education and Christian causes.
RANGE OF GRANTS Up to £20,000.
SAMPLE GRANTS Judd School (£15,000); Bronzefield Prison (£10,000); Sebastian's Action Trust (£5,000); Royal Horticultural Society (£3,000); Friends of the Family (£2,500); New Foundations (£1,400); Cancer Research UK and Youth for Christ (£1,000 each).
FINANCES *Financial year end 05/04/2022*
Income £203,000
Grants to organisations £154,900
Assets £9,700,000
TRUSTEES Jeremiah Colman; Lady Judith Colman; The Hon. Cynthia Colman; Oliver Colman; Sue Colman; Camilla Adeney; Louisa Mulvaney.
OTHER INFORMATION Only organisations that received grants of over £1,000 were listed as beneficiaries in the trust's accounts. Grants of under £1,000 totalled £42,800.
HOW TO APPLY Unsolicited applications are not accepted.
CONTACT DETAILS Rose Persson, Secretary and Administrator to the Trustees, Malshanger, Basingstoke, Hampshire RG23 7EY *Tel.* 01963 240260 *Email* rosepersson@btinternet.com

■ Col-Reno Ltd

CC NO 274896   **ESTABLISHED** 1977
WHERE FUNDING CAN BE GIVEN UK and Israel.
WHO CAN BENEFIT Jewish religious and educational institutions.
WHAT IS FUNDED The advancement of religion in accordance with the Orthodox Jewish faith.
RANGE OF GRANTS Up to £24,000 but typically between £1,000 and £10,000.
SAMPLE GRANTS Keren Shmuel (£24,500); The Jerusalem Foundation (£10,000); Lubavitch of Liverpool (£6,400); Chabad of Southgate (£4,300); Friends of Kol Torah Rabbinical College (£2,800); Hendon Adath Yisroel Congregation (£1,500); Tzivos Hashem (£360).
FINANCES *Financial year end 05/04/2022*
Income £135,100
Grants to organisations £100,100
Assets £2,290,000
TRUSTEES Keith Davis; Rhona Davis; Libbie Goldstein; Chaim Stern; Alan Stern; Martin Stern.
OTHER INFORMATION Grants were awarded to 40 organisations during the year.
HOW TO APPLY Apply in writing to the correspondent.
CONTACT DETAILS R. Davies, Secretary, Flat 54 Danescroft, Brent Street, London NW4 2QH *Tel.* 020 8202 7013

■ The Colt Foundation

CC NO 1190167   **ESTABLISHED** 1978
WHERE FUNDING CAN BE GIVEN UK.
WHO CAN BENEFIT Universities.
WHAT IS FUNDED Research projects in the field of occupational and environmental health, particularly those aimed at discovering the cause of illnesses arising from conditions at the place of work. The trustees are particularly keen to fund research that is likely to inform government policy or change working practices.

WHAT IS NOT FUNDED Applications for general funding; direct support for individuals; overseas projects.

TYPE OF GRANT Core costs; project funding.

SAMPLE GRANTS A list of beneficiaries was not included in the annual report and accounts. Previous beneficiaries have included: University of Edinburgh, Poland (£85,900); University College London/London School of Hygiene and Tropical Medicine (£64,900); Imperial College (£52,000); University of Southampton (£40,600); Imperial College (£27,700); British College – Nepal (£10,100); St Mary's Cathedral Workshop (£3,900).

FINANCES *Financial year end 31/12/2022*
Income £976,500
Grants to organisations £802,300
Assets £30,860,000

TRUSTEES Prof. Sir Anthony Newman Taylor; Clare Gilchrist; Prof. David Coggon; Prof. Ira Madan; Patricia Lebus; Christina Fitzsimons; Dr Alex Jones.

HOW TO APPLY Apply in writing to the correspondent. Full details of what should be included in an application can be found on the foundation's website. The trustees meet twice a year to review applications, in the spring and in the autumn, and applications normally need to be received approximately eight weeks beforehand to be considered at the meetings.

CONTACT DETAILS Tash Heydon, Director, Unit E, The Old Bakery, Petworth, West Sussex GU28 0AP *Tel.* 01798 342831 *Email* tash@coltfoundation. org.uk *Website* www.coltfoundation.org.uk

■ The Coltstaple Trust

CC NO 1085500   **ESTABLISHED** 2001
WHERE FUNDING CAN BE GIVEN Worldwide.
WHO CAN BENEFIT Charitable organisations.
WHAT IS FUNDED Social welfare; people who are at risk of or experiencing homelessness; overseas aid.
RANGE OF GRANTS Up to £500,000.
SAMPLE GRANTS Oxfam (£500,000); Shelter (£125,000); St Mungo's (£100,000); Emmaus UK (£25,000).
FINANCES *Financial year end 31/03/2022*
Income £912,100
Grants to organisations £750,000
Assets £17,020,000
TRUSTEES Elaine Colville; Matthew Oakeshott; Dr Philippa Oakeshott; Lord Stoneham of Droxford; Joseph Oakeshott; Leonard Baker.
OTHER INFORMATION Grants were awarded to four organisations during the year.
HOW TO APPLY Apply in writing to the correspondent. The trust tends to award grants to the same charities each year.
CONTACT DETAILS Jane Wells, 15 Queen Anne's Gate, London SW1H 9BU *Tel.* 020 7846 3252 *Email* jane.wells@olimproperty.co.uk

■ Colwinston Charitable Trust

CC NO 1049189   **ESTABLISHED** 1995
WHERE FUNDING CAN BE GIVEN UK, with a preference for Wales.
WHO CAN BENEFIT UK-registered charities; arts organisations; libraries; archives.
WHAT IS FUNDED The trust seeks to sustain and support high-quality artistic activities that add to the cultural life and experiences available in the UK and especially in Wales. Funding is particularly but not exclusively directed to the support of opera, music and the visual arts.

WHAT IS NOT FUNDED Organisations that are not registered with the Charity Commission; retrospective costs; individuals; research; general appeals; community or amateur arts groups; capital projects; commercial recordings (other than those benefitting emerging or mid-career Welsh composers).

TYPE OF GRANT Project funding; strategic funding.

RANGE OF GRANTS Up to £40,000 but mostly £5,000 to £20,000.

SAMPLE GRANTS Mousetrap Foundation for the Arts (£40,000); Valley Kids (£30,000); Buxton International Festival (£18,600); Benedetti Foundation (£10,000); Afan Arts (£7,000); Art UK (£5,000); Aberystwyth University (£4,800); NMC Recordings (£4,000).

FINANCES *Financial year end 05/04/2022*
Income £440,700
Grants to organisations £188,900
Assets £1,190,000

TRUSTEES Mathew Prichard; Martin Tinney; Sian Williams; Lucinda Prichard; Rebecca Evans.

OTHER INFORMATION The trust derives its income from the royalties from the West End production of The Mousetrap. Over 80% of funding goes to projects in Wales. In 2021/22 grants were awarded to 18 organisations.

HOW TO APPLY Application forms and application guidelines can be found on the trust's website.

CONTACT DETAILS The Trustees, 14 Hanover Court, Midhope Road, Woking, Surrey GU22 7UX *Tel.* 020 7842 2000 *Email* colwinston.trust@ ntlworld.com *Website* www.colwinston.org.uk

■ Colyer-Fergusson Charitable Trust

CC NO 258958   **ESTABLISHED** 1969
WHERE FUNDING CAN BE GIVEN Kent and Medway.
WHO CAN BENEFIT Registered charities; CICs; schools; hospices; individuals.
WHAT IS FUNDED Disadvantaged young people; disadvantaged families; community development; rehabilitation of offenders.
WHAT IS NOT FUNDED Individuals (unless applying to the Hardship Awards Programme); statutory bodies and anything deemed to be the responsibility of the state; nurseries, schools and colleges; hospitals and health authorities; medical care, equipment or research; academic research, scholarships or bursaries; animal charities; the promotion of religion; the restoration or conservation of buildings; annual or one-off events and festivals; work outside Kent; endowment appeals; retrospective expenditure; round-robin, widely circulated appeals; national charities without a base or planned project within Kent or Medway (unless applying to the Investing in Rehabilitation fund).
TYPE OF GRANT Project funding.
RANGE OF GRANTS Generally up to £100,000.
SAMPLE GRANTS National Literacy Trust (£88,000); The Amber Foundation (£56,000); Fine Cell Work (£34,000); Future Foundry (£15,000); Tree of Hope (£10,000); My Roots Go Deep (£2,500).
FINANCES *Financial year end 31/03/2022*
Income £662,300
Grants to organisations £1,880,000
Grants to individuals £76,000
Assets £33,690,000
TRUSTEES Nicholas Fisher; Ruth Murphy; Barbara Long; Rosalind Riley; James Thorne; Navprit Rai; Julia Megone.
OTHER INFORMATION Grants were broken down as follows: young people (£528,700); families

(£462,500); communities (£447,200); rehabilitation (£444,500); individuals (£76,000).

HOW TO APPLY Online application forms along with full guidance notes on each specific programme are available to download from the trust's website.

CONTACT DETAILS The Trustees, 34 Hill Street, Richmond, Surrey TW9 1TW *Tel.* 020 8948 3388 *Email* grantadmin@cfct.org.uk *Website* www.cfct.org.uk

■ Comic Relief

CC NO 326568   **ESTABLISHED** 1985

WHERE FUNDING CAN BE GIVEN UK and overseas.

WHO CAN BENEFIT UK-registered charities; voluntary organisations.

WHAT IS FUNDED Social welfare; social justice; people affected by climate change.

SAMPLE GRANTS A list of beneficiaries was not included in the annual report and accounts.

FINANCES *Financial year end 31/07/2022*
Income £4,990,000
Grants to organisations £25,240,000
Assets £93,940,000

TRUSTEES Dr Sue Black; Tom Shropshire; Tessy Ojo; Rupert Morley; Charlotte Moar; Matt Hyde; Jenny Hodgson; Jacqueline Onalo; Eric Salama; Fiona Campbell.

OTHER INFORMATION Grants awarded in the UK totalled £13.7 million and international grants totalled £11.54 million.

HOW TO APPLY Open funding opportunities are listed on the charity's website as they arise. Applications can made online via the charity's website, where full guidance is also provided.

CONTACT DETAILS The Trustees, 1st Floor, 89 Albert Embankment, London SE1 7TP *Tel.* 020 7820 2000 *Email* fundinginfo@comicrelief.com *Website* www.comicrelief.com

■ The Comino Foundation

CC NO 312875   **ESTABLISHED** 1971

WHERE FUNDING CAN BE GIVEN UK.

WHO CAN BENEFIT Registered charities; unregistered charities; universities; social enterprises.

WHAT IS FUNDED Educational activities for young people which: improve practical and personal capabilities; enrich learning in science, engineering and technology; transform services for young people with complex needs; and improve social opportunity.

WHAT IS NOT FUNDED Research; activities outside the UK; individuals.

TYPE OF GRANT Project funding.

RANGE OF GRANTS From £3,000 to £60,000.

SAMPLE GRANTS Knowle West Media Centre (£63,000); The Royal Society of Arts (£56,000); University of Manchester (£40,000); Centre for Real World Learning (£30,000); Potential Plus UK (£17,000); Potential Trust (£12,000); Craft Council (£5,000); Made Here Now (£2,000).

FINANCES *Financial year end 05/05/2022*
Income £98,300
Grants to organisations £347,400
Assets £3,630,000

TRUSTEES Anna Comino-James; David Perry; Mumtaz Bashir-Hanid; Amrit Singh; Prof. Jose Chambers.

OTHER INFORMATION The foundation awarded 19 grants to organisations.

HOW TO APPLY The foundation has a number of long-term funding commitments and a limited capacity to make grants. Potential applicants should refer to the foundation's website, where

advice is given about what is currently being considered by the trustees. If you think that your project is suitable, you should apply to the foundation's administrator, following the guidance on the website about what to include.

CONTACT DETAILS Sarah Mareschall, Administrator, 137 Thetford Road, Brandon, Suffolk IP27 0DB *Tel.* 07904 467625 *Email* administrator@cominofoundation.org.uk *Website* www.cominofoundation.org.uk

■ Community First

CC NO 288117   **ESTABLISHED** 1965

WHERE FUNDING CAN BE GIVEN Wiltshire and Swindon.

WHO CAN BENEFIT Charities; community organisations; parish or town councils.

WHAT IS FUNDED Community development; the arts; heritage; environmental projects; sport; transport; young carers.

WHAT IS NOT FUNDED Individuals; private companies.

TYPE OF GRANT Project funding; capital funding; core/revenue funding.

RANGE OF GRANTS Generally up to £20,000.

SAMPLE GRANTS Lyneham Village Hall (£52,100); Cricklade Rugby Football Club (£35,000); Swindon and Cricklade Railway (£30,000); Cricklade Petanque Club (£25,000); Purton and Cricklade Young Farmers Club (£20,000); St Sampson's Church – Cricklade (£12,000); Clarendon Juniors Football Club (£10,000).

FINANCES *Financial year end 31/03/2022*
Income £2,140,000
Grants to organisations £370,900
Grants to individuals £7,000
Assets £1,930,000

TRUSTEES Piers Dibben; Edward Heard; Steven Boocock; James Moody; Virginia Keen; Jane James; Sanjeen Payne-Kumar; Merope Sylvester; Leah Campbell; Victoria Walsh.

OTHER INFORMATION A total of 45 grants were awarded during the year. Only organisations that received grants of over £10,000 were listed as beneficiaries in the charity's accounts. Grants of under £10,000 totalled £85,000. There are five grant schemes: LEADER (heritage), Landfill Communities Fund, Lace Up Wiltshire (sport), Community Transport Development Fund and Building Bridges (young people). Three individuals received grants totalling £7,000.

HOW TO APPLY Each fund has a separate application process. See the charity's website for further details.

CONTACT DETAILS The Trustees, Unit C2 Brecon Business Centre, Hopton Park, Devizes, Wiltshire SN10 2EY *Tel.* 01380 722475 *Email* grants@communityfirst.org.uk *Website* www.communityfirst.org.uk

■ The Company of Actuaries Charitable Trust Fund

CC NO 280702   **ESTABLISHED** 1980

WHERE FUNDING CAN BE GIVEN UK, with a preference for the City of London.

WHO CAN BENEFIT Charitable organisations and individuals involved in, or training for, a career in actuary.

WHAT IS FUNDED The education of actuaries and research in the field of actuarial science; individuals studying to become an actuary; charities linked to members of the company; charities within the City of London.

SAMPLE GRANTS St Francis Hospice (£10,000); Exeter Mathematics School and The Lord

Think carefully about every application. Is it justified?

325

Mayor's Appeal Fund (£5,000 each); Edmonton Sea Cadets (£3,000); St John Ambulance (£500).

FINANCES *Financial year end 31/07/2022*
Income £135,900
Grants to organisations £108,100
Grants to individuals £38,900
Assets £296,100

TRUSTEES Peter Crutchett; Simon Dudley; Ian Farr; Christopher Green; Jay Stewart; Jennifer Segal; Gary Simmons; Robert Ross.

HOW TO APPLY Apply in writing to the correspondent.

CONTACT DETAILS Jerry Staffurth, Hon. Secretary and Assistant Treasurer, Three Greens, Branksome Park Road, Camberley GU15 2AE
Email almoner@actuariescompany.co.uk
Website www.actuariescompany.co.uk/charitable-trust

■ Douglas Compton James Charitable Trust

CC NO 1091125   **ESTABLISHED** 1997

WHERE FUNDING CAN BE GIVEN The Masonic Province of Northamptonshire and Huntingdonshire.

WHO CAN BENEFIT Registered charities, with a preference for Masonic charities; hospices; schools.

WHAT IS FUNDED General charitable purposes; education; social welfare; health, including mental health; children and young people; older people; arts. Some preference is given to Masonic charities.

TYPE OF GRANT Project funding; strategic funding.

RANGE OF GRANTS Mostly between £1,000 and £6,000, with the occasional larger grant.

SAMPLE GRANTS Beneficiaries include: Stephen Perse Foundation (£54,400); Wellingborough School (£32,700); Disasters Emergency Committee – Ukraine Humanitarian Appeal (£10,000); Lakelands Day Care Hospice, RNLI and Wildlife Trust for Beds, Cambs and Northants (£6,000 each); Food4Heroes, MND Association and Northampton Samaritans (£5,000 each); The 3 Pillars – Feeding the Homeless, Fermynwoods Contemporary Art Ltd and Palmer Court Masonic Housing Association (£3,000 each); Deafblind Centre, East Northants Headway and Nevill Holt Opera (£1,000 each).

FINANCES *Financial year end 05/04/2022*
Income £112,300
Grants to organisations £222,600
Assets £7,420,000

TRUSTEES Richard Ongley; Philip Humphrey; Thomas Reed; Keith Dickson.

OTHER INFORMATION Priority is given to public charities within Northamptonshire and Huntingdonshire. The trust's 2021/22 accounts demonstrate the trustees' preference to support charities with strategic and project funding rather than core costs.

HOW TO APPLY Apply in writing to the correspondent.

CONTACT DETAILS Louise Davies, Secretary, Montague House, Chancery Lane, Thrapston, Northamptonshire NN14 4LN *Tel.* 01832 732161 *Email* louise.davies@vshlaw.co.uk

■ Congleton Inclosure Trust

CC NO 244136   **ESTABLISHED** 1795

WHERE FUNDING CAN BE GIVEN Congleton Town Centre, High Town, Lower Heath, Mossley, West Heath and Buglawton, and the bordering Cheshire parishes of Bosley, Eaton, Hulme Walfield, Newbold Astbury, North Rode and Somerford.

WHO CAN BENEFIT Local organisations; UK organisations with projects in the area.

WHAT IS FUNDED Community development and engagement; religious organisations and festivals.

RANGE OF GRANTS Up to £10,000.

SAMPLE GRANTS Eaton Bank Academy (£20,000); Congleton RUFC (£10,000); Beartown Rickshaw (£5,000); Guide Dogs for the Blind (£5,000); The Green Tree House (£500); Congleton Live (£400).

FINANCES *Financial year end 31/12/2021*
Income £124,200
Grants to organisations £75,000
Assets £5,830,000

TRUSTEES John Beardmore; Janet Goodier; Mr J. S. Davies; Janet Hollins; Brenda Cook; Kenneth Wainwright; Anthony Curwen; Sion Raw-Rees; David Beech; Pamela Newman; John Hulse; Adele Cook.

HOW TO APPLY Applications can be made via the charity's website.

CONTACT DETAILS The Trustees, Congleton Town Hall, High Street, Congleton, Cheshire CW12 1BN *Tel.* 01260 270908 *Email* info@congletoninclosuretrust.org.uk *Website* www.congletoninclosuretrust.org.uk

■ Congregational and General Charitable Trust

CC NO 297013   **ESTABLISHED** 1987

WHERE FUNDING CAN BE GIVEN UK.

WHO CAN BENEFIT Churches; religious bodies.

WHAT IS FUNDED The overall care, upkeep and extension of churches; capital costs of church community projects; promotion of the Christian religion in particular, the United Reformed and Congregational denominations, and other churches of the Protestant tradition.

WHAT IS NOT FUNDED Running costs of the church organ and church bells restoration; conservation/restoration of works of art; manse works; graveyard maintenance; solar panels; projects with a total cost of over £1 million.

TYPE OF GRANT Capital costs; project funding.

RANGE OF GRANTS Typically £1,000 to £25,000, up to 25% of the total project cost.

SAMPLE GRANTS St Botolph (£15,000); All Saints Church – Laughton (£13,300); St Andrew's – Ewerby (£6,100); St Thomas' – Kidgrove (£4,100); Ballenon Reformed Presbyterian (£2,700).

FINANCES *Financial year end 31/12/2021*
Income £473,600
Grants to organisations £790,000
Assets £18,410,000

TRUSTEES Margaret Atkinson; The Revd Pamela Ward; John Holmes; The Revd David Coote; The Revd Margaret Tait; Alastair Forsyth; The Revd Richard Turnbull; Susan Austin; The Revd David Grosch-Miller.

HOW TO APPLY Application forms can be downloaded from the trust's website, where upcoming deadlines are also posted, along with guidance on what to include in your application.

CONTACT DETAILS Trish Thorpe, Trust Administrator, Congregational and General Charitable Trust, PO Box 1111, Lincoln, Lincolnshire LN5 0WJ *Email* enquiries@candgtrust.org.uk *Website* www.candgtrust.org.uk

■ The Connolly Foundation (UK) Ltd

CC NO 1109135　　**ESTABLISHED** 2005
WHERE FUNDING CAN BE GIVEN Bedfordshire.
WHO CAN BENEFIT Registered charities; schools.
WHAT IS FUNDED Education and young people; support for older people including the development of community facilities (including social care), hospice and end-of-life care and research into illnesses that principally affect older people.
SAMPLE GRANTS Redborne School (£525,000); Youthscape (£100,000); Keech Hospice (£50,000); Alzheimer's Research (£10,000); Chellingham Centre (£1,000).
FINANCES *Financial year end 31/05/2022*
Income £15,770,000
Grants to organisations £1,380,000
Assets £96,040,000
TRUSTEES Michael Callanan; Andrew Rowe; Shyam Ashoka; Vanessa Connolly; Simon White; David Wilkins.
HOW TO APPLY Apply via the foundation's website.
CONTACT DETAILS The Trustees, Manor Farm Court, Lower Sundon, Luton, Bedfordshire LU3 3NZ
Email enquiry@connollyfoundation.org.uk
Website www.connollyfoundation.org.uk

■ The Ernest Cook Trust

CC NO 1146629　　**ESTABLISHED** 1952
WHERE FUNDING CAN BE GIVEN UK.
WHO CAN BENEFIT State schools; registered charities; other recognised not-for-profit organisations.
WHAT IS FUNDED Education, particularly extra-curricular activities and outdoor learning.
SAMPLE GRANTS A list of beneficiaries was not included in the annual report and accounts. Previous beneficiaries have included: City of Bradford YMCA and Farms for City Children (£15,000 each); The Smallpeice Trust (£11,000); Earth Trust (£10,000); Future Roots (£8,400); City and Guilds of London Art School and Salisbury Cathedral (£4,000 each).
FINANCES *Financial year end 31/03/2022*
Income £9,960,000
Grants to organisations £1,890,000
Assets £215,860,000
TRUSTEES Mary Riall; Simon Eliot; Jenefer Greenwood; Harry Henderson; Ian Pigott.
OTHER INFORMATION No trustee information was available for this charity.
HOW TO APPLY See the trust's website for information on the application processes for each funding stream.
CONTACT DETAILS The Trustees, Fairford Park, Fairford, Gloucestershire GL7 4JH *Tel.* 01285 712492 *Email* grants@ernestcooktrust.org.uk
Website www.ernestcooktrust.org.uk

■ The Cooks Charity

CC NO 297913　　**ESTABLISHED** 1987
WHERE FUNDING CAN BE GIVEN UK; the City of London for community welfare grants.
WHO CAN BENEFIT Charitable organisations associated with the catering industry; individuals in the catering industry and their dependants.
WHAT IS FUNDED Education associated with the catering industry; skills and training associated with the catering industry; the general welfare of people associated with the City of London and/or the catering trade.
TYPE OF GRANT Project funding; capital costs.

SAMPLE GRANTS Royal Academy of Culinary Arts (£35,000); The Clink Charity (£32,000); Treloar Trust (£25,000); Bede House Association (£10,000); Beyond Food Foundation (£4,000).
FINANCES *Financial year end 30/06/2022*
Income £305,800
Grants to organisations £214,800
Assets £5,670,000
TRUSTEES Oliver Goodinge; Peter Wright; Cdre David Smith; Simon Fooks; Paul Budd.
OTHER INFORMATION Grants were broken down as follows: education (£124,400); general welfare (£65,200); City of London (£25,300).
HOW TO APPLY Applications should be submitted by email to the Clerk. Further information on what to include in an application can be found on the charity's website.
CONTACT DETAILS The Clerk, 3 Rock Lane, Warminster, Wiltshire BA12 9JZ *Tel.* 07518 138883 *Email* clerk@cookslivery.org.uk
Website www.cooks.org.uk

■ The Catherine Cookson Charitable Trust

CC NO 272895　　**ESTABLISHED** 1977
WHERE FUNDING CAN BE GIVEN UK, with a preference for the North East.
WHO CAN BENEFIT Charitable organisations.
WHAT IS FUNDED General charitable purposes, including: education and training; health; children and young people; religious activities; animal welfare; disability; art and culture.
WHAT IS NOT FUNDED Core funding; ongoing financing; work outside the UK; sports clubs/associations; personal appeals.
TYPE OF GRANT Capital costs; project funding.
RANGE OF GRANTS £100 to £100,000.
SAMPLE GRANTS Cancer Research UK (£250,000); King's College Hospital (£75,000); Bamburgh Pavilion Association (£60,000); Jesmond Dene Real Tennis Club (£50,000); Brain Tumour Research (£10,000); Newburn Sea Cadets (£14,000); Tyne Rivers Trust (£1,500); The Scottish SeaBird Centre (£500); Richmond Fellowship (£250).
FINANCES *Financial year end 05/04/2022*
Income £1,040,000
Grants to organisations £713,500
Assets £35,730,000
TRUSTEES Peter Magnay; David Hawkins; Daniel Sallows; Pamela Mallen.
OTHER INFORMATION In 2021/22, the trust awarded grants to 92 organisations, which were broken down as follows: medical causes, health and sickness (£417,900): other charities (£200,600); children and young people (£26,900); disability (£16,800); animal welfare (£15,000); religious activities (£14,000): education and training (£13,100); art and culture (£9,300).
HOW TO APPLY Applications can be made online through the trust's website. Alternatively, written applications can be submitted by post, enclosing an sae.
CONTACT DETAILS The Trustees, c/o Thomas Magnay and Co., 8 St Mary's Green, Whickham, Newcastle upon Tyne, Tyne and Wear NE16 4DN *Tel.* 0191 488 7459
Email enquiries@thomasmagnay.co.uk
Website http://catherinecookson.com/trust

■ The Keith Coombs Trust

CC NO 1149791   **ESTABLISHED** 2012
WHERE FUNDING CAN BE GIVEN UK, with a preference for the West Midlands.
WHO CAN BENEFIT Registered charities.
WHAT IS FUNDED General charitable purposes; children and young people; health; education.
SAMPLE GRANTS A list of beneficiaries was not included in the annual report and accounts.
FINANCES *Financial year end* 12/09/2021
Income £78,000
Grants to organisations £73,800
Assets £9,200
TRUSTEES Anthony Coombs; Graham Coombs; Demetrios Markou; Christine Ingram; Chris Redford; Manjeet Bhogal.
OTHER INFORMATION The 2020/21 accounts were the latest available at the time of writing (June 2023).
HOW TO APPLY Apply in writing to the correspondent.
CONTACT DETAILS Christine Ingram, Trustee, c/o S&U plc, 2 Stratford Court, Cranmore Boulevard, Solihull, West Midlands B90 4QT *Tel.* 0121 705 7777 *Email* christineingram@suplc.co.uk

■ Co-op Foundation

CC NO 1093028   **ESTABLISHED** 2000
WHERE FUNDING CAN BE GIVEN UK.
WHO CAN BENEFIT Registered charities and community groups.
WHAT IS FUNDED Community enterprise; community development; health; community safety; sustainability.
TYPE OF GRANT Unrestricted.
SAMPLE GRANTS A list of beneficiaries was not included in the annual report and accounts. Previous beneficiaries have included: Envision (£132,500); The Children's Society (£69,800); Women's Technology Centre (£50,000); White Rock Neighbourhood Ventures (£40,000); Changing Our Lives (£35,000); Scotswood Garden (£21,200); UK Youth (£20,000).
FINANCES *Financial year end* 31/12/2021
Income £4,540,000
Grants to organisations £2,530,000
Assets £28,920,000
TRUSTEES Jamie Ward-Smith; Sheila Malley; Sharon Jones; Hope Levy-Shepherd; Ewansiha Imafidon; Peter Batt; Latefa Mansarit; Mahalia Flasz.
HOW TO APPLY Funding rounds for specific programmes open periodically during the year and are advertised on the foundation's website.
CONTACT DETAILS The Trustees, 9th Floor, 1 Angel Square, Manchester M60 0AG *Email* foundation@coop.co.uk *Website* www.coopfoundation.org.uk

■ Mabel Cooper Charity

CC NO 264621   **ESTABLISHED** 1972
WHERE FUNDING CAN BE GIVEN UK, with a possible interest in South Devon.
WHO CAN BENEFIT Charitable organisations.
WHAT IS FUNDED General charitable purposes.
WHAT IS NOT FUNDED Individuals.
SAMPLE GRANTS A list of beneficiaries was not included in the annual report and accounts. Previous beneficiaries have included: Devon Air Ambulance (£10,000); Alzheimer's Research UK, Crisis, Cancer Research, Macmillan Cancer Support, St Luke's Hospice and St Peter's Hospice (£5,000 each); Rowcroft House Foundation, The Salvation Army, and Shelter

(£2,500 each); Future Trees and Young Lives vs Cancer (£1,000 each).
FINANCES *Financial year end* 30/06/2022
Income £287,300
Grants to organisations £119,700
Assets £5,840,000
TRUSTEES Ian Harbottle; David Harbottle; Alison Barrett.
HOW TO APPLY Apply in writing to the correspondent.
CONTACT DETAILS The Trustees, Middle Manor, Lascot Hill, Wedmore, Somerset BS28 4AF *Tel.* 01934 712102

■ The Alice Ellen Cooper-Dean Charitable Foundation

CC NO 273298   **ESTABLISHED** 1977
WHERE FUNDING CAN BE GIVEN UK, with a preference for Dorset and West Hampshire, and occasionally overseas.
WHO CAN BENEFIT Local and national UK-registered charities.
WHAT IS FUNDED General charitable purposes; education; religion; social welfare.
WHAT IS NOT FUNDED Individuals; non-UK-registered charities.
TYPE OF GRANT Project funding.
RANGE OF GRANTS Generally up to £40,000.
SAMPLE GRANTS Pilsdon Community (£40,000); Melplash Agricultural Society (£22,000); Poole Refuge (£20,000); Pathways for All People and Royal Agricultural Benevolent Institution (£15,000 each); Purbeck Youth and Community Foundation and Read Easy UK (£10,000); Roy Castle Lung Cancer Foundation (£5,000); Police Community Clubs of Great Britain (£2,000); Living Paintings Trust (£1,000).
FINANCES *Financial year end* 31/03/2022
Income £1,250,000
Grants to organisations £1,170,000
Assets £39,350,000
TRUSTEES Emma Blackburn; John Bowditch; Linda Bowditch; Douglas Neville-Jones; Richard Wedgwood; Richard King.
OTHER INFORMATION Grants were awarded to 143 organisations during the year.
HOW TO APPLY Apply in writing to the correspondent. Applicants are asked to provide a summary of the project together with costings, financial accounts and details of fundraising activities.
CONTACT DETAILS The Trustees, c/o Edwards and Keeping, Unity Chambers, 34 High East Street, Dorchester, Dorset DT1 1HA *Tel.* 01305 251333 *Email* cooperdean@edwardsandkeeping.co.uk

■ Marjorie Coote Animal Charity Trust

CC NO 208493   **ESTABLISHED** 1954
WHERE FUNDING CAN BE GIVEN Worldwide but mostly the UK.
WHO CAN BENEFIT Registered charities; research institutions such as universities.
WHAT IS FUNDED The welfare of horses, dogs, birds and other animals.
WHAT IS NOT FUNDED Individuals.
TYPE OF GRANT Research; general funding; project funding.
RANGE OF GRANTS Mostly between £500 and £5,000, with the occasional smaller or larger grant.
SAMPLE GRANTS Sheffield PDSA (£10,000); African Forest Elephant Foundation, Nature's SAFE and The Royal Veterinary College Animal Care Trust

(£5,000 each); The Guide Dogs for the Blind Association, Ren's Rescue and The Wildfowl and Wetlands Trust (£2,000 each); Fauna and Flora International, Forever Hounds Trust and World Animal Protection (£1,000 each); Cuan Wildlife Rescue, Himalaya Animal Treatment Centre UK and Wetheriggs Animal Rescue and Conservation (£500 each).

FINANCES *Financial year end* 05/04/2022
Income £163,600
Grants to organisations £139,600
Assets £4,180,000

TRUSTEES Se Browne; Jill Holah; Lady Neill; Sarah Neill; Nicola Baguley.

OTHER INFORMATION The charity deed names five registered charities as the original beneficiaries; however, the trust supports other charities as well. Of the grant total, £49,900 was awarded to recurrent beneficiaries and £89,700 was awarded in one-off grants.

HOW TO APPLY Apply to the correspondent via email during September. See the website for a checklist of information that must be included.

CONTACT DETAILS Jill Holah, Trustee, End Cottage, Terrington, York, North Yorkshire YO60 6PU *Tel.* 01759 322102 *Email* admin@mcacharity.org.uk *Website* www.neillcharities.com/mcac

■ The Helen Jean Cope Charity

CC NO 1125937　　　**ESTABLISHED** 1998

WHERE FUNDING CAN BE GIVEN East Midlands, with a particular preference for Leicestershire.

WHO CAN BENEFIT Registered charities.

WHAT IS FUNDED General charitable purposes.

WHAT IS NOT FUNDED Individuals; unregistered charities; requests for ongoing funding.

TYPE OF GRANT One-off grants for capital costs.

RANGE OF GRANTS £500 to £5,000.

SAMPLE GRANTS The David Clarke Railway Trust (£5,000); Charnwood Christmas Toy Appeal (£3,000); All Hallows PTA (£1,500); Baby Basics, Holy Trinity Church – Hinckley, Scropton Riding and Driving Centre and Together for Short Lives (£1,000 each); Leicester Cathedral Music Foundation (£750); Living Painting (£500).

FINANCES *Financial year end* 31/12/2021
Income £161,600
Grants to organisations £57,800
Assets £6,900,000

TRUSTEES Lindsay Brydson; Malcolm Carrington; Graham Freckelton; Alan Roberts; Matthew Freckelton; Anthony Benskin.

OTHER INFORMATION Grants were awarded to 52 charities during the year.

HOW TO APPLY Apply by post to the correspondent including the following: the full name and address of the charity to which correspondence should be sent and cheques made payable in the event of a grant being made; your charity number; a brief description of your charity and its activities if this is a first application; what the grant is for; who will benefit; how much any specific items will cost; other fundraising activities being carried out and the amount raised so far; a set of audited accounts, where available; and a copy of your reserves policy. The trustees meet about five times a year.

CONTACT DETAILS Malcolm Carrington, Secretary, 1 Woodgate, Loughborough, Leicestershire LE11 2TY *Tel.* 01509 218298 *Email* info@thehelenjeancopecharity.co.uk *Website* www.thehelenjeancopecharity.co.uk

■ The J. Reginald Corah Foundation Fund

CC NO 220792　　　**ESTABLISHED** 1953

WHERE FUNDING CAN BE GIVEN Leicester; Leicestershire; Rutland.

WHO CAN BENEFIT Charitable organisations. However, particular favour is given to organisations benefitting employees and ex-employees of hosiery firms in Leicester and Rutland and their dependants.

WHAT IS FUNDED Children; disability; education; community; medical causes; social welfare.

WHAT IS NOT FUNDED Applications from individuals are not considered unless made by, or supported by, a recognised charitable organisation.

RANGE OF GRANTS Typically up to £3,000.

SAMPLE GRANTS LOROS (£2,000); Dove Cottage Day Hospice (£1,800): CF Dream Holidays (£1,700); Gorse Hill City Farm, Leicester Samaritans, Listening Books and Police Community Clubs of Great Britain (£1,500 each).

FINANCES *Financial year end* 31/03/2022
Income £111,300
Grants to organisations £93,000
Assets £6,480,000

TRUSTEES Roger Bowder; David Corah; Jonathan Pears.

OTHER INFORMATION During 2021/22, grants were distributed as follows: appeal grants (£64,800); annual list grants (£28,200).

HOW TO APPLY Apply in writing to the correspondent.

CONTACT DETAILS The Trustees, 20 Welby Road, Asfordby Hill, Melton Mowbray, Leicestershire LE14 3RB *Tel.* 07771 542099 *Email* jrcfoundationfund@gmail.com

■ The Gershon Coren Charitable Foundation

CC NO 257615　　　**ESTABLISHED** 1968

WHERE FUNDING CAN BE GIVEN UK; Israel; financially developing countries.

WHO CAN BENEFIT Charitable organisations, particularly Jewish organisations.

WHAT IS FUNDED General charitable purposes; social welfare; Jewish causes.

RANGE OF GRANTS Mostly up to £12,000, with a few larger grants.

SAMPLE GRANTS JNF Charitable Trust (£285,000); Gategi Village Self Help Group (£90,000); Jewish Futures Trust (£15,000); Jewish Childs Day (£10,000); Jewish Renaissance, Shalom Foundation and The Together Plan (£5,000 each).

FINANCES *Financial year end* 05/04/2022
Income £1,090,000
Grants to organisations £647,000
Assets £63,400,000

TRUSTEES Anthony Coren; Graham Weinberg.

OTHER INFORMATION In 2021/22 the foundation awarded grants to 22 organisations.

HOW TO APPLY Contact the correspondent for further information.

CONTACT DETAILS Graham Weinberg, Correspondent, c/o Manna UK, Winston House, 303 Dollis Park, London N3 1HF *Tel.* 020 7429 4100

■ Michael Cornish Charitable Trust

CC NO 1107890   **ESTABLISHED** 2005

WHERE FUNDING CAN BE GIVEN Worldwide, with a preference for Lincolnshire and Jersey.

WHO CAN BENEFIT Charities and not-for-profit organisations.

WHAT IS FUNDED General charitable purposes, with a preference for: children and young people; people with disabilities; economic and community development; amateur sport; health.

TYPE OF GRANT Project funding.

RANGE OF GRANTS Up to £5,000 but typically £1,000.

SAMPLE GRANTS Christian Partners in Africa (£30,000); St Barnabas Hospice and RNLI (£5,000 each); Bat Conservation Trust, Child Brain Injury Trust, Dogs for Autism, Prisoners' Education Trust, Samaritans and Versus Arthritis (£1,000 each); Carlton Scroop Village Hall (£500).

FINANCES *Financial year end* 31/12/2021
Income £78,000
Grants to organisations £105,500
Assets £19,470,000

TRUSTEES Michael Cornish; Richard Vigar; Harriet Cornish-Sheasby; Stephen Cornish; Susan Cornish.

OTHER INFORMATION Grants were awarded to 61 organisations in 2021.

HOW TO APPLY Applications can be made through the trust's website, where there is a detailed list of what to include and how to use the application portal. Upcoming application deadlines are listed on the trust's website. The trustees typically meet in March, June, September and December to review applications. Applicants should expect to hear the outcome within 30 days of the given review date.

CONTACT DETAILS Phillipa Cridland, Trust Administrator, c/o Wright Vigar Ltd, 15 Newland, Lincoln, Lincolnshire LN1 1XG *Tel.* 01522 531341 *Website* www.michaelcornishcharity.org.uk

■ The Evan Cornish Foundation

CC NO 1112703   **ESTABLISHED** 2005

WHERE FUNDING CAN BE GIVEN UK, with a preference for the north of England, and overseas. International applicants must have a registered UK office.

WHO CAN BENEFIT Registered charities; not-for-profit organisations; CICs.

WHAT IS FUNDED Human rights; social and economic equality; education; health; the criminal justice system; older people; refugees and asylum seekers; homelessness; international projects which promote tolerance and equality for women or combat human rights violations.

WHAT IS NOT FUNDED Academic research; animal welfare; building work or repairs; flight costs; holiday club providers; individuals/gap year students; medical research; microfinance (unless the beneficiaries themselves control the finance and repayments); political activities and purpose.

TYPE OF GRANT Project funding.

RANGE OF GRANTS £1,000 to £50,000. First-time applicants should not apply for more than £5,000.

SAMPLE GRANTS Centre for Applied Human Rights University of York (£25,000); Whitehaven Community Trust Ltd (£10,000); Liverpool Cares (£5,000); Dementia UK (£2,000).

FINANCES *Financial year end* 05/04/2022
Income £179,200
Grants to organisations £628,600
Assets £10,470,000

TRUSTEES Sally Cornish; Rachel Cornish; Barbara Ward.

OTHER INFORMATION Organisations with projects in other areas of England or the UK (i.e. not based in the north of England) may still apply if their project: is unique in the UK; involves advocacy/policy work; or affects people in the UK prison system.

HOW TO APPLY Applications must be made through the foundation's website. Your application should include: a copy of your most recent accounts; a copy of your project budget; details of an independent, UK-based referee not affiliated to your organisation; supporting information about your project. The trustees meet three times a year. Check the website for application deadlines.

CONTACT DETAILS The Trustees, The Innovation Centre, 217 Portobello, Sheffield, South Yorkshire S1 4DP *Tel.* 0114 224 2230 *Email* contactus@evancornishfoundation.org.uk *Website* www.evancornishfoundation.org.uk

■ Cornwall Community Foundation

CC NO 1099977   **ESTABLISHED** 2003

WHERE FUNDING CAN BE GIVEN Cornwall and the Isles of Scilly.

WHO CAN BENEFIT Registered charities; voluntary or community groups; social enterprises; CICs; individuals.

WHAT IS FUNDED General charitable purposes.

WHAT IS NOT FUNDED Detailed eligibility criteria can be found on the foundation's website.

TYPE OF GRANT Programme dependent.

RANGE OF GRANTS Programme dependent.

SAMPLE GRANTS A list of successfully funded projects can be found on the foundation's website.

FINANCES *Financial year end* 31/12/2021
Income £3,740,000
Grants to organisations £2,420,000
Assets £10,600,000

TRUSTEES Jane Hartley; Daphne Skinnard; Timothy Smith; Toby Ashworth; Stamford Galsworthy; Kim Conchie; Jane Trahair; The Rt Revd Bishop Mounstephen; Gillian Pipkin; Daiman Baker; Jeremy Sharp; Mary Hosking; Verity Perham; Thomas Oss; Joseph Turnbull.

OTHER INFORMATION This is one of the 47 UK community foundations, which distribute funding for a wide range of purposes. As with all community foundations, there are a number of donor-advised funds managed on behalf of individuals, families and charitable trusts. Grant schemes tend to change frequently – consult the foundation's website for details of current programmes and up-to-date deadlines. Note that the grant total includes amounts awarded to individuals.

HOW TO APPLY Potential applicants are advised to visit the community foundation's website or contact its grants team to find the most suitable funding stream.

CONTACT DETAILS The Grants Team, 1 Sheers Barton, Lawhitton, Launceston, Cornwall PL15 9NJ *Tel.* 01566 779333 *Email* office@cornwallfoundation.com *Website* www.cornwallcommunityfoundation.com

■ The Corporation of Trinity House of Deptford Strond

CC NO 211869   **ESTABLISHED** 1514
WHERE FUNDING CAN BE GIVEN UK.
WHO CAN BENEFIT Charitable organisations related to seafarers.
WHAT IS FUNDED The education, safety, support and welfare of seafarers and their dependants.
TYPE OF GRANT Capital costs; project funding; strategic funding; development funding.
RANGE OF GRANTS £5,500 to £120,000.
SAMPLE GRANTS A list of beneficiaries was not included in the annual report and accounts. Previous beneficiaries have included: The Shipwrecked Mariners' Society (£110,000); Royal Alfred Seafarers' Society (£100,000); Sailors' Children's Society (£68,200); London Nautical School (£40,000); Combat Stress (£25,000); Care for Veterans (£10,000).
FINANCES *Financial year end* 31/03/2022
Income £10,690,000
Grants to organisations £1,570,000
Assets £275,480,000
TRUSTEES Capt. Roger Barker; Capt. Ian McNaught; Capt. Nigel Hope; Capt. Stephen Gobbi; Cdre William Walworth; Malcolm Glaister; Cdre Robert Dorey; Cdr Nigel Hare; Rear Admiral Ian Moncrieff; Lance Batchelor.
OTHER INFORMATION In 2021/22, grants were broken down as follows: youth opportunities and training (£720,000); lighthouse service (£320,000); other (£145,000); welfare (£15,000).
HOW TO APPLY Full information on how to apply for a grant can be found on the charity's website.
CONTACT DETAILS Vikki Muir, Head of Charitable Giving, Trinity House, Tower Hill, London EC3N 4DH *Tel.* 020 7481 6914 *Email* victoria.muir@trinityhouse.co.uk *Website* www.trinityhouse.co.uk/supporting-seafarers/maritime-charity

■ Corra Foundation

OSCR NO SC009481   **ESTABLISHED** 1986
WHERE FUNDING CAN BE GIVEN Scotland; Africa; Pakistan.
WHO CAN BENEFIT Charitable organisations.
WHAT IS FUNDED Social welfare; children and young people; homelessness; families affected by substance abuse; international development (Zambia, Rwanda, Malawi and Pakistan).
WHAT IS NOT FUNDED Exclusion criteria differ between grant programmes. See the website for further details.
TYPE OF GRANT Core costs; salaries; project funding.
SAMPLE GRANTS A list of beneficiaries was not included in the annual report and accounts.
FINANCES *Financial year end* 31/12/2021
Income £37,280,000
Grants to organisations £35,500,000
Assets £32,530,000
TRUSTEES Luke McCullough; Jude Turbyne; Joy Barlow; Nosheen Ahmed; Claire Gibson; David Johnson; Fiona Sandford; Richard Martin; Christine McLaughlin; Mildred Zimunya; Michaela Collins.
OTHER INFORMATION The foundation was previously known as Lloyds TSB Foundation for Scotland until it rebranded in August 2017. The foundation received its last payment from Lloyds Banking Group in February 2018 and now receives a large proportion of its income from the Scottish Government.
HOW TO APPLY Applications can be made via the foundation's website.

CONTACT DETAILS Grants Team, Office Suite 30, 4 Lochside Way, Edinburgh EH12 9DT *Tel.* 0131 444 4020 *Email* hello@corra.scot *Website* www.corra.scot

■ The Corton Hill Trust

CC NO 1186843   **ESTABLISHED** 2019
WHERE FUNDING CAN BE GIVEN Dorset; East Devon; Somerset.
WHO CAN BENEFIT Charitable organisations.
WHAT IS FUNDED General charitable purposes.
SAMPLE GRANTS A list of beneficiaries was not included in the annual report and accounts.
FINANCES *Financial year end* 13/11/2021
Income £5,120,000
Grants to organisations £704,600
Assets £12,850,000
TRUSTEES Ludlow Trust Company Ltd; Catherine Robinson; Nicholas Robinson.
OTHER INFORMATION The 2020/21 accounts were the latest available at the time of writing (June 2023).
HOW TO APPLY Apply in writing to the correspondent. The trust's Charity Commission record states that it is open to applications.
CONTACT DETAILS The Trustees, c/o Ludlow Trust Co. Ltd, Tower Wharf, Cheese Lane, Bristol BS2 0JJ *Tel.* 0117 313 8200 *Email* charitabletrusts@ludlowtrust.com

■ The Costa Family Charitable Trust

CC NO 221604   **ESTABLISHED** 1959
WHERE FUNDING CAN BE GIVEN UK.
WHO CAN BENEFIT Christian organisations; places of worship; hospitals; educational institutions; individuals.
WHAT IS FUNDED General charitable purposes; Christian causes.
RANGE OF GRANTS Mostly between £500 and £5,000, with the occasional larger grant.
SAMPLE GRANTS The Ecclesiastical Parish of St Paul – Hammersmith (£37,500); Alpha International (£15,000); British Red Cross and Grange Park Opera (£5,000 each); Royal Hospital Chelsea Appeal and St Paul's – Hammersmith (£2,000 each); Audacious Church and the Bible Reading Fellowship (£500 each).
FINANCES *Financial year end* 05/04/2022
Income £313,300
Grants to organisations £87,200
Grants to individuals £14,300
Assets £191,700
TRUSTEES Kenneth Costa; Ann Costa.
OTHER INFORMATION Eight individuals received grants during the year.
HOW TO APPLY Unsolicited applications are not accepted.
CONTACT DETAILS The Trustees, 35 Tite Street, London SW3 4JP *Tel.* 07785 467441

■ The Cotton Industry War Memorial Trust

CC NO 242721   **ESTABLISHED** 1947
WHERE FUNDING CAN BE GIVEN UK.
WHO CAN BENEFIT Individuals; organisations.
WHAT IS FUNDED The aid and assistance of employees, former employees and students of the textile industry.
RANGE OF GRANTS Up to £40,000.

SAMPLE GRANTS Huddersfield Textile Centre of Excellence (£40,000); Children's Adventure Farm Trust (£29,500); Seashell Trust (£25,000); Manchester University (£15,000); Blesma (£10,000); Orchid (£6,000); Chrysalis Holiday and SEN Manchester (£5,000 each).
FINANCES *Financial year end 31/12/2021*
Income £340,800
Grants to organisations £193,000
Grants to individuals £1,000
Assets £7,250,000
TRUSTEES Christopher Trotter; Peter Reid; Dr Michael Bartle; Alan Robinson; Adrian Abel; Peter Booth; Malcolm Jarvis; Peter Davey.
OTHER INFORMATION One individual was supported during the year.
HOW TO APPLY Apply in writing to the correspondent.
CONTACT DETAILS The Trustees, Stables Barn, Coldstones Farm, Bewerley, Harrogate, North Yorkshire HG3 5BJ *Tel.* 01706 341731 *Email* theciwmt@btinternet.com

■ The Coulthurst Trust

CC NO 209690   **ESTABLISHED** 1947
WHERE FUNDING CAN BE GIVEN UK, with a strong preference for the north of England, predominantly West and North Yorkshire and County Durham.
WHO CAN BENEFIT Registered charities.
WHAT IS FUNDED General charitable purposes.
WHAT IS NOT FUNDED Individuals.
SAMPLE GRANTS A list of beneficiaries was not available.
FINANCES *Financial year end 05/04/2022*
Income £21,900
Grants to organisations £87,000
TRUSTEES Iain Blair; Phillipa Dickens.
OTHER INFORMATION Full accounts were not available to view on the Charity Commission's website due to the trust's low income. Therefore, we have estimated the grant total based on the trust's total expenditure.
HOW TO APPLY Apply in writing to the correspondent.
CONTACT DETAILS The Trustees, Winterburn Grange, Winterburn, Skipton, North Yorkshire BD23 3QR *Tel.* 01756 700110 *Email* mail@ fosterlawsolicitors.com

■ The County Council of Dyfed Welsh Church Fund

CC NO 506583   **ESTABLISHED** 1977
WHERE FUNDING CAN BE GIVEN Carmarthenshire; Ceredigion; Pembrokeshire.
WHO CAN BENEFIT Churches and chapels; charitable organisations benefitting people in the local area; individuals.
WHAT IS FUNDED Maintenance of places of worship; the advancement of education; arts and culture; social welfare; the advancement of religion; general charitable purposes that benefit the local community.
TYPE OF GRANT Project funding; capital costs; core costs.
RANGE OF GRANTS Up to £10,000, but mostly £1,000 to £3,000.
SAMPLE GRANTS St Elli Parish Church (£10,000); St John's The Baptist Church (£6,800); St Mary's Church – Carew (£5,000); Carmarthen and District Youth Opera and Cilycwm Community Centre (£3,000 each); Pontyates Welfare Hall (£2,500); Pontyates RFC (£2,000); Marish Congregational Chapel (£1,200).

FINANCES *Financial year end 31/03/2022*
Income £88,500
Grants to organisations £57,000
Assets £5,470,000
TRUSTEES Jonathan Haswell; Stephen Johnson; Chris Moore.
OTHER INFORMATION The breakdown of grants awarded throughout 2021/22 by region is as follows: Carmarthenshire (£36,500); Ceredigion (£16,900); Pembrokeshire (£3,600).
HOW TO APPLY Apply in writing to the correspondent.
CONTACT DETAILS The Trustees, Corporate Services, County Hall, Carmarthen, Carmarthenshire SA31 1JP *Tel.* 01267 224180 *Email* AParnell@ carmarthenshire.gov.uk

■ County Durham Community Foundation

CC NO 1047625   **ESTABLISHED** 1995
WHERE FUNDING CAN BE GIVEN County Durham.
WHO CAN BENEFIT Registered charities; unregistered charities; CICs; social enterprises; PTAs; individuals.
WHAT IS FUNDED General charitable purposes including: social welfare; the environment; arts and culture; sport and recreation; community development; health; education.
WHAT IS NOT FUNDED Programme-specific exclusions can be found on the foundation's website.
TYPE OF GRANT Capital costs; core/revenue costs; project funding; seed funding/start-up funding.
RANGE OF GRANTS Programme dependent.
SAMPLE GRANTS A list of beneficiaries was not included in the annual report and accounts.
FINANCES *Financial year end 31/03/2022*
Income £3,850,000
Grants to organisations £4,580,000
Grants to individuals £172,900
Assets £19,460,000
TRUSTEES Prof. Ray Hudson; Stephen Hall; James Fenwick; Ann Dolphin; Emily Burns; Rebecca Armstrong; Emma O'Rourke; Emma Glover.
OTHER INFORMATION This is one of the 47 UK community foundations, which distribute funding for a wide range of purposes. As with all community foundations, there are a number of donor-advised funds managed on behalf of individuals, families and charitable trusts. Grant schemes tend to change frequently – consult the foundation's website for details of current programmes and up-to-date deadlines.
HOW TO APPLY Potential applicants are advised to visit the community foundation's website or contact its grants team to find the most suitable funding stream.
CONTACT DETAILS The Grants Team, Victoria House, Whitfield Court, St John's Road, Meadowfield Industrial Estate, Durham, County Durham DH7 8XL *Tel.* 0191 378 6340 *Email* info@cdcf. org.uk *Website* www.cdcf.org.uk

■ Countypier Ltd

CC NO 295399
WHERE FUNDING CAN BE GIVEN UK.
WHO CAN BENEFIT Mainly Jewish charitable organisations.
WHAT IS FUNDED Promotion of the Orthodox Jewish faith; social welfare.
TYPE OF GRANT Unrestricted funding.
RANGE OF GRANTS £13,000 to £63,800.
SAMPLE GRANTS Friends of Sanz Institutions (£63,000); Chevras Mo'oz Ladol (£37,200); Friends of Boyan Trust (£36,500); Friends of

Mercaz Hatorah Belz Macnivka (£25,000); Beth Midrash Lemoroth (£13,000).
FINANCES *Financial year end* 31/03/2022
Income £858,900
Grants to organisations £263,500
Assets £7,010,000
TRUSTEES Ahron Halpern; Esther Halpern; Chana Klein.
OTHER INFORMATION In 2021/22, seven grants were awarded.
HOW TO APPLY Apply in writing to the correspondent.
CONTACT DETAILS The Trustees, Greenwood Student House, 29–31 Station Road, London N22 6UX *Tel.* 020 8881 3080

■ Coutts Charitable Foundation

CC NO 1150784   **ESTABLISHED** 2013
WHERE FUNDING CAN BE GIVEN UK.
WHO CAN BENEFIT Charitable organisations.
WHAT IS FUNDED The prevention of poverty (particularly focused on women and girls in the UK).
RANGE OF GRANTS Typically £90,000 to £150,000.
SAMPLE GRANTS The Preston Road Women's Centre (£150,000); Travelling Light (£105,000); WomenCentre Ltd (£50,000); End Violence Against Women (£40,000).
FINANCES *Financial year end* 01/04/2022
Income £561,300
Grants to organisations £796,800
Assets £3,800,000
TRUSTEES Lord Waldegrave of North Hill; Dr Linda Yueh; Alison Rose-Slade; Peter Flavel; Rachel Harrington; Judith McNeill; Laura Lines; Linda Urquhart; Lord Philip Remnant.
OTHER INFORMATION Grants were made to 11 organisations during the year.
HOW TO APPLY The foundation does not accept unsolicited applications. However, its website states the following: 'if you wish to bring information about your organisation or programmes that fit with our funding priorities to our attention, complete the information submission form and either email it to us or post it.' The foundation will then be in touch if the trustees wish to learn more. Refer to the foundation's website for more details.
CONTACT DETAILS The Trustees, c/o Coutts & Co., 440 Strand, London WC2R 0QS *Tel.* 020 7753 1000 *Email* coutts.foundation@coutts.com *Website* www.coutts.com/coutts-foundation.html

■ Coventry Building Society Charitable Foundation

CC NO 1072244   **ESTABLISHED** 1998
WHERE FUNDING CAN BE GIVEN Coventry and Warwickshire.
WHO CAN BENEFIT Registered charities and community groups.
WHAT IS FUNDED General charitable purposes. Priority is given to groups or activities aimed at improving quality of life and opportunities in communities affected by disadvantage, deprivation and social exclusion.
TYPE OF GRANT One-off.
RANGE OF GRANTS £35,000 to £50,000.
SAMPLE GRANTS Coventry Citizens Advice, Grapevine and Positive Youth Foundation (£50,000 each); The Belgrade Theatre Trust and Central England Law Centre (£40,000 each); Age UK and St Francis Employability (£35,000 each).
FINANCES *Financial year end* 31/12/2021
Income £388,700
Grants to organisations £300,000
Assets £15,400
TRUSTEES Tina Jones; Matthew Mannings; Kevin Purvey.
OTHER INFORMATION This is the charitable foundation of Coventry Building Society. Grants are awarded to registered charities and community groups in Coventry and Warwickshire and are administered by the Heart of England Community Foundation. It has two funding streams for organisations: the Cost of Living Fund and Coventry Building Society Small Grants.
HOW TO APPLY To apply and for further information, visit www.heartofenglandcf.co.uk/available-grants.
CONTACT DETAILS Miss A. Thompson, Secretary, Coventry Building Society, Oak Tree Court, Harry Weston Road, Coventry, Warwickshire CV3 2UN *Tel.* 0800 121 8899 *Website* www.coventrybuildingsociety.co.uk/member/why-choose-us/in-the-community.html

■ The Noel Coward Foundation

CC NO 1178029   **ESTABLISHED** 2000
WHERE FUNDING CAN BE GIVEN UK.
WHO CAN BENEFIT Arts organisations.
WHAT IS FUNDED The arts.
WHAT IS NOT FUNDED Production costs; individuals.
TYPE OF GRANT Single grants for specific projects.
SAMPLE GRANTS Mousetrap Theatre Projects and New Adventure in Motion Pictures (£5,000 each); The Royal Court (£4,000); Traverse Theatre (£3,400); National Student Drama Festival (£3,000); The Mono Box (£2,300); English Touring Theatre (£2,200); Gate Theatre (£1,000).
FINANCES *Financial year end* 31/03/2022
Income £96,500
Grants to organisations £191,500
Assets £535,000
TRUSTEES Alan Brodie; Peter Kyle; Robert Lee.
OTHER INFORMATION Priority is given to organisations with a strong educational element and those with particular, but not exclusive, emphasis on supporting people entering or in the early stages of a career in the arts. During 2021/22, grants were distributed as follows: theatre (£116,700); education (£52,000); other (£14,500); workshops (£8,400).
HOW TO APPLY Application cover sheets can be downloaded from the foundation's website, where application deadlines can also be found. The foundation encourages interested organisations to get in touch before submitting an application to discuss suitability and ensure all the required information is provided.
CONTACT DETAILS The Grants Committee, 14 The Barbon Buildings, Red Lion Square, London WC1 4QH *Tel.* 020 7253 6226 *Email* ncf@alanbrodie.com *Website* www.noelcoward.org

■ The Sir Tom Cowie Charitable Trust

CC NO 1096936   **ESTABLISHED** 2003
WHERE FUNDING CAN BE GIVEN City of Sunderland and County Durham.
WHO CAN BENEFIT Registered charities.
WHAT IS FUNDED General charitable purposes including the natural environment; heritage; social welfare; the environment; children and young people.

WHAT IS NOT FUNDED Individuals; national or international charities seeking partial funding for large projects.

TYPE OF GRANT Capital costs; project funding.

RANGE OF GRANTS Usually up to £20,000.

SAMPLE GRANTS Foundation of Light (£50,000); University of Sunderland Development Trust (£20,000); Wear Rivers Trust (£16,800); St Mark's Community Centre (£10,000); Castletown Scout Group (£5,000); Sunderland Community Transport (£2,000); 7 Colombo Road (£200); Willow Hospice (£50).

FINANCES *Financial year end 31/08/2021*
Income £107,300
Grants to organisations £171,300
Assets £5,980,000

TRUSTEES Peter Blackett; Lady Diana Cowie; David Gray.

OTHER INFORMATION Grants were awarded to 20 organisations during the year. The 2020/21 accounts were the latest available at the time of writing (May 2023).

HOW TO APPLY Application forms can be completed and submitted on the trust's website, or downloaded and returned to the mailing address.

CONTACT DETAILS Emma Gray, Grants Administrator, Estate Office, Broadwood Hall, Lanchester, Durham, County Durham DH7 0TN *Tel.* 01207 529663 *Email* ecg@graysllp.co.uk *Website* www.stcct.co.uk

■ Dudley and Geoffrey Cox Charitable Trust

CC NO 277761   **ESTABLISHED** 1979

WHERE FUNDING CAN BE GIVEN UK, with a preference for London and the South East.

WHO CAN BENEFIT Registered charities; hospices; schools; universities.

WHAT IS FUNDED Medical research; young people; social welfare; education.

RANGE OF GRANTS Generally £5,000 to £10,000.

SAMPLE GRANTS Merchant Taylors' School (£50,000); University of Sheffield (£45,000); The Prince's Trust (£15,000); Mind (£10,000); Alzheimer's Society (£5,000); Anglia Ruskin University (£500).

FINANCES *Financial year end 31/12/2021*
Income £173,800
Grants to organisations £360,000
Assets £10,710,000

TRUSTEES Michael Boyle; Ian Ferres; John Wosner; Peter Watkins; Peter Magill.

OTHER INFORMATION Grants were broken down as follows: youth and welfare (£195,000); medical causes (£110,000); education (£55,000).

HOW TO APPLY Unsolicited applications are not accepted.

CONTACT DETAILS Charities Officer, Merchant Taylors' Company, 30 Threadneedle Street, London EC2R 8JB *Tel.* 020 7450 4440 *Email* charities@merchant-taylors.co.uk

■ The Sir William Coxen Trust Fund

CC NO 206936   **ESTABLISHED** 1940

WHERE FUNDING CAN BE GIVEN England.

WHO CAN BENEFIT Hospitals or charitable organisations carrying out orthopaedic work.

WHAT IS FUNDED Orthopaedic work.

WHAT IS NOT FUNDED Individuals; non-charitable institutions.

RANGE OF GRANTS £5,000 to £60,000.

SAMPLE GRANTS University of East Anglia (£70,000); Bone Canver Trust (£20,000); Kidscan (£2,000).

FINANCES *Financial year end 31/03/2022*
Income £98,800
Grants to organisations £155,300
Assets £2,790,000

TRUSTEES Alderman Masojada; Alderman Parmley; Sir Peter Estlin; Nicholas Lyons; John Garbutt; Christopher Makin.

HOW TO APPLY Apply in writing to the correspondent.

CONTACT DETAILS Lorraine Brook, Town Clerk, The Town Clerk's Office, Corporation of London, PO Box 270, Guildhall, London EC2P 2EJ *Tel.* 020 7332 1409 *Email* grants@cityoflondon.gov.uk

■ The Lord Cozens-Hardy Trust

CC NO 264237   **ESTABLISHED** 1972

WHERE FUNDING CAN BE GIVEN UK, with a preference for Norfolk.

WHO CAN BENEFIT Registered charities.

WHAT IS FUNDED General charitable purposes; medicine; health; social welfare; education.

WHAT IS NOT FUNDED Individuals.

TYPE OF GRANT Capital costs; core/revenue costs.

RANGE OF GRANTS Mostly £5,000 or less.

SAMPLE GRANTS Huntington's Disease Association (£20,000); The Guide Dogs for the Blind Association (£7,000); Priscilla Bacon Hospice and YMCA Norfolk (£5,000 each); Deafblind UK, International Spinal Research Trust, The Migraine Trust and Parkinson's UK (£1,000 each).

FINANCES *Financial year end 05/04/2022*
Income £59,700
Grants to organisations £100,000
Assets £3,850,000

TRUSTEES John Phelps; Linda Phelps; Justin Ripman; Benjamin Phelps.

OTHER INFORMATION Only organisations that received grants of over £1,000 were listed as beneficiaries in the trust's accounts. Grants of under £1,000 totalled £7,000.

HOW TO APPLY Apply in writing to the correspondent. Applications are reviewed annually, usually in January; applications should be made between October and December.

CONTACT DETAILS The Trustees, PO Box 28, Holt, Norfolk NR25 7WH *Tel.* 01603 693303

■ The CPF Trust

CC NO 1191787   **ESTABLISHED** 1971

WHERE FUNDING CAN BE GIVEN UK and overseas.

WHO CAN BENEFIT Charitable organisations.

WHAT IS FUNDED General charitable purposes.

RANGE OF GRANTS Mostly £500 to £3,000.

SAMPLE GRANTS Eton College (£27,500); Alzheimer's UK (£3,000); Age UK and Samaritans (£2,000 each); Anne Robson Trust, Classics for All and Woodland Trust (£1,000 each); Friends of the National Libraries (£500).

FINANCES *Financial year end 05/04/2022*
Income £123,900
Grants to organisations £80,000
Assets £2,160,000

TRUSTEES Sir Charles Matthew Farrer; Jenett Farrer; Dr Isobel Pinder; Nicola Guthrie.

HOW TO APPLY Apply in writing to the correspondent.

CONTACT DETAILS The Trustees, 6 Priory Avenue, London W4 1TX *Tel.* 020 8994 6052 *Email* jcfarrer@gmail.com

■ Craignish Trust

OSCR NO SC016882   **ESTABLISHED** 1961
WHERE FUNDING CAN BE GIVEN UK, with a preference for Scotland.
WHO CAN BENEFIT Registered charities.
WHAT IS FUNDED General charitable purposes; the environment; animal conservation; human rights, including refugees and asylum seekers; peace and conflict resolution.
RANGE OF GRANTS Mostly up to £5,000, with the occasional larger grant.
SAMPLE GRANTS Seawilding (£38,200); Dynamic Earth and Plantlife (£10,000 each); the Open Seas Trust (£8,400); Conservation Collective, Endangered Species Protection Agency and Scottish Environmental LINK (£5,000 each); Buglife Scotland, Environmental Funders Network and Refugee Survival Trust (£3,000 each); Association for the Protection of Rural Scotland, East Ayrshire Coalfield Environment Initiative and Edinburgh Remakery (£2,000 each); The Touring Network (£1,000).
FINANCES *Financial year end* 05/04/2022
Income £150,300
Grants to organisations £171,200
Assets £8,730,000
HOW TO APPLY Apply in writing to the correspondent.
CONTACT DETAILS The Trustees, c/o Geoghegans Chartered Accountants, 6 St Colme Street, Edinburgh EH3 6AD

■ CRASH

CC NO 1054107   **ESTABLISHED** 1996
WHERE FUNDING CAN BE GIVEN UK.
WHO CAN BENEFIT UK-registered charities; hospices.
WHAT IS FUNDED Homelessness charities and hospices' building projects.
WHAT IS NOT FUNDED Details on exclusions can be found on the charity's website.
TYPE OF GRANT Capital costs.
RANGE OF GRANTS Up to £40,000.
SAMPLE GRANTS Emmaus Village Carlton (£80,000); Emmaus Community South Lambeth and Surrey (£36,000); Herriot Hospice – Thirsk and Kairos Community Trust – London (£30,000 each); Emmaus Community Coventry and Warwickshire (£26,300); Winchester Churches Nightshelter (£20,000); Mary Stevens Hospice – Stourbridge (£15,000).
FINANCES *Financial year end* 31/03/2022
Income £871,300
Grants to organisations £186,500
Assets £949,900
TRUSTEES Alan Brookes; Kevin Corbett; Fiona Duncombe; Ian Bolster; Matthew Pullen; John O'Grady; James Wimpenny; David McGarry.
OTHER INFORMATION The charity provides grants, pro bono consultancy services and free-of-charge or discounted building materials. Project grants were awarded to seven organisations during 2021/22. An additional £217,900 was awarded as gifts in kind.
HOW TO APPLY Applications can be made through the charity's website. The charity's website states: 'Call us on 07951 446 531 and ask to speak to our Projects Manager who will discuss your project with you and determine whether your project is eligible.' The Project Manager will advise if further support is available and if so, in what form (i.e. professional expertise, construction products or grants).
CONTACT DETAILS Projects Manager, The Gatehouse, 2 Devonhurst Place, Heathfield Terrace, London W4 4JD   *Tel.* 020 8742 0717 or 07951 446 531 (ask to speak to the Projects Manager). *Email* info@crash.org.uk   *Website* www.crash.org.uk

■ Michael Crawford Children's Charity

CC NO 1042211   **ESTABLISHED** 1994
WHERE FUNDING CAN BE GIVEN England and Wales.
WHO CAN BENEFIT Registered charities.
WHAT IS FUNDED Children and young people; social welfare; health.
SAMPLE GRANTS Sick Children's Trust (£50,000); Strongbones (£15,000); Handicapped Children's Action Group (£10,000); DEMAND (£10,000); Designability (£5,000).
FINANCES *Financial year end* 31/10/2021
Income £67,500
Grants to organisations £100,000
Assets £6,550,000
TRUSTEES Alan Clark; Michael Crawford; Kenneth Dias; Natasha MacAller.
OTHER INFORMATION The 2020/21 accounts were the latest available to view at the time of writing (June 2023).
HOW TO APPLY Apply in writing to the correspondent.
CONTACT DETAILS The Trustees, Regina House, 124 Finchley Road, London NW3 5JS   *Tel.* 020 7433 2400

■ The Elizabeth Creak Charitable Trust

CC NO 286838   **ESTABLISHED** 1983
WHERE FUNDING CAN BE GIVEN UK, with a preference for Warwickshire.
WHO CAN BENEFIT Charities; training bodies; universities.
WHAT IS FUNDED Agricultural education and support; life sciences education.
SAMPLE GRANTS Warwick Hub (£71,800); Henry Plumb Foundation (£69,600); Studley College (£33,000); Newcastle University (£27,500); Sir Harold Hillier Gardens (£25,000).
FINANCES *Financial year end* 31/03/2022
Income £1,450,000
Grants to organisations £511,800
Assets £33,170,000
TRUSTEES John Hulse; Johnathan May; Nicholas Abell.
OTHER INFORMATION Grants were distributed as follows: life sciences education (£242,200); agricultural national support (£221,800); other local projects (£47,800). Only beneficiaries that received grants of over £25,000 were listed in the trust's accounts. Grants of less than £25,000 totalled £176,400.
HOW TO APPLY Apply in writing to the correspondent. The trustees usually meet every two months to consider grant applications.
CONTACT DETAILS The Trustees, 27 Widney Road, Knowle, Solihull, West Midlands B93 9DX   *Tel.* 01564 773951   *Email* creakcharity@hotmail.com

■ Creative Scotland

ESTABLISHED 2010
WHERE FUNDING CAN BE GIVEN Scotland.
WHO CAN BENEFIT Organisations and individuals.
WHAT IS FUNDED Arts, film and creative industries.

WHAT IS NOT FUNDED Most programmes have their own specific exclusions, details of which are available on the Creative Scotland website.

TYPE OF GRANT Project funding; core costs.

RANGE OF GRANTS Programme dependent.

SAMPLE GRANTS International Entertainment Holdings Ltd (£1.45 million); Aberdeen Stage Crew Ltd, Culture and Sport Glasgow and Shetland Arts Development Agency (£242,400 each); Sistema Scotland and Station House Media Unit (£150,000 each); The Glasgow Barons, Live Music Now Scotland and Take Me Somewhere Ltd (£100,000 each); David Dale Gallery and Studios (£80,000); Dumfries and Galloway Art Festival, Kelburn Arts Ltd and Utopia Costumes Ltd (£50,000 each); Beyond Presents Ltd, Glasgow Zine Library and NoFit State Community Circus Ltd (£25,000 each); Big Hand Events Ltd, Giant Step and Smalltown Audio Ltd (£10,000 each); African Connections and Tribute Act Entertainment (£5,000 each); Bunbury Banter (£1,000).

FINANCES *Financial year end 31/03/2022*
Income £35,870,000
Grants to organisations £153,760,000
Assets £27,100,000

TRUSTEES Malath Abbas; Yahya Berry; David Brew; Duncan Cockburn; Duncan Hendry; Stephanie Fraser; Philip Long; Carol Main; Sarah Munro; Elizabeth Partyka; David Strachan; Robert Wilson.

OTHER INFORMATION The grant total represents the net grants issued, taken from Creative Scotland's consolidated report. Note that the grant total may include grants awarded to individuals. Grants were broken down as follows: COVID-19 emergency fund (£69.24 million); targeted funding (£34.42 million); regular funding (£33.87 million); open project funding (£13.81 million); touring fund (£2.4 million).

HOW TO APPLY Visit Creative Scotland's website for information on how to apply.

CONTACT DETAILS Enquiries Service, Waverley Gate, 2–4 Waterloo Place, Edinburgh EH1 3EG *Tel.* 0345 603 6000 (unavailable at the time of writing in May 2023 due to office closure – email to request a call back). *Email* enquiries@creativescotland.com *Website* www.creativescotland.com

---

■ Credit Suisse EMEA Foundation

CC NO 1122472   **ESTABLISHED** 2007

WHERE FUNDING CAN BE GIVEN Countries where Credit Suisse has offices in Europe, the Middle East and Africa.

WHO CAN BENEFIT Registered charities; early-stage organisations and initiatives.

WHAT IS FUNDED The education and training of children and young people; financial inclusion.

WHAT IS NOT FUNDED Proposals that directly replace or subsidise statutory funding or for activities that are the responsibility of statutory bodies; administration and costs not directly associated with the application; individuals; promotion of religious or political causes; holidays; retrospective expenditure; general appeals; animal welfare; festivals, sports and leisure activities.

TYPE OF GRANT Project funding; multi-year partnerships (one to five years); development funding; salaries; core costs.

RANGE OF GRANTS Typically up to £250,000.

SAMPLE GRANTS City Year UK (£296,800); ThinkForward UK (£200,000); Learning with Parents (£100,000); Young Enterprise (£50,000); Cancer Research UK (£31,000).

FINANCES *Financial year end 31/12/2021*
Income £1,430,000
Grants to organisations £1,100,000
Assets £2,190,000

TRUSTEES Colin Hely-Hutchinson; Mark Ellis; Marc Pereira-Mendoza; Guy Varney; Sean Alleyne; Ian Hale; Karen Newton; Caroline Waddington; Matthew Weston; Katarzyna Jozefowicz; Mark Walsh; Katarzyna Sejwa; Jeremy Lewis; Samantha Ruston.

OTHER INFORMATION The foundation's core grant-making programme funds registered charities that fulfil its mission in Europe, the Middle East and Africa. Grants were made to 11 organisations during the year, some of which formed part of multi-year commitments.

HOW TO APPLY Credit Suisse coordinates grant-making on a regional basis within four regions of the world. Contact your local Credit Suisse office for further information.

CONTACT DETAILS Corporate Citizenship Team, Credit Suisse, 1 Cabot Square, London E14 4QJ *Tel.* 020 7888 8888 *Email* emea.corporatecitizenship@credit-suisse.com *Website* www.credit-suisse.com/about-us/en/our-company/corporate-responsibility/economy-society/emea.html

---

■ The Crerar Trust

CC NO 221335   **ESTABLISHED** 1903

WHERE FUNDING CAN BE GIVEN Areas where Crerar Hotels are based or have interests (mainly Scotland).

WHO CAN BENEFIT Charitable organisations.

WHAT IS FUNDED Disadvantaged groups; social welfare.

TYPE OF GRANT Capital costs; project funding.

SAMPLE GRANTS Isle of Mull Shore and Woodland Walk (£50,000); Springboard Charity (£10,000).

FINANCES *Financial year end 05/04/2022*
Income £90,600
Grants to organisations £60,000
Assets £11,780,000

TRUSTEES Crerar Trustee Company 1 Ltd; Crerar Trustee Company 2 Ltd.

HOW TO APPLY Apply in writing to the correspondent.

CONTACT DETAILS Claire Smith, General Secretary, The Mill House, Samuelston, East Lothian EH41 4HG *Tel.* 01620 822051 *Email* clerk@crerartrust.com

---

■ CRH Charitable Trust

CC NO 213579   **ESTABLISHED** 1842

WHERE FUNDING CAN BE GIVEN Cheshire East; Cheshire West; Chester; Cumbria; Greater Manchester; Lancashire.

WHO CAN BENEFIT Charitable organisations.

WHAT IS FUNDED Mental health; health; people with disabilities; children and young people; social welfare; medical research.

RANGE OF GRANTS Between £1,000 and £19,000.

SAMPLE GRANTS SPACE (£19,000); Cheshire Young Carers (£10,000); Growing Well (£7,500); Key Changes (£6,250); The Galaxy (£3,000); Pear Tree School (£1,000).

FINANCES *Financial year end 31/03/2022*
Income £136,400
Grants to organisations £210,100
Assets £9,840,000

TRUSTEES Peter Stafford; Dr Declan Hyland; Amanda Falk; Hugh Rylands; Diana Colquhoun.

OTHER INFORMATION A total of 33 grants were awarded in 2021/22.

HOW TO APPLY Apply in writing to the correspondent including a summary of your proposal.

CONTACT DETAILS B. Peak, Secretary, c/o Beyond Profit Ltd, G104 Bolton Arena, Arena Approach, Horwich, Bolton BL6 6LB *Tel.* 01204 414317 *Email* crhcharitabletrust@gmail.com

■ Cripplegate Foundation

CC NO 207499 **ESTABLISHED** 1891

WHERE FUNDING CAN BE GIVEN The London Borough of Islington and part of the City of London.

WHO CAN BENEFIT Registered charities; unregistered charities; CICs; social enterprises.

WHAT IS FUNDED Community work for disadvantaged residents including: advice and access to services; financial inclusion and capability; investing in young people; mental health and well-being; reaching isolated people; family support.

WHAT IS NOT FUNDED Political parties; political lobbying; churches or other religious bodies where the monies will be used for religious purposes/promotion of religion; work which does not benefit Islington residents; individuals (except through identified partners); medical or academic research; expenses that have already been incurred; projects that have already taken place; residential care services or residential facilities; general appeals; trips/outings (unless part of a bigger project); debts.

TYPE OF GRANT Core/revenue costs; project funding.

RANGE OF GRANTS £1,700 to £300,000.

SAMPLE GRANTS A list of beneficiaries was not included in the annual report and accounts.

FINANCES *Financial year end* 31/12/2021
Income £2,310,000
Grants to organisations £1,520,000
Assets £50,760,000

TRUSTEE Cripplegate Foundation Ltd.

OTHER INFORMATION Grants to organisations were made through three different programmes, some in partnership with Islington Giving and Islington Council.

HOW TO APPLY Funding programmes open at different times of the year. Application forms and guidance documents are made available on the foundation's website when programmes open. See the foundation's 'Support and Funding' webpage for more information.

CONTACT DETAILS Programme Team, 13 Elliott's Place, Islington, London N1 8HX *Tel.* 020 7288 6940 *Email* grants@cripplegate.org.uk *Website* www.cripplegate.org

■ Crisis UK

CC NO 1082947 **ESTABLISHED** 1967

WHERE FUNDING CAN BE GIVEN England; Scotland; Wales.

WHO CAN BENEFIT Registered charities; housing associations; individuals.

WHAT IS FUNDED Homelessness.

RANGE OF GRANTS Programme dependent.

SAMPLE GRANTS Ashley Community Housing; Birmingham and Solihull Women's Aid; Churches Housing Action Team; Emmaus Bristol; Justlife; Only a Pavement Away; Spitalfields Crypt Trust; YMCA Dulverton Group.

FINANCES *Financial year end* 30/06/2022
Income £64,830,000
Grants to organisations £279,000
Grants to individuals £58,000
Assets £39,450,000

TRUSTEES Charlotte Bates; Waqar Ahmed; Ezechi Britton; Kathleen Palmer; Sapna Dutta; Tristia Harrison; Alison Wallace; Robert Weston; Victoria Fox; Geetha Rabindrakumar; Terrie Alafat; Martin Cheeseman; Damien Regent.

OTHER INFORMATION Examples of beneficiaries are taken from the charity's website.

HOW TO APPLY Refer to the website for application forms and deadlines for any current grant schemes.

CONTACT DETAILS The Trustees, 66 Commercial Street, London E1 6LT *Tel.* 0300 636 1967 *Email* enquiries@crisis.org.uk *Website* www.crisis.org.uk

■ The Cross Trust

CC NO 1127046 **ESTABLISHED** 2008

WHERE FUNDING CAN BE GIVEN UK and overseas.

WHO CAN BENEFIT Registered charities; unregistered charities; schools; religious bodies/institutions; individuals.

WHAT IS FUNDED Social welfare; the advancement of religious and secular education; the advancement of the Christian faith in the UK and overseas.

RANGE OF GRANTS Up to £10,000, with the occasional larger grant.

SAMPLE GRANTS Beneficiaries include: Latimer Church Trust (£1.5 million); Luckley House (£764,700); SASRA (£125,000); Friends of JBC (£50,000); Presby Church and Tyndale House (£30,000 each); Mauritian Bible Training Institute and TNT Ministries (£10,000 each); EWS for Jesus (£7,000); Xcaliba Ltd (£220).

FINANCES *Financial year end* 05/04/2022
Income £4,750,000
Grants to organisations £4,530,000
Grants to individuals £8,500
Assets £2,540,000

TRUSTEES Michael Farmer; Jenny Farmer; Douglas Olsen; Antonia Richards.

HOW TO APPLY Apply in writing to the correspondent.

CONTACT DETAILS The Trustees, c/o Cansdales Audit LLP, St Mary's Court, The Broadway, Old Amersham, Buckinghamshire HP7 0UT *Tel.* 01494 765428 *Email* mailto@cansdales.co.uk

■ The Croydon Relief-in-Need Charity

CC NO 810114 **ESTABLISHED** 1962

WHERE FUNDING CAN BE GIVEN The London Borough of Croydon.

WHO CAN BENEFIT Local charities; individuals.

WHAT IS FUNDED Health; social welfare.

TYPE OF GRANT One-off project grants; core costs.

SAMPLE GRANTS Youth Zone (£75,000); Croydon Vision (£33,300); Age UK (£20,000); National Autistic Society (£2,400); PDSA (£1,000).

FINANCES *Financial year end* 31/12/2021
Income £200,000
Grants to organisations £211,700
Grants to individuals £2,000
Assets (£290)

TRUSTEE Croydon Almshouse Charities Trustee Company Ltd.

HOW TO APPLY Application forms are available from the charity's website.

CONTACT DETAILS Tessa Damer, Elis David Almshouses, Duppas Hill Terrace, Croydon CR0 4BT *Tel.* 020 8688 2649 *Email* tessadamer@croydonalmshouses.org.uk *Website* www.croydonalmshouses.org.uk

■ The Crucible Foundation

CC NO 1195787 **ESTABLISHED** 2021
WHERE FUNDING CAN BE GIVEN England and Wales.
WHO CAN BENEFIT Registered charities; community foundations.
WHAT IS FUNDED General charitable purposes.
RANGE OF GRANTS Mostly around £50,000.
SAMPLE GRANTS Susila Dharma Britain (£60,000); Community Foundation for Calderdale, Greencuisine Trust, London Community Foundation, Playback Theatre South West, Refugees at Home and Sussex Community Foundation (£50,000 each).
FINANCES *Financial year end 05/04/2022*
Income £50,340,000
Grants to organisations £360,000
Assets £46,940,000
TRUSTEE TLT Trustees Ltd.
HOW TO APPLY Apply in writing to the correspondent.
CONTACT DETAILS The Trustees, TLT Solicitors, 1 Redcliff Street, Bristol BS1 6TP *Tel.* 0333 006 0000 *Email* tltcharities@tltsolicitors.com

■ The Peter Cruddas Foundation

CC NO 1117323 **ESTABLISHED** 2006
WHERE FUNDING CAN BE GIVEN England and Wales.
WHO CAN BENEFIT Charitable organisations registered with The Charity Commission benefitting young people in England and Wales only.
WHAT IS FUNDED Projects supporting disadvantaged and disengaged young people (aged 16 to 30) with pathways into education, training and employment, including work experience/skills projects and youth work in London, especially evening work.
WHAT IS NOT FUNDED CICs; social enterprises; capital appeals; individuals; Scottish and Irish charities.
RANGE OF GRANTS Mostly up to £10,000.
SAMPLE GRANTS GOSH Charity (£35,000); Community Security Trust (£15,000); Ambitious about Autism (£10,000); Aspire Oxfordshire (£5,000); Cancer Research UK (£500).
FINANCES *Financial year end 31/03/2022*
Income £312,500
Grants to organisations £270,100
Assets £150,200
TRUSTEES Lord Peter Cruddas; Martin Paisner; The Rt Hon. Lord Young of Graffham.
OTHER INFORMATION Other forms of support are available to those the foundation cannot support financially, such as mentoring, business planning and networking events.
HOW TO APPLY The foundation operates an invitation-only application policy.
CONTACT DETAILS Stephen Cox, Company Secretary and Foundation Administrator, 133 Houndsditch, London EC3A 7BX *Tel.* 020 3003 8360 *Email* s.cox@petercruddasfoundation.org.uk *Website* www.petercruddasfoundation.org.uk

■ Cruden Foundation Ltd

OSCR NO SC004987 **ESTABLISHED** 1956
WHERE FUNDING CAN BE GIVEN Scotland.
WHO CAN BENEFIT Registered charities.
WHAT IS FUNDED Social welfare; medical causes; arts; education; heritage and conservation.
WHAT IS NOT FUNDED Individuals; capital development projects.
TYPE OF GRANT Capital costs; core/revenue costs; project funding.
RANGE OF GRANTS Up to £25,000.
SAMPLE GRANTS Edinburgh International Festival (£25,000); Pitlochry Festival Theatre (£15,000);

Street Soccer – Scotland (£10,000); Horatio's Garden (£5,000); Scottish Chamber Orchestra (£3,000); Borders Children's Charity, Sepsis Research – FEAT and St Andrew's Hospice (£2,500 each).
FINANCES *Financial year end 31/07/2022*
Income £391,600
Grants to organisations £346,700
Assets £13,430,000
TRUSTEES John Rafferty; Kevin Reid; Alison Paul; Dr Angus Campbell.
OTHER INFORMATION Grants were made to 164 organisations during the financial period. Grants were broken down as follows: social welfare (£132,000); medical causes (£104,200); the arts (£90,500); education (£11,000); heritage conservation (£9,000). Only organisations that received grants of over £2,500 were listed as beneficiaries in the foundation's accounts. Grants of less than £2,500 totalled £144,700.
HOW TO APPLY Applications can be made via the foundation's website at any time of the year. The trustees meet three times a year to consider applications, usually in November, February and June.
CONTACT DETAILS The Trustees, 16 Walker Street, Edinburgh EH3 7LP *Tel.* 0131 442 3862 *Email* info@crudenfoundation.org *Website* https://crudenfoundation.org

■ CSIS Charity Fund

CC NO 1121671 **ESTABLISHED** 2007
WHERE FUNDING CAN BE GIVEN UK.
WHO CAN BENEFIT Charitable organisations.
WHAT IS FUNDED Civil and public servants and their families with social welfare or health needs.
TYPE OF GRANT Unrestricted; core/revenue costs; development funding; service delivery.
RANGE OF GRANTS Up to £150,000.
SAMPLE GRANTS The Charity for Civil Servants (£150,000); BT Benevolent Fund (£40,000); Police Treatment Centres (£8,000); UNISON (£5,000).
FINANCES *Financial year end 31/12/2021*
Income £326,000
Grants to organisations £506,700
Grants to individuals £24,300
Assets £1,350,000
TRUSTEES Charles Cochrane; Rebecca Gooch; Sally Bundock; Ray Flanigan; Sun-Hee Park; Ian Albert; Gaby Glasener-Cipollone; Deborah Terry; Michael Duggan; Colin Birch; Mary Jeffrey; Christopher Smith.
HOW TO APPLY Potential applicants can use the enquiry from on the charity's website to check whether they are eligible for a grant.
CONTACT DETAILS Kevin Holliday, Secretary, 1st Floor, Gail House, Lower Stone Street, Maidstone, Kent ME15 6NB *Tel.* 07843 342889 *Email* secretary@csischarityfund.org *Website* www.csischarityfund.org

■ Cullum Family Trust

CC NO 1117056 **ESTABLISHED** 2006
WHERE FUNDING CAN BE GIVEN Surrey and Sussex.
WHO CAN BENEFIT Registered charities; unregistered charities; social enterprises; schools; universities; hospices.
WHAT IS FUNDED General charitable purposes; specialist education targeted at children in Surrey who are on the autistic spectrum. The trust's grant-making is mainly carried out in partnership with The National Autistic Society,

338

Does the funder you have chosen match your needs? Haphazard applications waste postage and time

Sussex Community Foundation and Bayes Business School.

TYPE OF GRANT Capital costs; project funding.

RANGE OF GRANTS £10,000 to £100,000, with larger awards to partner organisations.

SAMPLE GRANTS City University – Bayes Business School (£550,000); The National Autistic Society (£305,700); Save the Children Fund (£250,000); The Aldingbourne Trust (£125,000); Sussex Community Foundation (£100,000); Five Acre Wood School (£39,100).

FINANCES *Financial year end 05/04/2022*
Income £914,300
Grants to organisations £1,420,000
Assets £34,019,000

TRUSTEES Ann Cullum; Claire Cullum; Peter Cullum; Simon Cullum.

OTHER INFORMATION Grants to unspecified organisations totalled £45,600.

HOW TO APPLY Apply in writing to the correspondent.

CONTACT DETAILS Peter Cullum, Chair, Wealden Hall, Parkfield, Sevenoaks, Kent TN15 0HX
Tel. 01622 809471

■ Cumbria Community Foundation

CC NO 1075120   **ESTABLISHED** 1999

WHERE FUNDING CAN BE GIVEN Cumbria.

WHO CAN BENEFIT Registered and non-registered charities; CICs; social enterprises; PTAs; hospices; individuals.

WHAT IS FUNDED General charitable purposes including: disadvantaged children and families; skills and training; older people; health; community development; arts and culture; sport; the environment.

WHAT IS NOT FUNDED See the website for programme-specific exclusions.

TYPE OF GRANT Capital costs; core/revenue costs; project funding; seed funding/start-up funding.

RANGE OF GRANTS Mostly up to £20,000.

SAMPLE GRANTS Groundwork North East and Cumbria (£209,400); Hogwill Family Centre (£75,500); Together We CIC (£10,000); The Share Foundation (£5,000).

FINANCES *Financial year end 31/03/2022*
Income £5,410,000
Grants to organisations £4,020,000
Grants to individuals £93,800
Assets £33,880,000

TRUSTEES Richard Roberts; Anthony Keen; David Beeby; Jim Johnson; Susan Howorth; Alison Johnston; John Wilson; Kevin Walsh; Glenys Marriott; Col. Chris Sanderson; David Moore; Marcia Fotheringham; Lucy Cavendish; Michael Ditchburn; Suzanne Wilson.

OTHER INFORMATION This is one of the 47 UK community foundations, which distribute funding for a wide range of purposes. As with all community foundations, there are a number of donor-advised funds managed on behalf of individuals, families and charitable trusts. Grant schemes tend to change frequently – consult the foundation's website for details of current programmes and up-to-date deadlines. Grants to individuals and organisations were distributed as follows: health and well-being (£1.56 million); skills, education and employability (£850,300); disadvantaged children and families (£743,300); older people (£456,000); community development (£365,100); arts, sport, heritage and the environment (£133,300).

HOW TO APPLY Potential applicants are advised to visit the community foundation's website or contact its grants team to find the most suitable funding stream.

CONTACT DETAILS The Trustees, Dovenby Hall, Dovenby, Cockermouth, Cumbria CA13 0PN
Tel. 01900 825760 *Email* enquiries@cumbriafoundation.org *Website* www.cumbriafoundation.org

---

■ The Cunningham Trust

OSCR NO SC013499   **ESTABLISHED** 1984

WHERE FUNDING CAN BE GIVEN Scotland.

WHO CAN BENEFIT Universities; research institutions.

WHAT IS FUNDED Biomedical research.

TYPE OF GRANT Project funding; research.

SAMPLE GRANTS University of Dundee (£97,400); University of West of Scotland (£96,500); University of Aberdeen (£96,900); University of St Andrews (£96,800).

FINANCES *Financial year end 05/04/2022*
Income £311,400
Grants to organisations £387,300
Assets £12,520,000

HOW TO APPLY The trust's website states: 'There is an annual competition for funding, open to staff in all universities. Details will be announced on this site, usually around May from which you will be able to apply for application forms.'

CONTACT DETAILS David Harrison, Scientific Advisor, Kinburn Castle, Double Dykes Road, St Andrews, Fife KY16 9DR
Email cunninghamtrust@st-andrews.ac.uk or use the contact form on the website *Website* www.cunninghamtrust.org.uk

---

■ Itzchok Meyer Cymerman Trust Ltd

CC NO 265090   **ESTABLISHED** 1972

WHERE FUNDING CAN BE GIVEN UK and Israel.

WHO CAN BENEFIT Registered charities and, occasionally, individuals.

WHAT IS FUNDED The advancement of the Orthodox Jewish faith; education; social welfare; the relief of sickness; general charitable purposes.

RANGE OF GRANTS Up to £420,000.

SAMPLE GRANTS The M. D. and S. Charitable Trust (£182,000); Russian Immigrant Aid Fund Ltd (£122,000); Ichud Mosdos Gur Ltd (£117,600); Gur Foundation (£50,000); Colel Polen Kupath Ramban (£47,000); North London Welfare and Educational Foundation (£45,000); CMZ Ltd and Mercaz Hatorah Belz Machnovka (£40,000 each).

FINANCES *Financial year end 31/03/2022*
Income £1,720,000
Grants to organisations £1,190,000
Assets £18,370,000

TRUSTEES Mrs H. F. Bondi; Sara Heitner; Leonard Bondi; Ian Heitner; Bernard Hoffman; Michael Cymerman; Sylvia Cymerman.

OTHER INFORMATION Many grants are given to the same organisations each year. Grants in 2021/22 were distributed in the following categories: education (£420,400); relief of poverty (£372,500); advancement of religion (£292,100); medical causes £64,000); general charitable purposes (£22,600); social welfare (£18,200). Only grants of £40,000 or more were listed in the beneficiaries with other grants totalling £546,200.

HOW TO APPLY The trustees tend to select organisations to be supported based on their personal knowledge of the organisations' work. Although applications are not actively invited, the 2021/22 annual report states that the trustees 'are always prepared to accept any application which will be carefully considered and help given according to circumstances and funds then available.'

CONTACT DETAILS Mrs H. F. Bondi, Trustee and Secretary, 497 Holloway Road, London N7 6LE *Tel.* 020 7272 2255

■ The D. G. Charitable Settlement

CC NO 1040778   **ESTABLISHED** 1994
WHERE FUNDING CAN BE GIVEN UK.
WHO CAN BENEFIT Registered charities.
WHAT IS FUNDED General charitable purposes including: homelessness; older people; human rights; cancer; the environment; overseas aid; health and well-being.
RANGE OF GRANTS Generally £1,000 to £20,000, with some larger grants.
SAMPLE GRANTS Oxfam (£200,000); Crisis (£80,000); Shelter (£50,000); Amnesty International and Women for Refugee Women (£20,000 each); Liberty Choir (£10,000); Independent Digital Media (£6,000); The Folly Wildlife Rescue Trust (£1,000).
FINANCES *Financial year end* 30/06/2022
Income £250,000
Grants to organisations £509,000
Assets £19,100
TRUSTEES David Gilmour; Polly Samson.
OTHER INFORMATION Grants were awarded to 22 organisations during the year and broken down as follows: poverty overseas (£200,000); homelessness (£130,000); other (£74,000); human rights (£65,000); other medical causes (£30,000); cancer (£10,000).
HOW TO APPLY Apply in writing to the correspondent.
CONTACT DETAILS The Trustees, PO Box 90107, London SW6 9RR *Tel.* 07818 228523 *Email* emma@gilmour-dj.co.uk

■ The D. M. Charitable Trust

CC NO 1110419   **ESTABLISHED** 2005
WHERE FUNDING CAN BE GIVEN UK and Israel.
WHO CAN BENEFIT Jewish registered charities; Jewish educational institutions.
WHAT IS FUNDED Jewish causes; education; social welfare; relief of poverty and sickness.
SAMPLE GRANTS Employment Resource Centre (£100,000); WST Charity Ltd (£72,000); Keren Shabbos (18,000).
FINANCES *Financial year end* 30/06/2022
Income £82,000
Grants to organisations £190,000
Assets £735,600
TRUSTEES David Cohen; Stephen Goldberg; Patrice Klein; Deborah Dreyfuss.
OTHER INFORMATION All of the grant total was awarded to the alleviation of poverty, education and furtherance of the Jewish religion.
HOW TO APPLY Apply in writing to the correspondent.
CONTACT DETAILS Stephen Goldberg, Trustee, Sutherland House, 70–78 West Hendon Broadway, London NW9 7BT *Tel.* 020 8457 3258

■ The Daiwa Anglo-Japanese Foundation

CC NO 299955   **ESTABLISHED** 1988
WHERE FUNDING CAN BE GIVEN UK and Japan.
WHO CAN BENEFIT Schools; universities; individuals.
WHAT IS FUNDED UK–Japan relations, in particular the advancement of the UK and Japan in each other's institutions, culture, history, etc; scholarships or maintenance allowances to allow students and academics to travel to the UK/Japan to pursue their education; charitable organisations in the UK which promote, for public benefit, education in the UK or Japan; charitable organisations in the UK which conduct research into cultural, historical, medical and scientific subjects and the publication of all such research.
WHAT IS NOT FUNDED See the foundation's website for detailed exclusions for each grants programme.
TYPE OF GRANT Project funding.
RANGE OF GRANTS £2,000 to £18,000.
SAMPLE GRANTS South Eastern Regional College (£6,800); Belfast Photo Festival (£6,000); The Foundling Museum (£5,200); State of Trust (£4,000); Pierce (Festival) Ltd and Scottish Society for Art History (£3,000 each); Bounce Cinema (£2,000).
FINANCES *Financial year end* 31/03/2022
Income £136,400
Grants to organisations £234,100
Assets £45,710,000
TRUSTEES Yusuke Kawamura; Prof. Hirotaka Takeuchi; Stephen Barber; Yoko Dochi; Prof. Sachiko Kusukawa; Sir Tim Hitchens; Jessie Turnbull; Takashi Hibino; Sir Mark Walport; Rebecca Salter; Keiichi Hayashi; Dr Victoria Tuke.
OTHER INFORMATION Note that the grant total may include some grants to individuals. The foundation also awarded £257,200 in scholarships during 2021/22, but this has not been included in the grant total.
HOW TO APPLY Application forms are available to download from the foundation's website, where you can also find details of deadlines, further guidance and eligibility criteria.
CONTACT DETAILS The Trustees, Daiwa Foundation Japan House, 13/14 Cornwall Terrace (Outer Circle), London NW1 4QP *Tel.* 020 7486 4348 *Email* grants@dajf.org.uk *Website* www.dajf.org.uk

■ Oizer Dalim Trust

CC NO 1045296   **ESTABLISHED** 1994
WHERE FUNDING CAN BE GIVEN UK and overseas.
WHO CAN BENEFIT Registered charities.
WHAT IS FUNDED Orthodox Jewish causes; social welfare; education.
SAMPLE GRANTS A list of beneficiaries was not included in the annual report and accounts.
FINANCES *Financial year end* 30/06/2022
Income £111,600
Grants to organisations £141,700
Assets £800,200
TRUSTEES Mordechai Cik; Maurice Freund; Moishe Cohen.
OTHER INFORMATION Grants were broken down as follows: advancement of education (£64,500); relief of poverty (£28,100); advancement of religion (£22,500).
HOW TO APPLY Apply in writing to the correspondent.
CONTACT DETAILS The Trustees, 68 Osbaldeston Road, London N16 7DR *Tel.* 020 8806 9111

■ The Daniell Trust

CC NO 1176166
WHERE FUNDING CAN BE GIVEN England, Scotland and Wales, with a preference for Anglesey, Pembrokeshire, Shropshire and the West Highlands.

WHO CAN BENEFIT UK-registered charities and CICs with an annual turnover of above £250,000.

WHAT IS FUNDED The care and education of children with learning disabilities; environmental conservation.

TYPE OF GRANT Revenue costs; capital costs.

RANGE OF GRANTS £50,000 to £250,000.

SAMPLE GRANTS A list of beneficiaries was not included in the annual report and accounts.

FINANCES *Financial year end 05/04/2022*
Income £713,400
Grants to organisations £60,000
Assets £1,650,000

TRUSTEES William Prestwood; Odette Murray; Keith Bennett; Carmen Cullis; Katie Edwards.

OTHER INFORMATION The trust traditionally made small grants but is now looking to spend its remaining assets over the next few years with a series of more significant, sustainable projects which will leave a lasting legacy to the trust's founders, Tony and Noreen Daniell.

HOW TO APPLY Guidance notes and Expression of Interest forms can be downloaded from the trust's website.

CONTACT DETAILS The Trustees, c/o Dyke Yaxley Ltd, 1 Brassey Road, Shrewsbury SY3 7FA *Email* info@thedanielltrust.org.uk *Website* www.thedanielltrust.org.uk

■ The Danson Foundation

CC NO 1121928   **ESTABLISHED** 2010

WHERE FUNDING CAN BE GIVEN UK and overseas.

WHO CAN BENEFIT Registered charities.

WHAT IS FUNDED Education; mental health.

TYPE OF GRANT Core costs; project funding.

RANGE OF GRANTS Up to £150,000 but mostly £1,000 to £10,000.

SAMPLE GRANTS Highgate School (£150,000); Sealife Trust (£20,000); Anxiety UK (£7,000); Grace House Community Centre (£3,600); Twins Trust (£1,000).

FINANCES *Financial year end 31/12/2021*
Income £64,500
Grants to organisations £450,300
Assets £6,330,000

TRUSTEES Michael Danson; Ella Danson; Helen Danson.

HOW TO APPLY Full information on the foundation's application process can be found on its website.

CONTACT DETAILS The Trustees, John Carpenter House, John Carpenter Street, London EC4Y 0AN *Email* admin@thedansonfoundation.com *Website* www.thedansonfoundation.com

■ The Dashlight Foundation

CC NO 1184873   **ESTABLISHED** 2019

WHERE FUNDING CAN BE GIVEN UK, with a preference for Yorkshire, and Africa.

WHO CAN BENEFIT Charitable organisations.

WHAT IS FUNDED Mental health; wildlife conservation; general charitable purposes in Yorkshire; poverty relief and education in Africa; support for refugees.

RANGE OF GRANTS Up to £30,000,.

SAMPLE GRANTS Lighthouse Relief (£30,300); Vetlife (£25,000); The Honey Guide Foundation, The Shark Trust and Tiyeni (£20,000 each); Durrell Wildlife Conservation Trust (£15,000); Open Country (£5,000).

FINANCES *Financial year end 31/03/2022*
Income £1,120,000
Grants to organisations £349,000
Assets £2,140,000

TRUSTEES Owen Clarke; Jacqueline Clarke; Bethany Clarke; Dominic Clarke; Hannah Clarke.

OTHER INFORMATION Grants were distributed as follows: wildlife conservation (£170,000); relief of poverty (100,000); activities supporting mental health (£48,700); support for refugees (£30,300).

HOW TO APPLY Applications should be sent by email and be no longer than four pages. Unsuccessful applicants are not informed.

CONTACT DETAILS The Trustees, Flat G, 49 Wellington Street, London WC2E 7BN *Tel.* 01937 588826 *Email* dashlight.fdn@gmail.com

■ Baron Davenport's Charity

CC NO 217307   **ESTABLISHED** 1930

WHO CAN BENEFIT Registered charities; unregistered charities; CICs; social enterprises; hospices; religious bodies/institutions; uniformed groups; clubs; individuals.

WHAT IS FUNDED Almshouses; hospices; residential homes for older people; children and young people (under 25 years old); older people.

WHAT IS NOT FUNDED Statutory services; universities and further education colleges; nurseries and preschools; PTAs; uniformed groups participating in international camps or jamborees; start-up organisations; retrospective expenditure; capital appeals for places of worship (unless for community use); medical research.

TYPE OF GRANT Capital costs; core/revenue costs; project funding.

RANGE OF GRANTS Up to £20,000.

SAMPLE GRANTS The Hospice Charity Partnership (£20,000); Acorns Children's Hospice Trust and Compton Care (£12,000 each); Bromsgrove United Charities (£11,000); Age UK Birmingham (£10,000).

FINANCES *Financial year end 31/12/2022*
Income £580,200
Grants to organisations £567,000
Assets £33,070,000

TRUSTEES William Colacicchi; Gurvinder Samra; Clare Auty; Matthew Newbold; Lynn Redwood; Victoria Smith; Alec Jones; Lisa Bryan; Peter Horton; Mohammed Sajid; Victoria Milligan.

OTHER INFORMATION Only organisations that received grants of over £10,000 were listed as beneficiaries in the charity's accounts. Grants of under £10,000 totalled £370,000 and were awarded to 295 organisations.

HOW TO APPLY Applications can be made through the charity's website.

CONTACT DETAILS Louise Cotton, Grants Manager, Portman House, 5–7 Temple Row West, Birmingham, West Midlands B2 5NY *Tel.* 07712 862803 *Email* enquiries@barondavenportscharity.org *Website* www.barondavenportscharity.org

■ The David Family Foundation

CC NO 1123198   **ESTABLISHED** 2007

WHERE FUNDING CAN BE GIVEN UK.

WHO CAN BENEFIT Registered charities.

WHAT IS FUNDED Education; art and culture; the environment; animal welfare; people with disabilities; research into alternative energy sources.

RANGE OF GRANTS Up to £25,000 but mostly £1,000 to £10,000.

SAMPLE GRANTS Drake Music (£25,000); Age UK and Crisis (£10,000 each); Cruse Bereavement

(£5,000); Kirkwood Hospice (£4,000); Autism Inclusive (£2,500); Carers Forum (£1,000).
FINANCES *Financial year end* 31/12/2021
Income £47,300
Grants to organisations £646,900
Assets £7,940,000
TRUSTEES John Emerson; Jonathan David; Anna-Lisa Wright; Caroline David.
HOW TO APPLY Apply in writing to the correspondent.
CONTACT DETAILS The Trustees, Building One, 373 Kennington Road, London SE11 4PT *Tel.* 020 7820 1120

■ The Manny and Brigitta Davidson Charitable Foundation

CC NO 1175058　　　**ESTABLISHED** 2017
WHERE FUNDING CAN BE GIVEN UK and Israel.
WHO CAN BENEFIT Registered charities.
WHAT IS FUNDED Purchasing, holding, maintaining and exhibiting works of art; capital and infrastructure projects; social welfare.
TYPE OF GRANT Capital costs; collection and acquisition.
SAMPLE GRANTS The National Gallery (£100,000); London Academy of Music and Dramatic Art (£25,000); Tikva UK (£10,000).
FINANCES *Financial year end* 31/03/2022
Income £390,000
Grants to organisations £140,000
Assets £118,100
TRUSTEES Emanuel Davidson; Brigitta Davidson; Gerard Cohen; Richard Denton; Jeremy Sandelson; Ilan Rappaport; Lord Jonathan Kestenbaum.
HOW TO APPLY Apply in writing to the correspondent.
CONTACT DETAILS The Trustees, OGR Stock Denton LLP, 2nd Floor, Winston House, 2 Dollis Park, London N3 1HF *Tel.* 020 8349 5500

■ The Davidson Family Charitable Trust

CC NO 262937　　　**ESTABLISHED** 1971
WHERE FUNDING CAN BE GIVEN UK and overseas.
WHO CAN BENEFIT Mainly Jewish organisations.
WHAT IS FUNDED Jewish causes and general charitable purposes.
TYPE OF GRANT Grants are made towards larger capital projects.
SAMPLE GRANTS Previous beneficiaries have included: The Jerusalem Foundation (£308,200); Community Security Trust (£42,000); City Pregnancy Counselling and Psychotherapy (£20,000); Israel Philharmonic Orchestra Foundation UK (£10,000); Bodleian Libraries – University of Oxford (£5,000); The Chicken Soup Shelter (£1,000); Sinai Jewish Primary School (£500).
FINANCES *Financial year end* 05/04/2022
Income £37
Grants to organisations £165,000
TRUSTEES Gerald Davidson; Maxine Davidson.
OTHER INFORMATION Full accounts were not available to view on the Charity Commission's website due to the trust's low income. We have therefore estimate the trust's grant total based on its total expenditure.
HOW TO APPLY Apply in writing to the correspondent.
CONTACT DETAILS The Trustees, c/o Wolfe Property Services Ltd, Khiara House, 25/26 Poland Street, London W1F 8QN *Tel.* 020 7224 1030

■ Michael Davies Charitable Settlement

CC NO 1000574　　　**ESTABLISHED** 1990
WHERE FUNDING CAN BE GIVEN UK.
WHO CAN BENEFIT Charitable organisations.
WHAT IS FUNDED General charitable purposes.
SAMPLE GRANTS A list of beneficiaries was not included in the annual report and accounts. Previous beneficiaries have included: Architectural Association Foundation (£50,000); University of Sunderland Development Trust (£12,000); Marie Curie Hospice, Camden Arts Centre and Royal National Orthopaedic Hospital Trust (£10,000 each); Crisis (£5,000); Ebony Horse Club and North London Hospice (£1,000 each).
FINANCES *Financial year end* 05/04/2022
Income £364,700
Grants to organisations £185,000
Assets £989,000
TRUSTEES Michael Davies; Kenneth Hawkins.
HOW TO APPLY Apply in writing to the correspondent.
CONTACT DETAILS The Trustees, HW Lee Associates, New Derwent House, 69/73 Theobalds Road, London WC1X 8TA *Tel.* 020 7025 4600

■ Margaret Davies Charity

CC NO 235589　　　**ESTABLISHED** 1934
WHERE FUNDING CAN BE GIVEN Wales.
WHO CAN BENEFIT Registered charities; Welsh organisations; schools; universities; churches; hospices; PTAs; amateur sports clubs.
WHAT IS FUNDED General charitable purposes including: visual and performing arts; education; health; social welfare; provision for young people.
TYPE OF GRANT Our research suggests capital costs are supported.
RANGE OF GRANTS Mainly under £5,000.
SAMPLE GRANTS Brecon Festival of Ballet, Carers Trust Wales, Cwmparc Community Association, Hope House Charity, Mid Wales Opera, Nightingale House Hospice, Support Through Court and Wales Millennium Centre (£5,000 each).
FINANCES *Financial year end* 05/04/2022
Income £220,800
Grants to organisations £231,300
Assets £10,380,000
TRUSTEES Daniel Davies; Dr Denis Balsom; Dr Janet Lewis; Thomas Williams; Elinor Gilbey.
OTHER INFORMATION The charity made 14 awards of £5,000. Miscellaneous grants of under £5,000 totalled £161,300.
HOW TO APPLY Apply in writing to the correspondent. The trustees meet at least three times a year to consider new applications.
CONTACT DETAILS The Trustees, Plas Dolerw, Milford Road, Newtown, Powys SY16 2EH *Tel.* 01686 625228 *Email* daviescharities@gmail.com

■ The Crispin Davis Family Trust

CC NO 1150637　　　**ESTABLISHED** 2013
WHERE FUNDING CAN BE GIVEN Worldwide.
WHO CAN BENEFIT Registered charities; schools.
WHAT IS FUNDED Children and young people who are in need of help as a result of poverty, lack of education or illness.
SAMPLE GRANTS Optimus Foundation (£300,000); Whizz-Kidz (£100,000); Tushinde Children's Trust (£40,000); Game and Wildlife Conservation Trust (£7,500); Outdoor Adventure for Girls (£500).

FINANCES *Financial year end* 05/04/2022
Income £228,500
Grants to organisations £453,000
Assets £8,630,000
TRUSTEES Sir Crispin Davis; Lady Jean Davis; Julia Davis; Caroline King; Angela Spaid; Cripps Trust Corporation Ltd.
HOW TO APPLY Contact the correspondent for further information.
CONTACT DETAILS The Trustees, Heartwood Wealth Management, 77 Mount Ephraim, Tunbridge Wells, Kent TN4 8BS *Tel.* 01892 701801 *Email* info@heartwoodgroup.co.uk

■ The Davis Foundation

CC NO 1152998   ESTABLISHED 2013
WHERE FUNDING CAN BE GIVEN UK; overseas, including Israel and the Middle East.
WHO CAN BENEFIT Charitable organisations.
WHAT IS FUNDED Jewish causes; young people; older people; disability; the arts; horticulture; religious harmony; religious education; citizenship.
SAMPLE GRANTS A list of beneficiaries was not included in the annual report and accounts.
FINANCES *Financial year end* 05/04/2022
Income £1,060,000
Grants to organisations £1,220,000
Assets £273,300
TRUSTEES Sir Michael Davis; Lady Barbara Davis; Sarah Davis.
HOW TO APPLY Apply in writing to the correspondent.
CONTACT DETAILS The Trustees, 3 Beechworth Close, London NW3 7UT *Tel.* 020 7389 9512 *Email* applications@thedavisfoundation.com

■ The Henry and Suzanne Davis Foundation

CC NO 1153199   ESTABLISHED 2013
WHERE FUNDING CAN BE GIVEN England; Wales; Israel.
WHO CAN BENEFIT Charitable organisations.
WHAT IS FUNDED General charitable purposes.
SAMPLE GRANTS A list of beneficiaries was not included in the annual report and accounts.
FINANCES *Financial year end* 27/06/2022
Income £200,000
Grants to organisations £96,500
Assets £413,300
TRUSTEES Suzanne Davis; Henry Davis; Robert Craig.
HOW TO APPLY Unsolicited applications are not accepted.
CONTACT DETAILS R. Gallagher, Secretary, c/o Centreland Management LLP, Bolsover House, 5–6 Clipstone Street, London W1W 6BB *Tel.* 020 7460 5454 *Email* rgallagher@centreland.com

■ Dawat-E-Hadiyah Trust (United Kingdom)

CC NO 294807   ESTABLISHED 1986
WHERE FUNDING CAN BE GIVEN UK and overseas.
WHO CAN BENEFIT Registered charities; individuals.
WHAT IS FUNDED The advancement of the Islamic religion; education; social welfare; medical aid.
RANGE OF GRANTS Typically £3,000 to £8,000, with some much larger grants of over £600,000.
SAMPLE GRANTS Anjuman-e-Saifee – Leicester (£613,700); COVID-19 Healthcare Fund – Sri Lanka (£250,000); Anjuman-e-Hamidi – Manchester (£163,500); Silver Star Diabetes (£50,000); Anjuman-e-Burhani – London

(£8,800); Anjuman-e-Hamidi – Milton Keynes (£5,000); Anjuman-e-Burhani – Sydney (£1,300); Anjumane-e-Burhani – Singapore (£400).
FINANCES *Financial year end* 31/12/2021
Income £38,340,000
Grants to organisations £1,140,000
Grants to individuals £5,500
Assets £112,210,000
TRUSTEE The 53rd Dai Al-Mutlaq, His Holiness Syedna Mufaddal Saifuddin.
OTHER INFORMATION Grants to organisations were distributed as follows: UK-registered charities (£865,100); overseas charities (£268,800).
HOW TO APPLY Apply in writing to the correspondent.
CONTACT DETAILS The Trustees, 6 Mohammedi Park Complex, Rowdell Road, Northolt, Middlesex UB5 6AG *Tel.* 020 8839 0750 *Email* farazdaq@dawatuk.org

■ The Dawe Charitable Trust

CC NO 1060314   ESTABLISHED 1996
WHERE FUNDING CAN BE GIVEN UK and overseas, with a preference for Cambridgeshire.
WHO CAN BENEFIT Charitable organisations.
WHAT IS FUNDED Disadvantaged people and homelessness.
SAMPLE GRANTS A list of beneficiaries was not available.
FINANCES *Financial year end* 30/09/2021
Income £2,100
Grants to organisations £1,500
TRUSTEES Peter Dawe; Susan Dawe.
OTHER INFORMATION In previous years, the trust has awarded over £100,000 in grants. Full accounts were not available to view on the Charity Commission's website due to the trust's low income. We have therefore estimated the trust's grant total based on its total expenditure. The 2020/21 financial information was the latest available at the time of writing (May 2023).
HOW TO APPLY Apply in writing to the correspondent.
CONTACT DETAILS Peter Dawe, Trustee, F14 and 15, Lanwades Hall, Lanwades Park, Bury Road, Kentford, Cambridgeshire CB8 7UA *Tel.* 01353 634662 *Email* office@dawe.co.uk

■ The De Brye Charitable Trust

CC NO 326226   ESTABLISHED 1982
WHERE FUNDING CAN BE GIVEN England and Wales.
WHO CAN BENEFIT Charitable organisations.
WHAT IS FUNDED General charitable purposes; care and housing for older people; orphans and neglected children; aid for children with physical disabilities and blind people; charitable causes relating to woodlands, forests and wildlife.
RANGE OF GRANTS Between £1,000 and £5,000, with one payment of £10,000.
SAMPLE GRANTS Millfield Development (£10,000); Action for Child Trauma International, Facing the World and Family Rights Group (£5,000 each); Dogs for Good and Treloar Trust (£3,000 each); Disability Africa and Hope for Tomorrow (£2,000 each); YoungMinds (£1,500); Mencap (£1,000).
FINANCES *Financial year end* 05/04/2022
Income £104,100
Grants to organisations £89,300
Assets £3,090,000
TRUSTEES Alexander Brye; Phillip Sykes; Edward Reed.
HOW TO APPLY Contact the correspondent for further information.
CONTACT DETAILS The Trustees, Mercer and Hole, 72 London Road, St Albans, Hertfordshire AL1 1NS *Tel.* 01727 869141

■ The Roger De Haan Charitable Trust

CC NO 276274   **ESTABLISHED** 1978

WHERE FUNDING CAN BE GIVEN Folkestone.

WHO CAN BENEFIT Registered charities; schools; community organisations; churches; CICs.

WHAT IS FUNDED Arts and culture; education; health and welfare of older people; sports; community development, heritage and regeneration in Folkestone; social welfare; the environment.

WHAT IS NOT FUNDED See the trust's website for a full list of exclusions.

TYPE OF GRANT Capital costs; project funding; development funding.

RANGE OF GRANTS Typically up to £20,000.

SAMPLE GRANTS Creative Folkestone (£3.99 million); Shepway Sports Trust (£527,500); Art Fund – Prospect Cottage (£200,000); Kent Crime Stoppers (£54,500); British Red Cross (£50,000); Lower Leas Coastal Park Play Area (£20,000); Sunflower House (£10,000); St Luke's Church (£5,000); Romney Marsh Art Society (£500).

FINANCES *Financial year end* 05/04/2022
Income £231,000
Grants to organisations £5,400,000
Assets £8,430,000

TRUSTEES Sir Roger De Haan; Joshua De Haan; Benjamin De Haan; Lady De Haan.

OTHER INFORMATION Grants were awarded as follows: arts (4.56 million); sport (£538,000); community development (£117,000); health and welfare (£85,000); international (£52,000); education (£36,000); other sectors (£4,000). Seventy grants were awarded to organisations during the year.

HOW TO APPLY Applications can be made through the trust's website. Alternatively, applicants may download or print the form available on the website for completion and return to the trust by post. The trustees meet five times a year to consider grants; deadlines for the meetings can be found on the trust's website.

CONTACT DETAILS Roger De Haan, Trustee, Strand House, Pilgrims Way, Monks Horton, Ashford, Kent TN25 6DR *Email* use the contact form on the website *Website* www.rdhct.org.uk

■ The De Laszlo Foundation

CC NO 327383   **ESTABLISHED** 1978

WHERE FUNDING CAN BE GIVEN UK and worldwide.

WHO CAN BENEFIT Registered charities; universities; hospices.

WHAT IS FUNDED Promotion of the arts; general charitable purposes.

TYPE OF GRANT Research, project and capital costs; collections and acquisitions; scholarships and prizes.

RANGE OF GRANTS Up to £200,000.

SAMPLE GRANTS The de Laszlo Archive Trust (£200,000); Southampton University and City and Guilds of London Art School (£25,000 each); The David Nott Foundation (£5,000).

FINANCES *Financial year end* 05/04/2022
Income £1,410,000
Grants to organisations £386,000
Assets £3,930,000

TRUSTEES Lucy Birkbeck; Damon Laszlo; Robert Laszlo; William Laszlo.

OTHER INFORMATION The foundation was set up to support the advancement and promotion of education and interest in the visual arts, with special reference to encouraging knowledge of the works of contemporary painters, particularly the late Philip de Laszlo. In the 2021/22 accounts grants were broken down as follows: education (£188,200), medicine (£172,900), Archive Trust (£170,000), arts (£94,700), scholarships and grants (£62,500), science (£36,600), economics (£5,500) and other charities (£770).

HOW TO APPLY Apply in writing to the correspondent.

CONTACT DETAILS The Trustees, 5 Albany Courtyard, Piccadilly, London W1J 0HF *Tel.* 020 7437 1982 *Email* damon@delaszlo.com

■ William Dean Countryside and Educational Trust

CC NO 1044567   **ESTABLISHED** 1994

WHERE FUNDING CAN BE GIVEN UK, with a preference for Cheshire and also Derbyshire, Lancashire, Staffordshire and Wirral.

WHO CAN BENEFIT Charitable organisations; individuals.

WHAT IS FUNDED Education in natural history, ecology and the conservation of the natural environment.

RANGE OF GRANTS £150 to £16,000.

SAMPLE GRANTS Ruby's Fund (£25,000); Cheshire Wildlife Trust (£15,000); Congleton Building Preservation Trust (£3,000); Woodcock's Well Primary School (£2,000); Vauxhall City Farm (£1,000); Scottish Seabird Centre (£500); International Otter Survival Fund (£250).

FINANCES *Financial year end* 31/12/2021
Income £80,400
Grants to organisations £83,000
Assets £2,490,000

TRUSTEES John Ward; Rebecca Franklin; Patricia Pinto; David Crawford; Andrew Pear.

OTHER INFORMATION The trust regularly gives over £50,000 per year, mainly in small grants of under £1,000. During the year, the trust awarded 64 grants to organisations.

HOW TO APPLY Contact the correspondent for information. The trustees meet four times each year, in March, June, September and December, when applications for grants are considered.

CONTACT DETAILS Clare Amare, Co-ordinator, 51 Moss Road, Congleton CW12 3BN *Tel.* 01260 276970 *Email* williamdeantrust@gmail.com

■ The Miriam Dean Refugee Trust Fund

CC NO 269655   **ESTABLISHED** 1964

WHERE FUNDING CAN BE GIVEN Financially developing countries, particularly India and African countries.

WHO CAN BENEFIT Registered charities; schools; hospitals; hospices.

WHAT IS FUNDED People who are in need of assistance by reason of war, disaster, pestilence or otherwise, or any organisation engaged in the relief of human suffering abroad.

TYPE OF GRANT Capital costs; core/revenue costs; project funding.

RANGE OF GRANTS £1,200 to £30,400.

SAMPLE GRANTS Rural Area Development Trust (£30,300); Jeevan Jyothi Hospice (£29,400); DEEPAM (£28,500); Holy Cross Special School (£16,800); Loaves and Fishes Network (£12,500); CODI (£12,000); Tibetan Homes Foundation (£1,200).

FINANCES *Financial year end* 31/12/2021
Income £272,000
Grants to organisations £224,400
Assets £668,200

Think carefully about every application. Is it justified?

345

TRUSTEES Robert Buchanan; Jenny Buchanan; Sheila Moore; Andy Moore; Laura Buchanan.

HOW TO APPLY The trustees do not wish to receive any applications. The charity's funds are fully committed to projects and organisations already known to the trustees.

CONTACT DETAILS The Trustees, 3 Ladwell Close, Newbury, Berkshire RG14 6PJ *Tel.* 01635 34979 *Email* trustees@miriamdeanfund.org.uk *Website* www.miriamdeanfund.org.uk

■ Debmar Benevolent Trust Ltd

CC NO 283065   **ESTABLISHED** 1979

WHERE FUNDING CAN BE GIVEN UK and Israel.

WHO CAN BENEFIT Charitable organisations.

WHAT IS FUNDED Advancement of the Orthodox Jewish religion; the relief of poverty; general charitable purposes.

RANGE OF GRANTS Mostly up to £124,000 with the occasional larger grant.

SAMPLE GRANTS MW (RH) Foundation (£147,000); MW (CL) Foundation, MW (GK) Foundation and MK (HO) Foundation (£124,000 each).

FINANCES *Financial year end* 30/06/2022
Income £461,700
Grants to organisations £564,200
Assets £2,830,000

TRUSTEES Jacob Halpern; David Olsberg.

OTHER INFORMATION Three of the grants made to organisations were awarded to organisations described as 'related parties' in the trust's accounts: MW (RH) Foundation; MW (HO) Foundation; MW (CL) Foundation. Grants to other organisations totalled £169,200.

HOW TO APPLY Apply in writing to the correspondent.

CONTACT DETAILS The Trustees, 16 Stanley Road, Salford, Greater Manchester M7 4RW *Tel.* 0161 798 1660

■ William Delafield Charitable Trust

CC NO 328022   **ESTABLISHED** 1988

WHERE FUNDING CAN BE GIVEN Bedfordshire; Buckinghamshire; Oxfordshire.

WHO CAN BENEFIT Historical societies/bodies.

WHAT IS FUNDED Restoration of records or archives of historical societies/bodies.

TYPE OF GRANT One-off and ongoing grants.

RANGE OF GRANTS Up to £114,000.

SAMPLE GRANTS Ashmolean Museum and Bodleian Library (£113,600 each); Pitt Rivers Museum (£91,900); Brasenose College (54,100); Oxford Preservation Trust (£48,700).

FINANCES *Financial year end* 31/03/2022
Income £671,000
Grants to organisations £547,800
Assets £27,440,000

TRUSTEES Christopher Gee; Bianca Silva; Thomas Gilman.

HOW TO APPLY Apply in writing to the correspondent.

CONTACT DETAILS Tom Gilman, Trustee, Royds Withy King, Godstow Court, Minns Business Park, 5 West Way, Oxford OX2 0JB *Tel.* 01865 268664 *Email* tom.gilman@roydswithyking.com

■ The Delius Trust

CC NO 207324   **ESTABLISHED** 1935

WHERE FUNDING CAN BE GIVEN UK.

WHO CAN BENEFIT Registered charities; unregistered charities; individuals.

WHAT IS FUNDED The promotion of the works of the composer Frederick Delius and any other composer born, or at any time permanently resident, in Great Britain or Ireland from 1860 to the present day, with a preference for contemporaries of Delius.

WHAT IS NOT FUNDED Capital projects; individual performance, recording or publishing projects; retrospective projects.

TYPE OF GRANT Project funding.

RANGE OF GRANTS Mostly under £15,000.

SAMPLE GRANTS NMC Recordings Ltd (£30,000); Tommie Haglund Festival (£15,000); Villiers Quartet (£7,000); Royal Philharmonic Orchestra (£5,000); English Music Festival (£2,500); Lake District Summer Music Festival (£2,000); English Music Weekend at Hellens (£1,000).

FINANCES *Financial year end* 31/12/2021
Income £89,800
Grants to organisations £78,000
Assets £3,090,000

TRUSTEES Paul Guinery; Martin Williams; Musicians Benevolent Fund.

HOW TO APPLY Applications should be made in writing for consideration by the trustees and the advisers. See the trust's website for further details of what to include. The trustees meet three times a year, usually in February, June and October. Applications should be received early in the month before each meeting.

CONTACT DETAILS The Trustees, 13 Calico Row, London SW11 3YH *Tel.* 020 7924 4250 *Email* deliustrust@deliustrust.org.uk *Website* www.delius.org.uk

■ The Delves Charitable Trust

CC NO 231860   **ESTABLISHED** 1922

WHERE FUNDING CAN BE GIVEN UK and overseas.

WHO CAN BENEFIT Registered charities; CICs.

WHAT IS FUNDED Medical research; medical care and support; citizenship and community, particularly economic independence and self-sufficiency; the environment and biodiversity; social welfare; work outside the UK.

WHAT IS NOT FUNDED Non-UK organisations.

TYPE OF GRANT Project funding.

RANGE OF GRANTS Mostly between £5,000 and £15,000.

SAMPLE GRANTS Médecins Sans Frontières (£26,500); Client Earth and Macular Disease Society (£15,000 each); Alzheimer's Society – UK Dementia Research Institute, British Museum and Tree Aid (£10,000 each); the Forgiveness Project, Freedom from Torture and National Star (£8,000 each); Crisis, Motivation and Practical Action (£5,000 each).

FINANCES *Financial year end* 05/04/2022
Income £228,400
Grants to organisations £219,000
Assets £10,960,000

TRUSTEES Dr Elizabeth Breeze; Mark Breeze; Dr Charles Breeze; George Breeze; William Breeze; John Breeze.

HOW TO APPLY Unsolicited applications are not accepted.

CONTACT DETAILS The Trust Administrator, c/o Luminary Finance LLP, PO Box 135, Longfield, Kent DA3 8WF *Tel.* 01732 822114

■ Denman Charitable Trust

CC NO 326532   **ESTABLISHED** 1983

WHERE FUNDING CAN BE GIVEN Bristol; North East Somerset; South Gloucestershire.

WHO CAN BENEFIT Registered charities.

WHAT IS FUNDED General charitable purposes.

TYPE OF GRANT Project funding; pump-priming funding.

RANGE OF GRANTS Usually between £500 and £5,000.

SAMPLE GRANTS A list of beneficiaries was not included in the annual report and accounts.

FINANCES *Financial year end 05/04/2022*
Income £165,800
Grants to organisations £106,700
Assets £502,000

TRUSTEES Arnold Denman; Dorothy Denman; Joanna Denman; Sue Blatchford; Matthew Lee.

OTHER INFORMATION Grants were awarded to 38 local charities during 2021/22.

HOW TO APPLY Apply in writing by post or email. Details of what should be included in an application can be found on the trust's website. The trustees meet to consider applications four times a year, in March, June, September and December.

CONTACT DETAILS The Trustees, PO Box 1881, Old Sodbury, Bristol BS37 6WS *Email* enquiries@ denmancharitabletrust.org.uk *Website* www. denmancharitabletrust.org.uk/index.html

....

■ Dentons UK and Middle East LLP Charitable Trust

CC NO 1041204   **ESTABLISHED** 1994

WHERE FUNDING CAN BE GIVEN UK and Ireland.

WHO CAN BENEFIT Registered charities; hospices; community organisations.

WHAT IS FUNDED General charitable purposes.

RANGE OF GRANTS £200 to £6,500. A standard grant is of £1,500.

SAMPLE GRANTS Hackney Foodbank (£6,500); Afghanistan and Central Asian Association (£5,000); Glasgow's Pre-Loved Uniforms and Women's Aid Ireland (£3,000 each); Blind in Business, Children's Air Ambulance, Care After Prison – Dublin, Deptford Action Group for the Elderly, Edinburgh Young Carers, Family Carers Ireland, Irish Refuge Council, KEEN London, Pregnancy Counselling and Care and Women's Trust London (£1,000 each); Royal Marsden Cancer Charity (£250); The Lord Mayor's Appeal (£200).

FINANCES *Financial year end 30/04/2022*
Income £183,900
Grants to organisations £173,800
Assets £163,300

TRUSTEES Daniel Bodle; David Payton; Gareth Steen; Alison Bryce.

OTHER INFORMATION Preference is given to charities with a connection to Dentons UK and Middle East LLP or those that are local to its offices. Smaller and less known charities are also favoured. During 2021/22, a total of 136 grants were made.

HOW TO APPLY Apply in writing to the correspondent.

CONTACT DETAILS The Trustees, One Fleet Place, London EC4M 7WS *Tel.* 020 7246 4843 *Email* bernadette.osullivan@dentons.com

....

■ Foundation Derbyshire

CC NO 1039485   **ESTABLISHED** 1996

WHERE FUNDING CAN BE GIVEN Derbyshire and the City of Derby.

WHO CAN BENEFIT Charitable organisations.

WHAT IS FUNDED General charitable purposes including: community safety; the environment; mental health; disability access; social welfare;

art and culture; sport; education; social care; community safety; community cohesion.

TYPE OF GRANT Capital costs; core/revenue costs.

RANGE OF GRANTS Mostly up to £2,000.

SAMPLE GRANTS A list of beneficiaries was not included in the annual report and accounts.

FINANCES *Financial year end 31/03/2022*
Income £1,560,000
Grants to organisations £447,200
Grants to individuals £1,600
Assets £10,050,000

TRUSTEES Peter Pimm; Philip Bloxham; William Kerr; Paul Broadhead; Oliver Stephenson; Sheila Taylor; Nick Hodgson; David Palmer; Andrew Cochrane; Alison Williams; Jane Gerard-Pearse; Gurmail Raju; Stephen Gordon.

OTHER INFORMATION This is one of the 47 UK community foundations, which distribute funding for a wide range of purposes. As with all community foundations, there are a number of donor-advised funds managed on behalf of individuals, families and charitable trusts. Grant schemes tend to change frequently – consult the foundation's website for details of current programmes and up-to-date deadlines. Grants were made to 176 organisations during the year.

HOW TO APPLY Potential applicants are advised to visit the community foundation's website or contact its grants team to find the most suitable funding stream.

CONTACT DETAILS The Grants Team, Unit 2, Heritage Business Centre, Belper, Derbyshire DE56 1SW *Tel.* 01773 525860 *Email* hello@ foundationderbyshire.org *Website* www. foundationderbyshire.org

....

■ The J. N. Derbyshire Trust

CC NO 231907   **ESTABLISHED** 1944

WHERE FUNDING CAN BE GIVEN UK, with a strong preference for Nottingham and Nottinghamshire.

WHO CAN BENEFIT Charitable organisations; community groups.

WHAT IS FUNDED Health, including mental health; education; social relief; protection and welfare of children and vulnerable people; community; recreation and clubs; general charitable purposes.

WHAT IS NOT FUNDED Individuals; national charities with an income of more than £1 million; non-registered charities; organisations outside Nottinghamshire.

RANGE OF GRANTS Mostly up to £3,000 with the occasional slightly larger grant.

SAMPLE GRANTS Equation Nottinghamshire, Nottingham and Nottinghamshire Refugee Forum and PASIC (£5,000 each); FareShare Midlands and Imara CIO (£4,000 each); Ecoworks Nottingham, Nottingham Law Centre and Refugee Roots (£3,000 each).

FINANCES *Financial year end 05/04/2022*
Income £134,400
Grants to organisations £154,600
Assets £5,580,000

TRUSTEES William Carver; Georgia Cowan; Rose Whittle; Andrew Little; Charles George; Peter Moore.

OTHER INFORMATION Grants were broken down as follows: general charitable purposes (£45,900); social welfare (£29,400); education (£20,500); youth organisations (£20,000); welfare of women and children (£18,000); people with disabilities (£14,500); older people (£6,300). Only beneficiaries of grants of over £3,000 were listed in the accounts. Grants of under £3,000 totalled £79,000.

HOW TO APPLY Apply via the form available on the trust's website.

CONTACT DETAILS Emma Hanson, Secretary, c/o UHY, 14 Park Row, Nottingham, Nottinghamshire NG1 6GR *Tel.* 07800 617191 *Email* emma.hanson2022@outlook.com *Website* www.jnderbyshiretrust.com

······························

■ The Desmond Foundation

CC NO 1014352   **ESTABLISHED** 1992
WHERE FUNDING CAN BE GIVEN UK and overseas.
WHO CAN BENEFIT Charitable organisations.
WHAT IS FUNDED Social welfare; Jewish causes; children and young people.
RANGE OF GRANTS Up to £250,000 but mostly under £25,000.
SAMPLE GRANTS Royal Society for Blind Children (£250,000); Maggie's Cancer Centre (£25,000); London Hearts (£20,000); Hotline Meals (£5,000); Sick Children's Trust (£2,000); ADSO Charity (£500).
FINANCES *Financial year end 31/12/2021*
Income £987,300
Grants to organisations £1,040,000
Assets £45,400
TRUSTEES Richard Desmond; Northern & Shell Services Ltd; Northern & Shell plc.
OTHER INFORMATION Grants were awarded to 56 organisations during the year.
HOW TO APPLY Apply in writing to the correspondent.
CONTACT DETAILS Michael Downer, The Northern & Shell Building, 10 Lower Thames Street, London EC3R 6EN *Tel.* 020 7308 5320 *Email* michael. downer@norshell.co.uk

······························

■ Devon Community Foundation

CC NO 1057923   **ESTABLISHED** 1996
WHERE FUNDING CAN BE GIVEN Devon; Plymouth; Torbay.
WHO CAN BENEFIT Not-for-profit voluntary or community groups; registered charities; social enterprises; schools; individuals.
WHAT IS FUNDED General charitable purposes.
WHAT IS NOT FUNDED Individuals; grant-making organisations (where funding is requested for their own grant-making); sole traders; alcohol or medication; building works or large-scale refurbishment; capital purchases over £1,000; consultancy or feasibility studies; large projects where the link between a grant awarded and overall project outcomes are not clear; loss of income; organisations or activities that primarily support animal welfare; overseas travel; projects or activity that promote political or religious beliefs; retrospective expenditure; sponsorship or fundraising activities; organisations with outstanding end-of-grant evaluations for previously awarded grants from the community foundation; commercial or profit-making organisations; organisations with a reserves balance exceeding 12 months' equivalent turnover.
TYPE OF GRANT Core costs; project costs.
RANGE OF GRANTS Mainly between £1,000 and £10,000.
SAMPLE GRANTS Wellbeing Exeter – SE (£307,400); Devon County Council Household Support (£200,000); Wellbeing Exeter – BLF (£130,100); Let's Create Jubilee Fund (£93,200); TEF Revenue (£41,000); Babeleigh CE Turbine Ltd (£21,500); Blundell's (£7,200); North Devon Relief (£460).

FINANCES *Financial year end 31/03/2022*
Income £2,510,000
Grants to organisations £2,040,000
Grants to individuals £1,000
Assets £11,700,000
TRUSTEES Caroline Harlow; The Rt Revd Robert Atwell; Edward Burnand; Peter Holden; Sally Wace; Graham Howe; Dinah Cox; Ann Holman; The Revd Georgina Radford.
OTHER INFORMATION This is one of the 47 UK community foundations, which distribute funding for a wide range of purposes. As with all community foundations, there are a number of donor-advised funds managed on behalf of individuals, families and charitable trusts. Grant schemes tend to change frequently – consult the foundation's website for details of current programmes and up-to-date deadlines. During 20121/22, grants were awarded to 296 organisations and 1 individual.
HOW TO APPLY Potential applicants are advised to visit the community foundation's website or contact its grants team to find the most suitable funding stream.
CONTACT DETAILS The Trustees, The Factory, Leat Street, Tiverton, Devon EX16 5LL *Tel.* 01884 235887 *Email* grants@devoncf.com *Website* www.devoncf.com

······························

■ The Laduma Dhamecha Charitable Trust

CC NO 328678   **ESTABLISHED** 1990
WHERE FUNDING CAN BE GIVEN UK and overseas.
WHO CAN BENEFIT Charitable organisations.
WHAT IS FUNDED Health; education; general charitable purposes.
SAMPLE GRANTS A list of beneficiaries was not included in the annual report and accounts.
FINANCES *Financial year end 31/03/2022*
Income £1,730,000
Grants to organisations £1,520,000
Assets £2,880,000
TRUSTEES Pradip Dhamecha; Shantilal Dhamecha; Manish Dhamecha.
OTHER INFORMATION During 2021/22 grants to organisations in the UK totalled £179,700 and grants to overseas organisations totalled £1.34 million.
HOW TO APPLY Apply in writing to the correspondent.
CONTACT DETAILS Pradip Dhamecha, Trustee, c/o The Dhamecha Group, 2 Hathaway Close, Stanmore, Middlesex HA7 3NR *Tel.* 020 8903 8181 *Email* info@dhamecha.com

······························

■ Diabetes UK

CC NO 215199   **ESTABLISHED** 1934
WHERE FUNDING CAN BE GIVEN UK.
WHO CAN BENEFIT Research organisations; universities.
WHAT IS FUNDED To promote and fund research into the causes, treatment and alleviation of the effects of diabetes.
WHAT IS NOT FUNDED A full list of exclusions can be found on the charity's website.
TYPE OF GRANT Equipment; fellowships; research grants; small grants; studentships.
RANGE OF GRANTS Programme dependent.
SAMPLE GRANTS King's College London (£679,000); University of Bristol (£443,000); University of Manchester (£334,000); University of Surrey (£209,000); Academy of Medical Sciences (£184,000); University of Lincoln (£155,000);

Queen's University Belfast (£121,000); University of Aberdeen (£101,000).

FINANCES *Financial year end* 31/12/2021
Income £37,880,000
Grants to organisations £6,460,000
Assets £20,300,000

TRUSTEES Emma Foulds; Matthew Higham; Martin Dewhurst; Dr Sarah Neshat Ali; Dr Carol Homden; Michael Gibbs; Prof. Linda Bauld; Alexandra Morton Lewis; Dr Asiya Yunus; Melanie Stephenson Gray; Ian King; Prof. Mohamed Hanif; Janice Watson.

OTHER INFORMATION Only organisations that received grants of over £100,000 were listed as beneficiaries in the charity's accounts.

HOW TO APPLY Potential applicants are first advised to read the 'General guidelines for research grant applicants' on the charity's website. Information on the application process and deadlines for each specific scheme is also available on the website.

CONTACT DETAILS Research Department, Wells Lawrence House, 126 Back Church Lane, London E1 1FH *Tel.* 01345 123 239 *Email* research@diabetes.org.uk *Website* www.diabetes.org.uk/research/for-researchers/apply-for-a-grant

■ The Alan and Sheila Diamond Charitable Trust

CC NO 274312   **ESTABLISHED** 1977
WHERE FUNDING CAN BE GIVEN UK.
WHO CAN BENEFIT Registered charities only, places of worship.
WHAT IS FUNDED General charitable purposes, especially Jewish causes. The trust supports the same organisations every year.
RANGE OF GRANTS Generally, up to £10,000.
SAMPLE GRANTS Magen David Adom (£15,000); The Royal Society of Medicine (£10,000); Sidney Sussex College (£8,600); World Jewish Relief (£5,000); Jewish Community Secondary School (£2,500); British ORT (£2,000).
FINANCES *Financial year end* 05/04/2022
Income £312,500
Grants to organisations £140,500
Assets £3,950,000
TRUSTEES Sheila Diamond; Dr Alan Diamond; Jonathan Kropman; Jerrold Bennett; Nicholas Edmunds; Nicky Goldman.
HOW TO APPLY The trust states that it will not consider unsolicited applications. Preliminary telephone calls are not welcomed. There are no regular trustees' meetings, but the trustees frequently decide how the funds should be allocated. The trustees have their own guidelines, which are not published.
CONTACT DETAILS Carla Hobby, Morris Lane and Co., 31 Commercial Road, Poole, Dorset BH14 0HU *Tel.* 01202 715950 *Email* carla.hobby@morrislane.co.uk

■ The Dibden Allotments Fund

CC NO 255778   **ESTABLISHED** 1995
WHERE FUNDING CAN BE GIVEN Dibden; Fawley; Hythe; Marchwood.
WHO CAN BENEFIT Individuals; charitable organisations; schools and colleges; amateur sports clubs; hospitals and hospices.
WHAT IS FUNDED The charity distributes grants under the following areas of work: disability; schools/colleges; children and young people; community and medical welfare.

WHAT IS NOT FUNDED Churches and religious groups for the promotion of religion; religious activities; activities which are only available to members of a church or religious group.
TYPE OF GRANT It should be noted that the charity aims to pump-prime rather than commit to ongoing support and therefore does not normally provide ongoing support for longer than three years.
RANGE OF GRANTS Up to £45,000.
SAMPLE GRANTS Solent Mind (£45,700); Cadland Primary School (£25,500); National Coastwatch Institution – Calshot Tower (£7,500); Fawley Parish Council (£5,400); Healthy Haven Garden (£3,000); New Forest Academy (£2,000); Stop Domestic Abuse (£1,100); Residents Group Charles Ley Court (£250).
FINANCES *Financial year end* 31/03/2022
Income £415,200
Grants to organisations £151,200
Grants to individuals £138,100
Assets £11,640,000
TRUSTEES Pat Hedges; Judith Saxby; Jill Tomlin; Alan Alvey; Christina James; Sean Cullen; Simon Lodge; Daniel Poole; Sandra Delemare.
OTHER INFORMATION During 2021/22, grants were broken down as follows: community (£74,900); schools and colleges (£45,900); young people (£27,700); medical welfare (£2,700).
HOW TO APPLY Application forms are available to download from the charity's website.
CONTACT DETAILS The Trustees, 7 Drummond Court, Prospect Place, Hythe, Hampshire SO45 6HD *Tel.* 023 8084 1305 *Email* dibdenallotments@btconnect.com *Website* www.daf-hythe.org.uk

■ The Gillian Dickinson Trust

CC NO 1094362   **ESTABLISHED** 2002
WHERE FUNDING CAN BE GIVEN County Durham; Northumberland; Tyne and Wear.
WHO CAN BENEFIT Registered charities; museums; arts and theatre groups; CICs.
WHAT IS FUNDED The promotion of creativity in young people from disadvantaged backgrounds.
TYPE OF GRANT Capital grants; one-off revenue costs.
RANGE OF GRANTS Up to £90,000.
SAMPLE GRANTS Dance City (£90,000); National Youth Choir (£25,000); Young Pianist of the North (£10,000); Monkchester CIC (£2,800); Northern Chords (£2,500); Northern Steel Network (£730).
FINANCES *Financial year end* 05/04/2022
Income £50,300
Grants to organisations £101,100
Assets £1,510,000
TRUSTEES Alexander Dickinson; Piers Dickinson; Adrian Gifford; Col. James Ramsbotham.
OTHER INFORMATION Grants were made to six organisations in 2021/22.
HOW TO APPLY Applications can be made using the trust's online application form, available on its website, where criteria and guidelines are also posted.
CONTACT DETAILS The Trustees, c/o Womble Bond Dickinson, The Spark, Draymans Way, Newcastle Helix, Newcastle upon Tyne, Tyne and Wear NE4 5DE *Tel.* 0191 279 9000 *Email* grants@gilliandickinsontrust.org.uk *Website* www.gilliandickinsontrust.org.uk

■ Didymus

CC NO 1152432   ESTABLISHED 2013

WHERE FUNDING CAN BE GIVEN England; Wales; Africa; Central America; South America.

WHO CAN BENEFIT Registered charities.

WHAT IS FUNDED Social inclusion; education; the arts; equality and diversity; religious understanding.

WHAT IS NOT FUNDED Large national charities (those with an annual income in excess of £2 million); charities dedicated to issues deemed well-funded by the trustees; statutory authorities.

RANGE OF GRANTS Mostly up to £5,000.

SAMPLE GRANTS Bees for Development (£10,000); Hope in Action (£9,200); Blooming Blossoms Trust (£5,000); Compass Children's Charity (£4,000); Cherwell Theatre Company (£3,000); Iris Theatre (£2,000); Drama Express (£1,500); Dingley Family and Specialist Early Years Centres (£420).

FINANCES *Financial year end 01/12/2021*
Income £1,200,000
Grants to organisations £369,400
Assets £5,150,000

TRUSTEES Caroline Cummins; Alan Wall; The Revd Dr Daphne Green; Helen Wall.

OTHER INFORMATION During 2020/21, 86 grants were awarded to organisations. The 2020/21 annual report and accounts were the latest available at the time of writing (May 2023).

HOW TO APPLY Applications can be made via the charity's website. Applications for funding may be made at any time. Applications received within six weeks of a trustees' meeting will be considered at the following meeting.

CONTACT DETAILS Sheila Powell, Cresswell Crabtree and Sons, 12 Market Street, Hebden Bridge, West Yorkshire HX7 6AD *Tel.* 01422 842431 *Email* info@didymus-charity.org.uk *Website* www.didymus-charity.org.uk

■ Digital Extra Fund

OSCR NO SC047272   ESTABLISHED 2017

WHERE FUNDING CAN BE GIVEN Scotland.

WHO CAN BENEFIT Charitable organisations; schools; universities.

WHAT IS FUNDED Developing the digital skills of children and young people.

WHAT IS NOT FUNDED The fund will not award grants to organisations whose work is carried out outside Scotland.

TYPE OF GRANT Project funding.

RANGE OF GRANTS Up to £5,000.

SAMPLE GRANTS Heart of Midlothian FC and Logie Primary School (£5,000 each); Muirhouse Primary School and Nursery Class (£4,100); University of the Highlands and Islands (£4,500); James Hamilton Primary School (£3,600); Lourdes Secondary School (£3,200); East Lothian Council (£2,700); Hillside Primary School (£1,800).

FINANCES *Financial year end 31/03/2022*
Income £230,300
Grants to organisations £152,600
Assets £29,700

TRUSTEES Polly Purvis; David McNeil; Gina Wilson; Debbie McCutcheon; Karen Meechan; Lisa Imlach; Michael Hall; Paddy Burns.

OTHER INFORMATION The fund awarded 35 grants to organisations during 2021/22, totalling £152,600. Grants were awarded mostly to primary and secondary schools.

HOW TO APPLY Apply via the fund's website, where application deadlines can also be found.

CONTACT DETAILS The Trustees, c/o ScotlandIS, Oracle Campus, Blackness Road, Springfield, Edinburgh EH49 7LR *Tel.* 01506 472200 *Email* info@digitalxtrafund.scot *Website* www.digitalxtrafund.scot

■ Dinwoodie Charitable Company

CC NO 1151139   ESTABLISHED 1968

WHERE FUNDING CAN BE GIVEN UK.

WHO CAN BENEFIT Research fellowships; postgraduate medical centres.

WHAT IS FUNDED The provision of medical and healthcare education and training.

WHAT IS NOT FUNDED Basic scientific research unless related to medical education; the 'on-costs' of infrastructure projects (maintenance, refurbishment, replacement or salaries other than those directly relating to project management); undergraduate education (although consideration might be given to innovative proposals from new medical schools); projects in vulnerable institutions unless part of an agreed turn-around process.

TYPE OF GRANT Project funding; research.

RANGE OF GRANTS Up to £1 million.

SAMPLE GRANTS Faculty of Medical Leadership and Management (£136,900); Royal College of Surgeons – Oxford University (£36,300); Royal College of Obstetrics and Gynaecology (£25,000); Sandwell and Birmingham (£13,700); Royal College of Paediatrics and Child Healthcare (£3,300).

FINANCES *Financial year end 31/03/2022*
Income £815,300
Grants to organisations £181,200
Assets £8,330,000

TRUSTEES Ian Goalen; John Pears; Dr Elizabeth Hughes; Richard Miner; Christine Hall.

OTHER INFORMATION Grants were awarded to five organisations. Grants were broken down as follows: postgraduate medical centres (£178,800) and research fellowships (£36,300).

HOW TO APPLY Apply in writing to the correspondent.

CONTACT DETAILS Ian Goalen, Managing Trustee, 4 Tytherington Green, Macclesfield, Cheshire SK10 2FA *Tel.* 01625 610549 *Email* dinwoodie@irwinmitchell.com

■ The Dischma Charitable Trust

CC NO 1077501   ESTABLISHED 1999

WHERE FUNDING CAN BE GIVEN Worldwide, with a strong preference for London and Hampshire.

WHO CAN BENEFIT Charitable organisations.

WHAT IS FUNDED General charitable purposes, with a preference for: education; arts and culture; conservation; human and animal welfare.

WHAT IS NOT FUNDED Medical research charities.

RANGE OF GRANTS £4,000 to £10,000.

SAMPLE GRANTS Glass Door (£10,000); Hackney Migrant Centre and Womankind (£5,000 each); The Film and Television Charity and The Girls' Network (£2,000 each); Abortion Support Network and Age UK (£1,000 each); Surfers Against Sewage (£500); Care for Children (£400).

FINANCES *Financial year end 31/12/2021*
Income £26,000
Grants to organisations £107,000
Assets £8,020,000

TRUSTEES Virginia Robertson; Sir Simon Robertson; Lorna Timmis; Edward Robertson; Selina Robertson; Alana Robertson.

OTHER INFORMATION Grants were made to 50 organisations and broken down as follows: general medical causes, mental health and disability (£31,300); general (£23,400); wildlife and conservation (£13,500); homelessness (£13,000); children and youth welfare (£11,400); older people (£5,500); the arts, theatres and museums (£4,500); education (£2,500); animal welfare (£2,000).

HOW TO APPLY Apply in writing to the correspondent. The trustees meet half-yearly to review applications for funding. Only successful applicants are notified of the trustees' decision.

CONTACT DETAILS Linda Cousins, Secretary, Rathbones, 8 Finsbury Circus, London EC2M 7AZ *Tel.* 020 7399 0820 *Email* linda. cousins@rathbones.com

■ The Djanogly Foundation

CC NO 280500   **ESTABLISHED** 1980
WHERE FUNDING CAN BE GIVEN UK and Israel.
WHO CAN BENEFIT Registered charities; schools and universities.
WHAT IS FUNDED Jewish causes; arts and culture.
TYPE OF GRANT Project funding, particularly projects that are new and may require a number of years to establish.
RANGE OF GRANTS £200 to £100,000.
SAMPLE GRANTS National Portrait Gallery (£100,000); Imperial War Museum (£25,000); Jewish Care (£12,500); Nottingham City Academy (£10,000); United Synagogue (£2,500); Lina Paulione (£200).
FINANCES *Financial year end 05/04/2022*
Income £45,800
Grants to organisations £225,000
Assets £4,100,000
TRUSTEES Sir Harry Djanogly; Michael Djanogly; Jonathan Djanogly.
OTHER INFORMATION The foundation awarded grants to 18 organisations during the year.
HOW TO APPLY Contact the correspondent for further information.
CONTACT DETAILS The Trustees, 3 Angel Court, London SW1Y 6QF *Tel.* 020 7930 9845

■ The DLM Charitable Trust

CC NO 328520   **ESTABLISHED** 1990
WHERE FUNDING CAN BE GIVEN UK, mainly the Oxfordshire area.
WHO CAN BENEFIT Registered charities.
WHAT IS FUNDED General charitable purposes.
WHAT IS NOT FUNDED Individuals.
RANGE OF GRANTS Mostly under £5,000.
SAMPLE GRANTS Flourishing Families Leeds (£10,000); Child Autism UK and Thames Valley Air Ambulance (£5,000 each); Crisis – Skylight Oxford (£4,000); Aspire Oxford and Listening Books (£3,000 each); Cruse Bereavement Support and Wolvercote Young Peoples Club (£2,000 each).
FINANCES *Financial year end 05/04/2022*
Income £142,000
Grants to organisations £116,000
Assets £9,150,000
TRUSTEES Jeffrey Cloke; Jennifer Pyper; Philippa Sawyer.
HOW TO APPLY Apply in writing to the correspondent.
CONTACT DETAILS The Trustees, Stow House, Cotswold Road, Cumnor Hill, Oxford, Oxfordshire OX2 9JG *Tel.* 01865 709183 *Email* dlmcharitabletrust@gmail.com

■ William and Frances Dobie Charitable Foundation

CC NO 1172795   **ESTABLISHED** 2017
WHERE FUNDING CAN BE GIVEN England and Wales.
WHO CAN BENEFIT Charitable organisations.
WHAT IS FUNDED General charitable purposes; education/training; the advancement of health or saving of lives; religious activities.
SAMPLE GRANTS A list of beneficiaries was not included in the annual report and accounts.
FINANCES *Financial year end 05/04/2022*
Income £54,800
Grants to organisations £54,300
Assets £1,700,000
TRUSTEES Jonathan Parkin; Carl McColgan; Charles Platts.
HOW TO APPLY Apply in writing to the correspondent.
CONTACT DETAILS Carl McColgan, Trustee, 62 Bridge Lane, Bramhall, Stockport SK7 3AW *Tel.* 0161 834 9440

■ The Ken Dodd Charitable Foundation

CC NO 1179779   **ESTABLISHED** 2013
WHERE FUNDING CAN BE GIVEN UK, with a preference for Merseyside.
WHO CAN BENEFIT Charitable organisations.
WHAT IS FUNDED Performing arts; social welfare.
RANGE OF GRANTS Generally between £5,000 and £20,000, with some larger grants of up to £250,000.
SAMPLE GRANTS Shakespeare North Playhouse Trust (£250,000); St John the Evangelist Church – Knotty Ash (£120,000); Nextup Comedy Ltd (£25,000); Liverpool and Merseyside Theatres Trust Ltd and The Salvation Army (£20,000 each); Whitechapel Centre (£10,000); The Hammond School Ltd (£5,000); Worcester Operatic and Dramatic Society (£1,000).
FINANCES *Financial year end 31/03/2022*
Income £526,800
Grants to organisations £466,000
Assets £13,310,000
TRUSTEES Lady Anne Dodd; Peter Vaines; John Lewis.
OTHER INFORMATION Grants were awarded to ten organisations during the year.
HOW TO APPLY Apply in writing to the correspondent.
CONTACT DETAILS The Trustees, Barristers Chambers, 3 Field Court, London WC1R 5EP *Tel.* 020 3693 3700

■ Dollond Charitable Trust

CC NO 293459   **ESTABLISHED** 1986
WHERE FUNDING CAN BE GIVEN UK and Israel.
WHO CAN BENEFIT Jewish organisations.
WHAT IS FUNDED Jewish causes.
SAMPLE GRANTS A list of beneficiaries was not included in the annual report and accounts.
FINANCES *Financial year end 31/03/2022*
Income £1,170,000
Grants to organisations £1,800,000
Assets £53,030,000
TRUSTEES Adrian Dollond; Jeffrey Milston; Melissa Dollond; Brian Dollond; Rina Dollond.
OTHER INFORMATION Although the constitution of the charity is broad, the trustees have adopted a policy of principally assisting the Jewish communities in Britain and Israel. Grants to 180 organisations were distributed as follows: religious education (£520,000); education and training (£335,000); relief of poverty

(£327,500); health and medical causes (£270,000); disability (£225,000); other religious activities (£100,000).

HOW TO APPLY Apply in writing to the correspondent.

CONTACT DETAILS Brian Dollond, Trustee and Secretary, 3rd Floor, Hathaway House, Popes Drive, Finchley, London N3 1QF *Tel.* 020 8346 6446

■ Donibristle Trust

CCNI NO NIC101313 **ESTABLISHED** 2000

WHERE FUNDING CAN BE GIVEN Worldwide, but mainly financially developing countries.

WHO CAN BENEFIT Charitable organisations.

WHAT IS FUNDED Advancement of Christianity; education; health; relief of hardship and disadvantage; community development; overseas aid.

SAMPLE GRANTS A list of beneficiaries was not included in the annual report and accounts.

FINANCES *Financial year end* 30/04/2022
Income £265,100
Grants to organisations £303,500
Assets £256,400

TRUSTEES Ian MacCorkell; Heather MacCorkell; Cheryl Jenkins; Colin MacCorkell.

HOW TO APPLY Apply in writing to the correspondent.

CONTACT DETAILS Ian MacCorkell, Trustee, Unit 4 Garvey Studios, 8–10 Longstone Street, Lisburn, County Antrim BT28 1TP *Tel.* 028 9266 9777 *Email* donibristletrust@gmail.com

■ The Dorcas Trust

CC NO 275494 **ESTABLISHED** 1978

WHERE FUNDING CAN BE GIVEN UK.

WHO CAN BENEFIT Registered charities; retired missionaries and clergy who are in need.

WHAT IS FUNDED Christian causes; relief of poverty;advancement of education.

RANGE OF GRANTS Up to £23,000.

SAMPLE GRANTS Navigators (£23,000); Calderwood House (£5,000); Church Army (£3,000); Making a Difference to Maidstone (£2,500); Christian Heritage (£2,000); Azalea (£1,000); Bentley Beginners (£750); St Margaret's – Chippenham (£500).

FINANCES *Financial year end* 05/04/2022
Income £55,800
Grants to organisations £75,000
Grants to individuals £3,600
Assets £2,310,000

TRUSTEES Jan Broad; Peter Butler; James Broad; Paul Mangell.

OTHER INFORMATION The trustees will also consider making loans to organisations and individuals.

HOW TO APPLY Apply in writing to the correspondent.

CONTACT DETAILS James Broad, Trustee, 14 Albert Crescent, Bury St Edmunds, Suffolk IP33 3DY *Email* JamesBroad@cygnet.org.uk

■ The Dorfman Foundation

CC NO 1120714 **ESTABLISHED** 2007

WHERE FUNDING CAN BE GIVEN Worldwide.

WHO CAN BENEFIT Registered charities; educational and cultural establishments; hospitals.

WHAT IS FUNDED General charitable purposes, especially Jewish causes, education and training, health and the arts.

RANGE OF GRANTS Mostly up to £50,000.

SAMPLE GRANTS Nightingale Hammerson (£666,700); Royal Marsden Cancer Charity (£250,000); Community Security Trust (£100,000); Norwood Ravenswood (£35,000); Royal Academy Trust (£20,000); Dalaid (£15,000); Holocaust Educational Trust (£12,500); AJEX Charitable Foundation and World Jewish Relief (£10,000 each).

FINANCES *Financial year end* 05/04/2022
Income £142,600
Grants to organisations £1,060,000
Assets £4,650,000

TRUSTEES Amy Lux; Sophie Dorfman; Sir Lloyd Dorfman; Anthony Wagerman; Sarah Dorfman; Peter Leach; Charles Dorfman.

OTHER INFORMATION Grants of £5,000 or under totalled £23,000.

HOW TO APPLY The foundation does not accept unsolicited applications. Its website notes that the trustees tend to support charities that they 'have come to know over time'.

CONTACT DETAILS The Trustees, 22 Manchester Square, London W1U 3PT *Tel.* 020 7725 1221 *Email* charity.correspondence@bdo.co.uk *Website* http://dorfmanfoundation.org.uk

■ Dorset Community Foundation

CC NO 1122113 **ESTABLISHED** 2007

WHERE FUNDING CAN BE GIVEN The county of Dorset, including the authorities of Bournemouth and Poole.

WHO CAN BENEFIT Voluntary and community organisations; charities; CICs; individuals.

WHAT IS FUNDED General charitable purposes including: social welfare; the environment; community development.

WHAT IS NOT FUNDED A full list of exclusions can be found on the foundation's website.

TYPE OF GRANT Project funding; core/revenue funding; capital funding; strategic funding.

RANGE OF GRANTS Mostly up to £8,000.

SAMPLE GRANTS Citizens Advice Central (£30,000); Wimborne Community Theatre (£13,000); The Mowlem Institute Charity (£10,000); Access Dorset (£8,700); Christchurch Foodbank (£8,100).

FINANCES *Financial year end* 31/03/2022
Income £2,360,000
Grants to organisations £660,800
Grants to individuals £113,700
Assets £4,810,000

TRUSTEES Nick Fernyhough; Paul Sizeland; William Ansell; Simon Young; Terry Standing; Deborah Appleby; Louise Coulton; Tom Flood; Nick Lee.

OTHER INFORMATION This is one of the 47 UK community foundations, which distribute funding for a wide range of purposes. As with all community foundations, there are a number of donor-advised funds managed on behalf of individuals, families and charitable trusts. Grant schemes tend to change frequently – consult the foundation's website for details of current programmes and up-to-date deadlines. Only organisations that received grants of over £8,000 were listed as beneficiaries in the foundation's accounts. Grants of under £8,000 totalled £362,600.

HOW TO APPLY Applications can be made online through the foundation's website.

CONTACT DETAILS The Trustees, The Spire, High Street, Poole, Dorset BH15 1DF *Tel.* 01202 670815 *Email* grants@dorsetcf.org *Website* www.dorsetcommunityfoundation.org

■ The Dorset Historic Churches Trust

cc no 282790   **ESTABLISHED** 1960
WHERE FUNDING CAN BE GIVEN Dorset.
WHO CAN BENEFIT Churches.
WHAT IS FUNDED The restoration or preservation of Christian places of public worship, regardless of denomination.
WHAT IS NOT FUNDED Routine maintenance and decoration; works in the churchyard; heating and electrical maintenance; new buildings or extensions; new furniture or fittings; new bells or new bell frames; replacement or repair of organs; clocks or sound systems.
RANGE OF GRANTS From £1,000 to £12,000.
SAMPLE GRANTS St Mary – Stoke Abbott (£12,000); St Martin – Lillington and St Michael – Lyme Regis (£10,000 each); St Mary's – Sturminster Marshall (£7,000); St Nicholas – Worth Matravers (£6,000); St John the Baptist – Hawkchurch (£5,000); St Mary Magdelene – North Poorton (£1,000).
FINANCES *Financial year end 31/12/2021*
Income £158,900
Grants to organisations £85,700
Assets £692,700
TRUSTEES Col. Jeremy Selfe; Susan Bruce-Payne; Dr Timothy Connor; Susan Smith; Philippa Francis; James Smith; Steven Norman; Giles Sturdy; Maj. General John Stokoe; Thomas Wickson; Michael Warren; David Grant; The Revd Andrew Rowland; Sally-Anne Stanbury; Nicholas Head; Christopher Waite.
OTHER INFORMATION Grants were awarded to 42 churches in 2021.
HOW TO APPLY Applications should be made to the deanery representative of the trust in the area in which the church is located, on a form available to download, together with criteria and guidelines, from the website.
CONTACT DETAILS Grants Secretary, DHCT c/o Porter Dodson, Suite 1, Mey House, Bridport Road, Poundbury, Dorset DT1 3QY *Tel.* 01305 852138 *Email* grantssecretary@dhct.org.uk *Website* www.dorsethistoricchurchestrust.co.uk

■ The Dorus Trust

cc no 328724   **ESTABLISHED** 1990
WHERE FUNDING CAN BE GIVEN UK.
WHO CAN BENEFIT Registered UK charities.
WHAT IS FUNDED General charitable purposes; education and training; the advancement of health or saving of lives; disability; the prevention or relief of poverty; overseas aid/famine relief; accommodation and housing; arts, culture, heritage, science; amateur sport; the environment, conservation and heritage; economic, community development and employment.
WHAT IS NOT FUNDED Individuals.
TYPE OF GRANT Project and one-off grants.
RANGE OF GRANTS £3,000 to £10,000.
SAMPLE GRANTS Switchback (£10,000); St Raphael's Hospice (£8,000); Home-Start Merton (£7,000); Crisis (£6,000); Action for M.E. (£5,000); The Scar Free Foundation (£4,000); Royal Choral Society (£3,000).
FINANCES *Financial year end 31/12/2021*
Income £29,300
Grants to organisations £70,000
Assets £4,560,000
TRUSTEES Bettine Bond; Charles Peacock; Sarah Peacock.
OTHER INFORMATION The trust made grants to 12 organisations.

HOW TO APPLY Apply in writing to the correspondent.
CONTACT DETAILS Charles Peacock, Trustee, Charities Aid Foundation, 25 Kings Hill Avenue, Kings Hill, West Malling, Kent ME19 4TA *Tel.* 0300 012 3334

■ The Double 'O' Charity Ltd

cc no 271681   **ESTABLISHED** 1976
WHERE FUNDING CAN BE GIVEN UK.
WHO CAN BENEFIT Registered charities; educational institutions; individuals.
WHAT IS FUNDED General charitable purposes including: social welfare to reduce poverty; health; education.
RANGE OF GRANTS Mostly up to £10,000, with the occasional larger grant.
SAMPLE GRANTS De Tao Masters Academy (£56,100); Spirit of Recovery (£30,300); Royal British Legion (£10,000); John Badley Foundation (£5,000); The Salvation Army and Vineyard Community (£1,500 each); City of Westminster Charitable Trust and Sustainability Shrivenham (£500 each).
FINANCES *Financial year end 31/05/2022*
Income £188,500
Grants to organisations £115,900
Grants to individuals £51,000
Assets £29,600
TRUSTEES Peter Townshend; Rachel Townshend.
HOW TO APPLY Unsolicited applications are not accepted.
CONTACT DETAILS The Trustees, Crown Studios, 16–18 Crown Road, Twickenham TW1 3EE *Tel.* 020 8940 8171

■ The Doughty Charity Trust

cc no 274977   **ESTABLISHED** 1977
WHERE FUNDING CAN BE GIVEN England and Israel.
WHO CAN BENEFIT Jewish charitable organisations.
WHAT IS FUNDED Orthodox Jewish religious education; relief of poverty.
RANGE OF GRANTS Less than £50,000.
SAMPLE GRANTS A list of beneficiaries was not included in the annual report and accounts.
FINANCES *Financial year end 31/12/2021*
Income £315,900
Grants to organisations £459,100
Assets £735,700
TRUSTEES Mr G. Halibard; Mrs M. Halibard.
HOW TO APPLY The trustees have stated that the trust's funds are fully committed and therefore they do not accept unsolicited applications.
CONTACT DETAILS The Trustees, 22 Ravenscroft Avenue, London NW11 0RY *Tel.* 020 8209 0500

■ The D'Oyly Carte Charitable Trust

cc no 1112457   **ESTABLISHED** 1972
WHERE FUNDING CAN BE GIVEN UK.
WHO CAN BENEFIT UK-registered charities.
WHAT IS FUNDED The arts; health; social welfare; environmental protection or improvement.
WHAT IS NOT FUNDED A full list of exclusions can be found on the trust's website.
TYPE OF GRANT Project funding and core costs. Matched funding is also considered. The majority of the trust's grants are single grants awarded over a one-year period. Occasionally, longer-term grants (usually awarded for up to

three years) are agreed by the trustees when deemed to have particular merit.

RANGE OF GRANTS Up to £15,000 but typically between £500 and £6,000.

SAMPLE GRANTS Hospice UK (£15,000); Queen Elizabeth Scholarship Trust (£10,000); Sense (£5,000); Apollo Music Projects and Oxford Hospitals Charity (£4,000 each); Tourette Syndrome UK Association (£3,500); Special Stars Foundation (£2,000); Abbeyfield Reading Society (£1,000).

FINANCES *Financial year end 31/03/2022*
Income £1,180,000
Grants to organisations £1,800,000
Assets £66,470,000

TRUSTEES Henry Freeland; Andrew Jackson; Dr Michael O'Brien; Julia Sibley; Andrew Wimble; Amelia Beringer; Nina Camilleri; Prof. Frances Flinter.

OTHER INFORMATION Grants paid during the 2021/22 totalled £1.8 million. The following breakdown was provided (including grants committed but not yet paid): arts (£841,100); medical welfare (£722,400); the environment (£369,700).

HOW TO APPLY Apply online via the trust's website. The trust's website lists the relevant submission dates and has detailed guidelines on how to apply. The trustees usually consider applications three times a year in March, July and November.

CONTACT DETAILS Grants Administrator, 6 Trull Farm Buildings, Tetbury, Gloucestershire GL8 8SQ *Tel.* 020 3637 3003 *Email* info@doylycartecharitabletrust.org *Website* www.doylycartecharitabletrust.org

---

■ Dr. Martens Foundation

CC NO 1194513   **ESTABLISHED** 2021
WHERE FUNDING CAN BE GIVEN Worldwide.
WHO CAN BENEFIT Charitable organisations.
WHAT IS FUNDED Human rights; social justice; social welfare.
SAMPLE GRANTS A list of beneficiaries was not available.
FINANCES *Financial year end 31/03/2022*
Grants to organisations £753,800
TRUSTEES Emily Reichwald; Paul Armstrong; Tuze Schwank; Pamela Shores; Darren Campbell.
OTHER INFORMATION The charity is the corporate foundation of Dr. Martens plc. As the foundation is a newly registered charity, full accounts were not available to view on the Charity Commission's website. However, Dr. Martens plc's 2021/22 annual report states that the foundation made 41 grants during the year.
HOW TO APPLY The foundation is not accepting unsolicited applications as grant-making is currently by invitation only.
CONTACT DETAILS The Trustees, 28 Jamestown Road, Camden, London NW1 7BY *Tel.* 020 3995 2626 *Email* dmfoundation@drmartens.com *Website* www.drmartensplc.com/sustainability/people

---

■ Drapers Charitable Fund

CC NO 251403   **ESTABLISHED** 1959
WHERE FUNDING CAN BE GIVEN England, Wales and Northern Ireland, with a strong preference for disadvantaged areas of Greater London.
WHO CAN BENEFIT Registered or exempt charities; schools and universities.
WHAT IS FUNDED Social welfare including homelessness, prisoners, ex-Service personnel,

general welfare and disability; education and young people; textiles and heritage.

WHAT IS NOT FUNDED A comprehensive list of exclusions can be found on the charity's website.

TYPE OF GRANT Core costs (including salaries); project costs. Most grants are one-off payments but occasionally multi-year grants are awarded.

RANGE OF GRANTS Generally up to £15,000.

SAMPLE GRANTS Bancroft's School (£70,000 in two grants); Bangor University (£40,000); The Honorable Irish Society and Jamie's Farm (£30,000 each); Literacy Pirates and Prisoners' Education Trust (£25,000 each); Handel House Museum Trust (£20,000); The Textile Conservation Foundation (£15,500); Garden Classroom, Hackney Doorways and Young Women's Trust (£15,000 each).

FINANCES *Financial year end 31/07/2022*
Income £2,780,000
Grants to organisations £2,400,000
Grants to individuals £9,500
Assets £78,920,000

TRUSTEE The Drapers' Company.

OTHER INFORMATION Grants were awarded in the following categories: education and young people (£1.03 million in 88 grants); social welfare (£509,800 in 37 grants); prisoner support (£186,400 in 14 grants); homelessness (£191,800 in 14 grants); textiles and heritage (£94,300 in 14 grants); miscellaneous (£86,700); ex-Service personnel (£80,000 in 5 grants); disability (£51,600 in 4 grants); Northern Ireland (£30,000 in 1 grant).

HOW TO APPLY Applications can be submitted by email. You will need to send a detailed proposal explaining what your organisation does and how you intend to spend the funds, your most recent annual report and accounts, and a completed application summary sheet, which can be found on the charity's website alongside guidelines on how to apply.

CONTACT DETAILS Head of Charities, The Drapers' Company, Drapers' Hall, Throgmorton Avenue, London EC2N 2DQ *Tel.* 020 7588 5001 *Email* charities@thedrapers.co.uk *Website* https://thedrapers.co.uk/drapers-charitable-fund

---

■ Dromintee Trust

CC NO 1053956   **ESTABLISHED** 1996
WHERE FUNDING CAN BE GIVEN UK and overseas, with a preference for Leicestershire.
WHO CAN BENEFIT Charitable organisations.
WHAT IS FUNDED General charitable purposes; education/training; health; disability; the prevention or relief of poverty; overseas aid/famine relief; accommodation/housing; religious activities; arts/culture/heritage/science; the environment/conservation/heritage; economic/community; development/employment.
RANGE OF GRANTS £3,000 to £100,000.
SAMPLE GRANTS Consolata Fathers – Makiunga Hospital, Tanzania (£100,000); The Good Counsel Network (£50,000); Holy Cross Priory – Frassati Centre (25,000); Mary's Meals (£20,000); African Mission (£10,000) Leicestershire and Rutland Blood Bikes (£3,000).
FINANCES *Financial year end 31/03/2022*
Income £343,800
Grants to organisations £430,600
Assets £3,390,000
TRUSTEES Robert Smith; Hugh Murphy; Margaret Murphy; Paul Tiernan; Mary Middleton; Patrick Murphy; Joseph Murphy.

OTHER INFORMATION Grants were made to 18 organisations during the year.
HOW TO APPLY Apply in writing to the correspondent.
CONTACT DETAILS Hugh Murphy, Trustee, 1 Westmoreland Avenue, Thurmaston, Leicester, Leicestershire LE4 8PH *Tel.* 0116 260 3877 *Email* drominteetrust@gmail.com

■ The DS Smith Charitable Foundation
CC NO 1142817   **ESTABLISHED** 2011
WHERE FUNDING CAN BE GIVEN England and Wales.
WHO CAN BENEFIT Registered charities and voluntary organisations.
WHAT IS FUNDED Education and training; environmental conservation.
RANGE OF GRANTS A combination of small (less than £1,000) and larger donations each year. The foundation welcomes opportunities to develop multi-year partnerships with key selected charities.
SAMPLE GRANTS Previous beneficiaries have included: Ellen MacArthur Foundation (£150,000); Unicef (£42,600); The Royal Institute (£10,000); Litter Angels (£6,000); Earth Restoration (£2,000).
FINANCES *Financial year end* 30/04/2022 *Income* £11,600 *Grants to organisations* £350,000
TRUSTEES Mark Reeve; Emma Ciechan; Wouter Tol; Giulio Giannini; Diana Ciuraru.
OTHER INFORMATION The foundation's annual report and accounts were not available to view on the Charity Commission's website due to its low income. We have therefore estimated the foundation's grant total based on its total expenditure.
HOW TO APPLY Application forms are available from the foundation's website.
CONTACT DETAILS The Trustees, 7th Floor, 350 Euston Road, London NW1 3AX *Tel.* 020 7756 1823 *Email* charitablefoundation@ dssmith.com *Website* www.dssmith.com/ sustainability/building-strong-foundations/ looking-after-people-and-our-communities/ responsible-neighbour/charitable-foundation

■ Duchy Health Charity Ltd
CC NO 271957   **ESTABLISHED** 1976
WHERE FUNDING CAN BE GIVEN Cornwall and the Isles of Scilly.
WHO CAN BENEFIT Registered charities; other healthcare organisations.
WHAT IS FUNDED Health; well-being; the provision of health care.
TYPE OF GRANT Project costs; capital costs; equipment and services.
SAMPLE GRANTS The Chaos Group (£31,300); University of Exeter (£20,000); Clear (£10,000); The Hugs Foundation (£5,000); Drama Express (£1,000).
FINANCES *Financial year end* 31/03/2022 *Income* £216,000 *Grants to organisations* £152,700 *Assets* £6,170,000
TRUSTEES Sally-Jane Coode; Tim Guy; Carol O'Brien; Dr Barbara Vann; Graham Murdoch; Mark Williams; Aldyth Hambly-Staite; Jonathon Croggon; James Robinson; Dr John Evers; Dr Tamsyn Anderson; Katy Hutchinson.
OTHER INFORMATION Grants were made to 17 organisations during the year.

HOW TO APPLY The charity has an online application process – see the website for more information.
CONTACT DETAILS Helen Newton, Administrator, c/o Robinson Reed Layton LLP, Peat House, Newham Road, Truro, Cornwall TR1 2DP *Tel.* 01872 276116 *Email* mark.williams@ rrlcornwall.co.uk *Website* www. duchyhealthcharity.org

■ Duchy of Lancaster Benevolent Fund
CC NO 1026752   **ESTABLISHED** 1993
WHERE FUNDING CAN BE GIVEN Greater Manchester; Lancashire; Merseyside; elsewhere in the country where the Duchy of Lancaster has historical links.
WHO CAN BENEFIT Charitable organisations; schools; CICs; churches.
WHAT IS FUNDED Youth and education; people with disabilities; older people and people who are unwell; community help; religious causes.
RANGE OF GRANTS Mostly up to £5,000.
SAMPLE GRANTS Independence at Home (£10,000); Lancaster University Regional Heritage Trust (£9,000); Youth Action – Blackburn (£5,000); Manchester Cathedral (£3,500); Serve (£3,000); Cloughton Bowling Club (£2,000).
FINANCES *Financial year end* 31/03/2022 *Income* £510,900 *Grants to organisations* £594,000 *Assets* £18,410,000
TRUSTEES Lord Charles Shuttleworth; Sir Michael Stevens; Mark Blundell; Sonia Tolaney; The Hon. Justice Fancourt; Diane Hawkins.
OTHER INFORMATION Grants were broken down as follows: community help (£277,900); young people and education (£171,700); people with disabilities and older people (£91,200); religious causes (£48,800); miscellaneous (£4,500).
HOW TO APPLY Applicants in Lancashire, Greater Manchester and Merseyside should apply directly to their local Lieutenancy office. For eligible organisations outside these areas, an application form is available to download from the website and should be submitted by email to benfund@duchyoflancaster.co.uk, for consideration by the London panel.
CONTACT DETAILS The Secretary, 1 Lancaster Place, Strand, London WC2E 7ED *Tel.* 020 7269 1700 *Email* info@duchyoflancaster.co.uk *Website* www.duchyoflancaster.co.uk/about-the-duchy/duties-of-the-duchy/benevolent-fund

■ The Duke of Cornwall's Benevolent Fund
CC NO 269183   **ESTABLISHED** 1975
WHERE FUNDING CAN BE GIVEN UK, with a preference for Cornwall.
WHO CAN BENEFIT Charitable organisations.
WHAT IS FUNDED Social welfare; provision of almshouses, hospitals and hospices; education and training; arts and culture; religion; heritage and historic buildings.
RANGE OF GRANTS Up to £100,000 but generally £1,000 to £5,000.
SAMPLE GRANTS Cornwall Community Foundation – Environmental and Marine Fund (£100,000); Cornwall Community Foundation – Cornwall Crisis Fund (£40,000); Chapter of Truro Cathedral (£30,000); Cornwall Community Foundation – Young Carers Fund (£10,000);

Sea Sanctuary (£5,000); Trevuras Pond Restoration (£1,000).

FINANCES *Financial year end 30/06/2022*
Income £317,000
Grants to organisations £260,500
Grants to individuals £1,000
Assets £6,210,000

TRUSTEES Alastair Martin; Edward Harley.

OTHER INFORMATION Grants were awarded to 52 organisations and 1 individual during the year.

HOW TO APPLY Apply in writing to the correspondent.

CONTACT DETAILS The Trustees, Duchy of Cornwall, 10 Buckingham Gate, London SW1E 6LA *Tel.* 020 7834 7346

■ Duke of Devonshire's Charitable Trust

CC NO 213519   **ESTABLISHED** 1949

WHERE FUNDING CAN BE GIVEN Projects in areas which are local or relevant to Chatsworth, Bolton Abbey and the other Devonshire Group estates (Lismore Castle and Careysville Fishery in the Republic of Ireland).

WHO CAN BENEFIT UK-registered charities; CICs.

WHAT IS FUNDED General charitable purposes.

WHAT IS NOT FUNDED Requests made within 12 months of the outcome of a previously unsuccessful application; individuals or individual research or study; projects outside the UK; multi-year funding; organisations which cannot demonstrate significant progress with fundraising.

RANGE OF GRANTS Typically £250 to £10,000.

SAMPLE GRANTS British Red Cross (£10,000); Homes for the Homeless (£5,000); Martin House Children's Hospice (£1,800); Townend Community Garden (£1,000); Rude Mechanical (£500).

FINANCES *Financial year end 05/04/2022*
Income £118,800
Grants to organisations £264,100
Assets £1,670,000

TRUSTEES Duke of Devonshire Peregrine Andrew Morny Cavendish; Duchess of Devonshire; William Cavendish; Oliver Stephenson.

HOW TO APPLY Application forms can be found on the trust's website.

CONTACT DETAILS Mollie Moseley, Chatsworth, Bakewell, Derbyshire DE45 1PP *Email* mollie. moseley@chatsworth.org *Website* www.ddct.org. uk

■ The Dulverton Trust

CC NO 1146484   **ESTABLISHED** 1949

WHERE FUNDING CAN BE GIVEN UK (excluding Greater London and Northern Ireland); Kenya; Uganda.

WHO CAN BENEFIT Registered charities; CIOs. Particularly medium-sized charities (i.e. with an income of £200,000 to £3 million).

WHAT IS FUNDED Youth opportunities; general welfare; conservation; heritage; peace and humanitarian support; community development and conservation in Kenya and Uganda.

WHAT IS NOT FUNDED The trust is very unlikely to support work that focuses on research. Grants are not given to charities benefitting residents of Northern Ireland or London. Grants to UK charities operating in Kenya and Uganda are restricted to those with whom the trust has an existing relationship.

TYPE OF GRANT Capital costs; core/revenue costs; seed funding/start-up funding; project funding;

unrestricted funding. Single and multi-year grants are awarded.

RANGE OF GRANTS Typically between £25,000 and £35,000.

SAMPLE GRANTS Bumblebee Conservation Trust (£120,000); Future Trees Trust (£90,000); Coventry Cathedral (£40,000); Textile Conservation Foundation (£20,000); Child Bereavement UK (£10,000); RFEA – The Forces Employment Charity (£5,000); The Linking Network (£800).

FINANCES *Financial year end 31/03/2022*
Income £2,870,000
Grants to organisations £3,840,000
Assets £116,130,000

TRUSTEES Christopher Wills; Richard Howard; Lord Dulverton; Dame Mary Richardson; Tara Douglas-Home; Sir Malcolm Rifkind; Lord Hemphill; Robert Wills.

OTHER INFORMATION In 2021/22, grants in the UK were distributed as follows: youth opportunities (£1.56 million); community foundations (£772,300); general welfare (£734,400); conservation (£394,300); community foundations – Merseyside and Lancashire (£186,400); heritage (£156,000); Kent Community Foundation (£91,800); local appeals (£13,000).

HOW TO APPLY Apply online via the trust's website. Applications are accepted all year round, but the trustees make decisions in February, June and October.

CONTACT DETAILS Eleanor Hingley, Grants Manager, 5 St James's Place, London SW1A 1NP *Tel.* 020 7495 7852 *Email* grants@dulverton. org *Website* www.dulverton.org

■ Dumbreck Charity

CC NO 273070   **ESTABLISHED** 1976

WHERE FUNDING CAN BE GIVEN Warwickshire; the West Midlands; Worcestershire.

WHO CAN BENEFIT Charitable organisations.

WHAT IS FUNDED General charitable purposes including: animal welfare and conservation; children's welfare; older people; people with disabilities; health; social welfare; arts and culture.

WHAT IS NOT FUNDED Individuals.

RANGE OF GRANTS Mostly £500 to £2,000.

SAMPLE GRANTS Shipston Home Nursing (£3,000); Acorns and The British Horse Society (£2,000 each); Birmingham Hippodrome Theatre Trust and Straight Talking (£1,000 each); Pershore Civic Society (£750); Dog Assistance in Disability and YMCA Sutton Coldfield (£500 each).

FINANCES *Financial year end 05/04/2022*
Income £172,200
Grants to organisations £150,500
Assets £5,270,000

TRUSTEES Judith Melling; Jane Uloth; Hugh Carslake.

OTHER INFORMATION In 2021/22, grants were broken down as follows: miscellaneous (£37,500); medical causes (£30,000); older people and mental health (£19,000); social welfare (£19,000); culture and the arts (£15,000); children's welfare (£14,500); animal welfare and conservation (£13,500).

HOW TO APPLY Contact the correspondent for further information.

CONTACT DETAILS The Trustees, PS Accounting, 41 Sycamore Drive, Hollywood, Birmingham B47 5QX *Tel.* 07976 848390 *Email* psaccounting@hotmail.co.uk

■ Dumfriesshire East Community Benefit Group SCIO

OSCR NO SC047593
WHERE FUNDING CAN BE GIVEN East Dumfriesshire.
WHO CAN BENEFIT Charities and community groups.
WHAT IS FUNDED Education; citizenship and community development; arts, science, heritage and culture; recreational facilities; the environment.
TYPE OF GRANT Project funding.
RANGE OF GRANTS Typically up to £20,000.
SAMPLE GRANTS Longholm Playcare Ltd (£41,000); Middlebie Active Play (£31,500); Lockerbie Ice Rink (£24,000; Kirkpatrick Fleming Play Park Association (£20,000); Glenzier Hall Committee (£14,900); Hodom Parent Council (£9,800); Lockerbie Old School Community Hub (£4,500); Canonbie Tennis Club (£1,500).
FINANCES *Financial year end 31/07/2022*
Income £438,000
Grants to organisations £337,800
Assets £311,600
TRUSTEES D. Beattie; F. Carruthers; R. Dickson; A. Laird; C. Miles; T. Parker; A. Spence; M. Temple; P. Hands.
OTHER INFORMATION During the year, 21 grants were awarded to organisations.
HOW TO APPLY See the charity's website for information on the application process.
CONTACT DETAILS See website for relevant contact, c/o Southern Uplands Partnership, Studio 2 Lindean Mill, Galashiels TD1 3PE
Website www.decbg.org.uk

■ Dunard Fund

OSCR NO SC046889   **ESTABLISHED** 1986
WHERE FUNDING CAN BE GIVEN UK, mainly Scotland.
WHO CAN BENEFIT Registered charities.
WHAT IS FUNDED Classical music; architecture; visual arts; the environment.
TYPE OF GRANT Project funding; capital costs.
SAMPLE GRANTS Edinburgh International Festival (£570,400); Glyndeborne Music Festival, Monteverdi Choir and Orchestra and St Mary's Music School (£200,000 each); Dunedin Consort (£50,000).
FINANCES *Financial year end 31/03/2022*
Income £18,420,000
Grants to organisations £45,360,000
Assets £48,870,000
TRUSTEES Dr Carol Grigor; Colin Liddell; Catherine Hogel; Peter Thierfeldt; Elisabeth Lenz.
OTHER INFORMATION The charity has close links with Dunard Ltd and has previously received donations from the company. The trustees prefer to award grants for long-term projects. Grants were broken down as follows: architecture (£43.28 million); visual arts (£1.47 million); classical music (£583,600); the environment and other (£25,000).
HOW TO APPLY Unsolicited applications are not accepted.
CONTACT DETAILS The Trustees, c/o J. and H. Mitchell W. S., 51 Atholl Road, Pitlochry, Perthshire PH16 5BU *Tel.* 0131 556 4043

■ The Dunhill Medical Trust

CC NO 1140372   **ESTABLISHED** 1951
WHERE FUNDING CAN BE GIVEN UK.
WHO CAN BENEFIT Registered charities; CICs; social enterprises; universities; hospitals.
WHAT IS FUNDED Research into improving the quality of life, functional capacity and well-being of older people.
TYPE OF GRANT Capital costs; project funding; research; capacity building and development funding.
RANGE OF GRANTS Typically less than £30,000.
SAMPLE GRANTS TEC Services Association (£400,000); Housing Learning and Improvement Network (£84,000); Age UK Lancashire, Galloway's Society for the Blind and Linking Lives UK (£10,800 each); The Linking Network (£5,000).
FINANCES *Financial year end 31/03/2022*
Income £2,180,000
Grants to organisations £4,800,000
Assets £162,840,000
TRUSTEES Prof. Alison Petch; Deborah Dunn-Walters; James Lorigan; Keith Shepherd; Prof. Thomas Kirkwood; Michael Bellamy; Prof. Bernard Conway; Prof. Stuart Parker; Eren Osman; Dominic Jones; Prof. Carmel Hughes.
OTHER INFORMATION Grants were distributed as follows: academic research (£4.17 million); community organisations (£559,600); projects delayed by COVID-19 (£176,000); travel bursaries (£110).
HOW TO APPLY Applications can be made through the trust's online grants portal.
CONTACT DETAILS The Trustees, Thanet House, 231–232 Strand, London WC2R 1DA *Tel.* 020 7871 5402 *Email* admin@dunhillmedical.org.uk *Website* www.dunhillmedical.org.uk

■ Dunlossit and Islay Community Trust

OSCR NO SC047979
WHERE FUNDING CAN BE GIVEN Scotland, with a preference for Islay.
WHO CAN BENEFIT Charitable organisations.
WHAT IS FUNDED General charitable purposes including: health; social welfare; older people; children and young people; community development; citizenship; education; art, culture and heritage; the environment.
TYPE OF GRANT Multi-year grants.
RANGE OF GRANTS Up to £60,000.
SAMPLE GRANTS Venture Trust (£60,000); Scotland's Charity Air Ambulance (£50,000); Family Mediation Argyll and Bute (£7,500); Shopper Aide (£6,000); Environmental Funders Network (£4,000); Dochas Fund (£3,400); Islay Food Welfare Box Programme (£285).
FINANCES *Financial year end 31/10/2021*
Income £156,000
Grants to organisations £130,900
Grants to individuals £285
Assets £599,800
OTHER INFORMATION During 2020/21, the trust awarded grants totalling £130,900 to six organisations and one grant of £285 to individuals. The 2020/21 accounts were the latest available at the time of writing (May 2023).
HOW TO APPLY Contact the trust via the enquiries form on its website.
CONTACT DETAILS The Trustees, Turcan Connell, Princes Exchange, 1 Earl Grey Street, Edinburgh EH3 9EE *Email* use the contact form on the website *Website* www.dunlossit.org

■ The Dunn Family Charitable Trust

CC NO 297389   **ESTABLISHED** 1987
WHERE FUNDING CAN BE GIVEN UK, with a strong preference for Nottinghamshire.
WHO CAN BENEFIT Charitable organisations.
WHAT IS FUNDED General charitable purposes; health; social welfare.
RANGE OF GRANTS Between £500 and £7,500.
SAMPLE GRANTS Christ Church Fulwood (£7,500); Oakes Trust (£6,800); Nottingham Multiple Sclerosis Therapy Centre Ltd (£5,000); Sheffield Flourish (£1,000); Tearfund (£500).
FINANCES *Financial year end 31/03/2022*
Income £59,000
Grants to organisations £82,500
Assets £2,550,000
TRUSTEES Lisa Dunn; Jacky Chester; Peter Dunn; Nigel Dunn; Richard Dunn; Graham Dunn.
OTHER INFORMATION Grants were awarded to 32 organisations during the year.
HOW TO APPLY Apply in writing to the correspondent.
CONTACT DETAILS The Trustees, Rushcliffe Estates Ltd, Tudor House, 13–15 Rectory Road, West Bridgford, Nottingham, Nottinghamshire NG2 6BE *Tel.* 0115 945 5300 *Email* contact@rushcliffe.co.uk

■ The Charles Dunstone Charitable Trust

CC NO 1085955   **ESTABLISHED** 2001
WHERE FUNDING CAN BE GIVEN UK.
WHO CAN BENEFIT Registered charities.
WHAT IS FUNDED General charitable purposes including: arts and culture; children and young people; community care; education and training; health and disability; social welfare; heritage and restoration.
SAMPLE GRANTS Previous beneficiaries have included: Brighton Belle (£500,000); The Prince's Trust (£150,300); Royal Museum Greenwich (£100,000); Make a wish (£20,000); Lady Garden (£18,000); Comic Relief (£5,000); The Fulwood Academy (£2,200).
FINANCES *Financial year end 05/04/2022*
Income £0
Grants to organisations £400,000
TRUSTEES Adrian Bott; Denis Dunstone; John Gordon; Robert Clarkson.
OTHER INFORMATION Full accounts were not available to view on the Charity Commission's website due to the trust's low income. We have therefore estimated the trust's grant total based on its total expenditure.
HOW TO APPLY Unsolicited applications are not accepted.
CONTACT DETAILS The Trustees, HW Fisher and Co., Acre House, 11–15 William Road, London NW1 3ER *Tel.* 020 7388 7000 *Email* jtrent@hwfisher.co.uk

■ Dushinsky Trust Ltd

CC NO 1020301   **ESTABLISHED** 1992
WHERE FUNDING CAN BE GIVEN UK and Israel.
WHO CAN BENEFIT Jewish charitable organisations; individuals who are in need.
WHAT IS FUNDED Social welfare; furtherance of Orthodox Jewish education abroad.
RANGE OF GRANTS Up to around £173,000.
SAMPLE GRANTS Yeshivat Minchat Yitzchak (£172,900); United Institutions Maharitz Dushinsky (£103,200); Keren Habinyan Dushinsky (£59,000); Kahal Beis Yosef Dushinsky Jerusalem (£35,700); Mosdot Maharitz Dushinsky Bet Shemesh (£33,000); Ahavas Yakov (£30,000); Talmud Ohel Leah Bnei Brak (£24,000); Lachmei Simcha Fund (£23,500); Yachad Institutions (£20,000).
FINANCES *Financial year end 31/03/2022*
Income £744,900
Grants to organisations £708,500
Grants to individuals £45,000
Assets £29,000
TRUSTEES Simon Reisner; Zvi Levine; Mosche Schischa.
OTHER INFORMATION Grants were broken down into the following categories: advancement of education (£487,700); advancement of religion (£147,600); relief of poverty (£73,300). Only grants of £20,000 or more were listed in the annual report and accounts. Grants of below £20,000 totalled £157,200.
HOW TO APPLY The trust does not accept unsolicited applications.
CONTACT DETAILS Simon Reisner, Secretary, 23 Braydon Road, London N16 6QL *Tel.* 020 8802 7144

■ The Mildred Duveen Charitable Trust

CC NO 1059355   **ESTABLISHED** 1996
WHERE FUNDING CAN BE GIVEN UK and overseas.
WHO CAN BENEFIT Charitable organisations; universities, hospices and hospitals.
WHAT IS FUNDED General charitable purposes, including: animal welfare; children and young people; health and disability; education; social welfare; the environment.
WHAT IS NOT FUNDED Individuals.
RANGE OF GRANTS £500 to £10,000.
SAMPLE GRANTS Previous beneficiaries have included: Almeida Theatre (£10,000); Sparkles (£5,000); Bletchingly Skills Centre (£4,000); Palestine Trauma Centre (£2,000); National Advertising Benevolent Society (£1,500); ABF The Soldiers' Charity and Dogs Trust (£1,000 each); Canine Partners and Multiple Sclerosis Trust (£500 each).
FINANCES *Financial year end 05/04/2022*
Income £15,400
Grants to organisations £50,400
TRUSTEES Peter Holgate; Adrian Houstoun; Peter Loose; David Goepel.
OTHER INFORMATION Full accounts were not available to view on the Charity Commission's website due to the trust's low income. We have therefore estimated the trust's grant total based on its total expenditure. In previous years, grants were awarded to 50 organisations.
HOW TO APPLY Apply in writing to the correspondent.
CONTACT DETAILS The Trustees, c/o Moore Kingston Smith LLP, 9 Appold Street, London EC2A 2AP *Tel.* 020 4582 1000 *Email* pholgate@btinternet.com

■ The DWF Charitable Foundation

CC NO 1191347   **ESTABLISHED** 2014
WHERE FUNDING CAN BE GIVEN UK; Australia; Canada; France; Germany; India; Ireland; Italy; Poland; Qatar; Spain; United Arab Emirates; USA.
WHO CAN BENEFIT Registered charities.
WHAT IS FUNDED Homelessness; health and well-being; employability; education; the environment and sustainability.

WHAT IS NOT FUNDED Academic research; activities for which a statutory body is responsible; an activity taking place in school time that is a statutory responsibility; animal welfare; evaluation which is not related to the funded work; everyday running costs and core salaries; general fundraising appeals; individuals; loans or business finance; other grant-making bodies; professional fundraisers or bid writers; professional qualifications; recurrent funding; redundancy payments; religious or political causes; sponsorship/marketing appeals/ fundraising costs; start-up costs for new organisations; the advancement of religion; universities/higher education facilities; vehicles and minibuses; work that has already taken place.

TYPE OF GRANT Project funding.

RANGE OF GRANTS Mostly under £5,000.

SAMPLE GRANTS India Red Cross (£7,000); FareShare Yorkshire (£3,500); Friends of Dorothy (£2,500); CPotential (£1,000); Barnabus (£500).

FINANCES *Financial year end 31/03/2022*
Income £190,300
Grants to organisations £217,500
Assets £2,120,000

TRUSTEES James Davies; Lindsay Ogunyemi; Jewels Chamberlain; Sir Duncan Nichol; Mark Stanbury; Robert Binns; Edwin Oliver; Peter Holland; Sean Monks; Carolyn Ferber; Zelinda Bennett.

OTHER INFORMATION The foundation was established by DWF LLP, a multinational law firm based in Manchester. A list of the firm's office locations can be found on its website.

HOW TO APPLY Applications can be submitted using an online form on the foundation's website.

CONTACT DETAILS Clare Bevan, Foundation Manager, 5 St Paul's Square, Old Hall Street, Liverpool L3 9AE *Tel.* 07736 121046 *Email* clare. beavan@dwf.law *Website* https://dwfgroup. com/en/about-us/dwf-foundation

■ The Dyers' Company Charitable Trust

CC NO 289547   **ESTABLISHED** 1984
WHERE FUNDING CAN BE GIVEN UK.
WHO CAN BENEFIT Registered charities; schools; universities.
WHAT IS FUNDED Education; children and young people; health; social welfare; the armed forces; the arts; the dyeing industry.
WHAT IS NOT FUNDED Individuals; international charities.
TYPE OF GRANT One-off; project costs; recurrent.
RANGE OF GRANTS Typically up to £1,000.
SAMPLE GRANTS St Saviour's and St Olave's School (£109,800); Norwich School (£79,100); Boutcher Church of England Primary School (£62,500); The Trussell Trust (£20,000); Royal Navy Benevolent Trust (£14,000); The Passage (£5,000); Sight Research UK (£2,000); Berwick Swan and Wildlife Trust (£500).
FINANCES *Financial year end 31/10/2022*
Income £1,760,000
Grants to organisations £804,400
Assets £27,090,000
TRUSTEE The Dyers' Company.
OTHER INFORMATION During the year, 148 organisations were awarded grants.
HOW TO APPLY The trust does not accept unsolicited applications, but members of the company can nominate charities for support.

CONTACT DETAILS The Trustees, Dyer's Hall, 11–13 Dowgate Hill, London EC4R 2ST *Tel.* 020 7236 7197 *Email* office@ dyerscompany.com *Website* www. dyerscompany.co.uk/charitable-activity

■ The James Dyson Foundation

CC NO 1099709   **ESTABLISHED** 2002
WHERE FUNDING CAN BE GIVEN Worldwide, with a preference for the UK and in particular the local area around the Dyson company's UK headquarters in Malmesbury, Wiltshire.
WHO CAN BENEFIT Registered charities and educational organisations.
WHAT IS FUNDED Engineering education; medical research; scientific research; social and community welfare.
WHAT IS NOT FUNDED Animal welfare; loans or funding for individuals or companies; sports team sponsorship.
TYPE OF GRANT Project funding; research.
SAMPLE GRANTS A list of beneficiaries was not included in the annual report and accounts.
FINANCES *Financial year end 31/12/2021*
Income £1,110,000
Grants to organisations £2,340,000
Assets (£1,060,000)
TRUSTEES Lady Deirdre Dyson; Sir James Dyson; Valerie West.
OTHER INFORMATION During 2021, grants were distributed under the following categories: science and medical research (£1.16 million); education and training (£1.15 million); social and community welfare (£32,300).
HOW TO APPLY Complete the online contact form on the foundation's website. The foundation aims to respond within two weeks.
CONTACT DETAILS The Trustees, Tetbury Hill, Malmesbury, Wiltshire SN16 0RP *Tel.* 01666 746802 *Email* info@jamesdysonfoundation.com *Website* www.jamesdysonfoundation.com

■ The James and Deirdre Dyson Trust

CC NO 1160919   **ESTABLISHED** 2015
WHERE FUNDING CAN BE GIVEN England and Wales.
WHO CAN BENEFIT Charities; amateur sports clubs; schools.
WHAT IS FUNDED General charitable purposes including: health; education; cultural heritage; the arts; sport.
RANGE OF GRANTS Up to £22,000.
SAMPLE GRANTS Les Amis du Palais de Tokyo (£17,900); Cure EB (£15,000); Screw Cancer (£5,800); The Jubilee Sailing Trust (£500); Sheringham FC (£250); Hospitality Action (£100).
FINANCES *Financial year end 31/12/2021*
Income £58,300
Grants to organisations £92,600
Assets £4,890,000
TRUSTEES Lady Deirdre Dyson; Sir James Dyson.
OTHER INFORMATION During the year, nine grants totalling £46,100 were awarded for arts, culture, heritage and science, education and sport. Four grants were awarded for health care.
HOW TO APPLY Unsolicited applications are not accepted.
CONTACT DETAILS The Trustees, Dyson Ltd, Tetbury Hill, Malmesbury SN16 0RP *Tel.* 01666 827258 *Email* info@jamesanddeirdredysontrust. com *Website* www.jamesanddeirdredysontrust. com

■ E. B. M. Charitable Trust

CC NO 326186   ESTABLISHED 1982

WHERE FUNDING CAN BE GIVEN UK.

WHO CAN BENEFIT Charitable organisations; hospices; hospitals; educational organisations.

WHAT IS FUNDED General charitable purposes; animal welfare and research; youth development; social welfare.

TYPE OF GRANT Project funding; occasionally research.

RANGE OF GRANTS Typically £5,000 to £50,000, with some larger grants.

SAMPLE GRANTS The Prince's Trust (£75,000); The Salvation Army (£65,000); Wavertree Education Trust (£30,000); Young Lives vs Cancer (£25,000); The Porch Day Centre and Teenage Cancer Trust (£20,000 each); Re-Engage (£15,000); Orchid (£5,000).

FINANCES *Financial year end 30/06/2022*
Income £1,600,000
Grants to organisations £1,400,000
Assets £60,030,000

TRUSTEES Stephen Hogg; Michael MacFadyen; Richard Moore; Francis Moore; Lucy Forsyth.

OTHER INFORMATION Grants were awarded to 59 organisations during the year. The trust manages two funds, the Main Fund and Fitz' Fund. Fitz' Fund is a designated fund for animal charities.

HOW TO APPLY Unsolicited applications are not accepted.

CONTACT DETAILS Lynne Webster, Moore Family Office Ltd, 42 Berkeley Square, London W1J 5AW *Tel.* 020 7318 0845 *Email* ebm@moorefamilyofficegroup.com

■ EA Foundation

CC NO 1194169   ESTABLISHED 2021

WHERE FUNDING CAN BE GIVEN Worldwide.

WHO CAN BENEFIT Registered charities; NGOs.

WHAT IS FUNDED Education; basic services such as health care, clean water and electricity; social welfare; the environment; sustainable development.

SAMPLE GRANTS A list of beneficiaries was not included in the annual report and accounts.

FINANCES *Financial year end 31/12/2021*
Income £146,900
Grants to organisations £93,800
Assets £54,300

TRUSTEES Richard Bronze; Jessica Talbot; Lucy Mortimer; Fredrik Fosse; Amrita Sen; Dr Trevor Sikorski.

OTHER INFORMATION The foundation's website states: 'The EA Foundation supports projects around the world, with a particular focus on the least economically developed regions where the absolute need is greatest. Where we support organisations in the UK or other advanced economies we prioritise activities that have a strong international theme (e.g. support for refugees and asylum seekers).'

HOW TO APPLY Applications can be made via the foundation's website.

CONTACT DETAILS The Trustees, c/o Energy Aspects Ltd, 25 Canada Square, London E14 5LQ

Email info@ea-foundation.org.uk
Website https://ea-foundation.org.uk

■ Audrey Earle Charitable Trust

CC NO 290028   ESTABLISHED 1984

WHERE FUNDING CAN BE GIVEN UK.

WHO CAN BENEFIT Registered charities and voluntary organisations.

WHAT IS FUNDED General charitable purposes, with some preference for animal welfare and conservation charities.

SAMPLE GRANTS Action for Blind People, Age UK, Animal Care Trust, Burnham Overy Village Hall, Redwing Horse Sanctuary, Royal British Legion, SENSE and Wells Community Hospital Trust (£3,100 each).

FINANCES *Financial year end 05/04/2022*
Income £82,900
Grants to organisations £68,800

TRUSTEES Paul Sheils; Richard Fuller; Peter Turner.

OTHER INFORMATION Grants of just over £3,100 each were made to 22 organisations in 2021/22.

HOW TO APPLY Apply in writing to the correspondent; however, the trust tends to support the same beneficiaries year after year and, therefore, it appears unlikely that new applicants will receive support.

CONTACT DETAILS The Trustees, c/o Fladgate LLP, 16 Great Queen Street, London WC2B 5DG *Tel.* 020 3036 7000 *Email* fladgate@fladgate.com

■ The Earley Charity

CC NO 244823   ESTABLISHED 1820

WHERE FUNDING CAN BE GIVEN The Ancient Liberty of Earley (i.e. the central eastern and southern part of Reading, Earley and Lower Earley, northern Shinfield, Winnersh, Sonning and Lower Caversham).

WHO CAN BENEFIT Individuals; charitable and community organisations.

WHAT IS FUNDED General charitable purposes; social welfare; people with disabilities; education; sport and recreation; art and culture.

WHAT IS NOT FUNDED Open-ended salaries; running/core costs; general charitable appeals; public sector bodies; national organisations; religious activities.

TYPE OF GRANT Project funding; capital funding.

RANGE OF GRANTS £500 to £5,000.

SAMPLE GRANTS Readipop (£80,000); Berkshire Women's Aid (£41,100); Aspire 2 (£22,000); Launchpad Reading (£7,000); Me2 Club (£2,000); Readifolk (£500).

FINANCES *Financial year end 31/12/2021*
Income £283,200
Grants to organisations £329,600
Grants to individuals £13,200
Assets £11,930,000

TRUSTEES Philip Hooper; Dr Deborah Jenkins; David Sutton; Robert Ames; Mary Waite; Tahir Maher; Elizabeth Terry.

OTHER INFORMATION Grants were made to 33 organisations and 43 individuals during the year. Grants were also made to Earley Charity Workers (£116,300) and to Earley Crescent Community Association Resource Centre (£1.3 million).

HOW TO APPLY Application forms can be requested via email or by completing the online enquiry form. Application forms and supporting documents should be returned to the charity by post. Check the charity's website for application deadlines.

CONTACT DETAILS Jane Wittig, Clerk to the Trustees, St Nicolas Centre, Sutcliffe Avenue, Earley, Reading RG6 7JN *Tel.* 0118 926 1068 *Email* ec@earleycharity.org.uk *Website* www.earleycharity.org.uk

■ East End Community Foundation

CC NO 1147789   **ESTABLISHED** 1990

WHERE FUNDING CAN BE GIVEN The London boroughs of the City of London, Hackney, Newham and Tower Hamlets.

WHO CAN BENEFIT Registered charities; unregistered charities; CICs; social enterprises; schools.

WHAT IS FUNDED General charitable purposes; community development and cohesion; children and young people; employability skills; education.

TYPE OF GRANT Project funding; core/revenue costs.

RANGE OF GRANTS Mostly up to £10,000.

SAMPLE GRANTS Bromley by Bow Centre (£25,000); Stepney Community Trust (£2,900); Stifford Centre (£3,000); Supporting Humanity Ltd (£1,000); Canary Wharf Football Academy (£500).

FINANCES *Financial year end 31/03/2022*
Income £2,480,000
Grants to organisations £1,340,000
Assets £29,980,000

TRUSTEES Katherine Webster; Cllr Guy Nicholson; Rick Watson; Sahidur Rahman; The Revd Jeremy Fraser; Jim Machale; Atanu Bhattacherjee; Bronislaw Masojada; Alkhad Ali; Laurence Everitt; Catherine McGuinness.

OTHER INFORMATION This is one of the 47 UK community foundations, which distribute funding for a wide range of purposes. As with all community foundations, there are a number of donor-advised funds managed on behalf of individuals, families and charitable trusts. Grant schemes tend to change frequently – consult the foundation's website for details of current programmes and up-to-date deadlines. The foundation awarded 195 grants during the year.

HOW TO APPLY Potential applicants are advised to visit the community foundation's website or contact its grants team to find the most suitable funding stream.

CONTACT DETAILS Grants Team, Jack Dash House, 2 Lawn House Close, London E14 9YQ *Tel.* 020 7345 4444 *Email* admin@eastendcf.org *Website* www.eastendcf.org

■ Eastern Counties Educational Trust Ltd

CC NO 310038   **ESTABLISHED** 1922

WHERE FUNDING CAN BE GIVEN Cambridgeshire; Essex; Hertfordshire; Suffolk; Norfolk.

WHO CAN BENEFIT Charitable organisations; educational institutions.

WHAT IS FUNDED Support for people with special educational needs, particularly those under 25 who have emotional and behavioural difficulties.

RANGE OF GRANTS Up to £77,000 but typically between £5,000 and £10,000.

SAMPLE GRANTS St Edmundsbury and Ipswich MAT (£77,900); The Mix Stowmarket (£25,400); The Clare School (£23,600); The Gifted (£10,000); Grove Cottage (£9,400); Grove College, Castleton School (£5,000 each).

FINANCES *Financial year end 31/03/2022*
Income £66,600
Grants to organisations £200,700
Assets £5,600,000

TRUSTEES Harry Anderson; Deborah Reed; David Boyle; Ben Salmon; Robert Cowlin; Moira Usher; Deborah Hollister.

OTHER INFORMATION In 2021/22, grants were awarded to 11 organisations.

HOW TO APPLY Contact the correspondent for further information.

CONTACT DETAILS Verity Barclay, Secretary, 22 Brook Street, Coggeshall, Colchester CO6 1SH *Tel.* 01376 564025 *Email* ecet.secretary@yahoo.co.uk

■ Sir John Eastwood Foundation

CC NO 235389   **ESTABLISHED** 1964

WHERE FUNDING CAN BE GIVEN Nottinghamshire.

WHO CAN BENEFIT Local charitable organisations.

WHAT IS FUNDED General charitable purposes including children with special needs, older people and people with disabilities.

WHAT IS NOT FUNDED Individuals.

RANGE OF GRANTS Generally from £500 to £10,000.

SAMPLE GRANTS UK Med – Ukraine (£20,000); John Eastwood Hospice Trust and Warsop Youth Club (£10,000 each); Children's Air Ambulance, Mansfield Maulers and NSPCC (£5,000).

FINANCES *Financial year end 31/03/2022*
Income £291,700
Grants to organisations £311,000
Assets £10,960,000

TRUSTEES Valerie Hardingham; David Marriott; John Mudford; Victoria Cottingham.

OTHER INFORMATION Grants were awarded to 138 organisations. Only organisations that received grants of over £5,000 were listed in the foundation's accounts. Grants of under £5,000 totalled £211,000.

HOW TO APPLY Contact the correspondent for further information.

CONTACT DETAILS The Trustees, PO Box 9803, Handley Arcade, Leeming Street, Mansfield, Nottinghamshire NG18 9FT *Tel.* 07970 438740 *Email* sirjohneastwoodfoundation@talktalk.net

■ Ebenezer Trust

CC NO 272574   **ESTABLISHED** 1976

WHERE FUNDING CAN BE GIVEN UK and overseas.

WHO CAN BENEFIT Registered charities.

WHAT IS FUNDED Advancement of the evangelical tenets of the Christian faith.

RANGE OF GRANTS Mostly £500 to £2,000.

SAMPLE GRANTS CHESS (£302,500); Gunnersbury Baptist Church (£20,000); Christ Church – Stock (£9,000); Age UK (£4,000); Baptist Missionary Society (£3,000); Renew Counselling (£2,000); St Francis Hospice (£1,000); Rotary Club – Chelmsford (£100).

FINANCES *Financial year end 05/04/2022*
Income £360,900
Grants to organisations £389,700
Assets £745,200

TRUSTEES Ruth Davey; Nigel Davey.

OTHER INFORMATION Grants were made to 42 organisations during the year.

HOW TO APPLY According to our previous research, the trust is unlikely to accept unsolicited applications.

CONTACT DETAILS Nigel Davey, Trustee, Longwood Lodge, Longwood Lodge, Whites Hill, Stock, Ingatestone, Essex CM4 9QB *Tel.* 01277 829893 *Email* nigel.davey@live.co.uk

■ The Ecology Trust

CC NO 1099222   ESTABLISHED 2003
WHERE FUNDING CAN BE GIVEN UK and overseas.
WHO CAN BENEFIT Charitable organisations.
WHAT IS FUNDED The principal aim of the trust is to support ecological and environmental initiatives, particularly around the issues of agriculture, tropical forests and climate change. The trust also helps local community groups working on environmental issues in the UK and overseas, so as to empower people to contribute to policy development and to participate in planning and decision-making at the local level.
WHAT IS NOT FUNDED Retrospective work; part of general appeals or circulars; Outward Bound courses, expeditions or overseas travel; capital projects (i.e. buildings and refurbishment costs); conservation of already well-supported species or non-native species; recycling projects.
TYPE OF GRANT Project and core costs, including running costs such as salaries and overheads.
RANGE OF GRANTS Typically up to £50,000.
SAMPLE GRANTS Forum Konservasi Leuser (£64,000); Rainforest Action Network (£39,900); Environmental Paper Network (£37,300); Canopy Planet Society (£31,100); Bank Track (£29,000); Forest Peoples Programme (£24,700); The Gecko Project (£21,600).
FINANCES *Financial year end 31/03/2022*
Income £640,600
Grants to organisations £648,500
Assets £392,300
TRUSTEES Charles Filmer; Alexander Goldsmith; Benjamin Goldsmith; Charlotte Colbert.
OTHER INFORMATION Grants were awarded to 12 organisations during the year.
HOW TO APPLY Apply in writing to the correspondent. The trust rarely makes grants in response to unsolicited applications.
CONTACT DETAILS The Trustees, 48 Kidmore Road, Caversham, Reading, Berkshire RG4 7LU *Tel.* 0118 377 9085 *Email* info@jmgfoundation.org *Website* www.ecologytrust.org

■ The Economist Charitable Trust

CC NO 293709   ESTABLISHED 1986
WHERE FUNDING CAN BE GIVEN UK.
WHO CAN BENEFIT Charitable organisations.
WHAT IS FUNDED Education; communication; literacy and re-training for individuals and groups which are disadvantaged.
TYPE OF GRANT Project funding; one-off.
RANGE OF GRANTS Up to £20,000.
SAMPLE GRANTS Unicef (£47,000); Unicef Hong Kong (£4,600).
FINANCES *Financial year end 31/03/2022*
Income £119,300
Grants to organisations £89,500
Assets £29,800
TRUSTEES Ada Simkins; Kiran Malik; Susan Clark; Jamie Credland; Ursula Esling.
OTHER INFORMATION The trust is the corporate charity of The Economist Newspaper Ltd, a multinational media company specialising in international business and world affairs.
HOW TO APPLY The trust does not accept unsolicited applications.
CONTACT DETAILS The Trustees, The Adelphi, 1–11 John Adam Street, London WC2N 6HT *Tel.* 020 7576 8000

■ The Gilbert and Eileen Edgar Foundation

CC NO 241736   ESTABLISHED 1965
WHERE FUNDING CAN BE GIVEN UK and occasionally overseas.
WHO CAN BENEFIT Charitable organisations.
WHAT IS FUNDED General charitable purposes with preference towards medical research, care and support; fine arts; education in the fine arts; academic education; religion; recreation.
TYPE OF GRANT Full project funding; scholarships.
RANGE OF GRANTS Up to £9,000, but typically between £500 and £1,000.
SAMPLE GRANTS Royal College of Music (£9,000); Royal Academy of Arts (£6,000); Gurkha Welfare Trust (£1,000); Books Abroad and Victim Support (£500 each).
FINANCES *Financial year end 05/04/2022*
Income £84,000
Grants to organisations £63,500
Assets £1,820,000
TRUSTEES Simon Gentilli; Adam Gentilli.
OTHER INFORMATION In 2021/22, the foundation awarded 76 grants to organisations, distributed within the following categories: arts and music (£26,500); welfare (£17,500); medical and surgical science (£6,000); children (£4,500); overseas (£4,000); recreation and conservation (£3,000); the armed forces (£2,000); academia (£1,000).
HOW TO APPLY Apply in writing to the correspondent. According to the foundation's 2021/22 accounts: 'for a large number of years the trustees have concentrated on making annual grants to a range of charities. The trustees review the beneficiaries and from time to time amendments are made to the list. When funds allow the trustees occasionally make one-off grants.'
CONTACT DETAILS The Trustees, Greville Mount, Milcote, Stratford-upon-Avon, Warwickshire CV37 8AB *Tel.* 01491 639318 *Email* trustee@milcote.uk

■ Edinburgh Children's Holiday Fund

OSCR NO SC010312   ESTABLISHED 1912
WHERE FUNDING CAN BE GIVEN Edinburgh and Lothian.
WHO CAN BENEFIT Charitable organisations; schools; local councils.
WHAT IS FUNDED Children's welfare and holidays for children who are disadvantaged.
TYPE OF GRANT One-off grants.
RANGE OF GRANTS Mainly under £10,000.
SAMPLE GRANTS City of Edinburgh Council (£15,000); Hopscotch (£5,000); Edinburgh Young Carers Project (£3,000); Gilmerton Primary School (£2,500); Holy Cross Primary School and Spina Bifida Scotland (£1,500 each); React (Rapid Effective Assistance for Children with potentially Terminal illness) (£1,200); Hearts and Minds (£1,000).
FINANCES *Financial year end 31/10/2022*
Income £193,900
Grants to organisations £61,000
Assets £1,470,000
OTHER INFORMATION Of the grant total, £33,000 was awarded to four local councils to be distributed to individuals.
HOW TO APPLY Contact the correspondent for more information. Our previous research indicates that applications should be made on a form obtained from the correspondent and should be submitted in mid-December or mid-April.

CONTACT DETAILS The Trustees, c/o Bryce Wilson and Co., Hill Street Business Centre, 13 Hill Street, Edinburgh EH2 3JP

■ Edinburgh Trust No2 Account

CC NO 227897   **ESTABLISHED** 1959
WHERE FUNDING CAN BE GIVEN UK and overseas.
WHO CAN BENEFIT Registered charities.
WHAT IS FUNDED General charitable purposes; armed services; education.
RANGE OF GRANTS £1,000 to £2,500.
SAMPLE GRANTS King Edward VII's Hospital for Officers (£2,000); Honourable Company of Air Pilots, Muscular Dystrophy Group of Great Britain and NI, The Officers Association, Romsey Abbey Appeal Fund, Shaftesbury Young People SYP Trust, Tall Ships Youth Trust and The Zoological Society of London (£1,000 each).
FINANCES *Financial year end 31/03/2022*
Income £181,300
Grants to organisations £70,500
Assets £4,220,000
TRUSTEES Capt. Andrew Aspden; Samuel MacDonald; Alan Parker.
OTHER INFORMATION During 2021/22, grants were distributed as follows: general (£45,400); armed services (£22,700); education (£2,400).
HOW TO APPLY Apply in writing to the correspondent.
CONTACT DETAILS The Trustees, Office of the Earl of Wessex, St James's Palace, London SW1A 2BH *Tel.* 020 7024 5832

■ Edupoor Ltd

CC NO 1113785   **ESTABLISHED** 2005
WHERE FUNDING CAN BE GIVEN UK and overseas.
WHO CAN BENEFIT Charitable organisations.
WHAT IS FUNDED Education and training; the relief of poverty; older people; physical and mental health; disability; general charitable purposes.
SAMPLE GRANTS A list of beneficiaries was not included in the annual report and accounts.
FINANCES *Financial year end 30/06/2022*
Income £914,600
Grants to organisations £1,000,000
Assets £6,600
TRUSTEES Alan Shelton; Michael Shelton; Benjamin Levy.
HOW TO APPLY Apply in writing to the correspondent.
CONTACT DETAILS Meir Amitay, Secretary, Flat 10, 125 Clapton Common, Stamford Hill, London E5 9AB *Tel.* 07947 249515

■ Dr Edwards and Bishop King's Fulham Charity

CC NO 1113490   **ESTABLISHED** 1981
WHERE FUNDING CAN BE GIVEN The old metropolitan borough of Fulham.
WHO CAN BENEFIT Individuals; registered charities and community organisations. Applications from small, emerging and minority ethnic organisations are welcomed.
WHAT IS FUNDED Social welfare; support for people on low incomes.
WHAT IS NOT FUNDED A full list of exclusions can be found on the charity's website.
TYPE OF GRANT Core costs; project funding; capital costs.
RANGE OF GRANTS Generally up to £5,000 but higher awards can be considered.
SAMPLE GRANTS United Hammersmith and Fulham Charities (£21,000): The Smile Brigade

(£10,000); Turtle Key Arts (£6,000); Royal Trinity Hospice and St Alban's Church (£5,000 each); Acknowledging Youths (£4,200); Counselling Pastoral Trust (£1,000).
FINANCES *Financial year end 31/03/2022*
Income £459,700
Grants to organisations £159,900
Grants to individuals £177,100
Assets £9,560,000
TRUSTEES Carol Bailey; Michael Clein; Susan O'Neill; Zahra Beg; Helen Fagan; Ted Townsend; Robert Fryer; Iain Cassidy; John Shuffrey; Nikolaos Souslous; Genevieve Nwaogbe.
HOW TO APPLY Application forms are available to download from the charity's website and can be returned to the office by hand, post or email.
CONTACT DETAILS Clerk to the Trustees, Percy Barton House, 33–35 Dawes Road, Fulham, London SW6 7DT *Tel.* 020 7386 9387 *Email* clerk@ debk.org.uk *Website* www.debk.org.uk

■ W. G. Edwards Charitable Foundation

CC NO 293312   **ESTABLISHED** 1985
WHERE FUNDING CAN BE GIVEN UK.
WHO CAN BENEFIT Registered charities.
WHAT IS FUNDED Care for older people; improvement of well-being.
WHAT IS NOT FUNDED Buying or leasing transport; salaries; general campaigns; revenue funding; building projects in the planning stages; IT which is for the use of administration; retrospective items; rent; individuals.
TYPE OF GRANT Capital costs; project funding; innovative schemes for ongoing care.
RANGE OF GRANTS £1,000 to £3,000, with the average grant size being £1,500.
SAMPLE GRANTS St Wilfrid's Hospice (£3,000); The Together Project (£2,400); Arts 4 Dementia (£2,000); Rathfriland Historical Society (£1,700); Equal Arts (£1,600); Helpful Bureau (£1,000); Just Friends (£950); Cleveland Housing Advice (£540).
FINANCES *Financial year end 05/04/2022*
Income £144,100
Grants to organisations £125,100
Assets £3,790,000
TRUSTEES Prof. Wendy Savage; William Mackie; Sara Seymour-Savage; Lucy Polling.
OTHER INFORMATION During 2021/22, grants were made to 76 organisations.
HOW TO APPLY Detailed information outlining what should be included in grant applications and how applications should be structured is available from the foundation's website. Applications should be a maximum of four A4 pages and sent to the correspondent by email or post. There are four application deadlines each year – see the website for upcoming dates.
CONTACT DETAILS The Trustees, 14 Windsor Terrace, South Gosforth, Fernwood Road, Newcastle upon Tyne, Tyne and Wear NE3 1YL *Tel.* 07796 464802 *Email* wgedwardscharity@icloud.com *Website* www.wgedwardscharitablefoundation. org.uk

■ The Eight Foundation

CC NO 1174600   **ESTABLISHED** 2017
WHERE FUNDING CAN BE GIVEN Hampshire and the surrounding counties.
WHO CAN BENEFIT Individuals; registered charities.
WHAT IS FUNDED Education; health; social welfare.

WHAT IS NOT FUNDED Non-registered charities; charities outside the area of benefit or charitable focus; charities with an annual income in excess of £250,000 or with over £500,000 of assets; applicants with no connection or association with Eight Wealth Management; purposes for which the government has a statutory responsibility to provide.

RANGE OF GRANTS Up to £5,000.

SAMPLE GRANTS A list of beneficiaries was not included in the annual report and accounts.

FINANCES *Financial year end 30/06/2022*
Income £109,000
Grants to organisations £59,400
Assets £24,400

TRUSTEES Storm Shepherd-Riggs; Ian Riggs; Nathaniel Geddes.

OTHER INFORMATION This is the corporate foundation of Hampshire-based Eight Wealth Management. Note that the grant total includes amounts awarded to individuals.

HOW TO APPLY Applicants must be able to demonstrate their connection or association with Eight Wealth Management, or be referred by someone within the organisation. An online application form can be completed online.

CONTACT DETAILS The Trustees, 1460 Parkway, Whiteley, Fareham, Hampshire PO15 7AF
Email use the contact form on the website
Website www.eightfoundation.co.uk

■ Eight Strands Foundation

CC NO 1139841   **ESTABLISHED** 2018
WHERE FUNDING CAN BE GIVEN UK; India; Kenya; Pakistan; Tanzania.

WHO CAN BENEFIT Charitable organisations.

WHAT IS FUNDED Social welfare; health; education; water, sanitation and hygiene (WASH).

RANGE OF GRANTS Up to £600,000.

SAMPLE GRANTS Princeton University (£753,600); Donmar Warehouse (£100,000); Duke University Fund (£56,400); Felix Project (£30,000); Barnardo's (£25,000); Smithsonian Museum (£750).

FINANCES *Financial year end 31/12/2021*
Income £5,830,000
Grants to organisations £1,020,000
Assets £19,000,000

TRUSTEES Hardy McLain; Helle McLain; Ian Terry; Cameron McLain; Dr Carina McLain; Chelsea McLain; Chloe McLain.

OTHER INFORMATION Grants awarded to UK charities totalled £195,200 and grants awarded to US charities totalled £827,100.

HOW TO APPLY Apply in writing to the correspondent.

CONTACT DETAILS The Trustees, 6 New Street Square, New Fetter Lane, London EH4A 3AQ

■ The Eighteen Fund

CC NO 1135961   **ESTABLISHED** 2010
WHERE FUNDING CAN BE GIVEN Barnet.

WHO CAN BENEFIT Charitable organisations.

WHAT IS FUNDED General charitable purposes; education/training; advancement of health or saving of lives; disability; prevention or relief of poverty; religious activities.

SAMPLE GRANTS A list of beneficiaries was not included in the annual report and accounts.

FINANCES *Financial year end 31/03/2022*
Income £208,700
Grants to organisations £172,900
Assets £140,100

TRUSTEES Jacqueline Rashbass; Andrew Rashbass; Elie Rashbass.

OTHER INFORMATION In 2021/22 grants were made for the following causes: relief of poverty (£109,100); advancement of education (£41,100); advancement of religion (£14,600); relief of those in need (£4,600); advancement of health or the saving of lives (£850); other charitable purposes (£2,700). The grant total includes grants to organisations and individuals.

HOW TO APPLY Apply in writing to the correspondent.

CONTACT DETAILS Jacqueline Rashbass, Trustee, 17 Wykeham Road, London NW4 2TB
Tel. 07974 151494
Email jacquelinerrashbass@gmail.com

■ The Eighty Eight Foundation

CC NO 1149797   **ESTABLISHED** 2012
WHERE FUNDING CAN BE GIVEN UK; Ireland; South Africa.

WHO CAN BENEFIT Registered charities; unregistered charitable projects; individuals.

WHAT IS FUNDED Education and training; cancer and dementia research and care; social welfare; older people; disadvantaged artists and photographers.

RANGE OF GRANTS Generally £5,000 to £200,000, with some larger grants.

SAMPLE GRANTS UBS Optimus Foundation UK – Luminos (£236,900); UBS Optimus Foundation UK (£230,000); The Cares Family Ltd (£200,000); Royal Trinity Hospice (£139,000); UBS Optimus Foundation – Ukraine Appeal (£50,000); The Sutton Trust (£30,000); Chain of Hope and School of Hard Knocks SA (£5,000 each).

FINANCES *Financial year end 31/03/2022*
Income £1,940,000
Grants to organisations £1,820,000
Assets £20,630,000

TRUSTEES Edward Fitzmaurice; Ann Fitzmaurice; Claude Slatner; Stuart Walker; Neelesh Heredia; Barry Fine.

OTHER INFORMATION Grants were awarded to 16 organisations during the year totalling £1.82 million.

HOW TO APPLY The 2021/22 accounts state: 'The charity identifies worthy causes through its own research, the use of specialist research companies like NPC or the philanthropy units of UBS and Barclays. Once the potential charities are selected to progress to discussion by the trustees they need to submit a written proposal, showing how the grant will be spent, the phasing of the funds and the frequency and type of reporting. These proposals will then be discussed at meetings between the Board of Trustees with formal minutes being held.'

CONTACT DETAILS The Trustees, c/o Rawlinson and Hunter, Eighth Floor, 6 New Street Square, New Fetter Lane, London EC4A 3AQ *Tel.* 020 7842 2000 *Email* eighty.eight@rawlinson-hunter.com

■ The George Elias Charitable Trust

CC NO 273993   **ESTABLISHED** 1977
WHERE FUNDING CAN BE GIVEN UK and overseas.

WHO CAN BENEFIT Jewish organisations; registered charities.

WHAT IS FUNDED Education; relief of poverty; promotion of the Jewish faith.

TYPE OF GRANT Project funding; core costs.

SAMPLE GRANTS A list of beneficiaries was not included in the annual report and accounts.
FINANCES *Financial year end* 05/04/2022
Income £1,370,000
Grants to organisations £489,500
Assets £1,300,000
TRUSTEES Ernest Elias; Stephen Elias.
HOW TO APPLY Contact the correspondent for information regarding the application process.
CONTACT DETAILS Stephen Elias, Trustee, Shaws Fabrics Ltd, 1 Ashley Road, Altrincham, Cheshire WA14 2DT *Tel.* 0161 928 7171 *Email* textiles@kshaw.com

■ The Elie Trust

OSCR NO SC046848 **ESTABLISHED** 2016
WHERE FUNDING CAN BE GIVEN UK and overseas.
WHO CAN BENEFIT Registered charities; places of worship; individuals.
WHAT IS FUNDED Health; social welfare; education; Christian causes.
TYPE OF GRANT Project funding; development funding.
RANGE OF GRANTS Mostly up to £5,000, with the occasional larger grant.
SAMPLE GRANTS Teen Ranch Scotland (£100,000); Echoes International (£13,200); Open Doors and Scottish Bible Society (£6,000 each); Care for the Family, For Life Trust and Hope for Glasgow (£4,800 each); Scripture Union Scotland and The Leprosy Mission Scotland (£1,200 each).
FINANCES *Financial year end* 31/08/2022
Income £280,500
Grants to organisations £155,200
Grants to individuals £1,200
Assets £1,140,000
OTHER INFORMATION Some organisations that received a grant of under £2,000 were not listed as beneficiaries in the trust's 2021/22 accounts. Unlisted grants of under £2,000 totalled £6,600. Sometimes, the trust provides accommodation for missionaries.
HOW TO APPLY Apply in writing to the correspondent.
CONTACT DETAILS The Trustees, 72 Westermains Avenue, Kirkintilloch, East Dunbartonshire G66 1EH

■ The Wilfred and Elsie Elkes Charity Fund

CC NO 326573 **ESTABLISHED** 1984
WHERE FUNDING CAN BE GIVEN Staffordshire.
WHO CAN BENEFIT Charitable organisations.
WHAT IS FUNDED Children and young people, animal welfare, older people, health and churches of any denomination in Uttoxeter.
SAMPLE GRANTS Community Foundation for Staffordshire (£15,000); RSPCA Staffordshire North Branch (£11,000 in two grants);; The Hermitage Charity Care Trust (£10,000); Uttoxeter and District Old People's Housing Society Ltd (£6,000); Blind Veterans UK and Spinal Muscular Atrophy UK (£2,000 each); The Living Paintings Trust (£1,000).
FINANCES *Financial year end* 10/08/2021
Income £46,000
Grants to organisations £71,000
TRUSTEE Ludlow Trust Company Ltd.
OTHER INFORMATION The charity's 2020/21 accounts were the latest available to view at the time of writing (June 2023). Grants were awarded to 11 organisations.
HOW TO APPLY Apply in writing to the correspondent.

CONTACT DETAILS The Trustees, Ludlow Trust Company Ltd, 1st Floor Tower Wharf, Cheese Lane, Bristol BS2 0JJ *Tel.* 0117 313 8200 *Email* charitabletrusts@ludlowtrust.com

■ The Maud Elkington Charitable Trust

CC NO 263929 **ESTABLISHED** 1972
WHERE FUNDING CAN BE GIVEN Northamptonshire and Leicestershire.
WHO CAN BENEFIT Small registered charities.
WHAT IS FUNDED General charitable purposes; social welfare.
WHAT IS NOT FUNDED Generally, individuals.
TYPE OF GRANT Project funding.
RANGE OF GRANTS £500 to £5,000.
SAMPLE GRANTS A list of beneficiaries was not included in the annual report and accounts. Previous beneficiaries have included: Bromford Housing Association; Cancer Research UK; CARE Shangton; Charity Link – Northampton; Cynthia Spencer Hospice; Elizabeth Finn Care; Launde Abbey; Loughborough University; Multiple Sclerosis Society; Phoenix Furniture; Voluntary Action Northamptonshire.
FINANCES *Financial year end* 31/03/2022
Income £597,800
Grants to organisations £545,000
Grants to individuals £24,000
Assets £36,240,000
TRUSTEES Roger Bowder; Michael Jones; Katherine Hall.
OTHER INFORMATION The trust is committed to funding four pupils at Leicester Grammar School for the period of their education. Grants were given to 197 organisations.
HOW TO APPLY Apply in writing to the correspondent.
CONTACT DETAILS Helen Pole, Administrator, c/o Shakespeare Martineau LLP, Two Colton Square, Leicester, Leicestershire LE1 1QH *Tel.* 0116 257 4462 *Email* helen.pole@shma.co.uk

■ The Ellerdale Trust

CC NO 1073376 **ESTABLISHED** 1998
WHERE FUNDING CAN BE GIVEN UK, with a preference for Norfolk.
WHO CAN BENEFIT Registered charities; CICs; hospitals; schools. A small proportion of grants are made to overseas organisations.
WHAT IS FUNDED Children; families; disability and ill health; social welfare; respite for carers and children.
WHAT IS NOT FUNDED Individuals.
RANGE OF GRANTS Mostly between £1,000 and £5,000, with the occasional smaller or larger grant.
SAMPLE GRANTS NSPCC (£20,000); EACH and Home-Start Norfolk (£15,000 each); Sir Norman Lamb Mental Health and Wellbeing Fund (£10,000); Matthew's Friends, The Daisy Garland and The Matthew Project (£5,000 each); Asperger East Anglia, Community Action Norwich and ToysLikeMe (£2,000); The GEM Foundation and Great Yarmouth Pathway (£500 each).
FINANCES *Financial year end* 05/04/2022
Income £205,000
Grants to organisations £166,800
Assets £7,880,000
TRUSTEES Paul Kurthausen; Alistair MacFarlane; S. P. Moores; Clare Cairns; John Elliott; Samuel Moores.
HOW TO APPLY Apply in writing to the correspondent.

Think carefully about every application. Is it justified?

365

CONTACT DETAILS Mary Adlard, Director of Grant-making, The Parlour, The High Street, Ketteringham, Wymondham, Norfolk NR18 9RU *Tel.* 01603 813340 *Email* maryadlard7@gmail.com

■ John Ellerman Foundation

CC NO 263207 **ESTABLISHED** 1971
WHERE FUNDING CAN BE GIVEN England; UK-wide work; UK Overseas Territories (environmental work only).
WHO CAN BENEFIT Registered charities; museums; galleries.
WHAT IS FUNDED Performing arts; museums and galleries outside London; marine conservation; social action.
WHAT IS NOT FUNDED General and round-robin appeals; support for individuals, including student grants or bursaries; capital and equipment; promotion of religion or places of worship; arts organisations and projects whose main focus is supporting and developing individuals, rather than when new work is part of an artistic programme; learning and participation in the arts, where this is the primary focus of the application; leisure, individual holiday schemes or respite breaks; sport, where this is the core of the organisation's activities; boxing; education, such as initiatives linked to the curriculum, arts or environmental educational projects; animal welfare, captive breeding and animal rescue centres; medical research or treatment, including drug and alcohol rehabilitation services; work based in prisons that should receive statutory funding and does not pursue wider systems change; individual campaigns; one-off events, such as conferences, trips, seminars, master classes, summer schools, single commissions, productions or festivals.
TYPE OF GRANT Core/revenue costs; project funding.
SAMPLE GRANTS Refugee Action (£150,000); Opera Rara (£120,000); Carers UK (£100,000); North West Wildlife Trusts (£90,000); University of Oxford (£65,000); Local Trust (£25,000); Sheila McKechnie Foundation (£5,000).
FINANCES *Financial year end* 31/03/2022
Income £3,170,000
Grants to organisations £6,690,000
Assets £155,600,000
TRUSTEES Peter Kyle; Gary Steinberg; Geraldine Blake; Keith Shepherd; Tufyal Choudhury; Annika Small; Rebecca Bunce; Jonathan Hughes.
OTHER INFORMATION Grants were broken down as follows: social action (£1.72 million); the environment (£1.67 million); performing arts (£1.49 million); UK Overseas Territory Fund (£1.05 million); Museums and Galleries Fund (£491,300); other (£241,100).
HOW TO APPLY Apply via the foundation's website.
CONTACT DETAILS Kate Hitchcock, Senior Grants Manager, Aria House, 23 Craven Street, London WC2N 5NS *Tel.* 020 7930 8566 *Email* enquiries@ellerman.org.uk *Website* www.ellerman.org.uk

■ Ellinson Foundation Ltd

CC NO 252018 **ESTABLISHED** 1967
WHERE FUNDING CAN BE GIVEN London; the North East; overseas.
WHO CAN BENEFIT Jewish organisations.
WHAT IS FUNDED Jewish causes; relief of poverty; religious education; general charitable purposes.

RANGE OF GRANTS Up to £227,000.
SAMPLE GRANTS Achisomoch (£227,000); Three Pillars and Friends of Yeshivas Brisk (£10,000 each); Yeoidei Hatorah Schools (£5,000).
FINANCES *Financial year end* 31/03/2022
Income £334,600
Grants to organisations £252,000
Assets £5,880,000
TRUSTEES Uri Ellinson; Alexander Ellinson.
OTHER INFORMATION Only recipients of grants of over £5,000 were listed as beneficiaries. There were no grants of under £5,000 in 2022.
HOW TO APPLY Apply in writing to the correspondent.
CONTACT DETAILS Uri Ellinson, Company Secretary/Trustee, First Floor, Winston House, 349 Regents Park Road, London N3 1DH *Tel.* 020 3411 2001 *Email* u.ellinson@gmail.com

■ The Dorothy Whitney Elmhirst Trust

CC NO 1064069 **ESTABLISHED** 1997
WHERE FUNDING CAN BE GIVEN The South West, with a preference for Somerset.
WHO CAN BENEFIT Organisations and individuals.
WHAT IS FUNDED The trust continues to support the interests of the late Dorothy Whitney Elmhirst.
RANGE OF GRANTS Between £500 and £50,000.
SAMPLE GRANTS RNLI (£50,000); The Young Lives Foundation (£17,500); Healing Waves (£12,000); Love Thy Neighbour Jersey (£5,000); The Salvation Army Jersey Corps (£3,000); Porlock Weir Pilot Gig Club (£500).
FINANCES *Financial year end* 31/12/2022
Income £75,100
Grants to organisations £120,000
Assets £9,970,000
TRUSTEES Kathleen Burt; Nicholas Shattock; Chantelle Hibbs; Michelle Franklin.
HOW TO APPLY Apply writing to the correspondent.
CONTACT DETAILS The Trustees, PO Box 76, Minehead, Somerset TA24 9AR *Tel.* 07936 384190

■ The Elmley Foundation

CC NO 1004043 **ESTABLISHED** 1991
WHERE FUNDING CAN BE GIVEN Herefordshire and Worcestershire.
WHO CAN BENEFIT Constituted organisations and groups; individual artists from Herefordshire and Worcestershire; other individual artists whose proposals have been planned in conjunction with an organisation or body in Herefordshire or Worcestershire; students born and schooled in the two counties who are enrolled on nationally recognised specialist arts courses.
WHAT IS FUNDED A wide variety of projects and causes within the arts (including dance, film and media, literature, music, project development, theatre and visual arts and crafts); art events; art equipment.
WHAT IS NOT FUNDED Non-arts-related projects; projects not involving professional artists; arts events outside the beneficial area; arts events intended to raise funds for non-arts-related causes; general appeals; applications for retrospective funding.
TYPE OF GRANT Capital and core costs; start-up arts events; sponsorship. Funding awarded for up to, and over, three years will be considered. The foundation rarely covers full project costs; therefore, it partners with local authorities, businesses and arts development agencies.

Many of its grants are used as matched funding for Arts Council, National Lottery and local authority schemes.

RANGE OF GRANTS £250 to £25,000, but rarely more than £2,000 for unsolicited applications.

SAMPLE GRANTS Worcester City Council (£30,000); Worcester Cathedral (£21,000); 2Faced Dance Company (£14,500); Ledbury Poetry Festival (£12,000); Courtyard Centre For The Arts (£10,000); National Youth Orchestra of Great Britain (£5,000); Broadway Arts Festival (£2,500); The Linarol Consort of Viols (£750).

FINANCES *Financial year end 05/04/2022*
Income £396,100
Grants to organisations £245,700
Grants to individuals £32,800
Assets £4,600,000

TRUSTEES Diana Johnson; Sally Luton; Hugh Carslake.

OTHER INFORMATION The foundation has two funding schemes: the Main Programme, which supports proposals which promote the appreciation, knowledge and study of the arts and of artistic achievement in Herefordshire and Worcestershire; and the Small Grants Scheme (administered by Community First) which has two funds – one for arts events and activities and the other for arts equipment.

HOW TO APPLY Applicants to the Main Programme are strongly advised to contact the foundation before making a formal application. There is an application form available to download from the website or, alternatively, applicants can send a letter including details of: what the money is needed for; an estimate of the income and expenditure for the project/programme being planned; and, in particular, who will be benefitting from the project/programme. Applications can be made at any time. Application forms, deadlines and guidance notes for the Small Grants Scheme are available from the foundation's website.

CONTACT DETAILS The Trustees, West Aish, Morchard Bishop, Crediton, Devon EX17 6RX *Tel.* 01363 877433 *Email* foundation@elmley.org.uk *Website* www.elmley.org.uk

■ The Vernon N. Ely Charitable Trust

CC NO 230033   **ESTABLISHED** 1962

WHERE FUNDING CAN BE GIVEN The London Borough of Merton.

WHO CAN BENEFIT Charitable organisations.

WHAT IS FUNDED General charitable purposes; sport, particularly tennis.

SAMPLE GRANTS A list of beneficiaries was not included in the annual report and accounts.

FINANCES *Financial year end 05/04/2022*
Income £58,900
Grants to organisations £381,800
Assets £1,300,000

TRUSTEES Derek Howorth; Sarah Burdett; John Moyle.

OTHER INFORMATION The trustees decided in 2021 to close the trust within the following four or five years.

HOW TO APPLY Apply in writing to the correspondent.

CONTACT DETAILS Derek Howorth, Trustee, Copseham Rise, Lynx Hill, East Horsley, Leatherhead, Surrey KT24 5AX *Tel.* 07971 141316 *Email* derek.howorth@lta.org.uk

■ Emerton-Christie Charity

CC NO 262837   **ESTABLISHED** 1971

WHERE FUNDING CAN BE GIVEN UK.

WHO CAN BENEFIT UK-registered charities; voluntary organisations.

WHAT IS FUNDED Health, including mental health; disability; the arts; the environment; education.

WHAT IS NOT FUNDED Individuals.

TYPE OF GRANT One-off; project funding.

RANGE OF GRANTS Usually up to £3,000.

SAMPLE GRANTS Trinity Laban (£10,000); Freedom from Torture (£3,000); Alzheimer's Research, Autistica, Farming with Trees, The Pain Relief Foundation and Sunderland Women's Centre (£2,000 each); Royal National Institute of Blind People (£1,000).

FINANCES *Financial year end 05/04/2022*
Income £81,500
Grants to organisations £104,000
Assets £4,210,000

TRUSTEES Dr Claire Mera-Nelson; Lt Col. William Niekirk; Sally Walker.

HOW TO APPLY The charity's website notes that potential applicants should contact the correspondent by email (not post), detailing the following: 'Who you are, what you do, [and] the funding for which you are applying'.

CONTACT DETAILS The Trustees, 14 Silver Street, Bowness-on-Solway, Warminster, Wiltshire BA12 8PS *Tel.* 07887 397544 *Email* info@emertonchristie.org *Website* www.emertonchristie.org

■ EMI Music Sound Foundation

CC NO 1104027   **ESTABLISHED** 1997

WHERE FUNDING CAN BE GIVEN UK and Ireland.

WHO CAN BENEFIT Schools and individuals.

WHAT IS FUNDED The improvement of young people's access to music education. Support is given to: schools, teachers and individuals for the purchase of musical instruments and/or equipment. The foundation has also created bursaries at 11 conservatoires and music colleges to assist music students in need of financial support.

WHAT IS NOT FUNDED Music studios/businesses; private music centres; community projects.

TYPE OF GRANT Equipment costs; bursaries.

RANGE OF GRANTS Up to £1,500.

SAMPLE GRANTS A full list of beneficiaries was not available. Bursaries were paid to organisations including: English National Opera; Liverpool Institute for Performing Arts; National Children's Orchestra; Royal Conservatoire of Scotland.

FINANCES *Financial year end 31/07/2022*
Income £417,000
Grants to organisations £314,000
Grants to individuals £108,600
Assets £7,430,000

TRUSTEES Paul Gambaccini; Jo Hibbitt; Leslie Hill; Mr D. Hughes; Rupert Perry; Charles Ashcroft; Tony Wadsworth; Keith Harris; Adam Barker; Laura Arowolo.

HOW TO APPLY Application forms for instruments and equipment grants can be downloaded from the foundation's website, along with guidance notes.

CONTACT DETAILS The Trustees, Universal Music, 4 Pancras Square, Kings Cross, London N1C 4AG *Tel.* 020 3932 6101 *Email* umuksoundfoundation@umusic.com *Website* www.emimusicsoundfoundation.com

■ The Endrick Trust

OSCR NO SC012043   **ESTABLISHED** 1984

WHERE FUNDING CAN BE GIVEN The Glasgow postcode area.

WHO CAN BENEFIT Registered charities.

WHAT IS FUNDED Social welfare; citizenship and community development.

WHAT IS NOT FUNDED Individuals; animals; medical research; charities with an income of more than £2 million. Repeat applications within two years are less likely to be successful.

TYPE OF GRANT Core funding; project funding.

RANGE OF GRANTS Typically up to £5,000. Larger grants of up to £50,000 are made for exceptional projects.

SAMPLE GRANTS Amma Birth Companions and Glasgow City Mission (£5,000 each); NEMO Arts (£4,000); Move On (£3,000); PATH Scotland (£2,500); Stepping Stones for Families (£2,000); Occasional Cabaret (£1,700).

FINANCES *Financial year end 05/04/2022*
Income £126,300
Grants to organisations £105,600
Assets £5,310,000

OTHER INFORMATION Grants were awarded to 33 organisations during the year.

HOW TO APPLY Application forms are available to download from the trust's website and should be returned via email to the correspondent.

CONTACT DETAILS Alison Hempsey, Partner, c/o TC Young Solicitors, 7 West George Street, Glasgow G2 1BA *Tel.* 0141 225 2573 *Email* amh@tcyoung.co.uk *Website* www. tcyoung.co.uk/info/endrick-trust

■ England and Wales Cricket Trust

CC NO 1112540   **ESTABLISHED** 2005

WHERE FUNDING CAN BE GIVEN England and Wales.

WHO CAN BENEFIT Cricket clubs; county cricket boards; cricket-based charitable organisations.

WHAT IS FUNDED Encouragement of increased participation of amateur cricket (particularly among young people; supporting other charitable organisations associated with cricket.

TYPE OF GRANT Project funding; capital costs; core costs; development funding.

SAMPLE GRANTS A list of beneficiaries was not included in the annual report and accounts.

FINANCES *Financial year end 31/01/2022*
Income £45,460,000
Grants to organisations £22,640,000
Assets £67,300,000

TRUSTEES Scott Smith; Ian Lovett; James Wood; Peter Ackerley; Sancha Legg; Ruth Sienkiewicz; Forhad Hussain.

OTHER INFORMATION The trust mainly awards grants to cricket clubs and projects that promote community participation in cricket.

HOW TO APPLY Apply via the application form on the trust's website.

CONTACT DETAILS The Trustees, Lord's Cricket Ground, London NW8 8QZ *Tel.* 020 7432 1200 *Email* kate.hailstone@ecb.co.uk *Website* www. ecb.co.uk/be-involved/club-support/club-funding

■ The Englefield Charitable Trust

CC NO 258123   **ESTABLISHED** 1968

WHERE FUNDING CAN BE GIVEN Mainly the Berkshire area, as well as parts of Hackney and Inverness-shire which are connected with the Englefield Estate.

WHO CAN BENEFIT Mainly registered charities; some local schools and churches; individuals.

WHAT IS FUNDED General charitable purposes, including: churches and religion; agriculture and conservation; heritage and arts; young people; education; community; sport; social welfare; overseas projects; medical research; armed forces charities; work overseas.

WHAT IS NOT FUNDED Recipients of grants within the previous 12 months are advised not to re-apply.

TYPE OF GRANT Capital grants are preferred but revenue grants will be considered. Grants are generally one-off.

RANGE OF GRANTS Generally between £500 and £5,000.

SAMPLE GRANTS A list of beneficiaries was not included in the annual report and accounts.

FINANCES *Financial year end 31/03/2022*
Income £557,000
Grants to organisations £309,400
Assets £19,720,000

TRUSTEES Lady Elizabeth Benyon; Zoe Benyon; Lord Richard Benyon; Catherine Haig; Melissa Owston; Richard Bampfylde; Richard Griffiths; Andrew Hutton.

OTHER INFORMATION In 2021/22 the trust received 249 applications for funding and awarded 135 grants. Grants were made across seven categories: social welfare (£138,400); young people, education and community causes (£96,600); conservation, heritage and the arts (£22,500); churches and religion (£21,300); medical research and support (£15,000); overseas (£15,000). Applications from individuals are considered but are subject to a limit of £350 and full details are requested of what the money is needed for along with confirmation that all other relevant avenues have been explored.

HOW TO APPLY Apply in writing to the correspondent. Details of what to include can be found on the trust's website. Alternatively, applications can be submitted through the online fundraising platform The Good Exchange (www.thegoodexchange.com). Applications are considered in March and October.

CONTACT DETAILS The Trustees, Englefield Estate Office, Englefield Road, Theale, Reading, Berkshire RG7 5DU *Tel.* 07880 701138 *Email* charity@englefield.co.uk *Website* www. englefieldestate.co.uk/community/englefield-charitable-trust

■ The Enkalon Foundation

CCNI NO NIC103528   **ESTABLISHED** 1985

WHERE FUNDING CAN BE GIVEN Northern Ireland, particularly the Antrim area.

WHO CAN BENEFIT Charities, community groups and organisations working to improve the quality of life of people in Northern Ireland.

WHAT IS FUNDED Social welfare; animal welfare; arts, culture, heritage or science; amateur sport; health; education; citizenship and community development; healthcare equipment for ex-employees of British Enkalon in Antrim and their families.

WHAT IS NOT FUNDED Individuals (other than ex-British Enkalon employees); playgroups, PTAs, senior citizens' groups or sporting groups outside the former Antrim borough area; medical research; travel outside Northern Ireland; projects outside Northern Ireland.

TYPE OF GRANT Core costs; running costs; project costs; healthcare equipment.

RANGE OF GRANTS Usually up to £6,000 maximum, with the average grant being £1,000.

SAMPLE GRANTS A list of beneficiaries was not included in the annual report and accounts.

Previous beneficiaries have included: Muckamore Parish Dev Association (£20,000); Moving Forward Together (£4,000); Samaritans – Ballymena (£2,000); Prison Fellowship (£1,000); Adoption UK (£500).

FINANCES *Financial year end* 05/04/2022
Income £235,300
Grants to organisations £148,300
Grants to individuals £90,300
Assets £7,230,000

TRUSTEES Peter Dalton; John Wallace; Mark Patterson; Stephen Montgomery; Janet Hume.

HOW TO APPLY The trustees meet quarterly, in March, June, September and December. Applications should be submitted via the website along with supporting documentation (see details on the website).

CONTACT DETAILS Claire Cawley, Administrator, PO Box 126, Antrim BT41 9DF *Tel.* 028 9447 7131 *Email* info@enkelonfoundation.org *Website* www.enkalonfoundation.org

■ Entindale Ltd

CC NO 277052   **ESTABLISHED** 1978

WHERE FUNDING CAN BE GIVEN UK and Israel.

WHO CAN BENEFIT Orthodox Jewish organisations.

WHAT IS FUNDED Advancement of the Orthodox Jewish religion; education; the relief of poverty.

RANGE OF GRANTS Generally £50,000, with some larger grants.

SAMPLE GRANTS Keren Habinyan Ltd (£180,000); Kids Care London (£57,900); Achisomoch Aid Company Ltd (£50,200); Rowanville Ltd and Tchabe Kollel Ltd (£50,000 each).

FINANCES *Financial year end* 30/06/2022
Income £1,570,000
Grants to organisations £1,720,000
Assets £16,740,000

TRUSTEES Allan Becker; Barbara Peters; Joseph Pearlman.

OTHER INFORMATION Grants were awarded to more than five organisations during the year. Grants of £50,000 or less totalled £1.34 million.

HOW TO APPLY Apply in writing to the correspondent.

CONTACT DETAILS Joseph Pearlman, Chair, 8 Highfield Gardens, London NW11 9HB *Tel.* 020 8458 9266

■ Epilepsy Research UK

CC NO 1100394   **ESTABLISHED** 2007

WHERE FUNDING CAN BE GIVEN UK.

WHO CAN BENEFIT Hospitals; universities; other academic institutions.

WHAT IS FUNDED Scientific research investigating the causes, diagnosis and clinical management of epilepsy and associated conditions.

TYPE OF GRANT Project funding.

RANGE OF GRANTS Programme dependent.

SAMPLE GRANTS Newcastle University (£250,000); Aston University (£145,600); University of Liverpool (£88,500); Great Ormond Street Institute of Child Health (£10,000).

FINANCES *Financial year end* 31/03/2022
Income £2,990,000
Grants to organisations £1,570,000
Assets £2,710,000

TRUSTEES Barrie Akin; Prof. Matthew Walker; Prof. Mark Richardson; Judith Spencer-Gregson; Prof. Stephanie Schorge; Dr Rhys Thomas; Dr Anne Coxon; Prof. Michael Cousin; Joseph Brice; Prof. Nicholas Lench; Prof. Martin Elliott.

OTHER INFORMATION The charity offers three programmes: project grants (up to £200,000 to support a research project lasting a maximum of three years); fellowship awards (up to £300,000 over four years to support fellowships); pilot studies (up to £30,000 to support pilot or start-up studies lasting no more than two years). Further information on the grant programmes offered can be found on the charity's website.

HOW TO APPLY Application forms, together with criteria, guidelines and application deadlines are available to download from the charity's website.

CONTACT DETAILS Caoimhe Bennett, Head of Research, Can Mezzanine, 7–14 Great Dover Street, London SE1 4YR *Tel.* 020 3096 7887 *Email* caoimhe@eruk.org.uk *Website* www. epilepsyresearch.org.uk

■ The EQ Foundation

CC NO 1161209   **ESTABLISHED** 2015

WHERE FUNDING CAN BE GIVEN Worldwide, with a preference for the UK.

WHO CAN BENEFIT Charitable organisations.

WHAT IS FUNDED Projects that improve social mobility and support disadvantaged people.

WHAT IS NOT FUNDED The foundation has a preference for medium-sized charities, with annual expenditure of between £500,000 and £3 million.

TYPE OF GRANT Research funding; project funding.

RANGE OF GRANTS Typically up to £30,000.

SAMPLE GRANTS The Access Project (£50,000); The Big Issue (£31,000); Blue Marine Foundation and Sand Dams Worldwide (£28,400 each); Action Tutoring and Renewable World (£25,000 each); The Bike Project (£20,000).

FINANCES *Financial year end* 30/04/2022
Income £1,140,000
Grants to organisations £773,800
Assets £4,140,000

TRUSTEES Ian Barlow; Freddie Cleworth; Ben Faulkner; Mike Neumann; Catherine Deptford; Zoe Brett; Mark Kenner; John Spiers.

OTHER INFORMATION Grants were awarded to 46 organisations during the year. Twenty organisations received over £20,000 each.

HOW TO APPLY At the time of writing (August 2023) the foundation's website stated: 'Please note that we are not currently accepting unsolicited applications for funding as we are concentrating on our existing relationships.' Refer to the website for updates.

CONTACT DETAILS John Spiers, Trustee, Centennium House, 100 Lower Thames Street, London EC3R 6DL *Tel.* 020 7488 7110 *Email* info@ eqfoundation.org.uk *Website* https:// eqfoundation.org.uk

■ The Esfandi Charitable Foundation

CC NO 1103095   **ESTABLISHED** 2004

WHERE FUNDING CAN BE GIVEN UK and overseas.

WHO CAN BENEFIT Mainly Jewish organisations.

WHAT IS FUNDED General charitable purposes.

RANGE OF GRANTS Mostly up to £20,000, with the occasional larger grant.

SAMPLE GRANTS Side by Side Ltd (£310,000); Prism The Gift Fund and Rabbi Asaf Portal (£17,500 each); Variety, the Children's Charity (£10,000); Holocaust Educational Trust (£5,000); The Chicken Soup Shelter and Heichal Leah (£1,000 each); The Line (£500).

FINANCES *Financial year end* 05/04/2022
Income £900,000
Grants to organisations £845,000
Assets £21,600
TRUSTEES Denise Esfandi; Joseph Esfandi; Michael Esfandi; David Esfandi; Jonathan Esfandi.
HOW TO APPLY Apply in writing to the correspondent.
CONTACT DETAILS The Trustees, 4 Fitzhardinge Street, London W1H 6EG *Tel.* 020 7629 6666

■ Esher House Charitable Trust

CC NO 276183   **ESTABLISHED** 1978
WHERE FUNDING CAN BE GIVEN England and Wales.
WHO CAN BENEFIT Registered charities; hospices; hospitals; places of worship.
WHAT IS FUNDED Jewish causes; health; welfare; arts and culture; children and young people; education; community.
RANGE OF GRANTS Mostly less than £1,000.
SAMPLE GRANTS A list of beneficiaries was not included in the annual report and accounts.
FINANCES *Financial year end* 30/06/2022
Income £184,000
Grants to organisations £125,500
Assets £2,790,000
TRUSTEES Hadassa Conn; Michael Conn; Douglas Conn.
OTHER INFORMATION Grants were broken down as follows: community (£81,400); education (£31,000); health and welfare (£10,300); children and young people (£2,300).
HOW TO APPLY Apply in writing to the correspondent.
CONTACT DETAILS Michael Conn, Trustee, 845 Finchley Road, London NW11 8NA *Tel.* 020 8455 1111 *Email* michael@1stpolicy.co.uk

■ The Essex and Southend Sports Trust

CC NO 1092238   **ESTABLISHED** 2002
WHERE FUNDING CAN BE GIVEN Essex (including but not limited to the unitary authorities of Southend-on-Sea and Thurrock) and the London boroughs of Barking and Dagenham, Havering, Newham, Redbridge and Waltham Forest.
WHO CAN BENEFIT Registered charities; CICs; schools; amateur sports clubs; individuals.
WHAT IS FUNDED Sports; sports equipment; sports facilities; sports projects; coaching; training; education; children and young people; community projects; disability; older people.
TYPE OF GRANT Capital costs; seed funding/start-up funding.
RANGE OF GRANTS Up to £50,000.
SAMPLE GRANTS A list of beneficiaries was not included in the annual report and accounts. Previous beneficiaries have included: Southend United Community and Educational Trust (£25,000); Hadleigh and Thundersley Cricket Club (£8,000); Essex County Cricket Board and Harlow Cricket Club (£5,000 each); The Prince's Trust and Southend Rugby Club (£3,000 each); South East Essex District Cricket Board (£2,500); Giffords Primary School (£2,000); Richardsons-Trek cycling team (£1,500); RSPB (£1,200).
FINANCES *Financial year end* 30/06/2021
Income £315,000
Grants to organisations £160,600
Assets £7,100,000
TRUSTEES Linley Butler; Joseph Sims; Rachel Pearse; Simon Butler.
OTHER INFORMATION The trust's joint venture with Essex Community Foundation (the Essex and Southend Sports Charitable Fund, ESSCF) supports sporting activities for individuals. The 2020/21 annual report and accounts were the latest available at the time of writing (May 2023).
HOW TO APPLY Apply in writing to the correspondent via email. See the website for guidelines.
CONTACT DETAILS Joe Sims, Trustee, Red House, Larks Lane, Great Waltham, Chelmsford CM3 1AD *Tel.* 01245 360385 *Email* mail@easst.org.uk *Website* www.easst.org.uk

■ Essex Community Foundation

CC NO 1052061   **ESTABLISHED** 1995
WHERE FUNDING CAN BE GIVEN Essex, Southend-on-Sea; Thurrock.
WHO CAN BENEFIT Voluntary and community organisations and other not-for-profit organisations, with an interest in small grassroots organisations. Individuals can also be supported.
WHAT IS FUNDED General charitable purposes.
TYPE OF GRANT Core costs/revenue costs; new or continuing projects; one-off initiatives; capital costs.
RANGE OF GRANTS Mostly £250 to £10,000.
SAMPLE GRANTS Home-Start Essex (£127,600); Age Well East (£52,000); Havens Hospices (£30,000); Headway Essex (£22,200); Riverview Charitable Trust CIO (£20,300).
FINANCES *Financial year end* 30/06/2022
Income £5,380,000
Grants to organisations £4,460,000
Assets £47,500,000
TRUSTEES Charles Bishop; Benjamin Minter; Gemma Cartwright; Gail Cunningham; Nicholas Alston; Simon Hall; Joanna Wells; Claire Read; Sandra Hollis; Atul Manek; Soumya Kumar; Emma Goode.
OTHER INFORMATION This is one of the 47 UK community foundations, which distribute funding for a wide range of purposes. As with all community foundations, there are a number of donor-advised funds managed on behalf of individuals, families and charitable trusts. Grant schemes tend to change frequently – consult the foundation's website for details of current programmes and up-to-date deadlines. The grant total includes grants to individuals.
HOW TO APPLY Apply online via the foundation's website.
CONTACT DETAILS Grants Team, 3 Hoffmanns Way, Chelmsford, Essex CM1 1GU *Tel.* 01245 355947 *Email* hello@essexcf.org.uk *Website* www.essexcommunityfoundation.org.uk

■ The Essex Youth Trust

CC NO 225768   **ESTABLISHED** 1963
WHERE FUNDING CAN BE GIVEN UK.
WHO CAN BENEFIT Organisations, including youth clubs.
WHAT IS FUNDED Education; social welfare; people under the age of 25, particularly looked-after children. The trust's website explains that it awards grants 'which favour beneficiaries that develop young people's physical, mental and spiritual capacities through active participation in sports and indoor and outdoor activities.'
WHAT IS NOT FUNDED Individuals.
TYPE OF GRANT Core costs; running costs; capital expenditure; project funding; salaries.
RANGE OF GRANTS Mostly under £10,000.
SAMPLE GRANTS Essex Boys' and Girls' Clubs (£56,000); The Cirdan Sailing Trust (£50,000);

North Avenue Youth Centre (£32,600); The Ark Centre (£10,000).
FINANCES *Financial year end* 31/03/2022
Income £363,200
Grants to organisations £267,600
Assets £9,540,000
TRUSTEES Michael Biegel; Claire Cottrell; Lady Julia Denison-Smith; Michael Dyer; The Ven. Duncan Green; William Robson; Julie Rogers; Jonathan McEachern.
OTHER INFORMATION Grants were awarded to 29 organisations. Only organisations that received grants of over £10,000 were listed as beneficiaries in the charity's accounts. Grants of under £10,000 totalled £221,200.
HOW TO APPLY The trust's website has a downloadable application form, which should be emailed to the correspondent. Grant applications are considered by the trustees quarterly, in February, May, August and November. Applications made before the first day of the month in which a meeting is held will be considered at that meeting.
CONTACT DETAILS Jonathan Douglas-Hughes, Clerk, c/o Gepp and Sons, 58 New London Road, Chelmsford, Essex CM2 0PA *Tel.* 01245 228102 *Email* douglas-hughesj@gepp.co.uk *Website* https://sites.google.com/site/essexyouthtrust

■ The Ethos Foundation

CC NO 1166697   **ESTABLISHED** 2016
WHERE FUNDING CAN BE GIVEN UK.
WHO CAN BENEFIT Registered charities.
WHAT IS FUNDED General charitable purposes; community development.
SAMPLE GRANTS The Childhood Trust (£625,000); Thrive at Five (£333,000); The Cabrach Trust (£230,000); Beacon Fellowship (£20,000).
FINANCES *Financial year end* 30/09/2021
Income £1,000,000
Grants to organisations £1,370,000
Assets £563,400
TRUSTEES Grant Gordon; Brigitte Gordon; Lucy Blythe; Luka Gakic.
OTHER INFORMATION The foundation was previously called The Reekimlane Foundation. The 2020/21 annual report and accounts were the latest available to view at the time of writing (June 2023).
HOW TO APPLY Unsolicited applications are not accepted.
CONTACT DETAILS The Trustees, 18 Buckingham Palace Road, London SW1W 0QP *Tel.* 07802 208276 *Email* ethosfoundation.uk@gmail.com *Website* https://ethosfoundation.uk

■ Joseph Ettedgui Charitable Foundation

CC NO 1139615   **ESTABLISHED** 2010
WHERE FUNDING CAN BE GIVEN UK and overseas.
WHO CAN BENEFIT Registered charities.
WHAT IS FUNDED General charitable purposes.
RANGE OF GRANTS Mostly £5,000 to £10,000.
SAMPLE GRANTS David Rattray Foundation, Freedom from Torture and Great Ormond Street Hospital Children's Charity (£10,000 each); The Bike Project and Refugees at Home (£5,000 each); The Design Museum (£1,000).
FINANCES *Financial year end* 31/03/2022
Income £158,000
Grants to organisations £146,000
Assets £3,810,000

TRUSTEES Peter Ettedgui; Isabel Ettedgui; Paul Ettedgui; Genevieve Ettedgui; Matilda Ettedgui; Ludlow Trust Company Ltd.
OTHER INFORMATION Grants were made to 19 organisations during the year.
HOW TO APPLY Unsolicited applications are not accepted.
CONTACT DETAILS The Trustees, c/o Trustee Dept., 6th Floor, Trinity Quay 2, Avon Street, Bristol BS2 0PT *Tel.* 0345 304 2424

■ Euro Quality Foundation

CC NO 1119242   **ESTABLISHED** 2007
WHERE FUNDING CAN BE GIVEN Shropshire; UK; overseas.
WHO CAN BENEFIT Registered charities.
WHAT IS FUNDED Emergency response/relief; education; social welfare; sustainable living; social projects; health and medicine.
TYPE OF GRANT Project funding.
SAMPLE GRANTS A list of beneficiaries was not included in the annual report and accounts.
FINANCES *Financial year end* 30/06/2022
Income £717,800
Grants to organisations £627,600
Assets £1,580,000
TRUSTEES Rizvan Khalid; Sattar Khalid; Mr M. N. Mansha.
OTHER INFORMATION In 2021/22, grants were distributed as follows: education and training (£393,700); social community welfare (£133,800); emergency and health care (£100,100).
HOW TO APPLY Contact the correspondent for more information.
CONTACT DETAILS The Trustees, Euro House, Dale Street, Craven Arms, Shropshire SY7 9PA *Tel.* 01588 676318 *Email* hello@euroqualityfoundation.org *Website* https://sites.google.com/euroqualityfoundation.org/eqf/home

■ The Evelyn Trust

CC NO 232891   **ESTABLISHED** 1920
WHERE FUNDING CAN BE GIVEN Cambridgeshire.
WHO CAN BENEFIT Research organisations; registered charities; not-for-profit organisations.
WHAT IS FUNDED Medical research; health and well-being.
WHAT IS NOT FUNDED Each grants programme has different eligibility criteria; refer to the relevant funding guidelines on the trust's website for full details.
TYPE OF GRANT Research; project funding; pilot studies; capital costs; strategic costs.
RANGE OF GRANTS Small grants: £4,000 to £10,000; large grants: up to £250,000.
SAMPLE GRANTS The University of Cambridge (£630,600 in 11 grants); Young People's Counselling Service (£120,000); Cambridge Cyrenians Ltd (£87,000); Darwin College (£71,300); Caring Together Charity (£50,000); Myelopathy.org (£22,700); Jimmy's Cambridge (£20,700); Lives Set in Motion CIC (£14,000).
FINANCES *Financial year end* 31/03/2022
Income £833,000
Grants to organisations £1,090,000
Assets £30,540,000
TRUSTEES Amy Agnew; Will Dawkins; Adrian Frost; Jeremy Pemberton; Catherine Thomas; Prof. Rebecca Fitzgerald; Jeremy Newsum; Dr Trevor Baglin; Norest Mararike; Helena Jones.
OTHER INFORMATION Thirty-one grants were awarded during the year. Grants awarded of less than £10,000 were not listed and totalled £85,700.

HOW TO APPLY Visit the trust's website for full details regarding the grant application process.

CONTACT DETAILS Rebecca Wood, Charity Director, PO Box 1436, Willingham, Cambridgeshire CB24 5YX *Tel.* 01954 230389 *Email* rebeccawood@evelyntrust.com *Website* www.evelyntrust.com

■ The Eventhall Family Charitable Trust

CC NO 803178   **ESTABLISHED** 1989

WHERE FUNDING CAN BE GIVEN UK, with a preference for the North West.

WHO CAN BENEFIT Registered charities; hospitals; Jewish religious bodies/institutions.

WHAT IS FUNDED General charitable purposes including health, Jewish causes and social welfare.

TYPE OF GRANT Capital costs; project funding.

SAMPLE GRANTS A list of beneficiaries was not included in the annual report and accounts.

FINANCES *Financial year end* 05/04/2022 *Income* £69,900 *Grants to organisations* £196,800 *Assets* £2,380,000

TRUSTEES Julia Eventhall; David Eventhall; Emily Eventhall.

OTHER INFORMATION Grants were made to 33 organisations during the year.

HOW TO APPLY Apply in writing to the correspondent.

CONTACT DETAILS The Trustees, PO Box 490, Altrincham, Cheshire WA14 2ZT *Tel.* 01282 478200 *Email* efct@rectella.com

■ The Everard Foundation

CC NO 272248   **ESTABLISHED** 1976

WHERE FUNDING CAN BE GIVEN UK, with a preference for Leicestershire.

WHO CAN BENEFIT Registered charities; hospitals; places of worship; community groups.

WHAT IS FUNDED General charitable purposes, including: community development; education; social welfare; people with disabilities; the armed forces; the environment; health; religion.

RANGE OF GRANTS Mostly under £5,000, with the occasional larger grant.

SAMPLE GRANTS Leicester Hospitals Charity (£25,000); Semble Foundation (£20,000); British Heart Foundation (£5,000); St John's Church (£4,500); ABF The Soldier's Charity and Young Enterprise (£1,000 each); Charlie Waller Trust (£250); Young Leicestershire Ltd (£50).

FINANCES *Financial year end* 05/04/2022 *Income* £61,900 *Grants to organisations* £76,900 *Assets* £17,550,000

TRUSTEES Simon Atkinson; Richard Everard; Julian Everard; Charlotte Everard.

OTHER INFORMATION Grants were broken down as follows: health (£31,200); social welfare (£21,100); citizenship or community development (£14,300); education (£4,900); religion (£4,500); the armed forces (£1,000). During this period, no individuals were awarded grants.

HOW TO APPLY Apply in writing to the correspondent.

CONTACT DETAILS Richard Everard, Trustee, c/o Everards Brewery Ltd, Cooper Way, Everards Meadows, Glenfield, Enderby, Leicestershire LE19 2AN *Tel.* 0116 201 4307

■ Eversheds Sutherland (International) Charitable Trust

CC NO 1083594   **ESTABLISHED** 2000

WHERE FUNDING CAN BE GIVEN Charities local to the firm's UK offices.

WHO CAN BENEFIT Registered charities.

WHAT IS FUNDED General charitable purposes.

RANGE OF GRANTS Up to £109,000 but typically up to £25,000.

SAMPLE GRANTS End Youth Homelessness (£109,500); International Rescue Committee (£100,000); WaterAid (£70,000); Wildlife and Wetlands Trust (£25,000); Refuge and Refugee Legal Support (£15,000 each) Disasters Emergency Committee (£10,500).

FINANCES *Financial year end* 30/04/2022 *Income* £1,030,000 *Grants to organisations* £725,700 *Assets* £1,450,000

TRUSTEES Jonathan Bowley; Naeema Choudry; Peter Scurlock; Mark Fletcher; Kathryn Roberts; Michael Thompson.

OTHER INFORMATION The trust is the corporate charity of Eversheds Sutherland LLP, an international law firm. It receives its income from donations from the firm's partners and dormant client balances.

HOW TO APPLY The firm's website states: 'Each year the partners donate funds to the Eversheds Sutherland Business Lawyers Charitable Trust to create a significant pot of cash, the majority of which is allocated by reference to the number of people in each of our offices to support the various local charities chosen by each office.'

CONTACT DETAILS The Trustees, Eversheds, 1 Callaghan Square, Cardiff CF10 5BT *Tel.* 0845 498 7156 *Email* kathpring@ eversheds.com *Website* www.eversheds-sutherland.com/global/en/where/europe/uk/overview/csr/charitable-giving.page

■ The Eveson Charitable Trust

CC NO 1196672   **ESTABLISHED** 1993

WHERE FUNDING CAN BE GIVEN Herefordshire; the West Midlands (covering Birmingham, Coventry, Dudley, Sandwell, Solihull, Walsall and Wolverhampton); Worcestershire.

WHO CAN BENEFIT Mainly registered charities; however, some support is given, directly or indirectly, to statutory bodies for projects for which no statutory funding is available.

WHAT IS FUNDED People with disabilities; mental health; children in need; older people; people experiencing homelessness; hospitals; hospices.

WHAT IS NOT FUNDED Individuals; retrospective expenditure.

TYPE OF GRANT Core/running costs; project costs; capital costs.

RANGE OF GRANTS No set limit.

SAMPLE GRANTS Acorns Children's Hospice Trust (£197,000); Herefordshire Voluntary Organisations Support Service (£42,000); Marches Family Network (£20,000); Breast Cancer Now (£10,000); Herefordshire Growing Point (£8,000); Blind in Business (£2,000); Motor Neurone Disease Association (£5,000); Wheely Different Theatre Company (£650).

FINANCES *Financial year end* 31/03/2022 *Income* £1,670,000 *Grants to organisations* £3,430,000 *Assets* £110,820,000

TRUSTEES Richard Mainwaring; Louise Woodhead; Sir William Wiggin; Judith Millward; Vivien

Cockerill; Tamsin Clive; The Rt Revd Richard Jackson; Mark Taylor; Dr David Rees.

OTHER INFORMATION In 2021/22, the trust awarded 282 grants. Grants were distributed in the following categories: people with other Disabilities (£652,200); disadvantaged children (£546,500); hospices (£487,000); children with disabilities (£422,700); older people (£379,400); people experiencing homelessness (£328,500); people who are blind or deaf (£243,900); medical research (£163,200); hospitals (£151,000); causes fitting more than one category (£122,600).

HOW TO APPLY First-stage application forms can be completed on the trust's website. If eligible, applicants will receive a full application form. The trustees meet regularly to consider grant applications.

CONTACT DETAILS The Trustees, Office 7, Sansome Lodge, 6 Sansome Walk, Worcester WR1 1LH *Tel.* 01905 905085 or 07859 393380 or 07306 244624 (Monday to Thursday). *Email* grants@eveson.org.uk or use the contact form on the website *Website* www.eveson.org.uk

■ The Beryl Evetts and Robert Luff Animal Welfare Trust Ltd

CC NO 283944　　　**ESTABLISHED** 1981
WHERE FUNDING CAN BE GIVEN UK and sometimes overseas.
WHO CAN BENEFIT Registered animal charities.
WHAT IS FUNDED Veterinary research and the care and welfare of animals.
RANGE OF GRANTS £500 to £75,000.
SAMPLE GRANTS Royal Veterinary College (£60,000); Birds of Poole Harbour (£7,500); Oak Tree Animal Charity, Nowzad Dogs and Wildwood Trust (£5,000 each); Barkingside (£2,500); Cats Protection Birmingham (£2,000); Yorkshire Cat Rescue (£1,000).
FINANCES *Financial year end* 31/08/2021
Income £291,700
Grants to organisations £253,500
Assets £5,610,000
TRUSTEES Melanie Condon; Richard Price; The Revd Matthew Tomlinson; Lady Ruth Bodey; Sir Paul Coleridge; Dr Helen Hughes.
OTHER INFORMATION The 2020/21 annual report and accounts were the latest available at the time of writing (June 2023).
HOW TO APPLY Apply in writing to the correspondent.
CONTACT DETAILS Richard Price, Trustee, Waters Edge, Ferry Lane, Moulsford, Wallingford, Oxfordshire OX10 9JF *Tel.* 01491 652204 *Email* rpjprice@gmail.com

■ The Exilarch's Foundation

CC NO 275919　　　**ESTABLISHED** 1978
WHERE FUNDING CAN BE GIVEN Worldwide, with a preference for the UK, Israel, the USA and Iraq.
WHO CAN BENEFIT Charitable organisations, including Jewish organisations; hospitals; universities; schools.
WHAT IS FUNDED General charitable purposes including: social welfare; education; community development; hospitals, medical education and research; ethics.
RANGE OF GRANTS £4,000 to £900,000.
SAMPLE GRANTS Bevis Marks Synagogue Heritage Foundation (£900,000); Jewish Leadership Council (£50,000); Woolf Institute (£42,000);

University Jewish Chaplaincy (£20,000); Global Leadership Foundation (£5,000).
FINANCES *Financial year end* 31/12/2021
Income £7,030,000
Grants to organisations £6,130,000
Assets £102,810,000
TRUSTEES David Dangoor; Elie Dangoor; Michael Dangoor.
OTHER INFORMATION The foundation is the sponsor of Westminster Academy, to which it awarded £116,300 during the year.
HOW TO APPLY Apply in writing to the correspondent.
CONTACT DETAILS The Trustees, 4 Carlos Place, Mayfair, London W1K 3AW *Tel.* 020 7399 0850

■ The ExPat Foundation

CC NO 1094041　　　**ESTABLISHED** 2002
WHERE FUNDING CAN BE GIVEN UK.
WHO CAN BENEFIT Registered charities.
WHAT IS FUNDED Older people; young people and children; families.
WHAT IS NOT FUNDED Religious charities; animal welfare.
TYPE OF GRANT Project costs; core/revenue costs.
SAMPLE GRANTS St Giles Trust – SOS Royal London (£154,900); Enfield Carers Centre (£60,000); London Bubble Theatre Company (£50,000); Wear Valley Women's Aid (£45,000); Eikon (£36,000); Cirencester Housing for Young People (£20,000); Ringwood and District Community Association (£7,500); Rosehill Youth Theatre (£5,000).
FINANCES *Financial year end* 05/04/2022
Income £1,430,000
Grants to organisations £1,240,000
Assets £314,000
TRUSTEES Janet Cummins; Caroline Coombs; Jan Knight; Malcolm Stevens.
HOW TO APPLY At the time of writing (January 2023), new applications were not being accepted. The foundation's website stated: 'The ExPat Foundation has been the vehicle for our founder's charitable giving. Pat Wolfson died in August 2019, and the trustees have recently received her final legacy to the foundation. We expect this to allow us to give a final grant to a select number of charities with which we have worked with in the recent past. Therefore, we are not accepting applications from charities we have not funded in the last three years.'
CONTACT DETAILS Janet Cummins, Trustee and Administration, 127 Ellesmere Road, London NW10 1LG *Tel.* 020 3609 2105 *Email* expatfdn@gmail.com *Website* https://expatfoundation.org

■ Extonglen Ltd

CC NO 286230　　　**ESTABLISHED** 1982
WHERE FUNDING CAN BE GIVEN UK and Israel.
WHO CAN BENEFIT Orthodox Jewish charities.
WHAT IS FUNDED The advancement of the Orthodox Jewish religion; education; the relief of poverty.
SAMPLE GRANTS A list of beneficiaries was not included in the annual report and accounts.
FINANCES *Financial year end* 31/12/2021
Income £955,700
Grants to organisations £2,550,000
Assets £3,930,000
TRUSTEES Meir Levine; Chaya Levine; Isaac Katzenberg.
HOW TO APPLY Apply in writing to the correspondent.

Think carefully about every application. Is it justified?

373

CONTACT DETAILS Chaya Levine, Trustee and Secretary, New Burlington House, 1075 Finchley Road, London NW11 0PU *Tel.* 020 8731 0777 *Email* ml@rowdeal.com

■ G. F. Eyre Charitable Trust

CC NO 216040   ESTABLISHED 1960

WHERE FUNDING CAN BE GIVEN UK, with a focus on the South West.

WHO CAN BENEFIT National charities; local charities in the South West.

WHAT IS FUNDED General charitable purposes.

RANGE OF GRANTS Up to £10,000.

SAMPLE GRANTS DEBRA (£9,700); Holditch Village Hall (£5,000); Mercy Ships (£2,000); Axminster Choral Society (£1,000); The Trussell Trust (£500).

FINANCES *Financial year end* 05/04/2022
Income £121,000
Grants to organisations £117,500
Assets £504,500

TRUSTEES Carol Eyre; George Eyre; Rachael Young.

HOW TO APPLY Apply in writing to the correspondent. The trustees meet annually to consider applications. The 2021/22 annual report explains that 'In the interim, payments to good causes are nominated by individual Trustees'.

CONTACT DETAILS Andrew Richards, c/o Francis Clark LLP, Centenary House, Peninsula Park, Rydon Lane, Exeter, Devon EX2 7XE *Tel.* 01392 667000 *Email* andrew.richards@pkf-francisclark.co.uk

■ Esmée Fairbairn Foundation

CC NO 200051   **ESTABLISHED** 1961
WHERE FUNDING CAN BE GIVEN UK.
WHO CAN BENEFIT Charitable organisations.
WHAT IS FUNDED Preservation of species and habitat; fresh water; sustainable and ethical food; injustice and structural inequality; young leaders and artists; community development; local economies; art and culture.
WHAT IS NOT FUNDED Organisations with an annual turnover of less than £100,000 (as reflected in the latest set of accounts); organisations without at least three non-executive trustees or directors; grants of less than £30,000; social investments of less than £100,000 or more than £2 million; work that is not legally charitable; work that does not have a direct benefit in the UK; individuals; capital costs including building work, renovations and equipment (however, social investments can be made for these); academic research, unless it can demonstrate real potential for practical outcomes; health care with a clinical basis, including medical research, hospices, counselling and therapy, arts therapy, education about and treatment for drug and alcohol misuse; work that is primarily the responsibility of statutory authorities; the promotion of religion.
TYPE OF GRANT Core costs; project grants; unrestricted funding. Most grants are awarded for three years or more. Social investment is also available. Through the 'Grants Plus' scheme, recipients of grants and social investment are provided with a range of non-financial additional support.
SAMPLE GRANTS A list of beneficiaries was not included in the annual report and accounts. Previous beneficiaries have included: Soil Association (£675,500); Food Sense Wales (£234,200); Roots of Empathy (£195,000); The British Youth Council (£150,000); Best Beginnings (£60,000); Child Poverty Action Group (£39,900); UK Feminista (£17,500); Aurora Orchestra (£12,500); Friends of the Earth Scotland (£5,000).
FINANCES *Financial year end 31/12/2021*
Income £5,080,000
Grants to organisations £51,600,000
Assets £1,450,000,000
TRUSTEES Tom Chandos; John Fairbairn; Beatrice Hollond; Kate Lampard; Sir Jonathan Phillips; Joe Docherty; Eleanor Updale; Edward Carter; Prof. David Hill; Flora Fairbairn; Prof. Claire Alexander; Dr Wanda Wyporska.
OTHER INFORMATION The foundation has an informative website, where further information, guidelines and examples of giving can be found.
HOW TO APPLY An eligibility quiz is available on the foundation's website. Expressions of interest can be submitted via the website. Applicants should receive a response to their expression of interest within four weeks.
CONTACT DETAILS The Grants Team, Kings Place, 90 York Way, London N1 9AG *Tel.* 020 7812 3700 *Email* info@esmeefairbairn.org.uk *Website* www.esmeefairbairn.org.uk

■ The Fairness Foundation

CC NO 1044174   **ESTABLISHED** 1994
WHERE FUNDING CAN BE GIVEN UK.
WHO CAN BENEFIT Charitable organisations.
WHAT IS FUNDED Animal welfare; bullying; children; citizenship; domestic abuse; a fair society; human rights; LGBTQ+ rights; mental health and medical causes; migrants and refugees; older people; people with disabilities; support for prisoners; the environment; women.
RANGE OF GRANTS Up to £1 million, but most grants are of less than £20,000.
SAMPLE GRANTS Persula Foundation (£284,200); Hope and Homes for Children (£205,000); ASB Help (£80,000); Good Business Foundation (£40,000); Hickman and Rose (£7,500).
FINANCES *Financial year end 30/04/2022*
Income £661,100
Grants to organisations £1,130,000
Assets £34,200
TRUSTEES Julian Richer; Peter Gladwell; Emma Revie; Frances Crook.
OTHER INFORMATION The foundation changed its name from The Persula Foundation to The Fairness Foundation in December 2020. Grants were awarded in the following categories: a fair society (£439,200); children (£246,000); miscellaneous (£62,700); human welfare (£51,000); human rights (£48,000); prisoner support (£30,500); the environment (£30,000); other donations (£27,900); medical causes (£25,000); disability (£16,000); refugees (£9,000); support for women (£2,300); storytelling (£290).
HOW TO APPLY Apply in writing to the correspondent.
CONTACT DETAILS R. Bamforth, Secretary, Gallery Court, Hankey Place, London SE1 4BB *Tel.* 020 7173 4393 *Email* info@persula.org *Website* https://fairnessfoundation.com

■ The Fairstead Trust

CC NO 1096359   **ESTABLISHED** 2003
WHERE FUNDING CAN BE GIVEN UK.
WHO CAN BENEFIT Registered, excepted or exempt charities; hospices; hospitals.
WHAT IS FUNDED General charitable purposes; medical care; social welfare; children and young people; mental health and well-being.
RANGE OF GRANTS Mostly between £2,000 and £20,000.
SAMPLE GRANTS Previous beneficiaries have included: Castlehaven Community Association and React (Rapid Effective Assistance for Children with potentially Terminal illness) (£20,000 each); M and C Foundation (£15,000); Streatham Youth and Community Trust (£10,000); Ollie Foundation and Youth Talk (£5,000 each); Hopefield Animal Sanctuary (£2,000).
FINANCES *Financial year end 05/04/2022*
Income £8,800
Grants to organisations £126,100
TRUSTEES Edward Cox; Lucinda Cox; Wendy Cox.
OTHER INFORMATION The charity's 2021/22 annual report accounts were not available to view on the Charity Commission's website due to its low income. We have therefore estimated the charity's grant total based on its total expenditure.
HOW TO APPLY Apply in writing to the correspondent.
CONTACT DETAILS The Trustees, c/o New Quadrant Partners Ltd, 4th Floor, 5 Chancery Lane, London WC2A 1LG *Tel.* 020 7430 7161 *Email* charities@nqpltd.com

■ Family Philanthropy Ltd

CC NO 1181341
WHERE FUNDING CAN BE GIVEN UK and the USA.
WHO CAN BENEFIT Charitable organisations;
healthcare organisations, including nursing
homes and hospitals; schools; art groups;
museums; individuals.
WHAT IS FUNDED Art and culture; health and welfare;
environmental conservation and sustainability;
education.
SAMPLE GRANTS A list of beneficiaries was not
included in the annual report and accounts.
FINANCES *Financial year end 31/03/2022*
Income £34,500
Grants to organisations £153,800
Assets £576,200
TRUSTEES Richard Hayden; Susan Hayden; Spencer
Hayden; Lindsay Hayden.
OTHER INFORMATION During 2021/22, grants were
distributed as follows: global challenges
(£95,000); arts (£22,800); education
(£20,000); health (£10,000); other (£6,000).
HOW TO APPLY Apply in writing to the correspondent.
CONTACT DETAILS The Trustees, 17 Kensington Park
Gardens, London W11 3HD *Tel.* 020 7570
1460 *Email* info@familyphilanthropy.org.uk

■ Famos Foundation Trust

CC NO 271211   ESTABLISHED 1976
WHERE FUNDING CAN BE GIVEN UK and Israel.
WHO CAN BENEFIT Orthodox Jewish organisations.
WHAT IS FUNDED The promotion of Orthodox
Judaism; health; education; welfare.
SAMPLE GRANTS A list of beneficiaries was not
included in the annual report and accounts.
FINANCES *Financial year end 31/03/2022*
Income £109,200
Grants to organisations £143,200
Assets £1,770,000
TRUSTEES Fay Kupetz; Isaac Kupetz; Joseph Kupetz.
HOW TO APPLY Apply in writing to the correspondent.
CONTACT DETAILS The Trustees, 4 Hanover Gardens,
Salford M7 4FQ *Tel.* 0161 740 5735

■ The Lord Faringdon Charitable Trust

CC NO 1084690   ESTABLISHED 2000
WHERE FUNDING CAN BE GIVEN UK, with a preference
for Oxfordshire.
WHO CAN BENEFIT UK-registered national and local
charities; hospitals.
WHAT IS FUNDED General charitable purposes,
specifically: education; medical treatment; the
purchase of antiques and artistic objects for
museums and collections; older people; the arts
and sciences, physical recreation and drama;
relief of poverty.
WHAT IS NOT FUNDED Individuals.
TYPE OF GRANT Collections and acquisitions; project
costs; scholarships; research funding.
RANGE OF GRANTS From £500 to £10,000.
SAMPLE GRANTS Historic Houses Foundation
(£10,000); Disasters Emergency Committee –
Afghanistan Crisis Appeal (£7,500); FAI UK
Italian Heritage Trust (£5,000); Great Western
Air Ambulance Charity (£2,500); The Migraine
Trust, Prisoners' Advice Service and The
Salvation Army (£1,000 each); The Big Issue
Foundation, National Kidney Federation (£500
each).

FINANCES *Financial year end 05/04/2022*
Income £267,100
Grants to organisations £217,600
Assets £11,320,000
TRUSTEES Bernard Cazenove; The Hon.
J. H. Henderson; Mrs S. J. Robinson; Edward
Cottrell.
OTHER INFORMATION During 2020/21, grants were
given to 122 organisations.
HOW TO APPLY Apply in writing to the correspondent,
detailing information on the specific purpose
and expected beneficiaries of the grant.
CONTACT DETAILS Sharon Lander, Secretary, The
Estate Office, Buscot Park, Faringdon,
Oxfordshire SN7 8BU *Tel.* 01367 240786
Email estbuscot@aol.com

■ Samuel William Farmer Trust

CC NO 258459   ESTABLISHED 1928
WHERE FUNDING CAN BE GIVEN UK, primarily Wiltshire.
WHO CAN BENEFIT Registered charities; schools;
amateur sports clubs; hospital; hospices.
WHAT IS FUNDED Education; health; social welfare.
TYPE OF GRANT Capital costs; seed funding/start-up
funding.
RANGE OF GRANTS Generally between £1,000 and
£5,000.
SAMPLE GRANTS Royal Agricultural Benevolent
Institution (£10,000); Enford Parish Council and
Pennyhooks Farm Trust (£3,000 each); Evie's
Gift (£2,500) All Cannings Community Shop and
Wiltshire Museum (£2,000 each); Tall Ships
Youth Trust (£1,500); Wiltshire Bobby Van Trust
(£1,000).
FINANCES *Financial year end 31/12/2021*
Income £68,600
Grants to organisations £71,500
Grants to individuals £1,200
Assets £3,210,000
TRUSTEES Charles Brockis; Peter Fox-Andrews;
Jennifer Liddiard; Bruce Waight; Elaine Dewey.
HOW TO APPLY Contact the correspondent for
information regarding the application process.
The trustees normally meet half-yearly to
consider applications.
CONTACT DETAILS Melanie Linden-Fermor, Secretary,
71 High Street, Market Lavington, Devizes,
Wiltshire SN10 4AG *Tel.* 01380 813299

■ The Thomas Farr Charity

CC NO 328394   ESTABLISHED 1989
WHERE FUNDING CAN BE GIVEN Nottinghamshire.
WHO CAN BENEFIT Charitable organisations.
WHAT IS FUNDED Education; young people; health;
older people; community development; social
welfare; disability; homelessness.
WHAT IS NOT FUNDED Individuals; large national
charities with a large income; loans or business
finance; campaigning work and projects that are
primarily political; activities that have already
taken place; general or mailshot appeals;
activities that are the responsibility of local
health or education authorities.
TYPE OF GRANT Project funding.
RANGE OF GRANTS Mostly £1,000 to £5,000.
SAMPLE GRANTS Portland College (£25,000);
Mending Injured Minds (£6,000); Refugee Roots
(£5,000); The Wolfpack Project (£4,800); The
Phoenix Farm Open Door Project – The Ark
(£3,000); Arnold Swimming Club (£2,000); Read
for Good (£1,500); Mansfield District Corps of
Drums (£500).

FINANCES *Financial year end* 05/04/2022
Income £275,700
Grants to organisations £276,500
Assets £9,580,000

TRUSTEES Amanda Farr; Henry Farr; Philip Pruden; Rathbone Trust Company Ltd.

OTHER INFORMATION The charity awarded 84 grants during 2021/22. Grants were distributed as follows: community projects (£89,500); disability (£40,000); children (£36,900); youth organisations (£33,700); hospitals/health (£25,400); homelessness (£18,700); older people (£12,400); education (£11,500); sport (£5,300); museums/theatre (£3,000).

HOW TO APPLY Applications can be made via Nottinghamshire Community Foundation's website, a link to which can be found on the charity's website. The trustees meet three times a year to review applications, usually in March, July and November. For consideration in these meetings, applications must be received by 20 January, 20 May and 20 September, respectively.

CONTACT DETAILS The Trustees, c/o Nottinghamshire Community Foundation, Pine House B, Ransom Wood Business Park, Southwell Road West, Mansfield, Nottinghamshire NG21 0HJ *Tel.* 01623 620202 *Email* enquiries@nottscf.org.uk *Website* https://thomasfarrcharity.com

■ The Farthing Trust

CC NO 268066   **ESTABLISHED** 1974
WHERE FUNDING CAN BE GIVEN UK and overseas.
WHO CAN BENEFIT Charitable organisations; individuals.
WHAT IS FUNDED General charitable purposes, with a focus on the following: education; health; human rights; the reconciliation and promotion of religious and racial harmony, equality and diversity; relief of people in need.
RANGE OF GRANTS Priority is given to seedcorn funding for small projects.
SAMPLE GRANTS A list of beneficiaries was not included in the annual report and accounts.
FINANCES *Financial year end* 05/04/2022
Income £56,100
Grants to organisations £288,500
Grants to individuals £53,900
Assets £5,290,000
TRUSTEES J. Martin; A. White; Mr J. Martin; Ms E. Bell.
HOW TO APPLY Apply in writing to the correspondent. There are no financial or geographical restrictions placed on grant applicants.
CONTACT DETAILS The Trustees, PO Box 276, Newmarket CB8 1GW *Tel.* 07598 565623 *Email* thefarthingtrust@gmail.com

■ Fat Face Foundation

CC NO 1129392   **ESTABLISHED** 2009
WHERE FUNDING CAN BE GIVEN UK.
WHO CAN BENEFIT Registered charities.
WHAT IS FUNDED Social welfare; community development; the environment. Grants are made under the foundation's three pillars of: Life in the community; Life on land; Life underwater.
SAMPLE GRANTS A list of beneficiaries was not included in the annual report and accounts.
FINANCES *Financial year end* 31/05/2022
Income £649,900
Grants to organisations £230,200
Assets £343,200

TRUSTEES Nicola Amos; Matthew Prosser; Jodie Higgins; Robert Blackwood; Laura Praeger; William Crumbie; Ian Williams.
OTHER INFORMATION The foundation was established by the clothing retailer Fat Face Ltd.
HOW TO APPLY Only charities and projects brought forward by the trustees will normally be considered for funding. However, there are occasions on which the trustees will consider granting donations to new partners during a specifically appointed time period. Projects should have a link to FatFace or be close to where FatFace sources, manufactures, sells or distributes its products. See the foundation's website for further information.
CONTACT DETAILS The Trustees, 11–13 Meridian Shopping Centre, Havant PO9 1UN *Email* fatfacefoundation@fatface.com *Website* https://fatfacefoundation.org.uk

■ The February Foundation

CC NO 1113064   **ESTABLISHED** 2006
WHERE FUNDING CAN BE GIVEN UK.
WHO CAN BENEFIT Registered charities.
WHAT IS FUNDED General charitable purposes; health; end-of-life care; the environment; heritage.
WHAT IS NOT FUNDED Child care; Citizens Advice branches; community centres; higher education; housing associations; individuals; medical research; minibuses; NHS trusts; non-departmental government bodies; overseas projects; primary or secondary education; uniformed groups; single-faith organisations; special educational needs schools; amateur sports clubs, unless for people who have mental or physical disabilities; village halls; youth clubs and centres; charities which are party-politically driven or have a commercial bias for a particular product or company.
TYPE OF GRANT Capital costs; core costs; project costs.
RANGE OF GRANTS The average grant is usually £5,000 per award.
SAMPLE GRANTS A list of beneficiaries was not included in the annual report and accounts.
FINANCES *Financial year end* 28/02/2022
Income £12,760,000
Grants to organisations £27,120,000
Assets £70,850,000
TRUSTEES James Carleton; Mark Clarke; Michael Moody.
OTHER INFORMATION In 2021/22, grants were awarded to 207 organisations. Grants were broken down as follows: education (£25.58 million); health care and patient support (£916,600); end-of-life care (£490,200); other (£134,600).
HOW TO APPLY Apply in writing to the correspondent. Guidance notes on what to include in your application can be found on the foundation's website (note: for hospice applications, additional required information is listed). Applications should be submitted by email. There are no application deadlines and applicants are normally informed of the trustees' decision within 12 weeks of submission.
CONTACT DETAILS Richard Pierce-Saunderson, Chief Executive, 79 Cromwell Road, Norwich NR7 8XJ *Tel.* 01379 388200 *Email* rps@thefebruaryfoundation.org *Website* www.thefebruaryfoundation.org

■ George Fentham Birmingham Charity

CC NO 214487   **ESTABLISHED** 1906

WHERE FUNDING CAN BE GIVEN Birmingham.

WHO CAN BENEFIT Organisations providing services or facilities for people who are in need, hardship or distress; individuals who are long-term residents of Birmingham studying at a college or university.

WHAT IS FUNDED Organisational grants are given mainly in the following categories: children who are sick or who have disabilities; children's holidays and play schemes; young people's clubs and associations; adults who are sick or who have disabilities; social problems; community centres/neighbourhood groups; hospital charities; care for older people. Grants are given to individuals for educational purposes.

WHAT IS NOT FUNDED Salary costs; direct hardship grants to individuals.

TYPE OF GRANT Project funding.

RANGE OF GRANTS Mostly between £1,000 and £5,000.

SAMPLE GRANTS Birmingham Settlement (£17,000); St Basil's (£10,000); The Hospice Charity Partnership (£4,000); St Anne's Hostel (£3,200); Acorns Children's Hospice (£3,000); City of Birmingham Symphony Orchestra (£2,500); Whizz-Kidz (£2,000); Acacia Family Support (£1,000).

FINANCES *Financial year end 31/12/2021*
Income £187,500
Grants to organisations £89,700
Grants to individuals £19,900
Assets £8,360,000

TRUSTEES Martin Holcombe; Julie Scarratt; Paul Tunnadine; Suman Watts; Jelena Dukic; The Hon. Dr Cheuk Li.

HOW TO APPLY Application forms are available to download from the charity's website, where criteria and guidelines are also posted. These should be returned to the secretary by email or post. The meeting dates for general grants vary each year and applications are normally accepted up to one week prior to any scheduled meeting. Meetings are usually held three times a year.

CONTACT DETAILS J. Hobday, Secretary, Veale Wasbrough Vizards LLP, PO Box 3501, Bristol BS2 2FL *Tel.* 0121 227 3720 *Email* GeorgeFentham@vwv.co.uk *Website* www.georgefenthamcharity.org.uk

■ The A. M. Fenton Trust

CC NO 270353   **ESTABLISHED** 1975

WHERE FUNDING CAN BE GIVEN UK, with a preference for North Yorkshire.

WHO CAN BENEFIT Registered charities; places of worship; hospices.

WHAT IS FUNDED Health; people with disabilities; the environment, conservation and heritage.

WHAT IS NOT FUNDED Individuals.

RANGE OF GRANTS Mainly up to £10,000.

SAMPLE GRANTS Harrogate Homeless Project (£25,000); The Tweed Foundation (£8,000); St Peter's Church (£7,500); Yorkshire Cancer Research (£6,000); Wetherby in Support of the Elderly (£4,000); Yorkshire Children's Trust (£3,000); Harrogate and Knaresborough Toy Library (£2,000); War Memorials Trust (£1,000).

FINANCES *Financial year end 31/12/2021*
Income £198,500
Grants to organisations £180,500
Assets £7,740,000

TRUSTEES C. J. Fenton; Annalisa Fenton.

HOW TO APPLY Apply in writing to the correspondent.

CONTACT DETAILS The Trustees, The A. M. Fenton Trust, PO Box 788, Harrogate HG1 9RX *Tel.* 01423 564446

■ The Feoffees of St Michael's Spurriergate York

CC NO 1159025   **ESTABLISHED** 1599

WHERE FUNDING CAN BE GIVEN York.

WHO CAN BENEFIT Churches and charitable organisations.

WHAT IS FUNDED Church of England churches; general charitable purposes.

WHAT IS NOT FUNDED Individuals; causes or organisations outside the City of York.

TYPE OF GRANT Capital costs; project costs; core/revenue costs.

RANGE OF GRANTS Typically under £15,000.

SAMPLE GRANTS The Gateway Centre and St Luke the Evangelist (£15,000 each); St Edward the Confessor Church, St George's Roman Catholic Primary School and United Response (£10,000 each); The Hut and The Wilberforce Trust (£5,000 each); Age UK York (£2,700); Holy Trinity – Heworth (£2,500); York Oral History Society (£400).

FINANCES *Financial year end 31/12/2021*
Income £78,300
Grants to organisations £75,600
Assets £3,500,000

TRUSTEES Hannah Phillip; Laura Habgood-Joya; Stephen Hallett; Dr Robert Richards.

OTHER INFORMATION A map of the historic boundaries of York can be found on the charity's website.

HOW TO APPLY Apply in writing or by email to the correspondent. The feoffees (trustees) meet four times a year. Full details outlining what is required in an application are listed on the charity's helpful website.

CONTACT DETAILS Lyn Rickatson, Clerk, c/o Grays Solicitors, Duncombe Place, York, North Yorkshire YO1 7DY *Tel.* 01904 634771 *Email* LynRickatson@grayssolicitors.co.uk *Website* www.feoffeesofstmichaelsspurriergate.org.uk

■ Allan and Nesta Ferguson Charitable Settlement

CC NO 275487   **ESTABLISHED** 1977

WHERE FUNDING CAN BE GIVEN UK and overseas.

WHO CAN BENEFIT UK-registered charities; universities and individuals.

WHAT IS FUNDED Education; international friendship and understanding; world peace and development. Gap year students can also be supported.

WHAT IS NOT FUNDED Retrospective expenditure.

TYPE OF GRANT Project funding.

SAMPLE GRANTS Manchester University (£200,000); Loughborough University (£150,000); Amnesty International (£17,000); Hello World (£20,000); Pratham UK (£15,000).

FINANCES *Financial year end 31/12/2021*
Income £371,100
Grants to organisations £2,190,000
Grants to individuals £160,000
Assets £29,320,000

TRUSTEES Elizabeth Banister; Prof. David Banister; Letitia Glaister; Eleanor Banister; Edmund Cairns.

OTHER INFORMATION The charity's website explains that grants to organisations are given on a matched funding basis 'so that if the applicant has raised 50% of their budget the Trustees will consider awarding matching funding up to a maximum of 50%. If the applicant has raised less than 50% of their budget the Trustees will only consider awarding a maximum of 30% funding.' The website further explains, 'evidence of actively seeking funds from other sources is seen by the Trustees as being a beneficial addition to any application.'

HOW TO APPLY Apply online via the trust's website.

CONTACT DETAILS Letitia Glaister, Trustee, c/o Tees Law, John Street, Royston, Hertfordshire SG8 9BG *Tel.* 01763 295850 *Email* letitia. glaister@teeslaw.com *Website* www. fergusontrust.co.uk

■ The Fermanagh Trust

CC NO 102726   **ESTABLISHED** 1995
WHERE FUNDING CAN BE GIVEN County Fermanagh.
WHO CAN BENEFIT Voluntary organisations.
WHAT IS FUNDED General charitable purposes; community development.
WHAT IS NOT FUNDED See the grant-maker's website for a full list of exclusions.
TYPE OF GRANT Dependent upon funding stream.
RANGE OF GRANTS Up to £3,000.
SAMPLE GRANTS A list of beneficiaries was not included in the annual report and accounts.
FINANCES *Financial year end* 05/04/2022
Income £794,700
Grants to organisations £235,600
Assets £4,040,000
TRUSTEES Joanna McVey; Jim Ledwith; Aideen McGinley; Kevin Lunney; Ernie Fisher; Sue Bryson; Frank McManus; Anna Devlin; Robert Gibson.
OTHER INFORMATION The trust has number of funds which support a range of community and voluntary initiatives primarily in County Fermanagh. Although not an official UK community foundation, the trust operates in a very similar way, distributing funding for a wide range of purposes.
HOW TO APPLY Each fund has its own application procedure and guidelines. Check the trust's website for details.
CONTACT DETAILS The Trustees, Fermanagh House, Broadmeadow Place, Enniskillen, County Fermanagh BT74 7HR *Tel.* 028 6632 0210 *Email* info@fermanaghtrust.org *Website* www. fermanaghtrust.org

■ The Fidelio Charitable Trust

CC NO 1112508   **ESTABLISHED** 2005
WHERE FUNDING CAN BE GIVEN UK.
WHO CAN BENEFIT Registered charities; arts organisations; individuals.
WHAT IS FUNDED The arts, particularly music, including opera, lieder, composition and dance. Grants are made to enable beneficiaries to, for example: receive special tuition or coaching; participate in external competitions; be supported for a specially arranged performance; receive support for a special publication, musical composition or work of art.
WHAT IS NOT FUNDED Applications from individuals or groups seeking support for themselves or their children will not be considered. Applications are not generally considered for activities for people under the age of 21, or for course fees, capital items or retrospective expenditure.

TYPE OF GRANT Project funding.
RANGE OF GRANTS From £500 to £5,000.
SAMPLE GRANTS A list of beneficiaries was not available.
FINANCES *Financial year end* 31/03/2022
Income £9,200
Grants to organisations £77,700
TRUSTEES Robert Boas; Jennifer Wingate; Elizabeth Rantzen; Barbara Arnold; Dr Patricia Morison.
OTHER INFORMATION The trust's accounts were not available to view on the Charity Commission's website due to its low income. We have therefore estimated its grant total based on total expenditure.
HOW TO APPLY Application forms are available to download from the website, where guidelines can also be found. These should be completed and returned to the correspondent by email. Individuals and groups must be recommended by an appropriate organisation, college, arts festival or similar organisation. The trustees usually meet three times a year and provisional closing dates for applications are detailed on the website. The trustees aim to inform successful applicants within one month of the relevant closing date.
CONTACT DETAILS The Trustees, c/o Brian Cook Associates, Marine House, 151 Western Road, Haywards Heath, West Sussex RH16 3LH *Tel.* 020 8292 9975 *Email* admin@ fideliocharitabletrust.org.uk *Website* www. fideliocharitabletrust.org.uk

■ The Fidelis Foundation

CC NO 1192699   **ESTABLISHED** 2020
WHERE FUNDING CAN BE GIVEN England; Bermuda; Republic of Ireland.
WHO CAN BENEFIT Registered charities.
WHAT IS FUNDED General charitable purposes.
TYPE OF GRANT Unrestricted funding; one-off.
RANGE OF GRANTS Up to £100,000.
SAMPLE GRANTS International Care Ministries (£80,700); Big Brothers Big Sisters (£60,500); National Museum of Bermuda (£40,400); Irish Children's Rights Alliance (£37,700); Kalayaan (£28,200).
FINANCES *Financial year end* 31/12/2021
Income £1,470,000
Grants to organisations £796,300
Assets £660,000
TRUSTEES Richard Brindle; Alan Bossin; Charles Mathias; Belinda Tribley.
OTHER INFORMATION The foundation makes grants to organisations whose work reflects and is aligned to the values and interests of the people and businesses within the Fidelis Insurance Group. All financial information has been converted from USD using the exchange rate at the time of writing (January 2023).
HOW TO APPLY Apply in writing to the correspondent. The foundation's 2021 annual report and accounts state: 'The Foundation encourages members of staff of the Fidelis Insurance group to champion applications for grants from charities in which they have an interest or involvement.'
CONTACT DETAILS The Trustees, 42nd Floor, The Leadenhall Building, 122 Leadenhall Street, London EC3V 4AB *Email* foundation@ fidelisinsurance.com

■ The Fidelity UK Foundation

cc no 327899 ESTABLISHED 1988

WHERE FUNDING CAN BE GIVEN UK.

WHO CAN BENEFIT Registered charities. The foundation's website states that it 'focuses on supporting organisations that have annual budgets of over £1 million'.

WHAT IS FUNDED Disadvantaged children and young people; health and well-being; arts, culture and heritage.

TYPE OF GRANT Organisational development; IT projects; capital costs; core costs.

RANGE OF GRANTS Between £10,000 and £500,000.

SAMPLE GRANTS The Prince's Trust (£500,000); Asthma UK and British Lung Foundation Partnership (£450,000); Midlands Arts Centre (£332,300); MyBNK (£255,000); The Nelson Trust (£161,000); FARE – Scotland (£87,700); City Year UK (£52,000); Breaking Barriers (£10,000).

FINANCES *Financial year end* 31/12/2021
Income £4,340,000
Grants to organisations £9,510,000
Assets £338,800,000

TRUSTEES Anthony Bolton; John Owen; Sally Walden; Abigail Johnson; Elizabeth Johnson; Dr Malcolm Rogers; Sanjeev Gandhi; Peter Goldsbrough; Edward Johnson.

OTHER INFORMATION During the year, the foundation awarded 71 grants totalling £12.22 million, distributed as follows: disadvantaged children and young people (£6.37 million in 41 grants); health and well-being (£3.38 million in 14 grants); arts, culture and heritage (£1.81 million in 14 grants); cross-sector (£240,000 in 1 grant); the W. L. "Bill" Byrnes Global Scholarship (£129,100 in 1 grant).

HOW TO APPLY Unsolicited applications are not accepted. The foundation has an invitation-only application process.

CONTACT DETAILS The Trustees, Beech Gate, Millfield Lane, Lower Kingswood, Tadworth, Surrey KT20 6RP *Tel.* 01732 777364 *Email* foundation@fil.com *Website* https://filfoundations.fidelityinternational.com

■ Doris Field Charitable Trust

cc no 328687 ESTABLISHED 1990

WHERE FUNDING CAN BE GIVEN UK, with a particular interest in Oxfordshire.

WHO CAN BENEFIT Charitable organisations.

WHAT IS FUNDED General charitable purposes.

RANGE OF GRANTS Mostly from £500 to £1,000.

SAMPLE GRANTS Cancer Research UK (£5,000); University of Oxford – Motor Neuron Disease Research Group (£3,257); Laurence Home Nursing Team (£2,000); Asthma UK and The Sports Aid Trust (£1,000 each); Wantage Choral Society (£350).

FINANCES *Financial year end* 15/08/2022
Income £465,000
Grants to organisations £264,100
Assets £12,110,000

TRUSTEES John Cole; Mr N. Harper; Wilhelmina Church; Helen Fanyinka.

OTHER INFORMATION A total of 272 grants were made to organisations.

HOW TO APPLY Potential applicants can obtain an application form from the correspondent and submit it with the required information. The trustees meet three times a year to consider applications but can respond to urgent appeals if necessary.

CONTACT DETAILS Emily Greig, Correspondent, c/o Blake Morgan LLP, Seacourt Tower, West Way, Oxford, Oxfordshire OX2 0FB *Tel.* 01865 254286 *Email* emily.greig@blakemorgan.co.uk

■ Field Family Charitable Trust

cc no 259569 ESTABLISHED 1969

WHERE FUNDING CAN BE GIVEN The West Midlands and London (within the boundaries of the M25).

WHO CAN BENEFIT UK-registered charities.

WHAT IS FUNDED Disadvantaged children and young people (16 to 25 years old); older people.

WHAT IS NOT FUNDED The trustees do not consider applications from charities with an income of over £1 million and/or free unrestricted reserves to the value of more than one year of the applicant organisation's annual expenditure. Local charities are favoured over national ones.

TYPE OF GRANT Capital costs; core costs; project funding.

RANGE OF GRANTS £1,000 to £10,000.

SAMPLE GRANTS A list of beneficiaries was not included in the annual report and accounts.

FINANCES *Financial year end* 05/04/2022
Income £65,600
Grants to organisations £50,000
Assets £2,630,000

TRUSTEES John England; Paul England; Andrew Bidnell; Ruth Gibbins; Rachel Beatton.

HOW TO APPLY Applications should be made on an online form, which is available, together with criteria and guidelines, from the website. The trustees meet twice a year to consider applications for funding, in April and October. Application forms and supporting documentation must be submitted at least six weeks before the date of the next meeting.

CONTACT DETAILS Jayne Day, Administrator, c/o PWW Solicitors, The Office Group, Thomas House, 84 Eccleston Square, London SW1V 1PX *Email* use the contact form on the website *Website* https://pwwsolicitors.co.uk/charity-grants/field-family-charitable-trust

■ The Fieldrose Charitable Trust

cc no 1156644 ESTABLISHED 2014

WHERE FUNDING CAN BE GIVEN England and Wales.

WHO CAN BENEFIT Charitable organisations.

WHAT IS FUNDED General charitable purposes; health and medical research; humanitarian aid; the environment.

RANGE OF GRANTS Mostly between £1,000 and £5,000, with the occasional larger grant.

SAMPLE GRANTS The Duke of Edinburgh's International Awards Foundation (£42,000); Alzheimer's Research UK and International Spinal Research Trust (£20,000 each); Population Matters and Tibet Relief Fund (£10,000 each); Food for the Brain Foundation and National Star Foundation (£5,000 each); Down Ampney PCC (£1,000).

FINANCES *Financial year end* 05/04/2022
Income £308,200
Grants to organisations £236,000
Assets £8,160,000

TRUSTEES Angela Scott; Genevieve Kershaw; Louise Stoten; Paul Stibbard.

OTHER INFORMATION This trust normally awards grants to charities focusing on medical care and medical research but does offer grants towards other focus areas.

HOW TO APPLY Apply in writing to the correspondent.

CONTACT DETAILS The Trustees, c/o New Quadrant Partners Ltd, 4th Floor, 5 Chancery Lane, London WC2A 1LS *Tel.* 020 7430 7150 *Email* charities@nqpltd.com

■ The Fifty Fund

CC NO 214422 **ESTABLISHED** 1939
WHERE FUNDING CAN BE GIVEN Nottinghamshire.
WHO CAN BENEFIT Registered charities; individuals.
WHAT IS FUNDED Social welfare.
RANGE OF GRANTS From £500 to £23,000.
SAMPLE GRANTS Nottinghamshire Hospice
(£23,000); The Salvation Army (£7,300);
Radford Care Group (£5,300); React (Rapid
Effective Assistance for Children with potentially
Terminal illness) (£3,300); Portland College
(£2,200); Sense (£2,000); Open Minds
(£1,100); St Margaret's Church (£1,000); Rainy
Day Trust (£500).
FINANCES *Financial year end* 31/12/2021
Income £262,200
Grants to organisations £191,300
Grants to individuals £12,800
Assets £9,370,000
TRUSTEES The Revd Amanda Cartwright; Mark
Jenkinson; Dr David Hannah; Nigel Tamplin;
Jane Imrie.
OTHER INFORMATION Grants were made to 21
individuals and 87 charities during the year.
Forty-one applications from individuals and
charities were declined.
HOW TO APPLY Apply in writing to the correspondent.
The trustees meet quarterly to consider grant
applications.
CONTACT DETAILS Craig Staten-Spencer,
Correspondent, c/o Nelsons Solicitors, Pennine
House, 8 Stanford Street, Nottingham,
Nottinghamshire NG1 7BQ *Tel.* 0115 989 5251
Email craig.staten-spencer@nelsonslaw.co.uk

■ The Finborough Foundation

CC NO 1125130 **ESTABLISHED** 2007
WHERE FUNDING CAN BE GIVEN UK.
WHO CAN BENEFIT Registered charities.
WHAT IS FUNDED Education and training in the arts,
science and medicine; the environment;
homelessness.
RANGE OF GRANTS Up to £50,000.
SAMPLE GRANTS A list of beneficiaries was not
included in the annual report and accounts.
FINANCES *Financial year end* 31/12/2021
Income £240,500
Grants to organisations £136,000
Assets £8,220,000
TRUSTEES Charles Pettiward; Josephine Pettiward;
James Pettiward.
OTHER INFORMATION Grants were awarded to 18
registered charities during the year and included
a major grant to Treloar Trust, which receives
annual funding.
HOW TO APPLY Apply in writing to the correspondent.
CONTACT DETAILS Philip Hamilton, Trustee, 34 Ely
Place, London EC1N 6TD *Tel.* 07787 554962
Email nick@ruskinhouse.co.uk

■ Dixie Rose Findlay Charitable Trust

CC NO 251661 **ESTABLISHED** 1967
WHERE FUNDING CAN BE GIVEN UK.
WHO CAN BENEFIT Charitable organisations;
hospices.
WHAT IS FUNDED People with disabilities, especially
children and young people; health and medical
causes; sports and recreation for people with
disabilities; emergency response; social welfare
for disadvantaged people.
RANGE OF GRANTS £1,500 to £5,000.

SAMPLE GRANTS The Laura Centre (£5,000);
Infrosound and St Helena Hospice (£3,000
each); Challenging Mind, Maggs Day Centre and
Whoopsadaisy (£2,000 each); Beams, The
Listening Place and Shooting Stars (£1,500
each).
FINANCES *Financial year end* 05/04/2022
Income £5,040,000
Grants to organisations £57,700
Assets £5,710,000
TRUSTEE HSBC Trust Company (UK) Ltd.
HOW TO APPLY Apply in writing to the correspondent.
CONTACT DETAILS S. Hill, Trust Manager, c/o HSBC
Trust Company UK Ltd, 2nd Floor, 1 The Forum,
Parkway, Whiteley, Fareham, Hampshire
PO15 7PA *Tel.* 023 8072 2525

■ Fine & Country Foundation

CC NO 1160989 **ESTABLISHED** 2014
WHERE FUNDING CAN BE GIVEN UK and overseas.
WHO CAN BENEFIT Homelessness charities; poverty
prevention schemes; housing associations.
WHAT IS FUNDED Prevention of homelessness; care
of people experiencing homelessness; long-term
housing projects.
TYPE OF GRANT Project funding; core costs; capital
costs.
RANGE OF GRANTS Up to £3,000.
SAMPLE GRANTS A list of beneficiaries was not
included in the annual report and accounts.
FINANCES *Financial year end* 31/12/2021
Income £126,800
Grants to organisations £108,400
Assets £61,800
TRUSTEES Sean Newman; Emilie Despois; Jonathan
Cooke; Graham Wilson.
OTHER INFORMATION The foundation is more likely to
make grants to organisations that have a Fine
and Country office in their region.
HOW TO APPLY Potential applicants should first
request a nomination from their nearest Fine
& Country office and then complete an
application form, available on the website.
Applications are accepted in March and October
each year.
CONTACT DETAILS The Trustees, 121 Park Lane,
Mayfair, London W1K 7AG *Tel.* 020 7079 1415
Email grants@fineandcountry.com *Website* www.
fineandcountryfoundation.com

■ The Finnis Scott Foundation

CC NO 1121475 **ESTABLISHED** 2008
WHERE FUNDING CAN BE GIVEN UK and Ireland.
WHO CAN BENEFIT Registered charities; CICs; PTAs;
gardens; hospices. Preference is given to
smaller charities. Grants are made to individuals
by means of bursaries, traineeships or
apprenticeships but only through a sponsoring
educational establishment or registered charity.
WHAT IS FUNDED Horticulture; fine art; art history;
scientific plant projects; training of gardeners;
restoration of gardens; permanent art projects,
including the development of galleries, the
conservation and framing of pictures, the
purchase of works and the production of
exhibition catalogues.
WHAT IS NOT FUNDED Retrospective costs; newly
established organisations which do not yet have
a track record or accounts; individual salaries;
site-specific art installations; conceptual or
performance art; art created after 2000.
TYPE OF GRANT Capital and revenue costs.

RANGE OF GRANTS Typically £500 to £10,000, but larger grants may be made in exceptional circumstances.

SAMPLE GRANTS MK Gallery (£20,000); Professional Gardeners' Trust (£15,000); Fortescue Gardens (£10,000); Hartlebury Castle Preservation Trust (£4,200); Friends of Tower Hamlets Cemetery Park (£3,900); Ysgol Maes y Coed (£3,000); Lower Bush Farm CIC and Normandy Community Therapy Garden (£2,000 each); The Good Soil Trust and Suffolk Mind (£1,000 each); St George's Primary School (£500).

FINANCES *Financial year end 31/12/2021*
Income £345,400
Grants to organisations £226,200
Assets £12,030,000

TRUSTEES Ian Barnett; Dr William Elliott; David Laing; Lady Kathryn Robinson; The Hon. Ursula Wide; James Miller; Dr Patricia Morison; Lord Charles Scott.

OTHER INFORMATION Grants were awarded to 69 organisations during the year out of 106 applications considered. The foundation also runs The Botanical Art Prize – a £10,000 award awarded biennially to British and Irish botanical art groups and organisations in recognition of previous achievements and for the promotion of innovative ideas and projects.

HOW TO APPLY Applicants can download an application form from the foundation's helpful website and this should be sent to the grant administrator (by email or post) with accompanying documents. The trustees meet quarterly to discuss grant applications. Applications need to reach the grant administrator four weeks before a meeting. Further information on applications and deadlines is available on the website. Applicants for the Botanical Art Prize are asked to contact the administrator at botanicalartaward@finnis-scott-foundation.org.uk before making an application.

CONTACT DETAILS Angela Moon, Grant Administrator, c/o Hewitsons, Elgin House, Billing Road, Northampton, Northamptonshire NN1 5AU *Tel.* 01604 233233 *Email* angelamoon@hewitsons.com *Website* www.finnis-scott-foundation.org.uk

---

■ Sir John Fisher Foundation

CC NO 277844   **ESTABLISHED** 1979

WHERE FUNDING CAN BE GIVEN UK, with a strong preference for charities in the Furness peninsula and Cumbria.

WHO CAN BENEFIT Registered charities; CICs; community groups; museums; hospices; uniformed groups.

WHAT IS FUNDED General charitable purposes, with a preference for maritime causes, medicine, people with disabilities, education, music, the arts and community projects. The foundation gives priority to projects and causes in Barrow-in-Furness and the Furness peninsula.

WHAT IS NOT FUNDED Individuals; sponsorship; expeditions; the promotion of religion; places of worship; animal welfare; retrospective expenditure; pressure groups; community projects outside Barrow-in-Furness and surrounding area (except occasional projects in Cumbria or north Lancashire or if they fall within one of the other categories supported by the foundation).

TYPE OF GRANT Capital costs; revenue funding; occasionally, research grants.

RANGE OF GRANTS Mostly under £20,000.

SAMPLE GRANTS A list of beneficiaries was not included in the annual report and accounts. Previous beneficiaries have included: The Lady Maria Fisher Foundation (£1.2 million); University of Cumbria (£240,600); The Neurological Research Trust (£110,000); Cumbria Community Foundation (£50,000); Hospice of St Mary of Furness (£40,000); The Birchall Trust (£20,000); Word Market (£300).

FINANCES *Financial year end 31/03/2022*
Income £30,300
Grants to organisations £1,060,000
Assets £41,370,000

TRUSTEES Daniel Tindall; Michael Shields; Thomas Meacock; Christopher Batten; Chris Tomlinson; Dr David Jackson; Julie Barton.

OTHER INFORMATION Grants were broken down as follows: community (£398,600); education (£151,600); medical research (£151,100); music (£148,500); the arts (£100,500); medical causes (£90,400); maritime causes (£23,000).

HOW TO APPLY Application forms are available from the correspondent or to download from the website, where guidelines can also be found. Applications should be made by submitting a completed application form, together with all relevant information (set out on the application form) to the secretary by email or post. The trustees meet at the beginning of May and the beginning of November each year. The closing dates for applications are posted on the foundation's website.

CONTACT DETAILS David Dawson, Executive Officer, c/o Hart Jackson and Sons, 8–10 New Market Street, Ulverston, Cumbria LA12 7LW *Tel.* 07464 504756 *Email* eo@sirjohnfisherfoundation.org.uk *Website* www.sirjohnfisherfoundation.org.uk

---

■ Fishmongers' Company's Charitable Trust

CC NO 263690   **ESTABLISHED** 1972

WHERE FUNDING CAN BE GIVEN The City of London and the London boroughs of Camden, Hackney, Islington, Lambeth, Newham, Southwark, Tower Hamlets and Westminster.

WHO CAN BENEFIT Registered charities; social enterprises; CICs.

WHAT IS FUNDED Education in prisons; mental health; food and nutrition.

WHAT IS NOT FUNDED Individuals; charities with political purposes.

TYPE OF GRANT There is a preference for project funding.

RANGE OF GRANTS Between £15,000 and £30,000 a year, for up to three years.

SAMPLE GRANTS The Fishmongers' Company's Fisheries Charitable Trust (£806,000); The Gresham's Foundation (£134,000); The Listening Place (£47,000); No Going Back Pan-Livery Project (£30,000); Islington Mind (£15,000); Royal Academy of Music (£11,000); Game and Wildlife Conservation Trust (£3,000); Sheriffs' and Recorder's Fund (£1,000).

FINANCES *Financial year end 31/12/2021*
Income £1,340,000
Grants to organisations £1,790,000
Grants to individuals £48,000
Assets £40,560,000

TRUSTEES Michael Nicholson; The Fishmongers' Company.

OTHER INFORMATION During 2021, grants to organisations were broken down as follows: fisheries (£809,000); education (£559,000);

382

Does the funder you have chosen match your needs? Haphazard applications waste postage and time

health and well-being (£241,000); hardship (£136,000): civic grants (£45,000). Only organisations that received grants of over £1,000 were listed as beneficiaries in the trust's accounts.

HOW TO APPLY Visit the trust's website for information on open grant rounds and how to apply.

CONTACT DETAILS Philanthropy and Grants Team, The Fishmongers' Company, Fishmongers' Hall, London Bridge, London EC4R 9EL *Tel.* 020 7626 3531 *Email* charity@fishmongers.org.uk *Website* https://fishmongers.org.uk/grants

■ Marc Fitch Fund

CC NO 313303   **ESTABLISHED** 1956
WHERE FUNDING CAN BE GIVEN UK and Ireland.
WHO CAN BENEFIT Organisations and individuals.
WHAT IS FUNDED The publication of academic work on British and Irish history across several disciplines – see the website for more details.
WHAT IS NOT FUNDED Works principally concerned with the recent past (post-1979); new or revised editions of work already published; scientific or technical research; fieldwork; the costs of getting to the UK/Ireland from overseas; foreign travel or research outside the UK/Ireland (apart from in very exceptional circumstances); applications associated with vocational or educational courses (including postgraduate or doctoral research); building works, mounting or attending conferences; mounting exhibitions; general appeals.
TYPE OF GRANT Mainly publication costs and incidental research expenses. Also, special project grants and support for journal digitisation.
SAMPLE GRANTS Anglo-Saxon Charters of Worcester Cathedral (£27,500); Book Owners Online (£24,800); The Buildings of England: Staffordshire (£7,000); Coventry Historical Map (£2,600); Hadrian's Wall Cultural Resource Management 2022 (£1,200); Fragments of Bronze (£750); Frisians of the Early Middle Ages and The Guild Book of the Barbers and Surgeons of York (£500 each).
FINANCES *Financial year end* 05/04/2022
Income £244,200
Grants to organisations £80,900
Grants to individuals £30,100
Assets £8,850,000
TRUSTEES Lindsay Allason-Jones; Dr John Blair; Dr Helen Forde; Michael Hall; Andrew Murison; David White; Bernard Nurse; David Palliser; Christiana Payne; Roey Sweet.
OTHER INFORMATION The charity awarded 18 grants to organisations in 2021/22.
HOW TO APPLY Prospective applicants should submit a brief outline of their project by email. If the proposal meets the charity's criteria, the relevant application forms will be provided. The Council of Management meets in spring and autumn to consider applications. The deadlines for the receipt of completed applications and references are usually 1 March and 1 August.
CONTACT DETAILS Christopher Catling, Director, Flat 9, 13 Tavistock Place, London WC1H 9SH *Tel.* 020 7387 6580 *Email* mail2023@marcfitchfund.org.uk *Website* www.marcfitchfund.org.uk

■ The Earl Fitzwilliam Charitable Trust

CC NO 269388   **ESTABLISHED** 1975
WHERE FUNDING CAN BE GIVEN UK, with a preference for areas with historical Fitzwilliam family connections, chiefly in Cambridgeshire, Yorkshire and Denbighshire.
WHO CAN BENEFIT Charitable organisations linked to the Fitzwilliam Estates (Cambridgeshire and Yorkshire) and the Naylor-Leyland Estate (Nantclwyd in Denbighshire). Small and medium-sized charities that fall outside this criteria can also be supported.
WHAT IS FUNDED General charitable purposes.
RANGE OF GRANTS £100 to £65,000.
SAMPLE GRANTS Malton Amenity CIC (£65,000); Moorland Association (£10,000); Hunt Servants' Fund (£7,500); British Asian Trust and British Red Cross (£5,000 each); Nene Valley Railway and Newark Play Association (£2,500 each); Ovacome (£1,000); British Heart Foundation and St Peter's Church – Norton (£100).
FINANCES *Financial year end* 31/03/2022
Income £225,000
Grants to organisations £219,800
Assets £18,840,000
TRUSTEES Lady Isabella Naylor-Leyland; Sir Philip Naylor-Leyland.
OTHER INFORMATION Grants were awarded to 72 organisations during 2022.
HOW TO APPLY Apply in writing to the correspondent. Applications are considered at meetings throughout the year.
CONTACT DETAILS Mr R. W. Dalgliesh, Secretary, Estate Office, Milton Park, Peterborough, Cambridgeshire PE3 9HD *Tel.* 01733 267740 *Email* efct@miltonestate.co.uk

■ The Robert Fleming Hannay Memorial Charity

CC NO 1086811   **ESTABLISHED** 2000
WHERE FUNDING CAN BE GIVEN Scotland.
WHO CAN BENEFIT Charitable organisations.
WHAT IS FUNDED General charitable purposes, including: social welfare; education; religion; health; arts, culture heritage and science; human rights; disability; young people; older people.
RANGE OF GRANTS Mainly under £25,000.
SAMPLE GRANTS Cobbe Collection (£25,000); Holy Trinity Church – Brompton (£20,000); The Children's Society and Macmillan Cancer Support (£10,000 each); Help Musicians UK (£5,000); Christian Aid, Save the Children and Tearfund (£4,000 each).
FINANCES *Financial year end* 05/04/2022
Income £33,900
Grants to organisations £129,000
Assets £2,140,000
TRUSTEES Fiona Hannay; Christian Ward; Geoffrey Richards.
HOW TO APPLY The charity's 2021/22 annual report states that 'the Trustees consider applications and make grants they receive from various sources at the Trustees' meetings. However, due to constraints on income, unsolicited applications can no longer be considered. Although some donations may be made to the same charities each year none shall be either promised or guaranteed.'
CONTACT DETAILS The Trustees, RFT Management Services Ltd, 14 Buckingham Street, London WC2N 6DF *Tel.* 020 3696 6721 *Email* charities@rftrustee.com

■ The Joyce Fletcher Charitable Trust

CC NO 297901   **ESTABLISHED** 1987

WHERE FUNDING CAN BE GIVEN UK, with a very strong preference for the South West.

WHO CAN BENEFIT Registered charities.

WHAT IS FUNDED Music and arts education; music in a social and therapeutic context; children and young people.

WHAT IS NOT FUNDED Statutory organisations; professional arts or music organisations; medical research charities. Individuals, including students, are rarely supported.

TYPE OF GRANT Capital costs; core/revenue costs.

RANGE OF GRANTS Up to £6,000 but usually between £1,000 and £2,000.

SAMPLE GRANTS Drake Music (£5,000); English Touring Opera (£4,000); Holburne Museum (£3,500); Sound Waves South West (£3,000); Bath Play Area Project (£2,000); Magdalen Farm Strings (£1,500); Bath City Farm and Voice for Life (£1,000 each).

FINANCES *Financial year end* 05/04/2022
Income £129,800
Grants to organisations £85,500
Assets £2,570,000

TRUSTEES Stephen Fletcher; Robert Fletcher; William Fletcher; Susan Sharp.

OTHER INFORMATION Grants were broken down as follows: music in a social or therapeutic context (£39,500); music and arts education (£29,000); children and young people (£12,000); other (£5,000). Grants were made to 32 organisations in the South West and to 8 national charities.

HOW TO APPLY Apply in writing to the correspondent before 1 November each year. New applicants are advised to write in September. Applications are considered between September and November each year, with grants being made in early December. Telephone enquiries are accepted. Applications should include the purpose of the grant, an indication of the applicant organisation's history and viability and a summary of accounts. Applications sent by email and those including an sae will receive a response.

CONTACT DETAILS Robert Fletcher, Trustee, 68 Circus Mews, Bath, Somerset BA1 2PW *Tel.* 01225 314355 *Website* www.joyceflethercharitabletrust.co.uk

■ The Mrs Yvonne Flux Charitable Trust

CC NO 1136459   **ESTABLISHED** 2010

WHERE FUNDING CAN BE GIVEN UK.

WHO CAN BENEFIT Individuals and organisations.

WHAT IS FUNDED General charitable purposes.

SAMPLE GRANTS A list of beneficiaries was not included in the annual report and accounts.

FINANCES *Financial year end* 31/03/2022
Income £80,000
Grants to organisations £78,900
Assets £24,400

TRUSTEES Yvonne Flux; Timothy Flux.

OTHER INFORMATION Note that the grant total may include amounts awarded to individuals.

HOW TO APPLY Apply in writing to the correspondent.

CONTACT DETAILS The Trustees, c/o Stephenson Smart and Co., 22–26 King Street, King's Lynn, Norfolk PE30 1HJ *Tel.* 01553 774104

■ The Follett Trust

CC NO 328638   **ESTABLISHED** 1990

WHERE FUNDING CAN BE GIVEN UK and overseas, with a preference for Stevenage.

WHO CAN BENEFIT Organisations; individuals; hospitals; statutory authorities; social enterprises.

WHAT IS FUNDED General charitable purposes, including: education; the arts; medicine and health; work outside the UK; community services.

RANGE OF GRANTS Mostly up to £5,000, with the occasional larger grant.

SAMPLE GRANTS Donald Woods Foundation (£25,000); Impilo (£18,200); Stevenage Community Trust (£10,000); Canon Collins Educational Trust and The HALO Trust (£5,000 each); The Anne Robson Trust and Feed Up Warm Up (£2,000 each); City of Westminster Charitable Trust and Stevenage Pioneer Youth Trust (£1,000 each).

FINANCES *Financial year end* 30/06/2022
Income £82,500
Grants to organisations £118,000
Assets £41,000

TRUSTEES Barbara Follett; Ken Follett; Rebecca Hart.

OTHER INFORMATION Only organisations that received grants of over £1,000 were listed in the 2021/22 accounts. Grants of below £1,000 totalled £10,100. Note that the grant total may include amounts awarded to individuals.

HOW TO APPLY Apply in writing to the correspondent.

CONTACT DETAILS Rebecca Hart, Trustee, Kings Court, London Road, Stevenage, Hertfordshire SG1 2NG *Tel.* 01438 810400 *Email* folletttrust@thefollettoffice.com

■ Fonthill Foundation

CC NO 325071

WHERE FUNDING CAN BE GIVEN The South East and overseas.

WHO CAN BENEFIT Charitable organisations.

WHAT IS FUNDED The education of children and young people.

RANGE OF GRANTS Up to £25,700.

SAMPLE GRANTS Quicken Trust – Uganda (£25,700); Hindleap Warren (£20,900); Russell Martin Foundation (£15,800); Spear Brighton (£10,000); Brighton Table Tennis Club (£4,700); Sussex Clubs for Young People (£4,000); Audio Active and Herons Dale Primary School (£3,000 each).

FINANCES *Financial year end* 31/08/2022
Income £172,300
Grants to organisations £333,300
Assets £5,490,000

TRUSTEES Victoria Henley; Margaret Lloyd; Niki Cannon; Adrian Carver.

HOW TO APPLY The foundation's website states: 'We would love to hear about your organisation and the work you are doing. We're dynamic in constantly seeking out the best new partnerships, but note we don't take unsolicited applications for our UK or Overseas Programmes.' Application forms for the Small Community Grants Programme can be downloaded from the foundation's website.

CONTACT DETAILS The Trustees, PO Box 261, Lewes BN7 9LS *Tel.* 07479 921400 *Email* enquiry@fonthill-foundation.org.uk *Website* https://fonthill-foundation.org.uk

■ The Football Association National Sports Centre

CC NO 265132   **ESTABLISHED** 1972

WHERE FUNDING CAN BE GIVEN England.

WHO CAN BENEFIT County football associations; football clubs; sports associations.

WHAT IS FUNDED The charity offers clubs at step six and below of the National League System grants towards the provision of new floodlights and new or improved changing facilities. A separate scheme may be available to clubs at step three and below of the National League System to receive a grant towards the cost of materials for ground improvement projects where the club has the relevant trade skills within its membership.

TYPE OF GRANT Capital costs.

RANGE OF GRANTS Up to £10,000.

SAMPLE GRANTS Previous beneficiaries have included: Golcar United FC; Middlezoy Rovers FC and Roade Football Supporters Club (£10,000 each); Eccleshall FC (£8,000); Bottesford FC and Shirehampton AFC (£5,000 each); Tintwistle Athletic FC (£4,600); Walmer Bridge FC (£3,750).

FINANCES *Financial year end 31/12/2021*
Income £20
Grants to organisations £68,800

TRUSTEES Geoff Thompson; Mervyn Leggett; Brian Adshead.

OTHER INFORMATION We were unable to view the charity's annual report and accounts on the Charity Commission's website due to its low income. We have therefore estimated its grant total based on its total expenditure.

HOW TO APPLY Apply in writing to the correspondent.

CONTACT DETAILS Richard McDermott, Secretary to the Trustees, Wembley Stadium, PO Box 1966, London SW1P 9EQ *Tel.* 0800 169 1863 *Email* richard.mcdermott@thefa.com

■ The Football Foundation

CC NO 1079309   **ESTABLISHED** 1999

WHERE FUNDING CAN BE GIVEN England.

WHO CAN BENEFIT A wide range of organisations, including: football clubs (grassroots, professional and semi-professional) and their associated community charities; multi-sport clubs; leagues and county football associations; local authorities; educational establishments; schools; registered charities; not-for-profit companies.

WHAT IS FUNDED Improving community football facilities.

WHAT IS NOT FUNDED Facilities that are not available for community use; kit and equipment; projects intended for private gain; projects outside England; retrospective funding (for works that have already started or been completed); routine maintenance and repairs resulting from wear and tear and not part of a grass pitch improvement programme; facility hire.

TYPE OF GRANT Grants for football equipment, facilities and pitches.

RANGE OF GRANTS Programme dependent.

SAMPLE GRANTS London Borough of Barking and Dagenham (£6.2 million); Aston Villa Foundation (£1 million); Wirral Borough Council (£806,600); Community Action Derby (£525,000).

FINANCES *Financial year end 31/05/2022*
Income £78,700,000
Grants to organisations £95,950,000
Assets £4,530,000

TRUSTEES Peter McCormick; John Pearce; Jemima Bird; Tim Hollingsworth; William Bush; Mark Bullingham; Martin Glenn; Karen Taylor; Elena Narozanski.

OTHER INFORMATION The foundation receives income from The Football Association, the Premier League and the Department of Culture, Media and Sport via Sports England. It then uses this money to deliver a programme of new and improved community sports facilities in towns and cities across the country.

HOW TO APPLY Grant programmes open and close regularly, so potential applicants are advised to check the foundation's website for the latest information, including detailed application instructions and eligibility terms.

CONTACT DETAILS Grant Management Team, Wembley Stadium, Wembley Park, London HA9 0WS *Tel.* 0345 345 4555 *Email* enquiries@footballfoundation.org.uk *Website* www.footballfoundation.org.uk

■ The Forbes Charitable Foundation

CC NO 326476   **ESTABLISHED** 1983

WHERE FUNDING CAN BE GIVEN UK.

WHO CAN BENEFIT Registered or exempt charities; individuals; social enterprises. The foundation has a particular interest in supporting the development of new and innovative services or projects.

WHAT IS FUNDED Support for learning disabilities, including: residential care; supported living; day services; employment initiatives; skills training; support for informal carers; and transition services for young adults.

TYPE OF GRANT Capital costs; core/revenue costs; development funding; one-off and annual grants for up to three years.

RANGE OF GRANTS Up to £25,000.

SAMPLE GRANTS Linkage Community Trust and Oaklea Trust (£25,000 each); Avocet Trust (£21,500); Apuldram Centre (£16,000); Build Charity (£9,700); Style Acre (£8,300); Bentilee Volunteers (£3,000); Little Gate Farm (£2,000); Transitions UK (£1,000).

FINANCES *Financial year end 05/04/2022*
Income £236,000
Grants to organisations £248,300
Grants to individuals £3,800
Assets £8,730,000

TRUSTEES Ian Johnson; John Waite; Patrick Wallace; Helen Johnson; Mark Morris; Nigel Doggett; Julie Riley; Claire Rintoul.

OTHER INFORMATION During the year, the foundation awarded 19 grants to organisations.

HOW TO APPLY The foundation does not accept unsolicited applications. However, organisations with an annual turnover of between £1 million and £20 million should forward background information of their work to the correspondent.

CONTACT DETAILS The Trustees, 4 Market Place, Week St Mary, Holsworthy, Cornwall EX22 6XT *Tel.* 07749 642664 *Email* info@ theforbescharitablefoundation.org *Website* www. theforbescharitablefoundation.org

■ Ford Britain Trust

CC NO 269410   **ESTABLISHED** 1975

WHERE FUNDING CAN BE GIVEN The areas in close proximity to Ford Motor Company Ltd's locations in the UK, including: Bridgend; Daventry; Essex (including East London); Liverpool; Manchester; Southampton.

Think carefully about every application. Is it justified?

385

WHO CAN BENEFIT Registered charities; unregistered charities; schools; PTAs; hospices; wildlife trusts; sports clubs.

WHAT IS FUNDED Community; education and schools; people with special needs; people with disabilities; arts and culture; the environment; homelessness.

WHAT IS NOT FUNDED Individuals; CICs; local authorities, councils, government and government departments; core/running costs; major building works; sponsorship or advertising; research; overseas projects; travel; religious projects; political projects; purchase of second-hand vehicles; third-party fundraising initiatives.

TYPE OF GRANT New capital expenditure projects; refurbishment; IT equipment; contributions to vehicle purchases.

RANGE OF GRANTS Small grants: up to £250; large grants: £250 to £3,000.

SAMPLE GRANTS Bridgend Community Bereavement Support (£3,000); The Rose Road Association (£2,600); Samaritans Redbridge Branch (£2,000); Prevent 2 Protect (£1,000); Children With Cancer (£250).

FINANCES *Financial year end 31/03/2022*
Income £115,100
Grants to organisations £65,300
Assets £379,800

TRUSTEES David Russell; Dr June-Alison Sealy; Wendy James; Jane Skerry; Paul Bailey; Lara Nicoll; Jenny Ball.

OTHER INFORMATION This is the charitable trust of Ford Motor Company Ltd. Only organisations that received grants of over £2,000 were listed as beneficiaries in the trust's accounts. Grants of under £2,000 totalled £11,700.

HOW TO APPLY Application forms are available to download from the website, where guidance notes are also available. The trust's website states: 'The Ford Britain Trust particularly encourages applications supported by Ford employees, but is open to all, provided that the qualifying organisations meet our selection criteria.'

CONTACT DETAILS The Trustees, 15–02B D20-B, Ford Dunton Technical Centre, Laindon, Basildon, Essex SS15 6EE *Email* fbtrust@ford.com *Website* www.ford.co.uk/fbtrust

■ Oliver Ford Foundation

CC NO 1026551   **ESTABLISHED** 1993
WHERE FUNDING CAN BE GIVEN UK.

WHO CAN BENEFIT Registered charities; arts, culture and heritage organisations; students of the Victoria and Albert Museum, Royal Horticultural Society and Furniture History Society.

WHAT IS FUNDED Education, in particular interior design, the design of fabrics and decorative materials and landscape gardening, with particular reference to Oliver Ford.

TYPE OF GRANT Project funding; capital costs; salaries.

RANGE OF GRANTS Typically £1,000 to £50,000.

SAMPLE GRANTS The Fifth Trust (£29,000); The Mudlarks Community (£10,000); Time Out Group (£5,000); Walton Lea Partnership (£2,000).

FINANCES *Financial year end 05/04/2022*
Income £79,900
Grants to organisations £139,100
Assets £2,960,000

TRUSTEES Martin Levy; Lady Alison Wakeham; Matthew Pintus.

HOW TO APPLY Apply in writing to the correspondent.

CONTACT DETAILS The Trustees, c/o MacFarlanes LLP, 20 Cursitor Street, London EC4A 1LT *Tel.* 020 7831 9222

■ Fordeve Ltd

CC NO 1011612   **ESTABLISHED** 1992
WHERE FUNDING CAN BE GIVEN UK.

WHO CAN BENEFIT Orthodox Jewish organisations.

WHAT IS FUNDED The advancement of religion in accordance with the Orthodox Jewish faith; general charitable purposes.

SAMPLE GRANTS A list of beneficiaries was not included in the annual report and accounts.

FINANCES *Financial year end 31/03/2022*
Income £85,200
Grants to organisations £180,600
Assets £461,300

TRUSTEES Jeremy Kon; Helen Kon.

HOW TO APPLY Apply in writing to the correspondent.

CONTACT DETAILS Helen Kon, Trustee, Hallswelle House, 1 Hallswelle Road, London NW11 0DH *Tel.* 020 8209 1535

■ Forest Hill Charitable Trust

CC NO 1050862   **ESTABLISHED** 1995
WHERE FUNDING CAN BE GIVEN UK and overseas.

WHO CAN BENEFIT Charitable organisations.

WHAT IS FUNDED People with disabilities; social welfare; emergency aid; children and young people; addiction; carers; victims of torture; health and medical services; medical research; human trafficking and slavery; farming and fishing communities in the South West.

TYPE OF GRANT Core costs.

RANGE OF GRANTS Mostly between £500 and £2,500.

SAMPLE GRANTS LiNX (£20,000); Barnabas Fund and Scripture Union (£2,000 each); Emmaus School (£1,500); Family for Every Child and Hebron Trust (£1,000 each); Open Doors Exmouth (£500).

FINANCES *Financial year end 05/04/2022*
Income £39,000
Grants to organisations £187,500
Assets £3,500,000

TRUSTEES Ronald Pile; Patricia Pile; Marianne Tapper; Michael Thomas.

OTHER INFORMATION The trust supports around 130 charities on a monthly basis.

HOW TO APPLY The 2021/22 annual report states: 'The trust has been unable to accept new requests for some time and the situation is unlikely to change for the foreseeable future. However, when a charity previously supported by the Trust no longer needs our support, a new charity from an 'approved waiting list' is added to take their place.'

CONTACT DETAILS Patricia Pile, Secretary, Little Bluff, Treknow, Tintagel, Cornwall PL34 0EP *Tel.* 01840 779405 *Email* horacepilefhct@yahoo.co.uk

■ The Lady Forester Trust

CC NO 241187   **ESTABLISHED** 1979
WHERE FUNDING CAN BE GIVEN Shropshire.

WHO CAN BENEFIT Registered charities; individuals.

WHAT IS FUNDED Health and disability.

SAMPLE GRANTS A list of beneficiaries was not included in the annual report and accounts.

FINANCES *Financial year end 31/12/2021*
Income £229,400
Grants to organisations £87,000
Grants to individuals £78,500
Assets £7,130,000
TRUSTEES Henry Carpenter; Libby Collinson; Lady Catherine Forester; Lord Forester; The Hon. Alice Stoker; Janette Stewart; Lady Forester; Charles Whitaker.
HOW TO APPLY Apply in writing to the correspondent. The trustees meet on a quarterly basis to consider applications.
CONTACT DETAILS The Trustees, The Lady Forester Trust, The Estate Office, Willey, Broseley, Shropshire TF12 5JN *Tel.* 01952 884318 *Email* lft@willeyestates.co.uk

Forever Manchester

CC NO 1017504   **ESTABLISHED** 1993
WHERE FUNDING CAN BE GIVEN Greater Manchester.
WHO CAN BENEFIT Registered charities; unregistered charities; CICs; social enterprises; schools; PTAs.
WHAT IS FUNDED General charitable purposes including: older people; children and young people; stronger communities; the environment; health and well-being.
TYPE OF GRANT Core/revenue costs; project funding.
SAMPLE GRANTS A list of beneficiaries was not included in the annual report and accounts.
FINANCES *Financial year end 31/03/2022*
Income £158,200
Grants to organisations £2,090,000
Grants to individuals £50,900
Assets £8,980,000
TRUSTEES Alan Mackin; Nicholas Edmondson; Carl Austin-Behan; Rebecca Durrant; Christian Brooks; Dr Zoe Philips; Claire Ebrey; Samantha Booth; Sandra Lindsay.
OTHER INFORMATION This is one of the 47 UK community foundations, which distribute funding for a wide range of purposes. As with all community foundations, there are a number of donor-advised funds managed on behalf of individuals, families and charitable trusts. Grant schemes tend to change frequently – consult the foundation's website for details of current programmes and up-to-date deadlines.
HOW TO APPLY Potential applicants are advised to visit the charity's website or contact its grants team to find the most suitable funding stream.
CONTACT DETAILS Communities Team, Forever Manchester, 2nd Floor, 8 Hewitt Street, Manchester M15 4GB *Tel.* 0161 214 0940 *Email* awards@forevermanchester.com *Website* www.forevermanchester.com

The Forman Hardy Charitable Trust

CC NO 1000687   **ESTABLISHED** 1990
WHERE FUNDING CAN BE GIVEN Nottinghamshire.
WHO CAN BENEFIT Registered charities; community groups.
WHAT IS FUNDED General charitable purposes.
RANGE OF GRANTS Mostly up to £3,000.
SAMPLE GRANTS A list of beneficiaries was not available.
FINANCES *Financial year end 05/04/2022*
Income £11,300
Grants to organisations £128,100
TRUSTEES Nicholas Hardy; Jane Hardy; Dr Paul Sibley; Victoria Savile.

OTHER INFORMATION Full accounts were not available to view on the Charity Commission's website due to the trust's low income. We have therefore estimated the grant total based on the trust's total expenditure.
HOW TO APPLY Apply in writing to the correspondent.
CONTACT DETAILS The Trustees, 1st Floor, Toll Bar House, Landmere Lane, Edwalton, Nottingham, Nottinghamshire NG12 4DG *Tel.* 0115 950 8580 *Email* fhctrequest@formanhardy.co.uk

The Forrester Family Trust

CC NO 1190231   **ESTABLISHED** 1986
WHERE FUNDING CAN BE GIVEN UK and overseas.
WHO CAN BENEFIT Registered charities.
WHAT IS FUNDED General charitable purposes including: animals and birds; people with disabilities; children and young people; community care and social welfare; hospices and hospitals; medical relief and welfare; medical research; older people; Service and ex-Service personnel; overseas aid; people who are blind or deaf; education.
TYPE OF GRANT Capital costs; core/revenue costs; project funding; unrestricted funding.
RANGE OF GRANTS Up to £50,000 but mostly under £5,000.
SAMPLE GRANTS British Red Cross – Ukraine Crisis Appeal (£100,000); Eggcup (£40,000); Young Women's Trust (£30,000); Emmeline's Pantry (£28,000); Bowel Cancer UK (£25,000): HOPE International Development Agency (£10,000); National Back Pain Association (£5,000); St Michael's Hospice – North Hampshire (£1,300).
FINANCES *Financial year end 31/03/2022*
Income £1,320,000
Grants to organisations £1,380,000
Assets £43,790,000
TRUSTEES Wendy Forrester; Hilary Porter; Melissa Jones; Thomas Walker; Fiona Cole; Jonathan Kewley.
OTHER INFORMATION Grants were broken down as follows: theme of the year (£601,000); smaller grants (£343,300); term funding (£250,000); disaster relief (£185,000).
HOW TO APPLY Check the trust's website for information on how to apply.
CONTACT DETAILS The Trustees, 11 Whitecroft Way, Beckenham, Kent BR3 3AQ *Tel.* 020 8629 0089 *Email* admin@theforresterfamilytrust.org *Website* http://forrestertrusts.com/donald-forrester-trust

The Anna Rosa Forster Charitable Trust

CC NO 1090028   **ESTABLISHED** 1997
WHERE FUNDING CAN BE GIVEN UK and overseas.
WHO CAN BENEFIT Registered charities.
WHAT IS FUNDED Medical research; animal welfare; famine relief.
SAMPLE GRANTS A list of beneficiaries was not included in the annual report and accounts.
FINANCES *Financial year end 05/04/2022*
Income £65,200
Grants to organisations £52,500
Assets £2,720,000
TRUSTEES Andrew Morgan; Jonathan Heslop; Sarah Sinclair.
OTHER INFORMATION The trust divides its income equally between animal welfare, famine relief and medical research.
HOW TO APPLY Apply in writing to the correspondent.

CONTACT DETAILS Andrew Morgan, Trustee, 14 Bell Villas, Ponteland, Newcastle upon Tyne, Tyne and Wear NE20 9BE *Tel.* 01661 871012 *Email* amorgan@nicholsonmorgan.co.uk

■ The Fort Foundation

CC NO 1028639   **ESTABLISHED** 1993
WHERE FUNDING CAN BE GIVEN England and Wales, with a focus on Lancashire.
WHO CAN BENEFIT Charitable organisations and individuals.
WHAT IS FUNDED Health; amateur sport; education; art and culture; citizenship; community welfare; religion; environmental protection and improvement.
RANGE OF GRANTS Mostly between £5,000 and £20,000.
SAMPLE GRANTS The Outward Bound Trust (£20,000 each); Pendleside Hospice (£10,000); Lancaster University E-Racing Project (£6,000); Jubilee Sailing Trust (£5,000).
FINANCES *Financial year end 28/02/2022*
Income £338,900
Grants to organisations £163,900
Grants to individuals £8,700
Assets £1,840,000
TRUSTEES Ian Wilson; Edward Drury; John Hartley; Peter Fort; Edward Fort.
OTHER INFORMATION Grants awarded to organisations during the year were broken down as follows: health (£49,000); citizenship and community welfare (£47,200); education (£35,200); environmental protection and improvement (£17,100); amateur sport (£13,400); art and culture (£2,000).
HOW TO APPLY Apply in writing to the correspondent.
CONTACT DETAILS The Trustees, c/o Fort Vale Engineering Ltd, Calder Vale Park, Simonstone Lane, Simonstone, Burnley, Lancashire BB12 7ND *Tel.* 01282 440000 *Email* info@fortvale.com

■ The Lord Forte Foundation

CC NO 298100   **ESTABLISHED** 1987
WHERE FUNDING CAN BE GIVEN UK and overseas.
WHO CAN BENEFIT Educational establishments and charities.
WHAT IS FUNDED Training courses and research or other projects within the field of hospitality, encompassing the hotel, catering, travel and tourism industries within the UK and overseas.
TYPE OF GRANT Project funding.
RANGE OF GRANTS Up to £15,000.
SAMPLE GRANTS Queen Margaret University – Edinburgh, Springboard Charitable Trust (£15,000 each); Hotel School (£10,000) Edinburgh Napier University (£5,000); University of Strathclyde (£2,500).
FINANCES *Financial year end 31/03/2022*
Income £76,500
Grants to organisations £63,400
Assets £3,130,000
TRUSTEES Sir Rocco Forte; Andrew McKenzie; The Hon. Olga Sorrentino; Nick Scade; Geoff Booth.
OTHER INFORMATION Grants were made to eight organisations during the year.
HOW TO APPLY Apply in writing to the correspondent.
CONTACT DETAILS The Trustees, Rocco Forte Hotels Ltd, 70 Jermyn Street, London SW1Y 6NY *Tel.* 020 7321 2626 *Email* jlewendon@roccofortehotels.com

■ The Foster Wood Foundation

CC NO 1101364   **ESTABLISHED** 2003
WHERE FUNDING CAN BE GIVEN UK and overseas.
WHO CAN BENEFIT Registered charities.
WHAT IS FUNDED Advancement of Christianity; relief of poverty; advancement of education.
RANGE OF GRANTS £3,000 to £65,000.
SAMPLE GRANTS A list of beneficiaries was not included in the annual report and accounts.
FINANCES *Financial year end 05/04/2022*
Income £368,400
Grants to organisations £390,000
Assets £39,100
TRUSTEES Geoffrey Hill; Margaret Lodge; The Revd David Hodson.
HOW TO APPLY The foundation's annual report states the following: 'In the past applications have been invited from suitable charities able to demonstrate that they can use the funds they apply for in an effective manner to achieve their stated aims which must be consistent with the objects of the foundation. However, as it is the intention of the trustees to reduce the activities of the foundation, no applications are being sought from any other charity other than those already being supported.'
CONTACT DETAILS Geoffrey Hill, Trustee, 21–27 Lamb's Conduit Street, London WC1N 3GS *Tel.* 020 7935 3793 *Email* ghill@gsmaccountants.co.uk

■ Ian M. Foulerton Charitable Trust

CC NO 1164969   **ESTABLISHED** 2015
WHERE FUNDING CAN BE GIVEN England and Wales.
WHO CAN BENEFIT Buildings of historic, architectural, artistic or scientific interest.
WHAT IS FUNDED Arts and heritage, specifically: the preservation, conservation, protection and restoration of buildings, furniture, art, manuscripts and monuments of historic, architectural, artistic or scientific interest; advancement of education.
TYPE OF GRANT Maintenance costs; capital costs; bursaries and scholarships.
RANGE OF GRANTS From £1,500 to £20,000.
SAMPLE GRANTS Dean and Chapter of Exeter and Eartham PCC (£20,000 each); Sussex Heritage Trust Ltd (£15,000); St Andrew's Restoration Appeal (£11,000); St Philip and St James and Wincanton PCC (£10,000 each); Wethersfield PCC (£5,000); Church Council of Talaton Parish (£2,000); St Mary's Church (£1,500).
FINANCES *Financial year end 05/04/2022*
Income £48,400
Grants to organisations £167,500
Assets £1,760,000
TRUSTEES Duncan O'Kelly; John McEvoy; Thomas Eggar Trust Corporation Ltd.
OTHER INFORMATION Twenty-three grants were awarded during 2021/22.
HOW TO APPLY Apply in writing to the correspondent.
CONTACT DETAILS The Trustees, c/o Irwin Mitchell LLP, Thomas Eggar House, Friary Lane, Chichester, West Sussex PO19 1UF *Tel.* 01243 786111 *Email* foulerton@irwinmitchell.com

■ Four Acre Trust

CC NO 1053884   **ESTABLISHED** 1995
WHERE FUNDING CAN BE GIVEN Worldwide, with a preference for the UK.
WHO CAN BENEFIT Registered charities; organisations.

WHAT IS FUNDED Children and young people. Current programmes include support for schools' extracurricular projects, early intervention work, international eye and water projects.

WHAT IS NOT FUNDED Capital costs are rarely supported.

TYPE OF GRANT Revenue/core costs; salaries.

RANGE OF GRANTS Mostly £10,000 to £100,000.

SAMPLE GRANTS Dulverton Trust (£600,000); Tudor Trust (£399,000); Into University (£220,300); ReachOut Youth (£75,000); Farms for City Children (£35,000); Mission for Vision (£20,000); Young Carers Development Trust (£12,000); Kepplewray Trust (£6,000).

FINANCES *Financial year end* 31/03/2022
Income £121,500
Grants to organisations £3,190,000
Assets £2,230,000

TRUSTEES John Bothamley; Mary Bothamley; Stephen Ratcliffe.

HOW TO APPLY The trust's 2021/22 accounts state: 'Four Acre Trust (4AT) is essentially closed to new applications preferring to seek out relevant charities through thorough research.'

CONTACT DETAILS The Trustees, Treferanon, St Weonards, Hereford, Herefordshire HR2 8QF *Tel.* 01981 580002 *Email* info@fouracretrust.org.uk *Website* www.fouracretrust.org.uk

Foux Foundation

CC NO 1177520   **ESTABLISHED** 2018
WHERE FUNDING CAN BE GIVEN Worldwide.
WHO CAN BENEFIT Registered charities.
WHAT IS FUNDED Health; education; children and young people; the relief of poverty.
WHAT IS NOT FUNDED Charities with an income of over £3 million per annum.
SAMPLE GRANTS The Kids Network (£26,100); Garden Library (£20,900); Small Steps Project (£24,700); Disasters Emergency Committee – Ukraine Humanitarian Appeal (£10,000); Suicide&Co (£5,000).
FINANCES *Financial year end* 05/04/2022
Income £100,000
Grants to organisations £86,700
Assets £74,300
TRUSTEES Adam Ferguson; Mika Foux; Joshua Segal; Laura Ferguson.
OTHER INFORMATION The foundation made five grants during 2021/22.
HOW TO APPLY Proposals can be submitted via the foundation's website.
CONTACT DETAILS The Trustees, Gerald Edelman Chartered Accountant, 73 Cornhill, London EC3V 3QQ *Tel.* 020 7299 1400 *Email* hello@fouxfoundation.org.uk *Website* www.fouxfoundation.org.uk

Fowler Smith and Jones Trust

CC NO 1132249
WHERE FUNDING CAN BE GIVEN Essex.
WHO CAN BENEFIT Charitable organisations.
WHAT IS FUNDED Arts; churches; community; health; youth; general charitable purposes.
WHAT IS NOT FUNDED Individuals; animal charities; political activities; commercial ventures.
TYPE OF GRANT Capital costs; project funding; core/revenue costs.
SAMPLE GRANTS FACT, HARP Southend and Sawyers Church – Brentwood (£30,000 each); Brentwood Catholic Children's Society, SHARE Charity and Trust Links (£20,000 each).

FINANCES *Financial year end* 30/09/2022
Income £714,800
Grants to organisations £539,900
Assets £10,730,000

TRUSTEES Nicholas Charrington; Richard Furlonger; Philip Tolhurst; Lucy Bettley.

OTHER INFORMATION Grants were broken down as follows: young people (£156,700); medical/health (£96,200); capital projects (£95,000); community (£94,600); miscellaneous (£80,100); churches (£25,500); arts (£5,000); overseas (£3,000).

HOW TO APPLY Apply in writing to the correspondent. Details of what should be included in an application can be found on the trust's website.

CONTACT DETAILS Penny Langran, Grant Administrator, 3rd Floor, Marlborough House, Victoria Road South, Chelmsford, Essex CM1 1LN *Tel.* 01245 809899 *Email* plangran@fsjtrust.org.uk *Website* http://fsjtrust.org.uk

The Foxglove Trust

CC NO 1137839   **ESTABLISHED** 2010
WHERE FUNDING CAN BE GIVEN Worldwide, with a preference for Somerset.
WHO CAN BENEFIT Charitable causes.
WHAT IS FUNDED General charitable purposes, including: international and local causes; sports; the arts.
SAMPLE GRANTS Previous beneficiaries have included: Purple Community Fund (£45,000); The Open Door (£8,500); Baby Bank Bristol (£7,500); TLC Children's Trust (£6,800).
FINANCES *Financial year end* 30/04/2022
Income £18,400
Grants to organisations £135,000
TRUSTEES Kevin Austin; Ian Kelland; Helena Barry; Yasmin Woodland.
OTHER INFORMATION Full accounts were not available to view on the Charity Commission's website. We have therefore estimated the grant total based on the trust's total expenditure.
HOW TO APPLY Apply in writing to the correspondent. Previous annual reports have stated: 'Cases presented for consideration should, where possible, have concrete proposals and outcomes attached.'
CONTACT DETAILS Ian Kelland, Trustee, c/o Lentells Ltd, 17–18 Leach Road, Chard Business Park, Chard, Somerset TA20 1FA *Tel.* 01460 64441 *Email* ian.kelland@icloud.com

The Foyle Foundation

CC NO 1081766   **ESTABLISHED** 1999
WHERE FUNDING CAN BE GIVEN UK, particularly areas outside London and the South East.
WHO CAN BENEFIT Registered charities; state schools; universities.
WHAT IS FUNDED Arts, particularly the performing arts; education; literacy and literature; community support services.
WHAT IS NOT FUNDED Individuals; CICs; social enterprises; community amateur sports clubs; preschools/nurseries; independent schools; retrospective costs. See the foundation's website for specific exclusions for each funding stream.
TYPE OF GRANT Capital costs; core/revenue costs; project funding.
RANGE OF GRANTS Programme dependent.
SAMPLE GRANTS National Galleries of Scotland (£350,000); Institute of Contemporary Arts (£200,000); Aberystwyth University (£150,000); Help Musicians UK, Lord Leycester's Hospital

Think carefully about every application. Is it justified?

389

and The Salisbury and South Wiltshire Museum Trust (£100,000 each); The Poetry Society (£92,000); Cumbernauld Theatre and St Paul's Cathedral (£75,000 each).

FINANCES *Financial year end 31/12/2021*
Income £1,550,000
Grants to organisations £9,400,000
Assets £59,000,000

TRUSTEES Sir Peter Duffell; Michael Smith; Roy Amlot; James Korner; Vikki Heywood; Kathryn Ellison.

OTHER INFORMATION Only beneficiaries of grants of over £75,000 were listed in the accounts. The foundation made 664 grants in 2021.

HOW TO APPLY Guidelines and application forms for each of the foundation's grant schemes are available to download from its website, where specific contacts for each grants scheme may also be found. Applications need to be submitted online and are accepted all year round.

CONTACT DETAILS Grants Team, Rugby Chambers, 2 Rugby Street, London WC1N 3QU *Tel.* 020 7430 9119 *Email* info@foylefoundation.org.uk *Website* www.foylefoundation.org.uk

■ Mrs D. M. France-Hayhurst Foundation

CC NO 1160394   **ESTABLISHED** 2015
WHERE FUNDING CAN BE GIVEN UK.
WHO CAN BENEFIT Registered charities.
WHAT IS FUNDED Animal welfare.
TYPE OF GRANT Project costs and capital expenditure.
RANGE OF GRANTS Mostly up to £5,000.
SAMPLE GRANTS Mare and Foal Sanctuary (£5,000); HorseWorld Trust (£4,700); Angels for Animals Foundation (£2,500); Kenward Trust (£1,700); Wild at Heart Foundation (£900).
FINANCES *Financial year end 31/03/2022*
Income £465,500
Grants to organisations £112,400
Assets £21,860,000
TRUSTEES Andrew Wright; Jennifer Shearer; Peter Hunter; Christopher Henretty; Phillip Posnett; Penelope Sanders.
HOW TO APPLY Application forms are available to download from the foundation's website. The completed application form and any supporting documentation should be sent by post or email to the secretary. The trustees meet quarterly.
CONTACT DETAILS Penelope Byatt, Secretary, c/o Charles Russell Speechlys LLP, Compass House, Lypiatt Road, Cheltenham GL50 2QJ *Tel.* 01242 246311 *Email* Penelope.Byatt@ crsblaw.com *Website* www. francehayhurstcharitabletrust.org.uk

■ The Isaac and Freda Frankel Memorial Charitable Trust

CC NO 1003732   **ESTABLISHED** 1991
WHERE FUNDING CAN BE GIVEN UK and Israel.
WHO CAN BENEFIT Mainly organisations and institutions benefitting people of the Jewish faith.
WHAT IS FUNDED The advancement of religion in accordance with the Orthodox Jewish faith; the relief of poverty.
WHAT IS NOT FUNDED Individuals; students; expeditions; scholarships.
RANGE OF GRANTS £5,000 to £10,000.
SAMPLE GRANTS Achisomoch Aid Company Ltd (£28,000); North West Sephardish Synagogue

(£13,300); The New Girls School (£9,000); The Jewish Day Primary School (£5,000).

FINANCES *Financial year end 31/01/2022*
Income £78,800
Grants to organisations £73,000
Assets £453,700

TRUSTEES Geraldine Frankel; Mr J. Silkin; Mr J. Steinhaus; Montague Frankel.

OTHER INFORMATION Grants of less than £5,000 each totalled £17,200.

HOW TO APPLY Contact the correspondent for further information.

CONTACT DETAILS The Trustees, 117 Bridge Lane, London NW11 9JT *Tel.* 020 8458 4056

■ The Elizabeth Frankland Moore and Star Foundation

CC NO 257711   **ESTABLISHED** 1969
WHERE FUNDING CAN BE GIVEN UK.
WHO CAN BENEFIT Registered charitable organisations.
WHAT IS FUNDED General charitable purposes.
RANGE OF GRANTS From £1,000 to £20,000.
SAMPLE GRANTS Iceni Project and The Trussell Trust (£15,000 each); Age UK and The Salvation Army – Scotland (£10,000 each); Shelter (£5,000); Simon Community Scotland (£1,000); Saxmundham Museum (£500).
FINANCES *Financial year end 05/04/2022*
Income £384,200
Grants to organisations £345,500
Assets £15,440,000
TRUSTEES R. Griffiths; Anne Ely; Dr David Spalton; Janine Cameron.
OTHER INFORMATION In 2021/22 the foundation received 438 applications from UK-registered organisations, of which 48 were accepted. Grants were broken down as follows: vulnerable people (£89,200); medical research (£85,000); homelessness (£48,800); hospices (£44,000); education and the arts (£36,500); war veterans (£16,000); human rights (£15,000); National Star College (£10,000); other (£1,000).
HOW TO APPLY Apply in writing to the correspondent. The trustees meet twice a year.
CONTACT DETAILS The Trustees, c/o Neuhoff and Co., 11 Towcester Road, Whittlebury, Towcester, Northamptonshire NN12 8XU *Tel.* 01327 858171 *Email* info@neuhoffandco.com

■ Jill Franklin Trust

CC NO 1000175   **ESTABLISHED** 1988
WHERE FUNDING CAN BE GIVEN The North East (Cleveland, County Durham, Newcastle, Northumbria and Tyne and Wear).
WHO CAN BENEFIT Charitable organisations, particularly small charities; churches.
WHAT IS FUNDED Church restoration; self-help groups to support people with a mental illness or learning difficulties and their carers; help and support for refugees and asylum seekers coming to or in the UK; the restoration of churches of architectural importance; local schemes to help ex-offenders to resettle.
WHAT IS NOT FUNDED Building work (apart from church restoration); replacement of statutory funding; projects overseas; religious organisations set up for welfare, education, etc. whose services are not open and used by people from all denominations; animal charities; environmental charities; individuals, including students; medical research.

RANGE OF GRANTS Grants are typically of £1,000 for one to three years (apart from church restoration grants, which are usually of £500).

SAMPLE GRANTS Halo Project (£36,000); Mary Thompson Fund (£29,200); Fightback (£24,000); Wearside Women in Need (£24,000); The Bike Project (£14,400); Prisoners' Education Trust (£9,600).

FINANCES *Financial year end* 05/04/2022
Income £87,000
Grants to organisations £172,400
Assets £2,580,000

TRUSTEES Thomas Franklin; Dr Samuel Franklin; Andrew Franklin; Norman Franklin; Daniel Franklin.

OTHER INFORMATION Grants were made to ten organisations and were broken down as follows: refugees (£69,500); women's aid (£60,400); mental health (£32,800); desistance (£9,600).

HOW TO APPLY Apply by email to jft@jill-franklin-trust.org.uk in 500 words or less, detailing your project and aims. Preference will be given to smaller organisations (i.e. those with a turnover of less than £1 million). Applications will be acknowledged and are normally considered in the last month of the quarter.

CONTACT DETAILS The Trustees, Flat 5, 17–19 Elsworthy Road, London NW3 3DS *Email* jft@jill-franklin-trust.org.uk *Website* www.jill-franklin-trust.org.uk

■ The Gordon Fraser Charitable Trust

CC NO 260869   **ESTABLISHED** 1966
WHERE FUNDING CAN BE GIVEN UK, with a preference for Scotland.
WHO CAN BENEFIT Registered charities.
WHAT IS FUNDED General charitable purposes, with a preference for: performing arts, particularly for children, young people and people with disabilities; visual arts and museums; small medical and environmental charities, including those with a focus on the built environment.
WHAT IS NOT FUNDED Non-registered charities; individuals.
TYPE OF GRANT Capital costs; core/revenue costs; project funding; seed funding/start-up funding.
RANGE OF GRANTS Generally £500 to £2,500.
SAMPLE GRANTS Royal Scottish National Orchestra (£4,500); Bethany Christian Trust (£3,000); Artlink Central Ltd (£2,500); Cultural Perth and Kinross (£2,000); Abertay University (£1,500); Capital Carers (£1,000); Children 1st (£500).
FINANCES *Financial year end* 31/01/2022
Income £190,500
Grants to organisations £160,000
Assets £4,490,000
TRUSTEES Mrs M. A. Moss; Sarah Moss; Alexander Moss; Susannah Rae; Alison Priestley.
OTHER INFORMATION As well as its main grant-making, the trust also supports up to six projects per year through the Paper Conservation Fund which, according to the website, 'aims to help accredited museums in Scotland, in particular small and medium-sized independent ones, to work with conservators to undertake projects that conserve their collections of works on paper.' The website further explains, 'Projects can be treatment, surveys, training courses, and skills development workshops.' In 2021/22, 100 grants were awarded to organisations in total. Grants were broken down as follows: other (£60,100); arts and theatre (£48,900); health (£21,900); youth work (£14,500); relief of

poverty (£7,500); education (£6,000); animal welfare (£2,200); religion (£1,000).

HOW TO APPLY Applications can be made online on the trust's website or in writing to the correspondent. Applications are considered in January, April, July and October. According to the trust's website, applications for the Paper Conservation Fund are 'treated separately'; for this fund, applicants should contact the correspondent by email for an application form and guidance.

CONTACT DETAILS Claire Armstrong, Correspondent, Gaidrew Farmhouse, Drymen, Glasgow G63 0DN *Tel.* 01727 869141 *Email* enquiries@gfct.org.uk *Website* www.gfct.org.uk

■ The Hugh Fraser Foundation

OSCR NO SC009303   **ESTABLISHED** 1960
WHERE FUNDING CAN BE GIVEN Scotland.
WHO CAN BENEFIT Charitable organisations, principally hospitals; schools and universities; arts organisations; social welfare organisations.
WHAT IS FUNDED Medical facilities and research; relief of poverty; education and learning; older people; personal development and training of young people; music and the arts; other general charitable purposes.
WHAT IS NOT FUNDED Grants are only awarded to individuals in exceptional circumstances.
TYPE OF GRANT Project, capital and revenue grants for up to three years, sometimes longer; start-up costs.
SAMPLE GRANTS Burrell Collection (£100,000); Elsie Normington Foundation (£75,000); Dundee Heritage (£50,000).
FINANCES *Financial year end* 31/03/2022
Income £2,480,000
Grants to organisations £2,050,000
Grants to individuals £15,000
Assets £95,860,000
TRUSTEES Patricia Fraser; Dr Kenneth Chrystie; Belinda Hanson; Andrew Harrow.
OTHER INFORMATION The website notes that the trustees 'consider that grants to large, highly-publicised national appeals are not likely to be as effective a use of funds as grants to smaller, more focused charitable appeals'. There were 338 grants awarded to organisations and 3 to individuals during the year.
HOW TO APPLY Applications should be submitted in PDF format via email. Applications should include a description of the project and a budget, with a copy of your latest accounts or financial information. The trustees normally meet in March, June, September and December, with the cut-off date for applications being a month before.
CONTACT DETAILS The Trustees, c/o Turcan Connell, 180 St Vincent Street, Glasgow G2 5SG *Tel.* 0141 441 2111 *Email* hughfraserfoundation@turcanconnell.com *Website* www.turcanconnell.com/the-hugh-fraser-foundation

■ The Fraxinus Charitable Trust

CC NO 1175624   **ESTABLISHED** 2017
WHERE FUNDING CAN BE GIVEN England and Wales.
WHO CAN BENEFIT Charitable organisations.
WHAT IS FUNDED General charitable purposes.
SAMPLE GRANTS University of Leeds (£114,200 in two grants); Unicef UK (£100,000 in two grants); Tropical Health and Education Trust (£70,000); United World Schools (£55,000 in two grants).

FINANCES *Financial year end 24/10/2021*
Income £663,400
Grants to organisations £339,200
Assets £3,620,000

TRUSTEES Justinian Ash; Victoria Ash; Ludlow Trust Company Ltd.

OTHER INFORMATION The trust made four grants during the year. The 2020/21 accounts were the latest available at the time of writing (May 2023).

HOW TO APPLY Apply in writing to the correspondent.

CONTACT DETAILS The Trustees, c/o Ludlow Trust Co. Ltd, Tower Wharf, Cheese Lane, Bristol BS2 0JJ *Tel.* 0117 313 8200
Email charitabletrusts@ludlowtrust.com

■ The Joseph Strong Frazer Trust

CC NO 235311   **ESTABLISHED** 1939

WHERE FUNDING CAN BE GIVEN England and Wales.

WHO CAN BENEFIT Charitable organisations; hospitals; hospices; educational institutions; places of worship; statutory authorities.

WHAT IS FUNDED General charitable purposes, with a preference for the following: children and young people; older people; people with disabilities; medical research; maritime charities; the armed forces; education; religion; sport and recreation; social welfare; animals and wildlife; religion.

RANGE OF GRANTS Up to £4,000.

SAMPLE GRANTS Bobath Cymru, Coram Family and Childcare and Spinal Muscular Atrophy Support – UK (£4,000 each); Dementia UK and Versus Arthritis (£3,000); Breast Cancer Care, Cherry Trees and Royal Academy Trust (£2,500 each); Contact the Elderly – London, Tuberous Sclerosis Association and Women in Need (£2,000 each).

FINANCES *Financial year end 30/09/2021*
Income £648,300
Grants to organisations £531,100
Assets £15,790,000

TRUSTEES David Cook; Mr R. Read; William Reardon Smith; William Waites; Ugo Fagandini.

OTHER INFORMATION The 2020/21 accounts were the latest available at the time of writing (May 2023). Only beneficiaries of grants of £2,000 and above were listed in the trust's 2020/21 accounts. Grants of under £2,000 totalled £169,600 and were awarded to 153 organisations. Grants were broken down as follows: medical and other research (£125,000 – 70 organisations); care organisations (£70,500 – 49 organisations); children (£49,500 – 32 organisations); other trusts, funds and voluntary organisations (£45,500 – 29 organisations); leisure activities, animals and wildlife (£42,500 – 25 organisations); hospitals and home (£39,500 – 22 organisations); young people (£35,600 – 28 organisations); people who are deaf or blind (£33,000 – 17 organisations); people with physical disabilities (£22,500 – 12 organisations); maritime causes (£18,500 – 13 organisations); religion (£16,500 – 11 organisations); the armed forces (£14,000 – 7 organisations); people with mental disabilities (£8,000 – 5 organisations); people who are older or in ill health (£7,000 – 4 organisations); schools and colleges (£3,500 – 3 organisations).

HOW TO APPLY Apply in writing to the correspondent.

CONTACT DETAILS The Trustees, c/o Joseph Miller, Floor A, Milburn House, Dean Street, Newcastle upon Tyne NE1 1LE *Tel.* 0191 434 0830
Email jsf@joseph-miller.co.uk

■ The Louis and Valerie Freedman Charitable Settlement

CC NO 271067   **ESTABLISHED** 1976

WHERE FUNDING CAN BE GIVEN UK, especially Burnham.

WHO CAN BENEFIT Registered charities. The charity's 2021/22 accounts state that the trustees are 'normally minded to help those with a link to the Freedman family.'

WHAT IS FUNDED Medical research, health and sickness; children and young people; education.

TYPE OF GRANT Project costs; research funding.

RANGE OF GRANTS £5,000 to £20,000.

SAMPLE GRANTS Burnham Health Promotion Trust (£20,000); Disasters Emergency Committee – Ukraine Appeal, Medical Detection Dogs and Mind (£10,000 each); Revitalise (£5,000).

FINANCES *Financial year end 05/04/2022*
Income £124,100
Grants to organisations £55,000
Assets £4,940,000

TRUSTEES Michael Ferrier; Francis Hughes.

OTHER INFORMATION In 2021/22, grants were awarded to five organisations. Grants were given to projects relating to medical research, health, and sickness.

HOW TO APPLY Apply in writing to the correspondent. The trustees meet periodically. The trustees have a strong preference for helping those with a link to the Freedman family.

CONTACT DETAILS Francis Hughes, Trustee, c/o Bridge House, 11 Creek Road, East Molesey, Surrey KT8 9BE *Tel.* 020 8941 4455
Email francis@hughescollett.co.uk

■ The Freelands Foundation Ltd

CC NO 1162648   **ESTABLISHED** 2015

WHERE FUNDING CAN BE GIVEN UK.

WHO CAN BENEFIT UK-registered or exempt charities; CICs; galleries, museums and other arts organisations; universities.

WHAT IS FUNDED Artists and art organisations; access to the visual arts; art education; research exploring the value of art and culture.

WHAT IS NOT FUNDED Retrospective costs; building works or capital campaigns; individuals; work outside the UK; schools; projects that are solely artistic and do not centre education.

TYPE OF GRANT Project funding; research.

SAMPLE GRANTS Arts Council England (£540,000); MK Gallery (£101,000); Site Gallery (£79,500); Dundee Contemporary Arts (£77,600); Runnymede Trust (£61,900); Camden Art Centre (£32,500); Manchester Metropolitan University (£12,500).

FINANCES *Financial year end 31/12/2021*
Income £440,500
Grants to organisations £2,350,000
Assets £68,430,000

TRUSTEES Mark Devereux; Elisabeth Murdoch; Sarah von Schmidt; Keith Tyson.

OTHER INFORMATION Grants were awarded in the following categories: education (£1.56 million), artists and art organisations (£670,700), and research and publications (£115,200). The foundation awarded 27 grants during the year.

HOW TO APPLY The foundation's website publishes information on how to apply for its various calls for funding. Potential applicants are typically asked to send an expression of interest before completing a full application if it is successful. Full guidelines are released with each funding call – see the website for the most up-to-date information.

CONTACT DETAILS Mark James-Matthews, Grants Administrator, 113 Regent's Park Road, London NW1 8UR *Tel.* 020 3598 7081 *Email* grants@freelandsfoundation.co.uk *Website* http://freelandsfoundation.co.uk

■ Charles S. French Charitable Trust

CC NO 206476   **ESTABLISHED** 1959
WHERE FUNDING CAN BE GIVEN Essex and north-east London.
WHO CAN BENEFIT Registered charities; hospices.
WHAT IS FUNDED Older people; community and arts; people with disabilities; disadvantaged people; medical research; hospices; children and young people.
RANGE OF GRANTS Mostly £1,000 to £5,000 but sometimes larger grants are made for specific projects.
SAMPLE GRANTS Essex Boys and Girls Clubs (£22,400); Camp Knak (£10,000); Essex Dementia Care (£7,500); Healthy Generations (£5,000); Hackney Shed (£4,000); Horatio's Garden (£3,000); Half Moon Young People's Theatre (£2,500); Hearing Dogs for Deaf People (£2,000); Kids N'Action (£1,000); Lambourne End Centre for Outdoor Living (£500).
FINANCES *Financial year end* 31/03/2022
Income £392,400
Grants to organisations £580,000
Assets £11,620,000
TRUSTEES Michael Foster; William Noble; Joanna Thomas; Christopher Noble; James Foster; Antonia McLeod; Edwin Cook.
OTHER INFORMATION Grants were broken down as follows: medical causes (£98,400); disability (£91,400); sport/holiday (£90,700); education (£82,600); older people (£74,800); community (£70,900); disadvantaged (£58,200); hospice (£13,000).
HOW TO APPLY Application forms can be downloaded from the trust's website and should be returned to trustmanager@csfct.org.uk with a copy of your latest accounts.
CONTACT DETAILS The Trustees, 169 High Road, Loughton, Essex IG10 4LF *Tel.* 07936 802044 *Email* trustmanager@csfct.org.uk *Website* www.csfct.org.uk

■ Anne French Memorial Trust

CC NO 254567   **ESTABLISHED** 1963
WHERE FUNDING CAN BE GIVEN Diocese of Norwich (Norfolk).
WHO CAN BENEFIT Individuals; churches; local charities.
WHAT IS FUNDED General charitable purposes; the Anglican Church and clergy.
TYPE OF GRANT Capital cost.
SAMPLE GRANTS A list of beneficiaries was not included in the annual report and accounts.
FINANCES *Financial year end* 05/04/2022
Income £257,800
Grants to organisations £157,000
Grants to individuals £25,200
Assets £7,850,000
TRUSTEES The Ven. Steven Betts; John Jones; The Rt Revd Graham Usher.
OTHER INFORMATION Grants are mainly confined to the needs of the Anglican Church and clergy.
HOW TO APPLY Apply in writing to the correspondent.

CONTACT DETAILS Coraline Nicholls, Administrator, Bishop's House, Norwich, Norfolk NR3 1SB *Tel.* 01603 629001 *Email* coraline.nichols@dioceseofnorwich.org

■ The Freshfield Foundation

CC NO 1003316   **ESTABLISHED** 1991
WHERE FUNDING CAN BE GIVEN UK and overseas.
WHO CAN BENEFIT Registered charities.
WHAT IS FUNDED Climate change; sustainable development; health; education.
RANGE OF GRANTS Up to £100,000.
SAMPLE GRANTS Sustrans (£148,000 in two grants); Motor Neurone Disease Association (£19,800).
FINANCES *Financial year end* 05/04/2022
Income £1,400,000
Grants to organisations £167,800
Assets £31,580,000
TRUSTEES Paul Kurthausen; Patrick Moores; Elizabeth Potter; Noland Carter.
OTHER INFORMATION Grants were broken down as follows: sustainable development and climate change control (£100,000); education, health and general human well-being (£555,200).
HOW TO APPLY The foundation's 2021/22 annual report states: 'The trustees proactively research and identify those organisations and projects that will best achieve the Foundation's aims and objectives and make grants accordingly.'
CONTACT DETAILS Paul Kurthausen, c/o BWM Chartered Accountants Ltd, Suite 5.1, 12 Tithebarn Street, Liverpool L2 2DT *Tel.* 0151 236 1494 *Email* paul.k@bwm.co.uk

■ The Freshgate Trust Foundation

CC NO 221467   **ESTABLISHED** 1941
WHERE FUNDING CAN BE GIVEN South Yorkshire.
WHO CAN BENEFIT Registered charities; unregistered charities; social enterprises; CICs; schools; universities; amateur sports clubs; hospitals; hospices.
WHAT IS FUNDED Education (including travel and training); heritage, restoration and environment; music and the arts; recreation (including holidays and sport); welfare, health and social care.
WHAT IS NOT FUNDED See the foundation's website for a full list of exclusions.
TYPE OF GRANT Capital costs; core/revenue costs; seed funding/start-up funding.
RANGE OF GRANTS Typically between £100 and £2,000.
SAMPLE GRANTS A list of beneficiaries was not included in the annual report and accounts.
FINANCES *Financial year end* 31/12/2021
Income £94,800
Grants to organisations £81,000
Assets £3,950,000
TRUSTEES Holetta Dobson; Usha Fitch; Val Linnemann; Liz Murray; David Stone; Dr Geraldine Russell; Geoff Marston; Neil MacDonald; Alison Gaddes; Matthew Sibley; Jonathan Robinson.
OTHER INFORMATION In 2021, a total of 38 grants were made. Grants were distributed as follows: welfare, health and social care (£30,200); heritage, restoration and environment (£17,500); recreation (£16,600); education (£9,600); music and the arts (£7,000).
HOW TO APPLY Applications can be made online via the foundation's website.
CONTACT DETAILS Emma Legdon, Trust Secretary, The Hart Shaw Building, Europa Link, Sheffield Business Park, Sheffield, South Yorkshire

S9 1XU *Tel.* 0114 251 8850 *Email* emma.
legdon@hartshaw.co.uk *Website* www.freshgate.
org.uk

Friarsgate Trust

CC NO 220762   **ESTABLISHED** 1955

WHERE FUNDING CAN BE GIVEN UK, with a preference
for West Sussex.

WHO CAN BENEFIT Registered charities.

WHAT IS FUNDED Older people; community and family
services; people with disabilities; the education
and training of disadvantaged young people
under the age of 23.

WHAT IS NOT FUNDED Organisations that are not
registered charities; religious organisations;
environmental conservation; medical research;
work related to drug and alcohol addiction; work
related to HIV and AIDS; animal welfare;
projects taking place, or whose beneficiaries are
situated, outside the UK; or work that has
already taken place.

TYPE OF GRANT Capital costs; project funding; core
costs.

RANGE OF GRANTS Up to £20,000 but mostly £500
to £2,000.

SAMPLE GRANTS The JPK Sussex Project (£20,000);
Disabled Sailing (£8,000); Carers Support West
Sussex (£7,000); FitzRoy Support (£5,000);
Tuberous Sclerosis Association (£2,500);
Carousal Project (£750).

FINANCES *Financial year end* 05/04/2022
Income £111,700
Grants to organisations £133,700
Assets £4,400,000

TRUSTEES Sarah Bain; Gillian Livingstone; Robert
Newman; Diana Altman.

OTHER INFORMATION Grants were made to 43
organisations during the year.

HOW TO APPLY Application forms can be downloaded
from the trust's website. The trustees meet four
times a year and applications will normally be
considered at the next meeting following
submission of the application. The usual
quarterly meeting dates are the second Tuesday
of January, April, July and October.

CONTACT DETAILS Olga Powell, c/o Irwin Mitchell
LLP, Thomas Edgar House, Friary Lane,
Chichester, West Sussex PO19 1UF *Tel.* 01243
786111 *Email* friarsgate@irwinmitchell.com
Website http://friarsgatetrust.org.uk

Friends of Boyan Trust

CC NO 1114498   **ESTABLISHED** 2006

WHERE FUNDING CAN BE GIVEN Worldwide.

WHO CAN BENEFIT Orthodox Jewish organisations.

WHAT IS FUNDED Orthodox Jewish religious education
and the relief of poverty in the Orthodox Jewish
community.

RANGE OF GRANTS Up to £300,000.

SAMPLE GRANTS Yazoiree Boyan (£300,000);
Mesifta Tiferet Yisroel (£125,300); Bais Rizhin
Trust (£52,100); North London Cost Shop
(£11,100); Teens United (£7,500).

FINANCES *Financial year end* 31/12/2021
Income £768,500
Grants to organisations £677,100
Grants to individuals £130,100
Assets £28,500

TRUSTEES Jacob Getter; Mordechai Freund; Nathan
Kuflik.

HOW TO APPLY Apply in writing to the correspondent.

CONTACT DETAILS Jacob Getter, Trustee, 23 Durley
Road, London N16 5JW *Tel.* 020 8809 6051

Friends of Essex Churches Trust

CC NO 236033   **ESTABLISHED** 1951

WHERE FUNDING CAN BE GIVEN Essex (including
Thurrock and Southend-on-Sea) and the five
London boroughs formerly part of the county
(Barking and Dagenham, Havering, Newham,
Redbridge and Waltham Forest).

WHO CAN BENEFIT Christian churches.

WHAT IS FUNDED The preservation, repair,
maintenance and improvement of Christian
places of worship.

WHAT IS NOT FUNDED Electrical work (unless there is
a written report by a qualified electrician stating
that electrical installations are a fire hazard);
general lighting; redecoration (unless needed as
part of a scheme of eligible repairs); reseating;
liturgical reordering; the introduction of other
furnishings and fittings.

TYPE OF GRANT One-off grants.

SAMPLE GRANTS A list of beneficiaries was not
included in the annual report and accounts.

FINANCES *Financial year end* 31/12/2021
Income £294,500
Grants to organisations £114,600
Assets £487,200

TRUSTEES Martin Stuchfield; John Pickthorn; Jeremy
Beale; Catherine Leeder; Rachel Grainger; Dr
Francis Bettley; Joanna Pimblett; Gail Jones;
Clare Ford.

HOW TO APPLY Application forms can be downloaded
from the charity's website.

CONTACT DETAILS John Bloomfield, Secretary of the
Grants Committee, 39 Lake Rise, Romford,
Essex RM1 4DZ *Tel.* 01708 745273
Email john.bloomfield@btinternet.com
Website www.foect.org.uk

The Friends of Kent Churches

CC NO 207021   **ESTABLISHED** 1949

WHERE FUNDING CAN BE GIVEN Kent.

WHO CAN BENEFIT Churches.

WHAT IS FUNDED Churches undertaking repairs to
their fabric; church maintenance; church
facilities; roof alarms.

WHAT IS NOT FUNDED Work that has already started;
reordering; redecorating (except where required
for other eligible work); major new facilities;
bells; clocks; organs; churchyards and
churchyard walls (except for monuments of
special importance and works to paths, steps
and handrails necessary to facilitate access).

TYPE OF GRANT Capital grants.

RANGE OF GRANTS £500 to £20,000.

SAMPLE GRANTS St John – Tunstall (£12,500);
St Paulinus – Crayford (£10,000); All Saints –
Maidstone (£6,000); Christ Church –
Bexleyheath (£5,000); St Mary Magdelen –
Denton (£1,300); St Barnabus – Tunbridge
Wells (£1,000); St George – Ivychurch (£480).

FINANCES *Financial year end* 31/12/2021
Income £143,000
Grants to organisations £137,200
Assets £669,500

TRUSTEES Jane Bird; Mary Gibbins; Richard Latham;
Margaret Williams; Sir Paul Britton; The Ven.
Peter Lock; Rosemary Dymond; Raymond Hart.

HOW TO APPLY Application forms are available from
the charity's website, along with full guidelines.
Forms should be returned, preferably by email,
to the correspondent, along with a copy of the
latest audited church accounts and the
accounts of any associated bodies who have
the upkeep of the church as their main
objective. Further information on when to apply
can be found on the charity's website.

394

Does the funder you have chosen match your needs? Haphazard applications waste postage and time

CONTACT DETAILS Deb Sutch, Secretary, Parsonage Farm House, Hampstead Lane, Yalding, Maidstone, Kent ME18 6HG *Tel.* 01622 815569 *Email* debsutch@btinternet.com *Website* www.friendsofkentchurches.co.uk

■ Friends of the National Libraries

CC NO 313020 **ESTABLISHED** 1932
WHERE FUNDING CAN BE GIVEN UK.
WHO CAN BENEFIT The national libraries and the libraries of national museums; record offices and archive services; university and specialist libraries; any museum, gallery or collecting institution to which the public has reasonable access and which, in the opinion of the trustees, constitutes a proper repository for the proposed acquisition.
WHAT IS FUNDED Written and printed heritage.
WHAT IS NOT FUNDED The cost of an item already purchased; the costs of conservation or cataloguing.
TYPE OF GRANT Grants can be used towards the acquisition of: rare printed books; manuscripts; archives of historical, literary, artistic, architectural, musical or other interest; and fine bindings.
RANGE OF GRANTS £200 to £20,000.
SAMPLE GRANTS A list of beneficiaries was not included in the annual report and accounts. Previous beneficiaries have included: University College Cork (£500,000); Dorset History Centre (£18,200); The British Library (£15,000); Bangor University (£10,000); Ashmolean Museum – University of Oxford (£5,000); Cambridge University Library (£2,000); Balliol College (£900); Brighton and Hoe Record Office (£500).
FINANCES *Financial year end* 31/12/2021
Income £16,350,000
Grants to organisations £165,000
Assets £5,660,000
TRUSTEES Charles Sebag-Montefiore; Roland Keating; Prof. Richard Ovenden; Geordie Greig; Dr Jessica Gardner; Pedr Llwyd; Felix Oyens; Joan Winterkorn; Mark Storey; Alexandra Sitwell; Stephen Clarke; Peter Mimpriss; Natalie Livingstone; Richard Linenthal; Dr Amina Shah.
OTHER INFORMATION During the year, 38 grants were awarded totalling £165,000.
HOW TO APPLY Full information on the application process can be found on the charity's website.
CONTACT DETAILS Nell Hoare, Secretary, PO Box 4291, Reading, Berkshire RG8 9JA *Tel.* 01491 598083 *Email* admin@fnlmail.org.uk *Website* www.fnl.org.uk

■ Friends of Wiznitz Ltd

CC NO 255685 **ESTABLISHED** 1948
WHERE FUNDING CAN BE GIVEN Hackney; Haringey; Israel; USA.
WHO CAN BENEFIT Jewish organisations; individuals.
WHAT IS FUNDED Orthodox Jewish religious education; the advancement of the Orthodox Jewish religion; the relief of poverty.
RANGE OF GRANTS Up to £1.6 million.
SAMPLE GRANTS Mosdos Viznitz (£1.6 million); Lehachzikom UK (£164,000); Kollel Viznitz London (£66,000); Mosdos Imrei Chaim (£57,000); Ahavat Israel Synagogue (£53,800).
FINANCES *Financial year end* 31/03/2022
Income £2,960,000
Grants to organisations £2,470,000
Grants to individuals £26,000
Assets £2,970,000

TRUSTEES Shulom Feldman; Henrich Feldman; Ephraim Gottesfeld.
OTHER INFORMATION Grants were broken down as follows: religious education (£1.98 million); relief of poverty (£286,500); advancement of religion (£130,300); social welfare (£65,300). Grants of under £50,000 totalled £260,600.
HOW TO APPLY The 2021/22 annual report advises: 'In general the trustees select the institutions to be supported according to their personal knowledge of work of the institution. While not actively inviting applications, they are always prepared to accept any application which will be carefully considered and help given according to circumstances and funds then available. Applications by individuals must be accompanied by a letter of recommendation by the applicant's minister or other known religious leader.'
CONTACT DETAILS The Trustees, 8 Jessam Avenue, London E5 9DU *Tel.* 020 8806 0017

■ Friends Provident Charitable Foundation

CC NO 1087053 **ESTABLISHED** 2002
WHERE FUNDING CAN BE GIVEN UK.
WHO CAN BENEFIT Registered charities; social enterprise; organisations; community groups; universities.
WHAT IS FUNDED Projects that contribute to a more resilient, sustainable and fairer economic system. Grants have been awarded in the following areas: communicating economic ideas; investor/corporate behaviour; community energy; local development; a fair transition to a low-carbon economy; tax; community assets and convening; diversity, equity and inclusion.
WHAT IS NOT FUNDED Activity that is not based in or likely to have a tangible economic impact on the UK.
TYPE OF GRANT Core/revenue funding; project funding; development funding; capacity building; research; campaigning; unrestricted.
RANGE OF GRANTS Up to £200,000.
SAMPLE GRANTS New Economics Foundation (£200,000); Positive Money (£150,000); Institute for Welsh Affairs (£100,000); The Class Work Project (£88,000); Decolonising Economics (£75,000); Ethical Consumer Research Association (£25,000); The William and Flora Hewlett Foundation (£10,000); Power to Change (£5,000).
FINANCES *Financial year end* 30/09/2022
Income £689,800
Grants to organisations £1,790,000
Assets £23,880,000
TRUSTEES Joanna Elson; Paul Dickinson; Aphra Sklair; Kathleen Kelly; Stephen Muers; Abraham Baldry; Ann Bosco; Stephanie Maier; Paul Blyth; Caroline Taylor.
OTHER INFORMATION During 2021/22, grants totalling £1.79 million were awarded. Out of 161 first-stage applications, 32 were considered for funding. From these, 16 organisations were awarded grants, 3 of which had not previously received a grant from the foundation, and the remaining 13 were previous grant holders.
HOW TO APPLY The foundation has a two-stage application process. First, potential applicants should submit their proposal through an outline application online. These applications are reviewed by an expert advisory group. Successful proposals will then be invited to submit a full stage-two application. Applications can be submitted at any time. Further

information and guidance can be found on the foundation's website.

CONTACT DETAILS The Trustees, Blake House, 18 Blake Street, York YO1 8QG *Tel.* 01904 629675 *Email* enquiries@friendsprovidentfoundation.org.uk *Website* www.friendsprovidentfoundation.org

■ Frognal Trust

CC NO 244444 **ESTABLISHED** 1964
WHERE FUNDING CAN BE GIVEN UK.
WHO CAN BENEFIT Registered charities.
WHAT IS FUNDED Older people; children; disability; blindness; medical research; environmental heritage.
SAMPLE GRANTS A list of beneficiaries was not included in the annual report and accounts.
FINANCES *Financial year end* 05/04/2022
Income £99,900
Grants to organisations £125,200
Assets £3,670,000
TRUSTEES Jennifer Fraser; Caroline Philipson-Stow; Matthew Bennett; Simon Fraser.
OTHER INFORMATION Grants were broken down as follows: children (£37,700); medical research (£30,500); older people (£25,500); people with disabilities (£21,500); environmental heritage (£10,000).
HOW TO APPLY Apply in writing to the correspondent.
CONTACT DETAILS Joyce Salkeld, Correspondent, c/o Wilson Solicitors LLP, Alexandra House, St Johns Street, Salisbury, Wiltshire SP1 2SB *Tel.* 01722 412412 *Email* joyce.salkeld@wilsonsllp.com

■ The Patrick and Helena Frost Foundation

CC NO 1005505 **ESTABLISHED** 1991
WHERE FUNDING CAN BE GIVEN UK.
WHO CAN BENEFIT Registered charities; small organisations.
WHAT IS FUNDED General charitable purposes; social welfare.
WHAT IS NOT FUNDED Individuals.
RANGE OF GRANTS Between £2,000 and £45,000.
SAMPLE GRANTS Royal Marsden Cancer Charity (£45,000); Re-engage Ltd (£30,000); The Catholic Agency for Overseas Development and Ocean Youth Trust South (£20,000 each); Bowel Research UK (£15,000 each); The Gurkha Welfare, London Narrow Boat Project and Tools for Self Reliance Trust (£10,000 each); The Family Holiday Association (£8,000); The Forward Trust (£7,500); Acorn Christian Foundation (£5,000); Cinnamon Network (£3,000); The Fforest Uchaf Horse and Pony Rehabilitation Centre Charitable Trust (£2,000).
FINANCES *Financial year end* 05/04/2022
Income £480,500
Grants to organisations £762,500
Assets £23,970,000
TRUSTEES Dominic Tayler; Neil Hendriksen; Mark Hendriksen; Clare Armitage.
OTHER INFORMATION Grants were awarded to 63 organisations during 2021/22.
HOW TO APPLY The trustees proactively seek and select organisations they wish to support and therefore request that unsolicited applications are not submitted.
CONTACT DETAILS The Trustees, c/o Trowers and Hamlins LLP, 3 Bunhill Row, London EC1Y 8YZ *Tel.* 020 7423 8303 *Email* asorrell@trowers.com

■ The Fulmer Charitable Trust

CC NO 1070428 **ESTABLISHED** 1997
WHERE FUNDING CAN BE GIVEN UK and overseas.
WHO CAN BENEFIT Registered charities; charitable causes.
WHAT IS FUNDED The relief of suffering and hardship; education; religion; general charitable purposes.
TYPE OF GRANT Project funding.
RANGE OF GRANTS Up to £7,500 but mainly £900.
SAMPLE GRANTS Maternity Africa Co. Ltd (£7,500); Church Pastoral Aid Society, Hope For Tomorrow, John Fawcett Foundation and Rainbow Trust (£900 each); Alternatives to Violence Project (£500).
FINANCES *Financial year end* 31/12/2021
Income £357,200
Grants to organisations £216,600
Assets £16,900,000
TRUSTEES Caroline Mytum; John Reis; Sally Reis; The Revd Philip Bromiley; Julia Reis.
HOW TO APPLY Apply in writing to the correspondent.
CONTACT DETAILS The Trustees, 8 The Parade, Marlborough, Wiltshire SN8 1NE *Tel.* 01672 515691

■ The Funding Network

CC NO 1088315 **ESTABLISHED** 2002
WHERE FUNDING CAN BE GIVEN UK and overseas.
WHO CAN BENEFIT Not-for-profit organisations, including: registered charities; CICs; CIOs; social enterprises; grassroots organisations.
WHAT IS FUNDED General charitable purposes, including: human rights; health; education; livelihoods; inclusion; the environment; climate change; crime reduction; peacebuilding.
WHAT IS NOT FUNDED Organisations that are involved in the promotion of religion or a political party; organisations with a turnover of over £1.2 million; fundraising challenges; individuals.
TYPE OF GRANT Project costs; strategic; start-up.
RANGE OF GRANTS Up to £29,000, but mostly up to £10,000.
SAMPLE GRANTS Children Heard and Seen (£28,900); Human Milk Foundation (£25,000); Five Talents (£20,900); Greater Change (£17,800); Key4Life (£12,300); Cornerstone (£9,500); Vulcan Learning Centre (£3,300); Children with Voices (£580).
FINANCES *Financial year end* 31/03/2022
Income £811,000
Grants to organisations £487,800
Assets £177,800
TRUSTEES Michael Chuter; Adrian Coles; Samuel Lush; Kawika Solidum; Ailis Clarke; Fiona Johnston; Ofovwe Aig-Imoukhuede; Christina Chambers; Wendy Brierley; Alan Morton.
OTHER INFORMATION The charity invites non-profit organisations nominated by network members to apply for the opportunity to pitch for funds at its events. The funds raised are then passed on to the organisation by the network in the form of grants.
HOW TO APPLY Organisations must first be sponsored by a Funding Network member. A selection panel will shortlist the strongest candidates and interview these candidates over the phone. Applicants are notified within 48 hours whether they have been selected or not. The charity does not share the details of its current members; however, organisations that do not know a current network member can ask somebody to become a member with a view to nominating them. This could be a trustee, volunteer or someone close to the organisation, but it cannot be somebody who is in paid

employment of the organisation. Once they have signed up, new members are asked to attend and donate at a network event before being eligible to sponsor an organisation.

CONTACT DETAILS The Trustees, Toynbee Hall, 28 Commercial Street, London E1 6LS *Tel.* 020 7846 4070 *Email* info@thefundingnetwork.org. uk *Website* www.thefundingnetwork.org.uk

G

■ G. M. C. Trust

CC NO 288418   **ESTABLISHED** 1965
WHERE FUNDING CAN BE GIVEN West Midlands.
WHO CAN BENEFIT Registered charities.
WHAT IS FUNDED General charitable purposes;
mental health.
WHAT IS NOT FUNDED Individuals.
TYPE OF GRANT Capital costs; core/revenue costs;
seed funding/start-up funding; unrestricted
funding.
RANGE OF GRANTS £1,000 to £25,000.
SAMPLE GRANTS Sense International (£30,000);
Disasters Emergency Committee – Ukraine
Humanitarian Appeal (£12,000); Build It
International (£10,000); Marie Curie (£5,000);
The Bhopal Medical Appeal (£2,000).
FINANCES *Financial year end* 05/04/2022
Income £133,600
Grants to organisations £178,000
Assets £3,970,000
TRUSTEES B. E. S. Cadbury; M. J. Cadbury;
C. E. Fowler-Wright.
OTHER INFORMATION In 2021/22, the trust awarded
30 grants to organisations.
HOW TO APPLY Unsolicited applications are not
accepted.
CONTACT DETAILS Rodney Pitts, Secretary, c/o
Rodney Pitts Chartered Accountants, 4 Fairways,
1240 Warwick Road, Knowle, Solihull, West
Midlands B93 9LL *Tel.* 01564 779971
Email mail@rodneypitts.com *Website* www.
rodneypitts.com/pages/gmc_trust.html

■ The G. R. P. Charitable Trust

CC NO 255733   **ESTABLISHED** 1968
WHERE FUNDING CAN BE GIVEN England and Wales.
WHO CAN BENEFIT Charitable organisations already
known to the trustees.
WHAT IS FUNDED Jewish causes; general charitable
causes.
WHAT IS NOT FUNDED Individuals.
RANGE OF GRANTS From £200 to £39,500.
SAMPLE GRANTS Previous beneficiaries have
included: The A. M. Charitable Trust (£3 million);
UK Toremet Ltd (£500,000); West London
Synagogue (£200,000); Anglo-Israel Association
(£25,000); Institute for Policy Research
(£1,000).
FINANCES *Financial year end* 05/10/2021
Income £5,500
Grants to organisations £433,800
TRUSTEE SG Kleinwort Hambros Trust Company (UK)
Ltd.
OTHER INFORMATION Full accounts for 2020/21 were
not available to view on the Charity
Commission's website due to the trust's low
income. We have therefore estimated the grant
total based on the trust's total expenditure. The
2020/21 financial information was the latest
available information at the time of writing (May
2023).
HOW TO APPLY Unsolicited applications are not
accepted.
CONTACT DETAILS The Trustees, c/o SG Kleinwort
Hambros Bank Ltd, 1 Bank Street, London
E14 4SG *Tel.* 020 3207 7232

■ The Gale Family Charity Trust

CC NO 289212   **ESTABLISHED** 1984
WHERE FUNDING CAN BE GIVEN UK, with a preference
for Bedfordshire.
WHO CAN BENEFIT Registered charities; schools;
amateur sports clubs; hospitals; religious
bodies/institutions.
WHAT IS FUNDED General charitable purposes.
TYPE OF GRANT Project funding; unrestricted funding.
SAMPLE GRANTS A list of beneficiaries was not
included in the annual report and accounts.
FINANCES *Financial year end* 05/04/2022
Income £205,000
Grants to organisations £312,600
Assets £5,920,000
TRUSTEES John Tyley; Alistair Law; Doreen Watson;
Warwick Browning; Charles Codrington; David
Fletcher; Russell Beard; John Cleverley; Alison
Phillipson.
HOW TO APPLY Apply in writing to the correspondent.
The trustees meet every six months to award
grants.
CONTACT DETAILS The Trustees, Northwood House,
138 Bromham Road, Bedford, Bedfordshire
MK40 2QW *Tel.* 01234 354508
Email galefamilytrust@gmail.com

■ GambleAware

CC NO 1093910   **ESTABLISHED** 2002
WHERE FUNDING CAN BE GIVEN England; Scotland;
Wales.
WHO CAN BENEFIT Registered charities; research
organisations; NHS trusts.
WHAT IS FUNDED Education, prevention and
treatment services and research aimed at
minimising the impact of gambling.
TYPE OF GRANT Research.
RANGE OF GRANTS Up to £2 million.
SAMPLE GRANTS Citizens Advice – Gambling Support
Service (£1.78 million); Adferiad Residential
Rehab Complex (£1.76 million); Fast Forward –
Scottish Education Hub (£886,000); Ipsos Mori
(£300,000); Adferiad – Welsh Education Hub
(£297,000); Gordon Moody Association
(£251,000); IFF Research – Building Knowledge
Women's Lived Experience (£234,000).
FINANCES *Financial year end* 31/03/2022
Income £34,970,000
Grants to organisations £4,680,000
Assets £31,250,000
TRUSTEES Baroness Kathryn Lampard; Prof. Sian
Griffiths; Michelle Highman; Saffron Cordery;
Paul Simpson; Rachel Pearce; Marina Gibbs;
Mubin Haq; Dr Koravangattu Valsraj; The Rt
Hon. Baroness Hilary Armstrong.
OTHER INFORMATION During 2021/22, grants were
awarded to eight organisations. Grants were
distributed as follows: treatment (£2.01 million);
research (£560,000); education (£2.91 million).
HOW TO APPLY The 2021/22 annual report states:
'GambleAware does not offer funding in
response to speculative applications, but from
time to time does issue open tenders when
there is the opportunity to bid for funding for
innovative projects within a broader field.' See
the charity's website for more details.
CONTACT DETAILS The Trustees, Pennine Place, 2A
Charing Cross Road, London WC2H 0HF
Tel. 020 7287 1994 *Email* info@gambleaware.
org *Website* http://about.gambleaware.org

■ The Gannochy Trust

OSCR NO SC003133　　**ESTABLISHED** 1937

WHERE FUNDING CAN BE GIVEN Scotland, with a strong preference for the Perth and Kinross area.

WHO CAN BENEFIT OSCR-registered charities.

WHAT IS FUNDED Community development; social welfare; employability; education; the natural and built environment.

TYPE OF GRANT Core funding; project funding; capital costs. Funding may be awarded for up to three years.

SAMPLE GRANTS Live Active Leisure (£687,000); Aerospace Scientific Educational Trust (£250,000); Perth Autism Support (£150,000); Remake Scotland (£118,800).

FINANCES *Financial year end* 30/06/2022
Income £3,540,000
Grants to organisations £7,510,000
Assets £202,860,000

TRUSTEES Jane Mudd; David Gray; Stephen Hay; Bruce Renfrew; Roland Bean; Alisa Macmillan; Ruth Ogston; Karen Reid.

OTHER INFORMATION Grants were broken down as follows: improving quality of life for people – Perth and Kinross (£3.5 million); developing and inspiring young people – Scotland-wide including Perth and Kinross (£2.78 million); capital projects – Perth and Kinross (£1.21 million); other (£24,200). Only beneficiaries of grants of £100,000 and above were listed in the accounts.

HOW TO APPLY There are a number of documents that applicants must complete, including an application form. These are available to download from the trust's very informative website, where detailed guidance notes can also be found. Completed applications may be submitted by email. The trustees meet at least four times per year to consider applications, which may be submitted at any time.

CONTACT DETAILS Grants Team, Pitcullen Crescent, Perth, Perthshire PH2 7HX *Tel.* 01738 620653 *Email* grants@gannochytrust.org.uk *Website* www.gannochytrust.org.uk

■ Ganzoni Charitable Trust

CC NO 263583　　**ESTABLISHED** 1971

WHERE FUNDING CAN BE GIVEN Suffolk.

WHO CAN BENEFIT Registered charities; churches; hospices; hospitals; schools.

WHAT IS FUNDED General charitable purposes, including: relief of poverty; advancement of Christianity; education.

TYPE OF GRANT Mainly capital projects.

RANGE OF GRANTS Up to £5,000.

SAMPLE GRANTS Britten Pears Arts (£5,000); Future Inclusions Organisation (£4,000); Papworth Trust (£2,500); Colchester and Ipswich Hospitals Charity and Stradbroke Baptist Church (£2,000 each); Cardiac Risk in the Young and Young Women's Trust (£1,000 each); Cancer Support UK (£500); St Edmundsbury and Ipswich Diocesan Board of Finance (£250).

FINANCES *Financial year end* 05/04/2022
Income £224,800
Grants to organisations £140,500
Assets £5,450,000

TRUSTEES The Hon. Charles Boscawen; The Hon. Mary Ganzoni; John Pickering; Louise Long.

HOW TO APPLY Apply in writing to the correspondent.

CONTACT DETAILS The Trustees, c/o Birketts LLP, Providence House, 141–145 Princes Street, Ipswich, Suffolk IP1 1QJ *Tel.* 01473 232300 *Email* bill-white@birketts.co.uk

■ The Garrick Charitable Trust

CC NO 1071279　　**ESTABLISHED** 1998

WHERE FUNDING CAN BE GIVEN UK.

WHO CAN BENEFIT UK-registered charities.

WHAT IS FUNDED Theatre; music (including opera); dance; literature.

WHAT IS NOT FUNDED Drama, dance or music conservatoire training or academic studies; amateur productions; projects outside the UK; capital appeals.

TYPE OF GRANT Project funding.

RANGE OF GRANTS Usually £2,500 to £5,000.

SAMPLE GRANTS Previous beneficiaries have included: British Youth Opera (£5,000); Birmingham Hippodrome (£4,000); China Plate Theatre and London Symphony Orchestra (£2,500 each); Good Chance Theatre (£1,000).

FINANCES *Financial year end* 31/12/2021
Income £22,100
Grants to organisations £220,000

TRUSTEES Sir Stephen Waley-Cohen; John Coldstream; Dr Nigel Brown; Joseph Seelig; David Whelton.

OTHER INFORMATION Full accounts were not available to view on the Charity Commission's website due to the trust's low income. We have therefore estimated the trust's grant total based on its total expenditure.

HOW TO APPLY Details of the trust's two-stage application process can be found on its website. There is no deadline for applications but the trustees meet quarterly, usually in early March, June, September and December, and applications should be received in good time before a meeting to be considered.

CONTACT DETAILS The Trustees, Garrick Club, 15 Garrick Street, London WC2E 9AY *Email* charitabletrust@garrickclub.co.uk *Website* www.garrickclub.co.uk/charitable_trust

■ Garthgwynion Charities

CC NO 229334　　**ESTABLISHED** 1963

WHERE FUNDING CAN BE GIVEN Powys and the historic county of Montgomeryshire.

WHO CAN BENEFIT Charitable organisations; individuals.

WHAT IS FUNDED General charitable purposes.

SAMPLE GRANTS Derwenlas Community Centre; Dyfi Eco Valley Partnership; Harrow 450 Fund; The Machynlleth Tabernacle Trust.

FINANCES *Financial year end* 05/04/2022
Income £52,400
Grants to organisations £72,600
Assets £114,400

TRUSTEES Diana Walters; Rosie Lochiel-Owen; Elizabeth Frost.

HOW TO APPLY Apply in writing to the correspondent.

CONTACT DETAILS The Trustees, 9B Matham Road, East Molesey, Surrey KT8 0SX *Tel.* 020 8941 4088 *Email* Garthgwynioncharities@gmail.com

■ The Gatsby Charitable Foundation

CC NO 251988　　**ESTABLISHED** 1967

WHERE FUNDING CAN BE GIVEN Worldwide, with a preference for the UK and East Africa.

WHO CAN BENEFIT Registered charities only. Many beneficiary organisations are specialist research institutes.

WHAT IS FUNDED Plant science; neuroscience; STEM education; Africa; public policy; the arts.

TYPE OF GRANT Project funding; core costs, including salaries; research.

SAMPLE GRANTS Gatsby Africa (£15.18 million); University College London (£9.38 million); University of Cambridge (£8.41 million); Royal Academy of Music (£6 million); Backstage Trust (£2 million); Chamber Orchestra of Europe (£750,000); Imperial College London (£306,000); Cajal Advanced Neuroscience Training Program (£213,000); British Neuroscience Association (£150,000).

FINANCES *Financial year end* 05/04/2022
Income £142,720,000
Grants to organisations £77,830,000
Assets £604,400,000

TRUSTEES Sir Andrew Cahn; Judith Portrait; Joseph Burns.

OTHER INFORMATION The charity is one of the Sainsbury Family Charitable Trusts, which share a common administration – see www.sftc.org.uk for more information.

HOW TO APPLY The trustees take a proactive approach to grant-making; unsolicited applications are not considered.

CONTACT DETAILS The Trustees, The Peak, 5 Wilton Road, London SW1V 1AP *Tel.* 020 7410 0330 *Email* contact@gatsby.org.uk *Website* www.gatsby.org.uk

■ Gatwick Airport Community Trust

CC NO 1089683   **ESTABLISHED** 2001

WHERE FUNDING CAN BE GIVEN Parts of East and West Sussex, Kent and Surrey, but particularly communities directly affected by operations at Gatwick Airport.

WHO CAN BENEFIT Registered charities; unregistered charities; social Enterprises; schools; PTAs; hospices; religious bodies/institutions.

WHAT IS FUNDED Children and young people; art; sports facilities; the environment and conservation; community facilities; people with disabilities; older people; development of volunteering.

WHAT IS NOT FUNDED Projects or beneficiaries that are completely or largely outside the area of benefit; recurrent expenditure or running costs; ongoing costs maintenance or deficits; repeat annual applications for similar projects; costs that should be funded from other sources (e.g. public bodies); organisations that have statutory responsibilities (e.g. local authorities, hospitals and schools) unless the application is for a project that is over and above their core activities; the purchase of land or buildings; organisations that are working to make a profit for shareholders, partners or sole owners; individuals; salaries. Organisations with excess free reserves are not normally supported.

TYPE OF GRANT Capital costs; project funding; seed funding/start-up funding.

RANGE OF GRANTS Mostly up to £5,000.

SAMPLE GRANTS Crawley Youth Centre and Surrey East Girlguiding (£5,000 each); Crawley Film Initiative CIC (£3,500); Ifield Tennis Club and YMCA East Surrey (£3,000 each).

FINANCES *Financial year end* 31/12/2021
Income £236,000
Grants to organisations £205,700
Assets £50,400

TRUSTEES Richard Burrett; Julie Ayres; Alan Jones; Elizabeth McDermid; Joanna Rettie; Helyn Clack; Angela Baker; Andrew Lynch.

OTHER INFORMATION Grants were made to 96 organisations. Only organisations that received grants of over £3,000 were listed as beneficiaries in the charity's accounts.

HOW TO APPLY Application forms are available to download from the trust's helpful website along with more information about application guidelines.

CONTACT DETAILS Rosamund Quade, Administrator, GACT, PO Box 783, Chichester, West Sussex PO19 9TY *Tel.* 07444 737518 *Email* mail@gact.org.uk *Website* www.gact.org.uk

■ The Gaudio Family Foundation (UK) Ltd

CC NO 1157301   **ESTABLISHED** 2014

WHERE FUNDING CAN BE GIVEN England and Wales.

WHO CAN BENEFIT Registered charities.

WHAT IS FUNDED General charitable purposes including: relieving poverty, especially in urban areas; advancing and improving education, particularly for disadvantaged children.

RANGE OF GRANTS Mostly under £150,000.

SAMPLE GRANTS Gaudio Family Foundation (£2.17 million); St Giles Trust and West London Zone (£150,000 each); Just for Kids Law, Place2Be and Refugee Action (£75,000 each).

FINANCES *Financial year end* 31/12/2021
Income £11,360,000
Grants to organisations £3,670,000
Assets £43,210,000

TRUSTEES Julius Gaudio; Belma Gaudio; Alfred Cavallaro.

OTHER INFORMATION Grants were awarded to 14 organisations.

HOW TO APPLY Applications can be made in writing to the foundation. Grant recipients will be required to produce project reports.

CONTACT DETAILS The Trustees, c/o Withers LLP, Third Floor, 20 Old Bailey, London EC4M 7AN *Tel.* 020 7597 6000 *Email* ac@fultonvittoria.com

■ The Robert Gavron Charitable Trust

CC NO 268535   **ESTABLISHED** 1974

WHERE FUNDING CAN BE GIVEN UK.

WHO CAN BENEFIT Registered charities.

WHAT IS FUNDED General charitable purposes, in particular: access to the arts; education; social policy and research; prison reform; human rights; disability.

RANGE OF GRANTS Mostly up to £20,000.

SAMPLE GRANTS Mary Rose Trust (£60,000); House of Illustration (£50,000); Jackson's Lane Centre (£30,000); Open Democracy and University Jewish Chaplaincy (£5,000 each); Body Dysmorphic Disorder Foundation (£3,000).

FINANCES *Financial year end* 05/04/2022
Income £1,650,000
Grants to organisations £451,500
Assets £10,440,000

TRUSTEES Sarah Gavron; Charles Corman; Jessica Gavron; Dr Kate Gavron.

OTHER INFORMATION Only organisations that received grants of over £3,000 were listed as beneficiaries in the charity's accounts. Grants of under £3,000 totalled £25,300.

HOW TO APPLY Apply in writing to the correspondent. The trustees meet formally approximately four times a year.

CONTACT DETAILS The Trustees, 27 Maywin Drive, Hornchurch, Essex RM11 3ST *Tel.* 020 7400 4301 *Email* office@rgct.org.uk

◼ Martin Geddes Charitable Trust

cc no 1159776 **ESTABLISHED** 2014
WHERE FUNDING CAN BE GIVEN England and Wales.
WHO CAN BENEFIT Registered charities; charitable organisations.
WHAT IS FUNDED Support for people with a drug or alcohol dependency. According to the trust's website, preference is given to organisations that 'apply a 12-step philosophy'.
TYPE OF GRANT Project funding.
SAMPLE GRANTS 1 North East; Create Recovery; Foundation for Change; Hebron Trust; Kenward Trust; Pushing Change; New Note Orchestra; Recovery Through Nature; The Living Room.
FINANCES *Financial year end* 27/08/2021
Income £132,300
Grants to organisations £88,200
Assets £684,900
TRUSTEES Dr Sally Geddes; Michael Collins; Alexander Geddes; Judi Geisler; Jeremy Green; Catherine O'Connor.
OTHER INFORMATION Grants were awarded to ten organisations during the year. The 2020/21 accounts were the latest available at the time of writing (June 2023).
HOW TO APPLY Application forms can be downloaded from the trust's website. Completed forms should be returned to the correspondent by email.
CONTACT DETAILS The Trustees, Parkfield, Woodend, Styal, Wilmslow, Cheshire SK9 4HF *Tel.* 01625 540850 *Email* admin@ martingeddescharitabletrust.org *Website* http:// martingeddescharitabletrust.org

◼ Sir Robert Geffery's Almshouse Trust

cc no 219153 **ESTABLISHED** 1988
WHERE FUNDING CAN BE GIVEN UK.
WHO CAN BENEFIT Registered charities; schools.
WHAT IS FUNDED Education of disadvantaged children and young people.
WHAT IS NOT FUNDED Large projects towards which a contribution from the trust would have a limited impact; general appeals or circulars; replacement of statutory funding; general running costs (however, a reasonable proportion of overheads will be accepted as part of project costs); medical treatment, health care, counselling and therapy; course fees for professionals; research projects; bursaries; schools (unless a registered charity for children/ young people with disabilities); fundraising events and sponsorship; projects that begin before the date of the relevant committee meeting; building work; holidays.
TYPE OF GRANT Project funding.
RANGE OF GRANTS Up to £10,000.
SAMPLE GRANTS Make Believe Arts (£31,800); The Island Trust Ltd (£30,000); University of Oxford (£10,000); Guildhall School Trust and Imperial College (£5,000 each); College of Arms Trust (£500).
FINANCES *Financial year end* 31/03/2022
Income £8,950,000
Grants to organisations £602,800
Assets £44,450,000
TRUSTEE The Ironmongers' Trust Company.
OTHER INFORMATION The trust has five other linked charities collectively known as the Ironmongers' Charities.
HOW TO APPLY Application forms can be downloaded from the Ironmongers' website.
CONTACT DETAILS The Trustees, Ironmongers' Hall, Barbican, London EC2Y 8AA *Email* charities@ ironmongers.org *Website* www.ironmongers.org/ charitable-grants

◼ General Charity (Coventry)

cc no 216235 **ESTABLISHED** 1983
WHERE FUNDING CAN BE GIVEN Within the boundary of the city of Coventry.
WHO CAN BENEFIT Charitable organisations benefitting residents of Coventry.
WHAT IS FUNDED Social care and development including services for children and young people, older people, people with disabilities and people experiencing homelessness; education; medical research; health care including the prevention and treatment of specific diseases.
TYPE OF GRANT Core costs; capital costs; project funding.
RANGE OF GRANTS Between £5,000 and £90,000.
SAMPLE GRANTS Warwickshire and Northampton Air Ambulance (£90,000); Coventry Boys and Girls Club (£37,500); Macmillan Cancer Support (£10,000); Relate Coventry (£8,000); Langar Aid (£1,200).
FINANCES *Financial year end* 31/03/2022
Income £1,900,000
Grants to organisations £992,200
Assets £14,210,000
TRUSTEES Edward Curtis; David Evans; Michael Harris; Marcus Lapsa; David Mason; Terry Proctor; Richard Smith; Vivien Kershaw; Catherine Miks; Julia McNaney; Cllr Ram Lakha; Dr Roger Davies; Cllr Joseph Clifford; Cllr Tarlochan Singh Jandu; Simon Sharpe.
OTHER INFORMATION Grants were distributed as follows: social care and development (£587,700); health care (£231,500); medical causes (£96,400); education (£76,800).
HOW TO APPLY Apply in writing to the correspondent.
CONTACT DETAILS Susan Hanrahan, Clerk to the Trustees, Old Bablake, Hill Street, Coventry, Warwickshire CV1 4AN *Tel.* 024 7622 2769 *Email* cov.genchar@outlook.com

◼ The General Nursing Council for England and Wales Trust

cc no 288068 **ESTABLISHED** 1983
WHERE FUNDING CAN BE GIVEN England and Wales.
WHO CAN BENEFIT Universities and other public bodies benefitting nurses.
WHAT IS FUNDED Research into matters directly affecting nursing or the nursing profession.
WHAT IS NOT FUNDED Organisational overheads; purchase of equipment; dissemination costs such as conference attendance and publications.
TYPE OF GRANT Research costs.
RANGE OF GRANTS The normal maximum award is £40,000.
SAMPLE GRANTS University of South Wales (£39,900); University of York (£39,100); Oxford Brookes University (£38,400).
FINANCES *Financial year end* 31/03/2022
Income £89,900
Grants to organisations £117,400
Assets £3,700,000
TRUSTEES Prof. Kate Gerrish; Dr Susan Procter; Prof. Janice Sigsworth; Prof. Anne Topping; Prof. Lynne Wigens; Prof. Daniel Kelly.
OTHER INFORMATION Twenty-seven grant applications were received during 2021/22, of which three were successful. Each year there is a call for research grant applications with a specific focus – see the website for further information.

HOW TO APPLY Application forms can be downloaded from the trust's website.

CONTACT DETAILS The Trustees, 29 Beech Way, Blackmore End, Wheathamstead, Hertsfordshire AL4 8LY *Email* gnct@btinternet.com *Website* www.gnct.org.uk

■ The Generational Foundation

CC NO 1192397   **ESTABLISHED** 2020
WHERE FUNDING CAN BE GIVEN UK.
WHO CAN BENEFIT Charitable organisations.
WHAT IS FUNDED General charitable purposes including medical research, education and children and young people.
RANGE OF GRANTS Up to £60,000.
SAMPLE GRANTS The Sutton Trust (£60,000); The Outward Bound Trust (£50,000); Spinal Research (£5,000).
FINANCES *Financial year end 31/12/2021*
Income £1,250,000
Grants to organisations £115,000
Assets £1,130,000
TRUSTEES Meg Headley; Andrew Headley; Zoe Cronin.
HOW TO APPLY Apply in writing to the correspondent.
CONTACT DETAILS The Trustees, Withers LLP, 20 Old Bailey, London EC4M 7AN *Email* Generational. Foundation@outlook.com

■ The Generations Foundation

CC NO 1110565   **ESTABLISHED** 2005
WHERE FUNDING CAN BE GIVEN UK; the London Borough of Merton; financially developing countries.
WHO CAN BENEFIT Local charitable organisations in Merton; UK-registered charities working in the UK and in financially developing countries.
WHAT IS FUNDED The provision of a better quality of life for children who are disadvantaged, ill or who have disabilities; environmental protection and conservation projects.
TYPE OF GRANT Capital costs; project funding; development funding. Funding is often awarded for several years.
RANGE OF GRANTS £500 to £60,000.
SAMPLE GRANTS British Red Cross (£60,000); Jigsaw4u (£40,000); Home-Start Merton (£25,000); Rozmanita (£15,000) Down's South London (£12,500); Prodigal Bikes (£8,000); Wimbledon Guild (£5,000); Malawi Schools Trust (£2,000); Stem4 (£500).
FINANCES *Financial year end 05/04/2022*
Income £250,000
Grants to organisations £323,100
Assets £40,600
TRUSTEES Stephen Finch; Rohini Finch; Bob Finch.
OTHER INFORMATION Funding was awarded to 22 organisations during the year.
HOW TO APPLY Application forms are available to download from the website. Potential applicants should contact the foundation by email before applying, to gauge whether their application is likely to be successful.
CONTACT DETAILS The Trustees, 36 Marryat Road, Wimbledon, London SW19 5BD *Tel.* 07977 773365 *Email* generationstrust@mail.com *Website* www.generationsct.co.uk

■ The George Family Foundation

CC NO 1192385   **ESTABLISHED** 2020
WHERE FUNDING CAN BE GIVEN England and Wales.
WHO CAN BENEFIT Charitable organisations.
WHAT IS FUNDED General charitable purposes.
RANGE OF GRANTS Up to £25,000.
SAMPLE GRANTS Game and Wildlife Conservation Trust (£25,000); Northamptonshire County Cricket Club (£15,000); Royal Botanical Gardens Kew (£10,000); Country Food Trust (£1,500).
FINANCES *Financial year end 31/03/2022*
Income £100,000
Grants to organisations £83,300
Assets £13,600
TRUSTEES Martin George; Michael George; Simone George.
HOW TO APPLY Apply in writing to the correspondent.
CONTACT DETAILS The Trustees, Victoria Mills, London Road, Wellingborough NN8 2DT *Email* donations@thegeorgefamilyfoundation.org.uk

■ The Gertner Charitable Trust

CC NO 327380   **ESTABLISHED** 1987
WHERE FUNDING CAN BE GIVEN UK and overseas.
WHO CAN BENEFIT Jewish charities and individuals.
WHAT IS FUNDED Jewish charitable purposes, including: education; health; welfare.
RANGE OF GRANTS Between £500 and £79,700.
SAMPLE GRANTS Achisomoch Aid Company Ltd (£79,700); Diaspora Yeshiva New York (£41,500); Chasdei Aharon (£28,500); Torat Emet (£25,000); Keren Shabbos (£21,000); Torah (5759) Ltd (£6,900); Friends of Beis Yisroel Trust (£6,000); Merkas Hatzedaka (£1,700); Kef Kids (£500).
FINANCES *Financial year end 31/03/2022*
Income £790,100
Grants to organisations £278,300
Grants to individuals £35,000
Assets £4,310,000
TRUSTEES Michelle Gertner; Simon Jacobs; Mendi Gertner; Moises Gertner.
HOW TO APPLY Apply in writing to the correspondent. The trustees meet quarterly.
CONTACT DETAILS The Trustees, Fordgate House, Union House, 1 Allsop Place, London NW1 5LF *Tel.* 020 7224 1234

■ The Tara Getty Foundation

CC NO 1107895   **ESTABLISHED** 2004
WHERE FUNDING CAN BE GIVEN UK and overseas.
WHO CAN BENEFIT Charitable organisations.
WHAT IS FUNDED Conservation; the environment; climate change; community development; education; health and saving lives; medical research; mental health; disaster relief; children and young people; research.
SAMPLE GRANTS Africa Foundation; The Maven Project; Milton Abbey School; Ocean Family Foundation; Wellington College.
FINANCES *Financial year end 31/12/2021*
Income £324,800
Grants to organisations £326,300
Assets £49,200
TRUSTEES Patrick Maxwell; Tara Getty; Louise Creasey.
OTHER INFORMATION Grants were awarded to 16 organisations during the year in the following categories: education (£155,200); marine conservation (£107,100); community (£29,800); medical causes (£19,200); Young

People (£15,000). The individual grant amounts were not listed in the accounts. See the foundation's 2021 annual report for a detailed list of its updated objectives.

HOW TO APPLY Apply in writing to the correspondent. Shortlisted charities will be contacted for more detailed information. The foundation requests a full breakdown of the project, detailed financial statements and a breakdown of secured and projected income for the upcoming year.

CONTACT DETAILS The Trustees, 26 Curzon Street, London W1J 7TQ *Tel.* 020 7409 3900

······································

■ J. Paul Getty Jr General Charitable Trust

CC NO 292360 **ESTABLISHED** 1985

WHERE FUNDING CAN BE GIVEN UK.

WHO CAN BENEFIT Mainly registered charities. Priority is likely to be given to projects in less prosperous parts of the country, particularly outside London and the South East, and to those which cover more than one beneficial area.

WHAT IS FUNDED Social welfare; arts; conservation and the environment.

WHAT IS NOT FUNDED Individuals; organisations based outside the UK; schools; universities; or public sector organisations; routine maintenance, repairs, refurbishment or modernisation costs; large-scale development projects, such as church restoration work or the construction of new village halls and local community centres; medical care or general health and well-being programmes; one-off events; residential or adventure trips.

TYPE OF GRANT Capital or recurrent; core funding and salaries are considered.

RANGE OF GRANTS Small grants: up to £5,000; main grants: over £5,000.

SAMPLE GRANTS A list of beneficiaries was not available.

FINANCES *Financial year end 31/12/2021*
Income £90
Grants to organisations £285,000

TRUSTEES Lady Getty; Christopher Purvis; Zain Alatas.

OTHER INFORMATION This trust has no connection with the Getty Foundation in the USA. In accordance with the express wishes of Sir Paul Getty Jnr, the trustees decided in 2011 to wind down the trust. It is likely that the trust will close to new applications within the next two years, and at least six months' notice will be provided on the website. Full accounts were not available to view on the Charity Commission's website due to the trust's low income. We have therefore estimated the trust's grant total based on its total expenditure.

HOW TO APPLY The trust no longer accepts unsolicited applications.

CONTACT DETAILS Christopher Purvis, Trustee, 4 Queensborough Studios, London W2 3SQ *Tel.* 020 7262 1470 *Email* christopher@purvis.co.uk *Website* www.jpgettytrust.org.uk

······································

■ The Gibbons Family Trust

CC NO 290884 **ESTABLISHED** 1984

WHERE FUNDING CAN BE GIVEN Devon, with a preference for East Devon, and the Isle of Thanet in Kent.

WHO CAN BENEFIT Registered charities; not-for-profit organisations; individuals.

WHAT IS FUNDED Social welfare, education, and training and recreation of children and young people up to the age of 25.

WHAT IS NOT FUNDED Ongoing fees (e.g. regular payments for education); individuals taking trips overseas; retrospective expenditure; private schools, colleges and similar institutions.

TYPE OF GRANT Capital costs; project funding.

RANGE OF GRANTS £1,000 to £3,000.

SAMPLE GRANTS Honiton Town Youth Football Club (£4,800); Families for Children Adoption (£3,000); St Peter's Primary School – Budleigh (£2,500); Student Life (£2,000); Woodbury Salterton Church of England Primary School (£1,000); Friends of South Dartmoor Association (£350).

FINANCES *Financial year end 31/03/2022*
Income £94,000
Grants to organisations £88,900
Grants to individuals £6,000
Assets £2,300,000

TRUSTEES Dr John Frankish; Elizabeth Lee; Prof. Chris King; Dr Clive Stubbings.

OTHER INFORMATION Grants totalling £94,900 were awarded to organisations and individuals during the year. Grants were broken down as follows: charities in Devon (£66,400); charities in Isle of Thanet, Kent (£20,500); individuals (£6,000); charities in Devon and Isle of Thanet, Kent (£2,000).

HOW TO APPLY Applications can be made through an online form on the trust's website as well as the application criteria for each grant category. Only one application from any applicant will be considered in any financial year (April to March).

CONTACT DETAILS The Trustees, The Gibbons Trusts, 24 Philip Avenue, Barnstaple, Devon EX31 3AQ *Tel.* 07483 335759 *Email* enquiries@gibbonstrusts.org *Website* https://gibbonstrusts.org.uk

······································

■ The David Gibbons Foundation

CC NO 1134727

WHERE FUNDING CAN BE GIVEN Devon.

WHO CAN BENEFIT Registered charities; non-profit organisations; individuals.

WHAT IS FUNDED People with illnesses or disabilities; people who are experiencing financial hardship; older people.

WHAT IS NOT FUNDED Fees or payments of an ongoing nature (such as payments for education); trips overseas for any reason; private schools; retrospective expenditure.

RANGE OF GRANTS £500 to £5,000.

SAMPLE GRANTS Axe Valley Ring and Ride (£5,000); Homemaker South West (£4,000); Dartmouth Caring (£3,600); Axminster Community Shed (£3,000); Tarka Child Contact Centre (£2,000); Live Music Now – South West (£1,000); Budleigh Community Workshop Trust (£500).

FINANCES *Financial year end 31/03/2022*
Income £124,600
Grants to organisations £110,900
Grants to individuals £10,200
Assets £3,690,000

TRUSTEES John Frankish; Prof. Chris King; Simon Barnet; Elizabeth Lee.

HOW TO APPLY Application forms and further information on how to apply can be found on the foundation's website.

CONTACT DETAILS The Trustees, 24 Philip Avenue, Barnstaple, Devon EX31 3AQ *Tel.* 07483 335759 *Email* enquiries@gibbonstrusts.org *Website* https://gibbonstrusts.org.uk/david-gibbons-foundation

■ The Gibbs Charitable Trusts

CC NO 207997 ESTABLISHED 1946

WHERE FUNDING CAN BE GIVEN UK, with a preference for Wales, and overseas.

WHO CAN BENEFIT Registered charities; CICs.

WHAT IS FUNDED Methodist churches and organisations; health; welfare; arts and culture; education; international aid.

TYPE OF GRANT Buildings; capital and project grants.

RANGE OF GRANTS Mostly between £500 and £10,000.

SAMPLE GRANTS Christian Aid (£41,000); Welsh National Opera (£6,000); Brecon Baroque Festival (£5,000); Age UK (£4,000); Womankind (£1,000).

FINANCES *Financial year end 31/03/2022*
Income £100,800
Grants to organisations £219,000
Assets £3,660,000

TRUSTEES Elizabeth Gibbs; Dr John Gibbs; Andrew Gibbs; Dr John Gibbs; James Gibbs; William Gibbs; Rosetta Gibbs; James Gibbs; Rebecca Gibbs; Celia Gibbs; Dr Jessica Gibbs; Patience Gibbs; Timothy Gibbs.

OTHER INFORMATION Grants were broken down as follows: international (£122,700); arts, drama and music (£41,000); social, educational and medical need (£36,000); Methodist churches (£10,500); other Christian causes (£6,300); other Methodist initiatives (£2,500).

HOW TO APPLY Apply using the online portal available on the trust's website.

CONTACT DETAILS James Gibbs, Trustee, 8 Victoria Square, Bristol BS8 4ET *Tel.* 0117 973 6615 *Email* jamesgibbs@btinternet.com *Website* www.gibbstrust.org.uk

■ The G. C. Gibson Charitable Trust

CC NO 258710 ESTABLISHED 1968

WHERE FUNDING CAN BE GIVEN Worldwide (charities must be UK-registered).

WHO CAN BENEFIT Small and medium-sized charities operating in the UK.

WHAT IS FUNDED General charitable purposes, with grants falling within the following categories: civil society; health and medical research; education; nature conservation; care; art; music and entertainment; religion; hospices. The majority of support is already committed to existing beneficiaries; however, the trust supports around ten new applicants each year. New applications are focused on a particular theme, which can vary depending on the year.

WHAT IS NOT FUNDED The fabric of Christian churches; hospices; educational farms; riding and carriage driving for people with disabilities; cancer care and research; theatres; museums.

TYPE OF GRANT Mainly recurring grants for core costs; capital and one-off project costs are also supported.

RANGE OF GRANTS Normally £1,000 to £10,000, depending on the annual theme.

SAMPLE GRANTS A list of beneficiaries was not included in the annual report and accounts.

FINANCES *Financial year end 31/03/2022*
Income £583,000
Grants to organisations £563,900
Assets £17,300,000

TRUSTEES Anna Dalrymple; Martin Gibson; Lucy Kelly; Edward Gibson; Thomas Homfray.

OTHER INFORMATION In 2021/22, grants were broken down as follows: civil society (£224,200); health and medical research (£91,200); education (£73,000); nature

conservation (£49,000); care (£41,000); art, music and entertainment (£40,500); religion (£30,000); hospices (£15,000).

HOW TO APPLY For organisations new to the trust, applications must be made through the trust's online form, which is open yearly, usually from the start of August to the end of September. Prospective applicants are advised to read the guidelines before applying, as these may change with each funding round. Note that the trust will not respond to or acknowledge any correspondence made through post or telephone calls.

CONTACT DETAILS The Trustees, Durnsford Mill House, Mildenhall, Marlborough, Wiltshire SN8 2NG *Tel.* 07850 859824 *Email* gcgibsoncharity@gmail.com *Website* www.gcgct.org

■ The Simon Gibson Charitable Trust

CC NO 269501 ESTABLISHED 1975

WHERE FUNDING CAN BE GIVEN Cambridgeshire; Carmarthenshire; Hertfordshire; Glamorganshire; Gwent; Norfolk; Powys; Suffolk.

WHO CAN BENEFIT UK-registered charities and CICs. National charities are more likely to be considered if they support local causes in the areas listed above.

WHAT IS FUNDED General charitable purposes, with a preference for: young people and older people; conservation; education; religion.

WHAT IS NOT FUNDED Individuals or organisations applying on behalf of individuals; students for educational or gap year sponsorship; conferences, seminars or workshops; overseas charities (other than those working in conservation or previously known to the trustees).

TYPE OF GRANT Core costs; specific project funding.

RANGE OF GRANTS From £2,000 to £20,000, with most grants in the range of £3,000 to £5,000.

SAMPLE GRANTS Royal Welsh Agricultural Society Glamorgan Fund (£20,000); Wales Millennium Centre (£15,000); Baas Educational Trust UK (£10,000); University of Manchester Poverty Access Programme (£5,000); Cerebral Palsy Cymru (£4,000); Deafblind UK and Suffolk Philharmonic Orchestra (£3,000 each); St Mary's Burwell (£2,000).

FINANCES *Financial year end 05/04/2022*
Income £1,070,000
Grants to organisations £735,000
Assets £25,310,000

TRUSTEES Deborah Connor; George Gibson; John Homfray; Alicia Gibson; Virginia Lort.

HOW TO APPLY Application forms are available to download from the website and should be returned to the trust by post. Applications should be submitted between 1 January and 31 March each year.

CONTACT DETAILS The Trustees, SGCT Applications, PO Box 609, Welwyn Garden City AL7 9QQ *Tel.* 07798 515812 *Email* info@sgctrust.org.uk *Website* www.sgctrust.org.uk

■ The Girdlers' Company Charitable Trust

CC NO 328026 ESTABLISHED 1988

WHERE FUNDING CAN BE GIVEN England, with a preference for London, in particular Islington, Hammersmith and Peckham; New Zealand.

WHO CAN BENEFIT Registered and exempt charities; CIOs; community and amateur sports clubs.

WHAT IS FUNDED Employability through vocational training; support to carers; mental health; education; literacy; ex-offenders.

TYPE OF GRANT Grants to principal charities are for three years. One-off grants are awarded depending on available funds.

RANGE OF GRANTS Principal charities: up to £25,000 per year. One-off grants: up to £10,000.

SAMPLE GRANTS Ahoy Centre (£30,000); Country Trust (£20,000); Bosence Farm Community (£15,000); Crown and Manor Club (£12,500); Barons Court Project and The Vine Club (£10,000 each).

FINANCES *Financial year end 29/09/2022*
Income £140,300
Grants to organisations £836,200
Assets £3,640,000

TRUSTEE The Girdlers' Company.

OTHER INFORMATION Around half of the trust's annual grants are made to its principal charities, with many of which it maintains longstanding and close relationships. In 2021/22 grants totalling £373,500 were made to the principal charities.

HOW TO APPLY Applications for one-off grants of up to £10,000 can be made via the charity's website once an eligibility quiz has been completed. Applications are reviewed in mid-January and late June. Deadlines can be found on the trust's website. All applicants will be advised of the outcome, whether or not they have been successful. It appears that the trust does not accept unsolicited applications for its other funding streams.

CONTACT DETAILS M. Whiteside, Clerk, Girdlers' Hall, Basinghall Avenue, London EC2V 5DD *Tel.* 020 7638 0488 *Email* clerk@girdlers.co.uk *Website* www.girdlers.co.uk

■ The B. and P. Glasser Charitable Trust

CC NO 326571   **ESTABLISHED** 1984

WHERE FUNDING CAN BE GIVEN UK and worldwide.

WHO CAN BENEFIT UK-registered charities; community organisations; hospices; hospitals.

WHAT IS FUNDED General charitable purposes, including: health; disability; Jewish causes; social welfare; humanitarian aid; the environment.

WHAT IS NOT FUNDED Individuals, including students.

RANGE OF GRANTS Mostly up to £6,000, with the occasional larger grant.

SAMPLE GRANTS Wilstone Community Shop Ltd. (£50,000); Nightingale Hammerson and Practical Action (£12,000 each); Jewish Care and Sightsavers International (£10,000 each); Camphill Village Trust Ltd, Jewish Deaf Association and Rennie Grove Hospice Care (£5,000 each); Jewish Blind and Physically Disabled Society Ltd and Unicef UK (£4,000 each); ActionAid for Animals, Age UK and British Red Cross Society (£3,000 each); Samaritans – Chiltern Branch (£1,000).

FINANCES *Financial year end 31/10/2021*
Income £63,000
Grants to organisations £195,500
Assets £3,150,000

TRUSTEES Michael Glasser; John Glasser.

OTHER INFORMATION The 2020/21 accounts were the latest available at the time of writing (May 2023). According to the 2020/21 accounts, the trust would like to continue making grants 'at a similar, if no higher, level'.

HOW TO APPLY Apply in writing to the correspondent.

CONTACT DETAILS The Trustees, c/o Bruce Christer, 68 King William Street, London EC4N 7DZ *Tel.* 020 7486 5888 *Email* charity. correspondence@bdo.co.uk

■ The Glass-House Trust

CC NO 1144990   **ESTABLISHED** 2011

WHERE FUNDING CAN BE GIVEN UK, occasionally overseas.

WHO CAN BENEFIT Registered charities; activities with a clearly defined charitable purpose.

WHAT IS FUNDED The built environment; child development; social research/policy; the arts.

WHAT IS NOT FUNDED Individuals; education fees; expeditions.

TYPE OF GRANT Core costs; project funding; development funding; salaries; research.

RANGE OF GRANTS Up to £125,000.

SAMPLE GRANTS Raven Row (£125,000); Four Corner Books (£100,000); A Space (£55,000); Transform Drug Policy Foundation (£15,000); Concrete Action, Healing Justice London and The Sainsbury Archive (£5,000 each); F* Choir (£2,000).

FINANCES *Financial year end 05/04/2022*
Income £176,000
Grants to organisations £505,500
Assets £9,590,000

TRUSTEES Elinor Sainsbury; Alex Sainsbury; Judith Portrait.

OTHER INFORMATION The trust is one of the Sainsbury Family Charitable Trusts, which share a common administration – see www.sftc.org.uk for more information. According to the 2021/22 annual report and accounts, grants were awarded to 13 organisations during the year.

HOW TO APPLY Unsolicited applications are not accepted.

CONTACT DETAILS The Trustees, The Peak, 5 Wilton Road, London SW1V 1AP *Tel.* 020 7410 0330 *Email* info@sfct.org.uk *Website* www.sfct.org. uk/the-glass-house-trust/

■ The F. Glenister Woodger Trust CIO

CC NO 1187947   **ESTABLISHED** 1989

WHERE FUNDING CAN BE GIVEN West Wittering.

WHO CAN BENEFIT Registered charities; unregistered charities; social enterprises; schools; universities; PTAs; amateur sports clubs; hospitals; hospices; local authorities.

WHAT IS FUNDED General charitable purposes.

TYPE OF GRANT Capital costs; seed funding/start-up funding.

RANGE OF GRANTS From £1,000 to £161,500.

SAMPLE GRANTS Chichester University (£161,507); Manhood Wildlife and Heritage Group (£80,000); West Wittering PCC (£26,496); Rotary Club of Chichester Harbour (£10,000); Pregnancy Options Centre (£3,000); Calibre Audio (£1,000).

FINANCES *Financial year end 31/03/2022*
Income £1,530,000
Grants to organisations £699,900
Assets £50,750,000

TRUSTEES Rosamund Champ; William Craven; Maxine Pickup; Rosamund Gentle; Dr Adrian Gregory; Stuart Dobbin.

OTHER INFORMATION Grants were awarded to 31 organisations in 2021/22.

HOW TO APPLY Apply in writing to the correspondent. The trustees meet quarterly to review grant applications.

CONTACT DETAILS The Trustees, The Pavilion, Rookwood Road, West Wittering, Chichester, West Sussex PO20 8LT *Tel.* 01243 513116 *Email* office@fgwoodgertrust.org

■ The Gloag Foundation

OSCR NO SC035799   **ESTABLISHED** 2004

WHERE FUNDING CAN BE GIVEN UK and overseas.

WHO CAN BENEFIT Charitable organisations and individuals.

WHAT IS FUNDED Anti-people trafficking; advancement of Christianity; social welfare; health; education.

RANGE OF GRANTS Mostly up to £100,000.

SAMPLE GRANTS Freedom From Fistula Foundation (£703,400); Rotary Foundation (£25,000); Blue Sky (£20,000); Grassmarket Community Project (£5,000).

FINANCES *Financial year end 31/12/2021*
Income £726,000
Grants to organisations £866,500
Grants to individuals £26,400
Assets £7,460,000

HOW TO APPLY The foundation's website states that it 'no longer accepts unsolicited applications or requests. Applications are by invitation only.'

CONTACT DETAILS The Trustees, The Steading, Kinfauns, Perth, Perthshire PH2 7JU *Tel.* 01738 633264 *Website* www.gloagfoundation.org.uk

■ Global Charities

CC NO 1091657   **ESTABLISHED** 1978

WHERE FUNDING CAN BE GIVEN UK.

WHO CAN BENEFIT Registered charities.

WHAT IS FUNDED Health; mental health; domestic abuse; poverty; carers; loneliness; homelessness; isolation; bereavement.

TYPE OF GRANT Project funding; capital costs; core costs.

RANGE OF GRANTS £20,000 to £30,000.

SAMPLE GRANTS A list of beneficiaries was not included in the annual report and accounts.

FINANCES *Financial year end 31/03/2022*
Income £3,000,000
Grants to organisations £2,580,000
Assets £2,200,000

TRUSTEES Michael Connole; Jonathan Norbury; Joanne Kenrick; Ulrika Hogberg; Sally Cairns; Marcia Asare; Jennifer Stubbs; Shalni Sood; Martin Allen.

OTHER INFORMATION In 2021/22 the charity made 71 grants.

HOW TO APPLY The charity has a three-stage application process, details of which can be found on its website.

CONTACT DETAILS Grants Team, 30 Leicester Square, London WC2H 7LA *Tel.* 0345 606 0990 *Email* grants@makesomenoise.com *Website* www.makesomenoise.com

■ Gloucestershire Community Foundation

CC NO 900239   **ESTABLISHED** 1989

WHERE FUNDING CAN BE GIVEN Gloucestershire.

WHO CAN BENEFIT Charitable organisations, including CICs and social enterprises; individuals.

WHAT IS FUNDED General charitable purposes, including: social welfare; older people; children

and young people; carers; disadvantaged communities; families; minority communities.

WHAT IS NOT FUNDED See the website for programme-specific exclusions.

TYPE OF GRANT Project funding; core costs; salaries.

RANGE OF GRANTS £1,000 to £10,000.

SAMPLE GRANTS Read for Good (£16,000); Gloucester Cathedral (£8,000); Breakheart Community Project (£6,000); Charlea Community Gardens (£1,500); Forest Fighting Fit (£1,000).

FINANCES *Financial year end 31/12/2021*
Income £500,000
Grants to organisations £787,900
Assets £8,180,000

TRUSTEES His Hon. James Tabor; Jonathan Dunley; Tracy Clark; Richard Stephens; Richard Ingle; Rosina Tufnell; Charlie Sharp; Esme Lord; Sir Graham Miller.

OTHER INFORMATION This is one of the 47 UK community foundations, which distribute funding for a wide range of purposes. As with all community foundations, there are a number of donor-advised funds managed on behalf of individuals, families and charitable trusts. Grant schemes tend to change frequently – consult the foundation's website for details of current programmes and up-to-date deadlines. Grants were broken down as follows: children and young people (£231,900); health and disability (£122,000); carers (£121,300); social welfare (£79,600); disadvantaged communities (£76,900); older people (£71,100); families (£41,900); minority communities (£36,200).

HOW TO APPLY Potential applicants are advised to visit the community foundation's website or contact its grants team to find the most suitable funding stream.

CONTACT DETAILS The Grants Team, The Manor, Boddington, Cheltenham, Gloucestershire GL51 0TJ *Tel.* 01242 851357 *Email* use the contact form on the website *Website* www.gloucestershirecf.org.uk

■ The Gloucestershire Historic Churches Trust

CC NO 1120266   **ESTABLISHED** 1980

WHERE FUNDING CAN BE GIVEN Gloucestershire; North Bristol; South Gloucestershire.

WHO CAN BENEFIT Places of worship of all Christian denominations.

WHAT IS FUNDED Repair, maintenance and improvement of the fabric of religious buildings and their contents, as well as the surrounding churchyards.

WHAT IS NOT FUNDED Substantial repairs, unless the work has been specified by an architect or surveyor with appropriate conservation training.

TYPE OF GRANT One-off; capital costs.

RANGE OF GRANTS Up to £10,000.

SAMPLE GRANTS St Lawrence – Bourton-on-the-Hill (£13,000); St Mary's – Bitton (£10,000); Lechlade Baptist Church (£8,500); St Giles – Uley (£3,000); All Saints – Compton Greenfield (£1,500); St Andrew's – Awre (£500).

FINANCES *Financial year end 31/12/2021*
Income £245,800
Grants to organisations £150,000
Assets £2,000,000

TRUSTEES Helen Whitbread; David Kingsmill; Stephen Langton; Jonathan MacKechnie-Jarvis; James Drennan; Colin Senior; Ray Singleton.

OTHER INFORMATION Grants were made to 33 places of worship in 2021.

HOW TO APPLY Application forms and full guidelines can be downloaded from the trust's website. When an application is received, the trustees will arrange a meeting at your church to discuss your application and view the proposed work. The Grants Committee meets in June and December.

CONTACT DETAILS Jonathan MacKechnie-Jarvis, Chair of the Grants Committee, c/o Wenn Townsend, 5 Gosditch Street, Cirencester, Gloucestershire GL7 2AG *Tel.* 01452 502174 *Email* grants@ghct.org.uk *Website* www.ghct.org.uk

■ The Godinton Charitable Trust

CC NO 268321   **ESTABLISHED** 1974
WHERE FUNDING CAN BE GIVEN Kent.
WHO CAN BENEFIT The trust provides regular support for The Godinton House Preservation Trust, as well as supporting local registered charities, churches and hospices.
WHAT IS FUNDED General charitable purposes.
WHAT IS NOT FUNDED Individuals; organisations based outside Kent.
TYPE OF GRANT Capital costs; general funding.
RANGE OF GRANTS Generally £500 to £3,000.
SAMPLE GRANTS The Godinton House Preservation Trust (£70,400); Kent Autistic Trust (£3,000); Ashford Mediation Service (£2,500); KM Charity Team and St Francis Church – Ashford (£2,000 each); Music at Malling and The Rifles Officers' Fund (£1,000 each); Kent Association for the Blind (£500).
FINANCES *Financial year end 31/10/2021*
Income £186,900
Grants to organisations £109,600
Assets £7,170,000
TRUSTEES Michael Jennings; The Hon. John Leigh-Pemberton; The Hon. Wyndham Plumptre; Terence Bennett.
OTHER INFORMATION Grants were awarded to 27 organisations in total during the year. The 2020/21 accounts were the latest available at the time of writing (May 2023).
HOW TO APPLY Contact the correspondent for information regarding the application process.
CONTACT DETAILS The Trustees, Godinton House, Godinton Lane, Ashford, Kent TN23 3BP *Tel.* 01233 632652 *Email* office@godintonhouse.co.uk

■ Sydney and Phyllis Goldberg Memorial Charitable Trust

CC NO 291835   **ESTABLISHED** 1985
WHERE FUNDING CAN BE GIVEN UK and overseas.
WHO CAN BENEFIT Charitable organisations; hospitals; overseas organisations.
WHAT IS FUNDED Medical research; social welfare; health; disability.
WHAT IS NOT FUNDED Individuals.
TYPE OF GRANT Project funding.
RANGE OF GRANTS Typically £2,000 to £15,000.
SAMPLE GRANTS The British Stammering Association (£15,000); Nepal Earthquake Appeal (£10,000); Child Brain Injury Trust (£7,500); Friends of Children in Romania (£3,500); Chailey Heritage Enterprise Centre (£3,000); Inspire Foundation (£2,000).
FINANCES *Financial year end 05/04/2022*
Income £119,800
Grants to organisations £115,000
Assets £4,930,000
TRUSTEES Michael Church; Christopher Pexton.

OTHER INFORMATION In 2021/22, the trust made grants to 14 organisations totalling £115,000.
HOW TO APPLY Apply in writing to the correspondent. The trustees meet once a year.
CONTACT DETAILS The Trustees, Begbies, 9 Bonhill Street, London EC2A 4DJ *Tel.* 020 7628 5801

■ The Goldcrest Charitable Trust

CC NO 1147149   **ESTABLISHED** 2012
WHERE FUNDING CAN BE GIVEN UK.
WHO CAN BENEFIT Charitable organisations.
WHAT IS FUNDED General charitable purposes, including health.
RANGE OF GRANTS Up to £50,000.
SAMPLE GRANTS Wighton Recreation Hut Fund (£50,000); The Norfolk Accident Rescue Service (£10,000); The Excelsior Trust (£3,000).
FINANCES *Financial year end 30/04/2022*
Income £24,200
Grants to organisations £63,000
Assets £1,630,000
TRUSTEES Neil Dyson; Julie Dyson; Ludlow Trust Company Ltd.
OTHER INFORMATION During 2020/21, the charity made grants to three organisations.
HOW TO APPLY Apply by letter to the correspondent.
CONTACT DETAILS The Trustees, Coutts & Co. Trustee Department, 1st Floor, Trinity Quay 1, Avon Street, Bristol BS2 0PT

■ The Golden Bottle Trust

CC NO 327026   **ESTABLISHED** 1985
WHERE FUNDING CAN BE GIVEN Worldwide, with a preference for the UK.
WHO CAN BENEFIT Charitable organisations.
WHAT IS FUNDED General charitable purposes, including: the arts; religion; health; education; social welfare; citizenship and community development; human rights, racial harmony and equality; armed forces and emergency services; children; animal welfare; disability; the environment; overseas development; relief of poverty; culture, heritage and science.
RANGE OF GRANTS £250 to £10,000, with some larger grants.
SAMPLE GRANTS RefuAid (£120,000); Key 4 Life (£102,000); Think Forward UK (£100,000); Henry C. Hoare Charitable Trust (£60,000); Tree Council (£50,000); The Kids Network (£25,000); Dementia Adventure and Jubilee Centre (£10,000 each).
FINANCES *Financial year end 30/09/2021*
Income £1,640,000
Grants to organisations £1,400,000
Assets £18,160,000
TRUSTEE Hoare Trustees.
OTHER INFORMATION Only beneficiaries of grants of £10,000 and above were included in the accounts. The grant total does not include £186,600 given by the trust to match staff fundraising. Grants were made for a broad range of causes listed above. The 2020/21 accounts were the latest available at the time of writing (June 2023).
HOW TO APPLY The website states that the trust prefers to use trusted partners and networks to identify suitable causes to help. For this reason, unsolicited grant requests are not accepted.
CONTACT DETAILS Hoare Trustees, c/o C. Hoare and Co., 37 Fleet Street, London EC4P 4DQ *Tel.* 020 7353 4522 *Website* www.hoaresbank.co.uk/golden-bottle-trust

■ The Goldman Sachs Charitable Gift Fund (UK)

CC NO 1120148   **ESTABLISHED** 2007
WHERE FUNDING CAN BE GIVEN UK and overseas.
WHO CAN BENEFIT Registered charities; schools and universities.
WHAT IS FUNDED Education; relief of poverty; arts and culture; humanitarian relief; health; community; other charitable purposes.
TYPE OF GRANT Unrestricted.
SAMPLE GRANTS Princeton University (£896,000); Colombia University (£403,000); University of Pennsylvania (£169,000).
FINANCES *Financial year end* 30/06/2022
Income £2,290,000
Grants to organisations £3,160,000
Assets £25,630,000
TRUSTEES Jennifer Evans; Graham Shaw; Robert Katz; Peter Fahey.
OTHER INFORMATION This fund was established by Goldman Sachs International in 2007 as one of the vehicles for its charitable giving. It is also connected to Goldman Sachs Gives. A total of 47 grants were awarded during the year. Note that the financial information was converted from USD using the exchange rate at the time of writing (May 2023). Only organisations that received grants of over $100,000 were listed as beneficiaries in the charity's accounts. Grants of under $100,000 totalled $760,000 (£610,000).
HOW TO APPLY The annual report for 2021/22 explains that the fund 'operates as a donor-advised fund whereby the directors establish donor accounts for individual donors to make recommendations, although the ultimate decision for the distribution of funds tests solely with the directors of the fund.'
CONTACT DETAILS The Trustees, Goldman Sachs International, 25 Shoe Lane, London EC4A 4AU *Tel.* 020 7774 1000

■ Goldman Sachs Gives (UK)

CC NO 1123956   **ESTABLISHED** 2008
WHERE FUNDING CAN BE GIVEN Worldwide.
WHO CAN BENEFIT Registered charities; schools; universities.
WHAT IS FUNDED General charitable purposes including: arts and culture; community; education; humanitarian; medical.
TYPE OF GRANT Project costs.
SAMPLE GRANTS A list of beneficiaries was not included in the annual report and accounts. Previous beneficiaries have included: Greenhouse Sports Ltd (£854,000); Mind (£590,000); Fondation de l'Assistance Publique (£518,000).
FINANCES *Financial year end* 30/06/2022
Income £9,800,000
Grants to organisations £35,480,000
Assets £77,200,000
TRUSTEES Jenny Evans; Robert Katz; Graham Shaw; Peter Fahey.
OTHER INFORMATION Grants were broken down as follows: community (£13.42 million); education (£11.1 million); arts and culture (£3.41 million); medical causes (£3.19 million); other (£2.99 million); humanitarian (£1.38 million).
HOW TO APPLY The annual report for 2021/22 explains that the fund 'operates as a donor-advised fund whereby the directors establish donor accounts for individual donors to make recommendations, although the ultimate decision for the distribution of funds rests solely with the directors of the fund.'

CONTACT DETAILS The Trustees, Goldman Sachs, Peterborough Court, 133 Fleet Street, London EC4A 2BB *Tel.* 020 7774 1000 *Website* www.goldmansachs.com/citizenship/goldman-sachs-gives

■ The Goldsmiths' Company Charity

CC NO 1175593   **ESTABLISHED** 1961
WHERE FUNDING CAN BE GIVEN UK, with a preference for London.
WHO CAN BENEFIT Registered charities with a turnover of less than £5 million. National charities or charities operating in London can be supported.
WHAT IS FUNDED Prisoner resettlement; ageing population; young people; culture; education; mental health.
WHAT IS NOT FUNDED A comprehensive list of exclusions can be found on the charity's website.
RANGE OF GRANTS Up to £30,000.
SAMPLE GRANTS No Going Back – Pan-Livery Project (£50,000); Prisoners' Advice Service (£35,000); Islington Giving (£30,000); Hardman Trust (£20,000); Refugee Council (£15,000); Fulham Primary School (£8,000); Wiltshire Music Centre (£4,000); Middlesex Association for the Blind (£2,100); City of London Police Widows and Orphans (£1,000).
FINANCES *Financial year end* 31/03/2022
Income £3,170,000
Grants to organisations £3,130,000
Assets £170,420,000
TRUSTEES Lord Mark Bridges; Timothy Schroder; Edward Harley; Thomas Fattorini; George MacDonald; Dr Charles Mackworth-Young; Richard Reid; William Parente; Michael Prideaux; Edward Braham; Victoria Broackes; Judith Cobham-Lowe; Richard Fox; Dame Lynne Brindley; Arthur Drysdale; Arthur Galsworthy; Jane Goad; Joanna Hardy; Hector Miller; Michael Wainwright; Edward Butler; Richard Madeley; Neil Carson.
OTHER INFORMATION The charity also sponsors primary and secondary-level educational initiatives and awards grants in support of the goldsmithing trade and associated skills.
HOW TO APPLY At the time of writing (April 2023), applications for the charity's large grants category were by invitation only. Organisations are advised to check the website regularly for updates.
CONTACT DETAILS David Reddaway, Clerk and Correspondent, Goldsmiths' Hall, 13 Foster Lane, London EC2V 6BN *Tel.* 020 7606 7010 *Email* grants@thegoldsmiths.co.uk *Website* www.thegoldsmiths.co.uk/charities

■ The Golf Foundation

CC NO 285917   **ESTABLISHED** 1953
WHERE FUNDING CAN BE GIVEN UK.
WHO CAN BENEFIT Organisations providing formal golf tuition and informal introductory golfing experience to children and young people.
WHAT IS FUNDED The development, promotion and support of junior golf.
WHAT IS NOT FUNDED Individuals.
TYPE OF GRANT Full and partial recovery of costs incurred by the provision of golf tuition.
RANGE OF GRANTS Mostly up to £10,000.
SAMPLE GRANTS Road to the Open (£38,700); Golf Roots Centres and Wales Golf (£24,000 each);

Scottish Golf (£7,500); HSBC Golf Roots Plus (£5,100); Box of Tricks (£2,900); Doorstep Clubs (£2,000); Golf Development Wales (£1,200).

FINANCES *Financial year end 31/03/2022*
Income £1,420,000
Grants to organisations £111,000
Assets £3,680,000

TRUSTEES Sally Stewart; Nick Bragg; Stephen Lewis; Kevin Barker; Jeremy Tomlinson; Davinder Jhamat; Sanjit Atwal; James Brigden; Kim Wild; Robert Maxfield; Alan Watkins.

OTHER INFORMATION Grants were awarded to ten organisations during the year.

HOW TO APPLY Although the foundation states that it chooses its own beneficiaries each year, unsolicited applications from organisations that share its aims and objectives may be considered. Contact the foundation's representative in your area for further details on applying for funding – details can be found on the foundation's website.

CONTACT DETAILS The Trustees, Ambition Broxbourne Business Centre, Pindar Road, Hoddesdon, Hertfordshire EN11 0FJ *Tel.* 01992 449830 *Email* admin@golf-foundation.org *Website* www.golf-foundation.org

■ The Golsoncott Foundation

CC NO 1070885   **ESTABLISHED** 1998
WHERE FUNDING CAN BE GIVEN UK.
WHO CAN BENEFIT Arts organisations.
WHAT IS FUNDED The arts, including: performance, exhibition, artistic craft or education; music; ballet; theatre; museums; literature; fine arts; crafts; bursary funds.
WHAT IS NOT FUNDED Individuals for academic or vocational courses; schools; capital appeals from museums, galleries, theatres, arts complexes or other projects (except by invitation).
TYPE OF GRANT Project funding; bursaries.
RANGE OF GRANTS Grants rarely exceed £3,000.
SAMPLE GRANTS Contains Art (£2,500); Stringcredibles (£1,200); Lake District Music and OperaUpClose (£1,000 each); Debbie Hinds Production (£750); Berkshire Maestros (£500); Project One Theatre (£200); Ensemble Matters (£160).
FINANCES *Financial year end 30/06/2022*
Income £87,100
Grants to organisations £91,800
Assets £2,650,000
TRUSTEES Dr Harriet Wood; Jo Lively; Dame Penelope Lively; Steve Wick; Izzy Wick; Eliza Thompson; Emilio Salice.
OTHER INFORMATION In 2021/22 grants were awarded to 83 organisations or projects. The foundation sponsors the Society of Wood Engravers' Rachel Reckitt Open Prize.
HOW TO APPLY Applications should be submitted to the correspondent a few weeks before the trustees' meetings. Meetings are held quarterly to consider applications, usually in February, May, August and November. Details of what to include in the application can be found on the foundation's website. Applications must be submitted both in digital form and a hard copy.
CONTACT DETAILS Hal Bishop, Administrator, 53 St Leonard's Road, Exeter, Devon EX2 4LS *Tel.* 01392 252855 *Email* golsoncott@btinternet.com *Website* www.golsoncott.org.uk

■ Matthew Good Foundation

CC NO 1143550   **ESTABLISHED** 2011
WHERE FUNDING CAN BE GIVEN UK,.
WHO CAN BENEFIT Registered charities; CICs; social enterprises.
WHAT IS FUNDED General charitable purposes.
SAMPLE GRANTS Clean Planet, Creative Packs Cancer Charity and Market Field Farm, (£3,500 each); Diversified, Gleaning Cornwall Network and Tees River Rescue (£2,500 each); Girls Assemble and Make a Medic (£2,000 each); Kenya Recycling Centre, Leeds Bike Mill and Menai Straits Heritage Sailing (£1,000 each).
FINANCES *Financial year end 31/12/2022*
Income £229,700
Grants to organisations £130,000
Assets £207,000
TRUSTEES Seamus Jennings; Kevin Harrison; Tim Good; Jane Nash.
OTHER INFORMATION This is the corporate charity of the John Good Group and most grants are contributions towards employees' fundraising efforts. However, charities, CICs and social enterprises with an annual income of below £50,000 can apply for a share of £15,000 through the Grants for Good programme. Every three months, five shortlisted projects that demonstrate a positive impact on communities, people or the environment will be voted for by John Good Group employees.
HOW TO APPLY Applications can be made via the foundation's website.
CONTACT DETAILS The Trustees, Suite 1, Ground Floor, Parkgate House, Hesslewood Office Park, Hessle HU13 0LH *Email* michelle@matthewgoodfoundation.org. *Website* www.matthewgoodfoundation.org

■ Nicholas and Judith Goodison's Charitable Settlement

CC NO 1004124   **ESTABLISHED** 1991
WHERE FUNDING CAN BE GIVEN UK.
WHO CAN BENEFIT Registered charities.
WHAT IS FUNDED Arts and arts education.
WHAT IS NOT FUNDED Individuals.
TYPE OF GRANT Capital costs; arts acquisition; project costs.
RANGE OF GRANTS Up to £25,000, but mostly between £1,000 and £5,000.
SAMPLE GRANTS Courtauld Institute of Art (£25,000); Wigmore Hall (£7,200); Opera North (£5,000); English National Opera (£2,500); Westminster Abbey Foundation (£1,600).
FINANCES *Financial year end 05/04/2022*
Income £56,600
Grants to organisations £51,800
Assets £1,730,000
TRUSTEES Lady Judith Goodison; Katharine Goodison; Rachel Goodison; Adam Goodison.
HOW TO APPLY Apply in writing to the correspondent.
CONTACT DETAILS The Trustees, PO Box 2512, London W1A 5ZP *Email* goodisonn@btinternet.com

■ The Jane Goodman Charitable Trust

CC NO 1190940
WHERE FUNDING CAN BE GIVEN Worldwide.
WHO CAN BENEFIT Charitable organisations.
WHAT IS FUNDED General charitable purposes including health, education and Jewish causes.
RANGE OF GRANTS Up to £100,000.

SAMPLE GRANTS Girls' Day School Trust (£115,000); The Anthony Nolan Trust and Victim Support (£100,000 each); Diabetes UK (£50,000); Campaign Against Antisemitism (£10,000).

FINANCES *Financial year end 31/08/2021*
Income £980,000
Grants to organisations £958,500
Assets £12,900

TRUSTEES John Cohen; Lord Sherbourne; Baroness Sally Hamwee.

OTHER INFORMATION The 2020/21 accounts were the latest available at the time of writing (May 2023).

HOW TO APPLY Apply in writing to the correspondent.

CONTACT DETAILS The Trustees, c/o Clintons (ref: JC), 2 St Giles Square, London WC2H 8AP *Tel.* 020 7379 6080 *Email* jcohen@clintons.co.uk

■ The Goodman Foundation

CC NO 1097231   **ESTABLISHED** 2003
WHERE FUNDING CAN BE GIVEN UK and overseas.
WHO CAN BENEFIT Charitable organisations.
WHAT IS FUNDED General charitable purposes; the relief of poverty; older people; illness and disability; children; overseas assistance and disaster relief.

SAMPLE GRANTS A list of beneficiaries was not included in the annual report and accounts.

FINANCES *Financial year end 31/03/2022*
Income £11,360,000
Grants to organisations £3,310,000
Assets £85,220,000

TRUSTEES Laurence Goodman; Catherine Goodman; Philip Morgan.

OTHER INFORMATION Grants made during the year were broken down as follows: financially developing countries and disasters (seven grants totalling £2.77 million); help for people in financial need, older people and people with disabilities (ten grants totalling £254,500); children's charities (five grants totalling £202,300); other charitable causes deemed worthy (nine grants totalling £83,600).

HOW TO APPLY Apply in writing to the correspondent.

CONTACT DETAILS The Trustees, c/o ABP, Unit 6290, Bishops Court, Solihull Parkway, Birmingham Business Park, Birmingham B37 7YB *Tel.* 0121 717 2500

■ The Mike Gooley Trailfinders Charity

CC NO 1048993   **ESTABLISHED** 1995
WHERE FUNDING CAN BE GIVEN UK.
WHO CAN BENEFIT Charitable organisations.
WHAT IS FUNDED Medical research; youth community projects; education; armed forces.

SAMPLE GRANTS A list of beneficiaries was not included in the annual report and accounts.

FINANCES *Financial year end 30/06/2022*
Income £8,090,000
Grants to organisations £6,000,000
Assets £25,660,000

TRUSTEES Fiona Gooley; Tristan Gooley; Bernadette Gooley; Michael Gooley.

HOW TO APPLY Apply in writing to the correspondent.

CONTACT DETAILS The Trustees, 9 Abingdon Road, London W8 6AH *Tel.* 020 7938 3143

■ The Goshen Trust

CC NO 1119064   **ESTABLISHED** 2007
WHERE FUNDING CAN BE GIVEN England and Wales, with a preference for the North East.
WHO CAN BENEFIT Christian organisations; churches; charitable organisations.
WHAT IS FUNDED Christian causes. The trust's 2021/22 annual report and accounts describe its principal activity as follows: 'to encourage and develop Christian projects which otherwise would not be able to reach an effective operational conclusion.'

TYPE OF GRANT Project costs.
RANGE OF GRANTS From £1,000 to £60,000.
SAMPLE GRANTS United Christian Broadcasters (£60,000); Teen Challenge (£36,000); HOPE for Justice (£21,000); Angel Foundation (£7,500); Philo Trust (£5,000); African Pastors (£1,000).

FINANCES *Financial year end 05/04/2022*
Income £307,800
Grants to organisations £307,700
Assets £480,600

TRUSTEES Jonathan Dicken; Alison Dicken; Pauline Dicken; Albert Dicken; Rachel Dicken.

HOW TO APPLY Apply in writing to the correspondent. The trustees meet several times a year to consider applications. All applications are acknowledged; if applicants do not receive any further communication from the trust, they should assume that they have been unsuccessful.

CONTACT DETAILS Company Secretary, PO Box 275, Stanley, County Durham DH8 1HH *Email* admin@goshentrust.org

■ The Gosling Foundation Ltd

CC NO 326840   **ESTABLISHED** 1985
WHERE FUNDING CAN BE GIVEN UK.
WHO CAN BENEFIT Registered charities; CICs; CIOs; serving members of the Royal Navy and Royal Marines.
WHAT IS FUNDED Education; disability; young people; armed forces.
WHAT IS NOT FUNDED See the foundation's website for a full list of exclusions.
TYPE OF GRANT Project costs; capital costs.
RANGE OF GRANTS The minimum amount that can be applied for is £5,000.
SAMPLE GRANTS The Platinum Jubilee Pageant Ltd (£1.2 million); UK Sailing Academy (£100,000); HMS Heron Central Amenities Fund (£30,000); DEBRA (£10,000); The British Maritime Charitable Foundation (£6,000); The Tuberous Sclerosis Association (£5,200); The Sussex Association for Spina Bifida and Hydrocephalus (£1,000); Northwood Officers' Mess (£600).

FINANCES *Financial year end 31/03/2022*
Income £4,430,000
Grants to organisations £1,880,000
Assets £181,960,000

TRUSTEES Capt. the Hon. Adam Gosling; Peter Caplan; Nicholas Giles.

OTHER INFORMATION During 2021/22, grants paid to organisations were distributed as follows: Other (£1.21 million) Royal Navy/Royal Marines (£310,600); young people (£238,000); health (£191,200). A further £508,500 was committed for payment in future years.

HOW TO APPLY Applications should be made on the foundation's website. Applications are accepted all year round.

CONTACT DETAILS The Trustees, 2A Kempson Road, London SW6 4PU *Tel.* 020 3872 7723 *Email* office@thegoslingfoundation.com *Website* www.thegoslingfoundation.com

■ The Edward Gostling Foundation

CC NO 1068617   **ESTABLISHED** 1998
WHERE FUNDING CAN BE GIVEN UK.
WHO CAN BENEFIT UK-registered charities. The trustees have a preference for small and medium-sized charities.
WHAT IS FUNDED Disability; social welfare; illness. The foundation focuses on charities that have an impact across one or more of the following four 'life themes': health and well-being; independent living at home; respite; transition. The foundation's website expands on each theme.
WHAT IS NOT FUNDED Individuals; completed projects; political or religious causes; statutory services; universities, colleges or further education colleges (except where the organisation is wholly for students with additional needs; other grant-making charities or umbrella organisations; community centres and youth clubs (except those that benefit older people, people with disabilities or people with a long-term illness); overseas projects.
TYPE OF GRANT Project funding, unrestricted.
RANGE OF GRANTS Small fast-track grants: up to £5,000. Large grants: over £5,000.
SAMPLE GRANTS Family Fund (£1.02 million); Thames Hospice (£146,000); The Bodie Hodges Foundation (£50,000); The Meath Epilepsy Charity (£25,000); The Peter Pan Centre for Children with Special Needs (£20,000); The Eric Liddell Centre (£15,000); The Life Project (Bath) (£10,000).
FINANCES *Financial year end 31/03/2022*
Income £3,770,000
Grants to organisations £7,430,000
Assets £104,420,000
TRUSTEES John O'Sullivan; Denis Taylor; Robert White; Christine Erwood; Russell Meadows; Colin Clarkson; Stephen O'Sullivan; Victoria Hoskins; Carole Sawyers.
OTHER INFORMATION In 2021/22, 466 grants were awarded to organisations. The majority of grants (454) were of less than £25,000.
HOW TO APPLY Applicants are advised to visit the foundation's website in the first instance. The website provides detailed information on the application process and what to include in an application. The trustees meet four times a year and applications can be made at any time.
CONTACT DETAILS The Grants Manager, Suite 1, 61 Thames Street, Windsor, Berkshire SL4 1QW *Tel.* 01753 753900 *Email* info@theactfoundation.co.uk or use the contact form on the website. *Website* www.edwardgostlingfoundation.org.uk

■ Gowling WLG (UK) Charitable Trust

CC NO 803009   **ESTABLISHED** 1990
WHERE FUNDING CAN BE GIVEN UK in practice, but with a preference for: Birmingham; Coventry; Dudley; London; Sandwell; Solihull; Walsall.
WHO CAN BENEFIT Local and national charities.
WHAT IS FUNDED General charitable purposes, particularly: young people; older people; health; disability; social/economic circumstances.
WHAT IS NOT FUNDED The trust does not usually award grants to individuals or organisations which are not charities.
RANGE OF GRANTS £250 to £35,000.
SAMPLE GRANTS UK for UNHCR (£35,000); University of Birmingham (£24,000); The KEHS Trust (£7,000); Worcestershire Community Foundation and Working Families (£5,000 each); Suited for Success (£2,500); The Haven Wolverhampton. Lighthouse Construction Industry Charity and Support Through Court (£1,000 each); The Lily Mae Foundation, The Prince's Trust and The Story of Christmas (£500 each).
FINANCES *Financial year end 05/04/2022*
Income £162,800
Grants to organisations £164,800
Assets £103,300
TRUSTEES Lee Nuttall; Andreas Stylianou; Felicity Lindsay.
OTHER INFORMATION The trust is the corporate charity of Gowling WLG LLP.
HOW TO APPLY Apply in writing to the correspondent.
CONTACT DETAILS The Trustees, c/o Gowling WLG (UK) LLP, Two Snowhill, Snow Hill Queensway, Birmingham B4 6WR *Tel.* 0121 233 1000

■ The Hemraj Goyal Foundation

CC NO 1136483   **ESTABLISHED** 2010
WHERE FUNDING CAN BE GIVEN UK and overseas, particularly India.
WHO CAN BENEFIT Charitable organisations.
WHAT IS FUNDED Children and young people; social welfare; women's rights; education; disability; inter-faith understanding.
SAMPLE GRANTS Mukul Madhav Foundation UK (£100,000); iPartner India (£35,300); British Asian Trust (£35,000); Barnardo's (£27,000); Child Action (£25,000); Tommy's (£15,500); Aztecs Cricket Club (£14,300); The Outward Bound Trust (£12,000).
FINANCES *Financial year end 31/12/2021*
Income £407,200
Grants to organisations £362,400
Assets £32,800
TRUSTEES Avnish Goyal; Aneurin Brown; Anand Goyal; Sabrina Pervez; Anita Goyal.
OTHER INFORMATION Only beneficiaries of grants of over £10,000 were listed in the 2021 accounts. Grants of under £10,000 totalled £93,500.
HOW TO APPLY Contact the correspondent for information regarding the application process.
CONTACT DETAILS The Trustees, Unit 3, Woodbrook Crescent, Billericay, Essex CM12 0EQ *Tel.* 07960 136357 *Email* info@hgf.org.uk *Website* www.hgf.org.uk

■ Grace Baptist Trust Corporation

CC NO 251675   **ESTABLISHED** 1909
WHERE FUNDING CAN BE GIVEN UK.
WHO CAN BENEFIT Strict and Particular Baptist Chapels and their pastors.
WHAT IS FUNDED Building work or major renovation projects to churches.
TYPE OF GRANT Capital costs.
SAMPLE GRANTS A list of beneficiaries was not included in the annual report and accounts.
FINANCES *Financial year end 31/12/2021*
Income £403,900
Grants to organisations £220,800
Assets £6,530,000
TRUSTEES Jonathan Broome; Alan Copeman; Andrew Keen; Paul Relf; Kevin Wiltshire; Robert Powell; Matthew Gray; Darren Noller.
OTHER INFORMATION The trust administers a number of small trusts, the funds of which may be used to pay for capital projects. Grants are also made to pastors and members of the church who are in need. During 2021, grants totalling £141,100 were awarded to churches towards construction and maintenance. A further £79,700 was awarded to churches for ministry support.

HOW TO APPLY In the first instance, refer to the list of trust funds on the trust's website. If there is a suitable trust fund, applicants should then supply brief details about their church and the project for which they require assistance.

CONTACT DETAILS The Trustees, 19 Croydon Road, Caterham, Surrey CR3 6PA *Tel.* 01883 345488 *Email* admin@gbtc.org.uk or use the contact form on the website *Website* www.gbtc.org.uk

■ Grace Charitable Trust

CC NO 292984 **ESTABLISHED** 1985
WHERE FUNDING CAN BE GIVEN UK and overseas.
WHO CAN BENEFIT Registered charities; schools; hospitals; religious bodies/institutions.
WHAT IS FUNDED General charitable purposes; medical causes; Christian and church-based activities; education.
TYPE OF GRANT Capital costs; core/revenue costs; seeding funding/start-up funding.
SAMPLE GRANTS A list of beneficiaries was not included in the annual report and accounts.
FINANCES *Financial year end* 30/04/2022
Income £1,010,000
Grants to organisations £1,071,000
Assets £3,860,000
TRUSTEES Mark Mitchell; Eric Payne; Robert Quayle; Robert Wright; Angela Payne.
OTHER INFORMATION Grants were distributed as follows: Christian-based activities (£652,000); social and medical causes (£349,900); education (£60,500); general charitable purposes (£8,600).
HOW TO APPLY The trust's annual report for 2021/22 states that 'grants are only made to charities known to the settlors'.
CONTACT DETAILS The Trustees, Swinford House GCT Office, Nortons Lane, Great Barrow, Chester, Cheshire CH3 7JZ *Tel.* 01928 740773 *Email* gracecharitabletrust@live.co.uk

■ The Grace Trust

CC NO 257516 **ESTABLISHED** 1967
WHERE FUNDING CAN BE GIVEN UK and overseas.
WHO CAN BENEFIT Registered charities.
WHAT IS FUNDED Education; childcare; non-statutory emergency services and medical relief; disaster relief; medical research; humanitarian aid; relief of poverty; disability support; life preservation; advancement of Christianity.
RANGE OF GRANTS Mostly £100 to £5,000, with several particularly large grants awarded each year.
SAMPLE GRANTS OneSchool Global UK (£29.2 million); NAF UK (£8 million); Rapid Relief Team (£1.08 million); The Caledon Trust (£450,000); Little Hearts Matters (£2,000); Map action (£1,300); Road Victims Trust (£1,000); Kingswood Trust (£500).
FINANCES *Financial year end* 31/12/2021
Income £129,810,000
Grants to organisations £38,450,000
Assets £62,590,000
TRUSTEES Scribefort Ltd; Aller Brook Ltd.
OTHER INFORMATION A substantial amount of the grant total was awarded to OneSchool Global UK (£29.2 million).
HOW TO APPLY Apply in writing to the correspondent. The trust's 2021 annual report states 'all applications are considered carefully by a Grant-making Committee comprising individuals who are not directors. The Committee makes recommendations to the board, which makes the final decision on the approval of grants.'

CONTACT DETAILS The Trustees, Noble House, Eaton Road, Hemel Hempstead, Hertfordshire HP2 7UB *Tel.* 020 3301 3806
Email enquiries@thegracetrust.org.uk
Website www.thegracetrust.org.uk

■ The James Grace Trust

CC NO 1185450 **ESTABLISHED** 2019
WHERE FUNDING CAN BE GIVEN UK; Asia; the Middle East; North Africa.
WHO CAN BENEFIT Charitable organisations.
WHAT IS FUNDED Advancement of the Christian faith; social welfare; education.
RANGE OF GRANTS Mostly under £10,000.
SAMPLE GRANTS Anglican International Development (£28,000); Fountain of Life (£13,000); Caring for Life (£9,000); Anglican Consultative Council (£8,000); Interserve GB and Saltmine Trust (£4,000 each); Lighthouse Prayer Ministry and Stort Valley Schools Trust (£2,000).
FINANCES *Financial year end* 30/06/2022
Income £108,400
Grants to organisations £113,000
Grants to individuals £10,000
Assets £655,100
TRUSTEES Ian Sutherland; Janet Sutherland; Jyotir Banerjee.
HOW TO APPLY It is unlikely that unsolicited applications will be successful. Almost all grants are made to organisations already known to the trustees.
CONTACT DETAILS The Trustees, 23 Mill Lane, Saffron Walden, CB10 2AS *Email* ian@sutherlandviolin.com

■ Graff Foundation

CC NO 1012859 **ESTABLISHED** 1991
WHERE FUNDING CAN BE GIVEN UK.
WHO CAN BENEFIT Charitable organisations.
WHAT IS FUNDED General charitable purposes.
TYPE OF GRANT One-off and recurrent.
RANGE OF GRANTS Up to £763,000, with the average amount being £211,000.
SAMPLE GRANTS Chabad Jewish Community of Central London (£763,000); Facet Foundation (£598,000); The Museum of Contemporary Art (£73,100); Guggenheim Museum (£21,500); Tate Foundation (£10,000).
FINANCES *Financial year end* 31/12/2021
Income £743,800
Grants to organisations £1,480,000
Assets £2,540,000
TRUSTEES Alexander Molla; Mr L. Graff; Mr F. Graff.
OTHER INFORMATION Grants were made to seven organisations in 2021.
HOW TO APPLY Apply in writing to the correspondent.
CONTACT DETAILS Alexander Molla, Trustee, Kerman and Co. LLP, 28–29 Albemarle Street, London W1S 4JA *Tel.* 020 7584 8571

■ E. C. Graham Belford Charitable Settlement

CC NO 1014869 **ESTABLISHED** 1991
WHERE FUNDING CAN BE GIVEN Northumberland.
WHO CAN BENEFIT Smaller charities and branches of larger charities based in the area of benefit.
WHAT IS FUNDED General charitable purposes.
RANGE OF GRANTS Generally up to £15,000.
SAMPLE GRANTS Haltwhistle Youth Club (£25,000); Hexham Youth Initiative (£16,000); North Tyne Youth (£10,000); Calvert Trust (£5,000);

Depaul (£1,000); Berwick Educational Association (£750).

FINANCES *Financial year end* 05/04/2022
Income £71,500
Grants to organisations £109,000
Assets £10,310,000

TRUSTEES Anthony Thompson; Alison Burn.

OTHER INFORMATION Grants were made to 12 organisations during the year.

HOW TO APPLY Contact the correspondent for further information.

CONTACT DETAILS Anthony Thompson, Trustee, Forsters LLP, 31 Hill Street, London W1J 5LS
Tel. 020 7863 8333

■ The Gisela Graham Foundation

CC NO 1153514

WHERE FUNDING CAN BE GIVEN UK and overseas.

WHO CAN BENEFIT UK-registered charities.

WHAT IS FUNDED Health and medical research; people with learning disabilities; the education and care of children in the financially developing countries; the performing arts.

WHAT IS NOT FUNDED Individuals; retrospective expenditure.

TYPE OF GRANT One-off and recurrent.

RANGE OF GRANTS Up to £10,000.

SAMPLE GRANTS A list of beneficiaries was not included in the annual report and accounts. Previous beneficiaries have included: Shelter (£6,000); Crisis (£4,000); React (Rapid Effective Assistance for Children with potentially Terminal illness) (£3,000); London Handel Society (£2,500); Southmead Hospital (£2,000).

FINANCES *Financial year end* 31/05/2022
Income £250,200
Grants to organisations £115,500
Assets £216,400

TRUSTEES Andreas Graham; Paul Boys; Sir David Chapman; Richard Bailey; Piers Croke.

HOW TO APPLY Application forms can be downloaded from the foundation's website.

CONTACT DETAILS The Trustees, 12 Colworth Grove, Browning Street, London SE17 1LR
Email contact@ggrahamfoundation.org
Website http://ggrahamfoundation.org

■ The Graham Trust

OSCR NO SC038269   **ESTABLISHED** 2007

WHERE FUNDING CAN BE GIVEN UK, with a preference for Scotland.

WHO CAN BENEFIT Registered charities; individuals.

WHAT IS FUNDED General charitable purposes, with a preference for: the saving of lives; arts and heritage; relief of those in need; animal welfare.

RANGE OF GRANTS £500 to £20,000.

SAMPLE GRANTS Previous beneficiaries have included: Pancreatic Cancer Research (£22,500); RNLI and St Michael's Hospice (£15,000 each); Bethany Christian Trust (£10,000); Scotland Huntingdon Association (£5,000); Scotland's Charity Air Ambulance (£3,000).

FINANCES *Financial year end* 30/09/2022
Income £17,800
Grants to organisations £66,500

OTHER INFORMATION Full accounts were not available to view on the OSCR website due to the charity's low income. We have therefore estimated the trust's grant total based on its total expenditure.

HOW TO APPLY The trustees meet once a year in the autumn. Applications can be made online or by email. Relevant templates are available to download from the website. Only successful applicants will be contacted.

CONTACT DETAILS The Trustees, 14 Dirac Road, Ashley Down, Bristol BS7 9LP
Email thegrahamtrust@gmail.com
Website http://thegrahamtrust.co.uk

■ Grahame Charitable Foundation Ltd

CC NO 1102332   **ESTABLISHED** 2004

WHERE FUNDING CAN BE GIVEN UK and overseas.

WHO CAN BENEFIT Mainly Jewish charities and organisations.

WHAT IS FUNDED Education; social welfare; Jewish causes.

WHAT IS NOT FUNDED Individuals.

RANGE OF GRANTS £5,000 to £25,000.

SAMPLE GRANTS A list of beneficiaries was not included in the annual report and accounts. Previous beneficiaries have included: Jerusalem College of Technology and Keren Avraham Bezalel (£25,000 each); Emunah (£20,000); Partnership for Schools (£13,600); Charities Aid Foundation (£12,500); Beis Ruzhin Trust (£11,000); Yesodey Hatorah School (£10,000); Beit Almog (£6,000); Campaign Against Antisemitism and Kehilat Kadima (£5,000 each).

FINANCES *Financial year end* 31/12/2021
Income £338,700
Grants to organisations £327,900
Assets £96,500

TRUSTEES Alan Grahame; Joel Greenwood; Sara Shaw; Ethan Greenwood.

HOW TO APPLY Apply in writing to the correspondent.

CONTACT DETAILS The Trustees, Unit 102, 116 Ballards Lane, Finchley, London N3 2DN
Tel. 07710 221636

■ The Granada Foundation

CC NO 241693   **ESTABLISHED** 1965

WHERE FUNDING CAN BE GIVEN The North West.

WHO CAN BENEFIT Registered charities; not-for-profit organisations occasionally considered.

WHAT IS FUNDED The study, practice and appreciation of fine arts and science; engaging young people and adults to take an interest in science; provision of facilities for recreation or other leisure-time occupation in the interests of social welfare; education.

WHAT IS NOT FUNDED Salaries; long-term revenue funding; general appeals; individuals; courses of study; expeditions; overseas travel; youth clubs/ community associations; general appeals.

TYPE OF GRANT Project funding, including new projects; capital costs.

RANGE OF GRANTS £500 to £10,000, with the average grant being £2,000.

SAMPLE GRANTS Previous beneficiaries have included: Buxton Festival (£10,000); MusicLinks Ltd (£6,000); Engineering Development Trust (£4,000); Rule of Threes Arts Ltd (£3,000); Liverpool Arab Arts Festival and Streetwise Opera (£2,000 each); Manchester Literature Festival (£1,400); Grizedale Arts (£1,000).

FINANCES *Financial year end* 31/03/2022
Income £23,900
Grants to organisations £190,000

TRUSTEES Philip Ramsbottom; Robert Scott; Dr Virginia Tandy.

OTHER INFORMATION Full accounts were not available to view on the Charity Commission's website due to the foundation's low income. We have therefore estimated the grant total based on the foundation's total expenditure.

HOW TO APPLY In the first instance, organisations wishing to apply should provide a brief outline of the project for which funding is sought by completing the short enquiry form available on the foundation's website. If the project meets the funding criteria, a full application pack will be sent out by email. Dates of upcoming Advisory Council meetings, as well as relevant deadlines for applications, are detailed on the website.

CONTACT DETAILS Irene Langford, Administrator, PO Box 3430, Chester CH1 9BZ *Tel.* 01244 661867 *Email* enquiries@granadafoundation.org *Website* www.granadafoundation.org

■ Grand Charitable Trust of the Order of Women Freemasons

CC NO 1059151   **ESTABLISHED** 1996
WHERE FUNDING CAN BE GIVEN England and Wales.
WHO CAN BENEFIT Registered charities.
WHAT IS FUNDED Health; social welfare; older people; children and young people; people with disabilities.
SAMPLE GRANTS Adelaide Litten Charitable Trust; Flat Friends; London Air Ambulance; Smile Train; Sue Ryder; Unseen UK; Woodlands Academy.
FINANCES *Financial year end* 30/06/2022
  Income £88,000
  Grants to organisations £99,900
  Assets £759,300
TRUSTEES Zuzanka Penn; Dr Iris Boggia-Black; Sylvia Major; Elizabeth Keitch; Melanie Hooper; Dr Eileen Senior.
HOW TO APPLY The trust's 2021/22 annual report explains: 'Applications to receive support are made through lodges and individual members. Public applications are generally received through postal applications.'
CONTACT DETAILS The Trustees, 27 Pembridge Gardens, London W2 4EF *Tel.* 020 7229 2368 *Email* secretariat@owf.org.uk *Website* www.owf.org.uk/charitable-work

■ The Grand Trust CIO

CC NO 1179280   **ESTABLISHED** 2018
WHERE FUNDING CAN BE GIVEN England and Wales.
WHO CAN BENEFIT Charitable organisations; CICs.
WHAT IS FUNDED Supporting marginalised groups and those from disadvantaged backgrounds.
TYPE OF GRANT Project funding over three-year periods; strategic funding.
SAMPLE GRANTS A list of beneficiaries was not available.
FINANCES *Financial year end* 30/06/2022
  Income £1,300
  Grants to organisations £371,600
  Assets £180,000
TRUSTEES Steven Appleton; Dr Danielle Peet; Joanne Radcliff.
HOW TO APPLY Apply in writing to the correspondent.
CONTACT DETAILS The Trustees, c/o Brabners LLP, 55 King Street, Manchester M2 4LQ *Tel.* 0161 836 8949

■ The Grange Farm Centre Trust

CC NO 285162   **ESTABLISHED** 1984
WHERE FUNDING CAN BE GIVEN London Metropolitan Police District and Epping Forest in Essex.
WHO CAN BENEFIT Charitable organisations; amateur sports clubs; schools; churches.
WHAT IS FUNDED Recreation and leisure activities.
SAMPLE GRANTS EWCA Family Kung Fu; Live Unlimited; Spark (Loughton Youth Centre); Mill Hill Village Sports Club; St Mary the Virgin – Monken Hadley; Stubbers Adventure Playground; Sudbury Neighbourhood Centre; Surrey Docks Farm Provident Society; Theydon Bois Cricket Club; Vauxhall City Farms; Voluntary Action Epping Forest; Walthamstow Cricket Club.
FINANCES *Financial year end* 05/04/2022
  Income £466,600
  Grants to organisations £89,000
  Assets £17,900,000
TRUSTEES Peter Minoletti; Trevor Johnson; Robert Church; Mary Sartin; Marshall Vance; Richard Morgan; Javed Salim; Valerie Metcalfe; Rashni Holden.
OTHER INFORMATION During 2021/22, grants were awarded to 12 organisations.
HOW TO APPLY Contact the clerk for information regarding the application process.
CONTACT DETAILS L. Cleasby, Clerk, c/o 181 High Street, Epping, Essex CM16 4BQ *Tel.* 01992 578642 *Email* info@grangefarmcentre.co.uk *Website* www.grangefarmcentre.co.uk

■ William Grant Foundation

WHERE FUNDING CAN BE GIVEN Scotland.
WHO CAN BENEFIT Charitable organisations.
WHAT IS FUNDED People who are disadvantaged; community services and development; the natural and built environment; culture and heritage.
SAMPLE GRANTS A list of beneficiaries was not available.
FINANCES *Financial year end* 31/12/2022
  Grants to organisations £4,610,000
OTHER INFORMATION The foundation is not a registered charity and therefore full accounts were not available to view. Financial information has been taken from the foundation's annual review.
HOW TO APPLY The foundation's website states: The foundation does not invite unsolicited requests for funding. Instead it uses research and networks to proactively identify and select projects and organisations to support.' However, organisations local to company sites can get in touch to request grants and products (usually up to the value of £1,000) through the William Grant and Sons Local Giving scheme. Full information on how to apply to the Local Giving Scheme can be found on the foundation's website.
CONTACT DETAILS Giving Team, Strathclyde Business Park, Bellshill ML4 3AN *Email* foundation@wgrant.com *Website* www.williamgrantfoundation.org.uk

■ The Grantham Yorke Trust

CC NO 228466   **ESTABLISHED** 1963
WHERE FUNDING CAN BE GIVEN West Midlands.
WHO CAN BENEFIT Individuals aged under 25 who are in need and organisations working with them. A wide variety of organisations are supported including charities, museums, hospices, youth

414

Does the funder you have chosen match your needs? Haphazard applications waste postage and time

clubs, CICs, educational and religious organisations.

WHAT IS FUNDED Young people; education; physical and social training; rehabilitation; recreation and leisure; financial assistance; equipment for education or a profession.

TYPE OF GRANT General funding; capital costs (including school/professional equipment).

SAMPLE GRANTS A list of beneficiaries was not included in the annual report and accounts. Previous beneficiaries have included: Severn Valley Railway Charitable Trust (£10,000); Warley Baptist Church (£7,500); The Feast Youth Project and Touchstones Child Bereavement Support (£5,000 each); Birmingham Opera Company (£3,000); Kenelm Youth Trust and Shakespeare Hospice (£2,500 each); Queen Alexandra College (£1,500); 2nd Warwick Sea Scouts (£1,000).

FINANCES *Financial year end 05/04/2022*
Income £242,700
Grants to organisations £245,000
Grants to individuals £4,300
Assets £7,160,000

TRUSTEES Revd Matthew Thompson; Fred Rattley; Howard Belton; Philip Smiglarski; Sue Butler; Tim Clarke; Hugh Sherriffe; Ruth Burgess; Beverley Momenabadi.

OTHER INFORMATION During the year, the trust made 102 grants to organisations and 16 grants to individuals.

HOW TO APPLY Apply in writing to the correspondent. The trustees meet quarterly.

CONTACT DETAILS Chrissy Norgrove, Clerk to the Trustees, The Estate Office, Wharf Cottage, Broombank, Newham Bridge, Tenbury Wells, Worcestershire WR15 8NY *Tel.* 07940 160844 *Email* chrissy@granthamyorketrust.org.uk

■ GrantScape

CC NO 1102249   **ESTABLISHED** 2003

WHERE FUNDING CAN BE GIVEN UK.

WHO CAN BENEFIT Registered charities; community organisations, CICs.

WHAT IS FUNDED General charitable purposes including: the environment; community development; sports and recreation; social welfare.

WHAT IS NOT FUNDED Each fund is subject to its own exclusions, which are listed on the website.

TYPE OF GRANT Capital costs; project funding.

RANGE OF GRANTS Up to £100,000.

SAMPLE GRANTS Emerge Hub CIC (£50,000); Bee Wirral CIC (£9,600); Eggcup (£6,000); Making Space (£5,000); Inspired Equine Assisted Learning CIC (£1,300).

FINANCES *Financial year end 31/03/2022*
Income £4,390,000
Grants to organisations £3,580,000
Assets £2,530,000

TRUSTEES Antony Cox; Michael Clarke; Philippa Lyons; Michael Singh; John Mills; Thomas Walker; Stuart McAleese; Gillian French.

OTHER INFORMATION GrantScape administers community funds on behalf of developers, such as wind farms, landfill sites, solar farms and renewable energy plants.

HOW TO APPLY Applicants should visit the 'Grant and Project Finder' section of the charity's website to find information on all grant programmes currently available. Applications should be made online via the website.

CONTACT DETAILS Kim Wilkinson, Grant Administrator, Office E, Whitsundoles, Broughton Road, Salford, Milton Keynes, Buckinghamshire MK17 8BU *Tel.* 01908 247630 *Email* info@grantscape.org.uk *Website* www.grantscape.org.uk

■ The J. G. Graves Charitable Trust

CC NO 207481   **ESTABLISHED** 1930

WHERE FUNDING CAN BE GIVEN Sheffield.

WHO CAN BENEFIT Registered charities; charitable organisations; CICs; hospices.

WHAT IS FUNDED General charitable purposes; disadvantaged groups; community development; well-being and health; heritage; education; parks and open spaces; sports and recreation; art galleries and libraries for public use; medical research; recreational and sporting facilities; community projects connected to churches; special needs schools for non-mainstream educational expenditure.

WHAT IS NOT FUNDED A list of exclusions can be found on the trust's website.

TYPE OF GRANT Capital costs (preferred); seed funding; running costs. Grants are awarded for up to three years in exceptional circumstances.

RANGE OF GRANTS Typically £500 to £3,000.

SAMPLE GRANTS Sheffield Royal Society for the Blind (£5,000); Sheffield Maternity Cooperative (£4,500); Big Issue in the North Trust (£3,500); Grimesthorpe Family Centre and Sheffield Women's Counselling and Therapy Services (£3,000 each); Manor and Castle Development Trust (£2,500); Roundabout Ltd (£2,000 each); Park Community Action (£1,500).

FINANCES *Financial year end 31/12/2021*
Income £178,300
Grants to organisations £154,300
Assets £6,480,000

TRUSTEES John Bramah; Peter Clarkson; Dr Derek Cullen; Cllr Peter Price; Dona Womack; Roderick Plews; Cllr Jacqueline Drayton; Kim Streets; Adrian Graves; Prof. Solomon Tesfaye; Katie Hayward; Steven Cotton; Gavin Richards.

OTHER INFORMATION Grants were awarded to 73 organisations during 2020/21. Only organisations that received grants of over £1,000 were listed as beneficiaries in the trust's accounts. Grants of under £1,000 totalled £12,000.

HOW TO APPLY Applications can be made through the trust's website. The trustees meet quarterly to discuss applications. Applications should reach the secretary, usually by 31 March, 30 June, 30 September or 31 December – check the trust's website for current deadlines. Applicants should receive notification of the decision about their application within four weeks of the relevant meeting.

CONTACT DETAILS Jane Marshall, Secretary, c/o BHP Chartered Accountants, 2 Rutland Park, Sheffield, South Yorkshire S10 2PD *Tel.* 0114 266 7171 *Email* jane.marshall@bhp.co.uk *Website* http://jggravescharitabletrust.co.uk

■ Gordon Gray Trust

CC NO 213935   **ESTABLISHED** 1960

WHERE FUNDING CAN BE GIVEN England, with a preference for Gloucestershire and Worcestershire.

WHO CAN BENEFIT Registered charities.

WHAT IS FUNDED General charitable purposes, with a preference for medical charities, the welfare of children and older people, and environmental and local organisations.

WHAT IS NOT FUNDED Individuals.

RANGE OF GRANTS Mostly £500 to £4,000.

SAMPLE GRANTS Avon Navigation Trust (£10,000); Midlands Air Ambulance Charity (£6,000); Multiple Sclerosis Society (£4,000); Action Medical Research (£3,000); Dementia UK (£2,000); Organic Research Centre (£1,000); First Bredon Guides and Bredon Outward Bound Association (£500 each); Gloucestershire Historic Churches Trust (£50).

FINANCES *Financial year end* 30/09/2022
Income £139,200
Grants to organisations £145,600
Assets £6,120,000

TRUSTEES Edward Giles Akerman; Dr B. Gray; Dr Isabel Teague; Mr C. H. Wilder; Mrs S. Watson-Armstrong; Miss R. F. Holmes; Mrs M. M. Gray.

HOW TO APPLY Apply in writing to the correspondent. The trust's Charity Commission record notes that 'if you do not receive a reply to a request for funding, your application has been unsuccessful.'

CONTACT DETAILS Melanie Gray, Clerk to the Trustees, Grange Farm, Main Road, Bredon, Tewkesbury, Gloucestershire GL20 7EL

■ The Great Britain Sasakawa Foundation

CC NO 290766   **ESTABLISHED** 1985

WHERE FUNDING CAN BE GIVEN UK and Japan.

WHO CAN BENEFIT Voluntary, educational and cultural organisations; registered charities benefitting citizens of the UK and Japan. Emphasis is placed on innovative projects and those involving groups of people in both countries (especially young people) rather than individuals.

WHAT IS FUNDED Activities which support mutual understanding between Japanese and UK citizens in the following fields: arts and culture; the humanities and social issues; Japanese language and Japanese studies; medicine and health; science, technology and the environment; sport; young people and education.

WHAT IS NOT FUNDED Individuals; consumables; fees; salaries; purchase of materials; capital projects, such as the purchase, construction or maintenance of buildings; completed or current projects; student fees or travel for study, apart from PhD fieldwork in Japan (limited to £1,000 maximum).

TYPE OF GRANT Pump-priming funding; research funding. Grants are awarded for up to three years.

RANGE OF GRANTS Mostly between £1,500 and £2,000; grants do not normally exceed £5,000 to £6,000 for larger-scale projects. Butterfield Awards: around £5,000 for up to three years.

SAMPLE GRANTS A full list of beneficiaries can be found in the foundation's annual reports, available from its helpful website.

FINANCES *Financial year end* 31/12/2021
Income £1,450,000
Grants to organisations £267,300
Assets £46,580,000

TRUSTEES Prof. David Cope; Ambassador Fujii; Tatsuya Tanami; The Earl of St Andrews; Joanna Pitman; Prof. Yuichi Hosoya; Prof. Yoriko Kawaguchi; Prof. Janet Hunter; Prof. Ryuichi Teshima; Jeremy Scott; Prof. Izumi Kadono.

OTHER INFORMATION The grant total includes amounts awarded to 84 organisations and 1 individual during the year. The foundation also makes grants through its Butterfield Awards programme, for collaboration between qualified professionals in the fields of medical research and public health practice. Grants during the year were broken down as follows: arts and culture (£155,000); medicine and health (£44,500); young people and education (£28,000); humanities and social issues (£27,000); Japanese language (£7,000); science, technology and environment (£5,000). The 2021 accounts were the latest available at the time of writing (June 2023).

HOW TO APPLY Details on how to apply and application forms for the London office can be found on the website. To apply to the Tokyo office, the applicant must email tokyo@gbsf.org.uk before making an application. The trustees make their final decisions on awards at meetings held in London three times a year (normally March, May and November) and Tokyo twice a year (normally April and October). The deadline for London applicants are as follows: 15 December for a decision in March, 31 March for a decision in May and 15 September for a decision in November. The annual deadline for the Butterfield Awards is 15 December.

CONTACT DETAILS The Trustees, Lower Ground Floor, 24 Bedford Row, London WC1R 4TQ *Tel.* 020 7436 9042 *Email* grants@gbsf.org.uk *Website* www.gbsf.org.uk

---

■ The Great Stone Bridge Trust of Edenbridge

CC NO 224309   **ESTABLISHED** 1964

WHERE FUNDING CAN BE GIVEN Edenbridge, Kent.

WHO CAN BENEFIT Charitable organisations; clubs; societies; educational organisations; individuals.

WHAT IS FUNDED General charitable purposes.

TYPE OF GRANT Project funding; start-up funding; capital costs; revenue costs.

SAMPLE GRANTS A list of beneficiaries was not included in the annual report and accounts. Previous beneficiaries have included: Edenbridge Parish Church, Edenbridge Primary School, Eden Valley Museum and West Kent Extra.

FINANCES *Financial year end* 31/12/2021
Income £156,300
Grants to organisations £102,300
Assets £3,300,000

TRUSTEES Roy Cunnington; John Hodson; Giles Jackman; Ben Brownless; Julie Johnson; Julie Thompsett; Robert Todd; Alan Smart; Margot McArthur; Dr Simon Morrison; Peter Brook.

OTHER INFORMATION Grants were made to 32 organisations.

HOW TO APPLY Application forms can be downloaded from the website and should be returned by email to the correspondent.

CONTACT DETAILS Chloe Way, Clerk, Currie Accountancy Ltd, 1st Floor, 13A High Street, Edenbridge, Kent TN8 5AB *Tel.* 01732 381467 *Email* clerk@gsbtrust.org *Website* www.gsbt.co.uk

---

■ The Greater Manchester High Sheriff's Police Trust

CC NO 1040579   **ESTABLISHED** 1994

WHERE FUNDING CAN BE GIVEN Greater Manchester.

WHO CAN BENEFIT Charitable organisations; amateur sports clubs.

WHAT IS FUNDED Prevention of crime; community support; community and race-related initiatives; education relating to substance abuse.

WHAT IS NOT FUNDED Individuals; vehicles; salaries; professional fees.

TYPE OF GRANT Project funding.

RANGE OF GRANTS Mostly up to £5,000.

SAMPLE GRANTS Child Safety Media (£8,500); Stockport Lads Club (£7,500); Homeless Aid UK and Mustard Tree (£5,000 each); The Pankhurst Trust and Wythenshawe Community Farm (£3,500 each); The Destitution Project (£2,100).

FINANCES *Financial year end 31/03/2022* *Income* £264,600 *Grants to organisations* £242,000 *Assets* £5,380,000

TRUSTEES Stephen Watson; Lorraine Worsley-Carter; Diane Hawkins; Mark Adlestone; Eamonn O'Neal; Lady Joy Smith; Sharman Birtles; Nicholas Bird.

OTHER INFORMATION During 2021/22, grants of less than £2,000 totalled £83,300.

HOW TO APPLY Application forms can be downloaded from the trust's website. Once completed, these can be sent to the correspondent via email. The trustees meet four times a year to consider applications.

CONTACT DETAILS Glen Lockett, Head of Income Generation, Neighbourhoods, Confidence and Equality Team, Openshaw Complex, Lawton Street, Openshaw, Manchester M11 2NS *Tel.* 0161 856 8977 *Email* HighSheriff.Trust@gmp.police.uk *Website* www.gmhspt.org

■ The Freddie Green and Family Charitable Foundation

CC NO 1188083 **ESTABLISHED** 2020

WHERE FUNDING CAN BE GIVEN UK.

WHO CAN BENEFIT Registered charities.

WHAT IS FUNDED General charitable purposes.

RANGE OF GRANTS £5,000 to £10,000.

SAMPLE GRANTS Hospice in the Weald and Mental Health Matters (£10,000 each); Homeless Link, The Salvation Army and Tree of Hope (£5,000 each).

FINANCES *Financial year end 31/05/2022* *Income* £6,660,000 *Grants to organisations* £95,000 *Assets* £34,810,000

TRUSTEES John Nicol; Michael Edwards; John Goodchild.

HOW TO APPLY Unsolicited applications are not accepted.

CONTACT DETAILS The Trustees, Henry Streeter Group, Wolfelands Place, High Street, Westerham, Kent TN16 1RQ *Email* info@freddiegreenfoundation.com

■ The Kenneth and Susan Green Charitable Foundation

CC NO 1147248 **ESTABLISHED** 2012

WHERE FUNDING CAN BE GIVEN UK.

WHO CAN BENEFIT Charitable organisations.

WHAT IS FUNDED Social welfare; education; health; arts and culture; heritage; science.

WHAT IS NOT FUNDED Individuals.

RANGE OF GRANTS Up to £250,000.

SAMPLE GRANTS Royal Opera House Covent Garden Foundation (£250,000); Royal Ballet School (£50,000); Royal National Lifeboat Institution (£25,000); The Pepper Foundation (£20,000); Helford River Children's Sailing Trust and Royal Academy of Dance (£10,000 each).

FINANCES *Financial year end 31/12/2021* *Income* £2,210,000 *Grants to organisations* £432,600 *Assets* £9,730,000

TRUSTEES Kenneth Green; Philip Stokes; Susan Green; Sarah Scragg; Charlotte Garlick.

OTHER INFORMATION In 2021, grants were distributed as follows: arts, culture, heritage and science (£310,100); education, health and saving lives (£119,500); relief of poverty (£3,000). Grants of under £10,000 totalled £17,600.

HOW TO APPLY Apply in writing to the correspondent. Previous research suggests that the foundation supports a few specific charities and does not accept new applications.

CONTACT DETAILS The Trustees, c/o Kenneth Green Associates, Hill House, Monument Hill, Weybridge, Surrey KT13 8RX *Tel.* 01932 827 060

■ The Green Hall Foundation

CC NO 270775 **ESTABLISHED** 1976

WHERE FUNDING CAN BE GIVEN UK and overseas.

WHO CAN BENEFIT UK-registered charities only.

WHAT IS FUNDED The foundation makes grants to sustainably improve the lives of older people, young people in need, people with disabilities or illnesses and people who are experiencing homelessness.

WHAT IS NOT FUNDED Individuals; general running costs; salaries.

TYPE OF GRANT Capital costs and special project funding.

RANGE OF GRANTS Typically £1,000 to £10,000.

SAMPLE GRANTS The Salvation Army UK (£25,000); British Red Cross – Haiti Appeal (£10,000); The Children's Trust (£5,000); Warwickshire Wheelchair Basketball Academy (£4,000); Above and Beyond and Demelza House Children's Hospice (£3,000 each); Refreshing Minds and Thames Valley Air Ambulance (£2,000 each).

FINANCES *Financial year end 05/04/2022* *Income* £359,600 *Grants to organisations* £350,000 *Assets* £10,720,000

TRUSTEES Sue Collinson; Margaret Hall; Nigel Hall; Peter Morgan; Charlotte Footer.

HOW TO APPLY Applications must be made online through the foundation's website. The trustees meet twice a year, in May and November. In the May meeting, applications from charities in all income brackets will be considered. In the November meeting, only applications from charities with an annual income of £250,000 or less will be considered. Only the first 150 applications received by the foundation will be taken forward to be considered by the trustees. The opening dates for application cycles are detailed on the website and the cycles close when the 150th application has been received.

CONTACT DETAILS The Trustees, 2nd Floor, International House, 41 The Parade, St Helier, Jersey JE2 3QQ *Tel.* 01534 487757 *Email* greenhallfoundation@fcmtrust.com *Website* www.greenhallfoundation.org

■ The Green Room Charitable Trust

CC NO 1134766 **ESTABLISHED** 2010

WHERE FUNDING CAN BE GIVEN Mainly overseas.

WHO CAN BENEFIT Charitable organisations; social enterprises.

WHAT IS FUNDED General charitable purposes; human rights; social welfare and humanitarian aid; social enterprises; ethical and social impact investment; education overseas.

RANGE OF GRANTS Up to £55,000 with the occasional larger grant.

SAMPLE GRANTS Against Malaria Foundation (£81,200); International Rescue Committee – UK (£50,000); United World (£30,500); Renewable World (£2,000); Horsley, Bookham and Leatherhead Riding for the Disabled Association and The Felix Project (£1,000 each).

FINANCES *Financial year end* 01/10/2021
Income £891,700
Grants to organisations £860,900
Assets £7,910,000

TRUSTEES Tom Prickett; Kelly Prickett; Andrew Ferry.

OTHER INFORMATION The 2020/21 accounts were the latest available at the time of writing (May 2023).

HOW TO APPLY Apply in writing to the correspondent.

CONTACT DETAILS The Trustees, Piccards Wood, Sandy Lane, Guildford GU3 1HF *Tel.* 07855 697603 *Email* thegreenroomct@yahoo.co.uk

■ Philip and Judith Green Trust

CC NO 1109933   **ESTABLISHED** 2005

WHERE FUNDING CAN BE GIVEN UK and overseas.

WHO CAN BENEFIT Registered charities; Christian missionaries; churches; universities.

WHAT IS FUNDED Education in underprivileged communities; support for missionaries and Christian places of worship; health.

SAMPLE GRANTS A list of beneficiaries was not included in the annual report and accounts.

FINANCES *Financial year end* 31/03/2022
Income £68,100
Grants to organisations £125,300
Assets £41,600

TRUSTEES Philip Green; Judith Green.

OTHER INFORMATION Grants were awarded to 15 organisations.

HOW TO APPLY Apply in writing to the correspondent.

CONTACT DETAILS Philip Green, Trustee, c/o Dixon Wilson Chartered Accountants, 22 Chancery Lane, London WC2A 1LS *Tel.* 0118 984 5935 *Email* philipngreen@me.com

■ Greenham Trust Ltd

CC NO 1062762   **ESTABLISHED** 1997

WHERE FUNDING CAN BE GIVEN Newbury and the surrounding area.

WHO CAN BENEFIT Charitable organisations; individuals.

WHAT IS FUNDED General charitable purposes.

WHAT IS NOT FUNDED A list of exclusions can be found on the trust's website.

TYPE OF GRANT Project funding.

SAMPLE GRANTS Corn Exchange Newbury (£603,600); Community Youth Project (£150,000); The Watermill Theatre (£82,900); Hungerford Town Football Club (£75,000).

FINANCES *Financial year end* 31/03/2022
Income £10,540,000
Grants to organisations £1,790,000
Grants to individuals £30,200
Assets £101,430,000

TRUSTEES David Bailey; Graham Mather; Sir Peter Michael; Malcolm Morris; Julian Cazalet; Charles Brims; Biddy Hayward; Zoe Benyon; Robert Woods; Fiona Spencer-Jones; Justyn Waterworth; Justin Barnes; Sarah Scrope.

OTHER INFORMATION In 2021/22, grants were broken down as follows: community (£1.1 million); arts (£192,800); poverty relief (£151,700); young people (£121,700); education (£101,200); health (£52,000); sport

(£47,100); nature and conservation (£16,600); diversity (£9,000); older people (£140).

HOW TO APPLY All applications should be made through The Good Exchange. A link can be found on the trust's website.

CONTACT DETAILS Grants Team, Liberty House, The Enterprise Centre, Greenham Business Park, Newbury, Berkshire RG19 6HS *Tel.* 01635 736740 *Email* grantenquiries@greenhamtrust. com *Website* https://greenhamtrust.com

■ The Greenslade Family Foundation

CC NO 1178046   **ESTABLISHED** 2018

WHERE FUNDING CAN BE GIVEN UK.

WHO CAN BENEFIT Charitable organisations.

WHAT IS FUNDED Extracurricular activities for children and young adults; community recreation.

TYPE OF GRANT Project funding.

RANGE OF GRANTS Grants range from £10,000 to £80,000.

SAMPLE GRANTS Polka Children's Theatre (£80,000); Big Change Charitable Trust (£75,000); Barking and Dagenham Youth Zone, The Amber Foundation and The Prince's Foundation (£25,000 each); Catch 22 Charity and Power of Parenting (£10,000 each).

FINANCES *Financial year end* 05/04/2022
Income £227,900
Grants to organisations £250,000
Assets £5,170,000

TRUSTEES Carolyn Greenslade; Carol Bailey; James Wilcox.

HOW TO APPLY Contact the correspondent for further information.

CONTACT DETAILS The Trustees, 24 James Street West, Bath, London BA1 2BT *Email* laurence.barrat@floreat.com

■ The Greggs Foundation

CC NO 296590   **ESTABLISHED** 1987

WHERE FUNDING CAN BE GIVEN The North East (Durham, Northumberland, Teesside and Tyne and Wear).

WHO CAN BENEFIT Charitable organisations; community groups; not-for-profit organisations; schools; individuals.

WHAT IS FUNDED Social welfare; people with disabilities; homelessness; carers; older people; isolated people.

WHAT IS NOT FUNDED See the foundation's website for a full list of exclusions.

TYPE OF GRANT Core and running costs; project costs. Funding may be given for up to three years. The type of funding is dependent on the grants programme.

RANGE OF GRANTS Up to £60,000.

SAMPLE GRANTS A list of beneficiaries was not included in the annual report and accounts.

FINANCES *Financial year end* 31/12/2021
Income £3,310,000
Grants to organisations £1,840,000
Grants to individuals £1,690,000
Assets £29,020,000

TRUSTEE The Greggs Foundation Trustee.

HOW TO APPLY Apply online via the foundation's website. Each grants programme has its own criteria, guidelines and application process, all of which are available to view on the website.

CONTACT DETAILS The Trustees, Greggs House, Quorum Business Park, Newcastle upon Tyne, Tyne and Wear NE12 8BU *Tel.* 0191 212 7626 *Email* grants@greggsfoundation.org.uk *Website* www.greggsfoundation.org.uk

■ The Gretna Charitable Trust

CC NO 1020533   ESTABLISHED 1993

WHERE FUNDING CAN BE GIVEN UK, with a preference for Hertfordshire and London.

WHO CAN BENEFIT Registered charities; individuals.

WHAT IS FUNDED General charitable purposes.

SAMPLE GRANTS A list of beneficiaries was not included in the annual report and accounts. Previous beneficiaries have included: British Australia Society; Charlie Waller Memorial Trust; Garden Museum – Lambeth; Haileybury Youth Club; Mensah Recovery Support Agency; Royal Engineers Museum; The Globe Theatre; The Scout Association; World Sight Foundation.

FINANCES *Financial year end* 05/04/2022
Income £82,200
Grants to organisations £77,500
Assets £58,900

TRUSTEES Susan Walduck; Alexander Walduck; Alison Duncan.

OTHER INFORMATION Note that the grant total may include amounts awarded to individuals.

HOW TO APPLY Our previous research suggests that the trustees discourage unsolicited applications.

CONTACT DETAILS Alexander Walduck, Trustee, c/o Directors' Office, Imperial Hotel, 61–66 Russell Square, London WC1B 5BB *Tel.* 020 7691 2623 *Email* awalduck@imperialhotels.co.uk

■ The Grimmitt Trust

CC NO 801975   ESTABLISHED 1986

WHERE FUNDING CAN BE GIVEN Birmingham, Dudley, Walsall and Wolverhampton postcode areas.

WHO CAN BENEFIT Registered charities; unregistered charities; hospitals; hospices; individuals; PTAs; universities.

WHAT IS FUNDED Community development; children and youth; culture and education; health; older people; overseas aid.

WHAT IS NOT FUNDED National charities; CICs; social enterprises.

TYPE OF GRANT General funding; project funding; core/revenue costs; unrestricted funding.

RANGE OF GRANTS Mostly £1,000 to £5,000.

SAMPLE GRANTS Christian Aid (£20,000); All We Can (£10,000); St Martin's Youth Centre (£4,000); Birmingham Centre for Art Therapies and Brierley Hill Samaritans (£3,000 each); Age Concern Birmingham (£2,500); Sport4Life, The Cotteridge Church and West Midlands Care Team (£2,000 each).

FINANCES *Financial year end* 05/04/2022
Income £371,200
Grants to organisations £307,000
Grants to individuals £1,100
Assets £13,340,000

TRUSTEES Sue Day; Mr A. David Owen; Tim Welch; Sarah Wilkey; Phil Smith; Trevor Jones; Emma Pardoe; Catherine Chase.

OTHER INFORMATION Grants were made to 169 organisations and distributed as follows: community (£133,600); children and young people (£60,500); culture and education (£49,300); overseas (£30,800); medical and health (£23,500); older people (£11,900).

HOW TO APPLY Applicants should contact the secretary, who will advise on the best way to make a grant request and to ensure that all the necessary information is included. The trustees meet three times a year to consider applications.

CONTACT DETAILS Vanessa Welch, Secretary, 151B All Saints Road, Kings Heath, Birmingham, West Midlands B14 6AT *Email* admin@grimmitt-trust.org.uk

■ The Grocers' Charity

CC NO 255230   ESTABLISHED 1968

WHERE FUNDING CAN BE GIVEN UK.

WHO CAN BENEFIT UK-registered charities; churches.

WHAT IS FUNDED General charitable purposes, with a preference for children and young people, prevention of (re)offending, social welfare and reducing plastic waste and emissions.

WHAT IS NOT FUNDED Places of worship; educational establishments; hospices; charities whose beneficiaries are overseas; non-UK-registered charities; non-medical charities with a turnover of over £500,000; individuals.

TYPE OF GRANT Project funding; core costs.

RANGE OF GRANTS Mostly under £10,000.

SAMPLE GRANTS Oundle School (£150,000); Mental Health Research (£53,900); City and Guilds of London Art School (£22,500); The Brain Tumour Charity (£10,000); Teach the Future (£6,000); Almeida Theatre, Blind in Business Trust and St Mary-le-Bow – Cheapside (£5,000 each); International Otter Survival Fund (£4,500); Hackney Caribbean Elderly Organisation and High Barnet Chamber Music Festival (£2,500 each); ABF The Soldiers' Charity (£1,000).

FINANCES *Financial year end* 31/07/2022
Income £1,000,000
Grants to organisations £1,020,000
Assets £34,320,000

TRUSTEE The Grocers' Trust Company Ltd.

OTHER INFORMATION During 2021/22, 164 grants were awarded for the following purposes: education (£311,900); relief of poverty (£213,200); health (£161,900); young people (£100,500); disability (£54,300); the environment (£45,000); older people (£38,500); churches (£37,800); arts (£28,500); military (£26,000); heritage (£6,000).

HOW TO APPLY Applications can be made via the charity's website, where upcoming deadlines can be found. The Education and Charities Committee usually meets four times a year to consider applications.

CONTACT DETAILS Michelle Molyneux, Charity Manager, Grocers' Hall, Princes Street, London EC2R 8AD *Tel.* 020 7606 3113 *Email* charity@grocershall.co.uk *Website* www.grocershall.co.uk

■ M. and R. Gross Charities Ltd

CC NO 251888   ESTABLISHED 1967

WHERE FUNDING CAN BE GIVEN UK and overseas.

WHO CAN BENEFIT Jewish organisations.

WHAT IS FUNDED Orthodox Jewish educational and religious activities; the relief of Jewish people who are in need.

SAMPLE GRANTS United Talmudical Associates Ltd (£643,000); Asser Bishvil Foundation (£379,000); Congregation Sharei Sholom Tchabe Ltd (£143,000); Myrdle Charities (£122,500); British Friends of Rabbi Meir Baal Haness Charity (£110,000).

FINANCES *Financial year end* 31/03/2022
Income £4,930,000
Grants to organisations £3,240,000
Assets £54,560,000

TRUSTEES Rifka Gross; Sarah Padwa; Michael Saberski; Leonard Lerner.

HOW TO APPLY Apply in writing to the correspondent. Applications are assessed regularly and many smaller grants are dealt with through the grant-making agency United Talmudical Associates Ltd.

CONTACT DETAILS Rifka Gross, Secretary, c/o Cohen Arnold, New Burlington House, 1075 Finchley Road, London NW11 0PU *Tel.* 020 8731 0777 *Email* mail@cohenarnold.com

■ Groundwork UK

CC NO 291558   **ESTABLISHED** 1982

WHERE FUNDING CAN BE GIVEN UK.

WHO CAN BENEFIT Registered charities and community groups.

WHAT IS FUNDED Environmental conservation and protection; climate change; health and well-being; access to learning and work and opportunities; community development.

TYPE OF GRANT Capital costs; core/revenue costs; project funding.

SAMPLE GRANTS A list of beneficiaries was not included in the annual report and accounts.

FINANCES *Financial year end* 31/03/2022
Income £21,670,000
Grants to organisations £7,750,000
Assets £5,620,000

TRUSTEES Alan Smith; Graham Hartley; Graham Parry; Antony Nelson; Paul Roots; Jeff Greenidge; Jack White; Faiza Amin; Stuart Bonham; Anne-Marie Simpson; Andrew Thurston; Nigel Reader; Patrick Hughes; Claire Marshall; Karen Balmer; Margot Madin; Tina Cunliffe.

OTHER INFORMATION Groundwork UK manages a number of grant schemes on behalf of businesses, public sector and third sector partners.

HOW TO APPLY Check the Groundwork UK website for details of grant programmes currently being administered.

CONTACT DETAILS The Trustees, Suite B2, The Walker Building, 58 Oxford Street, Birmingham, West Midlands B5 5NR *Tel.* 0121 236 8565 *Email* info@groundwork.org.uk *Website* www.groundwork.org.uk

■ The Albert Gubay Charitable Foundation

CC NO 1193970   **ESTABLISHED** 2016

WHERE FUNDING CAN BE GIVEN England; Wales; Isle of Man; Republic of Ireland.

WHO CAN BENEFIT Registered charities.

WHAT IS FUNDED Amateur sport; care leavers; older people; people who have experience of the criminal justice system; homelessness; medical research; drug and substance misuse; people with cognitive or learning disabilities; people with terminal illnesses or life-limiting conditions; worship and community outreach; domestic abuse; slavery.

SAMPLE GRANTS Church Urban Fund (£172,000); Aber Morfa Mission Area (£100,000); Access Sport CIO (£21,200); Families United Network (£15,000); Recycling Lives (£8,000).

FINANCES *Financial year end* 31/03/2022
Income £40,790,000
Grants to organisations £4,030,000
Assets £630,980,000

TRUSTEE The Albert Gubay Trustee Ltd.

HOW TO APPLY To enquire about funding, contact enquiries@theagfoundation.org.

CONTACT DETAILS The Trustees, 3 Denmark Street, Goose Green, Altrincham WA14 2SS *Tel.* 0161 703 7992 *Email* enquiries@theagfoundation.org *Website* www.thederwentgroup.com/about-us/ag-foundation

■ The Walter Guinness Charitable Trust

CC NO 205375   **ESTABLISHED** 1968

WHERE FUNDING CAN BE GIVEN UK, with a preference for Wiltshire; India.

WHO CAN BENEFIT Registered charities and community groups.

WHAT IS FUNDED Medical research; projects relating to people with disabilities, older people, veterans, prisoners, children, families and young people.

RANGE OF GRANTS £1,000 to £5,000.

SAMPLE GRANTS Listening Books (£5,000); Salisbury Cathedral (£4,000); Wiltshire Air Ambulance (£3,000); Young Lives vs Cancer (£2,500); Brainwave and Brendon Care (£2,000 each); Tall Ships (£1,500); Revitalise (£1,100).

FINANCES *Financial year end* 05/04/2022
Income £154,700
Grants to organisations £160,600
Assets £11,230,000

TRUSTEES Catriona Guinness; Finn Guinness; Rosaleen Mulji.

OTHER INFORMATION In 2021/22, the trust awarded grants to 104 organisations.

HOW TO APPLY Apply in writing to the correspondent.

CONTACT DETAILS The Trustees, Biddesden House, Biddesden, Andover, Hampshire SP11 9DN *Tel.* 01582 439270 *Email* WGuinnessCT@tmf-group.com

■ Calouste Gulbenkian Foundation – UK Branch

ESTABLISHED 1956

WHERE FUNDING CAN BE GIVEN UK and the Republic of Ireland.

WHO CAN BENEFIT Registered charities; unregistered charities; CICs; social enterprises.

WHAT IS FUNDED The foundation's UK branch focuses on three themes: Valuing the Ocean – connecting and building relationships designed to help protect the oceans; Citizen Engagement on Climate – demonstrating what effective public engagement on climate looks like and creating conditions for its scaling; and The Civic Role of Arts Organisations – creating a movement of change-makers who want arts organisations to play a civic role in their communities.

TYPE OF GRANT Core/revenue costs; project funding; unrestricted funding.

SAMPLE GRANTS A list of beneficiaries was not available. Previous beneficiaries have included: Arts Homelessness International; Birmingham Royal Ballet; Climate Outreach; Common Vision; John Ellerman Foundation; Marine Alliance for Science and Technology for Scotland; Marine Conservation Society; Streetwise Opera; University of St Andrews; UK Health Alliance on Climate Change.

FINANCES *Financial year end* 31/03/2022
Grants to organisations £1,700,000

TRUSTEE Martin Essayan.

OTHER INFORMATION As the foundation is not a charity registered in the UK, it does not have a record on the Charity Commission's website. The foundation files an annual review on its website. The 2021/22 annual review states that 'outgoings' for the year were as follows (we have used the sum of these outgoings as the foundation's grant total for the year): climate (£644,700), the ocean (£561,100) and arts organisations (£494,500).

HOW TO APPLY Unsolicited applications are not accepted.

CONTACT DETAILS Louisa Hopper, Director, 50 Hoxton Square, London N1 6PB *Tel.* 020 7739 1961 *Email* info@gulbenkian.org.uk *Website* https://gulbenkian.pt/uk-branch

....

■ Dr Guthrie's Association

OSCR NO SC009302   **ESTABLISHED** 1986

WHERE FUNDING CAN BE GIVEN Scotland, with a preference for Edinburgh.

WHO CAN BENEFIT Not-for-profit organisations.

WHAT IS FUNDED The care and welfare of disadvantaged young people under the age of 22. Priority will be given to: organisations supporting economically and socially disadvantaged children and young people aged 10–21 years; small local organisations (as opposed to national organisations); creative and outdoor pursuits for disadvantaged children and young people; and organisations supporting young unemployed people.

WHAT IS NOT FUNDED Individuals; environmental or conservation projects; other grant-making or fundraising charities; endowment funds; building or restoration projects; retrospective expenditure. The application form gives further examples of what will not be supported.

TYPE OF GRANT One-off.

RANGE OF GRANTS £250 to £2,000.

SAMPLE GRANTS Children 1st (£2,000); Cyrenians and Edinburgh Young Carers (£1,500 each); Scottish Huntington's Association (£1,000); Hurlford and Crookedholm Early Learning and Childhood Centres (£900); Lothian Autistic Society (£500).

FINANCES *Financial year end* 31/03/2022
Income £37,200
Grants to organisations £96,400
Assets £2,150,000

HOW TO APPLY Application forms are available to download from the administrator's website.

CONTACT DETAILS The Grant Administrator, PO Box 28838, Edinburgh EH15 2XZ *Email* drguthrie16@gmail.com *Website* www.azets.co.uk/dr-guthrie-s-association

....

■ The Guy Foundation

CC NO 1178782

WHERE FUNDING CAN BE GIVEN Worldwide.

WHO CAN BENEFIT Universities; non-profit research organisations; individuals.

WHAT IS FUNDED Quantum biology research.

TYPE OF GRANT Project funding; research.

SAMPLE GRANTS A list of beneficiaries was not available.

FINANCES *Financial year end* 30/04/2022
Income £5,000
Grants to organisations £334,300
Grants to individuals £30,000
Assets £112,000

TRUSTEES Dr Geoffrey Guy; Katherine Guy; Jonathan Laughton; Richard Brass; Eric Dixon; Lord William Waldegrave of North Hill.

OTHER INFORMATION The foundation provides funding support for elite competitors in sports that are strongly influenced by neuropsychology, such as shooting and fencing.

HOW TO APPLY Contact the foundation for further information.

CONTACT DETAILS The Trustees, The Estate Office, Chedington Court, Chedington, Beaminster DT8 3HY *Tel.* 0151 600 3341 *Email* info@theguyfoundation.org *Website* www.theguyfoundation.org

■ H. and T. Clients Charitable Trust

CC NO 1104345   **ESTABLISHED** 2004
WHERE FUNDING CAN BE GIVEN UK and overseas.
WHO CAN BENEFIT Charitable organisations.
WHAT IS FUNDED General charitable purposes, including medical research and care.
SAMPLE GRANTS Helping Treating Cancer Together Committee (£152,700); Clarat LLP (£8,800); Ambulance Service (£250); Andy Sarsby Foundation (£180).
FINANCES *Financial year end 05/04/2022*
Income £311,500
Grants to organisations £245,300
Assets £929,000
TRUSTEES Ronnie Harris; Neville Newman; Charlotte Harris; Jamie Taylor.
HOW TO APPLY Apply in writing to the correspondent.
CONTACT DETAILS The Trustees, 64 New Cavendish Street, London W1G 8TB *Tel.* 020 7467 6300

■ H. P. Charitable Trust

CC NO 278006   **ESTABLISHED** 1979
WHERE FUNDING CAN BE GIVEN UK and overseas.
WHO CAN BENEFIT Orthodox Jewish charities.
WHAT IS FUNDED General charitable purposes; advancement of Orthodox Judaism; poverty relief.
RANGE OF GRANTS Typically £25,000 to £50,000, with some larger grants.
SAMPLE GRANTS Mercas Hatorah Belz Machnovke (£100,000); Kehal Yisroel D'Chasidei Gur (£62,000); CMZ Ltd and Friends of Beis Chinuch Lebonos (£50,000 each); Beis Ahron TT Activity Centre and C.M.A. Community Nursery (£25,000 each); Bais Rochel Dsatmer (£20,000).
FINANCES *Financial year end 30/06/2022*
Income £289,900
Grants to organisations £771,500
Assets £5,660,000
TRUSTEES Arthur Zonszajn; Aron Piller; Hannah Piller; Isaac Freilich.
HOW TO APPLY Apply in writing to the correspondent.
CONTACT DETAILS Aron Piller, Trustee, 26 Lingwood Road, London E5 9BN *Tel.* 020 8806 2432 *Email* apiller26@gmail.com

■ Hackney Parochial Charities

CC NO 219876   **ESTABLISHED** 1904
WHERE FUNDING CAN BE GIVEN Hackney.
WHO CAN BENEFIT Registered charities; CICs; schools; hospitals; hospices; religious bodies/institutions; individuals.
WHAT IS FUNDED Social welfare; older people; children and young people; support organisations.
WHAT IS NOT FUNDED A full list of exclusions can be found on the charity's website.
TYPE OF GRANT Core/revenue costs; project funding.
RANGE OF GRANTS Up to £40,000.
SAMPLE GRANTS Hackney Church (£40,000); East End Citizens Advice (£30,000); Choice in Hackney (£5,600); Hackney Shed (£5,000); Made in Hackney (£3,000).
FINANCES *Financial year end 31/03/2022*
Income £369,400
Grants to organisations £286,900
Grants to individuals £42,000
Assets £8,240,000
TRUSTEES Mary Cannon; Nicola Baboneau; Cllr Chris Kennedy; Allan Hilton; Irfan Malik; Rob Chapman; The Revd Alexander Gordon; Jacquie Driver; Cllr Sharon Patrick.
HOW TO APPLY Application forms are available to download from the charity's website.
CONTACT DETAILS The Trustees, Unit 11, 8–20 Well Street, London E9 7PX *Tel.* 01285 841900 *Email* ooffice@thetrustpartnership.com *Website* www.hackneyparochialcharities.org.uk

■ The Hadfield Charitable Trust

CC NO 1067491   **ESTABLISHED** 1997
WHERE FUNDING CAN BE GIVEN Cumbria.
WHO CAN BENEFIT Charitable organisations.
WHAT IS FUNDED Young people and employment; social welfare; older people; the arts; the environment.
TYPE OF GRANT Mainly one-off (occasionally for two to three years); project funding: capital costs preferred, revenue costs considered.
RANGE OF GRANTS Up to of £5,000, but mainly between £1,000 and £3,000.
SAMPLE GRANTS Always Another Way Cumbria Ltd CIC (£5,000); Eyes Open (£4,000); Houghton Village Hall and Howgill Village Hall (£3,000 each); MHA (£2,000); Penrith Cricket, Sport and Social Club (£1,000).
FINANCES *Financial year end 31/08/2021*
Income £298,100
Grants to organisations £281,200
Assets £9,760,000
TRUSTEES Andrew Morris; Roy Morris; William Rathbone; Andrew Forsyth; Caroline Addison; Duncan Bailey.
OTHER INFORMATION According to the 2020/21 accounts, grants were distributed as follows: social needs (£146,800); young people and employment (£90,200); the arts (£26,400); older people (£8,000); the environment (£7,800); other (£2,000). The 2020/21 accounts were the latest available at the time of writing (May 2023).
HOW TO APPLY Application forms are available from the trust's website. The completed application form should be sent to the administrator by post or email along with supporting documents, details of which are on the website. Application deadlines are usually 1 February, 1 June and 1 October; applications must be received by midday on these dates to be considered. Applicants are encouraged to contact the trust before applying to discuss their plans.
CONTACT DETAILS Susan Berriman, Trust Administrator, c/o Rathbone Investment Management, Port of Liverpool Building, Pier Head, Liverpool, Merseyside L3 1NW *Tel.* 01539 823112 *Email* admin@hadfieldtrust.org.uk *Website* www.hadfieldtrust.org.uk

■ The Hadley Trust

CC NO 1064823   **ESTABLISHED** 1997
WHERE FUNDING CAN BE GIVEN UK and overseas.
WHO CAN BENEFIT Registered charities; organisations with charitable purposes.
WHAT IS FUNDED Crime and justice; young people; disabilities; social investment; health; welfare reform; hospices.

422

Does the funder you have chosen match your needs? Haphazard applications waste postage and time

TYPE OF GRANT Core costs; project funding; capital costs; development funding.

RANGE OF GRANTS Up to £1.23 million.

SAMPLE GRANTS A list of beneficiaries was not included in the annual report and accounts.

FINANCES *Financial year end 31/03/2022*
Income £4,680,000
Grants to organisations £3,940,000
Assets £348,630,000

TRUSTEES Lady Janet Hulme; Sir Philip Hulme; Thomas Hulme; Katherine Prideaux; Sophie Swift; Juliet Lyon.

OTHER INFORMATION Grants were awarded to 73 organisations and were awarded in the following categories: crime and justice (£1.23 million); international (£1 million); young people (£721,400); local (£331,100); social investment (£300,000); disabilities (£124,000); medical causes (£100,000); hospices (£95,000).

HOW TO APPLY Apply in writing to the correspondent. Although the majority of the trust's funds are already committed, new applications are still considered.

CONTACT DETAILS Carol Biggs, Gladsmuir, Hadley Common, Barnet, Hertfordshire EN5 5QE *Tel.* 020 8447 4577 *Email* carol@hadleytrust.org

■ The Hadrian Trust

CC NO 272161   **ESTABLISHED** 1976

WHERE FUNDING CAN BE GIVEN Tyne and Wear, Northumberland and Durham, including Hartlepool.

WHO CAN BENEFIT Registered charities; CICs; social enterprises; PTAs; hospices.

WHAT IS FUNDED Social welfare; young people; disability; older people; women; ethnic minorities; education; the arts; the environment. There is a detailed list of areas of interest within each category on the website.

WHAT IS NOT FUNDED Capital projects for major building improvements; repair of buildings used solely for worship; animal protection charities; charities based outside the geographic area of benefit; national charities making general appeals; individuals.

TYPE OF GRANT Capital costs; project costs; part salaries; core/revenue costs; seed funding/start-up funding.

RANGE OF GRANTS Mostly between £500 and £2,000.

SAMPLE GRANTS A list of beneficiaries was not included in the annual report and accounts.

FINANCES *Financial year end 30/09/2022*
Income £256,500
Grants to organisations £234,600
Assets £8,730,000

TRUSTEES Pauline Dodgson; Jim Dias; Colin Fitzpatrick; Ian Brown; Catherine Wood; Dorothy Parker.

OTHER INFORMATION A total of 201 grants were made during 2021/22.

HOW TO APPLY Applications can be made online via the trust's website or by post. The trustees meet quarterly, usually in January, April, July and October. Applications must be received three weeks before the trustees' meeting. Refer to the website for application deadlines and information on what to include.

CONTACT DETAILS The Trustees, PO Box 785, Whitley Bay, Tyne and Wear NE26 9DW *Tel.* 07815 785074 *Email* enquiries@hadriantrust.co.uk *Website* www.hadriantrust.co.uk

■ Halifax Foundation for Northern Ireland

CCNI NO NIC101763   **ESTABLISHED** 1986

WHERE FUNDING CAN BE GIVEN Northern Ireland.

WHO CAN BENEFIT Registered charities with incomes of under £1 million.

WHAT IS FUNDED Social and community needs including: community services, advice services, people with special needs; health, civic responsibility, cultural enrichment; education and training.

WHAT IS NOT FUNDED See the foundation's website for a full list of exclusions.

TYPE OF GRANT Core costs; materials and equipment; salary costs; volunteer expenses; project costs; refurbishment; training; disabled access; transport costs.

RANGE OF GRANTS Programme dependent.

SAMPLE GRANTS A list of beneficiaries was not included in the annual report and accounts.

FINANCES *Financial year end 31/12/2021*
Income £1,600,000
Grants to organisations £1,040,000
Assets £2,830,000

TRUSTEES Barry Connolly; Gillian Boyd; Áine McCoy; Michael Prendergast; Ken Simpson; Melvin Slaine; Brenda Kelly; Dionne Darragh; Jenny Ebbage; Niall Parfitt; Becca Hume.

OTHER INFORMATION Grants were awarded to 227 organisations in 2021 in the following categories: social and community welfare (£701,400), education and training (£280,800) and matched giving (£59,600).

HOW TO APPLY All applications must be made online via the foundation's website, where full guidelines, including a list of supporting documentation required, are available. The Community Grants Programme is operated on a rolling basis.

CONTACT DETAILS The Trustees, Clifton House Heritage Centre, 2 North Queen Street, Belfast BT15 1ES *Tel.* 028 9032 3000 *Email* grants@halifaxfoundationni.org *Website* www.halifaxfoundationni.org

■ Hamamelis Trust

CC NO 280938   **ESTABLISHED** 1980

WHERE FUNDING CAN BE GIVEN UK, but with a special interest in the Godalming and Surrey areas.

WHO CAN BENEFIT Registered charities; universities.

WHAT IS FUNDED Medical research and ecological conservation.

WHAT IS NOT FUNDED Projects outside the UK.

RANGE OF GRANTS Up to £20,000 but typically less than £3,000.

SAMPLE GRANTS Disability Challengers (£4,000); Forest of Avon Trust, Somerset Wildlife Trust and The Barn Owl Trust (£3,000 each); Clowns in the Sky (£2,400).

FINANCES *Financial year end 05/04/2022*
Income £91,500
Grants to organisations £72,000
Assets £3,850,000

TRUSTEES Laura Dadswell; Dr Adam Stone; Lucy Mirouze.

OTHER INFORMATION In 2021/22, grants were made to 24 organisations. Each year grants are split equally between medical research and ecological conservation.

HOW TO APPLY Apply in writing to the correspondent. All applicants are asked to include a short summary of the project with estimated costings. Unsuccessful applications are not acknowledged. Medical applications are assessed by Dr Adam Stone, who is a medically qualified trustee.

CONTACT DETAILS Laura Dadswell, Trustee, c/o Penningtons Manches Cooper LLP, 31 Chertsey Street, Guildford, Surrey GU1 4HD *Tel.* 01483 791800

■ The Hamilton Davies Trust

CC NO 1106123   **ESTABLISHED** 2004
WHERE FUNDING CAN BE GIVEN Cadishead; Irlam; Rixton-with-Glazebrook.
WHO CAN BENEFIT Not-for-profit organisations with a governing body or committee, bank account and constitution (including registered charities, amateur sports clubs, parish councils, schools and colleges, CICs and voluntary/community groups); individuals.
WHAT IS FUNDED Community development and regeneration; education; recreation.
TYPE OF GRANT One-off grants; core costs; capital costs.
SAMPLE GRANTS A list of beneficiaries was not included in the annual report and accounts. Previous beneficiaries have included: Newton-le-Willows Boys' and Girls' Club (£270,000); Manchester Technology Trust (£180,000); Manchester United Foundation (£25,000); Lady James' Hall (£8,000); St Helen's Primary School (£6,200); 2nd Irlam Scout Group (£3,500); Preston Hall (£3,000); Hollins Green Bowling Club (£900); Irlam Junior Football Club (£500).
FINANCES *Financial year end* 05/04/2022
Income £120,700
Grants to organisations £562,400
Grants to individuals £3,800
Assets £2,630,000
TRUSTEES Frank Cocker; Graham Chisnall; Neil McArthur.
OTHER INFORMATION The trust also supports young people looking to develop practical and employability skills through the Chris Stocks Fund.
HOW TO APPLY There are three levels of grant available – see the trust's website for information on the application process and what to include. Smaller requests for under £150 are processed quicker than applications for larger amounts.
CONTACT DETAILS The Trustees, Hamilton Davies House, 117C Liverpool Road, Cadishead, Manchester M44 5BG *Tel.* 0161 222 4003 *Email* hello@hamiltondavies.org.uk *Website* www.hamiltondavies.org.uk

■ Paul Hamlyn Foundation

CC NO 1102927   **ESTABLISHED** 1987
WHERE FUNDING CAN BE GIVEN UK and India (Assam; Bihar; Chhattisgarh; Jharkhand; Madhya Pradesh; Odisha; West Bengal).
WHO CAN BENEFIT Registered charities and organisations; NGOs.
WHAT IS FUNDED Education; the arts; teacher development; people who are disadvantaged; children and young people; migration; communities in India; social change.
WHAT IS NOT FUNDED See the 'Exclusions' page of the foundation's website for full details of what will not be supported.
TYPE OF GRANT Programme dependent.
RANGE OF GRANTS Programme dependent.
SAMPLE GRANTS Esmée Fairbairn Foundation (£1 million); Coram Children's Legal Centre (£300,000); Touretteshero CIC (£120,000);

Youth Access (£50,000); Young Manchester (£7,000).
FINANCES *Financial year end* 31/03/2022
Income £5,050,000
Grants to organisations £37,130,000
Assets £915,130,000
TRUSTEES Tim Bunting; Michael Hamlyn; Jane Hamlyn; James Lingwood; Tom Wylie; Lord Anthony Hall; Charles Leadbeater; Dr Janet McKenley-Simpson; Claire Whitaker; Andrew Headley; Akeela Ahmed.
OTHER INFORMATION Grants were awarded to 463 organisations.
HOW TO APPLY Applications can only be submitted via the online application process. Information about available funds and grants can be found on the foundation's detailed website.
CONTACT DETAILS The Grants Team, 5–11 Leeke Street, London WC1X 9HY *Tel.* 020 7812 3300 *Email* information@phf.org.uk *Website* www.phf.org.uk

■ The Helen Hamlyn Trust

CC NO 1084839   **ESTABLISHED** 2000
WHERE FUNDING CAN BE GIVEN Worldwide, with a preference for the UK and India.
WHO CAN BENEFIT Charitable organisations, with a focus on innovative medium and long-term projects; small local and regional charities; museums; educational organisations.
WHAT IS FUNDED Medical innovation; education and welfare; arts and culture, including the professional development of musicians and performing artists; young people; young offenders; conserving heritage in India; international humanitarian affairs; older people.
TYPE OF GRANT Project funding; core costs; research; development costs.
RANGE OF GRANTS Up to £1 million; small grants of up to £10,000.
SAMPLE GRANTS The Royal College of Art (£1 million); University of Oxford Bodleian Libraries (£467,000); The Helen Hamlyn Centre for Design (£250,000); Pegasus Theatre Trust (£30,000); RAW Workshop (£10,000); Parenting Mental Health (£7,500); Oxfordshire Youth (£5,000); Autism Bedfordshire (£4,000).
FINANCES *Financial year end* 31/03/2022
Income £7,400,000
Grants to organisations £7,120,000
Assets £5,930,000
TRUSTEES Brendan Cahill; Dr Kate Gavron; Lady Hamlyn; Margaret O'Rorke; Dr Deborah Swallow; Dr Shobita Punja; Stephen Lewin; Dame Alison Peacock; Lord Ara Darzi; Baroness Gail Rebuck.
OTHER INFORMATION During 2021/22, grants were awarded for the following purposes: medical causes (£4.18 million); education and welfare (£1.2 million); arts and culture (£448,900); healthy ageing (£447,500); international humanitarian affairs (£10,000).
HOW TO APPLY The trust's website states: 'For further information, contact: The Helen Hamlyn Trust, 129 Old Church Street, London, SW3 6EB'.
CONTACT DETAILS John Roche, Director of Finance and Administration, 129 Old Church Street, London SW3 6EB *Tel.* 07969 811531 *Email* john.roche@helenhamlyntrust.org *Website* www.phf.org.uk/our-work-in-the-uk/helen-hamlyn-trust

■ Hammersmith United Charities

CC NO 205856   **ESTABLISHED** 1992

WHERE FUNDING CAN BE GIVEN The eight northern wards of Hammersmith and Fulham.

WHO CAN BENEFIT Registered charities; constituted organisations such as CICs; schools (for extracurricular activities and where the school can show that children experiencing some kind of disadvantage will benefit).

WHAT IS FUNDED Families and children; homelessness; social welfare; social mobility and inclusion; disabilities; community work.

WHAT IS NOT FUNDED Religious or political causes; animal welfare; environmental causes; work outside the beneficial area.

TYPE OF GRANT Core costs; project funding.

RANGE OF GRANTS Generally £250 to £10,000.

SAMPLE GRANTS Lido Foundation (£20,000); Bush Theatre (£15,000); Hammersmith Community Gardens Association (£10,000); Hammersmith and Fulham Age UK (£8,800); Fulham Reach Boat club (£6,500); This New Ground (£5,000); Grove Neighbourhood Folk Art Group (£3,000); The Upper Room (£250).

FINANCES *Financial year end 31/03/2022*
Income £1,160,000
Grants to organisations £405,000
Assets £34,780,000

TRUSTEE Hammersmith United Trustee Company.

OTHER INFORMATION In total, 57 grants were awarded during the year.

HOW TO APPLY The charity welcomes initial grant enquiries by phone or email. The charity's website states: 'We like to meet new applicants to develop a better understanding of what they are doing and we are happy to give advice about potential projects.' Application forms can be downloaded from the website. The charity has three grants committee meetings each year; the dates of these and the dates by which forms must be received for each meeting are advertised on the website. Once completed, application forms must be emailed to the correspondent. The charity's helpful website provides a number of documents relating to grant-making guidelines and the type of grants which the trustees are willing to award.

CONTACT DETAILS The Trustees, Sycamore House, Sycamore Gardens, London W6 OAS *Tel.* 020 8741 4326 *Email* grants@hamunitedcharities. com *Website* www.hamunitedcharities.org.uk

■ Hampshire and Isle of Wight Community Foundation

CC NO 1100417   **ESTABLISHED** 2002

WHERE FUNDING CAN BE GIVEN Hampshire and the Isle of Wight.

WHO CAN BENEFIT Charities; voluntary, community and faith groups; social enterprises; hospices; CICs.

WHAT IS FUNDED General charitable purposes.

WHAT IS NOT FUNDED See the website for programme-specific exclusions.

TYPE OF GRANT Programme dependent.

RANGE OF GRANTS Programme dependent.

SAMPLE GRANTS Countryside Education Trust (£25,000); It's Your Choice (£14,400); Suicide Prevention and Intervention (£16,000 in two grants); The Girls' Network (£9,000 in two grants); Romsey Young Carers Project (£5,100); Parenting Network CIC (£3,900); Solent Powerchair Football Club (£2,000); St Francis Church KraftiKids (£650); 3rd Ryde Girls' Brigade (£200); Polygon School (£86).

FINANCES *Financial year end 31/12/2021*
Income £1,600,000
Grants to organisations £1,800,000
Grants to individuals £12,500
Assets £17,940,000

TRUSTEES Dr Hugh Mason; Jane Sandars; Jo Ash; Rebecca Kennelly; Cllr Dan Putty; James Kennedy; Cllr Andrew Joy; Krysia Butwilowska; Sukanya Sitaram; Michael Smith; Richard Barton-Wood.

OTHER INFORMATION This is one of the 47 UK community foundations, which distribute funding for a wide range of purposes. As with all community foundations, there are a number of donor-advised funds managed on behalf of individuals, families and charitable trusts. Grant schemes tend to change frequently – consult the foundation's website for details of current programmes and up-to-date deadlines. A full list of beneficiaries can be downloaded from the website.

HOW TO APPLY Potential applicants should see the foundation's website for details of which grant programmes are currently open or contact the foundation directly. Application criteria, procedures and deadlines vary for each of the funds. Full details and separate application forms for each fund can be found on the foundation's website.

CONTACT DETAILS Catherine Gardner, Grants Administrator, The Orchard, White Hart Lane, Basingstoke, Hampshire RG21 4AF *Tel.* 01962 798695 *Email* grantsadmin@hiwcf.com *Website* www.hiwcf.com

■ The Hampstead Wells and Campden Trust

CC NO 1094611   **ESTABLISHED** 1971

WHERE FUNDING CAN BE GIVEN North Camden (the area comprising the old metropolitan borough of Hampstead; see the website for a map of the specific area and a list of street names in the trust's area of benefit).

WHO CAN BENEFIT Charitable organisations; voluntary groups; community projects; individuals.

WHAT IS FUNDED Social welfare; health.

WHAT IS NOT FUNDED Outings; trips; social events.

TYPE OF GRANT Core/revenue costs; project funding; occasionally capital costs.

RANGE OF GRANTS Mostly between £1,000 and £20,000.

SAMPLE GRANTS Citizens Advice Camden (£62,500); Sidings Community Centre (£10,000); West Hampstead Women's Centre (£7,500); Centre 404 (£5,000); Gingerbread (£3,000); Feast with Us (£2,000); KidsOut UK (£1,600).

FINANCES *Financial year end 30/09/2021*
Income £386,700
Grants to organisations £139,500
Grants to individuals £106,400
Assets £19,580,000

TRUSTEES Gaynor Humphreys; Stephen Bobasch; Tibor Gold; Jennifer Stevens; Christian Percy; The Revd Jeremy Fletcher; Simone Hensby; Fiona Dunsire; Jeremy Wells.

OTHER INFORMATION Grants were made to 20 organisations and 454 individuals during the year. Only grants of over £1,000 (16 grants totalling £136,500) were listed in the trust's accounts. The trust made four grants of less than £1,000 (totalling £3,000) in 2020/21. The 2020/21 accounts were the latest available at the time of writing (May 2023).

HOW TO APPLY It is recommended that you contact the correspondent for a discussion before starting an application. Refer to the trust's website for details of each grant category and application guidelines, including application deadlines. Application forms can be downloaded from the website.

CONTACT DETAILS Stuart Woltkamp-Moon, Director, The Hampstead Wells and Campden Trust, 344–354 Gray's Inn Road, London WC1X 8BP *Tel.* 020 7435 1570 *Email* grant@hwct.co.uk or stuart@hwct.co.uk *Website* www.hwct.org.uk

---

■ Hampton Fund

CC NO 211756   **ESTABLISHED** 1811

WHERE FUNDING CAN BE GIVEN Hampton; Hampton Hill; Hampton Wick; Teddington, Twickenham; Whitton.

WHO CAN BENEFIT Charities; voluntary sector organisations; community groups; individuals.

WHAT IS FUNDED Social welfare; arts, sport and recreation; carers; children and young people; community projects; disability; education; health; housing and homelessness; older people.

WHAT IS NOT FUNDED Holidays (except where there is a serious health-related need); services which are the responsibility of a statutory body; grants to individuals for private and post-compulsory education; retrospective expenditure, both capital and revenue; national general charitable appeals; endowment appeals; the advancement of religion and religious groups, unless they offer a non-religious service to the community; projects of a political nature; animal welfare; commercial and business activities; social enterprises, except CICs.

RANGE OF GRANTS Up to £60,000.

SAMPLE GRANTS Richmond Citizens Advice (£90,000 in two grants); Richmond upon Thames Crossroads Care (£40,000 in two grants); MTV Youth Hampton (£24,000); Kick London (£16,800); ADHD Richmond and Kingston (£10,000); OK Music Trust (£8,000); River Thames Boat Project (£4,800); Churches Together in Teddington (£900).

FINANCES *Financial year end 30/06/2022*
Income £1,900,000
Grants to organisations £1,550,000
Grants to individuals £1,170,000
Assets £59,410,000

TRUSTEES Dr James Brockbank; Dr Martin Duffy; Martin Seymour; The Revd Ben Lovell; David Meggitt; Geraldine Locke; Kim Loxton; Sharika Sharma; Adele Kimber; Laurence Sewell; Samantha Bailey; Richard Baker.

OTHER INFORMATION Grants were made to 81 organisations during the year.

HOW TO APPLY Application forms and guidance notes are available to download from the charity's website.

CONTACT DETAILS The Trustees, 15 High Street, Hampton, Middlesex TW12 2SA *Tel.* 020 8941 7866 *Email* use the contact form on the website *Website* www.hamptonfund.co.uk

---

■ The W. A. Handley Charity Trust

CC NO 230435   **ESTABLISHED** 1963

WHERE FUNDING CAN BE GIVEN County Durham; Cumbria; Northumberland; Tyne and Wear.

WHO CAN BENEFIT Registered charities.

WHAT IS FUNDED General charitable purposes including: social welfare; health; older people; young people; people with disabilities; education; employment; community support; historic and religious buildings; the environment;

music and the arts; volunteering and the voluntary sector.

TYPE OF GRANT One-off and recurrent grants.

RANGE OF GRANTS Generally between £1,000 and £10,000.

SAMPLE GRANTS Combat Stress and Newcastle Cathedral Trust (£10,000 each); Country Trust, SPLASH and United Against Dementia – Northumberland (£5,000 each); Contact Morpeth Health Group, Percy Park Women's Rugby Football Club and Tynemouth Volunteer Life Brigade (£2,000 each); Carols in Chelsea and Oasis Community Housing (£1,000 each).

FINANCES *Financial year end 31/03/2022*
Income £211,700
Grants to organisations £300,300
Assets £9,900,000

TRUSTEES Bill Dryden; Tony Glenton; David Milligan.

OTHER INFORMATION In 2021/22, the trust awarded grants to 130 organisations, among which 94 were annual grants totalling £154,300 and 36 were one-off grants totalling £146,000. Grants were awarded in the following categories: social care (£115,500); arts, culture and recreation (£55,800); health (£50,800); religious activities (£27,700); voluntary sector support (£23,500); the environment and animal care (£13,500); development and housing (£5,800); education (£5,000); civil society, law and advocacy (£3,300).

HOW TO APPLY Apply in writing to the correspondent, including your charity number.

CONTACT DETAILS Trust Secretary, c/o Ryecroft Glenton, 32 Portland Terrace, Newcastle upon Tyne, Tyne and Wear NE2 1QP *Tel.* 0191 281 1292 *Email* davidmilligan@ryecroft-glenton.co.uk

---

■ The Lennox Hannay Charitable Trust

CC NO 1080198   **ESTABLISHED** 2000

WHERE FUNDING CAN BE GIVEN England; Scotland; Wales.

WHO CAN BENEFIT Registered charities.

WHAT IS FUNDED General charitable purposes; education; disability; social welfare; health; animal welfare; arts and culture; the environment; the armed forces and emergency services; community development; human rights and equality.

RANGE OF GRANTS Up to £35,000.

SAMPLE GRANTS Able Stables (£35,000); Bristol University (£30,000); Missing Salmon Alliance (£25,000); Royal Horticultural Society (£21,600); The Branch Trust (£20,000).

FINANCES *Financial year end 31/03/2022*
Income £817,200
Grants to organisations £618,000
Assets £33,650,000

TRUSTEES Caroline Wilmot-Sitwell; Tara Douglas-Home; Joanne King; RF Trustee Co. Ltd.

OTHER INFORMATION During the year, the trust made 119 grants to UK-registered charities in support of a wide variety of causes. Only beneficiaries of grants of £25,000 and above were listed in the accounts. Grants of between £2,000 and £25,000 totalled £285,400. Grants of under £2,000 totalled £96,000.

HOW TO APPLY Apply in writing to the correspondent via post. There are no deadlines. The trustees meet twice a year to discuss applications.

CONTACT DETAILS The Trustees, 14 Buckingham Street, London WC2N 6DF *Tel.* 020 3696 6721 *Email* charities@rftrustee.com

■ The Kathleen Hannay Memorial Charity

CC NO 299600   **ESTABLISHED** 1988
WHERE FUNDING CAN BE GIVEN UK and worldwide.
WHO CAN BENEFIT Registered charities.
WHAT IS FUNDED General charitable purposes; health; children and young people; the arts.
WHAT IS NOT FUNDED Individuals; non-registered charities.
RANGE OF GRANTS Up to £50,000.
SAMPLE GRANTS The Harnhill Centre (£60,000); Disasters Emergency Committee – Afghanistan Crisis Appeal (£30,000); Museum of Music History and New English Ballet Theatre (£20,000 each); British Red Cross and Manchester Global Foundation (£15,000 each).
FINANCES *Financial year end 05/04/2022*
Income £129,500
Grants to organisations £383,300
Assets £16,870,000
TRUSTEES Simon Weil; Christian Ward; Jonathan Weil; Laura Watkins.
OTHER INFORMATION Only organisations that received grants of over £10,000 were listed as beneficiaries in the charity's accounts. Grants of under £10,000 totalled £103,300.
HOW TO APPLY Unsolicited applications are not accepted.
CONTACT DETAILS H. D'Monte, Secretary to the Trustees, c/o Charles Russell Speechlys LLP, 5 Fleet Place, London EC4M 7RD *Tel.* 01242 246311

■ The Happold Foundation

CC NO 1050814   **ESTABLISHED** 1995
WHERE FUNDING CAN BE GIVEN Worldwide.
WHO CAN BENEFIT UK-based organisations; students; engineers.
WHAT IS FUNDED Engineering and the built environment; human development and education.
TYPE OF GRANT Research funding; project funding; scholarships; education; pilot programmes.
RANGE OF GRANTS Grants are typically a £30,000 donation received over a three-year period.
SAMPLE GRANTS A list of beneficiaries was not included in the annual report and accounts.
FINANCES *Financial year end 30/04/2022*
Income £241,000
Grants to organisations £164,600
Assets £260,300
TRUSTEES Ian Liddell; Robert Okpala; Sarah Sachs; Thomas Newby; Anna Bruni; Andrew Daubney; Matthew Happold; Paul Rogers; Fergus Anderson; Steve Williamson; Celia Way; Ian Stewart; Ian Maddocks.
HOW TO APPLY Application forms may be downloaded from the foundation's website and should be completed and returned to the correspondent by email. A detailed set of guidance notes can also be found on the website. Recipients must have a UK bank account.
CONTACT DETAILS The Trustees, Buro Happold, 230 Lower Bristol Road, Bath, Somerset BA2 3DQ *Tel.* 020 7927 9745 *Email* info@happoldfoundation.org *Website* www.happoldfoundation.org

■ The Haramead Trust

CC NO 1047416   **ESTABLISHED** 1995
WHERE FUNDING CAN BE GIVEN UK and financially developing countries, with a preference for the East Midlands.
WHO CAN BENEFIT Registered charities; individuals.
WHAT IS FUNDED Children and young people; social and medical assistance; homelessness; education.
RANGE OF GRANTS Generally £10,000 to £75,000, with some larger grants.
SAMPLE GRANTS British Red Cross (£115,000); The Ireland Fund (£100,000); NSPCC (£75,000); ActionAid (£65,000); LOROS (£45,000); For Rutland, Inter Care and The Salvation Army (£25,000 each); Leicester Children's Hospital (£20,000); Narthex Sparkhill and Northwich Multi-Sports (£10,000 each).
FINANCES *Financial year end 31/03/2022*
Income £1,310,000
Grants to organisations £1,520,000
Assets £2,080,000
TRUSTEES Winifred Linnett; Robert Smith; Victoria Duddles; Dr Mary Hanlon.
OTHER INFORMATION During the year, a total of 146 grants were awarded, of which 95 were for less than £10,000.
HOW TO APPLY Apply in writing to the correspondent.
CONTACT DETAILS The Trustees, Park House, Park Hill, Gaddesby, Leicestershire LE7 4WH *Tel.* 01664 840908 *Email* harameadtrust@aol.com

■ Harbinson Charitable Trust

OSCR NO SC015248   **ESTABLISHED** 1984
WHERE FUNDING CAN BE GIVEN UK and overseas.
WHO CAN BENEFIT Charitable organisations, particularly those working in international development; schools and colleges; social enterprises.
WHAT IS FUNDED Social welfare; education; advancement of religion; humanitarian aid; the environment; general charitable purposes.
RANGE OF GRANTS Mostly up to £5,000 with the occasional larger grant.
SAMPLE GRANTS Pathway Centre for Hope (£31,000); Médecins Sans Frontières (£4,900); Practical Action and Rainforest Concern (£4,300 each); Renewable World (£4,000); Children on Edge (£3,500); Mvule Trust – Uganda and WaterAid (£2,700 each); ActionAid International, Farm Africa and Send a Cow (£1,000 each); Soil Association – Scotland (£300).
FINANCES *Financial year end 05/04/2022*
Income £135,800
Grants to organisations £123,000
Assets £8,000,000
HOW TO APPLY Apply in writing to the correspondent.
CONTACT DETAILS The Trustees, 190 St Vincent Street, Glasgow G2 5SP

■ Harborne Parish Lands Charity

CC NO 219031   **ESTABLISHED** 1576
WHERE FUNDING CAN BE GIVEN The ancient parish of Harborne, which includes parts of Harborne, Smethwick, Bearwood and Quinton (see the charity's website for a map outlining the beneficial area).
WHO CAN BENEFIT Charitable organisations; CICs; hospices; individuals.
WHAT IS FUNDED Social welfare; health; accommodation and housing. The charity has adopted the following grant priorities: provision for 16–24 year olds who are not in education, employment or training (NEET) or are at risk of becoming NEET; services for older people; debt and money management; food and household goods distribution.

TYPE OF GRANT Buildings and capital costs; core costs; project funding; salaries.

RANGE OF GRANTS Grants range from £2,000 to £20,000.

SAMPLE GRANTS A list of beneficiaries was not included in the annual report and accounts.

FINANCES *Financial year end 30/06/2022*
Income £1,570,000
Grants to organisations £163,700
Grants to individuals £41,900
Assets £21,810,000

TRUSTEE Harborne and Smethwick Charitable Trust.

HOW TO APPLY Application forms are available from the correspondent. An exact map of the beneficial area can be obtained from the charity (or can be viewed on its website) and should be consulted before an application is submitted. Details of the application process, including deadlines, are posted on the charity's website.

CONTACT DETAILS The Trustees, 109 Court Oak Road, Harborne, Birmingham, West Midlands B17 9AA *Tel.* 0121 426 1600 *Email* peter. hardisty@hplc.org.uk *Website* www.hplc.org.uk

■ The Harbour Foundation

CC NO 264927　　　　　**ESTABLISHED** 1970

WHERE FUNDING CAN BE GIVEN Worldwide; in practice, mostly the UK and Israel.

WHO CAN BENEFIT Registered charities; charitable organisations.

WHAT IS FUNDED Refugees; people experiencing homelessness; scientific and technical education and research; music; general charitable purposes.

RANGE OF GRANTS Up to £200,000.

SAMPLE GRANTS Ben Gurion University Foundation and British Friends of the Hebrew University of Jerusalem (£200,000 each); World Jewish Relief (£60,000); Alliance for Middle East Peace via New Israel Fund; (£50,000); Royal Society of Arts (£20,000); Royal Academy of Music (£15,000); British Red Cross and The Wigmore Hall Trust (£5,000 each).

FINANCES *Financial year end 31/05/2022*
Income £642,400
Grants to organisations £690,000
Assets £19,340,000

TRUSTEES Dr Daniel Harbour; Susan Harbour; Edmond Harbour; Gideon Harbour; Harry Rich; Richard Hermer.

OTHER INFORMATION In 2021/22, grants were made to 38 registered charities, in the following categories: education (£409,000); social organisations (£137,500); relief (£83,500); arts (£51,500); religious bodies (£5,500); medical causes (£3,000).

HOW TO APPLY Contact the correspondent for further information.

CONTACT DETAILS D. Abrahams, Secretary, 1 Red Place, London W1K 6PL *Tel.* 020 7456 8180

■ The Harding Trust

CC NO 328182　　　　　**ESTABLISHED** 1989

WHERE FUNDING CAN BE GIVEN Mainly, but not exclusively, Staffordshire and the surrounding areas.

WHO CAN BENEFIT Charitable organisations; theatres; hospices.

WHAT IS FUNDED Music, mainly by providing sponsorship or other support for public concerts, recitals and performances by both amateur and professional organisations.

TYPE OF GRANT Project funding; strategic costs. Mostly recurrent.

RANGE OF GRANTS Typically £1,000 to £6,000.

SAMPLE GRANTS Stoke-on-Trent Festival (£45,000); Harding Trust Piano Recitals (£25,000); Clonter Farm Music Trust (£6,000); Worcestershire Youth Theatre (£3,000); Katharine House Hospice (£1,500); St John Ambulance (£1,000).

FINANCES *Financial year end 05/04/2022*
Income £204,400
Grants to organisations £115,000
Assets £5,970,000

TRUSTEES John Fowell; Michael Lloyd; Geoffrey Wall; Richard Platt.

OTHER INFORMATION In 2021/22 grants for musical projects totalled £104,500 and grants to other causes totalled £10,500.

HOW TO APPLY Apply in writing to the correspondent.

CONTACT DETAILS Jane Fagan, Horton House, Exchange Flags, Liverpool, Merseyside L2 3YL *Tel.* 0151 600 3000 *Email* jane.fagan@ brabners.com

■ William Harding's Charity

CC NO 310619　　　　　**ESTABLISHED** 1719

WHERE FUNDING CAN BE GIVEN Aylesbury.

WHO CAN BENEFIT Registered charities; CICs; social enterprises; schools; amateur sports clubs; individuals.

WHAT IS FUNDED General charitable purposes, particularly social welfare and education and training.

TYPE OF GRANT Core/revenue costs; seed funding/ start-up funding; travel; unrestricted funding. Often recurrent.

RANGE OF GRANTS Mostly under £5,000.

SAMPLE GRANTS Bucks County Museum Trust (£65,000); Broughton Junior School (£36,100); Aylesbury Youth Action (£20,000); Queens Park Arts Centre (£14,000); Florence Nightingale Hospice (£4,500); Aylesbury Town Bowls Club (£2,000); Oakfield Ladies (£1,000).

FINANCES *Financial year end 31/12/2021*
Income £1,020,000
Grants to organisations £241,300
Grants to individuals £177,200
Assets £41,440,000

TRUSTEES Anne Brooker; William Chapple; Les Sheldon; Penni Thorne; Lennard Wakelam; Susan Hewitt; Roy Collis; Sherrilyn Bateman.

OTHER INFORMATION During 2021 grants to organisations were made for the following purposes: relief in need (£120,400); schools and education (£65,100); youth groups (£44,400); travel for clubs/societies/groups (£11,300).

HOW TO APPLY Application forms are available on request from the charity, either by collection or by sending an sae. The trustees meet on a regular basis to consider applications.

CONTACT DETAILS John Leggett, Clerk to the Trustees, c/o Parrott and Coales LLP, 14 Bourbon Street, Aylesbury, Buckinghamshire HP20 2RS *Tel.* 01296 318501 *Email* doudjag@ pandcllp.co.uk *Website* www.leapwithus.org.uk/ funding/william-hardings-charity

■ The Harebell Centenary Fund

CC NO 1003552　　　　　**ESTABLISHED** 1991

WHERE FUNDING CAN BE GIVEN UK.

WHO CAN BENEFIT Registered charities.

WHAT IS FUNDED General charitable purposes, including the education of young people; neurological and neurosurgical research; animal welfare.

WHAT IS NOT FUNDED Individuals.

TYPE OF GRANT Capital costs; core/revenue costs; unrestricted funding.

RANGE OF GRANTS Most grants are for £10,000.

SAMPLE GRANTS Alzheimer's Research UK, Dystonia UK, Grandparents Plus, Success After Stroke, The Tabor Centre and Talitha Arts (£10,000 each); Changing Faces (£5,000); Crathie School (£3,300).

FINANCES *Financial year end 31/12/2021*
Income £221,900
Grants to organisations £223,300
Assets £8,640,000

TRUSTEES Penelope Chapman; Michael Goodbody; Angela Fossick.

HOW TO APPLY Unsolicited applications are not accepted. The trustees prefer to make grants to charities whose work they have come across through their own research.

CONTACT DETAILS Penelope Chapman, Trustee, BDB Pitmans LLP, 1 Bartholomew Close, London EC1A 7BL *Tel.* 020 7783 3533 *Email* PennyChapman@bdbpitmans.com

■ The Hargreaves Foundation

CC NO 1187297

WHERE FUNDING CAN BE GIVEN UK.

WHO CAN BENEFIT Registered charities; CIOs; schools; further education colleges; NHS trusts.

WHAT IS FUNDED Supporting disadvantaged children and young people under the age of 18 through sport and education.

WHAT IS NOT FUNDED Feasibility studies/consultations; crisis funding; core costs; retrospective expenditure; items or projects which should be funded by statutory bodies; general activities such as after-school clubs, mentoring, youth clubs and counselling; individuals; social enterprises (including CICs); private companies; local authorities.

TYPE OF GRANT Project costs; capital costs; events; staff training.

RANGE OF GRANTS There is no minimum or maximum grant size.

SAMPLE GRANTS Reed's School (£180,700); Early Intervention Scheme – Ashcombe School (£143,800); The Literacy Pirates (£90,000); Action for Kids (£30,700); The Horse Rangers (£16,300); Dreams Come True (£13,400); Bidwell Brook School (£9,900); Square Food Foundation (£130).

FINANCES *Financial year end 31/01/2022*
Income £2,420,000
Grants to organisations £923,300
Assets £67,340,000

TRUSTEES Louisa Hargreaves; Robert Hargreaves; Nigel Bence; Peter Hargreaves; Rosemary Hargreaves.

HOW TO APPLY An online application form is available on the foundation's website.

CONTACT DETAILS Alexandra Butler, Managing Director, The Old Surgery, Swan Barton, Sherston, Malmesbury, Wiltshire SN16 0LJ *Tel.* 07768 935532 *Email* Alexandra.Butler@thehargreavesfoundation.org *Website* www.thehargreavesfoundation.org

■ The Harpur Trust

CC NO 1066861   **ESTABLISHED** 1566

WHERE FUNDING CAN BE GIVEN The borough of Bedford.

WHO CAN BENEFIT Registered charities; not-for-profit organisations; social enterprises; CICs; schools.

WHAT IS FUNDED Education; social welfare; health; recreation.

WHAT IS NOT FUNDED Businesses; projects that promote a particular religion; projects which are the responsibility of the local authority or national government; projects that do not benefit the residents of the borough of Bedford; costs already incurred; trips, except in exceptional circumstances.

TYPE OF GRANT Capital costs; project funding for up to three years.

RANGE OF GRANTS Up to £150,000. The majority of successful applications are for up to £20,000.

SAMPLE GRANTS Citizens Advice Bedford (£136,000); Project 229 (£49,200); Bedford Open Door (£32,000); Autism Bedfordshire (£25,000); Friends For Life Bedfordshire (£16,000); Laptop Scheme (£9,500); Modernian Swimming Club (£2,000); Advice Bedfordshire (£1,000).

FINANCES *Financial year end 30/06/2021*
Income £55,140,000
Grants to organisations £1,370,000
Grants to individuals £91,300
Assets £216,170,000

TRUSTEES Neil Harris; Abu Sultan; John Fordham; David Wilson; Mark Taylor; Linbert Spencer; Jennifer Sauboorah; Justin Phillimore; Harriett Mather; Clive Loader; Michael Womack; Tina Beddoes; Roger Rigby; Anne Egan; George Ratcliffe; Philip Wallace; Stephen Mayson; Rhian Castell; Murray Stewart; Shirley Jackson; Sarah Wheeler; Simon Lowe; Richard Wilson; Gary Cotton.

OTHER INFORMATION The 2020/21 accounts were the latest available to view at the time of writing (June 2023). Only organisations that received grants of over £1,000 were listed as beneficiaries in the trust's accounts. Grants for less than £1,000 totalled £2,100.

HOW TO APPLY Full details of how to apply can be found on the trust's website.

CONTACT DETAILS Grants Team, Princeton Court, The Pilgrim Centre, Brickhill Drive, Bedford, Bedfordshire MK41 7PZ *Tel.* 01234 369500 *Email* info@harpurtrust.org.uk *Website* www.harpurtrust.org.uk

■ The Peter and Teresa Harris Charitable Trust

CC NO 1161183   **ESTABLISHED** 2010

WHERE FUNDING CAN BE GIVEN England; Wales; overseas.

WHO CAN BENEFIT Charitable organisations; hospitals; hospices; places of worship; individuals.

WHAT IS FUNDED General charitable purposes; religion; medical care/medical research; humanitarian aid; the arts.

RANGE OF GRANTS Mostly between £1,000 and £3,000 with the occasional larger grant.

SAMPLE GRANTS Commonwealth Garden Woodland and Greenwich and Bexley Community Hospice (£10,000 each); Superkid2 (£6,000); Macmillan Cancer Support and Tools 4 Teens (£3,000 each); Royal Borough of Greenwich (£1.000); St Mark's United Church (£800).

FINANCES *Financial year end 05/04/2022*
Income £56,800
Grants to organisations £93,300
Grants to individuals £800
Assets £2,990,000

TRUSTEES Duncan Rabagliati; Tim Barnes.

HOW TO APPLY Apply in writing to the correspondent.

CONTACT DETAILS The Trustees, c/o Gregsons Solicitors, 19 Tabor Grove, London SW19 4EX *Tel.* 020 8946 1173 *Email* legal@rabagliati.com

■ The Harris Family Charitable Trust

CC NO 1064394 **ESTABLISHED** 1997
WHERE FUNDING CAN BE GIVEN England and Wales.
WHO CAN BENEFIT Charitable organisations.
WHAT IS FUNDED General charitable purposes; health.
SAMPLE GRANTS A list of beneficiaries was not available.
FINANCES *Financial year end 05/04/2022*
Income £22,000
Grants to organisations £234,500
TRUSTEES Charlotte Harris; Ronnie Harris; Loretta Harris; Sophie Harris; Toby Harris.
OTHER INFORMATION Full accounts were not available to view on the Charity Commission's website due to the trust's low income. We have therefore estimated the grant total based on the trust's total expenditure.
HOW TO APPLY Apply in writing to the correspondent.
CONTACT DETAILS The Trustees, 64 New Cavendish Street, London W1G 8TB *Tel.* 020 7467 6300

■ The Peter Harrison Foundation

CC NO 1076579 **ESTABLISHED** 1999
WHERE FUNDING CAN BE GIVEN UK, with some preference for the South East.
WHO CAN BENEFIT Registered charities; community amateur sports clubs.
WHAT IS FUNDED Access to sport for people with disabilities and people who are disadvantaged (UK-wide); enhancing the lives of children and young people with disabilities or who are disadvantaged (the South East).
WHAT IS NOT FUNDED Retrospective expenditure; activities that are primarily the responsibility of central or local government; individuals; CICs; overseas projects; adventure challenges or expeditions in the UK or abroad; religious projects.
TYPE OF GRANT Capital, revenue and project funding.
RANGE OF GRANTS Small grants of up to £5,000; major grants of £5,000 to £30,000.
SAMPLE GRANTS Loughborough University (£100,000); Rose Road Association (£30,000); Lifecentre (£19,400); Friends of Gibside School (£12,000); Glasgow Eagles Sports Club (£1,000).
FINANCES *Financial year end 31/05/2022*
Income £3,050,000
Grants to organisations £1,450,000
Assets £54,330,000
TRUSTEES Julia Harrison-Lee; Peter Lee; Nicholas Harrison.
OTHER INFORMATION Grants were broken down as follows: opportunities through sport (£888,100 in 56 grants); support for children and young people (£474,800 in 28 grants); trustees' discretion (£145,800).
HOW TO APPLY See the foundation's website for further information the application process and application deadlines. The foundation has a two-stage application process for major grant applications (£5,000 to £30,000) and a one-stage application process for small grant applications (up to £5,000).
CONTACT DETAILS The Trustees, Foundation House, 42–48 London Road, Reigate, Surrey RH2 9QQ *Tel.* 01737 228000 *Email* enquiries@peterharrisonfoundation.org *Website* www.peterharrisonfoundation.org

■ The Harrison-Frank Family Foundation (UK) Ltd

CC NO 1155149 **ESTABLISHED** 2013
WHERE FUNDING CAN BE GIVEN UK.
WHO CAN BENEFIT Registered charities.
WHAT IS FUNDED General charitable purposes, including: health; education; poverty; people with disabilities; housing; arts, culture, heritage and science; human rights.
RANGE OF GRANTS From £3,000 to £25,000.
SAMPLE GRANTS Médecins Sans Frontières (£25,000); Cancer Research (£15,000); Action for Stammering Children, Coram Beanstalk and Countess of Munster Musical Trust (£10,000 each); Changing Tunes (£6,000); Jewish Blind and Disabled, Macmillan Cancer Support and Rescare (£5,000 each); Prisoners' Education Trust (£3,000).
FINANCES *Financial year end 31/12/2021*
Income £4,210,000
Grants to organisations £173,000
Assets £15,160,000
TRUSTEES Fredrik Ulfsater; Richard Harrison; Michele Harrison; David Harrison; Louise Williams; Steven Marcovitch; Jeanne Harrison; Dominic Duffy; Simon Morris; Maurice Collins.
OTHER INFORMATION In 2021 grants were awarded to 21 organisations.
HOW TO APPLY Apply in writing to the correspondent.
CONTACT DETAILS The Trustees, Flat 17, 34 Seymour Place, London W1H 7NS *Tel.* 020 7724 1154 *Email* bfraharrison@hotmail.com

■ The Harry and Mary Foundation

CC NO 1148707 **ESTABLISHED** 2012
WHERE FUNDING CAN BE GIVEN West Yorkshire and Bradford.
WHO CAN BENEFIT Registered charities.
WHAT IS FUNDED The education of children and young people (under 25); health; social welfare.
RANGE OF GRANTS Usually between £1,000 and £10,000.
SAMPLE GRANTS St Gemma's Hospice (£185,900); Bradford Nightstop (£34,200); One in a Million (£18,000); Bradford FoodBank (£11,600); Marie Curie (£10,000); The Cellar Trust (£5,000); Health Action Local Engagement (£1,000).
FINANCES *Financial year end 31/03/2022*
Income £2,540,000
Grants to organisations £502,000
Assets £12,880,000
TRUSTEES Robert Walker; John Clough; Robert Bastow.
OTHER INFORMATION In 2021/22, grants were made to 29 organisations.
HOW TO APPLY Contact the correspondent for further information.
CONTACT DETAILS The Trustees, 11 Keighley Road, Cross Hills, Keighley BD20 7DA *Tel.* 01535 630298

■ Gay and Peter Hartley's Hillards Charitable Trust

CC NO 327879 **ESTABLISHED** 1988
WHERE FUNDING CAN BE GIVEN Forty-five towns in northern and central England – see the website for full list of towns supported.
WHO CAN BENEFIT Independent, locally managed, non-profit, voluntary and community-based organisations that provide social support to the communities once served by Hillards stores.

WHAT IS FUNDED Care for older people; children's welfare; education; physical/mental health; education; church-based projects with a proven outreach factor.

WHAT IS NOT FUNDED See the trust's website for a full list of exclusions.

TYPE OF GRANT One-off.

RANGE OF GRANTS Generally £100 to £1,000.

SAMPLE GRANTS Cancer Research UK (£1,200); Spencer Contact, Starseed Learning and The Hut (£1,000 each); The Prince of Wales Hospice (£920); ABF The Soldiers' Charity and The Cinnamon Trust (£500 each); Merchant Adventurers – York (£350); Multiple Sclerosis Society (£100).

FINANCES *Financial year end 31/12/2021*
Income £76,000
Grants to organisations £73,000
Assets £1,670,000

TRUSTEES Simon Hartley; Peter Hartley; Susan Hartley; George Hartley; Oscar Hartley; Norman Bettison.

OTHER INFORMATION Grants were awarded to 57 organisations during the year.

HOW TO APPLY Applicants can apply online via the trust's website, where there is also further application guidance and an eligibility checker.

CONTACT DETAILS Chris Hindle, Secretary to the Trustees, Shadwell Grange, 400 Shadwell Lane, Leeds, West Yorkshire LS17 8AW *Tel.* 07985 662840 *Email* secretary@hillardstrust.org *Website* www.hillardstrust.org

....

■ Edward Harvist Trust (The Harvist Estate)

CC NO 211970   **ESTABLISHED** 1994

WHERE FUNDING CAN BE GIVEN The London boroughs of Barnet, Brent, Camden, the City of Westminster and Harrow.

WHO CAN BENEFIT Charitable organisations.

WHAT IS FUNDED General charitable purposes including: health; social welfare; recreation and leisure; older people; education.

TYPE OF GRANT Mainly one-off awards for capital costs; project funding.

RANGE OF GRANTS Mostly from £1,000 to £5,000.

SAMPLE GRANTS English for Action, Living Way Ministries and Unique Community Charity (£5,000 each); Ashford Place (£4,800); The Avenues Youth Project (£4,000); Blind Aid (£3,500); Centrepoint (£3,000); Attend (£2,000); Barfield Allotment (£1,500); Friends of Barham Library (£1,100); St Mungo's (£1,000).

FINANCES *Financial year end 31/03/2022*
Income £390,300
Grants to organisations £277,000
Assets £11,440,000

TRUSTEES Cllr Heather Johnson; Cllr Pritesh Patel; Cllr Edith David; Cllr Concia Albert; Cllr Ihtesham Afzal.

HOW TO APPLY Applications must be made through the appropriate local authority, not through the correspondent. At the time of writing (May 2023) there was information about the trust (such as eligibility criteria and application procedures) available on each of the five borough councils' websites. This information could be found following a search for the trust's name using the websites' search bars. There may be different criteria and application procedures imposed by the five local authorities.

CONTACT DETAILS Hugh Peart, Hon. Secretary, London Borough of Harrow, Finance Department, PO Box 21, Civic Centre, Harrow, Middlesex

HA1 2XY *Tel.* 020 8424 1450
Email treasurymanagement@harrow.gov.uk

....

■ The Hasluck Charitable Trust

CC NO 1115323   **ESTABLISHED** 2006

WHERE FUNDING CAN BE GIVEN UK and overseas.

WHO CAN BENEFIT Registered charities.

WHAT IS FUNDED General charitable purposes; health; social welfare; disability; young people; older people; overseas aid.

WHAT IS NOT FUNDED Individuals.

TYPE OF GRANT One-off.

RANGE OF GRANTS Normally between £1,000 and £2,000.

SAMPLE GRANTS Anti-Slavery International, British Red Cross and Mustard Tree (£2,000 each); Just a Drop, Lucy Air Ambulance and Maytree Respite Centre (£1,000 each).

FINANCES *Financial year end 05/04/2022*
Income £160,300
Grants to organisations £111,000
Assets £2,600,000

TRUSTEES John Billing; Matthew Wakefield; Mark Wheeler.

OTHER INFORMATION According to the trust's 2021/22 accounts, half of the income received is awarded to eight charities of particular interest to the settlor (Barnardo's, International Fund for Animal Welfare, Macmillan Cancer Support, Mrs R. H. Hotblack's Michelham Priory Endowment Fund, Riding for the Disabled Association, RNLI, RSPB and Scope). During this period, these eight charities received £7,250 each. The remainder (£53,000 2021/22) is distributed to other charitable organisations, usually on a one-off basis.

HOW TO APPLY Apply in writing to the correspondent.

CONTACT DETAILS John Billing, Trustee, c/o Rathbone Trust Legal Services Ltd, 8 Finsbury Circus, London EC2M 7AZ *Tel.* 020 7399 0447 *Email* john.billing@rathbones.com

....

■ The Maurice Hatter Foundation

CC NO 1187823   **ESTABLISHED** 1987

WHERE FUNDING CAN BE GIVEN UK; Israel; overseas.

WHO CAN BENEFIT Registered charities and educational bodies, particularly those with links to the Jewish community.

WHAT IS FUNDED Education; medical research; social welfare and mobility; people with disabilities; general charitable purposes; the Jewish faith and community; international policy research.

SAMPLE GRANTS Southampton University (£393,000); Community Security Trust (£200,000); Chabad Hampstead Garden Suburb and Royal National Orthopaedic Hospital (£100,000 each).

FINANCES *Financial year end 05/04/2022*
Income £30,420,000
Grants to organisations £1,250,000
Assets £84,200,000

TRUSTEES Piers Barclay; Richard Hatter; Fausto Furlotti.

OTHER INFORMATION Grants were broken down as follows: medical research (£694,700); the Jewish faith and community (£346,500); other charitable purposes (£105,600); social welfare (£56,000); education (£22,000); people with disabilities (£20,000); international policy and research (£5,000). Only beneficiaries of grants of over £100,000 were included in the accounts.

HOW TO APPLY Apply in writing to the correspondent.

CONTACT DETAILS The Trustees, Onslow House, Onslow Street, Guildford, Surrey GU1 4TL *Tel.* 01483 407100 *Email* admin@mh-foundation.org

■ The Hawthorne Charitable Trust

CC NO 233921 **ESTABLISHED** 1964

WHERE FUNDING CAN BE GIVEN UK, particularly Hereford and Worcester.

WHO CAN BENEFIT Registered charities; hospices; places of worship; schools and colleges.

WHAT IS FUNDED General charitable purposes; people with disabilities; medical and health; animal welfare; social welfare; the environment; heritage and conservation; rural communities; emergency response or relief, including air ambulances.

WHAT IS NOT FUNDED Individuals.

RANGE OF GRANTS Between £500 and £7,500 with the occasional larger grant.

SAMPLE GRANTS Disasters Emergency Committee (£25,000); Southern Thailand Elephant Foundation (£10,000); Maggie's – Cheltenham and St Michael's Hospice – Hereford (£7,500 each); Museum of Royal Worcester (£5,000); Battersea Dogs and Cats Home, Different Strokes and Plant Heritage (£3,000 each); British Wireless for the Blind Fund, County Air Ambulance Trust and South Worcestershire Citizens Advice (£1,000 each); Stisted Charity Golf (£500).

FINANCES *Financial year end* 05/04/2022 *Income* £167,400 *Grants to organisations* £286,300 *Assets* £12,020,000

TRUSTEES Thomas Berington; Alexandra Berington; Richard White; Roger Clark.

OTHER INFORMATION Grants were broken down as follows: general charitable purposes (£110,500 in 36 grants); medical and health (£91,500 in 30 grants); the environment, heritage and conservation (£36,300 in 13 grants); people with disabilities (£24,800 in 9 grants); animal welfare (£17,300 in 5 grants); social welfare (£6,000 in 4 grants).

HOW TO APPLY Apply in writing to the correspondent.

CONTACT DETAILS Tatia Goldstone, c/o RSM UK Tax and Accounting Ltd, Priory Place, New London Road, Chelmsford, Essex CM2 0PP *Tel.* 01245 354402 *Email* tatia.goldstone@rsmuk.com

■ The Dorothy Hay-Bolton Charitable Trust

CC NO 1010438 **ESTABLISHED** 1992

WHERE FUNDING CAN BE GIVEN UK, with a preference for the South East.

WHO CAN BENEFIT Charities working with people who are blind or deaf, particularly children, young people and older people; hospitals.

WHAT IS FUNDED Health and disability; children and young people; older people.

WHAT IS NOT FUNDED Individuals.

TYPE OF GRANT One-off and recurrent.

RANGE OF GRANTS £1,000 to £5,000.

SAMPLE GRANTS Previous beneficiaries have included: Action for Blind People; British Blind Sport; East Kent Cycling Club; East Sussex Association for the Blind; Esther Benjamin's Trust; Eyeless Trust; Hearing Dogs for the Deaf; Seeing Ear; Sussex Lantern; Telephones for the Blind.

FINANCES *Financial year end* 05/04/2022 *Income* £8,700 *Grants to organisations* £63,000

TRUSTEES Clare Jeffries; Gary Hicks.

OTHER INFORMATION The 2021/22 annual report and accounts were not available to view on the Charity Commission's website due to the trust's low income. We have estimated the grant total based on the trust's expenditure.

HOW TO APPLY Apply in writing to the correspondent.

CONTACT DETAILS Gary Hicks, Trustee, c/o Kreston Reeves LLP, 2nd Floor, 168 Shoreditch High Street, London E1 6RA *Tel.* 020 7382 1820 *Email* Dorothy.Hay-BoltonTrust@krestonreeves.com

■ The Charles Hayward Foundation

CC NO 1078969 **ESTABLISHED** 1999

WHERE FUNDING CAN BE GIVEN The British Isles and the Commonwealth countries of Africa.

WHO CAN BENEFIT UK-registered charities.

WHAT IS FUNDED Social and criminal justice; heritage and conservation; older people; overseas aid, particularly WASH (water, sanitation and hygiene) initiatives and sustainable livelihoods.

WHAT IS NOT FUNDED Endowments; general appeals; grant-making charities; individuals; loans and deficits; retrospective expenditure; core costs; academic institutions. Individual programmes may have their own additional exclusions – see the programme-specific guidelines.

TYPE OF GRANT Capital costs; project funding; salaries.

RANGE OF GRANTS Up to £25,000. Projects can be funded over one to three years.

SAMPLE GRANTS Bletchley Park Trust (£50,000); NIACRO Belfast and Women in Prison (£25,000 each); Bounce Back (£18,000); African Child Trust (£15,000); Unlock (£5,000); Abused Men In Scotland (£4,000); Friends of Victoria Park Stretford (£3,000); Welsh Air Ambulance (£1,000); Chalke Valley History Trust (£730); St Raphael's Hospice (£500).

FINANCES *Financial year end* 31/12/2021 *Income* £60 *Grants to organisations* £2,350,000 *Assets* £83,540,000

TRUSTEES Julia Chamberlain; Susan Heath; Alexander Heath; Brian Insch; John Leuven; Caroline Donald; Richard Griffith.

OTHER INFORMATION Grants were paid to 185 organisations in the following categories: social and criminal justice (£1.62 million to 73 charities); overseas aid (£309,600 to 22 organisations); small grants (£241,600 to 51 charities); heritage and conservation (£140,500 to 5 charities); miscellaneous (£40,000 to 34 organisations).

HOW TO APPLY Details of how to apply are available on the foundation's website. Applications to the small grants programme are accepted on a rolling basis and are considered every two to three months. The main grants programme has a two-stage application process. Applications are first considered by the grants committee, which recommends applications to be considered by the trustees at the second stage of the process. Upcoming deadlines are listed on the website.

CONTACT DETAILS Jacinta Hamilton, Grants Assistant, Hayward House, 45 Harrington Gardens, London SW7 4JU *Tel.* 020 7370 7063 *Email* grants@charleshaywardfoundation.org.uk *Website* www.charleshaywardfoundation.org.uk

■ The Headley Trust

CC NO 266620   **ESTABLISHED** 1973
WHERE FUNDING CAN BE GIVEN UK; Central and Eastern Europe; Ethiopia; sub-Saharan anglophone Africa.
WHO CAN BENEFIT Registered charities; churches; museums; galleries.
WHAT IS FUNDED Arts and heritage; development projects in sub-Saharan anglophone Africa; education; health and social welfare. There is a small grant scheme to help local museums and galleries purchase objects for their collections. Small grants are also available to provide practical aids to people with disabilities (third-party referrals only).
WHAT IS NOT FUNDED Individuals; expeditions. For cathedrals/churches: education centres, conferences, exhibition or heritage space, organs, clocks, bells, plumbing, kitchens or heating. Note that for overseas projects priority will be given to locally led organisations employing local experts.
TYPE OF GRANT Capital and project costs; core costs; salaries; acquisitions costs; bursaries.
RANGE OF GRANTS Typically up to £50,000.
SAMPLE GRANTS British Museum Archaeological Research Collection (£250,000); Royal Opera House Covent Garden Foundation (£100,000); Bristol Museums Development Trust (£68,900); Hull Maritime Foundation (£50,000); Warburg Institute (£35,000); Watermill Theatre Trust (£25,000); Shropshire Skills Trust (£10,000); Orbis Charitable Trust (£5,000).
FINANCES *Financial year end 05/04/2022*
Income £2,160,000
Grants to organisations £2,930,000
Assets £79,670,000
TRUSTEES The Rt Hon. Sir Timothy Sainsbury; Timothy Sainsbury; Lady Susan Sainsbury; Camilla Woodward; Amanda McCrystal; Dominic Flynn; Charlotte Hatfield.
OTHER INFORMATION The trust is one of the Sainsbury Family Charitable Trusts, which share a common administration – see www.sftc.org.uk for more information. Grants approved during the year were broken down as follows: arts and heritage – UK (109 grants totalling £1.6 million); health and social welfare (107 grants totalling £740,200); financially developing countries (16 grants totalling £316,500); education (16 grants totalling £241,500); arts and heritage – overseas (8 grants totalling £82,500).
HOW TO APPLY Applications can be made online, by post to the Sainsbury Family Charitable Trusts, or by email to proposals@sfct.org.uk. Written applications should be no longer than two sides of A4 and provide the same information as the online form. Application forms for the trust's Museums Archaeological Acquisition Fund and Aids for Disabled People Programme are separate and can be found on the website.
CONTACT DETAILS The Trustees, c/o The Sainsbury Family Charitable Trusts, The Peak, 5 Wilton Road, London SW1V 1AP *Tel.* 020 7410 0330 *Email* info@sfct.org.uk *Website* www.sfct.org.uk/the-headley-trust/

■ The Health Foundation

CC NO 286967   **ESTABLISHED** 1983
WHERE FUNDING CAN BE GIVEN UK.
WHO CAN BENEFIT Registered charities; unregistered charities; NHS trusts; universities; hospitals; hospices; individuals.
WHAT IS FUNDED Healthcare and public health research; training and development.
WHAT IS NOT FUNDED See the foundation's website for a full list of exclusions.
TYPE OF GRANT Project funding; research; partnerships.
RANGE OF GRANTS Programme dependent.
SAMPLE GRANTS Children in Need (£1 million); Sheffield Teaching Hospitals NHS Foundation Trust (£499,500); University Hospitals Dorset NHS Foundation Trust (£435,200); BMJ Group (£164,100); Royal Cornwall Hospitals NHS Trust (£99,400); Nuffield Trust (£65,800); Equal Care Co-op (£60,000); Community Hospitals Association (£30,000); Mid and South Essex NHS Foundation Trust (£25,000); West of England Academic Health Science Networks (£20,000); Health Innovation Network (HIN) South London (£9,300).
FINANCES *Financial year end 31/12/2021*
Income £17,060,000
Grants to organisations £16,190,000
Assets £1,220,000
TRUSTEES Sir David Dalton; Branwen Jeffreys; Prof. Rosalind Smyth; Sir Hugh Taylor; Eric Gregory; Loraine Hawkins; Dr Ruth Hussey; David Smart; Prof. Dawn Edge; Katherine Blacklock; Ravi Gurumurthy.
OTHER INFORMATION The foundation runs a wide variety of funding programmes aimed at different organisations and individuals. The three main funding areas are improvement projects, research projects and fellowships. Funding is typically awarded for between one and four years. Note that the grant total includes amounts awarded to individuals.
HOW TO APPLY The foundation does not consider unprompted requests or proposals for funding. Programmes open for applications are advertised on the foundation's website. These are likely to change frequently and candidates are advised to visit the website for the most up-to-date information. You may sign up for a website account to receive alerts when new funding opportunities go live. Application forms are available online, together with full guidelines and specific requirements and deadlines for each of the programmes. There is also a helpful FAQs page, which should be consulted by potential applicants.
CONTACT DETAILS Programmes Team, Salisbury Square House, 8 Salisbury Square, London EC4Y 8AP *Tel.* 020 7257 8000 *Email* info@health.org.uk *Website* www.health.org.uk

■ Heart of England Community Foundation

CC NO 1117345   **ESTABLISHED** 1995
WHERE FUNDING CAN BE GIVEN Birmingham; Coventry; Dudley; Sandwell; Solihull; Walsall; Warwickshire; Wolverhampton.
WHO CAN BENEFIT Charitable organisations, including CICs and social enterprises; individuals.
WHAT IS FUNDED Social welfare; community development; education; health; general charitable purposes; the environment.
WHAT IS NOT FUNDED Applicants should check each funding programme for exclusions.
TYPE OF GRANT Project costs; capital costs; salaries; start-up costs.
SAMPLE GRANTS A list of beneficiaries was not included in the annual report and accounts.

Think carefully about every application. Is it justified?

433

FINANCES *Financial year end* 31/03/2022
Income £4,190,000
Grants to organisations £3,190,000
Assets £21,470,000

TRUSTEES Paul Belfield; Lucie Byron; Amrik Bhabra; Michelle Vincent; Christopher West; Daniel Worthing; Jude Jennison; Jasmin Koasha; Calum Nisbet; Cleopatra Morris; Alethea Fuller; Richard Port.

OTHER INFORMATION This is one of the 47 UK community foundations, which distribute funding for a wide range of purposes. As with all community foundations, there are a number of donor-advised funds managed on behalf of individuals, families and charitable trusts. Grant schemes tend to change frequently – consult the foundation's website for details of current programmes and up-to-date deadlines. A detailed breakdown of grants awarded is given in the foundation's annual grant-making report, which is available on its website.

HOW TO APPLY Potential applicants are advised to visit the community foundation's website or contact its grants team to find the most suitable funding stream.

CONTACT DETAILS The Grants Team, c/o Stellantis, Pinley House, Sunbeam Way, Coventry, Warwickshire CV3 1ND *Tel.* 024 7780 0520 *Email* info@heartofenglandcf.co.uk *Website* www.heartofenglandcf.co.uk

■ Heart Research UK

CC NO 1044821   **ESTABLISHED** 1967
WHERE FUNDING CAN BE GIVEN UK.
WHO CAN BENEFIT Community groups; voluntary organisations; hospitals; universities; CICs.
WHAT IS FUNDED Medical research; education; health; community projects.
WHAT IS NOT FUNDED Government organisations; local authority groups.
TYPE OF GRANT Project funding (including equipment and travel); research.
RANGE OF GRANTS Up to £250,000 for medical research grants; up to £10,000 for Healthy Heart grants.
SAMPLE GRANTS University of Glasgow (£250,000); University of Cambridge (£191,500); University of Dundee (£133,700); University of Edinburgh (£88,600); King's College London (£14,600); Leeds Teaching Hospital NHS Trust (£5,500); Ulster University (£1,000).
FINANCES *Financial year end* 31/12/2021
Income £2,730,000
Grants to organisations £2,040,000
Assets £6,830,000
TRUSTEES Richard Brown; Dr David Dickinson; Dr Catherine Dickinson; Anthony Knight; Kevin Watterson; Paul Rogerson; Peter Braidley; Julie Fenwick; Pierre Bouvet; Christopher Newman; James Breeze; Linda Musonza; James Andrews.
OTHER INFORMATION In total, 17 grants were awarded during the year.
HOW TO APPLY Application forms, full guidelines and up-to-date deadlines for each programme can be found on the charity's website or requested from the correspondent.
CONTACT DETAILS The Trustees, Suite 12D, Joseph's Well, Hanover Walk, Leeds, West Yorkshire LS3 1AB *Tel.* 0113 234 7474 *Email* info@heartresearch.org.uk *Website* www.heartresearch.org.uk

■ The Hearth Foundation

CC NO 1165540   **ESTABLISHED** 2016
WHERE FUNDING CAN BE GIVEN England and Wales, with a preference for the north of England and the Midlands.
WHO CAN BENEFIT Charitable organisations.
WHAT IS FUNDED General charitable purposes, in particular young people.
SAMPLE GRANTS A list of beneficiaries was not included in the latest set of accounts.
FINANCES *Financial year end* 05/04/2022
Income £153,700
Grants to organisations £96,000
Assets £2,890,000
TRUSTEES Chris Bosworth; Dr S. Bosworth; Michael Bosworth; Mrs H. E. Bosworth; Mrs V. M. Bosworth; Mrs J. Bosworth.
HOW TO APPLY Apply in writing to the correspondent. Applications are considered throughout the year and grants are awarded during the first quarter of each calendar year.
CONTACT DETAILS Michael Bosworth, Trustee, Monkstone, Main Street, Mowsley, Lutterworth, Leicestershire LE17 6NU *Tel.* 0116 240 2162 *Email* michael.bosworth@btopenworld.com

■ The Heathcoat Trust

CC NO 203367   **ESTABLISHED** 1945
WHERE FUNDING CAN BE GIVEN Local causes in and around Tiverton in Devon.
WHO CAN BENEFIT Local organisations to Tiverton and national charities working on projects in that area; educational bodies; employees and pensioners of the Heathcoat group of companies and their dependants.
WHAT IS FUNDED Social welfare; education and training; health; local causes.
RANGE OF GRANTS Up to £5,000.
SAMPLE GRANTS Holcombe Rogus Parish Council and Little Hero (£5,000); Tiverton Town FC and Westexe Sports and Social Club (£2,000); Bounce Brighter Future and Churches Housing Action Team (£1,000 each).
FINANCES *Financial year end* 05/04/2022
Income £878,700
Grants to organisations £511,000
Grants to individuals £104,800
Assets £29,720,000
TRUSTEES Mark Drysdale; Sir Ian Heathcoat-Amory; John Smith; Susan Westlake; Julian Morgan; Lee Sellens.
OTHER INFORMATION Only charitable organisations that received grants of £1,000 and above were listed in the accounts (26 organisations).
HOW TO APPLY Contact the correspondent for details regarding how to apply. The trustees meet regularly to consider applications for grants.
CONTACT DETAILS The Trustees, The Factory, West Exe, Tiverton, Devon EX16 5LL *Tel.* 01884 244296 *Email* heathcoattrust@heathcoat.co.uk

■ Heathrow Community Trust

CC NO 1183004   **ESTABLISHED** 2019
WHERE FUNDING CAN BE GIVEN The areas surrounding Heathrow Airport (Ealing, Hillingdon, Hounslow, Richmond, Runnymede, Slough, South Buckinghamshire, Spelthorne and the Royal Borough of Windsor and Maidenhead).
WHO CAN BENEFIT Local authorities; schools and colleges; hospices; charities; community groups; social enterprises; CICs; not-for-profit companies.

WHAT IS FUNDED The environment and sustainability; social welfare; recreation; young people; education and training; community cohesion; research and development projects.

WHAT IS NOT FUNDED Refer to the trust's website. Each of the grant programmes are subject to their own eligibility criteria and restrictions.

TYPE OF GRANT Restricted project-based funding for capital costs, revenue costs, direct project costs and overhead costs.

RANGE OF GRANTS Up to £25,000, but programme dependent.

SAMPLE GRANTS A list of beneficiaries was not included in the annual report and accounts. Previous beneficiaries have included: The Eikon Charity (£47,400); Fine Futures (£45,200); Oxfordshire Crossroads (£22,500); West London River Group (£20,900); Stanwell Village Hall (£17,000); Slough West Indian People's Enterprise (£15,000); Spark! (Hounslow Education Business Charity) (£9,400); Victoria Junior School (£5,000); The Manor Friends Charity (£2,100).

FINANCES *Financial year end 31/12/2021*
Income £431,400
Grants to organisations £194,700
Assets £343,500

TRUSTEES Dr Prabhjot Basra; Richard Belder; Gennie Dearman; David Cottrell; Alison Keeley; Jason Knight; Aled Patchett; Nigel Milton.

HOW TO APPLY Application forms and guidance notes for each of the grant programmes are available from the trust's website, where dates for application submissions and decision-making are also listed.

CONTACT DETAILS The Trustees, c/o Groundwork South, Colne Valley Park Centre, Denham Court Drive, Denham, Middlesex UB9 5PG *Tel.* 01895 839916 *Email* HCT@Groundwork.org.uk *Website* www.heathrowcommunitytrust.org

■ The Heathside Charitable Trust

CC NO 326959   **ESTABLISHED** 1985
WHERE FUNDING CAN BE GIVEN UK and overseas.
WHO CAN BENEFIT Charitable organisations. Our previous research suggests the trust has a preference for funding Jewish organisations.
WHAT IS FUNDED General charitable purposes; education; welfare; health care.
WHAT IS NOT FUNDED Individuals.
SAMPLE GRANTS A full list of beneficiaries was not available. One beneficiary was noted in the accounts: The Portland Trust (£50,000).
FINANCES *Financial year end 31/12/2021*
Income £390,700
Grants to organisations £450,400
Assets £5,320,000
TRUSTEES Geoffrey Jayson; Louise Jacobs; Juliet Solomon; Daniel Solomon; Sir Harry Solomon; Sam Jacobs; James Jacobs.
OTHER INFORMATION A total of 66 grants were made during the year, in the following categories: health care (46%); education (28%); other (24%); welfare (2%).
HOW TO APPLY Apply in writing to the correspondent.
CONTACT DETAILS The Trustees, 32 Hampstead High Street, London NW3 1QD *Tel.* 020 7431 7739

■ Heb Ffin (Without Frontier)

CC NO 1157947   **ESTABLISHED** 2014
WHERE FUNDING CAN BE GIVEN Africa and Wales.
WHO CAN BENEFIT Small charities; individuals.
WHAT IS FUNDED The advancement of the Christian religion, particularly evangelistic activities in South Wales and rural districts, as well as the promotion of theological, ministerial and lay training for Welsh ministers and African students; the relief of poverty, with a particular emphasis on Welsh projects that help homeless people, ex-offenders, those suffering from drug dependency and trafficked or sexually exploited people; the relief of poverty in Africa, particularly Christian initiatives that address health issues and education and support micro-businesses.

WHAT IS NOT FUNDED General appeals or circulars; campaigning or lobbying activity; political donations; animal welfare; grant-making organisations; uniformed groups such as Scouts and Guides; disaster relief funds.

TYPE OF GRANT Project costs; general funding.

RANGE OF GRANTS Up to £22,000, but typical grants range from £1,000 to £10,000.

SAMPLE GRANTS Jenga (£22,700); Forum of Christian Leaders (£15,200); Christian Heritage (£10,000); Heart for Africa and The Message Trust – Street Pastors (£5,000 each); Anglican International Development (£2,000); Educating the Children and Zambia Orphans Aid (£1,000 each).

FINANCES *Financial year end 05/04/2022*
Income £856,300
Grants to organisations £100,800
Grants to individuals £4,100
Assets £1,370,000

TRUSTEES Nigel Harris; Nick Davis; Dr Ruth Davis.

HOW TO APPLY Apply in writing to the correspondent by post or email. Full guidelines are available to download from the website.

CONTACT DETAILS Nick Davis, Trustee, 33 Ty Draw Road, Penylan, Cardiff CF23 5HB *Tel.* 07970 681560 *Email* NJSDavis@aol.com *Website* www.hebffin.com

■ The Charlotte Heber-Percy Charitable Trust

CC NO 284387   **ESTABLISHED** 1981
WHERE FUNDING CAN BE GIVEN UK and overseas.
WHO CAN BENEFIT Charitable organisations.
WHAT IS FUNDED General charitable purposes; education; children; animal welfare; the environment; health; hospices; medical research; arts and museums; overseas aid.
WHAT IS NOT FUNDED Individuals.
RANGE OF GRANTS Mostly between £1,000 and £10,000.
SAMPLE GRANTS Access Sport – Angus Irvine Playing Fields Fund (£25,000); Swell Church of England Primary School (£20,000); Addington Fund and Zimbabwe a National Emergency (£10,000 each); The Friends of Aphrodisias Trust (£7,000); Canine Partners for Independence, Marie Curie and UK Squirrel Accord (£5,000 each); Chipping Camden Music Festival (£4,000); Garsington Opera (£500).
FINANCES *Financial year end 05/04/2022*
Income £291,700
Grants to organisations £186,200
Assets £8,800,000
TRUSTEE Charlotte Heber-Percy.
OTHER INFORMATION In 2021/22, grants were awarded to 26 organisations and distributed in the following categories: other (£57,900); general charitable purposes (£42,000); education and children (£22,000); medical causes, cancer and hospices (£30,000); animal welfare and the local environment (£15,000); international charities (£10,000); the arts and museums (£9,300).

HOW TO APPLY Applications should be made in writing to the correspondent. According to the 2021/22 annual report, the trustees meet on an ad hoc basis to consider applications. Our research suggests that only successful applicants are notified.

CONTACT DETAILS Linda Cousins, c/o Rathbone Trust Company Ltd, 8 Finsbury Circus, London EC2M 7AZ *Tel.* 020 7399 0820 *Email* linda.cousins@rathbones.com

■ Ernest Hecht Charitable Foundation

CC NO 1095850   **ESTABLISHED** 2003
WHERE FUNDING CAN BE GIVEN UK.
WHO CAN BENEFIT UK-registered charities.
WHAT IS FUNDED Education; social welfare; health; disadvantaged people; arts and culture, particularly literature.
WHAT IS NOT FUNDED Individuals; charities whose primary area of benefit is outside the UK.
TYPE OF GRANT Project funding; core costs; capital costs.
RANGE OF GRANTS Up to £50,000.
SAMPLE GRANTS Chilterns MS Centre and Marie Curie Cancer Care (£50,000 each); The Felix Project (£45,500); Chickenshed (£37,200); Astor Community Arts Trust (£30,000); University of Westminster (£18,000); Mind in the City (£10,500); Crisis UK (£10,000); Wintercomfort for the Homeless (£5,000); Opera Circus (£4,000).
FINANCES *Financial year end* 31/12/2021 *Income* £2,000,000 *Grants to organisations* £631,700 *Assets* £5,400,000
TRUSTEES Barb Jungr; Robert Ward; Ben Barkow.
OTHER INFORMATION Grants were made to 18 organisations during the year.
HOW TO APPLY At the time of writing (May 2023) the foundation's website stated: 'The Ernest Hecht Charitable Foundation's applications process is closed and will remain closed until further notice.' See the website for the latest information on applications.
CONTACT DETAILS The Trustees, c/o Glazers, 843 Finchley Road, London NW11 8NA *Tel.* 020 8458 7427 *Email* info@ernesthechtcharitablefoundation.org *Website* https://ernesthechtcharitablefoundation.org

■ The Percy Hedley 1990 Charitable Trust

CC NO 1000033   **ESTABLISHED** 1990
WHERE FUNDING CAN BE GIVEN UK, with a preference for Northumberland and Tyne and Wear.
WHO CAN BENEFIT Registered charities.
WHAT IS FUNDED General charitable purposes.
TYPE OF GRANT Capital costs; core and revenue costs.
RANGE OF GRANTS Typically £500 to £1,000.
SAMPLE GRANTS Percey Hedley Foundation (£3,000); Marie Curie Hospice Newcastle (£1,500); Alzheimer's Research UK and Hospice Care Northumberland (£1,000 each); Tom's Trust (£500).
FINANCES *Financial year end* 05/04/2022 *Income* £46,400 *Grants to organisations* £53,500 *Assets* £1,940,000
TRUSTEES John Armstrong; Bill Meikle; Fiona Ruffman.

OTHER INFORMATION Grants were made to 61 organisations during the year.
HOW TO APPLY Apply in writing to the correspondent.
CONTACT DETAILS The Trustees, 10 Castleton Close, Newcastle upon Tyne, Tyne and Wear NE2 2HF *Tel.* 0191 281 5953 *Email* contact.phct@gmail.com

■ The Hedley Foundation

CC NO 262933   **ESTABLISHED** 1971
WHERE FUNDING CAN BE GIVEN UK.
WHO CAN BENEFIT Small to medium-sized registered charities.
WHAT IS FUNDED Disadvantaged young people; older people; people with terminal illnesses; disabilities; social welfare; carers; people experiencing homelessness; people who have experience of the criminal justice system.
WHAT IS NOT FUNDED Churches, cathedrals and museums; charities which only help people from specific groups; applications from individuals directly; appeals for general funding, salaries, deficit, core revenue or transport funding; appeals for building works or refurbishment projects.
TYPE OF GRANT Project funding; one-off (but multi-year grants can be considered).
RANGE OF GRANTS Typically between £250 and £5,000.
SAMPLE GRANTS A list of beneficiaries was not included in the annual report and accounts. Previous beneficiaries have included: In2Change South Yorkshire Ltd (£25,000); Edward James Foundation (£21,000); Young Musicians Symphony Orchestra (£15,000); English National Ballet School, Raleigh International and Tapping House Hospice (£10,000 each).
FINANCES *Financial year end* 31/03/2022 *Income* £1,280,000 *Grants to organisations* £610,100 *Assets* £42,560,000
TRUSTEES David Byam-Cook; Angus Fanshawe; Sir Andrew Ford; Patrick Holcroft; Lorna Stuttaford; Charles Bennett; Alexander Scully.
OTHER INFORMATION Grants were made to 173 charities during the year and were broken down as follows: disability (£206,400); young people (£184,600); other (£125,600); terminal illness and hospices (£93,500).
HOW TO APPLY Application forms are available to download from the foundation's website and should be returned by post with a copy of your latest accounts. Dates of trustees' meetings are listed on the foundation's website.
CONTACT DETAILS Lucy Janes, Appeals Secretary, Victoria House, 1–3 College Hill, London EC4R 2RA *Tel.* 020 7489 8076 *Email* ljanes@hedleyfoundation.org.uk *Website* www.hedleyfoundation.org.uk

■ The Michael Heller Charitable Foundation

CC NO 327832   **ESTABLISHED** 1988
WHERE FUNDING CAN BE GIVEN Worldwide.
WHO CAN BENEFIT Charitable organisations; research institutions; universities.
WHAT IS FUNDED Medical, scientific and educational research; humanitarian causes; education; general charitable causes.
WHAT IS NOT FUNDED Individuals.
TYPE OF GRANT Project funding; research.
SAMPLE GRANTS A list of beneficiaries was not included in the annual report and accounts.

FINANCES *Financial year end* 31/05/2022
Income £237,900
Grants to organisations £201,500
Assets £4,000,000

TRUSTEES Lady Morven Heller; Sir Michael Heller; WS Trustee Company Ltd.

OTHER INFORMATION Grants were broken down as follows: humanitarian causes (£166,500) and education (£35,000).

HOW TO APPLY Apply in writing to the correspondent.

CONTACT DETAILS The Trustees, 12 Little Portland Street, London W1W 8BJ *Tel.* 020 7415 5000

■ The Simon Heller Charitable Settlement

CC NO 265405   **ESTABLISHED** 1972
WHERE FUNDING CAN BE GIVEN UK and overseas.
WHO CAN BENEFIT Charitable organisations; research organisations; universities.
WHAT IS FUNDED Medical, scientific and educational research, as well as humanitarian support; the Jewish faith and community.
TYPE OF GRANT Project costs.
SAMPLE GRANTS A list of beneficiaries was not included in the annual report and accounts. Previous beneficiaries have included: Aish Hatora; Chief Rabbinate Charitable Trust; Institute for Jewish Policy Research; Jewish Care; Scopus; Spiro Institute.
FINANCES *Financial year end* 05/04/2022
Income £427,600
Grants to organisations £261,700
Assets £7,300,000
TRUSTEES Lady Morven Heller; Sir Michael Heller; WS Trustee Company Ltd.
OTHER INFORMATION In 2021/22, grants were distributed as follows: humanitarian causes (£213,100); education (£40,100); research (£8,500). The trustees of the charity also administer The Michael Heller Charitable Foundation (Charity Commission no. 327832), which has similar charitable purposes.
HOW TO APPLY Apply in writing to the correspondent.
CONTACT DETAILS The Trustees, 12 Little Portland Street, London W1W 8BJ *Tel.* 020 7415 5000

■ Help for Health

CC NO 1091814   **ESTABLISHED** 2002
WHERE FUNDING CAN BE GIVEN East Riding of Yorkshire, Hull and North and North East Lincolnshire.
WHO CAN BENEFIT Registered charities; medical and research bodies; universities.
WHAT IS FUNDED Healthcare provision (including facilities and equipment); medical research; medical education; people with disabilities.
TYPE OF GRANT Capital costs (healthcare facilities and equipment); research; project funding.
RANGE OF GRANTS Mostly up to £25,000.
SAMPLE GRANTS Linkage Community Trust (£47,000); Carers Plus Yorkshire (£30,000); Downright Special (£3,300); Hinge Centre (£3,000).
FINANCES *Financial year end* 30/06/2022
Income £27,600
Grants to organisations £210,400
Assets £5,360,000
TRUSTEES Prof. Peter Lee; Dr Andrew Milner; Andrew Mould; Stuart Smith; Richard Field; Victoria Winterton; Carol Hargreaves; Dr Emma Pinder; David Nuttall.

HOW TO APPLY Applications can be made via the charity's website, where application forms can also be downloaded.

CONTACT DETAILS The Trustees, Citadel House, 58 High Street, Wellington Street West, Hull HU1 1QE *Tel.* 01482 607200 *Email* info@helphealth.org.uk *Website* www.helphealth.org.uk

■ The Helping Foundation

CC NO 1104484   **ESTABLISHED** 2004
WHERE FUNDING CAN BE GIVEN UK.
WHO CAN BENEFIT Orthodox Jewish organisations; registered charities; occasionally individuals.
WHAT IS FUNDED The Orthodox Jewish faith and community.
TYPE OF GRANT Project funding.
SAMPLE GRANTS A list of beneficiaries was not included in the annual report and accounts.
FINANCES *Financial year end* 31/12/2021
Income £35,720,000
Grants to organisations £15,530,000
Assets £409,020,000
TRUSTEES David Neuwirth; Benny Stone; Rachel Weis; Rabbi Aubrey Weis; Sir Weis.
HOW TO APPLY Apply in writing to the correspondent.
CONTACT DETAILS Benny Stone, Secretary, 59 Kings Road, Prestwich, Manchester M25 0LQ *Tel.* 01617 40116

■ The Hemby Charitable Trust

CC NO 1073028   **ESTABLISHED** 1998
WHERE FUNDING CAN BE GIVEN Merseyside and Wirral.
WHO CAN BENEFIT Registered charities or organisations applying to become one.
WHAT IS FUNDED General charitable purposes; older people; the arts; social welfare; young people and employment; the environment.
WHAT IS NOT FUNDED Applicants from outside the area of benefit; sponsorship in any form; individuals; religious bodies; places of worship (unless there is significant non-worship community use); political organisations; pressure groups; feasibility studies; schools seeking specialist status; any form of memorial; repeat applicants within two years of a successful application.
TYPE OF GRANT Capital funding is preferred, although revenue requests may be considered.
RANGE OF GRANTS Mostly £500 to £2,000.
SAMPLE GRANTS Walton Centre (£20,000); James' Place Charity (£5,000); Huntington's Disease Association (£3,000); Bridge 2 (Liverpool) Ltd (£2,500); Bluecoat (£2,000); Foundation Years Trust (£1,500); Guide Dogs for the Blind (£1,000); Freshfields Animal Rescue (£500).
FINANCES *Financial year end* 31/01/2022
Income £103,700
Grants to organisations £103,700
Assets £3,590,000
TRUSTEES Andrew Morris; Roy Morris; Caroline Tod; David Fairclough; Stuart Keppie.
OTHER INFORMATION In 2021/22, the trust awarded 55 grants to organisations. Grants were distributed in the following categories: social needs (£72,500); young people and employment (£15,800); the arts (£10,300); older people (£5,200).
HOW TO APPLY Applications can be made using a form available from the trust's website. Completed application forms should be returned to the correspondent together with a copy of your most recent accounts. Up to two additional A4 sheets can be added if space is needed.

The deadlines for applications are normally midday on 1 February, 1 June and 1 October. Check the trust's website for the latest deadline dates. Applications are not acknowledged but applicants are welcome to email or telephone the correspondent to check if their submission has been received. The website advises potential applicants to get in touch via phone if they are unsure how to complete the application form (including the size of the grant to be requested).

CONTACT DETAILS Tom Evans, Administrator, c/o Rathbone Investment Management Ltd, Port of Liverpool Building, Pier Head, Liverpool, Merseyside L3 1NW *Tel.* 07503 319182 *Email* adminathembytrust@talktalk.net *Website* http://hembytrust.org.uk

■ The Trevor Hemmings Foundation

CC NO 1077311 **ESTABLISHED** 1999
WHERE FUNDING CAN BE GIVEN The North West; UK (national causes).
WHO CAN BENEFIT Charitable organisations.
WHAT IS FUNDED Social welfare, medical causes and racing welfare.
TYPE OF GRANT Mostly one-off.
RANGE OF GRANTS Generally £10,000 to £50,000, with some larger grants.
SAMPLE GRANTS Alder Hey Children's Charity (£105,000 in two grants); The Injured Jockeys Fund (£75,000); Noble's Hospital (£65,000); Spinal Injuries Association (£45,000 in two grants); Carers Trust (£32,500); The Cure Parkinson's Trust (£25,000); Manx Kidney Patients Association (£20,000); Manx Blind Welfare (£15,000); Stroke Association (£10,000).
FINANCES *Financial year end* 31/03/2022
Income £481,100
Grants to organisations £837,900
Assets £134,800
TRUSTEES Kathryn Revitt; Patrick Hemmings; Craig Hemmings; Mark Widders; Mark Tootell.
OTHER INFORMATION Grants were awarded to 35 organisations during the year.
HOW TO APPLY Apply in writing to the correspondent.
CONTACT DETAILS The Trustees, Dower House, Dawbers Lane, Euxton, Chorley PR7 6ED *Tel.* 01257 244720

■ Christina Mary Hendrie Trust

OSCR NO SC014514 **ESTABLISHED** 1975
WHERE FUNDING CAN BE GIVEN Scotland and Canada.
WHO CAN BENEFIT Registered charities with an annual turnover of less than £5 million; hospices.
WHAT IS FUNDED Young people; older people; veterans; hospices.
WHAT IS NOT FUNDED Individuals; building projects. See the trust's website for more information on eligibility criteria.
TYPE OF GRANT General funding; running costs (for hospices).
RANGE OF GRANTS The average award is £7,500.
SAMPLE GRANTS Super Power Agency (£35,000); St Andrew's Charitable Foundation (£25,400).
FINANCES *Financial year end* 31/03/2022
Income £102,600
Grants to organisations £366,300
Assets £8,570,000

TRUSTEES Anthony Cox; Charles Cox; Andrew Desson; Mary Grieve; Susie Hendrie; Laura Irwin; John Moncrieff; Alan Sharp.
OTHER INFORMATION Only beneficiaries of grants equating to more than 5% of the grant total were listed in the accounts. Other grants totalled £305,900.
HOW TO APPLY Applications can be made online via the trust's website.
CONTACT DETAILS The Secretary, 1 Rutland Court, Edinburgh EH3 8EY *Tel.* 0131 270 7700 *Email* support@email.com or use the contact form on the website *Website* www. christinamaryhendrietrust.co.uk

■ Henley Educational Trust

CC NO 309237 **ESTABLISHED** 1604
WHERE FUNDING CAN BE GIVEN Henley-on-Thames and the parishes of Bix and Rotherfield Greys in Oxfordshire and Remenham in Berkshire only.
WHO CAN BENEFIT State-maintained schools and colleges; youth and sports clubs; playgroups; charities; individuals under the age of 25.
WHAT IS FUNDED The education of children and young people (up to the age of 25), including related purposes such as extracurricular activities, sports, music, training, events, etc.
TYPE OF GRANT Project funding; capital costs.
RANGE OF GRANTS Mostly up to £9,000.
SAMPLE GRANTS Henley Schools Partnership (£45,200); Gillotts Academy (£19,800); The Henley College (£8,200); Trinity School (£6,600); Valley Road (£4,000); Henley Youth Festival (£2,800); AFC Henley (£600); Crazies Hill (£280).
FINANCES *Financial year end* 31/03/2022
Income £137,500
Grants to organisations £97,400
Grants to individuals £40,400
Assets £4,050,000
TRUSTEES Amanda Heath; Elizabeth Hodgkin; Kellie Hinton; Isobel Morrow; The Revd Jeremy Taylor; Michelle Mayor; Susan Bishop; Debbie Wermann; Tristan Arnison; Carly Watkins; John Print.
OTHER INFORMATION Grants were made to 12 organisations and 101 individuals during 2021/22. Grants were broken down as follows: promotion of education for children and young people (£89,600); individuals in need (£40,400); provision of special benefits for schools (£16,800).
HOW TO APPLY Contact the trust for more information.
CONTACT DETAILS Catherine Gosby, Clerk to the Trustees, 1A Coldharbour Close, Henley-on-Thames, Reading, Berkshire RG9 1QF *Tel.* 01491 524994 *Email* clerk@ henleyeducationaltrust.com *Website* www. henleyeducationaltrust.com

■ Henley Royal Regatta Charitable Trust

CC NO 299597 **ESTABLISHED** 1988
WHERE FUNDING CAN BE GIVEN UK.
WHO CAN BENEFIT Sports clubs and related organisations.
WHAT IS FUNDED Projects associated with, or promoting, rowing.
TYPE OF GRANT Project funding; scholarships.
RANGE OF GRANTS £500 to £100,000.
SAMPLE GRANTS London Youth Rowing (£100,000); Rowing Foundation (£51,500); Warrington Youth

Rowing (£17,300); National Junior Indoor Rowing Championships (£10,000); Oarsome Chance (£7,000); Runcorn Rowing Club (£1,500); Regatta for the Disabled (£500).

FINANCES *Financial year end 30/09/2021*
Income £62,800
Grants to organisations £187,800
Assets £9,020,000

TRUSTEES Chris Baillieu; R. C. Lester; Sir Steve Redgrave; Mr R. C. Stanhope; Sarah Winckless.

OTHER INFORMATION The trust is associated with the Henley Royal Regatta rowing event. Grants were made to seven organisations during the year. The 2020/21 accounts were the latest available at the time of writing (May 2023).

HOW TO APPLY Apply in writing to the correspondent. Full application guidelines, including the trust's application schedule, are available on the website.

CONTACT DETAILS The Trustees, Henley Royal Regatta Headquarters, Henley Bridge, Henley-on-Thames, Oxfordshire RG9 2LY *Tel.* 01491 572153 *Email* dgrist@regattahq.co.uk *Website* www.hrr.co.uk/charitable-trust

■ Tim Henman Foundation

CC NO 1161964   **ESTABLISHED** 2015
WHERE FUNDING CAN BE GIVEN England and Wales.
WHO CAN BENEFIT Registered charities; schools and educational establishments; hospices.
WHAT IS FUNDED Supporting disadvantaged and vulnerable children and young people by improving mental and physical health and creating sporting and educational opportunities.
TYPE OF GRANT Development funding; capital costs; projects; scholarships.
RANGE OF GRANTS £10,000 to £25,000.
SAMPLE GRANTS Reed's School Foundation (£5,000); Raynes Park High School (£750).
FINANCES *Financial year end 31/08/2022*
Income £275,700
Grants to organisations £5,800
Grants to individuals £5,300
Assets £794,600
TRUSTEES Jan Felgate; Lucy Henman; Tim Henman; Kevan Walsh; Andrew Hynard; Ashley Silverton; Mark Laurence; Trevor Alldridge; Dr Karl Altenburg.
OTHER INFORMATION The grant total was significantly lower than normal due to a change in reporting dates and returned funding following the disruption caused by the COVID-19 pandemic. Typically, grants to organisations total over £70,000.
HOW TO APPLY Contact the correspondent for more information.
CONTACT DETAILS The Trustees, c/o Menzies LLP, Ashcombe House, 5 The Crescent, Leatherhead, Surrey KT22 8DY *Tel.* 01372 849614 *Email* info@henmanfoundation.org *Website* www.henmanfoundation.org

■ The G. D. Herbert Charitable Trust

CC NO 295998   **ESTABLISHED** 1986
WHERE FUNDING CAN BE GIVEN UK.
WHO CAN BENEFIT Charitable organisations.
WHAT IS FUNDED General charitable purposes; medicine; health; social welfare; environmental causes.
TYPE OF GRANT Mainly recurrent, with occasional one-off awards (in the areas of health and welfare only).

RANGE OF GRANTS Up to £3,000.
SAMPLE GRANTS Red Cross – Ukraine Crisis Appeal (£5,000); Canterbury Oast Trust, Friends of the Elderly, Marie Curie Cancer Care and Queen Elizabeth's Foundation for Disabled People (£3,300 each); The Abbeyfield Society (£3,000); Cruse Bereavement Care (£2,500); Wiltshire Wildlife Trust (£900).
FINANCES *Financial year end 05/04/2022*
Income £53,100
Grants to organisations £90,300
Assets £2,690,000
TRUSTEES Mrs J. M. Cuxson; Caroline Beaumont.
OTHER INFORMATION The trust awarded regular grants to 25 organisations and 5 one-off grants to other charities.
HOW TO APPLY The annual report for 2021/22 states that the trustees 'review donations at their annual general meeting in February/March of each year and may make some adjustments but for the most part continue the donations to the beneficiaries listed year on year.'
CONTACT DETAILS The Trustees, c/o Veale Wasbrough Vizards LLP, 24 King William Street, London EC4R 9AT *Tel.* 020 7405 1234 *Email* mbyrne@vwv.co.uk

■ Herefordshire Community Foundation

CC NO 1094935   **ESTABLISHED** 2002
WHERE FUNDING CAN BE GIVEN Herefordshire.
WHO CAN BENEFIT Registered charities; unregistered charities; CICs; social enterprises; schools; hospices; individuals.
WHAT IS FUNDED General charitable purposes.
WHAT IS NOT FUNDED Animal welfare; arts projects with no community or charitable element; direct replacement of statutory funding; medical research; political groups or activities promoting political beliefs; religious groups seeking to influence people's religious choices; sports projects with no community or charitable element; general appeals.
TYPE OF GRANT Capital costs; core/revenue costs; seed funding/start-up costs; project funding.
RANGE OF GRANTS £1,000 to £10,000.
SAMPLE GRANTS Close House (£9,900); Leominster Festival (£6,000); Pembridge Amenity Trust (£3,500); Wellington Heath Parish Council (£1,500); Bromyard Community Arts (£1,200).
FINANCES *Financial year end 31/03/2022*
Income £1,170,000
Grants to organisations £900,500
Assets £6,330,000
TRUSTEES Frank Myers; Antony Lowther; Geoffrey Hughes; Laura Hughes; Shelagh Wynn; Philippa Spens; Karen Hall; Alex Davies; Nell Pearce-Higgins; Rachel Carr.
OTHER INFORMATION This is one of the 47 UK community foundations, which distribute funding for a wide range of purposes. As with all community foundations, there are a number of donor-advised funds managed on behalf of individuals, families and charitable trusts. Grant schemes tend to change frequently – consult the foundation's website for details of current programmes and up-to-date deadlines. During 2021/22 a total of 325 grants were made to organisations and individuals. Note that the grant total includes grants to individuals.
HOW TO APPLY Potential applicants are advised to visit the community foundation's website or contact its grants team to find the most suitable funding stream.

CONTACT DETAILS Grants Administrator, The Fred Bulmer Centre, Wall Street, Hereford, Herefordshire HR4 9HP *Tel.* 01432 272550 *Email* admin@herefordshirecf.org *Website* www.herefordshirecf.org

■ The Herefordshire Historic Churches Trust

CC NO 511181 **ESTABLISHED** 1954
WHERE FUNDING CAN BE GIVEN Herefordshire.
WHO CAN BENEFIT Churches of all denominations.
WHAT IS FUNDED Preservation, repair, maintenance and improvement of churches.
TYPE OF GRANT One-off awards for capital and core costs (primarily for repair and maintenance); project funding; loans of up to £10,000 are also available.
RANGE OF GRANTS £1,000 to £15,000.
SAMPLE GRANTS Kingsland (£15,000); Pembridge (£8,000); Leominster Priory (£3,000); Wellington (£1,500); Madley (£1,000).
FINANCES *Financial year end 31/12/2021*
Income £72,400
Grants to organisations £76,600
Assets £1,030,000
TRUSTEES David Furnival; Ali Jones; Jill Gallimore; Lady Susanna McFarlane; John Handby; Stephen Cheetham; Ben Furnival; The Ven. Derek Chedzey; Rod Barker.
HOW TO APPLY Application forms can be completed on the trust's website, where guidance notes can also be found. Potential applicants are encouraged to contact the trust at an early stage to discuss their project.
CONTACT DETAILS David Furnival, Chair, Coppice Barn, The Woodhouse Farm, Staplow, Ledbury, Herefordshire HR8 1NP *Email* david.furnival13@gmail.com *Website* www.hhct.co.uk

■ Heritage Lottery Fund

ESTABLISHED 1994
WHERE FUNDING CAN BE GIVEN UK.
WHO CAN BENEFIT Charitable organisations; heritage enterprises.
WHAT IS FUNDED Heritage projects.
TYPE OF GRANT Direct project costs including capital costs, salaries, training, repairs and maintenance.
RANGE OF GRANTS £3,000 to £5 million.
SAMPLE GRANTS A list of beneficiaries was not included in the annual report and accounts. Previous beneficiaries have included: Canterbury Cathedral; Historic England; Hull City Council; Imperial War Museums; National Maritime Museum; The British Library.
FINANCES *Financial year end 31/03/2022*
Income £362,090,000
Grants to organisations £163,150,000
Assets (£165,450,000)
TRUSTEES Baroness Kay Andrews; Maria Adebowale-Schwarte; Dr Claire Feehily; Prof. David Stocker; Mukesh Sharma; Julian Glover; Taryn Nixon; Ray Macfarlane; Carol Pyrah.
HOW TO APPLY All applications must be submitted via the online application portal.
CONTACT DETAILS The Grants Team, 4th Floor, Cannon Bridge House, 25 Dowgate Hill, London EC4R 2YA *Tel.* 020 7591 6044 *Email* enquire@heritagefund.org.uk

■ The Heritage of London Trust Ltd

CC NO 280272 **ESTABLISHED** 1980
WHERE FUNDING CAN BE GIVEN Greater London.
WHO CAN BENEFIT Buildings or monuments which are of architectural or historic interest; community organisations; local authorities; statutory bodies.
WHAT IS FUNDED The conservation and restoration of historic buildings and monuments which are in public or community use.
WHAT IS NOT FUNDED Buildings in private ownership that are not open or available for public use and enjoyment; roof replacements or repairs; restoration schemes where the work has already been completed; general maintenance or repairs.
TYPE OF GRANT Restoration grants, awarded over a period of three years.
RANGE OF GRANTS Typically between £1,000 and £15,000.
SAMPLE GRANTS Francis and C. Walters (£17,300); Tower Hamlets Market Barrows (£15,000); Wanstead Grotto (£14,000); The Jewish Memorial Fountain (£10,000); Boston Manor House (£9,300); Raine's House (£8,000); Friends of Ruskin Park (£5,000); St Pancras Church (£1,900).
FINANCES *Financial year end 31/03/2022*
Income £504,000
Grants to organisations £71,200
Grants to individuals £3,000
Assets £980,200
TRUSTEES Jamie Cayzer-Colvin; Kit Kemp; James Ritblat; Dora Dixon-Fyle; John Phillips; Richard Johnston; Prof. Pippa Catterall.
OTHER INFORMATION Buildings do not need to be listed in order to be eligible but must be considered of historic or architectural interest. During the year, £3,000 was awarded to individuals for education.
HOW TO APPLY In the first instance, applicants should contact the trust via phone, email or the online enquiry form to discuss the project. If a project is considered to be suitable for funding, the trustees will arrange a visit to discuss it further. The applicant will then be asked to complete the online application form. The trustees meet three times a year to consider applications.
CONTACT DETAILS The Trustees, 34 Grosvenor Gardens, London SW1W 0DH *Tel.* 020 7099 0559 *Email* info@heritageoflondon.com *Website* www.heritageoflondon.org

■ Hertfordshire Community Foundation

CC NO 1156082 **ESTABLISHED** 1988
WHERE FUNDING CAN BE GIVEN Hertfordshire.
WHO CAN BENEFIT Formally constituted community groups; charitable organisations; individuals.
WHAT IS FUNDED A wide range of charitable purposes including: social welfare; safer communities; youth social action; community transport; community development; children and young people.
WHAT IS NOT FUNDED See individual grant programmes for specific exclusions.
TYPE OF GRANT Project funding; capital costs.
SAMPLE GRANTS A list of beneficiaries was not included in the annual report and accounts.

FINANCES *Financial year end* 31/03/2022
Income £4,800,000
Grants to organisations £3,780,000
Grants to individuals £66,100
Assets £14,790,000

TRUSTEES Henry Hibbert; James Williams; Simon Tilley; Jill Burridge; John Saner; Terence Douris; Sally Burton; Anna Bates; Suzanne Westlake; Suzana Harvey; Augustus Machado; Jonathan Arrowsmith.

OTHER INFORMATION This is one of the 47 UK community foundations, which distribute funding for a wide range of purposes. As with all community foundations, there are a number of donor-advised funds managed on behalf of individuals, families and charitable trusts. Grant schemes tend to change frequently – consult the foundation's website for details of current programmes and up-to-date deadlines. Grants to organisations were broken down as follows: fairness (£2.53 million); strong communities (£648,500); Hertfordshire Community Foundation training and development (£237,500); emergency COVID-19 relief (£127,900); healthy living (£109,300); safety (£99,200); the environment (£22,400); and housing (£4,800).

HOW TO APPLY Potential applicants are advised to visit the community foundation's website or contact its grants team to find the most suitable funding stream.

CONTACT DETAILS Grants Team, Foundation House, 2–4 Forum Place, Fiddlebridge Lane, Hatfield, Hertfordshire AL10 0RN *Tel.* 01707 251351 *Email* grants@hertscf.org.uk *Website* www.hertscf.org.uk

---

■ **The Bernhard Heuberger Charitable Trust**

CC NO 294378   **ESTABLISHED** 1986
WHERE FUNDING CAN BE GIVEN England and Wales.
WHO CAN BENEFIT Charitable organisations. Preference may be given to Jewish organisations.
WHAT IS FUNDED The Jewish faith and community; general charitable purposes; education and training; health.
SAMPLE GRANTS A list of beneficiaries was not included in the annual report and accounts.
FINANCES *Financial year end* 05/04/2022
Income £77,700
Grants to organisations £213,000
Assets £2,220,000
TRUSTEES Stephen Heuberger; David Demby.
OTHER INFORMATION During 2021/22, grants were distributed in the following categories: general charitable purposes (£173,800); education and training (£28,100); health (£11,100).
HOW TO APPLY Apply in writing to the correspondent.
CONTACT DETAILS The Trustees, 77 Southover, London N12 7HG *Tel.* 020 8445 1627 *Email* d.demby@uhy-uk.com

---

■ **HFC Help for Children UK Ltd**

CC NO 1116081   **ESTABLISHED** 2006
WHERE FUNDING CAN BE GIVEN London and the South East; Hong Kong; Cayman Islands; Canada; USA.
WHO CAN BENEFIT Registered charities; CICs.
WHAT IS FUNDED The prevention of, or treatment for, child abuse.

WHAT IS NOT FUNDED Lobbying activities; annual fundraising drives; projects undertaken by individuals; multi-year grants.
TYPE OF GRANT Project funding; research.
RANGE OF GRANTS Typically less than £20,000.
SAMPLE GRANTS Dandelion Time, Redthread Youth Ltd, Safer London and The Mulberry Bush School (£18,000 each); Abianda (£17,000); Kids Inspire (£13,500).
FINANCES *Financial year end* 31/12/2021
Income £389,000
Grants to organisations £102,500
Assets £263,900
TRUSTEES Jack Edward; Louise Mourgues; Malcolm Goddard; Michael Merritt-Holmes; Catherine Streeter; Ashley Fuller; Robert Hughes; Sara Hall; Matthew Bloomfield; Robert Schultz; Jonathan Napora; Melanie Pittas; Christopher Radley-Gardner; Greg Gliner; Dan Petrovic; Damon Ambrosini; Jonathan May.
HOW TO APPLY Applicants should first complete a Letter of Intent, which can be downloaded from the application section of the Help for Children website. After review, selected organisations will be invited to complete a full proposal. Declined Letters of Intent are acknowledged. Visit the charity's website for current deadlines.
CONTACT DETAILS Kartika Fitrianingsih, Grants Manager, 106 W. 32nd Street, 2nd Floor, New York, USA NY 10001 *Email* kfitrianingsih@hfc.org or grants@hfc.org *Website* www.hfc.org

---

■ **P. and C. Hickinbotham Charitable Trust**

CC NO 216432   **ESTABLISHED** 1947
WHERE FUNDING CAN BE GIVEN Leicestershire; North Wales; Northern Ireland; Rutland.
WHO CAN BENEFIT Registered charities only.
WHAT IS FUNDED General charitable purposes; social welfare; people with disabilities; people experiencing homelessness; substance abuse; prisoners' education and rehabilitation; refugees and asylum seekers; sex workers; the arts; cultural and historic projects; children and young people; community development; the environment.
WHAT IS NOT FUNDED Individuals; large national charities (unless for a specific project); groups without charitable status; general running costs; repeat grants.
TYPE OF GRANT One-off grants; specialist equipment; premises purchase or renovation; start-up costs; salaries.
RANGE OF GRANTS Grants tend to range from £250 to £1,000, although there is no set upper limit.
SAMPLE GRANTS Leicester Charity Link (£7,500); Age UK Leicester Shire and Rutland and RNLI (£5,000 each); Dove Cottage Day Hospice (£2,500); Angels and Monsters, Cossington Project Group and Leicestershire Chorale (£2,000 each).
FINANCES *Financial year end* 05/04/2022
Income £196,100
Grants to organisations £53,400
Assets £5,930,000
TRUSTEES Rachel Hickinbotham; Roger Hickinbotham; Anna Steiger; Charlotte Palmer; Frances Hickinbotham; Alice Hickinbotham.
OTHER INFORMATION Grants of under £2,000 totalled £95,500.
HOW TO APPLY Apply in writing to the correspondent. The trustees meet quarterly to consider applications.
CONTACT DETAILS Roger Hickinbotham, Trustee, 9 Windmill Way, Lyddington, Oakham, Rutland

LE15 9LY *Email* roger@hickinbothamtrust.org.uk
Website www.hickinbothamtrust.org.uk

■ The Alan Edward Higgs Charity

CC NO 509367   **ESTABLISHED** 1979
WHERE FUNDING CAN BE GIVEN Within 25 miles of the
centre of Coventry only.
WHO CAN BENEFIT Registered charities; CICs;
formally constituted community organisations;
community amateur sports clubs.
WHAT IS FUNDED Disadvantaged young people,
families and children.
WHAT IS NOT FUNDED Visit the charity's website for a
detailed list of exclusions.
TYPE OF GRANT Capital costs; core/revenue costs;
seed funding/start-up costs.
RANGE OF GRANTS Mostly under £20,000.
SAMPLE GRANTS Roald Dahl's Marvellous Children's
Charity (£25,000); Sense (£10,000); Young
People First (£9,800); Whizz-Kidz (£6,000);
Stoke Community Club Ltd (£5,000); Level
Water (£3,000); Coventry City Mission (£2,500);
Holbrooks Community Centre (£1,000).
FINANCES *Financial year end 05/04/2022*
Income £583,300
Grants to organisations £216,000
Assets £20,410,000
TRUSTEES Marilyn Knatchbull-Hugessen; Rowley
Higgs; Emily Barlow; Mark Franklin; Steven
Cooke; Alexander Barrett; Emma Bates.
OTHER INFORMATION Grants were made to 35
organisations during 2021/22.
HOW TO APPLY Applications can be made online
through the charity's website, where detailed
guidelines are also available.
CONTACT DETAILS Marilyn Knatchbull-Hugessen,
Clerk, The Coventry Building Society Arena,
Judd's Lane, Longford, Coventry, Warwickshire
CV6 6GE *Tel.* 024 7622 1311 *Email* clerk@
higgscharity.org.uk *Website* www.higgscharity.
org.uk

■ The Highcroft Charitable Trust

CC NO 272684   **ESTABLISHED** 1975
WHERE FUNDING CAN BE GIVEN UK and overseas.
WHO CAN BENEFIT Jewish charitable organisations;
Jewish educational institutions.
WHAT IS FUNDED Social welfare for Jewish families;
Jewish religious education.
RANGE OF GRANTS Mostly up to £10,000 with the
occasional larger grant.
SAMPLE GRANTS BC Trust (£26,000); Tchabe Kollel
Ltd and Tevini Ltd (£10,000 each); Friends of
Torah Veyirah and Gateshead Talmudical
College (£5,000 each).
FINANCES *Financial year end 30/06/2021*
Income £151,500
Grants to organisations £118,700
Assets £1,300,000
TRUSTEES Richard Fischer; Alexander Eisner; Bella
Reicher.
OTHER INFORMATION The 2020/21 accounts were
the latest available at the time of writing (May
2023). Only organisations that received grants
of over £5,000 were listed as beneficiaries in
the trust's 2020/21 accounts. Grants of less
than £5,000 totalled £26,200.
HOW TO APPLY Apply in writing to the correspondent.
CONTACT DETAILS The Trustee, 13 Basing Hill,
London NW11 8TE *Tel.* 020 8458 5382

■ Highway One Trust

CC NO 1164753   **ESTABLISHED** 2016
WHERE FUNDING CAN BE GIVEN UK and overseas.
WHO CAN BENEFIT Registered charities (UK or
international); not-for-profit organisations.
WHAT IS FUNDED Disfiguring medical conditions;
mental health; prison and injustice; poverty;
homelessness; economic regeneration; online
safety (e.g. cyber abuse); singledom;
Christianity.
TYPE OF GRANT Multi-year funding; core costs; capital
costs; project funding.
RANGE OF GRANTS £5,000 to £10,000.
SAMPLE GRANTS Dose of Nature and Linking Lives
(£15,000 each); Changing Faces (£10,300);
Centre for Criminal Appeals, Christian Solidarity
Worldwide, Fair Trials International, Only
Connect and Mosaic Middle East (£10,000
each); Wilmslow Wells for Africa (£5,000).
FINANCES *Financial year end 31/12/2021*
Income £271,900
Grants to organisations £225,100
Assets £2,170,000
TRUSTEES Jacqueline Elton; Neil Maybin; Michael
Armstrong; Dr Sarah Rutherford.
OTHER INFORMATION Grants were awarded to 22
organisations in 2021.
HOW TO APPLY The policy of the trustees is to not
respond to unsolicited applications; however,
the website states: 'If you feel your work or
project meets our criteria, you may send an
email outlining the work or project in no more
than fifty words to the researcher at
info@highwayonetrust.com.'
CONTACT DETAILS The Trustees, 2nd Floor, Church
House, 86 Tavistock Place, London WC1H 9RT
Tel. 020 8878 0701 *Email* info@
highwayonetrust.com *Website* http://
highwayonetrust.com

■ The Hilden Charitable Fund

CC NO 232591   **ESTABLISHED** 1963
WHERE FUNDING CAN BE GIVEN UK; Malawi; Tanzania;
Uganda.
WHO CAN BENEFIT Registered charities; CICs;
voluntary organisations; NGOs; social
enterprises. Organisations should have an
income of under £250,000.
WHAT IS FUNDED In the UK: asylum seekers and
refugees; penal affairs. Overseas: projects
which support access to education for women
and girls; projects which enable rural and/or
displaced communities to become more self-
sufficient.
WHAT IS NOT FUNDED Individuals (including via
bursaries); non-charitable activities; promotion
of religion; party-political organisations or
campaigning; medical research; registered
social landlords (e.g. housing associations);
hospitals or primary healthcare provision;
fundraising-only posts; statutory services;
residential care.
TYPE OF GRANT Project funding; unrestricted core/
revenue costs; multi-year.
RANGE OF GRANTS Organisations can apply for up to
two years' funding with grants awarded usually
between £5,000 and £7,000 in value per year.
SAMPLE GRANTS Springfield Domestic Abuse Support
(£10,000); Devon and Cornwall Refugee
Support (£7,500); Aid Box Community (£5,000);
Kinship Care – Northern Ireland (£3,000);
Innovative Youth With Action – Uganda
(£1,500).

FINANCES *Financial year end* 05/04/2022
  Income £450,000
  Grants to organisations £426,300
  Assets £15,350,000
TRUSTEES Maggie Baxter; Prof. D. S. Rampton; Catherine Rampton; Prof. M. B. Rampton; Mr J. R. Rampton; A. J. M. Rampton; Prof. Charles Rodeck; Elizabeth Rodeck; Samia Khatun; Jonathan Branch; Robert Rampton; Bandi Mbubi; Emma Jenkins.
HOW TO APPLY Apply online via the charity's website.
CONTACT DETAILS Catherine Sotto, Office Manager, 34 North End Road, London W14 0SH *Tel.* 020 7603 1525 *Email* admin@hildencharitablefund.org *Website* www.hildencharitablefund.org

■ The Derek Hill Foundation

CC NO 801590   **ESTABLISHED** 1989
WHERE FUNDING CAN BE GIVEN UK.
WHO CAN BENEFIT Charitable organisations and individuals.
WHAT IS FUNDED Arts and culture; music; literature; education.
RANGE OF GRANTS Typically under £5,000.
SAMPLE GRANTS Previous beneficiaries have included: London Magazine (£10,000); Agenda Poetry (£7,500); National Youth Theatre (£5,000); Opera North Ltd (£2,000); Bampton Classical Opera and Lennox Berkeley Society (£1,000 each); The De Morgan Foundation (£500).
FINANCES *Financial year end* 09/05/2022
  Income £18,000
  Grants to organisations £119,000
TRUSTEES Ian Paterson; Bruce Newbigging; Rathbone Trust Company Ltd.
OTHER INFORMATION The foundation's accounts were not available to view on the Charity Commission's website due to its low income. We have estimated the grant total based on previous years' expenditure.
HOW TO APPLY Apply in writing to the correspondent.
CONTACT DETAILS The Trustees, c/o Rathbone Trust Company Ltd, 8 Finsbury Circus, London EC2M 7AZ *Tel.* 020 7399 0835 *Email* tracey.hazell@rathbones.com

■ The Hillier Trust

CC NO 1147629   **ESTABLISHED** 2012
WHERE FUNDING CAN BE GIVEN Worldwide.
WHO CAN BENEFIT Registered charities, mainly those which have a Christian ethos; individuals.
WHAT IS FUNDED Development and support work for disadvantaged groups; Christian causes.
RANGE OF GRANTS Typically £1,000 to £5,000, with some larger grants.
SAMPLE GRANTS The Family Trust (£165,000); Open Doors (£25,000); Embrace the Middle East (£20,000); Brogdale Collections (£12,000); The Loop (£4,000); The Salvation Army (£1,500); Age UK (£1,000).
FINANCES *Financial year end* 30/06/2022
  Income £45,500
  Grants to organisations £274,300
  Assets £3,090,000
TRUSTEES Anthony Hillier; Susan Hillier; Elizabeth Jordan; David Hillier.
OTHER INFORMATION Grants were made to 22 organisations in 2021/22. Each year a substantial grant is made to The Family Trust.
HOW TO APPLY Apply in writing to the correspondent. The trustees communicate regularly throughout the year to consider grant applications.

CONTACT DETAILS Anthony Hillier, Trustee, Loose Court Farmhouse, Old Drive, Maidstone, Kent ME15 9SE *Tel.* 07767 775792 *Email* tonyhillier@zen.co.uk

■ The Alison Hillman Charitable Trust

CC NO 1040855
WHERE FUNDING CAN BE GIVEN UK.
WHO CAN BENEFIT Charitable organisations.
WHAT IS FUNDED Epilepsy research; the care of people with epilepsy.
SAMPLE GRANTS A list of beneficiaries was not included in the annual report and accounts.
FINANCES *Financial year end* 05/04/2022
  Income £526,000
  Grants to organisations £259,400
  Assets £13,990,000
TRUSTEES Andrew Fisher; Ian Humphrey; Clare Wishart.
OTHER INFORMATION During the year, the trust made grants to 38 organisations.
HOW TO APPLY Apply in writing to the correspondent.
CONTACT DETAILS The Trustees, 153A Metchley Lane, Harborne, Birmingham B17 0JL

■ R. G. Hills Charitable Trust

CC NO 1008914   **ESTABLISHED** 1982
WHERE FUNDING CAN BE GIVEN UK and overseas, with a preference for Kent.
WHO CAN BENEFIT Registered charities.
WHAT IS FUNDED General charitable purposes with some preference for health, social welfare and education.
RANGE OF GRANTS Grants range from £1,000 to £2,500.
SAMPLE GRANTS Kent Search and Rescue (Lowland) (£2,500); Porridge and Pens Ghana (£2,000); Strong Men, Surfers Against Sewage and The Hill 112 Memorial Foundation (£1,000 each).
FINANCES *Financial year end* 31/03/2022
  Income £138,300
  Grants to organisations £100,000
  Assets £4,520,000
TRUSTEES Harvey Barrett; Kenneth Jones.
OTHER INFORMATION In 2021/22, grants were awarded to 77 organisations.
HOW TO APPLY Apply in writing to the correspondent.
CONTACT DETAILS The Trustees, c/o Furley Page, 39–40 St Margaret's Street, Canterbury CT1 2TX *Tel.* 01227 763939

■ Hinchley Charitable Trust

CC NO 1108412   **ESTABLISHED** 1973
WHERE FUNDING CAN BE GIVEN UK and Ireland; occasionally overseas.
WHO CAN BENEFIT Registered charities.
WHAT IS FUNDED Training of Christian leaders; holistic Christian mission in communities; Christian youth organisations; Christian influence in the public sphere.
WHAT IS NOT FUNDED Individuals.
TYPE OF GRANT Project funding; strategic funding; development funding; core costs; salaries.
RANGE OF GRANTS Up to £15,000.
SAMPLE GRANTS Sports Chaplaincy and Willowfield Parish Community (£10,000 each); Christians in Parliament (£7,500); Sutton Schools Work (£6,000); New Wine Ireland (£5,000).

FINANCES *Financial year end* 30/06/2022
Income £131,200
Grants to organisations £136,000
Assets £4,010,000

TRUSTEES John Levick; Roger Northcott; Dr Brian Stanley; Rebecca Corbett; Sarah Smith.

OTHER INFORMATION During the year, grants were made to 20 organisations and were distributed within the following categories: young people (£136,000); holistic mission (£55,000); training leaders (£37,500); the public sphere (£7,500).

HOW TO APPLY The trust's website states: 'Our aim is to work with a select number of charity partners and therefore we do not accept unsolicited applications.'

CONTACT DETAILS The Trustees, 2 Arnold Drive, Chessington, Surrey KT9 2GD *Email* info@ hinchleycharitabletrust.org.uk *Website* www. hinchleycharitabletrust.org.uk

■ The Lady Hind Trust

CC NO 208877   **ESTABLISHED** 1951

WHERE FUNDING CAN BE GIVEN Nottinghamshire and Norfolk.

WHO CAN BENEFIT Registered and exempt charities; CICs; churches; uniformed groups; educational organisations; hospices; community groups and clubs.

WHAT IS FUNDED General charitable purposes, particularly social welfare and health (including healthcare services, health education, social services and social preventive schemes); churches; education; arts and culture; the environment and heritage; accommodation.

WHAT IS NOT FUNDED Individuals; organisations working or based outside England; activities that are the responsibility of the local health authority, education authority or other statutory authority.

RANGE OF GRANTS Mostly under £5,000.

SAMPLE GRANTS National Rheumatoid Arthritis Society (£68,500); Reach Learning Disability (£25,000); Norwich Cathedral (£10,000); Framework Knitters Museum and Music in Country Churches (£5,000 each); Wild Things Ecological Education Collective (£2,000); SongBird Survival and Wherry Maud Trust (£1,000 each).

FINANCES *Financial year end* 31/12/2021
Income £443,800
Grants to organisations £422,000
Assets £24,960,000

TRUSTEES Charles Barratt; Timothy Farr; Nigel Savory; John Pears.

OTHER INFORMATION Only beneficiaries of grants of over £1,000 were listed in the accounts. Grants of under £1,000 totalled £7,800. Grants of over £1,000 were broken down as follows: medical and disability (£171,000); welfare (£115,500); churches (£46,500); education (£32,000); other (£21,500); the arts (£11,700); accommodation (£7,000); heritage (£6,000); groups/clubs (£2,000); the environment (£1,000).

HOW TO APPLY Applications should be made in writing via post to the correspondent. Applications must be received by 20 January, 20 May or 20 September, to be considered at the trustees' meetings held in March, July or November, respectively. Applicants should also provide their latest set of accounts.

CONTACT DETAILS Trust Administrator, PO Box 10455, Nottingham, Nottinghamshire NG5 0HR *Tel.* 07710 639946 *Email* ladyhind@btinternet. com *Website* www.ladyhindtrust.org.uk

■ The Hinduja Foundation

CC NO 802756   **ESTABLISHED** 1989

WHERE FUNDING CAN BE GIVEN UK and India.

WHO CAN BENEFIT Registered charities; educational and cultural organisations.

WHAT IS FUNDED Health and medicine; education; relief of poverty, hunger and sickness; interfaith understanding; arts and culture; social, economic and international development-related research.

TYPE OF GRANT Capital costs; project funding; research.

RANGE OF GRANTS £100 to £20,000.

SAMPLE GRANTS International Society for Krishna Consciousness (£36,700); St Paul's School (£11,100); The Caring Foundation (£2,500); Shelter UK (£400); Just Giving (£100).

FINANCES *Financial year end* 31/12/2021
Income £114,300
Grants to organisations £119,900
Assets (£10,700)

TRUSTEES G. P. Hinduja; Srichand Hinduja; Prakash Hinduja; Dheeraj Hinduja; Sanjay Hinduja.

OTHER INFORMATION Grants were broken down as follows: interfaith understanding (£55,900); social welfare (£47,600); education (£11,100); cultural awareness and the arts (£5,300).

HOW TO APPLY Apply in writing to the correspondent.

CONTACT DETAILS The Trustees, 12 Charles II Street, 1st Floor, London SW1Y 4QU *Tel.* 020 7839 4661 *Email* use the contact form on the website *Website* www.hindujafoundation.org/ index.html

■ The Stuart Hine Trust CIO

CC NO 1168500   **ESTABLISHED** 1985

WHERE FUNDING CAN BE GIVEN UK and overseas.

WHO CAN BENEFIT Evangelical Christian organisations, churches and missionary societies. Organisations supported by Stuart Hine during his lifetime, or by the trustees since his death, are favoured.

WHAT IS FUNDED Evangelical Christianity; missionary work.

TYPE OF GRANT Recurrent.

RANGE OF GRANTS Up to of £30,000.

SAMPLE GRANTS Wycliffe Bible Translators (£154,300); Retired Missionary Aid Fund (£31,700); Breadline (£20,000); European Mission Fellowship (£16,500); Scottish Bible Society (£15,000); Bible Text Publicity (£12,000); Stanton House Trust (£11,500); CLC International (£10,000).

FINANCES *Financial year end* 31/03/2022
Income £436,100
Grants to organisations £419,900
Assets £229,100

TRUSTEES Raymond Bodkin; Jonathan Juby; Leonard Chipping; Melanie Churchyard; Nigel Coltman; Robert Clark; Susan Wilmot.

HOW TO APPLY The trust has stated that 'unsolicited requests for funds will not be considered', as grants are normally made to the same people or organisations year after year, in accordance with the testator's wishes. The trustees maintain contact with all people and organisations supported.

CONTACT DETAILS Raymond Bodkin, Trustee, c/o Caladine Ltd, Chantry House, 22 Upperton Road, Eastbourne, East Sussex BN21 1BF *Tel.* 01323 843948 *Email* ray.bodkin@talktalk. net *Website* https://stuarthinetrust.com

■ The Hinrichsen Foundation

CC NO 272389   **ESTABLISHED** 1976
WHERE FUNDING CAN BE GIVEN UK.
WHO CAN BENEFIT Organisations and individuals.
WHAT IS FUNDED The performance of contemporary music, including the commissioning of new work, non-commercial recording and publication. The foundation's website explains that the trustees will occasionally fund musicological research projects 'not being conducted under the aegis of an academic institution'.
WHAT IS NOT FUNDED The purchase of musical instruments or equipment including the electronic or computer variety; retrospective expenditure; degree courses; applications for which there are existing official schemes of help. According to its website, the foundation will not usually support 'projects with a very large over-arching budget or where the budgeting is unclear or largely speculative.'
TYPE OF GRANT One-off project funding; multi-year partnerships; research.
RANGE OF GRANTS Small grants of £500 to £2,500; larger grants of £2,000 upwards.
SAMPLE GRANTS Previous beneficiaries have included: Huddersfield 2019 (£10,000); Vale of Glamorgan Festival (£5,000); London Contemporary Music Festival (£3,000); Sound Festival 2019 (£2,000); Dartington Summer School, Two Moors Festival and Wild Plum Arts (£1,000 each); 840 Concert Series (£750).
FINANCES *Financial year end 31/12/2021*
Income £4,830,000
Grants to organisations £15,800
Assets £2,580,000
TRUSTEES Tim Berg; Tabby Estell; Dr Linda Hirst; Prof. Stephen Walsh; Eleanor Gussman; Mark Bromley; Ed McKeon.
OTHER INFORMATION Grants paid during 2021 totalled £15,800; however, no new grants were approved. The 2021 accounts noted 'The impact of COVID-19 on the Peters Edition Group, the consequent lack of income, and the high levels of uncertainty that remained during 2021 meant that the Foundation did not make any grants during the year.'
HOW TO APPLY Application forms can be completed on the foundation's website, where upcoming deadlines can also be found.
CONTACT DETAILS The Trustees, 2–6 Baches Street, London N1 6DN *Tel.* 020 7553 4000 *Email* hinrichsen.foundation@editionpeters.com *Website* www.hinrichsenfoundation.org.uk

■ The Hintze Family Charity Foundation

CC NO 1101842   **ESTABLISHED** 2003
WHERE FUNDING CAN BE GIVEN UK and overseas.
WHO CAN BENEFIT Registered charities; churches; museums, galleries, libraries and other cultural bodies; educational organisations.
WHAT IS FUNDED Education; arts and culture; science and heritage; advancement of the Christian faith; health.
TYPE OF GRANT One-off or multi-year grants; capital and revenue funding, including salaries and core costs.
SAMPLE GRANTS Royal Navy and Royal Marines Charity (£120,000); Institute of Economic Affairs Ltd (£5,000).
FINANCES *Financial year end 31/12/2021*
Income £1,490,000
Grants to organisations £2,750,000
Assets £221,900

TRUSTEES Sir Michael Hintze; Sir Michael Peat; Duncan Baxter.
HOW TO APPLY The 2021 annual report explains that the foundation 'invites applications for grants from charities which further the objectives of the foundation. No specific format is required for applications. Applications and potential donations identified by the Chief Executive and the trustees are considered at trustees' meetings.'
CONTACT DETAILS Gemma Rooney, Secretary, 4th Floor, One Strand, London WC2N 5HR *Tel.* 020 7201 2444 *Email* enquiries@hfcf.org.uk

■ The Hiscox Foundation

CC NO 327635   **ESTABLISHED** 1987
WHERE FUNDING CAN BE GIVEN Worldwide, primarily the UK.
WHO CAN BENEFIT Registered charities.
WHAT IS FUNDED General charitable purposes; education; medical science; the arts; independent living for older people or disadvantaged or vulnerable members of society.
WHAT IS NOT FUNDED Scholarships; event sponsorship; new business start-up funding; carbon offset schemes; grant-making charities.
TYPE OF GRANT Usually one-off; occasionally unrestricted; multi-year.
RANGE OF GRANTS Mostly up to £30,000.
SAMPLE GRANTS German Red Cross (£100,000); MyBnk (£35,000); Social Ark (£30,000); Tall Ships Youth Trust (£3,000); Institute of Cancer Research (£2,500); Queenscourt Hospice (£500).
FINANCES *Financial year end 05/04/2022*
Income £827,800
Grants to organisations £866,500
Assets £9,710,000
TRUSTEES Craig Martindale; Robert Childs; Lee Turner; Nick Orton; Lucy Hensher; Keeley Davies; Vanessa Newbury.
HOW TO APPLY Applications can be made at any time using the foundation's online application form. Unsolicited applications are not accepted for multi-year grants.
CONTACT DETAILS The Trustees, Hiscox Underwriting Ltd, 1 Great St Helen's, London EC3A 6HX *Tel.* 020 7614 5299 *Website* www.hiscoxgroup.com/hiscox-foundation-uk

■ Historic Environment Scotland

OSCR NO SC045925
WHERE FUNDING CAN BE GIVEN Scotland.
WHO CAN BENEFIT Individuals and organisations.
WHAT IS FUNDED The protection of the historic environment.
TYPE OF GRANT Project funding; capital costs.
SAMPLE GRANTS A list of beneficiaries was not included in the annual report and accounts. Previous beneficiaries have included: East Ayrshire Council (£1.12 million); Glasgow Life (£500,000); Archaeology Scotland (£30,000); Society of Antiquaries of Scotland (£3,000); Leadhills Heritage (£530).
FINANCES *Financial year end 31/03/2022*
Income £96,400,000
Grants to organisations £15,950,000
Grants to individuals £64,000
Assets £22,520,000
HOW TO APPLY Apply via the charity's website. Applicants are required to submit a brief expression of interest form before making an application.

Think carefully about every application. Is it justified?

445

CONTACT DETAILS Grants Team, Longmore House, Salisbury Place, Edinburgh EH9 1SH *Email* use the contact form on the website *Website* www. historicenvironment.scot

■ Historic Houses Foundation

CC NO 1111049   ESTABLISHED 2005
WHERE FUNDING CAN BE GIVEN England and Wales.
WHO CAN BENEFIT Organisations; building preservation trusts; private owners.
WHAT IS FUNDED The repair and conservation of rural historic buildings and structures including, where appropriate, their gardens grounds and outbuildings; the conservation, maintenance and restoration of works of art and objects of outstanding artistic, scientific or historic interest.
WHAT IS NOT FUNDED A detailed list of exclusions can be found on the foundation's website.
TYPE OF GRANT Capital costs; project funding.
RANGE OF GRANTS Typically from £1,000 to £250,000.
SAMPLE GRANTS Haddon Hall (£350,300); Everingham Hall (£145,000); Calverley Old Hall (£40,000); Allerton Castle (£30,000); Turvey House (£10,000); Hedingham Castle (£6,000); Fulham Palace (£3,000); Bamburgh Church (£1,800); Sandon Hall (£1,400).
FINANCES *Financial year end 30/06/2022*
Income £3,660,000
Grants to organisations £2,680,000
Assets £14,220,000
TRUSTEES Nicholas Barber; Norman Hudson; Mary King; Sir John Parsons; Oliver Pearcey; Jeremy Musson; Sir Andrew Jardine; Richard Compton; Matthew Rice; Amicia De Moubray.
OTHER INFORMATION The Historic Houses Foundation was formerly known as The Country Houses Foundation. The foundation's website includes comprehensive case studies of previously funded projects.
HOW TO APPLY The foundation requires applicants to complete a pre-application form to confirm that their projects fit its criteria. Pre-application forms and application forms can be downloaded from the foundation's website.
CONTACT DETAILS David Price, Secretary, Sheephouse Farm, Uley Road, Dursley, Gloucestershire GL11 5AD *Tel.* 01453 547124 *Email* info@historichousesfoundation.org.uk *Website* www.historichousesfoundation.org.uk

■ The Henry C. Hoare Charitable Trust

CC NO 1088669   ESTABLISHED 2001
WHERE FUNDING CAN BE GIVEN UK.
WHO CAN BENEFIT Registered charities; statutory authorities.
WHAT IS FUNDED The environment; health; education; citizenship and community development; animal welfare; social welfare; religion.
RANGE OF GRANTS Mostly up to £10,000 with the occasional larger grant.
SAMPLE GRANTS Zeals Youth Trust (£40,000); Seeds 4 Success (£35,000); Somerset Community Foundation and Wincanton Community Venture (£20,000 each); Future Trees Trust, Mindfulness Initiative and Wessex Chalk Stream and Rivers Trust (£10,000 each).
FINANCES *Financial year end 30/09/2021*
Income £164,400
Grants to organisations £291,500
Assets £5,610,000

TRUSTEES Henry Hoare; Hoare Trustees.
OTHER INFORMATION The 2020/21 accounts were the most recent available from the Charity Commission at the time of writing (May 2023). Only beneficiaries of grants of £10,000 and above were listed in the accounts. Grants of under £10,000 totalled £126,500. Grants were broken down as follows: citizenship or community development (£111,000); the environment (£62,000); education (£46,000); health (£41,500); religion (£21,000); relief to older people; those with ill-health or disability (£5,000); prevention and relief of poverty (£3,000); animal welfare (£2,000).
HOW TO APPLY Unsolicited applications are not accepted.
CONTACT DETAILS Hoare Trustees, c/o C. Hoare and Co., 37 Fleet Street, London EC4P 4DQ *Tel.* 020 7353 4522

■ The Hobson Charity Ltd

CC NO 326839   ESTABLISHED 1985
WHERE FUNDING CAN BE GIVEN UK.
WHO CAN BENEFIT Registered charities; educational organisations; cultural organisations; churches; hospices.
WHAT IS FUNDED Community development; disability; domestic abuse; education; young people; older people; the environment; health and well-being; homelessness; hospices; medical research; mental health; culture and heritage; social welfare; rescue services; the armed forces.
WHAT IS NOT FUNDED Generally the charity will not support salaries, core costs or multi-year grants.
TYPE OF GRANT Project funding.
RANGE OF GRANTS No minimum or maximum, mostly up to £20,000.
SAMPLE GRANTS North London Hospice (£50,000); Bridge Church – Bolton (£20,000); Moorfields Eye Charity (£15,000); East Surrey Domestic Abuse Service (£7,000); Brain and Spinal Injury Centre Ltd (£5,000); Nomad Opening Doors (£3,000); Norwood Ravenswood (£1,600); Hampshire and Isle of Wight Air Ambulance (£810).
FINANCES *Financial year end 31/03/2022*
Income £1,380,000
Grants to organisations £570,200
Assets £47,670,000
TRUSTEES Lady Hobson; Deborah Hobson; Mrs J. Richardson; Emma Richardson; Elizabeth Kelsall.
HOW TO APPLY Applicants should first read the eligibility criteria and guidance on the charity's website. Applications may then be made using the online application form.
CONTACT DETAILS The Trustees, PO Box 57691, London NW7 0GR *Tel.* 020 3880 6425 *Email* Post@HobsonCharity.org.uk or use the contact form on the website *Website* https:// hobsoncharity.org.uk

■ Hockerill Educational Foundation

CC NO 311018   ESTABLISHED 1977
WHERE FUNDING CAN BE GIVEN UK and overseas, with a preference for the dioceses of Chelmsford and St Albans.
WHO CAN BENEFIT Registered charities; religious bodies/organisations; individuals; corporate bodies.
WHAT IS FUNDED Education on Christian principles.

WHAT IS NOT FUNDED General appeals; building projects; activities that are the clear responsibility of another body.

TYPE OF GRANT Seed funding/start-up funding; research; project funding.

SAMPLE GRANTS Diocese of Chelmsford and Diocese of St Albans (£110,000 each).

FINANCES *Financial year end 31/03/2022*
Income £329,000
Grants to organisations £229,000
Grants to individuals £61,500
Assets £8,390,000

TRUSTEES Colin Bird; Mrs H. Potter; Janet Scott; The Rt Revd Dr Alan Smith; Anthea Kenna; The Ven. Robin King; David Morton; The Ven. Janet Mackenzie; Judy King; David Lodge; The Rt Revd Dr Gulnar Francis-Dehqani.

OTHER INFORMATION Grants to organisations can be renewed for up to three years and, occasionally, for up to five years.

HOW TO APPLY Application forms and further information are available on the foundation's website.

CONTACT DETAILS The Trustees, 3 The Swallows, Harlow, Essex CM17 0AR *Tel.* 01279 420855 *Email* info@hockerillfoundation.org.uk *Website* www.hockerillfoundation.org.uk

■ The Jane Hodge Foundation

CC NO 216053   **ESTABLISHED** 1962
WHERE FUNDING CAN BE GIVEN UK and overseas.
WHO CAN BENEFIT Charitable organisations; hospices; educational organisations; churches.
WHAT IS FUNDED Medical care and research, in particular local hospices, children's care and research in the fields of cancer and mental health; education, including the arts and those with special educational needs; social welfare; religion, in particular facilities in church buildings and inclusive activities for the community.
TYPE OF GRANT Research; project funding.
RANGE OF GRANTS Usually under £200,000.
SAMPLE GRANTS Arts & Business Cymru; Cardiff Business School – Julian Hodge Institute of Applied Macroeconomics; Cardiff University – European Cancer Stem Cell Research Institute; Cardiff University – Hodge Centre for Neuropsychiatric Immunology; City Hospice; The Prince's Trust Cymru; Teenage Cancer Trust.
FINANCES *Financial year end 30/09/2021*
Income £6,020,000
Grants to organisations £2,710,000
Assets £52,060,000
TRUSTEES Ian Davies; J. Jonathan Hodge; Karen Hodge.
OTHER INFORMATION The 2020/21 accounts were the latest available to view at the time of writing (May 2023). In 2020/21, 66 grants were awarded to organisations in the following areas: care and welfare (£1.61 million); education (£766,800); medical research (£312,200); other (£22,400).
HOW TO APPLY Apply in writing via email. Full details of what should be included can be found on the foundation's website. Applications are not accepted by post.
CONTACT DETAILS The Foundation Administrator, One Central Square, Cardiff CF10 1FS *Tel.* 029 2078 7674 *Email* contact@hodgefoundation.org.uk *Website* www.hodgefoundation.org.uk

■ The Holbeck Charitable Trust

CC NO 1146205   **ESTABLISHED** 2006
WHERE FUNDING CAN BE GIVEN UK, with a preference for London and Yorkshire.
WHO CAN BENEFIT Registered charities; charitable organisations; community and voluntary organisations; excepted charities and exempt charities; individuals.
WHAT IS FUNDED General charitable purposes, including: medical research; education; Christian causes; social welfare; sports and recreation; relief for those affected by natural disasters; unemployment; buildings of historical importance; the arts.
WHAT IS NOT FUNDED See the website for a full list of exclusions.
TYPE OF GRANT Project costs; core funding; salaries; one-off grants.
SAMPLE GRANTS A list of beneficiaries was not included in the annual report and accounts. Previous beneficiaries have included: Cardinal Hume Centre; Helmsley Arts Centre; National Railway Museum; The Poppy Factory Ryedale Festival Trust Ltd; Tommy's; Wilberforce Trust; Yorkshire Ballet Seminars Charitable Trust.
FINANCES *Financial year end 05/04/2022*
Income £69,000
Grants to organisations £393,000
Grants to individuals £42,000
Assets £1,570,000
TRUSTEES Gordon Horsfield; Joshua Horsfield; Victoria Denman; Camilla Seligman; John Lane; Francesca Horsfield.
OTHER INFORMATION Grants were broken down as follows: education (£165,000); public amenities and recreation facilities (£132,000); medical research and palliative care (£62,000); social welfare (£28,000); children and young people (£6,000).
HOW TO APPLY Unsolicited applications are not accepted.
CONTACT DETAILS Gerry Morrison, Secretary, c/o Rollits LLP, Forsyth House, Alpha Court, Monks Cross, York, North Yorkshire YO32 9WN *Email* gerry.morrison@rollits.com *Website* www.holbecktrust.com

■ The Holden Charitable Trust

CC NO 264185   **ESTABLISHED** 1972
WHERE FUNDING CAN BE GIVEN UK.
WHO CAN BENEFIT Charitable organisations, primarily within the Jewish community.
WHAT IS FUNDED Orthodox Jewish education; the advancement of the Orthodox Jewish religion; the relief of poverty.
RANGE OF GRANTS £2,000 to £43,000.
SAMPLE GRANTS Broom Foundation (£45,000); King David School (£35,000); Hachno Kalo (£25,000); Teshuvoh Tefilloh Tzedokoh (£22,000); Friends of Beis Eliyohu Trust (£18,700).
FINANCES *Financial year end 05/04/2022*
Income £396,900
Grants to organisations £284,900
Assets £681,800
TRUSTEES Michael Lopian; Daniel Lopian.
HOW TO APPLY Apply in writing to the correspondent.
CONTACT DETAILS The Trustees, 1 Park Lane, Salford, Great Manchester M7 4HT *Tel.* 0161 832 8721 *Email* david.lopian@lopiangb.co.uk

■ The Hollands-Warren Fund

CC NO 279747 **ESTABLISHED** 1977
WHERE FUNDING CAN BE GIVEN Maidstone.
WHO CAN BENEFIT Individuals; organisations providing medical and nursing care.
WHAT IS FUNDED Temporary medical and nursing services and/or domestic help for residents in the borough of Maidstone.
RANGE OF GRANTS Up to 110,000.
SAMPLE GRANTS Blackthorn Trust (£110,000); The Heart of Kent Hospice (£17,000); Spadework Ltd (£10,000).
FINANCES *Financial year end 28/02/2022*
Income £95,500
Grants to organisations £137,000
Assets £3,630,000
TRUSTEES Daniel Bell; Kim Harrington; Anthony Palmer.
HOW TO APPLY Apply in writing to the correspondent.
CONTACT DETAILS Kim Harrington, Trustee, c/o Brachers Solicitors, Somerfield House, 57–59 London Road, Maidstone, Kent ME16 8JH *Tel.* 01622 690691 *Email* angelaJarvis@brachers.co.uk

■ The Iris Rose Holley Charitable Trust

CC NO 1189319 **ESTABLISHED** 2020
WHERE FUNDING CAN BE GIVEN England and Wales.
WHO CAN BENEFIT Charitable organisations.
WHAT IS FUNDED General charitable purposes.
SAMPLE GRANTS A list of beneficiaries was not available.
FINANCES *Financial year end 31/03/2022*
Income £4,000
Grants to organisations £108,000
TRUSTEES Christine Brown; Berenice Morris.
OTHER INFORMATION Full accounts for 2021/22 were not available to view on the Charity Commission's website due to the charity's low income. We have therefore estimated the charity's grant total based on its total expenditure.
HOW TO APPLY Apply in writing to the correspondent.
CONTACT DETAILS The Trustees, c/o Browns Solicitors, 51 Tweedy Road, Bromley, Greater London BR1 3NH *Tel.* 020 8464 7432 *Email* info@brownsols.co.uk

■ Hollick Family Foundation

CC NO 1060228 **ESTABLISHED** 1997
WHERE FUNDING CAN BE GIVEN There are no specific restrictions, although there is some preference for Camden, East Sussex, Kensington and Chelsea and Kent.
WHO CAN BENEFIT Registered small and medium-sized charities; community-led organisations.
WHAT IS FUNDED General charitable purposes; education and training; human rights; housing; mental health; women; young people; the arts.
TYPE OF GRANT Seed funding; one-off grants; long-term project funding.
RANGE OF GRANTS £1,000 to £15,000.
SAMPLE GRANTS A list of beneficiaries was not included in the 2021/22 accounts.
FINANCES *Financial year end 05/04/2022*
Income £5,460,000
Grants to organisations £166,600
Assets £33,367,000
TRUSTEES Caroline Kemp; The Hon. Georgina Hollick; David Beech; The Hon. Abigail Benoliel; Lady Sue Woodford-Hollick; Lord Clive Hollick; Lee Lambert.

HOW TO APPLY Apply in writing to the correspondent. The trustees meet at least twice a year.
CONTACT DETAILS David Beech, Trustee, Prager Metis LLP, 5A Bear Lane, Southwark, London SE1 0UH *Tel.* 020 7632 1400 *Email* dbeech@pragermetis.com

■ The Holliday Foundation

CC NO 1089931 **ESTABLISHED** 2001
WHERE FUNDING CAN BE GIVEN Worldwide.
WHO CAN BENEFIT Charitable organisations; individuals.
WHAT IS FUNDED General charitable purposes, with a particular interest in enabling children and young people to better themselves and supporting the arts.
TYPE OF GRANT Apprenticeships; bursaries; grants.
SAMPLE GRANTS Previous beneficiaries have included: Grange Park Opera (£100,000); Syria Relief (£20,000); Children in Crisis (£15,000); East Coast Sail Trust, Electric Umbrella and Sparkes Home Sri Lanka (£10,000 each); Protect Animals Greece (£5,000).
FINANCES *Financial year end 31/03/2022*
Income £22,200
Grants to organisations £235,300
TRUSTEES James Cave; David Garrett; Jane Garrett; Huw Llewellyn; Antony Wilson; Ashley Hurst; Tom Braiden.
OTHER INFORMATION Full accounts were not available to view on the Charity Commission's website due to the foundation's low income. We have therefore estimated the grant total based on the foundation's total expenditure.
HOW TO APPLY Contact the correspondent for information regarding the application process. The trustees normally meet at least four times a year and may visit applicants before deciding whether to make a payment.
CONTACT DETAILS Linda Wasfi, c/o Alvarium Investment Ltd, 10 Old Burlington Street, London W1S 3AG *Tel.* 020 7195 1400 *Email* linda.wasfi@alvariuminvestments.com

■ Hollyhock Charitable Foundation

CC NO 1186232
WHERE FUNDING CAN BE GIVEN UK and overseas.
WHO CAN BENEFIT UK-registered charities; CICs.
WHAT IS FUNDED Social welfare; health and well-being; education; the promotion of Christianity.
SAMPLE GRANTS Toy Like Me (£1.1 million); New Gate to Peace Foundation (£367,700); Magic Breakfast and Refuge UK (£50,000 each); Embracing Age (£22,500); Dame Vera Lynn Children's Charity (£18,600); Sense (£9,100); KidsOut (£5,000).
FINANCES *Financial year end 31/12/2021*
Income £3,850,000
Grants to organisations £2,640,000
Assets £1,240,000
TRUSTEES Simon Brooks; Berta Arienza; Rupert Elwes; Dr Simon Peck; Simon Jeffries.
HOW TO APPLY Application forms can be downloaded from the foundation's website.
CONTACT DETAILS The Trustees, c/o Rawlinson and Hunter LLP, 8th Floor, 6 New Street Square, London EC4A 3AQ *Tel.* 020 7842 2000 *Email* hollyhock@rawlinson-hunter.com *Website* www.hollyhockfoundation.co.uk

■ P. H. Holt Foundation

CC NO 1113708   **ESTABLISHED** 1955

WHERE FUNDING CAN BE GIVEN Merseyside.

WHO CAN BENEFIT Registered charities; universities.

WHAT IS FUNDED General charitable purposes in Merseyside, including community development, social welfare, education, the arts and the environment.

WHAT IS NOT FUNDED CICs, social enterprises or commercial endeavours; national charities and charities outside Merseyside; organisations enjoying high-profile support; activities of a statutory nature; work that has already taken place; umbrella charities that do not deliver direct services; grants to individuals and certain uniformed groups; scientific and medical research; one-off holidays, trips, sponsorship of individuals or events; religious and political causes; general charity appeals or mailshots.

TYPE OF GRANT Capital costs; seed/start-up funding; project funding.

RANGE OF GRANTS Typically between £5,000 and £10,000.

SAMPLE GRANTS Liverpool Domestic Abuse Service (£20,000); Wirral Women and Children's Aid (£15,600); Ferries Family Groups (£12,200); Barnstondale Centre and Deysbrook Village Centre (£10,000 each); Kindfulness Coffee Club (£8,900); The New Belve Youth and Community Sports Centre (£4,000); Huntington's Disease Association (£1,500).

FINANCES *Financial year end 31/03/2022*
Income £293,000
Grants to organisations £862,000
Assets £23,520,000

TRUSTEES Ken Ravenscroft; Elspeth Christie; Ian Matthews; Amy Joia; Ian Bakewell; Lesley Martin-Wright; Christopher Evered; Michael Furniss; Natan Levy.

OTHER INFORMATION During the year, 100 grants were awarded to organisations through the following programmes: resilience programme (£425,400); community and overcoming barriers (£388,000); engagement in the arts (£30,700); access to education (£10,000); care of the environment (£2,000).

HOW TO APPLY Application forms can be accessed on the foundation's helpful website and should be returned by email together with a copy of your latest annual report and accounts.

CONTACT DETAILS The Trustees, 151 Dale Street, Liverpool, Merseyside L2 2AH *Tel.* 0151 237 2663 *Email* administrator@phholtfoundation.org.uk *Website* www.phholtfoundation.org.uk

■ The Holywood Trust

OSCR NO SC009942   **ESTABLISHED** 1981

WHERE FUNDING CAN BE GIVEN Dumfries and Galloway.

WHO CAN BENEFIT Individuals; constituted charitable organisations which work with young people; voluntary organisations; statutory bodies; groups of young people within a constituted organisation.

WHAT IS FUNDED Young people, primarily those aged 15–25; personal development; sports; the arts; group development activities; education; health; social welfare; residential activities.

WHAT IS NOT FUNDED Retrospective expenditure.

TYPE OF GRANT One-off; capital and core costs; recurring funding; salaries; project costs.

RANGE OF GRANTS Programme dependent.

SAMPLE GRANTS Absolute Classics; Cample Line; DG Voice; Galloway Cricket Club Trust; Lochmabe Tennis Club; PAMIS.

FINANCES *Financial year end 05/04/2022*
Income £2,860,000
Grants to organisations £2,680,000
Grants to individuals £5,000
Assets £104,780,000

TRUSTEES Valerie McElroy; John Jencks; Ben Weatherall; Amy Agnew; Clara Weatherall.

OTHER INFORMATION During 2021/22, 120 grant awards were made. Grants of under £10,000 totalled £230,200.

HOW TO APPLY Applications can be made using a form available from the trust's website, where criteria and guidelines can also be found. The trustees meet quarterly to discuss applications for over £2,500; deadline dates are set prior to each meeting and advertised on the trust's website. Applications for under £2,500 or less can be submitted any time and should be processed within four to six weeks. Organisations may submit their applications electronically but the trustees also require a hard signed copy with all documents before the application form can be processed.

CONTACT DETAILS The Trustees, Hestan House, Crichton Business Park, Bankend Road, Dumfries, Dumfries and Galloway DG1 4TA *Tel.* 01387 269176 *Email* funds@holywood-trust.org.uk *Website* www.holywood-trust.org.uk

■ Homelands Charitable Trust

CC NO 214322   **ESTABLISHED** 1962

WHERE FUNDING CAN BE GIVEN UK.

WHO CAN BENEFIT Registered charities; hospices.

WHAT IS FUNDED General charitable purposes; the General Conference of the New Church; medical research; care and protection of children; hospices.

RANGE OF GRANTS Mostly £1,000 to £3,000.

SAMPLE GRANTS A list of beneficiaries was not included in the annual report and accounts. Previous beneficiaries have included: General Conference of New Church (£63,000); Broadfield Memorial Fund (£16,000); Friends of the Earth and RNLI (£3,000 each); Anorexia and Bulimia Care and SOS Children's Villages (£2,800 each); Benslow Music Trust, Edinburgh Young Carers Project, Riding for the Disabled and Sailors' Families Society (£1,800 each); St Luke's Hospice (£1,500); Womankind Worldwide (£1,000).

FINANCES *Financial year end 05/04/2022*
Income £169,200
Grants to organisations £321,000
Assets £9,580,000

TRUSTEES Nigel Armstrong; The Revd Clifford Curry; Robert Curry; Eleanor Maquire.

OTHER INFORMATION During 2021/22, grants were distributed as follows: other charities (£140,000); care and protection of children (£95,500); church (£93,000); medical causes (£25,500); hospices (£18,000).

HOW TO APPLY Contact the correspondent for further information.

CONTACT DETAILS The Trustees, 4th Floor, Imperial House, 8 Kean Street, London WC2B 4AS *Tel.* 020 7240 9971

■ Sir Harold Hood's Charitable Trust

CC NO 225870   **ESTABLISHED** 1962
WHERE FUNDING CAN BE GIVEN UK, with some work overseas.
WHO CAN BENEFIT Roman Catholic charitable organisations; places of worship; hospitals; hospices; educational institutions.
WHAT IS FUNDED Roman Catholic causes, including: social welfare, including homelessness; education and young people; medical and health; missionary work outside the UK; youth clubs.
RANGE OF GRANTS Mostly between £1,000 and £5,000 with the occasional larger grant.
SAMPLE GRANTS Downside Abbey (£60,000); Downside Fisher Youth Club and Duchess of Leeds Foundation (£30,000 each); Aid to the Church in Need UK, Diocese of Hexham and Newcastle and Youth 2000 (£10,000 each); Borderlands, Right to Life – Pro-Life Research Unit and St Wilfred's Centre (£5,000 each); Franciscan Missionary Sisters for Africa (£2,000); CAFOD and Growing Old Gracefully (£1,000 each).
FINANCES *Financial year end* 05/04/2022
Income £732,400
Grants to organisations £745,900
Assets £39,130,000
TRUSTEES Christian Elwes; Dom Hood; Margaret Hood; Lord True; Lady True.
HOW TO APPLY Apply in writing to the correspondent.
CONTACT DETAILS The Trustees, c/o haysmacintyre, Thames Exchange, 10 Queen Street Place, London EC4R 1AG *Tel.* 020 7969 5500 *Email* hoodcharitabletrust@yahoo.co.uk

■ Hope Trust

OSCR NO SC000987   **ESTABLISHED** 1912
WHERE FUNDING CAN BE GIVEN Worldwide, with a preference for Scotland.
WHO CAN BENEFIT Christian individuals and organisations; charitable organisations; places of worship.
WHAT IS FUNDED Christianity, including funding theology PhDs; temperance; addiction and substance abuse; education; health awareness.
RANGE OF GRANTS Mostly £3,000 to £3,500.
SAMPLE GRANTS Pittsburgh Theology Seminary Joint Programme (£10,000); Aberdeen Centre for Protestant Theology (£4,000); 3rd Hawick Battalion of the Girl's Brigade (£2,500); Theology in Scotland (£2,000).
FINANCES *Financial year end* 31/12/2021
Income £245,500
Grants to organisations £186,500
Assets £7,640,000
OTHER INFORMATION Grants were broken down as follows: to promote Christianity (£128,500) and to promote temperance and combat all forms of substance abuse (£58,000). Note that the grant figures include amounts awarded to individuals.
HOW TO APPLY Apply in writing to the correspondent.
CONTACT DETAILS The Trustees, Glenorchy House, 20 Union Street, Edinburgh EH1 3LR

■ The Thomas J. Horne Memorial Trust

CC NO 1010625   **ESTABLISHED** 1992
WHERE FUNDING CAN BE GIVEN UK and overseas.
WHO CAN BENEFIT Charitable organisations; hospices.
WHAT IS FUNDED Hospices, particularly children's hospices and related charities; disability; health; homelessness; self-help groups in financially developing countries.
RANGE OF GRANTS Mostly £5,000 to £10,000.
SAMPLE GRANTS North Yorkshire Hospice Care (£12,500); Demelza House Children's Hospice (£10,000); Acorns Children's Hospice Trust (£8,300); Grief Encounter (£8,000); Whitby Dog Rescue (£1,000).
FINANCES *Financial year end* 31/03/2022
Income £900,500
Grants to organisations £895,800
Assets £21,600,000
TRUSTEES Jeff Horne; Jon Horne; Emma Horne.
HOW TO APPLY Apply in writing to the correspondent.
CONTACT DETAILS The Trustees, Kingsdown, Warmlake Road, Chart Sutton, Maidstone, Kent ME17 3RP *Tel.* 01622 842638 *Email* cc@horne-trust.org.uk

■ The Horners Charity Fund

CC NO 292204   **ESTABLISHED** 1929
WHERE FUNDING CAN BE GIVEN London.
WHO CAN BENEFIT Registered charities; individuals; educational establishments.
WHAT IS FUNDED General charitable purposes; education; education related to the plastics industry; health.
RANGE OF GRANTS £500 to £6,000.
SAMPLE GRANTS Ralph Anderson Lecture (£6,200); Honeypot Children's Charity, Providence Row and Tower Hamlets Mission (£5,000 each); No Going Back, React (Rapid Effective Assistance for Children with potentially Terminal illness) and The Respite Association (£3,000 each); Livery Schools Showcase (£2,000); The Salvation Army (£1,700); 27 Squadron (£1,200); 1349 (Woking) Squadron Air Training Corps (£600).
FINANCES *Financial year end* 31/12/2021
Income £189,300
Grants to organisations £91,400
Grants to individuals £40,600
Assets £3,850,000
TRUSTEES Martin Muirhead; Dr David Giachardi; David Spofforth; Colin Freedman; Michael Birrell; John MacCabe; Hugh Moss; David Chitty; Dr Barry Maunders; Alan Price.
HOW TO APPLY Apply in writing to the correspondent.
CONTACT DETAILS R. Joyce, Clerk to the Trustees, Quarry Hill, Brassey Road, Oxted, Surrey RH8 0ET *Tel.* 07860 115585 *Website* www.horners.org.uk

■ The Horse Trust

CC NO 231748   **ESTABLISHED** 1886
WHERE FUNDING CAN BE GIVEN UK.
WHO CAN BENEFIT UK veterinary schools; other universities.
WHAT IS FUNDED Horses' health and welfare.
TYPE OF GRANT Research grants; PhD and postgraduate studentships; pump-priming; project grants.
SAMPLE GRANTS University of Liverpool (£248,000); The Animal Health Trust (£47,500); University of Nottingham (£34,400); University of Edinburgh (£28,000); University of Bristol (£22,700); Royal Veterinary College (£14,000); Moredun Research (£13,500); Roslin Institute (£6,600).
FINANCES *Financial year end* 31/12/2021
Income £1,900,000
Grants to organisations £418,200
Assets £25,650,000

TRUSTEES Christopher Marriott; Prof. Bruce McGorum; Lord Rupert Mauley; David Cook; Prof. Peter Clegg; Rupert Neal; Caroline Roddis; Laura McGillycuddy.

HOW TO APPLY Preliminary applications can be made in October each year. Applicants who are successful will be invited to complete a full application. Further details can be found on the trust's website.

CONTACT DETAILS Jan Rogers, Director of Research and Policy, Speen Farm, Slad Lane, Speen, Princes Riseborough, Buckinghamshire HP27 0PP *Tel.* 01494 488464 *Email* info@horsetrust.org.uk *Website* www.horsetrust.org.uk

■ Horwich Shotter Charitable Trust

CC NO 1068651 **ESTABLISHED** 1998

WHERE FUNDING CAN BE GIVEN UK, with a preference for Greater Manchester.

WHO CAN BENEFIT Individuals and charitable organisations.

WHAT IS FUNDED Education and the advancement of the Jewish faith.

SAMPLE GRANTS A list of beneficiaries was not included in the annual report and accounts.

FINANCES *Financial year end* 30/11/2021
Income £43,500
Grants to organisations £89,600
Assets £110,100

TRUSTEES Howard Horwich; Jeffrey Horwich; Maurice Horwich; Aharon Horwich.

OTHER INFORMATION The 2020/21 accounts were the latest available at the time of writing (June 2023).

HOW TO APPLY Apply in writing to the correspondent.

CONTACT DETAILS The Trustees, 13 Singleton Road, Salford, Greater Manchester M7 4NN *Tel.* 0161 792 2441

■ The Hosking Charitable Trust

CC NO 1183218

WHERE FUNDING CAN BE GIVEN UK.

WHO CAN BENEFIT Registered charities; CICs.

WHAT IS FUNDED Children and young people; education; social welfare; heritage.

RANGE OF GRANTS Up to £40,000 but mostly grants of £10,000 or £20,000.

SAMPLE GRANTS The Prince's Trust (£40,000); The Felix Project (£30,000); Sightsavers and Tempus Novo (£20,000 each); Hospice in the Weald and Together We Learn (£10,000 each).

FINANCES *Financial year end* 31/03/2022
Income £272,300
Grants to organisations £360,000
Assets £16,560,000

TRUSTEES Jeremy Hosking; Elizabeth Hosking; Thomas Hosking.

HOW TO APPLY Apply in writing to the correspondent.

CONTACT DETAILS Rachel Montgomery, c/o Arnold Hill and Co., 6th Floor Capital Tower, 91 Waterloo Road, London SE1 8RT *Email* rachel.montgomery@arnoldhill.co.uk

■ Hospice UK

CC NO 1014851/SC041112 **ESTABLISHED** 1984

WHERE FUNDING CAN BE GIVEN UK.

WHO CAN BENEFIT Hospices; other institutions related to hospices and hospice care; hospice staff.

WHAT IS FUNDED Support for hospices; projects that improve hospice care.

WHAT IS NOT FUNDED Exclusion criteria varies according to the programme being applied to; see the grant-maker's website for further information.

TYPE OF GRANT Core costs; project funding; capital costs; development funding; bursaries.

RANGE OF GRANTS Programme dependent.

SAMPLE GRANTS A list of beneficiaries was not available at the time of writing (June 2023).

FINANCES *Financial year end* 31/03/2022
Income £110,000,000
Grants to organisations £99,100,000
Assets £11,610,000

TRUSTEES Anthony Collins; Emma Reynolds; Stephen Roberts; Dr Michael Miller; Michelle Rollinson; David Smith; Paul Jennings; Chloe Chik; Sharon Allen; Terence O'Leary; Rhian Edwards.

OTHER INFORMATION The charity awarded 1,200 grants to 202 organisations during the year.

HOW TO APPLY Applications can be made via the grant-maker's website when the relevant programme is open for applications.

CONTACT DETAILS The Trustees, 34–44 Britannia Street, London WC1X 9JG *Tel.* 020 7520 8200 *Email* grants@hospiceuk.org *Website* www.hospiceuk.org

■ The Hospital of God at Greatham

CC NO 1123540 **ESTABLISHED** 2008

WHERE FUNDING CAN BE GIVEN County Durham; Darlington; Hartlepool; Gateshead; Newcastle upon Tyne; North Tyneside; Northumberland; South Tyneside; Stockton; Sunderland.

WHO CAN BENEFIT Charitable organisations; voluntary groups.

WHAT IS FUNDED Support for disadvantaged people in the following areas: asylum seekers; children; older people; victims of domestic violence and abuse; substance misuse; ex-offenders; homelessness; hospices; mental health; physical health; social welfare; community projects.

WHAT IS NOT FUNDED Capital works or money-raising appeals; statutory education and related travel or adventure projects; holidays (unless for personal or group development); national organisations (unless independently constituted and funded, delivering in the North East); conferences and feasibility studies; medical equipment and related projects; general appeals.

TYPE OF GRANT Project funding.

RANGE OF GRANTS Up to £3,000.

SAMPLE GRANTS A list of beneficiaries was not included in the annual report and accounts.

FINANCES *Financial year end* 31/10/2021
Income £5,030,000
Grants to organisations £96,600
Assets £47,250,000

TRUSTEES Philippa Sinclair; Margaret Bousfield; Lois Neal; Robert Eden; Dr Kai Sander; Patricia Hancock; The Revd Rick Simpson.

OTHER INFORMATION The charity also owns and manages 123 almshouses. The 2020/21 accounts were the latest available to view at the time of writing (June 2023).

HOW TO APPLY Application forms can be completed online through the charity's website. Applications can be submitted twice a year to be considered by the Grants Committee. Visit the website for upcoming deadlines.

CONTACT DETAILS Lawrence McAnelly, Director, The Estate Office, Greatham, Hartlepool, County Durham TS25 2HS *Tel.* 01429 870247 *Email* lawrence.mcanelly@hospitalofgod.org.uk *Website* www.hospitalofgod.org.uk

■ The Hospital Saturday Fund

CC NO 1123381   ESTABLISHED 1873
WHERE FUNDING CAN BE GIVEN UK; Republic of Ireland.
WHO CAN BENEFIT Registered health charities; hospitals; hospices; clinics; welfare organisations providing health services; individuals. Organisations must be registered with the Charity Commission or the appropriate regional body (outside England and Wales).
WHAT IS FUNDED Medical causes; health care; research; specialist equipment; welfare needs; scholarships to individuals.
WHAT IS NOT FUNDED Unregistered organisations; organisations carrying out activities not related to medicine; general fundraising appeals; projects outside the area of benefit.
TYPE OF GRANT Medical capital projects; medical care; research; support of medical training; running costs. Awards are mainly one-off.
RANGE OF GRANTS Up to £10,000, but mostly £2,000.
SAMPLE GRANTS Air Ambulance Northern Ireland; Autistica; Breast Cancer UK; Cerebral Palsy Cymru; Disabled Sailors Association; Forget Me Not Children's Hospice; Glasgow Children's Hospital Charity; Greenfingers Charity; Livability; Royal College of Emergency Medicine; Whizz-Kidz.
FINANCES *Financial year end 31/12/2021* *Income £31,900,000* *Grants to organisations £1,690,000* *Grants to individuals £124,000* *Assets £39,700,000*
TRUSTEES Jane Dalton; John Randel; David Thomas; John Greenwood; Dominic Fox; Mark Davies; Margaret Rogers; Cal Healy.
OTHER INFORMATION During the year, 326 grants were awarded to individuals and a further 534 grants were awarded to medical charities, hospices and hospitals.
HOW TO APPLY Applications should be made using the online system on the charity's website.
CONTACT DETAILS The Trustees, 24 Upper Ground, London SE1 9PD *Tel.* 020 7202 1365 *Email* charity@hsf.eu.com *Website* www. hospitalsaturdayfund.org

■ The Sir Joseph Hotung Charitable Settlement

CC NO 1082710   ESTABLISHED 2000
WHERE FUNDING CAN BE GIVEN UK and overseas, with some preference for London.
WHO CAN BENEFIT Charitable organisations.
WHAT IS FUNDED Medical causes; education; human rights; climate change.
SAMPLE GRANTS Fauna and Flora International (£1 million); St George's, University of London (£574,700); St Luke's Hospital – Oxford (£25,000); Strength and Learning Through Horses (£10,000); Spinal Research (£1,200 in 12 grants).
FINANCES *Financial year end 05/04/2022* *Income £1,000,000* *Grants to organisations £1,610,000* *Assets £1,780,000*

TRUSTEES Prof. Sir Robert Boyd; Henry Painton; Prof. Dame Jessica Rawson.
HOW TO APPLY Apply in writing to the correspondent.
CONTACT DETAILS Henry Painton, Trustee, c/o Penningtons Manches Cooper LLP, 125 Wood Street, London EC2V 7AW *Tel.* 020 8940 3827 *Email* henry.painton@blueyonder.co.uk

■ House of Industry Estate

CC NO 257079   ESTABLISHED 1988
WHERE FUNDING CAN BE GIVEN Borough of Bedford.
WHO CAN BENEFIT Third-sector organisations; rural organisations; voluntary and community groups.
WHAT IS FUNDED Social welfare.
WHAT IS NOT FUNDED Retrospective costs; capital expenditure cannot involve works to land or property.
TYPE OF GRANT One-off; capital costs; project funding; core costs.
RANGE OF GRANTS Up to £25,000 (capital items); up to £20,000 (core funding).
SAMPLE GRANTS A list of beneficiaries was not included in the annual report and accounts. Previous beneficiaries have included: Bedford Community Rights; Bedfordshire Garden Carers; Bedford Pilgrims Housing Association; Kempston Summer School; King's Arms Project.
FINANCES *Financial year end 31/03/2022* *Income £251,200* *Grants to organisations £302,900* *Assets £5,300,000*
TRUSTEES Cllr Tom Wootton; Cllr Colleen Atkins; Christine McHugh; Henry Vann; Carl Meader; Cllr Charles Royden.
HOW TO APPLY Application forms can be found on the charity's website and should be submitted via email. Guidelines for grants vary depending on what the grant is intended for; for a full list of guidelines, see the guidelines document on Bedford Borough Council's website.
CONTACT DETAILS Lee Phanco, Chief Officer for Customer Experience and Digital Services, Bedford Borough Council, Borough Hall, Cauldwell Street, Bedford MK42 9AP *Tel.* 01234 267422 *Email* Community.Welfare@ bedford.gov.uk *Website* www.bedford.gov.uk/ benefits-and-support/grants-and-funding/grants-and-funding-towns-and-organisations

■ Housing Pathways Trust

CC NO 211053   ESTABLISHED 1962
WHERE FUNDING CAN BE GIVEN Ealing and Brentford.
WHO CAN BENEFIT Community groups and small charities; individuals; places of learning; churches.
WHAT IS FUNDED Social welfare; health; education; homelessness; isolation; domestic abuse; counselling and support services; people with disabilities; social cohesion.
WHAT IS NOT FUNDED Exclusion criteria may vary according to the programme being applied to. See the trust's website for further information.
TYPE OF GRANT Main grants programme: project funding; start-up funding; core costs; for up to three years. See the website for types of funding awarded through other programmes.
RANGE OF GRANTS Programme dependent.
SAMPLE GRANTS Ealing Street Pastors (£8,000); MindFood (£5,000); The Login Cabin (£4,800); Into the Light (£3,900); St Nicholas – Perivale (£2,000); Woman's Trust (£1,500); Next Step Foundation (£1,000).

FINANCES *Financial year end* 31/03/2022
Income £1,560,000
Grants to organisations £56,000
Assets £16,050,000

TRUSTEES The Revd Mark Melluish; Isabella Rossi; Matthew Doyle; Andrea Joseph; Andrew Jefford; Joshua Reddaway.

OTHER INFORMATION The main grants programme is generally limited to small organisations, which are defined as those with an annual income of less than £100,000. During the year, 32 grants were awarded to organisations.

HOW TO APPLY Online application forms for the main grants programme are available on the trust's website. Other open programmes are also advertised on the website. For further information, contact the correspondent.

CONTACT DETAILS The Grants Officer, Housing Pathways, Unit 33, Dean Court, Bowmans Close, London W13 9YU *Tel.* 020 8579 7411 *Email* info@yourpathways.org.uk *Website* www.yourpathways.org.uk

---

■ The Keith Howard Foundation

CC NO 1127093   **ESTABLISHED** 2008
WHERE FUNDING CAN BE GIVEN Yorkshire.
WHO CAN BENEFIT Registered charities.
WHAT IS FUNDED The performing arts; animal welfare; amateur sport; social mobility.
WHAT IS NOT FUNDED Capital costs.
RANGE OF GRANTS Mostly under £25,000.
SAMPLE GRANTS Opera North (£150,000); Whitehall Dog Rescue (£120,000); Yorkshire Cricket Foundation (£50,000); Tia Greyhound and Lurcher Rescue (£30,000); Bradford Grammar School (£25,000); Moorview Rescue (£10,000); Bumble Bees Mixed Ability Rugby (£5,000); Keighley Imagination Library (£2,000).
FINANCES *Financial year end* 31/12/2021
Income £890,000
Grants to organisations £586,000
Assets £726,600
TRUSTEES Karen Fojt; Peter Meredith; Melissa Tomlinson; Martin Hasyn; Emma Tregenza; Howard Fojt; Vicky Williams.
OTHER INFORMATION Grants were awarded to 20 organisations across the following categories: performing arts (£222,000); animal welfare (£210,000); sport (£110,000); education (£44,000).
HOW TO APPLY Application forms can be completed online. The trustees meet three times a year (March, July and October) and applications are accepted between the beginning of March and the end of June.
CONTACT DETAILS Sylvia Hall, Secretary, KH Foundation, PO Box 379, Ilkley LS29 1JR *Tel.* 07908 426823 *Email* mtomlinson@khfoundation.co.uk *Website* www.keithhowardfoundation.co.uk

---

■ The Reta Lila Howard Foundation

CC NO 1041634   **ESTABLISHED** 1994
WHERE FUNDING CAN BE GIVEN UK and the Republic of Ireland.
WHO CAN BENEFIT Registered charities.
WHAT IS FUNDED Education and extracurricular activities for children and young people under the age of 16.
WHAT IS NOT FUNDED Individuals; organisations which are not registered charities; core costs; (sole) capital projects; annual charitable appeals;

general endowment funds; budget deficits; fundraising drives or events; conferences; student aid.
TYPE OF GRANT Short-term project funding.
RANGE OF GRANTS Mostly £5,000 to £50,000.
SAMPLE GRANTS Safe Passage (£70,000); YoungMinds (£50,000); Canal and River Trust (£45,000); ThinkForward (£40,000); Action for Conservation (£30,000); Walk Through the Bible UK (£25,000); Bibles for Children (£20,000); Countryside Education Trust (£15,000); New Forest Centre (£12,500); Young and Inspired (£10,000); Home-Start (£7,500); Boxing Academy (£5,000); It's Your Choice (£2,500).
FINANCES *Financial year end* 31/03/2022
Income £66,500
Grants to organisations £600,000
Assets £19,270,000
TRUSTEES Melissa Murdoch; Gregg Weston; Tamara Rebanks; Galvin Weston; Sarah Mitchell; Pilar Bauta.
OTHER INFORMATION During the year, 25 grants were awarded.
HOW TO APPLY The foundation has previously stated that it does not accept unsolicited applications as the trustees seek out and support projects they are interested in.
CONTACT DETAILS The Trustees, Horsmonden Business Centre, The Business Centre, Green Road, Horsmonden, Tonbridge, Kent TN12 8JS *Tel.* 07852 924412 *Email* retalilahoward@gmail.com

---

■ James T. Howat Charitable Trust

OSCR NO SC000201   **ESTABLISHED** 1989
WHERE FUNDING CAN BE GIVEN Primarily Glasgow, but support can also be given to UK-wide organisations.
WHO CAN BENEFIT Charitable organisations including: universities; cultural bodies; healthcare organisations; local community organisations; social groups; individuals.
WHAT IS FUNDED General charitable purposes.
WHAT IS NOT FUNDED Medical electives; second or further qualifications; payment of school fees; costs incurred at tertiary educational establishments; religious organisations seeking to grow rather than complement existing services.
TYPE OF GRANT Core costs; projects; research; running expenditure; start-up costs; educational support to individuals.
RANGE OF GRANTS Up to £10,000, but most grants are of £500.
SAMPLE GRANTS University of Strathclyde (£4,000 in four grants); East Park Home for Infirm Children (£3,000 in four grants); Brittle Bone Society (£2,000 in four grants); 4 Cancer Group, Crisis UK, Disability Snowsport UK and Families Outside (£500 each); Earlsferry Town Hall Ltd (£250).
FINANCES *Financial year end* 05/04/2022
Income £174,900
Grants to organisations £213,400
Grants to individuals £7,600
Assets £6,810,000
OTHER INFORMATION In 2021/22, grants were made to 13 individuals.
HOW TO APPLY Applications may be made in writing to the correspondent and should include: a summary of your request (no longer than one side of A4) backed up as necessary with schedules, a copy of your latest accounts and/or business plan, a breakdown of costs and financial needs (where possible), information on the effect the grant will have, details of other

Think carefully about every application. Is it justified?

453

grants applied for or awarded, and evidence that the project will help its beneficiaries and that they are involved in the decision-making. Applications should demonstrate potential impact. Unsuccessful applicants are not acknowledged due to the large number of applications received. The trustees meet to consider grants in March, June, September and December; applications should be received in the preceding month.

CONTACT DETAILS The Trustees, c/o Harper Macleod LLP, The Ca'd'oro, 45 Gordon Street, Glasgow G1 3PE

■ The Hudson Foundation

CC NO 280332   **ESTABLISHED** 1980
WHERE FUNDING CAN BE GIVEN Wisbech.
WHO CAN BENEFIT Charitable organisations.
WHAT IS FUNDED General charitable purposes, particularly the relief of older people.
TYPE OF GRANT Capital projects; revenue expenditure.
SAMPLE GRANTS Wisbech and Fenland Museum (£36,000); Wisbech Swimming Club (£10,000); Wisbech Table Tennis Club (£6,500); Meadowgate Academy (£1,000).
FINANCES *Financial year end 31/07/2022*
Income £701,800
Grants to organisations £106,300
Assets £2,830,000
TRUSTEES David Ball; Stephen Layton; Edward Newling; Michael Hutchinson.
HOW TO APPLY Apply in writing to the correspondent.
CONTACT DETAILS The Trustees, 1–3 York Row, Wisbech, Cambridgeshire PE13 1EA *Tel.* 01945 461456

■ The Huggard Charitable Trust

CC NO 327501   **ESTABLISHED** 1987
WHERE FUNDING CAN BE GIVEN UK, with a preference for South Wales.
WHO CAN BENEFIT Charitable organisations.
WHAT IS FUNDED Community support; homelessness; support for people who are disadvantaged, older, ill or who have disabilities.
WHAT IS NOT FUNDED Individuals.
TYPE OF GRANT Project funding.
SAMPLE GRANTS A list of beneficiaries was not included in the annual report and accounts.
FINANCES *Financial year end 31/03/2022*
Income £61,100
Grants to organisations £93,400
Assets £2,690,000
TRUSTEES Andrew Chiplen; Anne Helme; Stephen Thomas.
HOW TO APPLY The trustees do not accept unsolicited applications; they support a list of charities provided by the trust's founder.
CONTACT DETAILS The Trustees, 25 Harvey Crescent, Aberavon, Port Talbot, Neath Port Talbot SA12 6DF *Tel.* 07926 190632

■ The Hull and East Riding Charitable Trust

CC NO 516866   **ESTABLISHED** 1985
WHERE FUNDING CAN BE GIVEN Hull and the East Riding of Yorkshire.
WHO CAN BENEFIT Charitable organisations; schools.
WHAT IS FUNDED General charitable purposes.
WHAT IS NOT FUNDED Education; salaries of core staff; political purposes; religious purposes

(although requests for notable buildings with a good level of community use will be evaluated).
TYPE OF GRANT Project funding; capital costs; core costs.
RANGE OF GRANTS Generally between £100 and £10,000.
SAMPLE GRANTS Hull Children's University (£10,000); Riverside Special School (£8,900); Run With It (£5,000); Young Women's Trust (£2,300); Rotary Club of Humberside (£1,800); Portobello Methodist Scout Group (£1,000); Withernsea Carnival (£700); Bundles of Joy (£250).
FINANCES *Financial year end 05/05/2022*
Income £161,500
Grants to organisations £231,600
Assets £9,020,000
TRUSTEES Adrian Horsley; Matthew Fletcher; Victoria Carver.
OTHER INFORMATION The trust awarded 85 grants during the year to a range of organisations.
HOW TO APPLY Application forms can be downloaded from the trust's website. The trustees meet twice a year, usually in May and November. Appeals should be submitted by 20 April and 20 October, respectively.
CONTACT DETAILS Lynn Humphreys, Secretary, Greenmeades, 7 Westerdale, Swanland, East Riding of Yorkshire HU14 3PY *Tel.* 07821 166948 *Email* Lynn.Humphreys@herct.org.uk *Website* https://hullandeastridingtrust.org.uk

■ The Humanitarian Trust

CC NO 208575   **ESTABLISHED** 1946
WHERE FUNDING CAN BE GIVEN UK and Israel.
WHO CAN BENEFIT Mostly Jewish charitable organisations; individuals (via studentships).
WHAT IS FUNDED General charitable purposes.
WHAT IS NOT FUNDED Non-academic courses in art, music, theatre, youth work or sports; overseas courses; travel-related or fieldwork research projects; distance learning; correspondence; part-time or short-term courses.
TYPE OF GRANT Project funding; one-off grants.
RANGE OF GRANTS £2,000 to £10,000.
SAMPLE GRANTS World Jewish Relief (£25,000); Holocaust Educational Trust (£20,000); New Israel Fund and The Woolf Institute of Abrahamic Faiths (£15,000 each); Institute for Jewish Policy Research (£10,000); Nightingale Hammerson (£7,500); The Friends of Yeshivat Shefa (£6,000); Ohel Sarah (£5,500).
FINANCES *Financial year end 05/04/2022*
Income £232,400
Grants to organisations £223,500
Grants to individuals £23,000
Assets £5,890,000
TRUSTEES Emmanuelle Gunsbourg-Kasavi; Pierre Halban; Jacques Gunsbourg; Alexander Halban.
OTHER INFORMATION Grants were awarded to 25 organisations in the following categories: social service (£129,000), academic and educational (£66,000) and medical and charitable (£5,500).
HOW TO APPLY The trust does not accept unsolicited applications from organisations, although the trustees may occasionally invite charities to submit applications for consideration at board meetings.
CONTACT DETAILS The Trustees, 20 Gloucester Place, London W1U 8HA *Tel.* 020 7486 7760 *Email* humanitariantrust@prismthegiftfund.co.uk *Website* www.humanitariantrust.co.uk

■ Michael and Shirley Hunt Charitable Trust

CC NO 1063418　　　**ESTABLISHED** 1997
WHERE FUNDING CAN BE GIVEN UK and overseas.
WHO CAN BENEFIT Charitable organisations and individuals.
WHAT IS FUNDED People who have been in the criminal justice system or affected by it; animal welfare; general charitable purposes.
RANGE OF GRANTS Up to £7,000.
SAMPLE GRANTS Martlets Hospice (£7,000); Create (£4,300); Prison Advice and Care Trust (£3,000); Dogs Trust (£2,000); Animals in Need (£1,500); Crisis and Wild Futures (£1,000 each).
FINANCES *Financial year end 31/03/2022*
　Income £237,400
　Grants to organisations £85,700
　Grants to individuals £930
　Assets £7,870,000
TRUSTEES Wanda Baker; Chester Hunt; Deborah Jenkins; Kathy Mayberry.
OTHER INFORMATION During the year, 52 organisations received support. Grants of under £1,000 totalled £5,300 and were awarded to eight organisations. Grants were broken down as follows: animal welfare (30 grants totalling £34,900); general charitable purposes (8 grants totalling £25,300); prisoners and their families (13 grants totalling £24,600).
HOW TO APPLY Apply in writing to the correspondent. Applications are considered upon receipt and formal meetings are held as necessary, at least once a year.
CONTACT DETAILS Deborah Jenkins, Trustee, Ansty House, Henfield Road, Small Dole, Henfield, West Sussex BN5 9XH *Tel.* 01903 817116

■ The Albert Hunt Trust

CC NO 1180640　　　**ESTABLISHED** 1979
WHERE FUNDING CAN BE GIVEN UK.
WHO CAN BENEFIT Registered charities.
WHAT IS FUNDED Health and well-being; hospices; homelessness.
WHAT IS NOT FUNDED Adult mental health; animal welfare; air ambulances; arts/heritage; conservation/the environment; expeditions and overseas travel; medical research; NHS charities; organisations in the health and well-being sector with income levels above £250,000; promotion of religion; sport.
TYPE OF GRANT Single awards for capital projects; grants for core funding to include staff costs; ongoing running costs for specific projects.
RANGE OF GRANTS From £1,000 to £30,000, with most grants being between £1,000 and £5,000.
SAMPLE GRANTS Children's Hospices Across Scotland (£25,000); Forget Me Not Children's Hospice (£10,000); Hope into Action (£7,000); Petrus (£5,000); The Leanne Fund (£2,000).
FINANCES *Financial year end 05/04/2022*
　Income £900,800
　Grants to organisations £6,150,000
　Assets £59,730,000
TRUSTEES Stephen Harvey; Bridget McGuire; Ian Fleming; Kate McGuire.
HOW TO APPLY Applications can be made through the trust's website.
CONTACT DETAILS The Trustees, The Hermitage, 15A Shenfield Road, Brentwood, Essex CM15 8AG *Tel.* 0330 113 7280 *Email* info@ alberthunttrust.org.uk *Website* www. alberthunttrust.org.uk

■ The Hunter Foundation

OSCR NO SC027532　　　**ESTABLISHED** 1998
WHERE FUNDING CAN BE GIVEN UK and overseas.
WHO CAN BENEFIT Charitable organisations; schools; social enterprises.
WHAT IS FUNDED Education, entrepreneurship and poverty alleviation in the UK and internationally.
TYPE OF GRANT Project funding; strategic funding; development funding; start-up funding.
SAMPLE GRANTS Kiltwalk (£2.62 million); The Innovation Fund (£2.43 million); Social Innovation Partnership (£990,000); Children in Need (£770,000); Scottish Edge (£437,000); Remember Me Campaign (£250,000); STV Appeal (£150,000); Scale Up Scotland (£76,400).
FINANCES *Financial year end 31/03/2022*
　Income £2,360,000
　Grants to organisations £10,240,000
　Assets £64,200,000
TRUSTEES Sir Tom Hunter; Lady Marion Hunter; Jim McMahon.
OTHER INFORMATION In 2021/22, 14 organisations listed in the foundation's accounts received grants totalling £9.71 million. The remaining £528,700 was awarded in grants to organisations not listed.
HOW TO APPLY Contact the foundation using the contact form on the website. If your project appears to be of initial interest, the trustees will contact you to discuss taking the application further.
CONTACT DETAILS The Trustees, Marathon House, Olympic Business Park, Drybridge Road, Dundonald, Ayrshire KA2 9AE *Email* info@ thehunterfoundation.co.uk or use the contact form on the website *Website* www. thehunterfoundation.co.uk

■ Miss Agnes H. Hunter's Trust

OSCR NO SC004843　　　**ESTABLISHED** 1954
WHERE FUNDING CAN BE GIVEN Scotland.
WHO CAN BENEFIT OSCR-registered charities.
WHAT IS FUNDED Support for people with disabilities; education and training for disadvantaged people aged 16 or over who have left school.
WHAT IS NOT FUNDED A full list of exclusions can be found on the 'Restrictions' page of the trust's website.
TYPE OF GRANT Project funding; core costs.
RANGE OF GRANTS Mostly £5,000 to £10,000. The trust notes that it reserves a degree of flexibility on award values.
SAMPLE GRANTS Works+ (£45,000); Funding Auto Immune Research (£15,000); Move On (£14,000); Cancer Support (£12,000); Hear My Music (£6,000); Back Up (£5,000).
FINANCES *Financial year end 30/06/2022*
　Income £478,200
　Grants to organisations £550,800
　Assets £15,790,000
TRUSTEES Keith Burdon; Elaine Crichton; Norman Dunning; Duncan McEachran; Daljit Singh; Denise Spence.
OTHER INFORMATION The trust's website notes that it is particularly keen to hear from the following: smaller charities with a strong local community presence; causes that do not have a strong public profile, including start-up organisations; and charities developing innovative approaches, including pilot projects. Grants were awarded for education and training (28 grants totalling £342,400) and disability (14 grants totalling £208,500).

HOW TO APPLY Apply online via the trust's website. There are two grant decision meetings per year. Visit the trust's helpful website for exact deadlines, as well as further application guidance.
CONTACT DETAILS Sarah Wright, Trust Manger, Davidson House, 57 Queen Charlotte Street, Edinburgh EH6 7EY *Tel.* 0131 538 5496 *Email* s.wright@agneshunter.org.uk *Website* www.agneshunter.org.uk

■ The Hunting Horn General Charitable Trust
CC NO 1149358 **ESTABLISHED** 2012
WHERE FUNDING CAN BE GIVEN Worldwide, with a preference for the UK and the continent of Africa.
WHO CAN BENEFIT Charitable organisations; churches.
WHAT IS FUNDED General charitable purposes; Christianity; humanitarian work outside the UK, particularly across Africa.
TYPE OF GRANT General funding; in-kind support.
SAMPLE GRANTS Eden Baptist Church (£222,100); St Mary's Church – Cambridge (£80,200); CAMFED (£50,000); Sightsavers (£10,000); Wintercomfort (£5,000); South Sinai (£1,000).
FINANCES *Financial year end 31/05/2022 Income* £516,200 *Grants to organisations* £577,400 *Assets* £6,520,000
TRUSTEES Martin Oldfield; Sean Jackson.
OTHER INFORMATION Computer equipment (goods donated) accounted for £7,200 of the trust's grant total.
HOW TO APPLY Apply in writing to the correspondent.
CONTACT DETAILS The Trustees, 3 Adams Road, Cambridge, Cambridgeshire CB3 9AD *Tel.* 01223 476769

■ The Huntingdon Foundation Ltd
CC NO 286504 **ESTABLISHED** 1984
WHERE FUNDING CAN BE GIVEN UK and Israel.
WHO CAN BENEFIT Organisations benefitting Jewish people; Jewish schools, universities and other educational organisations.
WHAT IS FUNDED The Jewish faith and community; education and training.
RANGE OF GRANTS Up to £140,000.
SAMPLE GRANTS Achisomoch Aid Company (£140,000); Kehilas Adas Yisroel and MGS Charitable Trust (£25,000 each); North London Welfare (£11,000); Hasmonean Primary, Tiferes Shlomo and Yeshiva Gedola Nezer Hatorah (£10,000 each).
FINANCES *Financial year end 31/03/2022 Income* £551,600 *Grants to organisations* £401,100 *Assets* £16,470,000
TRUSTEES Rachel Jeidel; Dr Shoshanna Perl; Jonathan Perl; Naomi Tsorotzkin; Benjamin Perl; Adrian Jacobs.
HOW TO APPLY Apply in writing to the correspondent. The trustees meet several times a year.
CONTACT DETAILS The Trustees, Foframe House, 35–37 Brent Street, London NW4 2EF *Tel.* 020 3411 2001

■ Huntingdon Freemen's Trust
CC NO 1044573 **ESTABLISHED** 1993
WHERE FUNDING CAN BE GIVEN The area covered by Huntingdon Town Council, including Oxmoor, Hartford, Sapley, Stukeley Meadows and Hinchingbrooke Park.
WHO CAN BENEFIT Registered charities; individuals; students; churches; local groups and organisations involved in sports, hobbies and the arts.
WHAT IS FUNDED General charitable purposes including: recreation and leisure; social welfare; education.
TYPE OF GRANT Capital costs; project costs.
SAMPLE GRANTS A list of beneficiaries was not included in the annual report and accounts.
FINANCES *Financial year end 30/04/2022 Income* £551,600 *Grants to organisations* £332,400 *Assets* £19,700,000
TRUSTEES Brian Bradshaw; John Hough; Kate Parker; Juliet Cole; Tom Sanderson; Jonathan Hampstead; Marion Kadewere.
OTHER INFORMATION The grant total includes grants awarded to individuals.
HOW TO APPLY Application forms for organisations and individuals are available on the trust's website. Forms should be returned to the correspondent.
CONTACT DETAILS The Trustees, 37 High Street, Huntingdon, Cambridgeshire PE29 3AQ *Tel.* 01480 414909 *Email* info@huntingdonfreemen.org.uk *Website* www.huntingdonfreemen.org.uk

■ Hurdale Charity Ltd
CC NO 276997 **ESTABLISHED** 1978
WHERE FUNDING CAN BE GIVEN England and Wales.
WHO CAN BENEFIT Charitable organisations benefitting Jewish people.
WHAT IS FUNDED The Jewish faith and community.
RANGE OF GRANTS Up to £500,000.
SAMPLE GRANTS Springfield Trust Ltd (£495,000); Moundvilly Charities Ltd (£405,000); Fountain of Chessed (£264,000); Greenline Foundation (£130,000); Achisomoch Aid Company (£90,000); Wlodowa Charity and Rehabilitation Trust (£63,000); British Friends of Mishan L'Choleh (£32,000); Beis Aharon Trust (£27,000).
FINANCES *Financial year end 31/03/2022 Income* £1,800,000 *Grants to organisations* £2,370,000 *Assets* £29,710,000
TRUSTEES David Oestreicher; Benjamin Oestreicher; Jacob Oestreicher; Abraham Oestreicher.
OTHER INFORMATION Only beneficiaries of grants of £25,000 and above were listed in the 2021/22 accounts (16 organisations); grants of under £25,000 totalled £362,500.
HOW TO APPLY Apply in writing to the correspondent.
CONTACT DETAILS Abraham Oestreicher, Trustee, 162 Osbaldeston Road, London N16 6NJ *Tel.* 020 8731 0770

■ The Hutchinson Charitable Trust
CC NO 1155643 **ESTABLISHED** 2012
WHERE FUNDING CAN BE GIVEN UK, with a preference for Fenland, particularly Wisbech.
WHO CAN BENEFIT Charitable organisations.
WHAT IS FUNDED General charitable purposes; agriculture; disadvantaged people; education.

SAMPLE GRANTS Previous beneficiaries have included: Royal Agricultural Benevolent Institution (£50,000); The Addington Fund (£20,000); King's Lynn Samaritans and Send a Cow (£12,500 each).

FINANCES *Financial year end* 31/12/2021
Income £3,500
Grants to organisations £250,900

TRUSTEES Michael Hutchinson; David Hutchinson.

OTHER INFORMATION Full accounts were not available to view on the Charity Commission's website due to the trust's low income. We have therefore estimated the trust's grant total based on its total expenditure.

HOW TO APPLY Apply in writing to the correspondent.

CONTACT DETAILS The Trustees, 10 Victory Road, Wisbech, Cambridgeshire PE13 2PU *Tel.* 01945 586409

■ The Hutton Foundation

CC NO 1106521   **ESTABLISHED** 2004
WHERE FUNDING CAN BE GIVEN UK and overseas.
WHO CAN BENEFIT Charitable organisations.
WHAT IS FUNDED General charitable purposes.
RANGE OF GRANTS £2,400 to £70,000.
SAMPLE GRANTS Theological Institute (£69,800); Dr Wolfgang Kopf (£44,100); La Alegría de los Niños (£10,000); Cardinal Hume Centre (£5,000).
FINANCES *Financial year end* 31/12/2021
Income £194,900
Grants to organisations £192,200
Assets £1,480,000
TRUSTEES Graham Hutton; Amanda Hutton; James Hutton; Richard Hutton.
HOW TO APPLY Apply in writing to the correspondent.
CONTACT DETAILS Jaclyn Donnina, Secretary and Treasurer, The Old House, Bramley Road, Silchester, Reading, Berkshire RG7 2LU *Tel.* 07786 921033

■ The Nani Huyu Charitable Trust

CC NO 1082868   **ESTABLISHED** 2000
WHERE FUNDING CAN BE GIVEN UK, with a strong preference for Bristol and the surrounding areas.
WHO CAN BENEFIT Charitable organisations, particularly small local charities.
WHAT IS FUNDED Social and economic circumstances; health; young people (education, training and accommodation); older people (end-of-life medical care and assistance).
RANGE OF GRANTS £1,000 to £20,000.
SAMPLE GRANTS Womankind (£23,000); Young Bristol (£18,000); Young Carers (£16,000); Wellspring Counselling (£15,000); Brain Tumour Support (£11,000); Bristol Children's Help Society (£7,000); Age UK Bath (£5,000); Cerebral Palsy Plus (£2,000).
FINANCES *Financial year end* 31/10/2021
Income £199,600
Grants to organisations £196,000
Assets £5,970,000
TRUSTEES Ben Whitmore; Maureen Whitmore; Susan Webb; Jenny Wilson; Lucy Walford.
OTHER INFORMATION The 2020/21 accounts were the latest available to view at the time of writing (June 2023).
HOW TO APPLY Apply in writing to the correspondent.
CONTACT DETAILS The Trustees, 33 Ash Lane, Wells, Somerset BA5 2LR *Tel.* 01275 474433 *Email* maureensimonwhitmore@btinternet.com

---

■ The Harold Hyam Wingate Foundation

CC NO 264114   **ESTABLISHED** 1960
WHERE FUNDING CAN BE GIVEN UK and overseas.
WHO CAN BENEFIT Registered charities; academic organisations specialising in Jewish subjects; museums and libraries promoting Jewish culture.
WHAT IS FUNDED Jewish life and learning; performing arts; music; education and social exclusion; overseas aid; medical research (travel grants).
WHAT IS NOT FUNDED Individuals; gap years, Duke of Edinburgh's Awards or similar; large charities (including local branch offices of large organisations); funding for stage productions.
TYPE OF GRANT Project and development funding.
RANGE OF GRANTS Mostly up to £10,000.
SAMPLE GRANTS World ORT Trust (£17,500); Jasmin Vardinon Educational Co. Ltd (£10,000); Face Front Inclusive Theatre (£8,000); Brundibar Arts Festival (£6,500); Awards for Young Musicians (£5,000); Buxton International Festival (£3,000).
FINANCES *Financial year end* 05/04/2022
Income £50,100
Grants to organisations £375,800
Assets £6,120,000
TRUSTEES Prof. Robert Cassen; Jonathan Drori; Daphne Hyman; Emily Kasriel; Dr Richard Wingate; Roger Wingate; Barbara Arnold.
OTHER INFORMATION In 2021/22, grants were given to 36 organisations across the following categories: performing arts (37%); music (26%); Jewish life and learning (20%); education and social exclusion (10%); library prizes (5%); development project (1%); medical research including travel grants (1%).
HOW TO APPLY Application forms are available to download on the foundation's website. Once completed, forms should be returned to the administrator by email only. Applications should include supporting documentation and your most recent accounts. The trustees usually meet quarterly to consider grant applications. Details of upcoming meetings can be seen on the website.
CONTACT DETAILS Administrator, Somerset House, South Wing, Strand, London WC2R 1LA *Tel.* 020 3701 7479 *Email* admin@wingate.org. uk *Website* www.wingatefoundation.org.uk

---

■ Hyde Charitable Trust

CC NO 289888   **ESTABLISHED** 1984
WHERE FUNDING CAN BE GIVEN The areas in which the Hyde Group operates (London, the South East, the East of England and the East Midlands).
WHO CAN BENEFIT Community groups; individuals.
WHAT IS FUNDED Employability; young people; reducing isolation; mental health and well-being; food poverty; fuel poverty; reducing the impact of violence; community cohesion.
TYPE OF GRANT Project funding.
SAMPLE GRANTS A list of beneficiaries was not included in the annual report and accounts.
FINANCES *Financial year end* 31/03/2022
Income £445,000
Grants to organisations £1,150,000
Grants to individuals £662,000
Assets £14,960,000
TRUSTEES Patrick Law; Brid O'Dwyer; Katherine Rodgers; Junior Moka; Clare Ferguson; Jessica Skilbeck.
OTHER INFORMATION During 2021/22 grants were awarded to 39 organisations and 410 individuals.

HOW TO APPLY Contact the correspondent for further information.

CONTACT DETAILS The Trustees, Hyde Housing Association, 30 Park Street, London SE1 9EQ *Tel.* 020 3207 2762 *Email* zoe.ollerearnshaw@hyde-housing.co.uk *Website* www.hyde-housing.co.uk/corporate/our-social-purpose/hyde-charitable-trust

··

■ Hyde Park Place Estate Charity

CC NO 212439   **ESTABLISHED** 1914

WHERE FUNDING CAN BE GIVEN City of Westminster.

WHO CAN BENEFIT Charities and community organisations.

WHAT IS FUNDED Church maintenance; social welfare; health; education.

TYPE OF GRANT Capital costs.

RANGE OF GRANTS Mostly £1,000 to £5,000.

SAMPLE GRANTS Adventure Play Hub (£5,000); Cardboard Citizens (£3,000); Iris Theatre (£2,600); Mayfair Community Choir (£2,000); London Handel Society (£1,000).

FINANCES *Financial year end 31/03/2022*
Income £512,500
Grants to organisations £236,500
Assets £19,590,000

TRUSTEES The Revd Roderick Leece; Mark Hewitt; Graham Barnes.

HOW TO APPLY Apply in writing to the correspondent. The trustees meet four times a year.

CONTACT DETAILS Yvonne Eddy, Clerk to the Trustees, St George's Church, The Vestry, 2A Mill Street, London W1S 1FX *Tel.* 020 7629 0874

■ Ibrahim Foundation Ltd

cc no 1149438   **established** 2012
where funding can be given UK and overseas.
who can benefit Registered charities; educational organisations; community projects.
what is funded General charitable purposes including: community building; the environment; families; strengthening not-for-profit organisations.
what is not funded Applications from the same organisation in successive grant cycles.
type of grant Capital costs; core costs; project funding; unrestricted funding.
range of grants Up to £50,000 but usually between £500 and £10,000.
sample grants A list of beneficiaries was not included in the annual report and accounts.
finances *Financial year end 31/05/2022*
  Income £97,300
  Grants to organisations £91,200
  Assets £150
trustees Azeem Ibrahim; Adeel Ibrahim; Aadil Butt.
other information All grants were awarded for community-building initiatives.
how to apply Initial contact can be made via the foundation's website.
contact details The Trustees, 18 Little Street, Glasgow G3 8DQ *Tel.* 0141 416 1991 *Email* info@ibrahimfoundation.com *Website* www.ibrahimfoundation.com

■ The Iceland Foods Charitable Foundation

cc no 281943   **established** 1973
where funding can be given UK.
who can benefit Registered charities (mainly medical charities); hospices; universities.
what is funded General charitable purposes.
type of grant Capital costs; development funding; research.
sample grants Prostate Cancer UK (£500,000); Action for Children (£331,000); British Red Cross (£150,000); Maggie's (£75,000) The UK Sepsis Trust (£29,000); The Holroyd Foundation (£20,000); Alder Hey (£10,000); Christie Charity (£5,000); Chester Gang (£1,500); Welsh Ambulance (£100).
finances *Financial year end 05/04/2022*
  Income £958,900
  Grants to organisations £1,530,000
  Assets £3,270,000
trustees Tarsem Dhaliwal; Sir Malcolm Walker; Richard Walker; Paul Dhaliwal.
other information Each year the foundation chooses one principal charity partner as well as supporting causes nominated by Iceland employees.
how to apply Apply in writing to the correspondent.
contact details The Trustees, Second Avenue, Deeside Industrial Park, Deeside, Flintshire CH5 2NW *Tel.* 01244 842885 *Email* ifcf@iceland.co.uk *Website* www.ifcf.org.uk

■ The Idlewild Trust

cc no 268124   **established** 1974
where funding can be given UK.
who can benefit Registered charities; museums; galleries; churches that are excepted charities.
what is funded The arts, including programmes that improve opportunities for young professionals working within the arts, particularly at an early stage in their career; conservation of historic or artistically important objects and works of art.
what is not funded A full list of exclusions can be found in the funding guidelines document on the trust's website.
type of grant Project funding.
range of grants Up to £5,000.
sample grants Barbican Centre Trust, IMS Prussia Cove, London Symphony Orchestra and Talawa Theatre Company (£5,000 each); Studio Wayne McGregor (£4,900); English National Opera (£3,000); National Student Drama Festival (£2,500).
finances *Financial year end 31/12/2021*
  Income £140,100
  Grants to organisations £98,000
  Assets £7,320,000
trustees Helen McCabe; Dr Tessa Murdoch; Nancy Bell; James Turner; Serena Worthington; Rachael Williams.
other information The trustees considered 84 appeals and awarded 22 grants in 2021. The trust runs two grant programmes: Arts: Nurturing Early-Stage Professionals and Conservation: Objects and Works of Art.
how to apply Applications can be made via the trust's website. Applicants should note that there are separate forms for Arts and Conservation applications. The website has details of upcoming deadlines.
contact details Gail Devlin-Jones, Director, Marshall House, 66 Newcomen Street, London SE1 1YT *Email* info@idlewildtrust.org.uk *Website* www.idlewildtrust.org.uk

■ IGO Foundation Ltd

cc no 1148316   **established** 2012
where funding can be given Worldwide.
who can benefit Charitable organisations; educational institutions; places of worship.
what is funded The Jewish faith and community; relief of poverty; general charitable purposes.
range of grants Up to £10,000.
sample grants Friends of Beis Soroh Schneirer, Kehal Yisroel D'Chasidei Gur and The Rehabilitation Trust (£10,000 each); The TMC Trust Ltd (£6,800).
finances *Financial year end 30/06/2022*
  Income £239,200
  Grants to organisations £219,500
  Assets £1,260,000
trustees Abraham Lipschitz; Bernard Ost; Gita Ost.
other information A full list of beneficiaries was not available. Grants of less than £6,800 each totalled £82,700.
how to apply Apply in writing to the correspondent.
contact details The Trustees, 29 Grosvenor Gardens, London NW11 0HE *Tel.* 020 3411 2001

■ The Iliffe Family Charitable Trust

cc no 273437   established 1977
where funding can be given UK.
who can benefit Registered charities; hospices, hospitals.
what is funded General charitable purposes; social welfare; education; Christianity; conservation; health.
range of grants £1,000 to £10,000.
sample grants Country Food Trust (£15,000); Berkshire Community Foundation (£10,000); Lord Leycester Hospital (£5,000); Stem4 (£3,000); Sail 4 Cancer (£2,500); Hampshire and Isle of Wight Air Ambulance (£1,000).
finances *Financial year end 05/04/2022*
  Income £27,800
  Grants to organisations £134,000
  Assets £1,820,000
trustees Lord Iliffe; The Hon. Edward Iliffe; Catherine Fleming; Lady Iliffe.
other information In 2021/22, grants were broken down as follows: welfare (£45,000); conservation (£22,500); medical causes (£21,000); education (£20,000); heritage (£18,000); religion (£7,500).
how to apply Apply in writing to the correspondent.
contact details The Trustees, Barn Close, Burnt Hill, Yattendon, Berkshire RG18 0UX
  Tel. 01635 203929 *Email* ifct@yattendon.co.uk

■ Imagine Foundation

cc no 1152864   established 2013
where funding can be given UK.
who can benefit Registered charities.
what is funded Social welfare; unemployment; social exclusion; community development.
type of grant Ongoing partnerships; project funding.
range of grants Typically under £15,000.
sample grants Free to Be Kids and Luminary Bakery (£17,000 each); LS14 Trust and North East Young Dads and Lads (£15,000 each); The Women and Family Resource Centre (£10,000); Hear Me Out (£8,000); Monty's Community Hub (£7,500); Out Of Character (£5,000).
finances *Financial year end 31/12/2021*
  Income £218,000
  Grants to organisations £240,600
  Assets £804,900
trustees Steve Eyre; Diane Eyre; Kerry McLeish; Phil Stratton; Kerry Eyre.
other information The foundation mainly provides grants to charities with which it has ongoing partnerships. During 2021, grants were made to 22 organisations. Grants were awarded through the following programmes: capacity building (£80,000); using creativity to change the story (£65,100); supporting disadvantaged young people (£63,400); community development (£32,100).
how to apply Applications are invited through referrals from within the trustees' network of contacts.
contact details The Trustees, Lower Farm, Oakley Road, Chinnor, Oxfordshire OX39 4HR
  Tel. 07973 675257 *Email* info@if-trust.org
  Website www.if-trust.org

■ Impact Funding Partners Ltd

oscr no SC035037   established 2003
where funding can be given Scotland.
who can benefit Charitable organisations.
what is funded General charitable purposes; volunteering support; well-being; social isolation and loneliness.
what is not funded Programme dependent
type of grant Programme dependent
sample grants A list of beneficiaries was not included in the annual report and accounts.
finances *Financial year end 31/03/2022*
  Income £2,100,000
  Grants to organisations £1,670,000
  Assets £577,400
trustees Daphne Biliouri-Grant; Sarah Shanahan; Jim Nicol; Joanna McLaughlin; Ailsa Bruce; Carlos Alba; Dalvir Johal.
other information The charity manages a number of programmes on behalf of the Scottish Government and other funders.
how to apply Application forms and guidance notes for open programmes are available on the charity's website. Grant programmes may open and close so applicants should check the website for the most recent updates.
contact details The Trustees, Robertson House, 152 Bath Street, Glasgow G2 4TB *Tel.* 01383 620780 *Email* info@impactfundingpartners.com
  Website www.impactfundingpartners.com

■ Impetus

cc no 1152262   established 2013
where funding can be given UK.
who can benefit Registered charities.
what is funded Disadvantaged people aged 11–24; education and training; employment.
type of grant Long-term, unrestricted and core funding.
sample grants City Gateway (£486,400); Football Beyond Borders (£391,300); Tutor Trust (£245,000); ThinkForward (£154,000); Access Project (£125,000); Transforming Lives for Good (£75,000); Action Tutoring (£62,500); Career Ready (£50,000); Mama Youth (£30,000).
finances *Financial year end 31/12/2021*
  Income £10,000,000
  Grants to organisations £3,500,000
  Assets £8,240,000
trustees Hanneke Smits; Lisa Stone; Bill Benjamin; Shani Zindel; Rohan Haldea; Filippo Cardini; Charles Edwards; Natasha Porter; Joseph Schull; Andrew Thoms; Satwinder Singh; Alexander Walsh.
other information In addition to grants, the charity provides pro bono support to its partner organisations in the following areas: business planning, organisational structure, finance, leadership coaching and performance management. In 2021, grants paid to Youth Endowment Fund (YEF) interventions totalled £14 million; grants paid to charity partners totalled £3.5 million; and grants paid to research organisations totalled £2,600. We have not included the YEF figure in our grant total as, although the charity's sole corporate trustee is Impetus, it is an independent charity with its own grant-making criteria and application process. See entry on page 751 for more information.
how to apply For further information about funding and how to become a partner contact the Philanthropy Team.
contact details The Trustees, 1st Floor, Golden Cross House, 8 Duncannon Street, London

WC2N 4JF *Tel.* 07774 437701
Email philanthropy@impetus.org.uk
Website www.impetus.org.uk

■ The Indigo Trust

CC NO 1075920   **ESTABLISHED** 1999
WHERE FUNDING CAN BE GIVEN UK and sub-Saharan Africa.
WHO CAN BENEFIT Registered charities.
WHAT IS FUNDED Visual impairment in sub-Saharan Africa; access to justice in sub-Saharan Africa and in the UK.
TYPE OF GRANT Core and revenue costs; seed funding; start-up funding; project funding; unrestricted funding.
RANGE OF GRANTS Up to £260,000.
SAMPLE GRANTS Laws.Africa (£260,000); Access to Justice Foundation (£100,000); Vision Catalyst Fund (£75,000); Open Cities Lab (£50,000); Breakout Youth (£2,000).
FINANCES *Financial year end* 05/04/2022
Income £284,400
Grants to organisations £1,270,000
Assets £11,020,000
TRUSTEES Dominic Flynn; Francesca Perrin; William Perrin; Sameer Padania; Sonia Sodha.
OTHER INFORMATION The trust is one of the Sainsbury Family Charitable Trusts, which share a common administration – see www.sftc.org.uk for more information.
HOW TO APPLY The trust's website states the following: 'Indigo is not currently accepting unsolicited proposals. Experience has taught us that an open application process is burdensome for both sides and rarely results in new grants being awarded.'
CONTACT DETAILS The Trustees, The Peak, 5 Wilton Road, London SW1V 1AP *Email* indigo@sfct.org.uk *Website* https://indigotrust.org.uk

■ The Inflexion Foundation

CC NO 1179624   **ESTABLISHED** 2018
WHERE FUNDING CAN BE GIVEN England and Wales.
WHO CAN BENEFIT Registered charities.
WHAT IS FUNDED Social isolation and loneliness; health; environmental conservation.
SAMPLE GRANTS The Roundhouse Trust (£1.5 million), Impetus – The Private Equity Foundation (£142,900).
FINANCES *Financial year end* 31/03/2022
Income £5,000,000
Grants to organisations £2,430,000
Assets £4,660,000
TRUSTEES John Hartz; Simon Turner; James Goold.
HOW TO APPLY Apply in writing to the correspondent.
CONTACT DETAILS The Trustees, 47 Queen Anne Street, London WIG 9JG *Tel.* 020 7487 9827
Email manager@inflexionfoundation.com

■ The Ingram Trust

CC NO 1040194   **ESTABLISHED** 1994
WHERE FUNDING CAN BE GIVEN UK and overseas, with some preference for Surrey.
WHO CAN BENEFIT Registered charities.
WHAT IS FUNDED General charitable purposes.
WHAT IS NOT FUNDED Non-registered charities; individuals; charities specialising in overseas aid unless they are dedicated to encouraging self-help and providing more permanent solutions to problems; animal charities (except those concerned with wildlife conservation).
TYPE OF GRANT Project funding; capital costs.

RANGE OF GRANTS Up to £60,000 but mostly £5,000 to £25,000.
SAMPLE GRANTS WWF-UK (£60,000); NSPCC (£42,000); Age UK (£28,000); St Mungo's (£25,000); Scope (£20,000); Crimestoppers (£10,000); Cherry Trees (£5,000).
FINANCES *Financial year end* 05/04/2022
Income £140,500
Grants to organisations £700,000
Assets £10,910,000
TRUSTEES Janet Ingram; Clare Maurice; Jonathan Ingram; Sally Ingram; Christopher Ingram.
OTHER INFORMATION The majority of grants will be made for periods of three to four years at a time in order for the trustees to better assess grant applications and monitor progress.
HOW TO APPLY Apply in writing to the correspondent. The trustees consider grant applications from charities that they believe demonstrate concrete evidence of delivering public benefit.
CONTACT DETAILS The Trustees, c/o Rawlinson and Hunter LLP, 8th Floor, 6 New Street Square, London EC4A 3AQ *Tel.* 020 7842 2000
Email theingramtrust@rawlinson-hunter.com

■ The Inlight Trust

CC NO 236782   **ESTABLISHED** 1957
WHERE FUNDING CAN BE GIVEN UK.
WHO CAN BENEFIT Registered charities.
WHAT IS FUNDED Religious and spiritual development, healing and growth.
WHAT IS NOT FUNDED Individuals, including students; organisations which are not registered charities; general appeals from large national organisations; church buildings. Core funding and/or salaries are rarely considered.
TYPE OF GRANT Usually one-off for a specific project or part of a project.
RANGE OF GRANTS Between £2,000 and £18,000.
SAMPLE GRANTS Rowcroft House Foundation (£18,000); The Mary Stevens Hospice (£17,000); Corby and District Cancer Care (£14,000); Beachy Head Chaplaincy Team (£10,000); St Ethelburga's (£6,000); St Gemma's Hospice (£2,000).
FINANCES *Financial year end* 31/03/2022
Income £334,800
Grants to organisations £135,500
Assets £8,460,000
TRUSTEES Judy Hayward; Sharon Knight; Jane Dunham; Shirley Vening; Stephen Collins; Paul Summerfield.
HOW TO APPLY Previous research has shown that applications should be made in writing to the correspondent, including details of the need, the intended project to meet it, an outline of the budget, your most recent annual accounts and a copy of your trust deed or your entry on the Charity Commission register. Only applications from eligible bodies are acknowledged and only successful applicants are informed.
CONTACT DETAILS Clare Pegden, Administrator, PO Box 2, Liss, Hampshire GU33 6YP *Tel.* 07970 540015 *Email* inlight.trust01@ntlworld.com

■ The Inman Charity

CC NO 261366   **ESTABLISHED** 1970
WHERE FUNDING CAN BE GIVEN UK.
WHO CAN BENEFIT Charitable organisations.
WHAT IS FUNDED General charitable purposes, with a particular interest in: medical research; care of older people; social welfare; hospices; physical and mental disability including deafness and blindness; the armed forces.

WHAT IS NOT FUNDED Individuals; young children and infants; maintenance of buildings at a local level (e.g. churches and village halls); animal welfare; wildlife and environmental conservation; religious charities.

RANGE OF GRANTS Generally £2,000 to £5,000.

SAMPLE GRANTS Roy Castle Lung Cancer Foundation (£10,000); Bowel Cancer UK and All Of Us Versus Arthritis (£6,000 each); Changing Faces, Deafblind UK, Hot Line Meals Services and Listening Books (£5,000 each).

FINANCES *Financial year end 31/12/2021*
Income £163,100
Grants to organisations £230,000
Assets £6,790,000

TRUSTEES John Langdon; Michael Mathews; Belinda Strother; A. L. Walker; Neil Wingerath; Inman Charity Trustees Ltd.

OTHER INFORMATION The charity awards a regular grant of £25,000 to the Victor Inman Bursary Fund at Uppingham School.

HOW TO APPLY Applications should be made in writing to the correspondent. Full details of the application process can be found on the charity's website.

CONTACT DETAILS The Trustees, BM Box 2831, London WC1N 3XX *Tel.* 020 7465 4300 *Website* www.inmancharity.org

■ Inner London Magistrates Court Poor Box and Feeder Charity

CC NO 1046214   **ESTABLISHED** 1995

WHERE FUNDING CAN BE GIVEN Inner London.

WHO CAN BENEFIT Individuals; courts; probation services; organisations which provide relief of hardships faced by people who come into contact with the courts.

WHAT IS FUNDED Relief of need, hardship and distress of people concerned, directly or indirectly, in any proceedings at magistrates' courts in the London region, including family and youth courts.

WHAT IS NOT FUNDED Our previous research suggests that the charity will not fund the direct relief of rates, taxes or other public funds.

RANGE OF GRANTS £5,000 to £15,000.

SAMPLE GRANTS St Giles Trust (£15,000); Prison Advice and Care Trust (£12,500); Refuge (£7,500); The Margins Society and Toynbee Hall (£5,000 each).

FINANCES *Financial year end 31/03/2022*
Income £182,200
Grants to organisations £130,300
Assets £5,350,000

TRUSTEES Richard Kozak; Jane Richardson; Louise Moloney; Tanweer Ikram; Paul Goldspring; Nina Tempia.

OTHER INFORMATION Grants were made to 15 organisations during the year. The 2021/22 accounts were the latest available at the time of writing (May 2023).

HOW TO APPLY Apply in writing to the correspondent. The following was taken from the annual report for 2021/22: 'The trustees invite applications for grants from the courts themselves, the probation services and organisations involved in identifying and relieving need and hardship suffered in prison. The trustees are also aware that the needs and hardship of those who come into contact with the courts are often associated with homelessness, substance misuse, domestic violence and poverty and applications are invited from organisations which provide relief in those areas specifically to beneficiaries in the London region. The trustees

do not commit to repeat or renew a relief grant on any occasion.'

CONTACT DETAILS The Trustees, Ealing Magistrates' Court, 448 High Road, London NW10 2DZ *Tel.* 07901 822125 *Email* ilmcpbf@btinternet.com

■ The Innocent Foundation

CC NO 1104289   **ESTABLISHED** 2004

WHERE FUNDING CAN BE GIVEN Africa; South America; South Asia.

WHO CAN BENEFIT Community-based projects and NGOs in the countries where the Innocent Drinks company sources fruit. Generally, organisations must be UK-registered or have UK representation to receive funds.

WHAT IS FUNDED Food poverty worldwide, in particular projects which diagnose and treat children facing severe hunger; agricultural projects.

WHAT IS NOT FUNDED Individuals; religious or political causes; general appeals or circulars; events or conferences; seed funding is not given for core costs alone (but these can be included as overheads pro-rated to the project); major capital costs, such as buildings or machinery.

TYPE OF GRANT Most funds are allocated in multi-year partnerships but some one-off projects are supported. Development funding; project funding; research.

RANGE OF GRANTS Mostly up to £90,000.

SAMPLE GRANTS Save the Children (£144,500); Kickstart International (£120,000); Action Against Hunger (£100,000); Send a Cow (£17,400).

FINANCES *Financial year end 30/06/2022*
Income £1,000,000
Grants to organisations £882,000
Assets £2,340,000

TRUSTEES Adam Balon; Richard Reed; Christina Archer; Sarah-Jane Norman; Jonathan Wright; Camilla Clarke; Nicholas Canney.

OTHER INFORMATION The Innocent Foundation was set up by Innocent Drinks in 2004. Each year the company gives at least 10% of its profits to charity, the majority to the foundation. During the year, grants were distributed to 12 projects.

HOW TO APPLY Apply in writing to the correspondent.

CONTACT DETAILS Kate Franks, Foundation Director, The Innocent Foundation, 342 Ladbroke Grove, London W10 5BU *Tel.* 020 3235 0352 *Email* hello@innocentfoundation.org *Website* www.innocentfoundation.org

■ The Institute for Policy Research

CC NO 285143   **ESTABLISHED** 1982

WHERE FUNDING CAN BE GIVEN UK.

WHO CAN BENEFIT Think tanks; universities; other research institutions.

WHAT IS FUNDED Policy research and conferences that focus on social sciences, management studies and economic policy.

TYPE OF GRANT Research funding.

SAMPLE GRANTS TaxPayers' Alliance (£83,000); Centre for Policy Studies (£52,500); Politeia (£50,000).

FINANCES *Financial year end 30/09/2022*
Income £203,500
Grants to organisations £185,500
Assets £518,000

TRUSTEES Vincent Warner; Anthony Speaight; Jennifer Nicholson; Jeremy Bradshaw; Eric Koops.

HOW TO APPLY Apply in writing to the correspondent.

CONTACT DETAILS The Trustees, Flat 38, Charleston Court, 61 West Cliff Road, Broadstairs, Kent CT10 1RY *Tel.* 07815 502279 *Email* peter. orbelljones@yahoo.com

---

■ Integrated Education Fund

CCNI NO NIC104886   **ESTABLISHED** 1992

WHERE FUNDING CAN BE GIVEN Northern Ireland.

WHO CAN BENEFIT Schools undergoing or exploring the integration of pupils from the Catholic and Protestant communities; existing integrated schools; community/parent groups exploring integrated education for their area.

WHAT IS FUNDED Integrated education.

TYPE OF GRANT Research; evaluation; start-up costs; projects; development costs; training; salaries; capital costs.

FINANCES *Financial year end 31/03/2021*
Income £1,050,000
Grants to organisations £105,400
Assets £2,070,000

TRUSTEES David Cooke; Grainne Clarke; Michael McKernan; Ellen McVea; Mary Roulston; Barbara McAtamney; Kathleen O'Hare; Peter Osborne; Jane Morrice; Brandon McMaster; Patricia Murtagh; June Wilkinson; Sorcha Diver; Kenneth Cathcart.

OTHER INFORMATION The 2020/21 accounts were the latest available at the time of writing (June 2023).

HOW TO APPLY Each grant-making programme has its own rounds and deadlines for applications – see the charity's website for eligibility and closing dates.

CONTACT DETAILS The Trustees, Forestview, Purdy's Lane, Belfast BT8 7AR *Tel.* 028 9069 4099 *Email* info@ief.org.uk *Website* www.ief.org.uk

---

■ The International Bankers Charitable Trust

CC NO 1087630   **ESTABLISHED** 2001

WHERE FUNDING CAN BE GIVEN UK, with a preference for London.

WHO CAN BENEFIT Registered charities; schools; universities.

WHAT IS FUNDED Charities working with young people in education, financial literacy, employability, raising aspirations for education and employability; City of London and financial services-linked charitable initiatives.

TYPE OF GRANT Project funding; strategic funding.

RANGE OF GRANTS Typically up to £1,000 for new applicants, but larger awards may be considered.

SAMPLE GRANTS The Brokerage Citylink (£42,000); Dulwich College (£10,600); School-Home Support (£9,600); Mansion House Scholarship Scheme (£5,000); The Business School – City University (£4,300); Greenhouse Sports and King Henry's Walk Garden (£2,000 each); Bookmark Reading Charity (£1,000).

FINANCES *Financial year end 30/09/2021*
Income £118,000
Grants to organisations £97,800
Assets £1,180,000

TRUSTEE The Worshipful Company of International Bankers.

OTHER INFORMATION The 2020/21 accounts were the latest available at the time of writing (April 2023).

HOW TO APPLY Applications can be made online via the charity's website.

CONTACT DETAILS The Trustees, 3rd Floor, 12 Austin Friars, London EC2N 2HE *Tel.* 020 7374 0212 *Email* clerk@internationalbankers.co.uk *Website* http://internationalbankers.org.uk/ charity-education/charity-applications

---

■ The Inverforth Charitable Trust

CC NO 274132   **ESTABLISHED** 1977

WHERE FUNDING CAN BE GIVEN UK.

WHO CAN BENEFIT Charitable organisations.

WHAT IS FUNDED General charitable purposes including: health; hospices; young people and education; the armed forces; the arts; community development.

RANGE OF GRANTS Up to £10,000.

SAMPLE GRANTS St Minver Community Trust (£20,000); Allegra's Ambition, Childhood First and Teenage Cancer Trust (£10,000 each); Charlie Waller Memorial, Heritage Housing Caring Group, St Peter's PCC – Ropley and Welsh Air Ambulance (£5,000 each).

FINANCES *Financial year end 31/12/2021*
Income £43,600
Grants to organisations £130,000
Assets £7,510,000

TRUSTEES Jonathan Kane; Lady Elizabeth Inverforth; Lord Inverforth.

OTHER INFORMATION Grants were awarded to 14 organisations in 2021. The trust tends to support many of the same charities annually.

HOW TO APPLY Apply in writing to the correspondent.

CONTACT DETAILS Clarinda Kane, Secretary and Treasurer, 58A Flood Street, London SW3 5TE *Tel.* 020 7680 8100 *Email* clarindakane@ btopenworld.com

---

■ The Investindustrial Foundation

CC NO 1169179   **ESTABLISHED** 2011

WHERE FUNDING CAN BE GIVEN England; Wales; Italy; Spain; Switzerland; USA.

WHO CAN BENEFIT Charitable organisations.

WHAT IS FUNDED Education; diversity; environmental protection and conservation; arts, culture, heritage and science.

TYPE OF GRANT Project funding.

SAMPLE GRANTS A list of beneficiaries was not included in the annual report and accounts.

FINANCES *Financial year end 31/03/2022*
Income £744,400
Grants to organisations £101,200
Assets £8,490,000

TRUSTEES Oliver Dunn; Rohan Maxwell; Natalie Ramsden; Emanuele Bonomi.

OTHER INFORMATION All financial information was converted from EUR using the conversion rate at the time of writing (June 2023).

HOW TO APPLY Contact the correspondent for further information.

CONTACT DETAILS The Trustees, First Floor, One Hoopers Court, London SW3 1AF *Tel.* 020 7664 2121 *Website* www.investindustrial.com/social-responsibility/our-foundation.html

■ Investream Charitable Trust

CC NO 1097052 **ESTABLISHED** 2003

WHERE FUNDING CAN BE GIVEN Worldwide, with a preference for the UK and Israel.

WHO CAN BENEFIT Registered charities; educational organisations.

WHAT IS FUNDED The Jewish faith and community, with a focus on education, care for older people and medical causes.

SAMPLE GRANTS Achisomoch Aid Company (£212,000); Work Avenue (£50,000); The Belz Foundation (£45,000); Jay Education Trust (£37,000); Shaare Zedek (£36,000).

FINANCES *Financial year end* 30/04/2022
Income £1,410,000
Grants to organisations £911,200
Assets £1,190,000

TRUSTEES Mark Morris; Graham Morris.

OTHER INFORMATION Grants were broken down in the following categories: community care and care for older people (£514,200), education (£359,200) and medical causes (£37,800). Grants of under £30,000 totalled £521,200.

HOW TO APPLY Apply in writing to the correspondent.

CONTACT DETAILS The Trustees, Investream Ltd, 1 Portland Place, London W1B 1PN *Tel.* 020 7486 2800

■ The Invigorate Charitable Trust

CC NO 1162752 **ESTABLISHED** 2015

WHERE FUNDING CAN BE GIVEN UK and overseas.

WHO CAN BENEFIT Charitable organisations.

WHAT IS FUNDED General charitable purposes.

WHAT IS NOT FUNDED Health; amateur sport; environmental protection or improvement; animal welfare; the armed forces and emergency services.

SAMPLE GRANTS A list of beneficiaries was not included in the annual report and accounts.

FINANCES *Financial year end* 05/04/2022
Income £108,000
Grants to organisations £291,400
Assets £45,500

TRUSTEES Timothy Parr; Kate Aitchison.

OTHER INFORMATION During the year, grants were made to 22 organisations and ranged in size from £2,000 to £100,000. The figure includes grants totalling £75,000 that were approved by the trustees during the year ending 5 April 2022 but were not paid until after the year end.

HOW TO APPLY Contact the correspondent for more information regarding the application process.

CONTACT DETAILS Kate Aitchison, Trustee, 5th Floor, Central Square, 29 Wellington Street, Leeds, West Yorkshire LS1 4DL *Tel.* 0113 285 5000 *Email* kate.aitchison@rsmuk.com

■ The Ireland Fund of Great Britain

CC NO 327889 **ESTABLISHED** 1976

WHERE FUNDING CAN BE GIVEN UK, with a preference for Northern Ireland, and the Republic of Ireland.

WHO CAN BENEFIT Charities; community groups; voluntary groups.

WHAT IS FUNDED Education; community development; relief of poverty; the arts and culture; mental and physical health; older people; young people; peace and reconciliation.

TYPE OF GRANT Project funding.

RANGE OF GRANTS Mostly up to £20,000.

SAMPLE GRANTS Alexandra College (£35,200); Irish Sailing Foundation (£26,700); Integrated Education Fund (£20,000); Jack and Jill Foundation (£13,800); National Gallery of Ireland (£11,700); Luton Irish Forum (£8,000); Brent Adolescent Centre (£5,000); St Pat's Roof Appeal (£560).

FINANCES *Financial year end* 31/03/2022
Income £723,500
Grants to organisations £523,200
Assets £345,300

TRUSTEES Ruairi Conneely; Zach Webb; Rory Godson; Garrett Hayes; Eoin Bastible; Emily Bohill; Rachel Naughton; Declan Tiernan; Conor Hillery; John Feeney; Evelyn Bourke; Emer Finnan; Bridget Walsh; Susan Whelan; Susan O'Brien.

OTHER INFORMATION The Ireland Fund of Great Britain (IFGB) is one of 12 chapters of The Irish Funds. The IFBG makes grants through a donor-advised grants programme and an annual grant round. During 2021/22, 63 grants were awarded to organisations in the following areas: community development/the relief of poverty (£280,200); education (£151,300); sharing and developing Irish arts and culture (£12,500). The charity also has its own grant programmes for organisations in the Republic of Ireland and Northern Ireland, details of which can be found on the website.

HOW TO APPLY Guidelines, exclusions and full information on the application process are announced on the website when the relevant programme opens.

CONTACT DETAILS The Trustees, Level 17, Dashwood House, 69 Old Broad Street, London EC2M 1QS *Tel.* 07597 665646 *Email* ifgb@irelandfunds.org *Website* https://irelandfunds.org/chapters/worldwide/great-britain

■ Irish Youth Foundation (UK) Ltd (incorporating The Lawlor Foundation)

CC NO 328265 **ESTABLISHED** 1989

WHERE FUNDING CAN BE GIVEN UK.

WHO CAN BENEFIT Charities and community organisations.

WHAT IS FUNDED Projects that benefit young Irish people or enhance their personal and social development, especially if they are disadvantaged or in need. A wide range of projects are supported, including in the following areas: training/counselling; mental and physical health; substance and alcohol abuse rehabilitation; advice/advocacy; youth work; family support; homelessness; educational, cultural and social activities; cross-community initiatives; Irish Travellers; disability.

WHAT IS NOT FUNDED Projects for people over 25 (in Northern Ireland) and over 30 (in England, Scotland and Wales); general appeals; large/national charities; academic research; alleviating deficits already incurred; individuals (except for university students applying under The Lawlor Foundation's education programme); capital bids; overseas travel; multiple applications from a single organisation.

TYPE OF GRANT Programme development grants; seed funding; core costs and salaries; awards to upgrade premises and/or equipment. One-year grants only.

RANGE OF GRANTS In Northern Ireland: up to £10,000. In England, Scotland and Wales: small grants of up to £2,500; standard grants ranging from £2,500 to £10,000.

SAMPLE GRANTS Previous beneficiaries have included New Horizon Youth Centre – London (£9,500); Solace Women's Aid – London (£9,000); Brent Centre for Young People (£4,000); Birmingham

Irish Association and The Brandon Centre –
London (£3,000 each); Birmingham TradFest
(£2,000); Conradh na Gaeilge Glaschú –
Glasgow and Irish Arts Foundation – Leeds
(£1,000 each).
FINANCES *Financial year end 31/12/2021*
Income £213,300
Grants to organisations £205,500
Assets £2,920,000
TRUSTEES John Dwyer; Virginia Lawlor; June Trimble;
Richard Corrigan; Ciara Brett; Alan Byrne; Mark
Gough.
OTHER INFORMATION The Irish Youth Foundation (UK)
Ltd merged with The Lawlor Foundation in 2005.
HOW TO APPLY Application forms become available
during the annual funding round. Check the
website for current deadlines and detailed
guidelines. Unsolicited applications at other
times during the year are not accepted.
CONTACT DETAILS Linda Tanner, Company Secretary,
Irish Cultural Centre, 5 Blacks Road,
Hammersmith, London W6 9DT *Tel.* 020 8563
8232 *Email* linda@iyf.org.uk *Website* www.iyf.
org.uk

■ The Irving Memorial Trust
CC NO 1173441   **ESTABLISHED** 2017
WHERE FUNDING CAN BE GIVEN UK.
WHO CAN BENEFIT Charitable organisations.
WHAT IS FUNDED General charitable purposes.
RANGE OF GRANTS £100 to £20,000.
SAMPLE GRANTS Family First (£20,000); The London
Symphony Orchestra Endowment Trust
(£10,000); Barbaros Ensemble (£10,000);
Katharine House Hospice Trust (£5,000); Event
Mobility (£3,000); The Urology Foundation
(£1,000); The Liverpool Women's NHS
Foundation Trust (£1,000); Chaim V'Shalva
(£200); The Z.S.V. Trust (£100).
FINANCES *Financial year end 19/04/2022*
Income £280,000
Grants to organisations £272,400
Assets £725,000
TRUSTEES Pamela Huntingford; Andrew Huntingford;
Ludlow Trust Company Ltd.
HOW TO APPLY Contact the correspondent for further
information.
CONTACT DETAILS The Trustees, 1st Floor, Tower
Wharf, Cheese Lane, Bristol BS2 0JJ *Tel.* 0117
313 8200 *Email* charitabletrusts@ludlowtrust.
com

■ The J. Isaacs Charitable Trust
CC NO 1059865   **ESTABLISHED** 1996
WHERE FUNDING CAN BE GIVEN England and Wales.
WHO CAN BENEFIT Charitable organisations, including
those supporting Jewish people.
WHAT IS FUNDED General charitable purposes,
particularly care for children, education, the well-
being of older people, tolerance in the
community and health care.
RANGE OF GRANTS Up to £107,800.
SAMPLE GRANTS Noah's Ark Children's Hospice
(£107,500); Policy Exchange and Royal Society
for Blind Children (£50,000 each); UJIA
(£49,000).
FINANCES *Financial year end 31/03/2022*
Income £438,100
Grants to organisations £256,700
Assets £11,740,000
TRUSTEES Jeremy Isaacs: Joanne Isaacs; Helen
Eastick; Vincent Isaacs.
OTHER INFORMATION Grants were given in the
following categories: education (£160,100);

care for children (£112,500); health care
(£142,500); tolerance in the Jewish community
(£20,000); ad hoc/other (£2,500).
HOW TO APPLY Apply in writing to the correspondent.
CONTACT DETAILS The Trustees, JRJ Group, Mutual
House, 70 Conduit Street, London W1S 2GF
Tel. 020 7220 2305

■ The Isla Foundation
CC NO 1198389   **ESTABLISHED** 2013
WHERE FUNDING CAN BE GIVEN UK.
WHO CAN BENEFIT Charitable organisations with an
income of under £10 million.
WHAT IS FUNDED Social welfare; people who are
disadvantaged.
TYPE OF GRANT Project funding; staff costs; capital
costs; core costs.
SAMPLE GRANTS Voice 21 (£30,000); British Youth
Council (£29,900); Clear Sky (£29,100); Wider
World (£4,700).
FINANCES *Financial year end 31/12/2022*
Grants to organisations £171,000
TRUSTEES Farah Elemara; Flore de Taisne; Harriet
Williams; Charlotte Colbert.
OTHER INFORMATION The foundation was registered
with the Charity Commission in March 2022 and
therefore accounts were not available to view.
The grant total and beneficiaries have been
taken from the foundation's website.
HOW TO APPLY Apply online via the foundation's
website, where information on new funding calls
can also be found.
CONTACT DETAILS Grants Team, 6 Cobb Street,
London E1 7LB *Email* info@islafoundation.com
Website https://islafoundation.com

■ The Isle of Anglesey Charitable Association (Cymdeithas Elusennol Ynys Môn)
CC NO 1174536   **ESTABLISHED** 1990
WHERE FUNDING CAN BE GIVEN Isle of Anglesey.
WHO CAN BENEFIT Registered charities; constituted
community groups; social enterprises; other not-
for-profit organisations.
WHAT IS FUNDED General charitable purposes.
WHAT IS NOT FUNDED Political parties; party-political
campaigning or lobbying; non-charitable
activities; projects that do not comply with
charity law. See the website for full eligibility
criteria.
TYPE OF GRANT Core costs; capital costs.
RANGE OF GRANTS Small grants of £8,000 or less;
large grants of up to £30,000 with the
occasional larger amount.
SAMPLE GRANTS Menter Mechell (£35,000); Ardal
Chwarae Llangaffo and Parc y Plant Niwbwrch
(£30,000 each); Cwm Cadnant Community
Council and Mencap Môn (£20,000 each);
Amlwch Snooker Club, Girl Guiding Anglesey and
St Davids Hospice (£8,000 each).
FINANCES *Financial year end 30/09/2021*
Income £553,700
Grants to organisations £720,100
Assets £95,300
TRUSTEES Dr Edward Jones; Elen Jones; Trefor
Owen; Ann Tooze; Deborah Chafer; Dr Lowri
Hughes; Dafydd Roberts; Trefor Hughes; Gary
Pritchard; Non Dafydd; Neville Evans; Jackie
Lewis.
OTHER INFORMATION The 2020/21 accounts are the
latest available at the time of writing (May
2023).

Think carefully about every application. Is it justified?

465

HOW TO APPLY At the time of writing (July 2023), applications were not being accepted as a new online application system was being implemented. The charity was due to re-open to applications in autumn 2023 – refer to the website for updates. Full eligibility criteria and guidance are also available on the website.

CONTACT DETAILS Annwen Morgan, Trust Secretary, Cyngor Sir Ynys Mon, Swyddfeydd y Cyngor, Llangefni, Isle of Anglesey LL77 7TW
Tel. 01248 750057 *Email* post@elusennol.org
Website www.elusennol.org

■ Isle of Wight Foundation

CC NO 1163489   **ESTABLISHED** 2013
WHERE FUNDING CAN BE GIVEN Isle of Wight.
WHO CAN BENEFIT Registered charities; not-for-profit organisations; CICs; voluntary and community groups.
WHAT IS FUNDED Access to employment; community development and services; citizenship.
WHAT IS NOT FUNDED Projects or activities that do not meet any of the foundation's aims and criteria; any costs incurred when putting together a grant application; retrospective activities; political or religious activities; day-to-day operating costs (for example, utility bills, council tax, rent and insurance); land or building projects where the ownership or lease is not yet in place (including any planning permissions); ongoing staff costs; projects or activities that the state or a statutory body has a legal obligation to provide; projects that cannot be completed within 12 months of the date of the letter confirming the grant; individuals.
TYPE OF GRANT Project costs (including salaries related to the project); capital costs.
RANGE OF GRANTS £3,000 to £16,000.
SAMPLE GRANTS Wight Search and Rescue (£16,000); Pan Together (£15,600); Wessex Cancer Trust (£12,900); Havenstreet Community Association and Sandown and Shanklin Independent Lifeboat (£7,200 each); The Phoenix Project (£5,300); The Common Space (£5,000); Arreton Cricket Club (£4,900); St Helens Community Centre (£4,700); Home-Start (£3,500); Ryde Sea Cadets (£3,100).
FINANCES *Financial year end 31/12/2021*
Income £80,000
Grants to organisations £85,300
Assets £13,400
TRUSTEES Arnaud Judet; Robert Gillespie; Emma Scott; John Sunderland.
OTHER INFORMATION Grants were awarded to 11 organisations in 2021.
HOW TO APPLY Calls for applications are usually issued in February, with the closing date for applications falling around the beginning of May. Shortlisted projects are visited by a member of the funding panel between June and August. Grants are announced and awarded in December and paid the following January.
CONTACT DETAILS Samantha O'Rourke, Foundation Supervisor, Islands Roads, St Christopher House, 42 Daish Way, Newport, Isle of Wight PO30 5XJ *Tel.* 020 3006 4700
Email IWFoundation@IslandRoads.com
Website https://islandroads.com/iw-foundation

■ The ITF Seafarers Trust

CC NO 281936   **ESTABLISHED** 1981
WHERE FUNDING CAN BE GIVEN Worldwide.
WHO CAN BENEFIT Registered charities; educational institutions; trade unions; NGOs.
WHAT IS FUNDED The welfare, health and education of seafarers, their families and dependants.
WHAT IS NOT FUNDED Retrospective funding for completed projects; deficits which have already been incurred; projects which promote particular religious beliefs; recurring costs.
TYPE OF GRANT Capital costs; core costs; project funding; research.
RANGE OF GRANTS Small grants (£500 to £75,000); large grants (over £75,000).
SAMPLE GRANTS Associated Philippine Seafarers' Union (£1.5 million); World Maritime University (£532,000); Fondazione Centro Internazionale Radio Medico (£259,700); Independent Federation of Myanmar Seafarers (£87,600); The Chirp Charitable Trust (£60,000); Care Ashore (£40,000); Associazione Stella Maris Livorno (£26,000); Federazione Nazionale Stella Maris (£15,000).
FINANCES *Financial year end 31/12/2021*
Income £1,260,000
Grants to organisations £4,960,000
Assets £44,330,000
TRUSTEES Padraig Crumlin; Brian Orrell; Stephen Cotton; Jacqueline Smith; Dave Heindel; Maya Schwiegershausen-Guth.
OTHER INFORMATION Grants were awarded to around 71 organisations during the year.
HOW TO APPLY All applications must be made online. Refer to the funder's website for further information.
CONTACT DETAILS The Trustees, ITF House, 49–60 Borough Road, London SE1 1DR
Tel. 020 7403 2733 *Email* info@seafarerstrust.org *Website* www.seafarerstrust.org

■ The Ithaca Trust

CC NO 1145502   **ESTABLISHED** 2012
WHERE FUNDING CAN BE GIVEN Greater London.
WHO CAN BENEFIT Registered charities.
WHAT IS FUNDED Humanitarian causes; the environment and wildlife; arts productions and students.
SAMPLE GRANTS UNICEF (£45,000); Conservation Collective – Argolic Gulf Project (£8,700); The Quay Theatre (£5,000); Médecins Sans Frontières (£1,500); War Child UK (£1,200).
FINANCES *Financial year end 31/12/2021*
Income £58,700
Grants to organisations £69,400
Assets £1,560,000
TRUSTEES James Midgley; Ralph Fiennes; Julian Wadham.
HOW TO APPLY Apply in writing to the correspondent.
CONTACT DETAILS The Trustees, 6th Floor, 2 London Wall Place, London EC2Y 5AU *Tel.* 020 7429 4100

■ The J. A. R. Charitable Trust

CC NO 248418 **ESTABLISHED** 1966
WHERE FUNDING CAN BE GIVEN Worldwide.
WHO CAN BENEFIT Registered charities; places of worship.
WHAT IS FUNDED Advancement of the Roman Catholic Church; provision of education for people under 30; relief in need for people over 55.
WHAT IS NOT FUNDED Individuals.
RANGE OF GRANTS £500 to £5,000.
SAMPLE GRANTS The Passage (£4,000); Little Sisters of the Poor (£3,000); Marriage Care (£2,000); Maryvale (£1,000).
FINANCES *Financial year end 05/04/2022*
Income £117,700
Grants to organisations £76,500
Assets £5,620,000
TRUSTEES The Revd Canon Paschal Ryan; Benedict Noble; The Revd Martin Boland.
OTHER INFORMATION Grants were awarded to 26 organisations during the year.
HOW TO APPLY The trustees identify projects and organisations they wish to support; they do not accept unsolicited applications.
CONTACT DETAILS Wilfrid Vernor-Miles, c/o Hunters Solicitors, 9 New Square, London WC2A 3QN *Tel.* 020 7412 0050 *Email* wilfrid.vernormiles@hunterslaw.com

■ The J. and J. Benevolent Foundation

CC NO 1146602 **ESTABLISHED** 2012
WHERE FUNDING CAN BE GIVEN England.
WHO CAN BENEFIT Charitable organisations; individuals.
WHAT IS FUNDED Orthodox Jewish religious causes; education; social welfare.
RANGE OF GRANTS £10,000 to £30,000.
SAMPLE GRANTS Achisomoch Aid Company Ltd (£30,000); Friends of Mercaz Hatorah Belz Macnivka (£28,000); Tomchei Yotzei Anglia (£17,000); Friends of Mir Charitable Trust (£10,000).
FINANCES *Financial year end 31/03/2022*
Income £147,000
Grants to organisations £108,600
Assets £91,800
TRUSTEES Joseph Adler; Judi Adler.
OTHER INFORMATION In 2021/22, grants totalling £108,600 were made to five organisations.
HOW TO APPLY Apply to the trustees in writing.
CONTACT DETAILS The Trustees, c/o Cohen Arnold, New Burlington House, 1075 Finchley Road, London NW11 0PU *Tel.* 020 8731 0777 *Email* mail@cohenarnold.com

■ J. J. Charitable Trust

CC NO 1015792 **ESTABLISHED** 1989
WHERE FUNDING CAN BE GIVEN UK and overseas.
WHO CAN BENEFIT UK-registered charities.
WHAT IS FUNDED Literacy; sustainable lifestyles; environmental projects in the UK and Africa; innovative projects.

WHAT IS NOT FUNDED Individuals; educational fees; expeditions.
TYPE OF GRANT Seed funding; development funding; project funding; core costs.
RANGE OF GRANTS Up to £330,000, but typically between £1,000 and £60,000.
SAMPLE GRANTS Purpose Disruptors (£332,000); Perspectiva (£200,000); Client Earth (£83,000); Christian Aid and On Road Media (£50,000 each); People and Planet (£30,000); C40 Cities Climate Leadership Group (£25,000); The Social Change Nest (£10,000); Move Beyond Words CIC (£1,000).
FINANCES *Financial year end 05/04/2022*
Income £777,800
Grants to organisations £1,280,000
Assets £53,100,000
TRUSTEES Lucy Guard; John Sainsbury; Mark Sainsbury; Claudia Gonella.
OTHER INFORMATION The trust is one of the Sainsbury Family Charitable Trusts, which share a common administration – see www.sftc.org.uk for more information. During the year, grants were made for the following purposes: the environment – UK (£826,000), general charitable purposes (£60,000) and literacy (£30,000). The list of beneficiaries relates to grants approved (rather than paid) during the year, some of which are payable over multiple years.
HOW TO APPLY Funding enquiries can be submitted online. Generally applications should be sent by post to the Sainsbury Family Charitable Trusts, or by email to proposals@sfct.org.uk. Details of what to include can be found on the website. The website stresses that the vast majority of applications are unsuccessful. If your proposal is a candidate for support, you will hear from the trust within eight weeks.
CONTACT DETAILS Karen Everett, Chief Operating Officer, The Peak, 5 Wilton Road, London SW1V 1AP *Tel.* 020 7410 0330 *Email* info@sfct.org.uk *Website* www.sfct.org.uk/the-jj-charitable-trust

■ The Jabbs Foundation

CC NO 1128402 **ESTABLISHED** 2009
WHERE FUNDING CAN BE GIVEN UK, with a preference for the West Midlands, particularly Birmingham.
WHO CAN BENEFIT Registered charities; universities; educational and research institutions; women's centres.
WHAT IS FUNDED Medical research; education (including educational activities by arts organisations); family and community relationships in the West Midlands; supporting vulnerable members of society; the prevention of people entering the criminal justice system; research into the health of trees and forests.
TYPE OF GRANT Research; capital costs; core costs; salaries.
RANGE OF GRANTS Up to £5 million.
SAMPLE GRANTS Birmingham Institute of Forest Research (£5 million); University of Birmingham (£153,300); University of Birmingham – Acute Mountain Sickness (£71,500); St Basil's (£60,000); Recre8now (£26,100).
FINANCES *Financial year end 31/08/2021*
Income £6,040,000
Grants to organisations £5,380,000
Assets £1,110,000
TRUSTEES Robin Daniels; Alexander Wright; Ruth Keighley.
OTHER INFORMATION The 2020/21 accounts were the latest available at the time of writing (May 2023). Grants to organisations were broken

down as follows: tree/forest research and tree planting (£5.15 million); social welfare (£146,400); medical research (£71,500); work within the criminal justice system (£16,600); education (£10,000). Grants of less than £50,000 totalled £70,200.

HOW TO APPLY The foundation's 2020/21 annual report and accounts state: 'The JABBS Foundation does not encourage speculative grant requests, but the trustees read all applications that are received and consider these against the five priority areas'.

CONTACT DETAILS The Trustees, PO Box 16067, Birmingham, West Midlands B32 9GP *Tel.* 0121 428 2593 *Email* office@harborneoffice.co.uk

---

■ JAC Trust

CC NO 1189523
WHERE FUNDING CAN BE GIVEN UK and overseas.
WHO CAN BENEFIT Charitable organisations.
WHAT IS FUNDED Support for people forcibly displaced due to climate change, and their host communities.
SAMPLE GRANTS Afghan Relief and Sustainable Development (£59,900); Community Health and Sustainable Environment (CHASE) Africa (£30,000); Community Needs Initiative (£29,200); People's Planet Project (£27,600); Cameroon Gender and Environmental Watch (£26,400); Food for the Hungry (£26,000); Afghanistan and Central Asian Association and The Felix Project (£15,000 each).
FINANCES *Financial year end* 31/12/2021
Income £159,800
Grants to organisations £458,600
Assets £11,740,000
TRUSTEES Aidan Pelly; Odette Campbell; William Pym; Dulma Clark; Andrew Pym; David Linehan.
HOW TO APPLY Apply via the trust's website.
CONTACT DETAILS The Trustees, 43B Grange Road, Street BA16 0AY *Email* hello@jaclarktrust.org *Website* www.jaclarktrust.org

---

■ The Sir Barry Jackson County Fund

CC NO 517306   **ESTABLISHED** 1985
WHERE FUNDING CAN BE GIVEN Birmingham, Coventry, Dudley, Sandwell, Solihull, Walsall and Wolverhampton.
WHO CAN BENEFIT Registered charities; theatres; CICs; touring companies.
WHAT IS FUNDED Small-scale, touring and educational theatre projects. There are three different funds available: The County Fund, which funds productions of plays suitable for urban audiences with little or no previous theatre experience; The Hornton Fund, which develops talent (including acting and writing) in children and young people under the age of 25; and The Sir Barry Jackson Trust Fund, which commissions new work and supports Birmingham Repertory Theatre.
WHAT IS NOT FUNDED Individuals.
TYPE OF GRANT Project funding; capital costs.
RANGE OF GRANTS Typically up to £5,000.
SAMPLE GRANTS Birmingham Rep – Grimeboy (£65,000); Tour Park Bench (£5,000); Belgrade Theatre, Told by an Idiot and Vamos Theatre (£3,000 each); Box of Tricks Theatre (£2,500); Cloud Cuckoo Land Theatre Ltd (£2,000); Midland Actors Theatre with Purbanat Theatre (£1,500).

FINANCES *Financial year end* 05/04/2022
Income £95,500
Grants to organisations £94,200
Assets £2,380,000
TRUSTEES Roger Burman; Anthony Chorley; David Edgar; Ian King; Deborah Shaw; Graham Winteringham; Prof. Claire Cochrane; Linda Morgan; Graham Saunders; Amelia Ladbrook; Michael Hibbs.
OTHER INFORMATION Grants were made to 12 organisations in 2021/22.
HOW TO APPLY Application and contact details forms are available from the correspondent or to download from the website. Applications are usually considered twice a year, in January and June, and should be submitted no later than 1 December and 1 May, respectively. Further information and guidance on how to apply, the funds available and application guidelines can be found at www.birmingham-rep.co.uk/we-are-the-rep/the-sir-barry-jackson-trust.html.
CONTACT DETAILS Stephen Gill, Hon. Secretary, c/o Birmingham Repertory Theatre Ltd, Centenary Square, Broad Street, Birmingham, West Midlands B1 2EP *Tel.* 01983 617842 *Email* sbjt@outlook.com *Website* www.sirbarryjacksoncountyfund.org.uk

---

■ The Frank Jackson Foundation

CC NO 1007600   **ESTABLISHED** 1992
WHERE FUNDING CAN BE GIVEN South Africa and UK, with a preference for Suffolk.
WHO CAN BENEFIT Schools; colleges; universities; charitable organisations.
WHAT IS FUNDED Education; teacher training; environmental research.
TYPE OF GRANT Research; unrestricted.
RANGE OF GRANTS Up to £91,000 but typically between £7,500 and £50,000.
SAMPLE GRANTS Oriel College Development Trust (£91,700); Cordwalles Preparatory School (£81,400); Clifton Preparatory (£75,600); The Sozo Foundation (£36,000); The Learning Trust (£51,100); Western Cape Primary Science Programme (£23,900); Green Light Trust (£15,000); Winston Churchill Memorial Trust (£10,000); Protect PMB (£7,200).
FINANCES *Financial year end* 05/04/2022
Income £454,100
Grants to organisations £778,000
Assets £28,440,000
TRUSTEES Timothy Seymour; David Tennant; Mary-Anne Gribbon; Leila Brown; Mark Sargeantson.
OTHER INFORMATION Grants were made to 36 organisations during the year. Grants of less than £10,000 totalled £13,700.
HOW TO APPLY The foundation's website states that it does not accept unsolicited applications. However, the foundation does welcome enquiries if an organisation believes it meets the criteria. In this case, a short enquiry that summarises in a paragraph how your work meets the criteria should be emailed to the trustees.
CONTACT DETAILS Lisa Mills, Administrator, 24 Taylor Way, Great Baddow, Chelmsford, Essex CM2 8ZG *Email* frankjacksonfoundation@live.co.uk *Website* www.frankjacksonfoundation.org.uk

---

■ The Jagclif Charitable Trust

CC NO 1163459   **ESTABLISHED** 2015
WHERE FUNDING CAN BE GIVEN UK and overseas.
WHO CAN BENEFIT Charitable organisations.
WHAT IS FUNDED General charitable purposes.

SAMPLE GRANTS Ark (£2.82 million); Brainwaves (£100,000); British Fashion Council Foundation (£15,000); Macmillan Cancer Support (£10,000); Somerset House (£5,000).

FINANCES *Financial year end* 30/06/2022
Income £21,970,000
Grants to organisations £6,820,000
Assets £66,790,000

TRUSTEES Duncan Eriksen; Ernesto Fragomeni; Claudia Wace; Ian Wace; John Vincent; Robert Brown.

HOW TO APPLY Apply in writing to the correspondent.

CONTACT DETAILS The Trustees, c/o Marshall Wace Asset Management, George House, 131 Sloane Street, London SW1X 9AT *Tel.* 020 7316 2280 *Email* jagclif@mwam.com

---

■ John James Bristol Foundation

CC NO 288417   **ESTABLISHED** 1983

WHERE FUNDING CAN BE GIVEN Bristol.

WHO CAN BENEFIT Registered charities; exempt charities; social enterprises; CICs.

WHAT IS FUNDED Education; health; older people; general charitable purposes.

WHAT IS NOT FUNDED Individuals.

TYPE OF GRANT Capital costs; seed funding/start-up funding; unrestricted funding.

RANGE OF GRANTS Up to £250,000, but generally below £10,000.

SAMPLE GRANTS The Park (£250,000); Bristol Music Trust (£119,000); Royal West of England Academy (£76,300); Impermanence Dance (£45,000); Bristol Grammar School (£30,000); Lifeskills Learning (£20,000); Room 13 Hareclive (£7,000); Ups and Downs (£3,300).

FINANCES *Financial year end* 30/09/2022
Income £1,350,000
Grants to organisations £2,820,000
Assets £81,430,000

TRUSTEES Elizabeth Chambers; John Evans; Dr John Haworth; David Johnson; Joan Johnson; Andrew Jardine; Andrew Webley; Peter Goodwin; Nicola Parker; Julia Norton.

OTHER INFORMATION Grants were broken down as follows: education (£1.15 million); health (£1.13 million); older people (£536,000); general (£1,000). Only grants of over £3,000 were listed as beneficiaries in the foundation's accounts. Unlisted grants of £3,000 or less totalled £242,800.

HOW TO APPLY Apply in writing via post or email. Full information on what should be included in an application can be found on the foundation's website.

CONTACT DETAILS Louise O'Donnell, Chief Executive, 7 Clyde Road, Redland, Bristol BS6 6RG *Tel.* 0117 923 9444 *Email* info@johnjames.org.uk *Website* www.johnjames.org.uk

---

■ The Susan and Stephen James Charitable Settlement

CC NO 801622   **ESTABLISHED** 1988

WHERE FUNDING CAN BE GIVEN UK.

WHO CAN BENEFIT Charitable organisations.

WHAT IS FUNDED The Jewish faith and community; health.

SAMPLE GRANTS Community Security Trust (£20,000); Chai Cancer Care (£12,500); JW3 (£5,000); Lifelites (£1,000); Israel Guide Dog Centre (£800).

FINANCES *Financial year end* 31/12/2021
Income £98,500
Grants to organisations £101,800
Assets £17,000

TRUSTEES Stephen James; Susan James.

OTHER INFORMATION Grants were made to 17 organisations.

HOW TO APPLY Applications can be made in writing to the correspondent, although the charity has previously stated that unsolicited applications are not generally considered.

CONTACT DETAILS Stephen James, Trustee, 4 Turner Drive, London NW11 6TX *Tel.* 020 7486 5838

■ Lady Eda Jardine Charitable Trust

OSCR NO SC011599   **ESTABLISHED** 1960

WHERE FUNDING CAN BE GIVEN Scotland.

WHO CAN BENEFIT Charitable organisations; hospices; churches; universities.

WHAT IS FUNDED In addition to supporting a number of specific organisations (The Heriot-Watt College, University of Edinburgh, The Edinburgh Festival of Music and Drama and The National Trust in Scotland), the trustees select a different charitable sector to support each year. The trustees elected to support children and young people in 2019/20, heritage, conservation, the environment, gardens and the arts in 2020/21 and health and disability in 2021/22.

RANGE OF GRANTS Mostly up to £5,000.

SAMPLE GRANTS Seawilding (£10,000); University of Edinburgh (£6,000); National Trust for Scotland (£5,000); Alzheimer's Research UK (£3,000); Carer's Scotland (£2,000); Care for Carers (£1,000).

FINANCES *Financial year end* 05/04/2022
Income £53,500
Grants to organisations £81,500
Assets £2,290,000

OTHER INFORMATION Grants were made to 37 organisations during the year.

HOW TO APPLY Contact the correspondent regarding the funding focus for the year. Applications should be made in writing to the correspondent.

CONTACT DETAILS The Trustees, c/o Anderson Strathern LLP, 1 Rutland Court, Edinburgh EH3 8EY

■ Jay Education Trust

CC NO 1116458   **ESTABLISHED** 2006

WHERE FUNDING CAN BE GIVEN UK.

WHO CAN BENEFIT Jewish organisations; educational and religious establishments.

WHAT IS FUNDED The Jewish faith and community.

RANGE OF GRANTS Up to £200,500.

SAMPLE GRANTS CML (£200,500); Amud Hatzdoka (£58,400); Edupoor Ltd (£24,000); Rise and Shine (£19,000); Wlodowa Charity and Rehabilitation Trust (£10,000); Merkaz Hatorah and The ABC Trust (£7,500 each).

FINANCES *Financial year end* 31/07/2021
Income £1,290,000
Grants to organisations £489,200
Grants to individuals £95,400
Assets £5,970,000

TRUSTEES Aron Nezri; David Weis; Elimelech Bindinger; Rabbi Eli Schwartz.

OTHER INFORMATION The 2020/21 accounts were the latest available at the time of writing (May 2023).

HOW TO APPLY Apply in writing to the correspondent.

CONTACT DETAILS The Trustees, Jay Education Trust, 21 Grosvenor Way, London E5 9ND *Tel.* 0161 798 1660

CONTACT DETAILS The Trustees, 2 Copse Gate, Winslow, Buckingham, Buckinghamshire MK18 3HX *Tel.* 01296 715466

■ The JD Foundation

CC NO 1167090　ESTABLISHED 2015
WHERE FUNDING CAN BE GIVEN UK.
WHO CAN BENEFIT Registered charities.
WHAT IS FUNDED Disadvantaged children and young people including mental health and homelessness charities; the environment.
SAMPLE GRANTS Blueprint 4 All; Bolton Wanderers; Buddies of the Birches; Cardiac Risk in the Young; HideOut; Kidscape; Manchester Youth Zone; Mountain Rescue England and Wales; Once Upon A Smile; Papyrus; Sacriston Youth Project; Salford Foundation; Scottish Mountain Rescue; Smiling Families; Sport 4 Life UK; The Wellspring; YoungMinds.
FINANCES *Financial year end* 31/01/2022
Income £662,200
Grants to organisations £475,500
Assets £390,000
TRUSTEES Mawdsley Siobhan; Traci Corrie; Neil Greenhalgh; Nigel Keen; Christopher Stephenson.
OTHER INFORMATION Support is given to Mountain Rescue as well nominated youth and environmental charities. Grants were broken down as follows: young people (£225,200); health (£87,800); mountain rescue (£67,000); social services (£43,700); other (£29,400); education (£22,500).
HOW TO APPLY Contact the foundation for further information.
CONTACT DETAILS The Trustees, JD Sports Fashion, Edinburgh House, Hollins Brook Way, Bury BL9 8RR *Tel.* 0161 767 1000 *Email* thejdfoundation@jdplc.com *Website* www.jdsports.co.uk/page/jd-foundation

■ The Roger and Jean Jefcoate Trust

CC NO 1096211　ESTABLISHED 1983
WHERE FUNDING CAN BE GIVEN Milton Keynes, Buckinghamshire and the adjacent counties.
WHO CAN BENEFIT Registered charities.
WHAT IS FUNDED Health and well-being, especially advice and practical help for people with hidden disabilities such as dementia or mental health conditions; older people; carers.
TYPE OF GRANT Running costs; general funding; capital projects; project costs.
RANGE OF GRANTS Typically £3,000 to £10,000.
SAMPLE GRANTS Holy Trinity Church – Drayton Parslow (£10,000); West Cumbria Society for the Blind (£8,000); South Central Ambulance Charity (£7,000); Mind – Buckinghamshire (£6,000); Alive (£5,000) Winter Night Shelter – Milton Keynes (£4,000); Palz UK (£3,000).
FINANCES *Financial year end* 31/10/2022
Income £894,300
Grants to organisations £191,000
Assets £5,880,000
TRUSTEES Vivien Dinning; Roger Jefcoate; Carol Wemyss; Alistair Wemyss; Kathryn Hobbs; Catharine Parouty.
OTHER INFORMATION During 2021/22, grants were awarded to 34 charities.
HOW TO APPLY Apply in writing to the correspondent. The trustees meet at least twice annually to discuss applications.

■ The Jenour Foundation

CC NO 256637　ESTABLISHED 1968
WHERE FUNDING CAN BE GIVEN UK, with a special interest in Wales.
WHO CAN BENEFIT Registered charities only.
WHAT IS FUNDED General charitable purposes including: health causes; medical research; young people; arts and culture; animal welfare.
TYPE OF GRANT Capital projects.
RANGE OF GRANTS Up to £8,000 but typically between £1,000 and £5,000.
SAMPLE GRANTS UWC Atlantic College (£8,000); Macmillan Cancer Support (£6,000); The Prince's Trust in Wales (£5,000); Dreams and Wishes (£3,500); Crohn's and Colitis UK (£2,000); The Duke of Edinburgh's Award (£1,000).
FINANCES *Financial year end* 05/04/2022
Income £129,000
Grants to organisations £109,300
Assets £4,810,000
TRUSTEES James Zorab; Christopher Davies; Greer Hooper.
OTHER INFORMATION In 2021/22, the foundation awarded 42 grants to organisations.
HOW TO APPLY The trustees request that written applications are submitted to the registered office.
CONTACT DETAILS The Trustees, c/o Azets, Ty Derw, Lime Tree Court, Mulberry Drive, Cardiff Gate Business Park, Cardiff CF23 8AB *Tel.* 029 2054 9939 *Email* debbie.wassell@azets.co.uk

■ The Jephcott Charitable Trust

CC NO 240915　ESTABLISHED 1965
WHERE FUNDING CAN BE GIVEN Worldwide.
WHO CAN BENEFIT Charitable organisations.
WHAT IS FUNDED Health; education; the natural environment.
WHAT IS NOT FUNDED Organisations or charities where there are excessive administration costs; charities or organisations which have excessive reserves or liquid assets; heritage or preservation; projects solely focused on animal welfare and/or relief of poverty; general appeals for a large national charity or organisation; individuals and expedition groups; promotion of religion.
TYPE OF GRANT Capital costs; project funding.
RANGE OF GRANTS Grants range from £2,000 to £10,000 and, in exceptional cases, up to £20,000.
SAMPLE GRANTS Nick Weber Trust (£10,000); Eduspots (£7,000); Prodigal Bikes (£5,800); Karen Hill Tribes (£5,000); Child Action Nepal (£1,800).
FINANCES *Financial year end* 30/06/2022
Income £47,100
Grants to organisations £121,000
Assets £7,880,000
TRUSTEES Lady Mary Jephcott; Mark Jephcott; Keith Morgan; Dr David Thomas; James Parker; Christopher Parker; Stephen Lamdin; Corjanne Drimmelen.
OTHER INFORMATION Grants were made to 16 organisations during the year.
HOW TO APPLY Full and detailed guidelines and application forms can be downloaded from the trust's website. Applications are considered at

the trustees' meetings which are held in April and October.

CONTACT DETAILS The Secretary, The Threshing Barn, Ford, Kingsbridge, Devon TQ7 2LN *Website* www.jephcottcharitabletrust.org.uk

....

■ The Jerusalem Trust

CC NO 285696 **ESTABLISHED** 1982
WHERE FUNDING CAN BE GIVEN Worldwide.
WHO CAN BENEFIT Registered charities.
WHAT IS FUNDED Christian evangelism and relief work overseas; Christian media and education; evangelism and Christian mission in the UK. The trust also runs a small grants programme to commission new artwork for churches.
WHAT IS NOT FUNDED Building or repair work for churches; individuals.
TYPE OF GRANT Core costs; salaries; project funding; capacity building.
SAMPLE GRANTS Jerusalem Productions Ltd (£485,000); Tearfund (£295,000); Bristol CCRC Trust (£120,000); Youthscape (£100,000); Evangelical Alliance (£60,000); Transforming Lives for Good (£50,000); University of Durham – St John's College (£21,000); Biblica (£10,000).
FINANCES *Financial year end* 05/04/2022
Income £2,780,000
Grants to organisations £3,350,000
Assets £116,350,000
TRUSTEES Prof. Peter Frankopan; Lady Susan Sainsbury; Melanie Townsend; David Wright; Mark Browning.
OTHER INFORMATION The trust is one of the Sainsbury Family Charitable Trusts, which share a common administration – see www.sftc.org.uk for more information. During 2021/22, 113 grants were approved in the following categories: evangelism and Christian mission in the UK (£2 million); Christian evangelism and relief work overseas (£915,300); Christian media (£399,800); Christian education (£325,800).
HOW TO APPLY A funding enquiry can be made via the Sainsbury Family Charitable Trusts' website.
CONTACT DETAILS The Trustees, The Peak, 5 Wilton Road, London SW1V 1AP *Tel.* 020 7410 0330 *Email* info@sfct.org.uk *Website* www.sfct.org.uk/the-jerusalem-trust

....

■ Jewish Child's Day

CC NO 209266 **ESTABLISHED** 1947
WHERE FUNDING CAN BE GIVEN UK; Israel; overseas.
WHO CAN BENEFIT Registered charities providing equipment or services of direct benefit to Jewish children (up to the age of 18).
WHAT IS FUNDED Jewish children aged 18 and under who are living in difficult circumstances due to poverty, abuse, neglect, physical disabilities, learning challenges, educational barriers and emotional issues.
TYPE OF GRANT Items of equipment; project funding.
RANGE OF GRANTS Generally £1,000 to £5,000, with occasional larger grants.
SAMPLE GRANTS Grants awarded in the UK included: Ezra Umarpeh (£39,500); Hasmonean Charitable Trust (£10,000); Art Therapies and Teen Action (£5,000 each); Success Stories UK (£3,000); The London Reading Centre (£2,800); Blooming Blossoms (£1,100).
FINANCES *Financial year end* 30/06/2021
Income £1,130,000
Grants to organisations £783,900
Assets £2,100,000

TRUSTEES Virginia Campus; David Collins; Frankie Epstein; Gaby Lazarus; Joy Moss; Stephen Moss; Charles Spungin; Melvyn Orton; Gary Cohen.
OTHER INFORMATION Grants were distributed as follows: Israel (£255,400); UK (£126,700); the rest of the world (£27,800). The 2020/21 accounts were the latest available at the time of writing (May 2023).
HOW TO APPLY Contact the correspondent for further information on applying for a grant.
CONTACT DETAILS Adele Busse, Grants Manager, 1st Floor, Elscot House, Arcadia Avenue, London N3 2JU *Tel.* 020 8446 8804 *Email* adele.busse@jcd.uk.com *Website* https://jcd.uk.com/grants

....

■ The Jewish Youth Fund

CC NO 251902 **ESTABLISHED** 1937
WHERE FUNDING CAN BE GIVEN UK.
WHO CAN BENEFIT Jewish organisations.
WHAT IS FUNDED Jewish youth work projects.
TYPE OF GRANT Projects and equipment. Loans may be offered towards the cost of building. The charity can provide start-up costs as well as subsequent funding.
RANGE OF GRANTS Mostly up to £10,000.
SAMPLE GRANTS Union of Jewish Students (£12,500); University of Jewish Chaplaincy (£10,000); Federation of Zionist Youth (£7,500); Keren (£5,000); Lubavitch of Edgeware (£2,500); TAL (£1,000).
FINANCES *Financial year end* 30/09/2022
Income £61,900
Grants to organisations £113,800
Assets £3,640,000
TRUSTEES Adam Rose; Philippa Strauss; Joseph Woolf; Lea Helman; Robin Moss; Joshua Marks.
OTHER INFORMATION Grants awarded during the year were broken down as follows: recreation and leisure (£67,800); the advancement of religion (£27,500); the prevention or relief of poverty (£18,500).
HOW TO APPLY Applications can be made on a form available online. Applicants should enclose a copy of their latest accounts and annual report. For the most up-to-date submission deadline, consult the charity's website.
CONTACT DETAILS The Trustees, 35 Ballards Lane, London N3 1XW *Tel.* 07812 144576 *Email* info@jyf.org.uk *Website* www.jyf.org.uk

....

■ Joffe Charitable Trust CIO

CC NO 1180520 **ESTABLISHED** 1968
WHERE FUNDING CAN BE GIVEN Worldwide; lower-income countries.
WHO CAN BENEFIT Registered charities.
WHAT IS FUNDED Strengthening integrity in the UK's international financial systems; building stronger not-for-profit organisations.
TYPE OF GRANT Grants for up to three years; development funding; project costs; core costs; unrestricted funding; start-up funding.
RANGE OF GRANTS From £5,000 to £30,000 per year for up to three years.
SAMPLE GRANTS Good Jobs First (£50,000); Airwars (£30,000); Athena Foundation (£25,000); Death Penalty Project Charitable Trust (£15,000); Spotlight on Corruption (£5,000).
FINANCES *Financial year end* 31/12/2021
Income £231,800
Grants to organisations £910,000
Assets £10,670,000

TRUSTEES Dame Barbara Frost; Frances Longley; Nicholas Perks; Ruth Taylor; Jameela Raymond; Abigail Deffee; David Nussbaum.

HOW TO APPLY The charity is a relatively small charitable trust and can only make a few new grants each year. Most of the initiatives it funds come through its existing networks. However, the trust welcomes enquiries from applicants whose work is in line with the trust's objectives. Full details of how to approach the charity can be found on its website.

CONTACT DETAILS Abigail Prabhakar, Trust Manager, 4th Floor, Invicta House, 108–114 Golden Lane, London EC1Y OTL *Email* info@joffetrust.org *Website* https://joffetrust.org

■ The Elton John AIDS Foundation

CC NO 1017336   **ESTABLISHED** 1993
WHERE FUNDING CAN BE GIVEN Worldwide.
WHO CAN BENEFIT Registered charities; community-based organisations.
WHAT IS FUNDED HIV welfare and prevention; health and the saving of lives; the prevention or relief of poverty; overseas aid; LGBTQ+ rights; health advice and addiction; advocacy and campaigning.
WHAT IS NOT FUNDED Exclusions vary for each programme. Check the foundation's website for full details.
TYPE OF GRANT Programme dependent.
RANGE OF GRANTS Up to £3 million.
SAMPLE GRANTS Regional Public Fund (£2.99 million); Charity Foundation Tomsk-AntiAIDS (£2.11 million); Praekelt (£1.72 million); Lambeth Borough Council (£1.33 million); Triggerise (£1.08 million); Zipline (£756,000); AFEW International Uzbekistan (£412,600).
FINANCES *Financial year end* 31/12/2021
Income £10,020,000
Grants to organisations £9,640,000
Assets £11,600,000
TRUSTEES David Furnish; Dr Mark Dybul; Tracy Blackwell; Ilana Kloss; Ajaz Ahmed; Dr Eric Goosby; Samuel Segar; Sandra Lee; Emma Kane; Tani Austin; Kevin Martinez; Chris Cooper.
OTHER INFORMATION During the year, grants were awarded to 87 organisations in 54 countries.
HOW TO APPLY Application information and guidelines vary for each programme – see the foundation's website for full details.
CONTACT DETAILS The Trustees, Work.Life Hammersmith, Kings House, 174 Hammersmith Road, London W6 7JP *Tel.* 020 7603 9996 *Email* admin@eltonjohnaidsfoundation.org *Website* http://london.ejaf.org/grants

■ John Lewis and Partners Foundation

CC NO 1118162
WHERE FUNDING CAN BE GIVEN UK and overseas (particularly areas relevant to the John Lewis business).
WHO CAN BENEFIT Registered charities; non-registered voluntary organisations; CICs; hospices.
WHAT IS FUNDED Education and training; employability; health care; community development; the environment; children and young people; recreation facilities; childcare facilities.

SAMPLE GRANTS Grassmarket Community Project; Pop Up Enterprises; Smartworks; The Feed; Voices of Hope.
FINANCES *Financial year end* 31/01/2022
Income £853,600
Grants to organisations £475,000
Assets £1,020,000
TRUSTEES Margaret Porteous; Paul Buchanan; Sarah Gillard; Simon Bishop; Johnathan Marsh; Nyika Brain; Andrew Hoad; Marija Rompani; Louise Stuart.
HOW TO APPLY Application forms can be requested via email.
CONTACT DETAILS The Trustees, 171 Victoria Street, London SW1E 5NN *Tel.* 020 7592 5658 *Email* trustsandfoundations@johnlewis.co.uk *Website* www.johnlewisfoundation.org

■ Lillie Johnson Charitable Trust

CC NO 326761   **ESTABLISHED** 1984
WHERE FUNDING CAN BE GIVEN UK, with a preference for the West Midlands.
WHO CAN BENEFIT Charitable organisations; hospices; hospitals.
WHAT IS FUNDED General charitable purposes, particularly health, disability and children and young people.
WHAT IS NOT FUNDED Individuals.
RANGE OF GRANTS Up to £45,000; the vast majority of grants are of £1,000 or less.
SAMPLE GRANTS L.E.C. Worcester (£40,000); West House School (£10,000); Birmingham Youth Theatre (£5,000); Birmingham St Mary's Hospice (£2,000); Time 4 Hope (£1,200); Brain Tumour Support, Little Hearts Matter and Mary Stevens Hospice (£1,000 each).
FINANCES *Financial year end* 05/04/2022
Income £172,000
Grants to organisations £176,000
Assets £7,910,000
TRUSTEES Verena Adams; John Desmond; Victor Lyttle; Lynn Brookes; Alastair Lyttle; Daniel Adams.
OTHER INFORMATION A total of 221 organisations were supported in 2021/22. Only organisations that received grants of over £1,000 were listed as beneficiaries in the charity's accounts. Grants of under £1,000 totalled £96,300 and were awarded to 198 organisations.
HOW TO APPLY Apply in writing to the correspondent. Contact the correspondent for further information before making an application.
CONTACT DETAILS John Desmond, Trustee, 39 Rodbourne Road, Harborne, Birmingham, West Midlands B17 0PN *Tel.* 07854 175530 *Email* john.w.desmond@googlemail.com

■ Johnnie Johnson Trust

CC NO 200351   **ESTABLISHED** 1961
WHERE FUNDING CAN BE GIVEN UK, with a preference for the Midlands.
WHO CAN BENEFIT Charitable organisations which provide activities for children and young people, particularly those who are disadvantaged or who have disabilities.
WHAT IS FUNDED The trust supports activities which promote the development of individuals by being either physically and/or mentally challenging. Sailing and water sports for young people in the Midlands are a priority.
TYPE OF GRANT Usually one-off, for equipment or for specific purposes.
RANGE OF GRANTS £1,000 to £16,000.

SAMPLE GRANTS Marine Society and Sea Cadets (£16,000); Thomas Morley Trust (£7,500); London Youth Rowing Ltd (£6,000); Horse Rangers Association (£5,000); Edinburgh Young Carers and In Touch/Kids United (£3,000 each); Side by Side Children Ltd (£1,800).
FINANCES *Financial year end 31/12/2021*
Income £109,200
Grants to organisations £106,400
Assets £6,560,000
TRUSTEES Jane Fordham; Peter Johnson; Katherine Cross; Christopher Johnson; Alice Johnson.
HOW TO APPLY Apply in writing to the correspondent.
CONTACT DETAILS The Trustees, The Trust Partnership Ltd, 6 Trull Farm Buildings, Tetbury, Gloucestershire GL8 8SQ *Tel.* 01285 841900

■ The Christopher and Kirsty Johnston Charitable Trust

CC NO 1159433   **ESTABLISHED** 2014
WHERE FUNDING CAN BE GIVEN UK and overseas.
WHO CAN BENEFIT Charitable organisations.
WHAT IS FUNDED General charitable purposes.
TYPE OF GRANT General funding.
RANGE OF GRANTS Up to £46,000.
SAMPLE GRANTS All Saints Chiang Mai Mission (£46,000); The Royal Opera House Foundation (£30,000); International Nepal Fellowship (£22,500); Asthma UK and Keech Hospice Care (£1,000 each).
FINANCES *Financial year end 30/06/2022*
Income £125,000
Grants to organisations £100,500
Assets £105,000
TRUSTEES Christopher Johnston; Dr John Barber; Kirsty Johnston.
HOW TO APPLY Apply in writing to the correspondent. Note that the trust has limited sources of income.
CONTACT DETAILS The Trustees, 24 Tudor Gardens, Stony Stratford, Milton Keynes, Buckinghamshire MK11 1HX *Tel.* 01908 562113 *Email* candkjct@gmail.com

■ The Joicey Trust

CC NO 244679   **ESTABLISHED** 1965
WHERE FUNDING CAN BE GIVEN Eastern Scottish Borders; Northumberland; Tyne and Wear.
WHO CAN BENEFIT Registered charities; unregistered charities; CICs; places of worship.
WHAT IS FUNDED General charitable purposes.
WHAT IS NOT FUNDED Research and research costs within core funding applications; charities not registered within the beneficial area or with gross incoming resources exceeding £1 million.
TYPE OF GRANT Capital costs; core/revenue costs.
RANGE OF GRANTS Up to £15,000 but typically between £1,000 and £5,000.
SAMPLE GRANTS Greggs Foundation (£15,000); Charlotte Staker Project, Ellingham Willage Hall and Eyes Open Steering Group (£5,000 each); Ball View (£4,000); Circus Central and NE Youth (£3,000 each); Rothbury Recreation Club (£1,100); Seahouses Hostel (£400).
FINANCES *Financial year end 05/04/2022*
Income £246,200
Grants to organisations £294,200
Assets £8,740,000
TRUSTEES Lord Joicey; The Rt Hon. Lady Joicey; The Hon. Andrew Joicey; The Hon. Katherine Crosbie Dawson.
HOW TO APPLY Applications can be obtained by completing a contact form on the trust's

website. The trustees meet twice a year, usually in January/early February and late June/July. Applications should be submitted to the appeals secretary in time to allow for any queries to be resolved by 30 November or 31 May each year for consideration at the next trustees' meeting; early applications are therefore encouraged.
CONTACT DETAILS The Trustees, Womble Bond Dickinson, The Spark, Draymans Way, Newcastle Helix, Newcastle upon Tyne NE4 5DE *Tel.* 0191 279 9676 *Email* appeals@thejoiceytrust.org.uk *Website* www.thejoiceytrust.org.uk

■ The Jones 1986 Charitable Trust

CC NO 327176   **ESTABLISHED** 1986
WHERE FUNDING CAN BE GIVEN Primarily Nottinghamshire.
WHO CAN BENEFIT Charitable organisations; schools; CICs; hospices.
WHAT IS FUNDED Social welfare; health and disability; older people; children and young people.
WHAT IS NOT FUNDED Individuals; activities that are the responsibility of the local health authority, education authority or similar body.
TYPE OF GRANT Capital costs; core/revenue costs.
RANGE OF GRANTS Typical grants range from £20,000.
SAMPLE GRANTS Rainbows Children's Hospice (£243,000); Footprints (£135,000); R.E.A.L. Foundation (£105,000); Nottingham High School (£45,000); Emmanuel House Support Centre (£25,000); Safer Living Foundation (£15,000); Rosie May Foundation (£5,000); Sharewear Clothing Scheme (£2,000).
FINANCES *Financial year end 05/04/2022*
Income £1,390,000
Grants to organisations £1,070,000
Assets £51,960,000
TRUSTEES John Pears; Richard Stanley; David Lindley.
OTHER INFORMATION Grants were distributed as follows: relief of sickness and disability (£334,500); education (£302,500); community benefit (£205,000); young people's welfare (£122,500); older people's welfare (£60,500); accommodation (£40,700).
HOW TO APPLY Application forms can be found on the funder's website.
CONTACT DETAILS The Trustees, UHY Hacker Young LLP, 14 Park Row, Nottingham, Nottinghamshire NG1 6GR *Tel.* 0115 938 8762 *Email* enquiries@thejonescharitabletrust.org.uk *Website* www.thejonescharitabletrust.org.uk

■ The Muriel Jones Foundation

CC NO 1135107   **ESTABLISHED** 2010
WHERE FUNDING CAN BE GIVEN UK and overseas.
WHO CAN BENEFIT Charitable organisations.
WHAT IS FUNDED General charitable purposes.
RANGE OF GRANTS Typically between £25,000 and £100,000, with some larger grants.
SAMPLE GRANTS Crossflow Ltd (£132,100 in 11 grants); Animals Asia Foundation (£100,000); Epatoma Foundation (£70,400); Bath Cats and Dogs Home and Women for Women International (£50,000 each); Prader-Willi Syndrome Association UK (£25,000); Downside School (£13,600 in four grants); Forgotten Dogs Foundation (£390).
FINANCES *Financial year end 28/02/2022*
Income £778,700
Grants to organisations £769,100
Assets £3,710,000

TRUSTEES Ludlow Trust Company Ltd; Richard Brindle; Katie Brindle.

OTHER INFORMATION The foundation awarded a total of 27 grants to 13 organisations in 2021/22 totalling £769,100. Our research shows that the foundation has a preference for environmental, welfare and human rights charities.

HOW TO APPLY Apply by letter to the correspondent.

CONTACT DETAILS The Trustees, c/o Ludlow Trust Co. Ltd, Tower Wharf, Cheese Lane, Bristol BS2 0JJ *Tel.* 0117 313 8200

■ The Jordan Charitable Foundation

CC NO 1051507 **ESTABLISHED** 1995

WHERE FUNDING CAN BE GIVEN Herefordshire.

WHO CAN BENEFIT Registered charities.

WHAT IS FUNDED Children and young people; education.

TYPE OF GRANT Capital costs; core/revenue costs.

SAMPLE GRANTS Harris Federation (£4.26 million); IntoUniversity (£1.58 million); The Queen Elizabeth Scholarship Trust (£300,000); Next Step Foundation (£90,000); Herefordshire Growing Point (£5,000).

FINANCES *Financial year end* 31/12/2021
Income £26,680,000
Grants to organisations £9,250,000
Assets £165,680,000

TRUSTEES Anthony Brierley; Sir George Russell; Nicholas Fry; Parkdove Ltd; Snowport Ltd.

OTHER INFORMATION Grants were made to 21 organisations. The foundation used to support a variety of causes throughout Herefordshire but now focuses primarily on education.

HOW TO APPLY Applications may be made in writing to the correspondent. The trustees meet four times a year.

CONTACT DETAILS The Trustees, c/o Rawlinson and Hunter LLP, 8th Floor, 6 New Street Square, London EC4A 3AQ *Tel.* 020 7842 2000 *Email* jordan@rawlinson-hunter.com

■ The Joron Charitable Trust

CC NO 1062547 **ESTABLISHED** 1997

WHERE FUNDING CAN BE GIVEN UK.

WHO CAN BENEFIT Registered charities; hospitals.

WHAT IS FUNDED General charitable purposes; education; medical research.

TYPE OF GRANT Project funding; core/revenue costs; capital costs; one-off.

RANGE OF GRANTS Generally between £5,000 and £20,000, with some larger grants.

SAMPLE GRANTS The Gem Project (£400,000); The Wilderness Foundation (£70,000); The Society of Medicine (£30,000); Cosmic and Learning Disability Network (£20,000 each); Crisis UK and North Paddington Foodbank (£10,000 each); Justin Edinburgh 3 Foundation and Scotty's Little Soldiers (£5,000 each).

FINANCES *Financial year end* 31/03/2022
Income £750,800
Grants to organisations £670,000
Assets £419,300

TRUSTEES Bruce Jarvis; John Jarvis; Sandra Jarvis; Juliet Jarvis.

OTHER INFORMATION The trust awarded 20 grants during the year.

HOW TO APPLY Apply in writing to the correspondent.

CONTACT DETAILS The Trustees, c/o Ravensale Ltd, 26 New Broadway, London W5 2XA *Tel.* 020 8908 4655 *Email* info@ravensale.com

■ J. E. Joseph Charitable Fund

CC NO 209058 **ESTABLISHED** 1946

WHERE FUNDING CAN BE GIVEN London; Manchester; India; Israel.

WHO CAN BENEFIT Jewish charities.

WHAT IS FUNDED The relief of poverty and suffering; education; advancement of the Jewish religion; other charitable purposes beneficial to the Jewish community.

WHAT IS NOT FUNDED Individuals; large national charities with significant income; capital projects are generally not supported.

RANGE OF GRANTS £2,000 to £8,000.

SAMPLE GRANTS University Jewish Chaplaincy Board (£8,000); Jerusalem Conservatory Hassadna (£6,500); Carmel School Hong Kong (£5,000); The Future Generation Fund (£4,000); Kisharon Day School (£3,000); Jenetics (£2,500); Aish Ha'Torah (£2,000).

FINANCES *Financial year end* 05/04/2022
Income £93,800
Grants to organisations £152,000
Assets £6,150,000

TRUSTEE J. E. Joseph Trustee Company Ltd.

OTHER INFORMATION Grants were awarded to over 40 organisations during the year. According to the annual report for 2021/22, 'the trustees decided to reduce or not award grants to charities with large incomes and multimillion-pound budgets. Grants were directed more towards smaller charities, where the charity's grants made a difference and were relatively important to them.'

HOW TO APPLY Applications may be made in writing to the correspondent, including a copy of your latest accounts. The trustees respond to all applications, which are first vetted by the secretary.

CONTACT DETAILS Roger Leon, Secretary, 10 Compass Close, Edgware, Middlesex HA8 8HU *Tel.* 020 8958 0126 *Email* roger. leon@btinternet.com

■ The Cyril and Eve Jumbo Charitable Trust

CC NO 1097209 **ESTABLISHED** 2003

WHERE FUNDING CAN BE GIVEN UK and overseas.

WHO CAN BENEFIT Charitable organisations.

WHAT IS FUNDED General charitable purposes; overseas aid.

TYPE OF GRANT The website states that the trustees are 'less keen on capital projects'.

RANGE OF GRANTS £100 to £15,000.

SAMPLE GRANTS The Central British Fund for World Jewish Relief (£52,500); Action For Kids Charitable Trust (£41,600); PromiseWorks (£10,000); Humanity First UK (£5,000); Collage Arts (£4,500); Alzheimer's Society (£2,000); Great Ormond Street Hospital Children's Charity (£350); Friends of the Earth Charitable Trust (£200).

FINANCES *Financial year end* 05/04/2022
Income £186,800
Grants to organisations £310,100
Assets £1,880,000

TRUSTEES Rafiq Hayat; Geoffrey Margolis; Edward Engulu; Lorraine Margolis.

OTHER INFORMATION The trust's funding is equally divided between causes in the UK and overseas. Its website describes a preference for programmes for adolescents and post-adolescents in England and self-sufficiency projects in financially developing countries.

HOW TO APPLY The annual report states that applications can be submitted to the trustees and are considered regularly. Applications should be sent in writing and incorporate full details of the charity for which funding is requested.

CONTACT DETAILS The Trustees, Mumbo Jumbo World, 48 Great Marlborough Street, London W1F 7BB *Tel.* 020 7437 0879 *Email* charity@mjw13.com *Website* www.cejct.com

....

■ Anton Jurgens Charitable Trust

CC NO 259885 **ESTABLISHED** 1969
WHERE FUNDING CAN BE GIVEN UK.
WHO CAN BENEFIT UK-registered charities.
WHAT IS FUNDED People who are socially disadvantaged and/or have mental and/or physical disabilities.
WHAT IS NOT FUNDED Religious promotion; arts and culture (unless used for therapeutic purposes).
TYPE OF GRANT Generally one-off; project funding.
RANGE OF GRANTS £2,000 to £5,000.
SAMPLE GRANTS Street Soccer Scotland (£7,900); Linking Lives UK (£5,000); Quest for Learning (£4,500); Sharewear Clothing Scheme (£4,400); Hastings Furniture Service and Jubilee Sailing Trust (£4,000 each); Halpern Charitable Foundation (£3,500); Bristol Children's Help Society and ClearVision Project (£3,000 each).
FINANCES *Financial year end* 05/04/2022
Income £219,200
Grants to organisations £228,000
Assets £9,550,000
TRUSTEES Frans Jurgens; Paul Beek; Frans Tilman; Hans Veraart; Carlijn Bijvoet.
HOW TO APPLY Applications can be made via the trust's website. The trust no longer accepts postal applications. The trustees meet twice a year, in spring and autumn, to consider applications.
CONTACT DETAILS Vivienne Jurgens, Kellas Estate, Mains of Kellas, Kellas, Moray IV30 8TS *Tel.* 01343 890777 *Email* grants@ajct.org.uk *Website* www.antonjurgensfonds.nl/en/applications/ajct

....

■ The Jusaca Charitable Trust

CC NO 1012966 **ESTABLISHED** 1992
WHERE FUNDING CAN BE GIVEN UK and overseas, particularly Israel.
WHO CAN BENEFIT Registered charities; schools; universities; hospices; religious bodies/institutions.
WHAT IS FUNDED General charitable purposes; the Jewish faith and community; the relief of poverty; health; education; the arts; research; housing.
TYPE OF GRANT Capital costs; core and revenue costs; seed funding; start-up funding.
RANGE OF GRANTS Typically £40,000 to £150,000.
SAMPLE GRANTS New Israel Fund (£150,000); World Jewish Relief (£116,000); Practical Action (£50,000); Jewish Care (£40,000).
FINANCES *Financial year end* 31/03/2022
Income £5,890,000
Grants to organisations £836,000
Assets £8,800,000
TRUSTEES Ms C. Emanuel; Sara Emanuel; Maurice Emanuel; Dr Donald Franklin; Mrs D. Franklin; Rachel Paul; Miriam Emanuel; Jacob Emanuel.
HOW TO APPLY Apply in writing to the correspondent.
CONTACT DETAILS The Trustees, 17 Ashburnham Grove, London SE10 8UH *Tel.* 020 8692 2467

Kahal Chassidim Bobov

CC NO 278823   ESTABLISHED 1978
WHERE FUNDING CAN BE GIVEN Worldwide.
WHO CAN BENEFIT Jewish organisations, schools and charities.
WHAT IS FUNDED General charitable purposes, including education, health and the relief of poverty.
RANGE OF GRANTS Up to £124,000.
SAMPLE GRANTS Amud Hatzdokoh (£124,000); Keren Hatzolas Doros Alei Siach (£70,800); BC Trust (£47,000); Beis Aharon Trust (£38,200); Friends of Eidah Chareidis (£35,500).
FINANCES *Financial year end 31/12/2021*
Income £2,400,000
Grants to organisations £2,280,000
Assets £855,900
TRUSTEES Moshe Brinner; Mr L. Stempel.
OTHER INFORMATION Only recipients of over £35,000 were listed as beneficiaries. Grants of under £35,000 totalled £1.59 million.
HOW TO APPLY This charity is a donor-advised fund, with grants made to organisations according to the wishes of donors. The trustees may also make grants from the charity's unrestricted funds at their own discretion, based on their knowledge of organisations.
CONTACT DETAILS The Trustees, 87 Egerton Road, London N16 6UE *Tel.* 020 8880 8910

The Boris Karloff Charitable Foundation

CC NO 326898   ESTABLISHED 1985
WHERE FUNDING CAN BE GIVEN UK.
WHO CAN BENEFIT Charitable organisations; performing arts organisations.
WHAT IS FUNDED Performing arts; the promotion of cricket; young cricketers.
RANGE OF GRANTS Mostly £500 to £6,000.
SAMPLE GRANTS Royal Academy of Dramatic Art (RADA) – The Boris Karloff Scholarship Fund (£6,000); Arundel Castle Cricket Foundation (£5,000); Iris Theatre Company (£2,000); Masterclass (£1,500); Alive and Kicking Theatre (£1,000); Carousel (£750); Clowns in the Sky (£600); Sudden Productions (£500).
FINANCES *Financial year end 05/04/2022*
Income £71,800
Grants to organisations £51,500
Assets £3,370,000
TRUSTEES Owen Lewis; James Fairclough; Carole Fairclough.
OTHER INFORMATION During the year, the foundation awarded 34 grants to organisations.
HOW TO APPLY Contact the correspondent for further information.
CONTACT DETAILS The Trustees, c/o Russell Cooke Solicitors, 2 Putney Hill, London SW15 6AB *Tel.* 020 8394 6488

The Karlsson Játiva Charitable Foundation

CC NO 1168787   ESTABLISHED 2016
WHERE FUNDING CAN BE GIVEN UK; Sweden; Latin America (Peru, Bolivia, Ecuador and Colombia).
WHO CAN BENEFIT Registered charities; music schools; conservatories; orchestras; choirs; or other music establishments, with preference given to well-established charities.
WHAT IS FUNDED Music, including increasing access to music education; health; education; the relief of poverty.
RANGE OF GRANTS Generally £20,000 to £50,000.
SAMPLE GRANTS Latin American Children's Trust (£1.66 million); Signatur Foundation Sweden (£584,300); Birmingham Conservatoire (£55,000); Aurora Orchestra (£50,000); London Music Fund (£30,000); Music of Life (£20,000).
FINANCES *Financial year end 31/12/2021*
Income £454,700
Grants to organisations £2,600,000
Assets £32,330,000
TRUSTEES Erland Karlsson; Jeremy Arnold; Rose Karlsson; Martin Andersson; Annika Magnusson.
OTHER INFORMATION Through its Signature programmes in the UK and Sweden, the foundation awards grants to promote the advancement of music, particularly among young people. The foundation also makes an annual donation to the Latin American Children's Trust, a UK-registered charity. In 2021 grants were awarded to 12 organisations for poverty, health and education (£1.66 million) and music (£937,800).
HOW TO APPLY The trustees identify projects to be funded. Contact the foundation for further information.
CONTACT DETAILS Claire Miller, 2nd Floor, 78–79 Pall Mall, London SW1Y 5ES *Tel.* 020 3931 5210 *Email* info@kjcf.org.uk *Website* https://kjcf.org.uk

The Ian Karten Charitable Trust

CC NO 281721   ESTABLISHED 1980
WHERE FUNDING CAN BE GIVEN UK; Republic of Ireland; Israel.
WHO CAN BENEFIT Current Karten Centres; individuals wishing to enter and complete higher and postgraduate education.
WHAT IS FUNDED Improving the quality of life and independence of people with severe physical, sensory or cognitive disabilities or mental health problems; awareness and education of Jewish/non-Jewish relations.
TYPE OF GRANT Project funding; capital costs.
RANGE OF GRANTS Generally up to £25,000.
SAMPLE GRANTS Parkes Institute Southampton University (£50,400); Warwick University (£10,000); Langdon College – Salford (£24,500); Policy Connect (£20,000); Cantraybridge College (£17,500); British Friends of the Hebrew University (£2,000); The Anne Frank Educational Trust Ashkelon Foundation (£1,500).
FINANCES *Financial year end 30/09/2022*
Income £454,700
Grants to organisations £285,100
Assets £13,990,000
TRUSTEES Anthony Davis; Alexandra Moran; Sally Cooke; Edward Copisarow.
HOW TO APPLY At the time of writing (May 2023), the trust was not considering any new funding requests. Visit the trust's website for up-to-date information.

CONTACT DETAILS Ines Meza-Mitcher, Administrator, International House, 64 Nile Street, London N1 7SR *Tel.* 07720 931477 *Email* ines@ iankartencharitabletrust.org.uk or use the contact form on the website *Website* https://iankartencharitabletrust.org.uk

■ The Kasner Charitable Trust

CC NO 267510   ESTABLISHED 1973
WHERE FUNDING CAN BE GIVEN UK and overseas, with a preference for Israel, London and Manchester.
WHO CAN BENEFIT Charitable organisations; educational establishments; medical institutions; places of worship.
WHAT IS FUNDED The Jewish faith and community
SAMPLE GRANTS UK Toremet Ltd (£983,400); Herzog Memorial Hospital (£526,600); Dignity Organisation (£88,000); Ichud Talmudei Yesodey Hatorah (£47,900); Yesamach Levav (£35,000); Yeshuas Chaim Synagogue (£21,800).
FINANCES *Financial year end* 31/03/2022 *Income* £11,060,000 *Grants to organisations* £1,900,000 *Assets* £26,520,000
TRUSTEES Baruch Erlich; Judith Erlich; David Winegarten.
OTHER INFORMATION The following breakdown of grants has been taken from the accounts: medical advocacy and equipment (£551,700); relief of poverty (£522,800); 'development of the Land of Israel and its citizens' (£234,000); the furtherance of religion (£251,000); general charitable purposes (£184,600); the advancement of education (£158,700). Note that grants covering more than one category were classified under general charitable purposes. Grants of less than £45,000 totalled £94,000.
HOW TO APPLY Apply in writing to the correspondent. Most applications are successful.
CONTACT DETAILS Baruch Erlich, Trustee, 1A Gresham Gardens, London NW11 8NX *Tel.* 020 3637 2868

■ The Michael and Ilse Katz Foundation

CC NO 263726   ESTABLISHED 1971
WHERE FUNDING CAN BE GIVEN UK and overseas.
WHO CAN BENEFIT International and UK schemes and organisations benefitting Jewish people; at-risk groups or people who are disadvantaged by poverty or socially isolated.
WHAT IS FUNDED General charitable purposes, particularly the Jewish faith and community, health/disability and social welfare.
RANGE OF GRANTS £2,000 to £10,000.
SAMPLE GRANTS British Fund for World Jewish Relief (£10,000); Age Concern Enfield (£6,000); Deafblind UK (£5,000); Young Lives vs Cancer (£4,000); Camp Simcha for Sick Children (£2,000).
FINANCES *Financial year end* 05/04/2022 *Income* £120,000 *Grants to organisations* £93,000 *Assets* £3,140,000
TRUSTEES Lord Rupert Nathan; Jonathan Azis.
OTHER INFORMATION In 2021/22, the foundation awarded grants to 23 organisations.
HOW TO APPLY Apply in writing to the correspondent.

CONTACT DETAILS The Trustees, Westwood Manor, Lower Westwood, Bradford-on-Avon, Wiltshire BA15 2AF *Tel.* 07770 366930 *Email* osmanazis@btconnect.com

■ C. S. Kaufman Charitable Trust

CC NO 253194   ESTABLISHED 1967
WHERE FUNDING CAN BE GIVEN UK.
WHO CAN BENEFIT Organisations benefitting Jewish people.
WHAT IS FUNDED The promotion of the Jewish faith and education.
RANGE OF GRANTS Up to £60,000 but typically between £500 and £30,000.
SAMPLE GRANTS Keren Gemilas Chasodim (£60,000); Merkaz Hatorah Belz Machnovka (£30,000); Shir Chesed Beis Yisroel (£25,000); One Heart Lev Echod (£20,500); Friends of Beis Chinuch Lebonos (£15,000).
FINANCES *Financial year end* 05/04/2022 *Income* £396,000 *Grants to organisations* £229,100 *Assets* £1,510,000
TRUSTEES Mr J. J. Kaufman; Simon Kaufman; Mrs L. L. Kaufman.
HOW TO APPLY Contact the correspondent for further information.
CONTACT DETAILS The Trustees, c/o Haffner Hoff Ltd, 2nd Floor – Parkgates, Bury New Road, Prestwich, Manchester M25 0TL *Tel.* 0161 798 1660

■ The Kavli Trust

ESTABLISHED 1962
WHERE FUNDING CAN BE GIVEN UK; Asia; Finland; Norway; sub-Saharan Africa; Sweden.
WHO CAN BENEFIT Charitable organisations.
WHAT IS FUNDED Child and adolescent mental health, in particular preventive interventions, life skills and education; the climate and environment, with an emphasis on responsible consumption and production.
SAMPLE GRANTS UK beneficiaries included: Cedarwood Trust (£157,800); Mortal Fools and Children North East (£150,300 each); Curious Monkey (£112,700).
FINANCES *Financial year end* 31/12/2022 *Grants to organisations* £6,140,000
TRUSTEES Dag Opedal; Solfrid Lind; Lise Hammergren; Erik Volden.
OTHER INFORMATION The trust is not a UK-registered charity and therefore full financial information was not available. The financial figures have been taken from the trust's annual report and converted from Norwegian Kroner to GBP using the exchange rate at the time of writing (May 2023). Grants to UK organisations totalled £1.59 million.
HOW TO APPLY Apply in writing to the correspondent. The trust's website states: 'The Kavli Trust's general manager takes a proactive approach and largely identifies relevant projects, organisations and individuals herself. Projects can also receive support on the basis of an application, but this must then be specific, relevant, and clearly within the Kavli Trust's guidelines.'
CONTACT DETAILS Inger Elise Iversen, General Manager, Kavlifondet, Postboks 7360, N-5020 Bergen, Norway *Email* ingerelise.iversen@kavlifondet.no *Website* https://kavlifondet.no/en

■ The Emmanuel Kaye Foundation

CC NO 280281   **ESTABLISHED** 1980

WHERE FUNDING CAN BE GIVEN UK, with a preference for north-east Hampshire.

WHO CAN BENEFIT Registered charities; charitable organisations.

WHAT IS FUNDED General charitable purposes; medical research; penal reform; education; music; performing arts; the prevention of sexual exploitation; social welfare; community development.

RANGE OF GRANTS £10,000 to £50,000.

SAMPLE GRANTS Imperial College Trust (£50,000); City Harvest and Rosa Fund UK (£40,000 each); Cardinal Hume Centre and Lived Health (£30,000); Jewish Women's Aid and UK Music Masters (£25,000); Working Chance (£10,000); The Winchfield Festival – Outreach Programme (£10,000).

FINANCES *Financial year end 31/07/2022*
Income £489,900
Grants to organisations £666,000
Assets £4,400,000

TRUSTEES John Forster; Louise Kaye; Eleanor Kaye; Madeleine Hawes; Anton Sternberg.

OTHER INFORMATION Grants were made to 26 organisations during the year.

HOW TO APPLY The charity's 2021/22 accounts state: 'The foundation does not accept unsolicited requests for grants or donations, focusing its support for registered charities principally, but not exclusively, where a relationship with trustees has been established.'

CONTACT DETAILS The Trustees, PO Box 1540, Peterborough PE2 2YP *Tel.* 07585 341626 *Email* finance@ekf.org.uk

■ The Kelly Family Charitable Trust

CC NO 1102440   **ESTABLISHED** 2004

WHERE FUNDING CAN BE GIVEN UK.

WHO CAN BENEFIT Registered charities; CICs.

WHAT IS FUNDED Family support, in particular practical support, relationship counselling and mediation; families of offenders and ex-offenders; families suffering from the effects of sexual, physical, domestic or substance abuse.

WHAT IS NOT FUNDED Non-registered charities; individuals; national charities (only regional projects will be considered); general appeals; organisations with specific religious or political agendas.

TYPE OF GRANT Core/revenue costs; capital costs.

RANGE OF GRANTS Up to £5,000, but higher amounts may be considered.

SAMPLE GRANTS A list of beneficiaries was not included in the annual report and accounts. Previous beneficiaries have included: Acacia; Carefree Kids; Dadswork; Family Intervention Counselling; Parents Against Child Sexual Exploitation; Play Therapy Base; Public Initiative for the Prevention of Suicide and Self Harm; Relate; Women's Work Derbyshire.

FINANCES *Financial year end 31/03/2022*
Income £104,400
Grants to organisations £119,300
Assets £2,810,000

TRUSTEES Sheldon Cordell; Michael Field; Jenny Kelly; Annie Kelly; Brian Mattingley.

OTHER INFORMATION The trustees prefer to support charities whose income is below £500,000; however, larger charities with pioneering pilot projects will be considered.

HOW TO APPLY Application forms can be downloaded from the trust's website. Grants are awarded twice a year and appeals must be submitted by 1 March or 1 September.

CONTACT DETAILS Stuart Armstrong, Grants Administrator, 8 Mansfield Place, Edinburgh EH3 6NB *Email* mail@kfct.org *Website* https://kfct.org.uk

■ Kelsick's Educational Foundation

CC NO 526956   **ESTABLISHED** 1723

WHERE FUNDING CAN BE GIVEN Lakes parish (Ambleside, Grasmere, Langdale and part of Troutbeck).

WHO CAN BENEFIT Schools; sports clubs; individuals.

WHAT IS FUNDED The educational needs of individuals under the age of 25; school activities such as educational visits, field trips, music lessons, reading resources and items of necessary equipment; support for academic courses and apprenticeships, including equipment costs.

SAMPLE GRANTS Ambleside Primary School (£79,900); Langdale Primary School (£66,500); Grasmere Primary School (£59,100).

FINANCES *Financial year end 31/03/2022*
Income £407,500
Grants to organisations £205,900
Grants to individuals £61,700
Assets £10,510,000

TRUSTEES Linda Dixon; Nigel Hutchinson; Leslie Johnson; Nicholas Martin; Angela Renouf; Mark Blackburn; Paul Edmondson; The Revd Beverley Lock; William Clark; Dr Paul Davies; John Cunningham; Prof. Lois Mansfield.

HOW TO APPLY Application forms are available from the foundation's website.

CONTACT DETAILS Peter Frost, Clerk to the Trustees, The Kelsick Centre, St Mary's Lane, Ambleside, Cumbria LA22 9DG *Tel.* 01539 431289 *Email* john@kelsick.plus.com *Website* www.kelsick.org.uk

■ William Kendall's Charity (Wax Chandlers Company)

CC NO 228361   **ESTABLISHED** 1559

WHERE FUNDING CAN BE GIVEN Greater London and the London Borough of Bexley.

WHO CAN BENEFIT Registered charities; educational organisations.

WHAT IS FUNDED General charitable purposes; the relief of those in need, particularly inhabitants of Greater London and members of the company and their dependants.

WHAT IS NOT FUNDED Grants are not made directly to individuals.

RANGE OF GRANTS Up to £15,000.

SAMPLE GRANTS Stepney City Farm (£15,000); Jubilee Primary School (£5,000); Historic Royal Palaces (£2,500); St Paul's Cathedral (£2,200); Guildhall School of Music and Drama (£1,500).

FINANCES *Financial year end 31/03/2022*
Income £149,600
Grants to organisations £60,600
Assets £5,610,000

TRUSTEES Joan Beavington; Lt Col. John Chambers; Arthur Davey; Dr Jonathan Munday; John Sleeman; Peter Tompkins; Susan Green; Anthony Bickmore; Lynda Weston; Ian Appleton; Robert Holland; Dame Fiona Woolf; Jonathan Simpson; Margaret Ginman; Haydn Cole; Anthony Ward.

OTHER INFORMATION Grants were distributed through the following grant programmes: Greater London Fund (£31,300); Persons in Need Fund (£16,900); Bexley Fund (£12,300).

HOW TO APPLY The Bexley Small Grants Scheme is administered by the Bexley Voluntary Services Council – applicants may call 020 8304 0911 for more details. The Greater London Fund and Persons in Need Fund are operated on a commissioning basis and unsolicited applications are not accepted.

CONTACT DETAILS Richard Moule, Clerk, Wax Chandlers' Hall, 6 Gresham Street, London EC2V 7AD *Tel.* 020 7606 3591 *Email* clerk@waxchandlers.org.uk *Website* www.waxchandlers.org.uk/charity/index.php

■ The Kennedy Leigh Charitable Trust

CC NO 288293   **ESTABLISHED** 1983
WHERE FUNDING CAN BE GIVEN UK and Israel.
WHO CAN BENEFIT Registered charities.
WHAT IS FUNDED General charitable purposes; medicine and health; education; social welfare; human rights and equality; arts, culture and heritage.
WHAT IS NOT FUNDED Individuals.
TYPE OF GRANT Capital costs; core costs; seed/start-up funding.
SAMPLE GRANTS A list of beneficiaries was not included in the annual report and accounts. Previous beneficiaries have included: Magen David Adom UK (£250,000); Shaare Zedek (£65,000); CHAI-Lifeline (£22,500); British Friends of the Hebrew University (£16,300); New Israel Fund (£15,000); Jewish Association for the Mentally Ill (£5,000).
FINANCES *Financial year end* 31/03/2022
Income £482,600
Grants to organisations £316,300
Assets £25,440,000
TRUSTEES Alexander Sorkin; Angela Sorkin; Geoffrey Goldkorn; Carole Berman; Anthony Foux; Benjamin Goldkorn; Jacob Sorkin.
HOW TO APPLY The trust's 2021/22 annual report states: 'The funds available for distribution outside of Israel are all but committed for the foreseeable future to several UK charities. The Trustees are therefore unable to consider applications for funding from charitable organisations outside of Israel at this time.'
CONTACT DETAILS The Trustees, ORT House, 126 Albert Street, London NW1 7NE *Tel.* 020 7267 6500

■ The Kennedy Trust for Rheumatology Research

CC NO 260059   **ESTABLISHED** 1969
WHERE FUNDING CAN BE GIVEN England.
WHO CAN BENEFIT Registered charities; universities; research projects; hospitals.
WHAT IS FUNDED Basic and translational research into rheumatic and related musculoskeletal, immunological and inflammatory diseases.
TYPE OF GRANT Research.
SAMPLE GRANTS The Kennedy Institute (£2.5 million); University of Leeds (£2.43 million); University College London (£2.23 million); Versus Arthritis (£1 million).
FINANCES *Financial year end* 30/09/2022
Income £8,720,000
Grants to organisations £8,730,000
Assets £279,120,000

TRUSTEES Margaret Frost; Prof. Stephen Holgate; Prof. Andrew Cope; Edmund Buckley; Mark Dighero; Victoria White; Christopher Coombe; Prof. Michael Patton; Dr Paul Satchell; Richard Punt; Prof. Tracy Hussell.
OTHER INFORMATION The trust provides long-term funding to The Kennedy Institute.
HOW TO APPLY Visit the trust's website for information on current funding initiatives.
CONTACT DETAILS Zoe Montanaro, Grants and Office Manager, One Lyric Square, Hammersmith, London W6 0NB *Tel.* 020 8834 1562 *Email* z.montanaro@kennedytrust.org *Website* www.kennedytrust.org

■ The Kennel Club Charitable Trust

CC NO 327802   **ESTABLISHED** 1988
WHERE FUNDING CAN BE GIVEN UK.
WHO CAN BENEFIT Charitable organisations; re-homing organisations; universities and other research bodies.
WHAT IS FUNDED Research into canine diseases; canine welfare.
WHAT IS NOT FUNDED Individuals; political organisations; applications purely for building costs; requests from organisations that are not primarily focused on dogs (e.g. general animal shelters).
TYPE OF GRANT One-off and recurring grants; capital, core and project costs; research.
RANGE OF GRANTS £100 to 103,500.
SAMPLE GRANTS All Global Media (£80,000); Gifted Philanthropy Ltd (£69,100); Titman Firth Creative Marketing (£15,700); Autism at Kingwood (£9,300); Clymping Dog Sanctuary (£5,000).
FINANCES *Financial year end* 31/12/2021
Income £899,200
Grants to organisations £220,400
Assets £2,530,000
TRUSTEES Michael Herrtage; Jennifer Millard; Dr Andrew Higgins; Graham Hill; The Revd William King; Rosemary Smart.
OTHER INFORMATION Grants were awarded to 24 organisations during the year.
HOW TO APPLY Apply in writing to the correspondent. Provide your organisation's latest accounts (and registered charity number, if applicable). Detail the costs, purpose and length of the project. For scientific project proposals, apply using the application form on the trust's website. The trustees meet four times a year. Further guidance is given on the trust's website.
CONTACT DETAILS The Trust Administrator, 10 Clarges Street, Piccadilly, London W1J 8AB *Tel.* 020 7518 1061 *Email* kcct@thekennelclub.org.uk *Website* www.kennelclubcharitabletrust.org

■ The Kensington and Chelsea Foundation

CC NO 1125940   **ESTABLISHED** 2009
WHERE FUNDING CAN BE GIVEN Kensington and Chelsea.
WHO CAN BENEFIT Charities; community groups; organisations working within the borough; individuals.
WHAT IS FUNDED Children and young people; skills and employment; isolation and loneliness; vulnerable older people living in fuel poverty.
TYPE OF GRANT Project costs.
RANGE OF GRANTS Typically between £1,000 and £10,000.

SAMPLE GRANTS Earl's Court Youth Club (£34,000); Age UK Kensington and Chelsea (£20,600); Dalgarno Trust (£17,000); Hodan Somali Community (£10,000); Abundance Arts (£6,000); Dadihiye (£5,000); Latimer Community Art Therapy (£1,500).

FINANCES *Financial year end 31/03/2022*
Income £1,970,000
Grants to organisations £1,750,000
Assets £894,600

TRUSTEES Cynthia Dize; Lucinda Stafford-Deitsch; Jerome Raphaely; Martin Morgan; Clare Ferguson; Richard Briance; William Crone; Esma Dukali; Peter Winslow; Abdurahman Sayed; Abdi Aden; James Paradise.

OTHER INFORMATION During the 2021/22 financial period, grants totalling £1.48 million were awarded to 72 local charities and community groups. In addition, it awarded a further £264,300 to 34 organisations through the Grenfell Community Development Fund.

HOW TO APPLY In the first instance, applicants should consult the foundation's website, which details what funding is currently available.

CONTACT DETAILS The Trustees, 111–117 Lancaster Road, Ladbroke Grove, London W11 1QT *Tel.* 020 7229 5499 *Email* team@ thekandcfoundation.com *Website* https:// thekandcfoundation.com

■ Kent Community Foundation

CC NO 1084361   **ESTABLISHED** 2001
WHERE FUNDING CAN BE GIVEN The county of Kent and the borough of Medway.
WHO CAN BENEFIT Local charities, community groups and voluntary organisations; individuals.
WHAT IS FUNDED General charitable purposes.
TYPE OF GRANT Core, capital and project expenditure; one-off and recurrent.
SAMPLE GRANTS A list of beneficiaries was not included in the annual report and accounts. Previous beneficiaries have included: Sparks (£500,000); The J's Hospice (£75,000); Romney Marsh Day Centre (£34,000); Gap (£21,600); Carers FIRST (£17,400); Ellenor (£15,200); Blackthorn Trust (£13,000); Age Concern Sandwich Centre and Kent Cricket Development Trust (£10,500 each); Friends of Holcot (£10,100).
FINANCES *Financial year end 31/03/2022*
Income £6,100,000
Grants to organisations £3,780,000
Grants to individuals £287,100
Assets £33,170,000
TRUSTEES Sarah Hohler; Hugo Fenwick; Lord Robert Sackville-West; Melissa Murdoch; Dr Emilia Falcetti; Gail Hall; Russell Race; Samantha Cooper-Gray; Kruti Shrotri; Munyaradzi Badze.
OTHER INFORMATION This is one of the 47 UK community foundations, which distribute funding for a wide range of purposes. As with all community foundations, there are a number of donor-advised funds managed on behalf of individuals, families and charitable trusts. Grant schemes tend to change frequently – consult the foundation's website for details of current programmes and up-to-date deadlines.
HOW TO APPLY Potential applicants are advised to visit the community foundation's website or contact its grants team to find the most suitable funding stream.
CONTACT DETAILS Grants Team, Evegate Park Barn, Evegate, Ashford, Kent TN25 6SX *Tel.* 01303 814500 *Email* admin@kentcf.org.uk *Website* www.kentcf.org.uk/apply

■ The Kentown Wizard Foundation

CC NO 1163956   **ESTABLISHED** 2015
WHERE FUNDING CAN BE GIVEN Worldwide, with a preference for the UK.
WHO CAN BENEFIT UK-registered charities.
WHAT IS FUNDED Children and young people living with life-limiting conditions and disabilities, and their families.
TYPE OF GRANT Core costs; project funding; multi-year grants.
RANGE OF GRANTS Mostly up to £100,000, with exceptional grants of up to £3 million.
SAMPLE GRANTS Together for Short Lives (£3 million); Over the Wall (£980,000); Rainbow Trust Children's Charity (£575,000); The Jessie May Trust (£100,000); Cerebral Palsy Scotland (£49,500); Brian House Children's Hospice (£30,000); The Chronicle Sunshine (£15,200); Sight Support Derbyshire (£8,100).
FINANCES *Financial year end 31/03/2022*
Income £793,000
Grants to organisations £5,600,000
Assets £81,060,000
TRUSTEES David Bamber; Kenneth Townsley; Richard Ingle; Kathryn Graham.
OTHER INFORMATION During 2021/22, grants were awarded to 13 organisations.
HOW TO APPLY According to its website, the foundation seeks out potential charity partners and therefore does not accept unsolicited applications.
CONTACT DETAILS The Trustees, Metro House Ltd, Unit 14–17, Metropolitan Business Park, Preston New Road, Blackpool FY3 9LT *Tel.* 01253 446923 *Email* enquiries@ kentownwizard.org *Website* www.kentownwizard. org

■ The Nancy Kenyon Charitable Trust

CC NO 265359   **ESTABLISHED** 1972
WHERE FUNDING CAN BE GIVEN UK and overseas.
WHO CAN BENEFIT Registered small charities; individuals.
WHAT IS FUNDED General charitable purposes; Christian causes.
RANGE OF GRANTS Up to £10,500.
SAMPLE GRANTS Nancy Oldfield Trust (£15,000); Aylsham Care Trust (£5,000); Refuge, Information, Support and Education (RISE) UK (£4,200); Ashchurch PCC of St Nicholas (£3,500); Papworth Trust (£3,000); Laces Community Club (£1,000); Devon County Council (£600); Kiva (£30).
FINANCES *Financial year end 05/04/2022*
Income £77,000
Grants to organisations £81,100
Grants to individuals £2,500
Assets £2,160,000
TRUSTEES Sally Kenyon; Peter Kenyon; Lucy Phipps; Kieron Kenyon; Sarah Kenyon; David Kenyon; Emily Kenyon.
HOW TO APPLY Applications can be made in writing to the correspondent at any time. Previous research notes that applications for causes not known to the trustees are considered annually in December.
CONTACT DETAILS The Trustees, c/o Brook Financial Management Ltd, Meads Barn, Ashwell Business Park, Ashwell, Ilminster, Somerset TA19 9DX *Tel.* 01460 259852

■ Keren Association Ltd

CC NO 313119   **ESTABLISHED** 1961
WHERE FUNDING CAN BE GIVEN UK and overseas.
WHO CAN BENEFIT Charitable organisations, mainly those benefitting Jewish people.
WHAT IS FUNDED General charitable purposes, including the advancement of education and the provision of religious instruction and training in Orthodox Judaism.
TYPE OF GRANT Capital costs; project funding; development funding.
RANGE OF GRANTS Up to £1.6 million.
SAMPLE GRANTS Friends of Mercaz Hatorah Belz Macnivka (£1.6 million); China Vechisda (£693,900); Mosdot Toras Aharon (£480,300); M.L.T. Belz (£218,300); Ichud Mosdos Gur Ltd (£135,000); Friends of Mosdos Torah Veyirah (£63,000); Kollel Mishkon Yakov (£53,000); Side by Side School Ltd (£50,000).
FINANCES *Financial year end 31/03/2022*
Income £2,730,000
Grants to organisations £9,090,000
Assets £20,870,000
TRUSTEES A. Perlman; Mrs H. Weiss; Mr E. Englander; Mrs N. Weiss; J. Englander; S. Englander; J. Stern; Mr S. Englander; P. Englander.
OTHER INFORMATION Only beneficiaries of grants of over £50,000 were listed in the accounts Grants of under £50,000 totalled £930,100.
HOW TO APPLY Apply in writing to the correspondent.
CONTACT DETAILS The Trustees, 136 Clapton Common, London E5 9AG *Tel.* 020 8800 9677 *Email* mail@cohenarnold.com

■ E. and E. Kernkraut Charities Ltd

CC NO 275636   **ESTABLISHED** 1973
WHERE FUNDING CAN BE GIVEN UK and overseas.
WHO CAN BENEFIT Charitable organisations.
WHAT IS FUNDED The advancement of religion in accordance with the Orthodox Jewish faith; education; general charitable purposes.
RANGE OF GRANTS Generally up to £76,000, with grants of under £10,000 also given.
SAMPLE GRANTS Rookwood Foundation Ltd (£76,000); Noam Hatorah (£65,000); Vyoel Moshe Charitable Trust (£55,000); Beis Ruchel D'Satmar London (£43,000); United Talmudical Associates Ltd (£36,600); A T.I.M.E. Ltd (£30,000); CMZ Ltd (£28,000); UTRY Ltd (£26,000); Friends of Yeshiva Luzern (£24,000); Asser Bishvil Foundation (£24,000); Friends of Gur Foundation Israel (£18,000); Beis Aharon TT Activity Centre (£14,000); Kollel Viznitz London (£11,500); Ichud Mosdos Gur Ltd (£10,000).
FINANCES *Financial year end 31/03/2022*
Income £653,000
Grants to organisations £749,000
Assets £7,080,000
TRUSTEES Joseph Kernkraut; Jacob Kernkraut; Esther Kernkraut; Eli Kernkraut.
OTHER INFORMATION Grants were given to more than 24 organisations during the year, with grants of under £10,000 totalling £120,100.
HOW TO APPLY Contact the correspondent for further information. According to the annual report for 2021/22, when making grants, the trustees 'use their personal knowledge of the relevant institutions, their representatives, operational efficiency and reputation'.
CONTACT DETAILS The Trustees, The Knoll, Fountayne Road, London N16 7EA *Tel.* 020 8806 7947 *Email* mail@cohenarnold.com

■ The Peter Kershaw Trust

CC NO 268934   **ESTABLISHED** 1974
WHERE FUNDING CAN BE GIVEN Greater Manchester.
WHO CAN BENEFIT Registered charities; schools.
WHAT IS FUNDED Social welfare; health; people with disabilities; youth work.
WHAT IS NOT FUNDED Individuals (directly); loans; new building work (but payments for fitting out specialist premises may be made); long-term commitments (awards may be paid for up to three years); industrial and provident societies; CICs.
TYPE OF GRANT Salaries; seed funding/start-up funding; pump-priming; project funding; bursaries.
RANGE OF GRANTS Mostly between £1,000 and £3,000. Up to £50,000 over three years for the Peter Kershaw Memorial Bursary.
SAMPLE GRANTS N-Gage (£10,000); Manchester High School for Girls (£5,700); Reach Family Project (£2,000); St John Ambulance (£500); The Brain Tumor Charity (£250).
FINANCES *Financial year end 31/03/2022*
Income £105,800
Grants to organisations £84,700
Grants to individuals £27,300
Assets £7,660,000
TRUSTEES Rosemary Adams; Richard Kershaw; Tim Page; Bernard Lever; Jane Kershaw; Andrew Kershaw.
OTHER INFORMATION Each year, the trust awards the Peter Kershaw Memorial Bursary (£50,000 awarded over three years) to support innovative youth work by charitable organisations in Greater Manchester. Grants in 2021/22 were broken down as follows: memorial bursaries (£50,000); social welfare (£34,700); school bursaries (£27,300).
HOW TO APPLY Application forms can be downloaded from the trust's website.
CONTACT DETAILS The Trustees, Room G104, Bolton Arena, Arena Approach, Horwich, Bolton, Lancashire BL6 6LB *Tel.* 01204 414317 *Email* peterkershawtrust@gmail.com *Website* www.peterkershawtrust.org

■ The Ursula Keyes Trust

CC NO 517200   **ESTABLISHED** 1985
WHERE FUNDING CAN BE GIVEN Chester and surrounding areas.
WHO CAN BENEFIT Charitable organisations (including national charities if there is a link to a local beneficiary); medical and social care institutions; schools; individuals.
WHAT IS FUNDED General charitable purposes, particularly health and medical causes and social care. The trust's website further explains: 'A wide range of causes are supported, including cultural and leisure projects, particularly when matched by other fundraising efforts.'
TYPE OF GRANT Capital costs and equipment.
RANGE OF GRANTS Mostly £1,000 to £5,000.
SAMPLE GRANTS North West Air Ambulance (£7,700); DSL Mobility (£6,000); Chester Music Society and Young Enterprise (£2,000 each); Guide Dogs (£1,000).
FINANCES *Financial year end 31/12/2021*
Income £261,500
Grants to organisations £67,400
Assets £4,660,000
TRUSTEES John Brimelow; Mr J. R. Leaman; Dr Ian Russell; Dr Peter Reid; Euan Elliott; John McLintock; Elizabeth Redmond; Sian Preston.

HOW TO APPLY Applications should be made in writing to the correspondent, including a copy of the form available to download from the website. Appeals are considered at the trustees' quarterly meetings, which take place at the end of January, April, July and October (see the website for exact dates); they should reach the trustees at least two weeks before any particular meeting.

CONTACT DETAILS Mrs D. Lawless, c/o RSM Accountants, City Place, Queens Road, Chester CH1 3BQ *Email* use the contact form on the website *Website* www.ursula-keyes-trust.org.uk

■ KFC Foundation

CC NO 1163560   **ESTABLISHED** 2015
WHERE FUNDING CAN BE GIVEN UK.
WHO CAN BENEFIT Registered charities; CICs; unincorporated clubs or associations; unregistered charities. For Community Grants organisations must have a turnover of less than £300,000.

WHAT IS FUNDED Projects that benefit young people aged 11–25 years old, particularly those in a position of social disadvantage (i.e. care leavers, those experiencing homelessness, young carers, young parents, young people at risk of or with experience of the criminal justice system).

WHAT IS NOT FUNDED For Community Grants: general fundraising or sponsorship appeals; political campaigns; promotion of religion; overseas travel; curricular activities that take place during the school day; research; repayment of loans; purchase of vehicles; medical equipment; major capital projects; interventions which do not demonstrate long-term impact or support; one-off events; generic youth work activities (not tailored towards the priority groups).

TYPE OF GRANT Project funding; small capital costs.
RANGE OF GRANTS Partnerships: mostly up to £35,000. Community Grants: £200 to £2,000.
SAMPLE GRANTS Comic Relief (£990,000); Action for Youth, Childhood Trust, Focus Charity, Include Youth and Young Lives Foundation (£10,000 each).

FINANCES *Financial year end 27/12/2021*
Income £1,460,000
Grants to organisations £1,240,000
Assets £898,300

TRUSTEES James Fletcher; Simon Coates; Nichola Newman; Michael Williams; Daniel Carr; Clara Widdison.

OTHER INFORMATION Grants were awarded to 16 organisations during the year. A grant of £400,000 was awarded to Comic Relief (57% of the total grant expenditure). The foundation also awards Community Grants to support grassroots organisations in the heart of its restaurant's communities – see the website for details. The 2020/21 annual accounts were the latest available at the time of writing (June 2023).

HOW TO APPLY Apply via the foundation's website, where application deadlines and further guidance can be found.

CONTACT DETAILS The Trustees, Orion Gate, Guilford Road, Woking GU22 7NJ *Email* use the contact form on the website *Website* www.kfc.co.uk/kfc-foundation

■ The Kiawah Charitable Trust

CC NO 1107730   **ESTABLISHED** 2005
WHERE FUNDING CAN BE GIVEN UK and India.
WHO CAN BENEFIT Registered, excepted or exempt charities.

WHAT IS FUNDED Work outside the UK; humanitarian aid; children and young people; education and training; social welfare; social justice; women's rights; research, especially pertaining to gender inequality.

WHAT IS NOT FUNDED Individuals.
TYPE OF GRANT Development funding; capacity building; general funding; project funding; strategic funding.
RANGE OF GRANTS Mostly £15,000 with the occasional larger grant.
SAMPLE GRANTS Dasra and Population Services International (£730,000 each); Women's Budget Group (£20,000); Institute for Sustainable Philanthropy, Rosa and Women's Resource Centre (£15,000 each).

FINANCES *Financial year end 05/04/2022*
Income £579,600
Grants to organisations £211,300
Assets £6,500,000

TRUSTEES Lynne Smitham; Peter Smitham; Andrea Jackson.

HOW TO APPLY Apply in writing to the correspondent. The trustees also proactively approach organisations.

CONTACT DETAILS Lynne Smitham, Trustee, PO Box 76774, London WC1A 9RG *Tel.* 020 7836 1666 *Email* info@kiawahtrust.org

■ Kidney Research UK

CC NO 252892   **ESTABLISHED** 1967
WHERE FUNDING CAN BE GIVEN UK.
WHO CAN BENEFIT Recognised renal research establishments supporting medical professionals including universities and hospitals.

WHAT IS FUNDED The charity funds research with the aim of improving the understanding of kidney disease, its causes, treatment and management.

SAMPLE GRANTS A list of beneficiaries was not included in the annual report and accounts.

FINANCES *Financial year end 31/03/2022*
Income £12,770,000
Grants to organisations £5,220,000
Assets £13,680,000

TRUSTEES Dr Charles Tomson; Prof. Sunil Bhandari; Deirdre Jennings; Jill Norman; Adrian Akers; Prof. Jeremy Hughes; Dr Adnan Sharif; Prof. Elizabeth Lightstone; Dr David Hughes; Prof. Caroline Savage; Angela Watt; Ben Digby; Lisa Chan; Prof. Sir John Cunningham.

HOW TO APPLY Applications must be submitted through the online portal, which can be accessed via the charity's website.

CONTACT DETAILS Research Grants Committee, Nene Hall, Peterborough Business Park, Lynch Wood, Peterborough, Cambridgeshire PE2 6FZ *Tel.* 0300 303 1100 *Email* enquiries@kidneyresearchuk.org *Website* www.kidneyresearchuk.org

■ The Kildare Trust

CC NO 1148325   **ESTABLISHED** 2012
WHERE FUNDING CAN BE GIVEN Worcestershire.
WHO CAN BENEFIT Registered charities; hospices; churches.

WHAT IS FUNDED General charitable purposes, with a preference for music and health.

RANGE OF GRANTS Up to £250,000.

SAMPLE GRANTS The RGSW and AOS Foundation (£250,000); University of Birmingham – Kidney Research (£75,000); Megan Baker House (£25,000); Yana (£10,000); Worcester Breast Unit Haven (£3,000).

FINANCES *Financial year end 05/04/2022*
Income £4,930,000
Grants to organisations £608,500
Assets £6,080,000

TRUSTEES Martin Needham; Dawn Oliver; Ian Crockatt Smith; Anthony Champion; Geoffrey Probert.

OTHER INFORMATION During the year, the trust awarded grants to 14 organisations.

HOW TO APPLY Contact the correspondent for further information.

CONTACT DETAILS Louise Ruane, c/o Pear Tree Cottage, Yarrington Road, Alfrick, Worcester, Worcestershire WR1 2JG *Tel.* 07812 743485 *Email* info@kildaretrust.org.uk

---

■ Fraser Kilpatrick Charitable Trust

OSCR NO SC046233   **ESTABLISHED** 2016

WHERE FUNDING CAN BE GIVEN UK and overseas, with a preference for Scotland.

WHO CAN BENEFIT Registered charities; hospices; hospitals. Primarily Scottish organisations.

WHAT IS FUNDED Children and young people; medical research and support for older people and people with learning difficulties; cancer support and research; social inclusion; employability; social or economic disadvantage; community development; the arts, heritage, culture and science; sport and recreation.

TYPE OF GRANT Small-scale, targeted projects; provision of equipment.

RANGE OF GRANTS Mostly up to £5,000 with the occasional larger grant.

SAMPLE GRANTS Erskine Hospital (£10,400); Diabetes UK (£6,000); Gorilla Welfare Trust (£5,300).

FINANCES *Financial year end 31/03/2022*
Income £250,900
Grants to organisations £209,000
Assets £351,900

OTHER INFORMATION Only organisations that received grants of over £5,000 were listed as beneficiaries in the trust's accounts. Grants of under £5,000 totalled £169,700.

HOW TO APPLY Apply in writing to the correspondent.

CONTACT DETAILS The Trustees, c/o Brodies LLP, 110 Queen Street, Glasgow G1 3BX

■ The Kilroot Foundation

CC NO 1173150   **ESTABLISHED** 2017

WHERE FUNDING CAN BE GIVEN UK and overseas.

WHO CAN BENEFIT Registered, UK-based charities.

WHAT IS FUNDED Development and support of children and young people; conservation of the natural and built environment.

RANGE OF GRANTS Capital costs; project funding; one-off and recurrent awards (typically in three-year cycles).

SAMPLE GRANTS Eton College (£70,000); Game and Wildlife Conservation Trust (£40,000); Oxfordshire Historic Churches Trust (£20,000); Outward – Barclays Ukraine Appeal (£15,000); Salmon and Trout Conservation (£8,000); Catch

22 and National Gallery Trust (£5,000 each); Belvoir Cricket and Countryside Trust (£3,000).

FINANCES *Financial year end 05/04/2022*
Income £119,500
Grants to organisations £288,000
Assets £4,470,000

TRUSTEES Matthew Dobbs; Katharine Dobbs; Denis Clough.

OTHER INFORMATION Grants were made to 17 organisations.

HOW TO APPLY Apply in writing to the correspondent. The foundation's 2021/22 accounts state: 'Grants are made based on applications that have been made to the Trust and also charities nominated by Trustees as a result of research undertaken on specific organisations.'

CONTACT DETAILS The Trustees, Holywell Farm, Wigginton, Banbury, Oxfordshire OX15 4LG *Tel.* 07770 496973

■ The King Henry VIII Endowed Trust – Warwick

CC NO 232862   **ESTABLISHED** 1545

WHERE FUNDING CAN BE GIVEN The former borough of Warwick (CV34 postcode area).

WHO CAN BENEFIT Registered charities; unregistered charities; schools; PTAs; amateur sports clubs; hospitals; hospices; religious bodies/institutions; local authorities; individuals.

WHAT IS FUNDED General charitable purposes. Charitable expenditure is allocated in the following proportions: 50% to the five historic Anglican churches in Warwick; 30% to the Warwick Independent Schools Foundation; and 20% to causes benefitting inhabitants of the town.

TYPE OF GRANT Capital costs; core/revenue costs; seed funding/start-up funding; project funding; unrestricted funding.

RANGE OF GRANTS Up to £30,000.

SAMPLE GRANTS Lord Leycester Hospital (£30,000); Oken and Eyfiler Charity (£20,000); The Gap (£10,000); Warwick Cricket Club (£3,000); New Hope Counselling (£1,300).

FINANCES *Financial year end 31/12/2021*
Income £18,090,000
Grants to organisations £213,500
Assets £76,440,000

TRUSTEES John Edwards; Kathryn Parr; The Revd David Brown; Stephen Copley; Ian Furlong; Marie Ashe; Stephen Jobburn; Susan Grinnell; Stephen Cross; Vivienne Bosworth.

OTHER INFORMATION In 2021 the trust distributed a total of £1.52 million, with £843,600 being distributed to the five Anglican churches in the town and £60,600 to the Warwick Independent Schools Foundation. Grants from the Town Share were made to 38 different organisations and totalled £213,500. We have taken the Town Share figure as our grant total, as the other figures represent restricted funds from the trust's permanent endowment.

HOW TO APPLY Application forms are available to download from the trust's website. They should be returned by post or email. Detailed grant guidelines are also available to view on the website. The trustees consider applications on a quarterly basis, usually in March, June, September and November. Check the website for current deadlines.

CONTACT DETAILS Jonathan Wassall, 12 High Street, Warwick, Warwickshire CV34 4AP *Tel.* 01926 495533 *Email* jwassall@kinghenryviii.org.uk *Website* www.kinghenryviii.org.uk

---

■ King/Cullimore Charitable Trust

CC NO 1074928   **ESTABLISHED** 1999
WHERE FUNDING CAN BE GIVEN Worldwide.
WHO CAN BENEFIT Charitable organisations.
WHAT IS FUNDED General charitable purposes.
TYPE OF GRANT Capital, core and start-up costs; unrestricted funding; generally one-off.
RANGE OF GRANTS £5,000 to £2,000.
SAMPLE GRANTS A list of beneficiaries was not included in the annual report and accounts. Previous beneficiaries have included: Alexander Devine Children's Hospice (£500,000); RAFT (£25,000); Countryside Learning and Medical Detection Dogs (£20,000 each); Alzheimer's Research UK; Asthma UK, Demand, Mind and Sense (£10,000 each); Play Kenya (£9,000); Wired Cornwall (£8,000); Orangutan Foundation (£6,500); Drednought Centre, Everyday Art and Sussex Snowdrop Foundation (£5,000 each).
FINANCES *Financial year end 31/03/2022*
   Income £467,400
   Grants to organisations £512,000
   Assets £9,440,000
TRUSTEES Peter Cullimore; Christopher Gardner; Jill Pye; Richard Davies; Amanda Martin; Trudi Scrivener.
HOW TO APPLY At time of writing (July 2023) the trust's Charity Commission record stated: 'No new applications for funding are being accepted as funding is reserved for Charities already being assisted.'
CONTACT DETAILS The Trustees, 52 Ledborough Lane, Beaconsfield, Buckinghamshire HP9 2DF

■ The Kingsbury Charity

CC NO 205797   **ESTABLISHED** 1986
WHERE FUNDING CAN BE GIVEN Kingsbury, Brent.
WHO CAN BENEFIT Registered charities.
WHAT IS FUNDED Social welfare; health.
SAMPLE GRANTS St Luke's Hospice (£15,000); St Laurence's Larder (£14,000); Elders Voice and The Salvation Army (£10,000 each); Almshouse Associations (£50).
FINANCES *Financial year end 31/12/2021*
   Income £380,600
   Grants to organisations £132,600
   Assets £14,110,000
TRUSTEES Stephen Smails; Angela Hopkins; Siobhan Gilling; The Revd Sophie Schuil-Brewer; Ann Little.
HOW TO APPLY Apply in writing to the correspondent.
CONTACT DETAILS Philomena Hughes, Hon. Secretary, 29 Bowater Close, London NW9 0XD *Tel.* 020 8205 9712 *Email* info@kingsburycharity.org *Website* www.kingsburycharity.org

■ The Mary Kinross Charitable Trust

CC NO 212206   **ESTABLISHED** 1957
WHERE FUNDING CAN BE GIVEN UK.
WHO CAN BENEFIT Registered charities; CICs; social enterprises; universities.
WHAT IS FUNDED Medical research; young people; penal affairs; health, including mental health; community development.
WHAT IS NOT FUNDED Individuals.
TYPE OF GRANT Capital costs; core/revenue costs; seed funding/start-up funding; project funding; unrestricted funding.
RANGE OF GRANTS Generally £10,000 to £50,000.
SAMPLE GRANTS Max Planck UCL Centre for Computational Psychiatry and Ageing Research

(£100,000); Royal College of Surgeons of England (£75,000); Bendrigg Trust (£50,000); University of Edinburgh Development Trust (£45,000); Lucy Faithfull Foundation (£25,000); Play for Progress (£15,000); SIFA Fireside (£10,000).
FINANCES *Financial year end 31/03/2022*
   Income £1,220,000
   Grants to organisations £812,800
   Assets £64,810,000
TRUSTEES Dr Neil Cross; Gordon Hague; Elizabeth Shields; Lizzie Barber; Fiona Adams; Henrietta Shields.
OTHER INFORMATION During the year, 37 grants were awarded. Grants were broken down as follows: medical research (£220,000); young people (£213,500); penal affairs (£85,000); mental health (£80,000); health (£77,000); community development (£53,000); miscellaneous (£22,000).
HOW TO APPLY The majority of unsolicited applications are unsuccessful, as most new organisations are recommended by the trustees. Any correspondence must be in writing; telephone calls and emails are discouraged.
CONTACT DETAILS Fiona Adams, Trustee, 36 Grove Avenue, Moseley, Birmingham, West Midlands B13 9RY *Email* marykinrossct@gmail.com

■ Laura Kinsella Foundation

CC NO 1145325   **ESTABLISHED** 2011
WHERE FUNDING CAN BE GIVEN Worldwide.
WHO CAN BENEFIT Charitable organisations; individuals.
WHAT IS FUNDED General charitable purposes, including the arts, human rights and social welfare.
SAMPLE GRANTS A list of beneficiaries was not included in the annual report and accounts. Previous beneficiaries have included: Reprieve (£36,000); Camplin Trust, Centre for Criminal Appeals and Rock the Cotswolds (£10,000 each); Centre for European Reform and Stroud Valleys Support (£5,000 each); Crisis and Footsteps (£2,000 each); Arts Emergency and Alternative Theatre (£1,000 each); Solace Women's Aid (£100).
FINANCES *Financial year end 05/04/2022*
   Income £33,800
   Grants to organisations £230,224
   Grants to individuals £16,700
   Assets £2,910,000
TRUSTEES Alison Jolly; Michael Dickson; Stephen Kinsella.
HOW TO APPLY Apply in writing to the correspondent. Only successful applicants are notified in writing.
CONTACT DETAILS The Trustees, c/o Bates Wells and Braithwaite, 10 Queen Street Place, London EC4R 1BE *Tel.* 020 7551 7777

■ The Graham Kirkham Foundation

CC NO 1002390   **ESTABLISHED** 1991
WHERE FUNDING CAN BE GIVEN UK.
WHO CAN BENEFIT Registered charities; voluntary organisations; individuals.
WHAT IS FUNDED General charitable purposes; education, especially physical education and the study of literature, art, music or science; social welfare for those on low income; medical research and health; animal welfare; well-being of the armed forces; support for those who have misused substances; recreational facilities;

conservation of sites of heritage or historic interest and natural beauty.

TYPE OF GRANT Capacity building; research funding; in-kind support; core costs.

RANGE OF GRANTS Between £5,000 and £100,000.

SAMPLE GRANTS Outward Bound Trust and Worshipful Company of Furniture Makers Charitable Fund (£100,000 each); Penguins Against Cancer (£20,000); Friendly Band and Gloucestershire Academy of Music (£10,000 each); Arafest (£5,000); Sprotbrough Music Society (£500).

FINANCES *Financial year end 31/07/2022*
Income £313,500
Grants to organisations £304,000
Assets £25,800

TRUSTEES Lady Pauline Kirkham; Lord Kirkham; Hon. Michael Kirkham.

OTHER INFORMATION Grants were broken down as follows: welfare (£158,500 to five organisations); education (£100,000 to one organisation); health care (£25,000 to two organisations); culture (£20,500 to three organisations). Individuals can be supported; however, no individuals received grants during this period.

HOW TO APPLY Apply in writing to the correspondent.

CONTACT DETAILS The Trustees, 8 Ebor Court, Redhouse Interchange, Adwick-le-Street, Doncaster, South Yorkshire DN6 7FE *Tel.* 01302 573301

■ Robert Kitchin (Saddlers' Co.)

CC NO 211169   **ESTABLISHED** 1891

WHERE FUNDING CAN BE GIVEN Greater London, with a preference to those who are/have been resident or educated in the City of London.

WHO CAN BENEFIT Educational establishments; charitable organisations; individuals.

WHAT IS FUNDED The education of disadvantaged young people.

TYPE OF GRANT Project funding; bursaries for students.

SAMPLE GRANTS A list of beneficiaries was not included in the annual report and accounts. Previous beneficiaries have included: Beormund Primary School – Southwark; Capel Manor College – Enfield; City of London Academy – Islington; The XLP Project – Tower Hamlets.

FINANCES *Financial year end 31/03/2022*
Income £93,200
Grants to organisations £89,500
Assets £4,880,000

TRUSTEE Saddlers' Company.

OTHER INFORMATION Each year, 65% of the charity's net income is restricted to City University and St Ethelburga's Centre for Reconciliation and Peace. The remaining 35% is distributed at the discretion of the trustees.

HOW TO APPLY Contact the correspondent for more information.

CONTACT DETAILS The Clerk to the Trustees, Saddlers' Company, Saddlers' Hall, 40 Gutter Lane, London EC2V 6BR *Tel.* 020 7726 8661 *Email* clerk@saddlersco.co.uk *Website* www.saddlersco.co.uk

■ The Ernest Kleinwort Charitable Trust

CC NO 1197205   **ESTABLISHED** 1963

WHERE FUNDING CAN BE GIVEN UK, with a preference for Sussex; overseas.

WHO CAN BENEFIT Registered charities.

WHAT IS FUNDED Wildlife and environmental conservation; family planning; care of older and young people; disability; general social welfare; hospices; medical research; other charitable causes.

WHAT IS NOT FUNDED See the trust's website for a full list of exclusions.

TYPE OF GRANT Start-up funding; core/revenue costs; project costs; capital costs; conditionally renewable grants for up to three years may be agreed on occasion.

RANGE OF GRANTS Mostly of £20,000 or less.

SAMPLE GRANTS A list of beneficiaries was not included in the annual report and accounts. Previous beneficiaries have included: Tusk (£168,000); St Catherine's Hospice (£130,000); Off The Fence Trust (£35,000); Galapagos Conservation Trust (£30,000); The Sara Lee Trust (£10,000); The Chaseley Trust (£15,000); Education Training Consortium Sussex (£8,000); Whizz-Kidz (£5,000); Bristol Natural History Consortium (£1,100); React (Rapid Effective Assistance for Children with potentially Terminal illness) (£500).

FINANCES *Financial year end 31/03/2021*
Income £611,900
Grants to organisations £1,660,000
Assets £71,130,000

TRUSTEES Marina Rose Kleinwort; Sir Richard Kleinwort; Alexander Hamilton Kleinwort; The Rt Hon. Edmund Christopher; Lord Chandos; Charlie Mayhew.

OTHER INFORMATION The trust recently re-registered with the Charity Commission as a CIO; the financial information relates to the trust's previous registration (Charity Commission no. 229665).

HOW TO APPLY Firstly, potential applicants should complete the eligibility questionnaire. If eligible, application forms are available to be completed online on the trust's website. The trustees are unlikely to consider more than one application per year by any applicant. Deadlines for applications can also be found on the trust's website.

CONTACT DETAILS Andrina Murrell, Grants Officer, EKCT, c/o Knill James, 1 Bell Lane, Lewes BN7 1JU *Tel.* 07960 057742 *Email* grants@ekct.org.uk *Website* www.ekct.org.uk

■ Sir James Knott Trust

CC NO 1001363   **ESTABLISHED** 1990

WHERE FUNDING CAN BE GIVEN Durham; Gateshead; Hartlepool; Newcastle upon Tyne; North Tyneside; Northumberland; South Tyneside.

WHO CAN BENEFIT Registered charities; community groups; social enterprises.

WHAT IS FUNDED General charitable purposes, with special consideration for charitable activities known to have been of particular interest to Sir James Knott, including arts and culture; community issues and events; conservation and the environment; education and training; health and sport; heritage and historic buildings; housing, homelessness and hardship; maritime causes; the armed forces.

WHAT IS NOT FUNDED Individuals; research; activity which has already taken place or which takes place outside the trust's area of benefit.

TYPE OF GRANT Capital and core costs; salaries; start-up expenditure; matched funding.

RANGE OF GRANTS £5,000 to £15,000 per year, often over three years.

SAMPLE GRANTS A list of beneficiaries was not included in the annual report and accounts. Previous beneficiaries have included: University of Sunderland Development Trust (£250,000); YMCA North Tyneside (£30,000); Wearside Women in Need (£15,000); Hartlepool Stage Society and Northumberland Wildlife Trust Ltd (£10,000 each); Just Finance Foundation (£5,000); Smile for Life Children's Charity (£3,500); Northern Ballet Ltd (£2,000).

FINANCES *Financial year end* 31/03/2022
Income £2,940,000
Grants to organisations £2,320,000
Assets £68,970,000

TRUSTEES John Cresswell; Ben Speke; The Revd Fiona Sample; Sir Walter Riddell.

OTHER INFORMATION Grants were broken down as follows: health and active lifestyles (£871,700); arts and heritage (£673,000); employment, financial inclusion, debt management, education and training (£268,700); community development (£209,400); the armed forces and uniformed organisations (£137,300); strengthening a diverse charity sector (£103,500); crime prevention and rehabilitation of offenders (£60,500); the environment (£17,000).

HOW TO APPLY Check the eligibility criteria on the trust's website before applying. Applications can be made online via the website, which also has details on how to apply, application deadlines and FAQs.

CONTACT DETAILS The Trustees, Mea House, Ellison Place, Newcastle upon Tyne NE1 8XS *Tel.* 0191 432 8990 *Email* info@knott-trust.co.uk *Website* www.knott-trust.co.uk

■ The Kobler Trust

CC NO 275237 **ESTABLISHED** 1963
WHERE FUNDING CAN BE GIVEN UK.
WHO CAN BENEFIT Registered charities; hospices.
WHAT IS FUNDED General charitable purposes; the arts; the Jewish faith and community; health and disability; children and young people.
RANGE OF GRANTS From £300 to £25,000, but typically less than £1,000.
SAMPLE GRANTS Birmingham Rep – Nick Kent Productions (£25,000); West London Synagogue – Rainbow Refugees Project (£16,200); Smallpeice Trust Arkwright Scholarships (£4,400); English Touring Opera (£1,000); St Mungo's (£600); Interact Stroke Support and React (Rapid Effective Assistance for Children with potentially Terminal illness) and Thumbs Up Club (£500 each); The National Autistic Society (£300).
FINANCES *Financial year end* 05/04/2022
Income £89,700
Grants to organisations £73,500
Assets £3,420,000
TRUSTEES Joel Israelsohn; Joanne Evans; Andrew Stone; Antoine Xuereb.
HOW TO APPLY Applications should be made in writing to the trustees. Applications are considered by the trustees on a regular basis, both at the trustees' meetings and between meetings. Acknowledgements are generally not sent out to unsuccessful applicants.
CONTACT DETAILS The Trustees, c/o Lewis Silkin LLP, 10 Clifford's Inn Passage, London EC4A 1BL *Tel.* 020 7074 8000 *Email* info@lewissilkin.com

■ Kollel and Co. Ltd

CC NO 1077180 **ESTABLISHED** 1999
WHERE FUNDING CAN BE GIVEN Worldwide.
WHO CAN BENEFIT Charitable organisations with a Jewish focus.
WHAT IS FUNDED The Jewish faith and community; the relief of poverty; religious activities and education; medical needs; general charitable purposes.
TYPE OF GRANT Building, equipment and project costs.
SAMPLE GRANTS Amud Hatzdokoh Trust (£138,400); The Rehabilitation Trust (£126,700); Congregation Yetev Lev Dsatmar Antwerp Ltd (£70,800); Keren Hatzolas Doros Alei Siach (£25,000); Keren Chochmas Shloma Trust (£250).
FINANCES *Financial year end* 31/01/2022
Income £1,400,000
Grants to organisations £1,260,000
Assets £4,600,000
TRUSTEES Sam Low; Simon Low; Judith Weiss; Rachel Kalish.
OTHER INFORMATION The annual report and accounts for 2021/22 state that grants of under £50,000 totalled £672,500.
HOW TO APPLY Apply in writing to the correspondent.
CONTACT DETAILS Simon Low, Trustee, 7 Overlea Road, London E5 9BG *Tel.* 020 8806 1570

■ Kolyom Trust Ltd

CC NO 1112084 **ESTABLISHED** 2005
WHERE FUNDING CAN BE GIVEN Worldwide.
WHO CAN BENEFIT Registered charities; places of worship.
WHAT IS FUNDED Judaism; Jewish religious education; the alleviation of poverty in the Jewish community.
SAMPLE GRANTS Teshuvah Tefilloh Tzedokoh (£582,100); Bederech Kovod (£305,100); Academy for Talmudical Research (£136,400); Shir Bemosh Ltd (£112,400); Chessed Beis Yisroel (£111,000).
FINANCES *Financial year end* 31/05/2022
Income £3,490,000
Grants to organisations £3,420,000
Assets £1,890,000
TRUSTEES Michael Kaufman; Alan Klor; Victor Frankenhuis.
OTHER INFORMATION Grants were broken down as follows: education (£2.74 million); relief of poverty (£502,800); religion (£171,000). Only organisations that received grants of over £70,000 were listed as beneficiaries in the trust's 2021/22 accounts. Grants of under £70,000 totalled £2.17 million.
HOW TO APPLY Unsolicited applications are not accepted.
CONTACT DETAILS The Trustees, 134 Leicester Road, Salford, Greater Manchester M7 4GB *Tel.* 0161 740 1960 *Email* admin@kolyomtrust.org.uk

■ KPE4 Charitable Trust

OSCR NO SC047599
WHERE FUNDING CAN BE GIVEN North Edinburgh, primarily Pilton, Granton and Muirhouse (with specific support targeted towards children attending Craigroyston, Forthview, Granton, Leith and Pirniehall primary schools).
WHO CAN BENEFIT Scottish charities; schools and colleges.

WHAT IS FUNDED People who are disadvantaged; social welfare; children and young people; education.

RANGE OF GRANTS Mostly up to £10,000 with the occasional larger grant.

SAMPLE GRANTS Red Squirrel Accord (£20,000); Home Link Family Support (£15,000); Garvald Edinburgh and The Wave Project (£10,000 each); Fife Young Carers, LifeCare (Edinburgh) Ltd and Sunshine Wishes Children's Charity (£5,000 each); School of Hard Knocks (£2,000).

FINANCES *Financial year end* 05/04/2022
Income £5,940,000
Grants to organisations £106,400
Assets £7,800,000

OTHER INFORMATION According to its website, the trust mostly awards grants to its 'focus' charities that seek to improve the lives of people in northern Edinburgh. Each year the trust selects around 30 'focus' charities. There is a smaller pot for 'non-focused' charities which trustees would like to support.

HOW TO APPLY Application forms can be found on the trust's website.

CONTACT DETAILS The Trustees, 40 North Castle Street, Edinburgh EH2 3BN *Email* kpe4@revlab.com *Website* https://kpe4trust.wixsite.com/kpe4

■ The KPMG Foundation

CC NO 1194474   **ESTABLISHED** 2000

WHERE FUNDING CAN BE GIVEN UK.

WHO CAN BENEFIT Registered charities; social enterprises.

WHAT IS FUNDED Children and young people from disadvantaged communities in the UK.

TYPE OF GRANT Project funding.

RANGE OF GRANTS Mainly under £100,000.

SAMPLE GRANTS Education Endowment Foundation (£250,000); Reach Foundation (£100,000); Family Rights Group and School Home Support (£75,000 each); Lucy Faithfull Foundation (£59,500); Anna Freud Centre for Children and Families (£50,000); Family Action (£33,000); University of Oxford (£30,000); Buttle UK (£25,000).

FINANCES *Financial year end* 30/09/2021
Income £939,200
Grants to organisations £797,500
Assets £6,190,000

TRUSTEES Peter Sherratt; David Woodward; Corrine Harms; David Bartram; Kamini Mehta; Sherrylyn Peck.

OTHER INFORMATION The foundation is funded primarily by donations from KPMG LLP. The foundation has recently re-registered with the Charity Commission and therefore full financial information was not available. The financial information in this entry relates to the foundation's previous registration (Charity Commission no. 1086518).

HOW TO APPLY The foundation pro-actively identifies organisations to support and therefore does not accept unsolicited applications; however, the website states the following: 'if you share our purpose, priorities and approach, contact us with a brief description of your work and a link to your own website. Where there is a strong alignment, we will respond.'

CONTACT DETAILS Judith McNeill, Chief Executive, 15 Canada Square, Canary Wharf, London E14 5GL *Tel.* 020 7311 4217 *Email* kpmgfoundation@kpmg.co.uk *Website* https://kpmgfoundation.org.uk/index.html

---

■ Kreditor Charitable Trust

CC NO 292649   **ESTABLISHED** 1985

WHERE FUNDING CAN BE GIVEN UK.

WHO CAN BENEFIT Charitable organisations, Jewish organisations.

WHAT IS FUNDED The Jewish faith and community; general charitable purposes.

SAMPLE GRANTS A list of beneficiaries was not included in the annual report and accounts.

FINANCES *Financial year end* 05/04/2022
Income £185,000
Grants to organisations £75,800
Assets £226,700

TRUSTEES Sharon Kreditor; Paul Kreditor; Merle Kreditor.

OTHER INFORMATION In previous years, grants have been mostly for less than £100 and have been given mainly to Jewish organisations working in education and social and medical welfare.

HOW TO APPLY Apply in writing to the correspondent.

CONTACT DETAILS The Trustees, Hallswelle House, 1 Hallswelle Road, London NW11 0DH *Tel.* 020 8248 7500

■ The Kreitman Foundation

CC NO 269046   **ESTABLISHED** 1975

WHERE FUNDING CAN BE GIVEN UK.

WHO CAN BENEFIT Charitable organisations.

WHAT IS FUNDED Currently, the foundation's main focus is the climate crisis. Previously, support has also been given to supporting the rights of LGBTQ+ young people and addressing gender norms and stereotypes.

WHAT IS NOT FUNDED Individuals.

TYPE OF GRANT Project funding; one-off; multi-year.

RANGE OF GRANTS £5,000 to £20,000.

SAMPLE GRANTS Farming the Future Fund (£20,000); Project Seagrass (£15,000); Global Greengrants Fund UK (£10,000); SHE Changes Climate (£5,000); Nature-Friendly Farming Network (£2,500); SumOfUs (£500).

FINANCES *Financial year end* 05/04/2022
Income £31,200
Grants to organisations £114,300
Assets £3,540,000

TRUSTEES Richard Luck-Hille; Rowena Teall; James Belchamber.

OTHER INFORMATION In 2021/22, the foundation awarded 16 grants to organisations.

HOW TO APPLY In the first instance, potential applicants should contact the foundation via email, providing a brief introduction and their latest accounts. The trustees will then make contact if they wish to explore further. The 2021/22 annual report states: 'the trustees receive and assess unsolicited enquiries but generally adopt a largely strategic approach to funding.'

CONTACT DETAILS The Trustees, 5th Floor, Mariner House, 62 Prince Street, Bristol BS1 4QD *Tel.* 0117 971 3445 *Email* info@kreitmanfoundation.org.uk *Website* www.kreitmanfoundation.org.uk

---

■ Kupath Gemach Chaim Bechesed Viznitz Trust

CC NO 1110323   **ESTABLISHED** 2005

WHERE FUNDING CAN BE GIVEN UK and Israel.

WHO CAN BENEFIT Registered charities; religious institutions and places of worship; individuals.

WHAT IS FUNDED Social welfare for the Jewish community; Judaism; Jewish education.

TYPE OF GRANT General funding; interest-free loans.

RANGE OF GRANTS Mostly up to £20,000, with the occasional larger grant.

SAMPLE GRANTS Koel Ahavas Torah (£33,600); Bedside Kosher and Kollel Viznitz (£20,000 each); Colel Ahavat Israel and Wiznitz Institutions (£15,000 each).

FINANCES *Financial year end 31/05/2022*
Income £931,200
Grants to organisations £341,300
Grants to individuals £602,200
Assets £26,400

TRUSTEES Israel Kahan; Alexander Pifko; Saul Weiss.

OTHER INFORMATION Grants were broken down as follows: Judaism (£158,500); Jewish education (£143,200); medical causes (£16,700); relief of poverty (£15,400); social welfare (£7,500). Only organisations that received grants of over £10,000 were listed as beneficiaries in the trust's 2021/22 accounts. Grants of under £10,000 totalled £144,000.

HOW TO APPLY Apply in writing to the correspondent.

CONTACT DETAILS The Trustees, 171 Kyverdale Road, Stoke Newington, London N16 6PS *Tel.* 020 8442 9604

....

■ Kusuma Trust UK

CC NO 1126983   **ESTABLISHED** 2008

WHERE FUNDING CAN BE GIVEN UK (primarily London); Gibraltar; India.

WHO CAN BENEFIT Registered charitable organisations.

WHAT IS FUNDED Health and well-being; access to opportunities; community development and the environment.

TYPE OF GRANT Project funding; research.

SAMPLE GRANTS Natural History Museum (£1.5 million); Royal Brompton and Harefield Hospitals Charity (£250,100); St Paul's Girls' School (£100,000); Creative Futures (£54,300); Walworth Garden (£25,000); Migrants Organise (£15,000); Chelsea Theatre (£13,900); Photographers Gallery (£9,900); Butterfly Conservation (£9,300); The Inland Waterways Association (£5,800).

FINANCES *Financial year end 31/12/2021*
Income £3,400,000
Grants to organisations £2,790,000
Assets £494,900,000

TRUSTEES Dr Soma Pujari; Anurag Dikshit; Nitin Jain.

OTHER INFORMATION Grants were broken down as follows: UK projects (£2.13 million); Gibraltar projects (£456,600); India projects (£203,900).

HOW TO APPLY Typically the trust does not accept unsolicited applications; however, calls for funding are sometimes published on the trust's website and Twitter account. Details of what to include and the deadline for the funding round will be published alongside eligibility criteria.

CONTACT DETAILS Bethan Garfoot, Grants Assistant, 5th Floor, 55 New Oxford Street, London WC1A 1BS *Tel.* 020 7420 0650 *Email* info@kusumatrust.org *Website* www.kusumatrust.org

....

■ The Kyte Charitable Trust

CC NO 1035886   **ESTABLISHED** 1994

WHERE FUNDING CAN BE GIVEN UK.

WHO CAN BENEFIT Jewish charitable organisations.

WHAT IS FUNDED General charitable purposes; the Jewish faith and community.

SAMPLE GRANTS A list of beneficiaries was not included in the annual report and accounts. Previous beneficiaries have included: Maccabi London Brady Recreational Trust (£73,500);

Jewish Care and UJIA (£25,000); Jewish Community Secondary School Trust (£22,500); Community Security Trust (£20,000); Chai Cancer Care (£7,200); ORT (£500).

FINANCES *Financial year end 05/04/2022*
Income £187,500
Grants to organisations £162,500
Assets £52,604

TRUSTEES David Kyte; James Kyte; Tracey Kyte; Ilana Kyte; Max Kyte.

HOW TO APPLY Contact the correspondent for further information.

CONTACT DETAILS The Trustees, The Old Police Station, 1069 Finchley Road, London NW11 0PU *Tel.* 020 7123 6680

■ Ladbrokes Coral Trust

cc no 1101804 **established** 2003
where funding can be given UK.
who can benefit Registered charities, hospices, hospitals, community groups.
what is funded Health – principally research/ treatment, hospice services and disability support; education – supporting people with disabilities/who are disadvantaged and sports services in deprived areas or for disadvantaged people; community – focusing on projects for people who are homeless and for older people or social activity projects for those at risk; the environment and animals.
sample grants A list of beneficiaries was not included in the annual report and accounts.
finances *Financial year end 31/12/2021*
Income £224,700
Grants to organisations £155,100
Assets £286,000
trustees Karen Thraves; Nick Batram; Jay Dossetter; Craig Watson; Simon O'Halloran; Steve Humphries; Simon Burnell.
other information Grants were broken down as follows: medical causes (£103,700); hospices and hospitals (£17,600); other (£12,900); social welfare (£4,900); the environment and animals (£400).
how to apply Apply in writing to the correspondent. The trust's Charity Commission record states that the 'trustees meet every 4–6 weeks to consider grant requests from shop and head office fundraisers and registered charities.'
contact details The Trustees, c/o GVC Holdings plc, 3rd Floor, One New Change, London EC4M 9AF *Tel.* 020 3938 0000 *Email* charity@ ladbrokescoral.com

■ The K. P. Ladd Charitable Trust

cc no 1091493 **established** 2002
where funding can be given UK and overseas.
who can benefit Religious bodies; places of worship.
what is funded Christian causes; missionary work; overseas aid.
type of grant Capital costs; core and revenue costs; seed funding; start-up funding; project funding; unrestricted funding.
range of grants From £2,000 to £65,000.
sample grants London Institute for Contemporary Christianity (£65,000); London City Mission (£15,000); Church Army (£5,000); The Salvation Army (£5,000); Derby City Mission (£3,000); Livability and Mercy Ships (£2,000 each).
finances *Financial year end 30/04/2022*
Income £146,500
Grants to organisations £112,000
Assets £3,780,000
trustees Brian Ladd; Ian Creswick; Rosemary-Anne Ladd.
other information Grants were awarded to 16 organisations during 2021/22.
how to apply The trust has stated that it 'is fully committed and does not reply to unsolicited requests'. The trustees select charities known to them personally.

contact details Brian Ladd, Trustee, 34 St Mary's Avenue, Northwood, Middlesex HA6 3AZ *Tel.* 020 7399 9563 *Email* brian.ladd@licc.org. uk

■ John Laing Charitable Trust

cc no 236852 **established** 1962
where funding can be given UK and, occasionally, countries where the John Laing Group plc operates.
who can benefit Registered charities; CICs; NGOs; organisations outside the UK with a link to the John Laing Group; existing and former employees of John Laing Group plc who are in need.
what is funded Community; disadvantaged youth; education; homelessness.
what is not funded Individuals other than current or former employees of John Laing Group plc; organisations not aligned to the trust's strategic priorities; organisations whose main aim is animal welfare; sponsorships; projects that are not for public benefit.
type of grant Project funding; core funding; capital costs; single and multi-year funding.
sample grants A list of beneficiaries was not included in the annual report and accounts. Previous beneficiaries have included: FareShare (£100,000); The Silver Line (£50,000); Peace4Kids (£47,800); ReadEasy and Safer London (£25,000 each); Orminston Families (£7,500).
finances *Financial year end 31/12/2021*
Income £2,300,000
Grants to organisations £1,160,000
Assets £72,480,000
trustees Lynette Krige; Christopher Laing; Sir Martin Laing; Christopher Waples; Alexandra Gregory; Stewart Laing; Timothy Foster.
how to apply At the time of writing (March 2023) the trust's website stated: 'Note that applications to the Trust are currently closed. Until further notice, we only process invited applications.' Check the trust's website for further information.
contact details Helen Parker, Trust Director, 33 Bunns Lane, London NW7 2DX *Email* use the contact form on the website
Website https://johnlaingcharitabletrust.com

■ Maurice and Hilda Laing Charitable Trust

cc no 1058109 **established** 1996
where funding can be given UK and overseas, with a preference for sub-Saharan Africa.
who can benefit UK-registered charities.
what is funded The advancement of the Christian faith and values; people in the UK who are disadvantaged, vulnerable and/or socially isolated such as prisoners and ex-offenders, people who are homeless, children and young people and refugees; the relief of poverty overseas, with an emphasis on street children, education, sustainable livelihoods and people with disabilities.
what is not funded See the website for a full list of exclusions.
type of grant Project funding; capital costs.
range of grants Grants typically range between £5,000 and £25,000, although the trust has the capacity to make a small number of larger grants each year.

SAMPLE GRANTS Charities Aid Foundation (£130,000); Christians Against Poverty and Mission Aviation Fellowship (£50,000 each); Kids Matter (£10,000); The Woolf Institute (£5,000).

FINANCES *Financial year end 31/12/2021*
Income £782,700
Grants to organisations £964,500
Assets £27,670,000

TRUSTEES Andrea Currie; Charles Laing; Stephen Ludlow; Simon Martle; Dr Paul Bosch.

OTHER INFORMATION The trust made 52 grants which were broken down as follows: social welfare (£329,500); overseas aid (£201,000); religion (£199,000); children and young people (£35,000); health and medicine (£5,000).

HOW TO APPLY Apply in writing to the correspondent by post. Applicants are asked to download and complete an application cover sheet, which is available on the completion of an eligibility quiz. Full details of what should be included in an application can be found on the trust's website. This is one of four Laing Family Trusts. The Laing Family Trusts are run on a co-ordinated basis, which means that you do not need to make multiple applications to the individual trusts. Your application will automatically be directed to the most appropriate of the four trusts.

CONTACT DETAILS Belgin Wingrove, Grants Manager, 33 Bunns Lane, Mill Hill, London NW7 2DX *Tel.* 020 8238 8890 *Email* info@laingfamilytrusts.org.uk *Website* www.laingfamilytrusts.org.uk

■ Christopher Laing Foundation

CC NO 278460   **ESTABLISHED** 1979

WHERE FUNDING CAN BE GIVEN UK, with a preference for Hertfordshire and Oxfordshire.

WHO CAN BENEFIT Registered charities.

WHAT IS FUNDED Children and young people; education; culture; the environment; homelessness; disability.

TYPE OF GRANT Capital; core costs; project funding.

RANGE OF GRANTS Up to £100,000 but mostly from £1,000 to £50,000.

SAMPLE GRANTS The Duke of Edinburgh's Award (£52,800); Fields in Trust – National Playing Fields Association (£40,000); National Emergencies Trust (£20,000); Groundwork East (£12,500); Little Green Pig (£10,000); Make a Wish Foundation and Medical Detection Dogs (£5,000 each); Alzheimer's Society (£3,000).

FINANCES *Financial year end 05/04/2022*
Income £454,500
Grants to organisations £329,300
Assets £13,630,000

TRUSTEES John Keeble; Christopher Laing; Diana Laing; Michael Laing; Richard Haines; Carla Seale.

OTHER INFORMATION In 2021/22 grants were made to 20 organisations and were distributed for the following purposes: other (£163,000); children and young people (£69,800); culture and the environment (£62,500); Charities Aid Foundation (£44,000).

HOW TO APPLY Application forms can be made via the foundation's website. Applications are considered regularly by the trustees.

CONTACT DETAILS The Trustees, c/o TMF Global Services (UK) Ltd, 960 Capability Green, Luton, Bedfordshire LU1 3PE *Tel.* 01582 439200 *Email* info@christopherlaingfoundation.com *Website* www.christopherlaingfoundation.com

■ The David Laing Foundation

CC NO 278462   **ESTABLISHED** 1979

WHERE FUNDING CAN BE GIVEN Mainly Hertfordshire, Oxfordshire, Leicestershire, Northamptonshire with some UK-wide and worldwide grants.

WHO CAN BENEFIT Organisations benefitting children, including those who are adopted, fostered or in care; one-parent families; people with disabilities.

WHAT IS FUNDED General charitable purposes, with a focus on young people, disability and the arts.

WHAT IS NOT FUNDED Individuals.

TYPE OF GRANT One-off grants; capital costs.

RANGE OF GRANTS Up to £35,700.

SAMPLE GRANTS The Northamptonshire Community Foundation (£35,700); James Butler (£30,000); Northamptonshire Search and Rescue and Royal College of Music (£15,000 each); Adrenaline Alley and Crusader Community Boating (£5,000 each); Merry Opera Company (£3,500).

FINANCES *Financial year end 05/04/2022*
Income £189,700
Grants to organisations £244,400
Assets £6,570,000

TRUSTEES Francis Barlow; David Laing; Stuart Lewis; David Laing.

OTHER INFORMATION Grants were broken down as follows: arts and culture (£106,300); general charitable purposes (£50,000); children and young people (£38,500); disability/disadvantage/health and well-being (£30,200); social welfare/sports/recreation (£8,400); religion (£3,500); overseas aid (£2,700).

HOW TO APPLY Contact the correspondent for further information.

CONTACT DETAILS The Trustees, The Manor House, Grafton Underwood, Kettering, Northamptonshire NN14 3AA *Tel.* 01536 330404 *Email* david@david-laing.co.uk

■ The Kirby Laing Foundation

CC NO 264299   **ESTABLISHED** 1972

WHERE FUNDING CAN BE GIVEN UK and overseas, with a preference for Asia.

WHO CAN BENEFIT Registered charities; churches with exempt status.

WHAT IS FUNDED Christian causes; education, particularly STEM subjects and traditional crafts; medical welfare and research, particularly into dementia, stroke and other neurodegenerative diseases; opera and the performing arts; the environment; overseas development projects; children and young people; older people; people with disabilities.

WHAT IS NOT FUNDED See the website for a full list of exclusions.

TYPE OF GRANT Capital costs; programme development costs; endowment/capacity building; project costs; research funding; one-off and multi-year grants.

RANGE OF GRANTS £2,000 to £20,000 for small grants.

SAMPLE GRANTS Cicely Saunders International (£1.75 million); The Leprosy Mission (£236,800); St Albans Cathedral Trust (£150,000); The Duke of Edinburgh's Award (£100,000); Project Equinox (£45,000); National Portrait Gallery (£20,000); Tall Ships Youth Trust (£7,200); Royal Academy of Dramatic Art (RADA) (£5,000).

FINANCES *Financial year end 31/12/2021*
Income £2,100,000
Grants to organisations £4,170,000
Assets £66,430,000

TRUSTEES The Revd Charles Burch; David Laing; Simon Webley; Dr Frederick Lewis.

OTHER INFORMATION During 2021, grants were awarded to 76 organisations, including 5 grants of between £500 and £3,000 that were made through Charities Aid Foundation, totalling £12,600. Only organisations that received grants of over £5,000 were listed as beneficiaries in the foundation's accounts.

HOW TO APPLY The Laing Family Trusts are run on a co-ordinated basis; applications are directed to the most suitable of the four trusts, so multiple applications are not necessary. Full details on how to submit an application can be found on the foundation's website. Applications will not be accepted by email.

CONTACT DETAILS Belgin Wingrove, Grants Manager, 33 Bunns Lane, Mill Hill, London NW7 2DX *Tel.* 020 8238 8890 *Email* info@laingfamilytrusts.org.uk *Website* www.laingfamilytrusts.org.uk

■ The Martin Laing Foundation

CC NO 278461 **ESTABLISHED** 1979

WHERE FUNDING CAN BE GIVEN UK, with a preference for Essex, Hertfordshire and Norfolk; Malta.

WHO CAN BENEFIT Registered charities.

WHAT IS FUNDED The environment and conservation; projects benefitting disadvantaged young people or older people in Norfolk, Essex or Hertfordshire; development projects in Malta.

WHAT IS NOT FUNDED A list of exclusions can be found on the foundation's website.

TYPE OF GRANT One-off awards for capital costs; one-off and recurrent project grants.

RANGE OF GRANTS £500 to £10,000.

SAMPLE GRANTS Priscilla Bacon Norfolk Hospice Care (£25,000); Students Education Trust (£15,000); Welsh National Opera (£10,000); ABF The Soldiers' Charity and Hands Around The World (£5,000 each); Ware Museum Trust (£3,000); Crisis (£2,500); War Child (£2,000).

FINANCES *Financial year end* 05/04/2022
Income £409,100
Grants to organisations £548,800
Assets £14,350,000

TRUSTEES Colin Fletcher; Nicholas Gregory; Lady Laing; Sir Martin Laing; Edward Laing; Alexandra Gregory.

OTHER INFORMATION This is one of the Laing Family Trusts. Detailed information on this and the other Laing charities can be found on the website. There were 33 awards made in 2021/22 (including 7 through the Charities Aid Foundation). Grants were distributed in the following categories: religion (£330,000); health and medicine (£105,000); overseas development (£52,800); children and young people (£40,000); Charities Aid Foundation (£20,000); culture and the environment (£10,000); social welfare (£5,000).

HOW TO APPLY The Laing Family Trusts are administered and co-ordinated centrally; applications are directed to the most suitable of the four trusts, so multiple applications are not necessary. Detailed guidance on how to make an application can be found online. The majority of unsolicited applications are unsuccessful. Applications for overseas projects are by invitation only.

CONTACT DETAILS Belgin Wingrove, Grants Manager, Laing Family Trusts, 33 Bunns Lane, London NW7 2DX *Tel.* 020 8238 8890 *Email* info@laingfamilytrusts.org.uk *Website* www.laingfamilytrusts.org.uk

■ The Beatrice Laing Trust

CC NO 211884 **ESTABLISHED** 1952

WHERE FUNDING CAN BE GIVEN UK and anglophone countries in sub-Saharan Africa and parts of Asia.

WHO CAN BENEFIT Registered charities; Christian organisations; churches. Grants to overseas projects are normally made through a registered UK charity.

WHAT IS FUNDED Church building, extension or redevelopment projects; homelessness; older people; people who have experience of the criminal justice system; former members of the armed forces; people with disabilities; small-scale overseas development projects which improve educational opportunities and build sustainable livelihoods.

WHAT IS NOT FUNDED See the website for a full list of exclusions.

TYPE OF GRANT Mainly one-off, for capital costs; one-off or recurrent project expenditure.

RANGE OF GRANTS Mostly between £500 and £30,000.

SAMPLE GRANTS Coventry Cathedral Development Trust (£250,000); Off The Fence Trust (£25,000); Become (£3,000); Berkshire Vision (£2,500); Bryn Iwan Chapel (£1,000).

FINANCES *Financial year end* 05/04/2022
Income £2,870,000
Grants to organisations £2,030,000
Assets £75,380,000

TRUSTEES Paula Blacker; Alex Gregory; Christopher Laing; Charles Laing; Sir Martin Laing; David Laing.

HOW TO APPLY This is one of the Laing Family Trusts which are administered and co-ordinated centrally; applications are directed to the most suitable of the four trusts, so multiple applications are not necessary. Detailed guidance on how to make an application can be found on the website, along with an eligibility quiz.

CONTACT DETAILS Belgin Wingrove, Grants Manager, c/o Laing Family Trusts, 33 Bunns Lane, Mill Hill, London NW7 2DX *Tel.* 020 8238 8890 *Email* info@laingfamilytrusts.org.uk *Website* www.laingfamilytrusts.org.uk

■ The Leonard Laity Stoate Charitable Trust

CC NO 221325 **ESTABLISHED** 1950

WHERE FUNDING CAN BE GIVEN Bristol and Somerset (especially western Somerset); Cornwall; Devon; Dorset.

WHO CAN BENEFIT Registered charities; religious bodies/institutions.

WHAT IS FUNDED Methodism; general charitable purposes; social welfare; medical causes; disability; children and young people; community projects; the arts; overseas aid; the environment.

WHAT IS NOT FUNDED Individuals; non-registered charities; CICs; large projects; general appeals by national charities; running costs.

TYPE OF GRANT Capital costs; core/revenue costs; seed funding/start-up costs.

RANGE OF GRANTS Usually between £100 and £2,000.

SAMPLE GRANTS A list of beneficiaries was not included in the annual report and accounts. Previous beneficiaries have included: Methodist Homes for the Aged (£2,000); Devon in Sight and Farms for City Children (£1,000 each); Minehead Museum (£600); Countryside

Restoration Project and Deafblind UK (£500 each); St Mary's Church – Eversley (£200).

FINANCES *Financial year end* 31/03/2022
Income £97,300
Grants to organisations £70,700
Assets £2,250,000

TRUSTEES Dr Christopher Stoate; Dr Pam Stoate; Philip Stoate; The Revd Dr Jonathan Pye; Mark Harnden; Natasha Jones.

OTHER INFORMATION In 2021/22, grants were distributed in the following categories: disadvantaged people (£22,700); medical disabilities (£19,200); young people and children (£8,500); Methodist causes (£5,800); other churches (£5,500); overseas (£4,100); the environment (£1,800); community projects (£1,200); the arts (£1,000).

HOW TO APPLY Applications should be made in writing to the correspondent (not by email or telephone) and should include the information specified on the trust's website. There is no dedicated application form. There are no deadlines but the majority of grants are awarded at half-yearly meetings in April/May and October/November.

CONTACT DETAILS Philip Stoate, Secretary, 41 Tower Hill, Williton, Taunton, Somerset TA4 4JR *Email* secretary@stoate-charity.org.uk *Website* www.stoate-charity.org.uk

■ The Lake House Charitable Foundation

CC NO 1126293   **ESTABLISHED** 2008
WHERE FUNDING CAN BE GIVEN England.
WHO CAN BENEFIT Registered charities, with a preference for small and local charities.
WHAT IS FUNDED Support and care for sick and disadvantaged children and young people; older people.
WHAT IS NOT FUNDED Individuals; non-registered charities.
TYPE OF GRANT Project funding; core funding; one-off and repeat requests.
RANGE OF GRANTS Mostly £5,000 and under.
SAMPLE GRANTS The Big Give Trust (£35,400); Epsom College Development Fund (£13,500); The Change Foundation (£4,000); Action for Stammering Children (£1,000).
FINANCES *Financial year end* 05/04/2022
Income £265,900
Grants to organisations £119,600
Assets £161,000
TRUSTEES Sarah Mulford; Helen Perry; Timothy Perry; Marcus Platt; Sasha Platt; Alistair Candlish.
HOW TO APPLY Application forms can be downloaded from the foundation's website and should be returned via email to the correspondent. The trustees meet twice a year and applications can be sent at any time. Every application will receive a response. Full guidelines on applications can be found on the website.
CONTACT DETAILS The Trustees, PO Box 651, Weybridge, Surrey KT13 3EP *Tel.* 01932 848028 *Email* lakehouse.office@googlemail.com *Website* www.thelakehouse.org.uk

■ Community Foundations for Lancashire and Merseyside

CC NO 1068887   **ESTABLISHED** 1998
WHERE FUNDING CAN BE GIVEN Merseyside and Lancashire.
WHO CAN BENEFIT Registered charities; unregistered charities; social enterprises; CICs; schools.
WHAT IS FUNDED General charitable purposes including: social welfare; children and young people; community projects; health; older people; the environment.
TYPE OF GRANT Core costs; project funding; seed funding/start-up funding.
SAMPLE GRANTS A list of beneficiaries was not included in the annual report and accounts. Previous beneficiaries have included: dot-art Schools; Fire Support Network; Halton Voluntary Action; Jo Jo Mind and Body; Liverpool Academy of Art; Liverpool Greenbank Wheelchair Basketball Club; The Zero Centre.
FINANCES *Financial year end* 31/03/2022
Income £4,050,000
Grants to organisations £3,460,000
Assets £22,710,000
TRUSTEES Arthur Roberts; Andrew Myers; Chris Bliss; Amanda Meachin; Colin Wardale; George Mendoros; Nasima Zaman; Donna Howitt; Wiliam Wareing; Neil Welsh.
OTHER INFORMATION This is one of the 47 UK community foundations, which distribute funding for a wide range of purposes. As with all community foundations, there are a number of donor-advised funds managed on behalf of individuals, families and charitable trusts. Grant schemes tend to change frequently – consult the foundation's website for details of current programmes and up-to-date deadlines. During the year, 592 grants were awarded to community groups and individuals across Lancashire and Merseyside, as well as grants to 18 groups outside those regions. The foundation has separate websites for funding in Merseyside and funding in Lancashire.
HOW TO APPLY Potential applicants are advised to visit the community foundation's website or contact its grants team to find the most suitable funding stream.
CONTACT DETAILS Grants Team, 3rd Floor, Stanley Building, 43 Hanover Street, Liverpool, Merseyside L1 3DN *Tel.* 0330 440 4900 *Email* applications@cflm.org.uk *Website* www.cfmerseyside.org.uk or www.lancsfoundation.org.uk

■ Lancashire Environmental Fund Ltd

CC NO 1074983   **ESTABLISHED** 1998
WHERE FUNDING CAN BE GIVEN Lancashire (excluding the unitary authority districts of Blackpool and Blackburn). Projects must be located within ten miles of a landfill site.
WHO CAN BENEFIT Any not-for-profit organisation, charity, trust, community group, or voluntary organisation.
WHAT IS FUNDED Providing and maintaining public amenities and parks to the benefit of the natural, social or built environment. The charity's website states: 'Projects to date have included improvements to community facilities, general environmental improvements, creation and management of habitats, improvements to parks, gardens, open spaces, play areas, recreational facilities, ponds, canals and rivers and natural biodiversity.'

WHAT IS NOT FUNDED For a comprehensive list of exclusions, applicants are advised to refer to the guidance notes of the specific grants programme to which they intend to apply.

TYPE OF GRANT Project costs; capital costs.

RANGE OF GRANTS Green Grants of up to £1,000; Small Grants of up to £15,000; Main Grants of up to £30,000.

SAMPLE GRANTS Streetwise Youth Community Centre (£30,000); Boardwalk for All (£15,000); Clitheroe United Reformed Church (£14,100); Kelbrook and Sough Village Hall (£3,400); Whitworth Community Orchard (£1,000).

FINANCES *Financial year end 31/12/2021*
Income £1,300,000
Grants to organisations £1,040,000
Assets £1,270,000

TRUSTEES John Drury; Francis McGinty; Andrew Hughes; Shaun Turner.

OTHER INFORMATION Grants were broken down as follows: play areas and recreational facilities (£446,100); community facility improvements (£423,200); general environmental improvements (£209,300); parks, gardens and open spaces (£49,200); habitat creation and management (£30,000); Green Grants (£8,400).

HOW TO APPLY Detailed and helpful guidance notes and application forms for each funding strand can be found on the charity's website.

CONTACT DETAILS Andy Rowett, The Fund Manager, The Barn, Berkeley Drive, Bamber Bridge, Preston, Lancashire PR5 6BY *Tel.* 01772 317247 *Email* general@lancsenvfund.org.uk *Website* www.lancsenvfund.org.uk

■ The Lancashire Foundation

CC NO 1149184   **ESTABLISHED** 2012

WHERE FUNDING CAN BE GIVEN UK; Bermuda; worldwide.

WHO CAN BENEFIT Charitable organisations.

WHAT IS FUNDED General charitable purposes; young people; people who are disadvantaged; social isolation.

TYPE OF GRANT One-off and multi-year grants.

RANGE OF GRANTS Up to £60,000.

SAMPLE GRANTS The Family Centre (£60,000); St Giles Trust (£40,000); Cancer Research UK (£25,000); The Poppy Factory (£10,000); Victor Scott Primary School (£6,000); Carers Choice, The Living Paintings Trust and St Luke's Hospice (£4,000); BTA Youth Squad (£2,900); Macmillan Cancer Support (£2,000).

FINANCES *Financial year end 31/12/2021*
Income £196,600
Grants to organisations £515,800
Assets £1,930,000

TRUSTEES Derek Stapley; Louise Wells; Emma Grimes; Robert Kennedy.

OTHER INFORMATION This foundation is the corporate charity of the Lancashire Group of insurance companies which operates in Bermuda and London. It receives its income through an annual donation from the group. Grants were awarded to 57 organisations in 2021.

HOW TO APPLY Apply in writing to the correspondent. Grants are also made to organisations recommended by employees.

CONTACT DETAILS The Trustees, Lancashire Insurance Company (UK), Level 29, 20 Fenchurch Street, London EC3M 3BY *Tel.* 020 7264 4056 *Website* www.lancashiregroup.com/en/responsibility/lancashire-foundation.html

■ Lancaster Foundation

CC NO 1066850   **ESTABLISHED** 1997

WHERE FUNDING CAN BE GIVEN UK and Africa.

WHO CAN BENEFIT Christian registered charities only.

WHAT IS FUNDED Christianity; social welfare; health; children and young people.

SAMPLE GRANTS Message Trust (£212,100); Every Life International (£130,500); Love and Joy Ministries (£72,000); Visible Ministries (£42,500); Urban Saints (£25,000); Wren Bakery (£16,000); Noah Initiative (£5,000); Stonyhurst Charity Day (£1,000).

FINANCES *Financial year end 31/03/2022*
Income £3,410,000
Grants to organisations £2,560,000
Assets £67,920,000

TRUSTEES Julie Broadhurst; Dr John Lancaster; Steven Lancaster; Rosemary Lancaster.

OTHER INFORMATION Grants were awarded to 76 organisations during 2021/22.

HOW TO APPLY The foundation's annual report for 2021/22 states: 'Although many applications are received, the administrative structure of the charity does not allow for the consideration of unsolicited requests for grant funding.'

CONTACT DETAILS The Trustees, Text House, 152 Bawdlands, Clitheroe, Lancashire BB7 2LA *Tel.* 01200 444404

■ LandAid Charitable Trust Ltd (LandAid)

CC NO 295157   **ESTABLISHED** 1986

WHERE FUNDING CAN BE GIVEN UK.

WHO CAN BENEFIT Registered charitable organisations working in the UK.

WHAT IS FUNDED Youth homelessness.

WHAT IS NOT FUNDED Projects outside the UK; unrestricted grants toward running costs.

TYPE OF GRANT One-off grants; project funding; capital costs.

RANGE OF GRANTS £12,000 to £100,000.

SAMPLE GRANTS StreetSmart (£120,000); Andrew's Charitable Trust (£100,000); YMCA Thames Gateway (£75,000); New Horizon Youth Centre (£40,000); Centrepoint (£35,400); Segro Employability Fund (£20,000); Homeless Link (£15,300); YMCA Thames Gateway (£12,500).

FINANCES *Financial year end 31/03/2022*
Income £3,290,000
Grants to organisations £1,360,000
Assets £2,010,000

TRUSTEES Scott Parsons; Melanie Leech; Andrew Gulliford; Claire Milton; Gillian Bowen; Susan Hickey; Daniel Hughes; Anna Stewart; David Partridge; Neil Slater; Gemma Kataky; Damian Wild.

OTHER INFORMATION Grants were awarded to 25 organisations during the year.

HOW TO APPLY In the first instance, visit the LandAid website for full information of the charity's work. Open rounds of applications for funding are advertised online.

CONTACT DETAILS Grants Team, St Albans House, 5th Floor, 57–59 Haymarket, London SW1Y 4QX *Tel.* 020 3102 7190 *Email* enquiries@landaid.org *Website* www.landaid.org

■ The Allen Lane Foundation

CC NO 248031   ESTABLISHED 1966

WHERE FUNDING CAN BE GIVEN UK, excluding Greater London. Organisations with offices in London are eligible if the people who benefit from their work are not only in London.

WHO CAN BENEFIT Registered charities; unregistered charities; CICs; social enterprises.

WHAT IS FUNDED Asylum seekers and refugees; Gypsies and Travellers; offenders and ex-offenders; older people; people experiencing mental health problems; people experiencing violence or abuse; young people.

WHAT IS NOT FUNDED The foundation made 131 grants which were broken down as follows: older people (£188,000); offenders and ex-offenders (£173,800); refugees and asylum seekers (£119,000); people experiencing mental health issues (£99,600); people experiencing violence or abuse (£94,600); migrant communities (£27,600); social cohesion (£23,600); Gypsies and Travellers (£12,000).

TYPE OF GRANT Core/revenue costs; seed funding/start-up funding; unrestricted funding.

RANGE OF GRANTS The maximum grant size is £15,000 and the average grant size is around £5,000.

SAMPLE GRANTS Think Through Nutrition (£11,000); Lifesize CIC (£6,000); Survivors of Torture Activity Fund (£5,000); Always Community (£4,600); Earth23 (£1,500); N1M Trust (£1,000).

FINANCES *Financial year end 31/03/2022*
Income £637,100
Grants to organisations £738,200
Assets £21,710,000

TRUSTEES Fredrica Teale; Zoe Teale; Philip Walsh; Maurice Frankel; Justine Cadbury; Michael Firth; Claire Hitchcock.

HOW TO APPLY The foundation has an online application system where applicants can take an eligibility quiz. If the potential applicant is eligible to apply, they will be directed to the foundation's online application form.

CONTACT DETAILS Gill Aconley, Grants Officer, 90 The Mount, York, North Yorkshire YO24 1AR *Tel.* 01904 613223 *Email* info@allenlane.org.uk *Website* www.allenlane.org.uk

■ Langdale Trust

CC NO 215317   ESTABLISHED 1960

WHERE FUNDING CAN BE GIVEN UK, with some preference for Birmingham.

WHO CAN BENEFIT Registered charities, including those working overseas; hospices; museums and theatres.

WHAT IS FUNDED Animal welfare; conservation; health; social welfare; the environment; young people and older people.

WHAT IS NOT FUNDED Individuals.

TYPE OF GRANT One-off and recurrent.

RANGE OF GRANTS £1,000 to £6,000.

SAMPLE GRANTS Macmillan Cancer Support, Relate and YMCA – Sutton Coldfield (£5,000 each); Wildlife Trust Yorkshire (£4,000); St George's Youth Club (£3,000); Birmingham Royal Ballet and Ironbridge Gorge Museum Trust Ltd (£2,000 each); Galapagos Conservation Trust (£1,000).

FINANCES *Financial year end 30/11/2021*
Income £185,100
Grants to organisations £145,000
Assets £5,540,000

TRUSTEES Jethro Elvin; Teresa Wilson; Timothy Wilson; Naomi Rieley.

OTHER INFORMATION The 2020/21 accounts were the latest available to view at the time of writing (June 2023). Grants were awarded to 38 organisations during 2020/21.

HOW TO APPLY Apply in writing to the correspondent.

CONTACT DETAILS The Trustees, c/o Veale Wasbrough Vizards LLP, PO Box 3501, Bristol BS2 2FL *Tel.* 0121 227 3720 *Email* shiggins@vwv.co.uk

■ The LankellyChase Foundation

CC NO 1107583   ESTABLISHED 2005

WHERE FUNDING CAN BE GIVEN UK.

WHO CAN BENEFIT Charities; non-charitable organisations, provided the work itself has charitable purposes and there is no private benefit to non-charitable interests; individual consultants; private companies.

WHAT IS FUNDED Work that helps to change systems of injustice and oppression experienced by marginalised people.

TYPE OF GRANT Core costs; project costs; salaries; overheads; capital costs.

RANGE OF GRANTS Typically between £10,000 and £350,000.

SAMPLE GRANTS National Survivor User Network (£1.5 million); GM Spaces – Greater Manchester (£1.17 million); War on Want (£340,000); Living Rent (£120,000); Women's Community Matters (£100,000); Good Organisation CIC – York (£11,500); Arts at the Old Fire Station (£2,400); Institute of Development Studies (£1,500).

FINANCES *Financial year end 31/03/2022*
Income £2,420,000
Grants to organisations £11,040,000
Assets £143,860,000

TRUSTEES Darren Murinas; Robin Tuddenham; Myron Kellner-Rogers; Amanda Hailes; Asif Afridi; Baljeet Sandhu; Marai Larasi.

OTHER INFORMATION The LankellyChase Foundation is the amalgamation of two grant-making charities, the Lankelly Foundation and the Chase Charity.

HOW TO APPLY At the time of writing (February 2023) the foundation was not accepting unsolicited applications. Contact the foundation for more information.

CONTACT DETAILS The Trustees, Greenworks, Dog and Duck Yard, Princeton Street, London WC1R 4BH *Tel.* 020 3747 9930 *Email* enquiries@lankellychase.org.uk *Website* www.lankellychase.org.uk

■ The R. J. Larg Family Trust

OSCR NO SC004946   ESTABLISHED 1970

WHERE FUNDING CAN BE GIVEN Scotland, particularly Angus, Dundee, the north-east of Fife and Tayside.

WHO CAN BENEFIT Charitable organisations; hospices; uniformed groups.

WHAT IS FUNDED General charitable purposes including health and social welfare.

TYPE OF GRANT Generally one-off, some recurring.

RANGE OF GRANTS Grants range from £250 to £5,000 but are typically of around £1,000 to £2,000.

SAMPLE GRANTS RNLI Scotland (£4,500); Dundee Therapy Garden (£2,000); The Yard (£1,000); Cerebral Palsy Scotland (£500).

FINANCES *Financial year end 05/04/2022*
Income £125,900
Grants to organisations £93,500
Assets £4,520,000

494

Does the funder you have chosen match your needs? Haphazard applications waste postage and time

HOW TO APPLY Apply in writing to the correspondent.
CONTACT DETAILS The Trustees, Whitehall House, 33 Yeaman Shore, Dundee DD1 4BJ

■ Mrs M. A. Lascelles Charitable Trust

OSCR NO SC003495   **ESTABLISHED** 1968
WHERE FUNDING CAN BE GIVEN UK, particularly Scotland.
WHO CAN BENEFIT Charitable organisations, including those working overseas.
WHAT IS FUNDED General charitable purposes.
RANGE OF GRANTS Mostly up to £2,000.
SAMPLE GRANTS Dundee Women's Aid and Smallpeice Trust (£2,000 each); Edinburgh Young Carers and Give a Dog a Bone (£1,000 each); The Francis Bacon Research Trust (£750).
FINANCES *Financial year end* 05/04/2022
Income £62,400
Grants to organisations £66,800
Assets £2,930,000
HOW TO APPLY Apply in writing to the correspondent.
CONTACT DETAILS The Trustees, c/o Thorntons Law LLP, Whitehall House, 33 Yeaman Shore, Dundee DD1 4BJ

■ Laslett's (Hinton) Charity

CC NO 233696   **ESTABLISHED** 1879
WHERE FUNDING CAN BE GIVEN Worcestershire.
WHO CAN BENEFIT Charitable organisations; churches.
WHAT IS FUNDED The repair and restoration of churches and chapels connected with the established Church of England; social welfare; older people; children and young people; housing and homelessness.
WHAT IS NOT FUNDED Individuals (other than through a qualifying organisation); overseas charities; profit-based organisations.
SAMPLE GRANTS A list of beneficiaries was not included in the annual report and accounts.
FINANCES *Financial year end* 31/12/2021
Income £660,000
Grants to organisations £289,100
Assets £20,790,000
TRUSTEES Mr T. J. Bridges; Mr J. V. Panter; Mrs G. T. Newman; Michael Tarver; Peter Hughes; Douglas Dale; Colin Anstey; Kay Vincent; Lorraine Preece; Laura Baxter; Nicola Rogers.
HOW TO APPLY Applications can be made on a form available to download from the charity's website. Guidance notes can be also found on the charity's website. Applications are considered on a quarterly basis, in January, April, July and October. Upcoming deadlines are given on the website.
CONTACT DETAILS The Trustees, Kateryn Heywood House, Berkeley Court, The Foregate, Worcester, Worcestershire WR1 3QG
Email admin@lasletts.org.uk *Website* www.lasletts.org.uk

■ The Lauffer Family Charitable Foundation

CC NO 251115   **ESTABLISHED** 1967
WHERE FUNDING CAN BE GIVEN UK; other British Commonwealth countries; Israel; USA.
WHO CAN BENEFIT Charitable organisations; Jewish charities.

WHAT IS FUNDED The Jewish faith and community and general charitable purposes.
WHAT IS NOT FUNDED Individuals.
RANGE OF GRANTS Up to £36,000.
SAMPLE GRANTS Kehal Charedim Trust (£36,500); Shir Chesed Beis Yisroel (£27,000); Tomchei Yotzei Anglia (£16,000); Friends of Yeshivat Shaarei Shumuos (£12,000); College for Rabbinical Studies (£10,000); Gan Menachem (£3,900); Beit Halochem UK (£2,500); Holocaust Educational Trust and Project Seed (£1,000 each).
FINANCES *Financial year end* 31/03/2022
Income £121,300
Grants to organisations £480,900
Assets £4,720,000
TRUSTEES Gideon Lauffer; Jonathan Lauffer; Robin Lauffer.
OTHER INFORMATION Only beneficiaries that received grants of £1,000 or more were listed in the foundation's accounts. Grants of under £1,000 totalled £14,100.
HOW TO APPLY Apply in writing to the correspondent.
CONTACT DETAILS Jonathan Lauffer, Trustee, 123 Hampstead Way, London NW11 7JN
Tel. 020 7637 3210 *Email* jonathanlauffer13@gmail.com

■ Mrs F. B. Laurence Charitable Trust

CC NO 296548   **ESTABLISHED** 1976
WHERE FUNDING CAN BE GIVEN UK and overseas.
WHO CAN BENEFIT UK-registered charities; educational institutions; places of worship; hospices; community institutions; uniformed groups.
WHAT IS FUNDED General charitable purposes; social welfare; community facilities and services; the environment; animals; health and disability; older and young people; buildings and heritage; education.
WHAT IS NOT FUNDED Individuals; non-registered charities.
RANGE OF GRANTS Up to £4,000.
SAMPLE GRANTS Friends of St Nicholas School and The Halow Project (£4,000 each); Andrew Clark Trust, Friends of Newark Orchard and Salisbury Hospice Charity (£3,000 each); Blue Highlands Bird Rescue, Educate for Life and Phoenix Rehoming (£2,000 each); Over the Moon (£1,500).
FINANCES *Financial year end* 30/06/2021
Income £65,800
Grants to organisations £70,000
Assets £3,010,000
TRUSTEES Caroline Fry; William Hamilton; Payne Hicks Beach Trust Corporation.
OTHER INFORMATION The 2020/21 accounts were the latest available at the time of writing (May 2023). Only organisations that received over £1,000 were listed as beneficiaries in the trust's 2020/21 accounts. Grants of under £1,000 totalled £13,500. The trust aims to award at least £80,000 in grants per financial year.
HOW TO APPLY Apply in writing to the correspondent.
CONTACT DETAILS The Trustees, c/o Payne Hicks Beach LLP, 10 New Square, Lincoln's Inn, London WC2A 3QG *Tel.* 020 7465 4300
Email TheMrsFBLaurenceCharity@phb.co.uk

■ The Law Family Charitable Foundation

CC NO 1141997   **ESTABLISHED** 2011
WHERE FUNDING CAN BE GIVEN UK.
WHO CAN BENEFIT Registered charities; CICs; universities.
WHAT IS FUNDED General charitable purposes including education, health, disability, the arts, young people, the environment and sustainability.
RANGE OF GRANTS Mostly up to £50,000, with some exceptional larger grants.
SAMPLE GRANTS Speakers for Schools (£5.32 million); Place2Be (£2.72 million); Law Family Educational Trust (£1.5 million); Game and Wildlife Conservation Trust (£210,000); Lord Mayor's Appeal (£50,000); Devon Environment Foundation (£25,000); The Atlantic Partnership (£7,500); Maggie's at Marsden (£4,000).
FINANCES *Financial year end 31/03/2022*
Income £329,500
Grants to organisations £11,090,000
Assets £68,760,000
TRUSTEES Andrew Law; Roger Sadewsky; Zoe Law.
OTHER INFORMATION Grants of under £1,000 totalled £3,600. The foundation makes annual grants to The Law Family Educational Trust (Charity Commission no. 1169320) and in 2021/22 donated £1.5 million to the trust.
HOW TO APPLY A contact form is available on the website.
CONTACT DETAILS The Trustees, c/o Caxton Europe Asset Management, 3rd Floor, 40 Berkeley Square, London W1J 5AL *Tel.* 020 7647 4057 *Website* www.lawfamilycharitablefoundation.org

■ The Law Society Charity

CC NO 268736   **ESTABLISHED** 1974
WHERE FUNDING CAN BE GIVEN Worldwide.
WHO CAN BENEFIT Registered charities; CICs; schools; universities; local authorities; individuals.
WHAT IS FUNDED Law, legal education and access to justice. This includes: legal research; promotion of an increased understanding of the law; promotion of human rights and charities concerned with the provision of advice, counselling or mediation services connected with the law; welfare of solicitors, trainee solicitors and other legal and Law Society staff and their families.
TYPE OF GRANT Project funding; core/revenue costs. Grants are usually on a one-off basis but can occasionally be spread over two or three years.
RANGE OF GRANTS Typically £5,000.
SAMPLE GRANTS Margaret Clitherow (£10,000); Helena Kennedy (£6,000); Book Aid International, Here for Good and Reprieve (£5,000 each); Just Fair (£4,900); Prisoners of Conscience Appeal Fund (£4,000).
FINANCES *Financial year end 05/04/2022*
Income £111,800
Grants to organisations £64,900
Assets £333,800
TRUSTEE The Law Society Trustees Ltd.
OTHER INFORMATION During the year, 12 grants to organisations were awarded.
HOW TO APPLY Application forms and guidance notes are available from the charity's website.
CONTACT DETAILS The Trustees, 113 Chancery Lane, Holborn, London WC2A 1PL *Tel.* 020 7320 5739 *Email* lawsocietycharity@lawsociety.org.uk *Website* www.lawsociety.org.uk/charity

■ The Richard Lawes Foundation

CC NO 274042   **ESTABLISHED** 1977
WHERE FUNDING CAN BE GIVEN UK.
WHO CAN BENEFIT Charitable organisations, with a preference for registered charities, especially smaller charities or local branches of large charities.
WHAT IS FUNDED General charitable purposes, including medical research, bereavement support, mental health and young people.
TYPE OF GRANT Specific projects or capital costs.
SAMPLE GRANTS A list of beneficiaries was not included in the annual report and accounts.
FINANCES *Financial year end 05/04/2022*
Income £221,200
Grants to organisations £359,800
Assets £9,310,000
TRUSTEES William Lawes; Dr Dorothea Lawes; Janet Withers; David Northcroft.
HOW TO APPLY Contact the correspondent for further information.
CONTACT DETAILS Bobby Lawes, Trustee, Longhayes, Lowerdown, Bovey Tracey, Newton Abbot, Devon TQ13 9LF *Tel.* 07850 126351 *Email* Bobbylawes@aol.com

■ The Edgar E. Lawley Foundation

CC NO 201589   **ESTABLISHED** 1961
WHERE FUNDING CAN BE GIVEN UK, with a preference for the West Midlands.
WHO CAN BENEFIT Registered charities; charitable organisations; hospitals and hospices; schools and universities.
WHAT IS FUNDED General charitable purposes; education in the arts, commerce and industry; health and disability; medical care and research; older people; children and young people; community causes.
WHAT IS NOT FUNDED Individuals.
TYPE OF GRANT One-off, generally unrestricted funding.
RANGE OF GRANTS About £1,500 on average.
SAMPLE GRANTS Birmingham City Mission, The Disabled Sailors Association, Headway – The Brain Injury Association, Life Cycle UK, The Myton Hospice, National Literacy Trust, Teapot Trust and Thames Valley Air Ambulance (£1,500 each).
FINANCES *Financial year end 05/04/2022*
Income £205,700
Grants to organisations £231,000
Assets £5,120,000
TRUSTEES Philip Cooke; John Cooke; Francis Jackson; Katherine Coates; Laura Cooke.
OTHER INFORMATION There were 154 awards made during 2021/22.
HOW TO APPLY Application rounds typically open on 1 August and close on 31 October. Applications must be made through the foundation's online application form on its website. Note, the foundation receives approximately 800 applications per year for grants but in a normal year can only fund approximately 160 of them.
CONTACT DETAILS Frank Jackson, Administrative Trustee, PO Box 456, Esher, Surrey KT10 1DP *Tel.* 01372 805760 *Email* edgarelawley@gmail.com *Website* www.edgarelawleyfoundation.org.uk

■ The Herd Lawson and Muriel Lawson Charitable Trust

CC NO 1113220   **ESTABLISHED** 2006
WHERE FUNDING CAN BE GIVEN England and Wales, with a preference for Cumbria.
WHO CAN BENEFIT Charitable organisations.
WHAT IS FUNDED This trust supports a number of named organisations each year as well as organisations benefitting older people in need, particularly those who are members of evangelical or Christian Brethren churches.
TYPE OF GRANT Project funding; core costs.
RANGE OF GRANTS Typically between £1,500 and £20,000.
SAMPLE GRANTS British Red Cross and WWF (£37,500 each); Christian Workers Relief Fund (£28,900); Hospice at Home West Cumbria (£19,800); Hospice of St Mary of Furness (£13,800); Ambleside Welfare Charity and Spring Mount Christian Fellowship (£4,500 each); Sight Advice South Lakes (£3,000); Sandhill Lane Christian Brethren Church (£1,000).
FINANCES *Financial year end 05/04/2022*
Income £250,800
Grants to organisations £155,500
Assets £2,110,000
TRUSTEES Brian Herd; Dr Jenny Barker; William Corin; Andrew Hewitt; Ian Jenkinson; Paul Cookson.
OTHER INFORMATION There were ten awards made during the year.
HOW TO APPLY The trust receives more applications than it can deal with and does not seek further unsolicited appeals. The trust has previously informed us that 'the trustees have established a number of charities to whom they make grants each year and they very rarely make any donations to other charities.'
CONTACT DETAILS Robert Barker, Trustee, The Estate Office, 14 Church Street, Ambleside, Cumbria LA22 0BT *Tel.* 01539 434758 *Email* herdlawsontrust@gmail.com

■ Lawson Beckman Charitable Trust

CC NO 261378   **ESTABLISHED** 1970
WHERE FUNDING CAN BE GIVEN UK.
WHO CAN BENEFIT Charitable organisations.
WHAT IS FUNDED The Jewish faith and community.
WHAT IS NOT FUNDED Individuals.
RANGE OF GRANTS Up to £12,500.
SAMPLE GRANTS Jewish Care and Norwood Ravenswood (£12,500 each); Central Synagogue (£11,000); UK Friends of Yad Yisroel (£10,000); Community Security Trust and The Jewish Volunteering Network (£5,000 each); Teenage Cancer Trust and The Royal Free Charity (£1,000 each).
FINANCES *Financial year end 31/03/2022*
Income £137,100
Grants to organisations £92,500
Assets £4,970,000
TRUSTEES Francis Katz; Lynton Stock; Melvin Lawson.
OTHER INFORMATION Grants were distributed as follows: health/preservation of lives (£39,000); general charitable purposes (£22,000); education (£18,000); religious activities (£13,500).
HOW TO APPLY Apply in writing to the correspondent.

CONTACT DETAILS The Trustees, c/o AB Group Ltd, 2nd Floor, 25 Old Burlington Street, London W1S 3AN *Tel.* 020 7734 8111 *Email* bt@abplc.co.uk

■ The Lawson Trust CIO

CC NO 1171822   **ESTABLISHED** 1980
WHERE FUNDING CAN BE GIVEN Kent and Sussex.
WHO CAN BENEFIT Charitable organisations; registered charities, including those registered as a company limited by guarantee; CIOs. Preference is given to local organisations.
WHAT IS FUNDED The arts and heritage; education; the environment; health; social and economic disadvantage; children and young adults; older people; people with disabilities; the armed forces.
WHAT IS NOT FUNDED Individuals; non-registered charities; overseas charities; political parties; religious causes.
TYPE OF GRANT Project costs.
RANGE OF GRANTS Up to £10,000 but mostly £5,000 and under.
SAMPLE GRANTS Kent Community Foundation Environmental Fund (£25,000); Brighton Dome and Festival Ltd (£10,000); Martha Trust (£8,000); Achievement for All (£5,400); De La Warr Pavilion Charitable Trust and Medical Detection Dogs (£5,000 each); Carers Support West Sussex (£3,000); Multiple Sclerosis Trust (£2,500).
FINANCES *Financial year end 31/03/2022*
Income £664,700
Grants to organisations £930,200
Assets £22,350,000
TRUSTEES Philip Thomas; Michael Norrie; Sarah Hill; Paul Marsh; Sarah Playle; Antony Hooper; Robert Blundell; Katharine Lewis.
OTHER INFORMATION Grants were awarded to 101 organisations during 2021/22, of which 93 were grants of up to £10,000.
HOW TO APPLY Applicants based in Kent seeking funding of up to £5,000 can apply to the Lawson Endowment for Kent. Further information on this fund can be found on the Kent Community Foundation website. The trust also has an endowment with Sussex Community Foundation. Applicants based in Sussex with an annual income of under £1 million can apply to the foundation for a grant via its website. National charities or charities outside the criteria for the two community foundations can apply via the trust's online application process. Applicants should first complete the eligibility checker on the trust's website. Eligible organisations will then be provided with a link to the online application form. Applications can be made at any time. The trustees meet four times per year. Check the trust's website for meeting dates.
CONTACT DETAILS The Trustees, PO Box 506, Ramsgate CT11 1DZ *Email* enquiries@lawsontrust.co.uk *Website* https://lawsontrust.org

■ The Leach Fourteenth Trust

CC NO 204844   **ESTABLISHED** 1961
WHERE FUNDING CAN BE GIVEN UK, with some preference for the South West.
WHO CAN BENEFIT Registered charities based in the UK.
WHAT IS FUNDED General charitable purposes, including: health; the environment and

conservation; international development; the arts.

TYPE OF GRANT Project funding; one-off grants.

RANGE OF GRANTS Typically less than £3,000.

SAMPLE GRANTS Médecins Sans Frontières (£11,000); Alexander Devine's Children's Cancer Trust (£4,000); Durrell Wildlife Conservation Trust (£3,500); Kids for Kids (£2,000); Dog's for Good (£1,500); Become, The Mustard Tree and World Land Trust (£1,000 each).

FINANCES *Financial year end 05/04/2022*
Income £90,900
Grants to organisations £78,000
Assets £4,160,000

TRUSTEES John Henderson; Judith Nash; Roger Murray-Leach; Tamsin Murray-Leach; Grant Nash; Karen Brooking.

OTHER INFORMATION Grants were awarded to 55 organisations during the year. Only beneficiaries of grants of £1,000 and above were listed in the accounts. Grants of under £1,000 totalled £3,500.

HOW TO APPLY Contact the correspondent for further information.

CONTACT DETAILS The Trustees, c/o BHP LLP, Rievaulx House, 1 St Mary's Court, Blossom Street, York, North Yorkshire YO24 1AH *Tel.* 01904 628551

■ Ana Leaf Foundation

CC NO 1133255

WHERE FUNDING CAN BE GIVEN Worldwide, with a preference for UK and the Channel Islands.

WHO CAN BENEFIT Charitable organisations.

WHAT IS FUNDED Health; medical research; education.

SAMPLE GRANTS Previous beneficiaries have included: Summer Fields School (£100,000); Parent-Infant Foundation (£202,800); Mind Jersey (£20,000); Jersey Scout Association (£3,500); Brighter Futures (£550).

FINANCES *Financial year end 31/12/2021*
Income £2,500
Grants to organisations £130,000

TRUSTEES Hayley de Purton; Amanda Simmons.

OTHER INFORMATION Full accounts were not available to view on the Charity Commission's website due to the foundation's low income. We have therefore estimated the foundation's grant total based on its total expenditure.

HOW TO APPLY Apply in writing to the correspondent.

CONTACT DETAILS The Trustees, PO Box 155, Jersey JE4 5NS *Tel.* 07797 892310 *Email* queries@ana-leaf-foundation.co.uk

---

■ The Leathersellers' Foundation

CC NO 278072   **ESTABLISHED** 1979

WHERE FUNDING CAN BE GIVEN UK, particularly London.

WHO CAN BENEFIT UK-registered charities, including CIOs; educational establishments; individuals.

WHAT IS FUNDED General charitable purposes; education and training; social welfare; children and young people; leathercraft and the leather industry.

WHAT IS NOT FUNDED Medical research; capital restoration projects for the sole purpose of conservation/heritage; hospices; CICs.

TYPE OF GRANT One-off and multi-year grants; core, unrestricted funding; project expenditure; capital costs.

RANGE OF GRANTS Programme dependent.

SAMPLE GRANTS St Mary the Virgin Parish Church (£40,000); The Hardman Trust (£39,000); Football Beyond Borders and Tros Gynnal Plant (£25,000 each); Noa Girls (£23,000); London College of Fashion and Youth Adventure Trust (£22,000 each); Latin American Women's Aid, The Big House and Women's Work Derbyshire (£20,000 each).

FINANCES *Financial year end 31/07/2022*
Income £1,940,000
Grants to organisations £3,040,000
Grants to individuals £294,000
Assets £69,500,000

TRUSTEES Matthew Lawrence; The Leathersellers Company.

OTHER INFORMATION Grants were made to 91 individuals for educational purposes. Only beneficiaries of grants of £20,000 and above were listed in the accounts. Grants to organisations for less than £20,000 totalled £1.69 million. The foundation's charitable giving is led by a five-year strategy. This commits 80% of non-committed main grant funding to the alleviation of suffering caused by adverse childhood experiences (ACEs). Successful applicants are able to demonstrate evidence of the effectiveness of their approach, how lived experience informs and improves their work, and how the need for support is affected by location and demographics. The remaining 20% is allocated to the Responsive Fund (small grants).

HOW TO APPLY Applications can be made using the online form on the foundation's website during open funding periods. Applicants are advised to regularly check the foundation's website for up-to-date information and deadlines.

CONTACT DETAILS Natalia Rymaszewska, Grants Team, 7 St Helen's Place, London EC3A 6AB *Tel.* 020 7330 1452 *Email* charityapp@leathersellers.co.uk *Website* https://leathersellers.co.uk/foundation

---

■ The Leche Trust

CC NO 225659   **ESTABLISHED** 1963

WHERE FUNDING CAN BE GIVEN UK.

WHO CAN BENEFIT Registered charities; exempt charities; public authorities which are subject to financial regulation.

WHAT IS FUNDED The preservation and conservation of pre-Victorian historic objects, collections and features of buildings and designed landscapes; performing arts, particularly music, dance and theatre.

WHAT IS NOT FUNDED CICs; schools; social welfare; environmental or wildlife projects; health and medicine; buildings or objects in private ownership. See the website for a full list of exclusions.

TYPE OF GRANT Project funding; bursaries; acquisitions.

RANGE OF GRANTS Up to £5,000.

SAMPLE GRANTS Textile Conservation Foundation (£7,500); Ulster Orchestra (£3,000); JMK Trust, Mimbre and Southwark Playhouse (£2,000 each); The Gemini Trust (£500).

FINANCES *Financial year end 31/07/2022*
Income £149,300
Grants to organisations £224,800
Grants to individuals £50,500
Assets £7,540,000

TRUSTEES Thomas Howard; Robin Dhar; Dr Helen Jacobsen; Andrew Cameron; Diana Spiegelberg; Susan Sturrock; Regis Gautier-Cochefert.

HOW TO APPLY At the time of writing (May 2023) the trust's website stated: 'We are currently closed for applications while we install a new online

498

Does the funder you have chosen match your needs? Haphazard applications waste postage and time

application system. Check back in September 2023 for details of the next funding round.'

CONTACT DETAILS Rosemary Ewles, Grants Director, 105 Greenway Avenue, London E17 3QL *Tel.* 020 3233 0023 *Email* info@lechetrust.org *Website* www.lechetrust.org

■ The Arnold Lee Charitable Trust

CC NO 264437   **ESTABLISHED** 1972
WHERE FUNDING CAN BE GIVEN UK.
WHO CAN BENEFIT Registered charities; Jewish organisations.
WHAT IS FUNDED General charitable purposes; the Jewish faith and community.
RANGE OF GRANTS Mostly below £10,000. Larger grants are occasionally awarded.
SAMPLE GRANTS Jewish Futures Trust (£50,000); Friends of Ascent (£25,000); The Arts Council (£21,600); Mesila UK (£21,100); Chai Cancer Care (£15,000); North West London Jewish Day School (£10,000); Aish Hatorah (£12,500).
FINANCES *Financial year end* 05/04/2022
Income £895,700
Grants to organisations £244,300
Assets £2,360,000
TRUSTEES Alan Lee; Edward Lee.
OTHER INFORMATION Only organisations that received grants of over £10,000 were listed as beneficiaries in the trust's accounts. Grants of under £10,000 totalled £89,100.
HOW TO APPLY Applications in writing to the correspondent.
CONTACT DETAILS The Trustees, Palladium House, 1–4 Argyll Street, London W1F 7LD *Tel.* 020 7437 7666 *Email* PetronellaEvans@ princetonplc.com

■ The William Leech Charity

CC NO 1186957   **ESTABLISHED** 1972
WHERE FUNDING CAN BE GIVEN The North East and overseas.
WHO CAN BENEFIT UK-registered charities; CICs.
WHAT IS FUNDED General charitable purposes in the North East; support for volunteers. The charity's Lady Leech Fund also funds projects supporting children in financially developing countries.
WHAT IS NOT FUNDED Community care centres and similar (those in remote country areas may be supported); running expenses for youth clubs (capital projects are eligible); running expenses of churches (includes normal repairs, but churches engaged in social work or using their buildings largely for outside purposes may be supported); sport; the arts; individuals; organisations which have been supported in the last 12 months; holidays and travel; outings; minibuses (unless over 10,000 miles per year is expected); schools; housing associations.
TYPE OF GRANT One-off and recurring grants; interest-free loans; project funding; research funding.
RANGE OF GRANTS Mostly £500 to £10,000.
SAMPLE GRANTS St Oswald's (£35,000); Youth Ministry Trust (£10,000); Blyth Star Enterprises (£6,000); Heel and Toe (£5,000); Veterans at Ease (£4,000); Tyneside Hospice at Home (£2,500); Pelton Youth Project (£2,000); Headway Darlington (£1,000).
FINANCES *Financial year end* 31/03/2022
Income £499,700
Grants to organisations £189,300
Assets £22,610,000
TRUSTEES Richard Leech; The Revd Prof. David Wilkinson; David Stabler; Adrian Gifford; Barrie Wallace; Helen Short.

OTHER INFORMATION In 2021/22, grants awarded through the Main Fund totalled £176,300 and grants through the Lady Leech Fund totalled £13,000.
HOW TO APPLY Applications can be made online through the charity's website. The charity no longer accepts applications made by post.
CONTACT DETAILS The Trustees, c/o Robson Laidler, Fernwood House, Fernwood Road, Jesmond, Newcastle upon Tyne, Tyne and Wear NE2 1TJ *Tel.* 0191 281 8191 *Email* enquiries@ williamleechcharity.org.uk *Website* www. williamleechcharity.org.uk

■ Leeds Building Society Foundation

CC NO 1074429   **ESTABLISHED** 1999
WHERE FUNDING CAN BE GIVEN UK.
WHO CAN BENEFIT UK-registered charities. The foundation will only accept applications from UK-registered charities with a turnover of less than £1 million.
WHAT IS FUNDED General charitable purposes; community projects focusing on social welfare and relief in need; vulnerable people and disadvantaged individuals.
WHAT IS NOT FUNDED Religious, military or political projects; overseas charities; individuals (including sponsorship); animal welfare projects; medical research; general running costs, such as salaries or rent; general fundraising appeals; building restoration; items for staff use.
TYPE OF GRANT Capital expenditure.
RANGE OF GRANTS Typically under £1,000.
SAMPLE GRANTS A list of beneficiaries was not included in the annual report and accounts.
FINANCES *Financial year end* 31/12/2021
Income £152,100
Grants to organisations £142,200
Assets £3,200
TRUSTEES Gary Hetherington; Carla Marshall; Timothy Steere; Susan Moreland; Emma Woods-Bolger; Christopher Bell; Nicola Glover.
OTHER INFORMATION Grants were broken down as follows: mental or physical disability (£41,900); disadvantage (£27,500); social inclusion (£22,500); poverty (£20,900); homelessness (£14,300); caring responsibilities (£8,200); illness (£6,900).
HOW TO APPLY Apply online through the foundation's website, where information on trustees' meeting dates can also be found.
CONTACT DETAILS The Trustees, Leeds Building Society, 26 Sovereign Street, Leeds, West Yorkshire LS1 4BJ *Tel.* 0113 225 7518 *Email* foundation@leedsbuildingsociety.co.uk *Website* www.leedsbuildingsociety.co.uk/your-society/about-us/foundation

■ Leeds Community Foundation

CC NO 1096892   **ESTABLISHED** 2005
WHERE FUNDING CAN BE GIVEN Leeds and Bradford.
WHO CAN BENEFIT Community and voluntary groups; registered charities; not-for-profit organisations; social enterprises.
WHAT IS FUNDED General charitable purposes.
TYPE OF GRANT Capital costs; core costs; project funding.
RANGE OF GRANTS Programme dependant.
SAMPLE GRANTS Healthy Holidays (£1.12 million); Leeds Fund (£427,000); Local Care Direct (£267,000); Clubs in Crisis (£104,000); Leeds Civic Trust (£72,000); Stay Well This Winter

(£53,000); Bradford Children and Young People's Youth Fund (£23,000); No Child Cold (£1,000).

FINANCES *Financial year end* 31/03/2022
Income £4,580,000
Grants to organisations £4,040,000
Assets £28,654,000

TRUSTEES Roohi Collins; George Fox; Carolyn Cooper-Black; Anthony Cooke; Cleveland Henry; Sharon Orr; Deirdre Reid; Hugh Fairclough; Emily Jones; Carl Hawkes; William Clarke; Ruth Bromley.

OTHER INFORMATION This is one of the 47 UK community foundations, which distribute funding for a wide range of purposes. As with all community foundations, there are a number of donor-advised funds managed on behalf of individuals, families and charitable trusts. Grant schemes tend to change frequently – consult the foundation's website for details of current programmes and up-to-date deadlines.

HOW TO APPLY See the foundation's website for details of open grant programmes.

CONTACT DETAILS The Trustees, 1st Floor, 51A St Paul's Street, Leeds, West Yorkshire LS1 2TE *Tel.* 0113 242 2426 *Email* grants@leedscf.org.uk *Website* www.leedscf.org.uk

■ The Leeward Trust

OSCR NO SC047870   **ESTABLISHED** 2017
WHERE FUNDING CAN BE GIVEN UK; Africa; India; South America.
WHO CAN BENEFIT Charitable organisations.
WHAT IS FUNDED Social welfare; education; health and medical; citizenship and community development; arts, heritage and culture; science; recreation; equality and diversity; the environment; human rights; peace and conflict resolution; animal welfare.
SAMPLE GRANTS A list of beneficiaries was not included in the annual report and accounts.
FINANCES *Financial year end* 31/03/2022
Income £349,800
Grants to organisations £339,500
Assets £6,600
OTHER INFORMATION Grants were distributed as follows: poverty (£88,800); the environment (£49,000); age, ill health, disability, financial hardship or other disadvantage (£46,500); human rights, conflict resolution and reconciliation (£37,500); education (£28,800); citizenship and community development (£27,500); health (£27,500); saving lives (£17,500); recreation (£9,000); animal welfare (£5,000); religious or racial harmony (£2,500).
HOW TO APPLY Apply in writing to the correspondent.
CONTACT DETAILS The Trustees, c/o Gillespie Macandrew, 5 Atholl Crescent, Edinburgh EH3 8EJ

■ The Legal Education Foundation

CC NO 271297   **ESTABLISHED** 1962
WHERE FUNDING CAN BE GIVEN UK.
WHO CAN BENEFIT Legally constituted organisations undertaking charitable work in the UK, including charities, CICs, limited companies, private law firms and research institutions.
WHAT IS FUNDED Legal education, training and development; access to employment in the legal profession; public understanding of the law; the use of technology in legal education; research.
WHAT IS NOT FUNDED Individuals; work outside the UK; capital expenditure on buildings and

vehicles. A full list of exclusions can be found on the foundation's website.
TYPE OF GRANT Core costs; salaries; project funding; modest capital expenditure directly related to the work.
RANGE OF GRANTS Programme dependent.
SAMPLE GRANTS Child Poverty Action Group (£480,000); Central England Law Centre (£300,000); Citizens Advice Liverpool (£150,000); Access Social Care (£18,000).
FINANCES *Financial year end* 30/06/2022
Income £5,150,000
Grants to organisations £11,230,000
Assets £262,480,000
TRUSTEES Ailsa Beaton; Rupert Baron; Jonathan Freeman; Alison Pickup; Monica Risam; Vivek Luthra; Patricia Sloan; Rupen Shah; Hetan Shah; Alexander Temple.
HOW TO APPLY Apply using the online application form on the foundation's website. If you are successful at the first stage, you will be invited to make a full application – you will be sent a personalised link to a second-stage form. A grant timetable is posted on the foundation's website with up-to-date application deadlines.
CONTACT DETAILS The Trustees, 15 Alfred Place, London WC1E 7EB *Tel.* 020 3005 5695 *Email* use the contact form on the website *Website* http://thelegaleducationfoundation.org

■ Leicestershire and Rutland Masonic Charity Association

CC NO 234054   **ESTABLISHED** 1964
WHERE FUNDING CAN BE GIVEN Leicestershire and Rutland.
WHO CAN BENEFIT Registered charities, with a preference for small local charities; community clubs; Freemasons and their dependants.
WHAT IS FUNDED General charitable purposes; Masonry; support of Freemasons and their families.
RANGE OF GRANTS Mostly £2,000 and under.
SAMPLE GRANTS A list of beneficiaries was not included in the annual report and accounts. Previous beneficiaries have included: Masonic Charitable Foundation (£19,300); Rainbows (£7,800); Prostate Cancer Fund (£3,500); Hamilton Air Cadets and The Spark Arts for Children (£2,000 each); Leicestershire Rape Crisis (£1,600); 14th Nativity Scout Group (£1,500); Coping with Cancer (£1,000); Sunflowers Suicide Support (£500); LOROS (Leicester Hospice Charity) (£200).
FINANCES *Financial year end* 31/05/2022
Income £426,000
Grants to organisations £356,700
Assets £188,900
TRUSTEES Brent Goodwin; Ian Nesbitt; Peter Kinder; Brian Carruthers; Dr Andrew Green; Paul Wallace; Adrian Pearse; David Highton; Robert Mason; David Sandrovitch; John Peberdy.
OTHER INFORMATION Grants to organisations were broken down as follows: Masonic charities (£267,100); local non-Masonic charities (£89,600).
HOW TO APPLY The association encourages applications for grants from local non-Masonic charities. Apply in writing to the correspondent or use the contact form available on the website.
CONTACT DETAILS The Trustees, Freemasons' Hall, 80 London Road, Leicester, Leicestershire LE2 0RA *Tel.* 0116 223 6998 *Email* lrmca@pglleics.co.uk *Website* www.leicestershire-rutlandfreemasons.org.uk/charitable-work

■ Leicestershire, Leicester and Rutland Community Foundation

CC NO 1135322   **ESTABLISHED** 2002

WHERE FUNDING CAN BE GIVEN Leicester; Leicestershire; Rutland.

WHO CAN BENEFIT Charities and community groups, with some preference for smaller groups.

WHAT IS FUNDED General charitable purposes.

TYPE OF GRANT Running and project costs.

SAMPLE GRANTS A list of beneficiaries was not included in the annual report and accounts. Previous beneficiaries have included: Grimsby Town Football (£25,000); Room for Music Studios (£5,000); Sustainable Land Trust (£4,100); Leicester Stroke Club £4,000); Parish Community Hub (£3,500); Leicester City of Sanctuary (£3,000); Drum and Bass CIC (£2,500); Anstey Youth Cafe (£2,300); Ashby Arts Festival (£650).

FINANCES *Financial year end* 31/03/2022
Income £714,200
Grants to organisations £529,400
Assets £4,170,000

TRUSTEES Justine Flack; Stuart Dawkins; Trevor Shaw; Ian McCormack; Riaz Ravat; Richard Colton; Robin Clarke; Dr Vijay Sharma; David Andrews; Jennifer Hand; Mark Robinson.

OTHER INFORMATION This is one of the 47 UK community foundations, which distribute funding for a wide range of purposes. As with all community foundations, there are a number of donor-advised funds managed on behalf of individuals, families and charitable trusts. Grant schemes tend to change frequently – consult the foundation's website for details of current programmes and up-to-date deadlines.

HOW TO APPLY Potential applicants are advised to visit the community foundation's website or contact its grants team to find the most suitable funding stream.

CONTACT DETAILS Grants Team, 3 Wycliffe Street, Leicester, Leicestershire LE1 5LR *Tel.* 0116 262 4804 *Email* grants@llrcommunityfoundation.org.uk *Website* www.llrcommunityfoundation.org.uk

■ Sarah Jane Leigh Charitable Trust

CC NO 1189202

WHERE FUNDING CAN BE GIVEN UK.

WHO CAN BENEFIT Charitable organisations.

WHAT IS FUNDED Mental health.

SAMPLE GRANTS Jami (£50,000); Haringey She Ltd (£35,000).

FINANCES *Financial year end* 05/04/2022
Income £900,200
Grants to organisations £85,000
Assets £798,800

TRUSTEES Lindy Goldkorn; Leah Goldkorn; Sarah Whitney; Gabriella Brook.

HOW TO APPLY Apply in writing to the correspondent.

CONTACT DETAILS Lindy Goldkorn, Trustee, 21E Highgate Close, London N6 4SD *Email* lingoldkorn@aol.com

■ The Leigh Trust

CC NO 275372   **ESTABLISHED** 1976

WHERE FUNDING CAN BE GIVEN UK and overseas.

WHO CAN BENEFIT Registered charities.

WHAT IS FUNDED Drug and alcohol rehabilitation; criminal justice; asylum seekers; racial equality; education; young people at risk.

WHAT IS NOT FUNDED Individuals.

RANGE OF GRANTS Mostly £1,000 to £5,000.

SAMPLE GRANTS Disasters Emergency Committee (£25,000); Centre for Social Justice (£10,000); Prisoners Abroad (£7,500); The Amber Foundation (£5,000); Helen Bamber Foundation (£4,000); Faithwork Wessex (£3,000); Sapphire Community Trust (£2,000); All Saints Youth Project (£1,000).

FINANCES *Financial year end* 05/04/2022
Income £62,300
Grants to organisations £260,000
Assets £3,330,000

TRUSTEES The Hon. D. S. Bernstein; Ms C. Moorehead; Jonathon Bond.

OTHER INFORMATION In 2021/22, grants were distributed as follows: criminal justice and young people at risk (£108,100); other (£78,900); drug and alcohol rehabilitation (£37,000); asylum seekers and refugees (£36,000).

HOW TO APPLY The 2021/22 annual report states: 'Organisations applying for grants must provide their most recent audited accounts, a registered charity number and, most importantly, a cash flow statement for the next twelve months. Similarly all organisations to whom conditional commitments have been made must submit their annual report and accounts each year until these commitments have been fulfilled. All applications should have a stamped self-addressed envelope attached. The actual request for funds must be concise and preferably summarised on one side of A4 paper. The policy of the trustees is to support those organisations which they believe to be in greatest need. The trustees can only respond favourably to very few applicants.'

CONTACT DETAILS The Trustees, 9 Bonhill Street, London EC2A 4DJ *Tel.* 020 7628 5801 *Email* admin@begbiesaccountants.co.uk

■ Lempriere Pringle 2015

CC NO 1161516

WHERE FUNDING CAN BE GIVEN Bishop Auckland and the surrounding areas.

WHO CAN BENEFIT Registered charities; churches; individuals.

WHAT IS FUNDED Regeneration and community development.

SAMPLE GRANTS The Auckland Project (£5 million); SHED (£3.5 million); Eleven Arches Trust (£1 million); First Fruit (£500,000); Archbishop of Canterbury Discretionary Trust (£100,000); The Prince's Trust (£85,500); Stockton Project (£50,000).

FINANCES *Financial year end* 31/03/2022
Income £22,410,000
Grants to organisations £11,380,000
Assets £23,500,000

TRUSTEES Jonathan Ruffer; Dr Jane Ruffer; Ashe Windham; Harriet O'Rourke; Dr Norman Fraser; Elizabeth Booker; Richard Chartres.

OTHER INFORMATION Only grants of £5,000 or more were listed in the beneficiaries, with grants of under £5,000 totalling £8,000. Note that the grant total may include amounts awarded to individuals.

HOW TO APPLY The 2021/22 annual accounts state: 'The organisation is proactive in identifying projects, ministries, charities and individuals whose work relates to the organisation's objectives, but who generally are pursuing their causes without resorting to funding via professional fundraisers.' Contact the

Think carefully about every application. Is it justified?

501

correspondent for further information before making an application to the charity.

CONTACT DETAILS The Trustees, Ord House, Little Fencote, Northallerton, North Yorkshire DL7 0RR *Tel.* 01609 748284 *Email* ordhouse1@btinternet.com

■ Leng Charitable Trust

OSCR NO SC009285   **ESTABLISHED** 1989
WHERE FUNDING CAN BE GIVEN Dundee and Tayside.
WHO CAN BENEFIT Registered charities; churches; hospices; universities.
WHAT IS FUNDED General charitable purposes.
RANGE OF GRANTS Mostly up to £5,000.
SAMPLE GRANTS The Salvation Army (£40,000); Flexible Care Services Scotland (£20,000); Carnoustie Church and University of Dundee (£10,000 each).
FINANCES *Financial year end* 31/12/2021
Income £288,000
Grants to organisations £174,800
Assets £8,690,000
OTHER INFORMATION Grants of £5,000 or less totalled £134,800.
HOW TO APPLY Apply in writing to the correspondent.
CONTACT DETAILS The Trustees, c/o Thorntons Law LLP, Whitehall House, 33 Yeaman Shore, Dundee DD1 4BJ

■ The Mark Leonard Trust

CC NO 1040323   **ESTABLISHED** 1994
WHERE FUNDING CAN BE GIVEN Worldwide, but mainly the UK.
WHO CAN BENEFIT Registered charities.
WHAT IS FUNDED Environmental causes, particularly sustainable agriculture, food and climate change; young people, particularly those at risk of offending.
WHAT IS NOT FUNDED Individuals; educational fees; expeditions.
TYPE OF GRANT Core costs; capital costs; development funding; seed/start-up funding.
RANGE OF GRANTS Typical grants range between £1,000 and £50,000.
SAMPLE GRANTS Client Earth (£83,300); Global Legal Action Network (£60,000); On Road Media (£50,000); European Climate Foundation (£30,000); Centre for the Study of Existential Risk (£22,000); The Social Change Nest (£10,000); Torith y Tir (£5,000); Stump Up For Trees (£1,000).
FINANCES *Financial year end* 05/04/2022
Income £422,400
Grants to organisations £1,030,000
Assets £22,740,000
TRUSTEES John Sainsbury; Zivi Sainsbury; Mark Sainsbury.
OTHER INFORMATION The trust is one of the Sainsbury Family Charitable Trusts, which share a common administration – see www.sftc.org.uk for more information. Grants were awarded to 36 organisations.
HOW TO APPLY Unsolicited applications are not accepted.
CONTACT DETAILS The Trustees, The Sainsbury Family Charitable Trusts, The Peak, 5 Wilton Road, London SW1V 1AP *Tel.* 020 7410 0330 *Email* info@sfct.org.uk *Website* www.sfct.org.uk/the-mark-leonard-trust/

■ The Leri Charitable Trust

CC NO 1075107   **ESTABLISHED** 1999
WHERE FUNDING CAN BE GIVEN UK, with a preference for Manchester and the London Borough of Brent.
WHO CAN BENEFIT Registered charities.
WHAT IS FUNDED General charitable purposes, including: social welfare; human rights and economic justice; equality and diversity; education; the arts, culture, heritage and science; community development; health; refugees and asylum seekers; justice for Palestinians; the environment.
SAMPLE GRANTS A list of beneficiaries was not included in the annual report and accounts.
FINANCES *Financial year end* 02/03/2022
Income £215,800
Grants to organisations £582,000
Assets £12,710,000
TRUSTEES Alison Broadberry; Geoffrey Hellings; Leon Rosselson; Ruth Rosselson; John Ryan.
HOW TO APPLY The trust does not accept unsolicited applications.
CONTACT DETAILS Michael Reynolds, Administrator, c/o Edwin Coe LLP, 2 Stone Buildings, London WC2A 3TH *Tel.* 020 7691 4048 *Email* michael.reynolds@edwincoe.com

■ The Leverhulme Trust

CC NO 1159154   **ESTABLISHED** 1925
WHERE FUNDING CAN BE GIVEN UK.
WHO CAN BENEFIT Educational organisations; research bodies; charities; arts organisations; individuals.
WHAT IS FUNDED Scholarships, fellowships and prizes for education and research.
WHAT IS NOT FUNDED See the website for a full list of exclusions.
TYPE OF GRANT Research; project costs, including salaries.
RANGE OF GRANTS Dependent on grants programme.
SAMPLE GRANTS University of Cambridge (£19.8 million); University of Birmingham (£8.4 million); The Mandela Rhodes Foundation (£3 million); University of Glasgow (£1.44 million); Queen's University Belfast (£933,000); Guildhall School of Music and Drama (£755,000); London Contemporary Dance School (£522,000); University of Southampton (£506,000).
FINANCES *Financial year end* 31/12/2021
Income £95,090,000
Grants to organisations £137,500,000
Assets £3,580,000
TRUSTEES Rudy Markham; Steve Williams; Niall Fitzgerald; Christopher Saul; Doug Baillie; Prof. Keith Gull; Leena Nair; Mhairi McEwan; David Lewis; Alan Jope; Keith Weed.
OTHER INFORMATION During 2021, the trust received 3,640 applications, of which 664 were successful. The grant total includes grants to both individuals and organisations.
HOW TO APPLY Each programme, scholarship or award has its own individual application deadlines and procedures. Grant programmes open and close throughout the year. Full details and guidelines for each scheme are available from the trust directly or via its website.
CONTACT DETAILS Programme correspondent, 1 Pemberton Row, London EC4A 3BG *Tel.* 020 7042 9888 *Email* grants@leverhulme.ac.uk *Website* www.leverhulme.ac.uk

■ Lord Leverhulme's Charitable Trust

cc no 212431   **established** 1957

WHERE FUNDING CAN BE GIVEN UK, with a strong preference for Cheshire, Merseyside and South Lancashire.

WHO CAN BENEFIT Registered and exempt charities.

WHAT IS FUNDED Health; community; education; the arts; animal welfare; the environment; places of worship.

SAMPLE GRANTS Chester Cathedral (£237,900); Bolton School (£30,000); Lady Lever Art Gallery (£25,000); The Prince's Youth Trust (£21,400); Liverpool Heart and Chest Hospital (£20,000).

FINANCES *Financial year end* 05/04/2022
Income £861,400
Grants to organisations £614,300
Assets £42,960,000

TRUSTEES Anthony Hannay; Sir Algernon Heber-Percy; Henry Wilson.

OTHER INFORMATION Grants were made for the following purposes: religious establishments (£17,000); education (£23,000); health (£120,000); community (£120,000); the arts (£27,000); animal welfare (£31,000); the environment (£3,000).

HOW TO APPLY The trust states in its 2021/22 annual report: 'Priority is given [...] to applications from Cheshire, Merseyside and South Lancashire and the charities supported by the settlor in his lifetime. Others who do not meet those criteria should not apply without prior invitation but should, on a single sheet, state briefly their aims and apply fully only on being asked to do so. A handful of charities have heeded this warning and telephoned our administrator but the continuing volume of applications from charities which plainly do not meet the stated criteria suggests that many applicants do not concern themselves with their target's policies.'

CONTACT DETAILS The Trustees, Leverhulme Estate Office, Hesketh Grange, Manor Road, Thornton Hough, Wirral, Merseyside CH63 1JD *Tel.* 0151 336 4828 *Email* llctadmin@leverhulme.net

■ The Ralph Levy Charitable Company Ltd

cc no 200009

WHERE FUNDING CAN BE GIVEN UK and overseas.

WHO CAN BENEFIT Charitable organisations.

WHAT IS FUNDED Education, health, social welfare and the arts.

SAMPLE GRANTS A list of beneficiaries was not included in the annual report and accounts.

FINANCES *Financial year end* 05/04/2022
Income £460,400
Grants to organisations £469,100
Assets £129,200

TRUSTEES Daniel Levy; Stuart Levy; Christopher Andrews.

OTHER INFORMATION Grants were distributed as follows: education (£195,700); welfare (£189,500); medical causes (£82,500); the arts (£1,500).

HOW TO APPLY Apply in writing to the correspondent. The trustees meet monthly to discuss and approve grant applications.

CONTACT DETAILS The Trustees, 116 Piccadilly, London W1J 7BJ *Tel.* 020 7408 9333 *Email* charity@ralphtrustees.co.uk

■ Joseph Levy Foundation

cc no 1165225   **established** 1965

WHERE FUNDING CAN BE GIVEN UK and Israel.

WHO CAN BENEFIT Registered charities.

WHAT IS FUNDED From April 2021 to March 2022 the foundation focussed on two areas: youth disadvantage and cystic fibrosis.

WHAT IS NOT FUNDED Individuals.

TYPE OF GRANT Project costs; capital and core costs; research; salaries; start-up costs; up to and over three years.

RANGE OF GRANTS Generally between £1,000 and £30,000.

SAMPLE GRANTS Levy2 (£3.03 million); Cystic Fibrosis Holiday Fund (£123,500); Ambitious About Autism (£60,000); In2Out (£30,000); Gesher School (£20,000); Israel Guide Dog Centre (£10,000); Challenge Wales (£3,000); Community Trust (£1,500).

FINANCES *Financial year end* 31/03/2022
Income £844,600
Grants to organisations £3,450,000
Assets £21,090,000

TRUSTEES Jane Jason; James Jason; Katie Ellison; Mark Jason.

OTHER INFORMATION In 2021/22, the foundation awarded 14 grants to 13 organisations. Grants were broken down as follows: unrestricted funding (£3.03 million); cystic fibrosis (£202,400); disadvantaged young people (£120,000); autism (£60,000); small grants (£39,500).

HOW TO APPLY Unsolicited applications are not accepted. The foundation searches for opportunities where its funding could make a difference.

CONTACT DETAILS The Trustees, 1st Floor, 1 Bell Street, London NW1 5BY *Tel.* 020 7616 1200 *Email* info@jlf.org.uk *Website* www.jlf.org.uk

■ Cecil and Hilda Lewis Charitable Trust

cc no 258763   **established** 1962

WHERE FUNDING CAN BE GIVEN UK and overseas.

WHO CAN BENEFIT Charitable organisations; educational establishments; medical organisations; art institutions.

WHAT IS FUNDED General charitable purposes, including the following: social welfare; older people; education in the UK and Israel (focusing on children with disabilities); arts and culture; medical research; health; students and educational establishments; disaster relief.

TYPE OF GRANT One-year and multi-year grants.

RANGE OF GRANTS Mostly under £11,000.

SAMPLE GRANTS Contemporary Art Society (£20,000); University of Arts London (£12,000).

FINANCES *Financial year end* 31/12/2021
Income £278,100
Grants to organisations £224,400
Assets £7,550,000

TRUSTEES Robert Lewis; Catherine Wills; Roger Wise; Alan Mason.

OTHER INFORMATION Only organisations that received grants of over £11,000 were listed as beneficiaries in the charity's accounts. Grants of under £10,000 totalled £192,500 and were awarded to 43 organisations.

HOW TO APPLY Apply in writing to the correspondent. The trustees meet regularly to review grant applications.

CONTACT DETAILS Robert Lewis, Trustee and Secretary, Rotherwood, Jumps Road, Churt, Farnham, Surrey GU10 2JZ *Tel.* 01252 792189

■ Bernard Lewis Family Charitable Trust

cc no 1125035   **established** 2008
where funding can be given UK.
who can benefit Registered charities.
what is funded Child welfare; medical causes; older people; Jewish community support; education; general charitable purposes.
range of grants Up to £200,000 but mostly £10,000 to £50,000.
sample grants Newlife (£300,000); Meath Epilepsy (£100,000); Just for Kids Law (£30,000); WildTeam (£15,000); Lyra in Africa (£4,000); Westminster Synagogue (£3,000).
finances *Financial year end 31/12/2021*
Income £3,060,000
Grants to organisations £1,630,000
Assets £10,350,000
trustees Caroline Grainge; Bernard Lewis; Leonard Lewis; Clive Lewis.
other information Grants were broken down as follows: general charitable purposes (£831,800); child welfare (£508,800); medical causes (£264,300); Jewish support (£169,900); older people (£53,500).
how to apply The trust does not accept unsolicited applications.
contact details The Trustees, Chelsea House, Westgate, London W5 1DR *Tel.* 07730 091970

■ David and Ruth Lewis Family Charitable Trust

cc no 259892   **established** 1969
where funding can be given UK and overseas.
who can benefit Charitable bodies and research organisations.
what is funded General charitable purposes; medical research; Jewish religious support; child and social care; older people; education.
type of grant Most grants are one-off payments but some medical research grants can run for three years.
sample grants Hope for Tomorrow (£120,000); Community Security Trust (£100,000); Sense (£60,000); ActionAid, British Refugee Council and Jerusalem Foundation (£50,000 each).
finances *Financial year end 31/05/2022*
Income £3,240,000
Grants to organisations £2,250,000
Assets £25,500,000
trustees Benjamin Lewis; Simon Lewis; Rachel Lewis.
other information Grants were broken down as follows: general charitable funding (£1.83 million); children and social care (£137,800); medical research and support (£127,500); support for older people (£100,500); educational funding (£52,500).
how to apply Apply in writing to the correspondent.
contact details Benjamin Lewis, Trustee, Chelsea House, West Gate, Ealing, London W5 1DR *Tel.* 020 8991 4502

■ The Charles Lewis Foundation

cc no 1179185   **established** 2018
where funding can be given UK.
who can benefit Registered charities.
what is funded General charitable purposes, including children and young people and community.
type of grant Project funding; core costs.
range of grants £500 to £26,000.

sample grants Dandelion Time (£26,000); Free My Meal (£14,000); Little Stars Baby Bank (£8,800); Their Voice (£3,000); React (Rapid Effective Assistance for Children with potentially Terminal illness) (£2,500); The Respite Association (£2,000); The Hygiene Bank (£1,000); Holland Sports (£500).
finances *Financial year end 31/03/2022*
Income £125,000
Grants to organisations £187,000
Assets £42,000
trustees Della Skeates; Geoffrey Lewis.
other information Grants were made to 56 organisations.
how to apply Apply in writing to the correspondent.
contact details The Trustees, Unit 4, The Diamond, Holland Road, Oxted RH8 9BQ *Tel.* 07876 654045 *Email* office@tclf.org.uk

■ The Sir Edward Lewis Foundation

cc no 264475   **established** 1972
where funding can be given UK and overseas.
who can benefit Registered charities.
what is funded General charitable purposes.
what is not funded Individuals.
type of grant Capital costs; core/revenue costs.
range of grants Mostly up to £10,000.
sample grants Arnold Foundation for Rugby School (£25,000); Kent and Sussex Air Ambulance Trust (£10,000); The Childhood Trust and Duty to Care Trust (£5,000 each); Dogs Trust (£4,000); City Chamber Choir (£3,000); Listening Books (£2,000); The Pain Relief Foundation (£1,000).
finances *Financial year end 05/04/2022*
Income £277,100
Grants to organisations £214,500
Assets £12,140,000
trustees Sarah Dorin; Richard Lewis; Mark Harris; Christopher Lewis; David Lewis.
other information The trustees prefer to support charities known personally to them and those favoured by the settlor. During 2021/22, grants were awarded to 77 organisations. Small grants of less than £5,000 totalled £134,500 and grants of over £5,000 totalled £80,000. The foundation provides annual grants to a number of charities but new appeals are regularly considered.
how to apply Applications can be submitted to the correspondent by post or email. The trustees meet bi-annually, in May and December, to consider new applications.
contact details The Trustees, c/o Rawlinson and Hunter LLP, Eighth Floor, 6 New Street Square, London EC4A 3AQ *Tel.* 020 7842 2000 *Email* lewis.foundation@rawlinson-hunter.com

■ Liberum Foundation

cc no 1137475   **established** 2010
where funding can be given UK, with a preference for London.
who can benefit Registered charities.
what is funded Education and training; social welfare; recreation; community development; disadvantaged young people.
what is not funded Adult health; hospitals; animals; older people; the armed forces; housing; heritage; the environment; religion.
sample grants School-Home Support (£32,400); Place2Be (£25,000); Chance UK and Children's Burns (£5,000 each); Afghan Aid (£1,000).

FINANCES *Financial year end 31/12/2021*
Income £88,600
Grants to organisations £68,400
Assets £139,600

TRUSTEES Carolyn Doherty; Natalie Clarke; William Thomas; Christopher Metcalfe; Shane Le Prevost; Christopher Howlett; Timothy Medak.

OTHER INFORMATION In 2021 the foundation awarded grants to five organisations. It provides annual support to School-Home Support and Place2Be.

HOW TO APPLY Contact the correspondent for further information.

CONTACT DETAILS Justine Rumens, Company Secretary, Ropemaker Place, Level 12, 25 Ropemaker Street, London EC2Y 9LY *Tel.* 020 3100 2000 *Email* info@liberumfoundation.com *Website* www.liberum.com/about/corporate-responsibility

■ The Lightbulb Trust

CC NO 1187551
WHERE FUNDING CAN BE GIVEN UK.
WHO CAN BENEFIT Charitable organisations.
WHAT IS FUNDED Literacy and learning; mental health and well-being; digital inclusion; social infrastructure.
TYPE OF GRANT Grants and social investments.
SAMPLE GRANTS Doorstep Library (£80,000); West London Action for Children (£55,400); Solidarity Sports (£33,000); Kentish Town City Farm (£10,000).
FINANCES *Financial year end 31/05/2022*
Income £438,000
Grants to organisations £542,100
Assets £441,400
TRUSTEES Salome Holden-Leventis; Yu-Shuen Chan; Benjamin Holden; Siena Colgrave.
HOW TO APPLY Unsolicited applications are not accepted.
CONTACT DETAILS The Trustees, c/o MHA MacIntyre Hudson, 2 London Wall Place, 6th Floor, London EC2Y 5AU *Tel.* 020 7348 0395

■ The Limbourne Trust

CC NO 1113796   **ESTABLISHED** 2006
WHERE FUNDING CAN BE GIVEN UK and overseas.
WHO CAN BENEFIT Charitable organisations; community projects.
WHAT IS FUNDED The environment and sustainability; conservation; community projects; disadvantaged people; education, in particular in literature, music, drama and dance; health; the relief of poverty.
TYPE OF GRANT Capital costs; project funding.
RANGE OF GRANTS Typically up to £10,000.
SAMPLE GRANTS Rural Coffee Caravan and Suffolk Refugee Support (£15,000 each); Stepping Stones (£10,000); Buckingham Emergency Food Appeal and The Simon Community (£8,000 each); Kinda Education and Open Road (£5,000 each); Beccles Community Hub and Organic Research Centre (£3,000 each); Creekside Education Trust (£1,000).
FINANCES *Financial year end 05/04/2022*
Income £109,700
Grants to organisations £112,700
Assets £4,700,000
TRUSTEES Mrs E. A. Thistlethwayte; Katharine Thistlethwayte; Dr Andrew Eastaugh; Penelope Heath.
OTHER INFORMATION Grants were made to 14 organisations in 2021/22.
HOW TO APPLY According to the 2021/22 annual report, 'the trustees will seek to identify those projects where the greatest and widest benefit can be attained, and usually will only consider written applications and, where necessary, make further enquiries.'
CONTACT DETAILS The Trustees, Downs Farm, Homersfield, Harleston, Norfolk IP20 0NS *Tel.* 07572 966087

■ Limoges Charitable Trust

CC NO 1016178   **ESTABLISHED** 1991
WHERE FUNDING CAN BE GIVEN UK, with a preference for Birmingham.
WHO CAN BENEFIT Registered charities; universities; hospices; churches; community organisations; individuals (occasionally).
WHAT IS FUNDED General charitable purposes, including health, the environment, arts and heritage, community purposes, children and young people and animal welfare.
RANGE OF GRANTS Mostly up to £7,000.
SAMPLE GRANTS Young Careers Campaign (£7,200); Edward's Trust (£7,000); Birmingham Hospice and Elgar School of Music (£5,000 each); ACE Dance and Music and Elm Ballet School (£3,000 each); Christian Aid and Portsmouth Cathedral (£2,000 each); Royal Shakespeare Company and Samaritans Birmingham (£1,000 each); Dogs Trust and Dorothy Parkes Community Centre (£500 each).
FINANCES *Financial year end 05/04/2022*
Income £44,300
Grants to organisations £375,000
Assets £2,090,000
TRUSTEES Judy Dyke; Andrew Milner; Martin Dyke.
OTHER INFORMATION In 2021/22, a total of 60 grants were made.
HOW TO APPLY Apply in writing to the correspondent. The trustees usually meet four times a year to consider applications.
CONTACT DETAILS The Trustees, c/o Tyndallwoods Solicitors, 29 Woodbourne Road, Edgbaston, Birmingham, West Midlands B17 8BY *Tel.* 0121 693 2222 *Email* jdyke@tyndallwoods.co.uk

■ The Linbury Trust

CC NO 287077   **ESTABLISHED** 1983
WHERE FUNDING CAN BE GIVEN UK and overseas, particularly the Caribbean.
WHO CAN BENEFIT Charitable organisations; museums and galleries; educational organisations.
WHAT IS FUNDED Arts and culture (including visual arts, dance, historic buildings, museums and theatre); education; young people; older people; health and medical research; the environment; social welfare; overseas aid.
WHAT IS NOT FUNDED Our previous research suggests that support is not given for individuals, educational fees or expeditions.
TYPE OF GRANT Core and capital costs; project costs; collections and acquisitions; development funding.
RANGE OF GRANTS Mostly under £100,000.
SAMPLE GRANTS Royal Opera House Covent Garden Foundation (£1 million); University of Oxford – Ashmolean Museum (£312,500); Stowe House Preservation Trust (£125,000); Cardboard Citizens (£100,000); Mental Health Innovations (£75,000); Tate Britain (£70,000); Green Light Trust and YoungMinds (£50,000 each).
FINANCES *Financial year end 05/04/2022*
Income £4,280,000
Grants to organisations £6,530,000
Assets £143,600,000

TRUSTEES Lady Anya Sainsbury; Richard Adams; James Barnard; The Hon. Mark Sainsbury; John Sainsbury; Sarah Butler-Sloss.

OTHER INFORMATION The trust is one of the Sainsbury Family Charitable Trusts, which share a common administration – see www.sftc.org.uk for more information. A total of 95 organisations were supported during 2021/22. Grants were distributed as follows: culture (£2.38 million); COVID-19 (£1.47 million); social welfare (£878,000); the environment (£566,000); education and young people (£524,000); older people (£334,000); overseas and emergency relief (£220,000); small grants (£118,000); medical causes (£50,000).

HOW TO APPLY The trust's website states that it does not accept unsolicited applications but rather identifies potential organisations 'through partnership work and research'.

CONTACT DETAILS The Trustees, The Peak, 5 Wilton Road, London SW1V 1AP *Tel.* 020 7410 0330 *Email* linbury@sfct.org.uk *Website* www.linburytrust.org.uk

■ Lincolnshire Community Foundation

CC NO 1196448   **ESTABLISHED** 2002
WHERE FUNDING CAN BE GIVEN Lincolnshire.
WHO CAN BENEFIT Registered charities; unregistered charities; hospices; uniformed groups; CICs; social enterprises; schools; PTAs; amateur sports clubs; religious bodies/institutions; individuals.
WHAT IS FUNDED General charitable purposes including: the environment; social welfare; community projects.
TYPE OF GRANT Capital costs; core/revenue costs; seed funding/start-up funding; project funding; unrestricted funding.
SAMPLE GRANTS Citizens Advice Mid Lincolnshire; Crosby Community Association; Fusion Creative; Heart of Sleaford; Holbeach Hospital; Lincolnshire Action Trust; Responders to Warmth; St Giles Community Garden; St Luke's Community Choir.
FINANCES *Financial year end* 31/03/2020
Income £1,100,000
Grants to organisations £793,300
Assets £5,020,000
TRUSTEES Stephen Ryder; Lynnette Pryke; Danielle Budworth; Sarah Fletcher; Nicholas Danks; Paul Scott; John Maitland; Elizabeth Milligan-Manby; Paul Baumber.
OTHER INFORMATION This is one of the 47 UK community foundations, which distribute funding for a wide range of purposes. As with all community foundations, there are a number of donor-advised funds managed on behalf of individuals, families and charitable trusts. Grant schemes tend to change frequently – consult the foundation's website for details of current programmes and up-to-date deadlines. The community foundation has recently re-registered with the Charity Commission and therefore full financial information was not available. The financial information in this entry relates to the community foundation's previous registration (Charity Commission no. 1092328). Note that the grant total may include amounts awarded to individuals.
HOW TO APPLY Visit the foundation's website for details of current grant schemes.

CONTACT DETAILS The Trustees, 4 Mill House, Moneys Yard, Carre Street, Sleaford, Lincolnshire NG34 7TW *Tel.* 01529 305825 *Email* info@lincolnshirecf.co.uk *Website* www.lincolnshirecf.co.uk

■ The Linder Foundation

CC NO 267509   **ESTABLISHED** 1974
WHERE FUNDING CAN BE GIVEN UK.
WHO CAN BENEFIT UK-registered charities or exempt charities; universities and teaching hospitals; museums and arts charities.
WHAT IS FUNDED Medical research; funding for medical electives and hardship grants at selected universities; hospices and respite care; improving the mental health and development of young people, particularly teenagers, young offenders and those in care; the environment; the arts, including musical tuition and concerts.
WHAT IS NOT FUNDED Non-UK-registered charities/exempt charities.
TYPE OF GRANT Mainly one-off grants; project funding; seed funding; research funding.
RANGE OF GRANTS Generally up to £20,000.
SAMPLE GRANTS Royal College of Surgeons (£50,000); Victoria and Albert Museum (£32,200); Fields in Trust (£20,000); P3 (£16,000); Royal Trinity Hospice (£10,000); Oxford University (£8,000); Oxford Foundation for AI Research (£5,000); Katherine House Hospice (£3,500).
FINANCES *Financial year end* 31/03/2022
Income £634,600
Grants to organisations £493,700
Assets £18,470,000
TRUSTEES Michael Butler; Carole Cook; Jonathan Fountain; Jack Ladeveze; Audrey Ladeveze; Henrietta Buxton; Amanda Smith.
OTHER INFORMATION Grants were made to 36 organisations in 2021/22. The grant total includes £56,000 awarded in elective and hardship grants to seven university medical schools.
HOW TO APPLY Check the website for open funding rounds and apply using the online form on the foundation's website.
CONTACT DETAILS The Trustees, c/o The Trust Partnership, 6 Trull Farm Buildings, Trull, Gloucestershire GL8 8SQ *Tel.* 020 3997 4444 *Email* admin@thelinderfoundation.org.uk *Website* https://thelinderfoundation.org.uk

■ The Lister Charitable Trust

CC NO 288730   **ESTABLISHED** 1981
WHERE FUNDING CAN BE GIVEN Worldwide.
WHO CAN BENEFIT Charitable organisations.
WHAT IS FUNDED General charitable purposes; children and young people; environmental conservation; health.
TYPE OF GRANT Usually one-off for a specific project or part of a project.
SAMPLE GRANTS A list of beneficiaries was not included in the annual report and accounts. Previous beneficiaries have included: United Kingdom Sailing Academy (UKSA) (£75,000); Wildlife Media (£66,000); Fundatia Inocenti (£23,000); Brenda Phillips Photography (£13,000); Home-Start Ashford and Huntsham Village Hall (£10,000 each); Light Dragoons and Mount Carmel (£5,000 each); The Royal Marsden Cancer Charity (£4,000); The Ragamuffin Project (£2,500).

FINANCES *Financial year end* 05/04/2022
Income £128,800
Grants to organisations £209,300
Assets £7,260,000

TRUSTEES Penny Horne; Benjamin Horne; Samuel Horne; Tomas Horne; Joe Horne.

HOW TO APPLY Apply in writing to the correspondent. The trustees usually meet quarterly to review applications.

CONTACT DETAILS The Trustees, c/o Apperley Properties Ltd, 45 Welbeck Street, London W1G 8DZ *Tel.* 020 7486 0800 *Email* info@apperleylimited.co.uk

■ The Frank Litchfield Charitable Trust

CC NO 1038943 **ESTABLISHED** 1994
WHERE FUNDING CAN BE GIVEN Essex; Cambridgeshire; Hertfordshire.
WHO CAN BENEFIT Charitable organisations and projects.
WHAT IS FUNDED General charitable purposes, in particular health, disability, social welfare and medical research.
TYPE OF GRANT Project funding; research.
RANGE OF GRANTS Mostly between £500 and £27,500.
SAMPLE GRANTS Cambridge Community Foundation (£27,500); Sunny Days (£25,000); Disasters Emergency Committee (£15,000); University College London Hospitals Charitable Foundation (£2,000); Target Ovarian Cancer (£1,000); Transitions UK (£500).
FINANCES *Financial year end* 31/03/2022
Income £160,300
Grants to organisations £117,300
Assets £10,950,000
TRUSTEES David Chater; Michael Womack; Michael Hamilton.
HOW TO APPLY Apply in writing to the correspondent.
CONTACT DETAILS Michael Womack, Trustee, 12 De Freville Avenue, Cambridge, Cambridgeshire CB4 1HR *Tel.* 01223 358012 *Email* womack@btinternet.com

■ Little Lives UK

CC NO 1171884 **ESTABLISHED** 2017
WHERE FUNDING CAN BE GIVEN England.
WHO CAN BENEFIT Charitable organisations.
WHAT IS FUNDED General charitable purposes; disability; young people.
RANGE OF GRANTS Generally up to £2,200.
SAMPLE GRANTS Footsteps Foundation (£5,500); Harmony Youth Project and Moorvision (£2,200 each); East Anglia's Children's Hospices (£2,000); Wales Council for Deaf People (£1,600); Ronald McDonald House in Tooting (£1,000); Autism Unlimited (£500).
FINANCES *Financial year end* 31/03/2022
Income £199,000
Grants to organisations £113,300
Assets £192,600
TRUSTEES Lotta-Maija Salmi; Szonja Budai; Yauheni Sysoyeu.
HOW TO APPLY Contact the correspondent for more information.
CONTACT DETAILS The Trustees, Little Lives UK, Discovery Court Business Centre, 551–553 Wallisdown Road, Poole, Dorset BH12 5AG *Tel.* 020 7871 3059 *Email* info@littlelives.org.uk *Website* www.littlelives.org.uk

■ The Michael and Betty Little Trust

CC NO 1107412
WHERE FUNDING CAN BE GIVEN Hampshire; Surrey; West Sussex; overseas.
WHO CAN BENEFIT Registered charities and community organisations.
WHAT IS FUNDED General charitable purposes.
WHAT IS NOT FUNDED Political organisations; sponsored adventure holidays or trips abroad; local branches of national charities; education or health of individuals; commercial activity; one-off events.
TYPE OF GRANT Core costs; project funding.
RANGE OF GRANTS Up to £10,000.
SAMPLE GRANTS Over the Moon (£90,000); Crossover Youth Centre (£60,000); Life Centre (£30,000); First Give (£25,000); SJP Charity (£15,000).
FINANCES *Financial year end* 31/03/2022
Income £103,600
Grants to organisations £1,150,000
Assets £10,820,000
TRUSTEES Katherine Shipton; Martin Little; Christopher Little; Lucy Blackgrove; Elizabeth Moore; Dr Helen Little; Hilary Graham; Peter Little.
HOW TO APPLY Applications can be made via the trust's website.
CONTACT DETAILS The Trustees, 12 Stanton Drive, Chichester, West Sussex PO19 5QN *Email* contact@mbltrust.org *Website* www.mbltrust.org

■ The Charles Littlewood Hill Trust

CC NO 286350 **ESTABLISHED** 1978
WHERE FUNDING CAN BE GIVEN UK, with a preference for Nottinghamshire and Norfolk.
WHO CAN BENEFIT Charitable organisations; educational establishments; churches; community organisations.
WHAT IS FUNDED General charitable causes; social welfare; health and disability; the armed forces; the environment; education; religious activities; arts and culture.
WHAT IS NOT FUNDED Individuals; activities which are the responsibility of local authorities or similar bodies.
TYPE OF GRANT In practice, unrestricted funding, including capital and core costs. Applications for starter finance are encouraged, but grants are seldom made to endowment or capital funds.
RANGE OF GRANTS Generally £1,000 to £5,000.
SAMPLE GRANTS Priscilla Bacon Norfolk Hospice Care Ltd (£15,000); Nottinghamshire Community Foundation (£10,000); The Norfolk Churches Trust (£7,500); Bishops Fund for Refugees (£5,000); Eating Matters (£3,000); Holt Youth Project (£2,500); Age UK – Norwich (£2,000); Assist Trust (£1,000).
FINANCES *Financial year end* 31/12/2021
Income £150,400
Grants to organisations £110,000
Assets £6,180,000
TRUSTEES Charles Barratt; Tim Farr; Nigel Savory; John Pears.
OTHER INFORMATION Grants during the year were broken down as follows: medical/disability (£32,000); welfare (£20,500); other (£17,500); education (£15,000); churches (£7,500); the environment (£6,000); services (£4,000); arts (£2,500); groups (£1,000).
HOW TO APPLY Applications must be made in writing to the correspondent, including your latest set of audited accounts, at least one month before

trustees' meetings in March, July and November. Unsuccessful applicants will not be notified.

CONTACT DETAILS D. N. Lindley, Trust Administrator, PO Box 10454, Nottingham, Nottinghamshire NG5 0HQ *Tel.* 07710 639946 *Email* charles. hill@btinternet.com *Website* www.charleshill.org. uk

■ The Second Joseph Aaron Littman Foundation

CC NO 201892   **ESTABLISHED** 1961
WHERE FUNDING CAN BE GIVEN Worldwide.
WHO CAN BENEFIT Registered charities only.
WHAT IS FUNDED General charitable purposes; social welfare; education; the Jewish faith and community; academic and medical research.
WHAT IS NOT FUNDED Individuals.
TYPE OF GRANT General funding; research.
RANGE OF GRANTS Mostly up to £10,000, with exceptional grants of up to £100,000.
SAMPLE GRANTS The Littman Library of Jewish Civilisation (£100,000); Chabad Lubavitch (£47,500); Leo Baeck College (£15,000); PJ Library (£10,000); University College London (£6,000); Alyn Hospital (£5,000); African Rural Development (£4,000); Nightingale Homes (£2,500).
FINANCES *Financial year end 05/04/2022*
Income £429,600
Grants to organisations £249,000
Assets £9,170,000
TRUSTEES Mrs C. Littman; Joanna Littman; Rabbi Dr Thomas Salamon.
OTHER INFORMATION Only organisations that received grants of over £2,000 were listed as beneficiaries in the foundation's accounts. Grants of under £2,000 totalled £5,750. The foundation provides continuing substantial support to the Littman Library of Jewish Civilisation.
HOW TO APPLY Apply in writing to the correspondent.
CONTACT DETAILS The Trustees, Manor Farm, Mill Lane, Charlton Mackrell, Somerton, Somerset TA11 7BQ *Tel.* 01458 223650

■ The George John and Sheilah Livanos Charitable Trust

CC NO 1002279   **ESTABLISHED** 1985
WHERE FUNDING CAN BE GIVEN UK.
WHO CAN BENEFIT Registered charities.
WHAT IS FUNDED General charitable purposes.
RANGE OF GRANTS From £2,500 to £155,000.
SAMPLE GRANTS Previous beneficiaries have included: Gainsborough House (£155,000); Bletchley Park Trust (£15,000); Ekklesia Project Fakenham (£12,000); Whoopsadaisy (£3,300); Crackerjack's Children's Trust, Housing the Homeless and South East Cancer Help Centre (£2,500 each).
FINANCES *Financial year end 31/12/2021*
Income £6,700
Grants to organisations £219,200
TRUSTEES Timothy Cripps; Philip Harris.
OTHER INFORMATION Full accounts were not available to view on the Charity Commission's website due to the trust's low income. We have therefore estimated the grant total based on the trust's total expenditure.
HOW TO APPLY In the trust's accounts from 2018 (which were the latest available to view), it stated the following: 'Unsolicited applications are accepted, but the trustees do receive a very

high number of grant applications which, in line with the trustees' grant-making policy, are mostly unsuccessful. The trustees prefer to make donations to charities whose work they have researched and which is in accordance with the aims and objectives of the charity for the year. Financial circumstances will be relevant only in determining the amount of an award.'
CONTACT DETAILS The Trustees, c/o Longmores, 24 Castle Street, Hertford, Hertfordshire SG14 1HP *Tel.* 01992 300333

■ Liverpool Charity and Voluntary Services (LCVS)

CC NO 223485   **ESTABLISHED** 1970
WHERE FUNDING CAN BE GIVEN Merseyside.
WHO CAN BENEFIT Registered charities; CICs.
WHAT IS FUNDED General charitable purposes; health; education; community projects; children and young people; arts and culture.
WHAT IS NOT FUNDED Exclusions for each of the charity's grant programmes can be found on its website.
TYPE OF GRANT Capital costs; project funding; core costs (including salaries).
SAMPLE GRANTS A list of beneficiaries was not included in the annual report and accounts. Previous beneficiaries have included: Violence Reduction Unit (£285,200); Play Partnership (£260,000); UW Giving (£119,200); Wirral Council CAMHS (£41,800); Pen Natal Grants (£19,200); Liverpool and Merseyside Charities Funds (£10,000); Ways to Wellbeing (£3,000).
FINANCES *Financial year end 31/03/2022*
Income £6,830,000
Grants to organisations £4,140,000
Assets £8,790,000
TRUSTEES Michael Thomas; John Price; James Sloan; Kenneth Perry; Dorcas Akeju; Louise Scholes; Michael Salla; Neil Sturmey; Sonia Bassey; Maxine Ennis; Gemma Shone.
OTHER INFORMATION The charity acts in a similar manner to a community foundation, administrating the giving of much smaller charitable trusts. Comprehensive details of all of the grant programmes are available from the charity's website and details of new programmes or new funding rounds are posted as they come up.
HOW TO APPLY Apply online via the charity's website.
CONTACT DETAILS Grants Team, 151 Dale Street, Liverpool, Merseyside L2 2AH *Tel.* 0151 227 5177 *Email* info@lcvs.org.uk *Website* www.lcvs. org.uk

■ The Livingbridge Foundation

CC NO 1194565
WHERE FUNDING CAN BE GIVEN UK.
WHO CAN BENEFIT Charitable organisations.
WHAT IS FUNDED Equality; diversity; opportunity; entrepreneurship.
RANGE OF GRANTS Up to £250,000.
SAMPLE GRANTS upReach (£250,000); Action Tutoring (£200,000); Sutton Trust (£110,000); Greater Change (£75,000); Hideout Youth Zone (£50,000); Refugee Council (£1,000).
FINANCES *Financial year end 31/12/2021*
Income £757,000
Grants to organisations £948,100
Assets (£205,200)
TRUSTEES Xavier Woodward; Andrew Berwick; Christopher Hale; Amy Smith; Jeremy Dennison.

OTHER INFORMATION The foundation is the corporate charity of Livingbridge, a private equity firm based in London.

HOW TO APPLY Apply in writing to the correspondent.

CONTACT DETAILS The Trustees, 100 Wood Street, London EC2V 7AN *Tel.* 020 7506 5700 *Email* Foundation@livingbridge.com *Website* www.livingbridge.com

■ The Ian and Natalie Livingstone Charitable Trust

CC NO 1149025   **ESTABLISHED** 2012

WHERE FUNDING CAN BE GIVEN UK and Wales.

WHO CAN BENEFIT Registered charities.

WHAT IS FUNDED Children and young people; disadvantaged people.

WHAT IS NOT FUNDED Individuals.

TYPE OF GRANT Project funding; capital costs; core costs.

RANGE OF GRANTS Generally up to £50,000.

SAMPLE GRANTS Dalaid (£50,000); Highgate School (£20,000); Hasmonean High School and Make a Wish (£10,000 each); British Academy of Film and Television Arts (£6,300); Chicken Soup Shelter (£5,000); London Music Fund (£4,000).

FINANCES *Financial year end* 31/03/2022
Income £158,100
Grants to organisations £105,300
Assets £2,100

TRUSTEES Ian Livingstone; Natalie Livingstone; Mark Levitt.

OTHER INFORMATION The trustees will consider grant applications for up to £250,000.

HOW TO APPLY Apply in writing to the correspondent.

CONTACT DETAILS The Trustees, Blick Rothenberg Ltd, Palladium House, 1–4 Argyll Street, London W1F 7LD *Tel.* 020 7437 7666 *Email* email@blickrothenberg.com

■ Jack Livingstone Charitable Trust

CC NO 263473   **ESTABLISHED** 1971

WHERE FUNDING CAN BE GIVEN UK and worldwide, with a preference for the Manchester area.

WHO CAN BENEFIT Registered charities.

WHAT IS FUNDED General charitable purposes; the Jewish faith and community.

RANGE OF GRANTS Up to £115,000, but generally under £10,000.

SAMPLE GRANTS Manchester Art Gallery (£50,000); The Focus Foundation (£25,000); Federation Jewish Service (£10,000); The Lowry Centre Trust (£2,500); Royal Exchange Theatre (£1,800); Hale Barns Club and Southport New Synagogue (£1,000 each).

FINANCES *Financial year end* 05/04/2022
Income £52,100
Grants to organisations £147,100
Assets £2,140,000

TRUSTEES Janice Livingstone; Terence Livingstone; Brian White.

OTHER INFORMATION Only organisations that received grants of over £1,000 were listed as beneficiaries in the trust's accounts. Grants of under £1,000 totalled £4,400.

HOW TO APPLY Contact the correspondent for further information.

CONTACT DETAILS The Trustees, Apsley Cottage, Vale Road, Bowdon, Altrincham, Cheshire WA14 3AF *Tel.* 0161 928 0760 *Email* 2taf56@gmail.com

■ The Elaine and Angus Lloyd Charitable Trust

CC NO 237250   **ESTABLISHED** 1964

WHERE FUNDING CAN BE GIVEN UK, with a preference for Surrey and Kent.

WHO CAN BENEFIT Individuals; local, regional and UK-wide organisations.

WHAT IS FUNDED General charitable purposes; health; medical causes; disability; social welfare; Christianity.

TYPE OF GRANT Recurrent and one-off.

RANGE OF GRANTS Up to £12,000, but mostly around £1,000 to £3,000.

SAMPLE GRANTS What on Earth Foundation (£12,000); Rhema Bible College (£8,000); Spear Brighton (£5,000); Diabetes UK (£2,500); Policy Exchange (£1,000).

FINANCES *Financial year end* 05/04/2022
Income £138,300
Grants to organisations £98,400
Grants to individuals £5,400
Assets £4,100,000

TRUSTEES Virgina Best; Sir Michael Craig-Cooper; John Gordon; James Lloyd; Christopher Lloyd; Angus Lloyd; The Revd Richard Lloyd; Philippa Smith.

OTHER INFORMATION In 2021/22, grants of less than £1,000 each totalled £9,700.

HOW TO APPLY Grants are generally awarded to charities or for purposes known to one or more of the trustees, but applications may be made in writing to the correspondent. The trustees meet regularly to consider grants.

CONTACT DETAILS Ross Badger, Ground Floor, 45 Pall Mall, London SW1Y 5JG *Tel.* 020 7930 7797 *Email* ross.badger@hhLLP.co.uk

■ The W. M. and B. W. Lloyd Trust

CC NO 503384   **ESTABLISHED** 1974

WHERE FUNDING CAN BE GIVEN Darwen.

WHO CAN BENEFIT Charitable organisations, especially hospitals and hospices.

WHAT IS FUNDED General charitable purposes; education; medical science and the provision of medical equipment; the provision and improvement of public amenities; emergency support.

TYPE OF GRANT Capital costs.

SAMPLE GRANTS A list of beneficiaries was not included in the annual report and accounts.

FINANCES *Financial year end* 05/04/2022
Income £131,900
Grants to organisations £128,500

TRUSTEES John Jacklin; Dorothy Parsons; Jason Slack; Alan Slack.

OTHER INFORMATION The trust has previously stated that it has five committees: emergency, education, social amenities, medical and the T. P. Davies Fund. Each committee considers requests particular to its area of remit and reports to the trustees with its recommendations. The trust also administers the T. P. Davies Fund and Darwen Probation Volunteers Fund.

HOW TO APPLY Apply in writing to the correspondent either by post or email.

CONTACT DETAILS John Jacklin, Secretary and Trustee, Gorse Barn, Rock Lane, Tockholes, Darwen, Lancashire BB3 0LX *Tel.* 01254 771367 *Email* john.jacklin@btinternet.com

■ The Andrew Lloyd Webber Foundation

CC NO 1015648 **ESTABLISHED** 1992
WHERE FUNDING CAN BE GIVEN UK.
WHO CAN BENEFIT Registered charities; CICs.
WHAT IS FUNDED Arts; culture; heritage.
WHAT IS NOT FUNDED A full list of exclusions can be found on the foundation's website.
TYPE OF GRANT Project funding.
RANGE OF GRANTS Generally £3,000 to £30,000.
SAMPLE GRANTS Brit School (£143,300); Get into Theatre (£94,900); Mountview – Andre Ptaszynski Memorial Fund (£30,100); All Saints Church – King's Lynn (£10,000); Music Connect CIC (£5,100); Black British Theatre Awards (£3,000).
FINANCES *Financial year end 31/12/2021*
Income £338,100
Grants to organisations £292,100
Assets £40,640,000
TRUSTEES Louise Fennell; Philip Freedman; Lady Madeleine Webber; Dr Simon Thurley; Katherine Reardon; Emma Marsh.
OTHER INFORMATION Full details of all the foundation's current grant programmes are available on the website. During the year, grants were awarded to 31 organisations.
HOW TO APPLY At the time of writing (March 2023) the foundation was not accepting applications. See the foundation's website for further information.
CONTACT DETAILS Sarah Miller, Director, Sydmonton Court Estate, Burghclere, Newbury, Berkshire RG20 9NJ *Email* use the contact form on the website *Website* www.andrewlloydwebberfoundation.com

■ Lloyds Bank Foundation for England and Wales

CC NO 327114 **ESTABLISHED** 1986
WHERE FUNDING CAN BE GIVEN England and Wales.
WHO CAN BENEFIT Registered charities.
WHAT IS FUNDED Addiction and dependency; asylum seekers and refugees; care leavers; domestic abuse; homeless and vulnerably housed people; learning disabilities; mental health; offending, prison or community service; sexual abuse and exploitation; trafficking and modern slavery; young parents; racial equity.
WHAT IS NOT FUNDED CICs, or any other organisations that are not charities or CIOs registered in England and Wales; infrastructure or umbrella organisations; organisations whose primary purpose is to give funds to individuals or other organisations, i.e. organisations using more than 50% of annual expenditure as grants; hospitals, health authorities or hospices; rescue services; nurseries, pre-schools or playgroups; schools, colleges or universities; animal charities; charities working predominantly outside England and Wales; organisations that do not have a purpose/benefit beyond the promotion of religion.
TYPE OF GRANT Unrestricted.
RANGE OF GRANTS Grants of £50,000.
SAMPLE GRANTS Examples of projects the foundation has funded can be found on its website.
FINANCES *Financial year end 31/12/2021*
Income £19,360,000
Grants to organisations £15,880,000
Assets £33,480,000
TRUSTEES Catharine Cheetham; Joanna Harris; Dr Neil Wooding; Dame Gillian Morgan; Gareth Oakley; Rebecca Shaw; Darren Knight; Kamran Mallick; Ruth Sutherland; Dame Ann Limb; Bushra Ahmed.
OTHER INFORMATION Grants were made to 899 organisations in 2021.
HOW TO APPLY Applications can be made via the foundation's website.
CONTACT DETAILS Grants Team, Second Floor, Society Building, 8 All Saints Street, London N1 9RL *Tel.* 0370 411 1223 *Email* enquiries@lloydsbankfoundation.org.uk *Website* www.lloydsbankfoundation.org.uk

■ Lloyds Bank Foundation for the Channel Islands

CC NO 327113 **ESTABLISHED** 1986
WHERE FUNDING CAN BE GIVEN Channel Islands.
WHO CAN BENEFIT Registered charities.
WHAT IS FUNDED People with health issues or a disability; homelessness; alcohol or drug dependency; carers; discrimination and disadvantage; literacy; domestic violence; people leaving institutional care.
WHAT IS NOT FUNDED Organisations which are not registered charities; individual requests; sponsorship requests; international appeals; animal welfare; environmental charities; expeditions or overseas travel; the promotion of religion (charities which have a religious element but whose objectives demonstrate a wider benefit to people experiencing disadvantage may not be excluded); schools and colleges (except for projects that will benefit disadvantaged students and are clearly additional to statutory responsibilities); activities which are the responsibility of a statutory body or the islands' governments; activities which duplicate or overlap a service already provided; applications for salaries which would apply to the applicant; charities which have received a grant from the foundation in the previous 12 months or have received three years continuous funding.
TYPE OF GRANT Capital costs; core/revenue costs; salaries; project funding; seed funding/start-up funding.
SAMPLE GRANTS Guernsey's Rural Occupational Workshop (GROW) (£100,000); Autism Guernsey (£71,900); Jersey Childcare Trust (£59,400); The Shelter Trust (£35,000); Jersey Action Against Rape (£33,000); Centre Point Trust – Jersey (£28,900); Family First – Jersey (£25,000); Trauma Recovery Centre – Guernsey (£14,100).
FINANCES *Financial year end 31/12/2021*
Income £892,300
Grants to organisations £1,040,000
Assets £1,650,000
TRUSTEES John Henwood; Gavin Ferguson; Heather MacCallum; Tracey Johnson; Neil Fellows; Brian Heath; Alasdair Gardner; Philippa Stahelin; Poppy Murray.
HOW TO APPLY Applications can be made via the foundation's website. Applicants are encouraged to discuss their project with the Executive Director before completing an application form.
CONTACT DETAILS Johanna Le Poidevin, Executive Director, 1 Smith Street, St Peter Port, Guernsey GY1 4BD *Tel.* 01481 706360 *Email* jlepoidevin@lloydsbankfoundation.org.uk *Website* www.lloydsbankfoundationci.org.uk

■ Lloyd's of London Foundation

CC NO 207232   **ESTABLISHED** 1953

WHERE FUNDING CAN BE GIVEN Worldwide; UK, with a preference for East London.

WHO CAN BENEFIT Charitable organisations.

WHAT IS FUNDED Disasters and emergencies and humanitarian work; general charitable purposes.

TYPE OF GRANT One-off and recurrent grants; project costs; bursaries.

RANGE OF GRANTS £1,000 to £25,000.

SAMPLE GRANTS A list of beneficiaries was not included in the annual report and accounts.

FINANCES *Financial year end* 31/12/2021
Income £1,090,000
Grants to organisations £779,000
Grants to individuals £109,000
Assets £3,610,000

TRUSTEES Victoria Carter; David Ibeson; Andrew Brooks; Oliver Ferrari; Amy Bumstead; Mark Fidler; Caroline Klein; Claire O'Meara; Elizabeth Cabrera; Hannah-Polly Williams; Raza Hassan; Ola Jacob-Raji.

OTHER INFORMATION The Lloyd's Market Charity Awards are donations to charities supported by individuals working in the Lloyd's market. The Lloyd's Community Programme supports projects that tackle disadvantage. Grants are awarded to a small number of delivery partners each year to enable them to run projects. These projects provide volunteering opportunities to employees in the Lloyd's market.

HOW TO APPLY Applications for the Lloyd's Market Charity Awards can be made via the foundation's website, where guidelines and application deadlines can also be found. Details will be announced on the website.

CONTACT DETAILS The Trustees, Lloyd's Building, 1 Lime Street, London EC3M 7HA *Tel.* 020 7327 1000 *Email* responsiblebusiness@lloyds.com *Website* www.lloyds.com/about-lloyds/responsible-business/community-involvement/lloyds-charities-trust

■ Lloyd's Patriotic Fund

CC NO 210173   **ESTABLISHED** 1803

WHERE FUNDING CAN BE GIVEN England and Wales.

WHO CAN BENEFIT Registered charities.

WHAT IS FUNDED Armed forces. The fund focuses on 'improving the transition to civilian life for veterans and their families who need the most help.'

TYPE OF GRANT Project funding.

RANGE OF GRANTS Up to £200,000.

SAMPLE GRANTS Combat Stress and Regular Forces Employment Association (£50,000 each); Felix Fund (£11,000); Supporting Wounded Veterans (£10,000).

FINANCES *Financial year end* 30/06/2021
Income £470,000
Grants to organisations £170,000
Assets £2,690,000

TRUSTEES Richard Williams; Air Cdre Wendy Rothery; William Roscoe; Bruce Carnegie-Brown; Duncan Welham; Edward Butler; Caroline Sandeman-Allen; Michelle Alston; Neil Maidment.

OTHER INFORMATION The fund provides long-term support to a number of partner organisations as well as smaller one-off grants. The 2020/21 annual accounts were the latest available at the time of writing (June 2023).

HOW TO APPLY See the fund's website for the latest information on grants.

CONTACT DETAILS Corporate Social Responsibility Manager, Lloyd's, One Lime Street, London EC3M 7HA

Email globalcommunityengagement@lloyds.com
Website www.lloyds.com/lpf

■ Lloyd's Register Foundation

CC NO 1145988   **ESTABLISHED** 2012

WHERE FUNDING CAN BE GIVEN Worldwide.

WHO CAN BENEFIT Universities; research institutions; charitable organisations.

WHAT IS FUNDED Improving public safety at sea and in technology, food and infrastructure through engineering-related education, training and research; transportation; technology and engineering; sustainability.

WHAT IS NOT FUNDED One-off events, conferences or activities; capital works; infrastructure; school, college or university fees; retrospective expenditure; lobbying and campaigning; business or first-class travel; funding for a component of an already-funded project.

TYPE OF GRANT Research funding; project funding.

RANGE OF GRANTS Programme dependent.

SAMPLE GRANTS The Resilience Shift (£3.75 million); Station Biologique de Roscoff (£957,000); Imperial War Museum (£500,000); Foundation for the Global Compact (£250,000); TÜV SÜD Ltd and UNICEF (£100,000 each); Kindling Safety Organisation, National Safety Council and University of Southampton (£10,000 each).

FINANCES *Financial year end* 30/06/2022
Income £15,300,000
Grants to organisations £10,050,000
Assets £305,810,000

TRUSTEES Thomas Anderson; Madhavi Koya; Marina Wyatt; Sir Peter Gregson; Dame Una O'Brien; Andreas Sohmen-Pao; Rosemary Martin; Lambros Varnavides.

OTHER INFORMATION Grants were broken down as follows: safety for a sustainable future (£4.04 million); foundational (£2 million); safety of food (£1.1 million); skills for safety (£1.01 million); heritage and educational centre (£874,000); safety at sea (£477,000); evidence and insight (£410,000); safety of physical infrastructure (£134,000). Note that the foundation awarded a grant of £1.12 million to its trading arm, Lloyd's Register Group. Individuals can be supported but grants are awarded to institutions on their behalf.

HOW TO APPLY Unsolicited applications are not accepted; apply through the foundation's open calls only.

CONTACT DETAILS Michelle Davies, Company Secretary, 71 Fenchurch Street, London EC3M 4BS *Tel.* 020 7423 2783 *Email* michelle.davies@lr.org *Website* www.lrfoundation.org.uk

■ Localtrent Ltd

CC NO 326329   **ESTABLISHED** 1982

WHERE FUNDING CAN BE GIVEN UK, with some preference for Manchester.

WHO CAN BENEFIT Charities; educational or religious institutions.

WHAT IS FUNDED Education related to the Orthodox Jewish faith and the relief of poverty in the Jewish community.

RANGE OF GRANTS Generally, between £5,000 and £21,000.

SAMPLE GRANTS Zoreia Zedokos (£57,000); ABS Training Ltd (£21,000); Asser Bishvil (£20,000); Chasdei Yoel Charitable Trust (£10,400); Teshuva Tefilloh Tzedoka (£9,000); Cong Yetev Lev (£7,500); Merkaz Hatorah Belz Machnovke

(£7,000); Tchaba Kollel and Vyoel Moshe Charitable Trust (£5,000 each).

FINANCES *Financial year end 31/03/2022*
Income £554,500
Grants to organisations £229,700
Assets £1,480,000

TRUSTEES Hyman Weiss; Mina Weiss; Philip Weiss; Zisel Weiss; Yocheved Weiss; Bernardin Weiss.

HOW TO APPLY Apply in writing to the correspondent.

CONTACT DETAILS The Trustees, c/o Lopian Gross Barnett and Co., 1st Floor, Cloisters House, New Bailey Street, Manchester M3 5FS *Tel.* 0161 832 8721

■ The Locker Foundation

CC NO 264180   **ESTABLISHED** 1966

WHERE FUNDING CAN BE GIVEN UK and overseas (Israel).

WHO CAN BENEFIT Jewish organisations; hospices; places of worship; schools; registered charities.

WHAT IS FUNDED General charitable purposes, with a preference for the Jewish faith and community, health, disability and religious education.

TYPE OF GRANT Project funding.

SAMPLE GRANTS A list of beneficiaries was not included in the charity's 2021/22 accounts. Previous beneficiaries have included: Magen David Adam UK (£112,100); Tikva Children's Home (£58,000); Chai Cancer Care (£50,000); Noa Girls (£25,000); Community Security Trust and Norwood Ravenswood (£20,000 each); World Jewish Relief (£15,000); Jewish Deaf Association (£9,900); Chicken Soup Shelter (£9,000); Birmingham Hebrew Congregation (£3,000); Kef Kids (£1,000); Matilda Marks Kennedy School (£500); United Synagogue (£200).

FINANCES *Financial year end 05/04/2022*
Income £725,500
Grants to organisations £433,300
Assets £9,850,000

TRUSTEES Susannah Segal; Malcolm Carter.

OTHER INFORMATION Grants were made to 30 organisations during the year.

HOW TO APPLY Contact the correspondent for further information.

CONTACT DETAILS Malcolm Carter, Chair, 65 Flower Lane, Mill Hill, London NW7 2JN *Tel.* 07956 325198 *Email* thelockerfoundation@hotmail. com

■ The Lockwood Charitable Foundation

CC NO 1123272   **ESTABLISHED** 2008

WHERE FUNDING CAN BE GIVEN England and Wales.

WHO CAN BENEFIT Registered charities; educational organisations; cultural organisations.

WHAT IS FUNDED General charitable purposes including the following: health; education; culture and heritage; Christian causes.

RANGE OF GRANTS Up to £100,000.

SAMPLE GRANTS The Kensington and Chelsea Foundation (£75,000); Arthouse Unlimited (£50,000); Frome Medical Practice (£25,000); Sports Traider (£15,000); Surrey Drug and Alcohol Care (£10,000); Help2Read (£5,000); London Cares Family (£4,000); Phyllis Tuckwell Hospice (£1,000).

FINANCES *Financial year end 05/04/2022*
Income £363,000
Grants to organisations £246,000
Assets £5,920,000

TRUSTEES Richard Lockwood; Lesley Lockwood; Dr Rebecca Lockwood.

OTHER INFORMATION Grants were awarded to 14 organisations in the latest financial year for which accounts were available.

HOW TO APPLY Contact the correspondent for further information.

CONTACT DETAILS The Trustees, The Tithe Barn, The Avenue, Compton, Guildford, Surrey GU3 1JW *Tel.* 01483 415480

■ London Catalyst

CC NO 1066739   **ESTABLISHED** 1872

WHERE FUNDING CAN BE GIVEN Greater London, within the boundaries of the M25.

WHO CAN BENEFIT Registered charities; unregistered charities; CICs; hospices; churches.

WHAT IS FUNDED Health and well-being; social welfare.

WHAT IS NOT FUNDED Individuals; general appeals.

TYPE OF GRANT Capital costs; core/revenue costs; project funding; seed/start-up funding.

RANGE OF GRANTS Project grants range from £1,000 to £5,000.

SAMPLE GRANTS Work Rights Centre (£5,000); Room to Heal (£3,000); Listening Place (£2,000); Survivors Together (£1,500); Girls Rock London (£1,000).

FINANCES *Financial year end 31/12/2021*
Income £252,800
Grants to organisations £291,800
Assets £15,670,000

TRUSTEES Andrew Davidson; Philippe Granger; Dr Sarah Divall; Mark Palframan; Emma Whitby; Danny Daly; Joan Major; Ruby Sethna; Nicholas Durack; Glynis Berry; Alice Groux.

HOW TO APPLY Full guidance, including helpful FAQs, is available to download from the charity's website. The trustees usually meet four times a year, in February, May, September and November. Completed applications must be received at least four weeks in advance of meetings.

CONTACT DETAILS The Trustees, 45 Westminster Bridge Road, London SE1 7JB *Tel.* 07530 290476 *Email* london.catalyst@peabody.org.uk *Website* www.londoncatalyst.org.uk

■ The London Community Foundation (LCF)

CC NO 1091263   **ESTABLISHED** 2002

WHERE FUNDING CAN BE GIVEN London.

WHO CAN BENEFIT Charities and community groups; small and medium-sized organisations; social enterprises; CICs.

WHAT IS FUNDED General charitable purposes, in particular: arts, culture and heritage; life skills, employability and enterprise; stronger communities; physical and mental health, well-being and safety; the environment.

WHAT IS NOT FUNDED Political groups; activities which promote religion (faith groups may be assisted). Specific criteria may apply for different funds – check the foundation's website for further information.

TYPE OF GRANT Capital and core costs, feasibility studies, project funding, running costs, salaries and start-up costs.

RANGE OF GRANTS In 2021/22 the average grant was about £15,200.

SAMPLE GRANTS A list of beneficiaries was not included in the annual report and accounts. Previous beneficiaries have included: The

Dwayne Simpson Foundation (£50,000); The Show Crib (£47,000); Solidarity Sports and The Clement James Centre (£45,000 each); Homeless Link (£44,400); Music Fusion (£41,600); Migration Museum Project (£40,200 in two grants).

FINANCES *Financial year end 31/03/2022*
Income £12,180,000
Grants to organisations £9,430,000
Grants to individuals £33,000
Assets £33,130,000

TRUSTEES Gaynor Humphreys; Russell Prior; John Hume; Genine Whitehorne; Veesh Sharma; Natalie Creary-Aninakwa; Owen Jenkins; Urmi Dutta-Roy; Fiona Bickley; Dr Satnam Sagoo.

OTHER INFORMATION This is one of the 47 UK community foundations, which distribute funding for a wide range of purposes. As with all community foundations, there are a number of donor-advised funds managed on behalf of individuals, families and charitable trusts. Grant schemes tend to change frequently – consult the foundation's website for details of current programmes and up-to-date deadlines.

HOW TO APPLY Potential applicants are advised to visit the community foundation's website or contact its programmes team to find the most suitable funding stream.

CONTACT DETAILS Programmes Team, Unit 1.04, Piano House, 9 Brighton Terrace, London SW9 8DJ *Tel.* 020 7582 5117 *Email* info@londoncf.org.uk *Website* www.londoncf.org.uk

London Freemasons Charity

CC NO 1081205   **ESTABLISHED** 2000
WHERE FUNDING CAN BE GIVEN Greater London.
WHO CAN BENEFIT Charitable organisations.
WHAT IS FUNDED General charitable purposes; social welfare, particularly the relief of poverty and other forms of distress; education; emergency response.
TYPE OF GRANT Core costs; general funding.
RANGE OF GRANTS Mostly between £3,000 and £15,000 with the occasional larger grant.
SAMPLE GRANTS London Search and Rescue (£251,500); London Air Ambulance (£216,800); Seva Street (£15,000); Metropolitan Grand Lodge (£13,600); Lennox Children's Cancer Fund and Strongbones Children (£10,000 each); Tall Ships Youth Trust (£5,000); Heathrow Special Needs Centre (£3,000).
FINANCES *Financial year end 30/09/2022*
Income £253,200
Grants to organisations £555,200
Assets £1,930,000
TRUSTEES Michael Palmer; James Walker; Stratton Richey; Thomas Toumazis; Quentin Humberstone.
OTHER INFORMATION The charity supports both Masonic and non-Masonic organisations. During 2021/22, 98% of grants were awarded to non-Masonic organisations.
HOW TO APPLY Apply in writing to the correspondent.
CONTACT DETAILS The Trustees, 60 Great Queen Street, PO Box 29055, London WC2B 5AZ *Tel.* 020 7539 2930 *Email* c.hunt@metgl.com

London Housing Foundation Ltd (LHF)

CC NO 270178   **ESTABLISHED** 1975
WHERE FUNDING CAN BE GIVEN London.
WHO CAN BENEFIT Voluntary bodies; charities; housing and social care organisations.
WHAT IS FUNDED Housing and homelessness and work to prevent people from becoming homeless.
TYPE OF GRANT Project funding; research.
SAMPLE GRANTS A list of beneficiaries was not included in the annual report and accounts. Previous beneficiaries have included: Depaul International (£100,000); Hope Worldwide (£43,500); The Passage (£35,000); Cambridge House (£15,500).
FINANCES *Financial year end 31/03/2022*
Income £586,000
Grants to organisations £344,200
Assets £15,820,000
TRUSTEES Ian Brady; Simon Dow; Derek Joseph; Clare Miller; John Stebbing; Jeremy Swain; Eleanor Stringer; Nicholas Hardwick; Eloise Shepherd.
HOW TO APPLY Applicants are asked to complete a short application form on the foundation's website and wait for a response.
CONTACT DETAILS The Trustees, Altair Ltd, Tempus Wharf, 29A Bermondsey Wall West, London SE16 4SA *Tel.* 020 7934 0177 *Email* info@lhf.org.uk *Website* http://lhf.org.uk/programmes-and-grants

London Legal Support Trust (LLST)

CC NO 1101906   **ESTABLISHED** 2004
WHERE FUNDING CAN BE GIVEN London and the Home Counties.
WHO CAN BENEFIT Voluntary sector legal agencies and network organisations that support such agencies; registered charities.
WHAT IS FUNDED Free legal advice services.
WHAT IS NOT FUNDED Any non-charitable activity; organisations applying for general advice as opposed to specialist legal advice.
TYPE OF GRANT Core/revenue costs; capital costs; seed funding; development funding.
RANGE OF GRANTS Typically less than £10,000.
SAMPLE GRANTS Anti Trafficking and Labour Exploitation Unit (£46,500); South West London Law Centres (£28,700); Advocate (£18,400); Disability Law Service (£11,400); Bail for Immigration Detainees (£10,500); Prisoners' Advice Service and Working Families (£10,000 each); Reading Refugee Support Group (£3,400); Community Language Support Services (£870).
FINANCES *Financial year end 31/12/2021*
Income £1,200,000
Grants to organisations £773,300
Assets £379,600
TRUSTEES Richard Dyton; Sophie Hay; Melanie Pope; Conchita Anastasi; Candice Carboo-Ofulue; Amanda Illing; Katharine Pasfield; Emma Turnbull; Sarah McKeown; Joy Julien; Marc Sosnow; Alistair Woodland; Graham Huntley; Rodger Pressland; James Harper.
OTHER INFORMATION Only beneficiaries of grants of £5,000 and above were listed in the accounts. Grants of under £5,000 totalled £129,100. The trust also holds fundraising events and shares its sector knowledge and experience to help improve agencies' financial sustainability.
HOW TO APPLY See the trust's website for details about which grant programmes are currently accepting applications and how to apply.
CONTACT DETAILS Grants Team, 1 Lady Hale Gate, Gray's Inn, London WC1X 8BS *Tel.* 020 7092 3974 *Email* info@llst.org.uk *Website* https://londonlegalsupporttrust.org.uk

■ The London Marathon Charitable Trust Ltd

CC NO 283813   **ESTABLISHED** 1981

WHERE FUNDING CAN BE GIVEN London.

WHO CAN BENEFIT Charities; local authorities; community and voluntary sector organisations; amateur sports clubs, parish and town councils; educational organisations.

WHAT IS FUNDED The improvement of sports and recreation facilities; access to physical activity.

WHAT IS NOT FUNDED A full list of exclusions is available on the trust's website.

TYPE OF GRANT Capital costs; core costs; project funding.

RANGE OF GRANTS Small grants of £5,000 to £50,000; major grants of £50,000 to £250,000.

SAMPLE GRANTS Black Swimming Association (£550,000); Greenhouse Sports (£50,000); Livability (£33,000); Toynbee Hall (£30,000); London Borough of Ealing (£25,000); Repton Boxing Club (£20,000); London Borough of Tower Hamlets (£17,200); Purley Sports Club (£10,000); Coin Street Centre Trust (£4,000).

FINANCES *Financial year end 31/12/2021*
Income £35,750,000
Grants to organisations £819,800
Assets £14,200,000

TRUSTEES John Austin; Sir Rodney Walker; Charles Johnston; Alan Pascoe; Robert Rigby; Dawn Austwick; Gillian McKay; Clare Shepherd; Samantha Orde; Richard Henry; Terry Duddy; Lee Mason.

OTHER INFORMATION During the year, grants were awarded to 33 organisations.

HOW TO APPLY Application forms and full details of the application processes, funding guidelines, deadlines and FAQs can be found on the trust's website.

CONTACT DETAILS The Trustees, Marathon House, 190 Great Dover Street, London SE1 4YB *Tel.* 020 7902 0215 *Email* info@lmct.org.uk *Website* www.lmct.org.uk

■ Longleigh Foundation

CC NO 1169016   **ESTABLISHED** 2015

WHERE FUNDING CAN BE GIVEN England.

WHO CAN BENEFIT Registered charities; not-for-profit organisations; NGOs.

WHAT IS FUNDED Social welfare for people living in social housing, including projects that support their mental health and well-being.

TYPE OF GRANT Project grants; research funding; capital costs.

SAMPLE GRANTS Clean Slate (£180,000); Impact North (£40,000); Kaleidoscope Plus Group and Community Health Works (£30,000 each); Alcohol Education Trust (£26,000); Imagineer (£25,300); Justlife Foundation (£25,000).

FINANCES *Financial year end 30/06/2022*
Income £2,400,000
Grants to organisations £442,000
Grants to individuals £584,800
Assets £8,200,000

TRUSTEES Elizabeth Morris; Ron Williamson; Anne Dokov; John McLean Weguelin; Aisha Butera; Fiona Ellison.

OTHER INFORMATION In 2021/22 the foundation awarded £358,800 in project grants, £83,200 in research grants and an additional £584,800 to individuals living in social housing.

HOW TO APPLY The foundation puts out calls for applications about specific issues and then organisations can submit a response. The trustees then invite selected organisations to develop a full application – this is an in-principle approval of the work. Check the website for further information.

CONTACT DETAILS Charlotte Dicks, Grants Programme Manager, c/o Stonewater Ltd, Suite C, Lancaster House, Grange Business Park, Enderby Road, Whetstone, Leicester, Leicestershire LE8 6EP *Tel.* 020 7164 6199 *Email* charlotte@longleigh.org *Website* www.longleigh.org

■ Lords Group Foundation

CC NO 1193157   **ESTABLISHED** 2021

WHERE FUNDING CAN BE GIVEN Areas close to Lords Group Trading branches (within two miles of a site within the M25 or within five miles of a site outside the M25).

WHO CAN BENEFIT Registered charities and community groups. The trustees are keen to support smaller causes.

WHAT IS FUNDED Social welfare; community facilities.

TYPE OF GRANT Project funding.

RANGE OF GRANTS Up to £5,000.

SAMPLE GRANTS A list of beneficiaries was not included in the annual report and accounts.

FINANCES *Financial year end 31/12/2022*
Income £400,000
Grants to organisations £62,600
Assets £520,000

TRUSTEES Shanker Patel; Jess Harris; Christopher Day; Rachna Dewan.

HOW TO APPLY Apply via the foundation's website. The trustees meet quarterly.

CONTACT DETAILS The Trustees, 12–15 Hanger Green, London W5 3EL *Email* lordsfoundation@lordsgrouptrading.co.uk *Website* www.lordsgrouptradingplc.co.uk/about-us/lords-group-foundation

■ The Lord's Taverners

CC NO 306054   **ESTABLISHED** 1950

WHERE FUNDING CAN BE GIVEN UK.

WHO CAN BENEFIT Schools; organisations that cater for young people with disabilities under the age of 25; amateur sports clubs and organisations for young people.

WHAT IS FUNDED Sports programmes for children and young people with disabilities; specially adapted minibuses; adapted indoor and outdoor play equipment; sports wheelchairs for young people with disabilities.

WHAT IS NOT FUNDED Exclusion criteria may differ according to the grant being awarded. See the applications section of the charity's website for exclusion criteria for the relevant grants programme.

TYPE OF GRANT Capital costs; project funding.

SAMPLE GRANTS The Johnners Trust (£42,000).

FINANCES *Financial year end 30/09/2022*
Income £5,800,000
Grants to organisations £1,950,000
Assets £4,930,000

TRUSTEES Richard White; Alistair Row; Mike Gatting; Caj Sohal; Tim Luckhurst; Gordon Kennedy; Suzanne Farthing; Abeed Janmohamed; Paul Walker.

OTHER INFORMATION Grants in 2021/22 were made for the following purposes and organisations: cricket programmes – disability (£1 million); cricket programmes – disadvantage (£780,000); minibuses and other grants (£120,000); the Johnners Trust (£42,000).

514

Does the funder you have chosen match your needs? Haphazard applications waste postage and time

HOW TO APPLY Instructions on how to apply are available from the grant-maker's website. Applications are reviewed throughout the year.

CONTACT DETAILS Nicky Pemberton, Director of Programmes and Growth, 90 Chancery Lane, London WC2A 1EU *Tel.* 020 7025 0000 *Email* contact@lordstaverners.org *Website* www.lordstaverners.org

■ The Lower Green Foundation

CC NO 1137862　　　　**ESTABLISHED** 2010

WHERE FUNDING CAN BE GIVEN UK.

WHO CAN BENEFIT Charitable organisations.

WHAT IS FUNDED General charitable purposes; education for young people; youth apprenticeship schemes; medical research.

SAMPLE GRANTS First Give (£75,000); Motivation (£40,000); The Prince's Trust (£25,000); The Pelican Trust (£10,000); Dream Children's Home (£6,500); Hawkley Parish Hall (£550).

FINANCES *Financial year end* 30/04/2022 *Income* £156,300 *Grants to organisations* £256,400 *Assets* £10,800

TRUSTEES Laurence Billett; Marina Sajitz; Sinclair Beecham.

OTHER INFORMATION In 2021/22, grants were awarded to 16 organisations.

HOW TO APPLY Apply in writing to the correspondent.

CONTACT DETAILS Laurence Billett, Trustee, The Lower Green Foundation, 28 Eaton Avenue, Matrix Office Park, Buckshaw Village, Chorley, Lancashire PR7 7NA *Tel.* 01772 299888 *Email* info@lowergreen.com

■ The C. L. Loyd Charitable Trust

CC NO 265076　　　　**ESTABLISHED** 1973

WHERE FUNDING CAN BE GIVEN UK, with a preference for local causes in Oxfordshire.

WHO CAN BENEFIT National charities and local organisations known by or associated with the trustees.

WHAT IS FUNDED General charitable purposes including health, welfare, the arts and heritage.

RANGE OF GRANTS Mostly under £5,000.

SAMPLE GRANTS Country Buildings Protection Trust (£20,000); Mobility Trust (£10,000); Grange Festival (£5,200); Parkinsons.Me (£4,000); Grove PCC and The Tate Foundation (£2,000 each); The Earth Trust (£1,000); Arthur Rank Hospice (£100).

FINANCES *Financial year end* 05/04/2022 *Income* £57,600 *Grants to organisations* £49,300 *Assets* £3,570,000

TRUSTEES Alexandra Loyd; Thomas Loyd.

OTHER INFORMATION In 2021/22, the trust's grant total was £49,300; however, in previous years this has been much higher. Grants were awarded to 11 organisations during the financial period.

HOW TO APPLY Grants are only made to charities known to the trustees.

CONTACT DETAILS The Trustees, The Locking Estate Office, Ardington, Wantage, Oxfordshire OX12 8PP *Tel.* 020 7680 8100

■ LPW Ltd

CC NO 1148784　　　　**ESTABLISHED** 2012

WHERE FUNDING CAN BE GIVEN UK.

WHO CAN BENEFIT Charities and community groups.

WHAT IS FUNDED The advancement of the Orthodox Jewish religion and education; the relief of poverty.

RANGE OF GRANTS From £20,000 to £72,000.

SAMPLE GRANTS Kupath Gemach (£72,000); Aniyei Haolam Trust, British Friends of Chatzer Hakodesh Viznitz and Edupoor Ltd (£36,000 each); Kehal Chasidei Wiznitz Ltd and Keren Habinyan Ltd (£25,000 each).

FINANCES *Financial year end* 31/12/2021 *Income* £1,610,000 *Grants to organisations* £456,700 *Assets* £19,080,000

TRUSTEES Daniela Rosenthal; Monica Rosenthal; Nicholas Rosenthal; Talia Cohen; Ronny Rosenthal.

OTHER INFORMATION Grants were broken down as follows: relief of poverty (£201,700); advancement of education (£113,500); advancement of the Jewish religion (£100,300); other charitable purposes (£41,300). Only organisations that received grants of over £20,000 were listed as beneficiaries in the charity's accounts. Grants of under £20,000 totalled £80,700.

HOW TO APPLY Apply in writing to the correspondent.

CONTACT DETAILS The Trustees, c/o Cohen Arnold, New Burlington House, 1075 Finchley Road, London NW11 0PU *Tel.* 020 8731 0777

■ Robert Luff Foundation Ltd

CC NO 273810　　　　**ESTABLISHED** 1966

WHERE FUNDING CAN BE GIVEN UK.

WHO CAN BENEFIT Medical research charities and organisations, including hospices and hospitals.

WHAT IS FUNDED Medical research.

TYPE OF GRANT Research; normally recurrent.

RANGE OF GRANTS Generally £10,000 to £80,000, with some larger grants.

SAMPLE GRANTS Cystic Fibrosis Trust (£350,000); Rosetrees Trust (£182,000); Asthma UK (£90,000); International Spinal Research Trust (£45,000); The Cassel Hospital Charitable Trust and The Marriage Foundation (£40,000 each); Meningitis Now (£20,000); The Norman Laud Association (£5,000).

FINANCES *Financial year end* 31/08/2021 *Income* £683,100 *Grants to organisations* £2,040,000 *Assets* £42,070,000

TRUSTEES Melanie Condon; Richard Price; Revd Matthew Tomlinson; Lady Ruth Bodey; Sir Paul Coleridge; Dr Helen Hughes.

OTHER INFORMATION The 2020/21 accounts were the latest available at the time of writing (May 2023). Only organisations that received grants of £5,000 and above were listed as beneficiaries in the foundation's accounts (59 organisations). Grants of under £5,000 totalled £11,000.

HOW TO APPLY While the foundation tends to support the same charities on an annual basis, several new beneficiaries are funded each year. Contact the correspondent for more information regarding the application process.

CONTACT DETAILS Richard Price, Company Secretary, Waters Edge, Ferry Lane, Moulsford, Wallingford, Oxfordshire OX10 9JF *Tel.* 01491 652204 *Email* rpjprice@gmail.com

■ Lord and Lady Lurgan Trust

CC NO 297046   **ESTABLISHED** 1987
WHERE FUNDING CAN BE GIVEN Britain (mainly London); Northern Ireland; South Africa.
WHO CAN BENEFIT Registered charities; educational establishments; hospices.
WHAT IS FUNDED UK grants tend to be London-centric and have a bias towards the following: music and arts education and participation; deafness and other disabilities; older people; and medical relief, including hospice support and medical research. In Northern Ireland and South Africa, grants are not restricted by particular categories but rather by the trustees' perception of need.
WHAT IS NOT FUNDED Individuals; expeditions; core costs; emergency appeals.
TYPE OF GRANT Generally one-off payments.
RANGE OF GRANTS Between £1,000 and £5,000.
SAMPLE GRANTS Previous beneficiaries have included: Royal College of Music (£11,500); The Cure Parkinson's Trust (£3,000); English National Opera (£2,500); Cued Speech UK (£2,000); The Pushkin Trust (£1,600); Bampton Classical Opera (£1,500); Resources for Autism (£1,000).
FINANCES *Financial year end 31/12/2021*
Income £17,200
Grants to organisations £64,300
Assets £644,200
TRUSTEES Brendan Beder; Diana Graves; Andrew Stebbings.
OTHER INFORMATION The charity's latest accounts were not available to view on the Charity Commission's website due to its low income. We have therefore estimated the grant total based on the charity's total expenditure. The 2021 Charity Commission record was the latest available at the time of writing (June 2023).
HOW TO APPLY Application forms can be downloaded from the trust's website and should preferably be returned by email. Applicants should read the grant policy on the website before completing the form. The trustees meet twice a year, in December and July. Deadlines are published on the website. Applications must also include: your latest signed and audited accounts; a budget for the financial year in which the project falls, separating income which relates to the project; the budget for the project; and details about any other funding received or pending.
CONTACT DETAILS The Trustees, 45 Cadogan Gardens, London SW3 2TB *Tel.* 07368 652694 *Email* info@lurgantrust.org *Website* www.lurgantrust.org

■ The Lyndal Tree Foundation

CC NO 1125024   **ESTABLISHED** 2008
WHERE FUNDING CAN BE GIVEN UK, with a preference for Yorkshire and Scotland; overseas.
WHO CAN BENEFIT Registered, excepted or exempt charities; hospices.
WHAT IS FUNDED General charitable purposes; children and young people; social welfare; medical research/medical care; the environment; humanitarian aid; asylum seekers.
WHAT IS NOT FUNDED Non-UK charities.
TYPE OF GRANT One-off grants; regular support.
RANGE OF GRANTS Mostly between £2,000 and £8,000 with the occasional larger grant.
SAMPLE GRANTS Disasters Emergency Committee – Ukraine Appeal (£20,000); Marine Conservation (£12,000); Beamsley Project (£10,000); Beacon, Cancer Support Yorkshire and Lifelites (£8,000 each); Perth & Kinross Association of

Voluntary Service (PKAVS) (£5,000); Candlelighters, Lullaby Trust and Wheelpower (£3,000 each); Bradford Central Foodbank (£2,000).
FINANCES *Financial year end 05/04/2022*
Income £88,000
Grants to organisations £139,000
Assets £2,130,000
TRUSTEES Jennifer Brodie; Steven Duttine; Lynda Duttine; Susan Fidler.
OTHER INFORMATION The trustees aim to award 20% of the grant total to charities pertaining to the environment. Grants were broken down as follows: health and social welfare (£73,000); international (£35,000); the environment (£28,000); relief of sickness and injury (£3,000).
HOW TO APPLY Apply in writing to the correspondent.
CONTACT DETAILS The Trustees, Lyndal Tree, PO Box 330, Ilkley, West Yorkshire LS29 1GD *Tel.* 07725 900511

■ Sir Jack Lyons Charitable Trust

CC NO 212148   **ESTABLISHED** 1960
WHERE FUNDING CAN BE GIVEN UK; Canada; Israel.
WHO CAN BENEFIT Charitable organisations; Jewish charities; educational organisations.
WHAT IS FUNDED The Jewish faith and community; performing arts, especially music; education; humanitarian causes.
RANGE OF GRANTS Up to £53,000.
SAMPLE GRANTS Jerusalem Foundation (£29,800); Jerusalem Academy of Music and Dance (£22,400); Wigmore Hall Trust (£14,000); Jewish Music Institute (£7,500).
FINANCES *Financial year end 05/04/2022*
Income £99,000
Grants to organisations £143,400
Assets £3,640,000
TRUSTEES Mortimer Friedman; David Lyons; Belinda Lyons-Newman; Paul Mitchell; Simon Jackson.
OTHER INFORMATION Grants were made to 11 organisations.
HOW TO APPLY Applications may be made in writing to the correspondent.
CONTACT DETAILS Paul Mitchell, Trustee, Gresham House, 5–7 St Paul's Street, Leeds, West Yorkshire LS1 2JG *Tel.* 0113 297 6789 *Email* p.mitchell@sagars.co.uk

■ John Lyon's Charity

CC NO 237725   **ESTABLISHED** 1572
WHERE FUNDING CAN BE GIVEN The London boroughs of Barnet, Brent, Camden, the City of London, the City of Westminster, Ealing, Hammersmith and Fulham, Harrow and Kensington and Chelsea.
WHO CAN BENEFIT Registered and exempt charities; schools; local authorities (in limited circumstances).
WHAT IS FUNDED Children and young people up to the age of 25.
WHAT IS NOT FUNDED CICs; individuals; organisations that do not have charitable status or those acting as a conduit; national charities with no track record of delivery in the charity's beneficial area; grant-making organisations; not-for-profit organisations that are not registered charities; registered social landlords; schools that have not yet been inspected by Ofsted; hospitals, hospices or clinical commissioning groups; registered charities that have applied on behalf of organisations that are not registered with the Charity Commission.

TYPE OF GRANT Capital costs; core/revenue costs; project funding; unrestricted funding; capacity building; multi-year funding.

RANGE OF GRANTS A typical grant is in the range of £20,000 to £30,000 per annum for three years.

SAMPLE GRANTS A list of beneficiaries was not included in the annual report and accounts. Previous beneficiaries have included: Securing Success (£45,500); Belmont School (£40,000); Arts Depot (£30,000); National Youth Theatre (£25,000); The Listening Place (£14,000).

FINANCES *Financial year end 31/03/2022*
Income £8,720,000
Grants to organisations £13,000,000
Assets £436,000,000

TRUSTEE The Keepers and Governors of Possessions Revenues and Goods of Free Grammar School of John Lyon.

OTHER INFORMATION Grants were broken down as follows: arts and science (£1.78 million); education and learning (£1.69 million); capacity building (£1.62 million); youth clubs and youth activities (£1.6 million); bursaries (£1.53 million); emotional wellbeing (£1.29 million); special needs and disabilities (£940,000); children and families (£870,000); youth issues (£720,000); sport (£580,000); training (£310,000).

HOW TO APPLY Apply online via the charity's grants portal.

CONTACT DETAILS The Trustees, Savoy Strand, 105 Strand, London WC2R 0AA *Tel.* 020 7259 1700 *Email* info@jlc.london *Website* www.jlc. london

....

■ The Lyons Trust

CC NO 1188185

WHERE FUNDING CAN BE GIVEN UK, with a preference for Manchester and Cheshire; overseas.

WHO CAN BENEFIT Registered charities.

WHAT IS FUNDED General charitable purposes including social welfare and homelessness.

RANGE OF GRANTS Up to £60,000 but mostly £10,000 to £20,000.

SAMPLE GRANTS The Bread and Butter Thing (£50,000); Warrington Youth Club (£25,000); Project Luangwa (£10,700).

FINANCES *Financial year end 25/08/2022*
Income £30,700
Grants to organisations £85,800
Assets £806,600

TRUSTEES Carol Lyons; Fergus Lyons; Daniel O'Brien.

HOW TO APPLY Apply in writing to the correspondent.

CONTACT DETAILS The Trustees, Yew Tree Farm, Crouchley Lane, Lymm, Cheshire WA13 0TH *Email* lyonstrust2020@gmail.com

....

■ Sylvanus Lysons Charity

CC NO 202939   **ESTABLISHED** 1980

WHERE FUNDING CAN BE GIVEN Diocese of Gloucester.

WHO CAN BENEFIT Individuals; organisations; religious bodies; widows of clergy.

WHAT IS FUNDED The religious and charitable work of the Church of England, particularly work with disadvantaged young people and adults; children and young people; community initiatives.

WHAT IS NOT FUNDED Grants are not given for the repair or maintenance or improvement of churches or other buildings, other than in exceptional circumstances.

RANGE OF GRANTS Up to £30,000.

SAMPLE GRANTS The Rock Cheltenham (£30,000); Family Space Cheltenham (£25,000); St Phillip's and St James' (£20,000); Cheltenham Christians Against Poverty (CAP) Debt Centre (£15,000); Caleb's Mountain (£9,500); Amberley Shop on the Common (£5,000); University of Gloucestershire Chaplaincy (£3,500); Bishop of Tewkesbury Discretionary Fund (£2,000).

FINANCES *Financial year end 30/09/2021*
Income £465,200
Grants to organisations £266,400
Grants to individuals £36,100
Assets £15,290,000

TRUSTEES Mr G. V. Doswell; The Rt Revd Robert Springett; Ian Templeton; The Ven. Philip Andrew; The Revd Elizabeth Palin; Michael Angell; The Revd Lara Bloom; Stuart Hutton.

OTHER INFORMATION During the year, the charity awarded 115 grants to individuals and 20 grants to organisations. The 2020/21 accounts were the latest available at the time of writing (May 2023).

HOW TO APPLY Application forms can be downloaded from the charity's page on the Diocese of Gloucester website, where full guidance and application deadlines can also be found.

CONTACT DETAILS The Revd Helen Sammon, Grants Administrator, c/o Tayntons Solicitors, 8–12 Clarence Street, Gloucester, Gloucestershire GL1 1DZ *Tel.* 07554 992892 *Email* Sylvanuslysons@gmail.com *Website* https://gloucester.anglican.org/ support-services/parish-finance-gift-aid-legal-advice/sylvanus-lysons-charity/

M. and C. Trust

CC NO 265391   **ESTABLISHED** 1972
WHERE FUNDING CAN BE GIVEN UK.
WHO CAN BENEFIT Mainly Jewish organisations; educational establishments; health institutions.
WHAT IS FUNDED The Jewish faith and community; social welfare.
WHAT IS NOT FUNDED Individuals.
RANGE OF GRANTS Typically between £3,000 and £10,000.
SAMPLE GRANTS Jewish Women's Aid (£8,500); Freedom from Torture (£5,000); Deafblind UK and WaveLength (£4,500 each); Hot Line Meals Service (£3,000).
FINANCES *Financial year end 05/04/2022*
Income £164,200
Grants to organisations £153,000
Assets £4,800,000
TRUSTEES Rachel Lebus; Elizabeth Marks; Victoria Fairley; Matthew Bernstein.
OTHER INFORMATION In 2021/22, grants were broken down as follows: health (£36,000); relief of poverty (£31,000); community (£25,500); social care (£22,000); other (£16,500); youth work (£13,500); education (£8,500).
HOW TO APPLY Applications should be made via email. The trustees meet once a year to approve applications.
CONTACT DETAILS The Trustees, c/o Mercer and Hole Trustees Ltd, Gloucester House, 72 London Road, St Albans, Hertfordshire AL1 1NS *Tel.* 01727 869141 *Email* mandctrust@gmail.com

M. B. Foundation

CC NO 222104   **ESTABLISHED** 1965
WHERE FUNDING CAN BE GIVEN UK, with some preference for Greater Manchester.
WHO CAN BENEFIT Jewish organisations; individuals.
WHAT IS FUNDED The Jewish faith and community.
RANGE OF GRANTS Up to £170,000.
SAMPLE GRANTS KBS (£170,000); Kolyom Trust Ltd (£61,200); Asser Bishvil Foundation (£56,000); Bnos Yisroel School (£24,800); Kalloh Care (£16,500).
FINANCES *Financial year end 31/03/2021*
Income £436,700
Grants to organisations £603,700
Assets £5,460,000
TRUSTEES Elazer Dresdner; The Revd Martin Stamler.
OTHER INFORMATION The 2020/21 accounts were the latest available at the time of writing (May 2023). Grants were broken down as follows: education (£135,500), relief of poverty (£16,100) and religion (£20,200). Grants of less than £5,000 totalled £39,400.
HOW TO APPLY Apply in writing to the correspondent.
CONTACT DETAILS The Trustees, Fairways House, George Street, Prestwich, Manchester M25 9WS *Tel.* 0161 787 7898

The M. Y. A. Charitable Trust

CC NO 299642   **ESTABLISHED** 1987
WHERE FUNDING CAN BE GIVEN In practice, UK and Israel.
WHO CAN BENEFIT Charitable organisations and individuals.
WHAT IS FUNDED The Jewish faith and community.
SAMPLE GRANTS The Hiddur C.I.O (£672,265); Misgav Ladoch (£10,000); Ruzhin Sadigura Trust (£10,650); Mesifta Beis Medrash L'Torah, Israel (£16,645).
FINANCES *Financial year end 30/04/2022*
Income £190,000
Grants to organisations £807,000
Grants to individuals £2,100
Assets £1,410,000
TRUSTEES Joseph Pfeffer; Myer Rothfeld; Eve Rothfeld; Hannah Schraiber.
OTHER INFORMATION According to the annual report for 2021/22, the trust also provides short-term interest-free loans 'to assist individuals with financial hardship or charitable institutions with educational advancement'.
HOW TO APPLY Contact the correspondent for further information.
CONTACT DETAILS The Trustees, Medcar House, 149A Stamford Hill, London N16 5LL *Tel.* 020 8800 3582

The R. S. Macdonald Charitable Trust

OSCR NO SC012710   **ESTABLISHED** 1978
WHERE FUNDING CAN BE GIVEN Scotland.
WHO CAN BENEFIT Registered charities operating in Scotland and universities.
WHAT IS FUNDED Neurological conditions; visual impairment; child welfare; animal welfare; medical research; RNLI lifeboats.
TYPE OF GRANT Revenue or capital costs; project funding or core funding; one-off awards; multi-year awards for up to three years; seedcorn/ unrestricted funding.
SAMPLE GRANTS Alzheimer Scotland; Drake Music Scotland; Ecology Centre; Grampian Hospitals Art Trust; Home Link Family Support; MS Therapy Centre Lothian; South of Scotland Wildlife Hospital; Whale Arts.
FINANCES *Financial year end 31/03/2022*
Income £1,200,000
Grants to organisations £2,220,000
Assets £105,490,000
TRUSTEES James Baird; John Paterson; Robert Ross; Fiona Patrick; Frank Sullivan.
OTHER INFORMATION During 2021/22, the trust received 141 applications and awarded 84 grants. Grants were broken down as follows: neurological conditions (£889,000); tackling child abuse and neglect (£675,000); medical research (£348,000); visual impairment/sight loss (£199,000); animal welfare (£111,000). The trust's accounts did not provide the specific grant totals for each organisation supported.
HOW TO APPLY Applications can be made through the trust's website. Small grant applications can be submitted at any time. The main grants programme has specific deadlines for each area of work – check the website for the latest deadlines.
CONTACT DETAILS Katie Winwick, Grants and Relationships Manager, 21 Rutland Square, Edinburgh EH1 2BB *Tel.* 0131 228 4681 *Email* office@rsmacdonald.com *Website* www.rsmacdonald.com

518

Does the funder you have chosen match your needs? Haphazard applications waste postage and time

■ The Macdonald-Buchanan Charitable Trust

CC NO 209994   **ESTABLISHED** 1952

WHERE FUNDING CAN BE GIVEN Worldwide, with a preference for Northamptonshire.

WHO CAN BENEFIT Registered charities.

WHAT IS FUNDED General charitable purposes including health and disability, animal welfare, children and young people and older people.

RANGE OF GRANTS £5,000 to £30,000.

SAMPLE GRANTS Cure Parkinson's (£30,000); Orrin Charitable Trust (£25,000); Carriejo Charitable Trust, Oracle Cancer Trust and Stowe School (£10,000 each), The Goed Life and National Horse Racing Museum (£5,000 each).

FINANCES *Financial year end 31/12/2021*
Income £144,000
Grants to organisations £102,500
Assets £4,630,000

TRUSTEES Alastair MacDonald-Buchanan; Hugh MacDonald-Buchanan; Joanna Lascelles; Camilla Lascelles.

HOW TO APPLY Apply in writing to the correspondent. The annual report for 2021 states that the trustees will 'no longer consider appeals which are directed to the charity, preferring to consider appeals that have been received by them individually.'

CONTACT DETAILS Linda Cousins, Administrator, Rathbone Trust Co. Ltd, 8 Finsbury Circus, London EC2M 7AZ *Tel.* 020 7399 0820 *Email* linda.cousins@rathbones.com

■ Mace Foundation

CC NO 1150134   **ESTABLISHED** 2012

WHERE FUNDING CAN BE GIVEN UK.

WHO CAN BENEFIT Registered charities; schools; hospitals.

WHAT IS FUNDED Community development; homelessness; education and employment; health, particularly mental health.

TYPE OF GRANT Project funding; strategic funding.

SAMPLE GRANTS Mind and St Mungo's (£55,000 each); Dubai Cares (£20,000).

FINANCES *Financial year end 31/12/2021*
Income £442,700
Grants to organisations £130,000
Assets £91,200

TRUSTEES Mark Reynolds; Deborah Reynolds; Barbara Welch; Jason Millett; Rosario Abbate; Kirsten White.

OTHER INFORMATION This is the charitable foundation of the Mace Group, a construction and consultancy firm based in London. The foundation makes grants to its strategic partner charities and matches funds raised by Mace Group employees. Overall, three grants were made to strategic partner charities in 2021.

HOW TO APPLY The foundation does not accept unsolicited applications.

CONTACT DETAILS Ms C. Pate, Secretary, Mace Group, 155 Moorgate, London EC2M 6XB *Tel.* 020 3522 3385 *Email* mace.foundation@ macegroup.com *Website* www.macegroup.com/ about-us/a-responsible-business/mace- foundation

■ The Mackintosh Foundation

CC NO 327751   **ESTABLISHED** 1988

WHERE FUNDING CAN BE GIVEN Worldwide; in practice, mainly the UK.

WHO CAN BENEFIT Registered charities; educational establishments; individuals.

WHAT IS FUNDED Theatre and the performing arts; medical aid, particularly research into cancer and HIV; homelessness; community projects; the environment; general charitable purposes.

TYPE OF GRANT Capital costs; schools' core costs; research; project costs.

RANGE OF GRANTS Up to nearly £85,000.

SAMPLE GRANTS A list of beneficiaries was not included in the annual report and accounts. Previous beneficiaries have included: Theatre Development Trust (£625,900); Acting for Others (£177,400); NHS Charities Together (£88,300); The Royal Theatrical Fund (£25,000); Roundhouse Trust and Social Bite (£10,000 each); The National Student Drama Festival Ltd (£5,000).

FINANCES *Financial year end 31/03/2022*
Income £70,600
Grants to organisations £137,800
Assets £14,860,000

TRUSTEES Nicholas Allott; Sir Cameron MacKintosh; Nicholas MacKintosh; Robert Noble; Bart Peerless; Thomas Schonberg; Richard Pappas; Alan Finch; A. Constable.

OTHER INFORMATION Grants given during the year were broken down as follows: children and education (£72,900); theatre and the performing arts (£53,200); community projects (£5,000); medical causes (£6,700).

HOW TO APPLY Applications should be made in writing to the correspondent, outlining details of the applying organisation, the project for which funding is required and a breakdown of the costs involved. Supporting documents should be kept to a minimum and an sae enclosed (if materials are to be returned).

CONTACT DETAILS Richard Knibb, General Secretary, 1 Bedford Square, London WC1B 3RB *Tel.* 020 7637 8866 *Email* info@camack.co.uk

■ The John MacLeod Charitable Trust

CC NO 1192113

WHERE FUNDING CAN BE GIVEN UK and overseas.

WHO CAN BENEFIT Registered charities.

WHAT IS FUNDED General charitable purposes including social welfare and health.

RANGE OF GRANTS Up to £200,000.

SAMPLE GRANTS Médecins Sans Frontières (UK) (£207,000); Refugee Council (£50,000); Evolve Housing and Support (£13,000); Nepal Youth Foundation (UK) (£500).

FINANCES *Financial year end 31/01/2022*
Income £4,420,000
Grants to organisations £302,000
Assets £4,110,000

TRUSTEES Michael MacLeod; John MacLeod; Hannah MacLeod.

HOW TO APPLY Apply in writing to the correspondent.

CONTACT DETAILS The Trustees, c/o Gina Parker, 30–32 Lombard Street, London EC3V 9BQ *Tel.* 020 8042 2485

■ The Robin MacLeod Charitable Trust

CC NO 1192118

WHERE FUNDING CAN BE GIVEN England and Wales.

WHO CAN BENEFIT Registered charities.

WHAT IS FUNDED Health; social welfare; refugees, homelessness; animal welfare.

SAMPLE GRANTS The Ehlers Danlos Society (£247,100); The Refugee Council (£125,500);

Centrepoint (£14,400); Action Against Hunger UK (£8,000).

FINANCES *Financial year end 30/11/2021*
Income £1,080,000
Grants to organisations £407,400
Assets £749,200

TRUSTEES Michael MacLeod; Dr Melanie Macleod; Hannah MacLeod.

OTHER INFORMATION The 2020/21 accounts were the latest available to view at the time of writing (June 2023).

HOW TO APPLY Apply in writing to the correspondent.

CONTACT DETAILS Gina Parker, 30–32 Lombard Street, London EC3V 9BQ *Tel.* 0113 388 8268 *Email* robinmacleodcharity@yahoo.com

---

■ The MacRobert Trust 2019

OSCR NO SC049745   **ESTABLISHED** 1943
WHERE FUNDING CAN BE GIVEN UK, mainly Scotland.
WHO CAN BENEFIT Registered charities; universities and non-fee-paying schools; libraries; uniformed groups; local and regional charitable organisations in Tarland and the nearby area.
WHAT IS FUNDED Armed forces and seafarers; education and training; children and young people; science, engineering and technology; agriculture and horticulture.
TYPE OF GRANT Core costs; project expenditure; capital costs; building costs; research funding. One-off and three-year grants are available.
RANGE OF GRANTS Up to £300,000 but grants are usually of less than £44,500.
SAMPLE GRANTS The Outward Bound Trust and The Royal Air Forces Association (£50,000 each); 1016 ATC Squadron (£35,000); Black Watch Museum Trust (£10,000); Engineering Development Trust (£5,000); Perth Festival Of The Arts Ltd (£3,400); Cromar Parish Church (£1,500); Ballater and District Pipe Band (£500).
FINANCES *Financial year end 05/04/2022*
Income £4,530,000
Grants to organisations £599,500
Assets £97,740,000
TRUSTEES Sabrina Campbell; Charles Crole; Mr J. Fowlie; Group Capt. William Gibson; Prof. Gordon Masterton; Commodore Charles Stevenson; Jamie Montgomery; Dr Rebecca McCormick.
HOW TO APPLY See the trust's website for the latest information on applications.
CONTACT DETAILS Alison Donaldson, Charity Manager, Cromar, Tarland, Aboyne, Aberdeenshire AB34 4UD *Tel.* 01339 881444 *Email* alison@themacroberttrust.org.uk *Website* www.themacroberttrust.org.uk

---

■ The Mactaggart Third Fund

OSCR NO SC014285   **ESTABLISHED** 1968
WHERE FUNDING CAN BE GIVEN UK and overseas.
WHO CAN BENEFIT Registered charities.
WHAT IS FUNDED General charitable purposes.
RANGE OF GRANTS Grants range from £200 up to £81,800.
SAMPLE GRANTS Health Navigator (£39,600); Amazon Conservation Team (£17,100); London's Air Ambulance (£11,300); Islay Heritage (£5,200); Young Women's Christian Association (£3,200); Railway Children (£1,000); Jewish Blind and Disabled (£750); Age UK Oxfordshire (£350).

FINANCES *Financial year end 30/04/2022*
Income £761,900
Grants to organisations £432,300
Assets £20,430,000
TRUSTEES Alastair Mactaggart; Robert Gore; Fiona Mactaggart; Andrew Mactaggart; Sir John Mactaggart.
OTHER INFORMATION The charity is associated with The Ian Mactaggart Trust (OSCR no. SC012502).
HOW TO APPLY The charity does not accept unsolicited applications. The charity's website states 'The Directors are solely responsible for the choice of charitable organisations to be supported. They are proactive in seeking out charities to support and all projects are chosen on their initiative.'
CONTACT DETAILS The Trustees, 2 Babmaes Street, London SW1Y 6HD *Website* www. mactaggartthirdfund.org

---

■ The Ian Mactaggart Trust

OSCR NO SC012502   **ESTABLISHED** 1984
WHERE FUNDING CAN BE GIVEN UK and overseas.
WHO CAN BENEFIT Charitable organisations.
WHAT IS FUNDED General charitable purposes.
SAMPLE GRANTS Health Navigator (£44,300); Focusing Philanthropy (£38,000); Book Limited International (£11,600); Women's Support Services (£5,300); Hebridean Whale and Dolphin Trust (£3,500); The National Forest (£2,000); Centre for Alternative Technology (£1,000); The Penny Brohn Cancer Centre (£500).
FINANCES *Financial year end 30/04/2022*
Income £567,300
Grants to organisations £264,100
Assets £17,390,000
TRUSTEES Sir John Mactaggart; Robert Gore; Fiona Mactaggart; Jane Mactaggart; Philip Mactaggart; Leora Armstrong.
HOW TO APPLY The charities supported are found proactively by the trust's directors. The trust does not accept unsolicited applications.
CONTACT DETAILS The Trustees, 30 Mansfield Place, Port Ellen, Isle of Islay, Argyll and Bute PA42 7BJ *Website* www.ianmactaggarttrust.org

---

■ The Magdalen and Lasher Charity (General Fund)

CC NO 211415   **ESTABLISHED** 1837
WHERE FUNDING CAN BE GIVEN Hastings.
WHO CAN BENEFIT Individuals; charitable organisations.
WHAT IS FUNDED Social welfare.
WHAT IS NOT FUNDED Debt repayment; minibuses.
TYPE OF GRANT One-off, for specific projects.
SAMPLE GRANTS A list of beneficiaries was not included in the annual report and accounts. Previous beneficiaries have included: 4th Hastings Guides; Amicus Horizon; Association of Carers; Broomgrove Play Scheme; Counselling Plus; Hastings Advice and Representation Centre; The Salvation Army – St Andrews Square; St Clement and All Saints; Surviving Christmas; Snowflake Trust Night Shelter; White Rock Theatre.
FINANCES *Financial year end 31/03/2022*
Income £517,900
Grants to organisations £360,000
Assets £16,470,000
TRUSTEES Gareth Bendon; Keith Donaldson; Michael Foster; Sue Phillips; Ian Steel; Judith Rogers;

Ann Wing; Clive Galbraith; Cllr James Bacon; Dr Patricia Lock; John Bilsby; Judith Cubison; The Revd Paul Hunt.

OTHER INFORMATION The origins of the charity go back to 1294, when land was donated in support of a local leper and pest house. It merged with another charity in 1691, but the Mayor and Hastings Corporation controlled the funds. In 1837, the charity was placed under independent trusteeship and in 1877, the charity was divided into three main branches: a pensions branch, an eleemosynary (alms) branch and an education branch.

HOW TO APPLY See the charity's website for the latest information on applications.

CONTACT DETAILS Marcia Woolf, Administrator, Old Hastings House, 132 High Street, Hastings, East Sussex TN34 3ET *Tel.* 01424 452646 *Email* mlc@oldhastingshouse.co.uk *Website* http://magdalenandlasher.co.uk

■ The Magen Charitable Trust

CC NO 326535   **ESTABLISHED** 1984
WHERE FUNDING CAN BE GIVEN UK.
WHO CAN BENEFIT Registered charities, especially Jewish organisations.
WHAT IS FUNDED The Jewish faith and community.
WHAT IS NOT FUNDED Grant contracts.
SAMPLE GRANTS A list of beneficiaries was not included in the annual report and accounts.
FINANCES *Financial year end* 31/03/2022
Income £223,100
Grants to organisations £231,800
Assets £1,760,000
TRUSTEES Rosa Halpern; Jacob Halpern.
HOW TO APPLY Apply in writing to the correspondent.
CONTACT DETAILS The Trustees, New Riverside, 439 Lower Broughton, Salford, Greater Manchester M7 2FX *Tel.* 0161 792 2626

■ The Mageni Trust

CC NO 1070732   **ESTABLISHED** 1998
WHERE FUNDING CAN BE GIVEN UK and overseas.
WHO CAN BENEFIT Registered charities; hospitals and hospices.
WHAT IS FUNDED General charitable purposes including international development and the arts.
TYPE OF GRANT One-off and recurrent.
RANGE OF GRANTS £500 to £10,000.
SAMPLE GRANTS Afghanistan and Central Asia Association (£5,000); African Promise (£2,500); Oxfam (£1,000); World Child Cancer (£750); Mind (£500).
FINANCES *Financial year end* 31/05/2022
Income £147,000
Grants to organisations £133,900
Assets £114,100
TRUSTEES Garf Collins; Gillian Collins; Alex Collins; Tom Collins.
OTHER INFORMATION Grants were awarded to 98 organisations during the year.
HOW TO APPLY The trustees identify the causes they want to work with.
CONTACT DETAILS The Trustees, Leslie Cottage, The Promenade, Pevensey Bay, East Sussex BN24 6HE *Tel.* 01323 460770 *Email* garfcollins@gmail.com

■ Magnify Foundation

CC NO 1194854
WHERE FUNDING CAN BE GIVEN UK.
WHO CAN BENEFIT Registered charities; community groups; churches; individuals.
WHAT IS FUNDED Advancement of the Christian faith; social welfare.
RANGE OF GRANTS Mostly £1,000 to £25,000.
SAMPLE GRANTS The Message Trust (£50,000); Pioneer (£17,500); Tough Talk (£12,500); Beyond Ourselves (£4,000); Kingdom Living Ministries (£3,000).
FINANCES *Financial year end* 31/12/2021
Income £604,400
Grants to organisations £127,700
Assets £474,800
TRUSTEES Benjamin Collins; Susanna Blustin; Nicholas Davis; Megan Collins.
HOW TO APPLY Applications can be made via the foundation's website.
CONTACT DETAILS The Trustees, c/o Wilkes Tranter and Co. Ltd, Brook House, Moss Grove, Kingswinford, West Midlands DY6 9HS *Tel.* 07392 551683 *Email* hello@magnify. foundation *Website* www.magnify.foundation

■ The Mahoro Charitable Trust

CC NO 1151200   **ESTABLISHED** 2013
WHERE FUNDING CAN BE GIVEN UK.
WHO CAN BENEFIT Charitable organisations.
WHAT IS FUNDED General charitable purposes, with a preference for health and social welfare charities.
SAMPLE GRANTS A list of beneficiaries was not available.
FINANCES *Financial year end* 05/04/2022
Income £0
Grants to organisations £700,300
TRUSTEES Holly Ellis; Jenny Ellis; Luke Ellis; Rory Ellis.
OTHER INFORMATION Full accounts were not available to view on the Charity Commission's website due to the trust's low income. We have therefore estimated the grant total based on the trust's total expenditure.
HOW TO APPLY Apply in writing to the correspondent.
CONTACT DETAILS The Trustees, Flat 25, Sir John Lyon House, 8 High Timber Street, London EC4V 3PA *Tel.* 01892 701847 *Email* mahorotrust@gmail.com

■ Makers of Playing Cards Charity

CC NO 232876   **ESTABLISHED** 1943
WHERE FUNDING CAN BE GIVEN London and the home counties.
WHO CAN BENEFIT Registered charities with an income of under £1 million.
WHAT IS FUNDED Education, health and well-being of people under the age of 25; members of the Worshipful Makers of Playing Cards Livery Company and their close dependants.
WHAT IS NOT FUNDED Start-up charities; housing associations; places of worship; one-off events such as festivals; general appeals and circulars; large projects; course fees for professionals; schools and PTAs; Citizens Advice.
RANGE OF GRANTS Generally up to £1,000.
SAMPLE GRANTS Bloomfield Learning Centre; Clear Sky; Family Trust; Scorchers Basketball Foundation; Sunbeams; Young and Inspired.

FINANCES *Financial year end* 05/04/2022
Income £103,900
Grants to organisations £72,700
Assets £1,130,000

TRUSTEES Mark Winston; Nicholas Prentice; Capt. Michael Davis-Marks; Barbara Ide; Dr Paul Bostock; David Hussey; Lance Whitehouse; Neil Green; Linda Whitlam; Suzanne Nichols; Anthony Blower.

OTHER INFORMATION Grants were broken down as follows: hardship (£36,800); education (£23,100); children's charities (£12,800).

HOW TO APPLY Apply to the correspondent via email. The application should be no longer than one side of A4, set out how you would spend a grant of £1,000, explain briefly how the work for which you seek funds meets the Makers of Playing Cards Charity's charitable objects and include a copy of your most recent annual report and accounts.

CONTACT DETAILS The Prime Almoner, 35 Ascot Way, Bicester, Oxfordshire OX26 1AG *Tel.* 020 7531 5990 *Email* charityalmoners@makersofplayingcards.co.uk *Website* www.makersofplayingcards.co.uk

■ Making a Difference Locally Ltd

CC NO 1123800   **ESTABLISHED** 2008

WHERE FUNDING CAN BE GIVEN UK, in areas local to Nisa Retail Ltd stores (see the store locator on the website).

WHO CAN BENEFIT Registered charities or good causes with a dedicated business bank account. Organisations should ideally be located within ten miles of a Nisa Retail store.

WHAT IS FUNDED General charitable purposes; community projects and causes spanning health and well-being, education, employment, good food and nutrition, shelter and security.

WHAT IS NOT FUNDED See the charity's website for a full list of exclusions.

RANGE OF GRANTS Mostly up to £1,000.

SAMPLE GRANTS The Trussell Trust (£17,500).

FINANCES *Financial year end* 30/06/2021
Income £1,200,000
Grants to organisations £1,060,000
Assets £1,450,000

TRUSTEES David Stokes; Andrew Barber; Mohammed Aslam; Valerie Aston; Michael Gisby; John McNeill; Kathryn Marsden.

OTHER INFORMATION The foundation awarded 1,725 grants during the year. Grants were distributed as follows: retailers' nominated organisations (£868,600); national organisations (£137,800); local organisations (£51,700). The 2020/21 annual accounts were the latest available at the time of writing (June 2023).

HOW TO APPLY Use the store locator on the Nisa website to contact your local store. Individual retailers can then submit a form to the charity's committee for approval. Enquiries should be sent via the contact form on the website.

CONTACT DETAILS The Trustees, Waldo Way, Normanby Enterprise Park, Scunthorpe, North Lincolnshire DN15 9GE *Tel.* 01724 282028 *Email* makingadifference@nisaretail.com *Website* www.nisalocally.co.uk/community

■ The Mallinckrodt Foundation

CC NO 1058011   **ESTABLISHED** 1996

WHERE FUNDING CAN BE GIVEN UK and overseas.

WHO CAN BENEFIT Charitable organisations; universities.

WHAT IS FUNDED General charitable purposes.

RANGE OF GRANTS Up to £20,000.

SAMPLE GRANTS Royal Botanical Gardens Kew – Friends and Supporters (£15,000); The Woolf Institute (£14,000); Harvard Kennedy School of Government (£18,200); Christian Responsibility in Public Affairs, Foundation of the College of St George and The Royal Chapel of All Saints (£5,000 each).

FINANCES *Financial year end* 05/04/2022
Income £199,400
Grants to organisations £62,200
Assets £6,660,000

TRUSTEES Charmaine Mallinckrodt; Claire Howard; Philip Mallinckrodt; Edward Mallinckrodt.

OTHER INFORMATION In 2021/22 grants were awarded to six organisations.

HOW TO APPLY The 2021/22 annual report states: 'The Trustees identify projects and organisations they wish to support. The Foundation does not make grants to people or organisations that apply speculatively.'

CONTACT DETAILS The Trustees, 81 Rivington Street, London EC2A 3AY *Tel.* 020 3170 5793

■ Man Group plc Charitable Trust

CC NO 275386   **ESTABLISHED** 1978

WHERE FUNDING CAN BE GIVEN UK.

WHO CAN BENEFIT Small to medium-sized registered charities.

WHAT IS FUNDED Literacy, numeracy and programmes that support disadvantaged people to engage with education and build the necessary vital life skills to improve life chances and employment prospects.

WHAT IS NOT FUNDED Large national charities (unless in relation to a specific education project); charities which use external fundraising agencies; charities primarily devoted to promoting religious beliefs; endowment funds; requests to directly replace statutory funding; individual beneficiaries; general media campaigns or campaigning or advocacy work to influence policy debates; applicants which have been successful during the last 12 months; work which has already been completed; capital projects and appeals; sponsorship or funding towards marketing appeals or fundraising events; organisations or projects whose primary purpose is political; charities with high administration costs relative to the services provided.

TYPE OF GRANT Core costs, including salaries and overheads; project costs.

RANGE OF GRANTS Up to £100,000.

SAMPLE GRANTS Man US Charitable Foundation (£136,900); The Auditory Verbal Centre (£50,000); Read Easy UK (£41,600); Greenhouse Sports Ltd (£40,500); NSPCC (£35,000); Tower Hamlets Education Business Partnership (£28,800); Children's Discovery Centre East London (£25,000); Middlesbrough Football Club Foundation (£10,000).

FINANCES *Financial year end* 31/12/2021
Income £3,090,000
Grants to organisations £702,800
Assets £2,920,000

TRUSTEES Carol Ward; Lydia Bosworth; Keith Haydon; Steven Desmyter; Christopher Pyper; Angus Jacobs; Abby King.

OTHER INFORMATION Grants were made to 16 charities.

HOW TO APPLY In the first instance, see the foundation's page on the Man Group website, where a document detailing eligibility criteria and guidelines on how to apply is available. The document states that the trust has a two-stage application process. The trustees usually meet twice a year to consider applications.

CONTACT DETAILS The Trustees, Man Group plc, Riverbank House, 2 Swan Lane, London EC4R 3AD *Tel.* 020 7144 1734 *Email* charitable.trust@man.com *Website* www. man.com/responsibility

---

■ The Manackerman Charitable Trust

CC NO 326147   **ESTABLISHED** 1982

WHERE FUNDING CAN BE GIVEN UK, with a preference for Brent, Bury, Hackney, Salford and Scotland; Israel.

WHO CAN BENEFIT Jewish organisations; educational establishments; hospitals.

WHAT IS FUNDED The Jewish faith and community; education; health and medicine; disability; the relief of poverty.

RANGE OF GRANTS Generally up to £25,000.

SAMPLE GRANTS Federation of Great Britain and Ireland (£25,000); Seed UK (£15,000); Emunah UK (£10,000); Broughton Jewish Primary School and Friends of Alyn Orthapedic Hospital Jerusalem (£5,000 each).

FINANCES *Financial year end* 31/03/2022 *Income* £75,300 *Grants to organisations* £80,600 *Assets* £257,700

TRUSTEES Vanessa Marks; Jonathan Marks; Aryeh Marks.

OTHER INFORMATION Grants of less than £5,000 totalled £8,100.

HOW TO APPLY Apply in writing to the correspondent.

CONTACT DETAILS Jonathan Marks, Trustee, 3 Park Lane, Salford, Greater Manchester M7 4HT *Tel.* 0161 832 3434

■ Manchester Airport Community Trust Fund

CC NO 1071703   **ESTABLISHED** 1997

WHERE FUNDING CAN BE GIVEN Within a ten-mile radius of Manchester airport, concentrating on the areas most exposed to aircraft noise.

WHO CAN BENEFIT Community groups, voluntary groups, self-help groups, community charities or local branches of national charities.

WHAT IS FUNDED The environment; social welfare; community development and services.

TYPE OF GRANT Anything which is tangible and long lasting, i.e. equipment.

RANGE OF GRANTS Up to £3,000.

SAMPLE GRANTS Whalley Range Cricket and Lawn Tennis Club (£3,000); Plastic Shed (£2,600); Once Upon A Smile (£1,800); Knutsford Football Club (£490).

FINANCES *Financial year end* 31/03/2022 *Income* £117,000 *Grants to organisations* £89,200 *Assets* £51,700

TRUSTEES Cllr Don Stockton; Bill Fairfoull; Paul Andrews; John Taylor; Robert Pattison.

OTHER INFORMATION Grants were made to 55 organisations during the financial year.

HOW TO APPLY Apply online via the fund's website. The trustees meet four times a year and application deadlines are published on the fund's website.

CONTACT DETAILS The Trustees, Manchester Airport plc, Olympic House, Manchester Airport, Manchester M90 1QX *Tel.* 0161 489 3853

Email trust.fund@manairport.co.uk *Website* www.manchesterairport.co.uk/community/working-in-our-community/community-trust-fund

---

■ The Manchester Guardian Society Charitable Trust

CC NO 515341   **ESTABLISHED** 1984

WHERE FUNDING CAN BE GIVEN Greater Manchester.

WHO CAN BENEFIT Charities; uniformed groups; arts organisations; community associations. Preference is usually shown to smaller charities and community groups in the Greater Manchester area.

WHAT IS FUNDED General charitable purposes, especially children and young people, ill health and disability, older people, disadvantaged individuals, education, the arts and community causes.

WHAT IS NOT FUNDED Individuals; substitution of statutory funding; political groups; religious groups; salaries; recurrent costs; other funding bodies; core funding for public sector services; the purchase of computers and associated equipment.

TYPE OF GRANT Primarily small, one-off awards.

RANGE OF GRANTS Mostly up to £3,500.

SAMPLE GRANTS A list of beneficiaries was not included in the annual report and accounts. Previous beneficiaries have included: DEBRA Charity North West Office; Dogs for the Disabled; Freedom from Torture; Hand on Heart Charity; Greater Manchester Scouts; Manchester YMCA; New Hope Ashton; Northwood Youth Advice Service; React (Rapid Effective Assistance for Children with potentially Terminal illness); Sense.

FINANCES *Financial year end* 05/04/2022 *Income* £108,900 *Grants to organisations* £154,200 *Assets* £5,430,000

TRUSTEES Diane Hawkins; Warren Smith; Lorraine Worsley; Sharman Birtles; Lt Col. Shauna Dixon; Paul Griffiths; Philip Horton.

OTHER INFORMATION In 2021/22 grants were awarded to 82 organisations.

HOW TO APPLY Application forms can be downloaded from the charity's website along with guidelines on how to complete them. Applicants should submit the completed application by email. Only one application will be accepted from an organisation within a two-year period.

CONTACT DETAILS The Trustees, c/o Beyond Profit Ltd, Bolton Arena, Arena Approach, Horwich, Bolton, Greater Manchester BL6 6LB *Tel.* 01204 414317 *Email* manchesterguardiansociety@gmail.com *Website* www.manchesterguardiansociety.org.uk

---

■ The W. M. Mann Foundation

OSCR NO SC010111   **ESTABLISHED** 1992

WHERE FUNDING CAN BE GIVEN Mainly Scotland but UK-wide organisations may be assisted.

WHO CAN BENEFIT Charitable organisations; universities; hospices; hospitals; uniformed groups.

WHAT IS FUNDED General charitable purposes, including the arts, social welfare, education and medical causes.

WHAT IS NOT FUNDED Individuals.

RANGE OF GRANTS Generally between £500 and £2,000.

SAMPLE GRANTS Ayrshire Hospice (£10,000); University of St Andrews (£4,000); Edinburgh Food Social (£1,500); Hearts and Minds (£1,000); Home-Start Aberdeen (£750).

FINANCES *Financial year end 05/04/2022*
Income £187,600
Grants to organisations £124,900
Assets £9,930,000

OTHER INFORMATION Grants were made to 101 organisations.

HOW TO APPLY Apply in writing to the correspondent and include your organisation's latest annual report and accounts.

CONTACT DETAILS The Trustees, 201 Bath Street, Glasgow G2 4HZ *Tel.* 0141 248 4936
Email mail@wmmanngroup.co.uk

■ R. W. Mann Trust

CC NO 1095699   **ESTABLISHED** 1959

WHERE FUNDING CAN BE GIVEN The east of Newcastle city; Cramlington; Ashington; Blyth; south-east Northumberland; North Tyneside.

WHO CAN BENEFIT Local registered charities; youth groups (uniformed and non-uniformed); schools; hospitals; CICs; social enterprises; voluntary groups.

WHAT IS FUNDED General charitable purposes, including the following: social welfare; education; health; children and young people; people with disabilities; older people.

WHAT IS NOT FUNDED Large, well-established national charities; individuals; church buildings, except those used for community groups; projects which can attract public funds except where there is a particular part of the project which other sources would be unlikely to fund; replacement of statutory funding; retrospective expenditure; projects south of the River Tyne; medical research.

TYPE OF GRANT One-off and recurrent grants; capital project costs.

RANGE OF GRANTS £100 to £10,000 (the average grant is £1,000).

SAMPLE GRANTS A list of beneficiaries was not included in the annual report and accounts. Previous beneficiaries have included: CVA Blyth Valley (£5,000); Northumberland CVA (£4,000); Acorn Community Church and St Paul's Community Partnership (£2,000); Mind – Tyneside and Northumberland (£1,000); Grainger Park CIO (£750); The Jack Charlton Disabled Anglers Association (£500); Penrith and District Red Squirrel Group (£250).

FINANCES *Financial year end 31/03/2022*
Income £104,400
Grants to organisations £119,300
Assets £2,810,000

TRUSTEES Judith Hamilton; Monica Heath; Guy Javens.

HOW TO APPLY Applications should be made in writing to the correspondent – consult the trust's website for a full list of what should be included. The trustees meet regularly and applicants usually hear if their application has been successful within four weeks.

CONTACT DETAILS John Hamilton, Secretary, PO Box 119, Gosforth, Newcastle upon Tyne, Tyne and Wear NE3 4WF *Tel.* 0191 284 2158 *Email* rwmanntrust57@gmail.com *Website* www.rwmanntrust.org.uk

■ The Manoukian Charitable Foundation

CC NO 1084065   **ESTABLISHED** 2000

WHERE FUNDING CAN BE GIVEN UK and overseas.

WHO CAN BENEFIT Registered charities, with a preference for Armenian organisations.

WHAT IS FUNDED General charitable purposes, particularly social welfare, education, medical causes and arts and culture.

RANGE OF GRANTS Up to £200,000.

SAMPLE GRANTS Action Innocence (£196,100); Chronic Care Centre (£82,600); BASSMA (£73,900); St Yeghiche's Armenian Church Parish (£40,000); Mission Enfrance (£9,400 each).

FINANCES *Financial year end 31/12/2021*
Income £871,600
Grants to organisations £717,700
Grants to individuals £74,700
Assets £214,700

TRUSTEES Tamar Manoukian; Steven Press; Dr Armen Sarkissian.

HOW TO APPLY According to the foundation's Charity Commission record, the trustees do not accept unsolicited applications.

CONTACT DETAILS Steven Press, Trustee, St Yeghiche's Armenian Church, 13B Cranley Gardens, London SW7 3BB *Tel.* 020 7341 4444

■ The Manson Family Charitable Trust

CC NO 1168888   **ESTABLISHED** 2015

WHERE FUNDING CAN BE GIVEN UK and Israel.

WHO CAN BENEFIT Established charities, especially smaller organisations in the UK and overseas.

WHAT IS FUNDED General charitable purposes, particularly education, religion, health and social well-being; the Jewish faith and community.

RANGE OF GRANTS Mostly under £10,000.

SAMPLE GRANTS Previous beneficiaries have included: Ma'ayan Project (£35,000); Jerusalem Foundation (£19,100); The Langdon Foundation (£17,700); MGS Trust (£10,000); The Friendship Circle (£8,000); Gesher and Manchester Jewish Museum (£5,000 each); Leuka (£4,300); Community Security Trust (£3,500); Aish UK, Designability, Manchester Jewish School for Special Education and StandWithUs (£1,000 each).

FINANCES *Financial year end 31/12/2021*
Income £21,000
Grants to organisations £112,300
Assets £2,130,000

TRUSTEES Jonathan Manson; Avril Manson; Lauren Ornstein; Edward Manson; Hannah Peters.

OTHER INFORMATION Full accounts were not available to view on the Charity Commission's website. We have therefore estimated the charity's grant total based on its total expenditure.

HOW TO APPLY Apply in writing to the correspondent.

CONTACT DETAILS Jonathan Manson, Chair, 4 Parklands, Whitefield, Manchester M45 7WY *Tel.* 0161 245 1201

■ The Marandi Foundation

CC NO 1172282   **ESTABLISHED** 2017

WHERE FUNDING CAN BE GIVEN UK.

WHO CAN BENEFIT Registered charities.

WHAT IS FUNDED Education and training; mental health and well-being support services; arts and culture.

TYPE OF GRANT Project funding.

SAMPLE GRANTS Centre Point (£937,800); The Watercolour World (£60,000); The Latymer Foundation (£2,500); Walkabout Foundation (£2,400).

FINANCES *Financial year end 05/04/2022*
Income £925,700
Grants to organisations £902,600
Assets £48,300

TRUSTEES Narmina Marandi; Javad Marandi; Michael Lockett.

OTHER INFORMATION Grants were awarded to four organisations during 2021/22.

HOW TO APPLY Apply in writing to the correspondent.

CONTACT DETAILS The Trustees, 103 Mount Street, London W1K 2TJ *Tel.* 07771 787730 *Email* info@themarandifoundation.org *Website* www.themarandifoundation.org

---

■ **Marbeh Torah Trust**

CC NO 292491   **ESTABLISHED** 1985

WHERE FUNDING CAN BE GIVEN UK and overseas, particularly Israel.

WHO CAN BENEFIT Jewish charitable organisations, especially educational establishments; individuals.

WHAT IS FUNDED The advancement of Orthodox Jewish religious education and the relief of poverty.

RANGE OF GRANTS £5,000 to £180,000.

SAMPLE GRANTS Yeshiva Marbeh Torah (£182,300); Chazon Avraham Yitzchak (£80,700); Margenita DeAvraham (£23,800); Ponovezh Yeshiva (£20,000); Beis Dovid (£5,000).

FINANCES *Financial year end 31/12/2021*
Income £306,500
Grants to organisations £316,800
Assets £2,100

TRUSTEES Naftoli Elzas; Moishe Elzas; Simone Elzas.

OTHER INFORMATION The trustees made grants to six organisations in 2021, primarily for Jewish education.

HOW TO APPLY Contact the correspondent for further information.

CONTACT DETAILS The Trustees, 116 Castlewood Road, London N15 6BE *Tel.* 020 8802 9842

■ **The Marchig Animal Welfare Trust**

CC NO 802133   **ESTABLISHED** 1989

WHERE FUNDING CAN BE GIVEN Worldwide, excluding the USA and Canada.

WHO CAN BENEFIT Charitable organisations and veterinarians.

WHAT IS FUNDED Animal welfare.

TYPE OF GRANT Project funding; capital costs.

SAMPLE GRANTS Worldwide Veterinary Service – UK (£662,400); Friendicoes SECA and Wildlife SOS (£70,500 each); Chats du Quercy – France (£33,900); Help in Suffering – India (£33,100).

FINANCES *Financial year end 31/12/2021*
Income £364,900
Grants to organisations £297,100
Assets £16,230,000

TRUSTEES Les Ward; Janice McLoughlin; Fraser Symon; Matthew Tickle.

OTHER INFORMATION A total of 42 grants were awarded during the year, of which 16 were of less than £5,000.

HOW TO APPLY Application forms can be downloaded from the trust's website.

CONTACT DETAILS The Trustees, Caledonian Exchange, 19A Canning Street, Edinburgh EH3 8HE *Tel.* 0033 (0) 555 608055 *Email* applications@marchigtrust.org *Website* www.marchigtrust.org

---

■ **The Stella and Alexander Margulies Charitable Trust**

CC NO 220441   **ESTABLISHED** 1962

WHERE FUNDING CAN BE GIVEN UK and Israel.

WHO CAN BENEFIT Charitable organisations, particularly those benefitting Jewish people.

WHAT IS FUNDED Arts and culture; education; medical research; the Jewish faith and community.

SAMPLE GRANTS Royal Opera House Foundation (£175,000); Barbican Centre Arts and Culture (£65,000); Royal National Theatre Arts and Culture (£24,000); Food Bank Aid and Women Wage Peace Mozrahi Tefahot (£1,000 each).

FINANCES *Financial year end 05/04/2022*
Income £88,500
Grants to organisations £289,800
Assets £11,511,000

TRUSTEES Marcus Marguiles; Alexander Sorkin; Martin Paisner; Leslie Michaels; Sir Stuart Lipton.

OTHER INFORMATION Grants were made to eight organisations and were broken down as follows: arts and culture (£276,000); education (£10,000); relief for individuals of faith (£1,800); general charitable purposes (£1,000); religious activities (£1,000).

HOW TO APPLY Contact the correspondent for further information.

CONTACT DETAILS The Trustees, 27 Berkeley Square, London W1J 6EL *Tel.* 020 7343 7200 *Email* jill.tyrrell@timeproducts.co.uk

---

■ **The Michael Marks Charitable Trust**

CC NO 248136   **ESTABLISHED** 1966

WHERE FUNDING CAN BE GIVEN UK and overseas.

WHO CAN BENEFIT Registered charities; galleries, museums and libraries; educational institutions.

WHAT IS FUNDED Arts and culture; the environment and conservation.

WHAT IS NOT FUNDED Grants are not made to individuals or profit-making organisations.

RANGE OF GRANTS £500 to £25,000.

SAMPLE GRANTS Oxford Philharmonic Orchestra (£46,500); Wordsworth Trust (£26,000); National Theatre (£10,000); Manchester City Galleries Trust (£5,000); Orchestra of the Age of Enlightenment (£4,000); Etaireia Messeniakon Spoudon (£3,000).

FINANCES *Financial year end 31/01/2022*
Income £127,900
Grants to organisations £130,900
Assets £5,730,000

TRUSTEES Noel Annesley; Lady Marina Marks; Sir Christopher White.

OTHER INFORMATION In 2021/22, grants were awarded to 17 organisations.

HOW TO APPLY Applications should be made in writing to the correspondent and include audited accounts, information on other bodies approached and details of any funding obtained. The trustees meet twice a year, usually in January and July, to consider applications. Applicants will not receive a response unless they have been successful. The trustees will only accept written correspondence by regular mail.

Think carefully about every application. Is it justified?

525

CONTACT DETAILS Marina Marks, Trustee, 5 Elm Tree Road, London NW8 9JY *Tel.* 020 7286 4633 *Email* michaelmarkscharitabletrust@hotmail.co.uk

The Marks Family Charitable Trust

CC NO 263776   ESTABLISHED 1971
WHERE FUNDING CAN BE GIVEN Mostly the UK but also overseas.
WHO CAN BENEFIT Registered charities.
WHAT IS FUNDED The Jewish faith and community; children and young people; health care; education; the arts; refugees.
TYPE OF GRANT One-off; recurrent.
RANGE OF GRANTS Typically £5,000 to £20,000.
SAMPLE GRANTS Royal Horticultural Society (£50,000); Exeter College Oxford (£17,500); National Literacy (£15,000); Parochial Church (£8,400); London Music Fund (£4,000); Jewish Child's Day (£2,500); West London Synagogue (£1,000); British Heart Foundation (£500).
FINANCES *Financial year end* 05/04/2022
Income £98,400
Grants to organisations £115,400
Assets £7,020,000
TRUSTEES Lord Marks of Broughton; Lady Marks of Broughton; The Hon. Michael Marks; The Hon. Miriam Cooper.
OTHER INFORMATION During 2021/22, the trust awarded 11 grants.
HOW TO APPLY An online application form can be found on the trust's website.
CONTACT DETAILS The Trustees, c/o HW Fisher and Co., Acre House, 11–15 William Road, London NW1 3ER *Tel.* 020 7388 7000 *Email* office@marksfamilycharitabletrust.com *Website* www.marksfamilycharitabletrust.com

Marmot Charitable Trust

CC NO 1106619   ESTABLISHED 2004
WHERE FUNDING CAN BE GIVEN Worldwide.
WHO CAN BENEFIT 'Green' organisations; educational institutions.
WHAT IS FUNDED General charitable purposes; the environment; environmental research; conflict resolution; energy; disarmament; peace and mediation; renewable and sustainable energy; sustainability.
TYPE OF GRANT Project funding; core costs.
RANGE OF GRANTS The average grant size is £10,500.
SAMPLE GRANTS A list of beneficiaries was not included in the annual report and accounts.
FINANCES *Financial year end* 05/04/2022
Income £33,900
Grants to organisations £326,800
Assets £2,550,000
TRUSTEES Jean Barlow; Jonathan Gillett; Martin Gillett.
OTHER INFORMATION The 2021/22 annual report states that the trust prioritises organisations that are 'green' and which centre on sustainability. Grants were broken down as follows: the environment and sustainability (£139,600); peace and security (£95,300); general charitable purposes (£91,900).
HOW TO APPLY Unsolicited applications are not accepted.
CONTACT DETAILS The Trustees, c/o BM Marmot, London WC1N 3XX *Tel.* 07707 996220 *Email* marmot.trust@gmail.com

The Marque Foundation

CC NO 1174823   ESTABLISHED 2017
WHERE FUNDING CAN BE GIVEN UK.
WHO CAN BENEFIT Registered charities; Jewish organisations.
WHAT IS FUNDED The relief of poverty; education; religion; medical care.
RANGE OF GRANTS Mostly between £5,000 and £36,900, with the occasional smaller grant.
SAMPLE GRANTS Friends of Mosdos Torah Veyirah (£36,900); Torah Chesed Refuah CIO (£18,500); The Ruzin Sadagora Trust (£10,000); MGS Charitable Trust (£5,000).
FINANCES *Financial year end* 31/03/2022
Income £200,000
Grants to organisations £79,900
Assets £107,600
TRUSTEES Alexander Schimmel; Benjamin Schimmel; Leopold Schimmel.
OTHER INFORMATION Grants of under £5,000 totalled £9,500.
HOW TO APPLY Apply in writing to the correspondent.
CONTACT DETAILS The Trustees, 121 Princes Park Avenue, London NW11 0JS *Tel.* 020 8455 0100

The Michael Marsh Charitable Trust

CC NO 220473   ESTABLISHED 1958
WHERE FUNDING CAN BE GIVEN Birmingham, Staffordshire, Worcestershire, Warwickshire, Coventry, Wolverhampton and associated towns in the Black Country.
WHO CAN BENEFIT Registered charities; CICs; schools; universities; hospitals; hospices; religious bodies and institutions.
WHAT IS FUNDED General charitable purposes; education/training; disabilities; children/young people; the relief of poverty; older people.
WHAT IS NOT FUNDED Animals; entertainment charities; replacement of statutory funding; running costs. Grants to individuals are only given through charitable institutions on their behalf.
TYPE OF GRANT Capital costs; seed funding/start-up funding; project funding.
RANGE OF GRANTS Usually between £1,000 and £5,000.
SAMPLE GRANTS University of Birmingham (£75,000); Prison Advice and Care Trust (£10,000); Marine Society and Sea Cadets (£5,000); Age UK Birmingham (£3,000); Ackers Adventure (£2,500); Maryvale Community Project (£2,000); Frozen Light (£1,500); Thrive (£1,000); St Basil's (£500).
FINANCES *Financial year end* 05/04/2022
Income £109,000
Grants to organisations £227,900
Assets £3,020,000
TRUSTEES Peter Barber; Susan Bennett; Lee Nuttall.
OTHER INFORMATION Grants were broken down as follows: education and training (£99,000); general (£40,900); young people (£33,500); relief of poverty (£27,800); disability (£16,800); older people (£10,000).
HOW TO APPLY Apply in writing to the correspondent. The trustees meet around four times a year to consider applications.
CONTACT DETAILS Louise Ruane, Clerk to the Trustees, Pear Tree Cottage, Yarrington Road, Alfrick, Worcester, Worcestershire WR6 5EX *Tel.* 07812 743485 *Email* louise.ruane@michaelmarsh.org.uk

■ The Marsh Christian Trust

CC NO 284470   **ESTABLISHED** 1981
WHERE FUNDING CAN BE GIVEN UK.
WHO CAN BENEFIT Registered charities.
WHAT IS FUNDED General charitable purposes, with a preference towards the following: arts and heritage; social welfare; environmental causes; animal welfare; education and training.
WHAT IS NOT FUNDED Individuals; churches; hospices or hospitals; start-up costs; project costs; sponsorship proposals.
TYPE OF GRANT Core/revenue costs; unrestricted funding.
RANGE OF GRANTS Usually £300 to £2,000.
SAMPLE GRANTS Engage (£2,300); The Leprosy Mission (£1,400); Listening Books (£1,100); Environmental Investigation Agency (£800); British Thyroid Foundation (£500); Little Troopers (£300); Zoological Society of London (£150); British Hedgehog Preservation Society (£50).
FINANCES *Financial year end* 05/04/2022
Income £1,030,000
Grants to organisations £262,000
Grants to individuals £110,800
Assets £18,490,000
TRUSTEES Brian Marsh; Natalie Collings; Antonia Marsh; Charles Micklewright; Nicholas Carter; Alice Foulk.
OTHER INFORMATION The trust awarded 460 grants totalling £262,000 to organisations in 2021/22. Grants were distributed in the following categories: social welfare (£192,800); arts and heritage (£25,800); health care and medical research (£20,300); the environment and animal welfare (£14,000); education and training (£9,100). The trust also maintains the Marsh Awards Scheme, which recognises individual and group achievements in the charity sector. A further £110,800 was awarded to individuals and groups through this scheme. Full details are available on the website.
HOW TO APPLY Apply in writing to the correspondent – there is no standard application form. The trust requires a cover letter and a full copy of the applicant's annual report and accounts. There are no deadlines for applications. Further information can be found on the trust's website.
CONTACT DETAILS Annie McCarthy, Trust Manager, 4 Matthew Parker Street, London SW1H 9NP *Tel.* 07766 391674 *Email* mccarthy@bpmarsh.co.uk *Website* www.marshchristiantrust.org

■ Charity of John Marshall

CC NO 206780   **ESTABLISHED** 1631
WHERE FUNDING CAN BE GIVEN England and Wales (for parsonage grants); Canterbury, Guildford, Lincoln, Rochester and Southwark (for church restoration grants).
WHO CAN BENEFIT Anglican parish churches and cathedrals.
WHAT IS FUNDED Support for parsonage buildings throughout England and Wales; help with the upkeep of Anglican churches and cathedrals in Kent, Surrey and Lincolnshire (as the counties were defined in 1855), including the installation of CCTV and burglar alarms; support for the parish of Christ Church in Southwark; education.
WHAT IS NOT FUNDED Parsonage grants cannot be applied for by individual clergy or other denominations. Full exclusions can be found on the charity's website.
TYPE OF GRANT Building and other capital works.
RANGE OF GRANTS Grants to churches: typically between £4,000 and £20,000; awards to parsonages: typically between £2,000 and £20,000.
SAMPLE GRANTS St Luke with Holy Trinity – Charlton (£20,000); St Paul's – Thornton Heath (£15,000); St Matthew's – Croydon (£11,000); St John the Baptist – Tunstall (£10,000); St James – Skillington (£9,000); St Mary's – Willesborough (£8,000); St Helen's – East Keal (£7,000); St Barnabas – Sutton (£5,000); Holy Trinity – London (£3,000).
FINANCES *Financial year end* 31/12/2021
Income £1,270,000
Grants to organisations £805,300
Assets £24,350,000
TRUSTEES Lesley Bosman; Stephen Clark; William Eason; Col. Antony Guthrie; John Heawood; Surbhi Malhotra-Trenkel; The Revd Jonathan Rust; Alastair Moss; Charles Ledsam; Eleanor Lang; Rebecca Shilling; Ian Maxwell-Scott.
OTHER INFORMATION Restoration grants were made to 39 churches during 2021 totalling £359,900, and 40 dioceses received grants for the purchase, improvement or improved security of parsonages, totalling £233,800. Funds made available to Marshall's Educational Foundation totalled £33,100 and individual grants were made to Christ Church – Southwark (£155,700) and All Saints Church – Stamford (£8,300).
HOW TO APPLY Applications must be submitted through the charity's website. Applications for parsonages must be made through the relevant Diocesan Parsonage Board. Further information on applying can be found on the charity's website. The Grants Committee meets three times per year to shortlist applications for the full board of trustees to approve.
CONTACT DETAILS Catherine de Cintra, Clerk to the Trustees, 66 Newcomen Street, London SE1 1YT *Tel.* 020 7407 2979 *Email* grantoffice@marshalls.org.uk *Website* www.marshalls.org.uk

■ Charlotte Marshall Charitable Trust

CC NO 211941   **ESTABLISHED** 1962
WHERE FUNDING CAN BE GIVEN UK.
WHO CAN BENEFIT Registered charities; educational institutions benefitting Roman Catholics; hospices.
WHAT IS FUNDED Two-thirds of the trust's income is allocated to support educational, religious and other charitable purposes for Roman Catholics and the remainder is distributed at the trustees' discretion.
RANGE OF GRANTS Mostly up to £1,500.
SAMPLE GRANTS NOAH Enterprise (£2,000); Cantos Anchor House (£1,500); Carousel Project, Charity For Kids and The Oliver Curd Trust (£570 each); Kent Multiple Sclerosis Therapy Centre and Winston's Wish (£500 each); The JPK Sussex Project (£450).
FINANCES *Financial year end* 05/04/2022
Income £81,800
Grants to organisations £76,900
Assets £455,400
TRUSTEES Joseph Cosgrave; Rachel Cosgrave; Kevin Page; John Russell.
HOW TO APPLY Contact the correspondent to request an application form.
CONTACT DETAILS The Trustees, c/o C. and C. Marshall Ltd, 55–65 Castleham Road, St Leonards-on-Sea, East Sussex TN38 9NU *Tel.* 01424 856655 *Email* christinac@marshall-tufflex.com

■ The Martin Charitable Trust

OSCR NO SC028487 **ESTABLISHED** 1998
WHERE FUNDING CAN BE GIVEN Scotland, particularly Glasgow and Strathclyde; UK; overseas.
WHO CAN BENEFIT Charitable organisations; individuals; hospices; places of worship.
WHAT IS FUNDED General charitable purposes.
SAMPLE GRANTS A list of beneficiaries was not included in the annual report and accounts. Previous beneficiaries have included: Ardgowan Hospice (£8,000); Tenovus Scotland (£6,000); Kelvinside Academy (£5,000); Glasgow Care Foundation (£4,000); British Red Cross Society, Cancer Research UK and Christian Aid Scotland (£3,000 each); The National Trust for Scotland (£2,000); Seafarers UK and St Columba Church of Scotland (£1,000 each).
FINANCES *Financial year end* 30/11/2021
Income £88,200
Grants to organisations £115,500
Assets £3,110,000
OTHER INFORMATION The 2020/21 accounts were the latest available at the time of writing (May 2023).
HOW TO APPLY Apply in writing to the correspondent.
CONTACT DETAILS The Trustees, c/o Miller Beckett and Jackson Solicitors, 190 St Vincent Street, Glasgow G2 5SP *Tel.* 0141 204 2833

■ The Kristina Martin Charitable Trust

CC NO 249913 **ESTABLISHED** 1966
WHERE FUNDING CAN BE GIVEN UK.
WHO CAN BENEFIT Registered and exempt charities.
WHAT IS FUNDED General charitable purposes, particularly mental health, suicide prevention and care following bereavement.
TYPE OF GRANT One-off grants.
RANGE OF GRANTS Mostly up to £15,000.
SAMPLE GRANTS Time to Talk West Berkshire (£20,000); Place2Be, STEM4, Suffolk Mind, Waterloo Uncovered and YoungMinds Trust (£15,000 each); St Barnabas Church (£1,300).
FINANCES *Financial year end* 05/04/2022
Income £251,900
Grants to organisations £366,300
Assets £9,820,000
TRUSTEES Andrew Parry; Peter Tompkins.
OTHER INFORMATION During 2021/22 grants were made to 24 organisations.
HOW TO APPLY The 2021/22 annual report states that the trust is 'seldom able to make grants in response to unsolicited applications'; however, applications can be made using the form on the trust's website. Grants are usually made by 31 January and 30 June each year.
CONTACT DETAILS The Trustees, c/o Irwin Mitchell LLP, Davidson House, Forbury Square, Reading, Berkshire RG1 3EU *Tel.* 07766 714420 *Email* info@kmct.org.uk *Website* https://sites. google.com/kmct.org.uk/kmct/home

■ Sir George Martin Trust

CC NO 223554 **ESTABLISHED** 1956
WHERE FUNDING CAN BE GIVEN North and West Yorkshire.
WHO CAN BENEFIT Registered charities; churches; educational establishments; hospices; museums.
WHAT IS FUNDED Children and young people; church appeals; community centres; the countryside and the environment; hospices; LGBTQ+ communities; mental health; music, arts and heritage involving people in local disadvantaged communities; older people; physical and learning disabilities; schools which have a capital need related to a 'special' community-related project; social welfare; sports for disadvantaged communities.
WHAT IS NOT FUNDED Voluntary and community groups which are not a registered charity; social enterprises; CICs; appeals outside the area of benefit; individuals; applications from overseas seminars or exchange visits by individuals or groups; medical appeals of a capital or revenue nature; medical research projects; playgroups, nurseries and pre-schools which are not a charity and are not located in a disadvantaged area; restoration schemes of church roofs, spires, etc.
TYPE OF GRANT Capital costs; core/revenue costs; project funding.
RANGE OF GRANTS Mostly from £1,000 to £3,000.
SAMPLE GRANTS Sedbergh Community Centre (£7,500); Cougarmania Foundation, Hunslet Club, Kirkwood Hospice and Overgate Hospice (£5,000 each).
FINANCES *Financial year end* 05/04/2022
Income £513,500
Grants to organisations £227,200
Assets £10,720,000
TRUSTEES Martin Bethel; David Coates; Marjorie Martin; Roger Marshall; Paul Taylor; Morven Whyte; Sarah Blenkinsop; Andrew Wriglesworth; Sir George Martin Trust Company Ltd.
OTHER INFORMATION Grants of £3,000 and under totalled £189,700 and were awarded to 94 organisations.
HOW TO APPLY Visit the trust's website for details regarding the application process. Applicants should contact the Trust Manager by email or telephone, who can provide an application form.
CONTACT DETAILS Carla Marshall, Trust Manager, Harlig House, Skipton Road, Ilkley LS29 9RP *Tel.* 01943 605372 *Email* info@ sirgeorgemartintrust.org.uk *Website* www. sirgeorgemartintrust.org.uk

■ John Martin's Charity

CC NO 527473 **ESTABLISHED** 1714
WHERE FUNDING CAN BE GIVEN Evesham and surrounding villages only.
WHO CAN BENEFIT Individuals and charitable or voluntary organisations and schools benefitting the residents of Evesham.
WHAT IS FUNDED Religious support – to assist the vicars and PCCs within the town of Evesham; relief in need – to assist individuals and organisations within the town of Evesham who are in conditions of need, hardship and distress; the promotion of education – to promote education to those residing within the town of Evesham and to provide benefits to the schools and college within Evesham; health – to support people with chronic health problems and other related health issues.
TYPE OF GRANT One-off capital costs, general expenditure and project costs.
RANGE OF GRANTS Up to £50,000.
SAMPLE GRANTS Caring Hands in the Vale (£50,000); Evesham and District Mental Health Support Services (£20,000); St Richard's First School (£4,400); DIAL South Worcestershire (£2,900).
FINANCES *Financial year end* 31/03/2022
Income £711,500
Grants to organisations £265,300
Grants to individuals £267,800
Assets £28,800

TRUSTEES The Revd Mark Binney; Cyril Scorse; John Smith; Julie Westlake; John Wilson; Stuart Allerton; Valerie Butler; Philip Airdrie; Janet Osborne; Alan Booth; Sherraden Murphy.

OTHER INFORMATION Grants were broken down as follows: relief in need (£125,500); religious support (£53,800); health (£49,000); education (£37,000).

HOW TO APPLY Application forms are available on the charity's website. Applications are considered once per quarter.

CONTACT DETAILS John Daniels, Clerk to the Trustees, 16 Queens Road, Evesham, Worcestershire WR11 4JN *Tel.* 01386 765440 *Email* enquiries@johnmartins.org.uk *Website* www.johnmartins.org.uk

■ The Dan Maskell Tennis Trust

CC NO 1133589   **ESTABLISHED** 2009
WHERE FUNDING CAN BE GIVEN UK.
WHO CAN BENEFIT Individuals; disability groups and programmes; tennis clubs and associations; schools.
WHAT IS FUNDED Promotion of physical health, fitness and general well-being of people with disabilities through the sport of tennis.
WHAT IS NOT FUNDED Clothing or individual transport costs; 'luxury' items such as electronic equipment, e.g. videos; publicity, promotions or advertising; general administration; catering at tournaments and events.
TYPE OF GRANT The purchase of wheelchairs, tennis equipment and grants for coaching.
RANGE OF GRANTS Up to £1,500 for a group, club or project and £500 for an individual.
SAMPLE GRANTS A list of beneficiaries was not included in the annual report and accounts.
FINANCES *Financial year end 31/12/2021*
Income £80,900
Grants to organisations £69,200
Assets £577,500
TRUSTEES Robin Charlton; John James; Sue Wolstenholme; Noel McShane; Robert McCowen; Geraint Richards; Lesley Cundy.
OTHER INFORMATION In 2021, grants were made to 76 organisations and individuals. A financial breakdown of grants awarded was not available.
HOW TO APPLY The trustees meet at least three times a year, usually around May, July and November. Application forms are available from the trust's website and should be submitted in advance to the meeting, the exact dates of which are specified on the website. Completed application forms can be returned by post or scanned and emailed to the correspondent. It is requested that applicants provide as much information as possible and include details of the costs for each item or facility. The guidelines also note: 'before applying for assistance, you are advised to consult The Tennis Foundation and/or your local County Tennis Association.'
CONTACT DETAILS The Trustees, c/o Sport Wins, PO Box 238, Tadworth, Surrey KT20 5WT *Tel.* 01737 831707 *Email* info@ danmaskelltennistrust.org.uk *Website* www. danmaskelltennistrust.org.uk

■ Masonic Charitable Foundation

CC NO 1164703   **ESTABLISHED** 2015
WHERE FUNDING CAN BE GIVEN England and Wales.
WHO CAN BENEFIT Registered charities; research bodies; hospices (those receiving 60% or less of their funding from the NHS).
WHAT IS FUNDED Disadvantaged children and young people; isolation in later life; medical research into degenerative diseases; hospice care; disaster relief.
WHAT IS NOT FUNDED Each grants programme has its own exclusions; consult the foundation's website for details.
TYPE OF GRANT Project costs; core costs; PhD studentships.
RANGE OF GRANTS Small grants of £1,000 to £15,000; large grants of £10,000 to £60,000.
SAMPLE GRANTS Age UK (£290,000); Carers in Bedfordshire (£62,500); The Royal Leicestershire Rutland and Wycliffe Society for the Blind (£53,200); Southend Blind Welfare Organisation (£30,000); The Third Age Project (£15,000); Bedford Hospital Charity and Friends (£10,000); Headway Guernsey (£2,000); Children's Hospice South West – Little Harbour (£1,000); Clay Cross Foodbank (£250).
FINANCES *Financial year end 31/03/2022*
Income £72,920,000
Grants to organisations £11,820,000
Grants to individuals £12,590,000
Assets £416,230,000
TRUSTEES Sir Paul Williams; Antony Harvey; Michael Heenan; Christopher Head; John Boyington; Simon Duckworth; Andrew Wauchope; Howard Wilson; Clive Emerson; Alan Graham; Sinead Brophy; Dr Simon Fellerman; Stephen Robinson; David Southern; Bruce Walker.
OTHER INFORMATION The foundation was established in 2015 to bring together the previous work of four national Masonic charities: The Freemasons' Grand Charity; the Royal Masonic Trust for Girls and Boys; the Masonic Samaritan Fund; and the Royal Masonic Benevolent Institution. 'Non-Masonic' grants awarded in 2021/22 were broken down as follows: Royal Masonic School (£3.17 million); health and disability (£2.01 million); early interventions – children and families (£1.71 million); other charitable purposes (£999,000); hospices (£836,000); COVID-19 (£833,000); isolation in later life (£828,000); medical and social research programme (£519,000); The Duke of Edinburgh's Award (£300,000); disaster relief (£256,000); education and employability (£154,000); festival grants (£80,000); air ambulance and rescue services (£49,000); armed forces (£25,000); arts, culture and sports (£18,000); the environment, heritage and conservation (£13,000).
HOW TO APPLY Applications can be made through the foundation's website. Grants for medical research and disaster relief are for invited applicants only.
CONTACT DETAILS Grants Team, Freemasons' Hall, 60 Great Queen Street, London WC2B 5AZ *Tel.* 020 3146 3337 *Email* charitygrants@mcf. org.uk *Website* http://mcf.org.uk

■ Nancie Massey Charitable Trust

OSCR NO SC008977   **ESTABLISHED** 1989
WHERE FUNDING CAN BE GIVEN Scotland, particularly the City of Edinburgh.
WHO CAN BENEFIT Registered charities.
WHAT IS FUNDED Medical research and care; the arts; education; the community.
WHAT IS NOT FUNDED Individuals.
RANGE OF GRANTS Typically £2,500 to £10,000.
SAMPLE GRANTS Tenovus Scotland (£19,600); Hearts and Minds Charity (£10,000); Dunedin School (£6,000); Age Scotland and Bethany Christian Trust (£5,000).

FINANCES *Financial year end* 05/04/2022
Income £308,400
Grants to organisations £305,500
Assets £7,500,000

OTHER INFORMATION The trust made grants to 75 organisations.

HOW TO APPLY Contact the correspondent for further information.

CONTACT DETAILS The Trustees, c/o Chiene and Tait LLP, 61 Dublin Street, Edinburgh EH3 6NL

■ The Master Charitable Trust

CC NO 1139904   **ESTABLISHED** 2009

WHERE FUNDING CAN BE GIVEN UK and overseas.

WHO CAN BENEFIT Registered charities.

WHAT IS FUNDED Education; poverty; religion; health; community development; arts and culture; heritage; science; human rights; the environment; social welfare; animal welfare; the armed forces; children and young people; older people.

RANGE OF GRANTS Mostly £10,000 to £500,000.

SAMPLE GRANTS Royal Opera House Covent Garden Foundation (£2.66 million); Passage 2000 (£2 million); Forward Trust (£1.12 million); National Gallery Trust (£753,200); Mail Force Charity CIO (£500,000); Greenhouse Sports (£320,000); Action on Addiction (£287,100); Bradfield Foundation (£250,000).

FINANCES *Financial year end* 30/09/2021
Income £88,600,000
Grants to organisations £58,180,000
Assets £236,760,000

TRUSTEE Hoare Trustees.

OTHER INFORMATION Grants were awarded to 1,125 charities during the year. The 2020/21 accounts were the latest available at the time of writing (May 2023).

HOW TO APPLY Apply in writing to the correspondent. Charities and organisations are usually chosen at the donor's request.

CONTACT DETAILS Hoare Trustees, 37 Fleet Street, London EC4P 4DQ *Tel.* 020 7353 4522 *Website* www.hoaresbank.co.uk/master-charitable-trust

■ Matchroom Sport Charitable Foundation

CC NO 1167276   **ESTABLISHED** 2016

WHERE FUNDING CAN BE GIVEN UK.

WHO CAN BENEFIT Registered charities; hospices; hospitals.

WHAT IS FUNDED Sports and recreation for children and young people with disabilities or specific health conditions; health and medical; hospices and hospitals; heritage; animal welfare.

RANGE OF GRANTS Mostly between £5,000 and £20,000 with the occasional larger grant.

SAMPLE GRANTS Alexandra Park and Palace Charitable Trust (£110,000); Addenbrooke's Charitable Trust (£100,000); Haven House Children's Hospice and St Francis Hospice (£50,000 each); Royal Society for Blind Children and Strongbones Children's Charitable Trust (£20,000 each); British Disabled Angling Association, Cyclists Fighting Cancer and England and Wales Blind Golf (£10,000 each); Hopefield Animal Sanctuary and KEEN London (£5,000 each).

FINANCES *Financial year end* 30/06/2022
Income £361,700
Grants to organisations £491,500
Assets £155,000

TRUSTEES Susan Hearn; Jason Ferguson; Edward Lowy; Catherine Godding; Chloe Hearn.

HOW TO APPLY Apply in writing to the correspondent via email.

CONTACT DETAILS W. Barker, The Secretary, Mascalls, Mascalls Lane, Brentwood, Essex CM14 5LJ *Tel.* 01277 359900 *Email* mcf@matchroom.com *Website* www.matchroomsport.foundation

■ Material World Foundation

CC NO 266746   **ESTABLISHED** 1968

WHERE FUNDING CAN BE GIVEN UK; overseas.

WHO CAN BENEFIT Charitable organisations; individuals.

WHAT IS FUNDED The arts; people with disabilities; social welfare.

SAMPLE GRANTS War Child (£50,000); UNICEF (£33,300); Henley Music School (£20,000); Alexandria House (£19,200); Florence Immigrant and Refugee Rights (£18,400); Vets Aid (£7,300); Exodus Project (£7,200); Macmillan Cancer Support (£1,000).

FINANCES *Financial year end* 31/12/2021
Income £181,600
Grants to organisations £357,400
Assets £929,400

TRUSTEES Linda Arias; Leslie Boss; Dhani Harrison; Olivia Harrison; Deborah Owen; Ken Roberts.

OTHER INFORMATION The foundation was established by George Harrison in 1973 and is funded by the royalties from his album Living in the Material World.

HOW TO APPLY Contact the correspondent for further information.

CONTACT DETAILS The Trustees, c/o Shipleys, 10 Orange Street, London WC2H 7DQ *Tel.* 020 7312 0000 *Email* advice@shipleys.com *Website* www.materialworldfoundation.com

■ The Mather Family Charitable Trust

CC NO 1180415   **ESTABLISHED** 2018

WHERE FUNDING CAN BE GIVEN UK with some preference for Greater Manchester.

WHO CAN BENEFIT Registered charities; individuals.

WHAT IS FUNDED General charitable purposes.

TYPE OF GRANT One-off and recurrent.

RANGE OF GRANTS Typically £100 to £10,000.

SAMPLE GRANTS Pankhurst Trust (£42,500); East Cheshire Hospice (£20,000); Dogs for Autism (£10,000); Maggie's (£5,700); Forever Manchester (£1,200).

FINANCES *Financial year end* 05/04/2022
Income £951,500
Grants to organisations £134,000
Assets £9,220,000

TRUSTEES Trevor Mather; Suzanne Mather; Aimee Mather; Harry Mather; Kara Mather.

HOW TO APPLY Apply in writing to the correspondent.

CONTACT DETAILS The Trustees, c/o Brightside Planning, Atlas 3, St George's Square, Bolton BL1 2HB *Tel.* 0330 223 3833 *Email* issey@gobrightside.co.uk

■ Mathew Trust

OSCR NO SC016284   **ESTABLISHED** 1936

WHERE FUNDING CAN BE GIVEN City of Dundee; Angus; Perth and Kinross; Fife.

WHO CAN BENEFIT Registered charities; social enterprises; CICs; schools and colleges;

universities; individuals; local authorities; museums.

WHAT IS FUNDED Adult education; vocational and professional training; employment; social welfare.

TYPE OF GRANT Project funding.

RANGE OF GRANTS Mostly between £10,000 and £15,000 with the occasional smaller or larger grant.

SAMPLE GRANTS The Unicorn (£25,000); Helm Training (£20,000); Abertay University, Dundee Museum of Transport and the Venture Trust (£15,000 each); Alexander Community Development and Showcase the Street (£12,500 each); Launch It, Scottish Crannog Centre and Women's Business Station 10 by 30 (£10,000 each); Glenesk Folk Museum and Uppertunity (£5,000 each); Dundee Carers Centre (£3,700).

FINANCES *Financial year end 30/04/2022*
Income £320,000
Grants to organisations £196,100
Grants to individuals £2,000
Assets £10,790,000

OTHER INFORMATION In 2021/22, two individuals were awarded grants.

HOW TO APPLY Apply in writing to the correspondent.

CONTACT DETAILS The Trustees, c/o Henderson Loggie, The Vision Building, 20 Greenmarket, Dundee DD1 4QB *Tel.* 01382 200055

■ The Matliwala Family Charitable Trust

CC NO 1012756   **ESTABLISHED** 1992

WHERE FUNDING CAN BE GIVEN UK and India.

WHO CAN BENEFIT Charitable organisations.

WHAT IS FUNDED The advancement of education for pupils at Matliwala School of Baruch in Gujarat, India; the advancement of the Islamic religion; the relief of sickness and poverty; the advancement of education in the UK.

SAMPLE GRANTS A list of beneficiaries was not included in the annual report and accounts.

FINANCES *Financial year end 24/03/2022*
Income £547,000
Grants to organisations £896,500
Grants to individuals £10,000
Assets £7,590,000

TRUSTEE The Matliwala Foundation.

OTHER INFORMATION During the year, £844,800 was awarded in the UK and £61,600 was awarded overseas.

HOW TO APPLY Applications may be made in writing to the correspondent. The trustees meet monthly to assess grant applications and approve awards. The annual report for 2022 states: 'The charity welcomes applications for grants from all quarters and these are assessed by the trustees on their individual merits. Awards are given according to the individual needs of the applicant, depending on the funds available.'

CONTACT DETAILS Ayyub Bux, Trustee, Barton Hall, Garstang Road, Broughton, Preston, Lancashire PR3 5BT *Tel.* 01772 709090 *Email* info@mam.uk

■ Maudsley Charity

CC NO 1175877   **ESTABLISHED** 1996

WHERE FUNDING CAN BE GIVEN South London.

WHO CAN BENEFIT Registered charities; unregistered charities; CICs; social enterprises; schools; universities; hospitals; hospices; religious bodies/institutions; local authorities.

WHAT IS FUNDED Mental health projects across south London.

TYPE OF GRANT Project funding.

SAMPLE GRANTS South London and Maudsley NHS Foundation Trust (£10.8 million in 20 grants); Bethlem Art and History Collections Trust (£413,000); Bethlem Gallery Projects Ltd (£293,000); Football Beyond Borders and Lewisham and Southwark Mind (£30,000 each); Croydon Voluntary Action (£29,000); King's College London (£16,000); InHealth Associates (£3,000).

FINANCES *Financial year end 31/03/2022*
Income £9,700,000
Grants to organisations £11,760,000
Assets £171,900,000

TRUSTEES Nicola Byrne; Trevor Goode; Nigel Keen; Catherine Lee; David Bradley; Beatrice Butsana-Sita; Daniel Acquah; Josephine Namusisi-Riley; Peter Baffoe; Frances Corner.

OTHER INFORMATION Grants were awarded to 34 organisations during 2021/22.

HOW TO APPLY See the charity's website for the latest information on open funding programmes.

CONTACT DETAILS Grants Team, ORTUS Centre, 82–96 Grove Lane, London SE5 8SN *Tel.* 020 3696 9760 *Email* Rebecca.gray@maudsleycharity.org *Website* https://maudsleycharity.org

■ The Violet Mauray Charitable Trust

CC NO 1001716   **ESTABLISHED** 1990

WHERE FUNDING CAN BE GIVEN UK.

WHO CAN BENEFIT Registered charities.

WHAT IS FUNDED General charitable purposes, including health and the Jewish faith and community.

TYPE OF GRANT One-off.

RANGE OF GRANTS Under £15,000.

SAMPLE GRANTS Disasters Emergency Committee Ukraine Appeal (£15,000); CWPLUS and Keech Hospice Care (£12,000 each); Against Malaria Foundation and WaterAid (£6,000 each); Childhood Trust (£5,000); RNLI and UNICEF (£2,000 each).

FINANCES *Financial year end 05/04/2022*
Income £53,800
Grants to organisations £88,000
Assets £2,620,000

TRUSTEES Paul Stephany; Lisa Curtis; Samuel Karlin; Emma Ross.

OTHER INFORMATION Grants were made to 15 organisations during 2022.

HOW TO APPLY Apply in writing to the correspondent. The trustees meet regularly to consider applications. Grants are made on an ad hoc basis.

CONTACT DETAILS The Trustees, PO Box 76480, London N10 9FB *Tel.* 07841 048997 *Email* violetmauraytrust@gmail.com

■ The Theodore Maxxy Charitable Trust

CC NO 1188372   **ESTABLISHED** 2020

WHERE FUNDING CAN BE GIVEN England and Wales.

WHO CAN BENEFIT Charitable organisations.

WHAT IS FUNDED General charitable purposes.

SAMPLE GRANTS A list of beneficiaries was not included in the annual report and accounts.

FINANCES *Financial year end* 05/04/2022
Income £240,100
Grants to organisations £151,800
Assets £7,570,000
TRUSTEES Patricia Anne Bell; Charlotte Keating.
HOW TO APPLY Apply in writing to the correspondent.
CONTACT DETAILS Charlotte Keating, Trustee, c/o Prosperity Law LLP, Vantage Point, 4 Hardman Street, Manchester M3 3HF *Tel.* 0161 464 7595 *Email* charlottek@prosperitylaw.com

■ Mayfair Charities Ltd

CC NO 255281   **ESTABLISHED** 1968
WHERE FUNDING CAN BE GIVEN UK and overseas (particularly Israel).
WHO CAN BENEFIT Registered charities benefitting the Orthodox Jewish community; educational institutions; religious organisations.
WHAT IS FUNDED The Orthodox Jewish faith and community.
TYPE OF GRANT One-off awards for capital and running costs.
SAMPLE GRANTS Beth Jacob Grammar School for Girls Ltd (£1.6 million); Mifal Hachesed Vehatzedokoh (£60,000); The Rehabilitation Trust (£32,000); The Friends of the Bobover Yeshivah and Friends of Mercaz Hatorah Belz Macnivka (£29,000 each); Edupoor Ltd (£20,000).
FINANCES *Financial year end* 31/03/2022
Income £5,320,000
Grants to organisations £3,180,000
Assets £88,300
TRUSTEES D. Davis; Solomon Freshwater; Benzion Freshwater; Richard Fischer.
OTHER INFORMATION Grants were made in the following categories: the advancement of religion and education (£2.95 million) and the relief of poverty (£226,000).
HOW TO APPLY Apply in writing to the correspondent.
CONTACT DETAILS The Trustees, Freshwater Group of Companies, Freshwater House, 158–162 Shaftesbury Avenue, London WC2H 8HR *Tel.* 020 7836 1555

■ The Mayfield Valley Arts Trust

CC NO 327665   **ESTABLISHED** 1987
WHERE FUNDING CAN BE GIVEN UK, with a special preference for Yorkshire.
WHO CAN BENEFIT Charitable organisations; schools.
WHAT IS FUNDED Young artists; music education; the arts and music.
WHAT IS NOT FUNDED The education of individual students; the purchase of musical instruments for individuals, schools or organisations; capital appeals.
TYPE OF GRANT Recurrent.
RANGE OF GRANTS £10,000 to £30,000.
SAMPLE GRANTS Music in the Round (£29,800); Live Music Now (£21,000); York Early Music Foundation (£14,700); IMS Prussia Cove (£13,300); Leeds Leider (£7,500).
FINANCES *Financial year end* 05/04/2022
Income £123,600
Grants to organisations £86,300
Assets £2,310,000
TRUSTEES David Brown; James Thornton; David Whelton; Sarah Derbyshire; James Williams.
OTHER INFORMATION Grants were awarded to five organisations during 2021/22.
HOW TO APPLY Application forms can be found on the trust's website. The trustees meet once a year, usually in autumn. Applications should be

received at least three months in advance. See the trust's website for current application dates.
CONTACT DETAILS The Trustees, 14 Abbots Drive, Abbotswood, Ballasalla, Isle of Man IM9 3EB *Tel.* 0114 266 7141 *Email* jthornton@mayfieldartstrust.org.uk *Website* www.mayfieldartstrust.org.uk

■ Mayheights Ltd

CC NO 1112291   **ESTABLISHED** 2005
WHERE FUNDING CAN BE GIVEN Barnet, Hackney and Israel.
WHO CAN BENEFIT Registered charities; voluntary organisations; schools.
WHAT IS FUNDED The advancement of the Orthodox Jewish religion; Jewish education; the relief of poverty; medical purposes.
RANGE OF GRANTS Up to £355,000.
SAMPLE GRANTS Congregation Yetev Lev Synagogue (£355,000); Hichal Ahron (£172,000); Congregation Min (£95,000); The Kolel Ltd (£60,000); Rookwood Foundation (£50,000); Yeitev Lev Eretz Israel Ltd (£40,200).
FINANCES *Financial year end* 31/03/2022
Income £1,850,000
Grants to organisations £1,790,000
Assets £18,470,000
TRUSTEES Menashe Eichenstein; Rachel Low; Oscar Low; Chaim Klein.
OTHER INFORMATION Grants for the year were broken down into the following categories: advancement of religion (£828,700); religious education (£377,100); relief of poverty (£430,700); general purposes (£88,000); social welfare (£68,800). Grants of £30,000 or less totalled £538,500.
HOW TO APPLY Apply in writing to the correspondent. The charity's 2021/22 accounts note that while not actively inviting applications, the trustees consider all requests received.
CONTACT DETAILS The Trustees, 36 Gilda Crescent, London N16 6JP *Tel.* 020 8806 1234

■ Mazars Charitable Trust

CC NO 1150459   **ESTABLISHED** 2012
WHERE FUNDING CAN BE GIVEN UK.
WHO CAN BENEFIT Registered charities; voluntary organisations; hospices; colleges and schools.
WHAT IS FUNDED General charitable purposes including: mental health; research and support for physical health conditions; the arts; palliative care and hospices; food banks; sport.
RANGE OF GRANTS Up to £25,000.
SAMPLE GRANTS A list of beneficiaries was not included in the annual report and accounts. Previous beneficiaries have included: Friends of Asha (£25,000); Erskine Hospital Ltd (£14,400); Muntada Aid (£10,000); King's Arms Project Bedford (£9,000); Burning Nights CRPS Support (£5,000); The RAF Association (£2,000).
FINANCES *Financial year end* 31/03/2022
Income £657,200
Grants to organisations £501,600
Assets £628,600
TRUSTEES Tracey Marshall; Lesley Fox; Philip Verity; Kim Hurst; Janine Fox; Jonathan Bennett.
OTHER INFORMATION Grants were broken down as follows: major grants (£289,600); office grants (£109,500); emergency grants (£67,500); charity partner grants (£35,000).
HOW TO APPLY The trustees do not respond to unsolicited applications. All nominations for grants have to be proposed by staff members of

Mazars LLP and no grant applications should be submitted directly to the trust.

CONTACT DETAILS The Trustees, Mazars LLP, Merck House, Seldown Lane, Poole, Dorset BH15 1TW *Tel.* 07756 323888 *Email* mazarscharitabletrust@gmail.com

....

■ MBNA General Foundation

CC NO 1065515 **ESTABLISHED** 1997
WHERE FUNDING CAN BE GIVEN Within a 30-mile radius of the company's Chester campus.
WHO CAN BENEFIT Charities; community groups; schools.
WHAT IS FUNDED General charitable purposes including the following: children and young people; older people; people with disabilities; schools.
RANGE OF GRANTS Between £500 and £100,000.
SAMPLE GRANTS Poverty Truth Commission Event (£100,000); Chester FC Community Trust (£32,500); Chester Community Fund Brighter Future (£25,000); Northgate Church Trust (£10,000); Pontblyddyn Cricket Club (£500).
FINANCES *Financial year end* 31/12/2021
Income £68,100
Grants to organisations £291,700
Assets £963,200
TRUSTEES Ian O'Doherty; Mr Stables; Sean Humphreys; Elyn Corfield; Mark Elliott.
HOW TO APPLY Apply in writing to the correspondent. The foundation considers both internal requests (those considered to have a connection to an employee of MBNA Ltd or a historic relationship/connection to MBNA Ltd) and external requests (no connection to MBNA Ltd) for funding.
CONTACT DETAILS The Trustees, Chester Business Park, Chester CH4 9FB *Tel.* 07719 382421 *Email* mbnageneralfoundation@lloydsbanking. com

....

■ The Robert McAlpine Foundation

CC NO 226646 **ESTABLISHED** 1963
WHERE FUNDING CAN BE GIVEN UK.
WHO CAN BENEFIT Registered charities; schools; hospices; hospitals.
WHAT IS FUNDED General charitable purposes; medical research; social welfare; children with disabilities; older people; young people.
WHAT IS NOT FUNDED Fundraising activities.
TYPE OF GRANT Capital costs; running costs; project funding; research.
RANGE OF GRANTS £5,000 to £10,000.
SAMPLE GRANTS A list of beneficiaries was not included in the annual report and accounts.
FINANCES *Financial year end* 31/03/2022
Income £819,400
Grants to organisations £625,800
Assets £22,150,000
TRUSTEES Adrian McAlpine; The Hon. David McAlpine; Cullum McAlpine; Gavin McAlpine.
HOW TO APPLY Apply in writing or via email to the correspondent. Appeals should be no more than two A4 pages and include a copy of your most recent accounts. Visit the foundation's website for details on what to include. The trustees meet annually in November to approve grants – applications must be received no later than 31 August to be considered in the next meeting. The foundation is unable to accept any appeal requests by telephone.

CONTACT DETAILS Appeals Manager, Eaton Court, Maylands Avenue, Hemel Hempstead, Hertfordshire HP2 7TR *Tel.* 0333 566 2069 *Email* foundation@srm.com *Website* www. robertmcalpinefoundation.org

....

■ The McCarthy Stone Foundation

CC NO 1191504
WHERE FUNDING CAN BE GIVEN UK.
WHO CAN BENEFIT Small charities and community groups.
WHAT IS FUNDED Older people.
TYPE OF GRANT Core costs.
RANGE OF GRANTS Up to £6,000.
SAMPLE GRANTS British Red Cross (£25,000); Medway Volunteer Centre (£5,000); Greener Peebles (£4,000); Journey Enterprises (£3,000); Age Concern Bentham (£2,700).
FINANCES *Financial year end* 31/10/2022
Income £342,200
Grants to organisations £215,100
Assets £86,300
TRUSTEES John Tonkiss; Elizabeth Marsh; Dr Kimberley Smith; Sarah Allport; Martin Edwards; Paul Teverson; Paula Jordan.
OTHER INFORMATION The foundation made 109 grants during the year.
HOW TO APPLY Applications can be made through the foundation's website.
CONTACT DETAILS The Trustees, 4th Floor, 100 Holdenhurst Road, Bournemouth, Dorset BH8 8AQ *Email* use the contact form on the website *Website* https:// mccarthyandstonefoundation.org

....

■ Gemma and Chris McGough Charitable Foundation CIO

CC NO 1173373 **ESTABLISHED** 2017
WHERE FUNDING CAN BE GIVEN Worldwide.
WHO CAN BENEFIT Registered charities.
WHAT IS FUNDED The environment; child poverty; education; disaster relief; human rights.
SAMPLE GRANTS Pipal Tree Bhatighadi (£100,000); FSC Nederlands (£50,000).
FINANCES *Financial year end* 30/06/2022
Income £3,200
Grants to organisations £159,400
Assets £700,500
TRUSTEES Gemma McGough; Clare MacBeth; Jennifer Kerr.
OTHER INFORMATION The foundation's website states: 'Around 80% of our funding is reserved for environmental causes, with the remaining 20% going to charities supporting children and their families and disaster relief.'
HOW TO APPLY Apply in writing to the correspondent. Full details on what should be included in an application can be found on the foundation's website.
CONTACT DETAILS Gemma McGough, Trustee, The Rosery, Ilmer, Princes Risborough, Buckinghamshire HP27 9QZ *Email* use the contact form on the website *Website* www. mcgoughfoundation.org

■ D. D. McPhail Charitable Settlement

CC NO 267588 **ESTABLISHED** 1973

WHERE FUNDING CAN BE GIVEN UK.

WHO CAN BENEFIT Mainly small and medium-sized registered charities; hospices; educational institutions and research centres.

WHAT IS FUNDED Medical research; people with disabilities, particularly children; older people.

TYPE OF GRANT Research funding; project funding.

RANGE OF GRANTS Small grants: up to £4,000; large grants: typically up to £100,000.

SAMPLE GRANTS Spitalfields Crypt Trust (£125,000); Milton Keynes Community Foundation (£25,000); The Lewy Body Society (£4,000); UK Community Foundations (£3,000); Clacton Foodbank (£2,000); Child Autism UK (£1,000).

FINANCES *Financial year end* 05/04/2022
Income £129,100
Grants to organisations £372,200
Assets £10,910,000

TRUSTEES Mary Meeks; Olivia Hancock; George Courcy-Wheeler; Helene Jelman; Jane Brake; Edward Coley; Ben Smith.

OTHER INFORMATION In 2021/22, large grants totalled £372,200 and small grants totalled £31,000.

HOW TO APPLY The 2021/22 annual report states the following: 'Trustees identify potential projects for assessment by the Executive Director. The Trust makes no commitment to respond to unsolicited applications.'

CONTACT DETAILS Katharine Moss, Executive Director, PO Box 78190, Wimbledon, London SW19 9QL *Tel.* 07523 440550 *Email* director.ddmcphail@gmail.com *Website* www.ddmcphailcharitablesettlement.co.uk

■ Medical Research Foundation

CC NO 1138223 **ESTABLISHED** 2011

WHERE FUNDING CAN BE GIVEN UK; Africa.

WHO CAN BENEFIT Universities; research institutions.

WHAT IS FUNDED Medical research.

TYPE OF GRANT Research grants; infrastructure and equipment grants; fellowships and studentships; skill-sharing and collaborations; dissemination of research results.

RANGE OF GRANTS Up to £1 million.

SAMPLE GRANTS University of Copenhagen (£45,000); Institute of Hygiene and Tropical Medicine at NOVA University Lisbon (£36,000); University of Oxford (£27,000); Usmanu Danfodiyo University, Sokoto (£22,000); Noguchi Institute for Medical Research at the University of Ghana (£12,000); University of Kabianga (£4,000); Kenya Medical Research Institute (£3,000).

FINANCES *Financial year end* 31/03/2022
Income £5,710,000
Grants to organisations £5,550,000
Assets £69,680,000

TRUSTEES Prof. Nicholas Lemoine; Prof. Daniel Altmann; Susan Wilkinson; Dr Hans Haitchi; Prof. Patricia Kingori; Kristen Gallagher; Prof. Rosalind Smyth; Prof. Richard Coward; Jonathan Beck.

OTHER INFORMATION In 2021/22, grants were awarded to 41 institutions.

HOW TO APPLY Applications can be made via the foundation's website, where details of open programmes and application deadlines can also be found.

CONTACT DETAILS The Trustees, 99 Charterhouse Street, London EC1M 6HR *Tel.* 020 7250 8216 *Email* research@medicalresearchfoundation.org.uk *Website* www.medicalresearchfoundation.org.uk

■ Medical Research Scotland

OSCR NO SC014959 **ESTABLISHED** 1953

WHERE FUNDING CAN BE GIVEN Scotland.

WHO CAN BENEFIT Universities; research institutions.

WHAT IS FUNDED Medical research.

TYPE OF GRANT PhD studentships; undergraduate scholarships; fellowships.

SAMPLE GRANTS University of Edinburgh (£338,300 in 17 grants); University of Strathclyde (£88,500 in 3 grants); Heriot-Watt University (£86,400 in 3 grants); University of Aberdeen (£62,900 in 2 grants); University of Dundee (£62,700 in 2 grants); Glasgow Caledonian University (£31,700); University of St Andrews (£14,000); University of Glasgow (£750).

FINANCES *Financial year end* 31/03/2022
Income £1,810,000
Grants to organisations £2,040,000
Assets £46,890,000

TRUSTEES Prof. Heather Wallace; Linda Duncan; Alasdair Gill; Fiona Gillespie; Dr Michael Roberts; Barry Rose; Prof. Martin Denvir.

HOW TO APPLY Detailed information regarding the charity's grant programmes, guidance notes, deadlines for applications and more is available from the charity's website.

CONTACT DETAILS The Trustees, c/o Turcan Connell, Princes Exchange, 1 Earl Grey Street, Edinburgh EH3 9EE *Tel.* 0131 659 8800 *Email* enquiries@medicalresearchscotland.org.uk or use the contact form on the website *Website* www.medicalresearchscotland.org.uk

■ The Medicash Foundation

CC NO 257636

WHERE FUNDING CAN BE GIVEN The North West, Derbyshire and North Wales.

WHO CAN BENEFIT NHS and health-related charities; children's charities; educational organisations.

WHAT IS FUNDED Health and well-being.

SAMPLE GRANTS Northern Vision (£17,500); St Helens Christian Life Centre (£10,000); The Hope Centre (£7,500); Compassionate Friends (£6,000); Roy Castle Lung Cancer Foundation and Voice for Change Domestic Violence Support (£5,000 each); Henshaws Society for Blind People (£2,000); Litherland High School (£1,000); Radio City Cash for Kids (£480).

FINANCES *Financial year end* 31/12/2021
Income £924,900
Grants to organisations £371,900
Assets £2,030,000

TRUSTEE Medicash Health Benefits Ltd.

HOW TO APPLY Application forms can be downloaded from the foundation's website.

CONTACT DETAILS Linda Traynor, Medicash Ltd, 1 Derby Square, Liverpool L2 1AB *Tel.* 0151 702 0334 *Email* linda.traynor@medicash.org *Website* www.medicash.org/charity

■ The Medlock Charitable Trust

cc no 326927 **established** 1985

where funding can be given UK with a strong preference for Somerset and Lincolnshire.

who can benefit Registered charities, preferably smaller charities; educational establishments; local community groups.

what is funded Education; health and social care; housing; sports and recreation; arts and culture; the environment and conservation; community services; employment.

what is not funded Individuals; animal charities; competitions; events; educational institutions where only a privileged elite will benefit.

type of grant Project funding.

range of grants Generally from £5,000 to £15,000.

sample grants St John Ambulance (£1 million); Access Sport (£90,000); Turn to Starboard (£30,000); Centrepoint Outreach (£25,000); Bath Recreation Ltd (£10,000).

finances *Financial year end 31/07/2022*
Income £1,530,000
Grants to organisations £3,880,000
Assets £35,550,000

trustees Jacqueline Medlock; David Medlock; Mark Goodman; Peter Medlock; Steven Medlock.

other information Grants of under £25,000 totalled £1.51 million.

how to apply Apply through the online application form available on the trust's website.

contact details The Trustees, St George's Lodge, 33 Oldfield Road, Bath, Somerset BA2 3NE *Tel.* 01225 946226 *Email* office@medlockcharitabletrust.org *Website* https://medlockcharitabletrust.org

■ The Meikle Foundation

oscr no SC009842 **established** 1972

where funding can be given Scotland, with a preference for the Fife and Aberdeen areas.

who can benefit Predominately Scottish charities or charities with a Scottish connection.

what is funded General charitable purposes, particularly children and young people, older people, medical causes and culture.

what is not funded Individuals.

range of grants Generally up to £2,000.

sample grants RNLI (£4,000); Chest Heart, Mary's Meals and Stroke Scotland (£3,000 each); Scottish Mountain Rescue and Woodland Trust (£2,000 each); Blood Bikes Scotland, Care for Carers, Whale and Dolphin Conservation Programme (£1,000 each).

finances *Financial year end 05/04/2022*
Income £246,300
Grants to organisations £326,000
Assets £10,630,000

other information The foundation has been renamed from the Martin Connell Charitable Trust to The Meikle Foundation to reflect the family name of the four sisters who established it in 1973.

how to apply Contact the foundation's administrator for information on the application process. The trustees meet twice a year to consider appeals.

contact details Sandra Graham, Administrator, Shepherd and Wedderburn LLP, 1 West Regent Street, Glasgow G2 1RW *Tel.* 0141 566 7268 *Email* Sandra.MGraham@shepwedd.com *Website* www.themeiklefoundation.com

■ Melodor Ltd

cc no 260972 **established** 1970

where funding can be given UK and overseas.

who can benefit Orthodox Jewish institutions; Jewish educational institutions and charities.

what is funded General charitable purposes, especially education and religion, with a focus on the Orthodox Jewish faith and community; the relief of poverty; health.

range of grants Up to £52,000.

sample grants Machzikei Hadass (£52,500); Zorea (£20,000); Chasdei Yoel (£17,500); Bederech Kovod (£6,800); Cong Yetev Lev and Keser Torah (£5,000 each).

finances *Financial year end 31/03/2022*
Income £86,900
Grants to organisations £149,300
Assets £428,600

trustees Janet Bleier; Rebecca Delange; Miriam Friedlander; Esther Henry; Pesha Kohn; Pinchas Neumann; Maurice Neumann; Eli Neumann; Henry Neumann; Rivka Ollech; Rivka Rabinowitz; Yocheved Weiss; Hyman Weiss; Philip Weiss; Zisel Weiss.

other information Only grants of over £5,000 were listed as beneficiaries. Grants of under £5,000 totalled £19,900 in 2022.

how to apply Apply in writing to the correspondent. The charity's annual report for 2021/22 states: 'The governors receive many applications for grants, mainly by mail, but also verbally. Each application is considered against the criteria established by the charity. Although the charity does not advertise, it is well known within its community and there are many requests received for grants.'

contact details H. Neumann, Company Secretary, 10 Cubley Road, Salford, Greater Manchester M7 4GN *Tel.* 0161 720 6188

■ The Melow Charitable Trust

cc no 275454 **established** 1978

where funding can be given UK and overseas.

who can benefit Mainly Jewish charities.

what is funded The Jewish faith and community; general charitable purposes.

range of grants Up to £200,000, with an average of £82,000.

sample grants Congregation Supporters of Torah and Tchabe Kollel Ltd (£200,000 each); Friends of Beis Sorah Schneirer (£100,000); Start Upright (£83,000); The Rehabilitation Trust (£50,000); Inspirations (£150).

finances *Financial year end 31/12/2021*
Income £997,800
Grants to organisations £1,630,000
Assets £11,610,000

trustees Miriam Spitz; Ester Weiser.

other information Grants of under £30,000 totalled £61,000.

how to apply Apply in writing to the correspondent.

contact details The Trustees, 21 Warwick Grove, London E5 9HX *Tel.* 020 8806 1549

■ Menuchar Ltd

cc no 262782 **established** 1971

where funding can be given UK.

who can benefit Jewish organisations and religious establishments.

what is funded The advancement of religion in accordance with the Orthodox Jewish faith and the relief of people in need.

SAMPLE GRANTS A list of beneficiaries was not available.

FINANCES *Financial year end 31/03/2022*
Income £0
Grants to organisations £93,100

TRUSTEES Ruth Bude; Raphael Bude.

OTHER INFORMATION Full accounts were not available to view on the Charity Commission's website due to the charity's low income. We have therefore estimated the grant total based on the charity's total expenditure.

HOW TO APPLY Apply in writing to the correspondent.

CONTACT DETAILS Helena Bude, Secretary, Barry Flack and Co. Ltd, The Brentano Suite, Prospect House, 2 Athenaeum Road, London N20 9AE *Tel.* 020 8369 5170

....

■ Mercaz Torah Vechesed Ltd

CC NO 1109212   **ESTABLISHED** 2005

WHERE FUNDING CAN BE GIVEN Worldwide, with a preference for Barnet, Hackney and Israel.

WHO CAN BENEFIT Charitable organisations; individuals.

WHAT IS FUNDED The advancement of the Orthodox Jewish faith, Orthodox Jewish religious education and the relief of poverty and illness among members of the Orthodox Jewish community.

RANGE OF GRANTS £50,000 to £400,000.

SAMPLE GRANTS Ohr Haganuz Maseh Rokeach (£399,000); Adnei Hakodesh (£388,100); Parshat Mordchai (£306,500).

FINANCES *Financial year end 31/01/2022*
Income £1,250,000
Grants to organisations £1,220,000
Assets £146,800

TRUSTEES Joseph Ostreicher; Mordche Rand.

OTHER INFORMATION There were no grants made to individuals directly in this financial year. Grants of less than £50,000 amounted to £129,900.

HOW TO APPLY Apply in writing to the correspondent.

CONTACT DETAILS Joseph Ostreicher, Trustee, 28 Braydon Road, London N16 6QB *Tel.* 020 8880 5366 *Email* umarpeh@gmail.com

....

■ The Brian Mercer Charitable Trust

CC NO 1076925   **ESTABLISHED** 1999

WHERE FUNDING CAN BE GIVEN UK, Blackburn and overseas.

WHO CAN BENEFIT UK-registered charities.

WHAT IS FUNDED Art in the North West; causes local to Blackburn; health and welfare (UK and overseas).

WHAT IS NOT FUNDED Individuals; medical research projects; interventions that discriminate on gender, religion, sexual orientation, disability, race, colour or ethnicity; UK initiatives for specific local areas other than Blackburn, Lancashire.

TYPE OF GRANT Project funding.

SAMPLE GRANTS Médecins Sans Frontières (£300,000); Against Malaria Foundation (£150,000); Blackburn with Darwen Borough Council (£120,000); Blackburn Youth Zone (£75,000); Legs4Africa (£30,000); Blackburn Food Bank (£20,000); Intercare (£10,000); Chifundo UK (£2,000).

FINANCES *Financial year end 05/04/2022*
Income £1,320,000
Grants to organisations £918,200
Assets £38,010,000

TRUSTEES Christine Clancy; Mary Clitheroe; Roger Duckworth; Kenneth Merrill.

OTHER INFORMATION Within the broad objectives of the charity, grant-making is focused on the following areas: the prevention and relief of human suffering (80%), arts in the North West (10%) and causes local to Blackburn (10%).

HOW TO APPLY Application forms and deadlines can be found on the trust's website. At the time of writing (April 2023) the trust's website stated: 'We regret that due to an unprecedented number of current applications, no further grant requests for Prevention and Relief of Human Suffering are being accepted. Grants for this category will be made on an invitation only basis.'

CONTACT DETAILS The Trustees, c/o Beever and Struthers, Central Buildings, Richmond Terrace, Blackburn BB1 7AP *Tel.* 01254 686600 *Email* info@brianmercertrust.org *Website* www.brianmercertrust.org

....

■ The Mercers Charitable Foundation

CC NO 326340   **ESTABLISHED** 1982

WHERE FUNDING CAN BE GIVEN London; County Durham; Tyne and Wear; Northumberland; Tees Valley; Norfolk; Lincolnshire.

WHO CAN BENEFIT Registered charities; charities exempt from registration; churches.

WHAT IS FUNDED Disadvantaged communities; social welfare; refugees; homelessness; older people; disadvantaged young people; education; literacy; families; carers.

TYPE OF GRANT Core costs; project funding; salaries.

SAMPLE GRANTS Brentford Football Club Community Sports Trust (£110,000); College of Richard Collyer (£50,000); Almshouse Association (£15,000); Homelink Day Respite Care (£10,000); Lilian Baylis School (£1,000).

FINANCES *Financial year end 31/03/2022*
Income £6,730,000
Grants to organisations £2,610,000
Assets £21,940,000

TRUSTEE The Mercers' Company.

OTHER INFORMATION Grants were broken down as follows: young people and education (£1.6 million); communities and churches (£497,000); older people and housing (£417,000).

HOW TO APPLY Applications can be made via the foundation's website.

CONTACT DETAILS The Trustees, The Mercers' Company, 6 Frederick's Place, London EC2R 8AB *Tel.* 020 7776 7200 *Email* use the contact form on the website *Website* www.mercers.co.uk/philanthropy

....

■ Merchant Navy Welfare Board

CC NO 212799/SC039669 **ESTABLISHED** 1962

WHERE FUNDING CAN BE GIVEN UK and its overseas territories.

WHO CAN BENEFIT Charitable organisations related to sailors and seafarers. Grants are only made to the charity's constituent organisations.

WHAT IS FUNDED The welfare of merchant seafarers, fishermen and their dependants.

WHAT IS NOT FUNDED Individuals.

TYPE OF GRANT Capital costs; start-up costs.

RANGE OF GRANTS Up to £30,000.

SAMPLE GRANTS Nautilus Welfare Fund (£30,000); Sailors' Children's Society (£20,000); Marine Society and Sea Cadets (£10,000); Mission to

Seafarers – Newport (£5,000); Mediterranean Mission to Seafarers (£1,300); Lighthouse Seafarers Mission (£1,100); Fawley Seafarers' Centre (£950); Stella Maris (£80).

FINANCES *Financial year end* 31/12/2021
Income £416,700
Grants to organisations £87,500
Assets £15,460,000

TRUSTEES Mark Dickinson; Graham Lane; Timothy Springett; Andrew Cassels; Mark Carden; Alison Godfrey; David Appleton; Justin Osmond; Darren Procter; Adrian Hodgson; Richard Ballantyne; Brian Boxall-Hunt; Louise Sara.

HOW TO APPLY Applications can be made through the application portal on the charity's website.

CONTACT DETAILS The Trustees, 8 Cumberland Place, Southampton, Hampshire SO15 2BH *Tel.* 023 8033 7799 *Email* grants@mnwb.org. uk *Website* www.mnwb.org

....

■ The Merchant Taylors' Foundation

CC NO 1161568
WHERE FUNDING CAN BE GIVEN Lewisham; Hackney; Southwark; Tower Hamlets; UK.
WHO CAN BENEFIT Charities and community organisations.
WHAT IS FUNDED Social welfare in Lewisham, Hackney, Southwark and Tower Hamlets; education throughout the UK.
RANGE OF GRANTS Mostly up to £30,000.
SAMPLE GRANTS St Saviour's and St Olave's School (£133,400); Disasters Emergency Committee – Ukraine Appeal (£110,000); Merchant Taylors' Oxfordshire Academy Trust (£86,000); United St Saviour's Charity (£38,700); Merchant Taylors' School, Crosby (£16,600); Pembroke College (£10,000); Fine Cell Work (£5,000); Acheinu Cancer Support (£500).
FINANCES *Financial year end* 31/07/2022
Income £1,700,000
Grants to organisations £970,400
Assets £16,940,000
TRUSTEES Christopher Keville; Richard Nourse; Lissa Gillott; Peregrine Massey; Ralph Godsall; David Jackson; Richard Sullivan; Sarah Morgan; Rupert Bull.
OTHER INFORMATION Merchant Taylors' defines disadvantage as any form of limiting factor that prevents an individual from reaching their full potential or enjoying a fulfilled life. Grants have previously been made to organisations tackling housing insecurity, prisoners' rehabilitation, food poverty, domestic abuse, or which support mental and physical health. Educational support has previously included transformational bursaries and well-being initiatives in schools, community-based music-making and training programmes for ex-offenders.
HOW TO APPLY Apply via the charity's website.
CONTACT DETAILS The Trustees, Merchant Taylors' Hall, 30 Threadneedle Street, London EC2R 8JB *Tel.* 020 4511 6285 *Email* charities@merchant-taylors.co.uk *Website* www.merchant-taylors.co.uk/philanthropy/foundation

....

■ The Merchant Venturers Charity

CC NO 264302   **ESTABLISHED** 1972
WHERE FUNDING CAN BE GIVEN Greater Bristol area.
WHO CAN BENEFIT Local and regional charitable organisations; local branches of national organisations.

WHAT IS FUNDED Social welfare; children and young people; education; the environment; social enterprise; health care; culture and the arts; projects that will benefit Greater Bristol and its economic development.
WHAT IS NOT FUNDED Individuals; political activities; the promotion of religious beliefs; animal welfare; art or sports projects with no community or charitable element; medical research, equipment or treatment; statutory organisations or the direct replacement of statutory funding; retrospective costs; activities that are intended to raise funds for other organisations. Grants are unlikely to be made towards the cost of an existing salaried position.
TYPE OF GRANT Capital equipment or ongoing revenue costs.
RANGE OF GRANTS Generally between £500 and £5,000.
SAMPLE GRANTS Royal West of England Academy (£50,000); Black South West Network (£25,000); Collegiate School (£14,700); Hartcliffe and Withywood Community Partnership (£13,000); Bristol Future Talent Partnership (£10,000); The Art, Play and Environment Project, Genesis Trust Bath and Victoria Park Action Group (£5,000 each).
FINANCES *Financial year end* 31/12/2021
Income £407,300
Grants to organisations £281,300
Assets £8,440,000
TRUSTEE SMV Trustee Company Ltd.
OTHER INFORMATION In 2021, grants were distributed in the following categories: community and social (£194,700) and education (£86,600). Only organisations that received grants of over £5,000 were listed as beneficiaries in the charity's accounts. Grants of under £5,000 totalled £59,800.
HOW TO APPLY Application forms and detailed guidelines are accessible on the charity's website. Once completed, forms can be returned via email. The members of the Charity Committee meet four times a year, typically in January, April, July and October, to consider applications for funding.
CONTACT DETAILS Lisa Holyoake, Merchants' Hall, The Promenade, Clifton, Bristol BS8 3NH *Tel.* 0117 973 8058 *Email* enquiries@merchantventurers.com *Website* www.merchantventurers.com

....

■ Merchants House of Glasgow

OSCR NO SC008900   **ESTABLISHED** 1605
WHERE FUNDING CAN BE GIVEN Glasgow and the west of Scotland (map on website).
WHO CAN BENEFIT Registered charities working in Glasgow and the west of Scotland; individuals.
WHAT IS FUNDED General charitable purposes; social welfare; older people; children and young people; health; the arts; education.
TYPE OF GRANT Project funding; capital costs; core/revenue costs.
RANGE OF GRANTS Between £500 and £10,000.
SAMPLE GRANTS Say Women (£11,200); Ocean Youth Trust (£10,000); Launch Foods Foundation (£7,500); MediCinema (£6,000); Children's Wood (£5,000).
FINANCES *Financial year end* 31/12/2022
Income £1,130,000
Grants to organisations £218,100
Grants to individuals £96,100
Assets £10,700,000
HOW TO APPLY At the time of writing (May 2023) the charity was temporarily closed for applications

while it reviewed its grant criteria. See the charity's website for further information.

CONTACT DETAILS The Directors, Collectors Office, 0/1, 7 West George Street, Glasgow G2 1BA *Tel.* 0141 221 8272 *Email* info@merchantshouse.org.uk *Website* www.merchantshouse.org.uk

■ Merriman Charitable Foundation

CC NO 1080946

WHERE FUNDING CAN BE GIVEN Worldwide.

WHO CAN BENEFIT Registered charities.

WHAT IS FUNDED Children and young people; education; hospices; homelessness; medical causes; conservation and the environment.

RANGE OF GRANTS Up to £10,000 but mostly £1,000 to £5,000.

SAMPLE GRANTS Fauna and Flora International (£10,000); Five Talents (£3,000); Tree Aid (£2,500); Children Heard and Seen (£2,000); Artis Foundation (£1,500); My Life Films (£500).

FINANCES *Financial year end* 31/12/2021 *Income* £116,300 *Grants to organisations* £110,300 *Assets* £2,700,000

TRUSTEES Lindsay Merriman; Nicholas Merriman; Saskia Restorick.

HOW TO APPLY Apply in writing to the correspondent.

CONTACT DETAILS The Trustees, 48 College Road, London SE21 7BA *Tel.* 020 8693 2182

■ T. and J. Meyer Family Foundation Ltd

CC NO 1087507   **ESTABLISHED** 2000

WHERE FUNDING CAN BE GIVEN Worldwide.

WHO CAN BENEFIT Charitable organisations.

WHAT IS FUNDED Education; health care; conservation.

TYPE OF GRANT Core costs.

SAMPLE GRANTS African Visionary Fund (£82,600); Jacaranda Health (£62,000); Komo Learning Centres (£49,600); PIVOT (£41,300); Gardens for Health (£16,500).

FINANCES *Financial year end* 31/12/2021 *Income* £441,400 *Grants to organisations* £886,400 *Assets* £17,680,000

TRUSTEES Jane Meyer; Edwin Falkman; Dr Della Drees.

OTHER INFORMATION During the year, the foundation awarded 15 grants. The financial information has been converted from USD using the exchange rate at the time of writing (March 2023).

HOW TO APPLY The foundation does not accept unsolicited applications.

CONTACT DETAILS The Trustees, 5/6 Kendrick Mews, London SW7 3HG *Tel.* 020 7581 9900 *Email* info@tjmff.org

■ The Mickel Fund

OSCR NO SC003266   **ESTABLISHED** 1970

WHERE FUNDING CAN BE GIVEN Scotland; overseas.

WHO CAN BENEFIT Registered charities.

WHAT IS FUNDED Education; social welfare; health; arts, heritage, culture and science; sport.

WHAT IS NOT FUNDED Events such as conferences, seminars and exhibitions; fee-charging residential homes, nurseries and care facilities; fundraising events; individuals; loans or the repayment of loans; religious promotion;

replacement of statutory funds; schools, other than pre-school and afterschool clubs and activities promoting parental and community involvement.

TYPE OF GRANT Capital costs; core costs; project funding.

SAMPLE GRANTS Merci Corps (£15,000); Médecins Sans Frontières (£10,000); Hearts and Minds (£6,000); Carers Scotland (£5,000); Glasgow Women's Aid (£3,600); With Kids (£2,700).

FINANCES *Financial year end* 05/04/2022 *Income* £147,000 *Grants to organisations* £117,600 *Assets* £4,460,000

TRUSTEES Bruce Mickel; Mairi Mickel; Oliver Bassi; Alan Hartley; Finlay Mickel; Mandy Graham.

HOW TO APPLY Apply via the charity's website.

CONTACT DETAILS The Trustees, 1 Atlantic Quay, 1 Robertson Street, Glasgow G2 8JB *Tel.* 0141 242 7527 *Email* admin@mickelfund.org.uk *Website* www.mickelfund.org.uk

■ The Mickleham Trust

CC NO 1048337   **ESTABLISHED** 1995

WHERE FUNDING CAN BE GIVEN UK, with a preference for Norfolk.

WHO CAN BENEFIT Registered charities.

WHAT IS FUNDED Social welfare; health and disability; blind or partially sighted people; children and young people; older people.

RANGE OF GRANTS Usually between £1,000 and £5,000 with some significantly larger grants.

SAMPLE GRANTS Priscilla Bacon Hospice (£1 million); Age UK (£540,000); East Anglia's Children's Hospices (£435,000); Norfolk and Norwich University Hospital (£179,500 in two grants); Orbis International and RNIB (£5,000 each); BEAT, Home-Start and Leeway (£2,000 each).

FINANCES *Financial year end* 31/03/2022 *Income* £315,700 *Grants to organisations* £2,310,000 *Assets* £4,020,000

TRUSTEES Philip Norton; Revd Sheila Nunney; Anne Richardson.

OTHER INFORMATION Grants were made to 85 organisations. During the year, £2.31 million was awarded to social welfare and medical charities and £20,000 was awarded in support of people living with blindness or partial sightedness.

HOW TO APPLY Apply in writing to the correspondent.

CONTACT DETAILS Phillip Norton, Trustee, c/o Hansells Solicitors and Financial Advisers, 13–14 The Close, Norwich, Norfolk NR1 4DS *Tel.* 01603 615731 *Email* philipnorton@hansells.co.uk

■ The Gerald Micklem Charitable Trust

CC NO 802583   **ESTABLISHED** 1988

WHERE FUNDING CAN BE GIVEN Hampshire and West Sussex.

WHO CAN BENEFIT UK-registered charities; hospices.

WHAT IS FUNDED Adults and children with physical and learning disabilities; carers for older people and people with disabilities, especially young carers; the environment and wildlife; hospices; medical conditions affecting both adults and children; support for older people, including those with Alzheimer's or dementia.

WHAT IS NOT FUNDED Individuals; charities that are not registered in the UK; churches; drug/alcohol abuse and counselling; disadvantaged children and young people; education/schools (except those for children with disabilities); homelessness and housing; local community groups; medical research; mental health; museums, galleries and heritage; overseas aid; performing arts and cultural organisations.

TYPE OF GRANT Core costs; capital projects.

RANGE OF GRANTS Typically between £3,000 and £10,000.

SAMPLE GRANTS Hope Farm Trust (£73,000); Dementia Support (£10,000); The Rosemary Foundation (£7,000); Treloar Trust (£5,000); Dystonia UK (£2,500).

FINANCES *Financial year end 31/12/2021*
Income £290,960,000
Grants to organisations £315,000
Assets £2,850,000

TRUSTEES Helen Ratcliffe; Joanna Scott-Dalgleish; Susan Shone.

OTHER INFORMATION Grants were made to 32 organisations.

HOW TO APPLY There is no formal application form and applications should be made in writing to the correspondent by post (not email). Applicants must also provide a copy of their latest annual report and accounts. Enquiries prior to any application may be made by email. Appeals received up to 30 November are considered by the trustees at their meeting early in the calendar year. The trustees recommend that appeals are submitted close to the cut-off date (i.e. in October or November) so that the information is as up to date as possible when considered. Appeals are not carried forward.

CONTACT DETAILS Mrs S. J. Shone, Trustee, Bolinge Hill Farm, Buriton, Petersfield, Hampshire GU31 4NN *Email* mail@geraldmicklemct.org.uk *Website* www.geraldmicklemct.org.uk

■ The Mikheev Charitable Trust

CC NO 1162591 **ESTABLISHED** 2015

WHERE FUNDING CAN BE GIVEN England and Wales.

WHO CAN BENEFIT Charitable organisations; arts organisations; universities; schools; places of worship.

WHAT IS FUNDED General charitable purposes; the advancement of education, science, religion and the arts; humanitarian aid.

RANGE OF GRANTS Between £3,000 and £10,000 with the occasional larger grant.

SAMPLE GRANTS London School of Jewish Studies (£33,000); Red Cross – Ukraine Appeal (£20,000); The Winchester Project (£11,000); University of Cambridge (£5,000); University of Copenhagen and Westminster Synagogue (£3,500 each).

FINANCES *Financial year end 05/04/2022*
Income £322,400
Grants to organisations £84,500
Assets £6,380,000

TRUSTEES Natalia Mikheev; Lev Mikheev; Katerina Woolhouse; Dr Adrian Weller.

OTHER INFORMATION The trust focuses in particular on projects aimed at the advancement of education, science, religion and the arts. Grants are generally made to established charitable organisations with a track record for delivering benefit to the public. Grants were broken down as follows: religion (£36,500); community outreach (£21,000); humanitarian aid (£20,000); relief of poverty (£9,000); arts (£5,300).

HOW TO APPLY Unsolicited applications are not accepted.

CONTACT DETAILS The Trustees, c/o Withers LLP, 20 Old Bailey, London EC4M 7AN *Tel.* 020 7597 6000

■ The Mila Charitable Organisation

CC NO 1169936

WHERE FUNDING CAN BE GIVEN UK; overseas.

WHO CAN BENEFIT Charitable organisations.

WHAT IS FUNDED General charitable purposes including education, the arts, culture, heritage, heritage, science and the environment.

RANGE OF GRANTS £5,000 to £60,000.

SAMPLE GRANTS Oxford Botanic Garden and Arboretum (£60,000); Arcola Theatre Production (£35,000); Studio Voltaire (£20,000); Britten Pears Arts (£15,000); SienAgosto (£10,000); King Edward VI Grammar (£5,900).

FINANCES *Financial year end 31/12/2021*
Income £1,210,000
Grants to organisations £240,900
Assets £8,210,000

TRUSTEES Prof. Kim Nasmyth; Anna Nasmyth; Laura Nasmyth; Kate Nasmyth; Dr David Bentley; Hamish Forsyth; Polly Phipps; Mark Francis.

OTHER INFORMATION During the year, the charity awarded grants to nine organisations.

HOW TO APPLY Apply in writing to the correspondent.

CONTACT DETAILS The Trustees, 71 Queen Victoria Street, London, EC4V 4AY *Tel.* 020 7395 3000

■ The Millennium Oak Trust

CC NO 1083384 **ESTABLISHED** 2000

WHERE FUNDING CAN BE GIVEN Worldwide, mainly UK.

WHO CAN BENEFIT Charitable organisations; schools; youth organisations; hospices.

WHAT IS FUNDED General charitable purposes; social welfare; medical and health, including mental health; education; the environment, including climate change; animals; work outside the UK, including humanitarian aid and human rights.

SAMPLE GRANTS Abbeyfields; British Heart Foundation; Chrysalis Holidays; Deafkidz International; Greenpeace; Knowl Hill School; Liberty International; Shooting Star Hospice; WaterAid; Whale and Dolphin Conservation.

FINANCES *Financial year end 31/07/2022*
Income £188,000
Grants to organisations £181,700
Assets £1,920,000

TRUSTEES Nicholas Roads; Alexander Roads; Dawn Roads; Andrew Armiger.

HOW TO APPLY Unsolicited applications are not accepted.

CONTACT DETAILS The Trustees, 26 Vicarage Road, Kingfield, Woking, Surrey GU22 9BH *Tel.* 01483 762859

■ Millennium Stadium Charitable Trust (Ymddiriedolaeth Elusennol Stadiwm y Mileniwm)

CC NO 1086596 **ESTABLISHED** 2001

WHERE FUNDING CAN BE GIVEN Wales.

WHO CAN BENEFIT Charitable organisations; constituted voluntary organisations; not-for-profit organisations; voluntary groups working with local authorities.

WHAT IS FUNDED The arts, especially the performing and visual arts; community cohesion; people with disabilities; the environment and sustainability; sport.

WHAT IS NOT FUNDED Projects outside Wales; day-to-day running costs; projects that seek to redistribute grant funding for the benefit of third-party organisations; repayment of debts or overdrafts; retrospective requests; requests from individuals; payment to profit-making organisations; applications made solely in the name of a local authority.

TYPE OF GRANT Capital costs; project funding.

RANGE OF GRANTS Regional grants: up to £7,500; local grants: up to £2,500.

SAMPLE GRANTS A list of beneficiaries was not included in the annual report and accounts.

FINANCES *Financial year end* 31/03/2022
Income £49,300
Grants to organisations £0
Assets £248,800

TRUSTEES Ian Davies; Russell Goodway; Gerallt Hughes; John Lloyd-Jones; Andrew Walker; John Rawlins; Cllr Peter Bradbury; David Hammond; Jonathan Day; David Young; Momena Ali; Christopher Jones.

OTHER INFORMATION Grants were not distributed in 2021/22 due to the impact of the COVID-19 pandemic; however, previous years' grants have totalled over £400,000.

HOW TO APPLY Applications can be made via the trust's website.

CONTACT DETAILS Sarah Fox, Trust Administrator, c/o Fox SE Consultancy, Cardiff House, Cardiff Road, Vale of Glamorgan CF63 2AW *Tel.* 029 2002 2143 *Email* info@millenniumstadiumtrust.org.uk *Website* www.millenniumstadiumtrust.org.uk

---

■ Hugh and Mary Miller Bequest Trust

OSCR NO SC014950   **ESTABLISHED** 1976
WHERE FUNDING CAN BE GIVEN Scotland.
WHO CAN BENEFIT Registered charities.
WHAT IS FUNDED General charitable purposes, including: medical research and health; education; disability.
RANGE OF GRANTS Up to £7,700.
SAMPLE GRANTS Haven Products Ltd (£16,300); Action Medical Research for Children, Hansel Foundation and Music in Hospitals and Care – Scotland (£7,700 each); Disasters Emergency Committee Ukraine Humanitarian Appeal (£5,000); Finchale Training College, Lodging House Mission and Quarriers (£3,300 each); Calibre Audio and The Salvation Army (£1,100 each).
FINANCES *Financial year end* 05/04/2022
Income £132,100
Grants to organisations £116,800
Assets £3,480,000
OTHER INFORMATION Haven Products Ltd is a primary and recurrent beneficiary for this trust.
HOW TO APPLY Apply in writing to the correspondent.
CONTACT DETAILS The Secretaries to the Trust, c/o Shepherd and Wedderburn LLP, 1 West Regent Street, Glasgow G2 1RW

■ The Ronald Miller Foundation

OSCR NO SC008798   **ESTABLISHED** 1979
WHERE FUNDING CAN BE GIVEN UK, with a preference for Scotland.
WHO CAN BENEFIT Registered charities.
WHAT IS FUNDED General charitable purposes including: children and young people, animal welfare; health; education.
WHAT IS NOT FUNDED Individuals.

SAMPLE GRANTS A list of beneficiaries was not included in the annual report and accounts.
FINANCES *Financial year end* 05/04/2022
Income £194,100
Grants to organisations £164,800
Assets £7,020,000
OTHER INFORMATION Grants were broken down as follows: medical causes (£50,800); general (£36,500); education (£28,100); children (£26,000); animals (£23,500).
HOW TO APPLY Contact the correspondent for further information.
CONTACT DETAILS The Trustees, c/o Shepherd and Wedderburn LLP, 1 West Regent Street, Glasgow G2 1RW

■ The Millfield House Foundation (1)

CC NO 1158914   **ESTABLISHED** 1976
WHERE FUNDING CAN BE GIVEN The North East.
WHO CAN BENEFIT Registered charities; universities.
WHAT IS FUNDED Social and economic inequality projects; policy work and research.
TYPE OF GRANT One-off grants; core costs; project funding; research.
SAMPLE GRANTS Citizens Advice, Newcastle University and VONNE (£126,000 each); IPPR North (£42,000); Regional Refugee Forum North East (£3,500); Third Sector Trends (£3,000).
FINANCES *Financial year end* 05/04/2022
Income £108,700
Grants to organisations £426,500
Assets £7,330,000
TRUSTEES Laura Seebohm; Dr Yvonne Gale; John McCabe; Jonathan Walker; Allan Brownrigg.
OTHER INFORMATION Grants were paid to six organisations during the year.
HOW TO APPLY The foundation funds a small number of strategic partner organisations on a regular basis. While occasional one-off grants are made at the trustees' discretion, unsolicited grant applications are not accepted.
CONTACT DETAILS Cullagh Warnock, Trust Manager, 7 Lesbury Road, Heaton, Newcastle upon Tyne, Tyne and Wear NE6 5LB *Tel.* 07595 280401 *Email* cullagh@mhfdn.org.uk *Website* www.mhfdn.org.uk

---

■ The Millfield Trust

CC NO 262406   **ESTABLISHED** 1971
WHERE FUNDING CAN BE GIVEN UK and overseas.
WHO CAN BENEFIT Charitable and religious organisations; individuals; missionary societies.
WHAT IS FUNDED Religious or other charitable work; missionary work; relief in need.
TYPE OF GRANT Unrestricted but primarily eligible expenditure and project funding.
RANGE OF GRANTS Up to £12,500.
SAMPLE GRANTS Previous grants have included: Good News for Everyone (£12,500); Ambassadors Bible Church (£5,500); Belief in Action (£3,000); Speak Life (£2,000); Billy Graham Evangelical Association (£1,500).
FINANCES *Financial year end* 23/04/2022
Income £57,300
Grants to organisations £82,500
Grants to individuals £3,200
Assets £78,600
TRUSTEES Andrew Bunce; Stephen Bunce; Rita Bunce; Philip Bunce.
HOW TO APPLY Unsolicited applications are not accepted.

CONTACT DETAILS Rita Bunce, Trustee, Millfield House, Bell Lane, Liddington, Swindon, Wiltshire SN4 0HE *Tel.* 01793 790181 *Email* millfield@liddington.myzen.co.uk

■ The Millichope Foundation

CC NO 282357   **ESTABLISHED** 1993
WHERE FUNDING CAN BE GIVEN Worldwide. Mainly UK, with a preference for Shropshire.
WHO CAN BENEFIT Charitable organisations.
WHAT IS FUNDED The arts and culture; conservation projects and the environment; heritage; disaster relief; general charitable purposes.
WHAT IS NOT FUNDED Individuals.
RANGE OF GRANTS Mostly up to £5,000.
SAMPLE GRANTS Global Canopy Foundation (£20,000); Ocalenie Foundation (£12,700); Médecins Sans Frontières (£10,000); Shropshire Historic Churches Trust (£5,000); Conservation Trust for St Laurence, Ludlow (£2,000); Armonico Consort (£1,000); Gordon Wright Trust (£500).
FINANCES *Financial year end* 07/01/2022
Income £499,400
Grants to organisations £203,500
Assets £8,040,000
TRUSTEES Lindsay Bury; Mrs S. A. Bury; Bridget Marshall; Frank Bury; Mrs H. M. Horne.
OTHER INFORMATION Grants were awarded to 106 organisations during the year.
HOW TO APPLY Apply in writing to the correspondent. The trustees meet several times a year to consider applications.
CONTACT DETAILS Sarah Bury, Trustee, The Old Rectory, Tugford, Craven Arms, Shropshire SY7 9HS *Tel.* 01584 841234 *Email* sarah@millichope.com

■ Millie's Watch

CC NO 1179664
WHERE FUNDING CAN BE GIVEN England and Wales.
WHO CAN BENEFIT Charitable organisations.
WHAT IS FUNDED General charitable purposes.
SAMPLE GRANTS Queen Elizabeth Hospital – University Hospitals Birmingham (£25,000); Canal and River Trust, Family Care Trust and The Prince's Trust (£10,000 each); Acacia Family Support, Alopecia UK, FareShare and Let's Feed Brum Ltd (£5,000 each).
FINANCES *Financial year end* 06/08/2021
Income £51,600
Grants to organisations £135,000
Assets £313,400
TRUSTEES Mary Ayres; Rachel Harrod; Julie Stretton; Rebecca Ayres; Ludlow Trust Company Ltd.
OTHER INFORMATION The charity's 2020/21 accounts were the latest available to view at the time of writing (June 2023). Grants were awarded to 18 organisations.
HOW TO APPLY Apply in writing to the correspondent.
CONTACT DETAILS The Trustees, Ludlow Trust Co. Ltd, Tower Wharf, Cheese Lane, Bristol BS2 0JJ *Tel.* 0117 313 8200

■ Mills and Reeve Charitable Trust

CC NO 326271   **ESTABLISHED** 1982
WHERE FUNDING CAN BE GIVEN UK, with a preference for charities based near the offices of Mills and Reeve LLP.
WHO CAN BENEFIT Charitable organisations; universities.
WHAT IS FUNDED General charitable purposes with a preference for medical research and social welfare.
TYPE OF GRANT One-off and recurrent for research; project funding.
RANGE OF GRANTS Generally up to £6,000.
SAMPLE GRANTS British Ukrainian Aid (£10,000); YoungMinds (£6,700); Whitechapel Mission (£3,300); Life Lifts (£1,600); Welcome Charity (£1,600).
FINANCES *Financial year end* 31/05/2022
Income £141,000
Grants to organisations £131,200
Assets £273,500
TRUSTEES Greg Gibson; Tom Pickthorn; Sarah Seed; Alison Bull; Justin Ripman; Clive Levontine; Neil Howes; Stuart Thompson; Richard Santy.
OTHER INFORMATION The trust is the corporate charity of Mills and Reeve LLP, which provides a substantial proportion of the charity's income and each trustee is a member or a former member of the company. Only organisations that received grants of over £1,000 were listed as beneficiaries in the trust's accounts. Grants of under £1,000 totalled £16,800.
HOW TO APPLY Apply in writing to the correspondent.
CONTACT DETAILS The Trustees, Botanic House, 100 Hills Road, Cambridge CB2 1PH *Tel.* 01223 222273 *Website* www.mills-reeve.com/about-us/making-a-positive-impact

■ The Millward Charitable Trust

CC NO 328564   **ESTABLISHED** 1990
WHERE FUNDING CAN BE GIVEN UK and overseas.
WHO CAN BENEFIT Charitable organisations; churches.
WHAT IS FUNDED Social welfare; the performing arts; religion; animal welfare; education.
RANGE OF GRANTS Typically up to £40,000.
SAMPLE GRANTS City of Birmingham Symphony Orchestra (£40,000); National Trust (£28,000); Music in the Round (£15,000); Leamington Music, Cancer Research UK (£5,000).
FINANCES *Financial year end* 05/04/2022
Income £27,600
Grants to organisations £103,000
Assets £1,910,000
TRUSTEES John Hulse; Maurice Millward; Rachel Millward.
OTHER INFORMATION Grants were awarded in the following categories: performing arts (four grants totalling £70,000); conservation (one grant totalling £28,000); social welfare (one grant totalling £5,000). Only grants of less than £1,000 were listed in the beneficiaries.
HOW TO APPLY Apply in writing to the correspondent. The trustees meet regularly to consider applications.
CONTACT DETAILS Maurice Millward, Trustee, 23–25 Waterloo Place, Warwick Street, Leamington Spa, Warwickshire CV32 5LA *Tel.* 01926 451000 *Email* maurice@mauricemillward.co.uk

■ The Milne Family Foundation

OSCR NO SC046335   **ESTABLISHED** 2016
WHERE FUNDING CAN BE GIVEN UK, with a preference for Scotland; overseas.
WHO CAN BENEFIT Registered charities; places of worship; individuals.
WHAT IS FUNDED Christianity; education; health; community development, including citizenship; social welfare.

Think carefully about every application. Is it justified?

541

RANGE OF GRANTS Mostly up to £5,000 with the occasional larger grant.

SAMPLE GRANTS The Cruden Trust (£250,000); Worldlink (£96,000); Truth for Today (£44,000); Bensham Gospel Hall (£30,000); Bible Educational Services, Go! Youth Trust and The Lord's Work Trust (£24,000 each); Eagles Wings Trust, Seaton Community Church and UCCF: The Christian Unions (£12,000 each); Our Daily Bread (£6,000).

FINANCES *Financial year end 31/12/2021*
Income £1,630,000
Grants to organisations £1,180,000
Grants to individuals £434,000
Assets £31,900

TRUSTEES Sir James Milne; William Main; John McArthur.

OTHER INFORMATION The foundation receives the majority of its funding from Balmoral Group Holdings and its related companies. Individuals can be supported. Only organisations that received more than £5,000 were listed as beneficiaries in the foundation's accounts. Grants of under £5,000 totalled £14,800 and were awarded to 22 organisations. The 2021 accounts were the latest available at the time of writing (May 2023).

HOW TO APPLY Apply in writing to the correspondent.

CONTACT DETAILS Julie Lowden, Secretary, Balmoral Park, Loirston, Aberdeen AB12 3GY

■ The Clare Milne Trust

CC NO 1191010   **ESTABLISHED** 1999

WHERE FUNDING CAN BE GIVEN The South West, with a preference for Devon and Cornwall.

WHO CAN BENEFIT Local and regional charities.

WHAT IS FUNDED Disability projects, especially those for adults.

WHAT IS NOT FUNDED Individuals; national charities are not normally supported.

TYPE OF GRANT Generally a partial contribution towards the total cost of a project.

RANGE OF GRANTS Typically, grants range between £2,000 and £25,000, or from £30,000 to £50,000 for building projects.

SAMPLE GRANTS Community Equality Disability Action (CEDA) (£36,000); Plymouth Highbury Trust (£19,500); Helford River – Children's Sailing Trust (£15,000); Carers UK (£10,000); The Wave Project (£9,000); Get Changed (£8,400); Exmouth Town Council (£7,500); Listening Books (£4,500); Conquest Centre (£2,000).

FINANCES *Financial year end 31/12/2021*
Income £901,000
Grants to organisations £611,000
Assets £45,830,000

TRUSTEES Christine Kirk; Margaret Rogers; Eavan McCafferty; Kevin Underwood; Jacqueline Southon; Lynda Williams.

HOW TO APPLY Application forms can be downloaded from the trust's website. The form should be returned to the secretary along with a covering letter (on your letterhead), details regarding your proposal (up to two sides of A4) and a budget for the project. The trustees usually meet four times a year and aim to contact applicants within two weeks from the date of the meeting. Check the trust's website for the latest information on application deadlines and detailed guidelines on how to apply.

CONTACT DETAILS Emma Houlding, Secretary, Claypitts, Ladram Road, Otterton, Devon EX9 7HT *Tel.* 01395 270418 *Email* secretary@claremilnetrust.com *Website* www.claremilnetrust.com

■ The James Milner Foundation

CC NO 1146768   **ESTABLISHED** 2011

WHERE FUNDING CAN BE GIVEN UK, with a preference for the north of England.

WHO CAN BENEFIT Charitable organisations.

WHAT IS FUNDED Children and young people; sport and recreation, particularly football, rugby and cricket; education; health.

TYPE OF GRANT Project costs; development funding.

SAMPLE GRANTS Previous grants have included: Bloodwise, Help for Heroes and NSPCC (£100,000 each); Motor Neurone Disease Association (£50,000); Darby Rimmer MND Foundation (£30,000); Liverpool FC Foundation (£25,000); Leeds Rhinos Foundation (£15,000).

FINANCES *Financial year end 31/12/2021*
Income £28,500
Grants to organisations £0
Assets £20,900

TRUSTEES Christopher Hudson; Mark Hovell; Marie-Christine Bouchier.

OTHER INFORMATION The foundation's main source of income is through its annual fundraising ball. The trustees were unable to host the ball due to the COVID-19 pandemic and as such the foundation's income and grant-making capacity was impacted in 2021. In 2020, the foundation made grants totalling £420,000 to seven organisations, listed above. The foundation provides annual support to Bloodwise, Help for Heroes and the NSPCC.

HOW TO APPLY Contact the correspondent for further information.

CONTACT DETAILS Mark Hovell, Trustee, c/o Mills and Reeve LLP, 1 New York Street, Manchester M1 4HD *Tel.* 0161 235 5420 *Email* mark.hovell@mills-reeve.com *Website* www.thejamesmilnerfoundation.com

■ Milton Keynes Community Foundation Ltd

CC NO 295107   **ESTABLISHED** 1987

WHERE FUNDING CAN BE GIVEN Milton Keynes unitary authority.

WHO CAN BENEFIT Registered charities; not-for-profit community groups; social enterprises; amateur sports clubs; faith groups; CICs; voluntary sector organisations.

WHAT IS FUNDED Social welfare; community; health; children and young people; people with disabilities; older people; arts and culture.

WHAT IS NOT FUNDED Exclusion criteria differ between funds – see the foundation's website for further information.

TYPE OF GRANT Start-up costs; project extension or development core costs; pilot projects; equipment and resources.

SAMPLE GRANTS SOFEA (£60,000); Q:alliance (£37,500); Aylesbury Vale and Milton Keynes Sexual Assault and Abuse Support Service (£16,200); Baby Basics (£15,000); The Milton Keynes Rose (£10,000); Tinkers Bridge Residents Association (£2,800); Stony Stratford in Bloom (£1,100); 26th Milton Keynes Scout Group (£300).

FINANCES *Financial year end 31/03/2022*
Income £5,800,000
Grants to organisations £1,360,000
Assets £61,710,000

TRUSTEES Shaun Lee; Jill Heaton; Kurshida Mirza; Shirley Jones; Dr Devdeep Ahuja; Sean O'Reilly; Precious Lwanga; Christopher Shaw; Radhika Srinivasan; Syeda Sidra Mehdi; Richard Forman.

OTHER INFORMATION This is one of the 47 UK community foundations, which distribute funding for a wide range of purposes. As with all community foundations, there are a number of donor-advised funds managed on behalf of individuals, families and charitable trusts. Grant schemes tend to change frequently – consult the foundation's website for details of current programmes and up-to-date deadlines. In 2021/22, the foundation awarded 127 grants to 109 organisations.

HOW TO APPLY Potential applicants are advised to visit the community foundation's website or contact its programmes team to find the most suitable funding stream.

CONTACT DETAILS The Programmes Team, Acorn House, 381 Midsummer Boulevard, Milton Keynes, Buckinghamshire MK9 3HP *Tel.* 01908 690276 *Email* info@mkcommunityfoundation. co.uk *Website* www.mkcommunityfoundation.co.uk

■ The Peter Minet Trust

CC NO 259963   **ESTABLISHED** 1969
WHERE FUNDING CAN BE GIVEN Lambeth and Southwark.
WHO CAN BENEFIT UK-registered charities with offices, beneficiaries and work in Lambeth or Southwark.
WHAT IS FUNDED Community cohesion; social welfare.
WHAT IS NOT FUNDED Local branches of charities that have main offices outside Lambeth or Southwark; charities that also work with beneficiaries outside Lambeth and Southwark; individuals; nurseries, schools, colleges, higher education institutions, universities and associated charities, including PTAs; places of worship; one-off events.
TYPE OF GRANT Unrestricted funding of up to £30,000 per year for up to three years.
RANGE OF GRANTS £5,000 to £30,000.
SAMPLE GRANTS Home-Start Southwark, St Matthew's Project and Loughborough Junction Action Group (£30,000 each); Southside Young Leaders Academy (£25,000); Brixton Wings (£5,000); Institute for Voluntary Action Research (£1,000).
FINANCES *Financial year end* 30/09/2022
Income £158,500
Grants to organisations £391,000
Assets £4,990,000
TRUSTEES Anne Young; Tracey Fletcher; Thomas Gayfer; Patricia Okonkwo; Joseph Howell; Georgina Awoonor-Gordon; Ayodeji Bamidele.
OTHER INFORMATION The trust has two grant programmes; the Strategic Fund is by invitation only and the Open Grants Fund is available to charities working to support 'severe and multiple challenges' of Lambeth or Southwark residents.
HOW TO APPLY The Open Grants Fund has a three-stage application process consisting of an online 'Tell Us About You' form, an application form and an in-person meeting.
CONTACT DETAILS The Trustees, Marshall House, 66 Newcomen Street, London SE1 1YT *Tel.* 020 8037 0300 *Email* info@peterminet.org.uk *Website* www.peterminet.org.uk

■ Minton Charitable Trust

CC NO 1112106   **ESTABLISHED** 2005
WHERE FUNDING CAN BE GIVEN UK.
WHO CAN BENEFIT Registered, excepted or exempt charities; individuals.

WHAT IS FUNDED Education; social welfare; sports and recreation.
TYPE OF GRANT Capital costs; project funding.
RANGE OF GRANTS Between £50,000 and £200,000.
SAMPLE GRANTS Impetus Private Equity Foundation (£200,000); UKSA (£120,000); St Giles Trust (£100,000).
FINANCES *Financial year end* 05/04/2022
Income £50,500
Grants to organisations £420,000
Assets £2,150,000
TRUSTEES Richard Edmunds; Sir Anthony Greener; Charles Greener; Claire Greener.
OTHER INFORMATION St Giles Trust is the principal beneficiary of this trust, of which Sir Anthony Greener is a former trustee.
HOW TO APPLY Apply in writing to the correspondent.
CONTACT DETAILS Sir Anthony Greener, Trustee, Dores Hill, North Sydmonton, Newbury, Berkshire RG20 9AF *Tel.* 07720 271183 *Email* greenera@mintontrust.com

■ The Laurence Misener Charitable Trust

CC NO 283460   **ESTABLISHED** 1981
WHERE FUNDING CAN BE GIVEN UK.
WHO CAN BENEFIT Registered charities; hospitals; hospices.
WHAT IS FUNDED General charitable purposes; health; seafarers; culture.
TYPE OF GRANT One-off and recurrent.
RANGE OF GRANTS £5,000 to £25,000.
SAMPLE GRANTS Alzheimer's Research UK (£25,000); Royal Marsden Hospital (£18,000); Fight for Sight (£13,000); Imperial War Museum Development Trust (£10,000); Sussex Stroke and Circulation Fund (£5,000).
FINANCES *Financial year end* 05/04/2022
Income £68,600
Grants to organisations £192,000
Assets £1,620,000
TRUSTEES Jillian Legane; Capt. George Swaine.
OTHER INFORMATION In 2021/22, grants were made to 12 organisations. The trust appears to award grants to the same organisations every year.
HOW TO APPLY Contact the correspondent for further information.
CONTACT DETAILS The Trustees, 1 Printing Yard House, London E2 7PR *Tel.* 020 7739 8790 *Email* enquiries@leonardjones.co.uk

■ The Mishcon Family Charitable Trust

CC NO 213165   **ESTABLISHED** 1961
WHERE FUNDING CAN BE GIVEN UK.
WHO CAN BENEFIT Registered charities, particularly Jewish organisations.
WHAT IS FUNDED General charitable purposes; the Jewish faith and community; social welfare; health and disability; children and young people.
RANGE OF GRANTS £100 to £10,300.
SAMPLE GRANTS World Jewish Relief (£6,600); One to One Children's Fund (£4,700); United Synagogue (£3,400); The Trussell Trust (£1,000); The Kensington and Chelsea Foundation (£500); Avondale Extra (£100).
FINANCES *Financial year end* 05/04/2022
Income £48,800
Grants to organisations £73,500
Assets £1,840,000
TRUSTEES Jane Landau; Peter Mishcon; Russell Mishcon; Russell Orde Mishcon.
HOW TO APPLY Apply in writing to the correspondent.

CONTACT DETAILS The Trustees, 2 Prince Arthur Mews, London NW3 1RD *Tel.* 020 7794 2137

50 Bedford Street, Belfast BT2 7FW *Tel.* 028 9024 3141 *Email* trusts@cfrlaw.co.uk

■ The Brian Mitchell Charitable Settlement

CC NO 1003817 ESTABLISHED 1989
WHERE FUNDING CAN BE GIVEN UK.
WHO CAN BENEFIT Charitable organisations.
WHAT IS FUNDED General charitable purposes, including the arts, education, health, social welfare and disability.
RANGE OF GRANTS Up to £475,000.
SAMPLE GRANTS Glyndebourne (£475,000); Orchestra of the Age of Enlightenment (£50,000); Myeloma UK (£15,000); Trinity Theatre (£6,000); Taylor Made Dreams (£3,000).
FINANCES *Financial year end 31/03/2022* *Income* £103,900
Grants to organisations £702,500
Assets £3,090,000
TRUSTEES John Andrews; Andy Buss; Maxine Pancaldi.
OTHER INFORMATION Grants of less than £5,000 totalled at £31,000.
HOW TO APPLY Apply in writing to the correspondent; however, note that the charity has several regular beneficiaries.
CONTACT DETAILS The Trustees, 14 Hackwood, Robertsbridge, East Sussex TN32 5ER *Tel.* 07860 628597 *Email* john@aas.uk.net

■ The Esmé Mitchell Trust

CCNI NO NIC101659 ESTABLISHED 1965
WHERE FUNDING CAN BE GIVEN Northern Ireland.
WHO CAN BENEFIT Charitable organisations; places of worship; schools and colleges; universities; museums, libraries and galleries.
WHAT IS FUNDED Arts, culture and heritage; animal conservation; disability; children and young people; health; social welfare; general charitable purposes.
WHAT IS NOT FUNDED Individuals.
RANGE OF GRANTS Mostly between £1,000 and £5,000 with the occasional smaller or larger grant.
SAMPLE GRANTS NI Opera (£40,000); Belfast Philharmonic Society, RSPB and Ulster Historical Foundation (£20,000); Annagh Social Farm, Charles Wood Summer School and National Churches Trust (£10,000 each); Cahoots NI, National Autistic Society NI and Northern Ireland Museums Council (£5,000 each); Adopt NI, Carers NI and Future Trees (£3,000 each); Carrickfergus and Larne Child Contact Centre, The Guide Dogs for the Blind Association and Irish Georgian Foundation (£1,000 each); DU Dance NI (£500).
FINANCES *Financial year end 05/04/2022* *Income* £254,300
Grants to organisations £310,800
Assets £9,000,000
TRUSTEE Cleaver Fulton Rankin Trustees Ltd.
OTHER INFORMATION The trust has two funds: the general fund and the heritage fund. During this period, grants from the general fund totalled £221,800 and were awarded to 49 organisations. Grants from the heritage fund totalled £89,000 and were awarded to eight organisations.
HOW TO APPLY Apply in writing to the correspondent.
CONTACT DETAILS The Trustees, c/o Cleaver Fulton Rankin Trustees Ltd, Cleaver Fulton Rankin,

■ The MITIE Foundation

CC NO 1148858 ESTABLISHED 2012
WHERE FUNDING CAN BE GIVEN UK.
WHO CAN BENEFIT Charities and community groups.
WHAT IS FUNDED General charitable purposes; education and training; community and economic development; unemployed people; people with disabilities; older people; working with young people.
SAMPLE GRANTS A list of beneficiaries was not included in the annual report and accounts.
FINANCES *Financial year end 31/03/2022* *Income* £227,600
Grants to organisations £174,200
Assets £91,400
TRUSTEES Rebecca Faulkiner; Jasmine Hudson; Philippa Couttie; Pradyumna Pandit; Andrew Eastwood; Navinder Kalley; Michael Gibson.
HOW TO APPLY Contact the correspondent for more information.
CONTACT DETAILS The Trustees, MITIE Group plc, Level 12, The Shard, 32 London Bridge Street, London SE1 9SG *Email* Foundation@mitie.com *Website* www.mitie.com/mitie-foundation

■ The Mittal Foundation

CC NO 1146604 ESTABLISHED 1993
WHERE FUNDING CAN BE GIVEN UK, USA and India.
WHO CAN BENEFIT Registered charities; universities.
WHAT IS FUNDED General charitable purposes, especially education and training, the arts, the prevention of poverty and malnutrition, and children and young people.
SAMPLE GRANTS A list of beneficiaries was not included in the annual report and accounts. Previous beneficiaries have included: Boston Children's Hospital; Harvard University; The British Asian Trust; The Prince's Trust; University of Pennsylvania.
FINANCES *Financial year end 31/12/2021* *Income* £113,100
Grants to organisations £263,400
Assets £730,900
TRUSTEES Usha Mittal; Megha Mittal; Vanisha Bhatia; Aditya Mittal.
HOW TO APPLY The foundation does not accept unsolicited applications. The trustees research and use their personal contacts to identify suitable grantees.
CONTACT DETAILS The Trustees, c/o Mittal Investments Ltd, Floor 3, Berkeley Square House, Berkeley Square, London W1J 6BU *Tel.* 020 7659 1033

■ The MK Charitable Trust

CC NO 260439 ESTABLISHED 1966
WHERE FUNDING CAN BE GIVEN Worldwide; in practice, mainly the UK.
WHO CAN BENEFIT Orthodox Jewish organisations.
WHAT IS FUNDED General charitable purposes; the Jewish faith and community.
SAMPLE GRANTS A list of beneficiaries was not available.
FINANCES *Financial year end 05/04/2022* *Income* £20,700
Grants to organisations £151,900
Assets £342,200
TRUSTEES A. Piller; David Katz; Simon Kaufman.

OTHER INFORMATION Full accounts were not available to view on the Charity Commission's website due to the trust's low income. We have therefore estimated the trust's grant total based on its total expenditure.

HOW TO APPLY Applications can be made in writing to the correspondent. The trust accepts applications for grants from representatives of Orthodox Jewish charities, which are reviewed by the trustees on a regular basis.

CONTACT DETAILS Simon Kaufman, Trustee, 50 Keswick Street, Gateshead, Tyne and Wear NE8 1TQ *Tel.* 0191 490 0140

■ Mobbs Memorial Trust Ltd

CC NO 202478   **ESTABLISHED** 1963

WHERE FUNDING CAN BE GIVEN Stoke Poges and district within a 35-mile radius of St Giles' Church.

WHO CAN BENEFIT Charitable organisations; churches; schools and colleges.

WHAT IS FUNDED St Giles' Church and other charitable purposes including sports and recreation, health, conservation and the environment and community services.

WHAT IS NOT FUNDED The following applications are not normally supported: those from or for individuals or private companies; those from national charitable organisations unless a specific need arises within the local area; those that should be funded by national or local government; those for running costs, apart from exceptional cases within a four-mile radius of Stoke Poges.

TYPE OF GRANT One-off capital projects.

RANGE OF GRANTS Usually £500 to £10,000.

SAMPLE GRANTS Stoke Pages PCC St Giles' Church (£5,000); Windsor Christian Action (£4,000); Age UK Berkshire (£3,300); South Bucks Hospice (£3,000); Bucks Vision (£2,500); Wokingham in Need (£2,000); CreateEd (£1,500); Reading Association for the Blind (£250).

FINANCES *Financial year end* 31/03/2022
Income £109,100
Grants to organisations £153,900
Assets £3,450,000

TRUSTEES Sandra Greenslade; Dr Charles Mobbs; Chris Mobbs; Alexander Mobbs; Will Greenslade.

OTHER INFORMATION Grants were awarded to 56 organisations in 2021/22.

HOW TO APPLY Apply in writing to the correspondent via email. The trustees meet quarterly, normally in March, June, September and December. Full guidelines are available to view on the trust's website.

CONTACT DETAILS Sandra Greenslade, Chair, Victoria House, 26 Queen Victoria Street, Reading, Berkshire RG1 1TG *Tel.* 0118 957 3238 *Email* applications@mobbsmemorialtrust.com. *Website* www.mobbsmemorialtrust.com

■ The Modiano Charitable Trust

CC NO 328372   **ESTABLISHED** 1989

WHERE FUNDING CAN BE GIVEN England and Wales.

WHO CAN BENEFIT Charitable organisations and educational institutions, with some preference for Jewish groups.

WHAT IS FUNDED The arts; the Jewish faith and community; education; the relief of poverty.

TYPE OF GRANT One-off and recurrent.

RANGE OF GRANTS £50 to £20,000.

SAMPLE GRANTS A list of beneficiaries was not included in the annual report and accounts. Previous beneficiaries have included: Philharmonic Orchestra (£20,000); Weiznam Institute Foundation £10,000); Disasters Emergency Committee Haiti Appeal, St Paul's School and UJIA (£5,000 each); World Jewish Relief (£4,000); Life Action Trust (£3,500); CCJ and The Holocaust Educational Trust (£2,500 each); The Reform Research Trust and YMCA (£1,000 each); British Forces Association, Jami and St John of Jerusalem Eye Hospital (£100 each).

FINANCES *Financial year end* 05/04/2022
Income £200,000
Grants to organisations £83,500
Assets £491,800

TRUSTEES Michael Modiano; Liora Modiano.

HOW TO APPLY Apply in writing to the correspondent.

CONTACT DETAILS Michael Modiano, Trustee, Broad Street House, 55 Old Broad Street, London EC2M 1RX *Tel.* 020 7012 0000

■ The Mohn Westlake Foundation

CC NO 1170045   **ESTABLISHED** 2016

WHERE FUNDING CAN BE GIVEN England and Wales.

WHO CAN BENEFIT Organisations that support young people.

WHAT IS FUNDED Young people; education; recreation and leisure; the arts and science; research; general charitable purposes.

WHAT IS NOT FUNDED Individuals; projects outside the UK; animal welfare; faith/places of worship charities; campaigning and lobby work.

TYPE OF GRANT Project costs.

RANGE OF GRANTS Generally £100,000 to £1.5 million.

SAMPLE GRANTS Royal National Theatre (£3.34 million); Book Trust (£1.68 million); Screen Academy Foundation (£555,000); The Brilliant Club (£300,000); Full Fact (£250,000); Chance UK (£200,000); Centre for Public Data Practice CIC (£100,000); Team Oasis (£10,000); Royal Opera House Covent Garden (£30).

FINANCES *Financial year end* 31/12/2021
Income £19,150,000
Grants to organisations £8,850,000
Assets £13,280,000

TRUSTEES Marit Mohn; Robert Westlake; Stian Westlake; Diana Gerald.

OTHER INFORMATION During the year, grants were awarded to 14 organisations.

HOW TO APPLY The foundation's website provides detailed information on how registered charities or social enterprises can apply. Applications should be made in writing and include the following: the purpose of the funding, evidence of need, outcomes, the amount sought and a set of your latest accounts. Although unsolicited applications are accepted, most funding is allocated through specific call-outs. Where appropriate, the website will carry details of this.

CONTACT DETAILS Chris Thurlow, Ludlow Trust Co. Ltd, Centric House, 390–391 Strand, London WC2R 0LT *Tel.* 020 4534 2750 *Email* chris. thurlow@ludlowtrust.com *Website* www. themohnwestlakefoundation.co.uk

Think carefully about every application. Is it justified?

545

■ Mole Charitable Trust

CC NO 281452   ESTABLISHED 1980

WHERE FUNDING CAN BE GIVEN UK, with a preference for Manchester.

WHO CAN BENEFIT Registered charities; schools and colleges; universities.

WHAT IS FUNDED The Jewish faith and community; educational purposes; the relief of poverty; organisations working with children.

RANGE OF GRANTS Typically between £1,000 and £10,000.

SAMPLE GRANTS The Shaarei Torah Trust (£143,000); Three Pillars Trust (£60,000); Broughton Jewish Primary School and UK Friends of Yad Yisroel (£10,000 each); Asser Bishvil Foundation (£5,000); Torah Temimah (£1,000).

FINANCES *Financial year end 31/03/2022*
Income £81,300
Grants to organisations £235,600
Assets £2,400,000

TRUSTEES Leah Gross; Martin Gross; Dov Black; Jonathan Brodie.

OTHER INFORMATION In 2021/22, grants were awarded to eight organisations. Grants were distributed as follows: religious institutions (£154,000); educational institutions and relief of poverty (£81,600).

HOW TO APPLY Contact the correspondent for further information.

CONTACT DETAILS The Trustees, 2 Okeover Road, Salford, Greater Manchester M7 4JX *Tel.* 0161 832 8721 *Email* martin.gross@lopiangb.co.uk

■ The Alexander Moncur Trust

OSCR NO SC008863   ESTABLISHED 1946

WHERE FUNDING CAN BE GIVEN Dundee and the surrounding areas.

WHO CAN BENEFIT Registered charities.

WHAT IS FUNDED Cultural, health, educational and social projects.

TYPE OF GRANT General funding; revenue costs; one-off and recurrent grants.

RANGE OF GRANTS Generally, up to £5,000. Multi-year grants in the range of £10,000 per year for up to three years.

SAMPLE GRANTS The Eden Project (£52,100); Fife Young Carers and The Yard (£5,000 each); The Attic (£4,000); Sepsis Research (£3,000); Parent to Parent (£2,000).

FINANCES *Financial year end 29/12/2021*
Income £260,500
Grants to organisations £227,100
Assets £9,910,000

OTHER INFORMATION The 2020/21 accounts were the latest available at the time of writing (May 2023).

HOW TO APPLY Application forms are available to download from the trust's helpful website and should be returned to Miller Hendry Solicitors. Forms can also be requested from Miller Hendry Solicitors on 01382 200000. The application deadlines are 31 March and 30 September each year.

CONTACT DETAILS Ernest Boath, Administrator, c/o Miller Hendry Solicitors, 13 Ward Road, Dundee DD1 1LU *Tel.* 01382 200000 *Email* info@moncurtrust.org *Website* www.moncurtrust.org

■ The Monday Charitable Trust

CC NO 1174232

WHERE FUNDING CAN BE GIVEN UK.

WHO CAN BENEFIT UK-registered charities.

WHAT IS FUNDED Disadvantage, mainly in the fields of housing, education, welfare and social mobility.

RANGE OF GRANTS Generally between £10,000 and £150,000 with some larger grants.

SAMPLE GRANTS The Big Give (£212,000); Barts Charity, Chance to Shine Foundation Ltd and Think Through Nutrition (£150,000 each); Refugee Education (£70,000); Toynbee Hill (£47,500); Fine Cell Work, Injured Jockeys Fund and Social Change Nest CIC (£10,000 each); Cambridge University Land Society (£6,200).

FINANCES *Financial year end 31/03/2022*
Income £3,340,000
Grants to organisations £1,950,000
Assets £6,340,000

TRUSTEES Elspeth Lane; Sarah Baxter; Jonathan Brinsden; Douglas Blausten; Andrew Johnston.

OTHER INFORMATION During 2021/22, 24 organisations were supported.

HOW TO APPLY Unsolicited applications are not accepted.

CONTACT DETAILS The Trustees, c/o BDB Pitmans, One Bartholomew Close, London EC1A 7BL *Tel.* 020 7783 3685

■ The Monmouthshire County Council Welsh Church Act Fund

CC NO 507094   ESTABLISHED 1996

WHERE FUNDING CAN BE GIVEN Blaenau Gwent, Caerphilly, Monmouthshire, the City of Newport and Torfaen.

WHO CAN BENEFIT Organisations; religious organisations; libraries and museums; individual residents.

WHAT IS FUNDED General charitable purposes, including the following: education; religion; social welfare; art and heritage; community benefit.

TYPE OF GRANT Capital costs; core costs.

SAMPLE GRANTS Caerphilly County Borough Council (£45,000); Monmouthshire County Council (£34,000); Newport City Council (£32,600); Torfaen County Borough Council (£26,400); Blaenau Gwent County Borough Council (£25,000).

FINANCES *Financial year end 31/03/2022*
Income £193,900
Grants to organisations £163,300
Grants to individuals £4,500
Assets £5,680,000

TRUSTEE Monmouthshire County Council.

OTHER INFORMATION Grants are paid to five local authorities, which administer grants to organisations and individuals on behalf of the charity (see the beneficiary list). During the year, grants to organisations were distributed as follows: religion (£75,600); social welfare (£42,000); community (£39,400); education (£6,500). Grants to individuals for the advancement of education totalled £4,500.

HOW TO APPLY Applications are considered seven times a year. Application forms are available from the website. Applications from groups/organisations will only be considered with a copy of their financial statements.

CONTACT DETAILS The Trustees, Monmouthshire County Council, County Hall, The Rhadyr, Usk,

Gwent NP15 1GA *Tel.* 01633 644657 *Email* davejarrett@monmouthshire.gov.uk *Website* www.monmouthshire.gov.uk/welsh-church-fund

■ Moondance Foundation

cc no 1139224   **established** 2010
where funding can be given Wales.
who can benefit Registered charities; constituted community groups; social enterprises; community interest organisations; CICs; other not-for-profit organisations.
what is funded Children; education; older people; the environment; health; social welfare; women.
what is not funded Political activity; religious activity; research (medical or social); schools (primary and secondary) or their PTAs; sports clubs.
type of grant Project funding.
sample grants BBC Studios (£1 million); Moondance Cancer Initiative (£746,000); Purple Shoots (£250,000); Safer Wales (£125,000); St Kentigern Hospice (£100,000); Hospice of the Valleys (£50,000); Dementia UK (£25,000); Follow your Dreams (£7,300).
finances *Financial year end* 30/11/2021
Income £77,330,000
Grants to organisations £18,190,000
Assets £485,390,000
trustees Diane L'Isle-Engelhardt; Henry Engelhardt; Louisa Scadden; Damien Engelhardt; Adrian Engelhardt; Shanna Engelhardt; Tara Engelhardt.
other information The 2020/21 accounts were the latest available at the time of writing (May 2023). During the year, 658 grants were awarded. Grants were broken down as follows: other causes in Wales (£5.05 million); other causes (£3.87 million); children and young people (£3.32 million); health (£3.10 million); the environment (£2.05 million); education (£727,500). Unlisted grants of less than £20,000 totalled £2.71 million.
how to apply Apply via the foundation's website.
contact details The Trustees, c/o Azets, Ty Derw, Lime Tree Court, Cardiff Gate Business Park, Cardiff CF23 8AB *Email* moondancefoundation@gmail.com *Website* https://moondancefoundation.org.uk

■ The Janet and Brian Moore Charitable Trust

cc no 1189019
where funding can be given Warwickshire; Oxfordshire; Northamptonshire.
who can benefit Charitable organisations.
what is funded Projects which help unite local rural communities.
type of grant Salaries; capital expenditure; contributions to the cost of overheads.
range of grants The maximum amount of support per project is £20,000.
sample grants A list of beneficiaries was not included in the annual report and accounts.
finances *Financial year end* 31/03/2022
Income £125,100
Grants to organisations £87,800
Assets £107,000
trustees Janet Moore; Andrew Pinney; James Copeman.
how to apply Applications can be made via the trust's website.
contact details The Trustees, Kings Barn, Ladbroke, Southam CV47 2DF

Email bryjan4344@hotmail.com *Website* www.janetandbryanmooretrust.org.uk

■ The George A. Moore Foundation

cc no 262107   **established** 1970
where funding can be given Yorkshire.
who can benefit Registered charities.
what is funded General charitable purposes.
what is not funded Individuals; courses of study; overseas travel; holidays; purposes outside the UK.
type of grant Project funding.
range of grants Typically £500 to £2,500; larger grants may be considered for selected projects.
sample grants Knaresborough Museum Association (£100,000); The Forest School – Knaresborough (£50,000); Boston Spa Village Hall (£10,800); St Aidan's Church of England High School – Harrogate (£7,500); Parkinson's UK (£3,000); Samaritans of Leeds (£2,400); Wetherby in Support of the Elderly (£1,500); Leeds Hospitals Charity (£500).
finances *Financial year end* 05/04/2022
Income £117,600
Grants to organisations £420,000
Assets £7,430,000
trustees Jonathan Moore; Paul Turner; Charlotte Lowe.
other information Grants were awarded to 79 organisations, ranging from £150 to £50,000.
how to apply Apply in writing to the correspondent. The trustees meet quarterly. Full details of what should be included in an application and application deadlines can be found on the foundation's website.
contact details Elena Duke, Administrator, 4th Floor, 10 South Parade, Leeds, West Yorkshire LS1 5QS *Tel.* 0113 386 3393 *Email* info@gamf.org.uk *Website* www.gamf.org.uk

■ The Henry Moore Foundation

cc no 271370   **established** 1977
where funding can be given UK and overseas.
who can benefit Not-for-profit organisations; arts organisations; educational bodies; individuals (research and travel grants only).
what is funded Fine arts, in particular, sculpture; the development of collections through acquisitions, conservation, cataloguing and display.
what is not funded Revenue expenditure; individuals (except research and travel grants or fellowships); retrospective expenditure. No grant (or part of any grant) may be used to pay any fee or to provide any other benefit to any individual who is a trustee of the foundation.
type of grant One-off and long-term funding; publication; research; development; collections; exhibitions; fellowships; conferences and lectures.
range of grants Up to £20,000, depending on grant category.
sample grants Victoria and Albert Museum (£20,000); British Council (£17,000); Hepworth Wakefield (£15,000); Hood Museum of Art at Dartmouth College (£14,000); National Life Stories (£12,000); Glasgow Museums and Yorkshire Sculpture Park (£10,000 each).
finances *Financial year end* 31/03/2022
Income £3,170,000
Grants to organisations £404,200
Assets £125,970,000
trustees Peter Wienand; Charles Asprey; William Edgerley; Prof. Antony Griffiths; Nigel Carrington;

Pamela Raynor; Martin Barden; Courtney Martin; Ella Snell; Leonard Dunne; Lesley Sherratt; Hammad Nasar.

OTHER INFORMATION During 2021/22, 77 grants were awarded in the following categories: exhibitions and new projects (£250,200); collections (£94,500); research (£27,500); fellowships (£21,000); conferences, publications and workshops (£11,000). A list of previously supported projects is available on the foundation's website. Grants of less than £10,000 were not listed and totalled (£232,000).

HOW TO APPLY Applications can be completed on the foundation's website. The grants committee considers applications four times a year. Check the website for further guidance and current deadlines.

CONTACT DETAILS Grants Commitee, Dane Tree House, Perry Green, Much Hadham, Hertfordshire SG10 6EE *Tel.* 01279 843333 *Email* admin@henry-moore.org or use the enquiry form on the website *Website* www.henry-moore.org

....

■ John Moores Foundation

CC NO 253481   **ESTABLISHED** 1963

WHERE FUNDING CAN BE GIVEN Merseyside (including Skelmersdale, Halton and Ellesmere Port) and Northern Ireland.

WHO CAN BENEFIT Registered charities; unregistered charities; social enterprises; CICs.

WHAT IS FUNDED Social welfare; mental health; minority ethnic communities; refugees; women and girls; children and young people; discrimination; families; people who are homeless; carers; adult education.

WHAT IS NOT FUNDED Individuals; projects that are not substantially influenced by their target beneficiaries; national organisations or groups based outside the Merseyside region even if some of the service users come from the area; statutory bodies or work previously done by them; education (schools, colleges, universities and supplementary schools); faith-based projects exclusively for members of that faith, or for the promotion of religion; capital building costs; festivals, carnivals and fêtes; medicine or medical equipment; holidays and expeditions; gifts, parties, etc.; organising conferences; sport; vehicles; animal charities; the creative industries; heritage or local history projects; employability and enterprise schemes; academic or medical research; credit unions – except for the training of management committee members or the development of a new business plan; veterans; uniformed groups; sponsorship, advertising or fundraising events; counsellors not registered with the British Association for Counselling and Psychotherapy or the UK Council for Psychotherapy.

TYPE OF GRANT Running costs; capacity building; volunteer expenses; one-off projects; equipment (if part of a wider project).

SAMPLE GRANTS A list of beneficiaries was not included in the annual report and accounts. Previous beneficiaries have included: Mencap Wirral (£30,000); In Another Place (£22,500); Knowsley Disability Concern (£15,000); Liverpool Bereavement Service (£10,000); Glencolin Residents Association and Jus Kidz (£5,000 each); Tuebrook Hope Group (£1,000); Stockbridge Disability Group (£150).

FINANCES *Financial year end* 06/09/2022
Income £545,000
Grants to organisations £725,600
Assets £30,750,000

TRUSTEES Nicola Eastwood; Kevin Moores; Barnaby Moores; Christina Mee; John Davis.

OTHER INFORMATION In 2021/22, grants were awarded to 139 organisations. Grants awarded to organisations in Merseyside were broken down as follows: grassroots social health (£311,700); children and young people (£309,200); local community groups (£181,500); women (£99,300); equality and diversity (£97,200); advice (£60,700); carers (£54,400); minority ethnic organisations (£51,700).

HOW TO APPLY Applicants should first check their eligibility on the foundation's website. Following this, applicants can contact the foundation via email, letter, or phone to obtain an application form.

CONTACT DETAILS Phil Godfrey, Grants Director, 96 Bold Street, Liverpool, Merseyside L1 4HY *Tel.* 0151 707 6077 *Email* info@johnmooresfoundation.com *Website* www.jmf.org.uk

....

■ The Morel Charitable Trust

CC NO 268943   **ESTABLISHED** 1973

WHERE FUNDING CAN BE GIVEN Worldwide, with a preference for Bristol, Leeds, Brecon, London, Ghana, Zambia, Malawi and the Solomon Islands.

WHO CAN BENEFIT Charitable organisations.

WHAT IS FUNDED Arts and culture, particularly drama; race relations; inner-city projects; international development.

TYPE OF GRANT Project funding.

RANGE OF GRANTS Mostly £3,000 and under.

SAMPLE GRANTS Christian Aid (£10,000); Tree Aid (£5,000); Partners UK (£4,000); Excellent Development (£2,000); Retreat House Chester (£1,000).

FINANCES *Financial year end* 31/03/2022
Income £59,300
Grants to organisations £133,500
Assets £2,180,000

TRUSTEES Simon Gibbs; William Gibbs; James Gibbs; Dr Thomas Gibbs; Benjamin Gibbs; Abigail Keane; Dr Emily Parry; Susanna Coan.

OTHER INFORMATION Grants were awarded to 41 organisations and broken down as follows: international (£87,500); UK social (£29,500); UK arts (£16,500).

HOW TO APPLY Apply in writing to the correspondent. Grants are normally made to aid projects of which the trustees have personal knowledge.

CONTACT DETAILS Simon Gibbs, Trustee, 34 Durand Gardens, London SW9 0PP *Tel.* 020 7582 6901 *Email* simoned.gibbs@yahoo.co.uk

....

■ The Morgan Charitable Foundation

CC NO 283128   **ESTABLISHED** 1981

WHERE FUNDING CAN BE GIVEN UK.

WHO CAN BENEFIT Charitable organisations.

WHAT IS FUNDED General charitable purposes; social welfare; health; overseas aid; disability; homelessness; the Jewish faith and community.

WHAT IS NOT FUNDED Individuals.

SAMPLE GRANTS A list of beneficiaries was not made available in the 2021 accounts but can be requested from the trustees.

FINANCES *Financial year end* 31/12/2021
  Income £136,900
  Grants to organisations £88,000
  Assets £6,370,000
TRUSTEES Carmen Gleen; Leslie Morgan; Nelly Levene; Molly Tiroche; Ronnie Morgan.
OTHER INFORMATION The trustees maintain a list of charitable organisations which they regularly support and the list is reviewed half-yearly at the directors' meetings.
HOW TO APPLY Applications have to be made in writing to the correspondent and include a copy of the latest annual report and accounts. The trustees meet twice a year. The foundation has previously requested not to receive telephone enquiries.
CONTACT DETAILS The Trustees, PO Box 57749, London NW11 1FD *Tel.* 07970 056111

■ The Steve Morgan Foundation

CC NO 1087056   ESTABLISHED 2000
WHERE FUNDING CAN BE GIVEN North Wales, Merseyside and Cheshire.
WHO CAN BENEFIT Registered charities; CICs; social enterprises; individuals.
WHAT IS FUNDED Children and young people; families; older people; health and disability; people who are socially isolated. The foundation's website states: 'All requests which would result in a positive effect on people's welfare or quality of life or improves opportunities and life choices, are considered.'
WHAT IS NOT FUNDED Application guidelines and criteria for each funding programme can be found on the foundation's website.
TYPE OF GRANT Capital costs; core costs; revenue costs.
SAMPLE GRANTS Diabetes UK/Juvenile Diabetes Research Foundation (£50 million); Reader Organisation (£120,000); The Duke of Edinburgh's Award Scheme (£100,000); Creating Adventures (£60,000); Warrington Youth (£50,000).
FINANCES *Financial year end* 31/03/2022
  Income £6,510,000
  Grants to organisations £52,680,000
  Grants to individuals £172,800
  Assets £255,150,000
TRUSTEES Vincent Fairclough; Stephen Morgan; Rhiannon Walker; Ashley Lewis; Sally Morgan; Jonathan Masters; Brian Clark.
OTHER INFORMATION The foundation also funds specialised equipment for people in need through its Enable programme.
HOW TO APPLY For regional, major and Smiley Bus grants, applicants are requested to first check their eligibility against the criteria listed on the foundation's website. Eligible organisations are then asked submit an expression of interest via email.
CONTACT DETAILS The Trustees, PO Box 3517, Chester CH1 9ET *Tel.* 01829 782800 *Email* hello@stevemorganfoundation.org.uk *Website* https://stevemorganfoundation.org.uk

■ Morgan Stanley International Foundation

CC NO 1042671   ESTABLISHED 1994
WHERE FUNDING CAN BE GIVEN Europe, Middle East and Africa. Local projects in Tower Hamlets and Glasgow.
WHO CAN BENEFIT Registered charities; state-funded schools.
WHAT IS FUNDED Children's health; education.
WHAT IS NOT FUNDED See the foundation's website for a list of exclusions.
TYPE OF GRANT Project funding; capital costs.
RANGE OF GRANTS Up to £250,000.
SAMPLE GRANTS Place2Be – London (£252,700); GOSH – London (£107,400); Save the Children (£91,000); CHAS – Glasgow (£90,000); PEEK – Glasgow (£84,300).
FINANCES *Financial year end* 31/12/2021
  Income £2,690,000
  Grants to organisations £2,130,000
  Assets £3,450,000
TRUSTEES Clare Woodman; Stephen Mavin; Sue Watts; Oliver Stuart; Jamie Glynn; Norbert Fogarasi; Marco Gregotti; Aidan Armstrong; Sacha Anselm; Caroline Nicholls; Zoe Parish; Dorothee Fuhrmann; Emily Laino; Josephine Harriman.
OTHER INFORMATION The foundation is the corporate charity of Morgan Stanley and Co. International plc, the financial services corporation. The foundation matches any contribution, either monetary or through volunteering, by employees to a maximum of £500 per employee in one given year. Employees are encouraged to take on up to ten weeks' pro bono work for NGOs and charities.
HOW TO APPLY The foundation takes a proactive approach to grant-making and therefore does not accept unsolicited proposals. However, the foundation's website does state that you can make contact via email if you think your charity is a match with its funding criteria. Details of what should be included in the email can be found on the charity's website.
CONTACT DETAILS The Trustees, Morgan Stanley and Co. International plc, 20 Bank Street, London E14 4AD *Email* communityaffairslondon@morganstanley.com *Website* www.morganstanley.com/pub/content/msdotcom/en/about-us/giving-back/msif-guidelines.html

■ The Morris Charitable Trust

CC NO 802290   ESTABLISHED 1989
WHERE FUNDING CAN BE GIVEN UK and overseas, with strong preference for Islington.
WHO CAN BENEFIT Registered charities; local Islington community projects. The trustees select national and international charities to support on an ad hoc basis.
WHAT IS FUNDED Social welfare; health; education; community.
WHAT IS NOT FUNDED Individuals; annual core costs (e.g. staffing, salaries or equipment hire); repeat applications within one year; non-registered charities.
TYPE OF GRANT One-off project and capital grants for one year.
RANGE OF GRANTS Usually up to £5,000.
SAMPLE GRANTS A list of recent beneficiaries can be found on the trust's website.
FINANCES *Financial year end* 31/03/2022
  Income £100,000
  Grants to organisations £154,700
  Assets £122,900
TRUSTEES Dominic Jones; Jack Morris; Paul Morris; Alan Stenning; Linda Morris; Lucie Grant; Kate Simpson; Carly King; Marc Morris.
OTHER INFORMATION Grants were made to 29 organisations during the year.
HOW TO APPLY Application forms are available to complete online on the trust's website. The trustees meet throughout the year to consider applications. Grants are generally not repeated within a 12-month period.

CONTACT DETAILS Linda Morris, Secretary, Business Design Centre, 52 Upper Street, Islington Green, London N1 0QH *Tel.* 020 7359 3535 *Email* info@morrischaritabletrust.com *Website* www.morrischaritabletrust.com

■ G. M. Morrison Charitable Trust

CC NO 261380 ESTABLISHED 1970
WHERE FUNDING CAN BE GIVEN UK.
WHO CAN BENEFIT Registered charities operating in the UK and abroad; hospitals; hospices; universities; places of worship.
WHAT IS FUNDED General charitable purposes; medicine and health; social welfare; education and training.
WHAT IS NOT FUNDED Activities or projects that are generally regarded as the responsibility of statutory authorities; individuals; short-term projects; one-off capital grants (except for emergency appeals); commercial or business activities; retrospective grant applications.
TYPE OF GRANT Mostly recurrent annual awards for core/revenue costs.
RANGE OF GRANTS £1,000 to £5,000.
SAMPLE GRANTS Save the Children Emergency Appeal – COVID India (£5,000); Royal College of Surgeons (£3,300); Shelterbox (£3,200); Age UK (£2,100); Bowel and Cancer Research (£1,800); Alternatives to Violence Project, Care for the Family and Zoological Society of London (£1,700 each); Opera North (£1,600); Mental Health Foundation (£1,500); Catch 22 (£1,400); Prostate Cancer UK (£1,200); Migraine Trust and The Tree Register (£1,000 each).
FINANCES *Financial year end 05/04/2022*
Income £289,300
Grants to organisations £275,400
Assets £16,190,000
TRUSTEES Jane Hunt; Elizabeth Morrison; Felicity Rice.
OTHER INFORMATION In 2021/22 the trust made 195 grants to organisations. The average grant size was around £1,400. Grants were distributed as follows: medical causes and health (£114,100 in 86 grants); social welfare (£74,100 in 56 grants); other (£64,000 in 37 grants); education and training (£23,200 in 16 grants).
HOW TO APPLY To apply, write to the charity's address; however, note that new applications are only considered in exceptional circumstances. Beneficiaries are ordinarily selected based on the trustees' personal knowledge and supported on a long-term basis. Applications are not acknowledged. Grants are distributed annually in January.
CONTACT DETAILS The Trustees, c/o Currey and Co. LLP, 33 Queen Anne Street, London W1G 9HY *Tel.* 020 7802 2700 *Email* gen@curreyandco.co.uk

■ The Ken and Edna Morrison Charitable Trust

CC NO 327639 ESTABLISHED 1987
WHERE FUNDING CAN BE GIVEN UK, with a preference for Yorkshire.
WHO CAN BENEFIT Registered charities.
WHAT IS FUNDED General charitable purposes, including the following: support for people with a disability or special educational needs; education and training.
TYPE OF GRANT One-off.
RANGE OF GRANTS £5,000 to £40,000.

SAMPLE GRANTS Forget Me Not Children's Hospice (£40,000); Marie Curie (£40,000); Mind in Bradford (£20,000); Sense Bradford and Lifelites (£10,000 each); Addington Fund and Autism Angels (£5,000 each).
FINANCES *Financial year end 05/04/2022*
Income £172,500
Grants to organisations £194,000
Assets £2,500,000
TRUSTEES Eleanor Kernighan; William Morrison.
OTHER INFORMATION Grants were awarded to 16 organisations during the year.
HOW TO APPLY Apply in writing to the correspondent. The trust's 2021/22 accounts state: 'Future grants will include small donations (on application) to causes within the objectives and also larger donations to projects or organisations that the trustees have identified.'
CONTACT DETAILS The Trustees, c/o Progeny Private Law, Progeny House, 46 Park Place, Leeds, North Yorkshire LS1 2RY *Tel.* 0113 467 1742

■ The Ken and Lynne Morrison Charitable Trust

CC NO 1125586 ESTABLISHED 2008
WHERE FUNDING CAN BE GIVEN Yorkshire.
WHO CAN BENEFIT Registered charities; individuals; hospices.
WHAT IS FUNDED General charitable purposes; people with disabilities or special educational needs; education and training; medical care.
TYPE OF GRANT One-off grants.
RANGE OF GRANTS Up to £10,000 with the occasional larger grant.
SAMPLE GRANTS Marie Curie – Bradford Hospice (£140,000); Candlelighters and Centrepoint (£100,000 each); Age UK Bradford District (£40,000); Bradford Nightstop and Designability (£10,000 each); Clothing Solutions and Sudden Unexpected Death in Epilepsy (£5,000 each); Bradford Inclusive Disability Service (£2,400).
FINANCES *Financial year end 05/04/2022*
Income £491,300
Grants to organisations £594,300
Assets £17,920,000
TRUSTEES Lady Lynne Morrison; Andrea Shelley.
HOW TO APPLY The trust's 2021/22 annual report states that the trust normally does not accept unsolicited applications, other than in cases where the speculative applicant is considered as 'pertinent to the trust's objectives', particularly those associated with the Yorkshire region.
CONTACT DETAILS The Trustees, Myton Hall, Myton-on-Swale, Helperby, York, North Yorkshire YO61 2QX *Tel.* 01423 360258

■ The Morrisons Foundation

CC NO 1160224/SC045634 ESTABLISHED 2014
WHERE FUNDING CAN BE GIVEN England; Wales; Scotland.
WHO CAN BENEFIT Charities that have been registered for a minimum of one year.
WHAT IS FUNDED General charitable purposes; community; health; education; social welfare; the arts and culture.
WHAT IS NOT FUNDED Non-registered charities; individuals; salaries and running costs; part-funding. A full list of exclusions can be found on the foundation's website.
TYPE OF GRANT Capital costs and project funding.
RANGE OF GRANTS Up to £25,000.

SAMPLE GRANTS A list of beneficiaries was not included in the annual report and accounts. Previous beneficiaries have included: Ickle Pickles and The Children's Trust (£25,000 each); Dentaid (£20,000); Emmaus Oxford (£18,400); Lincolnshire Emergency Blood Bikes Service (£14,700); British Disabled Angling Association (£7,400); Pinpoint (£5,000); Disability Snowsport UK (£4,600).

FINANCES *Financial year end* 04/02/2021
Income £3,690,000
Grants to organisations £3,040,000
Assets £2,270,000

TRUSTEES Guy Mason; Jonathan Burke; Charles Jones; David Scott; Sarah Wilkinson; Kate Bratt-Farrar; Charles Dacres.

OTHER INFORMATION This is the corporate charity of the supermarket chain Morrisons. In addition to grants the foundation also matches employees' fundraising efforts. The 2020/21 accounts were the latest available at the time of writing (June 2023).

HOW TO APPLY Applications can be completed online through the foundation's website. Applications are accepted and reviewed on a continual basis. Applicants will be notified of a decision by telephone or email, even if the application is unsuccessful.

CONTACT DETAILS The Trustees, Hilmore House, Gain Lane, Bradford, West Yorkshire BD3 7DL *Tel.* 0845 611 5364 *Email* foundation. enquiries@morrisonsplc.co.uk *Website* www. morrisonsfoundation.com

---

■ The Mosawi Foundation

CC NO 1157269   **ESTABLISHED** 2014
WHERE FUNDING CAN BE GIVEN UK, with a preference for Oxfordshire; overseas.
WHO CAN BENEFIT Charitable organisations.
WHAT IS FUNDED Children and young people; community development; education; health care and trauma relief; social welfare.
RANGE OF GRANTS Up to £600,000.
SAMPLE GRANTS Royal Welsh College of Music and Drama (£553,900); Reading Rep Theatre (£50,000); St James Church (£60,000); Kids Alive International (£35,000); Unicorn Trust (£25,000); Hereford Cathedral School (£22,100); Berin Centre (£20,000).
FINANCES *Financial year end* 05/04/2022
Income £2,020,000
Grants to organisations £1,070,000
Assets £2,110,000
TRUSTEES Anthony Mosawi; Shannon Mosawi; Eleanor Mosawi; Mrs E. M. Mosawi; Mr A. Mosawi.
HOW TO APPLY Apply in writing to the correspondent.
CONTACT DETAILS Ali Mosawi, Trustee, PO Box 4822, Henley-on-Thames, Oxfordshire RG9 9HB *Email* alimosawi.tmf@gmail.com

---

■ The Moshal Charitable Trust

CC NO 284448   **ESTABLISHED** 1982
WHERE FUNDING CAN BE GIVEN UK.
WHO CAN BENEFIT Charitable and educational organisations.
WHAT IS FUNDED General charitable purposes; education; the Jewish faith and community.
SAMPLE GRANTS A list of beneficiaries was not included in the annual report and accounts.
FINANCES *Financial year end* 31/12/2022
Income £52,800
Grants to organisations £78,800
Assets £788,900

TRUSTEES Lea Halpern; David Halpern.
HOW TO APPLY Apply in writing to the correspondent.
CONTACT DETAILS The Trustees, New Riverside House, 439 Lower Broughton Road, Salford M7 2FX *Tel.* 0161 792 2626

■ Vyoel Moshe Charitable Trust

CC NO 327054   **ESTABLISHED** 1986
WHERE FUNDING CAN BE GIVEN UK and overseas, including Israel, USA and Europe.
WHO CAN BENEFIT Registered charities; religious bodies; synagogues; individuals.
WHAT IS FUNDED The Jewish faith and community. Awards made to religious bodies are given to synagogues for the preservation of cemeteries, Jewish culture and heritage.
RANGE OF GRANTS £3,000 to £25,000.
SAMPLE GRANTS A list of beneficiaries was not included in the annual report and accounts. Previous beneficiaries have included: Mishkanos Haroyim; Mosdos Yetyev Lev Antwerp; Talmud Torah Tuv Yerushalaim; Talmud Tora Hamekoris Remoh; Toldos Aharon; Yeshivas Kol Aryeh; Yetev Lev Institutions.
FINANCES *Financial year end* 31/01/2022
Income £961,000
Grants to organisations £907,700
Assets £138,400
TRUSTEES Jacob Frankel; Berish Berger; Shulom Cik.
OTHER INFORMATION The grant total includes amounts awarded to organisations and to individuals; a breakdown was not available.
HOW TO APPLY Apply in writing to the correspondent. The 2021/22 annual report states that 'the trustees select the institutions to be supported according to their personal knowledge of work of the institution. Individuals are referred to the charity by local rabbis.'
CONTACT DETAILS The Trustees, 63A Lampard Grove, London N16 6XA *Tel.* 07975 952011

■ The Alexander Mosley Charitable Trust

CC NO 1142898   **ESTABLISHED** 2011
WHERE FUNDING CAN BE GIVEN UK and overseas.
WHO CAN BENEFIT Mainly UK-registered charities; unregistered charities; hospices.
WHAT IS FUNDED General charitable purposes; the armed forces; heritage projects.
WHAT IS NOT FUNDED Large national charities (i.e. those with an annual income in excess of £10 million or with over £100 million in assets); charities dedicated to issues deemed by the trustees to be already well funded within the UK; charities dedicated to purposes for which the UK government has a statutory responsibility to provide.
TYPE OF GRANT One-off; recurrent.
RANGE OF GRANTS Up to £60,000.
SAMPLE GRANTS Independent Press Regulation Trust (£7 million); The 353 Trust (£60,000); Inside Justice (£25,000); Asthall Swinbrook and Widford Church (£12,000); Willow Foundation (£5,000).
FINANCES *Financial year end* 05/04/2022
Income £290,000
Grants to organisations £7,100,000
Assets £6,120,000
TRUSTEES Horatio Mortimer; Max Mosley; Emma Mosley.
HOW TO APPLY Apply in writing to the correspondent.

CONTACT DETAILS The Trustees, 10 New Square, Lincoln's Inn, London WC2A 3QG *Tel.* 020 7465 4300

■ The Mosselson Charitable Trust

CC NO 266517   **ESTABLISHED** 1974
WHERE FUNDING CAN BE GIVEN UK.
WHO CAN BENEFIT Charitable organisations.
WHAT IS FUNDED Education; medicine and medical research; women and children's support and welfare; religion; social welfare.
SAMPLE GRANTS Previous beneficiaries have included: ChildLine; Holocaust Education Trust; Jewish Women's Week; Family Housing Association; Nightingale House; Shaare Zedek Medical Centre.
FINANCES *Financial year end 30/09/2021*
Income £3,100
Grants to organisations £69,200
TRUSTEES Marian Mosselson; Dr Jacqueline Mosselson.
OTHER INFORMATION Full accounts were not available to view due to the trust's low income. Therefore, we have estimated the grant total based on the trust's total expenditure. The 2020/21 Charity Commission record was the latest available at the time of writing (June 2023).
HOW TO APPLY Apply in writing to the correspondent.
CONTACT DETAILS The Trustees, Denmoss House, 10 Greenland Street, London NW1 0ND *Tel.* 020 7428 1929

■ Motability

CC NO 299745
WHERE FUNDING CAN BE GIVEN UK.
WHO CAN BENEFIT Charitable organisations and disabled individuals.
WHAT IS FUNDED Disability.
TYPE OF GRANT Capital costs.
SAMPLE GRANTS A list of beneficiaries was not included in the annual report and accounts.
FINANCES *Financial year end 31/03/2022*
Income £183,750,000
Grants to organisations £4,110,000
Grants to individuals £53,850,000
Assets £1,700,000,000
TRUSTEES Charles Manby; Tony Davis; Sukhi Clark; Hannah Barham-Brown; Richard Cartwright; Robin Hindle-Fisher; Dr Juliana Onwumere; Prof. William Webb; David Hunter; Ed Humpherson.
OTHER INFORMATION In 2021/22, grants to organisations were broken down as follows: Family Fund (£1.8 million); Designability – charging points (£1.14 million); Designability – Wizzybugs (£605,000); user research (£539,000); scholarships (£23,000).
HOW TO APPLY Potential applicants should contact the Charitable Grants Team on 0800 500 3186.
CONTACT DETAILS Charitable Grants Team, Warwick House, Roydon Road, Harlow, Essex CM19 5PX *Tel.* 0800 500 3186 *Email* communications@ motability.co.uk *Website* www.motability.co.uk

■ Moto Foundation

CC NO 1111147   **ESTABLISHED** 2005
WHERE FUNDING CAN BE GIVEN UK. Organisations should be within a 15-mile radius of a Moto site.
WHO CAN BENEFIT Registered charities; schools; CICs; not-for-profit groups.
WHAT IS FUNDED Community development; the environment; general charitable purposes.

WHAT IS NOT FUNDED Overseas organisations; projects or organisations that are of a religious or political nature.
RANGE OF GRANTS Grants of up to £1,000 but mostly under £500.
SAMPLE GRANTS The Woodland Trust (£50,000); The Wetland and Wildfowl Trust (£25,000); 451 Stourbridge Squadron Royal Air Force Air Cadets and Cardiff Women's Aid (£1,000 each); Fairhaven Primary School (£500); Wessex Cancer Trust (£450); Tamworth Literary Festival (£240); Spirit and Soul Equine Therapy (£170); Digital Skills Training CIC and Garstang Community First Responders (£150 each).
FINANCES *Financial year end 31/12/2021*
Income £854,100
Grants to organisations £372,900
Grants to individuals £22,500
Assets £482,000
TRUSTEES Louise Hughes; Julie Donovan; Amy Procter; Robert O'Connell; Kayleigh Clarke; Samantha Peacock; Stephen Rac; Guy Latchem; Coral Brodie.
HOW TO APPLY Applications should be made through the online application form. Applications should have the endorsement of a Moto colleague.
CONTACT DETAILS Caroline Campbell, Administrator, PO Box 218, Toddington, Bedfordshire LU5 6QG *Tel.* 01525 878500 *Email* motofoundation@ moto-way.co.uk *Website* https://moto-way.com/ about-us/moto-foundation

■ Motor Neurone Disease Association

CC NO 294354   **ESTABLISHED** 1986
WHERE FUNDING CAN BE GIVEN UK and overseas.
WHO CAN BENEFIT Universities; hospitals; research institutions; charitable organisations; individuals.
WHAT IS FUNDED Research into motor neurone disease; support for individuals diagnosed with motor neurone disease.
WHAT IS NOT FUNDED Programme-specific exclusions can be found on the website.
TYPE OF GRANT Project funding; capital costs; core/ revenue funding; research grants.
RANGE OF GRANTS Grants vary according to the programme.
SAMPLE GRANTS King's College London (£1.08 million); LifeArc (£800,000); My Name'5 Doddie Foundation (£200,000); The Betty Messenger Charitable Foundation (£100,000); Darby Rimmer MND Foundation (£50,000); Netherby Trust (£40,000); The William Brake Foundation (£25,000); Malcolm Gunter Foundation (£20,000); The Harris Family Charitable Trust (£15,000); Frank Brake Charitable Trust (£10,000); Sir Samuel Scott of Yews Trust (£5,000); University of Edinburgh (£1,000).
FINANCES *Financial year end 31/12/2021*
Income £28,940,000
Grants to organisations £10,020,000
Grants to individuals £1,710,000
Assets £25,890.00
TRUSTEES Siobhan Rooney; Katy Styles; Catherine Knights; Shaun Gee; Debra Martin; Elizabeth Ellis; Dr Usman Khan; James Marshall; Simon Croxford; Dr Katherine Jackson; Kirrie Todd; Ian Lev; Susan Watts.
OTHER INFORMATION During the year, grants for care and care centres totalled £6.92 million and research grants totalled £4.8 million. The grant total includes grants made to individuals and organisations.

HOW TO APPLY The application process may vary according to the programme being applied to. Further information on each programme, including the application process, is available on the grant-maker's website.

CONTACT DETAILS Research Grants Team, Francis Crick House, 6 Summerhouse Road, Moulton Park Industrial Estate, Northampton, Northamptonshire NN3 6BJ *Tel.* 01604 611873 *Email* research.grants@mndassociation.org *Website* www.mndassociation.org/research/for-researchers

■ The Moulding Foundation

CC NO 1192727
WHERE FUNDING CAN BE GIVEN The north of England.
WHO CAN BENEFIT Charitable organisations.
WHAT IS FUNDED Social exclusion; young people with disabilities; health; education.
SAMPLE GRANTS A list of beneficiaries was not included in the annual report and accounts.
FINANCES *Financial year end 31/12/2021*
Income £88,130,000
Grants to organisations £2,440,000
Assets £32,010,000
TRUSTEES Jodie Moulding; Angela Richards; Rebecca Morris Adams.
HOW TO APPLY See the foundation's website for further information on applications.
CONTACT DETAILS The Trustees, c/o ICON 1, 7 Sunbank Lane, Ringway, Altrincham, Cheshire WA15 0AF *Email* enquiries@mouldingfoundation.com *Website* www.themouldingfoundation.com

■ J. P. Moulton Charitable Foundation

CC NO 1109891 **ESTABLISHED** 2004
WHERE FUNDING CAN BE GIVEN UK.
WHO CAN BENEFIT Registered charities; research institutions; universities; hospitals and hospices.
WHAT IS FUNDED Medical research and care, particularly non-commercial clinical trials; health education and training; counselling; community health projects.
TYPE OF GRANT Research; capital costs; project funding.
SAMPLE GRANTS Great Ormond Street Hospital Children's Charity (£100,000); Exeter University (£97,900); Royal Papworth Hospital NHS Foundation Trust (£89,100); University of Sheffield (£50,200); University of Manchester (£34,900); King's College London (£30,900); Scar Free Foundation (£30,000); Prostate Cancer UK (£22,200); Institute of Cancer Research (£5,300).
FINANCES *Financial year end 31/12/2021*
Income £177,100
Grants to organisations £460,400
Assets £553,000
TRUSTEES Jon Moulton; Dr Helen Critchley; Spencer Moulton.
OTHER INFORMATION Grants were made to nine organisations in 2021. According to the foundation's 2021 annual report, 'a new charity has been established in Guernsey, The Jon Moulton Charity Trust', which is continuing the foundation's work. The foundation 'will continue to fund its existing financial commitments' but future calls for funding and grants will be made via the new charity.

HOW TO APPLY Details of how to apply and what to include in an application can be found on The Jon Moulton Charity Trust's web page. Funding calls are not annual – the last call was in 2019 and the next one is anticipated to be towards the end of 2023.

CONTACT DETAILS Jon Moulton, Trustee, c/o Perscitus LLP, 10 Buckingham Street, London WC2N 6DF *Tel.* 020 3727 6601 *Email* Jon.Moulton@jonmoulton.gg *Website* www.perscitusllp.com/moulton-charity-trust

■ The Edwina Mountbatten and Leonora Children's Foundation

CC NO 228166 **ESTABLISHED** 1960
WHERE FUNDING CAN BE GIVEN UK and overseas.
WHO CAN BENEFIT Registered charities; hospitals; hospices.
WHAT IS FUNDED Health care; nursing; paediatric cancer.
TYPE OF GRANT Project funding.
RANGE OF GRANTS £5,000 to £70,000.
SAMPLE GRANTS LOOK (£70,000); Countess Mountbatten of Burma Romsey Memorial Trust (£50,000); Brecknock Hospice and St John of Jerusalem Eye Hospital (£25,000 each); Gift of Sight (£10,000); Andover Young Carers and Hope for Tomorrow (£5,000 each).
FINANCES *Financial year end 31/12/2021*
Income £111,000
Grants to organisations £200,000
Assets £7,350,000
TRUSTEES Lady Mary Fagan; Lady Alexandra Knatchbull; Peter Mimpriss; Myrddin Rees; Rt Hon. Penelope Meridith Mary the Countess Mountbatten of Burma.
OTHER INFORMATION Grants were made to nine organisations during the year.
HOW TO APPLY Apply in writing to the correspondent.
CONTACT DETAILS Richard Jordan-Baker, Trust Secretary, The Estate Office, Broadlands, Romsey, Hampshire SO51 9ZE *Tel.* 01794 505080 *Email* narahguy@broadlandsestates.co.uk

■ The Mowgli Trust

CC NO 1173842 **ESTABLISHED** 2017
WHERE FUNDING CAN BE GIVEN UK.
WHO CAN BENEFIT Registered charities; hospices; hospitals.
WHAT IS FUNDED General charitable purposes.
RANGE OF GRANTS £6,000 to £48,500.
SAMPLE GRANTS A list of beneficiaries was not included in the annual report and accounts. Previous beneficiaries have included: Tearfund (£48,500); Action Against Hunger (£33,300); Maggie's (£24,100); The Clatterbridge Cancer Charity (£22,000); Bobath Children's Therapy Centre Wales (£9,000); Rainbows Hospice for Children and Young People (£6,400).
FINANCES *Financial year end 31/03/2022*
Income £426,700
Grants to organisations £304,400
Assets £107,800
TRUSTEES Nisha Katona; Matthew Peck; Jane Lake.
OTHER INFORMATION Charities supported are typically local to a branch of Mowgli Street Food.
HOW TO APPLY Unsolicited applications are not accepted.
CONTACT DETAILS The Trustees, 18 Queen Avenue, Castle Street, Liverpool L2 4TX *Tel.* 01517 08505 *Email* matthewpeck@mowglistreetfood.com *Website* https://mowglitrust.com

■ The MSE Charity

cc no 1121320   **established** 2008
where funding can be given UK.
who can benefit Registered charities; CICs; credit unions; non-profit organisations with a constitution.
what is funded Financial literacy; debt, money and consumer issues education.
what is not funded Individuals; statutory organisations; organisations with an annual income over £500,000 and with more than six months' free reserves. For a full list of exclusions, see the FAQs section of the charity's website.
type of grant Project costs.
range of grants Up to £7,500.
sample grants Hull Kingston Rovers Community Trust (£7,500); Kith and Kin Financial Wellbeing CIC (£6,600); Citizens Advice Wokingham (£5,800); The Family Trust (£5,000); Transitions UK (£4,500); Happy Days Ministries UK (£3,000); CAP Larne (£2,100).
finances *Financial year end 31/03/2022*
Income £121,400
Grants to organisations £172,900
Assets £21,100
trustees Katie Davies; Vanessa Bissessur; Tony Tesciuba; Teej Dew; Clarissa Coleman; Marcus Herbert.
other information The charity provides two rounds of grants per year, focusing on four themes through a two-year cycle. See the website for the most up-to-date information.
how to apply Applicants should complete an online application form when the relevant funding round opens. A template can be found on the website which previews the questions that will need to be answered. Each grant round is limited to the first 40 applicants. An eligibility quiz is available on the charity's website. Full application details can be found on the website.
contact details Katie Davies, Operations Manager, c/o Tesciuba Ltd, 72 Cavendish Road, Salford M7 4WA *Tel.* 0161 211 0205 *Email* info@ msecharity.com *Website* www.msecharity.com

■ The Mulberry Trust

cc no 263296   **established** 1971
where funding can be given UK, with a preference for Essex.
who can benefit Charitable organisations; hospices; arts organisations; environmental organisations; Christian organisations.
what is funded General charitable purposes, particularly parenting and family welfare, children, older people, homelessness, debt relief and counselling, community development, education and research, religious and interfaith work, health, the arts and the environment.
what is not funded Individuals.
range of grants £500 to £20,000.
sample grants Harlow PCC (St Mary's Church) (£20,000); Hospice at Home Carlisle and North (£18,000); Inclusion Ventures (£15,000); Jigsaw Trust (£10,000); Magic Lantern (£8,000); National Youth Choirs of Great Britain (£1,100); Dr Edwin Doubleday Trust (£500).
finances *Financial year end 05/04/2022*
Income £73,700
Grants to organisations £407,300
Assets £4,260,000
trustees Timothy Marks; Ann Marks; Chris Marks; Rupert Marks; William Marks; Charles Woodhouse; Susan Gow; Leonie Marks.

other information Grants were awarded to 64 organisations for a wide variety of causes, the vast majority of which were located in the Essex area.
how to apply The trust does not accept unsolicited applications.
contact details The Trustees, c/o Farrer and Co., 65–66 Lincoln's Inn Fields, London WC2A 3LH *Tel.* 020 3375 7000 *Email* secretarialservices@ farrer.co.uk

■ The Mulchand Foundation

cc no 1181826   **established** 2019
where funding can be given England and Wales.
who can benefit Registered charities.
what is funded General charitable purposes.
sample grants A list of beneficiaries was not included in the annual report and accounts.
finances *Financial year end 28/02/2022*
Income £256,600
Grants to organisations £120,800
Assets £344,100
trustees Venika Mulchand; Rajan Mulchand; Sanjay Mulchand.
how to apply Apply in writing to the correspondent.
contact details Carl Price, Secretary, c/o Laltex Group, Leigh Commerce Park, Green Fold Way, Leigh, WN7 3XH *Tel.* 01942 687000 *Email* sanjay@laltex.com

■ The Frederick Mulder Foundation

cc no 296019   **established** 1986
where funding can be given UK and overseas.
who can benefit Registered and non-registered charities; social enterprises.
what is funded Social change philanthropy; climate change; global poverty.
type of grant Project funding; seed funding/start-up funding; core/revenue costs. One-off and multi-year grants.
range of grants Usually £1,000 to £20,000.
sample grants Cyber Tracker (£32,000); Global Witness (£25,000); Valence Solutions (£20,000); CEA Ltd (£15,000); Greenpeace Environmental Trust (£10,000); Roots and Wings Foundation (£4,200); One to One Africa Children's Fund (£2,500).
finances *Financial year end 31/03/2022*
Income £52,800
Grants to organisations £500,200
Assets £5,470,000
trustees Hannah Carteret; Dr Frederick Mulder; Robin Bowman.
other information The foundation supports many small social change organisations around the world through The Funding Network, which was founded by Frederick Mulder. In 2021/22, grants were awarded to 38 organisations.
how to apply The foundation does not accept unsolicited applications.
contact details Brynn Higgs, Director, 83 Belsize Park Gardens, London NW3 4NJ *Tel.* 07958 464373 *Email* brynn@ frederickmulderfoundation.org.uk *Website* www. frederickmulderfoundation.org.uk

■ Multiple Sclerosis Society

CC NO 1139257 **ESTABLISHED** 2010
WHERE FUNDING CAN BE GIVEN UK.
WHO CAN BENEFIT Recognised NHS & UK academic institutions.
WHAT IS FUNDED Multiple sclerosis research.
TYPE OF GRANT Research funding; PhD studentships; project grants.
SAMPLE GRANTS University College London (£1.48 million); University of Cambridge (£715,000); University of Nottingham (£313,000); International Progressive MS Alliance (£243,000); Association of British Neurologists (£105,000); University of Glasgow (£89,000); UKRI Medical Research Council (£71,000); Leeds General Infirmary (£64,000).
FINANCES *Financial year end* 31/12/2021
Income £29,500,000
Grants to organisations £4,600,000
Grants to individuals £235,000
Assets £21,000,000
TRUSTEES Christopher Murray; David Silver; Prof. Sir Paul Curran; Bayan Thaker; Mohini Raichura-Brown; Dr Shewly Choudhury; Nwanyieke Oluwayemi; Stuart Secker; Marion King; Sarah Schol; Polly Williams; Emily Revess.
OTHER INFORMATION There are separate grant programmes to support individuals with multiple sclerosis and their carers.
HOW TO APPLY Applications can be made through the society's website, where details of open funding programmes and application deadlines can also be found.
CONTACT DETAILS Grants Team, Carriage House, 8 City North Place, London N4 3FU *Tel.* 020 8438 0700 *Email* research@mssociety.org.uk *Website* www.mssociety.org.uk

■ The Mumford Memorial Trust

CC NO 1188517
WHERE FUNDING CAN BE GIVEN Herefordshire.
WHO CAN BENEFIT Registered charities.
WHAT IS FUNDED General charitable purposes including community development, churches and wildlife.
RANGE OF GRANTS Up to £55,000.
SAMPLE GRANTS Three Choirs Festival (£55,000); The Herefordshire Wildlife Trust (£44,000); Bromyard Community (£10,000); Blind Veterans UK (£2,000).
FINANCES *Financial year end* 28/03/2022
Income £208,600
Grants to organisations £195,700
Assets £275,300
TRUSTEES Ludlow Trust Company Ltd; Robin Bone; Susan Melville; Cythia Comyn.
HOW TO APPLY Apply in writing to the correspondent.
CONTACT DETAILS The Trustees, Ludlow Trust Co. Ltd, Tower Wharf, Cheese Lane, Bristol BS2 0JJ *Tel.* 0117 313 8200 *Email* charitabletrusts@ ludlowtrust.com

■ Edith Murphy Foundation

CC NO 1026062 **ESTABLISHED** 1993
WHERE FUNDING CAN BE GIVEN UK, with a preference for Leicestershire and the East Midlands.
WHO CAN BENEFIT National registered charities and organisations based in Leicestershire and the East Midlands.
WHAT IS FUNDED Social welfare; disability; older people; young people; animal welfare; research; education.
TYPE OF GRANT Project and research funding.

RANGE OF GRANTS The majority of grants are of under £20,000.
SAMPLE GRANTS Leicestershire Cares (£50,000); Natural History Museum (£30,000); Healing Little Hearts (£20,000); Age UK and Combat Stress (£10,000 each).
FINANCES *Financial year end* 31/03/2022
Income £562,800
Grants to organisations £1,120,000
Assets £37,150,000
TRUSTEES Richard Adkinson; Christopher Blakesley; David Tams; Dr Charlotte Blakesley; Julian Tams; Ludlow Trust Company Ltd.
OTHER INFORMATION Grants were broken down as follows: welfare (£444,200); research (£265,000); children (£154,800); heritage (£80,000); education (£67,200); disability (£61,700); animals (£43,800).
HOW TO APPLY Apply in writing to the correspondent. Visit the foundation's website for information on what to include. The foundation's trustees meet four times a year to consider grant applications, usually in January, April, July and October.
CONTACT DETAILS The Trustees, c/o Ludlow Trust Company Ltd, 1st Floor, Tower Wharf, Cheese Lane, Bristol BS2 0JJ *Tel.* 0117 457 2210 *Email* charitabletrusts@ludlowtrust.com *Website* https://edithmurphy.co.uk

■ Murphy-Neumann Charity Company Ltd

CC NO 229555 **ESTABLISHED** 1963
WHERE FUNDING CAN BE GIVEN UK.
WHO CAN BENEFIT Registered charities.
WHAT IS FUNDED Health; social welfare; medical research.
WHAT IS NOT FUNDED Individuals.
TYPE OF GRANT Research funding; capital costs.
RANGE OF GRANTS £750 to £2,000.
SAMPLE GRANTS Acorn Villages Ltd (£2,000); The Respite Association (£1,800); Changing Faces (£1,300); Camphill Village Trust (£1,000).
FINANCES *Financial year end* 05/04/2022
Income £75,500
Grants to organisations £53,500
Assets £1,950,000
TRUSTEES Mark Lockett; Marcus Richman; Paula Christopher; Supamon Holmes.
OTHER INFORMATION In 2021/22, the charity made grants to 42 charities.
HOW TO APPLY Apply in writing to the correspondent. In the past, the charity has mentioned that it does not welcome telephone calls. There are no application forms, guidelines, or deadlines and grants are usually given in November and December. A printed copy of the grant criteria is available upon request.
CONTACT DETAILS The Trustees, Hayling Cottage, Upper Street, Stratford St Mary, Colchester, Essex CO7 6JW *Tel.* 01206 323685 *Email* murphy-neumann@hayling-cottage.org.uk

■ The John R. Murray Charitable Trust

CC NO 1100199 **ESTABLISHED** 2003
WHERE FUNDING CAN BE GIVEN UK.
WHO CAN BENEFIT Registered charities.
WHAT IS FUNDED Arts, culture, literature and science; amateur sport; citizenship and community development; health; education; the environment; religion; social welfare.
RANGE OF GRANTS Up to £1 million, with an average of £26,000.

SAMPLE GRANTS Friends of National Libraries (£1.02 million); University of Cambridge (Fitzwilliam) (£65,000); University of Edinburgh Development Trust and The Foundling Museum Trust (£30,000 each); Enterprising Youth Education and Music for Youth (£5,000 each); Lennox Children's Cancer Fund (£2,000).

FINANCES *Financial year end 31/12/2021*
Income £295,200
Grants to organisations £2,640,000
Assets £301,860,000

TRUSTEES Charles Murray; Virginia Murray; John R. Murray; Hallam Murray; John Murray.

OTHER INFORMATION A total of 110 grants were made in 2021. The trust's annual report for that year states that 'the scope of [the trust's] giving is determined only by the extent of [its] resources; it is not otherwise restricted either geographically or by the type of activity carried on by prospective beneficiaries or applicants.'

HOW TO APPLY The trustees will not consider unsolicited applications for grants.

CONTACT DETAILS The Trustees, 50 Albemarle Street, London W1S 4BD *Tel.* 020 7493 4361

■ Brian Murtagh Charitable Trust

CC NO 1105099   **ESTABLISHED** 2004
WHERE FUNDING CAN BE GIVEN UK and overseas.
WHO CAN BENEFIT Registered charities with an income below £350,000. Applications from individuals are considered in certain circumstances.
WHAT IS FUNDED Education, training and development for young adults and children with physical and learning disabilities; social disadvantage; poverty; sickness and trauma.
WHAT IS NOT FUNDED Overseas capital projects.
SAMPLE GRANTS A list of beneficiaries was not included in the annual report and accounts.
FINANCES *Financial year end 31/01/2022*
Income £909,700
Grants to organisations £609,100
Assets £6,960,000
TRUSTEES Mary Noble; Brian Murtagh; Matthew Hahn; Anthony Michael Ryde; Benjamin Rencher.
OTHER INFORMATION Applications from individuals are considered in certain circumstances.
HOW TO APPLY Application forms are available from the trust's website. The trustee board meets four times a year, in March, June, September and November, to consider applications.
CONTACT DETAILS The Trustees, 9 Hanson Drive, Fowey, Cornwall PL23 1ET *Tel.* 07759 367222 *Email* admin@brianmurtaghct.org.uk *Website* www.brianmurtaghct.org.uk

■ Music Sales Charitable Trust

CC NO 1014942   **ESTABLISHED** 1992
WHERE FUNDING CAN BE GIVEN UK, with a preference for London and Bury St Edmunds.
WHO CAN BENEFIT Registered charities.
WHAT IS FUNDED General charitable purposes, including: health; the arts and culture; education and training; religion; overseas aid and famine relief; disability.
RANGE OF GRANTS Mostly under £5,000.
SAMPLE GRANTS Médecins Sans Frontières (£5,000); East Anglia's Children's Hospices (£5,000); St Nicholas Hospice Care (£5,000); LIFEM (£5,000); Westminster Synagogue (£5,000).
FINANCES *Financial year end 31/12/2021*
Income £102,400
Grants to organisations £165,100
Assets £223,100

TRUSTEES Christopher Butler; Ian Morgan; Robert Wise; Mildred Wise; Mr M. Wise; Nicholas Kemp; David Stock.

OTHER INFORMATION Grants were awarded to 80 organisations in the following categories: general (£76,700); disability (£37,400); art and culture (£22,100); religion (£11,000); medical health and sickness (£7,600); education and training (£6,300); overseas and famine relief (£4,000). Grants of under £5,000 totalled £130,100 and were awarded to 73 organisations.

HOW TO APPLY Contact the correspondent for further information.

CONTACT DETAILS The Trustees, c/o Music Sales Ltd, 14–15 Berners Street, London W1T 3LJ *Tel.* 020 7612 7400 *Email* neville.wignall@musicsales.co.uk

■ The Mutley Foundation

CC NO 326303   **ESTABLISHED** 1983
WHERE FUNDING CAN BE GIVEN Worldwide, with a preference for Barnet, Trafford and Israel.
WHO CAN BENEFIT Registered charities.
WHAT IS FUNDED General charitable purposes; the Jewish faith and community.
TYPE OF GRANT Project funding.
SAMPLE GRANTS A list of beneficiaries was not included in the annual report and accounts.
FINANCES *Financial year end 31/12/2021*
Income £133,600
Grants to organisations £99,200
Assets £2,360,000
TRUSTEES David Marks; Ashley Marks; Ann Marks; Marcelle Palmer; Dr Gillian Marks.
OTHER INFORMATION The foundation has a number of regular commitments and prefers to distribute to charities known to the trustees.
HOW TO APPLY The trustees do not welcome unsolicited applications.
CONTACT DETAILS The Trustees, Mutley Properties, Churchill House, 137–139 Brent Street, London NW4 4DJ *Tel.* 020 8203 8598

■ The Mutual Trust Group

CC NO 1039300   **ESTABLISHED** 1994
WHERE FUNDING CAN BE GIVEN Israel; UK; USA.
WHO CAN BENEFIT Jewish organisations.
WHAT IS FUNDED Orthodox Jewish religion and education; the relief of poverty; general charitable purposes.
TYPE OF GRANT Development funding.
RANGE OF GRANTS Up to £98,000.
SAMPLE GRANTS Yeshivas Shaar Hashamaym (£98,400); Yeshivat Kesser Hatalmud (£20,000).
FINANCES *Financial year end 31/12/2021*
Income £195,300
Grants to organisations £121,600
Assets £263,600
TRUSTEES Rabbi Benzion Weitz; Adrian Weisz; Michael Weitz.
OTHER INFORMATION Smaller grants towards education and the relief of poverty totalled £3,200.
HOW TO APPLY Contact the correspondent for further information.
CONTACT DETAILS Benzion Weitz, Chair, 12 Dunstan Road, London NW11 8AA *Tel.* 020 8458 7549

■ MW (CL) Foundation

CC NO 1134917   **ESTABLISHED** 2010
WHERE FUNDING CAN BE GIVEN Worldwide, with a preference for the UK.
WHO CAN BENEFIT Charitable organisations and education providers.
WHAT IS FUNDED Projects which promote education, the relief of poverty and the advancement of the Orthodox Jewish faith.
RANGE OF GRANTS Up to £35,000.
SAMPLE GRANTS Ateres Mordechai (£30,000); Achisomoch Aid Company (£25,000); Beis Soroh Schenirer (£19,000); Comet CT (£10,000); Tiferes High School (£7,000); Menorah Primary School (£5,800); Theo Radcliffe Memorial Fund (£5,300); WST Charity Ltd (£2,000).
FINANCES *Financial year end* 30/11/2021
Income £307,200
Grants to organisations £189,200
Assets £3,250,000
TRUSTEES Vivienne Lewin; Hilary Olsberg; Gerald Lewin.
OTHER INFORMATION The foundation is closely linked with the MW (RH) Foundation, MW (GK) Foundation and MW (HO) Foundation and shares the same charitable objectives. The 2020/21 accounts were the latest available at the time of writing (May 2023).
HOW TO APPLY Apply in writing to the correspondent.
CONTACT DETAILS The Trustees, 38 Princes Park Avenue, London NW11 0JT *Tel.* 020 8458 2933

■ MW (GK) Foundation

CC NO 1134916   **ESTABLISHED** 2010
WHERE FUNDING CAN BE GIVEN Worldwide, with a preference for the UK.
WHO CAN BENEFIT Charitable organisations and education providers.
WHAT IS FUNDED Projects which promote education, the relief of poverty and the advancement of the Orthodox Jewish faith.
RANGE OF GRANTS From £1,500 to £94,000.
SAMPLE GRANTS Mercaz Hatorah Belz Machnovk (£94,000); Friends of Beis Soroh Schenirer (£66,000); Mifal Hachesed Vehatzdoko (£52,000); Chasdei Devorah (£10,000); Mifal Hachesed Vehatzdoko (£3,300); Tov Vochesed (£1,500).
FINANCES *Financial year end* 30/11/2021
Income £235,700
Grants to organisations £348,600
Assets £2,700,000
TRUSTEES Shlomo Klein; Gella Klein.
OTHER INFORMATION The 2020/21 accounts were the latest available at the time of writing (June 2023). The foundation was initially known as the Weisz Children Foundation and is closely linked with the MW (CL) Foundation, MW (RH) Foundation and MW (HO) Foundation.
HOW TO APPLY Contact the correspondent for further information.
CONTACT DETAILS The Trustees, 15 Brantwood Road, Salford, Greater Manchester M7 4EN *Tel.* 0161 792 2330

■ MW (HO) Foundation

CC NO 1134919   **ESTABLISHED** 2010
WHERE FUNDING CAN BE GIVEN Worldwide, with a preference for Manchester.
WHO CAN BENEFIT Charitable organisations and education providers.

WHAT IS FUNDED Projects which promote education, the relief of poverty and the advancement of the Orthodox Jewish faith.
SAMPLE GRANTS A list of beneficiaries was not included in the annual report and accounts.
FINANCES *Financial year end* 30/11/2021
Income £518,300
Grants to organisations £514,800
Assets £2,410,000
TRUSTEES Hilary Olsberg; David Olsberg.
OTHER INFORMATION The 2020/21 accounts were the latest available at the time of writing (June 2023). The foundation was initially known as the Meir Weisz Foundation and is closely linked with the MW (CL) Foundation, MW (GK) Foundation and MW (RH) Foundation. Grants were distributed as follows: community projects (£226,700); religious grants (£125,500); education (£117,700); the relief of poverty (£63,600). Other grants of under £1,000 totalled £8,300.
HOW TO APPLY Contact the correspondent for further information.
CONTACT DETAILS The Trustees, 2nd Floor Parkgates, Bury New Road, Prestwich M25 0TL *Tel.* 0161 798 1660

■ MW (RH) Foundation

CC NO 1134918   **ESTABLISHED** 2010
WHERE FUNDING CAN BE GIVEN Worldwide, with a preference for the UK.
WHO CAN BENEFIT Charitable organisations and education providers.
WHAT IS FUNDED Education; relief of poverty; and advancement of the Orthodox Jewish faith.
SAMPLE GRANTS A list of beneficiaries was not included in the annual report and accounts.
FINANCES *Financial year end* 30/11/2021
Income £1,710,000
Grants to organisations £778,400
Assets £5,540,000
TRUSTEES Rosalind Halpern; Jacob Halpern; Abraham Halpern.
OTHER INFORMATION The 2020/21 accounts were the latest available at the time of writing (June 2023). This foundation was initially known as the Deborah Weisz Foundation and is closely linked with the MW (CL) Foundation, MW (GK) Foundation and MW (HO) Foundation. Grants were distributed as follows: community (£522,500); relief of poverty (£176,800); education (£51,200); religion (£22,600). Grants of less than £1,000 totalled £5,400.
HOW TO APPLY Contact the correspondent for further information.
CONTACT DETAILS The Trustees, 5 Park Hill, Bury Old Road, Prestwich, Greater Manchester M25 0FX *Tel.* 0161 737 7779

■ The National Churches Trust

cc no 1119845 **established** 1953

where funding can be given UK including the Channel Islands; Isle of Man and the Scilly Isles.

who can benefit Listed and unlisted churches, chapels and meeting houses that are open for regular public worship.

what is funded The repair, restoration and modernisation of Christian places of worship.

what is not funded See the website's FAQs page for more information on exclusions.

type of grant Capital costs.

range of grants Programme dependent, ranging from £500 to £50,000.

sample grants Friends Meeting House – Kendal (£284,500); St Lawrence – Bigbury, Devon (£132,700); St Michaels and All Angels – Hughenden, Buckinghamshire (£96,100); St James – Skillington, Lincolnshire (£42,100); Knock St Columba – Belfast (£25,000); St Collen – Llangollen (£7,500); Rye Lane Baptist Church – Peckham (£5,000); Yorkshire Historic Churches Trust (£1,900); All Saints – Nynehead, Somerset (£380).

finances *Financial year end 31/12/2021*
Income £6,450,000
Grants to organisations £5,140,000
Assets £6,160,000

trustees Sir Paul Britton; The Revd Lucy Winkett; Dr Stephen Sklaroff; Shirley Adams; Henry Stanford; Catherine McDonald; Catherine Pepinster; Sir Philip McDougall Rutnam; Dr Robert Muir; Gerald Corbett; Nigel Walter; Sarah Stewart.

how to apply Applications can be made through the trust's website. Each grants programme has a unique application form, as well as its own deadlines.

contact details The Trustees, 7 Tufton Street, London SW1P 3QB *Tel.* 020 7222 0605 *Email* info@nationalchurchestrust.org *Website* www.nationalchurchestrust.org/our-grants

■ The National Express Foundation

cc no 1148231 **established** 2012

where funding can be given The former West Midlands county boundary and the Medway, Gravesend and Longfield areas of Kent served by Kings Ferry and Clarke's commuter coach services (postcodes ME1–12, ME14, DA3, DA11, DA12 and DA13).

who can benefit Registered charities; unregistered charities; CICs; social enterprises; universities; religious bodies/institutions.

what is funded Young people aged 15 to 24; education, especially bursaries for disadvantaged students; social welfare; sport; community development; general charitable purposes.

what is not funded Short-term or one-off projects; sponsorship; projects that cannot be evaluated; projects that only benefit a small number of people.

type of grant Project funding.

range of grants Up to £20,000.

sample grants Employability UK, Friar Park Millennium Centre and Loaves n Fishes (£10,000 each); Blessed to Bless, Excite Active CIC and Longford Short Football (£5,000 each); Inspired2Connect (£2,500).

finances *Financial year end 31/12/2021*
Income £240,000
Grants to organisations £202,700
Assets £13,800

trustees Ian Fraser; Ian Austin; Thomas Stables.

other information Grants are given for two categories: community and education. The foundation funds student bursaries for individuals with challenging personal and financial circumstances. These grants are paid to academic partners – no grants are paid directly to individuals.

how to apply Application forms and guidance can be downloaded from the foundation's website when funding rounds open. The website provides further information on deadlines and successful projects.

contact details The Trustees, c/o National Express Ltd, National Express House, Mill Lane, Birmingham B5 6DD *Tel.* 0121 803 5650 *Email* foundation@nationalexpress.com *Website* www.nationalexpressgroup.com/our-way/national-express-foundation

■ The National Garden Scheme

cc no 1112664 **established** 1927

where funding can be given England, Wales, Northern Ireland and the Channel Islands.

who can benefit Charitable organisations.

what is funded Nursing and health care; gardening and horticulture.

what is not funded See the relevant grant scheme on the website for exclusion criteria.

type of grant Project funding; development funding.

range of grants Programme dependent.

sample grants Hospice UK, Macmillan Cancer Support and Marie Curie (£475,000 each); Carers Trust (£355,000); Parkinson's UK (£300,000); Horatio's Garden (£90,000); ABF the Soldier's Charity (£80,000); Greenfingers (£50,000); Professional Gardener's Trust and National Botanic Garden Wales (£20,000 each); Garden Museum (£10,000).

finances *Financial year end 31/12/2022*
Income £4,780,000
Grants to organisations £3,230,000
Assets £1,100,000

trustees Susan Phipps; Peter Clay; Richard Thompson; Susan Copeland; Andrew Ratcliffe; Mark Porter; Maureen Kesteven; Atty Beor-Roberts; Rupert Tyler; Lucy Hall; Alison Wright; Richard Barley; Susan Paynton; Vernon Sanderson; Arit Anderson.

other information Grants were awarded in the following categories: nursing beneficiary organisations (£2.43 million), garden and health beneficiary organisations (£290,000), support for gardeners (£290,000), community garden awards (£183,500) and donations to local charities by garden owners (£42,200).

how to apply Openings for the Community Gardens Awards are advertised on the charity's website along with an online application form. Other grant schemes open and close throughout the year – check the charity's website to see which are currently accepting applications and how to apply.

contact details Each county has its own contact (see the website for details), East Wing

Hatchlands Park, East Clandon, Guildford, Surrey GU4 7RT *Tel.* 01483 211535 *Email* hello@ngs.org.uk *Website* www.ngs.org.uk

....

■ The National Hockey Foundation

CC NO 1015550   **ESTABLISHED** 1992
WHERE FUNDING CAN BE GIVEN England with a preference for Milton Keynes.
WHO CAN BENEFIT Sports clubs; limited companies; registered charities.
WHAT IS FUNDED Sport, particularly hockey, for people under the age of 21.
WHAT IS NOT FUNDED See the foundation's website for a full list of exclusions.
TYPE OF GRANT Project funding; capital costs; equipment.
SAMPLE GRANTS A list of beneficiaries was not available.
FINANCES *Financial year end* 31/03/2022
Income £30
Grants to organisations £133,000
TRUSTEES Janet Baker; David Billson; John Cove; David Darling; Mr A. P. Dransfield; Michael Fulwood; David Laing; Benjamin Rea; John Waters; Keith McLean; Jane Carr.
OTHER INFORMATION Full accounts were not available to view on the Charity Commission's website due to the foundation's low income. We have therefore estimated the foundation's grant total based on its total expenditure.
HOW TO APPLY The foundation's website states: 'Note that the trustees are no longer inviting applications. If you have an interest in applying for a grant contact the administrator at nathockeyfoundation@gmail.com – you may then be asked to submit an application form.'
CONTACT DETAILS The Trustees, 19 The Avenue, Northampton, Northamptonshire NN5 7AJ *Email* nathockeyfoundation@gmail.com *Website* www.thenationalhockeyfoundation.com

....

■ The National Lottery Community Fund

                         ESTABLISHED 2004
WHERE FUNDING CAN BE GIVEN UK.
WHO CAN BENEFIT Registered charities; CICs; social enterprises; schools; amateur sports clubs; hospices; religious bodies/institutions; local authorities.
WHAT IS FUNDED The National Lottery Community Fund runs a range of different programmes aimed at improving communities and people's lives. Some are UK-wide and others are region-specific. New programmes are introduced from time to time and others close. Potential applicants are advised to check the funder's website for up-to-date information on current and upcoming programmes.
WHAT IS NOT FUNDED There are specific and detailed conditions for each separate programme – see the funder's website for more information.
TYPE OF GRANT Capital costs; core/revenue costs; seed funding/start-up funding; project funding; unrestricted funding.
RANGE OF GRANTS Up to £10,000 through Awards for All. Larger grants are available through other funding programmes.
SAMPLE GRANTS Details of all previous grants made by the fund can be found on its website or on 360Giving.

FINANCES *Financial year end* 31/03/2022
Income £726,990,000
Grants to organisations £595,400,000
Assets £437,340,000
OTHER INFORMATION The National Lottery Community Fund made 14,611 grants during the year. Grants were broken down as follows: England (£458.63 million); Scotland (£43.83 million); UK (£36.42 million); Wales (£34.79 million); Northern Ireland (£21.74 million).
HOW TO APPLY Full details on current programmes, contacts, application forms and guidance are available on the National Lottery Community Fund website.
CONTACT DETAILS The Grants Team, Apex House, 3 Embassy Drive, Edgbaston, Birmingham B15 1TR *Tel.* 0345 410 2030 *Email* general. enquiries@tnlcommunityfund.org.uk *Website* www.tnlcommunityfund.org.uk

....

■ The National Manuscripts Conservation Trust

CC NO 802796   **ESTABLISHED** 1990
WHERE FUNDING CAN BE GIVEN UK.
WHO CAN BENEFIT Record offices; libraries; other publicly funded institutions including local authorities, universities and specialist record repositories; owners of manuscript material that is available to members of the public.
WHAT IS FUNDED The conservation of manuscripts, documents and archives.
WHAT IS NOT FUNDED Public records; photographic, audio-visual or printed material; capital costs; equipment; loan collections; official archives of applicant institutions. Other exclusions can be found on the trust's website.
TYPE OF GRANT Salaries; training costs; repair, binding and preservation costs; digitisation (as part of conservation).
RANGE OF GRANTS Up to £25,000, but mostly between £2,000 and £10,000.
SAMPLE GRANTS A list of beneficiaries was not included in the annual report and accounts. Previous beneficiaries have included: British Glass Foundation (£25,000); The Ruskin Library Museum and Research Centre (£16,800); Doncaster Archives (£10,000); Royal Welsh College of Music and Drama (£8,500); Barnsley Archives (£5,000); Croxteth Hall (£3,200); Harris Manchester College (£1,800).
FINANCES *Financial year end* 31/12/2021
Income £129,100
Grants to organisations £96,200
Assets £2,670,000
TRUSTEES Charles Sebag-Montefiore; Caroline Checkley-Scott; Dr Norman James; Prof. David McKitterick; Caroline Taylor.
HOW TO APPLY Application forms are available to download from the website, along with guidance notes. Applicants are advised to contact the secretary for further advice. The deadlines are usually 1 April and 1 October – full details of how to apply are given on the charity's website.
CONTACT DETAILS Nell Hoare, Secretary, PO Box 4291, Reading, Berkshire RG8 9JA *Email* info@ nmct.org.uk *Website* www.nmct.co.uk

....

■ The Nationwide Foundation

CC NO 1065552   **ESTABLISHED** 1997
WHERE FUNDING CAN BE GIVEN UK.
WHO CAN BENEFIT Charitable organisations; universities; research organisations.

WHAT IS FUNDED Affordable housing; community-led housing schemes; projects working to build an understanding of life in the rented sector; homelessness; social welfare.

WHAT IS NOT FUNDED Religious or political causes; applications that do not comply with the foundation's funding criteria.

TYPE OF GRANT Project and capital costs; core costs; research; pilot projects; multi-year.

SAMPLE GRANTS Town and Country Planning Association (£259,100); Indigo House (£127,400); Affordable Housing Commission (£10,000); Shelter (£1,700).

FINANCES *Financial year end 31/03/2022*
Income £1,880,000
Grants to organisations £1,760,000
Assets £3,870,000

TRUSTEES Sarah Mitchell; Antonia Bance; Saphie Ashtiany; Terrie Alafat; Judith McNeill; Gill Leng; Baroness Usha Prashar; Robert Collins; Christopher Beazley; Rachael Sinclair.

OTHER INFORMATION Grants were made to 24 organisations.

HOW TO APPLY At the time of writing (May 2023) the foundation was focusing on current partnerships and therefore not accepting new applications. However, future invitations for new applicants will be advertised on the website.

CONTACT DETAILS The Trustees, Nationwide House, Pipers Way, Swindon, Wiltshire SN38 2SN *Tel.* 0330 460 0709 *Email* enquiries@nationwidefoundation.org.uk *Website* www.nationwidefoundation.org.uk

■ The NDL Foundation

CC NO 1133508   **ESTABLISHED** 2009
WHERE FUNDING CAN BE GIVEN Worldwide.
WHO CAN BENEFIT UK-registered charities.
WHAT IS FUNDED General charitable purposes; education; medicine; the arts; women and children in financially developing countries.
RANGE OF GRANTS Typically up to £50,000.
SAMPLE GRANTS Don Bosco Bangalore Girls' School (£50,000); Tate (£5,400); KAA Intrepidus Trust (£17,000).
FINANCES *Financial year end 05/04/2022*
Income £101,000
Grants to organisations £72,400
Assets £17,345
TRUSTEES Laura Destribats; Sylviane Destribats; Diane Destribats; Nicolas Destribats; Claude Marion.
HOW TO APPLY Contact the correspondent for further information.
CONTACT DETAILS The Trustees, 24 Chemin Des Moines, 1640 Rhode St Genese, Brussels, Belgium SW10 9LW *Tel.* 0322 358 1202 *Email* lucy@thendlfoundation.com

■ The Gareth Neame Foundation

CC NO 1178930   **ESTABLISHED** 2018
WHERE FUNDING CAN BE GIVEN England and Wales.
WHO CAN BENEFIT Charitable organisations.
WHAT IS FUNDED Improving the conditions and lives of people through education, advice and training.
RANGE OF GRANTS Generally between £2,000 and £10,000 with some slightly larger grants.
SAMPLE GRANTS Royal Central School of Speech and Drama (£12,500); University of Birmingham (£11,000); Fishmongers Campaign, National Youth Jazz Orchestra and Trinity Laban Conservatoire (£10,000 each); South Downs

National Park Trust (£2,500); Romney Marsh Historic Churches Trust (£500).
FINANCES *Financial year end 31/03/2022*
Income £713,100
Grants to organisations £86,200
Assets £1,130,000
TRUSTEES Gareth Neame; Brian Williams; William Townrow; Christopher Stothard.
OTHER INFORMATION During the year, 14 organisations were supported.
HOW TO APPLY Apply in writing to the correspondent.
CONTACT DETAILS The Trustees, SRLV, 20–22 Great Titchfield Street, London W1W 8BE *Tel.* 020 8079 8888

■ Near Neighbours

CC NO 1142426   **ESTABLISHED** 2011
WHERE FUNDING CAN BE GIVEN UK with local hubs in Birmingham, east and south London, Lancashire, Leicester, Luton and West Yorkshire.
WHO CAN BENEFIT Registered charities; CICs; social enterprises; schools; PTAs; religious bodies/institutions.
WHAT IS FUNDED Inter-faith and multi-ethnic community projects.
WHAT IS NOT FUNDED Consult the application guidelines for a full list of exclusions; these will become available on the charity's website when funding rounds open.
TYPE OF GRANT Project funding.
RANGE OF GRANTS £250 to £5,000.
SAMPLE GRANTS Examples of successful projects can be found on the charity's website.
FINANCES *Financial year end 31/12/2021*
Income £2,300,000
Grants to organisations £820,000
Assets £150,000
TRUSTEES Richard Sudworth; Susan Chalkley; The Revd Malcolm Brown; The Revd Jessica Foster; The Revd Catherine Allison; Katherine Hodkinson; The Revd Rogers Govender.
OTHER INFORMATION The charity runs a number of other initiatives, including a leadership programme for young people, a network of community groups and spaces, and practical advice on fundraising and marketing for community groups. See the charity's website for details.
HOW TO APPLY Full application details can be found on the charity's helpful website when funding rounds open. Join the charity's mailing list for notifications on openings.
CONTACT DETAILS Local Near Neighbours Co-ordinator, The Foundry, 17 Oval Way, London SE11 5RR *Tel.* 020 3752 5651 *Email* hello@nearneighbours.org.uk *Website* www.near-neighbours.org.uk

■ Nemoral Ltd

CC NO 262270   **ESTABLISHED** 1971
WHERE FUNDING CAN BE GIVEN Worldwide.
WHO CAN BENEFIT Jewish organisations.
WHAT IS FUNDED Jewish religious education; the relief of poverty in the Jewish community.
WHAT IS NOT FUNDED Individuals.
RANGE OF GRANTS £40,000 to £60,000.
SAMPLE GRANTS Asser Bishvil Foundation, The Great Club Charitable Trust Ltd (£60,000 each); Notzar Chesed (£40,000).
FINANCES *Financial year end 30/12/2021*
Income £75,000
Grants to organisations £160,000
Assets £721,800

TRUSTEES Rivka Gross; Michael Saberski.

OTHER INFORMATION The 2020/21 accounts were the latest at the time of writing (June 2023).

HOW TO APPLY Apply in writing to the correspondent.

CONTACT DETAILS The Trustees, c/o Cohen Arnold, New Burlington House, 1075 Finchley Road, London NW11 0PU *Tel.* 020 8731 0777

■ Ner Foundation

CC NO 1104866   **ESTABLISHED** 2004

WHERE FUNDING CAN BE GIVEN UK and Israel.

WHO CAN BENEFIT Orthodox Jewish organisations; community projects; Jewish educational institutions; places of worship.

WHAT IS FUNDED Orthodox Jewish religion and education; the relief of poverty in the Jewish community.

RANGE OF GRANTS Mostly up to around £20,000 with the occasional larger grant.

SAMPLE GRANTS Community Projects (£110,300); Kolyom Trust (£27,400); Choimel Dalim (£22,000); Shir Chesed Beis Yisroel (£20,000); Brewers' Company General Charitable Trust (£16,300); Yeshivos and Seminaries (£8,000).

FINANCES *Financial year end* 30/06/2022
Income £437,400
Grants to organisations £427,700
Assets £591,600

TRUSTEES Arnold Henry; Esther Henry; Henry Neumann.

OTHER INFORMATION Only organisations that received grants of over £1,000 were listed as beneficiaries in the foundation's 2021/22 accounts. Grants of under £1,000 totalled £29,000. Individuals can be supported but this is rare.

HOW TO APPLY Apply in writing to the correspondent.

CONTACT DETAILS The Trustees, 2nd Floor Parkgates, Bury New Road, Prestwich, Manchester M25 0TL *Tel.* 0161 772 0099

■ Nesta

CC NO 1144091   **ESTABLISHED** 2011

WHERE FUNDING CAN BE GIVEN UK.

WHO CAN BENEFIT Registered charities; social enterprises; research institutions; universities; businesses; public organisations; CICs.

WHAT IS FUNDED The priority areas of innovation (2021–30 strategy) are: narrowing educational inequality, with a focus on early childhood and secondary education; narrowing health inequalities, with a focus on tackling food environments and loneliness; improving sustainability, with a focus on reducing household emissions and increasing productivity.

WHAT IS NOT FUNDED Each funding programme has its own exclusions; refer to the website for further information.

TYPE OF GRANT Programme dependent.

SAMPLE GRANTS Flintshire County Council (£1.15 million); Digital Mums (£200,000); Education Datalab (£100,000); Youth Federation (£60,000); Attain Oxford (£50,000).

FINANCES *Financial year end* 31/03/2022
Income £21,610,000
Grants to organisations £8,730,000
Assets £53,470,000

TRUSTEES Anthony Lilley; Judy Gibbons; Heider Ridha; Christina McComb; Sarah Hunter; Jimmy Wales; Ian Gomes; Edward Richards; Seun Akindele; Jeremy King; Catherine Brien; Elizabeth Ditchburn.

OTHER INFORMATION Nesta provides financial and practical support, often in partnership with other organisations, through a mix of grants, direct investment and challenge prizes. Funding programmes open and close on a regular basis and potential applicants should refer to the website for up-to-date information.

HOW TO APPLY Information on current funding programmes is available to view on Nesta's website, including details of how to apply.

CONTACT DETAILS The Trustees, 58 Victoria Embankment, London EC4Y 0DS *Tel.* 020 7438 2500 *Email* information@nesta.org.uk *Website* www.nesta.org.uk

■ Network for Social Change Charitable Trust

CC NO 295237   **ESTABLISHED** 1986

WHERE FUNDING CAN BE GIVEN UK and overseas.

WHO CAN BENEFIT Registered charities; CICs; social enterprises.

WHAT IS FUNDED Peace; human rights; arts and education; the environment; health; economic and racial justice.

WHAT IS NOT FUNDED Disaster appeals; most types of building projects; direct contributions to political parties. Non-charitable projects are required to use the trust's money for non-violent and legal purposes only.

TYPE OF GRANT Capital costs; core/revenue costs; seed funding/start-up funding; project funding; unrestricted funding.

RANGE OF GRANTS Mostly up to £30,000.

SAMPLE GRANTS The Green Alliance Trust (£258,000); Permaculture Association (£153,000); Working Families (£35,000); The Association for Coastal Ecosystem Services (£29,300); Tees Valley Women's Centre (£22,600); Social Workers Without Borders (£22,100); Participation and Practice of Rights Project (£20,000); Peace Direct (£16,600); Community Arts North West (£15,000).

FINANCES *Financial year end* 31/08/2022
Income £1,620,000
Grants to organisations £1,460,000
Assets £210,200

TRUSTEES Carol Freeman; Annie Schiff; Mark Tucker; Patricia Horrocks; Gillian Howarth; Roger Manser.

HOW TO APPLY All applications to the trust must be sponsored by a network member; unsolicited applications are not accepted. However, project summaries can be submitted on the trust's project noticeboard on its website and if a member is interested they will get in touch. Visit the website for further information.

CONTACT DETAILS The Trustees, BM 2063, London WC1N 3XX *Tel.* 01647 61106 *Email* thenetwork@gn.apc.org *Website* http://thenetworkforsocialchange.org.uk

■ Newby Trust Ltd

CC NO 227151   **ESTABLISHED** 1937

WHERE FUNDING CAN BE GIVEN UK.

WHO CAN BENEFIT Registered charities.

WHAT IS FUNDED Education; health; social welfare.

WHAT IS NOT FUNDED Statutory bodies; large national charities enjoying widespread support; organisations not registered with the Charity Commission; exhibitions, conferences or events; individuals volunteering overseas; the promotion of religion; work outside the UK; large capital appeals; endowment appeals.

Think carefully about every application. Is it justified?

561

TYPE OF GRANT Capital costs; core/revenue costs; project funding; unrestricted funding.

RANGE OF GRANTS Typically £1,000 to £30,000.

SAMPLE GRANTS A list of beneficiaries was not included in the annual report and accounts. Previous beneficiaries have included: Yes Futures (£30,000); Empire Fighting Chance and The Wave Project (£20,000 each); Feeding Families, St Chad's Sanctuary and The Access Project (£10,000 each); Beyond the Horizon Charity, Freedom from Torture and White City Youth Theatre (£5,000 each); Riding for the Disabled (£1,000).

FINANCES *Financial year end 05/04/2022*
Income £423,000
Grants to organisations £493,000
Assets £20,000,000

TRUSTEES Evelyn Montgomery; Anna Foxell; Ben Gooder; David Charlton; Duncan Reed; Dr Stephen Gooder; Antonia Gooder; Kate Callaghan; Katherine Bartholomew; Daniel Callaghan.

OTHER INFORMATION Grants were awarded in the following categories: education (£127,900); health (£161,500, including grants in the special category); welfare (£151,200); the environment (£49,200). The annual special category has included support for refugees or asylum seekers, young people's mental health, and palliative care and bereavement.

HOW TO APPLY Unsolicited applications are not accepted, but charities – particularly those associated with the annual special category – are invited to make their activities known by email to the trust.

CONTACT DETAILS Annabel Grout, Company Secretary, PO Box 87, Petworth GU28 8BH *Email* info@newby-trust.org.uk *Website* www.newby-trust.org.uk

■ Newcomen Collett Foundation

CC NO 312804　　　**ESTABLISHED** 1988

WHERE FUNDING CAN BE GIVEN London Borough of Southwark.

WHO CAN BENEFIT Registered charities; unregistered charities; CICs; social enterprises; schools; PTAs; individuals.

WHAT IS FUNDED The education of young people under 25 years of age; extracurricular activities.

TYPE OF GRANT Core/revenue costs; seed funding/start-up funding; equipment.

RANGE OF GRANTS Up to £5,500, but mostly up to £2,000.

SAMPLE GRANTS St Peter's Primary School (£5,500); Southwark Playhouse (£2,200); Cathedral School and Glazier's Foundation (£2,000 each); John Keats Primary School (£1,500); St Giles Trust (£1,000).

FINANCES *Financial year end 30/09/2022*
Income £137,800
Grants to organisations £81,000
Assets £4,980,000

TRUSTEES Robert Ashdown; Alexander Leiffheidt; Robin Lovell; Janet Goodland; Peter MacFarlane; The Revd Michael Rawson; Neha Jain; Amir Eden; Timothy McNally; Janet Simpson; Edward Wingfield.

OTHER INFORMATION The grant total includes the figures for individuals and organisations.

HOW TO APPLY Application forms are available to download, together with criteria and guidelines, from the website. The governors consider requests four times a year. The closing dates for applications are listed on the website.

CONTACT DETAILS The Governors, Marshall's House, 66 Newcomen Street, London Bridge, London SE1 1YT *Tel.* 020 7407 2967 *Email* grantoffice@newcomencollett.org.uk *Website* www.newcomencollett.org.uk

■ The Frances and Augustus Newman Foundation

CC NO 277964　　　**ESTABLISHED** 1978

WHERE FUNDING CAN BE GIVEN UK.

WHO CAN BENEFIT Medical colleges; academic institutions; major research centres.

WHAT IS FUNDED Medical research projects and other medical charitable causes.

TYPE OF GRANT Research core costs; salaries; buildings and equipment. Grants made can be for one to three years.

RANGE OF GRANTS Up to £55,000.

SAMPLE GRANTS Royal College of Surgeons (£55,000); British Heart Foundation (£50,000); Bowel Cancer UK (£42,600); The Royal Hospital for Neuro Disability (£30,000); Wellbeing of Women Cancer Institute (£21,600); The Migrane Trust (£19,600).

FINANCES *Financial year end 31/03/2022*
Income £611,800
Grants to organisations £278,800
Assets £17,760,000

TRUSTEES John Williams; Stephen Cannon; David Sweetnam; Mark Rushton.

OTHER INFORMATION Grants were awarded to six organisations during the year.

HOW TO APPLY The annual report for 2021/22 states that the trustees 'invite applications for research grants from individuals ... [and in] respect of the limited number of other grants made, they favour projects submitted from major research centres.'

CONTACT DETAILS Ben Haines, Administrator, c/o RSM, Hartwell House, 55–61 Victoria Street, Bristol BS1 6AD *Tel.* 0117 945 2000 *Email* ben.haines@rsmuk.com

■ Newpier Charity Ltd

CC NO 293686　　　**ESTABLISHED** 1985

WHERE FUNDING CAN BE GIVEN UK and Israel.

WHO CAN BENEFIT Jewish organisations.

WHAT IS FUNDED The advancement of the Orthodox Jewish faith; the relief of poverty; general charitable purposes.

RANGE OF GRANTS Up to £66,000.

SAMPLE GRANTS Bluzhev Charitable Trust (£41,000); Yad Vochesed (£36,000); Yad Vochesed (£16,500); Side by Side Kids (£12,000); TS Trust (£11,000).

FINANCES *Financial year end 30/06/2022*
Income £677,000
Grants to organisations £499,600
Assets £318,600

TRUSTEES Charles Marguiles; Rachel Marguiles; Harvey Freudenberger; Michael Just; Bernard Stern.

HOW TO APPLY Apply in writing to the correspondent. The trustees meet on a regular basis to consider applications.

CONTACT DETAILS C. Margulies, Secretary, 186 Lordship Road, London N16 5ES *Tel.* 020 8802 4449

■ Alderman Newton's Educational Foundation

CC NO 527881   **ESTABLISHED** 1983

WHERE FUNDING CAN BE GIVEN Diocese of Leicester.

WHO CAN BENEFIT Schools; individuals.

WHAT IS FUNDED Educational projects.

WHAT IS NOT FUNDED Equipment or costs that would normally be met from the school's budget set by the local education authority.

TYPE OF GRANT Capital costs; project funding.

SAMPLE GRANTS A list of beneficiaries was not included in the annual report and accounts.

FINANCES *Financial year end* 31/03/2022
Income £179,000
Grants to organisations £178,600
Assets £5,470,000

TRUSTEES Charles Franks; Dr Richard Harries; Madan Kallow; Wendy Martin; Malcolm Unsworth; Cheryl Pharoah; The Revd Canon Philip O'Reilly; Suzanne Uprichard; Guy Newbury; The Revd Jonathan Surridge; Pauline Hinitt; Damini Hansrani; Gordon Springall.

OTHER INFORMATION The grant total includes grants to individuals and organisations.

HOW TO APPLY Application forms and guidelines are available to download from the charity's website.

CONTACT DETAILS The Trustees, c/o Charity Link, 20A Millstone Lane, Leicester, Leicestershire LE1 5JN *Tel.* 0116 222 2200 *Email* info@charity-link.org *Website* http://anef.org.uk

■ The NFU Mutual Charitable Trust

CC NO 1073064   **ESTABLISHED** 1998

WHERE FUNDING CAN BE GIVEN UK, with a preference for rural areas.

WHO CAN BENEFIT Charitable organisations; organisations with charitable aims.

WHAT IS FUNDED Agriculture; rural development; research; education; relief of poverty in rural areas; social welfare of the inhabitants of rural communities; insurance.

WHAT IS NOT FUNDED University fees; salaries; overseas appeals; multi-year funding.

TYPE OF GRANT One-off; project funding.

RANGE OF GRANTS Typical grants range from £10,000 to £100,000.

SAMPLE GRANTS FareShare (£150,000); Farming Community Network, Rural Support and Samaritans (£100,000 each); Royal Scottish Agricultural Benevolent Institution (£80,000); Young Farmers Club of Ulster (£30,000); Farms for City Children and Open Farm Weekend – Northern Ireland (£10,000 each); Wales Federation of Young Farmers Club (£7,000).

FINANCES *Financial year end* 31/12/2021
Income £1,110,000
Grants to organisations £1,100,000
Assets £285,300

TRUSTEES Meurig Raymond; Dr Harriet Kennedy; Minette Batters; James McLaren; Nicholas Turner; Martin Kennedy; David Brown; Aled Jones.

OTHER INFORMATION Grants were made to 31 organisations during the year.

HOW TO APPLY Application forms are available from the trust's website and should be sent to the correspondent either via post or email. Details of what to include can be found on the website. The trustees meet twice a year to consider applications, currently in June and November.

CONTACT DETAILS Jim Creechan, Secretary to the Trustees, Tiddington Road, Stratford-upon-Avon, Warwickshire CV37 7BJ *Tel.* 01789 204211 *Email* nfu_mutual_charitable_trust@nfumutual.co.uk *Website* www.nfumutual.co.uk/about-us/charitable-trust

■ The Nine Incorporated Trades of Dundee General Fund Charity

OSCR NO SC047218

WHERE FUNDING CAN BE GIVEN Dundee.

WHO CAN BENEFIT Charities; community groups; schools; occasionally individuals.

WHAT IS FUNDED The advancement of the arts, heritage, culture or science to include support appropriate to the nine trades (see the website for more information about the nine different trades); citizenship and community development; social welfare; education; health; the advancement of religion; health.

WHAT IS NOT FUNDED Retrospective expenditure; funding for grant-making charities; individuals generally.

RANGE OF GRANTS Mostly up to £10,000.

SAMPLE GRANTS Dundee Science Centre (£11,000); Rotary Club of Dundee (£10,000); Dyer Craft (£7,400); Dundee Bairns and St Andrew's Parish Church (£5,000 each); Unicorn Preservation Society (£3,000); Dundee Starter Packs (£1,000); Women's Business Station (£500).

FINANCES *Financial year end* 30/04/2021
Income £176,400
Grants to organisations £188,200
Assets £880,100

OTHER INFORMATION The charity does not generally fund individuals, though occasionally makes exceptions. The 2020/21 accounts were the latest available at the time of writing (May 2023).

HOW TO APPLY Apply via the charity's website. The charity operates a rolling grants programme and applications are reviewed every three months.

CONTACT DETAILS David Craig, Charities Convener, 11 South Tay Street, Dundee DD1 1NY *Email* charities.convener@ninetradesofdundee.co.uk *Website* www.ninetradesofdundee.co.uk/funding

■ The Nineveh Charitable Trust

CC NO 256025   **ESTABLISHED** 1968

WHERE FUNDING CAN BE GIVEN UK.

WHO CAN BENEFIT Registered charities; CICs; individual applicants (if the outcome benefits are clearly defined).

WHAT IS FUNDED Health; social welfare; education, in particular agriculture, silviculture, ecology and land management; conservation of the countryside.

WHAT IS NOT FUNDED Expeditions; personal educational needs; animal sanctuaries and care; work overseas; general appeals; projects unrelated to the trust's objects.

TYPE OF GRANT Capital costs; project funding; research; development funding; salaries. Matched funding is also available.

RANGE OF GRANTS Mainly between £500 and £10,000.

SAMPLE GRANTS Thomas Morley Trust Disabled Sailors Association (£14,100); Dyfed Archaeological Trust (£6,000); Ashford Volunteer Centre (£5,300); Apple Tree Farm Services (£3,000); Bethnal Green Nature Reserve (£2,000); Awbridge Parent Teacher

Association (£1,700); Ferryhill Station PTA (£1,000); Penumbra (£500).

FINANCES *Financial year end* 05/04/2022
Income £238,000
Grants to organisations £445,600
Assets £10,260,000

TRUSTEES Dr Michael James; Robert Lewis; John MacGregor.

OTHER INFORMATION Grants were made to 140 organisations during 2021/22.

HOW TO APPLY Apply in writing to the correspondent. Three copies of the proposal should be sent along with an sae. Applications should be no longer than two sides. Further information on what to include in the application can be found on the trust's website.

CONTACT DETAILS The Trustees, Park Farm, Frittenden Road, Ashford TN27 8LG *Tel.* 07710 998829 *Email* robert@ninevehtrust.org.uk *Website* www.ninevehtrust.org.uk

■ The Nisbet Trust

CC NO 1143496   **ESTABLISHED** 2011

WHERE FUNDING CAN BE GIVEN Bristol; North Somerset; South Gloucestershire.

WHO CAN BENEFIT Registered charities; exempt charities; not-for-profit social enterprises; CICs.

WHAT IS FUNDED Community cohesion; disadvantaged young people; the arts; homelessness.

WHAT IS NOT FUNDED Medical research; single-condition medical charities; individuals; animal welfare charities; sponsorship; CICs whose core business model is substantially grant-reliant; national charities.

TYPE OF GRANT Project funding; capital costs; core costs.

RANGE OF GRANTS Typically up to £30,000.

SAMPLE GRANTS The Park Community Centre Ltd (£250,000); Bristol Music Trust (£200,000); Royal West of England Academy (£50,000); Youth Moves (£35,000); South Bristol Consortium for Young People (£25,000); CHAS (Bristol) Housing Advice Service (£20,000); Somerset and Avon Rape and Sexual Abuse Support (£15,000); Bristol North West Foodbank, Bristol Refugee Rights and St Paul's Carnival CIC (£10,000 each); The Greenhouse Bristol (£5,000).

FINANCES *Financial year end* 31/12/2021
Income £1,500,000
Grants to organisations £1,360,000
Assets £755,700

TRUSTEES Andrew Nisbet; Anne Nisbet; Joseph Nisbet; Emily Nisbet; Zoe Joyner; Henry Bothamley.

HOW TO APPLY Application forms and guidance are available from the trust's website. Forms should be returned by email. The trustees meet quarterly to consider applications in January, April, July and October. Deadlines for applications are posted on the trust's website.

CONTACT DETAILS Gemma Roberts, Trust Administrator, 22 Clifton Road, Bristol BS8 1AQ *Email* admin@nisbettrust.co.uk *Website* www. nisbettrust.co.uk

■ NNS Foundation

CC NO 1184159   **ESTABLISHED** 2018

WHERE FUNDING CAN BE GIVEN Worldwide with a focus on the UK, USA, Egypt and the rest of Africa.

WHO CAN BENEFIT Charitable organisations.

WHAT IS FUNDED Health; education.

SAMPLE GRANTS Sawiris Foundation for Social Development (£8.48 million); African Mission Healthcare (£898,400); Egyptian Education Foundation (£622,700); University of Pennsylvania (£499,200).

FINANCES *Financial year end* 31/12/2021
Income £17,130,000
Grants to organisations £14,230,000
Assets £5,680,000

TRUSTEE NNS Foundation Ltd.

OTHER INFORMATION Financial information has been converted from USD using the exchange rate at the time of writing (March 2023).

HOW TO APPLY Unsolicited applications are not accepted.

CONTACT DETAILS The Trustees, Third Floor, 20 Old Bailey, London EC4 7AN *Tel.* 020 7597 6000

■ The Nomura Charitable Trust

CC NO 1130592   **ESTABLISHED** 2009

WHERE FUNDING CAN BE GIVEN London.

WHO CAN BENEFIT Charitable organisations.

WHAT IS FUNDED Education and training of young people.

RANGE OF GRANTS Up to £50,000.

SAMPLE GRANTS Previous beneficiaries have included: East London Business and IntoUniversity (£52,000 each); The Brokerage City (£51,100).

FINANCES *Financial year end* 31/03/2022
Income £9,500
Grants to organisations £125,000

TRUSTEES Breda Forrest; Gary Hyman; Iris Hinterberger; Clare Jarrett; Kevin Clark.

OTHER INFORMATION Full accounts were not available to view on the Charity Commission's website due to the foundation's low income. We have therefore estimated the grant total based on the foundation's expenditure.

HOW TO APPLY Organisations are nominated by a Nomura employee and are then invited to apply by a member of the Community Affairs team. Unsolicited applications are not accepted.

CONTACT DETAILS Samantha Barnwell, Grants Manager, 1 Angel Lane, London EC4R 3AB *Tel.* 020 7102 2005 *Email* communityaffairs@ nomura.com *Website* www.nomuraholdings. com/csr/society/foundation/nct.html

■ The Norfolk Churches Trust Ltd

CC NO 271176   **ESTABLISHED** 1976

WHERE FUNDING CAN BE GIVEN The Diocese of Norwich and the county of Norfolk.

WHO CAN BENEFIT Christian places of worship.

WHAT IS FUNDED Church renovation and repair including; structural repairs to building fabric; the repair and restructuring of rainwater goods and drainage; window repairs – glazing and tracery; repairs to fixtures and fittings including pews, monuments, organs and ledgerstones; the conservation of wall paintings and stonework; the renewal of interior plaster; repairs to floors and pew platforms; repairs and refurbishment of bell frames; the renewal of switchgear for electrics; interior decoration when it is part of internal wall repairs and replastering.

WHAT IS NOT FUNDED Reordering projects, extensions to buildings or the installation of new facilities.

TYPE OF GRANT Capital costs; surveys and reports on areas causing concern.

RANGE OF GRANTS Up to £10,000.

SAMPLE GRANTS St Andrew – Saxthorpe (£10,000); St Mary – Surlingham (£7,000); St John –

Terrington (£5,000); St Peter – Ringland (£2,000); All Saints – Tacolneston (£750).
FINANCES *Financial year end* 31/03/2022
Income £542,400
Grants to organisations £131,500
Assets £2,010,000
TRUSTEES Countess of Leicester Sarah Elizabeth Mary Leicester; Michael Sayer; Lt Col. Ian Lonsdale; Patrick Lines; Amelia Courtauld; Peter Sheppard; Dr John Maddison; Charles Inglis; Rosabelle Batt; Lauren Parker.
OTHER INFORMATION In 2021/22, the trust made grants to 31 churches.
HOW TO APPLY Application forms can be downloaded from the trust's website.
CONTACT DETAILS The Trustees, Manor Farm House, Diss Road, Tibenham, Norwich, Norfolk NR16 1QF *Tel.* 01379 677272
Email secretary@norfolkchurchestrust.org.uk
Website http://norfolkchurchestrust.org.uk

■ Norfolk Community Foundation

CC NO 1110817 **ESTABLISHED** 2004
WHERE FUNDING CAN BE GIVEN Norfolk.
WHO CAN BENEFIT Registered charities; local community groups; town and parish councils; CICs; social enterprises; individuals.
WHAT IS FUNDED General charitable purposes.
TYPE OF GRANT Programme dependent.
RANGE OF GRANTS Programme dependent.
SAMPLE GRANTS Priscilla Bacon Hospice (£200,000 in two grants); The Salvation Army (£93,100); Norwich City Football Club (£75,000); MensCraft (£51,100); Norfolk and Waveney Mind (£50,000); The Magdalene Group Norfolk (£46,000); Norfolk Citizens Advice (£28,800); Caring Together Charity and Norfolk Deaf Association (£25,000 each); The Purfleet Trust (£20,000).
FINANCES *Financial year end* 31/12/2021
Income £4,380,000
Grants to organisations £4,170,000
Grants to individuals £44,600
Assets £26,870,000
TRUSTEES Stephen Allen; Simon Bailey; Simon Brickles; Dr Rosalyn Proops; Jenny Watson; Jessica Middleton; Fiona McDiarmid; Richard Ross.
OTHER INFORMATION This is one of the 47 UK community foundations, which distribute funding for a wide range of purposes. As with all community foundations, there are a number of donor-advised funds managed on behalf of individuals, families and charitable trusts. Grant schemes tend to change frequently – consult the foundation's website for details of current programmes and up-to-date deadlines. The foundation made grants to 813 organisations and 191 individuals in 2021. Grants of £2,500 and under represent 56% of all grants made during the year. Only beneficiaries of grants of over £20,000 are listed in the accounts.
HOW TO APPLY Potential applicants are advised to visit the community foundation's website or contact its programmes advisors to find the most suitable funding stream.
CONTACT DETAILS Programmes Advisors, St James Mill, Whitefriars, Norwich, Norfolk NR3 1TN *Tel.* 01603 623958 *Email* grants@ norfolkfoundation.com *Website* www. norfolkfoundation.com

■ Educational Foundation of Alderman John Norman

CC NO 313105 **ESTABLISHED** 1962
WHERE FUNDING CAN BE GIVEN Norfolk.
WHO CAN BENEFIT Educational organisations; descendants of Alderman John Norman; Old Catton residents.
WHAT IS FUNDED The education and training of children and young people, including those descended from Alderman John Norman.
RANGE OF GRANTS Up to £10,000 but mostly from £1,000 to £5,000.
SAMPLE GRANTS YMCA Norfolk (£10,200); Break (£10,000); Connects and Co and University of East Anglia (£5,000 each); Wymondham Youth Bus (£3,000); Benedetti Foundation and 9th Norwich Rangers (£1,000 each); 31st Norwich Rainbows (£500).
FINANCES *Financial year end* 31/03/2022
Income £288,000
Grants to organisations £68,200
Grants to individuals £158,300
Assets £10,680,000
TRUSTEES Christopher Brown; Roger Sandall; Tracey Hughes; Dr Julia Leach; The Revd Philip Butcher; Francis Whymark; Roy Hughes; David Nobbs; The Revd Andrew Parsons; Timothy Lawes.
HOW TO APPLY Applications can be made in writing or through the foundation's website.
CONTACT DETAILS Nick Saffell, Clerk, The Atrium, St George's Street, Norwich, Norfolk NR3 1AB *Tel.* 01603 629871 *Email* nick.saffell@brown-co.com *Website* https://normanfoundation.co. uk

■ The Norman Family Charitable Trust

CC NO 277616 **ESTABLISHED** 1979
WHERE FUNDING CAN BE GIVEN Cornwall, Devon and Somerset. Preference is given to Exeter and East Devon.
WHO CAN BENEFIT Registered charities; unregistered charities; CICs; social enterprises; schools; universities; PTAs; hospital; hospices.
WHAT IS FUNDED General charitable purposes.
WHAT IS NOT FUNDED Individuals; organisations which use live animals for experimental or research purposes; the maintenance or repair of religious buildings; national charities will only be supported for projects which will help the area of benefit.
TYPE OF GRANT Core/revenue costs; capital costs.
RANGE OF GRANTS Grants are typically of less than £5,000.
SAMPLE GRANTS A list of beneficiaries was not included in the annual report and accounts. Previous beneficiaries have included: Wadebridge Foodbank (£10,000); Exmouth Community College (£5,300); Budleigh Relief In Need Charity and St Peter's Primary School (£3,000 each); TCR Radio Productions CIC (£2,000).
FINANCES *Financial year end* 31/03/2022
Income £428,400
Grants to organisations £855,000
Assets £10,810,000
TRUSTEES Sarah Gillingham; Cathy Houghton; Christopher Davis; William Tee; Liz Low; Stephen Green; John Bain; Fiona Ross.
OTHER INFORMATION Grants were made to 278 organisations during the year. Grants were broken down as follows: children (£222,100); homelessness social welfare (£135,800);

Think carefully about every application. Is it justified?

565

community projects (£126,700); medical causes (£112,600); mental health and learning disabilities (£70,200); senior welfare (£55,600); blind, deaf and physically handicapped (£45,100); sport and leisure (£28,400); animals, the environment and conservation (£20,000); youth (£13,500); the armed forces and emergency services (£5,200); crime prevention and rehabilitation (£1,000).

HOW TO APPLY See the trust's website for the latest information on applications.

CONTACT DETAILS Emma Le Poidevin, Grants Administrator, 14 Fore Street, Budleigh Salterton, Devon EX9 6NG *Tel.* 01395 446699 *Email* info@nfct.org *Website* www.nfct.org

Normanby Charitable Trust

CC NO 252102 **ESTABLISHED** 1966

WHERE FUNDING CAN BE GIVEN Mainly North Yorkshire and the North East.

WHO CAN BENEFIT Registered charities; hospices; hospitals; places of worship; PCCs; schools and colleges; universities; museums, libraries and galleries; uniformed groups.

WHAT IS FUNDED General charitable purposes, particularly arts, culture, heritage and social welfare.

WHAT IS NOT FUNDED Non-UK charities; individuals (apart from in exceptional circumstances).

RANGE OF GRANTS Up to £250,000 with an average grant of £10,800.

SAMPLE GRANTS Eskdale School (£250,000); Captain Cook Memorial Museum (£27,500); Sash (£2,500); The Small Piece (£1,250); Passage (£1,000); Chester-le-Street United (£500).

FINANCES *Financial year end 05/04/2022*
Income £158,000
Grants to organisations £396,600
Assets £14,190,000

TRUSTEES Lady Henrietta Burridge; Lady Peronel Cruz; Lady Lepel Kornicki; The Marquis of Normanby; Nicholas Buchan.

HOW TO APPLY Apply in writing to the correspondent. The trustees meet two to three times a year to award grants.

CONTACT DETAILS The Trustees, 52 Tite Street, London SW3 4JA *Tel.* 020 7352 3174 *Email* nct@normanby.org

North Berwick Trust

OSCR NO SC048462

WHERE FUNDING CAN BE GIVEN North Berwick.

WHO CAN BENEFIT Charities; community groups; individuals.

WHAT IS FUNDED Public recreational facilities and gardens; education; social welfare.

TYPE OF GRANT Project funding.

RANGE OF GRANTS Up to £32,000.

SAMPLE GRANTS Fringe by the Sea and Scottish Seabirds Centre (£30,000 each); North Berwick Community Skate Park (£20,000); Stepping Out (£15,400); North Berwick Highland Games (£10,000); Five in a Row (£5,000); North Berwick Pipe Band (£3,000); North Berwick Playgroup (£1,500).

FINANCES *Financial year end 31/03/2022*
Income £290,300
Grants to organisations £274,400
Grants to individuals £21,600
Assets £17,160,000

HOW TO APPLY Application forms and deadlines can be found on the trust's website.

CONTACT DETAILS The Trustees, The Lighthouse, Heugh Road Industrial Estate, North Berwick, East Lothian EH39 5PX *Email* use the contact form on the website *Website* www.northberwicktrust.co.uk

North London Charities Ltd

CC NO 312740 **ESTABLISHED** 1964

WHERE FUNDING CAN BE GIVEN North London.

WHO CAN BENEFIT Registered charities.

WHAT IS FUNDED Advancement of the Jewish Orthodox faith; general charitable purposes.

SAMPLE GRANTS A list of beneficiaries was not available.

FINANCES *Financial year end 31/03/2022*
Income £14,970,000
Grants to organisations £5,940,000
Assets £30,260,000

TRUSTEES Shulom Feldman; Dwora Feldman; Sara Friedman.

HOW TO APPLY Apply in writing to the correspondent.

CONTACT DETAILS Heinrich Feldman, North London Hospice, 47 Woodside Hospice, London N12 8TT *Tel.* 020 8557 9557

North West Cancer Research

CC NO 519357 **ESTABLISHED** 2012

WHERE FUNDING CAN BE GIVEN The North West and North Wales.

WHO CAN BENEFIT Universities.

WHAT IS FUNDED Cancer research.

WHAT IS NOT FUNDED Direct clinical care; buildings. See the website for the exclusion criteria of the relevant funding call.

TYPE OF GRANT Project funding; research; capital costs.

SAMPLE GRANTS A list of beneficiaries was not included in the annual report and accounts.

FINANCES *Financial year end 30/09/2021*
Income £4,900,000
Grants to organisations £1,950,000
Assets £5,410,000

TRUSTEES Catherine Jones; Catherine Bond; Hilary Atherton; Mark Haig; Philip Robertshaw; Michael Carter; Michael Ore; Philip Webster; Dr Sharvari Kothari-Short; John Willis; Frances Hewison; Paul Moonan; Sandeep Anantharaman; Andrew Stalker.

OTHER INFORMATION Formerly known as Clatterbridge Cancer Research (CCR), the charity in its current set-up was formed in 2012, when CCR merged with the North West Cancer Research Fund. The charity finances cancer research, primarily at the University of Liverpool, Lancaster University and Bangor University. Open calls for funding are advertised on the website. The 2020/21 accounts were the latest available at the time of writing (May 2023).

HOW TO APPLY Application guidance and deadlines are made available on the website as open funding calls arise.

CONTACT DETAILS The Trustees, North West Cancer Research Centre, 200 London Road, Liverpool, Merseyside L3 9TA *Tel.* 0151 709 2919 *Email* info@nwcr.org *Website* www.nwcr.org

■ Northamptonshire Community Foundation

CC NO 1094646   **ESTABLISHED** 2001
WHERE FUNDING CAN BE GIVEN Northamptonshire.
WHO CAN BENEFIT Registered charities; unregistered charities; CICs; social enterprises; amateur sports clubs; religious bodies/institutions; individuals.
WHAT IS FUNDED General charitable purposes including the following: education and training; older people; crime prevention; sport; health; children and young people; people with disabilities; women and girls.
TYPE OF GRANT Project funding; capital costs.
RANGE OF GRANTS Mostly up to £30,000.
SAMPLE GRANTS Groundwork Northamptonshire (£67,300); Rushton Parish Council (£27,000); Warts and All Theatre (£19,700); Screen Northants Ltd (£15,100); Revolution Zero (£13,000); Picture the Difference CIC (£9,900); Punjabi Fusion CIC (£5,000); Winchester Street Reach (£1,000).
FINANCES *Financial year end 31/03/2022*
Income £1,220,000
Grants to organisations £1,120,000
Grants to individuals £19,500
Assets £20,540,000
TRUSTEES David Knight; Hassan Shah; Joanna Gordon; Janine Jepson; Debra Charles; Peter Borley-Cox; Rachel Mallows; Liam Condron; Richard Dimbleby; Edward Caswell; Syrah Nazir; Nancy Stewart.
OTHER INFORMATION This is one of the 47 UK community foundations, which distribute funding for a wide range of purposes. As with all community foundations, there are a number of donor-advised funds managed on behalf of individuals, families and charitable trusts. Grant schemes tend to change frequently – consult the foundation's website for details of current programmes and up-to-date deadlines.
HOW TO APPLY Visit the foundation's website to view available open grant programmes and application criteria.
CONTACT DETAILS The Trustees, 18 Albion Place, Northampton, Northamptonshire NN1 1UD *Tel.* 01604 230033 *Email* enquiries@ncf.uk.com *Website* www.ncf.uk.com

■ Northcott Trust

CC NO 239754   **ESTABLISHED** 1963
WHERE FUNDING CAN BE GIVEN UK, with a preference for Hampshire.
WHO CAN BENEFIT Charitable organisations; schools and colleges.
WHAT IS FUNDED General charitable purposes; education.
SAMPLE GRANTS Previous beneficiaries have included: Baby Fund Trading; BACUP; Barnardo's; Hampshire Association for the Blind; National Blind Children's Society; Society for Welfare of Horses and Ponies; St Thomas' Centre; Youth Club Hampshire.
FINANCES *Financial year end 05/04/2021*
Income £8,000
Grants to organisations £109,600
TRUSTEES Francis Northcott; Kirsten Northcott; Rosemary Sharpe.
OTHER INFORMATION Full accounts were not available to view on the Charity Commission's website due to the charity's low income. We have therefore estimated the charity's grant total based on its total expenditure. The 2020/21 Charity Commission record was the latest available at the time of writing (June 2023).
HOW TO APPLY Apply in writing to the correspondent.
CONTACT DETAILS The Trustees, c/o Dixon Wilson, 22 Chancery Lane, London WC2A 1LS *Tel.* 020 7680 8100

■ Northern Consortium

CC NO 1018979
WHERE FUNDING CAN BE GIVEN UK.
WHO CAN BENEFIT Charities; not-for-profit organisations.
WHAT IS FUNDED The promotion of and access to international education; educational engagement, particularly for students from disadvantaged groups.
TYPE OF GRANT Research funding; project funding.
SAMPLE GRANTS A list of beneficiaries was not included in the annual report and accounts.
FINANCES *Financial year end 31/08/2022*
Income £4,970,000
Grants to organisations £36,400
Assets £2,070,000
TRUSTEES Dr Malcolm Butler; Prof. Ian Wood; Dr Janice Allan; Joseph Rossiter; Prof. Laura Bishop; Sarah Darch; Cathryn Webster; Nicholas Smith; Andrew Ryder; Prof. Alistair Sambell; Stuart McKinnon-Evans; Richard Cotton; Prof. Jennifer Watling; James Richardson.
OTHER INFORMATION In 2022, the charity finalised a new funding strategy and for the next funding year (2022/23) the trustees earmarked a grants budget of £130,000.
HOW TO APPLY Application forms for grant funding can be downloaded from the charity's website. When completed, forms should be emailed to grants@nccharity.org.uk. To apply for research funding, a written submission (no more than six sides of A4) should be submitted via email to grants@nccharity.org.uk, details of what to include can be found on the charity's website. Applications are accepted throughout the year. Following an initial assessment, completed applications are reviewed by a committee that meet three times a year, usually in February, July and November.
CONTACT DETAILS Diane Leicester, Executive Director, 667–669, Stockport Road, Manchester M12 4QE *Tel.* 07309 926751 *Email* grants@nccharity.org.uk *Website* https://nccharity.org.uk

■ Community Foundation for Northern Ireland

CCNI NO NIC105105   **ESTABLISHED** 1979
WHERE FUNDING CAN BE GIVEN Northern Ireland.
WHO CAN BENEFIT Community groups; voluntary organisations; CICs; individuals.
WHAT IS FUNDED General charitable purposes including: education, social welfare, health and community development.
SAMPLE GRANTS A list of beneficiaries was not included in the annual report and accounts.
FINANCES *Financial year end 31/03/2022*
Income £37,500,000
Grants to organisations £11,530,000
Assets £50,210,000
TRUSTEES David McCurley; Mary McKee; David Gavaghan; Dr Adrian Johnston; Dr Jane Wilde; Ciaran Moynagh; John Gerard Gordon; Suzanne Lagan; Dr Sophie Long; Rhyannon Blythe; Caolan Ward; Mr Justin Kouame; Gerard Deane.

OTHER INFORMATION This is one of the 47 UK community foundations, which distribute funding for a wide range of purposes. As with all community foundations, there are a number of donor-advised funds managed on behalf of individuals, families and charitable trusts. Grant schemes tend to change frequently – consult the foundation's website for details of current programmes and up-to-date deadlines.

HOW TO APPLY Potential applicants are advised to visit the community foundation's website or contact its grants team to find the most suitable funding stream.

CONTACT DETAILS The Grants Team, Community House, Citylink Business Park, 6A Albert Street, Belfast BT12 4HQ *Tel.* 028 9024 5927 *Email* info@communityfoundationni.org *Website* www.communityfoundationni.org

■ Northern Pharmacies Ltd Trust Fund

CCNI NO NIC101560   **ESTABLISHED** 1977
WHERE FUNDING CAN BE GIVEN Northern Ireland.
WHO CAN BENEFIT Charitable organisations; hospices; social enterprises; individuals, in particular pharmacists and healthcare professionals.
WHAT IS FUNDED Health, with a focus on pharmacology; research; education and training of pharmacology students; public health awareness.
TYPE OF GRANT Training, research and education costs; salaries; project funding.
SAMPLE GRANTS Health and Social Care Board (£54,400); Ulster Chemists' Association – leadership pre-reg course (£14,300).
FINANCES *Financial year end* 05/04/2022
Income £30,100
Grants to organisations £71,900
Assets £1,100,000
TRUSTEES Sarah Burrows; Gerard Greene; Dr Sheelagh Hillan; Sarah Mawhinney; Michael Hamill; Dr Martin Kerr; Paul Kelly; Patrick Slevin; Dr Terry Maguire.
HOW TO APPLY Apply in writing to the correspondent.
CONTACT DETAILS Sarah Mawhinney, Trustee, c/o 5 Annadale Avenue, Belfast BT7 3JH *Tel.* 028 9069 0444 *Email* kdouglas@communitypharmacyni.co.uk

■ The Northumbria Historic Churches Trust

CC NO 511314   **ESTABLISHED** 1980
WHERE FUNDING CAN BE GIVEN Dioceses of Durham and Newcastle.
WHO CAN BENEFIT Christian churches of any denomination.
WHAT IS FUNDED Repairs to church buildings.
WHAT IS NOT FUNDED The repair of lighting systems; bells; clocks; organs; stone cleaning; work which should be carried out as part of routine maintenance such as gutter clearing, slipped roof tile replacement and redecoration.
TYPE OF GRANT Capital costs.
RANGE OF GRANTS Grants of up to £5,000.
SAMPLE GRANTS Blaydon Methodist Church and St Mary's – Middleton (£5,000 each); Holy Cross – Ryton (£3,000); St Michael and All Angels – Felton (£2,500); St Helen's – Cornhill (£2,000); St Giles – Birtley (£1,000).
FINANCES *Financial year end* 31/01/2022
Income £23,000
Grants to organisations £58,500

TRUSTEES Lt General Brims; The Revd Canon Robert McTeer; Dr Margaret Stewart; Lawrence McLeman; William Heslop; Joanna Pullan; John Anderson; Elizabeth Walford; Edward Tulasiewicz; Matthew Sinclair; Dennis Parker; The Revd Christopher Wardale.
OTHER INFORMATION Full accounts were not available to view on the Charity Commission's website due to the trust's low income. We have therefore estimated the grant total based on the trust's total expenditure.
HOW TO APPLY Application forms are available from the trust's website.
CONTACT DETAILS Kim Pearson, Secretary to the Trust, 7 Strothers Road, High Spen, Rowlands Gill, Tyne and Wear NE39 2HR *Tel.* 07761 803408 *Email* Secretary@NorthumbriaHCT.org.uk *Website* www.northumbriahct.org.uk

■ The Northwick Trust

CC NO 285197   **ESTABLISHED** 1982
WHERE FUNDING CAN BE GIVEN UK and overseas.
WHO CAN BENEFIT Registered charities.
WHAT IS FUNDED Conservation and the natural environment; social welfare; disability; young people and citizenship.
RANGE OF GRANTS £1,000 to £50,000.
SAMPLE GRANTS Forest School Camps (£65,000); Woodland Trust (£20,000); Calvert Trust (£16,000); Clean Rivers Trust (£12,000); Action for Refugees in Lewisham, Aid Box Community and Alzheimer's Society (£10,000 each); Full Circle Docklands (£8,000); Asylum Welcome and Birth Companions (£5,000 each); Soundabout (£3,000); Pledgeball (£1,000).
FINANCES *Financial year end* 31/03/2022
Income £285,700
Grants to organisations £480,000
Assets £12,470,000
TRUSTEES Mary Morgan; Lady Rachel Willcocks; Anne Willcocks; Kate Willcocks; Xanthe Williams; Peter McCarthy; Andrew Laurie.
OTHER INFORMATION In 2021/22, grants were made to 47 organisations.
HOW TO APPLY Contact the correspondent for further information.
CONTACT DETAILS Peter McCarthy, Trustee, 13 Queensway, Wellingborough, Northamptonshire NN8 3RA *Tel.* 01933 222986 *Email* petermc1711@btinternet.com

■ Northwood Charitable Trust

OSCR NO SC014487   **ESTABLISHED** 1972
WHERE FUNDING CAN BE GIVEN Dundee and Tayside.
WHO CAN BENEFIT Charitable organisations; registered charities; universities; churches; CICs.
WHAT IS FUNDED The relief of poverty and inequality; advancing educational attainment; improving physical and mental health and well-being; and supporting community, heritage and cultural enrichment.
RANGE OF GRANTS Mostly up to £50,000, with some larger grants of up to £150,000.
SAMPLE GRANTS University of Abertay (£150,000); Dundee Science Centre (£20,500); Countryside Learning (£20,600); Brittle Bone Charity (£20,000).
FINANCES *Financial year end* 05/04/2022
Income £3,450,000
Grants to organisations £3,040,000
Assets £3,630,000
OTHER INFORMATION Grants were awarded to 115 organisations during the year. Only the

beneficiaries of the 50 largest grants were listed in the charity's accounts.

HOW TO APPLY The trust's 2021/22 accounts state: 'Unsolicited applications for donations are not encouraged and will not normally be acknowledged.'

CONTACT DETAILS The Trustees, 22 Meadowside, Dundee DD1 1LN *Website* www.dcthomson.co.uk/our-communities

■ The Norton Foundation

CC NO 702638 **ESTABLISHED** 1990
WHERE FUNDING CAN BE GIVEN Birmingham, Coventry and Warwickshire.
WHO CAN BENEFIT Registered and unregistered charitable organisations; schools; community groups; individuals.
WHAT IS FUNDED Children and young people under the age of 25.
TYPE OF GRANT Project and capital grants.
RANGE OF GRANTS Up to £15,000.
SAMPLE GRANTS The Bryntail Cottage Charity (£15,000); Ecobirmingham and Young People First (£5,000 each); Big Brum Theatre in Education and Happy Days Children's Charity (£3,000 each); BE Festival CIC (£2,800); Family Connection Association (£2,500); Stage 2 Youth Theatre Company (£1,000).
FINANCES *Financial year end* 05/04/2022
Income £149,200
Grants to organisations £120,900
Grants to individuals £31,700
Assets £6,030,000
TRUSTEES Alan Bailey; Michael Bailey; Jane Gaynor; Brian Lewis; Louise Sewell; The Hon. Graham Suggett; William Pusey; Gurandan Jaspal.
OTHER INFORMATION During 2021/22, 30 grants were made to organisations.
HOW TO APPLY Application forms can be found on the foundation's website. Completed applications should be submitted along with the latest financial statements. Grants to organisations are considered quarterly.
CONTACT DETAILS The Trustees, Carleton House, 266–268 Stratford Road, Shirley, Solihull, West Midlands B90 3AD *Tel.* 0121 733 1111 *Email* correspondent@nortonfoundation.org *Website* www.nortonfoundation.org

■ The Norton Rose Fulbright Charitable Foundation

CC NO 1102142 **ESTABLISHED** 2004
WHERE FUNDING CAN BE GIVEN Worldwide.
WHO CAN BENEFIT Registered charities; charitable organisations.
WHAT IS FUNDED Education; social welfare; medical causes; disaster relief.
RANGE OF GRANTS Grants are typically under £15,000.
SAMPLE GRANTS South West London Law Centres (£60,000); Missing People Ltd (£15,000); Breaking Barriers, City Solicitors and Hand in Hand (£10,000 each).
FINANCES *Financial year end* 30/04/2022
Income £450,000
Grants to organisations £426,200
Assets £35,200
TRUSTEES Patrick Farrell; Ffion Flockhart.
OTHER INFORMATION Grants were made in the following categories: social welfare (£400,200); education (£13,400); medical causes (£12,600).

HOW TO APPLY Apply in writing to the correspondent. The foundation tends to support the same charities each year, but new charities are considered at trustees' meetings. The trustees also meet on an ad hoc basis to consider specific urgent requests such as the support of major disaster relief appeals.
CONTACT DETAILS The Trustees, c/o Norton Rose Fulbright, 3 More London Riverside, London SE1 2AQ *Tel.* 020 7283 6000 *Website* www.nortonrosefulbright.com/corporate-responsibility

■ Norwich Consolidated Charities

CC NO 1094602 **ESTABLISHED** 2002
WHERE FUNDING CAN BE GIVEN Norwich.
WHO CAN BENEFIT Registered charities; CICs; PCCs.
WHAT IS FUNDED Social welfare; social housing and homelessness; financial advice and support services; health; people experiencing discrimination or exclusion.
TYPE OF GRANT Project funding.
RANGE OF GRANTS Typically less than £50,000.
SAMPLE GRANTS Norwich Samaritans and Priscilla Bacon Hospice (£100,000 each); St Barnabas Counselling Centre (£55,000); New Routes Integration (£29,900); VCSE Hive CIC (£24,700); Norfolk Family Carers (£21,100); NR2 Community Skills Share (£12,400); Norwich Puppet Theatre (£7,100); Marie Curie (£1,500).
FINANCES *Financial year end* 31/12/2022
Income £2,380,000
Grants to organisations £1,220,000
Grants to individuals £100,900
Assets £37,340,000
TRUSTEES David Fullman; Jeanne Southgate; Michael Flynn; Cllr Karen Davis; Boyd Taylor; Philip Davies; John Garside; Jacqueline Hanlon; Laura McCartney-Gray; Cllr Adam Giles; Sally Button; Prof. Eneida Mioshi; Vivien Thomas; Ashley Ford-McAllister.
OTHER INFORMATION This charity is one of three grant-making charities operating as Norwich Charitable Trusts. Grants were made to 28 organisations in 2022.
HOW TO APPLY Organisations that wish to apply should first contact the correspondent by email. A meeting will then be set up to discuss the potential application. After the meeting, organisations may then be invited to complete an application. Application deadlines can be found online. Unsolicited applications will not be considered prior to a meeting.
CONTACT DETAILS David Hynes, CEO of Norwich Charitable Trusts, 1 Woolgate Court, St Benedicts Street, Norwich NR2 4AP *Tel.* 01603 621023 *Email* david.hynes@norwichcharitabletrusts.org.uk *Website* www.norwichcharitabletrusts.org.uk

■ Norwich Town Close Estate Charity

CC NO 235678 **ESTABLISHED** 1892
WHERE FUNDING CAN BE GIVEN Within a 20-mile radius of Norwich Guildhall.
WHO CAN BENEFIT Charitable organisations; schools.
WHAT IS FUNDED Education; sport and recreation; art and culture.
TYPE OF GRANT Capital costs; project funding; capacity building.
RANGE OF GRANTS £1,000 to £100,000.
SAMPLE GRANTS The Samaritans (£100,000); Norfolk Museum Service (£49,000); Norfolk and

Norwich Festival (£60,000); St Giles Trust (£15,000); Happy Days (£2,000).

FINANCES *Financial year end* 31/03/2022
Income £1,070,000
Grants to organisations £610,000
Grants to individuals £130
Assets £30,330,000

TRUSTEES Nigel Back; David Fullman; Michael Quinton; John Rushmer; Jeanne Southgate; Stuart Lamb; Owen Gibbs; Elspeth Jones; Cynthia Cooke; Melanie Kent; Jacqueline Hanlon; Boyd Taylor; John Garside; Vivien Thomas; Jennifer Plunkett.

OTHER INFORMATION This charity is one of three grant-making charities operating as Norwich Charitable Trusts. It operates under the name 'Norwich Freemen's Charity'.

HOW TO APPLY In the first instance, read the information on the website. After that, the correspondent can be contacted by email to arrange a discussion about your potential application.

CONTACT DETAILS David Hynes, CEO of Norwich Charitable Trusts, 1 Woolgate Court, St Benedicts Street, Norwich, Norfolk NR2 4AP *Tel.* 01603 621023 *Email* david.hynes@norwichcharitabletrusts.org.uk *Website* www.norwichcharitabletrusts.org.uk

■ The Norwood and Newton Settlement

CC NO 234964   **ESTABLISHED** 1952
WHERE FUNDING CAN BE GIVEN England and Wales, with a preference for Romford and the surrounding area.
WHO CAN BENEFIT Methodist and other free churches; Anglican churches in Havering; small charities in Havering.
WHAT IS FUNDED The promotion of Christianity.
WHAT IS NOT FUNDED Repairs and maintenance; salaries and running costs; equipment; appeals for which lottery funding has been received or an application is being processed; churches operating a policy of closed communion table; individuals; small schemes where the cost could be covered by the church or charity; small schemes made up of individual elements that could be undertaken as and when funding is available; small schemes that are purely to comply with the Equalities Acts (e.g. ramps and toilets); schemes where building work has already been completed.
TYPE OF GRANT One-off capital building projects.
RANGE OF GRANTS Up to £30,000.
SAMPLE GRANTS Calvary Baptist Church (£30,000); Godmanchester Baptist Church – Cambridgeshire (£25,000); Ainon Baptist Church – Cardiff (£20,000); Hope Church – Rhydyfelin (£15,000); Kidlington Methodist Church – Oxfordshire (£10,000); Edale Methodist Chapel – Derby (£5,000); Sawyers Church – Brentwood (£2,000).
FINANCES *Financial year end* 31/03/2022
Income £395,900
Grants to organisations £285,000
Assets £12,180,000
TRUSTEES Stella Holland; Susan Bed; Alan Gray; Rodney Eborn; Trevor Marlow.
OTHER INFORMATION In 2021/22, 18 grants were awarded to organisations.
HOW TO APPLY Apply in writing to the correspondent. In normal circumstances, applicants are sent either a refusal or an application form inviting further information within a few days. Once satisfactory information has been received,

applications are considered by the trustees at quarterly meetings. Applicants are kept informed of the trustees' timescale at all times.
CONTACT DETAILS The Trustees, 5 Convent Close, Upminster, London RM14 2FA *Tel.* 01708 226618 *Email* norwoodandnewton@btinternet.com or use the contact form on the website *Website* http://norwoodandnewton.co.uk

■ The Notgrove Trust

CC NO 278692   **ESTABLISHED** 1979
WHERE FUNDING CAN BE GIVEN Gloucestershire.
WHO CAN BENEFIT Registered charities.
WHAT IS FUNDED General charitable purposes.
WHAT IS NOT FUNDED Individuals; medical research; major national charities.
SAMPLE GRANTS Cheltenham Festivals (£60,000); YG Ltd (£30,000); Lumbs Foundation (£24,000); Brockworth House Residents Fund (£10,000); Mulberry Bush School (£5,000); Wootton Drama School (£3,000); The Guiting Music Festival (£2,500); Allsorts (£1,000).
FINANCES *Financial year end* 30/09/2021
Income £169,300
Grants to organisations £239,000
Assets £10,810,000
TRUSTEES Elizabeth Acland; Harry Acland; Diana Acland; Lucy Morris; Nigel Rowbotham.
OTHER INFORMATION The 2020/21 accounts were the latest available at the time of writing (May 2023). Grants were made to 27 organisations during the year.
HOW TO APPLY Apply in writing to the correspondent, including a full copy of your latest accounts. Applications are not acknowledged. If you have heard nothing within a month, you can assume that your application has been unsuccessful. Applications by email are not accepted or acknowledged. The trustees meet annually to review applications.
CONTACT DETAILS Diana Acland, Trustee, The Manor, Notgrove, Cheltenham, Gloucestershire GL54 3BT *Tel.* 01451 850239 *Email* diana@notgrove.com *Website* https://notgroveholidays.com/notgrove-estate/#trust

■ Nottinghamshire Community Foundation

CC NO 1069538   **ESTABLISHED** 1998
WHERE FUNDING CAN BE GIVEN Nottinghamshire.
WHO CAN BENEFIT Registered charities; unregistered charities; CICs; social enterprises; PTAs; amateur sports clubs; hospices; individuals.
WHAT IS FUNDED General charitable purposes including the following: health; welfare; older people; children and young people; homelessness; art and music.
RANGE OF GRANTS £1,000 to £5,000.
SAMPLE GRANTS Small Steps Big Changes (£146,000); Wheatcroft Fund (£91,800); Made by Sport (£69,600); Samuel Fox Foundation (£50,000); Sir George Earl (£25,200); Starr Consulting (£10,000); Miner2Major (£7,600); Roshni Legacy (£100).
FINANCES *Financial year end* 31/03/2022
Income £993,100
Grants to organisations £600,200
Assets £3,340,000
TRUSTEES The Rt Hon. Simon Tipping; Lady Diana Meale; Kevin Price; Nikki Weston; Lynn Betts; Mark Goldby; Kevin Hyland; Nadeem Raza; Heather Parker; Robert Moyle.

OTHER INFORMATION This is one of the 47 UK community foundations, which distribute funding for a wide range of purposes. As with all community foundations, there are a number of donor-advised funds managed on behalf of individuals, families and charitable trusts. Grant schemes tend to change frequently – consult the foundation's website for details of current programmes and up-to-date deadlines. Note that the grant total may include amounts awarded to individuals.

HOW TO APPLY Potential applicants are advised to visit the community foundation's website or contact the foundation team to find the most suitable funding stream.

CONTACT DETAILS The Trustees, Pine House B, Southwell Road West, Rainworth, Mansfield, Nottinghamshire NG21 0HJ *Tel.* 01623 620202 *Email* enquiries@nottscf.org.uk *Website* www.nottscf.org.uk

···

■ The Nuffield Foundation

CC NO 206601   **ESTABLISHED** 1943

WHERE FUNDING CAN BE GIVEN Predominantly in the UK.

WHO CAN BENEFIT Universities; independent research institutions; voluntary sector organisations; think tanks; primary care trusts.

WHAT IS FUNDED Science and social science research into education, justice and welfare.

WHAT IS NOT FUNDED See the foundation's website for a full list of exclusions.

TYPE OF GRANT Project funding; research funding; seed funding; strategic funding.

RANGE OF GRANTS Programme dependent – see website.

SAMPLE GRANTS University of Oxford (£2.85 million); National Institute of Economic and Social Research (£498,700); University of York (£295,200); London School of Economics and Political Science (£151,800); Centre for Evidence and Implementation Global – CEI (£33,500); Coram (£10,000); Fatherhood Institute (£6,800); University of London (£1,800).

FINANCES *Financial year end* 31/12/2021
Income £11,670,000
Grants to organisations £15,960,000
Assets £514,530,000

TRUSTEES Prof. James Banks; The Rt Hon. Sir Ernest Ryder; Sir Keith Burnett; Prof. Ash Amin; John Pullinger; Prof. Ann Phoenix; Prof. Lorraine Dearden; Dame Clare Tickell.

OTHER INFORMATION According to the foundation's application guidelines, all grants are awarded to organisations (host institutions) rather than individuals. In 2021 the foundation received 358 initial applications from research, development and analysis projects and considered 65 full applications. Many of the foundation's funding programmes have individual funding criteria and guidelines which are not listed here. Consult the foundation's website before applying.

HOW TO APPLY Applicants should firstly read the 'Guide for applicants' for the relevant funding programme. The first stage is to submit an outline application for consideration and then the proposal may be shortlisted for consideration by trustees. At this point, shortlisted applicants will be asked to submit a full application. A timetable of application deadlines can be found on the foundation's website.

CONTACT DETAILS Grants Team, 100 St John Street, London EC1M 4EH *Tel.* 020 7631 0566 *Email* info@nuffieldfoundation.org *Website* www.nuffieldfoundation.org

■ The Oakdale Trust

CC NO 218827   ESTABLISHED 1950
WHERE FUNDING CAN BE GIVEN UK, with a preference for Wales; overseas.
WHO CAN BENEFIT Registered charities; unregistered charities; CICs.
WHAT IS FUNDED Welsh social and community projects; medical support groups in Wales; UK-based medical research projects; Welsh environmental conservation projects; the arts (where there is a Welsh connection); UK-based and registered charities working in financially developing countries; penal reform.
WHAT IS NOT FUNDED Individuals; holiday schemes; sport activities; expeditions.
TYPE OF GRANT Capital costs; core and revenue costs; seed funding/start-up funding; project funding; unrestricted funding.
RANGE OF GRANTS Grants range from £250 up to £2,000; the average grant is £1,000.
SAMPLE GRANTS Bipolar UK (£10,000); Narberth Energy Ltd (£6,000); Children Change Colombia (£4,000); Alternatives To Violence (AVP) Britain (£3,000); Motor Neurone Disease Association (£2,000); Terrence Higgins Trust (£1,000); Wessex Social Ventures (£500).
FINANCES *Financial year end 05/04/2022*
Income £374,100
Grants to organisations £237,300
Assets £18,820,000
TRUSTEES Rupert Cadbury; Dr Rebecca Cadbury; Bruce Cadbury; Olivia Tatton-Brown.
OTHER INFORMATION Repeat applications are not normally accepted within a two-year period.
HOW TO APPLY Applications can be submitted using the online form (preferred) or sent in by post. Full guidelines, including closing dates for applications, are published on the website. The trust states that it will accept telephone calls; however, messages should not be left on the answerphone as this is for private use only.
CONTACT DETAILS The Trustees, Tansor House, Main Street, Tansor, Peterborough, Cambridgeshire PE8 5HS *Tel.* 01832 226386 *Email* oakdale@tanh.co.uk *Website* www.oakdaletrust.org.uk

■ The Oakley Charitable Trust

CC NO 233041   ESTABLISHED 1963
WHERE FUNDING CAN BE GIVEN UK, with a preference for the West Midlands region.
WHO CAN BENEFIT UK-registered charities.
WHAT IS FUNDED The arts; heritage; social welfare; education.
WHAT IS NOT FUNDED Individuals; overseas charities; non-registered charities.
TYPE OF GRANT Core costs, project, research, recurring costs and buildings.
RANGE OF GRANTS Mostly £500 to £3,000.
SAMPLE GRANTS Marie Curie (£4,000); Acorn Children's Hospice (£2,500); Royal Birmingham Society of Artists (£1,500); Asthma Relief (£500); Sports Driving Unlimited (£100).
FINANCES *Financial year end 05/04/2022*
Income £69,400
Grants to organisations £66,100
Assets £3,190,000

TRUSTEES Christine Airey; Geoffrey Oakley; Simon Sharp.
OTHER INFORMATION Grants were made to 56 organisations during the year.
HOW TO APPLY Apply in writing to the correspondent, including the details of the project and the amount you need. Applications cannot be made by email. The trustees meet in March, July and November.
CONTACT DETAILS Grants Administrator, 10 St Mary's Road, Harborne, Birmingham, West Midlands B17 0HA *Tel.* 0121 427 7150 *Website* www.oakleycharitabletrust.org.uk

■ Ocean Family Foundation

CC NO 1174759
WHERE FUNDING CAN BE GIVEN Worldwide.
WHO CAN BENEFIT Charitable organisations.
WHAT IS FUNDED Marine conservation.
TYPE OF GRANT Project funding.
SAMPLE GRANTS A Plastic Free Planet Ltd (£125,000); The Africa Foundation (£133,800); Worldrise ONLUS (£88,800); UK Sailing Academy (£50,000); Fundacion Save The Med (£42,600); Bristol University (£30,000) Boat International Media (£25,000); Trash Hero World (£14,100).
FINANCES *Financial year end 28/02/2022*
Income £714,100
Grants to organisations £510,900
Assets £85,200
TRUSTEES Peter Dubens; David Till; Jessica Getty; Clare-Louise Creasey.
HOW TO APPLY Contact the foundation for further information. The foundation's website states: 'We welcome all funding proposals.'
CONTACT DETAILS The Trustees, 3 Cadogan Gate, London SW1X 0AS *Email* hello@oceanfamilyfoundation.org *Website* www.oceanfamilyfoundation.org

■ Odin Charitable Trust

CC NO 1027521   ESTABLISHED 1993
WHERE FUNDING CAN BE GIVEN UK.
WHO CAN BENEFIT UK-registered charities.
WHAT IS FUNDED General charitable purposes, with a preference for: the arts; care for people with disabilities; disadvantaged people; hospices; homelessness; prisoners' families; refugees; Roma and Travellers; tribes; indigenous peoples; research into false memories and dyslexia.
TYPE OF GRANT Mostly recurrent.
RANGE OF GRANTS Usually between £1,000 and £5,000, but occasionally up to £10,000.
SAMPLE GRANTS Dorothy House Hospice Care (£90,000); The Trussell Trust (£40,000); Crisis UK and Refuge (£10,000 each); Independent Age (£5,000).
FINANCES *Financial year end 05/04/2021*
Income £627,100
Grants to organisations £375,000
Assets £10,380,000
TRUSTEES Pia Cherry; Donna Kelly; Payne Hicks Beach Trust Corporation Ltd.
OTHER INFORMATION The 2020/21 annual report and accounts were the latest available at the time of writing (June 2023). Grants were committed to 23 organisations during the year.
HOW TO APPLY Applications should be submitted in the form of a letter or email and contain the following information: the aims and objectives of the charity, the nature of the appeal, the total target (if for a specific project), the charity's

registration number and any other relevant information. Letters should be accompanied by a set of the charity's latest report and full accounts.

CONTACT DETAILS The Trustees, 10 New Square, London WC2A 3QG *Tel.* 020 7465 4300

■ The Ofenheim Charitable Trust

CC NO 286525   **ESTABLISHED** 1983

WHERE FUNDING CAN BE GIVEN Worldwide but in practice UK and Wales with some preference for East Sussex.

WHO CAN BENEFIT Registered charities.

WHAT IS FUNDED General charitable purposes, particularly: older people; hospices; medical research; music; education; the arts; social welfare; wildlife preservation.

WHAT IS NOT FUNDED Individuals.

RANGE OF GRANTS Grants range from £7,000 to £30,000.

SAMPLE GRANTS Barnardo's and Royal Trinity Hospice (£30,000 each); Friends of the Elderly (£24,000); The Hepworth Wakefield and St Wilfrid's Hospice Eastbourne (£20,000 each); Enham Trust (£13,000); Longborough Festival Opera and Mildmay Hospital (£9,000 each); SongBird Survival (£7,000).

FINANCES *Financial year end 31/03/2022*
Income £540,500
Grants to organisations £987,000
Assets £18,000,000

TRUSTEES Fiona Byrd; Roger Clark; Dr Alexander Clark; Rory McLeod.

OTHER INFORMATION Grants were made to 72 organisations during the year.

HOW TO APPLY Apply in writing to the correspondent. The trustees tend to support the same organisations each year and prefer to support organisations of which they have prior knowledge.

CONTACT DETAILS The Trustees, c/o RSM UK Tax and Accounting Ltd, The Pinnacle, 170 Midsummer Boulevard, Milton Keynes, Buckinghamshire MK9 1BP *Tel.* 01908 687800

■ The Ogle Christian Trust

CC NO 1061458   **ESTABLISHED** 1938

WHERE FUNDING CAN BE GIVEN Worldwide.

WHO CAN BENEFIT Registered charities.

WHAT IS FUNDED The advancement of the Christian faith; evangelism worldwide; support for missionary enterprises; Bible student training; help for retired missionary workers and famine and relief organisations.

WHAT IS NOT FUNDED Individuals; building projects; general appeals from large national organisations; salaries.

RANGE OF GRANTS From £1,000 to £25,000 but typically less than £5,000.

SAMPLE GRANTS Savannah Education Trust (£20,000); Bethany Trust (£10,000); The Breakout Trust (£3,000); Yeldall Christian Centres (£2,000).

FINANCES *Financial year end 31/12/2021*
Income £91,500
Grants to organisations £191,200
Assets £2,390,000

TRUSTEES Ronald Goodenough; Dr David Harley; Fiona Putley; Stephen Procter; Dr Carol Walker; Paul Bigmore.

HOW TO APPLY Apply in writing to the correspondent and include an sae. Our previous research suggests that the trustees meet in May and November.

CONTACT DETAILS The Trustees, Here for Good – Community Centre, 17 Sydenham Road, London SE26 5EX *Tel.* 07857 043212
Email oglectrust@rockuk.net

■ The Hamish Ogston Foundation

CC NO 1185978

WHERE FUNDING CAN BE GIVEN UK and worldwide.

WHO CAN BENEFIT Registered charities.

WHAT IS FUNDED Health (eliminating disparities in access to treatment); heritage (preservation of buildings and craftsmanship with historic value); music (supporting the UK's musical traditions through training programmes).

TYPE OF GRANT Project funding.

SAMPLE GRANTS National Trust (£6.17 million); Cathedral's Workshop Fellowship (£2.28 million); Diocese of Leeds Grant (£869,300); Commonwealth Heritage Forum (£781,700); Global Snakebite Initiative (£95,700); Venoms and Toxins 2021 (£61).

FINANCES *Financial year end 30/06/2022*
Income £1,580,000
Grants to organisations £10,000,000
Assets (£545,000)

TRUSTEES Isabella Ogston; Hamish Ogston.

OTHER INFORMATION In 2021/22 grants were awarded for heritage (£9.24 million) and music (£871,600). Grants of less than £1,000 totalled £5,500.

HOW TO APPLY Application forms can be downloaded from the foundation's website. Once completed, applications should be returned by email only. The foundation aims to respond within a week; however, the website states that due to the high volume of applications, acknowledgements cannot be guaranteed in all circumstances.

CONTACT DETAILS The Trustees, Dixon Wilson, 6th Floor, 22 Chancery Lane, London WC2A 1LS *Tel.* 020 3696 1447 *Email* office@hamishogstonfoundation.org *Website* www.hamishogstonfoundation.org

---

■ Oizer Charitable Trust

CC NO 1014399   **ESTABLISHED** 1992

WHERE FUNDING CAN BE GIVEN UK, with a preference for Greater Manchester.

WHO CAN BENEFIT Jewish organisations.

WHAT IS FUNDED The provision of Orthodox Jewish education and the advancement of religion according to the Orthodox Jewish faith.

TYPE OF GRANT Typically recurrent.

RANGE OF GRANTS Up to £37,600.

SAMPLE GRANTS Bikur Cholim and Gemiluth Chesed Trust (£49,000); Friends of Boyan Trust (£37,600); Teshivoh Tefilloh Tzedokoh (£20,300); Chevras Mo'oz Ladol (£17,500); Shaarei Orah Ltd (£15,800).

FINANCES *Financial year end 31/03/2022*
Income £743,400
Grants to organisations £316,100
Assets £5,210,000

TRUSTEES Joshua Halpern; Cindy Halpern.

HOW TO APPLY Apply in writing to the correspondent.

CONTACT DETAILS The Trustees, 1st Floor, Cloister House, Riverside, New Bailey Street, Manchester M3 5FS *Tel.* 0161 832 8721

■ Old Possum's Practical Trust

CC NO 328558 **ESTABLISHED** 1990
WHERE FUNDING CAN BE GIVEN UK.
WHO CAN BENEFIT Registered charities; schools; arts, culture and heritage organisations; places of worship.
WHAT IS FUNDED Literary, artistic, musical and theatrical projects; historical conservation; social welfare.
WHAT IS NOT FUNDED Retrospective expenditure; capital building projects; personal training and education; medical care; national charities with substantial other funding; feasibility studies.
TYPE OF GRANT Project funding.
RANGE OF GRANTS Typically £2,500 to £30,000.
SAMPLE GRANTS The T.S. Elliot Foundation (£1 million); Garsington Opera – Arts Hub (£50,000); National Theatre (£25,000); English National Ballet (£15,000); British Library (£10,500); Imperial War Museum (£5,000); Wild Plum Arts (£2,500); Achievement for All (£1,500).
FINANCES *Financial year end 31/03/2022 Income £265,400 Grants to organisations £1,330,000 Assets £8,870,000*
TRUSTEES Judith Hooper; Clare Reihill; Deirdre Simpson.
OTHER INFORMATION Grants typically last for three years. In 2021/22 the trust made grants to 48 organisations across the following areas: the arts and historical conservation (£1.21 million); educational support (£61,200); support for people living with disabilities or disadvantage (£61,200).
HOW TO APPLY Grant applications can only be made online, via the trust's website: applications by email, fax, letter or by telephone are no longer accepted.
CONTACT DETAILS The Trustees, c/o RSM, The Pinnacle, 170 Midsummer Boulevard, Milton Keynes, Buckinghamshire MK9 1BP *Tel.* 01908 662255 *Email* generalenquiry@old-possums-practical-trust.org.uk *Website* www.old-possums-practical-trust.org.uk

■ Henry Oldfield Trust

CC NO 1156496 **ESTABLISHED** 2014
WHERE FUNDING CAN BE GIVEN Kent and Medway.
WHO CAN BENEFIT Registered charities; galleries; museums; hospices.
WHAT IS FUNDED The promotion of entrepreneurship; people experiencing homelessness and addiction; programmes which reduce offending and re-offending; children and young people.
RANGE OF GRANTS Mostly £1,000 to £50,000.
SAMPLE GRANTS The Amber Foundation (£1.65 million); King's Rochester (£160,000); Justice Defenders (£50,000); Save the Children UK (£100,000); Royal Marsden Cancer Charity and Unlocked Graduates (£40,000 each); Primal Roots (£30,000); AMAR Foundation (£25,000); Hypo Hounds (£19,000); New Philanthropy Capital Onward (£7,500); Mvule Trust (£1,000).
FINANCES *Financial year end 31/03/2022 Income £1,320,000 Grants to organisations £2,630,000 Assets £14,970,000*
TRUSTEES Richard Oldfield; Leonora Philipps; Amicia Oldfield; Christopher Oldfield; Edward Oldfield; Baroness Jenkin.
OTHER INFORMATION During the year, grants were awarded to 62 organisations.
HOW TO APPLY Apply in writing to the correspondent.

CONTACT DETAILS The Trustees, Doddington Place, Church Lane, Doddington, Sittingbourne, Kent ME9 0BB *Tel.* 01795 886385

■ The Olwyn Foundation

CC NO 1179306 **ESTABLISHED** 2018
WHERE FUNDING CAN BE GIVEN UK and overseas.
WHO CAN BENEFIT Registered charities.
WHAT IS FUNDED The empowerment, education and protection of women and girls.
TYPE OF GRANT Project funding; campaign funding; core/revenue costs; salaries. One-off and recurrent funding.
SAMPLE GRANTS A list of beneficiaries was not included in the annual report and accounts. Previous beneficiaries have included: ActionAid, Child's i Foundation, Orchid Project and Women for Women International.
FINANCES *Financial year end 31/12/2021 Income £200,000 Grants to organisations £182,000 Assets £20,500*
TRUSTEES Samantha Rowe-Beddoe; Antonia Deeson; Patricia Green; Samantha Merry.
HOW TO APPLY Unsolicited applications are not accepted.
CONTACT DETAILS Antonia Deeson, Trustee, 38 Market Place, Folkingham, Sleaford, NG34 0SF *Email* antonia@olwynfoundation.org *Website* www.olwynfoundation.com

■ One Community Foundation Ltd

CC NO 1135258 **ESTABLISHED** 2009
WHERE FUNDING CAN BE GIVEN Kirklees.
WHO CAN BENEFIT Registered charities; unregistered charities; CICs; schools; PTAs; amateur sports clubs; individuals.
WHAT IS FUNDED General charitable purposes; community development; the environment; sports; arts and social welfare.
WHAT IS NOT FUNDED Political activity; the promotion of religion; replacement of statutory funding; projects that have already started; groups which have not complied with previous monitoring requirements; animal welfare organisations.
TYPE OF GRANT Capital costs; core/revenue costs; project funding; unrestricted funding.
RANGE OF GRANTS Typically between £350 and £5,000.
SAMPLE GRANTS Local Care Direct (£137,200); Household Fund (£90,000); Made by Sport (£41,500); Bright Green Community Trust Fund (£25,700); The Charlesworth Fund (£13,200); Surviving Winter (£7,600); The Hirst Brierley Fund (£5,300); Collective Power Fund (£4,700); Heckmondwike Fund for the Needy Sick (£3,300); The Kirklees Police Fund (£2,100).
FINANCES *Financial year end 31/03/2022 Income £613,500 Grants to organisations £705,300 Grants to individuals £15,200 Assets £4,420,000*
TRUSTEES Sir John Harman; Judith Charlesworth; Eric Firth; Jeremy Garside; Jonathan Thornton; Joanne Bell; Nigel Taylor; Ian Brierley; Brendan Sykes.
OTHER INFORMATION This is one of the 47 UK community foundations, which distribute funding for a wide range of purposes. As with all community foundations, there are a number of donor-advised funds managed on behalf of individuals, families and charitable trusts. Grant schemes tend to change frequently – consult the foundation's website for details of current

programmes and up-to-date deadlines. During 2021/22, 249 grants were awarded.

HOW TO APPLY Potential applicants are advised to visit the community foundation's website or contact its grants team to find the most suitable funding stream.

CONTACT DETAILS Grants Team, c/o Chadwick Lawrence Solicitors, 13 Railway Street, Huddersfield, West Yorkshire HD1 1JS *Tel.* 01484 468397 *Email* info@one-community.org.uk *Website* www.one-community.org.uk

---

■ Open House Trust Ltd

CCNI NO NIC101352   **ESTABLISHED** 2015
WHERE FUNDING CAN BE GIVEN Worldwide.
WHO CAN BENEFIT Missionary organisations; individuals; schools and colleges; places of worship.
WHAT IS FUNDED Christianity; education; medical research; social welfare; health, including: water, sanitation and hygiene; citizenship and community development; overseas aid.
SAMPLE GRANTS Stauros Foundation (£42,000).
FINANCES *Financial year end* 31/12/2022
  Income £257,900
  Grants to organisations £175,500
  Assets £2,480,000
TRUSTEES Tom Eakins; Brendan Jones; Fred Charters; James Johnston; Stephen Williamson; Philip Hewitt.
HOW TO APPLY Apply in writing to the correspondent.
CONTACT DETAILS James Johnston, Trustee, 87 Ardlougher Road, Moynaghan South, Irvinestown, Enniskillen, County Fermanagh BT94 1SA *Tel.* 07973 149356 *Email* info@openhousetrust.org

---

■ Orange Tree Trust

CC NO 1183882
WHERE FUNDING CAN BE GIVEN UK and overseas.
WHO CAN BENEFIT Charitable organisations.
WHAT IS FUNDED Community development; refugees; homelessness; mental health; medical research; academic study and research in the arts, humanities and social sciences.
TYPE OF GRANT Capital projects; core costs; project funding.
RANGE OF GRANTS Up to £10,000.
SAMPLE GRANTS Waterloo Community Counselling (£10,000); Royal Court Theatre (£8,600); Gatwick Detainees Welfare Group, Lido Foundation and Veterans' Aid (£5,000 each); Lifelites (£4,000).
FINANCES *Financial year end* 31/07/2021
  Income £240,000
  Grants to organisations £67,600
  Assets £174,700
TRUSTEES Ghalia Al-Qattan; Omar Al-Qattan; David Freeman.
OTHER INFORMATION The trust awarded ten grants to organisations during the year. The trust has previously made grants to individuals, although none were awarded during the year. The 2020/21 accounts were the latest available at the time of writing (June 2023).
HOW TO APPLY Apply via the trust's website. Board meetings are held quarterly from January.
CONTACT DETAILS The Trustees, Tower House, 226 Cromwell Road, London SW5 0SW *Tel.* 020 7370 9990 *Email* info@orangetreetrust.org *Website* https://orangetreetrust.org

---

■ The Orrin Charitable Trust

CC NO 274599   **ESTABLISHED** 1977
WHERE FUNDING CAN BE GIVEN UK and occasionally overseas.
WHO CAN BENEFIT Registered charities.
WHAT IS FUNDED General charitable purposes.
WHAT IS NOT FUNDED Individuals.
RANGE OF GRANTS From £1,000 to £7,000, but typically up to £5,000.
SAMPLE GRANTS A list of beneficiaries was not included in the annual report and accounts. Previous beneficiaries have included: Atlantic Salmon Trust (£7,000); King Edward VII's Hospital and The National Playing Fields Association (£5,000 each); Fishmongers' Company Charitable Trust and Young Musicians Symphony Orchestra (£4,000 each); Scots Guards Association (£3,000); Project Malawi and The Wheelyboat Trust (£2,000 each); Church of the Most Holy Redeemer (£1,000).
FINANCES *Financial year end* 05/04/2022
  Income £37,600
  Grants to organisations £60,000
  Assets £772,000
TRUSTEES Hugh MacDonald-Buchanan; James MacDonald-Buchanan; Alexander MacDonald-Buchanan.
HOW TO APPLY Apply in writing to the correspondent.
CONTACT DETAILS The Trustees of The Orrin Charitable Trust, The Hedley Foundation, Victoria House, 1–3 College Hill, London EC4R 2RA *Tel.* 020 7489 8076

■ Orthopaedic Research UK

CC NO 1111657   **ESTABLISHED** 1989
WHERE FUNDING CAN BE GIVEN UK.
WHO CAN BENEFIT Universities; medical research organisations; NHS trusts; start-ups.
WHAT IS FUNDED Medical research, in particular orthopaedic research; education and training; publishing; start-ups.
TYPE OF GRANT Research, including PhD, postdoctoral and start-up funding; project funding; seed funding/start-up funding.
RANGE OF GRANTS Typically around £75,000.
SAMPLE GRANTS Newcastle University (£110,000); University of East Anglia (£109,400); Nottingham University (£97,900); South West London Elective Orthopaedic Centre (£50,000); University of Bath (£34,900); Queen Mary University of London (£30,000).
FINANCES *Financial year end* 31/03/2022
  Income £1,340,000
  Grants to organisations £776,000
  Assets £29,880,000
TRUSTEES Peter Harrison; Keith Tucker; Prof. Matteo Santin; Martin Gouldstone; Sarah Harkness; Adrian Downing; Dr Catherine Ball; Prof. Neil Rushton.
OTHER INFORMATION During 2021/22, 11 organisations received research grants.
HOW TO APPLY The application process, deadlines and eligibility vary for research grants, research fellowships (RCS/ORUK Research Fellowship and RAEng/ORUK Research Fellowship) and start-up funding. Pre-submission enquiries are welcomed. Visit the funder's website for full details.
CONTACT DETAILS Arash Angadji, Chief Executive, Furlong House, 10A Chandos Street, London W1G 9DQ *Tel.* 020 7637 5789 *Email* info@oruk.org *Website* www.oruk.org

■ Ostro Fayre Share Foundation

CC NO 1090985   **ESTABLISHED** 2000
WHERE FUNDING CAN BE GIVEN UK and overseas, with a preference for Myanmar.
WHO CAN BENEFIT Registered charities.
WHAT IS FUNDED Philanthropy and voluntary sector collaboration; interfaith relations; conflict resolution.
SAMPLE GRANTS A list of beneficiaries was not included in the annual report and accounts.
FINANCES *Financial year end 31/12/2021*
Income £1,800,000
Grants to organisations £1,680,000
Assets £1,010,000
TRUSTEES Maurice Ostro; Katy Ostro; Lyddon Simon; Hetty Maher.
OTHER INFORMATION In 2021 grants were distributed across the following areas: community champions (£914,000); strengthening faith institutions (£694,400); Rank and Peer Network (£37,800); educational (£15,300); religious and inter-faith (£9,800); entrepreneurial giving scheme (£2,100); medical causes (£2,100); children's welfare (£2,000).
HOW TO APPLY The foundation does not accept unsolicited requests for funding. However, it may consider offers of partnership in its key priority areas of philanthropy, collaboration, interfaith relations and conflict resolution.
CONTACT DETAILS The Trustees, 77–79 Charlotte Street, London W1T 4PW *Tel.* 020 7569 9093 *Email* info@fayresharefoundation.org *Website* www.ostro.com/foundation

■ The Sir Peter O'Sullevan Charitable Trust

CC NO 1078889   **ESTABLISHED** 1999
WHERE FUNDING CAN BE GIVEN UK.
WHO CAN BENEFIT Registered charities.
WHAT IS FUNDED Animal welfare; horses; the racing industry.
TYPE OF GRANT Capital and building costs; service delivery; project funding.
RANGE OF GRANTS Typically £2,000 to £30,000.
SAMPLE GRANTS Injured Jockeys Fund (£225,000); Horseback UK (£50,000); National Horseracing College (£30,000); Painted Horse (£24,000); British Horse Society (£16,800); Hopton Rehab (£10,000); Racing Together and Reanimate (£2,000).
FINANCES *Financial year end 30/04/2022*
Income £1,020,000
Grants to organisations £1,010,000
Assets £3,330,000
TRUSTEES Michael Dillon; Geoffrey Hughes; Nigel Payne; John McManus; Michael Kerr-Dineen; Sir Anthony McCoy; Dierdre Flood.
OTHER INFORMATION The trust has an ongoing commitment to the following six animal welfare charities: Blue Cross, British Thoroughbred Retraining Centre, Brooke, Compassion in World Farming, Racing Welfare and World Horse Welfare. These charities receive £30,000 each per annum. The grant total includes the £180,000 distributed equally between the six charities named above as well as £952,900 to other charities.
HOW TO APPLY Apply in writing to the correspondent. Further guidance is available on the trust's website. Applications need to be received by the last day of November each year and will be discussed in detail by the trustees to reach a decision by the end of January.
CONTACT DETAILS Nigel Payne, Trustee, The Old School, Bolventor, Launceston, Cornwall PL15 7TS *Tel.* 07768 025265 *Email* nigel@earthsummit.demon.co.uk *Website* www.thevoiceofracing.com

■ The O'Sullivan Family Charitable Trust

CC NO 1123757   **ESTABLISHED** 2008
WHERE FUNDING CAN BE GIVEN UK.
WHO CAN BENEFIT Registered charities.
WHAT IS FUNDED The care of people who have disabilities, especially children and young people; genetic research.
TYPE OF GRANT Research; project funding.
RANGE OF GRANTS Generally £3,000 to £10,000, with some larger grants.
SAMPLE GRANTS The Playhouse Foundation (£94,200); DEBRA (£15,000); Hampshire Cultural Trust (£25,000); British Asian Trust (£14,000); Shepherds Down School Fund and The Brickworks (£10,100); Stable Family Home Trust and Step by Step (£3,000 each).
FINANCES *Financial year end 30/06/2022*
Income £146,100
Grants to organisations £301,000
Assets £4,990,000
TRUSTEES Diana O'Sullivan; Finian O'Sullivan; Emily O'Sullivan; Sophie O'Sullivan; Tessa Cartwright.
OTHER INFORMATION Grants were awarded to 27 institutions during the year, with a substantial grant awarded to The Playhouse Foundation.
HOW TO APPLY Apply in writing to the correspondent.
CONTACT DETAILS The Trustees, 36 Edge Street, London W8 7PN *Tel.* 020 7131 4000

■ Otsar Trust

OSCR NO SC046456   **ESTABLISHED** 2016
WHERE FUNDING CAN BE GIVEN UK and overseas.
WHO CAN BENEFIT Charitable organisations.
WHAT IS FUNDED Advancement of the Christian faith; social welfare.
SAMPLE GRANTS A list of beneficiaries was not included in the annual report and accounts.
FINANCES *Financial year end 30/04/2022*
Income £141,900
Grants to organisations £240,500
Assets £505,800
HOW TO APPLY Apply in writing to the correspondent.
CONTACT DETAILS The Trustees, Kirkside, Kirkton of Tealing, Dundee, Angus DD4 0RD

■ The Ouseley Church Music Trust

CC NO 527519   **ESTABLISHED** 1989
WHERE FUNDING CAN BE GIVEN England, Wales and Ireland.
WHO CAN BENEFIT Registered charities; unregistered charities; schools; religious bodies/institutions.
WHAT IS FUNDED Projects that promote and maintain to a high standard the choral services and choir schools of the Church of England, the Church in Wales or the Church of Ireland.
WHAT IS NOT FUNDED Organs; applications for projects that will be substantially completed by the closing date; grants for building projects, recordings, the purchase of furniture, clothing or liturgical objects, instrument repairs or purchases (including organs) or for tours and visits; endowment or capital grants to endow choristerships or lay clerks' places.
TYPE OF GRANT Capital costs; seed funding/start-up funding.

RANGE OF GRANTS Up to £50,000; for fees, £5,000 maximum.

SAMPLE GRANTS Carlisle Cathedral (£16,000); Newcastle Cathedral (£12,500); Liverpool Cathedral (£2,500); The Alleyn Singers (£750).

FINANCES *Financial year end 31/12/2021*
Income £148,600
Grants to organisations £90,000
Assets £5,840,000

TRUSTEES The Very Revd Mark Boyling; Gillian Perkins; Dr John Rutter; Dr Stephen Darlington; Canon Paul Mason; Dr Jo Spreadbury; Simon Hirtzel; David Lowe; Samantha Bradburne; Richard Whymark; Carl Jackson.

OTHER INFORMATION During 2021, the trustees considered 35 applications and authorised 24 grants.

HOW TO APPLY Apply via the trust's website.

CONTACT DETAILS Neil Parsons, Clerk to the Trustees, PO Box 281, Stamford, Lincolnshire PE9 9BU *Tel.* 07912 696852 *Email* ouseleytrust@btinternet.com *Website* www.ouseleytrust.org.uk

■ Ovingdean Hall Foundation

CC NO 1052478   **ESTABLISHED** 2012

WHERE FUNDING CAN BE GIVEN UK.

WHO CAN BENEFIT Registered charities; non-profit organisations; universities.

WHAT IS FUNDED The education of children and young people with a hearing impairment.

WHAT IS NOT FUNDED Overseas charities or projects; other grant-making charities; charities that use external fundraising agencies; projects the reinforce negative stereotypes of children and young people with disabilities; activities or projects which a statutory authority is responsible for.

TYPE OF GRANT Project funding; salaries; research; capital costs; scholarships for individuals.

RANGE OF GRANTS Up to £35,000.

SAMPLE GRANTS British Association of Teachers of the Deaf (Con Powell Scholarships) (£39,200); School of Sexuality Education Ltd (£30,000); Panathlon (£25,000); Signhealth (£20,700); Mousetrap (£10,000); National Sensory Impairment Partnership (NATSIP) (£5,000); The Island Trust Grant (£2,000).

FINANCES *Financial year end 31/03/2022*
Income £80,000
Grants to organisations £205,700
Assets £1,660,000

TRUSTEES Ian Johnson; Edward Moore; Pauline Hughes; Hamish McAlpine; Lindsey Rousseau.

OTHER INFORMATION Grants were made to 19 listed organisations during 2021/22. Small grants of under £2,000 were not listed and totalled £2,500.

HOW TO APPLY The foundation's website states that applications are accepted from UK-registered charities and not-for-profit organisations. The trustees meet three times a year to discuss applications. The website states that potential applicants should first read the eligibility criteria for each grant programme, as well as the guidelines, before completing an application.

CONTACT DETAILS The Trustees, c/o Ovingdean Hall Foundation, 15 Great College Street, London SW1P 3RX *Tel.* 01273 301929 *Email* info@ ovingdeanhall.org.uk *Website* www. ovingdeanhall.org

■ The Ovo Charitable Foundation

CC NO 1155954   **ESTABLISHED** 2014

WHERE FUNDING CAN BE GIVEN UK and overseas.

WHO CAN BENEFIT Registered charities.

WHAT IS FUNDED Sustainability; the environment; climate change; children and young people; increased access to green spaces and opportunities in education, employment and health.

TYPE OF GRANT Project funding.

RANGE OF GRANTS Mainly under £50,000.

SAMPLE GRANTS Energy 4 Impact (£202,600); Energy Sparks (£114,200); Action for Conservation (£55,000); The Wildlife Trusts (£48,000); Roundabout Ltd (£35,900); End Youth Homelessness (£20,600); FareShare (£8,300); Doorstep Library (£3,000).

FINANCES *Financial year end 31/12/2021*
Income £999,700
Grants to organisations £799,100
Assets £1,770,000

TRUSTEES Gina Cicerone; Katherine Goldsmith; Phillip Kerry; Oluwakemi Akindele; Thomas Wilson; Charlotte Eaton.

OTHER INFORMATION The foundation is the corporate charity of Ovo Energy. During 2021, grants were made to 14 organisations.

HOW TO APPLY Calls for funding are advertised on the foundation's website.

CONTACT DETAILS The Trustees, 1 Rivergate, Bristol BS1 6ED *Tel.* 0800 599 9440 *Email* hello@ ovofoundation.org.uk *Website* www. ovofoundation.org.uk

■ The Owen Family Trust

CC NO 251975   **ESTABLISHED** 1967

WHERE FUNDING CAN BE GIVEN UK, with a strong preference for West Midlands.

WHO CAN BENEFIT Registered charities; schools (independent and church); Christian youth centres; churches; museums; community associations.

WHAT IS FUNDED General charitable purposes, including education and training, health and medicine, religious activities, arts, culture, heritage, and economic and community development.

WHAT IS NOT FUNDED Individuals.

RANGE OF GRANTS Mainly up to £5,000.

SAMPLE GRANTS A list of beneficiaries was not included in the annual report and accounts. Previous beneficiaries have included: Black Country Living Museum (£10,000); Lichfield Cathedral, Seven Valley Railway Charitable Trust, Shrewsbury Abbey and The Ironbridge Gorge Museum (£5,000 each); Bournville BookFest (£2,500); Birmingham Royal Ballet (£2,000); Serbian Orthodox Church (£1,000).

FINANCES *Financial year end 05/04/2022*
Income £30,100
Grants to organisations £84,100
Assets £588,800

TRUSTEES Mr A. David Owen; Ethne Owen; Nicholas Owen; Jeremy Owen; Virginia Allen.

HOW TO APPLY Apply in writing to the correspondent. Our previous research suggests that applications should include an annual report, a project budget, general information regarding the application and an sae. The trustees meet quarterly.

CONTACT DETAILS David Owen, Trustee, Mill Dam House, Mill Lane, Aldridge, Walsall WS9 0NB *Tel.* 0121 353 1221 *Email* owenmdh@ btinternet.com

■ Oxfordshire Community Foundation

CC NO 1151621   **ESTABLISHED** 2013

WHERE FUNDING CAN BE GIVEN Oxfordshire.

WHO CAN BENEFIT Community-based non-profit organisations based in Oxfordshire.

WHAT IS FUNDED General charitable purposes; social welfare.

SAMPLE GRANTS A list of beneficiaries was not included in the annual report and accounts. Previous beneficiaries have included: South Oxfordshire Food and Education Alliance (£45,500); Oxford Hub (£35,000); Oxfordshire Youth (£25,000); Blackbird Leys Neighbourhood Support Scheme (£10,000); Community Album (£4,000); Action for Carers Oxfordshire (£3,250); Museum of Oxford Development Trust (£3,180); Digital for Good (£2,000); Oxfordshire Bengali Cultural Society (£1,000); Hinksey Park Football Club (£500).

FINANCES *Financial year end 31/03/2022*
Income £2,540,000
Grants to organisations £2,060,000
Assets £10,850,000

TRUSTEES Anne Davies; Neil Preddy; Estella Wild; Julian Phillips; Ian Busby; Imam Hussain.

OTHER INFORMATION This is one of the 47 UK community foundations, which distribute funding for a wide range of purposes. As with all community foundations, there are a number of donor-advised funds managed on behalf of individuals, families and charitable trusts. Grant schemes tend to change frequently – consult the foundation's website for details of current programmes and up-to-date deadlines.

HOW TO APPLY Potential applicants are advised to visit the community foundation's website or contact its grants team to find the most suitable funding stream.

CONTACT DETAILS The Trustees, 3 Woodin's Way, Oxford, Oxfordshire OX1 1HD *Tel.* 01865 798666 *Email* ocf@oxfordshire.org *Website* www.oxfordshire.org

■ Oxfordshire Historic Churches Trust (2016)

CC NO 1168567   **ESTABLISHED** 2016

WHERE FUNDING CAN BE GIVEN Oxfordshire.

WHO CAN BENEFIT Religious bodies/institutions.

WHAT IS FUNDED Churches and chapels; repairs to the fixtures, fittings and structure of churches, chapels or meeting houses used as places of public worship; new work, such as the installation of toilets and kitchens, disabled access, security systems and electrics.

WHAT IS NOT FUNDED Routine maintenance; the removal or replacement of pews; liturgical reordering; church or parish halls; car parks; buildings of less than 50 years old; work that has already started.

TYPE OF GRANT Capital costs.

RANGE OF GRANTS £1,500 to £20,000.

SAMPLE GRANTS St Thomas – Goring (£20,000); St Mary – Pyrton (£10,500); New Road Baptist Church – Oxford (£6,000); St Martin's – Sandford (£3,000); St Olave's – Fritwell (£1,500); Christ the King – Sonning Common and Dorchester Abbey (£1,000 each); St Peter – Wolvercote (£500).

FINANCES *Financial year end 31/03/2022*
Income £450,900
Grants to organisations £221,000
Assets £5,680,000

TRUSTEES Giles Dessain; Hilary Hall; Cynthia Robinson; Michael Sibly; Dr Stephen Goss; Prof. Malcolm Airs; Richard Hughes; Dr Imogen Coldstream; Stephen Slack.

OTHER INFORMATION During 2021/22, grants were distributed as follows: 30 all-purpose grants (£212,000) and 2 roof alarms (£9,000).

HOW TO APPLY Applications can be made by downloading an application form from the trust's helpful website and returning it to the grants officer. The trust advises that you contact the area representative before applying.

CONTACT DETAILS The Secretary, 4 Haslemere Gardens, Oxford, Oxfordshire OX2 8EL *Tel.* 01865 559305 *Email* secretary@ohct.org. uk *Website* http://ohct.org.uk

578

Does the funder you have chosen match your needs? Haphazard applications waste postage and time

■ P. F. Charitable Trust

CC NO 220124   **ESTABLISHED** 1951
WHERE FUNDING CAN BE GIVEN England; Scotland; Wales.
WHO CAN BENEFIT Charitable organisations.
WHAT IS FUNDED General charitable purposes.
WHAT IS NOT FUNDED Individuals; non-registered charities; salaries of staff members.
TYPE OF GRANT One-off and recurring costs; buildings; core costs; project costs; research; running costs.
RANGE OF GRANTS Up to £100,000 but mostly under £30,000.
SAMPLE GRANTS ABF The Soldiers' Charity (£80,000); Helen and Douglas House (£75,000); Game and Wildlife Conservation Trust (£70,000); Foundation Scotland (£56,000); Institute of Cancer Research (£50,000); Scar Free Foundation (£40,000); British Heart Foundation (£35,000).
FINANCES *Financial year end* 31/03/2022
Income £2,610,000
Grants to organisations £2,030,000
Assets £144,140,000
TRUSTEES Philip Fleming; Rory Fleming; Matthew Fleming.
OTHER INFORMATION During 2021/22, grants were made to 368 organisations. Grants of between £20,000 and £30,000 totalled £150,000, grants of between £5,000 and £20,000 totalled £503,000 and grants of under £5,000 totalled £972,300. Only organisations that received grants of over £35,000 were listed as beneficiaries in the trust's accounts.
HOW TO APPLY Apply in writing to the correspondent. Applications should be sent to the Secretary at the principal office. The trustees usually meet monthly to consider applications and approve grants.
CONTACT DETAILS The Secretary, RFT Management Services Ltd, 14 Buckingham Street, London WC2N 6DF *Tel.* 020 3696 6721
Email charities@rftrustee.com

■ The P27 Trust

CC NO 1182660
WHERE FUNDING CAN BE GIVEN UK and overseas.
WHO CAN BENEFIT Christian charities.
WHAT IS FUNDED The advancement of the Christian faith.
RANGE OF GRANTS Up to £650,000.
SAMPLE GRANTS Stewardship (£650,000); Equipping Nurturing Young People (ENYP) (£12,500); Open Doors and The Archbishop of York Youth Trust (£10,000 each); Homes of Promise (£5,000).
FINANCES *Financial year end* 31/03/2022
Income £410,000
Grants to organisations £687,500
Assets £230,400
TRUSTEES Angus Wielkopolski; Kathleen Wielkopolska; Suzanne Patrick; Timothy Nelson.
OTHER INFORMATION Grants were awarded to five organisations during the year.
HOW TO APPLY Apply in writing to the correspondent.
CONTACT DETAILS The Trustees, The Farm Offices, St Helens Farm, Seaton Ross, York YO42 4NP
Email admin@thep27trust.org.uk

■ The Doris Pacey Charitable Foundation

CC NO 1101724   **ESTABLISHED** 2003
WHERE FUNDING CAN BE GIVEN UK.
WHO CAN BENEFIT Charitable organisations.
WHAT IS FUNDED The Jewish faith and community.
SAMPLE GRANTS World Jewish Relief (£605,000); Jewish Women's Aid (£80,000); Shobana Jeyasingh Dance Company (£50,000).
FINANCES *Financial year end* 05/04/2022
Income £61,900
Grants to organisations £735,000
Assets £2,510,000
TRUSTEES Ray Locke; Leslie Powell; Linda Courtney.
OTHER INFORMATION Grants were made to three organisations during the year.
HOW TO APPLY Contact the correspondent for further information.
CONTACT DETAILS The Trustees, West Wake Price LLP, The Mezzanine Floor, 68 Cornhill, London EC3V 3QX *Tel.* 020 7588 3541
Email paceyandbrynberg@westwakeprice.co.uk

■ The Paget Charitable Trust

CC NO 327402   **ESTABLISHED** 1986
WHERE FUNDING CAN BE GIVEN UK and overseas.
WHO CAN BENEFIT Registered charities; hospices.
WHAT IS FUNDED General charitable purposes. Previously, support has been given towards international aid and development, disadvantaged children, education, older people, animal welfare and environmental projects.
WHAT IS NOT FUNDED Our previous research indicates that support is not given to individuals, people with mental disabilities, medical research or HIV projects.
TYPE OF GRANT Capital costs; core/revenue costs; unrestricted funding.
SAMPLE GRANTS A list of beneficiaries was not included in the annual report and accounts. Previous beneficiaries have included: Second Chance (£15,000); Tibet Relief Fund (£7,300); Animals Asia Foundation and Farming Community Network (£5,000 each); Childhood First and Freedom from Torture (£4,000 each); Butterfly Hospice, Oxfam, Quaker Social Action and Southwark Community Education Council (£2,000 each); Contact the Elderly and Students' Education Trust (£1,000 each); Headway – Leicestershire and Rutland, Hospices of Hope Romania and St Andrew's Evangelical Mission (£500 each).
FINANCES *Financial year end* 05/04/2022
Income £192,300
Grants to organisations £144,500
Assets £12,530,000
TRUSTEES Joanna Herbert-Stepney; Vivienne Matravers; Laura Woodhead.
OTHER INFORMATION The trust is also known as The Joanna Herbert-Stepney Charitable Settlement. During 2021/22, grants were made to 130 organisations. Grants to organisations totalled £231,000, of which £144,500 was awarded in the UK.
HOW TO APPLY Apply in writing to the correspondent.
CONTACT DETAILS The Trustees, The Old Village Stores, Dippenhall Street, Crondall, Farnham, Surrey GU10 5NZ *Tel.* 01252 850253

■ The Gerald Palmer Eling Trust Company

CC NO 1100869   **ESTABLISHED** 2003
WHERE FUNDING CAN BE GIVEN West Berkshire and neighbouring counties.
WHO CAN BENEFIT Registered charities.
WHAT IS FUNDED Christian religion, particularly the Greek and Russian Orthodox Churches; community and education facilities; social welfare.
TYPE OF GRANT Project costs.
RANGE OF GRANTS Up to £30,000.
SAMPLE GRANTS Brendoncare (£30,000); Recovery In Mind (£15,000); The Royal Marsden Cancer Charity (£10,000); Autism Berkshire (£7,000); Newlife, Sue Ryder and Support Through Court (£5,000 each).
FINANCES *Financial year end 31/03/2022*
Income £1,790,000
Grants to organisations £285,100
Assets £89,700,000
TRUSTEES Desmond Harrison; Robin Broadhurst; James Gardiner; Kenneth McDiarmid; Angela Cropley.
OTHER INFORMATION The list of beneficiaries only includes grants of over £5,000. These grants made up 57% of the total amount awarded by the charity during the year.
HOW TO APPLY Apply in writing to the correspondent including a copy of your charity's latest accounts.
CONTACT DETAILS The Trustees, Eling Estate Office, Wellhouse, Hermitage, Thatcham, Berkshire RG18 9UF *Email* charities@elingestate.co.uk *Website* www.elingestate.co.uk/charitable-works

■ The Panacea Charitable Trust

CC NO 227530   **ESTABLISHED** 1926
WHERE FUNDING CAN BE GIVEN Bedford.
WHO CAN BENEFIT Registered charities; social enterprises; not-for-profit companies limited by guarantee; unincorporated clubs and associations; CICs.
WHAT IS FUNDED Social welfare; health; education; mental health.
WHAT IS NOT FUNDED Political parties or political lobbying; pressure groups; commercial ventures; non-charitable activities; the replacement of statutory funding.
TYPE OF GRANT Capital and revenue costs.
RANGE OF GRANTS £5,000 to £100,000.
SAMPLE GRANTS A list of beneficiaries was not included in the annual report and accounts.
FINANCES *Financial year end 31/12/2021*
Income £683,600
Grants to organisations £130,500
Assets £41,020,000
TRUSTEES Dr Justin Meggitt; Charles Monsell; Evan Jones; Sarah Cowls; Dr Philip Lockley; Dr Naomi Hilton; Dr Ian Beavis.
HOW TO APPLY Application forms can be downloaded from the trust's website.
CONTACT DETAILS David McLynn, Executive Officer, 14 Albany Road, Bedford, Bedfordshire MK40 3PH *Tel.* 01234 359737 *Email* admin@panaceatrust.org *Website* http://panaceatrust.org

■ The Pantheon Charitable Trust

CC NO 1174839   **ESTABLISHED** 2017
WHERE FUNDING CAN BE GIVEN England and Wales.
WHO CAN BENEFIT Charitable organisations.
WHAT IS FUNDED General charitable purposes.

RANGE OF GRANTS Up to £25,000.
SAMPLE GRANTS Blue Ventures Conservation (£25,000); World Land Trust (£20,000); British Red Cross, Cirencester Housing for Young People, Microloan Foundation, Teenage Cancer Trust and UNICEF (£5,000 each); Brent Adolescent Centre (£3,000).
FINANCES *Financial year end 05/04/2022*
Income £324,800
Grants to organisations £164,000
Assets £238,900
TRUSTEES Paul Thomas; Jocelyn Thomas; Jemma Potter; Alexander Thomas; Ludlow Trust Company Ltd.
OTHER INFORMATION Grants were awarded to 17 organisations in 2021/22.
HOW TO APPLY Apply in writing to the correspondent.
CONTACT DETAILS The Trustees, Ludlow Trust Co. Ltd, 1st Floor, Tower Wharf, Cheese Lane, Bristol BS2 0JJ *Tel.* 0117 313 8200 *Email* charitabletrusts@ludlowtrust.com

■ The James Pantyfedwen Foundation (Ymddiriedolaeth James Pantyfedwen)

CC NO 1069598   **ESTABLISHED** 1998
WHERE FUNDING CAN BE GIVEN Wales.
WHO CAN BENEFIT Registered charities; unregistered charities; religious bodies/institutions; individuals.
WHAT IS FUNDED Support is given in three main areas: to individual churches for the improvement and repair of fabric, to local and national eisteddfodau and to postgraduate students.
WHAT IS NOT FUNDED Exclusions vary according to the type of grant being applied for. See the appropriate guidance document on the website for details.
TYPE OF GRANT Unrestricted funding.
RANGE OF GRANTS Up to £18,000.
SAMPLE GRANTS National Eisteddfod of Wales (£13,000); Ainon Baptist Church (£10,000); Hope Church (£8,000); Capel Bro Tegla (£4,000); St Dunwyd Church (£3,000); Trinity Church (£1,500); St Marc's Church (£500); St David's Church (£300).
FINANCES *Financial year end 31/03/2022*
Income £514,000
Grants to organisations £167,600
Grants to individuals £365,600
Assets £17,370,000
TRUSTEES Gwerfyl Jones; William Jones; Amanda Roberts; Kevin Holland; Dr Eurfyl Gwilym; Sian Jones; Alun Charles; Arall Aaron; Wyn Jones; David Lewis; The Revd Alun Evans; Dr William Griffiths; Dr Eryn White.
HOW TO APPLY Guidelines and application forms for students, local eisteddfodau and churches can be found on the website. The trustees meet three times a year to consider applications.
CONTACT DETAILS Gwenan Creunant, Executive Secretary, Pantyfedwen, 9 Market Street, Aberystwyth, Ceredigion SY23 1DL *Tel.* 01970 612806 *Email* post@jamespantyfedwen.cymru *Website* www.jamespantyfedwenfoundation.org.uk

■ The Paphitis Charitable Trust

CC NO 1112721   **ESTABLISHED** 2005
WHERE FUNDING CAN BE GIVEN UK, occasionally overseas.
WHO CAN BENEFIT Registered charities.

WHAT IS FUNDED Children and young people.

RANGE OF GRANTS Typically less than £1,000.

SAMPLE GRANTS A list of beneficiaries was not included in the annual report and accounts.

FINANCES *Financial year end 30/06/2022*
Income £138,000
Grants to organisations £82,800
Assets £209,600

TRUSTEES Ian Childs; Malcolm Cooke; Kypros Kyprianou; Ann Mantz; Richard Towner.

OTHER INFORMATION The trust was established by entrepreneur and Dragon's Den panellist Theo Paphitis. It is funded by Theo's TV appearances, speeches and book sales.

HOW TO APPLY Apply in writing to the correspondent.

CONTACT DETAILS The Trustees, 1 St Georges Road, London SW19 4DR *Email* charitabletrust@tprg.com *Website* www.theopaphitis.com/charity-patronages

■ Parabola Foundation

CC NO 1156008   **ESTABLISHED** 2013

WHERE FUNDING CAN BE GIVEN England and Africa.

WHO CAN BENEFIT Registered charities; universities.

WHAT IS FUNDED General charitable purposes; poverty relief; the arts, culture and music.

TYPE OF GRANT One-off and recurrent project costs.

SAMPLE GRANTS Kings Place Music Foundation (£475,000); Ruwenzori (£36,000); Poverty Relief Foundation (£24,000).

FINANCES *Financial year end 31/03/2022*
Income £500,000
Grants to organisations £612,400
Assets (£979,900)

TRUSTEES Deborah Jude; Anne Millican; Peter Millican.

OTHER INFORMATION Grants awarded in support of creative arts totalled £582,800 and other grants totalled £29,600.

HOW TO APPLY Apply in writing to the correspondent.

CONTACT DETAILS The Trustees, Broadgate Tower, 20 Primrose Street, London EC2A 2EW *Tel.* 0191 500 8571

■ The Paragon Trust

CC NO 278348   **ESTABLISHED** 1979

WHERE FUNDING CAN BE GIVEN UK and overseas.

WHO CAN BENEFIT Registered charities; individuals; hospices; hospitals; places of worship.

WHAT IS FUNDED General charitable purposes.

RANGE OF GRANTS £500 to £5,000.

SAMPLE GRANTS Carers Trust (£3,000); British Heart Foundation and Emmaus (£2,000 each); Changing Faces (£1,500); Arthur Rank Hospice Charity, Good Neighbour Project and YoungMinds (£1,000 each); Terence Higgins Trust (£500).

FINANCES *Financial year end 22/08/2022*
Income £86,500
Grants to organisations £97,000
Assets £1,920,000

TRUSTEES Dr Fiona Cornish; Philip Cunningham; Patricia Russell; Lucy Whistler; Kathleen Larter.

HOW TO APPLY The trust does not accept or acknowledge unsolicited applications.

CONTACT DETAILS The Trustees, c/o Thomson Snell and Passmore LLP, Heathervale House, 2–4 Vale Avenue, Tunbridge Wells, Kent TN1 1DJ *Tel.* 01892 510000

■ The Pargiter Trust

CC NO 1157779   **ESTABLISHED** 2005

WHERE FUNDING CAN BE GIVEN England and Guernsey.

WHO CAN BENEFIT Registered charities.

WHAT IS FUNDED Social welfare and social inclusion projects for older people.

SAMPLE GRANTS Community Foundation Tyne and Wear, Kent Community Foundation and Suffolk Community Foundation (£80,000 each); Quartet Community Foundation (£50,000); Kissing It Better (£19,800 in two grants); Guernsey Voluntary Service (£10,500); In Deep Community Task Force (£5,800).

FINANCES *Financial year end 31/12/2021*
Income £748,200
Grants to organisations £486,200
Assets £14,200,000

TRUSTEES Suzanne Gardiner; Victoria Westhorp; Martyn Mogford; Mike Starkey; Paul Metcalfe; Ella Gardiner.

OTHER INFORMATION The trust tends to make grants through the following eight community foundations: Community Foundation for Surrey, Suffolk Community Foundation, Guernsey Community Foundation, Kent Community Foundation, Berkshire Community Foundation, Wiltshire Community Foundation, Tyne and Wear and Northumberland and Quartet Community Foundation.

HOW TO APPLY Apply in writing to the correspondent. Most applications are received through one of the community foundations with which the trust has a partnership with.

CONTACT DETAILS David McManus, Secretary, c/o AC Mole and Sons, Stafford House, Blackbrook Park Avenue, Taunton, Somerset TA1 2PX *Tel.* 07980 932716 *Email* admin@pargitertrust.org.uk *Website* https://pargitertrust.org.uk

■ The Parivar Trust

CC NO 1032529   **ESTABLISHED** 1993

WHERE FUNDING CAN BE GIVEN India; UK, with a preference for Bristol, Gloucestershire and Herefordshire.

WHO CAN BENEFIT Charitable organisations.

WHAT IS FUNDED Social welfare; health; provision of education, preservation and protection of good health among children, young people and women.

SAMPLE GRANTS Sarada Mission – India (£230,900); Ramakrishna Mission – India (£80,500); Eastside Community Trust and One25 (£2,000 each); Changing Tunes and Triple 'H' Trust (£1,000 each); Life Cycle UK (£500).

FINANCES *Financial year end 30/11/2022*
Income £317,400
Grants to organisations £321,900
Assets £520,900

TRUSTEES Dr Pramila Ramani; Nigel Rogers; Andrew Jennings.

OTHER INFORMATION A large proportion of the trust's grants were awarded to organisations in India.

HOW TO APPLY Apply in writing to the correspondent.

CONTACT DETAILS The Trustees, Wye Cottage, Fawley, Hereford, Herefordshire HR1 4SP *Tel.* 07879 856200

■ The Samuel and Freda Parkinson Charitable Trust

CC NO 327749   **ESTABLISHED** 1987

WHERE FUNDING CAN BE GIVEN UK, with a preference for Cumbria and north Lancashire.

WHO CAN BENEFIT Registered charities specified by the founder of the trust.

WHAT IS FUNDED General charitable purposes.

RANGE OF GRANTS £7,500 to £30,000.

SAMPLE GRANTS The Leonard Cheshire Foundation (£45,000); RNLI (£20,000); The Salvation Army (£15,000); Animal Concern Cumbria, Animal Rescue Cumbria, Animal Welfare and RSPCA (£10,000 each).

FINANCES *Financial year end* 02/11/2022
Income £119,000
Grants to organisations £130,000
Assets £3,840,000

TRUSTEES John Crompton; William Waterhouse; Margaret Jobling; Jane Brown.

OTHER INFORMATION Grants were awarded to eight organisations during the year.

HOW TO APPLY The trust's 2021/22 accounts state: 'Each year the Trustees approach potential beneficiaries, especially in the north Lancashire and Cumbria areas, in order to ascertain their current financial position and enquire whether any of them are considering any specific projects. With these facts to hand, distributions are made, bearing in mind the Trust's investment position.'

CONTACT DETAILS The Trustees, Regent House, 25 Crescent Road, Windermere, Cumbria LA23 1BJ *Tel.* 01539 446585 *Email* info@thwlegal.co.uk

■ Parkinson's UK

CC NO 258197   **ESTABLISHED** 1969

WHERE FUNDING CAN BE GIVEN Mainly UK; occasionally, the USA and Canada.

WHO CAN BENEFIT UK universities; NHS trusts; statutory social care organisations or other research institutions.

WHAT IS FUNDED Research into Parkinson's disease.

TYPE OF GRANT Research funding.

SAMPLE GRANTS University of Sheffield (£1.2 million); Oxford Parkinson's Disease Centre (£477,000); North Cumbria Integrated Care NHS Foundation Trust (£382,000); City University London (£200,000); Newcastle University (£64,000); Southport and Ormskirk Hospital NHS Trust (£51,000); Eurofins Integrated Discovery UK Ltd (£40,000); Medgenesis Therapeutix Inc. (£33,000).

FINANCES *Financial year end* 31/12/2021
Income £37,590,000
Grants to organisations £4,450,000
Grants to individuals £100,000
Assets £51,900,000

TRUSTEES Kyle Alexander; Matthew Durdy; Paresh Thakrar; Gary Shaughnessy; Dr Andrew Cavey; Peter Miller; Helen Burston; Elaine Evans; Katrina Green; Ann McCallum; Samantha Aylieff; Sally Bromley; Brian Carson.

OTHER INFORMATION During 2021, research grants totalled £3.98 million. In addition, grants made to organisations for Parkinson's nurses and service improvements totalled £473,000.

HOW TO APPLY Each grants programme has its own specific deadlines and application process. See the charity's website for more information.

CONTACT DETAILS The Trustees, 215 Vauxhall Bridge Road, London SW1V 1EJ *Tel.* 020 7963 3930 *Email* researchapplications@parkinson's.org.uk *Website* www.parkinson's.org.uk

■ Miss M. E. S. Paterson's Charitable Trust

OSCR NO SC004835   **ESTABLISHED** 1989

WHERE FUNDING CAN BE GIVEN Scotland.

WHO CAN BENEFIT Charitable organisations and the Church of Scotland.

WHAT IS FUNDED General charitable purposes; Church of Scotland; children and young people; older people; health and disability; sport; the environment; social welfare.

TYPE OF GRANT Capital costs for churches; project funding for all other organisations.

SAMPLE GRANTS Ayrshire Hospice (£25,000); Nairn Free Church of Scotland (£5,000); Glasgow City Mission (£3,000); Befriend a Child (£2,000); Norton Park SCIO (£600).

FINANCES *Financial year end* 05/04/2022
Income £37,100
Grants to organisations £188,200
Assets £940,600

HOW TO APPLY Unsolicited applications are not accepted.

CONTACT DETAILS The Trustees, c/o Lindsays, Caledonian Exchange, 19A Canning Street, Edinburgh EH3 8HE *Tel.* 0131 656 5670 *Email* mail@swintonpatersontrust.org.uk *Website* www.swintonpatersontrust.org.uk

■ The Patrick Trust

CC NO 213849   **ESTABLISHED** 1962

WHERE FUNDING CAN BE GIVEN West Midlands.

WHO CAN BENEFIT Charitable organisations.

WHAT IS FUNDED Children and young people; older people; cultural and pastoral activities in the West Midlands.

RANGE OF GRANTS Up to £2,500.

SAMPLE GRANTS A list of beneficiaries was not included in the annual report and accounts. Previous beneficiaries have included: Muscular Dystrophy Group of Great Britain and Northern Ireland (£37,500); The Hall for Cornwall Trust (£25,000); Performance Birmingham Ltd (£2,500); Home-Start Walsall (£500).

FINANCES *Financial year end* 05/04/2022
Income £3,010,000
Grants to organisations £123,000
Assets £11,970,000

TRUSTEES William Bond-Williams; Heather Cole; Graham Wem; Laura Pritchard; Amanda Pillinger; Julian Pritchard.

HOW TO APPLY Contact the trust to request a funding request information leaflet, which will contain details of how to progress the application.

CONTACT DETAILS The Trustees, The Lakeside Centre, 180 Lifford Lane, Birmingham, West Midlands B30 3NU *Tel.* 0121 486 3399 *Email* thepatricktrust@aol.com *Website* www.thepatricktrust.org.uk

■ The Jack Patston Charitable Trust

CC NO 701658   **ESTABLISHED** 1989

WHERE FUNDING CAN BE GIVEN Leicestershire and Cambridgeshire.

WHO CAN BENEFIT Registered charities; unregistered charities; hospices; religious bodies/institutions.

WHAT IS FUNDED The preservation of wildlife and the environment; the advancement of religion; the preservation of rural church fabric.

WHAT IS NOT FUNDED Individuals.

TYPE OF GRANT Capital costs (church fabric); general funding.

RANGE OF GRANTS £2,000 to £5,000.

SAMPLE GRANTS Leicestershire Historic Churches Trust (£5,000); National Churches Trust (£3,000); British Trust for Ornithology, Bumblebee Conservation Trust and The Bythams Community Shop (£2,000 each).

FINANCES *Financial year end* 05/04/2022
Income £120,400
Grants to organisations £94,000
Assets £5,590,000

TRUSTEES Charles Applegate; Stephen Knipe; Duncan Jackson.

OTHER INFORMATION Grants were made to 34 organisations during the year.

HOW TO APPLY Apply in writing to the correspondent.

CONTACT DETAILS The Trustees, Buckles Solicitors LLP, Grant House, 101 Bourges Boulevard, Peterborough, Cambridgeshire PE1 1NG *Tel.* 01733 888888 *Email* deborah.lewsley@buckles-law.co.uk

■ The J. G. W. Patterson Foundation

CC NO 1094086   **ESTABLISHED** 2002

WHERE FUNDING CAN BE GIVEN Tyne and Wear, Northumberland, Durham and Cumbria.

WHO CAN BENEFIT Universities; medical research institutions; hospices.

WHAT IS FUNDED Education and research.

TYPE OF GRANT Project funding; research.

RANGE OF GRANTS Mostly from £1,000 to £25,000.

SAMPLE GRANTS Newcastle University (£526,000); Marie Curie Hospice (£25,000); St Cuthbert's Hospice Durham (£20,100); St Oswald's Hospice and Tynesdale Hospice at Home (£15,000 each); Hospice Care North Northumberland (£12,000); Eden Valley Hospice (£6,500); Willow Foundation (£3,000).

FINANCES *Financial year end* 31/03/2022
Income £954,000
Grants to organisations £646,100
Assets £18,990,000

TRUSTEES Prof. Timothy Cawston; Prof. Sir Alan Craft; Stephen Gilroy; Mr D. R. Gold; James Dias; Prof. David Young; Prof. Steven Clifford.

OTHER INFORMATION A total of 24 grants were awarded in 2021/22. Of those grants, 12 were awarded to Newcastle University and the rest divided between 10 other organisations.

HOW TO APPLY Applications can be made through the foundation's website. The trustees meet quarterly, in February, May, September and November. Completed applications for funding must be received at least one month prior to a quarterly meeting. Applications are usually then sent out for peer review and discussed again at the subsequent quarterly meeting of the trustees.

CONTACT DETAILS Pippa Aitken, Secretary, c/o Sintons LLP, The Cube, Arngrove Court, Barrack Road, Newcastle upon Tyne, Tyne and Wear NE4 6DB *Tel.* 0191 226 7878 *Email* info@jgwpattersonfoundation.co.uk *Website* http://jgwpattersonfoundation.co.uk

■ Payne-Gallwey 1989 Charitable Trust

CC NO 1016286   **ESTABLISHED** 1987

WHERE FUNDING CAN BE GIVEN Berkshire with a preference for Newbury.

WHO CAN BENEFIT Registered charities. There is a preference for smaller charities.

WHAT IS FUNDED Horse racing; the Services; rural life and field sports; disadvantaged children and young people; medical research; Church of England; hospices; people who are deaf; people who are blind.

WHAT IS NOT FUNDED Any appeal with a target of over £10 million; capital projects, schools, hospitals, community centres or church restorations outside Berkshire; any charity primarily administered or funded by the government, a local authority or a quango; charities whose policies conflict with the interests of The National Farmers Union or The Country Land Business Group; any charity that campaigns against field sports.

RANGE OF GRANTS £100 to £15,000.

SAMPLE GRANTS Sight Research UK (£10,000); Game and Wildlife Trust (£7,500); Footsteps Foundation (£5,000); The Greatwood Charity (£4,000); 4 Cancer Group (£3,000).

FINANCES *Financial year end* 05/04/2022
Income £174,000
Grants to organisations £251,100
Assets £9,020,000

TRUSTEES Edward Leigh-Pemberton; Miss E. L. Nutt; Caroline Todhunter; Charles Leigh-Pemberton.

OTHER INFORMATION Only organisations that received grants of over £3,000 are listed as beneficiaries in the charity's accounts. Grants of under £3,000 totalled £59,100.

HOW TO APPLY Applicants should complete an application form, which can be found on the trust's website. The trust does not have an email address and does not deal with telephone requests.

CONTACT DETAILS The Trustees, c/o The Estate Office, Manor Farm, Little Coxwell, Faringdon, Oxfordshire SN7 7LW *Website* www.pgct.co.uk

■ Peacock Charitable Trust

CC NO 257655   **ESTABLISHED** 1968

WHERE FUNDING CAN BE GIVEN UK.

WHO CAN BENEFIT Registered charities; hospices.

WHAT IS FUNDED General charitable purposes, with a preference for: the education of young people; poverty relief and social welfare; medical and health; the environment; augmenting the income of other charities.

WHAT IS NOT FUNDED Individuals.

TYPE OF GRANT Mostly recurring.

RANGE OF GRANTS Mostly between £5,000 and around £25,000 with the occasional smaller or larger grant.

SAMPLE GRANTS The Prince's Trust (£103,000); the Jubilee Sailing Trust (£50,000); Alzheimer's Research Trust, HelpForce and MS Society (£20,000 each); Barnardo's and We Are With You (£15,000 each); ABF The Soldiers' Charity, Centrepoint and Royal Trinity Hospice (£10,000 each); Blood Cancer UK, Fields in Trust and Woodland Trust (£5,000 each); Endeavour Club (£4,000).

FINANCES *Financial year end* 05/04/2022
Income £490,100
Grants to organisations £1,390,000
Assets £50,380,000

TRUSTEES Bettine Bond; Charles Peacock; Dr Clare Sellors.

HOW TO APPLY Unsolicited applications are not accepted.

CONTACT DETAILS The Trustees, c/o Charities Aid Foundation, 25 Kings Hill Avenue, Kingshill, West Malling, Kent ME19 4TA *Tel.* 0300 012 3334 *Email* info@peacockct.org

■ Susanna Peake Charitable Trust

CC NO 283462   **ESTABLISHED** 1981

WHERE FUNDING CAN BE GIVEN Worldwide, with a preference for the South West, particularly Gloucestershire.

WHO CAN BENEFIT Registered charities.

WHAT IS FUNDED General charitable purposes.

WHAT IS NOT FUNDED Individuals.

RANGE OF GRANTS Up to £50,000. Typically between £1,000 and £5,000.

SAMPLE GRANTS Auditory Verbal UK (£50,000); The Retreat (£15,000); Disasters Emergency Committee (£10,000); Carers Centre and Cotswold Friends (£5,000 each); Listening Books (£4,000); London Reading Centre (£3,000); Keep Britain Tidy (£1,000).

FINANCES *Financial year end* 05/04/2022
Income £179,800
Grants to organisations £228,000
Assets £9,850,000

TRUSTEES Susanna Peake; Katharine Loyd.

OTHER INFORMATION In 2021/22 grants were broken down as follows: general charities (£18,500); medical causes and hospices (£87,500); older people and people with disabilities (£25,500); education and children (£32,500); international (£25,500); local charitable organisations (£33,500); animals and the environment (£1,000).

HOW TO APPLY Apply in writing to the correspondent. The trustees meet on a frequent, ad hoc basis to consider applications.

CONTACT DETAILS The Trustees, Rathbone Trust Company Ltd, 8 Finsbury Circus, London EC2M 7AZ *Tel.* 020 7399 0820 *Email* linda.cousins@rathbones.com

■ John Pearce Foundation

CC NO 1181348

WHERE FUNDING CAN BE GIVEN UK and Hong Kong.

WHO CAN BENEFIT Registered charities; hospices; charitable organisations.

WHAT IS FUNDED Current and former participants (equine and human) in horseracing and thoroughbred breeding who are in need, palliative care services.

TYPE OF GRANT Project funding; research funding; capital costs; one-off and multi-year.

RANGE OF GRANTS Up to £1 million.

SAMPLE GRANTS Priscilla Bacon Norfolk Hospice Care Ltd (£1 million); Racing Welfare (£131,400); Marie Curie (£39,000); Greatwood Charity Ltd (£10,900).

FINANCES *Financial year end* 31/12/2021
Income £2,500,000
Grants to organisations £1,480,000
Assets £2,490,000

TRUSTEES Michael Winarick; Nicolas Bentley; Rupert Bentley.

HOW TO APPLY Apply via the foundation's website.

CONTACT DETAILS The Trustees, c/o Bentley Reid and Co. UK Ltd, 29 Queen Anne's Gate, London SW1H 9BU *Email* JPFoundation@johnpearce.org *Website* www.johnpearce.org

■ David Pearlman Charitable Foundation

CC NO 287009   **ESTABLISHED** 1983

WHERE FUNDING CAN BE GIVEN UK.

WHO CAN BENEFIT Charitable organisations; Jewish organisations; places of worship; educational institutions; museums.

WHAT IS FUNDED Judaism; social welfare, particularly relief of poverty; education; medicine and health; community and citizenship development; arts, culture and heritage; science; general charitable purposes.

RANGE OF GRANTS Mostly up to £20,000 with the occasional larger grant.

SAMPLE GRANTS St Paul's Cathedral Foundation (£50,000); Cure Parkinson's Trust (£30,000); Aiming High – London, The Duke of Edinburgh's Award and Keren Hatzolas Doros Alei Siach (£20,000 each); Care All Ltd, Museum of London and Support The Charity Worker (£10,000 each).

FINANCES *Financial year end* 30/09/2021
Income £346,200
Grants to organisations £286,200
Assets £6,540,000

TRUSTEES Michael Goldberger; Stuart Appleman; David Pearlman; Jonathan Hager; H. Pearlman.

OTHER INFORMATION The 2020/21 accounts were the latest available at the time of writing (May 2023). Only organisations that received grants of over £5,000 were listed as beneficiaries in the accounts. Grants of under £5,000 totalled £42,700.

HOW TO APPLY Apply in writing to the correspondent.

CONTACT DETAILS Michael Goldberger, Secretary, New Burlington House, 1075 Finchley Road, London NW11 0PU *Tel.* 020 8731 0777

■ The Pears Family Charitable Foundation

CC NO 1009195   **ESTABLISHED** 1991

WHERE FUNDING CAN BE GIVEN UK and overseas.

WHO CAN BENEFIT Charitable organisations; educational organisations; youth organisations.

WHAT IS FUNDED The Jewish faith and community; holocaust education; young people; education and training; international development; youth social action; special educational needs and disability; palliative care; research; community health services.

TYPE OF GRANT Capital costs; core funding; unrestricted.

RANGE OF GRANTS Mostly from £50,000 to £1 million, with some larger grants.

SAMPLE GRANTS University College London (£1.15 million); Place2Be (£300,000); Young Citizens (£160,000); Carers UK and YoungMinds (£100,000 each).

FINANCES *Financial year end* 31/03/2022
Income £19,700,000
Grants to organisations £19,020,000
Assets £28,610,000

TRUSTEES David Pears; Sir Trevor Pears; Mark Pears.

HOW TO APPLY Unsolicited applications are not accepted.

CONTACT DETAILS The Trustees, Haskell House, 152 West End Lane, London NW6 1SD *Tel.* 020 7433 3333 *Email* contact@pearsfoundation.org.uk *Website* www.pearsfoundation.org.uk

■ The Pebbles Trust

CC NO 1129132   **ESTABLISHED** 2009
WHERE FUNDING CAN BE GIVEN Brighton and Hove.
WHO CAN BENEFIT UK-registered charities; CICs; individuals.
WHAT IS FUNDED Community projects; social welfare; support for young people with talent in sport, music, performing arts and academia.
TYPE OF GRANT Project funding; capital costs; bursaries; recurrent and one-off.
RANGE OF GRANTS Mostly up to £5,000.
SAMPLE GRANTS Brighton Dome and Brighton Fringe (£375,000); Sussex Wildlife Trust (£250,000); Little Green Pig (£5,000); Kennedy Street CIO (£2,000); Martlets Hospice (£1,400).
FINANCES *Financial year end 31/03/2022*
Income £1,110,000
Grants to organisations £894,800
Grants to individuals £25,500
Assets £117,900
TRUSTEES James Arnell; Louise Arnell; Louise Stoten.
OTHER INFORMATION Grants were awarded to 20 organisations during the year.
HOW TO APPLY Applications can be made via the trust's website. There are three application deadlines each year - in February, June and October.
CONTACT DETAILS The Trustees, c/o New Quadrant Partners Ltd, 4th Floor, 5 Chancery Lane, London WC2A 1LG *Tel.* 020 7430 7159 *Email* use the contact form on the website *Website* www.pebbletrust.org

■ The Dowager Countess Eleanor Peel Trust

CC NO 214684   **ESTABLISHED** 1951
WHERE FUNDING CAN BE GIVEN UK (medical grants); Cheshire, Cumbria, Greater Manchester, Lancashire and Merseyside (general grants).
WHO CAN BENEFIT Small and medium-sized UK-registered charities; universities.
WHAT IS FUNDED Medical research; older people; social welfare.
WHAT IS NOT FUNDED Charities primarily devoted to children; charities under the control of central or local government.
TYPE OF GRANT Capital costs and project funding (general grants); pilot studies and equipment (medical research); fellowships.
RANGE OF GRANTS £5,000 to £10,000.
SAMPLE GRANTS Blackpool Carers Centre Ltd (£10,000); Cumbria Drug and Alcohol Advisory Service (£7,500); Emerge 3Rs and Launchpad (£5,000 each); Adullam Programme (£2,500).
FINANCES *Financial year end 31/03/2022*
Income £751,300
Grants to organisations £580,900
Assets £21,270,000
TRUSTEES Prof. Margaret Pearson; Prof. Richard Ramsden; Michael Parkinson; Prof. Colin Sibley; David Parkinson.
OTHER INFORMATION Grants were broken down as follows: medical causes (£381,000); people in need (£199,900).
HOW TO APPLY Apply via the trust's website.
CONTACT DETAILS The Secretary, Hill Dickinson LLP, 50 Fountain Street, Manchester M2 2AS *Tel.* 0161 838 4977 *Email* secretary@peeltrust. com *Website* www.peeltrust.com

■ The Pell Charitable Trust

CC NO 1135398   **ESTABLISHED** 2010
WHERE FUNDING CAN BE GIVEN UK, with a preference for southern England.
WHO CAN BENEFIT Charitable organisations.
WHAT IS FUNDED The performing arts, particularly music.
RANGE OF GRANTS £500 to £21,000.
SAMPLE GRANTS Royal Opera House Covent Garden Foundation (£21,200); University of Southampton (£11,000); Garsington Opera Ltd (£9,800); Buckinghamshire Music Trust (£5,000); Barnardo's, Benslow Music Trust and British Heart Foundation (£1,000 each).
FINANCES *Financial year end 31/01/2022*
Income £10,500
Grants to organisations £160,000
TRUSTEES Marian Pell; Gordon Pell; Oliver Pell; Victoria Lundgren; Messrs Hoare Trustees.
OTHER INFORMATION Full accounts were not available to view on the Charity Commission's website due to the trust's low income. We have therefore estimated the grant total based on the trust's total expenditure.
HOW TO APPLY Apply in writing to the correspondent.
CONTACT DETAILS Messrs Hoare Trustees, C. Hoare and Co., 37 Fleet Street, London EC4P 4DQ *Tel.* 020 7353 4522

■ The Penchant Foundation

CC NO 1188402
WHERE FUNDING CAN BE GIVEN UK, with a possible preference for the East of England.
WHO CAN BENEFIT Registered charities.
WHAT IS FUNDED General charitable purposes; social welfare and community development; medical.
RANGE OF GRANTS Mostly £1,000 to £5,000.
SAMPLE GRANTS Birdlife International (£20,000); Arthur Rank Hospice Charity (£10,000); Open Trust (£5,000); Resurgo Trust (£1,000).
FINANCES *Financial year end 30/06/2022*
Income £37,000
Grants to organisations £242,400
Assets £4,900,000
TRUSTEES Sir Charles Chadwyck-Healey; Lady Angela Chadwyck-Healey; Catherine Davies; Edward Chadwyck-Healey; Faith Miller.
OTHER INFORMATION Grants were broken down as follows: social and community (£81,500); biodiversity and conservation (£70,000); education (£32,000); overseas relief (£27,800); arts and culture (£6,000).
HOW TO APPLY Apply in writing to the correspondent.
CONTACT DETAILS The Trustees, 5 Madingley Road, Cambridge CB3 0EE *Tel.* 01223 316766 *Email* ch@dwyck.com

■ The Pennycress Trust

CC NO 261536   **ESTABLISHED** 1970
WHERE FUNDING CAN BE GIVEN UK, with a preference for Cheshire and Norfolk.
WHO CAN BENEFIT Smaller charities.
WHAT IS FUNDED General charitable purposes.
WHAT IS NOT FUNDED Individuals.
RANGE OF GRANTS Typically £100 to £500.
SAMPLE GRANTS A list of beneficiaries was not included in the annual report and accounts.
FINANCES *Financial year end 05/04/2022*
Income £72,100
Grants to organisations £71,000
Assets £2,570,000

TRUSTEES Charles Cholmondeley; Rose Cholmondeley; Lady Margot Huston; Priscilla Dicketts.

OTHER INFORMATION Grants were made to 148 organisations in 2021/22.

HOW TO APPLY Apply in writing to the correspondent.

CONTACT DETAILS The Trustees, 46 Warwick Road, Bishop's Stortford, Hertfordshire CM23 5NW *Tel.* 07941 069823 *Email* nwestcott@ westcottwills.co.uk

■ People's Health Trust

CC NO 1125537   **ESTABLISHED** 2008

WHERE FUNDING CAN BE GIVEN England, Scotland and Wales.

WHO CAN BENEFIT Registered charities; CICs; community groups; constituted groups or voluntary organisations with a social/charitable purpose.

WHAT IS FUNDED Health and well-being; communities; social welfare; tackling inequality.

WHAT IS NOT FUNDED See the grant-maker's website for full eligibility criteria.

TYPE OF GRANT Capital costs; project funding; strategic funding.

RANGE OF GRANTS £5,000 to £40,000.

SAMPLE GRANTS Community Action Suffolk (£55,000); Community Renewal Trust (£44,500); Shoots of Hope (£35,100); Made by Morals (£33,100); Scotswood Natural Community Garden (£25,800); Open Minds Active (£23,600).

FINANCES *Financial year end* 30/09/2021
Income £5,750,000
Grants to organisations £3,330,000
Assets £10,200,000

TRUSTEES Barbara Simmonds; Paul Ballantyne; Prof. Elizabeth Dowler; Duncan Stephenson; Jacqueline Lodge; Thomas McIlravey; Leandra Box; Shavanah Taj; Jennifer Edwards; Joe Leigh.

OTHER INFORMATION The 2020/21 accounts were the latest available at the time of writing (May 2023).

HOW TO APPLY Applications can be submitted online. The trust funds organisations nationwide, in areas in which the Health Lottery operates. Check the website to see if a grant scheme is open in your area. Schemes open and close throughout the year.

CONTACT DETAILS The Trustees, 2 Bath Place, Rivington Street, London EC2A 3DR *Tel.* 020 4548 0939 *Email* enquiries@ peopleshealthtrust.org.uk *Website* www. peopleshealthtrust.org.uk

■ People's Postcode Trust

OSCR NO SC040387   **ESTABLISHED** 2009

WHERE FUNDING CAN BE GIVEN Scotland.

WHO CAN BENEFIT Registered charities; CICs; social enterprises.

WHAT IS FUNDED Mental health and well-being; enabling participation in physical activity; the arts; social welfare; marginalised groups; inequality; biodiversity and climate change; improving green spaces and increasing access to the outdoors.

WHAT IS NOT FUNDED A comprehensive list of exclusions can be found in the trust's funding guide on its website.

TYPE OF GRANT Project funding.

RANGE OF GRANTS Mostly £2,500 to £25,000.

SAMPLE GRANTS The Alma Project (£25,000); Scottish Detainee Visitors (£15,000); Grangemouth Old Peoples Welfare (£9,000);

Interest Link Borders (£6,000); Social Good Connect (£2,500).

FINANCES *Financial year end* 31/12/2021
Income £8,010,000
Grants to organisations £2,510,000
Assets £324,900

TRUSTEES Rob Flett; David Sharrod; Gareth Hill.

HOW TO APPLY Funding rounds open each month and close when either the maximum number applications have been submitted or by the dates found on the trust's website. An online application form becomes available on the trust's website when funding rounds open. Full details, including guidance notes and deadlines, are available from the trust's website.

CONTACT DETAILS The Trustees, 28 Charlotte Square, Edinburgh EH2 4ET *Tel.* 0131 322 9377 *Email* info@postcodetrust.org.uk *Website* www.postcodetrust.org.uk

■ Dina Perelman Trust Ltd

CC NO 274165

WHERE FUNDING CAN BE GIVEN UK and overseas.

WHO CAN BENEFIT Orthodox Jewish institutions.

WHAT IS FUNDED The Jewish faith and community; Jewish education and places of worship for the Jewish community.

RANGE OF GRANTS Generally around £10,000 to £50,000 with some larger grants.

SAMPLE GRANTS The Friends of Alexander Institutions Trust (£497,700); British Friends of Mishan L'choleh (£50,000); Ahavat Yisroel UK (£40,000); Chevras Mo'oz Ladol (£18,100); One Heart – Lev Echod (£13,500); Amud Hatzdokoh Trust (£12,800); Friends of Beis Chinuch Lebonos Trust (£11,000); Friends of Beis Soroh Schneirer (£10,000).

FINANCES *Financial year end* 31/03/2022
Income £1,100,000
Grants to organisations £824,000
Assets £9,610,000

TRUSTEES Asher Perelman; Jonah Perelman; Sara Perelman.

OTHER INFORMATION Grants were broken down into the following categories: advancement of education (£606,800); prevention or relief of poverty (£94,800); advancement of health and saving lives (£85,400); grants to other grant-making charities (£16,900); advancement of religion (£10,900); advancement of community development (£9,200).

HOW TO APPLY Apply in writing to correspondent.

CONTACT DETAILS The Trustees, 39 Overlea Road, London E5 9BG *Tel.* 020 8809 2345

■ The Performing Right Society Foundation

CC NO 1080837   **ESTABLISHED** 2000

WHERE FUNDING CAN BE GIVEN UK.

WHO CAN BENEFIT Organisations, with a preference for not-for-profit organisations (the foundation's definition of an 'organisation' also includes projects led by promoters, talent development organisations, festivals, venues, curators and large performance groups); individuals.

WHAT IS FUNDED The creation and performance of outstanding new music in any genre and the development of artists and audiences.

WHAT IS NOT FUNDED See the relevant funding programme on the website for exclusion criteria.

TYPE OF GRANT Project funding.

RANGE OF GRANTS Programme dependent.

SAMPLE GRANTS A list of beneficiaries was not included in the annual report and accounts. Previous beneficiaries have included: Apples and Snakes; Chamber Music Scotland; Horniman Museum and Gardens; Dante or Die Theatre; Kings Place Music Foundation; National Youth Orchestra of Great Britain; Presteigne Festival; The Belfast Ensemble; The Old Vic Theatre Trust 2000.

FINANCES *Financial year end* 31/12/2021
Income £4,180,000
Grants to organisations £1,930,000
Grants to individuals £1,240,000
Assets £1,220,000

TRUSTEES Richard King; Mark Poole; Caroline Norbury; Chris Butler; Susannah Simons; Lorna Clarke; Michelle Escoffery; Christine Geissmar; Nitin Sawhney; Yolanda Brown.

OTHER INFORMATION According to the foundation's 2021 accounts, grants were awarded to 222 organisations and 235 individuals. A list of beneficiaries for the year was not available; however, details of previous beneficiaries are available on the foundation's website.

HOW TO APPLY Apply via the foundation's website where full guidelines for each programme are available. Deadlines for applications vary from programme to programme. Note, organisations can only apply once per calendar year to the Open Fund.

CONTACT DETAILS Fiona Harvey, Secretary, 41 Streatham High Road, Streatham, London SW16 1ER *Tel.* 020 3741 4233 *Email* info@prsfoundation.com *Website* www.prsfoundation.com

The Persimmon Charitable Foundation

CC NO 1163608 **ESTABLISHED** 2015
WHERE FUNDING CAN BE GIVEN Areas of company presence in England, Scotland and Wales.
WHO CAN BENEFIT Charitable organisations.
WHAT IS FUNDED General charitable purposes, including: community and economic development; sustainable development; education; the arts; the environment; youth work; sport; health; social welfare.
TYPE OF GRANT Project costs; matched funding; capital costs.
RANGE OF GRANTS Building Futures programme: £5,000 to £100,000. Community Champions programme: up to £1,000.
SAMPLE GRANTS Change of Scene, The Children's Hospital Charity and Wotton Community Sports Foundation (£100,000 each); Great Melton Cricket Club, Senses Wellbeing Centre C.I.C and Warren Association Trust (£50,000 each); Islastones Foundation, Newcastle Powerchair Football Club and Sandwell Young Carers (£20,000 each).
FINANCES *Financial year end* 31/12/2021
Income £1,550,000
Grants to organisations £1,810,000
Assets (£177,500)
TRUSTEES Roger Devlin; Joanna Place; Dean Finch; Tracy Davison; Anthony Vigor.
OTHER INFORMATION This foundation is the corporate charity of Persimmon plc, a property development company. There are currently two programmes, the Community Champions campaign, which supports small local charities and community groups with matched funding and the Building Futures campaign, which supports children's health, sport, education and the arts with prizes of £1,000, £5,000, £20,000, £50,000 and £100,000.
HOW TO APPLY Applicants need to complete the relevant online form. Check the website for the Building Futures programme deadlines. For the Community Champions programme the foundation needs to know how much you have already raised and how much money you need. Applications are accepted each month and charities and groups that were previously unsuccessful can apply again. The trustees prefer to support local charities. Go to www.persimmonhomes.com/contact to find your nearest Persimmon office.
CONTACT DETAILS The Trustees, Persimmon plc, Persimmon House, Fulford, York, North Yorkshire YO19 4FE *Tel.* 01904 642199 *Email* contact@persimmonhomes.com *Website* www.persimmonhomes.com/charity

Personal Assurance Charitable Trust

CC NO 1023274 **ESTABLISHED** 1993
WHERE FUNDING CAN BE GIVEN Worldwide.
WHO CAN BENEFIT Registered charities; restricted to organisations recommended by policyholders of Personal Assurance plc, their employers and employees of Personal Group Holdings plc.
WHAT IS FUNDED General charitable purposes; social welfare; health.
WHAT IS NOT FUNDED Individuals.
RANGE OF GRANTS The majority of grants are under £10,000.
SAMPLE GRANTS Memusi Foundation (£66,400); Winter Night Shelter MK (£17,700); MK Community Foundation (£10,000); Willen Hospice (£3,300); Children in Need (£3,000); Victory Outreach (£2,100); St Luke's Hospice (£1,100); Wolverhampton Wanderers Foundation (£1,000).
FINANCES *Financial year end* 31/12/2021
Income £169,900
Grants to organisations £116,700
Assets £146,100
TRUSTEES Sarah Mace; Justine Woolf; Julie Stayte.
OTHER INFORMATION Only organisations that received grants of over £1,000 were listed as beneficiaries in the trust's accounts. Grants of under £1,000 totalled £12,100.
HOW TO APPLY Apply in writing to the correspondent.
CONTACT DETAILS The Trustees, c/o Personal Group Holdings plc, John Ormond House, 899 Silbury Boulevard, Milton Keynes, Buckinghamshire MK9 3XL *Tel.* 01908 605000 *Email* hayley.wheatley@personalgroup.com

Jack Petchey Foundation

CC NO 1176221 **ESTABLISHED** 1999
WHERE FUNDING CAN BE GIVEN London and Essex.
WHO CAN BENEFIT Registered charities; state schools and colleges; local authority youth clubs; other charitable organisations; individuals.
WHAT IS FUNDED Support for young people aged between 11 and 25.
WHAT IS NOT FUNDED Profit-making companies; statutory bodies (except for local authority youth clubs); private schools; political or religious activities.
TYPE OF GRANT Project funding. The foundation also funds internships, award schemes and educational visits for small groups.
RANGE OF GRANTS Programme dependent.

SAMPLE GRANTS Speakers Trust (£860,400); First Give (£150,000); Talk the Talk (£75,000); Anthony Nolan (£23,400); Wize Up Financial Education (£6,000).

FINANCES *Financial year end 31/12/2021*
Income £7,610,000
Grants to organisations £7,340,000
Assets £2,480,000

TRUSTEES Ronald Mills; Matthew Rantell; Raymond Rantell; Sonia Sinclair; Lewis Hooper; Robert McArthur; Amanda Galanopoulos.

HOW TO APPLY Applications can be made via the foundation's website. See the website for the eligibility criteria of the relevant programme.

CONTACT DETAILS Grants Team, Dockmaster's House, 1 Hertsmere Road, London E14 8JJ *Tel.* 020 8252 8000 *Email* mail@jackpetcheyfoundation.org.uk *Website* www.jackpetcheyfoundation.org.uk

---

■ Petplan Charitable Trust

CC NO 1032907   **ESTABLISHED** 1994
WHERE FUNDING CAN BE GIVEN UK and overseas.
WHO CAN BENEFIT Registered animal charities; research organisations.
WHAT IS FUNDED The promotion and improvement of the welfare of animals (dogs, cats, horses or rabbits) and the relief of their suffering; veterinary research and education.
WHAT IS NOT FUNDED Individuals; non-registered charities; studies involving experimental or invasive surgery; funding for overheads.
TYPE OF GRANT Project funding; capital costs; animal housing and repairs; research, including pump-priming/pilot grants.
RANGE OF GRANTS Scientific grants: up to £150,000 (unless for pump-priming grants where the maximum is £10,000); welfare grants: up to £20,000; special grants: up to £25,000.
SAMPLE GRANTS Bransby Horses (£25,000); Dogs Trust (£20,000); Ebony Horse Club (£15,000); Redwings Horse Sanctuary (£7,500); Help in Suffering UK and Woodlands Animal Sanctuary (£5,000 each).
FINANCES *Financial year end 30/06/2022*
Income £1,400,000
Grants to organisations £1,210,000
Assets (£74,300)
TRUSTEES Clarissa Baldwin; John Bower; Ted Bvetmed; David Simpson; Kathryn Willis; Jamie Crittall; Lord Prof. Lord Trees; Alan Farkas; Irene Santos; Isabella Mesterhazy.
OTHER INFORMATION Grants were broken down as follows: scientific grants (£647,000); welfare grants (£455,600); special grants (£28,100).
HOW TO APPLY Application forms, eligibility criteria and the dates for application rounds for each grants programme are available via the trust's website.
CONTACT DETAILS Catherine Bourg, Trust Administrator, Great West House (GW2), Great West Road, Brentford, Middlesex TW8 9EG *Email* info@petplancharitabletrust.org.uk *Website* https://petplancharitabletrust.org.uk

---

■ The Pets at Home Foundation

CC NO 1104152   **ESTABLISHED** 2004
WHERE FUNDING CAN BE GIVEN UK.
WHO CAN BENEFIT Registered charities; unregistered charities; CICs.
WHAT IS FUNDED Activities which improve the welfare of UK domestic pets in rescue or reduce the number of domestic pets in rescue.

WHAT IS NOT FUNDED Salaries, uniforms, or expenses; the cost of leasing a vehicle, road tax, insurance, or petrol costs; the purchase of land or buildings; any costs associated with a charity shop; fundraising costs such as marketing materials.
TYPE OF GRANT Capital costs; core/revenue costs; project funding.
RANGE OF GRANTS £250 to £240,000.
SAMPLE GRANTS Birmingham Dogs Home (£242,700); RSPCA (£193,100); Canine Partners (£55,700); Support Dogs (£51,900); Dogs for Autism (£41,600); HorseWorld Trust (£37,200); Dog Assistance in Disability (£30,000); Appledown Rescue and Rehoming Kennels (£27,300); Seeing Dogs Alliance (£20,000); London Inner City Kittens (£10,000).
FINANCES *Financial year end 25/03/2022*
Income £5,690,000
Grants to organisations £2,980,000
Assets £4,390,000
TRUSTEES George Lingwood; Jill Shields; Adrian Bates; Andrew Bickerton; Dr Catriona Curtis; Robert Kent.
OTHER INFORMATION The Pets at Home Foundation (formerly known as Support Adoption for Pets) was established in 2006 by Pets at Home, a pet supplies retailer.
HOW TO APPLY Prospective applicants should first check the grant criteria to confirm their eligibility and then complete the online request for an application form and provide the required supporting documentation. The charity's website notes that a 'virtual' visit to the rescue to learn more about your organisation may be requested.
CONTACT DETAILS The Charity Team, c/o Pets at Home, Chester House, Epsom Avenue, Stanley Green Trading Estate, Handforth, Cheshire SK9 3DF *Tel.* 0161 486 6688 *Email* info@petsathomefoundation.co.uk *Website* www.petsathomefoundation.co.uk

---

■ The Pharsalia Charitable Trust

CC NO 1120402   **ESTABLISHED** 2007
WHERE FUNDING CAN BE GIVEN UK and overseas, with a preference for Oxfordshire, Buckinghamshire and Wiltshire.
WHO CAN BENEFIT Charitable organisations.
WHAT IS FUNDED In the Oxford region: health care and social welfare. Nationally: medical research, higher education and health. Internationally: disaster relief.
RANGE OF GRANTS Mostly £500 to £2,000, with some larger grants.
SAMPLE GRANTS St Luke's Nursing Home (£12,000); Age UK (£10,800); Oxford Hospital Charity (£10,000); Wantage Silver Brand (£5,000); Disasters Emergency Committee – Ukraine Appeal (£3,000); Helen and Douglas House, Oxfordshire Youth and The Salvation Army (£2,000 each); Lifelines (£1,000); Oxford Samaritans (£500); Rotary Club of Machynnleth (£250).
FINANCES *Financial year end 31/03/2022*
Income £127,000
Grants to organisations £72,000
Assets £1,630,000
TRUSTEES Nigel Blackwell; Trudy Sainsbury; Nigel Roots.
OTHER INFORMATION Grants were awarded to 49 organisations during the year, with many grants given to charities in Oxford.
HOW TO APPLY Apply in writing to the correspondent.
CONTACT DETAILS The Trustees, The Ham, Ickleton Road, Wantage, Oxfordshire OX12 9JA *Tel.* 01235 426524

■ The Phillips and Rubens Charitable Trust

cc no 260378   **established** 1970
where funding can be given UK.
who can benefit Charitable organisations, including schools and places of worship.
what is funded General charitable causes; medical research and other medical causes; social welfare; education; disability; older people; sheltered accommodation; the arts; the Jewish faith and community.
what is not funded Individuals.
range of grants Mostly up to £15,000, with some larger grants awarded.
sample grants A list of beneficiaries was not included in the annual report and accounts. Previous beneficiaries have included: The Phillips Family Charitable Trust (£100,000); The Jewish Book Trust (£14,000); London School of Jewish Studies and St John's Hospice (£10,000 each); British Friends of the Jaffa Institute (£8,000); Lionel Rosenfeld Testimonial Fund and Work Avenue (£5,000 each); Charities Aid Foundation (£4,000); Cystic Fibrosis Trust (£3,000); Jewish Leadership Council and RAF Museum (£2,500 each).
finances *Financial year end 05/04/2022*
Income £494,200
Grants to organisations £357,900
Assets £13,930,000
trustees Carolyn Mishon; Martin Paisner; Ruth Phillips; Michael Phillips; Gary Phillips; Paul Phillips.
how to apply Apply in writing to the correspondent.
contact details The Trustees, 67–69 George Street, London W1U 8LT *Tel.* 020 7487 5757 *Email* psphillips@aol.com

■ Betty Phillips Charitable Trust

cc no 1158964   **established** 2014
where funding can be given UK.
who can benefit Registered charities.
what is funded Animal welfare.
sample grants Birmingham Dogs Home, Farplace Animal Rescue and Woodfield Animal Sanctuary (£10,000 each); The Mayhew Home and Redwings Horse Sanctuary (£5,000 each); Teckels Animal Sanctuaries (£3,000).
finances *Financial year end 31/12/2021*
Income £116,600
Grants to organisations £98,000
Assets £4,460,000
trustees Andrew Jones; Michael Vines; Andrew Holloway; Helen Wayman; Miss H. L. Mansfield; Andrew Ollerenshaw.
how to apply Apply in writing to the correspondent.
contact details Andrew Ollerenshaw, Trustee, c/o Tayntons Solicitors, 8–12 Clarence Street, Gloucester, Gloucestershire GL1 1DZ *Tel.* 01452 522047 *Email* andrew.ollerenshaw@tayntons.co.uk

■ The Phillips Family Charitable Trust

cc no 279120   **established** 1979
where funding can be given UK.
who can benefit Registered charities; Jewish organisations.
what is funded General charitable purposes, with a preference for the Jewish faith and community.
what is not funded Individuals.
range of grants Mostly up to £5,000.

sample grants The Holocaust Educational Trusts (£10,000); New Israel Fund (£2,500); Ohel Sarak UK (£250).
finances *Financial year end 05/04/2022*
Income £100,000
Grants to organisations £94,900
Assets £28,600
trustees Martin Paisner; Ruth Phillips; Michael Phillips; Gary Phillps; Paul Phillips.
other information During the year, 62 grants were awarded to organisations.
how to apply Apply in writing to the correspondent.
contact details The Trustees, 67–69 George Street, London W1U 8LT *Tel.* 020 7487 5757 *Email* psphillipsbsh@aol.com

■ The Philip and Connie Phillips Foundation

cc no 1189984
where funding can be given The Kent County Council area; Medway.
who can benefit Registered charities with an annual income between £10,000 and £1 million.
what is funded Health and social welfare with priority given to: older and isolated people; homelessness; strengthening local communities; people with long-term health conditions or disabilities.
what is not funded Contributions to capital appeals, including the restoration and conservation of buildings; equipment (unless as a percentage of project costs); individuals; academic research, scholarships or bursaries; nurseries, schools and colleges; work which has already taken place.
type of grant General running costs, volunteer costs, salaries and project costs.
range of grants £5,000 to £10,000.
sample grants 21 Together (£10,000); Catching Lives (£8,500); Kent Coast Volunteering (£5,000); GAP Thanet (£4,200).
finances *Financial year end 31/03/2022*
Income £30,600
Grants to organisations £211,500
Assets £2,330,000
trustees Deborah Wilkes; John Austin; Patrick DuCasse; Laura Hollands; Jane Davies.
other information Grants were made to 32 organisations during the year.
how to apply Applications can be made via the foundation's website. The foundation has three grant rounds per year.
contact details The Trustees, c/o Simpson Wreford and Partners, Suffolk House, George Street, Croydon CR0 0YN *Email* info@pcphillipsfoundation.org *Website* https://pcphillipsfoundation.org

■ The Pickwell Foundation

cc no 1149424   **established** 2012
where funding can be given UK, with a preference for the South West; overseas.
who can benefit Registered charities and community groups.
what is funded Displaced people; climate change.
type of grant Unrestricted funding; core costs; project funding.
range of grants Typically £1,000 to £25,000.
sample grants Client Earth (£28,000); Uplift (£10,000); Plastic Free North Devon (£5,000); Environmental Funders Network (£1,000).

FINANCES *Financial year end* 05/04/2022
Income £193,700
Grants to organisations £98,000
Assets £71,300

TRUSTEES Stephen Baker; Richard Elliott; Susannah Baker; Tracey Elliott.

OTHER INFORMATION The foundation also supports Community Sponsorship in north Devon, a programme which helps resettle refugees in local communities.

HOW TO APPLY Unsolicited applications are not accepted. The foundation makes invitations to apply for funding.

CONTACT DETAILS The Trustees, Pickwell Manor, Georgeham, Braunton, Devon EX33 1LA *Tel.* 01271 649108 *Email* use the contact form on the website *Website* www.thepickwellfoundation.org.uk

■ The Bernard Piggott Charitable Trust

CC NO 1154724   **ESTABLISHED** 1969
WHERE FUNDING CAN BE GIVEN Birmingham and North Wales.
WHO CAN BENEFIT Registered charities.
WHAT IS FUNDED Care for older people; education of youth; theatre and arts; buildings and heritage; Christianity; community development; health, medical and disability; social welfare; animals and the environment; the armed forces.
WHAT IS NOT FUNDED Individuals; organisations outside Birmingham and North Wales; unregistered charities.
TYPE OF GRANT Research; general funding.
RANGE OF GRANTS Between £250 and £5,000.
SAMPLE GRANTS A list of beneficiaries was not included in the annual report and accounts. Previous beneficiaries have included: St Mary's Church – Caerhun (£2,000); Stroke Association (£1,500); Dyffryn Parish Church (£1,200); Crisis Skylight Birmingham and Sunfield Children's Homes (£1,000 each); Resources for Autism (£900); Birmingham Contemporary Music Group and Northfield Eco Centre (£750 each); Kingsbury Training Centre (£400); Montgomeryshire Youth Theatre (£250).
FINANCES *Financial year end* 30/09/2021
Income £129,500
Grants to organisations £64,500
Assets £2,080,000
TRUSTEES Mark Painter; Richard Easton; Nigel Lea; Geoffrey Hall; Archdeacon of Bangor.
OTHER INFORMATION The 2020/21 annual report was the latest available at the time of writing (May 2023).
HOW TO APPLY Applications can be made via the trust's website.
CONTACT DETAILS Jenny Whitworth, Secretary, 5 Heydon Road, Finstall, Bromsgrove, Worcestershire B60 3DA *Tel.* 01527 575105 *Email* enquiries@bernardpiggotttrust.org.uk *Website* https://bernardpiggotttrust.org.uk

■ The Pilgrim Trust

CC NO 206602   **ESTABLISHED** 1930
WHERE FUNDING CAN BE GIVEN UK.
WHO CAN BENEFIT UK-registered charities; organisations exempt from registration; recognised public bodies; registered friendly societies.
WHAT IS FUNDED The preservation of architecturally or historically important buildings; the preservation of historically significant artefacts or documents; social welfare; vulnerable women and girls.
WHAT IS NOT FUNDED There is an extensive list of exclusions, which can be found in the funding guidelines document on the trust's website.
TYPE OF GRANT Revenue costs; salaries; project funding; capital costs; development funding; research.
RANGE OF GRANTS Mostly £3,000 to £60,000, with some outlying grants of much higher values. The trust's small grants programme is reserved for requests of £5,000 or less.
SAMPLE GRANTS The Archbishops' Council (£185,000); Asian Development Association Bury (£90,000); Friends of Tarlair Community Group (£30,000); Birmingham Museums Trust (£22,000); Mount Zion Apostolic Church, (£15,000); 1st Godstone Scout Group (£10,000); Eating Matters (£5,000); SAVE Britain's Heritage (£4,800); The Bedford Park Society (£3,600).
FINANCES *Financial year end* 31/12/2021
Income £1,630,000
Grants to organisations £2,790,000
Assets £87,180,000
TRUSTEES Sir Mark Jones; Caroline Butler; David Barrie; Joan Winterkorn; Atulkumar Patel; Marie Staunton; Alexander Sturgis; Alice Weston; Cullagh Warnock; Matthew Ridley; Asif Afridi; Dr Anna Keay.
OTHER INFORMATION Grants fall into two categories: preservation and scholarship grants (typically 60% of annual expenditure) and social welfare grants (typically 40% of annual expenditure). Preservation and scholarship grants include grants for historic buildings, care of collections, training and research. In 2021, grants for preservation and scholarship totalled £1.77 million and social welfare grants totalled £1.03 million.
HOW TO APPLY Applications can be made via the trust's website using a two-stage online application form. Applicants should read the funding guidelines document prior to making an application.
CONTACT DETAILS The Trustees, New Wing, Somerset House, Strand, London WC2R 1LA *Tel.* 020 7834 6510 *Email* info@thepilgrimtrust.org.uk *Website* www.thepilgrimtrust.org.uk

■ Cecil Pilkington Charitable Trust

CC NO 249997   **ESTABLISHED** 1966
WHERE FUNDING CAN BE GIVEN UK.
WHO CAN BENEFIT Charitable organisations.
WHAT IS FUNDED General charitable purposes including: the environment; medical causes; the arts; education; welfare.
RANGE OF GRANTS Mostly £3,000 and £5,000 with the occasional smaller or larger grant.
SAMPLE GRANTS The Big Give (£70,000); Psychiatry Research Trust (£40,000); Greenpeace, National Museum Liverpool and Rainbow for Africa (£10,000 each); Alzheimer's Research UK, Full Facts and Oxford Hospital Charity (£5,000 each); Bat Conservation Trust, Compliments of the House and Pegasus Theatre (£3,000 each); Countryside Learning and Sunningwell School of Art (£2,000 each).
FINANCES *Financial year end* 05/10/2022
Income £466,600
Grants to organisations £453,000
Assets £24,020,000
TRUSTEES Mark Feeny; Arnold Pilkington; Dr Vanessa Pilkington; Heloise Pilkington.

OTHER INFORMATION Grants were broken down as follows: welfare (£177,000); medical causes (£114,000); the environment (£91,000); medical causes (£54,000); education (£12,000); general charitable purposes (£5,000).

HOW TO APPLY Apply in writing to the correspondent.

CONTACT DETAILS The Trustees, c/o Duncan Sheard Glass, Castle Chambers, 43 Castle Street, Liverpool, Merseyside L2 9TL *Tel.* 0151 243 1200

■ Elise Pilkington Charitable Trust

CC NO 1170847

WHERE FUNDING CAN BE GIVEN UK.

WHO CAN BENEFIT Registered charities; hospices.

WHAT IS FUNDED Older people; equine welfare.

WHAT IS NOT FUNDED Equine welfare grants are normally only considered from charities that are members of the National Equine Welfare Council (NEWC) or charities that are proactively working towards NEWC membership.

TYPE OF GRANT Project funding; salaries; capital costs.

RANGE OF GRANTS £1,500 up to £15,000.

SAMPLE GRANTS SPANA (£15,000); Moorland Mousie Trust (£14,500); Glasgow's Golden Generation and Rice (£10,000 each); St Clare Hospice (£7,200); GL11 (£5,000); North Northumberland Hospice (£2,000); Teesside Hospice (£1,500).

FINANCES *Financial year end* 05/04/2022 *Income* £62,400 *Grants to organisations* £163,400 *Assets* £3,160,000

TRUSTEES The Revd Robert Merchant; Ruth Tarry; Dr David Shipway; Claire Gordon; Gemma Walpole; Dr Alison Pyatt; Mark Kerr; Dr Rachael Trenaman.

OTHER INFORMATION Grants were distributed as follows: equine grants (£71,700); older people and hospices (£91,800).

HOW TO APPLY Application forms can be downloaded from the trust's website.

CONTACT DETAILS The Trustees, Ridgecot, Lewes Road, Horsted Keynes, Haywards Heath, RH17 7DY *Tel.* 01825 790304 *Email* admin@elisepilkingtontrust.org.uk *Website* https://elisepilkingtontrust.org.uk

■ Pilkington Charities Fund

CC NO 225911 **ESTABLISHED** 1950

WHERE FUNDING CAN BE GIVEN Merseyside.

WHO CAN BENEFIT Registered charities.

WHAT IS FUNDED Support for people affected by poverty, old age or ill health.

TYPE OF GRANT Capital costs; core costs; project funding; funding for two or three years will be considered in exceptional circumstances.

RANGE OF GRANTS Typically between £1,000 and £10,000, but occasionally larger.

SAMPLE GRANTS Alzheimer's Society (£10,000); PDSA (£7,500); Aspire (£5,000); Caudwell Children and KIND (£3,000 each); Caring Connections (£1,000).

FINANCES *Financial year end* 30/06/2022 *Income* £600,000 *Grants to organisations* £775,500 *Assets* £25,590,000

TRUSTEES Neil Jones; Arnold Pilkington; Eleanor Ashton.

HOW TO APPLY Applications can be made in writing or by email to the correspondent. Deadlines fall on 1 May and 1 October, although urgent applications may be considered at other times. Clear instructions detailing what to include are available from the charity's website.

CONTACT DETAILS The Trustees, Rathbones Investment Management, Port of Liverpool Building, Pier Head, Liverpool, Merseyside L3 1NW *Tel.* 0151 236 6666 *Email* pilkingtoncharitiesfund@rathbones.com *Website* http://pilkingtoncharitiesfund.org.uk

■ The Sir Harry Pilkington Fund

CC NO 206740 **ESTABLISHED** 1962

WHERE FUNDING CAN BE GIVEN Merseyside and St Helens.

WHO CAN BENEFIT Charitable organisations: CICs; community groups; hospices; places of worship.

WHAT IS FUNDED General charitable purposes; arts and culture; youth work; health; social welfare; education.

RANGE OF GRANTS Under £10,000, mostly between £1,000 and £3,000.

SAMPLE GRANTS Acronym Community Empowerment and Voice of Nations (£9,000 each); Amadudu Women's Refuge, Crawford House Community Partner and Zero Carbon Liverpool City Region (£7,500 each); Ready Generations (£5,000); Autism in Motion Liverpool, Dingle Multi Agency Centre and Strengthening Wellbeing Together (£2,000 each); Holistic Harmonies, Kurdish Saturday School and Thred (£1,000 each); Greek School of St Nicholas (£800).

FINANCES *Financial year end* 30/06/2022 *Income* £174,000 *Grants to organisations* £224,200 *Assets* £8,100,000

TRUSTEE Liverpool Charity and Voluntary Services.

HOW TO APPLY Apply in writing to the correspondent.

CONTACT DETAILS The Trustees, Liverpool Charity and Voluntary Services, 151 Dale Street, Liverpool, Merseyside L2 2AH *Tel.* 0151 227 5177

■ The Austin and Hope Pilkington Trust

CC NO 255274 **ESTABLISHED** 1967

WHERE FUNDING CAN BE GIVEN UK.

WHO CAN BENEFIT UK-registered charities only.

WHAT IS FUNDED The trust focuses on supporting a different funding priority each year. In 2023, it will support the rehabilitation of prisoners, ex-prisoners, those at risk of offending and children and young people in/leaving care. Support in 2024 will be focused on disability.

WHAT IS NOT FUNDED Capital appeals, including equipment; charities involved with religion; animal charities; holidays; individual hospices (but national organisations can apply); individuals; minibuses and vehicles; overseas projects; schools including activities; Scouts, Cubs, Guides and Brownies; Sea Cadets; Shopmobility; students; village halls.

TYPE OF GRANT Project funding.

RANGE OF GRANTS Up to £5,000.

SAMPLE GRANTS NOAH Enterprise, Nordoff Robbins Music Therapy, The Whitechapel Centre and Welsh Housing Aid (£5,000 each); Baobab Centre for Young Survivors in Exile, Devon and Cornwall Refugee Support and Pukar Disability Resource Centre (£1,000 each).

FINANCES *Financial year end* 31/12/2021 *Income* £249,300 *Grants to organisations* £306,200 *Assets* £12,520,000

TRUSTEES Penny Badowska; Eleanor Stride; Harry Shankar; Louis Shankar.

OTHER INFORMATION Each grant round has different eligibility; consult the trust's website for more information.

HOW TO APPLY Apply via the trust's website.

CONTACT DETAILS The Trustees, Rathbones, Port of Liverpool Building, Pier Head, Liverpool, Merseyside L3 1NW *Email* admin@austin-hope-pilkington.org.uk *Website* www.austin-hope-pilkington.org.uk

---

■ Miss A. M. Pilkington's Charitable Trust

OSCR NO SC000282   **ESTABLISHED** 1972

WHERE FUNDING CAN BE GIVEN UK, with a preference for Scotland.

WHO CAN BENEFIT Registered charities.

WHAT IS FUNDED General charitable purposes.

WHAT IS NOT FUNDED Grants are not given to overseas projects or political appeals.

RANGE OF GRANTS Almost all grants are for £1,000.

SAMPLE GRANTS Aberlour Child Care Trust, Bumblebee Conservation Trust, Fife Girl Guide Association, Pitlochry Theatre, RockSolid Dundee, Sight Savers International, Teapot Trust and World Horse Welfare (£1,000 each).

FINANCES *Financial year end* 05/04/2022
Income £86,100
Grants to organisations £91,000
Assets £4,480,000

HOW TO APPLY Apply in writing to the correspondent.

CONTACT DETAILS The Trustees, EQ Chartered Accountants, Pentland House, Saltire Centre, Glenrothes, Fife KY6 2AH *Tel.* 01334 654044

■ PIMCO Foundation Europe

CC NO 1139109   **ESTABLISHED** 2010

WHERE FUNDING CAN BE GIVEN London and overseas.

WHO CAN BENEFIT Registered charities.

WHAT IS FUNDED Arts and culture; children; disability; education; the environment; health; homelessness; overseas aid.

SAMPLE GRANTS MyBnk (£110,600); House of St Barnabas (£110,600); Passage 2000 (£104,600); FareShare and UNICEF (£100,000 each); Wonder Foundation (£61,000).

FINANCES *Financial year end* 31/12/2021
Income £1,340,000
Grants to organisations £870,300
Assets £6,550,000

TRUSTEES Thomas Rice; Vishalakshi Ananthanarayanan; Ryan Blute; Craig Dawson; Ketishweran Pothalingam.

OTHER INFORMATION Grants to the six organisations listed as beneficiaries represent 73% of the total grants made.

HOW TO APPLY Unsolicited applications are not accepted.

CONTACT DETAILS Daisy Grehan, EMEA Programme Manager, 11 Baker Street, London W1U 3AH *Tel.* 020 7872 1300 *Email* daisy.grehan@pimco.com or emeacorporatesecretary@pimco.com *Website* www.pimco.co.uk/en-gb/our-firm/purpose/foundation

---

■ The Pinchbeck Charitable Trust

CC NO 1152723   **ESTABLISHED** 2013

WHERE FUNDING CAN BE GIVEN Worldwide.

WHO CAN BENEFIT Charitable organisations.

WHAT IS FUNDED General charitable purposes.

RANGE OF GRANTS £1,000 to £15,000.

SAMPLE GRANTS Previous beneficiaries have included: Clear Trust; Cure Parkinson's Trust; Friends of Royal Marsden; Médecins Sans Frontières; National Portrait Gallery; RAFT; St Peter's Hospice.

FINANCES *Financial year end* 11/06/2021
Income £2,000
Grants to organisations £51,000

TRUSTEES Robin Pinchbeck; Bridget Pinchbeck; Oliver Pinchbeck; Alexia Pinchbeck; Alan Catling.

OTHER INFORMATION The 2020/21 financial information was the latest available at the time of writing (June 2023). The trust's annual report and accounts were not available to view on the Charity Commission's website due to its low income. We have therefore estimated the grant total based on the trust's total expenditure.

HOW TO APPLY Apply in writing to the correspondent.

CONTACT DETAILS The Trustees, The Mead House, Taynton, Burford, Oxfordshire OX18 4UH *Tel.* 01993 824475

■ Pink Ribbon Foundation

CC NO 1080839   **ESTABLISHED** 2000

WHERE FUNDING CAN BE GIVEN UK and overseas.

WHO CAN BENEFIT UK-registered charities; hospitals; hospices.

WHAT IS FUNDED Relief for people who are suffering from or have been affected by breast cancer; work to advance the understanding of breast cancer and its early detection and treatment.

WHAT IS NOT FUNDED Individuals.

TYPE OF GRANT Capital costs; research; core/revenue costs; seed funding/start-up funding; project funding; unrestricted funding.

RANGE OF GRANTS Mostly up to £5,000.

SAMPLE GRANTS Something to Look Forward to (£46,800); Breast Cancer UK (£16,000); Liverpool NHS (£7,000); Primrose Centre (£6,000); Langan Dragons (£5,000); Paul's Cancer Support Centre (£4,000); Primrose Hospice (£2,500); Think Pink (£2,000).

FINANCES *Financial year end* 30/09/2022
Income £519,400
Grants to organisations £307,100
Assets £769,800

TRUSTEES Angela Brignall; Jonathan Prince; Elizabeth MacBean.

OTHER INFORMATION Grants were awarded to 63 organisations during the year.

HOW TO APPLY Application forms can be downloaded from the foundation's website or requested by email or phone. Grant applications must be sent to the correspondent as a hard copy, along with a set of your organisation's most current accounts. The annual deadline is late May, with grants being awarded in July; check the website for exact dates. If applying from a general cancer charity, the grant must be specifically for those with or affected by breast cancer.

CONTACT DETAILS The Trustees, Crofton House, 5 Morley Close, Orpington, Kent BR6 8JR *Tel.* 01689 858877 *Email* enquiries@pinkribbonfoundation.org.uk *Website* www.pinkribbonfoundation.org.uk

---

■ The Pixel Fund

CC NO 1191052   **ESTABLISHED** 2011

WHERE FUNDING CAN BE GIVEN UK.

WHO CAN BENEFIT Registered charities. The trustees have a strong preference for organisations with an annual income of under £10 million.

WHAT IS FUNDED The mental health and well-being of children and young people (under 26).

WHAT IS NOT FUNDED Individuals; non-UK-registered charities; projects/services delivered overseas; projects not related to mental health matters; independent schools (other than those supporting children with special educational needs); religious organisations.

TYPE OF GRANT Project funding.

RANGE OF GRANTS First grants are normally between £2,500 and £5,000.

SAMPLE GRANTS CHUMS Trauma Service; Clear Sky Children's Charity; Freedom from Torture; Gloucestershire Counselling Service; Meningitis Now; Rainbow Trust Children's Charity; Support Dogs; The Guild of Psychotherapists; The Listening Place; York Mind.

FINANCES *Financial year end* 05/04/2022
Income £210,200
Grants to organisations £165,300
Assets £2,000,000

TRUSTEES James Hitch; Katherine Ferrie; Sandra Thomson.

HOW TO APPLY Potential applicants are first advised to familiarise themselves with the charity's application checklist, which includes details of eligibility criteria. If eligible, contact the charity using the online contact form with a brief outline of your organisation, what you do and your reason for requesting a grant.

CONTACT DETAILS The Trustees, 9 Southlands Road, Bromley, Kent BR2 9QR *Email* use the contact form on the website *Website* www.pixelfund.org.uk

■ Charles Plater Trust

CC NO 309719

WHERE FUNDING CAN BE GIVEN UK.

WHO CAN BENEFIT Registered charities; churches.

WHAT IS FUNDED Projects that deepen the awareness of Catholic social teaching and Catholic social thought to better equip people to take on leadership roles in tackling poverty, exclusion, economic inequality and environmental concerns; projects that deliver tangible outcomes to tackle poverty, exclusion, economic inequality and environmental concerns for marginalised people and communities; projects that develop and apply Catholic social teaching and Catholic social thought.

WHAT IS NOT FUNDED See the trust's website for a full list of exclusions.

RANGE OF GRANTS Up to £60,000.

SAMPLE GRANTS Mustard Tree (£50,000); Prison Advice and Care Trust (£26,000); Soundabout (£12,400); Heart of Tamworth (£5,000); Street Doctors (£4,500).

FINANCES *Financial year end* 31/03/2022
Income £221,600
Grants to organisations £137,500
Assets £8,630,000

TRUSTEES The Rt Revd Richard Moth; Stephen Hargrave; Brian Mooney; Oliver Smith; Andrew Haines; Catherine Corcoran; Bishop Paul McAleenan; Michael Walsh; Richard Hooper.

HOW TO APPLY Apply online via the trust's website.

CONTACT DETAILS The Trustees, 39 Eccleston Square, London SW1V 1BX *Tel.* 020 7901 1907 *Email* plater@plater.org.uk *Website* www.plater.org.uk

■ The Players Foundation

CC NO 1150458 **ESTABLISHED** 2013

WHERE FUNDING CAN BE GIVEN UK.

WHO CAN BENEFIT Registered charities; sports organisations; individuals.

WHAT IS FUNDED Education on the development and social impact of football; sport, recreation and leisure facilities; equality and the elimination of discrimination; physical health; social welfare; access to football for people who are disadvantaged and socially excluded; health and welfare of footballers, both professional and amateur.

WHAT IS NOT FUNDED Private medical premiums; funds to establish a business; income; debt payment; court fines.

TYPE OF GRANT Capital costs; development funding; project funding; strategic funding; pro bono; bursaries.

RANGE OF GRANTS Mostly under £400,000 with the largest grant during this period being £2.8 million.

SAMPLE GRANTS The English Football League Trust (£2.8 million); Football Conference Community (£1.2 million); Premier League Professional Footballers' Association Community Fund and Sporting Chance (£400,000 each); Capital City Academy (£175,000); Show Racism the Red Card (£50,000); Fair Play Awards (£7,500).

FINANCES *Financial year end* 30/06/2022
Income £1,360,000
Grants to organisations £5,830,000
Grants to individuals £1,800,000
Assets £46,210,000

TRUSTEES Jonathon Walters; Martin Prothero; Jacqueline Newcombe; Monica Shafaq; Gareth Griffiths; Brendon Batson; Garth Crooks.

OTHER INFORMATION Grants were distributed as follows: community (£4.58 million); education (£1.33 million); player welfare (£1.1 million); benevolence (£316,300); equality (£305,400); coaching (£18,000). Note that the breakdown includes grants awarded to individuals. A full list of organisational beneficiaries was not available in the foundation's 2021/22 accounts. 'Sundry grants' totalled £19,000. This foundation has been issued with an official warning by the Charity Commission for mismanagement.

HOW TO APPLY Apply in writing to the correspondent.

CONTACT DETAILS The Trustees, 20 Oxford Court, Bishopsgate, Manchester M2 3WQ *Tel.* 0161 236 0575 *Email* info@theplayersfoundation.org or info@pfa.co.uk *Website* https://theplayersfoundation.org

■ Thomas Pocklington Trust

CC NO 1113729

WHERE FUNDING CAN BE GIVEN UK.

WHO CAN BENEFIT Charitable organisations.

WHAT IS FUNDED Research into sight loss; support for people with sight loss.

WHAT IS NOT FUNDED Charities registered overseas; construction projects such as playgrounds, village halls and disabled access; educational fees; general school appeals; hospices; individuals; medical research; parish facilities; requests for vehicles.

TYPE OF GRANT Research, project and development funding.

RANGE OF GRANTS Mainly up to £10,000.

SAMPLE GRANTS London Vision (£290,000); Metro Blind Sports (£100,000); Sense (£53,000); Henshaws Society for Blind People (£37,000); Angel Eyes NI (£22,000); Bradbury Fields (£16,000); British Blind Sport (£7,000).

FINANCES *Financial year end* 31/03/2022
Income £5,230,000
Grants to organisations £1,920,000
Assets £170,330,000

TRUSTEES Mervyn Williamson; Philip Longworth; Matt Wadsworth; Graham Findlay; Rashmikant Mehta; Judith Potts; Helen Mitchell; Robert Holl; Simon Curtis; Adam Youatt; Louise Robertshaw.

OTHER INFORMATION Grants were awarded to 32 organisations during the year.

HOW TO APPLY Applications can be made through the trust's grants portal on its website.

CONTACT DETAILS The Trustees, Pocklington Hub, 3 Queen Square, London WC1N 3AR *Tel.* 020 8995 0880 *Email* grants@pocklington-trust.org. uk *Website* www.pocklington-trust.org.uk

··

■ Polden-Puckham Charitable Foundation

CC NO 1003024   **ESTABLISHED** 1991
WHERE FUNDING CAN BE GIVEN UK and overseas.
WHO CAN BENEFIT Registered charities; non-governmental organisations.
WHAT IS FUNDED Peace and security; environmental sustainability.
WHAT IS NOT FUNDED Consult the foundation's website for a detailed list of grant exclusions.
TYPE OF GRANT Core/revenue costs; seed funding/start-up funding; project funding; unrestricted funding.
RANGE OF GRANTS Typically £5,000 to £30,000 per year, for up to three years.
SAMPLE GRANTS Climate 2025 (£174,000); Green New Deal UK (£150,000); Stop Ecocide International (£122,500); Corporate Europe Observatory (£122,500); Resourcing Racial Justice and Platform (£30,000 each); Promoting Economic Pluralism (£20,000); Faith for the Climate Network (£10,000); Energy Democracy Project (£7,500); #endperiodplastic campaign (£1,500).
FINANCES *Financial year end* 05/04/2022
Income £280,600
Grants to organisations £1,750,000
Assets £15,160,000
TRUSTEES Jonathan Gillett; Angela Seay; Dorothy Ball; Simon Fisher; Stephen Pittam; Fiona Duggan; Cindy Forde.
OTHER INFORMATION In 2021/22, the charity made 58 grants to charitable organisations: 38 under environmental sustainability (£978,000) and 20 under peace and security (£775,000).
HOW TO APPLY Guidelines on applications, deadlines and concept notes as well as an eligibility test can be accessed on the charity's website; formal submissions should be made via the online application form.
CONTACT DETAILS Christine Oliver, Trust Secretary, BM PPCF, London WC1N 3XX *Tel.* 020 7193 7364 *Email* ppcf@polden-puckham.org.uk *Website* www.polden-puckham.org.uk

··

■ The George and Esme Pollitzer Charitable Settlement

CC NO 212631   **ESTABLISHED** 1960
WHERE FUNDING CAN BE GIVEN UK.
WHO CAN BENEFIT Registered charities.
WHAT IS FUNDED Parenting, the family and children; the armed forces; people with disabilities and older people; homelessness; the community; the environment; education; health and medical research.
RANGE OF GRANTS Typically £5,000.

SAMPLE GRANTS The Virtual Doctors (£10,000); Greenwich Night Shelter, Level Trust, The Sreepur Village and West London Equality Centre (£5,000 each).
FINANCES *Financial year end* 05/04/2022
Income £112,400
Grants to organisations £120,000
Assets £4,240,000
TRUSTEES Richard Pollitzer; Catherine Charles; Frances Pollitzer; Joseph Pollitzer.
OTHER INFORMATION Grants were distributed as follows: other (£45,000); community and the environment (£20,000); health and medical research (£20,000); homelessness (£15,000); education (£10,000); parenting, the family and children (£10,000).
HOW TO APPLY Apply in writing to the correspondent.
CONTACT DETAILS The Trustees, Saffery Champness, St Catherine's Court, Berkeley Place, Clifton, Bristol BS8 1BQ *Tel.* 0117 915 1617

··

■ The Polonsky Foundation

CC NO 291143   **ESTABLISHED** 1985
WHERE FUNDING CAN BE GIVEN UK; Israel; USA; France; Italy.
WHO CAN BENEFIT Universities; arts and cultural institutions.
WHAT IS FUNDED Cultural heritage and digitisation (at major libraries and museums); education and research in the humanities and social sciences; innovation and excellence in the (performing) arts.
RANGE OF GRANTS Up to £90,000 but typically between £1,000 and £30,000.
SAMPLE GRANTS University of Oxford (£91,200); University of Cambridge (£84,500); Aspen Music Festival and School (£51,100); Consortium of European Research (£34,800); Classics for All (£27,000); Old Vic Trust (£5,000); Van Leer Institute (£2,100).
FINANCES *Financial year end* 31/03/2022
Income £425,000
Grants to organisations £415,400
Assets £14,630,000
TRUSTEES Dr Georgette Bennett; Dr Leonard Polonsky; Marc Polonsky; Hannah Whitney; Joshua-Marc Tanenbaum.
OTHER INFORMATION In 2021/22, grants were awarded to 12 organisations.
HOW TO APPLY The foundation does not accept unsolicited applications.
CONTACT DETAILS The Trustees, 8 Park Crescent, London W1B 1PG *Tel.* 020 7436 1997 *Website* https://polonskyfoundation.org

··

■ The Porta Pia 2012 Foundation

CC NO 1152582   **ESTABLISHED** 2013
WHERE FUNDING CAN BE GIVEN UK.
WHO CAN BENEFIT Registered charities.
WHAT IS FUNDED General charitable purposes; poverty relief; economic and community development and employment; recreation.
RANGE OF GRANTS Up to £33,500.
SAMPLE GRANTS St Vincent Depaul Society (£35,000); Crisis, Depaul UK, The Passage and The Samaritans (£20,000 each); Maytree, Papyrus, Streetchild and Why me? UK (£10,000 each); Depaul International and Help Musicians (£5,000 each).
FINANCES *Financial year end* 31/12/2021
Income £28,700
Grants to organisations £205,000
Assets £2,990,000

TRUSTEES James O'Shea; Joanne Sennitt; Helen O'Shea.

OTHER INFORMATION Grants were awarded to 15 organisations during the year. Only grants of over £3,000 were listed as beneficiaries. In 2021, no grants were made of under £3,000. Grants were awarded for a wide range of causes.

HOW TO APPLY The 2021 accounts state that unsolicited applications to the foundation are considered at the trustees' quarterly meetings. 'However most grants made are to a variety of charities of which the Trustees have prior and personal knowledge.' Apply in writing to the correspondent.

CONTACT DETAILS The Trustees, c/o Investment Quorum Ltd, Guild Hall House, 85 Gresham Street, London EC2V 7NQ *Tel.* 020 7337 1390

■ The Portal Trust

CC NO 312425   **ESTABLISHED** 1748

WHERE FUNDING CAN BE GIVEN Camden, the City of London, Greenwich, Hackney, Hammersmith and Fulham, Islington, Kensington and Chelsea, Lambeth, Lewisham, Newham, Southwark, Tower Hamlets, Wandsworth and Westminster.

WHO CAN BENEFIT Charitable organisations; schools; individuals.

WHAT IS FUNDED Education, particularly widening participation, truancy and prisoners' education. Applications should benefit children and young people under the age of 25 who are residents of the named inner London boroughs and are from a low-income or disadvantaged background.

WHAT IS NOT FUNDED Projects that do not meet a trust priority; supplementary schools or mother-tongue teaching; youth and community groups, or projects taking place in these settings; general fundraising campaigns or appeals; costs for equipment or salaries that are the statutory responsibility of education authorities; costs to substitute the withdrawal or reduction of statutory funding; costs for work or activities that have already taken place prior to the grant application; costs already covered by core funding or other grants; capital costs that are exclusively for the purchase, repair or furnishing of buildings, or the purchase of vehicles, computers, sports equipment or improvements to school grounds.

TYPE OF GRANT Project funding, capital costs, development funding, running programmes/workshops, maintenance, core costs for schools. Funding may be available for up to three years.

RANGE OF GRANTS Generally up to £50,000.

SAMPLE GRANTS Stepney All Saints Church of England Secondary School (£72,000); The World Reimagined (£40,100); Independent Film Trust, Saracens Sports Foundation and University of Westminster (£30,000 each); Ministry of Stories (£15,000); Fitzrovia Youth in Action (£5,000); Building Crafts College (£370).

FINANCES *Financial year end 31/03/2022*
Income £7,950,000
Grants to organisations £5,160,000
Grants to individuals £25,000
Assets £264,590,000

TRUSTEES His Honour Brian Barker; David Hogben; The Revd Laura Jorgensen; The Revd Trevor Critchlow; Jennifer Moseley; Sophie Fernandes; John Hall; Dr Denise Jones; Helen Folorunso; Sarwar Zaman; Ratidzo Starkey; Fancy Sinantha.

OTHER INFORMATION In 2021 the foundation changed its name from the Sir John Cass's Foundation to The Portal Trust due to Sir John Cass's links with the slave trade.

HOW TO APPLY The trust operates a multi-stage application process, details of which can be found on its website.

CONTACT DETAILS The Trustees, 31 Jewry Street, London EC3N 2EY *Tel.* 020 7480 5884 *Email* hello@portaltrust.org *Website* https://portaltrust.org

■ Porter Foundation

CC NO 261194   **ESTABLISHED** 1970

WHERE FUNDING CAN BE GIVEN UK and Israel.

WHO CAN BENEFIT Registered charities; organisations with charitable objects which are exempt from registration.

WHAT IS FUNDED Education; the environment; arts and culture; health; social welfare; the Jewish faith and community.

WHAT IS NOT FUNDED Charities that redistribute funds to other charities; third-party organisations raising money on behalf of other charities; covering general running costs; general appeals like direct mail circulars.

TYPE OF GRANT Project funding; capital costs; development funding.

RANGE OF GRANTS £1,400 to £5,000 with the occasional larger grant.

SAMPLE GRANTS Previous beneficiaries have included: Victoria and Albert Museum (£750,000); Anglo Israel Association and Community Security Trust (£5,000 each); Norwood (£3,000); University Jewish Chaplaincy (£2,500); Anthony Nolan (£1,000).

FINANCES *Financial year end 05/04/2023*
Income £11,000
Grants to organisations £100,000

TRUSTEES Prof. Sir Walter Bodmer; Steven Porter; Linda Streit; Brian Padgett.

OTHER INFORMATION Full accounts were not available to view on the Charity Commission's website due to the foundation's low income. We have estimated the grant total based on the foundation's total expenditure.

HOW TO APPLY Apply in writing to the correspondent.

CONTACT DETAILS Sarah Hunt, 63 Grosvenor Street, London W1K 3JG *Tel.* 020 7499 1957 *Email* Sarah.Hunt@princapital.com

■ The Portishead Nautical Trust

CC NO 228876   **ESTABLISHED** 1986

WHERE FUNDING CAN BE GIVEN Bristol, North Somerset, Portishead, South Gloucestershire and the South West.

WHO CAN BENEFIT Charitable organisations; individuals.

WHAT IS FUNDED Projects and activities to assist young people (under the age of 25) who need help due to deprivation, poverty, financial hardship, parental neglect, lack of control, or other misfortune.

RANGE OF GRANTS Mostly under £5,000 with the exception of the continuation of large grants to Portishead Youth Centre.

SAMPLE GRANTS Portishead Youth Centre (£20,000); Caring in Bristol Ltd (£5,000); Young Lives vs Cancer (£3,500); Bridge Foundation and Wellspring Counselling (£3,000 each); Living Paintings Trust (£2,500); Evergreen Equestrian Centre and Keynsham and District Mencap Society (£1,500 each).

FINANCES *Financial year end* 31/03/2022
Income £96,900
Grants to organisations £83,400
Grants to individuals £13,100
Assets £2,490,000
TRUSTEES Colin Crossman; Peter Dingley-Brown; Anne McPherson; Patricia Margerison; Conrad Woodhead; Alison Stone.
OTHER INFORMATION Grants were awarded to 24 organisations and 46 individuals during the year.
HOW TO APPLY Apply in writing to the correspondent. The trustees usually meet four times per annum.
CONTACT DETAILS Mrs E. Knight, Secretary, 108 High Street, Portishead, Bristol BS20 6AJ
Tel. 01275 847463
Email portisheadnauticaltrust@gmail.com

....

■ The Portrack Charitable Trust

CC NO 266120   **ESTABLISHED** 1973
WHERE FUNDING CAN BE GIVEN UK and overseas.
WHO CAN BENEFIT UK-registered charities; educational institutions.
WHAT IS FUNDED Education; overseas humanitarian aid for those suffering the consequences of violence and conflict; the environment; social welfare and support for disadvantaged people, including survivors of abuse and people who are homeless or at risk of homelessness; health and medicine; arts and culture.
WHAT IS NOT FUNDED Individuals; CICs; non-UK-registered charities.
RANGE OF GRANTS Mostly between £3,000 and £5,000 with the occasional larger grant.
SAMPLE GRANTS The Jencks Foundation and Screen Academy Foundation (£100,000 each); Disasters Emergency Committee – Afghanistan Appeal and Islington Giving (£50,000 each); Disasters Emergency Committee – Ukraine Appeal (£20,000); Blue Marine Foundation (£15,000); Maggie's and Red Cross Ukraine Appeal (£10,000 each); British Red Cross – Yemen Crisis Appeal, Human Rights Watch and Unlocked Graduates (£5,000 each); Canonbury School Foundation, Thornhill School Foundation and William Tyndale School Association (£3,000 each).
FINANCES *Financial year end* 05/04/2022
Income £388,400
Grants to organisations £494,000
Assets £14,190,000
TRUSTEES John Jencks; Lily Jencks; Chris Barnes.
OTHER INFORMATION The trust asks to be contacted by email only.
HOW TO APPLY Unsolicited applications are not accepted.
CONTACT DETAILS Lucy Dare, Administrator, The Old Stable, 15A Huntingdon Street, London N1 1BU
Email portrackcharitabletrust@gmail.com

....

■ Postcode Community Trust

OSCR NO SC044772   **ESTABLISHED** 2014
WHERE FUNDING CAN BE GIVEN Wales.
WHO CAN BENEFIT Registered charities; constituted community organisations such as CICs or CIOs; social enterprises; not-for-profit organisations.
WHAT IS FUNDED Mental well-being; participation in arts and sports; social welfare; supporting disadvantaged people; biodiversity and green space; the climate emergency and sustainability; access to the outdoors.
WHAT IS NOT FUNDED A comprehensive list of exclusions can be found on the trust's website.

TYPE OF GRANT Project funding; capital costs.
RANGE OF GRANTS From £250 to £25,000. Grants of more than £2,000 are for registered charities only.
SAMPLE GRANTS Creations of Cymru Film and Media (£25,000); Action for Elders Trust (£22,400); Resolven Building Blocks (£18,600); Tintern Recreation Centre and Village Hall (£15,000); Headway Cardiff and South East Wales (£7,500); Caldicot Town Team (£2,500); Happy Go Lucky Theatrical Company (£1,600); Cardiff Writers' Circle (£1,400).
FINANCES *Financial year end* 31/12/2021
Income £8,010,000
Grants to organisations £2,390,000
Assets £460,200
TRUSTEES David Sharrod; Gareth Hill; Hannah Woods; Rahul Bissoonauth; John Robson.
OTHER INFORMATION During 2021, under the Community Grants Programme, 165 grants were awarded across the following categories: improving mental well-being (£613,400); supporting marginalised groups and promoting equality (£362,000); enabling community participation in the arts (£247,800); preventing or reducing the impact of poverty (£227,900); enabling participation in physical activity (£204,700); responding to the climate emergency and promoting sustainability (£137,000); increasing community access to outdoor space (£111,500); improving biodiversity and green spaces (£90,500).
HOW TO APPLY There are several funding rounds each year, with deadlines detailed on the trust's website alongside guidance and tips for submissions. Applications can be made using the trust's online form.
CONTACT DETAILS The Trustees, 28 Charlotte Square, Edinburgh EH2 4ET *Tel.* 0131 322 9399 *Email* info@postcodecommunitytrust.org. uk *Website* www.postcodecommunitytrust.org.uk

....

■ Postcode Local Trust

OSCR NO SC045504   **ESTABLISHED** 2015
WHERE FUNDING CAN BE GIVEN Western England.
WHO CAN BENEFIT Registered charities; constituted voluntary or community groups; CICs; CIOs; not-for-profit organisations; social enterprises.
WHAT IS FUNDED Mental well-being; participation in arts and sports; social welfare; supporting disadvantaged people; biodiversity and green space; the climate emergency and sustainability; access to the outdoors.
WHAT IS NOT FUNDED A comprehensive list of exclusions can be found on the trust's website.
TYPE OF GRANT Project funding; capital costs.
RANGE OF GRANTS From £500 to £25,000.
SAMPLE GRANTS Avon Needs Trees and Berkeley Educational Swimming Trust (£20,000 each); The Burrough Harmony Centre (£14,700); Action for ME (£10,900); The Dorchester Trust for Counselling and Psychotherapy (£5,000); Manor Park Sailing Club (£2,000); PCC of Holy Trinity Church, Barnstaple (£560).
FINANCES *Financial year end* 31/12/2021
Income £8,010,000
Grants to organisations £2,420,000
Assets £370,400
TRUSTEES David Sharrod; Gareth Hill; Hannah Woods; Rahul Bissoonauth; John Robson.
OTHER INFORMATION In 2021, the trust awarded 160 projects through its community fund.
HOW TO APPLY There are several funding rounds each year, with deadlines detailed on the trust's website alongside guidance and tips for

submissions. Applications are made using the trust's online form.

CONTACT DETAILS The Trustees, 28 Charlotte Square, Edinburgh EH2 4ET *Tel.* 0131 322 9388 *Email* info@postcodelocaltrust.org.uk *Website* www.postcodelocaltrust.org.uk

....

■ Postcode Society Trust

OSCR NO SC044911   **ESTABLISHED** 2014
WHERE FUNDING CAN BE GIVEN Southern England.
WHO CAN BENEFIT Registered charities; constituted community organisations such as CICs or CIOs; social enterprises; not-for-profit organisations.
WHAT IS FUNDED Mental well-being; participation in arts and sports; social welfare; supporting disadvantaged people; biodiversity and green space; the climate emergency and sustainability; access to the outdoors.
WHAT IS NOT FUNDED A comprehensive list of exclusions can be found on the trust's website and includes: individuals; statutory activities; nurseries, schools, colleges or universities; organisations with annual income over £1 million.
TYPE OF GRANT Project funding; core costs.
RANGE OF GRANTS £500 to £25,000.
SAMPLE GRANTS Exeter Science Centre (£25,000); Activating Creative Talent CIC (£24,200); Citizens Advice Mendip (£18,400); Guardian Ballers CIC (£16,400); Gympanzees (£13,000); Moonstruck Astronaut CIC (£10,900); Bristol Association for Neighbourhood Daycare (£5,000); Manor Park Sailing Club (£2,000).
FINANCES *Financial year end* 31/12/2021
Income £610,680,000
Grants to organisations £2,990,000
Assets £400,700
TRUSTEES Frank Fletcher; Miranda Wixon; Rita Chadha; Rob Flett.
OTHER INFORMATION This trust is funded by players of the People's Postcode Lottery. The list of beneficiaries above includes grants awarded in 2022 from the Community Grants Programme, taken from the trust's website.
HOW TO APPLY There are several funding rounds each year, with deadlines detailed on the trust's website alongside guidance and tips for submissions. Applications are made using the trust's online form.
CONTACT DETAILS The Trustees, 28 Charlotte Square, Edinburgh EH2 4ET *Tel.* 0131 322 9430 *Email* info@postcodesocietytrust.org.uk *Website* www.postcodesocietytrust.org.uk

....

■ The Mary Potter Convent Hospital Trust

CC NO 1078525   **ESTABLISHED** 1999
WHERE FUNDING CAN BE GIVEN Nottinghamshire.
WHO CAN BENEFIT Charitable organisations; CICs; social enterprises; schools; universities; hospitals; hospices; PTAs; religious bodies/institutions; local authorities; individuals.
WHAT IS FUNDED Medical causes and health care.
TYPE OF GRANT Capital costs; core and revenue costs; seed funding; start-up funding; project funding.
RANGE OF GRANTS Up to £10,000.
SAMPLE GRANTS Lifelites (£7,000); Macmillan Charity Trust (£5,000); Maggie's (£4,000).

FINANCES *Financial year end* 30/06/2022
Income £171,300
Grants to organisations £84,600
Grants to individuals £66,500
Assets £3,630,000
TRUSTEES Mervyn Jones; Martin Witherspoon; Sr Jeannette Connell; Shaun Finn; Aidan Goulding; Godfrey Archer; Margaret Hollingworth; Simon Clunie.
OTHER INFORMATION The trust awarded 67 grants in 2021/22.
HOW TO APPLY Apply in writing to the correspondent.
CONTACT DETAILS Martin Witherspoon, Trustee, c/o Massers Solicitors, Rossell House, Tudor Square, West Bridgford, Nottingham, Nottinghamshire NG2 6BT *Tel.* 0115 851 1603 *Email* martinw@massers.co.uk

....

■ David and Elaine Potter Foundation

CC NO 1078217   **ESTABLISHED** 1999
WHERE FUNDING CAN BE GIVEN UK and South Africa.
WHO CAN BENEFIT Registered charities; universities.
WHAT IS FUNDED Education; civil society; social research; the arts.
WHAT IS NOT FUNDED Individuals; CICs; retrospective costs; full economic costs for universities; political organisations; clinical trials; religious organisations that work only for the benefit of members of their own religion; non-profit companies; capital works; building or rebuilding schools; individual schools or school projects; school equipment; scaling-up projects; bursaries for individuals; civic education/citizenship education programmes.
TYPE OF GRANT Core/revenue costs; project funding; unrestricted funding; pilot funding.
RANGE OF GRANTS £5,000 to £100,000.
SAMPLE GRANTS IntoUniversity, Nuffield College University of Oxford and Trust for the Bureau of Investigative Journalism (£100,000 each); Philharmonia and Transparency International UK (£50,000 each); Death Penalty Project and Spotlight on Corruption (£35,000 each); Almeida Theatre (£10,000).
FINANCES *Financial year end* 31/12/2021
Income £271,200
Grants to organisations £794,100
Assets £16,580,000
TRUSTEES Michael Langley; Dr Elaine Potter; Dr David Potter; Samuel Potter; Michael Polonsky.
OTHER INFORMATION In 2021 the foundation awarded grants to 16 organisations.
HOW TO APPLY Applications are by invitation only: unsolicited applications are not accepted. The website notes that organisations that believe their work may align with the foundation's should contact the foundation by email to discuss their potential eligibility.
CONTACT DETAILS Ben Stewart, Director, 6 Hamilton Close, London NW8 8QY *Tel.* 020 3915 9283 *Email* info@potterfoundation.com *Website* www.potterfoundation.com

....

■ The Potton Consolidated Charity

CC NO 201073   **ESTABLISHED** 1964
WHERE FUNDING CAN BE GIVEN The parish of Potton.
WHO CAN BENEFIT Charitable organisations; schools; individuals.
WHAT IS FUNDED Projects that further the religious and other charitable work of the Church of England in Potton; maintenance and upkeep of

communal buildings/recreation areas; general charitable purposes for the residents of Potton.
TYPE OF GRANT Capital costs; project funding.
RANGE OF GRANTS Mostly up to £10,000.
SAMPLE GRANTS Potton Tennis Club (£47,500); Bedfordshire Rural Communities Charity (£22,400); Potton Jubilee Project (£12,000); Potton Lower School (£10,000); Sue Ryder Care (£7,300).
FINANCES *Financial year end 31/03/2022*
Income £161,900
Grants to organisations £150,800
Grants to individuals £26,600
Assets £5,930,000
TRUSTEES Charles Belcher; Alan Leggatt; Andre Allison; Michael O'Keefe; Angus MacDonald; Anna Adnitt; George Howe; Terry Woods; The Revd Alex Wheatley.
HOW TO APPLY Apply in writing to the correspondent.
CONTACT DETAILS Dean Howard, Clerk, 69 Stotfold Road, Arlesey, Bedfordshire SG15 6XR *Tel.* 01462 735220 *Email* clerk@potton-consolidated-charity.co.uk *Website* www.potton-consolidated-charity.co.uk

■ Poundland Foundation

CC NO 1194291   **ESTABLISHED** 2021
WHERE FUNDING CAN BE GIVEN UK.
WHO CAN BENEFIT Registered charities; constituted groups or clubs; CICs.
WHAT IS FUNDED Community projects; children's sports.
SAMPLE GRANTS A list of beneficiaries was not available.
FINANCES
Grants to organisations £300,000
TRUSTEES Simon Wells; Mark Pym; Roger Wendt; Ben Jenner; Olivia McLoughlin; Sharon Jackson; Laura Yonish; Mark Woodruff; Krista Wright; Helen Walker; Lee Renshaw.
OTHER INFORMATION The foundation was registered with the Charity Commission in April 2021; therefore, full financial information was not available at the time of writing (June 2023). The foundation's website states: 'Since our launch in May 2021 we've awarded £300,000 to over 430 local kids' sports clubs across the UK'.
HOW TO APPLY Apply via the foundation's website.
CONTACT DETAILS The Trustees, Poundland CSC, Midland Road, Walsall, Walsall South WS1 3TX *Tel.* 0121 568 7000 *Email* foundation@poundland.co.uk *Website* https://poundlandfoundation.org.uk

■ Premierquote Ltd

CC NO 801957   **ESTABLISHED** 1985
WHERE FUNDING CAN BE GIVEN UK.
WHO CAN BENEFIT Jewish organisations; schools.
WHAT IS FUNDED The advancement of the Orthodox Jewish faith; the relief of poverty.
SAMPLE GRANTS A list of beneficiaries was not included in the latest annual report and accounts.
FINANCES *Financial year end 30/09/2021*
Income £1,010,000
Grants to organisations £700,000
Assets £11,110,000
TRUSTEES Henry Last; Morris Wiesenfeld.
OTHER INFORMATION The 2020/21 accounts were the most recent available on the Charity Commission's website at the time of writing (May 2023).
HOW TO APPLY Apply in writing to the correspondent.

CONTACT DETAILS Henry Last, Trustee, 18 Green Walk, London NW4 2AJ *Tel.* 020 8203 0665

■ The Pret Foundation

CC NO 1050195   **ESTABLISHED** 1995
WHERE FUNDING CAN BE GIVEN UK, in communities local to Pret shops.
WHO CAN BENEFIT Registered charities.
WHAT IS FUNDED Homelessness; social welfare; food poverty; education, training and employment.
TYPE OF GRANT Project costs; pay for support workers, rent, course supplies, counselling and drop-in centres.
RANGE OF GRANTS Up to £20,000.
SAMPLE GRANTS The 999 Club, Genisis Trust, InHope, Off the Fence Trust and Shelter from the Storm (£10,000 each); Salford Loaves and Fishes (£9,400); Street Connect (£7,000).
FINANCES *Financial year end 31/12/2021*
Income £803,000
Grants to organisations £190,000
Assets £1,370,000
TRUSTEES Clive Schlee; Andrea Wareham; Pano Christou; Valerie Cuminet; Dilys Winterkorn; Dulcie McDermott.
OTHER INFORMATION Only organisations that received grants of over £5,000 were listed as beneficiaries in the charity's accounts. Grants of under £5,000 totalled £3,800 and were awarded to four organisations.
HOW TO APPLY Apply in writing to the correspondent.
CONTACT DETAILS The Trustees, 10 Bressenden Place, London SW1E 5DH *Tel.* 07584 213354 *Email* pret.foundationuk@pret.com *Website* www.pret.co.uk/en-GB/the-pret-foundation

■ The William Price Charitable Trust

CC NO 307319
WHERE FUNDING CAN BE GIVEN Hampshire, with a preference for Fareham.
WHO CAN BENEFIT Charitable organisations and individuals under 25.
WHAT IS FUNDED Education and training; the prevention or relief of poverty; religious activities; arts/culture/heritage/science; amateur sport.
RANGE OF GRANTS £1,000 to £30,000.
SAMPLE GRANTS Fareham College (£32,500); St Columba CofE Primary Academy (£24,000); Orchard Lee Junior (£20,000); Wallisdean Infant (£13,800); Wicor Primary (£10,000); St Peter and St Paul Church (£5,000); Harrison Primary (£4,100); Wallisdean Junior (£1,600).
FINANCES *Financial year end 31/03/2022*
Income £171,100
Grants to organisations £295,500
Grants to individuals £31,800
Assets £8,220,000
TRUSTEES Derek Marlow; David Foot; Louise Clubley; Lucy Docherty; William Price Trust Company; Nicholas Groves; Peter Latham; Neale Fray; David Luckett; Sara Heaysman; Margaret Chappell; Tina Ellis; Timothy Geoghegan; Bruce Deans; Rodger Jackson; Phillip Reynolds; Pamela Bryant; Donna Irving; Anne Butcher.
HOW TO APPLY Apply in writing to the correspondent.
CONTACT DETAILS Christopher Thomas, Clerk, 8 Earl Godwin Close, Fareham, Hampshire PO16 0DW *Tel.* 01329 829602 *Email* ClerkWPT1721@gmail.com

■ Sir John Priestman Charity Trust

CC NO 209397 **ESTABLISHED** 1931

WHERE FUNDING CAN BE GIVEN Sunderland; County Durham; churches in the county of York.

WHO CAN BENEFIT Charitable organisations; churches; schools.

WHAT IS FUNDED Social welfare; older people; education; hospitals and convalescent homes; nurses; social welfare; upkeep of Church of England institutions, including the purchase of organs.

TYPE OF GRANT Project costs; equipment and building costs.

RANGE OF GRANTS Up to £15,000.

SAMPLE GRANTS St Leonard's Parish Church – Loftus-in-Cleveland and Middleton Tyas Parish Church Committee (£10,000 each); Durham Association of Boys and Girls Clubs (£7,500); Young Women's Trust (£5,000); Calverley Parish Church (£3,000); Willow (£1,000).

FINANCES *Financial year end* 31/12/2021
Income £550,100
Grants to organisations £390,300
Assets £16,550,000

TRUSTEES Peter Taylor; Timothy Norton; Thomas Greenwell; Jean Majer; Frank Nicholson.

OTHER INFORMATION Only in special circumstances are grants awarded outside the specified geographical area or to individuals. A number of charities are supported by way of annual grants.

HOW TO APPLY Apply in writing to the correspondent. The trustees meet on a quarterly basis to consider applications and award grants.

CONTACT DETAILS The Trustees, 47 John Street, Sunderland, Tyne and Wear SR1 1QU *Tel.* 0191 567 4857

■ The Primrose Trust

CC NO 800049 **ESTABLISHED** 1986

WHERE FUNDING CAN BE GIVEN UK.

WHO CAN BENEFIT Registered charities.

WHAT IS FUNDED General charitable purposes, with a strong preference for animal welfare.

TYPE OF GRANT Core costs; capital costs; project funding.

RANGE OF GRANTS £5,000 to £35,000.

SAMPLE GRANTS Free the Bears (£35,000); Animals Asia (£30,000); British Hen Welfare Trust (£15,000); Goatacre Farm for Animal Health and Welfare (£5,000).

FINANCES *Financial year end* 05/04/2021
Income £131,800
Grants to organisations £110,000
Assets £5,180,000

TRUSTEES Susan Boyes-Korkis; Malcolm Clark.

OTHER INFORMATION The 2020/21 accounts were the latest available at the time of writing (May 2023).

HOW TO APPLY Apply in writing and send your application to the registered office. The trustees meet annually to consider applications.

CONTACT DETAILS The Trustees, c/o Deloitte LLP, 5 Callaghan Square, Cardiff CF10 5BT *Tel.* 029 2026 4257 *Email* lham@deloitte.co.uk

■ The Prince of Wales's Charitable Foundation

CC NO 1127255 **ESTABLISHED** 1979

WHERE FUNDING CAN BE GIVEN UK.

WHO CAN BENEFIT UK-registered not-for-profit organisations that have been active for at least two years.

WHAT IS FUNDED Heritage and conservation; education; health and well-being; social inclusion; the environment; the countryside.

WHAT IS NOT FUNDED Individuals; public bodies; organisations that mainly distribute grants to other organisations; organisations that are looking to support similar projects delivered by the Prince of Wales's core charities (Prince's Foundation and The Prince's Trust); organisations with political associations or interests; capital expenditure with the exception of community-based heritage conservation and restoration projects.

TYPE OF GRANT Core costs; project funding; strategic funding.

RANGE OF GRANTS Small grants of up to £5,000 per year.

SAMPLE GRANTS A list of beneficiaries was not included in the annual report and accounts. Previous beneficiaries have included: Erskine Hospital; In Kind Direct; PIPS Suicide Prevention; Soil Association; Trees for Cities; Woodland Heritage.

FINANCES *Financial year end* 31/03/2022
Income £10,390,000
Grants to organisations £5,000,000
Assets £11,760,000

TRUSTEES Dame Julie Moore; Sir Ian Cheshire; Dame Louise Casey; Kristin Rechberger; The Hon. Sarah Butler-Sloss; Sir Kenneth Olisa.

HOW TO APPLY For the small grants programme, an online application form and further guidance is available from the foundation's website. Applications to the major grants and Strategic grant programmes are by invitation only.

CONTACT DETAILS Small Grants Committee, 3 Orchard Place, Broadway, London SW1E 5RS *Email* use the contact form on the website *Website* www.pwcf.org.uk

■ The Prince's Countryside Fund

CC NO 1136077 **ESTABLISHED** 2010

WHERE FUNDING CAN BE GIVEN UK.

WHO CAN BENEFIT Community organisations; charities; CIC's; community benefit societies; not-for-profit organisations; companies limited by guarantee; social enterprises; unincorporated associations.

WHAT IS FUNDED Projects that support the sustainability of British farming rural communities and the countryside.

TYPE OF GRANT Project and resource funding; capital costs (equipment); core costs.

RANGE OF GRANTS Up to £50,000.

SAMPLE GRANTS Grizedale Arts (£25,000); Hollesley Village Hall and Ropley Village Shop CIC (£10,000 each); Raasay Development Trust (£8,800); The Square Shop (£3,000).

FINANCES *Financial year end* 31/03/2022
Income £2,380,000
Grants to organisations £439,800
Assets £1,770,000

TRUSTEES Edwin Booth; Elizabeth Buchanan; Mark Duddridge; John Wilkinson; Rob Collins; Lord Jamie Lindsay; Edward Fursdon; Meurig Raymond; Janet McCollum; Heather Hancock; Baroness Kate Rock; Steven Murrells.

HOW TO APPLY Applications should be made online through the charity's website. Check the website for updates on when the next funding round will open.

CONTACT DETAILS The Trustees, 13th Floor, 33 Cavendish Square, London W1G 0PW *Email* grants@countrysidefund.org.uk *Website* www.princescountrysidefund.org.uk

■ The Princess Anne's Charities

CC NO 277814   ESTABLISHED 1979
WHERE FUNDING CAN BE GIVEN UK.
WHO CAN BENEFIT Registered charities.
WHAT IS FUNDED Social welfare; medical causes; the armed forces; children and young people; the environment and wildlife.
WHAT IS NOT FUNDED Individuals.
SAMPLE GRANTS A list of beneficiaries was not included in the annual report and accounts. Previous beneficiaries have included: Butler Trust, Canal Museum Trust, Cranfield Trust, Dogs Trust, Dorothy House Foundation, Durrell Wildlife Conservation Trust, Evelina Children's Hospital Appeal, Farms for City Children, Farrer and Co. Charitable Trust, Fire Services National Benevolent Fund, Home Farm Trust, Intensive Care Society and International League for the Protection of Horses.
FINANCES *Financial year end 05/04/2022*
Income £229,000
Grants to organisations £325,500
Assets £8,320,000
TRUSTEES Vice-Admiral Sir Tim Laurence; Sally Tennant; Christopher Morgan; Julian Smith.
OTHER INFORMATION Grants were made to 57 organisations during 2021/22. Grants were distributed within the following categories: social welfare (£152,200); children and young people (£74,000); medical causes (£44,300); the armed forces (£29,000); the environment and wildlife (£26,000).
HOW TO APPLY Apply in writing to the correspondent. Applications are considered by the trustees at their meetings.
CONTACT DETAILS The Trustees, c/o Farrer and Co. LLP, 66 Lincoln's Inn Fields, London WC2A 3LH *Tel.* 020 7024 4199 *Email* charles.davies@ royal.uk

■ The Priory Foundation

CC NO 295919   ESTABLISHED 1986
WHERE FUNDING CAN BE GIVEN UK and overseas. In the UK, preference is given to Essex and Hertfordshire.
WHO CAN BENEFIT Registered charities; individuals; schools; amateur sports clubs.
WHAT IS FUNDED General charitable purposes, in particular: sport; mental health; education; overseas relief.
RANGE OF GRANTS Generally between £1,000 and £20,000.
SAMPLE GRANTS Saracens Sport Foundation (£158,500); Woodlarks Camp Site Trust (£21,000); Cancer Council Western Australia (£10,000); Tennis Swansea (£7,500); Harrogate Grammar School (£4,500); The Kidney Fund (£1,200).
FINANCES *Financial year end 31/12/2021*
Income £170,000
Grants to organisations £275,600
Assets £4,000,000
TRUSTEES David Poutney; Nigel Wray; Lucy Mercey; Gordon Banks.
OTHER INFORMATION During 2021, grants were made to 11 organisations.
HOW TO APPLY Apply in writing to the correspondent. Details of the eligibility criteria can be obtained by contacting the foundation.
CONTACT DETAILS The Trustees, Flat 3, Grace Court, Totteridge Green, London N20 8PY *Tel.* 020 8445 7012

■ Prison Service Charity Fund

CC NO 1189519   ESTABLISHED 1989
WHERE FUNDING CAN BE GIVEN UK.
WHO CAN BENEFIT Charitable organisations; individuals. Applications must be sponsored by Prison Service staff who are also fundraising for the cause.
WHAT IS FUNDED Social welfare, medical treatment and equipment.
WHAT IS NOT FUNDED Organisations or individuals outside the UK.
TYPE OF GRANT One-off.
RANGE OF GRANTS Typically up to £2,000.
SAMPLE GRANTS Paul Keats Appeal (£2,500); Gemma Walker Appeal (£2,000); The Queens Centre (£1,200); Different Strokes (£780); Treetops Hospice Whatton (£500); Dementia UK (£450); Ronald Macdonald House (£250); Daft as a Brush Cancer Patient Care (£50).
FINANCES *Financial year end 31/12/2021*
Income £172,400
Grants to organisations £118,700
Assets £1,090,000
TRUSTEES Kenneth Wingfield; Victoria Sampey; Sara Musker; Emily Boardman; Philip Boardman; John White; Denise Bolton.
OTHER INFORMATION In 2021, the charity supported 198 appeals.
HOW TO APPLY Applicants must be a member of the Prison Service staff. For more information, contact the correspondent.
CONTACT DETAILS The Trustees, HM Prison, 68 Hornby Road, Liverpool, Merseyside L9 3DF *Tel.* 0151 530 4000 *Website* www. prisonservicecharityfund.co.uk

■ The Privy Purse Charitable Trust

CC NO 296079   ESTABLISHED 1987
WHERE FUNDING CAN BE GIVEN UK and overseas.
WHO CAN BENEFIT Charities of which the monarch is a patron; ecclesiastical organisations associated with the monarch.
WHAT IS FUNDED General charitable purposes; ecclesiastical causes; national and international disasters.
TYPE OF GRANT Core costs.
RANGE OF GRANTS Up to £162,000.
SAMPLE GRANTS City of London School – Choristers (£162,000); Sandringham Group of Parishes (£61,100); Chapel Royal – Hampton Court Palace (£52,100); Game and Wildlife Conservation Trust (£35,500); Chapel Royal – Windsor Great Park (£22,800).
FINANCES *Financial year end 31/03/2022*
Income £177,700
Grants to organisations £659,900
Assets £5,200,000
TRUSTEES Sir Michael Stevens; Sir Edward Young; Jane Graham.
OTHER INFORMATION The trust awarded grants to organisations within the following categories: ecclesiastical (£209,200); education (£226,800); other (£224,000). Only organisations that received grants of over £20,000 were listed as beneficiaries in the trust's accounts. The trust awards an annual grant to St James's Palace Chapel Royal Choir.
HOW TO APPLY The trust does not accept unsolicited applications.
CONTACT DETAILS The Trustees, Buckingham Palace, London SW1A 1AA *Tel.* 020 7930 4832 *Email* mike.stevens@royal.uk

■ The Progress Foundation

CC NO 1123219   **ESTABLISHED** 2008
WHERE FUNDING CAN BE GIVEN UK, with a strong preference for Greater London.
WHO CAN BENEFIT Registered charities; voluntary organisations; social enterprises.
WHAT IS FUNDED Young people (normally those aged 14–21) who are not in employment, education or training (NEET), or who are at risk of becoming so.
WHAT IS NOT FUNDED Individuals; organisations that promote a particular religious belief, unless the work is not for religious purposes and meets the foundation's funding guidelines; medical organisations; replacing or subsidising statutory funding.
TYPE OF GRANT Project funding; core costs; development funding.
RANGE OF GRANTS Up to £25,000 but typically between £10,000 and £15,000. Larger grants may be made; however, these grants are not open to applications.
SAMPLE GRANTS Envision (£68,000); Future Frontiers (£45,000); Art Against Knives (£20,000); Getting into Tech (£15,000); Goldsmiths College (£10,000); New Horizons (£8,300); Stamma (£4,000); Felix Project (£3,000).
FINANCES *Financial year end 31/03/2022*
Income £76,200
Grants to organisations £236,000
Assets £2,420,000
TRUSTEES Roger Pilgrim; Nadine Majaro; Nigel Hamway.
OTHER INFORMATION The foundation states that it typically supports up to five new projects or organisations each year. During 2021/22, grants were made to 12 organisations. A total of £216,000 was awarded through the main grants programme, the remaining £20,000 was awarded as a core funding unrestricted grant.
HOW TO APPLY Application forms and details of application deadlines are available on the foundation's website. The trustees meet three times a year to consider grants, usually in March, May and September. Applications made outside the set times will not be accepted.
CONTACT DETAILS The Trustees, c/o New Quadrant Partners Ltd, 5 Chancery Lane, London WC2A 1LG *Tel.* 020 7431 6608 *Email* use the contact form on the website *Website* www.progressuk.org

■ Prostate Cancer UK

CC NO 1005541   **ESTABLISHED** 1991
WHERE FUNDING CAN BE GIVEN UK.
WHO CAN BENEFIT Universities; NHS sites; research institutions.
WHAT IS FUNDED Prostate cancer research; education; training; campaigning.
TYPE OF GRANT Research; project funding.
SAMPLE GRANTS University of Manchester (£546,000); Queen's University (£280,000); The Institute of Cancer Research (£130,000).
FINANCES *Financial year end 31/03/2022*
Income £35,210,000
Grants to organisations £958,000
Assets £36,340,000
TRUSTEES Prof. David Neal; Lynne Robb; Simon Peck; Cristian Cussen; Samia Qadhi; Henry Obi; Kenneth Towle; Prof. Richard Neal; Dr Nicholas Hicks; Prof. Paul Stewart; Caroline Artis; Michael McGrath; Jennifer Liebenberg; Doris Olulode.
OTHER INFORMATION Grants were made to three organisations. The charity's research strategy focuses on three key areas: better treatment, better diagnosis and smarter data.
HOW TO APPLY Applications can be made online using the charity's grant management system. Each grants programme has its own guidelines and deadline dates; applicants should check the charity's helpful website for further information.
CONTACT DETAILS The Research Team, 4th Floor, The Counting House, 53 Tooley Street, London SE1 2QN *Email* info@prostatecanceruk.org *Website* www.prostatecanceruk.org

■ Provincial Grand Charity of the Province of Derbyshire

CC NO 701963   **ESTABLISHED** 1989
WHERE FUNDING CAN BE GIVEN Derbyshire.
WHO CAN BENEFIT Charitable organisations; Masons and their dependants; hospices; individuals.
WHAT IS FUNDED General charitable purposes including: health; disability; community projects; social welfare; children and young people.
SAMPLE GRANTS A list of beneficiaries was not included in the annual report and accounts.
FINANCES *Financial year end 30/06/2022*
Income £120,200
Grants to organisations £83,600
Assets £1,470,000
TRUSTEES Graham Sisson; Arthur Varley; John Acton.
OTHER INFORMATION Note that the grant total may include amounts awarded to individuals.
HOW TO APPLY Apply in writing to the correspondent.
CONTACT DETAILS The Secretary, Derby Masonic Hall, 457 Burton Road, Littleover, Derby, Derbyshire DE23 6XX *Tel.* 01332 272202 *Email* secretary@derbyshiremason.org *Website* www.derbyshiremason.org

■ The Prudence Trust

CC NO 1187700
WHERE FUNDING CAN BE GIVEN UK.
WHO CAN BENEFIT UK-registered or exempt charities.
WHAT IS FUNDED The mental health and well-being of disadvantaged young people aged between 11 and 25.
TYPE OF GRANT Programme costs; salaries; equipment; core costs.
RANGE OF GRANTS £30,000 to £50,000.
SAMPLE GRANTS Place2Be (£152,000); The Prince's Trust (£146,900); Sustainable Food Trust (£100,000); Core Arts (£90,000); Ebony Horse Club (£16,000); Roundhouse Trust (£15,000).
FINANCES *Financial year end 31/12/2021*
Income £49,490,000
Grants to organisations £3,950,000
Assets £190,250,000
TRUSTEE The Prudence Trust Company Ltd.
OTHER INFORMATION During 2021, grants were distributed as follows: mental health research (£1.6 million); mental health (£1.2 million); arts (£853,700); general (£200,000); disadvantaged people (£93,000).
HOW TO APPLY Contact the foundation for more information.
CONTACT DETAILS The Trustees, 16 Berkeley Street, London W1J 8DZ *Email* hello@theprudencetrust.org *Website* https://theprudencetrust.org

■ The Puebla Charitable Trust

CC NO 290055   ESTABLISHED 1984
WHERE FUNDING CAN BE GIVEN Worldwide.
WHO CAN BENEFIT Charitable organisations.
WHAT IS FUNDED Community development initiatives; social welfare.
WHAT IS NOT FUNDED Individuals.
TYPE OF GRANT Up to three years.
RANGE OF GRANTS Up to £30,000.
SAMPLE GRANTS A list of beneficiaries was not included in the annual report and accounts. Previous beneficiaries have included: Survivors Fund (£30,000); South West London Law Centres (£20,000); Hamlin Fistula (£7,500).
FINANCES *Financial year end 05/04/2022*
Income £86,600
Grants to organisations £3,100
Assets £3,090,000
TRUSTEES Justin Phipps; Martin Penrose; John Moore.
OTHER INFORMATION A total of £3,100 was awarded in 2021/22; however, the trust's accounts state: 'Grants totalling £142,500 were approved to five charities during the previous year. Of the total grants awarded, four of the grants are payable in equal instalments over a period of 3 years. The second instalment of these grants were paid during the current year and the final instalments are due in the next financial year.'
HOW TO APPLY Apply in writing to the correspondent.
CONTACT DETAILS John Moore, Trustee, 18 Hyde Gardens, Cardinal House, Eastbourne, East Sussex BN21 4PT *Tel.* 01323 431200 *Email* Puebla@p-p.uk

■ The Purey Cust Trust CIO

CC NO 1159079   ESTABLISHED 1950
WHERE FUNDING CAN BE GIVEN York.
WHO CAN BENEFIT Registered charities; organisations; individuals (only through third-party organisations). CICs are only supported in exceptional circumstances.
WHAT IS FUNDED Health; disability; mental health and well-being; health education; medical equipment.
WHAT IS NOT FUNDED Core costs; building projects.
TYPE OF GRANT One-off; equipment; service provision.
RANGE OF GRANTS Up to £10,000.
SAMPLE GRANTS St Leonard's Hospice (£10,000); National Axial Spondyloarthritis Society (£4,300); Teenage Cancer Trust (£3,000); York Women's Counselling (£2,500); York Bike Belles (£1,500); Lord Deramore's School (£1,000).
FINANCES *Financial year end 05/04/2022*
Income £72,500
Grants to organisations £100,300
Grants to individuals £23,700
Assets £2,970,000
TRUSTEES Dr David Heseltine; Geraldine Casswell; Dr John Hamilton; Phillip Bodmer; Michael Green; Marcella Sykes; Dr Michael Cust; Antonia Moore.
OTHER INFORMATION Grants were made to 25 organisations.
HOW TO APPLY Application can be made online or by downloading an application form and returning by post.
CONTACT DETAILS Trust Secretary, c/o Construction House, James Nicolson Link, Monks Cross, York, North Yorkshire YO30 4GR *Email* pureycusttrust@btinternet.com *Website* www.pureycusttrust.org.uk

■ The PwC Foundation

CC NO 1144124   ESTABLISHED 2011
WHERE FUNDING CAN BE GIVEN UK.
WHO CAN BENEFIT Registered charities; CICs; social enterprises.
WHAT IS FUNDED Social inclusion through employability and education; mental health and health care; the environment; general charitable purposes.
WHAT IS NOT FUNDED Political organisations; lobbying groups; animal rights groups; religious bodies.
RANGE OF GRANTS Typically £10,000 to £90,000.
SAMPLE GRANTS The British Red Cross Society (£385,700); Hospice UK (£178,200); Tech She Can (£100,000); The Sutton Trust (£10,000); Scottish Association for Mental Health (£8,200).
FINANCES *Financial year end 30/06/2022*
Income £2,410,000
Grants to organisations £2,580,000
Assets £3,300,000
TRUSTEES Kevin Ellis; David Adair; Zelf Hussain; Kalee Talvitie-Brown; David Walters; Emma Cox.
OTHER INFORMATION The PwC Foundation is the corporate charity of PricewaterhouseCoopers LLP (PwC). As well as grants, it also provides matched funding to support the charitable activities of PwC employees. Grants were broken down as follows: social mobility (£1.17 million); environmental and other charitable activities (£730,000); health care (£384,300); education (£164,900); matched funding (£123,700). The foundation made 564 grants during the year.
HOW TO APPLY The foundation's 2021 accounts state: 'there is no current requirement for a formal open grant application process. The Steering Committee and trustees can independently identify recipients for funding who meet the charitable objectives of the Foundation. Recipients are approved by the trustees.'
CONTACT DETAILS Community Engagement Team, PriceWaterhouseCoopers, 1 Embankment Place, London WC2N 6RH *Tel.* 07764 902846 *Email* uk_pwcfoundation@pwc.com *Website* www.pwc.co.uk/corporate-sustainability/the-pwc-foundation.jhtml

■ The Pye Foundation

CC NO 267851   ESTABLISHED 1974
WHERE FUNDING CAN BE GIVEN Cambridgeshire and the immediate surrounding area.
WHO CAN BENEFIT Registered charities and retired employees of the former Pye/Phillips group of companies.
WHAT IS FUNDED Social welfare.
WHAT IS NOT FUNDED Animal welfare; ecclesiastical buildings; faith-enhancing projects; independent schools and international projects.
RANGE OF GRANTS Mostly £1,000 to £6,000.
SAMPLE GRANTS The PYE Association (£26,500); Alzheimer's Society – Cambridge (£5,500); Care Network (£4,000); St Columba Foundation (£1,500); Happy Days (£3,000); Cambridge Talking News (£1,500).
FINANCES *Financial year end 31/03/2022*
Income £69,000
Grants to organisations £186,500
Grants to individuals £8,800
Assets £3,090,000
TRUSTEES Bob Bates; Roger Crabtree; John Hemming; Richard McMullan; Rick Mitchell; Douglas Irish; Dr Anil Chhabra; Dr Michael

Wassall; Rachel Hayden; Hilary Seaward; Linda Sinclair; Caroline Revitt.

OTHER INFORMATION Grants were broken down as follows: annual grants (£171,500); one-off grants (£10,000); welfare grants to individuals (£8,800); Pye History Trust (£5,000).

HOW TO APPLY Application forms can be downloaded from the foundation's website.

CONTACT DETAILS Rasik Kotecha, 70 Bishops Road, Trumpington, Cambridge, Cambridgeshire CB2 9NH *Email* pyefoundationcamb@gmail.com *Website* www.pye-foundation.org/home

■ Mr and Mrs J. A. Pye's Charitable Settlement

CC NO 242677   **ESTABLISHED** 1965

WHERE FUNDING CAN BE GIVEN Oxfordshire.

WHO CAN BENEFIT Registered charities.

WHAT IS FUNDED General charitable purposes including: education; the environment; social welfare.

WHAT IS NOT FUNDED Individuals; non-recognised charities; animal welfare; the promotion of religion.

RANGE OF GRANTS Generally up to £10,000.

SAMPLE GRANTS Music At Oxford (£100,000); Magdalen College School (£30,000); Style Acre (£10,000); SeeSaw (£5,000); Pusey House (£2,500); Lifelites (£1,000).

FINANCES *Financial year end* 31/12/2021
Income £616,100
Grants to organisations £452,100
Assets £15,210,000

TRUSTEES Patrick Mulcare; Graham Flint; Valerie Buzzard.

OTHER INFORMATION Grants were made to 108 organisations.

HOW TO APPLY All applications should be sent to the administrative office. The charity does not have an application form, but details on the information required is available on its website.

CONTACT DETAILS Lucy McCallum-Toppin, Grants Manager, Springfield, Farringdon Road, Southmoor, Oxfordshire OX13 5BG *Email* pyecharitablesettlement@gmail.com *Website* www.pyecharitablesettlement.org

■ Q Charitable Trust
cc no 1186920
WHERE FUNDING CAN BE GIVEN England and Wales.
WHO CAN BENEFIT Registered charities; universities.
WHAT IS FUNDED General charitable purposes.
RANGE OF GRANTS Typically £1,000 to £100,000.
SAMPLE GRANTS Alzheimer's Research (£3 million); Mull and Iona Community Trust (£140,000); Royal National Springboard (£50,000); Action for Kids Charitable Trust (£4,200); ActionAid (£1,000).
FINANCES *Financial year end 31/12/2021*
Income £666,600
Grants to organisations £3,920,000
Assets £38,530,000
TRUSTEES Ludlow Trust Company Ltd; Alexia Jane Quin; Jonathan Quin.
HOW TO APPLY Apply in writing to the correspondent.
CONTACT DETAILS The Trustees, c/o Ludlow Trust Co. Ltd, Tower Wharf, Cheese Lane, Bristol BS2 0JJ *Tel.* 0117 313 8200
Email charitabletrusts@ludlowtrust.com

■ QBE European Operations Foundation
cc no 1143828   **ESTABLISHED** 2011
WHERE FUNDING CAN BE GIVEN UK and Europe.
WHO CAN BENEFIT Registered charities.
WHAT IS FUNDED Health care; education; social welfare.
WHAT IS NOT FUNDED Non-registered charities; political, local authority, union-affiliated and religious organisations; schools and associated parent teacher organisations; animal welfare charities (not including those whose objectives are to support people); charities whose beneficiaries are predominantly outside the foundation's operating areas; salaries.
TYPE OF GRANT Project funding; one-off funding.
RANGE OF GRANTS Typically less than £10,000.
SAMPLE GRANTS Crisis UK (£149,400); Mind (£146,100); Ripple Suicide Prevention Charity (£50,400); Save the Children UK (£48,600); Alzheimer's Society (£33,000); Autism Parents Together (£14,200); Afghanistan and Central Asian Association and Against Violence and Abuse (£10,000 each); Youth Without Shelter (£6,900); Breast Cancer Now (£1,300); FareShare and Winston's Wish (£30 each).
FINANCES *Financial year end 31/12/2021*
Income £952,500
Grants to organisations £872,400
Assets £70,600
TRUSTEES Grant Clemence; Alexandra Smith; Benjamin McBean; Philippe Gueret; Naintara Agarwal; Catherine Davidson; Laura Dobbyn.
HOW TO APPLY At the time of writing (February 2023), the foundation was not accepting grant applications. See the foundation's website for the latest information.
CONTACT DETAILS Sophie Wraith-Lee, Foundation Adviser, QBE Insurance, 30 Fenchurch Street, London EC3M 3BD *Tel.* 01245 343253 *Email* sophie.wraith@uk.qbe.com *Website* https://qbeeurope.com/sustainability/qbe-foundation

■ Quartet Community Foundation
cc no 1080418   **ESTABLISHED** 1987
WHERE FUNDING CAN BE GIVEN Bristol, North Somerset, South Gloucestershire, Bath and North East Somerset.
WHO CAN BENEFIT Registered charities; unregistered charities; CICs; social enterprises; schools; PTAs; amateur sports clubs; hospices.
WHAT IS FUNDED General charitable purposes; community development; safety; homelessness; health; learning and education; arts, culture and heritage; the environment.
WHAT IS NOT FUNDED See the foundation's website for a list of exclusions.
TYPE OF GRANT Capital costs; core/revenue costs; seed funding/start-up costs; project funding.
SAMPLE GRANTS A list of beneficiaries can be found on the foundation's website.
FINANCES *Financial year end 31/03/2022*
Income £6,760,000
Grants to organisations £4,850,000
Assets £66,280,000
TRUSTEES Annie Kilvington; Ben Silvey; Christopher Johnson; Joanna Turner; Jonathon Baker; Susan Blatchford; Susan Mountstevens; Raj Kakar-Clayton; Nicholas Lee; Matthew Lee; Oliver Delany; Sheikh Abdulhamid.
OTHER INFORMATION This is one of the 47 UK community foundations, which distribute funding for a wide range of purposes. As with all community foundations, there are a number of donor-advised funds managed on behalf of individuals, families and charitable trusts. Grant schemes tend to change frequently – consult the foundation's website for details of current programmes and up-to-date deadlines.
HOW TO APPLY Applicants should refer to the foundation's website for details on how to apply to each grants programme.
CONTACT DETAILS Grants Team, Royal Oak House, Royal Oak Avenue, Bristol BS1 4GB *Tel.* 0117 989 7700 *Email* info@quartetcf.org.uk *Website* www.quartetcf.org.uk

■ The Queen Anne's Gate Foundation
cc no 1108903   **ESTABLISHED** 2005
WHERE FUNDING CAN BE GIVEN UK and Asia.
WHO CAN BENEFIT Registered charities.
WHAT IS FUNDED Education; health; rehabilitation. There is some preference for Christian organisations and those working with children and young people.
TYPE OF GRANT Multi-year grants for projects and service delivery.
RANGE OF GRANTS £5,000 to £25,000.
SAMPLE GRANTS Previous beneficiaries have included: English National Opera, Exeter Deaf Academy and Families for Children (£25,000 each); Horatio's Garden and Safelives (£20,000 each); The Two Moors Festival (£15,000); Christian Friends of Korea (£14,500); Churches Housing Action Trust and City of Exeter YMCA Community Projects (£10,000 each); Aanchal Women's Aid (£5,000).
FINANCES *Financial year end 30/04/2022*
Income £3,300
Grants to organisations £164,000
TRUSTEES Nicholas Allan; Jonathan Boyer; Deborah Fisher.
OTHER INFORMATION Full accounts were not available to view on the Charity Commission's website due to the foundation's low income. We have therefore estimated the grant total based on the foundation's total expenditure.

HOW TO APPLY Apply in writing to the correspondent. The trustees meet twice a year.

CONTACT DETAILS Deborah Fisher, Trustee, Unit 4 Hill Farm, Kirby Road, Kirby Bedon, Norwich, Norfolk NR14 7DU *Tel.* 01508 480100 *Email* info@fisherlegal.co.uk

■ Queen Mary's Roehampton Trust

CC NO 211715

WHERE FUNDING CAN BE GIVEN UK, Scotland and Wales.

WHO CAN BENEFIT Charitable organisations.

WHAT IS FUNDED The reception, accommodation, treatment or aftercare of ex-Service people who acquired disabilities during their service, their dependants, and medical or surgical research associated with this group.

TYPE OF GRANT Recurring and one-off; capital costs; core costs; project funding.

SAMPLE GRANTS Combat Stress and Poppy Factory (£30,000 each); Defence Medical Welfare Service and Royal British Legion's Industries (£25,000 each); RAF Association (£20,000); Broughton House (£15,000); Gurkha Welfare Trust (£14,000); Canine Partners (£8,100); Spinal Injuries Association (£7,500); Kart Force (£5,000); Queen Alexandra Hospital Trust (£4,000).

FINANCES *Financial year end 31/03/2022*
Income £491,500
Grants to organisations £477,100
Assets £15,030,000

TRUSTEES Col. Paul Cummings; Colin Green; James MacNamara; Sir Barry Thornton; Anne Child; Dr Rakesh Bhabutta; Miranda Thompson-Schwab; Heather Betts; Harvey Tilley; Air Cdre Barbara Cooper; Ian Nicoll; Alison Wyman; Benjamin Marshall.

HOW TO APPLY Apply in writing to the correspondent.

CONTACT DETAILS S. Rowland-Jones, Clerk to the Trustees, 2 Sovereign Close, Quidhampton, Salisbury, Wiltshire SP2 9ES *Tel.* 01722 501413 *Email* qmrt@hotmail.co.uk

■ The Quilter Foundation

CC NO 1175555 **ESTABLISHED** 2018

WHERE FUNDING CAN BE GIVEN UK and Isle of Man.

WHO CAN BENEFIT Registered charities; not-for-profit organisations.

WHAT IS FUNDED Young people's financial education and empowerment; sustainable employment; health and well-being support for young carers.

WHAT IS NOT FUNDED Political, religious or profit-making organisations.

SAMPLE GRANTS Carers Trust (£286,400); Local Community (£50,000); Safe New Futures (£7,700); Street League (£3,800); Crossroads Care (£3,700); Vivid Life (£1,200).

FINANCES *Financial year end 31/12/2021*
Income £521,900
Grants to organisations £362,700
Assets £9,750,000

TRUSTEES Philippa Back; Timothy Childe; Prof. Richard Breen; Tosin James-Odukoya; Stephen Gazard; Steven Levin.

HOW TO APPLY The foundation makes grants to selected charity partners. Contact the correspondent for further information.

CONTACT DETAILS The Trustees, c/o Quilter plc, Senator House, 85 Queen Victoria Street, London EC4V 4AB *Tel.* 020 7778 9614 *Email* responsiblebusiness@quilter.com *Website* www.quilter.com/responsible-business/the-quilter-foundation

■ Quintessentially Foundation

CC NO 1144584 **ESTABLISHED** 2008

WHERE FUNDING CAN BE GIVEN UK.

WHO CAN BENEFIT UK-registered charities.

WHAT IS FUNDED The education, health and welfare of disadvantaged children.

TYPE OF GRANT Project funding.

SAMPLE GRANTS The Childhood Trust (£114,900); Grief Encounter and Ruth Strauss Foundation (£81,900 each); The Felix Project (£6,500).

FINANCES *Financial year end 31/12/2021*
Income £1,060,000
Grants to organisations £290,900
Assets £420,300

TRUSTEES Dr Peter Crowther; Benjamin Elliot; Sebastian Lee; Emma McCarthy; Andrew Crawley; Rory Brooks.

OTHER INFORMATION The foundation partners with three to five charities per year, hosting events for their benefit. Often, these events are run in collaboration with the charity partner and the proceeds are awarded to the charity as a grant.

HOW TO APPLY Contact the correspondent for information on how to become a partner.

CONTACT DETAILS The Trustees, 29 Portland Place, London W1B 1QB *Tel.* 0845 388 7985 *Email* info@quintessentiallyfoundation.org *Website* www.quintessentiallyfoundation.org

■ Quothquan Trust

CC NO 1110647 **ESTABLISHED** 2004

WHERE FUNDING CAN BE GIVEN Birmingham and the surrounding area.

WHO CAN BENEFIT Christian organisations and individuals.

WHAT IS FUNDED Promotion of the Christian faith through specific projects and initiatives aimed at relieving poverty and sickness; the advancement of religious education.

WHAT IS NOT FUNDED Activities that are primarily the responsibility of central or local government or another responsible body; animal welfare; church buildings; the conservation and protection of wildlife and landscapes; expeditions and overseas trips; hospitals, hospices and health centres; individuals whose work is not well known to the trustees; large national charities; local projects run by large national charities; loans and business finance; medical research projects; overseas appeals; the promotion of any religion other than Christianity.

TYPE OF GRANT One-off project costs.

RANGE OF GRANTS £50 to £300.

SAMPLE GRANTS A list of beneficiaries was not included in the annual report and accounts.

FINANCES *Financial year end 31/12/2021*
Income £86,700
Grants to organisations £118,900
Grants to individuals £45,500
Assets £1,280,000

TRUSTEES Janet Gilmour; Susan Robinson.

OTHER INFORMATION In 2021 grants were awarded to 14 organisations and 24 individuals.

HOW TO APPLY Applications should be made in writing to the correspondent and should include a brief description of your organisation's activities, details of the project and its total cost, funds already raised and how you intend to raise the remaining funds, a copy of your organisation's latest accounts (including any associated or parent organisation) and any other supporting documentation. Applications by email are not accepted. Unsuccessful applicants are not notified and do not receive feedback or details – if you do not hear back within six months, you should assume that your application was unsuccessful. The trustees aim to consider applications on a quarterly basis.

CONTACT DETAILS Grant Applications Team, Dale Farm, Worcester Lane, Sutton Coldfield, West Midlands B75 5PR *Tel.* 0121 323 3236 *Website* www.quothquantrust.org.uk

606

Does the funder you have chosen match your needs? Haphazard applications waste postage and time

R. S. Charitable Trust

CC NO 1053660   **ESTABLISHED** 1996
WHERE FUNDING CAN BE GIVEN UK and Israel.
WHO CAN BENEFIT Registered Jewish charitable organisations.
WHAT IS FUNDED Jewish schools; education; social welfare, especially for Jewish people.
RANGE OF GRANTS Mostly up to £8,000 with the occasional larger grant.
SAMPLE GRANTS String of Pearls (£25,000); Mercaz Hatorah Belz Machnovka (£14,000); Friends of Galanta and Start Upright (£8,000 each); Rehabilitation Trust (£7,000); Manchester Yeshiva Kollel (£6,500); Beis Aharon Trust, Notzar Chesed and One Hart Lev Echod (£5,000 each).
FINANCES *Financial year end 05/04/2022*
Income £250,000
Grants to organisations £164,500
Assets £2,880,000
TRUSTEES Stuart Freudenberger; Harvey Freudenberger; Charles Margulies; Andre Freudenberger.
OTHER INFORMATION Only organisations that received grants of over £5,000 were listed as beneficiaries in the trust's 2021/22 accounts. Grants of under £5,000 totalled £39,500.
HOW TO APPLY Apply in writing to the correspondent.
CONTACT DETAILS The Trustees, 138 Stamford Hill, London N16 6QT *Tel.* 020 8455 6789

Rachel Charitable Trust

CC NO 276441   **ESTABLISHED** 1978
WHERE FUNDING CAN BE GIVEN Worldwide.
WHO CAN BENEFIT Charitable organisations. Our research suggests that the trust primarily funds Jewish organisations.
WHAT IS FUNDED General charitable purposes; the advancement of religion and religious education; the relief of poverty.
SAMPLE GRANTS The Kemach Foundation (£686,100).
FINANCES *Financial year end 30/06/2022*
Income £5,850,000
Grants to organisations £2,700,000
Assets £26,680,000
TRUSTEES Leo Noe; Susan Noe; Steven Noe; Simon Kanter.
OTHER INFORMATION Only organisations that received grants of over £300,000 were listed as beneficiaries in the charity's accounts. Grants of under £300,000 totalled £2.02 million. Grants were broken down as follows: education and training (£1.47 million); the prevention and relief of poverty (£624,600); other charitable purposes (£329,200); religious activities (£179,200); the advancement of health (£100,300).
HOW TO APPLY Apply in writing to the correspondent.
CONTACT DETAILS Robert Chalk, Charity Secretary, 30 Market Place, London W1W 8AP *Tel.* 020 7846 3036

The Racing Foundation

CC NO 1145297   **ESTABLISHED** 2011
WHERE FUNDING CAN BE GIVEN UK.
WHO CAN BENEFIT Registered, unregistered and exempt charities; charities regulated by another body including universities and higher education institutions; registered Industrial and Provident Societies; registered Friendly Societies.
WHAT IS FUNDED The welfare of members of the horseracing industry; education and training connected with the horseracing industry; racehorse and thoroughbred welfare; equine science research.
WHAT IS NOT FUNDED Work that does not benefit the horseracing and thoroughbred breeding industry in the UK; religious causes; fundraiser salaries; individuals or causes which will benefit only one person; gambling addiction work (unless it specifically focuses on participants within the horseracing and thoroughbred industry); retrospective costs.
TYPE OF GRANT Project costs; core costs; capital projects; research grants. Multi-year grants, usually up to three years, are considered.
RANGE OF GRANTS Programme dependent.
SAMPLE GRANTS Horse Welfare Board (£335,000); National Horseracing College (£147,000); Professional Jockeys Association (£123,000); British Thoroughbred Rehabilitation Centre (£105,000); Diversity in Racing Steering Group (£45,000); Concussion Foundation (£30,000); British Horseracing Authority (£25,000); Exeter University (£19,000); Newmarket Academy (£1,000).
FINANCES *Financial year end 31/12/2021*
Income £1,670,000
Grants to organisations £6,800,000
Assets £94,500,000
TRUSTEES Julia Budd; Rishi Persad; James Boyle; Edward Smith-Maxwell; Alice Page; Louise Kemble; Susannah Gill; Linda Bowles.
OTHER INFORMATION The grant total includes two grants to the Horseracing Betting Levy Board totalling £3.2 million, of which £3 million was to support the wider industry response to COVID-19.
HOW TO APPLY For all grant applications, apart from those for equine science research, there is a three-stage process. Applicants should submit a first-stage application using the online form, providing basic details about their organisation. Guidelines, along with dates of application deadlines, are available from the website. For equine science research applications, the website requests that applicants register to use the Horserace Betting Levy Board's equine grants system. After registration, a grant application form can be built and submitted. Further details can be found on the foundation's website.
CONTACT DETAILS Tansy Challis, Head of Grants and Programmes, c/o British Horseracing Authority, Holborn Gate, 26 Southampton Buildings, London WC2A 1AN *Tel.* 07741 035907 *Email* tansy.challis@racingfoundation.co.uk *Website* www.racingfoundation.co.uk

The Radcliffe Trust

CC NO 209212   **ESTABLISHED** 1714
WHERE FUNDING CAN BE GIVEN UK.
WHO CAN BENEFIT Registered or exempt charities; organisations and projects benefitting musicians and those involved in the crafts.
WHAT IS FUNDED Classical music performance and training especially chamber music, composition

and music education. Particular interests within music education are music for children and adults with special needs, youth orchestras and projects at secondary and higher levels, including academic research. Heritage and crafts are also supported, especially the development of the skills, knowledge and experience that underpin the UK's traditional cultural heritage and crafts sectors.

WHAT IS NOT FUNDED Generally, individuals, retrospective grants, general appeals, endowment funds and mainstream schools. See the trust's website for scheme-specific exclusions.

TYPE OF GRANT Project funding, for up to three years.

RANGE OF GRANTS Grants generally range between £2,500 and £7,500.

SAMPLE GRANTS Church Buildings Council (£20,000); Queen Elizabeth Scholarship Trust (£12,000); Birmingham Industrial Therapy Association (£5,000); Britannia Sailing Trust (£4,500); Cogges Manor Farm (£2,500).

FINANCES *Financial year end 31/03/2022*
Income £590,100
Grants to organisations £389,600
Assets £22,840,000

TRUSTEES Sir Christopher Butcher; The Hon. Felix Warnock; Timothy Wilson; Ellen Schroder; Richard Morrison; Margaret Casely-Hayford; Melanie Howse; David Whelton; Countess Howe.

HOW TO APPLY Applications can only be submitted via the online application form. The trustees meet twice yearly to oversee the charity's activities and to make decisions on grants. The deadlines are typically 31 January and 31 July, for consideration by the trustees in June and in December, respectively. Visit the trust's website for further details.

CONTACT DETAILS The Trustees, 6 Trull Farm Buildings, Trull, Tetbury, Gloucestershire GL8 8SQ *Tel.* 01285 841900 *Email* radcliffe@thetrustpartnership.com *Website* www.theradcliffetrust.org

---

■ Richard Radcliffe Trust

CC NO 1068930   **ESTABLISHED** 1998
WHERE FUNDING CAN BE GIVEN UK.

WHO CAN BENEFIT Charitable organisations; hospices; theatres.

WHAT IS FUNDED General charitable purposes, with a preference for education; health; citizenship; social welfare; disability; young people; nature conservation.

TYPE OF GRANT Mainly recurrent.

RANGE OF GRANTS Up to £5,000.

SAMPLE GRANTS St Peter and St James Hospice (£4,000); Martlets Hospice and Wildlife Trust (£3,000 each); The English Stage Company (£2,500); Buglife and Future Trees (£2,000 each); Kiln Theatre and Project Street Life (£1,000 each).

FINANCES *Financial year end 31/08/2022*
Income £45,400
Grants to organisations £56,500
Assets £2,110,000

TRUSTEES Adrian Bell; Penelope Radcliffe; Dr Paul Radcliffe; Richard Trust.

HOW TO APPLY Apply in writing to the correspondent.

CONTACT DETAILS The Trustees, 77 Moreton Road, Buckingham MK18 1JZ *Tel.* 01280 813352

■ The Bishop Radford Trust

CC NO 1113562   **ESTABLISHED** 2006
WHERE FUNDING CAN BE GIVEN UK and overseas.

WHO CAN BENEFIT Registered charities; religious bodies/institutions.

WHAT IS FUNDED Church-related projects; the education of priests, future priests and church workers; support of church ministry.

WHAT IS NOT FUNDED Organisations not registered as charities in the UK; building or capital projects; individuals; core funding; campaigns or lobbying; research; retrospective expenditure.

TYPE OF GRANT Project funding.

RANGE OF GRANTS Programme dependent, but typically under £10,000.

SAMPLE GRANTS The Friends of the Archbishop of Canterbury's Anglican Communion Fund (£130,000); Bible Reading Fellowship (£50,000); Kick London (£20,000); Mary's Meals (£10,000); Middle East Media (£5,000); Sorted Magazine (£3,000); Friends of the Holy Land (£2,000); Lighthouse Central (£500).

FINANCES *Financial year end 31/03/2022*
Income £1,350,000
Grants to organisations £505,500
Assets £25,190,000

TRUSTEES Dr Ruth Dare; Lady Janian Green; Suzannah O'Brien; Lord Stephen Green.

OTHER INFORMATION In 2021/22 the trust awarded grants to 58 organisations. Grants to UK organisations totalled £261,700.

HOW TO APPLY Applicants must check their eligibility online before making an application through the online form.

CONTACT DETAILS Suzannah O'Brien, Trustee, Devonshire House, 1 Devonshire Street, London W1W 5DR *Tel.* 020 7304 2000 *Email* enquiries@bishopradfordtrust.org.uk *Website* http://bishopradfordtrust.org.uk

---

■ The Raindance Charitable Trust

CC NO 1172166
WHERE FUNDING CAN BE GIVEN England, Wales and Africa (particularly Uganda).

WHO CAN BENEFIT Charitable organisations.

WHAT IS FUNDED General charitable purposes; social welfare; homelessness; children and young people; charitable work in Africa.

RANGE OF GRANTS £3,000 to £6,000.

SAMPLE GRANTS Singing Gorilla (£10,000); Caring in Bristol (£6,000); St Mungo's Bristol (£5,000); Bristol Children's Help Society and The Children's Society (£2,000 each).

FINANCES *Financial year end 31/12/2021*
Income £100,000
Grants to organisations £90,000
Assets £25,000

TRUSTEES Anthony Watson; Rukshana Watson; Alisha Watson; Amelia Watson; Alastair Young.

OTHER INFORMATION Grants were awarded to 19 organisations during the year.

HOW TO APPLY Contact the correspondent for further information.

CONTACT DETAILS The Trustees, Thrings LLP, 2 Queen Square, Bath, Somerset BA1 2HQ *Tel.* 01225 340093

■ The Rainford Trust

CC NO 266157   **ESTABLISHED** 1973
WHERE FUNDING CAN BE GIVEN Worldwide, with a preference for areas where Pilkington Brothers plc operates, or has operated, especially St Helens and Merseyside.

WHO CAN BENEFIT Registered and non-registered charitable and voluntary organisations; hospices; individuals.

WHAT IS FUNDED General charitable purposes; social welfare; medical research and health; education, including the arts and humanities; the environment; conservation; the arts; community services.

WHAT IS NOT FUNDED Individuals not based in St Helens; individuals not applying for an education-related grant.

TYPE OF GRANT Core costs; capital costs; project funding.

RANGE OF GRANTS Mostly between £1,000 and £5,000 with the occasional smaller or larger grant.

SAMPLE GRANTS Clonter Opera (£16,000); Disasters Emergency Committee – Ukraine Appeal and The World of Glass (£10,000 each); Group B Strep Support, Prevent to Protect and Sense International (£5,000 each); Home-Start St Helens, Street Child and Zoë's Place Baby Hospice (£3,000 each); Educate for Life, St Helens Youth Brass Band and Tools for Self Reliance (£2,000 each); Friends of Kipkelion, Linking Environment and Farming, and School-Home Support Service (£1,000 each); KIND Liverpool (£500).

FINANCES *Financial year end 31/07/2022*
Income £272,500
Grants to organisations £191,600
Assets £12,980,000

TRUSTEES Simon Pilkington; David Bricknell; John Pilkington; Andrew Pilkington; Dr Clarissa Pilkington; Louisa Walker; David Pilkington; Lady Kirsty Pilkington; Annabel Moseley.

OTHER INFORMATION Grants to organisations were split between welfare (£164,600) and education (£27,000).

HOW TO APPLY Apply via the application form on the trust's website.

CONTACT DETAILS Shirley Robinson, Secretary, c/o Brabners LLP, Horton House, Exchange Flags, Liverpool L2 3YL *Tel.* 0151 600 3362 *Email* shirley.robinson@brabners.com *Website* www.therainfordtrust.org

■ The Rambourg Foundation

CC NO 1140347   **ESTABLISHED** 2011

WHERE FUNDING CAN BE GIVEN UK, Tunisia, France and USA.

WHO CAN BENEFIT Charitable organisations.

WHAT IS FUNDED Arts and culture, children's welfare and education, medical causes; disability; social responsibility and human rights.

TYPE OF GRANT Project funding.

SAMPLE GRANTS Human Rights Watch (£100,000); Mouratoglou Tennis Academy (£47,200); Noah's Ark Children's Hospice (£14,000); Rambourg Prize for Art and Culture (£12,200).

FINANCES *Financial year end 31/12/2021*
Income £38,100
Grants to organisations £746,500
Assets £6,650,000

TRUSTEES Olfa Rambourg; Guillaume Rambourg.

HOW TO APPLY The foundation has previously stated that it prefers to fund organisations with which it already has a strategic partnership. Contact the correspondent for more information.

CONTACT DETAILS Guillaume Rambourg, Trustee, 1401 Scott House, 23 Circus Road West, London SW11 8EJ *Tel.* +33 9 51 76 28 92 *Email* contact@fondationrambourg.tn *Website* www.rambourgfoundation.org

■ The Randal Charitable Foundation

CC NO 1176129   **ESTABLISHED** 2017

WHERE FUNDING CAN BE GIVEN UK; overseas (lower and middle-income countries).

WHO CAN BENEFIT UK-registered charities.

WHAT IS FUNDED Health; mental health; social disadvantage; addiction; education.

TYPE OF GRANT One-off and recurrent.

RANGE OF GRANTS Smaller grants (under £3,000) as well as large-scale funding.

SAMPLE GRANTS Mental Health Innovations (£50,000); Centre for Social Justice (£40,000); The Forward Trust (£31,500); Shama Women's Centre (£16,000); Home From Hospital Care (£10,000); Hot Line Meals Service and Tiny Tims (£5,000 each).

FINANCES *Financial year end 31/12/2021*
Income £3,050,000
Grants to organisations £829,500
Assets £9,730,000

TRUSTEES Dr Nik Kotecha; Moni Kotecha; Yanyan Huang; Matthew Thompson; Christopher Hobson.

HOW TO APPLY The foundation's website states that to begin the application process, applicants must first make an enquiry. If the enquiry is approved, the organisation will then be invited to complete an application form. Full details of what should be included in the initial enquiry can be found on the foundation's website.

CONTACT DETAILS The Trustees, 5 Pavilion Way, Loughborough, Leicestershire LE11 5GW *Tel.* 01509 217705 *Email* grants@ randalfoundation.org.uk *Website* www. randalfoundation.org.uk

■ The Joseph and Lena Randall Charitable Trust

CC NO 255035   **ESTABLISHED** 1967

WHERE FUNDING CAN BE GIVEN UK; France.

WHO CAN BENEFIT Registered charities; educational institutions; hospices; hospitals.

WHAT IS FUNDED Social welfare, particularly of minorities; medical and health; education; cultural facilities; the Jewish faith and community.

WHAT IS NOT FUNDED Individuals.

RANGE OF GRANTS Mostly between £1,000 and £3,000 with the occasional smaller or larger grant.

SAMPLE GRANTS Community Security Trust (£5,000); Nightingale House (£3,000); Norwood and RNIB (£2,500 each); Cancer Research UK, Great Ormond Street Hospital Children's Charity and Queen Elizabeth Hospital Birmingham (£2,000 each); Brain and Spine Foundation (£1,500); Aldenham School, Listening Books and Not Forgotten Association (£1,000 each); Église Orthodoxe Russe (£830).

FINANCES *Financial year end 05/04/2022*
Income £69,800
Grants to organisations £70,600
Assets £1,920,000

TRUSTEE Rofrano Trustee Services Ltd.

OTHER INFORMATION Only organisations that received grants of over £750 were listed as beneficiaries in the trust's 2021/22 accounts. Grants of under £750 totalled £1,400.

HOW TO APPLY Apply in writing to the correspondent.

CONTACT DETAILS The Trustees, Europa Residence, Place des Moulins, Monte-Carlo, Monaco MC 98000 *Tel.* +377 93 50 03 82 *Email* rofrano.jlrct@hotmail.fr

Think carefully about every application. Is it justified?

609

■ Randeree Charitable Trust

CC NO 1171689   **ESTABLISHED** 2017

WHERE FUNDING CAN BE GIVEN UK.

WHO CAN BENEFIT Charitable organisations; individuals; schools and colleges; universities.

WHAT IS FUNDED Education; inclusion and empowerment of disadvantaged young people; humanitarian aid; community development; cultural equality through research; Islam; interfaith; sports.

RANGE OF GRANTS Up to between £10,000 and £20,000 with the occasional larger grant.

SAMPLE GRANTS Cambridge Muslim College (£48,400); Woolf Institute (£30,000); Azhar Academy and Muslim Aid (£20,000 each); Faith Belief Forum, Islamic Relief and The Muslim Cultural Heritage Trust (£10,000 each).

FINANCES *Financial year end 31/12/2021*
Income £804,500
Grants to organisations £164,900
Grants to individuals £5,400
Assets £4,400,000

TRUSTEES Shireen Randeree; Zaid Randeree; Faisal Randeree; Simon Mitchell; Norman Waller.

OTHER INFORMATION Grants of under £10,000 totalled £13,000.

HOW TO APPLY Apply in writing to the correspondent.

CONTACT DETAILS The Trustees, 85 Strand, London WC2R 0DW *Tel.* 020 7324 2000

■ The Rank Foundation Ltd

CC NO 276976   **ESTABLISHED** 1953

WHERE FUNDING CAN BE GIVEN UK.

WHO CAN BENEFIT Registered charities with an annual income of less than £500,000; churches.

WHAT IS FUNDED Christian communication; young people; education; older people; general charitable purposes.

SAMPLE GRANTS A list of beneficiaries was not included in the annual report and accounts. Previous beneficiaries have included: Venture Trust (£25,000); Making the Leap (£20,000); First Give (£15,000); Dementia Adventure (£10,000); Dundee Comics Creative Space (£3,000); Family Links (£750).

FINANCES *Financial year end 31/12/2021*
Income £4,280,000
Grants to organisations £10,480,000
Assets £300,930,000

TRUSTEES Nicholas Buxton; Jason Chaffer; Rose Fitzpatrick; Joey Newton; Johanna Ropner; Daniel Simon; William Wyatt; Andrew Fleming; Lindsey Clay; Joel Davis; Stuart Cowen.

HOW TO APPLY Applications to the Pebble Grant scheme can be made via the foundation's website.

CONTACT DETAILS The Trustees, 21 Garden Walk, London EC2A 3EQ *Email* contactus@rankfoundation.com *Website* www.rankfoundation.com

■ The Joseph Rank Trust

CC NO 1093844   **ESTABLISHED** 2002

WHERE FUNDING CAN BE GIVEN UK; Republic of Ireland; Channel Islands.

WHO CAN BENEFIT Registered charities; places of worship.

WHAT IS FUNDED Improvement of Church properties; Christian causes and evangelism.

WHAT IS NOT FUNDED A full list of exclusions can be found on the trust's website.

TYPE OF GRANT One-off grants for capital expenditure; three-year grants for core costs or project funding.

RANGE OF GRANTS Up to £50,000.

SAMPLE GRANTS The Exodus Project (£50,000); Prison Fellowship Scotland (£45,000); Survivors of Human Trafficking in Scotland (£37,500); Child Evangelism Fellowship – Belfast (£35,000); York Schools and York Trust (£30,000); Bray Methodist Church (£23,000); Gwithian Chapel (£10,000); Capel Bryn Iwan (£5,000).

FINANCES *Financial year end 31/12/2021*
Income £2,480,000
Grants to organisations £2,500,000
Assets £99,700,000

TRUSTEES James Rank; Gay Moon; Colin Rank; Sue Warner; The Revd John Irvine; The Revd Darren Holland; The Revd Carole Holmes; Joseph Jennings.

HOW TO APPLY Refer to the funder's website for detailed information on how to make an application.

CONTACT DETAILS Dr John Higgs, Secretary, Worth Corner, Turners Hill Road, Crawley, West Sussex RH10 7SL *Tel.* 01293 873947 *Email* secretary@ranktrust.org *Website* www.ranktrust.org

■ The Ranworth Trust

CC NO 292633   **ESTABLISHED** 1985

WHERE FUNDING CAN BE GIVEN UK, with a preference for East Norfolk; lower and middle-income countries.

WHO CAN BENEFIT Registered charities.

WHAT IS FUNDED Social welfare; work overseas; health; medical research; education; the environment; the arts.

WHAT IS NOT FUNDED Individuals.

RANGE OF GRANTS Grants range from £1,000 to £10,000.

SAMPLE GRANTS Norfolk Community Foundation (£50,000); University of East Anglia Scholarship (£10,700); Cancer Research UK (£10,000); Ormiston Families (£6,000); Norfolk Wildlife Trust (£5,000); Matthew Project (£2,500); Benedetti Foundation (£2,000); East Anglian Arts Foundation (£1,000).

FINANCES *Financial year end 05/04/2022*
Income £136,600
Grants to organisations £230,200
Assets £5,780,000

TRUSTEES Mark Cator; Jane Cator; The Hon. Isabel Cator.

OTHER INFORMATION In 2021/22, grants were made for the following purposes: social and welfare (£129,500); financially developing countries (£40,000); health and medical causes (£37,000); education (£12,700); the environment (£6,000); arts (£5,000). In 2010 a grant of £350,000 was given to Norfolk Community Foundation to establish The Ranworth Grassroots Fund. The fund will support a wide range of charitable, voluntary and community activities across Norfolk. The trust also offers loans.

HOW TO APPLY Apply in writing to the correspondent. The trustees meet four times a year to review grant applications.

CONTACT DETAILS The Trustees, Reedside, Farm Lane, Ranworth, Norwich, Norfolk NR13 6HY *Tel.* 01603 663300

610

Does the funder you have chosen match your needs? Haphazard applications waste postage and time

■ The Ratcliff Foundation

CC NO 222441   **ESTABLISHED** 1959
WHERE FUNDING CAN BE GIVEN UK, with a preference for the Midlands and Wales.
WHO CAN BENEFIT Charitable organisations; hospices; hospitals; places of worship.
WHAT IS FUNDED General charitable purposes; medical and health; the environment; wildlife conservation; sports and recreation.
WHAT IS NOT FUNDED Individuals.
RANGE OF GRANTS Up to £6,000.
SAMPLE GRANTS Giving Hands Mission and St David's Hospice (£6,000 each); Bromyard Choral Society, Kidney Research UK and Worcestershire Animal Rescue Centre (£5,000 each); Bike for the Future, Carers Trust Wales and Heart of England Forest (£4,000 each); Birmingham Centre for Arts Therapies, Cardiff Wheelchair Tennis Club and Surfers Against Sewage (£3,000 each); Adiscombe Hockey Club, Maggs Day Centre and RNLI – Swanage (£2,500 each).
FINANCES *Financial year end* 05/04/2022
Income £178,700
Grants to organisations £171,000
Assets £4,410,000
TRUSTEES David Ratcliff; Pauline Key; Christopher Gupwell; Carolyn Ratcliff; Gillian Thorpe.
OTHER INFORMATION Grants of over £2,500 totalled £151,000 and were awarded to 41 organisations. Grants of under £2,500 totalled £20,000 and were awarded to 12 organisations.
HOW TO APPLY Apply in writing to the correspondent.
CONTACT DETAILS Christopher Gupwell, Trustee, Woodlands, Earls Common Road, Stock Green, Redditch, Worcestershire B96 6TB *Tel.* 01386 792116 *Email* chris.gupwell@btinternet.com

■ The Eleanor Rathbone Charitable Trust

CC NO 233241   **ESTABLISHED** 1947
WHERE FUNDING CAN BE GIVEN UK, with the major allocation for Merseyside; also international projects in sub-Saharan Africa, the Indian sub-continent, Afghanistan and Palestine.
WHO CAN BENEFIT Registered charities; unregistered charities; CICs; social enterprises.
WHAT IS FUNDED Women and girls; orphaned children; young people and families who are economically deprived and/or socially excluded; unpopular and neglected causes; human rights; refugee support; education; social inclusion; holidays and outings provided by charities helping disadvantaged children and adults from Merseyside; overseas humanitarian aid.
WHAT IS NOT FUNDED Activities which are the responsibility of a statutory body; individuals; medical research; gap-year projects; lobbying or campaigning organisations; organisations that primarily exist to promote a religion, church or sect; local charities based outside Merseyside.
TYPE OF GRANT Core/revenue costs; seed funding/start-up funding; project funding; unrestricted funding. Most grants are for one year, although requests for two and three-year grants will be considered.
RANGE OF GRANTS From £1,000 to £3,000 for national and international grants and up to £5,000 for Merseyside grants. In exceptional cases grants may be higher.
SAMPLE GRANTS Greenbank (£7,000); In Your Shoes and Porchfield Community Association (£5,000 each); The New Belve (£4,000); Triple C

(£3,000); The Belvidere Centre (£2,000); Hello World (£1,000).
FINANCES *Financial year end* 05/04/2022
Income £475,900
Grants to organisations £355,500
Assets £13,180,000
TRUSTEES Lady Angela Morgan; Andrew Rathbone; Mark Rathbone; Jenny Rathbone; Joan Bonenfant.
OTHER INFORMATION Grants were awarded to 147 organisations during the year and were distributed as follows: Merseyside (£221,100); international (£61,500); national (£61,000); holidays – Merseyside (£11,900).
HOW TO APPLY Apply using the online form available on the website. In addition, supporting documents (listed on the website) must be sent as an email attachment. Applications are accepted at any time and are considered at trustees' meetings held three times a year.
CONTACT DETAILS The Trustees, 546 Warrington Road, Rainhill, Prescot, Merseyside L35 4LZ *Tel.* 07837 656314 *Email* eleanorrathbonetrust@gmail.com *Website* www.eleanorrathbonetrust.org.uk

■ Elizabeth Rathbone Charity

CC NO 233240   **ESTABLISHED** 1921
WHERE FUNDING CAN BE GIVEN Merseyside.
WHO CAN BENEFIT Registered charities; community organisations.
WHAT IS FUNDED Education; women; social welfare; the arts; community projects; health.
WHAT IS NOT FUNDED Individuals; sponsorship; political organisations; pressure groups; feasibility studies; annual applications.
RANGE OF GRANTS Mostly £1,000 to £3,000.
SAMPLE GRANTS Hooves For Healing (£3,200); Autism Together (£3,000); The Girls' Network (£1,500); Changing Faces (£1,300); Crohn's and Colitis UK (£680).
FINANCES *Financial year end* 05/04/2022
Income £83,200
Grants to organisations £86,700
Assets £2,830,000
TRUSTEES Susan Rathbone; Caroline Rathbone; Megan Rathbone; Richard Rathbone.
OTHER INFORMATION Grants were distributed as follows: health, well-being and disability (£33,300); social welfare and community (£30,500); children and young people (£22,900).
HOW TO APPLY Application forms can be downloaded from the trust's website.
CONTACT DETAILS Liese van Alwon, Secretary, 546 Warrington Road, Rainhill, Prescot, Merseyside L35 4LZ *Tel.* 07837 656314 *Email* elrathbonetrust@gmail.com *Website* www.elizabethrathbonetrust.org

■ The Rathbones Group Foundation

CC NO 1150432   **ESTABLISHED** 2012
WHERE FUNDING CAN BE GIVEN Areas where the company has an office.
WHO CAN BENEFIT Charitable organisations.
WHAT IS FUNDED The main objective of the foundation is to help disadvantaged young people in the areas the company has a presence.
TYPE OF GRANT Capital, development and project funding.
RANGE OF GRANTS Grants are mostly under £10,000.

SAMPLE GRANTS Paul Lavelle Foundation (£14,300); Envision (£10,000); Their Voice (£6,000); Teenage Cancer Trust (£5,000); Sussex Snowdrop Trust (£4,000); Winchester Young Carers (£2,000); Brathay Trust (£1,500); We Can Dance (£200).

FINANCES *Financial year end* 31/12/2021
Income £325,200
Grants to organisations £205,200
Assets £1,430,000

TRUSTEES Geoffrey Powell; Paul Stockton; Rathbone Trust Company Ltd; Richard Lanyon; Stuart Furzer.

HOW TO APPLY Apply in writing to your local Rathbone's office or directly to the trustees.

CONTACT DETAILS Sophie Boyd-Willis, Head of Communications, Rathbone Bros plc, 8 Finsbury Circus, London EC2M 7AZ *Tel.* 020 7399 0000 *Email* rathbonefoundation@rathbones.com

■ The Julia and Hans Rausing Trust

WHERE FUNDING CAN BE GIVEN UK.
WHO CAN BENEFIT Charitable organisations.
WHAT IS FUNDED Health and well-being; welfare and education; arts and culture.
SAMPLE GRANTS UK Youth (£10 million); The Prince's Trust (£1 million); Glass Door (£200,000); Earls Court Youth Club (£90,000); Relate North and South West Sussex (£3,000).
FINANCES *Financial year end* 31/12/2021
Grants to organisations £44,460,000
OTHER INFORMATION The trust is not a registered charity and therefore full financial information was not available. The financial information has been taken from the Julia and Hans Rausing Trust's Funding Allocation 2021 document.
HOW TO APPLY The trust does not accept unsolicited applications. However, the trust's website does state that time-limited opportunities that may be announced from time to time.
CONTACT DETAILS The Trustees, 250 King's Road, London SW3 5UE *Website* www.juliahansrausingtrust.org

■ The Sigrid Rausing Trust
CC NO 1194828   **ESTABLISHED** 1995
WHERE FUNDING CAN BE GIVEN Central and eastern Europe and Eurasia; north Africa; South Africa.
WHO CAN BENEFIT Charitable or voluntary organisations.
WHAT IS FUNDED The trust runs ten programmes that fall under the following categories: human rights, fairness and inclusion and the environment. See the website for more information.
TYPE OF GRANT Core costs; project funding.
RANGE OF GRANTS No minimum or maximum grant.
SAMPLE GRANTS A full list of organisations supported by the trust can be found on its website.
FINANCES *Financial year end* 31/12/2021
Income £119,930,000
Grants to organisations £16,640,000
Assets £102,790,000
TRUSTEES Sigrid Rausing; Andrew Puddephatt; Chris Stone; Sir Jeffrey Jowell; Hosh Ibrahim; Ruth Rogers; Joshua Mailman; Geoffrey Budlender; Mabel Oranje.
HOW TO APPLY The trust does not accept unsolicited applications for funding but rather invites applications from organisations that it has proactively identified. However, the trust's

website states: 'The Sigrid Rausing Trust does not accept unsolicited applications for funding, but you can contact us on: info@srtrust.org. If you wish to let us know about the work of your organisation, write to: research@srtrust.org. All emails are regularly reviewed.'
CONTACT DETAILS The Trustees, 12 Penzance Place, London W11 4PA *Email* info@srtrust.org *Website* www.sigrid-rausing-trust.org

■ The Ravensdale Trust
CC NO 265165   **ESTABLISHED** 1973
WHERE FUNDING CAN BE GIVEN Merseyside, particularly St Helens.
WHO CAN BENEFIT Registered charities.
WHAT IS FUNDED General charitable purposes, particularly young people, older people and disadvantaged groups.
TYPE OF GRANT Core costs; project funding.
RANGE OF GRANTS Grants range from £700 up to £5,000.
SAMPLE GRANTS Previous beneficiaries have included: Derbyshire Hill Family and Community Association, Halton Autistic Family Support Group, Home-Start St Helens, Mersey Regional Epilepsy Association, National Museums Liverpool and Newfield School.
FINANCES *Financial year end* 05/04/2022
Income £6,800
Grants to organisations £356,300
TRUSTEES Mrs J. Fagan; Mark Feeny; Karen Toseland.
OTHER INFORMATION The trust's full 2021/22 accounts were not available to view on the Charity Commission's website due to its low income. We have therefore estimated the trust's grant total based on previous years' expenditure.
HOW TO APPLY Apply in writing to the correspondent.
CONTACT DETAILS Jane Fagan, Trustee, c/o Brabners, Horton House, Exchange Flags, Liverpool, Merseyside L2 3YL *Tel.* 0151 600 3000 *Email* jane.fagan@brabners.com

■ The Roger Raymond Charitable Trust
CC NO 262217   **ESTABLISHED** 1971
WHERE FUNDING CAN BE GIVEN UK.
WHO CAN BENEFIT Registered charities.
WHAT IS FUNDED General charitable purposes.
WHAT IS NOT FUNDED Individuals.
RANGE OF GRANTS Typically less than £2,000.
SAMPLE GRANTS Bloxham School (£101,400); Sightsavers (£10,000); Practical Action and WaterAid (£5,000 each); The Smallpeice Trust (£4,400); British Red Cross (£4,000); Shelter and Stokenchurch Dog Rescue (£2,000 each).
FINANCES *Financial year end* 05/04/2022
Income £519,700
Grants to organisations £165,300
Assets £19,480,000
TRUSTEES Michael Raymond; Alasdair Thomson; Clive Sutton.
OTHER INFORMATION Bloxham School receives the majority of the grant total each year. Only organisations that received grants of over £2,000 were listed as beneficiaries in the charity's accounts. Grants of under £2,000 totalled £1,500.
HOW TO APPLY The trust does not accept unsolicited applications.
CONTACT DETAILS The Trustees, Forest Edge, Hangersley Hill, Ringwood, Hampshire

BH24 3JS *Tel.* 01425 471679 *Email* admin@
rrct.org.uk

■ The Rayne Foundation

CC NO 1179912   **ESTABLISHED** 1962
WHERE FUNDING CAN BE GIVEN UK.
WHO CAN BENEFIT Small and medium-sized
registered charities; not-for-profit organisations.
WHAT IS FUNDED Health; education; social welfare;
the arts; mental health, specifically for young
people; carers; older people; social change.
WHAT IS NOT FUNDED Medical research (including
cancer research); retrospective expenditure;
capital appeals; campaigning and lobbying work;
endowments; one-off events (including
performances, festivals, conferences, holidays,
respite breaks and residential trips); community
transport schemes and vehicle purchases;
church halls and community centres; running
costs of local organisations; feasibility studies
or scoping work; individuals; organisations
working or based outside the UK; brand new
organisations; organisations which have applied
and been rejected within the last 12 months;
charities supporting Service personnel.
TYPE OF GRANT Salaries and all types of project
costs plus a reasonable contribution to
overheads (there is no fixed percentage);
general running or core costs (normally for a
maximum of three years); capital costs of
buildings and equipment (unless specifically
stated in certain sectors); 'seed corn' projects
which are likely to attract other funding, if
successful; social investment loans.
RANGE OF GRANTS Typically up to £60,000.
SAMPLE GRANTS Hope for Justice (£80,000); Pure
Insight 1628 (£75,000); Open Up Music
(£60,000); Partnership for Children (£30,000);
Resurgo Trust (£20,000); The Bluecoat
(£10,000); Flora Cultura (£5,000); Displaced
People in Action (£1,900).
FINANCES *Financial year end* 30/11/2021
Income £1,990,000
Grants to organisations £1,760,000
Assets £102,240,000
TRUSTEES Lady Hilary Browne-Wilkinson; Lady Jane
Rayne; Prof. Sir Anthony Taylor; Sir Emyr Parry;
Baroness Julia Neuberger; The Hon. Robert
Rayne; The Hon. Natasha Rayne; The Hon.
Nicholas Oxon.
OTHER INFORMATION During 2020/21, the foundation
awarded COVID-19 grants totalling £418,300
and main grants totalling £1.34 million. The
2020/21 accounts were the latest available at
the time of writing (May 2023).
HOW TO APPLY Application forms and guidelines can
be downloaded from the foundation's website.
CONTACT DETAILS Morin Carew, Grants Administrator,
3 Bromley Place, London W1T 6DB *Tel.* 020
7487 9657 *Email* info@raynefoundation.org.uk
Website www.raynefoundation.org.uk

■ The Sir James Reckitt Charity

CC NO 225356   **ESTABLISHED** 1921
WHERE FUNDING CAN BE GIVEN Hull and the East
Riding of Yorkshire; UK (Quaker causes).
WHO CAN BENEFIT Community organisations; Quaker
organisations; national and regional charities;
CICs; uniformed groups; schools; individuals.
WHAT IS FUNDED General charitable purposes
including: older people; children and young
people; the environment; health; social work;
Quaker causes.

TYPE OF GRANT Start-up and core costs; project
funding; unrestricted; equipment; training costs.
RANGE OF GRANTS Generally up to £10,000, although
larger applications may be considered.
SAMPLE GRANTS Quaker United Nations Office
(£50,000); The University of Hull (£30,000);
North Humberside Hospice Project (£20,000);
Age UK (£12,000); Scholarships for Street Kids
(£8,000); Ditto (£2,000).
FINANCES *Financial year end* 31/12/2021
Income £1,710,000
Grants to organisations £1,410,000
Grants to individuals £131,000
Assets £59,230,000
TRUSTEES Sarah Craven; Rebecca Holt; Caroline
Jennings; Charles Maxsted; William Upton;
Robin Upton; Simon Upton; Simon Upton;
Edward Upton; James Atherton; Oliver Jennings;
Ondine Upton; Michelle Fisher; Nicholas Butler-
Watts.
OTHER INFORMATION Grants were distributed as
follows: social work (£736,200); education
(£287,500); religion (£176,500); medical
causes (£132,500); children (£118,300); young
people (£57,400); older people (£19,500); the
environment (£15,000).
HOW TO APPLY Apply via the charity's website.
CONTACT DETAILS Kelly Sykes-Moody,
4 Summergangs Drive, Thorngumbald, Hull
HU12 9PW *Email* kelly@
thesirjamesreckittcharity.org.uk *Website* www.
thesirjamesreckittcharity.org.uk

■ Red Hill Charitable Trust

CC NO 307891   **ESTABLISHED** 1948
WHERE FUNDING CAN BE GIVEN The South East
including East Anglia, London and the Home
Counties.
WHO CAN BENEFIT Charitable organisations.
WHAT IS FUNDED People under the age of 25 with
emotional or behavioural difficulties; education.
WHAT IS NOT FUNDED Individuals.
TYPE OF GRANT One-off; project funding, primarily for
capital costs.
RANGE OF GRANTS £1,000 to £5,000.
SAMPLE GRANTS Children's House Montessori
(£8,400); Challenger Troop (£6,600); Cycle
Community (£5,000); The Music Well (£5,000);
The Countryside Alliance (£3,000); East Stour
Primary School (£2,500); Bethersden Playschool
(£2,100); Sunbeams (£2,000); Goldilocks
Sittingbourne (£1,700).
FINANCES *Financial year end* 31/08/2022
Income £49,400
Grants to organisations £99,500
Assets £2,960,000
TRUSTEES Roger Barton; Antony Bunting; Bob Law;
John Moore; Michael Startup; Kevin Moule; Allan
Adams; Pam Jones; Nicola Clark.
OTHER INFORMATION Grants were awarded to 27
organisations in 2021/22.
HOW TO APPLY Application forms may be downloaded
from the trust's website and, once completed,
must be returned to the correspondent by email
as a Word-processed document. Supporting
materials may be sent electronically or as a
hard copy. The trustees hold meetings twice
yearly, in March and October. Applications for
these meetings should reach the correspondent
by 15 February and 15 September, respectively.
CONTACT DETAILS The Clerk to the Trustees,
3 Thurnham Oast, Aldington Lane, Thurnham,
Kent ME14 3LL *Email* clerk@redhilltrust.org
Website www.redhilltrust.org

■ C. A. Redfern Charitable Foundation

CC NO 299918 **ESTABLISHED** 1988
WHERE FUNDING CAN BE GIVEN England and Wales.
WHO CAN BENEFIT Registered charities; hospices.
WHAT IS FUNDED General charitable purposes; health and medical care and research; social welfare.
RANGE OF GRANTS Generally between £1,000 and £10,000, with one grant of £30,000.
SAMPLE GRANTS South Bucks Riding for the Disabled (£30,000); The Saints and Sinners Trust Ltd and White Ensign (£10,000 each); Create, Rewilding Britain and St Michael's Hospice (£5,000 each); St George's Hospital Charity and Crisis (£4,000 each); Redthread Youth Ltd (£3,000); Ben and Breast Cancer Heaven (£2,000 each); BRACE (£1,000).
FINANCES *Financial year end 05/04/2022*
Income £165,300
Grants to organisations £205,000
Assets £6,300,700
TRUSTEES William MacLaren; David Redfern; Simon Ward; Julian Heslop.
OTHER INFORMATION In 2021/22 grants were made to 58 organisations.
HOW TO APPLY Unsolicited applications are not accepted.
CONTACT DETAILS The Trustees, c/o PricewaterhouseCoopers, 3 Forbury Place, 23 Forbury Road, Reading, Berkshire RG1 3JH *Tel.* 0118 938 3128

■ The Reece Foundation

CC NO 1121325 **ESTABLISHED** 2007
WHERE FUNDING CAN BE GIVEN UK with a strong preference for the North East including Northumberland, Tyne and Wear and County Durham.
WHO CAN BENEFIT Registered charities; schools; universities.
WHAT IS FUNDED The development of maths, science and engineering skills; STEM employment opportunities.
SAMPLE GRANTS Beamish Museum (£160,600); Northumberland National Park (£100,000); Nissan (£64,000); Starlight Education (£33,000); Mission Discovery (£27,500); Newcastle University (£22,400).
FINANCES *Financial year end 31/12/2021*
Income £754,900
Grants to organisations £2,560,000
Assets £35,200,000
TRUSTEES Simon Gilroy; Eric Morgan; Anne Reece; Prof. David Sandbach.
OTHER INFORMATION Only the beneficiaries of grants of over £20,000 were listed in the 2021 accounts (12 organisations). Grants of less than £20,000 totalled £198,500. In 2021 the foundation also made a one-off exceptional grant of £2.02 million to the Northumberland Wildlife Trust.
HOW TO APPLY Application forms are available to download from the foundation's website. Forms should be returned by post or email (applications@reece-foundation.org). Applications can be made at any time and are considered at quarterly meetings. Decisions may take up to six months.
CONTACT DETAILS The Trustees, 40 Grosvenor Place, Newcastle upon Tyne, Tyne and Wear NE2 2RE *Tel.* 07704 076703 *Email* enquiries@reece-foundation.org *Website* www.reece-foundation.org

■ Rees Jeffreys Road Fund

CC NO 217771 **ESTABLISHED** 1950
WHERE FUNDING CAN BE GIVEN UK.
WHO CAN BENEFIT Registered charities; unregistered charities; CICs; universities; individuals.
WHAT IS FUNDED Education and research in transport; projects that improve the roadside environment for motorists and other road users.
TYPE OF GRANT Capital costs; project funding.
RANGE OF GRANTS £5,000 to £25,000.
SAMPLE GRANTS The 150 Competition (£25,000); Transport for London (£18,000); Engineering Development Trust (£8,000); Cycle Streets (£6,100).
FINANCES *Financial year end 31/12/2022*
Income £244,900
Grants to organisations £341,900
Assets £6,900,000
TRUSTEES David Tarrant; Sarah Clarke; Prof. Glenn; Stephen Gooding; Hilary Chipping; Andrew Graham; Leon Daniels; Dr Suzanne Green.
OTHER INFORMATION Note that the grant total includes amounts awarded to individuals.
HOW TO APPLY Visit the charity's website for full details regarding the application process.
CONTACT DETAILS The Trustees, Flat 22, Jetty Court, Old Bellgate Place, London E14 3SX *Tel.* 05603 849370 *Email* secretary@reesjeffreys.co.uk *Website* www.reesjeffreys.co.uk

■ Richard Reeve's Foundation

CC NO 1136337 **ESTABLISHED** 1706
WHERE FUNDING CAN BE GIVEN Camden, City of London and Islington.
WHO CAN BENEFIT Registered charities; unregistered charities; CICs; social enterprises; schools; local authorities; individuals.
WHAT IS FUNDED Education and training for children and young people (up to the age of 25).
TYPE OF GRANT Project funding; unrestricted funding; up to three years.
SAMPLE GRANTS A list of beneficiaries was not included in the annual report and accounts.
FINANCES *Financial year end 30/06/2022*
Income £1,310,000
Grants to organisations £591,700
Grants to individuals £578,900
Assets £48,580,000
TRUSTEES Mark Jessett; Gerald Rothwell; Alistair Wilson; Elizabeth Gallagher; Benjamin Musgrave Monaghan; Tracey Shackle; Charlotte Hilton; The Revd Nicholas Mottershead; Ian Seaton; Gulcin Ozdemir.
OTHER INFORMATION Grants were awarded for the following purposes: GCSE Maths support (£211,800); tuition programmes (£168,400); family support (£115,400); careers education services (£75,000); books (£21,100).
HOW TO APPLY The foundation is not currently accepting unsolicited applications. Check the foundation's website for further information.
CONTACT DETAILS Frances Wells, Clerk and Company Secretary, 20–22 Wenlock Road, London N1 7GU *Tel.* 020 8323 2662 *Email* clerk@richardreevesfoundation.org.uk *Website* www.richardreevesfoundation.org.uk

■ The Max Reinhardt Charitable Trust

cc no 264741   established 1972
where funding can be given UK.
who can benefit Charitable organisations.
what is funded Arts education; social welfare; health.
sample grants Engage in the Visual Arts (£38,100); Pro Corda (£25,000); The Trussell Trust (£3,000); Magdalen College School Oxford (£2,000).
finances *Financial year end 05/04/2022*
  Income £29,600
  Grants to organisations £68,100
  Assets £5,760,000
trustees Veronica Reinhardt; Magdalen Wade.
other information During 2021/22, grants were awarded to four organisations in the following categories: art and culture (£63,100) and relief of poverty/welfare and advancement of health (£5,000).
how to apply Apply in writing to the correspondent.
contact details The Trustees, Crown Chambers, Bridge Street, Salisbury, Wiltshire SP1 2LZ *Tel.* 01722 327801 *Email* charity@fletchpart. co.uk

■ Rentrust Foundation Ltd

cc no 1163817   established 2014
where funding can be given UK.
who can benefit Charitable organisations; Jewish educational institutions.
what is funded Education; welfare; the Jewish faith and community.
type of grant One-off and multi-year.
range of grants Up to £133,000.
sample grants United Talmudical Associates Ltd (£133,000); Toldos Aharon Trust Ltd (£20,000).
finances *Financial year end 31/07/2022*
  Income £105,200
  Grants to organisations £154,500
  Assets £213,800
trustees Esther Wosner; Pessi Eisenbach; Chavi Simon.
other information Only beneficiaries of grants of over £10,000 were listed in the accounts. Grants of under £10,000 totalled £1,500.
how to apply Apply in writing to the correspondent.
contact details The Trustees, Sarah House, 214/218 High Road, London N15 4NP *Tel.* 020 3137 9885 *Email* cf@nuenterprise.co.uk

■ The Resolution Trust

cc no 1123128   established 2007
where funding can be given UK.
who can benefit Charitable organisations.
what is funded Research/education in economic and social sciences with a particular focus on the causes, prevention or relief of poverty.
type of grant Project funding; research.
sample grants Prospect Magazine (£1.1 million); The Old Vic (£300,000); The Resolution Foundation (£95,400); Bristol Cultural Development Partnership (£20,000).
finances *Financial year end 30/09/2021*
  Income £664,800
  Grants to organisations £1,540,000
  Assets £47,430,000
trustee The Resolution Trust (Trustee) Ltd.
other information The trust made grants to four organisations. A large proportion of the grant total was awarded to Prospect Magazine. The

2020/21 accounts were the latest available at the time of writing (May 2023).
how to apply Contact the correspondent for further information. Funding is primarily given to the trust's existing partners.
contact details The Trustees, 2 Queen Anne's Gate, London SW1H 9AA *Tel.* 020 3372 2960 *Email* info@resolutiontrust.org *Website* http:// resolutiontrust.org

■ Reuben Foundation

cc no 1094130   established 2002
where funding can be given UK and overseas (particularly Israel).
who can benefit Charitable organisations, including universities and Jewish organisations; individuals.
what is funded Health care; education; general charitable purposes.
range of grants Typically less than £25,000. Several large grants of over £100,000 are made per year.
sample grants Reuben College, University of Oxford (£1.5 million); Sephardic Academy of Manhattan (£1.3 million); Centrepoint (£472,400); British Film Institute (£120,000); Design Museum (£50,000); Holocaust Educational Trust (£25,000); Juvenile Diabetes Research Foundation (£20,000); Fauna and Flora International (£10,000); National Horse Racing College (£8,000).
finances *Financial year end 31/12/2021*
  Income £4,200,000
  Grants to organisations £5,470,000
  Grants to individuals £75,500
  Assets £12,360,000
trustees Richard Stone; Malcolm Turner; James Reuben; Simon Reuben; Dana Reuben; Eileen Sawyer; Reuben.
other information Included in the grants to organisations total is £1.04 million awarded in response to the COVID-19 pandemic. The foundation supports a number of scholarship initiatives including the Reuben Scholarship programme alongside the University of Oxford, University College London, ARK Schools and the University of Cambridge.
how to apply The foundation's website states that applications for grants are made by invitation only.
contact details The Trustees, 4th Floor, Millbank Tower, 21–24 Millbank, London SW1P 4PQ *Tel.* 020 7802 5000 *Email* contact@ reubenfoundation.com *Website* www. reubenfoundation.com

■ The Revere Charitable Trust

cc no 1117369   established 2006
where funding can be given UK.
who can benefit Registered charities; hospices.
what is funded Medical research, in particular research into asthma and cancer; the environment; arts and culture; animal welfare; children and young people; people with disabilities.
range of grants £5,000 to £50,000.
sample grants Alzheimer's Research UK (£50,000); Woodlands Trust (£30,200); Asthma UK (£30,000); Hitchin Scouts Council (£10,000), Disasters Emergency Committee – Ukraine Humanitarian Appeal and St John Ambulance (£5,000 each).

FINANCES *Financial year end* 05/04/2022
Income £477,600
Grants to organisations £360,200
Assets £8,010,000
TRUSTEES John Donaldson; Peter Willmott; Richard Willmot.
OTHER INFORMATION During 2021/22, 15 organisations received grants.
HOW TO APPLY Contact the correspondent for further information.
CONTACT DETAILS Rick Willmott, Trustee, Westbury Farm House, West End Ashwell, Baldock, Hertfordshire SG7 5PJ *Tel.* 01462 742462 *Email* rick.willmott@willmottdixon.co.uk

---

■ Rhodi Charitable Trust

CC NO 1082915   **ESTABLISHED** 2000
WHERE FUNDING CAN BE GIVEN UK and overseas. Preference for Preston and India.
WHO CAN BENEFIT Charitable organisations; individuals.
WHAT IS FUNDED Poverty relief; social welfare; the advancement of religion; education; health.
SAMPLE GRANTS A list of beneficiaries was not included in the annual report and accounts.
FINANCES *Financial year end* 31/12/2022
Income £142,400
Grants to organisations £91,700
Assets £1,390,000
TRUSTEES Hamida Bux; Ibrahim Bux.
OTHER INFORMATION According to its 2022 accounts, the charity operates and finances five multi-faith facilities at motorway service stations across the UK.
HOW TO APPLY Apply in writing to the correspondent.
CONTACT DETAILS The Trustees, 1 Fishwick Park, Mercer Street, Preston, Lancashire PR1 4LZ *Tel.* 01772 562288

■ The Rhododendron Trust

CC NO 267192   **ESTABLISHED** 1974
WHERE FUNDING CAN BE GIVEN UK and overseas.
WHO CAN BENEFIT Registered charities.
WHAT IS FUNDED Overseas aid; disability; mental health; prisoners and ex-offenders; homelessness; older people; disadvantaged children; the arts and culture; wildlife; the environment.
WHAT IS NOT FUNDED Individuals, for example on gap-year projects with another charity; restoration work on individual churches and other buildings; local branches of national societies; medical or academic research; missionary charities.
TYPE OF GRANT Project costs.
RANGE OF GRANTS £500 to £1,500.
SAMPLE GRANTS A list of beneficiaries was not included in the annual report and accounts. Previous beneficiaries have included: African Revival, Book Aid International, Hardman Trust, Minority Rights Group and Womankind Worldwide (£1,000 each); Build IT International, English Touring Opera, Historic Chapels Trust, Prison Me No Way and Solar Aid (£500 each).
FINANCES *Financial year end* 05/04/2022
Income £112,000
Grants to organisations £66,000
Assets £2,890,000
TRUSTEES Sarah Oliver; Sarah Ray; Elizabeth Baldwin; Wendy Anderson.
OTHER INFORMATION Around 50% of grants are given to overseas charities, 40% are awarded to UK charities for social welfare purposes and 10% are given to UK charities supporting culture.

HOW TO APPLY Apply in writing to the correspondent. Guidelines are available on the website. Grants are awarded once a year, typically in February or March after the trustees' meeting in January. Applicants will be informed within about a month if they have been unsuccessful.
CONTACT DETAILS The Grants Officer, 6 Bridge Street, Richmond, North Yorkshire DL10 4RW *Tel.* 07495 752060 *Email* mail@rhododendron-trust.org.uk *Website* www.rhododendron-trust.org.uk

---

■ Riada Trust

OSCR NO SC028314   **ESTABLISHED** 1998
WHERE FUNDING CAN BE GIVEN UK and overseas.
WHO CAN BENEFIT Charitable organisations; registered charities; hospices; hospitals.
WHAT IS FUNDED General charitable purposes, including: health; Christianity; the armed forces; sport and recreation; disability; young people.
WHAT IS NOT FUNDED Individuals.
TYPE OF GRANT Capital costs; general funding.
RANGE OF GRANTS Mostly £1,000 to £5,000 with the occasional larger grant.
SAMPLE GRANTS Euan's Guide (£12,500); Children's Hospice Association Scotland, DEBRA and Scottish Love in Action (£5,000 each); Burnturk and Kettlehill Community Trust, Gurkha Welfare Trust and Scotland Yard Adventure Centre (£2,000 each); Bethany Christian Trust, Erskine Hospital and The Brain Tumour Charity (£1,000 each).
FINANCES *Financial year end* 31/12/2021
Income £109,500
Grants to organisations £56,000
Assets £1,970,000
OTHER INFORMATION The 2021 accounts were the latest available at the time of writing (May 2023).
HOW TO APPLY Apply in writing to the correspondent.
CONTACT DETAILS The Trustees, c/o Jeffree Crawford and Co., 25 Castle Terrace, Edinburgh EH1 2ER

■ Daisie Rich Trust

CC NO 236706   **ESTABLISHED** 1964
WHERE FUNDING CAN BE GIVEN Isle of Wight.
WHO CAN BENEFIT Charitable and community organisations and individuals (particularly former employees, or their spouses, of Upward and Rich Ltd).
WHAT IS FUNDED General charitable purposes; social welfare; community development; young people; health; arts and culture; the environment.
TYPE OF GRANT Running costs; project funding.
RANGE OF GRANTS Typically between £250 and £5,000.
SAMPLE GRANTS UKSA (£8,000); Isle of Wight Youth Trust (£6,100); Isle of Wight Citizens Advice (£5,000); West Wight Churches Youth Project (£3,000); Quay Arts (£2,000); Parkinson's UK Isle of Wight Group (£1,500); Motor Neurone Disease Association Isle of Wight (£1,000); British Epilepsy Association Isle of Wight (£200).
FINANCES *Financial year end* 05/04/2022
Income £158,000
Grants to organisations £121,600
Grants to individuals £21,600
Assets £3,900,000
TRUSTEES Maurice Flux; Ann Medley; James Attrill; Claire Locke; Naomi Keyte; Dawn Haig-Thomas.
OTHER INFORMATION In 2021/22, grants were made to 63 organisations. Grants to organisations and individuals (not including grants made to ex-

employees of Upward and Rich Ltd – £21,600) were broken down as follows: young people (£38,500); welfare (£29,100); services to the community (£25,500); health (£23,800); arts, culture and the environment (£6,300).

HOW TO APPLY Application forms are available on the trust's website. The trustees hold regular meetings to decide on grant applications and are assisted by information gathered by the administrator. Each application is considered on its own merits and the amounts granted vary.

CONTACT DETAILS Lyn Mitchell, Administrator, The Hawthorns, Main Road, Arreton, Newport, Isle of Wight PO30 3AD *Tel.* 07866 449855 *Email* info@daisierichtrust.org.uk *Website* www. daisierichtrust.org.uk

---

■ The Sir Cliff Richard Charitable Trust

CC NO 1096412   **ESTABLISHED** 1969
WHERE FUNDING CAN BE GIVEN UK.
WHO CAN BENEFIT Registered charities.
WHAT IS FUNDED General charitable purposes that reflect the support, Christian commitment and interests of Sir Cliff Richard.
RANGE OF GRANTS £10,000 to £20,000.
SAMPLE GRANTS Depaul UK, London's Air Ambulance, Mid Surrey Mencap, Noah's Ark Children's Hospice and The Rainbow Trust Children's Charity (£20,000 each); Tearfund (£10,000).
FINANCES *Financial year end 30/04/2022*
Income £462,800
Grants to organisations £191,000
Assets £385,600
TRUSTEES Malcolm Smith; Sir Cliff Richard; Tania Hogan.
OTHER INFORMATION Grants of £2,000 or less totalled £61,000 in 2021/22.
HOW TO APPLY Apply in writing to the correspondent.
CONTACT DETAILS The Trustees, PO Box 423, Leatherhead, Surrey KT22 2HJ *Tel.* 01372 467752 *Email* general@cliffrichard.org

---

■ The Clive Richards Foundation

CC NO 327155   **ESTABLISHED** 1986
WHERE FUNDING CAN BE GIVEN Within a 100-mile radius of the centre of Hereford city centre (see the website for a map); Africa; India.
WHO CAN BENEFIT Registered charities; individuals; religious bodies/institutions; hospitals; hospices; schools.
WHAT IS FUNDED General charitable purposes, but there is a preference for education, community, health care, heritage, art and culture; religion.
WHAT IS NOT FUNDED National charities. Operating costs (e.g. revenue costs, salaries) and costs that are or were the responsibility of a statutory organisation are not normally supported.
TYPE OF GRANT Capital costs; seed funding/start-up funding.
SAMPLE GRANTS Childhood Eye Cancer Trust (£50,000). Previous beneficiaries have included: Queen Elizabeth High School (£150,000); Sir Thomas Rich's School (£70,000); Bristol Aero Collection Trust (£50,000).
FINANCES *Financial year end 31/03/2022*
Income £450,500
Grants to organisations £147,400
Grants to individuals £24,800
Assets £1,400,000

TRUSTEES Sylvia Richards; Peter Dines; David Iddon; Peregrine Banbury; Gareth Davies; Liz Deutsch; James Kemp; Penelope Lovell.
OTHER INFORMATION The 2021/22 annual report provides the following breakdown of grants awarded: education (£51,200); medical, health and well-being (£50,800); community and general charitable purposes (£27,600); religion (£7,500); arts, culture and heritage (£950). Only organisations that received grants of over £50,000 were listed as beneficiaries in the foundation's accounts. Grants of under £50,000 totalled £122,100.
HOW TO APPLY Visit the foundation's website for information on how to apply.
CONTACT DETAILS Peter Henry, Stage One Grants Adviser, Lower Hope Estate, Ullingswick, Hereford, Herefordshire HR1 3JF *Tel.* 01432 820663 *Email* admin@cliverichardsfoundation. com *Website* http://csrcharity.com

---

■ Richmond Parish Lands Charity

CC NO 200069   **ESTABLISHED** 1786
WHERE FUNDING CAN BE GIVEN Richmond; Ham; Sheen; Mortlake; and Barnes (the SW13, SW14, TW9 and TW10 postcode areas).
WHO CAN BENEFIT Registered charities; not-for-profit organisations; CICs and CIOs; sports associations; social enterprises; schools; places of worship; individuals.
WHAT IS FUNDED General charitable purposes, including the following: education; sport and recreation; health; community services; younger and older people; social welfare.
WHAT IS NOT FUNDED Private companies.
TYPE OF GRANT Both one-off and recurring grants; core costs; project funding; salaries; capital costs; seed funding/start-up funding.
RANGE OF GRANTS Typically £400 to £60,000.
SAMPLE GRANTS Achieving for Children (£119,500); Citizens Advice Richmond (£55,600); Barnes Community Arts Centre (£20,000); Beautifully Made Foundation (£13,800); Darell Primary School (£5,900); Pensford Tennis Club (£2,000); Windham Nursery (£1,050); Westerley Ware Association (£250).
FINANCES *Financial year end 30/06/2022*
Income £2,720,000
Grants to organisations £2,160,000
Grants to individuals £266,100
Assets £115,170,000
TRUSTEES Owen Carew-Jones; Paul Lawrence; Jerome Misso; Carol Fletcher; Dr Joanna Nakielny; Chris Phillips; Cllr Richard Pyne; Ruth Scott; Claire O'Donnell; Duncan Richford; Stephen Speak; David Herring.
OTHER INFORMATION Grants were awarded to 137 organisations and 305 organisations.
HOW TO APPLY There are separate application forms and guidelines for the various types of grants, all of which can be found on the foundation's helpful website. The foundation welcomes enquiries to discuss ideas for applications. The trustees consider applications at quarterly meetings.
CONTACT DETAILS Cally Ballack-Naude, Grants Manager, Vestry House, 21 Paradise Road, Richmond, Surrey TW9 1SA *Tel.* 020 8948 5701 *Email* use the contact form on the website *Website* www.rplc.org.uk

Think carefully about every application. Is it justified?

617

■ Ridgesave Ltd

cc no 288020   **ESTABLISHED** 1983
WHERE FUNDING CAN BE GIVEN UK and overseas.
WHO CAN BENEFIT Charitable organisations.
WHAT IS FUNDED The advancement of the Jewish religion; education; social welfare.
RANGE OF GRANTS Typically up to £150,000.
SAMPLE GRANTS Keren Association (£150,000); Beis Aharon Trust (£132,600); Kollel Mishkon Yakov (£70,600); Kolel Belz Machnovkeh (£70,600); Friends of Mercaz Hatorah Belz Macnivka (£48,100).
FINANCES *Financial year end 31/03/2022*
Income £601,300
Grants to organisations £604,600
Assets £383,000
TRUSTEES E. Englander; Zelda Weiss; Joseph Weiss; Aaron Hoffman; Menachem Reichman.
OTHER INFORMATION Grants of below £30,000 totalled £109,800.
HOW TO APPLY Apply in writing to the correspondent.
CONTACT DETAILS The Trustees, 141B Upper Clapton Road, London E5 9DB *Tel.* 020 8806 4271 *Email* mail@cohenarnold.com

■ Rigby Foundation

cc no 1011259   **ESTABLISHED** 1992
WHERE FUNDING CAN BE GIVEN UK.
WHO CAN BENEFIT Registered charities; individuals; hospitals; theatres.
WHAT IS FUNDED General charitable purposes; health and the saving of lives; education; arts, culture and heritage; social welfare; the armed forces.
RANGE OF GRANTS From £4,000 up to £150,000.
SAMPLE GRANTS Fly Harrier Trust (£150,000); SWFT (£129,600); Cranfield University and Royal British Legion (£50,000 each); St Mary's Hospice (£20,000); Smiling Families (£5,000); Costford Primary School (£4,000).
FINANCES *Financial year end 05/04/2022*
Income £3,510,000
Grants to organisations £510,400
Assets £6,460,000
TRUSTEES Sir Peter Rigby; Patricia Rigby; Steven Rigby; James Rigby.
OTHER INFORMATION Grants to unnamed beneficiaries totalled £6,000 during 2021/22.
HOW TO APPLY Contact the correspondent for further information.
CONTACT DETAILS The Trustees, Bridgeway House, Bridgeway, Stratford-upon-Avon, Warwickshire CV37 6YX *Tel.* 01789 610000

■ The Sir John Ritblat Family Foundation

cc no 262463   **ESTABLISHED** 1971
WHERE FUNDING CAN BE GIVEN UK.
WHO CAN BENEFIT Charitable organisations.
WHAT IS FUNDED General charitable causes, with some preference for the arts and culture.
WHAT IS NOT FUNDED Individuals.
RANGE OF GRANTS Up to £81,000.
SAMPLE GRANTS United Synagogue (£81,100); Weizmann UK (£25,000); British Ski and Snowboard National Foundation (£20,000); Jewish Interactive (£18,100); The Gold Standard Charitable Trust (£14,000); The Design Museum (£4,600); The Royal Institute of Great Britain (£670); The British Institute of Florence (£500).

FINANCES *Financial year end 05/04/2022*
Income £46,400
Grants to organisations £191,500
Assets £5,510,000
TRUSTEES J. W. J. Ritblat; N. S. J. Ritblat; Sir John Ritblat; Michael Cohen.
OTHER INFORMATION Grants were made to 16 organisations during the year.
HOW TO APPLY Apply in writing to the correspondent.
CONTACT DETAILS The Trustees, c/o Delancey Group plc, Lansdowne House, 57 Berkeley Square, London W1J 6ER *Tel.* 020 7448 1956

■ The River Farm Foundation

cc no 1113109   **ESTABLISHED** 2006
WHERE FUNDING CAN BE GIVEN UK and overseas.
WHO CAN BENEFIT Charitable organisations.
WHAT IS FUNDED General charitable purposes, in particular: health and well-being; education; community development; children; homelessness; disadvantaged groups.
RANGE OF GRANTS Up to £790,000 but mostly under £25,000.
SAMPLE GRANTS Busoga Trust (£790,000); St Edmund Hall – Tutorial Fellowship (£713,000); Ensemble Pour la Différence (£72,000); Helen and Douglas House and NSPCC (£20,600 each); Royal British Legion (£7,300).
FINANCES *Financial year end 05/04/2022*
Income £455,000
Grants to organisations £1,950,000
Assets £64,380,000
TRUSTEES Mark Haworth; Nigel Langstaff; Deborah Fisher.
OTHER INFORMATION During 2021/22, grants were made to 14 organisations. Grants were distributed in the following categories: education (£949,300); community development (£862,000); health and welfare (£121,400); the environment and heritage (£18,200).
HOW TO APPLY Contact the correspondent for further information.
CONTACT DETAILS Deborah Fisher, Trustee, Unit 4, Hill Farm, Kirby Road, Kirby Bedon, Norwich, Norfolk NR14 7DU *Tel.* 01508 480100 *Email* info@fisherlegal.co.uk

■ The River Trust

cc no 275843   **ESTABLISHED** 1977
WHERE FUNDING CAN BE GIVEN UK, with a preference for Sussex.
WHO CAN BENEFIT Charitable organisations; missionaries.
WHAT IS FUNDED Evangelical Christian causes.
WHAT IS NOT FUNDED Individuals; repairs of church fabric; funding towards capital expenditure.
RANGE OF GRANTS Mostly up to £10,000.
SAMPLE GRANTS Barcombe PCC (£12,000); Youth with a Mission (£8,700); CARE (£6,500); Scripture Union (£5,000); Stewards Trust (£4,500); Church Pastoral Aid Society (£3,000); St Stephen's Society (£2,000); African Enterprise (£1,000).
FINANCES *Financial year end 31/10/2021*
Income £116,800
Grants to organisations £122,700
Assets £443,400
TRUSTEES Davina Irwin-Clark; S. G. Kleinwort Hambros Trust Company (UK) Ltd.
OTHER INFORMATION During the year, 42 grants were awarded within the following categories: the advancement of the Christian faith (£28,700 in six grants); miscellaneous (£19,500 in nine

grants); religious welfare work (£18,000 in nine grants); religious education (£27,500 in nine grants); church funds (£12,000 in one grant); missionary work (£17,000 in eight grants). The 2020/21 accounts were the latest available at the time of writing (May 2023).

HOW TO APPLY Apply in writing to the correspondent. Only successful applicants are notified of the trustees' decision. The 2020/21 annual report states: 'Donations are decided periodically, and it is unusual for the trustees to respond favourably to unsolicited appeals.'

CONTACT DETAILS The Trustees, SG Kleinwort Hambros Trust Company (UK) Ltd, 5th Floor, 8 St James's Square, London SW1Y 4JU *Tel.* 020 3207 7041 *Email* scott.rice@kleinworthambros.com

■ Rivers Foundation

CC NO 1078545   **ESTABLISHED** 1999
WHERE FUNDING CAN BE GIVEN UK and overseas.
WHO CAN BENEFIT Charitable organisations, with a preference for small charities.
WHAT IS FUNDED Education; social welfare.
TYPE OF GRANT Project costs; capital costs; educational fees; overseas trips.
SAMPLE GRANTS Grenfell Athletics Club; Hua Hin Charity; Madex; Music Masters; Navy Wings; St Vincent de Paul Society; The Longford Trust.
FINANCES *Financial year end 31/03/2022*
  Income £76,500
  Grants to organisations £86,600
  Assets £670,400
TRUSTEES Christine Bolton; Keith Constable; Alan Rivers; Cass Farrar; Susan Rivers; Euan Macmillan.
HOW TO APPLY Contact the correspondent for further information on the application process.
CONTACT DETAILS The Trustees, 190 Campden Hill Road, London W8 7TH *Tel.* 020 7792 1234 *Email* ajrultra@btinternet.com

■ Riverside Charitable Trust Ltd

CC NO 264015   **ESTABLISHED** 1972
WHERE FUNDING CAN BE GIVEN England and Wales, strong preference for Rossendale, Lancashire.
WHO CAN BENEFIT Charitable organisations; individuals.
WHAT IS FUNDED Education; relief of sickness for older people; relief of poverty for people employed or formerly employed in the shoe trade; general charitable purposes.
SAMPLE GRANTS A list of beneficiaries was not included in the annual report and accounts.
FINANCES *Financial year end 05/04/2022*
  Income £30,900
  Grants to organisations £85,500
  Grants to individuals £13,000
  Assets £1,790,000
TRUSTEES Mark Butterworth; Ian Dearing; Barry Lynch; Angela O'Gorman; Brian Terry; Nicholas Green.
OTHER INFORMATION During 2021/22, the trust awarded over 147 grants to organisations and individuals, totalling £98,500. Grants were distributed as follows: relief of poverty (£38,600); general charitable public benefit (£28,700); relief of sickness (£18,200); retired employees (£8,000); death grants (£5,000). A specific breakdown was not available, but we believe at least £13,000 was awarded to individuals.
HOW TO APPLY Apply in writing to the correspondent.

CONTACT DETAILS Mark Butterworth, Trustee/Secretary, c/o E. Suttons and Sons Ltd, PO Box 2, Bacup, Lancashire OL13 0DT *Tel.* 01706 874961 *Email* mark.butterworth@esutton.co.uk

■ The Rix-Thompson-Rothenberg Foundation

CC NO 285368   **ESTABLISHED** 1982
WHERE FUNDING CAN BE GIVEN England; Wales; Northern Ireland.
WHO CAN BENEFIT Registered charities; CICs; museums; theatres; arts organisations.
WHAT IS FUNDED People with learning disabilities and their carers; projects involving the arts that will enhance social interaction.
RANGE OF GRANTS £1,000 to £7,000.
SAMPLE GRANTS RIX Research and Media (£14,000); Sussex Association for Spina Bifida and Hydrocephalus (£7,000); Conwy Connect (£6,700); Breakthrough (£5,000); Birmingham Royal Ballet (£4,000); Mousetrap Theatre (£3,100).
FINANCES *Financial year end 31/12/2021*
  Income £125,700
  Grants to organisations £151,300
  Grants to individuals £6,000
  Assets £1,800,000
TRUSTEES Barrie Davis; Fred Heddell; Prof. Jonathan Rix; Suzanne Marriott; Prof. Andy Minnion; Bob Rothenberg; Simon Fox; Rory Kinnear.
OTHER INFORMATION The 2021 accounts were the latest available at the time of writing (June 2023). In 2021 the foundation made grants to 32 organisations and 4 individuals.
HOW TO APPLY Applicants must discuss the proposed work (either by telephone, email or letter) with the correspondent at least four months before a board meeting, which occur twice per annum (June and December). An application form must be accompanied by a copy of the organisation's latest audited accounts. Requests received without going through the correct process will not be acknowledged or considered.
CONTACT DETAILS The Administrator, c/o Pamis, University of Dundee, 15/16 Springfield, Dundee DD1 4JE *Tel.* 07532 320138 *Email* rtrfoundation@gmail.com

■ RJM Charity Trust

CC NO 288336   **ESTABLISHED** 1983
WHERE FUNDING CAN BE GIVEN England and Wales.
WHO CAN BENEFIT Charitable organisations.
WHAT IS FUNDED General charitable purposes.
SAMPLE GRANTS A list of beneficiaries was not available.
FINANCES *Financial year end 05/04/2022*
  Income £0
  Grants to organisations £273,500
TRUSTEES Joshua Rowe; Michelle Rowe.
OTHER INFORMATION Full accounts were not available to view on the Charity Commission's website due to the charity's low income. We have therefore estimated the grant total based on the charity's total expenditure.
HOW TO APPLY Apply in writing to the correspondent.
CONTACT DETAILS The Trustees, 84 Upper Park Road, Salford M7 4JA *Tel.* 0161 720 8787 *Email* JR@broomwell.com

■ RNID (The Royal National Institute for Deaf People)

CC NO 207720 **ESTABLISHED** 1962
WHERE FUNDING CAN BE GIVEN UK.
WHO CAN BENEFIT Research institutions; universities; hospitals.
WHAT IS FUNDED Research into hearing loss and tinnitus.
TYPE OF GRANT Research funding; fellowships; studentships.
RANGE OF GRANTS Up to £25,000.
SAMPLE GRANTS University College London (£206,000); Stanford University (£130,000); University of Sheffield (£118,000); University of Cambridge (£90,000); University of Manchester (£65,000); King's College London (£50,000); Cardiff University (£15,000); University Medical Centre Groningen (£10,000).
FINANCES *Financial year end 31/03/2022*
Income £22,620,000
Grants to organisations £1,320,000
Assets £7,350,000
TRUSTEES Dr Brian Caul; Claire Bailey; Gideon Hoffman; Lindsay Foster; Sally Harris; Ita Murphy; Nicholas Waring; Julian Meekings; Gillian Budd; Ewen Stevenson.
OTHER INFORMATION In 2021/22, the charity awarded 37 grants to 22 organisations.
HOW TO APPLY Details on current grant programmes, along with application opening/closing dates, can be found on the website. Alternatively, email research@rnid.org.uk to be notified of new grant calls.
CONTACT DETAILS The Trustees, Brightfield Business Hub, Bakewell Road, Orton Southgate, Peterborough PE2 6XU *Tel.* 0808 808 0123 *Email* research@rnid.org.uk *Website* https://rnid.org.uk

■ The Roan Charitable Trust

CC NO 1122851 **ESTABLISHED** 2008
WHERE FUNDING CAN BE GIVEN UK and overseas.
WHO CAN BENEFIT Registered charities.
WHAT IS FUNDED General charitable purposes including the following: social welfare; medical research; overseas aid; education.
RANGE OF GRANTS Mainly between £5,000 and £25,000, with some larger grants.
SAMPLE GRANTS Cancer Research UK (£100,000); RNIB (£75,000); Royal Opera House Covent Garden Foundation (£55,250); React (Rapid Effective Assistance for Children with potentially Terminal illness) (£50,000); The Royal Marsden Cancer Charity (£25,000); Mind (£20,000); Volunteering Matters (£15,000) Basingstoke and North Hampshire Medical Trust Fund (£10,000); Parkinson's UK (£5,000); SAFE (£1,000).
FINANCES *Financial year end 31/03/2022*
Income £204,300
Grants to organisations £447,300
Assets £8,750,000
TRUSTEES Amelia Harris; Susan Swete; Lady Margaret Jarvis; Trevor Swete.
OTHER INFORMATION Grants were awarded to 19 organisations during 2021/22.
HOW TO APPLY Apply in writing to the correspondent. The trust's 2021/22 accounts state: 'There is no formal grant application procedure. The trustees retain the services of a charitable grants advisor and take account of [their] advice when deciding on grants.'

CONTACT DETAILS The Trustees, c/o Solid Management Ltd, PO Box 2696, Woodford Green, London IG8 1UF *Tel.* 07771 711188 *Email* jeff@solidmanagement.co.uk

■ The Robertson Trust

OSCR NO SC002970 **ESTABLISHED** 1961
WHERE FUNDING CAN BE GIVEN Scotland.
WHO CAN BENEFIT Registered charities; constituted community groups.
WHAT IS FUNDED The trust has four funding strands aimed at alleviating poverty and trauma: financial well-being, emotional well-being and relationships, educational pathways and work pathways. The trust has specific priorities within these four strands – see the website for details.
WHAT IS NOT FUNDED Funding is aimed at organisations with an annual income of under £2 million. However, each of the grant types has its own eligibility criteria specifying the type and annual income levels of organisations that can apply. Consult the trust's website for full exclusion criteria.
TYPE OF GRANT Capital funding; revenue funding (unrestricted and restricted); project costs; salaries; capacity building; one-off and recurrent grants (up to five years).
RANGE OF GRANTS Dependent on grant type – see the website for full details.
SAMPLE GRANTS The trust publishes a full list of grants it has awarded to organisations on its website.
FINANCES *Financial year end 31/03/2022*
Income £21,880,000
Grants to organisations £21,310,000
Grants to individuals £2,540,000
Assets £848,850,000
TRUSTEES Mark Batho; Andrew Walls; Campbell Robb; Donald Workman; Edel Harris; Fiona Larg; Garry Coutts; Gerry McLaughlin; Heather Lamont; John Loughton; Judy Cromarty; Ligia Teixeira; Lorne Crerar; Prof. Morag Treanor.
HOW TO APPLY Applications can be made through the trust's website where further guidance is also available.
CONTACT DETAILS The Trustees, Robertson House, 152 Bath Street, Glasgow G2 4TB *Tel.* 0141 353 7300 *Email* funding@therobertsontrust.org.uk *Website* www.therobertsontrust.org.uk

■ The Dezna Robins Jones Charitable Foundation

CC NO 1104252 **ESTABLISHED** 2004
WHERE FUNDING CAN BE GIVEN UK, with a preference for South Wales and Rhondda Cynon Taff.
WHO CAN BENEFIT Local charitable organisations; hospitals; hospices; educational institutions.
WHAT IS FUNDED Medical and health; education, including arts and sports education; general charitable purposes.
RANGE OF GRANTS £200 to £62,000.
SAMPLE GRANTS Previous beneficiaries have included: Neil Boobyer Rugby Solutions Ltd (£62,500); Mid Rhondda Band (£27,500); Sporting Marvels (£15,000); ActionAid (£10,000); Costas Lazarou Medical Costs (£6,000); Kids Cancer Charity and Velindre Hospital (£5,000 each); Cerebra (£1,000); Macmillan Cancer Support (£500); Breast Cancer Campaign (£250).
FINANCES *Financial year end 31/03/2022*
Income £15,000
Grants to organisations £85,600

TRUSTEES Louise Boobyer; Alexia Cooke.

OTHER INFORMATION Full accounts for 2021/22 were not available to view on the Charity Commission's website due to the charity's low income. We have therefore estimated the charity's grant total based on its total expenditure.

HOW TO APPLY Apply in writing to the correspondent.

CONTACT DETAILS The Trustees, Greenacres, Laleston, Bridgend CF32 0HN *Tel.* 01656 768584 *Email* alexia.cooke@yahoo.co.uk

---

■ The Rock Foundation

CC NO 294775   **ESTABLISHED** 1986

WHERE FUNDING CAN BE GIVEN Worldwide.

WHO CAN BENEFIT Charitable organisations, especially those which are built upon a clear biblical basis and which, in most instances, receive little or no publicity. Individuals are also supported.

WHAT IS FUNDED Christian ministries and causes.

RANGE OF GRANTS Most grants are of less than £5,000.

SAMPLE GRANTS Word One to One (£123,800); Saffires (£40,900); Escale (£26,100); Cranleigh Baptist Church (£9,900); Institute of Bible Teaching (£6,300); Baltic Reformed Theological Seminary (£5,000).

FINANCES *Financial year end 05/04/2022*
Income £450,500
Grants to organisations £471,200
Grants to individuals £19,600
Assets £320,000

TRUSTEES Richard Borgonon; Jane Borgonon; Nancy Benham; Nicholas Marsh; David Burt.

OTHER INFORMATION Grants of under £5,000 totalled £490,800. During the year, grants were awarded to 89 individuals.

HOW TO APPLY Unsolicited applications are not accepted.

CONTACT DETAILS The Trustees, Park Green Cottage, Barhatch Road, Cranleigh, Surrey GU6 7DJ *Tel.* 07887 752159

■ Rockcliffe Charitable Trust

CC NO 274117   **ESTABLISHED** 1977

WHERE FUNDING CAN BE GIVEN UK.

WHO CAN BENEFIT Registered charities; educational establishments; hospitals and hospices; museums.

WHAT IS FUNDED General charitable purposes, in particular: health and health research; education; social welfare, particularly that of children; arts, culture and heritage.

WHAT IS NOT FUNDED Individuals.

RANGE OF GRANTS Typically up to £25,000.

SAMPLE GRANTS Swell Church of England Primary School (£105,000); Oxford Hospitals Charity (£50,000); Turquoise Mountain Trust (£25,300); Kate's Home Nursing (£25,000); London Youth (£20,000); The National Horseracing Museum (£10,000); Operation Smile United Kingdom (£5,000); The Royal Horticultural Society (£4,300); The Sunbeam Children's Trust (£2,000); Red Squirrel Survival Trust and The Royal Marsden Cancer Charity (£1,000 each); Clapton Common Boys Club (£500).

FINANCES *Financial year end 05/04/2022*
Income £330,700
Grants to organisations £312,600
Assets £12,160,000

TRUSTEES Emma Keswick; Simon Keswick; Nicholas Goodson.

OTHER INFORMATION A total of 31 grants were awarded to 28 organisations in 2021/22.

HOW TO APPLY Apply in writing to the correspondent. The 2021/22 annual report and accounts state that 'grant applications are reviewed by the trustees on a regular basis'.

CONTACT DETAILS The Trustees, c/o Matheson and Co. Ltd, Scottish Provident Building, 3 Lombard Street, London EC3V 9AQ *Tel.* 020 7816 8137

■ The Rockspring Charitable Trust

CC NO 1175442   **ESTABLISHED** 2017

WHERE FUNDING CAN BE GIVEN England and Wales.

WHO CAN BENEFIT Charitable organisations.

WHAT IS FUNDED General charitable purposes; education/training; the advancement of health or saving of lives; the arts, culture, heritage and science.

RANGE OF GRANTS £10,000 to £240,000.

SAMPLE GRANTS Chipping Campden School (£240,000); The Kensington and Chelsea Foundation (£106,700); Norwich-Dedza Partnership (£10,500); Reach Arts (£5,500).

FINANCES *Financial year end 31/12/2021*
Income £473,800
Grants to organisations £362,700
Assets £5,130,000

TRUSTEES Richard Plummer; Fiona Plummer; Graham Carter; Susan Floyd.

OTHER INFORMATION Grants were awarded to four organisations in 2021.

HOW TO APPLY Apply in writing to the correspondent.

CONTACT DETAILS Susan Floyd, Trustee, Wright Hassall, Olympus Avenue, Tachbrook Park, Warwick CV34 6BF *Tel.* 01926 883016 *Email* susan.floyd@wrighthassall.co.uk

---

■ The Roddick Foundation

CC NO 1061372   **ESTABLISHED** 1997

WHERE FUNDING CAN BE GIVEN UK and overseas.

WHO CAN BENEFIT Charitable and non-charitable organisations.

WHAT IS FUNDED Arts and culture; the environment; human rights; health/medical causes; social justice; education; the media; humanitarian aid.

WHAT IS NOT FUNDED Sport projects; fundraising events or conferences; sponsorship of any kind.

TYPE OF GRANT Project costs; core costs; capital costs.

RANGE OF GRANTS £1,000 to £150,000.

SAMPLE GRANTS Choose Love (£150,000); Abortion Access Front (£57,300); AHA! (£60,000); Appeal (£30,000); Associacao Dos Ashanika Do Rio Amonia Apiutxa (£25,000); CARIS Families (£17,100); Common Ground Relief (£13,600); Environmental Funders Network (£1,500).

FINANCES *Financial year end 31/03/2022*
Income £267,900
Grants to organisations £1,570,000
Assets £17,190,000

TRUSTEES Justine Roddick; Mr G. Roddick; Samantha Roddick; Tina Schlieske.

OTHER INFORMATION The foundation made 46 grants to organisations during the year. Grants were distributed as follows: poverty and social justice (£678,300); human rights (£373,100); the environment (£269,200); education and media (£173,200); art and culture (£73,600).

HOW TO APPLY The foundation does not accept unsolicited applications.

CONTACT DETAILS Karen Smith, The Roddick Foundation, PO Box 838, Chichester PO19 9XP *Email* karen@theroddickfoundation.org *Website* www.theroddickfoundation.org

■ The Rofeh Trust

cc no 1077682 **established** 1999
where funding can be given UK and Israel.
who can benefit Charitable organisations.
what is funded General charitable purposes and religious activities, with a possible preference for Jewish organisations.
sample grants A list of beneficiaries was not included in the annual report and accounts.
finances *Financial year end* 31/03/2022
Income £187,600
Grants to organisations £162,600
Assets £1,440,000
trustees Ruth Dunitz; Sir Henry Eder; Martin Dunitz; Vivian Wineman; Katya Dunitz.
how to apply Apply in writing to the correspondent.
contact details The Trustees, 44 Southway, London NW11 6SA *Tel.* 020 8458 7832

■ The Sir James Roll Charitable Trust

cc no 1064963 **established** 1997
where funding can be given UK.
who can benefit Registered charities; individuals.
what is funded General charitable purposes; interfaith understanding; IT education; research into specific learning disorders; children and young people.
range of grants Up to £10,000 but typically between £800 and £1,000.
sample grants Disasters Emergency Committee Ukraine Appeal (£10,000); Disasters Emergency Committee Afghanistan Crisis Appeal (£5,000); 3H Fund, Acid Survivors Trust International, Carers UK and City Escape (£1,000 each); Able Kidz, Action Medical Research and Church Homeless Trust Ltd (£800) each).
finances *Financial year end* 31/03/2022
Income £230,700
Grants to organisations £174,800
Assets £5,080,000
trustees Brian Elvy; Jonathan Liddiard; Nicholas Wharton.
other information In 2021/22, grants were awarded to 154 organisations.
how to apply Applications should be made in writing to the correspondent. The trustees usually meet around four times a year to assess grant applications.
contact details The Trustees, Downs Farm, Pilgrims Way, Wouldham, Rochester, Kent ME1 3RB *Tel.* 01634 668167
Email rolltrustees@gmail.com

■ The Helen Roll Charity

cc no 299108 **established** 1988
where funding can be given UK.
who can benefit Registered (or exempt) charities.
what is funded General charitable purposes. One of the trustees' aims is to support work for which charities find it difficult or impossible to obtain funds from other sources.
what is not funded Individuals.
type of grant Project funding, often on a start-up basis; most charities receive long-term support.
range of grants Up to £15,000 but mostly between £1,000 and £10,000.
sample grants West Oxfordshire Community Tran (£15,000); Oxford University Botanic Garden (£11,100); Oxford University Ashmolean Museum (£10,000); Pembroke College Oxford (£7,000); Sick Children's Trust Cambridge (£6,000); Our Special Friends (£5,000);

Oxfordshire Association for the Blind (£4,000); Snowden Award Scheme (£2,000); Read Easy (£1,000).
finances *Financial year end* 30/09/2022
Income £90,200
Grants to organisations £201,400
Assets £3,010,000
trustees Christine Reid; Paul Strang; Patrick Stopford; Stephen Williamson; Fiona Weiss; Jessica Mannix; Catherine Staples; Sarah Gunn.
other information The charity aims to distribute around £150,000 to £200,000 annually. The trustees work with the charities and often continue to make grants over a longer period of time. Due to this, there is limited capacity for new grant recipients each year.
how to apply Apply in writing to the correspondent by email or post. Applications are accepted from 1 December to 15 February.
contact details The Trustees, c/o Wenn Townsend Accountants, 30 St Giles, Oxford, Oxfordshire OX1 3LE *Tel.* 01865 559900
Email helenrollapplication@gmail.com

■ The Romney Marsh Historic Churches Trust

cc no 284909 **established** 1982
where funding can be given Kent and East Sussex.
who can benefit Churches.
what is funded The preservation and maintenance of the fabric of churches.
type of grant Mainly one-off grants, but occasional interest-free loans.
range of grants £2,000 to £15,000.
sample grants Mosacis for Snave (£15,600); St Peter and St Paul – Dymchurch (£12,100); St Dunstan – Snargate (£11,500); St Mary – East Guldeford (£7,800); All Saints – Lydd (£6,000); All Saints – Hope (£4,500); St Thomas Becket – Fairfield (£2,500).
finances *Financial year end* 31/12/2021
Income £138,500
Grants to organisations £108,000
Assets £986,400
trustees Peter Anwyl-Harris; David Hanbury; George Staple; Elizabeth Marshall; The Revd Patricia Fogden; Dr Nicholas Hudd; Judge Maple; John Hendy; Joanna Thompson; Celia Heritage; Georgia Small; David Williams; William Barham; Heather Maple.
other information In 2021, grants were awarded to 16 churches.
how to apply Apply in writing to the correspondent.
contact details The Trustees, Lansdell, High Street, Rolvenden, Cranbrook TN17 4LW *Tel.* 01580 241529 *Email* secretary@ romneychurches.org.uk *Website* https:// romneymarshchurches.org.uk

■ The Gerald and Gail Ronson Family Foundation

cc no 1111728 **established** 2005
where funding can be given UK; Israel; USA.
who can benefit Registered charities.
what is funded General charitable purposes; the Jewish faith and community; health; social welfare.
type of grant Capital projects; research.
range of grants Typically less than £15,000.
sample grants Maggie's Centres (£1.23 million); Community Security Trust (£300,000); Imperial War Museum (£50,000); Unlocking Potential (£30,000 in two grants); British Paralympic

Association (£25,000); United Synagogue (£15,000); Art Therapy for Children (£10,000); Grief Encounter (£6,000); Wolfson Hillel Primary School (£2,000); UK Jewish Film (£1,000); Fight for Peace UK (£830).

FINANCES *Financial year end* 31/12/2021
Income £48,200,000
Grants to organisations £7,070,000
Assets £343,420,000

TRUSTEES Alan Goldman; Jonathan Goldstein; Gerald Ronson; Lisa Althasen; Dame Gail Ronson; Nicole Allalouf; Marc Zilkha; Jeffrey Shear; Ian Rosenblatt; Amanda Ronson; Hayley Ronson.

HOW TO APPLY Applications for funding can be made on the foundation's website, although the annual report for 2021 states that the trustees 'do not generally invite unsolicited grant applications, rather relying on the Trustees' connections within the sector to bring relevant projects to the foundation's attention'.

CONTACT DETAILS Jeremy Trent, Secretary, c/o HW Fisher and Co., Acre House, 11–15 William Road, London NW1 3ER *Tel.* 020 7388 7000 *Email* jtrent@hwfisher.co.uk *Website* https://ronsonfoundation.org

---

■ Mrs L. D. Rope's Third Charitable Settlement

CC NO 290533   **ESTABLISHED** 1984
WHERE FUNDING CAN BE GIVEN UK and overseas, with a particular interest in East Suffolk.
WHO CAN BENEFIT Small registered charities that have a large volunteer force.
WHAT IS FUNDED The relief of poverty; homelessness; families; people with disabilities; education for young people; the Roman Catholic religion and ecumenical work; international aid; general charitable purposes.
WHAT IS NOT FUNDED Overseas projects; national charities; buildings; medical research/health care (outside the beneficial area); schools (outside the beneficial area); environmental charities and animal welfare; the arts; matched funding; repayment of debts for individuals.
TYPE OF GRANT For unsolicited requests, grants are usually one-off and small scale.
RANGE OF GRANTS Up to £24,000.
SAMPLE GRANTS Ipswich Academy (£24,400); Suffolk Young People's Health Project (£20,000); Médecins Sans Frontières UK (£15,000); Chaplaincy Benevolent Fund (£12,000); International Rescue Committee (£10,000).
FINANCES *Financial year end* 05/04/2022
Income £2,340,000
Grants to organisations £492,300
Grants to individuals £771,600
Assets £77,000,000
TRUSTEES Jeremy Heal; Ellen Jolly; Catherine Scott; Stephen Serpell.
OTHER INFORMATION Grants were broken down as follows: relief of poverty (£252,700); other (£150,000); advancement of education (£81,600); advancement of religion (£8,000).
HOW TO APPLY Send a concise letter (preferably one side of A4) explaining the main details of your request and include your most recent accounts and a budgeted breakdown of the sum you are looking to raise. The charity will also need to know whether you have applied to other funding sources and whether you have been successful elsewhere. Your application should say who your trustees are and include a daytime telephone number.

CONTACT DETAILS The Trustees, Lucy House, St William Court, Kesgrave, Ipswich, Suffolk IP5 2QP *Tel.* 01473 333288 *Email* ropetrust@lucyhouse.org.uk *Website* www.theropetrust.org.uk

---

■ Rosa Fund

CC NO 1124856   **ESTABLISHED** 2008
WHERE FUNDING CAN BE GIVEN UK.
WHO CAN BENEFIT Charitable organisations.
WHAT IS FUNDED Women's organisations and projects supporting women; women's safety; economic justice; health and well-being; representation in society.
WHAT IS NOT FUNDED Applicants should consult the guidance document on each funding programme's web page for a detailed list of funding exclusions.
TYPE OF GRANT Grant types are programme dependent but include: unrestricted funding; project funding; core/revenue costs.
RANGE OF GRANTS Up to £40,000.
SAMPLE GRANTS Smallwood Trust (£807,000); Coventry Panahghar Project (£50,000); Argyll and Bute Rape Crisis (£14,000); The Hull Lighthouse Project (£5,400); Craft Collective (£1,500).
FINANCES *Financial year end* 31/03/2022
Income £2,370,000
Grants to organisations £2,130,000
Assets £3,010,000
TRUSTEES Sheila Malley; Kay Ali; Catherine Dovey; Gillian Green; Lisa Raftery; Beverley Huie; Sarah Jackson; Sarah Barber; Shanta Assani; Memento Charinga; Claudia Dickens; Esmeralda Gambelli.
HOW TO APPLY Consult the charity's website for information on open programmes. Applications can be made through the charity's online application form before the specific deadline for each programme.
CONTACT DETAILS The Trustees, 4th Floor, Resource for London, 356 Holloway Road, London N7 6PA *Tel.* 020 7697 4013 *Email* info@rosauk.org *Website* https://rosauk.org

---

■ Rosca Trust

CC NO 259907   **ESTABLISHED** 1966
WHERE FUNDING CAN BE GIVEN Southend-on-Sea, Castle Point and Rochford local authority areas.
WHO CAN BENEFIT Registered charities; CICs; voluntary and community groups; churches; hospices. The trust has a stated preference for small, grassroots organisations.
WHAT IS FUNDED Social welfare; community development; people who are disadvantaged; older people; people with disabilities; minority ethnic groups; asylum seekers and refugees; young people.
WHAT IS NOT FUNDED Causes outside the area of benefit; individuals.
TYPE OF GRANT One-off; capital costs; project funding; requests for administration and salary costs are considered low priority.
RANGE OF GRANTS Typically £500 to £5,000.
SAMPLE GRANTS Southend YMCA (£5,000); Belchamps Scout Activity Centre (£4,800); Family Action (£3,300); Southchurch Park Bowling Club (£2,000); Panathlon Foundation (£750).
FINANCES *Financial year end* 31/03/2022
Income £155,500
Grants to organisations £141,900
Assets £174,700

TRUSTEES Nigel Gayner; Christine Sternshine; Anthony Quinn; Judith Bailey; John Harland.

HOW TO APPLY Apply in writing to the correspondent. Full details of what should be included in an application can be found on the trust's website. The trust will only consider one application from each organisation every 12 months. The trustees meet three times a year, in January, May and September. To be considered in any of these months, applications must be submitted before the end of the previous month.

CONTACT DETAILS The Trustees, 1 Moat End, Thorpe Bay, Southend-on-Sea, Essex SS1 3QA *Email* roscatrust@gmail.com *Website* www.roscatrust.org.uk

■ The Rose Animal Welfare Trust CIO

CC NO 1169516

WHERE FUNDING CAN BE GIVEN UK, with a preference for Yorkshire and the Humber.

WHO CAN BENEFIT Registered charities.

WHAT IS FUNDED Animal welfare.

RANGE OF GRANTS From £2,000 up to £20,000.

SAMPLE GRANTS Hull Animal Welfare Trust (£20,000); Humanimal Trust (£15,000); Dogs Trust and The Donkey Sanctuary (£10,000 each); Four Paws and Mare and Foal (£5,000 each): Cruelty Free International Trust (£2,000).

FINANCES *Financial year end 31/10/2021*
Income £2,290,000
Grants to organisations £465,000
Assets £2,830,000

TRUSTEES Antoinette Tomkinson; Nigel Shaw; Elizabeth Webb.

OTHER INFORMATION In 2020/21, 54 organisations were awarded grants. The 2020/21 accounts were the latest available at the time of writing (June 2023).

HOW TO APPLY Apply in writing to the correspondent. Grants are made each year in May and November.

CONTACT DETAILS The Trustees, Triune Court, Monks Cross Drive, Huntington, York YO1 7PR *Tel.* 01274 593779 *Email* npshaw63@gmail.com

■ The Rose Foundation

CC NO 1167144   **ESTABLISHED** 1978

WHERE FUNDING CAN BE GIVEN London.

WHO CAN BENEFIT Registered charities; exempt bodies; museums; theatres; educational institutions; community groups.

WHAT IS FUNDED Building projects where the cost is of less than £200,000. This could be a general refurbishment or a specific project.

WHAT IS NOT FUNDED The purchase of equipment; the purchase of a building or site; seed money required to draw up plans; fees.

TYPE OF GRANT Part-funding of building projects.

RANGE OF GRANTS Typically between £5,000 and £10,000.

SAMPLE GRANTS St John Ambulance (£613,000); New Amsterdam Charitable Foundation (£73,700); The Variety Club (£28,000); Soho Theatre Company (£10,000); Zoological Society of London (£7,500); Old Vic Theatre (£5,000); Nightingale Hammerson (£2,500).

FINANCES *Financial year end 31/10/2021*
Income £1,220,000
Grants to organisations £1,020,000
Assets £29,940,000

TRUSTEES Martin Rose; Alan Rose; John Rose; Paul Rose.

OTHER INFORMATION The 2020/21 accounts were the latest available at the time of writing (May 2023.) The foundation made grants to 46 organisations during the year.

HOW TO APPLY Applications should be made in writing to the correspondent including details of the organisation and the registered charity number, together with the nature and probable approximate cost of the scheme and its anticipated start and completion dates. Applications can be submitted any time between 1 July and 31 March the following year. The trustees hope to inform applicants of their decision by the second week in July. Further information can be found on the foundation's website.

CONTACT DETAILS Martin Rose, Trustee, 28 Crawford Street, London W1H 1LN *Tel.* 020 7262 1155 *Website* www.rosefoundation.co.uk

■ The Roseline Foundation

CC NO 1192886

WHERE FUNDING CAN BE GIVEN The North East, with a preference for Sunderland.

WHO CAN BENEFIT UK-registered charities; museums and galleries.

WHAT IS FUNDED Social welfare; youth; community development; arts; faith; the environment; education; health; museums and heritage.

TYPE OF GRANT Unrestricted; multi-year.

SAMPLE GRANTS Foundation of Light (£800,000).

FINANCES *Financial year end 31/12/2021*
Income £12,020,000
Grants to organisations £800,000
Assets £11,710,000

TRUSTEES Philip Cronin; James Cronin; Robert Cronin; Alison Cronin; Sophie Cronin; Michael Moran; Susanne Kennedy; Michael Cronin; Graham Purvis.

HOW TO APPLY Apply in writing to the correspondent.

CONTACT DETAILS Susanne Kennedy, Trustee, Fernwood House, Fernwood Road, Jesmond, Newcastle upon Tyne NE2 1TJ *Email* susanne.kennedy@roselinefoundation.co.uk

■ The Cecil Rosen Foundation

CC NO 247425   **ESTABLISHED** 1966

WHERE FUNDING CAN BE GIVEN UK and Israel.

WHO CAN BENEFIT Registered charities; universities; religious bodies/institutions.

WHAT IS FUNDED The Jewish faith and community; people with disabilities, including people who are blind; health; education; medical research; social welfare; international disaster appeals.

WHAT IS NOT FUNDED Individuals.

TYPE OF GRANT Capital costs.

SAMPLE GRANTS A list of beneficiaries was not included in the annual report and accounts. Previous beneficiaries have included: Alma Primary School; British Heart Foundation; Cancer Research UK; Great Ormond Street Hospital Children's Charity; Heart Cells Foundation; Jewish Deaf Society; National Institute for the Blind; Yesodeh Hatorah Primary School.

FINANCES *Financial year end 05/04/2022*
Income £489,800
Grants to organisations £400,800
Assets £6,730,000

TRUSTEES Malcolm Ozin; John Hart; Peter Silverman; Simon Lever.

HOW TO APPLY The annual report for 2021/22 states: 'The trustees consider all applications received and give special attention to those which were originally chosen by the Settlor, Cecil Rosen.'

CONTACT DETAILS The Trustees, 35 Langstone Way, Mill Hill East, London NW7 1GT *Tel.* 020 8346 8940 *Email* contact@cecilrosenfoundation.org

---

■ Rosetrees

CC NO 1197546   **ESTABLISHED** 1988
WHERE FUNDING CAN BE GIVEN UK.
WHO CAN BENEFIT Medical research organisations.
WHAT IS FUNDED Medical research.
WHAT IS NOT FUNDED Detailed eligibility criteria for each funding programme can be found on the trust's website.
TYPE OF GRANT Project and research funding; seed funding for preliminary studies; PhD, postdoctoral and fellowship funding; salaries and consumables.
RANGE OF GRANTS Programme dependent.
SAMPLE GRANTS Previous beneficiaries have included: UCL8 Royal Free (£1.42 million); Imperial College London (£622,000); University of Oxford (£509,300); Queen Mary University of London (£358,100); Imperial College London (£178,300); University of Southampton (£62,300).
TRUSTEES Debra Fox; Richard Ross; Sam Howard; Dr Jane Mitchell; Lee Mesnick; Hayley Katz; Mark Stewart.
OTHER INFORMATION Financial information was not available as the charity had recently re-registered with the Charity Commission as a CIO; however, in 2020/21 the charity's grant-making totalled over £5 million.
HOW TO APPLY Application forms and guidelines for each grants programme are available to download from the website. Refer to the website for the dates of application rounds.
CONTACT DETAILS The Trustees, Russell House, 140 High Street, Edgware, Middlesex HA8 7LW *Tel.* 020 8951 2588 *Email* info@rosetreestrust.co.uk *Website* https://rosetreestrust.co.uk

---

■ The Ross Foundation

CC NO 1121871   **ESTABLISHED** 2007
WHERE FUNDING CAN BE GIVEN UK.
WHO CAN BENEFIT Registered charities.
WHAT IS FUNDED The foundation's main focus is young people. Areas of work include education, sport, heritage and the arts.
TYPE OF GRANT One-off.
SAMPLE GRANTS National Portrait Gallery (£1 million); Nottingham University (£307,500); Blackwater Music Festival (£10,000); Lady Garden Fund (£250); Bone Cancer (£100).
FINANCES *Financial year end* 31/03/2022
Income £3,420,000
Grants to organisations £1,880,000
Assets £12,670,000
TRUSTEES Mark Bolland; Anita Bott; David Ross; Marcia Mercier; Lady Caroline Ryder; Ottilie Windsor; Henry Carling; Carl Ross.
HOW TO APPLY Apply in writing to the correspondent. The foundation's website states that applications should include an outline of your project (its purpose and activities), financial information about your project (the total budget, fundraising strategy and the level of funding you are asking for), who the beneficiaries are (community support) and details of the sustainability and legacy of your project.

CONTACT DETAILS Joanne Hoareau, Operations Manager, 10 St James's Place, London SW1A 1NP *Tel.* 020 7534 1551 *Email* joanne@rossfoundation.com *Website* www.davidrossfoundation.co.uk

---

■ The Rothermere Foundation

CC NO 314125   **ESTABLISHED** 1956
WHERE FUNDING CAN BE GIVEN UK.
WHO CAN BENEFIT Registered charities; hospices; hospitals; places of worship; universities; schools; individual graduates of the Memorial University of Newfoundland.
WHAT IS FUNDED General charitable purposes, including: medical research; education; children; arts; sports; religion; armed forces and memorial.
TYPE OF GRANT Bursaries; general funding.
RANGE OF GRANTS Mostly up to £10,000 with the occasional larger grant.
SAMPLE GRANTS Royal Society for Blind Children and Wildlife Conservation Trust (£100,000 each); The Platinum Jubilee Pageant Ltd (£50,000); Oxford University Development Fund (£30,000); Alzheimer's Research and St Mary's School Summer Fields (£10,000 each); Blandford Forum PCC, Dorset and Somerset Air Ambulance and Hands Up Foundation (£5,000 each); The Caring Family and The Dominican Count (£2,000 each); Journalists' Charity, Wild Waves and World Horse Welfare (£1,000 each).
FINANCES *Financial year end* 30/09/2021
Income £1,180,000
Grants to organisations £453,700
Grants to individuals £165,200
Assets £1,920,000
TRUSTEES Vyvyan Harmsworth; The Rt Hon. Viscount Jonathon Rothermere; Viscountess Claudia Rothermere; Gilbert Holbourn.
OTHER INFORMATION Grants totalling £165,2000 were made to support four Rothermere Fellows during the year. Grants to organisations were broken down as follows: general charitable purposes (£281,100); education and children (£184,900); medical research (£30,000); arts and sports (£5,000). The 2020/21 accounts were the latest available at the time of writing (May 2023).
HOW TO APPLY Apply in writing to the correspondent.
CONTACT DETAILS Vyvyan Harmsworth, Trustee, Memory House, Seaton, Ickham, Ickham, Kent CT3 1SL *Tel.* 01227 721279

■ Rothesay Foundation

CC NO 1189490   **ESTABLISHED** 2019
WHERE FUNDING CAN BE GIVEN UK.
WHO CAN BENEFIT Charitable organisations.
WHAT IS FUNDED Older people.
SAMPLE GRANTS Food Train (£190,000); GoodGym (£125,000).
FINANCES *Financial year end* 31/12/2021
Income £257,000
Grants to organisations £315,000
Assets £1,860,000
TRUSTEES Prof. Dame Carol Black; Antigone Loudiadis; James Dickson.
OTHER INFORMATION This is the corporate charity of Rothesay, one of the UK's largest pensions insurance specialists.
HOW TO APPLY Contact the correspondent for further information.
CONTACT DETAILS The Trustees, The Post Building, 100 Museum Street, WC1A 1PB

Email enquiries@rothesaylife.com *Website* www.rothesay.com/about-us/giving-back

······································

■ The Rothley Trust

CC NO 219849   **ESTABLISHED** 1959
WHERE FUNDING CAN BE GIVEN Northumberland; Tyne and Wear; Durham; Cleveland.
WHO CAN BENEFIT Registered charities; CICs; voluntary groups (these must be properly constituted and must find a registered charity to act as a cheque handler).
WHAT IS FUNDED General charitable purposes, with a preference for: children and young people; disability; community projects; education; energy saving projects; ex-Service people; medical causes; humanitarian aid.
WHAT IS NOT FUNDED Further education; the repair of buildings solely used for worship; religious purposes; arts, heritage or science; amateur sport; human rights, conflict resolution or reconciliation (except family mediation); environmental protection or improvement; animal welfare; residents associations; parish councils; University of the Third Age.
TYPE OF GRANT Mainly one-off towards specific projects. Buildings, equipment, website start-up/development costs, resources and capital grants will also be considered.
RANGE OF GRANTS Typically £2,000 and under, with some larger grants.
SAMPLE GRANTS Durham Association of Boys and Girls Clubs (£6,000); Citizens Advice Northumberland (£5,000); Combat Stress (£4,000); Percy Hedley Foundation (£3,000); Community Action Northumberland (£2,000).
FINANCES *Financial year end* 31/03/2022
Income £197,900
Grants to organisations £157,700
Grants to individuals £9,700
Assets £9,480,000
TRUSTEES Julia Brown; Anne Galbraith; David Holborn; Alice Brunton; Gerard Salvin; Donna Anderson.
OTHER INFORMATION Grants for less than £2,000 totalled £117,200. Grants were broken down as follows: children and young people (£39,100); disability (£26,000); medical causes (£20,400); education (£9,700); armed forces (£9,100); world in need (£3,000); energy (£900); older people (£750).
HOW TO APPLY The trust prefers to receive applications by email, although it will also accept applications by post. Full details can be found on the trust's website, where criteria, guidelines and closing dates for applications are posted.
CONTACT DETAILS Gillian Allsopp, Trust Secretary, PO Box 224, Bedlington, Northumberland NE63 3FJ *Email* mail@rothleytrust.co.uk *Website* www.rothleytrust.org.uk

······································

■ The Rothschild Foundation

CC NO 1138145
WHERE FUNDING CAN BE GIVEN UK, with a preference for the area within ten miles of the Waddesdon Estate in Buckinghamshire.
WHO CAN BENEFIT Charitable organisations; registered charities; CICs which are limited by guarantee may apply following confirmation from the Grants Manager.
WHAT IS FUNDED The arts and humanities; heritage; education; the environment; social welfare.
WHAT IS NOT FUNDED Individuals; major capital projects; medical equipment and research; academic research and bursaries; animal charities; projects outside the UK; projects promoting religion; overseas travel; charities and organisations without charitable status.
TYPE OF GRANT Project and core costs.
RANGE OF GRANTS Mostly up to £150,000.
SAMPLE GRANTS Screen Academy Foundation (£250,000); University of Cambridge (£210,000); Sustainable Food Trust (£200,000); Transitions UK (£120,000); The Platinum Jubilee Pageant Ltd (£100,000); Signdance Collective (£61,000); The Mayor's Fund for London (£50,000).
FINANCES *Financial year end* 28/02/2022
Income £44,310,000
Grants to organisations £7,040,000
Assets £864,200,000
TRUSTEES The Hon. Janet Botton; The Hon. Hannah Rothschild; Lord Rothschild Om; Francesco Goedhuis; The Hon. Emily Freeman-Attwood; Peter Troughton; Christopher Kemp; S. J. P. Trust Corporation Ltd.
OTHER INFORMATION Grants were made to 225 organisations during the year. Grants were distributed as follows: education and social welfare (£3.58 million); the arts and humanities (£2.24 million); energy and the environment (£1.22 million).
HOW TO APPLY Application processes may vary depending on the programme being applied to. Check the website for open programmes and relevant application details.
CONTACT DETAILS Ellie Stout, Head of Grants, Windmill Hill, Silk Street, Waddesdon, Aylesbury Vale HP18 0JZ *Tel.* 01296 653208 *Email* grants@rothschildfoundation.org.uk or info@rothschildfoundation.org.uk *Website* https://rothschildfoundation.org.uk

······································

■ The Eranda Rothschild Foundation

CC NO 255650   **ESTABLISHED** 1967
WHERE FUNDING CAN BE GIVEN UK and overseas; for charities working locally, priority is given to those in Buckinghamshire and Bedfordshire.
WHO CAN BENEFIT Registered charities; CIOs.
WHAT IS FUNDED Medical research; education; the arts; social welfare (especially work known to the trustees).
WHAT IS NOT FUNDED Individuals; organisations which are not registered charities; capital appeals (unless of personal significance to the trustees).
RANGE OF GRANTS Up to £150,000.
SAMPLE GRANTS Hygienebank (£150,000); Royal College of Art (£125,000); Global Greengrants (£90,000); McCain Institute Foundation (£76,500); School Readers Buckinghamshire (£28,500); Creative Dimensions Trust (£25,000); Somerset House Trust (£20,000); London School of Economics (£10,000).
FINANCES *Financial year end* 05/04/2022
Income £5,130,000
Grants to organisations £737,900
Assets £147,440,000
TRUSTEES Sir Evelyn Rothschild; Anthony Rothschild; Lady De Rothschild; Jessica Rothschild; Sir John Peace; Benjamin Elliot.
OTHER INFORMATION In 2021/22, grants were awarded to 12 organisations and broken down as follows: education (£317,900); health, welfare and medical research (£250,000); the arts (£170,000).
HOW TO APPLY The trustees prefer applications to be made using the online form on the foundation's website. Applications are considered at

meetings held three times a year, usually in February/March, June/July and October/November. Charities should make only one application per year. Online applications are acknowledged automatically and every applicant will be notified of the trustees' decision (this may take several months). The foundation's website notes that it always receives more applications than it is able to fund.

CONTACT DETAILS The Secretary, PO Box 6226, Leighton Buzzard, Bedfordshire LU7 0XF *Tel.* 01296 689157 *Email* secretary@erandarothschild.org *Website* www.erandarothschild.org

······································

■ Rothschild Foundation (Hanadiv) Europe

CC NO 1083262   **ESTABLISHED** 2000
WHERE FUNDING CAN BE GIVEN UK; Europe; Israel.
WHO CAN BENEFIT Registered charities; universities; individuals.
WHAT IS FUNDED Jewish heritage: Jewish community welfare; Jewish education; academic research into Judaism.
WHAT IS NOT FUNDED See the website for a comprehensive list of general and programme-specific exclusions.
TYPE OF GRANT Core/revenue costs; project funding; research; unrestricted funding.
RANGE OF GRANTS Typically under £100,000.
SAMPLE GRANTS Gesher L'Europa (£590,000); Bodleian Libraries (£133,300); Oxford Centre for Hebrew and Jewish Studies (£115,400); Jewish Care (£100,000); Wiener Holocaust Library (£93,800); Tyne and Wear Archives and Museums (£80,000); Community Security Trust (£75,000); Trinity College Dublin (£53,600).
FINANCES *Financial year end* 31/12/2021
Income £486,100
Grants to organisations £5,590,000
Assets £147,000,000
TRUSTEES Adam Karni-Cohen; David Landau; Madame Beatrice Rosenberg; Lord Rothschild; Sir Maurice Blank; The Hon. Beth Rothschild; Nicola Cobbold; Nicola Loftus; Bradley Fried; Ben Avigdori.
OTHER INFORMATION The grant total includes grants made in the UK and Europe, as well as six grants to European organisations working in the US and Israel. Only beneficiaries of grants of over £50,000 were listed in the accounts. Grants of less than £50,000 totalled £1.13 million. Note that the grant total includes amounts awarded to individuals.
HOW TO APPLY Applications must be submitted via the online application process. Refer to the website for application forms, deadlines and guidance for each programme.
CONTACT DETAILS Grant Programmes Manager, 15 St James's Place, London SW1A 1NP *Tel.* 01296 658778 *Email* info@rothschildfoundation.eu *Website* www.rothschildfoundation.eu

······································

■ The Roughley Charitable Trust

CC NO 264037   **ESTABLISHED** 1972
WHERE FUNDING CAN BE GIVEN Birmingham and overseas.
WHO CAN BENEFIT Registered charities, with priority given to small and medium-sized organisations.
WHAT IS FUNDED Community work (including church-based projects); social welfare for children and young people, older people, people with disabilities, offenders, people with addiction and other marginalised groups; homelessness; health and well-being; education; arts and leisure; heritage; the environment (particularly environmental improvement and green projects); development projects (overseas).
WHAT IS NOT FUNDED Birmingham-based medical charities; church fabric appeals; CICs; social enterprises; church-based projects which are essentially about the teaching of religion; animal charities; national charities, even if the charity has a Birmingham project or branch (unless the branch is a registered charity in its own right). Applications for projects outside the Birmingham city boundary are not normally accepted.
TYPE OF GRANT Core and revenue costs; seed funding; start-up funding.
RANGE OF GRANTS Mostly £1,000 to £3,000. Larger grants are made to projects where trustees have special knowledge.
SAMPLE GRANTS Practical Action (£10,000); Spitfire Advice and Support Services (£5,000); Entraide Mutual Aid (£4,000); Acacia Family Support (£3,000); St Mark's Community Hub (£2,000); Birmingham Boys and Girls Union (£1,500); Big Brum – Theatre in Education and Birmingham Bach Choir (£1,000 each).
FINANCES *Financial year end* 05/04/2022
Income £268,100
Grants to organisations £196,300
Assets £8,200,000
TRUSTEES Martin Smith; John Smith; Verity Owen; Rachel Richards; Benjamin Newton; Camilla Newton; Caroline Ward.
OTHER INFORMATION Grants were made to 39 organisations in 2021/22. During the year, grants were broken down as follows: Birmingham area – larger grants (£66,300); international grants (£65,500); Birmingham area – smaller grants (£64,500).
HOW TO APPLY Unsolicited applications are only accepted for charitable work in Birmingham. Applications should be made using the form available to download on the trust's website, where the trust's eligibility criteria, guidelines and key dates are also available. Application forms should be returned to the trust by email, along with a signed letter on headed paper, two or three photographs which give a good idea of what the project is about, and any other supporting material.
CONTACT DETAILS Adam Wilkins, Correspondent, 562 Kenilworth Road, Balsall Common, Coventry CV7 7RZ *Email* correspondent@roughleytrust.org.uk *Website* www.roughleytrust.org.uk

······································

■ The Row Fogo Charitable Trust

OSCR NO SC009685   **ESTABLISHED** 1970
WHERE FUNDING CAN BE GIVEN Edinburgh.
WHO CAN BENEFIT Registered charities; local charitable groups.
WHAT IS FUNDED Medical research projects; local projects; care of older people.
RANGE OF GRANTS Mostly £1,000 to £5,000.
SAMPLE GRANTS RNLI (£9,000); Erskine Hospital (£7,000); Cancer Support Scotland (£3,000); Deafblind Scotland and Penumbra (£1,500 each).
FINANCES *Financial year end* 05/04/2022
Income £183,800
Grants to organisations £89,500
Assets £5,910,000
HOW TO APPLY Apply in writing to the correspondent.
CONTACT DETAILS The Trustees, c/o Brodies LLP Solicitors, Capital Square, 50 Morrison Street, Edinburgh EH3 8BP

■ Rowanville Ltd

CC NO 267278 **ESTABLISHED** 1973
WHERE FUNDING CAN BE GIVEN UK, Israel and overseas.
WHO CAN BENEFIT Charitable organisations; Jewish religious and educational organisations.
WHAT IS FUNDED The advancement of the Orthodox Jewish faith.
RANGE OF GRANTS Up to £85,000.
SAMPLE GRANTS Tchabe Kollel Ltd (£85,000); Start Upright (£40,300); Zlotchiv (£40,000).
FINANCES *Financial year end 30/06/2022*
Income £970,700
Grants to organisations £621,900
Assets £11,860,000
TRUSTEES Joseph Pearlman; Ruth Pearlman; Allan Becker.
OTHER INFORMATION Grants of £40,000 or less totalled £456,600.
HOW TO APPLY Apply in writing to the correspondent.
CONTACT DETAILS The Trustees, 8 Highfield Gardens, London NW11 9HB *Tel.* 020 8458 9266

■ The Rowlands Trust

CC NO 1062148 **ESTABLISHED** 1996
WHERE FUNDING CAN BE GIVEN Primarily the West Midlands with a preference for Birmingham, Gloucestershire, Herefordshire, Shropshire, Warwickshire and Worcestershire.
WHO CAN BENEFIT Registered charities; CICs; museums; hospices; schools; Anglican churches; universities; uniformed groups; community groups.
WHAT IS FUNDED General charitable purposes, with a preference for: medical and scientific research; the Services; health; social welfare; older people; people with disabilities; music; the arts; the environment; the maintenance and restoration of Anglican church buildings.
WHAT IS NOT FUNDED Individuals; animal charities; annual running costs; projects eligible for state funding.
TYPE OF GRANT Capital expenditure including buildings, projects and research.
RANGE OF GRANTS Mostly up to £7,000, occasionally larger.
SAMPLE GRANTS Belgrade Theatre (£10,000); Side by Side Theatre Company (£3,000); Brampton Abbotts Village Hall (£2,500); Ataxia UK (£2,000).
FINANCES *Financial year end 31/12/2021*
Income £77,600
Grants to organisations £383,600
Assets £2,490,000
TRUSTEES Gary Barber; Diana Crabtree; Ian Smith; Rebecca Widdowson; Patrick Wrixon.
HOW TO APPLY Application forms are available from the correspondent. The trustees meet to consider grants four times a year.
CONTACT DETAILS Louise Ruane, Administrator, c/o Bishop Fleming LLP, 1–4 College Yard, Worcester, Worcestershire WR1 2LB *Tel.* 07812 743485 *Email* louise.ruane@therowlandstrust.org.uk

■ The Joseph Rowntree Charitable Trust

CC NO 210037 **ESTABLISHED** 1904
WHERE FUNDING CAN BE GIVEN UK and overseas.
WHO CAN BENEFIT Registered charities; unregistered charities; CICs; social enterprises; universities; religious bodies/organisations; individuals.
WHAT IS FUNDED Peace and security; power and accountability; rights and justice; sustainable future; Northern Ireland.
WHAT IS NOT FUNDED A full list of exclusions can be found on the trust's website.
TYPE OF GRANT Core/revenue costs; seed funding/start-up funding; project funding; unrestricted funding.
RANGE OF GRANTS Up to £300,000.
SAMPLE GRANTS Two Ridings Community Foundation (£330,000); Generation Rent (£198,200); Article 36 (£86,800); Peaceful Change Initiative (£39,100); Aston University (£21,300); Centre for Knowledge Equity (£14,700); The Commonweal Trust (£9,600); The HUBB Community Development Resource Centre (£5,000).
FINANCES *Financial year end 31/12/2021*
Income £1,880,000
Grants to organisations £10,750,000
Assets £348,660,000
TRUSTEES Helen Carmichael; Hannah Torkington; Jennifer Amery; Linda Batten; John Fitzgerald; Huw Davies; David Newton; Janet Slade; Hannah Darton; Marghuerita Remi-Judah.
HOW TO APPLY Apply via the trust's website, where application deadlines can also be found.
CONTACT DETAILS The Trustees, The Garden House, Water End, York, North Yorkshire YO30 6WQ *Tel.* 01904 627810 *Email* enquiries@jrct.org.uk *Website* www.jrct.org.uk

■ The Joseph Rowntree Foundation

CC NO 1184957 **ESTABLISHED** 1904
WHERE FUNDING CAN BE GIVEN UK.
WHO CAN BENEFIT Registered charities; CICs; social enterprises; universities.
WHAT IS FUNDED Research and policy work related to solving poverty.
WHAT IS NOT FUNDED See the website for a full list of exclusions.
TYPE OF GRANT Project funding; research.
RANGE OF GRANTS Up to £315,000.
SAMPLE GRANTS Heriot-Watt University (£494,000); Poverty Truth Network (£120,000); Citizens UK (£55,000); Shelter (£35,000); The Poverty Alliance (£25,000).
FINANCES *Financial year end 31/12/2021*
Income £34,230,000
Grants to organisations £3,660,000
Assets £596,520,000
TRUSTEES William Haire; Prof. Carol Tannahill; Deborah Cadman; Dr Saphie Ashtiany; David Lunts; Paul Jenkins; Hilary Cottam; Zeinab Elahi; Lesley Russell; Kenechukwu Umeasiegbu; Prof. Joanna Swaffield.
OTHER INFORMATION Grants of under £25,000 totalled £315,000. At the time of writing (May 2023), the foundation's website stated that it was in a transition period regarding its strategy and funding opportunities. Check the foundation's website for up-to-date information.
HOW TO APPLY Apply for funding by responding to a call for proposals. Applicants should submit a completed budget form (available to download from the foundation's website) and a proposal for the project. Unsolicited proposals outside open calls are not accepted.
CONTACT DETAILS The Trustees, The Homestead, 40 Water End, York, North Yorkshire YO30 6WP *Tel.* 01904 629241 *Email* info@jrf.org.uk *Website* www.jrf.org.uk

■ Royal Artillery Charitable Fund

CC NO 210202 **ESTABLISHED** 1964
WHERE FUNDING CAN BE GIVEN UK.
WHO CAN BENEFIT Service charities; regiments; individuals.
WHAT IS FUNDED The welfare, relief and assistance of any past or present members of the Royal Artillery, their dependants and families, who are in need.
TYPE OF GRANT Capital costs, typically on a recurrent basis; hardship grants to individuals.
RANGE OF GRANTS Typically £1,000 to £65,000. Grants to individuals average £700.
SAMPLE GRANTS ABF The Soldiers' Charity (£79,500); Royal Artillery Sports (£51,900); Gunner Magazine (£3,900). Previous beneficiaries have included: King Edward VII Hospital and Veterans Aid (£3,000 each); Army Widows' Association and Not Forgotten Association (£1,000 each).
FINANCES *Financial year end 31/12/2021*
Income £1,320,000
Grants to organisations £224,900
Grants to individuals £523,500
Assets £39,370,000
TRUSTEES Maj. Andrew Dines; Mr C. Fletcher-Wood; Maj. James Leighton; Maj. General David Cullen; Col. Christopher Comport; Col. Michael Relph; Brigadier Mark Pountain; Col. Craig Palmer; Col. Graham Taylor; Col. Mark Dornan; Lt Col. Simon Howe; Col. Robert Christopher; Col. Darren Bishop; Col. Richard Harmer; WO1 (RSM) Len Sanders.
HOW TO APPLY Contact the correspondent for more information. Applications for funding on behalf of individuals can be made through the charity's online application form.
CONTACT DETAILS The Trustees, RHQRA, Artillery House, Royal Artillery Barracks, Larkhill, Salisbury, Wiltshire SP4 8QT *Tel.* 01980 845233 *Email* RAA-Asstsec@artycen.ra.mod.uk *Website* www.thegunners.org.uk

■ The Royal British Legion

CC NO 219279 **ESTABLISHED** 1921
WHERE FUNDING CAN BE GIVEN UK.
WHO CAN BENEFIT Charitable organisations; individuals.
WHAT IS FUNDED Projects and services benefitting current and ex-Service personnel and/or their families not already provided by the Royal British Legion and in line with its funding priorities (see the website for up-to-date information).
WHAT IS NOT FUNDED See the website for up-to-date information on exclusions.
TYPE OF GRANT Core costs; capital costs; project funding; capacity building.
RANGE OF GRANTS Mostly up to £1.5 million.
SAMPLE GRANTS Combat Stress (£5.89 million); National Memorial Arboretum (£1.48 million); Shelter (£847,000); The Matthew Project (£621,000); Royal Commonwealth Ex-Services League (£514,000); Poppyscotland (£303,000); Army Families Federation (£467,000); X-Forces (£160,000); Never Such Innocence (£123,000).
FINANCES *Financial year end 30/09/2021*
Income £120,860,000
Grants to organisations £6,130,000
Grants to individuals £8,140,000
Assets £337,290,000
TRUSTEES Jason Coward; Steven Lee; Vice Admiral Sir Clive Johnstone; James Lambert; Philip Davies; Paul Astruc; Lynda Atkins; John Boisson; Patsy Wilkinson; Heather Spence; Monica Risam; Helen Owen; Elizabeth Butler; Debbie Sorkin; Paul Harris; Anny Reid.
OTHER INFORMATION Grant-making is one of many charitable activities the Royal British Legion undertakes. The 2020/21 accounts were the latest available to view at the time of writing (June 2023). In total, 27 organisations were awarded grants during the year.
HOW TO APPLY Contact the charity for further information.
CONTACT DETAILS The Trustees, 199 Borough High Street, London SE1 1AA *Tel.* 0808 802 8080 *Email* info@britishlegion.org.uk *Website* www. britishlegion.org.uk

■ Royal Docks Trust (London)

CC NO 1045057 **ESTABLISHED** 1995
WHERE FUNDING CAN BE GIVEN The area of the London Borough of Newham that lies between the A13 trunk road (Newham Way) and the River Thames.
WHO CAN BENEFIT Registered charities; not-for-profit organisations; voluntary organisations; religious institutions carrying out charitable work.
WHAT IS FUNDED Community development; social welfare; education and training; recreation and leisure; housing; the arts; disability; heritage; religious charitable work; the environment.
WHAT IS NOT FUNDED Individuals; general appeals; revenue, top-up or retrospective funding is not given through the minor grants programme.
TYPE OF GRANT Project funding for a maximum of three years, with a preference for matched funding; start-up/seed funding; capital costs.
RANGE OF GRANTS Typically £10,000 to £30,000.
SAMPLE GRANTS Royal Docks Learning and Activity Centre and Community Food Enterprise (£35,000 each); Drew Primary School (£21,000); Middlesex University (£20,000); Skills Enterprise Digital Learning (£11,000); Caritas Anchor House (£10,000).
FINANCES *Financial year end 31/03/2022*
Income £261,900
Grants to organisations £218,200
Assets £10,550,000
TRUSTEES Stephen Nicholas; Eric Sorensen; Amanda Williams; Katie Carter; James Kenworth; Belinda Vecchio; Sandra Erskine.
OTHER INFORMATION In 2021/22 the trust made grants to 11 charitable organisations totalling £218,200. There is a preference for applications which access other resources, offer the possibility of matched funding, complement regeneration initiatives and support the provision of services and resources locally through an active community and voluntary sector.
HOW TO APPLY Application forms, along with guidance information and an outline of the schedule for submitting applications, are available from the trust's website.
CONTACT DETAILS John Johnson, Grants Development, Olive Cottage, Station Road, St Margarets-at-Cliffe, Dover, Kent CT15 6AY *Tel.* 020 7277 8667 *Email* john.d.johnson@ btinternet.com *Website* www.royaldockstrust. org.uk

■ The Royal Foundation of The Prince and Princess of Wales

CC NO 1132048 **ESTABLISHED** 2009

WHERE FUNDING CAN BE GIVEN UK and overseas.

WHO CAN BENEFIT Registered charities.

WHAT IS FUNDED Conservation; children (early years); mental health; emergency responders.

TYPE OF GRANT Seed funding; capital funding; project funding.

SAMPLE GRANTS Mind (£450,000 in two grants); The Ambulance Staff Charity (£134,200); Hospice UK (£50,500); Al-Manaar – Muslim Cultural Heritage Centre (£47,700); Place2Be (£46,100); Best Beginnings (£29,700); The Felix Project (£28,500); London School of Economics (£16,300); Mountain Rescue England and Wales (£6,500).

FINANCES *Financial year end 31/12/2021*
Income £20,430,000
Grants to organisations £6,030,000
Assets £12,500,000

TRUSTEES Simon Patterson; Lady Demetra Pinsent; Claire Wills; Lord Hague of Richmond William Hague; Alice Webb; Zeinab Badawi-Malik; Jean-Christophe Gray; Rohinton Kalifa.

OTHER INFORMATION During the year, grants were awarded to 51 organisations in the following categories: conservation (£5.16 million); COVID-19 response fund (£560,500); emergency responders (£206,500); empowering communities (£76,200); early years (£16,300); others (£9,700).

HOW TO APPLY Contact the foundation for further information.

CONTACT DETAILS The Trustees, c/o Kensington Palace, Palace Green, London W8 4PU *Tel.* 020 7101 2963 *Email* reception@royalfoundation.com *Website* www.royalfoundation.com

■ Royal Masonic Trust for Girls and Boys

CC NO 1170336 **ESTABLISHED** 2016

WHERE FUNDING CAN BE GIVEN England and Wales.

WHO CAN BENEFIT Registered charities (at least one year of published accounts); hospices; individual children/grandchildren of Freemasons.

WHAT IS FUNDED Children and young people; relief of poverty; education and training; primarily, the trust supports children of Freemasons but also makes grants to non-Masonic registered charities.

WHAT IS NOT FUNDED See the 'Grants to charities' section of the Masonic Charitable Foundation's website for full details of eligibility requirements and exclusions with respect to activities and types of organisations.

TYPE OF GRANT Core/revenue costs; project funding; salaries; activities and materials; small grants are unrestricted. Grants are awarded for one to three years.

RANGE OF GRANTS £1,000 to £5,000 for small grants; £10,000 to £60,000 for large grants.

SAMPLE GRANTS The Duke of Edinburgh Tribute Fund (£300,000); Anne Frank Trust UK (£67,700); The Honeypot Children's Charity (£40,800); Home-Start South Leicestershire (£15,000); Tiny Tim's Children's Centre (£9,000); Gloucestershire Deaf Association (£1,800); Great Ayton District Girl Guides (£730); York Food Bank (£200).

FINANCES *Financial year end 31/03/2022*
Income £3,150,000
Grants to organisations £2,870,000
Grants to individuals £4,560,000
Assets £158,490,000

TRUSTEES Paul Williams; Masonic Charitable Foundation.

OTHER INFORMATION During 2021/22, non-Masonic donations amounted to £2.87 million (386 grants), alongside Masonic donations to support Freemasons and their families, totalling £4.56 million (1,884 grants).

HOW TO APPLY Applications are made online through the Masonic Charitable Foundation's website. Application guidelines and eligibility criteria are available for each grants programme.

CONTACT DETAILS The Trustees, Freemasons' Hall, 60 Great Queen Street, London WC2B 5AZ *Tel.* 020 3146 3333 *Email* info@mcf.org.uk *Website* www.mcf.org.uk

■ The Royal Navy and Royal Marines Charity

CC NO 1117794 **ESTABLISHED** 2007

WHERE FUNDING CAN BE GIVEN UK.

WHO CAN BENEFIT Registered charities; CICs; social enterprises; individuals.

WHAT IS FUNDED Organisations supporting serving or ex-serving personnel from the Royal Navy and the Royal Marines, and their dependants.

WHAT IS NOT FUNDED Organisational fundraising activities; retrospective costs; trading ventures; research; projects that could be funded by the Service, the state or other public bodies.

TYPE OF GRANT Capital costs; core and revenue costs; seed funding; start-up funding; project funding.

RANGE OF GRANTS Programme dependent.

SAMPLE GRANTS Resilience Centre (£1.3 million); Kings Foundation (£330,200); Relate (£229,700); HMS Drake (£100,800); Veterans Outreach Support (£80,000); Home-Start (£63,500); Age UK Portsmouth (£45,800); Fighting With Pride (£36,500); Poppyscotland, Portsmouth Naval Gliding Centre and Winter Sports Association (£25,000 each).

FINANCES *Financial year end 31/12/2021*
Income £11,720,000
Grants to organisations £8,290,000
Grants to individuals £1,910,000
Assets £53,100,000

TRUSTEES Dr Brian Gilvary; Steven Brunton; Dr Josephine Pabari; Jim Wright; Barry Firth; Dr Joanna Keogh; Kathryn Phipps-Wiltshire; Michelle Westwood; John Bartlett; Simon Black; Andrew Robinson; Roderic Birkett; Michael Tanner; Lt Harriet Delbridge.

OTHER INFORMATION Beneficiaries of grants of under £25,000 were not listed.

HOW TO APPLY Apply via the charity's online application portal. If applicants have any questions they can contact the Grants Team on 023 9387 4654 or mygrant@rnrmc.org.uk.

CONTACT DETAILS The Trustees, Building 37, HMS Excellent, Whale Island, Portsmouth, Hampshire PO2 8ER *Tel.* 023 9387 1520 *Email* theteam@rnrmc.org.uk *Website* www.rnrmc.org.uk

■ RSM UK Foundation

cc no 1179349
where funding can be given UK and overseas.
who can benefit Registered charities.
what is funded The environment; citizenship and community development; the advancement of education and relief of poverty in the context of access to employment.
what is not funded Grants are not normally made to individuals or for projects in countries in which another RSM Group corporate charity is based.
sample grants Anthony Nolan (£239,200); The Duke of Edinburgh's Award (£204,500); Unicef (£169,100); Leadership Through Sport and Business (£20,000); Trees for Cities (£15,000).
finances *Financial year end* 31/03/2022
Income £398,000
Grants to organisations £724,500
Assets £72,400
trustees David Gwilliam; Nicholas Sladden; Kelly Adams; John Taylor; Joy Welch; Catherine Riches.
other information The foundation supports its four core charities each year but also accepts applications from other organisations.
how to apply Apply by email to the correspondent. Application deadlines can be found on the foundation's website.
contact details The Trustees, 6th Floor, 25 Farringdon Street, London EC4A 4AB *Tel.* 020 3201 8313 *Email* info@rsmukfoundation.com *Website* www.rsmukfoundation.com

■ The Rubin Foundation Charitable Trust

cc no 327062   **established** 1986
where funding can be given UK.
who can benefit Registered charities; universities; Jewish organisations.
what is funded General charitable purposes.
range of grants Up to £150,000.
sample grants UJIA (£150,000); Lancaster University (£125,000); Jewish Care (£110,000); University College London Development Fund (£52,600); Chai Lifeline Cancer Care and The Prince's Trust (£50,000 each).
finances *Financial year end* 05/04/2022
Income £89,800
Grants to organisations £810,300
Assets £6,880,000
trustees Alison Mosheim; Angela Rubin; Robert Rubin; Andrew Rubin; Carolyn Rubin.
other information Grants of under £50,000 totalled £272,700.
how to apply Contact the correspondent for more information. According to previous research, the foundation gives grants to charities known to members of the Rubin family and those associated with Pentland Group Ltd; therefore, unsolicited applications are unlikely to succeed.
contact details The Trustees, The Pentland Centre, Lakeside House, Squires Lane, Finchley, London N3 2QL *Tel.* 020 8346 2600 *Email* amcmillan@pentland.com

■ The Ruddock Foundation for the Arts

cc no 1134994   **established** 2010
where funding can be given UK.
who can benefit Registered charities; museums, libraries and galleries; independent theatre groups; individuals.
what is funded The conservation of and research into pre-1800 performing, literary and decorative arts.
type of grant Collections and acquisitions; project funding; research.
sample grants Metropolitan Museum – New York (£810,000); British Museum (£52,000); Courtauld Institute (£350,000); Afrikids (£43,300); Almeida Theatre (£28,900).
finances *Financial year end* 05/04/2022
Income £584,200
Grants to organisations £4,310,000
Assets £24,640,000
trustees Sir Paul Ruddock; Lady Jill Ruddock; Michael Fullerlove; Sophie Ruddock; Isabella Ruddock.
other information Grants were made for the following purposes: museum and gallery projects (£3.32 million); research and curatorial support (£726,200); other charitable purposes (£254,000); museum acquisitions (£7,300).
how to apply Apply in writing to the correspondent. The trustees meet twice a year to discuss applications.
contact details Paul Ruddock, Trustee, 10 Colville Mews, London W11 2DA *Tel.* 020 7313 9350 *Email* nikita@ruddockfamily.com

■ The Rugby Group Benevolent Fund Ltd

cc no 265669   **established** 1955
where funding can be given Barrington (Cambridgeshire); Chinnor (Oxfordshire); Kensworth (Bedfordshire); Lewes (Sussex); Rochester (Kent); Rugby and Southam (Warwickshire); South Ferriby (North Lincolnshire); and Tilbury (Essex).
who can benefit Registered charities; schools; uniformed groups; community groups; amateur sports clubs.
what is funded Community projects.
what is not funded Organisations operating outside the areas of benefit; support is not normally given for day-to-day revenue costs.
type of grant Capital costs for specific projects.
range of grants Up to £30,000.
sample grants The Friends of St Cross (£20,000); Parenting Project – Rugby (£10,000); The Friends of Barrington School (£7,000); Rugby Theatre (£5,000); Winterton Bowls Club (£4,000); Muscular Dystrophy Support Centre (£3,000); Southam Albion FC (£2,000); Woodland Singers (£1,000).
finances *Financial year end* 31/12/2021
Income £36,700
Grants to organisations £162,600
Grants to individuals £5,300
Assets £1,100,000
trustees Nigel Appleyard; Graeme Fuller; Norman Jones; Ian Southcott; Geoff Thomas; John Brooks; David Holton; Kevin Murch.
other information This charity was established in 1955 with the aim of supporting employees and former employees of Rugby Group Ltd, and their dependants. The Rugby Group is now a part of CEMEX UK, a global cement manufacturer, but the charity has kept its independence and is

managed by a group of employees and former employees. During 2021, 42 grants were made to organisations. Only organisations that received grants of over £1,000 were listed as beneficiaries in the charity's accounts. Grants of under £1,000 totalled £3,600 and were awarded to eight organisations. In addition, grants were made to six individuals.

HOW TO APPLY Potential applicants must first complete an expression of interest form, available to download from the charity's website. Applicants must be able to demonstrate that the project has been properly costed and that any other support funding is in place or in prospect. Evidence of self-help is important. The trustees meet several times a year to consider applications.

CONTACT DETAILS The Trustees, Cemex UK, Cemex House, Evreux Way, Rugby, Warwickshire CV21 2DT *Tel.* 01788 517000 *Email* info@rugbygroupbenevolentfund.org.uk *Website* www.rugbygroupbenevolentfund.org.uk

■ Russell Trust

OSCR NO SC004424   **ESTABLISHED** 1985
WHERE FUNDING CAN BE GIVEN UK, especially Scotland and primarily Fife.
WHO CAN BENEFIT Charitable organisations and voluntary bodies.
WHAT IS FUNDED General charitable purposes.
WHAT IS NOT FUNDED Individuals.
TYPE OF GRANT Typically one-off. Preference is given to new, local projects that require initial funding.
RANGE OF GRANTS Mostly up to £2,000. Several larger grants (£4,000 to £30,000) are awarded each year.
SAMPLE GRANTS Fife College (£15,000); The Wave Project Scotland (£4,000); Scottish Book Trust (£3,000); Birthlink, Kids Come First and The Salvation Army (£2,000 each).
FINANCES *Financial year end* 05/04/2022
Income £207,900
Grants to organisations £166,600
Assets £6,970,000
OTHER INFORMATION Only organisations that received grants of over £2,000 were listed as beneficiaries in the trust's accounts. Grants of under £2,000 totalled £58,300.
HOW TO APPLY Apply in writing to the correspondent.
CONTACT DETAILS The Secretary, 2.19, 2nd, Block B, 1 Summerhall, Edinburgh EH9 1PL

■ The RWS Foundation

CC NO 1127138   **ESTABLISHED** 2008
WHERE FUNDING CAN BE GIVEN Worldwide.
WHO CAN BENEFIT Charitable organisations.
WHAT IS FUNDED Sustainable community and economic development; overseas aid; social welfare; education and training.
WHAT IS NOT FUNDED The foundation does not support political or religious causes. The projects it funds tend to be small but with lasting impact.
TYPE OF GRANT Mostly muti-year grants.
RANGE OF GRANTS £1,000 to £100,000.
SAMPLE GRANTS University of Manchester (£200,000); Outward Bound Trust (£26,000); International Red Cross (£15,000); Innovations for Learning (£6,000); The Sheffield Children's Hospital Foundation (£310).
FINANCES *Financial year end* 30/09/2022
Income £268,700
Grants to organisations £289,100
Assets £21,100

TRUSTEES Maria Schnell; David Shrimpton; James McHugh; Dorte Schou; Candida Davies; Emma Crarer; Emma Fisher; Kathleen Matthews.
OTHER INFORMATION The RWS Foundation is the corporate charity of RWS plc, which provides filing and search services, technical and commercial translation and localisation, and develops and supports translation productivity and management software. The foundation prefers to support projects where RWS employees can complement support with their own fundraising initiatives.
HOW TO APPLY Only causes supported and sponsored by RWS employees will be considered by the RWS Foundation. Contact the foundation by email for further information on how to request the support of staff and application procedures.
CONTACT DETAILS The Trustees, Europa House, Chiltern Park, Chalfont St Peter SL9 9FG *Tel.* 01753 480200 *Email* connect@rws.com *Website* www.rws.com/about/corporate-sustainability/social/community

■ The Ryvoan Trust

OSCR NO SC040707
WHERE FUNDING CAN BE GIVEN Scotland.
WHO CAN BENEFIT Registered charities.
WHAT IS FUNDED Children and young people; people with disabilities; mental health.
TYPE OF GRANT Capital projects; core costs.
RANGE OF GRANTS Multi-year grants of £5,000 to £50,000 per year for a minimum of three years; one-off grants of £5,000 to £10,000.
SAMPLE GRANTS Maggie's Centre (£110,000); Harmeny Education Trust (£60,000); Children 1st (£10,000); Earthtime for All (£2,000); Willow Foundation (£1,000).
FINANCES *Financial year end* 30/09/2021
Income £95,500
Grants to organisations £540,000
Assets £9,650,000
OTHER INFORMATION The 2020/21 accounts were the latest available at the time of writing (May 2023).
HOW TO APPLY Applications can be made via the trust's website where information on funding cycles can also be found.
CONTACT DETAILS The Secretary, 41 Northumberland Street, Edinburgh EH3 6JA *Email* secretary@ryvoantrust.com *Website* www.ryvoantrust.com

◾ S. and R. Charitable Trust

cc no 1098326   **established** 2003
where funding can be given England.
who can benefit Registered charities; individuals.
what is funded General charitable purposes; health; poverty relief.
range of grants Generally up to £25,000.
sample grants Chabad Lubavitch UK (£25,000); King's College London (£10,000); H. Stepic CEE Charity (£8,300); The Independent Jewish Day School Foundation (£8,200); Hasmonean High School Charitable Trust (£5,000).
finances *Financial year end 31/03/2022*
Income £40,100
Grants to organisations £79,400
Assets £126,800
trustees Rochelle Davis; Stephen Davis; Lee Rhodes.
other information Only organisations that received grants of over £2,000 were listed as beneficiaries in the charity's accounts. Grants of under £2,000 totalled £13,900. Note that the grant total may include amounts awarded to individuals.
how to apply Apply in writing to the correspondent.
contact details The Trustees, 14 Deacons Hill Road, Elstree, Borehamwood, Hertfordshire WD6 3LH *Tel.* 020 8953 5226

◾ The S. M. B. Trust

cc no 263814   **established** 1962
where funding can be given UK and overseas.
who can benefit Charitable organisations.
what is funded Christian faith; social and medical care in the UK and abroad; famine relief and emergency aid; the environment and wildlife; education; medical research.
what is not funded Individuals.
range of grants Generally between £1,000 and £4,000.
sample grants Hospice of Hope (£4,000); All Nations Christian College (£3,500); The Salvation Army and Speakers for Schools (£3,000 each); YMCA National Council (£2,500); London School of Theology (£2,000); Fisherman's Mission (£1,500); WaterAid and YoungMinds (£1,000 each).
finances *Financial year end 31/03/2021*
Income £502,300
Grants to organisations £347,200
Assets £12,180,000
trustees Jeremy Anstead; Barbara O'Driscoll; Ian Wilson.
other information The 2020/21 accounts were the latest at the time of writing (June 2023). Grants were awarded to 183 organisations for the following purposes: social and medical welfare (£100,100); religion (£91,300); relief of poverty (£62,500); education and research (£38,900); famine relief and emergency aid (£35,800); the environment and wildlife (£9,000).
how to apply Apply in writing to the correspondent.
contact details The Trustees, 15 Wilman Road, Tunbridge Wells, Kent TN4 9AJ *Tel.* 01892 537301 *Email* smbcharitabletrust@googlemail.com

◾ The Jeremy and John Sacher Charitable Trust

cc no 206321   **established** 1957
where funding can be given UK and Israel.
who can benefit Registered charities.
what is funded General charitable purposes, with a preference for the following: arts and culture; education, science and technology; community and welfare; children and youth; health and disability; Jewish organisations and causes.
what is not funded Individuals.
range of grants £500 to £50,000.
sample grants The Royal Philatelic Society London (£100,000); The London Symphony Orchestra Ltd (£50,000); Community Security Trust (£20,000); British Friends of The Hebrew University of Jerusalem (£15,000); St John Ambulance (£5,000); St Clements and St James School Trust (£500).
finances *Financial year end 31/01/2022*
Income £48,500
Grants to organisations £337,000
Assets £7,380,000
trustees Rosalind Sacher; Elisabeth Sacher; Jeremy Sacher.
other information Grants were awarded to 19 organisations.
how to apply Contact the correspondent for further information.
contact details The Trustees, HW Fisher and Co., Acre House, 11–15 William Road, London NW1 3ER *Tel.* 020 7388 7000 *Email* info@hwfisher.co.uk

◾ The Michael and Nicola Sacher Charitable Trust

cc no 288973   **established** 1984
where funding can be given UK.
who can benefit Registered charities.
what is funded General charitable purposes with a preference for arts, education, animal welfare, the Jewish faith and community, health and social welfare.
what is not funded Individuals; organisations which are not registered charities.
range of grants Generally up to £10,000.
sample grants A list of beneficiaries was not included in the annual report and accounts. Previous beneficiaries have included: New College (£17,000); National Railway Museum (£10,000); Natural History Museum (£5,000); Jewish Care (£3,000); The Zoological Society of London (£2,500); United Synagogue (£490).
finances *Financial year end 28/02/2022*
Income £49,800
Grants to organisations £138,700
Assets £3,280,000
trustees Michael Sacher; Nicola Sacher.
other information Grants were made to 18 organisations during 2021/22.
how to apply Apply in writing to the correspondent.
contact details The Trustees, 64 New Cavendish Street, London W1G 8TB *Tel.* 020 7467 6300 *Email* mail@harrisandtrotter.co.uk

◾ The Dr Mortimer and Theresa Sackler Foundation

cc no 1128926   **established** 2009
where funding can be given England; Wales; overseas, including the USA.
who can benefit Registered charities and universities.

Think carefully about every application. Is it justified?

633

WHAT IS FUNDED Research; medical research; education; the arts; science.

RANGE OF GRANTS Mostly under £65,000.

SAMPLE GRANTS King's College London (£750,000).

FINANCES *Financial year end 31/12/2021*
Income £115,900
Grants to organisations £936,300
Assets £26,570,000

TRUSTEES Dr Kathe Sackler; Michael Sackler; Sophia Dalrymple; Mortimer Sackler; Mrs I. Sackler Lefcourt; Dame Theresa Sackler; Marissa Sackler; Samantha Hunt; Anthony Collins.

OTHER INFORMATION During the year, the foundation awarded a large grant of £750,000 (approx. 80% of the grant total) to one organisation, as well as 12 grants of under £65,000.

HOW TO APPLY Apply in writing to the correspondent.

CONTACT DETAILS The Trustees, 83 Cambridge Street, Pimlico, London SW1V 8LU *Tel.* 020 7930 4944

■ The Sackler Trust

CC NO 1132097 **ESTABLISHED** 1988

WHERE FUNDING CAN BE GIVEN UK.

WHO CAN BENEFIT Charitable organisations.

WHAT IS FUNDED Visual and performing arts; heritage; medical research; education; the environment.

WHAT IS NOT FUNDED Individuals.

TYPE OF GRANT Typically one-off, although multi-year grants can also be considered.

RANGE OF GRANTS Typically less than £50,000.

SAMPLE GRANTS Chelsea and Westminster Hospital NHS Foundation Trust (£250,000); The Amber Foundation (£150,000); JW3 Trust and Priscilla Bacon Hospice (£100,000 each); Spitalfields Crypt Trust (£90,000); Galapagos Conservation Trust (£75,000); Britten Pears Arts (£70,000); Berkshire Youth Trust (£50,000).

FINANCES *Financial year end 31/12/2021*
Income £597,100
Grants to organisations £1,320,000
Assets £51,920,000

TRUSTEES Dame Theresa Sackler; Marissa Sackler; Sophia Dalrymple; Michael Sackler; Marianne Mitchell; Anthony Collins.

OTHER INFORMATION In 2021, the trust made 90 grants of less than £50,000 which totalled £432,000.

HOW TO APPLY Apply in writing to the correspondent, providing a brief description of the project. The trustees meet in June and November.

CONTACT DETAILS The Trustees, 83 Cambridge Street, Pimlico, London SW1V 4PS *Tel.* 020 7930 4944 *Email* contact@sacklertrust.org *Website* www.sacklertrust.org

■ The Saddlers' Company Charitable Fund

CC NO 261962 **ESTABLISHED** 1970

WHERE FUNDING CAN BE GIVEN UK, with a preference for the City of London.

WHO CAN BENEFIT Registered charities; educational organisations; religious organisations; individuals.

WHAT IS FUNDED General charitable purposes; education; equestrian charities; disadvantaged young people; disability; the armed forces; music; religious activities and churches; saddlery and leathercraft.

TYPE OF GRANT Project funding; capital costs.

SAMPLE GRANTS A list of beneficiaries was not included in the annual report and accounts.

FINANCES *Financial year end 31/03/2022*
Income £332,700
Grants to organisations £353,700
Grants to individuals £23,300
Assets £14,880,000

TRUSTEE Saddlers' Company.

HOW TO APPLY If you believe your activities are aligned with the charity's priorities, potential applicants should register their interest by way of an introductory email to the Charities Administrator at tc@saddlersco.co.uk who will advise whether the bid will be taken forward.

CONTACT DETAILS The Charities Administrator, Saddlers' Company, Saddlers' Hall, 40 Gutter Lane, London EC2V 6BR *Tel.* 020 7726 8661 *Email* clerk@saddlersco.co.uk *Website* www. saddlersco.co.uk

■ Erach and Roshan Sadri Foundation

CC NO 1110736 **ESTABLISHED** 2005

WHERE FUNDING CAN BE GIVEN Worldwide, but mainly India and the UK.

WHO CAN BENEFIT Registered charities; community groups; religious institutions; individuals.

WHAT IS FUNDED The main objects of the foundation are: providing financial assistance for education and welfare purposes; relieving poverty by alleviating homelessness; and assisting members of the Zoroastrian religious faith.

WHAT IS NOT FUNDED Applications are unlikely to be successful if they involve animal welfare or heritage or are a general appeal from large UK organisations.

TYPE OF GRANT One-off grants for project costs.

SAMPLE GRANTS A list of beneficiaries was not available.

FINANCES *Financial year end 31/03/2022*
Income £0
Grants to organisations £128,500
Assets £1,140,000

TRUSTEES Darius Sarosh; Peter Dudgeon.

OTHER INFORMATION Full accounts were not available to view on the Charity Commission's website due to the charity's low income. We have therefore estimated the charity's grant total based on its total expenditure.

HOW TO APPLY Unsolicited applications are not accepted. However, if invited by a trustee to make an application, there are detailed guidelines on the website.

CONTACT DETAILS Mark Cann, Administrator, 10A High Street, Pewsey, Wiltshire SN9 5AQ *Tel.* 01672 569131 *Email* markcann@ersf.org. uk *Website* www.ersf.org.uk

■ The Jean Sainsbury Animal Welfare Trust

CC NO 326358 **ESTABLISHED** 1982

WHERE FUNDING CAN BE GIVEN UK and overseas.

WHO CAN BENEFIT UK-registered national and international animal welfare charities.

WHAT IS FUNDED Animal welfare and wildlife.

WHAT IS NOT FUNDED The trust's website provides a full list of exclusions, which includes individuals.

TYPE OF GRANT Core costs; capital costs; project funding.

RANGE OF GRANTS Up to £35,000.

SAMPLE GRANTS Ape Action Africa (£11,500); Tree of Life for Animals and WeCare Worldwide (£10,000 each); Rain Rescue (£8,000); Rabbit

Residence Rescue (£7,000); Hugs Foundation (£6,000); Pawprints Dog Rescue (£5,000); Linbee Dog Rehoming (£3,000); Munchkins Miniature Shetland Rescue (£2,000); Hedgehog Rescue Blackpool (£1,500).

FINANCES *Financial year end* 31/12/2021
Income £417,800
Grants to organisations £441,200
Assets £33,170,000

TRUSTEES Mrs Allen; Mr Spurdens; Valerie Pike; Mr Keliher; Jacqui Sharp; Jill Inglis; Madeleine Orchard.

OTHER INFORMATION During the year, grants were awarded to 59 organisations in the UK and 17 overseas.

HOW TO APPLY Application forms can be downloaded from the trust's website. The trustees meet three times a year to consider applications. Applications should be received by 10 January, 1 May and 1 September. More details are available on the trust's website.

CONTACT DETAILS Barbara Georgiou, Administrator, PO Box 469, London W14 8PJ *Tel.* 020 7602 7948 *Email* jsawt7@gmail.com *Website* http://jeansainsburyanimalwelfare.org.uk

■ The Alan and Babette Sainsbury Charitable Fund

CC NO 292930   **ESTABLISHED** 1953

WHERE FUNDING CAN BE GIVEN UK, with some preference for Southwark; Africa.

WHO CAN BENEFIT Registered charities; theatres; community organisations; universities; research organisations.

WHAT IS FUNDED Arts and education projects for young people in Southwark, London; civil liberties and human rights charities in the UK; educational and employment opportunities for young people overseas, especially in Africa; scientific and medical research on type 1 diabetes.

WHAT IS NOT FUNDED Individuals; educational fees; expeditions.

TYPE OF GRANT Research; core/revenue costs; project funding; occasionally capital costs.

RANGE OF GRANTS Up to £70,000.

SAMPLE GRANTS Ashden Climate Solutions (£70,000); The Linking Network (£40,000); Community InfoSource and The Unity Project (£30,000 each); Kentish Town City Farm (£25,500); The Advocacy Academy (£20,000); Bede Housing Association (£10,000); National Holocaust Centre and Museum (£5,000).

FINANCES *Financial year end* 05/04/2022
Income £500,200
Grants to organisations £404,800
Assets £18,200,000

TRUSTEES Lindsey Anderson; John Sainsbury; Jessica Sainsbury.

OTHER INFORMATION The charity is one of the Sainsbury Family Charitable Trusts, which share a common administration – see www.sftc.org.uk for more information. In 2021/22 the charity made grants to 21 organisations.

HOW TO APPLY Unsolicited applications are not accepted; the trustees instead take a proactive approach to identifying organisations to support.

CONTACT DETAILS The Trustees, The Peak, 5 Wilton Road, London SW1V 1AP *Tel.* 020 7410 0330 *Email* info@sfct.org.uk *Website* https://abscharitablefund.org.uk/

■ Saint Sarkis Charity Trust

CC NO 215352   **ESTABLISHED** 1954

WHERE FUNDING CAN BE GIVEN UK and overseas.

WHO CAN BENEFIT Registered charities.

WHAT IS FUNDED Primarily, charitable causes within the Armenian community and charities developing innovative projects to support prisoners in the UK. The trust also funds the Armenian Church of Saint Sarkis in London and the Gulbenkian Library at the Armenian Patriarchate in Jerusalem on an annual basis.

TYPE OF GRANT Often recurrent.

SAMPLE GRANTS Association Arménienne d'Aide Sociale (£48,500); London Armenian Poor Relief Society Trust (£9,000); Armenian Summer Festival (£5,000); Armenian Church of St Sarkis (£2,000).

FINANCES *Financial year end* 31/03/2022
Income £170,800
Grants to organisations £207,500
Assets £12,320,000

TRUSTEES Martin Essayan; Rita Vartoukian; Alec D'Janoeff; Teni Shahiean.

OTHER INFORMATION In 2021/22 the trust made eight grants to organisations, including £58,000 to the Barrow Cadbury Trust, which, on behalf of the trust, recommends and administers a small number of projects connected with reducing prisoner re-offending. The trust is no longer accepting unsolicited applications for prisoner support projects.

HOW TO APPLY Apply in writing to the correspondent. There is no standard application form, so applicants should write a brief covering letter including an explanation of the exact purpose of the grant, how much is needed, with details of how the budget has been arrived at, details of any other sources of income (firm commitments and those still being explored), the charity's registration number, the latest annual report and audited accounts and any plans for monitoring and evaluating the work. The trust is no longer accepting unsolicited applications for prisoner support projects.

CONTACT DETAILS Chris Holmes, Secretary to the Trustees, 50 Hoxton Square, London N1 6PB *Email* info@saintsarkis.org.uk *Website* www.saintsarkis.org.uk

■ The Saintbury Trust

CC NO 326790   **ESTABLISHED** 1985

WHERE FUNDING CAN BE GIVEN West Midlands, Warwickshire, Worcestershire and North Gloucestershire. See website for eligible postcodes.

WHO CAN BENEFIT Registered charities.

WHAT IS FUNDED General charitable purposes, including the following: arts, culture, heritage and science; the environment; disability; social welfare; education; health; children and young people; older people; community development; homelessness.

WHAT IS NOT FUNDED Individuals; animal charities; religious charities; unregistered charities; national charities; uniformed groups; village halls; local churches; repair, maintenance, improvement; general running costs; start-up costs; organisations based outside the area of benefit.

RANGE OF GRANTS Typically between £1,000 and £5,000.

SAMPLE GRANTS Alzheimer's Research UK (£20,000); B:Music (£15,000); Foundation for Conductive Education (£10,000); Disability Challengers (£5,000); Ackers Adventures

(£3,000); Walsall Bereavement Support Services (£2,000); Bentley Beginnings (£1,000).
FINANCES *Financial year end 31/12/2021*
Income £290,800
Grants to organisations £263,000
Assets £15,600,000
TRUSTEES Mrs A. E. Atkinson-Willes; Harry Forrester; Mrs V. K. Houghton; Mrs A. R. Thomas; Mrs C. E. Brogan; Anita Bhalla; Mrs J. P. Lewis; Benjamin Atkinson-Willes; Dr Sarah Wareing; Jake Houghton; Kabir Sonhdi.
OTHER INFORMATION Grants were awarded to 68 organisations in 2021.
HOW TO APPLY Applications can be made through the trust's website. From January 2022, the trust reduced the geographical area from which they accept applications. Visit the trust website to see if your area is supported. The trust does not respond to telephone enquiries — all correspondence should be by email or post.
CONTACT DETAILS The Trustees, PO Box 464, Dorking, Surrey RH4 9AF *Tel.* 01223 460222 *Email* saintburytrust@btinternet.com *Website* www.thesaintburytrust.co.uk

■ The Salamander Charitable Trust

CC NO 273657   **ESTABLISHED** 1977
WHERE FUNDING CAN BE GIVEN UK.
WHO CAN BENEFIT Registered charities.
WHAT IS FUNDED General charitable purposes including the following: education and training; the promotion of health; social welfare; overseas aid; Christianity; arts and culture; medical research.
WHAT IS NOT FUNDED Individuals.
RANGE OF GRANTS £1,000 up to £6,500.
SAMPLE GRANTS A list of beneficiaries was not included in the annual report and accounts.
FINANCES *Financial year end 05/04/2022*
Income £54,800
Grants to organisations £157,500
Assets £1,950,000
TRUSTEES Robert Douglas; Alison Hardwick; Catharine Douglas.
HOW TO APPLY The trust's income is fully allocated each year, mainly to regular beneficiaries. The trustees do not wish to receive any new requests.
CONTACT DETAILS Catharine Douglas, Trustee, The Old Rectory, 5 Stamford Road, South Luffenham, Oakham, Rutland LE15 8NT *Tel.* 01782 847952 *Email* salamanderct@btinternet.com

■ Salisbury Pool Charity

CC NO 272626   **ESTABLISHED** 1976
WHERE FUNDING CAN BE GIVEN Dorset and Hertfordshire with a preference for Hatfield and Cranborne.
WHO CAN BENEFIT Registered charities; churches; schools; museums; libraries; local organisations.
WHAT IS FUNDED General charitable purposes, with a preference for heritage and conservation, social welfare and agricultural and scientific education.
RANGE OF GRANTS Typically less than £5,000.
SAMPLE GRANTS Eton College (£12,000); International Organ Festival Society Ltd (£7,000); The Malala Fund UK (£5,000); Hatfield Foodback (£2,000); The Grenadier Guards Association (£1,000); Alderholt PCC (£750); PCC of Hatfield Hyde (£360).

FINANCES *Financial year end 05/04/2022*
Income £67,500
Grants to organisations £65,900
Assets £2,000,000
TRUSTEES Viscount Cranborne; The Most Hon. the Marquess of Salisbury.
OTHER INFORMATION Grants were made to 26 organisations during the year for the following purposes: social welfare (£42,000); education (£12,000); churches (£5,800); other (£100).
HOW TO APPLY Apply in writing to the correspondent.
CONTACT DETAILS The Trustees, The Estate Office, Hatfield Park, Hatfield, Hertfordshire AL9 5NB *Tel.* 01707 287000 *Email* j.green@gascoyneholdings.co.uk

■ Salters' Charitable Foundation

CC NO 328258   **ESTABLISHED** 1989
WHERE FUNDING CAN BE GIVEN UK; Greater London.
WHO CAN BENEFIT Charitable organisations with an established connection to the foundation or to the City of London.
WHAT IS FUNDED London citizenship and community development; science education at school and university level; armed forces; emergency appeals.
TYPE OF GRANT Project funding; one-off grants; long-term core support.
SAMPLE GRANTS Harris Westminster School (£18,000); YMCA London City (£10,000); Circle Community (£2,500); Treloar's (£1,500); HMS Vengeance Welfare Fund (£300).
FINANCES *Financial year end 30/06/2022*
Income £208,700
Grants to organisations £95,600
Assets £2,430,000
TRUSTEE The Salters Company.
HOW TO APPLY The foundation does not accept unsolicited applications.
CONTACT DETAILS Anna-Maria Mullen, Head of Development, The Salters' Company, Salters' Hall, 4 London Wall Place, London EC2Y 5DE *Tel.* 020 7588 5216 ext. 235 *Email* charities@salters.co.uk *Website* www.salters.co.uk

■ Samjo Ltd

CC NO 1094397   **ESTABLISHED** 2002
WHERE FUNDING CAN BE GIVEN Greater Manchester.
WHO CAN BENEFIT Jewish organisations. The charity appears to support the same core group of beneficiaries each year, but it also makes grants to other organisations. Individuals with disabilities or experiencing poverty may also be supported.
WHAT IS FUNDED Jewish charitable causes, including the following: the advancement of the Orthodox Jewish faith; education; health and disability; social welfare; older people; vulnerable individuals and children.
RANGE OF GRANTS Generally between £5,000 and £25,000, with some larger grants.
SAMPLE GRANTS Shemtov Charitable Trust (£156,300); Teshivoh Tefilloh Tzedokoh (£130,000); Friends of Boyan Trust (£83,500); Oizer Charitable Trust (£74,000); Kolyom Trust Ltd (£34,500); Manchester Talmudical College and Theological Seminary (£25,000); Asser Bishvil Foundation (£15,000); Min Hameitzar (£10,000); Chevras Mo'oz Ladol (£6,000); Friends of Beis Chinuch Lebonos Trust (£5,000).

FINANCES *Financial year end* 31/03/2022
Income £3,390,000
Grants to organisations £634,500
Assets £30,960,000
TRUSTEES Rabbi Yisroel Friedman; Joshua Halpern; Samuel Halpern.
OTHER INFORMATION Grants were awarded to 19 organisations during the year.
HOW TO APPLY Apply in writing to the correspondent.
CONTACT DETAILS The Trustees, c/o Lopian Gross Barnett and Co., 1st Floor, Cloister House, New Bailey Street, Manchester M3 5FS *Tel.* 0161 832 8721 *Email* D.Stewart@ prestburymanagement.co.uk

■ The Basil Samuel Charitable Trust

CC NO 206579   **ESTABLISHED** 1959
WHERE FUNDING CAN BE GIVEN UK.
WHO CAN BENEFIT Registered charities.
WHAT IS FUNDED General charitable purposes, including health, social welfare, education and culture.
SAMPLE GRANTS A list of beneficiaries was not available.
FINANCES *Financial year end* 05/04/2022
Income £8,900
Grants to organisations £551,200
TRUSTEES Richard Peskin; William Furber.
OTHER INFORMATION Full accounts were not available to view on the Charity Commission's website due to the charity's low income. We have therefore estimated the grant total based on the charity's total expenditure.
HOW TO APPLY Contact the correspondent for further information.
CONTACT DETAILS The Trustees, c/o Smith and Williamson, 25 Moorgate, London EC2R 6AY *Tel.* 020 7131 4376

■ The M. J. Samuel Charitable Trust

CC NO 327013   **ESTABLISHED** 1985
WHERE FUNDING CAN BE GIVEN UK and overseas.
WHO CAN BENEFIT Charitable organisations.
WHAT IS FUNDED General charitable purposes with a preference for health, environmental causes, the arts and overseas aid.
RANGE OF GRANTS Up to £550,000.
SAMPLE GRANTS Civic (£550,000); King's College London (£25,000); Anna Freud Centre (£15,000); Historic Royal Palace (£5,000); Somerset Community Foundation (£500).
FINANCES *Financial year end* 05/04/2022
Income £65,600
Grants to organisations £508,200
Assets £3,230,000
TRUSTEES Hon. Michael Samuel; Hon. Julia Samuel; Lord Bearsted.
OTHER INFORMATION In 2021/22, the trust made 14 grants to organisations, including 5 grants of less than £1,000, totalling £1,500.
HOW TO APPLY Contact the correspondent for further information.
CONTACT DETAILS The Trustees, Mells Park, Mells, Frome, Somerset BA11 3QB *Tel.* 020 7402 0602 *Email* claire@mellspark.com

■ The Peter Samuel Charitable Trust

CC NO 269065   **ESTABLISHED** 1975
WHERE FUNDING CAN BE GIVEN UK, with some preference for local organisations in South Berkshire, Highlands of Scotland and East Somerset.
WHO CAN BENEFIT Charitable organisations.
WHAT IS FUNDED General charitable purposes, in particular: medical sciences; people's quality of life in the local areas; heritage and forestry/land restoration; the Jewish faith and community.
RANGE OF GRANTS Mostly £500 to £5,000, with some larger grants.
SAMPLE GRANTS Civic Ltd (£70,000); Henry Jackson Society (£15,000); AJEX Charitable Foundation (£5,000); Marie Curie Cancer Care (£1,000); Highland and Island Blood Bikes (£500).
FINANCES *Financial year end* 31/03/2022
Income £130,200
Grants to organisations £147,500
Assets £6,820,000
TRUSTEES Viscount Bearsted; The Hon. Michael Samuel.
OTHER INFORMATION Grants were awarded to 25 organisations during the year.
HOW TO APPLY Apply in writing to the correspondent.
CONTACT DETAILS The Trustees, The Estate Office – Farley Estate, Farley Hall, Castle Road, Farley Hill, Reading, Berkshire RG7 1UL *Tel.* 0118 973 0047 *Email* pa@farleyfarms.co.uk

■ The Samworth Foundation

CC NO 265647   **ESTABLISHED** 1973
WHERE FUNDING CAN BE GIVEN Worldwide.
WHO CAN BENEFIT Registered charities.
WHAT IS FUNDED Modern slavery and exploitation; the environment and climate change.
TYPE OF GRANT Project costs; core costs; unrestricted funding. Grants are often given over a three-year period.
RANGE OF GRANTS £1,000 to £500,000.
SAMPLE GRANTS Uppingham School (£500,000); Climate Outreach and Information Network (£244,400); University of Bedfordshire (£138,300); New Futures Project (£100,000); Tearfund (£90,000); WWF-UK (£70,000); Green New Deal UK Ltd (£50,000); Climate Alliance CIC (£30,000); Médecins Sans Frontières (£25,000); Climate Emergence (£1,000).
FINANCES *Financial year end* 05/04/2022
Income £516,100
Grants to organisations £5,110,000
Assets £70,910,000
TRUSTEES Mark Samworth; Susan Ralphs; Dr Daniela Lloyd-Williams; Belinda Gordon; Sarah-Jane Kerr; Prof. Neil Gorman.
OTHER INFORMATION Grants were awarded to 142 organisations. Only organisations that received grants of over £1,000 were listed as beneficiaries in the foundation's accounts. Grants were broken down as follows: core grants (£2.57 million); transformation and innovation fund (£2.18 million); family and exceptional donations (£869,800); humanitarian crisis response grants (£250,000); COVID-19 emergency response grants (£222,300).
HOW TO APPLY The foundation does not accept unsolicited applications.
CONTACT DETAILS The Trustees, Chetwode House, 1 Samworth Way, Melton Mowbray, Leicestershire LE13 1GA *Tel.* 01664 414500 *Email* admin@samworthfoundation.org.uk *Website* https://samworthfoundation.org.uk

Think carefully about every application. Is it justified?

637

■ The Sanderson Foundation

CC NO 1155744   **ESTABLISHED** 2014

WHERE FUNDING CAN BE GIVEN England and Wales.

WHO CAN BENEFIT Charitable organisation.

WHAT IS FUNDED General charitable purposes, including education.

RANGE OF GRANTS Up to £200,000.

SAMPLE GRANTS Royal Collection Trust (£200,000); University of Oxford (£100,000); Chalke Valley History Festival (£50,000); Erasmus Forum (£45,000); Venice in Peril Fund (£23,000); Remembrance Trust and Soil Association (£20,000); Eton College Collections (£15,000); Marston Church and The Georgian Group (£10,000 each); The Sixteen (£5,000); Opportunity International (£1,500).

FINANCES *Financial year end* 05/04/2022
Income £265,300
Grants to organisations £560,000
Assets £122,400

TRUSTEES Jonathan Azis; Timothy Sanderson; Damaris Sanderson.

OTHER INFORMATION Grants were made to 19 organisations during the year.

HOW TO APPLY Contact the correspondent for further information.

CONTACT DETAILS Jonathan Azis, Trustee, Westwood Manor, Lower Westwood, Bradford-on-Avon, Wiltshire BA15 2AF *Tel.* 01225 863374 *Email* jonathanazis@parkepartnership.com

■ The Sandhu Charitable Foundation

CC NO 1114236   **ESTABLISHED** 2006

WHERE FUNDING CAN BE GIVEN Worldwide.

WHO CAN BENEFIT UK-registered charities.

WHAT IS FUNDED General charitable purposes, with a preference for education, health and children and young people.

RANGE OF GRANTS Up to £75,000 but mostly £1,000 to £25,000.

SAMPLE GRANTS The Ehlers-Danlos Support UK (£75,000); The Anne Frank Trust UK (£50,000); Lullaby Trust (£25,000); The Pace Trust (£10,000); Mayor's Music Fund (£1,000).

FINANCES *Financial year end* 31/03/2022
Income £515,800
Grants to organisations £346,500
Assets £3,030,000

TRUSTEES Pardeep Sandhu; Bimaljit Sandhu.

OTHER INFORMATION In 2021/22, grants were made to 19 organisations.

HOW TO APPLY The trustees identify which charities they will support.

CONTACT DETAILS N. Steele, Administrator and Secretary to the Trustees, c/o The Santon Group, First Floor, Santon House, 53–55 Uxbridge Road, Ealing, London W5 5SA *Tel.* 020 3478 3900 *Email* nsteele@thesantongroup.com *Website* www.thesantongroup.com/charity/the-sandhu-charitable-foundation

■ Sandra Charitable Trust

CC NO 327492   **ESTABLISHED** 1987

WHERE FUNDING CAN BE GIVEN UK, with slight preference for the South East.

WHO CAN BENEFIT Charitable organisations; nurses.

WHAT IS FUNDED Animal welfare and research; environmental protection; the relief of poverty; youth development. Grants are also made to nurses and those studying to be nurses.

RANGE OF GRANTS Typically £1,000 to £30,000, with grants of up to £60,000.

SAMPLE GRANTS Florence Nightingale Foundation (£60,000); KIDS (£30,000); Leander Club (£15,000); Scope (£4,000); Royal Star and Garter, Royal Trinity Hospice and Sands (£4,000 each); Dorchester Festival (£1,500); Hurst Cricket Club (£1,000).

FINANCES *Financial year end* 30/06/2022
Income £828,400
Grants to organisations £562,000
Grants to individuals £146,000
Assets £25,440,000

TRUSTEES Michael MacFadyen; Richard Moore; Francis Moore; Lucy Forsyth.

OTHER INFORMATION Grants were made to 122 organisations. Only organisations that received grants of over £1,000 were listed as beneficiaries in the charity's accounts. Grants of under £1,000 totalled £2,000 and were awarded to two organisations. Grants were made to 236 individuals.

HOW TO APPLY The trust's 2021/22 annual report states: 'Unsolicited applications are not requested as the trustees prefer to support charities whose work they have researched and which is in accordance with the wishes of the Settlor. The trustees receive a very high number of grant applications which are mostly unsuccessful.' Applications may be considered from nurses and those training as nurses.

CONTACT DETAILS Lynne Webster, c/o Moore Family Office Ltd, 42 Berkeley Square, London W1J 5AW *Tel.* 020 7318 0845 *Email* Sandra@moorefamilyofficegroup.com

■ The Sands Family Trust

CC NO 1136909   **ESTABLISHED** 2010

WHERE FUNDING CAN BE GIVEN UK and overseas.

WHO CAN BENEFIT Charitable organisations; individuals.

WHAT IS FUNDED General charitable purposes, with a preference for education, health and the performing arts.

SAMPLE GRANTS Previous beneficiaries have included: United World Colleges (£65,700); Kay Mason Foundation (£15,000); Hackney Food Bank (£2,000).

FINANCES *Financial year end* 05/04/2022
Income £10,800
Grants to organisations £90,000

TRUSTEES Peter Sands; Jacqui Moseley; Rebecca Nicolson.

OTHER INFORMATION Full accounts were not available to view on the Charity Commission's website due to the trust's low income. We have therefore estimated its grant total based on its total expenditure.

HOW TO APPLY Contact the correspondent for further information.

CONTACT DETAILS The Trustees, Handelsbanken, 77 Mount Ephraim, Tunbridge Wells, Kent TN4 8BS *Tel.* 01892 701801 *Email* charities@heartwoodgroup.co.uk

■ Santander UK Foundation Ltd

CC NO 803655   **ESTABLISHED** 1990

WHERE FUNDING CAN BE GIVEN UK, including Guernsey, Jersey and the Isle of Man.

WHO CAN BENEFIT Registered charities; CICs; not-for-profit organisations.

WHAT IS FUNDED Financial and digital skills.

WHAT IS NOT FUNDED Charities principally for the benefit of a single religious or ethnic group;

638

Does the funder you have chosen match your needs? Haphazard applications waste postage and time

lobbying or political causes; causes outside the UK.

TYPE OF GRANT Project funding; matched fundraising for employees.

RANGE OF GRANTS Between £40,000 and £100,000.

SAMPLE GRANTS Code Your Future, Create Arts and Social Action for Health (£100,000 each); Share Community Ltd and Willowacre Trust (£75,000 each); Key Unlocking Futures (£40,000).

FINANCES *Financial year end 31/12/2021*
Income £3,680,000
Grants to organisations £2,120,000
Assets £21,800,000

TRUSTEES Sue Willis; Christopher Fallis; John Collins; Danny Jones; Judith Moran; Christopher Anderson.

HOW TO APPLY Visit the foundation's website for the most up-to-date information regarding open grant programmes.

CONTACT DETAILS The Trustees, Santander UK plc, Santander House, 201 Grafton Gate East, Milton Keynes, Buckinghamshire MK9 1AN *Email* grants@santander.co.uk *Website* www. santanderfoundation.org.uk

■ Sarum St Michael Educational Charity

CC NO 309456   **ESTABLISHED** 1980

WHERE FUNDING CAN BE GIVEN Salisbury; Devon; Dorset; Hampshire; Oxfordshire; Somerset; Wiltshire.

WHO CAN BENEFIT Schools; universities; individuals.

WHAT IS FUNDED Religious education; higher and postgraduate education; training of teachers.

WHAT IS NOT FUNDED Maintenance costs, unless they are an integral part of a residential course; grants for buildings, fixtures or fittings; retrospective grants; contributions to the general funds of any organisation.

TYPE OF GRANT Project costs; seed funding/start-up funding.

SAMPLE GRANTS A list of beneficiaries was not included in the annual report and accounts. Previous beneficiaries have included: Salisbury Diocesan Board of Education (£65,000); Diocese of Bristol (£10,000); National Association of Teachers of RE (£7,000); Bridge Youth Project (£5,000).

FINANCES *Financial year end 31/12/2021*
Income £163,000
Grants to organisations £90,500
Grants to individuals £72,000
Assets £6,890,000

TRUSTEES Jennifer Med; The Revd Jane Dunlop; The Revd Ann Keating; Mrs J. Molnar; Mrs J. Tubbs; Prof. Elizabeth Stuart; Jonathan Leigh; The Very Revd Nicholas Papadopulos; David Pain; Diane Wood; Tom Almond; The Rt Revd Stephen Lake.

OTHER INFORMATION During the year, 58 grants were awarded to organisations and individuals.

HOW TO APPLY Application forms for each funding stream are available from the charity's website. Completed application forms should be emailed to the correspondent. The trustees meet four or five times a year to determine grants.

CONTACT DETAILS Clerk to the Governors, Room 2, Suite 1, Second Floor North, Cross Keys House, 22 Queen Street, Salisbury, Wiltshire SP1 1EY *Tel.* 01722 422296 (in the mornings Monday to Thursday) *Email* clerk@sarumstmichael.org *Website* www.sarumstmichael.org

■ The Sasha Foundation

CC NO 1190822

WHERE FUNDING CAN BE GIVEN UK and overseas.

WHO CAN BENEFIT Charitable organisations.

WHAT IS FUNDED Young people suffering from depression and mental health issues or who are confronting drug abuse issues; education and health projects in financially developing countries.

TYPE OF GRANT Project funding.

RANGE OF GRANTS Typically up to £10,000 and no more than 50% of the total budgeted cost of the proposed project/programme.

SAMPLE GRANTS A list of beneficiaries was not included in the annual report and accounts.

FINANCES *Financial year end 31/12/2021*
Income £839,500
Grants to organisations £126,000
Assets £776,100

TRUSTEES Dr Mike Love; Nikolay Love; Ben Love; Pavla Love; Natasha Laird.

HOW TO APPLY Application forms can be downloaded from the foundation's website. They can be submitted by email or by post to the foundation's accountants, Richardson Swift. The trustees meet twice a year to consider applications. The annual application deadlines are 1 April and 1 October.

CONTACT DETAILS The Trustees, c/o Richardson Swift, 11 Laura Place, Bath BA2 4BL *Email* info@thesashafoundation.co.uk *Website* www.thesashafoundation.co.uk

■ The Savoy Educational Trust

CC NO 1161014   **ESTABLISHED** 2015

WHERE FUNDING CAN BE GIVEN UK.

WHO CAN BENEFIT Educational establishments; hospitality associations; charitable organisations/social enterprises; individuals.

WHAT IS FUNDED Hospitality-related projects and education.

TYPE OF GRANT Equipment; capital projects; project funding.

RANGE OF GRANTS Mostly up to £75,000.

SAMPLE GRANTS Hospitality Action (£150,000); Royal Academy of Culinary Arts (£78,000); Folkestone College (£60,000); University College Birmingham (£30,000); Wakefield College (£24,400); Brookvale Groby Learning Trust (£16,000); Be Inclusive Hospitality CIC (£10,000); The Federation Café (£1,300).

FINANCES *Financial year end 31/03/2022*
Income £1,170,000
Grants to organisations £1,560,000
Assets £66,090,000

TRUSTEES Robert Davis; Howard Field; Dr Sally Messenger; David Taylor; Prof. Peter Jones; Stephen Lowy; William Toner.

OTHER INFORMATION During the year, the trust awarded £1.53 million in grants to educational organisations and £24,400 in grants for competitions and prizes.

HOW TO APPLY See the trust's website for the latest information on how to apply including what to write before making an application, details on what to include in the application and application deadlines.

CONTACT DETAILS Margaret Georgiou, Administrator and Secretary to the Trustees, Office 5.23, 60 Cannon Street, London EC4N 6NP *Tel.* 020 4509 7445 *Email* info@savoyeducationaltrust. org.uk *Website* www.savoyeducationaltrust.org. uk

■ The Schmidt-Bodner Charitable Trust

cc no 283014 **established** 1981
where funding can be given UK and overseas.
who can benefit Jewish organisations and other registered charities.
what is funded General charitable purposes; the Jewish faith and community.
range of grants Up to £25,000.
sample grants Community Security Trust (£25,000); World Jewish Relief (£19,000); Chief Rabbinate Trust and Holocaust Educational Trust (£10,000); JW3 Development (£5,000); British Friends of Ohel Sarah and Magen David Adorn (£3,000 each).
finances *Financial year end* 05/04/2022
Income £26,200
Grants to organisations £88,000
Assets £2,160,000
trustees Daniel Dover; Martin Paisner; Harvey Rosenblatt.
other information The trust's latest accounts were not available to view on the Commission's website due to its low income. We have estimated the grant total based on previous years' figures.
how to apply Apply in writing to the correspondent. The trustees have previously stated in their annual report that 'all applications received are considered by the trustees on their own merit for suitability of funding'.
contact details The Trustees, 16 Caenwood Court, Hampstead Lane, London N6 4RU *Tel.* 07711 005151 *Email* charity.correspondence@bdo.co.uk

■ The Anthony Scholefield Foundation

cc no 1150446 **established** 2013
where funding can be given Worldwide, in practice UK.
who can benefit Registered charities.
what is funded General charitable purposes.
range of grants £2,500 to £10,000.
sample grants Aid to the Church in Need UK, Christian Blind Mission UK, Civitas and St Vincent de Paul Society (£5,000 each); INUK and Stella Maris (£2,500 each).
finances *Financial year end* 01/11/2021
Income £32,900
Grants to organisations £25,000
trustees Anthony Scholefield; Ludlow Trust Company Ltd.
other information The 2020/21 accounts were the latest available to view at the time of writing (June 2023). In 2020/21, grants totalled £25,000; however, in previous years, the figure has been much higher.
how to apply Apply in writing to the correspondent.
contact details The Trustees, Ludlow Trust Co. Ltd, Tower Wharf, Cheese Lane, Bristol BS2 0JJ *Tel.* 0117 313 8200 *Email* charitabletrusts@ludlowtrust.com

■ The Schreib Trust

cc no 275240 **established** 1977
where funding can be given UK.
who can benefit Charities, mainly Jewish organisations.
what is funded General charitable purposes including: the relief of poverty; the advancement of religion; religious education.

sample grants A list of beneficiaries was not included in the annual report and accounts. Previous beneficiaries have included: Lolev; Yad Eliezer; Ponovitz; Craven Walk Charity Trust; Shaar Hatalmud; Beis Rochel; Beth Jacob Building Fund; Toiras Chesed; Oneg Shabbos.
finances *Financial year end* 30/06/2023
Income £252,500
Grants to organisations £233,600
Assets £243,400
trustees Abraham Green; Rivka Niederman; Irene Schreiber; Jacob Schreiber.
how to apply Apply in writing to the correspondent.
contact details Rivka Niederman, Trustee, 147 Stamford Hill, London N16 5LG *Tel.* 020 8802 5492

■ Schreiber Charitable Trust

cc no 264735 **established** 1972
where funding can be given UK.
who can benefit Charitable organisations.
what is funded The Jewish faith and community; education and training; social welfare; medical causes.
sample grants A list of beneficiaries was not included in the annual report and accounts. Previous beneficiaries have included: Aish Hatorah UK Ltd; British Friends of Gesher; Friends of Rabbinical College Kol Torah; Gateshead Talmudical College; Mizrachi (UK) Israel Support Trust; SOFT.
finances *Financial year end* 05/04/2022
Income £153,000
Grants to organisations £264,700
Assets £6,920,000
trustees Graham Morris; Sara Schreiber; David Schreiber.
other information In 2021/22, grants were awarded in the following categories: education (£190,200); medical causes (£19,900); advancement of religion (£9,100); social welfare (£3,300).
how to apply Apply in writing to the correspondent.
contact details Graham Morris, Trustee, 9 Fernleigh Court, Wembley, Middlesex HA9 8PW *Tel.* 020 8457 6500 *Email* graham@schreibers.com

■ O. and G. Schreiber Charitable Trust

cc no 1073263 **established** 1998
where funding can be given UK and overseas.
who can benefit Registered charities, with a preference for Orthodox Jewish charities.
what is funded The Jewish faith and community; education; relief of poverty among the Jewish community.
range of grants Between £11,000 and £21,000.
sample grants Edupoor Ltd (£21,000); Care All Ltd (£20,000); Zoreya Tzedokos Ltd (£18,000); Chasdei Sorele (£14,000); Support The Charity Worker (£11,000).
finances *Financial year end* 31/12/2021
Income £150,000
Grants to organisations £148,100
Assets £1,781
trustees Osias Schreiber; Gyta Schreiber.
other information In 2021 the trust made grants to five listed organisations and an unknown number of other grants (under £10,000), totalling £64,100.
how to apply Apply in writing to the correspondent. The charity accepts applications for grants from

representatives of Orthodox Jewish charities, which are reviewed by the trustees on a regular basis.

CONTACT DETAILS Osias Schreiber, Trustee, 34 Jessam Avenue, London E5 9DU *Tel.* 020 8806 1842

■ The Schreier Foundation

CC NO 1187179
WHERE FUNDING CAN BE GIVEN UK.
WHO CAN BENEFIT UK mental health charities.
WHAT IS FUNDED Mental health.
WHAT IS NOT FUNDED Projects with a political element; sponsorship and general fundraising appeals or circulars; activities undertaken by public bodies or organisations contracted to carry out public services on their behalf; applications from individuals.
TYPE OF GRANT Grants to support the direct provision of services.
RANGE OF GRANTS £500 to £5,000. Grants are usually awarded to cover up to 50% of the cost of a proposed activity.
SAMPLE GRANTS Wycombe Youth Action (£4,500); 3H Fund (£3,000); Opening Doors (£2,500); Strong Men (£2,000); Rocking Horse (£1,000).
FINANCES *Financial year end 31/12/2021*
Income £83,600
Grants to organisations £127,600
Assets £4,550,000
TRUSTEES Iris Gibbor; John Smith; Dr Luke Gibbor; Mark Gibbor.
HOW TO APPLY Application forms can be downloaded from the foundation's website. The trustees meets quarterly, in April, July, October and January to consider grant applications. Applicants will be notified whether their request has been successful, or not, by email.
CONTACT DETAILS The Trustees, CP House, Otterspool Way, Watford WD25 8JJ *Email* info@schreierfoundation.com *Website* https://schreierfoundation.com

■ Schroder Charity Trust

CC NO 214050   **ESTABLISHED** 1946
WHERE FUNDING CAN BE GIVEN UK and overseas.
WHO CAN BENEFIT UK-registered charities.
WHAT IS FUNDED General charitable purposes; education; health; arts, culture and heritage; community work; the armed forces; the environment; international development.
WHAT IS NOT FUNDED Individuals; animal welfare organisations; political organisations; major capital appeals.
TYPE OF GRANT Project funding; core/revenue costs.
RANGE OF GRANTS Generally up to £5,000.
SAMPLE GRANTS Hope for Tomorrow and National Manuscripts Conservation Trust (£5,000 each); Eating Matters and Kennet Furniture Refurbiz (£4,000 each); Door Youth Project (£3,000); Colchester Gateway Clubs (£2,000); Ampney Crucis Church (£1,000); Royal Chapel Windsor (£400).
FINANCES *Financial year end 31/03/2022*
Income £560,600
Grants to organisations £399,400
Assets £14,500,000
TRUSTEES Leonie Schroder; Claire Howard; Mr T. B. Schroder; Charmaine Mallinckrodt; John Schroder.
OTHER INFORMATION In 2021/22, grants were made to 107 charities.
HOW TO APPLY Applications should be made online using a form on the website. There is a short

eligibility quiz that must be completed before applying for a grant. Applications can be made at any time as decisions are generally made bi-annually, around June and November. Applicants will be notified of the decision within nine months of submitting an application.
CONTACT DETAILS The Trustees, 81 Rivington Street, London EC2A 3AY *Tel.* 020 3170 5793
Email info@schrodercharitytrust.org
Website www.schrodercharitytrust.org

■ The Schroder Foundation

CC NO 1107479   **ESTABLISHED** 2005
WHERE FUNDING CAN BE GIVEN Worldwide in practice, but mainly UK.
WHO CAN BENEFIT Registered charities.
WHAT IS FUNDED General charitable purposes, mainly within the following areas: the environment; education; arts, culture and heritage; social welfare; community development; international aid. There is a separate grants programme for charities and community groups in Islay and Jura.
RANGE OF GRANTS £6,000 to £500,000.
SAMPLE GRANTS Moorfields Eye Charity and Museum of London (£500,000 each); University of Exeter (£50,000); Fauna and Flora International (£30,000); Amref Health Africa (£25,000); Disasters Emergency Committee (£6,000).
FINANCES *Financial year end 05/04/2022*
Income £5,600,000
Grants to organisations £2,270,000
Assets £15,440,000
TRUSTEES Leonie Schroder; Claire Howard; Philip Mallinckrodt; Charmaine Mallinckrodt; Richard Robinson.
OTHER INFORMATION The foundation shares a common administration with Schroder Charity Trust. In 2021/22, the foundation awarded 33 grants.
HOW TO APPLY The foundation does not respond to unsolicited applications.
CONTACT DETAILS The Trustees, 81 Rivington Street, London EC2A 3AY *Tel.* 020 3170 5793

■ The Scorpion Charitable Trust

CC NO 1094399
WHERE FUNDING CAN BE GIVEN England and Wales.
WHO CAN BENEFIT Charitable organisations.
WHAT IS FUNDED Social welfare; health; research; heritage and archaeology.
SAMPLE GRANTS A list of beneficiaries was not included in the annual report and accounts.
FINANCES *Financial year end 15/09/2022*
Income £1,580,000
Grants to organisations £103,000
Assets £4,680,000
TRUSTEE Ratbones Trust Company Ltd.
OTHER INFORMATION Grants were awarded for heritage and archaeology (£102,500) and research (£500).
HOW TO APPLY Apply in writing to the correspondent.
CONTACT DETAILS The Trustees, 8 Finsbury Circus, London EC2M 7AZ *Tel.* 020 7399 0820

■ Foundation Scotland

OSCR NO SC022910   **ESTABLISHED** 1995
WHERE FUNDING CAN BE GIVEN Scotland.
WHO CAN BENEFIT Charitable organisations.
WHAT IS FUNDED General charitable purposes including the following: health and well-being; art, culture and heritage; life skills, employability

and education; community cohesion; social welfare; access to transport; the environment.

TYPE OF GRANT Capital, revenue and project funding.

RANGE OF GRANTS Usually between £250 and £5,000, but occasionally larger.

SAMPLE GRANTS Scottish Refugee Council (£485,200 in two grants); George Watson's Family Foundation (£150,000); Edinburgh International Festival Endowment Fund (£72,000); Venture North Co-operative Ltd (£8,200); Tain and District Youth Cafe (£13,900); Montrose YMCA (£5,000); Scottish Enterprise Academy (£3,000); Macmillan Cancer Support – East of Scotland (£310).

FINANCES *Financial year end 31/03/2022*
Income £33,310,000
Grants to organisations £17,220,000
Assets £81,520,000

TRUSTEES Angus Tulloch; Barry Sillers; Ian Marr; James Hilder; Jen Gordon; Leslie Rance; Mamta Patel; Mamta Patel; Sharon Fairweather; Shona Smith; Stephen Connelly; Stewart Carruth; Tobias Jung; Toby Anstruther.

OTHER INFORMATION This is one of the 47 UK community foundations, which distribute funding for a wide range of purposes. As with all community foundations, there are a number of donor-advised funds managed on behalf of individuals, families and charitable trusts. Grant schemes tend to change frequently – consult the foundation's website for details of current programmes and up-to-date deadlines.

HOW TO APPLY Potential applicants are advised to visit the community foundation's website or contact its grants team to find the most suitable funding stream.

CONTACT DETAILS Grants Team, 15 Calton Road, Edinburgh EH8 8DL *Email* enquiries@foundationscotland.org.uk *Website* www.foundationscotland.org.uk

---

■ Scotland's Garden Scheme

OSCR NO SC049866   **ESTABLISHED** 1931

WHERE FUNDING CAN BE GIVEN Scotland.

WHO CAN BENEFIT Charitable organisations.

WHAT IS FUNDED Health and well-being; heritage and culture; horticulture and gardens; community development; general charitable purposes.

TYPE OF GRANT Unrestricted.

SAMPLE GRANTS Marie Curie (£9,200); Highland Hospice (£7,000); Canine Partners for Independence and Love Learning Scotland (£4,500 each); Mary's Meals and RNLI (£3,300 each); Médecins Sans Frontières (£2,400); Scotland's Charity Air Ambulance (£1,500); Abundant Borders (£1,000).

FINANCES *Financial year end 31/12/2021*
Income £360,600
Grants to organisations £203,500
Assets £655,400

TRUSTEES Dougal Philip; Sarah Landale; Peter Yellowlees; Colin Crosbie; Charlotte Hunt; David Buchanan-Cook; Stephen McCallum; Charlotte Halliday; Jonathan Cobb; Helen McMeekin.

OTHER INFORMATION The charity supports three core beneficiary charities: Maggie's, Perennial and The Queen's Nursing Institute Scotland. In 2021, each core charity received £11,000. Grants to other 254 charities chosen by garden owners totalled £170,500.

HOW TO APPLY At the time of writing (May 2023), there were no grant schemes open to organisations. Check the website or contact your local district team to see what is currently available.

CONTACT DETAILS Local District Team, 23 Castle Street, Edinburgh EH2 3DN *Tel.* 0131 226 3714 *Email* info@scotlandsgardens.org *Website* https://scotlandsgardens.org

---

■ The Scotshill Trust

CC NO 1113071   **ESTABLISHED** 2006

WHERE FUNDING CAN BE GIVEN UK and overseas.

WHO CAN BENEFIT Registered charities.

WHAT IS FUNDED General charitable purposes, particularly education; arts; animal welfare; relief of poverty and disadvantage; the environment; health; social welfare.

WHAT IS NOT FUNDED Individuals.

TYPE OF GRANT General funding; project funding.

RANGE OF GRANTS £10,000 to £110,000.

SAMPLE GRANTS Médecins Sans Frontières and Save the Children (£110,000 each); Disasters Emergency Committee – Ukraine Appeal (£50,000); New Israel Fund (£20,000); World Vision UK (£15,000); Care International, Oxfam and Shelter (£10,000 each).

FINANCES *Financial year end 05/04/2022*
Income £329,300
Grants to organisations £335,000
Assets £1,830,000

TRUSTEES Jeremy Burton; Deborah Hazan; Mark Burton.

OTHER INFORMATION The trust awarded ten grants to eight organisations during 2021/22. Of the grant total, £205,000 was awarded to causes outside the UK.

HOW TO APPLY Appeals should be in writing only to the trust managers. The annual report states that 'at present appeals will not be considered from charities not previously supported.' Unsuccessful appeals will not necessarily be acknowledged.

CONTACT DETAILS The Trustees, Castlegarth, Scott Lane, Wetherby, West Yorkshire LS22 6LH *Tel.* 01937 585558

■ Scott (Eredine) Charitable Trust

CC NO 1002267   **ESTABLISHED** 1990

WHERE FUNDING CAN BE GIVEN England and Wales.

WHO CAN BENEFIT Registered charities.

WHAT IS FUNDED General charitable purposes; armed forces/emergency service charities; people with disabilities.

TYPE OF GRANT Capital costs; project funding.

RANGE OF GRANTS Generally under £10,000.

SAMPLE GRANTS A list of beneficiaries was not included in the annual report and accounts. Previous beneficiaries have included: Alzheimer's Research UK (£40,000); Mental Health Research UK (£20,000); Combined Services Disabled Ski Team (£10,000); ABF The Soldiers' Charity (£6,000); The Gurkha Welfare Trust (£5,000); RNLI (£3,500); Send a Cow (£3,000); IT Schools Africa (£2,800); Woodworks Project (£1,000).

FINANCES *Financial year end 31/12/2021*
Income £584,600
Grants to organisations £525,500
Assets £15,490,000

TRUSTEES Keith Bruce-Smith; Amanda Scott; Col. Nick Wills; Lucy Gibson.

OTHER INFORMATION Grants were made to 92 organisations during the year.

HOW TO APPLY Apply in writing to the correspondent.

CONTACT DETAILS The Trustees, c/o Sinclair Gibson, Wises Farm House, Ampney St Mary, Cirencester GL7 5SN *Tel.* 01284 851244

■ The Scott Bader Commonwealth Ltd

CC NO 206391   **ESTABLISHED** 1951
WHERE FUNDING CAN BE GIVEN UK and areas near to where companies in the Scott Bader group are located.
WHO CAN BENEFIT Charitable organisations.
WHAT IS FUNDED Social welfare; education and training, overseas aid; conservation; children and young people; socially excluded and disadvantaged people; women; minority communities.
WHAT IS NOT FUNDED Charities concerned with animals; individual sponsorships; travel and adventure schemes; arts projects; any form of advertising; medical research and equipment; sports clubs; general charitable appeals; construction/renovation/maintenance of buildings in the UK.
TYPE OF GRANT Capital and core costs.
RANGE OF GRANTS Grants are typically under £10,000.
SAMPLE GRANTS Ace Africa (£10,000); Busy Bees Pre-school (£5,000); Action for Asperger's (£4,500); London Hearts (£3,000); Living Without Abuse (£2,900); Autism East Midlands (£2,000); Compassionate Friends (£750); Fondation René Verrier (£250).
FINANCES *Financial year end* 31/12/2021
Income £589,000
Grants to organisations £331,000
Assets £2,030,000
TRUSTEES Robert Gibson; David Harris; Hansi Manning; Agne Bengtsson; Paul Smith; Jessica Clark; David Black; Andrew Bell; Richard Tapp.
OTHER INFORMATION In 2021, the charity received around 240 applications and supported 114 of these.
HOW TO APPLY Details of how to apply and upcoming deadlines can be found on the company's website. When the application window is open, applications can be made online.
CONTACT DETAILS The Trustees, Scott Bader Commonwealth Ltd, PO Box 36, Wollaston, Wellingborough, Northamptonshire NN29 7RL *Tel.* 01933 663 100 or 01933 666 755 *Email* use the contact form on the website *Website* www.scottbader.com/humanity/our-society/how-to-access-funds

■ Francis C. Scott Charitable Trust

CC NO 232131   **ESTABLISHED** 1963
WHERE FUNDING CAN BE GIVEN Cumbria; north Lancashire (the Lancaster district to the west of the M6 and north of Galgate).
WHO CAN BENEFIT Registered charities; organisations which are pursuing charitable objectives and have not-for-profit aims/a constitution may be considered. A preference exists for small to medium-sized organisations (turnover less than £1 million).
WHAT IS FUNDED Organisations working with children and young people (up to 24 years old) in the following areas: raising aspirations and supporting personal development; inclusive practice; improving well-being and mental health; improving sector effectiveness.
TYPE OF GRANT Capital costs; project funding; core/revenue funding; start-up costs. The majority of grants are multi-year revenue grants for core costs.
SAMPLE GRANTS Better Tomorrows (£150,000); SAFA (Self-Harm Awareness for All) Cumbria (£22,000); Cumbria Youth Alliance (£4,000); The Laal Collective (£2,000); Wide Gilcrux Village Hall (£1,000).
FINANCES *Financial year end* 31/12/2021
Income £454,800
Grants to organisations £1,140,000
Assets £40,520,000
TRUSTEES Joanna Plumptre; Alexander Scott; Madeleine Scott; Melanie Wotherspoon; Christine Knipe; Peter Redhead; Sarah Dunning; Prof. Karen Stuart; Stephen Curl; Elizbeth Steinhart; Annalee Holliday; Ian Johnson.
HOW TO APPLY Application forms are available to download from the trust's website. Applicants are advised to contact the correspondent for an informal discussion before submitting an application for funding.
CONTACT DETAILS Helen Carter, Director, Stricklandgate House, 92 Stricklandgate, Kendal, Cumbria LA9 4PU *Tel.* 01539 742608 *Email* info@fcsct.org.uk *Website* www.fcsct.org.uk

■ The Frieda Scott Charitable Trust

CC NO 221593   **ESTABLISHED** 1974
WHERE FUNDING CAN BE GIVEN Cumbria, specifically the old county of Westmorland and the area covered by South Lakeland District Council.
WHO CAN BENEFIT Voluntary or charitable organisations; uniformed groups.
WHAT IS FUNDED Older people; people with disabilities; mental health; children and young people; family support work; domestic and sexual abuse; people recovering from substance misuse; people who have experience of the criminal justice system; carers; village hall and community centres; access to services for rural communities; voluntary sector support; arts and sports projects.
WHAT IS NOT FUNDED Retrospective expenditure; statutory bodies (including health and education); promotion of religion or places of worship; individuals; animal welfare, the environment or heritage causes; museums and art galleries; national charities ((with exceptions made for projects involving local volunteers/staff).
TYPE OF GRANT Project funding; revenue or capital costs; occasional larger grants; possible multi-year grants where required.
RANGE OF GRANTS Typically £4,500 to £20,000.
SAMPLE GRANTS Blackwell Sailing (£37,500); The Birchall Trust (£20,000); Keppleway Trust (£7,500); Kendal Lads and Girls Club (£1,200); Diabetes UK (£1,000).
FINANCES *Financial year end* 31/03/2022
Income £174,700
Grants to organisations £376,900
Assets £11,340,000
TRUSTEES Stuart Fairclough; Vanda Lambton; Samantha Scott; Hugo Pring; Laura Southern; Samuel Rayner; Simon Kirby; Alison Alger; Ian Baldwin; Frances Stokes; Gareth McKeever.
HOW TO APPLY Application forms can be requested from the correspondent either by post, email or phone. Alternatively, they can be downloaded from the trust's website. Applicants are welcome to contact the Trust Secretary for an informal discussion before applying. Applications are considered at meetings in March, June, September and December and should be sent at least five weeks in advance. Grants of less than £3,500 are considered by the Small Grants Committee, which meets between the main trustees' meetings. Charities

should not apply to this trust and the Francis C. Scott Charitable Trust at the same time.

CONTACT DETAILS Celia Forsyth, Trust Secretary, Stricklandgate House, 92 Stricklandgate, Kendal, Cumbria LA9 4PU *Tel.* 01539 742608 *Email* celia@fcsct.org.uk *Website* www. friedascott.org.uk

■ Sir Samuel Scott of Yews Trust

CC NO 220878   **ESTABLISHED** 1951
WHERE FUNDING CAN BE GIVEN UK.
WHO CAN BENEFIT Research institutions; hospitals; universities.
WHAT IS FUNDED Medical research and health.
TYPE OF GRANT Research.
RANGE OF GRANTS Between £1,000 and £10,000.
SAMPLE GRANTS Asthma UK, Designability Charity and Pancreatic Cancer UK (£10,000 each); Cure Parkinson's Trust, Motor Neuron Disease Association and Versus Arthritis (£5,000 each); Cerebra and Nottingham Trent University (£1,000 each).
FINANCES *Financial year end 05/04/2022*
  Income £205,100
  Grants to organisations £191,000
  Assets £7,790,000
TRUSTEES Felicity Rice; Hermione Stanford; Camilla Withington.
HOW TO APPLY Apply in writing to the correspondent.
CONTACT DETAILS The Trustees, c/o Currey and Co. LLP, 33 Queen Anne Street, London W1G 9HY *Tel.* 020 7802 2700 *Email* sirsamuelscottofyewstrust@curreyandco. co.uk

■ The Ina Scott Sutherland Charitable Foundation

OSCR NO SC046561   **ESTABLISHED** 2016
WHERE FUNDING CAN BE GIVEN Scotland, with a strong preference for Aberdeen and Aberdeenshire.
WHO CAN BENEFIT Charitable organisations, especially those with which the settlor had a connection; individuals, particularly those in further education.
WHAT IS FUNDED General charitable purposes; social welfare; emergency response; education; health.
RANGE OF GRANTS Mostly up to £10,000 with the occasional larger grant.
SAMPLE GRANTS Charlie House, Clan Cancer Support and VSA Aberdeen (£20,000 each); Aberdeen Endowments Trust and Camphill Schools Aberdeen (£15,000 each); Aberdeen Cyrenians, Befriend a Child and Maggie's Aberdeen (£10,000 each); Childline Aberdeen, Instant Neighbour, NSPCC and RNLI (£5,000 each); Guide Dogs Scotland, Meningitis Now and Sunrise Partnership (£2,000 each).
FINANCES *Financial year end 30/06/2022*
  Income £286,500
  Grants to organisations £252,000
  Assets £7,220,000
HOW TO APPLY Apply in writing to the correspondent.
CONTACT DETAILS The Trustees, c/o Peterkins Solicitors, 100 Union Street, Aberdeen, Aberdeenshire AB10 1QR

■ The John Scott Trust Fund

OSCR NO SC003297   **ESTABLISHED** 1984
WHERE FUNDING CAN BE GIVEN Scotland and other parts of the UK.
WHO CAN BENEFIT Registered, excepted or exempt charities; non-registered charities/voluntary groups; hospices.
WHAT IS FUNDED General charitable purposes including: health; social welfare; disability; children and young people; medical research; humanitarian aid; arts, culture and heritage.
WHAT IS NOT FUNDED Individuals.
RANGE OF GRANTS Mostly up to £5,000 with the occasional larger grant.
SAMPLE GRANTS Ayrshire Hospice (£50,000); The Salvation Army (£30,000); National Trust for Scotland and Royal Scottish National Opera (£20,000 each); Macmillan Cancer Support and Marie Curie Cancer Care (£15,000 each); Independence from Drugs and Alcohol Scotland and Save the Children (£10,000 each); Ayrshire Fiddle Orchestra, Boswell Book Festival and RNIB (£5,000 each); Cumnock Trust and Kincaidston Community Centre (£2,000 each).
FINANCES *Financial year end 30/04/2022*
  Income £51,700
  Grants to organisations £298,000
  Assets £1,920,000
HOW TO APPLY Apply in writing to the correspondent.
CONTACT DETAILS The Trustees, c/o Kilpatrick and Walker Solicitors, 4 Wellington Square, Ayr, Ayrshire KA7 1EN

■ Scottish Coal Industry Special Welfare Fund

OSCR NO SC001200   **ESTABLISHED** 1973
WHERE FUNDING CAN BE GIVEN Scotland.
WHO CAN BENEFIT People who are or have been employed in the mining industry and their families.
WHAT IS FUNDED Social welfare for those who are or have been employed in the mining industry and their families; recreation and respite; arts and culture; education.
SAMPLE GRANTS A list of beneficiaries was not available.
FINANCES *Financial year end 31/03/2022*
  Income £13,200
  Grants to organisations £360,000
OTHER INFORMATION Full accounts were not available to view on the OSCR website due to the charity's low income. We have therefore estimated the charity's grant total based on its total expenditure in 2021/22.
HOW TO APPLY Apply in writing to the correspondent.
CONTACT DETAILS The Trustees, c/o Scottish Mining Convalescent Trust, Blair Castle, Culross, Fife KY12 8JW

■ Scottish Property Industry Festival of Christmas (SPIFOX)

OSCR NO SC020660   **ESTABLISHED** 1983
WHERE FUNDING CAN BE GIVEN Scotland.
WHO CAN BENEFIT Registered charities.
WHAT IS FUNDED Financial assistance to charitable organisations providing relief to children and young people in need.
WHAT IS NOT FUNDED The charity's website states: 'It is not generally our policy to contribute to revenue or administrative needs, this having become our established practice from when our Charity was set up in 1983.'

TYPE OF GRANT Specific capital projects.

RANGE OF GRANTS Up to £36,000.

SAMPLE GRANTS Goodtrees Neighbourhood Centre (£36,000); Finding Your Feet (£20,000); The Yard (£18,000); React (Rapid Effective Assistance for Children with potentially Terminal illness) (£15,000); Music 4 U (£7,300); Riding for the Disabled Glasgow (£3,800); Wigtown Book Festival (£1,800); Amma Birth Partners (£1,000).

FINANCES *Financial year end 30/06/2022*
Income £366,700
Grants to organisations £110,800
Assets £267,900

TRUSTEES Christian Bruce; Alasdair Carlyle; Andy Clark; Ross Clephane; Bill Colville; Tom Cromar; Penny Hearn; Alasdair MacConnel; David Mackensie; Danny O'Neill; Frances Sim; Ronnie Urquhart; Craig Munro; David Kilgour; Chris Cuthbert; Paul Curran.

OTHER INFORMATION All grants are awarded to allow charities to purchase equipment or improve facilities.

HOW TO APPLY Contact the correspondent, or any of the trustees known to you, for an initial discussion. After this, the charity will seek further information on the project/cause to be supported, which will then be considered at the next Beneficiaries Subcommittee meeting. The charity responds to initial applications within a few weeks.

CONTACT DETAILS Alisdar Carlyle, Chair of Beneficiaries Committee, c/o Saffrey Champness LLP, Edinburgh Quay, 133 Fountainbridge, Edinburgh EH3 9BA *Email* alasdair@spifox.co.uk *Website* www.spifox.co.uk

■ ScottishPower Foundation

OSCR NO SC043862   **ESTABLISHED** 2013

WHERE FUNDING CAN BE GIVEN UK.

WHO CAN BENEFIT Registered charities.

WHAT IS FUNDED General charitable purposes; education; the environment; arts, heritage, culture and science; poverty relief; community development.

TYPE OF GRANT Project funding; capital costs.

RANGE OF GRANTS Typically between £10,000 and £150,000.

SAMPLE GRANTS Scottish Autism (£158,700); Museum of East Anglian Life (£122,000); The Single Homeless Project (£98,600); Dynamic Earth Charitable Trust (£76,000); Action for ME (£64,700); Street League (£56,100); Drake Music (£50,000); Dangerpoint Ltd (£36,600).

FINANCES *Financial year end 31/12/2021*
Income £1,370,000
Grants to organisations £1,570,000
Assets £71,700

TRUSTEES Mike Thornton; Melanie Hill; Sarah Mistry; Keith Anderson; Anita Longley; Revd Stuart MacQuarrie; Louise Smith.

HOW TO APPLY Check the website for updates on opening dates for grant programmes.

CONTACT DETAILS Rebecca Fairley, Secretary, 320 St Vincent Street, Glasgow G2 5AD *Email* scottishpowerfoundation@scottishpower.com *Website* www.scottishpower.com/pages/the_scottishpower_foundation.aspx

■ Scouloudi Foundation

CC NO 205685   **ESTABLISHED** 1962

WHERE FUNDING CAN BE GIVEN UK and overseas.

WHO CAN BENEFIT UK-registered charities.

WHAT IS FUNDED Historical research; the environment; social welfare; disability; the armed forces and sailors; children and young people; health; overseas aid.

WHAT IS NOT FUNDED Individuals; welfare activities of a purely local nature; loans.

TYPE OF GRANT Research and fellowships; recurrent; one-off.

RANGE OF GRANTS Typically £1,000 to £5,000.

SAMPLE GRANTS University of London Institute of Historical Research (£62,800); Straight Talking Peer Education and Together for Shorter Lives (£4,000 each); Fine Cell Work, Mental Health Foundation and Professional Classes Aid Council (£2,000 each); London Topographical Society and Tree Council (£1,300 each).

FINANCES *Financial year end 07/02/2022*
Income £178,400
Grants to organisations £107,000
Assets £8,850,000

TRUSTEES David Marnham; James Sewell; Sarah Baxter.

OTHER INFORMATION The foundation awards an annual grant to the Institute of Historical Research at the University of London for fellowships, research and publications. During 2021/22, grants were made to 20 organisations. Grants were broken down as follows: the environment and humanities (£69,000); medicine, health and hospices (£14,000); disability (£8,000); welfare (£8,000); children and young people (£4,000); overseas aid (£4,000).

HOW TO APPLY Applications are only open for Historical Grants fellowships. Copies of the regulations and application forms for 'Historical Awards' can be obtained from The Scouloudi Foundation Historical Awards Committee, c/o Institute of Historical Research, University of London, Senate House, Malet Street, London WC1E 7HU. The trustees meet annually to consider recommendations for grants.

CONTACT DETAILS The Trustees, c/o haysmacintyre, Thames Exchange, 10 Queen Street Place, London EC4R 1AG *Tel.* 020 7969 5500 *Email* pholden@haysmacintyre.com

■ The Screwfix Foundation

CC NO 1151375   **ESTABLISHED** 2013

WHERE FUNDING CAN BE GIVEN UK.

WHO CAN BENEFIT Registered charities and not-for-profit organisations, particularly those local to Screwfix Stores.

WHAT IS FUNDED The repair, maintenance, improvement or construction of homes, community facilities or other buildings for those in need.

WHAT IS NOT FUNDED Projects that will be used by members of the general public (e.g. sports clubs and associations); uniformed groups such as Scouts and Girl Guides; organisations that mainly benefit wildlife or animals. Further exclusions can be found on the foundation's website.

TYPE OF GRANT Capital costs.

RANGE OF GRANTS Typically up to £5,000; the average grant in 2021/22 was £5,100.

SAMPLE GRANTS Macmillan Cancer Support (£143,000).

FINANCES *Financial year end* 31/01/2022
Income £2,340,000
Grants to organisations £2,170,000
Assets £655,100

TRUSTEES Jonathan Mewett; Lindsay Haselhurst; Elizabeth Bell; Caroline Welsh; Darren Worth; Nicholas Boyd; Kelvin Jackson; Philip Barr.

OTHER INFORMATION The foundation was established in 2013 by Screwfix Ltd, a supplier of trade tools, plumbing, electrical, bathrooms and kitchens. During 2021/22, grants to local charities totalled £2.03 million.

HOW TO APPLY Applications can be made via the foundation's website. Applications are reviewed quarterly, usually in March, June, September and December.

CONTACT DETAILS The Trustees, Trade House, Mead Avenue, Houndstone Business Park, Yeovil, Somerset BA22 8RT *Tel.* 01935 414100 *Email* foundation@screwfix.com *Website* www. screwfix.com/help/screwfixfoundation

■ Seafarers UK (King George's Fund for Sailors)

CC NO 226446   **ESTABLISHED** 1917

WHERE FUNDING CAN BE GIVEN UK and the Commonwealth.

WHO CAN BENEFIT Registered charities; unregistered charities; CICs.

WHAT IS FUNDED The health, welfare and safety of seafarers.

TYPE OF GRANT Capital costs; core/revenue costs; seed funding/start-up funding; project funding; unrestricted funding.

SAMPLE GRANTS A list of beneficiaries was not included in the annual report and accounts. Previous beneficiaries have included: Fishermen's Mission (£195,000); Nautilus Welfare Fund (£118,400); Mission to Seafarers Africa (£60,000); Hull 4 Heroes (£10,000); Manx Marine Society (£1,500); Lord Kitchener Memorial Holiday Centre (£750).

FINANCES *Financial year end* 31/12/2022
Income £2,940,000
Grants to organisations £3,570,000
Assets £44,340,000

TRUSTEES Jeremy Monroe; Duncan Bain; Natalie Shaw; Paul Butterworth; William Lawes; Gerald Kidd; Robert Greenwood; Peter French; William Reid; Rear Admiral Iain Lower; Deborah Cavaldoro; Martyn Gray; Nigel Blazeby; Capt. Lee Clarke.

HOW TO APPLY Applications can be made through the charity's website.

CONTACT DETAILS Grants Team, 8 Hatherley Street, London SW1P 2QT *Tel.* 020 7932 0000 *Email* use the contact form on the website *Website* www.seafarers.uk

■ The Searchlight Electric Charitable Trust

CC NO 801644   **ESTABLISHED** 1988

WHERE FUNDING CAN BE GIVEN UK, with a preference for Manchester and the surrounding areas.

WHO CAN BENEFIT Registered charities.

WHAT IS FUNDED Teaching and understanding of the Jewish faith; social welfare and care of older people and those in ill health and their dependants.

WHAT IS NOT FUNDED Individuals.

SAMPLE GRANTS A list of beneficiaries was not included in the annual report and accounts. Previous beneficiaries have included: Bnei Akiva

Sefer Torah; Chabad Vilna; Community Security Trust; Guide Dogs for the Blind; Heathlands; Langdon College; Lubavitch Manchester; Manchester Eruv Committee; Nightingales; Sense; The Federation; UJIA; Young Israel Synagogue.

FINANCES *Financial year end* 05/04/2022
Income £70,200
Grants to organisations £89,600
Assets £1,680,000

TRUSTEES Morris Hamburger; Herzl Hamburger; David Hamburger; Daniel Hamburger.

HOW TO APPLY Apply in writing to the correspondent.

CONTACT DETAILS Daniel Hamburger, Trustee, 21 Brantwood Road, Salford, Greater Manchester M7 4EN *Tel.* 0161 203 3300

■ The Sam and Bella Sebba Charitable Foundation

CC NO 1191713   **ESTABLISHED** 1967

WHERE FUNDING CAN BE GIVEN UK, Israel and USA.

WHO CAN BENEFIT Registered charities; places of worship and Jewish organisations; universities; schools; hospices; social enterprises.

WHAT IS FUNDED Palliative and end-of-life care; refugees; homelessness; human rights; assistive technology.

WHAT IS NOT FUNDED Individuals; large organisations where the foundation does not believe a grant will significantly transform the organisation, except for specific programmes which address a need or sectoral gap that the foundation has identified; organisations which only provide services (sometimes exceptions are made when 'pump-priming'); organisations with unjustifiably large reserves.

TYPE OF GRANT Capital costs; core/revenue costs; project funding; strategic funding; development funding; capacity building; research.

RANGE OF GRANTS Mostly up to £50,000.

SAMPLE GRANTS Association for Civil Rights in Israel (£69,300); Compassion in Dying and Medical Justice (£40,000 each); Jewish Deaf Association (£25,000); Commons Law (£18,000); Halo Project (£15,000); Missing People (£12,500); University of Plymouth (£10,000).

FINANCES *Financial year end* 31/12/2021
Income £61,180,000
Grants to organisations £2,890,000
Assets £64,030,000

TRUSTEES Yoav Tangir; Odelia Sebba; Tamsin Doyle; Judith Sebba; Tali Emodi; Brian Parkinson; Ronit Armoni; Katherine Evans; Katie Waring.

OTHER INFORMATION The foundation also awards grants in the USA (homelessness, with a focus on Seattle) and Israel (tackling violence against women and girls, the environment, at-risk young people, human rights, disability, social justice and shared society). Only organisations that received grants of over £10,000 were listed as beneficiaries in the foundation's accounts.

HOW TO APPLY The foundation's website states that it does not accept unsolicited applications. However, it does provide information about the types of organisations and criteria that may be more likely to receive funding.

CONTACT DETAILS Amy Horne, UK Grants Manager, PO Box 864, Gillingham, Kent ME8 1FE *Tel.* 07809 702920 *Email* admin@ sebbafoundation.org *Website* https:// sebbafoundation.org

■ Seedfield Trust

CC NO 283463   **ESTABLISHED** 1981

WHERE FUNDING CAN BE GIVEN Worldwide.

WHO CAN BENEFIT Registered charities.

WHAT IS FUNDED Christian causes; disaster relief; social welfare.

WHAT IS NOT FUNDED Individuals; applications for multi-year, core funding and salaries are less likely to be successful.

TYPE OF GRANT One-off project funding.

RANGE OF GRANTS £100 to £10,000.

SAMPLE GRANTS Tearfund (£8,000); Missionary Aviation Fellowship (£5,100); Vision for Bangladesh (£4,000); The Message Trust (£3,000); The Leprosy Mission (£2,500); Zambia Orphans Aid (£1,500); Yeldall Christian Centre (£1,000); St Thomas' Church Community Connections Fund (£100).

FINANCES *Financial year end 31/12/2021*
Income £104,500
Grants to organisations £105,800
Assets £3,880,000

TRUSTEES David Ryan; Paul Vipond; Eric Proudfoot; Mervyn Hull; Linda Rigg.

OTHER INFORMATION Grants were made to 49 organisations in 2021.

HOW TO APPLY Application forms are available from the trust's website. The trustees meet twice each year, usually in March and November, to consider applications. Each section of the application should be completed so that it stands alone and does not refer to other documents. Additional information in relation to the project may be submitted if necessary.

CONTACT DETAILS The Trustees, PO Box 135, Keswick, Cumbria CA12 9AS
Email seedfieldtrust@yahoo.co.uk
Website https://seedfieldtrust.wordpress.com

■ The Segelman Trust

CC NO 1188686   **ESTABLISHED** 1992

WHERE FUNDING CAN BE GIVEN UK, occasionally overseas.

WHO CAN BENEFIT UK-registered charities.

WHAT IS FUNDED Vulnerable and disadvantaged children and families.

WHAT IS NOT FUNDED Individuals.

TYPE OF GRANT Core costs; project and development costs; start-up funding; multi-year; one-off.

RANGE OF GRANTS Up to £105,000. In 2021 the average grant was £72,000.

SAMPLE GRANTS Family Rights Group (£105,000); Carefree Cornwall (£90,000); Street Talk (£75,000); Just For Kids Law (£50,000); Clean Start (£35,000); National House Project 'Aspirational Awards' pilot (£25,000).

FINANCES *Financial year end 31/12/2021*
Income £52,230,000
Grants to organisations £1,020,000
Assets £52,590,000

TRUSTEES Wilson Cotton; Timothy White; Rebecca Eastmond; Christopher Graves.

HOW TO APPLY The trustees do not consider unsolicited applications but instead identify projects and organisations they wish to support.

CONTACT DETAILS Katy Golding, Grants Administrator, c/o White and Co., 190 Clarence Gate Gardens, Glentworth Street, London NW1 6AD *Tel.* 020 7759 1129 *Website* https://segelmantrust.org. uk

■ Leslie Sell Charitable Trust

CC NO 258699   **ESTABLISHED** 1969

WHERE FUNDING CAN BE GIVEN UK.

WHO CAN BENEFIT Scout and Guide associations and their members.

WHAT IS FUNDED The trust makes small grants to groups to help with the cost of small projects such as building work, transport or equipment. It also gives assistance to groups and individuals when they make trips in the UK or overseas.

WHAT IS NOT FUNDED The project or trip must be part of the Scouting or Guiding movement. The trust cannot award grants within three months of an event date or the date of departure for a trip.

TYPE OF GRANT Capital costs.

SAMPLE GRANTS A list of beneficiaries was not included in the annual report and accounts.

FINANCES *Financial year end 05/04/2022*
Income £119,700
Grants to organisations £186,500
Assets £5,540,000

TRUSTEES Adrian Sell; Nicola Coggins; Edward Wiltshire.

OTHER INFORMATION Note that the grant total may include amounts awarded to individuals.

HOW TO APPLY Application forms can be downloaded from the trust's website.

CONTACT DETAILS The Secretary, 1st Floor, 8–10 Upper Marlborough Road, St Albans, Hertfordshire AL1 3UR *Tel.* 01727 843603 *Email* admin@lesliesellct.org.uk *Website* www. lesliesellct.org.uk

■ Sellata Ltd

CC NO 285429   **ESTABLISHED** 1980

WHERE FUNDING CAN BE GIVEN UK and Israel.

WHO CAN BENEFIT Charitable organisations; individuals.

WHAT IS FUNDED Advancement of the Orthodox Jewish faith; relief of poverty.

RANGE OF GRANTS Up to £11,000.

SAMPLE GRANTS Ezrat Torah (£11,300); Chevras Machzikei Mesifta (£10,400); Alta Feige Trust (£7,400); Ohel Leah and Tomchei Yotzei Anglia (£6,000 each); Rays of Hope (£5,000).

FINANCES *Financial year end 31/12/2022*
Income £187,000
Grants to organisations £157,200
Assets £3,620,000

TRUSTEES Eliezer Benedikt; Aron Oberlander; Joseph Stern.

OTHER INFORMATION In 2022, grants of under £5,000 totalled £73,200.

HOW TO APPLY Apply in writing to the correspondent.

CONTACT DETAILS The Trustees, 29 Fountayne Road, London N16 7EA *Tel.* 020 8809 5051 *Email* management@abarisltd.co.uk

■ The Selwood Charitable Trust

CC NO 265974   **ESTABLISHED** 1973

WHERE FUNDING CAN BE GIVEN Hampshire.

WHO CAN BENEFIT Individuals and organisations.

WHAT IS FUNDED General charitable purposes.

SAMPLE GRANTS Minstead Trust (£40,400).

FINANCES *Financial year end 05/04/2022*
Income £118,400
Grants to organisations £118,400
Assets £6,050,000

TRUSTEES Simon Selwood; Timothy Selwood; Lorna Selwood; Kim Lazarou; Peter Stone.

OTHER INFORMATION Only one beneficiary was listed in the annual report and accounts. Grants to other organisations and individuals totalled £78,000; however, a breakdown was not available.

HOW TO APPLY Apply in writing to the correspondent.

CONTACT DETAILS The Trustees, Stone Osmond Ltd, 75 Bournemouth Road, Chandler's Ford, Eastleigh, Hampshire SO53 3AP *Tel.* 023 8057 8000

■ The Serco Foundation

CC NO 1150338

WHERE FUNDING CAN BE GIVEN Europe; Asia-Pacific; North America; the Middle East.

WHO CAN BENEFIT Charities; research bodies; social enterprises.

WHAT IS FUNDED Health care; transport; defence; prison management; immigration services; skills and training; waste collection and recycling.

SAMPLE GRANTS A list of beneficiaries was not included in the annual report and accounts.

FINANCES *Financial year end 31/12/2021*
Income £120,300
Grants to organisations £579,100
Assets £5,960,000

TRUSTEES Keith Archer-Jones; David Richardson; Brig. John Weller; Kate Steadman.

OTHER INFORMATION The Serco Foundation is the corporate charity of Serco Group plc, a government services contractor based in Hampshire.

HOW TO APPLY Application forms can be downloaded from the foundation's website. The trustees review applications for support quarterly, normally in February, May, September and December. The foundation has a strong preference for applications that are sponsored by a Serco employee or group of employees.

CONTACT DETAILS The Trustees, Serco House, 16 Bartley Wood Business Park, Bartley Way, Hook, Hampshire RG27 9UY *Email* info@ sercofoundation.org *Website* www. sercofoundation.org

■ The Seven Fifty Trust

CC NO 298886   **ESTABLISHED** 1988

WHERE FUNDING CAN BE GIVEN UK and worldwide.

WHO CAN BENEFIT Registered charities.

WHAT IS FUNDED General charitable purposes and advancement of the Christian religion. The trustees mainly give to causes they have supported for many years.

TYPE OF GRANT Strategic funding; project funding; campaigning.

SAMPLE GRANTS A list of beneficiaries was not included in the annual report and accounts.

FINANCES *Financial year end 05/04/2022*
Income £78,200
Grants to organisations £100,800
Assets £3,970,000

TRUSTEES The Revd Andrew Cornes; Katherine Cornes; The Revd Jonathan Clark; Dr Mary Clark.

OTHER INFORMATION Grants were made to 27 organisations and individuals during the year but a breakdown was not available.

HOW TO APPLY Unsolicited applications will not be considered.

CONTACT DETAILS The Trustees, 20 Gorringe Road, Eastbourne, East Sussex BN22 8XL *Tel.* 01323 732561

■ SF Foundation

CC NO 1105843   **ESTABLISHED** 2004

WHERE FUNDING CAN BE GIVEN UK and overseas.

WHO CAN BENEFIT Jewish organisations.

WHAT IS FUNDED Advancement of Jewish religion and religious education; relief of poverty to assist Jewish families in need.

RANGE OF GRANTS Up to £185,000.

SAMPLE GRANTS The Gilmoor Benevolent Fund Ltd (£185,000).

FINANCES *Financial year end 31/01/2022*
Income £913,900
Grants to organisations £2,510,000
Assets £41,550,000

TRUSTEES Hannah Lipschitz; Rifka Niederman; Miriam Schreiber.

OTHER INFORMATION In 2021/22, grants were distributed as follows: advancement of Jewish religion and education (£1.42 million); relief of poverty (£405,900); general charitable purposes (£364,000); other grant-making charities (£311,500). Grants of under £90,000 each totalled £2.32 million.

HOW TO APPLY Apply in writing to the correspondent.

CONTACT DETAILS Rifka Niederman, Company Secretary and Trustee, 143 Upper Clapton Road, London E5 9DB *Tel.* 020 8802 5492 *Email* sffoundation143@gmail.com

■ The Cyril Shack Trust

CC NO 264270   **ESTABLISHED** 1972

WHERE FUNDING CAN BE GIVEN England.

WHO CAN BENEFIT Charitable organisations.

WHAT IS FUNDED General charitable purposes; the Jewish faith and community.

SAMPLE GRANTS A list of beneficiaries was not included in the annual report and accounts.

FINANCES *Financial year end 28/09/2022*
Income £180,200
Grants to organisations £126,300
Assets £561,300

TRUSTEES Cyril Shack; Jonathan Shack.

HOW TO APPLY Apply in writing to the correspondent.

CONTACT DETAILS The Trustees, c/o Lubbock Fine Chartered Accountants, Paternoster House, 65 St Paul's Churchyard, London EC4M 8AB *Tel.* 020 7490 7766

■ Shaftoe Educational Foundation

CC NO 528101   **ESTABLISHED** 1685

WHERE FUNDING CAN BE GIVEN Parish of Haydon, Northumberland.

WHO CAN BENEFIT Groups working in Haydon with an educational initiative; students needing educational support; apprenticeships.

WHAT IS FUNDED Education and training.

TYPE OF GRANT Revenue support; development costs; capital costs.

SAMPLE GRANTS Shaftoe Wise Academies (£81,900); Haydon Bridge High School (£23,800); Haydon Bridge Playgroup and Tiny Tots (£4,500); Haydon Bridge Scout Group (£1,000).

FINANCES *Financial year end 31/03/2022*
Income £197,500
Grants to organisations £115,400
Grants to individuals £25,700
Assets £9,230,000

TRUSTEES Benedict Bates; Edward Brown; Paula Collis; John Drydon; Laura Gilhespy; John Wardle; Esmond Faulks; Doris Wardle; Kelly Richardson.

OTHER INFORMATION Grants were awarded to 6 organisations and 35 individuals.

HOW TO APPLY According to the foundation's website: 'Applications for grants for local groups should be submitted in writing to the Clerk stating: The initiative or activity, and its educational purpose; the cost, and if it is not for a 'one-off' grant then over what period the grant is requested, broken down into years or periods.'

CONTACT DETAILS The Clerk, The Office, Shaftoe Terrace, Haydon Bridge, Northumberland NE47 6BW *Tel.* 01434 684239 *Email* clerkshaftoecharities@outlook.com *Website* www.shaftoecharities.org.uk

---

■ The Jean Shanks Foundation

CC NO 293108   **ESTABLISHED** 1985

WHERE FUNDING CAN BE GIVEN UK.

WHO CAN BENEFIT Medical research institutions (i.e. medical schools), medical Royal Colleges and similar bodies; medical students.

WHAT IS FUNDED Medical research; education and training; grants for medical students.

WHAT IS NOT FUNDED Grants are not made for financial hardship or any project not having significant pathology research content.

TYPE OF GRANT Scholarships and research funding, for up to three years.

RANGE OF GRANTS From £14,700 to £146,700.

SAMPLE GRANTS The Jean Shanks Foundation and Pathological Society Clinical Research Training Fellowship (£150,000); Medical Research Council (£100,000); University College London (£59,900); Leeds Institute of Medical Research (£49,700); Academy of Medical Science (£25,000); University of Sheffield (£16,900).

FINANCES *Financial year end* 31/03/2022 *Income* £467,100 *Grants to organisations* £480,700 *Assets* £28,360,000

TRUSTEES Dr Julian Axe; Alistair Jones; Eric Rothbarth; Prof. Sir James Underwood; Prof. Sir Nicholas Wright; Prof. Adrienne Flanagan; Prof. Mark Arends.

OTHER INFORMATION Grants were made to 11 organisations.

HOW TO APPLY Application forms can be requested from the correspondent. Full grant guidelines are available on the foundation's website.

CONTACT DETAILS Eric Rothbarth, Chair, Peppard Cottage, Peppard Common, Henley-on-Thames, Oxfordshire RG9 5LB *Tel.* 01491 628232 *Email* administrator@jeanshanksfoundation.org *Website* www.jeanshanksfoundation.org

---

■ The Shanley Charitable Trust

CC NO 1103323   **ESTABLISHED** 2003

WHERE FUNDING CAN BE GIVEN Worldwide.

WHO CAN BENEFIT 'Recognised' international charities.

WHAT IS FUNDED Social welfare.

SAMPLE GRANTS Saber Education (£175,000); Disasters Emergency Committee – Afghanistan Crisis Appeal, India Coronavirus Appeal and Ukraine Humanitarian Appeal (£50,000 for each appeal).

FINANCES *Financial year end* 30/04/2022 *Income* £128,900 *Grants to organisations* £325,000 *Assets* £6,880,000

TRUSTEES Mr S. J. Atkins; Roger Lander; Miss C. Shanley.

OTHER INFORMATION Grants were made to two organisations during 2021/22.

HOW TO APPLY Apply in writing to the correspondent.

CONTACT DETAILS The Trustees, 13 Westbury Road, London N12 7NY *Tel.* 01582 731579

■ The Shanly Foundation

CC NO 1182155   **ESTABLISHED** 1997

WHERE FUNDING CAN BE GIVEN Buckinghamshire; Berkshire; Hertfordshire; Oxfordshire; West Sussex; parts of Surrey and Hampshire.

WHO CAN BENEFIT Registered charities; sports and social groups; community organisations; scout and guide groups; schools; woodland and environmental conservation organisations; outdoor activity centres for young people.

WHAT IS FUNDED General charitable purposes; local community benefit; children and young people; homelessness; health and disability.

WHAT IS NOT FUNDED Individuals; research; core costs; military charities; single-faith charities; animal welfare charities; organisations that have not been in existence for at least 12 months; organisations delivering services outside the area of benefit.

TYPE OF GRANT Generally project and capital costs; usually one-off but some organisations are supported on a long-term basis.

RANGE OF GRANTS Mostly under £5,000.

SAMPLE GRANTS King's College London (£59,000); Outward Bound Trust (£20,000); Jumbulance Trust and Windsor Lions (£10,000 each); Thames Hospice (£100).

FINANCES *Financial year end* 31/12/2021 *Income* £567,700 *Grants to organisations* £842,600 *Assets* £3,280,000

TRUSTEES Michael Shanly; Tamra Booth; Donald Tucker; Timothy Potter; Nicholas Young.

OTHER INFORMATION Grants were broken down as follows: community (£337,100); education (£152,800); health and welfare (£138,400); disability (£109,300).

HOW TO APPLY Applications should be made through the online portal on the foundation's website. The questions can be previewed before registration. General enquiries can be submitted via the online contact form.

CONTACT DETAILS The Trustees, Sorbon, Aylesbury End, Beaconsfield, Buckinghamshire HP9 1LW *Tel.* 01494 671331 *Email* info@shanlyfoundation.com *Website* www.shanlyfoundation.com

---

■ ShareGift (The Orr Mackintosh Foundation)

CC NO 1052686   **ESTABLISHED** 1995

WHERE FUNDING CAN BE GIVEN UK.

WHO CAN BENEFIT UK-registered charities; individuals.

WHAT IS FUNDED Charitable purposes, guided by the wishes of the donors of shares, from where the charity's income derives.

WHAT IS NOT FUNDED Charities not registered in the UK.

TYPE OF GRANT Unrestricted funding; core costs.

RANGE OF GRANTS £500 to £120,000.

SAMPLE GRANTS A list of beneficiaries was not included in the annual report and accounts. Previous beneficiaries have included: Tonbridge School Foundation (£150,000); Cambridge University (£86,000); Parkinson's UK (£65,000); ADHD Foundation (£30,000);

Transform Drug Policy Foundation (£25,000); ManKind Initiative (£15,000); Leeds Community Foundation and Wakefield Hospice (£10,000 each).

FINANCES *Financial year end* 31/03/2022
Income £4,030,000
Grants to organisations £3,770,000
Assets £2,610,000

TRUSTEES Paul Killik; Gillian Budd; Michael Kempe; Helen Baker; Lee Davis; Julian Baddeley.

OTHER INFORMATION In 2021/22, the foundation awarded 430 grants to 404 charities. The largest amount received by a single charity was £232,500.

HOW TO APPLY Applications for funding are not accepted and no response will be given to charities that send unsolicited applications. ShareGift supports a wide range of charities based on the value of shares donated and the number of suggestions it receives for a charity. Charities wishing to receive funding should encourage their supporters to donate unwanted shares to ShareGift. Further information is available on the foundation's website.

CONTACT DETAILS The Trustees, 4th Floor, 67–68 Jermyn Street, London SW1Y 6NY *Tel.* 020 7930 3737 *Email* help@sharegift.org *Website* www.sharegift.org

....

■ The Sharp Foundation

CC NO 1168241
WHERE FUNDING CAN BE GIVEN UK.
WHO CAN BENEFIT Charitable organisations.
WHAT IS FUNDED General charitable purposes, including the arts.
RANGE OF GRANTS Up to £50,000.
SAMPLE GRANTS Clibrary/Marnold and War Child (£10,000 each); Cliffside (£5,100).
FINANCES *Financial year end* 31/10/2021
Income £345,000
Grants to organisations £29,800
Assets £855,000
TRUSTEES Richard Sharp; Caroline Sharp.
OTHER INFORMATION The 2020/21 annual report and accounts were the latest available to view at the time of writing (June 2023). The foundation's grant total in 2020/21 was £29,800; however, in previous years, grants have totalled over £100,000. Only three organisations were listed as beneficiaries in the foundation's accounts.
HOW TO APPLY Apply in writing to the correspondent.
CONTACT DETAILS The Trustees, Finchley Park, Emmet Hill Lane, Kent ME18 6BG *Tel.* 020 3003 5370

....

■ The Shears Foundation

CC NO 1049907   **ESTABLISHED** 1994
WHERE FUNDING CAN BE GIVEN Worldwide, with a preference for the North East. In particular, Tyne and Wear, Northumberland, North and West Yorkshire and Greater Manchester.
WHO CAN BENEFIT Registered charities only.
WHAT IS FUNDED Community development, the environment, sustainable development, health and medicine, social welfare, education (adult and/or children), culture and the arts – all with a focus on education and raising awareness.
WHAT IS NOT FUNDED Capital projects; individuals; religious or political causes; single-identity groups where there is no evidence of integration; pre-school groups and playgroups; domestic pets.
TYPE OF GRANT Core and revenue costs; salaries; project funding.

RANGE OF GRANTS The average value of grants was about £10,100 in 2021/22. Grants to non-core groups are capped at £5,500.
SAMPLE GRANTS Community Foundation Linden Fund (£80,000); Bradford Grammar School, Royal College of Surgeons in England and St Oswald's Hospice Children's Service (£50,000 each); Samling Foundation (£45,000).
FINANCES *Financial year end* 31/03/2022
Income £385,400
Grants to organisations £747,000
Assets £17,130,000
TRUSTEES Mr G. Lyall; Mr P. J. Shears; Mrs L. G. Shears; Bruce Warnes; Mark Horner; Richard Shears; Louise Warnes; Georgie Shears; Nallely Cruz.
OTHER INFORMATION Grants were made to 74 organisations during the year. Grants for less than £25,000 were awarded to 68 organisations and totalled £422,000.
HOW TO APPLY In the first instance, consult the foundation's website, which provides clear details on the application process and when to make an application. At the time of writing (April 2023), the website stated: 'If you would like to apply for a £5,500 grant, we need to have a conversation with you, and find out a little more before you apply. Give us a call on 07544 380316. We normally work on Monday and Tuesday each week.'
CONTACT DETAILS Bruce Warnes, Trustee, c/o The Community Foundation, Philanthropy House, Woodbine Road, Gosforth, Newcastle upon Tyne, Tyne and Wear NE3 1DD *Tel.* 07544 380316 *Email* bruce@shearsfoundation.org *Website* www.shearsfoundation.org

....

■ The Sheepdrove Trust

CC NO 328369   **ESTABLISHED** 1989
WHERE FUNDING CAN BE GIVEN UK; there may be some preference for north Lambeth, London.
WHO CAN BENEFIT Registered charities; schools and universities; individuals.
WHAT IS FUNDED General charitable purposes, particularly the following: sustainability; biodiversity; organic farming and nutrition; health and medical research; education and research; spiritual care; arts and culture.
SAMPLE GRANTS A list of beneficiaries was not available.
FINANCES *Financial year end* 31/12/2022
Income £180
Grants to organisations £468,600
TRUSTEES Barnabas Kindersley; Juliet Kindersley; Peter Kindersley; Harriet Treuille; Anabel Kindersley.
OTHER INFORMATION Full accounts were not available to view on the Charity Commission's website due to the trust's low income. We have therefore estimated the grant total based on the trust's total expenditure.
HOW TO APPLY Contact the correspondent for further information.
CONTACT DETAILS The Trustees, Drove Farm, Sheepdrove, Lambourn, Hungerford, Berkshire RG17 7UN *Tel.* 01488 674726 *Email* helen. cravenjones@sheepdrove.com

....

■ The Sheffield Town Trust

CC NO 223760   **ESTABLISHED** 1297
WHERE FUNDING CAN BE GIVEN Sheffield.
WHO CAN BENEFIT Mainly local charities; national organisations will be supported if it can be demonstrated that the grants will be used

exclusively for the benefit of Sheffield or its inhabitants; CICs; uniformed groups; schools; not-for-profit organisations.

WHAT IS FUNDED General charitable purposes.

WHAT IS NOT FUNDED Individuals; organisations that do not benefit Sheffield or its inhabitants; animal charities; political organisations; religious groups. The trustees will consider support for church buildings as long as those buildings will be used by the local community.

TYPE OF GRANT Recurrent and one-off; project funding.

RANGE OF GRANTS Mainly under £5,000.

SAMPLE GRANTS Age UK Sheffield (£4,500); Ben's Centre for Vulnerable People (£3,000); Park Community Action (£2,000); Lowedges Community Festival Group (£1,000).

FINANCES *Financial year end 31/12/2021*
Income £437,700
Grants to organisations £258,500
Assets £10,790,000

TRUSTEES Jonathan Brayshaw; Jane Ferretti; James Fulton; Nicholas Hutton; Penelope Jewitt; Marian Rae; Adrian Staniforth; Oliver Stephenson; Prof. Sarah Thomas; Mark Swales; Zahid Hamid; Dr Julie MacDonald; Jason Heath.

OTHER INFORMATION One-off grants totalled £170,800.

HOW TO APPLY Application forms can be completed on the trust's website and need to be submitted with any supporting documents. Applicants are advised to draft their answers and documents before starting an application as the form must be completed in one go. The trustees meet four times a year in mid-February, mid-May, mid-August and mid-November. Applications should be submitted by the 15th of the preceding month.

CONTACT DETAILS The Law Clerk, Commercial House, 14 Commercial Street, Sheffield, South Yorkshire S1 2AT *Tel.* 0114 276 5555 *Email* sheffieldtowntrust2@knightsplc.com *Website* www.sheffieldtowntrust.org

····································

■ The Sheldon Trust

CC NO 242328 **ESTABLISHED** 1965

WHERE FUNDING CAN BE GIVEN UK, with a preference for West Midlands and Greater London.

WHO CAN BENEFIT Registered charities; CICs; uniformed groups; schools.

WHAT IS FUNDED Community projects in the West Midlands (mainly volunteer-led); support for special needs groups in the West Midlands (i.e. those facing disadvantage due to age, health, or disability); supporting 16 to 25-year-olds nationally, especially those not in education, employment or training; holidays for people who are disadvantaged living in the West Midlands or Greater London.

WHAT IS NOT FUNDED Costs of purchasing buildings or vehicles; charities with an annual income of over £1 million and/or free unrestricted reserves to the value of more than six months of their annual expenditure.

TYPE OF GRANT Projects; salaries; equipment; furnishings; refurbishments; and running costs. Multi-year grants are available up to three years.

RANGE OF GRANTS Up to £30,000 but typically between £1,000 and £10,000.

SAMPLE GRANTS Safeline (£30,000); Independent Advocacy (£9,100); Doorway (£30,000); Only Connect UK (£10,000); Input SCIO (£5,000); Sandwell Asian Development Association (£3,000); Play for Progress (£1,000); Parallel Youth Enterprise (£800).

FINANCES *Financial year end 05/04/2022*
Income £246,400
Grants to organisations £303,300
Assets £6,230,000

TRUSTEES Rachel Beatton; Andrew Bidnell; Paul England; John England; Ruth Gibbins.

OTHER INFORMATION In 2021/22, grants were made to 33 organisations. Grants were broken down as follows: youth development (£155,700); special needs group (£81,500); community projects (£59,400); holiday fund (£6,700).

HOW TO APPLY Applications should be submitted via the website, where further information and guidance is also provided. There is a separate application form for holidays. The trustees usually meet to consider applications in April and October. Queries should be emailed to the correspondent.

CONTACT DETAILS The Trustees, Pothecary Witham Weld Solicitors, The Office Group, Thomas House, 84 Eccleston Square, London SW1V 1PX *Tel.* 020 7821 8211 *Email* charities@pwwsolicitors.co.uk *Website* www.pwwsolicitors.co.uk/charity-grants/8-the-sheldon-trust

····································

■ The Patricia and Donald Shepherd Charitable Trust

CC NO 272948 **ESTABLISHED** 1973

WHERE FUNDING CAN BE GIVEN York.

WHO CAN BENEFIT Charitable organisations.

WHAT IS FUNDED General charitable purposes; young people.

WHAT IS NOT FUNDED Individuals; local authorities.

RANGE OF GRANTS Up to £105,000.

SAMPLE GRANTS York Theatre Royal (£105,000); British Red Cross – Ukraine Appeal (£10,000); Richard Shephard Music Foundation (£10,000).

FINANCES *Financial year end 05/04/2022*
Income £402,300
Grants to organisations £125,000
Assets £19,500,000

TRUSTEES Christine Shepherd; Iain Robertson; Jane Robertson; Michael Shepherd; Patrick Shepherd; Joseph Shepherd; Rory Robertson; Annabel Robertson; Carly Robertson.

OTHER INFORMATION During 2021/22, the trust made grants to 12 charities for a wide range of causes.

HOW TO APPLY Contact the correspondent for further information.

CONTACT DETAILS The Trustees, West Mount, 129 The Mount, York, North Yorkshire YO24 1DU

····································

■ The Sylvia and Colin Shepherd Charitable Trust

CC NO 272788 **ESTABLISHED** 1973

WHERE FUNDING CAN BE GIVEN North Yorkshire within a 25-mile radius of York.

WHO CAN BENEFIT Charitable organisations.

WHAT IS FUNDED General charitable purposes, particularly: health; social welfare; disability; older people; children and young people; the environment and conservation; heritage; the arts, science and culture.

WHAT IS NOT FUNDED Individuals.

TYPE OF GRANT Project funding.

SAMPLE GRANTS Forward Trust (£36,000); Outreach EMK (£24,000); Parrhesia Inc. (£12,000); Special Boat Service Association (£7,500); Howden AFC (£5,000); Acts 435 (£3,000);

Alzheimer's Society and Barnardo's (£1,000 each).

FINANCES *Financial year end* 05/04/2022
Income £390,000
Grants to organisations £279,800
Assets £1,050,000

TRUSTEES Sara Dickson; David Dickson; Lucy Dickson; Sophie Dickson; Harry Dickson.

OTHER INFORMATION During the year, grants of £1,000 or more were paid to 80 organisations and grants of under £1,000 were paid to 135 organisations. Grants of less than £1,000 totalled £66,600.

HOW TO APPLY Applications should be made in writing to the correspondent and should set out the purpose for which the funds would be used, the total amount required and other sources of finance available.

CONTACT DETAILS The Trustees, PO Box 730, York, North Yorkshire YO1 0HT *Tel.* 01904 619740 *Email* admin@scsctrust.co.uk

■ The Sherling Charitable Trust

CC NO 1079651   **ESTABLISHED** 1999

WHERE FUNDING CAN BE GIVEN UK, with a preference for Buckinghamshire and Dorset.

WHO CAN BENEFIT Charitable organisations.

WHAT IS FUNDED General charitable purposes, particularly education, sports, the arts and health.

TYPE OF GRANT Often recurrent.

RANGE OF GRANTS Grants range from £2,000 to £112,500.

SAMPLE GRANTS Chiltern MS Centre (£112,500); Friends of Liberty Woodland School (£35,000); Autism Wessex (£15,000); Zoological Society of London (£10,000); Flute Theatre (£6,000); Deafblind (£2,000).

FINANCES *Financial year end* 31/03/2022
Income £2,410,000
Grants to organisations £407,500
Assets £5,360,000

TRUSTEES Clive Sherling; Sally Sherling; Adrian Sherling; William Sherling.

OTHER INFORMATION Grants were made to 17 organisations during 2021/22, six of which had not been supported in the previous year.

HOW TO APPLY Apply in writing to the correspondent.

CONTACT DETAILS Clive Sherling, Chair of the Trustees, Lincoln House, Woodside Hill, Chalfont St Peter, Gerrards Cross, Buckinghamshire SL9 9TF *Tel.* 01753 887454 *Email* info@sherlingcharity.org

■ The Archie Sherman Charitable Trust

CC NO 256893   **ESTABLISHED** 1967

WHERE FUNDING CAN BE GIVEN UK and overseas.

WHO CAN BENEFIT Charitable organisations.

WHAT IS FUNDED General charitable purposes including the following: education and training; the Jewish faith and community; overseas aid; arts and culture; health.

TYPE OF GRANT Capital and buildings; project costs.

SAMPLE GRANTS Michael Gee Charitable Trust (£60,000); The Royal National Theatre (£20,000): The Royal Academy of Arts (£17,000); Tel Aviv University Trust (£2,500); Glyndebourne Productions Ltd (£2,100).

FINANCES *Financial year end* 05/04/2022
Income £1,080,000
Grants to organisations £373,200
Assets £18,860,000

TRUSTEES Michael Gee; Allan Morgenthau; Rhona Freedman.

OTHER INFORMATION During the year, 23 grants to organisations were awarded by the trust. Grants were broken down as follows in 2021/22: arts, culture and general charitable purposes (£315,000); health (£66,000); education and training (£29,100); overseas aid (£17,600). Previous research suggests that the trustees review all commitments on a forward five-year basis.

HOW TO APPLY Contact the correspondent for further information.

CONTACT DETAILS The Trustees, 274A Kentish Town Road, London NW5 2AA *Tel.* 020 7493 1904 *Email* trust@sherman.co.uk

■ The R. C. Sherriff Rosebriars Trust

CC NO 272527   **ESTABLISHED** 1976

WHERE FUNDING CAN BE GIVEN Elmbridge.

WHO CAN BENEFIT Charities, schools; constituted organisations; individuals.

WHAT IS FUNDED Arts development projects that work with one or more art form for the benefit of members of the local community, especially where a professional artist is involved. The trust has funded music, dance, drama, visual arts, crafts, literature, film and new media projects.

WHAT IS NOT FUNDED A full list of exclusions can be found on the trust's website.

TYPE OF GRANT Capital, one-off, event underwriting, project and school funds. Funding of up to three years will be considered.

RANGE OF GRANTS Project grants are unlikely to exceed £1,500, while underwriting grants are unlikely to exceed £1,000 and grants to individuals are unlikely to exceed £500.

SAMPLE GRANTS WOTCAT – Riverhouse Barn (£12,000); Vera Fletcher Hall (£5,000); Love of Learning (£2,000); The Barn Theatre Molesley (£1,700); Princess Alice Hospice/Music in Hospitals (£1,500); Rah Rah Community Theatre and The Young Pro School of Acting (£1,000 each).

FINANCES *Financial year end* 31/12/2021
Income £199,900
Grants to organisations £66,800
Assets £4,290,000

TRUSTEES Cllr Barry Cheyne; Elizabeth Cooper; Shweta Kapadia; Tannia Shipley; Wendy Smithers; James Vickers; Brian Nathan; Karen Randolph; Janet Turner; Tricia Bland.

OTHER INFORMATION It is expected that applicants find approximately 50% of the funding needed from other sources, except for underwriting grants. Only organisations that received grants of over £1,000 were listed as beneficiaries in the trust's accounts. Grants of under £1,000 totalled £10,500. The grant total includes amounts awarded to organisations and to individuals.

HOW TO APPLY Application forms can be downloaded from the website (together with a list of the year's deadlines for applications and decisions and full grant guidelines, including instructions for making an application). The trustees meet four times a year to consider applications. Applicants are advised to discuss their proposals and check their eligibility, with the Director, in advance. The website also gives information on past and current projects and successful applications.

CONTACT DETAILS Pete Allen, Director, The Sterling Suite, Hersham Technology Park, Molesey Road,

Hersham, Surrey KT12 4RZ *Tel.* 01932 229996 *Email* arts@rcsherrifftrust.org.uk *Website* www. rcsherrifftrust.org.uk

....

■ Shetland Charitable Trust

OSCR NO SC027025   **ESTABLISHED** 1976
WHERE FUNDING CAN BE GIVEN Shetland.
WHO CAN BENEFIT Charitable and voluntary organisations benefitting the community in Shetland.
WHAT IS FUNDED Arts projects for under 18s; activities for older people; social welfare; community development.
WHAT IS NOT FUNDED Exclusions can be found in the guidance notes on the trust's website.
TYPE OF GRANT Project costs; capital and building maintenance costs; running and recurring costs.
SAMPLE GRANTS Shetland Recreational Trust (£3.64 million); Support to Rural Care Model (£1.97 million); Shetland Amenity Trust (£1.17 million); Shetland Arts Development Agency (£950,000); COPE Ltd. (£225,000); Mind Your Head (£75,000); Gaada (£50,000); NSPCC Scotland (£4,000).
FINANCES *Financial year end* 31/03/2022
Income £6,600,000
Grants to organisations £8,870,000
Assets £450,620,000
TRUSTEES Andrew Cooper; Margaret Roberts; Ken Harrison; Yvette Hopkins; Robert Leask; Ian Napier; Ewen Adamson; Susan Gray; Ryan Leith; Emma Miller; Ryan Stevenson; Aaron Ferguson.
OTHER INFORMATION The trust awarded grants totalling £8.31 million through its Main Grants scheme and £51,200 through its Small Grants scheme. The remaining grant total was awarded through the trust's Contingency Fund.
HOW TO APPLY Application forms are available to download from the trust's website.
CONTACT DETAILS The Trustees, 22–24 North Road, Lerwick, Shetland ZE1 0NQ *Tel.* 01595 744990 *Email* mail@shetlandcharitabletrust.co.uk *Website* www.shetlandcharitabletrust.co.uk

....

■ SHINE (Support and Help in Education)

CC NO 1082777   **ESTABLISHED** 1999
WHERE FUNDING CAN BE GIVEN Northern England.
WHO CAN BENEFIT Registered charities; schools; CICs.
WHAT IS FUNDED Educational projects helping children and young people aged between 4 and 14 years who are disadvantaged to fulfil their academic potential. The charity's core priorities (up to 2025) are Ready for School, Bridging the Gap and Flying High. See the charity's website for further details.
WHAT IS NOT FUNDED Programmes that take place outside northern England; short-term or one-off projects; bursaries or any kind of student fees; direct replacement of statutory funding; capital build programmes for schools or other education institutions.
TYPE OF GRANT Project funding; seed funding/start-up funding; core/revenue costs.
RANGE OF GRANTS Mostly up to £50,000, but larger grants awarded in some cases.
SAMPLE GRANTS Wise Owl Trust (£100,000); St Patrick's Roman Catholic High School (£78,900); Vantage Academy Trust (£42,300); St Mary's Catholic Academy (£30,400); Boromi (£10,900); University of Manchester (£4,500);

Educational Diversity (£3,400); The Spencer Academies Trust (£750).
FINANCES *Financial year end* 31/08/2022
Income £878,900
Grants to organisations £1,500,000
Assets £6,370,000
TRUSTEES Cameron Ogden; Ann Mroz; Lord Jim O'Neill; Samantha Twiselton; Sarah Loftus; Mark Heffernan; Lorna Fitzsimons; Raksha Pattni; Kavita Gupta; Johnny Uttley; Paul Green.
OTHER INFORMATION The charity awarded 78 grants to organisations during the year, with a focus on literacy, maths, science and cross-curricular education.
HOW TO APPLY Applicants should use the enquiry form on the charity's website, outlining the following points in no more than three or four paragraphs: an overview of the project and its aims, specifically related to academic attainment in maths, literacy or science; how it would meet SHINE's core priorities; the number of beneficiaries and schools it would reach; the overall project budget and the size of the request to SHINE.
CONTACT DETAILS The Trustees, SHINE Trust, Princes Exchange, 2 Princes Square, Leeds, West Yorkshire LS1 4HY *Tel.* 0113 280 5872 *Email* info@shinetrust.org.uk *Website* www. shinetrust.org.uk

....

■ The Bassil Shippam and Alsford Trust

CC NO 256996   **ESTABLISHED** 1967
WHERE FUNDING CAN BE GIVEN UK, with a preference for West Sussex.
WHO CAN BENEFIT Charitable organisations; hospices; educational institutions; Christian institutions; individuals; statutory authorities.
WHAT IS FUNDED Medical research; education and training; the arts; social welfare; children and young people; older people; Christianity.
TYPE OF GRANT General funding; bursaries for individuals.
RANGE OF GRANTS Grants range from £200 up to £20,000.
SAMPLE GRANTS Christian Youth Enterprises Sailing Centre (£20,000); Tearfund – Ukraine Crisis (£5,000); 4Sight Vision Support (£2,500); Kent, Surrey and Sussex Community Rehabilitation Company Ltd (£2,000); Canine Partners, West Sussex County Council Voluntary Fund and Yeldall Christian Centre (£1,000 each); Hindleap Warren (£750); CICRA, Family Support Work and Over the Wall (£500 each); Church Pastoral Society, Elizabeth Finn Trust and Not Forgotten Association (£200 each).
FINANCES *Financial year end* 05/04/2022
Income £140,400
Grants to organisations £93,000
Grants to individuals £1,600
Assets £4,540,000
TRUSTEES Ian Macleod; Alison Swan; Janet Bailey; Simon Macfarlane; Richard Tayler; Susan Trayler; Molly Hanwell; Stanley Young; John Shippam; Christopher Doman.
OTHER INFORMATION Grants were broken down as follows: social welfare (£50,500); education (£38,500); performing arts (£3,300); medical research (£750).
HOW TO APPLY Apply in writing to the correspondent.
CONTACT DETAILS The Trustees, Thomas Eggar House, Friary Lane, Chichester, West Sussex PO19 1UF *Tel.* 01243 786111 *Email* shippam@irwinmitchell.com

....

■ The Shipwrights Charitable Fund

CC NO 262043   **ESTABLISHED** 1971
WHERE FUNDING CAN BE GIVEN UK, with a preference for the City of London.
WHO CAN BENEFIT Registered charities; unregistered charities; schools; universities; amateur sports clubs; individuals.
WHAT IS FUNDED Maritime training and education, seafarers' welfare; maritime heritage; young people.
TYPE OF GRANT Capital costs; core and revenue costs; seed funding; start-up funding; project funding.
RANGE OF GRANTS Programme dependent.
SAMPLE GRANTS Marine Society and Sea Cadets (£13,000); Seafarers' International Relief Fund (£5,000); Steamship Freshspring Trust (£1,000); Annual National Service for Seafarers (£500); Clergy Support Trust (£200).
FINANCES *Financial year end 30/04/2022*
Income £412,700
Grants to organisations £165,400
Assets £6,560,000
TRUSTEES John Denholm; Laura Bugden; R. H. Close-Smith; Richard Moore; Nicholas Shaw; Simon Beale; Andreas Bisbas; Sir George Zambellas; The Worshipful Company of Shipwrights.
OTHER INFORMATION The grant total includes grants made to individuals; we were unable to determine a breakdown.
HOW TO APPLY Applications can be submitted using the relevant online application form.
CONTACT DETAILS The Clerk, Ironmongers' Hall, 1 Shaftesbury Place, Barbican, London EC2Y 8AA *Tel.* 020 7606 2376 *Email* office@shipwrights.co .uk *Website* www.shipwrights.co.uk

■ Shlomo Memorial Fund Ltd

CC NO 278973   **ESTABLISHED** 1978
WHERE FUNDING CAN BE GIVEN Worldwide, with a preference for the UK, Israel and the USA.
WHO CAN BENEFIT Jewish organisations.
WHAT IS FUNDED Advancing Judaism through education; relief of poverty; general charitable purposes.
RANGE OF GRANTS Mostly up to £50,000 with the occasional larger or smaller grant.
SAMPLE GRANTS Ziv Hakehilla (£241,000); Dorshi Tzion Elit (£70,000); Arucha Chama Bechol Yom and Yachad Leman Kol Echod V'echod (£53,000 each); Ateret Avot, Kol HaChinuch and Shaarei Limud (£33,000 each); Chaim Vuchesed Organisation, Friends of Mosdos Torah and Reshet Mosdot Bakrayot Hadatiyot (£18,000 each); Igud Hakollelim (£10,000).
FINANCES *Financial year end 30/09/2021*
Income £10,780,000
Grants to organisations £2,280,000
Assets £71,690,000
TRUSTEES Amichai Toporowitz; Esther Hoffner; Meir Sulam; Chaim Kaufman; Eliyah Kleinerman; Channe Lopian; Hezkel Toporowitz.
OTHER INFORMATION The 2020/21 accounts were the latest available at the time of writing (May 2023). Only organisations that received grants of over £10,000 were listed as beneficiaries in the charity's 2020/21 accounts. Grants of under £10,000 totalled £20,300.
HOW TO APPLY Apply in writing to the correspondent.
CONTACT DETAILS Channe Lopian, Secretary, c/o Cohen Arnold, New Burlington House, 1075 Finchley Road, London NW11 0PU *Tel.* 0161 772 0444 *Email* info@olnato.com

■ The Shoe Zone Trust

CC NO 1112972   **ESTABLISHED** 2005
WHERE FUNDING CAN BE GIVEN Preference for Leicestershire and Rutland and for certain charities operating in the Philippines and elswhere.
WHO CAN BENEFIT Charitable organisations.
WHAT IS FUNDED Education and training; social welfare; children and young people.
RANGE OF GRANTS £10,000 to £73,000.
SAMPLE GRANTS Shepherd of the Hills (£73,600); CORD (£25,000); Amantani (£17,200); Leicester Charity UK (£10,000).
FINANCES *Financial year end 31/12/2021*
Income £319,900
Grants to organisations £237,600
Assets £336,900
TRUSTEES Anthony Smith; John Smith.
OTHER INFORMATION Grants were awarded to ten organisations during the year. No grants were awarded to individuals.
HOW TO APPLY Apply in writing to the correspondent.
CONTACT DETAILS The Trustees, c/o Shoe Zone, Haramead Business Centre, Humberstone Road, Leicester, Leicestershire LE1 2LH *Tel.* 0116 222 3000 *Website* www.shoezone.com/OurCharities

■ Shulem B. Association Ltd

CC NO 313654   **ESTABLISHED** 1961
WHERE FUNDING CAN BE GIVEN UK and overseas.
WHO CAN BENEFIT Jewish organisations.
WHAT IS FUNDED Jewish religion and education; general charitable purposes.
TYPE OF GRANT Capital and revenue costs.
RANGE OF GRANTS Up to £310,000.
SAMPLE GRANTS United Talmudical Associates Ltd (£310,000); Chevras Mo'oz Ladol (£87,000); Tchabe Kollel Ltd (£60,000); UTRY (£35,000); Palmcourt Ltd (£25,000); Yeshiva Gedolah Torah Veyirah Sevenoaks Ltd (£10,000).
FINANCES *Financial year end 30/09/2021*
Income £4,380,000
Grants to organisations £1,350,000
Assets £53,580,000
TRUSTEES Samuel Berger; Zelda Sternlicht; Sarah Klein.
OTHER INFORMATION The 2020/21 accounts were the latest available at the time of writing (May 2023). Grants were broken down as follows: general charitable purposes (£443,300); advancement of the Jewish religion (£475,300); advancement of Jewish education (£423,300). Grants were awarded to more than 11 institutions during the year.
HOW TO APPLY Applications should be made in writing to the trustees.
CONTACT DETAILS The Trustees, New Burlington House, 1075 Finchley Road, London NW11 0PU *Tel.* 020 8731 0777

■ The Florence Shute Millennium Trust

CC NO 1085358   **ESTABLISHED** 2001
WHERE FUNDING CAN BE GIVEN Chepstow, Monmouthshire and the Forest of Dean.
WHO CAN BENEFIT Charitable organisations, particularly health-related organisations.
WHAT IS FUNDED Health; local causes; general charitable purposes.
TYPE OF GRANT Generally one-off funding.
RANGE OF GRANTS £500 to £7,000.

SAMPLE GRANTS Great Oaks Hospice (£7,000); Bowel Cancer UK (£5,000); St David's Hospice Care (£4,000); Blind Veterans (£3,000); Cerebral Palsy Plus (£2,000); Buglife – The Invertebrate Conversation Trust (£500).
FINANCES *Financial year end* 05/04/2022
Income £86,300
Grants to organisations £96,700
Assets £2,360,000
TRUSTEES Richard O'Sullivan; Ursula Williams; James Zorab; Dr James Allison.
HOW TO APPLY Contact the correspondent for information regarding the application process.
CONTACT DETAILS The Trustees, St Maur Beaufort Square, Chepstow NP16 5EP *Tel.* 01291 622237 *Email* vickyc@francisandco.wales

....

■ The Simmons & Simmons Charitable Foundation

CC NO 1129643   **ESTABLISHED** 2009
WHERE FUNDING CAN BE GIVEN Worldwide, in areas local to the Simmons & Simmons' offices.
WHO CAN BENEFIT Registered charities, with a preference for smaller charities.
WHAT IS FUNDED General charitable purposes, particularly causes relating to social exclusion; legal support; access to justice.
RANGE OF GRANTS Typically from £5,000 to £20,000.
SAMPLE GRANTS Dementia UK (£300,000); Oceana UK (£62,500); Willing Hearts (£20,000); Lawyers Against Poverty and Pure Leapfrog (£10,000 each).
FINANCES *Financial year end* 30/04/2022
Income £2,300,000
Grants to organisations £2,300,000
Assets £88,300
TRUSTEES Richard Dyton; Fiona Loughrey; Devarshi Saksena; Stefania Bergia; Julian Taylor.
OTHER INFORMATION This is the corporate charity of Simmons & Simmons LLP. The foundation prioritises charities where the firm's employees can have some involvement. Grants were broken down as follows: COVID-19 (£1.95 million); other (£144,900); social inclusion (£105,700); pro bono (£54,900); access to justice (£45,300).
HOW TO APPLY Apply in writing to the correspondent by email.
CONTACT DETAILS The Trustees, Citypoint, 1 Ropemaker Street, London EC2Y 9SS *Tel.* 020 7628 2020 *Email* responsible.business@simmons-simmons.com *Website* www.simmons-simmons.com/en/about-us/responsible-business

....

■ Singer Foundation

CC NO 277364   **ESTABLISHED** 1979
WHERE FUNDING CAN BE GIVEN UK, with a preference for the the area within the Birmingham-Bristol-Reading triangle.
WHO CAN BENEFIT UK-registered charities.
WHAT IS FUNDED Supporting individuals through enterprise, employment and education.
TYPE OF GRANT One-off grants.
SAMPLE GRANTS A list of beneficiaries was not included in the annual report and accounts.
FINANCES *Financial year end* 05/04/2022
Income £119,500
Grants to organisations £72,600
Assets £4,790,000
TRUSTEES Roger Carter; Geoffrey Taylor; Christopher Powell; Susan Carrdus; Denise Lucas; Janis Langdon; Peter Hartley.

OTHER INFORMATION Grants were made to 12 organisations in 2021/22.
HOW TO APPLY Contact the foundation to request an application form.
CONTACT DETAILS D. E. Jones, Administrator, Hillcrest, Ragnal Lane, Nailsworth, Stroud GL6 0RU *Tel.* 07979 860136 *Email* admin@singer.foundation

....

■ The Sino-British Fellowship Trust

CC NO 1174487   **ESTABLISHED** 1948
WHERE FUNDING CAN BE GIVEN UK and China.
WHO CAN BENEFIT Universities, researchers and educational institutions.
WHAT IS FUNDED Education of teachers and researchers in China; grants to enable Chinese academics or students to carry out research or study in the UK; grants to enable UK academics to undertake research with Chinese colleagues; funding for academics to enhance their knowledge of Chinese languages.
TYPE OF GRANT Scholarships and grants for research and training.
RANGE OF GRANTS Grants range from £1,000 to £47,300.
SAMPLE GRANTS Great Britain China Educational Trust (£47,300); Royal Society (£37,500); Universities China Committee London (£29,800); British Academy (£26,000); Chinese University of Hong Kong (£20,000); Needham Research Institute (£3,900); Hong Kong University (£1,000).
FINANCES *Financial year end* 31/12/2021
Income £418,600
Grants to organisations £113,000
Grants to individuals £21,200
Assets £13,310,000
TRUSTEES Anne Ely; Peter Ely; Ling Thompson; Prof. Wayne Luk; Frances Wood; Prof. Rosemary Foot; Sir Christopher Hum.
OTHER INFORMATION During the year, seven grants were made to organisations and five grants were made to individuals.
HOW TO APPLY Apply in writing to the correspondent.
CONTACT DETAILS Anne Ely, Trustee, Flat 23, Bede House, Manor Fields, London SW15 3LT *Tel.* 020 8788 6252

....

■ The Skelton Bounty

CC NO 219370   **ESTABLISHED** 1934
WHERE FUNDING CAN BE GIVEN Greater Manchester, Lancashire and Merseyside (including the unitary authorities of Blackpool, Blackburn, Warrington and Halton).
WHO CAN BENEFIT Registered charities.
WHAT IS FUNDED Educational establishments supporting children who are disadvantaged; community facilities; holidays for disadvantaged children; older people; people with disabilities.
WHAT IS NOT FUNDED Core costs; large capital projects; individuals; unregistered charities; animal welfare charities; medical research charities; mainstream schools or NHS hospitals; national charities unless the requested funds directly benefit people in Greater Manchester, Merseyside or Lancashire.
TYPE OF GRANT Preference for small specific capital projects (particularly equipment) rather than general expenditure.
RANGE OF GRANTS £1,000 to £4,000.
SAMPLE GRANTS St Ann's Hospice (£4,000); Blackpool Boys and Girls Club (£3,500); Sefton Children's Trust and Vauxhall Community Law and Information Centre (£2,000 each); Liverpool

Cares, Manchester Jewish Community Care and Rochdale Connections Trust (£1,000 each).

FINANCES *Financial year end* 05/04/2022
Income £112,100
Grants to organisations £99,100
Assets £3,350,000

TRUSTEES Robert Hough; Sir Mark Hedley; Edith Conn; Gail Stanley; Sue Lomas; Carl Hankinson; Christine Reeves; Nabela Chaudhry; Gulab Singh.

OTHER INFORMATION Grants were awarded to 54 organisations during the year.

HOW TO APPLY Apply online via the Liverpool Charity and Voluntary Services website.

CONTACT DETAILS The Trustees, c/o Liverpool Charity and Voluntary Services, 151 Dale Street, Liverpool, Merseyside L2 2AH *Tel.* 0151 227 5177 ext. 3219 *Email* grants@lcvs.org.uk *Website* www.skeltoncharity.com

■ The Skerritt Trust

CC NO 1016701 **ESTABLISHED** 1992
WHERE FUNDING CAN BE GIVEN Within a ten-mile radius of Nottingham Market Square.
WHO CAN BENEFIT Registered charities.
WHAT IS FUNDED Housing for older people.
TYPE OF GRANT Capital costs.
SAMPLE GRANTS A list of organisations which received grants during the year 2021/22 was not available.
FINANCES *Financial year end* 05/04/2022
Income £102,000
Grants to organisations £74,000
Assets £2,750,000
TRUSTEES David Lowe; Roger Turner; Roy Taylor; Sandra Warzynska; Rona Harvie; Alma Davies; Charles Cullen; Teresa Clayton.
HOW TO APPLY Apply in writing to the correspondent, including annual accounts and details of the costs of the items or facilities required. The trustees consider applications at their quarterly meetings.
CONTACT DETAILS Anna Chandler, PO Box 11228, Nottingham, Nottinghamshire NG14 6YY *Tel.* 07354 875035 *Email* anna@chandler-cc.co.uk

■ The Charles Skey Charitable Trust

CC NO 277697 **ESTABLISHED** 1979
WHERE FUNDING CAN BE GIVEN UK, with a preference for Devon, Cornwall and Somerset.
WHO CAN BENEFIT Registered charities; churches; educational establishments; hospitals; museums.
WHAT IS FUNDED General charitable purposes, including the following: social welfare; education; Christianity; health; citizenship/community development; arts, culture, heritage and science; amateur sport; the armed forces and emergency services.
TYPE OF GRANT Capital costs; core/revenue costs; seed funding/start-up costs. Both annual and one-off awards.
RANGE OF GRANTS Up to around £200,000.
SAMPLE GRANTS Polka Theatre (£210,000); Almeida Theatre (£60,000); Imperial War Museum (£50,000); Centre for Enterprise Markets and Ethics (£35,000); On Course Foundation (£30,000); Help Musicians UK and Sherborne School Foundation (£25,000 each); Institute of Imagination (£20,000); Brasenose College – Oxford (£15,000); Dementia UK and French

Hospital (£10,000 each); St Andrew's Church – Ryde (£8,000).
FINANCES *Financial year end* 05/04/2022
Income £429,400
Grants to organisations £975,500
Assets £16,710,000
TRUSTEES Christopher Berkeley; John Leggett; The Revd James Leggett; David Berkeley; Edward Berkeley.
OTHER INFORMATION A total of 22 grants were awarded during the year. Grants were broken down as follows: arts, culture, heritage or science (£395,000); citizenship or community development (£315,000); amateur sport (£95,000); the armed forces and emergency services (£65,000); education (£40,000); health and saving lives (£25,000); social welfare (£22,500); religion (£18,000).
HOW TO APPLY Apply in writing to the correspondent.
CONTACT DETAILS The Trustees, Flint House, Park Homer Road, Colehill, Wimborne, Dorset BH21 2SP *Tel.* 01202 883778

■ Skipton Building Society Charitable Foundation

CC NO 1079538 **ESTABLISHED** 2000
WHERE FUNDING CAN BE GIVEN UK, with a preference for areas near the society's principal office or one of its branches.
WHO CAN BENEFIT Registered charities, with a focus on smaller, local organisations.
WHAT IS FUNDED The welfare and education of children (under 16); youth schemes and projects supporting those in their late teens and early 20s in socially deprived areas with literacy, numeracy and employment; supporting older people by reducing isolation and helping reduce the effects of dementia and Alzheimer's.
WHAT IS NOT FUNDED Applications for general ongoing funding, running costs, rent, utility costs medical research, sponsorship, payment of salaries, counselling or expenses; requests for administration equipment such as telephones, security systems or computers, for a charity's own use; the restoration and upkeep of buildings or maintenance of vehicles; causes serving only a specific sector of the community selected on the basis of ethnic, racial, political or religious grounds/advancement; overseas travel, expeditions or educational expenses, including causes that would otherwise qualify for support but require funds for activities outside the UK; non-registered charities, individuals or large national charities; support of activities which fall within an existing statutory funded budget or are the responsibility of central or local government even if the budget is insufficient to fund the activity applied for.
TYPE OF GRANT Specific items or activities.
RANGE OF GRANTS Up to £3,000.
SAMPLE GRANTS Frodsham Youth Association and Helping Disabilities (£3,000 each); Home-Start Kirklees (£2,500); Bolton Deaf Society (£2,300); The Happy and Healthy Trust (£1,300); Swansea Music Art Digital (£940); Willowbrook Hospice (£750); Walthew House – Cheshire (£470).
FINANCES *Financial year end* 28/02/2022
Income £200,200
Grants to organisations £236,800
Assets £48,300
TRUSTEES The Rt Revd and Rt Hon. Lord Hope of Thornes; Kitty North; Alison Davies; John Dawson; Amelia Vyvyan; Debra Ewing; Gregory Bell.

HOW TO APPLY Application forms can be downloaded on the website. The trustees usually meet at the beginning of March, June, September and December. Submission deadline dates are the first day of the month prior to each meeting.

CONTACT DETAILS The Trustees, The Bailey, Skipton, North Yorkshire BD23 1DN *Tel.* 01756 705000 *Email* charitablefoundation@skipton.co.uk *Website* www.skiptoncharitablefoundation.co.uk

■ The John Slater Foundation

CC NO 231145   **ESTABLISHED** 1963
WHERE FUNDING CAN BE GIVEN UK, with a preference for the North West and towns with which John Slater was connected.
WHO CAN BENEFIT Registered charities.
WHAT IS FUNDED General charitable purposes, including animal welfare, education and social welfare.
WHAT IS NOT FUNDED Individuals.
SAMPLE GRANTS Association for the Rights of Abandoned Animals (£18,700 in five grants); Sacred Heart Church (£10,000); The Blackpool Ladies' Sick Poor Association (£4,700 in two grants); Freshfields Animal Rescue (£2,000).
FINANCES *Financial year end* 05/04/2022
Income £4,380,000
Grants to organisations £129,100
Assets £4,850,000
TRUSTEE HSBC Trust Company (UK) Ltd.
OTHER INFORMATION During the year, 39 grants were made to 21 organisations.
HOW TO APPLY Apply in writing to the correspondent via email.
CONTACT DETAILS Nigel Miller, Secretary, c/o HSBC Trust Company (UK) Ltd, 2nd Floor, 1 The Forum, Parkway, Whiteley, Fareham, Hampshire PO15 7PA *Email* trust.management.account@ hsbc.com or nigel.millar@hsbc.com *Website* http://johnslaterfoundation.org.uk

■ The Slaughter and May Charitable Trust

CC NO 1082765   **ESTABLISHED** 2000
WHERE FUNDING CAN BE GIVEN UK and occasionally other parts of the world.
WHO CAN BENEFIT Charitable organisations.
WHAT IS FUNDED General charitable purposes, particularly causes relating to children and young people.
SAMPLE GRANTS St Luke's Community Centre (£65,800); Beam (£30,000); Internews (£15,000); Mencap (£5,000).
FINANCES *Financial year end* 05/04/2022
Income £573,600
Grants to organisations £568,100
Assets (£60,000)
TRUSTEE Slaughter and May Trust Ltd.
OTHER INFORMATION Grants were awarded to 22 organisations during the year.
HOW TO APPLY The trust does not generally accept unsolicited applications.
CONTACT DETAILS The Trustees, Slaughter and May (Trust Ltd), 1 Bunhill Row, London EC1Y 8YY *Tel.* 020 7090 5286
Email corporateresponsibility@slaughterandmay. com *Website* www.slaughterandmay.com

■ Kathleen Beryl Sleigh Charitable Trust

CC NO 1082136
WHERE FUNDING CAN BE GIVEN UK and overseas.
WHO CAN BENEFIT Charitable organisations.
WHAT IS FUNDED Older people; children and young people; people with disabilities (particularly loss of sight); music and culture.
RANGE OF GRANTS From £2,000 up to £10,0000.
SAMPLE GRANTS Royal College of Music, RSPB and The Salvation Army (£10,000 each); Blind Veterans UK, Mind and The Trussell Trust (£5,000 each), British Wireless for the Blind Fund (£2,000).
FINANCES *Financial year end* 05/04/2022
Income £186,900
Grants to organisations £202,000
Assets £1,220,000
TRUSTEES Hazel French; Jonathan Picken.
HOW TO APPLY Apply in writing to the correspondent.
CONTACT DETAILS Jonathan Picken, Trustee, c/o William Sturges Solicitors, 14–16 Caxton Street, London SW1H 0QY *Tel.* 020 7873 1000 *Email* jonathan.picken@williamsturges.co.uk

■ Sloane Robinson Foundation

CC NO 1068286   **ESTABLISHED** 1998
WHERE FUNDING CAN BE GIVEN England and Wales.
WHO CAN BENEFIT Universities; school; individuals.
WHAT IS FUNDED The advancement of education, particularly scholarships and bursaries to enable overseas students to study in the UK, or to enable UK students to study abroad, as well as to 'generally provide educational opportunities to students that would otherwise not be available to them'.
TYPE OF GRANT Recurrent.
RANGE OF GRANTS Generally £15,000 to £50,000, with some larger grants.
SAMPLE GRANTS Keble College – Oxford (£158,500); Lincoln College – Oxford (£150,400); Karta Initiative (£100,000); Tutor the Nation (£50,000); United World Schools (£45,100); Reuben College – Oxford (£30,000); Chase Africa (£15,000); Veerni Foundation (£9,100); Visitation Board Primary School (£230).
FINANCES *Financial year end* 28/02/2022
Income £847,800
Grants to organisations £681,600
Assets £16,490,000
TRUSTEES George Robinson; Hugh Sloane; Deborah Fisher.
OTHER INFORMATION During the year, ending 2021/22, grants were awarded to 15 organisations.
HOW TO APPLY Apply in writing to the correspondent. The foundation is very selective in its grant-making; therefore, to avoid increased administrative costs, only successful candidates will be notified of the outcome of their application.
CONTACT DETAILS The Trustees, c/o FisherLegal LLP, Unit 4 Hill Farm, Kirby Road, Kirby Bedon, Norwich, Norfolk NR17 7DU *Tel.* 01508 480100 *Email* info@fisherlegal.co.uk

■ Rita and David Slowe Charitable Trust

CC NO 1048209   **ESTABLISHED** 1995
WHERE FUNDING CAN BE GIVEN UK and overseas, in particular Africa.
WHO CAN BENEFIT Registered charities.

WHAT IS FUNDED General charitable purposes, in particular the following: homelessness; human trafficking; people who are disadvantaged overseas and overseas development, particularly in Africa.

WHAT IS NOT FUNDED Individuals.

TYPE OF GRANT Typically recurring.

RANGE OF GRANTS Usually £17,500.

SAMPLE GRANTS Campaign Against Living Miserably, Crisis, Excellent Development, Microloan Foundation, Re-Cycle, Unicef – Ukraine Appeal and Wiener Library (£17,500 each).

FINANCES *Financial year end 05/04/2022*
Income £43,600
Grants to organisations £120,000
Assets £2,510,000

TRUSTEES Jonathan Slowe; Elizabeth Slowe; Graham Weinberg; Robert Slowe.

OTHER INFORMATION Grants were made to seven organisations in 2021/22.

HOW TO APPLY Apply in writing to the correspondent.

CONTACT DETAILS The Trustees, 32 Hampstead High Street, London NW3 1JQ *Tel.* 020 7435 7800

■ Smallwood Trust

CC NO 205798   **ESTABLISHED** 1886

WHERE FUNDING CAN BE GIVEN UK.

WHO CAN BENEFIT Registered charities; social enterprises; not-for-profit organisations; individuals.

WHAT IS FUNDED Projects which enable women on low incomes to access new skills, training, confidence-building and employment opportunities; research and policy work relating to disadvantaged women.

WHAT IS NOT FUNDED Exclusions for specific grant programmes can be found on the trust's website.

TYPE OF GRANT Project funding.

RANGE OF GRANTS Dependent upon the funding programme. The average grant size is £37,000.

SAMPLE GRANTS Foleshill Women's Training (£211,100); Zinthiya Trust (£65,800); Women's Health in South Tyneside (£48,600); Cavell Nurses' Trust (£25,000); Deaf Ethnic Women's Association (£18,800); Fourth Action (£15,300); WomenZone Community Centre (£8,400); A Way Out (£5,000).

FINANCES *Financial year end 31/12/2021*
Income £2,090,000
Grants to organisations £2,810,000
Grants to individuals £657,500
Assets £35,280,000

TRUSTEE Smallwood Trust (Trustee) Ltd.

HOW TO APPLY The application process depends on the grants programme. Interested applicants should check the funder's website regularly for up-to-date information.

CONTACT DETAILS Grant Manager, Lancaster House, 25 Hornyold Road, Malvern, Worcestershire WR14 1QQ *Tel.* 01684 574645 *Email* info@smallwoodtrust.org.uk *Website* www.smallwoodtrust.org.uk

---

■ Ruth Smart Foundation

CC NO 1080021   **ESTABLISHED** 2000

WHERE FUNDING CAN BE GIVEN Worldwide, but mainly in the UK and USA.

WHO CAN BENEFIT Registered charities and charitable organisations.

WHAT IS FUNDED Animal welfare and conservation.

TYPE OF GRANT Normally recurrent.

RANGE OF GRANTS Up to £40,000.

SAMPLE GRANTS Monterey County SPCA (£39,900); Ventana Wildlife Society (£16,000); Mauritian Wildlife Foundation (£12,000); Durrell Wildlife Conservation and Endangered Species Protection Agency (£3,000 each); Pine Ridge Dog Sanctuary and Reef Conservation (£2,000 each); Belize Zoo (£1,500).

FINANCES *Financial year end 31/12/2021*
Income £140,900
Grants to organisations £170,600
Assets £7,210,000

TRUSTEES John Vernor-Miles; Wilfrid Vernor-Miles.

OTHER INFORMATION Many of the beneficiaries are supported year after year, particularly where trustees are informed of the benefits of the foundation's funding from previous grants. Of the 26 grantees in 2021, 21 were also funded the previous year.

HOW TO APPLY Apply in writing to the correspondent.

CONTACT DETAILS Wilfrid Vernor-Miles, Chair to the Board of Trustees, c/o Hunters, 9 New Square, Lincoln's Inn, London WC2A 3QN *Tel.* 020 7412 0050

■ The Mrs Smith and Mount Trust

CC NO 1009718   **ESTABLISHED** 1992

WHERE FUNDING CAN BE GIVEN Norfolk; Suffolk; Cambridgeshire; Hertfordshire; Essex; Kent; Surrey; London.

WHO CAN BENEFIT Registered charities.

WHAT IS FUNDED Mental health; disability; homelessness; community and economic development; care leavers; domestic abuse; food poverty; relief for individuals in need.

WHAT IS NOT FUNDED Exclusion criteria may vary between The Mount Fund and The Mrs Smith Fund. The Mount Fund will only consider appeals from national organisations at branch level where the branch is able to provide separate accounts and is responsible for its own finances. The Mount Fund will not consider applications for general counselling or from charities with an income of over £1 million, or £500,000 if the application relates to the trust's health in the community category.

TYPE OF GRANT Core costs; project funding; capital costs; development funding.

RANGE OF GRANTS Generally up to £5,000 unless the applicant meets the specific criteria for larger grants.

SAMPLE GRANTS STARS (£15,000); Family First and Fight Against Blindness (£10,000 each); Time Norfolk (£7,000); Aylsham and District Care (£6,000); Arts and Minds and Ascension Community Trust (£5,000 each); Home-Start Camden (£4,500); Essex Respite and Care Association (£3,000); Blooming Blossoms (£2,200).

FINANCES *Financial year end 31/01/2022*
Income £150,300
Grants to organisations £392,000
Grants to individuals £18,800
Assets £111,300

TRUSTEES Gillian Barnes; Timothy Warren; Sean Shepley; Christine McKenzie; Hannah Whitehead.

OTHER INFORMATION The trust offers two grant programmes. The Mount Fund focuses on mental health, homelessness and health in the community. The Mrs Smith Fund awards hardship funding for individuals via block grants to registered charities for a variety of circumstances which are noted on the website. Further information on each of the grant schemes is available on the website. In 2021/22, The Mount Fund gave 64 grants totalling £392,000. The Mrs Smith Fund gave three grants totalling £18,800. Grants to organisations were broken down as follows: mental health (£235,800); homelessness (£80,000); health in the community (£65,500).

HOW TO APPLY Applications for The Mount Fund can be made online on the trust's website. The trustees meet three times per year, in March, July and November, and applications and supporting documents must be submitted at least six weeks in advance of a meeting or by the date specified. For applications to The Mrs Smith Fund, email a one-page document providing initial details about your work to the correspondent. An application form will then be sent to you if there is an opportunity for funding.

CONTACT DETAILS The Trustees, 6 Trull Farm Buildings, Tetbury, Gloucestershire GL8 8SQ *Tel.* 01285 841900 *Email* admin@ mrssmithandmounttrust.org *Website* http:// mrssmithandmounttrust.org

■ The N. Smith Charitable Settlement

CC NO 276660   **ESTABLISHED** 1978
WHERE FUNDING CAN BE GIVEN UK.
WHO CAN BENEFIT Charitable organisations.
WHAT IS FUNDED General charitable purposes.
WHAT IS NOT FUNDED Individuals.
SAMPLE GRANTS A list of beneficiaries was not included in the annual report and accounts.
FINANCES *Financial year end* 05/04/2022
Income £159,000
Grants to organisations £63,800
Assets £5,500,000
TRUSTEES Anne Gregory; Janet Adam; Susan Darlington; Christine Yates.
HOW TO APPLY Contact the correspondent for further information. The trustees hold two or three meetings each year.
CONTACT DETAILS Charlotte Keating, c/o Linder Myers, Sale Point, 126–150 Washway Road, Sale, Greater Manchester M33 6AG *Tel.* 0161 832 6972 *Email* charlotte.keating@lindermyers. co.uk

■ The Peter Smith Charitable Trust for Nature

CC NO 328458   **ESTABLISHED** 1989
WHERE FUNDING CAN BE GIVEN UK.
WHO CAN BENEFIT Charitable organisations.
WHAT IS FUNDED Wildlife.
SAMPLE GRANTS A list of beneficiaries was not included in the annual report and accounts.
FINANCES *Financial year end* 31/12/2021
Income £125,000
Grants to organisations £311,100
Assets £803,000
TRUSTEES Paul Brittlebank; John Cowlishaw; Peter Smith; Sandra Smith.
HOW TO APPLY Contact the correspondent for further information.
CONTACT DETAILS The Trustees, The Old Rectory, Hills End, Eversholt, Milton Keynes, Buckinghamshire MK17 9DR *Tel.* 01525 280848

■ The Henry Smith Charity

CC NO 230102   **ESTABLISHED** 1628
WHERE FUNDING CAN BE GIVEN UK.
WHO CAN BENEFIT Registered charities (primarily small and medium sized); not-for-profit organisations; community-based organisations; social enterprises; schools; Christian organisations; individuals.
WHAT IS FUNDED Social welfare; community services and development; Christian projects; holiday grants for children.
WHAT IS NOT FUNDED See the charity's website for a full list of exclusions regarding each grants programme.
TYPE OF GRANT Running costs; salaries; project costs.
RANGE OF GRANTS Programme dependent.
SAMPLE GRANTS Aanchal Women's Aid (£180,000); ActionSpace (£120,000); Abigail's Footsteps (£16,000); Youth Plug In CIC (£2,500); 186th St Catherines Rainbow's (£530).
FINANCES *Financial year end* 31/12/2021
Income £11,000
Grants to organisations £38,710,000
Grants to individuals £1,440,000
Assets £1,386,860,000
TRUSTEES Piers Feilden; Emir Feisal; Vivienne Dews; Paul Hackwood; Lady Bella Colgrain; Mark Granger; Emma Davies; Jonathan Asquith; Faisel Rahman; George Roberts; Andrew Beeforth; Jan Garrill; Peter Wilson; Baldeesh Nahl.
OTHER INFORMATION A full list of grants awarded is available to view on the charity's website. Support is given to individuals descended from the family of Henry Smith through its Kindred grants.
HOW TO APPLY Application processes vary between grant programmes. Application details for a specific grant scheme, along with guidance, are available on the website.
CONTACT DETAILS The Trustees, 6th Floor, 65–68 Leadenhall Street, London EC3A 2AD *Email* there is a 'Request a call back' form on the website *Website* www.henrysmithcharity.org. uk

■ Arabella and Julian Smith Family Trust

CC NO 1174447   **ESTABLISHED** 2017
WHERE FUNDING CAN BE GIVEN England and Wales.
WHO CAN BENEFIT Registered charities.
WHAT IS FUNDED General charitable purposes; education; health; social welfare; animal welfare.
WHAT IS NOT FUNDED Individuals.
TYPE OF GRANT Project funding; research.
RANGE OF GRANTS Typically £3,000 to £20,000.
SAMPLE GRANTS Community Foundation for Surrey (£50,000); The Meath Epilepsy Charity (£26,000); The Eikon Charity (£10,000); Sense International (£500).
FINANCES *Financial year end* 31/08/2021
Income £45,900
Grants to organisations £102,100
Assets £1,110,000
TRUSTEES Julian Smith; Arabella Smith; Alexander Smith; Juliet Smith.
OTHER INFORMATION The 2020/21 accounts were the latest available at the time of writing (June 2023). In 2020/21 the trust made grants to four organisations.
HOW TO APPLY Apply in writing to the correspondent.
CONTACT DETAILS The Trustees, c/o Maris Interiors LLP, 65 Southwark Street, London SE1 0HR *Tel.* 020 7902 1760

■ The Leslie Smith Foundation

CC NO 250030   **ESTABLISHED** 1964
WHERE FUNDING CAN BE GIVEN UK.
WHO CAN BENEFIT Registered charities; schools, specifically special needs schools based in the UK; hospices.
WHAT IS FUNDED General charitable purposes in the UK; medical and health of children; orphans; special educational needs; social welfare; the environment, particularly climate change.
WHAT IS NOT FUNDED Individuals.
RANGE OF GRANTS Mostly between £5,000 and £7,000 with the occasional smaller or larger grant.
SAMPLE GRANTS Choose Love and Disasters Emergency Committee – Ukraine Appeal (£40,000 each); The Trussell Trust (£20,000); Honeypot Children's Charity and Phoenix Bereavement Support (£10,000 each); Access to Sport, Fairfield Farm Trust and Surfers Against Sewage (£7,000 each); Go Beyond, Mary Hare Foundation and Prior's Court Foundation (£5,000 each); Cancer Research UK and Kidney Research UK (£500).
FINANCES *Financial year end* 05/04/2022
Income £89,800
Grants to organisations £201,000
Assets £4,130,000
TRUSTEES Alice Hayles; Curtis Hayles; Emma Hayles; Matthew Hayles; Deborah Fisher.
OTHER INFORMATION Grants were broken down as follows: general welfare (£125,000); health (£40,000); education (£23,000); the environment (£13,000).
HOW TO APPLY Apply in writing to the correspondent.
CONTACT DETAILS The Trustees, c/o FisherLegal LLP, Unit 4, Hill Farm, Kirby Road, Kirby Bedon, Norwich, Norfolk NR14 7DU *Tel.* 01508 480100 *Email* info@fisherlegal.co.uk

■ The Martin Smith Foundation

CC NO 1150753   **ESTABLISHED** 2012
WHERE FUNDING CAN BE GIVEN UK.
WHO CAN BENEFIT Registered charities.
WHAT IS FUNDED General charitable purposes, in particular: the performing arts; education; ecology and the environment; recreational sport; the relief of poverty; and religion.
RANGE OF GRANTS £250 to £20,000.
SAMPLE GRANTS Oxford Lieder Ltd (£20,000); Garsington Opera Ltd (£15,000); Royal Academy of Music (£12,000); St Albans School (£10,000); Arcangelo (£6,000); International Musicians Seminar Prussia Cove (£3,000); Gloucestershire Wildlife Trust (£1,500); Cabinet of Wonders Project (£250).
FINANCES *Financial year end* 31/12/2021
Income £31,200
Grants to organisations £200,800
Assets £1,400,000
TRUSTEES Elizabeth Buchanan; Bartholomew Peerless; Lady Smith; Sir Martin Smith; Jeremy Smith; Katherine Wake.
HOW TO APPLY The foundation does not accept unsolicited applications.
CONTACT DETAILS The Trustees, 5 Park Town, Oxford, Oxfordshire OX2 6SN *Tel.* 01865 554554

■ Stanley Smith UK Horticultural Trust

CC NO 261925   **ESTABLISHED** 1970
WHERE FUNDING CAN BE GIVEN UK and overseas.
WHO CAN BENEFIT Charitable organisations; individuals.
WHAT IS FUNDED Horticulture, gardening and botany; the promotion of biodiversity; creation, development and maintenance of gardens accessible to the public; horticultural education, training, research and publications.
WHAT IS NOT FUNDED Projects relating to commercial agriculture initiatives, commercial crop production, or forestry; wages or salaries; training or tuition fees (except traineeships paid to organisations); pure gap year travel; modern slabbing, construction materials or equipment; social welfare, socio-economic development or physical or mental welfare (except legitimate horticultural therapy projects).
TYPE OF GRANT Project costs; research and publication costs; restoration costs.
RANGE OF GRANTS Typically £500 to £5,000.
SAMPLE GRANTS Professional Gardeners' Trust (£12,500); Chelsea Physic Garden (£5,000); Evesham Abbey Trust (£4,000); Fauna and Flora International (£3,500); Bannockburn House Trust (£2,500); Bloomin' Marvellous Rectory Park (£2,000); Atlantic Flowers – New Arcadian Journal (£1,000); Minehead Museum (£350).
FINANCES *Financial year end* 05/04/2022
Income £170,400
Grants to organisations £71,400
Assets £4,310,000
TRUSTEES Alexander Brye; Edward Reed; Phillip Sykes; Dr John David; Dr Sabina Knees; Dr Timothy Upson; William Watkins.
OTHER INFORMATION In 2021/22, grants were distributed as follows: 14 concerning restoration and development of gardens; 5 concerning publications; and 2 concerning research and conservation.
HOW TO APPLY Applications are submitted either via email or post to the correspondent. There is no application form; however, detailed guidance notes are available to download from the website. Grants are normally awarded twice a year. The upcoming deadlines for applications can be found in the guidance notes.
CONTACT DETAILS David Rae, Director, Royal Botanic Garden, 20A Inverleith Row, Edinburgh EH3 5LR *Tel.* 0131 248 2844 *Email* d.rae@rbge.org.uk *Website* www.horticulture.org.uk/careers/bursaries-and-grants

■ Philip Smith's Charitable Trust

CC NO 1003751   **ESTABLISHED** 1991
WHERE FUNDING CAN BE GIVEN UK, with a preference for Gloucestershire.
WHO CAN BENEFIT Registered charities; arts, culture and heritage organisations; hospices.
WHAT IS FUNDED General charitable purposes; the environment; older people; social welfare; the armed forces.
WHAT IS NOT FUNDED Individuals.
RANGE OF GRANTS £1,000 to £25,000.
SAMPLE GRANTS Previous beneficiaries have included: NSPCC (£25,000); Game and Wildlife Conservation Trust (£13,000); Royal Forestry Society, Salmon and Trout Conservation, and Soldiers of Shropshire Museum (£5,000 each); Friends of the Connection at St Martin-in-the-Fields and The Salvation Army (£2,500 each); Campden Home Nursing, Highland Hospice and Samaritans (£1,300 each).

FINANCES *Financial year end* 05/04/2022
Income £6,100
Grants to organisations £106,100
TRUSTEES The Hon. Philip Smith; Mary Smith.
OTHER INFORMATION The latest accounts were not available to view on the Charity Commission's website due to the trust's low income. We have therefore estimated the trust's grant total based on its total expenditure.
HOW TO APPLY Apply in writing to the correspondent.
CONTACT DETAILS The Trustees, c/o BDB Pitmans, One Bartholomew Close, London EC1A 7BL *Tel.* 020 7783 3685

....

■ The R. C. Snelling Charitable Trust

CC NO 1074776   **ESTABLISHED** 1999
WHERE FUNDING CAN BE GIVEN Within a 30-mile radius of the village of Blofield in Norfolk.
WHO CAN BENEFIT Registered charities; community groups; individuals.
WHAT IS FUNDED Medical causes; education; Christianity; social welfare; the environment.
WHAT IS NOT FUNDED Salaries; sponsorship for more than one year; general appeals where the need could be met several times over by grantors; national appeals; continued assistance with running costs.
TYPE OF GRANT Equipment; capital appeals; specific projects; local projects; assistance with running costs; seed funding; fundraising events.
RANGE OF GRANTS Up to £20,000.
SAMPLE GRANTS East Anglia's Children's Hospices (£20,000); Star Throwers (£6,000); Hear for Norfolk (£4,000); Blind Veterans UK (£3,000).
FINANCES *Financial year end* 30/04/2022
Income £14,390,000
Grants to organisations £226,300
Assets £14,550,000
TRUSTEES Philip Buttinger; Rowland Cogman; Toby Wise; Samuel Barratt; Nigel Savory; Stephan Phillips; Diana Jarrold; Mark Gook; Paul Giles.
HOW TO APPLY An online application form can be completed on the trust's website.
CONTACT DETAILS The Trustees, R. C. Snelling Ltd, Laundry Lane, Blofield Heath, Norwich, Norfolk NR13 4SQ *Tel.* 01603 712202 *Email* trustee@rcsnellingcharitabletrust.org *Website* www.rcsnellingcharitabletrust.org

....

■ Social Investment Business Foundation

CC NO 1117185   **ESTABLISHED** 2006
WHERE FUNDING CAN BE GIVEN UK.
WHO CAN BENEFIT Registered charities and social enterprises.
WHAT IS FUNDED General charitable purposes. The charity has a number of different funds; refer to the website for information on what is currently available. Funds often focus on enabling organisations to prepare for social investment or competing for contracts, or grow their scale or social impact.
WHAT IS NOT FUNDED Refer to the website for exclusions from each specific fund.
TYPE OF GRANT Grants, loans and other forms of social investment, as well as strategic support and advice.
RANGE OF GRANTS Programme dependent.
SAMPLE GRANTS A list of beneficiaries was not included in the annual report and accounts.

FINANCES *Financial year end* 31/03/2022
Income £9,070,000
Grants to organisations £5,120,000
Assets £49,020,000
TRUSTEES Jenny North; James Rice; Hazel Blears; Robert Hewitt; Sonali Siriwardena; Jagjit Dosanjh-Elton; Edward Wallis; Gavin Keyte.
HOW TO APPLY Applications can be made via the charity's website. Each fund has specific contact details to permit potential applicants to discuss the application process – full details can be found on the funder's website.
CONTACT DETAILS The Trustees, CAN Mezzanine Borough, 7–14 Great Dover Street, London SE1 4YR *Tel.* 020 3096 7900 *Email* enquiries@sibgroup.org.uk *Website* www.sibgroup.org.uk

....

■ Societe Generale UK Foundation

CC NO 1196579   **ESTABLISHED** 1994
WHERE FUNDING CAN BE GIVEN UK and overseas.
WHO CAN BENEFIT UK-registered charities working in the UK or overseas; charitable organisations including schools, hospitals and social enterprises.
WHAT IS FUNDED Inclusion through education and employability; general charitable purposes. The foundation also supports Shake Climate Change, a programme established to support entrepreneurs combatting climate change in agriculture and food production.
WHAT IS NOT FUNDED Organisations which work outside the scope of education and employment, including religious, political, research, drugs or animal welfare activities; non-UK-registered charities; organisations whose work could damage the reputation of the Societe Generale Group; requests for sponsorship, advertising, fees, gifts, prizes and personal appeals.
TYPE OF GRANT Matched funding for charitable organisations supported by Societe Generale employees; project funding – one-off and rolling donations.
SAMPLE GRANTS Previous beneficiaries have included: Young Lives vs Cancer (£198,500); East London Business Alliance (£41,000); National Emergencies Trust (£25,000); Alzheimer's Society (£11,100); Bristol Black Carers (£2,800); The Old Church (£2,000).
TRUSTEES Jasvant Singh; Ben Higgins; John Oberman; Elise Sabran; Hannah Mackenzie; Louise Redmond.
OTHER INFORMATION At the time of writing (May 2023), the foundation had not yet filed any annual report and accounts online with the Charity Commission as it had only recently registered. The foundation received funds transferred from its predecessor of the same name (Charity Commission no. 1039013) in August 2022.
HOW TO APPLY The foundation does not accept unsolicited applications.
CONTACT DETAILS The Trustees, 1 Bank Street, London E14 4SG *Tel.* 020 7597 3065 *Email* rachel.iles@sghambros.com *Website* https://www.societegenerale.co.uk/en/about/our-commitments/foundation

Think carefully about every application. Is it justified?

661

■ Sodexo Stop Hunger Foundation

CC NO 1110266 **ESTABLISHED** 2005
WHERE FUNDING CAN BE GIVEN UK and Ireland.
WHO CAN BENEFIT Charitable organisations.
WHAT IS FUNDED Hunger and malnutrition; healthy lifestyles; life skills such as cooking.
RANGE OF GRANTS £5,000 to £86,000.
SAMPLE GRANTS FareShare (£85,900); SSAFA, the Armed Forces charity (£35,000); Coram Life (£22,000); Wycombe Food Hub (£10,000); Alexander Rose Charity (£5,000).
FINANCES *Financial year end 31/08/2021*
Income £595,900
Grants to organisations £351,200
Assets £175,500
TRUSTEES Gareth John; David Mulcahy; Patrick Forbes; Sean Haley; Samantha Scott; Simon McCluskey; Laura Brimacombe; David Forbes.
OTHER INFORMATION The Sodexo Stop Hunger Foundation is the corporate charity of the food services and facilities management company, Sodexo Ltd. Grants were made to 20 organisations during the year. The 2020/21 accounts were the latest available at the time of writing (June 2023).
HOW TO APPLY Contact the foundation using the contact form available on its website.
CONTACT DETAILS The Trustees, Sodexo, 1 Southampton Row, London WC1B 5HA *Tel.* 020 7404 0110 *Email* stophunger@sodexo.com *Website* http://uk.stop-hunger.org/home.html

■ Sofronie Foundation

CC NO 1118621 **ESTABLISHED** 2008
WHERE FUNDING CAN BE GIVEN UK, France and the Netherlands.
WHO CAN BENEFIT Registered charities; non-profit organisations.
WHAT IS FUNDED Education and training for disadvantaged young people; STEM education.
TYPE OF GRANT Project funding; core costs.
RANGE OF GRANTS Typically £10,000 to £50,000.
SAMPLE GRANTS Codam (£1.08 million); JINC NL (£59,200); Stichting LeerKRACHT (£51,100); Zero Gravity (£50,000); Article 1 (£41,200); ESSEC Foundation (£30,700); Synlab (£25,400); Afghan Girls Assistance (£16,000).
FINANCES *Financial year end 31/12/2021*
Income £2,140,000
Grants to organisations £1,350,000
Assets £160,500
TRUSTEES Harold Goddijn; Corinne Goddijn-Vigreux; Ajay Soni; Boris Walbaum; Robert Wilne.
OTHER INFORMATION In 2021 the foundation made grants to eight charities, two of which were in the UK.
HOW TO APPLY Applications can be made at any time through the foundation's website but it may take up to three months to get a decision from the trustees.
CONTACT DETAILS Jacqueline Higgin, Head of Foundation, 16 Great Queen Street, London WC2B 5DH *Tel.* 020 7421 3330 *Email* enquiries@sofronie.org *Website* www.sofronie.org

■ David Solomons Charitable Trust

CC NO 297275 **ESTABLISHED** 1986
WHERE FUNDING CAN BE GIVEN UK.
WHO CAN BENEFIT Registered charities.
WHAT IS FUNDED Support for people with learning disabilities.
WHAT IS NOT FUNDED Individuals.
TYPE OF GRANT One-off grants.
RANGE OF GRANTS Generally between £500 and £1,000.
SAMPLE GRANTS Down's Syndrome Association (£10,000); The Pod (£1,500); The Bevern Trust and Upward Mobility (£1,000 each); Team Domenica (£800); Devon Link Up (£750); Orcadia Creative Learning Centre and Reach North West (£500).
FINANCES *Financial year end 05/04/2022*
Income £93,600
Grants to organisations £101,300
Assets £3,170,000
TRUSTEES Diana Huntingford; Jeremy Rutter; Dr Richard Solomons; Carol Boys; Andrew Penny; Zoe Solomons.
OTHER INFORMATION During 2021/22 the trust awarded 111 grants. An annual grant is awarded to the Down's Syndrome Association.
HOW TO APPLY Apply in writing to the correspondent. The trustees hold three meetings a year to consider grant applications.
CONTACT DETAILS The Trustees, 2 Highfield Road, Collier Row, Romford, Essex RM5 3RA *Tel.* 01708 502488 *Email* davidsolomonscharitabletrust@gmail.com

■ Somerset Community Foundation

CC NO 1094446 **ESTABLISHED** 2002
WHERE FUNDING CAN BE GIVEN Somerset.
WHO CAN BENEFIT Registered charities; unregistered charities; CICs; social enterprises; PTAs; amateur sports clubs; hospitals; hospices; individuals.
WHAT IS FUNDED General charitable purposes.
TYPE OF GRANT Capital costs; core/revenue costs; seed funding/start-up funding; project funding; unrestricted funding.
RANGE OF GRANTS Dependent upon grants programme. Generally up to £10,000.
SAMPLE GRANTS Community Council for Somerset and Taunton YMCA (£100,000 each); Diversity Voice (£60,000); The Magdalen Environmental Trust (£38,800); Somerset Parent Carer Forum (£26,400); Seed Sedgemoor (£10,000); The Bluebirds Theatre Company (£7,500); Wembdon Art Group (£850).
FINANCES *Financial year end 31/03/2022*
Income £5,670,000
Grants to organisations £2,120,000
Assets £14,240,000
TRUSTEES The Hon. Michael Samuel; Angela Kerr; Timothy Walker; Chris Bishop; John Lyon; Lucilla Nelson; Bruce McIntosh; David Taylor; Michelle Ferris; Giles Wood; Helen Gulvin; Kokila Lane; Kevin Whitmarsh.
OTHER INFORMATION This is one of the 47 UK community foundations, which distribute funding for a wide range of purposes. As with all community foundations, there are a number of donor-advised funds managed on behalf of individuals, families and charitable trusts. Grant schemes tend to change frequently – consult the foundation's website for details of current programmes and up-to-date deadlines. Only organisations that received grants of over £2,000 were listed as beneficiaries in the charity's accounts. Grants of under £2,000 totalled £9,800. Note that the grant total includes amounts awarded to individuals.
HOW TO APPLY Potential applicants are advised to visit the community foundation's website or

contact its grants team to find the most suitable funding stream.

CONTACT DETAILS The Trustees, Somerset Community Foundation, Yeoman House, The Bath and West Showground, Shepton Mallet, Somerset BA4 6QN *Tel.* 01749 344949 *Email* info@somersetcf.org.uk *Website* www.somersetcf.org.uk

....

■ Songdale Ltd

CC NO 286075   **ESTABLISHED** 1982
WHERE FUNDING CAN BE GIVEN England and abroad.
WHO CAN BENEFIT Charitable organisations.
WHAT IS FUNDED Advancement of Orthodox Jewish faith; relief of poverty and suffering; Jewish education.
RANGE OF GRANTS Up to £15,000.
SAMPLE GRANTS Friends of Shekel Hakodesh Ltd (£14,000); The New Rachmistrivke Synagogue Trust (£13,000); Mercaz Torah Vechesed Ltd (£8,100); Belz Mercazi and The J. and R. Margulies Charitable Trust (£4,000 each); Belz Foundation Ltd (£3,000).
FINANCES *Financial year end* 31/12/2022
Income £190,800
Grants to organisations £82,100
Assets £2,640,000
TRUSTEES Yechiel Grosskopf; Malka Grosskopf; Jacob Grosskopf; Pinchas Grosskopf.
OTHER INFORMATION Grants of less than £3,000 totalled £19,400.
HOW TO APPLY Apply in writing to the correspondent.
CONTACT DETAILS The Trustees, New Burlington House, 1075 Finchley Road, London NW11 0PU *Tel.* 020 8806 5010

....

■ The E. C. Sosnow Charitable Trust

CC NO 273578   **ESTABLISHED** 1977
WHERE FUNDING CAN BE GIVEN UK and overseas.
WHO CAN BENEFIT Charitable organisations.
WHAT IS FUNDED Education; the arts; social welfare; health; the Jewish faith and community.
TYPE OF GRANT Project costs.
RANGE OF GRANTS Up to £10,000.
SAMPLE GRANTS British Red Cross and Weizman UK (£10,000 each); Africa Educational Trust (£8,000); Doctors in Distress and Holocaust Educational Trust (£5,000 each); Mental Health Foundation (£3,000); S. and P. Shepardi Community and Supporting Wounded Veterans (£2,000 each).
FINANCES *Financial year end* 05/04/2022
Income £73,700
Grants to organisations £91,000
Assets £2,550,000
TRUSTEES Fiona Fattal; Elias Fattal; Alexandra Fattal; Richard Fattal.
OTHER INFORMATION Grants were made to 15 organisations during the year.
HOW TO APPLY Apply in writing to the correspondent.
CONTACT DETAILS The Trustees, c/o Bourner Bullock, 114 St Martin's Lane, Covent Garden, London, WC2N 4BE *Tel.* 020 7240 5821

....

■ Souter Charitable Trust

OSCR NO SC029998   **ESTABLISHED** 1992
WHERE FUNDING CAN BE GIVEN UK (with a preference for Scotland) and overseas.
WHO CAN BENEFIT UK-registered charities.

WHAT IS FUNDED The relief of human suffering, particularly projects with a Christian emphasis.
WHAT IS NOT FUNDED Capital projects and renovation works; individuals; organisations that are not UK-registered charities.
TYPE OF GRANT Core/revenue costs; project costs; one-off and multi-year.
RANGE OF GRANTS Mostly small grants of £1,000 to £3,000.
SAMPLE GRANTS Big Church Day Out; Centre for Social Justice; Christian Solidarity Worldwide; Safe Families for Children; Tearfund; Vine Trust.
FINANCES *Financial year end* 30/06/2022
Income £12,230,000
Grants to organisations £9,900,000
Assets £121,600,000
TRUSTEES Sir Brian Souter; Lady Elizabeth Souter; Ann Allen.
OTHER INFORMATION Only beneficiaries of grants of £15,000 and above were listed in the trust's accounts. Grants of under £15,000 totalled £4.21 million.
HOW TO APPLY Apply in writing to the correspondent via post or email. The trustees generally meet once a month and all applications whether successful or not will be acknowledged. Check the trust's website for further information on what to include and current deadlines.
CONTACT DETAILS Dion Judd, Trust Administrator, PO Box 7412, Perth, Perthshire PH1 5YX *Email* application@soutercharitabletrust.org.uk *Website* www.soutercharitabletrust.org.uk

....

■ The South Yorkshire Community Foundation

CC NO 1140947   **ESTABLISHED** 1986
WHERE FUNDING CAN BE GIVEN South Yorkshire, particularly Barnsley, Doncaster, Rotherham, Sheffield.
WHO CAN BENEFIT Community and voluntary organisations; CICs.
WHAT IS FUNDED General charitable purposes.
WHAT IS NOT FUNDED See individual grant programmes for specific exclusions.
TYPE OF GRANT Capital costs, core costs, project costs, salaries.
RANGE OF GRANTS Grants vary for each funding programme.
SAMPLE GRANTS A list of beneficiaries in 2020/21 was not available. Previous beneficiaries have included: Age UK Barnsley; Baby Basics and Little Miracles; FareShare Yorkshire; South Yorkshire Futures; St Wilfrid's Centre.
FINANCES *Financial year end* 30/09/2021
Income £1,910,000
Grants to organisations £1,910,000
Assets £14,830,000
TRUSTEES Revd David Bessue; The Earl of Scarbrough Richard Scarbrough; Paul Benington; Roderick Plews; Dr Julie MacDonald; Melvyn Lunn; Craig McKay; Zaidah Ahmed; John Holt; Alex Pettifer; Martin Ross; Michele Wightman; Dr Nicholas Kitchen; Yiannis Koursis; Prof. Christine Booth-Mayblin; Aref Mohammed; Racheal Blake.
OTHER INFORMATION This is one of the 47 UK community foundations, which distribute funding for a wide range of purposes. As with all community foundations, there are a number of donor-advised funds managed on behalf of individuals, families and charitable trusts. Grant schemes tend to change frequently – consult the foundation's website for details of current programmes and up-to-date deadlines. The

2020/21 accounts were the latest available at the time of writing (May 2023).

HOW TO APPLY Potential applicants are advised to visit the community foundation's website or contact its grants team to find the most suitable funding stream.

CONTACT DETAILS The Trustees, South Yorkshire's Community Foundation, The Campus, Pack Horse Lane High Green, Sheffield, South Yorkshire S35 3HY *Tel.* 0114 242 4857 *Email* grants@sycf.org.uk *Website* www.sycf.org.uk

---

■ The Stephen R. and Philippa H. Southall Charitable Trust

CC NO 223190   **ESTABLISHED** 1947

WHERE FUNDING CAN BE GIVEN UK, with a preference for Herefordshire.

WHO CAN BENEFIT Charitable organisations; hospices; places of worship; museums.

WHAT IS FUNDED General charitable purposes; education; conservation; the environment; cultural heritage; health; rural communities.

RANGE OF GRANTS Mostly £4,400 to £5,500 with the occasional larger grant.

SAMPLE GRANTS Mount Pleasant School Farm (£20,000); Prison Reform Trust and Waterworks Museum (£10,000 each); Hay and District Dial-a-Ride, Home-Start Herefordshire and Midlands Air Ambulance (£5,000 each); Clifford PCC, Hereford Historic Churches Trust and Society of Friends – Almeley (£4,000 each).

FINANCES *Financial year end* 05/04/2022
Income £116,200
Grants to organisations £98,500
Assets £6,420,000

TRUSTEES Anna Southall; Benjamin Compton; Henry Serle; Jack Serle; Timothy Compton; Candia Compton.

OTHER INFORMATION Out of the 16 recipients of grants in 2021/22, 15 also received grants in 2020/21. A significant proportion of the trust's grants are made in Herefordshire.

HOW TO APPLY Unsolicited applications are not accepted.

CONTACT DETAILS The Trustees, Beech Hill, Clifford, Hereford, Herefordshire HR3 5HE *Tel.* 01497 831765 *Email* beechhill48@gmail.com

---

■ W. F. Southall Trust

CC NO 218371   **ESTABLISHED** 1937

WHERE FUNDING CAN BE GIVEN UK and overseas.

WHO CAN BENEFIT Registered charities.

WHAT IS FUNDED Quaker work and witness; peace-making and conflict resolution; environmental action and sustainability; social action.

WHAT IS NOT FUNDED See the trust's website for a full list of exclusions.

TYPE OF GRANT Capital costs; core/revenue costs; seed funding/start-up funding.

RANGE OF GRANTS Mainly under £5,000.

SAMPLE GRANTS Britain Yearly Meeting (£50,000); Gatesbield Quaker Housing Trust (£6,500); Peace Museum £5,000); Quaker Congo Partnership (£4,000); Children of Rwanda, Down Syndrome International and Emmanuel International (£3,000 each).

FINANCES *Financial year end* 05/04/2022
Income £273,100
Grants to organisations £412,000
Assets £13,790,000

TRUSTEES Joanna Engelkamp; Hannah Engelkamp; Mark Holtom; A. Richard Maw; Andrew Southall; Philip Coventry; Lucy Greaves; Holly Wallis.

OTHER INFORMATION During 2021/22, grants were made to 114 organisations and were distributed in the following categories: social action (£260,300); Quaker work and witness (£68,500); peace and recognition (£43,400); the environment (£39,800).

HOW TO APPLY Applicants should first complete the trust's online eligibility checker; applicants that meet the criteria will then be provided with a link to the downloadable application form. The trustees do not accept postal applications. Any correspondence with the trust should be by phone or email (a contact form can be accessed on the trust's website).

CONTACT DETAILS Wil Berdinner, Trust Secretary, School House, Mytholm Bank, Hebden Bridge, West Yorkshire HX7 6DL *Tel.* 0300 111 1937 *Email* use the contact form on the website *Website* https://southalltrust.org

---

■ Southover Manor General Education Trust Ltd

CC NO 299593   **ESTABLISHED** 1988

WHERE FUNDING CAN BE GIVEN Sussex, Brighton and Hove.

WHO CAN BENEFIT Schools, colleges, nurseries, play groups, youth groups and any other educational organisations working with individuals under the age of 25; occasionally individuals are supported.

WHAT IS FUNDED Education and young people.

WHAT IS NOT FUNDED Salaries; transport costs; educational visits or attendance at conferences, expeditions or overseas travel; tuition fees; subsistence expenses, endowments or scholarships; retrospective expenditure; projects with the sole purpose of promoting a particular religion or faith (although applications from faith-based organisations are accepted where there is no faith restriction in the project or the educational objectives).

TYPE OF GRANT Capital and project costs.

RANGE OF GRANTS Up to £25,000.

SAMPLE GRANTS A full list of beneficiaries was not provided. The largest grant in the year was for £16,600 to Fletching Church of England Primary School.

FINANCES *Financial year end* 31/03/2022
Income £120,900
Grants to organisations £113,500
Assets £4,290,000

TRUSTEES Clare Duffield; John Farmer; Claire Pool; Marcus Hanbury; Susan Winn; Ian Jungius; Caroline Brand; Sophie Hepworth; Octavia Gilbert.

OTHER INFORMATION Grants were made to 22 organisations during the year.

HOW TO APPLY Application forms are available to download from the trust's website, where further guidance is also given. The trustees usually meet in May and November. To be considered, applications should be received by 31 March and 30 September, respectively.

CONTACT DETAILS A. M. Hepworth, The Secretary to the Trust, Woodmans Farmhouse, London Road, Ashington, Pulborough, West Sussex RH20 3AU *Tel.* 01903 893374 *Email* appn@southovermanortrust.org.uk *Website* http://southovermanortrust.org.uk

■ Peter Sowerby Foundation

cc no 1151978   ESTABLISHED 2013
WHERE FUNDING CAN BE GIVEN UK, with some preference for North Yorkshire.
WHO CAN BENEFIT Registered or exempt charities; CICs; universities; registered social and healthcare providers.
WHAT IS FUNDED Medical research; health and social care; education and learning; community development; the environment and conservation; the arts; 'innovative and catalytic' projects.
TYPE OF GRANT Mostly multi-year grants for project funding, research, development funding and capital costs.
RANGE OF GRANTS Mostly up to £100,000, with some exceptional larger grants.
SAMPLE GRANTS Alzheimer's Society (£1.85 million); Cancer Research UK (£230,000); Hospice Action (£148,000); York Arboretum (£50,000); Cultural Trust (£25,000); The Prospects Trust (£10,000); React (Rapid Effective Assistance for Children with potentially Terminal illness) (£5,500); West Kent Mind (£3,800).
FINANCES *Financial year end 30/09/2021*
Income £27,900,000
Grants to organisations £4,380,000
Assets £64,700,000
TRUSTEES Dr David Stables; David Aspinall; Sara Poulios; Prof. Carole Longson.
OTHER INFORMATION During the year, 72 grants of less than £50,000 that were unlisted in the foundation's accounts were awarded to organisations. The 2020/21 accounts were the latest available at the time of writing (May 2023).
HOW TO APPLY The foundation does not seek unsolicited applications. However, if you believe that your idea is closely aligned with the foundation's aims, you may fill in an online form on the charity's website, outlining your project, budget and proposed timeline. Occasionally, open calls for funding for health and social care projects are advertised on the website – sign up to the mailing list for updates.
CONTACT DETAILS The Trustees, 29 St John's Lane, Clerkenwell, London EC1M 4NA *Tel.* 0300 030 1151 *Email* info@petersowerbyfoundation.org.uk *Website* https://petersowerbyfoundation.org.uk

■ SPAR Charitable Fund

cc no 236252   ESTABLISHED 1964
WHERE FUNDING CAN BE GIVEN UK.
WHO CAN BENEFIT Registered charities, mostly well-known national organisations.
WHAT IS FUNDED General charitable purposes.
RANGE OF GRANTS Up to £50,000.
SAMPLE GRANTS Grocery Aid (£100,800); Drink Aware (£38,800); Marie Curie (£1,600).
FINANCES *Financial year end 30/04/2022*
Income £57,600
Grants to organisations £170,200
Assets £322,900
TRUSTEES Peter Dodding; Patrick Doody; Dominic Hall; Mohammed Sadiq; Paul Stone; Justin Taylor; Peter McBride; Mike Boardman; Julian Green; Mark Cleary; Louis Drake; Rodney Tucker; Steven Irons.
OTHER INFORMATION The fund is the corporate charity of the food retail chain SPAR. The fund makes grants to emergency appeals, as well as supporting the company's chosen charity and benevolent fund.
HOW TO APPLY Apply in writing to the correspondent.
CONTACT DETAILS The Trustees, SPAR (UK) Ltd, Hygeia Building, 66–68 College Road, Harrow, Middlesex HA1 1BE *Tel.* 020 8426 3670 *Email* michelle.geraghty@spar.co.uk

■ Sparquote Ltd

cc no 286232   ESTABLISHED 1982
WHERE FUNDING CAN BE GIVEN UK and overseas.
WHO CAN BENEFIT Charitable organisations.
WHAT IS FUNDED General charitable purposes; the relief of poverty; Jewish education; support for places of worship for the Jewish community.
SAMPLE GRANTS A list of beneficiaries was not included in the annual report and accounts. Previous beneficiaries have included: Achisomoch Aid Company Ltd (£212,300); Beis Aharon Trust (£50,000); The Rehabilitation Trust (£20,000); Friends of Ganei Geula Jerusalem Ltd (£6,400).
FINANCES *Financial year end 31/03/2022*
Income £997,300
Grants to organisations £167,000
Assets £18,410,000
TRUSTEES Dov Reichman; Anne-Mette Reichman; David Reichmann.
HOW TO APPLY Contact the correspondent for further information.
CONTACT DETAILS The Trustees, Cavendish House, 369 Burnt Oak Broadway, Edgeware, Middlesex HA8 5AW *Tel.* 020 8731 0777

■ The Spear Charitable Trust

cc no 1041568   ESTABLISHED 1962
WHERE FUNDING CAN BE GIVEN Mainly UK.
WHO CAN BENEFIT Registered charities; former employees of J. W. Spear and Sons plc and their dependants.
WHAT IS FUNDED General charitable purposes, with some preference for animal welfare, the environment, disability and health.
WHAT IS NOT FUNDED Appeals from individuals other than former employees of J. W. Spear and Sons plc and their dependants.
RANGE OF GRANTS Up to £30,000, with an average of £4,000.
SAMPLE GRANTS Nowzad UK (£30,000); Hertford Choral Society (£5,000) Lord Whiskey Sanctuary (£1,500); Bernese Rescue and Doctor Graham's Homes (£1,000 each).
FINANCES *Financial year end 31/12/2021*
Income £108,800
Grants to organisations £100,200
Grants to individuals £12,300
Assets £178,600
TRUSTEES Nigel Gooch; Philip Harris; Hazel Spear.
OTHER INFORMATION Grants were made to ten organisations and to eight individuals (former employees of J. W. Spear and Sons plc and their families and dependants).
HOW TO APPLY Apply in writing to the correspondent. The trustees state in their 2021 annual report that they will make grants without a formal application, but they encourage organisations to provide feedback on how grants are used. Feedback will be used for monitoring the quality of grants and will form the basis of assessment for any further applications.
CONTACT DETAILS Flora Gaughan, Adminstrator, Roughground House, Old Hall Green, Ware, Hertfordshire SG11 1HB *Tel.* 01920 823071

■ Spears-Stutz Charitable Trust

CC NO 225491   **ESTABLISHED** 1962

WHERE FUNDING CAN BE GIVEN Worldwide.

WHO CAN BENEFIT Registered charities.

WHAT IS FUNDED General charitable purposes; work outside the UK.

RANGE OF GRANTS Up to £25,000.

SAMPLE GRANTS Camfed International and Nashulai Maasai Conservancy (£25,000 each); One Goal (£19,500); Save the Elephants (£18,500); La Paz de Dios (£15,000); The Afghan Children's Trust (£10,000).

FINANCES *Financial year end 05/04/2022* Income £124,500 Grants to organisations £120,700 Assets £7,320,000

TRUSTEES Caroline Cooper; Emily Stutz.

OTHER INFORMATION Only organisations that received grants of over £5,000 were listed as beneficiaries in the trust's accounts. Grants of under £5,000 totalled £7,700.

HOW TO APPLY Apply in writing to the correspondent.

CONTACT DETAILS The Trustees, c/o Withers LLP, 20 Old Bailey, London EC4M 7AN *Tel.* 020 7597 6000

■ The SpeedoMick Foundation

CC NO 1189920

WHERE FUNDING CAN BE GIVEN UK.

WHO CAN BENEFIT Small, grass roots charities and community groups.

WHAT IS FUNDED Homelessness; education; social welfare; the rehabilitation and education of people who have offended.

SAMPLE GRANTS Bobby Colleran Trust; Diamonds in the Community; Steps to Hope; Team Oasis; Kids In The Spotlight; Up 'N Away; Tourettes Action.

FINANCES *Financial year end 31/03/2022* Income £429,100 Grants to organisations £215,500 Assets £415,500

TRUSTEES Paul Bibby; Andrew Moss; Andrew Bell; Adam Gough.

HOW TO APPLY Applications can be made through the foundation's website.

CONTACT DETAILS The Trustees, c/o DSG Chartered Accountants, Castle Chambers, 43 Castle Street, Liverpool L2 9TL *Email* use the contact form on the website *Website* www. thespeedomickfoundation.org

■ Michael and Sarah Spencer Foundation

CC NO 1184658

WHERE FUNDING CAN BE GIVEN Worldwide with a preference for the UK.

WHO CAN BENEFIT Charitable organisations; education institutions.

WHAT IS FUNDED Health; social welfare; education; the environment.

SAMPLE GRANTS A list of beneficiaries was not included in the annual report and accounts.

FINANCES *Financial year end 31/03/2022* Income £933,600 Grants to organisations £926,500 Assets £3,200

TRUSTEES Michael Spencer; Sarah Spencer; Marina Ritossa.

HOW TO APPLY Apply in writing to the correspondent. Applications are discussed quarterly.

CONTACT DETAILS The Trustees, 3rd Floor, 39 Sloane Street, London SW1X 9LP *Tel.* 020 7448 0377 *Email* office@spencerfoundation.com

■ The Jessie Spencer Trust

CC NO 219289   **ESTABLISHED** 1962

WHERE FUNDING CAN BE GIVEN UK, with some preference for the East Midlands.

WHO CAN BENEFIT Registered charities or CICs, with a preference for organisations that have significant volunteer support; hospices; churches.

WHAT IS FUNDED General charitable purposes.

WHAT IS NOT FUNDED Individuals; organisations that are not registered charities or CICs; endowment appeals; loans or business finance; sponsorship, marketing appeals or fundraising events; campaigning or projects that are primarily political; activities that are the responsibility of the local health or education authority or similar body; retrospective expenditure; general or mail shot appeals.

TYPE OF GRANT Grants are made towards both capital and revenue expenditure. They can be recurrent for up to ten years.

RANGE OF GRANTS Grants are generally between £500 and £5,000.

SAMPLE GRANTS Nottinghamshire Historic Churches Trust (£7,500); Rainbows Hospice For Children and Young People (£5,000); Beaumond House Hospice Care (£2,000); Age UK Nottingham and Nottinghamshire (£1,000); Notts County Foundation (£500).

FINANCES *Financial year end 05/04/2022* Income £164,000 Grants to organisations £84,600 Assets £5,560,000

TRUSTEES David Wild; Andrew Tiplady; Helen Lee; Dr Sharmini Krishanand; Peter Ellis.

OTHER INFORMATION In 2021/22, grants to organisations were broken down as follows: welfare (£40,400); medical causes/people with disabilities (£21,300); education (£8,500); churches (£8,500); arts (£2,500); services (£1,500); other (£1,500); groups (£500).

HOW TO APPLY Apply in writing to the correspondent. Guidance on what to include is provided on the trust's website. Applications should be received by 20 January, 20 April, 20 July or 20 October each year for consideration at trustees' meetings in March, June, September and December, respectively. To limit costs, only successful applicants are notified.

CONTACT DETAILS John Thompson, Trust Administrator, c/o 4 Walsingham Drive, Corby Glen, Grantham, Lincolnshire NG33 4TA *Tel.* 01476 552083 *Email* jessiespencer@ btinternet.com *Website* www.jessiespencertrust. org.uk

■ The Sperring Charity

CC NO 1048101   **ESTABLISHED** 1995

WHERE FUNDING CAN BE GIVEN The parishes situated within a five-mile radius of the church of St John the Baptist, Midsomer Norton.

WHO CAN BENEFIT Organisations and individuals.

WHAT IS FUNDED General charitable purposes.

TYPE OF GRANT Capital and project costs.

RANGE OF GRANTS £50 to £5,000.

SAMPLE GRANTS A list of beneficiaries was not included in the annual report and accounts.

FINANCES *Financial year end* 31/03/2022
 Income £264,200
 Grants to organisations £55,000
 Grants to individuals £2,100
 Assets £7,150,000
TRUSTEES Dr John Haxell; George Persson; William Weller; David Harvey; Catherine Bushill.
HOW TO APPLY Application forms can be downloaded from the charity's website.
CONTACT DETAILS The Trustees, c/o Thatcher and Hallam Solicitors, Island House, The Island, Midsomer Norton, Radstock, Somerset BA3 2HJ *Email* info@thesperringcharity.co.uk *Website* www.thesperringcharity.co.uk

■ Spielman Charitable Trust

CC NO 278306   **ESTABLISHED** 1979
WHERE FUNDING CAN BE GIVEN Bristol and the South West.
WHO CAN BENEFIT Registered charities; individuals.
WHAT IS FUNDED General charitable purposes; social welfare; disadvantaged children and young people; health; disability; education; the arts; older people; communities.
RANGE OF GRANTS Typically £2,000 to £5,000, but occasionally larger.
SAMPLE GRANTS Bristol Children's Help Society, Lord Mayor of Bristol Appeal and Royal Welsh College of Music (£20,000 each); The Wheels Project (£15,000); Creative Youth Network, Friends of Bristol Oncology and NSPCC (£10,000 each); Access Sport and St Peter's Hospice (£5,000 each); The Green House (£4,600); Dolphin Society and Whizz-Kidz (£3,000 each); Brainwave (£2,000); The Duke of Edinburgh's Award (£1,000).
FINANCES *Financial year end* 05/04/2022
 Income £282,400
 Grants to organisations £277,700
 Assets £6,290,000
TRUSTEES Chris Moorsom; Karen Hann; Paul Cooper; Amelia Hann; Anna MacCarthy.
OTHER INFORMATION Grants were broken down as follows: children who are disadvantaged (£150,600); arts and theatre (£40,000); children with disabilities or serious illnesses (£30,000); older people or people with disabilities (£22,000). A total of 35 grants were awarded.
HOW TO APPLY Apply in writing to the correspondent.
CONTACT DETAILS The Trustees, Whitefriars Business Centre, 2nd Floor, Whitefriars, Lewins Mead, Bristol BS1 2NT *Tel.* 0117 929 1929 *Email* spielmantrust@gmail.com

■ The Spoore, Merry and Rixman Foundation

CC NO 309040   **ESTABLISHED** 1958
WHERE FUNDING CAN BE GIVEN Maidenhead and Bray, covering the postcode area SL6 1–9 (see the map on the website).
WHO CAN BENEFIT Charitable organisations; schools; youth clubs and community organisations; individuals.
WHAT IS FUNDED Education and training; children and young people.
TYPE OF GRANT Capital costs; project costs.
SAMPLE GRANTS A list of beneficiaries was not included in the annual report and accounts.

FINANCES *Financial year end* 31/12/2021
 Income £327,200
 Grants to organisations £594,800
 Grants to individuals £323,900
 Assets £12,110,000
TRUSTEES Grahame Fisher; Tony Hill; Ann Redgrave; Ian Thomas; Barbara Wielechowski; Philip Love; David Coppinger; Cllr Gerry Clark; Donna Stimson; Mayor Christine Bateson.
OTHER INFORMATION According to the foundation's website, some of the grants made recently have included funding towards school buses, laptops for schools and individuals, new school library books and school uniform funding.
HOW TO APPLY Applications can be made online or via post. See the foundation's website for details on how to apply, as application forms differ depending on the purpose of the funding. The foundation asks that applications made by post are not sent via recorded or registered post.
CONTACT DETAILS Clerk to the Trustees, PO Box 4787, Maidenhead, Berkshire SL60 1JA *Tel.* 020 3286 8300 *Email* clerk@smrfmaidenhead.org *Website* www.smrfmaidenhead.org.uk

■ Spurrell Charitable Trust

CC NO 267287   **ESTABLISHED** 1960
WHERE FUNDING CAN BE GIVEN UK, with some preference for Norfolk.
WHO CAN BENEFIT UK-registered charities.
WHAT IS FUNDED General charitable purposes.
WHAT IS NOT FUNDED Individuals; CICs; not-for-profit organisations.
RANGE OF GRANTS Up to £10,000.
SAMPLE GRANTS East Anglian Air Ambulance (£10,000); Big C Appeal (£7,000); East Anglia Children's Hospital (£5,000); Royal Agricultural Benevolent Institution (£2,500); The Connection at St Martin-in-the-Fields (£2,000); Break (£1,500); Dog Aid (£1,000); Friends of Norwich Cathedral (£500).
FINANCES *Financial year end* 05/04/2022
 Income £69,200
 Grants to organisations £82,500
 Assets £3,220,000
TRUSTEES Ingeburg Spurrell; Martyn Spurrell; Christopher Spurrell.
OTHER INFORMATION Grants were made to 42 organisations during 2021/22.
HOW TO APPLY Apply in writing to the correspondent. The trustees meet annually to consider grants.
CONTACT DETAILS The Trustees, Harefields, Winslow Road, Little Horwood, Buckinghamshire MK17 0PD *Tel.* 01296 420113 *Email* spurrelltrust@icloud.com

■ The Geoff and Fiona Squire Foundation

CC NO 1085553   **ESTABLISHED** 2001
WHERE FUNDING CAN BE GIVEN UK.
WHO CAN BENEFIT Registered charities.
WHAT IS FUNDED General charitable purposes, particularly the following: medicine; education; disability; welfare and health care of children.
WHAT IS NOT FUNDED Large national charities (with an income of over £10 million or assets of more than £100 million); charities dedicated to issues that the trustees deem to be already well funded in the UK.
TYPE OF GRANT Mostly one-off.
RANGE OF GRANTS Up to £255,000.

SAMPLE GRANTS The Children's Trust (£255,000); Horatio's Garden (£110,000); Noah's Ark Children's Hospice (£78,500); Evelina London Children's Charity (£60,000); Stable Family Home Trust (£33,700); WheelPower (£20,000); Orpheus Centre (£16,450); Lord's Taverners (£10,000); Rockinghorse Children's Charity (£5,000); The Bren Project (£1,000).

FINANCES *Financial year end* 31/03/2022
Income £121,900
Grants to organisations £816,500
Assets £8,840,000

TRUSTEES Geoff Squire; Fiona Squire; Bartholomew Peerless.

OTHER INFORMATION Grants were made to 42 charities during the year.

HOW TO APPLY Apply in writing to the correspondent.

CONTACT DETAILS The Trustees, 18 Henry Moore Court, Manresa Road, London SW3 6AS *Tel.* 07759 636799 *Email* squirefoundation. temp@btinternet.com

■ The Squire Patton Boggs Charitable Trust

CC NO 1064028   **ESTABLISHED** 1997

WHERE FUNDING CAN BE GIVEN England and Wales with a preference for causes local to the firm's offices in Birmingham, London, Leeds and Manchester.

WHO CAN BENEFIT Registered charities only. National and international charities are supported, but there is a preference for smaller charities local to Squire Patton Boggs LLP offices.

WHAT IS FUNDED General charitable purposes, particularly: children and young people; older people; people with disabilities; health and medical research; disaster relief.

RANGE OF GRANTS Up to £10,000 but mostly £200 to £1,000. The average grant was approximately £400.

SAMPLE GRANTS Leeds Culture Trust (£10,000); Headlines Craniofacial Support (£3,000); LandAid Charitable Trust Ltd (£1,000); The Royal British Legion (£200).

FINANCES *Financial year end* 05/04/2022
Income £65,600
Grants to organisations £88,000
Assets £156,000

TRUSTEES Robert Elvin; Andrew Stones; Spencer McKay; Jane Haxby; Caroline Lumley; Matthew Giles.

OTHER INFORMATION Grants were awarded to 139 organisations during the year. Grants were broken down as follows: education and training (£30,800); general charitable purposes (£24,500); health (£22,100); disability (£3,900); social welfare (£3,300); overseas aid (£1,500); the advancement of education (£1,000); amateur sport (£500); arts, culture, heritage and science (£500).

HOW TO APPLY Apply in writing to the correspondent.

CONTACT DETAILS Liz Harris, c/o Squire Patton Boggs (UK) LLP, Rutland House, 148 Edmund Street, Birmingham, West Midlands B3 2JR *Tel.* 0121 222 3442 *Email* liz.harris@squirepb. com *Website* www.squirepattonboggs.com/en/ about/corporate-responsibility/squire-patton-boggs-charitable-trust

■ The Squires Foundation

CC NO 328149   **ESTABLISHED** 1989

WHERE FUNDING CAN BE GIVEN Mainly the North East and also Cumbria and Leeds.

WHO CAN BENEFIT Charitable organisations.

WHAT IS FUNDED Grants are given in the areas of social welfare; community development; children and young people; older people; local hospitals and hospices; Christian activities.

TYPE OF GRANT One-off or recurrent.

RANGE OF GRANTS Up to £25,000.

SAMPLE GRANTS The Prince's Trust (£25,000); Community Foundation (£20,000); Traidcraft Exchange (£15,000); Newcastle East End Mission and Newcastle Homeless Commission (£10,000 each).

FINANCES *Financial year end* 31/03/2022
Income £81,300
Grants to organisations £80,000
Assets £720

TRUSTEES Lynn Squires; Stephen Squires; John Squires; Malcolm Squires; Mark Squires.

HOW TO APPLY Apply in writing to the correspondent. The trustees meet twice a year, usually in May and November with applications to be received by the beginning of April or October respectively.

CONTACT DETAILS Lynn Squires, Trustee, The Community Foundation, Philanthropy House, Woodbine Road, Gosworth, Newcastle upon Tyne NE3 1DD *Tel.* 0191 222 0945 *Email* general@communityfoundation.org.uk

■ The Vichai Srivaddhanaprabha Foundation

CC NO 1144791

WHERE FUNDING CAN BE GIVEN Leicestershire; Rutland.

WHO CAN BENEFIT Charities; charitable organisations; community groups.

WHAT IS FUNDED General charitable purposes.

RANGE OF GRANTS Up to £800,000.

SAMPLE GRANTS Leicester Hospital (£1.01 million); The Royal British Legion (£18,500); Bodie Hodges Foundation (£11,300); iPads for Hospitals (£2,700).

FINANCES *Financial year end* 31/05/2022
Income £1,100,000
Grants to organisations £1,050,000
Assets £188,300

TRUSTEES Susan Whelan; Simon Capper; Tony Lander; Alan Birchenall.

OTHER INFORMATION This foundation is the corporate charity of Leicester City Football Club. During the year, grants were made to four organisations.

HOW TO APPLY See the foundation's website for further information.

CONTACT DETAILS The Trustees, King Power Stadium, Filbert Way, Leicester, LE2 7FL *Tel.* 0116 229 4737 *Email* VSFoundation@lcfc.co.uk *Website* www.lcfc.com/foundation-community/ foundation

■ The St Hilda's Trust

CC NO 500962   **ESTABLISHED** 1904

WHERE FUNDING CAN BE GIVEN The diocese of Newcastle (Newcastle upon Tyne, North Tyneside and Northumberland).

WHO CAN BENEFIT Organisations with charitable purposes (not exclusively registered charities); churches; community projects.

WHAT IS FUNDED Disadvantaged children and young people. Particular consideration is given to projects with a degree of church involvement.

TYPE OF GRANT Project funding.

SAMPLE GRANTS A list of beneficiaries was not included in the annual report and accounts.

FINANCES *Financial year end* 31/12/2021
Income £81,600
Grants to organisations £84,600
Assets £3,120,000

TRUSTEES Dr Margaret Wilkinson; The Revd Christine Brown; Julian Brown; Roger Styring; Helen Cooper; David Littlefield.

HOW TO APPLY Application forms can be obtained from the correspondent. The trustees meet at least three times a year to consider grant applications.

CONTACT DETAILS Ruth O'Hagan, Secretary, Church House, St John's Terrace, North Shields, Tyne and Wear NE29 6HS *Tel.* 0191 270 4100 *Email* r.o'hagan@newcastle.anglican.org *Website* www.newcastle.anglican.org/st-hildas-trust

---

■ St James's Place Charitable Foundation

CC NO 1144606   **ESTABLISHED** 1992

WHERE FUNDING CAN BE GIVEN UK and overseas.

WHO CAN BENEFIT Predominantly UK-registered charities and special needs schools. The small grants programme targets charities with an annual income of less than £1 million.

WHAT IS FUNDED The foundation's main themes are: supporting disadvantaged young people; combatting cancer; supporting hospices; mental health.

WHAT IS NOT FUNDED Charities with reserves of over 50% of income; administrative costs; activities which are the responsibility of statutory providers or replacement of statutory funding; research; events; advertising; holidays; sponsorship; contributions to large capital appeals; single-faith charities; charities that are fundraising on behalf of another charity.

TYPE OF GRANT Capital items; core/revenue grants including salaries; project funding.

RANGE OF GRANTS Up to £10,000 for small grants. Larger grants are made to selected beneficiaries on an invitation-only basis.

SAMPLE GRANTS Panathlon Foundation (£1 million); The OnSide Foundation (£500,000); School-Home Support (£120,000); Meningitis Now (£80,000); Centrestage Communities Ltd (£40,000); ThinkForward UK (£20,000); The Music Works (£5,000).

FINANCES *Financial year end* 31/12/2021
Income £8,570,000
Grants to organisations £6,190,000
Assets £6,110,000

TRUSTEES Malcolm Cooper-Smith; Andrew Croft; Ian Gascoigne; Sonia Gravestock; Andrew Humphries; Robert Edwards; Sir Mark Weinberg.

OTHER INFORMATION In 2021, the foundation supported 578 charities in the UK, Asia and other parts of the world. A list of beneficiaries was not published in the year's annual accounts; therefore, a sample of recent beneficiaries has been taken from the foundation's website.

HOW TO APPLY Applications for the small grants scheme should be made using the form on the foundation's website. Guidelines for each of the foundation's themes are also available to download on the website. There are no deadlines for the small grants scheme and applications are considered throughout the year, though the process can take between four and six months.

CONTACT DETAILS The Trustees, St James's Place House, 1 Tetbury Road, Cirencester, Gloucestershire GL7 1FP *Tel.* 01285 878037 *Email* sjp.foundation@sjp.co.uk *Website* www.sjpfoundation.co.uk

---

■ Sir Walter St John's Educational Charity

CC NO 312690   **ESTABLISHED** 1992

WHERE FUNDING CAN BE GIVEN The boroughs of Wandsworth or Lambeth, with a preference for Battersea.

WHO CAN BENEFIT Registered charities; CICs; social enterprises; PTAs; individuals; local community groups.

WHAT IS FUNDED The education and training of children and young people. The Small Education Grants scheme focuses on the following groups of local children and young people: those living in areas of particular social disadvantage; refugees and asylum seekers; carers; people with disabilities; looked after children and care leavers. The Strategic Grants scheme focuses on: refugees of secondary school age, particularly unaccompanied minors and those with little previous formal education; young carers; young people who are low achieving or at risk of dropping out of education.

TYPE OF GRANT Capital costs; project funding; start-up funding.

RANGE OF GRANTS Up to £1,500 for educational grants; up to £30,000 per year for Strategic Grants.

SAMPLE GRANTS CARAS (£90,000); Learn to Love to Read (£10,000); Carers Hub Lambeth (£9,900); South Thames College (£5,000); Caius House (£4,500); Parallel Youth Enterprise (£3,000); Sacred Heart (£2,000); South London Refugee Association (£1,500).

FINANCES *Financial year end* 05/04/2022
Income £216,600
Grants to organisations £149,400
Grants to individuals £5,000
Assets £6,250,000

TRUSTEES Daphne Daytes; Barry Fairbank; Sarah Rackham; Col. Julian Radcliffe; Godfrey Allen; Wendy Speck; Sheldon Wilkie; The Revd Canon Simon Butler; Michael Bates; Cllr Linda Bray; Col. Martin Stratton; Cllr Matthew Tiller; Victoria Asante; Cllr David Robson.

HOW TO APPLY Application forms, eligibility criteria and application deadlines can be found on the charity's website.

CONTACT DETAILS Susan Perry, Manager, c/o St Mary's Primary School, 7 St Joseph's Street, London SW8 4EN *Tel.* 020 7498 8878 *Email* manager@swsjcharity.org.uk *Website* www.swsjcharity.org.uk

---

■ St John's Foundation Est. 1174

CC NO 201476   **ESTABLISHED** 1174

WHERE FUNDING CAN BE GIVEN Bath and North East Somerset.

WHO CAN BENEFIT Charitable organisations.

WHAT IS FUNDED Health and well-being; housing; isolation; poverty; relationships; employment and skills.

RANGE OF GRANTS Generally £1,000 to £30,000.

SAMPLE GRANTS Brighter Futures (£230,100); HCRG Care Group (£78,000); Roundhill Primary School

Think carefully about every application. Is it justified?

669

(£72,200); Bath Recreation Ltd (£50,000); SARSAS (£30,000); HorseWorld Trust (£25,000); Designability (£20,000); Bath City FC Community Sports Foundation (£2,800); The Nest Project (£1,900).

FINANCES *Financial year end 31/12/2021*
Income £5,340,000
Grants to organisations £1,490,000
Assets £125,500,000

TRUSTEE St John's Hospital Trustee Ltd.

OTHER INFORMATION Grants were awarded to 45 organisations during the year.

HOW TO APPLY Contact the foundation for more information on the application process.

CONTACT DETAILS Louise Harvey, Director of Funding and Impact, St Johns Hospital, 4–5 Chapel Court, Bath BA1 1SQ *Tel.* 01225 486400 *Email* info@stjohnsbath.org.uk *Website* www.stjohnsbath.org.uk/funding-support

■ The St Lazarus Charitable Trust

CC NO 286918   **ESTABLISHED** 1983
WHERE FUNDING CAN BE GIVEN England; Wales.
WHO CAN BENEFIT Charitable organisations.
WHAT IS FUNDED The advancement of health or saving of lives; the prevention or relief of poverty; overseas aid/famine relief; religious activities.
RANGE OF GRANTS Typically between £100 and £10,000.
SAMPLE GRANTS The Leprosy Mission of England and Wales (£28,900); Aid to the Church in Need – Far East Asia Appeal (£25,000); LEPRA (£15,200); Samburu Trust (£2,000); Aid to the Church in Need – Lebanon Appeal (£1,000).
FINANCES *Financial year end 31/12/2021*
Income £112,900
Grants to organisations £76,400
Assets £529,800
TRUSTEES David Powell; Patrick Wilkins; Dr David Knox; Charles Betz; John Reid; Ivar Grey.
OTHER INFORMATION Grants were awarded to 28 organisations during the year.
HOW TO APPLY Apply using the form available to download from the website. After completion, the form, together with a copy of your most recent audited accounts, should be sent to the correspondent by post by 30 September.
CONTACT DETAILS Gareth Vaughan, Grants Secretary, Flat 2, The Glove Factory, Montacute Road, Tintinhull, Somerset BA22 8SL *Tel.* 01935 826723 *Email* ewsecretary@gmail.com *Website* www.stlazaruscharitabletrust.org.uk

■ St Monica Trust

CC NO 202151   **ESTABLISHED** 1925
WHERE FUNDING CAN BE GIVEN Bristol and the surrounding area.
WHO CAN BENEFIT Organisations; individuals and families.
WHAT IS FUNDED Improving facilities and opportunities for older people.
TYPE OF GRANT Capital items; running costs.
SAMPLE GRANTS A list of beneficiaries was not included in the annual report and accounts. Previous beneficiaries have included: Citizens Advice (£9,800); Headway Bristol, Motor Neurone Disease Association and St Peter's Hospice (£7,500 each); IT Help@Home (£5,000); The New Place (£3,900); Bristol and Avon Chinese Women's Group (£2,000); Bath Institute of Medical Engineering (£1,500); Western Active Stroke Group (£1,000).

FINANCES *Financial year end 31/12/2021*
Income £44,760,000
Grants to organisations £472,700
Grants to individuals £161,200
Assets £331,910,000
TRUSTEE St Monica Trustee Company Ltd.
OTHER INFORMATION The trust runs retirement villages in Bristol and North Somerset which offer sheltered accommodation, nursing homes and dementia care homes to older people. During 2021, 32 organisations were supported.
HOW TO APPLY Contact the trust for more information.
CONTACT DETAILS Community Fund Team, Cote Lane, Westbury-on-Trym, Bristol BS9 3UN *Tel.* 0117 949 4003 *Email* charitableimpact@stmonicatrust.org.uk *Website* www.stmonicatrust.org.uk

■ St Olave's and St Saviour's Schools Foundation CIO

CC NO 1181857
WHERE FUNDING CAN BE GIVEN Southwark.
WHO CAN BENEFIT Youth organisations and groups; schools; individuals.
WHAT IS FUNDED Activities for young people under the age of 25.
WHAT IS NOT FUNDED Retrospective expenditure.
RANGE OF GRANTS Up to £3,000.
SAMPLE GRANTS St Saviour's and St Olave's School (£7,000); Colombo Street Community and Sports Centre (£6,000); Downside Fisher Youth Club and Westminster House Youth Group (£3,000 each); Bridge the Gap Studios and Fairbeats Music (£2,000 each); Listening Books (£1,500); Afro-Brazilian Arts and Cultural Exchange (£1,000).
FINANCES *Financial year end 31/03/2022*
Income £1,200,000
Grants to organisations £122,800
Grants to individuals £33,000
Assets £27,400,000
TRUSTEES Robert Highmore; James de Sausmarez; Louise Harris; Adrian Boyd; Natalie Bell; James Rothwell; Dr Emma Sanderson-Nash; Stephen Parry; John Major; The Very Revd Andrew Nunn; Dr David Ryall; Elizabeth Edwards.
HOW TO APPLY Application forms can be downloaded from the foundation's website. The trustees meet four times a year and grant applications can be made at any time.
CONTACT DETAILS R. Walters, Clerk to the Governors, St Olave's and St Saviour's Schools Foundation, Europoint Centre, 5–11 Lavington Street, London SE1 0NZ *Tel.* 020 7401 2871 *Email* grants@stolavesfoundation.co.uk *Website* www.stolavesfoundationfund.org.uk

■ St Peter's Saltley Trust

CC NO 528915   **ESTABLISHED** 1980
WHERE FUNDING CAN BE GIVEN The dioceses of Worcester, Hereford, Lichfield, Birmingham and Coventry.
WHO CAN BENEFIT Charitable organisations, schools, colleges, individuals.
WHAT IS FUNDED Christianity; theological and religious education.
TYPE OF GRANT Project funding and development funding. Mostly one-off grants.
RANGE OF GRANTS Up to £10,000.
SAMPLE GRANTS The Feast (£20,000); Sandwell Churches Link (£9,300); Faith and Belief Forum (£4,500); Kingdom at Work Project (£200).

FINANCES *Financial year end* 31/03/2022
Income £157,500
Grants to organisations £64,200
Assets £5,140,000

TRUSTEES Gordon Thornhill; Dr Peter Kent; Michael Hastilow; The Revd Canon Dr Jonathan Kimber; The Revd Canon Dr Mark Pryce; David Owen; Julia Ipgrave; Daniel Martin.

OTHER INFORMATION Grants were awarded to eight projects.

HOW TO APPLY Full criteria and guidelines for each fund are available on the trust's helpful website. The trust asks that in the first instance you contact the correspondent to help determine if your proposal is suitable for a full application.

CONTACT DETAILS Ian Jones, Director, Gray's Court, 3 Nursery Road, Edgbaston, West Midlands B15 3JX *Tel.* 0121 427 6800 *Email* director@saltleytrust.org.uk *Website* www.saltleytrust.org.uk

■ Stadium Charitable Trust

CC NO 328522   **ESTABLISHED** 1989
WHERE FUNDING CAN BE GIVEN UK, with a preference for Yorkshire.
WHO CAN BENEFIT Charitable organisations, with a preference for local charities.
WHAT IS FUNDED General charitable purposes including: medical, health and sickness; sport and recreation.
RANGE OF GRANTS Mostly up to £10,000 with the occasional larger grant.
SAMPLE GRANTS Previous beneficiaries have included: Dove House Hospice (£500,000); Hey Smile Foundation (£200,000); Algarve Biomedical Centre (£50,000); Sincere Support (£20,000); Sailors Children's Society (£10,000); Asthma Relief (£3,000); Welton and Brough Sports Club (£1,000); The Children's Society (£500).
FINANCES *Financial year end* 05/04/2022
Income £10
Grants to organisations £130,300
TRUSTEES Susan Maxey; Anne Rozenbroek; Andrew Fish.
OTHER INFORMATION Full accounts were not available to view on the Charity Commission's website due to the trust's low income. We have therefore estimated the grant total based on its total expenditure.
HOW TO APPLY Apply in writing to the correspondent.
CONTACT DETAILS The Trustees, The Stadium Group, Welton Grange, Cowgate, Welton, East Riding of Yorkshire HU15 1NB *Tel.* 01482 667149 *Email* info@stadiumcity.co.uk

■ The Stafford Trust

OSCR NO SC018079   **ESTABLISHED** 1991
WHERE FUNDING CAN BE GIVEN UK, with a strong preference for Scotland.
WHO CAN BENEFIT UK-registered charities.
WHAT IS FUNDED General charitable purposes, including the following: social welfare; medical research; animal welfare; children and young people; community projects; sea rescue; welfare of Service personnel; overseas aid.
WHAT IS NOT FUNDED Religious organisations; political organisations; retrospective grants; student travel or expeditions; general appeals or mail shots.
TYPE OF GRANT Capital projects; core costs; salaries.
RANGE OF GRANTS Mostly between £500 and £5,000.

SAMPLE GRANTS Search and Rescue Aerial Association Scotland (£6,600); Live Music Now Scotland and St Andrews Environment Network (£5,000 each); Felix Fund (£4,000); Secret World Wildlife Rescue (£2,000); React (Rapid Effective Assistance for Children with potentially Terminal illness) (£1,900); The Krazy Kat Theatre Company (£1,700); Raploch Community Partnership (£500).

FINANCES *Financial year end* 05/04/2022
Income £493,300
Grants to organisations £390,500
Assets £31,860,000

TRUSTEES Gordon Wylie; Ian Ferguson; Robert Hogg; Fiona Gillespie.

OTHER INFORMATION During 2021/22, grants were broken down as follows: children and young people (£128,500); adult welfare (£96,400); community projects (£86,600); animal welfare (£35,300); medical research and support (£22,000); Service personnel welfare (£11,800); sea rescue (£9,900).

HOW TO APPLY An application form can be downloaded from the trust's website and should include the information specified on the website. The trustees usually meet twice a year in spring and autumn to review applications. Deadlines are posted on the website. Unsuccessful applicants should wait at least one year before re-applying.

CONTACT DETAILS Billy Russell, Trust Administrator, c/o Dickson Middleton CA, PO Box 14, 20 Barnton Street, Stirling, Stirlingshire FK8 1NE *Tel.* 01786 474718 *Email* staffordtrust@dicksonmiddleton.co.uk *Website* www.staffordtrust.org.uk

■ The Community Foundation for Staffordshire

CC NO 1091628   **ESTABLISHED** 2001
WHERE FUNDING CAN BE GIVEN Staffordshire.
WHO CAN BENEFIT Registered charities; community groups; CICs; individuals.
WHAT IS FUNDED General charitable purposes including: social welfare; community development, mental health, older people, health, children and young people and sport.
WHAT IS NOT FUNDED Each funding stream has its own set of exclusions – refer to the website for details.
TYPE OF GRANT Mainly project funding but some streams also give for core costs.
RANGE OF GRANTS Programme dependent.
SAMPLE GRANTS Realise Foundation (£30,000); Sir Stanley Matthews Foundation (£13,000); Rotten Park Road (£10,000); Rebalanced (£7,800); Frontline Dance (£6,800); Saltbox (£5,000).
FINANCES *Financial year end* 31/03/2022
Income £2,270,000
Grants to organisations £870,000
Grants to individuals £383,800
Assets £9,320,000
TRUSTEES Simon Price; Roger Lewis; Terry Walsh; Jonathan Andrew; Charlotte Almond; Adele Cope; Judy Scott-Moncrieff; Jeremy Lefroy; Ashley Brough; Charles Jewitt; Alan Durose.
OTHER INFORMATION This is one of the 47 UK community foundations, which distribute funding for a wide range of purposes. As with all community foundations, there are a number of donor-advised funds managed on behalf of individuals, families and charitable trusts. Grant schemes tend to change frequently – consult the foundation's website for details of current programmes and up-to-date deadlines.

HOW TO APPLY Potential applicants are advised to visit the community foundation's website or contact its grants team to find the most suitable funding stream.

CONTACT DETAILS The Grants Team, Communications House, University Court, Staffordshire Technology Park, Stafford, Staffordshire ST18 0ES *Tel.* 01785 339540 *Email* office@staffsfoundation.org.uk *Website* www.staffsfoundation.org.uk

---

■ Stanley Foundation Ltd

CC NO 206866   **ESTABLISHED** 1960
WHERE FUNDING CAN BE GIVEN UK.
WHO CAN BENEFIT Registered charities.
WHAT IS FUNDED General charitable purposes, including the following: education and training; arts, culture and heritage; medical care and research; community development; famine and disaster relief.
WHAT IS NOT FUNDED Individuals.
RANGE OF GRANTS Up to £15,000.
SAMPLE GRANTS King's College (£15,000); Bowel Cancer UK, Forget Me Not, Photoworks and Puzzle Centre (£5,000 each).
FINANCES *Financial year end 31/03/2022*
  Income £57,700
  Grants to organisations £59,000
  Assets £2,390,000
TRUSTEES Georgina Stanley; Charles Stanley; Isabelle Hirst; George Thompson.
HOW TO APPLY Apply in writing to the correspondent.
CONTACT DETAILS Nicholas Stanley, Trustee, c/o N. C. Morris and Co., 1 Montpelier Street, London SW7 1EX *Tel.* 07781 642750 *Email* edward.stanley.122@gmail.com

---

■ Staples Trust

CC NO 1010656   **ESTABLISHED** 1992
WHERE FUNDING CAN BE GIVEN UK and overseas; Oxfordshire.
WHO CAN BENEFIT Registered charities; universities; CICs; museums.
WHAT IS FUNDED Gender issues (domestic violence, women's rights and gender studies); overseas projects which support the rights of indigenous people; charities defending human rights and civil liberties. The trust also administers The Frankopan Fund, which makes small grants to Croatian students. The trustees also have an interest in supporting local charities in Oxfordshire.
WHAT IS NOT FUNDED Individuals.
TYPE OF GRANT Core costs; project funding; capital costs.
RANGE OF GRANTS Mostly £500 to £5,000.
SAMPLE GRANTS University of Oxford (£162,300); Insight Share (£70,000); One Small Thing (£8,000); The Felix Project and Twins Trust (£5,000 each); Oxford Food Hub and SWA (formerly Swindon Women's Aid) (£2,500 each); University of Nottingham (£1,000).
FINANCES *Financial year end 05/04/2022*
  Income £263,200
  Grants to organisations £392,100
  Assets £15,860,000
TRUSTEES Prof. Peter Frankopan; Timothy Sainsbury; Jessica Sainsbury.
OTHER INFORMATION The trust is one of the Sainsbury Family Charitable Trusts, which share a common administration – see www.sftc.org.uk for more information. During the year, grants to organisations were made for the following purposes: indigenous peoples (£290,000);

general charitable purposes (£22,500); gender (£42,500); local causes (£5,000). Grants for education totalled £23,000 and were made through The Frankopan Fund. The list of beneficiaries includes recipients of grants paid and committed.
HOW TO APPLY Unsolicited applications are not accepted.
CONTACT DETAILS The Trustees, The Peak, 5 Wilton Road, London SW1V 1AP *Tel.* 020 7410 0330 *Email* info@sfct.org.uk *Website* www.sfct.org.uk/the-staples-trust/

■ Starlow Charities Ltd

CC NO 1081386   **ESTABLISHED** 2000
WHERE FUNDING CAN BE GIVEN UK and overseas.
WHO CAN BENEFIT Jewish organisations.
WHAT IS FUNDED Causes affecting the Orthodox Jewish community, including the relief of poverty, religion and religious education; general charitable purposes.
RANGE OF GRANTS Up to £219,000.
SAMPLE GRANTS Chevras Mo'oz Ladol (£219,000); Ezer Bekovoid Ltd. (£154,200); Keren Ezra Mimeitzar (£132,000); Tchabe Kollel Ltd (£52,700).
FINANCES *Financial year end 31/07/2021*
  Income £737,600
  Grants to organisations £1,070,000
  Assets £8,170,000
TRUSTEES Eve Low; Abraham Low; Avraham Shwarts; Isaac Hochhauser; Benzion Rudzinski.
OTHER INFORMATION More than eight institutions received grants during the year, with only charities receiving £50,000 or more listed in the beneficiaries. Grants of less than £50,000 totalled £511,100. The 2020/21 accounts were the latest available at the time of writing (May 2023).
HOW TO APPLY Apply in writing to the correspondent.
CONTACT DETAILS The Trustees, 9 Craven Walk, London N16 6BS *Tel.* 020 8802 9517 *Email* mail@cohenarnold.com

---

■ The Peter Stebbings Memorial Charity

CC NO 274862   **ESTABLISHED** 1978
WHERE FUNDING CAN BE GIVEN UK (particularly London) and sub-Saharan Africa.
WHO CAN BENEFIT UK-registered charities. Generally grants go to charities where the trustees can see how the money is being used. The trustees prefer small to medium-sized charities with annual incomes of up to £5 million.
WHAT IS FUNDED UK charities are supported in the following areas: medical research and care; social welfare; homelessness; vulnerable families, women and children. Overseas charities are supported in the following areas: education; basic skills and tools; health; sanitation, irrigation, hygiene and access to clean water; women; help for marginalised communities.
WHAT IS NOT FUNDED Individuals; large national or international charities; animal welfare; publications and journals (unless as part of a supported project); general appeals; any charity whose beneficiaries are restricted to particular faiths; educational institutions (unless there is a particular project the trustees wish to support); arts organisations (unless there is a strong social welfare focus to the work); newly

registered charities (the application requires a year of audited accounts).

TYPE OF GRANT Project funding, although core costs will be considered for charities known to the trustees.

RANGE OF GRANTS Mostly between £3,000 and £10,000, with some larger grants made up to £50,000.

SAMPLE GRANTS Royal Marsden Hospital Charity (£50,000); Moorfields Eye Charity (£25,000); Tools with a Mission (£20,000); Target Ovarian Cancer (£15,000); The New Bridge Foundation (£10,000); Tools for Self Reliance Cymru (£5,000); Together We Learn (£2,500).

FINANCES *Financial year end 31/03/2022*
Income £39,800
Grants to organisations £606,600
Assets £8,260,000

TRUSTEES Jennifer Clifford; Nicholas Cosin; Andrew Stebbings; Nicolas Clifford; James Stebbings.

OTHER INFORMATION Grants were awarded to 79 charities during the year.

HOW TO APPLY Application forms can be filled in on the charity's website. The trustees meet twice a year to allocate grants. Upcoming meeting dates and deadlines can be found on the charity's website.

CONTACT DETAILS The Trustees, 45 Cadogan Gardens, London SW3 2AQ *Tel.* 07368 652694 *Email* info@peterstebbingsmemorialcharity.org *Website* http://peterstebbingsmemorialcharity.org

■ The Steel Charitable Trust

CC NO 272384   **ESTABLISHED** 1976

WHERE FUNDING CAN BE GIVEN UK; Luton and Bedfordshire.

WHO CAN BENEFIT UK-registered charities; exempt charities.

WHAT IS FUNDED Arts and heritage; education; the environment; health; social or economic disadvantage.

WHAT IS NOT FUNDED Charities not registered in the UK; individuals; political parties.

TYPE OF GRANT Capital costs; project funding; research programmes; core costs.

RANGE OF GRANTS Typically up to £20,000.

SAMPLE GRANTS A list of beneficiaries was not included in the annual report and accounts.

FINANCES *Financial year end 31/01/2022*
Income £24,850,000
Grants to organisations £1,270,000
Assets £51,860,000

TRUSTEES Wendy Bailey; Dr Natalie Briggs; Peter Day; Vanessa Fox; Philip Lawford; Nicholas Wright.

OTHER INFORMATION Grants were broken down as follows: social or economic disadvantage (35%); education (23%); health (18%); arts and heritage (18%); the environment (6%).

HOW TO APPLY Applicants must be made online using the form on the trust's website. The trustees meet quarterly (in March, June, September and December) to consider grant applications. See the trust's website for application deadlines.

CONTACT DETAILS Trust Manager, Suite 411, Jansel House, Hitchin Road, Stopsley, Luton, Bedfordshire LU2 7XH *Email* info@steelcharitabletrust.org.uk *Website* www.steelcharitabletrust.org.uk

■ The Steinberg Family Charitable Trust

CC NO 1045231   **ESTABLISHED** 1995

WHERE FUNDING CAN BE GIVEN The North West; Israel.

WHO CAN BENEFIT Registered charities.

WHAT IS FUNDED The Jewish faith and community; medical care and treatment, including respite care and hospices; education and care of people with disabilities; older people; children and young people.

WHAT IS NOT FUNDED Individuals.

SAMPLE GRANTS A list of beneficiaries was not included in the annual report and accounts.

FINANCES *Financial year end 05/04/2022*
Income £2,250,000
Grants to organisations £2,810,000
Assets £29,300,000

TRUSTEES Lynne Steinberg; Jonathan Steinberg.

OTHER INFORMATION Grants were broken down as follows: Torah (£1,670,000); education (£515,800); welfare (£365,000); community (£90,400); miscellaneous (£12,500).

HOW TO APPLY Applications can be made via the trust's website.

CONTACT DETAILS The Trustees, Lime Tree Cottage, 16 Bollinway, Hale, Altrincham, Cheshire WA15 0NZ *Tel.* 0161 903 8854 *Email* admin@sfct.co.uk *Website* www.sfct.co.uk

■ The Hugh Stenhouse Foundation

OSCR NO SC015074   **ESTABLISHED** 1968

WHERE FUNDING CAN BE GIVEN Mainly Scotland, with a preference for the West of Scotland.

WHO CAN BENEFIT Charitable organisations, preferably local organisations; hospices; places of worship.

WHAT IS FUNDED General charitable purposes including: social welfare; medical and health; youth; religion.

TYPE OF GRANT Project funding; core costs.

RANGE OF GRANTS Generally up to £2,000.

SAMPLE GRANTS Maxwelton Chapel Trust (£30,000); Birth Baby and Beyond, Moira Anderson Foundation and Roseberry Centre (£1,900 each); Fife Young Carers, Tron Theatre and Vics in the Community (£1,300 each); Butterfly Trust, Glasgow City Mission and Miracle Foundation (£630 each).

FINANCES *Financial year end 31/03/2022*
Income £81,100
Grants to organisations £59,400
Assets £2,300,000

OTHER INFORMATION Grants were broken down as follows: religion (£30,000 to one organisation); relief of poverty (£9,400 to seven organisations); medical causes (£8,800 to seven organisations); young people (£6,900 to six organisations); general charitable purposes (£4,400 to four organisations). The foundation has a long-term commitment to Maxwelton Chapel Trust, to which it awards recurrent funding.

HOW TO APPLY Apply in writing to the correspondent.

CONTACT DETAILS The Trustees, c/o Bell Ingram LLP, Durn, Isla Road, Perth, Perthshire PH2 7HF

■ C. E. K. Stern Charitable Trust

CC NO 1049157   **ESTABLISHED** 1992

WHERE FUNDING CAN BE GIVEN UK and overseas, particularly Israel.

WHO CAN BENEFIT Orthodox Jewish charities and religious organisations.

WHAT IS FUNDED Orthodox Jewish religion and education; the relief of poverty.

RANGE OF GRANTS Up to £77,000, but mostly for less than £25,000.

SAMPLE GRANTS Friends of Beis Soroh Schneirer (£42,500); Beis Chinuch Lebonos Ltd (£31,000); Friends of Mercaz Hatorah Belz Macnivka (£30,500); Mifal Hachesed Vehatzedokoh (£5,000).

FINANCES *Financial year end* 31/08/2021
Income £176,200
Grants to organisations £116,900
Assets £2,560,000

TRUSTEES Zvi Stern; Chaya Stern.

OTHER INFORMATION The 2020/21 accounts were the latest available at the time of writing (June 2023). Only organisations that received grants of over £3,500 were listed as beneficiaries in the charity's accounts. Grants of under £4,000 totalled £7,900.

HOW TO APPLY Apply in writing to the correspondent.

CONTACT DETAILS The Trustees, 92 Whitehall Road, Gateshead, Tyne and Wear NE8 4ET *Tel.* 0191 490 1241

■ The Sir Sigmund Sternberg Charitable Foundation

CC NO 257950   **ESTABLISHED** 1968

WHERE FUNDING CAN BE GIVEN Worldwide.

WHO CAN BENEFIT Registered charities.

WHAT IS FUNDED The foundation supports interfaith activities to promote racial and religious harmony. There is a particular focus on the Christian, Jewish and Muslim faiths, and the education in, and understanding of, their fundamental tenets and beliefs.

RANGE OF GRANTS Grants range from £3,500 to £145,200.

SAMPLE GRANTS The Faith and Belief Forum (£178,500 in two grants); Woolf Institute (£10,000); New Israel Fund (£5,000); World Congress of Faiths (£3,500).

FINANCES *Financial year end* 05/04/2022
Income £72,900
Grants to organisations £198,800
Assets £3,730,000

TRUSTEES The Revd Dr Marcus Braybrooke; Martin Paisner; Martin Slowe; Michael Sternberg; Noam Tamir.

HOW TO APPLY Contact the correspondent for further information.

CONTACT DETAILS The Trustees, c/o HW Fisher LLP, Acre House, 11–15 William Road, London NW1 3ER *Tel.* 020 7388 7000

■ The Sterry Family Foundation

CC NO 1143953   **ESTABLISHED** 2011

WHERE FUNDING CAN BE GIVEN UK; South Africa; Botswana; Zimbabwe; Mozambique; Zambia; Tanzania; Rwanda; Burundi; Malawi; Uganda; Kenya.

WHO CAN BENEFIT Registered charities and institutional applicants.

WHAT IS FUNDED Education; amateur sports; health; arts and culture.

RANGE OF GRANTS £2,000 to £6,000.

SAMPLE GRANTS Northern Ballet (£6,000); Rainbow Trust and Snow Camp (£4,000 each); Birmingham Ballet and Starlight Children's Foundation (£3,000 each); Get Set 4 Tennis and Help to Read (£2,000 each).

FINANCES *Financial year end* 05/04/2022
Income £72,400
Grants to organisations £90,000
Grants to individuals £3,600
Assets £3,900,000

TRUSTEES David Sterry; James Sterry; Nicola Clatworthy; Wendy Sterry.

OTHER INFORMATION Grants were awarded to 31 organisations and 3 individuals during the year.

HOW TO APPLY Apply in writing to the correspondent. The foundation's 2021/22 annual report states: 'The trust invites applications for charitable donations from other registered charities. Institutional applicants submit a summary of their proposals to the trustees in a specific format, together with outline appeals. Applications made in the correct format are reviewed against the Trust Deed and its objectives.'

CONTACT DETAILS The Trustees, c/o Rathbone Trust Company Ltd, 8 Finsbury Circus, London EC2M 7AZ *Tel.* 020 7399 0000

■ Stervon Ltd

CC NO 280958   **ESTABLISHED** 1980

WHERE FUNDING CAN BE GIVEN UK and Israel.

WHO CAN BENEFIT Charitable organisations, particularly Jewish organisations.

WHAT IS FUNDED Relief of poverty; advancement of Jewish religion.

RANGE OF GRANTS Mostly up to £10,000 with the occasional larger grant.

SAMPLE GRANTS Chasdei Aharon (£30,600); Satmar Kollel (£22,500); Erez Ltd, New Light Trust and Rayonhills Ltd (£10,000 each).

FINANCES *Financial year end* 31/12/2021
Income £200,700
Grants to organisations £214,700
Assets £284,100

TRUSTEES Gabriel Rothbart; Akiba Reich.

OTHER INFORMATION Only organisations that received grants of over £10,000 were listed as beneficiaries in the 2021 annual report. Grants of under £10,000 totalled £97,800.

HOW TO APPLY Apply in writing to the correspondent.

CONTACT DETAILS The Trustees, 109 St Annes Road, Prestwich, Manchester M25 9GE *Tel.* 0161 737 5000 *Email* charities@haffhoff.co.uk

---

■ The Stevenage Community Trust

CC NO 1000762   **ESTABLISHED** 1990

WHERE FUNDING CAN BE GIVEN The borough of Stevenage and the surrounding villages of Aston, Benington, Cromer, Datchworth, Graveley, Knebworth, Little Wymondley, Old Knebworth, Walkern, Watton-at-Stone, Weston and Woolmer Green.

WHO CAN BENEFIT Charitable organisations; community groups; individuals; schools; amateur sports clubs.

WHAT IS FUNDED General charitable purposes.

WHAT IS NOT FUNDED Charities pursuing political objectives; religious evangelism; pursuing trade union objectives save for the welfare functions of trade unions; animal welfare; any other purpose inconsistent with the trust's charitable objectives; retrospective grants (items or services already purchased); the supply and fitting of flooring materials, except in exceptional circumstances.

TYPE OF GRANT Capital costs; project costs.

SAMPLE GRANTS A list of beneficiaries was not included in the annual report and accounts. Previous beneficiaries have included: Age

Concern; Corey's Mill Lions Club; Great Ashby Youth Club; Headway Hertfordshire; Herts Area Rape Crisis Centre; Link Up Lunch Club; Phoenix Group for Deaf Children; Shaftesbury Court Sheltered Housing; St Nicholas School; Stevenage Arts Guild; The Breastfeeding Network; Track Autism.

FINANCES *Financial year end* 31/03/2022
Income £184,400
Grants to organisations £142,300
Assets £631,700

TRUSTEES Mike Phoenix; Robert Stewart; Jeannette Thomas; Robert Case; Sharon Brown; Claire Austin; Stephen McQueen.

OTHER INFORMATION The grant total includes grants given to both individuals and organisations; no breakdown was given in the 2021/22 accounts.

HOW TO APPLY Application forms can be downloaded from the trust's website.

CONTACT DETAILS Samantha Bush, Charity Grants Manager, Stewart House, Primmett Road, Stevenage, Hertfordshire SG1 3EE *Tel.* 01438 525390 *Email* enquiries@ stevenagecommunitytrust.org *Website* www. stevenagecommunitytrust.org

■ Stevenson Family's Charitable Trust

CC NO 327148   **ESTABLISHED** 1986
WHERE FUNDING CAN BE GIVEN UK.
WHO CAN BENEFIT Registered charities; universities; hospices; theatres; museums; libraries; galleries.
WHAT IS FUNDED General charitable purposes, in particular: education and training; health and medicine; arts and culture; overseas aid; heritage and conservation; the environment.
WHAT IS NOT FUNDED Individuals.
TYPE OF GRANT One-off and recurrent grants.
RANGE OF GRANTS Typically £250 to £20,000.
SAMPLE GRANTS University of Oxford (£151,000); Garsington Opera (£105,500); National Trust for Scotland (£25,000); The Sick Children's Trust (£10,000); Newbury Spring Festival (£5,000).
FINANCES *Financial year end* 05/04/2022
Income £385,300
Grants to organisations £590,600
Assets £2,560,000
TRUSTEES Sir Hugh Stevenson; Lady Stevenson; Joseph Stevenson.
OTHER INFORMATION In 2021/22 the trust made grants to 45 organisations totalling £590,600. Grants were distributed across the following areas of work: education and training (£194,500); general charitable purposes (£101,800); culture and arts (£180,500); conservation and heritage (£69,300); health and medicine (£44,500).
HOW TO APPLY Unsolicited applications are not considered.
CONTACT DETAILS Hugh Stevenson, Chair, Old Waterfield, Winkfield Road, Ascot, Berkshire SL5 7LJ *Tel.* 01344 620170 *Email* hugh. stevenson@oldwaterfield.com

■ Stewards Company Ltd

CC NO 234558   **ESTABLISHED** 1965
WHERE FUNDING CAN BE GIVEN UK and overseas.
WHO CAN BENEFIT Organisations involved with training people in religious education; Christian ministries; individuals. About one-third of the charity's funds are given for work overseas.

WHAT IS FUNDED Advancement of the Christian religion for charitable purposes. Substantial funds are also transferred to the Beatrice Laing Trust each year (see separate entry).
RANGE OF GRANTS Typically less than £25,000.
SAMPLE GRANTS Strategic Resource Group (£397,000); Tyndale (£250,000); Retired Missionary Aid Fund (£240,000); Beatrice Lang Trust (£163,800); Gospel Literature Outreach (£115,000).
FINANCES *Financial year end* 31/12/2021
Income £3,650,000
Grants to organisations £5,340,000
Grants to individuals £38,500
Assets £168,510,000
TRUSTEES Ian Childs; Keigh Bintley; Andrew Griffiths; Jennifer Michael; Huw Iley; Mr J. Aitken; Paul Young; Dr Joshua Fitzhugh; Simon Tomlinson; David Bingham; David Roberts; Dr John Burness; Michelangelo Leto; Philip Symons; Andrew Mayo; John Gamble; Alexander McIlhinney; Glyn Davies.
OTHER INFORMATION In 2021 the charity's grants to UK organisations totalled £3.39 million and those to overseas causes totalled £2 million. Grants were broken down as follows: over £100,000 (£2.23 million); £25,000 to £99,000 (£1.35 million); under £25,000 (£1.77 million). Only organisations that received grants of over £100,000 were listed as beneficiaries in the charity's accounts.
HOW TO APPLY Apply in writing to the correspondent.
CONTACT DETAILS Andrew Griffiths, Secretary and Director of Operations, 122 Wells Road, Bath, Somerset BA2 3AH *Tel.* 01225 427236 *Email* stewardsco@stewards.co.uk

■ Sir Halley Stewart Trust

CC NO 208491   **ESTABLISHED** 1924
WHERE FUNDING CAN BE GIVEN UK and overseas.
WHO CAN BENEFIT UK charitable organisations.
WHAT IS FUNDED Prevention of human suffering; education in priority areas: medical, social, religious projects.
WHAT IS NOT FUNDED Individuals; general appeals; purchase, erection or conversion of buildings; capital costs; university overhead charges. Visit the funder's website for further details regarding applications that are not usually considered.
TYPE OF GRANT Project grants; salaries; feasibility studies; research; start-up funding. Funding may be given for up to three years.
RANGE OF GRANTS Main grants: up to £60,000; small grants: up to £5,000.
SAMPLE GRANTS Church Urban Fund, Prison Advice and Care Trust, Respond and University of Bath (£60,000 each); EGA Institute for Women's Health and University College London (£56,000); York St John University (£50,000); Manchester Metropolitan University (£45,000); Theos Think Tank (£30,000); Religion Media Centre (£21,000); Bethnal Green Mission Church (£12,000).
FINANCES *Financial year end* 31/03/2022
Income £1,140,000
Grants to organisations £1,090,000
Assets £39,220,000
TRUSTEE Sir Halley Stewart Trustee Ltd.
OTHER INFORMATION Only beneficiaries of grants of £10,000 and above were listed in the trust's 2021/22 accounts. Grants of under £10,000 totalled £26,000.
HOW TO APPLY Applications can be made on the trust's website, but the trust recommends contacting the secretary first to discuss the suitability of a project before applying. Further

guidelines are provided on the trust's website, where the dates of the next trustees' meetings and deadlines are also provided.

CONTACT DETAILS Lorraine Faires, Grants Manager, The Trust Partnership Ltd, 6 Trull Farm Buildings, Trull, Tetbury GL8 8SQ *Tel.* 020 8144 0375 *Email* email@sirhalleystewart.org.uk *Website* www.sirhalleystewart.org.uk

■ The Stewarts Law Foundation

CC NO 1136714 **ESTABLISHED** 2010
WHERE FUNDING CAN BE GIVEN UK.
WHO CAN BENEFIT Charitable organisations.
WHAT IS FUNDED Alleviating poverty; access to justice; supporting disability; providing educational opportunity.
RANGE OF GRANTS Up to £50,000.
SAMPLE GRANTS Access to Justice Foundation (£251,000); Centrepoint (£50,000); Wheelpower (£30,000); Finito (£9,000); JUSTICE (£6,000).
FINANCES *Financial year end 30/04/2022*
Income £838,400
Grants to organisations £914,500
Assets £154,100
TRUSTEES Julian Chamberlayne; Stuart Dench; Stephen Foster; Daniel Herman; Clive Zietman; Emma Hatley; Debbie Chism; Keith Thomas; Ian Gatt; Kathryn Pollock; Mohan Bhaskaran; David Pickstone; James Price; Fiona Gillett; Sam Longworth; Richard Hogwood; Muiris Lyons; Sarah Stewart; Matthew Humphries; Peter Neenan.
OTHER INFORMATION Only organisations that received grants of over £3,000 were listed as beneficiaries in the foundation's accounts (20 organisations). Grants of under £3,000 totalled £9,100. The foundation has a partnership with the Access to Justice Foundation, to which it awards a large grant each year. In addition, employees of Stewarts Law are given the opportunity to vote for a charity to be supported each year.
HOW TO APPLY The foundation's annual report states that 'it is not the policy of the trustees to accept direct applications for funds.'
CONTACT DETAILS The Trustees, 5 New Street Square, London EC4A 3BF *Tel.* 020 7822 8000 *Website* www.stewartslaw.com/about/social-impact/the-stewarts-foundation

■ The Stobart Newlands Charitable Trust

CC NO 328464 **ESTABLISHED** 1989
WHERE FUNDING CAN BE GIVEN Worldwide.
WHO CAN BENEFIT Registered charities; missionary organisations.
WHAT IS FUNDED Christian and missionary causes.
RANGE OF GRANTS Up to £250,000.
SAMPLE GRANTS World Vision (£250,000); Operation Mobilisation (£142,000); Every Home Crusade (£28,500); Logos Ministries (£16,500).
FINANCES *Financial year end 31/12/2021*
Income £1,040,000
Grants to organisations £891,500
Assets £348,300
TRUSTEES Ronnie Stobart; Linda Rigg; Peter Stobart; Richard Stobart.
OTHER INFORMATION Only beneficiaries of grants of £10,000 and above were listed in the accounts. Grants of under £10,000 totalled £155,300.
HOW TO APPLY Unsolicited applications are unlikely to be successful.

CONTACT DETAILS The Trustees, Millcroft, Newlands, Hesket Newmarket, Wigton, Cumbria CA7 8HP *Tel.* 01697 478631

■ Stolkin Foundation

CC NO 1138476 **ESTABLISHED** 2007
WHERE FUNDING CAN BE GIVEN England and Wales; South Africa.
WHO CAN BENEFIT Registered charities; churches; hospitals; schools and colleges; universities.
WHAT IS FUNDED Public education in the performing and visual arts; health and social welfare; education; the furtherance of the Christian faith; architectural heritage.
TYPE OF GRANT Capital costs; project fudging; general funding.
SAMPLE GRANTS Previous beneficiaries have included: The PCC of the Ecclesiastical Parish of Holy Trinity with Saint Paul Onslow Square and St Augustine South Kensington (£198,300); Church Revitalisation Trust (£100,000); Care for Children (£62,500); St Peter's Church Brighton (£8,600); The Lambeth Trust (£6,000); The Art Academy (£2,000); Give Hope Trust (£1,800); Anne Frank Trust UK (£1,500); Crisis UK (£1,000).
FINANCES *Financial year end 05/04/2022*
Income £14,400
Grants to organisations £446,300
TRUSTEES Margeaux Stolkin; Mark Stolkin; Renate Lubert.
OTHER INFORMATION Full accounts were not available to view on the Charity Commission's website due to the charity's low income. We have therefore estimated the charity's grant total based on its total expenditure.
HOW TO APPLY Apply in writing to the correspondent.
CONTACT DETAILS The Trustees, 14–16 Egerton Gardens Mews, London SW3 2EH

■ The Stoller Charitable Trust

CC NO 285415 **ESTABLISHED** 1982
WHERE FUNDING CAN BE GIVEN The North West, with a preference for Manchester.
WHO CAN BENEFIT Charitable organisations.
WHAT IS FUNDED General charitable purposes including the following: children and young people; healthcare research and cancer relief.
WHAT IS NOT FUNDED Individuals.
RANGE OF GRANTS Mostly up to £20,000 with the occasional larger grant.
SAMPLE GRANTS Cancer Biomarker Sciences Centre (£5 million); Kingfisher Learning Trust (£450,000); Manchester Foundation Trust Charity (£200,000); Royal Northern College of Music (£25,000); Mayor's Appeal Fund (£10,000).
FINANCES *Financial year end 05/04/2022*
Income £1,320,000
Grants to organisations £6,340,000
Assets £10,240,000
TRUSTEES Roger Gould; KSL Trustees Ltd; Sir Norman Stoller; Richard Parkinson; Andrew Dixon.
HOW TO APPLY Apply in writing to the correspondent.
CONTACT DETAILS The Trustees, 24 Low Crompton Road, Royton, Oldham, Lancashire OL2 6YR *Tel.* 07902 857648 *Email* enquiries@ stollercharitabletrust.co.uk

■ The Stone Family Foundation

CC NO 1164682   **ESTABLISHED** 2005
WHERE FUNDING CAN BE GIVEN UK and overseas.
WHO CAN BENEFIT Charitable organisations.
WHAT IS FUNDED Mental health and disadvantaged young people in the UK; water and sanitation in sub-Saharan Africa and South-East Asia.
TYPE OF GRANT Core costs; development funding; project funding.
SAMPLE GRANTS 1001Fontaines (£775,300); Safe Water Network (£394,000); Hillside Clubhouse (£134,000); Beat (£144,600); Place2Be (£104,500); Bipolar UK (£55,000); On Purpose Careers (£50,000); Youth Moves (£35,000); Container-Based Sanitation Alliance (£14,000); SandONE (£2,800).
FINANCES *Financial year end* 31/12/2021
Income £8,410,000
Grants to organisations £5,150,000
Assets £50,030,000
TRUSTEES Charles Edwards; David Steinegger; John Stone.
OTHER INFORMATION In 2021, £2.34 million was awarded to organisations in the UK.
HOW TO APPLY The foundation does not accept unsolicited applications.
CONTACT DETAILS The Trustees, 201 Borough High Street, London SE1 1JA *Email* SFF@thinkNPC.org *Website* www.thesff.com

■ The Stoneygate Trust

CC NO 1119976   **ESTABLISHED** 2007
WHERE FUNDING CAN BE GIVEN UK.
WHO CAN BENEFIT Charities; universities; medical research institutions.
WHAT IS FUNDED Medical research, health, social welfare and education.
TYPE OF GRANT Research; project costs.
RANGE OF GRANTS Typically up to £100,000.
SAMPLE GRANTS Kidney Research UK (£954,200); LOROS (£264,700); University of Cambridge (£200,000); University of Nottingham (£111,000); King's College London (£75,800); University of Manchester (£42,500); Royal College of Psychiatrists (£26,100); Oxford Brookes University (£5,000).
FINANCES *Financial year end* 05/04/2022
Income £3,870,000
Grants to organisations £3,180,000
Assets £10,270,000
TRUSTEES Lady Nadine Adderley; Andrew Walden; Sir William Adderley; Timothy Slade.
OTHER INFORMATION Forty grants were given to organisations during 2021/22, primarily to universities and research institutions.
HOW TO APPLY Apply in writing to the correspondent.
CONTACT DETAILS The Trustees, Two Marlborough Court, Watermead Business Park, Syston, Leicestershire LE7 1AD *Tel.* 0116 296 2323 *Email* info@stoneygatetrust.org *Website* www.stoneygatetrust.org

■ The Samuel Storey Family Charitable Trust

CC NO 267684   **ESTABLISHED** 1974
WHERE FUNDING CAN BE GIVEN UK.
WHO CAN BENEFIT Charitable organisations.
WHAT IS FUNDED General charitable purposes.
WHAT IS NOT FUNDED Individuals.
RANGE OF GRANTS Mostly under £3,000.
SAMPLE GRANTS Winchester College (£17,300); Hope and Homes for Children (£10,100); All Saints' Church – Settrington (£4,000); Mid

Mediation and Counselling Ltd (£3,000); York Minster Fund (£2,000); Beverley Cherry Tree Community Centre (£600); ABF The Soldiers' Charity (£250); YoungMinds (£50).
FINANCES *Financial year end* 05/04/2022
Income £232,700
Grants to organisations £141,800
Assets £8,670,000
TRUSTEES Wren Abrahall; Kenelm Storey; Elisabeth Critchley; Melissa Stourton.
HOW TO APPLY Apply in writing to the correspondent.
CONTACT DETAILS The Trustees, c/o 33 Queen Anne Street, London W1G 9HY *Tel.* 020 7802 2700

■ Peter Stormonth Darling Charitable Trust

CC NO 1049946   **ESTABLISHED** 1995
WHERE FUNDING CAN BE GIVEN UK and overseas.
WHO CAN BENEFIT National and local charitable organisations.
WHAT IS FUNDED General charitable purposes, mainly in the following areas: education; health care; heritage; sports facilities.
WHAT IS NOT FUNDED Individuals.
RANGE OF GRANTS Mostly £1,000 to £10,000, with some larger grants.
SAMPLE GRANTS Winchester College (£81,000); St Bartholomew's Heritage (£30,000); Chelsea Academy Foundation, International Spinal Research Trust and London Library (£10,000 each); Hope of the Valley (£7,500); Barry and Martin's Trust and Bath Festivals (£5,000 each); Longlands Care Farm (£4,000); Countess of Brecknock Hospice (£2,500); Bath Mozartfest (£2,000).
FINANCES *Financial year end* 31/12/2021
Income £311,800
Grants to organisations £284,900
Assets £6,890,000
TRUSTEES Dr Elizabeth Cobb; Candis Taylor; Angus Darling; Oliver Cobb; Frederick Rosier.
OTHER INFORMATION During the year, 15 grants were awarded for health care and sporting facilities, 11 grants were awarded for heritage and 6 grants were given for education (32 grants in total).
HOW TO APPLY The trustees have stated that they do not respond to unsolicited applications.
CONTACT DETAILS Satvinder Mann, Administrator, 7 Lansdown Crescent, Bath BA1 5EX *Tel.* 020 7872 7042 *Email* satvinder.maan@soditic.co.uk

■ Peter Storrs Trust

CC NO 313804   **ESTABLISHED** 1970
WHERE FUNDING CAN BE GIVEN UK.
WHO CAN BENEFIT Registered charities.
WHAT IS FUNDED General charitable purposes; further education.
SAMPLE GRANTS A list of beneficiaries was not included in the annual report and accounts.
FINANCES *Financial year end* 05/04/2020
Income £155,600
Grants to organisations £149,000
Assets £2,650,000
TRUSTEES Arthur Curtis; Caroline Blake; Harriet Curtis.
OTHER INFORMATION The 2019/20 accounts were the latest available at the time of writing (May 2023).
HOW TO APPLY Apply in writing to the correspondent.
CONTACT DETAILS The Trustees, c/o Smithfield Accountants LLP, Suite 1, Unit 2, Stansted

Think carefully about every application. Is it justified?

677

Courtyard, Parsonage Road, Takeley, Essex CM22 6PU *Tel.* 020 7253 3757

....

■ Strand Parishes Trust

cc no 1121754   **established** 2007
where funding can be given City of Westminster.
who can benefit Community organisations; individuals.
what is funded Social welfare; education; young people.
what is not funded The trust's website provides a comprehensive eligibility guide.
type of grant Project funding; capital costs; core/revenue costs; start-up costs; matched funding.
range of grants Typically £2,500 to £5,000. Larger grants may be made in exceptional circumstances.
sample grants Avenues Youth Project (£25,000); St John and St Elizabeth Hospice (£12,000); FareShare and Paddington Law Centre (£10,000 each); Pimlico Toy Library (£8,600); Centre for Young Musicians (£8,300); Church Homeless Trust and Westminster Befriend a Family (£5,000 each); St Barnabas Primary School (£3,500).
finances *Financial year end 31/12/2021*
Income £242,600
Grants to organisations £221,800
Grants to individuals £10,900
Assets £7,820,000
trustees Jane Ker-Reid; Peter Maplestone; Margery Roberts; Julie Thomas; Mary Foster; The Revd Peter Babington; Akua Kyei-Mensah; Charles Spanton; Prof. Frank Keating; Christina Munday; Janet Crabtree.
other information The trust makes an annual grant to St Mary le Strand Church (£16,400 in 2021).
how to apply Application forms can be downloaded from the trust's website. A copy of your organisation's latest annual report and accounts and budget for the current year are requested as supporting information. Applications will be considered at the following trust board meeting (the trust's website states that the board meets in March, July and November). Following submission, representatives may meet with applicants for more in-depth discussion of the proposal.
contact details Roy Sully, Clerk to the Trustees, 169 Strand, London WC2R 2LS *Tel.* 020 7848 4275 *Email* sptwestminster@aol.com *Website* www.strandparishestrust.org.uk

....

■ The Strangward Trust

cc no 1036494   **established** 1993
where funding can be given East Anglia with a preference for Bedfordshire, Cambridgeshire and Northamptonshire.
who can benefit Charitable organisations.
what is funded The care and treatment of people with physical or mental disabilities.
range of grants Mostly under £5,000.
sample grants Rowan Humberstone (£5,000); Cambridgeshire Deaf Association (£4,000); Arthur Rank Hospice Charity (£2,500); Assist Trust (£2,000); Brainwave (£1,000).
finances *Financial year end 05/04/2022*
Income £241,500
Grants to organisations £120,600
Assets £10,750,000
trustees Ross Jones; Anne Allured; Paul Goakes; Clare O'Callaghan.

how to apply Application forms are available from the correspondent. A copy of your latest accounts (if relevant) and any other supporting documentation (e.g. copies of estimates, medical reports, etc.) should also be included. The trustees meet twice a year (March and September) to decide upon donations. Applications should be submitted by the end of February and August. The trustees will consider every application submitted to them that meets the criteria of the trust. It is important that applications on behalf of national charities identify a specific need for funding in the geographic area referred to above.
contact details The Trustees, Glebe House, Catworth, Huntingdon, Cambridgeshire PE28 0PA *Tel.* 01832 710230 *Email* strangwardtrust2@aol.com

....

■ Stratford-upon-Avon Town Trust

cc no 1088521   **established** 2001
where funding can be given Stratford-upon-Avon.
who can benefit Registered charities; community groups; CICs (limited by guarantee); schools; amateur sports clubs; hospitals; hospices; religious bodies/institutions.
what is funded Social welfare; health; education; recreation; Christianity; community development.
what is not funded Retrospective costs/activities.
type of grant Capital costs; core/revenue costs; project funding.
range of grants Up to £100,000.
sample grants Play House (£100,000); Citizens Advice South Warwickshire (£63,000); Stratford Toolshed (£25,000); The Parenting Project (£20,400); Street Arts Project (£10,000); TDC Stratford Youth Theatre (£6,300); Jubilee Club, National Childbirth Trust and Shottery United Football Club (£1,000 each); 1st Tiddington Scout Group (£900).
finances *Financial year end 31/12/2021*
Income £1,780,000
Grants to organisations £1,360,000
Assets £4,090,000
trustees Tony Jackson; Mark Tailby; Simon Littlejohns; Marion Homer; Jonathan Smith; Michael Rolfe; Dr Henry Lu; Timothy Bailey; Gillian Cleeve; Cllr Elizabeth Coles; Josephine Stevens.
other information Grants were awarded in the following categories: social welfare (£233,700); education (£184,400); recreation (£134,900); citizenship (£20,300); civic pride (£7,200); other (£2,400). The trust also made grants to two organisations (Entrust Care Partnership and Spring Housing) as part of its multi-year grant commitments. As well as its discretionary grant-giving, the trust is also required to make grants to the following: King Edward VI School, The Vicar of Holy Trinity Church and The Almshouses in Church Street.
how to apply Application forms and guidance for each grants programme are available on the trust's website. Questions regarding applications can be directed to the trust's Grants Team.
contact details James McHugh, Grants Team, 14 Rother Street, Stratford-upon-Avon, Warwickshire CV32 6LU *Tel.* 01789 207111 *Email* james.mchugh@stratfordtowntrust.co.uk *Website* www.stratfordtowntrust.co.uk

■ The W. O. Street Charitable Foundation

CC NO 267127   **ESTABLISHED** 1973

WHERE FUNDING CAN BE GIVEN UK, with a preference for Lancashire and Jersey.

WHO CAN BENEFIT For the W. O. Street Transformation Funds: constituted groups (including community groups, voluntary organisations, charities, CICs and social enterprises) with an annual income under £250,000.

WHAT IS FUNDED Education; relief of poverty; social and family welfare; illness and disability (particularly blindness); older people; children and young people; projects that can demonstrate engagement of the wider community.

WHAT IS NOT FUNDED Individuals. See the website for exclusion criteria for the W. O. Street Transformation Funds.

TYPE OF GRANT Development funding; project funding.

RANGE OF GRANTS Mostly up to £5,000.

SAMPLE GRANTS Community Foundations for Lancashire and Merseyside (£50,000); W. O. Street Jersey Charitable Trust (£40,000); Alex The Leukodystrophy Charity, The No Way Trust and Ulverston Inshore Rescue (£5,000 each); Manchester Cares (£3,500); Muma Nurture (£2,500); Walking with the Wounded (£1,500).

FINANCES *Financial year end* 31/12/2021
Income £323,200
Grants to organisations £422,100
Assets £22,270,000

TRUSTEES Chris Priestley; Zedra Trust Company (UK) Ltd.

OTHER INFORMATION Educational bursaries totalled £31,200. In 2011 the foundation established three W. O. Street Transformation Funds, which are administered by Forever Manchester (for Greater Manchester grants), the Community Foundation for Lancashire (for Lancashire grants) and the Community Foundation for Merseyside (for Merseyside grants). See the relevant website for the further information.

HOW TO APPLY Application forms are available from the correspondent. The foundation's 2021 accounts state: 'Applications are invited to Zedra Trust Company (UK) Ltd and an application form will be furnished for completion and subsequent consideration by the Trustees.' Applications to the W. O. Street Transformation Fund can be made via the Community Foundation for Lancashire website or the Community Foundation for Merseyside website.

CONTACT DETAILS The Trustees, c/o Zedra UK Trusts, Booths Hall, Booths Park 3, Chelford Road, Knutsford WA16 8GS *Tel.* 01565 748787 *Email* charities@zedra.com *Website* https://lancsfoundation.org.uk/funds/the-wo-street-transformation-fund

■ The Street Foundation

CC NO 1045229   **ESTABLISHED** 1995

WHERE FUNDING CAN BE GIVEN UK and overseas.

WHO CAN BENEFIT Registered charities; not-for-profit organisations.

WHAT IS FUNDED Children and young people with disabilities; social welfare; education; community development; human rights; advancement of religion.

RANGE OF GRANTS Up to £150,000.

SAMPLE GRANTS The New Culture Forum (£150,000); Civitas (£107,100); St Michael's Restoration Fund (£53,800); The Global Warming Policy Foundation (£50,000); The Natural History Museum (£42,000); Oxford University Museum of Natural History (£31,400); The Centre for Social Justice (£30,000); The Maggie Oliver Foundation (£20,000); Lower Teme Valley PCC (£18,700); Institute of Economic Affairs (£15,000).

FINANCES *Financial year end* 31/03/2022
Income £500,000
Grants to organisations £540,500
Assets £413,400

TRUSTEES Sarah Sharp-Smith; Susan Smith; Richard Smith; Lucinda Sharp-Smith.

OTHER INFORMATION Grants were broken down as follows: education (£426,000); human rights (£20,000); community (£88,500); disability (£5,000); poverty (£1,000). Other grants awarded totalled £22,500.

HOW TO APPLY Apply in writing to the correspondent.

CONTACT DETAILS The Trustees, Kingsland House, Kingsland, Leominster, Herefordshire HR6 9SG *Tel.* 01568 708744

■ Streetsmart – Action for the Homeless

CC NO 1071657   **ESTABLISHED** 1998

WHERE FUNDING CAN BE GIVEN UK. Grants are made to charities in the cities in which the Streetsmart campaign runs. A list is available on the charity's website.

WHO CAN BENEFIT Registered UK charities.

WHAT IS FUNDED Homelessness; employability; mental health and well-being. Projects that are aimed at getting people off the streets and 'onto their feet again'.

TYPE OF GRANT Project funding; capital costs.

SAMPLE GRANTS LandAid (£137,800); Centerpoint (£10,000); YMCA Cornwall (£3,000); Caritas Manchester (£2,000); Manna House – Cheshire (£1,500).

FINANCES *Financial year end* 31/05/2021
Income £362,000
Grants to organisations £242,000
Assets £274,900

TRUSTEES Rosie Boycott; William Sieghart; Mary Sturridge; Nicholas Emley.

OTHER INFORMATION The 2020/21 accounts were the latest available at the time of writing (June 2023).

HOW TO APPLY Applicants must submit their applications in writing during December.

CONTACT DETAILS Glenn Pougnet, Director, 1 St John's Lane, London EC1M 4BL *Tel.* 020 7292 5615 *Email* glenn.pougnet@streetsmart.org.uk *Website* www.streetsmart.org.uk

■ Suffolk Community Foundation

CC NO 1109453   **ESTABLISHED** 2005

WHERE FUNDING CAN BE GIVEN Suffolk.

WHO CAN BENEFIT Small and medium-sized registered charities; voluntary and community groups. Some funds are open to social enterprises and CICs.

WHAT IS FUNDED General charitable purposes, including: health and well-being; education; older people; children and young people; community safety; families; social welfare.

WHAT IS NOT FUNDED See the 'Guidelines and Policies' page of the website for a list of general exclusions. Each funding programme has further specific exclusions.

TYPE OF GRANT Core costs; project costs; one-off; capital costs.

RANGE OF GRANTS £100 to £225,000.

SAMPLE GRANTS A list of beneficiaries was not included in the annual report and accounts. Previous beneficiaries have included: Green Light Trust (£225,000); The Befriending Scheme (£180,000); BSC Multicultural Services (£69,900); Ipswich and District Citizens Advice (£35,000); Musicians' Union (£20,000); Woodbridge Town Council (£5,000); East Anglia's Children's Hospices (£2,000); Lighthouse Women's Aid (£1,000); Capel Parish Nurses (£500).

FINANCES *Financial year end* 30/06/2022
Income £6,390,000
Grants to organisations £4,870,000
Assets £23,670,000

TRUSTEES Terence Ward; Jonathan Agar; Neil Walmsley; Selina Hopkins; Peter Newnham; Susan Gull; William Kendall; George Vestey; Jordan Holder; Jane Millar; Gareth Wilson.

OTHER INFORMATION This is one of the 47 UK community foundations, which distribute funding for a wide range of purposes. As with all community foundations, there are a number of donor-advised funds managed on behalf of individuals, families and charitable trusts. Grant schemes tend to change frequently – consult the foundation's website for details of current programmes and up-to-date deadlines.

HOW TO APPLY The foundation's website has details of the grant schemes currently being administered and how to apply.

CONTACT DETAILS Grants Team, The Old Barns, Peninsula Business Centre, Wherstead, Ipswich, Suffolk IP9 2BB *Tel.* 01473 602602 *Email* info@suffolkcf.org.uk *Website* http://suffolkcf.org.uk

■ The Suffolk Historic Churches Trust

CC NO 267047   **ESTABLISHED** 1973

WHERE FUNDING CAN BE GIVEN Suffolk.

WHO CAN BENEFIT Churches and chapels which are in regular use as a place of worship.

WHAT IS FUNDED The preservation, repair, maintenance, restoration and improvement of churches.

WHAT IS NOT FUNDED Furnishings and fittings; brasses and bells; monuments; organs; redecoration (unless needed as part of an eligible project); new buildings or extensions to existing buildings.

TYPE OF GRANT Project costs; capital costs.

RANGE OF GRANTS £300 to £10,000.

SAMPLE GRANTS A list of beneficiaries was not included in the annual report and accounts. Previous beneficiaries have included: St John the Baptist – Needham Market (£10,000); St Mary – Bacton (£8,000); St Michael's – Beccles (£3,000); Felixstowe Methodist Church (£2,000); St Mary – Raydon (£500).

FINANCES *Financial year end* 05/04/2021
Income £326,000
Grants to organisations £108,900
Assets £981,300

TRUSTEES Geoffrey Probert; Loudon Greenlees; Arthur Norman; Simon Ronan; Rachel Sloane; Mary Luxmoore-Styles; David Gould; The Revd Anthony Redman; John Devaux; David King; Nicholas Pearson; Richard Bland; The Hon. Charles Boscawen; Christopher Spicer; Celia Stephens.

OTHER INFORMATION The 2020/21 accounts were the latest available to view at the time of writing (June 2023).

HOW TO APPLY Application forms can be downloaded from the trust's website. Grants committee meetings are held four times a year and deadlines for applications are posted on the trust's website.

CONTACT DETAILS Grants Secretary, Brinkleys, Hall Street, Long Melford, Suffolk CO10 9JR *Tel.* 01787 883884 *Email* shct@btconnect.com *Website* www.shct.org.uk

■ The Summerfield Charitable Trust

CC NO 802493   **ESTABLISHED** 1989

WHERE FUNDING CAN BE GIVEN Gloucestershire.

WHO CAN BENEFIT Registered charities; community groups; not-for-profit limited companies; voluntary groups; CICs.

WHAT IS FUNDED The arts; museums and built heritage; the environment; community projects; education; sport and recreation; social welfare.

WHAT IS NOT FUNDED Medical research; private education; animal welfare; trips abroad; retrospective projects; individuals; churches; charities which have already received a grant in the last two years. The trust is unlikely to support building projects.

TYPE OF GRANT Capital costs; seed funding; start-up funding; unrestricted funding.

RANGE OF GRANTS Typically under £10,000.

SAMPLE GRANTS A list of beneficiaries was not included in the annual report and accounts. Previous beneficiaries have included: Scrubditch Care Farm (£20,000); Art Couture Festival Ltd (£10,000); Cirencester Foodbank (£8,500); Court Barn Museum, Kempsford Village Hall and Make Believe CIC (£5,000 each); Contact the Elderly (£3,000); Future Trees Trust (£2,000); Charlton Kings Cricket Club (£1,000); Birdlip School PTA (£550).

FINANCES *Financial year end* 31/12/2021
Income £321,900
Grants to organisations £254,500
Assets £11,720,000

TRUSTEES Katrina Beach; Vanessa Arbuthnott; David Owen; Roger Mortlock; Antonia Shield.

OTHER INFORMATION Grants were made to 33 organisations during the year and distributed as follows: disadvantaged and vulnerable sectors (£213,000); the environment and natural heritage (£20,100); education, sport and recreation (£15,300); art, museums and built heritage (£6,200).

HOW TO APPLY Applications should be made using the trust's online application form.

CONTACT DETAILS The Trustees, PO Box 287, Cirencester, Gloucestershire GL7 9FB *Tel.* 01285 721211 *Email* admin@summerfield.org.uk *Website* www.summerfield.org.uk

■ The Bernard Sunley Foundation

CC NO 1109099   **ESTABLISHED** 1960

WHERE FUNDING CAN BE GIVEN England and Wales.

WHO CAN BENEFIT Registered charities; exempt charities; schools; hospices; religious bodies/institutions.

WHAT IS FUNDED The foundation's funding themes are community, education, health and social welfare.

WHAT IS NOT FUNDED A full list of exclusions is available on the foundation's website. It includes, but is not limited to: individuals; charities registered outside England or Wales or with an income over £10 million; core costs;

NHS hospitals or mainstream schools, colleges or universities; project costs of under £5,000 or over £5 million.

TYPE OF GRANT Capital costs; core funding.

RANGE OF GRANTS Programme dependent but typically up to £20,000.

SAMPLE GRANTS Country Trust (£100,000); Brecon Mountain Rescue Team (£75,000); The Exodus Project (£60,000); Rackets Cubed (£30,000); Emmaus Brighton and Hove (£20,000); The Forge Project (£10,000); Neighbours in Poplar (£5,000); Hawk Conservancy Trust (£100).

FINANCES *Financial year end* 31/03/2022
Income £2,720,000
Grants to organisations £3,280,000
Assets £160,920,000

TRUSTEES Anabel Knight; Dr Brian Martin; Bella Sunley; William Tice; Inigo Paternina; Lucy Evans.

OTHER INFORMATION During 2021/22 the foundation made 367 grants, which were distributed as follows: community (£2.12 million); education (£1.01 million); health (£607,000); social welfare (£545,000).

HOW TO APPLY The foundation invites applicants to discuss their project before applying. Applicants must undertake an online eligibility check before completing the online application form. There are no deadlines and the application process may take up to six months.

CONTACT DETAILS The Trustees, Green Park House, 15 Stratton Street, Mayfair, London W1J 8LQ *Tel.* 020 3036 0090 *Email* office@bernardsunley.org *Website* www.bernardsunley.org

....

■ The Sunrise Foundation CIO

CC NO 1172756   **ESTABLISHED** 2017

WHERE FUNDING CAN BE GIVEN UK, with a preference for Bristol; Peru.

WHO CAN BENEFIT Registered and unregistered charities; co-operatives; friendly societies; industrial and provident societies; not-for-profit companies; not-for-profit unincorporated associations; educational establishments; health bodies (including NHS hospital trusts, clinical commissioning groups and foundation hospitals).

WHAT IS FUNDED Health; social welfare.

WHAT IS NOT FUNDED General appeals or circulars; religious activity which is not for wider public benefit; public bodies to carry out their statutory obligations; activities which solely support animal welfare; activities which have already taken place; grant-making by other organisations; privately owned and profit-distributing companies or limited partnerships.

TYPE OF GRANT Project costs; salaries; unrestricted core costs; start-up costs for CICs.

SAMPLE GRANTS A list of beneficiaries was not included in the annual report and accounts. Previous beneficiaries have included: Asociación Yanapasun – Peru (£50,000); Caring in Bristol and Changes Bristol (£25,000 each); Newlife – Cannock (£23,500); Kids – Bristol (£15,400).

FINANCES *Financial year end* 30/06/2022
Income £149,600
Grants to organisations £241,900
Assets £1,360,000

TRUSTEES Maggie Glastonbury; Bryan Glastonbury; Paul Salmons; Sophie Brooke; Ben Glastonbury; Marta Glastonbury.

HOW TO APPLY Expressions of interest can be submitted by email or post. Full details of the application process can be found on the charity's website.

CONTACT DETAILS The Trustee, 8 Grange Road, Clifton, Bristol BS8 4EA *Tel.* 07950 809012 *Email* info@sunrisefoundation.org.uk *Website* http://sunrisefoundation.org.uk

....

■ Surgo Foundation UK Ltd

CC NO 1157510   **ESTABLISHED** 2014

WHERE FUNDING CAN BE GIVEN UK and the USA.

WHO CAN BENEFIT Charitable organisations; universities.

WHAT IS FUNDED Health care; education.

TYPE OF GRANT Project funding.

RANGE OF GRANTS Up to around £4 million.

SAMPLE GRANTS Surgo Ventures Inc. (£4.2 million); Harvard University (£81,400); Upstream Inc. (£20,300); Rare Village Foundation (£1,200).

FINANCES *Financial year end* 31/12/2021
Income £10,700,000
Grants to organisations £4,710,000
Assets £71,930,000

TRUSTEES Mala Gaonkar; Emmanuel Roman; Oliver Haarman; Malcolm Gladwell.

OTHER INFORMATION Grants were made to ten organisations during the year.

HOW TO APPLY Apply in writing to the correspondent.

CONTACT DETAILS The Trustees, c/o Withers LLP, Third Floor, 20 Old Bailey, London EC4M 7AN *Tel.* 020 7597 6000

....

■ Community Foundation for Surrey

CC NO 1111600   **ESTABLISHED** 2005

WHERE FUNDING CAN BE GIVEN Surrey.

WHO CAN BENEFIT Registered charities; unregistered charities; hospices; social enterprises; schools; CICs; PTAs; individuals.

WHAT IS FUNDED General charitable purposes including: health and well-being; arts, culture and heritage; education and employability; community cohesion; isolation and disadvantage; the environment and public spaces.

WHAT IS NOT FUNDED Visit the community foundation's website for a detailed list of exclusions.

TYPE OF GRANT Core/revenue costs; capital costs; project funding; seed funding/start-up funding.

RANGE OF GRANTS The average size grant to organisations was £6,200.

SAMPLE GRANTS Surrey Minority Ethnic Forum (£24,500); Age Concern – Mole Valley (£20,000); Merstham Mix Community Cafe and South West Surrey Domestic Abuse Outreach Service (£10,000 each); Love Me Love My Mind – Epsom (£4,000).

FINANCES *Financial year end* 31/03/2022
Income £3,300,000
Grants to organisations £2,710,000
Grants to individuals £42,800
Assets £13,090,000

TRUSTEES Julie Llewelyn; Peter Cluff; Emma Walker; Paul Downes; Holly Murnieks; Elaine Tisdall; William Dawson; Vibhaker Baxi; Sir Denis O'Connor; Carolyn Rich; Neelam Devesher.

OTHER INFORMATION This is one of the 47 UK community foundations, which distribute funding for a wide range of purposes. As with all community foundations, there are a number of donor-advised funds managed on behalf of individuals, families and charitable trusts. Grant schemes tend to change frequently – consult the foundation's website for details of current programmes and up-to-date deadlines. During

Think carefully about every application. Is it justified?

681

the year, grants were awarded to 106 individuals.

HOW TO APPLY Potential applicants are advised to visit the community foundation's website or contact its grants team to find the most suitable funding stream.

CONTACT DETAILS Grants Team, Suite 3, 1st Floor, Cleary Court, 169 Church Street, East Woking, Surrey GU21 6HJ *Tel.* 01483 478092 *Email* info@cfsurrey.org.uk *Website* www.cfsurrey.org.uk

■ The Sussex Community Foundation

CC NO 1113226 **ESTABLISHED** 2006

WHERE FUNDING CAN BE GIVEN East Sussex, West Sussex or Brighton and Hove.

WHO CAN BENEFIT Registered charities; CICs; social enterprises; PTAs; amateur sports clubs; hospices; individuals. There is a preference for supporting grassroots charities and community groups.

WHAT IS FUNDED General charitable purposes.

WHAT IS NOT FUNDED See the foundation's website for a detailed list of exclusions.

TYPE OF GRANT Capital costs; core costs; revenue costs; seed funding; start-up funding; project funding; unrestricted funding.

RANGE OF GRANTS Mostly up to £5,000; occasionally larger grants.

SAMPLE GRANTS Bognor Rugby Football Club (£59,000); Eastbourne Citizens Advice (£30,000); Carers Support Selsey and Free Shop Crawley (£20,000 each); South Downs National Park Trust (£12,500); Bognor Regis Foodbank, Breadwinners and Chichester District Foodbank (£10,000 each).

FINANCES *Financial year end* 31/03/2022
Income £4,380,000
Grants to organisations £4,260,000
Assets £28,200,000

TRUSTEES Pamela Stiles; Dr Margaret Burgess; His Honour Keith Hollis; Julia Carrette; Mark Spofforth; Martin Roberts; Patrick Stevens; David Hill; Brian Mills; Andrew Baird; Corinne Day; Mebrak Ghebreweldi; Guy Davison.

OTHER INFORMATION This is one of the 47 UK community foundations, which distribute funding for a wide range of purposes. As with all community foundations, there are a number of donor-advised funds managed on behalf of individuals, families and charitable trusts. Grant schemes tend to change frequently – consult the foundation's website for details of current programmes and up-to-date deadlines. Note that the grant total also includes grants made to individuals; we were unable to determine a breakdown.

HOW TO APPLY Applications should be made using the online application process, after checking the guidelines, eligibility criteria and deadlines for the relevant fund. Alternatively, email or call the office for a copy of the application form.

CONTACT DETAILS The Trustees, 15 Western Road, Lewes, East Sussex BN7 1RL *Tel.* 01273 409440 *Email* grants@sussexgiving.org.uk *Website* www.sussexgiving.org.uk

■ Sabina Sutherland Charitable Trust

CC NO 1163074 **ESTABLISHED** 2015

WHERE FUNDING CAN BE GIVEN Mostly in the UK; some overseas.

WHO CAN BENEFIT Charitable organisations; individuals.

WHAT IS FUNDED Religion; arts, culture, heritage and science; the environment and conservation; the prevention or relief of poverty; work outside the UK; general charitable purposes.

TYPE OF GRANT General funding; project funding.

RANGE OF GRANTS Up to £5,000.

SAMPLE GRANTS St Andrew's Church – Kettering, St John – Clevedon, and St Peter and St Paul – Wincanton (£5,000 each); Painshill Park Trust, St James the Less – Bethnal Green and St Peter – Ealing (£2,500 each); Bluecoat 'Out of the Blue' Project, Forest of Avon Trust and Village Water (£1,000 each); Clothing Solutions for Disabled People, English Symphony Orchestra and Young and Free (£500 each); Art Foundation (£110).

FINANCES *Financial year end* 30/06/2022
Income £32,600
Grants to organisations £105,300
Assets £897,400

TRUSTEES Julia Elton; Sophie Shepherd; Dr Peter Durrant.

OTHER INFORMATION Grants were broken down as follows: advancement of the arts, heritage or science (£59,100); relief or prevention of poverty (£35,200); the environment (£4,500); general charitable purposes (£4,500); religion (£2,000).

HOW TO APPLY Apply in writing to the correspondent.

CONTACT DETAILS The Trustees, 84 Beech Lane, Earley, Reading, Berkshire RG6 5QE *Tel.* 07940 266478

■ Sutton Coldfield Charitable Trust

CC NO 218627 **ESTABLISHED** 1528

WHERE FUNDING CAN BE GIVEN The former borough of Sutton Coldfield, comprising four electoral wards: New Hall, Four Oaks, Trinity and almost all of Vesey ward.

WHO CAN BENEFIT Organisations benefitting local residents; individuals.

WHAT IS FUNDED General charitable purposes including: social welfare; education; the arts, culture, heritage and science; religion; health; community development; amateur sport; environmental protection.

WHAT IS NOT FUNDED No awards are given to individuals or organisations outside the area of benefit, unless the organisations are providing essential services in the area.

TYPE OF GRANT Project funding.

SAMPLE GRANTS St Giles Hospice (£92,300); Wylde Green Primary School (£90,000 in two grants); Whitehouse Common Primary School (£45,000); Holy Trinity Parish Church (£43,500); Salus Fatigue Foundation (£35,000); Sutton Coldfield Methodist Church Centre (£33,700); Sutton Coldfield Community Games (£26,000); Sutton Coldfield Baptist Church (£20,000).

FINANCES *Financial year end* 30/09/2022
Income £1,760,000
Grants to organisations £876,000
Grants to individuals £80,000
Assets £72,230,000

TRUSTEES Andrew Burley; Henrietta Miles; Fahmida Ismail; Cllr David Pears; Cllr Jane Mosson; Cllr. Simon Ward; Jayne Luckett; Dr Francis Murray; Diane Donaldson; Inge Kettner-Wood; Andrew

Morris; Keith Dudley; Dr Stephen Martin; Anthony Andrews.

OTHER INFORMATION During 2021/22, 76 grants were awarded to organisations.

HOW TO APPLY Contact the Grants Manager to make an application or to discuss further details.

CONTACT DETAILS Grants Manager, Lingard House, Fox Hollies Road, Sutton Coldfield, West Midlands B76 2RJ *Tel.* 0121 794 0970 *Email* grantsmanager@suttoncharitabletrust.org *Website* www.suttoncoldfieldcharitabletrust.com

---

■ The Swann-Morton Foundation

CC NO 271925   **ESTABLISHED** 1976

WHERE FUNDING CAN BE GIVEN UK, with a preference for South Yorkshire.

WHO CAN BENEFIT Charitable organisations; hospitals; hospices; individual students; educational institutions; employees or former employees of W. R. Swann and Co. Ltd.

WHAT IS FUNDED Medical and surgical research; education; social welfare; ill health and disability; general charitable purposes.

TYPE OF GRANT Project funding; research; bursaries.

RANGE OF GRANTS Up to £8,000.

SAMPLE GRANTS Burton Street Foundation (£8,500); Bluebell Wood Children's Hospice (£7,300); Sheffield Children's Hospital (£5,500); St Luke's Hospice (£5,400); CBA projects (£3,500); University of Sheffield School of Medicine (£2,000); Whirlow Farm Trust (£1,000).

FINANCES *Financial year end* 30/06/2022
Income £85,000
Grants to organisations £60,800
Grants to individuals £13,500
Assets £109,600

TRUSTEES Judith Gilmour; Michael McGinley; George Rodgers.

OTHER INFORMATION A full list of beneficiaries was not provided in the 2021/22 annual report. 'Other donations' totalled £27,700, which may include grants awarded to individuals.

HOW TO APPLY Apply in writing to the correspondent.

CONTACT DETAILS The Trustees, c/o Swann-Morton Ltd, Owlerton Green, Sheffield, South Yorkshire S6 2BJ *Tel.* 0114 234 4231

■ Swansea and Brecon Diocesan Board of Finance Ltd

CC NO 249810   **ESTABLISHED** 1968

WHERE FUNDING CAN BE GIVEN Diocese of Swansea and Brecon (Neath Port Talbot, Powys and Swansea).

WHO CAN BENEFIT Places of worship and Christian organisations.

WHAT IS FUNDED Promoting Christian values and services for the benefit of the community; providing facilities for public worship; maintenance of church buildings; spiritual, moral and intellectual development.

WHAT IS NOT FUNDED Applications from outside the diocese.

TYPE OF GRANT Seed funding/start-up funding; project funding; development funding; capital costs.

RANGE OF GRANTS Fast-track grants (£100 to £500); small grants (£500 to £1,000); medium grants (£1,000 to £10,000); large grants (over £10,000).

SAMPLE GRANTS A list of beneficiaries was not included in the annual report and accounts.

FINANCES *Financial year end* 31/12/2021
Income £3,690,000
Grants to organisations £665,300
Assets £6,740,000

TRUSTEES Gwyn Lewis; The Ven. Alan Jevons; The Revd Albert Shackerley; The Ven. Jonathan Davies; Sonia Jones; The Rt Revd John Lomas.

OTHER INFORMATION We were unable to determine the charity's total figure for grants to organisations; however, using figures noted in the charity's accounts we have estimated it was around £665,300, broken down as follows: support for parishes (£336,600); other, including church repair, mission grants and so on (£202,300); material grants (£126,400).

HOW TO APPLY Applications are invited for the Mission Fund. Application forms can be downloaded from the charity's website as well as further information on what should be included with the application.

CONTACT DETAILS The Trustees, Diocesan Centre, Cathedral Close, Brecon, Powys LD3 9DP *Tel.* 01874 623716 *Email* diocese.swanbrec@ churchinwales.org.uk *Website* https:// swanseaandbrecon.churchinwales.org.uk/en/ resources/mission-and-transformation-grants

---

■ Swarovski Foundation

CC NO 1153618   **ESTABLISHED** 2012

WHERE FUNDING CAN BE GIVEN Worldwide.

WHO CAN BENEFIT Charitable organisations.

WHAT IS FUNDED Arts and culture; education and training; human rights; the environment.

TYPE OF GRANT Project costs.

SAMPLE GRANTS Central Saint Martins and Fashion Council Germany (£128,700 each); Design Museum and Equal Justice Initiative (£64,300 each); Conservation International and YoungMinds (£42,900 each); Womankind (£17,200); Room to Read (£4,500).

FINANCES *Financial year end* 31/12/2021
Income £1,750,000
Grants to organisations £905,100
Grants to individuals £98,300
Assets £9,400

TRUSTEES Helene von Damm; Marisa Schiestl-Swarovski; Mag Haim-Swarovski; Anouchka Rafail-Vogiatzakis.

OTHER INFORMATION The foundation awarded grants to 17 organisations in 2021.

HOW TO APPLY The foundation does not accept unsolicited grant requests.

CONTACT DETAILS Jakhya Rahmen-Corey, Director, 1st Floor, Building 4 – Chiswick Park, 566 Chiswick High Road, London W4 5YE *Tel.* 020 3640 8310 *Email* foundationoffice@ swarovskifoundation.org *Website* www. swarovskifoundation.org

---

■ The John Swire (1989) Charitable Trust

CC NO 802142   **ESTABLISHED** 1989

WHERE FUNDING CAN BE GIVEN UK.

WHO CAN BENEFIT Charitable organisations, universities, schools.

WHAT IS FUNDED General charitable purposes including: social welfare; health; the environment; arts.

RANGE OF GRANTS From £1,000 to £225,000.

SAMPLE GRANTS Kent Community Foundation (£225,000); Catching Lives (£45,000); Mind (£25,000); New Sussex Opera (£5,000);

University of London (£2,000); St Andrews Church (£1,000).

FINANCES *Financial year end* 31/12/2021
Income £6,030,000
Grants to organisations £2,250,000
Assets £1,930,000

TRUSTEES Mr B. Swire; Mr J. S. Swire; William Leigh-Pemberton.

OTHER INFORMATION The trust is one of the four organisations that make up the Swire Family Charitable Trusts, a group of charities that are managed by the same team as The Swire Charitable Trust (Charity Commission no. 270726).

HOW TO APPLY The 2021 annual report states: 'Although the Trustees make some grants without a formal application, they normally require organisations to submit a request explaining how the funds could be used and what would be achieved.'

CONTACT DETAILS The Trustees, Swire House, 59 Buckingham Gate, London SW1E 6AJ *Tel.* 020 7834 7717 *Email* info@scts.org.uk

----

■ The Swire Charitable Trust

CC NO 270726   **ESTABLISHED** 1975
WHERE FUNDING CAN BE GIVEN UK.
WHO CAN BENEFIT UK-registered charities.
WHAT IS FUNDED General charitable purposes, with a focus on opportunities for disadvantaged and marginalised people (specifically ex-Service people, victims of slavery and trafficking, and children and young people); the environment; heritage; education and training. For further detail on each of these areas, refer to the guidance on the website.
WHAT IS NOT FUNDED See the trust's website for a full list of exclusions to the core funding programmes. The trust's Discretionary Fund is not subject to the same exclusions.
TYPE OF GRANT Unrestricted; project costs; core costs; capital costs; salaries. Mostly for one year, occasionally for up to three years.
RANGE OF GRANTS Up to £40,000.
SAMPLE GRANTS Combat Stress (£40,000); Heritage Crafts Association (£30,000); Mission to Seafarers (£25,000); Chichester Ship Canal Trust (£20,000); E:Merge (£15,200); EP Youth Ltd (£10,000); Cathedral Music Trust (£2,500); Macmillan Cancer Support (£1,000).
FINANCES *Financial year end* 31/12/2021
Income £3,230,000
Grants to organisations £3,500,000
Grants to individuals £469,600
Assets £9,010,000
TRUSTEES Mr B. Swire; Mr J. S. Swire; Samuel Swire; Martha Allfrey; Rupert Hogg.
OTHER INFORMATION Grants were made to 240 organisations in 2021. Only organisations that received grants of over £1,000 were listed as beneficiaries in the trust's accounts. Grants to individuals represent scholarships awarded through universities and colleges affiliated with the trust. Alongside its core programmes, the trust's Discretionary Fund makes donations to charities that fall outside the funding criteria to causes championed by the staff and other stakeholders of John Swire & Sons Ltd.
HOW TO APPLY Applicants should read the guidelines and FAQs on the website first, then complete the eligibility test. If eligible, applications can be made using the online form. Requests for less than £25,000 are considered at monthly meetings, with larger requests being considered quarterly (usually in January, April, July and

October). Applications sent by post or email will not be considered.

CONTACT DETAILS Sarah Irving, Grants Manager, Swire House, 59 Buckingham Gate, London SW1E 6AJ *Tel.* 020 7834 7717 *Email* info@scts.org.uk *Website* www.swirecharitabletrust.org.uk

----

■ The Adrian Swire Charitable Trust

CC NO 800493   **ESTABLISHED** 1988
WHERE FUNDING CAN BE GIVEN Oxfordshire; Wiltshire; Somerset; Dorset.
WHO CAN BENEFIT Charitable organisations; schools and colleges; universities; hospitals; hospices.
WHAT IS FUNDED General charitable purposes including: music education; literacy; people who are disadvantaged; heritage and restoration; maritime and aviation heritage.
TYPE OF GRANT Unrestricted; core/revenue costs; capital costs; salaries.
RANGE OF GRANTS Around £1,000 to £50,000.
SAMPLE GRANTS Royal Trinity Hospice (£60,000); Armonico Consort (£25,000); Action4Youth (£15,000); Diverse Abilities (£10,000); Scottish Opera (£1,500).
FINANCES *Financial year end* 31/12/2021
Income £1,770,000
Grants to organisations £1,570,000
Assets £47,350,000
TRUSTEES Martha Allfrey; Merlin Swire; Lady Judith Swire; Samuel Swire; James Kidner.
OTHER INFORMATION The trust is one of four organisations that make up the Swire Family Charitable Trusts, a group of charities that are managed by the same team as The Swire Charitable Trust (Charity Commission no. 270726).
HOW TO APPLY The trust's 2021 annual accounts state: 'The Trust does not run open funding programmes or encourage unsolicited applications. Most potential grant holders are initially identified by the Trustees.'
CONTACT DETAILS The Trustees, Swire House, 59 Buckingham Gate, London SW1E 6AJ *Email* info@scts.org.uk *Website* www.swirecharitabletrust.org.uk

----

■ The Syder Foundation

CC NO 1119373   **ESTABLISHED** 2007
WHERE FUNDING CAN BE GIVEN The South East, with a preference for Berkshire and the surrounding counties.
WHO CAN BENEFIT Registered charities.
WHAT IS FUNDED General charitable purposes.
WHAT IS NOT FUNDED Animal welfare; research; individuals' education.
TYPE OF GRANT Capital funding is preferred.
RANGE OF GRANTS Programme dependent.
SAMPLE GRANTS A list of beneficiaries was not included in the 2020/21 accounts. Previous beneficiaries have included: Hampshire Medical Fund; National Horseracing Museum; The Prince's Countryside Fund; Salisbury Samaritans; The Wheelyboat Trust; Whitchurch Silk Mill.
FINANCES *Financial year end* 30/09/2021
Income £452,400
Grants to organisations £449,300
Assets £16,980,000
TRUSTEES Timothy Syder; Charlotte Syder.
OTHER INFORMATION Large grants of around £50,000 are awarded to ten or fewer organisations each

year. In addition, around £100,000 each year is awarded in small grants to charities in Berkshire, Hampshire and Wiltshire. Some Surrey, Oxfordshire and Buckinghamshire charities are also supported. National charities are unlikely to be funded. The 2020/21 accounts were the latest available at the time of writing (May 2023).

HOW TO APPLY For large grants the trustees prefer to proactively identify projects of interest; however, the foundation still welcomes contact from projects that fit the criteria (a formal application is not required). Applications for small grants should be no longer than two A4 pages and should include your most recent year's income and expenditure, the cost of raising funds annually and the intended impact of your project. Applications should preferably be emailed to the correspondent, with your latest accounts attached.

CONTACT DETAILS The Trustees, PO Box 6277, Newbury, Berkshire RG14 9PN
Email syderfoundation@gmail.com
Website www.syderfoundation.org

■ The Charles and Elsie Sykes Trust

CC NO 206926   **ESTABLISHED** 1954
WHERE FUNDING CAN BE GIVEN UK-wide for medical grants; Yorkshire for non-medical grants.
WHO CAN BENEFIT Registered charities only.
WHAT IS FUNDED A wide range of general charitable purposes, including: blind and partially sighted people; children and young people; cultural and environmental heritage; deaf or hard of hearing people and individuals with speech impairment; disability; education; medical research; medical welfare; mental health and well-being; older people; overseas aid; the armed forces; social welfare.
WHAT IS NOT FUNDED Individuals; building maintenance projects; projects without either a medical link or link to Yorkshire; recently established charities; applications for overseas work.
RANGE OF GRANTS Mainly under £5,000.
SAMPLE GRANTS Mathsworld UK (£10,000); Ripon Cathedral Music Trust (£7,000); Tang Hall Community Centre (£6,000); Leeds Baby Bank, Rosemere Cancer Foundation and The No Way Trust Ltd (£5,000 each); Woodmeadow Trust (£3,000); The Exodus Project (£2,000); York Hospital Radio (£1,000); Yorkshire Air Ambulance Ltd (£500).
FINANCES *Financial year end* 31/12/2021
Income £564,000
Grants to organisations £370,200
Assets £19,700,000
TRUSTEES R. Barry Kay; John Ward; Sara Buchan; Elaine Morrison; Sean Rushton; David Mead; Dr David Leinhardt.
OTHER INFORMATION A total of 354 applications were received during 2021. The trust has sub-committees to consider both medical and non-medical grants.
HOW TO APPLY Application forms can be downloaded from the website and should be sent by post along with a copy of the latest accounts and annual report and any other relevant information. Further guidance is given on the website. The trustees usually meet in March, June, September and December; applications should be submitted by the last Friday of January, April, July and October respectively.

CONTACT DETAILS Neil Shaw, Secretary, c/o LCF Law Ltd, First Floor, The Exchange, Harrogate, North Yorkshire HG1 1TS   *Tel.* 01423 502211
Email n.shaw@lcf.co.uk (Secretary) or helen. hawley@lcf.co.uk (Administrator) *Website* www. charlesandelsiesykestrust.co.uk

■ The Hugh Symons Charitable Trust

CC NO 1137778   **ESTABLISHED** 2010
WHERE FUNDING CAN BE GIVEN UK and overseas.
WHO CAN BENEFIT Registered charities.
WHAT IS FUNDED Health; social welfare; overseas development; the environment.
RANGE OF GRANTS Up to £200,000.
SAMPLE GRANTS British Red Cross (£200,000); Oxfam (£60,000); Christian Aid (£40,000); International Rescue Committee (£15,000); Lotus Flower Trust and Unicef (£5,000 each), Separated Child (£3,000), Carers Trust (£1,500).
FINANCES *Financial year end* 05/04/2022
Income £305,100
Grants to organisations £535,900
Assets £5,670,000
TRUSTEES Katherine Roper; Geoffrey Roper; Lester Aldridge Trust Company; Pauline Roper.
OTHER INFORMATION Grants were broken down as follows: overseas development and health care (£221,000); overseas health and welfare (£263,900); the environment (£51,000). Only organisations that received grants of over £10,000 were listed as beneficiaries in the charity's accounts. Grants of under £1,000 were awarded to four organisations.
HOW TO APPLY Contact the correspondent for further information.
CONTACT DETAILS The Trustees, Stubhampton House, Stubhampton, Blandford Forum DT11 8JU   *Tel.* 01258 830135

■ The Syncona Foundation

CC NO 1149202   **ESTABLISHED** 2012
WHERE FUNDING CAN BE GIVEN UK.
WHO CAN BENEFIT Registered charities.
WHAT IS FUNDED Medical causes, particularly oncology.
SAMPLE GRANTS The Listening Place (£33,300); Heritage of London Trust (£30,000); Matt Hampson Foundation (£30,000); Business Beats Cancer – Guernsey (£17,000); Trinity College Cambridge (£10,000).
FINANCES *Financial year end* 31/03/2022
Income £2,490,000
Grants to organisations £2,820,000
Assets £2,250,000
TRUSTEES James Maltin; Thomas Henderson; Rupert Adams; Nigel Keen; Lucie Kitchener.
OTHER INFORMATION This is the corporate charity of Syncona Ltd. Grants to core charities totalled £2.61 million and grants to other charities totalled £210,000.
HOW TO APPLY Grantees are chosen by shareholders. Unsolicited applications are unlikely to be successful.
CONTACT DETAILS The Trustees, c/o Couch Bright King and Co., 2 Tolherst Court Turkey Mill, Ashford Road, Kent ME14 5SF   *Tel.* 020 7387 4264   *Email* th@bacit.co.uk *Website* www. syncronaltd.com/about-us/charities

Think carefully about every application. Is it justified?

685

■ The William Syson Foundation

OSCR NO SC049635   **ESTABLISHED** 2012

WHERE FUNDING CAN BE GIVEN UK, with a particular focus on Scotland.

WHO CAN BENEFIT UK-registered charities; Scottish CIOs; public sector organisations and other not-for-profit organisations; individuals.

WHAT IS FUNDED Projects and activities that promote the advancement of the arts, heritage and culture, including those that promote, develop and ensure the practice and enjoyment of the arts, including visual and performing arts, poetry, literature, film-making, music, photography and digital arts.

WHAT IS NOT FUNDED Activities or projects that do not meet the charitable purposes of the foundation; capital development costs; retrospective expenditure; organisations supported by the foundation within the previous 12 months (except for beneficiaries of emergency funding); the promotion of political or religious beliefs; companies limited by shares.

RANGE OF GRANTS Mostly up to £10,000.

SAMPLE GRANTS Milport Town Hall (£28,800); National Theatre of Scotland (£20,000); Sonic Bothy (£16,500); Sistema Scotland (£10,000); East Neuk Festival (£7,500); Eric Liddell Centre (£5,000); Tunnell Trust (£2,000); Tain and District Development Trust (£500).

FINANCES *Financial year end 31/12/2021*
Income £322,800
Grants to organisations £416,300
Grants to individuals £5,600
Assets £14,500,000

TRUSTEES H. Cockburn; J. Holloway; M. Morrison; J. Syson; R. Doyle; I. Arnot; E. Ryder.

OTHER INFORMATION During the year, the foundation awarded grants to 75 organisations.

HOW TO APPLY See the foundation's website for full eligibility criteria and guidance on how to make an application.

CONTACT DETAILS The Trustees, 5 Atholl Crescent, Edinburgh EH3 8EJ *Email* hello@williamsysonfoundation.org.uk *Website* www.williamsysonfoundation.org.uk

■ T. and S. Trust Fund

CC NO 1095939   **ESTABLISHED** 2002

WHERE FUNDING CAN BE GIVEN UK, with a preference for Greater London, Gateshead and Manchester.

WHO CAN BENEFIT Jewish organisations; occasionally individuals.

WHAT IS FUNDED Advancement of the Orthodox Jewish religion and education; relief of poverty.

RANGE OF GRANTS Up to £57,900.

SAMPLE GRANTS Gateshead Kehillo (£10,000); British Friends of Igud Hakollelim, Kolyom Trust and Tomchei Yotzei Angliya (£8,400 each).

FINANCES *Financial year end 31/10/2021*
Income £139,000
Grants to organisations £111,700
Assets £92,400

TRUSTEES Shoshanna Sandler; Aharon Sandler; Vivienne Salomon.

OTHER INFORMATION The 2020/21 annual report and accounts were the latest available to view at the time of writing (June 2023). Grants of under £1,000 totalled £6,800.

HOW TO APPLY Apply in writing to the correspondent.

CONTACT DETAILS S. Sandler, Company Secretary and Trustee, 96 Whitehall Road, Gateshead, Tyne and Wear NE8 4ET *Tel.* 0191 482 5050

■ The T.K. Maxx and Homesense Foundation

CC NO 1162073   **ESTABLISHED** 2015

WHERE FUNDING CAN BE GIVEN UK, in communities local to T.K. Maxx stores.

WHO CAN BENEFIT National and local charities.

WHAT IS FUNDED Helping vulnerable children and young people in local communities achieve their potential.

TYPE OF GRANT Project funding; multi-year grants.

RANGE OF GRANTS up to £180,000.

SAMPLE GRANTS British Red Cross (£180,000); The Prince's Trust (£175,000); Retail Trust (£100,000); Stephen Lawrence Trust (£75,000); Mind (£50,000); School Without Racism (£40,000); Access UK (£35,000).

FINANCES *Financial year end 30/01/2022*
Income £2,240,000
Grants to organisations £1,480,000
Assets £7,480,000

TRUSTEES Deborah Dolce; Erica Farrell; Rachael Barber; Michael Munnelly; Maureen Dunn.

OTHER INFORMATION Formerly known as the TJX UK Foundation, this foundation is the charitable arm of TJX UK. The foundation supports charities that T.K.Maxx and Homesense staff are passionate about. In addition, a significant portion of grants is dedicated to charities supporting racial justice, mental health, disability and the LGBTQ+ community.

HOW TO APPLY Contact the correspondent for further information.

CONTACT DETAILS The Trustees, 73 Clarendon Road, Hertfordshire WD17 1TX *Tel.* 01923 47300 *Email* TJX_Foundation@tjxeurope.com *Website* www.tkmaxx.com/uk/en/tkmaxx-and-homesense-foundation

■ Tabeel Trust

CC NO 266645   **ESTABLISHED** 1974

WHERE FUNDING CAN BE GIVEN Worldwide, with a preference for Clacton (Essex).

WHO CAN BENEFIT Registered charities; religious bodies/institutions.

WHAT IS FUNDED Evangelical Christian charitable purposes, where the trustees have an existing interest.

WHAT IS NOT FUNDED Short-term gap year initiatives.

TYPE OF GRANT Capital costs; seed funding/start-up funding.

RANGE OF GRANTS Up to £20,000.

SAMPLE GRANTS Previous beneficiaries have included: BMS World Mission (£20,000); St Michael's – Paris (£18,000); Tearfund (£15,000); Gurnell Grove Community Trust (£9,000); Selkirk Baptist Church (£5,000); Evangelical Alliance (£4,000); Gideons (£800).

FINANCES *Financial year end 31/10/2021*
Income £22,900
Grants to organisations £84,700

TRUSTEES Douglas Brown; Barbara Carter; Dr Mary Clark; Nigel Davey; James Davey; Jean Richardson; Sarah Taylor; Edward Clark; Helen Hamer.

OTHER INFORMATION We were unable to view the trust's accounts due to its low income. We have therefore estimated its grant total using its total expenditure. The 2020/21 financial information was the latest available to view at the time of writing (June 2023).

HOW TO APPLY According to our previous research, only charities with which a trustee already has contact should apply. Grants are considered at trustees' meetings, which are usually in May and October.

CONTACT DETAILS The Trustees, East Dalcove House, Kelso, Scottish Borders TD5 7PD *Tel.* 01573 460395

■ The Tabhair Charitable Trust

OSCR NO SC043357   **ESTABLISHED** 2012

WHERE FUNDING CAN BE GIVEN UK and Ireland.

WHO CAN BENEFIT Registered charities.

WHAT IS FUNDED Education; training; community action; employability; social welfare.

WHAT IS NOT FUNDED Individuals; general charitable contributions.

TYPE OF GRANT Project funding, core costs.

RANGE OF GRANTS Mostly £500 to £5,000.

SAMPLE GRANTS Regenerate (£10,000); Cairns Counselling, Helm Training, The Larder West Lothian and Youth 2000 Project (£5,000 each); Whitburnlaw Community Resource Centre (£3,200); Smartworks (£3,000); Move On (£2,000).

FINANCES *Financial year end 30/09/2021*
Income £215,200
Grants to organisations £58,200
Assets £1,440,000

OTHER INFORMATION Grants were made to 12 organisations in 2020/21. The 2020/21 accounts were the latest available at the time of writing (June 2023). The trust's website states that it welcomes applications from charities that 'combine support services with enterprising mission to improve social well-being and employment opportunities in the lives of the disengaged and disadvantaged.'

HOW TO APPLY Applications can be made via the trust's website or in writing to the correspondent.

CONTACT DETAILS The Trustees, c/o Chiene and Tait LLP, 61 Dublin Street, Edinburgh EH3 6NL *Website* www.tabhair.org.uk

■ The Ashley Tabor-King Foundation

CC NO 1178634   **ESTABLISHED** 2018
WHERE FUNDING CAN BE GIVEN England and Wales.
WHO CAN BENEFIT Charitable organisations.
WHAT IS FUNDED Organisations and projects supporting first responders who suffer from post-traumatic stress disorder or physical harm associated with their employment; activities which develop young people's skills and enable them to participate in society as mature and responsible individuals.
RANGE OF GRANTS £20,000 to £200,000.
SAMPLE GRANTS The Royal Foundation of The Duke and Duchess of Cambridge (£500,000) and Taigh Mor Foundation (£20,000).
FINANCES *Financial year end 05/04/2022*
Income £500,000
Grants to organisations £520,000
Assets £126,600
TRUSTEES Ashley Tabor; Stephen Miron; The Lord Allen of Kensington; Emma Bradley.
OTHER INFORMATION Grants were awarded to two organisations during the year.
HOW TO APPLY Contact the correspondent for further information.
CONTACT DETAILS The Trustees, c/o Global Media and Entertainment Ltd, 29–30 Leicester Square, London WC2H 7LA *Tel.* 020 7766 6000

■ The Tajtelbaum Charitable Trust

CC NO 273184   **ESTABLISHED** 1974
WHERE FUNDING CAN BE GIVEN UK, with some preference given to London, Gateshead, Leeds, Manchester, Salford and Scotland.
WHO CAN BENEFIT Orthodox Jewish synagogues and educational establishments; care homes; UK-registered charities.
WHAT IS FUNDED Advancement of the Orthodox Jewish religion and education; relief of poverty and ill health.
SAMPLE GRANTS A list of beneficiaries was not included in the annual report and accounts.
FINANCES *Financial year end 05/04/2022*
Income £36,400
Grants to organisations £291,800
Assets £5,900,000
TRUSTEES Emanuel Tajtelbaum; Henry Frydenson; Shoshana Tajtelbaum; Hannah Prager.
HOW TO APPLY Contact the correspondent for further information.
CONTACT DETAILS The Trustees, PO Box 33911, London NW9 7ZX *Tel.* 020 8202 3464

■ The Gay and Keith Talbot Trust

CC NO 1102192   **ESTABLISHED** 2004
WHERE FUNDING CAN BE GIVEN Financially developing countries; UK.
WHO CAN BENEFIT Registered charities.
WHAT IS FUNDED Medical research, currently funding fistula work in particular; humanitarian aid; asylum seekers; general charitable purposes.
TYPE OF GRANT Capital costs; research and development; project funding.
SAMPLE GRANTS A list of beneficiaries was not included in the annual report and accounts.

FINANCES *Financial year end 28/02/2022*
Income £211,700
Grants to organisations £203,600
Assets £170,000
TRUSTEES Keith Talbot; Gay Talbot.
OTHER INFORMATION Grants were distributed in the following areas: fistula work (£79,000); maternity care (£40,000); research and development (£20,000); medical causes (£19,600); asylum seekers (£15,000); COVID-19 (£10,000).
HOW TO APPLY Apply in writing to the correspondent.
CONTACT DETAILS Gay Talbot, Trustee, Fold Howe, Kentmere, Kendal, Cumbria LA8 9JW *Tel.* 01539 821504 *Email* rktalbot@yahoo.co.uk

■ The Talbot Trusts

CC NO 221356   **ESTABLISHED** 1928
WHERE FUNDING CAN BE GIVEN Sheffield and immediate surrounding areas.
WHO CAN BENEFIT Registered charities; CICs; constituted community groups; social workers, GPs and practice nurses (see the trust's annual report for further detail).
WHAT IS FUNDED Health; people with cancer; mental health; disability; older people (social/physical isolation); children and young people; social welfare (including food poverty, domestic violence and homelessness); minority ethnic and refugee communities.
WHAT IS NOT FUNDED Research; educational projects; major fundraising and general appeals; non-registered charities or other organisations; individuals; recurrent grants.
TYPE OF GRANT One-off grants for items, services and facilities (capital and project funding).
RANGE OF GRANTS £500 to £5,000.
SAMPLE GRANTS South Yorkshire Eating Disorders Association (£5,000); Just Works (£4,600); Montgomery Theatre and Arts (£3,800); Speakup Self Advocacy Ltd (£3,500); The Bare Project and Sheffield Aspergers Group (£2,000 each); Sheffield Family Holiday (£1,000); Community Education Adult Disabilities CIC (£750).
FINANCES *Financial year end 31/03/2022*
Income £78,200
Grants to organisations £99,900
Assets £2,170,000
TRUSTEES Dr Zackary McMurray; Melanie Russell; Dr Mike Sawkins; Maria Flude; James Farmer; Sam Caldwell; Shasta Ashraf; Sarah Poulter.
HOW TO APPLY There are different application forms depending on the type of organisation applying. All application forms can be downloaded from the trust's website and should be returned via email. Further information and deadlines are also available on the website. The trustees meet twice a year, usually in July and December, to consider applications.
CONTACT DETAILS Gill Newman, Clerk to the Trustees, 3 Willow Tree Drive, Clowne, Chesterfield, North Derbyshire S43 4UP *Tel.* 07773 660552 *Email* admin@thetalbottrusts.com *Website* http://thetalbottrusts.com

■ The Talbot Village Trust

CC NO 249349   **ESTABLISHED** 1850
WHERE FUNDING CAN BE GIVEN Christchurch; Bournemouth; Poole; East Dorset; Isle of Purbeck.
WHO CAN BENEFIT Registered charities; faith-based organisations; education and properly

constituted not-for-profit organisations; grassroot organisations.

WHAT IS FUNDED Social welfare; local community projects; climate change awareness; mental health support; educational exclusion of children.

WHAT IS NOT FUNDED A full list of exclusions can be found on the trust's website. The trustees will not normally consider an application unless at least 25% of the total amount required has been raised or pledged.

TYPE OF GRANT Capital costs; revenue costs; core costs (only in exceptional circumstances).

RANGE OF GRANTS Recent grants have ranged from £900 to £150,000.

SAMPLE GRANTS Dorset Mental Health Forum (£67,700); 360 Skills for Life (£50,000): Creative Kids (£17,500); Grounded Community (£14,300); Crumbs (£5,000); Southbourne Tennis Club (£2,000); The Bus Stop Club (£1,500); Mudeford Wood Tiny Tots (£450).

FINANCES *Financial year end 31/12/2021*
Income £2,820,000
Grants to organisations £522,000
Assets £74,720,000

TRUSTEES Earl of Shaftesbury; James Fleming; Christopher Lees; George Meyrick; Mary Riall; Cecilia Bufton; Richard Cutler.

OTHER INFORMATION Grants were paid to 32 organisations during the year. A further 37 grants totalling £732,800 were authorised but unpaid.

HOW TO APPLY Applications can be made using the online application form or by post and must include the information specified in the guidelines on the website. The trustees meet twice a year to consider applications and applicants are notified of the outcome within a couple of weeks of a meeting.

CONTACT DETAILS The Trustees, c/o Savills (UK) Ltd, Wessex House, Priors Walk, Wimbourne BH21 1PB *Email* info@talbotvillagetrust.org *Website* www.talbotvillagetrust.org

■ Tallow Chandlers Benevolent Fund No 2

CC NO 246255   **ESTABLISHED** 1966

WHERE FUNDING CAN BE GIVEN London, mainly City of London.

WHO CAN BENEFIT Charitable organisations, schools and universities. There is a preference for charities where a liveryman or freeman is actively involved.

WHAT IS FUNDED Children and young people; education; health and medical research; people with disabilities; social welfare.

WHAT IS NOT FUNDED Large or national charities; charities operating overseas; charities that do not have a connection to London; individuals that apply to the charity directly.

TYPE OF GRANT One-off grants; three-year grants.

RANGE OF GRANTS One-off grants from £250 to £3,000; larger grants up to three years.

SAMPLE GRANTS Cubitt Town Junior School (£57,800); Greig City Academy (£50,000); The Halley Academy (£30,000); Treloar Trust (£15,000); IntoUniversity (£10,000); London Youth Choir (£3,000); Innovations for Learning (£2,000); The Sheriffs' and Recorder's Fund (£1,500).

FINANCES *Financial year end 05/04/2022*
Income £1,030,000
Grants to organisations £866,400
Assets £12,420,000

TRUSTEE The Worshipful Company of Tallow Chandlers.

OTHER INFORMATION In 2021/22, the charity awarded 65 grants to 55 organisations.

HOW TO APPLY Apply in writing to the correspondent, who considers all requests. Details of what to include in an application are available on the charity's website.

CONTACT DETAILS Education and Charity Manager, Tallow Chandlers Hall, 4 Dowgate Hill, London EC4R 2SH *Tel.* 020 7248 4726 *Email* estelle@ tallowchandlers.org *Website* www. tallowchandlers.org

■ The Talmud Torah Machzikei Hadass Trust

CC NO 270693   **ESTABLISHED** 1976

WHERE FUNDING CAN BE GIVEN UK and overseas; in practice, Hackney.

WHO CAN BENEFIT Orthodox Jewish organisations.

WHAT IS FUNDED The Orthodox Jewish religion and education.

RANGE OF GRANTS Up to £389,400.

SAMPLE GRANTS Moreshet Hatorah Ltd (£389,400); Dover Sholem Community Trust (£64,000); Belz Synagogue (£44,900).

FINANCES *Financial year end 31/03/2022*
Income £900,500
Grants to organisations £499,000
Assets £15,240,000

TRUSTEES Jehudah Baumgarten; Yitzchok Sternlicht; Mordechaj Wind.

OTHER INFORMATION Smaller grants totalled £730.

HOW TO APPLY Apply in writing to the correspondent.

CONTACT DETAILS The Trustees, 34 Heathland Road, London N16 5LZ *Tel.* 020 8800 6599

■ Talteg Ltd

CC NO 283253   **ESTABLISHED** 1981

WHERE FUNDING CAN BE GIVEN Worldwide.

WHO CAN BENEFIT Registered charities; Jewish organisations.

WHAT IS FUNDED Social welfare; health; education; the Jewish faith and community.

SAMPLE GRANTS Clive Jay Berkley Foundation and Westleague Ltd (£1 million); Magen David Adom (£40,000); UK Torement (£10,000).

FINANCES *Financial year end 30/06/2022*
Income £1,260,000
Grants to organisations £2,230,000
Assets £509,200

TRUSTEES Adam Berkley; Delia Berkley.

HOW TO APPLY Apply in writing to the correspondent.

CONTACT DETAILS The Trustees, 90 Mitchell Street, Glasgow G1 3NQ *Tel.* 0141 564 5155

■ The Tanlaw Foundation

CC NO 1094181

WHERE FUNDING CAN BE GIVEN UK and overseas.

WHO CAN BENEFIT Health charities; schools; environmental organisations; overseas aid organisations.

WHAT IS FUNDED Health and disability; medical research; overseas aid; the promotion of religion; education; wildlife and the environment; social welfare.

RANGE OF GRANTS £2,500 to £40,000.

SAMPLE GRANTS United World Schools (£100,000); The Trussell Trust (£40,000); Rainbow Trust (£30,000); Cancer Research UK (£20,000);

Think carefully about every application. Is it justified?

689

Borneo Rescue Centre (£10,000); Rokpa Trust (£5,000); Doorstep Library (£3,000).

FINANCES *Financial year end* 31/10/2022
Income £50,700
Grants to organisations £373,500
Assets £6,180,000

TRUSTEES Lady Tanlaw; The Hon. Asia Trotter; The Hon. Brooke Mackay; Lord Tanlaw.

OTHER INFORMATION Grants were made to 20 organisations.

HOW TO APPLY Apply in writing to the correspondent.

CONTACT DETAILS The Trustees, c/o Rathbone Investment Management Ltd, 8 Finsbury Circus, London EC2M 7AZ *Tel.* 020 7399 0134 *Email* Neil.Warman@rathbones.com

■ The David Tannen Charitable Trust

CC NO 280392   **ESTABLISHED** 1974

WHERE FUNDING CAN BE GIVEN Israel and the UK with a preference for Barnet, Hackney and Haringey.

WHO CAN BENEFIT Charitable organisations; schools.

WHAT IS FUNDED The Jewish faith and community; social welfare; education.

RANGE OF GRANTS Up to £55,000.

SAMPLE GRANTS Hendon Adath Yisroel Congregation (£55,000); WST Charity Ltd (£36,000); British Friends of United Hatzola Israel and Hasmonean High School Charitable Trust (£20,000 each); Hatzola Northwest Trust (£18,000); Achisomoch Aid Company Ltd (£16,000).

FINANCES *Financial year end* 30/06/2022
Income £2,630,000
Grants to organisations £319,200
Assets £24,540,000

TRUSTEES David Tannen; Jonathan Miller; Martin Irving Tannen; Daniel Asher Tannen.

OTHER INFORMATION Only grants of over £11,000 were listed in the annual report and accounts. Grants of under £11,000 totalled £154,200.

HOW TO APPLY Apply in writing to the correspondent.

CONTACT DETAILS The Trustees, c/o Sutherland House, 70–78 West Hendon Broadway, London NW9 7BT *Tel.* 020 8202 1066

■ Tanner Trust

CC NO 1021175   **ESTABLISHED** 1993

WHERE FUNDING CAN BE GIVEN UK and overseas, with a preference for the south of England.

WHO CAN BENEFIT Registered charities; hospitals; schools.

WHAT IS FUNDED Conservation and the countryside; youth projects; health; older people and people with disabilities; culture and preservation of buildings; overseas aid.

WHAT IS NOT FUNDED Individuals.

TYPE OF GRANT Development funding; project funding; capital costs.

RANGE OF GRANTS Typically £1,000 to £10,000, with some larger grants.

SAMPLE GRANTS Garden Museum (£60,000); Aberglasney Gardens (£50,000); Cathedral Music Trust and Help Tibet (£10,000 each); Conservation Foundation (£5,000); Mawran PTA (£1,100); Rotary Club of Falmouth Benevolent Fund (£1,000).

FINANCES *Financial year end* 31/03/2021
Income £405,700
Grants to organisations £493,800
Assets £10,890,000

TRUSTEES Alice Williams; Lucie Nottingham.

OTHER INFORMATION In 2020/21, a total of 75 grants were awarded to charitable organisations. The 2020/21 accounts were the latest available at the time of writing (March 2023).

HOW TO APPLY Unsolicited applications are not accepted.

CONTACT DETAILS The Trustees, c/o Blake Morgan LLP, New Kings Court, Tollgate, Chandler's Ford, Eastleigh, Hampshire SO53 3LG *Tel.* 023 9222 1122 *Email* Charity.Admin@blakemorgan.co.uk

■ The Taurus Foundation

CC NO 1128441   **ESTABLISHED** 2009

WHERE FUNDING CAN BE GIVEN UK.

WHO CAN BENEFIT Registered charities.

WHAT IS FUNDED Biodiversity, the environment and conservation; the arts; disadvantaged and marginalised members of society; mental health; domestic animal welfare; Jewish communities.

TYPE OF GRANT Unrestricted funding.

RANGE OF GRANTS £5,000 to £50,000.

SAMPLE GRANTS A list of beneficiaries was not included in the annual report and accounts.

FINANCES *Financial year end* 31/12/2021
Income £30,900
Grants to organisations £495,000
Assets £1,350,000

TRUSTEES Carole Cook; Alan Fenton; Denis Felsenstein; Priscilla Fenton; Antony Forwood; Wendy Pollecoff; Dominic Fenton; Anthony Felsenstein; Katherine Ekers; James Goodman; Charles Vermont.

OTHER INFORMATION Grants were made to 46 organisations during the year.

HOW TO APPLY The foundation does not accept unsolicited applications.

CONTACT DETAILS The Trustees, c/o Forsters LLP, 31 Hill Street, London W1J 5LS *Tel.* 020 7863 8580 *Email* cosmo.peach@taurus-foundation. org.uk *Website* http://taurus-foundation.org.uk

■ Tay Charitable Trust

OSCR NO SC001004   **ESTABLISHED** 1951

WHERE FUNDING CAN BE GIVEN UK, with a focus on Scotland, particularly Dundee and Tayside.

WHO CAN BENEFIT Registered charities in the UK; museums; schools; universities; individuals.

WHAT IS FUNDED General charitable purposes.

RANGE OF GRANTS Mostly up to £5,000 with the occasional larger grant.

SAMPLE GRANTS Grey Lodge Settlement and Scotland's Charity Air Ambulance (£55,000 each); Dundee Design Ltd – V&A, Maggie's Dundee and University of St Andrews (£50,000 each); British Red Cross and Culture and Sport Glasgow – Burrell (£10,000 each); Optimistic Sound and Sannox Christian Centre (£5,000 each); Braemar Castle, Community One Stop Shop and Fight for Sight (£3,000 each); Home-Start Dundee, Living Paintings and Royal British Legion Manufacturing (£2,000 each); Clean Rivers Trust, Epilepsy Scotland and Pittenween Tennis Club (£1,000 each).

FINANCES *Financial year end* 05/04/2022
Income £975,000
Grants to organisations £625,200
Grants to individuals £5,000
Assets £6,720,000

OTHER INFORMATION Only organisations that received grants of over £1,000 were listed as beneficiaries in the trust's 2021/22 accounts. Grants of under £1,000 totalled £4,700 and were awarded to 11 organisations. One individual was supported during this period.

HOW TO APPLY Apply in writing to the correspondent.
CONTACT DETAILS Z. Martin, Trustee, 87 Godstow Road, Wolvercote, Oxford OX2 8PF

....

■ C. B. and H. H. Taylor 1984 Trust

CC NO 291363　　**ESTABLISHED** 1964
WHERE FUNDING CAN BE GIVEN Birmingham and the West Midlands; Ireland; UK-based organisations working overseas. Quaker work is supported regardless of location.
WHO CAN BENEFIT Projects with a defined link to Quaker work; registered charities.
WHAT IS FUNDED Work of the Religious Society of Friends; social welfare including children and young people, older people, people with disabilities, homelessness, women-led initiatives, counselling and mediation and hospice and bereavement services; education including adult literacy schemes, employment training, youth work and mental health education; penal affairs including work with offenders and ex-offenders and their families, police-backed initiatives and youth projects. Aid for humanitarian emergencies is always considered.
WHAT IS NOT FUNDED Individuals; projects or groups outside the trust's geographical focus; general running costs/revenue costs; repeat applications within two years.
TYPE OF GRANT Project funding; development funding.
RANGE OF GRANTS Up to £70,000.
SAMPLE GRANTS Britain Yearly Meeting Of The Religious Society of Friends (£70,000); Quaker Social Action (£32,000); Woodbrooke (£24,000); Family Action (£8,000); The Trussell Trust (£5,000); All We Can (£4,000); Amateur Swimming Association and Youth Together for Higher Education (£1,000 each); Guy's Gift (£500).
FINANCES *Financial year end 05/04/2022*
Income £667,200
Grants to organisations £486,000
Assets £16,830,000
TRUSTEES Elizabeth Birmingham; Robert Birmingham; Clare Norton; Thomas Penny; Constance Penny; Simon Taylor; Camilla Middleton; Hannah Pattison; Lucy Taylor.
OTHER INFORMATION The trust's 2021/22 annual report states that around 60% of grants made are for the work of the Religious Society of Friends.
HOW TO APPLY Applications must be completed using the online form on the trust's website. The trustees usually meet in May and November each year. Upcoming deadlines will be advertised on the trust's website.
CONTACT DETAILS The Trustees, PO Box 282, Aberystwyth SY23 9BZ *Tel.* 07934 338005 *Email* admin@cbandhhtaylortrust.com. *Website* www.cbandhhtaylortrust.com

....

■ Humphrey Richardson Taylor Charitable Trust

CC NO 1062836　　**ESTABLISHED** 1997
WHERE FUNDING CAN BE GIVEN Surrey.
WHO CAN BENEFIT Schools; amateur music organisations; individuals.
WHAT IS FUNDED Music and allied performing arts.
TYPE OF GRANT Capital projects or items (instruments, sheet music, music computers, etc.); one-off grants; scholarships; music tuition; concerts and events; sponsorship.

RANGE OF GRANTS Up to £50,000 but typically between £1,000 and £5,000.
SAMPLE GRANTS Grey Court School (£42,500); Coombe Girls' School (£6,000); Guildford Opera (£5,000); Banstead Arts Festival (£3,000); Epsom Chamber Choir (£1,000); Meath Choir (£500).
FINANCES *Financial year end 31/12/2021*
Income £711,800
Grants to organisations £361,200
Grants to individuals £59,600
Assets £12,410,000
TRUSTEES Ian Catling; Colin Edgerton; William Malings; Michael Wood; Stephen Oliver.
OTHER INFORMATION During the year, grants were awarded in the following categories: schools (£233,600); societies (£69,100); partner organisations (£68,500); individuals (£59,600).
HOW TO APPLY Applications should be made by email to the correspondent. The trustees meet five times a year to consider applications. Applications should be no longer than four to six pages of A4 when printed. Specific application criteria and guidelines for schools, musical societies and individuals are available to view on the website.
CONTACT DETAILS Kate Perry, Administrator, 32 Chipstead Station Parade, Chipstead, Coulsdon, Surrey CR5 3TF *Email* admin@ hrtaylortrust.org.uk *Website* www.hrtaylortrust. org.uk

....

■ The Taylor Family Foundation

CC NO 1118032　　**ESTABLISHED** 2007
WHERE FUNDING CAN BE GIVEN UK. For smaller projects there is a particular focus on Merton.
WHO CAN BENEFIT Registered charities.
WHAT IS FUNDED Disadvantaged children and young people aged 11–25; the arts; social inclusion; cancer research.
TYPE OF GRANT Project funding.
RANGE OF GRANTS Generally £5,000 to £50,000, with some larger grants.
SAMPLE GRANTS The Institute of Cancer Research (£1 million); Royal Opera House Convent Garden Foundation (£250,000); Centrepoint (£30,000); The Brilliant Club (£20,000); Merton Mencap (£5,000).
FINANCES *Financial year end 31/03/2022*
Income £3,020,000
Grants to organisations £1,940,000
Assets £4,360,000
TRUSTEES Neville Shepherd; Cristina Taylor; Lisa Vaughan.
HOW TO APPLY Applicants should complete the contact form on the foundation's website with a summary of the project's aims, beneficiaries and location. The trustees will then arrange to discuss eligibility and whether the project is something they may fund. The applicant may then be asked to complete a full application form.
CONTACT DETAILS The Trustees, Hill Place House, 55A High Street, Wimbledon, London SW19 5BA *Email* info@ thetaylorfamilyfoundation.co.uk *Website* www. thetaylorfamilyfoundation.co.uk

....

■ Stephen Taylor Foundation

CC NO 1168032　　**ESTABLISHED** 2016
WHERE FUNDING CAN BE GIVEN Worldwide, mostly England.
WHO CAN BENEFIT Charitable organisations; educational institutions.

WHAT IS FUNDED Education; improving life chances in urban areas; inequality; the environment; young people; community.

TYPE OF GRANT Project funding; development funding; capital and building costs.

RANGE OF GRANTS Mostly up to £50,000.

SAMPLE GRANTS King's College, Cambridge (£12.84 million); Youth First Ltd (£200,000); Friends of the Earth (£100,000); Celia Hammond Animal Trust (£50,000); Thomas Tallis School and Toynbee Hall (£20,000 each); Prickles Hedgehog Rescue (£10,000).

FINANCES *Financial year end 31/07/2022*
Income £36,750,000
Grants to organisations £13,330,000
Assets £49,580,000

TRUSTEES Martin Taylor; Richard Walker; Lisa Taylor; Martin Taylor.

OTHER INFORMATION Grants were awarded to ten organisations in 2021/22. The vast majority of the foundation's grant total was awarded to King's College, Cambridge (£12.84 million).

HOW TO APPLY Contact the correspondent via email for information regarding the application process. The trustees will not reply to any queries received by post.

CONTACT DETAILS The Trustees, c/o Farrer and Co., 65–66 Lincoln's Inn Fields, London WC2A 3LH *Tel.* 020 3375 7000 *Email* contact@stf.london *Website* http://stf.london

■ The Tedworth Charitable Trust

CC NO 328524   **ESTABLISHED** 1990

WHERE FUNDING CAN BE GIVEN UK and overseas.

WHO CAN BENEFIT Registered charities; CICs; schools; universities.

WHAT IS FUNDED Parenting; child development; family welfare; the arts; rural arts; the environment; organic gardening; sustainable living; general charitable purposes.

WHAT IS NOT FUNDED Individuals.

TYPE OF GRANT Core/running costs; salaries; project funding; development and strategic funding.

RANGE OF GRANTS Up to £40,000.

SAMPLE GRANTS Global Canopy Programme (£40,000); Best Beginnings (£25,000); Royal Drawing School (£15,000); Home-Start Worldwide (£12,000); One Small Thing (£8,000); Two Moors Festival (£5,000); Institute of Imagination (£2,500); Fauna and Flora International (£1,000).

FINANCES *Financial year end 05/04/2022*
Income £47,200
Grants to organisations £236,000
Assets £11,960,000

TRUSTEES Timothy Sainsbury; Jessica Sainsbury; Margaret Sainsbury.

OTHER INFORMATION The trust is one of the Sainsbury Family Charitable Trusts, which share a common administration – see www.sfct.org.uk for more information. During 2021/22, the trust made grants to 20 organisations for the following purposes: arts and the environment (£136,000); parenting, family welfare and child development (£59,500); general charitable purposes (£47,000).

HOW TO APPLY Unsolicited applications are not accepted.

CONTACT DETAILS The Trustees, The Peak, 5 Wilton Road, London SW1V 1AP *Tel.* 020 7410 0330 *Email* info@sfct.org.uk *Website* www.sfct.org.uk/the-tedworth-charitable-trust/

■ Tees Valley Community Foundation

CC NO 1111222   **ESTABLISHED** 1988

WHERE FUNDING CAN BE GIVEN The former county of Cleveland, being the local authority areas of Hartlepool, Middlesbrough, Redcar and Cleveland, and Stockton-on-Tees.

WHO CAN BENEFIT Registered charities; constituted community groups; schools; CICs; individuals.

WHAT IS FUNDED General charitable purposes, benefitting communities in Tees Valley. The foundation makes grants from various different funds, each with its own criteria – refer to the website for information on current programmes.

WHAT IS NOT FUNDED Each fund has separate exclusions which are available on the foundation's website.

TYPE OF GRANT One-off.

RANGE OF GRANTS Usually up to £2,000.

SAMPLE GRANTS Peat Rigg (£65,000); Teesside University (£24,000); The Wharton Trust (£10,000 each); Norton Bowling Club, St Mark's Church and Teesside Community Action Group (£1,000); Ropner Park Bowling (£500); Orchard Eagles (£385).

FINANCES *Financial year end 31/03/2022*
Income £549,400
Grants to organisations £459,700
Grants to individuals £4,000
Assets £16,310,000

TRUSTEES Jeffrey Taylor; Keith Smith; Heather O'Driscoll; Nigel Williams; Emma Read.

HOW TO APPLY Application forms are available on the foundation's website.

CONTACT DETAILS Grants Administrator, Wallace House, Falcon Court, Preston Farm, Stockton-on-Tees, Durham TS18 3TX *Tel.* 01642 260860 *Email* info@teesvalleyfoundation.org *Website* www.teesvalleyfoundation.org

■ Tegham Ltd

CC NO 283066   **ESTABLISHED** 1981

WHERE FUNDING CAN BE GIVEN UK, with a preference for Barnet.

WHO CAN BENEFIT Registered charities; individuals.

WHAT IS FUNDED Promotion of the Orthodox Jewish faith and the relief of poverty.

SAMPLE GRANTS A list of beneficiaries was not included in the annual report and accounts.

FINANCES *Financial year end 31/03/2022*
Income £341,200
Grants to organisations £268,000
Assets £2,800,000

TRUSTEES Nizza Fluss; Daniel Fluss.

OTHER INFORMATION Grants were awarded to organisations and individuals during the year, but the breakdown was not specified in the accounts.

HOW TO APPLY The trustees have previously stated that the charity has enough causes to support and they do not welcome new applications.

CONTACT DETAILS The Trustees, 13 Garrick Avenue, London NW11 9AR *Tel.* 020 8209 1535 *Email* admin@geraldkreditor.co.uk

■ The Templeton Goodwill Trust

OSCR NO SC004177   **ESTABLISHED** 1938

WHERE FUNDING CAN BE GIVEN Glasgow and the west of Scotland (the Glasgow postal area).

WHO CAN BENEFIT Scottish registered charities.

WHAT IS FUNDED General charitable purposes.

WHAT IS NOT FUNDED Projects or organisations outside Scotland; individuals.

SAMPLE GRANTS A list of beneficiaries was not included in the annual report and accounts. Previous beneficiaries have included: Alzheimer Scotland; Church of Scotland Lodging House Mission; City of Glasgow Society of Social Services; Girl Guides Association; Glasgow Hospital Broadcasting Service; Muscular Dystrophy Group; Scottish Autistic Society; Scottish Furniture Trades Benevolent Association; The Urban Fox Programme.

FINANCES *Financial year end* 31/03/2022
Income £170,300
Grants to organisations £184,700
Assets £6,780,000

HOW TO APPLY Apply in writing to the correspondent, preferably including a copy of your latest accounts. The trustees have previously stated applications should be received by April as the trustees meet once a year, at the end of April or in May. An sae is required from applicants to receive a reply.

CONTACT DETAILS The Trustees, 2 Charnwood Avenue, Johnstone, Johnstone, Renfrewshire PA5 0AF

....

■ The Tennis Foundation

CC NO 298175   **ESTABLISHED** 1987
WHERE FUNDING CAN BE GIVEN UK.
WHO CAN BENEFIT Tennis clubs; schools; charitable organisations; individuals.
WHAT IS FUNDED People with disabilities – empowering and enabling; young people in education – building futures; young people in disadvantaged communities – transforming lives; supporting wider participation. Activities include competitions; education projects; community projects and outreach; tennis development projects; coaching.
TYPE OF GRANT Capital grants; revenue costs; project costs.
SAMPLE GRANTS A list of beneficiaries was not available.
FINANCES *Financial year end* 31/12/2021
Income £11,000
Grants to organisations £2,200,000
TRUSTEES Oliver Scadgell; Timothy Lawler.
OTHER INFORMATION The charity's latest accounts were not available to view on the Charity Commission's website due to its low income. We have therefore estimated the grant total based on the charity's total expenditure.
HOW TO APPLY Initial enquiries should be made by telephone.
CONTACT DETAILS Joanna Farquharson, Secretary, National Tennis Centre, 100 Priory Lane, London SW15 5JQ *Tel.* 0845 872 0522 *Email* info@tennisfoundation.org.uk *Website* www.tennisfoundation.org.uk

....

■ Tenovus Scotland

OSCR NO SC009675   **ESTABLISHED** 1967
WHERE FUNDING CAN BE GIVEN Scotland.
WHO CAN BENEFIT Universities, health bodies and research organisations; researchers and students.
WHAT IS FUNDED Research in the fields of medicine, dentistry, nursing, the medical sciences and allied professions. According to the charity's website, grants are given in the following categories: small pilot grants; large grants (Tayside only); scholarships and awards through universities and medical schools. Further details are provided on the website.

WHAT IS NOT FUNDED Applications which are not properly certificated; work outside the beneficial area; partial funding for projects; applications that fail to provide evidence of appropriate ethical permission or statistical justification for sample/cohort sizes (where appropriate); equipment for routine patient care or for assessment of new products, which the manufacturer might be expected to finance. The following are not usually funded: applications from established investigators for work within their usual field of expertise; applications from PhD students; applications for follow-on work previously funded by Tenovus Scotland, except in exceptional circumstances.
TYPE OF GRANT Research projects – equipment, consumables, running costs, salaries, studentships; evaluations or start-up costs.
RANGE OF GRANTS Small grants of up to £20,000; large grants of up to £100,000.
SAMPLE GRANTS A list of beneficiaries was not included in the annual report and accounts.
FINANCES *Financial year end* 31/03/2022
Income £976,200
Grants to organisations £948,300
Assets £3,200,000
TRUSTEES Prof. Derek Bell; Prof. Andrew Calder; Colin Black; Prof. John Connell; Prof. James Grieve; Prof. Alan Foulis; Prof. David Hamblin; Francis McCrossin; Bryant Paterson; Graham Philips.
OTHER INFORMATION The grant total includes the total expenditure on 'research projects and awards' during the year.
HOW TO APPLY An application form can be requested from the relevant regional correspondent – refer to the website for contact details. Application deadlines are also posted on the website.
CONTACT DETAILS The Trustees, The Royal College of Physicians and Surgeons of Glasgow, 232–242 St Vincent Street, Glasgow G2 5RJ *Tel.* 0141 221 6268 *Email* general.secy@tenovus-scotland.org.uk *Website* www.tenovus-scotland.org.uk

....

■ The Thales Charitable Trust

CC NO 1000162   **ESTABLISHED** 1990
WHERE FUNDING CAN BE GIVEN UK.
WHO CAN BENEFIT Registered charities.
WHAT IS FUNDED Young people; health, in particular, care for permanent or terminal conditions; general charitable purposes.
SAMPLE GRANTS British Heart Foundation; Civil Service Benevolent Fund; Combat Stress; Primary Engineers; Railway Benefit Fund; Railway Children.
FINANCES *Financial year end* 31/12/2021
Income £165,000
Grants to organisations £175,900
Assets £42,400
TRUSTEES John Howe; Michael Seabrook; Craig Stevenson; Stephen Murray.
OTHER INFORMATION This trust is the corporate charity of aerospace and defence company, Thales UK Ltd.
HOW TO APPLY The 2021 annual report states that the trust 'does not generally solicit requests other than for major donations'. The trustees meet on a quarterly basis.
CONTACT DETAILS Michael Seabrook, Trustee and secretary, c/o Thales UK Ltd, 350 Longwater Avenue, Green Park, Reading, Berkshire RG2 6GF *Tel.* 0118 943 4500 *Email* mike.seabrook@uk.thalesgroup.com *Website* www.thalesgroup.com/en/thales-solidarity-charitable-fund

the7stars Foundation

CC NO 1168240   **ESTABLISHED** 2016
WHERE FUNDING CAN BE GIVEN UK.
WHO CAN BENEFIT Registered charities; charitable organisations; individuals.
WHAT IS FUNDED Young people experiencing abuse, addiction, or homelessness; and young people who are carers.
WHAT IS NOT FUNDED See the website for programme-specific restrictions.
TYPE OF GRANT Project funding.
RANGE OF GRANTS Typically up to £2,500.
SAMPLE GRANTS A list of beneficiaries was not included in the annual report and accounts.
FINANCES *Financial year end* 31/03/2022
  Income £239,800
  Grants to organisations £83,800
  Assets £346,900
TRUSTEES Anuschka Clarke; Jenny Biggam; Nick Maddison; Liam Mullins; Rhiannon Murphy; Helen Rose.
HOW TO APPLY Apply using the form for the relevant funding stream on the foundation's website.
CONTACT DETAILS The Trustees, Bush House, North West Wing, Aldwych, London WC2B 4PJ *Email* info@the7starsfoundation.co.uk *Website* www.the7starsfoundation.co.uk

The Theatres Trust Charitable Fund

CC NO 274697   **ESTABLISHED** 1976
WHERE FUNDING CAN BE GIVEN UK.
WHO CAN BENEFIT Theatres.
WHAT IS FUNDED Capital improvements for theatres. See the website for details of current grant schemes.
TYPE OF GRANT Capital costs; capacity building.
RANGE OF GRANTS Up to £25,000. The grant size is dependent on the scheme.
SAMPLE GRANTS Royal Lyceum Edinburgh (£20,000); The Customs House (£16,500); The Courtyard Theatre (£12,100); Doncaster Grand Theatre (£11,500); King's Theatre Kirkcaldy (£7,000); Malvern Theatre (£5,000); Robin Hood Theatre (£3,000); Sheppey Little Theatre (£2,100).
FINANCES *Financial year end* 31/03/2022
  Income £1,050,000
  Grants to organisations £285,000
  Assets £1,190,000
TRUSTEES Paul Cartwright; Richard Johnston; Gary Kemp; Manpreet Gill; Truda Spruyt; Katherine Town; Jane Spiers; Willimina Hampson; James Dacre; Lucy Osborne; David Moutrey; Stephanie Hall; Suba Das.
OTHER INFORMATION This charity is the national advisory public body for theatres. It also provides advocacy, advice and other support.
HOW TO APPLY Application forms and eligibility guidelines for each scheme can be found on the charity's website.
CONTACT DETAILS The Trustees, 22 Charing Cross Road, London WC2H 0QL *Tel.* 020 7836 8591 *Email* info@theatrestrust.org.uk or tom. stickland@theatrestrust.org.uk *Website* www. theatrestrust.org.uk

The Thirty Percy Foundation

CC NO 1177514   **ESTABLISHED** 2018
WHERE FUNDING CAN BE GIVEN England and Wales.
WHO CAN BENEFIT Charitable organisations; CICs; social enterprises; research institutions; innovative projects; individuals.
WHAT IS FUNDED Sustainable development; environmental conservation and research; community development; social welfare.
TYPE OF GRANT Dependent on fund: core funding; project funding; rapid-response funding; development and strategic funding; flexible grants; multi-year grants.
RANGE OF GRANTS Mostly £2,000 to £160,000.
SAMPLE GRANTS The Maggie Keswick Jencks Cancer Caring Centres Trust (£600,000); Cheltenham Festivals (£160,000); Land Workers' Alliance (£110,000); The Rewild Project (£62,900); Menopause Support (£50,000); Gloucestershire Wildlife Trust (£31,200); Young Gloucestershire (£20,000); International Lawyers Project (£5,000).
FINANCES *Financial year end* 31/03/2022
  Income £5,100,000
  Grants to organisations £3,280,000
  Grants to individuals £295,000
  Assets £8,530,000
TRUSTEES Anne Mann; Katharine Hill; Derek Bardowell.
OTHER INFORMATION There is no open general fund, as the foundation is keen to explore and test new, innovative ideas and collaborate with others.
HOW TO APPLY Contact the correspondent for further information. There is also an option to subscribe to updates through the website.
CONTACT DETAILS Nikki Clegg, Director of Operations and Grants, 30 Percy Street, London W1T 2DB *Tel.* 020 7514 3052 *Email* hello@thirtypercy.org *Website* https://thirtypercy.org

The Thompson Family Charitable Trust

CC NO 326801   **ESTABLISHED** 1985
WHERE FUNDING CAN BE GIVEN UK.
WHO CAN BENEFIT Registered charities.
WHAT IS FUNDED General charitable purposes.
RANGE OF GRANTS Between £500 and £500,000.
SAMPLE GRANTS Kidney Research UK (£500,000); St John's College Oxford (£250,000); V&A (£100,000); Rose Paterson Trust (£10,000); Our Special Friends and St Mary's Church – Cheveley (£500 each).
FINANCES *Financial year end* 31/01/2022
  Income £6,810,000
  Grants to organisations £8,870,000
  Assets £111,070,000
TRUSTEES Patricia Thompson; Katharine Woodward; Roy Copus.
HOW TO APPLY Apply in writing to the correspondent. The trust's 2021/22 accounts state: 'The trustees meet as regularly as is necessary to assess grant applications. Applications for donations are invited from all categories of registered charity. Applications should be in writing in the first instance, and sent to the Trustees at the Charity's address.'
CONTACT DETAILS The Trustees, 15 Totteridge Commom, London N20 8LR *Tel.* 01608 676789 *Email* roycopus@btconnect.com

Scott Thomson Charitable Trust

OSCR NO SC004071   **ESTABLISHED** 1965
WHERE FUNDING CAN BE GIVEN UK and overseas.
WHO CAN BENEFIT Christian charitable organisations.
WHAT IS FUNDED General charitable purposes, including: relief of poverty; social welfare; education; advancement of the Christian religion.

RANGE OF GRANTS Up to £5,000.

SAMPLE GRANTS A list of beneficiaries was not included in the annual report and accounts. Previous beneficiaries have included: Scripture Union (£4,500); Glasgow City Mission (£3,000); St Luke's Church (£2,400); Habitat for Humanity (£2,000); Bethany Trust (£1,000); Leprosy Mission (£500); Global Justice Now (£100).

FINANCES *Financial year end 05/04/2022*
Income £275,300
Grants to organisations £52,600
Assets £670,600

HOW TO APPLY Apply in writing to the correspondent.

CONTACT DETAILS The Trustees, 0/1 68 Lauderdale Gardens, Glasgow G12 9QW

....

■ The Sue Thomson Foundation

CC NO 298808   **ESTABLISHED** 1988

WHERE FUNDING CAN BE GIVEN UK, Sussex, London and Surrey.

WHO CAN BENEFIT Organisations.

WHAT IS FUNDED Education and welfare.

RANGE OF GRANTS Mostly under £10,000.

SAMPLE GRANTS Christ's Hospital (£50,100); City of London Freemen's School (£38,800); Children's Trust (£10,000); Book Trade Benevolent Society (£5,000); City of London Prep School (£3,000); The Bridewell Foundation (£2,000); The Stationers' Foundation (£1,000).

FINANCES *Financial year end 31/08/2022*
Income £193,400
Grants to organisations £109,900
Grants to individuals £61,000
Assets £4,450,000

TRUSTEES Tim Binnington; Kathleen Duncan; Mary Ireland; Mike Barford; Dr Jeremy Monsen; Susannah Holliman.

OTHER INFORMATION The foundation's principal beneficiary is Christ's Hospital. During 2021/22, grants were made to Christ's Hospital pupils and pupils at City of London Freemen's School.

HOW TO APPLY Apply in writing to the correspondent. Our previous research notes that preliminary telephone or email enquiries are encouraged. Unsolicited applications are not acknowledged, unless accompanied by an sae or an email address.

CONTACT DETAILS Susannah Holliman, Administrator, 76C Reigate Hill, Reigate, Surrey RH2 9PD *Tel.* 07508 038632 *Email* stfsusannah@aol.com

....

■ Sir Jules Thorn Charitable Trust

CC NO 233838   **ESTABLISHED** 1964

WHERE FUNDING CAN BE GIVEN UK.

WHO CAN BENEFIT Registered charities; universities; hospitals; hospices.

WHAT IS FUNDED Medical research; medicine; serious illness; people who are disadvantaged; hospices.

WHAT IS NOT FUNDED Refer to the trust's website for exclusions from each specific grant scheme.

TYPE OF GRANT Capital costs; core and revenue costs; project funding; research.

SAMPLE GRANTS Imperial College London (£1.69 million); University of Sheffield (£112,000); Wallace and Gromit's Grand Appeal (£85,000); Isabel Hospice (£5,000); Horatio's Garden (£2,500).

FINANCES *Financial year end 31/12/2021*
Income £1,410,000
Grants to organisations £5,280,000
Assets £128,840,000

TRUSTEES Elizabeth Charal; Prof. Sir Ravinder Maini; Prof. David Russell-Jones; William Sporborg; John Rhodes; Julian Ide; Mark Lever; Timothy Harvey-Samuel.

OTHER INFORMATION Grants were broken down as follows: medical research grants (£2.89 million); medically related grants (£1.5 million); Hospice Fund (£471,300); Ann Rylands Small Donations programme (£421,200).

HOW TO APPLY Apply via the trust's website.

CONTACT DETAILS The Director, 24 Manchester Square, London W1U 3TH *Tel.* 020 7487 5851 *Email* donations@julesthorntrust.org.uk *Website* www.julesthorntrust.org.uk

....

■ The Thornton Trust

CC NO 205357   **ESTABLISHED** 1962

WHERE FUNDING CAN BE GIVEN UK and overseas.

WHO CAN BENEFIT Charitable organisations.

WHAT IS FUNDED Promotion and furthering of education and evangelical Christian faith; social welfare; health; young people.

TYPE OF GRANT Recurrent, one-off.

SAMPLE GRANTS A list of beneficiaries was not included in the annual report and accounts.

FINANCES *Financial year end 05/04/2022*
Income £66,300
Grants to organisations £91,400
Assets £897,300

TRUSTEES Catherine Awelan; Vivienne Thornton; James Thornton.

HOW TO APPLY The trust has previously stated that it identifies organisations and projects it wishes to support and does not respond to speculative grant applications.

CONTACT DETAILS The Trustees, 25 Castle Street, Hertford, Hertfordshire SG14 1HH *Tel.* 01992 584004 *Email* jim@AshbyPLC.com

....

■ The Three Guineas Trust

CC NO 1059652   **ESTABLISHED** 1996

WHERE FUNDING CAN BE GIVEN UK.

WHO CAN BENEFIT Charitable organisations; universities.

WHAT IS FUNDED Projects in the field of autistic spectrum disorder (ASD) which include service users in decision-making; disability; prevention of violence; access to justice.

WHAT IS NOT FUNDED Capital projects; individuals; research.

TYPE OF GRANT Project funding; research; core costs.

SAMPLE GRANTS Autism Bedfordshire (£15,000); Dreadnought Centre (£12,000); KIDS Lincolnshire (£10,000); WHISH (£3,300).

FINANCES *Financial year end 05/04/2022*
Income £1,640,000
Grants to organisations £1,460,000
Assets £27,450,000

TRUSTEES Clare Sainsbury; Dominic Flynn; David Wood.

OTHER INFORMATION The trust is one of the Sainsbury Family Charitable Trusts, which share a common administration – see www.sftc.org.uk for more information. Grants were awarded to 31 organisations under the following themes: disability, violence and access to justice (£1.9 million) and autism (£365,000). The trustees have an annual small grants programme for play schemes run in the summer school holiday which support children with ASD.

HOW TO APPLY The trustees will only consider applications for proposals in the field of ASD. Application forms can be completed on the Sainsbury Family Charitable Trusts' website.

CONTACT DETAILS The Trustees, The Sainsbury Family Charitable Trusts, The Peak, 5 Wilton Road, London SW1V 1AP *Tel.* 020 7410 0330 *Email* info@sfct.org.uk *Website* www.sfct.org.uk/the-three-guineas-trust/

....

■ The Three Oaks Trust

CC NO 297079   **ESTABLISHED** 1987
WHERE FUNDING CAN BE GIVEN UK and overseas, with a preference for West Sussex.
WHO CAN BENEFIT Charitable organisations; individuals, via statutory or voluntary organisations.
WHAT IS FUNDED Social welfare. The trustees tend to support the same organisations each year (see applications). Applications are accepted from individuals for relief-in-need purposes through local statutory or voluntary organisations.
WHAT IS NOT FUNDED No direct applications from individuals.
TYPE OF GRANT Core costs; project costs.
RANGE OF GRANTS Up to £17,500.
SAMPLE GRANTS Basildon Resource Centre (£17,500); BEAM (£15,000); Freedom from Torture (£10,000); Phoenix Stroke Club (£7,500); Islington People's Rights (£5,000); Macular Disease Society (£3,000).
FINANCES *Financial year end* 30/09/2021
Income £297,700
Grants to organisations £269,300
Grants to individuals £129,500
Assets £17,700,000
TRUSTEES Polly Hobbs; Sarah Kane; Dianne Ward; Giles Wilkinson; Pamela Wilkinson; Eugenia Chandy; Susan Ellery; Dr Paul Kane; Three Oaks Family Trust Company Ltd.
OTHER INFORMATION The 2020/21 accounts were the latest available at the time of writing (May 2023).
HOW TO APPLY An application form can be downloaded from the trust's website.
CONTACT DETAILS The Trustees, 65 Worthing Road, Horsham, West Sussex RH12 9TD *Email* contact@thethreeoakstrust.co.uk *Website* www.thethreeoakstrust.co.uk

....

■ The Thriplow Charitable Trust

CC NO 1025531   **ESTABLISHED** 1993
WHERE FUNDING CAN BE GIVEN Worldwide.
WHO CAN BENEFIT Registered charities; universities.
WHAT IS FUNDED The furtherance of higher education; research.
WHAT IS NOT FUNDED Capital projects; individuals; primary, secondary and early years education.
TYPE OF GRANT Core/revenue costs; seed funding/start-up funding; project funding.
RANGE OF GRANTS £1,000 to £5,000.
SAMPLE GRANTS A list of beneficiaries was not included in the annual report and accounts. Previous beneficiaries have included: Academy of Ancient Music; African Child Trust; British Council for the Prevention of Blindness; Open Book Publishers; Spinal Research; Royal Scottish Conservatoire; Textile Conservation Foundation; University of the West of England; Zoological Society of London.
FINANCES *Financial year end* 05/04/2022
Income £126,700
Grants to organisations £157,400
Assets £71,200

TRUSTEES Dr Harriet Crawford; Prof. Dame Jean Thomas; Prof. Lord Mair; Prof. David McKitterick; Prof. Dame Caroline Humphrey.
HOW TO APPLY Application forms are available to download from the trust's website and should be submitted by post together with a covering letter and any supporting material. The trustees meet regularly to consider and approve grants.
CONTACT DETAILS The Secretary, PO Box 225, Royston, Hertfordshire SG8 1BG *Email* contact@thriplowcharitabletrust.org *Website* www.thriplowcharitabletrust.org

....

■ Mrs R. P. Tindall's Charitable Trust

CC NO 250558   **ESTABLISHED** 1966
WHERE FUNDING CAN BE GIVEN UK and overseas.
WHO CAN BENEFIT Charitable organisations; churches; schools and colleges; individuals; members of the clergy.
WHAT IS FUNDED The Christian Church; education; music; health; social welfare; overseas aid. The trust also supports the welfare of Christian clergy and their dependants.
TYPE OF GRANT Project costs; capital costs; core/revenue costs.
RANGE OF GRANTS Typically up to £18,000.
SAMPLE GRANTS Salisbury Diocesan Board of Finance – Organ Lessons (£18,100); Salisbury Cathedral School (£18,000); Church of England Pensions Board and Salisbury Diocesan Board of Finance – Sudan Medical Link (£5,000 each); Save the Children (£2,000).
FINANCES *Financial year end* 31/12/2021
Income £115,200
Grants to organisations £115,600
Grants to individuals £3,100
Assets £4,270,000
TRUSTEES Giles Fletcher; Michael Newman; Nicola Halls; Claire Newman.
OTHER INFORMATION In 2021, 48 grants were made across the following categories: music (£42,100); welfare (£27,500); medical causes (£19,000); Christian Church (£12,500); Madagascar and Africa (£7,500); education (£7,000).
HOW TO APPLY According to the trust's annual report, the trustees invite applications for funding by advertising in charitable trusts' registers. Apply in writing to the correspondent.
CONTACT DETAILS The Trustees, Appletree House, Wishford Road, Middle Woodford, Salisbury, Wiltshire SP4 6NG *Tel.* 01722 782329

....

■ The Tolkien Trust

CC NO 1150801   **ESTABLISHED** 1977
WHERE FUNDING CAN BE GIVEN UK; Africa; USA; Europe.
WHO CAN BENEFIT Registered charities.
WHAT IS FUNDED Arts and culture; education; social welfare; the environment; homelessness; international relations and peace building; migration and refugees; prison reform; health; medical research.
WHAT IS NOT FUNDED Individuals.
RANGE OF GRANTS Typically less than £100,000.
SAMPLE GRANTS Médecins Sans Frontières (£400,000); Client Earth (£200,000); Trust for Research and Education on the Arms Trade (£145,000); Asylum Welcome (£80,000); Marine Mammal Centre (£40,000); Alzheimer Research UK (£30,000); Be Free Young Carers (£20,000); Cutteslowe and District Community

Association (£15,000); Oxford Playhouse Trust (£10,000).
FINANCES *Financial year end* 31/12/2021
Income £4,180,000
Grants to organisations £5,470,000
Assets £36,290,000
TRUSTEES Baillie Tolkien; Michael Tolkien; Simon Tolkien.
OTHER INFORMATION The total number of grants awarded in 2021 was 78.
HOW TO APPLY Unsolicited applications are not accepted.
CONTACT DETAILS Cathleen Blackburn, Secretary, Prama House, 267 Banbury Road, Oxford, Oxfordshire OX2 7HT *Tel.* 01865 339330 *Email* nerissa.martin@outlook.com *Website* www.tolkientrust.org

■ The Tomoro Foundation
CC NO 1178061   **ESTABLISHED** 2018
WHERE FUNDING CAN BE GIVEN UK and overseas.
WHO CAN BENEFIT Registered charities.
WHAT IS FUNDED General charitable purposes; children and young people's education; the environment; social welfare.
RANGE OF GRANTS Mostly up to £25,000.
SAMPLE GRANTS Earthwatch (£41,000); Synchronicity Earth (£34,000); Place2Be (£30,000); Surfers Against Sewage (£25,000); Cranbrook Scholarship – Australia (£22,800); Arts for Dementia, Pets as Therapy, Riding for the Disabled and Working Chance (£10,000 each).
FINANCES *Financial year end* 05/04/2022
Income £1,320,000
Grants to organisations £232,800
Assets £5,760,000
TRUSTEES Michael Rembaum; Tanya Rembaum; Nadine Jayes.
OTHER INFORMATION A total of 12 organisations were supported in 2021/22.
HOW TO APPLY Apply in writing to the correspondent.
CONTACT DETAILS Martin Pollock, Administrator, Moore Family Office Ltd, 42 Berkeley Square, London W1J 5AW *Tel.* 020 7318 0845

■ The Tompkins Foundation
CC NO 281405   **ESTABLISHED** 1980
WHERE FUNDING CAN BE GIVEN UK, with a preference for the parish of Hampstead Norreys in Berkshire and the parish of West Grinstead in West Sussex.
WHO CAN BENEFIT Registered charities; schools; theatres; hospitals; hospices; places of worship.
WHAT IS FUNDED General charitable purposes; education and training; recreation; religious causes; health.
WHAT IS NOT FUNDED Individuals.
TYPE OF GRANT One-off and recurring.
RANGE OF GRANTS Mostly, up to £25,000.
SAMPLE GRANTS Royal National Orthopaedic Hospital Charity (£550,000); British Red Cross, Childhood First, The Foundation of Nursing Studies and The Police Foundation (£25,000 each); Guide Dogs for the Blind (£20,000); Douglas Macmillan Hospice and Hotline Meals Service (£5,000 each); The Living Paintings Trust (£2,500).
FINANCES *Financial year end* 05/04/2022
Income £269,600
Grants to organisations £862,500
Assets £14,320,000
TRUSTEES Peter Vaines; Elizabeth Tompkins; Victoria Brenninkmeijer.

OTHER INFORMATION Grants were made to 17 organisations in 2021/22.
HOW TO APPLY Apply in writing to the correspondent. Our research suggests that unsolicited applications are unlikely to be successful, as the foundation has a list of charities that regularly receive support.
CONTACT DETAILS The Administrator, 7 Belgrave Square, London SW1X 8PH *Tel.* 020 7235 9322

■ The Tory Family Foundation
CC NO 326584   **ESTABLISHED** 1984
WHERE FUNDING CAN BE GIVEN Worldwide with a preference for East Kent.
WHO CAN BENEFIT Charitable organisations.
WHAT IS FUNDED General charitable purposes; education and training; Christian causes; social welfare; medical causes.
TYPE OF GRANT Capital costs; research.
SAMPLE GRANTS A list of beneficiaries was not included in the annual report and accounts. Previous beneficiaries have included: Pilgrims Hospice (£4 million); RSPCA (£50,000); Lyminge Youth Action (£10,000); Kent Search and Rescue (£1,000); Canterbury Cathedral (£1,500); Royal British Legion Industries (£1,000); British Liver Trust (£500); Tree of Hope (£250).
FINANCES *Financial year end* 30/04/2022
Income £4,670,000
Grants to organisations £4,100,000
Assets £7,900,000
TRUSTEES James Tory; S. A. Tory; Mr P. N. Tory; David Callister; Steven Coates.
HOW TO APPLY Apply in writing to the correspondent. Only successful applicants will be notified.
CONTACT DETAILS Paul Tory, Trustee, Etchinghill Golf Club, Canterbury Road, Etchinghill, Folkestone, Kent CT18 8FA *Tel.* 01303 862280

■ The Tottenham Grammar School Foundation
CC NO 312634   **ESTABLISHED** 1989
WHERE FUNDING CAN BE GIVEN Haringey.
WHO CAN BENEFIT Schools and colleges; charities; voluntary groups; organisations working with young people; individuals.
WHAT IS FUNDED Education of young people (under 25 years old).
WHAT IS NOT FUNDED The employment of staff; the construction, adaptation, repair and maintenance of school buildings; the repair and maintenance of school equipment; the direct delivery of the national curriculum; the purchase of vehicles.
TYPE OF GRANT Project costs; capital costs; equipment.
RANGE OF GRANTS Mostly under £20,000.
SAMPLE GRANTS Haringey Sports Development Trust (£143,400); Activiteens (£15,800); Alexandra Park and Palace Charitable Trust (£10,300); The Trove Market CIC (£8,800); Blooming Blossoms Trust (£7,000); West Green Primary School (£6,600); Bernie Grant Arts Centre (£6,000); The Literacy Pirates (£5,000).
FINANCES *Financial year end* 31/08/2022
Income £342,600
Grants to organisations £806,100
Grants to individuals £254,000
Assets £25,000,000
TRUSTEES Keith Brown; Terry Clarke; Frederick Gruncell; Lorna Reith; Andrew Krokou; Graham

Kantorowicz; John Fowl; Derek Levy; David Kaplan; Barbara Blake; Ann Waters.

HOW TO APPLY Application packs can be requested by email from grantsform@tgsf.info. Upcoming deadlines can be found on the foundation's website.

CONTACT DETAILS G. Chappell, Clerk to the Foundation, PO Box 34098, London N13 5XU *Tel.* 020 8882 2999 *Email* info@tgsf.info *Website* www.tgsf.info

■ Tower Hill Trust

CC NO 206225   **ESTABLISHED** 1934

WHERE FUNDING CAN BE GIVEN Tower Hill and Tower Hamlets.

WHO CAN BENEFIT Charities; community organisations; schools.

WHAT IS FUNDED The development and provision of gardens and open spaces; biodiversity projects by schools and community groups in school grounds, around housing estates or in community gardens. Grants are also occasionally made for sport and leisure facilities, education and social welfare.

WHAT IS NOT FUNDED Activities that do not directly benefit Tower Hill and the London Borough of Tower Hamlets.

TYPE OF GRANT Preference is given for equipment/capital costs. Project funding is also available.

RANGE OF GRANTS Biodiversity grants: £100 to £2,000. Main grants: generally around £1,000 to £15,000.

SAMPLE GRANTS City of London School for Girls (£197,500); Butterfly Conservation (£6,000); E1 Community Gardens (£1,900); Wider Communities (£1,000).

FINANCES *Financial year end* 30/04/2022 *Income* £211,100 *Grants to organisations* £297,600 *Assets* £7,740,000

TRUSTEES Davina Walter; Susan Wood; Ken Clunie; Jonathan Solomon; Les Chapman; Edward Walter; Col. Richard Harrold.

OTHER INFORMATION There were 21 grants awarded under the Main Grant Programme during the year and 11 grants awarded under the Biodiversity Grant Programme. The trust also pays for three bursaries for pupils from Tower Hamlets at the City of London School for Girls. The trust prioritises projects that meet two or more of its objects.

HOW TO APPLY Applications for both grant programmes can be made through the application portal on the trust's website. Applications will not be accepted by post or email. Grant deadlines can be found on the website.

CONTACT DETAILS Elaine Crush, Grant Officer, Marshall House, 66 Newcomen Street, London SE1 1YT *Email* enquiries@towerhilltrust.org.uk *Website* www.towerhilltrust.org.uk

■ The Toy Trust

CC NO 1001634   **ESTABLISHED** 1991

WHERE FUNDING CAN BE GIVEN UK and Ireland; overseas.

WHO CAN BENEFIT Small children's charities registered in the UK and Ireland that have been operating for at least one year; international organisations with a UK office.

WHAT IS FUNDED The welfare of disadvantaged children (up to 13 years old); emergency aid for any crisis involving children.

WHAT IS NOT FUNDED Salaries; research; running costs; books, publishing or individual cases (unless there is a compelling reason).

TYPE OF GRANT Equipment; project funding.

RANGE OF GRANTS Mainly under £5,000. Occasionally larger grants are made.

SAMPLE GRANTS A list of beneficiaries was not included in the annual report and accounts. Previous beneficiaries have included: Action for kids and Over The Wall (£30,000 each); Bag Books (£5,100); The Children's Foundation (£4,600); Yorda Playhouse Adventurers (£3,000); Children in Hunger and Three Ways School (£2,500 each).

FINANCES *Financial year end* 31/12/2021 *Income* £145,600 *Grants to organisations* £169,500

TRUSTEES Phil Ratcliffe; Graham Canning; Jon Diver; Simon Pilkington; British Toy and Hobby Association Ltd.

OTHER INFORMATION This trust was registered in 1991 to centralise the giving of the British Toy and Hobby Association. During 2021, grants were made to 48 organisations.

HOW TO APPLY Application forms can be found on the trust's website. Completed applications should be sent to the trust's office, along with a photocopy, to be considered at the next meeting. The trustees meet four times a year. Application guidelines and upcoming deadlines can be found on the trust's website.

CONTACT DETAILS Tracey Butcher, Office and Services Manager, British Toy and Hobby Association, BTHA House, 142–144 Long Lane, London SE1 4BS *Tel.* 020 7701 7271 *Email* tracey@btha.co.uk *Website* https://toytrust.co.uk

■ Toyota Manufacturing UK Charitable Trust

CC NO 1124678   **ESTABLISHED** 2008

WHERE FUNDING CAN BE GIVEN Burnaston; Deeside.

WHO CAN BENEFIT Registered charities; local community groups; sports and leisure clubs.

WHAT IS FUNDED Community development; road safety; social inclusion; social welfare; health and medical research. Support may also be given to charities with which Toyota employees are involved.

WHAT IS NOT FUNDED Full exclusion criteria for Member Grants can be found on the website.

RANGE OF GRANTS Generally up to £5,000.

SAMPLE GRANTS The Welsh Ambulance Charitable Trust (£5,000); Derbyshire Mind (£3,000); Quarrydale Utd (£2,000); Neston Nomads (£1,500); Prostate Cancer UK (£800).

FINANCES *Financial year end* 31/12/2021 *Income* £217,300 *Grants to organisations* £144,300 *Assets* £402,300

TRUSTEES Kevin Reader; Sarah Overson; Kevin Potter; Tim Freeman; Gary Shrimpton; Sharon Wilson.

OTHER INFORMATION This is the charitable trust of Toyota Motor Manufacturing (UK) Ltd. Income is largely derived from company employees through fundraising activities and the trust supports matched funding for its employees ('members'). Grants were broken down as follows: Community Grants (£86,300); Member Grants (£55,300); Member Match Funding (£12,400). Funding was also awarded for three apprentice volunteering projects (£2,800).

HOW TO APPLY Application forms for Member Grants can be downloaded from the website.

698

Does the funder you have chosen match your needs? Haphazard applications waste postage and time

Beneficiaries of Community Grant Awards are nominated by company employees. Contact the trust for further information.

CONTACT DETAILS The Trustees, c/o Toyota Motor Manufacturing (UK) Ltd, Derby, Derbyshire DE1 9TA *Tel.* 01332 283611 *Email* charitabletrust@toyotauk.com *Website* www.toyotauk.com/the-toyota-charitable-trust/charitable-trust-overview.html

....

■ The Trades House of Glasgow

OSCR NO SC040548 **ESTABLISHED** 1920
WHERE FUNDING CAN BE GIVEN Glasgow.
WHO CAN BENEFIT Charitable organisations; individuals.
WHAT IS FUNDED General charitable purposes; children and young people; social welfare; education.
WHAT IS NOT FUNDED Funding is not provided outside Glasgow and the surrounding areas (there is a postcode checker available on the charity's website indicating eligible areas).
TYPE OF GRANT Project costs; capital costs.
RANGE OF GRANTS The majority of grants are for under £3,000.
SAMPLE GRANTS Voluntary Tutors Organisation (£20,000); Cultivating Mindfulness (£6,400); Evening Times Charity Awards and Glasgow Care (£5,000); Moira Anderson Foundation (£4,800); Articulate Cultural Trust (£4,300); Impact Arts (£4,100); Junction 12 and Wing Hong Chinese Centre (£3,500 each).
FINANCES *Financial year end* 30/09/2021
Income £1,200,000
Grants to organisations £143,200
Grants to individuals £254,600
Assets £23,650,000
TRUSTEES Tom McInally; Ken Dalgleish; Dr Alistair Dorward; Bruce Reidford; Billy Birse-Stewart; Ewen Mackie; Richard Paterson.
OTHER INFORMATION Grants were made to 49 organisations in 2020/21. Only organisations that received grants of over £3,000 were listed as beneficiaries in the charity's accounts. Grants of under £3,000 totalled £71,600. The 2020/21 accounts were the latest available at time of writing (June 2023).
HOW TO APPLY Application forms are available to download from the website, where further guidance about what to include and upcoming deadlines are also provided.
CONTACT DETAILS The Trustees, Trades Hall, 85 Glassford Street, Glasgow G1 1UH *Tel.* 0141 553 1605 *Email* info@tradeshouse.org.uk *Website* www.tradeshouse.org.uk

....

■ Annie Tranmer Charitable Trust

CC NO 1044231 **ESTABLISHED** 1989
WHERE FUNDING CAN BE GIVEN Suffolk and adjacent counties.
WHO CAN BENEFIT Charitable organisations; individuals.
WHAT IS FUNDED General charitable purposes; education and training; children and young people.
RANGE OF GRANTS Up to £5,000 but mostly £500 to £2,000.
SAMPLE GRANTS East Anglian Air Ambulance (£5,000); 1st Kesgrave Scout Group (£2,800); Young Lives vs Cancer (£2,000); Age Well East (£1,000); Alzheimer's Research (£500).

FINANCES *Financial year end* 05/04/2022
Income £144,300
Grants to organisations £105,500
Grants to individuals £15,200
Assets £4,090,000
TRUSTEES Nigel Bonham-Carter; Valerie Lewis; Patrick Grieve; Mary Allen; Hector Wykes-Sneyd.
HOW TO APPLY Apply in writing to the correspondent. The 2021/22 accounts state: 'The charity receives applications for funding from institutions and individuals. The trustees review the applications against the objectives of the charity before deciding whether or not to authorise the application and make the grant.'
CONTACT DETAILS A. Williams, Trust Administrator, 55 Dobbs Lane, Kesgrave, Ipswich, Suffolk IP5 2QA *Tel.* 07801 556002 *Email* amwilliams7903@gmail.com

....

■ The Constance Travis Charitable Trust

CC NO 294540 **ESTABLISHED** 1986
WHERE FUNDING CAN BE GIVEN UK and overseas, with a preference for Northamptonshire.
WHO CAN BENEFIT Registered charities.
WHAT IS FUNDED General charitable purposes including: health; social welfare; housing; arts and culture; animal welfare; economic and community development; education and training; disability; overseas aid; religious activities; sport and recreation; the environment, conservation and heritage.
WHAT IS NOT FUNDED Individuals.
TYPE OF GRANT One-off grants for core, capital and project support.
RANGE OF GRANTS From £20,000 to £150,000.
SAMPLE GRANTS Age UK Northamptonshire (£150,000); Unicef (£100,000); Northamptonshire Historic Churches Trust, The Sutton Trust and Woodland Trust (£50,000 each); All Saints Church – Northampton and Royal Opera House (£20,000 each).
FINANCES *Financial year end* 31/12/2021
Income £3,590,000
Grants to organisations £2,590,000
Assets £188,520,000
TRUSTEES Ernest Travis; Peta Travis; Matthew Travis.
HOW TO APPLY Apply in writing to the correspondent. The trustees meet at least quarterly to consider grants. The trustees do not welcome contact prior to application.
CONTACT DETAILS Ernest Travis, Chair of Trustees, 86 Drayton Gardens, London SW10 9SB *Email* travistrust86@yahoo.co.uk

....

■ The Trelix Charitable Trust

CC NO 1124952
WHERE FUNDING CAN BE GIVEN Worldwide.
WHO CAN BENEFIT Charitable organisations.
WHAT IS FUNDED General charitable purposes including health and social welfare.
RANGE OF GRANTS £500 to £4,000.
SAMPLE GRANTS Previous beneficiaries have included: Mission Aviation Fellowship (£4,000); The Bromley Christian Workers Trust (£3,000); Alzheimer's Society (£2,000); IT Schools Africa (£1,000); Innovista (£500).
FINANCES *Financial year end* 05/04/2022
Income £53,100
Grants to organisations £265,000
Assets £1,580,000

TRUSTEES Matthew Hanning; Christopher Hanning; Sarah Walker; Elizabeth Hanning; Graham Benwell.

OTHER INFORMATION Full accounts were not available to view on the Charity Commission's website due to the trust's low income. We have therefore estimate the trust's grant total based on its total expenditure.

HOW TO APPLY Apply in writing to the correspondent.

CONTACT DETAILS The Trustees, Blandy and Blandy, 1 Friar Street, Reading RG1 1DA *Email* trelix@newburyweb.net

■ The Triangle Trust (1949) Fund

CC NO 222860　　**ESTABLISHED** 1949

WHERE FUNDING CAN BE GIVEN UK, with some preference for Northern Ireland, Scotland and Wales.

WHO CAN BENEFIT UK-registered or exempt charities; community and voluntary organisations; retired employees of the pharmaceutical industry.

WHAT IS FUNDED Young carers; work supporting young people with criminal convictions.

WHAT IS NOT FUNDED Organisations that are not registered in the UK; organisations working entirely outside the UK; general appeals; emergency funding (unless an advertised opportunity); capital projects; academic research; promotion of religion; international development work; disaster relief; organisations which have more than one year's worth of unrestricted reserves; organisations which have made an unsuccessful application to the trust in the last two years.

TYPE OF GRANT Core/revenue costs; seed funding/start-up funding; development funding.

RANGE OF GRANTS Up to £30,000 per year for up to two years.

SAMPLE GRANTS Turnaround Project (£33,600 in two grants); Recoop (£30,000); Safe Welcome After Prison (£23,700); Inside Connections (£15,000); Harrow Carers (£13,600); Clean Sheet (£10,000); Signpost Stockport for Carers (£9,500); Promas Caring for People CIC (£7,500).

FINANCES *Financial year end* 31/03/2022
Income £700,700
Grants to organisations £556,000
Grants to individuals £8,800
Assets £24,200,000

TRUSTEES Alison Hope; Karen Drury; Doreen Foster; David Loudon; James Marshall; Sarah Cutler.

OTHER INFORMATION In total, 32 grants were awarded to organisations during 2021/22 in two categories: rehabilitation (£399,700) and carers (£156,300). Grants were awarded to eight individuals for the relief of poverty.

HOW TO APPLY There are two rounds of funding each year: one for organisations working with young carers and another for organisations working with young offenders/ex-offenders. Opening and closing dates for each round of funding are published on the trust's website. There is also a mailing list that organisations can sign up to be notified when applications open. The application process is in two stages. Following the submission of an initial online application, shortlisted applicants will be asked to host a visit from the trust where they will be required to present their strategic plan for the next few years.

CONTACT DETAILS Fran Box, Grants Assistant, Brighton Eco Centre, 39–41 Surrey Street, Brighton BN1 3PB *Tel.* 07716 378564 *Email* info@triangletrust.org.uk or use the contact form on the website *Website* www.triangletrust.org.uk

■ The Troutsdale Charitable Trust

CC NO 1165224　　**ESTABLISHED** 2015

WHERE FUNDING CAN BE GIVEN England.

WHO CAN BENEFIT Charitable organisations; children and young people.

WHAT IS FUNDED Medical research; social welfare; children and young people; religious buildings; animal welfare; education; arts; sports.

SAMPLE GRANTS A list of beneficiaries was not included in the annual report and accounts.

FINANCES *Financial year end* 05/04/2022
Income £363,300
Grants to organisations £218,200
Assets £2,670,000

TRUSTEES Leslie Guthrie; Richard Guthrie; Peter Guthrie; John Guthrie.

OTHER INFORMATION Grants were broken down as follows: medical research (£122,400); education and training (£66,000); social welfare (£28,900); animal welfare (£500); performing arts (£500). All grants paid during 2021/22 were awarded to organisations.

HOW TO APPLY Apply in writing to the correspondent.

CONTACT DETAILS The Trustees, c/o Moore Stephens, 12–13 Alma Square, Scarborough YO11 1JU *Tel.* 01723 360361

■ The True Colours Trust

CC NO 1089893　　**ESTABLISHED** 2001

WHERE FUNDING CAN BE GIVEN UK and Africa.

WHO CAN BENEFIT Registered charities.

WHAT IS FUNDED Improving access to palliative care for babies, children and young people in the UK: enabling children and young people with disabilities to live their lives to the full; the development of pain relief and palliative care in Africa.

TYPE OF GRANT Small grants: one-off capital costs. Large grants: project funding; development funding; core costs; capital costs.

RANGE OF GRANTS Small grants of up to £10,000.

SAMPLE GRANTS Jessie May Trust (£195,000); Palliative Care Association of Malawi (£30,800); Little Village (£23,000); The Very Inclusive Play Club CIC (£1,500).

FINANCES *Financial year end* 05/04/2022
Income £929,000
Grants to organisations £1,650,000
Assets £10,470,000

TRUSTEES Dominic Flynn; Mr T. G. Price; Lucy Sainsbury; David Wood.

OTHER INFORMATION The trust is one of the Sainsbury Family Charitable Trusts, which share a common administration – see www.sftc.org.uk for more information. Grants were made for the following purposes: UK – children with disabilities or receiving palliative care (£940,500); Africa – palliative care (£212,600); UK small grants and Sainsbury Archive (£201,600).

HOW TO APPLY The trustees only consider unsolicited applications for their Small Grants programme. Applications can be made via the trust's website.

CONTACT DETAILS The Trustees, The Peak, 5 Wilton Road, London SW1V 1AP *Tel.* 020 7410 0330 *Email* info@truecolourstrust.org.uk *Website* www.truecolourstrust.org.uk

■ Truedene Co. Ltd

CC NO 248268   **ESTABLISHED** 1966
WHERE FUNDING CAN BE GIVEN UK and overseas.
WHO CAN BENEFIT Jewish organisations.
WHAT IS FUNDED Jewish religious education; support for Jewish people who are in need.
RANGE OF GRANTS Generally £5,000 to £10,000 with some larger grants.
SAMPLE GRANTS Chevras Mo'oz Ladol (£25,000); Vyoel Moshe Charitable Trust (£17,000); Beis Ruchel D'Satmar (London) Ltd, Bnois Jersusalem Schools, Ora Vesimcha, Yetev Lev London Jerusalem Trust and Yeshiva Gedola Seminar (£10,000 each).
FINANCES *Financial year end 31/03/2022*
Income £175,700
Grants to organisations £345,600
Assets £11,380,000
TRUSTEES Sije Berger; Samuel Berger; Sarah Klein; Solomon Laufer; Zelda Sternlicht.
OTHER INFORMATION Grants of under £10,000 totalled £138,600.
HOW TO APPLY Apply in writing to the correspondent.
CONTACT DETAILS The Trustees, Cohen Arnold, New Burlington House, 1075 Finchley Road, London NW11 0PU *Tel.* 020 8731 0777

■ The Truemark Trust

CC NO 265855   **ESTABLISHED** 1973
WHERE FUNDING CAN BE GIVEN UK.
WHO CAN BENEFIT Registered charities, with a preference for small local charities.
WHAT IS FUNDED Social welfare and disadvantage. There is a preference for neighbourhood-based community projects and innovative work with less popular groups.
RANGE OF GRANTS £1,000 up to £10,000.
SAMPLE GRANTS No Way Trust (£10,000); Without Walls Christian Fellowship (£9,000); Waterlily Project (£3,500); space2grow and Sudden Productions (£1,000 each).
FINANCES *Financial year end 05/04/2022*
Income £674,700
Grants to organisations £300,500
Assets £19,550,000
TRUSTEES Sharon Knight; Judy Hayward; Jane Dunham; Shirley Vening; Paul Summerfield; Stephen Collins.
OTHER INFORMATION During the year, grants were awarded to 60 organisations.
HOW TO APPLY Contact the correspondent for further information.
CONTACT DETAILS The Trustees, PO Box 2, Liss, Hampshire GU33 6YP *Tel.* 07970 540015 *Email* truemark.trust01@ntlworld.com

■ Truemart Ltd

CC NO 1090586   **ESTABLISHED** 1984
WHERE FUNDING CAN BE GIVEN UK.
WHO CAN BENEFIT Charitable organisations.
WHAT IS FUNDED Orthodox Jewish faith; relief of poverty; general charitable purposes.
TYPE OF GRANT Capital costs, project costs, strategic funding, development funding.
SAMPLE GRANTS Achisomoch Aid Company Ltd (£18,500); Yeshuos Shabbos (£10,500); Low Cost Living (£10,000); Chevras Mo'oz Ladol, Tsechenov Institutions and Talmud Torah D'Chasidei Gur (£5,000 each).
FINANCES *Financial year end 31/03/2022*
Income £163,500
Grants to organisations £143,300
Assets £77,000

TRUSTEES Ian Heitner; Mrs S. Heitner.
OTHER INFORMATION Grants of less than £4,000 totalled £66,300.
HOW TO APPLY Apply in writing to the correspondent.
CONTACT DETAILS The Trustees, 34 The Ridgeway, London NW11 8QS *Tel.* 020 8455 4456

■ Trumros Ltd

CC NO 285533   **ESTABLISHED** 1982
WHERE FUNDING CAN BE GIVEN UK and Israel.
WHO CAN BENEFIT Charitable organisations.
WHAT IS FUNDED The Jewish faith and community; education and training; social welfare; health.
TYPE OF GRANT Capital costs; development funding; project funding; strategic funding.
RANGE OF GRANTS Generally £1,000 to £20,000.
SAMPLE GRANTS Beit Hamidrash Abarbanel Ashdod (£264,000); Torah Vochessed (£171,400); Chevras Mo'oslodol (£26,000); Beth Yosef Zvi (£12,000); Yeshivat Chochamt Shlomo (£9,000).
FINANCES *Financial year end 31/12/2021*
Income £1,140,000
Grants to organisations £791,500
Assets £10,310,000
TRUSTEES Hannah Hofbauer; Ronald Hofbauer.
OTHER INFORMATION Grants were awarded to more than 21 organisations during the year. Grants of under £5,000 totalled £104,100.
HOW TO APPLY Apply in writing to the correspondent.
CONTACT DETAILS Hannah Hofbauer, Trustee/ Secretary, 282 Finchley Road, London NW3 7AD *Tel.* 020 7431 3282 *Email* r.hofbauer@btconnect.com

■ Trust for London

CC NO 205629   **ESTABLISHED** 2004
WHERE FUNDING CAN BE GIVEN London.
WHO CAN BENEFIT Voluntary, community and other not-for-profit organisations; registered charities; bodies providing advice, information and advocacy; educational and training institutions; new initiatives; shelters and re-settlement homes; CICs and social enterprises. While most recipients are registered charities this is not a requirement. Priority is given to smaller and medium-sized organisations with an income of under £2 million.
WHAT IS FUNDED Relief and prevention of poverty; social welfare; disability; cultural equality; religion.
WHAT IS NOT FUNDED Work outside London; applications for funding of services which are the primary responsibility of statutory funders or to subsidise services delivered through statutory contracts; schools and hospitals; individuals; organisations with fewer than three people on their governing body; promotion of religion; organisations seeking to distribute grants on the trust's behalf; work that has already taken place; general appeals; large capital appeals; applicants rejected in the last 12 months. See the trust's guidelines for a full list of exclusions and preferences.
TYPE OF GRANT Campaigning; research; core/ revenue costs; salaries; small capital costs.; project costs.
RANGE OF GRANTS Usually up to £150,000.
SAMPLE GRANTS Citizens UK (£4.8 million); Crowdfunder (£242,600); Women into Construction (£130,000).

Think carefully about every application. Is it justified?

701

FINANCES *Financial year end* 31/12/2021
  Income £9,410,000
  Grants to organisations £35,440,000
  Assets £358,520,000
TRUSTEE Trust For London Trustee.
OTHER INFORMATION During 2021, 199 grants were awarded to organisations from the Central Fund for the relief of poverty, totalling £20.03 million. At the time of writing (June 2023), the Central Fund's priority areas were: good homes and neighbourhoods; better work; decent living standards; shared wealth; pathways to settlement; stronger voices; connected communities. Note that the trust is in the process of updating its funding strategy so priority areas may differ. Grants made for the furtherance of religion, including from the City Church Fund, totalled £15.41 million. A full list of beneficiaries can be downloaded from the website. The sample of beneficiaries includes grants to be paid over multiple years.
HOW TO APPLY Applications can be made through the trust's website when funding rounds are open. Visit the website for more information.
CONTACT DETAILS The Trustees, 4th Floor, 4 Chiswell Street, London EC1Y 4UP *Tel.* 020 7606 6145 *Email* info@trustforlondon.org.uk *Website* www.trustforlondon.org.uk

■ The Trusthouse Charitable Foundation
CC NO 1063945   **ESTABLISHED** 1997
WHERE FUNDING CAN BE GIVEN UK.
WHO CAN BENEFIT Charitable organisations including CICs, social enterprises, not-for-profit registered companies and voluntary organisations.
WHAT IS FUNDED The foundation has two overarching themes – rural issues and urban deprivation. Within these themes, the foundation's major grants programme currently focuses on family support projects (e.g. early intervention, work with families coping with addiction and prisoners' families). The foundation's small grants programme currently focuses on community support projects (see the foundation's website for examples). Projects must be based in areas of high deprivation (see website for details).
WHAT IS NOT FUNDED A full list of exclusions can be found on the foundation's website.
TYPE OF GRANT General costs including core costs, salaries and project costs.
RANGE OF GRANTS Major grants: £10,000 to £100,000. Small grants: £2,000 to £10,000.
SAMPLE GRANTS Springboard Charity (£500,000); Aiming Higher for the Disabled Community (£100,000); Barlow Moor Community Association Ltd (£65,100); Think Children (£27,600); Advice At Hart (£10,000); Kids Kabin (£8,800); Vision Care for Homeless People (£5,000); Liberty Choir UK (£1,000).
FINANCES *Financial year end* 30/06/2022
  Income £1,450,000
  Grants to organisations £3,000,000
  Assets £82,870,000
TRUSTEES The Hon. Olga Polizzi; Philippa Hardwick; Crispian Collins; Nicholas Melhuish; Carole Milner; Charlie Peyton; Patrick Reeve; The Revd Paul Gismondi; Nicholas Acland; Salma Shah; Sharon Rich.
OTHER INFORMATION In 2021/22, the foundation awarded 98 grants. Major grants totalled £2.06 million, small grants totalled £359,100 and trustee-nominated grants totalled £78,500. Additionally, the foundation awarded an anniversary grant of £500,000 to Springboard Charity.
HOW TO APPLY Applications can be made through the foundation's website, following the completion of a brief eligibility questionnaire, which also identifies which type of grant may be most suitable. Eligible organisations will be directed to an online application portal. Applications are accepted year-round.
CONTACT DETAILS Jessica Brown, Grants Director, Kings Buildings, 16 Smith Square, London SW1P 3HQ *Tel.* 020 3150 4517 *Email* grants@trusthousecharitablefoundation.org.uk *Website* www.trusthousecharitablefoundation.org.uk

■ The Trysil Charitable Trust
CC NO 1107309   **ESTABLISHED** 2004
WHERE FUNDING CAN BE GIVEN UK and overseas.
WHO CAN BENEFIT Charitable organisations.
WHAT IS FUNDED Children and young people, particularly social welfare and health; general charitable purposes.
RANGE OF GRANTS £1,000 to £10,000.
SAMPLE GRANTS A list of beneficiaries was not available.
FINANCES *Financial year end* 31/12/2021
  Income £20
  Grants to organisations £213,000
TRUSTEES David Lumley; Corinna Schumacher; Jonathan Dudman; Edward Porter.
OTHER INFORMATION Full accounts were not available to view on the Charity Commission's website due to the trust's low income. We have therefore estimated the trust's grant total based on its total expenditure.
HOW TO APPLY Apply in writing to the correspondent.
CONTACT DETAILS Jonathan Dudman, Trustee, c/o MSM, 24 Boulevard Princesse Charlotte, Immeuble Est-Ouest, 5e etage, Monaco MC 98000 *Tel.* +377 931 04250

■ The James Tudor Foundation
CC NO 1105916   **ESTABLISHED** 2004
WHERE FUNDING CAN BE GIVEN UK and overseas.
WHO CAN BENEFIT Registered charities; charities with exempt status; CIOs.
WHAT IS FUNDED Palliative care; medical research; health education; relief of human sickness.
WHAT IS NOT FUNDED A full list of exclusions can be found in the foundation's application guidelines, which are available to download from the website.
TYPE OF GRANT Core costs; project funding.
RANGE OF GRANTS Mostly up to £20,000.
SAMPLE GRANTS University of Nottingham (£62,000); St Peter's Hospice (£22,000); Southend Hospital Charity (£15,000); Kent Autistic Trust (£10,000); Myceloma UK (£7,000); Teenage Cancer Trust (£5,000); Listening Post (£2,000); The Anchor Society (£500).
FINANCES *Financial year end* 30/09/2021
  Income £866,200
  Grants to organisations £600,800
  Assets £35,540,000
TRUSTEES Richard Esler; Anne McPherson; Stephanie Wren; Linda Hooper.
OTHER INFORMATION A total of 93 grants were awarded to organisations during the year. Grants were distributed as follows: relief of sickness (£242,100); health education (£106,900); palliative care (£100,700); medical research (£92,300); overseas (£58,800). A full list of beneficiaries is available to view on the

foundation's website. The 2020/21 accounts were the latest available at the time of writing (May 2023).

HOW TO APPLY In the first instance, applicants should use the eligibility checker on the foundation's website. If eligible, applicants should then submit a one-page summary and a completed application cover sheet. Further information and a breakdown of the application process are available from the foundation's website.

CONTACT DETAILS The Trustees, Trym Lodge, 1 Henbury Road, Westbury-on-Trym, Bristol BS9 3HQ *Tel.* 0117 440 7340
Email admin@jamestudor.org.uk
Website www.jamestudor.org.uk

■ The Tudor Trust

CC NO 1105580   **ESTABLISHED** 1955
WHERE FUNDING CAN BE GIVEN UK and Africa.
WHO CAN BENEFIT Registered charities; unregistered charities; CICs; social enterprises; religious bodies/institutions.
WHAT IS FUNDED Work that makes a direct difference to the lives of marginalised people.
TYPE OF GRANT Core/revenue costs; capital costs; project funding; development funding.
RANGE OF GRANTS There is no minimum or maximum grant; grants are usually £10,000 or more.
SAMPLE GRANTS A list of beneficiaries was not included in the annual report and accounts. Previous beneficiaries have included: Corra Foundation (£200,000); Barrow Cadbury Trust (£150,000); Asylum Justice (£130,000); Growing Sudley CIC (£88,000); London Renters Union (£60,000); Road to Recovery Trust (£50,000); Voice of Domestic Workers (£40,000); Sustainable Living Initiative (£30,000); Hope House Church (£25,000); Local Trust (£15,000); The School and Family Works (£3,000).
FINANCES *Financial year end* 31/03/2022
Income £4,730,000
Grants to organisations £20,210,000
Assets £274,710,000
TRUSTEES Catherine Antcliff; Monica Barlow; Nell Buckler; Louise Collins; Elizabeth Crawshaw; Matt Dunwell; Ben Dunwell; Christopher Graves; James Long; Francis Runacres; Rosalind Dunwell; Holly Baine; Shilpa Shah; Jonathan Bell.
OTHER INFORMATION Grants were broken down as follows: community (£10.48 million); relationships (£1.93 million); young people (£1.65 million); mental health (£1.31 million); criminal justice (£1.09 million); housing (£914,000); substance abuse (£895,000); overseas (£820,000); older people (£530,000); learning (£330,000); financial security (£260,000).
HOW TO APPLY At the time of writing (May 2023) the trust was closed to new applications. The trust's website states: 'We are reducing our direct grant-making in this way to create time and space for Tudor's staff and trustees to re-think how the Trust operates.' See the trust's website for further information.
CONTACT DETAILS The Grants Team, 7 Ladbroke Grove, London W11 3BD *Tel.* 020 7727 8522
Email There is no email address for general enquiries as the trust prefers contact via telephone; however, if you have communication difficulties, email access@tudortrust.org.uk.
Website www.tudortrust.org.uk

■ The Tudwick Foundation

CC NO 1184459   **ESTABLISHED** 2019
WHERE FUNDING CAN BE GIVEN Essex; Suffolk.
WHO CAN BENEFIT Charitable organisations.
WHAT IS FUNDED Health; social welfare; education.
WHAT IS NOT FUNDED General appeals to directly promote religious or political agendas; charities registered outside the UK.
TYPE OF GRANT Project funding; core funding.
RANGE OF GRANTS £300 to £3,000.
SAMPLE GRANTS CHAPS and Music in Our Bones (£3,000 each); SEND the Right Message (£2,800): Stansfield Village Hall (£2,500); Little Heroes ASD Support Group (£1,800); Riding for the Disabled (£1,300); Great Barton Free Church (£1,000); Tsunami ESU Chelmsford Scouts (£500).
FINANCES *Financial year end* 31/03/2022
Income £198,400
Grants to organisations £75,000
Assets £2,600,000
TRUSTEES Colin Bennett; Valerie Shaikly; Julia Endacott; Timothy Bennett.
OTHER INFORMATION The foundation typically supports charities with an income under £500,000. New organisations are encouraged to apply.
HOW TO APPLY Application forms can be downloaded from the foundation's website.
CONTACT DETAILS The Trustees, 17 James Chester Road, Colchester CO3 9XA *Tel.* 01206 587000
Email thetudwickfoundation@gmail.com
Website www.tudwickfoundation.org.uk

■ The Tufton Charitable Trust

CC NO 801479   **ESTABLISHED** 1989
WHERE FUNDING CAN BE GIVEN UK.
WHO CAN BENEFIT Charitable organisations; churches.
WHAT IS FUNDED Christian causes, general charitable activities.
RANGE OF GRANTS Up to £250,000, with an average of £57,000.
SAMPLE GRANTS Stowe School Foundation (£250,000); Church Revitalisation Trust (£150,000); The London City Mission (£30,000); Mission Aviation Fellowship and Off The Fence (£15,000 each); Bob Champion Cancer Trust (£5,000).
FINANCES *Financial year end* 31/12/2021
Income £345,900
Grants to organisations £694,600
Assets £437,700
TRUSTEE Wates Charitable Trustees Ltd.
OTHER INFORMATION Only organisations that received grants of £5,000 and above were listed as beneficiaries in the 2021 accounts (12 organisations). Grants of under £5,000 totalled £9,000. The trust also provides accommodation for Christian retreats.
HOW TO APPLY Apply in writing to the correspondent.
CONTACT DETAILS The Trustees, Tufton Place, Tufton Lane, Northiam, Rye TN31 6HL *Tel.* 01797 253311

■ The Tuixen Foundation

CC NO 1081124   **ESTABLISHED** 2000
WHERE FUNDING CAN BE GIVEN UK.
WHO CAN BENEFIT Registered charities; unregistered charities; hospitals; hospices; CICs; schools; universities; social enterprises. Charities receiving grants will usually have a turnover in the range of £500,000 to £5 million.

WHAT IS FUNDED Children and young people; education; people with physical or learning disabilities; mental health; hospices; homelessness; relief of poverty.

TYPE OF GRANT Core/revenue costs; unrestricted funding; project funding.

RANGE OF GRANTS Mostly £500 to £50,000.

SAMPLE GRANTS Fight for Peace (£100,000); Leap Confronting Conflict (£50,000); Richard House Hospice (£40,000); Royal National Theatre (£10,000).

FINANCES *Financial year end* 05/04/2022
Income £589,700
Grants to organisations £1,120,000
Assets £66,070,000

TRUSTEES Paul Clements; Peter Englander; Dr Leanda Kroll; Stephen Rosefield; Simon Englander; William Englander; Thomas Englander.

OTHER INFORMATION In total, 34 grants were awarded to organisations during the year. The foundation's helpful website provides a detailed breakdown of the grants awarded and specifies to what purpose they were given. According to the website, approximately 20 charities are selected to receive a donation each year and some donations will be ongoing.

HOW TO APPLY The website states that unsolicited applications are not sought and correspondence will not be replied to.

CONTACT DETAILS The Trustees, 440 Strand, London WC2R 0QS *Tel.* 020 7649 2903 *Email* Jandoole@tuixen.org.uk *Website* http://tuixen.org.uk

....

■ The Roger and Douglas Turner Charitable Trust

CC NO 1154467   **ESTABLISHED** 2013

WHERE FUNDING CAN BE GIVEN Birmingham, the Black Country (Dudley, Sandwell, Walsall and Wolverhampton), Herefordshire and Worcestershire.

WHO CAN BENEFIT Registered charities; hospices.

WHAT IS FUNDED Children and young people; disability; health; the environment and heritage; the arts; community projects; older people; social welfare.

WHAT IS NOT FUNDED Individuals; grant-making charities; CICs; social enterprises or other not-for-profit organisations; charities that have large investment portfolios or excessive reserves; charities with a large defined-benefit pension fund deficit; large national and international organisations.

TYPE OF GRANT Capital costs; core and revenue costs; unrestricted funding.

RANGE OF GRANTS Typically between £1,000 and £5,000.

SAMPLE GRANTS Severn Valley Railway Charitable Trust (£25,000); St Richard's Hospice (£20,000); Severn Area Rescue Association (£15,000); The Stonehouse Gang (£12,000); Birmingham Botanical and Horticultural Society (£7,000); Listening Books (£5,000); Newlife, Prisoners' Education Trust, Sophie Hayes Foundation and Target Ovarian Cancer (£3,000 each).

FINANCES *Financial year end* 31/12/2022
Income £2,360,000
Grants to organisations £720,000
Assets £65,010,000

TRUSTEES Ronald Middleton; Geoffrey Thomas; Peter Millward; Dawn Long; Amanda McGeever; Sharon De Souza-Stotts.

OTHER INFORMATION Grants were made to 192 organisations during the year. There were 51 grants of less than £5,000 which totalled £361,000. The trust has a number of regular beneficiaries which it supports on a long-term basis. Applications from new charities, if successful, tend to lead to an initial grant award of up to £3,000, often for capital appeals or specific projects.

HOW TO APPLY Application forms and guidelines can be downloaded from the trust's website. The website notes that it prefers to receive applications by email. Deadlines for applications can be found online.

CONTACT DETAILS Jenny Harris, Grants and Compliance Officer, Arley House, Lion Lane, Upper Arley, Bewdley, Worcestershire DY12 1SQ *Tel.* 01299 861368 *Email* jenny@turnertrust.co.uk *Website* www.turnertrust.co.uk

....

■ G. J. W. Turner Trust

CC NO 258615   **ESTABLISHED** 1969

WHERE FUNDING CAN BE GIVEN Birmingham.

WHO CAN BENEFIT Charitable organisations.

WHAT IS FUNDED General charitable purposes.

SAMPLE GRANTS A list of beneficiaries was not included in the annual report and accounts.

FINANCES *Financial year end* 05/04/2022
Income £368,700
Grants to organisations £377,500
Assets £182,400

TRUSTEES Lesley Davis; Kate Honeyborne; Hugh Carslake.

OTHER INFORMATION In 2021/22 the trust made 115 grants.

HOW TO APPLY Contact the correspondent for further information.

CONTACT DETAILS Chrissy Norgrove, Clerk to the Trustees, The Estate Office, Wharf Cottage, Broombank, Tenbury Wells, Worcestershire WR15 8NY *Tel.* 07940 160844

....

■ The Florence Turner Trust

CC NO 502721   **ESTABLISHED** 1973

WHERE FUNDING CAN BE GIVEN UK, with a strong preference for Leicestershire.

WHO CAN BENEFIT Charitable organisations. Smaller charities are favoured. Grants to national charities are made only when there is a clear and direct benefit to the people of Leicestershire. Grants can be made for the benefit of individuals through a referring agency such as social services, NHS trusts or similar responsible bodies.

WHAT IS FUNDED General charitable purposes.

SAMPLE GRANTS A list of beneficiaries was not included in the annual report and accounts.

FINANCES *Financial year end* 31/03/2022
Income £218,600
Grants to organisations £155,200
Assets £8,460,000

TRUSTEES Roger Bowder; Michael Jones; Katherine Hall.

HOW TO APPLY Contact the correspondent for information regarding the application process. The trustees meet on a bi-monthly basis to consider grant applications.

CONTACT DETAILS Helen Pole, Administrator, c/o Shakespeare Martineau, Two Colton Square, Leicester, Leicestershire LE1 1QH *Tel.* 0116 257 4462 *Email* helen.pole@shma.co.uk

■ The Turtleton Charitable Trust

OSCR NO SC038018   **ESTABLISHED** 2007
WHERE FUNDING CAN BE GIVEN Scotland.
WHO CAN BENEFIT Registered charities.
WHAT IS FUNDED Arts, culture and heritage; welfare; education.
WHAT IS NOT FUNDED Individuals.
RANGE OF GRANTS Mostly between £5,000 and £25,000.
SAMPLE GRANTS The Trimontium Trust (£38,400); Paisley Museum Reimagined Ltd (£25,000); Edinburgh International Festival (£10,000); Krazy Kat Theatre Company (£3,600).
FINANCES *Financial year end* 30/06/2022
Income £234,200
Grants to organisations £198,000
Assets £6,070,000
HOW TO APPLY Apply using the online application form on the trust's website.
CONTACT DETAILS The Trustees, c/o Turcan Connell, Princes Exchange, 1 Earl Grey Street, Edinburgh EH3 9EE *Email* enquiries@turcanconnell.com *Website* www.turcanconnell.com/the-turtleton-charitable-trust

■ The Tweed Family Charitable Foundation

CC NO 1192366
WHERE FUNDING CAN BE GIVEN England and Wales.
WHO CAN BENEFIT Registered charities.
WHAT IS FUNDED The promotion of life enhancing opportunities to socially disadvantaged young people under the age of 25.
WHAT IS NOT FUNDED Individuals or organisations applying on behalf of individuals; capital projects relating to building or refurbishment; large and national charities; statutory bodies, universities, colleges, schools, nurseries, playgroups or crèches; one-off events such as holidays, trips, festivals and concerts; sports and leisure projects without a strong social welfare focus; retrospective expenditure.
RANGE OF GRANTS Grants are typically £10,000 per year for up to three years.
SAMPLE GRANTS Inspiring Minds, Lads Need Dads and Youth Cafe Cornwall (£10,000 each).
FINANCES *Financial year end* 31/12/2021
Income £435,400
Grants to organisations £120,000
Assets £341,400
TRUSTEES Clare Kendall; Barbara Tweed; Andrew Tweed; Christopher Tweed; Jayne Woods.
OTHER INFORMATION The foundation states that it is only able to fund a limited number of projects each year.
HOW TO APPLY Applicants should first submit an enquiry form on the foundation's website.
CONTACT DETAILS The Trustees, 5 High Ridge, Cuffley, Potters Bar, Hertfordshire EN6 4JH *Email* tweedfcf@gmail.com *Website* www.tweedfamilycharitablefoundation.org.uk

■ Two Magpies Fund

CC NO 1189451
WHERE FUNDING CAN BE GIVEN Haringey, Westminster; Camden; Islington.
WHO CAN BENEFIT Charitable organisations; not-for-profit organisations; community groups; clubs; hostels; food banks.
WHAT IS FUNDED Women who have experienced abuse; disadvantaged children.
WHAT IS NOT FUNDED Individuals; faith-based organisations; research.

TYPE OF GRANT Project costs; core costs; one-off equipment costs.
SAMPLE GRANTS A list of organisations that have received funding from the charity can be found on its website.
FINANCES *Financial year end* 31/03/2022
Income £314,200
Grants to organisations £311,400
TRUSTEES Stian Westlake; Kirsten Westlake.
HOW TO APPLY At the time of writing (April 2023), the charity's website stated that it had fully committed its funding and was not accepting new applications. However, the website also noted that it plans to accept new applications again at the end of the year. Consult the charity's website for up-to-date information.
CONTACT DETAILS The Trustees, 35 Stormont Road, London N6 4NR *Tel.* 020 8341 7689 *Email* info@twomagpiesfund.co.uk *Website* www.twomagpiesfund.co.uk

■ Two Ridings Community Foundation

CC NO 1166471   **ESTABLISHED** 2000
WHERE FUNDING CAN BE GIVEN North and East Yorkshire.
WHO CAN BENEFIT Charitable organisations and community groups. The foundation focuses mainly on smaller and grassroots organisations (larger organisations should contact the foundation before applying). Individuals can also be supported.
WHAT IS FUNDED General charitable purposes.
WHAT IS NOT FUNDED Each of the foundation's funding programmes has specific criteria, which can be found on the website. In general, grants are not given to: private businesses; general appeals or sponsorship; national organisations and their affiliates (this does not include locally constituted and managed branches of national or large charities); statutory agencies, including parish councils and schools, in the discharge of their statutory obligations; organisations that have substantial unrestricted funds; previous grant recipients who have outstanding monitoring information; organisations that mainly give funds to other organisations or individuals. Grants are not given for: the advancement of religion; activities solely benefitting animals; overseas holidays or trips; political campaigning; medical research, equipment or treatment.
TYPE OF GRANT See individual grant programmes.
RANGE OF GRANTS Mostly from £500 to £10,000.
SAMPLE GRANTS Bellerby Parish Council (£38,000); Humber and World's Rural Action and York CVS (£30,000 each); Active Humber (£17,000); Hull CVS and Best Hope CIC (£10,000 each); Concrete Youth and Igbo Union Yorkshire CIC (£5,000 each).
FINANCES *Financial year end* 02/03/2022
Income £4,670,000
Grants to organisations £2,170,000
Grants to individuals £57,600
Assets £10,830,000
TRUSTEES Hannah Harris; Alison Pearson; Harriet Reid; Eric Downey; Andrew Wilson; Venetia Wrigley; Christopher Legard; Deborah Rosenberg; The Revd Richard Frith; Dr Gillian Hughes; Rolline Frewen; Sheila Crennell; Elizabeth Wild; Emma Kissack.
OTHER INFORMATION This is one of the 47 UK community foundations, which distribute funding for a wide range of purposes. As with all community foundations, there are a number of

Think carefully about every application. Is it justified?

705

donor-advised funds managed on behalf of individuals, families and charitable trusts. Grant schemes tend to change frequently – consult the foundation's website for details of current programmes and up-to-date deadlines. During the year, grants were awarded to 429 organisations. In addition, grants were awarded to 94 individuals.

HOW TO APPLY Potential applicants are advised to visit the community foundation's website or contact its grants team to find the most suitable funding stream.

CONTACT DETAILS The Trustees, Pavilion 2000, Amy Johnson Way, York, North Yorkshire YO30 4XT *Tel.* 01904 929500 *Email* info@tworidingscf. org.uk *Website* www.tworidingscf.org.uk

---

■ Community Foundation serving Tyne and Wear and Northumberland

CC NO 700510   **ESTABLISHED** 1988
WHERE FUNDING CAN BE GIVEN Tyne and Wear and Northumberland.

WHO CAN BENEFIT Charitable organisations; CICs; social enterprises; individuals.

WHAT IS FUNDED General charitable purposes. The foundation has a range of different grant programmes, which change frequently – refer to the website for information on grants currently available.

WHAT IS NOT FUNDED Contributions to general appeals or circulars; religious activity which is not for wider public benefit; replacement of statutory funding; activities where the primary benefit is the advancement of animal welfare; activities which have already taken place; grant-making, or equivalent gifts in kind, by other organisations; privately owned and profit-distributing companies or limited partnerships.

TYPE OF GRANT Projects costs; equipment and capital developments; running costs (including salaries and overheads).

RANGE OF GRANTS Mostly under £5,000.

SAMPLE GRANTS A list of beneficiaries was not included in the annual report and accounts.

FINANCES *Financial year end* 31/03/2022
Income £6,370,000
Grants to organisations £8,460,000
Grants to individuals £108,000
Assets £104,800,000

TRUSTEES Andrew Haigh; Patrick Melia; Lucy Winskell; Paul Farquhar; Dr Laura Warwick; Claire Malcolm; Gillian Baker; Michael Brodie; Philip Moorhouse; Colin Hewitt; Sarah Glendinning; Fiona Standfield; Stella Simbo.

OTHER INFORMATION This is one of the 47 UK community foundations, which distribute funding for a wide range of purposes. As with all community foundations, there are a number of donor-advised funds managed on behalf of individuals, families and charitable trusts. Grant schemes tend to change frequently – consult the foundation's website for details of current programmes and up-to-date deadlines. Grants were awarded to 1,133 organisations and 123 individuals during the year.

HOW TO APPLY Potential applicants are advised to visit the community foundation's website or contact its grants team to find the most suitable funding stream.

CONTACT DETAILS The Grants Team, Philanthropy House, Woodbine Road, Gosforth, Newcastle upon Tyne NE3 1DD *Tel.* 0191 222 0945 *Email* general@communityfoundation.org.uk *Website* www.communityfoundation.org.uk

---

■ Tzedakah

CC NO 251897   **ESTABLISHED** 1966
WHERE FUNDING CAN BE GIVEN Worldwide, in practice mainly UK and Israel.

WHO CAN BENEFIT Charitable organisations.

WHAT IS FUNDED The Jewish faith and community; education and training; relief of poverty.

WHAT IS NOT FUNDED Individuals.

SAMPLE GRANTS A list of beneficiaries was not included in the annual report and accounts. Previous beneficiaries have included: Gertner Charitable Trust; Hasmonean High School Charitable Trust; Hendon Adath Yisroel Synagogue; Medrash Shmuel Theological College; Sage Home for the Aged; Society of Friends of the Torah; Tiferes Girls' School; Torah Movement of Great Britain; Torah Temimoh; Willow Foundation; Wizo.

FINANCES *Financial year end* 31/03/2022
Income £29,800
Grants to organisations £578,900
Assets £97,000

TRUSTEES Leonard Finn; Michael Lebrett.

OTHER INFORMATION The trustees' annual report for 2021/22 states: 'The grant-making programme helps over 300 smaller charities develop themselves each year. The charities are chosen by the individual members.'

HOW TO APPLY Apply in writing to the correspondent.

CONTACT DETAILS The Trustees, Brentmead House, Britannia Road, London N12 9RU *Tel.* 020 8446 6767 *Email* lfinnco@aol.com

■ UBS Optimus Foundation UK

CC NO 1153537
WHERE FUNDING CAN BE GIVEN UK and overseas.
WHO CAN BENEFIT Charitable organisations.
WHAT IS FUNDED Children's health and welfare; the environment.
SAMPLE GRANTS Absolute Return for Kids (Ark) (£6.5 million); OnSide Youth Zones (£2.78 million); Common Seas (£1.1 million); Transparentem (£928,600); For Baby's Sake (£825,000); Hope and Homes for Children (£500,500); Social Impact Fund (£250,000); Last Mile Health (£79,600); Healthy Me Healthy Sea (£18,600); We Care Solar (£11,000); Education Portfolio (£720).
FINANCES *Financial year end* 31/12/2021
Income £30,640,000
Grants to organisations £29,300,000
Assets £9,060,000
TRUSTEES Eva-Kristiina Ispahani; Edoardo Rulli; Paul Vail; Vineet Bewtra; Maria Rocafort-Varela.
OTHER INFORMATION Grants were awarded to 50 organisations in 2021.
HOW TO APPLY Contact the foundation for further information on how to make an application.
CONTACT DETAILS The Trustees, UBS AG London Branch, 5 Broadgate, London EC2M 2QS *Tel.* 020 7567 8000 *Email* use the contact form on the website *Website* www.ubs.com

■ The Udlington Trust

CC NO 1129443　　**ESTABLISHED** 2009
WHERE FUNDING CAN BE GIVEN UK and overseas.
WHO CAN BENEFIT Registered charities.
WHAT IS FUNDED General charitable purposes.
SAMPLE GRANTS A list of beneficiaries was not included in the annual report and accounts.
FINANCES *Financial year end* 31/12/2021
Income £71,500
Grants to organisations £120,600
Assets £23,200
TRUSTEES Rebecca Blackledge; Richard Blackledge; Bruce Blackledge; Robert Blackledge.
HOW TO APPLY Apply in writing to the correspondent.
CONTACT DETAILS The Trustees, c/o Arrow County Supplies, Arrow House, Longden Road, Shrewsbury, Shropshire SY3 9AE *Tel.* 01743 283600

■ Ufi VocTech Trust

CC NO 1081028　　**ESTABLISHED** 2000
WHERE FUNDING CAN BE GIVEN UK.
WHO CAN BENEFIT Charities; trade bodies; learning providers; employers; private companies; CICs; and other not-for-profit organisations.
WHAT IS FUNDED Projects that use digital methods to widen access to adult (over 16) vocational learning.
WHAT IS NOT FUNDED See the trust's FAQs web page (www.ufi.co.uk/faqs) for a full list of exclusions.
TYPE OF GRANT Seed funding; development funding; project funding.
RANGE OF GRANTS Programme dependent.
SAMPLE GRANTS Bodyswaps; Bridgend College; Career Matters; Game Academy; Into Games

CIC; NIACRO; Renaissance Management; Skills for Logistics; University of Sheffield; West College Scotland.
FINANCES *Financial year end* 31/12/2021
Income £533,000
Grants to organisations £2,350,000
Assets £52,730,000
TRUSTEES Dominic Gill; Julia Lambdon; Charlotte Kirby; Jonathan Scott; Anthony Bravo; Alexandra Cullen; Jeffrey Greenidge; David Chapman.
OTHER INFORMATION Each year the trust operates funding calls for a specific type of project or 'Challenge' calls where it combines funding types.
HOW TO APPLY Grant funding calls are advertised on the website and applications can be made via an online portal on the trust's website. The trust usually uses a two-stage application process, where you first give a summary of your idea (stage one), and if suitable you will be invited to submit a more detailed, full application (stage two).
CONTACT DETAILS The Trustees, 1st Floor, 10 Queen Street Place, London EC4R 1BE *Tel.* 020 7551 7777 *Email* info@ufi.co.uk *Website* www.ufi.co.uk

■ UJIA (United Jewish Israel Appeal)

CC NO 1060078
WHERE FUNDING CAN BE GIVEN Israel and UK.
WHO CAN BENEFIT Registered charities; schools and colleges; universities.
WHAT IS FUNDED The Jewish faith and community.
RANGE OF GRANTS Up to £626,000.
SAMPLE GRANTS Jewish Agency for Israel (£626,000); UJIA Israel (£586,000); Carmiel Youth Village (£216,000); B'Nei Akiva (£102,000); Union of Jewish Students (£80,000); Maccabi GB (£50,000); Kemach (£32,000); Atidim (£20,000).
FINANCES *Financial year end* 30/09/2021
Income £7,470,000
Grants to organisations £3,430,000
Assets £7,240,000
TRUSTEES Marc Lester; Melvin Berwald; Louise Jacobs; Karen Goodkind; Brian May; Hilton Nathanson; Steven Kaye; Nicola Wertheim; Miles Webber; Raphael Addlestone; David Pliener.
OTHER INFORMATION Grants were awarded to 125 organisations during the year. Of the grant total, £2.03 million was given to organisations in Israel and £1.4 million was given to organisations in the UK. No grants were given to individuals. The 2020/21 accounts were the latest available at the time of writing (May 2023).
HOW TO APPLY For further information, email the correspondent.
CONTACT DETAILS The Trustees, 4th Floor Amelie House, 221 Golders Green Road, London NW11 9DQ *Tel.* 020 7424 6400 *Email* info@ujia.org *Website* www.ujia.org

■ The UK Youth Fund: Thriving Minds

CC NO 1110590　　**ESTABLISHED** 2005
WHERE FUNDING CAN BE GIVEN UK.
WHO CAN BENEFIT Registered charities with an annual income of less than £500,000 whose primary purpose is to benefit young people.

WHAT IS FUNDED General charitable purposes; registered charities focused on young people's mental health; youth organisations; organisations that provide non-formal education to young people.

RANGE OF GRANTS From £15,000 up to £50,000.

SAMPLE GRANTS A list of beneficiaries was not included in the annual report and accounts.

FINANCES *Financial year end* 31/03/2022
Income £14,620,000
Grants to organisations £10,220,000
Assets £6,930,000

TRUSTEES Wayne Bulpitt; Aaron D'Souza; Benjamin Jessup; Iain McDougall; Kamara Bennett; Matthew Price; Yui Chan; Obumneke Ekeke; David Thomlinson; Jonathan Yates; Lanai Collis-Phillips; Dr Gabrielle Mathews; Godfrey Junior.

OTHER INFORMATION Grants were awarded in 2021/22 for the following causes: Non-formal education programmes (£7.7 million); Avon Tyrell Outdoor Activity Centre (£1.79 million); other non-formal education (£451,000); communications and policy (£280,000).

HOW TO APPLY Applications can be made via The UK Youth Fund's website.

CONTACT DETAILS The Trustees, Avon Tyrrell Activity Centre, Avon Tyrrell, Bransgore, Christchurch, Dorset BH23 8EE *Tel.* 020 3137 3817 *Email* funding@ukyouth.org *Website* www.ukyouth.org/thriving-minds

....

■ UKH Foundation

CC NO 1160507   **ESTABLISHED** 2014
WHERE FUNDING CAN BE GIVEN The North West.
WHO CAN BENEFIT Registered charities.
WHAT IS FUNDED Health, including mental health; disability.
WHAT IS NOT FUNDED Non-registered charities; individuals; large national charities.
RANGE OF GRANTS £1,000 to £15,000.
SAMPLE GRANTS A list of beneficiaries was not included in the annual report and accounts. Previous beneficiaries have included: Royal Manchester Children's Hospital (£40,000); Chorley Youth Zone (£20,000); Bolton Community Transport (£10,000); Friends for Leisure and The Epiphany Trust (£5,000 each); West Coast Crash Rugby (£2,000); Bolton Hospice (£1,000).
FINANCES *Financial year end* 31/12/2021
Income £111,400
Grants to organisations £200,000
Assets £3,470,000
TRUSTEES Andrew Redfern; David Udall; Julie Hulme; Sarah Boustoller.
OTHER INFORMATION Grants were awarded to 42 organisations during the year.
HOW TO APPLY Applications can made through the foundation's website and are considered at quarterly meetings.
CONTACT DETAILS The Trustees, Lancashire Gate, 21 Tiviot Dale, Stockport, Cheshire SK1 1TD *Tel.* 07955 197310 *Email* info@ukhfoundation.com *Website* https://ukhfoundation.org

....

■ Ulster Garden Villages Ltd

CCNI NO NIC101248   **ESTABLISHED** 1946
WHERE FUNDING CAN BE GIVEN Northern Ireland.
WHO CAN BENEFIT Registered charities; hospices; hospitals; educational organisations; local authorities.
WHAT IS FUNDED Health; disadvantaged sections of society; young people; culture and heritage; the environment.

WHAT IS NOT FUNDED Retrospective expenditure; office expenses; administrative staff salaries; replacement of statutory funding.
TYPE OF GRANT Project costs; loans; capital costs.
RANGE OF GRANTS Mostly up to £60,000.
SAMPLE GRANTS A list of beneficiaries was not included in the annual report and accounts. Previous beneficiaries have included: Northern Ireland Children's Hospice (£100,000); Cancer Fund for Children (£70,000); Action Cancer and Greenhill YMCA (£50,000 each).
FINANCES *Financial year end* 31/12/2021
Income £2,010,000
Grants to organisations £1,270,000
Assets £52,850,000
TRUSTEES Martie Boyd; Erskine Holmes; Kevin Baird; Dr Anthony Hopkins; Susan Crowe; Brian Garrett; William Webb; Dame Rotha Johnston; Colin Walsh.
OTHER INFORMATION Grants were awarded to 38 organisations during the year in the following categories: community (£867,300); education and training (£239,100); health (£67,000); culture and heritage (£65,000); people with disabilities (£31,500).
HOW TO APPLY Applications can be made via the charity's website. The most recent annual report and accounts will also be required. Applicants should first complete a short eligibility quiz in order to access the application form.
CONTACT DETAILS The Trustees, Forestview, Purdy's Lane, Newtownbreda, Belfast BT8 7AR *Tel.* 028 9049 1111 *Email* admin@ulstergardenvillages.co.uk *Website* www.ulstergardenvillages.co.uk

....

■ Ulting Overseas Trust

CC NO 294397   **ESTABLISHED** 1986
WHERE FUNDING CAN BE GIVEN UK; financially developing countries (mostly, but not exclusively, Asia, Africa and South and Central America).
WHO CAN BENEFIT Christian training organisations; individuals.
WHAT IS FUNDED Theological training and work in majority world countries.
TYPE OF GRANT Bursaries and training costs.
RANGE OF GRANTS £1,000 to £16,000.
SAMPLE GRANTS International Fellowship of Evangelical Students (£16,100); Langham Scholarships (£13,700); Oxford Centre for Mission Studies (£7,000); Pan Africa Christian College (£5,700); Latin Link (£4,800); Cornerstone Christian College – Cape Town (£2,500); Atiri Bible School (£1,600); Centro de Capacitación Misionera Transcultural (£1,000).
FINANCES *Financial year end* 05/04/2022
Income £86,500
Grants to organisations £125,500
Grants to individuals £7,600
Assets £4,740,000
TRUSTEES John Heyward; The Revd Joseph Kapolyo; Tim Warren; Nicholas Durlacher; Dr Carol Walker; John Whitfield; Jennifer Brown; Dr Sue Brown; Jennifer Stewart; William Clark; Philip Greenwood.
OTHER INFORMATION In total, 40 grants were awarded to organisations during the year.
HOW TO APPLY Apply in writing to the correspondent. Grants are reviewed and awarded on an annual basis.
CONTACT DETAILS The Trustees, Goosehill Hall, Buxton Road, Castleton, Derbyshire S33 8WP *Tel.* 01433 621826

....

■ The Ulverscroft Foundation

CC NO 264873 **ESTABLISHED** 1972
WHERE FUNDING CAN BE GIVEN UK and overseas.
WHO CAN BENEFIT Registered charities; unregistered charities; social enterprises; CICs; schools; universities; hospitals.
WHAT IS FUNDED Projects that help visually impaired people.
WHAT IS NOT FUNDED The foundation does not fund staff salaries or ongoing running costs for an organisation.
TYPE OF GRANT Capital costs; project funding.
RANGE OF GRANTS Grants range from £1,000 to £5,000 with some larger grants.
SAMPLE GRANTS University of Leicester (£202,000); University of Liverpool (£31,000); Open Sight – Hampshire (£5,000); Walsall Society for the Blind (£1,000).
FINANCES *Financial year end 30/04/2022*
Income £8,630,000
Grants to organisations £437,000
Assets £20,860,000
TRUSTEES Roger Crooks; Robert Gent; John Sandford-Smith; Geoffrey Woodruff; Ian Moon; Christopher Ashton; Richard Clarke.
HOW TO APPLY Applications can be made online using a form on the foundation's website. Alternatively, applicants may wish to download a copy of the form and once completed, return by post. The trustees meet quarterly (in January, April, July and October) to consider grant applications. Application deadlines, along with guidance notes, can be seen on the website.
CONTACT DETAILS The Trustees, The Green, Bradgate Road, Anstey, Leicester, Leicestershire LE7 7FU *Tel.* 0116 236 1595 *Email* foundation@ulverscroft.co.uk *Website* www.ulverscroft-foundation.org.uk

■ The Underwood Trust

CC NO 266164 **ESTABLISHED** 1973
WHERE FUNDING CAN BE GIVEN UK.
WHO CAN BENEFIT Charitable organisations.
WHAT IS FUNDED Medicine and health; social welfare; education; arts and culture; the environment and wildlife.
WHAT IS NOT FUNDED Individuals; political activities; commercial ventures or publications; the purchase of vehicles including minibuses; overseas travel, holidays and expeditions.
TYPE OF GRANT Capital costs; core costs; project funding.
RANGE OF GRANTS Up to £150,000 but typically between £10,000 and £25,000.
SAMPLE GRANTS Bristol Speech and Language Therapy Research Unit (£150,000); Bristol Children's Hospital (£114,700); Swindon Women's Aid (£30,000); Music for Youth (£25,000); Ebony Horse Club (£22,500); Separated Child Foundation (£10,000).
FINANCES *Financial year end 05/04/2022*
Income £17,660,000
Grants to organisations £1,320,000
Assets £35,340,000
TRUSTEES Robin Clark; Briony Wilson; Richard Bennison.
OTHER INFORMATION Grants were broken down into the following categories: medicine and health (£439,700); the environment and wildlife (£425,000); social welfare (£362,500); education and arts (£90,000).
HOW TO APPLY The trust's website states: 'The trustees have decided to give annual support to a number of charities and proactively seek out certain projects. This restricts the funds available for general applications and as such the Trust is closed to unsolicited applications.' Only make an application if you have been invited to do so. The application form is available to download on the website. Once completed, you can either post or email it to the trust's office. The trustees meet on a regular basis to consider applications during the year.
CONTACT DETAILS Michele Judge, Manager, Ground Floor, 20 York Street, London W1U 6PU *Tel.* 020 7486 0100 *Email* michelej@taylorclark.co.uk *Website* www.theunderwoodtrust.org.uk

■ The Union of Orthodox Hebrew Congregations

CC NO 1158987 **ESTABLISHED** 1966
WHERE FUNDING CAN BE GIVEN UK.
WHO CAN BENEFIT Charitable organisations; individuals.
WHAT IS FUNDED The Jewish faith and community.
SAMPLE GRANTS UOHC Foundation Ltd (£1.31 million); Bris Brucha (£83,100); Support The Charity Worker and Vishnitz Girls' School Ltd (£18,000 each); Kollel Torah Veyirah Ltd (£15,000); Interlink (£12,000); Shaarei Orah Ltd (£10,800).
FINANCES *Financial year end 31/12/2021*
Income £1,370,000
Grants to organisations £1,890,000
Grants to individuals £7,800
Assets £927,900
TRUSTEES Ahron Klein; Benzion Freshwater; Sydney Sinitsky; Moses Bibelman; Jacob Goldman; Michael Lobenstein; Benjamin Roth; Myer Rothfeld; Nathan Bindinger; Victor Brinner; Aron Goldman; Chaim Goldman; Benzion Goldstein; Robert Grussgott; Michael Just; Joshua Muller; Daniel Ost; Ahron Rand; Schloime Rand; Zalman Roth; Abraham Schreiber; Shalom Seidenfeld; Mordechai Steren; Benjamin Stern; Chaim Pinter; Jehudah Baumgarten.
OTHER INFORMATION Grants of under £7,500 to organisations totalled £50,400.
HOW TO APPLY Apply in writing to the correspondent. The trustees meet regularly to review applications.
CONTACT DETAILS The Trustees, 140 Stamford Hill, London N16 6QT *Tel.* 020 8800 6833

■ The Union of the Sisters of Mercy of Great Britain

CC NO 288158 **ESTABLISHED** 1991
WHERE FUNDING CAN BE GIVEN England; Wales; Scotland; South Africa; Lebanon; Romania.
WHO CAN BENEFIT Charitable organisations; individuals.
WHAT IS FUNDED Catholic mission work; education; health; social welfare.
RANGE OF GRANTS Up to £50,000 but typically between £5,000 and £10,000.
SAMPLE GRANTS Daniel's Corporation – Romania (£50,900); Sagesse High School – Lebanon (£25,000); Addo – South Africa (£14,600); Diocese of Westminster (£12,000); Weldmar Hospicecare (£10,000); WaterAid (£5,000).
FINANCES *Financial year end 03/03/2022*
Income £5,550,000
Grants to organisations £310,600
Grants to individuals £121,500
Assets £74,270,000

TRUSTEES Sr Geraldine Lawlor; Sr Margaret Jones; Sr Mary McGrath; Sr Annette McCartan; Sr Johanna Moloney.

OTHER INFORMATION The grant-maker states that it is inspired by gospel values to benefit the public, particularly women and children and those who are poor. During the year, 56 grants were awarded to organisations and 11 grants were awarded to individuals.

HOW TO APPLY Apply in writing to the correspondent.

CONTACT DETAILS The Trustees, Mercy Union Generalate, 11 Harewood Avenue, London NW1 6LD *Tel.* 020 7723 3221 *Email* admin@mercyunion.org.uk *Website* http://sistersofmercyunion.org.uk

·····················

■ The United Reformed Church (Wessex) Trust Ltd

CC NO 282729   **ESTABLISHED** 1980

WHERE FUNDING CAN BE GIVEN UK.

WHO CAN BENEFIT Churches of the United Reform Church; Christian organisations, particularly the Wessex Synod of the United Reform Church.

WHAT IS FUNDED Christian activities.

TYPE OF GRANT Capital costs; core costs; project funding; strategic funding.

RANGE OF GRANTS Generally £400 to £15,000.

SAMPLE GRANTS Mission Development Group (£107,800); Twyford (Buckinghamshire) URC (£85,000); Banbury URC – The Haven (£30,000); Trinity Learning – Abingdon (£15,000); Avenue St Andrew's URC – Southampton (£12,000); South Hayling URC (£3,000); St Martin's URC – West Moors (£1,500); Christ Church URC – Windsor (£420).

FINANCES *Financial year end* 31/12/2021
Income £2,770,000
Grants to organisations £526,100
Assets £48,560,000

TRUSTEES Margaret Smith; Raymond Dunnett; The Revd Julian Macro; The Revd Nigel Appleton; The Revd Clare Downing; Colin MacBean; Susan Brown; Andrew Gibb; The Revd Dr Romilly Micklem; John Sinclair; The Revd Glyn Millington.

OTHER INFORMATION Grants were awarded to 25 churches during the year. Some examples of projects for which grants were awarded include building works; renovation works; employment of a children's worker; audio-visual installation.

HOW TO APPLY Apply in writing to the correspondent.

CONTACT DETAILS The Trustees, 120 Alma Road, Southampton, Hampshire SO14 6UW *Tel.* 023 8067 4515 *Email* trust@urcwessex.org.uk *Website* www.urcwessex.org.uk

·····················

■ United St Saviour's Charity

CC NO 1103731   **ESTABLISHED** 2004

WHERE FUNDING CAN BE GIVEN North Southwark and Bermondsey.

WHO CAN BENEFIT Local charitable organisations, including: charities; social enterprises; companies limited by guarantee (with a social purpose); faith-based organisations (where activities are not specifically connected with religion); tenants' and residents' associations; CICs.

WHAT IS FUNDED Social welfare; community development; older people.

WHAT IS NOT FUNDED Projects where the main beneficiaries are living or working outside the charity's area of benefit; individuals (including sole traders); for-profit private companies; local

authorities; purely religious activity; political or animal welfare activity.

TYPE OF GRANT Project funding; capital costs; core funding; strategic funding.

SAMPLE GRANTS Bede House Association (£30,000); Southside Young Leaders Academy (£25,000); Silvefit (£20,000); The Black Society (£10,000); Young Futures CIC (£5,000).

FINANCES *Financial year end* 31/03/2022
Income £1,510,000
Grants to organisations £414,400
Assets £53,000,000

TRUSTEES Shane Holland; Stephen Burns; Lord Roy Kennedy; Nicola Steuer; Claire Treanor; Dr Ben Johnson; Lucinda Glover; Kathryn Ogunbona; Izabela Szmidt; Dwight Pile-Gray.

OTHER INFORMATION The charity awards grants on the basis of three priority themes: positive ageing; strong resilient communities; levelling the playing field. There are two open-access grant programmes: large grants of over £3,000 and small grants of under £3,000.

HOW TO APPLY Apply via the link on the charities helpful website to the 'Flexigrant' online portal.

CONTACT DETAILS The Trustees, 16 Crucifix Lane, London SE1 3JW *Tel.* 020 7089 9014 *Email* info@ustsc.org.uk *Website* www.ustsc.org.uk

·····················

■ United Utilities Trust Fund

CC NO 1108296   **ESTABLISHED** 2004

WHERE FUNDING CAN BE GIVEN The area supplied by United Utilities Water plc (predominantly the North West).

WHO CAN BENEFIT Mainly individuals, but also organisations.

WHAT IS FUNDED Money advice; debt counselling; financial literacy.

RANGE OF GRANTS £3,800 to £32,900.

SAMPLE GRANTS A list of beneficiaries was not included in the annual report and accounts. Previous beneficiaries have included: Citizens Advice Halton (£15,100); Citizens Advice Preston (£13,100); The Oaks (£11,100); Liverpool Community Advice (£9,200); Institute of Money Advisors (£3,400).

FINANCES *Financial year end* 31/03/2022
Income £3,500,000
Grants to organisations £117,300
Grants to individuals £3,120,000
Assets £323,200

TRUSTEES Deborah Morton; Alastair Richards; Lynne Heath; Jo-Anne Boswell; Martin Crowhurst.

HOW TO APPLY Details of open funding rounds can be found on the fund's website.

CONTACT DETAILS Company Secretary, c/o Auriga Services Ltd, Emmanuel Court, 12–14 Mill Street, Sutton Coldfield, West Midlands B72 1TJ *Email* communitygrants@aurigaservices.co.uk *Website* www.uutf.org.uk/information-for-organisations/organisational-grant-funding/grant-funding

·····················

■ UnLtd (Foundation for Social Entrepreneurs)

CC NO 1090393   **ESTABLISHED** 2001

WHERE FUNDING CAN BE GIVEN UK.

WHO CAN BENEFIT Social entrepreneurs and those looking to start a social enterprise project; social businesses.

WHAT IS FUNDED Health ageing; access to employment.

TYPE OF GRANT Award winners receive a complete, tailored package of funding, training and advice for their project; social investment.

SAMPLE GRANTS A list of beneficiaries was not included in the annual report and accounts.

FINANCES *Financial year end* 31/03/2022
Income £11,040,000
Grants to organisations £4,280,000
Assets £7,580,000

TRUSTEES Nicolas Farhi; Susan Charteris; Nicholas Petford; Rachel Barton; Krishna Vishnubhotla; Lynne Berry; Elizabeth Sideris; James Lawson; Stephen Bediako; Tim Davies-Pugh; Anne Glover; Amma Mensah.

HOW TO APPLY Applications can be made via the application portal on the charity's website.

CONTACT DETAILS The Trustees, 123 Whitecross Street, Islington, London EC1Y 8JJ *Tel.* 020 7566 1100 *Email* use the contact form on the website *Website* www.unltd.org.uk

---

■ UPP Foundation

CC NO 1166323   **ESTABLISHED** 2015
WHERE FUNDING CAN BE GIVEN UK.

WHO CAN BENEFIT Registered UK charities; universities and other higher educational organisations; non-registered groups with a clear social purpose, social enterprises, community groups and other charitable bodies.

WHAT IS FUNDED Student welfare; sustainable universities; higher education.

WHAT IS NOT FUNDED Individuals.

TYPE OF GRANT Project funding.

RANGE OF GRANTS Between £5,000 and £25,000; applications outside that scale will not be considered.

SAMPLE GRANTS A list of beneficiaries was not included in the annual report and accounts.

FINANCES *Financial year end* 31/08/2022
Income £270,000
Grants to organisations £32,000
Assets £405,000

TRUSTEES Prof. Mary Stuart; Jonathan Wakeford; Christopher Skidmore; Karen Morgon.

OTHER INFORMATION The UPP Foundation was created in 2016 by University Partnerships Programme (UPP) the leading provider of on campus student accommodation infrastructure and support services in the UK. UPP is the sole funder of the UPP Foundation. The UPP Foundation is an autonomous charity and all of its grants are reviewed and authorised by its Board of Trustees. In previous years grants have totalled over £200,000.

HOW TO APPLY Application forms can be downloaded from the foundation's website. Check the website for upcoming deadlines and further information on eligibility.

CONTACT DETAILS The Trustees, 12 Arthur Street, London EC4R 9AB *Tel.* 020 7398 7200 *Email* upp-foundation@upp-ltd.com *Website* http://upp-foundation.org

---

■ The Michael Uren Foundation

CC NO 1094102   **ESTABLISHED** 2002
WHERE FUNDING CAN BE GIVEN UK and overseas.

WHO CAN BENEFIT Registered charities; hospitals; universities.

WHAT IS FUNDED The armed forces; medical research; animal welfare; education; heritage.

TYPE OF GRANT Project funding; research.

SAMPLE GRANTS Imperial College Trust (£6.08 million); Royal Naval Benevolent Trust (£500,000); Combat Stress (£200,000); The Salvation Army (£100,000); Friends of Oxford Botanical Garden (£25,000); Tenterden Mindfulness Group (£15,000).

FINANCES *Financial year end* 05/04/2022
Income £51,560,000
Grants to organisations £9,070,000
Assets £252,580,000

TRUSTEES Anne Gregory-Jones; Roger Gould; Janis Bennett; Robert Uren.

OTHER INFORMATION Grants were made to 17 organisations in 2021/22.

HOW TO APPLY The foundation does not consider unsolicited applications.

CONTACT DETAILS The Trustees, c/o haysmacintyre, Thames Exchange, 10 Queen Street Place, London EC4R 1AG *Tel.* 020 7969 5500 *Email* mpattenden@haysmacintyre.com

---

■ The Utley Foundation

CC NO 1157399   **ESTABLISHED** 2014
WHERE FUNDING CAN BE GIVEN UK and overseas.

WHO CAN BENEFIT Charitable organisations.

WHAT IS FUNDED General charitable purposes; music and dementia; veterans; children and young people; international aid.

SAMPLE GRANTS A list of beneficiaries was not included in the annual report and accounts.

FINANCES *Financial year end* 31/03/2022
Income £622,100
Grants to organisations £1,410,000
Assets £25,620,000

TRUSTEES Melvyn Sims; Nicky Utley; Neil Utley; Raja Balasuriya.

OTHER INFORMATION In 2021/22, grants were broken down as follows: music and dementia (£1.12 million); children (£158,000); international aid (£75,100); other (£11,900). Of the total £1.41 million awarded, £1.03 million was awarded to UK-registered charities.

HOW TO APPLY Unsolicited applications are not accepted; however, the foundation's website states that new grant enquiries should be sent via email or post.

CONTACT DETAILS The Trustees, Larkins Farm, 199 Nine Ashes Road, Ingatestone, Essex CM4 0JY *Tel.* 01277 821338 *Email* Peyton@utleyfoundation.org.uk *Website* http://utleyfoundation.org.uk/index.html

■ Valencia Communities Fund

CC NO 1096538   **ESTABLISHED** 2003
WHERE FUNDING CAN BE GIVEN England and Scotland, specifically areas near Viridor landfill sites.
WHO CAN BENEFIT Charitable organisations; places of worship.
WHAT IS FUNDED Community development; heritage; biodiversity.
WHAT IS NOT FUNDED A list of exclusions can be found in the guidance notes for applicants available on the grant-maker's website.
TYPE OF GRANT Capital costs; project funding.
RANGE OF GRANTS Up to £100,000.
SAMPLE GRANTS Dinnington Community Centre (£100,000); Welbeck Street Recreation Ground (£80,900); Middlezoy Rovers FC (£60,000); Wickham Community Hall (£50,000).
FINANCES *Financial year end 31/03/2022*
Income £5,820,000
Grants to organisations £4,510,000
Assets £2,620,000
TRUSTEES Peter Renshaw; Simon Catford; David Robertson; Mary Prior.
OTHER INFORMATION Grants made may require a contributing third-party payment, which is the equivalent of 10% of any funds awarded. See the 'Contributing Third Party' section of the grant-maker's website for further information. Grants awarded in England totalled £4.19 million and grants awarded in Scotland totalled £321,900.
HOW TO APPLY Applicants should check the availability of funding in their area using the postcode checker on the charity's website, before submitting a stage one application form.
CONTACT DETAILS Grants Officer, PO Box 977, Taunton, Somerset TA1 9PQ *Tel.* 01823 476476 *Email* enquiries@ valenciacommunitiesfund.co.uk *Website* www. valenciacommunitiesfund.co.uk

■ The Valentine Charitable Trust

CC NO 1001782   **ESTABLISHED** 1990
WHERE FUNDING CAN BE GIVEN UK and overseas, with a preference for Dorset.
WHO CAN BENEFIT Registered charities; hospitals; hospices; CICs; educational institutions; museums.
WHAT IS FUNDED General charitable purposes; local projects in Dorset; medical research and health; the environment; community development; arts and culture.
TYPE OF GRANT Core costs; development funding; project funding; strategic funding; medical research; matched funding.
RANGE OF GRANTS Up to £20,000.
SAMPLE GRANTS Dorset Country Museum, Lewis-Manning Hospice and MacDougall Trust (£20,000 each); Anthony Nolan, Pathways for All People and Safewise (£15,000 each); Chase Africa, Citizens Advice Purbeck and Game and Wildlife Conservation Trust (£10,000 each); Bourne Academy, Faithworks Wessex and SAYes (£5,000 each); Swanage and Purbeck Development Trust and Wimborne Community Theatre (£1,000 each).

FINANCES *Financial year end 30/09/2021*
Income £986,100
Grants to organisations £710,500
Assets £39,580,000
TRUSTEES Roger Gregory; Peter Leatherdale; Douglas Neville-Jones; Susan Patterson; Wing Cdr Donald Jack; Susan Ridley; Fiona Normington-Smith.
OTHER INFORMATION The 2020/21 accounts were the most recent available at the time of writing (May 2023). The trust states that it mostly awards grants recurrently but may award grants to new organisations. Applications from speculative applicants may be accepted, especially if the applicant is local.
HOW TO APPLY Apply in writing to the correspondent.
CONTACT DETAILS The Trustees, Hinton House, Hinton Road, Bournemouth, Dorset BH1 2EN *Tel.* 01202 292424

■ The Valiant Charitable Trust

CC NO 1135810   **ESTABLISHED** 2010
WHERE FUNDING CAN BE GIVEN Hitchin and surrounding areas.
WHO CAN BENEFIT Registered charities.
WHAT IS FUNDED General charitable purposes.
TYPE OF GRANT Project funding; capital costs.
RANGE OF GRANTS Grants range from £5,000 to £100,000.
SAMPLE GRANTS Keech Hospice (£200,000); Herts Homeless (£106,000); The Prince's Trust (£50,000); Stirling and Trossachs Scouts (£37,000); Garden House Hospice (£25,000); Daisychains (£20,000); Kids in Action (£10,000).
FINANCES *Financial year end 05/04/2022*
Income £697,000
Grants to organisations £370,300
Assets £5,840,000
TRUSTEES Lady Valerie Dixon; Roger Woolfe; Paul Brenham.
OTHER INFORMATION Grants were made to 13 organisations throughout the year.
HOW TO APPLY Contact the correspondent for further information.
CONTACT DETAILS Jonathon Goldstone, c/o Collyer Bristow LLP, 140 Brompton Road, London SW3 1HY *Tel.* 020 7470 4407 *Email* jonathon. goldstone@collyerbristow.com

■ The Albert Van Den Bergh Charitable Trust

CC NO 296885   **ESTABLISHED** 1987
WHERE FUNDING CAN BE GIVEN UK and overseas.
WHO CAN BENEFIT Charitable organisations.
WHAT IS FUNDED General charitable purposes, particularly medical research and care for patients with cancer, multiple sclerosis, Parkinson's and other diseases and disabilities. Organisations that care for older people and children's charities are also supported.
SAMPLE GRANTS A list of beneficiaries was not included in the annual report and accounts.
FINANCES *Financial year end 05/04/2022*
Income £124,300
Grants to organisations £240,000
Assets £4,040,000
TRUSTEES Jane Hartley; Glover Nicola; David Webster.
OTHER INFORMATION Grants were awarded in the following categories: help in the community (£125,500); conservation (£27,000); overseas (£24,000); disability (£13,000); medical

research, care and support (£12,000); disadvantaged people (£10,000); cultural charities (£9,000); mental health (£7,000); hospices (£5,000); homelessness (£4,000); churches (£3,000); Service personnel (£500).

HOW TO APPLY Contact the correspondent for further information.

CONTACT DETAILS The Trustees, Trevornick Farmhouse, Holywell Bay, Newquay, Cornwall TR8 5PW *Tel.* 01637 830272 *Email* trustees@albertvandenbergh.org

■ The Van Mesdag Fund

CC NO 1166453   **ESTABLISHED** 2015
WHERE FUNDING CAN BE GIVEN UK and overseas.
WHO CAN BENEFIT Charitable organisations.
WHAT IS FUNDED General charitable purposes; health and disability; education; animal welfare; social welfare.
SAMPLE GRANTS A list of beneficiaries was not included in the annual report and accounts.
FINANCES *Financial year end* 30/06/2022
  Income £108,100
  Grants to organisations £219,600
  Assets £4,870,000
TRUSTEES Rozemarijn Mesdag; Ewen Gilmour; Savanna Mesdag; Milo Mesdag.
OTHER INFORMATION Grants were distributed as follows: general charitable purposes (£73,300); prevention or relief of poverty (£57,000); health and disability (£53,100); animal welfare (£27,000); education (£16,000).
HOW TO APPLY Apply in writing to the correspondent.
CONTACT DETAILS Rozemarijn Mesdag, Trustee, Flat G/1, 112 Cloch Road, Gourock, Renfrewshire PA19 1FN *Tel.* 01475 639861 *Email* rvmesdag@gmail.com

■ The Van Neste Foundation

CC NO 201951   **ESTABLISHED** 1959
WHERE FUNDING CAN BE GIVEN UK and financially developing countries.
WHO CAN BENEFIT Registered charities; CICs.
WHAT IS FUNDED Children and young people; community projects focusing on marginalised people and environmental improvement.
WHAT IS NOT FUNDED National appeals; large NGOs.
RANGE OF GRANTS Typical grants range from £1,000 up to £10,000.
SAMPLE GRANTS CHAS (£22,500); Climate Change All Charge (£15,000); Bristol Ensemble (£10,000); Universal Church and Wonder Foundation (£5,000 each); Friends of Hanover School (£4,000); Bristol Hub (£3,300); Mendip Schools PTA (£1,680).
FINANCES *Financial year end* 05/04/2022
  Income £233,700
  Grants to organisations £346,400
  Assets £10,780,000
TRUSTEES Benedict Appleby; Tom Appleby; Jeremy Lyons; Joanna Dickens; Anthony Delaney; Lucy Appleby; Jessica Lyons.
OTHER INFORMATION Grants were made to 53 organisations during the year.
HOW TO APPLY Application forms can be downloaded from the foundation's website. Grant applications are assessed three times a year, usually in January, June and October.
CONTACT DETAILS The Trustees, 15 Alexandra Road, Clifton, Bristol BS8 2DD *Tel.* 07711 186057 *Email* secretary@vanneste.org.uk *Website* http://vanneste.org.uk

■ The Vandervell Foundation

CC NO 255651   **ESTABLISHED** 1968
WHERE FUNDING CAN BE GIVEN UK.
WHO CAN BENEFIT Charitable organisations.
WHAT IS FUNDED General charitable purposes, particularly education, medical care and research, the performing arts, environmental regeneration and social welfare.
WHAT IS NOT FUNDED Individuals.
RANGE OF GRANTS Between £5,000 and £18,000.
SAMPLE GRANTS City and Guilds (£18,000); University of Nottingham, Arts Education School Tring Park, British Exploring Society, King's College London School of Medicine (£15,000 each); London's Air Ambulance (£7,000); Roy Castle Lung Cancer Foundation, Prisoner's Education Trust and St Joseph's Hospice (£5,000 each).
FINANCES *Financial year end* 31/12/2021
  Income £248,100
  Grants to organisations £364,500
  Assets £8,130,000
TRUSTEE The Vandervell Foundation Ltd.
OTHER INFORMATION In 2021, 106 grants were made to organisations.
HOW TO APPLY Apply in writing to the correspondent. The trustees meet every other month to consider grant applications.
CONTACT DETAILS Valerie Kaye, Administrator, Hampstead Town Hall Centre, 213 Haverstock Hill, London NW3 4QP *Tel.* 020 7435 7546 *Email* vandervell@btconnect.com

■ The Vardy Foundation

CC NO 328415   **ESTABLISHED** 1987
WHERE FUNDING CAN BE GIVEN UK and overseas, with a preference for the North East.
WHO CAN BENEFIT Registered charities; individuals.
WHAT IS FUNDED Education; religion; the arts; rehabilitation of offenders; families; social welfare; homelessness; addiction.
RANGE OF GRANTS Grants range from £25,000 up to £900,000.
SAMPLE GRANTS Mercy Ships (£900,000); Biblica Europe (£100,000); Good Shepherd (£286,000); Kids Operating Room (£125,000); Revelation Trust (£30,000); The Message Trust and The Moses Project (£25,000 each).
FINANCES *Financial year end* 05/04/2022
  Income £1,240,000
  Grants to organisations £2,660,000
  Grants to individuals £35,640
  Assets £35,810,000
TRUSTEES Richard Vardy; Lady Margaret Vardy; Peter Vardy; Sir Peter Vardy; Victoria Vardy.
OTHER INFORMATION In 2021/22, the foundation distributed 151 grants as follows: welfare (£1.79 million); religion (£528,200); education (£24,900); arts (£10,000). Grants of under £25,000 totalled £439,800. The foundation has two designated funds – Peter Vardy Foundation and The Jigsaw Foundation – which are primarily focused on charitable activities in Scotland but also support some international programmes.
HOW TO APPLY Apply in writing to the correspondent. The trustees meet every three months to review grants.
CONTACT DETAILS The Trustees, 110 George Street, Edinburgh EH2 4LH *Tel.* 0131 374 7144

■ Variety, the Children's Charity

CC NO 209259   ESTABLISHED 1962
WHERE FUNDING CAN BE GIVEN UK.
WHO CAN BENEFIT Charitable organisations; youth clubs; hospitals; hospices; individuals.
WHAT IS FUNDED Support children and young people: disability; health; social and economic disadvantage.
WHAT IS NOT FUNDED The charity does not fund: standard household equipment or furnishings; repayment of loans; garden adaptations; garden sheds or summerhouses; the cost of a family/wheelchair adapted vehicle; computer hardware; maintenance or ongoing costs; travel costs; therapy sessions; reimbursement of funds already paid out; hire/rental costs or down payments; trikes/bikes or buggies; trips abroad or holiday costs; trampolines; medical treatment; or education or tuition fees. Application guidelines are available to download from the website.
TYPE OF GRANT Capital costs.
RANGE OF GRANTS £5,000 to £72,000.
SAMPLE GRANTS Shenstone School – Crayford (£72,500); Green Meadows School – Leeds (£45,400); Hazelbeck School – Bingley (£41,300); Twydall Primary School – Kent (£36,700); West Road Primary – Doncaster (£30,700); The Pines School – Birmingham (£28,400); Manor Green College – Crawley (£21,600); Muntham House School – Horsham (£16,600); The Golf Trust (£5,300).
FINANCES *Financial year end 31/12/2021*
Income £3,690,000
Grants to organisations £1,320,000
Grants to individuals £602,300
Assets £3,790,000
TRUSTEES Stanley Salter; Prof. Jonathan Shalit; Tushar Prabhu; Dilaram Kitchlew-Williamson; Tesula Mohindra; Guy Remond; Benjamin Whittle.
OTHER INFORMATION In total, 330 grants were awarded during the year. Grants are generally awarded for the purposes of providing equipment for organisations that fit the criteria of Variety's charitable objectives.
HOW TO APPLY Download the relevant application form from the charity's website, where guidelines are also available. Applications should be returned to the correspondent by post or email to grants@variety.org.uk. There are no deadlines.
CONTACT DETAILS Grants Programme Manager, Variety Club House, 93 Bayham Street, London NW1 0AG *Tel.* 020 7428 8100 *Email* info@variety.org.uk or grants@variety.org.uk *Website* www.variety.org.uk

■ Veg Trust (incorporating the Matthew Eyton Animal Welfare Trust)

CC NO 1195550
WHERE FUNDING CAN BE GIVEN Worldwide.
WHO CAN BENEFIT Individuals; non-profit organisations; registered charities.
WHAT IS FUNDED Animal welfare, with a preference for farm animals; educating the public in veganism.
WHAT IS NOT FUNDED Large, well-funded national charities (i.e. those with an annual income in excess of £5 million or with assets of more than £50 million) or charities dedicated to issues deemed by the trustees to be already well funded; activities which appear to, or actively seek to, influence public opinion in favour of a particular political party or promote political partisanship; organisations or individuals who deny the human rights of others, commit acts of cruelty/subjugation of animals, coerce or force others to change their beliefs, promote or support violence, aggression or oppression towards others.
RANGE OF GRANTS £200 to £5,000.
SAMPLE GRANTS Veganuary (£48,400); Vegan Outreach Scotland (£35,000); ProVeg CIC (£20,800); Casa Animal (£11,300); ProVeg Spain (£5,000).
FINANCES *Financial year end 05/04/2022*
Income £28,600
Grants to organisations £261,500
Assets £4,780,000
TRUSTEES Kathryn Fowler; Richard Constant; Graeme Wotherspoon.
OTHER INFORMATION The charity was registered with the Charity Commission in August 2021 and incorporates the Matthew Eyton Animal Welfare Trust (Charity Commission no. 1003575). Full financial information for the Veg Trust Ltd was not available due to its recent registration and we have therefore used financial information from the Matthew Eyton Animal Welfare Trust. Grants were made to 14 organisations during the year.
HOW TO APPLY Guidelines and FAQs are available on the trust's website. At the time of writing (August 2023), the website stated that the trust had temporarily paused accepting applications (until September 2023) to allow existing applications to be processed and evaluated. See the website for updates.
CONTACT DETAILS The Trustees, Westgate House, 87 St Dunstan's Street, Canterbury, Kent CT2 8AE *Email* hello@vegtrust.com *Website* https://vegtrust.com

■ The Velvet Foundation

CC NO 1169789   ESTABLISHED 2015
WHERE FUNDING CAN BE GIVEN England; Wales; Israel.
WHO CAN BENEFIT Charitable organisations; individuals; medical institutions; educational establishments.
WHAT IS FUNDED General charitable purposes; social welfare; health and medical; education; the Jewish faith and community.
TYPE OF GRANT In-kind support; capital costs; general funding.
RANGE OF GRANTS Mostly between £7,000 and £35,000 with the occasional larger grant.
SAMPLE GRANTS Netivei Itzhak (£179,400); Enhance Reviews (£35,800); Friends of I.D.C. (£22,000); Institute for Higher Rabbinical Studies (£15,000); Chabad of Hampstead Garden Suburb, Kollell Beis Aharon and Yeshaya Adler Memorial Fund (£10,000 each); Aish Hatorah UK Ltd and Tikva UK (£7,000 each).
FINANCES *Financial year end 30/09/2021*
Income £1,150,000
Grants to organisations £616,200
Grants to individuals £800
Assets £723,500
TRUSTEES David Rodney; Chee Cheah; Michael Aaronson.
OTHER INFORMATION The foundation's 2020/21 accounts were the latest available information at the time of writing (May 2023). Grants were broken down as follows: education (£436,000); health and medical causes (£94,000); relief of poverty (£87,000). Only organisations that received grants of over £7,000 were listed as beneficiaries in the foundation's 2020/21

accounts. Grants of under £7,000 totalled £54,400.

HOW TO APPLY Apply in writing to the correspondent.

CONTACT DETAILS David Rodney, Trustee, 1st Floor, Winston House, 349 Regents Park Road, London N3 1DH *Tel.* 020 8458 9223 *Email* davidrodney@velvetfoundation.org.uk

■ The William and Patricia Venton Charitable Trust

CC NO 1103884   **ESTABLISHED** 2004

WHERE FUNDING CAN BE GIVEN UK.

WHO CAN BENEFIT Charitable organisations.

WHAT IS FUNDED Relief in need for older people, particularly day centre provision; and the prevention of cruelty and suffering among animals.

SAMPLE GRANTS Age UK Plymouth (£52,600).

FINANCES *Financial year end* 31/03/2022
Income £93,800
Grants to organisations £52,600
Assets £3,320,000

TRUSTEES Christopher Saunby; Martin Hill; Stephen Hone.

OTHER INFORMATION During the year, the charity supported one organisation. The 2021/22 accounts note that the trust had a quiet year due to the ill health of the Chair.

HOW TO APPLY Apply in writing to the correspondent. Following an initial approach, eligible applicants will be sent the relevant application forms, to be returned with the appropriate documentation and then reviewed by trustees. The trustees favour applications from charities with which the trust's founders had a connection, but all applications meeting the trust's objectives are considered.

CONTACT DETAILS The Trustees, Broadlands Gate, Broadlands Road, Brockenhurst, Hampshire SO42 7SX *Tel.* 01590 623818 *Email* johngriffiths@wpventontrust.org.uk

■ The Veolia Environmental Trust

CC NO 1064144   **ESTABLISHED** 1997

WHERE FUNDING CAN BE GIVEN UK. Projects should be near a Veolia site. Postcode checker on website.

WHO CAN BENEFIT Constituted not-for-profit groups or charitable organisations.

WHAT IS FUNDED Community and environmental projects. More specifically, capital projects in the following categories: community buildings and rooms; outdoor spaces; play and recreation spaces; environmental improvements; biodiversity.

WHAT IS NOT FUNDED Each programme has its own specific exclusions. See the trust's website for further information.

TYPE OF GRANT Capital projects with a total cost of less than £250,000.

RANGE OF GRANTS Typically under £50,000.

SAMPLE GRANTS Durham Wildlife Trust (£570,000); Gasworks Dock Partnership (£270,000); Madeley Town Council (£75,000); Knowsley Metropolitan Borough Council (£70,000); London Wildlife Trust (£60,000); Alt Valley Community Trust (£50,000).

FINANCES *Financial year end* 31/03/2022
Income £5,430,000
Grants to organisations £5,310,000
Assets £4,010,000

TRUSTEES Caroline Schwaller; Donald MacPhail; Joanne Demetrius; Ruth Forbes; James

Dennison; Luke Bailey; Richard Hulland; Dean More; Rituja Rao; Rachel Titchen.

OTHER INFORMATION In 2021/22, grants were made to 98 organisations and broken down as follows: community hall centres (£1.72 million); sporting facilities (£989,300); playgrounds (£878,300); nature reserves (£676,500); community gardens (£209,800); footpaths/ bridges (£179,400); parks (£167,200); places of worship (£128,900); cycle paths (£120,000); village greens (£36,900); community farms (£28,100).

HOW TO APPLY After completing the online postcode checker and eligibility checker, a stage one application can be made using the form on the trust's website, where guidelines are also provided. See the trust's website for application deadlines.

CONTACT DETAILS The Trustees, Ruthdene, 1 Station Road, Four Ashes, Wolverhampton, West Midlands WV10 7DG *Tel.* 020 3567 6820 *Email* UK.EnvironmentalTrustInfo@veolia.com *Website* www.veoliatrust.org

■ Versus Arthritis

CC NO 207711   **ESTABLISHED** 2017

WHERE FUNDING CAN BE GIVEN UK.

WHO CAN BENEFIT Universities; research institutions.

WHAT IS FUNDED Research into the cure and prevention of arthritis and related musculoskeletal diseases.

TYPE OF GRANT Project funding; research funding; capital costs; salaries.

SAMPLE GRANTS Medical Research Council (£12.5 million); University of Oxford (£1.22 million in four grants); University of Nottingham (£355,000); Imperial College London (£14,000).

FINANCES *Financial year end* 31/03/2022
Income £30,610,000
Grants to organisations £19,970,000
Assets £152,580,000

TRUSTEES Dr Rodger Macmillan; Karin Hogsander; Juliette Scott; Phillip Gray; Prof. Martijn Steultjens; Dr Andrew Holford; Vincent Noinville; John Isaacs; Jonathan Rodgers; Iain McInnes.

OTHER INFORMATION Only beneficiaries of grants of £10,000 and above were listed in the charity's accounts. Grants of under £10,000 totalled £370,000.

HOW TO APPLY Details of all open grant programmes can be found on the 'Types of grants' section of the charity's website. All applications should be made via the online application portal.

CONTACT DETAILS Research Department, Copeman House, St Mary's Court, St Mary's Gate, Chesterfield S41 7TD *Tel.* 0300 790 0400 *Email* research@versusarthritis.org *Website* www.versusarthritis.org

■ The Veterans' Foundation

CC NO 1166953   **ESTABLISHED** 2016

WHERE FUNDING CAN BE GIVEN UK.

WHO CAN BENEFIT Registered charities; not-for-profit organisations, including CICs limited by guarantee; community groups; individuals.

WHAT IS FUNDED The armed forces community.

WHAT IS NOT FUNDED Organisations that do not support the armed forces or seafaring communities; gap years; study trips; fundraising expeditions; sponsorship; housing associations and corporations (unless activities and costs are clear and charitable); activities that result in profit; organisations requiring payments to be sent to bank accounts outside the UK.

TYPE OF GRANT Project funding; capital costs; multi-year awards.

RANGE OF GRANTS Up to £30,000.

SAMPLE GRANTS Age Cymru Dyfed; Bulldogs Boxing and Community Activities; Citizens Advice Hillingdon Ltd; Defence Gardens Scheme CIC; Little Troopers; Mid Ulster Victims' Empowerment Project; The Military Wives Choirs Foundation; West Lancashire Crisis and Information Centre.

FINANCES *Financial year end* 30/06/2022
Income £9,020,000
Grants to organisations £4,400,000
Grants to individuals £8,100
Assets £518,000

TRUSTEES Bruce Walker; Peter Mountford; Eline Lofgren; Guy Gibson Cartwright; Mungo Tulloch; Simon Banks-Cooper; Gillian Brewer.

OTHER INFORMATION During 2021/22, 202 grants were awarded to 160 organisations, the majority of which were registered charities. Grants were also made to three individuals. Priority is given to small and medium-sized charities.

HOW TO APPLY Applications can be made online after creating an account on the foundation's website. Completed applications should be submitted by the end of the month preceding the grants committee meeting. Check the website for current deadlines. Full guidelines are also available to download from the foundation's website.

CONTACT DETAILS The Trustees, Thistle Court (Room 5), Thistle Street, Edinburgh EH2 1DD *Tel.* 0333 999 3899 *Email* grants@veteransfoundation.org.uk *Website* www.veteransfoundation.org.uk

....

■ VHLT Ltd

CC NO 1101241   **ESTABLISHED** 2002
WHERE FUNDING CAN BE GIVEN London and Israel.
WHO CAN BENEFIT Registered charities; individuals.
WHAT IS FUNDED The Jewish faith and community.
RANGE OF GRANTS Up to £877,600.
SAMPLE GRANTS Vaad Harabonim Israel (£861,600); Olam Chesed Yiboneh and Sharei Marpeh (£10,000 each).
FINANCES *Financial year end* 31/08/2021
Income £1,060,000
Grants to organisations £896,100
Grants to individuals £62,000
Assets £210,000
TRUSTEES Yehiel Frand; Yoel Marmorstein; Avrohom Streicher; Raymond Frand.
OTHER INFORMATION The 2020/21 accounts were the latest available at the time of writing (May 2023). Grants were broken down as follows: relief of poverty £877,600; social welfare (£10,000); advancement of education (£5,600); advancement of religion (£2,900). Other grants of under £10,000 totalled £14,500.
HOW TO APPLY Apply in writing to the correspondent.
CONTACT DETAILS The Trustees, 61 Fairholt Road, London N16 5EW *Tel.* 020 8809 5700

....

■ VINCI UK Foundation

CC NO 1171871
WHERE FUNDING CAN BE GIVEN Projects near to VINCI offices throughout the UK and Republic of Ireland.
WHO CAN BENEFIT Small and medium-sized registered community interest or non-profit organisations.

WHAT IS FUNDED Access to employment; housing; mobility; community development.
WHAT IS NOT FUNDED Individuals; for-profit organisations; statutory bodies; federations; political or religious organisations/groups.
TYPE OF GRANT Capital costs.
RANGE OF GRANTS £3,000 to £20,000.
SAMPLE GRANTS A list of beneficiaries was not included in the annual report and accounts. Previous beneficiaries have included: Raw Workshop (£15,000); Chelmsford Chess (£12,600); Friends of the Castle (£10,000); The Daisy Garland (£8,200).
FINANCES *Financial year end* 31/12/2021
Income £176,000
Grants to organisations £175,000
Assets £37,400
TRUSTEES Philip Hines; Scott Wardrop; Francois Pogu; Jean-Yves Cojean; Russell Matthews; Pascal Mercier; Tom Jones; Robert Gillespie; Scott Vord.
OTHER INFORMATION The foundation is the UK corporate charity of the VINCI Group, a construction company based in France. Projects should actively involve VINCI employees. Only beneficiaries that received grants of over £7,500 were listed in the annual report and accounts. During the year, the foundation awarded 39 grants to organisations.
HOW TO APPLY The foundation has detailed guidance for potential applicants, including deadlines, eligibility criteria and examples of past projects, on its website.
CONTACT DETAILS Ayyub Dedat, Unit 2050 The Crescent, Birmingham Business Park, Birmingham B37 7YE *Tel.* 0121 717 1820 *Email* contact@vinci-uk-foundation.co.uk *Website* www.vinci-uk-foundation.co.uk

....

■ Nigel Vinson Charitable Trust

CC NO 265077   **ESTABLISHED** 1972
WHERE FUNDING CAN BE GIVEN UK.
WHO CAN BENEFIT Charitable organisations; universities; religious organisations; statutory authorities.
WHAT IS FUNDED Education, including research bodies; citizenship and community development; religion; animal welfare; environmental protection or improvement; previously, arts, culture, heritage or science.
WHAT IS NOT FUNDED Individuals.
RANGE OF GRANTS Mostly between £1,000 and £5,000 with the occasional smaller or larger grant.
SAMPLE GRANTS Foundation for the History of Totalitarianism (£75,000); Buckingham University (£45,000); Institute of Economic Affairs (£25,000); Adam Smith Research Trust and Radley Foundation (£5,000 each); Global Warming Policy Foundation, Ilderton PCC and SongBird Survival (£2,000 each).
FINANCES *Financial year end* 30/06/2022
Income £140,000
Grants to organisations £204,400
Assets £4,010,000
TRUSTEES Hoare Trustees; Hon. Antonia Bennett; Bettina Witheridge; Thomas Harris; Lord Nigel Vinson; Hon. Rowena Cowen.
OTHER INFORMATION Only organisations that received grants of over £1,000 were listed as beneficiaries in the trust's 2021/22 accounts. Grants of under £1,000 totalled £11,000. Grants were broken down as follows: education (£175,400 to six organisations); citizenship or community development (£12,000 to three organisations); animal welfare (£2,000 to one

....

organisation); the environment (£2,000 to one organisation); religion (£2,000 to one organisation).

HOW TO APPLY Apply in writing to the correspondent.

CONTACT DETAILS Hoare Trustees, c/o C. Hoare and Co., 37 Fleet Street, London EC4Y 1BT *Tel.* 020 7353 4522

■ The Vintners' Foundation

CC NO 1015212   **ESTABLISHED** 1992

WHERE FUNDING CAN BE GIVEN Greater London with a preference for inner London.

WHO CAN BENEFIT Registered charities; schools. There is a preference for smaller charities.

WHAT IS FUNDED People who are homeless or disadvantaged in Greater London; alleviating the social effects of alcohol abuse; young people, youth projects and educational establishments in London.

WHAT IS NOT FUNDED Applications relating to the rest of the UK or overseas; medical research; restoration of buildings; individuals.

TYPE OF GRANT Project funding is preferred though general running costs are sometimes supported.

RANGE OF GRANTS Normally in the range of £3,000 to £5,000.

SAMPLE GRANTS A list of beneficiaries was not included in the annual report and accounts. Previous beneficiaries have included: The Drinks Trust (£100,000); City Harvest (£33,200); Spitalfields Trust (£17,500); School-Home Support (£15,000); New Regent's College (£10,000); Future Frontiers (£9,000); ABF The Soldiers' Charity (£6,500); St James Garlickhythe (£5,500).

FINANCES *Financial year end 31/03/2022*
Income £1,710,000
Grants to organisations £500,600
Assets £9,820,000

TRUSTEES Sophia Bergqvist; Edward Berry; Anthony Fairbank; Richard Wilson.

OTHER INFORMATION The foundation states that most of the grants it awards are to its current selected charities. However, some limited funds are available for new organisations. Only organisations that received grants of over £1,000 were listed as beneficiaries in the foundation's accounts. Grants of under £1,000 totalled £3,000 and were awarded to seven organisations.

HOW TO APPLY Applications can be made via the foundation's website. The grants committee meets four times a year, usually in March, June, September and December.

CONTACT DETAILS Charity Secretary, The Vintners' Company, Vintners' Hall, Upper Thames Street, London EC4V 3BG *Tel.* 020 7651 0753 *Email* charity@vintnershall.co.uk *Website* www.vintnershall.co.uk

---

■ Virgin Atlantic Foundation

CC NO 1097580   **ESTABLISHED** 2003

WHERE FUNDING CAN BE GIVEN UK and overseas.

WHO CAN BENEFIT Registered charities.

WHAT IS FUNDED Education; health; social welfare.

TYPE OF GRANT Capital costs; development funding; project funding.

RANGE OF GRANTS £5,000 up to £75,000.

SAMPLE GRANTS UNHCR (£313,500); Speakers for Schools (£78,600); World Health Organization (£74,500); Save the Children (£65,100); Cranfield University (£50,000); Smallpeice Trust (£44,600); The Trussell Trust (£7,800); Chestnut Treehouse (£5,500).

FINANCES *Financial year end 30/04/2022*
Income £251,100
Grants to organisations £639,500
Assets £350,300

TRUSTEES Suzanne Roddie; Estelle Hollingsworth; Philip Wardlaw; Edward Taplin; Kerry McNally.

OTHER INFORMATION In total, eight grants were awarded during the year, totalling £639,500. Of this, £313,500 was awarded to UNHCR for the provision of aid to refugees.

HOW TO APPLY Apply in writing to the correspondent.

CONTACT DETAILS K. Bristoll, Secretary, c/o Virgin Atlantic Airways Ltd, The VHQ, Fleming Way, Crawley, West Sussex RH10 9DF *Tel.* 01293 747128 *Email* community.investment@fly.virgin.com *Website* https://corporate.virginatlantic.com/gb/en/sustainability/programme-overview/partners.html

---

■ The Virgin Foundation (Virgin Unite)

CC NO 297540   **ESTABLISHED** 1987

WHERE FUNDING CAN BE GIVEN England; Australia; Canada; Jamaica; South Africa; the USA.

WHO CAN BENEFIT Organisations; individuals; innovative and entrepreneurial projects.

WHAT IS FUNDED Entrepreneurial approaches to social and environmental issues. The foundation has four aims: changing business for good; market solutions to address climate change and conserve natural resources; the power of entrepreneurs; human dignity. The foundation achieves this through a wide range of initiatives, which are categorised as follows: uniting leaders; uniting entrepreneurs; uniting voices; uniting communities. Many initiatives bring together different organisations in 'disruptive collaborations' to tackle global issues. Further information is given on the foundation's website.

TYPE OF GRANT Grants; loans; non-financial support.

RANGE OF GRANTS Generally £4,000 to £100,000.

SAMPLE GRANTS Sightsavers (£2.66 million); Last Mile/Living Goods (£2.11 million); The End Fund (£760,000); The Elders Foundation (£100,000); Emergency Fund (£63,000); Criminal Justice Reform (£30,000); JUST Capital (£18,000); Maldives Coral Reef (£4,000).

FINANCES *Financial year end 31/12/2021*
Income £11,950,000
Grants to organisations £7,890,000
Assets £8,970,000

TRUSTEES Holly Branson; Vanessa Branson; Ajaz Ahmed; Jean Oelwang; Nathalie Richards; Jillian Brady; Nicola Humphrey.

OTHER INFORMATION Grants were broken down as follows: Audacious Ideas (£5.54 million); other (£1.18 million); large-scale collaborative initiatives (£1.09 million); Virgin Unite local entity programmes (£82,000).

HOW TO APPLY The website states the following: 'Unlike some other charities, we do not run an open grant application process. On most of our initiatives, we either work with an already established circle of partners or identify new partners we think are best placed to deliver in line with our strategy and with whom we can leverage initial investments for significant impact.'

CONTACT DETAILS C. M. Howes, Secretary, 66 Porchester Road, London W2 6ET *Tel.* 020 7313 2000 *Email* contact@virginunite.co.uk *Website* www.virginunite.com

Think carefully about every application. Is it justified?

717

■ The Virgin Money Foundation

CC NO 1161290 **ESTABLISHED** 2014

WHERE FUNDING CAN BE GIVEN UK, with a preference for Glasgow, Sheffield, Edinburgh, Norwich, Manchester, Cardiff, London, Leeds and the North East.

WHO CAN BENEFIT Registered charities; social enterprises; CICs.

WHAT IS FUNDED The sustainable regeneration of communities; social enterprise; children and young people. See the website for current funding programmes.

WHAT IS NOT FUNDED See individual grant programmes for specific exclusions.

TYPE OF GRANT Running costs/core costs; project costs.

RANGE OF GRANTS £500 to £50,000.

SAMPLE GRANTS Baltic Centre for Contemporary Art (£34,000); Annexe Communities (£26,000); The Big League CIC (£8,000); Whitley Bay FC Juniors (£400).

FINANCES *Financial year end 30/09/2022*
Income £1,880,000
Grants to organisations £1,280,000
Assets £2,210,000

TRUSTEES Joanne Curry; Lorna Bennie; Keith Burge; Hannah Underwood; Edward Younger; Keith Merrin; Amanda Jordan; Alison Kidd; Abigail Walker; Laura Christer.

OTHER INFORMATION In 2020/21, grants were awarded to 140 organisations.

HOW TO APPLY Some grant programmes are open to applications and others are by invitation only. For those open to applications, an online form can be accessed through the foundation's application portal on its website. The foundation's website provides further information on each fund, including application deadlines and detailed eligibility criteria.

CONTACT DETAILS Richard Walton, Programme Manager, Jubilee House, Gosforth, Newcastle upon Tyne, Tyne and Wear NE3 4PL *Tel.* 0330 123 3624 *Email* info@virginmoneyfoundation. org.uk *Website* https://virginmoneyfoundation. org.uk

■ Vision Foundation

CC NO 1074958 **ESTABLISHED** 1999

WHERE FUNDING CAN BE GIVEN London.

WHO CAN BENEFIT Registered CIOs; charitable companies; CICs limited by guarantee.

WHAT IS FUNDED Projects that are collaborative and designed in partnership with blind and partially sighted people. Services that have been proven to be effective, are valued by their users or can demonstrate evidence for demand. New, innovative and untested work that has a significant positive impact on people living with or are at risk of sight loss.

WHAT IS NOT FUNDED Educational establishment charities and individuals are not supported.

TYPE OF GRANT Project costs; core costs; one-off awards.

RANGE OF GRANTS £10,000 to £50,000.

SAMPLE GRANTS Middlesex Association for the Blind (£55,000); Deafblind UK (£50,000); Blind in Business (£25,000); Look UK (£20,000); Talking News Islington (£1,500).

FINANCES *Financial year end 31/03/2022*
Income £1,170,000
Grants to organisations £402,000
Assets £2,340,000

TRUSTEES Keith Felton; Sharon Petrie; Robert Hughes; Heather Goodhew; Elizabeth Honer; Susanette Mansour; Ly Lam; Victoria Currey; Darren Barker; Dr Amit Patel.

OTHER INFORMATION Grants were awarded to 22 organisations during the year. At the time of writing (May 2023) the foundation's website stated that the organisation was merging with Fight for Sight.

HOW TO APPLY See the foundation's website for details of open grant programmes.

CONTACT DETAILS Steven Smith, Grants Manager, Sir John Mills House, 12 Whitehorse Mews, 37 Westminster Bridge Road, London SE1 7QD *Tel.* 020 7620 2066 *Email* hello@ visionfoundation.org.uk *Website* www. visionfoundation.org.uk

■ Vivdale Ltd

CC NO 268505 **ESTABLISHED** 1974

WHERE FUNDING CAN BE GIVEN UK.

WHO CAN BENEFIT Jewish organisations.

WHAT IS FUNDED Advancement of the Orthodox Jewish faith.

SAMPLE GRANTS A list of beneficiaries was not included in the annual report and accounts. Previous beneficiaries have included: Achisomach Aid Company Ltd; Beis Soroh Schneirer; Beis Yaakov Town; Beis Yisroel Tel Aviv; Comet Charities Ltd; Friends of Harim Bnei Brak; Jewish Teachers Training College Gateshead; Mosdos Bnei Brak; Torah Vechesed Ashdod; Woodstock Sinclair Trust.

FINANCES *Financial year end 05/04/2022*
Income £182,100
Grants to organisations £89,500
Assets £4,280,000

TRUSTEES Loretta Marks; Gary Sinclair; Norman Blum.

HOW TO APPLY Apply in writing to the correspondent.

CONTACT DETAILS The Trustees, 133 Leeside Crescent, Golders Green, London NW11 0JN *Tel.* 020 8458 0900 *Email* aepton@goldwins. co.uk

■ The Vodafone Foundation

CC NO 1089625 **ESTABLISHED** 2001

WHERE FUNDING CAN BE GIVEN UK and overseas (where Vodafone operates).

WHO CAN BENEFIT Charitable organisations.

WHAT IS FUNDED Projects which use mobile connectivity and technology to promote a healthier, safer and more sustainable society.

TYPE OF GRANT Project funding.

SAMPLE GRANTS United Nations Children's Fund (£2 million); The African Vaccine Acquisition Trust (£823,200); Touch Foundation (£110,400); Tusk Trust (£99,200).

FINANCES *Financial year end 31/03/2022*
Income £17,640,000
Grants to organisations £8,480,000
Assets £5,600,000

TRUSTEES Nick Land; Elizabeth Filkin; Patricia Ithau; Amparo Moraleda; Rosemary Martin; Joakim Reiter; John Otty; Leanne Wood.

HOW TO APPLY The foundation usually approaches charitable organisations which it believes can help with the delivery of its charitable aims.

CONTACT DETAILS The Trustees, 1 Kingdom Street, Paddington Central, London W2 6BY *Tel.* 07824 342833 *Email* groupfoundation@vodafone.com *Website* www.vodafonefoundation.org

■ Volant Charitable Trust

OSCR NO SC030790 **ESTABLISHED** 2000
WHERE FUNDING CAN BE GIVEN Scotland.
WHO CAN BENEFIT Registered charities; CICs; community organisations.
WHAT IS FUNDED Social deprivation, particularly where it affects women, children and young people.
WHAT IS NOT FUNDED A full list of exclusions can be found on Foundation Scotland's website (www.foundationscotland.org.uk).
TYPE OF GRANT Project funding; core costs.
RANGE OF GRANTS Up to £15,000 per year for three years.
SAMPLE GRANTS Disasters Emergency Committee (£2.05 million); Gingerbread (£1 million); The Message Trust (£30,000); Scottish Autism (£20,000); Glasgow Children's Hospital Charity (£15,000).
FINANCES *Financial year end* 05/04/2022
Income £5,180,000
Grants to organisations £9,050,000
Assets £73,340,000
OTHER INFORMATION This trust was established by the author J. K. Rowling. Grants were broken down as follows: COVID-19 Response Fund (£7.3 million); social deprivation (£1.54 million); international aid relief (£200,000).
HOW TO APPLY Applications can be made online via the Foundation Scotland website.
CONTACT DETAILS Jennifer Malcolmson, Fund Advisor, c/o Turcan Connell, Princes Exchange, 1 Earl Grey Street, Edinburgh EH3 9EE *Tel.* 0141 341 4964 *Email* jennifer@ foundationscotland.org.uk *Website* www. volanttrust.org

■ The Georg and Emily von Opel Foundation

CC NO 1172977 **ESTABLISHED** 2017
WHERE FUNDING CAN BE GIVEN UK and overseas.
WHO CAN BENEFIT UK-registered charities; charities in Switzerland.
WHAT IS FUNDED Sport; social welfare; health; education; nature and the environment; the advancement of the Roman Catholic faith; general charitable purposes.
RANGE OF GRANTS Up to £1 million, with an average grant of £162,000.
SAMPLE GRANTS Latymer Foundation at Hammersmith (£1 million); Natare West London Swimming Club (£500,000); WaterAid (£125,000); Collateral Global (£100,000); Westminster Roman Catholic Diocese Trustee (£34,700).
FINANCES *Financial year end* 31/12/2021
Income £1,770,000
Grants to organisations £2,130,000
Assets £288,800
TRUSTEES Georg von Opel; Emily von Opel; Viscountess Candida Petersham.
OTHER INFORMATION Georg von Opel is a German-born Swiss billionaire and great-grandson of Adam von Opel, founder of the German car manufacturer.
HOW TO APPLY Apply in writing to the correspondent.
CONTACT DETAILS Emily von Opel, Trustee, GVO Asset Management AG, Bundesplatz 14, 6300 Zug, Switzerland *Tel.* +41 526 470 219

■ The VTCT Foundation

CC NO 1155360 **ESTABLISHED** 2013
WHERE FUNDING CAN BE GIVEN UK.
WHO CAN BENEFIT UK-based organisations; medical research organisations; universities.
WHAT IS FUNDED Medical research in the field of disfigurement; providing support to organisations helping those living with visible difference.
WHAT IS NOT FUNDED Projects that have commercial interests.
TYPE OF GRANT Project funding; research; capacity building; seed funding; one-off; multi-year.
RANGE OF GRANTS Small grants up to £25,000; larger grants are awarded through the main grants scheme.
SAMPLE GRANTS University of the West of England/ Centre for Appearance Research (£930,800); Changing Faces (£123,100); University of Oxford (£94,600); NF2 BioSolutions (£25,000); Facial Palsy UK (£12,500); The Appearance Collective (£3,000).
FINANCES *Financial year end* 31/07/2022
Income £52,900
Grants to organisations £1,380,000
Grants to individuals £33,800
Assets £4,130,000
TRUSTEES Rosanna Preston; Anthony Walker; Prof. Nichola Rumsey; Prof. Naiem Moiemen; Dr Wendy Edwards; Angela Cross-Durrant.
OTHER INFORMATION Grants were awarded to nine organisations and one individual during 2021/22. Grants awarded were broken down in the foundation's annual report and accounts as career development grants (£176,500) and other grants (£1.15 million).
HOW TO APPLY To request further information and/or an application form, contact the correspondent.
CONTACT DETAILS Amanda Shepard, Grant Manager, Aspire House, Annealing Close, Eastleigh, Hampshire SO50 9PX *Tel.* 07968 130339 *Email* amanda.shepard@vtctfoundation.org.uk *Website* www.vtctfoundation.org.uk

■ Sylvia Waddilove Foundation UK

CC NO 1118097   **ESTABLISHED** 2006

WHERE FUNDING CAN BE GIVEN UK.

WHO CAN BENEFIT Registered charities; registered societies; CICs.

WHAT IS FUNDED Education, particularly in organic farming, non-domestic animal husbandry and veterinary science; visual and performing arts; medical research; the relief of disability or illness; architectural heritage; accommodation for those in need.

WHAT IS NOT FUNDED Individuals; 'friends of' charities; not-for-profit companies (which are not charities); social enterprises; schools or religious organisations.

TYPE OF GRANT Capital costs; staff costs and overheads (only for COVID-19 emergency funding).

RANGE OF GRANTS Typically £1,000 to £5,000.

SAMPLE GRANTS Crohn's and Colitis UK and Hogarth House (£5,000 each); Southern Domestic Abuse (£4,000); Haworth Riding for the Disabled Group (£3,500); The Bernard Leach Trust (£2,000); Bridge the Gap Mental Health CIC, Glenview Farm Equine Learning Centre CIC, Haemochromatosis UK, Music 24 and Pateley Bridge Dramatic Society (£1,000 each); Iris Theatre (£500).

FINANCES *Financial year end 31/12/2021*
Income £115,500
Grants to organisations £252,500
Assets £2,800,000

TRUSTEES Gerald Kidd; Peter Spencer; Christopher Perkins.

OTHER INFORMATION In 2021, the foundation made grants to 112 organisations.

HOW TO APPLY Application forms, alongside guidance notes, are available from the foundation administrator's website and must be returned by email; applications or correspondence by post are not accepted. Typically, the trustees meet quarterly.

CONTACT DETAILS Foundation Administrator, c/o Pothecary Witham Weld Solicitors, The Office Group, Thomas House, 84 Eccleston Square, London SW1V 1PX *Tel.* 020 7821 8211 *Email* waddilove@pwwsolicitors.co.uk *Website* www.pwwsolicitors.co.uk/charity-grants/13-the-sylvia-waddilove-foundation-uk

■ Wade's Charity

CC NO 224939   **ESTABLISHED** 1530

WHERE FUNDING CAN BE GIVEN Leeds, within the pre-1974 boundary of the city (approximately LS1 to LS17 postcode areas).

WHO CAN BENEFIT Registered charities; unregistered charities; charitable organisations.

WHAT IS FUNDED Recreational activities; the preservation of public open spaces. The main grants programme (£300 or above) considers applications supporting all or any section of the community, including: children and young people; older people; the arts; open spaces. There is also a small grants programme (up to £300) for small community groups and charities.

WHAT IS NOT FUNDED Applications from outside the beneficial area; applications from individuals or non-charitable organisations; applications for church repairs (except where there is evidence of significant community use); circulars or general appeals from high profile national charities; applications which do not offer benefit within the charity's terms; applications for activities which are the responsibility of statutory or local authority funding, particularly within health or education; applications to fund salaries or core costs.

TYPE OF GRANT Capital costs; seed funding/start-up funding; project funding; unrestricted funding.

RANGE OF GRANTS Mostly £1,000 to £5,000.

SAMPLE GRANTS Friends of Temple Newsam (£7,500); Lippy People Charitable Trust (£2,000); Live Music Now (£1,500); People in Action (£1,000).

FINANCES *Financial year end 31/12/2021*
Income £284,000
Grants to organisations £148,600
Assets £10,760,000

TRUSTEES Bernard Atha; Hilary Finnigan; Mark Pullan; Susan Reddington; John Stoddart-Scott; John Tinker; John Pike; David Richardson; Nicholas Mercer; Timothy Ward; Tim Barber; Cllr Jacqueline Shemilt; Cllr Jonathan Bentley; Cllr Denise Ragan; Peter Lewis.

OTHER INFORMATION Grants were distributed as follows: provision of facilities for recreation (£129,800); provision and maintenance of open spaces (£18,700).

HOW TO APPLY Applications to the main grants programme should preferably be submitted by email, including all the required information given in the guidelines on the charity's website. Applicants will then be contacted by the Grants Adviser to arrange a meeting, after which applications are considered by the trustees at meetings in April, July and November. Early applications are encouraged as it can take four to six weeks to process an application. The charity welcomes contact to discuss ideas before submitting an application. Applications to the small grants programme should be made through Voluntary Action Leeds (https://doinggoodleeds.org.uk/wades-charity-small-grants).

CONTACT DETAILS Kathryn Hodges, Grants Adviser and Administrator, Mount Villa, 306 Tadcaster Road, York, North Yorkshire YO24 1HE *Tel.* 01904 702384 *Email* info@wadescharity.org *Website* www.wadescharity.org

■ The Scurrah Wainwright Charity

CC NO 1002755   **ESTABLISHED** 1991

WHERE FUNDING CAN BE GIVEN England with a preference for Yorkshire, South Africa and Zimbabwe.

WHO CAN BENEFIT Registered charities; unregistered charities; CICs; social enterprises.

WHAT IS FUNDED Social reform.

WHAT IS NOT FUNDED Individuals; large and national charitable organisations unless specifically working in the Yorkshire region and providing local control and access to the grant; organisations with an annual income/expenditure that exceeds around £250,000; animal welfare; buildings; medical research or support for individual medical conditions; substitution for government funding (e.g. in education and health); unsolicited general appeal letters; activities that have already taken place; organisations without a UK bank account into which a grant can be paid.

TYPE OF GRANT Capital costs; core and revenue costs; seed funding; start-up funding; unrestricted funding.

RANGE OF GRANTS Typically £1,000 to £5,000, but in exceptional cases larger grants may be awarded.

SAMPLE GRANTS Bring Us Together (£9,600); South Yorkshire Refugee Law and Justice (£7,000); Complete Woman (£3,600); The Old Fire Station (£1,000); Sir George Martin Trust (£50).

FINANCES *Financial year end* 05/04/2022
Income £75,700
Grants to organisations £162,100
Assets £2,970,000

TRUSTEES Hugh Scott; Penny Wainwright; Tessa Wainwright; Hilary Wainwright; Martin Wainwright.

OTHER INFORMATION Grants were distributed as follows: north of England (£142,900); Zimbabwe and South Africa (£14,200); UK national projects (£5,000). The Wainwright family also runs The Andrew Wainwright Reform Trust Ltd, a non-charitable organisation that focuses on 'work for a just and democratic society and to redress political and social injustices'.

HOW TO APPLY In the first instance, check the eligibility criteria and deadlines on the charity's website. Applicants should then submit a preliminary registration form to register their interest, which can be found on the website. If the trustees are interested in the proposal, applicants will be asked to submit their most recent audited accounts together with a full application to the correspondent via post or email. The trustees usually meet in March, July and November and applications should be submitted by 14 January, 14 May or 14 September, respectively. Applicants may contact the administrator by email with any queries.

CONTACT DETAILS Kerry McQuade, Administrator, 19 Wadsworth Lane, Hebden Bridge, West Yorkshire HX7 8DL *Email* admin@wainwrighttrusts.org.uk *Website* www.wainwrighttrusts.org.uk

---

■ The Bruce Wake Charity

CC NO 1018190   **ESTABLISHED** 1993

WHERE FUNDING CAN BE GIVEN UK.

WHO CAN BENEFIT Charities; not-for-profit organisations; CICs; individuals.

WHAT IS FUNDED Grants to fund leisure activities for people with disabilities, particularly activities which aim to improve access to sport or leisure activities for people who use a wheelchair.

WHAT IS NOT FUNDED For-profit companies.

RANGE OF GRANTS Mostly under £5,000.

SAMPLE GRANTS Motor Neurone Disease Association (£30,000); Wheelpower (£25,000); Disability Snowsports UK (£10,000); South London Special League (£7,500); Charity Link – Northampton (£6,000).

FINANCES *Financial year end* 05/04/2022
Income £124,900
Grants to organisations £689,100
Grants to individuals £128,500
Assets £7,480,000

TRUSTEES Peter Hems; Robert Rowley; Penny Wake; John Gilboy.

OTHER INFORMATION Grants were made to 254 organisations during the year.

HOW TO APPLY Apply via the website using the online application form.

CONTACT DETAILS The Trustees, 9 Spring Back Way, Uppingham, Oakham, Rutland LE15 9TT

Email info@brucewaketrust.co.uk *Website* www.brucewaketrust.co.uk

---

■ Wakefield and Tetley Trust

CC NO 1121779   **ESTABLISHED** 2008

WHERE FUNDING CAN BE GIVEN Tower Hamlets, Southwark and the City of London.

WHO CAN BENEFIT Registered charities; unregistered charities; CICs.

WHAT IS FUNDED Marginalised individuals and communities experiencing disadvantage in particular: carers, people with disabilities, people from Black, Asian and minority ethnic communities, refugees, people with no recourse to public funds, people in manual or insecure work, families affected by domestic violence and abuse, people experiencing poor mental health, people living alone who may be isolated.

WHAT IS NOT FUNDED See the trust's website for a full list of exclusions.

TYPE OF GRANT Core/revenue costs; seed funding/start-up funding; project funding; unrestricted funding.

RANGE OF GRANTS Between £500 and £6,000.

SAMPLE GRANTS East End Citizens Advice (£35,000); East London Cares (£12,500); Burdett FC and Legal Advice Centre (£10,000 each); Bubble CIC (£5,800); Chain Reaction Theatre (£4,700); Ocean Women's Association (£4,600); Carers Centre Tower Hamlets (£4,400); Latin America Disabled People's Project and Southwark Day Centre for Asylum Seekers (£2,000 each).

FINANCES *Financial year end* 31/12/2021
Income £463,600
Grants to organisations £301,600
Assets £8,900,000

TRUSTEES The Ven. Peter Delaney; Patrick Kelly; Stuart Morganstein; Clare Murphy; Sue Smith; Dawn Plimmer; Tim McNally; Clare Payne; Mohima Kamaly.

OTHER INFORMATION The trust makes an annual grant to All Hallows by the Tower Church.

HOW TO APPLY Details of how to apply are available on the trust's website.

CONTACT DETAILS Elaine Crush, Joint Clerk to the Trustees (with Cherry Bushell), Marshall House, 66 Newcomen Street, London SE1 1YT *Email* enquiries@wakefieldtrust.org.uk *Website* www.wakefieldtrust.org.uk

---

■ The Walcot Foundation

CC NO 312800   **ESTABLISHED** 1990

WHERE FUNDING CAN BE GIVEN The London Borough of Lambeth.

WHO CAN BENEFIT Schools; registered charities, social enterprises, community groups and other voluntary organisations; individuals.

WHAT IS FUNDED Social welfare and education. The aim of the foundation is to help individuals along the key paths of educational achievement, employment/employability and financial self-sufficiency.

WHAT IS NOT FUNDED Activities that are the responsibility of central or local government, or schools; organisations that cannot show they are working with Lambeth residents in financial need; debt repayments; crisis funding to solve an organisation's financial problems; research; capital projects; organisations with fewer than three trustees or directors.

TYPE OF GRANT Revenue funding; project funding.

RANGE OF GRANTS Up to £25,000 per year for three years.

SAMPLE GRANTS Groundwork London (£54,000); Unity Works Social Enterprises (£42,000); Solace Women's Aid (£25,000); The Kids Network (£20,000); Young Futures (£19,000); Art4Space (£14,000); Walnut Tree Walk Primary School (£10,000).

FINANCES *Financial year end* 31/03/2022
Income £3,040,000
Grants to organisations £2,510,000
Grants to individuals £312,800
Assets £127,040,000

TRUSTEE The Walcot and Hayle's Trustee.

OTHER INFORMATION The Walcot Foundation, also known as the Lambeth Endowed Charities, has roots dating back to the 17th century. It is an umbrella title for three charities: The Walcot Educational Foundation, Hayle's Charity and The Walcot Non-Educational Charity. In 2021/22, grants were awarded to 139 organisations and 252 individuals.

HOW TO APPLY Refer to the website to check if the grants scheme for organisations is currently open. Potential applicants should initially contact a member of the Grants Team to discuss whether their proposal is eligible and obtain an application form. Deadlines are posted on the website.

CONTACT DETAILS Daniel Chapman, Grants Manager, 127 Kennington Road, London SE11 6SF *Tel.* 020 7735 1925 *Email* grants@walcotfoundation.org.uk *Website* www.walcotfoundation.org.uk

■ The Community Foundation in Wales

CC NO 1074655   **ESTABLISHED** 1999
WHERE FUNDING CAN BE GIVEN Wales.

WHO CAN BENEFIT Registered charities, community groups and other voluntary organisations; individuals.

WHAT IS FUNDED General charitable purposes; community development.

RANGE OF GRANTS The majority of grants awarded are under £5,000.

SAMPLE GRANTS Examples of projects supported by the foundation can be found on its website.

FINANCES *Financial year end* 31/03/2022
Income £2,380,000
Grants to organisations £1,570,000
Grants to individuals £152,500
Assets £14,480,000

TRUSTEES Kathryn Morris; Lt Col. Andrew Tuggey; Samsunear Ali; Alun Evans; Emma Beynon; Tanwen Grover; Nigel Annett; Sarah Jennings; Annabel Lloyd; Sarah Corser; Elizabeth James; Gaenor Howells; Ian Thomas; Derek Howell.

OTHER INFORMATION This is one of the 47 UK community foundations, which distribute funding for a wide range of purposes. As with all community foundations, there are a number of donor-advised funds managed on behalf of individuals, families and charitable trusts. Grant schemes tend to change frequently – consult the foundation's website for details of current programmes and up-to-date deadlines.

HOW TO APPLY Potential applicants are advised to visit the community foundation's website or contact its grants team to find the most suitable funding stream.

CONTACT DETAILS Grants Team, St Andrews House, 24 St Andrews Crescent, Cardiff CF10 3DD *Tel.* 029 2037 9580 *Email* info@communityfoundationwales.org.uk *Website* www.cfiw.org.uk

■ The Walker Trust

CC NO 215479   **ESTABLISHED** 1897
WHERE FUNDING CAN BE GIVEN Shropshire.

WHO CAN BENEFIT Registered charities; unregistered charities; hospices; individuals.

WHAT IS FUNDED Health and people with disabilities; education.

TYPE OF GRANT Capital costs.

RANGE OF GRANTS Up to £50,000 but mostly £500 to £15,000.

SAMPLE GRANTS Flaxmill Shrewsbury (£50,000); University Centre Shrewsbury (£15,000); Ironbridge Gorge Museum Trust (£7,500); VCH – Shropshire (£5,000); Educating Kids Outdoors (£3,800); Shrewsbury and Oswestry Crucial Crew (£2,000); Engineering Development Trust (£1,500); The Police Community Clubs (£1,000); Shropshire Council (£500).

FINANCES *Financial year end* 31/03/2022
Income £142,000
Grants to organisations £119,100
Grants to individuals £16,700
Assets £57,010,000

TRUSTEES Sir Algernon Heber-Percy; Carolin Paton-Smith; Shirley Reynolds; Lady Lydia Forester; Vince Hunt; Brian Williams.

OTHER INFORMATION In 2021/22 a total of £191,300 was awarded to schools and other organisations and £27,900 was awarded to health and disability organisations.

HOW TO APPLY Apply in writing to the correspondent. The trustees meet four times a year to consider applications; however, urgent decisions may be made between meetings.

CONTACT DETAILS Edward Hewitt, Clerk, 2 Breidden Way, Bayston Hill, Shrewsbury, Shropshire SY3 0LN *Tel.* 01743 873866 *Email* edward.hewitt@btinternet.com

■ Wallace and Gromit's Children's Foundation

CC NO 1043603   **ESTABLISHED** 2003
WHERE FUNDING CAN BE GIVEN UK.

WHO CAN BENEFIT Children's hospitals, hospices and healthcare organisations.

WHAT IS FUNDED Examples of projects which the trustees will fund include: arts, music, play and leisure programmes; facilities to support families of children treated in hospitals or hospices; welcoming and accessible environments; care and facilities in hospices; promoting education and information programmes; supporting children with physical and emotional difficulties; medical equipment (when it can be shown that funding is not available from statutory sources).

WHAT IS NOT FUNDED Charities not supporting children's health care; organisations that are not registered charities; animal, religious or international charities; retrospective expenditure; organisations that do not work in a hospice or hospital; organisations providing away days, holidays or excursions; individuals; clown doctors.

RANGE OF GRANTS £100 to £10,000.

SAMPLE GRANTS A list of beneficiaries was not included in the annual report and accounts.

FINANCES *Financial year end* 31/03/2022
Income £3,080,000
Grants to organisations £243,100
Assets £9,880,000

TRUSTEES Geoff Meagher; Dervla Owens; Catherine Cotrell; Mary Robinson; Hadi Husani.

OTHER INFORMATION During the year, grants were awarded to Bristol Children's Hospital

722

Does the funder you have chosen match your needs? Haphazard applications waste postage and time

(£213,100) and support for special care baby unit/Cots for Tots (£30,000).

HOW TO APPLY Full guidelines and an application form are available on the charity's website. Applicants are encouraged to check that their organisation meets the criteria set out in the guidelines before making an application. Applications from organisations working within a hospice or hospital will require a supporting reference from the hospice or hospital. An application form should be completed and sent via email to the correspondent. Supporting documentation may be sent by post, but annual reports and accounts should not be sent unless requested. Grant recipients are required to send a grant report and case study within ten months of receiving a grant. Check the charity's website for current information on grant application deadlines.

CONTACT DETAILS Anna Shepherd, Deputy Director, 30–32 Upper Maudlin Street, Bristol BS2 8DJ *Tel.* 0117 927 3888 *Email* info@ wallaceandgromitcharity.org or use the contact form on the website *Website* https:// wallaceandgromitcharity.org

■ Walton Foundation

OSCR NO SC004005 **ESTABLISHED** 1965
WHERE FUNDING CAN BE GIVEN Glasgow and the West of Scotland.
WHO CAN BENEFIT Charitable organisations.
WHAT IS FUNDED Education; medical causes; the Jewish faith and community.
RANGE OF GRANTS Up to £15,000 per year.
SAMPLE GRANTS Previous beneficiaries have included: University of Strathclyde (£100,000); Cosgrove Care (£15,100); UJIA (£10,200); Friends of Lubavitch Scotland and Kinship Care Initiative (£5,000 each); Jewish Care Scotland (£1,500); Canine Partners (£500).
FINANCES *Financial year end* 31/12/2022
Income £16,000
Grants to organisations £115,000
OTHER INFORMATION Full accounts were not available to view on the OSCR website due to the charity's low income. We have therefore estimated the grant total based on the charity's total expenditure.
HOW TO APPLY Apply in writing to the correspondent.
CONTACT DETAILS The Trustees, c/o Martin Aitken and Co., Caledonia House, 89 Seaward Street, Glasgow G41 1HJ

■ Walton-on-Thames Charity

CC NO 1185959 **ESTABLISHED** 1963
WHERE FUNDING CAN BE GIVEN Borough of Elmbridge, Surrey.
WHO CAN BENEFIT Registered charities; social enterprises; schools; CICs; individuals.
WHAT IS FUNDED Social welfare. The charity's Community Grants programme offers grants to organisations which provide a range of services to the local community. There is a particular focus on the following themes: child poverty; alleviating financial poverty; promoting personal health and well-being, particularly mental health; addressing isolation and loneliness for those on low incomes; facilitating access to affordable housing; and improving educational attainment. Further guidance is given on the charity's website.
TYPE OF GRANT Project funding; core/revenue costs; seed funding/start-up funding; capacity building; development costs.

RANGE OF GRANTS Up to £10,000; small grants up to £5,000.
SAMPLE GRANTS A list of beneficiaries was not included in the annual report and accounts. Previous beneficiaries have included: Burwood Pre-school; Citizens Advice Elmbridge West; Elmbridge Borough Council; Elmbridge Youth Support Services; Surrey Fire and Rescue Service; Surrey SATRO; Thames Riverboat Project; Walton Oak School.
FINANCES *Financial year end* 31/03/2022
Income £2,160,000
Grants to organisations £516,000
Grants to individuals £45,000
Assets £37,680,000
TRUSTEES Elizabeth Kennedy; Nicholas Stuart; Paul Tajasque; David Easson; Kellie Scott; Robert Mills; Sarah Tomkins; Alexandra Fitzpatrick.
OTHER INFORMATION The charity also provides sheltered housing as well as offering other support to local voluntary sector organisations, such as office space, training and advice. Grants were broken down as follows: community grants (£406,000); delegated fund (£67,000); school opportunities fund (£43,000).
HOW TO APPLY To request an application, contact the correspondent.
CONTACT DETAILS Caroline Davies, Head of Community Programmes, Charities House, 1–2 The Quintet, Churchfield Road, Walton-on-Thames, Surrey KT12 2TZ *Tel.* 019 3222 0242 or 07359 018 643 *Email* cdavies@ waltoncharity.org.uk *Website* www.waltoncharity.org.uk

■ War Memorials Trust

CC NO 1062255
WHERE FUNDING CAN BE GIVEN UK; Channel Islands; Isle of Man.
WHO CAN BENEFIT Individuals; organisations; councils.
WHAT IS FUNDED The repair and conservation of war memorials.
WHAT IS NOT FUNDED See the trust's website for a full list of exclusions.
RANGE OF GRANTS Grants are usually 25% to 75% of eligible costs up to a maximum of £30,000.
FINANCES *Financial year end* 31/03/2022
Income £306,300
Grants to organisations £132,300
Assets £429,600
TRUSTEES Peter McCormick; John Peat; Russell Walters; Lord Rupert Mauley; Randolph Churchill; Margaret Goodall.
OTHER INFORMATION During the year, grants were awarded to 34 organisations. The grant total also includes grants made to individuals for conservation and protection projects.
HOW TO APPLY Applications can be submitted via the trust's website.
CONTACT DETAILS The Grants Team, 1st Floor, 14 Buckingham Palace Road, London SW1W 0QP *Tel.* 020 7834 0200 *Email* grants@warmemorials.org *Website* www.warmemorials.org

■ The Barbara Ward Children's Foundation

CC NO 1089783 **ESTABLISHED** 2001
WHERE FUNDING CAN BE GIVEN UK and overseas.
WHO CAN BENEFIT Charitable organisations, particularly smaller charities.

WHAT IS FUNDED Children and young people who are disadvantaged in some respect; adults with learning disabilities.

WHAT IS NOT FUNDED Religious charities.

TYPE OF GRANT One-off and multi-year grants; project costs for up to five years.

RANGE OF GRANTS Up to £15,000.

SAMPLE GRANTS Daisy Garland Trust (£13,800); Strongbones and Tracks Autism (£10,000 each); Arts for All and Families First St Andrews (£7,000 each); Anaphylaxis Campaign, Communigrow and Norfolk Carers Support (£5,000 each); Sensory Soft Play (£4,000); The Therapy Garden (£3,000); Pontllanfraith Children's Contact Centre (£1,500).

FINANCES *Financial year end 31/12/2022*
Income £504,300
Grants to organisations £464,500
Assets £12,200,000

TRUSTEES David Bailey; John Banks; Kenneth Parker; Brian Walters; Barbara Ward; Christopher Brown; Mark Waight.

OTHER INFORMATION Grants were made to 85 organisations in 2022.

HOW TO APPLY Apply in writing to the correspondent detailing the purpose for which the grant is requested. Your application should also include the latest annual report and set of audited financial statements. Beneficiaries or applicants may be visited by trustees, who usually meet on a quarterly basis to review and award grants.

CONTACT DETAILS The Trustees, c/o Weightmans LLP, 100 Old Hall Street, Liverpool L3 9QJ *Tel.* 0345 073 9900 *Email* info@bwcf.org.uk *Website* www.bwcf.org.uk

■ Warwick Relief-in-Need Charity

CC NO 256447　　　　**ESTABLISHED** 1976

WHERE FUNDING CAN BE GIVEN Warwick.

WHO CAN BENEFIT Charitable organisations; individuals.

WHAT IS FUNDED Social welfare.

TYPE OF GRANT Project costs.

SAMPLE GRANTS The Percy Estate – The Gap (£49,900); Citizens Advice South Warwickshire (£19,000); Lord Leycester Hospital (£5,000); Chase Meadow Community (£4,000); Music of Life Foundation (£2,500); Happy Days (£1,100); Woodloes Primary (£1,000); Myton Hospices (£290).

FINANCES *Financial year end 31/12/2021*
Income £180,200
Grants to organisations £99,200
Grants to individuals £23,300
Assets £4,580,000

TRUSTEES Sheila Brown; Janet Honnoraty; The Revd Dr Vaughan Roberts; The Revd Linda Duckers; John Atkinson; Sarah Hunt; Cllr Martyn Ashford; Cllr Richard Edgington; The Revd Diane Thompson; Cllr Parminder Birdi; Amanda Littlejohn; Janette Eslick.

HOW TO APPLY Apply in writing to the correspondent or by downloading an application form from the charity's website.

CONTACT DETAILS Christopher Houghton, Clerk to the Trustees, c/o Moore and Tibbits, Solicitors, 34 High Street, Warwick, Warwickshire CV34 4BE *Tel.* 01926 491181 *Email* choughton@moore-tibbits.co.uk *Website* www.warwickreliefinneed.org.uk

■ The Warwickshire Masonic Charitable Association Ltd

CC NO 211588　　　　**ESTABLISHED** 1945

WHERE FUNDING CAN BE GIVEN Warwickshire.

WHO CAN BENEFIT Charitable organisations; Masonic organisations.

WHAT IS FUNDED Masonic organisations; general charitable purposes.

RANGE OF GRANTS £250 to £6,500.

SAMPLE GRANTS Warwickshire and Solihull Blood Bikes (£6,500); Acorns Children's Hospice (£5,000); Shakespeare Hospice (£4,000); Birmingham Crisis Centre (£3,000); Warwickshire Young Carers (£2,000); Acacia Family Support (£750); Warwickshire and Northamptonshire Air Ambulance (£250).

FINANCES *Financial year end 31/12/2021*
Income £323,000
Grants to organisations £205,400
Assets £10,170,000

TRUSTEES Peter Britton; Stanley Butterworth; Christopher Grove; Gordon Law; Michael Morris; Eric Rymer; Nigel Burton; John Hayward; William Clark; Richard Barker; Philip Hall; David Greenwood; Mervyn Kimberley; Peter Manning; John Harris; Geoffrey Walker; Stephen Tranter; Nigel Hawkins; Howard Smith; David Butcher.

OTHER INFORMATION Grants were awarded to 137 non-Masonic charities and through the Woodthorpe Trust.

HOW TO APPLY Applications can be made through the association's website.

CONTACT DETAILS John Harris, Provincial Grand Almoner, Yenton Assembly Rooms, 73–75 Gravelly Hill North, Erdington, Birmingham, West Midlands B23 6BJ *Tel.* 0121 454 0554 *Email* dalec@warwickshirepgl.org *Website* www.warwickshirefreemasons.org.uk/charity

■ The Watches of Switzerland Group Foundation

CC NO 1196714

WHERE FUNDING CAN BE GIVEN UK.

WHO CAN BENEFIT Registered charities.

WHAT IS FUNDED Social welfare.

RANGE OF GRANTS Up to £475,000.

SAMPLE GRANTS The Prince's Trust (£325,000); Fuel Bank Foundation (£200,000); Crisis UK (£175,000); British Red Cross and The Prince and Princess of Wales Hospice (£100,000 each).

FINANCES *Financial year end 30/04/2022*
Income £4,520,000
Grants to organisations £1,380,000
Assets £3,110,000

TRUSTEES John Hannah; Hugh Duffy; David Gandy; Ruth Benford; Terence Parris.

HOW TO APPLY Apply in writing to the correspondent.

CONTACT DETAILS The Trustees, The Watches of Switzerland Group plc, Aurum House, 2 Elland Road, Braunstone, Leicester LE3 1TT *Tel.* 020 7317 4600 *Email* thefoundation@thewosgroup.com *Website* www.thewosgrouppdc.com/esg/community

■ Mrs Waterhouse Charitable Trust

CC NO 261685　　　　**ESTABLISHED** 1967

WHERE FUNDING CAN BE GIVEN UK, with an interest in the North West, particularly the Lancashire area.

WHO CAN BENEFIT Charitable organisations.

WHAT IS FUNDED General charitable purposes, particularly: medical causes and health; social welfare; the environment and wildlife; churches and heritage.

WHAT IS NOT FUNDED Individuals.

RANGE OF GRANTS £1,000 to £30,000.

SAMPLE GRANTS Amend (£30,000); Caritas (£20,000); North West Air Ambulance Service (£19,000); Francis House (£15,000); UK-Med (£5,000).

FINANCES *Financial year end* 05/04/2022
Income £345,400
Grants to organisations £349,500
Assets £10,710,000

TRUSTEES Alistair Dunn; Helen Dunn.

OTHER INFORMATION In 2021/22 the trust made 32 grants.

HOW TO APPLY Apply in writing to the correspondent.

CONTACT DETAILS The Trustees, 2nd Floor, Parkgates, Bury New Road, Prestwich, Manchester M25 0TL *Tel.* 0161 904 9942 *Email* houghtondunnct@gmail.com

---

■ The Waterloo Foundation

CC NO 1117535   **ESTABLISHED** 2007

WHERE FUNDING CAN BE GIVEN UK and overseas, with a preference for Wales.

WHO CAN BENEFIT Charitable organisations.

WHAT IS FUNDED Globally: marine conservation; tropical rainforests; child development. Overseas: water, sanitation and hygiene (WASH) initiatives; nutrition services; sexual and reproductive health services. Wales: unpaid carers; education and training.

WHAT IS NOT FUNDED Individuals; religious or political causes; general appeals or circulars.

TYPE OF GRANT Research and research dissemination; project costs; one-off and multi-year up to five years.

RANGE OF GRANTS Programme dependent.

SAMPLE GRANTS A list of beneficiaries was not included in the annual report and accounts.

FINANCES *Financial year end* 31/12/2021
Income £14,340,000
Grants to organisations £10,700,000
Assets £246,370,000

TRUSTEES Caroline Oakes; David Stevens; Heather Stevens.

OTHER INFORMATION During the year, the foundation received 563 applications and made 299 grants. We were unable to determine the figure for grants given in the UK.

HOW TO APPLY Application guidelines and deadlines for each of the grant programmes are available on the foundation's website. There is no application form and all applications should be submitted via email to applications@waterloofoundation.org.uk. Details of what should be included in the application are specific to each grants programme and can be found on the foundation's website.

CONTACT DETAILS The Trustees, c/o 46–48 Cardiff Road, Llandaff, Cardiff CF5 2DT *Tel.* 029 2083 8980 *Email* info@waterloofoundation.org.uk *Website* www.waterloofoundation.org.uk

---

▨ G. R. Waters Charitable Trust 2000

CC NO 1091525   **ESTABLISHED** 2000

WHERE FUNDING CAN BE GIVEN UK mainly, also overseas.

WHO CAN BENEFIT Registered charities; human rights organisations; individuals.

WHAT IS FUNDED General charitable purposes; community services and development; education; human rights, including civil liberties; work outside the UK; media.

TYPE OF GRANT Core costs; project funding; capital costs.

RANGE OF GRANTS Between £7,000 and £75,000.

SAMPLE GRANTS 3DCentre (£75,200); Independent Media Institute (£56,000); Tools For Solidarity (£10,000); Unicorn School (£7,100).

FINANCES *Financial year end* 05/04/2022
Income £72,300
Grants to organisations £148,300
Grants to individuals £18,300
Assets £1,090,000

TRUSTEES Mark Fenwick; Christopher Organ.

OTHER INFORMATION This trust replaced Roger Waters 1989 Charitable Trust (Charity Commission no. 328574). All assets were transferred to the successor trust (the 2000 in the title refers to when the declaration of trust was made). Like the former trust, it receives a share of Pink Floyd's royalties as part of its annual income. According to its 2021/22 accounts, the trust gives grants to organisations and individuals that address 'humanitarian, religious, equality, animal and environmental issues'.

HOW TO APPLY Unsolicited applications are not accepted.

CONTACT DETAILS The Trustees, 7 Melbray Mews, 158 Hurlingham Road, London SW6 3NS *Tel.* 020 7499 7275

■ Wates Family Enterprise Trust

CC NO 1126007   **ESTABLISHED** 2008

WHERE FUNDING CAN BE GIVEN UK.

WHO CAN BENEFIT Registered charities; unregistered charities; schools; universities; social enterprises; CICs; sports clubs; hospices; religious bodies/institutions.

WHAT IS FUNDED General charitable purposes, including: communities; education, training and employment; sustainability; social enterprise; thought leadership.

TYPE OF GRANT Core/revenue costs; project funding; unrestricted funding.

RANGE OF GRANTS Mostly up to £30,000.

SAMPLE GRANTS The Difference (£100,000); Look Ahead (£30,000); Smith Institute (£27,500); Starlight Children's Charity (£10,000); Bridge the Gap and Carlisle Key (£5,000 each); Brixton Soup Kitchen and The Sick Children's Fund (£1,000 each).

FINANCES *Financial year end* 31/12/2021
Income £825,000
Grants to organisations £478,500
Assets £478,500

TRUSTEES Andrew Wates; Andy Wates; Tim Wates; Charles Wates; Jonathan Wates; Sir James Wates; Paul Wates; Michael Wates.

OTHER INFORMATION The trust runs the Wates Giving programme, which supports causes with which Wates employees or the Wates family are involved.

HOW TO APPLY Unsolicited applications are not considered – the trust only supports organisations where a Wates employee has direct involvement on a regular basis.

CONTACT DETAILS Rebecca Ray, Grants Officer, Wates House, Station Approach, Leatherhead, Surrey KT22 7SW *Email* director@ watesfoundation.org.uk *Website* www.wfet.org. uk

Think carefully about every application. Is it justified?

725

■ The Wates Foundation

CC NO 247941   ESTABLISHED 1966

WHERE FUNDING CAN BE GIVEN Southern England.

WHO CAN BENEFIT Registered charities; social enterprises; community groups.

WHAT IS FUNDED Building social values; education and employment; community health; life transitions; safer communities; strengthening the charitable and voluntary sector.

WHAT IS NOT FUNDED Promotion of religion; individuals; statutory bodies; other grant-makers; organisations with an income over £3 million; capital projects; general appeals; continuation funding or new bids on behalf of organisations already in receipt of a foundation award.

TYPE OF GRANT Core costs; salaries; project funding.

RANGE OF GRANTS £200 to £20,000.

SAMPLE GRANTS Northleigh House (£21,000); Birth Trauma Association (£10,000); Different Planet Arts (£7,000); GASP Motor Project (£6,000); Migrants Organise (£5,000); Highreach Holidays (£250).

FINANCES *Financial year end 31/12/2021*
Income £357,700
Grants to organisations £279,400
Assets £24,480,000

TRUSTEES Jonathan Heynes; Victoria Tanner; Luke Wates; Nichola Adams; Christian Brodie; Jonathan Wates.

OTHER INFORMATION Grants were distributed as follows: community health (£128,000); education and employment (£76,000); life transition (£28,000); the environment (£16,600); building family values (£16,600); strengthening the voluntary sector (£14,300).

HOW TO APPLY Unsolicited applications are not accepted. The foundation is a proactive grant-maker.

CONTACT DETAILS Rebecca Ray, Grants Officer, Wates House, Station Approach, Leatherhead, Surrey KT22 7SW *Tel.* 01372 861000 *Email* director@watesfoundation.org.uk *Website* www.watesfoundation.org.uk

■ The William Wates Memorial Trust

CC NO 1011213

WHERE FUNDING CAN BE GIVEN London and the South East. The trust will also support projects throughout the UK proposed by their Le Loop riders.

WHO CAN BENEFIT Registered charities and not-for-profit enterprises.

WHAT IS FUNDED Projects that encourage young people (5–19 years old) experiencing severe disadvantage to keep away from anti-social behaviour and criminal activity, enabling them to fulfil their potential.

TYPE OF GRANT Project funding.

RANGE OF GRANTS Typically £30,000 over three years.

SAMPLE GRANTS Palace for Life (£90,000); West London Zone (£50,000); Abram Wilson Foundation (£35,000); YMCA East Surrey (£27,000); Hounslow Action for Youth (£22,000); Community Cycle Works (£10,000); Manorfield Charitable Foundation (£5,000); Sleep Pod (£2,000).

FINANCES *Financial year end 31/08/2021*
Income £421,800
Grants to organisations £477,300
Assets £636,200

TRUSTEES Susan Laing; Andrew Wates; Timothy Wates; Jonathon Wates; Richard Wates; Monty Wates; Sarah Wates.

OTHER INFORMATION The 2021/22 accounts were the latest available at the time of writing (May 2023). During the year, grants were made to 18 organisations and were distributed within the following themes: personal development (£279,800); mentoring (£145,500); arts (£35,000); sports (£12,000); educational support (£5,000). The trust's primary fundraising event, Le Loop, gives riders the opportunity to tackle up to 21 stages of the Tour de France.

HOW TO APPLY Applications can be made through the trust's website, where information about current submission dates can be found. Applications made before submission dates are announced will not be processed.

CONTACT DETAILS Jane Lowe, Administrator, Wates House, Station Approach, Leatherhead, Surrey KT22 7SW *Tel.* 01372 861051 *Email* wwmt@wates.co.uk *Website* https://wwmt.rideleloop.org

■ The Geoffrey Watling Charity

CC NO 1025258   ESTABLISHED 1993

WHERE FUNDING CAN BE GIVEN Norfolk and the Waveney area of Suffolk.

WHO CAN BENEFIT Charitable organisations.

WHAT IS FUNDED Social welfare; churches and historic buildings; education; the arts; health; sport; the environment.

WHAT IS NOT FUNDED Organisations which have not submitted their annual accounts/annual return to the Charity Commission or Companies House.

TYPE OF GRANT Project funding.

RANGE OF GRANTS Up to £50,000.

SAMPLE GRANTS Priscilla Bacon Norfolk Hospice Care Ltd (£50,000); University of East Anglia (£16,000); NORCA and Sistema in Norwich Ltd Education and Arts (£15,000); Norfolk Community Law Service (£12,000); SOUL Church and St Martin's (£10,000).

FINANCES *Financial year end 30/09/2022*
Income £747,800
Grants to organisations £553,800
Assets £15,640,000

TRUSTEES Alan Watling; Susan Watling; Richard Marks; David Lundean; Alexandra Haswell.

OTHER INFORMATION The charity made 118 grants, which were broken down as follows: social and welfare (£247,100); education and arts (£67,700); medical causes (£109,500); churches and historic buildings (£76,500); the environment (£47,000); sport (£15,000); infrastructure (£4,000).

HOW TO APPLY Applications can be made via the charity's website, where there are detailed guidelines for prospective applicants. The trustees meet quarterly to consider applications and make decisions on the grants to be awarded in accordance with the charity's objectives. The guidelines for applicants state that applications for funding 'towards a specific project are more likely to be looked on favourably by the trustees than those to help core costs or salaries'.

CONTACT DETAILS The Trustees, 8A Ber Street, Norwich, Norfolk NR1 3EJ *Tel.* 01603 766736 *Email* enquiries@geoffreywatling.org.uk *Website* www.geoffreywatling.org.uk

■ John Watson's Trust

OSCR NO SC014004
WHERE FUNDING CAN BE GIVEN Scotland.
WHO CAN BENEFIT Schools; educational organisations; individuals.
WHAT IS FUNDED Educational purposes including: school trips; equipment; performances and more.
WHAT IS NOT FUNDED Recurrent running costs; salaries.
TYPE OF GRANT Equipment; one-off costs.
RANGE OF GRANTS £100 to £2,000.
SAMPLE GRANTS Canal St Primary School (£5,900); East Lothian Council (£2,900); ABC Creative Music (£2,000); Lyra Artspace (£1,800); Live Music Now (£1,200); Gracemount High School, Living Paintings Trust, Positive Help and Young Speakers Scotland (£1,000 each).
FINANCES *Financial year end* 31/12/2022
Income £164,800
Grants to organisations £86,700
Grants to individuals £59,900
Assets £4,800,000
TRUSTEES Amanda Laurie; Andrew Cochrane; Cllr Alison Dickie; Robin Garrett; John Harding-Edgar; Susie Jamieson; Kenneth Mackay; Janet Morton; Richard Murray; Karen Phillips; Gordon Wylie.
HOW TO APPLY Applications can be made online via the trust's website, where upcoming deadlines can also be found.
CONTACT DETAILS James Hamilton, The Signet Library, Parliament Square, Edinburgh EH1 1RF *Tel.* 0131 220 3249 *Email* jhamilton@ wssociety.co.uk *Website* www.wssociety.co.uk/charities/jwt

■ We Love MCR Charity

CC NO 1066972   **ESTABLISHED** 1997
WHERE FUNDING CAN BE GIVEN The City of Manchester.
WHO CAN BENEFIT Community groups and grassroots charities; individuals.
WHAT IS FUNDED Social welfare and community development for the City of Manchester; children and young people; loneliness and social exclusion.
WHAT IS NOT FUNDED A full list of exclusions can be found in the guidance notes document on the charity's website.
TYPE OF GRANT One-off; project funding.
RANGE OF GRANTS Up to £4,000.
SAMPLE GRANTS Groundwork GM (£12,000); Sale Sharks Community Trust (£5,000); Friends of MCR's Gay Village (£4,400); Easy Peel Studio CIC (£3,900); Feelgood Theatre (£2,500); Manchester South District Scout Council (£1,800); Gorton Heritage Trail (£800); Church of Fire, Faith and Salvation (£500).
FINANCES *Financial year end* 31/03/2022
Income £229,300
Grants to organisations £192,100
Grants to individuals £98,700
Assets £1,150,000
TRUSTEES Anne Unwin, Deputy Lord Mayor; Fiona Ledden; Lord Mayor Cllr Tommy Judge; Michelle Rothwell; Aneel Mussarat; Hassan Hassan; Donna Ludford; Andreas Georgiou; Debra Cooper.
OTHER INFORMATION Grants are made to individuals through the charity's Rising Stars Fund.
HOW TO APPLY Application forms can be downloaded from the charity's website, along with guidance notes and upcoming deadlines. The trustees meet monthly to assess applications.
CONTACT DETAILS The Trustees, We Love MCR Charity, Lord Mayor's Office, Room 412, Town Hall, Manchester M60 2LA *Tel.* 0161 234 3229 *Email* welovemcrcharity@manchester.gov. uk *Website* www.welovemcrcharity.org

■ The Weavers' Company Benevolent Fund

CC NO 266189   **ESTABLISHED** 1973
WHERE FUNDING CAN BE GIVEN UK.
WHO CAN BENEFIT Charitable organisations.
WHAT IS FUNDED The charity lists the following as areas of interest: young offenders (particularly those under 30 years of age); prisoners and ex-prisoners; young disadvantaged people, especially those at risk of criminal involvement.
WHAT IS NOT FUNDED Long-term support; general appeals (sponsorship, marketing or other fundraising activities); endowment funds; grant-giving charities; retrospective expenditure; replacement funding; building projects; capital projects to provide access in compliance with the Disability Discrimination Act; personal appeals; umbrella bodies or large established organisations; overseas organisations/projects.
TYPE OF GRANT Project funding; core costs; capital costs.
RANGE OF GRANTS Typically up to £15,000.
SAMPLE GRANTS C2C Social Action (£15,000); South West Community Chaplaincy Trust (£10,200); Middleton Popstars Academy (£6,000); Code 4000 (£7,000); Innercity Films (£3,500); Koestler Award Trust (£1,000); St Paul's Cathedral (£500); City of London Police Widows and Orphans Fund (£150).
FINANCES *Financial year end* 31/12/2021
Income £663,500
Grants to organisations £451,700
Assets £17,590,000
TRUSTEE Bailiffs Wardens and Assistants of The Worshipful Company of Weavers.
OTHER INFORMATION The grant-maker is composed of four funds: the Charitable Grants Fund, which is administered by the Charitable Grants Committee; the Millennial Fund, which was launched in 1995 with the aim of building a significant new charitable fund by 2130; the Primary Schools Fund, which is administered by the Primary Schools Committee; and the Textile Fund, which is administered by the Textile Committee.
HOW TO APPLY Application forms can be downloaded from the charity's website. Once completed, applications should be submitted by post along with supporting documents. The Charitable Grants Committee meets three times a year, usually in February, June and October. Any late applications will be held over for consideration at the next closing date.
CONTACT DETAILS Anne Howe, Charities Officer, Saddlers Hall, 40 Gutter Lane, London EC2V 6BR *Tel.* 020 7606 1155 *Email* charity@ weavers.org.uk *Website* https://weavers.org. uk/charity/charitable-grants

■ The David Webster Charitable Trust

CC NO 1055111   **ESTABLISHED** 1995
WHERE FUNDING CAN BE GIVEN UK.
WHO CAN BENEFIT Charitable organisations.
WHAT IS FUNDED Environmental and conservation causes, including wildlife; heritage; general charitable causes.

RANGE OF GRANTS £500 to £100,000.

SAMPLE GRANTS Isabel Hospice (£65,900); Bat Conservation Trust (£2,000).

FINANCES *Financial year end* 27/11/2021
Income £49,800
Grants to organisations £67,900
Assets £1,830,000

TRUSTEES Nikola Thompson; Thomas Webster.

OTHER INFORMATION The 2020/21 accounts were the latest available to view at the time of writing (May 2023). During this period, the trust gave grants to two organisations. In previous years it has given to more organisations.

HOW TO APPLY Apply in writing to the correspondent.

CONTACT DETAILS Nikola Thompson, Trustee, Marshalls, Marshalls Lane, High Cross, Ware, Hertfordshire SG11 1AJ *Tel.* 01920 462001

■ The William Webster Charitable Trust

CC NO 259848   **ESTABLISHED** 1969

WHERE FUNDING CAN BE GIVEN The North East, principally Northumberland, Tyne and Wear, Durham and Cleveland.

WHO CAN BENEFIT Registered charitable organisations.

WHAT IS FUNDED General charitable purposes.

TYPE OF GRANT One-off grants for capital projects.

RANGE OF GRANTS £1,000 to £5,000.

SAMPLE GRANTS Ellingham Village Hall (£5,000); Blyth Star Enterprises (£3,000); The Charlotte Straker Project (£2,500); Eden Network NE (£1,500); Baby Equipment Loan Service (£1,000).

FINANCES *Financial year end* 05/04/2022
Income £68,700
Grants to organisations £54,000
Assets £2,700,000

TRUSTEE Zedra Trust Company (UK) Ltd.

OTHER INFORMATION In 2021/22, the trust awarded grants to 24 organisations.

HOW TO APPLY Apply in writing to the correspondent. Our previous research suggests that applications should include details of the costings of capital projects and of funding already raised, a set of the latest annual accounts and details of the current charity registration.

CONTACT DETAILS The Trustees, Zedra UK Trusts, Booths Hall, Booths Park 3, Chelford Road, Knutsford, Cheshire WA16 8GS *Tel.* 01565 748813 *Email* charities@zedra.com

■ The Linda and Michael Weinstein Charitable Trust

CC NO 1000637   **ESTABLISHED** 1990

WHERE FUNDING CAN BE GIVEN UK and Israel.

WHO CAN BENEFIT Charitable organisations.

WHAT IS FUNDED The Jewish faith and community; general charitable purposes.

RANGE OF GRANTS Up to £22,000.

SAMPLE GRANTS United Synagogue (£21,500); Friends of Bnei Akiva (£15,000); Camp Simcha (£7,500); Chai Cancer Care (£5,500); Jenetics and London School of Jewish Studies (£4,000 each); Ezras Hakohol Trust (£2,300).

FINANCES *Financial year end* 05/04/2022
Income £69,900
Grants to organisations £110,200
Assets £519,900

TRUSTEES Philip Keane; Linda Weinstein; Michael Weinstein.

HOW TO APPLY Apply in writing to the correspondent.

CONTACT DETAILS The Trustees, 32 Fairholme Gardens, London N3 3EB *Tel.* 020 8346 1257

■ The Weinstock Fund

CC NO 1150031   **ESTABLISHED** 2012

WHERE FUNDING CAN BE GIVEN UK.

WHO CAN BENEFIT Registered charities.

WHAT IS FUNDED Medical care and treatment, including respite care and hospices; care for adults and children with disabilities; education and training for adults and children with disabilities; care and support of older people; care and support of children; social welfare; music and the arts.

TYPE OF GRANT Capital costs; core/revenue costs; unrestricted funding.

SAMPLE GRANTS A list of beneficiaries was not included in the annual report and accounts.

FINANCES *Financial year end* 05/04/2022
Income £892,500
Grants to organisations £663,400
Assets £20,580,000

TRUSTEES Susan Lacroix; The Hon. Laura Weinstock; The Hon. Clare Renton.

OTHER INFORMATION Grants were made to 157 organisations and were broken down as follows: arts (£177,800); disability (£140,200); medical treatment and care (£128,800); education (£69,800); social welfare (£64,500); culture and the environment (£35,000); community (£33,200); hardship alleviation (£14,000).

HOW TO APPLY Applications can be made via the charity's website.

CONTACT DETAILS The Trustees, PO Box 5369, Wincanton BA9 0BG *Email* enquiries@weinstockfund.org.uk *Website* www.weinstockfund.org.uk

■ The Colin Weir Charitable Foundation

OSCR NO SC049161   **ESTABLISHED** 2019

WHERE FUNDING CAN BE GIVEN Scotland.

WHO CAN BENEFIT Charitable organisations; individuals.

WHAT IS FUNDED General charitable purposes.

RANGE OF GRANTS Mostly £2,000 to £25,000 with the occasional larger grant.

SAMPLE GRANTS Royal Marines Association (£35,000); Men Matter Scotland (£20,000); Abused Men in Scotland, Share Alike and The Underheugh Ark Rescue (£10,000 each); Help the Homeless (£6,000).

FINANCES *Financial year end* 31/03/2022
Income £500,000
Grants to organisations £236,000
Assets £232,200

OTHER INFORMATION Only organisations that received grants of over £6,000 were listed as beneficiaries in the foundation's 2021/22 accounts. Grants of under £6,000 totalled £88,000 and were awarded to 29 organisations. Previously, the foundation has supported individuals.

HOW TO APPLY Apply in writing to the correspondent.

CONTACT DETAILS The Trustees, c/o Murray Beith Murray, 3 Glenfinlas Street, Edinburgh EH3 6AQ

■ The Weir Charitable Trust

OSCR NO SC043187   **ESTABLISHED** 2012

WHERE FUNDING CAN BE GIVEN Scotland.

WHO CAN BENEFIT Small Scottish charities and community groups with an income of less than £125,000.

WHAT IS FUNDED Sport; recreational facilities; animal welfare; health; Scottish culture.

WHAT IS NOT FUNDED Individuals; commercial activities; educational costs; social enterprises; governing bodies; public sector bodies; sponsorship; sports strips; one-off events such as Gala Days and exhibitions.

TYPE OF GRANT Capital projects; running costs; one-off projects; core costs; salaries. All awards are for one year or less.

RANGE OF GRANTS Less than £25,000.

SAMPLE GRANTS Four Pillars (£19,500); Nature Scotland (£14,000); The Folan Trust (£13,800); Ochil Youths Community Improvement (£11,800); Nevis Ensemble (£10,000); Fostering Compassion (£8,000); Feral Cats Scotland (£6,000); SupportED (£5,000).

FINANCES *Financial year end 19/12/2021*
Income £202,400
Grants to organisations £201,200
Assets £5,260,000

OTHER INFORMATION In 2020/21, the trust awarded 33 grants, which were broken down as follows: health (£89,800); The Robert Hartness Awards (£29,000); sport (£22,400); recreational facilities (£22,200); culture (£19,800); animal welfare (£18,000).

HOW TO APPLY Applications can be made through the trust's website or on an application form available from the website. Details of application deadlines are also published on the website. Applications for grants of over £25,000 will not be considered.

CONTACT DETAILS Trust Manager, Unit 201, Ettrick Riverside, Dunsdale Road, Selkirk, Scottish Borders TD7 5EB *Email* enquiries@ weircharitabletrust.com *Website* www. weircharitabletrust.com

■ The James Weir Foundation

CC NO 251764   **ESTABLISHED** 1967

WHERE FUNDING CAN BE GIVEN UK, with a preference for Ayrshire and Glasgow.

WHO CAN BENEFIT UK-registered charities.

WHAT IS FUNDED General charitable purposes including: education and training; health; disability.

WHAT IS NOT FUNDED Individuals; overseas organisations.

TYPE OF GRANT Capital costs; core/revenue costs.

RANGE OF GRANTS £1,000 to £5,000.

SAMPLE GRANTS Youth Sport Trust (£202,000); National Brain Appeal (£8,000); Ardgowan Hospice and Mission to Seafarers (£5,000 each); Asthma UK, Foodtrain and St Andrew's First Aid (£3,000 each); The Prince's Trust (£1,000).

FINANCES *Financial year end 31/12/2021*
Income £345,300
Grants to organisations £292,000
Assets £10,600,000

TRUSTEES Elizabeth Bonham; William Ducas; Simon Bonham.

HOW TO APPLY Applications should be sent by post with supporting evidence and a copy of the applicant's latest annual report. Emailed applications will not be considered.

CONTACT DETAILS Louisa Lawson, Secretary to the Trustees, PO Box 72361, London SW18 9NB *Tel.* 01727 869141 *Email* info@ jamesweirfoundation.org *Website* http:// jamesweirfoundation.org

■ The Welland Trust

CC NO 1181775

WHERE FUNDING CAN BE GIVEN England and Wales.

WHO CAN BENEFIT Charitable organisations; individuals.

WHAT IS FUNDED Care experienced adults.

TYPE OF GRANT Project funding.

SAMPLE GRANTS A list of beneficiaries was not included in the annual report and accounts.

FINANCES *Financial year end 31/12/2021*
Income £125,700
Grants to organisations £807,800
Grants to individuals £54,800
Assets £12,190,000

TRUSTEES Sarah Saunders; Polly Jones; Janet Rees; Isabelle Murphy.

HOW TO APPLY Contact the charity via email or using the form available on its website. Applicants will need to provide a full project plan indicating how the grant will be used and the expected outcomes and benefits for adults who have experienced care.

CONTACT DETAILS The Trustees, Craftsman House, De Salis Drive, Hampton Lovett, Droitwich, Worcestershire WR9 0QE *Email* enquiries@ thewellandtrust.org *Website* www. thewellandtrust.org

■ Wellbank Foundation

CC NO 1192329

WHERE FUNDING CAN BE GIVEN Northumberland; Tyne and Wear.

WHO CAN BENEFIT Registered charities with a turnover of no more than £1 million.

WHAT IS FUNDED People who are disadvantaged. The foundation prefers projects that have an educational, environmental or sporting benefit.

WHAT IS NOT FUNDED Research projects; the advancement of a religious or political causes; retrospective expenditure.

TYPE OF GRANT Project funding.

RANGE OF GRANTS £500 to £25,000.

SAMPLE GRANTS A list of beneficiaries was not included in the annual report and accounts.

FINANCES *Financial year end 31/03/2022*
Income £225,000
Grants to organisations £120,800
Assets £104,200

TRUSTEES Andrew Robson; Ruth Robson; Emilia Robson; Lauren Robson.

HOW TO APPLY Application forms are available to download from the foundation's website.

CONTACT DETAILS The Trustees, PO Box 320, Morpeth NE61 9GX *Email* wellbankfoundation@ gmail.com *Website* www.wellbankfoundation. com

■ Wellbeing of Women

CC NO 239281   **ESTABLISHED** 1964

WHERE FUNDING CAN BE GIVEN UK and Ireland.

WHO CAN BENEFIT Medical research organisations, primarily universities; individuals.

WHAT IS FUNDED Research into women's reproductive and gynaecological health.

WHAT IS NOT FUNDED See the charity's website for a full list of exclusions for each scheme.

TYPE OF GRANT Research projects; training and research fellowships; scholarships.

RANGE OF GRANTS Grants range up to £255,300.

SAMPLE GRANTS University College London (£255,300); University of Sheffield (£19,500); University of Birmingham (£8,500); University of Oxford (£6,200); Glasgow Caledonian University (£1,000).

FINANCES *Financial year end 31/12/2021*
Income £1,820,000
Grants to organisations £916,800
Assets £2,350,000

TRUSTEES Philip Jansen; Debra White; Sir Ian Powell; Margaret Horvath; Lady Helen Ward; Prof. Lesley Regan; Ranee Thakar; Sacha Nathan; Gill Walton.

OTHER INFORMATION The charity runs various grant programmes, including: research grants; research training fellowships; entry-level research scholarships; postdoctoral research fellowships.

HOW TO APPLY Application forms are available to download from the charity's website, where you will also find research guidelines and dates of open application periods for each scheme.

CONTACT DETAILS The Trustees, 10–18 Union Street, London SE1 1SZ *Tel.* 020 3697 7000 *Email* hello@wellbeingofwomen.org.uk *Website* www.wellbeingofwomen.org.uk

■ The Wellcome Trust

CC NO 210183   **ESTABLISHED** 1936

WHERE FUNDING CAN BE GIVEN UK and overseas.

WHO CAN BENEFIT Academic researchers; research institutions; charitable organisations.

WHAT IS FUNDED Medical research including research into: mental health; infectious disease; the effects of climate change on health.

WHAT IS NOT FUNDED Specific criteria and exclusions for each funding programme are detailed on the trust's website.

TYPE OF GRANT A wide range of grants including: research grants; fellowships; starter grants; funding for PhD and master's degrees; undergraduate scholarships; equipment and resources.

SAMPLE GRANTS University of Oxford (£124.2 million); European Bioinformatics Institute (£22.6 million); Francis Crick Institute (£19.3 million); University of Liverpool (£16 million); Medical Research Council (£11.4 million).

FINANCES *Financial year end 30/09/2021*
Income £410,260,000
Grants to organisations £847,900,000
Assets £36,260,600,000

TRUSTEE The Wellcome Trust Ltd.

OTHER INFORMATION The Wellcome Trust is one of the world's leading biomedical research charities and is the UK's largest non-governmental source of funds for biomedical research. The grant total is taken from the organisation's consolidated accounts and refers to grants awarded by the trust. Grants were broken down as follows: science (£598.3 million); innovations (£104.1 million); priority areas (£102.4 million); culture and society (£43.1 million). The 2020/21 accounts were the latest available at the time of writing (June 2023).

HOW TO APPLY Applications can be made via the trust's website.

CONTACT DETAILS The Grants Team, Gibbs Building, 215 Euston Road, London NW1 2BE *Tel.* 020 7611 8888 *Email* use the contact form on the website *Website* www.wellcome.ac.uk

■ Wellington Management UK Foundation

CC NO 1167369   **ESTABLISHED** 2016

WHERE FUNDING CAN BE GIVEN UK; Germany; Luxembourg; Switzerland.

WHO CAN BENEFIT Registered charities.

WHAT IS FUNDED Improvement of academic performance and behaviour, reduction in absenteeism and development of life skills for economically disadvantaged young people (up to 26).

WHAT IS NOT FUNDED The foundation does not support scholarship programmes.

TYPE OF GRANT Unrestricted (although not scholarship programmes).

RANGE OF GRANTS £11,000 to £51,000.

SAMPLE GRANTS Action Tutoring and London Music Masters (£51,000 each); Debate Mate, Future Frontiers and London Youth Rowing (£46,000 each); London Thunder Basketball Club and Nova New Opportunities (£20,000 each); Street League and Westminster City School (£10,000 each).

FINANCES *Financial year end 31/12/2021*
Income £1,100,000
Grants to organisations £1,000,000
Assets £105,000

TRUSTEES Nicola Staunton; Damian Bloom; Joanne Carey; Richard Lienden; Anna Lunden; James Stoll; Thomas Horsey; Gemma MacDonald.

OTHER INFORMATION Grants were awarded to 28 organisations during the year.

HOW TO APPLY There is more information about the grant-making process and application deadlines on the foundation's website. Email wmukf@wellington.com with any questions about the application process.

CONTACT DETAILS The Trustees, c/o Wellington Management International Ltd, 80 Victoria Street, London SW1E 5JL *Tel.* 020 7126 6000 *Email* wmukf@wellington.com *Website* www.wellington.com/en-gb/community-engagement

■ The Welsh Church Act Fund

CC NO 506658   **ESTABLISHED** 1976

WHERE FUNDING CAN BE GIVEN Rhondda Cynon Taff, Bridgend and Merthyr Tydfil County Borough Councils.

WHO CAN BENEFIT Charitable organisations; churches.

WHAT IS FUNDED General charitable purposes; education; social welfare; health; arts, culture and heritage; social and recreational activities; medical and social research; probation; older people; blind people; places of worship; emergency and disaster relief.

WHAT IS NOT FUNDED Students; individuals; clubs with a liquor licence; projects operating outside the area of benefit; regular running expenses.

TYPE OF GRANT Capital costs; project costs.

RANGE OF GRANTS Typically up to £10,000, with one-off grants of up to £48,600.

SAMPLE GRANTS Lee Gardens Pool (£48,600); Gelligaled Park Community Action Group (£39,800); Hope Rescue (£12,100); Rock Community Church – Abercynon (£9,300); St Thomas Church – Rhondda Area (£8,500); Hetty Pit the Great Western Colliery Preservation Trust (£6,000); Bridge Mentoring Scheme – Bridgend (£5,000); Bridgend Society of Friends/Quakers (£4,100).

FINANCES *Financial year end 31/03/2022*
Income £376,300
Grants to organisations £384,700
Assets £13,900

TRUSTEES Christopher Lee; Rhondda Cynon Taff County Borough Council.

OTHER INFORMATION Grants of more than £2,000 require a minimum of 10% matched funding from non-Welsh Church Fund sources (20% for grants exceeding £10,000). Those grants which are structural in nature are only considered where a professional assessment for the necessary works has been made. Grants were made to 38 organisations in 2021/22, of which three were under £2,000 and together totalled £5,700. Grants of more than £2,000 were awarded to 38 organisations and totalled £379,000.

HOW TO APPLY Apply in writing to the correspondent, submitting your application together with your estimates, accounts and constitution. The 2021/22 annual report states: 'Recommendations for grant awards are made by officers in an Assessment Round Report, which is considered at special meetings regularly throughout the year on approximately a monthly basis.'

CONTACT DETAILS Chris Bradshaw, Chief Executive, c/o Rhondda Cynon Taff County Borough Council, Council Offices, Bronwydd, Porth, Rhondda Cynon Taf CF39 9DL *Tel.* 01443 680734 *Email* treasurymanagement@rctcbc.gov.uk

---

■ Wembley National Stadium Trust

CC NO 1072392 **ESTABLISHED** 1998

WHERE FUNDING CAN BE GIVEN England, with a strong preference for the London Borough of Brent.

WHO CAN BENEFIT Registered charities; local authorities; schools, colleges and educational establishments; amateur sports clubs; CICs; not-for-profit organisations; social enterprises; community groups.

WHAT IS FUNDED Sports and recreation; disability sports projects; football projects for women and girls.

WHAT IS NOT FUNDED Individuals; items already purchased or ordered, or works already undertaken; core PE curricular activities; activities which promote religion; trips abroad; the purchase of a vehicle.

TYPE OF GRANT Capital grants; strategic funding; projects; core costs.

RANGE OF GRANTS Mostly up to £36,000.

SAMPLE GRANTS Middlesex Football Association (£25,000); Wembley Football (£20,000); Active Sporting Communities, Brent Punjabi Association, Garryowen Gaelic Football Club, London Basketball Association, Sudbury Court Running Club and Young Roots (£2,500 each).

FINANCES *Financial year end* 31/03/2022
Income £892,000
Grants to organisations £90,000
Assets £911,000

TRUSTEES Baroness Tanni Grey-Thompson; Peter Ackerley; Andrew Douglass; Lynsey Edwards; Khilna Shah; Nayim Ahmed; Ellis Clark; Kawsar Zaman; Marilyn Okoro.

HOW TO APPLY See the trust's website for information on programme opening dates.

CONTACT DETAILS The Trustees, Wembley Stadium, Wembley, Middlesex, London HA9 0WS *Tel.* 07944 518065 *Email* info@wnst.org.uk *Website* www.wnst.org.uk

---

■ West Derby Waste Lands Charity

CC NO 223623 **ESTABLISHED** 1753

WHERE FUNDING CAN BE GIVEN West Derby, Merseyside.

WHO CAN BENEFIT Charitable organisations; amateur sports clubs; uniformed groups; individuals.

WHAT IS FUNDED General charitable purposes; community development; social welfare; older people; children and young people.

RANGE OF GRANTS Grants range from £430 to £6,000.

SAMPLE GRANTS Bradbury Fields (£6,000); Bridge Community Centre (£4,000); Roscoe Primary School (£3,000); Ronald McDonald House (£2,000); Beautiful New Beginnings (£1,000); Christ Church – Tuebrook (£600); 446th St Paul's Brownies (£430).

FINANCES *Financial year end* 31/12/2021
Income £69,800
Grants to organisations £71,300
Grants to individuals £4,400
Assets £2,170,000

TRUSTEES Derek Corlett; Joan Driscoll; Brenda Antrobus; Anthony Heath; Barbara Kerr; Peter North; Barbara Shacklady; John Hudson; Jennifer Driscoll; Stephen Pye.

HOW TO APPLY Apply in writing to the correspondent. Individuals can download an application form from the website.

CONTACT DETAILS Lawrence Downey, Secretary, Ripley House, 56 Freshfield Road, Formby, Liverpool, Merseyside L37 3HW *Tel.* 01704 879330 *Email* lawrencedowney@btconnect.com *Website* www.westderbywastelands.co.uk

---

■ West Herts Charity Trust Ltd

CC NO 278891 **ESTABLISHED** 1992

WHERE FUNDING CAN BE GIVEN Hertfordshire.

WHO CAN BENEFIT Charities and community groups.

WHAT IS FUNDED Vehicles and minibuses.

SAMPLE GRANTS A list of beneficiaries was not included in the annual report and accounts. Previous beneficiaries have included: Abbotts Langley Primary School; Batchworth Sea Scouts; Brockswood Primary and Nursery School.

FINANCES *Financial year end* 31/07/2022
Income £209,000
Grants to organisations £96,200
Assets £3,620,000

TRUSTEES Paul Miller; Michael Humphreys; Peter Miller; Mr R. D. Minashi; Matthew Humphreys.

HOW TO APPLY Applications can be made through the charity's website.

CONTACT DETAILS The Trustees, Ver House, Park Industrial Estate, Frogmore, St Albans, Hertfordshire AL2 2WH *Email* info@whct.org.uk *Website* www.whct.org.uk

---

■ The Westfield Health Charitable Trust

CC NO 246057 **ESTABLISHED** 1965

WHERE FUNDING CAN BE GIVEN UK.

WHO CAN BENEFIT Registered charities.

WHAT IS FUNDED Health, well-being and medical causes.

TYPE OF GRANT Capital costs; project funding.

RANGE OF GRANTS Typically up to £30,000.

SAMPLE GRANTS Age UK Sheffield (£40,000); The Children's Hospital Charity and St Luke's Hospice (£30,000 each); Paces and St Wilfrid's Centre (£20,000 each); British Blind Sport (£10,000); Sheffield Area Kidney Association (£1,000); Hope Trauma Support Charity (£500).

FINANCES *Financial year end 05/04/2022*
Income £210,900
Grants to organisations £264,900
Assets £455,400

TRUSTEES Graham Moore; David Whitney; Lynn Clarke.

OTHER INFORMATION The trust was previously known as The Sheffield and District Hospital Services Charitable Fund. During 2021/22, the trust awarded 16 grants to organisations.

HOW TO APPLY An application form can be downloaded from the trust's 'Apply for Funding' webpage. The form includes all the required details for an application, which should be submitted by email to charity@westfieldhealth.com. There are no deadlines and submissions are considered throughout the year.

CONTACT DETAILS The Trustees, Westfield House, 60 Charter Row, Sheffield, South Yorkshire S1 3FZ *Tel.* 0114 250 2079 *Email* charity@westfieldhealth.com *Website* www.westfieldhealth.com/charitable-trust

■ Westhill Endowment

CC NO 1104736

WHERE FUNDING CAN BE GIVEN Worldwide, with a preference for the UK.

WHO CAN BENEFIT Registered charities; churches.

WHAT IS FUNDED Formal and informal religious education projects and faith-motivated activities that enable people to transform their lives and the life of their communities.

WHAT IS NOT FUNDED See the charity's website for a detailed list of exclusions.

TYPE OF GRANT Project funding, mostly for a one-year period; capacity building.

RANGE OF GRANTS Up to £21,000, mostly between £2,000 and £5,000.

SAMPLE GRANTS British and Foreign Bible Society (£21,000); Entraide and Prison Advice and Care Trust (£20,000 each); NASACRE (£16,000); Chaplaincy – University of Birmingham (£12,900); Swansea Sacre (£12,000); Total Insight Theatre and Trinity Church (£10,000 each).

FINANCES *Financial year end 31/07/2022*
Income £486,400
Grants to organisations £287,300
Assets £15,260,000

TRUSTEES The Revd Edward Coleman; Sarah Evans; Peter Ullathorne; Philip White; David Slade; Lorna Hewitt; Andrew Morris; Dr Rachael Royal; Dr Aisha Ahmad; Shivaji Shiva; The Revd Neil Roberts.

OTHER INFORMATION Grants were awarded to 53 organisations. Only organisations that received grants of over £10,000 were listed as beneficiaries in the charity's accounts. Grants of under £10,000 totalled £137,500 and were awarded to 31 organisations.

HOW TO APPLY See the charity's website for details on how to apply.

CONTACT DETAILS The Trust Office Manager, The Lodge Westhill, South Drive, Selly Oak, Birmingham, West Midlands B29 6WE *Tel.* 0121 472 8000 *Email* info@westhillendowment.org *Website* www.westhillendowment.org

■ Westminster Almshouses Foundation

CC NO 226936   **ESTABLISHED** 2007

WHERE FUNDING CAN BE GIVEN City of Westminster.

WHO CAN BENEFIT Charitable organisations and individuals.

WHAT IS FUNDED Relief in need, particularly for social isolation; education/training for young people on low.

WHAT IS NOT FUNDED Organisations with large financial reserves will not be funded.

TYPE OF GRANT Project funding; capital grants; one-off grants for individuals.

RANGE OF GRANTS Up to £30,000 for organisations and up to £500 for individuals.

SAMPLE GRANTS Harris Academy 6th Form (£27,000); St Matthew's Primary School (£19,900); I Can and North Paddington Foodbank (£10,100 each); St Andrew's Club (£7,000); Avenues Youth Project (£5,000); Westminster Medical School Schools Science Conference (£2,600).

FINANCES *Financial year end 31/12/2021*
Income £769,200
Grants to organisations £214,200
Grants to individuals £39,300
Assets £43,530,000

TRUSTEES Lady Joanna Knatchbull; Cllr Rachael Robathan; Charles Lillis; The Revd Graham Buckle; Lucy Slater; Dr Robert Linton; Susan Ford; Cllr Jim Glen; Cllr Selina Short; Xavier Villers.

HOW TO APPLY Apply in writing to the correspondent. Large grants are considered by the grants committee, who meet four times a year in January, April, July and October.

CONTACT DETAILS The Clerk, Palmer's House, 42 Rochester Row, London SW1P 1BU *Tel.* 020 7828 3131 *Email* clerk@westminsteralmshouses.com *Website* www.westminsteralmshouses.com

■ Westminster Foundation

CC NO 267618   **ESTABLISHED** 1974

WHERE FUNDING CAN BE GIVEN Westminster (parts of the old metropolitan borough of Westminster); Cheshire West and Cheshire; north-west rural Lancashire (near Forest of Bowland); and north-west Sutherland.

WHO CAN BENEFIT Registered charities.

WHAT IS FUNDED Social welfare. The foundation is currently focusing its grant-making on issues around poverty in UK, in the following themes: supporting communities in need; vulnerable groups; building resilience; crisis intervention. Further detail on eligibility criteria is given on the foundation's website. The foundation also makes some grants overseas, but these are not open to application.

WHAT IS NOT FUNDED Requests for individuals including student fees and bursaries; projects benefitting only one school or college; holidays or trips including respite programmes; projects that are overtly political or religious; gifts and prizes for events and auctions; organisations that have applied to us unsuccessfully within the previous 12 months; capital costs in isolation.

TYPE OF GRANT One-off grants; core costs; project grants.

RANGE OF GRANTS Grants range from £10,000 up to £250,000.

SAMPLE GRANTS NHS Charities Together (£5 million); The Prince's Trust (£250,000); The Country Trust (£190,000); Future Men and YoungMinds

(£100,000 each); Chester Schools Together (£65,000); The Mix (£50,500); Cheshire West Citizens Advice (£20,000).

FINANCES *Financial year end 31/12/2021*
Income £13,420,000
Grants to organisations £5,690,000
Assets £121,800,000

TRUSTEES The Duke of Westminster; James Hanbury; Victoria Hornby.

OTHER INFORMATION Only organisations that received grants of over £20,000 were listed as beneficiaries in the charity's accounts. Grants of under £20,000 totalled £364,000.

HOW TO APPLY Check the foundation's website for details on eligibility. Applications for the Small Grant Programme can be made online. Charities can also join the waiting list for office space online. Partnership grants are by invitation only.

CONTACT DETAILS Oliver Woodford, Grants Manager, The Grosvenor Office, 70 Grosvenor Street, London W1K 3JP *Tel.* 020 7408 0988 *Email* westminster.foundation@grosvenor.com *Website* www.westminsterfoundation.org.uk

···

■ The Galen and Hilary Weston Foundation

CC NO 1167260   **ESTABLISHED** 2015
WHERE FUNDING CAN BE GIVEN UK; Canada; the Netherlands; Republic of Ireland.

WHO CAN BENEFIT Medical research institutions; universities; registered charities.

WHAT IS FUNDED Medical research into brain diseases.

WHAT IS NOT FUNDED The foundation's objects are restricted specifically to the advancement of such charitable purposes as the trustees see fit, provided that they do not include the promotion of any religion.

TYPE OF GRANT Research funding.

RANGE OF GRANTS £21,500 to £137,500.

SAMPLE GRANTS King's College London (£137,500); Rare Dementia Support Centre (£50,000); Age Action Ireland and Alzheimer Society Ireland (£40,000 each); Swansea University (£39,000); Stichting Katholieke Universiteit (£21,500).

FINANCES *Financial year end 31/12/2021*
Income £1,130,000
Grants to organisations £573,000
Assets £1,390,000

TRUSTEES Anthony Edwards; Alannah Cochrane; Paul Kelly; Adam Batty; Alexandria Forbes.

HOW TO APPLY Applications can be made via the Weston Brain Institute.

CONTACT DETAILS The Trustees, Selfridges Group, Nations House, 103 Wigmore Street, London W1U 1QS *Tel.* 020 7318 2318

···

■ The Garfield Weston Foundation

CC NO 230260   **ESTABLISHED** 1958
WHERE FUNDING CAN BE GIVEN UK.

WHO CAN BENEFIT Registered charities; schools; universities; CICs; hospitals; hospices.

WHAT IS FUNDED Social welfare; the arts; young people; community development; faith; the environment; education; health; museums and heritage.

WHAT IS NOT FUNDED Individuals; CICs; social enterprises without UK Charity Commission registration; sporting associations without UK Charity Commission registration; work that does not deliver a direct benefit in the UK, even if the organisation is registered with the Charity Commission; animal welfare charities; charities

that spend the majority of their income outside the UK; local authorities and councils.

TYPE OF GRANT Capital costs; core/revenue costs; project funding.

RANGE OF GRANTS £1,000 to several millions.

SAMPLE GRANTS Zoological Society of London (£1.5 million); Imperial College London (£1 million); Theatr Clwyd Trust (£500,000); Redhills CIO (£250,000); Media Trust (£200,000); The RSA (£150,000); The Gesher Trust (£100,000); Chefs in Schools (£75,000); Hull and East Yorkshire Children's University (£40,000); Newport Girls' High School Academy Trust (£25,000); Wyldwood Arts (£20,000); Shakespeare at the Tobacco Factory (£15,000); Under the Edge Arts (£2,500).

FINANCES *Financial year end 05/04/2022*
Income £84,000,000
Grants to organisations £89,880,000
Assets £7,192,480,000

TRUSTEES Kate Hobhouse; Jana Khayat; Sophia Weston; Eliza Mitchell; Melissa Murdoch; George Weston; Guy Weston; Geordie Dalglish; Alannah Weston.

OTHER INFORMATION In 2021/22, the foundation made 1,988 grants to charities. Grants were broken down as follows: young people (£18.6 million); welfare (£14.43 million); museums and heritage (£11.45 million); health (£11.42 million); education (£9.84 million); the environment (£7.4 million); community (£6.88 million); arts (£5.07 million); faith (£4.49 million); other (£205,000).

HOW TO APPLY Apply via the foundation's website.

CONTACT DETAILS The Trustees, Weston Centre, 10 Grosvenor Street, London W1K 4QY *Tel.* 020 7399 6565 *Email* admin@ garfieldweston.org *Website* www.garfieldweston. org

···

■ Westway Trust

CC NO 1123127   **ESTABLISHED** 2008
WHERE FUNDING CAN BE GIVEN The Royal Borough of Kensington and Chelsea, with a particular focus on north Kensington, in and around the Westway.

WHO CAN BENEFIT Social enterprises; charitable, voluntary and community organisations.

WHAT IS FUNDED Isolation; spaces for young people; recreation and exercise; economic participation; arts and culture; the environment.

WHAT IS NOT FUNDED See the grant-maker's website for exclusions relevant to each grants programme.

TYPE OF GRANT Projects costs; capital costs; core costs.

RANGE OF GRANTS Grants range from £500 to £32,660.

SAMPLE GRANTS Association for Cultural Advancement through Visual Art (£25,100); Bike Works CIC (£10,800); All Saints Catholic College (£1,000); The West London Turkish School (£500).

FINANCES *Financial year end 31/03/2022*
Income £6,770,000
Grants to organisations £541,800
Assets £63,600,000

TRUSTEES Dr Marwan Elnaghi; Thomas Fitch; Tobias Belson; Huey Walker; Eve Wedderburn; Sheraine Williams; Marie-Therese Rossi; Jonathan Kelly; Minal Patel; Niamh Graham.

HOW TO APPLY When grant programmes open, a link to an online application portal is made available on the trust's website. Applicants will need to create an account and login to make an

Think carefully about every application. Is it justified?

········

733

application. Guidelines are also made available for each open funding programme.

CONTACT DETAILS The Trustees, 1 Thorpe Close, London W10 5XL *Tel.* 020 8962 5720 *Email* info@westway.org *Website* www.westway.org

---

■ The Barbara Whatmore Charitable Trust

CC NO 283336　　　　**ESTABLISHED** 1981
WHERE FUNDING CAN BE GIVEN UK, with some preference for East Anglia.
WHO CAN BENEFIT Registered charities.
WHAT IS FUNDED Arts, music and relief of poverty, focusing mainly on cultural and heritage projects, particularly in East Anglia. Eligible areas of support include: classical music education; conservation and crafts training; education projects in museums, the theatre and poetry; conservation of endangered historic artefacts and of the natural heritage environment, as well as preventative projects to protect historic or natural collections.
WHAT IS NOT FUNDED Repair work to the fabric of buildings or structures; the purchase of musical instruments or works of art; choral societies; festivals; individuals; organisations without registered charitable status.
TYPE OF GRANT Project funding; general funding.
RANGE OF GRANTS Up to £5,000.
SAMPLE GRANTS London Philharmonic Orchestra and City and Guilds of London Art School (£4,000 each); Orange Tree Theatre and The Prince's Foundation (£3,000 each); Wonderful Beast Theatre (£2,000); Sherborne Douzelage (£500); St Nicholas – Woodrising (£200).
FINANCES *Financial year end* 05/04/2022
Income £82,800
Grants to organisations £70,500
Assets £2,190,000
TRUSTEES Denis Borrow; Sally Carter; David Eldridge; Luke Gardiner; Gillian Lewis; Edmund Gardiner.
OTHER INFORMATION Grants were awarded to 24 organisations in 2021/22.
HOW TO APPLY Apply in writing to the correspondent, either by post or email. Applications can be submitted at any time but no later than 15 March or 15 September for consideration at the meetings in April and October, respectively.
CONTACT DETAILS Denise Gardiner, 3 Honeyhanger, Hindhead Road, Hindhead, Surrey GU26 6BA *Tel.* 07762 942914 *Email* denise@bwct.org

---

■ The Which? Fund

WHERE FUNDING CAN BE GIVEN UK.
WHO CAN BENEFIT UK-registered charities; universities; not-for-profit CICs.
WHAT IS FUNDED Research projects aiming to improve understanding of the specific consumer harms experienced by diverse and disadvantaged communities and the development of evidence-based solutions to tackle these harms.
SAMPLE GRANTS The Bevan Foundation; London South Bank University; Money and Mental Health Policy Institute; National Energy Action; The Pensions Policy Institute; Samaritans; The Social Market Foundation.
FINANCES *Financial year end* 30/06/2023
Grants to organisations £75,000

OTHER INFORMATION Which? is a not-for-profit organisation wholly owned by the Consumers' Association (Charity Commission no. 296072). The Which? Fund is funded by the Consumers' Association.
HOW TO APPLY Apply via the fund's website, where further guidance and information on application deadlines can be found.
CONTACT DETAILS Raveene-Jonelle Dompreh, 2 Marylebone Road, London NW1 4DF *Email* funding@which.co.uk *Website* www.which.co.uk/policy-and-insight/the-which-fund

---

■ The Whinfell Charitable Fund

CC NO 267333　　　　**ESTABLISHED** 1973
WHERE FUNDING CAN BE GIVEN UK, in particular Bolton and Manchester.
WHO CAN BENEFIT Registered charities and charitable organisations. The charity has specific regular beneficiaries, including the RNLI, with opportunities to add further charities.
WHAT IS FUNDED General charitable purposes; the advancement of the Christian religion; education; the advancement of health; saving lives.
TYPE OF GRANT Mainly recurrent grants to established beneficiaries.
SAMPLE GRANTS A list of beneficiaries was not included in the annual report and accounts.
FINANCES *Financial year end* 31/01/2022
Income £99,200
Grants to organisations £80,000
Assets £6,420,000
TRUSTEES Jennifer Mitchell; Katherine Duff; Sarah Bowles.
OTHER INFORMATION Grants were awarded to charitable organisations in the fields of health and local social impact.
HOW TO APPLY Apply in writing to the correspondent.
CONTACT DETAILS The Trustees, 35 Westgate, Huddersfield HD1 1PA *Tel.* 01484 423691

■ The Whitaker Charitable Trust

CC NO 234491　　　　**ESTABLISHED** 1964
WHERE FUNDING CAN BE GIVEN UK, with a preference for Nottinghamshire, the East Midlands and Scotland.
WHO CAN BENEFIT Registered charities.
WHAT IS FUNDED General charitable purposes with a preference for: local charities in Nottinghamshire and the East Midlands; music; agricultural and silvicultural education; countryside conservation; Scottish charities.
RANGE OF GRANTS Up to £20,000 but mostly £1,000 to £2,000.
SAMPLE GRANTS School of Artisan Food (£20,000); Atlantic College (£10,000); Nottinghamshire and Nottingham Refugee Forum (£5,000); Bassetlaw Hospice (£3,000); Criminon UK (£1,000).
FINANCES *Financial year end* 31/03/2022
Income £224,100
Grants to organisations £172,000
Assets £11,620,000
TRUSTEES Edward Perks; Lady Elizabeth Whitaker; Sir Jack Whitaker.
HOW TO APPLY Apply in writing to the correspondent. The trustees meet regularly to review grant applications.
CONTACT DETAILS The Trustees, 33 Queen Anne Street, 33 Queen Anne Street, London W1G 9HY *Tel.* 020 7802 2700

■ Colonel W. H. Whitbread Charitable Trust

CC NO 210496   **ESTABLISHED** 1953
WHERE FUNDING CAN BE GIVEN UK.
WHO CAN BENEFIT Charitable organisations; educational organisations; sports organisations.
WHAT IS FUNDED The trust supports: education, particularly for those who are disadvantaged, as well as for pupils at Aldenham School and in support of Corpus Christi College, Cambridge; amateur sports, particularly those enjoyed by the settlor (ocean racing, Finn Class sailing, National Hunt racing, flying, field sports, eventing and polo); health and welfare of service personnel; conservation projects.
SAMPLE GRANTS A list of beneficiaries was not included in the annual report and accounts. Previous beneficiaries have included: 1st Queen's Dragon Guards Regimental Trust; ABF The Soldiers' Charity; Disasters Emergency Committee; Friends of Alderman Knight School – Gloucestershire; Historic Churches Trust; Great Ormond Street Hospital Children's Charity; Household Cavalry Museum Appeal; Queen Mary's Clothing Guild; Royal Hospital Chelsea; St Richard's Hospice.
FINANCES *Financial year end* 31/12/2021
Income £234,800
Grants to organisations £160,700
Assets £14,590,000
TRUSTEES Jeremy Barkes; Rupert Foley; Mr H. F. Whitbread.
HOW TO APPLY Apply in writing to the correspondent.
CONTACT DETAILS Susan Smith, Secretary, Fir Tree Cottage, World's End, Grimley, Worcestershire WR2 6NN *Tel.* 07812 454321
Email whwhitbread.trust@googlemail.com

■ The Melanie White Foundation Ltd

CC NO 1077150   **ESTABLISHED** 1999
WHERE FUNDING CAN BE GIVEN Mainly UK.
WHO CAN BENEFIT Charitable organisations.
WHAT IS FUNDED General charitable purposes, particularly: health; medicine; social welfare.
SAMPLE GRANTS Tiger Woods Charity (£109,400); Disasters Emergency Committee Ukraine Humanitarian Appeal (£50,000); Waves for Inclusion (£30,000); Alfred Dunhill Foundation (£25,000); Saints Foundation (£16,250); Holy Trinity Claygate PCC (£5,000); Windsor Academy – Nassau (£3,220).
FINANCES *Financial year end* 05/04/2022
Income £171,600
Grants to organisations £298,000
Assets £14,050,000
TRUSTEES Melanie White; Paul Reynolds.
HOW TO APPLY The foundation does not accept unsolicited applications as the trustees proactively identify beneficiaries themselves.
CONTACT DETAILS The Trustees, 61 Grosvenor Street, London W1K 3JE *Tel.* 020 3011 1100
Email melaniewhitefoundation@gmail.com

■ The Norman Whiteley Trust

CC NO 226445   **ESTABLISHED** 1963
WHERE FUNDING CAN BE GIVEN Worldwide, with a preference for Cumbria.
WHO CAN BENEFIT Christian evangelical organisations; individuals.
WHAT IS FUNDED Evangelical Christian causes. The trust's objects are to fund activities which further the spread of the Gospel, relieving poverty and assisting with education.
RANGE OF GRANTS Up to £8,000, typically less than £3,000.
SAMPLE GRANTS Christian and Missionary Alliance (£3,600); Passion Trust and Through the Roof (£2,000 each); Sports Reach (£1,600); Bibles for Children (£1,500); Christian Fellowship School (£1,300); The Lighthouse Cafe (£400).
FINANCES *Financial year end* 28/02/2022
Income £798,700
Grants to organisations £83,100
Assets £3,990,000
TRUSTEES Derek Dickson; Paul Whiteley; Pippa Guidera.
OTHER INFORMATION The grant total includes grants to organisations and individuals.
HOW TO APPLY Apply in writing to the correspondent.
CONTACT DETAILS The Trustees, Overdale, Dunny Lane, Chipperfield, Kings Langley, Hertfordshire WD4 9DE *Tel.* 01253 798812
Email normanwhiteleytrust@gmail.com

■ Whitley Animal Protection Trust

CC NO 236746   **ESTABLISHED** 1964
WHERE FUNDING CAN BE GIVEN UK and overseas.
WHO CAN BENEFIT Registered charities only.
WHAT IS FUNDED Animal welfare.
WHAT IS NOT FUNDED Grants are not made to non-registered charities.
TYPE OF GRANT Core and project grants. One-off grants are made, but most are recurrent grants that last for several years.
RANGE OF GRANTS Generally £2,500 to £25,000, although larger grants may also be awarded.
SAMPLE GRANTS Whitley Fund for Nature (£132,500); Game and Wildlife Conservation Trust (£20,000); Blue Marine Trust, COAST and Fauna and Flora International (£5,000 each); Association for the Protection of Rural Scotland and Scottish Seabirds Centre (£2,500 each).
FINANCES *Financial year end* 31/12/2021
Income £370,800
Grants to organisations £223,000
Assets £11,930,000
TRUSTEES Jeremy Whitley; Edward Whitley; Penelope Whitley; Edward Whitley; Vivien Thompson.
HOW TO APPLY The trust's 2021 annual report states: 'A majority of the grants undertaken are repeat donations, however, the Trustees do provide essential core funding to these smaller charities without which they would find it hard to maintain their activities. The Charity does also make one-off grants, but a majority of the grants are in respect of longer-term commitments.' Contact the correspondent for more information.
CONTACT DETAILS The Trustees, 9 Corve Street, Ludlow, Shropshire SY8 1DE *Tel.* 01952 641651

■ WHSmith Trust

CC NO 1013782   **ESTABLISHED** 1992
WHERE FUNDING CAN BE GIVEN UK.
WHO CAN BENEFIT Charitable organisations and schools.
WHAT IS FUNDED General charitable purposes; community services and development.
TYPE OF GRANT Project funding.
RANGE OF GRANTS Typical size of grants is £1,000.
SAMPLE GRANTS Young Readers Programme 2021 (£80,000); Read Easy UK (£5,000); The White Horse Federation (£2,000); 1st Lydiate Scout Group, Anthony Nolan Trust and Macmillan Cancer Support (£1,000 each).

FINANCES *Financial year end* 31/12/2021
  Income £93,400
  Grants to organisations £90,400
  Assets £170,600
TRUSTEES Sharon Appleton; Nicki Woodhead; Clare O'Grady; Paul Johnson; Mitchell Hunt; Wendy Stroud; John Pouton; Danielle Richards; Debbi Clapham.
HOW TO APPLY Apply in writing to the correspondent.
CONTACT DETAILS The Trustees, W. H. Smith Ltd, Greenbridge Road, Swindon, Wiltshire SN3 3JE *Tel.* 01793 616161 *Email* corporate. responsibility@whsmith.co.uk *Website* www. whsmithplc.co.uk/corporate_responsibility/ whsmith_trust

■ Wickens Family Foundation

CC NO 1190456
WHERE FUNDING CAN BE GIVEN UK and overseas.
WHO CAN BENEFIT UK-registered charities.
WHAT IS FUNDED Disadvantaged young people and adults.
SAMPLE GRANTS A list of beneficiaries was not included in the annual report and accounts.
FINANCES *Financial year end* 31/03/2022
  Income £236,100
  Grants to organisations £212,900
  Assets £144,000
TRUSTEES Rebecca Foster Wickens; Sarah Foster Wickens; Roger Foster Wickens.
OTHER INFORMATION Grants were made to 24 organisations.
HOW TO APPLY Apply in writing to the correspondent.
CONTACT DETAILS Sarah Wickens, Trustee, Farr House, 4 New Park Road, Chichester PO19 7XA *Tel.* 01243 836666 *Email* sarah@wffoundation. co.uk

■ The Wigoder Family Foundation

CC NO 1086806   **ESTABLISHED** 2000
WHERE FUNDING CAN BE GIVEN England and Wales.
WHO CAN BENEFIT Registered charities.
WHAT IS FUNDED General charitable purposes; the Jewish faith and community.
RANGE OF GRANTS Grants range from under £5,000 up to £55,000.
SAMPLE GRANTS The Jewish Learning Exchange (£55,000); South Hampstead Synagogue (£50,000); The Prince's Teaching Institute and UJIA (£25,000 each); The Chicken Soup Shelter (£10,000); Camp Simcha (£6,000).
FINANCES *Financial year end* 30/11/2021
  Income £2,390,000
  Grants to organisations £532,300
  Assets £65,060,000
TRUSTEES Elizabeth Wigoder; Charles Wigoder; Martin Rose.
OTHER INFORMATION The 2020/21 annual accounts were the latest available at the time of writing (June 2023).
HOW TO APPLY Apply in writing to the correspondent. According to the 2020/21 annual report, 'the trustees meet as many times as deemed appropriate but not less than twice a year to discuss grants, based on applications received throughout the year'.
CONTACT DETAILS The Trustees, c/o Network HQ, 508 Edgware Road, The Hyde, Colindale, London NW9 5AB *Tel.* 020 8955 5000

■ The Felicity Wilde Charitable Trust

CC NO 264404   **ESTABLISHED** 1972
WHERE FUNDING CAN BE GIVEN UK.
WHO CAN BENEFIT Charitable organisations; hospices.
WHAT IS FUNDED Children's charities; medical research, particularly into the causes of and cures for asthma.
RANGE OF GRANTS Mostly between £1,000 and £3,000.
SAMPLE GRANTS Brainwave Centre Ltd (£3,500); NARA – The Breathing Charity (£3,000); Hope House Children's Hospice (£2,500); Children with Cancer (£2,200); Bentley Beginnings (£1,500); Listening Books, Strathfoyle Women's Centre, Think Children, Wallace and Gromit's Grand Appeal, Wiltshire Music and Wirral Community Narrowboat Trust (£1,000 each).
FINANCES *Financial year end* 09/05/2022
  Income £61,200
  Grants to organisations £58,300
  Assets £2,340,000
TRUSTEE Zedra Trust Company (UK) Ltd.
OTHER INFORMATION In 2021/22, a total of 30 organisations received grants.
HOW TO APPLY Apply in writing to the correspondent.
CONTACT DETAILS The Trustees, Zedra UK Trusts, Booths Hall, Booths Park, 3 Chelford Road, Knutsford, Cheshire WA16 8GS *Tel.* 01565 748814 *Email* charities@zedra.com

■ The Will Charitable Trust

CC NO 801682   **ESTABLISHED** 1989
WHERE FUNDING CAN BE GIVEN UK.
WHO CAN BENEFIT UK-registered or exempt charities.
WHAT IS FUNDED Care of and services for blind people; the prevention and cure of blindness; the long-term care of people with learning disabilities; care of and services for people suffering from cancer and their families.
WHAT IS NOT FUNDED A full list of exclusions can be found on the trust's website.
TYPE OF GRANT Capital costs; project funding; one-off.
RANGE OF GRANTS Grants range from £3,000 to £30,000.
SAMPLE GRANTS L'Arche (£90,000); Orchid Cancer Appeal (£40,000); Stanley Grange Community Association (£30,000); Target Ovarian Cancer (£22,000); Northdale Horticulture (£19,000); MySight York (£10,000); Southend in Sight (£7,000); Compass Disability Services (£5,000).
FINANCES *Financial year end* 05/01/2022
  Income £490,600
  Grants to organisations £721,000
  Assets £21,750,000
TRUSTEES Rodney Luff; Vanessa Reburn; Joanna Dyson; Robert Boddington.
OTHER INFORMATION Grants were made to 45 organisations during the year and distributed as follows: care of cancer patients (£256,500); care of blind people (£233,500); care of people with learning disabilities (£141,000); exceptional grants fund (£90,000). The trustees may occasionally consider larger exceptional grants, but this is unusual and generally confined to charities that the trustees know well and have supported for some time.
HOW TO APPLY Applications should be made in writing to the correspondent and sent by post – emailed applications will not be accepted. Guidance on what to include in your application is given on the trust's website, along with more

detailed eligibility criteria. There are separate deadlines for each area of focus.

CONTACT DETAILS The Grants Administrator, Bridge House, 11 Creek Road, East Molesey KT8 9BE *Tel.* 020 8941 0450 *Email* admin@ willcharitabletrust.org.uk *Website* http:// willcharitabletrust.org.uk

---

■ Alfred Williams Charitable Trust

CC NO 266652 **ESTABLISHED** 1974
WHERE FUNDING CAN BE GIVEN Suffolk.
WHO CAN BENEFIT Registered charities; CICs.
WHAT IS FUNDED Environmental and heritage causes including repair and development, conservation and restoration. Social causes are also supported. This includes voluntary care, education, theatre, music, youth projects and community projects. The trust has a preference for the preservation or regeneration of the built heritage, amenity and landscape of Suffolk.
TYPE OF GRANT Capital costs; seed funding/start-up funding.
RANGE OF GRANTS £100 to £4,000.
SAMPLE GRANTS Museum of East Anglian Life (£4,000); Higham PCC (£3,000); Brome and Oakley PCC (£2,500); St Andrew's PCC – Great Finborough (£2,000); Olive AP Academy (£1,000); Suffolk Historic Churches Trust (£150).
FINANCES *Financial year end* 05/04/2022 *Income* £76,700 *Grants to organisations* £65,100 *Assets* £3,820,000
TRUSTEES Jonathan Penn; Paul Clarke; Robert Williams; Dr Luke Williams.
OTHER INFORMATION In 2021/22, the trust awarded 37 grants to organisations. Grants were broken down as follows: churches (£38,600); heritage (£13,500); social welfare (£10,000); music, literary and drama (£2,500); the environment (£500).
HOW TO APPLY Application forms can be downloaded from the trust's website. The trustees meet three times a year to consider grant applications. Applications must be received by the end of January, May and September.
CONTACT DETAILS Kate Bowe, Administrator, Haughley Park, Stowmarket, Suffolk IP14 3JY *Tel.* 07899 662200 *Email* alfredwilliamscharitabletrust@gmail.com *Website* https://alfredwilliamscharitabletrust.org

---

■ The Williams Family Foundation

CC NO 1157478 **ESTABLISHED** 2014
WHERE FUNDING CAN BE GIVEN Cheshire West and Chester; Denbighshire; Flintshire; Wrexham.
WHO CAN BENEFIT Registered charities.
WHAT IS FUNDED Health; the arts and culture; social welfare; young people; older people; people with disabilities or illnesses.
WHAT IS NOT FUNDED General appeals from national charities; small contributions to large appeals for vehicles or buildings; animal charities; religious organisations; any part of a request for a grant that would involve the payment of salaries or remuneration.
TYPE OF GRANT Project funding; equipment.
SAMPLE GRANTS A list of beneficiaries was not included in the annual report and accounts.
FINANCES *Financial year end* 31/12/2021 *Income* £150,000 *Grants to organisations* £87,600 *Assets* £33,200

TRUSTEES John Gregory; Amy Sheppard; Thomas Williams; Mark Williams; Barbara Williams.
OTHER INFORMATION Grants were awarded to 19 organisations in 2021.
HOW TO APPLY Applications can be made through the foundation's website. Alternatively, application forms can be downloaded from the website to be completed and returned to applications@williamsfamilyfoundation.org.uk.
CONTACT DETAILS The Trustees, PO Box 3809, Chester CH1 9ZW *Tel.* 01244 570292 *Email* enquiries@williamsfamilyfoundation.org.uk *Website* www.williamsfamilyfoundation.org.uk

---

■ The H.D.H Wills 1965 Charitable Trust

CC NO 1117747 **ESTABLISHED** 1965
WHERE FUNDING CAN BE GIVEN UK (predominantly) and overseas.
WHO CAN BENEFIT Registered, exempt or excepted charities only.
WHAT IS FUNDED General charitable purposes; the environment; wildlife.
WHAT IS NOT FUNDED Organisations that have been supported in the previous 24 months; individuals.
TYPE OF GRANT Revenue, capital or project expenditure.
RANGE OF GRANTS Grants from the small fund are typically £250 to £2,000, occasionally up to £5,000. Large grants range from £5,000 to £50,000.
SAMPLE GRANTS 21st Century Trust (£40,000); Sandford St Martin Cricket Club (£10,000); Médecins Sans Frontières (£9,000); British Red Cross (£8,000); Over Worton and Nether Worton PCC and The National Horseracing Museum (£2,000 each); Britten Pears Arts, Leith School of Art and The Turquoise Mountain Trust (£1,000 each).
FINANCES *Financial year end* 31/03/2022 *Income* £3,220,000 *Grants to organisations* £1,630,000 *Assets* £100,510,000
TRUSTEES John Carson; Charles Francklin; Martin Fiennes; Thomas Nelson; Richard Tulloch.
OTHER INFORMATION Only organisations that received grants of over £1,000 were listed as beneficiaries in the trust's accounts. Grants of under £1,000 totalled £55,000 and were awarded to 111 organisations. The trust makes two types of grants: small and large. Small grants are used to make grants for general charitable purposes, the environment and wildlife conservation; large grants operate on a seven-year funding priority cycle. In years one, two, five, six and seven of this cycle, grants are made to specified organisations; in years three and four, favour is given to environmental and wildlife conservation and external applications are accepted.
HOW TO APPLY Monthly grants can be applied for at any time using the online form on the trust's website. Applications should be accompanied by supporting documents. Details on what should be included are given on the trust's website. For large grants, visit the website for details of current funding rounds.
CONTACT DETAILS Sue Trafford, Trust Administrator, Henley Knapp Barn, Fulwell, Chipping Norton, Oxfordshire OX7 4EN *Tel.* 01608 678051 *Email* suetrafford@hdhwills.org or trust@ hdhwills.org *Website* www.hdhwills.org

■ Dame Violet Wills Will Trust

cc no 262251 **ESTABLISHED** 1965
WHERE FUNDING CAN BE GIVEN Bristol;
Gloucestershire; Somerset.
WHO CAN BENEFIT Registered charities.
WHAT IS FUNDED General charitable purposes, with a
preference for projects for children and medical
causes.
RANGE OF GRANTS £500 to £4,000.
SAMPLE GRANTS A list of beneficiaries was not
included in the annual report and accounts.
FINANCES *Financial year end 31/03/2022*
Income £116,800
Grants to organisations £83,800
Assets £3,910,000
TRUSTEES Tim Baines; Guy Biggin; Mark Naughton.
OTHER INFORMATION The trust made 45 grants
during the year.
HOW TO APPLY Apply in writing to the correspondent.
CONTACT DETAILS The Trustees, Red Roofs, Station
Road, Flax Bourton, Bristol BS48 1UA
Tel. 07367 095245

■ The Wilmcote Charitrust

cc no 503837 **ESTABLISHED** 1974
WHERE FUNDING CAN BE GIVEN Midlands.
WHO CAN BENEFIT Registered charities and voluntary
organisations.
WHAT IS FUNDED Social welfare; health; older people;
religion; education; ex-Service personnel.
RANGE OF GRANTS Mostly £250, £500 or £1,000.
SAMPLE GRANTS Previous beneficiaries have
included: England and Wales Blind Golf and
Sunny Days Children's Fund (£1,000 each);
Troop Aid, Wide Horizons and Willow Foundation
(£500 each); Dudley Hospital Radio and Marine
Conservation Society (£250 each).
FINANCES *Financial year end 05/04/2022*
Income £14,200
Grants to organisations £63,500
TRUSTEES Graham Beach; Anabel Murphy;
Roseamond Whiteside; Jean King.
OTHER INFORMATION Full accounts were not available
to view on the Charity Commission's website
due to the charity's low income. We have
therefore estimated the charity's grant total
based on its total expenditure.
HOW TO APPLY Apply in writing to the correspondent.
CONTACT DETAILS Graham Beach, Trustee, Warren
Chase, Billesley Road, Wilmcote, Stratford-upon-
Avon, Warwickshire CV37 9XG *Tel.* 01789
298472 *Email* graham@leighgraham.co.uk

■ Brian Wilson Charitable Trust

cc no 1059736 **ESTABLISHED** 1996
WHERE FUNDING CAN BE GIVEN Cheshire.
WHO CAN BENEFIT Charitable organisations.
WHAT IS FUNDED General charitable purposes.
SAMPLE GRANTS A list of beneficiaries was not
included in the annual report and accounts.
Previous beneficiaries have included: Leonard
Cheshire Disability Support (£115,000); Help for
Heroes (£25,000); The Friends of Russett
School (£10,000); Cross Roads Care – North
Wales (£7,000); St Luke's Cheshire Hospice
(£5,000).
FINANCES *Financial year end 31/12/2021*
Income £127,000
Grants to organisations £106,700
Assets £4,300,000
TRUSTEES John Pickup; Vivien Roberts; Ruth
Downes; Margaret Occleston.

OTHER INFORMATION The trust made 27 grants in
2021.
HOW TO APPLY Apply in writing to the correspondent.
The trustees meet on a quarterly basis to
consider requests and approve grants.
CONTACT DETAILS The Trustees, 36 Landswood Park,
Hartford, Northwich, Cheshire CW8 1NF
Tel. 01606 74970

■ Sumner Wilson Charitable Trust

cc no 1018852 **ESTABLISHED** 1992
WHERE FUNDING CAN BE GIVEN UK.
WHO CAN BENEFIT Registered charities.
WHAT IS FUNDED Charitable organisations.
TYPE OF GRANT Capital costs; general funding.
RANGE OF GRANTS £1,000 to £30,000.
SAMPLE GRANTS Hope and Homes for Children
(£29,900); The Branch Trust (£20,000); Chailey
Heritage Foundation and The Charlie Waller
Foundation (£10,000 each); Jemima Layzell
Trust and St James's Place Foundation (£5,000
each); Mental Health Foundation (£1,000).
FINANCES *Financial year end 05/04/2022*
Income £125,300
Grants to organisations £142,600
Assets £6,990,000
TRUSTEES Amanda Christie; Anne-Marie Challen;
Davina Longsdon.
OTHER INFORMATION Grants were distributed as
follows: health (£67,000); international
(£41,000); community development (£20,000);
human services (£9,600); education (£5,000).
HOW TO APPLY The trust will not be making any
grants or donations to unsolicited applications
for the foreseeable future.
CONTACT DETAILS The Trustees, Mercer and Hole,
72 London Road, St Albans AL1 1NS
Tel. 01727 869141
Email sumnerwilsoncharity@gmail.com
Website www.sumnerwilson.uk

■ J. and J. R. Wilson Trust

OSCR NO SC007411 **ESTABLISHED** 1989
WHERE FUNDING CAN BE GIVEN Scotland, particularly
Glasgow and the west coast of Scotland.
WHO CAN BENEFIT Registered charities; hospices.
WHAT IS FUNDED Older people; care of both domestic
and wild animals and birds.
TYPE OF GRANT Capital costs; core/revenue costs;
general funding; project funding; seed funding/
start-up funding; unrestricted funding.
RANGE OF GRANTS £1,000 to £10,000.
SAMPLE GRANTS Glasgow's Golden Generation
(£6,000); Alzheimer's Scotland (£5,000); The
Pershal Trust (£2,000); Penumbra and Shelter
Scotland (£1,000 each).
FINANCES *Financial year end 09/02/2022*
Income £138,900
Grants to organisations £129,900
Assets £4,750,000
OTHER INFORMATION Grants were distributed as
follows: care of older people (£80,900) and
charities in support of animals and birds
(£55,000).
HOW TO APPLY Apply in writing to the correspondent.
The 2021/22 annual report states: 'Requests
for donations are investigated carefully and,
where appropriate, the Trustees visit the
charities concerned to check the carrying out of
the purposes of the donation.'
CONTACT DETAILS The Trustees, c/o Bartys, 61 High
Street, Dunblane, Perthshire FK15 0EH

■ Wiltshire Community Foundation

CC NO 1123126   **ESTABLISHED** 1991

WHERE FUNDING CAN BE GIVEN Wiltshire and Swindon.

WHO CAN BENEFIT Registered charities; unregistered charities; individuals.

WHAT IS FUNDED General charitable purposes including: health; social welfare; community development; education and training; the environment; arts, culture and heritage.

WHAT IS NOT FUNDED Each programme has specific exclusions.

TYPE OF GRANT Capital costs; core/revenue costs; unrestricted funding; project funding.

RANGE OF GRANTS See individual grant programmes.

SAMPLE GRANTS Age UK Wiltshire (£65,600); Action for the River Kennet (£20,000); Julia's House (£15,000); Bravo Medics (£13,300); Wiltshire Citizens Advice (£12,600).

FINANCES *Financial year end* 31/03/2022
Income £2,000,000
Grants to organisations £1,310,000
Grants to individuals £351,500
Assets £29,850,000

TRUSTEES Steve Wall; Susan Webber; Lisa Lewis; Oliver Jones-Davies; David Wray; Samantha O'Sullivan; Angus MacPherson; Junab Ali; Mark Barnett; David Coombs.

OTHER INFORMATION This is one of the 47 UK community foundations, which distribute funding for a wide range of purposes. As with all community foundations, there are a number of donor-advised funds managed on behalf of individuals, families and charitable trusts. Grant schemes tend to change frequently – consult the foundation's website for details of current programmes and up-to-date deadlines. In 2021/22, the foundation awarded 197 grants to organisations and 128 grants to individuals. Only organisations that received grants of over £12,000 were listed as beneficiaries in the foundation's accounts. Grants of under £10,000 totalled £417,800.

HOW TO APPLY Potential applicants are advised to visit the community foundation's website or contact its grants team to find the most suitable funding stream.

CONTACT DETAILS Grants Team, Sandcliff House, 21 Northgate Street, Devizes, Wiltshire SN10 1JT *Tel.* 01380 729284 *Email* info@ wiltshirecf.org.uk *Website* https://wiltshirecf.org.uk

■ The Wimbledon Foundation

CC NO 1156996   **ESTABLISHED** 2014

WHERE FUNDING CAN BE GIVEN Merton, Wandsworth and overseas.

WHO CAN BENEFIT Registered charities; community groups; amateur sports clubs.

WHAT IS FUNDED The three main focus areas of the foundation are: the London boroughs of Merton and Wandsworth; charities associated with or promoted by key groups involved in The Championships; projects and charities that use the power of sport (and particularly tennis) to provide opportunities to assist people, especially young individuals, with education and personal development.

SAMPLE GRANTS WaterAid (£463,000); Youth Sport Trust (£255,000); Magic Bus (£100,000).

FINANCES *Financial year end* 31/07/2022
Income £3,140,000
Grants to organisations £2,550,000
Assets £1,480,000

TRUSTEES I. L. Hewitt; Sir Nicholas Young; Sir Keith Ajegbo; Henry Weatherill; Nicholas Bitel; Kevin Havelock; Anne Bretherton.

OTHER INFORMATION During the year, grants were distributed through the following funds: Wimbledon Foundation Community Fund (£499,000); The Emergency Relief Fund (£300,000); The Championships and Club-related grants (£250,000); The Health and Wellbeing Fund (£197,000); A Roof for All (£175,000); Strengthening Our Local Community (£83,000); Get Set, Get Active Fund (£43,000). Check the website for open funding programmes.

HOW TO APPLY Details of open funding rounds and application procedures are published on the foundation's website as they arise.

CONTACT DETAILS The Trustees, Church Road, Wimbledon, London SW19 5AE *Tel.* 020 8971 2702 *Email* foundation@aeltc.com *Website* www.wimbledon.com/en_GB/foundation/index.html

■ The Windfall Foundation

CC NO 1176650   **ESTABLISHED** 2018

WHERE FUNDING CAN BE GIVEN UK; Africa.

WHO CAN BENEFIT Charitable organisations.

WHAT IS FUNDED Health; education; social welfare; the environment.

TYPE OF GRANT One-off and multi-year grants.

SAMPLE GRANTS Beneficiaries in the UK included: Inspiring Teachers; Resurgo Trust; Stand Out.

FINANCES *Financial year end* 30/06/2022
Income £368,000
Grants to organisations £308,700
Assets £5,990,000

TRUSTEES Andrew Elder; Linsay Elder; Thomas Elder; Geoff Stead.

OTHER INFORMATION The foundation's Charity Commission record states: 'The Foundation has an interest in projects that provide sustainable, long-term income generation and self-sufficiency, especially those making a demonstrable positive impact on marginalised communities currently beyond the reach of traditional government or market-based solutions.'

HOW TO APPLY Apply in writing to the correspondent.

CONTACT DETAILS The Trustees, 13 Hammersmith Terrace, London W6 9TS *Tel.* 020 8563 0240

■ The Benjamin Winegarten Charitable Trust

CC NO 271442   **ESTABLISHED** 1976

WHERE FUNDING CAN BE GIVEN UK.

WHO CAN BENEFIT Jewish organisations; individuals.

WHAT IS FUNDED Jewish religious education; the Jewish faith and community; social welfare.

SAMPLE GRANTS A list of beneficiaries was not included in the annual report and accounts. Previous beneficiaries have included: Hechal Hatovah Institute; the Jewish Educational Trust; the Mechinah School; Merkaz Lechinuch Torani Zichron Ya'akov; Ohr Someach Friends; Or Akiva Community Centre; Yeshivo Hovomo Talmudical College; ZSVT.

FINANCES *Financial year end* 05/04/2022
Income £235,500
Grants to organisations £204,000
Assets £2,320,000

TRUSTEES Esther Winegarten; Miriam Schwab; Leah Chontow; Simon Winegarten.

OTHER INFORMATION No grants were awarded to individuals during the year.

HOW TO APPLY Apply in writing to the correspondent.
CONTACT DETAILS The Trustees, 25 St Andrews Grove, Stoke Newington, London N16 5NF *Tel.* 07817 212952

■ W. Wing Yip and Brothers Foundation

CC NO 1187265   **ESTABLISHED** 1985
WHERE FUNDING CAN BE GIVEN Within 25 miles of Wing Yip stores in Birmingham, Manchester, Croydon and Cricklewood.
WHO CAN BENEFIT Registered charities (preference for small charities); educational organisations; community bodies. Our previous research suggests there is a preference for those organisations with a Chinese connection.
WHAT IS FUNDED General charitable purposes, including: education; community welfare; medical research; care for people with illnesses.
WHAT IS NOT FUNDED Large charitable organisations; projects and travel undertaken by individuals or religious organisations; individuals; applications that fall within two calendar months of proposed events.
RANGE OF GRANTS Up to £42,000.
SAMPLE GRANTS Chinese Community Health and Wellbeing Service (£42,000); Loughborough University (£39,000); Birmingham Chinese School and Home from Hospital (£3,000 each); The Honeypot Children's Charity (£1,000).
FINANCES *Financial year end 31/07/2022*
Income £121,000
Grants to organisations £90,000
Assets £1,880,000
TRUSTEES Sujinda Munputkul; David Wing Yip; Joseph Bates; Ennevor Yap; Jenny Loynton; Albert Wing Yip; Brian Wing Yip.
OTHER INFORMATION During 2021/22, grants were distributed as follows: medical research and relief of suffering (£45,000); educational (£42,000); community welfare (£3,000). Note that the grant total may include grants to individuals.
HOW TO APPLY At the time of writing (June 2023), the foundation's website stated the following: 'At this time, we are not taking any more applications for donations. Note that we are also unable to accept applications from individuals for donations.'
CONTACT DETAILS The Trustees, W. Wing Yip plc, The Wing Yip Centre, 375 Nechells Park Road, Birmingham B7 5NT *Tel.* 0121 327 6618 *Email* foundation@wingyip.com

■ The Francis Winham Foundation

CC NO 278092   **ESTABLISHED** 1979
WHERE FUNDING CAN BE GIVEN England.
WHO CAN BENEFIT Registered charities; exempt charitable organisations.
WHAT IS FUNDED Welfare of older people.
RANGE OF GRANTS Typically between £5,000 and £20,000.
SAMPLE GRANTS SSAFA, the Armed Forces charity (£440,400 in eight grants); Royal British Legion Industries (£15,000); Unite – Carers in Mid Devon (£15,000); St Christopher's Hospice and Vista (£5,000 each).
FINANCES *Financial year end 05/04/2022*
Income £381,300
Grants to organisations £859,500
Assets £4,140,000
TRUSTEES Elsa Peters; Josephine Winham; Desmond Corcoran; Fuschia Peters.

OTHER INFORMATION The foundation made 134 grants to organisations during 2021/22. Only organisations that received grants of more than £5,000 were listed as beneficiaries in the foundation's accounts. Grants of under £5,000 were made to 46 organisations and totalled £90,900.
HOW TO APPLY Apply in writing to the correspondent.
CONTACT DETAILS The Trustees, 18 Gilston Road, London SW10 9SR *Tel.* 020 7795 1261 *Email* francinetrust@outlook.com

■ The Michael and Anna Wix Charitable Trust

CC NO 207863   **ESTABLISHED** 1955
WHERE FUNDING CAN BE GIVEN UK.
WHO CAN BENEFIT UK-registered charities.
WHAT IS FUNDED General charitable purposes, particularly medical causes and social welfare.
WHAT IS NOT FUNDED Individuals.
TYPE OF GRANT Unrestricted.
RANGE OF GRANTS Between £100 and £5,000.
SAMPLE GRANTS British Friends of the Hebrew University (£1,500); Tuberous Sclerosis Association (£1,000); Brain Tumour Research, Care for Veterans and Macular Society (£500 each); Activiteens and Clapton Common Boys Club (£200 each); Dolphin Society and Support Dogs (£100 each).
FINANCES *Financial year end 05/04/2022*
Income £80,500
Grants to organisations £70,900
Assets £2,210,000
TRUSTEES Janet Bloch; Dominic Flynn; Judith Portrait.
OTHER INFORMATION Grants were awarded to 325 organisations in 2021/22.
HOW TO APPLY Apply in writing to the correspondent. Applications are considered half-yearly. According to our previous research, only applications from registered charities are acknowledged.
CONTACT DETAILS The Trustees, c/o BDB Pitmans LLP, 1 Bartholomew Close, London EC1A 7BL *Tel.* 020 7783 3125

■ The Wixamtree Trust

CC NO 210089   **ESTABLISHED** 1949
WHERE FUNDING CAN BE GIVEN Bedfordshire.
WHO CAN BENEFIT Registered or exempt charities; mainly local charities, with a small number of national charities supported.
WHAT IS FUNDED Social welfare; the environment and conservation; sport and leisure; the arts; education; training and employment.
RANGE OF GRANTS Usually between £1,000 and £10,000.
SAMPLE GRANTS A list of beneficiaries was not included in the annual report and accounts.
FINANCES *Financial year end 05/04/2022*
Income £508,200
Grants to organisations £726,900
Assets £32,530,000
TRUSTEES Charles Whitbread; Paul Patten; Harry Whitbread; Marion Stern; Arthur Polhill.
OTHER INFORMATION Grants were made to 126 organisations and broken down as follows: social welfare (£340,200); the environment and conservation (£135,000); sport and leisure (£57,200); the arts (£50,300); education (£24,400); training and employment (£16,000).

HOW TO APPLY Applications can be made via the trust's website where deadlines and guidance can also be found.

CONTACT DETAILS The Trust Administrator, 6 Trull Farm Buildings, Tetbury, Gloucestershire GL8 8SQ *Tel.* 020 8777 4140 *Email* wixamtree@thetrustpartnership.com *Website* www.wixamtree.org

■ The Maurice Wohl Charitable Foundation

CC NO 244519   **ESTABLISHED** 1965
WHERE FUNDING CAN BE GIVEN UK; Israel; Europe.
WHO CAN BENEFIT Jewish organisations; registered charities.
WHAT IS FUNDED Employment; Jewish education; medical advancement; care and welfare; arts and culture; Jewish and communal life.
WHAT IS NOT FUNDED Ongoing maintenance projects; individuals; scholarships.
SAMPLE GRANTS The Golders Green Beth Hamedrash Congregation (£600,000); The Follicular Lymphoma Foundation (£400,000); The Langdon Foundation (£300,000); Noa Girls (£156,100); The United Synagogue (£18,500).
FINANCES *Financial year end* 31/12/2021
Income £1,290,000
Grants to organisations £2,850,000
Assets £88,420,000
TRUSTEES Daniel Dover; Sir Ian Gainsford; Prof. David Latchman; Ella Latchman; Martin Paisner.
OTHER INFORMATION The foundation is part of the Wohl Legacy, a group of three charitable foundations established by Maurice and Vivienne Wohl.
HOW TO APPLY The foundation does not accept unsolicited applications, as the trustees work with full-time staff to identify suitable projects.
CONTACT DETAILS Penelope Rudge, Secretary, Fitzrovia House, 2nd Floor, 153–157 Cleveland Street, London W1T 6QW *Email* info@wohl.org. uk *Website* www.wohl.org.uk

■ The Charles Wolfson Charitable Trust

CC NO 238043   **ESTABLISHED** 1960
WHERE FUNDING CAN BE GIVEN Worldwide, mainly UK.
WHO CAN BENEFIT Registered charities, hospitals, schools or other similar charitable organisations.
WHAT IS FUNDED Medicine; education; welfare. The 2021/22 annual report states that 'particular, but not exclusive, regard is given to the needs of the Jewish community'.
WHAT IS NOT FUNDED Individuals.
TYPE OF GRANT Mostly capital or fixed-term projects. Occasionally, the trust also provides rent-free premises and loans to charities.
RANGE OF GRANTS Mostly up to £50,000, with some larger grants.
SAMPLE GRANTS Maudsley Charity Fundraising (£666,700); Music in Secondary Schools Trust (£350,000); Follicular Lymphoma Foundation, Jewish Learning Exchange and London School of Hygiene and Tropical Medicine (£125,000 each); Churchill Lines Foundation, Community Security Trust and Wolfson Hillel Primary School (£100,000 each); Jewish Agency for Israel and The National Holocaust Centre (£50,000 each).
FINANCES *Financial year end* 05/04/2022
Income £8,330,000
Grants to organisations £6,090,000
Assets £216,210,000

TRUSTEES Lord Simon Wolfson; Dr Sara Levene; The Hon. Andrew Wolfson; Deborah Edwards; Lord Jonathan Mendelsohn.
OTHER INFORMATION Grants are made to registered charities, hospitals, schools or other similar charitable institutions. Grants are typically made towards capital and project costs in the following areas: medicine; education; welfare. Only organisations that received grants of over £50,000 were listed as beneficiaries in the charity's accounts. Grants of under £50,000 totalled £1.49 million. The grant total includes £196,900 distributed by the trust's subsidiary Benesco Charity Ltd. Grants were broken down as follows: welfare (£2.48 million); education (£2.25 million); medicine (£1.36 million). Occasionally, the trust also provides rent-free premises and loans to charities; however, according to its 2021/22 annual report 'there were no such items this year'.
HOW TO APPLY Apply in writing to the correspondent.
CONTACT DETAILS Joanne Cowan, Administrator, 8/10 Hallam Street, London W1W 6NS *Tel.* 020 7079 2506 *Email* admin@cwctcharity.org.uk

■ The Wolfson Family Charitable Trust

CC NO 228382   **ESTABLISHED** 1958
WHERE FUNDING CAN BE GIVEN UK and Israel.
WHO CAN BENEFIT Universities and hospitals in Israel; UK organisations serving the Jewish community. Applicants should be registered charities or organisations with equivalent charitable status, and have an income of more than £50,000.
WHAT IS FUNDED In the UK: culture and heritage (especially historic synagogues), education, older people and people with disabilities. In Israel: science, medicine, health, cultural organisations and people with disabilities.
WHAT IS NOT FUNDED The purchase of land or existing buildings (including a building's freehold); grants direct to individuals; grants through conduit organisations; overheads, maintenance costs, VAT; non-specific appeals (including circulars) and endowment funds; costs of meetings, exhibitions, concerts, expeditions, conferences, etc.; film or promotional materials; repayment of loans; projects that have already been completed or will be by the time of award.
TYPE OF GRANT Capital projects (new buildings, refurbishment or specialist equipment).
RANGE OF GRANTS Programme dependent but generally £10,000 to £50,000. Applicants are expected to provide matched funding for grants exceeding £50,000.
SAMPLE GRANTS Weizmann Institute of Science (£240,000); The Gesher Trust (£154,000); Yad Chaim Herzog Memorial Foundation (£100,000); Tel Aviv University (£90,000); Magen David Adom (£50,000); Jewish Deaf Association (£25,000); Institute for Jewish Policy Research (£15,000); Get Set Girls (£5,000).
FINANCES *Financial year end* 31/03/2022
Income £950,000
Grants to organisations £1,500,000
Assets £44,190,000
TRUSTEES Sir Ian Gainsford; Martin Paisner; Sir Bernard Rix; Lord Turnberg; The Hon. Laura Townsley; Dame Janet Botton; The Hon. Elizabeth Peltz; Alexandra Halamish; Sir Michael Pepper.
OTHER INFORMATION Grants were committed to 17 organisations during the year. Grants paid

during the year were broken down as follows: science and medicine (£1 million); health and disability (£304,000); arts and humanities (£150,000); education (£77,000).

HOW TO APPLY There is a two-stage application process for grants in the UK. A stage-one application can be submitted on the trust's website, where guidance is also provided. All requests are responded to and eligible organisations will be invited to submit a stage-two application. Unsolicited applications are not accepted for grants in Israel.

CONTACT DETAILS The Trustees, 8 Queen Anne Street, London W1G 9LD *Tel.* 020 7323 5730 *Email* grants@wolfson.org.uk *Website* www.wfct. org

■ The Wolfson Foundation

CC NO 1156077   **ESTABLISHED** 1955
WHERE FUNDING CAN BE GIVEN UK.
WHO CAN BENEFIT Charities; hospices; places of worship; libraries, museums, galleries and libraries; schools, colleges and universities.
WHAT IS FUNDED Disability; mental health; older people; historic buildings and landscapes; hospices and palliative care; places of worship; libraries and archives; museums and galleries; performing arts; public engagement with science; secondary schools and sixth forms colleges; special needs schools and colleges; universities and research institutions.
WHAT IS NOT FUNDED Exclusions differ for each grants programme. A full list of exclusions is available on the foundation's website.
TYPE OF GRANT Capital infrastructure (new buildings, refurbishment and equipment).
RANGE OF GRANTS Grant sizes vary depending on programme.
SAMPLE GRANTS University of Birmingham (£1.5 million); The Natural History Museum (£500,000); Magna Academy (£74,500); Crisis (£25,000); Samaritans – Ewell (£3,000).
FINANCES *Financial year end 31/03/2022*
Income £20,390,000
Grants to organisations £35,520,000
Assets £927,500
TRUSTEES Dame Janet Wolfson de Botton; The Hon. Laura Wolfson Townsley; Prof. Sir David Cannadine; Dame Hermione Lee; Sir Michael Pepper; Prof. Dame Jean Thomas; Lord Turnberg of Cheadle; Sir Peter Ratcliffe; Rebecca Marks; Charles Wolfson Townsley; Allegra Berman.
OTHER INFORMATION The grant total includes bursaries, scholarships, fellowships and prizes paid to organisations on behalf of individuals. Grants were broken down as follows: science (£17.02 million); education (£8.96 million); arts and humanities (£7.35 million); health (£4.2 million).
HOW TO APPLY There is a two-stage application process. A stage-one application can be submitted on the foundation's website, where guidance is also provided. Eligible organisations will be invited to submit a stage-two application. Applications can usually be submitted at two points during the year. Check the foundation's website for the latest application deadlines.
CONTACT DETAILS The Trustees, 8 Queen Anne Street, London W1G 9LD *Tel.* 020 7323 5730 *Email* grants@wolfson.org.uk *Website* www. wolfson.org.uk

■ The Lord Leonard and Lady Estelle Wolfson Foundation

CC NO 1148663   **ESTABLISHED** 2012
WHERE FUNDING CAN BE GIVEN UK.
WHO CAN BENEFIT Universities; hospitals; registered charities; arts organisations; cultural organisations.
WHAT IS FUNDED Medical research and related initiatives in preventative health care. The foundation states that an area of focus is the role that art, music and literature can play in preventing and mitigating certain illnesses and in creating innovative healthcare delivery mechanisms.
WHAT IS NOT FUNDED The foundation outlines a list of exclusions via the grant application information document on the foundation's website.
TYPE OF GRANT Research funding; project funding.
RANGE OF GRANTS £10,000 to £150,000.
SAMPLE GRANTS Great Ormond Street Hospital Children's Charity (£1 million); University College Hospital (£150,000); Royal Society of Medicine (£45,000); Nightingale Hammerson (£25,000).
FINANCES *Financial year end 31/03/2022*
Income £416,600
Grants to organisations £1,320,000
Assets £30,360,000
TRUSTEES Lady Estelle Wolfson; Lord Ara Darzi; Ian Burman; Sir Ian Gilmore; Antoinette Jackson.
OTHER INFORMATION In 2021/22, £1.32 million in grants were awarded to organisations. Grants were broken down as follows: medical research (£1.23 million); well-being (£90,000).
HOW TO APPLY An application information document can be found on the foundation's website.
CONTACT DETAILS M. S. Feldman, Administrator, 74 Portland Place, London W1B 1NR *Tel.* 020 7636 6446 *Email* admin@lordandladywolfson. org.uk *Website* https://lordandladywolfson.org. uk

■ Women's Fund for Scotland

OSCR NO SC049217
WHERE FUNDING CAN BE GIVEN Scotland.
WHO CAN BENEFIT Charities and community groups with an annual income of less than £1 million, with priority given to those with an income of less than £500,000.
WHAT IS FUNDED Projects that encourage women's growth, self-sufficiency and social economic equality.
TYPE OF GRANT Project funding.
RANGE OF GRANTS Up to £5,000.
SAMPLE GRANTS FNY Collective and Period Place (£5,000 each); Al Masaar (£4,500); Adventure Circus SCIO (£4,100); Maryhill Integration Network (£3,400); North West Women's Centre (£3,000); Yusuf Youth Initiative (£2,500); Jubilee House (£1,900).
FINANCES *Financial year end 31/03/2022*
Income £123,300
Grants to organisations £99,900
Assets £218,600
TRUSTEES Sue Robertson; Judy Russell; Adrian Bell; Anne Meikle; Jan Torrance; Rebecca Bonnington; Beth Edberg.
HOW TO APPLY Information regarding eligibility and the application process can be found on the fund's website.
CONTACT DETAILS Shona Blakeley, Executive Director, 17–21 East Mayfield, Edinburgh EH9 1SE *Email* shona@womensfundscotland. org *Website* www.womensfundscotland.org

■ The James Wood Bequest Fund

OSCR NO SC000459   **ESTABLISHED** 1932
WHERE FUNDING CAN BE GIVEN Scotland.
WHO CAN BENEFIT Charitable organisations.
WHAT IS FUNDED Christianity; health; social welfare; community development; emergency response; general charitable purposes.
WHAT IS NOT FUNDED Individuals.
RANGE OF GRANTS £500 to £4,000.
SAMPLE GRANTS The Church of Scotland's Fabric Fund (£4,000); The Church of Scotland's Missionaries Fund (£3,000); Multiple Sclerosis Charity, Renfrewshire Food Bank and Roseberry Centre (£2,000 each); Braid Health and Wellbeing and Listening Books (£1,500 each); British Liver Trust, Bethany Liver Trust and Westbourne Music (£1,000 each); Lanarkshire Epilepsy (£500).
FINANCES *Financial year end* 30/06/2022
  Income £74,800
  Grants to organisations £58,500
  Assets £2,000,000
HOW TO APPLY Apply in writing to the correspondent.
CONTACT DETAILS The Trustees, c/o Mitchells Roberton Solicitors, George House, 36 North Hanover Street, Glasgow G1 2AD

■ The Wood Foundation

OSCR NO SC037957   **ESTABLISHED** 2007
WHERE FUNDING CAN BE GIVEN Scotland and sub-Saharan Africa.
WHO CAN BENEFIT Charitable organisations; individuals.
WHAT IS FUNDED Economic development; venture philanthropy; young people.
TYPE OF GRANT Project funding.
SAMPLE GRANTS A list of beneficiaries was not included in the annual report and accounts.
FINANCES *Financial year end* 31/03/2022
  Income £6,390,000
  Grants to organisations £4,560,000
  Assets £97,760,000
TRUSTEES Sir Ian Wood; Lady Helen Wood; Graham Good.
HOW TO APPLY Unsolicited applications are not accepted. The foundation independently seeks beneficiaries rather than inviting open applications.
CONTACT DETAILS The Trustees, Blenheim House, Fountainhall Road, Aberdeen, Aberdeenshire AB15 4DT *Tel.* 01224 619862 *Email* info@thewoodfoundation.org.uk *Website* www.thewoodfoundation.org.uk

■ The Victoria Wood Foundation

CC NO 1170494   **ESTABLISHED** 2016
WHERE FUNDING CAN BE GIVEN UK, with a preference for the north of England and London.
WHO CAN BENEFIT Charitable organisations.
WHAT IS FUNDED The arts.
WHAT IS NOT FUNDED Individuals; courses of study; expeditions and foreign travel; general appeals; youth and community associations; retrospective expenditure; statutory bodies; places of worship or which promote religion; animal, wildlife, heritage and environmental causes.
RANGE OF GRANTS Up to £5,000.
SAMPLE GRANTS A list of beneficiaries was not included in the annual report and accounts.
FINANCES *Financial year end* 05/04/2022
  Income £141,600
  Grants to organisations £164,400
  Assets £4,090,000
TRUSTEES Roger Glossop; Charlotte Scott; Piers Wenger; Jane Wymark; Nigel Lilley; Lucy Ansbro; Davina Walter.
OTHER INFORMATION The foundation was established in memory of comedian Victoria Wood, who died from cancer in April 2016.
HOW TO APPLY Applications can be made by using the form found on the foundation's website. Alternatively, contact the administrator who will take you through the application process.
CONTACT DETAILS Catherine Edis, Trust Administrator, Plumpton House, Bents Drive, Sheffield, South Yorkshire S11 9RN *Tel.* 07715 593995 *Email* cathyedis@gmail.com *Website* https://victoriawoodfoundation.org.uk

■ Wooden Spoon Society

CC NO 326691   **ESTABLISHED** 1983
WHERE FUNDING CAN BE GIVEN UK and Ireland.
WHO CAN BENEFIT Organisations with a legal status such as charities, schools or clubs.
WHAT IS FUNDED Transforming young people's lives through rugby. Projects must enhance and support the lives of children and young people under the age of 25 who are disadvantaged physically, mentally or socially. Grants are given in the following categories: special equipment and facilities; playground; education, skills and training; sensory rooms and gardens; health and well-being; transport.
WHAT IS NOT FUNDED See the charity's website for exclusions relating to different types of projects.
TYPE OF GRANT Mostly capital costs and equipment; project costs; some salaries and core costs.
RANGE OF GRANTS Grants are unlikely to be less than £5,000.
SAMPLE GRANTS Blackpool Carers Centre and Friars Multi Academy Trust (£40,000 each); Hexham Priory School (£30,000); Brunstane Primary School (£28,000); We Are Beams and The Sheiling Ringwood (£25,000 each).
FINANCES *Financial year end* 31/03/2022
  Income £2,420,000
  Grants to organisations £819,600
  Assets £2,020,000
TRUSTEES John Gibson; Mark McCafferty; Quentin Smith; Joanna Coombs; Jane Harwood; Brett Bader; Christine Braithwaite; Graham Allen; Adrian Alli.
HOW TO APPLY The charity recommends first submitting an Expression of Wish form, which can be completed on its website. Eligible applicants may then complete an application form, which can also be downloaded from the website. Applications will be sent to the regional committee for approval.
CONTACT DETAILS Projects Team, Sentinel House, Ancells Business Park, Harvest Crescent, Fleet, Hampshire GU51 2UZ *Tel.* 01252 773720 *Email* projects@woodenspoon.org.uk *Website* www.woodenspoon.org.uk

■ Woodlands Green Ltd

CC NO 277299   **ESTABLISHED** 1979
WHERE FUNDING CAN BE GIVEN Worldwide.
WHO CAN BENEFIT Charitable organisations.
WHAT IS FUNDED Orthodox Jewish faith; relief of poverty.
WHAT IS NOT FUNDED Individuals, expeditions or scholarships.

RANGE OF GRANTS Typically up to £10,000.

SAMPLE GRANTS Mercaz Chasidei Wiznitz Trust (£20,000); Edupoor Ltd and Tchernobel Foundation Ltd (£10,000 each); Moreshet Hatorah Ltd (£8,600); Tchabe Kollell Ltd (£6,000); The TMC Trust Ltd (£5,400); Bnois Jerusalem Schools and Gateshead Hatzola (£5,000 each).

FINANCES *Financial year end 05/04/2022*
Income £331,700
Grants to organisations £193,700
Assets £2,800,000

TRUSTEES A. Hepner; J. Ost; Daniel Ost.

OTHER INFORMATION Grants of under £5,000 totalled £42,500. Thirteen grants of above £5,000 were awarded to organisations.

HOW TO APPLY Apply in writing to the correspondent.

CONTACT DETAILS The Trustees, 75 Woodlands, London NW11 9QS *Tel.* 020 8209 1458

■ **Woodroffe Benton Foundation**

CC NO 1075272   **ESTABLISHED** 1988

WHERE FUNDING CAN BE GIVEN UK.

WHO CAN BENEFIT UK-based charitable and educational organisations.

WHAT IS FUNDED Relief of hardship; care of older people; education and youth development; the environment and conservation; physical well-being.

WHAT IS NOT FUNDED Organisations operating outside the UK; places of worship needing restoration or upgrading of facilities; grants for further education; grants for gap years; grants for educational activities taking place outside Derbyshire; palliative care; non-registered organisations; organisations that have operated for less than 12 months; animal welfare organisations whose primary purpose is not environmental conservation; national organisations and their local branches.

TYPE OF GRANT Core costs; project costs.

RANGE OF GRANTS £500 to £2,500.

SAMPLE GRANTS A list of beneficiaries was not included in the annual report and accounts.

FINANCES *Financial year end 02/12/2022*
Income £213,200
Grants to organisations £242,700
Assets £8,810,000

TRUSTEES James Hope; Richard Page; Jill Wesley; Edward White; Chiyo Rimington; William White.

OTHER INFORMATION The foundation's annual report states that 140 grants were paid during the year in the following categories: substantial ongoing support (£111,700); small grants programme (£118,000); trustees' grants (£13,000).

HOW TO APPLY Apply via the application form on the foundation's website.

CONTACT DETAILS Joanna Noles, Secretary to the Trustees, PO Box 309, Cirencester, Gloucestershire GL7 9HA *Email* secretary@woodroffebenton.org.uk *Website* www.woodroffebenton.org.uk

■ **Woodsmith Foundation Ltd**

CC NO 1163127   **ESTABLISHED** 2013

WHERE FUNDING CAN BE GIVEN North York Moors National Park; Scarborough; Redcar and Cleveland.

WHO CAN BENEFIT Charitable organisations.

WHAT IS FUNDED Community services and development; education and training; the environment; social welfare; recreational facilities.

TYPE OF GRANT Programme dependent.

RANGE OF GRANTS Programme dependent.

SAMPLE GRANTS A list of beneficiaries was not included in the annual report and accounts.

FINANCES *Financial year end 31/05/2022*
Income £1,000,000
Grants to organisations £1,060,000
Assets £2,510,000

TRUSTEES Neil Irving; Ian Swales; Jacqueline Flynn; Jonathan Samuel; Dr Elizabeth Walmsley; Sir Martin Narey; William Woods.

HOW TO APPLY Applications can be made via the foundation's website.

CONTACT DETAILS Gemma Sciré, Grant and Programme Manager, Resolution House, Lake View, Scarborough, YO11 3ZB *Email* info@woodsmithfoundation.org.uk *Website* https://woodsmithfoundation.org.uk

■ **The Woodstock Family Charitable Foundation**

CC NO 1156449   **ESTABLISHED** 2014

WHERE FUNDING CAN BE GIVEN England and Wales.

WHO CAN BENEFIT Charitable organisations.

WHAT IS FUNDED Projects to assist young people who are at risk of offending, through guidance, coaching and life skills.

SAMPLE GRANTS A list of beneficiaries was not available.

FINANCES *Financial year end 31/03/2022*
Income £3,100
Grants to organisations £74,900

TRUSTEES Peter Harris; Thomas Harris; Paul Harris; Alison Swinburn; Margaret West; Nevena Harris.

OTHER INFORMATION Full accounts were not available to view on the Charity Commission's website due to the foundation's low income. We have therefore estimated the grant total based on the foundation's total expenditure.

HOW TO APPLY Apply in writing to the correspondent.

CONTACT DETAILS Peter Woodstock Harris, Trustee, Sallow Copse, Ringshall, Berkhamsted, Hertfordshire HP4 1LZ *Tel.* 01442 842480

■ **The Woodward Charitable Trust**

CC NO 299963   **ESTABLISHED** 1988

WHERE FUNDING CAN BE GIVEN UK.

WHO CAN BENEFIT UK-registered charities; CICs. The trustees favour small-scale, locally based initiatives.

WHAT IS FUNDED Children and young people; prisoners and ex-offenders; disadvantaged women and families; community cohesion particularly among minority groups including refugees and Travellers; disability; arts outreach. A budget is set aside each year for summer play schemes that take place during the summer holidays for disadvantaged children and young people (aged 5–16).

WHAT IS NOT FUNDED Charities whose annual income exceeds £200,000; charities only registered or working overseas; construction projects such as playgrounds, village halls and disability access; hospices; individuals; medical research; exclusively education-based charities; arts organisations without a social purpose. For summer play schemes, the trustees will also not fund: trips that are only social (the trustees prefer to fund trips that are educational and motivational); organisations with an annual turnover exceeding £100,000; overseas projects; playgroups.

TYPE OF GRANT Core costs.

RANGE OF GRANTS Small grants (up to £3,000); large grants (over £3,000 and only given to charities known to the trustees); children's summer playscheme grants (£250 to £1,000).

SAMPLE GRANTS University of West London (£25,000); Glyndebourne Productions Ltd (£10,000); British Red Cross (£6,000); The Access Project (£5,000); Birmingham City Clubs for Young People (£3,000); Empowr-U CIC (£2,000); Jacari (£1,000); Evolving Mindset CIC (£500).

FINANCES *Financial year end* 05/04/2022
Income £107,200
Grants to organisations £239,500
Assets £13,010,000

TRUSTEES The Rt Hon. Shaun Woodward; Camilla Woodward; Eleanor Mills; Thomas Hunniwood; Olivia Woodward; Katherine Woodward.

OTHER INFORMATION The trust is one of the Sainsbury Family Charitable Trusts, which share a common administration – see www.sftc.org.uk for more information. In 2021/22, grants were made for the following purposes: children and young people (£95,300); disadvantaged families (£48,900); summer schemes (£29,900); prisoners and ex-offenders (£10,900); other charitable purposes (£54,500).

HOW TO APPLY Applications must be completed using the online form on the trust's website. Applications can only be made during open grant rounds, details of which can be found on the 'diary' page on the website. General grants are allocated following the trustees' meetings, which usually happen in February/March and October/November each year. Children's summer play scheme grants are considered in April/May. Full criteria and guidelines can be found on the trust's website.

CONTACT DETAILS The Trustees, The Peak, 5 Wilton Road, London SW1V 1AP *Tel.* 020 7410 0330 *Email* contact@woodwardcharitabletrust.org.uk *Website* www.woodwardcharitabletrust.org.uk

■ The Woosnam Foundation

CC NO 1171136   ESTABLISHED 2016
WHERE FUNDING CAN BE GIVEN UK.
WHO CAN BENEFIT Charitable organisations.
WHAT IS FUNDED Education; research, with some preference for medical research; animal welfare.
TYPE OF GRANT Research.
RANGE OF GRANTS £1,000 to £150,000.
SAMPLE GRANTS University College London Hospitals Charitable Foundation (£150,000); Rays of Sunshine (£5,000).
FINANCES *Financial year end* 31/12/2021
Income £66,300
Grants to organisations £168,500
Assets £3,700,000
TRUSTEES Ian Burman; Michael Feldman.
OTHER INFORMATION During the year, the foundation made six grants to organisations.
HOW TO APPLY Contact the correspondent for more information.
CONTACT DETAILS Ian Burman, Trustee, Penthouse 2, Mount Tyndal, Spaniards Road, London NW3 7JH *Tel.* 020 7636 6446 *Email* ian. burman@laytons.com

■ Worcestershire Community Foundation

CC NO 1102266   ESTABLISHED 2003
WHERE FUNDING CAN BE GIVEN Worcestershire.
WHO CAN BENEFIT Organisations and individuals.
WHAT IS FUNDED Projects that promote the well-being of the local communities in Worcestershire.
WHAT IS NOT FUNDED Each funding programme has its own set of exclusions; refer to the foundation's website for further information.
RANGE OF GRANTS Programme dependent, but typically up to £10,000.
SAMPLE GRANTS A list of beneficiaries was not included in the annual report and accounts. Previous beneficiaries have included: Eastham Memorial Hall; Footsteps; Jestaminute; Malvern Community Forest; Redditch Boxing Academy; St Mary's Pickersleigh.
FINANCES *Financial year end* 30/09/2021
Income £1,100,000
Grants to organisations £620,600
Assets £2,340,000
TRUSTEES Robert Sykes; Prof. Tamar Thompson; Roger Britton; David Shaw; Nick Stanley; Mark Yates; Jonathan Chenevix-Trench; Kathleen Leather; Edward Lloyd.
OTHER INFORMATION This is one of the 47 UK community foundations, which distribute funding for a wide range of purposes. As with all community foundations, there are a number of donor-advised funds managed on behalf of individuals, families and charitable trusts. Grant schemes tend to change frequently – consult the foundation's website for details of current programmes and up-to-date deadlines. The 2020/21 accounts were the latest available at the time of writing (May 2023).
HOW TO APPLY Potential applicants are advised to visit the community foundation's website or contact its grants team to find the most suitable funding stream. Application forms are available on the foundation's website. Each funding programme has its own set of exclusions and deadlines, refer to the website for further information. The grants panel will usually meet within eight weeks of the grant programme's application deadline.
CONTACT DETAILS Emma Buckingham, Grants and Communications Officer, c/o Community First, 1st Floor, Unit 3, Harmac House, Chequers Close, Enigma Business Park, Malvern, Worcestershire WR14 1GP *Tel.* 01684 892666 *Email* emmab@comfirst.org.uk *Website* www. worcscf.org.uk

■ The Worshipful Company of Glovers of London Charitable Trust

CC NO 269091   ESTABLISHED 1975
WHERE FUNDING CAN BE GIVEN UK, with a preference for London.
WHO CAN BENEFIT Charitable organisations; educational institutions; individuals; hospitals.
WHAT IS FUNDED General charitable purposes; education; social welfare, especially for Liverymen, Freemen and their family; in-kind support in the form of provision of gloves; prosthetics.
TYPE OF GRANT Projects; bursaries; prizes; in-kind support.
RANGE OF GRANTS Up to around £8,000.
SAMPLE GRANTS King Edward's School – Witley (£6,000); City of London School, City of London School for Girls and St Paul's Cathedral School

Think carefully about every application. Is it justified?

745

(£5,500 each); gloves for homeless charities (£4,200); Church of St Margaret – Lothbury, Lord Mayor's Charities and The PACE Centre (£2,000 each).

FINANCES *Financial year end* 05/04/2022
Income £107,600
Grants to organisations £51,400
Grants to individuals £8,400
Assets £950,000

TRUSTEE The Worshipful Company of Glovers of London.

OTHER INFORMATION Two individuals were supported during this period in the form of the provision of bionic arms. A total of £27,000 was awarded to the trust's related charity, the Worshipful Company of Glovers Charitable Endowment; this is not included in the grant total. Only organisations and individuals that received grants of over £1,500 were listed as beneficiaries in the trust's 2021/22 accounts. Grants of under £1,500 totalled £7,000.

HOW TO APPLY Apply in writing to the correspondent.

CONTACT DETAILS Mark Butler, Clerk, c/o Knox Cropper and Co., 65 Leadenhall Street, London EC3A 2AD *Tel.* 01747 851887 *Email* clerk@thegloverscompany.org *Website* www.thegloverscompany.org/philanthropy

---

■ Worshipful Company of Gold and Silver Wyre Drawers Second Charitable Trust Fund

CC NO 802491   **ESTABLISHED** 1969

WHERE FUNDING CAN BE GIVEN London.

WHO CAN BENEFIT Registered charities.

WHAT IS FUNDED General charitable purposes, including: medical causes; education; music; children and young people; the armed forces; the gold and silver wire trade.

SAMPLE GRANTS A list of beneficiaries was not included in the annual report and accounts. Previous beneficiaries have included: Tilehouse Counselling (£12,600); Royal School of Needlework Goldwork and Bursary (£6,000); Goldsmiths Craft and Design Council Jewellery Awards (£3,000); 101 Squadron Centenary (£1,100); Action for ME and Queen Alexandra's Hospital Home (£1,000 each); Bexley Heath Young People's Service (£200); City and Guilds of London Institute (£50).

FINANCES *Financial year end* 31/12/2021
Income £83,800
Grants to organisations £81,000
Assets £1,760,000

TRUSTEES Brian Turner; Air Cdre Cynthia Fowler; Roger Carter; Catherine Carr; Anneliese Edgcumbe; David Utting.

HOW TO APPLY Apply in writing to the correspondent.

CONTACT DETAILS The Trustees, 40 Woodcote Road, Lye Green, Wanstead, London E11 2QA *Email* clerk@gswd.co.uk *Website* www.gswd.co.uk

---

■ The Worshipful Company of Information Technologists

CC NO 1113488   **ESTABLISHED** 2006

WHERE FUNDING CAN BE GIVEN UK.

WHO CAN BENEFIT Registered charities; educational organisations; organisations with a formal not-for-profit constitution, such as CICs.

WHAT IS FUNDED Education; digital skills; information technology; social welfare.

WHAT IS NOT FUNDED Individuals; local authorities or councils; private companies; core costs; political/lobbying work; loans/debt repayments; retrospective costs; consultancy costs; work overseas; or projects that seek to build an endowment.

TYPE OF GRANT Project costs.

RANGE OF GRANTS Up to £15,000.

SAMPLE GRANTS Campaign Against Living Miserably (£75,000); Thames Reach (£22,100); Gresham College (£11,300); Community TechAid, Restorative Justice for All International Institute and TeenTech Charity (£9,800 each); Apps for Good (£9,300); Lifelites (£5,400); AbilityNet and Cyber Girls First (£5,000 each).

FINANCES *Financial year end* 31/12/2021
Income £832,400
Grants to organisations £229,200
Assets £7,790,000

TRUSTEES Bill Kennair; Elizabeth Sparrow; Dr Stefan Fafinski; Richard Pone; Jonathan Soar; Bryan Parkinson; Augustus Machado; Serena Pandey; David Berry.

OTHER INFORMATION The charity also provides pro bono IT support for charities and social enterprises.

HOW TO APPLY Online application forms can be accessed via the charity's online portal on its website. Applications are considered four times a year in February, May, September and November, See the charity's website for deadlines.

CONTACT DETAILS Lindsay Wratten, Charity Co-ordinator, 39A Bartholomew Close, London EC1A 7JN *Tel.* 020 7600 1992 *Email* charity@wcit.org.uk *Website* https://wcitcharity.org.uk

---

■ Worshipful Company of Needlemakers Charitable Fund

CC NO 288646   **ESTABLISHED** 1952

WHERE FUNDING CAN BE GIVEN City of London.

WHO CAN BENEFIT Charitable organisations, including those associated with the needle-making industry.

WHAT IS FUNDED Education; religion; social welfare; general charitable purposes.

RANGE OF GRANTS £50 up to £12,800.

SAMPLE GRANTS King Edward's School (£12,800); Florence Nightingale Foundation (£11,500); Old Palace School (£7,000); City of London School for Girls (£5,000); City and Guilds of London Institute (£3,500); Pembroke College (£1,000); The Paraorchestra (£300); Lady Eleanor Hollis School (£50).

FINANCES *Financial year end* 30/09/2021
Income £120,100
Grants to organisations £88,300
Assets £3,430,000

TRUSTEE Master, Wardens, and Commonalty of The Art or Mystery of Needlemakers of the City of London.

OTHER INFORMATION Grants were awarded to 29 organisations during the year and were broken down as follows: education (£40,100); welfare (£24,100); focus grants (£14,600); by virtue of office (£9,000); religion (£500). The 2020/21 accounts were the latest available at the time of writing (June 2023).

HOW TO APPLY Apply in writing to the correspondent.

CONTACT DETAILS The Trustees, PO Box 73635, London SW14 9BY *Tel.* 07908 521731 *Email* needlemakers.clerk@yahoo.com *Website* www.needlemakers.org.uk

■ Worth Waynflete Foundation

CC NO 1068892   **ESTABLISHED** 1986
WHERE FUNDING CAN BE GIVEN UK, with a strong preference for Lincolnshire.
WHO CAN BENEFIT Lincolnshire-based charities and organisations (including schools, churches, sports clubs and community groups); national charities and organisations benefitting Lincolnshire residents; individual projects and initiatives.
WHAT IS FUNDED General charitable purposes particularly in South Lincolnshire; community projects; rural projects that enhance the landscape and ecology; heritage preservation; school initiatives (including IT equipment).
WHAT IS NOT FUNDED Individuals.
TYPE OF GRANT Training of existing staff; training of new volunteers; core costs, running costs and special requirements.
SAMPLE GRANTS Previous beneficiaries have included: Lincolnshire Blind Society (£6,000); Canine Partners, Lincolnshire and Nottinghamshire Air Ambulance and the Order of St John (£4,000 each); Deafblind UK (£2,500); Action for Kids, Gurkha Welfare Trust and Marine Conservation Society (£1,000); Braille Chess Association, Children's Safety Education Foundation and Royal National Lifeboat Fund (£500 each); Mouth and Foot Painting Artists (£100).
FINANCES *Financial year end 31/12/2022*
Income £0
Grants to organisations £420,000
TRUSTEES Graham Scrimshaw; Michael Worth; Hubert Lewczuk-Tilley.
OTHER INFORMATION Full accounts were not available to view on the Charity Commission's website due to the foundation's low income. We have therefore estimated the foundation's grant total based on its total expenditure.
HOW TO APPLY Applicants should contact the foundation by email or post, providing their name, address, organisation, contact details and a brief outline of their activities and proposal. Alternatively, contact one of the foundation managers, details of which can be found on the website.
CONTACT DETAILS Margaret Dawson, Foundation Manager, PO Box 9986, Grantham, Lincolnshire NG31 0FJ *Tel.* 01400 250210 *Email* info@waynfletecharity.com *Website* www.waynfletecharity.com

■ The Worwin UK Foundation

CC NO 1037981   **ESTABLISHED** 1994
WHERE FUNDING CAN BE GIVEN UK; Canada.
WHO CAN BENEFIT Registered charities.
WHAT IS FUNDED General charitable purposes; relief of poverty; disability; education; health and medicine; young and disadvantaged people; arts and culture; community development; human rights; animal conservation.
RANGE OF GRANTS £20,000 to £30,000.
SAMPLE GRANTS Previous beneficiaries have included: Momentum Community Economic Society (£31,000); Big Brothers Big Sisters – Calgary (£29,500); Multicultural Arts For Schools and Communities (£28,000); Operation Come Home (£23,500); Family Dynamics – Winnipeg (£22,000); SEED Winnipeg (£21,500).
FINANCES *Financial year end 31/12/2021*
Income £40
Grants to organisations £7,130,000
Assets £168,860,000

TRUSTEES Anthony Graham; Brian Moore; Oliver McGinley; Dr Emily Braun; Dr Nancy Marcus; Heather McCourt; James Meekison.
OTHER INFORMATION Full accounts were not available to view on the Charity Commission's website due to the charity's low income. We have therefore estimated the charity's grant total based on its total expenditure.
HOW TO APPLY Unsolicited applications are not accepted.
CONTACT DETAILS The Trustees, Farrer and Co., 65–66 Lincoln's Inn Fields, London WC2A 3LH *Tel.* 020 3375 7000

■ WPG Charitable Trust

OSCR NO SC042134
WHERE FUNDING CAN BE GIVEN Scotland.
WHO CAN BENEFIT Registered charities; individuals.
WHAT IS FUNDED Sport; the arts; culture; education.
SAMPLE GRANTS A list of beneficiaries was not included in the annual report and accounts.
FINANCES *Financial year end 31/03/2022*
Income £127,000
Grants to organisations £118,400
Assets £3,600
OTHER INFORMATION Note that the grant total includes amounts awarded to individuals.
HOW TO APPLY Application forms can be downloaded from the trust's website. Applications can be submitted at any time but are only considered at the end of February, April, June, August, October and December.
CONTACT DETAILS The Trustees, c/o Witherby Publishing Group Ltd, Navigation House, 3 Almondvale Business Park, Almondvale Way, Livingston EH54 6GA *Email* use the contact form on the website *Website* https://wpgtrust.com

■ The Edward and Catherine Wray Charitable Trust

CC NO 1160375
WHERE FUNDING CAN BE GIVEN UK; South Africa.
WHO CAN BENEFIT Charitable organisations.
WHAT IS FUNDED General charitable purposes.
SAMPLE GRANTS Coach Core Foundation (£100,000); The Onside Foundation (£100,000 in two grants); Headington School Oxford Ltd (£40,000).
FINANCES *Financial year end 13/01/2022*
Income £95,400
Grants to organisations £240,000
TRUSTEES Edward Wray; Catherine Wray; Ludlow Trust Company Ltd.
OTHER INFORMATION During 2021/22 four grants were made to three organisations.
HOW TO APPLY Apply in writing to the correspondent. Applications or enquiries should be made by post.
CONTACT DETAILS The Trustees, Tower Wharf, Cheese Lane, Bristol BS2 0JJ *Tel.* 0117 313 8200

■ The Eric Wright Charitable Trust

CC NO 1002966
WHERE FUNDING CAN BE GIVEN UK, with a preference for the North West.
WHO CAN BENEFIT Community and voluntary service organisations.

WHAT IS FUNDED Young people; older people; education and training; health; mental health; carers' support.

TYPE OF GRANT Revenue costs; and specific service delivery project costs; capacity building. In exceptional circumstances, the trust may fund capital costs.

RANGE OF GRANTS Major grants from £20,000 to £35,000; community grants from £5,000 to £20,000; and minor grants from £500 to £5,000.

SAMPLE GRANTS A list of beneficiaries was not included in the annual report and accounts. Previous beneficiaries have included: Galloway Society for the Blind (£50,000); Age UK Lancashire, Blackburn Youth Zone, Lancashire Mind, The Children's Adventure Farm Trust and Wigan Boys and Girls Club (£25,000 each).

FINANCES *Financial year end* 31/12/2021
Income £176,790,000
Grants to organisations £1,270,000
Assets £92,830,000

TRUSTEES Michael Collier; Hugh MacDonald; Alan Sturrock; Alison Wright; Janette Collier; Martin Newsholme; Catherine Wilson.

OTHER INFORMATION A high volunteer involvement in the applicant organisation is likely to be influential although not essential.

HOW TO APPLY Major grants are by invitation only. In regards to applications for community grants and minor grants the trust's website states: 'If you would like to apply, we would strongly advise you in the first instance to contact the Trust to discuss the nature of your application and the process involved.'

CONTACT DETAILS The Trustees, Sceptre House, Sceptre Way, Bamber Bridge, Preston, Lancashire PR5 6AW *Tel.* 01772 694613 *Email* rebeccam@ericwright.co.uk *Website* www.ericwright.co.uk/charitable-trust

---

■ WWDP (World Day of Prayer National Committee for England, Wales and Northern Ireland)

CC NO 233242   **ESTABLISHED** 1964
WHERE FUNDING CAN BE GIVEN Worldwide.
WHO CAN BENEFIT Christian charities.
WHAT IS FUNDED Christian causes.
TYPE OF GRANT Project costs; core grants; development funding. Mostly one-off but also some recurrent awards.
RANGE OF GRANTS Mostly £5,000 and under.
SAMPLE GRANTS Women on the Frontline Ministries (£3,000); Hope for Kids International (£2,000); Army Cadet Charitable Trust UK (£1,200); Wales Sunday Schools Council (£400).
FINANCES *Financial year end* 31/12/2021
Income £308,700
Grants to organisations £69,400
Assets £427,500
TRUSTEES Dr Elizabeth Burroughs; Nicola Hoskin-Stone; The Revd Carole Bourne.
HOW TO APPLY Contact the correspondent to find out whether your organisation is eligible for a grant.
CONTACT DETAILS The Trustees, WDP Office, Commercial Road, Tunbridge Wells, Kent TN1 2RR *Email* office@wwdp.org.uk *Website* www.wwdp.org.uk/grants

---

■ Wychville Ltd

CC NO 267584   **ESTABLISHED** 1973
WHERE FUNDING CAN BE GIVEN UK and overseas.
WHO CAN BENEFIT Charitable organisations.
WHAT IS FUNDED The advancement of the Orthodox Jewish faith; education; general charitable purposes.
RANGE OF GRANTS Up to £174,100.
SAMPLE GRANTS Friends of Mercaz Hatorah Belz Machnivka (£174,100); Friends of Beis Soroh Schneirer (£101,000); One Heart Lev Echod (£81,000); Friends of Beis Chinuch Lebonos Trust (£67,000); Mifal Hachesed Vehatzdokoh (£58,000); Bnois Jerusalem Girls' School (£22,500).
FINANCES *Financial year end* 31/03/2022
Income £570,000
Grants to organisations £565,000
Assets £211,500
TRUSTEES Mr E. Englander; Mrs B. R. Englander.
OTHER INFORMATION Grants were awarded to more than six organisations, with smaller grants totalling £61,500.
HOW TO APPLY Apply in writing to the correspondent.
CONTACT DETAILS The Trustees, 44 Leweston Place, London N16 6RH *Tel.* 020 8802 3948

■ The Wyfold Charitable Trust

CC NO 1157483   **ESTABLISHED** 2014
WHERE FUNDING CAN BE GIVEN England and Wales.
WHO CAN BENEFIT UK-registered charities.
WHAT IS FUNDED General charitable purposes, including: social welfare; health; arts, culture, heritage or science; education; citizenship or community development; sports; the armed forces; the environment; animal welfare; religion.
RANGE OF GRANTS Up to £30,000.
SAMPLE GRANTS British Heart Foundation (£30,000); The Fleming-Wyfold Art Foundation (£25,000); British Red Cross (£20,000); Chronic Disease Research Foundation, Global Warming Policy Foundation, Red Squirrel Survival Trust and Supporting Wounded Veterans (£10,000 each).
FINANCES *Financial year end* 31/03/2022
Income £331,200
Grants to organisations £225,000
Assets £10,400,000
TRUSTEES Roderick Fleming; Adam Fleming; Nicholas Powell; Angus Fleming; Hermione Fleming.
OTHER INFORMATION During 2021/22, grants were made to 38 organisations. Only organisations that received grants of over £10,000 were listed as beneficiaries in the trust's accounts. Grants of under £10,000 totalled £110,000.
HOW TO APPLY Our previous research suggests that applications should be made in writing on no more than two sides of A4 and sent to the correspondent by post along with any supporting documentation. The Wyfold Charitable Trust should be referenced in the application. The trustees meet twice during the year to consider applications.
CONTACT DETAILS The Trustees, 14 Buckingham Street, London WC2N 6DF *Tel.* 020 3696 6721 *Email* charities@rftrustee.com

---

■ Sir Graham Wylie Foundation

CC NO 1165447   **ESTABLISHED** 2017
WHERE FUNDING CAN BE GIVEN The North East.
WHO CAN BENEFIT Charities; voluntary or community groups; not-for-private profit companies.

WHAT IS FUNDED Educational and recreational projects for disadvantaged young people; children and young people's health; social welfare.

TYPE OF GRANT Recurrent up to three years.

SAMPLE GRANTS Youth Ministry Trust (£48,600); North East Homeless (£22,000); Children's Heart Unit Fund (£10,000); Teenage Cancer Trust (£4,000); Gateshead Leam Rangers Football Club (£2,000).

FINANCES *Financial year end* 31/12/2021
Income £279,100
Grants to organisations £86,600
Assets £647,400

TRUSTEES Graham Wylie; Rachael Garden; Andrea Wylie.

OTHER INFORMATION Grants were made to five organisations in 2021.

HOW TO APPLY Application forms can be downloaded from the 'Who we help' page of the foundation's website and should be returned by post.

CONTACT DETAILS The Trustees, Nelson House, Burdon Terrace, Newcastle upon Tyne, Tyne and Wear NE2 3AE *Tel.* 0191 212 5140 *Email* info@grahamwyliefoundation.org.uk *Website* www.grahamwyliefoundation.org.uk

······································

■ The Wyndham Charitable Trust

CC NO 259313   **ESTABLISHED** 1969

WHERE FUNDING CAN BE GIVEN UK and financially developing countries.

WHO CAN BENEFIT Registered charities; universities; hospitals; hospices; religious bodies/institutions.

WHAT IS FUNDED General charitable purposes including the elimination of modern-day slavery.

TYPE OF GRANT Unrestricted funding; capital costs; core/revenue costs.

RANGE OF GRANTS Mostly under £10,000.

SAMPLE GRANTS A list of beneficiaries was not included in the annual report and accounts. Previous beneficiaries have included: Anti-Slavery International (£16,000); Institute of Cancer Research (£8,000); The Royal College of Surgeons of England (£4,000); Liverpool School of Tropical Medicine (£1,200); Church Mission Society (£800); Asthma UK (£700); Boldre PCC (£45).

FINANCES *Financial year end* 20/06/2022
Income £234,900
Grants to organisations £102,600
Assets £2,040,000

TRUSTEES John Gaselee; Julie Gaselee; Sarah Gaselee; David Gaselee.

HOW TO APPLY The trustees have previously stated that they do not encourage unsolicited requests.

CONTACT DETAILS The Trustees, 34A Westfield Road, Lymington, Hampshire SO41 3QA *Email* wyndham_ct@yahoo.co.uk *Website* www.wyndham-ct.org

······································

■ The Wyseliot Rose Charitable Trust

CC NO 257219   **ESTABLISHED** 1968

WHERE FUNDING CAN BE GIVEN UK.

WHO CAN BENEFIT Registered charities; hospices; hospitals.

WHAT IS FUNDED Charities of national significance; health and medicine; social welfare; arts and culture; general charitable purposes.

WHAT IS NOT FUNDED Individuals; non-registered charities.

TYPE OF GRANT Recurrent funding.

RANGE OF GRANTS £2,000 to £6,000.

SAMPLE GRANTS Mind (£6,000); Alzheimer's Research UK, Royal College of Music and Time and Talents Association (£5,000 each); Cystic Fibrosis Trust, Musicians Benevolent Fund and Trinity Hospice (£4,000 each); Brains Trust, Prostate Cancer UK and Trail Blazers (£3,000 each); Andover Child Contact Centre, Runnymede Trust and University College Hospitals (£2,000 each).

FINANCES *Financial year end* 05/04/2022
Income £110,500
Grants to organisations £118,000
Assets £2,990,000

TRUSTEES Adam Raphael; Jonathan Rose; William Rose; Lucy Rose.

HOW TO APPLY Contact the correspondent for further information. Note that it is unlikely new organisations will be supported as most grants are recurrent.

CONTACT DETAILS The Trustees, 17 Chelsea Square, London SW3 6LF *Tel.* 01273 562563

■ Yankov Charitable Trust

CC NO 1106703 **ESTABLISHED** 2004
WHERE FUNDING CAN BE GIVEN Worldwide.
WHO CAN BENEFIT Charitable organisations, particularly Jewish organisations.
WHAT IS FUNDED Jewish religion, culture and education.
SAMPLE GRANTS Riosan (£50,000); Chevras Maoz Ladol (£13,600); Yeshivas Toras Moshe (£11,000).
FINANCES *Financial year end 30/09/2021*
Income £306,100
Grants to organisations £93,000
Assets £690,800
TRUSTEES Jacob Schonberg; Aryeh Schonberg; Julian Lewin.
OTHER INFORMATION The 2020/21 annual report was the latest available information at the time of writing (May 2023). Only organisations that received grants of over £10,000 were listed as beneficiaries in the 2020/21 annual report. Grants of under £10,000 totalled £18,400.
HOW TO APPLY Apply in writing to the correspondent.
CONTACT DETAILS The Trustees, 158 Albert Avenue, Prestwick, Manchester M25 0HE *Tel.* 020 8202 7948

■ The Yapp Charitable Trust

CC NO 1076803 **ESTABLISHED** 1999
WHERE FUNDING CAN BE GIVEN England and Wales.
WHO CAN BENEFIT Registered charities.
WHAT IS FUNDED Older people; children and young people (aged 5–25); people with physical disabilities, learning disabilities or mental health challenges; social welfare, particularly people trying to overcome life-limiting problems of a social nature (such as addiction, relationship difficulties, abuse and offending); education and learning, particularly adults or children who are educationally disadvantaged.
WHAT IS NOT FUNDED There is a detailed list of exclusions on the trust's website.
TYPE OF GRANT Core/revenue costs.
RANGE OF GRANTS £2,000 to £9,000.
SAMPLE GRANTS High Peak Homeless Help (£9,000); Amber Crisis Pregnancy Care (£7,500); Friends of Heavitree Health Centre and Phoenix Counselling Services (£6,000 each); Radio Bronglais (£4,000); New Child Centre (£3,000); Maun Refuge (£2,000).
FINANCES *Financial year end 30/09/2022*
Income £168,900
Grants to organisations £187,000
Assets £6,760,000
TRUSTEES Jane Fergusson; Alfred Hill; Lisa Bone; Jacqui Orchard; John Kisenyi; Sheona Evans.
OTHER INFORMATION The trust gives priority to work that is 'unattractive' to the general public or 'unpopular' with other funders, particularly when it helps improve the lives of marginalised, disadvantaged or isolated people. Preference is also given to charities that can demonstrate the effective use of volunteers, an element of self-sustainability, or preventative work which aims to create change through raising awareness and campaigning. Grants were made to 32 organisations and distributed as follows:

disability (£64,500 in 11 grants); children and young people (£42,000 in six grants); older people (£38,000 in seven grants); social welfare (£36,500 in six grants); education (£11,000 in two grants).
HOW TO APPLY An application form and further guidelines are available on the trust's website. Pre-application enquiries can be made to the correspondent via phone or email.
CONTACT DETAILS The Trustees, 1st Floor, Mile House, Bridge End, Chester-le-Street, County Durham DH3 3RA *Tel.* 0191 389 3300
Email info@yappcharitabletrust.org.uk
Website www.yappcharitabletrust.org.uk

■ Yorkshire Building Society Charitable Foundation

CC NO 1069082 **ESTABLISHED** 1998
WHERE FUNDING CAN BE GIVEN UK, with a preference for areas local to society branches.
WHO CAN BENEFIT UK-registered charities.
WHAT IS FUNDED General charitable purposes, with priority areas: alleviating poverty; improving health/saving lives. There is a particular focus on beneficiary groups that are vulnerable or disadvantaged, such as children, people with disabilities or serious illness, older people and people facing homelessness.
WHAT IS NOT FUNDED Charities serving only a specific sector of the community selected on the basis of political or religious grounds/advancement; animal welfare charities; charities with beneficiaries not in the UK; CICs, community or voluntary organisations that are not registered charities; individuals. See the charity's guidance notes for full exclusions.
TYPE OF GRANT Specific projects; purchase of specific capital items.
RANGE OF GRANTS Typically up to £2,000.
SAMPLE GRANTS Refugee Action (£30,000); Smart Works – Leeds (£28,000); Canopy Housing and Groundwork – North England and Cumbria (£21,000); Give Bradford – No Child Cold (£10,000); Ace, Age UK and Autism Angels (£2,000 each).
FINANCES *Financial year end 31/12/2021*
Income £406,700
Grants to organisations £407,400
Assets £70,200
TRUSTEES Vanessa White; Gordon Rogers; Lloyd Latibeaudiere; Erin Fuller.
OTHER INFORMATION During the year, grants were made to 215 organisations. Only organisations that received grants of £2,000 and above were listed as beneficiaries in the charity's accounts.
HOW TO APPLY To be eligible for a grant you must be recommended by one of the building society's members or colleagues. If you are a member and would like the foundation to consider supporting a charity, an online application form can be found on the foundation's webpage. All applications are reviewed on a quarterly basis by the trustees. Deadlines are 31 March, 30 June, 30 September and 31 December annually. You can expect to hear back within three months of submitting an application.
CONTACT DETAILS D. Colley, Secretary, Yorkshire House, Yorkshire Drive, Bradford, West Yorkshire BD5 8LJ *Tel.* 0345 166 9271
Email corporateresponsibility@ybs.co.uk
Website www.ybs.co.uk/your-society/charitable-foundation/index.html

■ Yorkshire Cancer Research

CC NO 516898   **ESTABLISHED** 1985
WHERE FUNDING CAN BE GIVEN Yorkshire.
WHO CAN BENEFIT Universities; research organisations; health bodies.
WHAT IS FUNDED Research and services to help prevent, diagnose and treat cancer.
WHAT IS NOT FUNDED Refer to the guidance notes on the website for specific exclusions.
TYPE OF GRANT Research projects, programmes and facilities; development funding; strategic funding.
RANGE OF GRANTS Dependent on funding call.
SAMPLE GRANTS University of Leeds (£3.91 million in 17 grants); University of Hull (£1.63 million in 3 grants); Lynparza Legacy Fund (£400,000); Leeds City Council (£337,600); University of Nottingham (£281,300); Northumbria University (£84,500); Leeds Teaching Hospitals NHS Trust (£15,400).
FINANCES *Financial year end 31/03/2022*
Income £25,830,000
Grants to organisations £9,950,000
Assets £84,050,000
TRUSTEES Graham Berville; Sandra Dodson; Dr Yvette Oade; Bobby Ndawula; Elizabeth Richards; Clare Field; Dr James Rice; Craig Bonnar; Samuel Jenner; Matthew Johnson; The Hon. Sir Robert Langlands; Heather Jackson.
OTHER INFORMATION During 2021/22, the charity awarded 48 grants.
HOW TO APPLY See the charity's website for information on current funding rounds, as well as deadlines, guidance and application forms.
CONTACT DETAILS Research Team, Jacob Smith House, 7 Grove Park Court, Harrogate, North Yorkshire HG1 4DP *Tel.* 01423 501269 *Email* hq@ycr.org.uk *Website* https://yorkshirecancerresearch.org.uk

■ The Yorkshire Dales Millennium Trust

CC NO 1061687   **ESTABLISHED** 1996
WHERE FUNDING CAN BE GIVEN The Yorkshire Dales.
WHO CAN BENEFIT Voluntary organisations; community groups; farmers and other individuals; Yorkshire Dales National Park Authority; estates; parish councils and district councils.
WHAT IS FUNDED The environment; conservation; heritage; rural communities; climate and sustainability.
TYPE OF GRANT Project funding; capital costs; core costs.
SAMPLE GRANTS A list of beneficiaries was not included in the annual report and accounts.
FINANCES *Financial year end 31/03/2022*
Income £1,740,000
Grants to organisations £111,700
Grants to individuals £132,300
Assets £1,720,000
TRUSTEES Carl Lis; Thomas Wheelwright; Prof. Christine Leigh; Eileen Spencer; Tracy Walker; Mark Cunliffe-Lister; Eloise Brown; Claire Brightley; William Downs; Jonathan Page; Kelsey Williamson; Thomas Pratt.
HOW TO APPLY Application processes may vary depending upon the specific programme. Guidance and application forms for all current grant programmes can be downloaded from the trust's website. The trustees meet at regular intervals – six times for full board plus additional meetings during the financial year.
CONTACT DETAILS Josephine Boulter, Company Secretary, Main Street, Clapham, Lancaster, Lancashire LA2 8DP *Tel.* 01524 251002 *Email* info@ydmt.org *Website* www.ydmt.org

■ The Yorkshire Historic Churches Trust

CC NO 1175099   **ESTABLISHED** 1988
WHERE FUNDING CAN BE GIVEN Yorkshire (pre-1974 boundaries).
WHO CAN BENEFIT Churches.
WHAT IS FUNDED Maintenance of Christian churches; also, the preservation of individual items such as bells, monuments and organs.
WHAT IS NOT FUNDED Facilities for people with disabilities; heating or electrical installations (including up-grading); improvements or re-ordering, including extensions; projects where work has either commenced or been completed.
TYPE OF GRANT Capital costs.
RANGE OF GRANTS £250 to £112,500.
SAMPLE GRANTS Liz and Terry Bramall Foundation (£60,000); St Mary the Virgin – Oxenhope (£10,000); St Giles – Pontefract (£6,000); All Saints North Street – York (£5,000); All Saints – North Ferriby (£4,000); St Peter – Leeds (£3,500); St Mary – Carlton (£2,000); St Mary – Long Preston (£500).
FINANCES *Financial year end 31/12/2021*
Income £118,700
Grants to organisations £121,500
Assets £1,240,000
TRUSTEES Thomas Ramsden; Rory Wardroper; Sylvia Johnson; Richard Bailey; Jane Crease; Christopher Wildblood; Moira Fulton; Clive Lloyd; Dr Katherine Giles; Robert Beaumont.
OTHER INFORMATION The 2021 accounts were the latest available at the time of writing (June 2023).
HOW TO APPLY Apply via the application form on the trust's website.
CONTACT DETAILS J. K. Stamp, Grants Secretary, Yorkshire Historic Churches Trust, 2 Dalton Terrace, York YO24 4DA *Tel.* 07594 578665 *Email* vanbarassociates@gmail.com *Website* www.yhct.org.uk

■ Youth Endowment Fund (YEF)

CC NO 1185413   **ESTABLISHED** 2019
WHERE FUNDING CAN BE GIVEN England and Wales.
WHO CAN BENEFIT Registered charities; CICs; statutory authorities.
WHAT IS FUNDED Violence prevention projects for children and young people, particularly those aged between 10 and 14 years old and those from marginalised backgrounds.
WHAT IS NOT FUNDED Eligibility criteria are released with each funding round – see the charity's website for more information.
TYPE OF GRANT Project costs; research and evaluation.
RANGE OF GRANTS Project dependent.
SAMPLE GRANTS South London and Maudsley NHS Foundation Trust (£1.9 million); Lives Not Knives (£575,000); Wakefield Council Youth Work Team (£418,200); ASSIST Trauma Care (£318,100); Imperial College London (£287,800); RISE Mutual CIC (£163,400); Young Persons Advisory Service (£159,400); Volunteering Matters (£92,800); Brandon Centre for Counselling (£75,000).
FINANCES *Financial year end 31/12/2021*
Income £10,820,000
Grants to organisations £13,950,000
Assets £195,600,000

TRUSTEE Impetus – The Private Equity Foundation.

OTHER INFORMATION Only grants of above £75,000 were listed in the 2021 accounts.

HOW TO APPLY Details of how to apply can be found on the charity's website, including details around the evaluation and reporting expectations. Projects must be co-designed with an independent evaluator before being awarded funding – the charity has a list of approved evaluation partners on its website. Applicants will be assigned a YEF Programme Manager who will support them throughout the entire process, from applying to finishing the project.

CONTACT DETAILS Grants Team, 1st Floor, 64 Great Eastern Street, London EC2A 3QR
Email grants@youthendowmentfund.org.uk
Website https://youthendowmentfund.org.uk

···

■ Youth Music

CC NO 1075032   ESTABLISHED 1999

WHERE FUNDING CAN BE GIVEN England, Wales and Scotland.

WHO CAN BENEFIT Registered charities; CICs; constituted community groups; schools.

WHAT IS FUNDED Youth Music funds projects that provide musical opportunities and activities for children and young people (under 25), working towards greater inclusion of young people in musical activities, across all genres and styles.

WHAT IS NOT FUNDED See the charity's website for a full list of funding exclusions relevant to the fund being applied to.

TYPE OF GRANT Project costs; core costs; salaries; capital costs; development funding (programme dependent). Funding can be given for projects lasting from one year up to three years and beyond.

RANGE OF GRANTS £2,000 to £200,000.

SAMPLE GRANTS A list of beneficiaries was not included in the annual report and accounts.

FINANCES *Financial year end* 31/03/2022
Income £13,350,000
Grants to organisations £12,530,000
Assets £3,270,000

TRUSTEES Rachel Lindley; Rachel Nelken; Yolanda Brown; Samuel Ross; Sophia Hall; Robert Aitken; Nathifa Jordan; Samuel Denniston; Mirjana Buac.

OTHER INFORMATION This trust is funded each year by the National Lottery, channelled through Arts Council England and the People's Postcode Lottery.

HOW TO APPLY The four main funds from which grants are awarded each differ in their funding criteria and application process. Potential applicants are advised to refer to the Youth Music Network website for up-to-date criteria, priorities, guidelines and deadlines. Applications can be made online, via the Youth Music Network website.

CONTACT DETAILS Angela Linton, Chief Operating Officer, Studio LG01, The Print Rooms, 164–180 Union Street, London SE1 0LH
Tel. 020 7902 1060 *Email* use the contact form on the website *Website* www.youthmusic.org.uk

■ The Elizabeth and Prince Zaiger Trust

CC NO 282096　　　**ESTABLISHED** 1981
WHERE FUNDING CAN BE GIVEN UK with some preference for Somerset, Dorset and the South West.
WHO CAN BENEFIT Registered charities; hospitals; hospices; occasionally individuals.
WHAT IS FUNDED General charitable purposes; social welfare; older people; people with disabilities; education of children and young people; care and protection of animals.
RANGE OF GRANTS £3,000 to £26,500.
SAMPLE GRANTS Variety, the Children's Charity (£26,500); Centre 70 (£20,000); King's College Hospital Charity (£15,000); Macmillan Cancer Support (£12,000); St Margaret's Hospice (£11,000); Springboard Opportunity Group (£3,000).
FINANCES *Financial year end 31/03/2022*
Income £619,800
Grants to organisations £652,500
Assets £21,660,000
TRUSTEES John Davidge; Peter Harvey; Derek Long; Edward Parry; Dr Robin Keyte.
OTHER INFORMATION The trust awarded 96 grants to organisations during 2021/22.
HOW TO APPLY The trust's Charity Commission record states: 'This trust does not respond to unsolicited applications for funds. Don't apply – it wastes your time and money.'
CONTACT DETAILS The Trustees, Gatesmoor, Hawkridge, Spaxton, Bridgwater, Somerset TA5 1AL *Tel.* 01278 671353

■ Zephyr Charitable Trust

CC NO 1003234　　　**ESTABLISHED** 1991
WHERE FUNDING CAN BE GIVEN UK and overseas.
WHO CAN BENEFIT Charitable organisations.
WHAT IS FUNDED Community development; the environment; social welfare; human rights; cultural equality.
WHAT IS NOT FUNDED Individuals.
TYPE OF GRANT Recurrent; direct costs; project funding; strategic funding; development funding; capital costs.
RANGE OF GRANTS Mostly under £5,000.
SAMPLE GRANTS The Mango Tree Trust (£100,000); Farm for City Children (£35,000); Pesticide Action Network UK (£20,000); Freedom from Torture and Womankind (£10,000 each); Friends of the Earth Trust, Intercare and Quaker Action Social Group (£5,000 each); Crisis (£4,000).
FINANCES *Financial year end 05/04/2022*
Income £55,700
Grants to organisations £269,000
Assets £1,310,000
TRUSTEES David Baldock; Dr Elizabeth Breeze; Marigo Harries; Donald Watson.
OTHER INFORMATION According to its 2021/22 annual report, the trust plans to close within the next few years; therefore, it is 'spending-out' its capital.
HOW TO APPLY Unsolicited applications are not accepted.

CONTACT DETAILS Trust Administrator, c/o Luminary Finance LLP, PO Box 135, Longfield, Kent DA3 8WF *Tel.* 01732 822114

■ The Marjorie and Arnold Ziff Charitable Foundation

CC NO 249368　　　**ESTABLISHED** 1964
WHERE FUNDING CAN BE GIVEN UK, with a preference for Leeds.
WHO CAN BENEFIT Jewish organisations.
WHAT IS FUNDED General charitable purposes, including education, health care, the arts and social welfare; in practice, the Jewish faith and community.
TYPE OF GRANT Capital costs.
SAMPLE GRANTS Maccabi GB (£102,500); Leeds Hospital Charity (£66,700); Leeds Jewish Welfare Board (£50,300); Western Marble Arch Synagogue (£16,900); United Hebrew Congregation (£6,500).
FINANCES *Financial year end 05/04/2022*
Income £214,000
Grants to organisations £484,500
Assets £7,370,000
TRUSTEES Ann Manning; Michael Ziff; Edward Ziff; Dr Marjorie Ziff.
HOW TO APPLY Apply in writing to the correspondent. The trustees have previously stated that funds available are limited and requests not previously supported are unlikely to be successful. Initial telephone calls are welcome but applicants should note the foregoing comments. Replies will only be given to a request accompanied by an sae.
CONTACT DETAILS The Trustees, Town Centre House, The Merrion Centre, Leeds, West Yorkshire LS2 8LY *Tel.* 0113 222 1234

■ The Zochonis Charitable Trust

CC NO 274769　　　**ESTABLISHED** 1978
WHERE FUNDING CAN BE GIVEN UK (particularly Greater Manchester) and overseas (particularly Africa).
WHO CAN BENEFIT Registered charities only.
WHAT IS FUNDED A range of charitable purposes including: welfare; education; children and young people; homelessness; community work; armed forces; older people; rescue services.
SAMPLE GRANTS A list of beneficiaries was not included in the annual report and accounts.
FINANCES *Financial year end 05/04/2022*
Income £3,840,000
Grants to organisations £4,420,000
Assets £130,790,000
TRUSTEES Archibald Calder; Paul Milner; Paul Evans.
OTHER INFORMATION Grants were distributed as follows: education (£1.33 million); health (£1.31 million); children and young people (£468,500); overseas (£402,000); homelessness (£265,000); social provision (£205,000); community (£120,000); emergency (£120,000); family (£74,000); armed forces (£60,500); rescue services (£35,000); older people (£30,500).
HOW TO APPLY Apply in writing to the correspondent.
CONTACT DETAILS The Trustees, Manchester Business Park, 3500 Aviator Way, Manchester M22 5TG *Tel.* 0161 435 1005
Email enquiries@zochonischaritabletrust.com

....

■ Zurich Community Trust (UK) Ltd

CC NO 266983   **ESTABLISHED** 1973

WHERE FUNDING CAN BE GIVEN UK and overseas, with priority given to locations where the company has offices.

WHO CAN BENEFIT Registered charities; community groups; voluntary organisations; NGOs.

WHAT IS FUNDED Communities and people who are disadvantaged.

WHAT IS NOT FUNDED See the trust's website for a full list of exclusions for each funding programme.

TYPE OF GRANT Multi-year partnership grants; project costs; core cost; salaries; seed funding; capital.

RANGE OF GRANTS Mostly £100 to £5,000 for UK grants; £2,000 to £10,000 for grants overseas. Strategic grants may be much larger.

SAMPLE GRANTS TeachFirst (£200,000); The GoodGym (£160,000); Mind in Haringey (£115,000); The Soup Kitchen (£56,000); SIFA Fireside (£43,000); 2 Wish Upon A Star (£35,000); The Diana Award (£30,000); The Openwork Foundation (£16,000).

FINANCES *Financial year end 31/12/2021*
Income £3,360,000
Grants to organisations £2,330,000
Assets £5,010,000

TRUSTEES Tim Culling; Wayne Myslik; Andrew Jepp; Richard Peden; Stephen Collinson; Timothy Bailey.

OTHER INFORMATION Only organisations that received over £30,000 were listed as beneficiaries in the trust's accounts. Grants of under £30,000 totalled £1.26 million. The trust's grant-making comes under a number of programmes. The Zurich Cares programme provides grants at a national level to three partner charities chosen by employees; at a local level to charities in the communities local to Zurich offices and employees, with local and regional grant funds available (refer to the website for further information on eligibility); and overseas, through applications from UK-registered charities. The Strategic Funding programmes are specific targeted projects, funded by the annual donation made to the trust by Zurich UK (applications for this scheme are by invitation only).

HOW TO APPLY Application processes vary between grant schemes and different locations. Prospective applicants should see the website for details on how to apply for a given scheme. Application opening/closing dates are also published on the website.

CONTACT DETAILS Steve Grimmett, Head of ZCT (UK), PO Box 1288, Swindon, Wiltshire SN1 1FL *Tel.* 07875 886341 *Email* steve.grimmett@zct.org.uk or zct@zct.org.uk. *Website* www.zct.org.uk